W9-CNP-215

The Question & Answer Book

OUR AMAZING SUN

OUR AMAZING SUN

By Richard Adams
Illustrated by Patti Boyd

Troll Associates

Library of Congress Cataloging in Publication Data

Adams, Richard Craig.
Our amazing sun.

(The Question and answer book)
Summary: Questions and answers provide basic information about the central body of the solar system, including its distance from the earth, solar storms, and sunspots.
1. Sun—Juvenile literature. [1. Sun. 2. Questions and answers] I. Boyd, Patti, ill. II. Title
III. Series.
QB521.5.A34 1983 523'.7 82-17419
ISBN 0-89375-890-6
ISBN 0-89375-891-4 (pbk.)

Copyright © 1983 by Troll Associates, Mahwah, New Jersey

All rights reserved. No part of this book may be used or reproduced in any manner whatsoever without written permission from the publisher.

Printed in the United States of America
10 9 8 7 6 5 4 3 2

How was the sun born?

Once upon a time, billions of years ago, there was no sun. Where the sun is now, there were only great clouds of dust and gas. As these clouds collected, they formed a huge swirling mass. Gravity pulled the dust and gas closer and closer together. This produced heat. The center of the huge mass grew hotter and hotter. It grew so hot that it began to glow. The sun had been born.

At about the same time, the nine planets that now travel around the sun were born, too. Scientists believe the planets were formed from dust and gas that collected around the sun's great, swirling mass. The sun and the planets are called the *solar system.*

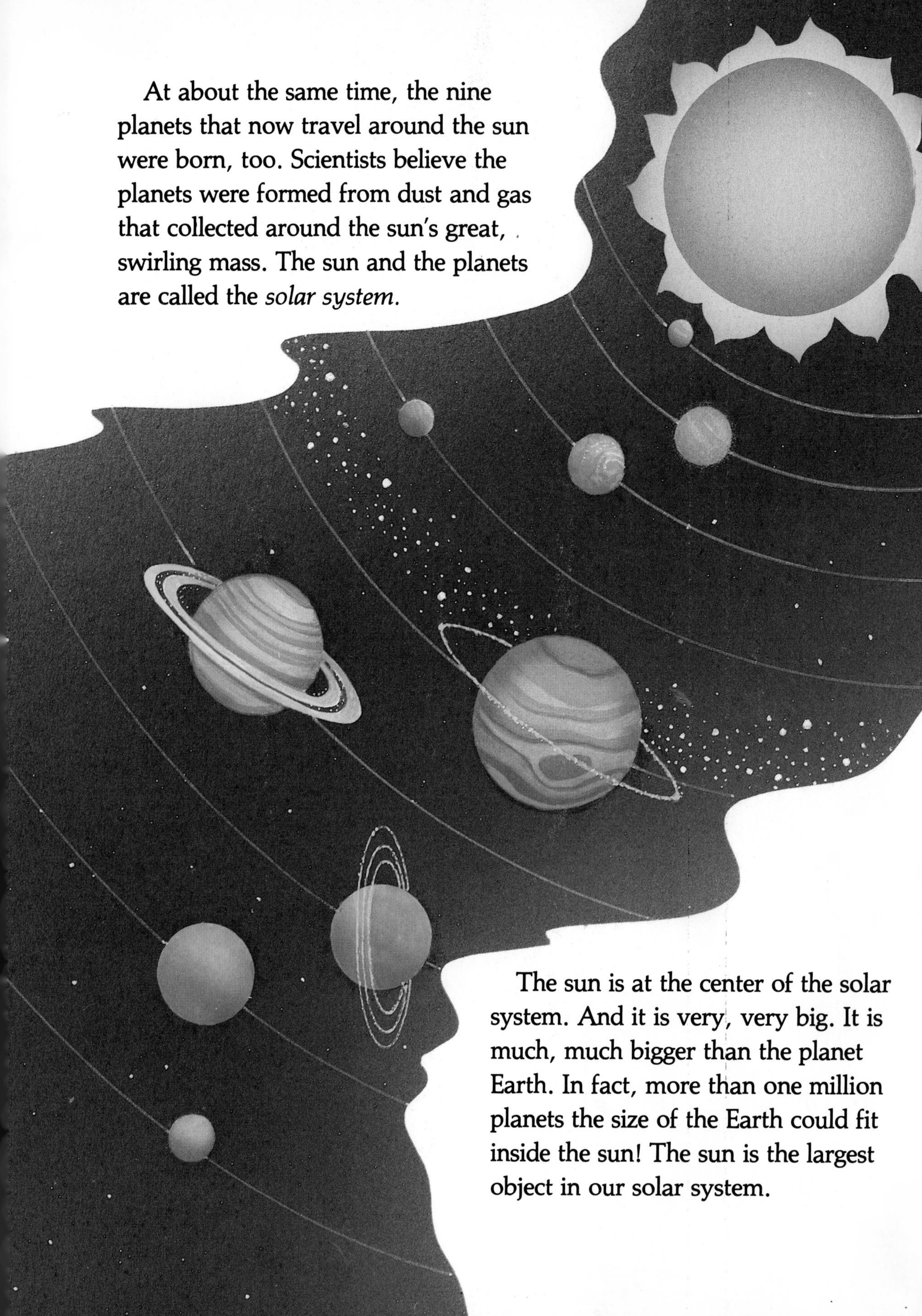

The sun is at the center of the solar system. And it is very, very big. It is much, much bigger than the planet Earth. In fact, more than one million planets the size of the Earth could fit inside the sun! The sun is the largest object in our solar system.

Why is the sun important?

The sun is the most important object in the solar system. It supplies energy to the planets—in the form of light and heat. Our own Earth is one of these planets. The sun gives us daylight and provides the energy needed by all living things. Green plants use the sun's energy directly. They use the energy in sunlight to make food.

Try this experiment.

Try this experiment to see what happens when a plant does not receive sunlight. Take two healthy plants. Keep one on a sunny windowsill. Put the other in a dark closet. Give them both the same amount of water. The plant in the sun will stay green and healthy. The plant in the closet will slowly lose its green color. After a while, it will die.

If there were no sunlight, all plants would die. Then there would be no carrots, no apples, no corn, and no beans. There would be no grass for cows to eat. So cows would die. In fact, all animals that eat plants would die. And animals that eat the plant-eating animals would die, too. So would people! We would have nothing left to eat.

Without the sun, the Earth would be so cold that no plants, animals, or people could survive. You can see how important the sun is. Of all the objects in the sky, the sun is most important to us. For life on Earth could not continue without the sun.

The sun is a star.

The sun is really a star. It looks bigger than the other stars because it is closer to us. Look out the window. Can you see any parked cars? Look at one that is parked nearby. Now look at one that is parked several blocks away. The one nearer to you looks bigger than the other, doesn't it? In the same way, a nearby star looks bigger than a faraway star. Our sun looks big to us because it is the closest star to the Earth. But compared to other stars, the sun is only a medium-sized star.

How far away is the sun?

How far away do you think the sun might be? A thousand miles or kilometers? A million? Ten million? The sun is about 93 million miles (150 million kilometers) away from the Earth. It is just the right distance from us to warm and light our planet. The next nearest star is over 25 trillion miles (40 trillion kilometers) away from the Earth. It is much too far away to give us heat or light.

How hot is the sun?

The surface of the sun is very, very hot. It is much hotter than the flame in a stove or oven. The temperature on the sun's surface is about 10,000° Fahrenheit (5,500° Celsius). That's hot enough to melt anything on Earth—stoves, brick buildings, steel bridges, and concrete sidewalks. In fact, if the Earth were close to the sun's surface, the heat would burn up the entire planet. Fortunately, the Earth is far enough away from the sun so we don't feel all that heat.

Then how do we know how much heat the sun really has? No one has ever visited the sun to measure its temperature directly. But scientists have measured the sunlight that reaches the Earth and calculated the sun's temperature. They believe that the temperature at the center of the sun is about 27,000,000°F (15,000,000°C).

The sun is made mostly of two kinds of gases—hydrogen and helium. All gases are made of tiny, tiny bits called atoms. Atoms are too small to see, but scientists know that they exist. The center of each atom is called a nucleus.

Because of the extremely high temperature at the center of the sun, something happens inside the nucleus of each hydrogen atom. We call this happening a nuclear reaction. Because of it, the hydrogen gas changes into helium gas.

Every nuclear reaction produces energy. The nuclear reactions in the sun produce several forms of energy, including x-rays, ultraviolet rays, and radio waves. But most of the sun's energy is in the form of heat and light. Every second, billions of nuclear reactions happen inside the sun. That's why the sun gives off the great amount of heat and light that it does.

What is a solar storm?

Other things are always happening on the sun, too. These happenings are called solar storms. By sending satellites into space, scientists have learned a lot about solar storms. These storms are very different from storms here on Earth. They have no wind, no rain, and no snow. Have you ever seen a picture of a dragon with flames shooting out of its mouth? Those dragon flames are very much like two kinds of solar storms—*prominences* and *flares*.

What is a prominence?

Prominences are great sheets of hot gases that shoot out from the sun. Then they flow back into the sun again. Prominences may last for a few hours, a few days, or a few months. They are thousands of miles thick. They may extend 20,000 miles (32,000 kilometers) above the surface of the sun.

What is a flare?

Flares are a lot like prominences. Flares are bright bursts of light that shoot out from the sun. But flares are smaller than prominences and don't usually last as long. However, flares are more powerful. They pour out great amounts of energy, in the form of heat, light, and cosmic rays. Cosmic rays from large solar flares contain large amounts of radiation. These rays are dangerous to astronauts traveling in space. Therefore, stations have been set up around the world to watch the sun's activities. If reports show possible danger, astronauts in space may be ordered to stop some of their activities. Or space flights may be postponed.

Sunspots

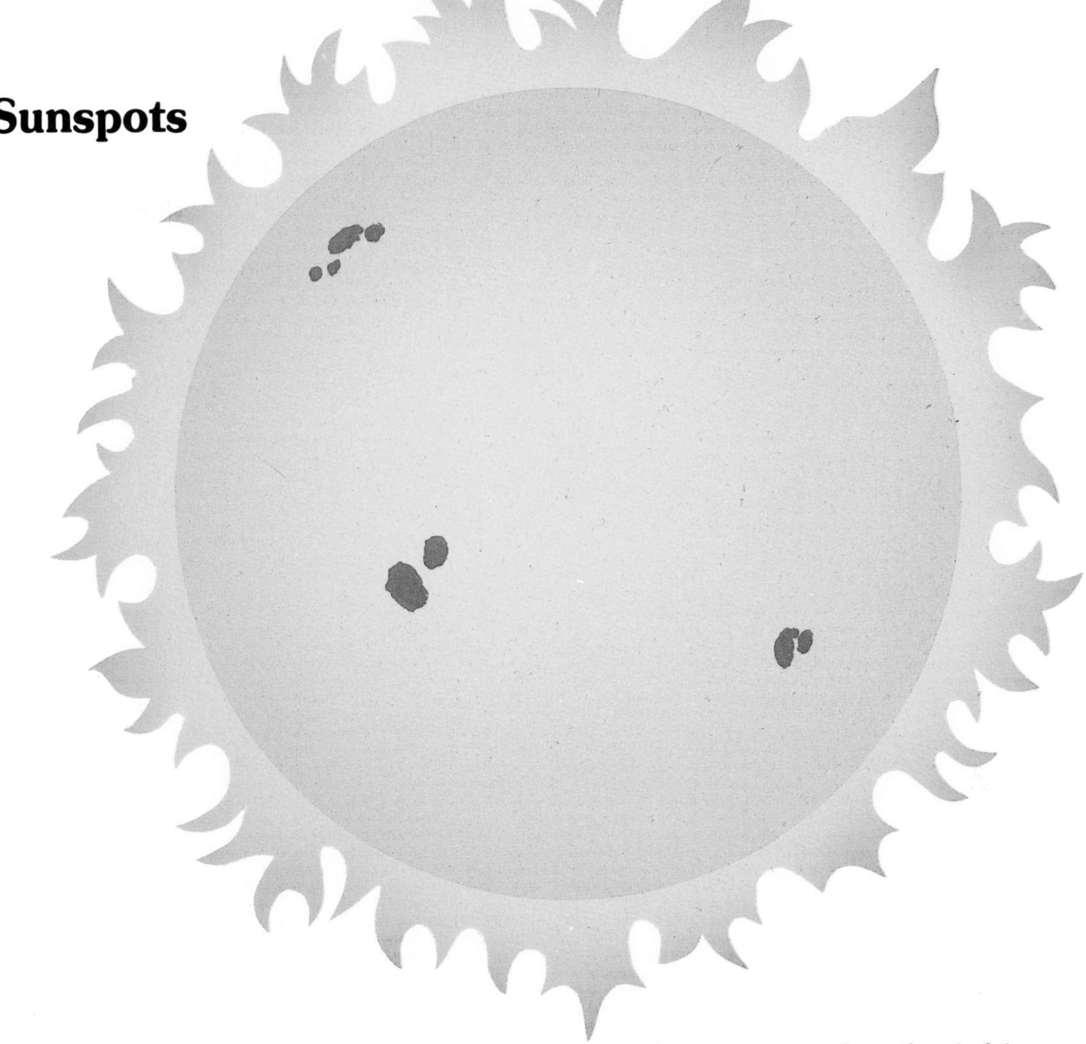

Sunspots are a third kind of solar storm. They look like round, dark patches on the sun. Scientists think they are caused by magnetic activity on the sun's surface. Sunspots are usually found in pairs. They vary in size, but the average width is over 20,000 miles (32,000 kilometers). Sunspots may last for only two days or as long as forty days or more. Sometimes one sunspot breaks up into a few. But all sunspots eventually fade away.

The number of sunspots changes from year to year. But scientists have found that the number of sunspots follows a pattern that seems to repeat itself every eleven years. This is called the sunspot cycle. During the eleven-year cycle, the number of sunspots increases to as many as one hundred, and then decreases again. Then a new sunspot cycle begins.

What is solar wind?

The sun's storms have no wind, but there is such a thing as a *solar wind*. It is a constant movement of very thin gases. These gases stream out from the sun in all directions. When the solar wind passes the Earth, the gases are moving at tremendous speed—between 1 and 2 million miles an hour (1.6 to 3.2 million kilometers an hour).

The solar wind moves even faster when solar flares occur. This can make strange things happen on Earth. Have you ever heard static on your radio? It may have been caused by solar wind. And if you are ever trying to find your way in the woods, and your compass needle starts to swing wildly, you'll know that the solar wind is probably the cause. If you wait a while, your compass will return to normal.

What is the sun's corona?

The gases that make up the solar wind come from the sun's corona. The corona is an area above the surface of the sun. It is like a crown that circles the sun. But it can only be seen during a solar eclipse.

What is a solar eclipse?

A solar eclipse happens whenever the moon passes directly between the sun and the Earth. The moon blocks out the sun's rays, and the sky gets dark for a short time. At this time, the corona's circle of light is visible around the dark area where the sun and moon are lined up. Then, when the moon moves out of the way, the sun's rays again reach the Earth.

If the moon blocks only part of the sun, we call it a partial eclipse. If the moon blocks all of the sun, we call it a total eclipse.

Of course, the sun is much bigger than the moon. Its diameter is about 400 times as wide as the diameter of the moon. But the sun is about 400 times farther away from the Earth than the moon is. So the sun and the moon look as if they are about the same size.

Here is an experiment that will show how this happens. Hold an eraser between your forefinger and your thumb. Look across the room at someone's head. Now close one eye. Move the eraser up close to your other eye. Keep looking at the person's head. What happened? The eraser blocked out the head, even though the head is much bigger than the eraser. In much the same way, the moon blocks the sun during a solar eclipse.

No one should ever look directly at the sun—even during an eclipse. Looking directly at the sun will damage your eyes. So if you get the chance to watch a solar eclipse, you will need a special kind of projector called a pinhole projector.

How to make a pinhole projector

To make a pinhole projector, take two pieces of cardboard, each about 10 inches square. Push a pin through the center of one piece of cardboard. Move the pin around until the hole is smooth.

Now turn your back to the sun. Hold the cardboard with the hole at your right shoulder. Hold the other cardboard in your left hand about a foot away. Move the two cardboards around until you see a tiny image of the sun on the second cardboard. You can watch the whole eclipse in this way, and never hurt your eyes.

How does the sun affect the weather?

One of the biggest effects of the sun on the Earth is on our weather. You know that the sun keeps us warm when it shines on us. But did you know that the sun also causes the wind? In sunny places on Earth, the air is warmed by the sun's rays. Warm air is lighter than cold air, so it rises. As the warm air rises, cooler air moves in from cloudy areas. This movement of air is called the wind.

When warm air rises, something else happens. Clouds form! All air has tiny bits of water in it. We call this kind of water "water vapor." As warm air rises and begins to cool, it can't hold as much water vapor. The tiny bits of water vapor join together into water droplets. A large group of these droplets forms a cloud.

As more air rises, more water droplets form. They join together in the cloud to form big drops. When they get too heavy to float in the air, they fall as raindrops.

After the rain falls, the sun "dries it up," or turns it back into water vapor. The water is back in the air again! Without sunshine, there would be no wind and no rain.

Why do we have day and night?

Each morning, the sun rises. Each night, the sun sets, or goes down. Does this mean the sun is moving from one side of the Earth to the other? People used to believe this. But today we know that the Earth rotates, or spins like a top. As it turns, only part of the Earth's surface receives the sun's rays. It is daytime in that part of the world.

It is nighttime where the sun's rays cannot reach. As your part of the Earth moves from darkness into the sun's rays, you see the sun "rise." Then, when your part of the Earth moves into darkness again, you see the sun "set." The sun seems to move across the sky because of the Earth's rotation. The Earth takes one day to make one rotation. (The sun also rotates. But it takes the sun about a month to make one rotation.)

The Earth moves in another way. It revolves, or travels in an orbit. The Earth's orbit is a path around the sun. The sun also travels in an orbit. The sun's orbit is a path around the center of the Milky Way galaxy. A galaxy is a large group of neighboring stars.

The sun is one of billions of stars that make up the Milky Way galaxy. All the stars in the Milky Way move around the center of the galaxy. The sun takes about 200 million years to travel once around the center of the Milky Way.

What is solar energy?

Energy from the sun is called *solar energy*. The sun is very important to every living thing on Earth. It provides heat and light. It causes the weather. It supplies the energy plants need in order to make food. Animals eat these plants, and people eat both plants and animals. So people receive energy indirectly from the sun.

Solar energy can also be used instead of coal, gas, or oil to produce heat for homes. This is very important in today's energy-conscious world, where supplies of these fuels are limited. Scientists are constantly searching for other ways to harness the sun's energy and put it to work.

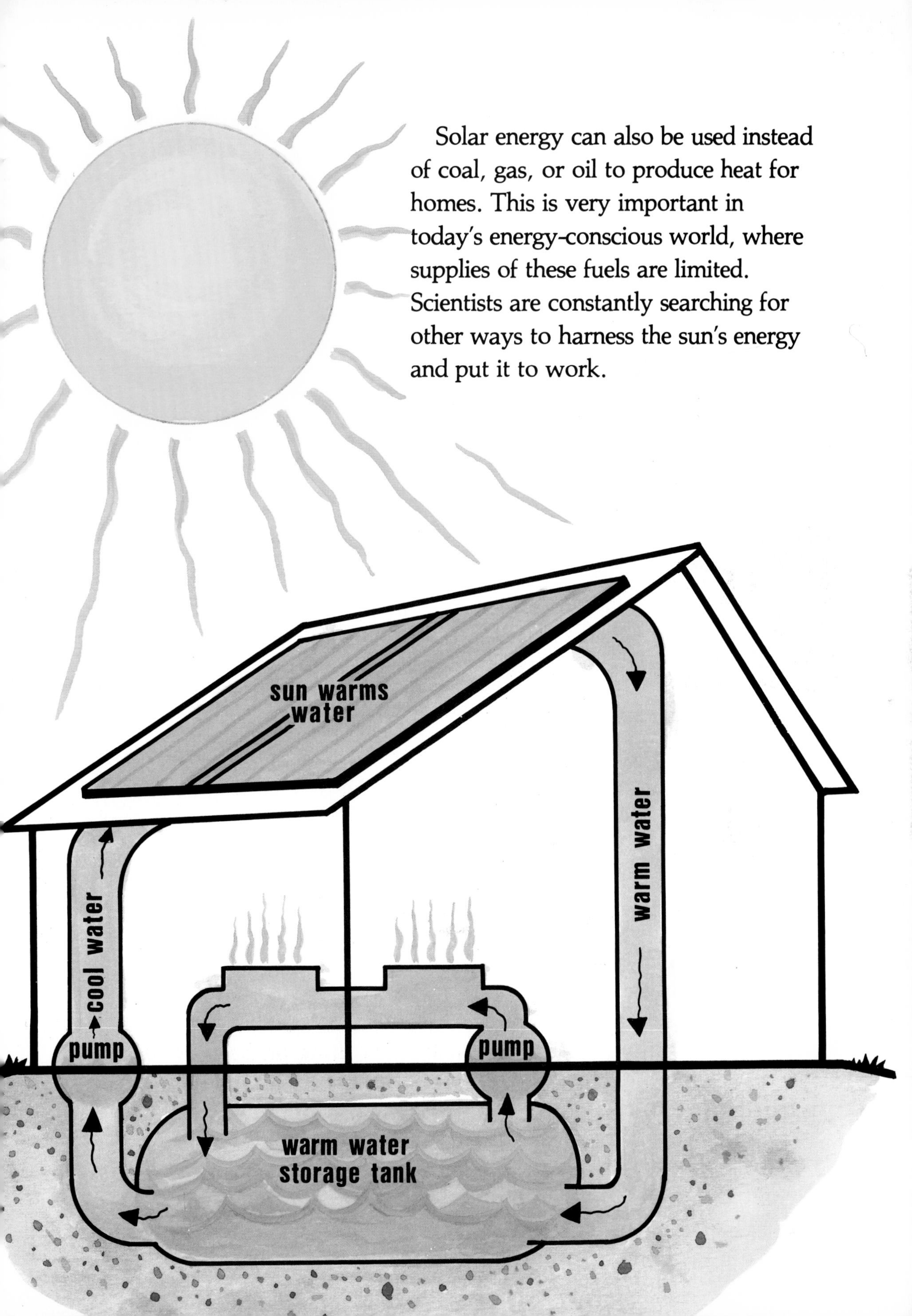

The search continues.

Long ago, people worshiped the sun because of its importance to their lives. Today, more than ever, we know how important the sun is to life on the planet Earth. By studying the sun, we may find the answers to questions that will help us understand our universe and how it began. There is so much to discover and to learn about that faraway star we call the sun.

SOLAR PATROLLER

W9-ANM-304

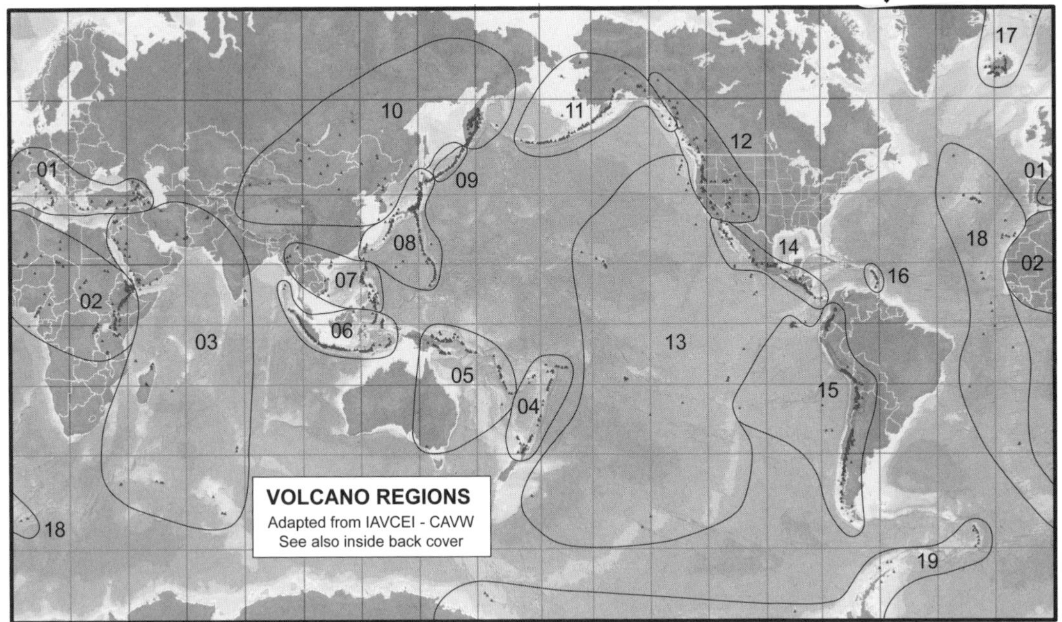

CODE AFTER DATE (Uncertainty) (p. 15)

Code		±Years	±Days	Code		±Years	±Days	
a	=	1	1	o	=	18	25	
b	=	2	2	p	=	20	30	(1 mo)
c	=	3	3	q	=	25	45	
d	=	4	4	r	=	30	60	(2 mo)
e	=	5	5	s	=	40	75	
f	=	6	6	t	=	50	90	(3 mo)
g	=	7	7	u	=	75	120	
h	=	8	8	v	=	100	150	
i	=	9	9	w	=	150	180	(6 mo)
j	=	10	10	x	=	200	270	
k	=	12	12	y	=	300	365	(1 yr)
m	=	14	15	z	=	500	545	
n	=	16	20	*	=	1000	730	(2 yr)

>	=	eruption after date listed
<	=	eruption before date listed
?	=	date uncertain (no data)

EXAMPLES:

1731<	=	on or before 1731
1731a	=	between 1730 and 1732
1731 1105d	=	between Nov 1 & 9
1750t	=	18th century
1790j	=	late 18th century
1778 02?	=	February (?) 1778

CODE BEFORE DATE (p. 16-24)

Code		Method	Count
A	=	Anthropology	39
C	=	Radiocarbon (uncorrected)	1000
D	=	Dendrochronology (tree ring)	18
E	=	Surface Exposure	25
F	=	Fission Track	3
G	=	Radiocarbon (corrected)	758
H	=	Hydration Rind	12
I	=	Ice Core	116
K	=	Potassium-Argon (K-Ar)	21
L	=	Lichenometry	2
M	=	Magnetism	54
N	=	Thermoluminescence	12
R	=	Argon-Argon (Ar-Ar)	17
S	=	SOFAR (hydrophonic)	63
T	=	Tephrochronology	1027
U	=	Uranium-Series	29
V	=	Varve Counts	35
-	=	BC date	2221
?	=	Eruption uncertain	1120
@	=	Eruption location uncertain	57
X	=	Discredited Eruption	179

VOLUME (p. 30-31)

L/T = volume of lava erupted (left column) / volume of tephra (right column)

7/- = 10^7 m^3 lava, no recorded tephra voume

-/**9** = 10^9 m^3 tephra, no recorded lava volume

7/8 = 10^7 m^3 lava, 10^8 m^3 tephra

ABBREVIATIONS

CAVW = Catalog of Active Volcanoes of the World

IAVCEI = International Association of Volcanology and Chemistry of the Earth's Interior

SEAN = Scientific Event Alert Network

GVN = Global Volcanism Network

METRIC CONVERSIONS

m = meter (3.28 ft)

km = kilometer (0.6214 miles)

km^3 = cubic kilometers (0.24 cubic miles)

ROCK TYPES

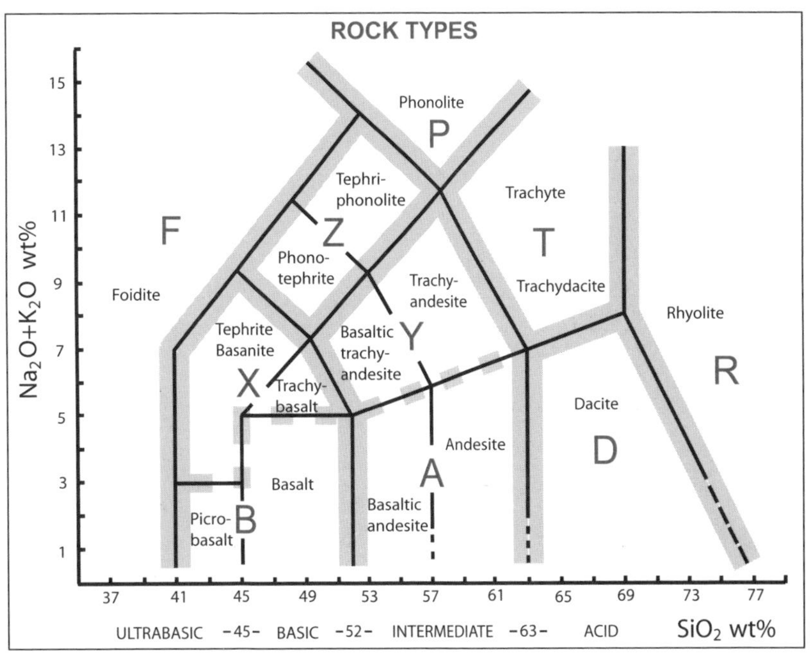

VOLCANOES OF THE WORLD

VOLCANOES

OF THE

WORLD

THIRD EDITION

LEE SIEBERT, TOM SIMKIN, AND PAUL KIMBERLY

SMITHSONIAN INSTITUTION | *Washington, D.C.*

UNIVERSITY OF CALIFORNIA PRESS | *Berkeley Los Angeles London*

University of California Press, one of the most distinguished university presses in the United States, enriches lives around the world by advancing scholarship in the humanities, social sciences, and natural sciences. Its activities are supported by the UC Press Foundation and by philanthropic contributions from individuals and institutions. For more information, visit www.ucpress.edu.

Digital edition available on the University of California Press website.

University of California Press
Berkeley and Los Angeles, California

University of California Press, Ltd.
London, England

© 2010 by the Smithsonian Institution

Library of Congress Cataloging-in-Publication Data

Siebert, Lee.
Volcanoes of the world.—3rd ed. / Lee Siebert, Tom Simkin, and Paul Kimberly.
p. cm.
Earlier edition entered under this title.
Includes bibliographical references.
ISBN 978-0-520-26877-7 (cloth : alk. paper)
1. Volcanoes. I. Simkin, Tom. II. Kimberly, Paul. III. Title.
QE522.V92 2010
551.21—dc22
2010026805

19 18 17 16 15 14 13 12 11 10

10 9 8 7 6 5 4 3 2 1

The paper used in this publication meets the minimum requirements of ANSI/NISO Z39.48-1992 (R 1997)(Permanence of Paper).

Cover: Strombolian eruption in June 2009 from Indonesia's Anak Krakatau (Child of Krakatau) volcano. Photograph by Marco Fulle, Stromboli Online.

Contents

Preface

Few geologic processes both capture the popular imagination and fuel scientists' quest for knowledge about our planet more than active volcanism. Volcanoes span an enormous spectrum: from topographically inconspicuous fissures to majestic peaks and from mild steaming to terrifying paroxysms. To understand volcanism, essential to either avoid its dangers or to utilize its resources, we must document its full breadth. Volcanology, more than most disciplines, depends upon history. The range of behavior is extremely broad, and the intervals between events can be long enough that it is essential to mine the contemporary and historical records to understand the dynamic aspects that are difficult or impossible to obtain for prehistoric eruptions. Well-documented examples from the past can be enormously helpful in interpreting a current volcanic crisis, and understanding the processes of the present is a long-established geological key for unlocking secrets of the past.

For more than four decades our group at the Smithsonian has been both documenting the older eruptions that have built the record of our planet's volcanism and aggressively seeking descriptions of ongoing volcanism. Even in the 21st century, unless eruptions are documented at the time of their occurrence, essential data may be lost to science. We endeavor to ask the right questions while the answers are still available, integrate data from diverse sources, and share this information with an ever-broadening community interested in volcanism.

Even the most basic volcanological information can be widely scattered, making it difficult to answer the first questions asked when confronted by a newly active volcano (Where is it?, What is its history?, Who has studied it?). Consequently, we started a database back in the keypunch card era nearly four decades ago. Since the publication of our first edition in 1981, and including the 2nd in 1994, the number of eruptions documented has nearly doubled to more than 10,400, and the number of "new" volcanoes has grown by more than 200. These additions cumulatively reflect incorporation of data on old and new eruptions, reviews of our data by regional specialists, and gratifying contributions from readers all over the world, including more than 250 personal communications cited in our database. Published references have more than doubled since the 2nd edition, and the number of names and synonyms listed in the Gazetteer increased by half, in part because of the inclusion of preliminary data from Pleistocene volcanoes. We believe that quality has increased along with quantity, but must emphasize, as we do throughout the following text, that the record of volcanism documented here remains far from complete.

It is a pleasure to thank the many people who have contributed to the data presented in this and previous volumes during the past four decades. We owe a particular debt of gratitude to Chris Newhall, formerly of the U.S. Geological Survey and now of the Earth Observatory of Singapore. This long-term collaboration began prior to our first edition and has continued through the years. He reviewed much of the first two editions and contributed his invaluable Volcanic Explosivity Index (VEI) data on explosive magnitude (with Steve Self). Another very profitable long-term collaboration was with John Latter of New Zealand, who contributed his painstaking compilations on the world's volcanoes; we also acknowledge Dan Shackelford for his contributions to the 2nd edition from correspondence with international volcanologists. Long-term collaboration with the U.S. Geological Survey Volcano Hazards Program under the successive leadership of Marianne Guffanti, John Pallister, Jim Quick, and John Eichelberger has greatly benefited our program, as has interactions with USGS geoscience advisors to the USAID-Office of Foreign Disaster Assistance, Tina Neal, Jim Smith, and Gari Mayberry. Ongoing collaboration with Steve Sparks and colleagues Laura Hobbs, Natalie Oritz, Natalia Delinge, and Sian Crosweller from Bristol University has contributed to the large-volume Pleistocene eruption list and will lead to future enhancement of these important data.

We have benefited from funding supplied by the U.S. Department of Energy (Office of Geothermal Technologies), NASA (Volcano-Climate Interaction Program), and the U.S. Geological Survey (Volcano Hazards Program), and we thank these organizations for their support. Our greatest support has come directly from the U.S. Congress in the form of line-item funding for the Smithsonian's Global Volcanism Program. This support has enhanced our eruption reporting, helped establish a permanent archive for maps, photographs, and documents, and greatly improved our intensive information technology needs. Funds for this project were provided by the Atherton Seidell Endowment Fund of the Smithsonian Institution.

It is a pleasure to acknowledge the significant contributions of Jenny Wapner and Kate Hoffman of the University of California Press for skilled guidance through the publication process and Lia Tjandra for design of the front and back covers. Dick Fiske reviewed the full text, and his input and encouragement along with that of external reviewers Bob Tilling and Bill Rose is greatly appreciated.

Archivist Stacia Largen and volunteer Mig Dooley Johnson processed the greatly increased number of images used in this edition. Giuseppina Kysar Mattietti and Diane Hanley earlier laid the groundwork for the extensive image database. Stacia Largen also worked on the bibliography. Pamela Melser helped with the greatly improved two-color maps in this edition, and Ken Brown assisted with graphics and figures. John Norton crafted the figures of eruption types and cheerfully incorporated comments from numerous iterations that greatly improved this figure from that used in the first two editions. Ed Venzke, Sorena Sorensen, Cheryl Siebert, Sally Kuhn Sennert, Stacia Largen, Bruce Lederer, and Steve Bentley performed the painstaking but invaluable role of proofing many sections of the book.

Below, we list some of the many people who have contributed data or reviews to parts of or full regions. An asterisk after the name singles out the friends who have reviewed large segments (in a few cases all) of their region's entries or provided major data streams. We also would like to acknowledge the important roles of many other contributors (not mentioned here) who sent reprints or otherwise alerted us to additions and corrections to individual entries.

Europe and Middle East Vicente Arana, Guy Camus*, Frank Clover, Oskar Ermann, Jean Feraud*, Jörg Keller*, Josep-María Mallarach, James Mellaart, Claudia Principe*, Romolo Romano, Roberto Scandone*, Jean-Claude Tanguy*.

Africa Peter Dunkley, Craig Feibel, Jörg Keller, Paul Mohr, Celia Nyamweru*, Martin Smith*, Pierre Vincent*, Giday Woldegabriel*, Chuck Wood*.

Indian Ocean Reginald Briggs, Guy Camus*, JP Poirer, Laurent Stieltjes*, Alta Walker, Graeme Wheller, Chuck Wood.

New Zealand to Fiji Jim Cole*, Stan Hart, Bruce Houghton*, John Latter*, Peter Rodda, Brad Scott, Paul Taylor, Colin Wilson*.

Melanesia to Australia Jean-Philippe Eissen, Wally Johnson*, Chris McKee, Malcom Sheard.

Indonesia Dali Ahmad, Sutikno Bronto, Tom Casadevall*, George de Neve*, Pat Dobson, Eddie Effendi, Ruska Hadian, Peter Jezek, Kaswanda, Chris Newhall, Liek Pardyanto, Nanang Rahardja, Haroun Said, Adjat Sudradjat, I Supriatman, David Sussman, Roy Torley*, Pierre Vetch.

Philippines and SE Asia Maricar Carmen Arpa*, Toti Corpuz*, Espie Del Mundo*, Chris Newhall*, Olimpio Peña*, Jim Whitford-Stark*, John Wolfe*.

Japan, Taiwan, Marianas Toshio Higashino*, Yukio Hayakawa*, Hiroki Kamata, Yasuo Miyabuchi, Dick Moore, Makoto Nishiwaki, T Nota, Yoshiro Sawada, Masaki Takahashi*, Toki Tiba.

Kuriles A Antonov, Ed Erlich, Genrich Steinberg*, Andre Tsvetkov.

Kamchatka and Mainland Asia Alexander Belousov, Oleg Dirksen, Yuri Doubik, Ed Erlich*, Jim Gill, William Kidd, Jiaqui Lui, Xiang Liu, Jim Luhr, P Novograblenof, Maria Pevzner, Vera Ponomareva*, Sergei Rasskazov, Oleg Volynets, Geoff Wadge, Jim Whitford-Stark*, Ming Zhang.

Alaska Cheryl Cameron, Klaus Jacob, Juergen Kienle, Bruce Marsh, Game McGimsey, Steve McNutt, Tom Miller, Tina Neal, Chris Nye*, John Reeder, Janet Schaefer.

Canada Neil Church, Ben Edwards, Cathy Hickson*.

Continental United States Roy Bailey, Michael Clynne, William Elston, Dan Miller, Frank Monastero, Michael Ort, Dave Sherrod*.

Hawaii and Pacific Islands Hans Barsczus, Jack Lockwood*, Dave Sherrod, Jacques Talandier, Tom Wright.

Mexico and Central America Guillermo Alvarado*, Jorge Aranda, Jorge Barquero*, Sam Bonis, Andrei Borgia, Mike Carr*, Gerardo Carrasco-Núñez, Mark Defant, C Demetrio Escobar, Jaime Incer*, Larry Feldman*, Jim Luhr*, Alfredo MacKenney, Eduardo Malavassi, William Melson, Steve Nelson, Carlos Pullinger, Jim Reynolds, Antonio Rivera, Bill Rose*, Dick Stoiber, Ben van Wyk de Vries.

South America Norm Banks, Bernardo Beate*, Shan de Silva*, Tui De Roy, José Egred, Moyra Gardeweg, John Guest, Pete Hall*, BA Klinck, Hugo Moreno*, Alberto Parodi-I, Maria Eugenia Petit-Breuilh*, Steve Porter, Guido Salas, Cindy Stine, Gerhard Wörner.

West Indies Philippe Bouysse, Jan Lindsay, Keith Rowley*, John Shepherd, Haraldur Sigurdsson, Alan Smith*.

Iceland and Jan Mayen Páll Einarsson, Ármann Höskuldsson, Paul Imsland, Gudrun Larsen*, Thor Siggerud, Sigurdur Steinthorsson*, Thor Thordarson*.

Atlantic Ocean Klaus Mehl*, Dick Moore*, Paco Pérez, Steve Self.

Antarctica Phil Kyle, Wes LeMasurier.

Over the years, the GVP has been supported within the Smithsonian's Department of Mineral Sciences during the successive terms of chairs Brian Mason, Bill Melson, Dan Appleman, Jeff Post, Glen MacPherson, Jim Luhr, Sorena Sorensen, and Tim McCoy. This project ultimately dates back to 1971, when Barbara Radovich, working as a Smithsonian student intern under the direction of Bill Melson, outlined the basic framework of the data file. Many in the Department of Mineral Sciences participated in the initial entry of data from the Catalog of Active Volcanoes of the World (CAVW), the Smithsonian Center for Short-Lived Phenomena, and independent data sets kindly supplied by John Latter, Bob Decker, and Fred Mauk.

Our first Information Technology (IT) specialists, Jon Dehn and Tom Stein, facilitated our mainframe database migration to the desktop environment, giving greater control over content and output. Their successor, Roland Pool, played a critical and time-consuming role in the full spectrum of production of the 2nd edition at a time when IT resources were considerably less robust than today. He furthermore spearheaded the migration of our database from the Pick operating system to Paradox, with late assistance from Genyong Peng. Additional IT assistance during preparation of the 2nd edition was welcomed from Ed Venzke and Genyong Peng of GVP, Dan Cole of our museum's GIS center, and Ken McCormick of the Smithsonian's main IT center; interns Scott Chaney and Pavan Khoobchandani provided help with regional maps.

The essential contributions of GVN Bulletin editors Lindsay McClelland, Ed Venzke, and Rick Wunderman through the years deserve special thanks for seeking out the new eruption information that helps build our record. McClelland led SEAN/GVN for 17 years, and Wunderman has now done so for an equal amount of time. This group has included David Squires, Elizabeth Nielsen, Marge Summers, Lisa Wainger, Katherine Duncker Romanak, Genyong Peng, David Lescinsky, and Tom Murray (on detail from the Cascades Volcano Observatory before becoming Scientist-in-Charge of the Alaska Volcano Observatory). A host of additional short-term employees and interns (both short and long-term) have also been essential in contributing to the monthly Bulletins, and we acknowledge their critical contributions in the "About GVP" section of our website. Gari Mayberry and Sally Kuhn Sennert have written the Weekly Volcanic Activity Reports over the past decade in a collaborative program with the USGS Volcano Hazards Program initiated by Marianne Guffanti, a long-term USGS colleague of GVP. Rick Wunderman also continues to play a major role in interactions with the volcano and aviation communities in response to volcanic ash and aviation safety issues. In addition to Bulletin work, Ed Venzke has spearheaded efforts to make Bulletin reports and our broader volcano data widely available on the GVP website. Translation assistance throughout the years has come from Virginia Wong, Boris Behncke, Cheerie Magalit, Gene Jarosewich, Joe Nelen, Luigi Mancini, Liudmila Eichelberger, and Russell Ross, in addition to several already named under the region headings above.

Additional Smithsonian colleagues have helped make this and earlier editions of this book a reality. First among these is Ellen Thurnau, who has solved and prevented a host of administrative problems over the years. A succession of archivists (Elizabeth Nielsen, Courtenay Wilkerson, Julia Lewis, and currently Stacia Largen) have organized resources on which we all draw. We also acknowledge the many Smithsonian co-workers who contributed to the first edition. These include Mary McGuigan, Geneva McClain and Edna Montford (for years of typing and keypunching), Cindy Hilmoe (map draft), Ken McCormick (computer graphics), Peter Kauslick (bibliographic programming), David Bridge and Kim Clark (database programming), Kathy Auer and Daphne Ross (literature review and other tasks), and over the term of all three editions, our museum library staff (for tracking down obscure references).

Curatorial colleagues in the department's Petrology and Volcanology Division, Dick Fiske, Jim Luhr, Bill Melson, and Sorena Sorensen, have contributed advice and encouragement. More distant colleagues Chris Newhall, Wally Johnson, John Latter, Bob Smith, and Grant Heiken have given us thoughtful, helpful counsel on the database through most of its life. Russell Blong instigated, and contributed importantly to, the initial version of the Fatality table. Visiting historian Howard Plotkin helpfully reviewed the historical content of regional Directory text.

We also owe thanks to the families of Maurice and Katia Krafft for facilitating access to the Krafft's magnificent collections after their tragic deaths at Unzen volcano. Maurice and Katia contributed substantively to the first two editions of this book by their reports and published work, and the welcome addition of their illustrations here, as in previous editions, is a small measure of the large contributions they made to volcanology. We also gratefully acknowledge the many other volcanologists and contributors to our image archive that were the sources of most of the 193 images that convey the breadth of volcanism covered here.

Finally, we ask for your help and offer some in return. Please continue to send us PDFs or reprints, copies of old documents, maps, photographs, specimens, and feedback on how we can improve our record of your favorite volcano. This is surely the best way to build the better record of global volcanism that will benefit us all, and we have valued every communication received. Please keep the information flowing and we will do our best to incorporate it accurately in our database as it grows. In return, we expect to be able to be more responsive to data requests, and will be working to make our data more directly accessible, including more robust search capabilities on our website.

We dedicate this book to two former Directors of the Global Volcanism Program, Jim Luhr (1953–2007) and Tom Simkin (1933–2009). Jim Luhr served as Director of GVP for a dozen years beginning in 1995. Jim was a volcano petrologist known widely in the volcanological community for his painstaking efforts to integrate the petrological context of volcanic rocks with detailed stratigraphic studies of volcanoes around the world, but primarily in México, where his footprints covered much of its volcanic landscape.

Tom Simkin was the founding Director of GVP and its antecedents dating back to 1968 and was Director until 1995. Tom was a pioneer in quantitative volcanology and recognized the utility of applying digital databases to issues of global volcanism. His distinguished career in volcanology spanned four decades and is reflected in his vision for GVP. Tom completed work on the 3rd edition of the This Dynamic Planet map project in retirement and was participating in the early work on this book in emeritus status. Tom was the heart and soul of GVP for many years, and much of his handiwork in the first two editions is reflected in this one.

Data Criteria and Context

Introduction

Volcanoes and their eruptions are among the most awe-inspiring expressions of the natural world. Volcanic activity has shaped the history of many different worlds, Earth as well as other planets and moons in our Solar System. Volcanic eruptions have played a major role in the evolution of Earth, creating the first crust of our planet 4.54 billion years ago; degassing of the Earth led to formation of the atmosphere, water, and life itself. Volcanoes provide both a window into the deep Earth, bringing mantle xenoliths to the surface, and explosive eruptions that impact the atmosphere above the Earth. These fundamental processes continue today: volcanic eruptions add new land to the Earth's surface, submersible expeditions have documented ongoing eruptions on the deep sea floor, and large-volume explosive eruptions produce ash and aerosols that transit the globe.

Violent volcanic eruptions can cause widespread destruction. However, volcanoes also benefit mankind by providing rich agricultural soils, geothermal heat, economically valuable ore deposits and construction materials, as well as some of our planet's most spectacular and beautiful terrain. Volcanoes have fascinated humans from time immemorial, and the study of volcanic phenomena has a rich history (Krafft, 1993; Sigurdsson, 1999; and Table 1). We present here the results of more than four decades of data compilation on the world's volcanoes and their eruptions by the Smithsonian's Global Volcanism Program (GVP), which resides in the National Museum of Natural History.

This introductory chapter discusses the column headings of our data tables (printed here in mixed-case bold letters, e.g., **Status**), the standardized data elements used in the tables (bold letters within quotation marks, e.g., "**Historical;**" sometimes in red for emphasis), and the guidelines that we have followed in building the data file. Use of all-capital bold letters identifies the main data tables of the book and text section titles (e.g., **DIRECTORY, PREVIOUS SUMMARIES**).

We have attempted to leaven this discussion and later regional summaries with some of the more interesting examples from the volcanological record, incorporating data through late 2009 and summary statistics that might both help readers searching for data on specific manifestations of volcanism and help place these data in the context of global volcanism. Volcanology textbooks (e.g., Macdonald, 1972; Williams and McBirney, 1979; Marti and Aranja, 1993; Sigurdsson et al., 2000; Francis and Oppenheimer, 2003; Schmincke, 2004; Decker and Decker, 2005) provide valuable background, but we have here included brief explanations of some additional subjects, such as age-dating techniques, essential to our tables yet not covered in most volcanology texts. Our extensive volcano image archive illustrates more sections of this book than in previous editions, including a color plate section. Photos by Smithsonian and international volcanologists, as well as others who have graciously contributed to our archive of more than 23,000 photos, depict many of the volcano types and eruptive processes discussed here and illustrate both renowned and more obscure volcanoes. We conclude with some comments on the nature of the historical record, cautions on use of the data set, and discussion of some insights these data provide about Earth's volcanism.

PREVIOUS SUMMARIES

Volcano lists go back nearly 2000 years. Pliny the Elder's renowned *Natural History*, finished two years before his death in the famous 79 AD eruption of Vesuvius, mentioned Etna, Lipari, and volcanoes in East Africa, Turkey, and the Middle East. The geographer Varenius (Bernhard Varen) published a list in 1650 that was brief (Table 1) but notable for containing representatives of most major volcanic regions known today. Nineteenth century publications, including two volumes each by Scrope and Daubeney, expanded the number of known volcanoes and eruptions. Quantitative volcano documentation took a quantum leap in the early 20th century with the compilations of German volcanologists Karl Schneider and Karl Sapper, who added systematic eruption data (including indicators of eruption magnitude) while doubling the number of recognized active volcanoes. Since Sapper's compilations, the major growth has been geological rather than historical, as field investigations have recognized more and more volcanoes with obviously recent, but usually not historical, activity.

In the years following World War II, volcano catalogs took another major leap with the onset of the International Association of Volcanology and Chemistry of the Earth's

REFERENCE	DATE	PAGES	VOLCANOES WITH DATED ERUPTIONS	ALL "RECENT" VOLCANOES	DATED ERUPTIONS
Varenius	1650	3	5	27	5
Scrope-I	1825	16	150	194	86
Daubeney-I	1826	466	33	73	130
von Hoff	1841	876	52	341	56
Daubeny-II	1848	743	85	247	275
Landgrebe	1855	949	133	320	269
Scrope-II	1862	171	191	217	214
Fuchs	1865	82	270	672	-
Humboldt	1869	237	225	407	?
Mercalli	1907	90	231	415	-
Schneider	1911	176	298	367	1440
Sapper-I	1917	297	430	486	2039
Sapper-II	1927	58	436	971	2428
CAVW	1951-75	2139	441	714	3542
Katsui (ed.)	1971	160	527	829	-
Macdonald	1972	20	516	735	-
Gushchenko	1979	474	609	933	5150
Smithsonian-I	1981	76	627	1343	5564
Smithsonian-II	1994	125	719	1511	7886
Smithsonian-III	2010	165	858	1545	10,415

Table 1. Growth of global volcanic data. Variable definitions of both "volcano" and "eruption" preclude close comparisons. Page totals are for volcano data, not full reference. Sapper-II data for recent volcanoes include those plotted on maps but not mentioned in text. Pleistocene volcanoes with continuing thermal activity included with Holocene volcanoes in our 2nd edition are not included here.

Interior (IAVCEI) Catalog series described below and, in the 1960s, regular annual reporting of volcanic activity around the world initiated by the Volcanological Society of Japan. These catalogs were the invaluable building blocks of later Smithsonian compilations.

Although the value of a standardized global volcano catalog compiled by regional specialists had been recognized by volcanologists as early as during the 1922 meeting of the International Union of Geodesy and Geophysics (IUGG) in Rome, it was not until after World War II that a catalog format was accepted. The first volume of the *Catalog of Active Volcanoes of the World* (hereinafter *CAVW*) was published in 1951, and the current set of 22 volumes has been an invaluable reference source for volcanologists as well as the initial source of data for our file. A compilation for Alaska (Miller et al., 1998) was published by the U.S. Geological Survey, and an unpublished draft of the Iceland catalog was compiled by Steinthorsson et al. (2002). We have not attempted to digitize the full *CAVW*, but we have largely retained its regional numbering system and have also used many other organizational elements of the *CAVW* as the basic format for our digital file.

By 1960, nearly half of the regional *CAVW* volumes had been published, but new eruptions were quickly making the earlier volumes out of date. Consequently, the catalog organizers met at the IUGG meeting in Helsinki that year and implemented a *Bulletin of Volcanic Eruptions* to cover global volcanism on an annual basis. These bulletins, produced by the Volcanological Society of Japan since 1960 and published until 1996 in the IAVCEI journal *Bulletin of Volcanology*, were based on thorough enquiries to individual volcanologists around the world and normally appeared several years after the eruptions that they reported.

In an effort to gain faster reporting of volcanic (and other) natural events, the Smithsonian *Center for Short-Lived Phenomena* (CSLP) was founded in 1968 in Cambridge, Massachusetts. Individual event cards were generated shortly after learning of an event, and a worldwide network of correspondents was developed. In 1975, the CSLP was reconstituted as the *Scientific Event Alert Network* (SEAN) at the National Museum of Natural History in Washington, D.C., with a substantially revised emphasis on the types of events being reported. From October of 1975 through 1989, a monthly *SEAN Bulletin* was published for its correspondents, and the first 10 years of reporting was reorganized and indexed in book form (McClelland et al., 1989). By the end of 1989, SEAN had nearly ceased reporting non-volcanological events, and its name was changed to *Global Volcanism Network* (GVN) to better reflect its work. Monthly reporting continued unchanged, but under the name of the *GVN Bulletin*. From 1977 to 1999 the Smithsonian summarized these monthly reports in *Geotimes*, the monthly journal of the American Geological Institute, and since 1986 in the IAVCEI journal *Bulletin of Volcanology* (itself the subject of a name change, from *Bulletin Volcanologique*, in 1986). The GVN Bulletin is also posted electronically on the Smithsonian's GVP website (www.volcano.si.edu) and on Arizona State University's volcano email list (volcano@asu.edu).

Since the publication of the first two editions of this book, expansion of web-based technologies has allowed much broader dissemination of scientific data. Recognizing the value of timelier reporting of volcanic activity, the U.S. Geological Survey and the Smithsonian have collaborated in producing Weekly Volcanic Activity Reports of volcanic activity and unrest that are posted on the GVP website and available using automated RSS feeds.

Any compilation of dynamic data streams such as volcanoes and their eruptions is by definition dated by the time of publication. Much of the data in this 3rd edition of *Volcanoes of the World* are also available on the GVP website (Siebert and Simkin, 2002-), and readers of this volume are referred there (www.volcano.si.edu/gvp/world/) to see the most current data. Smithsonian volcano data are also accessible in volcano layers on *Google Earth* and *Google Maps*, which allow map-driven access to information on individual volcanoes.

SOURCES

The above sources–the *Catalog of Active Volcanoes*, the *Bulletin of Volcanic Eruptions*, and the Smithsonian *SEAN-GVN Bulletin*–have been the basic building blocks of our data file. In addition, several other global compilations have been helpful: among them are IAVCEI data sheets of Post-Miocene volcanoes (1973-80); Gustav Hantke's papers covering the period 1937-1959; *Volcano Letter* reports from 1926-55 (Fiske et al., 1987); the Newhall and Dzurisin (1988) caldera monograph; and the independent compilations of Latter (1975) and Gushchenko (1979). A number of volcanoes from these compilations have not been included here, however, either because of direct evidence against, or insufficiently strong evidence for, eruptive activity during the last 10,000 years (see discussion of **Status** on p. 15-16). We have added information new to us and attempted to cover name (or grouping) differences in our **GAZETTEER**. Specific volcano or eruption descriptions from the scientific literature have been incorporated and these, plus broader global summaries such as those mentioned above, are listed in the **REFERENCES** at the end of this volume.

We emphasize that our search of the voluminous and ever expanding literature on volcanism is by no means complete, but it benefits from the invaluable assistance of the reviewers acknowledged in the Preface and the many readers of our first two editions who have kindly called specific papers to our attention and otherwise improved our database.

YEARS COVERED

The primary focus of this compilation is on volcanoes likely to have been active in Holocene, or Recent, time–the geologic terms for postglacial or post-Pleistocene time. Almost all compilers of the *CAVW* limited their coverage to historical time, but we extended our coverage to allow more equal treatment for regions where the historical record spans only a few hundred years, and further to cover the Holocene. Major eruptions may be separated by thousands of years, and postglacial time is often a convenient limit of volcanic history in higher latitudes where evidence of Pleistocene glaciation is clear. The

Pleistocene/Holocene boundary (Fairbridge, 1968) was defined as 10,000 years Before Present (BP) at the 1969 International Union for Quaternary Research (INQUA) Congress. More recent work with precise tree-ring chronologies has confirmed the 10,000 ^{14}C year boundary (Becker et al., 1991; see also Harland et al., 1989), and we use it as the time period covered by our data file. Note, however, that conversion of radiocarbon dates (measured in years BP from 1950) to calendar years results in some dates earlier than 8000 BC, which we have included.

Although only 21% of the eruptions listed in this compilation are older than 2000 years, they form an important and rapidly growing part of our file. Between the first and current editions of this book, the number of BC dates increased by more than a factor of 13, from 166 to 2221, reflecting the growth of detailed stratigraphic studies essential to determine the eruptive history of Earth's volcanoes.

Because of the lack of widespread prehistoric dating of recent volcanism, nearly half of the Holocene volcanoes listed here have no dated eruption. Most of these volcanoes are listed because they show clear evidence of eruption(s) within the last few thousand years (e.g., uneroded volcanic ash cones, eruptive products overlying young glacial debris, young unvegetated lava flows in regions where revegetation should be rapid). However, we have also followed the compilers of the *CAVW* in including volcanoes now in the fumarolic stage. These volcanoes are without (to this point) specifically dated Holocene eruptions, but volcanic gas or fumes signal either a pause between eruptions or residual degassing of a volcano that has not erupted for many thousands of years.

Finally, we have included volcanoes in our Holocene listing for which Holocene activity is only uncertain. At some volcanoes it has not been possible to determine whether eruptive activity ceased in the very latest Pleistocene, or the early Holocene, but we have attempted to clarify that uncertainty under both **Status** and date headings.

The distinction between volcanoes that last erupted during the early Holocene and those that ceased activity during the latest Pleistocene, however, is not volcanologically significant. Smith and Leudke (1984) pointed out that terrestrial volcanoes may be intermittently active over 10 million years; studies of the ocean floor suggest that individual volcanoes may remain active for 20 million years (Menard, 1969); and the IAVCEI data sheet project set a post-Miocene (approximately 5.3 million years) limit in order to capture all volcanoes that might still be active. The 10,000 years time frame clearly does not include all active volcanoes, and we thus have begun expanding our coverage into the Pleistocene (the last 1.8 million years). Because of the varying completeness of the Holocene and Pleistocene data, we present them here in separate tables.

Mud volcanoes, which reach diameters of 2½ km in Alaska (Reitsema, 1979) have been included by some volcanological compilers, but are excluded by us. Some mud-volcano eruptions, such as the 1951 California event that distributed fine debris over 6 km from the source (White, 1955), take place in hot spring areas, but their cause has no direct relation to new volcanic magma, and most mud volcanoes, in fact, result from methane generation in thick sequences of Cenozoic sediments distant from regions of true volcanism (Hedberg, 1974).

MAPS and REGIONAL NUMBERING SCHEME

World maps on the inside covers introduce the regional numbering scheme used throughout the book for both sequencing and cross-referencing, and each region is introduced in the **DIRECTORY** by detailed maps showing the relative positions of individual volcanoes. These maps serve as visual indexes to the volume. The numbering system, developed by the *CAVW* in the late 1930s and used in all catalogs, is geographic and hierarchical. The first two numerals identify region, the next two identify subregion, and the last two or three (after the hyphen) identify individual volcanoes in that subregion. Original *CAVW* volcano numbers have been retained, where possible, to aid cross-referencing, but this has required, for the many volcanoes added since *CAVW* publication, the interpolation of 3-digit volcano numbers between 2-digit-plus-equal-sign *CAVW* numbers. This potentially confusing practice is discussed below (p. 15), but readers are alerted to it here at the start. Our **DIRECTORY** is sequenced by volcano numbers for easy location on maps and allowing cross-referencing to other tables, such as the **CHRONOLOGY and GAZETTEER**. The regional numbers generally proceed east and south from Europe through the Indian Ocean and then across to New Zealand, beginning a clockwise circle around the Pacific margin, and ending with the Atlantic and Antarctic regions.

We have assigned new subregion numbers where the *CAVW* has no listings and have renumbered subregions in some areas, such as the western United States and Canada, where work of recent decades has increased the number of recognized Holocene volcanoes from the 12 listed in the 1960 *CAVW* compilation to the 78 listed here. We have also expanded several regions to cover volcanoes not listed by the *CAVW*. For example, region 05 (Melanesia) now includes Holocene volcanism in Australia, region 10 includes newly recognized Holocene centers in Mainland Asia, region 13 (Hawaii) has been widened to include most of the Pacific Ocean (not already included by the *CAVW* in other regions), and region 17 (Iceland) has been expanded to include the Arctic Ocean. We have substantially renumbered volcanoes in several regions since our first edition, particularly in Iceland and New Zealand where work with regional specialists has provided simplification based on the concept of volcano systems. Additional discussion of this and other aspects of volcano numbers follows on p. 15.

Red symbols give some indication of each volcano's activity status as well as location. For the detailed maps in the **DIRECTORY**, the 590 volcanoes with known eruptions since 1500 AD are shown by solid triangles with black outlines; 162 with earlier AD eruptions by solid triangles, and 541 with BC or undated Holocene eruptions by open triangles. For this latter group (often identified by uneroded, youthful cones or fresh, unvegetated lava flows), the lack of dated eruptions generally reflects a weak historical record rather than a lack of geologically recent volcanism.

The final group, the 243 locations marked by very small open triangles, represent distinctly less certain activity during the last 10,000 years. These include questionable submarine eruptions and other accounts of doubtful reliability, plus the fumarolic fields that are included in the *CAVW* as evidence of late-stage volcanic development. This group is made up of volcanoes in our "*Uncertain*" status (including those for which the only dated eruptions are questionable), and those for which our volcano **Type** designation is no more than a thermal feature (such as fumarolic field or hydrothermal region). On the inside back cover map, all volcanoes with dated eruptions are shown by one symbol and probable Holocene volcanoes without explicitly dated eruptions by another.

We chose the volcano categories (increasingly long time periods since the last known eruption) because unusually long periods of volcanic quiet are often ended by unusually violent eruptions, and this symbol convention helps identify volcanoes that have been apparently quiet for long periods of time. Volcanoes are also quiet, of course, when they are dead, and there is no simple means of distinguishing dormant from extinct volcanoes.

The maps introducing each region in the **DIRECTORY** are designed to show the relative positions of every volcano at a level of detail not possible in the world map. In addition to volcano information in red, political boundaries are shown and capital cities are named for volcano nations, along with selected major cities, often with populations exceeding 1 million. Names are entered for all volcanoes having: (1) confirmed eruptions since 1500 AD; (2) ≥10 dated eruptions; (3) eruption(s) with VEI ≥4 or producing ≥1 km^3 of lava; (4) fatal eruptions or recent evacuations; (5) Holocene volcanoes with documented Pleistocene eruptions producing ≥1km^3 of lava or tephra, discussion in this text; or (6) other noteworthy characteristics. Volcanoes in adjacent regions are shown by smaller gray triangles (without age distinctions).

Readers wishing a larger world map of volcanoes might be interested in the *This Dynamic Planet* produced by the U.S. Geological Survey in collaboration with the Smithsonian and the U.S. Naval Research Lab (Simkin et al., 2006). This wall map uses similar volcano symbols as those in the detailed **DIRECTORY** maps here, but also shows tectonic features, seismicity, and impact craters. The bathymetric and topographic base and plate boundary data of this map are also used for the regional maps in the **DIRECTORY** and the maps on the inside covers of this book. Our volcano data also appear on a three-series Plate Tectonics, Geodynamics, & Hazards map set published beginning in 1981 by the Circum-Pacific Map Project. These maps and *This Dynamic Planet* map are available from the U.S. Geological Survey, Map Distribution, Box 25256, Federal Center, Denver, CO 80225 (I-800-USA-MAPS). An interactive on-line version of the *This Dynamic Planet* map can be accessed through the GVP website (mineralsciences.si.edu/tdpmap/).

Smithsonian volcano data can also be seen on the interactive global satellite imagery of *Google Earth* and *Google Maps*. Users can zoom in and click on icons of about 1300 Holocene volcanoes (excluding those with uncertain **Status**) to see brief geologic summaries, photos, and links to our website for more detailed information, including current eruption chronologies.

Data Table Summaries

The content and formats for the 7 data tables that make up most of this book are briefly summarized below. The many codes and abbreviations used in the tables also appear on the inside front cover and on the opening pages of each section for easy reference. These data table summaries are followed by introductory text beginning on page 8 discussing the volcano and eruption data in more detail in sequence of the column headings used in the tables.

DIRECTORY

This section, the largest in the book, is basically a condensed and updated version of the *CAVW*, but with its time frame expanded to 10,000 years. We have compressed the geographic data, morphology, activity status, and known eruptive history of 1545 volcanoes into 165 pages of tables. Such an attempt suffers from a very uneven historical record, inconsistent use of important terms ("volcano," "eruption"), and the many uncertainties of reducing subjective, human accounts to a rigid, tabular format. Although it must be recognized as an inescapably incomplete record, we provide it as a summary and guide to the literature for all readers interested in volcanism. As we found after publishing the first two editions, such readers supply additions and corrections that can be incorporated to provide more accurate and complete future editions of this work.

Maps introduce each region, along with a few words about its history, tectonic setting, geography, and noteworthy volcanological features to provide context for the records that follow. The following references were particularly helpful: Fernandez-Armesto (1991); Schnauble (1993); Trager (1992); Webster's New Geographical Dictionary (1988); Wright (1993). Differences between the robustness of the volcanological record of regions are often large, and the aim of these brief introductions is to increase appreciation for the strengths and weaknesses of each regional data set.

The **DIRECTORY** consists of a single line of information for each volcano and another for each known Holocene eruption. The basic geographical and geological data for each volcano are arranged in columns on a single line, and they are sequenced regionally by volcano number (see maps and discussion of numbering system on p. 15).

Under each volcano, dated eruptions are chronologically summarized, including the book's only coverage of eruptive characteristics. The **DIRECTORY** thus provides a concise summary of the known eruptive history for each volcano and region. Discussion of the conventions used and information shown will follow under the main sections **VOLCANO DATA** and **ERUPTION DATA** (p. 8-31).

CHRONOLOGY

This section arranges all 10,415 eruptions in a chronological sequence by **START** date **(YEAR M-Dy)**, displaying all volcanism known to have taken place in each year. The record begins with a few eruptions older than 8000 BC (because of the 10,000 BP radiocarbon years as discussed above) and ends with the first day of 2010. For any given year, those eruptions known to be continuing from the previous year are listed first (sequenced by volcano number). These are followed by eruptions known only to have taken place sometime during the year (also sequenced by volcano number), and finally by eruptions starting in a known month or day. However, attention must be paid, particularly with older dates, to the uncertainty code (p. 19-20) and to the uncorrected radiocarbon dates (p. 21-22). An eruption listed simply as "seventeenth century" will be shown only *once* as "1650t" (1650 ± 50 years), and radiocarbon dates preceded by "C" may be as much as 900 years from the true calendar date.

When the date of an eruption's end is known, we have displayed the **Duration** (in days), but for the 7% of all eruptions exceeding ~999 days we have simply listed "**>3yr**." **VOLCANO NAME** is then listed, followed by **Subregion** name (truncated after some longer names). **NUMBER** allows cross-reference to map or directory, for additional information, and both **VEI** and volume data (**Vol-L/T**) indicate eruption size. When more than one **VEI** is assigned for an eruption, as for a paroxysmal explosion following the onset of the eruption, the two dates appear separately in chronologic sequence. Thus the catastrophic eruption of Tambora in Indonesia appears on April 5, 1815, but the eruption's start is also entered in 1812, and its continuing lower-level activity is noted for 1813 and 1814. The renowned 1980 eruption of Mount St. Helens is listed for its March 27 start, its May 18 paroxysmal eruption, and 5 subsequent events that produced ash cloud heights of 13 km or more.

Art work and photographs are interspersed through the **CHRONOLOGY** to illustrate eruptions and show the processes and features treated in the book. Their sequence attempts to convey a sense of history, as a reminder that our record of volcanism is largely a human record and, as such, is subject to many shortcomings.

LARGE-VOLUME HOLOCENE ERUPTIONS

There is substantial interest in the larger-volume eruptions that have affected our planet. This section highlights those eruptions, both explosive and effusive, in separate tables. The **Explosive Eruptions** table includes all Holocene explosive eruptions with a **VEI** of 4 or larger (≥0.1 km^3 of tephra). Data are shown in the same format as in the **CHRONOLOGY** tables, except that only dates of eruptive events of VEI 4 or larger are displayed, whenever they may occur during the course of an eruption. The start date of an eruption is displayed only when there is a single VEI assignment for the full eruption. The associated data for the eruption duration and the lava volume, however, are for the full eruption. This gives context for the eruption as a whole, while noting the magnitude (VEI and tephra volume) of the sometimes more specifically dated explosive event. Thus the **VEI** 7 eruption of Tambora volcano, the largest in historical time, appears only under its April 10, 1815 date, but the **Duration** column indicates that the eruption lasted for more than three years. As with the **DIRECTORY** and **CHRONOLOGY** tables, explosive eruptions without tephra volumes that are described as "plinian" or caldera-forming are shown with a "P" or "C," respectively, in the **VEI** column.

The ensuing **Effusive Eruptions** table includes all eruptions producing ≥0.1 km^3 (or 10^8 m^3) of lava. In contrast to the **Explosive Eruptions** table, all data in the **Effusive Eruptions** table, including the eruption duration, VEI, and lava and tephra volumes, provide context for the eruption as a whole and are listed under the start date of the eruption. This means that the lava volume, even for long-duration eruptions, is applied to the first year of the eruption. The compound Santiaguito lava dome at Santa María volcano in Guatemala, for example, still in eruption after almost 90 years, has now produced more than 1 km^3 of lava, but its lava volume of 9 (10^9 m^3) appears only with its 1922 start date.

As with the **CHRONOLOGY** listing discussed above, it must be emphasized that these "Large Eruption" tables include dates with large dating uncertainties and incorporate both corrected and uncorrected radiocarbon dates (discussed in more detail later under **Dating Technique**). Consequently, events do not always appear in strict chronological sequence. It must also be noted that these tables are clearly substantially incomplete, as deposits of many Holocene eruptions have not been studied in sufficient detail to determine their volumes.

FATALITIES and EVACUATIONS

Volcanic hazards have received increased attention in the past decades (Blong, 1984; Latter, 1989; UNDRO, 1985; Scarpa and Tilling, 1989; Tilling, 1989). Because of widespread interest in the subject, we include here an extended table of all known fatal eruptions (see also Tanguy et al., 1998; Simkin et al., 2001; Witham, 2005). These tragic events carry important lessons to everyone who is (or should be) concerned with volcanoes, and their sobering toll gives these lessons a power not found in more theoretical treatments.

The fatality table is arranged in the sequence of the preceding **DIRECTORY**. Volcano name (and number) is followed by entries for each fatal eruption, carrying date (**YEAR M-Dy**), number of **Deaths**, the proportion that can be assigned to principal **Agents** or causes, and **Remarks**, a free-form description of the event. For cross-referencing to other parts of the book, both volcano number and eruption **Start date** are shown. More detailed descriptions of table elements appear in a box immediately preceding the table (p 330).

Fatalities have been recorded from nearly 400 eruptions, with the most deadly being the roughly 60,000 estimated fatalities from the 1815 Tambora eruption. Large numbers of people live in proximity to active volcanoes, and three densely populated countries on the western side of the Pacific Ring of Fire (Indonesia, the Philippines, and Japan) account for half of the pages in this fatality listing.

A fatality table, however, places unfair emphasis on the negative side of volcano hazard work. Increased understanding of, and attention to, volcanic hazards in recent decades has resulted in many successful evacuations and the saving of thousands of lives. Therefore, we follow the fatality table with a shorter listing of known evacuations since 1975. This covers the time period of regular Smithsonian reporting by SEAN and GVN. The number of evacuees is accompanied by the number of fatalities and the type of volcanic activity causing the fatalities or evacuations. Since 1975, more than 150 eruptions, averaging 4 to 5 per year, have documented evacuations; the many eruptions during this interval with no fatalities underscore the success of evacuation efforts.

PRELIMINARY LIST of PLEISTOCENE VOLCANOES

The focus of the volcano data in the first two editions of this book has been on Holocene volcanoes. However, increasingly detailed field studies of volcanoes have shown that they can remain dormant for very long periods of time, even beyond the 10,000 year period of the Holocene, and then resume eruptive activity. This complicates considerations of volcanic hazards, and we have begun to expand our data into the Pleistocene to allow coverage of a broader period of volcanism. This significantly enlarges the time span covered from 10,000 years to 1.81 million years, the Pliocene/Pleistocene boundary as defined by dating of deep-water marine strata exposed in Italy (Van Couvering, 2004).

Obtaining representative global coverage for the entire Pleistocene will be a long-term project, and we have emphasized the very preliminary nature of these data in the title of this section. One of early building blocks was a compilation on *Post-Miocene Volcanoes of the World* (IAVCEI, 1973-80). These data sheets have been supplemented by many papers from the scientific literature, but the coverage is regionally quite variable. For some regions, such as Japan (Nakano et al., 2001-) and the West Indies (Lindsay et al., 2005), volcanologists have compiled comprehensive lists of Quaternary volcanoes, but in many other regions only a small percentage of Pleistocene volcanoes are listed. For this reason we have not integrated Pleistocene volcanoes with our Holocene listing to avoid creating the impression that regional volcano listings are of comparable completeness.

In the first two editions of this book, we included some Pleistocene volcanoes with continuing vigorous thermal activity, such as Long Valley and Valles calderas, in the Holocene list. Expansion of data into the Pleistocene has now allowed us to move these volcanoes into their proper Pleistocene category. This has dropped the total number of volcanoes in the Holocene listing from 1587 to the 1545 listed here, but the Pleistocene thermal activity is still noted in the Pleistocene volcano listing. Detailed field studies since the 2nd edition have demonstrated that some volcanoes thought to have erupted during the Holocene actually ceased eruption during the late Pleistocene. This is particularly the case in arid regions, where weathering processes are slowed, and apparently youthful volcanoes have been found to be inactive since the late Pleistocene. Some familiar volcanoes, such as Amboy and Capulin in the SW United States, which would otherwise have disappeared from this compilation, can now be found in the Pleistocene volcano listing and also appear in the **GAZETTEER**.

PRELIMINARY LIST of LARGE-VOLUME PLEISTOCENE ERUPTIONS

The recognition of global-scale impacts of large-volume eruptions has promoted interest in expanding documentation of these eruptions into the Pleistocene. Compilation of these data was begun independently at the Smithsonian and has continued as a collaborative "Volcano Global Risk Identification and Analysis" project (VOGRIPA) with Steve Sparks of Bristol University and colleagues to assess the impact of large-volume eruptions. This list partially mirrors that of the **LARGE-VOLUME HOLOCENE ERUPTIONS**, but has a higher threshold of **VEI** 5 for explosive eruptions (≥1 km^3 of tephra) or effusive eruptions that produced ≥1 km^3 of lava. Data are listed chronologically, first in thousands of years (ka) Before Present and then in millions of years (Ma) Before Present. Thus 22.6 ka = 22,600 years BP, and 0.58 Ma = 580,000 years BP. We include eruptions dated as early as the beginning of the Pleistocene (1.81 million years).

We have included all Pleistocene eruptions known to us that meet the criteria of being dated, either explicitly or within a reasonable stratigraphic range (the latter are flagged by an "*"), and have an estimated volume for either tephra ejection or lava effusion in excess of 1 km^3. There are two exceptions: one is that explosive eruptions known to have resulted in caldera formation, but without a volume calculation, are included with a **C** in the **VEI** field; the other is that we have included some eruptions without volume calculations where a VEI value has been assigned by our data source. Unlike in the **CHRONOLOGY**, the dating technique is not listed, but radiocarbon dates appear as uncorrected radiocarbon dates, unless only a corrected date is known (flagged by a "י"). To help identify eruptive units, we have listed their names. References are listed regionally by author(s) and year at the end of the list; full citations can be found in the pertinent regional section of the **REFERENCES** at the end of this book.

Volume calculations can vary significantly depending on the density of thickness measurements and the calculation technique used; we display published volumes, but users should be aware that considerable uncertainties are attached to these data. As the table title indicates, this is a preliminary list, and both volumes and dates are subject to change as more detailed studies are conducted.

GAZETTEER

Volcano names are commonly confused by synonyms, official geographic name changes, subsidiary feature names, and the grouping of nearby features in different ways. We have attempted to reduce this confusion by listing alphabetically all 15,872 names in our file, stating their relationship to the 2870 volcano names used here. We have expanded the **GAZETTEER** from the 2nd edition by including Pleistocene volcanoes; these can easily be distinguished from Holocene volcanoes by the absence of a volcano number. Including the names and subsidiary features of both Holocene and Pleistocene volcanoes more than doubles the length of the previous edition **GAZETTEER**. We have attempted to leaven its telephone book appearance by interspersing images of volcanic features with names beginning with each letter of the alphabet.

Names of primary volcanoes are bolded to distinguish them from unbolded subsidiary features and synonyms. The morphologic type of each primary volcano is listed with each mention of it (see detailed description of **TYPE** on p. 14-15). Under its main entry (bolded **NAME** and **NUMBER**) we further identify the primary volcano by listing its total number of certain dated Holocene eruptions, its year of most recent confirmed eruption, and its **STATUS**. Such information can be helpful when choosing between several features with similar names or synonyms (there are, for example, 5 "Ploskys" in Kamchatka, and "Pan de Azucars" in Alaska, Colombia, Ecuador, and the Canary Islands).

Many volcanoes carry words such as "Mount," "Cerro," or "Volcán" before the proper name by which they are uniquely known, and the use of such modifiers is often uncertain or confusing (e.g., "Mount Lassen," "Lassen Peak," or "Lassen volcanic center"). Therefore we have either dropped these frequently used modifiers, or placed them, with comma, behind the proper name (e.g., "Azul, Cerro"), with appropriate cross-references in the **GAZETTEER**.

We have tended to group nearby volcanic vents under one **VOLCANO** entry, following the model of Mauna Loa, Hawaii (where eruptions 50 km from the volcano's summit are clearly linked to it) rather than that of the Canary Islands (where the *CAVW* listed vents separated by only a few kilometers as distinct "volcanoes"). This tendency toward grouping is likely to continue as understanding of regional volcanism increases. In Iceland, for example, the 70 volcanoes of our first edition have been reduced to 33, based on the concept of "volcanic systems" linked by detailed petrologic and tectonic characteristics (Johannesson and Saemundsson, 1998; Jakobsson et al., 2008; Thordarson and Hoskuldsson, 2008). Such changes enhance the value of a gazetteer, linking various volcanic features and the names by which they have been known.

We have not, however, assigned names to unnamed volcanoes based on nearby geographic features. This means that 72 Holocene and 100 Pleistocene volcanoes are listed under "unnamed" (48 of them submarine). Their positions can be determined from geographic coordinates, and more detailed geographic locations are entered in our data file for most. The guide on p. 374 introducing the **GAZETTEER** points out some common alternative spellings that greatly reduce the number of synonyms that we need to list in the **GAZETTEER**.

REFERENCES

The more than 4800 references that are the source documents used in our compilation are arranged by region in the same *CAVW* sequence used in volcano numbering, map, and **DIRECTORY**. This scheme should enable the reader to find references for a specific volcano, group, or eruption, but attention must also be paid to the *CAVW* series and the initial "global" references. Major regional references are highlighted with those words in bold italics at the end of the reference to more easily identify these more comprehensive compilations. Many eruptions subsequent to the *CAVW* date can be found in the global references section at the beginning of the References list and include those by Hantke (to 1959), the Volcanological Society of Japan (1960-1996), and the Smithsonian Institution (since 1968). The other references listed under "global" have been searched for volcanological data not found elsewhere, and the coverage of additional regional references is clear from their titles in most cases. For some we have added clarification in square brackets. References used for each volcano and eruption are entered with the appropriate data in our data file, but we have not attempted to cross-reference all sources in the tabular summaries presented here. Some references are listed because we have added data for a single eruption, but we may not have exhaustively searched the full reference for other possible additions to our file. Users will note that our references do not display special characters, (e.g., diacritical marks, superscripts or subscripts), and we include doi (Digital Object Identifier) citations only for those publications lacking standard volume and page number formats. In contrast to the first two editions, we display references alphabetically within region, rather than chronologically. Users looking for chronological data can find references on our website entry for each volcano.

Although these listings are a helpful guide to the literature for each region, they do not form a definitive bibliography. These are simply the references we have used in entering the data presented here. It is also the case that we have not consulted all the available literature, and our coverage is particularly weak in non-English journals. We urge readers to help us by sending references (reprints or PDF files if possible) of papers that are missing in our listings.

More detailed discussion of individual data elements, and how we have dealt with them, follows. Most section titles are keyed to the headings of the tables described briefly above, and data headings appear in bold-faced letters in the text.

Volcano Data

One of the most difficult problems of standardization has been the varying usage of the word "volcano." Definitions of "volcano" range from individual vents, measured in meters, through volcanic edifices measured in kilometers or tens of kilometers, to volcanic fields measured in hundreds of kilometers. In a compilation such as this one, the disadvantage of the narrowest definition is not so much the multiplicity of names introduced, as the dismembering of a single volcanic plumbing system's history into apparently unrelated separate records. The interiors of ancient volcanoes, now eroded and exposed for geologic study, show us that most subsurface magma chambers (the suppliers of lavas to overlying volcanoes) can be at least several kilometers in diameter. We also know that many contemporary volcanoes grow by additions from countless flank vents as well as activity at its summit. Consequently, we have tended to group closely spaced "volcanoes" such as the historical vents of the Canary Islands (many listed as separate volcanoes in the *CAVW*) by the major volcanic edifice on which they are located. The names of historical vents are retained under the **Area of activity** heading in the **DIRECTORY** and are alphabetically listed in the **GAZETTEER**. Volcanoes listed here are rarely closer than 10 km to their nearest neighbor, and are commonly separated by at least 20 km (Vogt, 1974).

Another problem is simply the identification of volcanoes. Prominent, steaming cones are easy to recognize, but water, ice, erosion, collapse processes, or dense vegetation can mask very dangerous volcanoes. Lake Taupo, in the center of New Zealand's North Island, is beautifully tranquil, with no obvious features alerting non-geologists to its particularly violent history. In the Alaskan summer of 1975, two volcanologists traced an ever-thickening ash layer to a vent now covered by the Hayes Glacier, and a "new" volcano was added to the NE end of the Aleutian arc (Miller and Smith, 1976). Also in Alaska, 5 decades passed before the true source of the largest eruption of the 20th century was recognized. Subsurface magma connections led to prominent collapse of Mount Katmai in 1912, and this was assumed to be the eruption's source until careful fieldwork showed it to be Katmai's inconspicuous neighbor, Novarupta (Curtis, 1968). These examples illustrate why the listings below must be recognized as incomplete. Inclusion in this compilation may depend on thoroughness of mapping (quite variable through the world's volcanic regions), and the most dangerous volcanoes may be those not yet recognized by compilers.

VOLCANO NAME

With few exceptions, we have used the **VOLCANO NAME** listed by the compilers of the *CAVW*, the contributors to the IAVCEI Post-Miocene data sheets, and individual volcanologists documenting additional volcanoes. We have preferred broader island names, locatable on standard maps, rather than crater names locally used to identify the full island volcano, and we have dropped modifiers, such as "Mount," when they seemed unnecessary. For Japanese volcanoes, we have listed the more widely used Hepburn style of spelling, although all Japanese *CAVW* names appear alphabetically as synonyms in the **GAZETTEER**. We have in a few cases used square brackets, however, to indicate alternative names that are widely encountered in the literature (e.g., "Azul, Cerro [Quizapu]" in Chile). Readers familiar with older spellings of Indonesian names will note that newer official names are used here with the older names appearing as synonyms in the **GAZETTEER**. With the new names, TJ, DJ, J, and OE appear as C, J, Y, and U, respectively.

Unlike the first two editions of this book, we have begun the process of adding special characters to volcano names from other languages. This has not been done systematically for all languages because some characters still elude our database capabilities, but diacritical marks for Spanish-language names, for example, covering a large percentage of the world's volcanic features, have been incorporated. We have also switched to mixed-case names throughout this book, which has increased legibility.

A few names have also been changed from the *CAVW* to reflect the broader time coverage of this compilation. Historically active features that are clearly part of a larger volcanic construct active in Holocene time have been listed under the larger feature. For example, the *CAVW* lists volcano number 0603-31= as Bromo; however, Bromo is but one of several youthful features in Tengger caldera, so we have used the caldera name for 0603-31= and indicated Bromo both as the area of historical activity in the **DIRECTORY** and as a subsidiary feature in the **GAZETTEER**. An extension of the time coverage problem is the volcano grouping issue mentioned above. Amboy, a solitary late Pleistocene cinder cone 200 km east of Los Angeles, is entered as a single volcano, and so is the Michoacán-Guanajuato Field, made up of nearly 1,000 cinder cones dotting a 200 x 200 km area in México (Hasenaka and Carmichael, 1985). Clearly not all "volcanoes" are equal, and caution must be used in any serious tabulation of them.

SUBREGION

A more general geographic location appears in parentheses after the volcano name in all tables. This normally consists of the **Subregion** designated by the *CAVW* compilers (and identified by the third and fourth digits of the *CAVW* volcano number system continued here; see map on inside back cover), but we have added a more general location name where useful for identification. Not all of these locations are fully displayed, some subregion names and a few unusually long volcano names have necessarily been abbreviated. In the **DIRECTORY** (where formal subregions are often clear from the regional sequence) we have often substituted a more specific location, such as island name, after the volcano name.

LATITUDE and LONGITUDE

Geographic coordinates are listed in decimal parts of a degree. This facilitates both digital manipulation of data and rapid estimation of distances between points (one degree of latitude being equal to 111 km). To retain some indication of the accuracy of original locations when converting from minutes and seconds, we have listed 3 digits to the right of the decimal point only where seconds were originally specified. We list 2 digits if only degrees and minutes were given in the original (e.g., 71° 41' = 71.68° whereas 71° 41' 01" = 71.684°). Readers should also beware of obviously generalized locations such as X.00° or Y.50°. If different references give different positions for the same volcano, we include each (with references) in the database, attempt to determine which is most reliable, and list that location here. For some regions, where our growing archive of topographic maps permits, we have obtained more precise locations than given in older sources. Maps for the Kuriles and Kamchatka, for example, have permitted correction of deliberately mislocated volcano positions that were a Cold War artifact. An asterisk (*) following the **LAT**itude entry warns the reader that the location is the center point of a broad volcanic field. The absence of an asterisk, however, does not mean that the coordinates given match the eruption site. Tens of kilometers may separate eruptive centers of a single volcano, particularly in large caldera complexes and rift zone settings.

Location data shown here are typically derived directly or indirectly from topographic maps. Regional topographic mapping does not utilize a standardized global datum, or a surface defined as "zero elevation" with respect to local gravity fields. Consequently, the European Datum, North American Datum, and Tokyo Datum, for example, do not provide an integrated global standard. Efforts to provide a world geodetic system to reference elevations and locations to an ellipsoidal model rather than to the geoid began in the 1950s. The current standard World Geodetic System, WGS84, was developed in the early 1980s and is now used by the Global Positioning System (GPS). The discrepancies between regional and global datums can often result in volcano summit locations offset from those on satellite imagery using the World Geodetic System.

Distribution of the world's volcanoes with respect to latitude has gained wide interest because of the relationship between large volcanic eruptions and climate, prompting the generation of climate-related eruption lists (Lamb, 1970; LaMarche and Hirschboeck, 1984). Major explosive eruptions drive volcanic ash and gas tens of kilometers into the

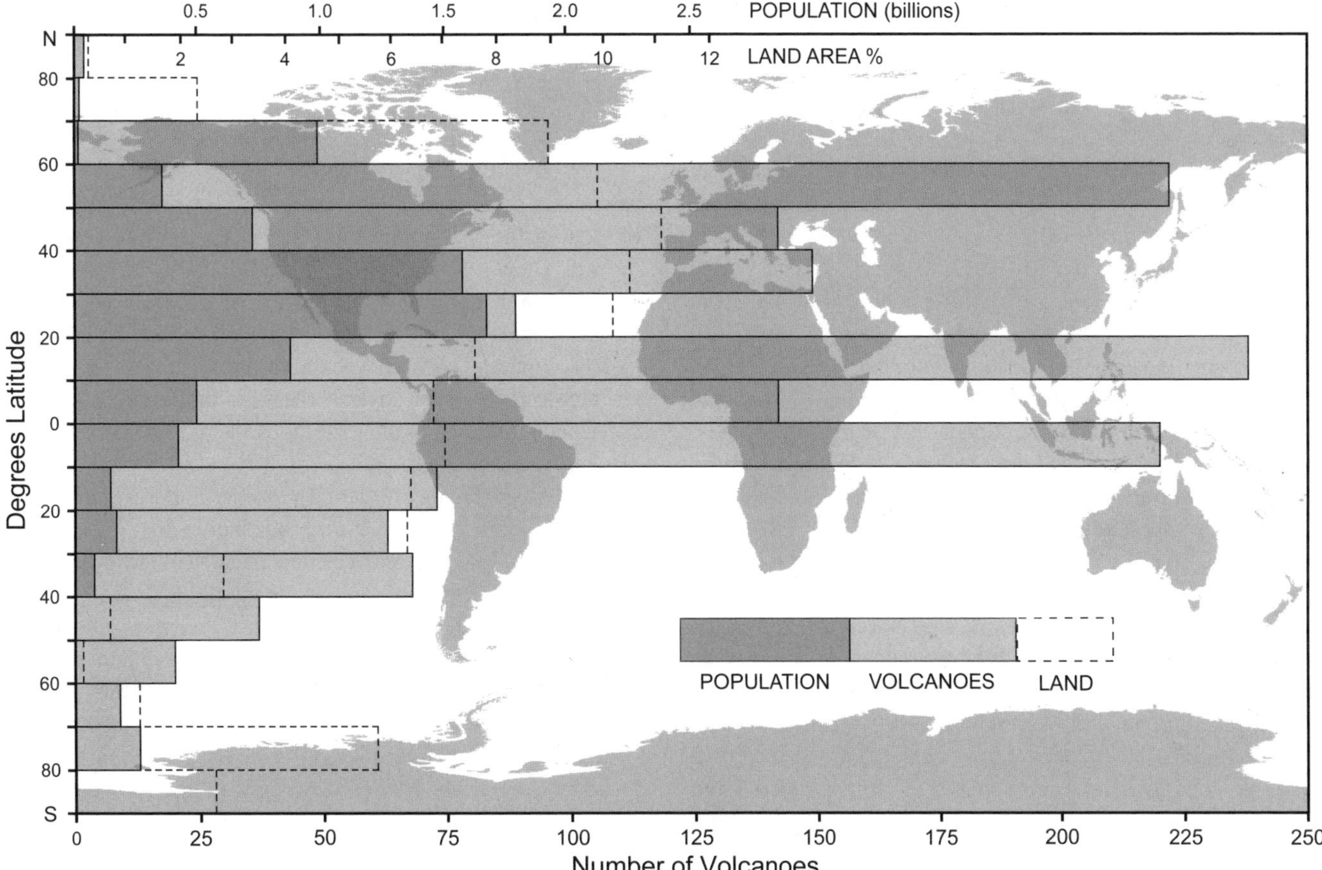

Figure 1. Distribution of known Holocene volcanoes per 10 degrees of latitude. The thin dashed line shows the percentage of land area per 10 degrees of latitude (Kossinna, 1933). Population numbers are 2008 data from LandScan.

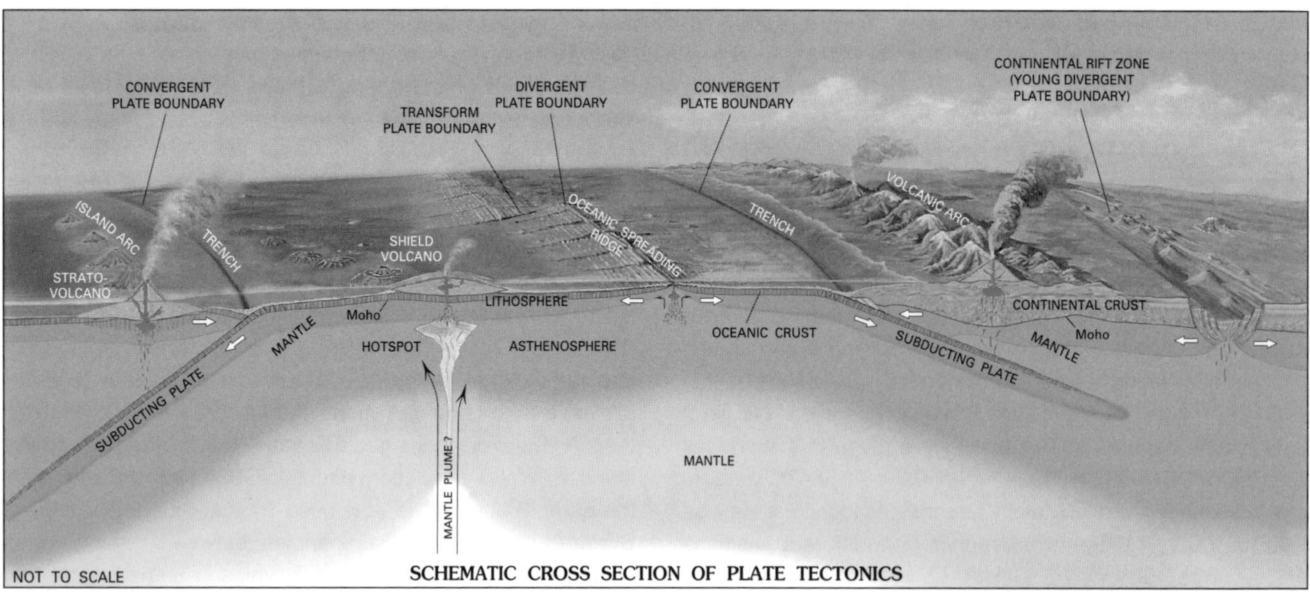

Figure 2. Plate Tectonics: schematic cross-section illustrating processes (modified from Simkin et al., 2006). Artists José F. Vigil and Robert I. Tilling.

stratosphere where, because fine ash and aerosol particles settle slowly and are not washed out by rain, they may be distributed around the globe by stratospheric circulation. For months or years before settling back to Earth, this layer of volcanic aerosol acts as a solar radiation filter, lowering temperatures on the Earth below it. The extent to which this process has affected global climate in the past is a matter of considerable scientific debate (Rampino et al., 1979, 1988; Bryson and Goodman, 1980; Sigurdsson and Laj, 1992; Robock, 1991; Simarski, 1992), but the fact that individual eruptions can affect climate is established. The catastrophic eruption of Indonesia's Tambora in 1815, for example, contributed to a lowering of global temperatures that brought June snow-storms to New England and widespread crop failure to northern latitudes (Stommel and Stommel, 1983; Harington, 1992). The decade of 1810-1819 was the coldest during the past 500 years, and a major eruption from an unknown tropical volcano in 1809 documented in polar ice cores may have contributed to global cooling prior to the 1815 eruption of Tambora and enhanced the effect of that eruption (Cole-Dai et al., 2009).The Earth's rotation strongly influences stratospheric circulation patterns, and therefore any concentration of the world's volcanoes by latitude is important in assessing their effect on global climate.

Figure 1 shows the distribution of the world's known volcanoes by latitude. Two thirds of the volcanoes are in the northern hemisphere and only 19% are between 10º S and the South Pole. The northern hemisphere concentration reflects the fact that two-thirds of the world's land area is also north of the equator, but nevertheless indicates the greater vulnerability of the northern hemisphere to volcanically induced climate change. This potential human impact is greatly exacerbated because 87% of Earth's population resides in the northern hemisphere.

The most northerly volcano in our list is an unnamed submarine volcano in the Arctic Ocean only 192 km from the North Pole. Three eruptions have been attributed to this site. The next most northerly volcano, on Jan Mayen Island and 2104 km from the pole, has been recently quite active with vigorous eruptions in 1970 and early 1985.

The southernmost historically active volcano is Mount Erebus, 1387 km from the South Pole on Ross Island, Antarctica. This volcano was erupting violently when first seen by Ross, in 1841, and is active today with a molten lava lake that has been circulating in its summit crater since at least 1972. Ash layers of probable Holocene age have been found in glaciers adjacent to the many young cinder cones of the Royal Society Range, 80 km closer to the pole, but no eruptions have been dated.

No significant concentration of volcanoes by **LONG**itude is obvious, but nearly 1000 volcanoes (or nearly two-thirds of those listed) lie around the Pacific Ocean margin forming the well known "Ring of Fire." If the Sunda arc of Indonesia, resulting from subduction of Indian Ocean crust NE under the Eurasian Plate, is included, the Ring of Fire figure rises to 70%. Arcuate belts of volcanoes are a striking feature of the planet (see inside cover maps) and they reflect, in most cases, convergence of the major tectonic plates that make up the Earth's outer shell.

These vast plates (Figure 2), moving at speeds of only a few centimeters per year, form a shifting jig-saw puzzle with the major earthquake and volcano belts marking the unrest at plate boundaries (e.g., Cox and Hart, 1986; Sullivan, 1991; Kious and Tilling, 1996). Where plates converge, the more dense plate normally descends beneath the less dense plate, and a line of volcanoes grows above. Because this type of volcanism is normally both explosive and near (if not on) land, where eruptions or their deposits are visible, these roughly two-thirds of known Holocene volcanoes account for more than four-fifths of confirmed Holocene eruptions (Figure 3).

The spreading apart of major plates, however, is characterized by the relatively nonexplosive outpouring of fluid lava and commonly takes place one or more kilometers below sea level. Consequently we have a very incomplete record of this

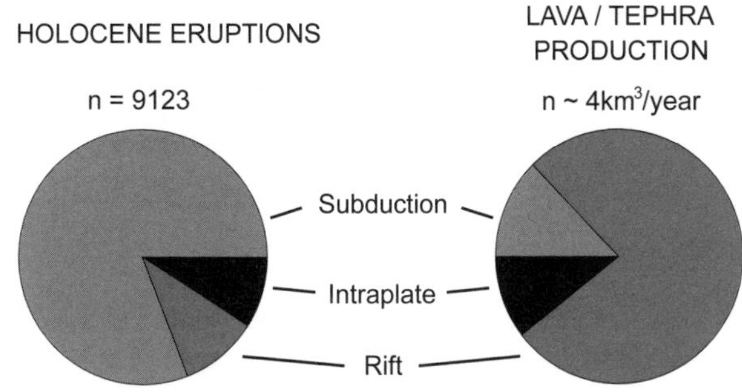

Figure 3. Pie diagrams contrasting the volcanism that we see with that we don't. Left diagram from Smithsonian data shows proportion of confirmed Holocene eruptions from subduction zones, mid-ocean ridges, and hotspot settings. Right diagram (Crisp, 1984), building on earlier work of Nakamura (1974), shows proportion of estimated annual magma budget in the same settings.

important type of volcanism. Rift volcanism forms only about a tenth of our eruption file and is dominated by those few regions, such as East Africa and Iceland, where the spreading apart of plates takes place on land.

A similar percentage (about 9%) represents volcanism within major plates rather than at their boundaries. This takes place where deep "hot spots" penetrate the overlying crust, and old volcanic products are carried slowly away from the volcanic center by the moving plate. This record of intraplate volcanism is considerably better than that for the volcanism of spreading ocean ridges, which is significantly underrepresented.

The numbers for rift eruptions are even lower when data are restricted to historical eruptions, as they were in our 2nd edition. The sharp contrast between the volcanism we see and the submarine volcanism we largely don't see shows up dramatically in the estimates of annual magma budgets (Crisp, 1984) that reveal that more than ¾ of the world's magma output is estimated to originate from rift environments.

ELEVATION

ELEVation of each volcano's highest point is listed in meters above or below sea level. Elevation for the same volcano may differ because of different surveying techniques or because of volcanological changes (e.g., the 400 m reduction in Mount St. Helens' summit height due to edifice collapse at the onset of the 1980 eruption). As with latitude and longitude, when separate values for the same feature appear in different references, we list both (with reference) in the database and display here the one that seems most reliable. If we are unable to resolve a difference any other way, we normally display the more recent figure. Most elevations, both in the *CAVW* and original references, are given in meters, but when we have had to convert from other units we have attempted to retain a measure of the original's accuracy by rounding the conversion to the same number of significant figures as in the original. Thus a 2,600 ft elevation, apparently rounded to the nearest 100 ft, is listed here as 790 m rather than the 792 m figure that is the exact metric equivalent (but implies greater accuracy than in the original measurement).

Fewer than 2% of the listed volcanoes, most of them submarine, have **ELEV**ations unknown to us. Submarine volcano elevations (or depths) are particularly unreliable because changes are often rapid, dramatic, and unrecorded. We normally list the most recent elevation when several are given, but caution should be used with *all* submarine volcano elevations.

The summits of roughly 24% of the subaerial volcanoes in our list are within 1000 m of sea level, 64% are within 2000 m and 82% are within 3000 m of sea level (Figure 4). Only 76 volcanoes, or 5% of our file, have elevations above 5000 m (16,400 ft): 86% of these are in the South American Andes and most of those are in that chain's central segment (15-28° S).

The highest volcano with historical eruptions is Llullaillaco (volcano number 1505-11=) in the northern Chilean Andes. Its elevation is 6739 m, and three eruptions were recorded there in the second half of the 19th century. Nevado Ojos del Salado, 267 km to the south of and 148 m higher than Llullaillaco, has erupted during the Holocene, and its youthful nature suggests that its lack of historical eruptions stems only from its remote location, and that it is rightfully the world's highest volcano above sea level. The only higher mountain in the Americas, Argentina's Aconcagua at 6962 m, was listed as active by Darwin during the voyage of the *Beagle*, but subsequent geologic studies have shown that its volcanic rocks date back to the Miocene and its height results from imbricate thrust faulting.

A very different picture of the highest volcano emerges when considering the height of volcanic edifices themselves, as measured from their constructional bases rather than from sea level. Massive oceanic shield volcanoes, such as Hawaii's Mauna Loa, rise as much as 9000 m above the sea floor. These volcanoes are by far the world's largest by volume, dwarfing the continental-margin stratovolcanoes of the Andes. Furthermore, the weight of the countless overlapping lava

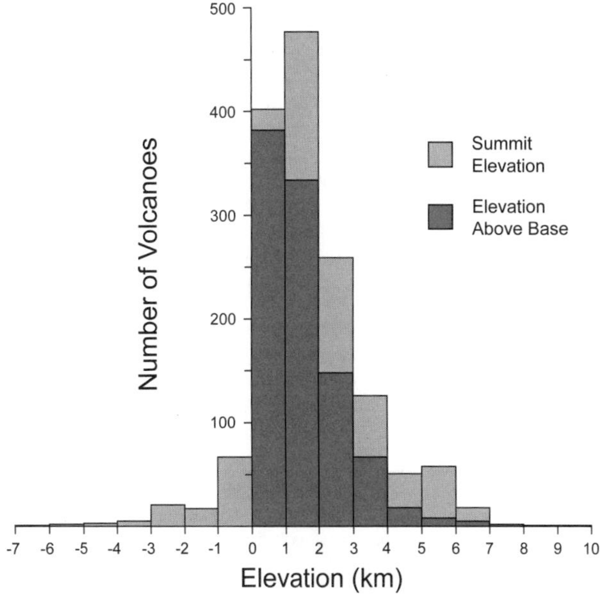

Figure 4. Distribution of known volcanoes by elevation of summit (lighter fill) and elevation above their constructional base (darker fill). Addition of the many unknown volcanoes of the sea floor would greatly alter this distribution.

flows forming these shield volcanoes substantially depresses the oceanic crust beneath them. Geophysical evidence indicates that the full height of Mauna Loa above its base is an astounding 17 kilometers (Lipman, 1995), nearly twice the height of Mount Everest above sea level. Nevados Ojos del Salado, the world's highest volcano above sea level, rises only about 2000 m above its base. The broad summit of Mauna Loa shield volcano is 2700 m lower than Nevados Ojos del Salado, but it's height above base is almost 10 times that of the Andean volcano.

The deepest submarine volcano in our list has less significance because the record is so poor. Seawater not only hides eruptions from view, but its weight also provides enormous pressure on the deep-sea floor, inhibiting (and often prohibiting) the explosive release of volcanic gases that frequently calls attention to shallow submarine eruptions. A few historical reports, however, give some credence to explosive volcanism on the deep-sea floor: 1955 activity at 4000 m near Hawaii (1302-10=), 1865 activity at 4200 m west of the Azores (1801-04=), uncertain 1852 activity at 5300 m in the central mid-Atlantic (1805-04=), and an 1850 event at about 6000 m depth off Taiwan. Non-explosive volcanism regularly takes place at great depths on the ocean floor, as shown by photography of fresh volcanic features at depths of ~5 km in the Cayman Trough, Caribbean Sea (Ballard, 1976), but our record of these deep submarine events is exceedingly scant. Recent submersible expeditions sponsored by NSF and NOAA, however, have permitted extremely close range documentation of long-term explosive and effusive eruptions from volcanoes in the Mariana and Tonga arcs (Embley et al., 2006; Chadwick et al., 2008; Rubin et al., 2009).

As noted above, the height of a volcano above its regional

VPI	Population	Criteria
VPI_5	~47 million	Potentially lethal proximal volcanic effects from small-to-moderately large eruptions (VEI 1-3). Probability of pyroclastic flows to 5 km, 0.7 for VEI 3; probability of >10 cm ash at 5 km, 0.55 for VEI 3.
VPI_{10}	~58 million	Evacuation may be needed for moderately large eruptions (VEI 3-4). Probability of pyroclastic flows to 10 km, 0.2 for VEI 3, 0.6 for VEI 4-5; probability of >10 cm ash at 10 km, 0.4 for VEI 3 and 0.9 for VEI ≥4.
VPI_{30}	~201 million	Infrastructure-threatening tephra accumulations and distally diminishing pyroclastic flows from moderately large-to-large eruptions (VEI 4-5). Probability of pyroclastic flows to >15 km, 0.3 at VEI 4-5; probablity of >10 cm ash at 30 km, 0.8 for VEI ≥4.
VPI_{100}	~757 million	Significant potential impact even in distal areas from tephra accumulation from large-volume eruptions (VEI 5-6). Probability of >10 cm of ash at 100 km, 0.55 at VEI ≥4; >70 cm of ash at 100 km, 0.1.

Table 2. Population data criteria, modified from Ewert and Harpel (2004) and Ewert et al. (2005), with probability data from Newhall and Hoblitt (2002).

0 - 0	5 - >10,000
1 - <10	6 - >100,000
2 - >10	7 - >1,000,000
3 - >100	8 - >10,000,000
4 - >1000	

Table 3. Population data codes.

base is of more volcanological interest than its absolute elevation above sea level, but data are unavailable for 37% of the listed volcanoes and are often a highly subjective measurement, particularly in the case of oceanic volcanoes. With neighboring volcanoes, for example, it is often impossible to state what proportion of each summit elevation is the result of its own plumbing system and how much is contributed by its neighbor (or a now-buried, older volcano). Furthermore, lava flows and volcaniclastic aprons can disguise the buried morphology of the substrate over which the volcanoes are constructed, making the volcanoes appear higher than they actually are. We thus do not include data on the relative heights of volcanic edifices above their base in the **DIRECTORY**, but existing data are displayed by the darker bars in Figure 4. This implies that nearly three-fourths of volcanoes are less than 2000 m high, and nearly 9 out of 10 are less than 3000 m high. These numbers are skewed at both ends, however, by the fact that the most common volcano type, low-elevation cinder cones, is included only once in the data for volcanic fields, and elevation data for large submarine volcanoes are likewise underrepresented.

Volcanoes vary widely in size, and similar problems are associated with volume estimates of volcanic edifices. The morphology of the buried base of a volcano can be difficult to determine, and as noted above, flank deposits can extend the apparent base of a volcano to elevations well below its exposed substrate. Consequently, relatively few volcanoes have had accurate volume estimates. We have volume data for less than a quarter of the Holocene volcanoes in our file, and thus do not display them in this compilation. The existing data indicate that volcano volumes vary over a half dozen orders of magnitude, ranging from less than a cubic kilometer for small cinder cones to the 95,300 km^3 estimated volume of the massive Mauna Loa shield volcano. The median volume is just under 100 km^3, but meaningful comparisons are problematical because, as with data for the heights of volcanoes, determining the base of a volcano is difficult and the numbers of small volume edifices (such as cinder cones) are significantly underestimated.

POPULATION

The number of people living in proximity to volcanoes has clear volcanic hazards implications, and new population datasets help assess volcanic risk. The LandScan population dataset produced by the Oak Ridge National Laboratory apportions census counts to each grid cell based on likelihood coefficients incorporating proximity to roads, slope, land cover, nighttime lights, and other data. The LandScan 2008 data set was applied to the Smithsonian Holocene volcano database

Rock Type	Code	Rock Names
Basaltic	B	**Basalt, Picro-basalt**, Alkali-basalt, Alkali-olivine-basalt, Subalkaline-basalt, Tholeiitic basalt, Mid-Ocean Ridge basalt (MORB), Ankaramite, Kulaite, Picrobasalt, Picrite, Oceanite
	X	**Tephrite, Basanite, Trachybasalt**, Hawaiite, Minette, Ankaramite, Basanitoid, Nepheline-basanite, Leucite-basanite, Kivite, Trachydolerite, Limburgite, Basaltic-latite
Andesitic	A	**Andesite, Basaltic-andesite**, Lati-andesite, Boninite, Bajaite, Icelandite, Spessartite
	Y	**Trachyandesite, Basaltic trachyandesite**, Mugearite, Shoshonite, Benmoreite, Latite, Quartz-latite, Hornblende-lamprophyre, Banakite, Absarokite, Tristanite, Doreite
Dacitic	D	**Dacite**, Rhyodacite
Rhyolitic	R	**Rhyolite**, Peralkaline rhyolite, Comendite, Pantellerite, Liparite
Trachytic	T	**Trachyte**, Trachydacite, Peralkaline trachyte, Pantelleritic-trachyte, Comenditic-trachyte, Eutaxite
Phonolitic	P	**Phonolite**, Trachyphonolite
	Z	**Phonotephrite, Tephriphonolite**, Tahitite
Foiditic	F	**Foidite**, Nephelinite, Melilite-Nephelinite, Melilitite, Leucitite, Melilite-Leucitite, Carbonatite, Ankaratrite, Etindite, Katungite, Melilite-basalt, Analcine-basalt, Analcimite, Sövite
Unknown	U	No known chemical analyses or rock-type descriptions

Table 4. Dominant rock types for volcanoes. Bolded red names mark fields of the total alkali-silica (TAS) diagrams of Le Bas et al. (1986) and Le Maitre et al. (2002), with other rock type names from the literature in black.

to calculate population densities surrounding volcanoes at radii of 5, 10, 30, and 100 km (Siebert et al., 2008). This builds on Volcano Population Index (VPI) data calculated by Ewert and Harpel (2004) at VPI_5 and VPI_{10} radii for Central American volcanoes and at VPI_{30} radii for U.S. volcanoes (Ewert et al., 2005) as a component of the National Volcanic Early Warning System (NVEWS). Calculations were made here for individual volcanoes at VPI_5, VPI_{10}, VPI_{30}, and VPI_{100} radii (Table 2) and are displayed in order of magnitude values at each radius (Table 3).

The number 4 at VPI_5 indicates that more than 1000 people reside within 5 km of the volcano's summit, the number 7 at VPI_{100} indicates that more than 1 million people live within 100 km of the volcano. Data also factor population densities at volcanic fields with large numbers of vents over broad areas, oceanic shield volcanoes with large footprints, and large silicic calderas. For volcanic fields, minimum population densities were calculated for those living within a rectangle encompassing the known footprint of the volcanic field or a circle of 20 km radius (the average radius of database volcanic fields with documented dimensions). Similarly, 20 km minimum radii were used for large oceanic shield volcanoes and large silicic calderas that could erupt from vents in broad areas over their flanks.

These data do not account for non-resident visitors to national parks, forests, or other recreational areas in volcanic regions, which form an unknown, but sometimes non-trivial component of persons at risk from volcanic eruptions.

ROCK TYPE

This field fills in an important gap in the first two editions of *Volcanoes of the World* and summarizes the lithologic character of Earth's volcanoes. It provides a broad-brush summary of up to five of the most common rock types at a volcano, listed in general order of abundance. Rock types of younger-stage edifices of long-term volcanic systems are given precedence, however, even if not volumetrically dominant. Pre-Quaternary lithologies may also be included.

Single-letter, mnemonic codes are used (B = Basalt, A = Andesite, etc.), although this was not possible for three subdivided alkalic fields, labeled "X," "Y," and "Z," respectively (Figure 5). Capital letters are used for codes, unless a rock type is described as "minor," "rare," or, if quantified, consists of less than 10% of the total volume, in which case lower case letters are used. The ten fields used in this compilation are based on the total alkali-silica (TAS) diagrams of Le Bas et al. (1986), which represent the conclusions of three decades' deliberation of the Subcommission on the Systematics of Igneous Rocks of the International Union of Geological Sciences (IUGS), as summarized in Le Maitre et al. (2002).

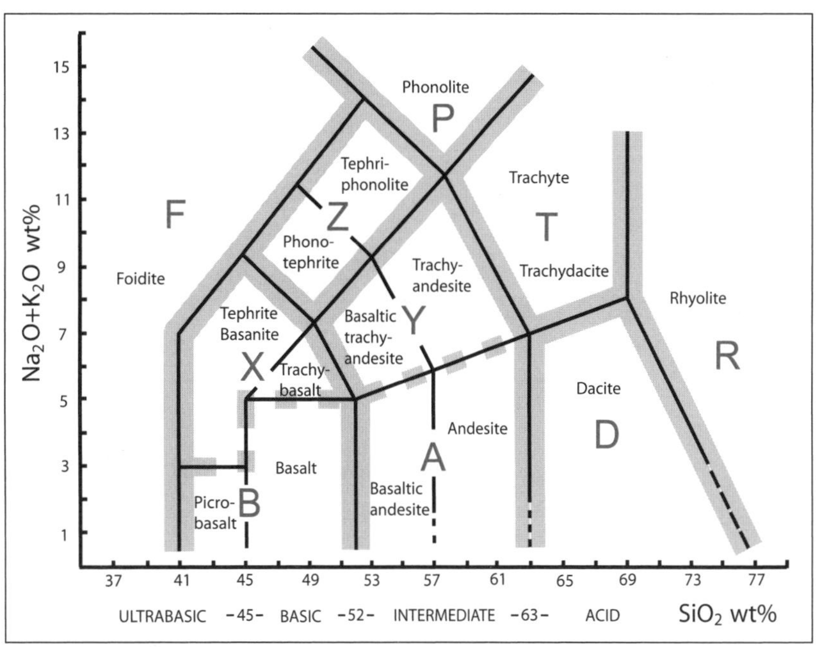

Figure 5. Dominant rock types for volcanoes. Bolded red letters mark fields used in the Directory tables of the total alkali-silica (TAS) diagrams of Le Bas et al. (1986) and Le Maitre et al. (2002).

Published TAS plots, when available, were used to determine the rock-type assignments. In the absence of published normalized geochemical analyses or TAS plots, the rock names assigned by authors of individual papers are shown.

Although the **Rock Type** field summarizes lithological variation at a volcano, its limitations should be kept in mind. Many volcanoes have not been studied in sufficient detail to accurately document their petrologic variation. In the absence of available petrological papers, data from earlier compilations, which may list only the most dominant rock type(s), were used. Even petrologically oriented papers often do not contain TAS diagrams, and rock-name usage has varied considerably; a plethora of published rock names, many of which have had variable definitions and can overlap TAS fields, complicates standardized summary of geochemical variation. Table 4 is only a partial list of rock-type names falling within (or sometimes straddling) TAS fields, whose names appear in red type. Users should note that for many volcanoes, published geochemical analyses are not available, and authors may have used broad definitions of basalt and andesite, for example, that do not distinguish more alkalic basalts and andesites that would otherwise be assigned codes "X" or "Y," respectively.

Although an attempt was made to infer relative abundance from descriptions of the volcanic history, the proportion of rock types at a volcano is rarely quantified, and the sequence of rock-type codes should be considered an approximation. Incorporation of this generalized petrological data is a new component of our database, and we have conducted only a preliminary search for petrologically oriented papers. These fields are consequently subject to modification as new (and previously unseen) data are incorporated, but we felt that these preliminary petrological summaries provide valuable context for the accompanying volcano and eruption data.

TYPE (MORPHOLOGY)

Volcanoes come in a variety of shapes and sizes. Under the heading of **Type**, we have attempted to characterize the morphology of each volcano. Several features may be entered into our database in descending order of size, but only an abbreviated version of the major feature is printed in the **DIRECTORY** and **GAZETTEER**. If, for example, a stratovolcano contains a caldera that is itself filled by lava domes and pyroclastic cones, this will typically appear only as "**Stratovolcano**" in the **DIRECTORY** and **GAZETTEER**. We have mostly followed the *CAVW* entry, and inspection of the table of types (see inside front cover) shows the lack of standardized usage. Figure 6 illustrates the main profiles shown, but the reader should consult volcanological textbooks mentioned above and those dealing more specifically with morphology (e.g., Cotton, 1969; Ollier, 1969) for further description (and recognize that different volcanologists have

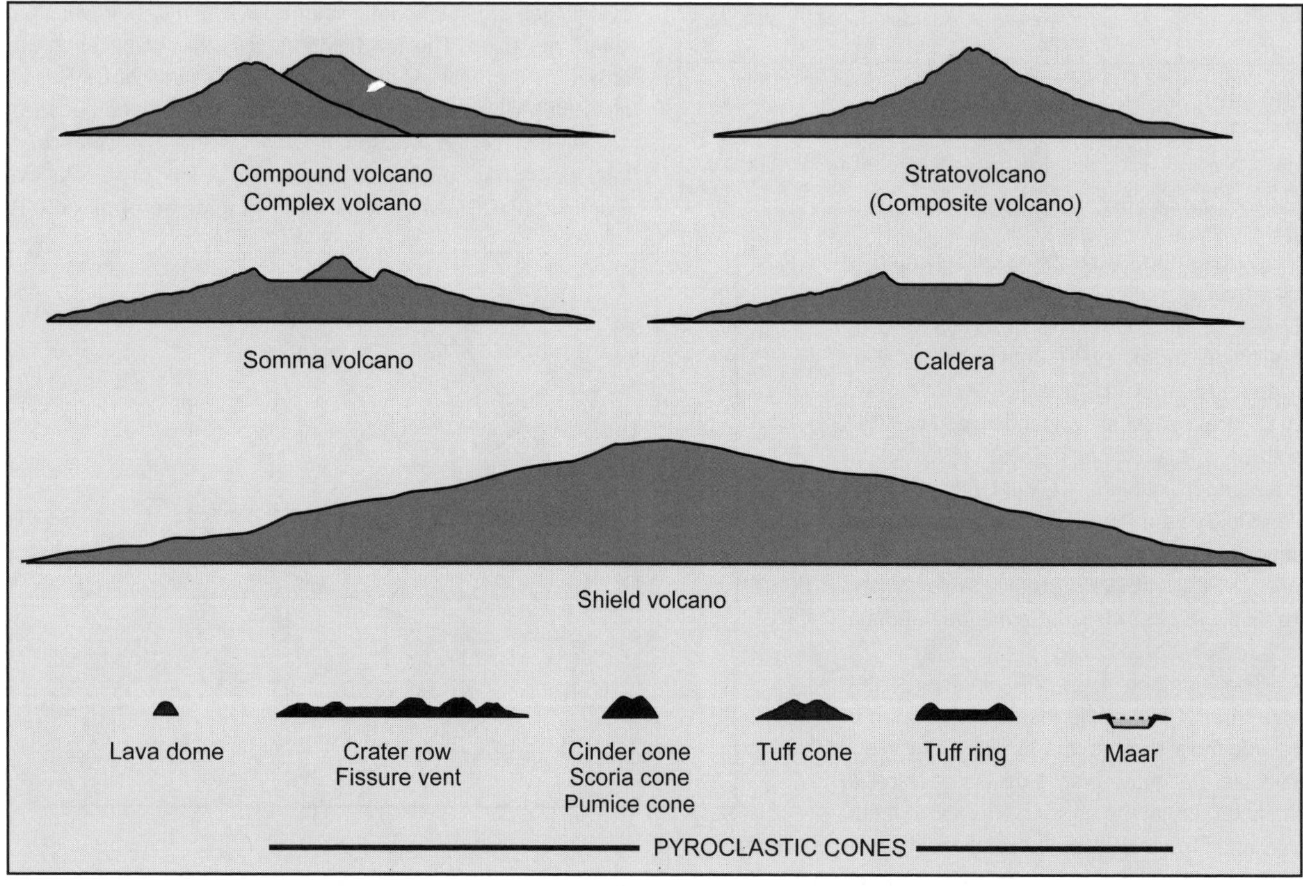

Figure 6. Types of volcanoes. Schematic profiles are vertically exaggerated by 2:1 (colored fill) and 4:1 (black fill) from the data of Pike (1978). Relative sizes are only approximate, as dimensions vary within each group.

used different terms for the same features). Interest in the landforms of other planets has prompted a more quantitative approach to the morphology of Earth's volcanoes (Pike, 1978). Lacking a standardized nomenclature, however, we have generally listed the volcano types as given in the various sources used in our compilation. This data element is not suitable for a search for all examples of a given volcano type. A tuff cone, for example, might be listed under "**Cone**," "**Pyroclastic cone**," "**Tuff cone**," "**Maar**," or possibly "**Explosion crater**" or "**Pumice cone**," and would not be listed at all in the **DIRECTORY** if it is a subsidiary feature of a larger volcanic landform. These data, however, provide helpful information about the size and shape of each volcano listed.

VOLCANO NUMBER

The volcano number consists of a 4-digit number identifying region and subregion, followed (after a hyphen) by a 2- or 3-digit individual volcano number. This scheme follows that of the *CAVW* and has already been discussed above under **MAPS and REGIONAL NUMBERING SCHEME** (p. 3). The **DIRECTORY** is sequenced by volcano **Number**, which is repeated as the basic cross-referencing device in the **CHRONOLOGY** and **GAZETTEER** sections as well. We have followed the exact *CAVW* numbering where possible, and volcanoes bearing numbers identical to those used by the *CAVW* (including an unpublished draft of the Iceland catalog) carry an "=" symbol at the end of the number to facilitate reference to the *CAVW* for fuller descriptions. When we have added a volcano between those already numbered, we have added a third numeral. Thus Panarea and Lipari, between Stromboli (0101-04=) and Vulcano (0101-05-), are given the numbers 0101-041 and 0101-042, respectively, rather than the next available two-digit number at the end of the Italian subregion. This scheme permits natural geographic sequencing of volcanoes while broadly retaining original *CAVW* numbering. When adding numbers in regions not previously numbered by the *CAVW*, and when renumbering in regions such as the Canary Islands and the western United States, we have used only two numerals for the individual volcano number but have designated the fact that it cannot be found under this number in the *CAVW* by adding a "-" in the last place.

STATUS

This element states, essentially, the most persuasive reason for including each volcano in this compilation. A "**Historical**" **Status**, used for eruptions documented during or shortly after their occurrence, is the best evidence for inclusion. We list 570 volcanoes with historical eruptions, the criterion used by many people terming a volcano "active." Thirty volcanoes had their first historical eruption since our 2nd edition in 1994, including three effusive eruptions in the East African Rift from 2005-2008, submarine eruptions on the Juan de Fuca ridge, and the Mariana and Tonga arcs. The scale of these eruptions ranges from the relatively modest phreatic eruptions from Four-Peaked volcano in Alaska in 2006 to the vigorous explosive activity from Anatahan in the Marianas in 2003 and Chaitén in southern Chile in 2008.

The length of the historical record varies widely regionally, however, from BC dates in the Mediterranean, to only a few hundred years in sparsely populated regions like Kamchatka and the Aleutians. In our second edition we considered a wall mural at the Catal Hayuk excavation near Hasan Dagi and Karapinar volcanoes in Central Turkey to represent the first documented historical eruption (Mellaart, 1967), but this interpretation has been controversial (Meece, 2006). The regionally variability of the historical record led us to expand our data to include volcanoes with eruptions during the last 10,000 years, as determined by techniques, such as "**Radiocarbon**" dating. For volcanoes with different eruptions dated by different techniques, we have entered under **Status** the technique that seemed to confirm Holocene activity most certainly. These techniques are listed on the inside front cover and summarized below under **DATING TECHNIQUES** (p. 20-24). We should mention, however, that the "**Anthropology**" status covers volcanoes with undated (but recent) activity described in native legends as well as activity dated by buried artifacts.

The remaining **Status** categories cover the many volcanoes (45% of our file) for which Holocene eruptions have not been dated, but are either likely or possible. These status categories will be discussed in order of decreasing certainty.

First in certainty for undated eruptions comes the variety of general evidence lumped together under "**Holocene**" status. These locations, although without dated products, are considered likely to have been active in postglacial time. Evidence includes volcanic products overlying latest Pleistocene glacial debris, youthful volcanic landforms in areas where erosion should have been pronounced in many thousands of years, and vegetation patterns that would have been far richer if the volcanic substrates were more than a few thousand (or hundred) years old. We have included in this category volcanoes mapped by original authors simply as "Holocene" or "postglacial." Some subjectivity is involved in this assignment, and the compiler is dependent upon the field experience of the original author. Many early investigators, unaware of slow erosion rates in arid regions, described lava flows as "extremely fresh, probably erupted within the last few hundred or few thousand years," but later radiometric dating has shown them to be Pleistocene or even older. We have generally required relatively strong evidence for entry under this category, and 381 volcanoes bear "**Holocene**" status in our file, with another 193 (with distinctly less certainty) are identified as "**Holocene?**." This group includes locations for which equally reliable sources disagree over the existence of Holocene volcanism. Also included are those for which uncertainty is expressed by the original author (e.g., "perhaps Holocene age"), and line straddlers (e.g., "late Pleistocene or early Holocene"). We emphasize the uncertainties attending these age assignments by printing their **Status** in a less prominent regular font. The number of volcanoes in this category has increased in this edition as more precise dating of volcanoes in regions such as Kamchatka has called into question the age of many of those volcanoes thought to have been Holocene in age due to their youthful morphological appearance.

Many volcanoes with obviously recent, but undated, eruptions are still visibly internally hot, as evidenced by surface thermal features. For 67 volcanic locations, or 4% of our file, one or more of the following thermal features are displayed in the **Status** category. "**Fumarolic**" locations are those characterized by steam and volcanic gas, or fume, reaching the surface. Temperatures are near the boiling point of water, and a substantial supply of groundwater is necessary. In our 1981 edition, we used the word "**Solfataric**" for **Status** when sulfur dominated the volcanic gases, but we have since encountered inconsistencies with this usage and have combined it with "**Fumarolic**" here. When the volume of water is large compared to steam and gas, however, the words "**Hot springs**" are used. A "**Fumarolic**" or "**Hot springs**" status is assigned, however, only where we have seen no explicit evidence for Holocene ***eruptive*** activity. Recent bathymetric exploration has found evidence for vigorous thermal activity at young submarine volcanoes in subduction-related arc settings such as the Kermadec-Tonga (Stoffers et al., 2006) and Mariana (Embley et al., 2006; Chadwick et al., 2008) arcs. Although many subaerial thermal features require only a high local heat flow and groundwater, we have not included such features unless they are clearly related to Holocene volcanism, and for deep-sea, mid-ocean ridge volcanism we have only entered thermally active centers with dated Holocene volcanism.

Our least certain **Status** category, "**Uncertain**," is used for 48 volcanoes: with possible Holocene activity, but with sufficiently questionable documentation that we wanted to draw attention to that uncertainty. These entries include mariner's equivocal reports of submarine volcanism and volcanoes known only by uncertain reports of historical activity (with no other evidence of Holocene eruptions). As with volcanoes classified as "**Holocene?**," we emphasize the uncertainties attending these age assignments by printing their **Status** in a less prominent regular font. The nature of this uncertainty is normally described in the free-form "remarks" category of our database, but cannot be displayed in the tabular formats presented here.

One significant change from the previous editions with respect to **Status** needs to be mentioned. In the first two editions of this book we followed the *CAVW* in including some thermal features, such as fumarolic fields, despite absence of other evidence for their Holocene volcanism. In fact, some areas, such as the Valles and Long Valley calderas in the western United States, show good evidence precluding eruptions in the last 10,000 years (but equally good evidence of still-molten magma below the surface). In these cases the word "**Pleistocene**" preceded the appropriate thermal feature listed above. For 7 of these, the designation "**Pleistocene-Geysers**" was used to identify uncommon variations of hot springs from which steam and water are periodically erupted. These volcanoes are no longer included with the Holocene volcanoes, but are listed with the Pleistocene volcanoes discussed below and also appear in the **GAZETTEER**.

P	Pleistocene
P?	Uncertain Pleistocene
Q	Quaternary (Pleistocene or Holocene)
PT	Pleistocene-thermal
PM	Post-Miocene

Table 5. Pleistocene status codes.

Finally, we should comment on the "youthful" volcanoes that we have ***not*** included in the Holocene file. A volcano mapped as "Quaternary" would not be entered unless more specific Holocene age data were available. When a group of volcanoes is listed in a region of "Pleistocene-Holocene volcanism," we have entered only those for which Holocene evidence is available. Volcanoes listed as Holocene, or "active," in previous compilations, but later found to be Pleistocene or older, have also been excluded from the Holocene file. For a few "volcanoes," well established in the literature (such as the *CAVW*, or our first two editions) but later found to be misidentifications, we have entered "**Not a Volcano**" under **Status**. These have not been entered in any volcano totals and do not appear on our map, but we thought it best to include them in the **DIRECTORY** and **GAZETTEER** to avoid confusion when making comparisons with earlier lists.

In summary, the **Status** category conveys the following hierarchical progression from high to low certainty of Holocene volcanism: (1) "**Historical**," (2) dated eruptions based on a spectrum of techniques from "**Hydrophonic**" through "**Radiocarbon**" to "**Anthropology**," which is transitional to (3) "**Holocene**," (4) thermal features such as "**Fumarolic**," (5) "**Holocene?**," and (6) "**Uncertain**." Any entry can (and probably does) carry evidence to be found under lower **levels** of this hierarchy, but we have entered the highest **Status** category indicated by the data known to us. Furthermore, the **Status** listed is that of the ***most recent eruptive*** activity. A major Pleistocene center with only a single Holocene flank vent, for example, would have a "**Holocene**" status.

For Pleistocene volcanoes a different **Status** assignment is used (Table 5). These are shown in the **PRELIMINARY LIST OF PLEISTOCENE VOLCANOES** only by a one or two column code, but their **Status** is spelled out in the **GAZETTEER**. The "**P?**" **Status** indicates volcanoes whose age is considered to be either early Pleistocene or late Pliocene. A "**Q**" Status is used for volcanoes that are likely Pleistocene in age, but could be as young as Holocene. "**PT**" indicates volcanoes that ceased eruptive activity during the Pleistocene, but currently display thermal activity in the form of fumaroles, hot springs, or geysers. The "**PM**" status is reserved for volcanoes in the IAVCEI (1973-80) Post-Miocene listing for which no age is stated and for which we have not seen subsequent information as to their age. An unknown number of these volcanoes are of Pliocene age, but a few could be as young as Holocene. As with the Holocene volcanoes, the **Status** listed for Pleistocene volcanoes is that of the ***most recent eruptive*** activity.

Eruption Data

The arrival of volcanic products at the Earth's surface is termed an eruption. At first glance it might appear surprising that the ambiguity regarding what constitutes a volcano extends to eruptions as well. Some definitions of the word include purely gaseous expulsions, but we confine the term to events that involve the explosive ejection of fragmental material, the effusion of molten lava, or both. Other definitions restrict eruptions to magmatic events, but the fragmental material ejected may be old as well as new. The explosive interaction of volcanically generated heat and near-surface water can cause dramatic eruptions without any fresh volcanic material reaching the surface, and from a volcanic hazards perspective are as important to document as magmatic events.

Eruptions vary widely both in magnitude and duration, with some eruptions over in minutes and others going on for centuries. They also display a wide variety in eruptive styles and processes. Volcanologists traditionally have described eruptions in terms of characteristic activity at particular volcanoes or volcanic regions. Although we do not document these descriptive terms in our database, we illustrate common eruption types in Figure 7.

Two terms originated from volcanoes in Italy's Aeolian Islands. **Strombolian** eruptions derive their name from the long-term eruptions at Stromboli volcano. Discrete, sometimes rhythmic explosions common at low-viscosity, basaltic to basaltic-andesite volcanoes eject incandescent lava fragments that can form spectacular night-time displays. The nearby island of Vulcano lent its name to more energetic **vulcanian** eruptions, common at stratovolcanoes and lava domes, which eject blocks, bombs and tephra, accompanied by atmospheric shock waves.

Shallow submarine eruptions where water has access to the vent are named **surstseyan** after the 1963-1967 eruptions that formed the island of Surtsey off the south coast of Iceland. These explosive bursts eject a column of ash, mud, and steam, with individual ejected blocks characteristically trailing cockscomb sprays of ash and steam, and are sometimes accompanied by base surges (laterally driven clouds of gas and ash expanding outward above the sea surface from the base of the eruption column). This type of magma-water interaction is common at shallow submarine eruptions and at crater lakes.

Pelean eruptions were named from the renowned 1902 eruption of Pelée volcano on the West Indies island of Martinique, when explosive eruptions accompanying collapse of summit lava domes produced pyroclastic flows that devastated the town of St. Pierre and its 28,000 inhabitants. These dome-collapse pyroclastic flows are often referred to as Merapi-type pyroclastic flows, which are common at that very active Indonesian volcano on the island of Java.

Much larger explosive eruptions are named not for a volcano, but from the observations of Pliny the Younger during the 79 AD eruption of Italy's Vesuvius volcano. **Plinian** eruptions, the most powerful known, are magmatic eruptions with convective eruption columns that eject large volumes of ash to high altitudes that are dispersed by winds over huge areas. Quantification of grain-size characteristics has led to subdivision into subplinian, plinian, phreatoplinian (major interaction with external water), and ultraplinian eruptions.

Dominantly effusive eruptions are named after two volcano-rich regions, Hawaii and Iceland. **Hawaiian** eruptions can produce long-term activity feeding summit crater lava lakes and the effusion of lava flows fed by sustained lava fountains along radial fissures. **Icelandic** eruptions display similar activity, but from regional fissures such as those that produced the voluminous lava flows of the 1783 "Laki fires" eruption from Grímsvötn volcano. Icelandic eruptions may also include explosive activity from often ice-covered summit craters of central volcanoes.

These varied eruption types produce characteristic deposits that allow identification of their eruptive processes for both historical and prehistorical eruptions. Even in historical time, however, eruptions vary from those at volcanoes rich with sensing instruments and trained observers to remote volcanoes that are often hidden by clouds from their highly infrequent visitors. These variations cause problems for compilers (particularly when using a digital format devoid of the subjective words with which we commonly express variations) and render true standardization impossible on a global scale.

A common problem through much of the historical record is the popular tendency to describe a volcano as "smoking" or "steaming." The full spectrum of steam venting ranges from normal fumarolic emission (with steam clouds many hundreds of meters above the volcano under some meteorological conditions) to very large steam columns that can rapidly rise to more than 10 km above the vent. We have not included vigorous steam plumes without ash emission in our data. Some large steam plumes may contain ash, however, and we have placed a question mark before the date to indicate the uncertainty of large steam emissions with questionable ash content. We have also used the question mark in this way to mark volcanoes noted simply as "smoking," since this description might refer to either ash eruptions or steam emission. There has been no uniformity in treatment of such reports by previous compilers, and it is certain that an unknown number of simple steam clouds have entered the historical record as "eruptions" (Miller et al., 1998). Many recent uncertain eruptions result from reports of discolored water often observed during reconnaissance flights over the waters of volcanic arcs south of Japan.

Although some false eruptions have entered the historical record without the confirmation of solid volcanic products, many more true eruptions have been altogether missed simply because nobody was present to document them. This is easy to understand for remote volcanoes or the distant past, but eruptions can be missed even today on well-monitored

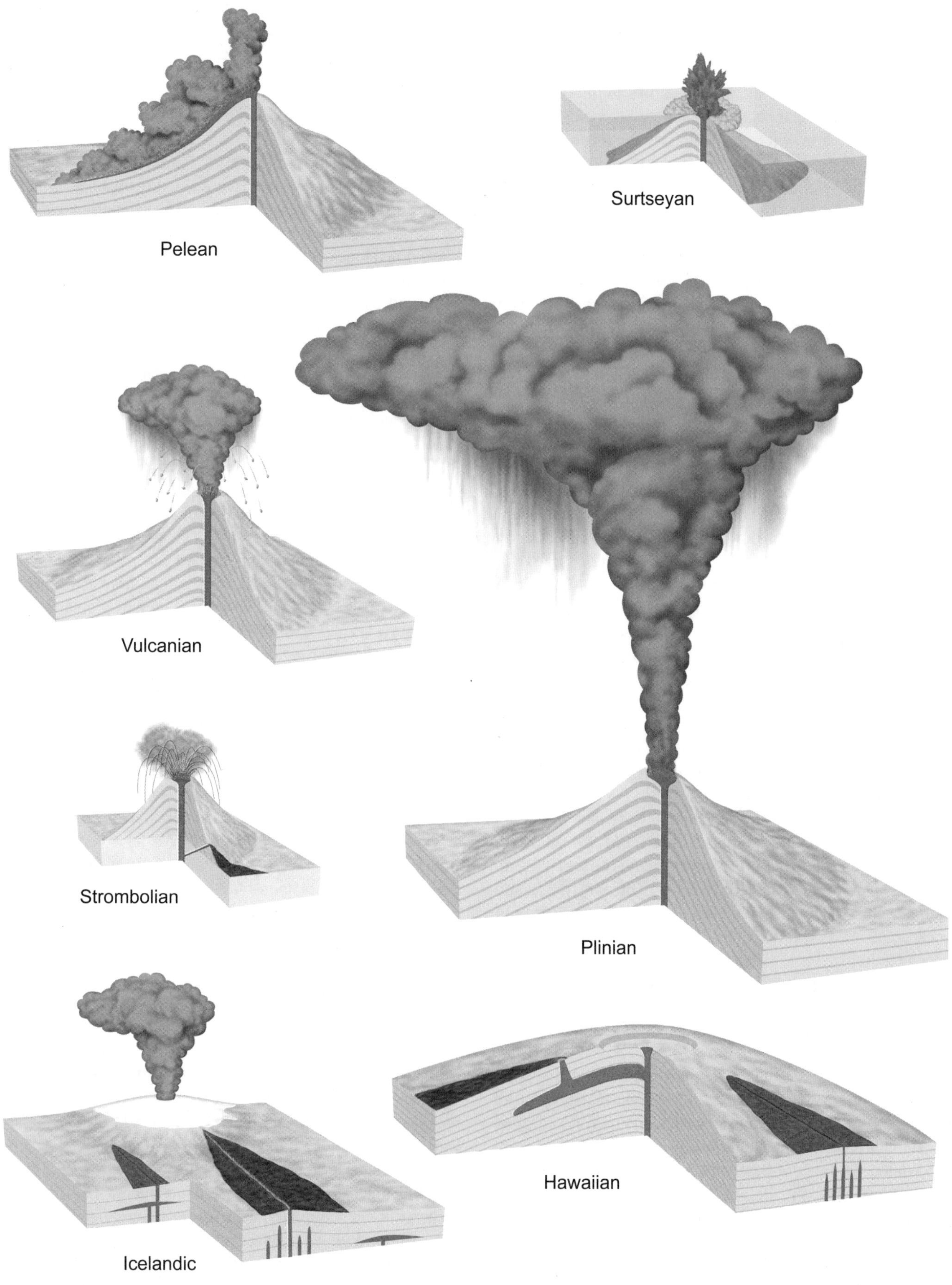

Figure 7. Types of eruptions. The great range in explosivity depends upon many factors, particularly the magma's gas content and viscosity. Artist John Norton.

volcanoes. In 1982, volcanologists on Kilauea, probably the world's best instrumented volcano, recognized a tiny deposit of fresh scoria (<3 m^3) that had not been present at this rarely visited East Rift site two years earlier (Banks, 1982 pers. comm.; Peterson and Moore, 1987). The eruption has been tied to a seismic swarm recorded on the rainy night of March 10-11, 1980. Larger eruptions have been recognized after the fact in the Galápagos Islands, at least two since tour boats began regular operation in late 1969, and even larger eruptions have no doubt been missed in more remote regions. In recent decades, however, atmospheric monitoring has advanced so well that any moderately large sulfur-producing eruption is soon recognized. In early 1982, laser imaging radar (LIDAR) stations around the world reported a new volcanic aerosol layer, and spectacular "volcanic" sunsets were being observed. The responsible volcano was not known, and the aerosol layer was dubbed "the mystery cloud," but retrospective work with SO_2-sensing satellite images later showed the source to have been Zaire's Nyamuragira. The eruption had been recognized and studied, but its remarkable gas component was surprising.

Eruptions are particularly easy to miss when, as in the 1980 Kilauea example, they take place during a period of frequent *intrusive* activity. Following a major earthquake in 1975, and continuing through 1981, scientists at the Hawaiian Volcano Observatory documented 15 episodes of intrusion (when magma moved laterally below the surface) and only two significant surface eruptions. The rift earthquake made room available below the surface, and magma filled it before returning to the more familiar style of eruptions in 1983. Similar intrusive activity was well documented in Iceland during an episode of rifting covering the same years, and offering a fascinating example of spreading processes at major plate boundaries. Here, repeated cycles of inflation at Krafla were punctuated by brief episodes of rifting, with magma generally moving laterally below the surface. This pattern suggests that plate divergence takes place during intense episodes of several meters separation over several years, followed by perhaps 100 years of quiet, rather than steady-state separation of a few cm per year (Bjornsson et al., 1977).

Well-studied eruptions are commonly recognized as having distinct phases of activity, often including quiet periods lasting for days or months between more vigorous bursts of activity that are clearly part of a single, long eruptive period. Untrained observers, however, commonly report these bursts of activity as separate eruptions and these, in turn are difficult to distinguish in the historical record from the observations of travelers witnessing an ongoing remote eruption at separate times. A 1970s review of well-studied, longer eruptions showed us that quiet periods are commonly measured in days and weeks but rarely exceed 3 months. We also looked at the intervals between eruptions of each individual volcano in our file, finding a disproportionately large number in the 0-to-3 month range. Most of these apparently closely spaced eruptions have not been studied, but we believe that careful volcanological investigation would group most of them as phases in longer eruptions. Accordingly, in order to simplify our file, we have arbitrarily treated an eruption following its predecessor by less than 3 months as a phase of the earlier eruption, unless careful work has shown it to be distinct. All phase data remain in our file, but only the start and stop dates are shown in this publication. However, major explosions during the lifetime of an eruption (if assigned a specific VEI—see discussion below) are shown in our **CHRONOLOGY** table.

AREA of ACTIVITY

For the simple volcano with a central summit vent, we have normally not specified the location of eruptions from that vent other than to place an X in the first **Eruptive Characteristic** (designated by "**Central**," for central vent eruption location, and present for 54% of the eruptions in our file). For flank eruptions, however, and those from named subsidiary features, we have listed the location under **Area of activity** where possible. We have also used this part of the **DIRECTORY** to call attention to uncertainties in eruption location (see below). For this edition we have expanded the **Area of Activity** to include (in parentheses) information on the names of eruptive units.

DATES: START and STOP

For each of the 10,415 eruptions in the file we have entered the **Start** date by year, month, and day (**YEAR M-Dy**), where known. Some ancient eruptions are known only to the century and many only to the year. Of the eruptions in our file, 53% are known to the month and 41% to the day. Only 9% are known to the hour or minute, but these times are not displayed here. All dates (and times) are local, as used in virtually all volcanological reporting, but conversions to Greenwich, or Universal, time are in our database. BC dates are indicated by a "**-**" before the year and appear chronologically in all tables.

Readers should be cautioned that the **DIRECTORY** does not list the dates of paroxysmal eruptions occurring after the start of eruptive activity. These dates are, however, listed in the **CHRONOLOGY**, and as detailed below under VEI, an "*****" symbol in the **VEI** column of the **DIRECTORY** indicates the existence of an additional event, between the start and stop dates shown, which can be found in the **CHRONOLOGY**.

The end of an eruption is usually less dramatic than its start, and the commonly gradual decline in eruptive activity makes precise "stop dates" difficult to determine. Other eruptions, not recognized until well after they ended, are entered only with an approximate start date. These factors combine to explain the absence of a listed stop date for 59% of the eruptions in our file.

UNCERTAINTIES

Uncertainties of time, place, and event surround an unfortunately large proportion of the volcanological literature. If the eruption's location is uncertain, as when a mariner's report fails to specify which of an island's several volcanoes was erupting, we have listed it with the most likely volcano but prefaced the date with the commercial "at" sign ("@") to indicate location uncertainty. Only 56 of the eruptions (<1%) carry this uncertainty, and we briefly describe the problem under the **Area of Activity** heading. If the existence of the eruption itself is uncertain, however, as with questionable submarine eruption reports, or subaerial activity that may have been nothing more than increased fumarolic emission, we place a question mark ("**?**") *before* the date (11% of the file). If the eruption is certain but the date is not, we indicate this uncertainty by a question mark *after* the date (17% of the file), but only when no further information exists on the extent of the uncertainty. Some radiocarbon dates are listed by authors without their often considerable dating uncertainties.

Date uncertainty is expressed in several ways. If the eruption is known only to year or month, we simply leave the following columns blank. But if the size of the uncertainty is known, we indicate this by a letter code (Table 6). This code allows us to deal with eruption dates known only as falling between two observations ("after May 10 but before May 24" becomes **0517g**, or May 17 ± 7), more general ranges ("17th century" becomes **1650t** or 1650 ± 50), or specific analytical uncertainties (a corrected radiocarbon date of "1750 BC ± 150" becomes G**-1750w;** see Table 7). If original sources list an uncertainty not exactly matched by our letter code, we use the closest available letter.

If we have been unable to determine the type of uncertainty intended by the original reporter, we have placed a question mark after the date. An undated ash layer sandwiched between two layers of known age is assigned an age midway between the two, and preceded by a "**T**," indicating that the age is determined by tephrochronology. Such dates may have a greater uncertainty than that listed, however, because the two dated layers may themselves have dating uncertainties of substantial (but unknown) size.

Also following some dates is the "greater than" (>) or "less than" (<) symbol. The most common use of the ">" symbol is in designating "**stop date**" for the 105 eruptions believed to be continuing at the time of the report used in our compilation. The ">" symbol is also used for eruptive products known only to be younger than a dated object or horizon, such as lava flows covering earthen dams constructed 800-1200 BC in Yemen (this date, for Jabal Hylan, becomes A**-1200>**). The "<" symbol is used when it is the **date** that is younger than the **eruption** (but it is the only date available and is generally believed to be close to the true start date). Examples are observation dates for "new" volcanic features if earlier, pre-eruption observation dates are not known. We have used these symbols as little as possible, but felt it better to include such "maximum" or "minimum" dates, with appropriate symbols, than to ignore them. The "<" symbol, though, should be used more often than the historical record permits: many older dates listed by us under **Start**, for example, may have been reports by travelers, who witnessed an eruption that had been underway for some time.

Code	± Years	± Days	Code	± Years	± Days	
a	1	1	o	18	25	
b	2	2	p	20	30	(1 mo)
c	3	3	q	25	45	
d	4	4	r	30	60	(2 mo)
e	5	5	s	40	75	
f	6	6	t	50	90	(3 mo)
g	7	7	u	75	120	
h	8	8	v	100	150	
i	9	9	w	150	180	(6 mo)
j	10	10	x	200	270	
k	12	12	y	300	365	(1 yr)
m	14	15	z	500	545	
n	16	20	*	1000	730	(2 yr)

> eruption after date listed
< eruption before date listed
? date uncertain (no data)

Table 6. Eruption dating uncertainty codes.

DATING TECHNIQUES

More than 3000 eruptions in this compilation are pre-historical in age, and these are dated using a variety of radiometric and other techniques. Such eruptions are distinguished from historical eruptions by the presence of a letter code immediately preceding the start year, which indicates the type of dating technique. These codes are listed on the inside front cover, at the beginning of the data tables, and in Table 7. The dating techniques are briefly described alphabetically below, along with discussion of their accuracy. Dating uncertainties can range from as low as to the season of the year for some events dated by dendochronological techniques, to hundreds or even thousands of years for radiocarbon or other radiometric dating techniques such as argon-argon ($^{40}Ar/^{39}Ar$), or potassium-argon (K-Ar). One dating method code is used to flag contemporary submarine eruptions detected using low-frequency sound waves traveling in the SOFAR channel and detected by hydrophones.

A = "ANTHROPOLOGY." About half of these 30 dates reflect oral history. Some are entered without an uncertainty code (e.g., Bedouin legends of a 640 AD Arabian eruption), whereas other uncertainties range from ± 5 to ± 50 years (the "11th century" eruption in México's Michoacán-Guanajuato field). However, all should be treated with some caution, recognizing the human difficulty to accurately recall an undocumented date. Some "**Anthropology**" dates come from buried artifacts and others from dated structures (temples, dams) affected by an eruption. An eruption date in the Galápagos Islands is based on marmalade pots. The pots were stashed by English buccaneers in 1683, and fragments were later found by Heyerdahl (1963) in a lava flow recognized as "young" by Darwin during his historic visit of 1835. The eruption from Santiago volcano on Isabela Island is therefore dated here as "A 1759u," or midway between 1683 and 1835, ± 76 years. Other dates have been obtained by anthropologists but entered directly in our file under the dating technique used (commonly ^{14}C).

C = "^{14}C" or *uncorrected* radiocarbon. Most of the prehistoric dates in our file result from this technique, at least

A	Anthropology	M	Magnetism
C	Radiocarbon (uncorrected)	N	Thermoluminescence
D	Dendrochronology (tree ring)	R	Argon-Argon (Ar-Ar)
E	Surface Exposure	S	SOFAR (hydrophonic)
F	Fission Track	T	Tephrochronology
G	Radiocarbon (corrected)	U	Uranium-Series
H	Hydration Rind	V	Varve Counts
I	Ice Core	@	Eruption location uncertain
K	Potassium Argon (K-Ar)	?	Uncertain eruption
L	Lichenometry	X	Discredited eruption

Table 7. Eruption dating method codes.

indirectly, and an even 1000 carry the designation "**C**," up 29% from the number in our 2nd edition. The technique is based upon the late 1940s discovery that wood and other organic matter contains minute amounts of carbon's radioactive isotope (of atomic weight 14). When the organism dies, its radioactive carbon is no longer replenished and the proportion of ^{14}C in its carbon begins to decrease by radioactive decay. Because this decay rate is accurately known, careful laboratory measurement of the $^{14}C/^{12}C$ ratio in prehistoric wood can accurately date vegetation death. Although the half-life of ^{14}C is about 5,730 years, and its initial concentration is only one part in a trillion (10^{12}) of ^{12}C, ages to 40,000 years are measured routinely (e.g., Taylor 1987; Michael and Ralph, 1971).

Radiocarbon dates are normally expressed in years BP ("Before Present"), and we have followed the standard convention of treating 1950 as "present" (unless otherwise stated) in converting to calendar year dates. Some uncertainty in radiocarbon dates is guaranteed by analytical error and the fact that the ^{14}C decay rate is known only to within ± 30 years. Most authors combine these and other factors in a single uncertainty, or "±" value, after each radiocarbon date presented. We then accept the author's reported date and attach the appropriate uncertainty code upon entry to our file, but see discussion in the next paragraphs for important cautions against mistaking these dates for calendar dates. Uncertainties for uncalibrated radiocarbon dates listed here range from ± 10 to more than ± 1000 years, but most are between ± 50 and ± 300 years. We have rounded calendar dates to the nearest 10 years to avoid creating the impression of a more accurate date than exists. The youngest radiocarbon dates are from Cabalián in the Philippines, Pagan in the Marianas, and Canada's Iskut-Unuk River Cone Group (around 1800 AD). Over 500 uncorrected radiocarbon dates in this compilation would have been "**historical**" if they had taken place in southern Italy, where the written record extends to 1500 BC.

D = "DENDROCHRONOLOGY." The annual character of tree rings was recognized by the ancient Greeks, and use of tree rings to reconstruct the past goes back at least to Leonardo da Vinci (Baillie, 1982). The accuracy of the date depends upon that of the tree-ring time scale developed for the region (Fritts, 1977). Dendrochronology has been used in volcanology both for indirect evidence of climate change from huge eruptions and for more direct reconstruction of nearby events. For example, tree-ring data have been used to distinguish (to the season of the year) two major explosive eruptions from Mount St. Helens within two years of each other about 1480 AD (Yamaguchi, 1985).

Interest is strong in the proxy record of eruptions large enough to have influenced global climate. Distant but long-lived trees bear frost rings from known historical eruptions, and research suggests that tree-ring chronologies will help establish a more detailed record of the planet's largest eruptions (LaMarche and Hirshboeck, 1984).

Other paleobotanical techniques can also be useful to volcanology. The famous eruption that created Oregon's Crater Lake, for example, is dated only to ± 50 years (nearly 6,000 years ago), but careful study of pollen associated with its volcanic ash in a far-away Montana bog showed that the eruption began in the autumn and apparently continued for at least 3 years (Mehringer et al., 1977). Analysis of annual layers in Irish peat bogs has yielded detailed records (including fine particles of volcanic ash) from Icelandic eruptions, and leaf impressions beneath Japanese ash layers have dated prehistoric eruptions to the exact season of the year (Pilcher and Hall, 1992; Hayakawa et al., 1994). In New Zealand, insect remains preserved by the famous Taupo eruption of the second century AD have shown that the eruption took place in the early afternoon (D. Lowe, 1993 pers. comm.). The application of biology to eruptive deposits holds great promise for unraveling the recent histories of many volcanoes.

E = "SURFACE EXPOSURE." This relatively new technique measures the exposure ages of rocks at the Earth's surface to cosmic-ray production. Cosmic-ray production rates are dependent on both elevation and latitude, but if local cosmogenic helium (^{3}He) production rates can be constrained, helium isotopes can be used to determine the ages of rocks exposed at the surface since their formation. Chlorine isotopes (^{36}Cl) have also been used to date very young volcanic rocks. Careful sampling is required, but surface exposure procedures have been used to date late-Pleistocene and Holocene lava flows. The technique has somewhat larger uncertainties (many hundreds to more than a thousand years) than ages from calibrated radiocarbon dating (see below). Although relatively infrequently used, it is useful if organic material for radiocarbon dating is unavailable and correlates fairly well with radiocarbon ages in cases that compare both techniques.

F = "FISSION TRACK." This technique depends upon the natural spontaneous fission decay of uranium. The resulting heavy fission particles leave minute damage tracks in volcanic glass that are revealed by chemical etching of a cut and polished surface. The number of tracks per unit area, counted microscopically, is proportional to the age of the glass (for any given uranium content) and can therefore provide eruption ages. Although the technique is capable of better accuracy, one (of only 4) fission track ages included here—1000 BP from Canada's Mount Edziza (Aumento and Souther, 1973)—carries one of the largest uncertainties in the file: ± 6000 years.

G = "^{14}C," or corrected radiocarbon. Careful radiocarbon dating has been done on selected portions of long-lived bristlecone pine trees that can be independently dated by tree-ring techniques. This work shows generally close agreement (<80 years) between the two methods for the last 2,500 years, but they then start to diverge until "true" tree-ring dates exceed radiocarbon dates by 700-900 years for the last 4,000 years of the Holocene. The reason for this divergence is apparent variation in past content of atmospheric radiocarbon. For many years there was substantial disagreement between different laboratories, but a common calibration program for correcting raw radiocarbon dates has gained wide acceptance (Stuiver et al., 1998). If a corrected date is available we have preceded it by the letter "**G**" (which can be thought of, mnemonically, as a slightly altered "**C**"). However, we have not attempted to correct the uncorrected dates of other workers. Many published dates are not accompanied by all the information required (e.g., laboratory precision, relation of dated material to eruption, number of independent dates, contamination of sample) for an accurate correction, and we have chosen not to risk confusion by publishing incorrect dates not reported by original authors. At the time of the 2nd edition, only 14% of our radiocarbon dates were corrected; that figure has now tripled to more than 43%. The mixing of uncorrected dates with a growing number of calendar dates remains, however, very misleading to readers who do not pay attention to the letter code in front of prehistoric dates, particularly those in the BC part of the **CHRONOLOGY**. It is imperative that readers be aware of the significant age difference between "**C**" and "**G**" dates: to 100-150 years during the last 2500 years, rising to 900 years in the early Holocene.

H = "HYDRATION RIND." Obsidian flows were molten liquids with unusually high viscosity inhibiting nucleation and growth of the crystals that make up most volcanic rocks. The resulting glass is unstable and gradually decomposes by the addition of moisture from the atmosphere. The thickness of the hydration rind on an obsidian flow surface is proportional to the time that it has been exposed to the atmosphere, and this property has been used to date a dozen flows in our file, mainly from Oregon's Newberry Caldera and California's Mono Craters (Friedman, 1977, 1981). Uncertainties are large for this technique, ranging from ± 200 to ± 1740 years for the dates included here, and hydration rates are affected by regional climatic variations.

I = "ICE CORE." The far-traveled aerosol of major eruptions eventually settles to the Earth's surface, leaving a chemical trace in glaciers and ice caps that grow by annual accumulation of snow layers. Cores through these annual layers then provide an important record of past volcanism that can extend, as with the cores from Greenland, over 250,000 years (Hammer, 1977; Hammer et al., 1980). Whereas tree ring studies give an unequivocal link to volcanism only if close to the source, strongly acidic layers have been formed in the ice of both polar regions by major historical eruptions. Even more pronounced layers in prehistoric portions of the core point clearly to volcanism with global distribution as the cause. This gives the exciting potential of establishing a complete chronology of large, sulfur-producing eruptions, but the difficulty lies in determining which volcano was responsible for a specific acidic layer.

Aerosols move swiftly around the globe but their spread to the north and south is relatively slow. Thus an eruption from high northern latitudes (Iceland, Alaska, Kamchatka) leaves a relatively large volcanic deposit in Greenland, whereas a comparable eruption from low latitudes leaves a much smaller record, and one from the southern hemisphere may leave none at all. Small volcanic ash particles have been found in some cores, allowing petrologic correlation with individual volcanoes (Palais et al., 1990), but substantial uncertainty surrounds the identification of most eruptive sources. Added to this problem is the danger of misinterpreting the completeness of volcanism's recent historical record. Very large eruptions may well have been missed only a few hundred years ago in some parts of the world, so the matching of acidity spikes with poorly constrained dates from the volcanic record requires caution. This technique holds great promise, particularly in local icecaps in Iceland, where 35 eruptions have been dated by this technique. Elsewhere we have entered only 7 ice core dates in the **DIRECTORY** (3 from North America and 4 from Antarctica).

In the **CHRONOLOGY**, however, we list some dates of major eruptions documented by ice core data for which the source is unknown. These dates cover much of the Holocene, but are chronologically well constrained and unequivocally volcanic. The entry at 1259 AD, for example, is based on acidity spikes in cores from both polar regions (Langway et al., 1988; Palais et al., 1992) and is regarded as one of the largest eruptions of the Holocene, although surprisingly for such a large and recent eruption, its source remains unknown (Oppenheimer, 2003). The source volcanoes for some ice-core spikes even in recent historical time remain unknown. A major eruption from an unknown tropical volcano as recently as 1809 AD was also recorded in both polar regions and was considered to have contributed to global cooling prior to the 1815 eruption of Tambora (Cole-Dai et al., 2009). We have not attempted to compile a comprehensive listing of ice core dates, however, and readers are referred to more recent papers, such as those of Castellano et al. (2005) and Kurbatov et al. (2006) for discussion of ice core dates and possible correlations with specific eruptions.

K = "K-Ar," or Potassium-Argon, is one of the most widely used geochronometers. Like radiocarbon dating, it depends upon the relative proportions of parent (^{40}K) to daughter (^{40}Ar) isotopes, and the well-established half-life of that constant decay. It has been used to date rocks approaching the age of the Earth (4.54 x 10^9 years), but is less frequently used on materials younger than 100,000 years (Dalrymple and Lanphere, 1969). Of the 22 K-Ar dates listed here, none is younger than 2000 BP. Uncertainties given in the original reports range from ± 1000 to ± 7000 years, the latter, the largest in our file, is for a 9000 BP date from Loihi volcano.

L = "LICHENOMETRY." The slow but rather regular growth rate of lichens on a lava flow surface has been used to date two eruptions on Penguin Island, Antarctica (Birkenmajer, 1979). The technique is useful for establishing relative ages on young lava flows, but absolute ages require accurate baseline growth rates, under comparable conditions of climate and substrate, that are rarely available over more than a century. This technique is used relatively infrequently and only appears twice in this compilation.

M = "MAGNETISM." As lava cools from its molten state, it may capture an accurate "memory" of the Earth's magnetic field at that time. Secular variation, or historical wander of the Earth's magnetic poles, has been large enough that careful study of a lava's magnetic "memory" may reveal its approximate date of cooling. The number of dates in our file based on this technique has increased dramatically from the 2 in our 1981 book to 49 here. Most carry uncertainties in the ± 50-150-year range. The accuracy of the technique decreases greatly for events older than a few thousand years.

N = "THERMOLUMINESCENCE" dating depends on the effects of radioactive decay (like **"U"** and **"F"**) rather than direct counts of isotopic ratios (like **"C," "K,"** and **"R"**). Some electrons emitted during decay are trapped in crystal defects, and laboratory heating frees them, producing light in the process. The amount of light depends, in part, on the age of the crystal. This technique is much used by archeologists, and is represented here by a dozen dates from Italy, Africa, Papua New Guinea, and Japan; dates typically have a large uncertainty (to a thousand years or more).

R = "ARGON-ARGON" (^{40}Ar/^{39}Ar) dating was first developed in the late 1980s. Similar in many ways to K-Ar dating, it offers greater precision and requires much smaller amounts of material. Following irradiation by nutrons, stepwise heating yields a spectrum of apparent ages shown by changing isotopic ratios that reflect contamination until reaching a plateau that represents the crystal's cooling age. The technique is particularly useful for relatively young materials, and is bringing new order to geologic time scales over the past few tens of millions of years. Only 2 dates using this technique were listed in the 2nd edition, but 17 are listed here; ^{40}Ar/^{39}Ar dates for Holocene eruptions typically have fairly large dating uncertainties, often in the several thousand year range.

S = "SOFAR," or submarine "**Hydrophone**" detection. Explosive eruptions on the sea floor send out shock waves through the water in much the same way that earthquakes send shock waves through Earth's solid crust. The velocities are slower, about 5300 km/hr, but these low-frequency sound waves travel for long distances through the SOFAR channel (a discrete sub-surface layer of water within 1200 m of the surface where sound energy is concentrated), and their arrival times at submarine hydrophones can be used to locate the eruption in the same way that seismologists locate earthquake epicenters. Study of hydrophone records from observed submarine eruptions has shown features characteristic of volcanism, and when these features appear on records from more remote parts of the sea floor they have been used to locate and to date (often to the hour and minute) volcanism that would otherwise have been completely missed.

Although the quiet, non-explosive effusion of lava that typifies most seafloor volcanism is difficult to detect by hydrophones, earthquake swarms commonly accompany these more gentle eruptions in places such as Hawaii and Iceland, and such swarms from submerged seamounts have been interpreted as submarine eruptions. We have entered 4 volcanoes (one off of Hawaii and three near Tahiti) because of earthquake swarms (**STATUS** entered as "**Seismicity**") and the fresh glass dredged from their submerged summits. However, the earthquake swarms might represent magma movement without eruption, so we have preceded these dates with a question mark rather than a symbol representing the "seismic" dating technique.

T = "TEPHROCHRONOLOGY." Aristotle used the Greek word for ash, "tephra," in describing an eruption on the island of Vulcano. Because modern volcanologists define "ash" as particles smaller than 2 mm in diameter, a broader term is useful for describing material of *all* sizes explosively ejected by volcanoes. In 1944, Sigurdur Thorarinsson proposed the word "tephra" for this purpose, and it is widely accepted today (Westgate and Gold, 1974; Self and Sparks, 1981). Tephra from large explosive eruptions may be distributed over enormous distances, forming a distinctive layer that later constitutes a "marker" horizon within layers of sediment. Careful mapping of such layers throughout a volcanic area can develop a *relative* sequence of overlapping ash layers. If some of these ash layers are dated, either historically or by some other technique, dates can be assigned to the intervening layers in their relative sequence. The technique is a broad one, embracing a variety of field geologic and stratigraphic methods, and we have used this designation to cover prehistoric eruptions for which our source specified no technique (as, for example, a date placed midway between two radiocarbon-dated eruptions). Uncertainties are commonly large, ranging from 10 to 3000, with a median around 500 years.

U = "URANIUM-SERIES." Several dating techniques utilize Uranium-series disequilibrium ratios. The Uranium-Thorium disequilibrium series is often used to date carbonate materials such as speleothems, travertines, corals, deep sea sediments, bones, teeth, peat, or evaporites. More complex applications of this technique have also been applied to volcanic rocks. ^{230}Thorium, part of the ^{238}Uranium decay series, has a half-life of about 75,000 years, in comparison to the half-life of ^{238}Uranium of 4,470,000,000 years. If the amounts of Uranium and Thorium isotopes are compared, an estimate of the age of a specimen can be obtained. This technique has been applied to volcanic rocks as young as the end of the Pleistocene and the beginning of the Holocene and has relatively large uncertainties (from hundreds to a few thousand years) during these time intervals. Other Uranium-series nuclides have dramatically shorter half-lives. ^{226}Ra-^{230}Th ratios have been used to date eruptions during the mid-Holocene, and ^{210}Po-^{210}Pb ratios have been applied to eruptions on the sea floor as young as a few decades or even less. No eruptions dated with this technique appeared in our 2nd edition, but 29 dates from 14 volcanoes are listed here.

V = "VARVE COUNT." Seasonal changes affect sediment accumulation in many small lakes, particularly those in which the spring melting of ice adds an annual layer of coarse sandy particles to the lake floor, in contrast to the finer clay deposited during the rest of the year. These layers, or varves, can later be counted to establish the date for a layer of volcanic ash in their midst. Like tree rings, these annual layers provide very accurate dates under ideal conditions and careful work, but uncertainty increases with age and non-ideal conditions. The sediments of Turkey's Lake Van provide a remarkable record of 22 eruptions of nearby Nemrut Dagi volcano since the beginning of the Holocene (Degens et al., 1984; Ulusoy et al., 2008).

Two codes used in the dating methods column are not dating techniques, but indicate varying degrees of uncertainty about the eruption.

? = "UNCERTAIN ERUPTION." Historical eruption reports of uncertain validity are flagged by a question mark preceding the eruption year. These uncertain eruptions appear in both the **DIRECTORY** and **CHRONOLOGY**, and are further distinguished by appearing in italics.

X = "DISCREDITED ERUPTION." Eruptive events that, although once established in the volcanological literature such as the *CAVW* but have since been discredited, are marked by an "X" preceding the eruption year. These are included in none of our totals, but great effort is often invested in proving a reported eruption to be false, and we thought it better to retain these 177 "non-events", in a form that allows easy identification (and removal), rather than have them appear to readers of earlier compilations as mistaken omissions. A discredited eruption appears in the **DIRECTORY** but not in the **CHRONOLOGY**.

DURATION

Duration information exists for fewer than 40% of the eruptions in our file. Data quality suffer from the difficulty of recognizing the gradual end of an eruption that may have begun quite dramatically, but is also affected by the large number of radiometrically dated eruptions, for which duration data are unavailable, as well as by inconsistent definition of the word "eruption." At Stromboli, for example, references to volcanism go back at least 2400 years, and more or less continual activity has been inferred since. However, the record is clearly uneven, and recent work (Rosi et al., 2000) has demonstrated periods of quiescence during this interval. With these cautions in mind, however, it is interesting to examine the distribution of known eruption durations.

Of the 3929 eruptions in our file with duration data, about 12% ended in less than a day and 18% within two days. One quarter ended within a week, 44% within a month, and more than half (54%) within two months (Figure 8). Only 15% of eruptions lasted more than a year, 3.4% more than five years, and only 1% lasted more than two decades. The median duration was about 7 weeks. Again demonstrating the unremarkable nature of the most eruption endings, fewer than 10% of durations are accurately known to the day.

An eruption's stop date is a useful indicator of reporting quality. Prior to 1500 AD, stop dates (and thus durations) were known from only 62 eruptions, with a median uncertainty of about three weeks. The subsequent onset of western explorations, the increase in populations living near (and observing) volcanoes, and development of the printing press and communication technologies have progressively increased the number of eruptions described accurately enough to assign a stop date. Since the 1968 onset of regular Smithsonian reporting, more than 86% of eruptions have known durations, with a median uncertainty of ± 1 day.

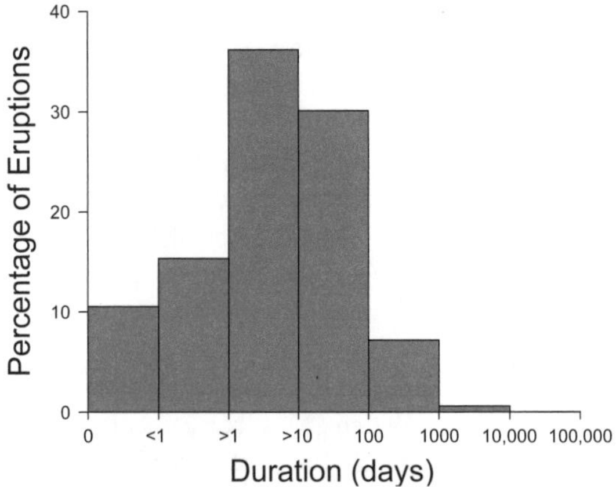

Figure 8. Duration of 3935 eruptions for which stop (as well as start) date is known. Median duration is about 7 weeks.

Although several very brief explosive eruptions have been recorded (such as the minutes-long Krafla borehole eruption described below under **VOLUMES,** p. 31), the shortest major eruption known to us is the fatal event in 1977, when the long-lived molten lava lake of Nyiragongo, Zaire, drained in less than one hour, flooding the outer flanks with 20 million cubic meters of exceptionally fluid lava that moved downslope at speeds reaching 60-100 km/hr (Tazieff, 1976-77; Krafft, 1990). Such brief eruptions must be balanced against long-term eruptions lasting several centuries or longer from Stromboli, Fogo, Sangay, and Yasur volcanoes, the latter active in Vanuatu since it was first discovered by Captain Cook in 1774. Nearly a dozen volcanoes (Italy's Stromboli, Erta Ale in Ethiopia, Yasur, Semeru and Dukono in Indonesia, Japan's Sakura-jima, Kilauea in Hawaii, Santa María in Guatemala, Arenal in Costa Rica, Ecuador's Sangay, and Erebus in Antarctica) have been erupting for more than two decades and could remain active for some time.

A good indication of a new eruption's likely duration would seem to be the previous history of that volcano, but the record is rarely extensive enough, and even the better records often defy simple generalization. On Hawaii's Kilauea, for example, 1 out of every 4 historical eruptions ended in 2 days or less, 14 of them lasted less than 24 hours. Yet Kilauea also has had 4 of the longest eruptions in our file (43, 27, 27, and 17 years), including the East Rift activity that began in January of 1983 and is continuing at the time of this writing.

Perhaps the most sobering lessons about eruption duration (and about the wide range of behavior in a single eruption) come from Indonesia's Tambora in 1815. More than three full years of mild eruptive activity preceded a dramatic eruption, with cloud height estimated at 33 km. Such paroxysmal explosions end many eruptions, and reasonable people might have concluded that the eruption had ended. But they would have been wrong. After a lull of 5 days came history's largest explosive eruption: the culminating blast reached heights estimated at 44 km, caused three days of total darkness 500 km from the volcano, and ultimately resulted in an estimated 60,000 fatalities (Sigurdsson and Carey, 1989; Tanguy et al., 1998). Predicting an eruption's end is no easier than predicting its beginning.

ERUPTIVE CHARACTERISTICS

In the first two editions of our **DIRECTORY**, we indicated the presence, when known, of 20 characteristics selected by the originators of the *CAVW* and shown throughout those volumes. We do the same here, but have substituted one eruptive characteristic (**Caldera** formation) for the original CAVW **Fumarolic** characteristic, as further discussed below. Our data file contains a larger list of characteristics, and we have modified some of the older *CAVW* entries, but we have not yet systematically revised the full file. We therefore present only these basic 20 characteristics that have been reasonably well standardized. This compressed format is designed to provide a swift summary of the behavior common to a particular volcano or region, but also to allow a systematic search for eruptions of a particular type. No such search can be complete, however, because most of the eruptions in the file were neither documented adequately at the time, nor studied sufficiently since, to enable us to list all characteristics with confidence. Many eruptions have no characteristics listed at all, and many more carry only a single entry, such as "normal explosions," despite the likelihood of other characteristics having accompanied them. Positive identification of a particular characteristic is indicated by an "X" in that column, uncertainty is shown by a "?," and negative (absence of information as well as absence of that characteristic) by a "-." Photographs of many of these eruptive characteristics are scattered throughout this book.

The first 4 characteristics describe where the eruption took place (see also discussion of **Area of Activity** on p. 19). **Central crater** is entered for 61% of the eruptions listed here; Japan's Aso has the most central crater eruptions in the file with 181, followed by Italy's Etna with 139. **Flank vent**, or parasitic crater eruptions have been noted for 277 volcanoes, and Piton de la Fournaise, on the Indian Ocean island of Reunion, leads the list with 53 such eruptions. Some volcanoes, such as Alaska's Trident and Chile's Cerro Azul (Quizapu), have recorded eruptions from parasitic craters only. **Radial fissure** eruptions are listed for 137 volcanoes. Etna (83) and Hawaii's Mauna Loa (82) lead in radial fissure eruptions, but Piton de la Fournaise (65), and Kilauea (48) have had frequent eruptions of this type. Although eruptions also take place from fissures circumferential to the volcano, they were not among the eruptive characteristics chosen for *CAVW* and are not designated here. **Regional fissure** eruptions are entered for only 78 volcanoes. One third of these are in Iceland, where eruptions fill new linear fissures created by the spreading of the Atlantic Ocean, although Taveuni in Fiji has the second highest total (34). Icelandic eruptions, led by Hekla/Vatnafjöll (51), Krafla (23), Grímsvötn (21), and Bardarbunga (17) make up one-quarter of the regional fissure eruptions in the file.

The next 4 characteristics deal with eruptions that interact with water. **Submarine** eruptions are the most common, with 397 eruptions from 123 locations, a substantial jump from the 289 in our 2nd edition due to heightened emphasis on mid-ocean rift and submarine arc volcano research, but these recorded events are nevertheless only a small fraction of all submarine eruptions. Kavachi, in the Solomon Islands has had 30 known submarine eruptions since 1938. Seawater unquestionably complicates eruption reporting. An Icelandic volcanologist once balanced simultaneous telephone calls concerning a nearby submarine eruption (K. Grönvold, 1984 pers. comm.). One was from a policeman in a mainland phone booth looking out at the eruption column and describing its red interior. The other was from an airplane pilot circling the site and declaring emphatically that there was no eruption. Apparently a confluence of currents had caused a waterspout-like cloud and sunset glint gave it a red glow. Some skepticism is called for in evaluating ocean eruption reports, and we have eliminated from our listings an 1853 submarine event 55 km off the coast of California. This was entered in the *CAVW* on the basis of high water spouting and shoal soundings, but the ocean floor bedrock is 15 million years old and the shoals are frequented by whales. We have also rejected submarine eruption events such as the shock waves and sulfurous smells reported from a Soviet ship (Gushchenko, 1979) in the middle of the Gulf of Alaska in 1964, on the day of the famous Good Friday earthquake, one of this century's largest.

A specific type of submarine eruption—**New island**, or Island Building—was added to the original *CAVW* list of characteristics in 1953. These events have special importance for biologists interested in colonization, as on Iceland's new island of Surtsey, formed from 1963 to 1967. We record 99 new islands, but the fact that they are from only 41 locations shows that many of the islands were short-lived; eroded by the sea soon after they were formed, only to be followed by other islands built by later eruptions. The famous Greek island of Santorini had 7 island-forming eruptions between 197 BC and 1866 AD, and Kavachi has built itself above sea-level at least 12 times since 1950. We have used this characteristic for eruptions forming islands in caldera lakes (e.g., Taal, Askja) as well as the open ocean, but the former are identified by the absence of an X in the column for submarine eruptions. **Subglacial** eruptions represent a special interaction with water. Most are not recorded, but in Iceland the sudden release of water from such eruptions forms tremendous floods ("jökulhlaups" or glacier bursts) with flow rates that have exceeded those of the Amazon River. These are marked by a "**J**" rather than an "**X**" in the **Mudflow** column (see below). Only a quarter of the 26 volcanoes that have produced subglacial eruptions are from Iceland, but they have produced 237 of the 268 documented subglacial eruptions, with Katla at 128 leading the way. Most are in high latitudes, but one is from Ecuador's Antisana, just 55 km from the equator, and 8 more are from other Andean volcanoes.

Crater lake eruptions are recorded from 73 volcanoes.

Water and hot magma make an explosive combination, and a summit crater lake on an active volcano places these two components in dangerous proximity. Lake water adds to the danger by contributing, in an eruption, to mudflows that can devastate the volcano's outer slopes and beyond. The Costa Rican volcano Poás has had at least 44 crater lake eruptions, with one (in 1910) reportedly shooting a fountain of water 4 km in the air. Ruapehu, in New Zealand, has recorded the most crater lake eruptions (58), with Aso (50) close behind, but the most devastating has been Java's Kelut, where extensive efforts to drain the lake have successfully reduced its danger after 13 fatal highly explosive eruptions claimed many thousands of lives. Not all crater lake eruptions are explosive, however. An eruption in 2009 at Kelut saw a lava dome quietly extrude in the crater lake, as also occurred at Soufrière St. Vincent volcano in the West Indies in 1971-72. A very few of the 410 crater lake eruptions are from regional rather than summit lakes, but these should be clear from the initial "place" characteristic.

The next 4 characteristics deal with explosive volcanism. **Explosive** eruptions (or "normal explosions" in the original *CAVW* terminology) is the single most common characteristic, appearing in 74% of all eruptions. Explosive eruptions and their products have received increasing attention in volcanic textbooks (e.g., Fisher and Schmincke, 1984; Heiken and Wohletz, 1985). Etna leads the list with 181 in the past 8000 years, and Aso has recorded 162 since 553 AD. As noted below under discussion of **Phreatic** eruptions, an 'X' in the Explosive column does not necessarily imply magmatic explosions.

Pyroclastic flows are hot glowing avalanches that can move down slopes at hurricane speeds, devastating all living things in their paths. They are recorded from 306 volcanoes and 1290 eruptions, a substantial increase over the 763 eruptions recorded in our 2nd edition, reflecting input from detailed stratigraphic studies. Java's Merapi has had pyroclastic flows in 30 of its 66 historical eruptions since 1548 AD, and nearly half of these 30 have been fatal. The famous West Indian volcano Mont Pelée has had more pyroclastic flow eruptions dated (50), and more than 90% of its eruptions have produced pyroclastic flows. Only 3 have been in historical time, but that of 1902 claimed 28,000 lives in only a few minutes. The term nuée ardente has been used in the *CAVW*, and by us (in the 1st edition), to cover a variety of pyroclastic-flow phenomena, including pyroclastic surges and Merapi-type dome collapse flows. Our current use of the term pyroclastic flow covers the same broad range.

Phreatic explosions result from the mixing of cold water and hot rock. The products of these explosions contain only fragmented older rock, but the source of the heat is normally near-surface magma, and this may appear in the products as small proportions of fresh glass. As the proportion of fresh material increases to dominance, either in a different phase of the eruption or in a different eruption, the words "phreatic" or "phreatomagmatic" no longer apply. We list this characteristic for 1217 eruptions from 282 volcanoes, but usage of the term is variable and most explosions are too poorly studied to know their phreatic component. Thus the presence of an "X" in the **Explosive** column does not necessarily imply a magmatic eruption. Nevertheless, phreatic eruptions are commonly associated with the "water" characteristics discussed above, and the expected relationship with crater lake eruptions is particularly clear. The 13 volcanoes with the greatest number of phreatic explosions (35% of the total) also account for nearly half of all crater lake eruptions.

In the first two editions of this book we followed the *CAVW* in using the last of four characteristics grouped with explosive activity to refer to instances of non-eruptive fumarolic (or solfataric) gas emission. Because over 100 events listed by the *CAVW* were solely fumarolic, we had restricted this entry to cases in which distant observations of apparent eruptions carried cautionary phrases such as "possibly only fumarolic activity," or different sources disagreed on whether an "eruption" emitted any solid material.

Because almost all eruptions have associated fumarolic activity, however, it seems more useful to assign the last of the four characteristics associated with explosive activity to **Caldera**-forming eruptions, which we have done in this edition. The ejection of large amounts of explosive material can leave the summit of a volcano unsupported, causing inward collapse, forming calderas (Lipman, 2000) typically one to many km in diameter. We have documented 79 such events with an "**X**" in the **Caldera** column. Caldera collapse can also occur during mostly non-explosive eruptions due to the effusion of large amount of lava, seen most commonly in basaltic shield volcanoes such as those on Hawaii. We have distinguished 8 of these more mafic (low-silica) collapse events with an "**M**" in this column.

A third type of collapse occurs when large segments of a volcano's summit collapse gravitationally, producing large-volume debris avalanches that can travel tens of km or more from the volcano and create large horseshoe-shaped collapse scarps. Volcanologists recognized the significance of these events after the 1980 eruption of Mount St. Helens and observed that they were not uncommon in the life cycle of volcanoes (Siebert, 1984; Ui et al., 2000). Often referred to as sector collapse, 71 such events are flagged with an "**A**" in the caldera column. We restrict this characteristic to edifice-collapse events of 0.1 km^3 or larger. Large debris avalanches can also occur in the absence of eruptions, and we only include these events in association with documented eruptions.

The next 4 characteristics deal with the eruption of fluid lava, the most common being **Lava flows**. Lava flows occurred in only 24% of the listed eruptions, but nearly half of the volcanoes with dated eruptions have dated flows, and of course a much higher proportion have prehistoric flows. Lava flows are the dominant eruptive product around the global rift system, where new material is being added to the crust, and within the deep ocean basins. They are overwhelmed by explosive eruption products near continental margins, where crustal material is being consumed. Of the 858 volcanoes with dated eruptions, 142 have had lava flows with all eruptions and 381 have had them with none. The leading producers are Piton de la Fournaise with 148 recorded eruptions with lava flows, Etna with 130, and Mauna Loa with 109. **Lava lakes** are a particularly spectacular type of lava flow, forming molten lakes over submerged vents that may keep them circulating colorfully for tens of years. Lava lakes are known from 31 volcanoes, with Kilauea having 26 of the 142 recorded lava lake eruptions. The Nyiragongo lake (0203-03=) also provided useful information during its 49 year existence, and lava lakes were still active at Erta Ale (0201-08=) and Erebus (1900-02=) in 2009. We have followed the *CAVW* in also applying this characteristic to eruptions that ponded lava in pre-existing pit craters or calderas. Drilling through the crusts of such lakes as they solidified has provided valuable data on the cooling history and fractionation of magma (Wright et al., 1976; Peck et al., 1979; Helz and Thornber, 1987).

Lava **Domes** form if lava is too viscous and too limited in volume to spill substantially over the rim of its crater and move down slope as a lava flow. These steep-sided viscous masses are commonly extruded after the explosive discharge of more gas-rich magma, and may grow to make up much of the volcanic edifice. The upper 800 m of California's Lassen Peak, for example, is a dome with a basal diameter of about 2.5 km. Most lava domes are smaller and some (such as those recently active at Japan's Usu volcano) are cryptodomes that have grown largely below the surface, uplifting the ground above. Santiaguito dome, on Volcán Santa María, Guatemala, began growing in 1922, and activity continues today. We list 606 dome-forming eruptions from 201 volcanoes, led by Shiveluch with 45 and Bezymianny, also in Kamchatka, and Merapi in Java with 41. **Spines** are a minor (but sometimes spectacular) subdivision of domes, forming when a slender column of nearly solid lava is thrust upward from the top of a growing dome. After the tragic 1902 eruption at Mont Pelée, a celebrated spine was thrust 311 m high (at rates to 25 m/day) before it crumbled. We list 27 spine-forming eruptions from 18 volcanoes, but this is not a significant data field, and many smaller undocumented spines have been produced during the 606 dome-forming eruptions in the file.

The final group of 4 characteristics deals with the effects of eruptions on humans. **Fatalities** are recorded for 384 eruptions from 167 volcanoes; not a large percentage of either total, but some eruptions have been calamitous and these have not been evenly distributed in either space or time. Indonesia's Kelut and Merapi, Japan's Asama, and the Philippines' Mayon have had 15, 14, 14, and 12 fatal eruptions, respectively. These three nations, among the most densely populated in the world, are host to 44% of the world's fatal volcanoes and 54% of history's fatal eruptions. More detailed information about fatalities and their causes as well as the successes of vigorous volcano hazards programs in these and other countries in reducing fatalities can be found in the **Fatalities and Evacuations** tables (p. 329-347).

The world's population doubled in the 130 years prior to 1903, and more than 200,000 deaths resulted from volcanism, most of them in 5 major eruptions with death tolls exceeding 10,000. Since the last of these, the Mont Pelée disaster of 1902, the world's population had again doubled by the mid 1960s, but volcanism had claimed fewer than 16,000 lives. In the first edition of this book, we suggested that one reason for this dramatic reduction was increased monitoring and understanding of volcanoes, but another was simply good luck. That luck ran out, and in the last quarter century more than 26,000 lives have been lost to eruptions. Population densities continue to increase exponentially in many volcanic regions, and careful, instrumental monitoring (Ewert and Swanson, 1992) is the best defense against eruption surprises.

Damage to property or other human infrastructures, such as roads, bridges, and buildings, has been recorded for 1018 eruptions from 274 volcanoes. As with the fatality data, there is a strong association with population density, and the 3 most destructive volcanoes are Etna, Aso, and Merapi (with 70, 32, and 23 eruptions, respectively). Volcanic **mudflows**, or lahars, are a major cause of this destruction. Mudflows form in several different ways, but many large explosive volcanoes bring together their three essential components: steep slopes, extensive ash deposits, and abundant water (in crater lakes, swiftly melted ice, or the rains commonly associated with both mountain peaks and eruptions). These often combine to form dense mudflows sweeping down slope with enormous momentum that can carry them for tens of kilometers across flat arable land beyond the foot of the volcano. Volcanic mudflows are reported from 787 eruptions from more than 200 volcanoes, with 31 having come from Cotopaxi in the Ecuadorian Andes and 26 from Mayon in the Philippines. Pyroclastic flows from Cotopaxi's 1877 eruption swiftly melted the perennial ice at its 5897 m summit and soon turned the vast, fertile inter-Andean valley below into a roiling sea of mud, moving at speeds averaging 70 km/hr. The 1985 eruption of Nevado del Ruiz, destroying the town of Armero and killed 22,000 people, and the 1991 mudflows from Pinatubo in the Philippines (which continued for a number of years after the eruption) are more recent examples. Mudflows directly associated with glacier bursts, or jökulhlaups (see above), are identified in the **DIRECTORY** by a **J**, rather than the **X** used to indicate other characteristics.

Tsunami are long-period sea waves (often mistakenly called tidal waves) that travel at speeds up to 800 km/hour in the open ocean and may build to devastating heights as they slow and approach land. They form when huge masses of water are suddenly displaced, either by earthquake or by eruption. One of the most powerful eruptions of recent centuries, at Krakatau in 1883, produced lethal waves with each major explosion, killing more than 34,000 Javanese and Sumatrans. The largest wave, an estimated 15 m high in the open ocean, reached heights to 40 m on the heavily populated coast, carrying a steamship 2½ km inland and stranding it 24 m above sea level. This tsunami immediately followed the largest explosion, heard 4653 km away, which hurled ash into the stratosphere (Simkin and Fiske, 1983). The even larger eruption of Santorini, around 1600 BC, is likewise thought to have produced a major tsunami affecting the eastern Mediterranean (perhaps contributing to flood legends and the end of the Minoan civilization). Many tsunami result when large parts of the seafloor are displaced by tectonic earthquakes, some of which may also trigger eruptions. We list tsunami from 51 volcanoes and 80 eruptions, with the largest number from Taal in the Philippine Islands (6) and 4 each from Italy's Stromboli and Ritter Island in Melanesia. The active Volcano Island cones of Taal lie in a large lake, rather than an ocean, and damaging waves have accompanied 6 of its historical eruptions, all but one of them fatal. The Japanese word "tsunami" means "long wave in the harbor" and has the same spelling for singular and plural.

VOLCANIC EXPLOSIVITY INDEX (VEI)

The reported size, or "bigness," of historical eruptions depends very much on both the experience and vantage point of the observer. Volcanology, unfortunately, has no instrumentally determined magnitude scale, like that used successfully by seismologists for earthquakes, and it is easy to understand why one observer's "major" eruption might be another's "moderate," or even "small" event. However, there are several size measurements that can aid quantitative ranking of eruptions, such as height of eruptive cloud, volume of eruptive products, distances to which objects of a particular size were thrown, and explosive energy coupled into the air wave (measured by recording barographs). Walker (1980) has provided a thoughtful discussion of the various measures of "bigness" and both the Volcanological Society of Japan and the Smithsonian's SEAN/GVN have been attempting to gather the quantitative data needed from contemporary eruptions. However, these data exist for an unfortunately small proportion of contemporary eruptions, and that proportion decreases dramatically as one goes back in the historical record. To meet the need for a meaningful magnitude measure that can be easily applied to the past, Newhall and Self (1982) integrated quantitative data with the subjective descriptions of observers, building on an earlier scale introduced in Japan (Tsuya, 1955). The result is the Volcanic Explosivity Index (VEI), and we have assigned VEIs since Chris Newhall generously provided his data in 1979.

The VEI has some similarities to the Richter magnitude scale for earthquakes. It is a simple 0-to-8 index of increasing explosivity, each interval representing an increase of about a factor of ten. The VEI combines total volume of explosive products, eruptive cloud height, descriptive terms, and other measures (Table 8, with examples of VEI assignments in Table 9). Note that there is some intentional overlap in criteria for VEI assignments, and a combination of data is used whenever possible. Attention is paid to the records of nearby volcanoes in estimating VEI for poorly described eruptions, and a correction has been made for the fact that only the relatively important eruption records survive in the early history of most regions. Eruptions before a certain date—generally 1700 AD for most regions but different in some (1000 AD for Iceland, Europe, and Japan; 1500 for parts of Central America and México; and 1800 AD for Tonga-Samoa, Melanesia, and Kamchatka) depending on regional history—have had some VEI values increased by 1 unit and these upgraded values are indicated in our tables by an up-arrow (e.g. 3↑).

Eruptions that were definitely explosive, but carry no other descriptive information in their record, have been assigned a default VEI of 2, leading to a disproportionate number of eruptions bearing this VEI, but this also reflects that fact that the large majority of explosive eruptions are of small-to-moderate size.

The counterpart of VEI upgrading described above is the

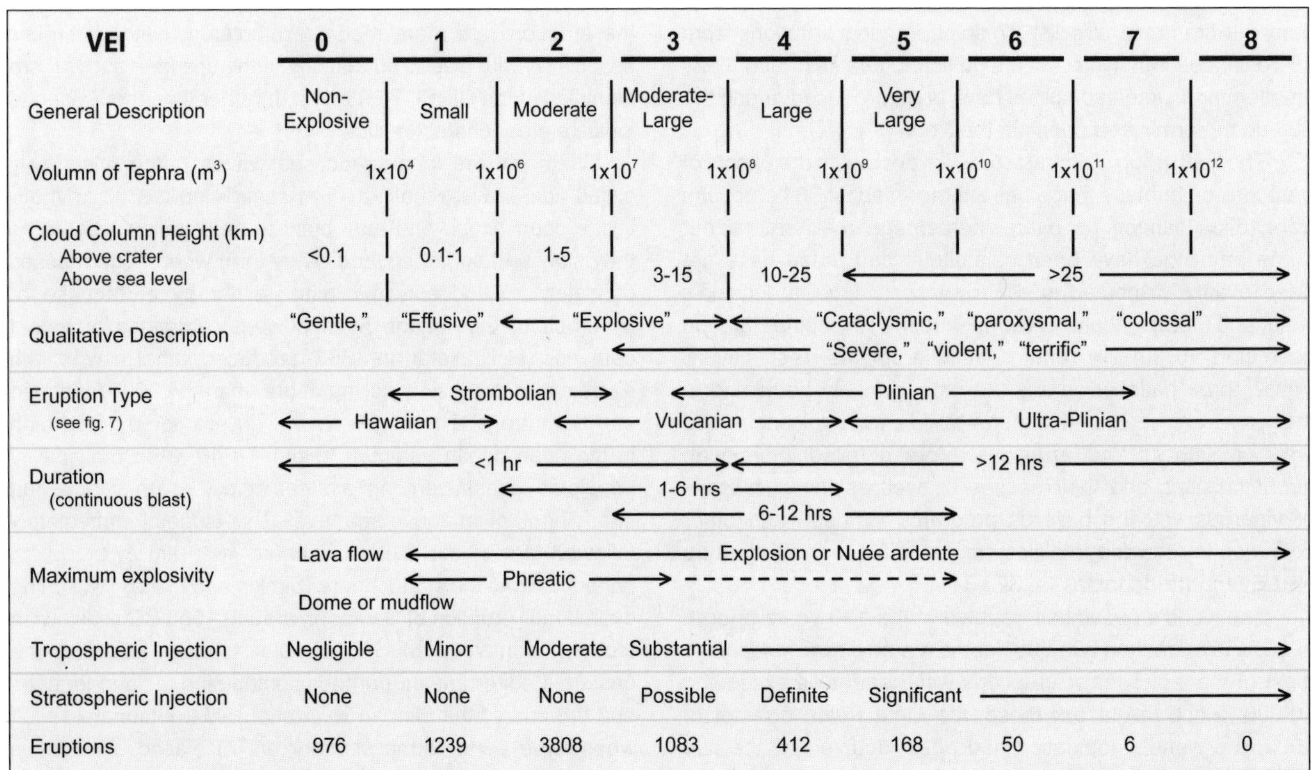

VEI	0	1	2	3	4	5	6	7	8
General Description	Non-Explosive	Small	Moderate	Moderate-Large	Large	Very Large			
Volumn of Tephra (m^3)	$1x10^4$	$1x10^6$	$1x10^7$	$1x10^8$	$1x10^9$	$1x10^{10}$	$1x10^{11}$	$1x10^{12}$	
Cloud Column Height (km) Above crater	<0.1	0.1-1	1-5						
Above sea level				3-15	10-25	← >25 →			
Qualitative Description	"Gentle,"	"Effusive"	← "Explosive" →		← "Cataclysmic," "paroxysmal," "colossal" →				
				← "Severe," "violent," "terrific" →					
Eruption Type (see fig. 7)		← Strombolian →		← Plinian →					
	← Hawaiian →		← Vulcanian →		← Ultra-Plinian →				
Duration (continuous blast)	← <1 hr →				← >12 hrs →				
			← 1-6 hrs →						
				← 6-12 hrs →					
Maximum explosivity	Lava flow	← Explosion or Nuée ardente →							
		← Phreatic → - - - - →							
	Dome or mudflow								
Tropospheric Injection	Negligible	Minor	Moderate	Substantial →					
Stratospheric Injection	None	None	None	Possible	Definite	Significant →			
Eruptions	976	1239	3808	1083	412	168	50	6	0

Table 8. Volcanic Explosivity Index (VEI) criteria (Newhall and Self, 1982).

VEI	Tephra Vol. (km^3)	Volcano	Region	Year
0	Effusive	**Masaya**	Nicaragua	1570
1	>0.00001	**Poás**	Costa Rica	1991
2	>0.001	**Ruapehu**	New Zealand	1971
3	>0.01	**Nevado del Ruiz**	Colombia	1985
4	>0.1	**Pelée**	West Indies	1902
5	>1	**St. Helens**	United States	1980
6	>10	**Krakatau**	Indonesia	1883
7	>100	**Tambora**	Indonesia	1815
8	>1000	**Yellowstone**	United States	Pleistocene

Table 9. Holocene eruptions in VEI size classes.

downgrading (by one VEI unit) for those eruptions in which substantial tephra volumes were accumulated over long periods of time and/or much of that volume was in near-vent cone construction. Parícutin, the volcano born in a Mexican cornfield, is a good example: it produced 1.3 km^3 of tephra (VEI 5 magnitude), but over a 9-year eruption, and is consequently assigned a VEI of 4. The VEI emphasizes explosivity, and eruptions that produce their tephra over a long period normally have less impact than those producing an equivalent volume in a shorter, more violent lifetime. Recent observations at Redoubt and Pinatubo volcanoes have shown that, although pyroclastic flows are emplaced along the surface, elutriating ash clouds can produce ash columns comparable to those of large, vertically directed explosions. Pyroclastic-flow deposit volumes are thus included with tephra-fall volumes as indicators of eruption magnitude.

The VEI was developed, in fact, to aid studies of climatic impact from volcanism. It was conceived by volcanologists as a purely volcanological measure of explosive eruption magnitude, in order to avoid the circularity of using climatic effects to measure eruptions and then using that measure to confirm the influence of volcanism on climate. It has proved to be a helpful approximation of eruption size, particularly useful in allowing assignments based on incomplete information from the historical record, but it had barely been introduced when it quickly showed its limitations as a measure of climatic influence. The 1982 eruption of México's El Chichón, although very close to the 1980 eruption of Mount St. Helens by VEI measures, produced a dramatically larger aerosol cloud. Because of the many sophisticated tools available in the 1980s for monitoring the atmosphere and stratosphere, it was soon recognized that the critical difference between these two events was that El Chichón contributed roughly 10 times the SO_2 that St. Helens did to higher altitudes. SO_2 reacts with stratospheric H_2O to produce an aerosol of H_2SO_4, and it is this fine mist, distributed as a broad stratospheric layer, that acts as a shield to solar radiation, thereby cooling the Earth's surface below. The lesson of these two eruptions showed that eruptive volume, cloud height, and the other eruption descriptors of the VEI provide an inadequate measure of climatic impact. What is needed is the incorporation of an eruption's SO_2 production into its magnitude, but that is proving difficult to do. Although SO_2 can be measured in contemporary eruptions (e.g., Bluth et al., 1992), it is difficult to assess for the past, so we have retained the VEI here as the most useful measure available for eruptions through the full Holocene record.

An "*" following a VEI unit indicates that there are two or more VEI assignments for that eruption, as in the common example of a short, paroxysmal eruption accompanied by lower level activity over months or years. In the **DIRECTORY**, the "*" follows the maximum VEI for an eruption, and alerts the reader that more information on the eruption can be found in the **CHRONOLOGY** section. An italicized line in the **CHRONOLOGY** warns the reader that this event is part of a longer eruption, and that preceding, and possibly succeeding, VEI data may be found in the **CHRONOLOGY** between the start and stop dates listed in the **DIRECTORY**. VEI data for paroxysmal phases are entered mainly for the large, well-studied eruptions, and the data used to establish VEIs for separate eruptive phases are not available for the vast majority of eruptions in our file. Italics are used in the **CHRONOLOGY** to identify lesser entries; only the single largest event during an eruption is listed in normal type. If the level of activity differs significantly from year to year (in a continuing eruption), the VEI assigned to that year is entered as a separate line and no **Cont**inuing year entry appears.

A "**?**" accompanies those VEIs that were particularly difficult to assign or are based on purely circumstantial evidence. For example, a VEI of 1? might have been assigned to an undescribed eruption because a nearby contemporaneous eruption received sufficient historical comment to confidently assign a VEI of 2. For roughly a quarter of the eruptions in our file, there was simply no evidence on which to base a VEI, and this column was left empty.

A "**+**" following a VEI indicates an eruption volume in the upper third of the range for that particular VEI designation. It shows those eruptions known to be larger than most others with the same VEI numeral, but its absence does not necessarily indicate a relatively small event. The designation is used only for VEIs ≥4, and volume data permit adding it to only 54 events, but it is helpful to identify the obviously larger events in volume ranges that span a full order of magnitude.

Bold type is used in both **DIRECTORY** and **CHRONOLOGY** listings to emphasize VEIs of 5 and above. We have also used letters in the VEI column to identify eruptions known to have been large (probably VEI ≥4) but lacking the reported data necessary to assign a specific VEI. Eruptions associated with caldera collapse are normally large, and those for which we have been unable to assign a VEI are here indicated by a bold "**C**" in the VEI column. The same is true for plinian deposits and, in the absence of more quantitative data, we have marked such eruptions with "**P**" in the VEI column. When both caldera collapse and plinian eruptions occur, the letter "**C**" takes precedence, but in neither case (and particularly with plinian eruptions) can these letters be used as a comprehensive listing of such characteristics. Finally, as mentioned above under **DATING TECHNIQUES**, we have entered in the **CHRONOLOGY** some of the largest eruptions known only from ice core research. These are marked by an "**I**" before the date and "Source unknown" message under "**VOLCANO NAME**." These 78 dates are largely from the Zielinski et al. (1994, 1996) reports on the GISP2 core from Greenland. They represent SO_4^{2-} residuals ≥90 ppb, a figure chosen (somewhat arbitrarily) to include some historical low-latitude events with VEI ≥4 while excluding high-latitude events of VEI ≤3 from Iceland and Alaska. Several dates marked with SP (South Pole) are primarily from the work of Delmas et al., 1992. These are sulfate levels >200 ng/g (not directly comparable to the GISP2 measurements). This limit was chosen because several historical eruptions as close to GISP2 as to the South Pole failed to exceed the 90 ppb cutoff used there, and were in the 100-190 ng/g range at the South Pole. Despite the apparent precision of ice-core dates, they are accompanied by dating uncertainties of often unstated magnitude.

The largest Holocene eruptions were of VEI 7 magnitude, and only one of these, Indonesia's Tambora in 1815, was recorded historically. Other Holocene VEI 7 eruptions include Changbaishan (or Baitoushan) on the China/Korea border ca. 1000 AD, Santorini in Greece, ca. 1610 BC, Kikai in Japan ca. 4350 BC, Crater Lake in Oregon ca. 5677 BC (ice core date), and Kuril Lake in Kamchatka ca. 6440 BC. Even larger volume eruptions (VEI 8) have been recorded during the Pleistocene, but only two of these have currently been documented during the past 100,000 years. The well-known Toba eruption about 74,000 years ago produced 2500-3000 km^3 of magma (Chesner and Rose, 1991), and the latest known VEI 8 eruption, at Taupo volcano in New Zealand, produced the Kawakawa (Oruanui) Tephra about 22,600 years ago (Wilson, 1993). VEI's of 5 or more have been assigned to 225 Holocene eruptions from 118 volcanoes. At the time of our 2nd edition, New Zealand, with a relatively small number of volcanoes but a well-developed tephrochronologic record, led the list with 9% of these eruptions, but vigorous stratigraphic studies of Kamchatka volcanoes have pushed this region to the top of the list, with 17% of the world's total. Shiveluch volcano alone has nearly half of these. Taupo's youngest VEI 5 eruption (ca. 230 AD) was thought by Walker (1980) to be the most powerful eruption known (80% of its products—or 20 km^3 of tephra—having been distributed farther than 220 km from its source). At least 635 eruptions carry a VEI of 4 or more. As with VEI 5 eruptions, Shiveluch volcano dominates this list, with 43 eruptions of VEI 4 or higher. Fully half of the volcanoes for which we have VEI data have had "large" eruptions in the VEI range 3-7. Magnitude and frequency of eruptions is discussed in more detail below.

One further limitation of the VEI must be mentioned. Radar measurements of cloud heights, such as those made of the eruptions following the May 18 paroxysm at Mount St. Helens in 1980, have shown that rather small events can produce plumes that reach quite high altitudes, and these observations have been supported by grain-size measurements and the modeling of eruption dynamics (Sigurdsson, 1991). The upper limits of cloud height used in the original VEI designations (Table 8) are too low, with the result that some VEIs assigned on the basis of cloud height are one (or even two) units higher than they would have been on the basis of tephra volume. If both measures are known, volume is used to assign VEI, but for many events in recent decades only cloud height is available. This means that some VEIs, particularly in the 3-4 range, are higher than they should be. The VEI structure has not been revised, however, and we have not undertaken the large job of rechecking VEI assignments based on cloud height. Instead, we use the VEI as a helpful guide to explosive magnitude for three-fourths of known Holocene eruptions. It should not be used to indicate size of effusive, lava-producing eruptions, its limitations in assessing climatic impact have been discussed above, and some assignments are no doubt off by one or even two units. Because no alternative measure can be applied to more than a small proportion of Holocene events, if used with reasonable caution, it is a valuable indicator of eruptive magnitude.

VOLUME of PRODUCTS (Vol L/T)

Accurate measurement of eruptive volumes requires careful field work and is often subject to irresolvable uncertainties. The many difficulties of making accurate measurements have, unfortunately, inhibited the reporting of even rough estimates, and we have volume information for fewer than a fifth of the eruptions in our file. Volume estimates can be made, however, thousands of years after the eruption, and the number of these estimates is increasing rapidly as volcanologists piece together the Holocene histories of important volcanoes. We have tephra volume data (**VT**) for 1338 eruptions and lava volume data (**VL**) for 1023 eruptions, 13% and ~10%, respectively, of all eruptions. We have volume data from 394 volcanoes, although more than a quarter of the volumes are from 7 vigorous, well studied volcanoes: Shiveluch (89), Etna (85), Kilauea and Fournaise (54 each), Oshima (39), Mauna Loa (32), and Merapi (31).

Although full volume data, including references, are entered in the database, only the order of magnitude is displayed here. Thus a lava volume of 1,300,000 cubic meters, or 1.3×10^6 m^3, appears in the appropriate "**V/L**" column simply as "6." This means that an eruption volume may be nearly 10 times larger than the exponent value shown, but there is such large initial uncertainty in most eruptive volumes that we preferred to display, in the limited space available, at least this order-of-magnitude estimate as a crude indication of both eruption size and the availability of volume estimates. In a relatively few number of cases the original source lists only order of magnitude data.

Volumes of 10^9 m^3 (1 km^3) or larger are emphasized in the **DIRECTORY** and **CHRONOLOGY** by use of bold type. VEIs of 5 and above have received this treatment (see above), so doing the same for non-explosive, effusive eruptions assures that all events likely to have produced a cubic kilometer of material are emphasized by bold type in the VEI or Volume columns on the right-hand side of our tables.

The measurements needed to determine volume are difficult to make in the field. Thick deposits often hide their own true thickness, and thin, distal deposits are by nature ephemeral (although often comprising a significant proportion of the total volume). Much ash falls in the sea, where measurements are difficult, costly, and often rendered inaccurate by sea-floor processes such as bioturbation. In addition to these uncertainties, tephra volumes are generally listed without correction for three important factors: (a) vesicularity (the void space occupied by air bubbles, or vesicles, in pumiceous material); (b) the extraneous fragments of older rock included accidentally in the deposit; or (c) compaction of ash layers with time. The tephra volume displayed, therefore, may be substantially larger than the volume of new magma emitted.

The volume figures listed here vary widely in size. Iceland accounts for both the smallest and largest historical lava volumes known; from the 26 m^3 of magma extruded from a Krafla borehole in 1977 (Larsen et al., 1979) to the ~15 km^3 of lava from Lakagigar in 1783 (Thordarson and Self, 1993). The largest historical lava flows, however, are dwarfed by some in the prehistoric, geologic record. Fifteen million years ago, single flows measuring 700 km^3 flooded a 1000 km^2 area of the northwestern United States in only a few days (Swanson and Wright, 1978). The same is true of large explosive eruptions. Tephra from history's largest eruption, Tambora 1815, exceeded 100 km^3, but only about 21,600 radiocarbon years ago about 1170 km^3 of tephra was erupted from Taupo volcano (Wilson, 1993), and 74,000 years ago another Indonesian volcano, Toba, erupted 2,800 km^3 of rhyolitic magma (Chesner and Rose, 1991; Ninkovich et al., 1978). Two million years ago a Yellowstone eruption produced 2,500 km^3 of magma in devastating ash flows, the like of which have (fortunately) never been seen in history (Izett and Wilcox, 1982; Christiansen, 2001). A much more recent eruption from Yellowstone, 0.64 million years ago (Ma), was nearly as large, and numerous Oligocene eruptions in the western U.S. were even larger (G. Izett, 1992 pers. comm.).

Volume data are available for fewer than one-fifth of the eruptions in our file and a far smaller proportion of all eruptions, unrecorded as well as recorded, in Holocene time. This fact should caution against misuse of volume data, and the reader should also be cautioned about a possibly confusing convention that we have used for volume data in the **CHRONOLOGY** section. The volume data for the whole eruption has been repeated when a continuing eruption is repeated in a following year or years. These repetitions are clear because the line is italicized (see also discussion in VEI section above), and we have deleted some repeated volumes that we know are inapplicable (such as the early volumes for the Tambora eruption that began in 1812 but produced its major tephra volume in April of 1815). For most eruptions, however, we have not been able to apportion the volume in successive years, and we have thought it better to repeat the total (with cautionary italics) than to assign it arbitrarily to the eruption's start date.

Historical Record: Trends and Cautions

The past four decades of Smithsonian compilation of volcano and eruption data provide context for assessing issues of regional and global volcanism; the tables and references presented here and on the on-line version of *Volcanoes of the World* provide windows into temporal or spatial evaluation of our planet's volcanism. The events of the present provide some of our best clues in interpreting Earth's past volcanism. The detailed documentation of volcanic processes and events at historical eruptions from eyewitness accounts, photographs, and instrumental documentation all build a picture of the processes, rates, and interrelationships of events that cannot be found from the products alone. This context is essential in understanding volcanism and assessing the likelihood and character of future activity.

The value of documentation of the recent volcanological record is clear. However, its limitations are not as apparent and require continued emphasis to caution anyone brash enough to mistake the record for the reality. Perhaps the best illustration of the record's limitations come from the data themselves. In Figure 9, the last 600 years of apparent global volcanism are shown by the number of volcanoes known to have been active each year. At first glance the nearly exponential increase through recent centuries suggests that the planet may soon be overwhelmed by volcanic activity, but this increase tracks the striking growth of global population that has spread potential observers of eruptions over much of the Earth and the technological advances that have facilitated reporting of those eruptions.

Another indicator of the growth of the volcanic record is the increase in number of historically active volcanoes around the world (Figure 9). If a list of such volcanoes had been continuously kept, it would, at the time of Christ, have contained only the names of 9 Mediterranean volcanoes and West Africa's Mount Cameroon. In the next ten centuries the list would have grown by only 30 names, 18 of them Japanese. Although newly settled Iceland soon added 7 volcanoes, the list totaled only 63 by 1400 AD, where Figure 9 begins.

A dramatic, roughly 5-fold increase in both the number of historically active volcanoes and their recorded eruptions took place about 1500 AD. These increases resulted in part from the great Spanish/Portuguese marine Age of Discovery explorations around the end of the 15th century, when Columbus, Balboa, Vasco da Gama, Magellan, and others opened Latin America and much of the western Pacific to European record-keeping. But perhaps equally important was the development and widespread distribution of the printing press in the late 15th century, markedly increasing the likelihood that new volcanological records would survive. Through the 17th and into the early 18th century, the identification of new volcanoes outpaced the list of reported eruptions, but by the 18th century global trade was flourishing, the Industrial Revolution was under way, and the reporting of new eruptions swiftly dominated the discovery of new volcanoes. The list has continued to grow, with several important volcanic regions such as New Zealand, Alaska, and Hawaii being unrepresented until the last 250 years.

Examination of the geologic record for many regions shows major periods of Earth history in which volcanism is clearly concentrated (e.g., Kennett, 1981; Kennett et al., 1977; Vogt, 1979). The last 200 years, with humans distributed over most of the globe and relatively efficient communication lines in use, would seem to be the best suited to search for episodic, or cyclical, trends in global volcanism. However, even in the last two centuries, we find historical trends in reporting overshadowing any real trends in volcanism.

Figure 10 shows the detailed record of volcanism over the last 200 years. The overall trend of increased reporting, so dominant in Figure 9, is evident, but we notice that the two most prominent drops below that rising trend correspond precisely with the two world wars of this century. In times of great international instability, the people (and presses) that might otherwise have reported natural phenomena were preoccupied with other things. In the years 1941-45, for example, the number of volcanoes reported active in the western Pacific and Indonesia dropped by nearly one-third from the preceding 5 years, while regions less affected by the war showed little change. With more observers in more unusual areas during World War II, it seems likely that more eruptions than normal were actually witnessed, but it is easy to appreciate why many of these eruptions were never recorded in the scientific literature.

Great economic crises, like wars, might also be expected to interfere with the reporting of natural events. One of the most precipitous drops in reported volcanism took place following the stock market collapse of 1929 and during the ensuing Great Depression. From the late 1920's to the early 1930's, every volcanic region in the world (except those of Russia, Melanesia, and the West Indies) showed a drop in the number of volcanoes reported active. Because reporting of volcanism depends on humans, it seems reasonable to expect that widespread preoccupation with war or economic depression would have decreased reporting effectiveness, resulting in apparent reductions in global volcanism. For the same reason, it seems reasonable to expect that times of increased global sensitivity to volcanism would result in enhanced reporting of eruptions. Two of the most notorious eruptions of recent centuries were at Krakatau in 1883 (more than 36,000 victims) and Mont Pelée in 1902 (about 29,000 victims). They received widespread global publicity for years afterwards and the resulting increased sensitivity to volcanism may be at least partially responsible for the relatively high level of reported volcanism for 5-to-7 years after each eruption occurred (Figure 10).

More recent major eruptions, such as Mount St. Helens in

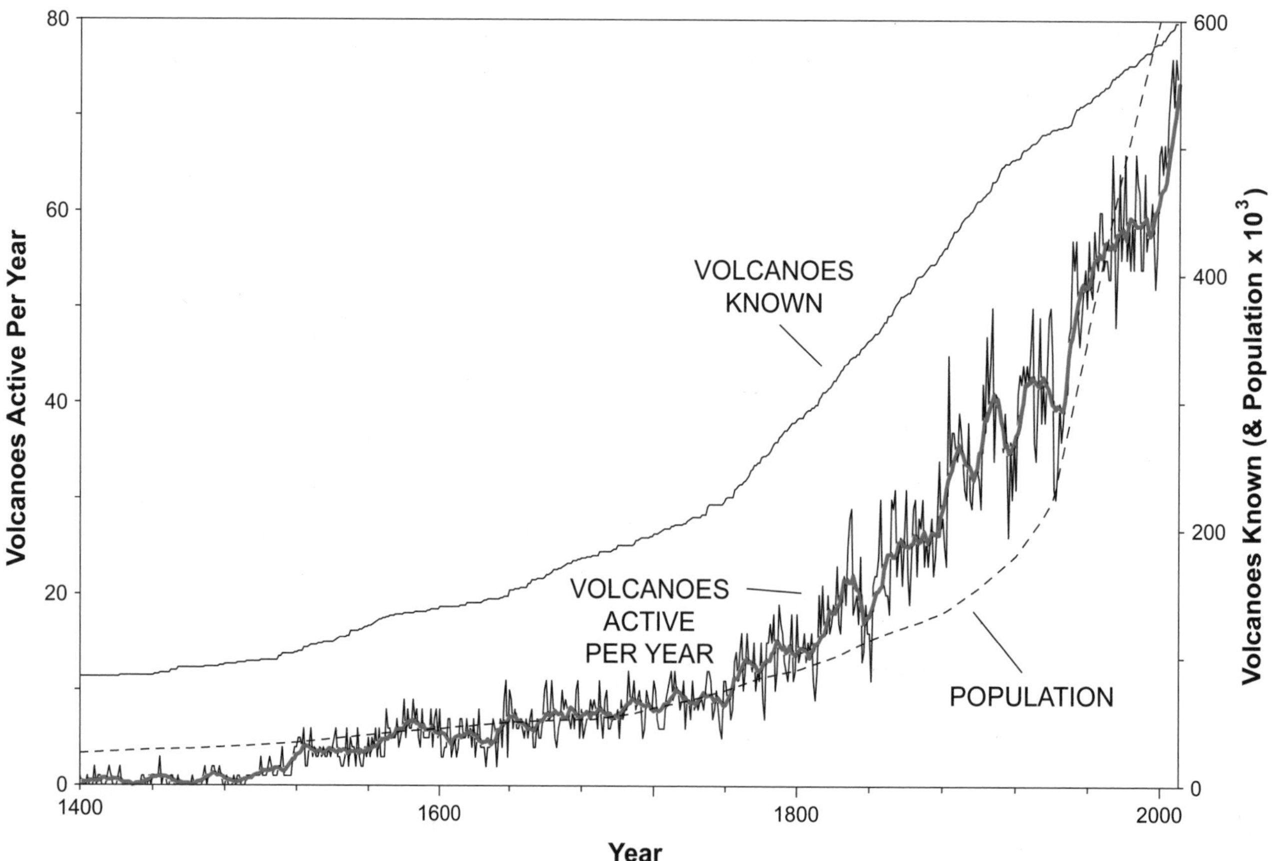

Figure 9. 600 years of volcano reporting. Total number of volcanoes erupting per year (black line) and 10-year running mean of same data (red line). Eruption dates with an uncertainty >1 year or uncertain eruptions (those preceded by a "?" in the tables that follow) have not been included. A volcano with more than one eruption recorded in a year is counted only once. "Volcanoes known" is the total number with a historically recorded eruption by any given year. World's estimated human population data from McEvedy and Jones (1978) and (since 1750) Population Reference Bureau, Washington, D.C.

1980, have not had this effect, in part due to more systematic cataloging and media focus on volcanic events. The newsworthiness of an eruption depends more on its location and human impact than on its size. The 1980 eruption of Mount St. Helens, for example, generated enormous media attention, while the remarkably similar 1956 eruption of Bezymianny in sparsely populated Kamchatka, in which no lives were lost, was hardly noticed by the world press. Similarly, the 1991 eruption of Mt. Pinatubo, with its many fatalities and effects on nearby military bases, was front page news, but the eruption of Cerro Hudson that year in isolated southern Chile created barely a ripple in international interest.

This leaves the peak in the late 1820s and the sharp rise in the early 1950s (Figure 10) as the most prominent changes in apparent volcanism with no obvious relationship with historic events likely to influence eruption reporting either positively or negatively. The Alaskan peak reflects the observations of Lutke's exploring expedition to the Aleutians covered in their subsequent 1834-36 reports, which dramatically increased by a factor of four or more the number of reported Aleutian eruptions from the years bracketing the expedition. The distinct change in eruption documentation that occurred during the 2nd half of the 20th century was marked by a sharp rise in eruptions followed by a transition from the previous pattern of peaks and valleys to a more uniform one. This corresponds to the combined onset of three venues of global eruption documentation—the beginning of the *Catalog of Active Volcanoes of the World* series with eruption-rich Indonesia in 1951, publication of the annual *Bulletin of Volcanic Eruptions* of the Volcanological Society of Japan in 1960, and Smithsonian cataloging beginning in 1968.

At the time of our 2nd edition, the annual number of eruptions appeared to have plateaued for the previous three decades, suggesting that documentation of a uniform global eruption rate may have been realized. The new data of Figure 10, however, show an unanticipated rise in eruptions since about 2000 AD. Several new reporting effects appear to have contributed to this increase. These include the increased utilization of remote-sensing satellite data from volcano observatories, the onset of systematic reporting of volcanic ash plumes by the Volcanic Ash Advisory Centers (VAACs) to mitigate aircraft-ash interactions, and the deployment of NASA's first Earth Observing System (EOS) satellite 'Terra,' which was launched in December 1999. The SOEST MODIS thermal alerts have detected volcanic eruptions in sparsely populated or rarely visited regions, such as the effusive and explosive activity from glacier-covered Montagu Island in the South Sandwich Islands. These collective "eyes in the skies" have detected eruptions that might otherwise go unreported. Another contributing reporting factor may have been the onset of more systematic weekly documentation of current volcanism by the Smithsonian and USGS in 2000.

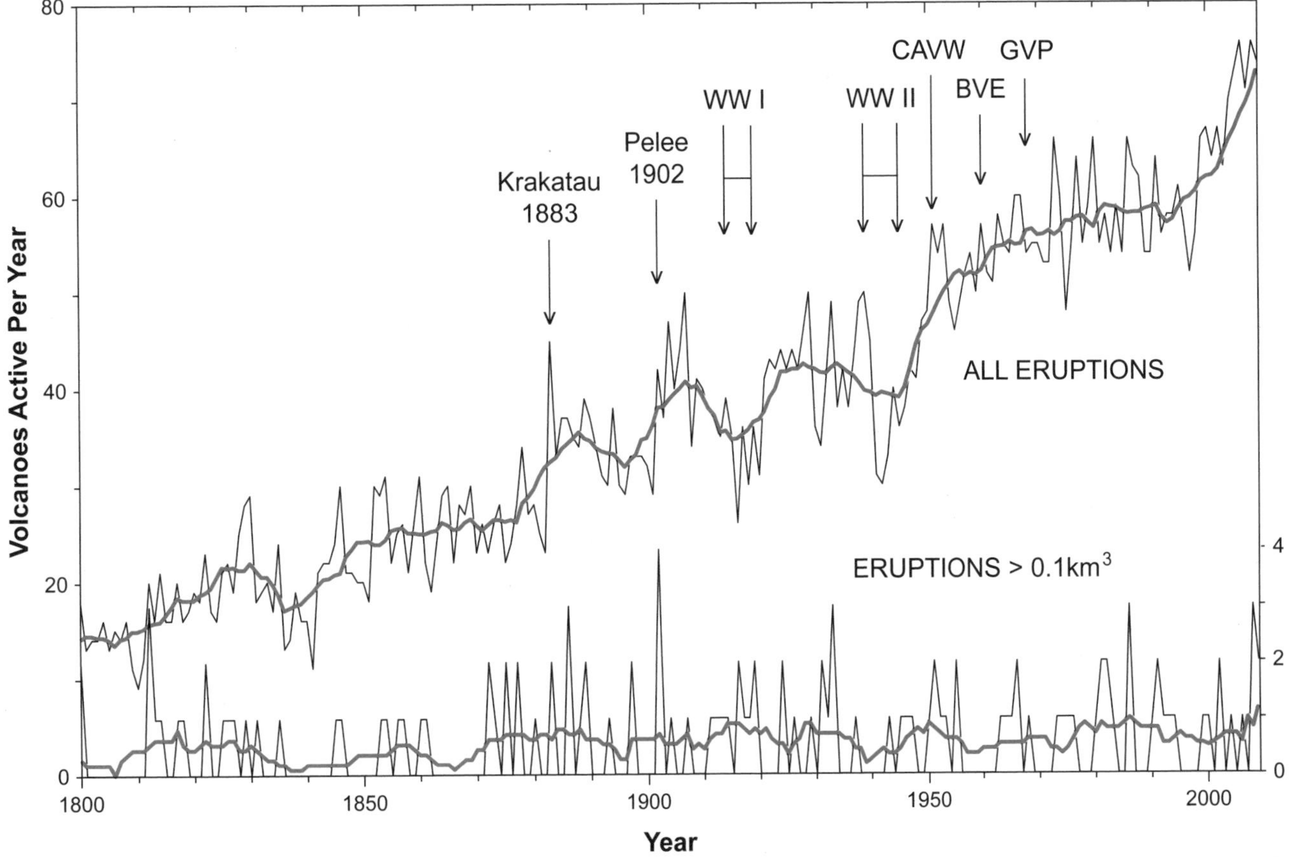

Figure 10. Last 200 years of volcano reporting. Total number of volcanoes erupting per year (upper black line) and 10-year running mean of same data (upper red line). Lower plot shows the annual number of volcanoes producing large eruptions (≥0.1 km^3 of tephra) and scale is enlarged (on right axis) with lower red line showing a 10-year running mean.

Thus all major trends in our recent volcanological record can be reasonably explained by socioeconomic and exploration influences. The apparent increase in activity reflects increases in people living near volcanoes to observe eruptions and improvements in communication technologies to report those eruptions. However, the best evidence that these trends are apparent rather than real comes from the record of large eruptions alone. At the base of Figure 10 we plot the data for eruptions producing more than 0.1 km^3 of tephra, using the same conventions as the plot of *all* eruptions above it (but at an expanded vertical scale). The effects of these large (VEI ≥4) eruptions are far reaching and thus they are less likely to escape documentation even in remote areas. Their constancy over the past two centuries is a better indicator of the global frequency of eruptions than the apparent increase of smaller eruptions.

VOLCANOES and HUMANS

The number of people living in proximity to volcanoes has risen commensurate with increases in global population. New global population data sets allow regional and global assessment of persons living near volcanoes. The LandScan population dataset produced by the Oak Ridge National Laboratory was applied to the Smithsonian Holocene volcano database to calculate a Volcano Population Index (VPI) surrounding volcanoes at radii of 5, 10, 30, and 100 km (Table 2). Calculations were made here for individual volcanoes at VPI_5, VPI_{10}, VPI_{30}, and VPI_{100} radii; regional comparisons were then made, compensating for overlapping intersecting radii of individual volcanic centers to avoid double-counting of persons living within proximity to more than one volcano (Siebert et al., 2008). The data also factor population densities at volcanic fields with large numbers of vents over broad areas, oceanic shield volcanoes with large footprints, and large silicic calderas. For volcanic fields, minimum population densities were calculated for those living within a rectangle encompassing the known footprint of the volcanic field or a circle of 20 km (the average radius of database volcanic fields with documented dimensions). Volcanoes with uncertain Holocene eruptions were excluded from these calculations. It must be emphasized that radial point-source data such as these do not take into account regional/seasonal tephra wind-dispersal factors or topographically controlled volcaniclastic flowage phenomena and thus represent relative risk.

Preliminary data show that >47 million people reside within a VPI_5 radius of ~1300 Holocene volcanoes (or volcanic-field vents). Persons living within this distance are subject to potentially lethal volcanic effects from even small to moderately large eruptions (VEI 2-3) and are most likely to require evacuation measures. About 58 million live within a VPI_{10} radius, where evacuation may be needed for small-to-moderately large eruptions. More than 200 million live within a VPI_{30} radius, subject to infrastructure-threatening tephra accumulations and distally diminishing pyroclastic flows from VEI 4-5 eruptions (Newhall and Hoblitt, 2002). About 753 million (>11% of the 6.5 billion world population) live within a VPI_{100} radius, with significant potential impact even in distal areas from tephra accumulation from large-volume (VEI 5-6) eruptions. Regional VPIs mimic global population distribution and are highest at VPI_5 and VPI_{10} in México/Central America and at VPI_{30} and VPI_{100} in Indonesia (Table 10).

These data allow assessment of global volcanic risk with respect to specific volcanic processes. More than 12 million people live within 10 km of 314 volcanoes or volcanic fields that have had documented pyroclastic flows during the Holocene, with the largest number of these being in México and Central America. This hazard is widespread, with 13 of the world's 19 regions containing volcanoes for which half or more of their eruptions (of volcanoes with at least 5 documented eruptions) have produced these devastating flows. The greatest number of people living near an individual pyroclastic-flow-producing volcano are the nearly one million residing within 10 km of El Salvador's Volcán San Salvador, which overlooks the capital city of the same name. San Salvador overtops deposits from the major caldera-forming eruptions of Ilopango volcano to the west. The 12 million global figure does not include the roughly 5.7 million people living within the massive Michoacán-Guanajuato volcanic field in México, which has produced small pyroclastic flows.

Nearly 17 million people live within 30 km of 65 volcanoes

Volcanoes with Post-1500 AD Eruptions (n = 589)

VPI_5 Region	Popl	VPI_{10} Region	Popl	VPI_{30} Region	Popl	VPI_{100} Region	Popl
Mexico/Central America	8,963,970	Mexico/Central America	10,067,371	Indonesia	48,543,028	Indonesia	173,900,211
Philippines & SE Asia	2,588,904	Indonesia	4,947,238	Mexico/Central America	24,192,929	Japan	80,710,010
Europe	2,384,784	Philippines & SE Asia	3,463,392	Philippines & SE Asia	10,651,359	Philippines & SE Asia	73,743,688
Indonesia	2,111,700	Europe	2,802,081	Japan	9,703,526	Mexico/Central America	73,584,057
Arabia/Indian Ocean	1,360,511	Arabia/Indian Ocean	1,360,511	Europe	6,002,350	Africa	41,427,447

Holocene Volcanoes (n = 1295)

VPI_5 Region	Popl	VPI_{10} Region	Popl	VPI_{30} Region	Popl	VPI_{100} Region	Popl
Mexico/Central America	12,855,939	Mexico/Central America	15,073,682	Indonesia	63,540,182	Indonesia	179,374,526
Philippines & SE Asia	8,291,857	Indonesia	10,051,210	Mexico/Central America	40,215,827	Philippines & SE Asia	110,799,197
Indonesia	5,895,487	Philippines & SE Asia	9,969,791	Philippines & SE Asia	31,817,156	Africa	99,846,719
Arabia/Indian Ocean	5,637,008	Africa	6,584,494	Africa	19,636,196	Japan	93,601,463
Africa	5,377,753	Arabia/Indian Ocean	5,641,014	Japan	13,800,588	Mexico/Central America	89,104,387

Table 10. Volcano Population Index (VPI) data by region. Volcanoes with post-1500 eruptions as a proxy for "historically active" volcanoes. Holocene volcanoes exclude those with uncertain Holocene eruptions. Totals may include residents of the adjacent region living within the pertinent radius of a region's volcano.

that have had dated Holocene caldera-forming eruptions; about half of these are in Europe/W Asia and the Philippines. Almost 5 million people live within 30 km of Vesuvius and Etna volcanoes, which had relatively small caldera-forming eruptions during the Holocene, and Campi Flegrei caldera, which partially underlies the city of Naples, had a major caldera-forming eruption about 12,000 years ago. About 2.4 million people in the greater Manila area live in proximity to Taal volcano, which had a caldera-forming eruption about 5500 years ago, and more than a million more reside near Pinatubo volcano, where successful monitoring by Philippine and USGS volcanologists prevented major fatalities during its 1991 caldera-forming eruption. The numbers of people susceptible to caldera-forming eruptions would be much higher were it not that many regions with large numbers of caldera-forming volcanoes, such as Kamchatka and the Aleutians, are fortuitously sparsely populated.

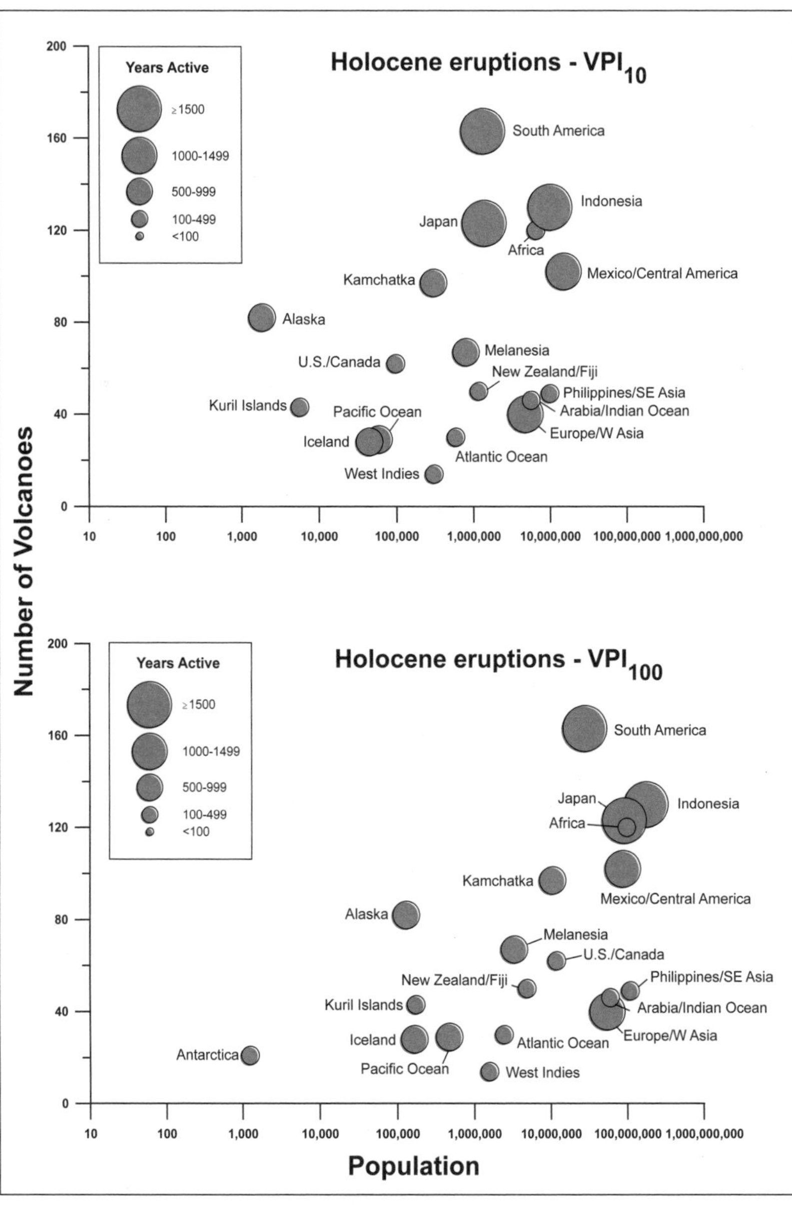

Figure 11. Regional population data for Holocene volcanoes at 10 km radius (top) and 100 km radius (bottom). Circle size indicates number of cumulative Holocene years active within each region.

The five highest regions with population within VPI_5, VPI_{10}, VPI_{30}, and VPI_{100} radii are shown with post-1500 eruptions as a proxy for "historically active" volcanoes and for Holocene volcanoes (Table 10), excluding those with uncertain Holocene eruptions. Population data are discriminated to eliminate duplicate counting for overlapping radii.

Only three regions (Indonesia, Philippines and SE Asia, and México/Central America) make the top five in all categories shown here, and only seven of the world's 19 volcanic regions populate the top 5 list in any category. México/Central America is the region with the highest potential risk for residents in close proximity to volcanoes or volcanic-field vents (VPI_5 and VPI_{10}). Indonesia has the highest risk from larger-volume eruptions affecting broader areas (VPI_{30} and VPI_{100}); in fact the entire more than 130 million population of Java, the world's most populated island, lies within 100 km of a Holocene volcano. Only 7 of 19 global regions from the IAVCEI volcano catalog make the top five in any of the categories, with Africa and Arabia/Indian Ocean making perhaps non-intuitive appearances reflecting the proximity of volcanoes or large volcanic fields to large African rift cities, such as Adis Abeba in Ethiopia and Nairobi in Kenya, the Saudi Arabia cities of Al Madinah and Makkah (Mecca), and the Yemeni capital of Sana'a.

We examined population densities near volcanoes with respect to the degree of activity of those volcanoes. Population in volcanic regions residing within 10 km (top) and 100 km (bottom) of Holocene volcanoes is shown in Figure 11 and for "historically active" volcanoes with eruptions since 1500 AD in Figure 12. The data are corrected to eliminate multiple counting of residents living within 10 and 100 km radii of more than one volcano. The diameters of the circles are proportional to "years active," the cumulative number of eruption years during the Holocene (Figure 11) and the cumulative years active since 1500 AD (Figure 12).

All plots show a similar trend, somewhat disturbing from a volcanic hazards perspective, with the largest populations at risk from volcanoes living adjacent to the most active volcanoes. Densely populated Indonesia, Japan, México/Central America, and Europe/W Asia, along with South America (with its higher number of volcanoes) are all regions with the most frequently active volcanoes (those with more than 1000 cumulative years active). Several factors could contribute to these trends. Ash from volcanic eruptions provides soil nutrients, increasing the numbers of persons working and living on their flanks, and volcaniclastic deposits can create flat land in otherwise more mountainous terrain, providing favorable topography to construct towns and cities. The now-destroyed capital city of the island of Montserrat was constructed on virtually the island's only flat terrain (provided by previous eruptions of Soufrière Hills volcano), and the city of Armero, devastated by mudflows from Nevado del Ruiz volcano, was built on mudflow deposits from an eruption a little more than a century earlier.

VOLCANOES and AIRCRAFT

In recent decades, interactions between aircraft and volcanic ash emphasize the fact that hazards from volcanic eruptions are not restricted to people living near volcanoes, but also include those in transit over volcanic or even non-volcanic areas. The 1982 near-catastrophic jumbo jet ash encounter at Galunggung volcano in Indonesia, in which a commercial aircraft temporarily lost power in all four engines and glided silently for an agonizing 13 minutes before the engines were successfully restarted at lower altitude, kick-started interest in assessing and averting this risk. A similar incident over Redoubt, in Alaska in 1989, resulted in $80 million damage to the aircraft.

The impact of aircraft/ash interaction extends beyond physical damage of aircraft to the severe economic disruption caused by diversion and cancellation of flights. The sparse population of volcanic regions such as Alaska, Kamchatka, and the Kuriles does not immunize them from volcanic hazard, because their explosive volcanoes directly threaten heavily traveled great-circle air routes over the north Pacific. Aircraft-ash interactions are furthermore not restricted to volcanic regions. By September 19, 1992 an ash cloud erupted days earlier from Alaska's Mt. Spurr had drifted 5,000 km to northern Ohio (among the busiest airspaces in the world) and diversions around this very visible cloud resulted in major costs of rerouting delays. Volcanic ash drifts into air routes at altitudes greater than 30,000 ft for roughly 20 days per year worldwide (Miller and Casadevall, 2000), and by the end of 2003, 105 interactions between aircraft and ash had been recognized (Casadevall, 1994; Miller and Casadevall, 2000; Guffanti et al., 2004). More recently, the 2009 eruption of Redoubt volcano caused cancellation of hundreds of flights at Anchorage International Airport, highlighting the importance of volcanic monitoring by the USGS Alaska Volcano Observatory to detect explosive eruptions in this major international air corridor. An even more dramatic aviation/ash event took place during this writing (but after the eruption chronology included in this book) when Eyjafjallajökull volcano in Iceland erupted, producing ash plumes that drifted over Europe, causing cancellation of more than 100,000 flights, with severe economic ramifications.

Volcanologists, meteorologists, and the civil aviation industry have devoted much effort to mitigating the impact of volcanic ash plumes. In 2007 NOAA issued a multi-agency *National Volcanic Ash Operations Plan for Aviation*, of which the Smithsonian's Global Volcanism Program was a signatory, to help eliminate aircraft encounters with ash by improving the ability to detect, track, and forecast hazardous ash clouds and to provide adequate warnings to the aviation community on the known and projected transport of the ash cloud. An issue of the *Journal of Volcanology and Geothermal Research* (Webley and Mastin, 2009) was recently devoted to multi-agency efforts to improve prediction and tracking of volcanic ash clouds.

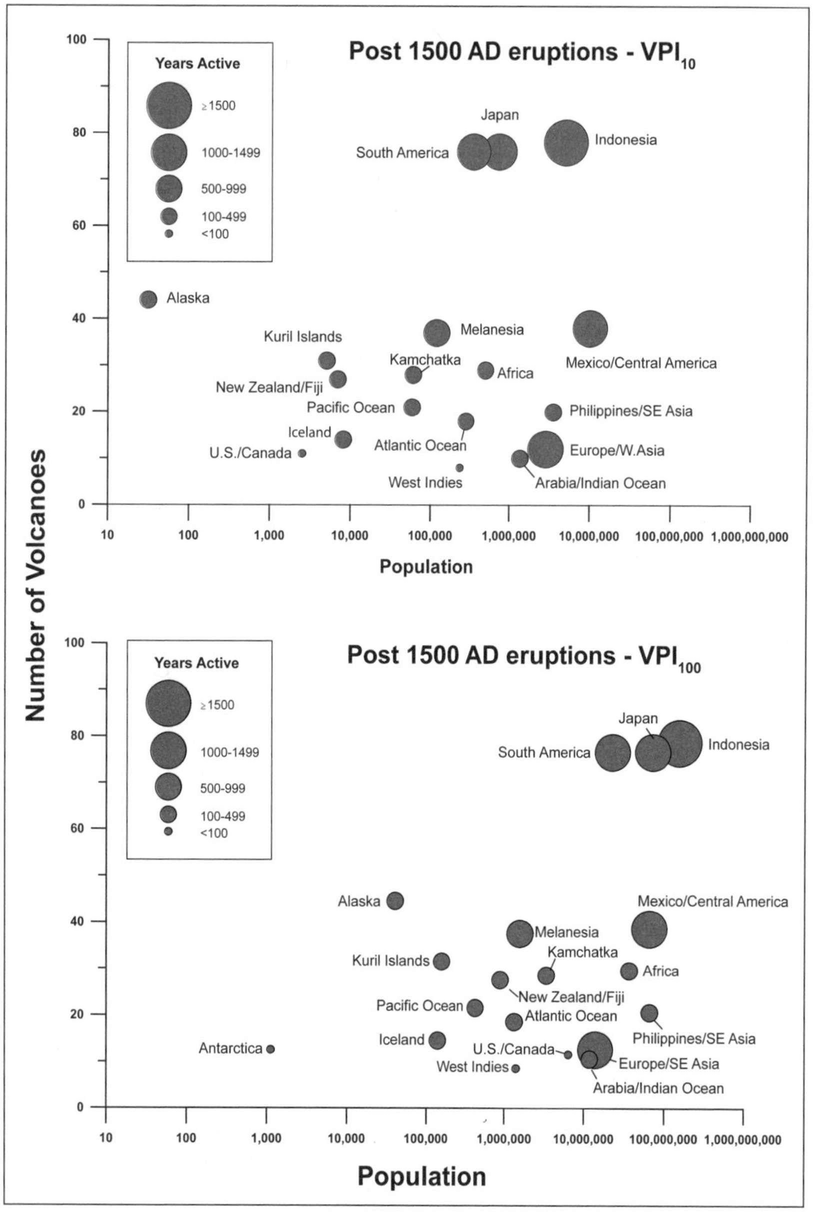

Figure 12. Regional population data for volcanoes with "historical" (post-1500 AD eruptions) at 10 km radius (top) and 100 km radius (bottom). Circle size indicates number of cumulative post-1500 AD years active within each region.

VOLCANIC PROCESSES

Volcanoes deliver material to the Earth's surface in a wide variety of ways. Eruptive processes are influenced by the "three Vs," volatiles, viscosity, and volume. The significance of volatiles is seen in the high percentage of eruptions that are explosive in character. More than four-fifths of all documented Holocene eruptions are explosive. In contrast, only slightly more than a quarter of all eruptions (27%) produced documented lava flows. Their effusion rates and distribution reflect magma chemistry, viscosity, and volume, which span many orders of magnitude. Highly viscous lava domes are erupted at a greatly reduced rate (only 6.5% of eruptions).

Of particular interest from a volcanic hazards perspective are high-impact eruptive processes such as pyroclastic flows. These have been documented at 14% of all confirmed Holocene eruptions. This drops to 8.7% when restricted to eruptions since 1500 AD, reflecting the lack of preservation of products of smaller-volume eruptions not likely to produce pyroclastic flows in the stratigraphic record of prehistoric eruptions. Percentages of eruptions with other eruptive processes can be found in the **Eruptive Characteristics** table on the inside front cover.

Also of concern from a hazards perspective are high-impact events that cause collapse of volcanoes, documented for the first time in this edition. Large-scale collapse of volcanic edifices can occur as a result of magma chamber evacuation following highly explosive eruptions, or from gravitational collapse that produces massive, highly mobile debris avalanches and leaves large breached collapse scarps. These two high-impact, low-frequency events have been recorded in roughly comparable numbers (79 and 71, respectively). Both are recorded in less than 1% of all known Holocene eruptions, but many prehistorical events remain undocumented.

Although the Holocene data would imply these two mechanisms of large-scale collapse of volcanic edifices occur at comparable rates, large-scale gravitational edifice collapse (also known as sector collapse) often occurs in the absence of eruptive activity, and would thus not be included in this compilation. A better temporal comparison would be the last 500 years, when both processes would be more likely to have been documented. Eleven major explosive eruptions producing caldera collapse have been recorded since 1500 AD (most recently at Pinatubo in 1991). During this same period, 20 syn-eruptive sector collapse events have occurred. An additional 4 likely non-eruptive sector collapse events since 1500 AD imply that gravitational sector collapse during this interval has been the dominant mechanism of large-scale volcano collapse, occurring at a rate twice that of caldera collapse resulting from explosive eruptions.

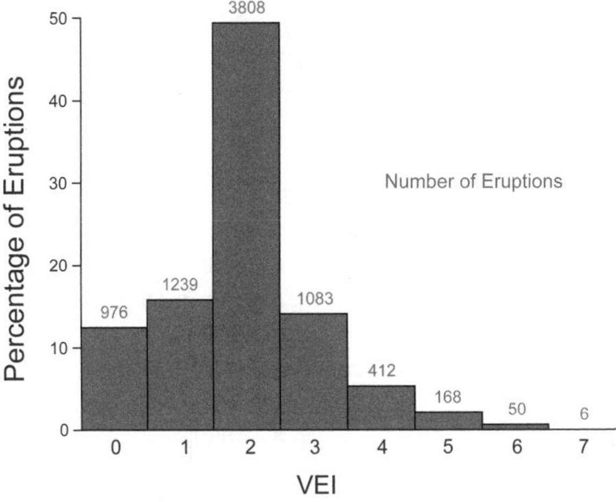

Figure 13. Volcanic Explosivity Index (VEI) (Newhall and Self, 1982). Percentage of VEI assignments on vertical axis, and number of assignments for each VEI labeled. VEI assignments are available for 75% of Holocene eruptions.

VOLCANISM: MAGNITUDE, FREQUENCY, and GLOBAL IMPACTS

The magnitude of the next eruption is of direct concern to those living in the shadow of volcanoes, but many factors influence an eruption's intensity. The past few decades have seen great strides in the ability to predict when an eruption will occur at well-monitored volcanoes, but anticipating the size of a pending eruption remains elusive. Volcanic eruptions vary dramatically in intensity over many orders of magnitude, with commensurate hazards implications.

The past record at individual volcanoes provides a perspective on potential future eruptions at that volcano, but some generalizations can be made from the global volcanic record. The explosive magnitude as expressed by the Volcanic Explosivity Index has a strong peak at VEI 2 (Figure 13), with nearly half of all eruptions with VEI assignments being of this magnitude. Although this peak is intensified somewhat by the default VEI assignment of 2 for explosive eruptions lacking other information, plume height data for recent eruptions support the strong dominance of VEI 2 eruptions. Small eruptions of VEI 0 to VEI 2 account for nearly four-fifths of all Holocene eruptions, and small-to-moderate magnitude eruptions of VEI 0 to VEI 3 for more than 90%. Only 6% of eruptions are VEI 4 or larger (the size of the devastating 1902 eruption of Pelée in the West Indies), and only 2.4% of explosive eruptions (224 in total) are VEI 5 or larger, the size of the 1980 eruption of Mount St. Helens. This implies that the vast majority of eruptions are fairly modest affairs, although proximal effects can still be considerable.

Explosive magnitude can be assessed by volcano as well as by eruption, and we have calculated data for the average VEI of the 299 volcanoes with 5 or more VEI assignments. Although average VEIs at the higher end can be biased by the difficulty of adequately documenting smaller volume tephra layers during stratigraphic studies, this nevertheless provides an indication of the relative explosivity of many of Earth's volcanoes. The highest documented average VEI is 4.62, from Japan's Towada volcano in northern Honshu. This lake-filled andesitic-to-rhyolitic caldera complex is one of Japan's most prolific tephra producers, and its Holocene explosive record (5 of 7 eruptions of VEI 5 magnitude) is a continuation of activity during the Pleistocene, when it produced as many as 14 explosive eruptions of VEI 5 and 6 magnitude. Other volcanoes with average VEIs of 4 or larger include, in decreasing order, El Chichón in México, Pinatubo in the Philippines, Ksudach in Kamchatka, Furnas in the Azores, Aniakchak in Alaska, Cerro Bravo in Colombia, and Mashu in Hokkaido. Not surprisingly, all these, with the exception of Furnas in the Azores, are subduction zone volcanoes.

Nearly half of all volcanoes have average VEIs of between 2 and 3 (the median value is 2.0), and nearly 90% of volcanoes have average VEIs of less than 3 (Figure 14). This figure increases to more than 97% when only historical eruptions are considered due to the more comprehensive documentation of smaller volume eruptions. The 37 volcanoes (only one eighth of the total) with average Holocene VEIs greater than 3 are from 14 of the world's 19 volcanic regions, but are dominated by Japan, Kamchatka, and México/Central America. These highly explosive volcanoes are of obvious concern in volcanic hazards assessments, but volcanoes with lower average VEIs that have produced occasional large volume eruptions must also be considered.

VEI assessments are based on both qualitative and quantitative data, and eruptions with documented volumes provide a somewhat similar perspective on eruption magnitude. The 1339 eruptions with documented tephra volumes peak at higher values (VEI 3 or 4 equivalent) than the VEI 2 peak of the full data set. This, however, reflects the fact that tephra volumes for smaller magnitude eruptions are rarely calculated, skewing the data towards the larger-volume eruptions.

The data of Figure 10 show that the larger eruptions (VEI ≥4) have taken place at a reasonably constant rate of nearly 1 per year for at least the last 140 years and that all eruptions have averaged about 50-70 per year for the last 60 years. These data reinforce our intuition that, like earthquakes, the frequency of eruptions decreases with increasing size: there are many small, fewer medium-sized, and far fewer large eruptions. Furthermore, the data and the historical argument marshaled above, suggest that the record for small eruptions is valid for only a few recent decades, whereas the record for larger events is accurate for more than a century.

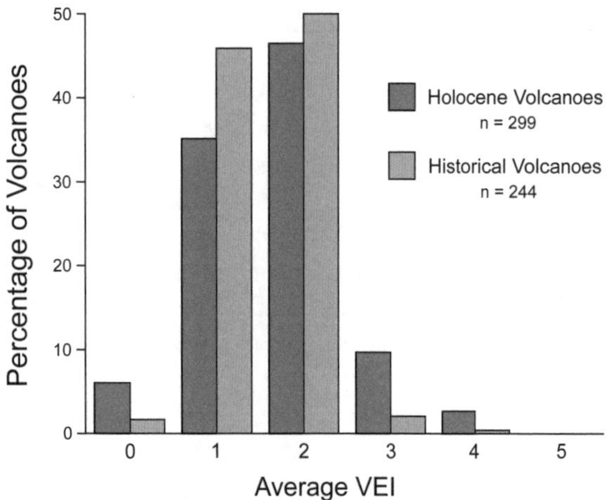

Figure 14. Average VEI of 299 volcanoes with more than 5 Holocene VEI assignments (darker fill), and 244 volcanoes with more than 5 historical VEI assignments (lighter fill).

Subaerial eruptions that produce at least 10^6 m^3 of tephra (VEI 2) take place at an average rate of once every few weeks somewhere on Earth. Those that produce ≥10^7 m^3 of tephra, such as the VEI 3 Ruiz event that generated such fatal mudflows in 1985, take place several times a year. Eruptions of VEI 4 (≥10^8 m^3 tephra), such as at Mount Pelée in 1902, occur on average every 1-2 years. Eruptions the size of St. Helens 1980 (≥10^9 m^3, or 1 km^3 and VEI 5) occur perhaps once a decade, those such as Krakatau 1883 (≥10 km^3) about every two centuries (50 total during the Holocene), and VEI 7 (≥100 km^3) eruptions, such as those of Tambora in 1815, 1-2 per millennium. Neither the historical or Holocene record, however, prepare us for the even larger eruptions of the past. The Toba eruption, only 74,000 years ago in Indonesia, produced nearly 10,000 times more magma (2700 km^3) than the St. Helens eruption (Chesner and Rose, 1991), and even larger eruptions are known from the older geologic record. There are, however, no known eruptions of VEI 9, or ≥10^4 km^3 of tephra, and magma chambers of such dimensions are virtually unknown in the geologic record. Ongoing efforts to flesh out the record of large volume Pleistocene eruptions are underway, and though we display a preliminary list on pages 361-371, we have not revised an earlier plot including rough estimates of these large-volume eruptions because of the still considerable uncertainties of volumes and frequencies of these very large events.

It is useful, however, to look at the known effect of large historical eruptions. The 1980 eruption of Mount St. Helens (VEI 5, or 1 per decade) was a *local* catastrophe with devastation over hundreds of km^2. The 1883 eruption of Krakatau (VEI 6, or 1 per century) was a *regional* catastrophe, with 36,000 dead, one as far away as India. Another order of magnitude larger, the 1815 eruption of Tambora (VEI 7) caused global cooling, with summer snowstorms and crop failures on the opposite side of the globe (Harington, 1992; Stommel and Stommel, 1983). A New England farmer in 1816 would be justified in calling it a global catastrophe. The effects of a VEI 8 event, such as Toba about 74 ka and the Lava Creek Tuff from Yellowstone about 0.64 Ma, must have been *global* by any definition.

Nearly 40% of 1023 documented Holocene lava flow volumes were of 10^7 m^3 volume (equivalent to a VEI 3 tephra volume). More than four-fifths (84%) of all documented lava flow volumes were 10^6 to 10^8 m^3 (less than 1 km^3 in volume), and only about a tenth of lava flows exceeded 1 km^3. Eleven Holocene lava flows exceeded 10 km^3 in volume, and 8 of these were in Iceland. The largest of these is the early Holocene Thjorsarhraun lava flow from Iceland's Bárdarbunga volcano, which covered an area of around 950 km^2 with a volume of more than 21 km^3 and traveled at least 140 km down the Thorsa River to the sea (Hjartarson, 1988). The Pleistocene Undara and Toomba alkalic lava flows in north Queensland, Australia also exceeded 100 km in length (Stephenson et al., 1998), and the longest known Quaternary lava flow, the 33 km^3 Pampas Onduladas lava flow from Payún Matru volcano in Argentina, traveled 181 km (Pasquarè et al., 2008). More viscous silicic lava flows, although having shorter travel distances, can have larger volumes; Pleistocene rhyolitic lava flows at Yellowstone have volumes up to about 70 km^3 (Christiansen et al., 2007).

DURATIONS and PAROXYSMS

Although volcanic eruptions can vary widely in duration from minutes to centuries (Figure 15 top), of more interest from a perspective of volcanic hazard mitigation is the interval between the start of an eruption and its paroxysmal phase. Eruptive activity is rarely distributed evenly throughout the full duration, and an eruption's paroxysmal phase may come at any time. Several prominent eruptions, such as Krakatau 1883, Mount St. Helens 1980, and Pinatubo 1991 reached their peak months after lower-level activity began, prompting the erroneous impression that volcanoes provide their own warning, and that observatory monitoring of volcanoes is therefore unnecessary.

We thus examined the time interval between the onset of an eruption and its paroxysmal phase for the most explosive eruptions (≥VEI 3) for which we have adequate data (Figure 15 bottom). These data contrast dramatically with the bell-shaped curve of eruption durations. The sobering implication is that many catastrophic eruptions provide little advance warning, and it is a mistake to assume that days, weeks, or months are available to prepare for an eruption's paroxysmal phase. More than half of the 288 eruptions studied reached their climax within the first week, and more than 40% peaked within the eruption's first *day*. Furthermore, several major eruptions (e.g., Tarawera 1886, Bandai-san 1888, Hekla 1947, Shiveluch 1964, Usu 1977) reached their climax within an *hour* of their start (Simkin and Siebert, 1984, 2000).

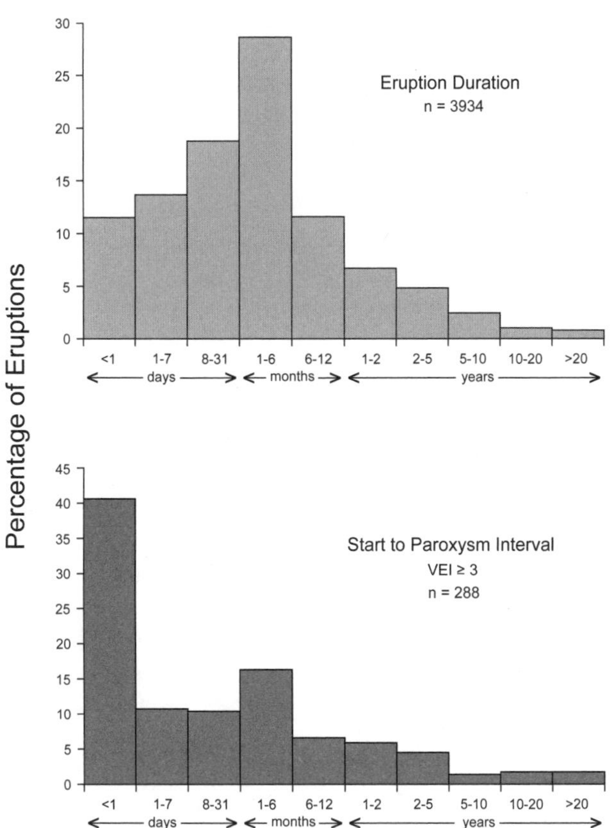

Figure 15. Eruption durations (top) and interval between onset of an eruption and its paroxysmal phase (bottom).

The other side of this coin is that eruptive behavior varies widely, and some eruptions continue at relatively low levels for years and even decades before reaching their climax. History's largest eruption, Tambora in Indonesia in 1815, did not reach its paroxysmal phase until three years after the onset of low-level eruptive activity. This catastrophic eruption produced an eruptive cloud that rose to an estimated 44 km, pyroclastic flows that swept much of the island of Sumbawa; more than 60,000 persons lost their lives. It is understandably difficult to sustain public awareness of hazards during long-term, low-level eruptive activity. It is dangerous, however, to assume that the worst is over after the initial explosive phase.

EPISODICITY and PERIODICITY

None of the historical discussion above excludes the probability that real fluctuations are present in the recent volcanic record. Fluctuations are to be expected in a random distribution, but the record contains some intriguing episodic concentrations of volcanism. The famous 1902 eruption of Mount Pelée was preceded, only one day earlier, by an equally explosive eruption on St. Vincent, 165 km to the south and much too far to consider subsurface plumbing connections. These were followed 5 months later by an even larger eruption of Guatemala's Santa María, 3260 km to the west on the opposite side of the Caribbean Plate. In no other year have three explosive eruptions of this magnitude and impact (more than 40,000 cumulative fatalities) been recorded, and it is tempting to link them to plate tectonic movement (Rose, 1972). Within an 8 month period in 1974, 5 of the 7 historically active volcanoes in the western Bismarck arc erupted, several for the first time in the 20th century (Cooke et al., 1976). On an even shorter time scale, Darwin (1840) noted simultaneous eruptions of several Andean volcanoes (and in the Juan Fernandez Islands) around the time of the great 1835 earthquake that he experienced in Chile. Furthermore, fortnightly earth tide cycles clearly have influenced the timing of some eruptions (Mauk and Johnston, 1973; Dzurisin, 1980), and cycles of activity have been shown for many volcanoes (Newhall, 1979; Luhr and Carmichael, 1990; Scandone et al., 1993).

Although episodic volcanism has clearly been demonstrated on a local and even regional scale, evidence of global synchronicity is lacking and certainly none has been found in our own work with this Holocene data set. Going much farther back in time, and concentrating on the Cordillera of western North America, Armstrong and Ward (1991) assessed a huge data set with great care. They concluded that "although magmatism is always locally episodic, the episodes blur into a continuum of magmatic activity when the whole Cordilleran region is viewed during later Cenozoic time." Statistical approaches have been applied with seeming success, only to be contradicted by other workers using different approaches and data. Gudmundsson and Saemundsson (1980), for example, have analyzed the eruptions of Iceland

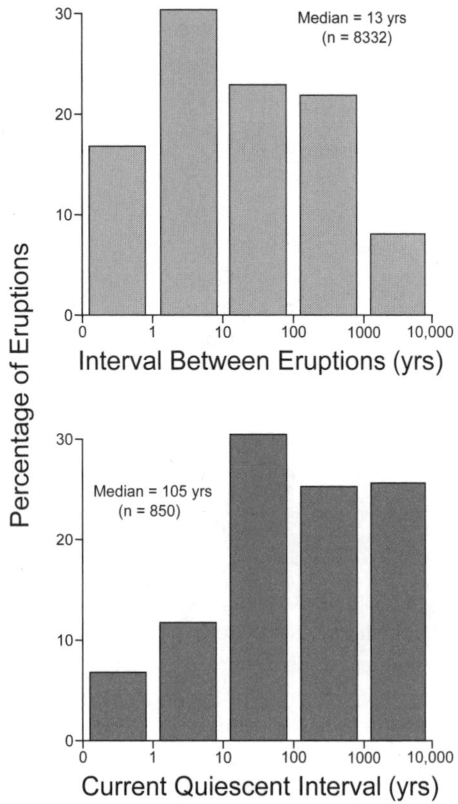

Figure 16. Global distribution of intervals between successive eruptions of Holocene volcanoes (top) and length of current quiescence (bottom).

from 1550 to 1978 and found neither statistical clustering nor periodicity, although Bjornsson et al. (1977) called attention to a ca. 100-year periodicity for the recently active Krafla region, and Thorlaksson (1967) found non-random behavior in two Icelandic volcanoes.

Large-scale magmatic episodicity is difficult to confirm, given the inherently incomplete nature of the geologic record, and demonstrating periodicity in these episodes is, inescapably, even more difficult (Simkin, 1993). The development of more complete ice-core records of volcanism, though often difficult to correlate with specific eruptions, provides some input into global rates of volcanic activity during the Holocene. Greenland ice cores show elevated volcanic events during the early Holocene attributed to unloading of the lithosphere due to deglaciation of the northern hemisphere (Zielinski et al., 1994, 1996), and Antarctic ice-core data show a distinct increase in volcanic events during the past 2000 years (Castellano et al., 2005; Kurbatov et al., 2006). Huybers and Langmuir (2009) noted a two- to six-fold increase in subaerial volcanism between about 12,000 and 7000 yrs BP, which they attributed to decompresssional melting of the mantle resulting from ablation of glaciers and icecaps during the last deglaciation.

Plate motions, major earthquakes, tides, glacial unloading, and no doubt other factors affect volcanism in ways that are only just beginning to be appreciated. However, we have stressed the historical factors that have influenced the *reporting* of volcanism in order to emphasize the many frailties of the historical record. Users of the data tabulated in this book should keep these historical factors in mind, and remember that chronological records of deep-sea rift eruptions, volumetrically the dominant form of global volcanism (Figure 3), are virtually unknown. The degradation of the volcanic record with time must be also be considered; the small-to-moderate eruptions that make up the bulk of the world's eruptions, now close to being adequately documented, are largely absent in the earlier Holocene record. Extrapolating data from the past half century to the beginning of the Holocene is a sobering reminder that fewer than 2% of the world's Holocene eruptions are currently known.

INTERVALS BETWEEN ERUPTIONS and ASSOCIATED HAZARD IMPLICATIONS

To assess the length of quiescent intervals between eruptions at individual volcanoes, we have calculated both the interval between start times of successive eruptions and the repose period between the end of the previous eruption and the start of the next. The latter is the better measure of the duration of quiescent periods, and we have used these data here rather than the interval between eruption starts used in the 2nd edition. The quiescent interval varies widely between volcanoes, but the median interval between successive volcanic eruptions from the same volcano is only about a dozen years (Figure 16 top). About two-fifths of eruptions follow quiet intervals of more than a half century, often placing the last eruption outside the direct memory of those living near the volcano.

For volcanoes with dated Holocene eruptions, more than three-fifths have currently been in repose for more than a half century (Figure 16 bottom), and the median period of current inactivity is slightly more than a century. Many volcanoes have thus currently been quiescent for significantly longer periods of time than is typical, but as seen below, this is not necessarily

Year	Volcano	First Historical?	VEI	Fatalities
1991	**Cerro Hudson** (Chile)	no	5+	0
1991	**Pinatubo** (Philippines)	yes	6	800
1982	**El Chichón** (México)	no	5	2000
1980	**Mount St. Helens** (US)	no	5	57
1963	**Agung** (Indonesia)	no	5	1148
1956	**Bezymianny** (Kamchatka)	yes	5	0
1933	**Kharimkotan** (Kuril Is)	no	5	2
1932	**Cerro Azul/Quizapu** (Chile)	no	5+	0
1913	**Colima** (México)	no	5	8?
1912	**Novarupta/Katmai** (Alaska)	yes	6	2
1907	**Ksudach** (Kamchatka)	yes	5	0
1902	**Santa María** (Guatemala)	yes	6?	>10,000
1886	**Tarawera** (New Zealand)	yes	5	153
1883	**Krakatau** (Indonesia)	no	6	36,417
1875	**Askja** (Iceland)	yes	5	0
1854	**Shiveluch** (Kamchatka)	yes	5	0
1835	**Cosigüina** (Nicaragua)	no	5	5-10
1822	**Galunggung** (Indonesia)	yes	5	4011
1815	**Tambora** (Indonesia)	yes	7	60,000
1800	**Mount St. Helens** (US)	no	5	0

Table 11. Eruptions of VEI ≥5 since 1800 AD. Fatality data include deaths from indirect effects.

a reason for reassurance.

A more complex pattern emerges by considering quiescent intervals with respect to explosive magnitude. In Figure 17 we show, for each VEI class, the length of the quiescent interval since the previous eruption. Human memories are short, and the interval between large eruptions can often be longer than the historical record in many parts of the world. A clear correlation is seen among increasing explosive magnitudes (higher VEI numbers), the length of the preceding repose period, and the likelihood of fatalities. The repose period influences the magnitude of eruptions, as magma differentiation and recharge rates imply longer intervals prior to larger eruptions. Repose periods of centuries to millennia typically precede the larger eruptions that inevitably cause the most fatalities. In regions with short historical records the human population is commonly unprepared, with often tragic results.

This illustration would be even more dramatic if pre-eruption intervals were known for more of the large explosive events. Some of the most calamitous eruptions of recent decades have been from volcanoes with no previously known historical volcanism (Table 11), where nearby residents are often unaware of the potential impact of future eruptions, or in some cases, that they are even living next to a volcano. This was the case at Lamington volcano in Papua New Guinea, where there were no local legends of eruptive activity, and the forested mountain was not recognized as a volcano prior to the devastating 1951 eruption in which pyroclastic flows killed 2942 people. Similarly, the volcanic character of forest-covered, relatively low-relief Pinatubo volcano in the Philippines was largely unknown prior to its major eruption in 1991.

Volcanological research tends to concentrate on renowned volcanoes with frequent or destructively large eruptions, but we must not neglect the poorly known, thickly vegetated, long-quiescent volcanoes that have had no historical activity. Like Lamington and Pinatubo, they may be the most dangerous of all.

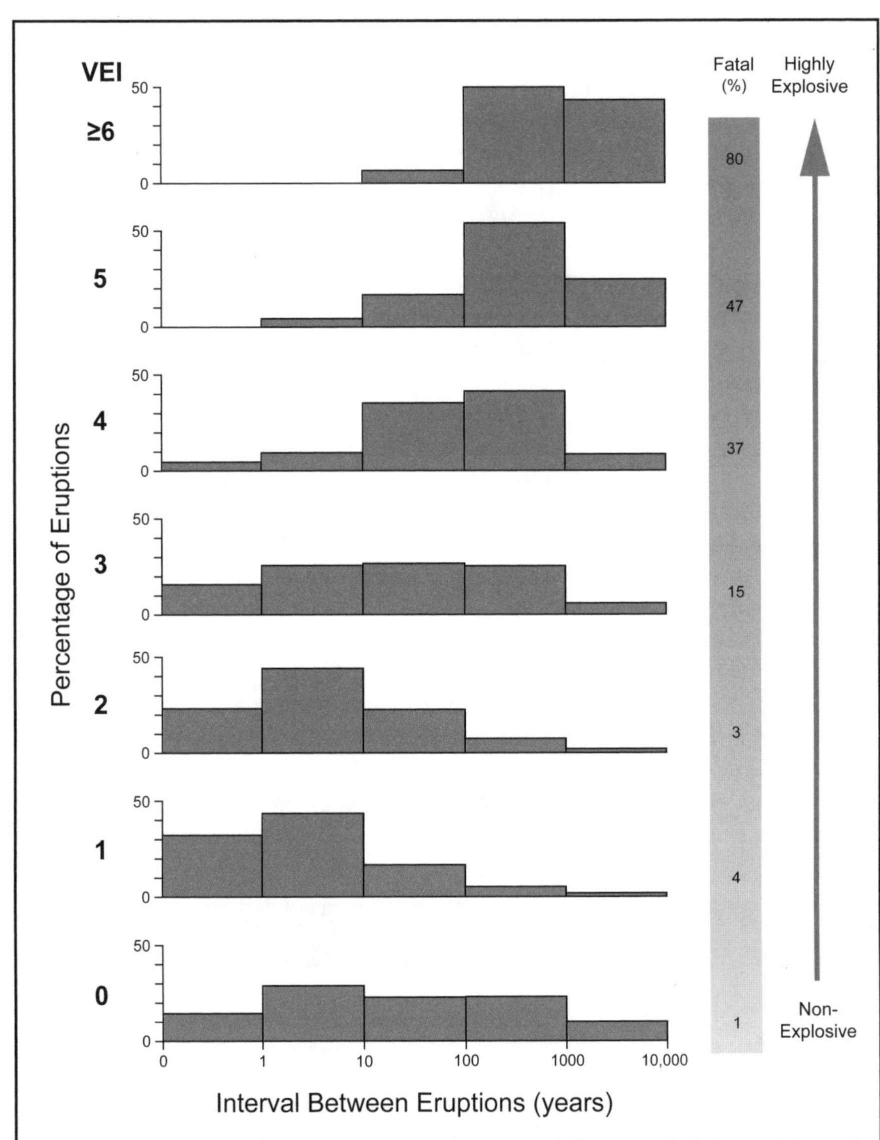

Figure 17. Explosivity and time intervals between eruptions. For each VEI unit, eruptions are grouped by time interval from start of previous eruption. The number of eruptions (6502, compared to 5100 in the 2nd edition) in VEI groups 0 to ≥6 are, respectively: 635, 1031, 3383, 970, 376, 137, 30. For each group, the percentage of fatal historical eruptions is also shown to emphasize the danger of large explosive eruptions from volcanoes apparently quiet for hundreds to thousands of years.

Conclusions

Volcanoes are among the most dramatic geologic features of our dynamic planet. Humankind has had an uneasy co-existence with Earth's volcanoes, which have been the object of both fascination and understandable concern from those living in their proximity. The past few decades have seen a heightened awareness of volcanic hazards. The number of volcanoes with volcanic hazards maps prepared through careful geologic mapping has increased significantly, and scientists at the many volcano observatories under the umbrella of the IAVCEI-commissioned *World Organization of Volcano Observatories* have installed instrumentation to monitor those volcanoes and help mitigate their hazards. Successful prediction of volcanic eruptions is now possible at well-instrumented volcanoes, although determination of the magnitude of anticipated eruptions remains elusive, as does knowing how long an eruption will last.

Evaluation of the historical and Holocene volcanological record provides invaluable context for Earth's volcanism. The historical record implies that the global rate of volcanism, both for total eruptions and for larger-magnitude eruptions (VEI ≥4), appears to be relatively constant at about 70 eruptions per year and 1 per decade, respectively. Apparent increases and fluctuations in historical eruption rates are largely attributable to reporting and communication factors.

The Holocene record shows that although there is a wide range of eruptive magnitudes, the vast majority of explosive eruptions are relatively modest affairs. Explosive eruption magnitudes display a bell-shaped distribution strongly peaking at ≥0.001 km^3 of tephra (VEI 2). These eruptions are not likely to have major distal effects, although their proximal impact can still be considerable. Only 8% of documented eruptions were VEI 4 or larger (≥0.1 km^3), but these large-volume eruptions are responsible for the vast majority of fatalities and human impact.

The relatively small increase (1511 to 1545) of volcanoes with known or possible Holocene eruptions from our 2nd edition to this one would imply that scientists are close to identifying all of the Earth's Holocene volcanoes. This goal remains elusive, however. "New" Holocene volcanoes identified as a result of the considerable emphasis in recent years on strengthening the stratigraphic record of volcanoes have been offset by precise dating that shows that many volcanoes previously thought to be Holocene based primarily on morphologic evidence actually ceased eruptive activity during the late Pleistocene.

New techniques, along with heightened awareness of volcanic hazards, are contributing to a rapid increase in volcanological data independent of the historical record. Painstaking field mapping, modern petrologic analysis of volcanic products, laboratory experiments at the high temperatures and pressures of volcano interiors, theoretical modeling of eruptive processes utilizing interdisciplinary approaches, are all needed, along with the chronological record, to understand the history and hazards of active volcanoes. It is the chronological record, though, that teaches the hard lesson that a volcano's long repose is more likely to be a cause for concern than reassurance. Differentiation processes act slowly in a magma chamber deep below a seemingly quiet volcano, steadily concentrating volatiles in increasingly siliceous magma, on a time scale that dwarfs human memory and most record-keeping. The application of more precise dating techniques such as $^{39}Ar/^{40}Ar$ has shown that volcanoes can remain quiescent for tens or even hundreds of thousands of years before resuming activity. The repeat interval between gigantic ashflow eruptions of VEI 8 magnitude (fortunately not yet known in the historical record) is even longer and can reach millions of years (Smith, 1979).

Although documentation of historical eruptions has significantly improved during the past half century, even in the 21st century eruptions can occur unnoticed in sparsely populated and poorly instrumented areas. Ongoing efforts to improve documentation of eruptive activity at both ends of the time continuum are essential in understanding our planet's volcanism and anticipating what future volcanic events might be in store. Recognition that volcanoes can resume activity after very long periods of quiescence even exceeding the full duration of the Holocene underscores the importance of extending the record back into the Pleistocene to include all volcanoes that could erupt next year. That effort has begun, and in concert with application of new instrumentation to document current activity, new techniques to date older eruptions, and the continuing contributions of those from many disciplines, will result in increasingly more comprehensive compilations in the years to come.

References

Armstrong R L, Ward P, 1991. Evolving geographic patterns of Cenozoic magmatism in the North American Cordillera: the temporal and spatial association of magmatism and metamorphic core complexes. *J Geophys Res,* 96: 13,201-13,224

Aumento F, Souther J G, 1973. Fission track dating of Late Tertiary and Quaternary volcanic glass from the Mount Edziza volcano, British Columbia. *Can J Earth Sci,* 10: 1156-1163

Baillie M G L, 1982. *Tree-ring Dating and Archaeology.* Chicago: Univ Chicago Press, 274 p

Ballard R D, 1976. Window on Earth's interior. *Natl Geog,* 150: 228-249

Becker B, Kromer B, Trimborn P, 1991. A stable-isotope tree-ring timescale of the Late Glacial/Holocene boundary. *Nature,* 353: 647-49

Birkenmajer K, 1979. Age of the Penguin Island volcano, South Shetland Islands (West Antarctica), by the lichenometric method. *Bull Acad Polonaise, Sci Ser, Sci Terre, 27: 69-76*

Bjornsson A, Saemundsson K, Einarsson P, Truggvason E, Gronvold K, 1977. Current rifting episode in North Iceland. *Nature,* 266: 318-323

Blong R J, 1984. *Volcanic Hazards.* Sydney: Academic Press, *427 p*

Bluth G J S, Doiron S D, Schnetzler C C, Krueger A J, Walter L S, 1992. Global tracking of the SO_2 clouds from the June, 1991 Mount Pinatubo eruptions. *Geophys Res Lett,* 19: 151-55

Bryson R A, Goodman B M, 1980. Volcanic activity and climatic changes. *Science*, 207: 1041-1044

Casadevall T J (ed), 1994. Volcanic ash and aviation safety: Proc First Internat Symp Volc Ash Aviation Safety, Seattle, WA, July 1991. *U S Geol Surv Bull,* 2047: 1-450

Castellano E, Becagli S, Hansson M, Hutterli M, Petit J R, Rampino M R, Severi M, Steffensen J P, Traversi R, Udisti R, 2005. Holocene volcanic history as recorded in the sulfate stratigraphy of the European Project for Ice Coring in Antarctica Dome C (EDC96) ice core. *J Geophys Res,* 110: D06114, doi:10.1029/2004JD005259

CAVW, 1951-1975. *Catalog of Active Volcanoes of the World and Solfatara Fields.* Rome: Internat Assoc Volc Geochem Earth's Interior [Regional catalogs cited and flagged separately in Reference list at end of this volume]

Chadwick W W Jr, Cashman K V, Embley R, Matsumoto H, Dziak R P, de Ronde C E J, Lau T A, Deardorff N D, Merle S M, 2008. Direct video and hydrophone observations of submarine explosive eruptions at NW Rota-1 volcano, Mariana Arc. *J Geophys Res*, doi:10.1029/2007JB005215

Chesner C A, Rose W I, 1991. Stratigraphy of the Toba tuffs and the evolution of the Toba caldera complex, Sumatra, Indonesia. *Bull Volc,* 53: 343-356

Christiansen R L, 2001. The Quaternary and Pliocene Yellowstone Volcanic Field of Wyoming, Idaho, and Montana. *U S Geol Surv Prof Pap*, 729-G: 1-145

Christiansen R L, Lowenstern J B, Smith R B, Heasler H, Morgan L A, Nathenson M, Mastin L G, Muffler L J P, Robinson J E, 2007. Preliminary assessment of volcanic and hydrothermal hazards in Yellowstone National Park and vicinity. *U S Geol Surv, Open-File Rpt*, 2007-1071: 1-94

Cole-Dai J, Ferris D, Lanciki A, Savarino J, Baroni M, Thiemens M H, 2009. Cold decade (AD 1810-1819) caused by Tambora (1815) and another (1809) stratospheric volcanic eruption. *Geophys Res Lett*, 36: L22703, doi:10.1029/2009GL040882

Cooke R J S, Baldwin J T, Sprod T J, 1976. Recent volcanoes and mineralization in Papua New Guinea. 25th Internatl Geol Cong, Sydney, Excur Guide, 53: 1-30

Cotton, C.A., 1969. *Volcanoes as Landscape Forms* (2nd ed) New York: Hafner, 416 p

Cox A, Hart R B, 1986. *Plate Tectonics: How it Works*: Palo Alto, California, Blackwell Sci Publ, 392 p

Crisp J, 1984. Rates of magma emplacement and volcanic output. *J Volc Geotherm Res.* 20: 177-211

Curtis G H, 1968. The stratigraphy of the ejecta from the 1912 eruption of Mount Katmai and Novarupta, Alaska. *Geol Soc Amer Mem,* 116: 153-210

Dalrymple G B, Lanphere M A, 1969. *Potassium-Argon Dating: Principles, Techniques, and Applications to Geochronology*. San Francisco: W H Freeman, 240 p

Darwin C, 1840. On the connexion of certain volcanic phenomena in South America; and on the formation of mountain chains and volcanos, as the effect of the same power by which continents are elevated. *Trans Geo. So. London,* 5(2nd ser): 601-31

Daubeny C, 1826. *A Description of Active and Extinct Volcanoes.* London: Phillips, 467 p

Daubeny C, 1848. *A Description of Active and Extinct Volcanoes* (2nd ed), London: R. & J.E. Taylor, 743 p

Decker R W, Decker B B, 2005. *Mountains of Fire* (4th edition). New York: W.H. Freeman, 326 p

Degens E T, Wong H K, Kempe S, Kutman F, 1984. A geologic study of Lake Van, eastern Turkey. *Geol Rundschau,* 73: 701-734

Dzurisin D, 1980. Influence of fortnightly earth tides at Kilauea volcano, Hawaii. *Geophys Res Lett,* 7: 925-928

Embley R W, Chadwick W W Jr, Baker E T, Butterfield D A, Resing J A, de Ronde C E J, Tunnicliffe V, Lupton J E, Juniper S K, Rubin K H, Stern R J, Lebon G T, Nakamura K, Merle S G, Hein J R, Wiens D A, Tamura Y, 2006. Long-term eruptive activity at a submarine arc volcano. *Nature*, 441: 494-497

Ewert J W, Guffanti M, Murray T L, 2005. An Assessment of Volcanic Threat and Monitoring Capabilities in the United States: Framework for a National Volcano Early Warning System. *U S Geol Surv, Open-File Rep, 2*005-1164: 1-62

Ewert J W, Harpel C J, 2004. In harm's way: population and volcanic risk. *Geotimes*, May, 2004, p 14-17

Ewert J W, Swanson D A (eds), 1992. Monitoring volcanoes: techniques and strategies used by the staff of the Cascades Volcano Observatory, 1980-90. *USGS Bull,* 1966: 204 & 223 p

Fairbridge R W, 1968. "Holocene, postglacial or Recent epoch." *In*: Fairbridge R W (ed). *Encyclopedia of Geomorphology*. Encyclopedia of Earth Sciences Series, Stroudsburg, Pennsylvania: Dowden, Hutchinson & Ross, 3: 5252D36

Fernandez-Armesto F (ed), 1991. *Atlas of World Exploration*. London: Times Books, 285 p

Fisher R V, Schmincke H-U, 1984. *Pyroclastic Rocks*. Berlin: Springer-Verlag, 472 p

Fiske R S, Simkin T, Nielsen E A (eds), 1987. *The Volcano Letter*. Washington, DC: Smithsonian Inst Press, 1536 p

Francis P, Oppenheimer C, 2003. *Volcanoes* (2nd edition). Oxford: Oxford Univ Press, 536 p

Friedman I, 1977. Hydration rind dates rhyolite flows. *Science*, 159: 878-880

Friedman I, 1981. Obsidian hydration dates in the Newberry volcano area, Oregon. *U S Geol Surv Prof Pap*, 750-A: A-117

Fritts H C, 1977. *Tree Rings and Climate*. New York: Academic Press, 562 p

Fuchs C W C, 1865. *Die Vulkanischen Erscheinungen der Erde*. Heidelberg: C F Winter'sche Verlagshandlung, 582 p

Gudmundsson G, Saemundsson K, 1980. Statistical analysis of damaging earthquakes and volcanic eruptions in Iceland from 1550-1978. *J Geophys Res, 47: 99-109*

Guffanti M, Casadevall T J, Mayberry G, 2004. Reducing encounters of aircraft with volcanic-ash clouds. *Proc 2nd Internat Conf Volcanic Ash Aviation Safety, June 21-24, 2004, Alexandria, VA.* U S Dept Commerce/NOAA, session 1, p 17-19

Gushchenko I I, 1979. *Eruptions of Volcanoes of the World: A Catalog.* Moscow: Nauka Pub, Acad Sci USSR Far Eastern Sci Center, 474 p (in Russian)

Hammer C U, 1977. Past volcanism revealed by Greenland Ice Sheet impurities. *Nature*, 270: 482-85

Hammer C U, Clausen H B, Dansgaard W, 1980. Greenland ice sheet evidence of post-glacial volcanism and its climatic impact. *Nature*, 288: 230-235

Harington C R (ed), 1992. *The Year Without a Summer: World Climate in 1816.* Ottawa: Canadian Museum of Nature, 578 p

Harland W B, Armstrong R L, Cox A V, Craig L E, Smith A G, Smith D G, 1989. *A geologic time scale 1989.* Cambridge: Cambridge Univ Press, 263 p

Hasenaka T, Carmichael I S E, 1985. The cinder cones of Michoacán-Guanajuato, central Mexico: their age, volume, and distribution, and magma discharge rate. *J Volc Geotherm Res,* 25: 105-124

Hayakawa Y, Soda T, Arai F, 1994. Asama and Haruna volcanoes: recent eruptions and hazards. *Climatic impact of explosive volc conf, Tokyo, Dec 3-4, 1993,* 28 p guidebook

Hedberg H D, 1974. Relation of methane generation to undercompacted shales, shale diapirs, and mud volcanoes. *Amer Assoc Petroleum Geol Bull*, 58: 661-673

Heiken G, Wohletz K, 1985. *Volcanic Ash.* Berkeley: Univ Calif Press, 245 p

Helz R T and Thornber C R, 1987. Geothermometry of Kilauea Iki lava lake, Hawaii. *Bull Volc,* 49: 651-668

Heyerdahl T, 1963. Archeology in the Galapagos Islands. *Occ Pap Calif Acad Sci*, 44: 45-51

Hjartarson A, 1988. The Thorsa lava - the largest Holocene lava flow on earth. Natturufraedingurinn, 58: 1-16 (in Icelandic with English summary)

Humboldt A von, 1869. *Cosmos: A Sketch of a Physical Description of the Universe, I.* New York: Harpers Brothers, 375

Huybers P, Langmuir P, 2009. Feedback between deglaciation, volcanism, and atmospheric CO_2. *Earth Planet Sci Lett*, doi:10.1016/j.espl.2009.07.014

IAVCEI, 1973-80. Post-Miocene Volcanoes of the World. *IAVCEI Data Sheets, Rome: Internatl Assoc Volc Chemistry Earth's Interior*

Izett G A, Wilcox R E, 1982. Map showing localities and inferred distributions of the Huckleberry Ridge, Mesa Falls, and Lava Creek ash beds (Pearlette family ash beds) of Pliocene and Pleistocene age in the western United States and southern Canada. *U S Geol Surv Misc Invest Ser Map* I-1325

Jakobsson S P, Jonasson K, Sigurdsson I A, 2008. The three igneous rock series of Iceland. *Jokull,* 58: 117-138

Johannesson H, Saemundsson K, 1998. Geological map of Iceland, 1:500,000. Tectonics. *Icelandic Inst Nat Hist, Reykjavik*

Katsui Y (ed), 1971. *List of the World Active Volcanoes.* [Volc Soc Japan draft ms, limited circulation], 160 p

Kennett J P, 1981. Marine tephrochronology. *In*: C. Emiliani (ed), *The Sea: The Oceanic Lithosphere.* New York: John Wiley, 7: 1373-1435

Kennett J P, McBirney A R, Thunnell R C, 1977. Episodes of Cenozoic volcanism in the circum-Pacific region. *J Volc Geotherm Res,* 2: 145-63.

Kious W J, Tilling R I, 1996. *This Dynamic Earth: the Story of Plate Tectonics.* U S Geol Surv, 56 p

Kossinna E, 1933. Die Erdoberflache; *in* Gutenberg B (ed), *Handbuch der Geophysik*, 2: 869-954, Berlin: Borntraeger

Krafft M, 1990. *Fuhrer zu den Vlrunga-Vulkanen.* Stuttgart: Ferdinand Enke, 187 p

Krafft M, 1993. *Volcanoes: Fire from the Earth* [English translation]: New York: Harry N. Abrams, Inc., 207 p

Kurbatov A V, Zielinski G A, Dunbar N W, Mayewski P A, Meyerson E A, Sneed S B, Taylor K C, 2006. A 12,000 year record of explosive volcanism in the Siple Dome ice core, West Antarctica. *J Geophys Res,* 111: D12307, doi:10.1029/2005JD006072

LaMarche V C, Hirschboeck K K, 1984. Frost rings as records of major volcanic eruptions. *Nature,* 307: 121-26

Lamb H H, 1970. Volcanic dust in the atmosphere: with a chronology and assessment of its meteorological significance. *Phil Trans Roy Soc London, Ser A,* 256: 425-533

Landgrebe G, 1855, *Naturgeschichte der Vulcane*, Gotha: Justus Perthes, 499 & 450 p in two parts

Langway C C, Clausen H B, Hammer C U, 1988. An interhemispheric volcanic time-marker in ice cores from Greenland and Antarctica. *Ann. Glaciol,* 10: 102-08

Larsen G, Gronvold K, Thorarinsson S, 1979. Volcanic eruption through a geothermal borehole at Namafjall, Iceland. *Nature,* 278: 707-710

Latter J H, 1975. The history and geography of active and dormant volcanoes. A worldwide catalog and index of active and potentially actives volcanoes, with an outline of their eruptions. Unpub ms

Latter J H (ed), 1989. *Volcanic Hazards — Assessment and Monitoring.* Berlin: Springer-Verlag, 635 p

Le Bas M J, Le Maitre R W, Streckeisen A, Zanettin B, 1986. A chemical classification of volcanic rocks based on the total alkali-silica diagram. *J Petr,* 27: 745-750

Le Maitre R W (ed), Streckeisen A, Zanettin B, Le Bas M J, Bonin B, Bateman P, Bellieni G, Dudek A, Efremova S, Keller J, Lameyre J, Sabine P A, Schmid R, Sorensen H, Woolley A R, 2002. *Igneous Rocks: A classification and Glossary of Terms. Recommendations of the International Union of Geological Sciences Subcommission on the Systematics of Igneous Rocks,* 2nd ed. Cambridge, UK: Cambridge Univ Press, 236 p

Lindsay J M, Robertson R E A, Shepherd J B, Ali S (eds), 2005. *Volcanic Hazard Atlas of the Lesser Antilles.* Trinidad and Tobago, Seismic Res Unit, Univ West Indies, 279 p

Lipman P W, 1995. Declining growth of Mauna Loa during the last 10,000 years: rates of lava accumulation vs. gravitational subsidence. *In:* Rhodes J M, Lockwood J P (eds), *Mauna Loa Revealed. Structure, Composition, History, and Hazards.* Geophys Monogr, 92: 45-80

Lipman P W, 2000. Calderas, *In*: Sigurdsson H (ed) *Encyclopedia of Volcanoes*, San Diego: Academic Press, p 643-662

Luhr J F, Carmichael I S E, 1990. Petrologic monitoring of cyclical eruptive activity at Volcan Colima, Mexico. *J Volc Geotherm Res,* 42: 235-260

Macdonald G A, 1972, *Volcanoes.* Englewood Cliffs, New Jersey: Prentice-Hall, 510 p

Marti J, Aranya V, 1993. *La Volcanologia Actual.* Madrid: Consejo Superior de Investigationes Cientificas, 578 p

Mauk F J, Johnston M J S, 1973. On the triggering of volcanic eruptions by earth tides. *J Geophys Res,* 78: 3356-3362.

McClelland L, Simkin T, Summers M, Nielsen E, Stein T C (eds), 1989. *Global Volcanism 1975-1985.* Englewood Cliffs, New Jersey: Prentice Hall and Washington, DC: Amer Geophys Union, 655 p

McEvedy C, Jones R, 1978. *Atlas of World Population History.* Harmondsworth: Penguin Books, 368 p

Meece S, 2006. A bird's eye view - of a leopard's spots, The Catalhoyuk 'map' and the development of cartographic representation in prehistory. Anatolian Studies, 56: 1-16

Mehringer P J, Blinman E, Petersen K L, 1977. Pollen influx and volcanic ash. *Science,* 198: 257-261

Mellaart J, 1967. *Catal Huyuk a Neolithic Town in Anatolia.* New York: McGraw Hill, 232 p

Menard H W, 1969. Growth of drifting volcanoes. *J. Geophys Res*, 74: 4827-4837

Menard H W, Smith S M, 1966. Hypsometry of ocean basin provinces. *J Geophys Res,* 71: 4305-4325

Mercalli G, 1907. *Vulcani Attivi della Terra.* Milan: Ulrico Hoepli, 421 p

Michael H N, Ralph E K, 1971. *Dating Techniques for Archeologists.* Cambridge: M.I.T. Press, 227 p

Miller T P, Casadevall T J, 2000. Volcanic ash hazards to aviation. In: Sigurdsson H, Houghton B F, McNutt S R, Rymer H, Stix J (eds), *Encyclopedia of Volcanoes*, Academic Press, San Diego (2000), p 915-930.

Miller T P, McGimsey R G, Richter D H, Riehle J R, Nye C J, Yount M E, Dumoulin J A, 1998. Catalogue of the historically active volcanoes of Alaska. *U S Geol Surv Open-File Rpt*, 98-582: 1-104

Miller T P, Smith, R L, 1976. "New" volcanoes in the Aleutian arc. *U S. Geol Surv. Circ, 733*, p11

Nakamura K, 1974. Preliminary estimate of global volcanic production rate. p 273-86 *in* Colp J, Furimoto A S, (eds) *Utilization of volcanic energy*, Hilo: Univ. Hawaii & Sandia Corp

Nakano S, Yamamoto T, Iwaya T, Itoh J, Takada A, 2001-. *Quaternary Volcanoes of Japan.* Geol Surv Japan, AIST, http://www.aist.go.jp/RIODB/strata/VOL_JP/

Newhall C G, 1979. Temporal variation in the lavas of Mayon volcano, Philippines. *J Volc Geotherm Res,* 5: 61-84

Newhall C G, Dzurisin D, 1988. Historical unrest at large calderas of the world. *U S Geol Surv Bull,* 1855: 1108 p, 2 vol

Newhall C G, Hoblitt R P, 2002. Constructing event trees for volcanic crises. *Bull Volc,* 64: 3-20

Newhall C G, Self S, 1982. The volcanic explosivity index (VEI): an estimate of explosive magnitude for historical volcanism. *J Geophys Res (Oceans & Atmospheres),* 87: 1231-1238

Ninkovich D, Sparks R S J, Ledbetter M T, 1978. The exceptional magnitude and intensity of the Toba eruption, Sumatra: an example of the use of deep-sea tephra layers as a geological tool. *Bull Volc*, 41: 286-298.

Ollier C D, 1969. *Volcanoes.* Cambridge: M.I.T. Press, 177 p

Oppenheimer C, 2003. Ice core and palaeoclimatic evidence for the timing and nature of the great mid-13th century volcanic eruption. Internatl J Climatology, 23: 417-426

Palais J M, Germani M S, Zielinski G A, 1992. Inter-hemispheric transport of volcanic ash from a 1259 A.D. volcanic eruption to the Greenland and Antarctic ice sheets. *Geophys Res Lett,* 19: 801-804

Palais J M, Kirchner S, Delmas R J, 1990. Identification of some global volcanic horizons by major element analysis of fine ash in Antarctic ice. *Annu Glaciol* 14: 216-20

Pasquarè G, Bistacchi A, Francalanci L, Bertotto G W, Boari E, Massironi M, Rossotti A, 2008. Very long pahoehoe inflated basaltic lava flows in the Payena volcanic province (Mendoza and La Pampa, Argentina). *Rev Asso Geol Argentina*, 63: 131-149

Peck D L, Wright T L, Decker R W, 1979. The lava lakes of Kilauea. *Sci Amer,* 241: 114-28

Peterson D W, Moore R B, 1987. Geologic history and evolution of geologic concepts, island of Hawaii. *U S Geol Surv Prof Pap,* 1350: 395-404

Pike, R.J., 1978. Volcanoes on the inner planets: some preliminary comparisons of gross topography. *Proc. 9th Lunar Planet. Sci Conf*, p. 3239-3273

Pilcher J R, Hall V A, 1992. Toward a tephrochronology for the Holocene of the north of Ireland. *The Holocene,* 2,3: 255-59

Rampino M R, Self S, Fairbridge R W, 1979. Can rapid climatic change cause volcanic eruptions? *Science,* 206: 826-829

Rampino M R, Self S, Stothers R B, 1988. Volcanic winters. *Annu Rev Earth Planet Sci,* 16: 73-99

Reitsema R H, 1979. Gases of mud volcanoes in the Copper River Basin, Alaska. *Geochim. Cosmochim. Acta*, 43: 183-187

Robock A, 1991. The volcanic contribution to climate change of the past 100 years; *in* Schlesinger M E (ed), *Greenhouse-Gas-Induced Climatic Change*, Amsterdam: Elsevier, p 429-41

Rose W I, 1972. Notes on the 1902 eruption of Santa Maria volcano, Guatemala. *Bull Volc,* 36: 29-45

Rosi M, Bertagnini A, Landi P, 2000. Onset of the persistent activity at Stromboli volcano (Italy). *Bull Volc, 62: 294-300*

Rubin K H, Embley R W, Clague D A, Resing J A, Michael P J, Keller N S, Baker E T, 2009. Lavas from active boninite and very recent basalt eruptions at two submarine NE Lau Basin sites. Eos, *Trans Amer Geophys Union*, 89: Fall Meet Suppl, abstr V43I-05

Sapper K, 1917. *Katalog der Geshichtlichen Vulkanausbruche.* Strasbourg: Karl J Trubner, 358 p

Sapper K, 1927. *Vulkankunde.* Stuttgart: J Engelhorns Nacht, 424 p

Scandone R, Giacomelli L, Gasparini P, 1993. Mount Vesuvius : 2000 years of volcanological observations. *J Volc Geotherm Res,* 58:5-26

Scarpa R, Tilling R I (eds), 1989. *Monitoring and Mitigation of Volcanic Hazards.* Berlin: Springer-Verlag, 841 p

Schmincke H-U, 2004. *Volcanism.* Heidelberg: Springer Verlag, 324 p

Schnauble J (ed), 1993. *The SBS World Guide.* Melbourne, Australia: The Text Pub. Co., 611 p

Schneider K, 1911. *Die Vulkanischen Ercheinungen der Erde.* Berlin: Gebruder Borntraeger, 272 p

Scrope G P, 1825. *Considerations on Volcanoes.* London: W Phillips, 270 p

Scrope G P, 1862. *Volcanoes: The Character of Their Phenomena, Their Share in the Structure and Composition of the Surface of the Globe and Their Relation to its Internal Forces.* London: Longman, Green, Longmans & Roberts (2nd edition), 490 p

Self S, Sparks R S J (eds), 1981. *Tephra Studies.* Dordrecht: Reidel, 481 p

Siebert L, 1984. Large volcanic debris avalanches: characteristics of source areas, deposits, and associated eruptions. *J Volc Geotherm Res,* 22: 163-197

Siebert L, Ewert J W, Kimberly P, Schilling S P, 2008. Population in proximity to volcanoes: a global perspective. *IAVCEI 2008 Gen Assembly, Reykjavík, Iceland, Aug 17-22, 2008,* Abs

Siebert L, Simkin T, 2002-. *Volcanoes of the World: an Illustrated Catalog of Holocene Volcanoes and their Eruptions.* Smithsonian Inst, Global Volcanism Prog Digital Inf Ser GVP-3 (http://www.volcano.si.edu/world/).

Sigurdsson H, 1991. The intensities and magnitudes of volcanic eruptions. *Earthq Volc,* 22(3): 142-146

Sigurdsson H, 1999. *Melting the Earth: The History of Ideas on Volcanic Eruptions.* New York: Oxford Univ Press, 260 p

Sigurdsson H, Carey S, 1989. Plinian and co-ignimbrite tephra fall from the 1815 eruption of Tambora volcano. *Bull Volc,* 51: 243-270

Sigurdsson H, Houghton B, McNutt S R, Rymer H, Stix J, (eds), 2000. *Encyclopedia of Volcanoes.* San Diego: Academic Press, 1415 p

Sigurdsson H, Laj P, 1992. Atmospheric effects of volcanic eruptions; *In:* Nierenberg W A (ed), *Encyclopedia Earth Systems Science.* San Diego: Academic Press, 1: 183-199

Simarski L T, 1992. *Volcanism and Climate Change.* Washington, DC: Amer Geophys Union Spec Rep, 27 p

Simkin T, 1993. Terrestrial volcanism in space and time. *Annu Rev Earth Planet. Sci,* 21: 427-452

Simkin T, Fiske R S, 1983. Krakatau 1883: The Volcanic Eruption and its Effects. Washington, DC: Smithsonian Inst Press, 464 p

Simkin T, Siebert L, 1984. Explosive eruptions in space and time: durations, intervals, and a comparison of the world's volcanic belts. p 110-21 *In:* Boyd F R (ed). *Explosive Volcanism: Inception, Evolution, and Hazards.* Washington, D C: Natl Acad, 176 p

Simkin T, Siebert L, 1994. *Volcanoes of the World* (2nd ed), Tucson: Geoscience Press, 349 p

Simkin T, Siebert L, 2000. Earth's volcanoes and eruptions: an overview, *In*: Sigurdsson H (ed) *Encyclopedia of Volcanoes*, San Diego: Academic Press, p 249-261

Simkin T, Siebert L, Blong R, 2001. Volcano fatalities: lessons from the historical record. *Science*, 291: 255

Simkin T, Siebert L, McClelland L, Bridge D, Newhall C, and Latter J H, 1981. *Volcanoes of the World.* Hutchinson-Ross, Stroudsburg, Pennsylvania, 232 p

Simkin T, Tilling R I, Vogt P R, Kirby S H, Kimberly P, Stewart D B, 2006. This Dynamic Planet: World map of volcanoes, earthquakes, impact craters, and plate tectonics: U S Geol Surv Geol Invest Ser Map I-2800, 1 two-sided sheet, scale 1:30,000,000 (URL: http://mineralsciences.si.edu/tdpmap/)

Smith R L, 1979. Ash-flow magmatism. *Geol Soc Amer Spec Pap,* 180: 5-27

Smith R L, Luedke R G, 1984. Potentially active volcanic lineaments and loci in western conterminous United States. P 96-109 *In*: Boyd, F. R. (ed). *Explosive Volcanism: Inception, Evolution, and Hazards.* Washington, D C: Natl Acad, 176 p

Steinthorsson S, et al., 2002. Catalog of Active Volcanoes of the World - Iceland. Unpublished manuscript

Stephenson P J, Burchjohnston A T, Stanton D, Whitehead P W, 1998. Three long lava flows in north Queensland. *J Geophys Res,* 103: 27,359-27,370

Stoffers P, Worthington T J, Schwarz-Schampera U, Hannington M D, Massoth G J, Hekinian R, Schmidt M, Lundsten L J, Evans L J, Vaiomo'unga R, Kerby T, 2006. Submarine volcanoes and high-temperature hydrothermal venting on the Tonga arc, southwest Pacific. *Geology*, 34: 453-456

Stommel H, Stommel E, 1983, *Volcano Weather.* Newport, RI: Seven Seas Press, 177 p

Stuiver M, Reimer P J, Bard E, Beck J W, Burr G S, Hughen K A, Kromer B, McCormac F G, van der Plicht J, Spurk M, 1998. INTCAL98 radiocarbon age calibration, 24000-0 cal B.P. Radiocarbon 40, 1041-1083

Sullivan W, 1991. *Continents in Motion (*2nd ed), New York: Amer Inst Phys, 430 p

Swanson D A, Wright T L, 1978. "Bedrock geology of the Northern Columbia Plateau and adjacent areas." p 37-58 *In*: Baker V R, Nummadal D (eds), *The Channeled Scabland*, Washington, DC: NASA.

Tanguy J C, Ribiere C, Scarth A, Tjetjep W S, 1998. Victims from volcanic eruptions: a revised database. *Bull Volc,* 60: 137-144

Taylor R E, 1987. *Radiocarbon Dating: an Archeological Perspective.* Orlando: Academic Press, 212 p

Thorlaksson J E, 1967. A probability model of volcanoes and the probability of eruptions of Hekla and Krafla, *Bull. Volc,* 31: 97-106

Tilling R I (ed), 1989. *Volcanic Hazards.* Washington, DC: Amer Geophys Union, 123 p

Tazieff H, 1976-77. An exceptional eruption: Mt. Niragongo, Jan 10th, 1977. *Bull Volc,* 40: 189-200

Thordarson T, Hoskuldsson A, 2008. Postglacial eruptions in Iceland. *Jokull,* 58: 197-228

Thordarson T, Self S, 1993. The Laki (Skaftar Fires) and Grimsvotn eruptions in 1783-1785. *Bull Volc,* 55: 233-263

Trager J, 1992. *The People's Chronology.* New York: Henry Holt, 1237 p

Tsuya H, 1955. Geological and petrological studies of volcano Fuji, Part 5: on the 1707 eruption of volcano Fuji. *Bull Earthq Res Inst, Univ Tokyo,* 33: 341-383

Ui T, Takarada S, Yoshimoto M, 2000. Debris avalanches. *In*: Sigurdsson H (ed) *Encyclopedia of Volcanoes*, San Diego: Academic Press, p 617-626

Ulusoy I, Labazuy P, Aydar E, Ersoy O, Cubukcu E, 2008. Structure of the Nemrut caldera (Eastern Anatolia, Turkey) and associated hydrothermal fluid circulation. *J Volc Geotherm Res*, 174: 269-283

UNDRO, 1985, *Volcanic Emergency Management.* New York: United Nations, 86 p

Van Couvering J A (ed), 2004. *The Pleistocene Boundary and the Beginning of the Quaternary.* London: Cambridge Univ Press, 318 p

Varenius B, 1650. *Geographia generalis, in qua affectiones generales tell Uris explicantur.* Amstelodami Apud L Elzevirium, 786 p

Vogt P R, 1974. Volcanic spacing, fractures, and the thickness of the lithosphere. *Earth Planet Sci Lett,* 21:235-52

Vogt P R, 1979. Global magmatic episodes: new evidence and implications for the "steady state" mid-oceanic ridge. *Geology* , 7: 93-98

von Hoff K E A, 1841. *Chronik der Erdbeben und Vulcan-ausbruche*, Gotha: Justus Perthes, 405 p

Walker G P L, 1980. The Taupo pumice: product of the most powerful known (ultraplinian) eruption? *J Volc Geotherm Res,* 8: 69-94

Webley P, Mastin L (eds), 2009. Improved Prediction and Tracking of Volcanic Ash Clouds *J Volc Geotherm Res,* 186: 1-132

Webster's New Geographical Dictionary, 1988. Springfield, Mass: Merriam-Webster, 1376 p

Westgate J A, Gold C M (eds), 1974. *World Bibliography and Index of Quaternary Tephrochronology.* Calgary: Univ Alberta, 528 p

White D E, 1955. Violent mud-volcano eruption of Lake City Hot Springs, Northeastern California. *Geol Soc Amer Bull*, 66: 1109-1130

Williams H, McBirney A R, 1979. *Volcanology.* San Francisco: Freeman Cooper & Co, 397 p

Wilson C J N, 1993. Stratigraphy, chronology, styles and dynamics of late Quaternary eruptions from Taupo volcano, New Zealand. *Phil Trans Roy Soc London, Ser A,* 343: 205-306.

Witham C S, 2005. Volcanic disasters and incidents: a new database. *J Volc Geotherm Res,* 148: 191-233

Wright J W (ed), 1993. *The Universal Almanac, 1994.* Kansas City: Universal Press Syndicate Co, 716 p

Wright T L, Peck D L, Shaw H R, 1976. Kilauea lava lakes: natural laboratories for study of cooling, crystallization, and differentiation of basaltic magma. *AGU Monograph,* 19: 375-90

Yamaguchi D K, 1985. Tree-ring evidence for a two-year interval between Recent prehistoric explosive eruptions of Mount St. Helens. *Geology*, 13: 554-557

Zielinski G A, Mayewski P A, Meeker L D, Whitlow S, Twickler M S, 1996. A 11,000-yr record of explosive volcanism from the GISP2 (Greenland) ice core. *Quat Res,* 45: 109-118

Zielinski G A, Mayewski P A, Meeker L D, Whitlow S, Twickler M S, Morrison M, Meese D A, Gow A J, Alley R B, 1994. Record of volcanism since 7000 B.C. from the GISP2 Greenland ice core and implications for the volcano-climate system. Science, 264: 948-952

Directory of Volcanoes

Volcano Regions

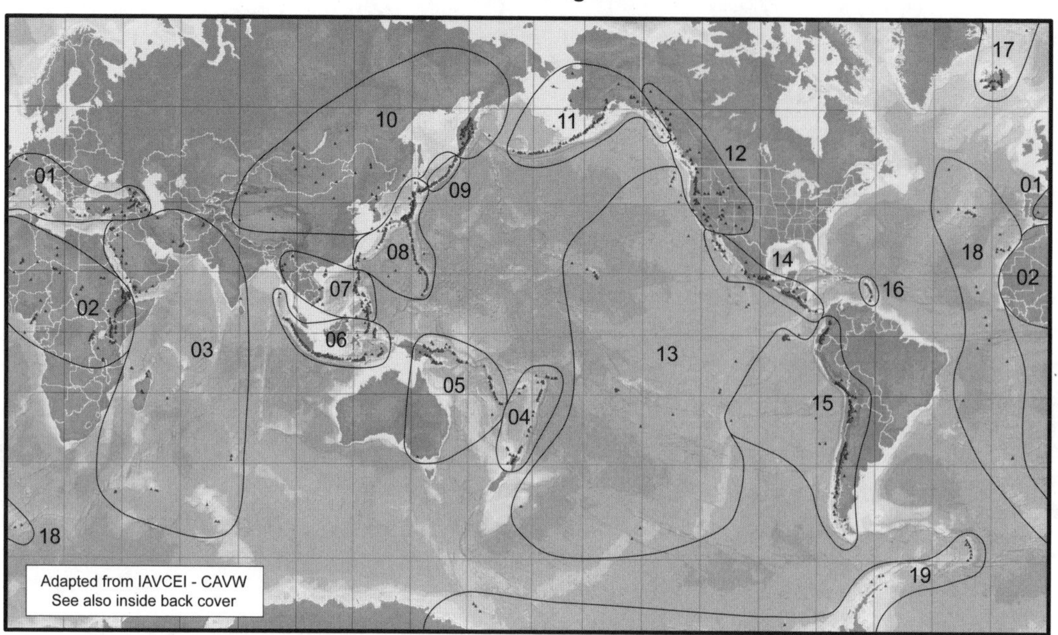

CODE BEFORE DATE

A = Anthropology
C = Radiocarbon (uncorrected)
D = Dendrochronology (tree ring)
E = Surface Exposure
F = Fission Track
G = Radiocarbon (corrected)
H = Hydration Rind
I = Ice Core
K = Potassium-Argon (K-Ar)
L = Lichenometry
M = Magnetism
N = Thermoluminescence
R = Argon-Argon (Ar-Ar)
S = SOFAR (hydrophonic)
T = Tephrochronology
U = Uranium-Series
V = Varve Counts

- = BC date
? = Eruption uncertain
@ = Eruption location uncertain
X = Discredited Eruption

CODE AFTER DATE (Uncertainty)

Code		±Years	±Days	Code		±Years	±Days	
a	=	1	1	o	=	18	25	
b	=	2	2	p	=	20	30	(1 mo)
c	=	3	3	q	=	25	45	
d	=	4	4	r	=	30	60	(2 mo)
e	=	5	5	s	=	40	75	
f	=	6	6	t	=	50	90	(3 mo)
g	=	7	7	u	=	75	120	
h	=	8	8	v	=	100	150	
i	=	9	9	w	=	150	180	(6 mo)
j	=	10	10	x	=	200	270	
k	=	12	12	y	=	300	365	(1 yr)
m	=	14	15	z	=	500	545	
n	=	16	20	*	=	1000	730	(2 yr)

> = eruption after date listed
< = eruption before date listed
? = date uncertain (no data)

VOLUME

L/T = volume of lava erupted (left column) / volume of tephra (right column)
7/- = 10^7 m³ lava, no recorded tephra voume
-/9 = 10^9 m³ tephra, no recorded lava volume
7/8 = 10^7 m³ lava, 10^8 m³ tephra

POPULATION CODES

0	- 0	**5**	- >10,000
1	- <10	**6**	- >100,000
2	- >10	**7**	- >1,000,000
3	- >100	**8**	- >10,000,000
4	- >1000		

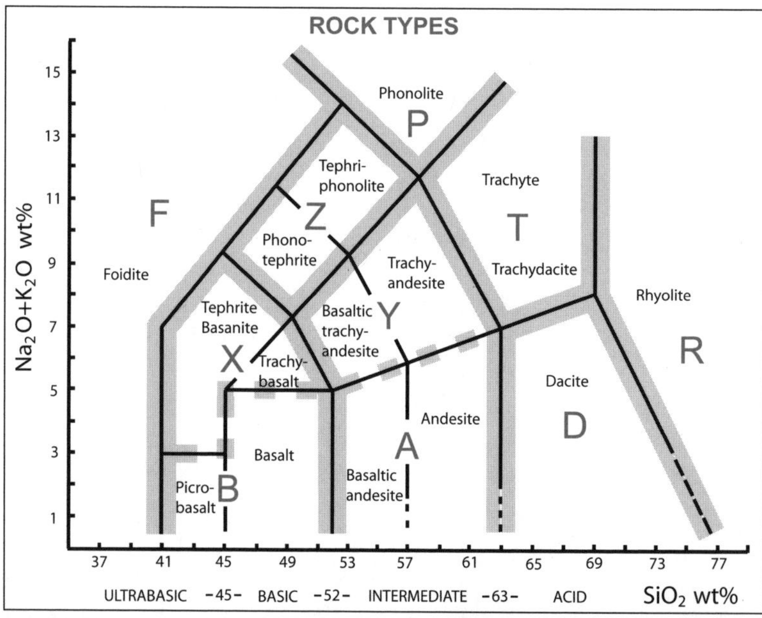

Europe to Caucasus (01)

This is the first of 19 regions covered in the classic *Catalog of Active Volcanoes of the World* (CAVW) published by the International Association of Volcanology and Chemistry of the Earth's Interior (IAVCEI) beginning in the mid-20th century. Two-color maps such as the ones on the facing page and the inside covers delineate volcanic regions and serve as a graphic guide to the global numbering scheme originating with the CAVW. The CAVW began with Italian volcanoes and included those in Greece, Turkey, and the Caucasus. We have subsequently added Holocene volcanoes to this region in West Germany, France, and Spain and expanded coverage of West Asia volcanoes, while moving volcanoes in Iran to region 03.

Often called "The Cradle of Western Civilization," this region is also very much the cradle of volcanology. The vigorous historical record of Etna in Sicily goes back to about 1500 BC; and the catastrophic eruption of Vesuvius in 79 AD, with the burial of Pompeii and Herculaneum, continues to serve today as an object lesson in volcanism. The region has given us the first documented "new mountain" (Monte Nuovo, a pyroclastic cone that formed in the Campi Flegrei caldera in 1538), the first "new island" at Santorini in 197 BC, and the word "volcano" itself (derived from Vulcan, the Roman god of fire, and applied to the island of Vulcano).

The volcanism of this broad region, stretching from Spain to the Caucasus, is largely the result of convergence between the Eurasian Plate and the northward-moving African Plate. The geology is diverse and complex, with microplates defying easy tectonic generalizations. However, subduction under the Greek islands (Hellenic arc) and southern Italy (Calabrian arc) explains the region's principal volcanic centers.

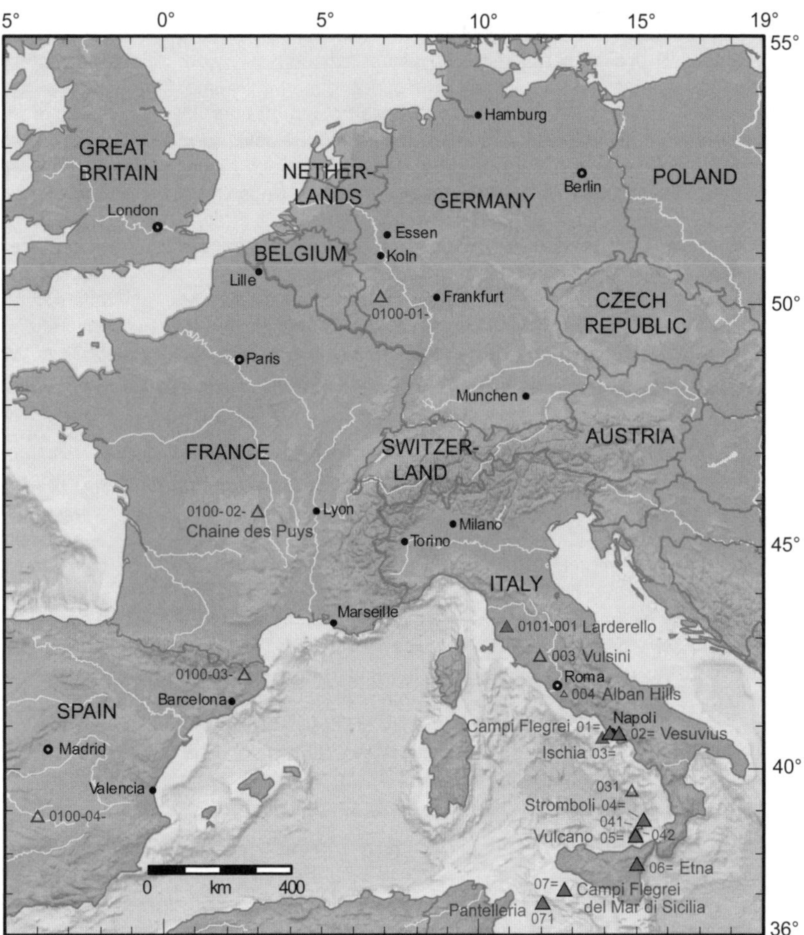

The historical and cultural richness of the Mediterranean region has led to the most robust historical record of volcanism of any region. Traditions of record-keeping go back thousands of years and generations of historians and geologists have mined those records. This work is ongoing; the largely traditional historical eruptive record shown here for Etna does not yet fully reflect the application of new techniques such as archeomagnetic dating, which has raised questions about the traditional interpretations of the roughly 3500-year-long historical record of Mount Etna that correlated written eruption reports with specific lava flows based largely on the morphology of the flows. Etna and Stromboli are two of Earth's most

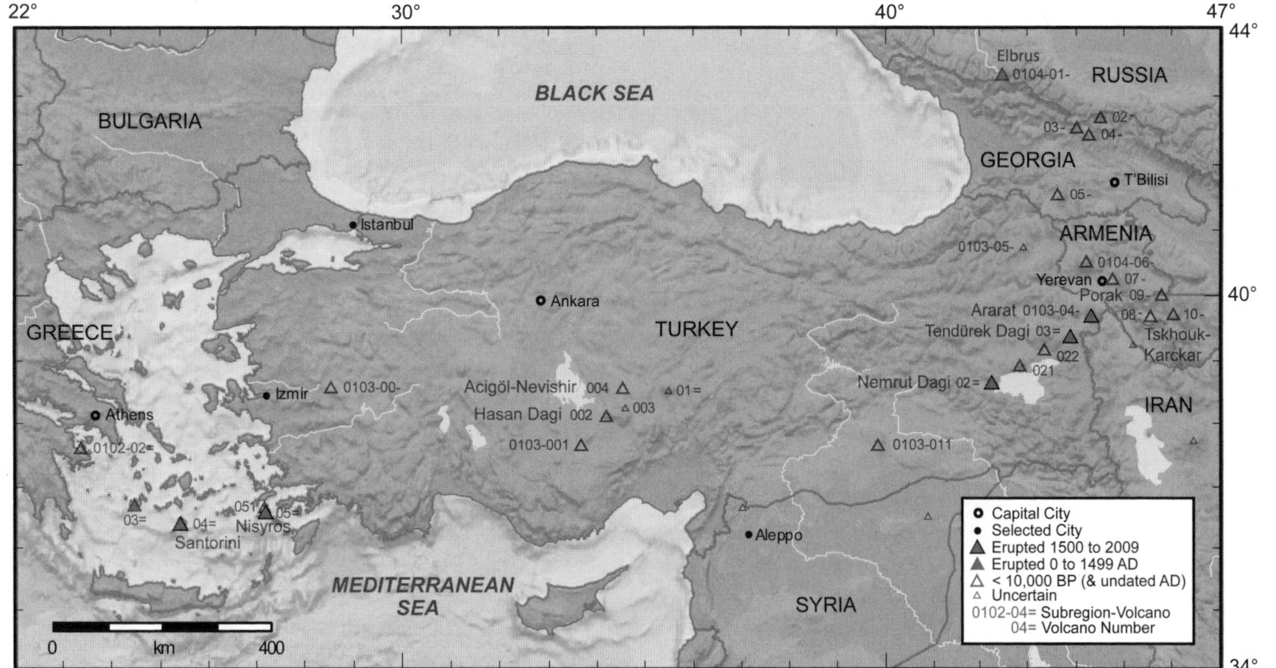

active volcanoes, with documented eruptions for several millennia; Stromboli's persistent pyrotechnic activity has lent its name to a type of eruptive activity (strombolian) characterized by frequent small-scale magmatic explosions. Stromboli has been considered to have been continually active for at least 2500 years, although new work has demonstrated some periods of quiescence during this time, and we have modified our eruption chronologies from that in our 2nd edition to reflect this. Vesuvius towers over the Bay of Naples, and its eruptions have affected those living in its shadow since before the Roman era. Regular documentation of volcanism began with Vesuvius: Lord Hamilton's systematic observations from 1766 through 1794, the world's first volcano observatory in 1845, and Palmieri's seismographic monitoring of the 1872 eruption.

Santorini volcano in the Aegean Sea is renowned for its Minoan era eruption that left its current spectacular caldera, largely flooded by the sea, which draws legions of tourists. In 1879, Fouque's monograph on Santorini explained the fundamentals of caldera collapse 4 years before the Krakatau eruption–on the other side of the globe–gave the world a dramatic example of the process. The mid-18th century work of Guettard and Desmerest on pre-historic volcanoes of central France, and Hutton's work on older volcanics in Scotland, taught the world that contemporary processes explain the volcanic landforms and rocks of the past. And the continuing vigor of both volcanism and volcanology in this important region adds to our understanding of volcanoes every year.

The lengthy historical record of this region also reflects the large numbers of people living in proximity to volcanoes. Nearly 15 million people live within 30 km of a Holocene volcano in this region. Of these, more than 2,200,000 reside within 20 km of the center of the Campi Flegrei caldera, which partly overlaps the city of Naples, and more than 675,000 live within 10 km of Vesuvius volcano. Italian and other volcanologists have devoted considerable efforts to documenting the past eruptive record of these volcanoes and working with public officials to develop hazard plans in the event of future eruptions.

Italian volcanoes display both vigorous explosive activity, even more prominent when the record of caldera formation in the Roman Magmatic Province is extended into the Pleistocene, and a relatively high percentage of Earth's documented Holocene effusive activity, much of which has blanketed the summit and flanks of Etna volcano. The volcanoes of Italy and Greece are prominent in this region, but impressive volcanism lies elsewhere as well. The lava domes and maars of the Chaîne des Puys range in France have produced vigorous Holocene volcanism, and Nemrut Dagi caldera in Turkey has more documented Holocene eruptions than any in this region outside Italy and erupted as recently as the 17th century. Explosive activity has recently been documented accompanying a collapse and lahar from storied Mount Ararat on the Turkey/Georgia border in 1840. At 5633 m, Mount Elbrus in SW Russia near the Georgia border is by far the highest volcano in this region, and lava flows overlying human settlements have recently been documented from volcanic fields along the Armenia/Azerbaijan border.

This region's eruptive record is easily the longest of any. Roughly half of its 47 volcanoes have dated eruptions and more than half of these begin with BC events. Many of these were dated by radiocarbon or other techniques, but a remarkably large number were documented by humans. By 500 AD–85% of the way through the Holocene–59 eruptions had been historically documented globally, and 54 of them were from region 01. Frequent lava effusion during the 3500 year history of Etna contributes to this region accounting for, along with Kamchatka and Japan, 30% of the world's eruptions with lava flows. The large number of coastal and island volcanoes places this region at the top of the list of tsunami-producing eruptions, and the large numbers of people living in proximity to its volcanoes is reflected in the high number of eruptions causing damage to human infrastructures.

VOLCANO NAME (Subregion) / **ERUPTION** — Area of Activity	LAT	LONG	ELEV (m)	POPL (5 km, 10, 30, 100)	ROCK TYPE	VOLC TYPE / — Start — Year M-Dy	NUMBER / — Stop — Year M-Dy	STATUS	ERUPTIVE CHARACTERISTICS (Central, Flank vent, Radial fiss, Regional / Submarine, New island, Subglacial, Crater lake / Explosive, Pyro flow, Phreatic, Caldera / Lava flow, Lava lake, Dome, Spine / Fatal, Damage, Mudflow, Tsunami)	VEI	Vol L/T
EUROPE - W											
West Eifel Volc Field (Germany)	**50.17** N*	**6.85** E	**600**	5567	**Fxp**	**Maars**	**0100-01-**	**Radiocarbon**			
Ulmener Maar						G-**8740**w	....		x--- ---- x--- ---- ----		
Strohn, Pulvermaar						C-**8300**y	....		x--- ---- x--- ---- ----		
Chaîne des Puys (France)	**45.775** N*	**2.97** E	**1464**	6667	**BXyt**	**Cinder cones**	**0100-02-**	**Radiocarbon**			
Western Puy de Dôme						C-**7840**x	....		---- ---- x--- --x- ----		
Puy Mey						N-**7740**?	....		---- ---- x--- x--- ----		
(Taphanel tephra)						C-**7020**v	....		---- ---- x--- ---- ----		
Puys Chopine, Vasset, Cratère Kilian						C-**6550**?	....		---- ---- xx-- --x- ----		
Puy de Pariou						N-**6250**?	....		---- ---- xxx- xx-- ----		
Puy de Lassolas, Puy de la Vache						C-**6020**w	....		---- ---- x--- x--- ----		
Puy de Come, Puy Montchier						N-**5760**?	....		---- ---- x--- ---- ----		
Montcineyre, Estivadoux, Pavin						C-**4040**w	....		---- ---- xx-- x--- ----		-/7
Olot Volc Field (Spain)	**42.17** N*	**2.53** E	**893**	5567	**XB**	**Pyroclastic cones**	**0100-03-**	**Holocene**			
Calatrava Volc Field (Spain)	**38.87** N*	**4.02** W	**1117**	6666	**BFX**	**Pyroclastic cones**	**0100-04-**	**Radiocarbon**			
Columba						G-**3600**z	....		x--- ---- xx-- ---- ----		
ITALY											
Colli Euganei Group (Italy)	45.32 N*	11.75 E	600				0101-00-	Not a Volcano			
Larderello (Italy)	**43.25** N	**10.87** E	**500**	4567	**U**	**Explosion craters**	**0101-001**	**Historical**			
Lago Vecchienna						**1282**<	....		x--- ---x x-x- ---- -x--	3?	
Vulsini (Italy)	**42.60** N	**11.93** E	**800**	5567	**TXPFZ**	**Caldera**	**0101-003**	**Historical**			
						-0104	....		---- ---- ---- ---- ----		
Alban Hills (Italy)	**41.73** N	**12.70** E	**949**	6677	**FZx**	**Caldera**	**0101-004**	Holocene?			
Ariccia crater						*?-0600*	....		x--- ---- --?- ---- ----		
(ashfall, stone ejection report unlikely)						*X-0540*?	....		---- ---- ---- ---- ----		
(ashfall, fire report likely forest fire)						*X-0114*	....		---- ---- ---- ---- ----		
Campi Flegrei (Italy)	**40.827** N	**14.139** E	**458**	7777	**TPYxz**	**Caldera**	**0101-01=**	**Historical**			
(Agnano Pomici Principali tephra)						G-**8480**v	....		x--- ---- xx-- ---- ----	4	
Soccavo, Minapoli, Pisani & other vents						T-**7980**z	....		x--- x--- xx-- ---- ----	3	-/7
NE part of NYT caldera (Pisani 3 tephra)						C-**7590**t	....		x--- x--- xx-- ---- ----		
Fondi di Baia, Sartania						C-**6650**v	....		x--- x--- xx-- ---- ----	4	-/8
Eastern part of NYT caldera						T-**6490**?	....		x--- x--- x--- ---- ----	3?	-/7
N part of NYT caldera (San Martino)						C-**6300**t	....		x--- x--- xx-- ---- ----		
East part of NYT caldera (Agnano 1 tephra)						C-**2890**	....		x--- ---- x--- ---- ----		
(Averno 1, Agnano 2 tephras)						C-**2580**t	....		x--- ---- xx-- ---- ----		
Cigliano						T-**2500**?	....		x--- ---- xx-- ---- ----	4	-/8
Agnano-Monte Sant'Angelo						C-**2440**?	....		x--- ---- xx-- ---- ----		
(Paleoastroni 1 tephra)						T-**2330**w	....		x--- ---- xx-- ---- ----	3	
Eastern NYT caldera (Paleoastroni 2 tephra)						C-**2220**t	....		x--- ---- xx-- ---- ----		
Agnano Monte Spina						C-**2150**z	....		x--- ---- xx-- x--- ----	**5**	-/9
Monte Olibano-Accademia						T-**2080**u	....		x--- ---- x--- x-x- ----	2	7/-

VOLCANO NAME (Subregion) / ERUPTION	LAT / LONG / ELEV (m) / POPL / ROCK TYPE / VOLC TYPE / NUMBER / STATUS — Area of Activity	Start Year	Start M-Dy	Stop Year	Stop M-Dy	Central / Flank vent / Radial fiss / Regional	Submarine / New island / Subglacial / Crater lake	Explosive / Pyro flow / Phreatic / Caldera	Lava flow / Lava lake / Dome / Spine	Fatal / Damage / Mudflow / Tsunami	VEI	Vol L/T
Campi Flegrei (Italy) *continued*	Solfatara	T -**2040**?	....	....	....	x---	----	x---	----	----	3	-/7
	Averno	T -**2000**w	....	....	....	x---	----	xx--	x-x-	----	4	-/8
	Astroni	C-**1870**t	....	....	....	x---	----	xx--	x-x-	----	4	-/9
	Fossa Lupara (Monte Senga)	T -**1650**?	....	....	....	x---	----	xx--	x---	----	4	-/8
	Solfatara	**1198**	....	....	....	x---	----	--x-	----	-x--	1	
	Monte Nuovo	**1538**	0929	**1538**	1006	x---	----	xxx-	xx--	xx--	3	-/7
Vesuvius (Italy)	**40.821 N 14.426 E 1281** 5677 **ZPYXT Somma volcano 0101-02= Historical**											
	(Mercato Pumice)	G-**6940**v	....	....	....	x---	----	xx-x	----	--x-	**5**	-/9
	(Avellino eruption)	G-**2420**s	....	....	....	x---	----	xx-x	----	xxx-	**5**	-/9
	(AP1 tephra layer)	G-**1550**u	....	....	....	x---	----	xx--	----	----	4	-/8
	(AP2 tephra layer)	G-**1430**y	....	....	....	x---	----	xx--	----	----	4	-/8
	(AP3 tephra layer)	G-**0880**t	....	....	....	x---	----	x---	----	-xx-	4	-/8
		A-**0600**<	....	....	....	x---	----	x---	----	----	3	
	(AP6 tephra layer)	**-0217**	....	**-0216**	....	x---	----	x---	----	--x-	3?	
	(Pompeii eruption)	**0079**	1024?	**0079**	1028a	x---	----	xx-x	----	xxxx	**5?**	-/9
		0172	....	....	....	x---	----	x---	----	----	3?	
		0203	....	....	....	x---	----	x---	----	----	**P**	
		0222	....	**0235**	....	x---	----	x---	----	----	2	
		? *0303*	....	....	....	x---	----	?---	?---	----	*2?*	
		0379	....	**0395**	....	x---	----	x---	?---	----	2	
		0472	1105	**0472**	1106?	x-?-	----	xx--	?---	-xx-	**5**	-/9
		? *0505*	*1109*	....	....	x---	----	?---	?---	----	*2?*	
		0512	0708	....	....	x---	----	xx--	----	-x--	4?	
		0536	....	....	....	x---	----	x---	----	-x?-		
		0685	02	**0685**	03	x---	----	x---	?---	-x--	4	-/8
	Summit and south flank	**0787**	1015q	**0788**	0115q	x-x-	----	x?--	x---	?x--	3	
	South flank	M **0860**t	....	....	....	--x-	----	----	x---	----	0?	
	South and west (Tironi) flanks	M **0900**s	....	....	....	--x-	----	----	x---	----	0?	
		0968	1201p	....	....	x---	----	x---	x---	-?--	4	-/8
		0991	....	....	....	x---	----	x---	----	----	3	
	Summit and south flank (Fossamonaca)	**0999**	....	....	....	x-x-	----	x---	x---	----	3	
		1006	1231y	....	....	x---	----	x---	?---	----	3	
	Summit and south flank (I Monticelli?)	**1037**	0127	....	....	x-x-	----	x---	x---	----	3	
		? *1049*	....	....	....	x---	----	----	?---	----	*1*	
		? *1073*e	....	....	....	x-?-	----	?---	?---	----	*3*	
		1139	0601	**1139**	0609	x---	----	x---	x---	----	3	
		1150	....	....	....	x---	----	x---	----	----	3?	
		? *1270*	....	....	....	x---	----	x---	----	----	*2?*	
		? *1347*	....	....	....	x---	----	?---	----	----	*2?*	
		1500	....	....	....	x---	----	x-x-	----	----	2?	
		1570<	....	**1572**a	....	x---	----	x-x-	----	----	1?	
	Summit, SW and S flanks	**1631**	1216	**1632**	0131?	x-x-	----	xx-x	----	xxxx	**5?**	-/9
		1637	0701	**1652**	12	x---	----	x---	----	--x-	2*	
		1654	0225	**1680**	0328	x---	----	x---	?---	-xx-	3*	
		1682	0812	**1682**	0822	x---	----	x---	x---	x---	3	-/6
		1685	1003	**1694**	0429	x---	----	x---	x---	-x--	3*	
		1696	0731	**1696**	0814?	x---	----	x---	x---	----	2	
		1697	0915	**1698**	07	x---	----	x---	x---	-xx-	3*	
	Summit and SW flank	**1701**	0701	**1707**	0822	x-x-	----	x---	x---	-xx-	3*	-/6
	Summit, upper east and south flanks	**1708**	0814	**1723**	0708	x-x-	----	x---	x---	-x--	3*	-/6
		1724	0904	**1730**	0401?	x---	----	x---	x---	----	3*	-/6
	Summit and SW flank	**1732**	1225	**1737**	0604	x-x-	----	x---	x---	xxx-	3?	7/-
		1742	....	**1743**	....	x---	----	x---	----	----	1	
	Summit, upper SE, E and lower S flanks	**1744**	11 ?	**1761**	0106	x-x-	----	x---	x---	-x--	3*	6/-
	Summit, upper SW, SE, and NNW flanks	**1764**	....	**1767**	1027	x-x-	----	x---	x---	-x--	3*	7/6
	Summit, N, NE, SE and E flanks	**1770**	0215	**1779**	1004?	x-x-	----	x---	x---	xxx-	3?	7/6
	Summit and SW flank (550-300 m)	**1783**	0818	**1794**	0705	x-x-	----	x---	x---	xxx-	3?	7/8
	Summit and upper flanks	**1796**	01	**1822**	1116	x-x-	----	x---	x---	xxx-	3?	6/7
	Summit, upper E and S flanks	**1824**	0702	**1834**	0902	x-x-	----	x---	x---	-xx-	3*	7/-
	Summit, upper east and west flanks	**1835**	01	**1839**	0103	x-x-	----	x---	x---	----	3*	7/-
	Summit, upper N and E flanks	**1841**	0920	**1850**	0216	x-x-	----	x---	x---	-x--	2*	7/-
	Summit and upper N flank	**1854**	1214	**1855**	0527	x-x-	----	x---	x---	-x--	3*	7/-
	Summit and SW flank (300-225 m)	**1855**	1219	**1861**	1231	x-x-	----	x---	x---	-x--	3*	8/-
	Summit and upper SE flank	**1864**	0210	**1868**	1126	x-x-	----	x---	x---	----	2*	6/-
	Summit and upper NW and south flanks	**1870**	12	**1872**	0430	x-x-	----	x---	x---	xx--	3*	7/7
		? *1874*	*01*	....	....	x---	----	?---	?---	----	*1*	
	Summit and upper flanks	**1875**	1218	**1906**	0422	x-x-	----	xx--	x---	xxx-	4?	8/8
	Summit and upper flanks	**1913**	0705	**1944**	0404	x-x-	----	xx--	x---	xx--	3*	8/7
Ischia (Italy)	**40.73 N 13.897 E 789** 5567 **TYPxz Complex volcano 0101-03= Historical**											
	Selva del Napolitano, Piedmonte	K-**7550***	....	....	....	x---	----	----	--x-	----		
	Zaro, Marecocco, Spiaggia degli Inglesi	M-**3880**x	....	....	....	x---	----	x---	x-x-	----		
	Submarine SE flank (Secca d'Ischia)	G-**3580**y	....	....	....	-x--	x---	xx--	----	----		
	Cantariello	K-**3050***	....	....	....	x---	----	x---	x---	----		
	Punta della Cannuccia	T-**2700***	....	....	....	x---	----	x---	----	----		
	Costa Sparaina	K-**2350***	....	....	....	x---	----	x---	--x-	----		
	Castiglione	M-**1480**y	....	....	....	x---	----	----	x---	-x--		
	SE of Selva del Napolitano (CaT tephra)	G-**0930**w	....	....	....	x---	----	xx--	----	----		
	Costa del Lenzuolo	T-**0700**u	....	....	....	x---	----	xx--	----	----		
	Case Balestrieri?, Cava Nocelle?	M-**0490**w	....	....	....	x---	----	x---	x---	----		
	Bosco dei Conti and Fondo Ferraro ?	**-0470**?	....	....	....	x---	----	x---	--x-	----		
	Ischia Porto (San Pietro)	M-**0370**w	....	....	....	x---	----	x---	x---	---x		
	Ischia Porto (Spiaggia dei Pescatori)	M-**0200**x	....	....	....	x---	----	x---	x---	----		
		-0091	....	....	....	x---	----	?---	?---	----		
		-0006p	....	....	....	x---	----	----	----	----		
	Cretaio Tephra (near Bosco della Maddalena)	G **0040**u	....	....	....	x---	----	xx--	----	----	3	-/7
		? *0069*	....	....	....	----	----	?---	--?-	----		
		0080a	....	....	....	x---	----	?---	--?-	----		
		0145?	....	....	....	x---	----	?---	--?-	----		
	Vateliero, Molara-Cava Nocelle, Rotaro	**0295**j	....	....	....	x---	----	x---	x---	----		
	Montagnone-Moschiata area (BCT tephra)	G **0540**w	....	....	....	x---	----	xx--	----	----		
	Near Arso (FiT tephra layer)	G **0820**y	....	....	....	x---	----	xx--	----	----		
	(FBT tephra; preceded 1302 Arso eruption)	G **1290**?	....	....	....	----	----	xx--	----	----		
	Arso	**1302**	0118	**1302**	03	x---	----	x---	x---	xx--		

VOLCANO NAME (Subregion) / ERUPTION — Area of Activity	LAT	LONG	ELEV (m)	POPL (5 km, 10, 30, 100)	ROCK TYPE	VOLC TYPE / Start Year	Start M-Dy	NUMBER / Stop Year	Stop M-Dy	STATUS	Central / Flank vent / Radial fiss / Regional	Submarine / New island / Subglacial / Crater lake	Explosive / Pyro flow / Phreatic / Caldera	Lava flow / Lava lake / Dome / Spine	Fatal / Damage / Mudflow / Tsunami	VEI	Vol L/T
Palinuro (Italy)	**39.48 N**	**14.83 E**	**-70**	0006	**PTZ**	**Submarine volc**		**0101-031**		**Radiocarbon**							
						G-**8040**v	....	....	....		----	x---	x---	----	----		
Stromboli (Aeolian Islands)	**38.789 N**	**15.213 E**	**924**	4447	**YABtx**	**Stratovolcano**		**0101-04=**		**Historical**							
Northern flank (Vallonazzo)						M-**6050**?	....	....	....		--x-	----	----	x---	----	0	
NE flank (Nel Camnestrà lava flow)						M-**5800**y	....	....	....		--x-	----	----	x---	----	0	
Northern flank (Labronzo)						M-**5550**?	....	....	....		--x-	----	----	x---	----	0	
Northern flank (Vallonazzo lava flow)						M-**5050**?	....	....	....		--x-	----	----	x---	----	0	
Northern flank						M-**4800**y	....	....	....		--x-	----	x---	x---	----	2?	
Northern flank (Vallonazzo)						M-**4550**?	....	....	....		--x-	----	----	x---	----	0	
NE flank (Punta Lena lava flow)						M-**4250**?	....	....	....		--x-	----	x---	x---	----	2?	
(Secche di Lazzaro pyroclastics)						C-**4050**?	....	....	....		x---	----	xx-A	----	--xx	3?	
						-0350t	....	....	....		x---	----	x---	----	----	2	
						-0210j	....	....	....		x---	----	x---	----	----	2	
						-0050t	....	....	....		x---	----	x---	----	----	2	
						0050t	....	....	....		x---	----	x---	----	----	2	
						0150t	....	....	....		x---	----	x---	----	----	2	
						0250t	....	....	....		x---	----	x---	----	----	2	
						0550t	....	....	....		x---	----	x---	----	----	3	
						0950t	....	....	....		x---	----	x---	----	----	2	
Summit craters and Sciara del Fuoco						**1558**<	....	**1857**	....		x-x-	x---	x---	x---	-x--	3*	
Summit craters and Sciara del Fuoco						**1857**	....	**1889**	0626		x-x-	----	x---	x---	---x	3*	4/-
						1890	....	**1907**	0529		x---	----	x---	x---	-x--	3*	4/-
Summit craters and Sciara del Fuoco						**1910**	05	**1931**	07		x-x-	----	xx--	x---	xx-x	3*	5/-
						1932	0603	**1932**	0603		x---	----	x---	----	----	2	
Summit craters and Sciara del Fuoco						**1934**	0202	**2010**>	....		x-x-	xx--	xx--	x---	xx-x	2*	7/-
Panarea (Aeolian Islands)	**38.63 N**	**15.07 E**	**421**	4457	**ADryb**	**Stratovolcano**		**0101-041**		Holocene?							
Lipari (Aeolian Islands)	**38.48 N**	**14.95 E**	**602**	5557	**RAYBD**	**Stratovolcanoes**		**0101-042**		**Radiocarbon**							
(Gabellotto-Fiumebianco, E-1 tephra)						G-**5820**u	....	....	....		x---	----	xx--	x-x-	----		
Monte Pelato						G **0780**v	....	....	....		x---	----	xx--	x-x-	----		
Pelato (Forgia Vecchia, Rocche Rossi)						M **1230**s	....	....	....		x---	----	x---	x---	----		
Vulcano (Aeolian Islands)	**38.404 N**	**14.962 E**	**500**	4557	**XYTRB**	**Stratovolcanoes**		**0101-05=**		**Historical**							
NW side (Lentia)						K-**6550**?	....	....	....		-x--	----	----	--x-	----		
(Monte Saraceno tephra)						K-**6350***	....	....	....		x---	----	x---	x---	----		
Fossa (Punte Nere lava flow)						K-**3550***	....	....	....		x---	----	----	x---	----	0	6/-
Fossa (Campo Sportivo eruptive cycle)						K-**2650***	....	....	....		x---	----	xx--	x---	----	3	6/7
Fossa						T-**1300**?	....	....	....		x---	----	xx--	----	----	3	-/7
Fossa						U-**0950**z	....	....	....		x---	----	----	x---	----	0	
Fossa						**-0475**?	....	....	....		x---	----	x---	----	----		
Fossa						**-0360**j	....	....	....		x---	----	x---	----	----	2	
Fossa						**-0300**	....	....	....		----	----	x---	----	----	2	
Offshore vent						**-0215**	....	....	....		----	x---	----	----	----		
Vulcanello						**-0183**	....	....	....		-x--	xx--	x---	----	----	4	
						U-**0150**y	....	....	....		----	----	xx--	----	----		
Vulcanello						**-0126**	06	....	....		----	xx--	----	----	---x		
Vulcanello						**-0091**	....	....	....		-x--	----	x---	----	----	3?	
(no 43 BC eruption)						*X-0043*	....	....	....		----	----	----	----	----		
Vulcanello ?						**-0024**e	....	....	....		-x--	----	----	----	----		
Vulcanello						*? -0010*j	....	....	....		-x--	----	----	x---	----		
Fossa						**0050**t	....	....	....		x---	----	x---	----	----		
Fossa						**0144**	....	....	....		x---	----	?---	?---	----		
Fossa and Vulcanello III?						**0526**?	....	....	....		xx--	----	x---	----	----	3	
Fossa						**0729**	....	....	....		x---	----	x---	----	----		
						0925q	....	....	....		----	----	x---	----	----	3?	
						M **1040**u	....	....	....		-x--	?---	x---	x---	----	2?	
Vulcanello						M **1200**u	....	....	....		-x--	----	----	x---	----	2?	
Fossa (Palizzi lava flow)						M **1230**p	....	....	....		x---	----	----	x---	----	0	
						1444	0204	....	....		----	?---	x---	----	----	3	
Vulcanello III						**1550**	....	....	....		-x--	----	x---	----	----	3	
						1618	....	....	....		----	----	x---	----	----		
						1626	03	**1626**	04		----	----	x---	----	----	3	
						1631	....	....	....		----	----	x---	----	----		
Fossa						**1651**	....	....	....		x---	----	x---	----	----		
Fossa						**1688**	....	....	....		x---	----	x---	----	----		
Forgia Vecchia II and Fossa						**1727**	....	....	....		xx--	----	xxx-	----	--x-	3	
Fossa						**1731**	....	**1739**	....		x---	----	x---	x---	--x-	3*	6/7
Fossa						**1771**	0217	**1771**	05		x---	----	x---	----	----	3	
Fossa						*? 1775*	....	....	....		x---	----	?---	----	----		
Fossa						**1780**	....	....	....		x---	----	x---	----	----	2	
Fossa						*? 1786*	....	....	....		x---	----	x---	----	----	*3*	
Fossa						*? 1812*	....	....	....		x---	----	?---	----	----	*1?*	
Fossa						*? 1822*	....	*?1823*	....		x---	----	?---	----	----	*2?*	
Fossa						*? 1831*	....	....	....		x---	----	?---	----	----	*1?*	
Fossa						**1873**	09	**1879**	....		x---	----	x---	----	----	3*	
Fossa						**1886**	0105d	....	....		x---	----	x---	----	----	3	
Fossa						**1888**	0802	**1890**	0322		x---	----	xx--	----	-xx-	3*	
5 km east of Vulcanello						*? 1892*	*1214*	....	....		----	?---	----	----	----	*0*	
(smoke clouds not due to eruption)						*X 1968*	*0711*	....	....		----	----	----	----	----		
Etna (Sicily)	**37.734 N**	**15.004 E**	**3330**	2477	**XYBtz**	**Stratovolcanoes**		**0101-06=**		**Historical**							
						C-**6190**x	....	....	....		----	----	x---	----	----		
						C-**5150**w	....	....	....		----	----	x---	----	----		
						C-**4150**w	....	....	....		----	----	x---	----	----		
						C-**3510**w	....	....	....		----	----	x-x-	----	--x-		
(Tufo varicolori tephra layer)						C-**3390**t	....	....	....		----	----	x---	----	----		
						C-**3050**w	....	....	....		----	----	x---	----	----		
						C-**2330**v	....	....	....		----	----	x---	----	----		
(FS tephra layer)						C-**1980**t	....	....	....		----	----	x---	----	----		
						-1500t	....	....	....		--?-	----	x---	x---	-x?-	**5?**	
(confused with ca. 1500 BC eruption)						*X-1470*	....	....	....		----	----	----	----	----		
(FL tephra layer)						G-**1420**u	....	....	....		----	----	xx--	----	----		
South flank (Monte Salto del Cane)						C-**1050**u	....	....	....		--x-	----	x---	x---	----		
						? -0735	....	....	....		----	----	----	----	----		
South ?, Mt. Mompilieri ?						**-0695**b	....	....	....		--x-	----	x---	x---	-x--		
						? -0565	....	....	....		----	----	----	----	----		

Etna (Sicily) *continued*

VOLCANO NAME (Subregion) / ERUPTION — Area of Activity		Start Year	Start M-Dy	Stop Year	Stop M-Dy	Central / Flank vent / Radial fiss / Regional	Submarine / New island / Subglacial / Crater lake	Explosive / Pyro flow / Phreatic / Caldera	Lava flow / Lava lake / Dome / Spine	Fatal / Damage / Mudflow / Tsunami	VEI	Vol L/T
South flank ?		**-0479**	08 ?	**-0475**?	....	--x-	----	x---	x---	-x--		
South flank (Monte Arso)		**-0425**	0315m	**-0424**?	....	--x-	----	?---	x---	-x--		
SE flank (700 m, Monte Gorna)		**-0396**?	0415q	....	....	--x-	----	x---	x---	-x--		
(no ca. 350 BC eruption)	*X*	*-0350*?	....	....	....	----	----	----	----	----		
		-0141	1231y	....	....	?---	----	x---	x---	----		
		-0135	....	....	....	--?-	----	x---	x---	-x--		
		-0126	06 <	....	....	x-?-	----	x---	?---	----		
S flank, summit (Cratere del Piano caldera)		**-0122**	....	....	....	x-x-	----	xx-x	x---	-x--	**5**	-/**9**
	?	*-0061*	....	....	....	?---	----	x---	----	----		
	?	*-0056*	....	....	....	----	----	----	----	----		
West flank and summit ?		**-0049**	....	....	....	?-x-	----	x---	x---	----		
(FF tephra layer)		**-0044**	03 ?	....	....	x-?-	----	x---	x---	-x--	3?	
East side ?		**-0036**	0715q	**-0035**	....	x-?-	----	x---	x---	----		
		-0032	1231y	....	....	----	----	----	?---	----		
	?	*-0010*?	....	....	....	x---	----	?---	?---	----		
		0010?	....	**0020**?	....	x---	----	x---	----	----		
		0039a	....	....	....	x---	----	x---	----	----		
(description of Etna, not eruption)	*X*	*0050*	....	....	....	----	----	----	----	----		
(incorrect eruption report)	*X*	*0072*	....	....	....	----	----	----	----	----		
	?	*0080*?	....	....	....	x---	----	x---	?---	----		
(FV tephra layer)	T	**0100**v	....	....	....	----	----	x---	----	----		
(no 165 AD eruption)	*X*	*0165*	....	....	....	----	----	----	----	----		
South flank (Monpeloso)		**0252**	0201	**0252**	0209	x-x-	----	?---	x---	-x--	3?	
(incorrectly interpreted as eruption)	*X*	*0400*	....	....	....	----	----	----	----	----		
(incorrectly interpreted as eruption)	*X*	*0410*	....	....	....	----	----	----	----	----		
		0417?	....	....	....	----	----	x---	----	----		
(no specific eruptions AD 500-560)	*X*	*0500*	....	....	....	----	----	----	----	----		
(no specific eruptions AD 500-560)	*X*	*0560*	....	....	....	----	----	----	----	----		
(incorrect reference to eruption)	*X*	*0604*	....	....	....	----	----	----	----	----		
	?	*0644*	....	....	....	----	----	----	----	----		
South flank (1200 m, S of Mt. Sona)	*?*	*0812*?	....	....	....	--x-	----	x---	x---	----		8/5
	?	*0814*	....	....	....	----	----	----	----	----		
	?	*0859*	....	....	....	----	----	----	----	----		
	?	*0911*	....	....	....	----	----	----	----	----		
	?	*1004*	....	....	....	----	----	----	----	----		
	?	*1044*	....	....	....	----	----	----	----	----		
WSW flank (1500 m) ?		**1063**a	....	....	....	--?-	----	x---	x---	----		
		1157	....	....	....	----	----	----	----	----	2?	
		1160	....	....	....	----	----	----	----	----	2?	
		1164?	....	....	....	----	----	----	----	----	2?	
(tectonic earthquake, eruption uncertain)	*?*	*1169*	*0204*	....	....	--?-	----	?---	?---	-?--		
(probably confused with 1169 events)	*X*	*1175*	....	....	....	----	----	----	----	----		
		1194	....	....	....	----	----	----	----	----	2?	
(incorrect inference of date)	*X*	*1222*	....	....	....	----	----	----	----	----		
SE flank		**1224**	08 ?	....	....	--x-	----	----	x---	-x--		
		1250	....	....	....	----	----	----	----	----	2?	
East flank (Valle del Bove)		**1284**	....	**1285**	01 ?	--x-	----	----	x---	----		
(confused with 1329 eruption)	*X*	*1321*	....	*X1328*	....	----	----	----	----	----		
SE flank		**1329**	0628	**1329**	0804d	x-x-	----	x---	x---	?x-x	3?	7/6
		1333	....	....	....	?---	----	x---	x---	----	2	
(confused with 1329 eruption)	*X*	*1334*	....	....	....	----	----	----	----	----		
		1350	....	....	....	x---	----	x---	----	----	2	
SSE (370 m), Mts. Pomiciari, Arsi?		**1381**?	0806?	....	....	--x-	----	?---	x---	-x--	2	7/6
Summit, south flank (M. Piniteddu)		**1408**	1108	**1408**	1125?	x-x-	----	x---	x---	-x--	3	
South (N of Mt. Arso and 950 m)		**1444**	....	....	....	x-x-	----	x---	x---	-x--	2	
East (Valle del Bove, 1630 or 1825 m)		**1446**	0925	....	....	--x-	----	----	x---	----	1	
		1447	0921	....	....	x---	----	x---	x---	----	1	
(no 1470 eruption)	*X*	*1470*	....	....	....	----	----	----	x---	----		
		1493?	....	**1500**?	....	x---	----	?---	?---	----	1	
(no activity recorded 1494-1533)	*X*	*1533*	....	....	....	----	----	----	----	----		
(probably same as 1536 eruption)	*X*	*1535*	....	....	....	----	----	----	----	----		
Summit, S, N & W flanks (1400-2500 m)		**1536**	0322	**1536**	12 ?	x-x-	----	x---	x---	xxx-	3	7/5
Summit, south flank (1800-1500 m)		**1537**	03 ?	**1537**	07	x-x-	----	x---	x---	-x--	2	7/6
		1540	07	....	....	x---	----	x---	----	----	1	
		1541	07 ?	....	....	x---	----	x---	----	----	2	
(no 1550 eruption)	*X*	*1550*	....	....	....	----	----	----	----	----		
	?	*1554*	....	....	....	x---	----	----	----	----	*2*	
NE flank		**1566**	1101?	**1566**	12	x-x-	----	x---	x---	-x--	2	7/5
	?	*1578*	....	....	....	--?-	----	----	----	----		
SE flank		**1579**	0909?	**1580**?	....	--x-	----	x---	x---	-x--		
(1595 eruption report discredited)	*X*	*1595*	....	....	....	----	----	----	----	----		
Central Crater (SW and S slope)		**1603**	07	**1610**	....	x---	----	x---	x---	----	2	6/-
SW flank (2250-1950 m)?		**1607**	0628	**1608**?	....	--x-	----	x---	x---	----	2	8/6
(confused with 1607 eruption)	*X*	*1609*	*07*	....	....	----	----	----	----	----		
SW flank (2500-1700 m)		**1610**	0206	**1610**	0815	x-x-	----	x---	x---	-x--	2	8/6
NNE flank (2800-2400 m), Monti Deserti		**1614**	0701?	**1624**	....	x-x-	----	x---	x---	-x--	2	**9**/6
Central Crater	*?*	*1633*	*0221*	....	....	x-?-	----	?---	?---	----		
SE (2100-1950 m), Little Mt. Pecorara		**1634**	1219?	**1638**	0427	x-x-	----	x---	x---	-x--	1	8/5
(1640 is error for 1643 eruption)	*X*	*1640*	....	....	....	----	----	----	----	----		
N flank (2100-1275 m), Monte Pomiciaro		**1643**	0220	**1643**	0228	--x-	----	x---	x---	----	1	6/5
NNE (2000 m, 1800 m), Mt. Nero		**1646**	1120	**1647**	0117	--x-	----	x---	x---	-x--	2	8/6
West (2600-1770 m), east (1875-1815 m)		**1651**	0117	**1653**	07 ?	x-x-	----	x---	x---	-x--	1	8/5
Central Crater		**1654**	0101	**1656**?	....	x---	----	x---	x---	----	1	
S flank (950-625 m, Monti Rossi)		**1669**	0311	**1669**	0711?	x-x-	----	x---	x---	-x--	3?	**9**/8
East flank (Valle del Bove, 2900 m)		**1682**	0901	**1682**	10 ?	?-x-	----	?---	x---	----	2	
East slope of Central Crater		**1688**	....	....	....	x---	----	x---	x---	----	1	
East flank (Valle del Bove, 2300 m?)		**1689**	0314	....	....	x-x-	----	x---	x---	xx--	1	7/-
(tectonic earthquake, eruption doubtful)	*?*	*1693*	*0109*	....	....	x---	----	?---	?---	----		
Central Crater		**1693**	12	**1694**	11 ?	x---	----	x---	----	-x--	3?	
East flank (Valle del Bove, 2075-1875 m)		**1702**	0308	**1702**	0508	x-x-	----	x---	x---	-x--	1	7/-
(confused with 1727-1728 eruption?)	*?*	*1723*	*1122*	*?1724*	*05 ?*	x---	----	x---	x---	-x--	*2*	
Central Crater (SW slope)		**1727**	1122	**1728**	0510?	x---	----	x---	x---	-x--	2?	
Central Crater		**1732**	1209	**1765**	....	x---	----	x---	x---	-x--	2*	7/-
East flank (Valle del Bove, 1750 m)		**1755**	0309	**1755**	0315	x-x-	----	x---	x---	-xx-	3	6/-

VOLCANO NAME (Subregion) / ERUPTION	Area of Activity	Start Year	Start M-Dy	Stop Year	Stop M-Dy	Central, Flank vent, Radial fiss, Regional	Submarine, New island, Subglacial, Crater lake	Explosive, Pyro flow, Phreatic, Caldera	Lava flow, Lava lake, Dome, Spine	Fatal, Damage, Mudflow, Tsunami	VEI	Vol L/T
Etna (Sicily) *continued*	Central Crater, south flank (3000 m)	1758	1103?	1759	0801	x---	----	x---	x---	----	2*	
	West flank (1725-1580 m, Mt. Nuovo)	1763	0206	1763	0310?	--x-	----	x---	x---	-x--	2	7/6
	South flank (2500-1925 m, Montagnola)	1763	0618	1763	0910	--x-	----	x---	x---	-x--	3	8/7
	NW flank (3125-2500 m?)	1764	....	1765?	....	--x-	----	x---	x---	----	1	8/5
	South flank (2100-1950 m, M. Calcarazzi)	1766	0427	1766	1106	x-x-	----	x-?-	x---	-x--	2	8/6
	Central Crater	1767	0502	....	....	x---	----	x---	----	----		
	Central Crater	? *1770*	*0528*a	....	....	x---	----	?---	----	----		
	Central Crater	1776	....	....	....	x---	----	x---	----	----		
	Summit, S & SSW flanks (2360-1850 m)	1780	0420?	1780	07 ?	x-x-	----	x---	x---	-x--	2*	7/4
	Central Crater	1781	03	1781	0510	x---	----	x---	x---	----	2	
	Central Crater	1787	0604d	1787	0811	x---	----	x---	x---	-x--	4*	6/-
	Central Crater	1791	02	1791	09	x---	----	x---	----	----	2	
	Central Crater, west slope	1792	03	1792	0524	x---	----	x---	x---	----	2	6/-
	Summit, SE flank (2825-1500 m)	1792	0525	1793	0526e	x-x-	----	x-x-	x---	-x--	3	7/5
	Central Crater	1793?	....	1802?	....	x---	----	x---	x---	----	3?	
	Central Crater, E flank (1950-1700 m)	1802	1115	1802	1118	x-x-	----	x---	x---	----	2	7/-
	Central Crater	1803	0101	1819?	....	x---	----	x---	x---	----	2*	
	Central Crater, N & NE flanks (3000-1325 m)	1809	0327	1809	0409	x-x-	----	x---	x---	-x--	2	7/6
	East (Valle del Bove 3000-1975 m)	1811	1027	1812	05 ?	--x-	----	x---	x---	----	2*	7/6
	Offshore from Aci-Castello	? *1816*	*0306*	....	....	----	?---	----	----	----	*0*	
	(Valle del Bove 2850-2375 m), Central Crater	1819	0527	1819	0805	x-x-	----	x---	x---	----	2?	7/5
	Central Crater	1820	12 ?	1833	....	x---	----	x---	x---	----	2*	
	SSE, W flanks (3000-1700? m), Mt. Nunziata	1832	1031	1832	1122	--x-	----	x---	x---	xx--	2	7/6
	Central Crater	1838	0708	1839	02	x---	----	x---	x---	----	2	7/-
	Central Crater (south & east slopes)	1842	1118	1842	1229?	x---	----	x---	x---	----	2	6/-
	West flank (2400-1900 m), Central Crater	1843	1117	1843	1216?	x-x-	----	x---	x---	xx--	2	7/6
	East (Valle del Bove 1950-1700 m)	1852	0820	1853	0527	x-x-	----	x---	x---	-x--	2	8/6
	Central Crater	? *1857*	*0906*	....	....	x---	----	?---	----	----	*1?*	
	Central Crater	1863	0501	1863	0725?	x---	----	x---	x---	-x--	3?	
	Central Crater	1864	0805d	1864	0919	x---	----	x---	x---	----	2	
	NE flank (1865-1690 m, Mt. Sartorius)	1865	0130	1865	0628	x-x-	----	x---	x---	-x--	2	7/6
	Central Crater	1868	1126?	1868	1208	x---	----	x---	----	----	3	
	East flank (W wall of Valle del Bove)	1869	0926	1869	0926	--x-	----	----	x---	----	0	6/-
	Central Crater	1874	05	....	....	x---	----	x---	----	----	2	
	North flank (2520-2110 m), Central Crater	1874	0829	1874	0831	x-x-	----	x---	x---	----	2	6/6
	Central Crater	1878	1223	1883	0331>	x-x-	----	x---	x---	-x--	2	
	SSW (2650-2300 m), NNE (2450-1690 m)	1879	0526	1879	0607	--x-	----	x---	x---	-x--	3	7/7
	South flank (1200-950 m, Mt. Leone)	1883	0322	1883	0324	--x-	----	x---	x---	----	2	4/5
	Central Crater	1884	....	1886	04	x---	----	x---	----	----	1	
	S flank (1525-1320 m), Mt. Gemmellaro	1886	0518	1886	0607	x-x-	----	x---	x---	-x--	3	7/6
	Central Crater	1887	0531	1887	08	x---	----	x---	----	----	1	
	Central Crater	1888	0413<	1889	08	x---	----	x---	----	----	2	
	Central Crater	1890	05	1890	1017?	x---	----	x---	----	----	2*	
	Central Crater	1891	0220	1891	12	x---	----	x---	?---	----	2*	
	Central Crater	1892	0620	1892	0708?	x---	----	x---	----	----	2*	
	South flank (2045-1800 m), Mt. Silvestri	1892	0709	1892	1229	--x-	----	x---	x---	-x--	2	8/6
	Central Crater	1893	0426	1898	06	x---	----	x---	x---	----	1	
	Central Crater	1899	0719	1899	0805	x---	----	x-x-	----	-x--	3	
		1899	1115	1907	08	x---	----	x---	x---	----	2*	
	SE flank (Valle del Bove 2800-2275 m)	1908	0429	1908	0501a	x-x-	----	x---	x---	----	2	6/5
	Central Crater	1908	0520	1909	0928	x---	----	x---	----	----	2	
	Central Crater	1910	0221	1910	0221	x---	----	x---	----	----	1	
	South flank (2300-1900 m, Mt. Ricco)	1910	0323	1910	0418	x-x-	----	x---	x---	-x--	2	7/5
	Central Crater	1910	1227	1911	0217	x---	----	x---	?---	----	2	
	(collapse forming NE Crater: no eruption)	X *1911*	*0527*	....	....	----	----	----	----	----		
	Central Crater, NE Crater?	1911	08	1911	0926d	x---	----	x---	----	----	2	
	NE flank (2550-1625 m)	1911	0910	1911	0922	--x-	----	x---	x---	-x--	1	7/6
	Central Crater	1912	0804	1912	08	x---	----	x---	x---	----	3	
	Central Crater, NE Crater	1913	1113	1917	03	x---	----	x---	x---	----	2	
	NE Crater, Central Crater	1917	0624	1917	0705d	x---	----	x---	x---	-x--	2	
	NE Crater, Central Crater	1918	03	1918	11	x---	----	x---	x---	----	2*	
	North flank (3110-2025 m)	1918	1130?	1918	1201?	--x-	----	x---	x---	----	1?	6/-
	Central Crater, NE Crater	1919	0315	1923	07 ?	x---	----	x---	x---	----	2	6/-
	NE flank (2500-1800 m)	1923	0617	1923	0718	x-x-	----	x---	x---	-x--	2	7/5
	Central Crater	1923	1009	1925	02	x---	----	x---	----	----	1	
	NE Crater	1926	0102	1926	06	x---	----	x---	----	----	1	
	Central Crater	1928	0731	1928	0820	x---	----	x---	----	----	1	
	East flank (3000-1200 m), NE Crater	1928	1102	1928	1120	x-x-	----	x---	x---	xx--	1	7/6
	NE Crater	1929	0802	....	....	x---	----	x---	----	x---	1	
	NE Crater	1930	1101	....	....	x---	----	x---	----	----	1	
	Central Crater, NE Crater	1931	0726e	1933	09	x---	----	x---	----	----	2	
	NE Crater	1934	0105	1934	03	x---	----	x---	----	----	1	
	Central Crater, NE Crater	1935	0707	1941	0127?	x---	----	x---	x---	-x--	3*	
	Central Crater, NE Crater	1941	10 ?	1944	0426d	x---	----	x---	----	----	2	
	SW flank (2780-2240 m)	1942	0630	1942	0701	--x-	----	x---	x---	----	2	6/5
	NE Crater	1945	0605d	1945	10	x---	----	x---	----	----	1	
	NE Crater	1946	02	1946	10	x---	----	x---	----	----	1	
	NE Crater, Central Crater	1947	0129	1947	0224	x---	----	x---	----	----	3?	
	NE flank (3050-2150 m)	1947	0224	1947	0310	--x-	----	x---	x---	-x--	1	7/4
	Central Crater and NW flank (2420-1900 m)	1949	1202	1949	1205	x-x-	----	x-x-	x---	-x--	2	7/5
	NE Crater	1949	1203	1950	11	x---	----	x---	----	----	1	
	East flank (2820-2200 m)	1950	1125	1951	1202	--x-	----	x-x-	x---	-x--	2	8/6
	NE Crater	1951	0921	1952	0530	x---	----	x---	----	----	1	
		? *1953*	*0730*	....	....	----	----	?---	----	----	*2*	
	NE Crater, Central Crater	1955	0405	1956	0407	x---	----	x---	x---	----	2*	6/6
	NE Crater	1957	0205	1957	0507	x---	----	x---	x---	----	2	6/7
	NE Crater	1957	0825	1958	0503	x---	----	x---	x---	----	2	
	NE Crater, Central Crater	1958	11	1958	12	x---	----	x---	----	----	1	
	Central Crater	1959	0323	1959	0425e	x---	----	x---	----	----	1	
	Central and NE Craters, NNE (3100 m)	1959	1017	1964	1231	x-x-	----	x---	x---	-x--	3*	7/-
	NE Crater, Central Crater	1966	0110	1971	03 ?	x---	----	x---	x---	----	2	7/-
	SE flank (2550 m)	1968	0107	1968	0504	--x-	----	----	x---	----	0	6/-
	SE flank (3050 m), E flank (2880-1800 m)	1971	0405	1971	0612	x-xx	----	x---	x---	-x--	2	7/6
	Central Crater	1971	0919	1979	03 ?	x---	----	x---	----	----	2	6/-

VOLCANO NAME (Subregion) / ERUPTION — Area of Activity	LAT		LONG		ELEV (m)	POPL 5 km 10 30 100	ROCK TYPE	VOLC TYPE	NUMBER	STATUS	Start Year	Start M-Dy	Stop Year	Stop M-Dy	Central Flank vent Radial fiss Regional	Submarine New island Subglacial Crater lake	Explosive Pyro flow Phreatic Caldera	Lava flow Lava lake Dome Spine	Fatal Damage Mudflow Tsunami	VEI	Vol L/T
Etna (Sicily) *continued*																					
West flank (1670 m and 1650 m)											**1974**	0130	**1974**	0329	--x-	----	x---	x---	-x--	2	6/6
NE Crater											**1974**	0929?	**1978**	0329	x---	----	x---	x---	----	2	7/-
North flank (2625 m)											**1975**	0224	**1975**	0829	--x-	----	x---	x---	----	1	6/-
SE Crater, SE and ENE flanks (3050-1675 m)											**1978**	0429	**1978**	1130	--x-	----	x---	x---	----	2*	7/-
Central Crater											**1979**	0703	**1992**	12	x---	----	x-x-	----	xx--	2*	
SE Crater, SE, E and NE flanks											**1979**	0716	**1980**	0901e	x-x-	----	x---	x---	-x--	3?	6/-
NE Crater											**1980**	0708	**1980**	0926	x---	----	x---	x---	----	3*	6/-
NE Crater											**1981**	0126e	**1981**	0305d	x---	----	x---	x---	----	2	6/-
NNW flank (2550-1140 m)											**1981**	0317	**1981**	0323	--x-	----	x---	x---	-x--	2	7/6
NE Crater											**1981**	1126	**1981**	1126	x---	----	x---	----	----	2	
South flank (2680-2250 m)											**1983**	0328	**1983**	0806	--x-	----	x-x-	x---	-x--	1	7/5
SE Crater											**1984**	0428	**1984**	1018	x---	----	x---	x---	----	1	7/5
NE Crater											**1984**	0720	**1986**	0924	x---	----	xx--	x---	xx--	3*	5/6
SE Crater, south flank (2620-2480 m)											**1985**	0308	**1985**	0713	x-x-	----	x-x-	x---	-xx-	1	7/4
SE Crater and SE flank (2750-2420 m)											**1985**	1219	**1985**	1231	x-x-	----	x---	x---	x---	1	5/4
SE Crater											**1986**	03	**1986**	1031?	x-x-	----	x---	x---	----	2?	
Valle del Bove (3050-2180 m)											**1986**	1030	**1987**	0301	--x-	----	x---	x---	----	2	7/6
NE and SE Craters											**1987**	0308h	**1987**	0516	x---	----	x-x-	----	x---	2*	
SE Crater											**1988**	1002	**1989**	0630	x---	----	x---	x---	----	1	
SE Crater, SE and NE flanks											**1989**	0911	**1989**	1009	x-x-	----	x---	xx--	-x--	2	7/-
SE and NE Craters											**1989**	1216	**1992**	0523	x---	----	x---	x---	----	3*	6/7
SE flank (3100-2800 m and 2400-2100 m)											**1991**	1214	**1993**	0330	--x-	----	x---	x---	-x--	2	8/-
NE Crater											**1993**	0203	**1993**	0203	x---	----	x-x-	----	----	1	
Central Crater, NE Crater											**1993**	0803	**1993**	1013	x---	----	x---	----	----	1	
Central Crater, NE Crater, SE Crater											**1994**	0617	**2001**	0717	x-x-	----	xx--	x-x-	-x--	3*	7/8
S to NE flanks (3100-2100 m)											**2001**	0717	**2001**	0809	--x-	----	x---	x---	-x--	2*	7/6
Central Crater, NE Crater											**2001**	12 ?	**2002**	1030?	x---	----	x---	----	----	1	
NE Rift (3100-1900 m), S flank (2850-2600 m)											**2002**	1026	**2003**	0128	--x-	----	x---	x---	-x--	3	7/7
NE Crater											**2003**	0308c	**2003**	1109	x---	----	x---	----	----	1	
Central Crater											**2004**	0212	**2004**	0214	x---	----	x---	----	----	1?	
SE Crater, SE flank (3000-2320 m)											**2004**	0907	**2005**	0308	x-x-	----	x---	x---	----	1*	7/-
Bocca Nuova											**2005**	1216	**2005**	1222	x---	----	x---	----	----	1	
SE Crater & flank vents; NE Crater											**2006**	0714	**2006**	1215	x-x-	----	xx--	x---	----	2*	7/-
Bocca Nuova, SE Crater and flank vents											**2007**	0319	**2008**	05 ?	x---	----	x---	x---	----	2*	
East base of NE Crater (3000-2650 m)											**2008**	0513	**2009**	0704	--x-	----	x---	x---	----	1	
Campi Flegrei Mar Sicilia (Italy)	**37.10**	**N***	**12.70**	**E**	**-8**	6666	**XB**	**Submarine volcs**	**0101-07=**	**Historical**											
											-0253k	....	....	....	----	x---	----	----	----		
Giulia Ferdinandeo											**1632**	....	....	....	----	x---	----	----	----	0	
Giulia Ferdinandeo											*? 1701*	....	....	....	----	??--	----	----	----	*2*	
Giulia Ferdinandeo (Graham Island)											**1831**	0628>	**1831**	0811d	---x	xx--	x---	----	----	3*	-/8
Pinne											**1846**	1004	**1846**	1005	----	x---	----	----	----	2	
Giulia Ferdinandeo											**1863**	0812	....	....	----	xx--	----	----	----	2	
Pinne											**1867**	....	....	....	----	x---	----	----	----	0	
Pinne											*? 1911*	*0930*	....	....	----	?---	----	----	----	*1?*	
Pantelleria (Italy)	**36.77**	**N**	**12.02**	**E**	**836**	4556	**RTBXy**	**Shield volcano**	**0101-071**	**Historical**											
Cuddia di Mida, Valenza											K-**7050**?	....	....	....	x---	----	x---	x---	----		
Cuddia Patite ?											C-**6130**u	....	....	....	x---	----	x---	----	----		
Punta Tracino											C-**5610**v	....	....	....	-x--	----	x---	----	----		
Cuddia Randazzo											C-**3640**y	....	....	....	x---	----	x---	x---	----		
Hingeline vent system											C-**1080**y	....	....	....	x---	----	x---	----	----		
Off the northern coast											*? 1831*	....	....	....	----	?---	----	----	----		
Foerstner (4 km NNW of Pantelleria)											**1891**	1017	**1891**	1025	---x	x---	x---	----	----	1	
South of Pantelleria											*? 1891*	*12*	....	....	----	?---	----	----	----		

Romolo Romano (IIV-CNR, Italy)

1986 eruption

GREECE

VOLCANO NAME (Subregion) / ERUPTION — Area of Activity	LAT		LONG		ELEV (m)	POPL	ROCK TYPE	VOLC TYPE	NUMBER	STATUS	Start Year	Start M-Dy	Stop Year	Stop M-Dy	Central Flank vent Radial fiss Regional	Submarine New island Subglacial Crater lake	Explosive Pyro flow Phreatic Caldera	Lava flow Lava lake Dome Spine	Fatal Damage Mudflow Tsunami	VEI	Vol L/T
Susaki (Greece)	37.935	N	23.073	E	180				0102-01=	Not a Volcano											
Methana (Greece)	**37.615**	**N**	**23.336**	**E**	**760**	3457	**AD**	**Lava domes**	**0102-02=**	**Historical**											
Kameno Vouno											**-0258**o	....	....	....	----	----	x---	x-x-	----	3	7/-
											? 1922	*08*	....	....	----	----	?---	----	----		
Mílos (Greece)	**36.699**	**N***	**24.439**	**E**	**751**	4445	**RAD**	**Stratovolcanoes**	**0102-03=**	**Radiocarbon**											
SE Mílos, east of Fyriplaka tuff ring											G **0140**y	....	....	....	x---	----	x-x-	----	-xx-	1?	
Santorini (Greece)	**36.404**	**N**	**25.396**	**E**	**367**	4555	**DABTr**	**Shield volcanoes**	**0102-04=**	**Historical**											
											G-**1610**m	....	....	....	x--x	x---	xxxx	----	xxxx	**7?**	-/10
Hiera Island											**-0197**	....	....	....	x--x	xx--	x---	----	----	3	
(eruption took place in 46 A.D.)											*X 0019*	....	....	....	----	----	----	----	----		
Thia Island											**0046**	1231	**0047**	0201p	x--x	xx--	x---	x-x-	---x	3	
NE side of Thia Island											**0726**	0715q	....	....	x--x	xx--	x---	x-x-	-x--	4?	7/-
Mikri Kameni											**1570**	....	**1573**	....	x--x	xx--	x---	x-x-	----	3	6/-
Colombo Bank (6.5 km NE of Thera)											**1650**	0927	**1650**	1206	-x-x	xx--	x---	x---	xx-x	4?	-/8
Nea Kameni											**1707**	0523	**1711**	0914	x--x	xx--	x---	x-x-	-x--	3	7/-
Georgios, Afroessa and Reka domes											**1866**	0126	**1870**	1015	x--x	xx--	x---	x-x-	xx--	2	8/-
Nea Kameni (Dafni dome)											**1925**	0811	**1926**	05	x--x	x---	xxx-	x-x-	?---	2*	8/-
Nea Kameni (Naftilos dome)											**1928**	0123	**1928**	0317	x--x	----	x-x-	x-x-	----	2	4/-
Nea Kameni (Triton, Ktenas, Fouque domes)											**1939**	0820	**1941**	0702a	x--x	x---	x-x-	x-x-	-x--	2	7/-
Nea Kameni (Liatsikas dome)											**1950**	0110	**1950**	0202	x--x	----	x-x-	x-x-	----	2	4/-
Nisyros (Greece)	**36.586**	**N**	**27.160**	**E**	**698**	3356	**DAR**	**Stratovolcano**	**0102-05=**	**Historical**											
											1422	....	....	....	x---	----	?-x-	?---	----	2	
Plegathon and Polyvotis											**1871**	....	....	....	x---	----	x-x-	----	-x--	2	
Plegathon and Polyvotis											**1873**	06	**1873**	0926	x---	----	x-x-	----	--x-	2	
Polyvotis Micros											**1888**	0925d	....	....	x---	----	--x-	----	----	2	
Yali (Greece)	**36.671**	**N**	**27.140**	**E**	**180**	1356	**R**	**Lava domes**	**0102-051**	**Holocene**											

TURKEY

VOLCANO NAME (Subregion) / ERUPTION — Area of Activity	LAT		LONG		ELEV (m)	POPL	ROCK TYPE	VOLC TYPE	NUMBER	STATUS	Start Year	Start M-Dy	Stop Year	Stop M-Dy	Central Flank vent Radial fiss Regional	Submarine New island Subglacial Crater lake	Explosive Pyro flow Phreatic Caldera	Lava flow Lava lake Dome Spine	Fatal Damage Mudflow Tsunami	VEI	Vol L/T
Kula (Turkey-W)	**38.58**	**N***	**28.52**	**E**	**750**	5567	**XZbyf**	**Cinder cones**	**0103-00-**	**Holocene**											
Karapinar Field (Turkey-C)	**37.67**	**N***	**33.65**	**E**	**1302**	5557	**YXb**	**Cinder cones**	**0103-001**	**Holocene**											
Hasan Dagi (Turkey-C)	**38.13**	**N**	**34.17**	**E**	**3253**	3467	**DARBY**	**Stratovolcano**	**0103-002**	**Holocene**											
											*? -7550*t	....	....	....	?---	----	??-?	----	----		
											*? -6750*t	....	....	....	?---	----	?---	?---	----		
Göllü Dag (Turkey-C)	**38.25**	**N**	**34.57**	**E**	**2143**	3567	**RDB**	**Lava dome**	**0103-003**	Holocene?											

VOLCANO NAME (Subregion) / ERUPTION — Area of Activity	LAT	LONG	ELEV (m)	POPL 5 km 10 30 100	ROCK TYPE	VOLC TYPE / —Start— Year	NUMBER / M-Dy	STATUS / —Stop— Year	M-Dy	ERUPTIVE CHARACTERISTICS: Central / Flank vent / Radial fiss / Regional	Submarine / New island / Subglacial / Crater lake	Explosive / Pyro flow / Phreatic / Caldera	Lava flow / Lava lake / Dome / Spine	Fatal / Damage / Mudflow / Tsunami	VEI	Vol L/T
Acigöl-Nevsehir (Turkey-C)	**38.57** N	**34.52** E	**1689**	6667	RDBA	**Caldera**	**0103-004**	**Anthropology**								
(tephra layer T10)						C-**7810**?	....	....	....	x---	----	x---	----	----		
(tephra layer T13)						C-**6230**?	....	....	....	x---	----	x---	----	----		
(tephra layer T15)						C-**3500**?	....	....	....	x---	----	x---	----	----		
(tephra layer T17)						C-**2370**x	....	....	....	x---	----	x---	----	----		
						A-**2080**x	....	....	....	----	----	x---	----	-x--		
Erciyes Dagi (Turkey-C)	**38.52** N	**35.48** E	**3916**	4467	DARYT	**Stratovolcano**	**0103-01=**	**Radiocarbon**								
						G-**6880**s	....	....	....	----	----	x---	----	----		
						? 0253<	....	....	....	-x--	----	?---	----	----		
Karaca Dag (Turkey-E)	**37.67** N	**39.83** E	**1957**	4457	B	**Shield volcano**	**0103-011**	**Holocene**								
Nemrut Dagi (Turkey-E)	**38.65** N	**42.23** E	**2948**	3467	RTYBX	**Stratovolcano**	**0103-02=**	**Historical**								
						V-**9950**w	....	....	....	----	----	x---	----	----		
						V-**7769**?	....	....	....	----	----	x---	----	----		
						V-**7579**?	....	....	....	----	----	x---	----	----		
						V-**7087**?	....	....	....	----	----	x---	----	----		
						V-**6471**?	....	....	....	----	----	x---	----	----		
						V-**6213**?	....	....	....	----	----	x---	----	----		
						V-**5745**?	....	....	....	----	----	x---	----	----		
						V-**5320**?	....	....	....	----	----	x---	----	----		
						V-**5242**u	....	....	....	----	----	x---	----	----		
						V-**5152**?	....	....	....	----	----	x---	----	----		
						V-**5085**?	....	....	....	----	----	x---	----	----		
						V-**4938**u	....	....	....	----	----	x---	----	----		
						V-**4849**?	....	....	....	----	----	x---	----	----		
						V-**4615**?	....	....	....	----	----	x---	----	----		
						V-**4321**?	....	....	....	----	----	x---	----	----		
						V-**4055**t	....	....	....	----	----	x---	----	----		
						V-**1662**?	....	....	....	----	----	x---	----	----		
						V-**1396**?	....	....	....	----	----	x---	----	----		
						V-**0787**q	....	....	....	----	----	x---	----	----		
						V-**0657**q	....	....	....	----	----	x---	----	----		
						V-**0531**?	....	....	....	----	----	x---	----	----		
East flank (Lake Van)						**1111**	....	....	....	-x--	---x	x---	----	---x		
						V **1402**?	....	....	....	----	----	x---	----	----		
North flank (Nemrut Boynu)						**1441**	....	....	....	--x-	----	x---	x---	----		
						1597<	....	....	....	--x-	----	----	x---	----		
East flank (Lake Van)						**1650**	1027	....	....	-x--	---x	x---	----	----		
						? 1692	*0413*	....	....	----	----	?---	----	----		
Süphan Dagi (Turkey-E)	**38.92** N	**42.82** E	**4158**	3467	YTRDX	**Stratovolcano**	**0103-021**	**Holocene**								
						T-**8050**?	....	....	....	-x--	----	?---	?---	----		
Girekol Tepe (Turkey-E)	**39.10** N	**43.42** E		4467	AD	**Shield volcano**	**0103-022**	**Holocene**								
Tendürek Dagi (Turkey-E)	**39.37** N	**43.87** E	**3584**	3467	BTYPZ	**Shield volcano**	**0103-03=**	**Historical**								
Lower SE flank						C-**0550**?	....	....	....	-x--	----	----	x---	----		
						1855	....	....	....	----	----	x---	----	----		
Ararat (Turkey-E)	**39.70** N	**44.30** E	**5165**	2467	ADBXR	**Stratovolcano**	**0103-04-**	**Historical**								
NW flank						A-**2450**t	....	....	....	-x--	----	xx--	x---	xx--		
Summit (?) and north flank						A-**0550**	....	....	....	?x--	----	----	x---	----		
						? 1450	....	....	....	----	----	----	----	----		
						? 1783	....	....	....	----	----	----	----	----		
Upper northern flank						**1840**	0702	....	....	--x-	----	xx-A	----	xxx-	3?	
Kars Plateau (Turkey-E)	**40.75** N*	**43.25** E	**3000**	7777	AYDBR	**Volcanic field**	**0103-05-**	Holocene?								
						*? 1450*t	....	....	....	----	----	----	----	----	*2?*	
						? 1959	*07*	....	....	x---	----	--?-	----	----	*2*	

Nemrut Dagi caldera

NASA Space Shuttle image ISS001-E-6354

CAUCASUS & ARMENIA

VOLCANO NAME (Subregion) / ERUPTION — Area of Activity	LAT	LONG	ELEV (m)	POPL	ROCK TYPE	VOLC TYPE / Start Year	NUMBER / M-Dy	STATUS / Stop Year	M-Dy	Central / Flank vent / Radial fiss / Regional	Submarine / New island / Subglacial / Crater lake	Explosive / Pyro flow / Phreatic / Caldera	Lava flow / Lava lake / Dome / Spine	Fatal / Damage / Mudflow / Tsunami	VEI	Vol L/T
Elbrus (Russia-SW)	**43.33** N	**42.45** E	**5633**	2347	DART	**Stratovolcano**	**0104-01-**	**Tephrochronology**								
						T **0050**t	....	....	....	----	----	x---	x---	----		
Kasbek (Georgia)	**42.70** N	**44.50** E	**5050**	0147	AD	**Stratovolcano**	**0104-02-**	**Tephrochronology**								
						C-**4000**t	....	....	....	----	----	----	x---	----		
						T-**0750**t	....	....	....	----	----	----	----	----		
Kabargin Oth Group (Georgia)	**42.55** N*	**44.00** E	**3650**	4447	AD	**Cinder cones**	**0104-03-**	**Holocene**								
Unnamed (Georgia)	**42.45** N*	**44.25** E	**3750**	3357	AD	**Cinder cones**	**0104-04-**	**Holocene**								
Unnamed (Georgia)	**41.55** N*	**43.60** E	**3400**	5557	ABRD	**Lava cones**	**0104-05-**	**Holocene**								
Aragats (Armenia)	**40.53** N	**44.20** E	**4095**	0367	ABDR	**Stratovolcano**	**0104-06-**	**Holocene**								
Ghegam Ridge (Armenia)	**40.275** N*	**44.75** E	**3597**	7777	ARD	**Volcanic field**	**0104-07-**	**Anthropology**								
North part of eastern cone cluster						A-**1900***	....	....	....	---x	----	----	x---	----	0	
Dar-Alages (Armenia)	**39.70** N*	**45.542** E	**3329**	5557	A	**Pyroclastic cones**	**0104-08-**	**Anthropology**								
Vaiyots-Sar						A-**2000***	....	....	....	----	----	----	x---	----		
						? 0753	....	....	....	----	----	?---	----	----		
Porak (Armenia)	**40.02** N	**45.78** E	**2800**	3357	A	**Stratovolcano**	**0104-09-**	**Anthropology**								
						T-**4510**y	....	....	....	x---	----	x---	x---	----		
SW flank						A-**0778**e	....	....	....	-x--	----	x---	x---	xx--		
						*?-0740*b	....	....	....	----	----	?---	?---	x---		
Tskhouk-Karckar (Armenia)	**39.73** N	**46.02** E	**3000**	2357	ADR	**Pyroclastic cones**	**0104-10-**	**Tephrochronology**								
						T-**3000**y	....	....	....	x---	----	x---	x---	-x--		

Africa & Red Sea (02)

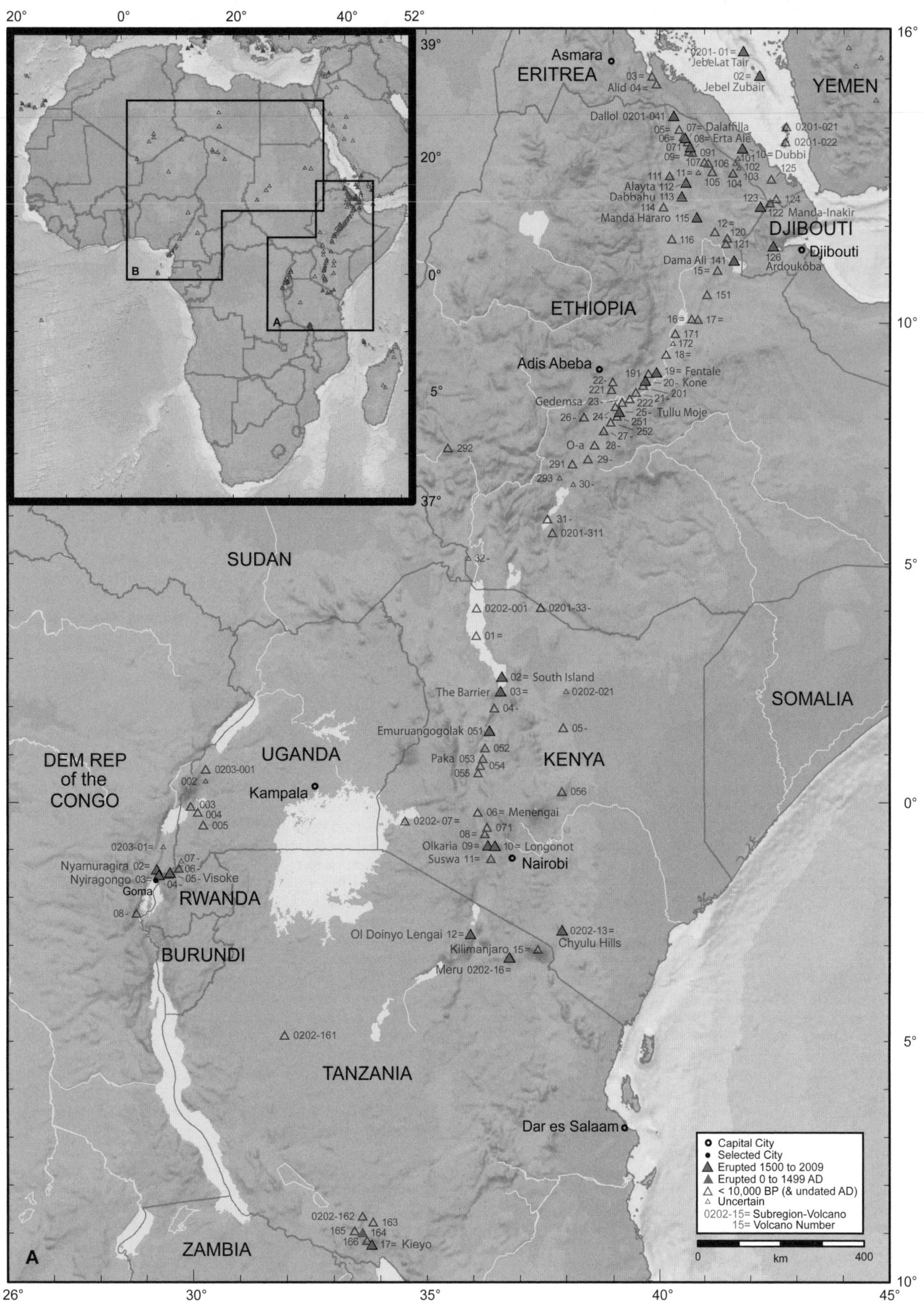

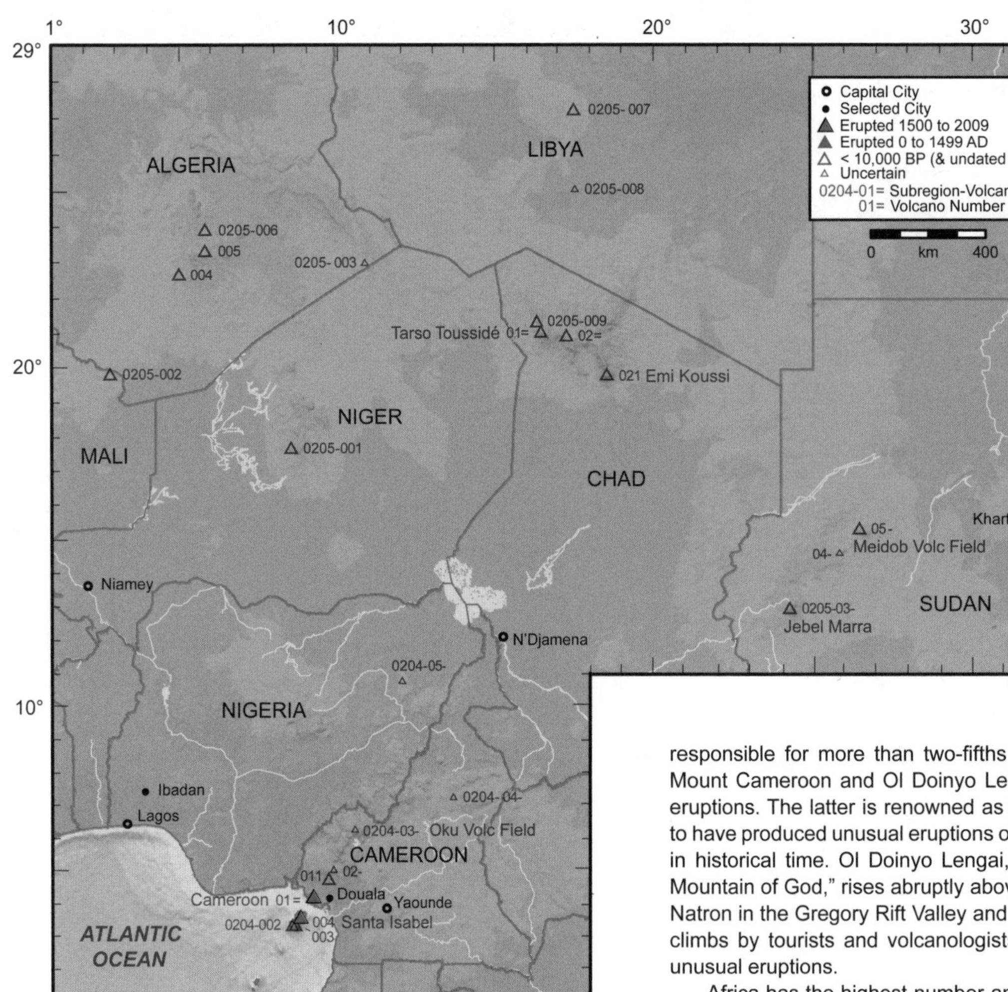

Africa's historical record is relatively brief, but it is the only region other than the Mediterranean with a historically dated BC eruption (at Mt. Cameroon, observed by a passing Carthaginian navigator in the 5th century BC). By the 15th century AD, however, when Portuguese exploration of Africa had begun and Vasco de Gama sailed to India via the Cape of Good Hope, only 2 more historical eruptions had been recorded (both from Ethiopia), and the main historical record of the continent did not begin until the opening of the Suez Canal at the end of 1869, and the heyday of African exploration that followed. More than 85% of the region's 155 historical eruptions are since 1870.

Most African volcanoes result from the rifting in E Africa, hotspots, or a combination of the two. The East African Rift, one of the world's most dramatic extensional structures, has produced the continent's highest and lowest volcanoes, ranging from massive Kilimanjaro to vents in Ethiopia's Danakil Depression that lie below sea level. Young fissure-fed lava flows blanket large areas along the floor of the East African Rift. Recent eruptions in 2007 and 2009 from closely spaced fissures of the Manda Hararo complex in Ethiopia mark an episode of extension and lava effusion analogous to rifting episodes along the Mid-Atlantic Ridge in Iceland at Krafla volcano in the 18th and 20th centuries. Four African volcanoes are its most active, accounting for nearly two-thirds of the continent's historical eruptions. Two neighboring volcanoes in Zaire's Virunga National Park, Nyamuragira and Nyiragongo, have 64 historical eruptions between them, and are responsible for more than two-fifths of Africa's historical eruptions. Mount Cameroon and Ol Doinyo Lengai have another 37 historical eruptions. The latter is renowned as the world's only known volcano to have produced unusual eruptions of high-calcium carbonatitic lavas in historical time. Ol Doinyo Lengai, known to the Maasai as "The Mountain of God," rises abruptly above the broad plain south of Lake Natron in the Gregory Rift Valley and has been the focus of repeated climbs by tourists and volcanologists to observe and document its unusual eruptions.

Africa has the highest number and percentage of volcanoes that are undated but known or thought to be Holocene, reflecting the early stage of detailed geologic studies. The continent, consequently has recorded relatively few large (VEI ≥4) eruptions in the Holocene, also reflecting the typical milder eruptions of many rift zone volcanoes. However, rift zone volcanoes are bimodal in chemistry, and many large-volume caldera-forming eruptions have occurred from East-African Rift volcanoes during the early Holocene and late Pleistocene. Africa leads the world in the rate of lava lake production, with 10% of its eruptions (most at Erta Ale, Nyiragongo, and Nyamuragira) having exhibited this relatively uncommon characteristic. Dramatic draining of long-term lava lakes at the summit crater of Nyiragongo volcano through fissures on its southern flanks in 1977 and 2002 produced lava flows that reached inhabited areas and caused many fatalities. The 1977 flows were particularly fluid and traveled at unusually high velocities, estimated at 60-100 km/hr. The 2002 lava flows traveled through the city of Goma, exacerbating the pre-existing humanitarian crisis due to long-term political turmoil.

Africa, somewhat surprisingly, consistently ranks in the top five volcanic regions in numbers of people living in proximity to volcanoes within distances of 5-100 km. This largely reflects the high number of broad volcanic fields and calderas in proximity to cities such as Adis Abeba, Nairobi, and Goma in the East African Rift and along the Cameroon Line of SW Africa. The latter area has become known for a relatively unusual type of volcanic hazard resulting from lethal gas emissions from overturn of stratified volcanic lake waters. Lake Monoun and Lake Nyos both produced catastrophic carbon-dioxide gas release events in 1984 and 1986, respectively; the Lake Nyos disaster caused at least 1700 fatalities when the denser-than-air CO_2 flowed down inhabited valleys.

VOLCANO NAME (Subregion) / ERUPTION — Area of Activity	LAT	LONG	ELEV (m)	POPL (5 km, 10, 30, 100)	ROCK TYPE	VOLC TYPE / Start Year	NUMBER / Start M-Dy	STATUS / Stop Year	Stop M-Dy	Central, Flank vent, Radial fiss, Regional	Submarine, New island, Subglacial, Crater lake	Explosive, Pyro flow, Phreatic, Caldera	Lava flow, Lava lake, Dome, Spine	Fatal, Damage, Mudflow, Tsunami	VEI	Vol L/T
ETHIOPIA & RED SEA																
Tair, Jebel at (Yemen)	**15.55 N**	**41.83 E**	**244**	0005	**XB**	**Stratovolcano**	**0201-01=**	**Historical**								
						1750t	....	....	....	----	----	x---	----	----	2	
						1833	1231y	....	....	----	----	x---	----	----	2	
						1863	....	....	....	----	----	?---	----	----	2	
						1883	....	....	....	----	----	?---	----	----	2	
						2007	0930	**2008**	06 ?	x-x-	----	x---	x---	x---	3?	
Zubair, Jebel (Yemen)	**15.05 N**	**42.18 E**	**191**	1116	**BX**	**Shield volcano**	**0201-02=**	**Historical**								
Saddle Island						**1824**	....	....	....	----	----	x---	----	----	2	
Saddle Island						*? 1846*	*0814*	....	....	----	----	?---	----	----	*2*	
Zukur (Yemen)	**14.02 N**	**42.75 E**	**624**	3347	**BXYT**	**Shield volcano**	**0201-021**	**Holocene**								
Hanish (Yemen)	**13.72 N**	**42.73 E**	**422**	3336	**BXY**	**Shield volcano**	**0201-022**	**Holocene**								
Jalua (Eritrea)	**15.042 N**	**39.82 E**	**713**	4557	**B**	**Stratovolcano**	**0201-03=**	**Holocene**								
Alid (Eritrea)	**14.88 N**	**39.92 E**	**904**	3457	**RBAYT**	**Stratovolcano**	**0201-04=**	**Holocene**								
Dallol (Ethiopia)	**14.242 N**	**40.30 E**	**-48**	3346	**U**	**Explosion craters**	**0201-041**	**Historical**								
						1926	....	....	....	----	----	--x-	----	----	1	
Gada Ale (Ethiopia)	**13.975 N**	**40.408 E**	**287**	3346	**BYT**	**Stratovolcano**	**0201-05=**	**Holocene**								
Alu (Ethiopia)	**13.825 N**	**40.508 E**	**429**	0156	**BATR**	**Fissure vents**	**0201-06=**	**Holocene**								
Dalaffilla (Ethiopia)	**13.792 N**	**40.55 E**	**613**	0156	**BATR**	**Stratovolcano**	**0201-07=**	**Historical**								
W and NW of Dalaffilla						**2008**	1103	**2008**	12 ?	---x	----	x---	x---	----	3?	
Borale Ale (Ethiopia)	**13.725 N**	**40.60 E**	**668**	0056	**BATR**	**Stratovolcano**	**0201-071**	**Holocene**								
Erta Ale (Ethiopia)	**13.60 N**	**40.67 E**	**613**	4446	**BA**	**Shield volcano**	**0201-08=**	**Historical**								
						? 1873	....	....	....	----	----	?---	----	----	*2*	
						? 1903	....	....	....	----	----	?---	----	----	*2*	
						? 1904	*1101r*	....	....	----	----	?---	----	----	*2*	
						1906	05	....	....	x---	----	?---	?x--	----	0	
						1940	....	....	....	x---	----	----	-x--	----	0	
						1960	01	....	....	x-x-	----	----	x---	----	0	
						1967<	....	**2010**>	....	x---	----	----	xx--	----	0	
Ale Bagu (Ethiopia)	**13.52 N**	**40.63 E**	**1031**	1346	**BTR**	**Stratovolcano**	**0201-09=**	**Holocene**								
Hayli Gubbi (Ethiopia)	**13.50 N**	**40.72 E**	**521**	0246	**BTR**	**Shield volcano**	**0201-091**	**Holocene**								
Dubbi (Eritrea)	**13.58 N**	**41.808 E**	**1625**	0025	**BXytr**	**Stratovolcano**	**0201-10=**	**Historical**								
						1400	0715q	....	....	x-x-	----	x---	x---	----	2?	
						1861	0508	**1861**	10 ?	x-x-	----	x?--	x---	xx--	3?	9/-
(perhaps confused with 1861 eruption)						*? 1863*	....	....	....	----	----	?---	----	----	*2*	
						? 1900?	....	....	....	----	----	----	?---	----		
Nabro (Eritrea)	**13.37 N**	**41.70 E**	**2218**	2345	**TRB**	**Stratovolcano**	**0201-101**	Holocene?								
Mallahle (Ethiopia/Eritrea)	**13.27 N**	**41.65 E**	**1875**	3445	**TRB**	**Stratovolcano**	**0201-102**	Holocene?								
Sork Ale (Ethiopia/Eritrea)	**13.18 N**	**41.725 E**	**1611**	3345	**BT**	**Stratovolcano**	**0201-103**	Holocene?								
Asavyo (Ethiopia)	**13.07 N**	**41.60 E**	**1200**	2345	**BR**	**Shield volcano**	**0201-104**	**Holocene**								
Mat Ala (Ethiopia)	**13.10 N**	**41.15 E**	**523**	2245	**BAXY**	**Shield volcano**	**0201-105**	**Holocene**								
Tat Ali (Ethiopia)	**13.28 N**	**41.07 E**	**700**	2246	**BXYRT**	**Shield volcano**	**0201-106**	**Holocene**								
Borawli (Ethiopia)	**13.30 N**	**40.98 E**	**812**	2346	**BTR**	**Stratovolcano**	**0201-107**	**Holocene**								
Afderà (Ethiopia)	**13.08 N**	**40.85 E**	**1295**	2446	**Rbxa**	**Stratovolcano**	**0201-11=**	Holocene?								
Ma Alalta (Ethiopia)	**13.02 N**	**40.20 E**	**1815**	4557	**RTbxa**	**Stratovolcano**	**0201-111**	**Holocene**								
Alayta (Ethiopia)	**12.88 N**	**40.57 E**	**1501**	3356	**BTY**	**Shield volcano**	**0201-112**	**Historical**								
SE flank						**1907**	06	**1907**	0804>	---x	----	x---	x---	xx--	2	
						1915	....	....	....	----	----	x---	----	----	2	
Dabbahu (Ethiopia)	**12.60 N**	**40.48 E**	**1442**	3456	**RTBXY**	**Stratovolcano**	**0201-113**	**Historical**								
NE flank (Da'Ure)						**2005**	0926	**2005**	0929	--x-	----	x---	--x-	----	3?	
Dabbayra (Ethiopia)	**12.38 N**	**40.07 E**	**1302**	3457	**BR**	**Shield volcano**	**0201-114**	**Holocene**								
Manda Hararo (Ethiopia)	**12.17 N**	**40.82 E**	**600**	3346	**B**	**Shield volcanoes**	**0201-115**	**Historical**								
						2007	0812	**2007**	0917?	---x	----	x---	x---	----	2	
						2009	0628	**2009**	0701?	---x	----	----	x---	----	2?	
Groppo (Ethiopia)	**11.73 N**	**40.25 E**	**930**	4557	**R**	**Stratovolcano**	**0201-116**	**Holocene**								
Kurub (Ethiopia)	**11.88 N**	**41.208 E**	**625**	1156	**BX**	**Shield volcano**	**0201-12=**	**Holocene**								
Manda Gargori (Ethiopia)	**11.75 N**	**41.48 E**		3456	**BR**	**Fissure vents**	**0201-120**	**Anthropology**								
Borawli (Ethiopia)	**11.63 N**	**41.45 E**	**875**	3566	**R**	**Lava domes**	**0201-121**	**Holocene**								
Manda-Inakir (Ethiopia/Djibouti)	**12.38 N**	**42.20 E**	**600**	3456	**BX**	**Fissure vents**	**0201-122**	**Historical**								
Kammourta						**1928**	1231y	....	....	---x	----	x---	x---	----	2?	
Mousa Alli (Ethiopia/Eritrea/Djibouti)	**12.47 N**	**42.40 E**	**2028**	3456	**RTB**	**Stratovolcano**	**0201-123**	**Holocene**								
Gufa (Eritrea/Djibouti)	**12.55 N***	**42.53 E**	**600**	4446	**B**	**Volcanic field**	**0201-124**	**Holocene**								
Assab Volc Field (Eritrea)	**12.95 N***	**42.43 E**	**987**	1126	**B**	**Volcanic field**	**0201-125**	**Holocene**								
Ardoukôba (Djibouti)	**11.58 N***	**42.47 E**	**298**	4446	**BXR**	**Fissure vents**	**0201-126**	**Historical**								
						1978	1107	**1978**	1114	---x	----	x---	xx--	----	1	7/-
Dama Ali (Ethiopia)	**11.28 N**	**41.63 E**	**1068**	2456	**BTR**	**Shield volcano**	**0201-141**	**Historical**								
						@ 1631	0214?	....	....	----	----	x---	----	----		
Gabillema (Ethiopia)	**11.08 N**	**41.27 E**	**1459**	3356	**RBXY**	**Stratovolcano**	**0201-15=**	**Holocene**								
Yangudi (Ethiopia)	**10.58 N**	**41.042 E**	**1383**	2356	**RBXY**	**Complex volcano**	**0201-151**	**Holocene**								
Ayelu (Ethiopia)	**10.082 N**	**40.702 E**	**2145**	3457	**R**	**Stratovolcano**	**0201-16=**	**Holocene**								
						? 1928	....	....	....	----	----	?---	----	----	*2*	
Adwa (Ethiopia)	**10.070 N**	**40.840 E**	**1733**	3357	**RBT**	**Stratovolcano**	**0201-17=**	**Holocene**								
						? 1828	....	....	....	----	----	?---	----	----	*2*	
						? 1928	....	....	....	----	----	?---	----	----	*2*	
Hertali (Ethiopia)	**9.78 N**	**40.33 E**	**900**	3457	**B**	**Fissure vent**	**0201-171**	**Holocene**								
Liado Hayk (Ethiopia)	**9.57 N***	**40.28 E**	**878**	5557	**U**	**Maars**	**0201-172**	Holocene?								
Dofen (Ethiopia)	**9.35 N**	**40.13 E**	**1151**	4557	**R**	**Stratovolcano**	**0201-18=**	**Holocene**								
Fentale (Ethiopia)	**8.975 N**	**39.93 E**	**2007**	4567	**RTXA**	**Stratovolcano**	**0201-19=**	**Historical**								
						1250t	....	....	....	-x--	----	----	x---	-x--		
Caldera floor and SW flank						**1820**?	....	....	....	---x	----	----	x---	----	0	7/-
Beru (Ethiopia)	**8.95 N**	**39.75 E**	**1100**	4567	**B**	**Volcanic field**	**0201-191**	**Holocene**								
Kone (Ethiopia)	**8.80 N**	**39.692 E**	**1619**	4567	**RTB**	**Calderas**	**0201-20-**	**Historical**								
East margin of Gariboldi caldera						**1820**j	....	....	....	x--x	----	x---	x---	----	1	
Unnamed (Ethiopia)	**8.70 N***	**39.63 E**	**1300**	6667	**B**	**Pyroclastic cones**	**0201-201**	**Holocene**								
Boset-Bericha (Ethiopia)	**8.558 N**	**39.475 E**	**2447**	4567	**RTBXY**	**Stratovolcanoes**	**0201-21-**	**Holocene**								
Bishoftu Volc Field (Ethiopia)	**8.78 N***	**38.98 E**	**1850**	6667	**BR**	**Fissure vents**	**0201-22-**	**Holocene**								
Unnamed (Ethiopia)	**8.62 N***	**38.95 E**	**1800**	6667	**B**	**Fissure vents**	**0201-221**	**Holocene**								

VOLCANO NAME (Subregion) / ERUPTION — Area of Activity	LAT	LONG	ELEV (m)	POPL (5 km, 10, 30, 100)	ROCK TYPE	VOLC TYPE	NUMBER	STATUS	Start Year	Start M-Dy	Stop Year	Stop M-Dy	Central, Flank vent, Radial fiss, Regional	Submarine, New island, Subglacial, Crater lake	Explosive, Pyro flow, Phreatic, Caldera	Lava flow, Lava lake, Dome, Spine	Fatal, Damage, Mudflow, Tsunami	VEI	Vol L/T
Sodore (Ethiopia)	8.43 N*	39.35 E	1765	6667	B	Pyroclastic cones	0201-222	Holocene											
Gedamsa (Ethiopia)	8.35 N	39.18 E	1984	6667	RTb	Caldera	0201-23-	Holocene											
Bora-Bericcio (Ethiopia)	8.27 N	39.03 E	2285	4567	R	Pumice cones	0201-24-	Holocene											
Tullu Moje (Ethiopia)	8.158 N	39.13 E	2349	5567	RTBX	Pumice cone	0201-25-	Anthropology											
Giano									A 1775q	....	....	....	---x	----	----	x---	----		
Wonji fault belt, SE of Lake Koka									1900?	....	....	....	---x	----	x---	x---	-x--		
Unnamed (Ethiopia)	8.07 N*	39.07 E	1800	6667	B	Fissure vents	0201-251	Holocene											
East Zway (Ethiopia)	7.95 N*	38.93 E	1889	5567	B	Fissure vents	0201-252	Holocene											
Butajiri-Silti Field (Ethiopia)	8.05 N*	38.35 E	2281	6667	B	Fissure vents	0201-26-	Holocene											
Alutu (Ethiopia)	7.77 N	38.78 E	2335	4567	RDB	Stratovolcano	0201-27-	Radiocarbon											
									C-0050?	....	....	....	----	----	x---	x---	----		
O'a Caldera (Ethiopia)	7.47 N	38.58 E	2075	6667	RTb	Caldera	0201-28-	Holocene											
Corbetti Caldera (Ethiopia)	7.18 N	38.43 E	2320	6677	RB	Caldera	0201-29-	Holocene											
(fumarolic activity only)									X 1957	....	X1964	....	----	----	----	----	----		
Bilate River Field (Ethiopia)	7.07 N*	38.10 E	1700	6677	U	Maars	0201-291	Holocene											
Tepi (Ethiopia)	7.42 N*	35.43 E	2728	5567	B	Shield volcano	0201-292	Holocene											
Hobicha Caldera (Ethiopia)	6.78 N	37.83 E	1800	6677	B	Caldera	0201-293	Holocene?											
Chiracha (Ethiopia)	6.65 N	38.12 E	1650	5567	RB	Stratovolcano	0201-30-	Holocene?											
Tosa Sucha (Ethiopia)	5.93 N*	37.57 E	1650	6667	B	Cinder cones	0201-31-	Holocene											
Unnamed (Ethiopia)	5.65 N*	37.67 E	1200	5567	B	Cinder cones	0201-311	Holocene											
Korath Range (Ethiopia)	5.10 N*	35.88 E	912	5556	XBZ	Tuff cones	0201-32-	Holocene?											
Mega Basalt Field (Ethiopia/Kenya)	4.08 N*	37.42 E	1067	4446	B	Pyroclastic cones	0201-33-	Holocene											

AFRICA - KENYA to DEMOCRATIC REPUBLIC of the CONGO

VOLCANO NAME (Subregion) / ERUPTION — Area of Activity	LAT	LONG	ELEV (m)	POPL (5 km, 10, 30, 100)	ROCK TYPE	VOLC TYPE	NUMBER	STATUS	Start Year	Start M-Dy	Stop Year	Stop M-Dy	Central, Flank vent, Radial fiss, Regional	Submarine, New island, Subglacial, Crater lake	Explosive, Pyro flow, Phreatic, Caldera	Lava flow, Lava lake, Dome, Spine	Fatal, Damage, Mudflow, Tsunami	VEI	Vol L/T
North Island (Kenya)	4.07 N	36.05 E	520	2246	YBT	Tuff cones	0202-001	Holocene											
Central Island (Kenya)	3.50 N	36.042 E	550	2256	BYT	Tuff cones	0202-01=	Holocene											
East side of Central Island									? 1974	0722?	?1974	0727a	----	----	--?-	----	----	1	
South Island (Kenya)	2.63 N	36.60 E	800	0045	BXZY	Stratovolcano	0202-02=	Historical											
									1888	....	....	....	x---	----	x---	----	----	1	
Marsabit (Kenya)	2.32 N	37.97 E	1707	5556	BX	Shield volcano	0202-021	Holocene?											
Barrier, The (Kenya)	2.32 N	36.57 E	1032	2346	TPBYX	Shield volcano	0202-03=	Historical											
North (Abili Agituk) and south flanks									T-7710x	....	....	....	-x--	----	x---	x---	----		
North flank									M 1030w	....	....	....	-x--	----	----	x---	----	0	
North flank									M 1050w	....	....	....	-x--	----	----	x---	----	0	
North flank									M 1090t	....	....	....	-x--	----	----	x---	----	0	
North flank (Teleki's Cone)									1871c	....	....	....	-x--	----	x---	x---	----	2	
North flank (Teleki's Cone)									1888	....	....	....	-xx-	----	----	x---	----	0	
North flank (Teleki's Cone)									1895	....	....	....	-x--	----	x---	x---	----	2	
North flank (Teleki) and Likaiu									1897	05 <	....	....	xx--	----	x---	----	----	2?	
Andrew's or Teleki's Cones									? 1906	....	....	....	-x--	----	----	----	----		
Andrew's or Teleki's Volcanoes									1917	....	....	....	-x--	----	x---	----	----	2	
South flank (Andrew's Volcano)									? 1920c	....	....	....	-x--	----	?---	----	----		
North flank (Teleki)									1921	1231y	....	....	-x--	----	x---	x---	----	2	
Namarunu (Kenya)	1.98 N	36.43 E	817	2346	BTR	Shield volcano	0202-04-	Tephrochronology											
Lower eastern flanks									T-6550*	....	....	....	-x--	----	?---	?---	----		
Segererua Plateau (Kenya)	1.57 N*	37.90 E	699	4456	BT	Pyroclastic cones	0202-05-	Holocene											
Emuruangogolak (Kenya)	1.50 N	36.33 E	1328	2346	TB	Shield volcano	0202-051	Radiocarbon											
North flank									C-8050*	....	....	....	-x--	----	----	x---	----		
North flank									T-6550*	....	....	....	-x--	----	x---	x---	----		
North flank									M 1120w	....	....	....	-x--	----	----	x---	----	0	
NE flank									M 1160w	....	....	....	-x--	----	----	x---	----	0	
NE flank									M 1230w	....	....	....	-x--	----	----	x---	----	0	
NE flank									M 1300w	....	....	....	-x--	----	----	x---	----	0	
South caldera rim									C 1700v	....	....	....	x---	----	----	x---	----	0	
South caldera rim									M 1910t	....	....	....	x---	----	----	x---	----	0	
Silali (Kenya)	1.15 N	36.23 E	1528	3356	TBx	Shield volcano	0202-052	Ar/Ar											
Upper east flank									R-7050*	....	....	....	-x--	----	x---	x-x-	----		
Eastern part of caldera									R-6050*	....	....	....	x-x-	----	x---	x---	----		
Upper east flank									R-5050*	....	....	....	-x--	----	----	x-x-	----		
Paka (Kenya)	0.92 N	36.18 E	1697	3457	TBy	Shield volcano	0202-053	Ar/Ar											
									R-7550*	....	....	....	x---	----	xx-x	----	--x-	C	
Korosi (Kenya)	0.77 N	36.12 E	1446	4457	TBY	Shield volcano	0202-054	Holocene											
Ol Kokwe (Kenya)	0.62 N	36.075 E	1130	3467	BT	Shield volcano	0202-055	Holocene											
Nyambeni Hills (Kenya)	0.23 N	37.87 E	750	5667	BPXYR	Shield volcano	0202-056	Holocene											
Menengai (Kenya)	0.20 S	36.07 E	2278	4667	TRB	Shield volcano	0202-06=	Tephrochronology											
									T-7350*	....	....	....	x---	----	x-x-	----	----		
									C-6050?	....	....	....	x---	----	xx-x	----	----	6+	-/10
Homa Mountain (Kenya)	0.38 S	34.50 E	1751	5568	FP	Complex volcano	0202-07=	Holocene											
Elmenteita Badlands (Kenya)	0.52 S*	36.27 E	2126	6667	B	Pyroclastic cones	0202-071	Holocene											
Eburru, Ol Doinyo (Kenya)	0.65 S	36.22 E	2856	3467	RPT	Complex volcano	0202-08=	Holocene											
Olkaria (Kenya)	0.904 S*	36.292 E	2434	5567	RTBx	Pumice cones	0202-09=	Radiocarbon											
NE side (Gorge Farm)									T-6050?	....	....	....	x---	----	----	x---	----		9/-
									T-4050?	....	....	....	x---	----	----	x---	----		
Ololbutot									C 1770t	....	....	....	--x-	----	xx--	x---	----		
Longonot (Kenya)	0.914 S	36.446 E	2776	3567	TX	Stratovolcano	0202-10=	Anthropology											
									C-7200v	....	....	....	----	----	x---	----	----		
									C-1330v	....	....	....	----	----	x---	----	----		
Northern flank									A 1863e	....	....	....	-x--	----	----	?---	----	0	7/-
Suswa (Kenya)	1.175 S	36.35 E	2356	3467	PTx	Shield volcano	0202-11=	Holocene											
Lengai, Ol Doinyo (Tanzania)	2.764 S	35.914 E	2962	3456	FP	Stratovolcano	0202-12=	Historical											
									T-1550*	....	....	....	----	----	x---	----	----		
(BTA Tuffs)									T-0050?	....	....	....	----	----	x---	----	----		
(Namrod Ash)									T 0700?	....	....	....	----	----	x---	----	----		
(Footprint Tuff)									T 1350?	....	....	....	----	----	x---	----	----		
North Crater									1880	12	....	....	x---	----	x---	----	----	2	
North Crater									1882	....	1883	....	x---	----	x---	?---	----	2	
(fumarolic activity only)									X 1894	....	....	....	----	----	----	----	----		
North Crater									1904	....	....	....	x---	----	----	x---	----	0	
North Crater									1907c	....	1910	0804>	x---	----	----	x---	----	0	

VOLCANO NAME (Subregion)	LAT	LONG	ELEV (m)	POPL (5 km / 10 / 30 / 100)	ROCK TYPE	VOLC TYPE	NUMBER	STATUS	ERUPTION — Area of Activity	Start Year	Start M-Dy	Stop Year	Stop M-Dy	Central / Flank vent / Radial fiss / Regional	Submarine / New island / Subglacial / Crater lake	Explosive / Pyro flow / Phreatic / Caldera	Lava flow / Lava lake / Dome / Spine	Fatal / Damage / Mudflow / Tsunami	VEI	Vol L/T
Lengai, Ol Doinyo (Tanzania) *continued*									North Crater	**1914**	0815x	**1915**	....	x---	----	----	x---	----	0	
									North Crater	**1916**	1201p	**1917**	06	x---	----	x---	x---	-x--	3*	
									North Crater	**1921**	02	....	....	x---	----	x---	----	--x-	2	
									North Crater	**1926**	....	....	....	x---	----	x---	----	----	2	
									North Crater	**1940**	0724	**1941**	02	x---	----	x-x-	----	-xx-	3*	
									North Crater	**1954**	0726e	**1954**	09	x---	----	x---	----	----	2	
									North Crater	**1955**	0119	**1955**	0120	x---	----	x---	----	----	2	
									North Crater	**1958**	0206<	....	....	x---	----	x---	?---	----	1	
									North Crater	**1960**	03 <	**1966**	1128p	x---	----	x---	x---	-x--	3*	
									North Crater	**1967**	0708	**1967**	0904	x---	----	x---	----	-x--	3	
										? *1969*	*07 ?*	....	....	x---	----	?---	----	----		
									(1974 eruption report incorrect)	X *1974*	*08*	X*1974*	*09*	----	----	----	----	----		
									North Crater	**1983**	0101	**1993**	0924	x---	----	x---	xx--	----	2*	7/-
									North Crater	**1994**	0918	**2006**	07 ?	x---	----	x---	xx--	----	1	5/-
										2007	06	**2010**>	....	x---	----	xx--	xx--	-x--	3*	
Chyulu Hills (Kenya)	2.68 S*	37.88 E	2188	5557	XBF	**Volcanic field**	0202-13=	**Anthropology**												
									Umani	C **1470**x	....	....	....	----	----	----	x---	----		
									Shaitani and Chaimu	A **1855**e	....	....	....	x---	----	x---	x---	----	2	
Kilimanjaro (Tanzania)	3.07 S	37.35 E	5895	0067	PZXYF	**Stratovolcano**	0202-15=	**Holocene**												
Meru (Tanzania)	3.25 S	36.75 E	4565	0467	PFZTB	**Stratovolcano**	0202-16=	**Historical**												
									Meru caldera	C-**5850**?	....	....	....	x---	----	x--A	----	--x-	**P**	
									Dome NW of Ash Cone	**1878**a	....	....	....	x---	----	x---	x---	----	2	
									Dome NW of Ash Cone	**1886**?	....	....	....	x---	----	----	x---	----	0	
									Ash Cone	**1910**	1026	**1910**	1222	x---	----	x---	----	----	2	
Igwisi Hills (Tanzania)	4.87 S*	31.92 E		5566	F	**Tuff cones**	0202-161	**Holocene**												
Unnamed (Tanzania)	8.63 S	33.57 E		4457	B	**Pyroclastic cone**	0202-162	**Holocene**												
SW Usangu Basin (Tanzania)	8.75 S*	33.80 E	2179	5557	P	**Lava domes**	0202-163	**Holocene**												
Ngozi (Tanzania)	8.97 S	33.57 E	2622	6667	TPYB	**Caldera**	0202-164	**Radiocarbon**												
									(Kitulo Pumice)	G-**8250**?	....	....	....	x---	----	x--x	----	----	**C**	
										G **1450**s	....	....	....	----	----	xx--	----	----		
Izumbwe-Mpoli (Tanzania)	8.93 S	33.40 E	1568	5667	F	**Pyroclastic cones**	0202-165	**Holocene**												
Rungwe (Tanzania)	9.13 S	33.67 E	2961	3567	TB	**Stratovolcano**	0202-166	**Radiocarbon**												
									(Rungwe Pumice)	G-**2400**?	....	....	....	x---	----	x---	----	----	**P**	
									(Isongole Pumice)	G-**0050**v	....	....	....	x---	----	x---	----	----		
									(Aphyric Pumice)	G **1350**s	....	....	....	----	----	x---	----	----		
Kieyo (Tanzania)	9.23 S	33.78 E	2175	4567	TYBX	**Stratovolcano**	0202-17=	**Historical**												
									Sarabwe and Fiteko	**1800**?	....	....	....	x---	----	x---	x---	xx--	2	
Fort Portal (Uganda)	0.70 N*	30.25 E	1615	6667	F	**Tuff cones**	0203-001	**Radiocarbon**												
										C-**2750**u	....	....	....	x---	----	x---	----	----		
										C-**2120**v	....	....	....	x---	----	x---	----	----		
Kyatwa (Uganda)	0.45 N*	30.25 E	1430	6667	F	**Tuff cones**	0203-002	Holocene?												
Katwe-Kikorongo (Uganda)	0.08 S*	29.92 E	1067	6667	F	**Tuff cones**	0203-003	**Holocene**												
Bunyaruguru (Uganda)	0.20 S*	30.08 E	1554	6667	F	**Maars**	0203-004	**Holocene**												
Katunga (Uganda)	0.471 S	30.191 E	1707	4667	F	**Tuff cone**	0203-005	**Holocene**												
May-ya-moto (Dem Rep Congo)	0.93 S	29.33 E	950	4567	U	**Fumarole field**	0203-01=	**Fumarolic**												
Nyamuragira (Dem Rep Congo)	1.408 S	29.20 E	3058	4567	XZ	**Shield volcano**	0203-02=	**Historical**												
										G **1550**v	....	....	....	x?--	----	---M	?---	----		
										1865	....	....	....	----	----	----	----	----		
									North flank	**1882**	....	....	....	-x--	----	----	----	----		
										1894	06	....	....	x---	----	x---	x---	----	2	
										1896	....	....	....	----	----	x---	----	----	1	
									NNW fissure zone	**1899**	02	....	....	-xx-	----	x---	x---	----	1	
									East flank (Singiro)	**1901**	....	....	....	-x--	----	x---	x---	----	2	7/6
									SSE fissure zone	**1902**	0422?	....	....	-xx-	----	----	x---	----	0	
									SW flank (Nahimbi)	**1904**	04	**1904**	0516?	-x--	----	x---	x---	----	2	7/7
									East flank (Kanamaharagi)	**1905**	0722	**1905**	0925>	-x--	----	x---	x---	----	2	7/7
									Summit caldera	? *1906*	....	....	....	x---	----	x---	----	----	*1*	
									Summit caldera	**1907**	04	**1907**	05	x---	----	x---	----	----	1	
									Summit caldera	**1907**	1107	**1907**	1205	x---	----	x---	----	----	3	
									Summit caldera	**1908**	....	....	....	x---	----	?---	----	----		
									Summit caldera	**1909**	05	**1909**	05	x---	----	?-?-	----	----	1?	
									SW flank (Rumoka), and summit	**1912**	1203	**1913**	04	xx--	----	x---	x---	xx--	3	7/7
									SSW flank (Lake Kivu)	**1920**	....	....	....	--x-	---x	?---	----	----	0	
									Caldera	**1921**	....	**1938**	0117c	x---	----	x---	xx--	----	0	8/-
									Summit, SE and SW flanks (Tshambene)	**1938**	0128	**1940**	0625e	xxx-	----	x-x-	xx--	-x-x	1	8/-
									SW flank (Gituro, Muhuboli), N flank	**1948**	0301	**1948**	0715e	-xx-	----	x---	xx--	----	2	7/7
									SW flank (Gituro)	**1951**	0725	**1951**	0728	-x--	----	x---	----	----	1	-/4
									NNW fissure zone (Shabubembe-Ndakaza)	**1951**	1116	**1952**	0116	xxx-	----	x---	xx--	----	2	7/5
									SSE fissure zone (Mihaga)	**1954**	0221	**1954**	0528	-xx-	----	x---	x---	----	1	7/6
									Summit caldera and NNW fissure zone	**1956**	1117	**1956**	1118	x-x-	----	x---	x---	----	1	5/4
									Summit caldera and SSE fissure zone	**1957**	1228	....	....	x-x-	----	----	x---	----	0	6/-
									North flank (Kitsimbanyi), NNW rift	**1958**	0807	**1958**	1121	-xx-	----	x---	x---	----	2	7/6
									North flank (Gakararanga)	**1967**	0423	**1967**	0509	-xx-	----	x---	x---	----	2	7/7
									WNW flank (Rugarama)	**1971**	0324	**1971**	0505d	-x--	----	x---	x---	-x--	3	7/7
									SSW flank (Murara and Harakandi)	**1976**	1223	**1977**	0615e	-xx-	----	x---	xx--	----	1	7/7
									North flank (Gasenyi)	**1980**	0130	**1980**	0224	-xx-	----	x---	x---	-x--	3	7/7
									SE flank (Rugarambiro)	**1981**	1225	**1982**	0114	-xx-	----	x---	x---	-x--	3	7/7
									NW flank (Kivandimwe)	**1984**	0223	**1984**	0314	-xx-	----	x---	x---	-x--	2	7/7
									South flank (near Kitazungurwa)	**1986**	0716	**1986**	0820	-x-x	----	x---	xx--	-x--	2	7/7
									North Flank (Gafuranindi)	**1987**	1230	**1988**	0104	--x-	----	x---	x---	----	1	6/6
									Summit, SE and East flank	**1989**	0424	**1989**	0815e	xxx-	----	x---	x---	----	3	7/7
									NE flank 1530 m (Mikombe)	**1991**	0920	**1993**	0208	--x-	----	x---	x---	-x--	3*	-/7
									West flank (Kimera) and summit	**1994**	0704	**1994**	0825>	--x-	----	x---	x---	-x--	2?	
										1996	1201	**1996**	1205>	----	----	x---	x---	----	3	
										1998	1017	**1998**	1025>	----	----	x---	x---	----	2?	
									SE flank (Ngerageze)	**2000**	0127	**2000**	0210>	--x-	----	x---	x---	----	2?	
									North and SSE flanks	**2001**	0206	**2001**	0405d	--x-	----	x---	x---	-x--	2?	
									Summit caldera, north & south flanks	**2002**	0725	**2002**	09 ?	x-x-	----	x---	x---	----	2?	
									Summit and NNW flank	**2004**	0508	**2004**	0528c	x-x-	----	x---	xx--	----	2?	
									South flank	**2006**	1127	**2006**	1205?	--x-	----	x---	x---	----	2	
Nyiragongo (Dem Rep Congo)	1.52 S	29.25 E	3470	4577	Fb	**Stratovolcano**	0203-03=	**Historical**												
									Southern pit	**1884**	....	....	....	x---	----	x---	----	----	1	
									(probably Nyiragongo)	@ **1891**<	....	....	....	x---	----	----	----	----		

VOLCANO NAME (Subregion) / ERUPTION — Area of Activity	LAT	LONG	ELEV (m)	POPL 5 km 10 30 100	ROCK TYPE	VOLC TYPE / —Start— Year	NUMBER / M-Dy	STATUS / —Stop— Year	M-Dy	Central Flank vent Radial fiss Regional	Submarine New island Subglacial Crater lake	Explosive Pyro flow Phreatic Caldera	Lava flow Lava lake Dome Spine	Fatal Damage Mudflow Tsunami	VEI	Vol L/T
Nyiragongo (Dem Rep Congo) continued																
						1894	....	....	....	x---	----	----	-x--	----	1	
						1898	....	....	....	x---	----	----	----	----	1	
						1899	....	....	....	x---	----	x---	----	----	1	
						1900	....	....	....	x---	----	x---	----	----	1	
						1901	....	....	....	x---	----	x---	----	----	1	
						1902	....	....	....	x---	----	----	----	----	1	
						1905	....	....	....	x---	----	----	-x--	----	1	
						1906	....	....	....	x---	----	----	----	----	1	
Southern craters						? *1908*	*1201*p	....	....	?---	----	----	----	----		
Southern pit						**1911**	08	**1911**	10	x---	----	----	----	----	1	
						1918	....	....	....	x---	----	----	-x--	----	1	
						1920	....	**1921**	....	x---	----	x---	----	----	1	
						1927	03	**1977**	0110	x---	----	----	xx--	----	1	
North, south, and west flanks						**1977**	0110	**1977**	0110	x-x-	----	x---	x---	xx--	1	7/4
						1982	0621	**1982**	1017m	x---	----	--x-	xx--	----	1	7/-
						1994	0623	**1996**	03 ?	x---	----	x---	xx--	----	1	7/-
South flank (2800-1570 m), summit crater						**2002**	0117	**2002**	0203>	x-x-	----	x---	x---	xx--	1	7/-
						2002	0517?	**2010>**	....	x---	----	x---	xx--	-x--	2*	
Karisimbi (D. R. Congo/Rwanda)	**1.50 S**	**29.45 E**	**4507**	4578	**XYT**	**Stratovolcano**	**0203-04-**	**Potassium-Argon**								
						K-**8050**?	....	....	....	----	----	----	x---	----		
Visoke (Dem Rep Congo/Rwanda)	**1.47 S**	**29.492 E**	**3711**	5578	**Y**	**Stratovolcano**	**0203-05-**	**Historical**								
						@ **1891**	....	....	....	----	----	----	----	----		
11 km north of summit (Mugogo)						**1957**	0801	**1957**	0803	-x--	----	x---	x---	----	1	5/5
Muhavura (Uganda/Rwanda)	**1.38 S**	**29.67 E**	**4127**	5678	**XY**	**Stratovolcano**	**0203-06-**	**Holocene**								
Bufumbira (Uganda)	**1.23 S***	**29.72 E**	**2440**	6668	**ZYXTF**	**Cinder cones**	**0203-07-**	Holocene?								
Tshibinda (Dem Rep Congo)	**2.32 S***	**28.75 E**	**1460**	6667	**BF**	**Cinder cones**	**0203-08-**	**Holocene**								
AFRICA - W & N																
Sao Tome (Sao Tome)	**0.20 N**	**6.58 E**	**2024**	4566	**BXytp**	**Shield volcano**	**0204-001**	Holocene?								
San Carlos (Bioko)	**3.35 N**	**8.52 E**	**2260**	0356	**BX**	**Shield volcano**	**0204-002**	**Holocene**								
San Joaquin (Bioko)	**3.35 N**	**8.63 E**	**2009**	3456	**BX**	**Shield volcano**	**0204-003**	**Holocene**								
Santa Isabel (Bioko)	**3.58 N***	**8.75 E**	**3007**	5566	**BX**	**Shield volcano**	**0204-004**	**Historical**								
SE flank						**1898**?	....	....	....	-x--	----	----	----	----		
SE flank, near Bahu						**1903**	....	....	....	-x--	----	----	----	----		
SE flank						**1923**	....	....	....	-x--	----	----	----	----		
Cameroon (Cameroon)	**4.203 N**	**9.170 E**	**4095**	3567	**XBYtf**	**Stratovolcano**	**0204-01=**	**Historical**								
						-**0450**t	....	....	....	----	----	?---	?---	-?--	3	
						1650t	....	....	....	----	----	?---	----	----	3↑	
South flank (2600 m)						**1807**h	....	....	....	-x--	----	x---	x---	-?--	3	
						1825j	....	....	....	----	----	?---	----	----	2	
Near Fako						**1838**	1231y	....	....	----	----	x---	x---	----	2	
West flank						**1852**	....	....	....	-x--	----	x---	x---	----	2	
						1865	....	....	....	x---	----	x---	----	----	2	
						1866	01 ?	....	....	----	----	?---	----	----	2	
SW flank (2250 m) and NW flank						**1868**	....	....	....	-x--	----	x---	----	----	2	
						1871	....	....	....	----	----	?---	----	----	2	
NE flank (2400 m; Okoli Craters)						**1909**	0428	**1909**	06 ?	-x--	----	x---	x---	----	2	6/-
Mateer (W, 3300 m), Waldau (SW, 1300 m)						**1922**	0203	**1922**	0824	-x--	----	x---	x---	-x--	2	7/-
Near Fako						**1925**	....	....	....	x---	----	----	----	----		
Immediately south of summit						**1954**	0628	**1954**	0726	x---	----	x-x-	x---	----	2	
NE flank (3000-1500 m)						**1959**	0123	**1959**	0319	-x--	----	x---	x---	-x--	2	6/-
SW flank (2500 m)						**1982**	1016	**1982**	1112	--x-	----	x---	x---	-xx-	2	7/5
NE flank (2860 m)						**1989**	0529	**1989**	0529	-x--	----	--x-	----	----	1?	
South flank (2650 and 1500 m)						**1999**	0328	**1999**	0417	--x-	----	x---	x---	-x--	2	7/6
Upper SW flank (4000, 3470-3220, 2750 m)						**2000**	0528	**2000**	0915e	---x	----	x---	xx--	----	2?	6/-
Tombel Graben (Cameroon)	**4.75 N***	**9.67 E**	**500**	6667	**XB**	**Cinder cones**	**0204-011**	**Holocene**								
Manengouba (Cameroon)	**5.03 N**	**9.83 E**	**2411**	4567	**BXYTr**	**Stratovolcano**	**0204-02-**	Holocene?								
Oku Volc Field (Cameroon)	**6.25 N***	**10.50 E**	**3011**	6667	**BXYRT**	**Stratovolcano**	**0204-03-**	Holocene?								
Lake Nyos						? *1550*v	....	....	....	x---	----	xxx-	----	----	*3*	-/7
Lake Nyos						? *1986*	*0821*	*?1986*	*1230*?	----	---?	--?-	----	xx--		
Ngaoundere Plateau (Cameroon)	**7.25 N***	**13.67 E**		5556	**XBTPZ**	**Volcanic field**	**0204-04-**	Holocene?								
Biu Plateau (Nigeria)	**10.75 N***	**12.00 E**		5567	**B**	**Volcanic field**	**0204-05-**	Holocene?								
Todra Volc Field (Niger)	**17.68 N***	**8.50 E**	**1780**	3336	**BTP**	**Cinder cones**	**0205-001**	**Holocene**								
Tin Zaouatene Volc Field (Mali)	**19.83 N***	**2.83 E**		2234	**X**	**Volcanic field**	**0205-002**	**Holocene**								
In Ezzane Volc Field (Algeria/Niger)	**23.00 N***	**10.83 E**		2224	**X**	**Volcanic field**	**0205-003**	Holocene?								
Tahalra Volc Field (Algeria)	**22.67 N***	**5.00 E**	**1467**	0035	**XFytr**	**Pyroclastic cones**	**0205-004**	**Holocene**								
Atakor Volc Field (Algeria)	**23.33 N***	**5.83 E**	**2918**	0006	**XTPyz**	**Scoria cones**	**0205-005**	**Holocene**								
Manzaz Volc Field (Algeria)	**23.92 N***	**5.83 E**	**1672**	4444	**XB**	**Scoria cones**	**0205-006**	**Holocene**								
Haruj (Libya)	**27.25 N***	**17.50 E**	**1200**	0013	**B**	**Volcanic field**	**0205-007**	**Holocene**								
Wau-en-Namus (Libya)	**25.05 N***	**17.55 E**	**547**	2223	**B**	**Caldera**	**0205-008**	Holocene?								
Tôh, Tarso (Chad)	**21.33 N***	**16.33 E**	**2000**	0004	**B**	**Volcanic field**	**0205-009**	**Holocene**								
Toussidé, Tarso (Chad)	**21.03 N**	**16.45 E**	**3265**	0034	**TYDRb**	**Stratovolcano**	**0205-01=**	**Holocene**								
Voon, Tarso (Chad)	**20.92 N**	**17.28 E**	**3100**	0004	**TPXyr**	**Stratovolcano**	**0205-02=**	**Fumarolic**								
Koussi, Emi (Chad)	**19.80 N**	**18.53 E**	**3415**	0124	**TRBA**	**Pyroclastic shield**	**0205-021**	**Holocene**								
Marra, Jebel (Sudan)	**12.95 N**	**24.27 E**	**3042**	3466	**BTXYP**	**Volcanic field**	**0205-03-**	**Radiocarbon**								
Deriba caldera						G-**2000**?	....	....	....	x---	----	x--x	----	----	**C**	
Kutum Volc Field (Sudan)	**14.57 N***	**25.85 E**		5556	**B**	**Scoria cones**	**0205-04-**	Holocene?								
Meidob Volc Field (Sudan)	**15.32 N***	**26.47 E**	**2000**	4445	**XBpty**	**Scoria cones**	**0205-05-**	**Holocene**								
NE crater of vent VF 57						N-**6050***	....	....	....	x---	----	xx--	----	----	**P**	
Central Meidob volcanic field						N-**5250**z	....	....	....	x---	----	x---	----	----		
Central Meidob volcanic field						T-**4150***	....	....	....	x---	----	xx--	----	----	**P**	
SW crater of vent VF 57						T-**3050**?	....	....	....	x---	----	xx--	----	----	**P**	
Central Meidob volcanic field						T-**3000**?	....	....	....	x---	----	x---	----	----	**P**	
Vent VF 214						N-**2950**z	....	....	....	x---	----	----	x---	----	0	
Bayuda Volc Field (Sudan)	**18.33 N***	**32.75 E**	**670**	4446	**X**	**Cinder cones**	**0205-06-**	**Radiocarbon**								
						C **0850**t	....	....	....	----	----	----	x---	----		
Umm Arafieb, Jebel (Sudan)	**18.17 N***	**33.83 E**		5566	**X**	**Shield volcano**	**0205-07-**	Holocene?								

Middle East & Indian Ocean (03)

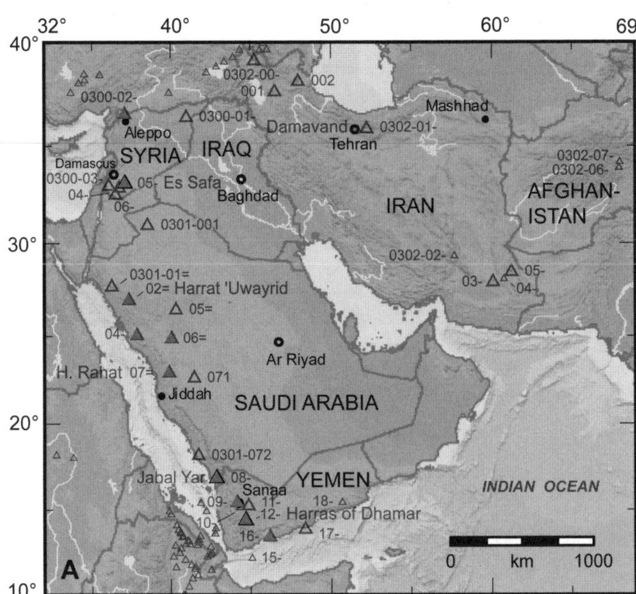

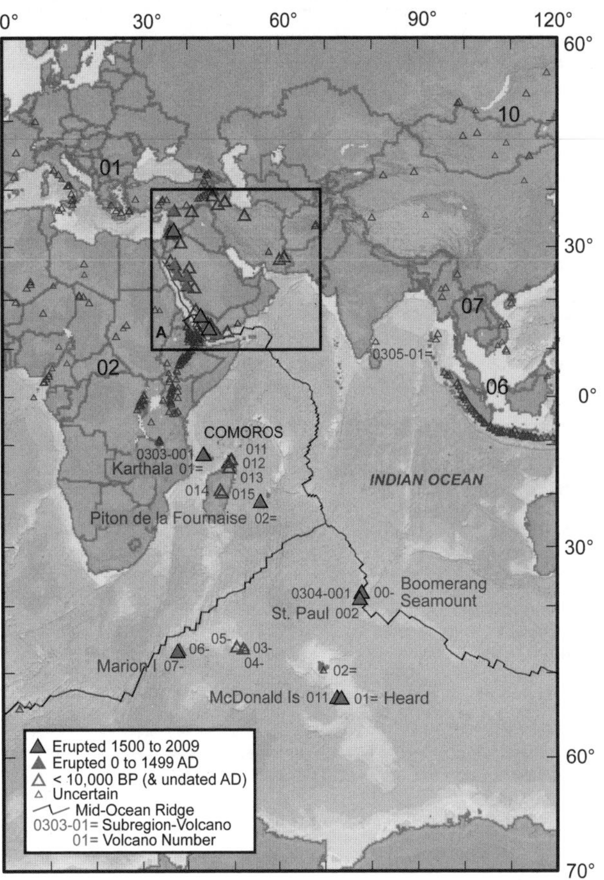

This region is a mixture of continental, rift-influenced volcanoes of the Middle East and island oceanic intraplate and island hotspot volcanoes of the Indian Ocean. We have moved Iranian volcanoes of region 01 in the *CAVW* to this region and added coverage of volcanoes in Afghanistan to create a broader "Middle East" region extending from Syria to Saudi Arabia and then from Iran to Afghanistan. The Comoros Islands and Reunion heavily dominate the eruption record (more than four-fifths of dated events) in contrast to the Middle Eastern volcanoes that dominate volcano listings (>60% of the region), population, and land area (both 99%).

The early historical record extends back to the 5th century AD. The region's earliest recorded eruption, a 9 km-long lava flow, bears the date 0500 AD (± 100) and, like the next 7, was from the Middle East, where the new religion of Islam unified Arabia in the 7th century. The first reported eruption of the region's most active volcano, Piton de la Fournaise on the island of Reunion, was not until the 17th century, and by then half of the 16 historically active volcanoes in the region had recorded their first known eruptions. All were from the Middle East, with the exception of an account written in the 10th to 12th centuries describing a summit eruption on Grand Comore Island.

In the last few centuries, though, the Indian Ocean has dominated the volcanic record of the region, and two new historically active volcanoes have been documented since the 2nd edition. An active submarine volcano named Boomerang Seamount with a 2-km-wide summit caldera 18 km NE of Amsterdam Island was first discovered during a bathymetric survey in 1996. Very short half-life radionuclide dating of fresh volcanic glass samples indicated that it had erupted only about 5 months earlier. Boomerang Seamount lies along the axis of the Southeast Indian Ridge and marks the site of the Amsterdam-St. Paul hotspot. A possible nearby active submarine center was inferred from phonolitic pumice that washed up on Heard Island in 1992, and volcanic plumes were observed from the MacDonald Islands, 75 km to the west of Heard, in December 1996. Possible pyroclastic deposits and lava were seen in 1997, and a satellite image taken in November 2001 showed the island to have more than doubled in area in the past year.

Reunion was known to the Arabs and visited by the Portuguese in the early 1500s. The first of its 172 known historical eruptions was in 1640, and France claimed the island around 1662. It has been French virtually continuously since then. Settlers moved in from 1715, and more than 700,000 people now live on the 2510 km^2 island. The Piton de la Fournaise volcanological observatory, one of the three French observatories along with those at Soufrière de Guadeloupe and Montagne Pelèe (Martinique), was established in 1980.

The Comoros were controlled by Moslem Sultans until acquired by the French in the latter half of the last century. After the 10th-12th century eruption mentioned above, no further reports are known until the early 19th century. The Comoros became a French overseas territory in 1947 and declared independence in 1975.

Madagascar's first settlers are believed to have arrived in the 5th century, but no historical eruptions are known from their youthful volcanoes. The French settled in 1626, and the island became a colony in 1896. The independent Malagasy Republic was declared in 1960, but ended in a 1972 coup, and the island is again called Madagascar.

The Kerguelen Archipelago was first visited in 1772 and has been occupied since 1950 by a small research station staff. Uninhabited neighboring islands St. Paul and Amsterdam are also Overseas Territories of France. The glacier-covered and unoccupied island of Heard is owned by Australia, and Marion Island belongs to South Africa. A small research station is maintained on Marion.

Fully 95% of region 03's dated eruptions have been historically documented, a proportion exceeded only by Indonesia. This region, along with Africa and Antarctica, is distinguished by having few known Holocene eruptions of substantial size (VEI ≥4 or ≥1 km^3 of lava), reflecting the relative absence of detailed stratigraphic studies of their volcanoes. Surprisingly, this region ranks second in subglacial eruptions. Although the Indian Ocean is far behind Iceland in this category, the 2745-m-high summit of Heard volcano has a large permanent ice cap, and eruptions from its summit vent have often produced partially subglacial lava flows.

VOLCANO NAME (Subregion) / ERUPTION — Area of Activity	LAT	LONG	ELEV (m)	POPL 5 km 10 30 100	ROCK TYPE	VOLC TYPE	NUMBER	STATUS	Start Year	Start M-Dy	Stop Year	Stop M-Dy	ERUPTIVE CHARACTERISTICS (Central vent, Flank vent, Radial fiss, Regional / Submarine, New island, Subglacial, Crater lake / Explosive, Pyro flow, Phreatic, Caldera / Lava flow, Lava lake, Dome, Spine / Fatal, Damage, Mudflow, Tsunami)	VEI	Vol L/T
SYRIA															
Sharat Kovakab (Syria)	**36.53** N*	**40.85** E	**534**	6667	**B**	**Volcanic field**	**0300-01-**	**Holocene**							
Unnamed (Syria)	**36.67** N*	**37.00** E		6667	**BA**	**Volcanic field**	**0300-02-**	**Historical**							
									1222	....	....	....	---- ---- ---- x--- ----	0?	
Golan Heights (Syria)	**33.10** N*	**35.97** E	**1197**	6668	**XBayt**	**Volcanic field**	**0300-03-**	**Holocene**							
Unnamed (Syria)	**33.00** N*	**36.63** E	**1050**	5567	**BX**	**Volcanic field**	**0300-04-**	**Radiocarbon**							
Kra lava field									G-**2670**x	....	....	....	---x ---- x--- x--- -x--		
Es Safa (Syria)	**33.25** N*	**37.07** E	**979**	6667	**BX**	**Volcanic field**	**0300-05-**	**Historical**							
Jabal Druse									**1850**j	....	....	....	---- ---- ---- -x-- ----	0	
Druze, Jabal ad (Syria)	**32.658** N*	**36.425** E	**1803**	7778	**XBayt**	**Volcanic field**	**0300-06-**	**Holocene**							
ARABIA															
Harrah, Al (Saudi Arabia)	**31.08** N*	**38.42** E	**1100**	6666	**B**	**Volcanic field**	**0301-001**	**Holocene**							
Rahah, Harrat ar (Saudi Arabia)	**27.80** N*	**36.17** E	**1950**	2236	**B**	**Volcanic field**	**0301-01=**	**Anthropology**							
'Uwayrid, Harrat (Saudi Arabia)	**27.08** N*	**37.25** E	**1920**	3335	**BX**	**Volcanic field**	**0301-02=**	**Anthropology**							
Hala-'l-Bedr, Hala-'l-'Ishqua or both									A **0640**?	....	....	....	---- ---- x--- x--- xx--	2?	
Lunayyir, Harrat (Saudi Arabia)	**25.17** N*	**37.75** E	**1370**	3335	**BX**	**Volcanic field**	**0301-04-**	**Historical**							
									1000<	....	....	....	---- ---- ---- x--- ----		
Ithnayn, Harrat (Saudi Arabia)	**26.58** N*	**40.20** E	**1625**	4445	**BX**	**Volcanic field**	**0301-05=**	**Holocene**							
Khaybar, Harrat (Saudi Arabia)	**25.00** N*	**39.92** E	**2093**	5557	**BXYTR**	**Volcanic field**	**0301-06=**	**Historical**							
Harrat Lali									**0650**t	....	....	....	---- ---- ?--- ?--- ----	2?	
Rahat, Harrat (Saudi Arabia)	**23.08** N*	**39.78** E	**1744**	7776	**BXYt**	**Volcanic field**	**0301-07=**	**Historical**							
West of Madinah									**0641**	....	....	....	---x ---- x--- ---- ----	2	
Fissure 20 km SE of Madinah									**1256**	0605	**1256**	0727?	---x ---- x--- x--- ----	3	8/-
Near Madinah									*? 1292*	....	....	....	---- ---- ---- ?--- ----		
Kishb, Harrat (Saudi Arabia)	**22.80** N*	**41.38** E	**1475**	4445	**XBPZ**	**Volcanic field**	**0301-071**	**Holocene**							
Birk, Harrat al (Saudi Arabia)	**18.37** N*	**41.63** E	**381**	5556	**BX**	**Volcanic field**	**0301-072**	**Holocene**							
Yar, Jabal (Saudi Arabia)	**17.05** N*	**42.83** E	**305**	6667	**B**	**Volcanic field**	**0301-08-**	**Historical**							
									1810j	....	....	....	---- ---- ?--- ?--- ----	2	
Arhab, Harra of (Yemen)	**15.63** N*	**44.08** E	**3100**	6667	**XBy**	**Volcanic field**	**0301-09-**	**Historical**							
East flank of Jabal Zebib									A **0200**>	....	....	....	-x-- ---- x--- x--- -x--	2?	
South flank of Kaulet Hattab									**0500**v	....	....	....	-x-- ---- ---- x--- -x--	0	
Marha, Jabal el- (Yemen)	**15.245** N	**44.236** E	**2506**	4677	**B**	**Tuff cone**	**0301-10-**	Holocene?							
Haylan, Jabal (Yemen)	**15.43** N*	**44.78** E	**1550**	6667	**B**	**Volcanic field**	**0301-11-**	**Anthropology**							
West of Sirwan									A-**1200**>	....	....	....	---- ---- ---- x--- ----	0?	
Dhamar, Harras of (Yemen)	**14.57** N*	**44.67** E	**3500**	6667	**BR**	**Volcanic field**	**0301-12-**	**Historical**							
Near the town of Dhamar									**1937**	....	....	....	---- ---- ?--- ---- ----	2	
Hamman Demt, Jabal (Yemen)	14.05 N	44.75 E	2000				0301-13-	Not a Volcano							
Nar, Jabal an (Yemen)	13.33 N	43.73 E					0301-14-	Not a Volcano							
Unnamed (Gulf of Aden)	**12.25** N	**45.00** E		0006	**U**	**Submarine volc**	**0301-15-**	Uncertain							
Sawâd, Harra es- (Yemen)	**13.58** N*	**46.12** E	**1737**	5556	**XB**	**Volcanic field**	**0301-16-**	**Historical**							
									1253	....	....	....	---- ---- ?--- ---- ----	3	
Bal Haf, Harra of (Yemen)	**14.05** N*	**48.33** E	**233**	4446	**B**	**Volcanic field**	**0301-17-**	**Holocene**							
Bir Borhut (Yemen)	**15.55** N*	**50.63** E		3346	**B**	**Volcanic field**	**0301-18-**	Holocene?							
									? 0950?	....	....	....	---- ---- ?--- ?--- ----		
Ormus Islands (Oman-E of)	26.00 N	56.50 E					0301-19-	Not a Volcano							
(earthquake uplift?, not eruption)									*X 1945*	*12*	....	....	---- ---- ---- ---- ----		
IRAN & AFGHANISTAN															
Unnamed (Iran)	**39.25** N*	**45.17** E		4567	**U**	**Volcanic field**	**0302-00-**	**Holocene**							
Sahand (Iran)	**37.75** N	**46.43** E	**3707**	3457	**A**	**Stratovolcano**	**0302-001**	**Holocene**							
Sabalan (Iran)	**38.25** N	**47.92** E	**4811**	3367	**A**	**Stratovolcano**	**0302-002**	**Holocene**							
Damavand (Iran)	**35.951** N	**52.109** E	**5670**	2458	**Ybt**	**Stratovolcano**	**0302-01-**	**Uranium-series**							
									U-**5350**x	....	....	....	---- ---- ---- x--- ----	0	
Qal'eh Hasan Ali (Iran)	**29.40** N*	**57.57** E		4456	**X**	**Maars**	**0302-02-**	Holocene?							
Bazman (Iran)	**28.07** N	**60.00** E	**3490**	1246	**AB**	**Stratovolcano**	**0302-03-**	**Fumarolic**							
Unnamed (Iran)	**28.17** N*	**60.67** E		4456	**B**	**Volcanic field**	**0302-04-**	Holocene?							
Taftan (Iran)	**28.60** N	**61.13** E	**3940**	1346	**A**	**Stratovolcano**	**0302-05-**	**Holocene**							
									? 1902	*01*	....	....	x--- ---- ---- ---- ----		
(perhaps sulfur flow rather than lava flow)									*? 1993*	*0425*	....	....	---- ---- ---- ?--- -x--		
Dacht-i-Navar Group (Afghanistan)	**33.95** N*	**67.92** E	**3800**	5557	**YAD**	**Lava domes**	**0302-06-**	Holocene?							
Vakak Group (Afghanistan)	**34.25** N*	**67.97** E	**3190**	5567	**DT**	**Volcanic field**	**0302-07-**	Holocene?							
INDIAN OCEAN															
Grille, La (Grand Comore I)	**11.47** S	**43.33** E	**1087**	6666	**XB**	**Shield volcano**	**0303-001**	**Holocene**							
Karthala (Grand Comore I)	**11.75** S	**43.38** E	**2361**	6666	**BX**	**Shield volcano**	**0303-01=**	**Historical**							
									1050w	....	....	....	---- ---- ?--- ?--- ----		
									1808	....	....	....	---- ---- ---- ---- ----		
									1814	1231y	....	....	---- ---- ---- ---- ----		
									1821	1231y	....	....	---- ---- ---- ---- ----		
									1828	05	....	....	-x-- ---- x--- ---- ----	2?	
									1830	....	....	....	-?-- ---- x--- ---- ----	2?	
Summit caldera ?									**1833**	....	....	....	?--- ---- ---- ---- ----		
SE flank									**1848**	....	....	....	--x- ---- ---- x--- ----	0	
West-SW flank (400 m)									**1850**?	....	....	....	--x- ---- ---- x--- ----	0	
SE flank									**1855**	0701p	....	....	-xx- ---- x--- x--- -x--	2	
SE flank (Badjini Massif) & summit									**1857**	....	....	....	x-x- ---- x--- x--- ----	2	
Upper NE flank (2200 m)									**1858**	....	....	....	-xx- ---- x--- x--- ----	2	
NW flank (Diboini Plateau fissures)									**1859**	....	....	....	--x- ---- x--- x--- ----	2	
SE flank (Badjini Massif, 1200 m)									**1860**	1229	....	....	--x- ---- ---- x--- ----	0	
(date perhaps confused with 1860)									*? 1862*	....	....	....	-x-- ---- x--- x--- ----	*2*	
									1865	....	....	....	-?-- ---- ?--- ---- ----	2?	

VOLCANO NAME (Subregion)	LAT	LONG	ELEV (m)	POPL (5 km 10 30 100)	ROCK TYPE	VOLC TYPE	NUMBER	STATUS	ERUPTION — Area of Activity	Start Year	Start M-Dy	Stop Year	Stop M-Dy	ERUPTIVE CHARACTERISTICS (Central Flank vent Radial fiss Regional / Submarine New island Subglacial Crater lake / Explosive Pyro flow Phreatic Caldera / Lava flow Lava lake Dome Spine / Fatal Damage Mudflow Tsunami)	VEI	Vol L/T
Karthala (Grand Comore I) *continued*									NW flank (Diboini Plateau)	**1872**	....	....	....	-xx- ---- x--- x--- ----	2	
									SE flank (Badjini Massif)	**1876**	....	....	....	-xx- ---- ---- x--- -x--	0	
									SE flank (Badjini Massif)	**1880**	....	....	....	--x- ---- x--- x--- ----	2	
									SE flank	**1883**	03	**1884**	....	-xx- ---- x--- x--- xx--	2	
									North flank (1300 m)	**1904**	0225	**1904**	04	--x- ---- x--- x--- xx--	2	
									North flank (1300 m)	**1910**	03	**1910**	03	--x- ---- x--- ---- ----	1	
									NE flank, Changomeni, NE Chahalé	**1918**	0811	**1918**	0826	x-x- ---- x-x- x--- ----	3*	
										1928b	....	....	....	x--- ---- ---- ---- ----	1?	
									Cheminee Nord (Changomeni)	**1948**	0422	**1948**	0616	x?-- ---- x--- -x-- ----	2	
									Chahalé crater	**1952**	0210?	**1952**	0212	x--- ---x x--- ---- ----	2	
									Chahalé crater	**1956**	0601?	....	....	x--- ---- ?--- ?--- ----	2?	
									Between Changomeni & Chahalé Craters	**1965**	0712	**1965**	0712	x--- ---- x--- xx-- ----	2?	5/-
									North end of summit crater	**1972**	0908	**1972**	1005	x--- ---- x--- xx-- ----	1	6/-
									SW flank	**1977**	0405	**1977**	0410	--x- ---- x--- x--- ?x--	1	6/5
									Choungou-Chahalé (Choungou-Chamadji)	**1991**	0711	**1991**	0711	x--- ---- x-x- ---- ----	2	-/6
									Chahalé crater	**2005**	0416	**2005**	0418	x--- ---x x-x- -x-- --x-	2?	
									Chahalé crater	**2005**	1124	**2005**	1208	x--- ---- x-x- -x-- xx--	3	
									Chahalé crater	**2006**	0528	**2006**	0603?	x--- ---- ---- -x-- ----	0	
									Chahalé crater	**2007**	0112	**2007**	0115?	x--- ---- x--- -x-- ----	2	
Ambre-Bobaomby (Madagascar)	12.60 S*	49.15 E	1475	5556	BRTPF	Volcanic field	0303-011	Holocene								
Nosy-Be (Madagascar)	13.32 S*	48.48 E	214	5556	FBR	Cinder cones	0303-012	Holocene								
Ankaizina Field (Madagascar)	14.30 S*	48.67 E	2878	4456	B	Cinder cones	0303-013	Holocene								
Itasy Volc Field (Madagascar)	19.00 S*	46.77 E	1800	6667	TXP	Scoria cones	0303-014	Radiocarbon								
										C-**7130**v	....	....	....	x--- ---- x--- ---- ----		
										C-**6050**<	....	....	....	---- ---- ---- x--- ----		
Ankaratra Field (Madagascar)	19.40 S*	47.20 E	2644	6667	XFATP	Cinder cones	0303-015	Holocene								
Fournaise, Piton de la (Reunion I)	21.231 S	55.713 E	2632	5566	BX	Shield volcano	0303-02=	Historical								
										C-**2800**w	....	....	....	x--- ---- x--- ---- ----		
									(Bellecombe Ash Member)	G-**2700**?	....	....	....	x--- ---- XXXA ---- ----	**5?**	-/9
										C-**1790**v	....	....	....	x--- ---- x--- ---- ----		
									Upper NW flank (Cratère Commerson)	G **0120**?	....	....	....	-x-- ---- ---- x--- ----	0	
										C **0460**?	....	....	....	---- ---- ---- x--- ----	0	
									Upper NW flank (Piton Gîte)	G **0600**?	....	....	....	-x-- ---- ---- x--- ----	0	
									Upper W flank (Piton Chisny)	G **0960**?	....	....	....	-x-- ---- ---- x--- ----	0	
									South rift zone (Brulé du Baril)	G **1340**?	....	....	....	--x- ---- ---- x--- ----	0	
									Upper NW flank (Petit Cratère)	G **1440**?	....	....	....	-x-- ---- ---- x--- ----	0	
									S rift zone (Piton Taye Poule)	G **1600**?	....	....	....	--x- ---- ---- x--- ----	0	
										1640	....	....	....	---- ---- x--- x--- ----	2	
										1649	....	....	....	---- ---- x--- x--- ----	2	
										1669	....	....	....	---- ---- x--- x--- ----	2	
										1671	....	....	....	---- ---- x--- x--- ----	2	
										1672	....	....	....	---- ---- x--- x--- ----	2	
										1703<	....	**1705**	....	---- ---- ---- x--- ----	0	
									NE rift zone	**1708**	04	**1708**	04	--x- ---- ---- x--- ----	0	7/-
										1709	....	....	....	---- ---- ?--- x--- ----	2	
										1721	06	....	....	---- ---- x--- ---- ----	2	
									L'Enclos and NE rift zone	**1733**?	....	....	....	--x- ---- ---- x--- -x--	0	
										1734	0101	**1734**	0306	---- ---- ---- x--- ----	2	
										1734	12	**1734**	12	---- ---- ---- x--- ----	2	
										1751	06	**1751**	06	---- ---- x--- x--- ----	2	
										1753	....	....	....	---- ---- --x- x--- ----	2	
										1759	....	....	....	---- ---- ---- ---- ----		
									East flank	**1760**	1215	**1760**	1229	--x- ---- x-x- ---- ----	2	
										1766	03	**1766**	0526e	x-x- ---- x-x- ?-x- ----	2	
									Formica Leo	**1768**	....	....	....	-x-- ---- x--- x--- ----	2	
										1771	....	....	....	---- ---- ?--- ---- ----		
										1772	02	....	....	x--- ---- x--- ---- ----	2	
										1772	1118	....	....	x--- ---- x--- x--- ----	2	
									SE rift zone	**1774**	....	....	....	--x- ---- ---- x--- -x--	0	7/-
									East side of summit cone	**1775**	....	....	....	--x- ---- x--- x--- ----	2	
									SE rift zone (Piton Takamaka)	**1776**	....	....	....	--x- ---- ---- x--- -x--	0	6/-
										1784	....	**1785**	....	x--- ---- x--- ---- ----	2	
										1786	0605?	**1786**	0804>	---- ---- x--- x--- ----	2	
									Bory	**1787**	0614	**1787**	0801	x?-- ---- x--- x--- ----	2	7/-
									East side of summit cone and Bory crater	**1789**	06	**1789**	07	xx-- ---- ---- x--- ----	2	
									Dolomieu, Mamelon Central ?	**1791**	0605d	**1791**	0727?	x-x- ---- x-x- x-x- ----	2*	7/-
										1792	1219?	....	....	---- ---- ---- x--- ----	0	
										1794	01	**1794**	01	---- ---- ---- x--- ----	0	
										1795	....	....	....	---- ---- ---- ?--- ----		
										1797?	....	....	....	---- ---- ---- x--- ----	0	
									SE rift zone	**1800**	1102	**1800**	1108	--x- ---- ---- x--- ----	0	7/-
									Mammelon Central	**1801**	1027	**1802**	0428g	x--- ---- x-x- xx-- ----	2	
										1802	12	....	....	x-x- ---- --x- x--- ----	2	
										1807	0323	**1807**	0613	xx-- ---- x--- x--- ----	2	
										1809	0717	**1809**	0808	x--- ---- x--- ---- ----	2	
										1810	1120	**1810**	1128	x--- ---- x--- ---- ----	2	
									Summit and above Piton de Crac	**1812**	0805d	**1812**	12	xxx- ---- x-x- x--- ----	2	
										1813	0926	**1813**	1126	x--- ---- x--- x--- ----	2	
										1814	0910	**1814**	1013	x--- ---- x--- x--- ----	2	
										1815	0121	**1815**	0127	x--- ---- x--- ---- ----	2	
									Summit and Plaine des Osmondes	**1815**	0815	**1815**	0816	xx-- ---- x--- x--- ----	2	
										1816	1215	....	....	xx-- ---- ---- x--- ----	0	
										1817	01	**1817**	04	x--- ---- ---- ---- ----	0	
									NW rift zone	**1820**	01	**1820**	02	--x- ---- x--- x--- ----	2	
										1821	0227	**1821**	0410	x--- ---- x-x- x--- ----	2	
										1824	02	....	....	---- ---- ---- x--- ----	0	
										1824	12	....	....	---- ---- ---- x--- ----	0	
									Cratere Faujas	**1830**	10	....	....	-x-- ---- ---- x--- ----	0	
									L'Enclos and NE rift zone	**1832**	03	....	....	--x- ---- ---- x--- ----	0	
										1842	04	....	....	---- ---- ---- x--- ----	0	
										1843	....	....	....	---- ---- ---- x--- ----	0	
									Summit and Piton de Crac	**1844**	0319	**1844**	0511	x-x- ---- x--- x--- ----	2	
										1844	12	....	....	---- ---- x--- x--- ----	2	

VOLCANO NAME (Subregion)..... **LAT** **LONG** **ELEV** (m) **POPL** (5 km, 10, 30, 100) **ROCK TYPE** **VOLC TYPE** **NUMBER** **STATUS**

ERUPTION — Area of Activity

Fournaise, Piton de la (Reunion I) *continued*

Area of Activity		Start Year	Start M-Dy	Stop Year	Stop M-Dy	Central / Flank vent / Radial fiss / Regional	Submarine / New island / Subglacial / Crater lake	Explosive / Pyro flow / Phreatic / Caldera	Lava flow / Lava lake / Dome / Spine	Fatal / Damage / Mudflow / Tsunami	VEI	Vol L/T
		1845	....	....	....	----	----	----	x---	----	0	
		1846	....	....	....	----	----	----	x---	----	0	
		1847	....	....	....	----	----	----	x---	----	0	
		1848	....	....	....	----	----	----	x---	----	0	
		1849	....	....	....	----	----	----	x---	----	0	
		1850	1103	**1850**	1112	----	----	----	x---	----	0	
Brulant, l'Enclos Velain		**1851**	....	....	....	x---	----	----	-x--	----	0	
Brulant		**1852**	....	....	....	x---	----	----	-x--	----	0	
		1858	1103	**1859**	01	x---	----	x---	x---	-x--	2	7/-
		1859	0508	**1859**	0523>	x---	----	x---	x---	----	2	
Dolomieu and l'Enclos		**1860**	0122	**1860**	0320	x-x-	----	x-x-	x---	----	2	-/5
Brulant		**1861**	0319	**1861**	0319	x---	----	x---	----	----	2	
		1863	1220	**1864**	0129	x---	----	----	x---	-x--	0	
		1865	0205	**1865**	0210	x---	----	x---	x---	----	2	
		1868	03	....	....	----	----	----	x---	-x--	0	
		1869?	....	....	....	----	----	----	?---	----	2?	
	?	*1870*	*0201*p	....	....	----	----	----	?---	----	*0*	
		1871	0621	**1871**	0705	x---	----	----	x---	----	0	
	?	*1872*	*0201*p	....	....	----	----	----	?---	----	*0*	
		1874	0201p	....	....	----	----	----	----	----		
		1874	0629	**1874**	1107>	x---	----	x-x-	x---	----	2	
		1875	1126	**1875**	1211?	----	----	----	x---	----	0	
		1876	1211	**1876**	1211?	----	----	----	?---	----		
		1878	0314	**1878**	0330	-x--	----	----	x---	----	0	
	?	*1882*	....	....	....	----	----	----	?---	----	*0*	
		1884	0204	**1884**	0205	----	----	----	x---	----	0	
Grandes Pentes and summit		**1889**	06	**1889**	0811>	xx--	----	x---	x---	-x--	2	
Summit, Grandes Pentes		**1890**	02	**1891**	0204	xx--	----	x-x-	x---	-x--	2	
		1894	08	....	....	----	----	----	x---	-x--	2	
		1897	0105d	**1897**	0124	--x-	----	----	x---	----	0	
		1898	0114	**1898**	0120	----	----	----	x---	----	2	
		1898	1126	....	....	x---	----	x---	x---	----	2	
		1899	0213	**1899**	0718>	xxx-	----	x---	x---	-x--	2	
East of Dolomieu		**1900**	0511	**1900**	0530	-x--	----	----	x---	----	0	
East of Dolomieu		**1901**	0221	**1901**	0225	-x--	----	----	x---	----	2	
NE flank (above Piton de Crac)		**1901**	0704	**1901**	0706	-x--	----	x---	x---	----	2	
		1902	0813	**1902**	0818	x-x-	----	x---	x---	----	2	
		1903?	....	....	....	----	----	----	x---	----	0	
NE flank (above Piton de Crac)		**1904**	0819	**1904**	1017	-x--	----	x---	x---	----	2	
		1905	0215	**1905**	0216	x---	----	x-x-	x---	----	2	
		1907	1129	**1907**	1205d	-x--	----	----	x---	----	0	
	?	*1908*	....	....	....	----	----	----	?---	----	*0*	
East of Cratère Faujas		**1909**	04	....	....	-x--	----	x---	x---	----	2	
		1910	1116	**1910**	1212	-x--	----	x---	x---	----	2	
		1913	0710	**1913**	0803	--x-	----	x---	x---	----	2	
Summit, N and NE of Crater Velain		**1915**	0722	**1915**	1121	xx--	----	x---	x---	----	2	
NE flank (above Piton de Crac)		**1917**	0429	**1917**	0429	-x--	----	----	x---	----	0	
		1920	0628	**1920**	1018	-x--	----	----	x---	----	0	
		1921	1127	**1921**	1203	xx--	----	?---	x---	----	2	
		1924	0519	**1924**	0523>	----	----	----	x---	----	0	
		1924	0903	**1924**	0913	x---	----	?---	x---	----	2	
		1925	1230	**1926**	0420	?-x-	----	x---	x---	----	2	
North flank		**1926**	0918	**1927**	0615	--x-	----	----	x---	----	2	
		1929	1223	**1929**	1231	xx--	----	x---	x---	----	2	
		1930	0523	**1930**	0524	x---	----	----	x---	----	0	
Summit, NE flank (Cratère Haug)		**1931**	0122	**1931**	0826e	xxx-	----	x---	x---	-x--	2	8/-
		1932	11	**1932**	11	----	----	----	----	----		
Dolomieu, upper and SE flanks		**1933**	0607	**1934**	0401	xx--	----	x---	x---	----	2	
		1935?	....	....	....	----	----	x---	----	----	2	
Near 1933 crater		**1936**	09	....	....	--x-	----	----	x---	----	0	
Bory, flanks of Bory and Dolomieu		**1937**	0813	**1937**	1125	x-x-	----	x---	x---	----	2	6/-
		1938	0725	**1938**	0729	-x--	----	x---	x---	----	1	
ESE and SW flanks, Dolomieu		**1938**	1207	**1939**	0115	xxx-	----	x---	x---	-x--	2	7/-
		1941?	....	....	....	----	----	x---	----	----	1	
Bory, rim of Dolomieu		**1942**	1005	**1942**	1025	x-x-	----	x---	x---	----	2	6/-
SE of Dolomieu, lower Grandes Pentes		**1943**	0330?	**1943**	0526e	-xx-	----	x---	x---	-x--	2	7/-
		1944	0411	**1944**	0501	-x--	----	x---	x---	----	2	
SE flank near Nez Coupe du Tremblet		**1945**	0415	**1945**	0506	xx--	----	x---	x---	----	2	6/-
Dolomieu crater and upper flanks		**1946**	0618	**1946**	0705	xx--	----	x---	x---	----	2	6/-
Dolomieu, Grand Brule		**1947**?	....	....	....	x-x-	----	x---	x---	----	2	
South flank (le Chateau Fort)		**1948**	0214	**1948**	0308	-x--	----	x---	x---	----	2	6/-
	?	*1949*	*10*	....	....	-?--	----	?---	?---	----	*2*	
South flank (2080 m)		**1950**	0225	**1950**	0402	-xx-	----	x---	x---	----	2	6/-
SE of Bory		**1950**	0830	**1950**	0905	-x--	----	x---	?---	----	2	
North part of Grand Brule	?	*1951*	*06*	....	....	-x--	----	----	x---	----	*0*	
		1951	0910	**1951**	0920	-x--	----	x---	----	----	1	
NE flank near north rim (1500 m)		**1952**	0519	**1952**	0720	-x--	----	x---	x---	----	2	6/-
South, NW & N flanks, Dolomieu, Bory		**1953**	0313	**1953**	0708	-xx-	----	x---	x---	----	2	7/-
		1954	01	**1954**	12	-x--	----	----	----	----		
Dolomieu, Bory, S, SE & ESE flanks		**1955**	0706	**1957**	0316	xxx-	----	x---	x-x-	-x--	2*	7/-
Bory, N of Bory, NE of Dolomieu		**1957**	0902	**1957**	1116	xxx-	----	x---	x---	----	2	6/-
Dolomieu		**1958**	0530	**1958**	0920	xx--	----	x---	x---	----	2	
Bory		**1959**	0311	**1959**	0806	x---	----	x---	x---	----	2	6/-
Bory, south flank (2030 m)		**1960**	0111	**1960**	0310	xxx-	----	x---	x---	----	2	6/-
NE flank (east of Cratère Picard)		**1961**	0405	**1961**	0425	-x--	----	----	x---	-x--	0	7/-
Dolomieu, upper east flank (2410 m)		**1963**	1107	**1963**	1121	x-x-	----	x---	----	----	2	-/7
Dolomieu, upper east and NE flanks		**1964**	0430	**1964**	0508	x-x-	----	x---	x---	----	2	
East flank (1930 m)		**1964**	1221	**1965**	0215	-xx-	----	x---	x---	----	2?	7/-
SE flank (Cratere Maillard, 2400 m)		**1966**	0315	**1966**	0515	--x-	----	x---	x---	----	2?	7/-
South, ENE, north and SE of Dolomieu		**1972**	0609?	**1973**	0116?	-xx-	----	x---	xx--	----	2	7/5
Dolomieu (SSW wall)		**1973**	0510	**1973**	0905?	x---	----	x---	x---	----	2	6/-
Dolomieu and SE flank (1320-2350 m)		**1975**	1104	**1976**	0406	-xx-	----	x---	xx--	-x--	1	7/5
North of Dolomieu (2250-2330 m)		**1976**	1102	**1976**	1104?	--x-	----	x---	x---	----	1	5/4
NE and SE of Dolomieu, NE rift zone		**1977**	0324	**1977**	0416	--x-	----	x---	x---	-x--	0	7/-

VOLCANO NAME (Subregion)	LAT	LONG	ELEV (m)	POPL (5 km / 10 / 30 / 100)	ROCK TYPE	VOLC TYPE	NUMBER	STATUS	ERUPTION — Area of Activity	Start Year	Start M-Dy	Stop Year	Stop M-Dy	Central / Flank vent / Radial fiss / Regional	Submarine / New island / Subglacial / Crater lake	Explosive / Pyro flow / Phreatic / Caldera	Lava flow / Lava lake / Dome / Spine	Fatal / Damage / Mudflow / Tsunami	VEI	Vol L/T
Fournaise, Piton de la (Reunion I) *cont*									ENE flank (2050-2200 m, 1850-1920 m)	**1977**	1024	**1977**	1117	-xx-	----	x---	x---	----	1	7/-
									SE, SW and N flanks, Dolomieu & Bory	**1979**	0528	**1979**	0714	x-x-	----	x---	x---	----	1	5/-
									Bory, SW, N & NE of Dolomieu	**1981**	0203	**1981**	0505	x-x-	----	x-x-	xx--	----	2	7/-
									SSW flank of Dolomieu (2110-2300 m)	**1983**	1204	**1984**	0218	--x-	----	x---	x---	----	2	7/-
									Dolomieu and flanks, SE rift zone	**1985**	0614	**1988**	1229	xxx-	----	x-x-	xx--	-x--	1	8/-
									Dolomieu and SE flank	**1990**	0118	**1990**	0508	x-x-	----	----	x---	----	0	6/-
									Dolomieu and upper east flank	**1991**	0719	**1991**	0720	--x-	----	----	x---	----	0	6/-
									Dolomieu and upper SE flank	**1992**	0827	**1992**	0923	x-x-	----	----	x---	----	1	6/-
									N and WSW of Dolomieu, outer N flank	**1998**	0309	**1998**	0920?	--x-	----	x---	x---	-x--	1	7/-
									Dolomieu, E (2500-2100) &S flanks (1900 m)	**1999**	0719	**1999**	1023	x-x-	----	x---	x---	----	1	6/-
									North flank of Dolomieu (2490-2250 m)	**2000**	0214	**2000**	0304	--x-	----	x---	x---	----	1	6/-
									SE flank (2100-1800 m), E flank (2260-2000 m)	**2000**	0623	**2000**	1113	--x-	----	x---	xx--	----	1	7/-
									South flank (below Dolomieu at ~2500 m)	**2001**	0327	**2001**	0404	--x-	----	----	x---	----	1	6/-
									ESE flank (2500 m), East flank (1800-2000 m)	**2001**	0611	**2001**	0707	--x-	----	----	x---	-x--	1	6/-
									NE part of l'Enclos Fouqué caldera	**2002**	0105	**2002**	0116	--x-	----	x---	x---	-x--	1	7/-
									East flank of Dolomieu (1850-1540 m)	**2002**	1116	**2002**	1203	--x-	----	x---	x---	-x--	2	6/-
									Dolomieu, Bory, N, NW, and SSW flanks	**2003**	0530	**2004**	0110	x-x-	----	x---	x---	----	1	7/-
									SSW of Bory, Dolomieu and east flank	**2004**	0502	**2004**	1016	x-x-	----	----	x---	-x--	0	7/-
									North side of caldera (1600, 1200, & 450 m)	**2005**	0217	**2005**	0226	--x-	----	----	x---	-x--	0	7/-
									Dolomieu, N and NE flanks	**2005**	1004	**2006**	0118	--x-	----	----	x---	----	0	7/-
									Dolomieu, S, E, and SE flanks	**2006**	0720	**2007**	0501	--x-	----	x--M	x---	-x--	1?	8/-
									Dolomieu crater	**2008**	0921	**2009**	0204	x-x-	----	x---	xx--	----	1	6/-
									Dolomieu crater and east flank	**2009**	1105	**2010**	0101>	x-x-	----	x---	x---	----	1?	
Boomerang Seamount (Indian O.)	**37.721 S**	**77.825 E**	**-650**	0000	**B**	**Submarine volc**	**0304-00-**	**Historical**												
										U **1995**	1201p	....	....	x---	x---	----	----	----	0	
Amsterdam Island (Indian O.-S)	**37.83 S**	**77.52 E**	**881**	0000	**B**	**Stratovolcano**	**0304-001**	**Holocene**												
St. Paul (Indian O.-S)	**38.72 S**	**77.53 E**	**268**	0000	**B**	**Stratovolcano**	**0304-002**	**Historical**												
									SW flank (near Cape West)	**1793**	....	....	....	-x--	----	x---	----	----	2	
Heard (Indian O.-S)	**53.106 S**	**73.513 E**	**2745**	0000	**XBYTZ**	**Stratovolcano**	**0304-01=**	**Historical**												
										? 1881	*0602*	....	....	-x--	--x-	?---	----	----	*2*	
									Mawson Peak	**1910**	03	**1910**	04	x---	--x-	x---	----	----	2	
									Mawson Peak	**1950**	0124	**1952**	0312?	x?--	--x-	x---	x---	----	2	
									Mawson Peak	**1953**	0820	**1953**	1118	x---	--x-	x---	----	----	2	
									Mawson Peak	**1954**	0413?	**1954**	0613?	x---	--x-	x---	?---	----	2	
									Mawson Peak	**1985**	0114	**1987**	01 ?	x?--	--x-	x---	xx--	----	2?	
									Mawson Peak	*? 1992*	*0117*	*?1992*	*0118*	x---	----	?---	----	----		
									Mawson Peak	**1992**	0529?	....	....	x---	--x-	----	----	----	0	
									Mawson Peak	**1993**	0102m	....	....	x---	--x-	x---	x---	----	2?	
									Mawson Peak and upper south flank	**2000**	0307?	**2001**	02	x-x-	--x-	x---	x---	----	2*	
									Mawson Peak	**2003**	0609	**2004**	0614	x---	--x-	----	-x--	----	0	
									Mawson Peak	**2006**	0311	**2008**	0303	x---	--x-	----	xx--	----	0	
McDonald Islands (Indian O.-S)	**53.03 S**	**72.60 E**	**230**	0000	**PZ**	**Complex volcano**	**0304-011**	**Historical**												
									Submarine vent near McDonald Islands	**1992**	12	....	....	----	x---	x---	----	----	0	
									Northern part of McDonald Island	**1996**	12	**1997**	0210p	x---	----	x---	?---	----	1?	
										2001	0503v	....	....	x---	----	x---	x-x-	----	1?	
										? 2004	*1114*	*?2004*	*1114*	?---	----	----	----	----	*1?*	
										2005	0712<	....	....	x---	----	----	x---	----	0	
Kerguelen Islands (Indian O.-S)	**49.58 S**	**69.50 E**	**1840**	0000	**YTZ**	**Stratovolcanoes**	**0304-02=**	Holocene?												
Est, Ile de l' (Indian O.-S)	**46.43 S**	**52.20 E**	**1090**	0000	**BX**	**Stratovolcano**	**0304-03-**	Holocene?												
Possession, Ile de la (Indian O.-S)	**46.42 S**	**51.75 E**	**934**	0000	**BPXY**	**Stratovolcano**	**0304-04-**	**Holocene**												
Cochons, Ile aux (Indian O.-S)	**46.10 S**	**50.23 E**	**775**	0000	**B**	**Stratovolcano**	**0304-05-**	**Holocene**												
Prince Edward Island (Indian O.)	**46.63 S**	**37.95 E**	**672**	0000	**BXt**	**Shield volcano**	**0304-06-**	**Holocene**												
Marion Island (Indian O.-S)	**46.90 S**	**37.75 E**	**1230**	0000	**BXy**	**Shield volcanoes**	**0304-07-**	**Historical**												
									E-W fissure from summit to W coast	**1980**	09 ?	....	....	-xx-	--x-	x---	x---	----	1	6/-
									South side of island	**2004**	0624	**2004**	0624?	-x--	----	x---	----	----	1	
Unnamed (Indian O.-E)	**11.75 N**	**80.75 E**		0005	**U**	**Submarine volc ?**	**0305-01=**	Uncertain												
										? 1757	....	....	....	----	??--	----	----	----	*0*	

Dolomieu crater (center) caps the summit lava shield of Piton de la Fournaise volcano. Two large calderas formed by eastward landsliding of the summit of the volcano lie beyond Dolomieu; the more distant formed about 65,000 years ago, and the closer one, inside which the modern lava shield was constructed, originated less than 5000 years ago. Unvegetated fissure-fed lava flows mantle the flanks of the lava shield. The deeply dissected Pleistocene Piton des Neiges shield volcano forms the western horizon.

New Zealand to Fiji (04)

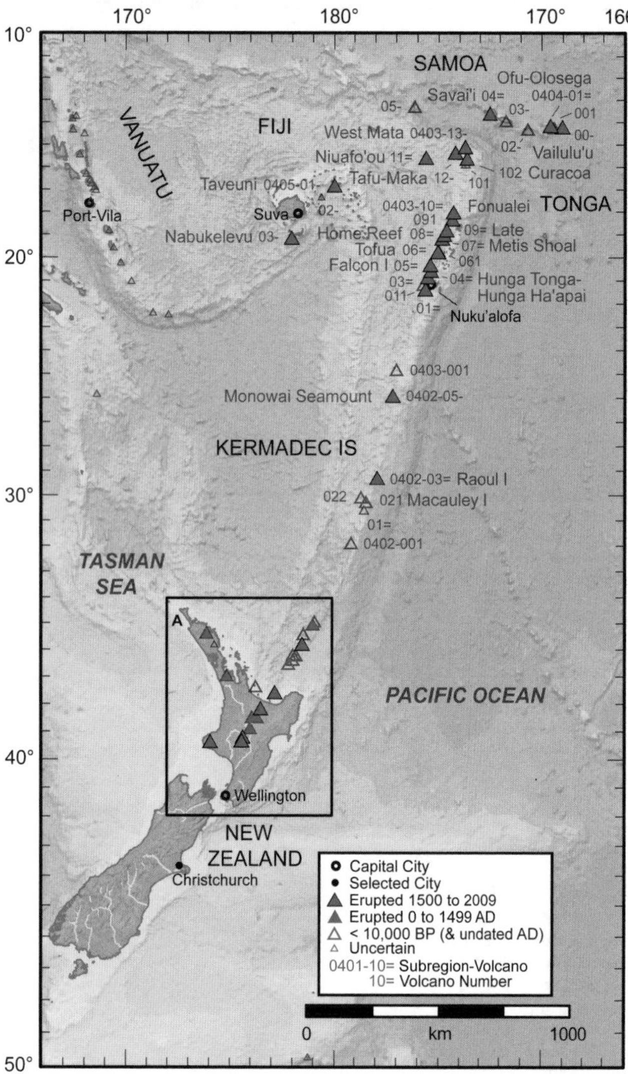

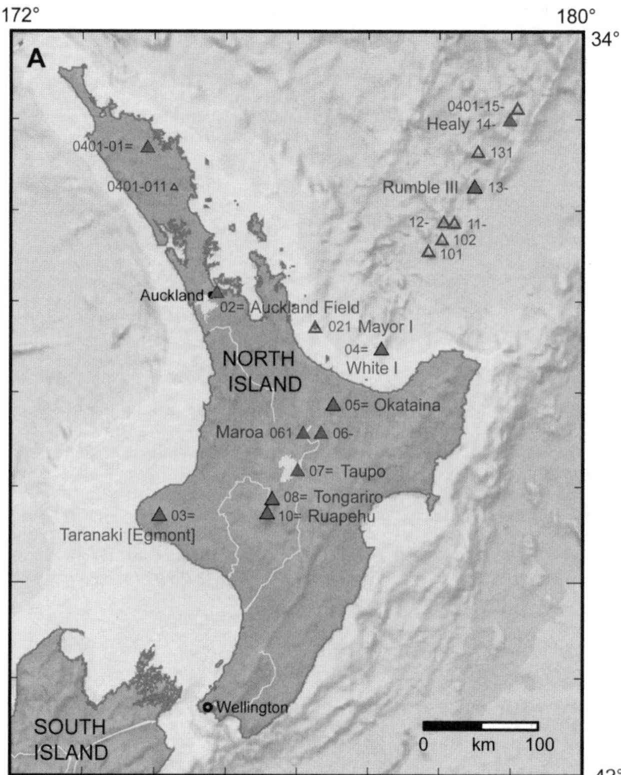

After the Indian Ocean, the *CAVW* regions begin a long clockwise circuit around the Pacific Rim starting with New Zealand. The Pacific's "Ring of Fire" has produced about two-thirds of the world's Holocene volcanoes and their dated eruptions, largely by subduction of the huge Pacific plate and several smaller plates. The New Zealand to Fiji region is geographically small but volcanologically important. Its total land area is only 292,000 km^2 (the size of Arizona) and its population of 5.4 million is roughly comparable to greater Philadelphia. New Zealand makes up 92% of the land area and three-fourths of the region's population, but its Holocene volcanoes are restricted to North Island and offshore areas north to the Kermedec Islands.

Estimates of Maori arrival in New Zealand range from 800 AD to 1350 AD, and the first European to sight the islands was probably Tasman in 1642. Written records, however, were not kept until whalers started to land in the 1790s, and detailed record-keeping began with the missionaries in the late 1810s. The earliest historically-dated eruption in New Zealand was at White Island in 1826. The first permanent settlement (Wellington) and the Maori treaty (ceding sovereignty to England) came in 1840. The Kermadec Islands, totaling 34 km^2 in area, were annexed to New Zealand in 1887, and a small research station is maintained there.

New Zealand contains the world's strongest concentration of youthful rhyolitic volcanoes, and voluminous ignimbrite sheets of the many calderas of the Taupo volcanic zone marking the boundary of the Australian and Pacific tectonic plates blanket much of North Island. Taupo volcano itself, a topographically subdued caldera largely filled by Lake Taupo, produced one of Earth's largest Holocene eruptions in about 180 AD, as well as Earth's most recent VEI 8 eruption that ejected more than 1100 km^3 of ash and pyroclastic flows about 23,000 years ago. A strong emphasis on tephrochronology has documented the Quaternary volcanic history of this active island in unusual detail. This region has a high percentage of eruptions producing pyroclastic flows (nearly 10%, mostly on New Zealand's North Island), which underscores the potential risk for New Zealand eruptions. It is also near the top of regions with crater lake eruptions, primarily due to the frequent eruptions from Ruapehu's crater lake. In collaboration with New Zealand colleagues, we have reorganized the North Island volcanoes in an effort to achieve a closer genetic identification of each center.

The Kingdom of Tonga is an archipelago of two parallel island belts: that to the east is low, fertile, coralline, and well populated, while that to the west is young, volcanic, and ranges from steep cones to ephemeral islands. The unbroken line of subduction, from NZ through the Kermadecs and Tonga, ends abruptly and the trench swings west north of the remarkable, donut-shaped island of Niuafo'ou, a basaltic shield volcano with a large, lake-filled caldera. European contact with Tonga began in the 17th century and Captain Cook named them the Friendly Isles in 1773; the first recorded eruption was in the next year.

The Samoan islands are formed by a hotspot to the NE of the Tonga-Kermadec-NZ subduction zone, and are volcanically distinct from their neighbors. They were invaded by Fijians in the early 13th century, but may well have been settled thousands of years earlier. European contact was first made by the Dutch in 1722, but detailed record keeping began with the arrival of missionaries from London in 1830. The 1725 eruption of Savai'i, covering 190 km^2 with 2 km^3 of lava, was the first historical volcanism in region 04. In 1900 the islands were divided, with the smaller western islands going to the US and the larger, more populated, and more volcanic western islands going to Germany. New Zealand annexed Western Samoa and administered it from 1914 to 1962, when it became independent.

The three Holocene centers of Fiji form smaller islands NE to S of the two largest islands that support 90% of the population. The archipelago was populated for thousands of years by Polynesians, but the Dutch began European exploration in 1643, and it became a British crown colony in 1874 before achieving independence in 1970. Although not in the *CAVW* for Region 04, Fiji was added by us in 1981 upon recognition of its Holocene volcanism.

Much of the region north of New Zealand's North Island is made up of seamounts and small islands, including 16 submarine volcanoes with sufficiently recent activity to be included in the 2nd edition of this compilation. Many more seamounts exist along the Kermadec-Tonga arc, and we have added a half dozen more submarine volcanoes in this edition. Recent bathymetric studies have begun to document the widespread distribution of submarine volcanoes and discovered many with active hydrothermal activity. In 2009 an ongoing eruption was observed at a submarine volcano at the northern end of the Tonga arc, and a new lava flow from an eruption in late 2008 was documented at a vent on a nearby Lau Basin back-arc spreading center. This high level of submarine activity is seen in the fact that this region has the largest number of eruptions dated by SOFAR technology, or underwater sound, and no other region has a higher proportion of eruptions building new islands. More than one sixth of all eruptions in Tonga and the Kermadecs have produced new islands, most recently in 2006 at Home Reef and 2009 at Hunga Tonga-Hunga Ha'apai. Many of these "jack-in-the-box" islands are composed of pyroclastic deposits that are quickly eroded below sea level by wave action.

VOLCANO NAME (Subregion) / ERUPTION — Area of Activity	LAT	LONG	ELEV (m)	POPL (5 km, 10, 30, 100)	ROCK TYPE	VOLC TYPE / —Start— Year	NUMBER / M-Dy	STATUS / —Stop— Year	M-Dy	Central, Flank vent, Radial fiss, Regional	Submarine, New island, Subglacial, Crater lake	Explosive, Pyro flow, Phreatic, Caldera	Lava flow, Lava lake, Dome, Spine	Fatal, Damage, Mudflow, Tsunami	VEI	Vol L/T
NEW ZEALAND																
Kaikohe-Bay of Islands (N Zeal)	**35.30 S***	**173.90 E**	**388**	5556	**XBar**	**Volcanic field**	**0401-01=**	**Radiocarbon**								
Te Puke						C **0400**y	....	....	....	**xx-x**	----	**x---**	**x---**	----		
Whangarei (New Zealand)	**35.75 S***	**174.27 E**	**397**	5556	**XBadr**	**Cinder cones**	**0401-011**	Holocene?								
Auckland Field (New Zealand)	**36.90 S***	**174.87 E**	**260**	7777	**XBf**	**Volcanic field**	**0401-02=**	**Radiocarbon**								
Rangitoto						C **1350**?	....	....	....	**x---**	----	**x---**	**x---**	----		9/-
Mayor Island (New Zealand)	**37.28 S**	**176.25 E**	**355**	3336	**R**	**Shield volcano**	**0401-021**	**Radiocarbon**								
SE caldera rim						C-**6050**u	....	....	....	**x---**	----	**x---**	**x---**	----		
South end of caldera, Taratimi Bay						G-**5060**x	....	....	....	**xxx-**	**x---**	**xxxx**	----	----	5	-/9
Taranaki [Egmont] (New Zealand)	**39.30 S**	**174.07 E**	**2518**	3356	**Ab**	**Stratovolcano**	**0401-03=**	**Historical**								
(Kaponga-b tephra)						C-**7650**?	....	....	....	----	----	**x---**	----	----		
(Kaponga-e Tephra)						T-**7330**?	....	....	....	----	----	**x---**	----	----		
						C-**7270**t	....	....	....	----	----	**x---**	----	----		
(Kaponga-f Tephra)						C-**7000**v	....	....	....	**x---**	----	**x---**	----	----		
						T-**6050**?	....	....	....	**x---**	----	**xx--**	**x---**	----		
						C-**5120**t	....	....	....	----	----	**x---**	----	----		
(Waipuku Tephra)						T-**3250**?	....	....	....	----	----	**x---**	----	----		
						T-**2850**y	....	....	....	----	----	**x---**	----	----		
(Tariki Tephra)						T-**2700**?	....	....	....	----	----	**x---**	----	----		
(Mangatoki Tephra)						T-**2450**y	....	....	....	----	----	**x---**	----	----		
						C-**2400**s	....	....	....	----	----	**x---**	----	----		
(Korito Tephra)						T-**2150**?	....	....	....	----	----	**x---**	----	----		
(Inglewood Tephra)						C-**1700**v	....	....	....	----	----	**xx--**	----	----	5	-/9
						C-**1560**s	....	....	....	----	----	**x---**	----	----		
Southern Beehive						T-**1250**?	....	....	....	**-x--**	----	----	**--x-**	----		
						C-**1190**s	....	....	....	----	----	**x---**	----	----		
Fanthams Peak (Manganui Tephra)						T-**1130**x	....	....	....	**-x--**	----	**x---**	----	----		
						T-**0590**z	....	....	....	----	----	**x---**	----	----		
						C-**0420**r	....	....	....	----	----	**x---**	----	----		
						C-**0150**r	....	....	....	----	----	**x---**	----	----		
(Maketawa Tephra)						C-**0040**u	....	....	....	**x---**	----	**xx--**	**--x-**	----		
						C **0100**s	....	....	....	----	----	**x---**	----	----		
(Curtis Ridge episode)						T **0150**?	....	....	....	**xx--**	----	**xx--**	**--x-**	----	3?	-/7
						C **0390**s	....	....	....	----	----	**x---**	----	----		
						C **0520**w	....	....	....	----	----	**xx--**	----	----		
(Kaupokonui Tephra)						T **0550**?	....	....	....	----	----	**x---**	----	----		
						C **0820**r	....	....	....	----	----	**x---**	----	----		
						C **0970**r	....	....	....	----	----	**x---**	----	----		
						C **1070**s	....	....	....	----	----	**x---**	----	----		
						C **1300**t	....	....	....	----	----	**x---**	----	----		
						C **1340**s	....	....	....	----	----	**x---**	----	----		
						C **1400**t	....	....	....	**x---**	----	**xx--**	**x---**	----		
						C **1480**t	....	....	....	----	----	**x---**	----	----		
(Newall Ash)						C **1500**r	....	....	....	**x---**	----	**xx--**	**--x-**	**-x--**		
						C **1550**s	....	....	....	----	----	**x---**	----	----		
						C **1560**s	....	....	....	----	----	**x---**	----	----		
						C **1570**s	....	....	....	----	----	**x---**	----	----		
						C **1590**s	....	....	....	----	----	**x---**	----	----		
(Burrell Lapilli)						D **1655**?	....	....	....	**x---**	----	**xx--**	**--x-**	**-x--**	4	-/8
						C **1700**t	....	....	....	----	----	**x---**	----	----		
(Tahurangi Ash)						D **1755**?	....	....	....	**x---**	----	**x---**	----	----		
						T **1800**?	....	....	....	----	----	**x---**	----	----		
						1854	....	....	....	**x---**	----	**x---**	**--x-**	----		
White Island (New Zealand)	**37.52 S**	**177.18 E**	**321**	1116	**AD**	**Stratovolcanoes**	**0401-04=**	**Historical**								
						1826	1201	....	....	**x---**	----	**x---**	----	----	2	
						1836b	....	....	....	**x---**	----	?---	----	----	2	
						? *1856*h	....	....	....	**x---**	----	?---	----	----	*2*	
						? *1885*	*01*	....	....	**x---**	----	?---	----	----	*2*	
West end of crater						**1885**	10	....	....	**x---**	----	**x-x-**	----	----	2	
						? *1886*	*0610*	?*1886*	*0615*	**x---**	----	?---	----	----	*2*	
						1886	0916	**1886**	12 ?	**x---**	----	**x---**	----	----	2	
						? *1908*	*1128*	?*1908*	*1206*	**x---**	----	?---	----	----	*2*	
						1909	0513	....	....	**x---**	----	**x---**	----	----	2	
(landslide without eruption)						*X 1914*	*0910*?	....	....	**x---**	----	----	----	**xxx-**		
NW end of crater (Lot's Wife vent)						**1922**	....	....	....	**x---**	----	**x---**	----	----	2	
North end of crater (Schuberts Fairy?)						**1924**	....	....	....	**x---**	----	**x---**	----	----	2	
Little Donald vent						**1926**	0203	....	....	**x---**	----	**x---**	----	----	2	
Between Big Donald and Lot's Wife						**1928**	0901	**1928**	0903a	**x---**	----	**x---**	----	----	1	
						1930	0316	....	....	**x---**	----	**x---**	----	----	2	
Foot of crater ridge (1933 crater)						**1933**	0402	....	....	**x---**	----	**x---**	----	----	3	
Noisy Nellie Crater						**1947**	01 <	....	....	**x---**	----	**x---**	----	----	2	
						1955	01	....	....	**x---**	----	**x---**	----	----	2	
						1957	1211	....	....	**x---**	----	**x---**	----	----	2	
Noisy Nellie and 1933 craters						**1958**	12	....	....	**x---**	----	**x---**	----	----	1	

VOLCANO NAME (Subregion) LAT LONG ELEV (m) POPL (5 km, 10, 30, 100) ROCK TYPE VOLC TYPE NUMBER STATUS / ERUPTION — Area of Activity	Start Year	Start M-Dy	Stop Year	Stop M-Dy	Central / Flank vent / Radial fiss / Regional	Submarine / New island / Subglacial / Crater lake	Explosive / Pyro flow / Phreatic / Caldera	Lava flow / Lava lake / Dome / Spine	Fatal / Damage / Mudflow / Tsunami	VEI	Vol L/T
White Island (New Zealand) *continued* — Noisy Nellie Crater	**1959**	1214	**1959**	1220	x---	----	x---	----	----	2	
Big John Crater	**1962**	1215	....	....	x---	----	x---	----	----	3	
Gilliver Crater	**1966**	1113	**1967**	03	x---	----	xxx-	----	----	3	
Rudolf vent (back wall of 1933 crater)	**1968**	0127	**1969**	02	x---	----	x---	----	----	3*	
Rudolf vent	**1969**	08	**1969**	09	x---	----	x---	----	----	2	
Rudolf vent	**1970**	0630p	....	....	x---	----	x---	----	----	2	
Noisy Nellie Crater	**1971**	0409c	....	....	x---	----	x-x-	----	----	2	
South of Rudolf (1971 crater)	**1971**	0719	**1971**	0720	x---	----	x-x-	----	----	2	
SE of Donald Mound,	**1974**	0908j	....	....	x---	----	--x-	----	----	2	
Christmas, Gibrus, and 1978 craters	**1976**	1218	**1982**	0129	x---	----	xxx-	----	----	3*	-/7
(incorrect report of eruption)	*X 1982*	*0701*	....	....	----	----	----	----	----		
North margin of 1978 crater complex	**1983**	1226e	**1984**	0212e	x---	----	x---	----	----	2	
Congress and numerous other craters	**1986**	0201?	**1994**	0728	x---	----	x-x-	----	----	3*	
Wade Crater	**1995**	0628?	**1995**	0629?	x---	----	x---	----	----	1	
	1998	0328	**1998**	0329	x---	----	x-x-	----	----	1	
NW corner of 1978/90 crater complex	**1998**	0822	**1999**	08	x---	----	x-x-	----	----	2	
MH vent	**2000**	0307	**2000**	0905d	x---	----	x---	----	----	3?	
MH vent	**2001**	0219	**2001**	0219?	x---	----	x---	----	----	2	
Okataina (New Zealand) **38.12** S **176.50** E **1111** 2356 **Rbda** **Lava domes** **0401-05=** **Historical**											
West Rerewhakaaitu fissures	T -**8050**?	....	....	....	---x	----	--x-	----	----		
Rotoma caldera, Tuahu, Kawerau	G-**7560**o	....	....	....	---x	----	xxx-	x-x-	----	**5**	**9/9**
Haroharo (Te Horoa & other domes)	G-**6060**t	....	....	....	---x	----	xx--	x-x-	----	**5**	**10/9**
Mt. Edgecumbe	T-**5550**?	....	....	....	---x	----	----	x-x-	----	0	
Haroharo (Makatiti and other domes)	G-**3580**t	....	....	....	---x	----	xx--	x-x-	----	**5**	**9/9**
Haroharo (Rotokawau to Rotoatua)	G-**1750**?	....	....	....	--x-	----	x---	----	----	4+	8/8
Mt. Edgecumbe	G-**1330**u	....	....	....	----	----	xx--	----	----		
Mt. Edgecumbe	T-**0300**?	....	....	....	---x	----	----	x-x-	----	0	**9/-**
Te Kopia thermal area	T **0180**?	....	....	....	---x	----	--x-	----	----		
Tarawera (Kaharoa eruption)	G **1310**k	....	G**1315?**	....	---x	----	xxx-	--x-	--x-	**5**	**9/9**
Tarawera (Wahanga-Waimangu fissure)	**1886**	0610	**1886**	08	---x	----	xxx-	----	xxx-	**5**	-/9
Waimangu (Echo Crater)	**1896**	....	....	....	----	---?	--x-	----	----	1?	
Waimangu Geyser	**1900**	01	**1904**	1101	----	----	--x-	----	x---	1	
Waimangu (Echo Crater)	**1905**	0218	**1905**	0223	----	----	--x-	----	----	1	
Waimangu (Echo Crater)	**1905**	0617	**1905**	0617	----	----	--x-	----	----	1	
Waimangu (NW of Fairy Crater)	**1906**	0221	**1906**	0221	----	----	--x-	----	----	1	
Waimangu (Echo Crater)	**1908**	1001	**1908**	1001	----	----	--x-	----	----	1	
Waimangu (Echo Crater)	**1910**	0724	**1910**	0725	----	----	--x-	----	----	1	
Waimangu (Echo Crater)	**1912**	04	....	....	----	----	--x-	----	----	1	
Waimangu (Echo Crater)	**1913**	0127	**1913**	0127	----	----	--x-	----	----	1	
Waimangu (NW of Fairy Crater)	**1914**	0128	**1914**	02	----	----	--x-	----	----	1	
Waimangu (Echo Crater & NW of Fairy Crater)	**1915**	0204	**1915**	0413	----	----	--x-	----	----	1	
Waimangu (Echo Crater)	**1915**	1105	**1915**	1109	----	----	--x-	----	----	1	
Waimangu (Echo Crater)	**1917**	0324	**1917**	0404	----	----	-?x-	----	xx--	1	
Waimangu (Echo Crater)	**1918**	....	**1920**	....	----	---x	--x-	----	----	1	
Waimangu (Echo Crater)	**1924**	....	....	....	----	---x	--x-	----	----	1	
Rotomahana	**1926**	1117	**1926**	1118	----	---x	--x-	----	----	1	
Rotomahana	**1951**	06	....	....	----	---x	--x-	----	----	1	
Waimangu (Echo Crater)	**1973**	0222	**1973**	0222	---x	---x	--x-	----	----	1	-/3
Waimangu (Raupo Pond, Inferno Crater)	**1978**	0223	**1978**	0223	---x	---x	--x-	----	----	1	
Waimangu (Raupo Pond crater)	**1981**	05	**1981**	05	---x	---x	--x-	----	----	1	
Reporoa (New Zealand) **38.42** S **176.33** E **592** 4456 **RAd** **Caldera** **0401-06-** **Tephrochronology**											
Waiotapu thermal area	T **1180**?	....	....	....	---x	----	--x-	----	----		
Maroa (New Zealand) **38.42** S **176.08** E **1156** 3356 **Rba** **Calderas** **0401-061** **Tephrochronology**											
Orakeikorako	T-**7050**?	....	....	....	---x	----	--x-	----	----		
Orakeikorako	T **0180**?	....	....	....	---x	----	--x-	----	----		
Taupo (New Zealand) **38.82** S **176.00** E **760** 5556 **Rdb** **Caldera** **0401-07=** **Radiocarbon**											
East-central L. Taupo (Karapiti, Unit B)	G-**9460**x	....	....	....	x--x	---x	xx--	?---	----	**5**	-/9
4 km W Te Kohaiakahu Pt. (Poronui, Unit C)	G-**9240**u	....	....	....	x---	---x	x---	?---	----	**5**	-/9
Acacia Bay lava dome (Unit D)	T-**9210**?	....	....	....	x--x	----	x---	--x-	----	4	7/8
Central, E-central L. Taupo (Opepe, Unit E)	G-**8130**x	....	....	....	x---	----	xx--	----	----	**5**	-/9
SE Lake Taupo (Motutaiko Island) (Unit F)	G-**5100**?	....	....	....	x---	---x	x---	--x-	----	3	7/7
East-central Lake Taupo (Unit G)	G-**4700**?	....	....	....	x---	---x	x---	?---	----	4	-/8
4 km WNW of Kohaiakahu Point (Unit H)	G-**4100**?	....	....	....	x---	---x	x---	?---	----	4	-/8
(Unit I)	G-**4000**?	....	....	....	x---	---x	x---	?---	----	3	-/7
(Unit J)	G-**3420**?	....	....	....	x---	---x	x---	?---	----	3	-/7
4 km NW Te Kohaiaikahu Point (Unit K)	G-**3170**x	....	....	....	x---	---x	x---	?---	----	4	-/8
2 km W of Te Kohaiakahu Point (Unit L)	T-**3120**?	....	....	....	x---	---x	x---	?---	----	3	-/7
5 km NW Te Kohaiakahu Point (Unit M)	G-**3070**?	....	....	....	x---	----	x---	?---	----	4	-/8
5 km NW of Te Kohaiakahu Point (Unit N)	G-**2900**?	....	....	....	x---	---x	x---	?---	----	4	-/8
2 km S of Te Tuhi Point (Unit O)	G-**2850**?	....	....	....	x---	----	x---	?---	----	3	-/7
(Unit P)	T-**2800**?	....	....	....	x---	----	x---	?---	----	3	-/7
3 km NW of Te Kohaiakahu Point (Unit Q)	G-**2600**?	....	....	....	x---	----	x---	?---	----	4	-/8
3 km SW of Motutaiko Island (Unit R)	G-**2500**?	....	....	....	x---	---x	x---	----	----	3	-/7
Horomatangi Reefs? (Unit S)	G-**1460**s	....	....	....	x---	----	xx--	----	----	**6**	**-/10**
4 km W of Te Kohaiakahu Point (Unit T)	G-**1250**?	....	....	....	x---	---x	x---	?---	----	3	-/7
5 km NE of Motutaiko Island (Unit U)	G-**1050**?	....	....	....	x---	---x	x---	?---	----	4	-/8
4 km NW Te Kohaiakahu Point (Unit V)	G-**1010**x	....	....	....	x---	---x	x---	?---	----	4+	-/8
Ouaha Hills (Unit W)	T-**0800**?	....	....	....	x---	----	x---	x---	----	2	7/6
4 km NW of Te Kohaiakahu Point (Unit X)	G-**0200**?	....	....	....	x---	---x	x---	?---	----	4+	-/8
Horomatangi Reefs area (Unit Y)	G **0230**n	0315n	....	....	x--x	---x	xx-x	----	--x-	**6?**	**-/10**
East Lake Taupo (Horomatangi Reefs)	T **0260**?	....	....	....	x---	---x	----	--x-	----	0	8/-
Tongariro (New Zealand) **39.13** S **175.642** E **1978** 2345 **Ab** **Stratovolcanoes** **0401-08=** **Historical**											
	G-**9850**?	....	....	....	x---	----	x---	----	----		
Saddle Cone to Half Cone	T-**9650**?	....	....	....	x---	----	x---	----	----	**5**	-/9
Saddle cone area to Half Cone	G-**9450**?	....	....	....	x---	----	xx--	----	--x-	**5**	-/9
Tama Lakes to Te Mari	T-**9350**?	....	....	....	x---	----	xx--	x---	----	**5**	8/9
Ngauruhoe and Red Crater	C-**0550**x	....	....	....	xx--	----	x---	----	----	**5**	-/9
Upper Te Mari Craters	T **1500**t	....	....	....	-x--	----	----	x---	----		
Ngauruhoe	**1839**	02	**1839**	03	x---	----	x---	----	----	1?	
Ngauruhoe	**1841**	....	....	....	x---	----	x---	----	----	2	
Ngauruhoe	**1844**	10	**1845**	01	x---	----	x---	----	----	2	
SSE flank (Red Crater)	**1855**	....	....	....	-x--	----	x---	----	----	2	
Ngauruhoe	**1857**	02	**1857**	03	x---	----	x---	----	----	2	
SSE flank (Red Crater)	**1859**	0421	....	....	-x--	----	--x-	----	----	1?	

VOLCANO NAME (Subregion) / ERUPTION	LAT LONG ELEV (m) POPL ROCK TYPE VOLC TYPE NUMBER STATUS / Area of Activity	Start Year	Start M-Dy	Stop Year	Stop M-Dy	Central, Flank vent, Radial fiss, Regional	Submarine, New island, Subglacial, Crater lake	Explosive, Pyro flow, Phreatic, Caldera	Lava flow, Lava lake, Dome, Spine	Fatal, Damage, Mudflow, Tsunami	VEI	Vol L/T
Tongariro (New Zealand) *continued*	Ngauruhoe	**1862**	01	....	....	x---	----	x---	----	----	2	
	Ngauruhoe	**1863**	....	**1864**	04	x---	----	x---	----	----	2	
	Ngauruhoe	**1864**	12	**1865**	01	x---	----	x---	----	----	2	
	NE flank (Upper Te Mari Crater)	**1869**	....	....	....	-x--	----	x---	----	----	2	
	Ngauruhoe	**1869**	08	....	....	x---	----	x---	----	----	2	
	Ngauruhoe (NW sub-crater)	**1870**	04	**1870**	08	x---	----	x---	x---	----	2	5/-
	Ngauruhoe	? *1875*	*1001* t	....	....	x---	----	?---	----	----	*2*	
	Ngauruhoe (NW sub-crater)	**1878**	0901u	....	....	x---	----	x---	----	----	2	
	Ngauruhoe	**1881**	0706	....	....	x---	----	x---	----	----	2	
	Ngauruhoe (south sub-crater)	**1883**	0425e	....	....	x---	----	x---	----	----	2	
	SSE flank (Red Crater)	**1885**a	....	**1887**	....	-x--	----	--x-	----	----	1	
	NE flank (upper Te Mari Crater)	**1886**	06	....	....	-x--	----	x---	----	----	2	
	SSE flank (Red Crater)	? *1890*	*03*	....	....	-x--	----	--?-	----	----	*1*	
	Ngauruhoe	**1892**	02	**1892**	03	x---	----	x---	----	----	2	
	Ngauruhoe	**1892**	11	**1892**	12	x---	----	x---	----	----	2	
	NE flank (upper Te Mari Crater)	**1892**	1130	....	....	-x--	----	xx--	----	-x--	2	
	NE flank (upper Te Mari Crater)	**1896**	11	**1896**	1226e	-x--	----	x---	----	----	2	
	Ngauruhoe	**1897**	....	....	....	x---	----	x---	----	----	2	
	Ngauruhoe	**1898**	01	....	....	x---	----	x---	----	----	2	
	Ngauruhoe	**1904**	1122	....	....	x---	----	x---	----	----	2	
	Ngauruhoe	**1905**	....	....	....	x---	----	x---	----	----	2	
	Ngauruhoe	**1906**	03	....	....	x---	----	x---	----	----	2	
	Ngauruhoe (south sub-crater)	**1907**	02	**1907**	05	x---	----	x---	----	----	2	
	Ngauruhoe	**1907**	11	....	....	x---	----	x---	----	----	2	
	Ngauruhoe	**1909**	03	**1909**	07	x---	----	x---	----	----	2	
	Ngauruhoe	**1910**	01	....	....	x---	----	x---	----	----	2	
	Ngauruhoe	**1910**	10	**1911**	01	x---	----	x---	----	----	2	
	Ngauruhoe	**1913**	01	....	....	x---	----	x---	----	----	2	
	Ngauruhoe	**1913**	05	....	....	x---	----	x---	----	----	2	
	Ngauruhoe	**1914**	09	**1914**	10	x---	----	x---	----	----	2	
	Ngauruhoe	**1917**	10	**1917**	11	x---	----	x---	----	----	2	
	Ngauruhoe	**1924**	0109	**1924**	0130	x---	----	x---	----	----	2	
	Ngauruhoe	**1924**	0522	....	....	x---	----	x---	----	----	2	
	Ngauruhoe	**1924**	10	**1924**	11	x---	----	x---	----	----	2	
	Ngauruhoe	**1925**	11	**1925**	12	x---	----	x---	----	----	2	
	Ngauruhoe and Red Crater	**1926**	0416	**1926**	06	xx--	----	x---	----	----	2	
	Ngauruhoe	**1926**	1221	**1926**	1230?	x---	----	x---	----	----	2	
	North flank (Ketetahi)	? *1927*	....	....	....	-x--	----	--?-	----	----	*1?*	
	Ngauruhoe	**1928**	0303	....	....	x---	----	x---	----	----	2	
	Ngauruhoe	**1928**	07	....	....	x---	----	x---	----	----	2	
	Ngauruhoe	**1931**	02	**1931**	05	x---	----	x---	----	----	2	
	Ngauruhoe	**1934**	06	....	....	x---	----	x---	----	----	2	
	Ngauruhoe	**1934**	12	**1935**	02	x---	----	x---	----	----	2	
	Ngauruhoe	**1937**	01	....	....	x---	----	x---	----	----	2	
	Ngauruhoe	**1939**	08	....	....	x---	----	x---	----	----	2	
	Ngauruhoe	**1940**	09	**1940**	10	x---	----	x---	----	----	2	
	Ngauruhoe	**1948**	0430	**1948**	05	x---	----	x---	----	----	2	
	Ngauruhoe	**1948**	09	....	....	x---	----	x---	----	----	2	
	Ngauruhoe (south sub-crater)	**1949**	0209	**1949**	0303	x---	----	xx--	x-x-	----	2	5/-
	Ngauruhoe	**1950**	0616	....	....	x---	----	x---	----	----	2	
	Ngauruhoe	**1951**	05	....	....	x---	----	x---	----	----	2	
	Ngauruhoe (south sub-crater)	**1952**	1129	**1953**	07	x---	----	x---	----	----	2	
	Ngauruhoe (south sub-crater)	**1953**	1228<	....	....	x---	----	----	x---	----	0	
	Ngauruhoe (south sub-crater)	**1954**	0513	**1955**	0625	x---	----	xx--	x---	----	3	6/-
	Ngauruhoe (south sub-crater)	**1956**	0111	**1956**	0211	x---	----	x---	----	----	2	
	Ngauruhoe	**1958**	1105	**1958**	1118?	x---	----	x---	----	----	2	
	Ngauruhoe	**1959**	0601	....	....	x---	----	x---	----	----	2	
	Ngauruhoe	**1962**	0524	....	....	x---	----	x---	----	----	2	
	Ngauruhoe	**1968**	0818	....	....	x---	----	x---	----	----	2	
	Ngauruhoe	**1969**	0121	....	....	x---	----	x---	----	----	2	
	Ngauruhoe	**1972**	0319	**1972**	0606	x---	----	x-x-	----	----	2	
	Ngauruhoe	**1972**	1122	**1974**	0819	x---	----	xx--	----	----	3*	
	Ngauruhoe	**1975**	0212	**1975**	0223	x---	----	xx--	----	--x-	3	-/6
	Ngauruhoe	**1976**	0823	**1976**	0828	x---	----	x---	----	----	1	
	Ngauruhoe	**1977**	0704	**1977**	0704	x---	----	x---	----	----	1	
Ruapehu (New Zealand)	**39.28 S 175.57 E 2797** 2346 **Adb Stratovolcano 0401-10= Historical**											
	(UT1 tephra)	G-**9850**?	....	....	....	x---	----	x---	----	----		
	(UT2 tephra)	T-**9650**?	....	....	....	x---	----	x---	----	----		
	Upper north flank (Pinnacle Ridge)	C-**7840**<	....	....	....	-x--	----	x---	----	----	4	-/8
	North flank (Whakapapanui Gorge area)	C-**7590**v	....	....	....	-x--	----	?--A	--x-	----		
	NE flank (Whakapapa)	T-**5550***	....	....	....	-x--	----	x---	x---	----		
	(Tf5 tephra layer)	C **1210**w	....	....	....	x---	---x	x---	----	----	3	-/7
		1861	0213	**1861**	0516>	x---	----	x-?-	--x-	-xx-	2	
		1889	0501	....	....	x---	---x	--x-	----	--x-	2	
		1895	0310	**1895**	0314>	x---	---x	x-x-	----	--x-	2	
		1903	....	....	....	x---	---x	x-x-	----	--x-	2	
		1906	0315	....	....	x---	---x	x-x-	----	----	2	
		1918	0629	....	....	x---	---x	--x-	----	----	2	
		1921	10	....	....	x---	---x	--x-	----	----	2	
		1925	0122	....	....	x---	---x	--x-	----	-xx-	2	
		1934	0811	....	....	x---	---x	--x-	----	----	2	
		1934	12	**1935**	02	x---	---x	--x-	----	----	2	
		1936	0509?	**1936**	0513	x---	---x	x-x-	----	----	2	
		1940	04	....	....	x---	---x	--x-	----	----	2	
		1942	0810	....	....	x---	---x	--x-	----	----	2	
		1944	10	....	....	x---	---x	--x-	----	----	2	
		1945	0308	**1945**	12	x---	---x	x-x-	--x-	----	3*	7/-
		1946	04	**1946**	06	x---	---x	x-x-	----	----	2	
		1946	1121	**1947**	0531	x---	---x	x-x-	----	----	1	
		1948	0501	....	....	x---	---x	--x-	----	----	1	
		1950	0626	**1950**	0626	x---	---x	--x-	----	----	1	
		1951	0319	....	....	x---	---x	--x-	----	----	1	
		1952	07	....	....	x---	---x	--x-	----	----	1	
		1956	1118	**1956**	1118	x---	---x	--x-	----	----	1	
		1959	0521	**1959**	0831	x---	---x	?-x-	----	----	1	

Katia and Maurice Krafft

Blue Lake Crater, Red Crater, and conical Ngauruhoe. Ruapehu volcano in background.

VOLCANO NAME (Subregion) / ERUPTION — Area of Activity	LAT	LONG	ELEV (m)	POPL (5 km, 10, 30, 100)	ROCK TYPE	VOLC TYPE / Start Year	NUMBER / Start M-Dy	STATUS / Stop Year	Stop M-Dy	Central, Flank vent, Radial fiss, Regional	Submarine, New island, Subglacial, Crater lake	Explosive, Pyro flow, Phreatic, Caldera	Lava flow, Lava lake, Dome, Spine	Fatal, Damage, Mudflow, Tsunami	VEI	Vol L/T
Ruapehu (New Zealand) *continued*						1966	0404	1966	0927	x---	---x	x-x-	x---	----	1	
						1967	0722	1967	1004?	x---	---x	?-x-	----	----	1	
						1968	0406	1968	0610	x---	---x	--x-	----	--x-	2*	
						1969	0622	1969	0623	x---	---x	xxx-	----	-xx-	2	
						1970	0916	1970	0917	x---	---x	x---	----	----	1	
						1971	0403	1971	1101	x---	---x	x-x-	----	--x-	2*	-/6
						1972	1022	1973	0110	x---	---x	--x-	----	----	1	
						1973	1031	1974	1025	x---	---x	--x-	----	----	1	
						1975	0424	1975	0427	x---	---x	xxx-	----	-xx-	2	
						1975	1017<	1975	1017<	x---	---x	--x-	----	----	1	
						1976	0306	1976	0306	x---	---x	--x-	----	----	1	
						1976	0912<	1976	1122?	x---	---x	x-x-	----	----	1	
						1977	0716	1979	0117	x---	---x	xx--	----	--x-	2*	-/5
						1979	0630	1979	0715	x---	---x	--x-	----	----	1	
						1980	0115?	1980	0327?	x---	---x	x-x-	----	----	1	
						1980	1018	1980	1103	x---	---x	x-x-	----	----	1	
						1981	1025?	1982	0412c	x---	---x	x-x-	----	----	1	
						1984	0402	....	....	x---	---x	--x-	----	----	1	
						1984	1025?	1984	12	x---	---x	--x-	----	----	1	
						1985	0521<	1985	0609?	x---	---x	--x-	----	----	1	
						1985	1115	1985	1115	x---	---x	--x-	----	----	1	
						1986	0208	1986	0209?	x---	---x	--x-	----	----	1	
						1987	0824	1987	0830	x---	---x	--x-	----	----	1	
						1988	0320	1988	0525c	x---	---x	--x-	----	----	1	
						1988	1208	1989	0305?	x---	---x	x-x-	----	--x-	1	
						1989	0701	1989	0920?	x---	---x	--x-	----	----	1	
						1990	0107	1990	0126	x---	---x	--x-	----	----	1	
						1990	0617	?1990	0908<	x---	---x	--x-	----	----	0	
						1991	0705?	1991	0714?	x---	---x	x-x-	----	----	1	
						1992	0208	1992	0306	x---	---x	--x-	----	----	1	
						? 1994	0212	?1994	0401	x---	---x	--?-	----	----	1	
						1995	0111?	1995	1109	x---	---x	xxx-	--?-	-xx-	3*	-/7
						? 1996	0321<	....	....	x---	---x	----	?---	----	0	
						1996	0616	1996	0901	x---	---x	x-x-	----	--x-	3*	-/6
						1997	1009	1997	1018	x---	---x	--x-	----	----	1	
						2006	1004	2006	1004	x---	---x	--x-	----	----	1	
						2007	0925	2007	0925	x---	---x	x-x-	----	-xx-	1?	
Clark (New Zealand)	36.446 S	177.839 E	-860	0000	BD	Submarine volc	0401-101	Fumarolic								
Tangaroa (New Zealand)	36.321 S	178.028 E	600	0000	BA	Submarine volc	0401-102	Fumarolic								
Rumble V (New Zealand)	36.142 S	178.196 E	400	0000	A	Submarine volc	0401-11-	Fumarolic								
Rumble IV (New Zealand)	36.13 S	178.05 E	500	0000	A	Submarine volc	0401-12-	Fumarolic								
(Rumble III activity, not Rumble IV)						X 1966	04	X1966	12 >	----	----	----	----	----		
Rumble III (New Zealand)	35.745 S	178.478 E	-220	0000	AB	Submarine volc	0401-13-	Historical								
						S 1958	0709	S1962	....	----	x---	----	----	----	0	
						S 1963	01	S1966	12 >	----	x---	----	----	----	0	
						S 1970	....	....	....	----	x---	----	----	----	0	
						S 1973	1015	S1973	1017	----	x---	----	----	----	0	
						S 1986	0615	S1986	0805?	----	x---	----	----	----	0	
						2008a	....	....	....	----	x---	----	----	----	0	
Rumble II West (New Zealand)	35.353 S	178.527 E	1200	0000	ABd	Submarine volc	0401-131	Fumarolic								
Healy (New Zealand)	35.004 S	178.973 E	980	0000	Drb	Submarine volc	0401-14-	Radiocarbon								
Healy caldera						G 1360u	....	....	....	x---	x---	x--x	----	----		
Brothers (New Zealand)	34.875 S	179.075 E	-1350	0000	Db	Submarine volc	0401-15-	Fumarolic								

Steaming Crater Lake at summit of Ruapehu in 1986

Tom Simkin (Smithsonian)

KERMADECS

VOLCANO NAME (Subregion) / ERUPTION — Area of Activity	LAT	LONG	ELEV (m)	POPL	ROCK TYPE	VOLC TYPE / Start Year	NUMBER / Start M-Dy	STATUS / Stop Year	Stop M-Dy	Central, Flank vent, Radial fiss, Regional	Submarine, New island, Subglacial, Crater lake	Explosive, Pyro flow, Phreatic, Caldera	Lava flow, Lava lake, Dome, Spine	Fatal, Damage, Mudflow, Tsunami	VEI	Vol L/T
Volcano W (Kermadec Is)	31.85 S	179.18 W	-900	0000	B	Submarine volcs	0402-001	Fumarolic								
Curtis Island (Kermadec Is)	30.542 S	178.561 W	137	0000	ADR	Submarine volc	0402-01=	Uncertain								
(steaming not caused by an eruption)						X 1899	....	....	....	----	----	----	----	----		
						? 1936	0618	?1936	12	----	?---	----	----	----		
5-6 km NNE of Curtis Island						? 2009	0118	?2009	0119	----	?---	----	----	----	0	
Brimstone Island (Kermadec Is)	30.23 S	178.92 W	-2000				0402-02=	Not a Volcano								
Macauley Island (Kermadec Is)	30.20 S	178.47 W	238	0000	BRda	Caldera	0402-021	Radiocarbon								
(Sandy Bay Tuff)						C -4360x	....	....	....	-x--	x---	xx-x	----	----	6?	-/10
"Brimstone Island," W of Macauley Island						? 1825	0906	....	....	----	?---	----	----	----	0	
22 km NNE of Macauley Island						? 1887	1201	....	....	----	?---	----	----	----	0	
Giggenbach (Kermadec Is)	30.036 S	178.712 W	-65	0000	BDA	Submarine volc	0402-022	Fumarolic								
Raoul Island (Kermadec Is)	29.27 S	177.92 W	516	0000	ADB	Stratovolcano	0402-03=	Historical								
SE Raoul caldera (Matatirohia tephra)						C -2000v	....	....	....	x---	----	xx-x	----	----	4	-/8
SW part of Raoul caldera (Oneraki tephra)						C -1200w	....	....	....	x---	----	xx--	----	----	4	-/8
Denham caldera (Fleetwood tephra)						C -0250u	....	....	....	x---	x---	xx-x	----	----	6	-/10
Denham caldera? (Bell tephra)						T -0050?	....	....	....	----	?---	x---	----	----	3?	-/7
N flank Moumoukai volcano (Judith tephra)						T 0100?	....	....	....	-x--	----	xx--	----	----	4	-/8
S part Raoul Caldera (Raynor tephra)						T 0400?	....	....	....	x---	----	x---	----	----	4	-/8
Green Lake Pumice Crater						C 0550?	....	....	....	x---	----	x--x	----	----	4	-/8
Pukekohu Crater						T 0700?	....	....	....	x---	----	--x-	----	----	3	-/7
Expedition Crater						T 0850?	....	....	....	x---	----	--x-	----	----	4	-/8
NE of Raoul Island (Meyer Islands)						T 1450?	....	....	....	-x--	----	x---	----	----		
Rangitahua Crater						C 1630t	....	....	....	x---	----	x-x-	----	----	4	-/8
Denham Bay?, Tui Lake Crater						C 1720t	....	....	....	x---	x---	x---	----	----	4	-/8
Denham caldera and Smith Crater						1814	0309	....	....	x---	xx--	x-x-	----	----	3	-/7
Denham caldera, Green Lake						1870	0620d	1870	1003	x---	xx--	x-x-	----	----	3	-/7
(post-1870 eruption unsubstantiated)						X 1872	0201r	....	....	----	----	----	----	----		
NNE flank (7.5 km from Raoul Island)						1886	03	....	....	-x--	x---	x---	----	----	0	
West side of Green Lake, Denham caldera						1964	1119	1965	0425?	---x	x---	xxx-	----	----	2*	
NNE flank (7 km from Raoul Island)						? 1987	0325	?1987	0325	-x--	?---	----	----	----	0	
Green Lake crater						2006	0317	2006	0317	x---	---x	x-x-	----	x---	1?	
Monowai Seamount (Kermadec Is)	25.887 S	177.188 W	-132	0000	B	Submarine volc	0402-05-	Historical								
						? 1944	....	....	....	----	?---	----	----	----	0	
						S 1977	04	S1977	04	----	x---	----	----	----	0	
						1977	1017	1977	1027?	----	x---	x---	----	----	0	
						S 1978	02	S1978	07	----	x---	x---	----	----	0	

VOLCANO NAME (Subregion) / ERUPTION — Area of Activity	LAT	LONG	ELEV (m)	POPL (5 km, 10, 30, 100)	ROCK TYPE	VOLC TYPE / Start Year	NUMBER / Start M-Dy	STATUS / Stop Year	Stop M-Dy	Central vent, Flank vent, Radial fiss, Regional	Submarine, New island, Subglacial, Crater lake	Explosive, Pyro flow, Phreatic, Caldera	Lava flow, Lava lake, Dome, Spine	Fatal, Damage, Mudflow, Tsunami	VEI	Vol L/T
Monowai Seamount (Kermadec Is) *continued*						S **1979**	02 ?	S**1979**	0419?	----	x---	x---	----	----		
						S **1980**	01	S**1980**	01	----	x---	----	----	----	0	
						S **1982**	05	S**1982**	05	----	x---	----	----	----	0	
						S **1986**	06	S**1986**	06	----	x---	----	----	----	0	
						S **1988**	0908	S**1988**	0908	----	x---	----	x---	----	0	
						S **1990**	0530	S**1991**	0325	----	x---	x---	----	----	0	
						S **1995**	1127	S**1995**	1130	----	x---	x---	----	----	0	
						S **1996**	0920	S**1996**	0922	----	x---	x---	----	----	0	
						S **1997**	0418	S**1997**	0421	----	x---	x---	----	----	0	
						S **1997**	1215	S**1998**	0204?	----	x---	x---	----	----	0	
						S **1999**	0606	S**1999**	0611	----	x---	x---	----	----	0	
						S **2002**	0524	S**2002**	0524	----	x---	x---	----	----	0	
						S **2002**	1101	S**2002**	1124	----	x---	x---	----	----	0	
						S **2003**	0410	S**2004**	09	----	x---	x---	----	----	0	
						S **2005**	0302	S**2006**	0627	----	x---	x---	----	----	0	
						S **2006**	1212	S**2006**	1231?	----	x---	x---	----	----	0	
						S **2008**	0208?	....	....	----	x---	----	----	----	0	

TONGA

VOLCANO NAME (Subregion) / ERUPTION — Area of Activity	LAT	LONG	ELEV (m)	POPL	ROCK TYPE	VOLC TYPE / Start Year	NUMBER / Start M-Dy	STATUS / Stop Year	Stop M-Dy	Central vent, Flank vent, Radial fiss, Regional	Submarine, New island, Subglacial, Crater lake	Explosive, Pyro flow, Phreatic, Caldera	Lava flow, Lava lake, Dome, Spine	Fatal, Damage, Mudflow, Tsunami	VEI	Vol L/T
Unnamed (Tonga-SW Pacific)	**24.80 S**	**177.02 W**	**-385**	0000	**BA**	**Submarine volc**	**0403-001**	**Fumarolic**								
Unnamed (Tonga-SW Pacific)	**21.38 S**	**175.65 W**	**-500**	0005	**U**	**Submarine volc**	**0403-01=**	**Historical**								
						1907	07	....	....	----	x---	----	----	----	0	
						1932	1201p	....	....	----	x---	----	----	----	0	
Unnamed (Tonga-SW Pacific)	**21.15 S**	**175.75 W**	**-65**	0005	**A**	**Submarine volc**	**0403-011**	**Holocene**								
Unnamed (Tonga-SW Pacific)	21.07 S	175.33 W					0403-02=	Not a Volcano								
(date of depth sounding, not eruption)						*X 1943*	....	....	....	----	----	----	----	----		
Unnamed (Tonga-SW Pacific)	**20.85 S**	**175.53 W**	**-13**	0005	**U**	**Submarine volc**	**0403-03=**	**Historical**								
						1911	08	....	....	----	x---	----	----	----	0	
						1923	0701	....	....	----	x---	----	----	----	0	
						1999	0108<	**1999**	0114?	x---	xx--	x---	x---	----	1	
Hunga Tonga-Hunga Ha'apai	**20.57 S**	**175.38 W**	**149**	3335	**A**	**Submarine volc**	**0403-04=**	**Historical**								
						1912	0429	....	....	----	x---	x---	----	----	2	
						1937	....	....	....	----	x---	x---	----	----	2	
1 km SSE of Hunga Ha'apai						**1988**	0601	**1988**	0603>	----	x---	x---	----	----	0	
Hunga Ha'apai						**2009**	0317?	**2009**	0322a	----	xx--	xx--	----	----	2	
Falcon Island (Tonga-SW Pacific)	**20.32 S**	**175.42 W**	**-17**	3335	**AD**	**Submarine volc**	**0403-05=**	**Historical**								
						? *1781*	....	....	....	----	?---	----	----	----	*0*	
						? *1865*	....	....	....	----	?---	----	----	----	*0*	
						1877	....	....	....	----	x---	x---	----	----	2	
						1885	1012?	**1886**	....	---x	xx--	x---	----	----	3	-/8
						? *1894*	*12*	....	....	----	??--	?---	----	----	*0?*	
						? *1921*	*11*	....	....	----	??--	?---	----	----	*0?*	
						1927	1004	**1928**	09 >	x---	xx--	x---	----	----	2	-/7
						1933	04	....	....	----	----	x---	----	----	2	
						1936	06	....	....	x---	----	x---	----	----	2	
						? *1970*	*0103*	....	....	----	?---	----	----	----	*0*	
Tofua (Tonga-SW Pacific)	**19.75 S**	**175.07 W**	**515**	4444	**AD**	**Caldera**	**0403-06=**	**Historical**								
						1774	06	....	....	x---	----	x---	----	----	2	
						1792	....	....	....	x---	----	----	x---	----	0	
						1854	....	....	....	x---	----	x---	----	----	2	
						1885	10 <	....	....	x---	----	x---	----	----	2	
Northern part of caldera						**1906**	01	**1906**	02	xx--	----	x---	x---	----	2	
Northern part of caldera						**1906**	12	....	....	xx--	----	x---	x---	----	2	
Northern part of caldera						**1958**	1231u	**1960**?	....	x---	----	x---	?---	----	2	
Northern part of caldera						? *1993*	*0429*	....	....	x---	----	----	----	----	*0*	
						? *2004*	*0319*	?*2004*	*0529*	x---	----	----	-?--	----	*1?*	
Lofia crater						**2004**	10	....	....	x---	----	x---	----	----	1	
Lofia crater						**2006**	05	**2006**	06	x---	----	----	-x--	----	0	
Lofia crater						? *2008*	*0307*	?*2008*	*1121*	x---	----	----	-?--	----	*1?*	
Lofia crater						**2009**	03	**2009**	03	x---	----	x---	----	----	1	
Kao (Tonga-SW Pacific)	**19.67 S**	**175.03 W**	**1030**	3444	**A**	**Stratovolcano**	**0403-061**	**Holocene**								
Metis Shoal (Tonga-SW Pacific)	**19.18 S**	**174.87 W**	**43**	2224	**D**	**Submarine volc**	**0403-07=**	**Historical**								
						1781<	....	....	....	----	xx--	----	----	----	2?	
						1851	....	....	....	----	x---	?---	----	----	0	
						? *1852*	....	....	....	----	?---	----	----	----	*0*	
						1858	....	....	....	----	xx--	x---	----	----	2	
						1878	04 <	....	....	----	xx--	x---	----	----	2	
						1886	....	....	....	----	??--	x---	----	----	2	
						? *1894*<	....	....	....	----	??--	----	----	----	*2*	
						1967	1211<	**1968**	0104d	----	xx--	x-x-	----	----	2	
						1979	0510<	**1979**	0721>	----	xx--	x---	----	----	2	
						1991	0624<	....	....	----	x---	x---	----	----	0	
						1995	0606	**1995**	0623b	----	xx--	x---	--x-	----	2	6/-
Home Reef (Tonga-SW Pacific)	**18.992 S**	**174.775 W**	**-10**	0035	**D**	**Submarine volc**	**0403-08=**	**Historical**								
						1852	....	....	....	----	xx--	x---	----	----	2	
						? *1857*	....	....	....	----	??--	----	----	----	*2*	
						1984	0301	**1984**	0305	----	xx--	x---	----	----	3?	
						2006	0807	**2006**	0816?	----	xx--	x---	----	----	2?	
Late (Tonga-SW Pacific)	**18.806 S**	**174.65 W**	**540**	3335	**A**	**Stratovolcano**	**0403-09=**	**Historical**								
NE flank?						**1790**	....	....	....	-x--	----	x---	?---	----	2	
NE flank						**1854**	....	....	....	-x--	----	x---	?---	----	2	
Unnamed (Tonga-SW Pacific)	**18.325 S**	**174.365 W**	**-40**	0025	**D**	**Submarine volc**	**0403-091**	**Historical**								
						2001	0927	**2001**	0928?	----	x---	x---	----	----	2	
Fonualei (Tonga-SW Pacific)	**18.02 S**	**174.325 W**	**180**	2225	**DA**	**Stratovolcano**	**0403-10=**	**Historical**								
						? *1780*<	....	....	....	x---	----	?---	----	----		
						1791	....	....	....	x---	----	x---	----	----	2	
(major eruption in 1846, not 1847)						**1846**	0611?	**1846**	1010>	x---	----	x---	x---	-x--	4?	7/8
						1906	03	....	....	x---	----	----	----	----		
Summit, west and SE sides						**1939**	06	....	....	xx--	?---	x---	x---	----	2	
North-central part of the island						**1951**	0821	....	....	x---	----	x---	x---	----	2	
						1957	06	....	....	----	----	----	----	----		
						? *1974*	*0216*	....	....	x---	----	--?-	----	----	*1*	

VOLCANO NAME (Subregion) / ERUPTION — Area of Activity	LAT	LONG	ELEV (m)	POPL (5 km, 10, 30, 100)	ROCK TYPE	VOLC TYPE	NUMBER	STATUS	Start Year	Start M-Dy	Stop Year	Stop M-Dy	Central / Flank vent / Radial fiss / Regional	Submarine / New island / Subglacial / Crater lake	Explosive / Pyro flow / Phreatic / Caldera	Lava flow / Lava lake / Dome / Spine	Fatal / Damage / Mudflow / Tsunami	VEI	Vol L/T
Tafahi (Tonga-SW Pacific)	**15.85** S	**173.72** W	**560**	2244	AB	**Stratovolcano**	**0403-101**	Holocene?											
Curacoa (Tonga-SW Pacific)	**15.62** S	**173.67** W	**-33**	0024	D	**Submarine volc**	**0403-102**	**Historical**											
6.4 km SW of Curacoa Reef									**1973**	0711	**1973**	0716	----	x---	x---	----	----	3	
13 km north of Tafahi									**1979**	0514	....	....	----	x---	----	----	----	1	
Niuafo'ou (Tonga-SW Pacific)	**15.60** S	**175.63** W	**260**	3333	B	**Shield volcano**	**0403-11=**	**Historical**											
South end of caldera ?									**1814**	....	....	....	x---	---x	x-x-	x---	-x--	2	
(probably confused with 1853 erupt.)									*X 1840*	....	....	....	----	----	----	?---	----		
SW caldera rim (Ahau village area)									**1853**	0624	**1853**	0624?	-x--	----	----	x---	xx--	0	
SSW flank									**1867**	0412	....	....	-x--	----	x---	x---	-x--	1	
NE side of caldera									**1886**	0831	**1886**	0918?	x---	---x	x-x-	----	-xx-	4?	-/8
									1887	....	....	....	----	----	x---	----	----	2	
West side, near Alele 'Uta village									**1912**	1015e	....	....	-x--	----	x---	x---	-x--	2	
West flank									**1929**	0725	**1929**	0726	-x--	----	x---	x---	-x--	2	
South flank									**1935**	1207	**1936**	02 ?	-x--	----	x-x-	x---	-x--	2	
SW flank									**1943**	0926	**1943**	1016p	-x--	----	x-x-	x---	-x--	2	
North flank									**1946**	0909	**1946**	0917	-x--	----	x---	x---	-x--	2	
									? 1947	*01*	....	....	----	----	----	----	----		
									? 1959	....	....	....	----	----	----	----	----		
NE part of caldera lake (Vai Lahi)									**1985**	0321	**1985**	0322	x---	---x	x---	----	----	0	-/2
Tafu-Maka (Tonga-SW Pacific)	**15.37** S	**174.23** W	**-1400**	0004	B	**Submarine volc**	**0403-12-**	**Historical**											
Maka									**2008**	11 ?	**2008**	11 ?	----	x---	----	x---	----	0	
West Mata (Tonga-SW Pacific)	**15.10** S	**173.75** W	**-1174**	0004	A	**Submarine volc**	**0403-13-**	**Historical**											
Prometheus and Hades vents									**2008**	11 <	**2009**	05 >	----	x---	x---	x---	----	0	
SAMOA & W																			
Vailulu'u (American Samoa)	**14.215** S	**169.058** W	**-592**	0004	B	**Submarine volc**	**0404-00-**	**Historical**											
									S **1973**	0710	S**1973**	0710	----	x---	----	----	----	0	
									S **1995**	0109	S**1995**	0129	x---	x---	----	x---	----	0	
West side of caldera (Nafanua)									**2003**b	04	....	....	x---	x---	----	x---	----	0	
Ta'u (American Samoa)	**14.23** S	**169.454** W	**931**	2444	BX	**Shield volcano**	**0404-001**	**Holocene**											
Ofu-Olosega (American Samoa)	**14.175** S	**169.618** W	**639**	3344	BX	**Shield volcanoes**	**0404-01=**	**Historical**											
Submarine vent 3 km SE of Olosega									**1866**	0912	**1866**	1115e	---x	x---	x---	----	----	2	
Tutuila (American Samoa)	**14.295** S	**170.70** W	**653**	5555	BAT	**Tuff cones**	**0404-02-**	**Holocene**											
Upolu (Samoa)	**13.935** S	**171.72** W	**1100**	3566	Bayt	**Shield volcano**	**0404-03-**	**Holocene**											
Savai'i (Samoa)	**13.612** S	**172.525** W	**1858**	0256	B	**Shield volcano**	**0404-04=**	**Historical**											
North flank (Maugaloa)									G-**1990**w	....	....	....	-x--	----	x---	x---	----		
									G-**1150**w	....	....	....	-x--	----	----	x---	----		
									G-**0480**y	....	....	....	----	----	x---	?---	----		
									G **0170**v	....	....	....	-?--	----	----	x---	----		
									G **1040**w	....	....	....	-?--	----	----	x---	----		
									G **1240**r	....	....	....	x---	----	----	x---	----		
									G **1310**t	....	....	....	----	----	x---	x---	----		
Tafua Savai'i?									G **1350**t	....	....	....	-x--	----	x---	x---	----		
Le'ele									G **1610**x	....	....	....	-x--	----	x---	----	----		
Mauga Afi (west-central Toasivi ridge)									**1760**	....	....	....	x-x-	----	x---	x---	-x--	2	**9**/-
Mata Ole Afi (1649 m)									**1902**	1030	**1902**	1117d	x-x-	----	x---	x---	----	1	
Matavanu (north flank 402 m)									**1905**	0804	**1911**	11	-xx-	----	x---	xx--	-x-x	2	**9**/6
Wallis Islands (W of Samoa)	**13.30** S	**176.17** W	**143**	4555	BX	**Shield volcanoes**	**0404-05-**	**Holocene**											
FIJI																			
Taveuni (Fiji Is-SW Pacific)	**16.82** S	**179.97** W	**1241**	3456	Bxy	**Shield volcano**	**0405-01-**	**Radiocarbon**											
									G-**8040**t	....	....	....	---x	----	x---	x---	----	2	
									G-**6560**u	....	....	....	---x	----	x---	----	----	2	
									G-**5920**u	....	....	....	---x	----	x---	x---	----	2	
									G-**5230**v	....	....	....	---x	----	x---	----	----	2	
									G-**4800**v	....	....	....	---x	----	x---	x---	----	2	
									G-**3580**x	....	....	....	---x	----	x---	----	----	2	
									G-**3200**w	....	....	....	---x	----	x---	----	----	2	
									T-**1700**?	....	....	....	---x	----	x---	x---	----	2	
									T-**1450**?	....	....	....	---x	----	x---	x---	----	2	
									T-**1300**?	....	....	....	---x	----	x---	----	----	2	
									T-**1200**?	....	....	....	---x	----	x---	----	----	2	
									T-**1100**?	....	....	....	---x	----	x---	----	----	2	
									T-**1020**?	....	....	....	---x	----	x---	----	----	2	
									T-**0680**?	....	....	....	---x	----	x---	x---	----	2	
									T-**0600**?	....	....	....	---x	----	x---	x---	----	2	
									G-**0400**p	....	....	....	---x	----	x---	----	----	2	
									G-**0330**u	....	....	....	---x	----	x---	x---	----	2	
									T-**0200**?	....	....	....	---x	----	x---	x---	----	2	
									G-**0090**x	....	....	....	---x	----	x---	x---	-x--	2	
									G **0220**v	....	....	....	---x	----	----	x---	----	0	
Central Taveuni (west of Lake Tagimoucea)									T **0270**?	....	....	....	---x	----	x---	x---	-x--	1	
									G **0320**v	....	....	....	---x	----	x---	x---	----	2	
Central Taveuni (Des Voeux Peak area)									T **0350**?	....	....	....	---x	----	x---	----	----	2	
									G **0400**t	....	....	....	---x	----	x---	x---	----	2	
Central Taveuni (Tagimoucea area)									G **0480**u	....	....	....	---x	----	x---	x---	----	2	
South Taveuni (Tavuyaga, Ngatutu, Ngatavo)									G **0520**v	....	....	....	---x	----	x---	x---	-x--	2	
									G **0640**s	....	....	....	---x	----	x---	x---	----	2	
									T **0770**?	....	....	....	---x	----	x---	x---	----	2	
									T **0880**?	....	....	....	---x	----	x---	x---	----	2	
									T **1020**?	....	....	....	---x	----	x---	x---	----	2	
Southern Taveuni (Vana Kei Vuna)									G **1160**w	....	....	....	---x	----	x---	x---	-x--	2	
									T **1350**u	....	....	....	---x	----	x---	----	----	2	
Central Taveuni (Tutu area)									G **1420**p	....	....	....	---x	----	----	x---	-x--	0	
Near South Cape									G **1550**v	....	....	....	---x	----	----	x---	----	0	
Koro (Fiji Is-SW Pacific)	**17.32** S	**179.40** E	**522**	3446	B	**Cinder cones**	**0405-02-**	Holocene?											
Nabukelevu (Fiji Is-SW Pacific)	**19.12** S	**177.98** E	**805**	3445	AD	**Lava domes**	**0405-03-**	**Radiocarbon**											
Summit lava dome									G-**0580**y	....	....	....	x---	----	-?--	--x-	----		
West side of summit dome complex									G **0340**?	....	....	....	x---	----	xx--	----	----		
Dome NW of summit									G **1660**r	....	....	....	x---	----	xx-A	--x-	----		

Melanesia & Australia (05)

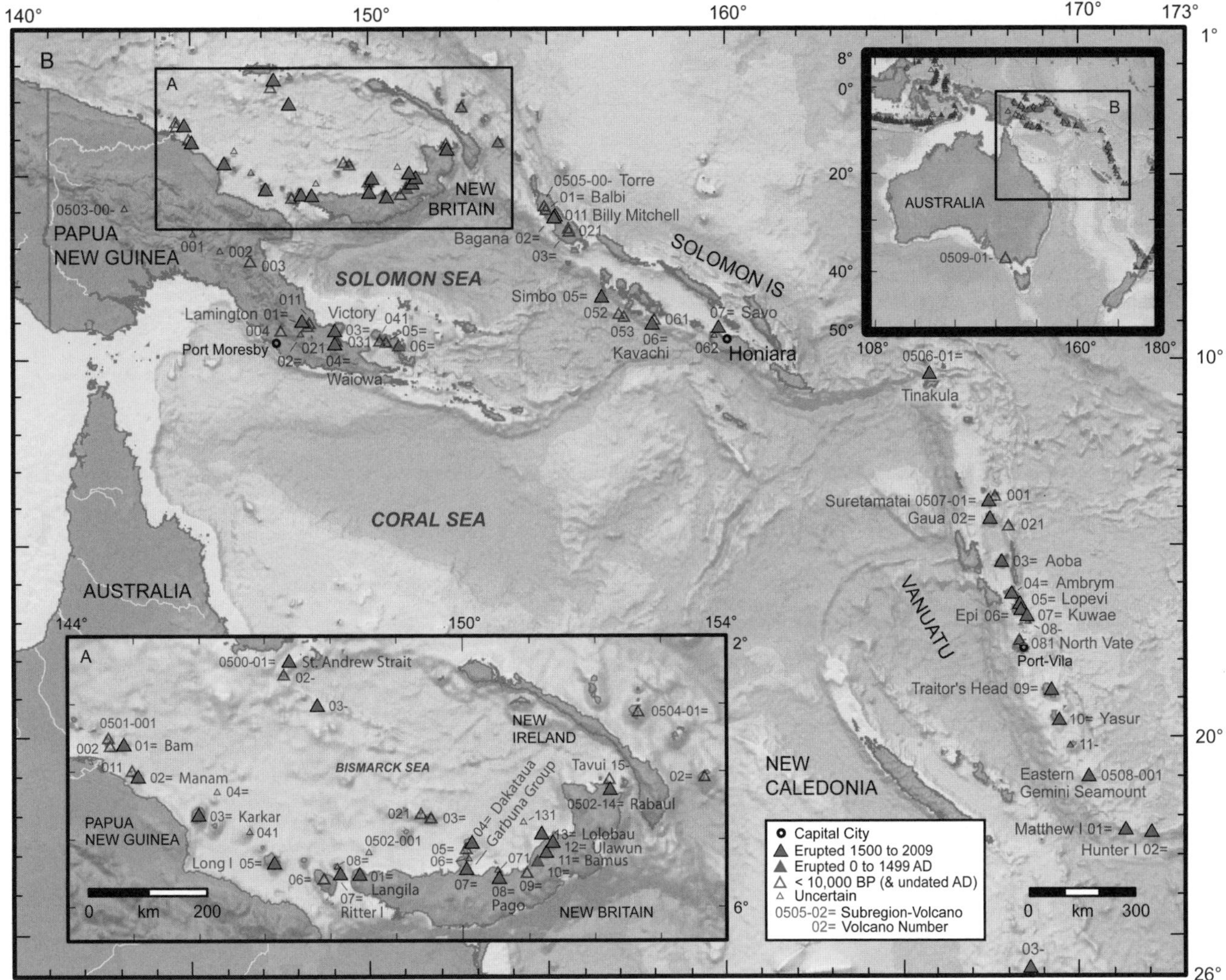

The islands of Melanesia have been inhabited for at least 3,000 years, but the first western contact was with sailors from Spain and Portugal who landed on New Guinea around 1526 AD. The Solomon Islands were discovered by westerners in 1568, when the region's first historical eruption was recorded on Savo. The New Hebrides (now Vanuatu) were discovered by Spaniards in 1606, a year after the Dutch sighted northernmost Australia. But it was not until Cook's historic voyage of 1770 that Australia's east coast was discovered, and its substantial settling did not begin until 1788. In 1884, Germany took possession of the northern part of New Guinea, and 3 days later Britain declared the southern section a protectorate, followed by outright annexation in 1888. The region's combined land area equals that of California, but many areas are sparsely settled and its population is only slightly greater than that of the cities of Los Angeles and San Diego.

In 1906 this British territory was transferred to newly independent Australia, which also took control of the northern portion of New Guinea during World War I (WW-I). With the exception of Japanese occupation in 1942-45, this situation prevailed until self-government was declared in 1973; full independence came to Papua New Guinea (PNG) two years later. The Solomon Islands had only sporadic contact with the west until Britain established a protectorate in the 1890s; the islands gained independence in 1978. Captain Cook extensively explored the southern islands in 1774, naming them the New Hebrides. Both France and Britain formed trading posts and missions in the last century, formalizing an Anglo-French Condominium in 1906, but the islands remained isolated despite considerable attention during WW-II. The Republic of Vanuatu was declared in 1980.

South of New Britain lies an oceanic trench that parallels its arcuate coast. Nearing the Solomons, the trench swings SE'ly, then down along the Vanuatu chain before turning east again and ending below Hunter Island. This trench system marks the subduction of oceanic crust–the Solomon and Coral Seas–moving N, NE, and E under the volcanic islands formed by this process. Tectonic complications in the form of two short oceanic spreading centers affect nearby volcanoes: One extends from SE New Guinea eastward to Kavachi, and the other runs broadly east-west below the Admiralty Islands at the north end of the region.

Of all historically documented eruptions now known from Melanesia, three-fourths have been recorded in the past century. Melanesia almost matches the Atlantic Ocean as the region with the highest proportion of its eruptions being submarine, and it has nearly a quarter of the world's documented island-building eruptions, many of these from Kavachi volcano. It also matches Indonesia as the region with the highest number of tsunami-producing eruptions; a tsunami accompanying the collapse of Ritter Island volcano in 1888 swept the coasts of Papua New Guinea and New Britain, causing about 700 fatalities. The explosive character of volcanism in this caldera-rich region places Melanesia at the top of the list of documented Holocene caldera-forming eruptions.

One of these calderas formed the magnificent natural harbor of Rabaul during a major eruption and collapse in the 6th century. Rabaul was the capital of PNG from 1910 through 1941, and site of a 1937 eruption that killed 441 people. This event led to the founding, in the same year, of one of the world's pre-eminent volcano centers, the Rabaul Volcanological Observatory (RVO), operated by the Geological Survey of Papua New Guinea. RVO covers all the volcanoes of PNG, and its work has been particularly valuable in major eruptions such as Lamington in 1951, only a year after RVO resumed operations following WW-II. A major eruption in 1994 destroyed much of Rabaul town and prompted moving the capital city of the province of East New Britain to Kokopo, 20 km away.

Australia overwhelms the island nations of the Melanesia region in size, but we list only one Holocene volcano. This "volcano" is actually one of Earth's largest volcanic fields, called the Newer Volcanics Province, which covers a broad 15,000 km² area of SE Australia with nearly 400 small shield volcanoes and explosive vents of Tertiary-to-Holocene age.

VOLCANO NAME (Subregion) / **ERUPTION** — Area of Activity	**LAT**	**LONG**	**ELEV** (m)	**POPL** (5 km, 10, 30, 100)	**ROCK TYPE**	**VOLC TYPE** / —Start— Year	M-Dy	**NUMBER** / —Stop— Year	**STATUS** / M-Dy	Central, Flank vent, Radial fiss, Regional	Submarine, New island, Subglacial, Crater lake	Explosive, Pyro flow, Phreatic, Caldera	Lava flow, Lava lake, Dome, Spine	Fatal, Damage, Mudflow, Tsunami	VEI	Vol L/T
OFFSHORE NEW GUINEA & ADMIRALTY ISLANDS																
St. Andrew Strait (Admiralty Is)	**2.38 S**	**147.35 E**	**270**	3345	**R**	**Complex volcano**		**0500-01=**	**Historical**							
Lou Island (Bedal volcano)						C-**0240**v	....	....	....	x---	----	xx--	----	----		
Lou Island (Bedal volcano)						C **0350**?	....	....	....	x---	----	x---	----	xx--		
Tuluman						**1883**	0328	....	....	----	x---	x---	----	----	2	
Tuluman						**1953**	0627	**1957**	0128	----	xx--	x---	x-x-	-x-x	2*	8/-
Baluan (Admiralty Is-SW Pacific)	**2.57 S**	**147.28 E**	**254**	3335	**B**	**Stratovolcano**		**0500-02-**	Holocene?							
						? 1931	....	....	....	----	?---	----	----	----	*0*	
Unnamed (Admiralty Is-SW Pacific)	**3.03 S**	**147.78 E**	**-1300**	0004	**U**	**Submarine volc**		**0500-03-**	**Hydrophonic**							
						S **1972**	0108	S**1972**	0112	----	x---	----	----	----	0	
Blup Blup (New Guinea-NE of)	**3.507 S**	**144.605 E**	**402**	3335	**AD**	**Stratovolcano**		**0501-001**	**Holocene**							
(Manam erupted in 1616, not Blup Blup)						*X 1616*	....	....	....	----	----	----	----	----		
(eruption report not valid)						*X 1830*	....	....	....	----	----	----	----	----		
Kadovar (New Guinea-NE of)	**3.630 S**	**144.631 E**	**365**	0046	**A**	**Stratovolcano**		**0501-002**	**Holocene**							
(Manam erupted in 1616, not Kadovar)						*X 1616*	....	....	....	----	----	----	----	----		
						? 1700	*04*	....	....	----	----	----	----	----		
Bam (New Guinea-NE of)	**3.613 S**	**144.818 E**	**685**	3336	**A**	**Stratovolcano**		**0501-01=**	**Historical**							
(eruption from Manam, not Bam)						*X 1616*	....	....	....	----	----	----	----	----		
(1700 activity at Kadovar, not Bam)						*X 1700*	*04*	....	....	----	----	----	----	----		
(eruption between 1868 and 1875)						*X 1868*	....	....	....	----	----	----	----	----		
						1872d	....	....	....	x---	----	x---	----	-x--	3	
						1874	0520	....	....	x---	----	x---	----	----	2	
						1877	1113	....	....	x---	----	x---	----	----	3	
						? 1883	*03*	....	....	----	----	----	----	----		
(date of Finsch observ. was May 1885)						*X 1884*	....	....	....	----	----	----	----	----		
						? 1885	*0520*	....	....	----	----	----	----	----		
						? 1888	....	....	....	----	----	----	----	----		
						? 1897	....	*?1898*	....	----	----	----	----	----		
						1907	11	....	....	x---	----	x---	----	----	2	
						1908	0712	....	....	x---	----	x---	----	----	2	
						1909	0419	**1909**	0913	x---	----	x---	----	----	2	
						1913	....	....	....	x---	----	?---	----	----		
						*? 1920*b	....	....	....	x---	----	----	----	----		
						1924	....	....	....	x---	----	x---	----	-x--	2	
						? 1936	*07*	*?1939*	*04*	x---	----	----	----	----		
(1941 & 1942 eruptions not verified)						*X 1941*	....	*X1942*	....	----	----	----	----	----		
						1944	....	....	....	x---	----	x---	----	----	2	
(this eruption took place in 1947)						*X 1946*	*1201*p	....	....	----	----	----	----	----		
						1947	0313s	....	....	x---	----	x---	----	----	2	
						1954	0803	**1957**	0102	x---	----	x---	----	-x--	2*	
						1957	1026	**1957**	1026	x---	----	x---	----	----	1	
						1958	0311j	**1958**	0419?	x---	----	x---	----	----	2	
						1958	0905	**1958**	0910	x---	----	x---	----	----	2	
						1959	0402	**1959**	1031	x---	----	x---	----	----	2	
						1960	0428	**1960**	0706	x---	----	x---	----	----	2	
Boisa (New Guinea-NE of)	**3.994 S**	**144.963 E**	**240**	3456	**BA**	**Stratovolcano**		**0501-011**	Holocene?							
Manam (New Guinea-NE of)	**4.080 S**	**145.037 E**	**1807**	4456	**BA**	**Stratovolcano**		**0501-02=**	**Historical**							
						1616	0706	....	....	x---	----	x---	----	----	2?	
(eruption in 1643, not 1642)						**1643**	0421	....	....	x---	----	x---	----	----	2	
South Crater						**1700**	0402	....	....	x---	----	?---	----	----		
						1830	....	....	....	x---	----	x---	----	----	2	
South Crater						**1877**	1029	**1877**	1113>	x---	----	x---	----	----	2	
						? 1884	....	....	....	----	----	----	----	----		
						1885	05	....	....	x---	----	x---	----	----		
						1887	06	**1895**	....	x---	----	x?--	x---	----	2	
Main Crater, South Crater						**1899**a	....	....	....	x---	----	x---	x---	x---	2?	
						? 1901	....	*?1902*	....	x---	----	?---	----	?---		
						1904	0430p	....	....	----	----	----	----	----		
						1904	1026	**1904**	1027	x---	----	x?--	?---	-x--	3?	
						? 1907	....	....	....	----	----	----	----	----		
						1909	....	**1914**?	....	x---	----	x---	x---	----	2	
						1917	....	....	....	x---	----	x---	----	----	2	
South Crater, Main Crater						**1919**	0811	....	....	x---	----	xx--	?---	-x--	4	
						1920	1205?	**1921**	03	x---	----	xxx-	?---	-x--	2	
						1922	....	....	....	x---	----	x---	----	----	3?	
						? 1923	....	....	....	----	----	----	----	----	*2?*	
						? 1924	....	....	....	----	----	----	----	----	*2?*	
						1925	....	....	....	x---	----	x---	----	----	2?	
						1926	03	**1928**	0301p	x---	----	x---	----	----	2	
						1932	....	**1934**	....	x---	----	x---	----	----	2	
Main Crater, South Crater						**1936**	09	**1939**	....	x---	----	xx--	x---	----	3*	
South Crater						**1946**	1201p	**1947**	09	x---	----	x---	x---	----	3	7/-
						1953	04	**1953**	08	x---	----	x---	----	----	2	
						1954	05	**1954**	06	x---	----	x---	----	----	2	
South Crater, Main Crater						**1956**	1208	**1958**	08	x---	----	xx--	x---	-xx-	3*	7/7
South Crater						**1959**	06	**1959**	07	x---	----	x---	----	----	2	
Main Crater, South Crater						**1959**	12	**1960**	12 >	x---	----	xx--	x---	----	2	6/-
South Crater						**1961**	07	**1961**	09	x---	----	x---	x---	----	2	
South Crater						**1962**	04	....	....	x---	----	x---	x---	----	2	

VOLCANO NAME (Subregion)	LAT	LONG	ELEV (m)	POPL (5 km / 10 / 30 / 100)	ROCK TYPE	VOLC TYPE	NUMBER	STATUS	ERUPTION — Area of Activity	Start Year	Start M-Dy	Stop Year	Stop M-Dy	Central / Flank vent / Radial fiss / Regional	Submarine / New island / Subglacial / Crater lake	Explosive / Pyro flow / Phreatic / Caldera	Lava flow / Lava lake / Dome / Spine	Fatal / Damage / Mudflow / Tsunami	VEI	Vol L/T
Manam (New Guinea-NE of) *continued*									South Crater	**1963**	02	**1963**	05 >	x---	----	x---	x---	----	2	
									South Crater	**1963**	1126	**1964**	04	x---	----	xx--	x---	----	2*	6/-
									South Crater	**1965**	....	**1966**	0125>	x---	----	xx--	x---	----	2	6/-
									South Crater, Main Crater	**1974**	0304?	**1999**	1109?	x---	----	xx--	x---	xx--	3*	7/7
									South Crater	**2000**	0603	**2000**	0604	x---	----	x---	----	----	2	
										2001	0614	**2001**	0625?	x---	----	x---	----	----	2	
									South Crater	**2002**	0113	**2002**	0521	x---	----	x---	----	----	3?	
										2002	1031	....	....	x---	----	x---	----	----	2	
									Main Crater	**2003**	0517	**2003**	0523	x---	----	x---	----	----	1	
									Main Crater	**2003**	1026e	**2004**	0328	x---	----	x---	----	----	1	
									South Crater, Main Crater	**2004**	1024	**2009**	12 >	x---	----	xx--	x---	xx--	4?	
Karkar (New Guinea-NE of)	**4.649 S**	**145.964 E**	**1839**	1456	**AB**	**Stratovolcano**	**0501-03=**	**Historical**												
										C -**7140**w	....	....	....	x---	----	xx-x	----	--x-	**C**	
										C -**0870**u	....	....	....	x---	----	x?--	----	--x-		
										C **0520**v	....	....	....	x---	----	xx-x	----	----	**C**	
										C **0730**?	....	....	....	x---	----	xx--	----	----	**P**	
									South flank (Patilo Cone)	C **1070**x	....	....	....	-x--	----	x---	----	----		
										1643	0420	....	....	x---	----	x---	----	----	3↑	
										? *1830*	....	....	....	----	----	?---	----	----		
										1885	....	....	....	x---	----	x---	----	----	2?	
										1895	0617	**1895**	08	x---	----	x---	x---	xx--	2	7/-
									Ulumam	? *1962*?	....	....	....	x---	----	?---	----	----	*2?*	
									Bagiai	**1974**	0214	**1974**	0808	x---	----	x---	x---	----	2	7/-
									Bagiai	**1974**	1230?	**1975**	0626	x---	----	x---	x---	----	2	6/-
									SE foot of Bagiai	**1979**	0112?	**1979**	0809	x---	---x	xxx-	----	x-x-	2*	-/7
										? *1980*	*0107*	?*1980*	*0117*	x---	----	?---	----	----	*1*	
										? *2009*	*0501*p	....	....	----	----	?---	----	----		
Unnamed (New Guinea-NE of)	**4.311 S**	**146.256 E**	**-2000**	0005	**U**	**Submarine volc ?**	**0501-04=**	Uncertain												
									(correct date is 1944, not 1945)	? *1944*	....	....	....	----	?---	----	----	----	*0*	
										? *1951*	*1124*	....	....	----	?---	----	----	----	*0*	
Yomba (New Guinea-NE of)	**4.90 S**	**146.75 E**		0005	**U**	**Submarine volc ?**	**0501-041**	Uncertain												
Long Island (New Guinea-NE of)	**5.358 S**	**147.12 E**	**1280**	3445	**AB**	**Complex volcano**	**0501-05=**	**Historical**												
										C -**2040**v	....	....	....	x---	----	xx-x	----	----	**6**	-/10
										C **1660**p	....	....	....	x---	----	xx-x	----	xxx-	**6**	-/10
									Lake Wisdom	**1933**	....	....	....	x---	---x	----	----	----		
									Lake Wisdom	**1938**	....	....	....	x---	---x	----	----	----		
									Motmot	**1943**	....	....	....	x---	---x	x---	----	----		
									Motmot	**1953**	0508	**1954**	0107	x---	---x	x-x-	----	----	3	
									Motmot	**1955**	0605	**1955**	0613	x---	---x	x---	----	----	3	
									Motmot	? *1961*	....	....	....	x---	----	?---	----	----		
									Motmot	**1968**	0316	**1968**	0612	x---	---x	x---	----	----	2	
									Motmot	**1973**	04	**1974**	0228	x---	----	x-x-	x---	----	2	3/-
									Motmot	**1976**	0102u	....	....	x---	----	x---	----	----	1	
									E-W fissure NNE of Motmot Island	**1993**	1103?	**1993**	1125e	x-x-	---x	x---	----	----	1	
Umboi (New Guinea-NE of)	**5.589 S**	**147.875 E**	**1548**	3445	**BAd**	**Complex volcano**	**0501-06=**	**Holocene**												
Ritter Island (New Guinea-NE of)	**5.52 S**	**148.121 E**	**140**	1245	**BA**	**Stratovolcano**	**0501-07=**	**Historical**												
										1700	0324	....	....	x---	----	x?--	----	----	3↑	
										1793	0629	....	....	x---	----	x?--	----	----	2	
										? *1848*	*0413*	?*1848*	*0710*?	x---	----	----	----	----		
										? *1878*	*1231*p	....	....	x---	----	----	----	----		
										? *1885*	*0113*?	....	....	x---	----	----	----	----		
									(probably Ritter or Langila: Cooke)	@ **1887**	0202	@**1887**	0205	----	----	x---	----	----	2	
										1888	0313	**1888**	0313	x---	----	x-xA	----	xx-x	2?	
									West of Ritter Island	**1972**	1009	**1972**	1009	x---	x---	x---	----	---x	1	
									600-900 m west of Ritter Is.	**1974**	1017	**1974**	1017	x---	x---	x---	----	---x	1	
										? *2002*	*0802*	?*2002*	*0802*	----	----	?---	----	----	*2?*	
										2006	1017	**2006**	1017?	x---	----	x---	----	----	1?	
										2007	0519	**2007**	0521?	x---	x---	x---	----	-x-x	1?	
Sakar (New Guinea-NE of)	**5.414 S**	**148.094 E**	**992**	3345	**BA**	**Stratovolcano**	**0501-08=**	Holocene?												

NEW BRITAIN

VOLCANO NAME (Subregion)	LAT	LONG	ELEV (m)	POPL (5 km / 10 / 30 / 100)	ROCK TYPE	VOLC TYPE	NUMBER	STATUS	ERUPTION — Area of Activity	Start Year	Start M-Dy	Stop Year	Stop M-Dy	Central / Flank vent / Radial fiss / Regional	Submarine / New island / Subglacial / Crater lake	Explosive / Pyro flow / Phreatic / Caldera	Lava flow / Lava lake / Dome / Spine	Fatal / Damage / Mudflow / Tsunami	VEI	Vol L/T
Unnamed (New Britain-N of)	**5.20 S**	**148.57 E**		0005	**U**	**Submarine volc ?**	**0502-001**	Uncertain												
										? *1983*	*0615*	?*1983*	*0616*	----	?---	----	----	----		
Langila (New Britain)	**5.525 S**	**148.42 E**	**1330**	3455	**BA**	**Complex volcano**	**0502-01=**	**Historical**												
									Crater 2	**1878**	....	....	....	x---	----	x---	x---	----	2	
										1884	....	....	....	----	----	x---	----	----	2	
										1890	....	....	....	----	----	----	x---	----	0	
									North Crater (crater 1)	**1900**	....	....	....	x---	----	x---	----	----	2	
									NE Crater (crater 2)	**1907**	....	....	....	x---	----	x---	----	----	2	
									Crater 2	? *1942*e	....	....	....	x---	----	x---	----	----	*1?*	
									Crater 2	**1954**	0518	**1954**	1113	x---	----	x---	----	----	3	
									Crater 2	**1955**	0215	**1955**	0217	x---	----	x---	----	----	2	
									Crater 2	**1955**	0601	**1955**	0616	x---	----	x---	----	----	2	
									Crater 2	**1956**	0325	**1956**	0331	x---	----	x---	----	----	2	
									Crater 2	**1958**	0421	**1958**	0604d	x---	----	x---	----	----	2	
									Crater 3, Crater 2	**1960**	1219	**1961**	0925e	xx--	----	x---	x---	----	2	4/-
									Crater 2, Crater 3	**1962**	03	**1963**	0811	xx--	----	x---	----	----	2	
									Crater 2, Crater 3	**1964**	1204d	**1966**	0923c	xx--	----	x---	----	----	2	
									Crater 2, Crater 3	**1967**	0119	**1968**	06	xx--	----	x---	x---	----	2	4/-
									Crater 2 or 3	**1969**	0929	**1969**	0929	x---	----	x---	----	----	2	
									Crater 2	**1970**	0520	**1970**	0922	x---	----	x---	----	----	2	
									Crater 2	**1971**	0126e	**1972**	0705d	x---	----	x---	----	----	2	
									Crater 3, Crater 2	**1973**	0224d	**2000**	10 >	xx--	----	xxx-	x-x-	----	3*	7/-
									Crater 2	**2002**	0525?	**2003**	0409?	x---	----	x---	----	----	2	
										2004	0120?	**2004**	0127?	x---	----	?---	----	----	2?	
										2004	1124?	**2004**	1225?	x---	----	x---	----	----	2?	
										2005	0419?	**2006**	0331?	x---	----	x---	x---	-x--	2	
										2006	0809	**2008**	0706?	x---	----	x---	----	----	2	
									Crater 2	**2009**	09 <	**2009**	11 ?	x---	----	x---	----	----	2	
Mundua (New Britain)	**4.63 S**	**149.35 E**	**179**	3344	**B**	**Complex volcano**	**0502-021**	**Holocene**												
Garove (New Britain)	**4.692 S**	**149.50 E**	**368**	4445	**ADBr**	**Stratovolcano**	**0502-03=**	**Holocene**												

VOLCANO NAME (Subregion) / ERUPTION — Area of Activity	LAT	LONG	ELEV (m)	POPL (5 km, 10, 30, 100)	ROCK TYPE	VOLC TYPE / Start Year	NUMBER / Start M-Dy	STATUS / Stop Year	Stop M-Dy	Central, Flank vent, Radial fiss, Regional	Submarine, New island, Subglacial, Crater lake	Explosive, Pyro flow, Phreatic, Caldera	Lava flow, Lava lake, Dome, Spine	Fatal, Damage, Mudflow, Tsunami	VEI	Vol L/T
Dakataua (New Britain)	**5.056 S**	**150.108 E**	**400**	4446	**ADB**	**Caldera**	**0502-04=**	**Anthropology**								
						C **0800**t	....	....	....	x---	----	xx-x	----	----	**6?**	-/10
Makalia						A **1895**e	....	....	....	x---	----	x---	x---	xx--	2	
Bola (New Britain)	**5.15 S**	**150.03 E**	**1155**	2346	**A**	**Stratovolcano**	**0502-05=**	**Holocene**								
Garua Harbour (New Britain)	**5.30 S***	**150.07 E**	**565**	5556	**RA**	**Volcanic field**	**0502-06=**	Holocene?								
Garbuna Group (New Britain)	**5.45 S**	**150.03 E**	**564**	2456	**ADB**	**Stratovolcanoes**	**0502-07=**	**Historical**								
Garbuna and Welcker						C **0150**?	....	....	....	----	----	----	----	----		
Central part of Garbuna complex						**2005**	1016	**2005**	1117>	x---	----	x---	----	--x-	2	
						2008	0311	**2008**	0313	x---	----	x---	----	----	1	
						2008	0713	**2008**	1004	x---	----	x---	----	----	2	
Lolo (New Britain)	**5.468 S**	**150.507 E**	**805**	4556	**AB**	**Stratovolcano**	**0502-071**	Holocene?								
Pago (New Britain)	**5.58 S**	**150.52 E**	**742**	5556	**DARb**	**Caldera**	**0502-08=**	**Historical**								
Witori						C **-7510**w	....	....	....	----	----	x---	----	----		
Witori (WK-1 tephra)						G **-4000**x	....	....	....	x---	----	xx-x	----	xx--	**6?**	-/10
Witori (WK-2 tephra)						G **-1370**v	....	....	....	x---	----	xx-x	----	-x--	**6**	-/10
Witori						C **-0640**y	....	....	....	x---	----	xx--	----	----		
Witori (WK-3 tephra)						G **0310**v	....	....	....	x---	----	x--?	----	-x--	**5**	-/9
Witori (WK-4 tephra)						G **0690**v	....	....	....	x---	----	xx-?	----	-x--	**5**	-/9
Witori (W-G tephra)						C **0710**u	....	....	....	x---	----	x--x	----	----	**6**	-/10
Witori (H1 tephra)						T **0950**?	....	....	....	x---	----	x---	----	----		
Witori (H2 tephra)						T **1050**v	....	....	....	x---	----	x---	----	----		
Witori (W-H3 tephra)						T **1450**?	....	....	....	x---	----	x---	----	----		
Witori (W-H4 tephra)						T **1550**?	....	....	....	x---	----	x---	----	----	**P**	
Witori (W-H5 tephra)						T **1730**q	....	....	....	x---	----	x---	----	----		
Witori (W-H6 tephra)						T **1800**?	....	....	....	x---	----	x---	----	----	**P**	
(same as 1911-1918 eruption)						*X 1900?*	....	....	....	----	----	----	----	----		
						1911	....	**1918**	05 ?	x---	----	x---	x---	-x--	3	
						1920b	....	....	....	x---	----	----	x---	----	0	8/-
						1933	07 ?	**1933**	08 ?	x---	----	x---	----	----	2	
Summit and NW flank						**2002**	0803	**2003**	0326o	x-x-	----	x---	x---	----	3	8/-
						? 2004	*0224*	*?2004*	*0224*	xx--	----	?---	----	----	*1?*	
						2007	0828	**2007**	0828	x---	----	x---	----	----	1?	
Sulu Range (New Britain)	**5.50 S**	**150.942 E**	**610**	3456	**ABDR**	**Stratovolcanoes**	**0502-09=**	**Fumarolic**								
Hargy (New Britain)	**5.33 S**	**151.10 E**	**1148**	2455	**DA**	**Stratovolcano**	**0502-10=**	**Radiocarbon**								
Galloseulo						C **-5050**?	....	....	....	x---	----	x---	x---	----		
Galloseulo						C **0950**?	....	....	....	x---	----	x---	----	----		
Bamus (New Britain)	**5.20 S**	**151.23 E**	**2248**	2355	**A**	**Stratovolcano**	**0502-11=**	**Anthropology**								
						C **-0350**u	....	....	....	----	----	xx--	----	----		
						C **-0270**t	....	....	....	----	----	xx--	----	----		
						C **1650**t	....	....	....	----	----	xx--	----	----		
						1886h	....	....	....	x---	----	xx--	--?-	----	3?	
Ulawun (New Britain)	**5.05 S**	**151.33 E**	**2334**	2455	**BA**	**Stratovolcano**	**0502-12=**	**Historical**								
						1700	0311	....	....	x---	----	x---	----	----	2	
						1878	....	....	....	x---	----	x---	----	----	2	
						1898	....	....	....	x---	----	xx--	----	----	3	
(no confirmed eruption in 1912)						*X 1912*	....	....	....	----	----	----	----	----		
						1915	04	....	....	x---	----	x---	----	-x--	3	
						1918	0721?	....	....	x---	----	x---	----	----	2	
						1919	0528?	....	....	x---	----	x---	----	----	2	
						1927	07	**1927**	0917>	x---	----	x---	----	----	2	
						? 1937	*05*	....	....	----	----	?---	----	----		
						1941	0126	**1941**	0126	x---	----	x---	----	----	2	
						? 1951	....	....	....	----	----	?---	----	----		
						1958	0201r	....	....	x---	----	x---	----	----	2	
						1960	0729c	**1962**	11	x---	----	x---	----	----	2	
						1963	0317	**1963**	0502?	x---	----	x---	----	----	2	
						1967	0122	**1967**	1228	x---	----	x---	----	-x--	2	
						1970	0115	**1970**	0211	x-x-	----	xx--	x---	----	3	6/6
						1973	1004	**1973**	1019	x---	----	xx--	x---	----	2	7/6
Summit, lower east flank						**1978**	0507	**1978**	0514	x-x-	----	xx--	x---	-x--	3	6/7
						1980	1006	**1980**	1007	x---	----	xx--	----	-x--	3	-/7
						1983	1106	**1984**	0313	x---	----	--x-	----	----	1	
						1984	0823	**1984**	0911	x---	----	x-x-	----	----	1	
						1984	1230	**1985**	0127	x---	----	x---	x-x-	----	1	5/-
						1985	1117	**1985**	1122	x---	----	xx--	x---	----	3*	6/6
						1989	0101	**1989**	12 ?	x---	----	x-x-	----	----	2	
						1993	0112	**1993**	0131?	x---	----	x-?-	?---	----	2	
						1994	0419?	**1994**	06	x---	----	x-x-	----	----	1	
						1999	1020	**1999**	1020	x---	----	x---	----	----	1	
						2000	0928	**2000**	1101	x---	----	xx--	----	-xx-	4*	
Summit and NNE flank						**2001**	0116?	**2001**	0503	xx--	----	xx--	x---	----	3*	
						2001	0828	**2001**	0828	x---	----	x---	----	----	2	
						2002	0822?	**2002**	1103	x---	----	x---	----	----	2*	
						2003	0414?	**2003**	1010	x---	----	x---	----	----	2*	
						2004	0412	**2004**	0414	x---	----	x---	----	----	2	
						2005	0327?	**2005**	0809?	x---	----	x---	----	----	2*	
						2006	0301	**2007**	0118	x---	----	x---	----	----	2*	
						2007	0501	**2007**	0501	x---	----	x---	----	----	2	
						? 2007	*1225*	....	....	x---	----	?---	----	----	*1?*	
Lolobau (New Britain)	**4.92 S**	**151.158 E**	**858**	4445	**BDA**	**Caldera**	**0502-13=**	**Historical**								
Hulu						C **1100**r	....	....	....	x---	----	x---	----	----	4	-/8
East flank (Sili, Malo), Hulu ?						**1904**	0809	**1905**	1018>	xx--	----	x---	x---	----	**P***	
						? 1908	....	....	....	----	----	----	----	----		
East flank (Sili)						**1911**	....	*?1912*	....	-xx-	----	x---	x---	----	4	8/8
Unnamed (New Britain-N of)	**4.75 S**	**150.85 E**		0015	**U**	**Submarine volc ?**	**0502-131**	Uncertain								
						? 1951	....	....	....	----	?---	----	----	----	*0*	
						? 1970	*0602*	*?1970*	*0613*	----	?---	----	----	----	*0*	
Rabaul (New Britain)	**4.271 S**	**152.203 E**	**688**	4566	**DABr**	**Pyroclastic shield**	**0502-14=**	**Historical**								
(Rabaul caldera-forming eruption)						C **0540**v	....	....	....	x---	----	xx-x	----	----	**6**	-/10
NE caldera rim (Rabalanakia)						T **1450**w	....	....	....	x---	----	x---	x---	----		
Tavurvur ?						**1767**	0910	....	....	x---	----	x---	----	----	2	

VOLCANO NAME (Subregion) / ERUPTION — Area of Activity	LAT	LONG	ELEV (m)	POPL (5 km, 10, 30, 100)	ROCK TYPE	VOLC TYPE / Start Year	NUMBER / Start M-Dy	STATUS / Stop Year	Stop M-Dy	Central, Flank vent, Radial fiss, Regional	Submarine, New island, Subglacial, Crater lake	Explosive, Pyro flow, Phreatic, Caldera	Lava flow, Lava lake, Dome, Spine	Fatal, Damage, Mudflow, Tsunami	VEI	Vol L/T
Rabaul (New Britain) *continued*																
Tavurvur						**1791**	0522	....	....	x---	----	x---	----	----	2?	
Sulfur Creek						**1850**?	....	....	....	x---	----	x-x-	----	xx--	2	
Vulcan Island and Tavurvur						**1878**	0130?	**1878**	0226b	x---	xx--	x-x-	----	xx-x	3	-/8
Vulcan and Tavurvur						**1937**	0529	**1937**	0602	xx--	xx--	xxx-	----	xxxx	4?	-/8
Tavurvur						**1940**	0204d	**1940**	0518	x---	---x	--x-	----	----	1	
Tavurvur						**1941**	0606	**1942**	0331p	x---	----	x---	x---	-x--	2	
Tavurvur						**1943**	1124	**1943**	1223>	x---	----	x---	----	----	2	
Tavurvur and Vulcan						**1994**	0919	**1995**	0416	xx--	----	xx--	x---	xxxx	4?	5/-
Tavurvur						**1995**	1128	**2001**	0905d	x---	----	xx--	x---	-x--	2	6/-
Tavurvur						**2002**	1006?	**2004**	0217	x---	----	x---	----	----	2*	
Tavurvur						**2005**	0125	**2006**	0217	x---	----	x---	----	----	2*	
Tavurvur						**2006**	0811	**2010>**	....	x---	----	x---	x-x-	-x--	4?	
Tavui (New Britain)	**4.12 S**	**152.20 E**	**200**	5566	**Rb**	**Caldera**	**0502-15-**	**Radiocarbon**								
(Raluan Ignimbrite)						N-**5150***	....	....	....	x---	x---	xx-x	----	----	**5**	-/9

NEW GUINEA & D'ENTRECASTEAUX ISLANDS

VOLCANO NAME (Subregion) / ERUPTION — Area of Activity	LAT	LONG	ELEV (m)	POPL	ROCK TYPE	VOLC TYPE / Start Year	NUMBER / Start M-Dy	STATUS / Stop Year	Stop M-Dy	Vent	Setting	Explosive	Lava	Effects	VEI	Vol L/T
Doma Peaks (New Guinea)	**5.90 S**	**143.15 E**	**3568**	4466	**Ax**	**Stratovolcano**	**0503-00-**	Holocene?								
Crater Mountain (New Guinea)	**6.58 S**	**145.08 E**	**3233**	3456	**XBAD**	**Stratovolcano**	**0503-001**	Holocene?								
Yelia (New Guinea)	**7.05 S**	**145.858 E**	**3384**	2456	**Ad**	**Stratovolcano**	**0503-002**	Holocene?								
Koranga (New Guinea)	**7.33 S**	**146.708 E**	**1500**	5556	**DA**	**Maar**	**0503-003**	**Holocene**								
Madilogo (New Guinea)	**9.20 S**	**147.57 E**	**850**	3356	**X**	**Pyroclastic cone**	**0503-004**	**Holocene**								
Lamington (New Guinea)	**8.95 S**	**148.15 E**	**1680**	3456	**AYX**	**Stratovolcano**	**0503-01=**	**Historical**								
(Owalama Ash)						C-**5980**y	....	....	....	----	----	x---	----	----		
(Dea Ash)						C-**4850**y	....	....	....	----	----	x---	----	----		
						1951	0117	**1956**	....	x---	----	xx--	--xx	xxx-	4*	8/-
Hydrographers Range (")	**9.00 S**	**148.37 E**	**1915**	3456	**Abd**	**Stratovolcano**	**0503-011**	**Holocene**								
Musa River (New Guinea)	**9.308 S**	**148.13 E**	**808**	3346	**A**	**Hydrothermal field**	**0503-02=**	**Hot Springs**								
Managlase Plateau (New Guinea)	**9.08 S***	**148.33 E**	**1342**	4456	**XYDB**	**Volcanic field**	**0503-021**	**Anthropology**								
Victory (New Guinea)	**9.20 S**	**149.07 E**	**1925**	2256	**Abd**	**Stratovolcano**	**0503-03=**	**Historical**								
						*? 1810*j	....	....	....	----	----	----	----	----	*2?*	
						1890?	....	**1935**e	....	x---	----	xx--	--x-	xx--	2	
Sessagara (New Guinea)	**9.48 S***	**149.13 E**	**370**	4446	**Y**	**Pyroclastic cones**	**0503-031**	**Holocene**								
Waiowa (New Guinea)	**9.57 S**	**149.075 E**	**640**	2356	**Y**	**Pyroclastic cone**	**0503-04=**	**Historical**								
(eruption began in 1943, not 1942)						**1943**	0918	**1944**	0831	xx--	----	xxx-	----	--x-	3*	
Goodenough (D'Entrecasteaux Is)	**9.48 S***	**150.35 E**	**220**	4456	**A**	**Volcanic field**	**0503-041**	**Holocene**								
Iamalele (D'Entrecasteaux Is)	**9.52 S**	**150.53 E**	**200**	3346	**ARB**	**Lava domes**	**0503-05=**	**Holocene**								
Dawson Strait Group (")	**9.62 S***	**150.88 E**	**500**	4445	**RTY**	**Volcanic field**	**0503-06=**	**Hydration Rind**								
Oiau						H **1350**?	....	....	....	----	----	----	----	----		

NEW IRELAND & BOUGAINVILLE

VOLCANO NAME (Subregion) / ERUPTION — Area of Activity	LAT	LONG	ELEV (m)	POPL	ROCK TYPE	VOLC TYPE / Start Year	NUMBER / Start M-Dy	STATUS / Stop Year	Stop M-Dy	Vent	Setting	Explosive	Lava	Effects	VEI	Vol L/T
Lihir (New Ireland)	**3.125 S**	**152.642 E**	**700**	3445	**XByz**	**Compound volcano**	**0504-01=**	**Holocene**								
Ambitle (New Ireland)	**4.08 S**	**153.65 E**	**450**	4445	**ZXYBT**	**Stratovolcano**	**0504-02=**	**Radiocarbon**								
East side of caldera						C-**0350**v	....	....	....	x---	----	x---	----	----		
Tore (Bougainville)	**5.83 S**	**154.93 E**	**2200**	2356	**A**	**Lava cone**	**0505-00-**	**Holocene**								
Balbi (Bougainville)	**5.92 S**	**154.98 E**	**2715**	3356	**A**	**Stratovolcano**	**0505-01=**	**Holocene**								
Crater B ?						*? 1825*q	....	....	....	x---	----	x---	----	x---		
Billy Mitchell (Bougainville)	**6.092 S**	**155.225 E**	**1544**	3346	**AD**	**Pyroclastic shield**	**0505-011**	**Radiocarbon**								
						C **1030**q	....	....	....	x---	----	x---	----	----	**5+**	-/9
						C **1580**p	....	....	....	x---	----	xx-x	----	----	**6**	-/10
Bagana (Bougainville)	**6.140 S**	**155.195 E**	**1750**	3346	**A**	**Lava cone**	**0505-02=**	**Historical**								
						1842	0315	....	....	x---	----	----	x---	----	1	
						1865c	....	**1883**	....	----	----	x---	----	----	2	
						1883	1231p	....	....	x---	----	x---	----	x---	3	
						1894	....	**1895**	....	x---	----	xx--	x---	----	2	
						1897	0516?	....	....	x---	----	x---	----	----	2	
						1899	....	....	....	----	----	----	----	----		
						1908	0715	....	....	x---	----	?---	?---	----	2?	
						? 1909	*07*	....	....	----	----	----	----	----		
						1937	0907	....	....	x---	----	x---	----	----	3	
						1938	0515	....	....	x---	----	xx--	----	----	3	
						1939	0130?	....	....	x---	----	x---	x---	----	2	
						1943	0407<	....	....	x---	----	----	x---	----	1	
						1945	....	**1947**	....	x---	----	x---	x---	----	2	
						1948	1201p	**1951**	1201p	x---	----	xx--	x-x-	----	3*	
						1952	0229	**1952**	10	x---	----	xx--	x-x-	----	4	
						1953	06	**1953**	09	x---	----	xx--	----	----	3*	
						1956	....	....	....	x---	----	x---	----	----	2	
						1959?	....	**1960**	05	x---	----	x---	x---	----	2	
						1961	0726	....	....	x---	----	x---	----	----	2	
						1962	0215	**1963**	....	x---	----	x---	x---	----	2	
						1964	0424	**1965**	....	x---	----	x-x-	x---	----	2	
						1966	0320	**1967**	1130	x---	----	xx--	x-x-	----	3*	
						1968	08	**1968**	08	x---	----	x---	----	----	2	
						1970	0521m	**1971**	08 >	x---	----	x---	x---	----	2	
						1972	....	**1995>**	....	x---	----	xx--	x-x-	----	2*	6/-
						2000	0916	**2010>**	....	x---	----	x?--	x---	----	2	
Takuan Group (Bougainville)	**6.442 S**	**155.608 E**	**2210**	2455	**AD**	**Compound volcano**	**0505-021**	**Holocene**								
Loloru (Bougainville)	**6.52 S**	**155.62 E**	**1887**	1355	**A**	**Pyroclastic shield**	**0505-03=**	**Radiocarbon**								
						C-**6950**?	....	....	....	x---	----	x---	----	----		
						C-**4150**?	....	....	....	x---	----	xx--	----	----		
						C-**3150**?	....	....	....	x---	----	xx--	----	----		
						C-**2150**?	....	....	....	x---	----	xx--	----	----		
						C-**1260**y	....	....	....	x---	----	xx--	----	----		
						C-**1050**?	....	....	....	x---	----	x---	----	----		

Wally Johnson ((Australian Bur. Min. Resour.)

Billy Mitchell caldera; Bagana (upper R)

SOLOMON ISLANDS & SANTA CRUZ

VOLCANO NAME (Subregion) / ERUPTION — Area of Activity	LAT	LONG	ELEV (m)	POPL (5 km, 10, 30, 100)	ROCK TYPE	VOLC TYPE	NUMBER	STATUS	Start Year	Start M-Dy	Stop Year	Stop M-Dy	Central / Flank vent / Radial fiss / Regional	Submarine / New island / Subglacial / Crater lake	Explosive / Pyro flow / Phreatic / Caldera	Lava flow / Lava lake / Dome / Spine	Fatal / Damage / Mudflow / Tsunami	VEI	Vol L/T
Simbo (Solomon Is-SW Pacific)	**8.292 S**	**156.52 E**	**335**	3335	**AB**	**Stratovolcanoes**	**0505-05=**	**Anthropology**											
Ngusuna crater?									A **1910**j	....	....	....	-?--	----	--?-	----	----		
Cook (Solomon Is-SW Pacific)	8.415 S	157.10 E	-1300				0505-051	Not a Volcano											
(no volcano at this location)									*X 1964*	*0525*	*X1964*	*0614*?	----	----	----	----	----		
Kana Keoki (Solomon Is-SW Pacific)	**8.75 S**	**157.03 E**	**-700**	0035	**D**	**Submarine volc**	**0505-052**	**Holocene**											
Coleman Seamount (Solomon Is)	**8.83 S**	**157.17 E**		0045	**U**	**Submarine volc**	**0505-053**	**Holocene**											
Kavachi (Solomon Is-SW Pacific)	**9.02 S**	**157.95 E**	**-20**	1135	**AB**	**Submarine volc**	**0505-06=**	**Historical**											
									1939	0430?	....	....	----	x---	x---	----	----	2	
									1942?	....	....	....	----	x?--	----	----	----	1	
									1950	1201p	....	....	----	x---	x---	----	----	2	
									1951	1201p	....	....	----	x---	x---	----	---x	2	
									1952	0416	**1953**	0131?	----	xx--	x---	x---	----	2	
									1957	0208	....	....	----	x---	--x-	----	----	0	
									1958	1121	**1958**	1202?	----	x?--	----	?---	----	0	
									1961	0328<	....	....	----	xx--	x---	x---	----	2	
									1962	01	**1962**	02	----	x---	x---	----	----	2	
(eruption Dec. 14, 1963, not 1961)									**1963**	1214	**1964**	0131?	----	xx--	--x-	x---	----	2*	
									1965	1211	**1965**	1213	----	xx--	--x-	x---	----	2	
									1966	0319	**1966**	0322>	----	x---	x-x-	----	----	2	
									1969	1028	**1970**	0206	----	xx--	x---	x---	----	2	
									1972	1024	....	....	----	x---	x---	----	----	0	
									1974	1112	**1974**	1212?	----	x---	x---	----	----	1	
									1975	08	....	....	----	x---	x---	----	----	1	
									1976	0824	**1976**	1013	----	xx--	x---	x---	----	1	
									1977	0222	....	....	----	x---	x---	----	----	1	
									1977	0717?	**1977**	0722	----	x---	x---	----	----	1	
									1978	0621	**1978**	0722f	----	xx--	x---	x---	----	2	
									1980	1007	**1981**	0225	----	x---	x---	----	----	1	
									? *1981*	*0915*e	....	....	----	?---	----	----	----	*0*	
									1982	0407	**1982**	0602a	----	x---	x---	----	----	2	
									1985	1209	**1986**	0228c	----	x---	x---	----	----	1	
									1986	0705	**1986**	0723	----	xx--	x-x-	----	----	1	
									1991	0504<	**1991**	09	----	xx--	x---	x---	----	2	
									1997	0116	**1997**	0117>	----	x---	x---	----	----	1	
									? *1998*	....	....	....	----	?---	----	----	----	*0*	
									1999	02	**1999**	05	----	x---	x---	----	----	1	
									1999	11 ?	**2003**	08	----	xx--	x---	----	----	1	
									2004	0315	....	....	----	x---	x---	----	----	1	
									2007	0402?	**2007**	0406>	----	x---	x---	----	----	1	
Unnamed (Solomon Is-SW Pacific)	**8.92 S**	**158.03 E**	**-240**	0145	**A**	**Submarine volcs**	**0505-061**	**Holocene**											
Gallego (Solomon Is-SW Pacific)	**9.35 S***	**159.73 E**	**1000**	5556	**A**	**Volcanic field**	**0505-062**	Holocene?											
Savo (Solomon Is-SW Pacific)	**9.13 S**	**159.82 E**	**485**	4446	**ADb**	**Stratovolcano**	**0505-07=**	**Historical**											
NE crater margin									**1568**<	....	....	....	x---	---x	xx--	--x-	xxxx	3	
									G **1650**p	....	....	....	x---	----	xx--	----	--x-		
									1835e	....	**1847**?	....	x---	---x	xx--	--?-	xxx-	3?	
									? *1865*p	....	....	....							
Tinakula (Santa Cruz Is-SW Pacific)	**10.38 S**	**165.80 E**	**851**	0225	**Abd**	**Stratovolcano**	**0506-01=**	**Historical**											
									C-**1050**?	....	....	....	----	----	x---	----	----		
									1595	....	....	....	x---	----	x---	x---	----	3↑	
									1768	08	....	....	----	----	x---	----	----	2	
									1797	....	....	....	----	----	x---	----	----	1?	
									1840?	....	....	....	x---	----	xx--	----	xx--	3?	
									1855	08	....	....	x---	----	x---	----	----	2	
									1857	08	....	....	----	----	x---	----	----	2	
									1869	03	....	....	----	----	x---	----	----	2	
									1871	....	....	....	----	----	x---	x---	----	2?	
									1886	....	....	....	----	----	----	----	----		
									1897	0326e	....	....	----	----	x---	----	-x-x	2?	
									1909	08	....	....	----	----	x---	x---	----	2	
									1951	1023	**1951**	1127p	x---	----	x---	x---	----	3	
									? *1955*	*08*	?*1955*	*1015*r	----	----	--?-	----	----	*2?*	
Upper NW flank									**1965**	1123	**1966**	0611	-x--	----	x-x-	x---	---x	3*	
Upper and lower NW flanks									**1971**	0906	**1971**	1211	-x--	----	xx--	x---	-x-x	2	
Upper NW flank									**1984**	0603<	**1985**	0613>	-x--	----	x---	----	----	2	
									1989	08 <	**1990**	02 >	x---	----	x---	----	----	1	
									1995	....	....	....	x---	----	x---	----	----	1?	
									1999	05	....	....	x---	----	x---	----	----	1?	
									2000	1102?	**2001**	0416?	----	----	?---	----	----	1?	
Upper NW flank									**2002**	04	....	....	-x--	----	x---	----	----	1	
									? *2002*	*11*	....	....	----	----	----	----	----	*1?*	
									2006	02 <	**2007**	11 >	x---	----	x---	----	----	2	
									2008	0919?	**2010**>	....	x---	----	x---	----	----	1?	

VANUATU & S

VOLCANO NAME (Subregion) / ERUPTION — Area of Activity	LAT	LONG	ELEV (m)	POPL (5 km, 10, 30, 100)	ROCK TYPE	VOLC TYPE	NUMBER	STATUS	Start Year	Start M-Dy	Stop Year	Stop M-Dy	Central / Flank vent / Radial fiss / Regional	Submarine / New island / Subglacial / Crater lake	Explosive / Pyro flow / Phreatic / Caldera	Lava flow / Lava lake / Dome / Spine	Fatal / Damage / Mudflow / Tsunami	VEI	Vol L/T
Motlav (Banks Is)	**13.67 S**	**167.67 E**	**411**	3344	**B**	**Stratovolcano**	**0507-001**	**Holocene**											
Suretamatai (Banks Is)	**13.80 S**	**167.47 E**	**921**	2444	**ABD**	**Complex volcano**	**0507-01=**	**Historical**											
									? *1841*	....	....	....	----	----	----	----	----		
(eruption 1856 or 1860)									**1856**?	....	....	....	x---	----	x---	----	----	2?	
(eruption 1861 or 1865)									**1861**?	....	....	....	x---	----	x---	----	----	2	
NW flank									**1965**	0809	**1966**	....	-x--	----	x-x-	----	----	2	
Gaua (Banks Is)	**14.27 S**	**167.50 E**	**797**	3444	**ABd**	**Stratovolcano**	**0507-02=**	**Historical**											
Mt. Garat									**1962**	07 <	....	....	x---	----	x---	----	----	2?	
Mt. Garat (upper SE flank)									**1963**	0915e	**1963**	1109>	x---	----	x---	----	----	2	
Mt. Garat									**1965**	0927	**1965**	0930>	x---	----	x---	----	----	3	
Mt. Garat									**1966**	....	....	....	x---	----	x---	----	----	2	
Mt. Garat									**1967**	07	....	....	x---	----	x---	----	----	2	
Mt. Garat (upper SE flank)									**1968**	....	**1968**	1201p	x---	----	x---	----	----	2	
Mt. Garat									**1969**	0922	....	....	x---	----	x---	----	----	2	

VOLCANO NAME (Subregion) / ERUPTION	LAT	LONG	ELEV (m)	POPL (5 km, 10, 30, 100)	ROCK TYPE	VOLC TYPE	NUMBER	STATUS	Area of Activity	Start Year	Start M-Dy	Stop Year	Stop M-Dy	Central vent, Flank vent, Radial fiss, Regional	Submarine, New island, Subglacial, Crater lake	Explosive, Pyro flow, Phreatic, Caldera	Lava flow, Lava lake, Dome, Spine	Fatal, Damage, Mudflow, Tsunami	VEI	Vol L/T
Gaua (Banks Is) *continued*									Mt. Garat (upper SE flank)	**1971**	0512	**1971**	0513	x---	----	x---	----	----	2	
									Mt. Garat (upper SE flank)	**1973**	1009	**1974**	0121	x---	----	x---	----	----	2*	
									Mt. Garat	**1976**	0115e	....	....	x---	----	x---	----	----	2	
									Mt. Garat	**1977**	0413	**1977**	0413	x---	----	x---	----	----	2	
									Mt. Garat	**1980**	....	....	....	x---	----	--?-	----	----	1?	
									Mt. Garat	**1981**	0709	**1981**	0709	x---	----	x-?-	----	----	1?	
									Mt. Garat	**1982**	0418	**1982**	0418	x---	----	x-?-	----	----	2	
									Mt. Garat	**2009**	0927	**2010**	0101>	x---	----	xx--	----	----	2	
Mere Lava (Banks Is)	**14.45 S**	**168.05 E**	**1028**	2225	**B**	**Stratovolcano**	**0507-021**	**Holocene**												
										? *1606*	....	....	....	----	----	----	----	----		
Aoba (Vanuatu-SW Pacific)	**15.40 S**	**167.83 E**	**1496**	2445	**B**	**Shield volcano**	**0507-03=**	**Historical**												
									Lakes Voui and Manaro Ngoru	C **1530**?	....	....	....	x---	----	x---	----	----		
									Lake Voui and upper west flank	A **1670**?	....	....	....	xxx-	----	x-x-	x---	xx--	2?	
									SE side Lake Manaro Lakua; Lake Voui?	**1870**?	....	....	....	x---	----	--x-	----	xxx-	2?	
										? *1915*a	....	....	....	--x-	----	?-?-	----	xxx-		
									Lake Voui	**1995**	0302	**1995**	0303?	x---	---x	x-x-	----	----	2	
									Lake Voui	**2005**	1127	**2006**	02	x---	---x	xxx-	----	----	2	
Ambrym (Vanuatu-SW Pacific)	**16.25 S**	**168.12 E**	**1334**	1355	**BAD**	**Pyroclastic shield**	**0507-04=**	**Historical**												
										C **0050**v	....	....	....	x---	----	xx-x	x---	----	**6+**	-/10
										1774	....	....	....	----	----	x---	----	----	2	
									West flank	**1820**?	....	....	....	--x-	----	----	x---	-x--		
										1863	....	**1864**	....	x---	----	x---	x---	----	2	
										? *1870*	....	....	....	----	----	?---	----	----		
										1871	....	....	....	----	----	x---	----	----	2	
									Marum	**1883**	....	....	....	x---	----	x---	----	----	2	
									Marum and/or Benbow	**1884**	....	....	....	x---	----	?---	----	----	2?	
										1886	07	....	....	x---	----	x---	----	----	2	
									SE flank (6 km from SE Point), Marum	**1888**	0224d	**1888**	04 ?	xx--	----	x---	x---	----	2	
									Benbow and west flank	**1894**	1015	**1895**	0210>	x-x-	----	x---	x---	xx--	3	
										1898	0326	....	....	----	----	?---	----	----	1?	
										1908	....	....	....	----	----	?---	----	----	2?	
										? *1909*	*0628*	....	....	----	----	?---	----	----		
									Base of Marum	**1910**	....	....	....	x---	----	----	x---	----	0?	
									Marum ?, west flank ?	**1912**	....	....	....	x?--	?---	?---	----	----		
									Benbow, west flank, Marum	**1913**	1014	**1914**	....	xxx-	----	x---	x---	xx--	3*	
									Marum, crater at SE point	**1915**	1020	....	....	xx--	----	x---	----	----	2	
									Benbow, west flank, Marum	**1929**	0628	**1929**	0701	xxx-	x---	x---	x---	-x--	2	
									Benbow	**1935**	09	**1936**	01	x---	----	x---	-x--	----	2	
									Benbow and west flank	**1937**	0327	**1937**	04	x-x-	----	x---	x---	----	2	
									Benbow, Marum ?	**1938**	....	....	....	x---	----	x---	----	----	2	
									NW flank of Benbow	**1942**	0606	....	....	x-x-	----	x---	x---	----	2	
									Benbow	**1950**	1206	**1951**	1125e	x---	----	x---	----	-xx-	4+	-/8
									Benbow	**1952**	0810	**1952**	1226e	x---	----	x---	----	-x--	2	
									Benbow, Mbuelesu, S flank of Benbow	**1953**	05	**1953**	1013?	xx--	----	x---	-x--	----	2	
									Benbow	**1954**	....	....	....	x---	----	x---	----	----	2	
									Benbow	**1955**	....	....	....	x---	----	x---	x---	----	2	
									Benbow, Marum	**1957**	0826e	**1957**	10	x---	----	x---	----	----	1?	
									Benbow and Marum	**1958**	1118	....	....	x---	----	?---	----	----	2?	
									Marum	**1959**	04	....	....	x---	----	x---	----	----	2	
									Mbuelesu, Benbow, near Marum	**1960**	0917	....	....	xx--	----	?---	-x--	----	1?	
									Benbow, Marum, south of Marum	**1961**	0815	**1963**	0403	xx--	----	x---	-x--	----	3*	
									Benbow, Marum	**1963**	0830	**1963**	0923>	x---	----	x---	----	----	2	
									Marum, Benbow	**1964**	02 ?	**1966**	09 >	xx--	----	x---	-x--	----	2	
									Marum, Benbow, Mbuelesu	**1967**	07	**1970**	0829	x---	----	x---	-x--	-x--	2	
									Marum, Benbow	**1971**	0203	**1971**	1105	x---	----	x---	-x--	----	2	
									Benbow, Marum	**1972**	0415	**1972**	0815	x---	----	x---	x---	-x--	3*	
									Benbow, Mbuelesu, Marum	**1973**	0415e	**1976**	1014	xx--	----	x---	-x--	----	3*	
										1977	0120e	**1977**	0128?	x---	----	x---	----	-x--	2	
										1977	08	**1977**	0930	x---	----	x---	----	----	2	
									Benbow	**1979**	0126e	**1979**	0218?	x---	----	x---	----	-x--	2	
									Benbow, Marum	**1979**	0606	**1979**	09 ?	x---	----	x---	----	----	2	
									Marum	**1980**	0516	**1980**	0818	x---	----	x---	----	----	3*	
									Benbow, Marum	**1981**	0220	**1981**	0930	x---	----	x-x-	x---	-x--	2	
									Marum	**1983**	....	....	....	x---	----	x---	----	----	2	
										1984	....	**1986**	0308>	x---	----	x---	----	----	2	
									New cone 3 km east of Marum	**1986**	1113	**1986**	1119?	x---	----	x---	x---	----	2	
									Benbow, Mbwelesu, Marum, Niri Taten	**1988**	0212?	**1988**	0823	xx--	----	x---	xx--	----	3	6/-
									Marum, Benbow, Niri Mbwelesu Taten	**1989**	0424	**1989**	1223	xx--	----	x---	xx--	-?--	2	
									Mbwelesu, Niri Mbwelesu, Niri Taten	**1990**	09 <	**1991**	07 >	x---	----	x---	-x--	----	2	
									Benbow and Marum	**1994**	12 <	....	....	x---	----	x---	-x--	----	1?	
									Benbow, Marum, Niri Mbelesu, Mbwelesu	**1996**	06 <	**2005**	08 >	x---	----	x---	-x--	----	1	
									Marum (Mbwelesu)	**2006**	1108	**2007**	1227>	x---	----	x---	-x--	----	2*	
									Benbow and Marum	**2008**	0523	**2010**>	....	x---	----	----	-x--	----	1	
Lopevi (Vanuatu-SW Pacific)	**16.507 S**	**168.346 E**	**1413**	3345	**BA**	**Stratovolcano**	**0507-05=**	**Historical**												
										1863	....	....	....	x---	----	x?--	----	----	2	
										1864	0609	....	....	x---	----	xx--	----	----	3	
										1874	....	....	....	----	----	----	----	----	2	
										1883	....	**1884**	....	----	----	----	----	----		
										1892	10	**1893**	....	----	----	x---	----	----	2?	
										1898	0603	**1898**	0724?	x---	----	x---	x---	-x--	2?	
										1908	....	....	....	?---	----	----	x---	----	2	
										1922	0628	**1922**	0701	----	----	?---	----	----	2	
										1933	....	....	....	----	----	----	----	----		
									NW and SE flanks	**1939**	0202	....	....	-xx-	----	x---	x---	-x--	2	
									NW and/or SW flanks	**1939**	1101	....	....	-xx-	----	xx--	x---	-x--	2	
									NW flank (640 m)	**1960**	0710	**1960**	09	-xx-	----	xx--	x---	-x--	3	
									NW flank	**1962**	07	**1962**	07 ?	-xx-	----	----	x---	----	0	
									Summit, NW, north, east and SE flanks	**1963**	0707	**1965**	....	xxx-	----	xx--	x---	-x--	3*	
									Summit and NW flank	**1967**	0127	**1969**	0331	xxx-	----	x---	x---	----	3*	
									Summit, NW and east flanks	**1970**	0509	**1972**	0807	xxx-	----	x---	x---	----	2*	
									Summit and NW flank	**1974**	01	**1974**	1007	x?--	----	x-?-	----	----	2	
									Summit and NW flank	**1975**	0306c	**1975**	0623	xx--	----	x---	----	----	2	
										1976	0501	**1976**	0905	x---	----	x---	----	----	1	

VOLCANO NAME (Subregion) / ERUPTION — Area of Activity	LAT	LONG	ELEV (m)	POPL (5 km, 10, 30, 100)	ROCK TYPE	VOLC TYPE	NUMBER	STATUS	Start Year	Start M-Dy	Stop Year	Stop M-Dy	Central / Flank vent / Radial fiss / Regional	Submarine / New island / Subglacial / Crater lake	Explosive / Pyro flow / Phreatic / Caldera	Lava flow / Lava lake / Dome / Spine	Fatal / Damage / Mudflow / Tsunami	VEI	Vol L/T
Lopevi (Vanuatu-SW Pacific) *continued* — Summit and NW flank									1978	1122	1979	03	xx--	----	x---	x---	----	2*	
NW flank									1979	0702	1979	0912	-x--	----	x---	----	----	2	
Summit, NW and SE flanks									1980	0415	1980	0820	xxx-	----	x---	x---	-x--	3	
									1982	1024	1982	1025	x---	----	x---	----	----	2	
1963 crater (NW flank 1000 m)									1998	07	2000	0425?	-x--	----	xx--	x---	----	3*	3/-
NW flank (200-400 m)									2001	0608	2001	0619>	-xx-	----	x---	x---	-x--	3	
									2003	0608	2003	0616?	x---	----	x---	x---	----	3	
									2004	09	2004	09	----	----	x---	----	----	2	
									2005	0130	2005	0331?	----	----	x---	----	----	2	
									2005	1027?	2006	0801?	x---	----	x---	x---	----	2	
									2007	0421	2007	0514?	x---	----	x---	?---	----	2	
									? 2008	0224	?2008	0224?	x---	----	?---	----	----	2	
Epi (Vanuatu-SW Pacific)	16.68 S	168.37 E	833	0345	BAD	Stratovolcanoes	0507-06=	Historical											
									1920	0122	....	....	----	xx--	----	----	----	2	
Epi B and other vents									1953	0212	1953	0219	x---	xx--	x---	----	----	3	
									? 1953	11	....	....	----	?---	----	----	----	0	
									1958	09 ?	1958	11 ?	----	x---	x---	----	----	2?	
									1960	07 ?	....	....	----	x---	----	----	----	0	
									? 1971	1028	?1971	1115?	----	?---	----	----	----	0	
									? 1972	0515e	?1972	0625e	----	?---	----	----	----	0	
									? 1973	0505d	?1973	1026e	----	?---	----	----	----	0	
Epi A and Epi B									? 1974	11	?1974	11	x---	?---	----	----	----	0	
South flank of Epi B									1979e	....	....	....	-x--	x---	----	----	----	0	
									? 1988	08	....	....	----	?---	----	----	----	0	
									1999?	0201p	....	....	----	x---	?---	----	----	1?	
									2002	03	2002	03	----	x---	x---	----	----	1?	
Epi B									2004	0216	2004	0224	----	x---	x---	----	----	2	
Kuwae (Vanuatu-SW Pacific)	16.829 S	168.536 E	-2	4445	BDA	Caldera	0507-07=	Historical											
									G 1430?	....	....	....	----	x---	xx--	----	-x--		
Karua									1897	0525?	1901	....	x---	xx--	x---	----	----	2*	
Karua									1923	....	1925	....	x---	xx--	----	----	----	2?	
Karua									1948	0922	1948	0929	x---	xx--	x---	----	----	2	
Karua									1949	04	....	....	x---	x---	x---	----	----	3	
Karua									1949	10	1949	12	x---	xx--	----	----	----	3	
Karua									1952	1003	....	....	x---	x---	x---	----	----	1	
Karua									1953	0212	....	....	x---	x---	----	----	----	1?	
Karua									1958	1007?	1958	1218	x---	xx--	x---	----	----	2?	
Karua									1959	0918?	1959	0920?	x---	xx--	----	----	----	2	
Karua									? 1970	0912	?1970	0920	x---	?---	----	----	----	0	
Karua									1971	0222	1971	0222	x---	xx--	x---	----	----	2	
Karua									? 1972	0305e	?1972	0515e	x---	?---	----	----	----	0	
Karua									? 1973	0505d	?1973	10	x---	?---	----	----	----	0	
Karua									1974	0204d	1974	09 ?	x---	xx--	----	----	----	0	
Karua									? 1977	0201	....	....	x---	?---	----	----	----	0	
Karua									? 1979	09	....	....	x---	?---	----	----	----	0	
Karua									? 1980	0820	....	....	x---	?---	----	----	----	0	
Unnamed (Vanuatu-SW Pacific)	16.992 S	168.592 E	216	4445	BD	Stratovolcanoes	0507-08-	Holocene?											
North Vate (Vanuatu-SW Pacific)	17.47 S	168.353 E	594	4455	BAT	Stratovolcanoes	0507-081	Holocene											
Traitor's Head (Vanuatu)	18.75 S	169.23 E	837	3345	BA	Stratovolcano	0507-09=	Historical											
NE flank submarine vent									1881	....	....	....	-x--	x---	----	----	----	0	
Four submarine vents N of Erromango									? 1959	....	....	....	----	?---	----	----	----		
Yasur (Vanuatu-SW Pacific)	19.53 S	169.442 E	361	4455	Ab	Stratovolcano	0507-10=	Historical											
									C 0550?	....	....	....	x---	----	x---	----	----		
									C 0850y	....	....	....	x---	----	x---	----	----		
									C 1150?	....	....	....	x---	----	x---	----	----	2	
									1774<	....	2010>	....	x---	----	x-x-	-x--	xx-x	3*	
Aneityum (Vanuatu-SW Pacific)	20.20 S	169.78 E	852	3335	BA	Stratovolcanoes	0507-11-	Holocene?											
Eastern Gemini Seamount	20.98 S	170.28 E	-80	0003	BA	Submarine volc	0508-001	Historical											
									1996	0218	1996	0222>	----	x---	x---	----	----	1	
Matthew Island (SW Pacific)	22.33 S	171.32 E	177	1111	AD	Stratovolcano	0508-01=	Historical											
									? 1828	01	....	....	----	----	----	----	----		
West-Matthew									1949<	....	....	....	x---	xx--	x---	x---	----	2	
West-Matthew (October 1954, not 1953)									1954	10 ?	....	....	x---	----	?---	----	----	2	
West-Matthew									1956b	....	....	....	x-x-	----	----	----	----	0?	
									? 1966	08	....	....	----	----	?---	----	----		
									? 1976	1127	....	....	x---	----	--?-	----	----	1?	
Hunter Island (SW Pacific)	22.40 S	172.05 E	297	0001	AD	Stratovolcano	0508-02=	Historical											
									? 1797	....	....	....	----	----	----	----	----		
									1835	....	....	....	----	----	----	x---	----		
									1841	0315	....	....	----	----	x---	----	----		
									? 1892	....	....	....	----	----	----	----	----		
East side									1895	1124	....	....	-x--	----	x---	x---	----		
Northern tip of island									1903	....	....	....	--x-	----	----	x---	----	0	
(eruption report not valid)									X 1983	0309<	....	....	----	----	----	----	----		
Unnamed (SW Pacific)	25.78 S	168.63 E	-2400	0000	U	Submarine volc	0508-03-	Hydrophonic											
Norfolk Island Ridge									S 1963	0911	S1964	....	----	x---	x---	----	----	0	

AUSTRALIA

VOLCANO NAME (Subregion) / ERUPTION — Area of Activity	LAT	LONG	ELEV (m)	POPL	ROCK TYPE	VOLC TYPE	NUMBER	STATUS	Start Year	Start M-Dy	Stop Year	Stop M-Dy	Central / Flank vent / Radial fiss / Regional	Submarine / New island / Subglacial / Crater lake	Explosive / Pyro flow / Phreatic / Caldera	Lava flow / Lava lake / Dome / Spine	Fatal / Damage / Mudflow / Tsunami	VEI	Vol L/T
Newer Volcanics Prov (Australia)	37.77 S*	142.50 E	1011	6666	XBtay	Shield volcanoes	0509-01-	Radiocarbon											
Red Rock									C-5850?	....	....	....	x---	----	x---	----	----		
Mt. Napier									C-5290<	....	....	....	x---	----	----	x---	----		
Mt. Schank									F-3000z	....	....	....	x--x	----	x-x-	x---	----		
Mt. Gambier									C-2900w	....	....	....	x---	----	x-x-	x---	----		

Indonesia & Andaman Is (06)

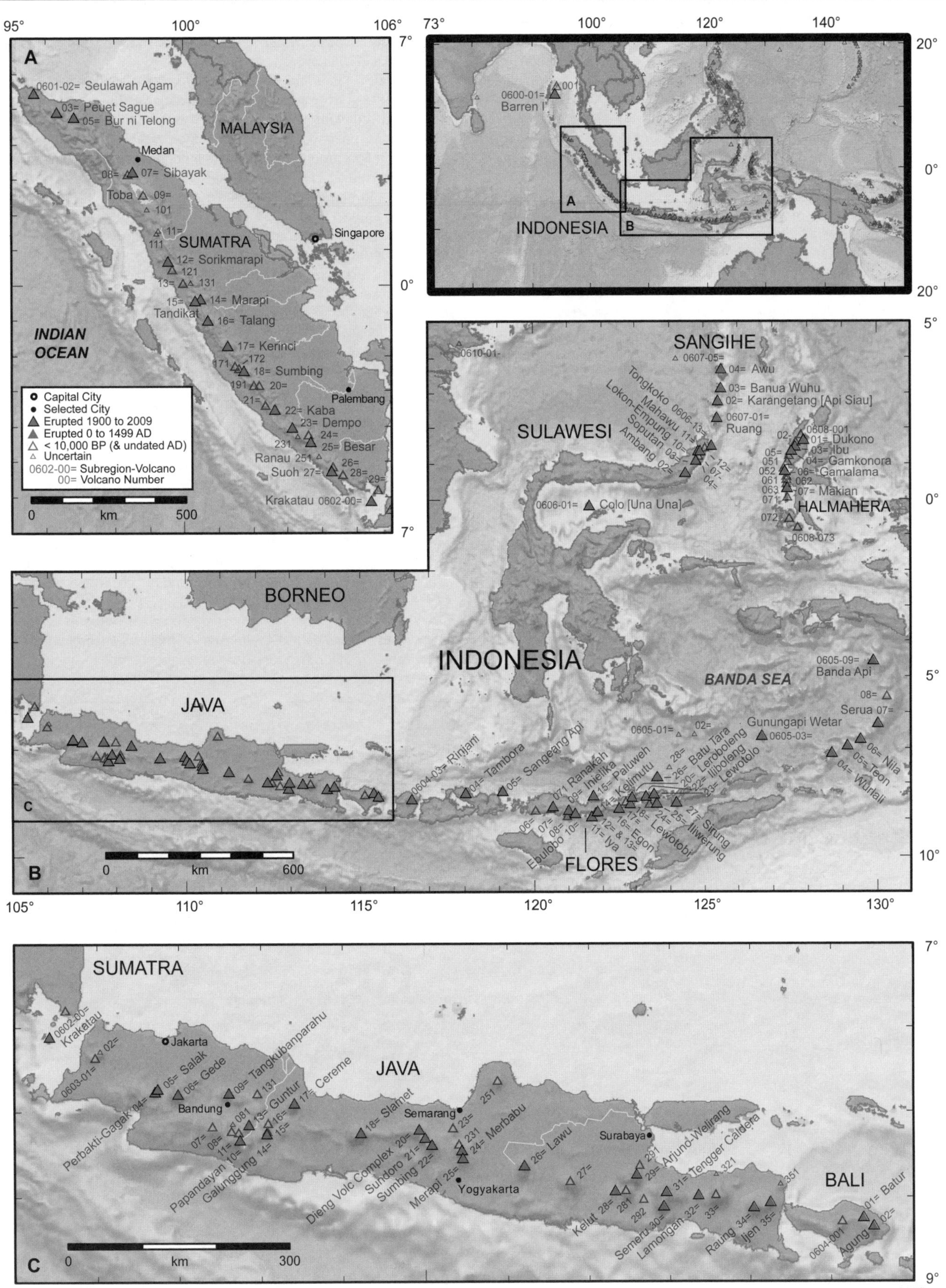

The vast Indonesian archipelago consists of more than 13,000 islands, spread over an area approximating that of the width of the conterminous United States. Its population of more than 237 million is three-fourths of the US's, but with only one-fifth of the land area. More than 75% of Indonesian residents live within 100 km of a Holocene volcano, the highest number of people of any of the world's volcanic regions. Indonesia was the subject of the first *CAVW* in 1951, authored in Holland by Meir Neumann van Padang, who had grown up in Indonesia and worked there as a geologist. He went on to spearhead the *CAVW* series, authoring or co-authoring 6 catalogs and overseeing publication of 21 before retiring, at the age of 73, in 1967.

Although Chinese records show a Krakatau eruption in the 3rd century AD, and some 20 additional historical eruptions are reported, mostly from Kelut as well as Krakatau, through the 15th century, uncertainty surrounds many of them. Europeans first began to document eruptions in 1512 (Sangeang Api and Gunungapi Wetar), about the time Portugal gained control of the Mollucan clove trade. The Dutch East India Company controlled the islands from 1602 through 1780, followed by the Dutch government. Britain took temporary control of the islands in the early 19th century, but the Dutch returned and unrest marked much of the century. The disastrous Krakatau eruption of 1883 was followed by several devastating eruptions on other islands and in 1920 a Volcano Survey was established by the government, leading to much improved volcano monitoring and reporting. The islands were occupied by Japan from early 1942, and WW-II was followed by a 4 year war of independence, with sovereignty gained at the end of 1949. The Volcanological Survey of Indonesia (VSI), now known as the Centre of Volcanology and Geological Hazard Mitigation (CVGHM), operates a network of 76 volcano observatories continuously monitoring 66 volcanoes.

The great sweep of the Sunda Arc, over 3000 km from NW Sumatra to the Banda Sea, results from the subduction of Indian Ocean crust beneath the Asian Plate. This arc includes 78% of the region's volcanoes, but those on either end are tectonically more complex. To the NNW, the basaltic volcanism of the Andaman Islands results from short spreading centers, and to the east the Banda Arc reflects Pacific Ocean crust subducted westward. North of this arc, tectonic complexity increases, with converging plate fragments forming multiple subduction zones, mainly oriented N-S, that in turn produce the Sulawesi-Sangihe volcanoes on the west and Halmahera on the east of the collision zone.

Indonesia leads the world in many volcano statistics. It has the largest number of historically active volcanoes (78), its total of 1250 confirmed eruptions is only exceeded by Japan's 1469, and these two regions have combined to produce nearly 1/3 of the known pyroclastic-flow producing eruptions. Indonesia easily leads the world in numbers of residents living within 30 and 100 km of a Holocene volcano, and has more than double the number of the next highest region of those within these distances of volcanoes with eruptions since 1500 AD. The combination of a densely packed population in a volcano-rich country has led to Indonesia suffering the highest numbers of eruptions producing fatalities (114) and damage to human infrastructure (195). In recent years, however, the VSI (now CVGHM) has compiled an enviable record of evacuating populations before eruption disasters occur. As shown in the evacuation table later in this compilation, Indonesia has had many more recent evacuations than any other nation, and fatalities have been avoided in all but a few eruptions. Indonesia also ranks at the top of regions with tsunamis and crater lake eruptions, the former best known for the major 1883 tsunami from the eruption of Krakatau that swept the coasts of Sumatra and Java, and the latter seen in the frequent eruptions from Kawah Ijen on Java and the renowned multi-hued crater lakes at Kelimutu on Flores Island. Indonesia lies near the top of the list in eruptions producing lava domes (second only to Kamchatka), and mudflows: the volcanological term *lahar* used for mudflows in volcanic terrain derives from Indonesia.

More than four-fifths of Indonesian volcanoes with dated eruptions have erupted since 1900 AD, and history shows the danger of volcanoes that have *not* erupted in recent centuries. Relatively few stratigraphic studies of older volcanic deposits have been completed in Indonesia, and only 0.4% of known Indonesian eruptions have been dated by other than historical techniques, emphasizing the need for more study of the prehistoric record in this region.

VOLCANO NAME (Subregion) / **ERUPTION** — Area of Activity	**LAT**	**LONG**	**ELEV** (m)	**POPL** (5 km, 10, 30, 100)	**ROCK TYPE**	**VOLC TYPE** / Start **Year**	Start M-Dy	**NUMBER** / Stop **Year**	**STATUS** / Stop M-Dy	Central, Flank vent, Radial fiss, Regional	Submarine, New island, Subglacial, Crater lake	Explosive, Pyro flow, Phreatic, Caldera	Lava flow, Lava lake, Dome, Spine	Fatal, Damage, Mudflow, Tsunami	VEI	Vol L/T
SUMATRA & ANDAMAN ISLANDS																
Narcondum (Andaman Is-Indian O)	**13.43 N**	**94.28 E**	**710**	0000	AD	**Stratovolcano**		**0600-001**	**Holocene**							
Barren Island (Andaman Is)	**12.278 N**	**93.858 E**	**354**	3334	BA	**Stratovolcano**		**0600-01=**	**Historical**							
(eruption May 12, 1787, not 1783)						**1787**	0512	....	....	x---	----	x---	----	----	2	
						1789	0324	....	....	x---	----	x---	----	----	2	
						1795	1220	**1795**	1221>	x---	----	x---	----	----	2	
						1803	11	**1804**	0131>	x---	----	x---	x---	----	2	
						1832	03	....	....	x---	----	?---	x---	----	2?	
(uncertain press report of activity)						*? 1852*	....	....	....	?---	----	?---	----	----	*2*	
Central cone summit and NE flank						**1991**	0329	**1991**	1031g	xx--	----	x---	x---	-x--	2	6/6
Central cone summit, SW & S flanks						**1994**	1220<	**1995**	0605h	xxx-	----	x---	x---	----	2	6/6
						? 2000	*01*	....	....	x---	----	?---	----	----	*1?*	
Central cone summit, N, S, and SW flanks						**2005**	0526	**2007**	1223?	x---	----	x---	x---	----	2	
						2008	0513	**2010>**	....	x---	----	x---	x---	----	2	
Seulawah Agam (Sumatra)	**5.448 N**	**95.658 E**	**1810**	3567	AD	**Stratovolcano**		**0601-02=**	**Historical**							
NNE flank						**1510**j	....	....	....	-x--	----	?-?-	----	----	2	
NNE flank (van Heutsz crater)						**1839**	0112	**1839**	0113	-x--	----	?-?-	----	----	2	
Peuet Sague (Sumatra)	**4.914 N**	**96.329 E**	**2801**	2357	AD	**Complex volcano**		**0601-03=**	**Historical**							
						1918	....	**1921**	....	x---	----	xx--	--x-	----	2	
						1979	....	....	....	x---	----	x---	----	----	2	
						1986	....	....	....	x---	----	x---	----	----	2	
						1991	....	....	....	x---	----	x---	----	----	2	
						1998	0419	**1998**	0426?	x---	----	x-x-	----	----	1	
						1999	0309?	**1999**	0430c	x---	----	x---	----	----	1	
						2000	1225	**2000**	1226>	x---	----	x---	x---	----	2	
Telong, Bur ni (Sumatra)	**4.769 N**	**96.821 E**	**2617**	4567	A	**Stratovolcano**		**0601-05=**	**Historical**							
						1837	0925e	....	....	x---	----	x---	----	----	2	
						1839	0112	**1839**	0113	x---	----	x---	----	----	2	
						1856	0414	....	....	x---	----	x---	----	----	2	
						1919	12	....	....	x---	----	x---	----	----	2	
						? 1924	*1207*	....	....	----	----	----	----	----	*2*	
						1937	....	....	....	----	----	----	----	----		
Sibayak (Sumatra)	**3.23 N**	**98.52 E**	**2212**	5567	AD	**Stratovolcanoes**		**0601-07=**	**Historical**							
						1881	....	....	....	----	----	x---	----	----		
Sinabung (Sumatra)	**3.17 N**	**98.392 E**	**2460**	3567	AD	**Stratovolcano**		**0601-08=**	**Holocene**							
						? 1881	....	....	....	----	----	x---	----	----		
Toba (Sumatra)	**2.58 N**	**98.83 E**	**2157**	6667	DRYA	**Caldera**		**0601-09=**	**Holocene**							

VOLCANO NAME (Subregion) / ERUPTION — Area of Activity	LAT	LONG	ELEV (m)	POPL (5 km, 10, 30, 100)	ROCK TYPE	VOLC TYPE	NUMBER	STATUS	Start Year	Start M-Dy	Stop Year	Stop M-Dy	Central / Flank vent / Radial fiss / Regional	Submarine / New island / Subglacial / Crater lake	Explosive / Pyro flow / Phreatic / Caldera	Lava flow / Lava lake / Dome / Spine	Fatal / Damage / Mudflow / Tsunami	VEI	Vol L/T
Imun (Sumatra)	**2.158 N**	**98.93 E**	**1505**	4567	**DR**	**Unknown**	**0601-101**	Holocene?											
Sibualbuali (Sumatra)	**1.556 N**	**99.255 E**	**1819**	4567	**DRAb**	**Stratovolcano**	**0601-11=**	Holocene?											
Lubukraya (Sumatra)	**1.478 N**	**99.209 E**	**1862**	3467	**Ab**	**Stratovolcano**	**0601-111**	Holocene?											
Sorikmarapi (Sumatra)	**0.686 N**	**99.539 E**	**2145**	3457	**AD**	**Stratovolcano**	**0601-12=**	**Historical**											
									1829?	....	....	....	x---	----	x-x-	----	----	2	
									? *1866*	....	....	....	----	----	----	----	----		
									1879	....	....	....	x---	----	--x-	----	----	2	
									? *1888*	*02*	....	....	----	----	----	----	----		
Summit and east flank (Jurang Siunik)									**1892**	0521	....	....	xx--	----	--x-	----	xxx-	2	
East flank (Sibanggor Julu)									**1893**	0104	**1893**	0104	-x--	----	--x-	----	----	2	
									1917	0520	**1917**	0520	x---	----	x-x-	----	----	2	
									1970	....	....	....	x---	----	x---	----	----	2	
									1986	0705	**1986**	0714	x---	----	x-x-	----	----	1	-/2
									? *1996*	*0505*	....	....	----	----	?---	----	----		
Malintang (Sumatra)	**0.47 N**	**99.67 E**	**1983**	2367	**Ad**	**Stratovolcano**	**0601-121**	**Holocene**											
Talakmau (Sumatra)	**0.079 N**	**99.98 E**	**2919**	2467	**AD**	**Complex volcano**	**0601-13=**	**Holocene**											
									? *1937*	*0908*	....	....	x---	----	----	----	----	*1*	
Sarik-Gajah (Sumatra)	**0.08 N**	**100.20 E**		4567	**ABD**	**Pyroclastic cones**	**0601-131**	Holocene?											
Marapi (Sumatra)	**0.381 S**	**100.473 E**	**2891**	3567	**AYB**	**Complex volcano**	**0601-14=**	**Historical**											
									1770	....	....	....	x---	----	x---	----	----	2	
									1807	....	....	....	x---	----	x---	----	----	2	
									1822	0723	**1822**	0731	x---	----	x---	x---	-x--	2	
									1833	....	**1834**	....	x---	----	x---	----	----	2?	
									1845	1116	**1845**	1118	x---	----	x---	----	----	2?	
									1854	0829>	....	....	x---	----	x---	----	----	2	
									1855	1002	**1856**	01	x---	----	x---	----	----	2	
									1861	04	....	....	x---	----	x---	----	----	2?	
									1863	0523	....	....	x---	----	x---	----	----	2?	
									1871	0424	....	....	x---	----	x---	----	----	2?	
									1871	0924	....	....	x---	----	x---	----	----	2?	
									1876	0404	....	....	x---	----	x---	----	----	2?	
									1876	08	**1877**	06	x---	----	x---	----	----	2?	
									? *1878*	*12*	....	....	x---	----	x---	----	----	*2?*	
									1883	0625	**1883**	0827	x---	----	--x-	----	----	1	
									1883	12	**1883**	12	x---	----	x---	----	----	1	
									1885	1112	....	....	x---	----	x---	----	----	2?	
									1886	0331	**1886**	0503	x---	----	x---	----	----	2	
									1888	0219	**1888**	0319	x---	----	x---	----	----	2?	
									1889	0327	**1889**	0417?	x---	----	x---	----	----	2?	
									1904	0418	**1904**	0418	x---	----	x---	----	----	1	
									1905	1101	....	....	x---	----	x---	----	----	2?	
									1907	1217	**1908**	09	x---	----	x---	----	----	2?	
									1910	....	....	....	x---	----	x---	----	----	2?	
									1911	1102	....	....	x---	----	x---	----	----	2?	
									1913	0623	**1913**	0731	x---	----	x---	----	----	2?	
									1914	0701	....	....	x---	----	x---	----	----	2?	
									1915	12	....	....	x---	----	x---	----	----	2?	
									1916	0505	**1916**	0707	x---	----	x---	----	----	1	
									1917	0616	**1917**	0916	x---	----	x---	----	----	2?	
									1918	0308	**1918**	0310	x---	----	x---	----	----	2?	
									1918	0815e	**1918**	0815e	x---	----	x---	----	----	2?	
									1919	0228	**1919**	0301	x---	----	x---	----	----	2?	
									1925	04 ?	....	....	x---	----	----	x---	----	0	
Kepundan Bongsu									**1927**	0205	**1927**	0803	x---	----	x---	----	----	2	
Kepundan Bongsu									**1929**	0622	**1929**	0622	x---	----	x---	----	----	2	
									1930	0409<	**1930**	1207	x---	----	x---	x-?-	----	2?	
									1932	....	....	....	x---	----	?---	----	----	2?	
Kepundan Kuniang, Kepundan Jinggo									**1943**e	....	....	....	x---	----	x---	----	----		
Kepundan Bongsu									**1949**	0429	**1949**	0430	x---	----	x---	----	----	2	
									1949	1015e	**1949**	1022e	x---	----	x---	----	----	2	
Kepundan Bongsu, Kuniang, Jinggo									**1950**	0927	**1952**	0614	x---	----	x---	----	----	2*	
Kepundan Bongsu, B and C Craters									**1954**	08	**1957**	12 >	----	----	x---	----	----	2?	
									1958	0623	**1958**	0623?	x---	----	x---	----	----	1	
									1958	1017	**1958**	1025	x---	----	x---	----	----	1	
B and C Craters, Kebun Bungo									**1966**	03	**1966**	06	x---	----	x---	----	----	1	
Crater C, Bungsu Crater									**1967**	04	**1967**	07	x---	----	x---	----	----	1	
Craters B and C									? *1968*	*12*	?*1968*	*12*	x---	----	--?-	----	----	*1*	
Bungo, Bongsu, Tuo, B and C Craters									**1970**	0726e	**1971**	0820	x---	----	x-?-	----	----	2	
Verbeek Crater									**1973**	0724	**1973**	0724	x---	----	x---	----	----	2	
Verbeek Crater, B and C Craters									**1975**	01	**1979**	0911	x---	----	x-x-	----	xxx-	2*	
									1980	0329	....	....	x---	----	x---	----	----	1	
									1982	0310<	**1982**	05	x---	----	x---	----	----	1	
									1982	12	**1982**	12	x---	----	x---	----	----	1	
Kepundan Tuo and Kepundan Verbeek									**1983**	....	....	....	x---	----	x---	----	----	1	
Kepundan Tuo, Kepundan B									**1984**	1115	**1984**	1115	x---	----	--x-	----	----	1	
Verbeek Crater									**1987**	0115	**1994**>	....	x---	----	x---	----	x---	2	
									1999	04 <	**1999**	09 >	x---	----	x---	----	----	2	
									2000	0311	**2000**	0403>	x---	----	x---	----	----	2	
Verbeek Crater									**2001**	0413	**2001**	0605	x---	----	x---	----	----	2	
									2004	0805	**2004**	0805?	x---	----	x---	----	----	2	
Tandikat (Sumatra)	**0.433 S**	**100.317 E**	**2438**	3567	**Ad**	**Stratovolcanoes**	**0601-15=**	**Historical**											
Summit crater and upper NE flank									**1889**	0219	**1889**	1204	xx--	----	x-x-	----	----	1	
									? *1892*	....	....	....	----	----	----	----	----		
									1914	0531	....	....	x---	----	x---	----	----	1	
									1924	04	**1924**	04 ?	x---	----	x-x-	----	----	1	
Talang (Sumatra)	**0.978 S**	**100.679 E**	**2597**	4567	**A**	**Stratovolcano**	**0601-16=**	**Historical**											
NE flank									**1833**	10	....	....	-x--	----	x---	----	----	2	
NE flank (some reports list 1842 date)									**1843**	1021	....	....	-x--	----	x---	----	----	2	
NE flank									**1845**	0422	....	....	-x--	----	x---	----	----	2	
									? *1868*c	....	....	....	----	----	?---	----	----		
NE flank									**1876**?	....	....	....	-x--	----	x---	----	----	2	
									1963	....	....	....	----	----	----	----	----	2	

VOLCANO NAME (Subregion) / ERUPTION — Area of Activity	LAT	LONG	ELEV (m)	POPL 5 km 10 30 100	ROCK TYPE	VOLC TYPE	NUMBER — Start — Year	M-Dy	STATUS — Stop — Year	M-Dy	Central Flank vent Radial fiss Regional	Submarine New island Subglacial Crater lake	Explosive Pyro flow Phreatic Caldera	Lava flow Lava lake Dome Spine	Fatal Damage Mudflow Tsunami	VEI	Vol L/T
Talang (Sumatra) *continued*																	
NE flank (200 m below summit)							**1967**	1010	**1967**	1010	--x-	----	?-?-	----	----	1	
NE flank							**1968**	0114	**1968**	0114?	--x-	----	x---	----	----	1	
NE flank							**1968**	09	**1968**	10	--x-	----	x---	----	----	2	
NE flank (Panjang Crater)							? *1986*	*0716*	?*1986*	*1013*	-x--	----	--?-	----	----	*1*	
Kepundan Panjang & Kabuo, Gabuo Atas							**2001**	0925	**2001**	1115c	-x--	----	--x-	----	----	1	
North & south flanks							**2005**	0412?	**2005**	0718?	-x--	----	x-x-	----	----	2	
							2006	0910	**2006**	0910	?---	----	x---	----	----	1	
Main crater							**2007**	0319	**2007**	0622c	x---	----	x---	----	----	2	
							2007	1127	**2007**	12 ?	x---	----	x---	----	----	2	
Kerinci (Sumatra)	**1.697 S**	**101.264 E**	**3800**	3567	**A**	**Stratovolcano**	**0601-17=**		**Historical**								
							1838	....	....	....	x---	----	x---	----	----	2	
							1842	....	....	....	x---	----	x---	----	----	2	
							1874?	....	....	....	x---	----	x---	----	----	2?	
							1878	1211	....	....	x---	----	--x-	----	----	2	
							1887	0323	**1887**	0330	x---	----	--x-	----	----	2?	
							1908	10	?*1909*	....	x---	----	x-?-	----	----	2	
							1921	05	**1921**	06	x---	----	x---	----	----	2	
							1923	09	**1923**	09	x---	----	--?-	----	----	1	
							1936	0429	**1936**	0429	x---	----	x-x-	----	----	2	
							1936	0830	**1936**	0830	x---	----	x-x-	----	----	2	
							1937	0908	....	....	x---	---x	--x-	----	----	2	
							1938	0119	**1938**	0318	x---	----	--x-	----	----	2	
							1952	01	**1952**	06	x---	----	x---	----	----	2	
							1960	07	....	....	x---	----	x---	----	----	2	
							1963	07	....	....	x---	----	x---	----	----	2	
							1964	0708	**1964**	0708?	x---	----	x---	----	----	2	
							1966	0609	**1966**	0630>	x---	----	x---	----	----	2	
							1967	1102	....	....	x---	----	x---	----	----	2	
							1968	0203	**1968**	0318	x---	----	x---	----	----	2	
							1969	....	**1970**	....	x---	----	x---	----	----	2	
							? *1971*	*06*	?*1971*	*06*	x---	----	--x-	----	----	*1?*	
							1990	1231y	....	....	x---	----	x---	----	----	2	
							1996	08	**1996**	10 ?	x---	----	x---	----	----	1	
							1998	0704	**1998**	0704	x---	----	x---	----	----	2	
							1998	1103	....	....	x---	----	x---	----	----	2?	
							1999	03 <	**1999**	09 >	x---	----	x---	----	----	2	
							2001	0512	**2002**	0827?	x---	----	x---	----	----	2	
							2004	0622?	**2004**	1024?	x---	----	x---	----	----	2*	
							2007	0909	**2007**	0909	x---	----	x---	----	----	1	
							2008	0324	....	....	x---	----	x---	----	----	1	
							2009	0401?	**2009**	0619?	x---	----	x---	----	----	1	
Kunyit (Sumatra)	**2.274 S**	**101.483 E**	**2151**	3457	**D**	**Stratovolcano**	**0601-171**		**Fumarolic**								
Hutapanjang (Sumatra)	**2.33 S**	**101.60 E**	**2021**	2357	**U**	**Stratovolcano**	**0601-172**		**Holocene**								
Sumbing (Sumatra)	**2.414 S**	**101.728 E**	**2507**	1357	**AD**	**Stratovolcano**	**0601-18=**		**Historical**								
							1909	0603	**1909**	07	x---	----	x---	----	----	2	
							1921	0523	**1921**	0603	-x--	----	x---	----	----	2	
Pendan (Sumatra)	**2.82 S**	**102.02 E**		3457	**U**	**Unknown**	**0601-191**		**Holocene**								
Belirang-Beriti (Sumatra)	**2.82 S**	**102.18 E**	**1958**	1257	**BA**	**Compound volc**	**0601-20=**		**Fumarolic**								
Daun, Bukit (Sumatra)	**3.38 S**	**102.37 E**	**2467**	4567	**BA**	**Stratovolcanoes**	**0601-21=**		**Fumarolic**								
Kaba (Sumatra)	**3.52 S**	**102.62 E**	**1952**	3567	**A**	**Stratovolcano**	**0601-22=**		**Historical**								
							1833	1124	**1833**	1125	x---	---x	x---	----	xxx-	2	
							1834	11	....	....	x---	----	x---	----	-x--	2	
							? *1838*	....	....	....	----	----	----	----	----		
							1853	11	....	....	x---	----	x---	----	-xx-	2	
Kaba Baru ? and Kaba Vogelsang							**1868**	10	**1869**	....	?x--	----	x---	----	----	2	
Kaba Volgelsang and Kaba Baru							**1873**	....	**1892**	1101p	xx--	----	x---	?---	----	2	
Kaba Baru							**1907**	....	....	....	x---	----	x---	----	----	2	
							? *1918*	*0809*	....	....	x---	----	--?-	----	----	*2?*	
Kaba Baru, Kaba Lama							**1939**	1119	**1941**	0314	x---	----	x-x-	----	----	2	
Kaba Vogelsang							**1950**	03	**1951**	04	-x--	----	x---	----	----	1*	
							1952	0401	**1952**	0428	x---	----	x---	----	----	2	
							1956	0322	**1956**	0328	x---	----	x---	----	----	2	
							2000	0822?	**2000**	0827?	x---	----	x---	----	----	1	
Dempo (Sumatra)	**4.03 S**	**103.13 E**	**3173**	3457	**A**	**Stratovolcanoes**	**0601-23=**		**Historical**								
							1817	1231y	....	....	x---	----	x---	----	----	2	
							1839?	....	....	....	x---	----	x---	----	----	2	
							1853	0101	....	....	x---	----	x---	----	----	2	
							1879	0518	....	....	x---	----	x---	----	----	2	
							1880	05	....	....	x---	----	--x-	----	----	2	
							1881	0216	....	....	x---	----	x---	----	----	2	
							1881	12	**1881**	12	x---	----	x---	----	----	2	
							1884	06	**1884**	07	x---	----	x---	----	----	2	
							1895	0702	**1895**	0930	x---	----	x---	----	----	2	
							1900	0604	**1900**	0604	x---	----	x---	----	----	2	
							1900	1026	**1900**	1027	x---	----	x---	----	----	2	
							1905	....	....	....	x---	---x	--x-	----	----	0	
							1908	0216	**1908**	0217	x---	----	x-?-	----	----	2	
							1921	04	**1921**	04	x---	---x	--x-	----	----	1	
							1923	0519?	**1923**	0519?	x---	---x	--x-	----	----	1	
							1926	0422	**1926**	0424	x---	---x	--x-	----	----	2	
							1934	0124	**1934**	0425	x---	----	x---	----	-x--	2	
							1936	1126	**1936**	1127	x---	----	x---	----	----	2	
							1939	0718	**1939**	0730	x---	---x	x-x-	----	-x--	2	
							1939	1219	**1940**	0221	x---	---x	x-x-	----	-xx-	2*	
							1940	07	....	....	x---	----	x---	----	----	2	
							1964	0214	**1964**	0214	x---	----	x---	----	----	2	
							1973	0124	**1973**	0125	x---	----	x-x-	----	----	2	
							1974	0226	**1974**	1020	x---	----	x-?-	----	-x--	2	
							1994	10	**1994**	10	x---	---x	x-x-	----	----	1	
							2006	0925	**2006**	0925	x---	---x	--x-	----	----	1	
							2009	0101	**2009**	0101	x---	----	x-x-	----	----	1?	
Patah (Sumatra)	**4.27 S**	**103.30 E**	**2817**	2357	**U**	**Unknown**	**0601-231**		**Fumarolic**								

UNOCAL

Dempo summit crater (upper L)

VOLCANO NAME (Subregion) / ERUPTION — Area of Activity	LAT	LONG	ELEV (m)	POPL (5 km / 10 / 30 / 100)	ROCK TYPE	VOLC TYPE	NUMBER	STATUS	Start Year	Start M-Dy	Stop Year	Stop M-Dy	Central / Flank vent / Radial fiss / Regional	Submarine / New island / Subglacial / Crater lake	Explosive / Pyro flow / Phreatic / Caldera	Lava flow / Lava lake / Dome / Spine	Fatal / Damage / Mudflow / Tsunami	VEI	Vol L/T
Lumut Balai, Bukit (Sumatra)	4.22 S	103.62 E	2055	2457	A	Stratovolcano ?	0601-24=	Fumarolic											
Besar (Sumatra)	4.43 S	103.67 E	1899	3457	A	Stratovolcano ?	0601-25=	Historical											
Marga Bayur (Gemurah Ilahan)									**1940**	04	....	....	-x--	----	--x-	----	----	1	
Ranau (Sumatra)	4.83 S	103.92 E	1881	5556	DA	Caldera	0601-251	Holocene?											
									? 1887	*1007*	*?1888*	*0120*	----	---?	----	----	----		
									? 1903	*1209*	*?1903*	*1209*	----	---?	----	----	----		
Sekincau Belirang (Sumatra)	5.12 S	104.32 E	1719	3457	ARD	Calderas	0601-26=	Fumarolic											
Suoh (Sumatra)	5.25 S	104.27 E	1000	3457	U	Calderas	0601-27=	Historical											
Pematang Bata									**1933**	0710	**1933**	0805	x---	----	-xx-	----	----	4	-/8
Hulubelu (Sumatra)	5.35 S	104.60 E	1040	5557	ADB	Caldera	0601-28=	Fumarolic											
Rajabasa (Sumatra)	5.78 S	105.625 E	1281	4667	A	Stratovolcano	0601-29=	Fumarolic											

KRAKATAU

VOLCANO NAME (Subregion) / ERUPTION — Area of Activity	LAT	LONG	ELEV (m)	POPL	ROCK TYPE	VOLC TYPE	NUMBER	STATUS	Start Year	Start M-Dy	Stop Year	Stop M-Dy	Central / Flank vent / Radial fiss / Regional	Submarine / New island / Subglacial / Crater lake	Explosive / Pyro flow / Phreatic / Caldera	Lava flow / Lava lake / Dome / Spine	Fatal / Damage / Mudflow / Tsunami	VEI	Vol L/T
Krakatau (Indonesia)	6.102 S	105.423 E	813	4447	ADBt	Caldera	0602-00=	Historical											
									0250t	....	....	....	x---	----	x---	----	----		
									0416	....	....	....	x---	----	x--x	----	xx-x	C	
									0850t	....	....	....	----	----	----	----	----		
									0950t	....	....	....	----	----	----	----	----		
									1050t	....	....	....	----	----	----	----	----		
									1150t	....	....	....	----	----	----	----	----		
									1320?	....	....	....	----	----	----	----	----		
									1530	....	....	....	----	----	----	----	----		
Perbuwatan									**1680**	05	**1681**	1119>	x---	----	x---	x---	----	3	-/8
									1684	0201	....	....	x---	----	x---	----	----	3↑	
Krakatau Island (Perbuwatan, Danan)									**1883**	0520	**1883**	1021?	x---	x---	xx-x	----	xxxx	**6***	**-/10**
Anak Krakatau									**1927**	1229	**1930**	0815	x--x	xx--	xxx-	----	----	2*	
Anak Krakatau									**1931**	0923	**1932**	0217	xx--	---x	x---	----	----	2	
Anak Krakatau									**1932**	1114	**1934**	0609	x---	---x	x---	----	----	3*	
Anak Krakatau									**1935**	0104	**1935**	0712	x---	x--x	x-x-	----	----	2	
Anak Krakatau									**1936**	1013	**1936**	11	x---	?---	x---	----	----	1	
Anak Krakatau									**1937**	0806	**1937**	1123	x---	---x	x---	----	----	2	
Anak Krakatau									**1938**	0704	**1940**	0702	x---	x--x	x-x-	----	----	3*	
Anak Krakatau									**1941**	0128	**1941**	0212	x---	---x	x---	----	----	2	
Anak Krakatau									**1942**	0129	**1942**	0130	x---	---x	x---	----	----	2	
Anak Krakatau									**1943**	....	....	....	x---	---?	?---	----	----	2	
Anak Krakatau									**1944**	....	....	....	x---	---?	?---	----	----	2	
Anak Krakatau									**1945**	....	....	....	x---	---?	?---	----	----	2	
Anak Krakatau									**1946**	0725	**1946**	0725	x---	---x	x---	----	----	1	
Anak Krakatau									**1946**	1226e	**1947**	0807>	x---	---x	x---	----	----	2	
Anak Krakatau									**1949**	0512	....	....	x---	---x	x---	----	----	2	
Anak Krakatau									**1950**	0703	**1950**	0707	x---	---x	x---	----	----	2	
Anak Krakatau									**1952**	1010	**1952**	1011	x---	---x	x---	----	----	2	
Anak Krakatau									**1953**	0317	**1953**	0501?	x---	---x	x---	----	----	2	
Anak Krakatau									**1953**	0921	**1953**	1125	x---	---x	x---	----	----	2	
Anak Krakatau									**1955**	0211	....	....	x---	----	x---	----	----	2	
Anak Krakatau									**1958**	1002	**1959**	0625d	x---	---x	x---	----	----	2	
Anak Krakatau									**1959**	12	**1963**	....	x---	---x	x---	x---	----	2	6/-
Anak Krakatau									**1965**?	....	....	....	x---	----	x-x-	?---	----	1?	
Anak Krakatau									*? 1969*	....	....	....	----	----	----	----	----	*2?*	
Anak Krakatau									**1972**	0610c	**1973**	0701p	xx--	----	x---	x---	----	2	6/-
Anak Krakatau									**1975**	0327	**1975**	1026e	x---	----	x---	x---	----	2	6/-
Anak Krakatau									**1978**	0710	**1978**	11	x---	----	x---	----	----	1	-/4
Anak Krakatau									**1979**	0715e	**1979**	11	x---	----	x---	x---	----	2	4/-
Anak Krakatau									**1980**	0315e	**1980**	12	x---	----	x---	x---	----	2	5/-
Anak Krakatau									**1981**	0424	**1981**	1020	x---	----	x---	----	----	1	
Anak Krakatau (S flank 1960-81 cone)									**1988**	0214e	**1988**	04 ?	xx--	----	x---	x---	----	2	5/-
Anak Krakatau									**1992**	1107	**1993**	10	x---	----	x---	x---	x---	1	6/-
Anak Krakatau									**1994**	0319	**1995**	06 >	x---	----	x---	----	----	2	
Anak Krakatau									**1996**	07 <	**1996**	10 >	x---	----	x---	x---	----	2	
Anak Krakatau									**1997**	03 <	**1997**	05 >	x---	----	x---	----	----	2	
Anak Krakatau									**1999**	0205	**1999**	08 >	x---	----	x---	----	----	2	
Anak Krakatau									**2000**	0529	**2000**	1030?	x---	----	x---	----	----	1	
Anak Krakatau									**2001**	0721	**2001**	0917?	x---	----	x---	----	----	1	
Anak Krakatau									**2007**	1023	**2008**	0830?	x---	----	xx--	x---	----	2	
Anak Krakatau									**2009**	0325?	**2009**	09 ?	x---	----	x---	x---	----	2	

JAVA

VOLCANO NAME (Subregion) / ERUPTION — Area of Activity	LAT	LONG	ELEV (m)	POPL	ROCK TYPE	VOLC TYPE	NUMBER	STATUS	Start Year	Start M-Dy	Stop Year	Stop M-Dy	Central / Flank vent / Radial fiss / Regional	Submarine / New island / Subglacial / Crater lake	Explosive / Pyro flow / Phreatic / Caldera	Lava flow / Lava lake / Dome / Spine	Fatal / Damage / Mudflow / Tsunami	VEI	Vol L/T
Pulosari (Java-W)	6.342 S	105.975 E	1346	4568	AB	Stratovolcano	0603-01=	Holocene											
Karang (Java-W)	6.27 S	106.042 E	1778	4578	AB	Stratovolcano	0603-02=	Holocene?											
Perbakti-Gagak (Java-W)	6.75 S	106.70 E	1699	4578	ARD	Stratovolcanoes	0603-04=	Historical											
Kiaraberes									C-**6450**?	....	....	....	-x--	----	--x-	----	----		
Kawah Cibodas									**1923**	06	....	....	-x--	----	--x-	----	----	1	
Cibeureum West									**1929**	....	....	....	-x--	----	--x-	----	----	1	
Kawah Cibodas									**1935**	0531p	....	....	-x--	----	--x-	----	----	1	
Cipanas Parabakti									**1936**	1026	**1936**	1028	-x--	----	--x-	----	----	1	
Kawah Parabakti									**1938**	12	....	....	-x--	----	--x-	----	----	1	
Kawah Parabakti									**1939**	0406<	....	....	-x--	----	--x-	----	----	1	
Salak (Java-W)	6.72 S	106.73 E	2211	4578	AB	Stratovolcano	0603-05=	Historical											
Salak 3.									*? 1699*	*0105*	....	....	x---	----	?---	----	-xx-		
Kawah Ratu									**1780**	....	....	....	-x--	----	x---	----	----	2	
Kawah Ratu									**1902**	....	**1903**	....	-x--	----	--x-	----	----	2	
Kawah Ratu									**1919**	....	....	....	-x--	----	--x-	----	----	2	
Kawah Cikaluwung Putri.									**1935**	02	....	....	-x--	----	--x-	----	----	2	
Kawah Cikaluwung Putri.									**1938**	0131e	....	....	-x--	----	--x-	----	----	2	
Gede (Java-W)	6.78 S	106.98 E	2958	4678	AB	Stratovolcano	0603-06=	Historical											
									1747	....	**1748**	....	x---	----	x---	?---	----	3	
									1761	....	....	....	x---	----	x---	----	----	2	
									1832	0829	**1832**	0829	x---	----	x---	----	----	3	
									? 1839	....	....	....	----	----	----	----	----		

VOLCANO NAME (Subregion) / ERUPTION — Area of Activity	LAT	LONG	ELEV (m)	POPL (5 km, 10, 30, 100)	ROCK TYPE	VOLC TYPE	NUMBER	STATUS	Start Year	Start M-Dy	Stop Year	Stop M-Dy	Central / Flank vent / Radial fiss / Regional	Submarine / New island / Subglacial / Crater lake	Explosive / Pyro flow / Phreatic / Caldera	Lava flow / Lava lake / Dome / Spine	Fatal / Damage / Mudflow / Tsunami	VEI	Vol L/T
Gede (Java-W) *continued*									**1840**	1112	**1840**	1211	x---	----	xx--	----	-x--	3*	
									1843	0728	....	....	x---	----	x---	----	----	2	
									1845	0123	**1845**	0305	x---	----	x---	----	----	2	
									1847	1017	**1847**	1018	x---	----	x---	----	----	2	
									1848	0508	....	....	x---	----	x---	----	----	2	
									1852	0528	**1852**	0528	x---	----	x---	----	-x--	2	
									1853	0314	**1853**	0314	x---	----	x---	----	----	3?	
									1866	0918	....	....	x---	----	x---	----	----	2	
									1870	08	**1870**	1003	x---	----	x---	----	----	2	
									? *1885*	*01*	?*1885*	*02*	x---	----	x---	----	----	*2?*	
									1886	0610	**1886**	0816	x---	----	x---	----	----	2	
									1887	1022	**1887**	1022	x---	----	x---	----	----	2	
									1888	....	....	....	x---	----	x---	----	----	2?	
									? *1889*	*0508<*	....	....	x---	----	----	----	----	*1*	
									1891	....	....	....	x---	----	x---	----	----	2	
									1899	0501	**1899**	0514	x---	----	x---	----	----	2	
									1909	0502	**1909**	0502	x---	----	x---	----	----	1	
Kawah Ratu?, Kawah Lanang									**1947**	0902	**1948**	0128	x---	----	x-x-	----	----	2	-/5
Kawah Leutik (Kawah Ratu)									**1948**	1115	**1949**	0205	x---	----	x---	----	----	2	-/5
									? *1955*	*0721*	?*1955*	*0802*	x---	----	--x-	----	----	*1*	
									1956	0428	**1956**	0428	x---	----	x---	----	----	2?	
									1957	0313	**1957**	0313	x---	----	x---	----	----	2	
Patuha (Java-W)	**7.160 S**	**107.40 E**	**2434**	5578	**A**	**Stratovolcano**	**0603-07=**	**Holocene**											
Wayang-Windu (Java-W)	**7.208 S**	**107.63 E**	**2182**	5678	**A**	**Lava dome**	**0603-08=**	**Fumarolic**											
Malabar (Java-W)	**7.13 S**	**107.65 E**	**2343**	5678	**A**	**Stratovolcano**	**0603-081**	Holocene?											
Tangkubanparahu (Java-W)	**6.77 S**	**107.60 E**	**2084**	6678	**AB**	**Stratovolcano**	**0603-09=**	**Historical**											
(tephra layer YT2)									C-**8020**t	....	....	....	x---	----	x---	----	----		
(tephra layer YT3)									C-**7500**t	....	....	....	x---	----	x---	----	----		
									1826	1011	**1826**	1011	x---	----	--?-	----	----	2	
Kawah Ratu and Kawah Domas									**1829**	0401	**1829**	0404?	x---	----	x-x-	----	----	2	
									1842	....	....	....	x---	----	--?-	----	----		
Kawah Ratu B									**1846**	0527	....	....	x---	----	x?--	----	xxx-	2	
Kawah Baru									**1896**	0522	**1896**	0523	x---	----	x-x-	----	----	2	
Kawah Ratu B									**1910**	0407	**1910**	05	x---	----	x-x-	----	----	2	
Kawah Ecoma									**1926**	0301	**1926**	0709	x---	----	x-x-	----	----	1?	
Kawah Ecoma									**1929**	0520	**1929**	0520	x---	----	--x-	----	----	0	
Kawah Ecoma									**1952**	0704?	**1952**	0711	x---	----	x-x-	----	----	1	
Kawah Baru									**1957**	01	**1957**	01	x---	----	--x-	----	----	1	
									1961	0716	**1961**	0801	x---	----	--x-	----	----	1	
									1965	02	**1965**	03	x---	----	--x-	----	----	1	
									1965	10	**1965**	10	x---	----	--x-	----	----	1	
Kawah Ecoma									**1967**	07	**1967**	07	x---	----	--x-	----	----	1	
Kawah Ecoma									**1969**	0720	**1969**	1021	x---	----	x-x-	----	----	1	
Kawah Ratu									**1983**	0914	....	....	x---	----	x-x-	----	----	1	
Kawah Baru									? *1985*	*1115*	?*1985*	*1115*	x---	----	--x-	----	----	*1*	
Papandayan (Java-W)	**7.32 S**	**107.73 E**	**2665**	4678	**A**	**Stratovolcanoes**	**0603-10=**	**Historical**											
									1772	0812	**1772**	0812	x---	----	x-xA	----	xx--	3	
Kawah Baru, Kawah Nangklak									**1923**	0311	**1925**	0309	x---	----	x-x-	----	x---	1	
									1942	0815	**1942**	0816	x---	----	--?-	----	----	1?	
Kawah Baru, Kawah Nangklak									**2002**	1111	**2002**	1219c	x---	----	x-x-	----	-xx-	2*	
Kendang (Java-W)	**7.23 S**	**107.72 E**	**2608**	4578	**AR**	**Stratovolcano**	**0603-11=**	**Holocene**											
Guntur (Java-W)	**7.143 S**	**107.840 E**	**2249**	4678	**AB**	**Complex volcano**	**0603-13=**	**Historical**											
									1690	....	....	....	x---	----	x---	----	xx--	3	
									1777	....	....	....	----	----	----	----	----	2?	
									1780	....	....	....	x---	----	x---	x---	----	2	
									1800	....	....	....	----	----	----	x---	?-?-		
									1803	0403	**1803**	0415	x---	----	x---	----	----	2	
									1807	0901	**1807**	0906	x---	----	x---	----	----	2	
									1809	0509	....	....	x---	----	x---	----	----	2	
									1815	0815	....	....	x---	----	x---	----	----	2	
									1816	0921	....	....	x---	----	x---	----	----	2	
									1818	1021	**1818**	1024	x---	----	x---	----	----	2	
									1825	0614	**1825**	0615	x---	----	x---	----	-x--	2	
									1827	0513	....	....	x---	----	x---	----	----	2	
									1828	0514	**1828**	0708	x---	----	x---	----	----	2	
									1829	....	....	....	x---	----	x---	----	xx--	2	
									1832	0116	....	....	x---	----	x---	----	----	2	
									1832	0808	**1832**	0813	x---	----	x---	----	----	2	
									1833	0901	....	....	x---	----	x---	----	----	2	
									1834	12	**1835**	01	x---	----	x---	----	-x--	2	
									1836	1011	....	....	x---	----	x---	----	----	2	
									1840	0520	**1840**	0524	x---	----	x---	x---	-x--	2	
									1841	1114	**1841**	1114	x---	----	x---	----	-x--	2	
									1843	0104	**1843**	0104	x---	----	x---	----	----	3	-/6
									1843	1126	**1843**	1126	x---	----	x---	----	-?--	2?	
									1847	1016	**1847**	1028	x---	----	x---	----	----	2	
(increased activity; not an eruption)									X *1849*	....	....	....	----	----	----	----	----		
									? *1885*	*0118*	....	....	----	----	----	----	----		
									? *1887*	....	....	....	----	----	----	----	----		
Tampomas (Java-W)	**6.77 S**	**107.95 E**	**1684**	5678	**A**	**Stratovolcano**	**0603-131**	**Holocene**											
Galunggung (Java-W)	**7.25 S**	**108.058 E**	**2168**	4578	**BAr**	**Stratovolcano**	**0603-14=**	**Historical**											
									C-**2250**w	....	....	....	x---	----	xx-A	----	--x-	**5?**	
									? *0850*t	....	....	....	----	----	----	----	----		
									1822	1008	**1822**	1201p	x---	----	xx--	--x-	xxx-	**5**	-/9
									1894	1017	**1894**	12	x---	----	xx--	----	-xx-	3	-/7
Gunung Jadi									**1918**	0717	**1918**	0730	x---	----	x---	--x-	----	1	7/-
New crater at Gunung Jadi location									**1982**	0405	**1983**	0108	x---	----	xx--	x---	xxx-	4*	-/8
									1984	0109	**1984**	0131?	x---	----	x-x-	----	----	1	
Talagabodas (Java-W)	**7.208 S**	**108.07 E**	**2201**	4578	**BA**	**Stratovolcano**	**0603-15=**	**Fumarolic**											
Karaha, Kawah (Java-W)	**7.12 S**	**108.08 E**	**1155**	5678	**A**	**Fumarole field**	**0603-16=**	**Fumarolic**											
									? *1861*	*05*	....	....	x---	----	--?-	----	----		

VOLCANO NAME (Subregion) / ERUPTION — Area of Activity	LAT	LONG	ELEV (m)	POPL (5 km, 10, 30, 100)	ROCK TYPE	VOLC TYPE	NUMBER / — Start — Year	M-Dy	STATUS / — Stop — Year	M-Dy	ERUPTIVE CHARACTERISTICS: Central, Flank vent, Radial fiss, Regional	Submarine, New island, Subglacial, Crater lake	Explosive, Pyro flow, Phreatic, Caldera	Lava flow, Lava lake, Dome, Spine	Fatal, Damage, Mudflow, Tsunami	VEI	Vol L/T
Cereme (Java-W)	**6.892S**	**108.40 E**	**3078**	3578	**A**	**Stratovolcano**	**0603-17=**		**Historical**								
							1698	0203	....	....	?---	----	x---	----	xxx-	3	
							1772	0811	1772	0812	x---	----	x---	----	----	2	
							1775	0104	....	....	?---	----	?---	----	----	2	
							1805	04	....	....	x---	----	x---	----	----	2	
Floor and north wall of East Crater							1937	0624	1938	0107	x-x-	----	x-x-	----	----	2	
							1951	0301	1951	0302	----	----	x---	----	----	2?	
Slamet (Java-C)	**7.242S**	**109.208E**	**3428**	3578	**BAd**	**Stratovolcano**	**0603-18=**		**Historical**								
							1772	0811	1772	0812	x---	----	x---	----	----	2	
							1825	10	....	....	x---	----	x---	----	----	2	
							1835	09	1835	09	x---	----	x---	----	----	2	
							1847	0320	....	....	x---	----	x---	----	----	2	
							1849	1201	....	....	x---	----	x---	----	----	2	
							1860	0319	1860	0411	x---	----	x---	----	----	2	
							1875	0529<	1875	0604d	x---	----	x---	----	----	2	
							1875	1102b	1875	1226e	x---	----	x---	----	----	2	
							1885	0321	1885	0330	x---	----	x---	----	----	2	
							1890	0806	1890	0829	x---	----	x---	----	----	2	
							1904	0714	1904	0809	x---	----	x---	----	----	2	
							1923	0602	1923	0602	x---	----	x---	----	----	2	
							1926	1123a	1926	1130	x---	----	x---	----	----	2	
							1927	0227	1927	0227	x---	----	x---	----	----	2	
							1928	0320	1928	0512	x-x-	----	x---	----	----	2	
							1929	0606	1929	0615	x---	----	x---	----	----	2	
							1930	0402	1930	0413	x---	----	x---	----	----	2	
							1932	0701	1932	0910	x---	----	x---	----	----	2	
							1933	0512	1933	0513	x---	----	x---	----	----	1?	
							? *1934*	....	....	....	----	----	----	----	----		
							1937	....	....	....	x---	----	----	----	----		
							1939	0329	1939	0715	x---	----	x---	----	----	2	
							1939	1204	1939	1204	x---	----	x---	----	----	2	
							1940	0315	1940	0415	x---	----	x---	----	----	2	
							? *1943*	*0318*	....	....	x---	----	----	----	----		
							1943	1002	1944	0105	x---	----	x---	----	----	2	
							1944	0509	1944	1030	x---	----	x---	----	----	2	
							1948	1114	1948	1215	x---	----	x---	----	----	2	
							1951	0211	....	....	x---	----	x---	----	----	2	
							1951	0626	1952	0101	x---	----	x---	----	----	2	
							1953	08	1953	10	x---	----	x---	----	----	2	
							1955	1112	1955	1220?	x---	----	x---	----	----	2	
							1957	0208	1957	0208	x---	----	x---	----	----	2	
							1958	0417	1958	0507	x---	----	x---	----	----	2	
							1958	0913	1958	1105d	x---	----	x---	----	----	2	
							1960	12	1961	01	x---	----	x---	----	----	2	
							1966	....	....	....	x---	----	x---	----	----	2	
							1967	0507	1967	07	x---	----	x---	----	----	2	
							1969	0623	1969	08	x---	----	x---	----	----	2	
							1973	08	....	....	x---	----	----	x---	----	1?	
							? *1974*	*0529*	*?1974*	*0529*	x---	----	----	----	----	*2*	
(eruption July 12-13, 1988, not 1989)							1988	0712	1988	0713	x---	----	x---	----	----	1	
							1999	0501?	1999	09 ?	x---	----	x---	----	----	1	
							? *2000*	*07 ?*	*?2000*	*10 ?*	x---	----	--?-	----	----	*1?*	
							2009	0421	2009	0622?	x---	----	x---	----	----	1	
Dieng Volc Complex (Java-C)	**7.20 S***	**109.92 E**	**2565**	7778	**AB**	**Complex volcano**	**0603-20=**		**Historical**								
Sikunang							C-6590w	....	....	....	x---	----	----	x---	----	0	
Sikidang-Siterus (Telaga Lumut)							C-0500u	....	....	....	----	----	--x-	----	----		
							C-0050v	....	....	....	x---	----	----	x---	----	0	
							C 1180v	....	....	....	x---	----	--x-	----	----		
Pakuwaja							1375u	....	....	....	x---	----	x---	----	----	3↑	
							? *1766*	....	....	....	----	----	----	----	----		
(perhaps confused with 1786 eruption)							? *1776*	....	....	....	----	----	--?-	----	----		
Butak Petarangan (Butak)							1786	....	....	....	x---	----	x-x-	----	xx--	2	
Pakuwaja							1825	....	....	....	x---	----	x-x-	----	----	2	
Pakuwaja							1826	1011	1826	1015	x---	----	x-x-	----	x---	2	
Pakuwaja							1847	1204	....	....	x---	----	x-x-	----	x---	2	
Sikidang							1883	1226e	1884	0318	----	----	--x-	----	----	1*	
Butak Petarangan (Timbang)							1928	0513	....	....	-x--	----	--x-	----	xxx-	2	
Butak Petarangan							1939	1013	1939	1015	-x-x	----	--x-	----	xxx-	1?	
Sileri							1943	1103	....	....	----	----	--x-	----	----	1	
Sileri							1944	1204	....	....	x---	----	x-x-	----	xx--	2	
							? *1952*	*07*	....	....	----	----	----	----	----	*1?*	
							1953	0324	1953	0325	----	----	x---	----	----	2	
Candradimuka area							1954	1206	1954	1206	----	----	--x-	----	----	0	
Sileri							1956	0602	1956	0602	----	----	--x-	----	----	1	
Sileri							1964	1213	1964	1213	----	----	x-x-	----	x---	1	
Sinila and Sigluduk							1979	0220	1979	0220	-x--	----	--x-	----	xxx-	1	-/5
Sikidang							1981	....	....	....	----	----	--x-	----	----	1?	
Sileri							1986	0806	1986	0806	x---	---x	--x-	----	----	1	
Near Pandawa Lima temples							1993	0123	1993	0123?	x---	----	--x-	----	----	1	
Near Padangsari crater							1996	1231	1996	1231	x---	----	--x-	----	----	1	
Sileri crater							2003	07	2003	07	x---	----	--x-	----	----	1?	
Sibanteng crater							2009	0115	2009	0115	x---	----	x-x-	----	----	1	
Sileri crater							2009	0927	2009	0927	x---	----	--x-	----	----	1	
Sundoro (Java-C)	**7.30 S**	**109.992E**	**3136**	5678	**AB**	**Stratovolcano**	**0603-21=**		**Historical**								
							C 0230?	....	....	....	x---	----	xx--	----	----		
							C 0470?	....	....	....	x---	----	xx--	----	----		
							1806?	....	....	....	x---	----	x---	----	----	2	
							1818	....	....	....	x---	----	x---	----	----	2	
Summit, NW and NE flanks							1882	0401	1882	0407	xx--	----	x---	x---	----	2	
							1883	08 ?	....	....	x---	----	x---	----	----	2	
							1887	1113	1887	1114	x---	----	x---	----	----	2	
							1902	0501	1902	0525	x---	----	--x-	----	----	1	
Upper NE and SW flanks (2850-2980 m)							1903	1017	1903	1021?	--x-	----	x---	----	----	2	
Summit crater K5							1906	0922	1906	1220	x-x-	----	x---	----	----	2	
							1971	1029	1971	1109	x---	----	--x-	----	----	2	

Tropenmuseum (Roy. Trop. Inst.)

Slamet summit crater

VOLCANO NAME (Subregion) / ERUPTION — Area of Activity	LAT	LONG	ELEV (m)	POPL 5 km 10 30 100	ROCK TYPE	VOLC TYPE / Start Year	NUMBER / Start M-Dy	STATUS / Stop Year	Stop M-Dy	Central Flank vent Radial fiss Regional	Submarine New island Subglacial Crater lake	Explosive Pyro flow Phreatic Caldera	Lava flow Lava lake Dome Spine	Fatal Damage Mudflow Tsunami	VEI	Vol L/T
Sumbing (Java-C)	**7.384 S**	**110.070 E**	**3371**	5678	**ABD**	**Stratovolcano**	**0603-22=**	**Historical**								
						1730?	....	....	....	x---	----	--x-	----	----	1	
Ungaran (Java-C)	**7.18 S**	**110.33 E**	**2050**	4678	**YXB**	**Stratovolcano**	**0603-23=**	**Holocene**								
Telomoyo (Java-C)	**7.37 S**	**110.40 E**	**1894**	5678	**AB**	**Stratovolcano**	**0603-231**	**Holocene**								
Merbabu (Java-C)	**7.45 S**	**110.43 E**	**3145**	5678	**BYA**	**Stratovolcano**	**0603-24=**	**Historical**								
						1560	....	....	....	----	----	x---	----	----		
						? *1570*	....	....	....	----	----	----	----	----		
(1586 eruption not from Merbabu)						*X 1586*	....	....	....	x---	----	x---	----	----		
						1797	....	....	....	x---	----	x---	----	----	2	
Merapi (Java-C)	**7.542 S**	**110.442 E**	**2968**	5678	**AYbx**	**Stratovolcano**	**0603-25=**	**Historical**								
Old Merapi						G-**8780**w	....	....	....	x---	----	xx--	----	----		
						G-**7310**y	....	....	....	x---	----	xx--	----	----		
						G-**4690**u	....	....	....	x---	----	xx--	----	----		
						G-**2910**w	....	....	....	x---	----	xx--	----	----		
						G-**1890**	....	....	....	x---	----	xx--	----	----		
						G-**1770**u	....	....	....	x---	----	xx--	----	----		
						G-**1410**t	....	....	....	x---	----	xx--	----	----		
(Bakalan Tephra)						C-**1180**u	....	....	....	x---	----	xx--	----	----	**P**	
						G-**1010**x	....	....	....	x---	----	xx--	----	----		
						G-**0700**w	....	....	....	x---	----	xx--	----	----		
(Ngrangkah Tephra)						G-**0340**z	....	....	....	x---	----	xx--	--x-	----	3	-/7
(Tegalsruni Tephra)						G **0020**y	....	....	....	x---	----	xx--	----	--x-	**P**	
(collapse of Old Merapi edifice?)						G **0120**u	....	....	....	x---	----	xx-A	----	----		
(New Merapi)						G **0190**y	....	....	....	x---	----	x---	----	----		
						G **0280**w	....	....	....	x---	----	xx--	----	----		
(Plalangan Tephra)						G **0410**w	....	....	....	x---	----	xx--	----	----	3	-/7
						G **0480**u	....	....	....	x---	----	x---	--x-	----		
						G **0540**t	....	....	....	x---	----	xx--	----	----		
						G **0630**r	....	....	....	x---	----	xx--	----	----		
						G **0680**x	....	....	....	x---	----	xx--	----	----		
						G **0870**v	....	....	....	x---	----	xx--	----	----		
(Selo Tephra)						G **0940**v	....	....	....	x---	----	xx--	--x-	----	3	-/7
(collapse of Old Merapi ~900 yrs earlier)						*X 1006*	....	....	....	----	----	----	----	----		
						G **1010**q	....	....	....	x---	----	xx--	----	----		
						G **1090**v	....	....	....	x---	----	xx--	----	-x--		
						G **1140**w	....	....	....	x---	----	xx--	----	----		
						G **1190**r	....	....	....	x---	----	xx--	----	----		
(Deles Tephra)						G **1230**x	....	....	....	x---	----	xx--	----	----		
						G **1300**u	....	....	....	x---	----	xx--	----	----		
(Sambisari Ash)						G **1380**y	....	....	....	x---	----	xx--	----	----		
						G **1440**v	....	....	....	x---	----	xx--	----	--x-		
(Sambisari Ash)						G **1480**y	....	....	....	x---	----	xx--	----	-xx-		
						1548	....	....	....	x---	----	x?--	----	----	3↑	
						1554	....	....	....	x---	----	x?--	----	----	3↑	
						1560	....	....	....	x---	----	x?--	----	----	3↑	
						1584	....	....	....	x---	----	x---	----	----	3↑	
						? *1586*	....	....	....	----	----	----	----	----		
						1587	....	....	....	x---	----	xx--	----	xxx-	3↑	
						1658	....	....	....	x---	----	x---	----	----	3↑	
						1663	1231y	....	....	x---	----	x---	----	----	3↑	
						1672	0804	....	....	x---	----	xx--	----	xxx-	3	
						1677	....	....	....	x---	----	x---	----	----	3↑	
						1678	0819	....	....	x---	----	x---	----	----	3↑	
						1745	....	....	....	x---	----	x---	----	----	2	
						1752	....	....	....	x---	----	x---	----	----	2	
						1755	....	....	....	x---	----	x---	----	----	2	
						1768	0819	....	....	x---	----	x---	x-x-	----	2?	
						1786	0717	....	....	x---	----	----	--x-	----	1?	
						1791<	....	....	....	x---	----	x---	--x-	----	2	
						1797	....	....	....	x---	----	----	--x-	----	1	
						1807	....	....	....	x---	----	x---	----	----	1?	
						1810	....	....	....	x---	----	----	--x-	----	1	
						1812	....	**1822**	....	x---	----	----	--x-	----	1	
						1822	1227	**1823**	0406	x---	----	xx--	x-x-	xxx-	3?	8/7
						1828	1218	**1828**	1219	x---	----	x---	----	----	2	
						1832	1225	**1836**	....	x---	----	xx--	x-x-	xxx-	2?	7/7
						1837	0810	**1838**	06	x---	----	xx--	x-x-	-x--	2?	7/7
						1840	0104	....	....	?---	----	?---	----	----	1	
						1846	0406	....	....	x---	----	x---	----	----	2	
Summit and upper SE flank (2600 m)						**1846**	0902	**1847**	10	xx--	----	xx--	x-x-	-xx-	3	
						? *1848*	*0108*	....	....	?---	----	?---	----	----		
						1849	0426	**1849**	0426	x---	----	xx--	----	----	2	-/6
						1849	0914	**1849**	0924	x---	----	xx--	----	-x--	3	-/7
						? *1854*	*09*	....	....	x---	----	----	----	----		
						1861	....	....	....	x---	----	x---	----	----	2	
						1862	0526	**1864**	....	x---	----	xx--	x-x-	----	2*	7/6
						1865	1024	**1871**	08 ?	x?--	----	xx--	x-x-	-x--	2*	7/7
						1872	0415	**1872**	0421	x---	----	xx--	----	xx--	4	-/8
						1872	1103	**1873**	01 ?	x---	----	x---	----	----	2	
						1878	....	**1879**	0620	x---	----	x---	x---	----	2	
East dome						**1883**	01 ?	**1884**	11	x---	----	----	--x-	----	1	7/-
						1885	0224d	**1887**	....	x---	----	--x-	--x-	----	1	
						1888	0818	**1888**	1220	x---	----	xx--	--x-	-xx-	2	
						1889	07	....	....	x---	----	--x-	----	----	1	
						1891	0825	**1892**	....	x---	----	x---	--x-	----	2?	
						1893	10	....	....	x---	----	----	--?-	----	1	
						1894	0127	**1894**	0202	x---	----	x---	--x?	-x--	2?	-/6
						1894	10	....	....	x---	----	----	--?-	----	1?	
						1897	....	....	....	x---	----	x---	----	----	2?	
						1902	0203	**1902**	0203	x---	----	x---	----	----	1	
						1902	12	**1904**	0620e	x---	----	xx--	x-x-	xx--	2*	6/6
						1905	01	**1905**	0601	x---	----	xx--	x-x-	----	2	-/6
Summit and upper east flank (2600 m)						**1906**	0126e	**1907**	0217	xx--	----	xx--	x-x-	----	2*	7/6

VOLCANO NAME (Subregion) / ERUPTION — Area of Activity	LAT	LONG	ELEV (m)	POPL (5 km, 10, 30, 100)	ROCK TYPE	VOLC TYPE	NUMBER	STATUS	Start Year	Start M-Dy	Stop Year	Stop M-Dy	Central, Flank vent, Radial fiss, Regional	Submarine, New island, Subglacial, Crater lake	Explosive, Pyro flow, Phreatic, Caldera	Lava flow, Lava lake, Dome, Spine	Fatal, Damage, Mudflow, Tsunami	VEI	Vol L/T
Merapi (Java-C) *continued*									**1908**	....	....	....	x---	----	----	--x-	----	1?	
West dome									**1909**	0201	**1913**	05	x---	----	xx--	x-x-	----	1*	6/-
									1915	0328	**1915**	0515	x---	----	x---	--x-	----	1	
									1918	01	....	....	x---	----	x---	----	----	1	
									1920	0725	**1921**	02	x---	----	xx--	--x-	xxx-	2	-/6
									1922	0218	**1922**	0808	x---	----	x---	--x-	--x-	1	6/-
									? *1923*	*09*	?*1923*	*11*	x---	----	----	----	----		
									1924	0910	**1924**	0912a	x---	----	xx--	----	----	1	
									1930	1125	**1931**	09	x-x-	----	xx--	x-x-	xxx-	3*	7/6
									1932	11	....	....	x---	----	x---	x-x-	--x-	1	
									1933	1001	**1935**	04	x---	----	xx--	x-x-	--x-	2*	6/6
									1939	1213	**1940**	09	x---	----	xx--	--x-	--x-	2*	6/-
									1942	0530	**1945**	05	x---	----	xx--	x-x-	-xx-	2*	6/6
									1948	0929	**1948**	12	x---	----	xx--	x-x-	----	2	6/-
									1953	0302	**1958**	12	x---	----	xxx-	x-x-	xxx-	2*	6/7
									1961	0411	**1961**	1128	x---	----	xx--	x-x-	xxx-	3*	7/7
Upper Batang breach (2600 m)									**1967**	0112	**1970**?	....	xx--	----	xx--	x-x-	xxx-	2*	7/7
									? *1971*	*01*	?*1971*	*0726*	x---	----	-?--	----	----	*1?*	
									1972	1006	**1985**	03	x---	----	xx--	x-x-	xxx-	2*	7/7
									1986	1010	**1990**	08 ?	x---	----	xx--	x-x-	--x-	2	6/-
NW of 1984 lava dome									**1992**	0120	**2002**	1019?	x---	----	xx--	--x-	xxx-	2*	7/-
									2006	03	**2007**	0809?	x---	----	xx--	x-x-	xx--	1	6/-
									? *2008*	*0519*	....	....	x---	----	?---	----	----		
Muria (Java-C)	**6.62 S**	**110.88 E**	**1625**	3478	**XTPBA**	**Stratovolcano**	**0603-251**	**Holocene**											
East flank (Gunung Bambang)									C-**0160**y	....	....	....	-x--	----	xx--	----	----		
Lawu (Java-C)	**7.625 S**	**111.192 E**	**3265**	4578	**AB**	**Stratovolcano**	**0603-26=**	**Historical**											
(1752 eruption was from Kelut volcano)									X *1752*	*0501*	....	....	----	----	----	----	----		
									1885	1128	**1885**	1128	----	----	x---	----	----	1	
Wilis (Java-C)	**7.808 S**	**111.758 E**	**2563**	3478	**A**	**Stratovolcano**	**0603-27=**	**Holocene**											
									? *1641*	....	....	....	----	----	----	----	----		
Kelut (Java-E)	**7.93 S**	**112.308 E**	**1731**	3578	**AB**	**Stratovolcano**	**0603-28=**	**Historical**											
									C-**0230**y	....	....	....	x---	----	x---	----	----		
									1000	....	....	....	x---	---x	x---	----	-??-	3	
									1311	....	....	....	x---	---x	x---	----	???-	3	
									1334	....	....	....	x---	---x	x---	----	xxx-	3	
									1376	....	....	....	x---	---x	x---	--x-	x---	3↑	
									1385	....	....	....	x---	---x	x---	----	xxx-	3↑	
									1395	....	....	....	x---	---x	x---	----	-??-	3↑	
									1411	....	....	....	x---	---x	x---	----	-??-	3↑	
									1450	....	....	....	x---	---x	----	----	----	3↑	
									1451	....	....	....	x---	---x	x---	----	-??-	3↑	
									1462	....	....	....	x---	---x	x---	----	-??-	3↑	
									1481	....	....	....	x---	---x	x---	----	-??-	3↑	
									? *1500?*	....	....	....	----	----	----	----	----		
									1548	....	....	....	x---	---x	x---	----	-xx-	3↑	
									1586	....	....	....	x---	---x	x---	----	xxx-	**5?**	-/9
									1641	....	....	....	x---	---x	x---	----	-??-	4?	-/8
									1716	0720	....	....	x---	---x	x---	----	xxx-	2	
									1752	0501	....	....	x---	---x	x---	----	-??-	2	
									? *1756*	....	....	....	x---	----	----	----	----		
									1771	0110	....	....	x---	---x	x---	----	-??-	2	
									1776	....	....	....	x---	---x	x---	----	-??-	2	
									1785	....	....	....	x---	---x	x---	----	-??-	2	
									1811	0605	....	....	x---	---x	x---	----	-??-	2	
									1825	....	....	....	x---	---x	x---	----	xxx-	2	
									1826	1011	**1826**	1025	x---	---x	xx--	----	xxx-	4?	-/8
									1835	....	....	....	x---	---x	x---	----	-xx-	2	
									1848	0516	**1848**	0517	x---	---x	xx--	----	xxx-	3	
									? *1849*	....	....	....	----	----	----	----	----		
									1851	0124	....	....	x---	---x	x---	----	-??-	2	
									1864	0104?	**1864**	0104?	x---	---x	xx--	----	xxx-	2	
(breach of crater wall: no eruption)									X *1875*	*0129*	....	....	----	----	----	----	xxx-		
									1901	0522	**1901**	0523	x---	---x	xx--	----	xxx-	3	-/6
									1919	0519	**1919**	0520	x---	---x	xx--	----	xxx-	4	-/8
									1920	1206	**1920**	1212	x---	---x	x---	--x-	----	2	5/-
									1951	0831	**1951**	0831	x---	---x	xx--	----	xxx-	4	-/8
									1966	0426	**1966**	0427	x---	---x	xx--	----	xxx-	4	-/7
									1967	0218	**1967**	0218	x---	----	--x-	----	----	1	
Crater floor at foot of Kelut Peak									**1967**	1211	**1967**	1211	x---	----	--x-	----	----	1	
									1990	0210	**1990**	0313q	x---	---x	xxx-	--x-	xxx-	4	-/8
									2007	10 ?	**2008**	04 <	x---	---x	x---	--x-	----	2*	7/-
Kawi-Butak (Java-E)	**7.92 S**	**112.45 E**	**2651**	3678	**U**	**Stratovolcanoes**	**0603-281**	**Holocene**											
Arjuno-Welirang (Java-E)	**7.725 S**	**112.58 E**	**3339**	4578	**AB**	**Stratovolcano**	**0603-29=**	**Historical**											
NW part of Gunung Welirang (2500 & 2700 m)									**1950**	1030	....	....	----	----	x---	----	----	2	
NW flank (Kawah Plupuh)									**1952**	0815e	....	....	-x--	----	--?-	----	--x-	0	
Gunung Welirang									? *1991*	*0913*	....	....	x---	----	?---	----	----		
Penanggungan (Java-E)	**7.62 S**	**112.63 E**	**1653**	5678	**AYB**	**Stratovolcano**	**0603-291**	**Holocene**											
									? *0200?*	....	....	....	----	----	----	----	----		
Malang Plain (Java-E)	**8.02 S***	**112.68 E**	**680**	7778	**U**	**Maars**	**0603-292**	**Holocene**											
Semeru (Java-E)	**8.108 S**	**112.92 E**	**3676**	4478	**AB**	**Stratovolcano**	**0603-30=**	**Historical**											
									1818	1108	....	....	x---	----	x---	x---	----	2	
									1829	02	....	....	x---	----	x---	----	----	2	
									1830	1215	**1830**	1216	x---	----	x---	----	----	2	
									1832	0418	....	....	x---	----	x---	?---	----	2	
									1836	0803	**1836**	0805	x---	----	x---	----	----	2	
									1838	07	**1838**	1018	x---	----	x---	----	----	2	
									1842	01	**1842**	03	x---	----	x---	----	----	2	
									1844	0925	**1844**	0927	x---	----	x---	x---	----	2	
									1845	01	**1845**	07	x---	----	x---	x---	----	2	
									1848	02	....	....	x---	----	x---	----	----	2	
									1848	0804	....	....	x---	----	x---	x---	----	2	
									? *1849*	....	....	....	----	----	----	----	----		

Dan Dzurisin (USGS/CVO)

Kelut crater lake, 1980

VOLCANO NAME (Subregion) / ERUPTION	LAT LONG ELEV (m) POPL ROCK TYPE VOLC TYPE NUMBER STATUS / Area of Activity		Start Year	Start M-Dy	Stop Year	Stop M-Dy	Central / Flank vent / Radial fiss / Regional	Submarine / New island / Subglacial / Crater lake	Explosive / Pyro flow / Phreatic / Caldera	Lava flow / Lava lake / Dome / Spine	Fatal / Damage / Mudflow / Tsunami	VEI	Vol L/T
Semeru (Java-E) *continued*			**1851**	01	....	....	x---	----	x---	----	----	2	
			1856	0910	....	....	x---	----	x---	x---	----	2	
			1857	0813	**1857**	09	x---	----	x---	----	----	2	
			1860	04	**1860**	06	x---	----	x---	----	-x--	2	
	(eruption probably from Lamongan)	X	*1864*	*0702*	....	....	----	----	----	----	----		
			1865	0415e	....	....	x---	----	x---	?---	----	2	
		?	*1866*	....	....	....	x---	----	?---	----	----	*2?*	
			1867	0415e	**1867**	05	x---	----	x---	----	----	2	
			1872	1023	**1872**	1023	x---	----	x---	----	----	2	
			1877	04	....	....	x---	----	x---	----	----	2	
			1877	09	....	....	x---	----	x---	----	----	2	
			1878	....	....	....	x---	----	x---	x---	----	2	
			1879	....	....	....	x---	----	x---	----	----	2	
			1884	1210?	**1885**	09	x---	----	xx--	x---	xxx-	2	
			1886	0125	**1886**	0826e	x---	----	x---	?---	----	2	
			1887	02	**1887**	03	x---	----	x---	----	----	2	
			1887	08 ?	**1887**	1011	x---	----	x---	x---	----	2*	
			1888	02	**1888**	10	x---	----	xx--	x---	----	2	
			1889	01	**1891**	0531>	x---	----	x---	x---	----	2*	
			1892	03	**1892**	04	x---	----	x---	----	----	2	
			1893	01	**1893**	05	x---	----	x---	----	----	2	
			1893	1211	**1894**	02	x---	----	x---	----	----	2*	
			1895	0522	**1895**	1001	x---	----	xx--	x---	xxx-	2	
			1896	05	**1896**	06	x---	----	x---	----	--x-	2	
			1897	0101	**1897**	0103	x---	----	x---	x---	----	2	
			1898	0223	....	....	x---	----	x---	x---	----	2	
			1899	0117	**1899**	0331?	x---	----	x---	----	----	2	
			1899	0811	....	....	x---	----	x---	----	----	2	
			1899	12	....	....	x---	----	x---	----	----	2	
			1900	0329	**1900**	0411>	x---	----	x---	x---	----	2	
			1901	0129	**1901**	0130>	x---	----	x---	----	----	2	
			1903	0326	**1903**	06	x---	----	x---	----	----	2	
			1904	0102	**1904**	0116	x---	----	x---	----	----	2	
			1905	0804	....	....	x---	----	x---	----	----	2	
			1907	0107	**1907**	0110	x---	----	x---	----	----	2	
			1907	0709<	....	....	x---	----	x---	----	----	2	
			1908	01	**1908**	12	x---	----	x---	----	----	2	
			1909	09	**1910**	0322	x---	----	xx--	----	xxx-	2*	
			1910	1116	**1911**	02	x---	----	x---	----	----	2	
			1911	1108	**1911**	12	x---	----	xx--	x---	-xx-	3*	
			1912	0828	....	....	x---	----	x---	----	----	2	
	Jonggring Seloko		**1913**	0623	**1913**	0626?	x---	----	x---	x---	-xx-	2	
			1915a	....	....	....	x---	----	?---	----	--x-	2?	
	ESE flank (1400-1775 m)		**1941**	0921	**1942**	02	--x-	----	x---	x---	-x--	2	7/-
	Jonggring Seloko		**1945**	0612	**1945**	0618	x---	----	x---	----	----	2	
	Jonggring Seloko		**1946**	02	**1946**	05	x---	----	xxx-	----	xxx-	2	
	Jonggring Seloko		**1946**	1029	**1947**	06	x---	----	xx--	--x-	-xx-	2	
	Jonggring Seloko		**1950**	0723	**1964**	12	x---	----	xx--	x-x-	-xx-	2*	
	Jonggring Seloko		**1967**	0831	**2010>**	....	x---	----	xxx-	x-x-	xxx-	3*	
Tengger Caldera (Java-E)	**7.942S 112.95 E 2329** 5578 YBA **Stratovolcanoes 0603-31= Historical**												
	Sandsea caldera	C	**-5260***	....	....	....	x---	----	xx--	----	----		
	Sandsea caldera	C	**-0830**t	....	....	....	x---	----	xx--	----	----	**P**	
	Widodaren	C	**0190**t	....	....	....	x---	----	x-x-	----	----	2	
	Segorowedi	C	**0330**t	....	....	....	x---	----	xxx-	x---	----	3?	
	Bromo	C	**1590**t	....	....	....	x---	----	x---	----	----	2	
	Bromo	?	*1767*	....	....	....	x---	----	----	----	----		
	Bromo	?	*1775*	....	....	....	x---	----	----	----	----		
	Bromo		**1804**	09	....	....	x---	----	x---	----	----	2	
	Bromo		**1815**	0405	**1815**	0417>	x---	----	x---	----	----	2	
	Bromo		**1820**	....	....	....	x---	----	?-?-	----	----	2	
	Bromo		**1822**	1228	**1823**	0105d	x---	----	x---	----	----	2	
	Bromo		**1825**	1105	**1825**	1108	x---	----	x---	----	----	2	
	Bromo		**1829**	1105	**1829**	1111	x---	----	x---	----	-x--	2	
	Bromo		**1830**	0303	....	....	x---	----	x---	----	----	2	
	Bromo		**1830**	1215	**1830**	1216	x---	----	x---	----	----	2	
	Bromo		**1835**	....	....	....	x---	----	x---	----	----	2	
	Bromo		**1842**	0124	**1842**	06	x---	---x	x---	----	----	2	
	Bromo		**1843**	01	....	....	x---	----	x---	----	----	2	
	Bromo		**1844**	1109	....	....	x---	----	x---	----	----	2	
	Bromo	@	**1856**	0910	....	....	x---	----	x---	----	----	2	
	Bromo		**1857**	....	....	....	x---	----	x---	----	----	2	
	Bromo		**1858**	0304	....	....	x---	----	x---	----	----	2	
	Bromo		**1858**	1018	....	....	x---	----	x---	----	----	2	
	Bromo		**1859**	0130	**1859**	0304d	x---	----	x---	----	----	2	
	Bromo		**1860**	0612	**1860**	0614	x---	----	x---	----	----	2	
	Bromo		**1865**	04	**1865**	05	x---	----	x---	----	----	2	
	Bromo		**1865**	1201	**1865**	1218	x---	----	x---	----	----	2	
	Bromo		**1866**	07	....	....	x---	----	x---	----	----	2	
	Bromo		**1867**	1213	**1868**	0112	x---	----	x---	----	----	2	
	Bromo		**1877**	0424?	....	....	x---	----	x---	----	----	2	
	Bromo		**1885**	06 ?	....	....	x---	----	x---	----	----	2	
	Bromo		**1885**	1031	**1886**	0110	x---	----	x---	----	-x--	2	
	Bromo		**1886**	0415	**1886**	0426	x---	----	x---	----	----	2	
	Bromo		**1886**	1111	**1887**	0125	x---	----	x---	----	----	2	
	Bromo	?	*1888*	*0227*	....	....	x---	----	--x-	----	----	*2*	
	Bromo		**1890**	05	**1890**	09	x---	----	x---	----	----	2	
	Bromo		**1893**	0113	**1893**	0327	x---	----	x---	----	----	2	
	Bromo		**1896**	....	....	....	x---	----	x---	----	----	2	
	Bromo		**1906**	0925	**1907**	0518	x---	----	x---	----	----	2	
	Bromo		**1907**	0828	....	....	x---	----	x---	----	----	2	
	Bromo		**1907**	1214	**1908**	0213	x---	----	x---	----	----	2	
	Bromo		**1909**	0112	**1909**	0114	x---	----	x---	----	----	2	
	Bromo		**1910**	0118	**1910**	0121	x---	----	x---	----	----	2	
	Bromo		**1915**	11	**1916**	06	x---	----	x---	----	-x--	3	

Tom Simkin (Smithsonian)

Tengger caldera, Bromo (foreground), Semeru (background)

VOLCANO NAME (Subregion) / ERUPTION	Area of Activity	LAT	LONG	ELEV (m)	POPL (5 km / 10 / 30 / 100)	ROCK TYPE	VOLC TYPE	NUMBER	STATUS	Start Year	Start M-Dy	Stop Year	Stop M-Dy	Central / Flank vent / Radial fiss / Regional	Submarine / New island / Subglacial / Crater lake	Explosive / Pyro flow / Phreatic / Caldera	Lava flow / Lava lake / Dome / Spine	Fatal / Damage / Mudflow / Tsunami	VEI	Vol L/T
Tengger Caldera (Java-E) *continued*	Bromo									1921	06	1921	1017	x---	----	x---	----	----	2	
	Bromo									1922	0205	1922	0620	x---	----	x---	----	----	2	
	Bromo									1928	0315e	1928	07	x---	----	x---	----	----	2	
	Bromo									1928	1216	....	....	x---	----	x---	----	----	2	
	Bromo									1929	0807	1929	0908	x---	----	x---	----	----	2	
	Bromo									1930	0530	1930	07	x---	----	x---	----	----	2	
	Bromo									1935	07	....	....	x---	----	x---	----	----	2	
	Bromo									1939	0624	1939	07	x---	----	x---	----	----	2	
	Bromo									1940	0425	1940	0703>	x---	----	x---	----	----	2	
	Bromo									1948	0215	1948	0425	x---	----	x---	----	-x--	3	
	Bromo									1950	0527	1950	08	x---	----	x---	----	----	2	
	Bromo									1955	1229	1955	1230	x---	----	x---	----	----	2	
	Bromo									1956	06	1956	07 ?	x---	----	x---	----	----	2	
	Bromo									1972	0126	1972	03	x---	----	x---	----	-x--	2	
	Bromo									1980	0605a	1980	0920	x---	----	x-x-	---?	----	2	
	Bromo									? *1983*	*0415*e	? *1983*	*0628*a	x---	----	--?-	----	----	*1*	
	Bromo									1983	1221	1983	1221	x---	----	x---	----	----	1	
	Bromo									1984	0512	1984	0531	x---	----	x---	----	----	1	
	Bromo									1995	0303	1995	0526e	x---	----	x---	----	----	1	
	Bromo									1995	0909	1995	12	x---	----	x---	----	----	1	
	Bromo									2000	1129	2001	0115>	x---	----	x---	----	----	2	
	Bromo									2004	0608	2004	0624c	x---	----	x-x-	----	x---	2	
Lamongan (Java-E)		7.979 S	113.342 E	1651	4578	Baxy	Stratovolcano	0603-32=	Historical											
										1799	....	....	....	x---	----	x---	----	----	2	
										1806	05	....	....	x---	----	x---	----	----	2	
										1808	1208	....	....	x---	----	x---	----	----	2	
										1817	....	....	....	x---	----	x---	----	----	2	
										1818	1008	....	....	x---	----	x---	----	----	2	
										1821	1215e	1822	0105	xx--	----	x---	x---	----	2	
										1824	0101?	1824	0131?	x---	----	x---	----	----	2	
										1826	....	....	....	x---	----	x---	----	----	2	
										1829	01	1829	02	x---	----	x---	x---	----	2	
										1830	02	1830	03	x---	----	x---	x---	----	2	
										1838	0704	1838	0706	x---	----	x---	----	----	2	
										1838	1018	....	....	x---	----	x---	----	----	2	
										1841	0716	1842	08	x---	----	x---	----	----	2	
										1843	08	1844	09	x---	----	x---	?---	xx--	2	
										1847	0326	1847	0626	xx--	----	x---	x---	----	2	
										1847	0925	....	....	xx--	----	x---	x---	----	2	
	Summit and north flank									1849	06	1849	09	xx--	----	x---	x---	----	2	
										1856	0301	1856	0614	x---	----	x---	----	----	2	
										1859	0227	1859	03	x---	----	x---	----	-x--	2	
										1861	....	....	....	x---	----	x---	----	----	2	
										1864	0609	1864	07	x---	----	x---	x---	----	2	
	Summit and south slope									1869	0406	1869	0504	xx--	----	x---	x---	-x--	2	
										1869	0912	....	....	x---	----	x---	x---	xx--	2	
										1870	0302	1870	0305	x---	----	x---	----	----	2	
	Summit and SW flank									1870	0818	1871	0205a	xx--	----	x---	----	----	2	
										1872	0815	1872	0918	x---	----	x---	----	----	2	
										1874	0520	1874	0821	x---	----	x---	----	----	2	
										1877	0424?	1877	0512?	xx--	----	x---	x---	-x--	3?	
										1883	0413	1883	0504a	xx--	----	x---	x---	-x--	2	7/-
										1884	0106	1884	0623	x---	----	x---	----	----	2	
										1885	0311	1886	1015e	x---	----	x---	x---	-x--	2	
										1887	0703a	1887	0709	x---	----	x---	----	----	2	
										1887	11	1888	0227	x---	----	x---	----	----	2	
										1888	09	1888	1006	x---	----	x---	----	----	2	
										1889	0907	1889	11	x---	----	x---	----	----	2	
										1890	0323h	1890	05	x---	----	x---	----	----	2	
										1890	0905d	1891	01 >	x---	----	x---	?---	----	2	
										1891	0925e	1891	1005d	x---	----	x---	x---	----	2	
										1893	1118	....	....	x---	----	x---	----	-xx-	2	
										1896	0905	1896	0919>	x---	----	x---	----	----	2	
	SW flank 400 m (Mt. Anyar)									1898	0205	1898	0215	-x--	----	x---	x---	-x--	2	
										? *1953*	*0404*	? *1953*	*06*	x---	----	----	----	----	*2?*	
Lurus (Java-E)		7.73 S	113.58 E	539	5668	AT	Complex volcano	0603-321	Holocene?											
Iyang-Argapura (Java-E)		7.97 S	113.57 E	3088	3578	AB	Complex volcano	0603-33=	Holocene											
										? *1597*	....	....	....	----	----	----	----	----		
Raung (Java-E)		8.125 S	114.042 E	3332	3367	AB	Stratovolcano	0603-34=	Historical											
	(may be same as 1593 eruption)									? *1586*	....	....	....	x---	---x	x---	----	xx--	*3*	
										1593	....	....	....	x---	---x	x---	----	xx--	**5?**	-/9
										1597	0117	1597	0202>	x---	---x	x---	----	xx--	3	
										1638	....	....	....	x---	---x	x---	----	xxx-	4?	-/8
										1730	....	....	....	x---	---x	x---	----	xxx-	3?	-/8
										1793f	....	....	....	x---	----	x---	----	----	2	
										1804d	....	....	....	x---	----	x---	----	----	2	
										1812	....	1814?	....	x---	----	x---	----	----	2	
										1815	1231y	....	....	x---	----	x---	----	----	2	
										1817	0116	1817	0210?	x---	---x	x---	----	xxx-	4?	-/8
										1838	....	....	....	x---	---x	x---	----	-xx-	2	
										1849	1201p	....	....	x---	----	----	----	----		
										1859	1214	....	....	x---	----	x---	----	----	2	
										1860	09 <	....	....	x---	----	x---	----	----	2	
										1864	0702	1864	12	x---	----	x---	----	----	2	
										1881	....	....	....	x---	----	?---	----	----		
										1885	0621	1885	0622	x---	----	x---	----	----	2	
										1890	07	1890	0915b	x---	----	x---	----	----	2	
										1896	08	....	....	x---	----	x---	----	----	2	
										1897	04	....	....	x---	----	x---	----	----	2	
										1902	0216	1902	0227>	x---	----	x---	x---	----	2	
										1903	1128	1904	01	x---	----	x---	----	----	2	
										1913	0510	1913	12	x---	----	x---	----	----	2	
										1915	05	....	....	x---	----	x---	----	----	2	

VOLCANO NAME (Subregion) / ERUPTION — Area of Activity	LAT	LONG	ELEV (m)	POPL (5 km / 10 / 30 / 100)	ROCK TYPE	VOLC TYPE	NUMBER / Start Year	Start M-Dy	STATUS / Stop Year	Stop M-Dy	Central / Flank vent / Radial fiss / Regional	Submarine / New island / Subglacial / Crater lake	Explosive / Pyro flow / Phreatic / Caldera	Lava flow / Lava lake / Dome / Spine	Fatal / Damage / Mudflow / Tsunami	VEI	Vol L/T
Raung (Java-E) *continued*							**1916**	11	**1916**	12	x---	----	x---	----	----	2	
							1917	0222	....	....	x---	----	x---	----	----	2	
1913 cone							**1921**	0214d	**1921**	04	x---	----	x---	x---	----	2	
							1924	02 <	....	....	x---	----	x---	x---	----	2	
							? *1924*	*0820*	....	....	x---	----	----	----	----	*2?*	
Central cone and NW crater wall							**1927**	0802	**1928**	03 ?	x---	----	x---	----	----	2	
							1928	11	....	....	x---	----	x---	----	----	2	
							1929	0427r	....	....	x---	----	x---	----	----	2	
							1933	1121	**1933**	1206	x---	----	x---	----	----	2	
							1936	0822	**1936**	1211	x---	----	x---	----	----	2	
							1937	1027	**1937**	1127	x---	----	x---	----	----	2	
							1938	0813	**1939**	0110>	x---	----	x---	----	----	2	
							1940	....	....	....	?---	----	?---	----	----	2	
							1941	1213	....	....	x---	----	x---	----	----	2	
							1943	0317	**1943**	0618	x---	----	x---	----	----	2	
							1944	0630	**1945**	0419	x---	----	x---	?---	----	2	
							1953	0131	**1953**	0415e	x---	----	x---	x---	-x--	3	8/-
							1955	0118	**1955**	0118	x---	----	x---	----	----	2?	
							1956	0213	**1956**	0325	x---	----	x---	----	----	3*	
							1971	0914	**1971**	0914	x---	----	--x-	----	----	1	
							1973	05	**1973**	10	x---	----	x---	----	----	1	
							1974	0615	**1974**	0717?	x---	----	x---	----	----	2	
							1975	03	**1975**	05	x---	----	x-x-	----	----	1	
							1976	0607	**1976**	1121	x---	----	x---	----	----	2	
							1977	0609	**1977**	0630	x---	----	xx--	----	----	2	
							1978	01	**1979**	12 >	x---	----	x-?-	----	----	1	
							1982	0718	**1982**	0720	x---	----	x---	----	-x--	3	
							1985	0823	**1986**	0228	x---	----	x---	----	----	2	
							1987	05	**1989**	0728c	x---	----	x---	----	----	1	
							1990	0116<	**1990**	12 >	x---	----	x---	----	----	2	
							1991	0910	**1991**	1112?	x---	----	x---	----	----	2	
							1993	0401t	....	....	x---	----	x---	----	----	1	
							1994	0714	**1994**	0714	x---	----	x---	----	----	1	
							1995	03	**1995**	03	x---	----	x---	----	----	1	
							? *1995*	*0815*	....	....	x---	----	?---	----	----	*2?*	
							1997	04 <	....	....	x---	----	x---	----	----	2	
							1999	0730	....	....	x---	----	x---	----	----	2	
							2000	0709	....	....	x---	----	x---	----	----	2?	
							2002	06 <	**2002**	0825>	x---	----	x---	----	----	2	
							? *2004*	*0415*?	?*2004*	*1008*?	x---	----	?---	----	----	*2?*	
							? *2005*	*0723*?	?*2005*	*0815*?	x---	----	?---	----	----	*2?*	
							2007	0726	**2007**	0826	x---	----	x---	----	----	2	
							2008	0612	**2008**	0617?	x---	----	x---	----	----	2	
Ijen (Java-E)	**8.058 S**	**114.242 E**	**2799**	4467	**ABd**	**Stratovolcanoes**	**0603-35=**		**Historical**								
Kawah Ijen							C-**0640**t	....	....	....	x---	----	xx--	----	----		
Kawah Ijen							**1796**	....	....	....	x---	---x	--x-	----	--x-	2	
Kawah Ijen							**1817**	0115	**1817**	0218?	x---	---x	x---	----	xxx-	2*	
Kawah Ijen							**1917**	0225	**1917**	0314	x---	---x	--x-	----	----	1	
Kawah Ijen							**1936**	1105	**1936**	1125	x---	---x	--x-	----	--x-	2	
Kawah Ijen							**1952**	0422	**1952**	0424a	x---	---x	x-x-	----	----	1	
Kawah Ijen							**1993**	0703	**1993**	0801	x---	---x	--x-	----	----	1	
Kawah Ijen							**1994**	0203	**1994**	0203	x---	---x	--x-	----	----	1	
Kawah Ijen							**1999**	0628	**1999**	0628	x---	---x	--x-	----	----	1?	
Kawah Ijen							? *2000*	*0901*e	?*2000*	*0910*c	x---	----	?-x-	----	----	*1*	
Kawah Ijen							? *2002*	*0729*	?*2002*	*0815*c	x---	----	?-?-	----	----	*1*	
Baluran (Java-E)	**7.85 S**	**114.37 E**	**1247**	4567	**A**	**Stratovolcano**	**0603-351**		Holocene?								

LESSER SUNDA ISLANDS

VOLCANO NAME (Subregion) / ERUPTION — Area of Activity	LAT	LONG	ELEV (m)	POPL	ROCK TYPE	VOLC TYPE	NUMBER / Start Year	Start M-Dy	STATUS / Stop Year	Stop M-Dy	Central / Flank vent / Radial fiss / Regional	Submarine / New island / Subglacial / Crater lake	Explosive / Pyro flow / Phreatic / Caldera	Lava flow / Lava lake / Dome / Spine	Fatal / Damage / Mudflow / Tsunami	VEI	Vol L/T
Bratan (Bali)	**8.28 S**	**115.13 E**	**2276**	6667	**AB**	**Caldera**	**0604-001**		**Holocene**								
Batur (Bali)	**8.242 S**	**115.375 E**	**1717**	6667	**ADYB**	**Caldera**	**0604-01=**		**Historical**								
Batur I							**1804**	....	....	....	x---	----	x---	----	----	2	
Batur I							**1821**	0316	....	....	x---	----	x---	----	----	2	
							? *1847*	....	....	....	----	----	----	----	----		
							1849	....	....	....	x---	----	x---	x---	----	2	
Batur I							**1854**	0428	....	....	x---	----	x---	----	----	1?	
SE flank of Batur I							**1888**	0530	**1888**	0531	x-x-	----	x---	x---	----	2	
Batur I							**1897**	....	....	....	x---	----	x---	----	----	2	
West caldera floor (Gunung Anti)							**1904**	....	....	....	-x--	----	x---	x---	----	2	
Batur I, Batur II, Batur III							**1905**	....	....	....	xx--	----	x---	x---	-x--	2	
SW flank (Batur II)							**1921**	0129	**1921**	0417	x---	----	x---	x---	----	2	
							1922	0830	....	....	x---	----	x---	----	----	2	
Batur II							**1923**	....	....	....	x---	----	x---	----	----	2	
Batur II							**1924**	03	**1924**	03 ?	x---	----	x---	----	----	2	
Batur II							**1925**	0105d	**1925**	0105d	x---	----	x---	----	----	2	
SW flank below Batur III							**1926**	0802	**1926**	0921	-xx-	----	x---	xx--	-x--	2	7/6
SW, W flanks (near Batur III, Butus)							**1963**	0905	**1964**	0510	-xx-	----	x---	x---	-x--	2	7/5
SW flank (near Batur III)							**1965**	0818	**1965**	12	-x--	----	x---	?---	-x--	1	
SW flank (west of 1965 vent)							**1966**	0428	....	....	-x--	----	x---	----	----	1	
SW flank (Batur III)							**1968**	0123	**1968**	0215	-x--	----	x---	x---	----	2	6/-
SW flank (1963 vent)							**1970**	0105d	**1970**	0115	-x--	----	x---	----	----	1	
							1971	0311	**1971**	0825>	x---	----	x---	----	----	1	
Batur III							**1972**	0119	**1972**	03	x---	----	x---	----	----	2	
							1973	....	....	....	----	----	----	----	----		
Batur III							**1974**	0312	**1974**	04	x---	----	x---	x---	----	2	
							? *1976*	*0326*	?*1976*	*0326*	----	----	--?-	----	----	*1?*	
Batur III							**1994**	0807	**1994**	0814>	x---	----	x---	?---	----	1	
							1998	0704c	....	....	----	----	x---	----	----	1	
							1999	0315	**2000**	06 ?	x---	----	x---	----	----	1	
Agung (Bali)	**8.342 S**	**115.508 E**	**3142**	4567	**A**	**Stratovolcano**	**0604-02=**		**Historical**								
							1808	....	....	....	x---	----	x---	----	----	2	
							? *1821*	*0316*	....	....	x---	----	x---	----	----	*2*	
							1843	....	....	....	x---	----	x---	----	----	2	
							1963	0218	**1964**	0127	x---	----	xx--	x---	xxx-	**5***	8/9

Lee Siebert (Smithsonian)

Raung volcano (upper L) beyond peaks of Ijen caldera

VOLCANO NAME (Subregion) / **ERUPTION** — Area of Activity	**LAT**	**LONG**	**ELEV** (m)	**POPL** 5 km 10 30 100	**ROCK TYPE**	**VOLC TYPE**	**NUMBER**	**STATUS**	**Start Year**	Start M-Dy	**Stop Year**	Stop M-Dy	Central / Flank vent / Radial fiss / Regional	Submarine / New island / Subglacial / Crater lake	Explosive / Pyro flow / Phreatic / Caldera	Lava flow / Lava lake / Dome / Spine	Fatal / Damage / Mudflow / Tsunami	**VEI**	**Vol L/T**
Rinjani (Lombok I)	**8.42** S	**116.47** E	**3726**	5577	**ABXDr**	**Stratovolcano**	**0604-03=**	**Historical**											
Gunung Barujari									**1847**	0910	**1847**	0912	x---	----	x---	----	----	2	
Gunung Barujari									**1884**	0808	**1884**	0810a	x---	----	x---	----	----	2	
Gunung Barujari									**1900**	1130	**1900**	1202	x---	----	x---	x---	----	2	
Gunung Barujari									**1901**	0601	**1901**	0602	x---	----	x---	----	----	2	
Gunung Barujari									**1906**	0429	....	....	x---	----	x---	----	----	1?	
Gunung Barujari									**1909**	1130	**1909**	1202	x---	----	x---	----	--x-	2	
Gunung Barujari (Segara Munjar)									**1915**	1104	....	....	x---	----	x---	----	----	2	
Rinjani summit									? *1941*	*0530*	....	....	x---	----	----	----	----		
NW flank of Barujari (Rombongan)									**1944**	1225	**1945**	0101?	xx--	---x	x---	x-x-	-x--	2	7/-
NW flank of Gunung Barujari									**1949**	....	**1950**	....	xx--	----	----	x---	----	0	
Gunung Barujari									**1953**	1015q	....	....	x---	----	----	----	----	0?	
Gunung Barujari									**1965**	09	....	....	-x--	----	----	?---	----	0	
East side of Barujari (2250 m)									**1966**	0328	**1966**	0808	x---	----	x---	x---	----	1	6/4
Gunung Barujari									**1994**	0603	**1994**	1121	x---	----	xx--	x---	x-x-	3?	
									? *1995*	*0912*	....	....	----	----	?---	----	----		
Summit and NE flank of Barujari									**2004**	1001	**2004**	1005>	xx--	----	x---	----	----	2	
NE flank of Gunung Barujari									**2009**	0502	**2009**	1220?	xx--	----	x---	x---	----	2	
Tambora (Sumbawa I)	**8.25** S	**118.00** E	**2850**	4557	**XYba**	**Stratovolcano**	**0604-04=**	**Historical**											
									C-**3910**x	....	....	....	x---	----	xx--	----	----		
									C-**3050**?	....	....	....	x---	----	xx--	----	----		
									C **0740**w	....	....	....	x---	----	x---	----	----		
									1812	....	**1815**	0715?	x---	----	xx-x	----	xx-x	**7***	-/11
									1819	08	....	....	x---	----	x---	----	----	2	
SW part of caldera (Doro Afi Toi)									**1880**r	....	....	....	x---	----	x---	x-x-	----	2	
NE part of caldera floor									**1967**p	....	....	....	x---	----	----	x---	----	0	
Sangeang Api (Lesser Sunda Is)	**8.20** S	**119.07** E	**1949**	3456	**XYb**	**Complex volcano**	**0604-05=**	**Historical**											
									1512	....	....	....	x---	----	x---	----	----	3↑	
									1715	....	....	....	x---	----	x---	----	----	2	
									1821	0323	....	....	x---	----	x---	----	----	2	
									1860	0911	**1860**	10	x---	----	x---	----	----	2	
Doro Api									**1911**	0213	**1911**	0302	x---	----	x---	x---	----	2	
									1912	04	....	....	x---	----	x---	----	----	2	
									1927	....	....	....	x---	----	x---	----	----	2	
Doro Api									**1953**	0319	**1953**	0515>	x---	----	x---	x---	--x-	3	
									1954	0426	....	....	x---	----	x---	----	----	2	
									1954	1104	....	....	x---	----	x---	----	----	2	
									1955	....	....	....	x---	----	--x-	----	----	1	
									1956	12	....	....	x---	----	--x-	----	----	1	
									1957	....	....	....	x---	----	--x-	----	----	1	
									1958	....	....	....	x---	----	x---	----	----	1?	
Doro Api									**1964**	0129	**1965**	1201p	x---	----	x---	x-x-	----	2	6/-
									1966	0228	**1966**	11	x---	----	x---	----	----	2	
Doro Api									**1985**	0730	**1988**	02	x---	----	xx--	x---	--x-	3*	7/-
									1997	....	**1999**	....	x---	----	x---	x-x-	----	2?	
									? *2009*	*0501*	?*2009*	*0603*	x---	----	----	----	----		
Sano, Wai (Flores I)	**8.72** S	**120.02** E	**903**	6666	**D**	**Caldera**	**0604-06=**	**Holocene**											
Poco Leok (Flores I)	**8.68** S	**120.48** E	**1675**	3566	**AD**	**Stratovolcano**	**0604-07=**	**Fumarolic**											
Ranakah (Flores I)	**8.62** S	**120.52** E	**2350**	4566	**AD**	**Lava domes**	**0604-071**	**Historical**											
Anak Ranakah									**1987**	1228	**1989**	04 >	-x--	----	xx--	x--x	----	3*	7/6
Anak Ranakah									**1991**	03 <	....	....	x---	----	x---	----	----	1	
Inierie (Flores I)	**8.875**S	**120.95** E	**2245**	4466	**AB**	**Stratovolcano**	**0604-08=**	**Radiocarbon**											
NE side (Wolo Bobo)									C-**8050**?	....	....	....	-x--	----	x---	----	----		
Inielika (Flores I)	**8.73** S	**120.98** E	**1559**	4566	**A**	**Complex volcano**	**0604-09=**	**Historical**											
									1905	11	**1905**	11	x---	----	x-x-	----	-x--	2	
Summit crater complex									**2001**	0111	**2001**	03 ?	x-x-	----	x-x-	----	----	2	
Ebulobo (Flores I)	**8.82** S	**121.18** E	**2124**	4566	**AB**	**Stratovolcano**	**0604-10=**	**Historical**											
									1830	....	....	....	x---	----	x---	x---	----	2	
									1888	....	....	....	x---	----	x---	----	----	2	
									1910	0410	....	....	x---	----	x---	----	----	2	
									1924	11	....	....	x---	----	xx--	----	----	2	
									1938	05	**1938**	06	----	----	----	----	----		
									1941	0823h	....	....	x---	----	----	x---	----	0?	
									1969	0227	....	....	x---	----	x---	----	----	2?	
Iya (Flores I)	**8.897**S	**121.645**E	**637**	5556	**BA**	**Stratovolcano**	**0604-11=**	**Historical**											
									? *1559*	....	....	....	----	----	----	----	----		
									1671?	....	....	....	x---	----	x---	----	----	3↑	
									1844	05	....	....	x---	----	x---	----	----	2	
									1867	01	....	....	x---	----	x---	----	----	2	
									1868	0504	....	....	x---	----	x---	----	----	2	
									1871	0901	....	....	x---	----	x---	----	----	2	
									1882	....	....	....	x---	----	x---	----	----	2	
									? *1888*	*12*	....	....	----	----	----	----	----		
									1953	0904	**1953**	0905	----	----	x---	----	----	2?	
Crater II (upper SW flank)									**1969**	0127	**1969**	0130	-x--	----	xx--	----	xx--	3	
									? *1971*	*06*	?*1971*	*06*	x---	----	--?-	----	----	*1*	
Sukaria Caldera (Flores I)	**8.792**S	**121.77** E	**1500**	5556	**U**	**Caldera**	**0604-12=**	**Fumarolic**											
Ndete Napu (Flores I)	**8.72** S	**121.78** E	**750**	4566	**U**	**Fumarole field**	**0604-13=**	**Fumarolic**											
Kelimutu (Flores I)	**8.77** S	**121.82** E	**1639**	3466	**AB**	**Complex volcano**	**0604-14=**	**Historical**											
									1865e	....	....	....	----	----	--?-	----	----	2	
									1938	05	**1938**	06	----	----	--x-	----	----	2	
Tiwu Nua Muri									**1968**	0603	**1968**	0729	x---	---x	x-x-	----	----	1	
Paluweh (Lesser Sunda Is)	**8.32** S	**121.708**E	**875**	3346	**AB**	**Stratovolcano**	**0604-15=**	**Historical**											
									1650t	....	....	....	x---	----	x---	----	----	3	
									? *1831*	....	....	....	----	----	----	----	----		
Rokatenda									**1928**	0804	**1928**	0925	x---	----	x---	--x-	xx-x	3	6/7
Rokatenda (1928 crater)									**1963**	1231	**1966**	0316	x---	----	xx--	x-x-	xx--	2*	7/-
Rokatenda									**1972**	1022	**1973**	0116	x---	----	x---	----	-x--	3*	
									1973	1027	**1973**	1028	x---	----	x---	----	----	2	
Rokatenda									**1980**	1105	**1981**	09	x---	----	xx--	--x-	-x--	2	6/-
Rokatenda (west side of lava dome)									**1984**	0509	**1984**	0521	x---	----	x---	----	----	2	
Rokatenda (west side of lava dome)									**1985**	0203	**1985**	0203	x---	----	x---	----	----	1	

VOLCANO NAME (Subregion) / ERUPTION — Area of Activity	LAT	LONG	ELEV (m)	POPL (5 km, 10, 30, 100)	ROCK TYPE	VOLC TYPE	NUMBER	STATUS	Start Year	Start M-Dy	Stop Year	Stop M-Dy	Central / Flank vent / Radial fiss / Regional	Submarine / New island / Subglacial / Crater lake	Explosive / Pyro flow / Phreatic / Caldera	Lava flow / Lava lake / Dome / Spine	Fatal / Damage / Mudflow / Tsunami	VEI	Vol L/T
Egon (Flores I)	8.67 S	122.45 E	1703	3566	A	Stratovolcano	0604-16=	Historical											
									? 1888	....	?1892	....	x---	----	----	----	----	2	
(confused with 1907 Lewotobi eruption)									X 1907	0928	....	....	----	----	----	----	----		
									2004	0129	2004	0205?	x---	----	x---	----	x---	1	
									2004	0703	2004	0916?	x---	----	x---	----	----	2*	
Summit and southern flank									2005	0206	2005	0227	x-x-	----	x---	----	----	1	
									2008	0415	2008	0428?	x---	----	x-x-	----	----	2	
Ilimuda (Flores I)	8.478 S	122.671 E	1100	5566	A	Stratovolcano	0604-17=	Fumarolic											
Lewotobi (Flores I)	8.542 S	122.775 E	1703	5566	A	Stratovolcanoes	0604-18=	Historical											
Lewotobi Lakilaki									1675q	....	....	....	x---	----	x---	x---	----	3↑	
Lewotobi Lakilaki									? 1859	07	....	....	----	----	----	----	----		
Lewotobi Lakilaki									1861	0504	1861	0518	x---	----	x---	----	----	2	
Lewotobi Lakilaki									1865	0504	....	....	x---	----	x---	----	----	2	
Lewotobi Lakilaki									1868	0713<	....	....	x---	----	x---	----	----	2	
Lewotobi Lakilaki									1868	1215	....	....	x---	----	x---	----	----	2	
Lewotobi Lakilaki									1869	0707	1869	0727	x---	----	x---	----	xx--	2	
Lewotobi Lakilaki									1889	....	....	....	x---	----	x---	----	----	2	
Lewotobi Lakilaki									1907	0928	1907	1030	x---	----	x---	x---	xx--	3	
Lewotobi Lakilaki									1909	0108	1910	0526	x---	----	x---	x---	----	2	
Lewotobi Lakilaki									1914	0629	....	....	x---	----	x---	x---	----	2	
Lewotobi Perempuan									1921	0101	1921	1220	x---	----	x---	--x-	----	2	5/-
Lewotobi Lakilaki									1932	0523	1933	1226e	x---	----	xx--	x-xx	----	3	5/-
Lewetobi Perempuan									1935	12	1935	1225>	x---	----	x---	----	----	2	
Lewotobi Lakilaki									1939	1217	1940	0421	x---	----	x---	----	----	2	
Lewotobi Lakilaki									1968	1128	1969	0202	x---	----	x---	----	----	2	
Lewotobi Lakilaki									1970	....	....	....	x---	----	x---	----	----	2	
Lewotobi Lakilaki									1971	01	....	....	x---	----	x---	----	----	2	
Lewotabi Lakilaki									1990	0128	1990	06	x---	----	x---	----	----	1	
Lewotobi Lakilaki									1991	0511	1992	1231>	x---	----	x---	----	----	1	
Lewotobi Lakilaki									1999	0331	1999	0701?	x---	----	x---	----	----	2*	
Lewotobi Lakilaki									2002	1012	2002	1012?	x---	----	x---	----	----	1	
Lewotobi Lakilaki									2003	0530	2003	0901>	x---	----	x---	----	-x--	2*	
Leroboleng (Flores I)	8.358 S	122.842 E	1117	4566	A	Complex volcano	0604-20=	Historical											
Burak (Kawah XXIV)									1873	....	....	....	x---	----	x---	----	----	2	
Burak (Kawah XXVI)									1876	....	....	....	x---	----	x---	----	----	2	
Burak (Kawah XXVII)									1881	0316	....	....	x---	----	x---	----	----	2	
									2003	0626	2003	0729	x---	----	x---	----	----	3*	
Iliboleng (Adonara I)	8.342 S	123.258 E	1659	5566	BA	Stratovolcano	0604-22=	Historical											
									1885	09	1885	10	x---	----	x---	----	----	2	
									1888	....	....	....	x---	----	x---	x---	----	2	
									1904	....	....	....	x---	----	x---	x---	----	2	
									1909	1109	....	....	x---	----	x---	----	----	2	
									1925	....	....	....	x---	----	x---	----	----	2	
									1927	....	....	....	x---	----	?---	----	----	2	
									1944	08	1944	10	x---	----	x---	----	----	2	
									1948	0429	....	....	x---	----	x---	----	----	2	
									1949	0204	....	....	x---	----	x---	----	----	2	
									1949	0612	....	....	x---	----	x---	----	----	2	
									1950	03	1950	08 ?	x---	----	x---	----	----	2	
									1951	....	....	....	----	----	x---	----	----	2?	
									1973	04	1974	04	x---	----	x---	----	-x--	2	
									1982	1117	1982	1117	x---	----	x---	----	----	2	
									1983	0511	1984	0413	x---	----	x---	----	----	2*	
									1986	0528	1986	1124	x---	----	x---	----	----	1	
									1987	1002	1987	1002	x---	----	x---	----	----	2	
									1991	0508	1991	0630>	----	----	x---	----	----	1	
									1991	1103	1991	1115	x---	----	x---	----	----	1	
									1993	06 ?	1993	07	x---	----	x---	----	----	1?	
Lewotolo (Lembata I)	8.272 S	123.505 E	1423	4566	AYB	Stratovolcano	0604-23=	Historical											
									1660	....	....	....	x---	----	x---	----	----	3↑	
									1819	....	....	....	x---	----	x---	----	----	2	
									1849	1006	....	....	x---	----	x---	----	----	2	
K2 crater									1852	1005	1852	1006	x---	----	x---	----	-x--	2	
									1864	....	....	....	x---	----	x---	----	----	2	
									1899	0602	....	....	x---	----	x---	----	----	2	
									1920	....	....	....	x---	----	x---	----	----	2	
									1951	1215	....	....	----	----	----	----	----	2	
Ililabalekan (Lembata I)	8.55 S	123.38 E	1018	4566	BA	Stratovolcano	0604-24=	Fumarolic											
Iliwerung (Lembata I)	8.53 S	123.57 E	1018	3456	BA	Complex volcano	0604-25=	Historical											
Iliwerung (Iliadowajo)									1870	....	....	....	x---	----	x---	--x-	x---	3	
Iliwerung									1910	....	....	....	x---	----	?---	----	----	2	
Iliwerung									1928	....	....	....	x---	----	x---	--x-	----	2	7/-
									? 1941	0605	....	....	----	----	----	----	----		
East flank (Iligripe)									1948	0407	1948	1126	xxx-	----	xx--	--x-	xx--	2	6/6
									1949	0409	1949	0429	x---	----	xx--	----	----	2	
									1950	0910	1950	1002	x---	----	xx--	x---	-x--	2	
									1951	1112	1951	1116	x---	----	xx--	----	-x--	2	
									1952	0324	....	....	x---	----	x---	----	----	1	
Hobal (submarine vent on SE flank)									1973	1205	1974	0822	-x--	xx--	x---	----	x--x	2*	
Hobal (submarine vent on SE flank)									? 1976	0308	....	....	-x--	?---	----	----	---x	0	
Hobal (submarine vent on SE flank)									1983	0817	1983	0818	-x--	x---	x---	----	x--x	1	
Hobal (submarine vent on SE flank)									1993	0915	1993	0919	-x--	x---	x---	----	----	2	
Hobal (submarine vent on SE flank)									1999	0522	1999	09 >	-x--	x---	x---	----	----	0	
Tara, Batu (Komba I)	7.792 S	123.579 E	748	3336	XY	Stratovolcano	0604-26=	Historical											
									1847	....	1852	0831>	x---	----	x---	x---	----	2	
									? 2006	0701	?2006	0701	x---	----	?---	----	----	1?	
									2007	0117?	2010>	....	x---	----	x---	x---	----	2	
Sirung (Pantar I)	8.508 S	124.13 E	862	4556	AB	Complex volcano	0604-27=	Historical											
									? 1852	....	....	....	x---	----	--?-	----	----	2	
									? 1899	03	?1899	04	x---	----	--?-	----	----	2	
									? 1927	....	....	....	x---	---?	--?-	----	----	2	
									1934	0614	1934	0715e	x---	----	x-x-	----	----	2	

VOLCANO NAME (Subregion) / ERUPTION — Area of Activity	LAT	LONG	ELEV (m)	POPL 5 km 10 30 100	ROCK TYPE	VOLC TYPE	NUMBER	STATUS	Start Year	Start M-Dy	Stop Year	Stop M-Dy	Central Flank vent Radial fiss Regional	Submarine New island Subglacial Crater lake	Explosive Pyro flow Phreatic Caldera	Lava flow Lava lake Dome Spine	Fatal Damage Mudflow Tsunami	VEI	Vol L/T
Sirung (Pantar I) *continued*									**1947**	04	**1947**	05	x---	----	--x-	----	----	2	
									1953	06	....	....	----	----	----	----	xx--		
									1960	0313	....	....	----	----	----	----	----	2?	
									1964	0208	**1964**	1005>	x---	---x	x-x-	----	----	1	
									1965	0507	**1965**	0518	x---	----	x-x-	----	----	1	
									1965	1102	**1965**	1102	x---	----	x-?-	----	----	1	
									1970	....	....	....	----	----	----	----	----	2?	
Yersey (Wetar I)	7.53 S	123.95 E	-3800	0006	U	**Submarine volc ?**	**0604-28=**	Uncertain											

BANDA SEA

VOLCANO NAME (Subregion) / ERUPTION — Area of Activity	LAT	LONG	ELEV (m)	POPL	ROCK TYPE	VOLC TYPE	NUMBER	STATUS	Start Year	Start M-Dy	Stop Year	Stop M-Dy	Central Flank vent Radial fiss Regional	Submarine New island Subglacial Crater lake	Explosive Pyro flow Phreatic Caldera	Lava flow Lava lake Dome Spine	Fatal Damage Mudflow Tsunami	VEI	Vol L/T
Emperor of China (Banda Sea)	6.62 S	124.22 E	-2850	0005	U	**Submarine volc ?**	**0605-01=**	Uncertain											
									? 1893<	....	....	....	----	?---	?---	----	----	*1?*	
									? 1927	*0301p*	....	....	----	?---	?---	----	----	*2*	
Nieuwerkerk (Banda Sea)	6.60 S	124.675 E	-2285	0004	U	**Submarine volc ?**	**0605-02=**	Uncertain											
									? 1893<	....	....	....	----	?---	?---	----	----	*1?*	
									? 1925	*0924*	....	....	----	?---	?---	----	----	*2*	
									? 1927	*0301p*	....	....	----	?---	?---	----	----	*2*	
Gunungapi Wetar (Banda Sea)	6.642 S	126.65 E	282	1111	A	**Stratovolcano**	**0605-03=**	**Historical**											
									1512	....	....	....	x---	----	?---	?---	----	3↑	
									1699	....	....	....	x---	----	x---	----	----	3↑	
Wurlali (Damar I)	7.125 S	128.675 E	868	3333	Ab	**Stratovolcano**	**0605-04=**	**Historical**											
									1892	0603	**1892**	0605	x---	----	x---	----	----	2	
Teon (Banda Sea)	6.92 S	129.125 E	655	2334	A	**Stratovolcano**	**0605-05=**	**Historical**											
									1659	1111	....	....	?---	----	?---	----	----	3↑	
									1660	02	....	....	x---	----	xx--	----	xx--	4?	-/8
									1663	0118	....	....	x---	----	x---	----	----	3↑	
									1693	....	....	....	x---	----	x---	----	----	3↑	
									1904	0603	....	....	x---	----	x---	----	----	2	
Nila (Banda Sea)	6.73 S	129.50 E	781	3334	Ab	**Stratovolcano**	**0605-06=**	**Historical**											
									1903	1208	....	....	x---	----	--x-	----	----	2	
SE flank									**1932**	0313	....	....	x-x-	----	x-x-	----	----	2	
									1964	03	**1964**	03	----	----	--?-	----	----	1?	
East flank									**1968**	0507	**1968**	06	-x-x	----	--x-	----	----	1	
Serua (Banda Sea)	6.30 S	130.00 E	641	2223	A	**Stratovolcano**	**0605-07=**	**Historical**											
									1683	....	....	....	x---	----	x---	----	----	3↑	
									1687	0615	....	....	x---	----	x---	----	----	3↑	
(perhaps same as 1693 eruption)									*? 1692*	*0604?*	....	....	?---	----	?---	----	----		
									1693	0604	**1693**	07	x---	----	x---	xx--	xx--	4?	-/8
									1694	....	....	....	x---	----	x---	----	----	3↑	
									1844	08	**1844**	09	x---	----	x---	x---	----	2	
									? 1845	....	....	....	?---	----	?---	----	----	*2*	
									1846	09 ?	....	....	?---	----	?---	----	----	2	
									1858	....	....	....	x---	----	x---	----	-x--	2	
									1859	....	....	....	x---	----	x---	?---	----	2	
									1919	11	....	....	x---	----	x---	?---	----	2	
Summit and south flank									**1921**	0918	....	....	xx--	----	x---	?---	----	2	
Manuk (Banda Sea)	5.53 S	130.292 E	282	0002	A	**Stratovolcano**	**0605-08=**	**Fumarolic**											
Banda Api (Banda Sea)	4.525 S	129.871 E	640	4444	DAB	**Caldera**	**0605-09=**	**Historical**											
									1586	0417	....	....	x---	----	x---	----	----	3↑	
									1598	....	**1602**	....	x---	----	x---	----	xx--	3	
									1609	....	....	....	x---	----	x---	----	----	3↑	
									? 1614	....	....	....	----	----	----	----	----		
									1615	0316	**1615**	04 ?	x---	----	x---	----	xx--	3	
									1632	1216	....	....	x---	----	x---	----	----	3↑	
									1635	1118	....	....	x---	----	x---	----	----	1?	
									1683	....	....	....	x-x-	----	x---	----	----	3	
									1690	....	**1696**	0522	x---	----	x---	----	x---	3↑	
									1712	05	**1712**	12	x---	----	x---	----	----	2	
									1722	....	....	....	x---	----	x---	----	----	2	
									1749	....	....	....	x---	----	x---	----	----	2	
									1762	....	....	....	x---	----	x---	----	----	2	
									1765	0419	**1766**	10	x---	----	x---	----	----	2	
									1773	0206	....	....	x---	----	x---	----	----	2	
									1775	....	....	....	?---	----	?---	----	----	2	
									1778	....	....	....	?---	----	?---	----	----	2	
									1816	1011	**1816**	12	x---	----	x---	----	----	2	
Summit, south and NNW flanks									**1820**	0611	**1820**	0808	x-x-	----	x---	x---	xx--	2	
North side									**1824**	0422	**1824**	0628	xx--	----	x---	x---	----	2	
									1825?	....	**1831**	....	x---	----	x---	----	----	1	
									? 1835	*10*	....	....	----	----	----	----	----		
									? 1855	*1229*	*?1855*	*1230*	----	----	----	----	----		
									1890	1123	**1890**	1123	x---	----	x---	----	----	2	
Summit and north flank									**1901**	0518	....	....	xx--	----	x---	x---	-x--	2	
									? 1902	*0320*	....	....	x---	----	----	----	----		
Summit, north and south flanks									**1988**	0509	**1988**	0517	xxx-	x---	xxx-	x---	xxx-	3?	6/-

SULAWESI

VOLCANO NAME (Subregion) / ERUPTION — Area of Activity	LAT	LONG	ELEV (m)	POPL	ROCK TYPE	VOLC TYPE	NUMBER	STATUS	Start Year	Start M-Dy	Stop Year	Stop M-Dy	Central Flank vent Radial fiss Regional	Submarine New island Subglacial Crater lake	Explosive Pyro flow Phreatic Caldera	Lava flow Lava lake Dome Spine	Fatal Damage Mudflow Tsunami	VEI	Vol L/T
Colo [Una Una] (Sulawesi)	0.17 S	121.608 E	507	4446	YT	**Stratovolcano**	**0606-01=**	**Historical**											
Gunung Colo									**1898**	0502	**1900?**	....	x---	---?	x---	----	-xx-	3?	-/7
Gunung Colo									**1938j**	....	....	....	x---	----	--x-	----	----	1	
Gunung Colo									**1983**	0718	**1983**	12	x---	----	xxx-	----	-x--	4*	
Ambang (Sulawesi)	0.75 N	124.42 E	1795	4567	A	**Complex volcano**	**0606-02=**	**Historical**											
									1845e	....	....	....	----	----	----	----	----		
Soputan (Sulawesi)	1.108 N	124.73 E	1784	4567	AB	**Stratovolcano**	**0606-03=**	**Historical**											
									1450j	....	....	....	----	----	x---	----	----	3↑	
									1785	1231y	....	....	x---	----	x---	----	----	2	
									1819	....	....	....	x---	----	x---	----	----	2	
									1833?	....	....	....	x---	----	x---	----	----	2	
									1845	0208	....	....	x---	----	x---	----	---x	2	

Tom Casadevall (USGS)

1988 fissure vents and lava flow

VOLCANO NAME (Subregion) / ERUPTION — Area of Activity	LAT	LONG	ELEV (m)	POPL 5 km 10 30 100	ROCK TYPE	VOLC TYPE	NUMBER	STATUS	Start Year	Start M-Dy	Stop Year	Stop M-Dy	ERUPTIVE CHARACTERISTICS (Central Flank vent Radial fiss Regional / Submarine New island Subglacial Crater lake / Explosive Pyro flow Phreatic Caldera / Lava flow Lava lake Dome Spine / Fatal Damage Mudflow Tsunami)	VEI	Vol L/T
Soputan (Sulawesi) *continued*									**1890**	....	....	....	?--- ---- ?--- ---- ----	2	
									1901	0204	....	....	-x-- ---- x-x- ---- ----	2	
NE flank (Aeseput)									**1906**	0617	**1906**	09	-x-- ---- x--- x--- ----	2	
NE flank (Aeseput)									**1907**	0605	**1907**	0625?	-x-- ---- x--- ---- ----	2	
NE flank (Aeseput)									**1908**	06	**1909**	06	-x-- ---- x--- x--- ----	2	
NE flank (Aeseput)									**1910**	1115q	....	....	-x-- ---- x--- x--- ----	2	
NE flank (Aeseput)									**1911**	11	**1912**	04	-x-- ---- x--- x--- ----	2	
NE flank (Aeseput)									**1913**	04	**1913**	07	-x-- ---- x--- ---- ----	2	
NE flank (Aeseput Weru)									**1915**	04	**1915**	06	-x-- ---- ---- x-x- ----	2	6/-
NE flank (Aeseput)									**1917**	11	....	....	-x-- ---- x--- ---- ----	2	
NE flank (Aeseput)									**1923**	1127	**1924**	0118	-x-- ---- x--- x--- ----	2*	7/-
NE flank (Aeseput)									**1947**	0822	**1947**	0827	-x-- ---- x--- ---- ----	2	
NE flank (Aeseput)									**1953**	11	....	....	-x-- ---- ?--- ---- ----	2	
Kawah Soputan									**1966**	0521	**1967**	11	x--- ---- xx-- x-x- -xx-	3*	7/-
									1968	07	**1968**	08	x--- ---- -x-- --x- ----	1	
									1970	02	**1970**	0526e	x--- ---- x--- ---- ----	2	
									1971	0519	**1971**	0519	x--- ---- --?- ---- ----	1	
									1973	0106	**1973**	0527	x--- ---- x--- ---- ----	2	
									1982	0826	**1982**	1110	x--- ---- x--- ---- -x--	3	-/6
									1984	0524	**1984**	0831	x--- ---- x--- ---- -x--	3*	-/7
									1985	0519	**1985**	0520	x--- ---- x--- ---- -x--	2	-/6
									1989	0422	**1989**	0423	x--- ---- x--- ---- -x--	2	
									1991	0522	**1996**	0929>	x--- ---- x--- x-x- ----	2*	7/-
									2000	0513	**2003**	0904?	x--- ---- xx-- x-x- -x--	2*	7/-
									2004	1018	**2004**	1227?	x--- ---- xx-- x--- -x--	3?	
									2005	0419	**2005**	0718?	x--- ---- xx-- --x- ----	2	
									2005	1226	**2006**	0124?	x--- ---- x--- --x- ----	1	
									2006	1214	**2006**	1226?	x--- ---- x--- ---- ----	1	
									2007	06 ?	**2007**	1109?	x--- ---- x--- x-x- ----	3*	
									2008	0606	**2008**	1102?	x--- ---- xx-- --x- -x--	3?	
Sempu (Sulawesi)	**1.13 N**	**124.758 E**	**1549**	6667	**U**	**Caldera**	**0606-04=**	**Fumarolic**							
									? 1819	....	....	....	---- ---- ---- ---- ----		
Tondano Caldera (Sulawesi)	**1.23 N**	**124.83 E**	**1202**	6667	**A**	**Caldera**	**0606-07-**	**Fumarolic**							
Lokon-Empung (Sulawesi)	**1.358 N**	**124.792 E**	**1580**	5567	**BDA**	**Stratovolcano**	**0606-10=**	**Historical**							
Empung									**1375**q	....	....	....	x--- ---- x--- ---- ----	3↑	
Empung									**1775**q	....	....	....	x--- ---- x--- ---- xx--	3	
Tompaluan									**1829**	03	....	....	-x-- ---- x--- ---- ----	2	
Tompaluan									**1893**	0329	**1894**	0814>	-x-- ---- x--- ---- ----	2	
Tompaluan									**1930**	08	....	....	-x-- ---- x-x- ---- ----	2	
Tompaluan									**1942**	0903	....	....	-x-- ---- x--- ---- ----	2	
Tompaluan									**1949**	0914	....	....	-x-- ---- --x- ---- ----	1	
Tompaluan									**1951**	0702	**1953**	03	-x-- ---- x--- --x- -x--	3*	
Tompaluan									**1958**	0219	**1959**	1223	-x-- ---- xx-- --x- -x--	2	
Tompaluan									**1961**	0519	**1961**	12	-x-- ---- x--- ---- ----	2	
Tompaluan									**1962**	04	**1962**	11	-x-- ---- --x- ---- ----	1	
Tompaluan									**1963**	1217	**1964**	04	-x-- ---- x--- ---- ----	2	
Tompaluan									**1965**	0710	**1965**	0710	-x-- ---- x--- ---- ----	1	
Tompaluan									**1966**	0924	**1966**	0930?	-x-- ---- x--- ---- ----	2	
Tompaluan									**1969**	1127	**1970**	1226e	-x-- ---x xx-- ---- -xx-	2	
Tompaluan									**1971**	0511	**1971**	1026e	-x-- ---- x--- --x- ----	2	2/-
Tompaluan									**1973**	0915	**1974**	12	-x-- ---- x--- ---- ----	1	
Tompaluan									**1975**	11 <	**1980**	....	-x-- ---- x?-- --x- ----	2*	4/-
Tompaluan									*? 1984*	*0605*d	*? 1984*	*11*	-x-- ---- --?- ---- ----	*1*	
Tompaluan									**1986**	0322	**1987**	0513	-x-- ---x x-x- ---- -xx-	2	
Tompaluan									**1988**	0421	**1988**	0501	-x-- ---- x--- ---- ----	1	
Tompaluan									**1991**	0517	**1992**	01	-x-- ---- xx-- x--- xx--	3*	5/7
Tompaluan									**2000**	0510c	**2001**	0818	-x-- ---- x--- ---- ----	2	
Tompaluan									**2002**	0209	**2002**	05 ?	-x-- ---- x--- ---- ----	2	
Tompaluan									**2002**	1223	**2003**	0401	-x-- ---- x--- ---- ----	2*	
Tompaluan									**2003**	0912	**2003**	0912	-x-- ---- x--- ---- ----	3	
Mahawu (Sulawesi)	**1.358 N**	**124.858 E**	**1324**	5667	**ADB**	**Stratovolcano**	**0606-11=**	**Historical**							
									1788<	....	....	....	x--- ---- x--- ---- ----		
									1789	1231y	....	....	x--- ---- x--- ---- -?--	2	
									1846	....	....	....	-x-- ---- --x- ---- ----	2	
									1904	1004<	....	....	x--- ---- x--- ---- --x-	2	
									1952	....	....	....	---- ---- ---- ---- ----	2?	
									1958	0712	**1958**	0729	x--- ---- x-x- ---- xxx-	2?	
									1977	1116	....	....	x--- ---x --x- ---- ----	0	
Klabat (Sulawesi)	**1.47 N**	**125.03 E**	**1995**	4567	**AB**	**Stratovolcano**	**0606-12=**	**Fumarolic**							
Tongkoko (Sulawesi)	**1.52 N**	**125.20 E**	**1149**	3567	**ABD**	**Stratovolcano**	**0606-13=**	**Historical**							
									1680	....	....	....	x--- ---- x--- ---- -x--	**5?**	**-/9**
									1683	....	....	....	x--- ---- x--- ---- ----	3↑	
									1694	....	....	....	x--- ---- x--- ---- ----	3?	
Summit and east flank (Batu Angus)									**1801**	....	....	....	xx-- ---x x--- x-x- -x--	2	6/-
Batu Angus Baru									**1821**	....	....	....	-x-- ---- ---- x--- ----	0	
Batu Angus									**1843**	....	**1846**	....	-x-- ---- x--- ---- ----	2	
Batu Angus									**1880**	....	....	....	-x-- ---- ---- x-x- ----	1	

SANGIHE ISLANDS

VOLCANO NAME (Subregion) / ERUPTION — Area of Activity	LAT	LONG	ELEV (m)	POPL 5 km 10 30 100	ROCK TYPE	VOLC TYPE	NUMBER	STATUS	Start Year	Start M-Dy	Stop Year	Stop M-Dy	ERUPTIVE CHARACTERISTICS	VEI	Vol L/T
Ruang (Sangihe Is)	**2.30 N**	**125.37 E**	**725**	3446	**AB**	**Stratovolcano**	**0607-01=**	**Historical**							
(eruption in 1808, not 1810 or 1811)									**1808**	....	....	....	x--- ---- xx-- ---- -x--	2	
									1836?	0422	**1836**?	0424	x--- ---- x--- ---- ----	2	
									1840	....	....	....	x--- ---- xx-- ---- ----	2	
									1856	09	....	....	x--- ---- x--- --x- ----	1	
									1870	0827	**1870**	0828	x--- ---- x--- ---- xx--	3?	
									1871	0302	**1871**	0314	x--- ---- xx-- ---- xx-x	2	
									1874	1115	....	....	x--- ---- xx-- ---- -x--	2	
									1889	06	....	....	x--- ---- ---- --x- ----	1	
									1904	0422	**1905**	0527	x--- ---- xx-- x-x- -xx-	3?	6/-
									1914	0529	**1915**	0228p	x--- ---- xx-- x--- ----	2	
(increased fumarolic activity only)									*X 1918*	*02*	....	....	---- ---- ---- ---- ----		

VOLCANO NAME (Subregion) / ERUPTION — Area of Activity	LAT	LONG	ELEV (m)	POPL (5 km 10 30 100)	ROCK TYPE	VOLC TYPE / Start Year	NUMBER / Start M-Dy	STATUS / Stop Year	Stop M-Dy	Central, Flank vent, Radial fiss, Regional	Submarine, New island, Subglacial, Crater lake	Explosive, Pyro flow, Phreatic, Caldera	Lava flow, Lava lake, Dome, Spine	Fatal, Damage, Mudflow, Tsunami	VEI	Vol L/T
Ruang (Sangihe Is) *continued*																
(increased fumarolic activity only)						X 1940	04	....	....	----	----	----	----	----		
(no eruption in 1946: NVP 1959)						X 1946	1013	X1946	1015	----	----	----	----	----		
						1949	0105	**1949**	0119>	x---	----	x---	x-x-	----	2	
						? 1996	0627	....	....	----	----	?---	----	----		
						2002	0925	**2002**	0929?	x---	----	xx--	----	-xx-	4?	
Karangetang [Api Siau] (Siau I)	**2.78 N**	**125.40 E**	**1784**	3455	**AB**	**Stratovolcano**	**0607-02=**	**Historical**								
						1675	....	....	....	x---	----	x---	----	----	3↑	
						1712	0116	....	....	x---	----	x---	----	----	2	
						1825	....	....	....	x---	----	x---	----	----	2	
						1864	0606	....	....	x---	----	x---	----	----	2	
Crater II?						**1883**	0825	**1883**	0826	x---	----	x---	----	----	2	
Crater III						**1886**	0425	**1886**	0619>	x---	----	x---	----	----	2	
						1887	0527	**1887**	0527	x---	----	x---	----	----	2	
						1892	0614?	....	....	x---	----	x---	----	--x-	2	
						1899	....	....	....	x---	----	x---	----	----	2	
						1900	....	....	....	x---	----	x---	----	----	2	
						1905	0521	**1905**	0522	x---	----	x---	----	----	2	
Crater V						**1921**	03	**1921**	06 >	x---	----	x---	--?-	----	2	
Crater IV						**1922**	0504	**1922**	1213	x---	----	x---	x---	----	2	
						1924	05	....	....	x---	----	x---	----	----	2	
						1926	10	....	....	x---	----	x---	----	----	2	
Crater IV						**1930**	0204	**1930**	0206	x---	----	x---	----	----	2	
						1930	11 ?	....	....	x---	----	x---	----	----	2	
						1935	0831	....	....	x---	----	x---	----	----	2	
						1940	0301	**1940**	0309	x---	----	x---	----	----	2	
						1940	0620	**1940**	0823	x---	----	x---	----	xx--	2	
						1941	1030	**1941**	1030	x---	----	x---	----	-x--	2	
						1947	0209	**1947**	0209	x---	----	x---	----	----	2	
						1947	1201	**1947**	1221	x---	----	x---	----	----	2	
						1948	12	....	....	x---	----	x---	----	----	2	
						1949	0914	....	....	x---	----	x---	----	----	2	
Craters I, II and III						**1952**	02	**1952**	0630	x---	----	x---	----	-x--	2	
						1953	....	....	....	----	----	x---	----	----	2	
						1961	0228	**1961**	04	x---	----	x---	----	----	2	-/6
						1961	1009	**1961**	1019>	x---	----	x---	----	----	2	-/6
						1962	0129	**1963**	12	x---	----	x---	----	-xx-	2	
						1965	0405d	**1967**	06	x---	----	x---	?---	----	2	
						1967	1129	**1967**	1202	x---	----	x---	----	----	2	
						1970	1127	**1971**	03	x---	----	xx--	x-x-	----	2	
						1972	01	**1976**	0405	x---	----	x-x-	x-x-	xxx-	3*	
South flank (1100 m) and summit						**1976**	0915	**1977**	09	xx--	----	xx--	x---	xx--	2	7/-
						1978	0222	**1978**	1218	x---	----	x---	----	----	1	
NNW flank, 1300 m (Kawah Maralebule)						**1979**	0531	**1979**	0531	-x--	----	x---	----	----	1	
						1980	0324	**1980**	0913	x---	----	x---	----	----	1	
						1982	....	....	....	x---	----	?---	----	----	1	
Summit and SW flank (1443 m)						**1983**	05	**1988**	1231>	xx--	----	xxx-	x---	-x--	3*	4/-
						1989	07	**1989**	07	----	----	x---	----	----	1	
						1991	0702<	**1993**	1231>	x---	----	xx--	x-x-	xx--	2*	6/6
						1995	1109	**1995**	1217	x---	----	x---	----	----	1	
						1996	1001<	**1997**	06 >	x---	----	xx--	----	x---	1	
						1998	0705d	....	....	x---	----	x---	----	----	1	
						1999	03 <	**2003**	1028	x---	----	xx--	x-x-	-xx-	3?	
						2004	0402?	**2005**	0805?	x---	----	x---	--x-	----	2*	
						2006	0703	**2007**	10 >	x---	----	xx--	x-x-	--x-	1	
						? 2008	0312	....	....	----	----	?---	----	----	1?	
						2008	1129?	**2010>**	....	x---	----	xx--	x---	--x-	2	
Banua Wuhu (Sangihe Is)	**3.138 N**	**125.491 E**	**-5**	3345	**A**	**Submarine volc**	**0607-03=**	**Historical**								
						1835	0423	**1835**	0426	x---	xx--	x---	x-x-	----	2	6/-
						1889	0906	**1889**	0909	x---	xx--	x---	--x-	---x	2	
						1895	07	**1895**	1226e	x---	x---	x---	----	----	2	
						1904	0417	**1904**	0418	x---	xx--	x---	----	----	2	
						1904	0827	....	....	x---	x---	x---	----	----	2	
						1918	0718	**1919**	1201p	x---	xx--	x---	--x-	-x-x	3*	
						? 1968	0905	?1968	0909d	----	?---	----	----	----	0	
Awu (Sangihe Is)	**3.67 N**	**125.50 E**	**1320**	4555	**AB**	**Stratovolcano**	**0607-04=**	**Historical**								
						? 1640	12	?1641	0104	x---	----	x-x-	----	--x-	3↑	
						1646e	....	....	....	x---	----	--x-	----	----	2?	
						? 1699	....	....	....	----	----	----	----	----		
						1711	1210	**1711**	1216	x---	---x	xxx-	----	xxx-	3	
						1812	0806	**1812**	0808	x---	----	xx--	----	xxx-	4?	-/8
						1856	0302	**1856**	0317	x---	----	xx--	----	xxxx	3?	-/8
						1875	08	**1875**	08	x---	----	--x-	----	----	2	
						1883	0825	**1883**	0826	x---	----	x---	----	----	2	
						1885	0818	....	....	x---	----	--x-	----	----	2	
						1892	0607	**1892**	0612?	x---	----	xx--	----	xxxx	3	
						1893	....	....	....	x---	----	--x-	----	----	2	
						1913	0314	**1913**	0314	x---	----	x-x-	----	----	2	
						1921	02	**1921**	1001t	x---	---x	--?-	--x-	----	0	
						1922	0620	**1922**	09	x---	---x	--?-	--x-	----	0	
						1930	12	**1931**	12	x---	---x	--x-	--x-	----	2*	6/-
						1966	0812	**1966**	10	x---	---x	xx--	----	xxx-	4	
						? 1968	08	?1968	09	----	----	----	----	----	2	
SE part of summit crater						**1992**	0407i	....	....	x---	----	--x-	----	----	1	
						2004	0602<	**2004**	08 ?	x---	----	x---	--x-	----	2*	
Unnamed (Sangihe Is)	**3.97 N**	**124.17 E**	**-5000**	0000	**U**	**Submarine volc ?**	**0607-05=**	Uncertain								
						? 1922	0201p	....	....	----	?---	----	----	----	0	
						? 1955	0213	....	....	----	?---	?---	----	----	0	

HALMAHERA

VOLCANO NAME (Subregion) / ERUPTION — Area of Activity	LAT	LONG	ELEV (m)	POPL	ROCK TYPE	VOLC TYPE / Start Year	NUMBER / Start M-Dy	STATUS / Stop Year	Stop M-Dy	Central, Flank vent, Radial fiss, Regional	Submarine, New island, Subglacial, Crater lake	Explosive, Pyro flow, Phreatic, Caldera	Lava flow, Lava lake, Dome, Spine	Fatal, Damage, Mudflow, Tsunami	VEI	Vol L/T
Tarakan (Halmahera)	**1.83 N**	**127.83 E**	**318**	5556	**B**	**Pyroclastic cones**	**0608-001**	**Holocene**								
Dukono (Halmahera)	**1.68 N**	**127.88 E**	**1335**	4466	**ATB**	**Complex volcano**	**0608-01=**	**Historical**								
						1550	1120n	....	....	x---	----	x---	x---	xx--	3	-/8

VOLCANO NAME (Subregion) / ERUPTION	Area of Activity	LAT	LONG	ELEV (m)	POPL (5 km, 10, 30, 100)	ROCK TYPE	VOLC TYPE	NUMBER	STATUS		Start Year	Start M-Dy	Stop Year	Stop M-Dy	Central / Flank vent / Radial fiss / Regional	Submarine / New island / Subglacial / Crater lake	Explosive / Pyro flow / Phreatic / Caldera	Lava flow / Lava lake / Dome / Spine	Fatal / Damage / Mudflow / Tsunami	VEI	Vol L/T
Dukono (Halmahera) *continued*	East flank of Tolo										**1719**w	....	....	....	-x--	----	----	x---	----		
											1868?	....	....	....	x---	----	x---	----	-?--	2	
											1901	....	....	....	x---	----	x---	----	----	2	
	Malupang Magiwe and Malupang Warirang										**1933**	0813	**2010**>	....	x---	----	x---	x---	-xx-	3*	
Tobaru (Halmahera)		**1.63** N	**127.67** E	**1035**	3456	**A**	**Unknown**	**0608-02-**	**Holocene**												
Ibu (Halmahera)		**1.488** N	**127.63** E	**1325**	4556	**AB**	**Stratovolcano**	**0608-03=**	**Historical**												
											1911	0830	**1911**	0901	x---	----	x---	----	----	2	
											1998	1218	**1999**	09 >	x---	----	x---	x-x-	----	2*	
											2001	0528?	**2001**	1003?	x---	----	----	--?-	----	0	
											2004	05 ?	**2005**	0222?	x---	----	----	--x-	----	0?	
											2008	0405	**2010**>	....	x---	----	x---	x-x-	----	1	
Gamkonora (Halmahera)		**1.38** N	**127.53** E	**1635**	4556	**A**	**Stratovolcano**	**0608-04=**	**Historical**												
											1564	1231y	....	....	x---	----	x---	x---	xx--	3↑	
											1673	0520	....	....	x---	----	x---	----	xx-x	**5?**	-/9
											1885e	....	....	....	x---	----	x---	----	----	2	
											1911	....	....	....	----	----	----	----	----	2?	
											1917	1018	**1917**	1018	x---	----	x---	----	----	2	
											1926	06	....	....	x---	----	x---	----	----	1?	
											1949	....	....	....	x---	----	x---	----	----	2	
											1950	10	....	....	x---	----	----	----	----	2	
											1951	....	....	....	----	----	x---	----	----	2	
											1952	0716	**1952**	0905d	x---	----	x---	----	----	2	
											1981	0304	**1981**	0725	x---	----	x-x-	----	----	1	-/5
											1987	0413	**1987**	0426	x---	----	x---	----	----	1	
											2007	0708	**2007**	0716?	x---	----	x-x-	----	----	2*	
Todoko-Ranu (Halmahera)		**1.25** N	**127.47** E	**979**	3556	**A**	**Calderas**	**0608-05=**	**Holocene**												
Jailolo (Halmahera)		**1.08** N	**127.42** E	**1130**	4556	**AB**	**Stratovolcano**	**0608-051**	**Holocene**												
Hiri (Halmahera)		**0.90** N	**127.32** E	**630**	4566	**BA**	**Stratovolcano**	**0608-052**	**Holocene**												
Gamalama (Halmahera)		**0.80** N	**127.33** E	**1715**	6666	**Ad**	**Stratovolcanoes**	**0608-06=**	**Historical**												
											1510j	....	....	....	x---	----	x---	----	----	3↑	
											1538	....	....	....	x---	----	x---	----	----	3↑	
											1561	1231y	....	....	xx--	---?	x---	----	--x-	2	
											1605	05	....	....	x---	----	x---	----	----	2	
	(eruption in 1608, not 1609)										**1608**	0718	**1608**	0719	x---	----	x---	----	-x--	3	
											1635	0329	....	....	x---	----	x---	----	----	2	
	(perhaps confused with 1648 eruption)									?	*1643*	*0615*	....	....	?---	----	?---	----	----	*2?*	
											1648	0615	**1648**	0618	x---	----	x---	?---	----	2	
											1653	1231y	....	....	x---	----	x---	----	-?--	3↑	
											1659	06	....	....	x---	----	x---	----	----	2	
	(earthquake: eruption at Gamkonora)									X	*1673*	*0812*	....	....	----	----	----	----	----		
											1676	1231y	....	....	x---	----	x---	----	----	2	
											1686	09 ?	**1686**	1013>	x---	----	x---	----	----	2	
											1687	0510	**1687**	0511	x---	----	x---	----	----	3↑	
											1737	0310	**1737**	0313	x---	----	x---	x---	----	2	
											1739	....	....	....	x---	----	x---	?---	----	2	
	North flank										**1763**	....	....	....	-x--	----	----	x---	----	2	7/-
											1770	0706	**1770**	1209	xx--	----	x---	----	-x--	3	
											1771	0828	**1772**	1009	x---	----	x---	----	xx--	3	
											1773	0202	**1773**	0207	x---	----	x---	----	----	2	
											1773	1021	**1774**	0122	x---	----	x---	----	xx--	2	
	Summit and NW flank (100 m)										**1775**	0820	**1775**	1106	xx--	----	xx--	----	xx--	3*	
										?	*1781*	....	....	....	----	----	----	----	----		
											1811	0201	**1811**	05	x---	----	x---	?---	----	2	
											1812	0907	**1812**	0907	x---	----	x---	----	----	2	
											1814	1127	**1814**	1128	x---	----	x---	----	----	2	
	(earthquakes, not eruption)									X	*1815*	....	....	....	----	----	----	----	----		
										?	*1821*	*0822*	....	....	x---	----	----	----	----	*1*	
										?	*1830*	....	....	....	----	----	----	----	----		
											1831	0527	**1831**	0627	x---	----	x?--	----	----	2	
											1833	0615	....	....	x---	----	x---	----	----	2	
											1835	0104	....	....	x---	----	x---	----	----	2	
											1838	0226	**1838**	05	x---	----	x---	----	x---	2	
											1839	0129	**1839**	0326	x---	----	x---	?---	----	2*	
											1840	0202	**1840**	0929	x---	----	x---	----	-xx-	3	
										?	*1841*	*0330*	?*1841*	*1120*	x---	----	----	----	----	*1*	
											1842	1006	**1842**	1231	x---	----	x---	----	----	1	
											1843	0410	**1843**	0527	x---	----	x?--	?---	----	2	
										?	*1844*	*0324*	?*1844*	*1114*	x---	----	----	----	----	*1*	
										?	*1845*	*0423*	?*1845*	*0903*	x---	----	----	----	----	*1*	
											1846	0519	**1846**	0519	x---	----	x---	----	-x--	2	
											1847	0207	**1847**	0207	x---	----	x---	?---	----	2	
											1847	0907	**1847**	0907	x---	----	----	----	----		
											1849	1127	**1850**	1119	x---	----	x---	----	----	2	
										?	*1858*	*11*	?*1859*	*09*	x---	----	----	----	----	*1*	
										?	*1860*	*06*	....	....	x---	----	----	----	----	*1*	
											1862	0715	**1862**	10	x---	----	x---	?---	--x-	2	
										?	*1863*	*0501?*	?*1863*	*06 ?*	x---	----	----	----	----	*2*	
											1864	0120	**1864**	0217	x---	----	x---	----	----	2	
										?	*1864*	*0604*d	?*1864*	*0625*e	x---	----	----	----	----	*1*	
											1864	1227	**1865**	0102	x---	----	x---	?---	----	2	
											1868	0313	**1868**	0313	x---	----	x---	----	----	1	
											1868	1113	**1869**	0210	x---	----	x---	----	----	2	
	(earthquakes, not eruption)									X	*1870*	....	....	....	----	----	----	----	----		
											1871	0807	**1871**	0925	x---	----	x---	?---	x---	2	
											1884	05	**1884**	05	x---	----	x---	----	--x-	2	
										?	*1884*	*1208*	?*1884*	*1209?*	x---	----	--?-	----	----	*1*	
											1895	1219	**1895**	1219	x---	----	x---	----	----	1	
										?	*1896*	*0803*	?*1896*	*0804?*	x---	----	x---	----	----	*1*	
											1897	0907	**1897**	0924	x---	----	x---	----	--x-	1	
											1898	0514	**1898**	0528?	x---	----	x---	----	----	2	
										?	*1900*	*05*	?*1900*	*0604*d	x---	----	x---	----	----	*1*	
											1907	1117	**1907**	1120	x---	----	x---	x---	--x-	2	
											1911	0902	**1911**	0906	x---	----	x---	----	----	1	

VOLCANO NAME (Subregion) / ERUPTION	Area of Activity	LAT	LONG	ELEV (m)	POPL (5 km, 10, 30, 100)	ROCK TYPE	VOLC TYPE	NUMBER	STATUS	Start Year	Start M-Dy	Stop Year	Stop M-Dy	Central / Flank vent / Radial fiss / Regional	Submarine / New island / Subglacial / Crater lake	Explosive / Pyro flow / Phreatic / Caldera	Lava flow / Lava lake / Dome / Spine	Fatal / Damage / Mudflow / Tsunami	VEI	Vol L/T
Gamalama (Halmahera) *continued*										**1918**	08	**1918**	0904	x---	----	x---	----	----	1	
										1923	0413	**1923**	0506	x---	----	x---	----	----	2	
										1932	1110	**1932**	1113	x---	----	x---	----	----	2	
										1933	1112	....	....	x---	----	x---	----	----	2	
										1938	0908	**1938**	0908	x---	----	x---	----	----	2	
	East flank									**1962**	1231	**1963**	0102?	-x--	----	x-x-	----	x---	2	
										1980	0904	**1980**	0923	x---	----	x---	----	-x--	2	-/6
										1983	0809	**1983**	0812	x---	----	x---	----	-x--	3	
										1988	0212	**1988**	03 ?	x---	----	x---	----	----	2	
										1990	0425	**1990**	0426	x---	----	x?--	----	-x--	3?	
										? *1991*	*0615*	?*1991*	*0615*	x---	----	--?-	----	----	*1?*	
										1993	0506	**1993**	0521	x---	----	x?--	----	----	2	
										1994	01	**1994**	1015>	x---	----	x---	----	----	2	
										1996	....	....	....	x---	----	xx--	----	----	2?	
										2003	0731	**2003**	1002c	x---	----	xx--	----	----	2	
										? *2007*	*0823*	....	....	x---	----	--?-	----	----	*1?*	
										? *2008*	*0510*	....	....	x---	----	?---	----	----	*1*	
Tidore (Halmahera)		**0.658** N	**127.40** E	**1730**	5566	**A**	**Stratovolcano**	**0608-061**	**Holocene**											
Mare (Halmahera)		**0.57** N	**127.40** E	**308**	3566	**A**	**Stratovolcano**	**0608-062**	**Holocene**											
Moti (Halmahera)		**0.45** N	**127.40** E	**950**	4456	**AB**	**Stratovolcano**	**0608-063**	**Holocene**											
	(confused with 1773 Gamalama eruption). . .									*X 1774*<	....	....	....	----	----	----	----	----		
Makian (Halmahera)		**0.32** N	**127.40** E	**1357**	4456	**AB**	**Stratovolcano**	**0608-07=**	**Historical**											
										1550<	....	....	....	x---	----	x---	?---	-x-?	3↑	
	(mistaken for 1608 Gamalama eruption?). . .									*X 1608*	....	*X1609*	....	----	----	----	----	----		
	(eruption in 1646, not 1648 or 1659<).									**1646**	0719	**1646**	0721	x-x-	----	x---	----	xx--	4?	-/8
										? *1660*	....	....	....	----	----	----	----	----		
										1760	0922	**1761**	0430>	x---	----	x---	----	xx--	4?	-/8
										? *1854*	*0618*	?*1854*	*0618*	x---	----	----	----	----	*1*	
										? *1860*	....	....	....	----	----	?---	----	----	*1*	
										1861	1228	**1862**	10	x---	----	xxx-	?---	xxx-	4?	-/8
										1863	0825	**1863**	0831	x---	----	--x-	----	----	1	
										1864	10	**1864**	10	x---	----	--x-	----	----	1	
										1890	0620	**1890**	0630	x---	----	x---	?---	xx--	2	
										1988	0729	**1988**	0805	x---	----	xx--	--x-	-x--	3	
Tigalalu (Kayoa I)		**0.07** N	**127.42** E	**422**	3446	**A**	**Stratovolcano**	**0608-071**	**Holocene**											
Amasing (Bacan I).		**0.53** S	**127.48** E	**1030**	2355	**A**	**Stratovolcanoes**	**0608-072**	**Holocene**											
Bibinoi (Bacan I)		**0.77** S	**127.72** E	**900**	2455	**A**	**Stratovolcanoes**	**0608-073**	**Holocene**											
Umsini (New Guinea-W).		1.18 S	134.00 E	2665				0609-01=	Not a Volcano											

BORNEO

VOLCANO NAME (Subregion)	LAT	LONG	ELEV (m)	POPL	ROCK TYPE	VOLC TYPE	NUMBER	STATUS
Bombalai (Borneo)	**4.40** N	**117.88** E	**531**	3466	**BAD**	**Pyroclastic cone**	**0610-01-**	Holocene?

Katia and Maurice Krafft

Merapi, one of Indonesia's most active volcanoes, towers above the major regional cultural and religious center of Yogyakarta in central Java. The prominent SW side breach seen here funnels rockfalls, pyroclastic flows, and lahars (mudflows) associated with long-term growth of summit lava domes onto populated agricultural lands beneath the volcano. Merapi eruptions have frequently produced major devastation during historical time.

Philippines & SE Asia (07)

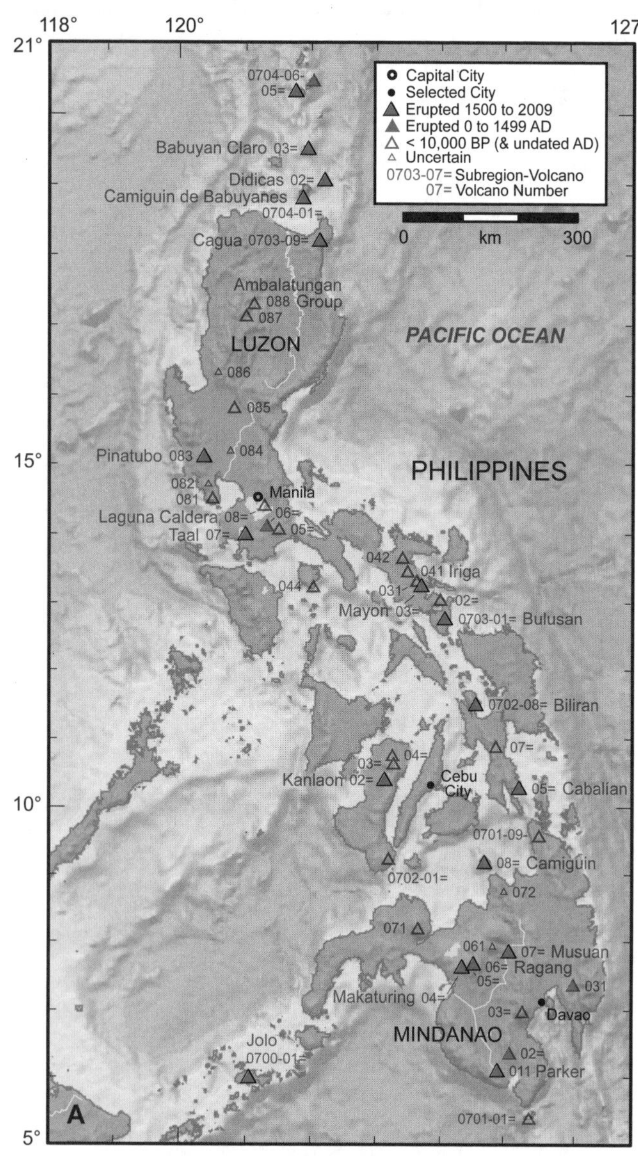

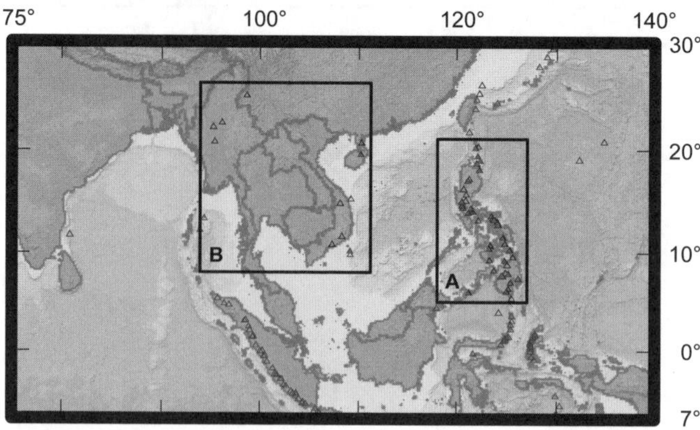

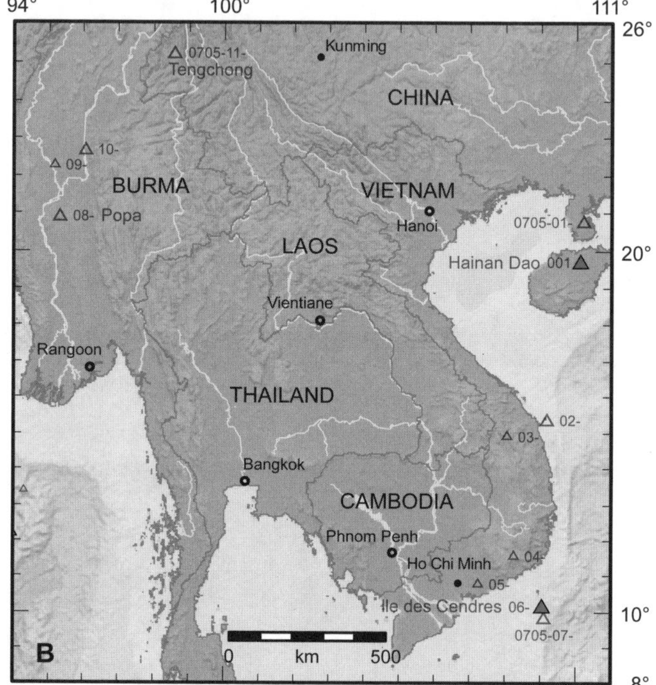

The Philippines is an archipelago of more than 7100 islands, most of which are of volcanic origin. After Magellan's death there in 1521, the Philippines were re-claimed for Spain by Lopez de Legazpi in 1564. The islands gained independence from Spain in mid-1898, but were soon occupied by the US and, from 1942 through 1944, by Japan. True independence did not come until 1946. The population of the Philippines has increased dramatically in recent years and now exceeds 91 million. Its land area approximates that of Italy.

The Philippines ranks relatively low in the total number of eruptions, but their impact has been high, reflecting its population density. More than 110 million people live within 100 km of a Holocene volcano in the Philippines and SE Asia, 2nd highest of the world's regions, trailing only Indonesia, and the Philippines and SE Asia consistently ranks within the top three globally of residents living with 5, 10, 30, and 100 km of both Holocene volcanoes and volcanoes with eruptions since 1500 AD. More than 13% of Philippine eruptions have resulted in fatalities, and more than 21% in damage, with the notable Taal and Mayon volcanoes having particularly high human impact. As with Indonesia, though, this record reflects the many years prior to the development of a strong government agency charged with the study of volcanism. The Philippine Institute of Volcanology and Seismology (PHIVOLCS) now maintains a modern monitoring program on most of the islands' volcanoes, and the evacuation table testifies to their effectiveness in dealing with recent eruptions.

The tectonics of the Philippines are not simple, but most volcanoes result from convergence of the Philippine Sea Plate and the Eurasian Plate. In the south the former is subducted westward under the latter, but in the north the opposite pattern prevails. Mudflows (lahars) are also frequently associated with Philippine eruptions, and remain a hazard long after the eruption ceases. Heavy rains in this typhoon-plagued archipelago regularly redistribute new volcanic tephra to surrounding lowlands. Secondary mudflows following the 1991 Pinatubo eruption have been especially devastating, partially or totally burying towns and villages and destroying the homes of more than 100,000 people. More than a half dozen primary or secondary lahars from Mayon volcano have caused fatalities, including most recently 1266 dead or missing due to post-eruptive lahars caused by a November 30, 2006 typhoon following the July to October 2006 eruption of Mayon. Tsunamis have accompanied 4.5% of eruptions in the Philippines, a proportion that is not itself high but one that exceeds all other regions.

Burma, only recently recognized as an area of Holocene volcanism, became part of the British Empire in 1886 after several wars. The British withdrew in WW-II and granted independence in 1948. Unrest has followed, and the country's 1988 name change to Myanmar has been widely but not universally accepted. Vietnam, another mainland part of Region 07 with several Holocene volcanoes, has also undergone political unrest. It was a province of China from the 1st century BC to 939 AD, and missionary work, particularly by the French, began in the 17th century. French troops captured Saigon in 1859, the rest of Cochin-China (South Vietnam) within 8 years, and North Vietnam by 1887. After Japanese occupation during WW-II, nationalist forces defeated the French in 1954 and the US in 1975.

The *CAVW* originally designated region 07 as Philippines only, but Cochin-China was added upon publication of the catalog in 1954, and our expansion to SE Asia followed recognition of Holocene volcanism in Burma (Myanmar) and SE China, where young volcanism has occurred at Tengchong near the border with Burma and in islands bordering the Gulf of Tonkin.

VOLCANO NAME (Subregion) / **ERUPTION** — Area of Activity	**LAT**	**LONG**	**ELEV** (m)	**POPL** 5 km 10 30 100	**ROCK TYPE**	**VOLC TYPE**	**NUMBER**	**STATUS**	**Start Year**	Start M-Dy	**Stop Year**	Stop M-Dy	Central / Flank vent / Radial fiss / Regional	Submarine / New island / Subglacial / Crater lake	Explosive / Pyro flow / Phreatic / Caldera	Lava flow / Lava lake / Dome / Spine	Fatal / Damage / Mudflow / Tsunami	VEI	Vol L/T
PHILIPPINES - S																			
Jolo (Sulu Is)	**6.013 N***	**121.057 E**	**811**	5666	**BA**	**Pyroclastic cones**	**0700-01=**	**Historical**											
(1641 eruption from Parker volcano)									*X 1641*	*0104*	....	....	----	----	----	----	----		
									1897	0921	....	....	----	?---	----	----	---x	0	
Balut (Mindanao)	**5.40 N**	**125.375 E**	**862**	4457	**AB**	**Stratovolcano**	**0701-01=**	**Fumarolic**											
Parker (Mindanao)	**6.113 N**	**124.892 E**	**1824**	3467	**AD**	**Stratovolcano**	**0701-011**	**Historical**											
									C-**1920**s	....	....	....	x---	----	xx--	----	--x-	P	
									G **1380**u	....	....	....	x---	----	xx--	----	--x-	P	
									1640	1226e	**1641**	0104	x---	----	xx-x	----	-xx-	5?	-/9
Matutum (Mindanao)	**6.37 N**	**125.07 E**	**2286**	3567	**AD**	**Stratovolcano**	**0701-02=**	**Radiocarbon**											
									C-**0400**t	....	....	....	----	----	?---	----	----		
									C-**0170**u	....	....	....	----	----	x---	----	----		
									C **1290**s	....	....	....	----	----	?---	----	----		
									? 1911	*0307*	....	....	----	----	--?-	----	----		
Apo (Mindanao)	**6.989 N**	**125.269 E**	**2938**	4467	**AD**	**Stratovolcano**	**0701-03=**	**Fumarolic**											
Leonard Range (Mindanao)	**7.382 N**	**126.047 E**	**1080**	3467	**AD**	**Stratovolcano**	**0701-031**	**Radiocarbon**											
									C-**4090**v	....	....	....	----	----	x---	----	----		
									C-**0080**t	....	....	....	----	----	x---	----	----		
									C **0120**v	....	....	....	----	----	x---	----	----		
Makaturing (Mindanao)	**7.647 N**	**124.32 E**	**1940**	4467	**B**	**Stratovolcano**	**0701-04=**	**Historical**											
									? 1856	....	....	....	----	----	----	----	----		
									? 1858	....	....	....	----	----	----	----	----		
									1865	....	....	....	x---	----	x---	----	----	2	
									1882	....	....	....	----	----	----	----	----		
Latukan (Mindanao)	**7.65 N**	**124.45 E**	**2338**	3467	**B**	**Stratovolcano**	**0701-05=**	Holocene?											
Ragang (Mindanao)	**7.70 N**	**124.50 E**	**2815**	3467	**BA**	**Stratovolcano**	**0701-06=**	**Historical**											
									1765	....	....	....	x---	----	?---	----	----	2	
									1834	....	....	....	x---	----	x---	----	----	2	
									1840	0120	**1840**	0405	x---	----	x---	----	----	2	
									1856	1101	....	....	x---	----	x---	----	----	2	
									1858	0218	....	....	x---	----	x---	----	----	2	
									1871	1208<	....	....	x---	----	x---	----	----	2	
									1873	0116	**1873**	04	x---	----	x---	----	??--	2	
									? 1915	....	....	....	x---	----	?---	----	----	*2?*	
									? 1916	*07*	....	....	----	----	?---	----	----		
Kalatungan (Mindanao)	**7.95 N**	**124.80 E**	**2824**	3567	**Bad**	**Stratovolcano**	**0701-061**	Holocene?											
Musuan (Mindanao)	**7.877 N**	**125.068 E**	**646**	5667	**AD**	**Lava dome**	**0701-07=**	**Historical**											
									1886	1231y	....	....	----	----	--?-	----	----	2	
Malindang (Mindanao)	**8.22 N**	**123.63 E**	**2404**	3567	**BAd**	**Stratovolcano**	**0701-071**	**Holocene**											
Balatukan (Mindanao)	**8.77 N**	**124.98 E**	**2450**	3467	**BA**	**Compound volc**	**0701-072**	Uncertain											
Camiguin (Camiguin I)	**9.203 N**	**124.673 E**	**1552**	5557	**ADbr**	**Stratovolcanoes**	**0701-08=**	**Historical**											
Hibok-Hibok									**1827**	....	....	....	?---	---?	?---	----	-xx-	2	
Hibok-Hibok									**1862**	....	....	....	?---	---?	?---	----	-xx-	2	
Lower NW flank of Hibok-Hibok (Mt. Vulcan)									**1871**	0430	**1875**	....	-x--	----	x---	--x-	xx--	2	8/-
(solfataric activity only)									*X 1897*	....	....	....	----	----	--?-	----	-x?-		
(solfataric activity only)									*X 1902*	*0727*	....	....	----	----	--?-	----	-x?-		
Upper NE flank of Hibok-Hibok									**1948**	0901	**1953**	07	-x--	----	xx--	x-x-	xxx-	3*	
Paco (Mindanao)	**9.593 N**	**125.520 E**	**524**	4567	**ADB**	**Stratovolcano**	**0701-09-**	**Anthropology**											
PHILIPPINES - C																			
Cuernos de Negros (Negros I)	**9.25 N**	**123.17 E**	**1862**	4567	**ADB**	**Complex volcano**	**0702-01=**	**Fumarolic**											
Kanlaon (Negros I)	**10.412 N**	**123.132 E**	**2435**	4567	**AY**	**Stratovolcano**	**0702-02=**	**Historical**											
									1866	....	....	....	x---	----	x-x-	----	----	2	
									? 1883	*07*	....	....	x---	----	x-x-	----	----	*2*	
									? 1884	*05*	*?1884*	*06*	x---	----	x---	----	----	*2*	
									1893	07	....	....	x---	----	x-x-	----	----	2	
									1894	05	**1894**	06	x---	----	x---	----	----	2	
									1902	0131	....	....	x---	----	x---	x---	----	2	
									1904	....	....	....	x---	----	x-x-	----	----	2	
									1905	1106	**1906**	0116>	x---	----	x-x-	----	----	2	
									1927	0320	....	....	x---	----	x-x-	----	----	2	
									1932	12	**1933**	01	x---	----	x-x-	----	----	2	
									1969	1010	**1969**	1029	x---	----	x-x-	----	--x-	2	
									1970	0605	**1970**	0824	x---	----	x-x-	----	----	1?	
									1978	0627	**1978**	0902	x---	----	x-x-	----	----	2	
									1980	0808	....	....	x---	----	x-x-	----	----	2	
									1985	0313	**1985**	0314	x---	----	x-x-	----	----	1	
									1985	1005	**1985**	1207	x---	----	x-x-	----	----	1	
									1986	0603	**1986**	0818	x---	----	x-x-	----	----	2	-/5
									1987	0330?	**1987**	0702	x---	----	x-x-	----	----	1	
									1988	0621	**1988**	0702	x---	----	x-x-	----	----	1	
									1989	1025	**1989**	1213>	x---	----	x-x-	----	----	2	
									1991	0214	**1991**	0214	x---	----	x-x-	----	----	2	
									1992	0108	**1992**	0108	x---	----	x-x-	----	----	1	
									1992	0610	**1992**	0610	x---	----	x-x-	----	----	2	
									1993	0825	**1993**	0903	x---	----	x-x-	----	----	2	
									1996	0810	**1996**	0810	x---	----	x-x-	----	x---	2	
									2002	1128	**2002**	1128	x---	----	x-x-	----	----	1	

VOLCANO NAME (Subregion) / ERUPTION — Area of Activity	LAT	LONG	ELEV (m)	POPL (5 km, 10, 30, 100)	ROCK TYPE	VOLC TYPE / —Start— Year	M-Dy	NUMBER / —Stop— Year	M-Dy	STATUS / ERUPTIVE CHARACTERISTICS: Central, Flank vent, Radial fiss, Regional	Submarine, New island, Subglacial, Crater lake	Explosive, Pyro flow, Phreatic, Caldera	Lava flow, Lava lake, Dome, Spine	Fatal, Damage, Mudflow, Tsunami	VEI	Vol L/T
Kanlaon (Negros I) *continued*						**2003**	0307	**2003**	0723	x---	----	x-x-	----	----	1	
						2005	0125	**2005**	0525	x---	----	x-x-	----	----	2*	
						2006	0603	**2006**	0725	x---	----	x-x-	----	----	2	
Mandalagan (Negros I)	**10.65 N**	**123.25 E**	**1885**	3467	ADB	**Complex volcano**		**0702-03=**		**Fumarolic**						
Silay (Negros I)..................	**10.77 N**	**123.23 E**	**1510**	3577	A	**Stratovolcano**		**0702-04=**		**Fumarolic**						
Cabalían (Leyte I)	**10.287 N**	**125.221 E**	**945**	5567	A	**Stratovolcano**		**0702-05=**		**Radiocarbon**						
						C **1820**r	....	....	....	----	----	xx--	----	----		
Mahagnao (Leyte I)..............	**10.896 N**	**125.87 E**	**860**	2456	AD	**Stratovolcano**		**0702-07=**		**Fumarolic**						
						? *1895*	....	....	....	----	----	----	----	----		
Biliran (Biliran I).................	**11.523 N**	**124.535 E**	**1301**	4567	AB	**Compound volc**		**0702-08=**		**Historical**						
						1939	0926	....	....	-x--	----	x-x-	----	----	1?	
PHILIPPINES - N																
Bulusan (Luzon)	**12.770 N**	**124.05 E**	**1565**	4567	ADbr	**Stratovolcanoes**		**0703-01=**		**Historical**						
						C **-3050**?	....	....	....	----	----	x---	----	--x-		
						C **0950**?	....	....	....	----	----	x---	----	--x-		
						? *1852*	....	....	....	----	----	----	----	----		
						1886	....	....	....	?---	----	?---	----	----	2	
						1889	....	....	....	----	----	----	----	----		
						1892	....	....	....	?---	----	?---	----	----	2	
						1894	....	....	....	?---	----	?---	----	----	2	
						1916	0118	**1916**	0122	x---	----	x-x-	----	----	2	
						1918	10	**1922**	05	x---	----	x?--	x-?-	----	2	
						1928	06	....	....	x---	----	x---	----	----	2	
						1933	1225	....	....	x---	----	x---	----	-x-x	2	
						1978	0729	**1978**	0814	x---	----	x-x-	----	-x--	2	-/5
						1979	1227	**1980**	0928	x-x-	----	x-x-	----	----	3*	
						1981	0409	**1981**	0427	x---	----	x-x-	----	----	3	
						1983	0625	**1983**	0629	x---	----	x-x-	----	----	2	
						1988	0220	**1988**	0308	x---	----	x-x-	----	--x-	2	-/4
						1994	1127	**1995**	0128>	x---	----	x-x-	----	----	2	
						2006	0321	**2006**	0628	x---	----	xxx-	----	x---	2	
						2006	1010	**2007**	1004	x-x-	----	x---	----	-xx-	2*	
Pocdol Mountains (Luzon).......	**13.05 N**	**123.958 E**	**1102**	4667	Adb	**Compound volc**		**0703-02=**		**Fumarolic**						
Mayon (Luzon)..................	**13.257 N**	**123.685 E**	**2462**	4677	Ab	**Stratovolcano**		**0703-03=**		**Historical**						
						C **-3100**y	....	....	....	----	----	----	----	----		
						C **0470**u	....	....	....	x---	----	xx--	----	----		
						1616	0219	**1616**	0223	x---	----	xx--	x---	--x-	3	
						1766	0720	**1766**	0725	x---	----	xx--	x---	xxx-	3	
(may be confused with 1766 lahar date) . . .						X *1767*	*1024*	....	....	----	----	----	----	----		
						1800	1030	**1800**	1031	x---	----	xx--	----	xx--	2	
						? *1811*	*1005*	?*1811*	*1006*	x---	----	x?--	----	----	*2*	
						1814	0201	**1814**	0215>	xx--	----	xx--	----	xxx-	4	-/8
						1827	0627	**1828**	0228	x---	----	x---	----	-xx-	2	
						1834	....	**1835**	05	x---	----	xx--	?---	--x-	3*	
						1839	....	....	....	x---	----	x---	----	----	2	
						1845	0120a	**1845**	0130a	x---	----	xx--	----	-xx-	3	
						1846	0511	**1846**	0511	x---	----	x---	----	----	3	
						1851	0526	**1851**	06	x---	----	x---	----	----	1	
						1853	0713	**1853**	0826	x---	----	xx--	----	xxx-	3	
						1855	0322	....	....	x---	----	x---	x---	----	2	
						1857	....	....	....	x---	----	x---	----	----	2	
						1858	01	**1858**	12	x---	----	xx--	x--?	xxx-	2	
						1859	....	....	....	x---	----	?---	---?	----		
						1860	....	....	....	x---	----	?---	----	----		
						1861	....	....	....	x---	----	x---	----	----	1	
						1862	....	....	....	x---	----	x---	----	--x-	2	
						? *1863*	*0530*	....	....	----	----	----	----	----		
						1868	1217	....	....	x---	----	x---	----	--x-	2	
						1871	1208	**1872**	01	x---	----	xx--	----	xx--	3	
						1872	0905	**1872**	0909	x---	----	x---	x---	----	1	
						1873	0620	**1873**	0722	x---	----	x---	x---	----	2	
						1876	04	....	....	x---	----	x---	----	----	1	
						1876	1126	**1876**	1126	x---	----	x---	----	----	1	
Summit and south and SW flanks						**1881**	0706	**1882**	08	x-x-	----	xx--	x---	--x-	3	
						1885	1121	**1885**	1202	x---	----	x---	x---	----	2	
						1886	0708	**1887**	0310	x---	----	xx--	x---	xxx-	3*	
						1888	1215	....	....	x---	----	x---	----	----	1	
						1890	0910	**1890**	0930	x---	----	x---	x---	----	2	
						1891	1003	**1892**	0229	x---	----	xx--	x---	-?--	2	
						1893	1003?	**1893**	1031	x---	----	x---	x---	--x-	1	
Summit and east flank.						**1895**	0720	**1895**	1126	x-x-	----	x---	x---	--x-	2	
						1896	0831	**1896**	0927	x---	----	x---	x---	--x-	2	
						1897	0523<	**1897**	0723	x---	----	xx--	x---	xxx-	4?	-/7
						1900	0301	**1900**	0306	x---	----	xx--	x---	--x-	2	
						1902	....	....	....	x---	----	x---	----	--x-	1	
						1928	01 ?	**1928**	0826e	x---	----	xx--	x---	xxx-	3*	7/7
						1938	0605	....	....	x---	----	xx--	x---	xxx-	2	-/6
						1939	0821	....	....	x---	----	x---	----	----	1	
						1941	0913	....	....	x---	----	x---	----	----	1	
						1943	....	....	....	x---	----	x---	----	----	1	
						1947	0108	**1947**	02	x---	----	xx--	x---	xxx-	2	
						1968	0421	**1968**	0520	x---	----	xx--	x---	xxx-	3	7/7
						1978	0307	**1978**	09 ?	x---	----	x---	x---	----	2*	7/-
						1984	0909	**1984**	1006	x---	----	xx--	x---	?xx-	3*	7/7
						1993	0202	**1993**	0404	x---	----	xx--	x---	xxx-	2?	7/6
						1999	0622	**2000**	0319	x---	----	xx--	x-x-	--x-	3*	
						2000	0716	**2000**	0831	x---	----	x-x-	----	----	2	
						2001	0108	**2001**	0808	x---	----	xx--	x-x-	----	3*	7/7
						2002	1011	**2002**	1011	x---	----	x---	----	----	1	
						2003	0317	**2003**	0514	x---	----	x-x-	----	----	2	

Kurt Fredrickson (Smithsonian)

Mayon 1968

VOLCANO NAME (Subregion) / ERUPTION — Area of Activity	LAT	LONG	ELEV (m)	POPL (5 km, 10, 30, 100)	ROCK TYPE	VOLC TYPE	NUMBER	STATUS	Start Year	Start M-Dy	Stop Year	Stop M-Dy	Central / Flank vent / Radial fiss / Regional	Submarine / New island / Subglacial / Crater lake	Explosive / Pyro flow / Phreatic / Caldera	Lava flow / Lava lake / Dome / Spine	Fatal / Damage / Mudflow / Tsunami	VEI	Vol L/T
Mayon (Luzon) *continued*									*? 2003*	*1008*	*?2003*	*1011?*	x---	----	----	?---	----	*0*	
									2004	0603	**2004**	0912?	x---	----	x-x-	----	----	1	
									2005	0817<	....	....	x---	----	----	--x-	----	0	
									2006	0221	**2006**	0223	x---	----	x---	----	----	1	
									2006	0713	**2006**	1001	x---	----	xxx-	x---	xxx-	1	7/-
									2008	0810	**2008**	0810	x---	----	x-x-	----	----	1	
									2009	0915	**2010**	0101>	x---	----	xx--	x---	----	2*	
Masaraga (Luzon)	**13.32 N**	**123.60 E**	**1328**	5677	ADR	**Stratovolcano**	**0703-031**	**Holocene**											
Iriga (Luzon)	**13.457 N**	**123.457 E**	**1196**	4677	AB	**Stratovolcano**	**0703-041**	**Holocene**											
(collapse and eruption prior to 1628 AD)									*X 1628*	....	....	....	x---	----	xxx-	----	xx?-		
Isarog (Luzon)	**13.658 N**	**123.38 E**	**1966**	3577	A	**Stratovolcano**	**0703-042**	**Fumarolic**											
Malindig (Marinduque I)	**13.240 N**	**122.018 E**	**1157**	4567	A	**Stratovolcano**	**0703-044**	**Hot Springs**											
Banahaw (Luzon)	**14.07 N**	**121.48 E**	**2158**	3578	ABD	**Complex volcano**	**0703-05=**	**Holocene**											
Banáhao									*? 1730*	....	....	....	x---	----	?---	----	-xx-		
Banáhao									*? 1743?*	....	....	....	----	----	?---	----	--x-		
Banáhao									*? 1843*	....	....	....	----	----	?---	----	--x-		
Banáhao									*? 1909*	....	....	....	----	----	?---	----	--x-		
San Pablo Volc Field (Luzon)	**14.12 N***	**121.30 E**	**1090**	7778	YRTA	**Stratovolcano**	**0703-06=**	**Anthropology**											
Sampaloc Lake									A **1350** v	....	....	....	x---	----	x---	----	----		
Taal (Luzon)	**14.002 N**	**120.993 E**	**311**	6678	ABDr	**Caldera**	**0703-07=**	**Historical**											
(Taal Scoria Flow)									C-**3580** x	....	....	....	x---	----	xx-x	----	----	**6**	-/10
									1572	....	....	....	x---	----	x---	----	-x--	3	
									1591	....	....	....	x---	----	--x-	----	----	3↑	
									1608 c	....	....	....	x---	----	?---	----	----	2?	
									1634	....	....	....	x---	----	?---	----	----	3↑	
									1635	....	....	....	x---	----	?---	----	----	3↑	
									1641	....	....	....	x---	----	x-x-	----	-x--	3	
									1645	....	....	....	x---	----	?---	----	----	3↑	
Binintiang Malaki									**1707**	....	....	....	-x--	----	--x-	----	----	2	
Binintiang Munti									**1709**	....	....	....	-x--	----	x---	----	-x--	2	
Binintiang Malaki									**1715**	....	....	....	-x--	----	x---	----	-x--	2	
Calauit (sublacustral SE flank)									**1716**	0924	**1716**	0927	--x-	---x	xx--	----	xx-x	4?	
Binintiang Munti									**1729**	....	....	....	-x--	----	x---	----	----	2	
Pira-piraso (NE flank)									**1731**	....	....	....	-x--	-x-x	xx--	----	-x-x	2	
									1749	0811?	**1749**	09	xx?-	---x	xx--	----	xx-x	4	-/8
Summit crater and SE flank									**1754**	0515	**1754**	1204	xxx-	----	x---	----	xx-x	4*	-/8
									1790	....	....	....	x---	----	?---	----	----	2	
									1808	02	**1808**	04	x---	----	x---	----	-x--	2	
									1825	....	....	....	x---	----	?---	----	----	2	
									1842	....	....	....	x---	----	?---	----	----	2	
									1873	....	....	....	x---	----	?---	----	-?--	2	
									1874	0719	....	....	x---	----	x---	----	?x--	2	
									1878	1112	**1878**	1115	x---	----	x-x-	----	----	2	
									? 1885	....	....	....	----	----	----	----	----		
									1903	04	....	....	x---	----	x---	----	----	2	
Base of south wall of main crater									**1904**	04	**1904**	0715e	x---	----	--x-	----	----	1	
									1911	0127	**1911**	0208	x---	----	xxx-	----	xx-x	3*	-/7
SW flank (near Mt. Tabaro)									**1965**	0928	**1965**	0930	-x--	-x-x	xxx-	----	xx-x	4	-/7
SW flank (near Mt. Tabaro)									**1966**	0705	**1966**	0804	-x--	---x	x-x-	----	-x--	3*	
SW flank (near Mt. Tabaro)									**1967**	0816	**1967**	0819	-x--	-x-x	x---	----	----	1	
SW flank (near Mt. Tabaro)									**1968**	0131	**1968**	0402	-xx-	---x	x-x-	x---	----	2	
SW flank (near Mt. Tabaro)									**1969**	1029	**1969**	1210	-x--	----	x-x-	x---	----	2	6/6
SW flank (near Mt. Tabaro)									**1970**	1109	**1970**	1113	--x-	----	x-x-	----	----	1	
SW flank (near Mt. Tabaro)									**1976**	0903	**1976**	1017	-x--	----	x-x-	----	-x--	2	-/6
SW flank (near Mt. Tabaro)									**1977**	1003	**1977**	1112?	-x--	----	x-x-	----	----	2	
Laguna Caldera (Luzon)	**14.42 N**	**121.27 E**	**743**	6678	ATDBR	**Caldera**	**0703-08=**	**Fumarolic**											
Mariveles (Luzon)	**14.52 N**	**120.47 E**	**1388**	3568	AB	**Stratovolcano**	**0703-081**	**Radiocarbon**											
									C-**2050**?	....	....	....	----	----	----	----	----		
Natib (Luzon)	**14.72 N**	**120.40 E**	**1253**	3478	ABD	**Stratovolcano**	**0703-082**	Holocene?											
Pinatubo (Luzon)	**15.13 N**	**120.35 E**	**1486**	3478	DAb	**Stratovolcano**	**0703-083**	**Historical**											
Tayawan caldera (Pasbul eruptive period)									G-**7460** w	....	....	....	x---	----	xx--	----	----	**6?**	
(Pasbul eruptive period)									G-**7030** y	....	....	....	----	----	xx--	----	----		
(Crow Valley eruptive period)									G-**3550**?	....	....	....	x---	----	xx--	----	--x-	**6**	-/10
(Maraunot eruptive period)									G-**1050** z	....	....	....	x---	----	xx--	----	--x-	**6**	-/10
(Baug eruptive period)									G **1450** t	....	....	....	x---	----	xx--	--x-	-xx-	**5?**	
Lower north flank and summit									**1991**	0402	**1991**	0902	xx--	----	xxxx	--x-	xxx-	**6***	-/10
Center of caldera lake									**1992**	0709<	**1992**	1030	x---	---x	x---	--xx	x-x-	1	6/-
Caldera floor									**1993**	02	**1993**	07 ?	x---	----	--x-	----	xx--	1	
Arayat (Luzon)	**15.20 N**	**120.742 E**	**1026**	4678	BYxa	**Stratovolcano**	**0703-084**	Holocene?											
Amorong (Luzon)	**15.828 N**	**120.805 E**	**376**	5678	Y	**Lava domes**	**0703-085**	**Fumarolic**											
Santo Tomas (Luzon)	**16.33 N**	**120.55 E**	**2260**	4677	A	**Stratovolcano**	**0703-086**	Uncertain											
Patoc (Luzon)	**17.147 N**	**120.980 E**	**1865**	4557	A	**Stratovolcano**	**0703-087**	**Fumarolic**											
Ambalatungan Group (Luzon)	**17.32 N**	**121.10 E**	**2329**	3457	DA	**Compound volc**	**0703-088**	**Fumarolic**											
Mt. Binuluan									*? 1952*	....	....	....	----	----	--?-	----	x-x-	*1?*	
Cagua (Luzon)	**18.222 N**	**122.123 E**	**1133**	2457	AB	**Stratovolcano**	**0703-09=**	**Historical**											
									1860	10	....	....	?---	----	x?x-	----	----	2	

N of LUZON

VOLCANO NAME (Subregion) / ERUPTION — Area of Activity	LAT	LONG	ELEV (m)	POPL (5 km, 10, 30, 100)	ROCK TYPE	VOLC TYPE	NUMBER	STATUS	Start Year	Start M-Dy	Stop Year	Stop M-Dy	Central / Flank vent / Radial fiss / Regional	Submarine / New island / Subglacial / Crater lake	Explosive / Pyro flow / Phreatic / Caldera	Lava flow / Lava lake / Dome / Spine	Fatal / Damage / Mudflow / Tsunami	VEI	Vol L/T
Camiguin de Babuyanes	**18.83 N**	**121.860 E**	**712**	3446	A	**Stratovolcano**	**0704-01=**	**Historical**											
SW flank									**1857**<	....	....	....	-x--	??--	--x-	----	----	2	
Didicas (Didicas I)	**19.077 N**	**122.202 E**	**228**	0035	A	**Compound volc**	**0704-02=**	**Historical**											
									1773	10	....	....	----	x---	--x-	----	----	1?	
									1856	0930p	**1860**	10 ?	----	xx--	----	--xx	----	2*	8/-
									1900	....	....	....	----	?---	----	--x-	----	0?	
									1952	0316<	**1953**?	....	-x--	xx--	x---	x-x-	----	2	8/-
North side									**1969**	0321	**1969**	06	-x--	----	x-x-	----	x--x	2	
NNE side									**1978**	0106	**1978**	0109	-x--	----	x---	----	----	2	
Babuyan Claro (Babuyan I)	**19.523 N**	**121.940 E**	**1080**	3335	AB	**Stratovolcanoes**	**0704-03=**	**Historical**											
Smith volcano									**1652**	....	....	....	-x--	----	x---	----	----	3↑	

VOLCANO NAME (Subregion) / ERUPTION	LAT	LONG	ELEV (m)	POPL (5 km, 10, 30, 100)	ROCK TYPE	VOLC TYPE	NUMBER	STATUS	Area of Activity	Start Year	Start M-Dy	Stop Year	Stop M-Dy	Central / Flank vent / Radial fiss / Regional	Submarine / New island / Subglacial / Crater lake	Explosive / Pyro flow / Phreatic / Caldera	Lava flow / Lava lake / Dome / Spine	Fatal / Damage / Mudflow / Tsunami	VEI	Vol L/T
Babuyan Claro (Babuyan I) *continued*									Babuyan Claro	**1831**	....	....	....	x---	----	x---	----	-x--	4?	-/8
									Babuyan Claro	**1860**	....	....	....	x---	----	x---	----	----	2	
									Smith volcano	**1907**	....	....	....	-x--	----	--x-	----	----	2	
									Babuyan Claro	? *1913*	....	....	....	x---	----	--?-	----	----	*2*	
									Smith volcano	**1917**	....	....	....	-x--	----	?---	----	----	2	
									Smith volcano	**1918**	0517	**1918**	0519	-x--	----	x---	----	----	2	
									Smith volcano	**1919**	05	....	....	-x--	----	?---	----	----	2	
									Smith volcano	**1924**	....	....	....	-x--	----	x---	----	----	2	
Unnamed (Batan Is)	**20.33** N	**121.75** E	**-24**	1345	U	**Submarine volc**	**0704-05=**	**Historical**												
										1773	10	....	....	----	?---	----	----	----	0	
										1850	....	....	....	----	?---	----	----	----	0	
										1854	0115	....	....	----	?---	----	----	----	0	
Iraya (Batan Is)	**20.469** N	**122.010** E	**1009**	4445	ABY	**Stratovolcano**	**0704-06-**	**Historical**												
										C **0250**x	....	....	....	----	----	x---	----	----		
										C **0470**t	....	....	....	x---	----	xx--	----	----		
										1454?	....	....	....	----	----	----	----	----		

SE ASIA (INDOCHINA)

VOLCANO NAME (Subregion) / ERUPTION	LAT	LONG	ELEV (m)	POPL (5 km, 10, 30, 100)	ROCK TYPE	VOLC TYPE	NUMBER	STATUS	Area of Activity	Start Year	Start M-Dy	Stop Year	Stop M-Dy	Central / Flank vent / Radial fiss / Regional	Submarine / New island / Subglacial / Crater lake	Explosive / Pyro flow / Phreatic / Caldera	Lava flow / Lava lake / Dome / Spine	Fatal / Damage / Mudflow / Tsunami	VEI	Vol L/T
Hainan Dao (China-SE)	**19.70** N*	**110.10** E		7777	B	**Pyroclastic cones**	**0705-001**	**Historical**												
									Lingao	**1883**	....	....	....	---x	----	x---	----	----		
									Nansheling ridge	**1933**	0626d	**1933**	0708>	---x	----	x---	----	----		
Leizhou Bandao (China-SE)	**20.78** N*	**110.17** E	**259**	7777	BX	**Volcanic field**	**0705-01-**	**Holocene**												
Cù-Lao Ré Group (Vietnam)	**15.38** N*	**109.12** E	**181**	3357	B	**Volcanic field**	**0705-02-**	**Holocene**												
Toroeng Prong (Vietnam)	**14.93** N	**108.00** E	**800**	3357	B	**Cinder cone**	**0705-03-**	Holocene?												
Haut Dong Nai (Vietnam)	**11.60** N*	**108.20** E	**1000**	6667	BXYA	**Volcanic field**	**0705-04-**	Holocene?												
Bas Dong Nai (Vietnam)	**10.80** N*	**107.20** E	**392**	6668	B	**Volcanic field**	**0705-05-**	Holocene?												
Cendres, Ile des (Vietnam-E of)	**10.158** N	**109.014** E	**-20**	0004	B	**Submarine volcs**	**0705-06-**	**Historical**												
										1923	0302	**1923**	0513	xx--	xx--	x---	x---	----	2	-/8
Veteran (Vietnam-E of)	**9.83** N	**109.05** E		0004	U	**Submarine volc**	**0705-07-**	**Fumarolic**												
										? *1880*?	....	....	....	----	?---	----	----	----	*0*	
										? *1928*	....	....	....	----	?---	----	----	----	*0*	
Popa (Burma)	**20.92** N	**95.25** E	**1518**	4567	BAYD	**Stratovolcano**	**0705-08-**	**Anthropology**												
										A-**0442**	....	....	....	----	----	----	----	----		
Lower Chindwin (Burma)	**22.28** N*	**95.10** E	**385**	6667	BRDA	**Volcanic field**	**0705-09-**	Holocene?												
Singu Plateau (Burma)	**22.70** N*	**95.98** E	**507**	5567	Y	**Fissure vents**	**0705-10-**	**Holocene**												
Tengchong (China-S)	**25.23** N*	**98.50** E	**2865**	6667	BAd	**Pyroclastic cones**	**0705-11-**	**Uranium-series**												
										U-**5750***	....	....	....	----	----	----	----	----		
									Dayingshan or Heikongshan	? *1609*	....	....	....	x---	---?	?---	----	?x--		

Chris Newhall (USGS)

The 15 x 20 km Taal caldera of Pleistocene and Holocene age is largely filled by a lake whose surface is only 3 m above sea level. The 5-km-wide Volcano Island in the north-central part of the caldera is constructed of coalescing small stratovolcanoes, tuff rings, and scoria cones. It has been the site of all historical eruptions at Taal, including powerful phreatomagmatic explosive eruptions with devastating pyroclastic surges.

Japan, Taiwan, & Marianas (08)

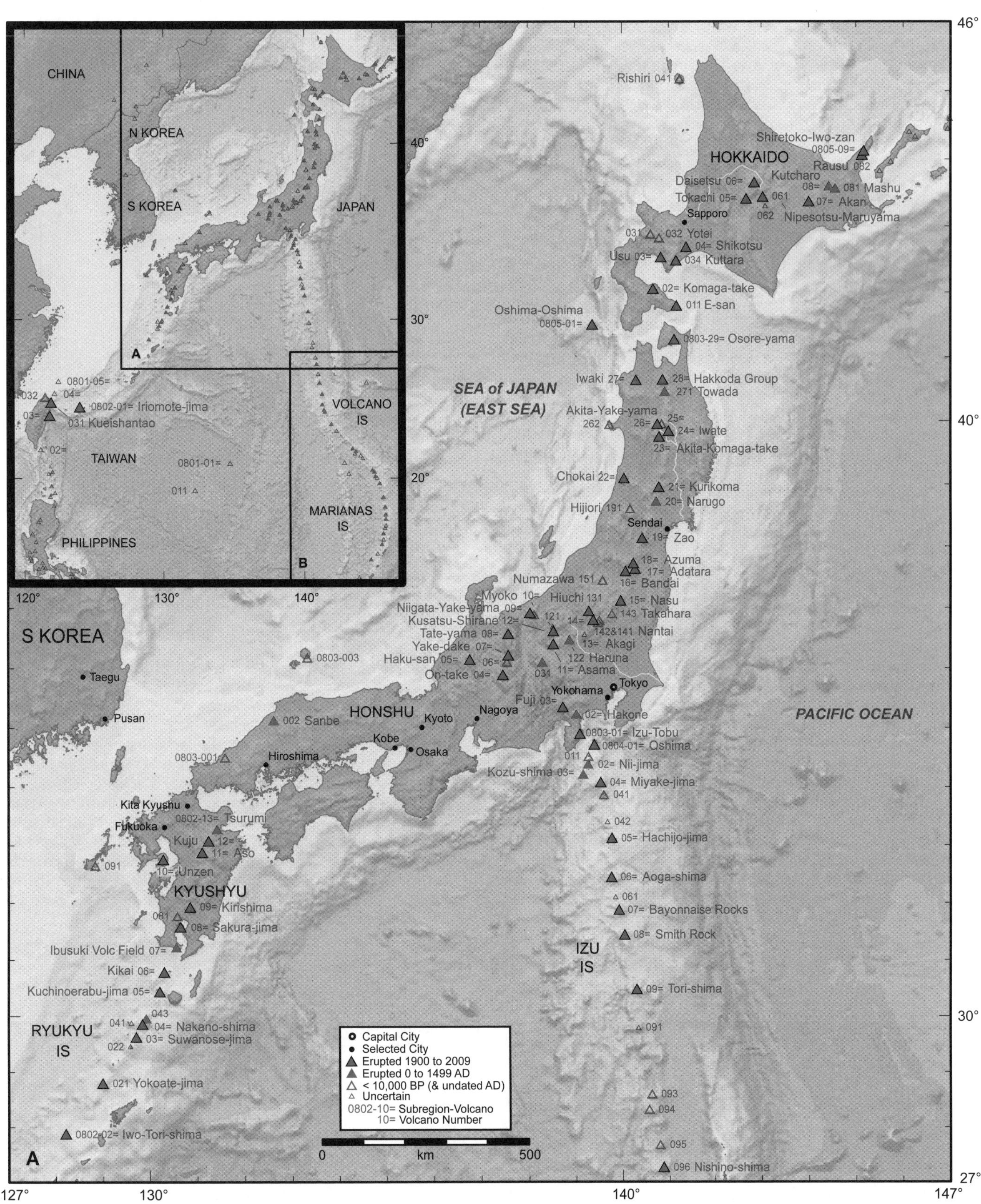
CHINA
N KOREA
S KOREA
JAPAN
TAIWAN
PHILIPPINES
VOLCANO IS
MARIANAS IS
0801-05=
04=
032
03=
0802-01= Iriomote-jima
031 Kueishantao
02=
0801-01=
011
40°
30°
20°
120°
130°
140°
A
B
HOKKAIDO
HONSHU
KYUSHYU
RYUKYU IS
IZU IS
SEA of JAPAN (EAST SEA)
PACIFIC OCEAN
Rishiri 041
Shiretoko-Iwo-zan
0805-09=
Rausu 082
Kutcharo
08=
081 Mashu
Daisetsu 06=
Tokachi 05=
061
062
07= Akan
Nipesotsu-Maruyama
Sapporo
031
032 Yotei
04= Shikotsu
Usu 03=
034 Kuttara
02= Komaga-take
011 E-san
Oshima-Oshima
0805-01=
0803-29= Osore-yama
Iwaki 27=
28= Hakkoda Group
271 Towada
Akita-Yake-yama
262
26=
25=
24= Iwate
23= Akita-Komaga-take
Chokai 22=
21= Kurikoma
20= Narugo
Hijiori 191
Sendai
19= Zao
18= Azuma
17= Adatara
16= Bandai
Numazawa 151
Myoko 10=
Hiuchi 131
15= Nasu
Niigata-Yake-yama 09=
121
143 Takahara
Kusatsu-Shirane 12=
14=
142&141 Nantai
Tate-yama 08=
13= Akagi
Yake-dake 07=
122 Haruna
Haku-san 05=
06=
031
11= Asama
On-take 04=
Tokyo
Yokohama
Fuji 03=
02= Hakone
0803-01= Izu-Tobu
0804-01= Oshima
011
02= Nii-jima
Kozu-shima 03=
04= Miyake-jima
041
042
05= Hachijo-jima
06= Aoga-shima
061
07= Bayonnaise Rocks
08= Smith Rock
09= Tori-shima
091
093
094
095
096 Nishino-shima
0803-003
S KOREA
Taegu
Pusan
002 Sanbe
Kyoto
Nagoya
Kobe
Osaka
0803-001
Hiroshima
Kita Kyushu
Fukuoka
0802-13= Tsurumi
Kuju
12=
11= Aso
091
10= Unzen
09= Kirishima
081
08= Sakura-jima
Ibusuki Volc Field 07=
Kikai 06=
Kuchinoerabu-jima 05=
043
041
04= Nakano-shima
03= Suwanose-jima
022
021 Yokoate-jima
0802-02= Iwo-Tori-shima
Capital City
Selected City
Erupted 1900 to 2009
Erupted 0 to 1499 AD
< 10,000 BP (& undated AD)
Uncertain
0802-10= Subregion-Volcano
10= Volcano Number
0
km
500
46°
40°
30°
27°
127°
130°
140°
147°

Human settlement of Japan can be traced for tens of thousands of years and through an unbroken line of emperors from 660 BC. In 552 AD, Buddhism was introduced from Korea, and Japan's first confirmed historical eruption was in 664 AD at Oshima. A fixed capital at the present location of Nara was first established in 710. By the time of Japan's largest historical eruption (Towada, 915 AD), 19 Japanese volcanoes had been documented in eruption, more than the rest of the world combined (including 10 in Europe). It was not until 1626, however, that history recorded an eruption from Japan's northern island of Hokkaido, and it was not formally made part of Japan until 1868. A feudal system had dominated all of Japan from 1192, but in 1868, 14 years after the nation was first opened to western trade, the Emperor Meiji overcame shogun power, and Edo (renamed Tokyo, or *Eastern Capital*) became Japan's capital city.

To the south, the Mariana Islands were populated from 1500 BC and explored by Spaniards in the 15th century AD, but the islands did not come under Spanish colonial rule until 1668. The first historical eruption was documented the following year. The northern volcanic islands were sold to Germany in 1898, occupied by Japan between the two World Wars, and named a Trust Territory by the UN in 1947 administered by the US. The islands became a self-governing US commonwealth in 1975. Region 08's total land area approximates California's, but its population is 4 times as large, and the Marianas constitute only 0.1% of each.

Most volcanoes in this region result from subduction of westward-moving oceanic crust under the Asian Plate. In the Izu-Mariana chain, however, the crust to the west is also oceanic, forming more basaltic island arcs (but with volcanoes that are far more explosive than oceanic hotspot volcanoes).

Japan's long history and careful attention to tephrochronology have produced an unusually detailed and balanced record of Holocene volcanism. One result of this work is that this region now leads all others in the total number of dated eruptions (1465) and number of volcanoes with dated eruptions (106). Several regions in which tephrochronology is emphasized, such as New Zealand and the Mediterranean, show a high proportion of their large eruptions (VEI ≥4) more than 2000 years ago. In contrast, regions such as Latin America, Indonesia, and the Philippines, show them concentrated in the last 200 years of historical records. Japan, however, (along with Kamchatka, Iceland, and Alaska) shows a balanced temporal distribution of large eruptions, reflecting *both* tephrochronology emphasis and vigorous explosive volcanism during recent centuries.

The volcanoes of this region are unusually explosive, and include Kikai in the Ryukyu Islands immediately south of Kyushu, which produced one of the earth's largest Holocene explosive eruptions about 6300 radiocarbon years ago. Lake-filled Towada volcano in northern Honshu has an average VEI of 4.42, the world's highest of those with 5 or more VEI assignments. Mashu, another caldera volcano in Hokkaido, is another of only 8 volcanoes globally with an average VEI of 4 or higher. Japan leads the world in volcanoes with average VEIs of 3 or larger, and no other region has documented more large (VEI ≥4) explosive eruptions (114), or approaches its total of 58 eruptions of this magnitude in the past 2000 years.

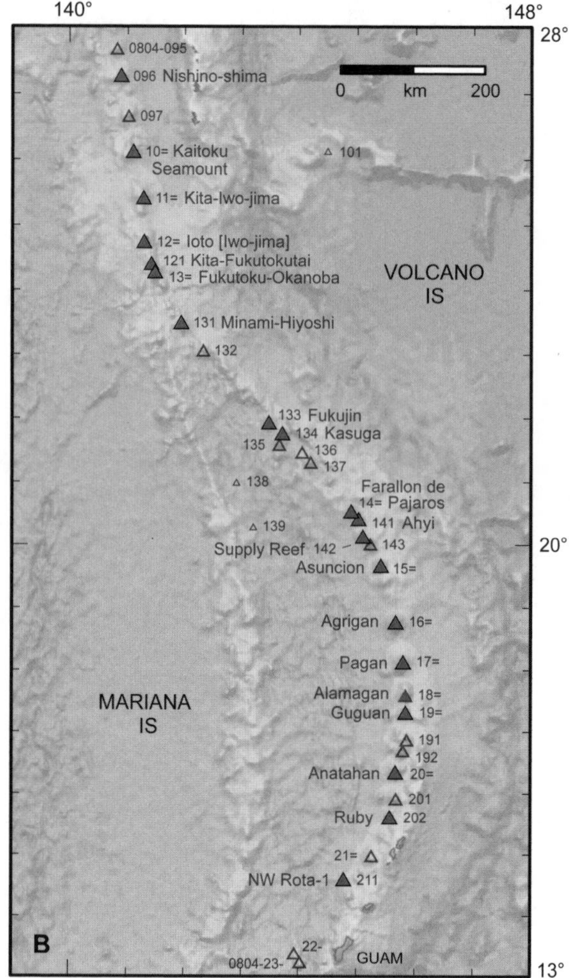

Region 08 has the largest number of submarine volcanoes, mostly extending down the Izu-Marianas arc, contributing the many submarine eruptions around the Pacific's "Ring of Fire." The many reports of water discoloration over submarine vents have also contributed to this region's record number (292) of eruptions preceded by a question mark, indicating uncertainty that the eruption actually took place. Recent bathymetric expeditions have uncovered evidence for young submarine volcanism in the Marianas arc, including first-hand observations of active explosive and effusive eruptions from NW Rota-I volcano beginning in 2004. Vigorous submarine activity in this region, in combination with that at Melanesia and the New Zealand to Fiji regions, accounts for more than half of the world's 100 documented eruptions that have built oceanic islands.

VOLCANO NAME (Subregion) / **ERUPTION** — Area of Activity	**LAT**		**LONG**		**ELEV** (m)	**POPL** (5 km / 10 / 30 / 100)	**ROCK TYPE**	**VOLC TYPE** / —**Start**— **Year**	**NUMBER** / M-Dy	**STATUS** / —**Stop**— **Year** M-Dy	Central / Flank vent / Radial fiss / Regional	Submarine / New island / Subglacial / Crater lake	Explosive / Pyro flow / Phreatic / Caldera	Lava flow / Lava lake / Dome / Spine	Fatal / Damage / Mudflow / Tsunami	VEI	Vol L/T
TAIWAN & RYUKYU ISLANDS																	
Unnamed (Taiwan-E of)...........	**20.93**	**N**	**134.75**	**E**	**-6000**	0000	**U**	**Submarine volc ?**	**0801-01=**	Uncertain							
								? 1850	....	....	----	?---	----	----	----	*0*	
(incorrect Lat-Long, see 0801-02=)								*X 1854*	*0115*	....	----	?---	----	----	----		
Unnamed (Taiwan-E of)...........	**19.17**	**N**	**132.25**	**E**	**-10**	0000	**U**	**Submarine volc ?**	**0801-011**	Uncertain							
								? 1955	*10*	....	----	?---	----	----	----	*0*	
Unnamed (Taiwan-E of)...........	**21.83**	**N**	**121.18**	**E**	**-115**	0006	**U**	**Submarine volc**	**0801-02=**	Uncertain							
								? 1854	*0115*	....	----	?---	----	----	----	*0*	
Unnamed (Taiwan-E of)...........	**24.00**	**N**	**121.83**	**E**		0066	**U**	**Submarine volc**	**0801-03=**	**Historical**							
								1853	1029	**1853** 11 ?	----	x---	x---	----	----	2?	
Kueishantao (Taiwan-E of)	**24.85**	**N**	**121.92**	**E**	**401**	1468	**A**	**Stratovolcano**	**0801-031**	**Historical**							
								1785j	....	....	----	----	----	x---	----	0	
Tatun Group (Taiwan)............	**25.17**	**N***	**121.52**	**E**	**1120**	7777	**Ab**	**Lava domes**	**0801-032**	**Radiocarbon**							
Cisingshan....................								G-**4100**s	....	....	--x-	----	--x-	?---	----	1?	

VOLCANO NAME (Subregion) / ERUPTION — Area of Activity	LAT	LONG	ELEV (m)	POPL (5 km / 10 / 30 / 100)	ROCK TYPE	VOLC TYPE	NUMBER	STATUS	Start Year	Start M-Dy	Stop Year	Stop M-Dy	Central / Flank vent / Radial fiss / Regional	Submarine / New island / Subglacial / Crater lake	Explosive / Pyro flow / Phreatic / Caldera	Lava flow / Lava lake / Dome / Spine	Fatal / Damage / Mudflow / Tsunami	VEI	Vol L/T
Unnamed (Taiwan-N of)	**25.40 N**	**122.20 E**	**-100**	0007	U	**Submarine volc**	**0801-04=**	Uncertain											
									? 1867	....	....	....	----	?---	----	----	----	*0*	
Zengyu (Taiwan-N of)	**26.18 N**	**122.458 E**	**-418**	0000	U	**Submarine volc**	**0801-05=**	Uncertain											
									? 1916	*0418*	....	....	----	?---	----	----	----	*0*	
Iriomote-jima (Ryukyu Is)	**24.558 N**	**124.00 E**	**-200**	0055	R	**Submarine volc**	**0802-01=**	**Historical**											
(eruption October 31, 1924, not 1925)									**1924**	1031	....	....	----	x---	x---	----	----	4?	-/9
Iwo-Tori-shima (Ryukyu Is)	**27.877 N**	**128.224 E**	**212**	0005	A	**Complex volcano**	**0802-02=**	**Historical**											
									1664	....	....	....	----	?---	----	----	xx-x		
Iwo-dake									**1796**	10	**1796**	11	x---	----	x---	----	----	2	
									1829	1201	**1829**	1216	x---	----	--?-	----	----	1?	
									1855	03	**1855**	05	----	----	x---	----	----	2	
									1868	02	**1868**	04	----	----	x---	----	----	1	
									1903	0315e	**1903**	0826e	x---	----	x---	----	----	2	
Iwo-dake									**1959**	0608	**1959**	07	x---	----	x---	----	----	2	
									1967	1125e	....	....	x---	----	--?-	----	----	1	
									1968	0718	**1968**	0718	x---	----	x-x-	----	----	1	
Yokoate-jima (Ryukyu Is)	**28.797 N**	**128.997 E**	**495**	2225	A	**Stratovolcanoes**	**0802-021**	**Historical**											
									1835r	....	....	....	x---	----	x---	----	----	2?	
Akuseki-jima (Ryukyu Is)	**29.461 N**	**129.597 E**	**584**	2233	AD	**Stratovolcanoes**	**0802-022**	Holocene?											
Suwanose-jima (Ryukyu Is)	**29.635 N**	**129.716 E**	**799**	3334	A	**Stratovolcanoes**	**0802-03=**	**Historical**											
									T **1600**?	....	....	....	x---	----	x---	----	----	4+	
SW ridge fissure and O-take									**1813**	....	**1814**	....	x-x-	----	xx-A	x---	----	4	
									1877	....	....	....	----	----	x---	----	----	4?	
Northeastern summit crater (O-take)									**1884**	....	....	....	x---	----	x---	x---	----	1	
O-take									**1885**	01	**1885**	05	x---	----	x---	----	----	2?	
O-take									**1889**	1002	**1889**	1013	x---	----	x---	----	----	4	
O-take									*? 1914*	*0321*	....	....	x---	----	----	----	----		
O-take									*? 1915*	*07*	*?1915*	*09*	x---	----	?---	----	----	*2?*	
O-take									**1921**	1208	**1922**	0126	x---	----	x---	----	----	2?	
O-take									**1925**	0513	....	....	x---	----	x---	----	----	2?	
O-take									*? 1934*	*0111*	....	....	x---	----	?---	----	----	*2?*	
O-take									**1938**	0311	**1938**	0311	x---	----	x---	----	----	2?	
O-take									**1940**	1129	....	....	x---	----	x---	----	----	2?	
O-take									**1949**	10	**1954**	....	x---	----	x---	----	-x--	2	
Submarine E flank (Suwanose-jima Oki)									**1954**?	....	....	....	----	x---	----	----	----	0	
O-take									**1956**	11	**1984**	05	x---	----	x---	----	-x--	2	
Submarine E flank (Suwanose-jima Oki)									**1960**?	....	....	....	----	x---	----	----	----	0	
O-take									**1984**	10	**1984**	10	x---	----	x---	----	----	2	
O-take									**1985**	09	**1987**	06	x---	----	x---	----	----	2	
O-take									**1988**	01	**1989**	12	x---	----	x---	----	----	2	
O-take									**1990**	04	**1996**	0714	x---	----	x---	----	----	2	
O-take									**1996**	1226	**1997**	0417	x---	----	x---	----	----	1	
O-take									**1999**	0105e	**1999**	0224d	x---	----	x---	----	----	1?	
O-take									**1999**	0615e	**1999**	0630d	x---	----	x---	----	----	1?	
O-take									**2000**	0224d	**2000**	0224d	x---	----	x---	----	----	2?	
O-take (Upper NE flank)									**2000**	1219	**2004**	0705?	xx--	----	x---	----	----	3?	
O-take									**2004**	1023	**2010>**	....	x---	----	x---	----	----	2	
Nakano-shima (Ryukyu Is)	**29.856 N**	**129.859 E**	**979**	3335	AD	**Stratovolcanoes**	**0802-04=**	**Historical**											
On-take									**1914**	01	....	....	x---	----	--x-	----	----	1	
On-take									*? 1949*	*10*	....	....	x---	----	----	----	----	*1?*	
Kogaja-jima (Ryukyu Is)	**29.879 N**	**129.625 E**	**301**	1234	A	**Lava domes**	**0802-041**	Holocene?											
Kuchino-shima (Ryukyu Is)	**29.964 N**	**129.927 E**	**628**	2335	A	**Stratovolcanoes**	**0802-043**	**Radiocarbon**											
Yoko-dake, Mae-dake									G-**6750**t	....	....	....	x---	----	xx--	--x-	----		
									C-**0900**?	....	....	....	----	----	--?-	----	----		
									G **0750**t	....	....	....	x---	----	xx--	--x-	----		
									G **1190**s	....	....	....	x---	----	----	----	----		
Kuchinoerabu-jima (Ryukyu Is)	**30.440 N**	**130.219 E**	**657**	4446	Ab	**Stratovolcanoes**	**0802-05=**	**Historical**											
Furu-take									G-**9520**y	....	....	....	x---	----	x---	----	----		
Furu-take									G-**3480**w	....	....	....	x---	----	x---	----	----		
Shin-take (N-m tephra)									G-**1450**u	....	....	....	----	----	x---	----	----		
Furu-take									G-**1140**w	....	....	....	x---	----	xx--	----	----		
Shin-take (N-6 tephra)									G **0600**u	....	....	....	----	----	x---	----	----		
Furu-take									G **0970**u	....	....	....	x---	----	--?-	x---	----		
Shin-take (N-5 tephra)									G **1100**v	....	....	....	----	----	x---	----	----		
Furu-take									G **1110**u	....	....	....	x---	----	x---	----	----		
Shin-take (N-1? tephra)									G **1440**t	....	....	....	----	----	x---	----	----		
Furu-take									G **1470**t	....	....	....	x---	----	x---	----	----		
Furu-take									G **1560**v	....	....	....	x---	----	x---	----	----		
Shin-take									**1840**<	....	....	....	x---	----	----	----	----	2?	
Shin-take									**1841**	0523	**1841**	0801	x---	----	x---	----	xx--	2*	
Shin-dake									*? 1906*	....	*?1907*	....	----	----	----	----	----		
Shin-dake									**1914**	0105	....	....	x---	----	--?-	----	----	2?	
SW flank of Shin-take									**1931**	0402	**1931**	0622	-x--	----	x-x-	----	-x--	3?	
Shin-take									*? 1932*	*0723*	*?1932*	*0723*	x---	----	?---	----	----	*1?*	
Shin-take									**1933**	1223	**1934**	0112	x---	----	x---	----	xx--	4?	
NNE-SSW fissure on E side of Shin-take									**1945**	1103	**1945**	1103	---x	----	x-x-	----	----	2	
Shin-take									**1966**	1122	**1966**	1122	x---	----	--x-	----	----	2	
Shin-take									**1968**	1221	**1969**	0310	x---	----	x-x-	----	----	3*	
Shin-take									**1972**	0902	**1972**	0902	x---	----	--x-	----	----	2	
Shin-take									**1973**	1105	**1973**	1119	x---	----	x-x-	----	----	2	
Shin-take									**1974**	0603	**1974**	0603	x---	----	x-x-	----	----	1	
Shin-take									**1976**	0402	**1976**	0402	x---	----	x-x-	----	----	2	
NNE-SSW fissure on E side of Shin-take									**1980**	0928	**1980**	0928	---x	----	x-x-	----	----	2	-/6
Kikai (Ryukyu Is)	**30.789 N**	**130.308 E**	**704**	3337	RBA	**Caldera**	**0802-06=**	**Historical**											
Kikai caldera (Akahoya tephra)									C-**4350**?	....	....	....	x---	----	xx-x	----	xx--	**7**	**-/11**
Old Iwo-dake (Olo1a,b tephras)									C-**3250**u	....	....	....	x---	----	xx--	----	----		
Old Iwo-dake (Olo2a,b tephras)									T-**2450***	....	....	....	x---	----	x---	----	----		
Inamura-dake (In-I tephra)									C-**1830**u	....	....	....	x---	----	x---	----	----		
Inamura-dake									C-**1090**v	....	....	....	x---	----	x---	----	----	2	
Iwo-dake									C-**0280**u	....	....	....	x---	----	x---	----	----		
Iwo-dake									C **0390**v	....	....	....	x---	----	x---	x---	----	3	
Iwo-dake									T **0750**?	....	....	....	x---	----	x---	x-x-	----	3	

VOLCANO NAME (Subregion) / ERUPTION	LAT / LONG / ELEV (m) / POPL (5 km, 10, 30, 100) / ROCK TYPE / Area of Activity	VOLC TYPE / NUMBER / Start Year	Start M-Dy	STATUS / Stop Year	Stop M-Dy	Central, Flank vent, Radial fiss, Regional	Submarine, New island, Subglacial, Crater lake	Explosive, Pyro flow, Phreatic, Caldera	Lava flow, Lava lake, Dome, Spine	Fatal, Damage, Mudflow, Tsunami	VEI	Vol L/T
Kikai (Ryukyu Is) *continued*	Iwo-dake (K-Iw-P1 tephra)	C **0830**s	....	....	....	x---	----	x---	----	----		
	Iwo-dake (K-Sk-u-3 tephra)	C **1010**s	....	....	....	x---	----	x---	----	----		
	Iwo-dake (K-Sk-u-4 tephra)	C **1030**s	....	....	....	x---	----	x---	----	----		
	Iwo-dake (K-Iw-P2 tephra)	C **1340**r	....	....	....	x---	----	x---	----	----		
	Iwo-dake	C **1430**u	....	....	....	x---	----	x---	----	----		
	Tokara-Iwo-jima	? *1914*	*0213*	....	....	----	----	----	----	----		
	2 km east of Tokara-Iwo-Jima	**1934**	0919	**1935**	08 ?	x---	xx--	x---	x-x-	----	2*	6/-
	Iwo-dake	**1988**	0118	**1988**	0118	x---	----	x-x-	----	----	1	
	Iwo-dake	**1997**	....	....	....	x---	----	x-x-	----	----	1?	
	Iwo-dake	**1998**	0425	**1999**	08	x---	----	x-x-	----	----	2	
	Iwo-dake	**2000**	01	**2000**	03	x---	----	x---	----	----	2?	
	Iwo-dake	**2000**	10	**2001**	12	x---	----	x---	----	----	1	
	Iwo-dake	**2002**	0511	**2002**	07	x---	----	x---	----	----	2	
	Iwo-dake	**2003**	02 ?	**2003**	10	x---	----	x---	----	----	2	
	Iwo-dake	**2004**	0305	**2004**	10	x---	----	x---	----	----	2	

KYUSHU

VOLCANO NAME (Subregion) / ERUPTION	LAT / LONG / ELEV (m) / POPL (5 km, 10, 30, 100) / ROCK TYPE / Area of Activity	VOLC TYPE / NUMBER / Start Year	Start M-Dy	STATUS / Stop Year	Stop M-Dy	Central, Flank vent, Radial fiss, Regional	Submarine, New island, Subglacial, Crater lake	Explosive, Pyro flow, Phreatic, Caldera	Lava flow, Lava lake, Dome, Spine	Fatal, Damage, Mudflow, Tsunami	VEI	Vol L/T
Ibusuki Volc Field (Kyushu)	**31.22** N* **130.57** E **922** 5567 **ARDB**	**Calderas** **0802-07=**		**Historical**								
	Unagi, Narikawa and Yamakawa maars	T-**5050**?	....	....	....	x---	----	x---	----	----		
	Ikeda-ko caldera (tephra layer Ikp)	C-**2690**u	....	....	....	x---	----	xx-x	----	----	**5**	-/**9**
	Kaimon (tephra layer Km-rho)	T-**2010**?	....	....	....	----	----	x---	----	-x--	4	-/8
	Kaimon (tephra set Km-pi)	T-**1780**?	....	....	....	----	----	x---	----	----	4	-/8
	Kaimon (tephra layer Km-omicron)	T-**1610**?	....	....	....	----	----	x---	----	----	3	-/7
	Nabeshima-dake	T-**1550**?	....	....	....	x---	----	----	--x-	----		
	Kaimon (tephra layer Km-xi)	T-**1500**?	....	....	....	----	----	x---	----	----	4	-/8
	Mizunashi, Kagami, Ikezoko maars	T-**1450**?	....	....	....	x---	----	x---	----	----		
	Kaimon (tephra layer Km-nu)	T-**0700**?	....	....	....	----	----	x---	x---	----	2	7/6
	Kaimon (tephra set Km-mu)	T-**0650**?	....	....	....	----	----	x---	----	----	4	-/8
	Kaimon (tephra set Km-lamda)	T-**0270**?	....	....	....	----	----	x---	----	----	4	-/8
	Kaimon (tephra set Km-kappa)	T-**0080**?	....	....	....	----	----	x---	----	----	4	-/8
	Kaimon (tephra set Km-iota)	T **0030**?	....	....	....	----	----	x---	----	----	3	-/7
	Kaimon (tephra set Km-theta)	T **0130**?	....	....	....	----	----	x---	x---	----	4	7/8
	Kaimon (tephra set Km-eta)	T **0150**?	....	....	....	----	----	x---	----	----	4	-/8
	Kaimon (tephra set Km-zeta)	T **0270**?	....	....	....	----	----	x---	----	----	3	-/7
	Kaimon (tephra set Km-epsilon)	T **0550**?	....	....	....	----	----	x---	----	----	2	-/6
	Kaimon (tephra set Km-delta)	T **0600**?	....	....	....	----	----	x---	x---	----	4	8/8
	Kaimon	T **0660**?	....	....	....	----	----	xx--	----	----	4+	
	Kaimon (tephra set Km-gamma)	T **0720**?	....	....	....	----	----	x---	----	----	4	-/8
	Kaimon (tephra set Km-beta)	T **0770**?	....	....	....	----	----	x---	----	----	4	-/8
	Kaimon	? *0860*	*04*	....	....	----	----	?---	----	----	*2?*	
	Kaimon	? *0866*	*05*	....	....	----	----	?---	----	----	*2?*	
	Kaimon	**0874**	0329	**0874**	07 ?	x---	----	x---	----	-x--	4	
	Kaimon	? *0882*	*11*	....	....	----	----	?---	----	----	*2?*	
	Kaimon	**0885**	0829	**0885**	0928	----	----	x---	x---	-x--	4	
	Kaimon	? *1615*	*0807*?	....	....	----	----	?---	----	----		
Sakura-jima (Kyushu)	**31.585**N **130.657**E **1117** 4667 **ADR**	**Stratovolcano** **0802-08=**		**Historical**								
	Kita-dake	C-**7750**?	....	....	....	x---	----	x---	----	----		
	Kita-dake	C-**6350**?	....	....	....	x---	----	x---	----	----		
	Wakamiko Caldera	C-**6200***	....	....	....	x---	x---	xx-x	----	----	**6**	-/**10**
	Kita-dake (tephra layer Sz-11)	C-**6050**?	....	....	....	x---	----	x---	----	----	**5**	
	Kita-dake	C-**5950**?	....	....	....	x---	----	x---	----	----		
	Kita-dake	C-**5400**?	....	....	....	x---	----	x---	----	----		
	Kita-dake	C-**4800**?	....	....	....	x---	----	x---	----	----		
	Kita-dake (tephra layer Sz-7)	C-**3050**?	....	....	....	x---	----	x---	----	----	4	
	Kita-dake (tephra layer Sz-5)	C-**2900**?	....	....	....	x---	----	x---	----	----	4	
	(Miyamoto lava)	M-**2050**?	....	....	....	----	----	----	x---	----		
	(Kannonzaki lava)	M-**1050**?	....	....	....	----	----	----	x---	----		
	Minami-dake	C-**0650**?	....	....	....	x---	----	x---	----	----		
		0708	....	....	....	----	xx--	?---	----	----	3↑	
		? *0712*	....	....	....	----	----	?---	----	----	*3?*	
		0716	....	**0718**	....	----	xx--	?---	----	----	3↑	
	East flank (Nabe-yama) (Sz-4 tephra)	**0764**	01	....	....	-x--	----	xxx-	x---	xx--	4	
		0766	0720	....	....	----	xx--	x---	----	x---	3↑	
		0778	....	....	....	----	x---	----	----	----	0?	
	Minami-dake	**1468**	....	....	....	x---	----	x---	----	----	2	
	NE and SW flanks, summit crater	**1471**	1103	**1476**	1008>	xxx-	----	xx--	x---	xx--	**5?**	8/**9**
	Minami-dake	**1478**	0923	....	....	x---	----	x---	----	-x--	2?	
	Minami-dake	**1642**	0406	....	....	x---	----	x---	----	----	2?	
		? *1670*	*0601*	....	....	----	----	----	----	----	*2?*	
	Minami-dake	**1678**	0301	....	....	x---	----	x---	----	----	2?	
	Minami-dake	**1706**	01	....	....	x---	----	x---	----	----	2?	
	Minami-dake	**1742**	0406	....	....	x---	----	x---	----	----	2?	
	Minami-dake summit, west flank?	**1749**	09	....	....	x?--	----	x---	?---	----	2	
	Minami-dake	**1756**	0909	....	....	x---	----	x---	----	----	2	
	(earthquake, but not eruption)	X *1766*	*0605*	....	....	----	----	----	----	----		
	NE flank, off NE coast, south flank	**1779**	1108	**1781**	05	-xx-	xx--	xx--	x---	xxxx	4*	**9**/8
	NE flank (offshore)	**1782**	0118	....	....	----	x---	----	----	----	2?	
		1783	0903	....	....	-x--	----	x---	----	----	3	
		1785	1120	....	....	-x--	----	x---	----	----	2	
	Minami-dake	**1790**	0729	....	....	x---	----	x---	----	----	2	
	Minami-dake	**1791**	0911	....	....	x---	----	x---	----	----	2	
	Minami-dake	? *1792*	....	....	....	x---	----	?---	----	----	*2?*	
	Minami-dake	**1794**	....	....	....	x---	----	x---	----	----	2	
	Minami-dake	**1797**	....	....	....	x---	----	x---	----	----	2	
	Minami-dake	**1799**	0327	....	....	x---	----	x---	----	----	2	
	Minami-dake	**1860**	....	....	....	x---	----	x---	----	----	1	
	Minami-dake	? *1899*	*0924*	?*1899*	*0925*	x---	----	----	----	----	*1?*	
	West, east and SE flanks	**1914**	0112	**1915**	05	-xx-	----	xx--	x---	xx--	4	**9**/8
	Minami-dake	**1935**	0920	**1935**	0924	x---	----	x---	----	----	1	
	Minami-dake	**1938**	0225	**1938**	0331	----	----	x-?-	----	----	2	
	East flank of Minami-dake (750 m)	**1939**	1026	**1939**	1112?	-x--	----	xx--	----	----	2	-/5
	Minami-dake and east flank (750 m)	**1940**	0424	**1940**	0709	xx--	----	x---	----	----	2	

VOLCANO NAME (Subregion)	LAT	LONG	ELEV (m)	POPL 5 km 10 30 100	ROCK TYPE	VOLC TYPE / ERUPTION — Area of Activity	NUMBER / Start Year	Start M-Dy	STATUS / Stop Year	Stop M-Dy	Central, Flank vent, Radial fiss, Regional	Submarine, New island, Subglacial, Crater lake	Explosive, Pyro flow, Phreatic, Caldera	Lava flow, Lava lake, Dome, Spine	Fatal, Damage, Mudflow, Tsunami	VEI	Vol L/T
Sakura-jima (Kyushu) *continued*						East flank of Minami-dake (750 m)	**1941**	0428	**1941**	0826	-x--	----	x---	----	----	2	
						East flank of Minami-dake (750 m)	**1942**	0716	**1942**	0716	-x--	----	x---	----	----	1	
						East flank of Minami-dake (750 m)	**1946**	01	**1946**	11	-x--	----	x---	x---	xxx-	2	8/7
						East flank of Minami-dake (750 m)	**1948**	0727	**1948**	0727	-x--	----	x---	----	----	1	
						Minami-dake	**1950**	0629	**1950**	0909	x---	----	x-x-	----	----	1	
						Minami-dake	? *1954*	*11*	?*1954*	*12*	x---	----	--?-	----	----	*1?*	
						Minami-dake and east flank (Showa crater)	**1955**	1013	**2010>**	....	xx--	----	xxx-	-xx-	xxx-	3*	
Sumiyoshi-ike (Kyushu)	**31.768 N**	**130.594 E**	**15**	5567	**B**	**Maars**	**0802-081**		**Radiocarbon**								
						Sumiyoshi-ike	T **-6250**?	....	....	....	x---	----	x-x-	----	----	2	-/6
						Yonemaru	T **-6200**?	....	....	....	x---	----	xxx-	----	----	3	-/7
Kirishima (Kyushu)	**31.931 N**	**130.864 E**	**1700**	3467	**ABD**	**Shield volcano**	**0802-09=**		**Historical**								
						Shinmoe-dake (Setao Pumice)	T **-7050***	....	....	....	x---	----	x---	----	----	3	-/7
						Old Takachiho (Uramuta Scoria)	T **-5700***	....	....	....	x---	----	x---	----	----	3	-/7
						Old Takachiho (Ushinosune Ash)	C **-4350**?	....	....	....	x---	----	x---	x---	----	4	-/8
						Takachiho-mine (Mojihara Ash)	T **-3550**?	....	....	....	x---	----	x---	----	----	3	-/7
						Takachiho-mine (Oji Scoria)	T **-3050**?	....	....	....	x---	----	x---	----	----	3	-/7
						Mi-ike (tephra layer Kr-M)	C **-2650**?	....	....	....	x---	----	xx--	----	----	4	
						Shinmoe-dake (Mae-yama Pumice)	C **-2050**?	....	....	....	x---	----	x---	----	----	3	-/7
						Ohachi (Araso tephra)	T **0700**?	....			x---	----	x---	----	----		
						Ohachi	**0742**	1228	....	....	x---	----	x---	?---	----	3	
						Ohachi (Katazoe Scoria)	**0788**	0418	....	....	x---	----	xx--	x---	-x--	4	-/8
						Ohachi	**0837**	....	**0839**?	....	x---	----	x---	----	----	3	
							0843	....	**0848**	....	x---	----	x---	----	----	2?	
							0857	....	....	....	x---	----	x---	----	----	2?	
							0858	....	....	....	x---	----	x---	----	----	2?	
							0945	....	....	....	x---	----	x---	----	----	2?	
						Ohachi (Miyasugi Tephra)	T **1000**?	....	....	....	x---	----	x---	x---	----		
						Ohachi	**1112**	0309	....	....	x---	----	x---	----	-x--	2?	
							1113	0227	....	....	x---	----	x---	----	-x--	2?	
						Ohachi	**1167**	....	....	....	x---	----	x---	----	-x--	2?	
							? *1175*	*01* ?	....	....	----	----	x---	----	----	*2?*	
						Ohachi	**1184**	0207	....	....	x---	----	x---	----	----	2?	
						Ohachi (Takahara Tephra)	**1235**	0125	....	....	x---	----	xx--	x---	-x--	**P**	
							? *1381*	....	....	....	----	----	?---	----	----	*2?*	
						Ohachi	**1524**	....	....	....	x---	----	x---	----	----	2?	
						Ohachi	**1554**	....	....	....	x---	----	x---	----	----	2?	
							1566	0506	....	....	x---	----	?---	----	----	2?	
						Ohachi	**1566**	1031	....	....	x---	----	x---	----	x---	3	
						Ohachi	**1574**	02	....	....	x---	----	x---	----	----	2?	
						Ohachi	**1576**	....	**1578**	....	x---	----	x---	----	----	2?	
						Ohachi	**1585**	11 ?	....	....	x---	----	x---	----	----	2?	
						Ohachi	**1587**	0524	....	....	x---	----	x---	----	----	2?	
						Ohachi	**1588**	0407	....	....	x---	----	x---	----	----	2?	
							1595	....	....	....	----	----	x---	----	----	2?	
							? *1596*	....	....	....	----	----	x---	----	----	*2?*	
						Ohachi	**1598**	....	**1600**	....	x---	----	x---	----	----	2?	
						Ohachi	**1613**	....	**1614**	....	x---	----	x---	----	----	2?	
						Ohachi	**1615**	....	**1618**	....	----	----	x---	----	----	2?	
							1620	....	....	....	----	----	x---	----	----	2?	
						Ohachi	**1628**	1026	....	....	x---	----	x---	----	----	2?	
						Shinmoe-dake	**1637**	....	**1638**	....	x---	----	x---	----	----	2?	
						Ohachi	**1659**	02	**1661**	....	x---	----	x---	----	----	2?	
						Ohachi	**1662**	09	**1664**	....	x---	----	x---	----	----	2?	
						Ohachi	? *1667*	....	....	....	x---	----	x---	----	----		
						Ohachi	**1677**	....	....	....	x---	----	x---	----	----	2?	
						Ohachi	**1678**	0229	....	....	x---	----	x---	----	----	2?	
						Ohachi	**1690**	....	....	....	x---	----	x---	----	----	2?	
						Ohachi	**1706**	0128	....	....	x---	----	x---	----	-x--	2	
						Shinmoe-dake	**1716**	0311	....	....	x---	---x	x-x-	----	--x-	3	-/7
						Shinmoe-dake	**1716**	1109	**1717**	0213	x---	----	xx--	----	xxx-	3*	-/8
						Shinmoe-dake (tephra layer Sm-KP7)	**1717**	0919	....	....	x---	----	xx--	----	----	3	-/7
						Shinmoe-dake	**1719**	....	....	....	x---	----	x---	----	----	2	
						Iwo-yama (NW flank of Karakuni-dake)	**1768**	....	....	....	-x--	----	----	x-x-	----	0	
						Ohachi	**1769**	....	....	....	x---	----	x---	----	----	2	
						Shinmoe-dake	**1771**	....	**1772**	....	x---	----	xx--	xx--	--x-	2	-/6
						Shinmoe-dake (tephra layer Sm-BP)	**1822**	0112	....	....	x---	---x	xx--	----	--x-	2	-/6
						Shinmoe-dake	**1832**	0420	....	....	x---	----	x---	----	----	2	
						Ohachi	**1880**	09	....	....	x---	----	x---	----	----	2	
						Ohachi	**1887**	05	....	....	x---	----	x---	----	----	2?	
						Ohachi	**1888**	0221	**1888**	0509	x---	----	x---	----	----	2	
						Ohachi	**1889**	1210	**1889**	1218	x---	----	x---	----	----	2	
						Ohachi	**1891**	0619?	....	....	x---	----	x---	----	----	2?	
						Ohachi	**1891**	1110	**1891**	1120?	x---	----	x---	----	----	2	
						Ohachi	**1894**	0225	**1894**	0228?	x---	----	x---	----	----	2	
						Ohachi	**1895**	0716	**1896**	0626	x---	----	x---	----	x---	2	
						Ohachi	**1896**	1221	....	....	x---	----	x---	----	----	2	
						Ohachi	**1897**	0503	**1897**	0904	x---	----	x---	----	----	2	
						Ohachi	**1898**	0208	**1898**	0311	x---	----	x---	----	----	2	
						Ohachi	**1898**	1226	**1898**	1230	x---	----	x---	----	----	2	
						Ohachi	**1899**	0728	**1900**	0216	x---	----	x---	----	x---	2	
						Ohachi	**1903**	0829	**1903**	1125	x---	----	x---	----	----	2	
						Ohachi	**1913**	1108	**1914**	0108	x---	----	x---	----	----	2	
						Ohachi	**1914**	1108	....	....	x---	----	x---	----	----		
						Ohachi	**1923**	07	**1923**	07	x---	----	x---	----	x---	2	
						(Shinmoe crater lake gas emission)	*X 1934*	....	....	....	----	----	----	----	----		
						Karakuni-dake ?	? *1946*	*04*	....	....	x---	----	?---	----	----	*2*	
						Shinmoe-dake	**1959**	0213	**1959**	0217	x-x-	---x	x-x-	----	--x-	2	-/6
						North foot, near Tearai hot springs	**1971**	0805	**1971**	0805	x---	----	x-x-	----	----	1	
						Shinmoe-dake	**1979**	0216r	....	....	x---	----	--x-	----	----	1	
						Shinmoe-dake	**1991**	1201	**1992**	0419	x---	----	x-x-	----	----	1	-/3
						Shinmoe-dake crater and W flank	**2008**	0822	**2008**	0822	--x-	----	x-x-	----	----	1	
Fukue-jima (Kyushu)	**32.653 N**	**128.851 E**	**317**	5556	**B**	**Shield volcanoes**	**0802-091**		**Tephrochronology**								
						Hino-take	G **-0400**?	....	....	....	x---	----	x---	----	----		

VOLCANO NAME (Subregion) / ERUPTION — Area of Activity	LAT	LONG	ELEV (m)	POPL (5 km, 10, 30, 100)	ROCK TYPE	VOLC TYPE / Start Year	Start M-Dy	NUMBER / Stop Year	Stop M-Dy	STATUS	Central, Flank vent, Radial fiss, Regional	Submarine, New island, Subglacial, Crater lake	Explosive, Pyro flow, Phreatic, Caldera	Lava flow, Lava lake, Dome, Spine	Fatal, Damage, Mudflow, Tsunami	VEI	Vol L/T
Unzen (Kyushu)	**32.757 N**	**130.294 E**	**1500**	4567	**AD**	**Complex volcano**		**0802-10=**		**Historical**							
Fugen-dake (Shimanomine)						F-4050*	....	....	....		x---	----	----	x-x-	----		
Fugen-dake						G-2720y	....	....	....		x---	----	xx--	----	----		
Mayu-yama (Shichimen-zan)						G-2640z	....	....	....		x---	----	-x--	--x-	----		
Mayu-yama (Tengu-yama)						N-2150*	....	....	....		x---	----	----	--x-	----		
Fugen-dake (Kazaana)						N-1450z	....	....	....		x---	----	----	--x-	----		
Fugendake-Sancho						N-1150z	....	....	....		x---	----	----	--x-	----		
						? 0860	....	....	....		----	----	----	----	----		
(eruption occurred in 1663, not 1657)						X 1657	....	....	....		----	----	----	----	----		
Fugen-dake (Tsukumo-jima Pond)						1663	04	1663	05		x---	----	x---	----	----	2?	
NE flank of Fugen-dake (1200 m)						1663	1211	1663	1227>		-x--	----	?---	x---	----	2?	6/-
						? 1690	....	?1692	....		----	----	?---	----	----		
Fugen-dake (summit, NNE), Mayu-yama						1792	0210	1792	0722		xx--	----	x--A	x---	xxxx	2	7/-
Fugen-dake						? 1798	1113	?1798	12		----	----	?---	----	----		
Fugen-dake						1990	1117	1995	02		x---	----	xxx-	--x-	xxx-	1	8/6
Fugen-dake						1996	0210	1996	0501		x---	----	-x--	----	----	2	
Aso (Kyushu)	**32.881 N**	**131.106 E**	**1592**	5567	**ADRB**	**Caldera**		**0802-11=**		**Historical**							
Jigoku explosion crater (Ikph2 tephra)						T-8050*	....	....	....		x---	----	x-x-	----	----	1	-/5
(N12 eruptive stage)						C-3610t	....	....	....		x---	----	x---	----	----		
Naka-dake						T-2850?	....	....	....		x---	----	----	x---	----	0	
Jigoku explosion crater (Ikph1 tephra)						T-2550?	....	....	....		x---	----	x-x-	----	----	1	-/5
(N9 eruptive stage)						C-2350u	....	....	....		x---	----	x---	----	----		
(N7 eruptive stage)						C-1830u	....	....	....		x---	----	x---	----	----		
(ACP-1 tephra layer)						C-1770w	....	....	....		x---	----	x---	----	----		
Kishima-dake (KsS tephra layer)						G-1700t	....	....	....		x---	----	x---	----	----	P	
(N5 eruptive stage)						C-1270u	....	....	....		x---	----	x---	----	----		
Ojo-dake (OjS tephra layer)						G-0950?	....	....	....		x---	----	x---	----	----	P	
(N3 eruptive stage)						C-0630t	....	....	....		x---	----	x---	----	----		
Kometsuka						T 0210?	....	....	....		x---	----	x---	x---	----	3	
Naka-dake (N2S tephra layer)						G 0440u	....	....	....		x---	----	x---	----	----		
Naka-dake						? 0553	....	....	....		x---	----	?---	----	----	3↑	
Naka-dake						? 0796	08	....	....		x---	---?	----	----	----	0?	
Naka-dake						0864	1109	....	....		x---	---x	x---	----	--x-	3?	
Naka-dake						0867	0620?	....	....		x---	----	x---	----	----	2	
Naka-dake						? 0986	0902	....	....		x---	---x	?---	----	----	2?	
Naka-dake						? 1229	1231y	....	....		x---	----	?---	----	----	2?	
Naka-dake						1239	0208	....	....		x---	----	x---	----	----	2	
Naka-dake						1240	....	....	....		x---	---x	x---	----	----	2	
Naka-dake						1265	1201?	....	....		x---	----	x---	----	----	2	
Naka-dake						1269	08	....	....		x---	---x	x---	----	----	2	
Naka-dake						1271	0105	....	....		x---	---x	x---	----	----	2	
Naka-dake						1272	0416	....	....		x---	---x	x---	----	--?-	2	
Naka-dake						1272	1129	....	....		x---	----	x---	----	----	2	
Naka-dake						1273	08	....	....		x---	----	x---	----	----	2	
Naka-dake						1274	....	....	....		x---	---x	x---	----	-x--	2	
Naka-dake						1281	07	1281	08		x---	---x	x---	----	----	2	
Naka-dake						1286	0830	....	....		x---	---x	x---	----	----	2	
Naka-dake						1305	0502	....	....		x---	---x	x---	----	----	2	
Naka-dake						1324	0907	....	....		x---	---x	x---	----	----	2	
Naka-dake						1331	04	1331	04		x---	----	x---	----	----	2	
Naka-dake						1331	12	1333	06		x---	---x	x---	----	?x--	2	
Naka-dake						1335	0207	1335	0326		x---	---x	x---	----	-x--	2	
Naka-dake						1340	0203	1340	0225		x---	---x	x---	----	-x--	2	
Naka-dake						1343	....	....	....		x---	----	x---	----	----	2	
Naka-dake						? 1346	....	....	....		x---	----	?---	----	----	2	
Naka-dake						? 1369	....	....	....		x---	----	?---	----	----	2	
Naka-dake						1375	1220	1376	0131		x---	---x	x---	----	--?-	2	
Naka-dake						1376	0620	....	....		x---	----	x---	----	----	2	
Naka-dake						1377	0506	....	....		x---	---x	x---	----	-xx-	2	
Naka-dake						1387	0619	....	....		x---	---x	x---	----	----	2	
Naka-dake						? 1388	1016	....	....		x---	---x	?---	----	----	2	
Naka-dake						? 1390	....	....	....		x---	----	----	----	-x--	2?	
Naka-dake						1434	0510	1434	0518		x---	---x	x---	----	--x-	2	
Naka-dake						1438	0109	1438	0218		x---	---x	x---	----	----	2	
Naka-dake						1473	0516	1474	0415q		x---	---x	x---	----	-x--	2	
Naka-dake						1485	0105	....	....		x---	---x	x---	----	x---	2	
Naka-dake						1505	02	....	....		x---	----	x---	----	----	2	
Naka-dake						1506	0406	....	....		x---	----	x---	----	----	2	
Naka-dake						1522	0215	....	....		x---	---x	x---	----	----	2	
Naka-dake						1533	0717	....	....		x---	---x	x---	----	--x-	2	
Naka-dake						1542	0429	....	....		x---	----	x---	----	----	2	
Naka-dake						1558	....	1559	....		x---	----	x---	----	-x--	2	
Naka-dake						1562	03	....	....		x---	----	x---	----	----	2	
Naka-dake						? 1563	0503	....	....		x---	----	?---	----	----	2?	
Naka-dake						1564	12	....	....		x---	----	x---	----	----	2	
Naka-dake						1573	....	....	....		x---	----	x---	----	----	2	
Naka-dake						1574	....	....	....		x---	----	x---	----	----	2	
Naka-dake						1576	1115	....	....		x---	----	x---	----	-?--	2	
Naka-dake						1582	0217	....	....		x---	----	x---	----	----	2	
Naka-dake						1583	1214	....	....		x---	---x	x---	----	-x?-	2	
Naka-dake						1584	08	....	....		x---	----	x---	----	-x--	2	
Naka-dake						1587	....	....	....		x---	---x	x---	----	----	2	
Naka-dake						1592	....	....	....		x---	----	x---	----	----	2	
Naka-dake						1598	12	1599	....		x---	----	x---	----	----	2	
Naka-dake						1611	....	....	....		x---	----	x---	----	----	2	
Naka-dake						1612	0812	....	....		x---	----	x---	----	----	2	
Naka-dake						1613	0808	....	....		x---	---x	x---	----	----	2	
Naka-dake						1620	0603	....	....		x---	---x	x---	----	----	2	
Naka-dake						1631	12	....	....		x---	---x	x---	----	--?-	2	
Naka-dake						1637	0929	1637	1005		x---	----	x---	----	----	2	
Naka-dake						1649	07	1649	08		x---	----	x---	----	----	2	
Naka-dake						1668	02	....	....		x---	----	x---	----	----	2	
Naka-dake						1668	08	1669	....		x---	---x	x---	----	----	2	
Naka-dake						? 1671	....	....	....		x---	----	x---	----	----	2	

VOLCANO NAME (Subregion) / ERUPTION	Area of Activity	Start Year	Start M-Dy	Stop Year	Stop M-Dy	Central / Flank vent / Radial fiss / Regional	Submarine / New island / Subglacial / Crater lake	Explosive / Pyro flow / Phreatic / Caldera	Lava flow / Lava lake / Dome / Spine	Fatal / Damage / Mudflow / Tsunami	VEI	Vol L/T
Aso (Kyushu) *continued*	Naka-dake	**1675**	0216	....	....	x---	----	x---	----	----	2	
	Naka-dake	**1683**	06	....	....	x---	----	--?-	----	----	2	
	Naka-dake	**1691**	04	**1691**	08	x---	----	x---	----	----	2	
	Naka-dake	? *1708*	*0917*	....	....	x---	---?	?---	----	----	*2*	
	Naka-dake	**1709**	0213	....	....	x---	---x	x---	----	----	2	
	Naka-dake	? *1753*	....	?*1754*	....	x---	----	?---	----	----	*2?*	
	Naka-dake	**1765**	01 ?	**1765**	10 ?	x---	----	x---	----	-xx-	3?	
	Naka-dake	**1772**	....	**1780**	....	x---	----	x---	----	-x--	2	
	Naka-dake	**1781**	....	**1788**	....	x---	----	x---	----	----	1	
	Naka-dake	**1804**	0905	....	....	x---	---x	x---	----	----	2	
	Naka-dake	**1806**	06 ?	**1806**	10 ?	x---	----	x---	----	-xx-	2	
	Naka-dake	**1814**	....	....	....	x---	----	x---	----	----	2	
	Naka-dake	**1815**	0210	**1815**	10	x---	----	x---	----	-x--	2	
	Naka-dake and west flank (Yunotani)	**1816**	0609	**1816**	0706	xx--	----	x-x-	----	xx--	2	
	Naka-dake	**1826**	1003	**1826**	1122	x---	----	x---	----	-x--	2	
	Naka-dake	**1827**	05	....	....	x---	----	x---	----	-x--	2	
	Naka-dake	**1827**	1112	**1828**	01	x---	----	x---	----	x---	2	
	Naka-dake	**1828**	06	....	....	x---	----	x---	----	-x--	2	
	Naka-dake	**1829**	06	....	....	x---	----	x---	----	----	2	
	Naka-dake	**1830**	0216	**1830**	03	x---	----	x---	----	-x--	2	
	Naka-dake	**1830**	0811	**1832**	08	x---	---x	x---	----	-x--	2	
	Naka-dake	**1835**	0501	....	....	x---	----	x---	----	----	2	
	Naka-dake	**1837**	1008	....	....	x---	----	x---	----	----	2	
	Naka-dake	**1838**	0304	....	....	x---	----	x---	----	----	2	
	Naka-dake	**1854**	0226	....	....	x---	---x	x---	----	x---	2	
	Naka-dake	**1856**	0318	**1856**	0613	x---	----	x---	----	----	2	
	Naka-dake	**1872**	1201	**1873**	0608	x---	---x	x---	----	xx?-	3*	
	Naka-dake	**1874**	0207	....	....	x---	----	x---	----	----	2	
	Naka-dake	**1884**	0321	**1884**	06	x---	----	x---	----	----	2	
	Naka-dake	**1894**	0306	**1894**	0830	x---	----	x---	----	----	2	
	Naka-dake	**1897**	0224d	....	....	x---	----	x---	----	----	2	
	Naka-dake	**1898**	08 ?	**1899**	04 >	x---	----	x---	----	----	2	
	Naka-dake	**1906**	0607	....	....	x---	----	x---	----	----	3	
	Naka-dake	**1907**	1212	....	....	x---	----	x---	----	----	2	
	Naka-dake	**1908**	0117	**1908**	0129?	x---	----	x---	----	----	2	
	Naka-dake	**1909**	04	....	....	x---	----	x---	----	----	2	
	Naka-dake	**1910**	0403	....	....	x---	----	?---	----	----	2	
	Naka-dake	**1911**	....	**1912**	....	x---	----	x---	----	----	2	
	Naka-dake	**1914**	0113	....	....	x---	----	x---	----	----	2	
	Naka-dake	**1916**	0419	....	....	x---	----	x---	----	----	2	
	Naka-dake	**1918**	0116	....	....	x---	----	x-x-	----	----	2	
	Naka-dake	**1919**	04	**1919**	05	x---	----	x---	----	----	2	
	Naka-dake	**1920**	....	....	....	x---	----	x---	----	----	2	
	Naka-dake	**1923**	01	**1923**	0917	x---	----	x---	----	----	2	
	Naka-dake	**1925**	0106	....	....	x---	----	x---	----	----	2	
	Naka-dake	**1926**	0921	**1928**	0113	x---	----	x---	----	-x--	2	
	Naka-dake	**1928**	0906	**1929**	1023	x---	----	x---	----	-x--	2	
	Naka-dake	**1930**	0903	**1930**	0906	x---	----	x---	----	----	2	
	Naka-dake	? *1931*	*1018*	....	....	x---	----	--?-	----	----	*1?*	
	Naka-dake	**1932**	06	**1933**	0928	x---	---x	x---	----	-x--	2	
	Naka-dake	**1934**	0716	....	....	x---	----	x---	----	----	2	
	Naka-dake	**1935**	0107	**1935**	1008	x---	----	x---	----	----	2	
	Naka-dake	**1936**	0205	**1936**	0205	x---	----	x---	----	----	2	
	Naka-dake	**1936**	0808	**1936**	0814	x---	----	x---	----	----	2	
	Naka-dake	**1937**	0113	**1937**	0113	x---	----	x---	----	----	2	
	Naka-dake	**1937**	0507	**1937**	0513	x---	----	x---	----	----	2	
	Naka-dake	**1938**	....	**1939**	0811	x---	----	x---	----	----	2	
	Naka-dake	**1940**	0420	**1941**	0808	x---	----	x---	----	-x--	2	
	Naka-dake	? *1942*	*0608*	?*1942*	*0622*	x---	----	----	----	----	*1?*	
	Naka-dake	**1943**	0621	**1943**	0624	x---	----	x---	----	----	2	
	Naka-dake	**1943**	1209	**1944**	02	x---	----	x---	----	----	2	
	Naka-dake	**1945**	0916	**1945**	0919	x---	----	x---	----	----	2	
	Naka-dake	**1946**	0429	**1946**	0624	x---	----	x---	----	----	2	
	Naka-dake	**1946**	1230	**1946**	1230	x---	----	x---	----	----	2	
	Naka-dake	**1947**	0526	**1947**	09	x---	----	x---	----	-x--	2	
	Naka-dake	**1948**	0409	**1948**	12	x---	----	x---	----	----	1	
	Naka-dake	**1949**	1226	**1950**	0415	x---	----	x---	----	----	2	
	Naka-dake	**1950**	11	**1951**	01	x---	----	x---	----	----	2	
	Naka-dake	**1951**	0504	**1951**	08	x---	----	x---	----	----	2	
	Naka-dake	? *1952*	....	....	....	x---	----	----	----	----		
	Naka-dake	**1953**	0427	**1953**	0730	x---	----	x---	----	xx--	2	
	Naka-dake	**1953**	12	**1953**	12	x---	----	x---	----	----	1	
	Naka-dake	**1954**	0526	**1954**	0526	x---	----	x---	----	----	1	
	Naka-dake	**1955**	0725	**1955**	0728	x---	----	x---	----	----	1	
	Naka-dake	**1956**	0103?	**1956**	0113	x---	----	x---	----	----	2	
	Naka-dake	**1956**	08	....	....	x---	----	x---	----	----	2	
	Naka-dake	**1956**	1221	**1956**	1221	x---	----	x---	----	----	1	
	Naka-dake	**1957**	0412	**1957**	0412	x---	----	x---	----	----	1	
	Naka-dake	**1957**	10	**1958**	12	x---	----	x---	----	xx--	2*	-/5
	Naka-dake	**1959**	07	**1959**	1002	x---	----	x---	----	----	1	
	Naka-dake	**1960**	01	**1960**	0409	x---	----	x---	----	----	2	
	Naka-dake	**1960**	09	**1962**	11	x---	----	x-x-	----	----	1	
	Naka-dake	**1963**	0421	**1963**	07	x---	----	x---	----	----	1	
	Naka-dake	**1963**	1110	**1964**	01	x---	----	x---	----	----	2	
	Naka-dake	**1964**	0514	**1964**	0514	x---	----	x---	----	----	1	
	Naka-dake	**1964**	10	**1966**	12	x---	---x	x-x-	----	-x--	2*	
	Naka-dake	**1967**	05	**1969**	12	x---	---x	x---	----	----	1	
	Naka-dake	**1970**	0421	**1972**	09	x---	---x	x---	----	----	2	
	Naka-dake	**1973**	01	**1975**	06	x---	----	x---	----	-x--	2	
	Naka-dake	**1975**	10	**1976**	0113	x---	----	x---	----	----	1	
	Naka-dake	**1977**	0411	**1978**	08	x---	---x	x---	----	-x--	2	
	Naka-dake	**1979**	0605d	**1980**	0308	x---	---x	x-x-	----	xx--	2*	
	Naka-dake	**1980**	0924	**1980**	0924	x---	---x	x-x-	----	----	1	
	Naka-dake	**1981**	0615	**1981**	0615	x---	---x	x-x-	----	----	1	

VOLCANO NAME (Subregion) / ERUPTION	— Area of Activity	LAT	LONG	ELEV (m)	POPL (5 km, 10, 30, 100)	ROCK TYPE	VOLC TYPE / Start Year	NUMBER / Start M-Dy	STATUS / Stop Year	Stop M-Dy	Central, Flank vent, Radial fiss, Regional	Submarine, New island, Subglacial, Crater lake	Explosive, Pyro flow, Phreatic, Caldera	Lava flow, Lava lake, Dome, Spine	Fatal, Damage, Mudflow, Tsunami	VEI	Vol L/T
Aso (Kyushu) *continued*	Naka-dake						**1983**	07	**1983**	10	x---	---x	--x-	----	----	1	
	Naka-dake						**1984**	0413c	**1985**	0624	x---	---x	x-x-	----	----	1	
	Naka-dake						**1988**	0526e	**1989**	01	x---	---x	--x-	----	----	1	
	Naka-dake						**1989**	0405	**1991**	0209	x---	---x	xxx-	----	-x--	2*	
	Naka-dake						**1992**	0423	**1993**	0610?	x---	---x	x-x-	----	----	2*	
	Naka-dake						**1994**	0502	**1995**	11	x---	---x	x-x-	----	----	2*	
	Naka-dake						**2003**	0710	**2003**	0714	x---	---x	x-x-	----	----	1	
	Naka-dake						**2004**	0114	**2004**	0114	x---	---x	x-x-	----	----	1	
	Naka-dake						**2005**	0414	**2005**	08	x---	---x	x-x-	----	----	1	
	Naka-dake						**2008**	0217	**2008**	0217	x---	---x	x-x-	----	----	1	
Kuju (Kyushu)		**33.083** N	**131.251** E	**1791**	4567	**ADb**	**Stratovolcanoes**	**0802-12=**	**Historical**								
	(tephra layer A2)						G-**9160***	....	....	....	x---	----	x---	--x-	----	4	8/8
	Sensui-zan						T-**7180***	....	....	....	x---	----	-x-A	--x-	----		8/-
	Tachi-san, Gakurokuji						T-**4490**z	....	....	....	x---	----	----	x---	----		8/-
	Taisen-Hokubu lava dome (tephra layer A1)						G-**3780**z	....	....	....	x---	----	x---	--x-	----	4	8/8
	Iwaigo-dake, Ogigahana, Hizengajo						T-**3110**z	....	....	....	x---	----	----	x-x-	----		8/-
	Danbaru (tephra layer DS)						G-**2440**y	....	....	....	x---	----	x---	x---	----	4	7/8
	Taisen-Minami						T-**1720**y	....	....	....	x---	----	----	x-x-	----		8/-
	Komekubo crater (tephra layer KA)						G-**0990***	....	....	....	x---	----	x---	x---	----	4	-/8
	Komekubo crater (tephra layer KB)						G-**0100**y	....	....	....	x---	----	x---	----	----	4	-/8
	Kuro-dake						G **0370**s	....	....	....	x---	----	xx--	--x-	----	3	**9**/7
							1662	0126?	....	....	x---	----	--x-	----	----	2?	
							1675	06 ?	....	....	----	----	?---	----	----	2?	
							? 1738	*0813*	....	....	----	----	--?-	----	----	*2?*	
	Hosho lava dome (east flank)						**1995**	1011	**1996**	0324	---x	----	x-x-	----	--x-	1	-/5
Tsurumi (Kyushu)		**33.28** N	**131.432** E	**1584**	5667	**AD**	**Lava domes**	**0802-13=**	**Historical**								
	Yufu-dake summit and N flank (Ikeshiro)						C-**0200**t	....	....	....	xx--	----	xx-A	x-x-	----	4	
							0771	....	....	....	x---	----	----	--x-	----	0	
							0867	0304	**0867**	0504m	x---	---?	x---	----	-x--	3	
HONSHU																	
Abu (Honshu)		**34.50** N	**131.60** E	**641**	4467	**ABD**	**Shield volcanoes**	**0803-001**	**Thermoluminescence**								
	Kasa-yama						N-**6850**?	....	....	....	x---	----	x---	----	----		
Sanbe (Honshu)		**35.13** N	**132.62** E	**1126**	4467	**DA**	**Stratovolcano**	**0803-002**	**Radiocarbon**								
							G-**3550**t	....	....	....	x---	----	xx--	----	----		
	Taihei-zan						T-**1920**?	....	....	....	x---	----	xx--	--x-	----	4	**9**/8
							G **0650**t	....	....	....	x---	----	x-?-	----	----		
Oki-Dogo (Honshu-W of)		**36.176** N	**133.334** E	**151**	4556	**B**	**Shield volcano**	**0803-003**	**Anthropology**								
Izu-Tobu (Honshu)		**34.900** N	**139.098** E	**1406**	4568	**BADr**	**Pyroclastic cones**	**0803-01=**	**Historical**								
	Akakubo						T-**8050**?	....	....	....	xx--	----	x---	x---	----	3	6/7
	Omuro-yama						G-**2100**v	....	....	....	xx--	----	x---	x-x-	--x-	4	8/8
	Yoichizaka						T-**2050**?	....	....	....	x---	----	x---	x---	----		6/-
	Kawagodaira						G-**1150**t	....	....	....	x---	----	xx--	x-x-	--x-	4+	8/8
	Iwano-yama, Iyuzan, and other vents						T-**0750**?	....	....	....	x--x	----	x-x-	x-x-	----	3	8/7
	3.6 km NE of Teishi-jima						*? 1930*	*0301*p	....	....	----	?---	----	----	----		
	Teishi-kaikyu (4 km NE of Ito City)						**1989**	0713	**1989**	0713	----	x---	--x-	----	----	1	-/5
Hakone (Honshu)		**35.230** N	**139.024** E	**1438**	5578	**ABD**	**Complex volcano**	**0803-02=**	**Radiocarbon**								
	Kami-yama (Hk-Km5 tephra)						G-**6000**v	....	....	....	x---	----	xx--	----	----	3	-/7
	Futago-yama						G-**3700**v	....	....	....	x---	----	-x--	--x-	----	1	8/5
	NW side of Kami-yama (Kanmuriga-take)						G-**1400**v	....	....	....	x---	----	--xA	----	----		
	NW side of Kami-yama (Kanmuriga-take)						G-**1200**?	....	....	....	x---	----	xxx-	--xx	----	2	8/6
	NE of Kamiyama (Hk-Ow1 tephra)						T-**1050**?	....	....	....	x-x-	----	x-x-	----	--x-		
	NE of Kamiyama (Hk-Ow2 tephra)						T-**0050**?	....	....	....	x-x-	----	xxx-	----	--x-		
	Owakudani (Hk-Ow 3-5 tephras)						G **1170**v	....	....	....	xx--	----	x-x-	----	----		
Fuji (Honshu)		**35.358** N	**138.731** E	**3776**	3468	**Bad**	**Stratovolcano**	**0803-03=**	**Historical**								
	South flank? (Mishima)						C-**8540**>	....	....	....	-x--	----	----	x---	----		9/-
	(tephra layer S-0-1)						C-**7820**x	....	....	....	x---	----	x---	----	----		
	(tephra layer S-0-2)						C-**7530**y	....	....	....	x---	----	x---	----	----		
	(Motomura-yama lava flow)						C-**7310**z	....	....	....	x---	----	----	x---	----		
	(Saruhashi and Shiraito lava flows)						C-**6580**<	....	....	....	x---	----	----	x---	----		
	(tephra layer S-0-3)						C-**6240**y	....	....	....	x---	----	x---	----	----		
	(Nashigahara lava flow)						T-**6050**?	....	....	....	----	----	----	x---	----		
	(tephra layer S-0-4)						C-**5540**x	....	....	....	x---	----	x---	----	----		
	(tephra layer I-7)						C-**5070**x	....	....	....	x---	----	x---	----	----		
	(tephra layer S-0-5)						T-**4730**z	....	....	....	x---	----	x---	----	----		
	(tephra layer S-0-6)						T-**4120**y	....	....	....	x---	----	x---	----	----		
							C-**3690**v	....	....	....	x---	----	x---	----	----		
	(tephra layer S-5)						C-**3050**?	....	....	....	x---	----	x---	----	----		
	(tephra layer S-6)						T-**2800**y	....	....	....	x---	----	x---	----	----		
	(Nihon-Land lava flow)						T-**2550**?	....	....	....	----	----	----	x---	----		
	(tephra layer SNG)						C-**2450**z	....	....	....	x---	----	x---	----	----		
							C-**2050**?	....	....	....	----	----	xx--	----	----		
							C-**1850**w	....	....	....	----	----	xx--	----	----		
	(tephra unit SYP1)						G-**1510**v	....	....	....	x---	----	xx--	----	----		
	(tephra layer S-10)						T-**1450**v	....	....	....	x---	----	x---	----	----		
	(tephra layer Os)						T-**1350**?	....	....	....	x---	----	x---	----	----	**5**	-/9
	(tephra unit SYP2)						G-**1300**w	....	....	....	x---	----	xx--	----	----		
	NW flank (Omuro-yama)						T-**1030**?	....	....	....	-x--	----	x---	x---	----	4+	-/8
	(tephra unit SYP3)						G-**1010**v	....	....	....	x---	----	xx--	----	----		
	Upper SE flank (tephra layer Zu)						C-**0930**>	....	....	....	-x--	----	x---	----	----	**5**	-/9
	(tephra layer SPY4)						G-**0780**z	....	....	....	x---	----	xx--	----	----		
	(tephra layer S-18)						G-**0520**y	....	....	....	x?--	----	x--A	----	----		
	(tephra layer Yu-2)						T-**0190**v	....	....	....	x---	----	x---	----	----		
	South flank						C-**0100**w	....	....	....	-x--	----	x---	x---	----		
	NW flank (Futatsuzuka)						T **0050**?	....	....	....	-x--	----	x---	----	----	2	
	NW flank (Ohira-yama)						T **0100**?	....	....	....	-x--	----	x---	----	----	2	
	NW flank (Sajiki-yama)						T **0200**?	....	....	....	-x--	----	x---	----	----	2	
	NE flank (Hinokimarubi lava flow)						T **0220**?	....	....	....	-x--	----	x---	x---	----	2	
	SE flank (tephra layer S-24-2)						C **0240**w	....	....	....	-x--	----	x?--	----	--?-		
	NW flank (Kita-Koriike)						T **0250**?	....	....	....	-x--	----	x---	----	----	2	
	NW flank (Oniwa-Okuniwa)						T **0300**?	....	....	....	-xx-	----	x---	x---	----	1	

VOLCANO NAME (Subregion) / ERUPTION	Area of Activity	LAT	LONG	ELEV (m)	POPL (5 km, 10, 30, 100)	ROCK TYPE	VOLC TYPE — Start — Year	M-Dy	NUMBER — Stop — Year	STATUS M-Dy	Central / Flank vent / Radial fiss / Regional	Submarine / New island / Subglacial / Crater lake	Explosive / Pyro flow / Phreatic / Caldera	Lava flow / Lava lake / Dome / Spine	Fatal / Damage / Mudflow / Tsunami	VEI	Vol L/T
Fuji (Honshu) *continued*	SE flank (Kurotsuka)						C **0350**y	....	....	....	-x--	----	x---	x---	----	3	
	SSE flank (Obuchi Craters)						C **0370**x	....	....	....	-x--	----	x---	x---	----		
	SE flank (Akatsuka)						T **0400**?	....	....	....	-x--	----	x---	x---	----	2	
	SE flank (Kita-Kansu-yama)						C **0470**v	....	....	....	-x--	----	x---	----	----	3?	
	SE flank (Makuiwa, Nishi-Futatsuzuka)						C **0520**v	....	....	....	-x--	----	x---	x---	----	2	
	South flank (Takabachi)						T **0530**?	....	....	....	-x--	----	x---	x---	----	3	
	NW flank (Kori-ike, Hakudairyuo)						C **0720**v	....	....	....	-x--	----	x---	x---	----	2	
							0781	07	**0781**	07	----	----	x---	----	----	3	
	Summit, NE and NW flanks (Tenjin-yama)						**0800**	0411	**0802**	0206>	xxx-	----	x---	x---	-x--	4	
							0826	1231p	....	....	----	----	?---	----	----	2?	
	NW flank (Koriana)						**0830**	....	....	....	--x-	----	x---	x---	----	2	
	NW flank (Nagao-yama, Kudari-yama)						**0864**	0612?	**0866**	0201p	-xx-	----	x---	x---	-x--	3	**9**/-
							0870	08	....	....	x---	----	x---	----	----	2?	
	North flank (Kenmarubi I)						**0932**	1119	....	....	--x-	----	x---	x---	-x--	2?	
	North flank (Kenmarubi II?)						**0937**	1218	....	....	--x-	----	x---	x---	----	2	
	NE flank						*? 0952*	*03 ?*	....	....	-x--	----	----	----	----		
							? 0993	*0901*p	....	....	----	----	----	----	----		
	South flank ?						**0999**	03	....	....	-x--	----	?---	?---	----	2?	
	North flank						*? 1017*	*1001*p	....	....	-x--	----	----	----	----		
	Summit, SSE flank (Nishi-Asakizuka)						**1033**	0119?	....	....	xx--	----	x---	x---	----	2	
							1083	0417	....	....	----	----	----	----	----	2?	
							? 1427	*0628*	....	....	----	----	?---	----	----		
	North flank (Onagare lava?)						**1435**	1231r	....	....	-x--	----	x---	x---	----	2?	
							1511	0901p	....	....	----	----	----	x---	----	2?	
	(possibly only non-eruptive lahar)						*? 1560*	*0104*	....	....	----	----	----	----	--x-		
	(possibly confused with 1707 eruption)						*? 1627*	....	....	....	----	----	----	----	----		
							1700	....	....	....	----	----	----	----	----	2?	
	SE flank (Hoei Craters)						**1707**	1216	**1708**	0224?	-xx-	----	x---	----	-xx-	**5**	-/9
							? 1708	*12*	*?1709*	*0116*?	----	----	?---	----	----		
	South flank?						*? 1770*	*0916*	....	....	-x--	----	?---	?---	----		
							? 1854	*1223*	*?1855*	*0109*	----	----	----	----	----		
Kita Yatsuga-take (Honshu)		**36.10 N**	**138.30 E**	**2530**	4567	ADB	**Stratovolcanoes**		**0803-031**	**Radiocarbon**							
	Yoko-dake (NYk-2 tephra)						G-**0400**>	....	....	....	x---	----	x---	----	----		
	Yoko-dake (NYk-1 tephra)						G **1200**v	....	....	....	x---	----	x---	x---	----		6/-
On-take (Honshu)		**35.890 N**	**137.48 E**	**3063**	3457	ABDR	**Complex volcano**		**0803-04=**	**Historical**							
							? 0774	....	....	....	----	----	----	----	----		
	200 m SW of Kengamine						**1979**	1028	**1980**	0425	x---	----	xxx-	----	-x--	1	
Haku-san (Honshu)		**36.152 N**	**136.774 E**	**2702**	3357	AD	**Stratovolcano**		**0803-05=**	**Historical**							
	(Hm-1 tephra)						G-**7550**t	....	....	....	x---	----	x-x-	----	----		
	(Hm-3 tephra)						T-**7050**z	....	....	....	x---	----	x-x-	----	----		
	(Hm-4 tephra)						G-**6550**t	....	....	....	x---	----	x-x-	----	----		
	(Hm-5 tephra)						C-**5000**?	....	....	....	x---	----	x-x-	----	----		
	(Hm-7 tephra)						G-**3900**x	....	....	....	x---	----	x-x-	----	----		
	(Hm-8 tephra)						T-**3550**z	....	....	....	x---	----	x-x-	----	----		
	(Hm-9 tephra)						G-**2550**w	....	....	....	x---	----	x-x-	----	----		
	Kengamine (Hm-10 tephra)						G-**0200**?	....	....	....	x---	----	x-x-	x-x-	----	4	8/8
	(Hm-11,12 tephras)						T **0200**?	....	....	....	x---	----	x-x-	----	----		
	(Hm-13 tephra)						G **0500**v	....	....	....	x---	----	x-x-	----	----		
							0706	09 ?	....	....	x---	----	x-x-	----	----		
	(Hm-14 tephra?)						*? 0853*	....	....	....	x---	----	x-?-	----	----		
							? 0859	....	....	....	----	----	?---	----	----		
							? 0884	....	....	....	----	----	----	----	----		
							? 0900?	....	....	....	----	----	?---	----	----		
	Midoriga-ike						**1042**	....	....	....	x---	----	--x-	----	-xx-	3?	
							? 1177	*0518*	....	....	x---	----	?-x-	----	----	*3?*	
							1239?	....	....	....	x---	----	xx--	--x-	----	3	-/7
							1547	0304	**1547**	10 ?	x---	----	x-x-	----	-x--	3	
							1548	....	....	....	x---	----	?-x-	----	----	3?	
	SW of Midoriga-ike						**1554**	05	**1556**	....	x---	----	xxx-	----	-x--	3	
	Jigoku-no-oana						**1579**	0927a	....	....	x---	---x	x-x-	----	-xx-	3	
							1582	....	....	....	x---	----	x---	----	----	2	
	(ashfall attributed to Komaga-take)						*X 1640*	*0802*?	....	....	----	----	----	----	----		
							1658	10 ?	....	....	x---	----	x---	----	----	2?	
	Midoriga-ike						**1659**	0421	**1659**	0808	x---	----	x-x-	----	----	2?	
Norikura (Honshu)		**36.103 N**	**137.557 E**	**3026**	3467	AD	**Stratovolcanoes**		**0803-06=**	**Radiocarbon**							
	Kengamine						G-**7700**w	....	....	....	x---	----	x-x-	----	----	3	-/7
	Ichino-ike (Kuraigahara tephra)						G-**7250**w	....	....	....	x---	----	x-x-	x---	----	3	8/7
							T-**0050**?	....	....	....	x---	----	x-x-	x---	----	3	8/7
Yake-dake (Honshu)		**36.224 N**	**137.590 E**	**2455**	3467	AD	**Stratovolcanoes**		**0803-07=**	**Historical**							
	Akandana-yama						T-**7450**?	....	....	....	----	----	----	x---	----	0	
							T-**2550**?	....	....	....	x---	----	----	x---	----	0	**9**/-
	(Ykd-Tl1 tephra)						T-**0850**?	....	....	....	x---	----	x-x-	----	----		
	(Ykd-Tl2 tephra)						T-**0400**?	....	....	....	x---	----	x-x-	----	----		
							G-**0350**?	....	....	....	x---	----	xxx-	x---	----	4	8/8
	(Ykd-Tu1 tephra)						T **0630**?	....	....	....	x---	----	x-x-	----	----	1	-/5
	(Ykd-Tu2 tephra)						**0686**	....	....	....	x---	----	x-x-	----	----	2	-/6
	(Ykd-Tu3 tephra)						T **1270**?	....	....	....	x---	----	x-x-	----	----		
	(Ykd-Tu4 tephra)						T **1440**?	....	....	....	x---	----	x-x-	----	----		
	(Ykd-Tu5 tephra)						T **1460**?	....	....	....	x---	----	x-x-	----	----	2	-/6
	(Ykd-Tu6 tephra)						**1585**	12 ?	....	....	x?--	----	--x-	----	-xx-	3↑	
	(Ykd-Tu7 tephra)						**1746**	0418	**1746**	0419	x---	----	x-x-	----	----	2	-/6
	Summit crater (Shoga-ike)						**1907**	1208	**1909**	0601	x---	----	x-x-	----	----	2	
	Summit crater (Shoga-ike)						**1910**	1111	**1910**	1130	x---	----	x-x-	----	----	2	
	New summit crater (Inkyo-ko)						**1911**	0506	**1911**	0823?	x---	----	x-x-	----	----	2	
							1912	0211	**1912**	09 ?	x---	----	x-x-	----	----	2	
	Inkyo-ko						**1913**	0901?	**1914**	0113	x---	----	x-x-	----	----	2	
							1915	02	**1915**	02	x---	----	x---	----	----	2?	
	1911 summit crater, SE flank (Taisho)						**1915**	0606	**1915**	0716	x-x-	----	x-x-	----	-xx-	2	-/6
	Taisho Crater, Inkyo-ko						**1916**	0317	**1916**	0412?	x-x-	----	x-x-	----	----	2	
	Taisho Crater						**1917**	....	....	....	--x-	----	--x-	----	----	1	
	Taisho crater						**1918**	....	....	....	--x-	----	--x-	----	----	1	
	NW flank (Kurodani Crater)						**1919**	1101	**1919**	1101	-x--	----	--x-	----	----	2	
							1920	....	....	....	----	----	--x-	----	----		

VOLCANO NAME (Subregion)	ERUPTION — Area of Activity	LAT	LONG	ELEV (m)	POPL (5 km, 10, 30, 100)	ROCK TYPE	VOLC TYPE	NUMBER	STATUS	Start Year	Start M-Dy	Stop Year	Stop M-Dy	Central / Flank vent / Radial fiss / Regional	Submarine / New island / Subglacial / Crater lake	Explosive / Pyro flow / Phreatic / Caldera	Lava flow / Lava lake / Dome / Spine	Fatal / Damage / Mudflow / Tsunami	VEI	Vol L/T
Yake-dake (Honshu) *continued*										**1921**	....	....	....	----	----	--x-	----	----		
	NW flank (Kurodani Crater), Inkyo-ko									**1922**	0310	**1922**	0319	xx--	----	x-x-	----	----	1?	
	NW flank (Kurodani Crater), Inkyo-ko									**1923**	0626	**1923**	0802	xx--	----	x-x-	----	----	2	
	Summit (Inkyo-ko), NW flank (Kurodani)									**1924**	1116	**1926**	0127	xx--	----	x-x-	----	----	2	
	Summit (Inkyo-ko), NW flank (Kurodani)									**1927**	0123	**1927**	0429	xx--	----	x-x-	----	----	2	
	Summit (Inkyo-ko), NW flank (Kurodani)									**1927**	1215	**1927**	1215	xx--	----	x-x-	----	----	2	
	Summit (Inkyo-ko), NW flank (Kurodani)									**1929**	0417	**1929**	0419	xx--	----	x-x-	----	----	2	
	Inkyo-ko									**1930**	0313	**1930**	0511?	x---	----	--x-	----	----	2	
										1931	0326	**1931**	0624	----	----	x-x-	----	-x--	2	
										1932	0206	**1932**	0206	----	----	x-x-	----	----	2	
										1935	0911	**1935**	1112	----	----	x-x-	----	----	2	
										1939	0604	**1939**	0604	----	----	x-x-	----	----	2	
	North flank (Kurodani and Nakao-toge)									**1962**	0617	**1963**	0629	--x-	----	x-x-	----	-xx-	2	-/6
	SE flank (Azusa-gawa)									**1995**	0211	**1995**	0211	-x--	----	--x-	----	xx--	1	-/3
Washiba-Kumonotaira (Honshu)		**36.408 N**	**137.594 E**	**2924**	2367	**ADB**	**Shield volcanoes**	**0803-071**	**Holocene**											
Tate-yama (Honshu)		**36.568 N**	**137.593 E**	**2621**	3367	**AD**	**Stratovolcano**	**0803-08=**	**Historical**											
	Jigoku-dani									T-**7300***	....	....	....	x---	----	x-x-	----	----		
	Jigoku-dani									T-**3200***	....	....	....	x---	----	x-x-	----	----		
	Jigoku-dani									T-**0900**?	....	....	....	x---	----	--x-	----	----		
										? 0704	....	....	....	----	----	----	----	----		
	Jigoku-dani									**1836**	0709	....	....	x---	----	--x-	----	----	1	-/5
	Jigoku-dani									**1839**	0610	....	....	x---	----	x-x-	----	----	2	
	(landslide, lahars; no eruption)									*X 1858*	*0408*	....	....	----	----	--?-	----	x-x-		
Niigata-Yake-yama (Honshu)		**36.918 N**	**138.039 E**	**2400**	2367	**AD**	**Lava dome**	**0803-09=**	**Historical**											
	(Koyaike Ash; tephra layer KG-e)									T-**1900***	....	....	....	?---	----	xx--	x-x-	--x-		
										G-**1750**?	....	....	....	?---	----	xx--	x---	--x-		
	(Koyaike Ash; tephra layer KG-d)									G-**0700**v	....	....	....	?---	----	xx--	----	----	3	
										0813?	....	....	....	?---	----	xxx-	x---	----		
	(Koyaike Ash; tephra layer KG-c)									**0887**	....	....	....	x---	----	xx--	x---	-xx-	4	-/8
	(Koyaike Ash; tephra layer KG-c?)									**0989**	....	....	....	x---	----	x?--	----	----		
	(Koyaike Ash; tephra layer KG-b)									**1361**	....	....	....	x---	----	xx--	x-x-	-xx-	3	8/7
	(Koyaike Ash; tephra layer KG-a)									**1773**	....	....	....	x---	----	xx--	----	-xx-	3	-/7
	NW flank									**1852**	1101	**1853**	05 ?	-x--	----	x-x-	----	----	2	
	NW flank									**1854**	....	....	....	-x--	----	--?-	----	----		
	NE-SW fissures, both sides of summit									**1949**	0205	**1949**	0913	--x-	----	x-x-	----	--x-	2	
										1962	0314	**1962**	0314	x---	----	x-x-	----	----	1	
										1963	0214	....	....	----	----	--x-	----	----	1	
										1963	0710	**1963**	0930	--x-	----	--x-	----	----	1	
	WNW and NNE side of lava dome									**1974**	0728	**1974**	0728	--x-	----	xxx-	----	xxx-	2	-/5
										1983	0414?	**1983**	0415?	x---	----	x-x-	----	----	1	
										1987	0425e	....	....	----	----	x-?-	----	----	1	
	Upper East flank									**1989**	0419	**1989**	0426	-x--	----	x-x-	----	----	1	
	Upper east flank									**1997**	1029	**1997**	1210	-x--	----	x-x-	----	----	1	
	Upper east flank									**1998**	0330	....	....	-x--	----	x-x-	----	----	1	
Myoko (Honshu)		**36.888 N**	**138.12 E**	**2446**	4567	**ADB**	**Stratovolcano**	**0803-10=**	**Radiocarbon**											
	(Akakura Ash; AK-a tephra)									G-**4750**y	....	....	....	x---	----	xxx-	?---	----	**5?**	-/9
										T-**4300**?	....	....	....	x---	----	x---	x---	----		
										T-**4000**?	....	....	....	x---	----	x-x-	----	----		
										T-**3700**?	....	....	....	x---	----	xx--	----	----		
										T-**3450**?	....	....	....	x---	----	xx--	----	----		
										T-**2900**?	....	....	....	x---	----	x-x-	----	----		
	(Otagirigawa Ash; OT-a tephra)									G-**2750**v	....	....	....	x---	----	xxx-	----	----	4	-/8
										T-**2100**z	....	....	....	----	----	x-x-	----	----		
										T-**1200**?	....	....	....	x---	----	-xx-	----	----		
										T-**0750**	....	....	....	x---	----	-xx-	----	----		
Asama (Honshu)		**36.403 N**	**138.526 E**	**2568**	3567	**AD**	**Complex volcano**	**0803-11=**	**Historical**											
										G-**7200**x	....	....	....	x---	----	x---	----	----		
										T-**6400***	....	....	....	x---	----	x---	----	----		
	(AM-10 tephra)									T-**4700**z	....	....	....	x---	----	x---	----	----		
										G-**4200**v	....	....	....	x---	----	xx--	----	----		
	(As-E tephra)									C-**3450**?	....	....	....	x---	----	x---	----	----	3	
	(As-D tephra layers)									A-**2550**z	....	....	....	x---	----	x---	----	----	4	
										T-**1130***	....	....	....	x---	----	x---	----	----		
	(As-C tephra)									A **0350**j	1115m	....	....	x---	----	xx--	x---	-x--	4	8/8
										@ **0685**	04	....	....	x---	----	x---	----	----	3	
	(eruption from Niigata-Yake-yama)									*X 0887*	....	....	....	x---	----	?---	----	----		
										1108	0829	**1108**	10	x---	----	xx--	x---	----	**5**	8/9
										? 1128	....	....	....	x---	----	x---	----	----		
										? 1281	*0703*	....	....	x---	----	xx--	----	----	*3*	
										? 1427	*0707*	....	....	x---	----	?---	----	----		
										? 1518	....	....	....	x---	----	?---	----	----		
										1527	05	....	....	x---	----	x---	----	----	2	
										1528	....	....	....	x---	----	x---	----	----	2	
										? 1532	*0114*	....	....	x---	----	?---	----	-??-		-/6
										? 1534	....	....	....	x---	----	----	----	----		
										1582	0216	....	....	x---	----	x---	----	----	2	
										1582	0703	....	....	x---	----	x---	----	----	2	
										1590	0415q	....	....	x---	----	x---	----	----	2?	
										1591	0415q	....	....	x---	----	x---	----	----	2?	
										1591	1129	....	....	x---	----	x---	----	----	3?	
										1595	0601	....	....	x---	----	?---	----	----	2?	
										1596	0501	**1596**	09	x---	----	x---	----	x---	3	-/7
										1597	0417	....	....	x---	----	x---	----	----	2	
										1598	0513	....	....	x---	----	x---	----	x---	2	
										1600	0114	**1600**	0128?	x---	----	x---	----	----	3?	
										? 1604	....	....	....	x---	----	?---	----	----	*2*	
										1605	12	**1606**	02	x---	----	x---	----	----	2	
										1609	0405	....	....	x---	----	x---	----	----	2	
										1644	0220	....	....	x---	----	x---	----	----	2	
										1645	0224?	**1645**	0521	x---	----	x---	----	----	2	
										1647	0218	**1647**	0325	x---	----	x---	----	----	2	
										1648	0320?	....	....	x---	----	x---	----	--x-	2	
										1648	0830?	....	....	x---	----	x---	----	----	2	

VOLCANO NAME (Subregion) / ERUPTION — Area of Activity	LAT	LONG	ELEV (m)	POPL (5 km, 10, 30, 100)	ROCK TYPE	VOLC TYPE		Start Year	Start M-Dy	Stop Year	Stop M-Dy	Central / Flank vent / Radial fiss / Regional	Submarine / New island / Subglacial / Crater lake	Explosive / Pyro flow / Phreatic / Caldera	Lava flow / Lava lake / Dome / Spine	Fatal / Damage / Mudflow / Tsunami	VEI	Vol L/T
Asama (Honshu) *continued*								1649	0817?	1649	0818?	x---	----	x---	----	----	2	
							?	*1650*	*0702*?	....	....	x---	----	?---	----	----	*2?*	
								1651	0412	....	....	x---	----	x---	----	----	2	
								1652	0412	....	....	x---	----	x---	----	----	2	
							?	*1653*	....	?*1654*	....	x---	----	?---	----	----	*2?*	
								1655	1125	....	....	x---	----	x---	----	----	2	
								1656	1210	....	....	x---	----	x---	----	----	2	
								1657	1125	....	....	x---	----	x---	----	----	2	
								1658	0724	....	....	x---	----	x---	----	----	2	
								1659	0724	....	....	x---	----	x---	----	----	2	
								1660	0408?	....	....	x---	----	x---	----	----	2	
								1661	0414	1661	0427	x---	----	x---	----	----	2	
								1661	1021	....	....	x---	----	x---	----	----	2	
								1669	0405	1669	0415	x---	----	x---	----	----	2	
								1695	0623	....	....	x---	----	x---	----	----	2	
								1703	....	....	....	x---	----	x---	----	----	2	
								1704	0205	1704	0209	x---	----	x---	----	----	2	
								1706	1120	....	....	x---	----	x---	----	----	2	
								1708	1229	1709	0108	x---	----	x---	----	----	2	
								1710	0325	1710	0413	x---	----	x---	----	----	2	
								1711	0413	....	....	x---	----	x---	----	----	2	
								1713	0629	....	....	x---	----	x---	----	----	2	
								1717	0923	....	....	x---	----	x---	----	----	2	
								1718	0926	....	....	x---	----	x---	----	----	2	
							@	1719	0610	@1719	0611	----	----	x---	----	----		
								1720	0606	....	....	x---	----	x---	----	----	2	
								1721	0622	....	....	x---	----	x---	----	x---	1	-/5
								1722	1118	1723	0205	x---	----	x---	----	----	2	
								1723	0820	....	....	x---	----	x---	----	----	2	
								1728	1110	....	....	x---	----	x---	----	----	2	
								1729	02	....	....	x---	----	x---	----	----	2	
								1729	11	1729	12	x---	----	x---	----	----	2	
								1731	....	....	....	x---	----	x---	----	----	2	
								1732	0730	....	....	x---	----	x---	----	----	2	
								1733	0730	....	....	x---	----	x---	----	----	2	
								1752	09	1752	10	x---	----	?---	----	----	2?	
								1754	0807	1754	0819	x---	----	x---	----	----	2	
								1755	0705	1755	0806	x---	----	x---	----	----	2	
								1762	04	....	....	x---	----	x---	----	----	2	
							@	1769	0806	....	....	----	----	x---	----	----		
								1776	0905	....	....	x---	----	x---	----	----	2	
								1777	....	....	....	x---	----	x---	----	----	2	
							?	*1779*	*09* ?	....	....	----	----	x---	----	----		
								1783	0509	1783	0805	x---	----	xx--	x---	xxx-	4*	8/8
								1803	0704	....	....	x---	----	x---	----	?---	2	
								1803	1107	1803	1121	x---	----	x---	----	?---	2	
								1815	0228	....	....	x---	----	x---	----	----	3	
								1869	05	1869	1023	x---	----	x---	----	----	2	
								1875	0614	....	....	x---	----	x---	----	----	2	
							?	*1878*	....	....	....	x---	----	x---	----	----	*2*	
								1879	0927	1879	0928	x---	----	x---	----	----	2	
								1889	1224	....	....	x---	----	x---	----	----	2	
								1891	10 ?	1891	11 ?	x---	----	?---	----	----		
							?	*1892*	....	....	....	x---	----	?---	----	----		
								1894	0406	1894	0614	x---	----	x---	----	----	2	
								1899	0311	....	....	x---	----	x---	----	----	2	
								1899	0710	1899	0807	x---	----	x---	----	----	2	
								1900	0122	1901	10	x---	----	x---	----	----	2	
								1902	0207	1902	0207	x---	----	x---	----	----	2	
								1902	0805	1902	0820?	x---	----	x---	----	----	2	
							?	*1903*	*0528*	?*1903*	*0630*	x---	----	?---	----	----	*2*	
								1904	0804	1904	0804	x---	----	x---	----	----	2	
							?	*1905*	....	....	....	----	----	?---	----	----		
								1906	0406	1906	0406	x---	----	x---	----	----	2	
								1907	0118	1907	0328	x---	----	x---	----	----	2	
								1907	0824	1907	0824	x---	----	x---	----	----	2	
								1908	0213?	1908	0219	x---	----	x---	----	----	2	
								1908	0805	1908	0923	x---	----	x---	----	----	2	
								1909	0129	1914	0624	x---	----	x---	----	xx--	1	-/5
								1914	1112	1914	1216	x---	----	x---	----	----	2	
								1915	0513?	1915	0827	x---	----	x---	----	----	1	
								1916	0512?	1916	1002	x---	----	x---	----	----	1	
								1917	0503?	1917	0731?	x---	----	x---	----	----	1	
							?	*1918*	....	....	....	?---	----	?---	----	----		
								1919	0314	1919	0827?	x---	----	x---	----	----	2	
								1920	1206	1922	0405	x---	----	x---	----	----	2	
								1924	0907	1924	0929	x---	----	x---	----	----	2	
								1927	03 ?	1928	0725	x---	----	x---	----	----	2	
								1929	0122	1929	0405	x---	----	x---	----	----	2	
								1929	0918	1929	1115	x---	----	x---	----	----	2	
								1930	0418	1930	1017	x---	----	x---	----	x---	2	
								1931	0331	1932	0921	x---	----	x---	----	xx--	3*	
								1933	0109	1933	0803	x---	----	x---	----	----	2	
								1934	0109	1934	0211	x---	----	x---	----	----	1	
								1934	06	1934	06	x---	----	x---	----	----	1	
								1934	1113	1937	07	x---	----	x?--	----	xx--	3*	
								1938	0325	1942	12	x---	----	x---	----	x---	1	-/5
								1944	01 ?	1945	11	x---	----	x---	----	----	2	
								1946	1029	1946	1030	x---	----	x---	----	----	2	
E corner of crater bottom								1947	06	1947	0814	x---	----	x---	----	xx--	1	-/5
								1949	0310	1949	1024	x---	----	x---	----	----	2	
								1950	0923	1951	0617	x---	----	x---	----	xx--	1	-/5
							?	*1952*	*01*	?*1952*	*01*	x---	----	?---	----	----	*1?*	
								1952	0607	1952	0614	x---	----	x---	----	----	2	

Richard Fiske (Smithsonian)

Temple on 1783 lava flow

VOLCANO NAME (Subregion) / ERUPTION	Area of Activity	LAT	LONG	ELEV (m)	POPL (5 km, 10, 30, 100)	ROCK TYPE	VOLC TYPE	NUMBER	STATUS	Start Year	Start M-Dy	Stop Year	Stop M-Dy	Central / Flank vent / Radial fiss / Regional	Submarine / New island / Subglacial / Crater lake	Explosive / Pyro flow / Phreatic / Caldera	Lava flow / Lava lake / Dome / Spine	Fatal / Damage / Mudflow / Tsunami	VEI	Vol L/T
Asama (Honshu) *continued*										**1953**	1227	**1955**	0802	x---	----	x---	----	----	3*	
	(no eruption in December 1955)									X *1955*	*12*	....	....	----	----	----	----	----		
										1958	1003	**1959**	0826e	x---	----	xx--	----	-x--	2*	-/5
										1961	0818	**1961**	1116	x---	----	xx--	----	xx--	2	-/4
										1965	0523	**1965**	0523	x---	----	x-x-	----	----	2	
										1973	0201	**1973**	0524	x---	----	xx--	----	----	2	
										1982	0426	**1982**	0426	x---	----	xxx-	----	-xx-	2	
										1982	1002	**1982**	1002	x---	----	x---	----	----	1	
										1983	0408	**1983**	0408	x---	----	x---	----	----	2	
										1990	0720	**1990**	0720	x---	----	x---	----	----	2	-/3
										2003	0206	**2003**	0418	x---	----	x---	----	----	1	-/2
										2004	0901	**2004**	1209	x---	----	x---	--x-	----	2	6/5
										2008	0810	**2008**	0814	x---	----	x-x-	----	----	1	
										2009	0121	**2009**	0502	x---	----	x---	----	----	2*	
Kusatsu-Shirane (Honshu)		**36.620 N**	**138.535 E**	**2171**	4567	**AD**	**Stratovolcanoes**	**0803-12=**	**Historical**											
	Shirane									G-**6550**?	....	....	....	x---	----	x---	x---	----	3	7/7
										C-**6270**x	....	....	....	----	----	x-x-	----	----		
	Shirane									G-**3750**?	....	....	....	x---	----	x-x-	----	----	2	-/6
	Moto-Shirane									C-**1120**w	....	....	....	x---	----	x-x-	x---	----	4	8/8
	Yu-gama (tephra layer 13D)									T-**0550**?	....	....	....	x---	----	x---	----	----	3	-/7
	Yu-gama (tephra layer 13.7D)									T **0050**?	....	....	....	x---	----	x---	----	----	2	-/6
										C **1470**w	....	....	....	----	----	x-x-	----	----		
	Yu-gama									**1805**	....	....	....	x---	----	x-x-	----	----	2	
	Yu-gama, NE end of Kara-gama									**1882**	0806	**1882**	0816>	x---	---x	x-x-	----	--x-	2	-/6
	NE part of Yu-gama									**1897**	0708	**1897**	0816	x---	---x	x-x-	----	----	2	
	NE part of Yu-gama									**1900**	1001	**1900**	1001	x---	----	--x-	----	----	1	
	North side of Yumi-ike									**1902**	0715	**1902**	0924	x---	----	x-x-	----	----	1	-/5
										? *1903*	....	....	....	----	----	----	----	----		
	Yu-gama									**1905**	10	**1905**	10	x---	---x	--x-	----	----	2	
	Northern part of Yu-gama									**1925**	0122?	**1925**	0130	x---	----	x-x-	----	----	2	-/6
	N Yu-gama & S outer rim (in 1927, not 1928)									**1927**	1229	**1927**	1231	x---	----	x-x-	----	----	2	
	NE part of Yu-gama, SE outer rim									**1932**	1001	**1932**	11	x---	----	--x-	----	xxx-	3*	-/4
										? *1933*	....	....	....	----	----	----	----	----		
										1934	....	....	....	x---	----	x-x-	----	----	2	
	Yu-gama									**1937**	1127	**1938**	0216?	x---	----	x-x-	----	----	1	
	Yu-gama									**1938**	0717?	**1938**	1005?	x---	----	--x-	----	----	1	
	Yu-gama									**1939**	02 ?	**1939**	0828?	x---	----	x-x-	----	----	1	
										1940	0407	**1940**	0913	x---	----	--x-	----	----	1?	
										1941	0119	**1941**	0119	x---	----	--x-	----	----	1?	
	Fissure east and south of Yu-gama									**1942**	0202	....	....	x---	----	x-x-	----	----	1	
	Yu-gama									**1958**	1231y	....	....	x---	----	x-x-	----	----	1	
	NE corner of Mizu-gama Crater									**1976**	0302	**1976**	0302	x---	----	x-x-	----	----	1	-/4
	Kara-gama, Yu-gama									**1982**	1026	**1982**	1229	x---	---x	x-x-	----	----	1	-/4
	Yu-gama, Kara-gama									**1983**	0726	**1983**	1221	x---	----	x-x-	----	----	1	
	NW part of Yu-gama									? *1989*	*0106*	?*1989*	*0106*	x---	---x	x-x-	----	----	*1*	
Shiga (Honshu)		**36.688 N**	**138.519 E**	**2041**	4467	**A**	**Shield volcanoes**	**0803-121**	Holocene?											
Haruna (Honshu)		**36.474 N**	**138.881 E**	**1449**	4578	**ADB**	**Stratovolcano**	**0803-122**	**Anthropology**											
	Futatsu-dake									T **0450**t	....	....	....	x---	----	x---	----	----	3	-/7
	Futatsu-dake									A **0520**j	0601p	....	....	x---	----	xx--	----	-xx-	4+	-/8
	Futatsu-dake									A **0550**j	0601p	....	....	x---	----	xx--	--x-	-xx-	**5**	8/9
Akagi (Honshu)		**36.557 N**	**139.196 E**	**1828**	3478	**Ad**	**Stratovolcano**	**0803-13=**	Holocene?											
										? *1251*	*0518*	....	....	----	----	----	----	----	*3?*	
										? *1938*	*0716<*	....	....	----	----	----	----	----		
Hiuchi (Honshu)		**36.952 N**	**139.289 E**	**2356**	3357	**AD**	**Stratovolcano**	**0803-131**	**Historical**											
	Akanagure lava dome									T-**6050**?	....	....	....	x---	----	x---	x-x-	----		
	Miike-dake lava dome									**1544**	0728	....	....	x---	----	x-x-	----	--x-	2	-/6
Nikko-Shirane (Honshu)		**36.796 N**	**139.379 E**	**2578**	3457	**A**	**Shield volcano**	**0803-14=**	**Historical**											
	(Nks-4 tephra)									G-**4150**x	....	....	....	----	----	x-x-	----	----		
	(Nks-3 tephra)									T-**2000**?	....	....	....	----	----	x-x-	----	----		
	(Nks-2 tephra)									T-**0400**?	....	....	....	x---	----	x---	----	----		
	(Nks-1 tephra)									T **0800**?	....	....	....	----	----	x-x-	----	----		
	Shirane-san									**1625**	....	....	....	----	----	--?-	----	----	3	
	Shirane-san									**1649**	02	....	....	x---	----	x-x-	----	----	2	-/6
	Shirane-san									? *1871*	*04*	....	....	----	----	----	----	----		
	Shirane-san (SW flank)									**1872**	0514	....	....	-x--	----	--x-	----	----	2	
	Shirane-san									**1873**	0312	....	....	----	----	x-x-	----	----	1	
	Shirane-san (west flank)									**1889**	1204	....	....	-x--	----	x-x-	----	----	1	
	Shirane-san									**1890**	0822	....	....	----	----	--x-	----	----	1	
	Shirane-san									**1952**	07	**1952**	09	----	----	x-x-	----	----	2	
Nantai (Honshu)		**36.762 N**	**139.494 E**	**2486**	3568	**ADB**	**Stratovolcano**	**0803-141**	**Radiocarbon**											
	(Bentengawara pyroclastic-flow deposit)									G-**9540**z	....	....	....	x---	----	xx--	----	----		
Omanago Group (Honshu)		**36.792 N**	**139.510 E**	**2367**	3568	**DA**	**Lava domes**	**0803-142**	**Radiocarbon**											
	Mitsu-dake									C-**3050**?	....	....	....	x---	----	----	--x-	----		
Takahara (Honshu)		**36.897 N**	**139.780 E**	**1795**	3467	**ABD**	**Stratovolcano**	**0803-143**	**Holocene**											
	Fuji-san lava dome (Tk-Ue tephra)									G-**4570**?	....	....	....	--x-	----	x-x-	--x-	----	4?	8/7
Nasu (Honshu)		**37.122 N**	**139.966 E**	**1915**	3467	**ABD**	**Stratovolcanoes**	**0803-15=**	**Historical**											
	Chausu-dake									T-**8550***	....	....	....	x---	----	--x-	----	----	2?	
	Chausu-dake (CH3 tephra)									G-**7850**?	....	....	....	x---	----	xxx-	x---	----	3	7/7
	Chausu-dake									T-**6050***	....	....	....	x---	----	--x-	----	----	2?	
	Chausu-dake (CH4 tephra)									G-**5550**z	....	....	....	x---	----	xxx-	x---	----	3	7/7
	Chausu-dake									T-**4350***	....	....	....	x---	----	--x-	----	----	2?	
	Chausu-dake									T-**2000***	....	....	....	x---	----	--x-	----	----	2?	
	Chausu-dake									T-**1440**z	....	....	....	x---	----	--x-	----	----	2?	
	Chausu-dake (CH5 tephra)									G-**0700**x	....	....	....	x---	----	x-x-	----	----	3	-/7
	Chausu-dake (Ns-12 to 9 tephras)									T-**0250**?	....	....	....	x---	----	--x-	----	----	2?	
	Chausu-dake (Ns-8 tephra)									G **0250**x	....	....	....	x---	----	x-x-	----	----	3	-/7
	Chausu-dake (Ns-7 to 5 tephras)									G **0330**x	....	....	....	x---	----	x-x-	----	----	2	
	Chausu-dake									**1397**	0217	....	....	x---	----	x-x-	----	-x--	3	
	Chausu-dake									**1404**	0211	....	....	x---	----	x-x-	----	----	3	
	Chausu-dake (CH6 tephra)									**1408**	0224	....	....	x---	----	x-x-	----	--x-	3	
	Chausu-dake									**1410**	0305	....	....	x---	----	xx--	x---	xxx-	3	6/7
	Chausu-dake									**1846**	08	....	....	x---	----	?-x-	----	----	1	-/5

VOLCANO NAME (Subregion) · LAT · LONG · ELEV (m) · POPL (5 km, 10, 30, 100) · ROCK TYPE · VOLC TYPE · NUMBER · STATUS

Nasu (Honshu) *continued*

ERUPTION — Area of Activity	Start Year	Start M-Dy	Stop Year	Stop M-Dy	Central / Flank vent / Radial fiss / Regional	Submarine / New island / Subglacial / Crater lake	Explosive / Pyro flow / Phreatic / Caldera	Lava flow / Lava lake / Dome / Spine	Fatal / Damage / Mudflow / Tsunami	VEI	Vol L/T
Chausu-dake (west and NW side of summit)	**1881**	0701	....	....	x---	----	x-x-	----	-x--	1?	-/5
Chausu-dake (1881 crater)	**1953**	1024	**1953**	1029	x---	----	x-x-	----	----	1	
Chausu-dake (50 m north of 1953 vent)	**1960**	1010?	....	....	x---	----	x-x-	----	----	1	
Chausu-dake	? *1963*	*0710*	?*1963*	*0711*	x---	----	--?-	----	----	*1*	
Chausu-dake (west side)	**1963**	1120	**1963**	1121	x---	----	x-x-	----	----	1	

Numazawa (Honshu) — **37.450N 139.579E 1100** 3467 **DRA Shield volcano 0803-151 Radiocarbon**

ERUPTION — Area of Activity	Start Year	Start M-Dy	Stop Year	Stop M-Dy	Central / Flank vent / Radial fiss / Regional	Submarine / New island / Subglacial / Crater lake	Explosive / Pyro flow / Phreatic / Caldera	Lava flow / Lava lake / Dome / Spine	Fatal / Damage / Mudflow / Tsunami	VEI	Vol L/T
(formation of Numazawako caldera)	G-**3400**?	....	....	....	x---	----	xxxx	----	--x-	**5**	-/9

Bandai (Honshu) — **37.598N 140.076E 1819** 4567 **A Stratovolcano 0803-16= Historical**

ERUPTION — Area of Activity	Start Year	Start M-Dy	Stop Year	Stop M-Dy	Central / Flank vent / Radial fiss / Regional	Submarine / New island / Subglacial / Crater lake	Explosive / Pyro flow / Phreatic / Caldera	Lava flow / Lava lake / Dome / Spine	Fatal / Damage / Mudflow / Tsunami	VEI	Vol L/T
(HA-2.01 tephra layer)	T-**7450**?	....	....	....	----	----	x---	----	----		
(HA-1.8 tephra layer)	T-**6350**?	....	....	....	----	----	x-x-	----	----		
(HA-1.7 tephra layer)	T-**5050**?	....	....	....	----	----	x-x-	----	----		
(HA-1.6 tephra layer)	T-**4650**?	....	....	....	----	----	x-x-	----	----		
(HA-1.5 tephra layer)	T-**3850**?	....	....	....	----	----	x-x-	----	----		
Numanotaira (RE4 tephra layer)	T-**1800***	....	....	....	x---	----	x-x-	----	----		
Numanotaira (RE3 tephra layer)	T-**0550**?	....	....	....	x---	----	x-xA	----	----		
O-Bandai (RE2 tephra layer)	**0806**	....	....	....	x---	----	x-x-	----	--?-	3	
	? *1611*	....	....	....	x---	----	--?-	----	--x-		
	? *1719*<	....	....	....	x---	----	----	----	----		
Mt. Hanzawa (Bandai foothills)	? *1767*n	....	....	....	-x--	----	--?-	----	--?-		
	1787<	....	....	....	x---	----	--?-	----	----	2?	
Numanotaira	**1808**?	....	....	....	x---	----	--?-	----	--x-	2	
Kobandai (RE1 tephra layer)	**1888**	0715	**1888**	0715	x---	----	xxxA	----	xxx-	4	-/8

Adatara (Honshu) — **37.644N 140.286E 1718** 3467 **Adb Stratovolcanoes 0803-17= Historical**

ERUPTION — Area of Activity	Start Year	Start M-Dy	Stop Year	Stop M-Dy	Central / Flank vent / Radial fiss / Regional	Submarine / New island / Subglacial / Crater lake	Explosive / Pyro flow / Phreatic / Caldera	Lava flow / Lava lake / Dome / Spine	Fatal / Damage / Mudflow / Tsunami	VEI	Vol L/T
Numanotaira (Ad-NT1 tephra)	T-**8050**?	....	....	....	x---	----	x---	----	----	3	-/7
Numanotaira (Ad-NT2 tephra)	G-**6650**v	....	....	....	x---	----	x---	----	----	3	-/7
Numanotaira (Ad-NT3 tephra)	G-**6150**v	....	....	....	x---	----	x---	----	----	3	-/7
Numanotaira (Ad-NT4 tephra)	T-**4300***	....	....	....	x---	----	x---	----	----	3	-/7
Numanotaira (Ad-NT5 tephra)	G-**2600**t	....	....	....	x---	----	x-x-	----	----	3	-/7
Numanotaira (Ad-p1, p2 tephras)	T-**1550***	....	....	....	x---	----	x-x-	----	----		
Numanotaira (Ad-NT6 tephra)	G-**0590**x	....	....	....	x---	----	--x-	----	--x-	3	-/7
Numanotaira (Ad-p3 tephra)	T-**0050***	....	....	....	x---	----	x-x-	----	----		
Numanotaira (Ad-p4 tephra)	T **0950**t	....	....	....	x---	----	x-x-	----	----		
Numanotaira	? *1813*	*0110*	....	....	x---	----	--?-	----	----	*1?*	
Numanotaira	**1899**	0824	**1899**	1112	x---	----	x-x-	----	-x--	2	
Numanotaira	**1900**	0717	**1900**	0717	x---	----	xxx-	----	xx--	2	-/6
Numanotaira	**1996**	0901	**1996**	0901	x---	----	--x-	----	----	1	

Azuma (Honshu) — **37.732N 140.248E 2035** 3367 **AB Stratovolcanoes 0803-18= Historical**

ERUPTION — Area of Activity	Start Year	Start M-Dy	Stop Year	Stop M-Dy	Central / Flank vent / Radial fiss / Regional	Submarine / New island / Subglacial / Crater lake	Explosive / Pyro flow / Phreatic / Caldera	Lava flow / Lava lake / Dome / Spine	Fatal / Damage / Mudflow / Tsunami	VEI	Vol L/T
Oke-numa (Az-OK tephra)	G-**5700**t	....	....	....	x---	----	x---	----	----	2	-/6
Goshiki-numa (Az-GS tephra)	G-**5400**x	....	....	....	x---	----	x-x-	----	----	1	-/5
Issaikyo-Minami (Az-JP1 tephra)	T-**4550***	....	....	....	-x--	----	x-x-	----	----		
Azuma Ko-Fuji (Az-KF tephra)	G-**4150**z	....	....	....	x---	----	x---	x---	----	3	8/7
Issaikyo (Az-IS tephra)	G-**3000**t	....	....	....	x---	----	x---	----	----	1	-/5
Issaikyo (Az-JP2 tephra)	G-**2750**x	....	....	....	x---	----	x-x-	----	----		
Issaikyo (Az-JP3 tephra)	G-**1800**t	....	....	....	x---	----	x-x-	----	----		
Issaikyo (Az-JP4 tephra)	G-**0950**v	....	....	....	x---	----	x-x-	----	----		
Issaikyo (Az-JP5 tephra)	G-**0150**x	....	....	....	x---	----	x-x-	----	----		
(Az-JP6 tephra)	G **0600**x	....	....	....	-x--	----	x-x-	----	----		
Issaikyo (Az-OA tephra)	**1331**	....	....	....	-x--	----	x-x-	----	----	1	-/5
Issaikyo (Oana area)	**1711**?	....	....	....	-x--	----	x-x-	----	----	1	-/5
Issaikyo (Oana)	**1800**?	....	....	....	-x--	----	--?-	----	----		
Issaikyo (Oana)	? *1844*	....	....	....	-x--	----	--x-	----	----	*1?*	
Issaikyo (west of Oana)	**1893**	0519	**1893**	0713	-x--	----	x-x-	----	x---	1	
Issaikyo	**1893**	1109	**1893**	1110	-x--	----	x---	----	----	1	
Issaikyo (near Oana)	**1894**	0316	**1894**	0412	-x--	----	x-x-	----	----	1	
Issaikyo (near Oana)	**1895**	0308	**1895**	0913	-x--	----	x-x-	----	-x--	1	
(dates may be confused with Sept 1895)	? *1896*	*0905*	?*1896*	*0919*	-x--	----	?-?-	----	----	*1*	
Issaikyo	? *1914*	*1112*	?*1914*	*1114*a	----	----	--?-	----	----	*1*	
Issaikyo (Oana and NW of Oana)	**1950**	0210	**1950**	0219	-x--	----	x-x-	----	----	1	
Issaikyo	? *1952*	*0618*	....	....	----	----	--x-	----	----	*1*	
Issaikyo (Oana)	? *1966*	*05*	?*1966*	*08*	-x--	----	x-x-	----	----	*1*	
Issaikyo (Oana)	**1977**	1207	**1977**	1207	-x--	----	x-x-	----	----	1	

Zao (Honshu) — **38.141N 140.443E 1841** 3467 **ABD Complex volcano 0803-19= Historical**

ERUPTION — Area of Activity	Start Year	Start M-Dy	Stop Year	Stop M-Dy	Central / Flank vent / Radial fiss / Regional	Submarine / New island / Subglacial / Crater lake	Explosive / Pyro flow / Phreatic / Caldera	Lava flow / Lava lake / Dome / Spine	Fatal / Damage / Mudflow / Tsunami	VEI	Vol L/T
Goshiki-dake area	G-**7600**?	....	....	....	x---	----	x-x-	----	----		
Goshiki-dake (Z-To5a tephra)	G-**5600**?	....	....	....	x---	----	x---	----	----		
Goshiki-dake area	G-**5500**?	....	....	....	x---	----	x-x-	----	----		
Goshiki-dake area (Z-To5b tephra)	G-**4150**x	....	....	....	x---	----	x-x-	----	----		
Goshiki-dake area (Z-To5 tephra)	G-**3850**x	....	....	....	x---	----	xx--	----	----		
Goshiki-dake area (Z-To6 tephra)	G-**3350**t	....	....	....	x---	----	x-x-	----	----		
Goshiki-dake area (Z-To7 tephra)	G-**2600**x	....	....	....	x---	----	x---	----	----		
Goshiki-dake area (Z-To8 tephra)	G-**2300**u	....	....	....	x---	----	x---	----	----		
Goshiki-dake	T-**2000**z	....	....	....	x---	----	x-x-	----	----		
Goshiki-dake	G-**1600**?	....	....	....	x---	----	x-x-	----	----		
Goshiki-dake area (Z-To9 tephra)	G **0300**x	....	....	....	x---	----	x-?-	----	----	4	-/8
Okama	? *0773*	*11 ?*	....	....	x---	----	----	----	----		
Okama (Z-To10 tephra?)	**0884**?	....	....	....	x---	----	x---	----	----	3	-/7
Okama	**1183**	0528?	....	....	x---	---x	?---	----	----	2?	
Okama	**1227**	10 ?	....	....	x---	----	x-?-	----	-x--	3	
Okama	**1230**	1129?	....	....	x---	----	x---	----	----	2?	
Okama	? *1331*	....	?*1333*	....	x---	----	--?-	----	----	*2?*	
Okama	? *1350*?	....	....	....	x---	----	--?-	----	----	*2?*	
Goshiki-dake area (Z-To11 tephra)	G **1400**v	....	....	....	x---	----	x-?-	----	----	3	-/7
Okama	**1620**	....	....	....	x---	---x	?---	----	----	2?	
Okama	**1622**	....	....	....	x---	----	?---	----	----	2?	
Okama	**1623**	0515?	**1624**	1115?	x---	---x	x---	----	----	3*	
Okama	**1630**	....	....	....	x---	----	?---	----	----	2?	
Okama	**1641**	....	....	....	x---	----	?---	----	----	2?	
Okama	**1668**	08	....	....	x---	----	?---	----	----	2?	
Okama	**1669**	....	....	....	x---	----	x---	----	-x--	3	
Okama	**1670**	0426	**1670**	0926	x---	----	x-x-	----	----	2*	
Okama	**1694**	0529	**1694**	0830?	x---	---x	?-x-	----	-xx-	2	
SE side of Okama	**1794**	0922	**1794**	12 >	x---	---x	x-?-	----	-x--	2	
Okama	**1796**	0324	....	....	x---	---x	--?-	----	----	2	
Okama	**1804**	05 ?	....	....	x---	---x	--?-	----	----	2	

VOLCANO NAME (Subregion) / ERUPTION — Area of Activity	LAT	LONG	ELEV (m)	POPL (5 km 10 30 100)	ROCK TYPE	VOLC TYPE / Start Year	Start M-Dy	NUMBER / Stop Year	Stop M-Dy	STATUS	Central Flank vent Radial fiss Regional	Submarine New island Subglacial Crater lake	Explosive Pyro flow Phreatic Caldera	Lava flow Lava lake Dome Spine	Fatal Damage Mudflow Tsunami	VEI	Vol L/T
Zao (Honshu) *continued*																	
Okama						**1806**	0712	....	....		x---	----	--?-	----	----	2	
Okama						**1809**	0612	**1809**	1229		x---	---x	x-?-	----	-?x-	2	
Okama						**1821**	0127	**1821**	0501		x---	---x	x---	----	--x-	2*	
						1822	0501	....	....		x---	----	--?-	----	----		
Okama						**1830**	....	....	....		x---	---x	--?-	----	----	2	
Okama						**1831**	1122	....	....		x---	---x	--?-	----	--?-	2	
Okama						**1833**	....	....	....		x---	---x	x-?-	----	----	2	
Okama						**1867**	1021	....	....		x---	---x	--?-	----	x?x-	2	
Okama						**1873**	08	**1873**	09		x---	----	--?-	----	----	1?	
Okama						? *1890*	....	....	....		x---	----	--?-	----	----	*1?*	
Okama						**1894**	0703	**1894**	0703		x---	---x	x-?-	----	----	2?	
Okama						**1895**	0215	**1895**	0322		x---	---x	x-?-	----	--x-	1	-/5
Okama						**1895**	0822	**1895**	0928		x---	---x	x-x-	----	-xx-	2	
Okama						**1896**	0308	**1896**	0308		x---	----	x-x-	----	----	1	
Okama						? *1896*	*0901*?	....	....		x---	---x	--?-	----	----	*1?*	
Okama						? *1897*	*0114*	?*1897*	*0114*		x---	----	--?-	----	----	*1?*	
Okama						**1905**	....	....	....		x---	----	--?-	----	----	1?	
(1906 report of eruption in 1905)						X *1906*	....	....	....		----	----	----	----	----		
Okama						? *1927*	....	....	....		x---	----	--?-	----	----	*1?*	
Okama						? *1939*	*07*	....	....		x---	---x	--?-	----	--x-	*1?*	
Okama						**1940**	0518	**1940**	0518		x---	---x	x-x-	----	----	1	-/5
Hijiori (Honshu)	**38.606 N**	**140.178 E**	**516**	5567	**D**	**Caldera**		**0803-191**		**Holocene**							
Narugo (Honshu)	**38.733 N**	**140.732 E**	**470**	5567	**RD**	**Caldera**		**0803-20=**		**Historical**							
						G-**4400**>	....	....	....		----	----	x---	----	----		
						T-**1400**<	....	....	....		----	----	--x-	----	----		
						G-**1350**t	....	....	....		----	----	x-x-	----	----		
						G-**0800**<	....	....	....		----	----	--x-	----	----		
						0837	0527	....	....		----	----	x---	----	--?-	1	
Kurikoma (Honshu)	**38.958 N**	**140.792 E**	**1628**	3467	**AD**	**Stratovolcano**		**0803-21=**		**Historical**							
						T-**3540***	....	....	....		----	----	--x-	----	----		
						T **1450**t	....	....	....		----	----	--x-	----	----	1	-/5
Tsurugi-yama						**1726**j	....	....	....		x---	----	--?-	----	----	1?	
						1744	0203	....	....		x---	----	--?-	----	----	2	
						? *1783*	....	....	....		x---	----	--?-	----	-x--		
						1944	1120	**1944**	12		x---	----	--x-	----	-xx-	1	-/4
SE of Tsurugi-yama						**1946**	1124	....	....		x---	----	--x-	----	--x-	2	
						1950	0115	....	....		x---	----	--x-	----	----	2	
Chokai (Honshu)	**39.096 N**	**140.052 E**	**2233**	3367	**AB**	**Stratovolcanoes**		**0803-22=**		**Historical**							
West flank (Saruana crater)						T-**1050**?	....	....	....		-x--	----	----	x---	----	0	8/-
Higashi-Chokai						C-**0650**?	....	....	....		x---	----	--?A	?-?-	----		
(OD-12 tephra layer)						T-**0450**?	....	....	....		----	----	x-x-	----	----		
						? *0573*	*03* ?	....	....		----	----	?---	----	----		
						? *0577*	*1201*p	?*0578*	*0715*q		----	----	?---	?---	----		
						? *0610*o	....	....	....		----	----	?---	----	----		
						0711c	....	....	....		x---	----	--x-	----	----		
						? *0717*	*07*	....	....		----	----	x---	----	----		
						? *0804*	....	?*0806*	....		x---	----	?---	----	----		
						0817g	....	....	....		x---	----	--x-	----	----		
						0830	01	....	....		x---	----	x-x-	----	--x-		
						? *0839*	*1014*	....	....		----	----	?---	----	----		
						? *0856*	....	....	....		----	----	----	----	----		
						? *0857*	*05*	....	....		----	----	----	----	----		
						? *0861*	*05*	....	....		----	----	?---	----	----	*3*	
						0871	0505	....	....		x---	----	x---	x---	--x-	2	7/6
						? *0884*	*0726*	?*0884*	*08*		----	----	?---	----	----		
(915 AD eruption was from Towada volcano)						X *0915*	*0823*	X*0915*	*0901*		----	----	----	----	----		
						0939	0515	....	....		x---	----	--x-	----	----		
						? *0948*	*1231*y	....	....		----	----	----	----	----		
						? *0999*	....	....	....		----	----	----	----	----		
						? *1477*	....	....	....		----	----	?---	----	----		
						? *1560*	....	....	....		----	----	?---	----	----		
						1659	04	**1663**a	....		x---	----	--x-	----	----		
						? *1735*	....	....	....		----	----	?---	----	----	*2*	
						? *1738*	*1231*y	....	....		x---	----	x---	----	----	*2*	
Small crater at foot of Kojin-yama						**1740**	06 ?	**1747**?	....		x---	----	x-x-	----	-x--	2?	
						? *1764*	....	....	....		x---	----	?---	----	----	*2*	
Shinzan (foot of Kojin-yama)						**1800**	12	**1804**	07 ?		x---	----	x-x-	x-x-	x-x-	2*	6/-
Near Shinzan and Shichiko-zan						**1821**	0523	....	....		x---	----	--x-	----	----	2?	
						1834	0709	**1834**	07		x---	----	--x-	----	--?-	2?	
E side of Shinzan, W of Kojin-yama						**1974**	0301	**1974**	0430		x-x-	----	x-x-	----	--x-	1	-/5
Akita-Komaga-take (Honshu)	**39.758 N**	**140.803 E**	**1637**	3467	**BA**	**Stratovolcanoes**		**0803-23=**		**Historical**							
(AK-11, AK-10 tephra layers)						T-**8800**y	....	....	....		x---	----	x---	----	----	3?	-/8
(AK-9, Arasawa tephra layer)						T-**8300**y	....	....	....		x---	----	x---	----	----	4	-/8
(AK-8, Horikiri tephra layer)						G-**7850**x	....	....	....		x---	----	x---	----	----	4	-/8
						T-**7100***	....	....	....		x---	----	x---	----	----		
(AK-7 tephra layer)						G-**6350**x	....	....	....		x---	----	x---	----	----	3	-/7
						T-**6150**y	....	....	....		x---	----	x---	x---	----		
(AK-6 tephra layer)						G-**5950**x	....	....	....		x---	----	x---	----	----	3	-/7
(AK-5, AK-4 tephra layers)						G-**1450**t	....	....	....		x---	----	x-x-	----	----		
(AK-3 tephra layer)						G-**0350**x	....	....	....		x---	----	x---	x---	----	3	-/7
Minami-dake, Ko-dake						G-**0200**x	....	....	....		x---	----	x-x-	x---	----		
(AK-2 tephra layer)						G-**0050**x	....	....	....		x---	----	x---	----	----	2	-/6
Me-dake						T **0400**z	....	....	....		x---	----	x---	x---	----		
(AK-1 tephra layer)						**0807**?	....	....	....		x---	----	x---	----	----	3	-/7
						T **1100**?	....	....	....		----	----	x---	----	----	2	
						1890	12	**1891**	01		x---	----	--x-	----	----	2	
Yoko-dake						**1902**	....	....	....		-x--	----	--?-	----	----	1?	
Ishibora (south flank of Me-dake)						**1932**	0721	**1932**	0724		x-x-	----	x-x-	--x-	--x-	2	
Me-dake						**1970**	0918	**1971**	0126		xx--	----	x---	x---	----	2	7/6
Iwate (Honshu)	**39.850 N**	**141.004 E**	**2041**	3567	**BA**	**Complex volcano**		**0803-24=**		**Historical**							
						T-**6450***	....	....	....		x---	----	x---	----	----		
Nishi-Iwate (PHD8 tephra layer)						G-**6300**v	....	....	....		x---	----	x-x-	----	----		
Nishi-Iwate (PHD7 tephra layer)						G-**5650**t	....	....	....		x---	----	x-x-	----	----		

VOLCANO NAME (Subregion) / ERUPTION	Area of Activity (LAT LONG ELEV (m) POPL ROCK TYPE VOLC TYPE NUMBER STATUS)	Start Year	Start M-Dy	Stop Year	Stop M-Dy	Central / Flank vent / Radial fiss / Regional	Submarine / New island / Subglacial / Crater lake	Explosive / Pyro flow / Phreatic / Caldera	Lava flow / Lava lake / Dome / Spine	Fatal / Damage / Mudflow / Tsunami	VEI	Vol L/T
Iwate (Honshu) *continued*	Higashi-Iwate	G-4900v	....	....	....	x---	----	xx--	----	----		
	Nishi-Iwate (PHD6 tephra layer)	G-4850t	....	....	....	x---	----	x-x-	----	----		
	Higashi-Iwate	T-4450z	....	....	....	x---	----	----	x---	----	0	
	Higashi-Iwate	T-4350z	....	....	....	x---	----	x---	----	----		
	Higashi-Iwate	T-3750v	....	....	....	x---	----	xx--	----	----		
		T-3250z	....	....	....	x---	----	----	x---	----	0	
	Higashi-Iwate	C-3050?	....	....	....	x---	----	x---	----	----		
	Nishi-Iwate (PHD5 tephra layer)	G-2950t	....	....	....	x---	----	x-x-	----	----		
	Higashi-Iwate (W6a-d tephra layers)	T-2700x	....	....	....	x---	----	x---	----	----		
	Higashi-Iwate (W5 tephra layer)	G-2050x	....	....	....	x---	----	xx--	----	----		
	Nishi-yama	G-2000?	....	....	....	x---	----	x-x-	----	----		
	Nishi-Iwate (O-jigokudani area)	G-1650?	....	....	....	x---	----	--x-	----	----		
	Higashi-Iwate	T-1500y	....	....	....	x---	----	x---	----	----		
	Higashi-Iwate	G-1250?	....	....	....	x---	----	x---	----	----	3	-/7
	Nishi-Iwate	C-1150?	....	....	....	x---	----	x-x-	----	----		
	Nishi-Iwate (O-jigokudani area)	G-0450?	....	....	....	x---	----	--x-	----	----		
	Higashi-Iwate	C-0350?	....	....	....	x---	----	x---	----	----		
	Higashi-Iwate	C 0150?	....	....	....	x---	----	x---	----	----		
	Higashi-Iwate (Myoko-dake)	T 1300t	....	....	....	x---	----	x---	----	----	3	-/7
	Nishi-Iwate and Higashi-Iwate	C 1450v	....	....	....	x---	----	x-x-	----	----		
		1686	0326	1686	0327	-x--	----	xx--	x---	-xx-	3	-/7
		? 1687	0414	?1687	07	----	----	x---	----	----	2?	
		? 1689	0622	....	....	----	----	x---	----	----	2?	
	(reported 1719 events occurred during 1732)	X 1719	02 ?	....	....	----	----	----	----	----		7/-
	NE flank of Yakushi-dake	1732	0122	1732	10 ?	-x--	----	x---	x---	----	2	
	(earthquake swarm, not eruption)	X 1823	....	....	....	----	----	----	----	----		
	W side of Onigajo caldera (O-jigokudani)	1919	0715?	1919	0715?	x---	----	x-x-	----	--x-	1	-/5
		? 1934	07	?1935	....	----	----	--?-	----	----		
Hachimantai (Honshu)	39.955 N 140.857 E 1614 3457 ABD Stratovolcano 0803-25= Radiocarbon											
		G-7900w	....	....	....	x---	----	--x-	----	----		
		T-5350?	....	....	....	x---	----	--x-	----	----		
Akita-Yake-yama (Honshu)	39.961 N 140.761 E 1366 3357 Ad Stratovolcano 0803-26= Historical											
	Onigajo lava dome	N-3050?	....	....	....	x---	----	----	--x-	----		
		G-1250x	....	....	....	----	----	x---	----	----		
	(Ay-2 tephra layer)	T 0570?	....	....	....	----	----	x---	----	----		
		? 0807	1101	....	....	----	----	x---	----	----		
		G 1390u	....	....	....	----	----	--x-	----	----		
	Karenuma	1678	0222?	....	....	x---	----	x-x-	----	----	2	-/6
		1867	....	....	....	x---	----	--?-	----	----		
	Karenuma	1887	....	....	....	x---	----	--x-	----	----	2	
		1890	0923	....	....	x---	----	x-x-	----	----	2	
		1929	09	....	....	x---	----	x-x-	----	----	2	
	Kare-numa	1948	....	....	....	x---	----	--x-	----	----	1?	
	Kare-numa	1949	0830	1949	0901	x---	----	x-x-	----	--x-	1	-/5
	Kare-numa	1950	....	....	....	x---	----	--x-	----	----	1	
	Kare-numa	1951	02	....	....	x---	----	--x-	----	----	1?	
		1957	....	....	....	x---	----	--x-	----	--x-	1	
	NE flank (Sumikawa-Onsen)	1997	0511	1997	0511	-x--	----	x-x-	----	-xx-	1	-/3
	Kare-numa	1997	0816	1997	0816	x---	----	x-x-	----	--x-	1	-/3
Megata (Honshu)	39.95 N 139.73 E 291 4457 ABDR Maars 0803-262 Tephrochronology											
		T-7050?	....	....	....	x---	----	xx--	----	----		
		T-2050?	....	....	....	x---	----	xx--	----	-x--		
Iwaki (Honshu)	40.653 N 140.307 E 1625 3567 A Stratovolcano 0803-27= Historical											
	Torinoumi lava dome	K-8050?	....	....	....	x---	----	----	--x-	----		
	West summit lava dome	T-4050?	....	....	....	x---	----	x---	--x-	----		
	Summit and central lava dome	T-1050?	....	....	....	x---	----	x---	--x-	----		
	Torinoumi lava dome	T-0550z	....	....	....	x---	----	----	--x-	----		
		? 1597	01	....	....	x---	----	--?-	----	----	2	
		? 1597	0613	....	....	x---	----	--?-	----	--x-	2	
	Torinoumi	1600	0222	....	....	x---	---x	--x-	----	--x-	2	
	Torinoumi	1600	0723	1600	0725	x---	---x	--x-	----	-xx-	2	
	Torinoumi	1604	0207	....	....	x---	---x	--x-	----	--x-	3?	
		? 1605	0410	....	....	x---	----	--x-	----	----	2?	
		1618	0131	....	....	x---	----	x-?-	----	----	2	
		? 1672	0712	?1672	0728	x---	----	--?-	----	----	2?	
		? 1694	0619	....	....	x---	----	--?-	----	----	2?	
		? 1709	0423	....	....	x---	----	--?-	----	----	2?	
		? 1769	....	....	....	----	----	--?-	----	----	2	
	South flank	? 1782	0412	....	....	-x--	----	--?-	----	----	2	
		1782	1201p	1783	0312	x---	----	--x-	----	----	2	
		? 1783	1203	....	....	x---	----	--?-	----	----	2?	
		1790	1009	....	....	x---	----	x-x-	----	----	2	
		? 1793	0402	....	....	x---	----	--?-	----	----	2	
		? 1794	0403	....	....	x---	----	--x-	----	----	2	
		? 1800	0511	....	....	x---	----	--?-	----	----	2	
		? 1807	0331	....	....	x---	----	--?-	----	----	2	
		? 1833	0411	....	....	x---	----	--?-	----	----	2	
	Summit and south flank?	1844	0407	....	....	x?--	----	--x-	----	----	2	
		1845	0404	....	....	x---	----	--x-	----	----	2	
		? 1848	0118	....	....	x---	----	--x-	----	----	2	
		? 1856	0520	....	....	x---	----	--?-	----	----	2	
		1863	0323	....	....	x---	----	--x-	----	----	1	
Towada (Honshu)	40.47 N 140.92 E 1159 5567 ADBR Caldera 0803-271 Historical											
	Nakanoumi (To-G tephra; Shingo Pumice)	G-9490?	....	....	....	x---	----	x---	----	----	3	-/7
	Goshikiiwa (To-F tephra)	G-8250?	....	....	....	x---	----	x---	----	----	**5**	-/9
	Goshikiiwa (To-E tephra; Nambu Pumice)	G-7250?	....	....	....	x---	----	x---	----	----	**5?**	-/9
	Goshikiiwa (To-D tephra; Oguni Pumice)	G-6250?	....	....	....	x---	----	x---	----	----	4	-/8
	Goshikiiwa (To-D' tephra)	G-5550?	....	....	....	x---	----	x---	----	----	3?	-/8
	Goshikiiwa (Nakanoumi) (To-C tephra)	G-4150?	....	....	....	x---	----	xx--	----	----	**5+**	-/9
	Nakanoumi (To-B tephra)	G-0750?	....	....	....	x---	---x	x---	----	----	4+	-/8
	Goshikiiwa (NE rim Nakanoumi crater)	0915	0817	....	....	x---	----	xx--	x-x-	-xx-	**5**	8/9
Hakkoda Group (Honshu)	40.656 N 140.881 E 1585 3367 ADBR Stratovolcanoes 0803-28= Radiocarbon											
	O-dake (Hk-5 tephra)	G-2850?	....	....	....	x---	----	x-x-	----	----	2	-/6

VOLCANO NAME (Subregion)	ERUPTION — Area of Activity	LAT	LONG	ELEV (m)	POPL (5 km, 10, 30, 100)	ROCK TYPE	VOLC TYPE	NUMBER	STATUS	Start Year	Start M-Dy	Stop Year	Stop M-Dy	Central / Flank vent / Radial fiss / Regional	Submarine / New island / Subglacial / Crater lake	Explosive / Pyro flow / Phreatic / Caldera	Lava flow / Lava lake / Dome / Spine	Fatal / Damage / Mudflow / Tsunami	VEI	Vol L/T
Hakkoda Group (Honshu) *continued*	O-dake (Hk-4 tephra)									G-**2250**?	....	....	....	**x**---	----	**x**-**x**-	----	----	3	-/7
	O-dake (Hk-3 tephra)									G-**1150**?	....	....	....	**x**---	----	**x**---	----	----	1	-/5
	O-dake (Hk-2 tephra)									G-**0050**?	....	....	....	**x**---	----	**x**-**x**-	----	----	1	-/5
	O-dake (Hk-1 tephra)									G **0450**?	....	....	....	**x**---	----	**x**-**x**-	----	----	1	-/6
	SW flank of O-dake (Jigoku-numa)									G **1340**u	....	....	....	-**x**--	----	--**x**-	----	----	1	
	SW flank of O-dake (Jigoku-numa)									G **1550**v	....	....	....	-**x**--	----	--**x**-	----	----	1	-/2
Osore-yama (Honshu)		**41.276 N**	**141.124 E**	**879**	5557	AD	**Stratovolcano**	**0803-29=**	**Historical**											
										1787<	....	....	....	----	----	----	----	----		

IZU & VOLCANO ISLANDS

VOLCANO NAME (Subregion)	ERUPTION — Area of Activity	LAT	LONG	ELEV (m)	POPL (5 km, 10, 30, 100)	ROCK TYPE	VOLC TYPE	NUMBER	STATUS	Start Year	Start M-Dy	Stop Year	Stop M-Dy	Central / Flank vent / Radial fiss / Regional	Submarine / New island / Subglacial / Crater lake	Explosive / Pyro flow / Phreatic / Caldera	Lava flow / Lava lake / Dome / Spine	Fatal / Damage / Mudflow / Tsunami	VEI	Vol L/T
Oshima (Izu Is-Japan)		**34.721 N**	**139.398 E**	**764**	4448	BAd	**Stratovolcano**	**0804-01=**	**Historical**											
	(tephra layer O47)									T-**8450**?	....	....	....	----	----	**x**---	----	----		
	(tephra layers O46, O45)									T-**8050**z	....	....	....	----	----	**x**---	----	----		
	(tephra layer O44)									T-**7650**?	....	....	....	----	----	**x**---	----	----		
	(tephra layers O43, O42)									T-**7150**z	....	....	....	----	----	**x**---	----	----		
	(tephra layer O41)									T-**6650**?	....	....	....	**x**---	----	**x**?**x**-	----	----		
	(tephra layer O40)									T-**6550**?	....	....	....	----	----	**x**---	**x**---	----		
	(tephra layers Osb39-2 to Osb38-1)									T-**6050**z	....	....	....	----	----	**x**---	----	----		
	(tephra layer Osb37-5)									T-**5550**?	....	....	....	----	----	**x**---	----	----		
	(tephra layers Osb37-4, Osb37-3)									T-**5450**u	....	....	....	----	----	**x**---	----	----		
	(tephra layers Osb37-2, Osb36-1)									T-**4920**z	....	....	....	----	----	**x**---	----	----		
	(tephra layer O35)									T-**4450**?	....	....	....	----	----	**x**---	----	----		
	(tephra layer O34)									T-**4250**?	....	....	....	----	----	**x**---	----	----		
	(tephra layers O32-2, O32-1, and O32)									T-**4000**y	....	....	....	----	----	**x**---	**x**---	----		
	(tephra layer O31)									T-**3750**?	....	....	....	----	----	**x**---	----	----		
	(tephra layer O30)									T-**3650**?	....	....	....	----	----	**x**---	----	----		
	(tephra layers O29 to O16)									T-**2550**?	....	....	....	----	----	**x**-**x**-	**x**---	----		
	(tephra layer O15)									T-**1450**?	....	....	....	----	----	**xxx**-	----	----		
	(tephra layer O14)									T-**1200**?	....	....	....	**x**---	----	**x**---	**x**---	----		
	(tephra layers O13 to O11)									T-**1050**x	....	....	....	----	----	**x**---	----	----		
	SE flank (tephra layer O10)									G-**0900**v	....	....	....	-**x**--	----	**x**?--	**x**---	----	2	5/6
	(tephra layers O9 to O5)									T-**0600**z	....	....	....	----	----	**x**---	----	----	3	
	(tephra layers O4, O3)									T-**0150**?	....	....	....	----	----	**x**---	----	----	3	
	(tephra layer O2)									G **0150**t	....	....	....	----	----	**x**---	----	----	3	
	(tephra layer O1)									T **0250**v	....	....	....	----	----	**x**---	----	----	3	
	Summit and east flank (tephra layer S2)									G **0340**x	....	....	....	**xx**-**x**	----	**xxxx**	**x**---	--**x**-	4	7/8
	(tephra layer S1.5)									V **0580**?	....	....	....	**x**---	----	**x**---	?---	----	3	-/7
	(tephra layer S1)									V **0600**?	....	....	....	**x**---	----	**x**-**x**-	----	----	3	-/7
	(tephra layer N4.8)									V **0625**?	....	....	....	**x**---	----	**x**---	----	----	3	-/7
	(tephra layer N4.6?)									**0654**?	....	....	....	**x**---	----	**x**---	----	----	3	-/7
	(tephra layer N4.4?)									**0680**?	....	**0681**	0326>	**x**---	----	**x**---	**x**---	----	4	-/8
										0684?	1129	....	....	-?--	----	----	**x**---	----		
	(tephra layer N4.2)									V **0700**?	....	....	....	**x**---	----	**x**---	----	----	3	-/7
	Summit, N & S flanks (tephra layer N4)									V **0713**?	....	....	....	**xx**--	----	**x**---	----	----	3	-/7
	(tephra layer N3.2)									V **0822**?	....	....	....	**x**---	----	**x**---	----	----	3	-/7
	Summit, SE flank (tephra layer N3.0)									**0838**?	08 ?	....	....	**xx**--	----	**x**---	----	----	3	-/7
	(tephra layer N2.0?)									**0854**?	0914?	**0856**?	....	**x**---	----	**x**-**x**-	----	----	4	-/8
	(tephra layer N1.0?)									**0886**?	0629?	....	....	**xx**--	----	**x**-**x**-	**x**---	----	4	4/8
										? *0936*	....	....	....	----	----	----	----	----		
										? *1112*	*1118*	?*1112*	*1226*e	**xx**--	----	**x**---	**x**---	----		
	(tephra layer Y6)									V **1183**?	....	....	....	**x**---	----	**x**---	----	----	4	-/8
	(tephra layer Y5.6)									V **1245**?	....	....	....	**x**---	----	**x**---	----	----	1	-/5
	NW flank (tephra layer Y5.2)									V **1307**?	....	....	....	---**x**	----	**x**---	**x**---	----	3	6/7
	(tephra layer 5)									**1338**	0915e	**1338**	1115e	**x**---	----	**x**---	----	----	3	-/7
										1415	0521	....	....	----	----	----	?---	----		
	(tephra layer 4.2)									**1416**	0902	V**1417**?	....	**x**---	----	**x**---	----	----	2	-/6
	Summit, S flank (tephra layer Y4)									**1421**	0514	....	....	**x**-**x**-	----	**x**---	**x**---	----	4	8/8
										1442	08	**1443**	....	----	----	?---	----	----		
	(tephra layer Y3.8)									V **1471**?	....	....	....	**x**---	----	**x**---	----	----	2	-/6
										1552	1007	**1552**	1015	**x**-**x**-	----	**x**---	**x**---	----	3	8/7
										1600	10 w	....	....	----	----	?---	----	----		
										1612	1015w	....	....	----	----	?---	----	----		
										1623	....	....	....	----	----	?---	----	----		
										1634	....	....	....	----	----	?---	----	----		
										1637	0826	**1638**	04	----	----	?---	----	----		
	(tephra layer Y2)									**1684**	0214	**1690**	....	**x**---	----	**x**-**x**-	**x**---	-**x**--	3	7/8
										1695	0412?	....	....	----	----	?---	----	----		
	Mihara-yama & flanks, (tephra layer Y1)									**1777**	0831	**1779**	....	**xx**--	----	**x**-**x**-	**x**---	----	3*	8/8
	Mihara-yama									**1783**	....	**1786**	....	**x**---	----	**x**---	----	-**x**--	2	
	Mihara-yama									**1789**	....	....	....	**x**---	----	**x**---	----	**xx**--	2	
	Mihara-yama									**1792**	....	....	....	**x**---	----	?---	----	----	2	
	Mihara-yama									**1803**	0926?	**1803**	1114	**x**---	----	**x**---	----	----	2	
	(tephra layer Y0.8)									V **1821**?	....	....	....	**x**---	----	**x**---	----	----	3	-/7
	Mihara-yama									**1822**	....	**1824**	....	**x**---	----	**x**---	----	----	2	
	Mihara-yama									? *1827*	....	....	....	**x**---	----	?---	----	----		
	Mihara-yama									? *1837*	....	?*1838*	....	**x**---	----	?---	----	----	*2*	
	Mihara-yama									**1846**	....	....	....	**x**---	----	**x**---	----	----	2	
	Mihara-yama									? *1868*	*1231*y	....	....	**x**---	----	----	----	----		
	Mihara-yama									**1870**	....	....	....	**x**---	----	**x**---	----	----	2	
	Mihara-yama									**1876**	1227	**1877**	0205	**x**---	----	**x**---	**x**---	----	2	6/6
	Mihara-yama									**1910**	12	....	....	**x**---	----	**x**---	----	----	1	-/4
	Mihara-yama									**1912**	0223	**1913**	0125	**x**---	----	**x**---	**x**---	----	1	7/5
	Mihara-yama									**1914**	0515	**1914**	0526	**x**---	----	**x**---	**x**---	----	2	7/6
	Mihara-yama									**1915**	1010	**1915**	1025?	**x**---	----	**x**---	----	----	2	
	Mihara-yama									**1919**	0518	**1919**	1223	**x**---	----	----	**x**---	----	0	
	Mihara-yama									? *1920*	....	....	....	**x**---	----	----	?---	----		
	Mihara-yama									**1922**	1208	**1923**	0130	**x**---	----	**x**-**x**-	**x**---	----	1	6/5
	Mihara-yama									**1928**	0807	**1928**	0808	**x**---	----	**x**---	----	----	2	
	Mihara-yama									**1933**	1014	**1933**	11	**x**---	----	----	**x**---	----	0	5/-
	Mihara-yama									**1934**	0415	**1934**	0425?	**x**---	----	----	**x**---	----	0	
	Mihara-yama									? *1934*	*09*	....	....	**x**---	----	----	?---	----		
	Mihara-yama									**1935**	0426	**1935**	0506?	**x**---	----	----	**x**---	----	0	

VOLCANO NAME (Subregion) / ERUPTION	Area of Activity	LAT	LONG	ELEV (m)	POPL (5 km, 10, 30, 100)	ROCK TYPE	VOLC TYPE	NUMBER	STATUS	Start Year	Start M-Dy	Stop Year	Stop M-Dy	Central / Flank vent / Radial fiss / Regional	Submarine / New island / Subglacial / Crater lake	Explosive / Pyro flow / Phreatic / Caldera	Lava flow / Lava lake / Dome / Spine	Fatal / Damage / Mudflow / Tsunami	VEI	Vol L/T
Oshima (Izu Is-Japan) *continued*	Mihara-yama									**1937**	0717	**1937**	08	x---	----	----	x---	----	0	
	Mihara-yama									**1938**	0811	**1938**	0811	x---	----	x---	x---	----	1	5/5
	Mihara-yama									**1939**	02	**1939**	02	x---	----	x---	----	----	1?	
	Mihara-yama									**1939**	0901	**1939**	0916	x---	----	x---	x---	----	1	5/-
	Mihara-yama									**1940**	0818	**1940**	0819	x---	----	x---	----	----	1	5/5
	Mihara-yama, south rim									**1950**	0716	**1951**	0628	x---	----	x---	xx--	----	2	7/6
	Mihara-yama									**1953**	1005	**1954**	0208	x---	----	x---	x---	x---	1	5/4
	Mihara-yama									**1956**	0103	**1956**	0106	x---	----	x---	----	----	1	
	Mihara-yama									? *1956*	*0825*	?*1956*	*0826*	x---	----	----	----	----	*1?*	
	Mihara-yama									**1957**	08	**1957**	12	x---	----	x---	----	x---	1	-/4
	Mihara-yama									**1958**	0417	**1958**	0613	x---	----	x---	----	----	1	-/4
	Mihara-yama									**1959**	01	**1959**	01	x---	----	x---	----	----	1	
	Mihara-yama									**1959**	10	**1960**	11	x---	----	x---	----	----	1	
	Mihara-yama									? *1961*	....	....	....	x---	----	----	----	----		
	Mihara-yama									**1962**	01	**1965**	05	x---	----	x-x-	----	----	1	
	Mihara-yama									**1965**	1125	**1966**	0613	x---	----	x---	----	----	1	
	Mihara-yama									**1967**	05	**1967**	08	x---	----	x---	----	----	1	
	Mihara-yama									**1968**	0119	**1968**	0119	x---	----	x---	----	----	1	
	Mihara-yama									**1968**	0728	**1968**	0728	x---	----	x---	----	----	1	
	Mihara-yama									**1969**	0119	**1969**	07	x---	----	x---	----	----	1	
	Mihara-yama									**1970**	0126	**1970**	0131	x---	----	x---	----	----	1	
	Mihara-yama									**1970**	0630	**1970**	1112	x---	----	x---	----	----	1	
	Mihara-yama									**1971**	0405	**1971**	0405	x---	----	x---	----	----	1	
	Mihara-yama									**1974**	0228	**1974**	0620	x---	----	x---	----	----	1	
	Mihara-yama, N part and NW of caldera									**1986**	1115	**1986**	1218	x-x-	----	x---	xx--	-x--	3*	7/7
	Mihara-yama									**1987**	1116	**1988**	0127	x---	----	x-x-	----	-x--	2*	-/4
	Mihara-yama (1987 summit crater)									**1990**	1004	**1990**	1004	x---	----	x-x-	----	----	2	
To-shima (Izu Is-Japan)		**34.517 N**	**139.283 E**	**508**	3357	**BA**	**Stratovolcano**	**0804-011**	**Tephrochronology**											
	Kajiana crater									T-**4550***	....	....	....	x---	----	----	x---	----	0	
Nii-jima (Izu Is-Japan)		**34.393 N**	**139.273 E**	**432**	4447	**Rb**	**Lava domes**	**0804-02=**	**Historical**											
										T-**5950**?	....	....	....	x---	----	?---	--x-	----		
	Niijima-yama									T-**4350**?	....	....	....	x---	----	x---	--x-	----		
	(Wakago tephra)									T-**1250**?	....	....	....	x---	----	xx--	----	----		
	Achi-yama									**0856**?	....	**0857**?	....	x---	----	xx--	--x-	----	2	7/6
	Mukai-yama									**0886**	0629	....	....	x---	x---	xx--	--x-	----	4+	8/8
Kozu-shima (Izu Is-Japan)		**34.216 N**	**139.156 E**	**572**	4446	**R**	**Lava domes**	**0804-03=**	**Historical**											
	Jogo-yama									T-**8050**?	....	....	....	x---	----	----	--x-	----		
	N tip of island (Anano-yama, Hanatabe)									H-**0750***	....	....	....	x---	----	----	x-x-	----		
	NW tip of island (Kobe-yama)									H-**0100***	....	....	....	x---	----	----	x-x-	----		
										? *0832*	....	....	....	----	----	----	?---	----		
	Tenjo-san									**0838**	0802?	....	....	x---	----	xx--	x-x-	----	4	8/8
Miyake-jima (Izu Is-Japan)		**34.079 N**	**139.529 E**	**815**	4445	**BA**	**Stratovolcano**	**0804-04=**	**Historical**											
	NW flank (Ofunata; OFB tephra layer)									T-**6450**z	....	....	....	-x--	----	x---	----	----	4	-/8
	(Igaya tephra layer)									T-**2900**z	....	....	....	x---	----	x---	x---	----	4	7/8
	(Igaya-Higashi tephra layer)									G-**2000**v	....	....	....	--x-	----	x---	----	----	3	-/7
	South flank (Mizutamari maar)									T-**1800**t	....	....	....	-x--	----	xx--	----	----	3	-/7
	NW flank (NGS scoria layer)									T-**1450**z	....	....	....	-x--	----	x---	----	----		
	(TBS tephra layer)									T-**1250**?	....	....	....	----	----	x---	----	----	3	-/7
	Hatchodaira caldera, S flank (Furumio maar)									T-**0950**x	....	....	....	xx--	----	x--x	----	--x-	4+	-/8
	(IZS scoria layer)									T-**0600**z	....	....	....	x---	----	x---	----	----	3	-/7
	Taira-yama (TYS tephra layer)									G-**0050**t	....	....	....	x---	----	x---	x---	----	3	6/7
	(TGS and TGA tephra layers)									T **0260**z	....	....	....	xx--	----	x---	----	----	4	-/8
	Sabigahama (SHB tephra layer)									T **0320**z	....	....	....	-x--	----	x---	x---	----	3?	5/7
	Daihannya-yama (DHS tephra layer)									G **0500**t	....	....	....	-x--	----	x---	----	----	3	-/7
	NE flank (MBS tephra layera)									G **0750**t	....	....	....	-xx-	----	x---	----	----	3	-/7
	(KHS tephra layer)									**0832**	0623	....	....	-x--	----	x---	----	----	3	-/7
	Oyama and East flank (Mi-ike maar)									**0850**?	....	....	....	xx--	----	xx--	x---	----	4	7/8
										1085	....	....	....	x---	----	x---	x---	----	2	6/-
	NE flank? (SBS tephra layer)									**1154**	11	....	....	-?--	----	x---	----	----	3	-/7
	Oyama									**1469**	1224	....	....	x-x-	----	x---	x---	----	3	6/-
	SE flank									**1535**	03	....	....	--x-	----	x---	x---	----	2	6/-
	SE flank									**1595**	1122	....	....	--x-	----	x---	x---	--?-	2	5/-
	SW flank (SE of Ako, Kuwanoki-daira?)									**1643**	0331	**1643**	04	-xx-	----	x---	x---	-x--	3	6/7
										? *1709*	*0423*	....	....	----	----	----	----	----		
	SW flank (Kuwanoki-daira)									**1712**	0204	**1714**	....	-xx-	x---	x---	x---	-xx-	3?	5/8
	Oyama, SSW flank (Shinmio maar)									**1763**	0817	**1769**	....	xxx-	----	x---	x---	-x--	4	5/8
	Summit and NE flank?									**1811**	0127	**1811**	0128	x-x-	----	x---	x---	----	2	-/6
	West flank (east and SE of Ako)									**1835**	1111?	....	....	-xx-	----	x---	x---	-x--	2	5/-
	NNE flank (560 m)									**1874**	0703	**1874**	0717?	--x-	----	x---	x---	xx--	3	
	Oyama, NE flank									**1940**	0712	**1940**	0805	x-x-	----	x---	x---	xx--	3	6/7
	NE flank									**1962**	0824	**1962**	0827	-xx-	----	x---	x---	-x--	2	6/6
	SW flank (4.5 km long NE-SW fissure)									**1983**	1003	**1983**	1004	-xx-	----	xxx-	x---	-x--	3	6/7
	Summit and submarine western flank									**2000**	0627	**2000**	0928	x-x-	x---	xxxM	----	-xx-	3*	-/7
										2001	0111	**2002**	1124	x---	----	x---	----	----	2*	
										2004	1130	**2004**	1209	x---	----	x---	----	----	1	
										2005	0412	**2005**	0518	x---	----	x---	----	----	1	
										2006	0217	**2006**	0217	x---	----	x-?-	----	----	1	
										2006	0823	**2006**	0823	x---	----	x-?-	----	----	1	
										2008	0107	**2008**	0107	x---	----	x-x-	----	----	1	
										2008	0508	**2008**	0508	x---	----	--x-	----	----	1	
										2009	0401	**2009**	0401	x---	----	x-x-	----	----	1	
Mikura-jima (Izu Is-Japan)		**33.871 N**	**139.605 E**	**851**	3345	**BA**	**Stratovolcano**	**0804-041**	**Tephrochronology**											
										T-**5050**?	....	....	....	x---	----	----	----	----		
	Tsubunegamori & Yasukajigamori domes									G-**4100**v	....	....	....	x---	----	xx--	--x-	----		7/-
Kurose Hole (Izu Is-Japan)		**33.40 N**	**139.68 E**	**-107**	0025	**D**	**Submarine volc**	**0804-042**	Holocene?											
Hachijo-jima (Izu Is-Japan)		**33.13 N**	**139.769 E**	**854**	5555	**BA**	**Stratovolcanoes**	**0804-05=**	**Historical**											
	Nishi-yama									T-**8020***	....	....	....	x---	----	xx--	----	----	4	-/8
	Nishi-yama									T-**7650***	....	....	....	----	----	x---	----	----		
	Higashi-yama south flank									T-**5020***	....	....	....	-x--	----	--x-	----	--x-	3	-/7
	Nishi-yama									T-**4650**?	....	....	....	?x--	----	xx--	----	----	**5**	-/9
	Nishi-yama									T-**3350***	....	....	....	----	----	x---	----	----		
	Between Nishi-yama & Higashi-yama									G-**2700**v	....	....	....	-x--	----	xx--	----	----	3	-/7
	S flank of Higashi-yama (Myohoji)									T-**2550**z	....	....	....	-x--	----	x---	----	----	3	-/7

VOLCANO NAME (Subregion) / ERUPTION	Area of Activity	LAT	LONG	ELEV (m)	POPL (5 km, 10, 30, 100)	ROCK TYPE	VOLC TYPE	NUMBER	STATUS	Start Year	Start M-Dy	Stop Year	Stop M-Dy	Central, Flank vent, Radial fiss, Regional	Submarine, New island, Subglacial, Crater lake	Explosive, Pyro flow, Phreatic, Caldera	Lava flow, Lava lake, Dome, Spine	Fatal, Damage, Mudflow, Tsunami	VEI	Vol L/T
Hachijo-jima (Izu Is-Japan) *continued*	Nishi-yama									T-**2450**z	....	....	....	----	----	**xx**--	----	----	4	-/8
	SE of Nishi-yama, NE of Higashi-yama									T-**2050**?	....	....	....	-**x**--	----	**xx**--	----	----	**5**	-/9
	Nishi-yama									T-**1250***	....	....	....	----	----	**x**---	----	----		
	SE flank of Nishi-yama (Kanda-yama)									T-**1150***	....	....	....	-**x**--	----	**xx**--	----	----		
	NW flank of Higashi-yama									T-**0350**z	....	....	....	-**x**--	----	**xx**--	----	----	3	-/7
	Nishi-yama									G-**0150**t	....	....	....	**x**---	----	**x**---	----	----		
	Nishi-yama summit and SE flank									G **0850**x	....	....	....	**xx**--	----	**x**---	**x**---	----		
	Nishi-yama									**1487**	1207	....	....	**x**---	----	**x**---	----	----	2	
	Nishi-yama									**1518**	02	**1523**	....	**x**---	----	**x**---	----	----	2	
	Nishi-yama SE flank									**1605**	1027	....	....	-**x**--	----	**x**---	**x**---	-**x**--	2	6/6
	Submarine flank									**1606**	0123	....	....	-**x**--	**xx**--	**x**---	----	----	2	
										? *1707*	....	....	....	----	----	?---	----	----	*2*	
Aoga-shima (Izu Is-Japan)		**32.454 N**	**139.762 E**	**423**	3334	**BA**	**Stratovolcano**	**0804-06=**	**Historical**											
	Northwest flank									G-**1800**v	....	....	....	--**x**-	----	**x**---	**x**---	----	2?	7/-
										G-**1200**t	....	....	....	**x**---	----	**xx**--	----	----		
	NNW flank									T-**1100**y	....	....	....	-**x**--	----	**x**---	**x**---	----		
	SE flank (Kintagaura)									C-**0600**x	....	....	....	-**x**--	----	**x**---	----	----	4	8/8
	Ikenosawa crater									**1652**	....	....	....	**x**---	----	**x**-?-	----	----	3	
	Ikenosawa crater									**1670**	....	**1680**	....	**x**---	---**x**	**x**---	----	----	2	
	Maru-yama, SW part of Ikenosawa crater									**1780**	0727	**1785**	05 ?	**x**---	---**x**	**x**---	**x**---	**xxx**-	3*	6/7
Myojin Knoll (Izu Is-Japan)		**32.10 N**	**139.85 E**	**360**	0003	**Ra**	**Submarine volc**	**0804-061**	Holocene?											
Bayonnaise Rocks (Izu Is-Japan)		**31.88 N**	**139.92 E**	**11**	0003	**DAR**	**Submarine volc**	**0804-07=**	**Historical**											
										@ **1869**	0506	....	....	----	**x**---	----	----	----	0	
	31.50 N 139.50 E (approx.)									@ **1871**	....	....	....	----	**x**---	----	----	----	0	
	14 km north of Bayonnaise Rocks									**1896**	....	....	....	----	**xx**--	----	----	----	2	
	9-15 km SE of Bayonnaise Rocks									**1906**	0407	**1906**	0414	----	**x**---	**x**---	----	----	1	
	11 km east, 19 km NE, 4 km SW									**1915**	02	**1915**	07	----	**x**---	**x**---	----	---**x**	0	
	9 km east of Bayonnaise Rocks									**1934**	05	....	....	----	**x**---	----	----	----	0	
	Island at 31.95 N 140.02 E									**1946**	0204d	....	....	----	**xx**--	----	--**xx**	----	2	7/-
	Myojinsho									**1952**	0916	**1953**	10	----	**xx**--	**xx**--	--**xx**	**xx**-**x**	2	7/-
	Myojinsho									**1954**	1104	**1954**	1105	----	**x**---	----	----	----	0	
	4 km north of Bayonnaise Rocks									**1955**	0625	....	....	----	**x**---	----	----	----	0	
										1957	0502	....	....	----	**x**---	----	----	----	0	
										1958	....	....	....	----	**x**---	----	----	----	0	
										1959	....	....	....	----	**x**---	----	----	----	0	
	Myojinsho									**1960**	0721	....	....	----	**x**---	----	----	----	2	
	Myojinsho									**1970**	0129	**1970**	06	----	**x**---	**x**---	----	----	2	
										? *1971*	*0318*	....	....	----	?---	----	----	----	*0*	
	Myojinsho									? *1979*	*0713*	....	....	----	?---	----	----	----	*0*	
	Myojinsho									? *1980*	*1115*	?*1980*	*1223*	----	?---	----	----	----	*0*	
	Myojinsho									? *1982*	*0810*	....	....	----	?---	----	----	----	*0*	
	Myojinsho									? *1983*	*0512*	....	....	----	?---	----	----	----	*0*	
	Myojinsho									? *1986*	*1024*	?*1986*	*1024*	----	?---	----	----	----	*0*	
	Myojinsho									? *1987*	*1021*	?*1987*	*1209*	----	?---	----	----	----	*0*	
	Myojinsho									? *1988*	*0318*	?*1988*	*0319*	----	?---	----	----	----	*0*	
Smith Rock (Izu Is-Japan)		**31.436 N**	**140.054 E**	**136**	0000	**DBRa**	**Submarine volc**	**0804-08=**	**Historical**											
	31.58 N 140.25 E									? *1672*?	....	....	....	----	?---	----	----	----	*0*	
	18 km SW of Smith Rock									**1870**	05	....	....	----	**xx**--	----	----	----	2	
	31.28 N 139.92 E									? *1873*	....	....	....	----	?---	----	----	----	*0*	
	Just west of Smith Rock									**1916**	0621	....	....	----	**x**---	----	----	----	0	
										? *1974*	*0706*	?*1974*	*0706*	----	?---	----	----	----	*0*	
										? *1975*	*0813*	?*1975*	*0926*	----	?---	----	----	----	*0*	
										? *1976*	*08*	?*1976*	*08*	----	?---	----	----	----	*0*	
										? *1977*	*10*	?*1977*	*10*	----	?---	----	----	----	*0*	
										? *1989*	*0118*	?*1989*	*0118*	----	?---	----	----	----	*0*	
										? *1989*	*0718*	?*1989*	*0718*	----	?---	----	----	----	*0*	
										? *1991*	*1105*	?*1991*	*1105*	----	?---	----	----	----	*0*	
	Shirane (7.5 km NE of Smith Rocks)									? *1992*	*0805*	?*1992*	*1007*	----	?---	----	----	----	*0*	
										? *1993*	*0908*	?*1993*	*0910*	----	?---	----	----	----	*0*	
										? *1994*	*0117*	?*1994*	*0117*	----	?---	----	----	----	*0*	
										? *1994*	*0727*	?*1994*	*0727*	----	?---	----	----	----	*0*	
										? *1995*	*0705*	?*1995*	*0707*	----	?---	----	----	----	*0*	
										? *1996*	*0122*	?*1996*	*0122*	----	?---	----	----	----	*0*	
										? *1997*	*1121*	?*1997*	*1121*	----	?---	----	----	----	*0*	
										? *1998*	*1027*	?*1999*	*0113*	----	?---	----	----	----	*0*	
										? *2000*	*1030*	?*2000*	*1030*	----	?---	----	----	----	*0*	
										? *2001*	*1031*	?*2002*	*0228*	----	?---	----	----	----	*0*	
										? *2002*	*0904*	?*2002*	*0904*	----	?---	----	----	----	*0*	
										? *2003*	*1106*	?*2003*	*1106*	----	?---	----	----	----	*0*	
										? *2005*	*0308*	?*2005*	*0308*	----	?---	----	----	----	*0*	
Tori-shima (Izu Is-Japan)		**30.480 N**	**140.306 E**	**394**	2222	**BDA**	**Stratovolcano**	**0804-09=**	**Historical**											
										1871	04	....	....	----	**x**---	----	----	----	0	
	Komochi-yama, N & SW offshore flanks									**1902**	0807	**1902**	0824	**xx**--	**x**---	**x**-**x**-	**x**---	**xx**--	3	-/7
	North side of 1902 crater (Iwo-yama)									**1939**	0817	**1939**	1226e	**x**---	----	**x**---	**x**---	**x**---	3	7/7
										S **1965**	1113	**1965**	1205d	----	**x**---	----	----	----	0	
	9 km south of Torishima									**1975**	1002	....	....	----	**x**---	----	----	----	2	
	Iwo-yama									**2002**	0812	**2002**	0820	**x**---	----	**x**---	----	----	2	
Sofugan (Izu Is-Japan)		**29.789 N**	**140.345 E**	**99**	0002	**BA**	**Stratovolcano**	**0804-091**	Uncertain											
										? *1975*	....	....	....	----	?---	----	----	----	*0*	
Omachi Seamount (Izu Is-Japan)		29.22 N	140.80 E	-1700		A		0804-092	Not a Volcano											
Suiyo Seamount (Izu Is-Japan)		**28.60 N**	**140.63 E**	**-1418**	0000	**ADB**	**Submarine volc**	**0804-093**	**Fumarolic**											
Mokuyo Seamount (Izu Is-Japan)		**28.32 N**	**140.57 E**	**-920**	0000	**A**	**Submarine volc**	**0804-094**	**Fumarolic**											
Doyo Seamount (Izu Is-Japan)		**27.68 N**	**140.80 E**	**-860**	0000	**BA**	**Submarine volc**	**0804-095**	**Fumarolic**											
Nishino-shima (Volcano Is-Japan)		**27.274 N**	**140.882 E**	**38**	0000	**A**	**Caldera**	**0804-096**	**Historical**											
	East of Nishino-shima									**1973**	0412	**1974**	0505d	----	**xx**--	**x**---	**x**---	----	2	
										? *1975*	....	?*1977*	....	----	?---	----	----	----	*0*	
	6.5 km NW of Nishino-shima									? *1978*	*1116*	?*1979*?	....	----	?---	----	----	----	*0*	
	South, east, and west sides									? *1980*	*0707*	?*1981*?	....	----	?---	----	----	----	*0*	
										? *1982*	*04*	?*1982*	*04*	----	?---	----	----	----	*0*	
										? *1983*	....	?*1984*	....	----	?---	----	----	----	*0*	
										? *1985*	*1202*	?*1985*	*1202*	----	?---	----	----	----	*0*	
										? *1986*	....	?*1990*	....	----	?---	----	----	----	*0*	
										? *2001*	*01*	....	....	----	?---	----	----	----	*0*	

VOLCANO NAME (Subregion) / ERUPTION — Area of Activity	LAT	LONG	ELEV (m)	POPL (5 km, 10, 30, 100)	ROCK TYPE	VOLC TYPE	NUMBER	STATUS	Start Year	Start M-Dy	Stop Year	Stop M-Dy	Central / Flank vent / Radial fiss / Regional	Submarine / New island / Subglacial / Crater lake	Explosive / Pyro flow / Phreatic / Caldera	Lava flow / Lava lake / Dome / Spine	Fatal / Damage / Mudflow / Tsunami	VEI	Vol L/T
Kaikata Seamount (Volcano Is)	**26.67** N	**141.00** E	**-162**	0000	**ABD**	**Submarine volc**	**0804-097**	**Fumarolic**											
Kaitoku Seamount (Volcano Is)	**26.122** N	**141.102** E	**-103**	0003	**BAD**	**Submarine volc**	**0804-10=**	**Historical**											
West flank of Nishi-Kaitokuba									**1543**	....	....	....	-x--	x---	----	----	----	0	
Higashi-Kaitokuba									**1984**	0308	**1984**	0326?	x---	x---	x---	----	----	0	
									? 1984	*1223*	*?1984*	*1223*	----	?---	----	----	----	*0*	
									? 1986	*0618*	*?1986*	*0618*	----	?---	----	----	----	*0*	
Unnamed (Volcano Is-Japan)	**26.13** N	**144.48** E	**-3200**	0000	**U**	**Submarine volc ?**	**0804-101**	Uncertain											
									? 1974	*03*	....	....	----	?---	----	----	----	*0*	
Kita-Iwo-jima (Volcano Is-Japan)	**25.424** N	**141.284** E	**792**	3334	**BA**	**Stratovolcano**	**0804-11=**	**Historical**											
Funka-Asane									**1780**	....	....	....	----	x---	----	----	----	0	
Funka-Asane									**1880**	....	**1889**	....	----	x---	x---	----	----	0	
Funka-Asane									**1930**	....	**1945**	....	----	x---	x---	----	----	2?	
Funka-Asane									*? 1953*	*05*	*?1953*	*05*	----	?---	----	----	----	*0*	
Funka-Asane									*? 1968*	*08*	*?1968*	*08*	----	?---	----	----	----	*0*	
Funka-Asane									*? 1982*	*06*	*?1982*	*06*	----	?---	----	----	----	*0*	
Funka-Asane									*? 1983*	*07*	*?1983*	*07*	----	?---	----	----	----	*0*	
Funka-Asane									*? 1987*	*08*	*?1987*	*08*	----	?---	----	----	----	*0*	
Funka-Asane									*? 1989*	*07*	*?1989*	*07*	----	?---	----	----	----	*0*	
Funka-Asane									*? 1997*	*0310*	*?1997*	*0310*	----	?---	----	----	----	*0*	
Funka-Asane									*? 1998*	*0521*	*?1998*	*0521*	----	?---	----	----	----	*0*	
Funka-Asane									*? 1998*	*1027*	*?1998*	*1027*	----	?---	----	----	----	*0*	
Funka-Asane									*? 1999*	*0907*	*?1999*	*0916*	----	?---	----	----	----	*0*	
Funka-Asane									*? 2000*	*0125*	*?2000*	*0126*	----	?---	----	----	----	*0*	
Funka-Asane									*? 2000*	*1030*	*?2000*	*1030*	----	?---	----	----	----	*0*	
Funka-Asane									*? 2001*	*1029*	*?2001*	*1029*	----	?---	----	----	----	*0*	
Funka-Asane									*? 2002*	*0228*	*?2002*	*0228*	----	?---	----	----	----	*0*	
Funka-Asane									*? 2003*	*0310*	*?2003*	*0310*	----	?---	----	----	----	*0*	
Funka-Asane									*? 2003*	*1104*	*?2003*	*1104*	----	?---	----	----	----	*0*	
Ioto [Iwo-jima] (Volcano Is-Japan)	**24.754** N	**141.290** E	**161**	4444	**YT**	**Caldera**	**0804-12=**	**Historical**											
Motoyama									G-**0850**t	....	....	....	x---	----	x---	x---	----		
Chidoriga-ana									**1889**	1231y	....	....	x---	----	--x-	----	----	1	
West side (Asodai)									**1922**	07	....	....	x---	----	--x-	----	----	1	
NW side near the coast									**1930**?	....	....	....	x---	----	--x-	----	----	1	
SW side at Chidoriga-hara									**1935**	....	....	....	x---	----	--x-	----	----	1	
North and west sides near the coast									**1944**	12	....	....	x---	----	--x-	----	----	1	
Chidoriga-hara									**1957**	0328	**1957**	0328	x---	----	x-x-	----	----	1	-/3
West side (Asodai)									**1967**	1223	**1967**	1223	x---	----	--x-	----	----	1	-/5
West side (Asodai)									**1969**	0112?	**1969**	0121?	x---	----	--x-	----	----	1	
									1969	1201p	**1969**	1201p	x---	----	--x-	----	----	1	
NW of Iwo-jima (Kaiseinishinoba)									*? 1974*	*01*	*?1974*	*0202*	-x--	?---	----	----	----	*0*	
West side (Asodai)									**1976**	01	....	....	x---	----	--x-	----	----	1	
West side (Asodai)									**1978**	1211	**1978**	1211	x---	----	--x-	----	----	1	
Kitanohara									**1980**	0313	**1980**	0313	x---	----	--x-	----	----	1	
NW side (Idogahama beach)									**1982**	0309	**1982**	0310	x---	----	--x-	----	----	1	
West side (Asodai)									**1982**	1128	**1982**	12 ?	x---	?---	--x-	----	----	1	
Asodai area and NE of Iwo-jima									*? 1993*	*1027?*	*?1993*	*1116?*	xx--	?---	--?-	----	----	*1?*	
NE side									**1994**	0822	**1994**	0822	x---	----	--x-	----	----	1	
Asodai area									**1999**	0910	**1999**	0910	x---	----	--x-	----	----	1	
Off SE coast and Idogahama (NW coast)									**2001**	0921	**2001**	1023	x---	xx--	x-x-	----	----	1	
Asodai area									*? 2004*	*0606*	*?2004*	*0608*	x---	----	?-?-	----	----	*1*	
Kita-Fukutokutai (Volcano Is)	**24.414** N	**141.419** E	**-73**	0024	**U**	**Submarine volc**	**0804-121**	**Historical**											
									? 1937	....	....	....	----	?---	----	----	----	*0*	
									? 1947	....	....	....	----	?---	----	----	----	*0*	
									1953	....	**1954**	....	----	x---	x---	----	----	0	
									? 1959	....	....	....	----	?---	----	----	----	*0*	
									? 1988	*0127*	....	....	----	?---	?---	----	----	*1?*	
24.443 N, 141.378 E.									*? 2001*	*1030*	*?2001*	*1030*	----	?---	----	----	----	*0*	
Fukutoku-Okanoba (Volcano Is)	**24.28** N	**141.485** E	**-14**	2223	**Y**	**Submarine volc**	**0804-13=**	**Historical**											
Shin-Iwo-jima									**1904**	1114	**1905**	0516?	----	xx--	x---	----	----	3	8/8
Shin-Iwo-jima									**1914**	0113	**1914**	0821>	----	xx--	x---	----	----	3	-/9
									? 1950	*0201*	*?1950*	*0201*	----	?---	----	----	----	*0*	
									? 1952	*0620*	*?1952*	*0620*	----	?---	----	----	----	*0*	
									? 1953	*1201*	*?1953*	*1201*	----	?---	----	----	----	*0*	
									? 1954	*0204d*	....	....	----	?---	----	----	----	*0*	
									? 1955	*0401*	*?1955*	*0401*	----	?---	----	----	----	*0*	
									? 1956	*0401*	*?1956*	*0501*	----	?---	----	----	----	*0*	
									? 1958	*0701*	*?1958*	*1001*	----	?---	----	----	----	*0*	
									? 1959	*0701*	*?1959*	*1001*	----	?---	----	----	----	*0*	
									? 1960	*0701*	*?1960*	*0901*	----	?---	----	----	----	*0*	
									? 1962	*0701*	*?1962*	*1001*	----	?---	----	----	----	*0*	
									? 1963	*1027*	....	....	----	?---	----	----	----	*0*	
									? 1967	*0701*	*?1967*	*0701*	----	?---	----	----	----	*0*	
									? 1968	*0209*	*?1968*	*0209*	----	?---	----	----	----	*0*	
									? 1968	*0814*	*?1968*	*0820*	----	?---	----	----	----	*0*	
									? 1972	*1001*	*?1972*	*1001*	----	?---	----	----	----	*0*	
3.8 km NNE of Minami-Iwo-jima									**1973**	1218	**1974**	0216	----	x---	x---	----	----	2*	
									1974	1224	*?1975*	*1113*	----	xx--	----	----	----	2	
									? 1976	*0802*	*?1985*	*1223*	----	?---	----	----	----	*0*	
									1986	0118	**1986**	0328?	----	xx--	x---	----	----	2	
									? 1986	*0407*	*?1987*	*0626*	----	?---	----	----	----	*0*	
									1987	0714	**1987**	0830?	----	x---	x---	----	----	0	
									? 1987	*0904*	*?1991*	*0206*	----	?---	----	----	----	*0*	
									? 1991	*0719*	*?1991*	*1018*	----	?---	----	----	----	*0*	
									1992	1110	*?1993*	*0909*	----	x---	x---	----	----	1	-/5
									? 1994	*0728*	*?1994*	*0728*	----	?---	----	----	----	*0*	
									? 1995	*1121*	*?1997*	*0728*	----	?---	----	----	----	*0*	
									? 1997	*1118*	*?1998*	*0521*	----	?---	----	----	----	*0*	
									? 1998	*1016*	*?1999*	*0112*	----	?---	----	----	----	*0*	
									? 1999	*0908*	*?2000*	*0218*	----	?---	----	----	----	*0*	
									? 2000	*0726*	*?2001*	*0613*	----	?---	----	----	----	*0*	
									? 2001	*1030*	*?2002*	*0619*	----	?---	----	----	----	*0*	
									? 2002	*1219*	*?2003*	*0311*	----	?---	----	----	----	*0*	
									2005	0702	**2005**	0721?	----	x---	x---	----	----	1	
									? 2005	*0911*	*?2010>*	....	----	?---	----	----	----	*0*	

VOLCANO NAME (Subregion)	LAT	LONG	ELEV (m)	POPL (5 km/10/30/100)	ROCK TYPE	VOLC TYPE	NUMBER	STATUS	ERUPTION — Area of Activity	Start Year	Start M-Dy	Stop Year	Stop M-Dy	Central/Flank vent/Radial fiss/Regional	Submarine/New island/Subglacial/Crater lake	Explosive/Pyro flow/Phreatic/Caldera	Lava flow/Lava lake/Dome/Spine	Fatal/Damage/Mudflow/Tsunami	VEI	Vol L/T
Minami-Hiyoshi (Volcano Is-Japan)	**23.497 N**	**141.940 E**	**-30**	0002	**Y**	**Submarine volc**	**0804-131**	**Historical**												
									(23.50 N 141.92 E)	**1975**	0825	....	....	----	x---	----	----	----	0	
										? 1976	02	....	....	----	?---	----	----	----	0	
									Hiyoshi-Okinoba (also 23.48 N 141.67 E)	? 1976	1220	?1977	0328	----	?---	----	----	----	0	
										? 1978	0126?	?1978	0324	----	?---	----	----	----	0	
										? 1992	0212	?1992	0304	----	?---	----	----	----	0	
										? 1996	0111	?1996	0112	----	?---	----	----	----	0	
Nikko (Volcano Is-Japan)	**23.075 N**	**142.308 E**	**-391**	0000	**BA**	**Submarine volc**	**0804-132**	**Fumarolic**												
										? 1979	0712	....	....	----	?---	----	----	----	0	
Fukujin (Volcano Is-Japan)	**21.93 N**	**143.47 E**	**-217**	0000	**A**	**Submarine volc**	**0804-133**	**Historical**												
										1951	0715q	**1951**	1015q	----	x---	x---	----	----	0	
										? 1952	....	....	....	----	?---	----	----	----	0	
										? 1958	08	?1958	09	----	?---	----	----	----	0	
										? 1959	08	?1959	10	----	?---	----	----	----	0	
										1968	09	....	....	----	x---	----	----	----	0	
									(21.93 N 143.46 E)	**1973**	0927	**1974**	0305	----	x---	x---	----	----	1	
									(21.95 N 143.45 E)	? 1976	0802	?1977	0421	----	?---	----	----	----	0	
										? 1977	1014	?1978	0324	----	x---	----	----	----	0	
										? 1978	0824	?1978	0825	----	?---	----	----	----	0	
										? 1979	0426	?1980	0512	----	?---	----	----	----	0	
										? 1981	0107	?1981	0108	----	?---	----	----	----	0	
										? 1982	0112	?1982	0316	----	?---	----	----	----	0	
										? 1982	1215	....	....	----	?---	----	----	----	0	
Kasuga (Volcano Is-Japan)	**21.765 N**	**143.710 E**	**-598**	0000	**A**	**Submarine volc**	**0804-134**	**Historical**												
										1959	0715q	....	....	----	x---	----	----	----	0	
									(21.78 N 143.71 E)	? 1975	11	....	....	----	?---	----	----	----	0	
Minami Kasuga (Volcano Is-Japan)	**21.60 N**	**143.637 E**	**-274**	0000	**BAYd**	**Submarine volc**	**0804-135**	**Holocene**												
NW Eifuku (Volcano Is-Japan)	**21.485 N**	**144.043 E**	**-1535**	0000	**BA**	**Submarine volc**	**0804-136**	**Fumarolic**												
Daikoku (Volcano Is-Japan)	**21.324 N**	**144.194 E**	**-323**	0000	**A**	**Submarine volc**	**0804-137**	**Fumarolic**												

MARIANA ISLANDS

VOLCANO NAME (Subregion)	LAT	LONG	ELEV (m)	POPL (5 km/10/30/100)	ROCK TYPE	VOLC TYPE	NUMBER	STATUS	ERUPTION — Area of Activity	Start Year	Start M-Dy	Stop Year	Stop M-Dy	Central/Flank vent/Radial fiss/Regional	Submarine/New island/Subglacial/Crater lake	Explosive/Pyro flow/Phreatic/Caldera	Lava flow/Lava lake/Dome/Spine	Fatal/Damage/Mudflow/Tsunami	VEI	Vol L/T
Unnamed (Mariana Is-C Pacific)	**21.00 N**	**142.90 E**		0000	**U**	**Submarine volc ?**	**0804-138**	Uncertain												
										? 1975	0910	....	....	----	?---	----	----	----	0	
Unnamed (Mariana Is-C Pacific)	**20.30 N**	**143.20 E**		0000	**U**	**Submarine volc ?**	**0804-139**	Uncertain												
										? 1975	0910	....	....	----	?---	----	----	----	0	
Farallon de Pajaros (Mariana Is)	**20.538 N**	**144.896 E**	**360**	0000	**A**	**Stratovolcano**	**0804-14=**	**Historical**												
									SW side	**1864**	0107	....	....	-x--	----	x---	----	----	2	
									(publication date of 1864 eruption)	X 1865	....	....	....	----	----	----	----	----		
									Summit, NE side	**1874**?	....	**1876**	0103>	xx--	----	x---	x---	----	2	
									Summit, east side	**1900**?	....	**1901**	05	xx--	----	x---	x---	----	2	
									North side ?	**1912**	....	....	....	-?--	----	x---	?---	----	2	
										1925	....	....	....	----	----	x---	----	----	2	
										1928	1215e	....	....	----	----	x---	----	----	2?	
									Summit, east side ?	**1932**	0907	**1932**	1007	x?--	----	x---	x---	----	2	
									Immediately south of Uracas	**1934**	0715q	....	....	-x--	x---	x---	----	----	0	
										1936	0415q	....	....	x---	----	x---	----	----	2	
									East side ?	**1939**	....	....	....	-?--	----	x---	?---	----	2	
										1941	0328	....	....	x---	----	x---	x---	----		
									Summit, south side	**1943**	....	....	....	xx--	----	x---	x---	----	2	
									North side	**1947**	01 ?	....	....	-x--	----	----	x---	----	0?	
										1951	08	....	....	x---	----	x---	----	----	2	
									Summit, east side	**1952**	1026e	**1953**	0415	xx--	----	x---	x---	----	2	
									SW of Uracas (Makhahnas seamount)	S **1967**	0327	S**1967**	0410	-x--	x---	----	----	----	0	
Ahyi (Mariana Is-C Pacific)	**20.42 N**	**145.03 E**	**-137**	0000	**AB**	**Submarine volc**	**0804-141**	**Seismicity**												
										? 1979	1115	....	....	x---	?---	----	----	----	0	
									20.34°N, 145.02°E.	S **2001**	0424	S**2001**	0425	-?--	x---	----	----	----	0	
Supply Reef (Mariana Is-C Pacific)	**20.13 N**	**145.10 E**	**-8**	0000	**A**	**Submarine volc**	**0804-142**	**Hydrophonic**												
									NW of Supply Reef (20.24 N, 145.02 E)	S **1969**	0311	S**1969**	0313	----	x---	----	----	----	0	
									25 km? NW of Supply Reef	? 1985	0902	....	....	----	?---	----	----	----	0	
									NW of Supply Reef (ca. 20.3 N 144.9E)	@ **1989**	0921	@**1989**	1227	----	x---	----	----	----	0	
Maug Islands (Mariana Is-C Pacific)	**20.02 N**	**145.22 E**	**227**	0000	**BAD**	**Stratovolcano**	**0804-143**	**Fumarolic**												
Asuncion (Mariana Is-C Pacific)	**19.671 N**	**145.406 E**	**857**	0000	**A**	**Stratovolcano**	**0804-15=**	**Historical**												
										? 1690j	....	....	....	----	----	----	----	----		
										? 1775j	....	....	....	----	----	?---	----	----	2	
									(same as 1775j eruption: Corwin)	X 1786	....	....	....	----	----	----	----	----		
									(no specific ref. to 1819 activity)	X 1819	....	....	....	----	----	----	----	----		
									(steaming only, no eruption)	X 1901	....	....	....	----	----	----	----	----		
									Upper SE and west flanks	**1906**	....	....	....	-x--	----	x---	x---	----	2	
										? 1924	....	....	....	--x-	----	-?--	----	--?-	2?	
Agrigan (Mariana Is-C Pacific)	**18.77 N**	**145.67 E**	**965**	0000	**BA**	**Stratovolcano**	**0804-16=**	**Historical**												
										1917	0409	....	....	x---	----	x---	----	-x--	4	
Pagan (Mariana Is-C Pacific)	**18.13 N**	**145.80 E**	**570**	0000	**BA**	**Stratovolcanoes**	**0804-17=**	**Historical**												
									North Pagan (west flank maar)	G **1340**v	....	....	....	-x--	----	xx--	----	----		
									North Pagan	**1669**	....	....	....	----	----	x---	?---	----		
									North Pagan (west flank maar)	C **1800**t	....	....	....	-x--	----	xx--	----	----		
									North Pagan	**1825**e	....	....	....	----	----	x---	----	----	2?	
									South Pagan	**1864**	....	....	....	----	----	x---	----	----	1?	
									North Pagan	**1873**?	....	....	....	x---	----	x---	x---	----	3?	
									North Pagan	**1909**	....	....	....	x---	----	x---	----	----	2	
									North Pagan	**1917**	....	....	....	x---	----	x---	----	----	2	
									North Pagan	**1923**	02 ?	**1923**	0326e	x---	----	x---	x---	----	3*	
										1925	02	**1925**	0505	x---	----	x---	x---	----	2	
									South Pagan, cone within caldera	? 1929	....	?1930	....	x---	----	?---	----	----		
									("eruption" actually a grassfire)	X 1966	0523	....	....	----	----	----	----	----		
									North Pagan (summit and north flank)	**1981**	0515	**1985**	0501>	xxx-	----	xx--	x---	-x--	4*	7/8
									North Pagan	**1987**	0904	**1987**	0904	x---	----	x---	----	----	1	
									North Pagan	? 1988	0216	....	....	x---	----	?---	----	----		
									North Pagan	**1988**	0824	**1988**	1012	x---	----	x---	----	----	2	
									North Pagan	**1992**	0413	**1992**	0413	x---	----	x---	----	----	1?	
									North Pagan	**1993**	0115e	**1993**	11 >	x---	----	x---	----	--x-	2	

VOLCANO NAME (Subregion) / **ERUPTION** — Area of Activity	**LAT**	**LONG**	**ELEV** (m)	**POPL** 5 km 10 30 100	**ROCK TYPE**	**VOLC TYPE** / — Start — **Year**	**NUMBER** / M-Dy	**STATUS** / — Stop — **Year**	M-Dy	ERUPTIVE CHARACTERISTICS: Central, Flank vent, Radial fiss, Regional	Submarine, New island, Subglacial, Crater lake	Explosive, Pyro flow, Phreatic, Caldera	Lava flow, Lava lake, Dome, Spine	Fatal, Damage, Mudflow, Tsunami	**VEI**	**Vol L/T**
Pagan (Mariana Is-C Pacific) *continued*																
North Pagan						**1996**	....	....	....	x---	----	x-x-	----	----	1	
North Pagan						**2006**	1204	**2006**	1208	x---	----	x---	----	----	1	
						? 2009	*0415*	....	....	x---	----	?---	----	----	*2*	
Alamagan (Mariana Is-C Pacific)	**17.60 N**	**145.83 E**	**744**	0000	**AB**	**Stratovolcano**	**0804-18=**	**Radiocarbon**								
						C **0540**u	....	....	....	x---	----	xx--	----	----		
						C **0870**v	....	....	....	x---	----	xx--	----	----	4	-/8
						? 1864	*01*	....	....	x---	----	?---	----	----		
						? 1887	*1129*	....	....	----	----	?---	----	----		
Guguan (Mariana Is-C Pacific)	**17.307 N**	**145.845 E**	**287**	0000	**AB**	**Stratovolcano**	**0804-19=**	**Historical**								
(solfataric activity only)						*X 1819*	....	....	....	----	----	----	----	----		
						1883a	....	....	....	x---	----	x---	x---	----	2?	
(solfataric activity only)						*X 1901*	....	....	....	----	----	----	----	----		
Zealandia Bank (Mariana Is)	**16.88 N**	**145.85 E**	**0**	0000	**BA**	**Stratovolcano**	**0804-191**	**Fumarolic**								
Sarigan (Mariana Is-C Pacific)	**16.708 N**	**145.78 E**	**538**	0000	**AB**	**Stratovolcano**	**0804-192**	**Holocene**								
Anatahan (Mariana Is-C Pacific)	**16.35 N**	**145.67 E**	**790**	0000	**ADby**	**Stratovolcano**	**0804-20=**	**Historical**								
East Crater						**2003**	0510	**2003**	0712c	x---	----	xxx-	x-x-	----	3	-/7
East Crater						**2004**	0412<	**2005**	0903?	x---	---x	xx--	x-x-	-x--	3?	
East Crater						**2006**	0320?	**2006**	0626?	x---	----	x---	----	----	2*	
						2007	1127c	**2008**	0809?	x---	----	x---	----	----	2*	
East Diamante (Mariana Is)	**15.93 N**	**145.67 E**	**-127**	0005	**D**	**Submarine volc**	**0804-201**	**Fumarolic**								
Ruby (Mariana Is-C Pacific)	**15.62 N**	**145.57 E**	**-230**	0005	**B**	**Submarine volc**	**0804-202**	**Historical**								
						S **1966**	0421g	S**1966**	05	----	x---	----	----	----	0	
						1995	1011?	**1995**	1025	----	x---	----	----	----	0	
Esmeralda Bank (Mariana Is)	**15.00 N**	**145.25 E**	**-43**	0005	**BA**	**Submarine volc**	**0804-21=**	**Fumarolic**								
						? 1944	*0820*j	....	....	----	?---	----	----	----	*0*	
						? 1964	*0414*	....	....	----	?---	----	----	----	*2*	
						*? 1970*a	....	....	....	----	?---	----	----	----	*0*	
						? 1975	*0426*	*?1975*	*0429*	----	?---	----	----	----	*0*	
						? 1982	*0406*	....	....	----	?---	----	----	----	*0*	
						? 1987	*0526*	....	....	----	?---	----	----	----	*0*	
NW Rota-1 (Mariana Is-C Pacific)	**14.601 N**	**144.775 E**	**-517**	0004	**BA**	**Submarine volc**	**0804-211**	**Historical**								
Upper South flank (Brimstone Pit)						**2003**?	....	**2009**	04 >	-x--	x---	x---	x---	----	0	
Forecast Seamount (Mariana Is)	**13.40 N**	**143.92 E**		0006	**U**	**Submarine volc**	**0804-22-**	**Fumarolic**								
Seamount X (Mariana Is-C Pacific)	**13.25 N**	**144.02 E**	**-1230**	0006	**B**	**Submarine volc**	**0804-23-**	**Fumarolic**								

HOKKAIDO

VOLCANO NAME (Subregion) / **ERUPTION** — Area of Activity	**LAT**	**LONG**	**ELEV** (m)	**POPL** 5 km 10 30 100	**ROCK TYPE**	**VOLC TYPE** / — Start — **Year**	**NUMBER** / M-Dy	**STATUS** / — Stop — **Year**	M-Dy	ERUPTIVE CHARACTERISTICS: Central, Flank vent, Radial fiss, Regional	Submarine, New island, Subglacial, Crater lake	Explosive, Pyro flow, Phreatic, Caldera	Lava flow, Lava lake, Dome, Spine	Fatal, Damage, Mudflow, Tsunami	**VEI**	**Vol L/T**
Oshima-Oshima (Hokkaido)	**41.507 N**	**139.371 E**	**737**	1115	**BA**	**Stratovolcano**	**0805-01=**	**Historical**								
Nishi-yama						C-**0800**v	....	....	....	x---	----	x---	----	----		
Nishi-yama						C **0250**w	....	....	....	x---	----	x---	----	----		
Nishi-yama						**1741**	0818?	**1742**	05	x---	----	x--A	x---	xx-x	4*	-/8
Nishi-yama						**1759**	0819	....	....	x---	----	x---	----	----	2	-/6
Nishi-yama						*? 1786*	....	....	....	x---	----	----	----	----	*2?*	
Nishi-yama						**1790**	01 ?	....	....	x---	----	x---	----	----	2	
E-san (Hokkaido)	**41.802 N**	**141.170 E**	**618**	4456	**A**	**Stratovolcano**	**0805-011**	**Historical**								
						G-**7050**?	....	....	....	x---	----	xx--	--x-	----	3	-/7
NW E-san (Es-1 tephra)						G-**3900**v	....	....	....	----	----	xx--	----	--x-		
NW E-san (Es-2 tephra)						T-**1050**?	....	....	....	----	----	x-x-	----	----		
(Es-3 tephra)						T-**0550**?	....	....	....	----	----	xx-A	----	----		
NW E-san (Es-4 tephra)						T **1350**?	....	....	....	----	----	-xx-	----	----		
(Es-5 tephra)						**1846**	1118	....	....	x---	----	--x-	----	xxx-	1	
(Es-6 tephra)						**1874**	0608	....	....	----	----	--x-	----	----	1	-/5
Komaga-take (Hokkaido)	**42.061 N**	**140.681 E**	**1131**	3566	**A**	**Stratovolcano**	**0805-02=**	**Historical**								
(tephra layer Ko-g)						G-**4600**t	....	....	....	x---	----	xx--	----	----	**5**	-/9
(NS1 and NS2 tephras)						T-**4500**w	....	....	....	x---	----	xx--	----	----		
(tephra layer Ko-f)						G-**4350**?	....	....	....	x---	----	xx--	----	----	**P**	
(tephra layer Ko-d)						**1640**	0731	**1640**	1009	x---	----	xxxA	----	xxxx	**5**	-/9
(tephra layer Ko-c2)						**1694**	0704	**1694**	0706	x---	----	xx--	----	----	4	-/8
						? 1710	*0627*	....	....	----	----	----	----	----		
						? 1765	....	....	....	x---	----	--x-	----	----	*2*	
						? 1784	*0208*	....	....	x---	----	--x-	----	----	*2*	
Ansei Crater (tephra layer Ko-c1)						**1856**	0925	....	....	x---	----	xx--	--x-	xx--	4	-/8
NW side of 1856 (Ansei) crater						**1888**	0414	....	....	x---	----	--x-	----	----	2	
South of Ansei Crater						**1905**	0819	**1905**	0901?	x---	----	--x-	----	-xx-	2	
SE of Ansei Crater						**1919**	0617	**1919**	0726	x---	----	x-x-	----	----	2	
						1922	0522	....	....	x---	----	--x-	----	----	2	
						1923	0227	**1923**	0315	x---	----	--x-	----	----	2	
						1924	0731	....	....	x---	----	x-x-	----	----	2	
						1928	0328	....	....	x---	----	x-?-	----	----	1	
SE and NE of Ansei Crater (layer Ko-a)						**1929**	0617	**1929**	0906	x---	----	xx--	----	xxx-	4	-/8
(fumarolic activity only)						*X 1935*	*0708*	....	....	----	----	----	----	----		
						? 1935	*1015*	*?1935*	*1015*	x---	----	--?-	----	----		
						1937	0317	**1937**	0319	x---	----	x-x-	----	----	1	
NW-SE 1.6-km fissure						**1942**	1116	**1942**	1118	x-x-	----	xxx-	----	--x-	3	-/6
1929 crater and summit crater fissure						**1996**	0305	**1996**	0312?	x-x-	----	x-x-	----	----	1	
1996 crater						**1998**	1025	**1998**	1025	x---	----	xxx-	----	----	2	
						2000	0904	**2000**	1108	x---	----	xxx-	----	----	1	
Usu (Hokkaido)	**42.541 N**	**140.843 E**	**737**	4567	**BADR**	**Stratovolcano**	**0805-03=**	**Historical**								
						T-**6550***	....	....	....	x---	----	----	x---	----		
(Zenkoji debris avalanche)						T-**5550**z	....	....	....	x---	----	--?A	----	----		
						? 1611	*10*	....	....	----	----	?---	----	----		
						1626	0519	**1626**	07 ?	----	----	?---	----	----		
						1638	0725	....	....	----	----	x---	----	----		
(Usu-b Pumice)						**1663**	0816	**1663**	0905d	x---	----	xxx-	----	xx--	**5**	-/9
						T **1690**j	....	....	....	x---	----	xxx-	----	----		
Ko-Usu						**1769**	0123	....	....	x---	----	xx--	--x-	-x--	4	7/8
Foot of Ko-Usu dome, Ogari-yama						**1822**	0312	**1822**	09	x---	----	xx--	--x-	xxx-	4	-/8
O-Usu						**1853**	0422	**1853**	09	x---	----	xx--	--x-	-x--	4	8/8
North flank (Meiji-Shinzan)						**1910**	0725	**1910**	11	-x--	----	x-x-	--x-	xxx-	2	-/6
East flank (Showa-Shinzan)						**1944**	0623	**1945**	0919	-x--	----	xxx-	--x-	xxx-	2	7/6
Usu-Shinzan						**1977**	0807	**1982**	03	x---	----	xxx-	--x-	xxx-	3*	-/8
North flank (Kompira-yama & W Nishi-yama)						**2000**	0331	**2001**	0915e	-x--	----	xxx-	----	-xx-	2	

VOLCANO NAME (Subregion) / ERUPTION — Area of Activity	LAT	LONG	ELEV (m)	POPL 5 km 10 30 100	ROCK TYPE	VOLC TYPE / Start Year	NUMBER / Start M-Dy	Stop Year	STATUS / Stop M-Dy	Central, Flank vent, Radial fiss, Regional	Submarine, New island, Subglacial, Crater lake	Explosive, Pyro flow, Phreatic, Caldera	Lava flow, Lava lake, Dome, Spine	Fatal, Damage, Mudflow, Tsunami	VEI	Vol L/T
Niseko (Hokkaido)	42.88 N	140.63 E	1154	3457	A	Stratovolcanoes	0805-031		Tephrochronology							
						T-4900?	....	....	....	----	----	x-x-	----	----		
Yotei (Hokkaido)	42.830 N	140.815 E	1898	3557	AD	Stratovolcano	0805-032		Tephrochronology							
						T-3550?	....	....	....	----	----	?---	----	----		
NW flank (Hangetsu-ko)						T-1050?	....	....	....	-x--	----	x---	----	----		
Kuttara (Hokkaido)	42.489 N	141.163 E	581	5567	BADR	Stratovolcanoes	0805-034		Tephrochronology							
Hiyori-yama lava dome						T-8050?	....	....	....	-x--	----	----	--x-	----		7/-
						G 0200u	....	....	....	----	----	x-x-	----	----		
West flank (Jigoku-dani)						T 1820v	....	....	....	-x--	----	--x-	----	----	1	-/5
Shikotsu (Hokkaido)	42.688 N	141.380 E	1320	6667	ADR	Caldera	0805-04=		Historical							
Tarumai (Ta-d tephra)						C-6950?	....	....	....	x---	----	xx--	----	----	5	-/9
Tarumai (Ta-c1, Ta-c2 tephras)						C-0550?	....	....	....	x---	----	xx--	----	----	5	-/9
Eniwa volcano (east side of summit)						G-0100v	....	....	....	x---	----	x---	----	----	2	
Tarumai (Ta-c3 tephra)						T-0050?	....	....	....	x---	----	x---	----	----	3	-/7
Eniwa (crater 1)						G 1500w	....	....	....	x---	----	x-x-	----	----	2	
Eniwa (crater 2)						G 1550u	....	....	....	x---	----	x-x-	----	--x-	2	
Tarumai (Ta-b tephra)						1667	0923	1667	0926?	x---	----	xx--	----	----	5	-/9
Eniwa (crater 3)						T 1707r	....	....	....	x---	----	x-x-	----	--x-	2	
Tarumai (Ta-a tephra)						1739	0819	1739	0831	x---	----	xx-x	----	----	5	-/9
Tarumai						1804	....	1817	....	x---	----	xx--	----	-x--	3	-/7
Tarumai						1867	0908	....	....	x---	----	x---	--x-	----	2	
Tarumai						? *1871*	*1225*	?*1871*	*1228*	x---	----	x---	----	----	*2*	
Tarumai						1874	0208	1874	0216	x---	----	xx--	----	----	3*	-/7
Tarumai						1883	1007	1883	1105	x---	----	x---	----	----	2	
Tarumai						1885	0104	1885	03	x---	----	x---	----	----	2	
Tarumai						1886	0413	1886	0428	x---	----	x---	----	----	2	
Tarumai						1887	0903	1887	1008	x---	----	x---	----	----	2	
Tarumai						1894	0208	1894	0208	x---	----	x---	----	----	2	
Tarumai						1894	0817	1894	0817	x---	----	x---	----	----	2	
Tarumai						1909	0111	1909	0422	x---	----	x---	--x-	----	3*	7/-
Tarumai (east-west summit fissure)						1917	0430	1917	0512	x-x-	----	x---	----	----	2	
Tarumai						1918	0613	1918	0731	x---	----	x---	----	----	1	
Tarumai						1919	0504	1919	0504	x---	----	x---	----	----	2	
Tarumai						1920	0717	1920	0723	x---	----	x---	----	----	1	
Tarumai						1921	0706	1921	0706	x---	----	x---	----	----	1	
Tarumai						1923	02	1923	0823	x---	----	x---	----	----	1	
Tarumai						1926	1019	1926	1030	x---	----	x---	----	----	2	
Tarumai						1928	0107	1928	0107	x---	----	x---	----	----	2	
Tarumai						1928	0906	1929	0210	x---	----	x---	----	----	1	
Tarumai						1931	1011	1931	1024	x---	----	x---	----	----	1	
Tarumai (east-west summit fissure)						1933	1201	1933	1214	x-x-	----	x---	----	----	2	
Tarumai						1936	0419	1936	0419	x---	----	x---	----	----	1	
Tarumai						1936	1115	1936	1126	x---	----	x---	----	----	1	
Tarumai						1944	0702	1944	0702	x---	----	x-x-	----	----	1	
Tarumai						? *1944*	*1125*	?*1944*	*1125*	x---	----	----	----	----	*1?*	
Tarumai						1951	0129	1951	0129	x---	----	x---	----	----	2	
Tarumai						1951	0728	1951	0728	x---	----	x---	----	--x-	2	
Tarumai						1953	0914?	1953	0914?	x---	----	x-x-	----	----	1	
Tarumai						1954	0502	1954	0502	x---	----	x---	----	--x-	1	
Tarumai						1954	1119	1955	0214	x---	----	x---	----	----	1	
Tarumai (SE foot of summit dome)						1978	0514	1978	0517	x---	----	xxx-	----	----	1	-/4
Tarumai (SE foot of summit dome)						1978	1212	1979	0511	x---	----	x-x-	----	----	1	
Tarumai						1981	0227<	....	....	x---	----	--x-	----	----	0	-/2
Rishiri (Hokkaido)	45.18 N	141.25 E	1721	3455	ADBr	Stratovolcano	0805-041		Radiocarbon							
(Rs-Ho tephra layer)						C-5830y	....	....	....	-x--	----	x---	----	----		
Tokachi (Hokkaido)	43.416 N	142.690 E	2077	2357	ABD	Stratovolcanoes	0805-05=		Historical							
(To-h tephra)						G-2650x	....	....	....	----	----	x-x-	----	----		
						G-1750t	....	....	....	----	----	-x--	----	----		
Ground Crater						G-1350?	....	....	....	x---	----	xx--	----	----	3	-/7
						G 0000t	....	....	....	----	----	x-x-	----	----		
(To-f tephra)						G 0350v	....	....	....	----	----	x---	----	----		
(To-d, To-e tephras)						T 0600y	....	....	....	----	----	x---	----	----		
(To-c tephra)						G 0950t	....	....	....	----	----	x---	----	----		
						T 1050x	....	....	....	----	----	x---	x---	----		
(To-b tephra)						G 1250?	....	....	....	x---	----	x-x-	----	----	3	-/7
Maru-yama						G 1570v	....	....	....	x---	----	x---	x---	----	2?	7/-
						1857	....	....	....	x---	----	x---	----	----	2	
Lower part of Maru-yama?						1887	06	....	....	-x--	----	x-?-	----	----	2	
Maru-yama (Yunuma)						1889	....	....	....	x---	----	?---	----	----	2	
Shin-funkako.						1925	1120	1927	09	x---	----	xxx-	----	xxx-	3*	
Shin-funkako.						1928	01	1928	0523	x---	----	x-x-	----	----	1	
Shin-funkako.						1928	1204	1928	1225	x---	----	--x-	----	----	1	
						1931	0516	1931	0516	----	----	x-x-	----	----	1	
NE of Shin-funkako (Showa Crater)						1952	0817	....	....	x---	----	--x-	----	----		
NE of Shin-funkako (Showa Crater)						1954	09	1954	09	x---	----	--x-	----	----	1	
NE of Shin-funkako (Showa Crater)						1956	06	1956	06	x---	----	--x-	----	----	1	
NE of Shin-funkako (Showa Crater)						? *1957*	*0820*	?*1957*	*0820*	x---	----	--x-	----	----	*1*	
NE of Shin-funkako (Showa Crater)						1958	1004	1958	1004	x---	----	--x-	----	----	1	
NE of Shin-funkako (Showa Crater)						1959	0815e	1959	1125	x---	----	--x-	----	----	1	
NW of Kami-Horokamettoku-yama						1961	0814	1961	0814	x---	----	--x-	----	----	1	
South of Shin-funkako						1962	0629	1962	09	x---	----	x---	----	xx--	3	-/7
East wall of 1962 crater						1985	0619	1985	0622	x---	----	x-x-	----	----	1	
1962 Crater						1988	1210?	1989	05	x---	----	xxx-	----	--x-	2*	-/5
1962-II Crater						2004	0225	2004	0419	x---	----	x-x-	----	----	1?	
Daisetsu (Hokkaido)	43.661 N	142.858 E	2290	2357	AD	Stratovolcanoes	0805-06=		Tephrochronology							
Asahi-dake (Asahi Scoria deposit)						G-3200u	....	....	....	----	----	x---	----	----		
Asahi-dake (As-A tephra)						G-2800v	....	....	....	----	----	x-x-	----	----		
Asahi-dake (As-B tephra)						G-1450t	....	....	....	----	----	x-x-	----	----		
Asahi-dake (Ash-b tephra)						T-0550z	....	....	....	----	----	x-x-	----	----		
Asahi-dake.						T 1739>	....	....	....	?-?-	----	x-x-	----	----		
Nipesotsu-Maruyama (Hokkaido)	43.453 N	143.036 E	2013	0147	ADR	Stratovolcanoes	0805-061		Historical							
Maru-yama (My-b tephra)						G-1700?	....	....	....	----	----	x-x-	----	----	2	-/6
Maru-yama (No. 1 crater)						1898	1203?	1898	1206	x-x-	----	x-x-	----	--x-	2	-/6

VOLCANO NAME (Subregion) / ERUPTION — Area of Activity	LAT	LONG	ELEV (m)	POPL 5 km 10 30 100	ROCK TYPE	VOLC TYPE / — Start — Year	NUMBER / M-Dy	STATUS / — Stop — Year	M-Dy	Central, Flank vent, Radial fiss, Regional	Submarine, New island, Subglacial, Crater lake	Explosive, Pyro flow, Phreatic, Caldera	Lava flow, Lava lake, Dome, Spine	Fatal, Damage, Mudflow, Tsunami	VEI	Vol L/T
Shikaribetsu Group (Hokkaido)	**43.312 N**	**143.096 E**	**1401**	2357	**AD**	**Lava domes**	**0805-062**	Holocene?								
Akan (Hokkaido)	**43.384 N**	**144.013 E**	**1499**	4446	**ADBR**	**Caldera**	**0805-07=**	**Historical**								
Me-Akan (Nakamachineshiri)						C-**7050**?	....	....	....	----	----	xx--	----	----	4	-/8
Me-Akan (Ponmachineshiri)						C-**4550**z	....	....	....	----	----	----	x---	----		
Me-Akan (Nakamachineshiri)						C-**3550**z	....	....	....	----	----	xx--	----	--x-	3	-/7
Nishi-yama, O-Akan						C-**3050**?	....	....	....	x---	----	x---	x---	----		
Kita-yama, Me-Akan (Ponmachineshiri)						C-**2050**?	....	....	....	----	----	x---	x---	----		
Me-Akan (Ponmachineshiri)						C-**0800**	....	....	....	----	----	x---	----	--x-		
Akan-Fuji (tephra layer AS-1)						T-**0550**?	....	....	....	----	----	x---	----	----		
Akan-Fuji (tephra layers AS-2-6, AL-1-3)						T-**0300**v	....	....	....	----	----	x---	x---	----		
Akan-Fuji (AS-7 tephra)						G-**0050**?	....	....	....	----	----	xx--	x---	----	**P**	
Akan-Fuji (AS-8,9 tephras)						T **0100**v	....	....	....	----	----	x---	----	----		
Akan-Fuji (AS-10 and AL-4 tephras)						G **0250**?	....	....	....	----	----	x---	x---	----		
Akan-Fuji (AS-11-17 tephras)						T **0600**y	....	....	....	----	----	x---	----	----		
Me-Akan (Ponmachineshiri)						T **0950**?	....	....	....	x---	----	x---	x---	----		
Me-Akan (Ponmachineshiri Po-29-15)						T **1250**y	....	....	....	----	----	x?x-	?---	----		
Me-Akan (Ponmachineshiri tephra Po-14)						T **1550**?	....	....	....	----	----	x-x-	----	----		
Me-Akan (Ponmachineshiri tephra Po-13,12)						T **1600**t	....	....	....	----	----	x-x-	----	----		
Me-Akan (Ponmachineshiri Po-11 tephra)						**1780**u	....	....	....	x---	----	x---	----	----	1	
Me-Akan						**1808**?	....	....	....	----	----	--?-	----	----		
Me-Akan						*? 1927*	*04*	*?1927*	*05*	x---	----	--?-	----	----	*1*	
Me-Akan (NE foot)						*? 1951*	*0731*	*?1952*	*03*	-x--	----	--?-	----	----	*1*	
Me-Akan (Nakamachineshiri)						**1954**	0107?	**1954**	0413	x---	----	x-x-	----	----	1*	
Me-Akan (Ponmachineshiri)						**1955**	1119	**1955**	1119	x---	----	x-x-	----	----	1	-/4
Me-Akan (Ponmachineshiri)						**1956**	0318	**1956**	1031	x---	----	x-x-	----	----	1	-/5
Me-Akan (Ponmachineshiri)						**1957**	0226	**1957**	0905	x---	----	x-x-	----	----	1	
Me-Akan (Ponmachineshiri)						**1958**	0223	**1958**	0223	x---	----	x-x-	----	----	1	
Me-Akan (Naka- and Ponmachineshiri)						**1959**	0515e	**1959**	10	x---	----	--x-	----	----	1	
Me-Akan (Ponmachineshiri)						**1960**	09	**1960**	09	x---	----	--x-	----	----	1	
Me-Akan (Nakamachineshiri)						**1962**	0428	**1962**	0428	x---	----	--x-	----	----	1	
Me-Akan (Nakamachineshiri)						**1964**	0618	**1964**	0704?	x---	----	--x-	----	----	1	
Me-Akan (Nakamachineshiri)						**1965**	0515e	**1965**	0515e	x---	----	--x-	----	----	1	
Me-Akan (Nakamachineshiri)						**1966**	0615e	**1966**	0615e	x---	----	--x-	----	----	1	
Me-Akan (Ponmachineshiri)						**1984**	0501	**1984**	0501	x---	----	x-x-	----	----	1	
Me-Akan (SE rim of Ponmachineshiri)						**1988**	0105	**1988**	0218?	x---	----	x-x-	----	----	1	
Me-Akan (Ponmachineshiri crater no. 4)						**1996**	1121	**1996**	1121	x---	----	x-x-	----	----	1	
Me-Akan (Ponmachineshiri crater)						**1998**	1109	**1998**	1109	x---	----	x-x-	----	----	1	
NE flank of Me-Akan						**2006**	0321	**2006**	0321	x---	----	x-x-	----	----	1	
Me-Akan (Ponmachineshiri crater)						**2008**	1118	**2008**	1128	x---	----	x-x-	----	----	1	
Kutcharo (Hokkaido)	**43.608 N**	**144.443 E**	**999**	4456	**DARB**	**Caldera**	**0805-08=**	**Tephrochronology**								
Atosanupuri						T-**5800***	....	....	....	x---	----	----	--x-	----		
Atosanupuri						T-**3550**?	....	....	....	x---	----	xx--	--x-	----		
Atosanupuri						T-**1550***	....	....	....	x---	----	----	--x-	----		
Atosanupuri (At-b tephra)						T **0450**?	....	....	....	x---	----	x-x-	----	----		
Atosanupuri						T **0700**?	....	....	....	x---	----	----	--x-	----		
Atosanupuri (At-a tephra)						T **1320**y	....	....	....	x---	----	x-x-	----	----		
Mashu (Hokkaido)	**43.570 N**	**144.565 E**	**855**	4456	**ADB**	**Caldera**	**0805-081**	**Radiocarbon**								
(tephra layers Ma-j-f)						G-**5550**v	....	....	....	x---	----	xx-x	----	----	**6**	-/10
Kamuinupuri (tephra layer Ma-e)						G-**3550**s	....	....	....	-x--	----	xx--	----	----	4	-/8
Kamuinupuri (tephra layer Ma-e')						T-**2800***	....	....	....	-x--	----	x---	----	----	3	-/7
Kamuinupuri (tephra layer Ma-d)						G-**2050**s	....	....	....	-x--	----	xx--	----	----	4	-/8
Kamuinupuri (tephra layers Ma-c4-c2)						G **0150**v	....	....	....	----	----	x---	----	----	4	-/8
Kamuinupuri (tephra layer Ma-c1)						G **0350**v	....	....	....	----	----	x---	----	----	2	-/6
Kamuinupuri (tephra layer Ma-b)						G **1080**v	....	....	....	-x--	----	x--x	----	----	**5**	-/9
Rausu (Hokkaido)	**44.073 N**	**145.126 E**	**1660**	2446	**AD**	**Stratovolcano**	**0805-082**	**Radiocarbon**								
(Ra3-Ra8 tephras)						G-**0270**v	....	....	....	x---	----	xx--	----	----		
SW flank (Tencho-zan; Ten-a tephra)						G **0080**t	....	....	....	--x-	----	x-x-	----	----	3	-/7
(Ra2 tephra)						G **0550**v	....	....	....	x---	----	xx--	----	----	4	-/8
(Ra1 tephra)						G **1350**v	....	....	....	x---	----	xx--	----	----	3	-/7
						T **1800**t	....	....	....	x---	----	xx--	----	----	3	
Shiretoko-Iwo-zan (Hokkaido)	**44.131 N**	**145.165 E**	**1563**	1446	**A**	**Stratovolcano**	**0805-09=**	**Historical**								
(St-1 tephra layer)						T **0850**z	....	....	....	----	----	x-x-	----	----		
						1857	....	**1858**	....	----	----	--?-	----	----		
NW flank						**1876**	0923	**1876**	0926	-x--	----	--x-	----	----	2	
						? 1880	*1124*	*?1880*	*1126*	----	----	--?-	----	----		
NW flank						**1889**	0809	**1889**	0825	-x--	----	--x-	----	----	2?	
NW flank						**1890**	0615	....	....	-x--	----	--x-	----	----	1	
NW flank						**1935**	12	**1936**	10	-x--	----	--x-	----	----	1	

Ichio Moriya (Kanazawa Univ.)

Historical eruptions of Hokkaido's Usu volcano, with multiple flank and summit lava domes rising above Lake Toya, have impacted the town of Toyako-Onsen at its base.

Yukio Hayakawa (Gunma Univ.)

The symmetrical post-caldera cone of Haruna-Fuji, rising above Haruna Lake, is one of many Japanese volcanoes named after the country's most renowned landmark.

Kuriles, Kamchatka, & Mainland Asia (09 &10)

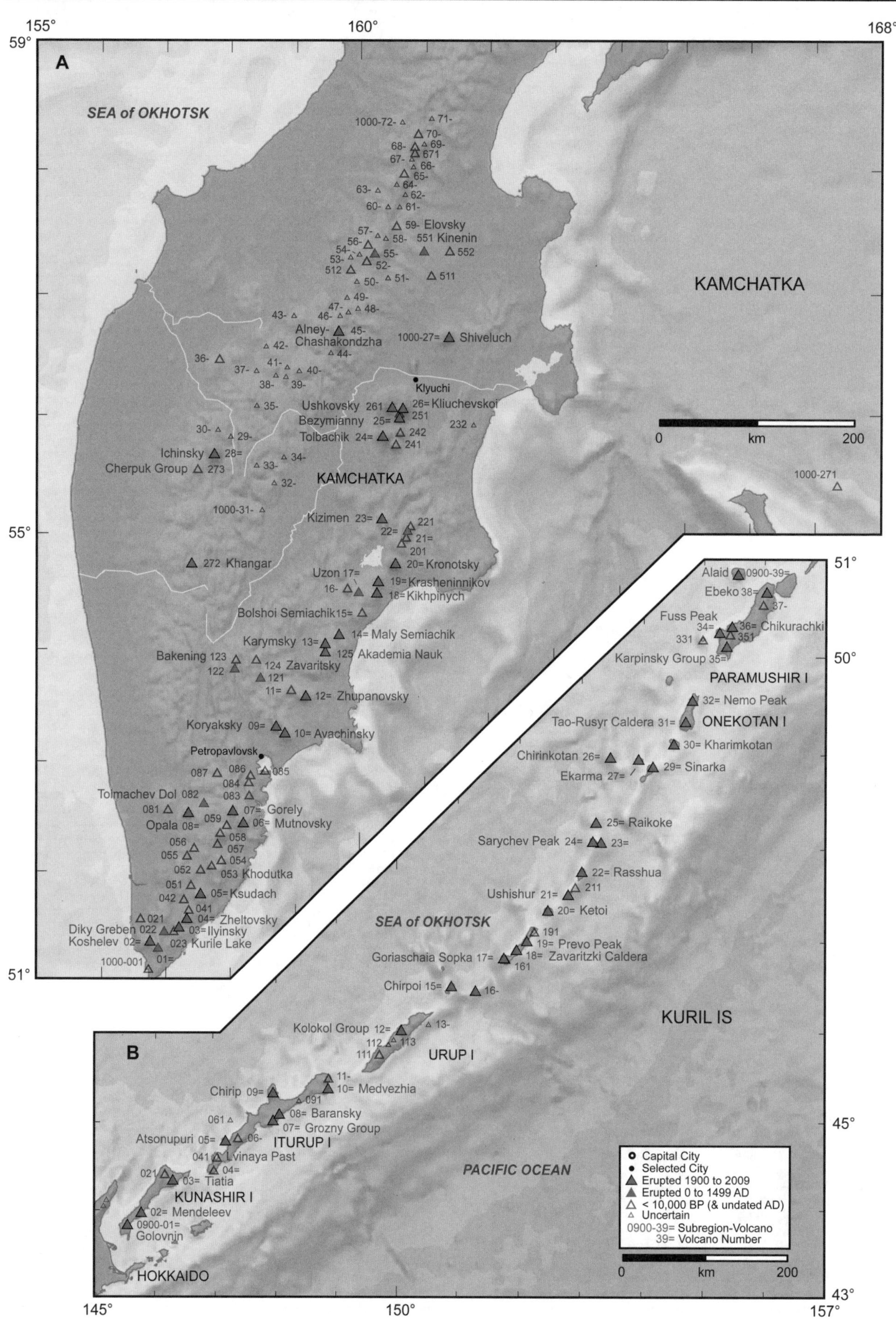

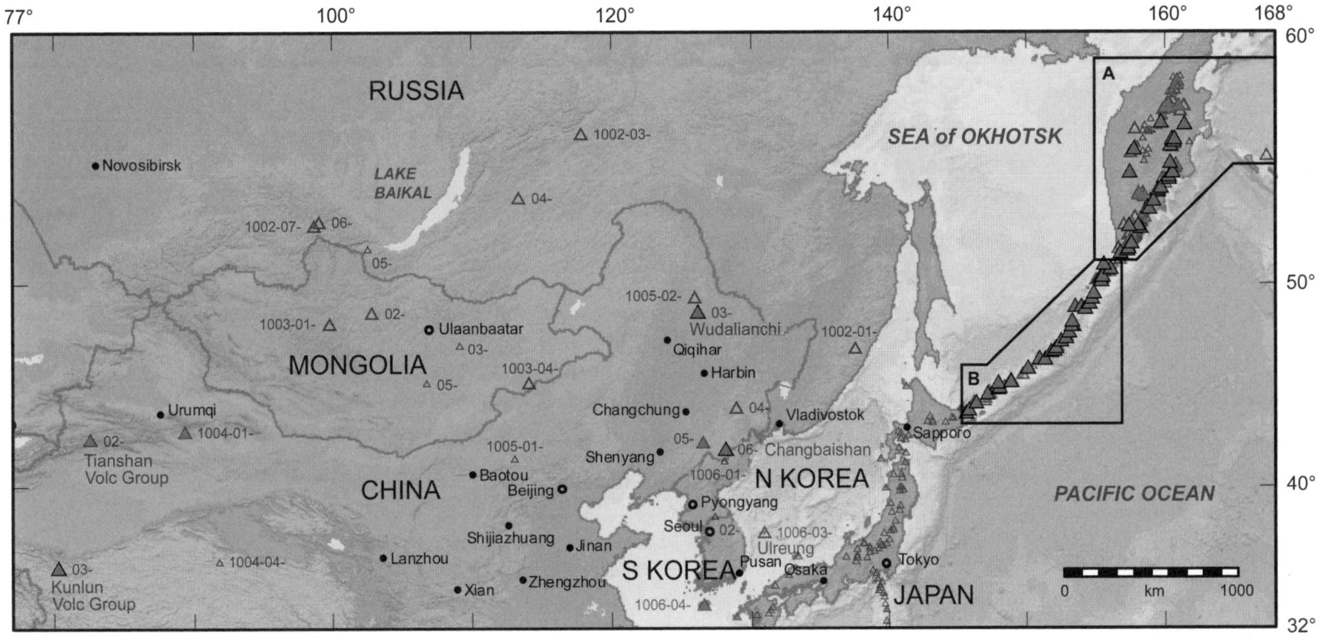

These two *CAVW* regions are combined here, since most of their volcanoes form a continuous arc with a shared history and tectonic setting. Although the *CAVW* organizers could have originally combined the Kuriles and Kamchatka as Region 09 and used 10 for the volcanoes of mainland Asia, few if any inland volcanoes were recognized at the time. The original *CAVW* grouping was "Kamchatka and Manchuria", but by the time of publication (1958) this had been widened to "Kamchatka and continental areas of Asia." Nevertheless, only 5 mainland volcanoes were listed in that catalog, as opposed to 26 here; an increase exceeded only by the gains in Region 12 (Western US and Canada).

Russian explorers reached Siberia's Pacific coast in 1637 and the Kamchatka Peninsula by 1697, also the year of its first eruption report (on Kliuchevskoi, the region's most vigorous volcano). Two other Kamchatkan volcanoes are known to have erupted in the 17th century, Mutnovsky and Koshelev, but the first historical eruptions from the Kurile Islands were early in the 18th. Peter the Great's epic exploring expedition, led by Vitus Bering from 1733 to 1742, mapped the east coast of Kamchatka, and La Perouse explored the Kuriles by sea in 1787. The Kuriles have been contested by Japan and Russia, and Japan held the islands from 1875 to the end of WW-II. Heavy colonization of Kamchatka began early in the 19th century, and in 1904 the Trans-Siberian Railroad opened, linking Europe to Vladivostok (and China). Of Kamchatka's 306 historically documented eruptions, nearly 90% have been since 1800 AD and nearly three-fourths since 1900.

As with the rest of the NW Pacific, subduction of the Pacific Plate has produced the vigorous explosive volcanism of the Kurile-Kamchatka arc, but tensional volcanism dominates the mainland part of the region. The Baikal rift, for example, includes young basaltic cinder cones as well as the world's deepest lake.

The contrast between Kamchatka and the mainland remains strong in the timing of historical volcanism, with that on the Asian mainland having begun early but been infrequent in recent centuries. Four volcanoes had erupted by mid-17th century (the time of the first historical Kamchatkan eruption), the first being the Tianshan Group in the 1st and 7th centuries AD. One of the world's largest Holocene eruptions, only recently receiving volcanological attention, took place at Changbaishan (Baitoushan) on the China/Korea border, in the 11th century AD. Mainland Asia's most recent eruptions are Wudalianchi in Manchuria in 1719-21 and 1776, Changbaishan in 1903, and the Kunlun volcano group in western China in 1951.

The Kuriles and Kamchatka are sparsely populated and among the 4 smallest *CAVW* regions. The Kamchatka peninsula holds about 450,000 people, most in its largest city, Petropavlovsk. The population of the Kuriles declined from about 30,000 to about 16,000 following a major earthquake in 1994, and most reside in the 3 southern islands of Kunishir, Iturup, and Urup. The addition of mainland Asia, however, makes region 10 easily the most heavily populated, and (with the possible exception of Antarctica) the largest.

Regular monitoring of Kamchatkan volcanoes began in 1935 when the Kamchatka Volcanological Station was founded in Petropavlovsk. This grew into the Institute of Volcanology, the largest in the world, and was split into the IV and the Institute for Volcanic Geology and Geophysics in 1991. Observation of Kurile volcanoes is largely done by the Institute of Volcanology and Geodynamics in Sakhalin.

This region currently has the third largest number of undated Holocene volcanoes (70) next to 87 for South America and 101 for Africa. This number for Kamchatka and Mainland Asia has gone down significantly since the 2nd edition (105) as detailed stratigraphic studies of Kamchatka volcanoes have refined the ages of Kamchatka volcanoes and led to the second highest regional totals for eruptions dated by radiocarbon or tephrochronology (448), trailing only Japan. Kamchatka and Mainland Asia is tied for third with Africa and Japan (140), and behind Indonesia (144) and South America (194) in total number of known or possible Holocene volcanoes, and trails only Japan (114) in the number of the number of volcanoes with average VEIs of 3 or larger and in large (VEI $\geq$4) eruptions (102). No other region has a higher proportion of explosive eruptions (95%) or a higher number of dated Holocene caldera-forming eruptions; Ksudach volcano with four leads the world in this category. Kamchatka leads the world in the number of eruptions forming lava domes, led by repeated dome growth at Bezymianny and Shiveluch volcanoes, both of which have undergone large-scale edifice collapse producing debris avalanches in historical time. Kamchatka also has the largest number of shield volcanoes (44), mostly in the Sredinny Range on the western side of the peninsula. Many volcanoes in this range were considered to be of Holocene age due to morphology and degree of glacial modification, but later work has cast doubt on the age of these volcanoes, many of which could be of late Pleistocene age. Their Status has been downgraded in this compilation to "Holocene?," reflecting the uncertainty of their age in the absence of dated eruptions.

VOLCANO NAME (Subregion) / ERUPTION — Area of Activity	LAT	LONG	ELEV (m)	POPL (5 km, 10, 30, 100)	ROCK TYPE	VOLC TYPE	NUMBER	STATUS	Start Year	Start M-Dy	Stop Year	Stop M-Dy	Central, Flank vent, Radial fiss, Regional	Submarine, New island, Subglacial, Crater lake	Explosive, Pyro flow, Phreatic, Caldera	Lava flow, Lava lake, Dome, Spine	Fatal, Damage, Mudflow, Tsunami	VEI	Vol L/T
KURILES																			
Golovnin (Kunashir I)	**43.841 N**	**145.509 E**	**543**	4446	ADB	**Caldera**	**0900-01=**	**Historical**											
(tephra layer Kn-IV-12)									T **-4550**?	....	....	....	----	----	x---	----	----		
Kipyascheye lake (tehra layer KnIV-4)									T **1290**P	....	....	....	x---	----	x-x-	----	----		
Eastern explosion crater									**1848**	....	....	....	x---	----	x---	----	----	1	
Mendeleev (Kunashir I)	**43.976 N**	**145.736 E**	**888**	3446	ADB	**Stratovolcano**	**0900-02=**	**Historical**											
West side of central cone (KnIV-10 tephra)									C **-2270**t	....	....	....	x---	----	xx-A	--x-	----		
NE solfatara field									**1880**	....	....	....	-x--	----	--x-	----	----	1	
									? *1900*	....	....	....	----	----	----	----	----	*2?*	
Smirnov (Kunashir I)	**44.420 N**	**146.135 E**	**1189**	0335	AD	**Stratovolcano**	**0900-021**	**Holocene**											
Tiatia (Kunashir I)	**44.351 N**	**146.256 E**	**1819**	1335	BA	**Stratovolcano**	**0900-03=**	**Historical**											
									1812	08	....	....	----	----	x---	----	----	2	
NNW and SSE flanks									**1973**	0714	**1973**	0728	-x--	----	x---	x---	----	4	-/8
(steam-gas columns: no solid ejecta)									X *1974*	....	X*1975*	....	----	----	----	----	----		
									1978	0720	....	....	----	----	--x-	----	----	2	
									1981	0610	**1981**	0625	??--	----	x---	----	----	2?	
									? *1982*	*0210*	?*1982*	*0214*	x---	----	--?-	----	----	*1*	
Berutarube (Iturup I)	**44.459 N**	**146.936 E**	**1221**	0334	AD	**Stratovolcano**	**0900-04=**	**Holocene**											
(probably only fumarolic activity)									? *1812*	....	....	....	----	----	?---	----	----	*1*	
Lvinaya Past (Iturup I)	**44.608 N**	**146.994 E**	**528**	0334	ABD	**Stratovolcano**	**0900-041**	**Radiocarbon**											
									C **-7480**t	....	....	....	x---	----	xx-x	----	----	**6+**	-/10
Atsonupuri (Iturup I)	**44.805 N**	**147.135 E**	**1206**	1334	AB	**Stratovolcano**	**0900-05=**	**Historical**											
									1812	0905d	....	....	----	----	x---	----	----	1	
									1932	....	....	....	----	----	?---	----	----	2	
Bogatyr Ridge (Iturup I)	**44.833 N**	**147.342 E**	**1634**	1344	AD	**Stratovolcano**	**0900-06-**	**Holocene**											
Unnamed (Iturup-NW of)	**45.03 N**	**147.208 E**	**-930**	0034	U	**Submarine volc**	**0900-061**	Uncertain											
17.5 km NW of Iturup Island									? *1967*	*0426*	....	....	----	?---	----	----	----		
Grozny Group (Iturup I)	**45.026 N**	**147.922 E**	**1211**	0244	A	**Complex volcs**	**0900-07=**	**Historical**											
Ivan Grozny									**1968**	02	**1968**	02	x---	----	x---	----	----	1	
Ivan Grozny									**1970**	....	....	....	x---	----	x---	----	----	1	
Ivan Grozny									**1973**	01	**1973**	01	x---	----	x---	----	----	1	
Ivan Grozny (N flank of cent. dome)									**1973**	0516	**1973**	0517	-x--	----	x---	----	----	2?	
Ivan Grozny									**1989**	0503	**1989**	0805d	x---	----	x---	----	--x-	2	
Baransky (Iturup I)	**45.097 N**	**148.024 E**	**1132**	0044	AD	**Stratovolcano**	**0900-08=**	**Historical**											
									C **1460**r	....	....	....	----	----	----	----	----		
									C **1570**r	....	....	....	----	----	----	----	----		
									1951	0715q	....	....	----	----	x---	----	----	1	
Chirip (Iturup I)	**45.338 N**	**147.925 E**	**1587**	2344	BAd	**Stratovolcanoes**	**0900-09=**	**Historical**											
									1843	....	....	....	----	----	x---	----	----	2?	
SE of Bogdan Khmelinitskii summit									**1860**?	....	....	....	-x--	----	x---	----	----	1	
Golets-Tornyi Group (Iturup I)	**45.25 N**	**148.35 E**	**442**	4444	AD	**Pyroclastic cones**	**0900-091**	Holocene?											
Medvezhia (Iturup I)	**45.387 N**	**148.843 E**	**1125**	2234	ABDR	**Somma volcano**	**0900-10=**	**Historical**											
									T **-0050**?	....	....	....	x---	----	x---	----	----		
Kudriavy									**1778**	1231y	....	....	x---	----	x---	----	----	2	
Kudriavy									**1883**	05	**1883**	06	x---	----	x---	x---	----	2	
Kudriavy									? *1946*	....	....	....	----	----	--?-	----	----	*2*	
Kudriavy									**1958**	....	....	....	----	----	x---	----	----	1	
Kudriavy									**1999**	1007	**1999**	1013	x---	----	x-x-	----	----	1	
Demon (Iturup I)	**45.50 N**	**148.85 E**	**1205**	2334	U	**Stratovolcano**	**0900-11-**	**Holocene**											
Ivao Group (Urup I)	**45.77 N**	**149.68 E**	**1426**	1223	U	**Cinder cones**	**0900-111**	**Holocene**											
Rudakov (Urup I)	**45.88 N**	**149.83 E**	**542**	2223	A	**Stratovolcano**	**0900-112**	Holocene?											
Tri Sestry (Urup I)	**45.93 N**	**149.92 E**	**998**	0023	A	**Stratovolcano**	**0900-113**	Holocene?											
Kolokol Group (Urup I)	**46.042 N**	**150.05 E**	**1328**	1133	A	**Somma volcs**	**0900-12=**	**Historical**											
									1780j	....	....	....	----	----	----	----	----	2?	
Berg									**1845**	....	**1846**	....	----	----	x---	----	----	2	
Berg ?									**1894**	0725	**1894**	0726	----	----	x---	----	----	2	
Trezubetz									**1924**	0313	....	....	-x--	----	x---	----	----	2?	
Berg									**1940**f	....	....	....	x---	----	----	--x-	----		7/-
Berg									**1946**	0415q	....	....	----	----	x---	----	----	2	
Berg									**1952**	0115q	....	....	x---	----	x---	----	----	2	
Berg									**1970**	02	**1970**	03	-x--	----	x---	----	----	3	
Berg (northern part of lava dome)									**1973**	0725	**1973**	0726?	x---	----	x---	----	----	1	
Berg									? *2005*	....	....	....	----	----	--?-	----	----	*1?*	
Berg									? *2009*	*0826*	....	....	x---	----	?---	----	----	*2*	
Unnamed (Urup-E of)	**46.10 N**	**150.50 E**	**-100**	0233	U	**Submarine volc ?**	**0900-13-**	Uncertain											
7.7 km E of Urup Island									? *1978*	*0331*	....	....	----	?---	----	----	----	*0*	
Chirpoi (Kuril Is)	**46.525 N**	**150.875 E**	**742**	1113	ABD	**Caldera**	**0900-15=**	**Historical**											
Cherny									**1712**	1231y	....	....	----	----	x---	----	----	4?	
Snow									**1790**p	....	....	....	----	----	x---	x---	----		
Snow									**1811**	0611	....	....	----	----	x---	----	----	2	
Snow (or Cherny)									**1854**	0624	....	....	----	----	x---	----	----	2	
Cherny									**1857**	07	....	....	----	----	x---	----	----	3	
Snow									**1879**	05	**1879**	06	----	----	x---	x---	----	2	
Snow									**1960**	1020	....	....	----	----	x---	----	----	2?	
Snow									**1982**	1122	....	....	x---	----	?---	----	----	2	
Unnamed (Kuril Is)	**46.47 N**	**151.28 E**	**-502**	0003	U	**Submarine volc**	**0900-16-**	**Hydrophonic**											
									S **1972**	0429	S**1972**	0430	----	x---	----	----	----	0	
Milne (Simushir I)	**46.82 N**	**151.78 E**	**1540**	2223	A	**Somma volcano**	**0900-161**	**Holocene**											
Goriaschaia Sopka (Simushir I)	**46.83 N**	**151.75 E**	**891**	2223	AB	**Stratovolcano**	**0900-17=**	**Historical**											
									1842	06	....	....	----	----	x---	----	----	3?	
									1849	....	....	....	----	----	x---	----	----	2	
									1881	09	....	....	----	----	x---	x---	----	2	
									1883	0415q	....	....	----	----	----	--?-	----	1	7/-
									1914	0604	**1914**	0604	x---	----	x---	----	----	2	
									? *1944*	....	....	....	----	----	?---	----	----	*2*	
Zavaritzki Caldera (Simushir I)	**46.925 N**	**151.95 E**	**624**	2223	ABD	**Caldera**	**0900-18=**	**Historical**											
North end of caldera lake									**1923**h	....	....	....	x---	----	x---	--x-	----	1	
North end of caldera lake									**1957**	1112	**1957**	1201	----	---x	x---	x-x-	--x-	3*	

VOLCANO NAME (Subregion) / ERUPTION — Area of Activity	LAT	LONG	ELEV (m)	POPL (5 km, 10, 30, 100)	ROCK TYPE	VOLC TYPE	NUMBER / —Start— Year	M-Dy	STATUS / —Stop— Year	M-Dy	Central / Flank vent / Radial fiss / Regional	Submarine / New island / Subglacial / Crater lake	Explosive / Pyro flow / Phreatic / Caldera	Lava flow / Lava lake / Dome / Spine	Fatal / Damage / Mudflow / Tsunami	VEI	Vol L/T
Prevo Peak (Simushir I)	**47.02** N	**152.12** E	**1360**	0123	BA	**Stratovolcano**	**0900-19=**		**Historical**								
							1765e	....	....	....	----	----	xx--	----	-x--	3↑	
							1825q	....	....	....	----	----	x---	----	----	2	
Urataman (Simushir I)	**47.12** N	**152.25** E	**678**	1122	A	**Somma volcano**	**0900-191**		**Holocene**								
Ketoi (Kuril Is)	**47.35** N	**152.475** E	**1172**	1222	AB	**Stratovolcano**	**0900-20=**		**Historical**								
Pallas Peak							**1843**	07	**1846**	....	----	----	x---	x---	----	2	
Pallas Peak							**1924**	....	....	....	----	----	x---	----	----	2	
Pallas Peak							**1960**	0927	....	....	----	----	x---	----	----	2	
Ushishur (Kuril Is)	**47.52** N	**152.80** E	**401**	0023	AD	**Caldera**	**0900-21=**		**Historical**								
							C-**7450**t	....	....	....	x---	----	x--x	----	----	C	
SE caldera wall							**1710**j	....	....	....	x---	----	--x-	----	----	1	
Center of caldera bay							**1769**>	....	....	....	x---	x---	x---	--x-	----		7/-
SE caldera wall							**1884**	07	....	....	x---	----	--x-	----	----	1	
Srednii (Ushishur-NW of)	**47.60** N	**152.92** E	**36**	0013	U	**Submarine volc**	**0900-211**		**Holocene**								
							? 1880?	*0712*	*?1880?*	*0712*	----	x---	----	----	----	*0*	
Rasshua (Kuril Is)	**47.77** N	**153.02** E	**956**	0113	AD	**Stratovolcano**	**0900-22=**		**Historical**								
Eastern cone ?							**1846**	....	....	....	x---	----	x---	----	----	3	
							1957	10	....	....	----	----	--x-	----	----	1	
Unnamed (Matua-E of)	**48.08** N	**153.33** E	**-150**	2333	U	**Submarine volc**	**0900-23=**		**Historical**								
Near Toporkovyi islet							**1924**	0215	....	....	----	x---	----	----	----	0	
Sarychev Peak (Matua I)	**48.092** N	**153.20** E	**1496**	2333	A	**Stratovolcano**	**0900-24=**		**Historical**								
							1765e	....	....	....	----	----	x---	----	----	2?	
							1805	....	....	....	----	----	----	----	----		
							1879	0115q	....	....	----	----	----	x---	----	0	
							1923	0117	**1923**	0122	----	----	x---	----	----	2	
							1927	....	....	....	----	----	----	----	----	2?	
							1928	0214	....	....	----	----	x---	----	----	2	
							1930	0213	**1930**	0213	----	----	x?--	----	----	3	
							? 1932?	....	....	....	x---	----	?---	----	----		
							1946	1109	**1946**	1119	x---	----	xx--	x---	----	4	
							1954	08	**1954**	10	----	----	x---	--x-	----	2	
							1960	0830	**1960**	0830	x---	----	x---	----	----	3	
							1965	1209	**1965**	1209	x---	----	x---	----	----	2	
							1976	0923	**1976**	1002	x---	----	x---	x---	----	2	6/-
							1986	09 ?	....	....	x---	----	x---	x---	----		
							1989	0113	**1989**	0114	x---	----	x---	----	----	1?	
							2009	0611	**2009**	0621	x---	----	xx--	----	----	4	-/8
Raikoke (Kuril Is)	**48.292** N	**153.25** E	**551**	0033	B	**Stratovolcano**	**0900-25=**		**Historical**								
							1765e	....	....	....	----	----	x---	----	----	2	
							1778	....	....	....	x---	----	x---	----	xx--	4↑	
							1924	0215	....	....	x---	----	x---	----	----	4	
Chirinkotan (Kuril Is)	**48.98** N	**153.48** E	**724**	0001	AD	**Stratovolcano**	**0900-26=**		**Historical**								
							? 1760?	....	....	....	----	----	?---	----	----	*2*	
North foot of inner summit cone							**1884**f	....	....	....	x---	----	----	x---	----	0	
							1900j	....	....	....	x---	----	x---	----	----		
Floor of summit explosion crater							**1955**?	....	....	....	x---	----	x---	x---	----	2?	
							1979	04	**1980**	1010	x---	----	x---	x---	----	2	
							1986	1011	**1986**	1012	x---	----	x-x-	----	----	1	
							2004	0720	**2004**	0720	x---	----	x---	----	----	2	
Ekarma (Kuril Is)	**48.958** N	**153.93** E	**1170**	0012	A	**Stratovolcano**	**0900-27=**		**Historical**								
Summit dome							**1767**	....	**1769**	....	x---	----	x---	--x-	----	2	
							1980	0524	....	....	----	----	x---	----	----	1	
Sinarka (Shiashkotan I)	**48.875** N	**154.175** E	**934**	0112	A	**Stratovolcano**	**0900-29=**		**Historical**								
							1725q	....	....	....	----	----	----	----	----	2?	
							1846	....	....	....	----	----	x---	----	----	3	
							1855	....	....	....	----	----	x---	----	----	2	
							1872	....	**1878**	....	x---	----	xx--	x-x-	-x--	4	7/-
Kharimkotan (Kuril Is)	**49.12** N	**154.508** E	**1145**	1112	ADB	**Stratovolcano**	**0900-30=**		**Historical**								
Severgin							**1713**	....	....	....	----	----	x---	----	----	3↑	
Severgin							**1846**	....	....	....	----	----	x---	----	----	2	
Severgin							**1848**	....	....	....	----	----	x---	----	----	2	
Severgin							**1883**	....	....	....	----	----	x---	----	----	3	
Severgin							**1931**	09	....	....	----	----	x---	----	----	1	
Severgin							**1933**	0108	**1933**	0414>	x---	----	xx-A	x-x-	xx-x	**5**	8/9
Tao-Rusyr Caldera (Onekotan I)	**49.35** N	**154.70** E	**1325**	0223	AB	**Stratovolcano**	**0900-31=**		**Historical**								
Tao-Rusyr							C-**5550**u	....	....	....	x---	----	xx-x	----	----	**6**	-/10
Krenitzyn Peak (east flank)							**1952**	1112	**1952**	1119	-x--	---x	x---	--x-	----	3	7/-
Nemo Peak (Onekotan I)	**49.57** N	**154.808** E	**1018**	2223	ABD	**Caldera**	**0900-32=**		**Historical**								
							T-**7550**?	....	....	....	x---	----	x---	x---	----		
							T-**7050**?	....	....	....	x---	----	x---	x---	----		
							T-**5550**?	....	....	....	x---	----	x---	x---	----		
							T-**3050**?	....	....	....	x---	----	x---	x---	----		
							T-**1850**?	....	....	....	x---	----	x---	x---	----		
							T-**0550**v	....	....	....	x---	----	x---	x---	----		
							T **0750**?	....	....	....	x---	----	x---	x---	----		
							T **1350**?	....	....	....	x---	----	----	--x-	----		
(eruption from Nemo, not Asyrmintar)							**1710**j	....	....	....	x---	----	x-x-	----	----	2	
							1906	....	....	....	x---	----	x-x-	--?-	----	2	
SE flank							*? 1932?*	....	....	....	-x--	----	?---	----	----		
(eruption from Nemo, not Asyrmintar)							**1938**	0812	....	....	----	----	x---	----	----	2	
Asyrmintar (Onekotan I)	49.60 N	154.90 E	570				0900-33=		Not a Volcano								
Shirinki (Kuril Is)	**50.20** N	**154.98** E	**761**	0024	A	**Stratovolcano**	**0900-331**		**Holocene**								
Fuss Peak (Paramushir I)	**50.27** N	**155.25** E	**1772**	0234	A	**Stratovolcano**	**0900-34=**		**Historical**								
							? 1742	....	....	....	----	----	----	----	---x		
							1854	0705	....	....	----	----	x---	----	----	3	
							? 1933	....	....	....	----	----	?---	----	----		
Karpinsky Group (Paramushir I)	**50.13** N	**155.37** E	**1345**	0334	A	**Cones**	**0900-35=**		**Historical**								
East side of Karpinsky Ridge							**1952**	1105	....	....	x---	----	x---	----	----	1	
Lomonosov Group (Paramushir I)	**50.25** N	**155.43** E	**1681**	0234	U	**Cinder cones**	**0900-351**		**Holocene**								

VOLCANO NAME (Subregion) / ERUPTION — Area of Activity	LAT	LONG	ELEV (m)	POPL (5 km, 10, 30, 100)	ROCK TYPE	VOLC TYPE	NUMBER	STATUS	Start Year	Start M-Dy	Stop Year	Stop M-Dy	Central / Flank vent / Radial fiss / Regional	Submarine / New island / Subglacial / Crater lake	Explosive / Pyro flow / Phreatic / Caldera	Lava flow / Lava lake / Dome / Spine	Fatal / Damage / Mudflow / Tsunami	VEI	Vol L/T
Chikurachki (Paramushir I)	50.325 N	155.458 E	1816	0234	BA	Stratovolcanoes	0900-36=	Historical											
Tatarinov									T 1690j	....	....	....	-x--	----	x---	----	----	4	
									1853	12	1859	....	x---	----	x?--	x---	----	3?	-/7
									? 1933	*0415*q	....	....	x---	----	?---	----	----		
									1957	05	....	....	x---	----	x---	----	----	2	
									1958	0526	1958	0527	x---	----	x---	----	----	2	
									1961	0502	1961	0810	x---	----	x---	----	--x-	1	
									1964	0201	1964	02	x---	----	x---	----	--x-	2	
									1967	0906	1967	0920	x---	----	x---	----	----	2	
									1973	0810	1973	0928	x---	----	x---	----	----	2	-/6
									1986	1118	1986	1207	x---	----	xxx-	x---	--x-	4*	7/8
SSE part of summit crater									2002	0125	2002	0422?	x---	----	x---	----	----	2	
									2003	0417	2003	0703?	x---	----	x---	----	----	2	
									2005	0312	2005	0407	x---	----	x---	----	----	1	
									2007	0304	2007	0418	x---	----	x---	----	----	2	
									2007	0819	2007	1101g	x---	----	x---	----	----	2	
									2008	0729	2008	0808?	x---	----	x---	----	----	2	
Vernadskii Ridge (Paramushir I)	50.55 N	155.97 E	1183	0134	AB	Cinder cones	0900-37-	Holocene											
Ebeko (Paramushir I)	50.68 N	156.02 E	1156	0344	A	Somma volcano	0900-38=	Historical											
									C-0390u	....	....	....	x---	----	x---	----	----		
									C 1600?	....	....	....	----	----	x---	----	----		
									C 1650?	....	....	....	----	----	x---	----	----		
									C 1670?	....	....	....	----	----	x---	----	----		
									1793	....	....	....	----	----	x---	----	--x-	2	-/5
									1833	1231y	....	....	----	----	x---	----	----	2	
									1859	0927	....	....	----	----	x---	----	----	2	
Sredniy crater									1934	1004	1935	1015q	x-x-	----	x---	----	----	2	-/5
North wall of east amphitheater									1963	0308	1964	....	-x--	----	x-x-	----	----	1	-/3
Middle Crater									1965	08 ?	1965	08 ?	x---	---x	--x-	----	----	1	
Northern crater									1967	01	1967	04 ?	x---	---x	x-x-	----	----	1	-/4
Northern crater									1969	02	1969	02 ?	x---	---x	x-x-	----	----	1	
Northern crater									*? 1971*	....	....	....	x---	----	--?-	----	----	*1*	
Northern crater									1987	1014	1988	01	x---	---x	x-x-	----	----	1	-/4
Northern crater and upper east flank									1989	0202	1990	0415e	xx--	---x	x-x-	----	--x-	2	-/6
Northern crater									1991	01	1991	01	x---	----	x-x-	----	----	1	
									2005	0129	2005	0216	x---	----	x---	----	----	2*	
									2009	0211	2009	0713?	x---	----	x---	----	----	1	
Alaid (Kuril Is)	50.858 N	155.55 E	2339	0224	BA	Stratovolcano	0900-39=	Historical											
									1790	....	1793	....	x---	----	x---	----	----	4↑	
									1854	0627	....	....	x---	----	x---	----	----	3	
									1860	0707	1860	0709	x---	----	x---	----	----	3	
									1894	....	....	....	x---	----	x---	----	----	2	
East submarine flank (Taketomi)									1933	1113	1934	08	-x--	xx--	x---	x---	----	2	
NW foot									1972	0618	1972	0911	-xx-	----	x---	x---	----	3	7/8
									? 1973	....	....	....	-x--	----	--?-	----	----		
									1981	0427	1981	0605	x---	----	x---	----	-xx-	4*	-/8
									1981	1125	....	....	x---	----	x---	----	----	2	
									1982	0329	1982	0329	x---	----	x---	----	----	2	
									1986	0525	1986	0528c	x---	----	x-x-	----	----	2?	
									1996	1203	....	....	----	----	x---	----	----	2	
									? 1997	*0823*	*?1997*	*0823*	----	----	?---	----	----		
KAMCHATKA																			
Mashkovtsev (Kamchatka-S)	51.10 N	156.72 E	503	1234	B	Stratovolcano	1000-001	Holocene											
Kambalny (Kamchatka-S)	51.30 N	156.87 E	2156	0234	BA	Stratovolcano	1000-01=	Historical											
									C 1350?	....	....	....	----	----	x-x-	----	----		
Koshelev (Kamchatka-S)	51.357 N	156.75 E	1812	0134	BAd	Stratovolcano	1000-02=	Historical											
Eastern cone									C-4550?	....	....	....	----	----	x---	x---	----		
NW flank (Gorely)									T-4050?	....	....	....	x---	----	x---	----	----		
Northern flank									C-1350?	....	....	....	-x--	----	x---	x---	----		
SE flank									1690j	....	....	....	-x--	----	x---	----	----	3↑	
									? 1741	....	....	....	----	----	----	----	----		
Yavinsky (Kamchatka-S)	51.57 N	156.60 E	705	2344	B	Stratovolcano	1000-021	Tephrochronology											
NW flank (Ukho)									T-4050?	....	....	....	-x--	----	x---	----	----		
Diky Greben (Kamchatka-S)	51.45 N	156.97 E	1070	0234	DAR	Lava domes	1000-022	Radiocarbon											
									T-5700v	....	....	....	x---	----	x---	x-x-	----		
									T-3050?	....	....	....	x---	----	x---	----	----		
									C-2250?	....	....	....	x---	----	x---	x---	----		
									T 0350y	....	....	....	x---	----	x---	x-x-	----		10/-
Kurile Lake (Kamchatka-S)	51.45 N	157.12 E	81	2234	DRa	Caldera	1000-023	Radiocarbon											
									T-7550z	....	....	....	x---	----	x---	----	----		
(tephra layer KO)									G-6440q	....	....	....	x---	---x	xx-x	--x-	--x-	7	-/11
Ilyinsky (Kamchatka-S)	51.490 N	157.20 E	1578	0034	ADB	Stratovolcano	1000-03=	Historical											
									T-5700t	....	....	....	x---	----	x--x	----	----	C	
									C-4550?	....	....	....	x---	----	x---	x---	----		
(ZLT tephra)									C-2850?	....	....	....	x---	----	x---	----	----	5	-/9
									C-2050?	....	....	....	x---	----	x---	----	----		
									C 0050?	....	....	....	-x--	----	----	x-x-	----		
NE flank									1901	....	....	....	-x--	----	x-x-	x---	----	3	
Zheltovsky (Kamchatka-S)	51.57 N	157.323 E	1953	0234	BAdr	Stratovolcano	1000-04=	Historical											
									T-7050*	....	....	....	x---	----	xx-x	----	----	5	-/9
									T-6050?	....	....	....	x---	----	x---	x---	----		
									C-3050?	....	....	....	----	----	x---	----	----	5	-/9
									*? 1823*e	....	....	....	----	----	----	----	----		
									1923	0211	1923	04	x---	----	x---	x---	----	3	
									? 1972	*03*	....	....	x---	----	--?-	----	----	*1?*	
Kell (Kamchatka-S)	51.65 N	157.35 E	900	0234	B	Stratovolcanoes	1000-041	Holocene											
Belenkaya (Kamchatka-S)	51.75 N	157.27 E	892	0134	B	Stratovolcano	1000-042	Holocene											
Ksudach (Kamchatka-S)	51.80 N	157.53 E	1079	0034	ADB	Stratovolcano	1000-05=	Historical											
Ksudach III caldera (tephra layer KS4)									G-7900?	....	....	....	x---	---x	xx-x	----	----	5	-/9

VOLCANO NAME (Subregion) / ERUPTION — Area of Activity	LAT	LONG	ELEV (m)	POPL (5 km, 10, 30, 100)	ROCK TYPE	VOLC TYPE	NUMBER	STATUS	Start Year	Start M-Dy	Stop Year	Stop M-Dy	ERUPTIVE CHARACTERISTICS (Central, Flank vent, Radial fiss, Regional / Submarine, New island, Subglacial, Crater lake / Explosive, Pyro flow, Phreatic, Caldera / Lava flow, Lava lake, Dome, Spine / Fatal, Damage, Mudflow, Tsunami)	VEI	Vol L/T
Ksudach (Kamchatka-S) *continued*									G-**5600**?	....	....	....	x--- ---- x--- ---- ----		
Ksudach IV caldera (tephra layer KS3)									G-**5200**?	....	....	....	x--- ---x xx-x ---- ----	**5?**	-/9
Ksudach IV caldera (tephra layer KS2)									G-**4900**?	....	....	....	x--- ---x xx-x ---- ----	**5+**	-/9
SW part of caldera IV (Paryashchiy Utes)									T-**4750**?	....	....	....	x--- ---- x--- --x- ----		8/-
									T-**4550**?	....	....	....	x--- ---- x--- ---- ----	3	
									T-**4100**?	....	....	....	x--- ---- x--- ---- ----	3	
(tephra layer KSbt)									T-**3000**?	....	....	....	x--- ---- xx-- ---- ----	4	-/8
									T-**0200**?	....	....	....	x--- ---- x--- ---- ----	3	-/7
Ksudach V caldera (tephra layer KS1)									G **0240**v	....	....	....	x--- ---x xx-x ---- ----	**6**	-/10
Stubel									G **0350**?	....	....	....	x--- ---- x--- --?- ----	2	-/6
									T **0700**?	....	....	....	x--- ---- x--- ---- ----		
Stubel (tephra layer KSht1)									G **1000**t	....	....	....	x--- ---- xx-- ---- ----	4+	-/8
Stubel (tephra layer KSht2)									G **1750**?	....	....	....	x--- ---- x--- ---- --x-	4	-/8
Stubel (tephra layer KSht3)									**1907**	0328?	....	....	x--- ---x xx-- ---- ----	**5**	-/9
Ozernoy (Kamchatka-S)	**51.88 N**	**157.38 E**	**562**	0124	B	**Shield volcano**	**1000-051**	**Holocene**							
Olkoviy Volc Group (Kamchatka-S)	**52.02 N***	**157.53 E**	**681**	2224	B	**Volcanic field**	**1000-052**	**Holocene**							
Khodutka (Kamchatka-S)	**52.063 N**	**157.703 E**	**2090**	0034	ADR	**Stratovolcanoes**	**1000-053**	**Radiocarbon**							
NW flank of Priemysh volcano									T-**1050**<	....	....	....	-x-- ---- x--- ---- ----	4+	-/8
WNW flank (Khodutkinsky maar; KHD tephra)									G-**0930**v	....	....	....	-x-- ---- xx-- x-x- ----	**5**	7/9
									T-**0300**y	....	....	....	x--- ---- ---- x--- ----	0	
Piratkovsky (Kamchatka-S)	**52.113 N**	**157.849 E**	**1322**	0135	U	**Stratovolcano**	**1000-054**	**Holocene**							
Ostanets (Kamchatka-S)	**52.146 N**	**157.322 E**	**719**	0024	B	**Shield volcanoes**	**1000-055**	**Holocene**							
Otdelniy (Kamchatka-S)	**52.220 N***	**157.428 E**	**791**	2224	B	**Shield volcanoes**	**1000-056**	**Holocene**							
Golaya (Kamchatka-S)	**52.263 N**	**157.787 E**	**858**	0025	B	**Stratovolcano**	**1000-057**	**Holocene**							
Asacha (Kamchatka-S)	**52.355 N**	**157.827 E**	**1910**	0026	BAdr	**Complex volcano**	**1000-058**	**Holocene**							
Visokiy (Kamchatka-S)	**52.43 N**	**157.93 E**	**1234**	0026	B	**Stratovolcano**	**1000-059**	**Holocene**							
Mutnovsky (Kamchatka-S)	**52.453 N**	**158.195 E**	**2322**	0026	Bad	**Complex volcano**	**1000-06=**	**Historical**							
									T-**7550**?	....	....	....	---- ---- x--- ---- ----	2	-/6
									T-**6000**?	....	....	....	---- ---- x-x- ---- ----	2	-/6
									T-**5900**?	....	....	....	---- ---- x-x- ---- ----	2	-/6
									T-**5800**?	....	....	....	---- ---- x-x- ---- ----	2	-/6
									T-**5450**?	....	....	....	---- ---- x-x- ---- ----	2	-/6
									T-**5350**?	....	....	....	---- ---- x-x- ---- ----	2	-/6
									T-**5250**?	....	....	....	---- ---- x-x- ---- ----	2	-/6
									T-**5050**?	....	....	....	---- ---- x--- ---- ----	3	-/7
									T-**5000**?	....	....	....	---- ---- x-x- ---- ----	2	-/6
									T-**4700**?	....	....	....	---- ---- x-x- ---- ----	2	-/6
									T-**4650**?	....	....	....	---- ---- x-x- ---- ----	2	-/6
									T-**4550**?	....	....	....	---- ---- x--- ---- ----	2	-/6
									T-**4050**?	....	....	....	---- ---- x-x- ---- ----	2	-/6
									T-**3650**?	....	....	....	---- ---- x-x- ---- ----	2	-/6
									T-**2900**?	....	....	....	---- ---- x-x- ---- ----	2	-/6
									T-**2150**?	....	....	....	---- ---- x-x- ---- ----	3	-/7
									T-**2050**?	....	....	....	---- ---- x-x- ---- ----	2	-/6
									T-**0450**?	....	....	....	---- ---- x-x- ---- ----	2	-/6
									T-**0200**?	....	....	....	---- ---- x-x- ---- ----	2	-/6
									T-**0100**?	....	....	....	---- ---- x-x- ---- ----	2	-/6
									T **0050**?	....	....	....	---- ---- x-x- ---- ----	2	-/6
									T **0250**?	....	....	....	---- ---- x-x- ---- ----	2	-/6
									T **0750**?	....	....	....	---- ---- x-xA ---- ----	3	-/7
									T **0950**?	....	....	....	---- ---- x-x- ---- ----	2	-/6
									T **1300**?	....	....	....	---- ---- x-x- ---- ----	2	-/6
									1650t	....	....	....	x--- ---- x--- ---- ----	2	
									1750t	....	....	....	x--- ---- x--- ---- ----	2	
									1848	....	....	....	x--- ---- x--- ---- ----	3	-/7
									1852	03	....	....	x--- ---- x--- ---- ----	2	
									1853	01	....	....	x--- ---- x--- ---- ----	2	
									1853	1218	**1854**	03	x--- ---- x--- ---- ----	2	
									1898	04	**1898**	0715q	x--- ---- x-x- ---- ----	2	-/6
									1904	0402	**1904**	0626>	x--- ---- x-x- x--- ----	2	
									1916	0715e	....	....	x--- ---- x--- ---- ----	2	
									1916	12	....	....	x--- ---- x--- ---- ----	2	
									1917	0705d	....	....	x--- ---- x--- ---- ----	3?	
									1927	01	**1927**	02	x--- ---- x-x- ---- ----	2	
									1928	0125	**1928**	02	x--- ---- x-x- ---- ----	2	
									1929	02	....	....	x--- ---- x-x- ---- ----	2	
									1938	11	....	....	x--- ---- x--- ---- ----	2	
									1939	05	....	....	x--- ---- x--- ---- ----	2	
									1945	0623	....	....	x--- ---- x--- ---- ----	2	
West wall of SW crater									**1960**	12	**1961**	01	x--- ---- x--- ---- ----	2	-/6
North crater									**2000**	0317	**2000**	0317	x--- ---- x-x- ---- ----	2	
									S **2000**	0630	S**2000**	0630	x--- ---- --x- ---- ----	1?	
Gorely (Kamchatka-S)	**52.558 N**	**158.03 E**	**1829**	0026	BAD	**Caldera**	**1000-07=**	**Historical**							
									T-**7400**w	....	....	....	x--- ---- ---- x--- ----	0	
									T-**7250**?	....	....	....	x--- ---- x--- ---- ----	2	
									T-**6050**?	....	....	....	x--- ---- ---- x--- ----	0	
									T-**5950**?	....	....	....	x--- ---- x--- x--- ----	3	-/7
									T-**5650**?	....	....	....	x--- ---- x--- x--- ----	3	-/7
									T-**5500**?	....	....	....	x--- ---- x--- x--- ----	3	-/7
									T-**5450**?	....	....	....	x--- ---- x--- x--- ----	3	-/7
									T-**5300**?	....	....	....	x--- ---- x--- ---- ----	2	
									T-**5150**?	....	....	....	x--- ---- x--- x--- ----	3	-/7
									T-**4950**?	....	....	....	x--- ---- x--- ---- ----	2	
									T-**4750**?	....	....	....	x--- ---- x--- x--- ----	3	-/7
									T-**4700**?	....	....	....	x--- ---- x--- ---- ----	2	
									T-**4650**?	....	....	....	x--- ---- x--- x--- ----	3	-/7
									T-**4600**?	....	....	....	x--- ---- x--- ---- ----	2	
									T-**4500**?	....	....	....	x--- ---- x--- ---- ----	2	
									T-**4450**?	....	....	....	x--- ---- x--- ---- ----	2	-/6
									T-**4350**?	....	....	....	x--- ---- x--- x--- ----	3	-/7
									T-**4300**w	....	....	....	x-x- ---- ---- x--- ----	0	
									T-**4150**?	....	....	....	x--- ---- x--- ---- ----	2	-/6

Oleg Volynets (Inst. Volc. Petropavlovsk)

Mutnovsky with Asacha in background

Oleg Volynets (Inst. Volc. Petropavlovsk)

1985 eruption

VOLCANO NAME (Subregion) / ERUPTION — Area of Activity	LAT	LONG	ELEV (m)	POPL (5 km / 10 / 30 / 100)	ROCK TYPE	VOLC TYPE / Start Year	NUMBER / Start M-Dy	STATUS / Stop Year	Stop M-Dy	Central / Flank vent / Radial fiss / Regional	Submarine / New island / Subglacial / Crater lake	Explosive / Pyro flow / Phreatic / Caldera	Lava flow / Lava lake / Dome / Spine	Fatal / Damage / Mudflow / Tsunami	VEI	Vol L/T
Gorely (Kamchatka-S) *continued*						T -3950?	....	....	....	x---	----	x---	----	----	2	-/6
						T -3900?	....	....	....	x---	----	x---	----	----	2	
(Gsh1 tephra layer)						C -3580v	....	....	....	x---	----	x---	----	----	2?	
						T -3550?	....	....	....	x---	----	----	x---	----	0	
						T -3450?	....	....	....	-x--	----	x---	x---	----	3	-/7
						T -2750?	....	....	....	-x--	----	x---	x---	----	2	-/6
						T -2450?	....	....	....	-x--	----	x---	x---	----	3	-/7
						T -2250?	....	....	....	----	----	x---	----	----	2	-/6
						T -2200?	....	....	....	----	----	x---	----	----	2	
						T -2050?	....	....	....	----	----	x---	----	----	2	-/6
						T -2000?	....	....	....	----	----	x---	----	----	2	-/6
						T -0700*	....	....	....	--x-	----	----	x---	----	0	8/-
						T -0350?	....	....	....	----	----	x---	x---	----	3	-/7
						T 0050?	....	....	....	----	----	x---	----	----	3	-/7
						T 0200?	....	....	....	----	----	x---	----	----	3	-/7
						T 0250?	....	....	....	----	----	x---	----	----	3	-/7
						T 0550?	....	....	....	----	----	x---	----	----	3	-/7
						T 1030q	....	....	....	----	----	x---	----	----	3	-/7
						T 1330q	....	....	....	----	----	x-x-	----	----	2?	
						T 1750t	....	....	....	x-x-	----	x-x-	xx--	----	2?	
						? 1821	....	....	....	----	----	----	----	----		
						1828	06	....	....	x---	----	x---	----	----	3	-/7
						1832	02	....	....	x---	----	x---	----	----	3	-/7
						? 1855	*04*	....	....	x---	----	?---	----	----	*2?*	
						1869	....	....	....	x---	----	x---	----	----	2	
						1929	0901	1930	04	x---	----	x---	----	----	3	-/7
						1930	09	1931	0117	x---	----	x---	----	----	3	-/7
						1931	05	1931	0715q	x---	----	x---	----	----	2	
						? 1932	....	....	....	----	----	----	----	----		
						1947	12	....	....	x---	----	x---	----	----	2	
						1961	01	....	....	x---	----	x---	----	----	2	
						1980	0615e	1981	0703	x---	----	xxx-	----	----	3*	-/7
						1984	0804	1986	0921?	x---	---x	x-x-	----	----	2	
Opala (Kamchatka-S)	**52.543 N**	**157.335 E**	**2475**	2225	**BAdr**	**Caldera**	**1000-08=**	**Historical**								
						T -3500?	....	....	....	----	----	x---	----	----		
						C -1550?	....	....	....	----	----	----	x---	--x-		
SE flank (Barany Amphitheater)						G 0610t	....	....	....	-x--	----	xx--	--x-	----	**5+**	8/**9**
						1776	1023	....	....	x---	----	x---	----	----	2?	
						? 1827	....	....	....	x---	----	?---	----	----		
(uncertain S flank eruption report)						*? 1854*	....	....	....	-x--	----	?---	----	----		
(S flank eruption report unlikely)						*X 1894*	....	....	....	-x--	----	----	----	----		
Unnamed (Kamchatka-S)	**52.57 N***	**157.02 E**	**610**	2235	**B**	**Cinder cone**	**1000-081**	**Holocene**								
Tolmachev Dol (Kamchatka-S)	**52.63 N***	**157.58 E**	**1021**	1126	**BR**	**Cinder cones**	**1000-082**	**Radiocarbon**								
Chasha crater (OPtr tephra layer)						C -2650?	....	....	....	x---	----	x---	----	----	4+	-/8
NW part of Tolmachev Dol						T 0300w	....	....	....	x---	----	x---	x---	----		
Vilyuchik (Kamchatka-S)	**52.70 N**	**158.28 E**	**2173**	0156	**AB**	**Stratovolcano**	**1000-083**	**Tephrochronology**								
						T -8050?	....	....	....	x---	----	x---	x---	----	2?	
Barkhatnaya Sopka (Kam.-S)	**52.823 N**	**158.27 E**	**870**	0356	**BADR**	**Lava domes**	**1000-084**	**Tephrochronology**								
						T -3550>	....	....	....	x---	----	x---	----	----		
Unnamed (Kamchatka-S)	**52.92 N**	**158.52 E**	**450**	2566	**BDR**	**Shield volcanoes**	**1000-085**	**Holocene**								
Unnamed (Kamchatka-S)	**52.88 N**	**158.30 E**	**700**	2566	**B**	**Shield volcanoes**	**1000-086**	**Holocene**								
Bolshe-Bannaya (Kamchatka-S)	**52.90 N**	**157.78 E**	**1200**	0246	**BARD**	**Lava domes**	**1000-087**	**Holocene**								
Koryaksky (Kamchatka-E)	**53.320 N**	**158.688 E**	**3456**	0266	**AB**	**Stratovolcano**	**1000-09=**	**Historical**								
						T -5050?	....	....	....	----	----	----	----	----		
South and SW flanks						C -1950y	....	....	....	--x-	----	----	x---	--x-		
South and SW flanks						C -1550?	....	....	....	--x-	----	----	x---	--x-		
Upper SW flank						1890c	....	....	....	--x-	----	--x-	----	----	1?	
(steam plumes only in 1895-96)						*X 1895*	*1015*q	*X 1896*	....	--x-	----	----	----	----		
						1926	1222	1926	1222	x---	----	x-x-	----	----	1?	
Summit and upper NW flank (3000 m)						1956	12	1957	06	x-x-	----	xx--	----	--x-	3*	
Upper NW flank (3000 m)						2008	1223?	2009	0827	--x-	----	x-x-	----	----	2*	
Avachinsky (Kamchatka-E)	**53.255 N**	**158.830 E**	**2741**	0066	**ABd**	**Stratovolcano**	**1000-10=**	**Historical**								
(tephra layer IAv1)						T -6100?	....	....	....	----	----	xx--	----	----		
(tephra layer IAv2)						G -5980v	....	....	....	----	----	x---	----	----	**5+**	-/**9**
(tephra layer IAv3)						T -5700?	....	....	....	----	----	x---	----	----		
(tephra layer IAv4)						T -5600?	....	....	....	----	----	x---	----	----		
(tephra layer IAv5)						T -5500?	....	....	....	----	----	x---	----	----		
(tephra layer IAv6)						T -5450?	....	....	....	----	----	x---	----	----		
(tephra layer IAv7)						G -4550x	....	....	....	----	----	xx--	----	----	4	-/8
(tephra layer IAv10; AV5)						G -4460v	....	....	....	----	----	x---	----	----	4	-/8
(tephra layer IAv11)						T -4400?	....	....	....	----	----	x---	----	----		
(tephra layer IAv12; AV4)						G -4340u	....	....	....	----	----	xx--	----	--?-	**5**	-/**9**
(tephra layer IAv13)						T -4250?	....	....	....	----	----	x---	----	----		
(tephra layer IAv14)						T -4200?	....	....	....	----	----	x---	----	----		
(tephra layer IAv15)						T -4050?	....	....	....	----	----	x---	----	----		
(tephra layer IAv16)						G -3790v	....	....	....	----	----	xx--	----	----	4	-/8
(tephra layer IAv17)						T -3700?	....	....	....	----	----	x---	----	----		
(tephra layer IAv18)						T -3500?	....	....	....	----	----	x---	----	----		
(tephra layer IAv19)						T -3400?	....	....	....	----	----	x---	----	----		
(tephra layer IAv20; AV3)						G -3200w	....	....	....	----	----	xx--	----	----	**5**	-/**9**
(tephra layer IAv21)						T -2950?	....	....	....	----	----	x---	----	----		
(tephra layer IAv22)						T -2900?	....	....	....	----	----	x---	----	----		
(tephra layer IAv23)						T -2650?	....	....	....	----	----	x---	----	----		
(tephra layer IAv24; AV2)						G -2530y	....	....	....	----	----	xx--	----	----	4	-/8
(tephra layer IAv25)						T -2500?	....	....	....	----	----	x---	----	----		
(tephra layer IAv26)						T -2300?	....	....	....	----	----	x---	----	----		
(tephra layer IAv27)						T -2100?	....	....	....	----	----	x---	----	----		
						T -1700?	....	....	....	----	----	x---	----	----		
(tephra layer AV1)						G -1500?	....	....	....	x---	----	xx--	----	--x-	**5**	-/**9**
(tephra layer IIAV3)						C -1350?	....	....	....	----	----	x---	----	----	**5**	-/**9**
						T 0100?	....	....	....	----	----	x---	----	----		
						T 0400?	....	....	....	----	----	x---	----	----		

VOLCANO NAME (Subregion)	ERUPTION — Area of Activity	LAT	LONG	ELEV (m)	POPL (5 km / 10 / 30 / 100)	ROCK TYPE	VOLC TYPE	NUMBER	STATUS	Start Year	Start M-Dy	Stop Year	Stop M-Dy	Central / Flank vent / Radial fiss / Regional	Submarine / New island / Subglacial / Crater lake	Explosive / Pyro flow / Phreatic / Caldera	Lava flow / Lava lake / Dome / Spine	Fatal / Damage / Mudflow / Tsunami	VEI	Vol L/T
Avachinsky (Kamchatka-E) *continued*										T 0700?	....	....	....	----	----	x---	----	----		
										T 0900?	....	....	....	----	----	x---	----	----		
										T 1100?	....	....	....	----	----	x---	----	----		
										T 1200?	....	....	....	----	----	x---	----	----		
										C 1400?	....	....	....	x---	----	x---	----	----		
										C 1550?	....	....	....	x---	----	x---	----	----		
										1737	08	1737	08	x-x-	----	x---	?---	---x	3	-/7
										1772	....	....	....	----	----	x---	----	----	2	
										1779	0615	1779	0616	x---	----	x---	----	----	3	-/7
										? *1789*	....	....	....	----	----	----	----	----		
										1827	0627	1827	0629	x---	----	xx--	----	--x-	4	-/8
										1828	0417	....	....	----	----	x---	----	----	2	
										? *1837*	....	....	....	----	----	----	----	----		
										1851	1126	1852	0214d	x---	----	x---	----	----	2	
										1853	1221	?*1854*	*0314*	x---	----	x---	----	----	2	
										1854	0813	....	....	x---	----	x---	----	----	2	
										1855	0528	1855	0904d	x---	----	x---	----	----	2	
										1878	....	....	....	x---	----	x---	----	----	2	
										1881	....	....	....	x---	----	x---	----	----	2	
										1894	10	1895	02	x---	----	x---	x---	----	2	7/6
										1901	0707	1901	0713	x---	----	xx--	----	----	2	-/6
										1909	08	....	....	x---	----	xx--	----	----	2	-/6
										? *1910*	....	....	....	----	----	----	----	----		
										1926	0327	1927	0314?	x---	----	xx--	x---	--x-	4*	6/8
										1938	0306	1938	1201>	x---	----	xx--	----	--x-	3	-/7
										1945	0225	1945	0225	x---	----	x---	----	--x-	4	-/8
										1991	0113	1991	0130	x---	----	x---	x-x-	--x-	2	7/5
										2001	1005	2001	1005	x---	----	x---	----	--x-	1	
Dzenzursky (Kamchatka-E)		53.637 N	158.922 E	2285	0036	AD	Compound volc	1000-11=	Holocene											
	(fumarolic activity only)									*X 1923*	*02*	....	....	----	----	----	----	----		
	(fumarolic activity only)									*X 1957*	*0128*	*X1957*	*0311*	----	----	----	----	----		
Zhupanovsky (Kamchatka-E)		53.590 N	159.147 E	2958	0036	ABD	Compound volc	1000-12=	Historical											
										T -5050?	....	....	....	----	----	x---	----	----		
										T -3050?	....	....	....	----	----	x---	----	----		
										C -0220t	....	....	....	----	----	xx--	----	----		
										T -0050?	....	....	....	----	----	x---	----	----		
										T 1000z	....	....	....	----	----	x---	----	----		
										1776	10	....	....	x---	----	x---	----	----	2	
										1882	....	....	....	x---	----	x---	----	----	2	
										1925	....	....	....	x---	----	x---	----	----	2	
										1929	....	....	....	x---	----	x---	----	----	2	
										1940	01	1940	02	x---	----	x---	----	----	2	
	Middle crater, east crater									1956	1227	1957	06	x---	----	x---	----	----	2	
										1959	....	....	....	x---	----	x---	----	----	2	
Veer (Kamchatka-E)		53.75 N	158.45 E	520	0126	BA	Cinder cones	1000-121	Tephrochronology											
										T 0390u	....	....	....	x---	----	x---	x---	----	2?	
	(Korenevski Ridge eruption ca. 1600 BP)									*X 1856*	....	....	....	----	----	----	----	----		
Kostakan (Kamchatka-E)		53.83 N*	158.05 E	1150	2246	BA	Cinder cones	1000-122	Holocene											
	Domashnii									T -8050*	....	....	....	x---	----	x---	----	----	3	-/7
	Ochkovy									T -6550z	....	....	....	x---	----	x---	x---	----	3	6/7
	Maar S of Lake Kostakan, Krasny cone									T 0800t	....	....	....	x---	----	x---	x---	----	3	7/7
	Serpovidny									T 1000t	....	....	....	x---	----	x---	x---	----	3	7/7
	Glavny									T 1200t	....	....	....	x---	----	x---	x---	----	2	7/6
	Glavny									T 1350?	....	....	....	x---	----	x---	----	----	1?	
Bakening (Kamchatka-E)		53.905 N	158.07 E	2278	0245	ADBR	Stratovolcano	1000-123	Tephrochronology											
	NE flank (Novo-Bakening)									T -7550z	....	....	....	-x--	----	x---	x-x-	----	2?	**9**/-
	West of Bakening									T -6550z	....	....	....	-x--	----	x---	----	----	3	-/7
										T -6300y	....	....	....	x---	----	xx-A	----	----		
	SE flank									T -1550?	....	....	....	-x--	----	----	x---	----		
	Western flank									T -0550	....	....	....	-x--	----	x---	----	----	2	-/6
Zavaritsky (Kamchatka-E)		53.905 N	158.385 E	1567	0026	B	Cinder cones	1000-124	Radiocarbon											
	Mt. Peschanaya and adjacent cones									C -0850?	....	....	....	xx--	----	x---	x---	----	4+	7/8
	14 km WNW of Zavaritsky									T -0800z	....	....	....	x---	----	x---	----	----	2	-/6
Akademia Nauk (Kamchatka-E)		53.98 N	159.45 E	1180	1135	ADbr	Stratovolcanoes	1000-125	Historical											
	N margin of caldera lake (Karymsky maar)									G -5500z	....	....	....	---x	---x	xx--	----	----	3?	
	North of Karymsky Lake (Lagerny cone)									G -3850?	....	....	....	---x	----	x---	--x-	----		
	North of Karymsky Lake (tephra layer SC)									G -0950?	....	....	....	---x	----	x---	----	----		
	North margin of Karymsky Lake									1996	0102	1996	0103	x--x	---x	xx--	----	--xx	3	-/7
Karymsky (Kamchatka-E)		54.05 N	159.45 E	1536	0035	AD	Stratovolcano	1000-13=	Historical											
	Karymsky caldera (tephra layer KRM)									G -6600?	....	....	....	x---	----	xx-x	x---	----	**6**	-/**10**
	(birth of Karymsky stratovolcano)									G -4150?	....	....	....	x---	----	x---	----	----		
										G -3450?	....	....	....	x---	----	x---	x---	----		8/-
	(tephra layer PM1)									G -3200?	....	....	....	x---	----	x---	x---	----	4	8/8
	(tephra layer PM2)									G -2350?	....	....	....	x---	----	x---	x---	----	3	7/7
	(tephra layer PM3)									G -2250?	....	....	....	x---	----	x---	x---	----	4	7/**9**
										G -2050?	....	....	....	x---	----	x---	----	----		
	(tephra layer PM4)									G -1400?	....	....	....	x---	----	x---	x---	----	2?	7/6
										G -1100?	....	....	....	x---	----	x---	x---	----		7/-
	(tephra layer SC)									G -0850?	....	....	....	x---	----	xx--	----	----	3	7/7
										G 0950?	....	....	....	x---	----	x---	----	----		
										G 1050?	....	....	....	x---	----	x---	----	----		
	(tephra layer PM6)									G 1150?	....	....	....	x---	----	x---	----	----	2	-/6
										G 1450?	....	....	....	x---	----	x---	----	----		
	(tephra layer PM7)									G 1550?	....	....	....	x---	----	x---	x---	----		8/-
	(tephra layer PM9)									G 1730q	....	....	....	x---	----	x---	x---	----		8/-
										1771	....	....	....	x---	----	x---	----	----	2	
										1830	....	....	....	x---	----	x---	----	----	2	
										1852	....	....	....	x---	----	x---	----	----	2	
										1854	09	....	....	x---	----	x---	----	----	2	
										1908	....	....	....	x---	----	x---	?---	----	2	
										1911	....	....	....	x---	----	x---	----	----	2	
										1912	01	....	....	x---	----	x---	----	----	2	

VOLCANO NAME (Subregion) / ERUPTION	Area of Activity	LAT	LONG	ELEV (m)	POPL (5 km, 10, 30, 100)	ROCK TYPE	VOLC TYPE	NUMBER	STATUS	Start Year	Start M-Dy	Stop Year	Stop M-Dy	Central / Flank vent / Radial fiss / Regional	Submarine / New island / Subglacial / Crater lake	Explosive / Pyro flow / Phreatic / Caldera	Lava flow / Lava lake / Dome / Spine	Fatal / Damage / Mudflow / Tsunami	VEI	Vol L/T
Karymsky (Kamchatka-E) *continued*										**1915**	....	....	....	x---	----	x---	----	----	2	
										1921	09	....	....	x---	----	x---	----	----	2	
										1923	02	....	....	x---	----	x---	----	----	2	
										1925	07	....	....	x---	----	x---	----	----	2	
										1929	....	....	....	x---	----	x---	----	----	2	
										1932	06	....	....	x---	----	x---	----	----	2	
										1933	09	**1933**	10	x---	----	x---	----	----	2	
	(tephra layer PM11?)									**1934**	11	**1935**	02	x---	----	x---	x---	----	2	8/-
										1938	10	....	....	----	----	--x-	----	----	2	
										1940	....	....	....	x---	----	x---	----	----	2	
										1943	0201p	....	....	x---	----	x---	----	----	2	
										1945	09	....	....	x---	----	x---	x---	----	2	
										1946	04	....	....	x---	----	x---	----	----	2	
										1946	09	**1946**	10	x---	----	x---	----	----	2	
										1947	04	....	....	x---	----	x---	----	----	2	
										1952	11	....	....	x---	----	x---	----	----	2	
										1953	....	....	....	x---	----	x---	----	----	2	
										1955	....	....	....	x---	----	x---	----	----	2	
										1956	03	**1957**	02	x---	----	x---	----	----	1	
										1960	04	**1964**	12	x---	----	x---	x---	----	3*	6/7
										1965	0515e	**1967**	02	x---	----	x---	x---	----	3	
										1967	11	**1967**	11	x---	----	x---	----	----	1	
										1970	0511	**1982**	1011	x---	----	xx--	x-x-	--x-	3	7/7
	(fumarolic activity only in 1985)									*X 1985*	*0503*?	....	....	----	----	----	----	----		
	New summit crater SW of 1970-82 crater									**1996**	0102	**2000**	1220?	x---	----	xx--	x---	----	3*	7/-
	Summit and upper south flank									**2001**	1115	**2010>**	....	x---	----	xx--	x-x-	----	3*	
Maly Semiachik (Kamchatka-E)		**54.13 N**	**159.67 E**	**1560**	2235	**BAd**	**Caldera**	**1000-14=**	**Historical**											
	Meso-Semiachik									C-**7550**?	....	....	....	x---	----	x---	x---	----		
	Meso-Semiachik east flank (Vostochny)									C-**6950**?	....	....	....	-x--	----	----	x---	----		
	Ceno-Semiachik									G-**6150**?	....	....	....	x---	----	x---	x---	----		
	Ceno-Semiachik									G-**5850**?	....	....	....	x---	----	x---	----	----		
	Ceno-Semiachik									G-**5750**?	....	....	....	x---	----	x---	----	----		
	Ceno-Semiachik									G-**5450**?	....	....	....	x---	----	x---	----	----		
	Ceno-Semiachik									G-**5050**?	....	....	....	x---	----	x---	----	----		
	Ceno-Semiachik									G-**4650**?	....	....	....	x---	----	x---	x---	----		
	Ceno-Semiachik flank (Yushny cone)									G-**4500**t	....	....	....	-x--	----	----	x---	----		
	Ceno-Semiachik flank (Obmanuvshy)									G-**3500**t	....	....	....	-x--	----	----	x---	----		
	Ceno-Semiachik (Crater IV)									G-**2450**?	....	....	....	x---	----	xx--	----	----		
	Ceno-Semiachik									G-**2250**?	....	....	....	x---	----	x---	----	----		
	Ceno-Semiachik (SW flank)									G-**1800**t	....	....	....	--x-	----	x---	x---	----		
	Ceno-Semiachik									G-**0850**?	....	....	....	x---	----	x---	xx--	----		
	Ceno-Semiachik									G-**0650**?	....	....	....	x---	----	x---	----	----		
	Ceno-Semiachik									G-**0550**?	....	....	....	x---	----	x---	----	----		
	Ceno-Semiachik (Crater V)									G **1400**t	....	....	....	x---	----	x---	xx--	----		
	Ceno-Semiachik (Crater VI--Troitsky)									G **1550**?	....	....	....	x---	----	x---	----	----	4	-/8
	Ceno-Semiachik (Troitsky Crater)									**1804**	....	....	....	x---	----	x-x-	----	----	3	
	Ceno-Semiachik (Troitsky Crater)									**1851**	09	....	....	x---	----	--x-	----	----	2	
	Ceno-Semiachik (Troitsky Crater)									**1852**	0415q	**1852**	07	x---	----	--x-	----	----	2	
	Ceno-Semiachik (Toitsky Crater)									**1945**	09 ?	**1946**	0415q	x---	----	?-x-	----	----	2	
	Ceno-Semiachik (Toitsky Crater)									**1952**	1205d	....	....	x---	----	--x-	----	----	2	
Bolshoi Semiachik (Kamchatka-E)		**54.32 N**	**160.02 E**	**1720**	0034	**BADR**	**Stratovolcanoes**	**1000-15=**	**Radiocarbon**											
	Ivanov lava dome									C-**6800**y	....	....	....	x---	----	----	--x-	----		
	Korona and Yezh lava domes									G-**4450**?	....	....	....	x---	----	----	--x-	----		
Taunshits (Kamchatka-E)		**54.53 N**	**159.80 E**	**2353**	0035	**A**	**Stratovolcano**	**1000-16-**	**Radiocarbon**											
										C-**5800**t	....	....	....	x---	----	xx-A	--x-	----		
										C-**0550**?	....	....	....	x---	----	xx--	x-x-	----		
Uzon (Kamchatka-E)		**54.50 N**	**159.97 E**	**1617**	0034	**ABDR**	**Calderas**	**1000-17=**	**Radiocarbon**											
										T-**5750**?	....	....	....	x---	----	x-x-	----	----		
	N part of caldera (Lake Dal'ny maar)									C-**5700**t	....	....	....	x---	----	x---	----	----		
	Bannoe Lake									T-**1550**?	....	....	....	x---	----	x-x-	----	----		
	Khloridnoe Lake									T **0200**y	....	....	....	x---	----	x-x-	----	----		
Kikhpinych (Kamchatka-E)		**54.487N**	**160.253E**	**1552**	0234	**BA**	**Stratovolcanoes**	**1000-18=**	**Radiocarbon**											
	Zapadny									G-**2850**?	....	....	....	x---	----	x---	x---	----	3	-/7
	Zapadny									G-**2780**q	....	....	....	x---	----	x---	x---	----	4	8/8
	East side of Zapadny, Savich cone									G **0550**?	....	....	....	xx--	---?	x---	x---	--x-	3	7/7
	Savich cone									C **0650**?	....	....	....	x---	----	x---	----	----		
	Savich cone									T **0830**q	....	....	....	x---	----	x---	x---	----		
	Savich cone									C **0900**t	....	....	....	x---	----	x---	----	----	3?	-/8
	Savich cone and north flank									C **1350**?	....	....	....	xx--	----	x---	x---	----	4	8/8
	East flank of Savich (Krab cone)									T **1550**?	....	....	....	-x--	----	----	x---	----		7/-
Krasheninnikov (Kamchatka-E)		**54.593N**	**160.273E**	**1856**	3334	**BAD**	**Caldera**	**1000-19=**	**Radiocarbon**											
	Southern cone & S outer flank fissure									C-**8050**?	....	....	....	x-x-	----	x---	x---	----		
	Southern cone & S outer flank fissure									C-**7250**?	....	....	....	x-x-	----	x-x-	x---	----		
	Southern cone summit, outer SW flank									C-**6550**?	....	....	....	x-x-	----	x---	x---	----		
	Southern cone summit and flank									C-**6350**?	....	....	....	x-x-	----	x---	x---	----		
	Northern outer flank fissure									C-**6250**?	....	....	....	--x-	----	x---	x---	----		
	Southern cone summit and flank									C-**6000**t	....	....	....	x-x-	----	x---	x---	----	4	**9**/8
	Southern cone summit and west flank									C-**5800**t	....	....	....	x-x-	----	x---	x---	----	4	7/8
	Southern cone									C-**5450**?	....	....	....	x---	----	x---	----	----		
	Northern outer flank fissure									G-**5250**?	....	....	....	--x-	----	x---	x---	----		
	Southern cone									C-**5050**?	....	....	....	x---	----	x---	----	----		
	Southern cone									C-**4850**?	....	....	....	x---	----	x---	----	----		
	Northern cone									G-**4450**?	....	....	....	x---	----	x---	----	----		
	Northern cone & N outer flank fissure									G-**3550**?	....	....	....	x-x-	----	x-x-	x---	----		
	Northern cone									G-**3250**?	....	....	....	x---	----	x---	----	----		
	Northern cone & N outer flank fissure									G-**2950**?	....	....	....	x-x-	----	x-x-	x---	----		
	Northern cone									G-**2250**?	....	....	....	x---	----	x---	----	----		
	Northern cone									G-**1650**?	....	....	....	x---	----	x---	----	----		
	N (Zametny) & S (Duga) flank fissures									G-**1350**?	....	....	....	--x-	----	x---	x---	----	3	8/7
	Northern cone									G-**1150**?	....	....	....	x---	----	x---	x---	----		
	Northern cone									G-**1050**?	....	....	....	x---	----	x---	x---	----		
	Northern cone									G-**1000**t	....	....	....	x---	----	x---	----	----	3	-/7
	Northern cone and southern cone flank									G-**0850**?	....	....	....	x-x-	----	x---	x---	----		7/-

VOLCANO NAME (Subregion) / ERUPTION — Area of Activity	LAT	LONG	ELEV (m)	POPL (5 km, 10, 30, 100)	ROCK TYPE	VOLC TYPE	NUMBER	STATUS	Start Year	Start M-Dy	Stop Year	Stop M-Dy	Central / Flank vent / Radial fiss / Regional	Submarine / New island / Subglacial / Crater lake	Explosive / Pyro flow / Phreatic / Caldera	Lava flow / Lava lake / Dome / Spine	Fatal / Damage / Mudflow / Tsunami	VEI	Vol L/T
Krasheninnikov (Kamchatka-E) *continued*																			
Northern cone and southern cone flank									G-0650?	....	....	....	x-x-	----	x---	x---	----		
Northern cone									G-0350?	....	....	....	x---	----	x---	----	----		
Northern cone									G-0250?	....	....	....	x---	----	x---	----	----		
Northern cone									G-0150?	....	....	....	x---	----	x--x	----	----	C	
NW flank and central northern cone									T 0650?	....	....	....	x-x-	----	x---	x-x-	----	2	-/6
Central N cone, SE flank of S cone									G 0750?	....	....	....	x-x-	----	x---	x---	----	3	-/7
Northern cone									G 0850?	....	....	....	x---	----	x---	----	----		
SW flank of southern cone									T 1350?	....	....	....	--x-	----	----	x---	----	0	7/-
Northern cone (Pauk) & SW of S cone									T 1550?	....	....	....	x-x-	----	x---	x---	----		7/-
Kronotsky (Kamchatka-E)	54.753 N	160.527 E	3528	0244	BA	Stratovolcano	1000-20=	Historical											
									T-0050?	....	....	....	----	----	x---	----	----		
South flank (3150 m)									1922	11	....	....	-x--	----	--x-	----	----	2	
Summit and/or south flank (3150 m)									1923	02	....	....	??--	----	?-x-	----	----	2	
Schmidt (Kamchatka-E)	54.92 N	160.63 E	2020	0034	BA	Shield volcano	1000-201	Holocene											
Gamchen (Kamchatka-E)	54.973 N	160.702 E	2576	0034	BA	Complex volcano	1000-21=	Tephrochronology											
SE flank (Barany)									T-1650?	....	....	....	-x--	----	x---	----	----		
SE flank (Barany, Lukovitsa)									T-0550?	....	....	....	-x--	----	x---	--x-	----		
Komarov (Kamchatka-E)	55.032 N	160.720 E	2070	0034	BA	Stratovolcano	1000-22=	Radiocarbon											
									C 0450?	....	....	....	x---	----	----	x---	----	0	
									C 0950>	....	....	....	----	----	----	----	----		
Vysoky (Kamchatka-E)	55.07 N	160.77 E	2161	0034	ABD	Stratovolcano	1000-221	Radiocarbon											
									C-0550?	....	....	....	x---	----	----	x---	----	0	
Kizimen (Kamchatka-E)	55.130 N	160.32 E	2376	0234	ABd	Stratovolcano	1000-23=	Historical											
									T-8050?	....	....	....	x---	----	xx--	x-x-	----	5	-/9
(tephra layer KZII)									C-6400t	....	....	....	x---	----	xx--	--x-	----	5	-/9
									T-5800t	....	....	....	x---	----	x---	--x-	----		8/-
									T-4450?	....	....	....	x---	----	x---	--x-	----	4	-/8
									T-4050?	....	....	....	x---	----	x---	--x-	----	2	-/6
									T-1010?	....	....	....	x---	----	x---	x-x-	----		
									C 0350u	....	....	....	x---	----	x---	x-x-	----		
									T 0700t	....	....	....	x---	----	xx--	--x-	----		
									T 0850?	....	....	....	x---	----	xx--	x-x-	----	3	7/7
									1927	12	1928	01	x---	----	x-x-	----	----	2	
Unnamed (Kamchatka-E)	55.92 N*	161.75 E		2224	U	Cinder cones	1000-232	Holocene?											
Tolbachik (Kamchatka-C)	55.830 N	160.330 E	3682	0035	BA	Shield volcano	1000-24=	Historical											
									G-7600	....	....	....	----	----	x---	----	----		
SW flank (Lesnaya)									C-6050?	....	....	....	x-x-	----	x---	x---	----		
SW flank (Bubochka)									T-5650?	....	....	....	-xx-	----	x---	x---	----		
SW flank									T-5600?	....	....	....	--x-	----	x---	x---	----		
SW flank and NE flank									T-5450?	....	....	....	--x-	----	x---	x---	----		
Plosky and Ostry Tolbachik calderas									T-4550?	....	....	....	x---	----	?--M	x---	----		
SW flank (Kruglenky)									T-2050?	....	....	....	-xx-	----	x---	x---	----	3	8/7
SW flank (Mokhnataya)									T-1750?	....	....	....	-xx-	----	x---	x---	----	3	
SW flank (Istochniky)									T-1650?	....	....	....	-xx-	----	x---	x---	----		
SW flank (Serga, Starichky)									T-0800?	....	....	....	-xx-	----	x---	x---	----		
SW flank (Tsepochka, Malishi)									T-0750?	....	....	....	-xx-	----	x---	x---	----		
SW flank (Buraya)									T-0700?	....	....	....	-xx-	----	x---	x---	----		
SW flank (Kust)									T-0200?	....	....	....	-xx-	----	x---	x---	----		
SW flank (Sosed, Malenky)									T-0100?	....	....	....	-xx-	----	x---	x---	----		
SW flank (Mt. 1004, Pra-Visokaya)									T 0050?	....	....	....	-xx-	----	x---	x---	----	4+	8/8
SW flank (Zapretny)									T 0150?	....	....	....	x-x-	----	x---	x---	----		
SW flank (Poteryanny, Yupiter)									T 0250?	....	....	....	-xx-	----	x---	x---	----		
SW flank (Zasipannie)									T 0350?	....	....	....	-xx-	----	x---	x---	----		
SW flank (Pelmen, Lagerny)									T 0400?	....	....	....	-xx-	----	x---	x---	----	4+	8/8
SW flank (Dvoinoy, Nedostupny, Dalny)									T 0450?	....	....	....	-xx-	----	x---	x---	----	3	9/7
SW flank (Kamenistaya)									T 0550?	....	....	....	-xx-	----	x---	x---	----	3	9/7
SW flank (Peschanie Gorky)									T 0900?	....	....	....	-xx-	----	x---	x---	----	4	9/9
SW flank (Alaid)									T 0950?	....	....	....	-xx-	----	x---	x---	----	4+	8/8
SW flank (Kleshnya, Rastaschenny)									T 1000?	....	....	....	-xx-	----	x---	x---	----	4+	9/8
SW flank (Visokaya, Treschina)									T 1050?	....	....	....	-xx-	----	x---	x---	----	3	9/7
SW flank (Zvezda)									T 1550?	....	....	....	-xx-	----	x---	x---	----	2	8/6
									? *1699*a	....	....	....	x---	----	?---	----	----	*2?*	
									1739	0201p	....	....	x---	----	x---	----	----	2?	
									1740	12	....	....	x---	----	x---	x---	----	2	
									1769	0215q	1769	1015q	x---	----	x---	----	----	2	
									1788	....	....	....	x---	----	x---	----	----	2	
									1789	....	....	....	x---	----	x---	----	----	2	
									1790	....	....	....	x---	----	x---	----	----	2	
									1793	....	....	....	x---	----	x---	----	----	2	
									1904	....	....	....	x---	----	x---	x---	----	2	
									1931	0304	1932	....	x---	----	x---	----	----	2	
									1936	0813<	1937	0302	x---	----	x---	----	----	2*	
									1939	0925	1939	0927	x---	----	x---	----	----	2	
									1940	02	1940	04	x---	----	x---	----	----	2	
Summit, SW flank (1950 m)									1940	11	1941	0715q	xx--	----	x---	x---	----	3*	7/7
									1947	01	....	....	--x-	----	x---	----	----	2?	
									1954	0221	1954	0613	x---	----	x---	----	----	2	
									1955	0107	1955	0209	----	----	x-?-	----	----	2	
									1955	1006	1955	1208	----	----	x-?-	----	----	2	
									1956	0928	1957	1128	x---	----	x---	----	----	2	
									1958	0713<	....	....	x---	----	x---	----	----	2?	
									1959	....	1960	....	x---	----	x---	----	----	2	
									1961	0324	1962	0216>	x---	----	x---	----	----	2	
									1962	08	1963	....	x---	----	x---	----	----	1	
									1964	03	1964	0424>	x---	----	x---	-x--	----	2	
									1965	....	....	....	x---	----	x---	----	----	1	
									1966	0415q	....	....	x---	----	x---	----	----	2	
									1967	03	1967	05	x---	----	x---	----	----	2	
									1967	10	1967	11	x---	----	x---	----	----	2	
									1968	....	1969	....	x---	----	--x-	----	----	1	
									1970	01	1970	04	x---	----	x---	----	----	1	
									1970	09	1970	1201p	x---	----	x---	x---	----	2*	

VOLCANO NAME (Subregion) / ERUPTION	Area of Activity	LAT	LONG	ELEV (m)	POPL (5 km, 10, 30, 100)	ROCK TYPE	VOLC TYPE / Start Year	Start M-Dy	NUMBER / Stop Year	STATUS / Stop M-Dy	Central, Flank vent, Radial fiss, Regional	Submarine, New island, Subglacial, Crater lake	Explosive, Pyro flow, Phreatic, Caldera	Lava flow, Lava lake, Dome, Spine	Fatal, Damage, Mudflow, Tsunami	VEI	Vol L/T
Tolbachik (Kamchatka-C) *continued*							*? 1973*	*10*	*?1974*	*12*	x---	----	x-x-	----	----	*1?*	
	South flank (18 & 28 km from summit)						**1975**	0628	**1976**	1210	xx-x	----	x--M	x---	----	4+	**9**/8
Udina (Kamchatka-C)		**55.755N**	**160.527E**	**2923**	0125	AB	**Stratovolcanoes**		**1000-241**	**Holocene**							
Zimina (Kamchatka-C)		**55.862N**	**160.603E**	**3081**	0025	AD	**Stratovolcanoes**		**1000-242**	**Holocene**							
Bezymianny (Kamchatka-C)		**55.978N**	**160.587E**	**2882**	0025	AD	**Stratovolcano**		**1000-25=**	**Historical**							
	Pra-Bezymianny						T-**7050***	....	....	....	x---	----	x---	----	----		
	Pra-Bezymianny						T-**5050**?	....	....	....	x---	----	x---	----	----		
							T-**2750**z	....	....	....	x---	----	x---	x-x-	----		
	Expeditsii and Exstrusivny Greben						T-**1550**z	....	....	....	-x--	----	----	--x-	----		
							T-**1350**?	....	....	....	x---	----	x---	x-x-	----		
	(tephra layer BZ)						G-**0450**?	....	....	....	----	----	x---	----	----	4	-/8
							T **0050**?	....	....	....	----	----	x---	----	----		
							T **0150**?	....	....	....	----	----	x---	x---	----		
							T **0250**?	....	....	....	----	----	x---	x---	----		8/-
							T **0600**?	....	....	....	----	----	x---	----	----		
	East summit region (Razrushenny dome)						T **0700**t	....	....	....	x?--	----	xx--	--x-	----	4?	-/8
							T **0850**?	....	....	....	----	----	x---	x---	----		
	Summit region and western flank						T **0950**?	....	....	....	xx--	----	xx--	x---	----	4?	-/8
							1955	1022	**1957**	0301	x---	----	xx-A	--x-	--xx	**5***	-/**9**
							1957	0731	**1957**	0731	x---	----	x---	----	----	2	
							1958	01	**1958**	0214	x---	----	x---	--x-	----	1	
							1958	0521	....	....	x---	----	x---	--x-	----	1	
							1958	1228	**1959**	0330	x---	----	x---	--x-	----	2*	
							1959	1015	**1959**	1104?	x---	----	x---	--x-	----	1	-/4
							1960	0413	**1960**	0414	x---	----	xx--	--x-	----	2	-/6
							1961	0325	**1961**	0326	x---	----	xx--	--x-	--x-	3	-/6
							1961	0521	**1961**	0606	x---	----	xx--	----	----	2	
							1961	1018	**1961**	1215	x---	----	x---	--x-	----	3	
							1962	1021	**1962**	1106	x---	----	x---	--x-	----	2	
							1963	05	**1963**	09 ?	x---	----	-x--	--x-	----	1	
							1964	0625	**1964**	0920	x---	----	-x--	--x-	----	2	6/-
							1964	1225	**1964**	1226	x---	----	-x--	--x-	----	1	
							1965	0309	**1970**	03	x---	----	xx--	x-xx	--x-	3*	7/7
							1971	03	**1974**	12 >	x---	----	xx--	--xx	----	3*	
							1976	0325	....	....	x---	----	xx--	x-x-	--x-	2	
							1977	0325	....	....	x---	----	xx--	x-x-	--x-	3	5/7
							1978	0908p	....	....	x---	----	x---	----	--x-	2	
							1979	0211	....	....	x---	----	xx--	x---	----	3	5/7
							1979	0918	....	....	x---	----	xx--	x---	----	2	5/6
							1980	0418	**1980**	0419	x---	----	xx--	x-x-	--x-	3	5/7
							1980	0821	**1980**	0827d	x---	----	xx--	x---	----	2	5/-
							1981	0612	**1983**	0522	x---	----	xxx-	x-xx	--x-	3*	6/7
							1984	0205	**1984**	12	x---	----	xx--	x-x-	----	3*	-/7
							1985	0612	**1985**	1214	x---	----	xx--	x-x-	-x--	3*	-/7
							1986	0326e	**1986**	0629	x---	----	xx--	x-x-	----	2*	6/5
							1986	1205d	**1988**	0726e	x---	----	xx--	x-x-	----	3*	
							1989	0801	**1989**	0804	x---	----	xx--	x-x-	----	2	
							1990	0129	**1991**	1129	x---	----	xx--	x-x-	----	3*	
							1992	0312	**1992**	0612	x---	----	x---	x-x-	----	2	
							1993	1021	**1994**	0204d	x---	----	xx--	x-x-	--x-	3	-/7
							1994	0707	**1994**	1005d	x---	----	x---	x-x-	----	2*	
							1995	09 <	**1995**	1008?	x---	----	x---	x-?-	----	3?	
							1996	0723?	**1996**	0901	x---	----	----	x-x-	----	0	
							1997	0508	**1997**	0516?	x---	----	xx--	x-x-	--x-	3*	-/7
							1997	1205	**1997**	1206	x---	----	x---	----	----	3	
							1998	0620?	**1998**	0622?	x---	----	----	--x-	----	0	
							1999	0225	**1999**	0225	x---	----	x---	----	----	2	
							2000	0314	**2000**	0326a	x---	----	x---	----	----	2	
							2000	0718	**2000**	1104>	x---	----	x---	--x-	----	2*	
							2001	0723?	**2001**	0810?	x---	----	x---	x-x-	----	3*	
							2001	1210	**2002**	0106?	x---	----	x---	--x-	----	2	
							2002	1225	**2002**	1228?	x---	----	x---	x-x-	----	2	
							2003	0726	**2003**	0801?	x---	----	x---	----	----	3	
							2004	0114	**2005**	02 ?	x---	----	xx--	x-x-	----	3*	
							2005	1129?	**2005**	1201>	x---	----	x---	?---	----	2*	
							2006	04 <	**2006**	1229?	x---	----	xx--	x-x-	----	3*	
							2007	0510?	**2007**	1224?	x---	----	xx--	x---	--x-	3?	
							2008	0711	**2008**	0823?	x---	----	x---	x-x-	----	3?	
							2009	1217	**2010**	0101>	x---	----	x---	?---	----	3?	
Kamen (Kamchatka-C)		**56.02 N**	**160.593E**	**4585**	0025	BA	**Stratovolcano**		**1000-251**	**Holocene**							
Kliuchevskoi (Kamchatka-C)		**56.057N**	**160.638E**	**4835**	0035	BA	**Stratovolcano**		**1000-26=**	**Historical**							
							C-**3950**?	....	....	....	x---	----	x---	----	----		
							T-**1050**?	....	....	....	-x--	----	x---	----	----		
							C **0550**?	....	....	....	-x--	----	x---	----	----		
							1697	....	**1698**	....	x---	----	x---	----	----	3↑	
							1720	....	**1721**	....	x---	----	x---	----	----	2	
							1727	....	**1731**	....	x---	----	x---	x---	----	2	
							1737	0925?	**1737**	1104?	x---	----	x---	x---	----	2	
							1740	....	....	....	----	----	----	----	----		
							1762	....	....	....	x---	----	x---	----	x---	2	
							1767	....	....	....	x---	----	x---	----	----	2	
							1770	05	....	....	x---	----	x---	----	----	2	
							1772	....	....	....	x---	----	x---	----	----	2	
							1785	11	....	....	x---	----	x---	----	----	2	
							1787	09	....	....	----	----	?---	----	----	2?	
							1788	02	....	....	x---	----	x---	----	----	2	
							1788	08	....	....	x---	----	x---	----	----	2	
							1789	1201	**1790**	02	x---	----	x---	----	----	2	
							1791	04	....	....	x---	----	x---	----	----	2	
							1791	08	....	....	x---	----	x---	----	----	2	
							1807	0201p	....	....	x---	----	x---	----	----	2	
							1812	09	....	....	x---	----	x---	----	----	2	
							1813	02	....	....	x---	----	x---	----	----	2	

Yuri Doubik (Inst. Volc. Petropavlovsk)

Novy lava dome in 1956 collapse scarp

VOLCANO NAME (Subregion) / ERUPTION — Area of Activity	LAT	LONG	ELEV (m)	POPL (5 km, 10, 30, 100)	ROCK TYPE	VOLC TYPE / Start Year	Start M-Dy	NUMBER / Stop Year	STATUS / Stop M-Dy	Central, Flank vent, Radial fiss, Regional	Submarine, New island, Subglacial, Crater lake	Explosive, Pyro flow, Phreatic, Caldera	Lava flow, Lava lake, Dome, Spine	Fatal, Damage, Mudflow, Tsunami	VEI	Vol L/T
Kliuchevskoi (Kamchatka-C) *continued*						**1819**	....	*?1822*	....	x---	----	x---	x---	----	2*	
						1829	0909	....	....	x-x-	----	x---	x---	----	4?	7/8
						1840	....	....	....	x---	----	x---	----	----	2	
						1848	....	....	....	x---	----	x---	----	----	2	
						1852	02	**1852**	03	x---	----	x---	----	----	2	
						1852	08	....	....	x---	----	x---	----	----	2	
						1853	10	**1854**	0217	x---	----	x---	----	----	2	
						1865	09	....	....	x---	----	x---	----	----	2	
						1877	....	....	....	x---	----	x---	----	----	2	
						1878	09	....	....	x---	----	x---	----	----	2	
						1879	....	....	....	x---	----	x---	----	----	2	
						1882	09	....	....	x---	----	x---	----	----	2	
						1883	07	**1883**	08	x---	----	x---	----	----	2	
						1890	04	....	....	x---	----	x---	----	----	2	
						1896	12	**1897**	11	x---	----	x---	x---	----	2	
						1898	0220	....	....	x---	----	x---	x---	----	2	
						1904	0131p	**1904**	0614>	x---	----	x---	x---	----	2	
Summit and east flank.						**1907**	08	....	....	xx--	----	x---	x---	----	2	
						1909	06	....	....	x---	----	x---	----	----	2	
						1910	08	....	....	x---	----	x---	----	----	2	
						1911	11	....	....	x---	----	x---	----	----	2	
						1913	01	....	....	-x--	----	x---	----	----	2	
						1915	01	....	....	-x--	----	x---	----	----	2	
						1922	05	....	....	x---	----	x---	----	----	2	
						1923	08	**1923**	09	x---	----	x---	----	----	2	
						1925	0404	**1925**	1010	x---	----	x---	----	----	2	
						1926	0323	**1926**	0407	x---	----	x---	----	----	2	
						1929	06	**1929**	09	x---	----	x---	----	----	2	
						1931	0325	**1931**	0327	x---	----	x---	----	----	4	
						1931	08	**1931**	09	x---	----	x---	----	----	2	
NE flank (Kirgurich, Tuyla, Biokos)						**1932**	0125	**1932**	1226e	-x--	----	x---	x---	----	2	7/6
						1935	0421	**1936**	1104>	x---	----	x---	----	----	3*	
Summit, east flank (Bilyukai)						**1937**	0403	**1939**	03	xxx-	----	x---	x---	----	3*	8/7
						1944	1209	**1945**	0120>	x-x-	----	x---	x---	----	3?	-/7
SE flank (Yubileinoye, 1000-1450 m)						**1945**	0619	**1945**	0707	--x-	----	x---	x---	----	3	7/7
SE flank (Apakhonchich, ca. 1600 m).						**1946**	1023	**1946**	1122?	-xx-	----	x-x-	x---	----	2	7/5
						1948	08	....	....	----	----	x---	----	----	2?	
						1949	05	....	....	x---	----	x---	----	----	2	
Summit, NE flank (Bylinkina, 950 m)						**1951**	1119	**1951**	1130	xxx-	----	x---	x---	----	2	7/6
Summit, NE flank (Belyankin Crater)						**1953**	0607	**1953**	0625	xxx-	----	x---	x---	----	2	7/6
						1954	0528	**1954**	09	x-x-	----	x---	----	----	2	
Summit and SE flank (1500 m)						**1956**	01	**1956**	0802	xxx-	----	x---	x---	----	2*	6/-
						1957	....	....	....	x---	----	x---	----	----	1	
East part of summit crater.						**1958**	0518	**1958**	0818>	x---	----	x---	----	----	1	
						1959	0103	....	....	x---	----	x---	----	----	1	
						1960	12	**1963**	0322>	x---	----	x---	----	----	3*	-/6
						1963	1113	**1964**	12 ?	x---	----	x---	----	----	1	
Summit, NE flank (Piip Crater)						**1965**	08	**1966**	1226	x-x-	----	x---	x---	----	3*	8/7
						1967	....	....	....	x---	----	x---	----	----	1	
						1968	0703	**1968**	0703	x---	----	x?--	----	----	3	
						1969	09	**1969**	12	x---	----	x---	----	----	2	
						1970	0526	**1970**	1227	x---	----	x---	----	----	2	
						1971	06	**1971**	07	x---	----	x---	----	----	1	
						1971	11	**1973**	12	x---	----	x-x-	----	----	1	
Summit and SW flank (3400-3600 m).						**1974**	0408	**1974**	12 ?	x-x-	----	x---	x---	----	3*	7/6
Summit, NE flank (1700 m)						**1977**	0802	**1980**	0312	x-x-	----	x---	x---	x---	3*	5/7
						1981	0125	**1981**	0804?	x---	----	x---	----	----	1	
						? *1981*	*1221*	....	....	----	----	----	----	----		
						1982	0324	**1982**	0502	x---	----	x-?-	----	----	1	
Summit and east flank (2875 m).						**1982**	1007	**1983**	0627	x-x-	--x-	x-x-	x---	x-x-	2*	7/-
						1984	0310	**1985**	0128	x---	----	x-x-	x---	--x-	3*	
Summit and NW flank (3100 m)						**1985**	0816	**1986**	0121	x-x-	----	x-x-	x---	--x-	3?	
						1986	0608	**1986**	0711	x---	----	x---	x---	--x-	2	
Summit, SE, SW, NE and east flanks						**1986**	1127	**1990**	09	x-x-	----	xx--	x---	--x-	4*	7/8
						1991	0408	**1991**	0624?	x---	----	x---	----	----	2	
						1992	0125	**1992**	0525?	x---	----	x---	----	----	2	
						1992	0912	**1993**	0912a	x---	----	x-x-	x---	-xx-	2*	
						1994	0908	**1995**	0114>	x-x-	----	xxx-	x---	-xx-	3*	7/7
						1996	1114	**1997**	0320k	x---	----	x---	----	----	2*	
						1997	0907	**1997**	0926	x---	----	x---	----	----	1	
						1998	0723	**1998**	0902?	x---	----	x-x-	----	----	2*	
						1999	0205	**1999**	0712	x---	----	x---	----	----	2	
						2000	0203	**2000**	0208?	x---	----	x---	----	----	2	
						2000	0728	**2000**	0922	x---	----	x---	----	----	2	
						2002	0409	**2002**	0609<	x---	----	x---	----	----	2	
						2002	1124	**2004**	0408	x---	----	x---	?---	--x-	2*	
						2004	0915	**2004**	0915	x---	----	x---	----	----	1	
						2005	0120<	**2005**	0407	x---	----	x---	x---	--x-	2*	
						2007	0215	**2007**	0715	x---	----	x---	x---	--x-	2*	
						2008	1008	**2009**	0416?	x---	----	x---	x---	----	1	
						2009	0801?	**2010**	0101>	x---	----	x---	x---	----	1	
Ushkovsky (Kamchatka-C).	**56.070** N	**160.470** E	**3943**	0035	**BA**	**Compound volc**		**1000-261**	**Historical**							
						C-7550?	....	....	....	----	----	x---	----	----		
Lavovy Shish cone group & summit caldera .						C-6670w	....	....	....	xx--	----	x--M	----	----		
						1890	04	....	....	x---	----	x---	----	----	2?	
Shiveluch (Kamchatka-C).	**56.653** N	**161.360** E	**3283**	0045	**AB**	**Stratovolcano**		**1000-27=**	**Historical**							
						T-8500?	....	....	....	x---	----	x---	--x-	----	3	-/7
						T-8450?	....	....	....	x---	----	x---	--x-	----	3	-/7
						T-8350?	....	....	....	x---	----	xx--	----	----	4	-/8
						T-8200?	....	....	....	x---	----	x---	----	----	4	-/8
						T-8100?	....	....	....	x---	----	xx--	----	----	4	-/8
						T-7950?	....	....	....	x---	----	x---	----	----	4	-/8
						T-7850?	....	....	....	x---	----	x---	--x-	----	3	-/7

VOLCANO NAME (Subregion)..... **LAT** **LONG** **ELEV** (m) **POPL** (5 km, 10, 30, 100) **ROCK TYPE** **VOLC TYPE** **NUMBER** **STATUS**

ERUPTION — Area of Activity

Shiveluch (Kamchatka-C) *continued*

Area of Activity	Start Year	Start M-Dy	Stop Year	Stop M-Dy	Central / Flank vent / Radial fiss / Regional	Submarine / New island / Subglacial / Crater lake	Explosive / Pyro flow / Phreatic / Caldera	Lava flow / Lava lake / Dome / Spine	Fatal / Damage / Mudflow / Tsunami	VEI	Vol L/T
	T -7750?	....	....	....	x---	----	x---	--x-	----	3	
	T -7700?	....	....	....	x---	----	xx--	----	----	4	-/8
	T -7630?	....	....	....	x---	----	x---	----	----	4	-/8
	T -7600?	....	....	....	x---	----	xx--	----	----	4	-/8
	T -7550?	....	....	....	x---	----	x---	--x-	----	3	-/7
	T -7500?	....	....	....	x---	----	xx--	----	----	4+	-/8
	G -7400w	....	....	....	x---	----	xx--	----	----	**5**	-/9
	T -7300?	....	....	....	x---	----	xx--	----	----	**5**	-/9
	T -7150?	....	....	....	x---	----	xx--	----	----	**5**	-/9
	T -7000?	....	....	....	x---	----	x---	--x-	----	3	-/7
	T -6800?	....	....	....	x---	----	xx--	----	----	**5?**	-/9
	T -6600?	....	....	....	x---	----	xx--	----	----	4	-/8
	T -6500?	....	....	....	x---	----	x---	--x-	----	3	-/7
	G -6400w	....	....	....	x---	----	x---	----	----	4	-/8
	T -6380?	....	....	....	x---	----	x---	----	----	4	-/8
	T -6350?	....	....	....	x---	----	x---	----	----	4	-/8
	T -6200?	....	....	....	x---	----	x---	--x-	----	3	-/7
	T -6100?	....	....	....	x---	----	x---	--x-	----	3	-/7
	T -6000?	....	....	....	x---	----	x---	--x-	----	3	-/7
	T -5500?	....	....	....	x---	----	xx--	----	----	**5**	-/9
	T -5400?	....	....	....	x---	----	x---	--x-	----	3	-/7
(SH6 tephra is from Khangar volcano)	*X -5050?*	....	....	....	----	----	----	----	----		
	T -4900?	....	....	....	x---	----	x---	--x-	----	3	-/7
	G -4530?	....	....	....	x---	----	xx-A	----	----	3	-/7
	G -4400?	....	....	....	x---	----	xx--	----	----	**5**	-/9
	G -4350?	....	....	....	x---	----	xx--	----	----	3	-/7
	T -4250?	....	....	....	x---	----	x---	--x-	----	3	-/7
	G -3650?	....	....	....	x---	----	x---	----	----	**5**	-/9
	G -3500?	....	....	....	x---	----	x---	----	----	**5**	-/9
	T -3200?	....	....	....	x---	----	xx--	----	----	4+	-/8
	T -3050?	....	....	....	x---	----	x---	--x-	----	3	-/7
	T -2900?	....	....	....	x---	----	x---	--x-	----	3	-/7
	T -2750?	....	....	....	x---	----	x---	--x-	----	3	-/7
(tephra layer SHdv)	G -2620y	....	....	....	x---	----	x---	----	----	**5**	-/9
	T -2530?	....	....	....	x---	----	x---	--x-	----	3	-/7
	G -2490?	....	....	....	x---	----	xx--	----	----	3	-/7
	T -2200?	....	....	....	x---	----	xx--	----	----	4+	-/8
	T -2150?	....	....	....	x---	----	x---	--x-	----	3	-/7
	G -2100?	....	....	....	x---	----	x---	----	----	**5**	-/9
(tephra layer SHsp)	G -2000?	....	....	....	x---	----	xx-A	----	----	**5**	-/9
	T -1700?	....	....	....	x---	----	xx--	----	----	4	-/8
	T -1650?	....	....	....	x---	----	x---	--x-	----	3	-/7
	T -1500?	....	....	....	x---	----	x---	--x-	----	3	-/7
	G -1330x	....	....	....	x---	----	xx--	----	----	3	-/7
	T -1010?	....	....	....	x---	----	x---	--x-	----	3	-/7
	G -0950?	....	....	....	x---	----	x---	----	----	**5**	-/9
	T -0900?	....	....	....	x---	----	x---	--x-	----	3	-/7
(tephra layer SH5)	G -0780y	....	....	....	x---	----	xx-A	----	----	4+	-/8
	T -0650?	....	....	....	x---	----	x---	--x-	----	3	-/7
	G -0500?	....	....	....	x---	----	x---	----	----	4	-/8
West flank (Karan)	T -0400?	....	....	....	-x--	----	x---	--x-	----	3	-/7
West flank (Karan)	G -0300?	....	....	....	-x--	----	xx--	--x-	----	4	-/8
West flank (Karan)	T -0150?	....	....	....	-x--	----	x---	--x-	----	3	-/7
(SH4 tephra is from Ksudach volcano)	*X -0050?*	....	....	....	----	----	----	----	----		
	T -0010?	....	....	....	x---	----	x---	--x-	----	3	-/7
	T 0100?	....	....	....	x---	----	x---	----	----	4	-/8
	G 0120?	....	....	....	x---	----	xx--	----	----	3	-/7
	G 0170p	....	....	....	x---	----	xx--	----	----	3	-/7
	T 0230?	....	....	....	x---	----	x---	----	----	3	-/7
	T 0250?	....	....	....	x---	----	xx--	--x-	----	4	-/8
	G 0380?	....	....	....	x---	----	xx--	----	----	3	-/7
	G 0500?	....	....	....	x---	----	xx-A	----	----	4+	-/8
	T 0530?	....	....	....	x---	----	x---	----	----	3	-/7
	T 0580?	....	....	....	x---	----	x---	----	----	4+	-/8
	G 0600?	....	....	....	x---	----	x---	----	----	**5**	-/9
Western flank (Karan)	T 0630?	....	....	....	-x--	----	x---	--x-	----	3	-/7
(tephra layer SH3)	G 0650s	....	....	....	x---	----	xx--	----	----	**5**	-/9
	T 0700?	....	....	....	x---	----	x---	--x-	----	3	-/7
	T 0750?	....	....	....	x---	----	x---	--x-	----	3	-/7
	G 0970?	....	....	....	x---	----	xx-A	----	----	4	-/8
	T 1000?	....	....	....	x---	----	x---	--x-	----	3	-/8
(tephra layer SH2)	G 1030v	....	....	....	x---	----	xx--	----	----	**5**	-/9
	T 1150?	....	....	....	x---	----	x---	--x-	----	3	-/7
(tephra layer SH2a)	G 1430?	....	....	....	x---	----	xx-A	----	----	4	-/8
	T 1550?	....	....	....	x---	----	x---	--x-	----	3	-/7
(tephra layer SH1)	G 1650j	....	....	....	x---	----	xx--	----	----	**5**	-/9
	T 1700?	....	....	....	x---	----	x---	--x-	----	3	-/7
	1739	....	....	....	x---	----	x---	--x-	----	3	-/7
	? *1800*j	....	....	....	x---	----	x---	--x-	----	*3*	-/7
	1854	0218	....	....	x---	----	xx--	--x-	-xx-	**5**	-/9
	1879	....	1883	....	x---	----	xx--	--x-	----	3	
	1897	....	1898	....	x---	----	x---	--x-	----	2	
	1905	....	....	....	----	----	----	----	----		
	1928	0127	1929	0415q	x---	----	----	--x-	----	1	
	1930	0201p	....	....	----	----	x---	----	----	1	
Suelich	1944	1105	1950	0406	x---	----	xx--	--xx	----	2	8/-
Molodoy Sheveluch summit domes	1964	1112	1964	1112	x---	----	xx-A	----	--x-	4+	-/8
Center of 1964 crater	1980	0823	1981	1201p	x---	----	xx--	--xx	--x-	1	7/-
	1984	0317	1984	0906	x---	----	x-x-	----	--x-	2?	
	1985	0526	1985	1025	x---	----	x-x-	----	----	2	
	1986	0328	1988	0228	x---	----	xxx-	----	--x-	3*	
	1988	1207	1988	1207	x---	----	xxx-	----	----	2?	
	1989	0407	1989	0626	x---	----	x-x-	----	--x-	2	
	1990	0110	1995	02	x---	----	xxx-	--xx	-xx-	3*	8/6

VOLCANO NAME (Subregion) / ERUPTION — Area of Activity	LAT		LONG		ELEV (m)	POPL (5 km, 10, 30, 100)	ROCK TYPE	VOLC TYPE	NUMBER	STATUS	Start Year	Start M-Dy	Stop Year	Stop M-Dy	Central / Flank vent / Radial fiss / Regional	Submarine / New island / Subglacial / Crater lake	Explosive / Pyro flow / Phreatic / Caldera	Lava flow / Lava lake / Dome / Spine	Fatal / Damage / Mudflow / Tsunami	VEI	Vol L/T
Shiveluch (Kamchatka-C) *continued*											**1997**	0308	**1997**	0404	x---	----	x---	--x-	----	2	
											1998	0530	**1998**	0903	x---	----	xx--	----	----	3*	
											1999	0403	**1999**	0412	x---	----	x---	----	----	2	
											1999	0815	**2010>**	....	x---	----	xx--	x-x-	-xx-	4?	8/-

KAMCHATKA - E of & W

VOLCANO NAME (Subregion) / ERUPTION — Area of Activity	LAT		LONG		ELEV (m)	POPL	ROCK TYPE	VOLC TYPE	NUMBER	STATUS	Start Year	Start M-Dy	Stop Year	Stop M-Dy	Central / Flank vent / Radial fiss / Regional	Submarine / New island / Subglacial / Crater lake	Explosive / Pyro flow / Phreatic / Caldera	Lava flow / Lava lake / Dome / Spine	Fatal / Damage / Mudflow / Tsunami	VEI	Vol L/T
Piip (Kamchatka-E of)	**55.42**	**N**	**167.33**	**E**	**-300**	0003	**DA**	**Submarine volc**	**1000-271**	**Tephrochronology**											
											T-**5050**?	....	....	....	----	x---	x---	----	----		
Khangar (Kamchatka-W)	**54.75**	**N**	**157.38**	**E**	**2000**	0025	**DARB**	**Stratovolcano**	**1000-272**	**Radiocarbon**											
											G-**9500**y	....	....	....	----	----	xx--	----	----	P	
											G-**8250**v	....	....	....	----	----	x---	----	----		
											G-**7100**v	....	....	....	----	----	x---	----	----		
											G-**6400**u	....	....	....	----	----	x---	----	----		
(KHG tephra)											G-**5700**n	....	....	....	x---	----	xx--	--x-	----	**6**	-/10
											G-**5500**q	....	....	....	----	----	xx--	----	----		
											G-**2700**q	....	....	....	----	----	x---	----	----		
											G-**0350**r	....	....	....	----	----	x---	----	----		
											G **1000**n	....	....	....	----	----	x---	----	----		
											G **1500**s	....	....	....	----	----	x---	----	----		
Cherpuk Group (Kamchatka-W)	**55.55**	**N**	**157.47**	**E**	**1868**	0024	**A**	**Pyroclastic cones**	**1000-273**	**Radiocarbon**											
North and South Cherpuk											C-**4550**?	....	....	....	x---	----	x---	x---	----		9/-
Ichinsky (Kamchatka-W)	**55.68**	**N**	**157.73**	**E**	**3621**	0024	**BAdr**	**Stratovolcano**	**1000-28=**	**Historical**											
											T-**6950**?	....	....	....	----	----	x---	----	----		
											G-**6150**t	....	....	....	----	----	xx--	----	----		
											T-**5850**?	....	....	....	----	----	x---	----	----		
											T-**5650**?	....	....	....	----	----	x---	----	----		
SW flank											T-**5400**?	....	....	....	-x--	----	xx--	x-x-	----	**5**	9/9
											G-**2850**y	....	....	....	----	----	xx--	----	----		
											G-**1950**y	....	....	....	----	----	xx--	----	----		
											T-**1200**?	....	....	....	----	----	x---	----	----		
											T-**0600**?	....	....	....	----	----	xx--	----	----		
											G **0050**y	....	....	....	----	----	xx--	----	----		
											T **0550**?	....	....	....	----	----	x---	----	----		
											G **0800**y	....	....	....	----	----	x---	----	----		
											G **1300**x	....	....	....	----	----	xx--	----	----		
SSW flank											**1740**	....	....	....	-x--	----	----	x---	----	0?	
Maly Payalpan (Kamchatka-W)	**55.82**	**N**	**157.98**	**E**	**1802**	0224	**AB**	**Shield volcanoes**	**1000-29-**	Holocene?											
Bolshoi Payalpan (Kamchatka-W)	**55.88**	**N**	**157.78**	**E**	**1906**	0024	**AB**	**Shield volcanoes**	**1000-30-**	Holocene?											
Plosky (Kamchatka-W)	**55.20**	**N**	**158.47**	**E**	**1236**	0234	**BA**	**Shield volcano**	**1000-31-**	Holocene?											
Akhtang (Kamchatka-W)	**55.43**	**N**	**158.65**	**E**	**1956**	0024	**BA**	**Shield volcano**	**1000-32-**	Holocene?											
Kozyrevsky (Kamchatka-W)	**55.58**	**N**	**158.38**	**E**	**2016**	0024	**BA**	**Shield volcano**	**1000-33-**	Holocene?											
Romanovka (Kamchatka-W)	**55.65**	**N**	**158.80**	**E**	**1442**	0124	**BA**	**Stratovolcano**	**1000-34-**	Holocene?											
Uksichan (Kamchatka-W)	**56.08**	**N**	**158.38**	**E**	**1692**	0124	**BAd**	**Shield volcano**	**1000-35-**	Holocene?											
Bolshoi-Kekuknaysky (Kam.-W)	**56.47**	**N**	**157.80**	**E**	**1401**	0034	**BAD**	**Shield volcanoes**	**1000-36-**	**Radiocarbon**											
N flank of Kekuknaysky (Kekuk Crater)											C-**5310**v	....	....	....	-x--	----	x---	x---	----	3	7/7
Kulkev (Kamchatka-W)	**56.37**	**N**	**158.37**	**E**	**915**	1234	**BA**	**Shield volcano**	**1000-37-**	Holocene?											
Geodesistoy (Kamchatka-W)	**56.33**	**N**	**158.67**	**E**	**1170**	0134	**BA**	**Shield volcano**	**1000-38-**	Holocene?											
Anaun (Kamchatka-W)	**56.32**	**N**	**158.83**	**E**	**1828**	1124	**BA**	**Stratovolcano**	**1000-39-**	Holocene?											
Krainy (Kamchatka-W)	**56.37**	**N**	**159.03**	**E**	**1554**	0024	**BA**	**Shield volcano**	**1000-40-**	Holocene?											
Kekurny (Kamchatka-W)	**56.40**	**N**	**158.85**	**E**	**1377**	0124	**BA**	**Shield volcanoes**	**1000-41-**	Holocene?											
Eggella (Kamchatka-W)	**56.57**	**N**	**158.52**	**E**	**1046**	0234	**BA**	**Shield volcano**	**1000-42-**	Holocene?											
Unnamed (Kamchatka-W)	**56.82**	**N**	**158.95**	**E**	**1185**	0134	**BA**	**Shield volcano**	**1000-43-**	Holocene?											
Verkhovoy (Kamchatka-W)	**56.52**	**N**	**159.53**	**E**	**1400**	0025	**BA**	**Shield volcano**	**1000-44-**	Holocene?											
Alney-Chashakondzha (Kam.-W)	**56.70**	**N**	**159.65**	**E**	**2598**	0015	**BArd**	**Stratovolcano**	**1000-45-**	**Radiocarbon**											
E of Chashakondzha (Levaya Belaya)											C-**0660**u	....	....	....	-x--	----	x---	x---	----	3	8/7
East flank of Alney (Kireunsky)											C-**0650**u	....	....	....	-x--	----	x---	x---	----	3	8/7
Alney volcano											C **1600**?	....	....	....	x---	----	x---	----	----		
Cherny (Kamchatka-W)	**56.82**	**N**	**159.67**	**E**	**1778**	0025	**BA**	**Stratovolcano**	**1000-46-**	Holocene?											
Pogranychny (Kamchatka-W)	**56.85**	**N**	**159.80**	**E**	**1427**	0014	**BA**	**Shield volcanoes**	**1000-47-**	Holocene?											
Zaozerny (Kamchatka-W)	**56.88**	**N**	**159.95**	**E**	**1349**	0025	**BA**	**Shield volcanoes**	**1000-48-**	Holocene?											
Bliznets (Kamchatka-W)	**56.97**	**N**	**159.78**	**E**	**1244**	0034	**BA**	**Stratovolcano**	**1000-49-**	Holocene?											
Kebeney (Kamchatka-W)	**57.10**	**N**	**159.93**	**E**	**1527**	0034	**BA**	**Shield volcano**	**1000-50-**	Holocene?											
Fedotych (Kamchatka-W)	**57.13**	**N**	**160.40**	**E**	**965**	0224	**B**	**Shield volcano**	**1000-51-**	Holocene?											
Shisheika (Kamchatka-W)	**57.15**	**N**	**161.08**	**E**	**379**	0134	**AD**	**Lava dome**	**1000-511**	**Radiocarbon**											
											C-**2240**?	....	....	....	x---	----	----	x-x-	----		8/-
Terpuk (Kamchatka-W)	**57.20**	**N**	**159.83**	**E**	**765**	0124	**B**	**Shield volcano**	**1000-512**	**Radiocarbon**											
											C-**0800**y	....	....	....	----	----	x---	x---	----		
Sedankinsky (Kamchatka-W)	**57.27**	**N**	**160.08**	**E**	**1241**	0024	**BA**	**Shield volcano**	**1000-52-**	**Radiocarbon**											
											C-**7050***	....	....	....	----	----	x---	x---	----		
Leutongey (Kamchatka-W)	**57.30**	**N**	**159.83**	**E**	**1333**	0024	**B**	**Shield volcano**	**1000-53-**	Holocene?											
Tuzovsky (Kamchatka-W)	**57.32**	**N**	**159.97**	**E**	**1533**	0034	**BA**	**Shield volcanoes**	**1000-54-**	Holocene?											
Gorny Institute (Kamchatka-W)	**57.33**	**N**	**160.20**	**E**	**2125**	0024	**ADB**	**Stratovolcano**	**1000-55-**	**Radiocarbon**											
South flank (Sedanka lava flow)											C-**4250**?	....	....	....	-x--	----	----	x---	----	0	
											C **1000**?	....	....	....	x---	----	xx--	----	----		
											C **1250**?	....	....	....	x---	----	x---	----	----		
Kinenin (Kamchatka-W)	**57.35**	**N**	**160.97**	**E**	**583**	0024	**BA**	**Maar**	**1000-551**	**Radiocarbon**											
											C **0850**t	....	....	....	x---	----	xx--	----	----	4	-/8
Bliznetsy (Kamchatka-W)	**57.35**	**N**	**161.37**	**E**	**265**	0134	**A**	**Lava cone**	**1000-552**	**Radiocarbon**											
											C-**1060**s	....	....	....	x---	----	x---	x---	----	1?	8/-
Titila (Kamchatka-W)	**57.40**	**N**	**160.10**	**E**	**1559**	0024	**B**	**Shield volcanoes**	**1000-56-**	**Radiocarbon**											
											C-**0550**?	....	....	....	x---	----	----	x---	----		
Mezhdusopochny (Kamchatka-W)	**57.47**	**N**	**160.25**	**E**	**1641**	0024	**B**	**Shield volcano**	**1000-57-**	Holocene?											
Shishel (Kamchatka-W)	**57.45**	**N**	**160.37**	**E**	**2525**	0024	**B**	**Shield volcano**	**1000-58-**	Holocene?											
Elovsky (Kamchatka-W)	**57.55**	**N**	**160.53**	**E**	**1381**	0024	**B**	**Shield volcanoes**	**1000-59-**	**Tephrochronology**											
NE side (Ozernovsky lava flow)											T-**7550**z	....	....	....	-x--	----	x---	x---	----	4	**9**/8

VOLCANO NAME (Subregion) / ERUPTION — Area of Activity	LAT		LONG		ELEV (m)	POPL (5 km, 10, 30, 100)	ROCK TYPE	VOLC TYPE	NUMBER	STATUS	Start Year	Start M-Dy	Stop Year	Stop M-Dy	Central / Flank vent / Radial fiss / Regional	Submarine / New island / Subglacial / Crater lake	Explosive / Pyro flow / Phreatic / Caldera	Lava flow / Lava lake / Dome / Spine	Fatal / Damage / Mudflow / Tsunami	VEI	Vol L/T
Alngey (Kamchatka-W)	**57.70**	**N**	**160.40**	**E**	**1853**	0034	**BA**	**Stratovolcano**	**1000-60-**	Holocene?											
Uka (Kamchatka-W)	**57.70**	**N**	**160.58**	**E**	**1643**	0024	**B**	**Shield volcano**	**1000-61-**	Holocene?											
Kaileney (Kamchatka-W)	**57.80**	**N**	**160.67**	**E**	**1582**	0024	**B**	**Shield volcano**	**1000-62-**	Holocene?											
Plosky (Kamchatka-W)	**57.83**	**N**	**160.25**	**E**	**1255**	0134	**B**	**Shield volcano**	**1000-63-**	Holocene?											
Bely (Kamchatka-W)	**57.88**	**N**	**160.53**	**E**	**2080**	0024	**B**	**Shield volcanoes**	**1000-64-**	Holocene?											
Nylgimelkin (Kamchatka-W)	**57.97**	**N**	**160.65**	**E**	**1764**	0024	**B**	**Shield volcanoes**	**1000-65-**	**Radiocarbon**											
											C-**3550**?	....	....	....							
Snezhniy (Kamchatka-W)	**58.02**	**N**	**160.80**	**E**	**2169**	0024	**B**	**Shield volcano**	**1000-66-**	Holocene?											
Iktunup (Kamchatka-W)	**58.08**	**N**	**160.77**	**E**	**2300**	0024	**BA**	**Shield volcanoes**	**1000-67-**	Holocene?											
Spokoiny (Kamchatka-W)	**58.13**	**N**	**160.82**	**E**	**2171**	0024	**DR**	**Stratovolcano**	**1000-671**	**Radiocarbon**											
											C-**3450**?	....	....	....	x---	----	?---	----	----		
Ostry (Kamchatka-W)	**58.18**	**N**	**160.82**	**E**	**2552**	0014	**BA**	**Stratovolcano**	**1000-68-**	**Holocene**											
SW flank cinder cone											C-**2050**?	....	....	....	-x--	----	x---	x---	----		
Snegovoy (Kamchatka-W)	**58.20**	**N**	**160.97**	**E**	**2169**	0014	**BA**	**Shield volcano**	**1000-69-**	Holocene?											
Severny (Kamchatka-W)	**58.28**	**N**	**160.87**	**E**	**1936**	0014	**BA**	**Shield volcano**	**1000-70-**	**Radiocarbon**											
WSW flank (Tobeltsen)											C-**1550**?	....	....	....	-x--	----	x---	x---	----		
Iettunup (Kamchatka-W)	**58.40**	**N**	**161.08**	**E**	**1340**	0014	**BA**	**Shield volcanoes**	**1000-71-**	Holocene?											
Voyampolsky (Kamchatka-W)	**58.37**	**N**	**160.62**	**E**	**1225**	0024	**BA**	**Shield volcanoes**	**1000-72-**	Holocene?											

MAINLAND ASIA

VOLCANO NAME (Subregion) / ERUPTION — Area of Activity	LAT		LONG		ELEV (m)	POPL (5 km, 10, 30, 100)	ROCK TYPE	VOLC TYPE	NUMBER	STATUS	Start Year	Start M-Dy	Stop Year	Stop M-Dy	Central / Flank vent / Radial fiss / Regional	Submarine / New island / Subglacial / Crater lake	Explosive / Pyro flow / Phreatic / Caldera	Lava flow / Lava lake / Dome / Spine	Fatal / Damage / Mudflow / Tsunami	VEI	Vol L/T
Sikhote-Alin (Russia-SE)	**47.00**	**N***	**137.50**	**E**		5556	**BA**	**Volcanic field**	**1002-01-**	**Holocene**											
Udokan Plateau (Russia-SE)	**56.28**	**N***	**117.77**	**E**	**2180**	2224	**XBTFY**	**Pyroclastic cones**	**1002-03-**	**Radiocarbon**											
Sini											C-**7290**v	....	....	....	---x	----	x---	x---	----		
Khangura											C-**6210**v	....	....	....	---x	----	x---	x---	----		
Dolinnyi											C-**5990**v	....	....	....	---x	----	----	x---	----		
Aku											C-**2670**v	....	....	....	---x	----	----	x---	----		
Chepe											C-**0220**t	....	....	....	---x	----	x---	----	----		
Vitim Plateau (Russia-SE)	**53.70**	**N***	**113.30**	**E**	**1250**	3335	**BXa**	**Cinder cones**	**1002-04-**	**Holocene**											
Tunkin Depression (Russia-SE)	**51.50**	**N***	**102.50**	**E**	**1200**	3345	**XB**	**Volcanic field**	**1002-05-**	Holocene?											
Oka Plateau (Russia-SE)	**52.70**	**N***	**98.98**	**E**	**2077**	0014	**B**	**Cinder cones**	**1002-06-**	**Holocene**											
Azas Plateau (Russia-SE)	**52.52**	**N***	**98.60**	**E**	**2765**	3334	**XZb**	**Volcanic field**	**1002-07-**	**Holocene**											
Taryatu-Chulutu (Mongolia)	**48.17**	**N***	**99.70**	**E**	**2400**	4445	**XZBYA**	**Volcanic field**	**1003-01-**	**Radiocarbon**											
Khorog											C-**2980**w	....	....	....	x---	----	x---	x---	----		
Khanuy Gol (Mongolia)	**48.67**	**N***	**102.75**	**E**	**1886**	4445	**YX**	**Volcanic field**	**1003-02-**	**Holocene**											
Bus-Obo (Mongolia)	**47.12**	**N**	**109.08**	**E**	**1162**	3445	**B**	**Cinder cone**	**1003-03-**	Holocene?											
Dariganga Volc Field (Mongolia)	**45.33**	**N***	**114.00**	**E**	**1778**	5555	**BXF**	**Cinder cones**	**1003-04-**	**Holocene**											
Middle Gobi (Mongolia)	**45.28**	**N***	**106.70**	**E**	**1120**	4445	**B**	**Cinder cones**	**1003-05-**	Holocene?											
Turfan (China-W)	**42.90**	**N**	**89.25**	**E**		4566	**U**	**Cone**	**1004-01-**	**Historical**											
											1120w	....	....	....	x---	----	x---	----	----		
Tianshan Volc Group (China-W)	**42.50**	**N***	**82.50**	**E**		4446	**U**	**Volcanic field**	**1004-02-**	**Historical**											
Pechan											**0050**t	....	....	....	----	----	?---	----	----		
Pechan											**0650**t	....	....	....	----	----	?---	----	----		
Kunlun Volc Group (China-W)	**35.52**	**N***	**80.20**	**E**	**5808**	4445	**S**	**Pyroclastic cones**	**1004-03-**	**Historical**											
											*? 1850*t	....	....	....	----	----	----	----	----		
Ashi Shan											**1951**	0527	....	....	x---	----	x---	----	----	2	
Unnamed (China-W)	**35.85**	**N***	**91.70**	**E**	**5400**	0024	**PFDYA**	**Volcanic field**	**1004-04-**	Uncertain											
(plume probably of meteorol. origin)											*X 1973*	*0716?*	....	....	----	----	----	----	----		
Honggeertu (China-E)	**41.47**	**N***	**113.00**	**E**	**1700**	5567	**B**	**Cinder cones**	**1005-01-**	Holocene?											
Arshan (China-E)	**47.50**	**N***	**120.70**	**E**		4446	**B**	**Cinder cones**	**1005-011**	**Radiocarbon**											
											C **0000**w	....	....	....	x---	----	x---	----	----		
Keluo Group (China-E)	**49.37**	**N***	**125.92**	**E**	**670**	5556	**XF**	**Pyroclastic cones**	**1005-02-**	**Holocene**											
Wudalianchi (China-E)	**48.72**	**N***	**126.12**	**E**	**597**	5567	**X**	**Volcanic field**	**1005-03-**	**Historical**											
Laoheishan and Huoshaoshan											**1720**	0114	**1721**	06	x-x-	----	x-x-	x---	----	3	**9**/8
Laoheishan											**1776**	....	....	....	x---	----	x---	x---	----	2?	
Jingbo (China-E)	**44.08**	**N***	**128.83**	**E**	**1000**	5567	**XZBf**	**Volcanic field**	**1005-04-**	**Radiocarbon**											
											C-**3550**?	....	....	....	x---	----	xx--	x---	----		
											C-**1540**w	....	....	....	x---	----	x---	x---	----		
											C-**0520**v	....	....	....	x---	----	x---	x---	----		
Longgang Group (China-E)	**42.33**	**N***	**126.50**	**E**	**1000**	5567	**BX**	**Cinder cones**	**1005-05-**	**Radiocarbon**											
Jinlongdingzi											C **0350**?	....	....	....	x---	----	x---	----	----		
Changbaishan (China/Korea)	**41.98**	**N**	**128.08**	**E**	**2744**	3457	**TRByx**	**Stratovolcano**	**1005-06-**	**Historical**											
											C-**2160**v	....	....	....	x---	----	xx--	----	----	**P**	
											A-**1000**?	....	....	....	----	----	xx--	?---	----		
											C-**0180**u	....	....	....	x---	----	xx--	----	----	**P**	
											G **1000**s	....	....	....	x---	----	xx--	----	--x-	**7?**	-/**10**
											? 1413	....	....	....	----	----	----	----	----		
											? 1597	*1006*	....	....	----	----	?---	----	----		
											1668	06	....	....	----	----	x---	----	----		
											1702	0609	....	....	x---	----	xx--	?---	----		
											1898	....	....	....	x---	---x	x---	----	----	2?	
											1903	0415q	....	....	----	----	x---	----	----		
Xianjindao (Korea)	**41.33**	**N**	**128.00**	**E**		4567	**U**	**Unknown**	**1006-01-**	Uncertain											
											? 1597	*1008*	....	....	----	----	x---	----	-x--		
											? 1724	....	....	....	----	----	----	----	----		
Sanjiangdao											*? 1898*	....	....	....	----	----	----	----	----		
Ch'uga-ryong (Korea)	**38.33**	**N**	**127.33**	**E**	**452**	4568	**B**	**Shield volcano**	**1006-02-**	Holocene?											
Ulreung (Korea)	**37.50**	**N**	**130.87**	**E**	**984**	4444	**YP**	**Stratovolcano**	**1006-03-**	**Radiocarbon**											
(Ulreungdo-Oki tephra layer; U-4)											G-**8750**?	....	....	....	x---	----	xx--	----	----	**6**	-/**10**
(U-3 tephra)											G-**6450**?	....	....	....	----	----	x---	----	----		
(U-2 tephra)											C-**2990**s	....	....	....	----	----	x---	----	----		
Halla (Korea)	**33.37**	**N**	**126.53**	**E**	**1950**	3466	**BXYt**	**Shield volcano**	**1006-04-**	**Historical**											
NE flank (Ilchulbong tuff cone)											C-**2830**t	....	....	....	-x--	x---	xx--	----	----		
SW flank (Songaksan tuff ring)											C-**2050**x	....	....	....	-x--	----	xx--	x---	----		
											1002	....	....	....	-x--	----	x---	----	----		
											1007	....	....	....	-x--	----	x---	----	----		

Alaska (11)

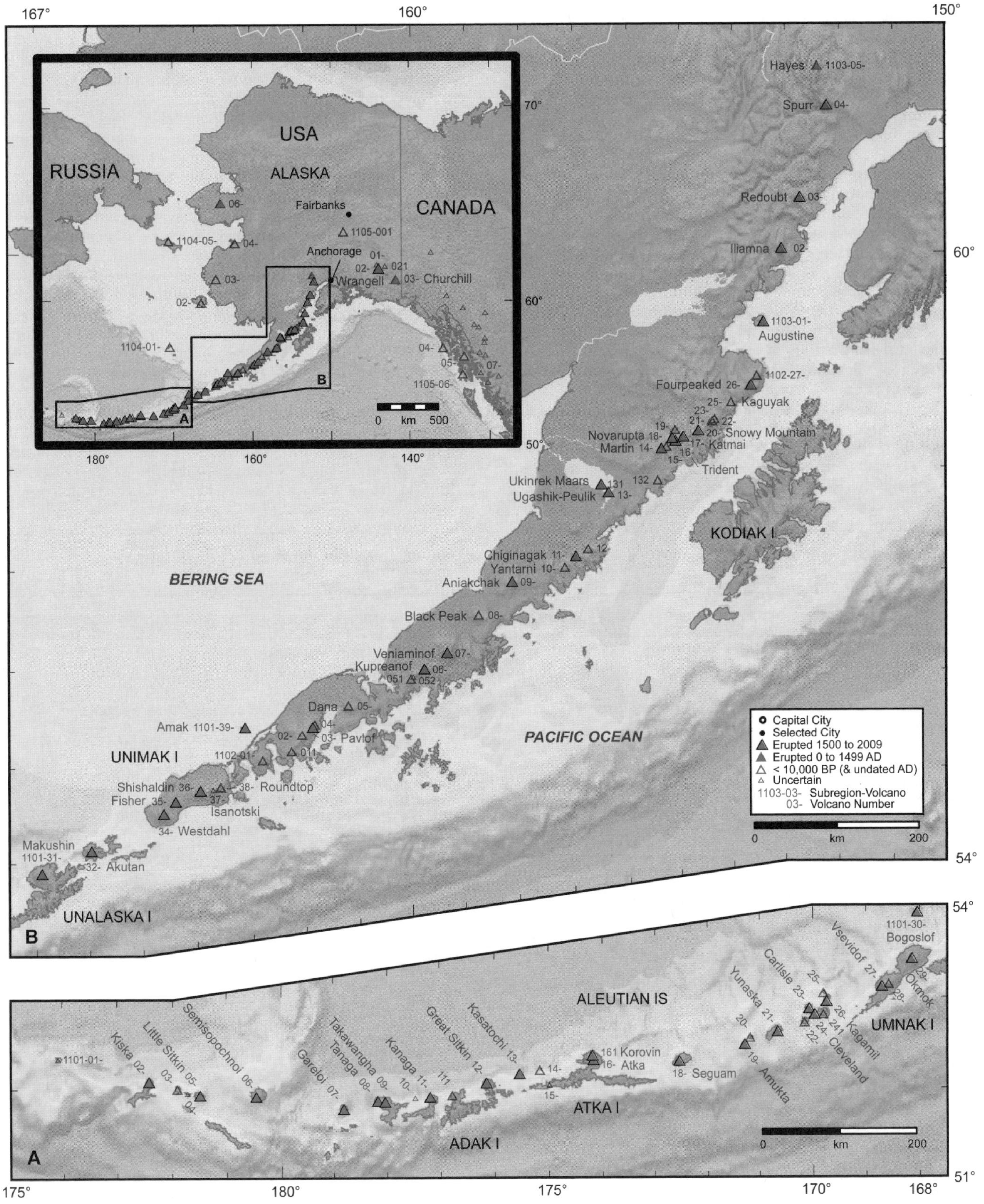

USA
ALASKA
RUSSIA
CANADA
Fairbanks
Anchorage
Wrangell
Churchill
BERING SEA
PACIFIC OCEAN
KODIAK I
UNIMAK I
UNALASKA I
ALEUTIAN IS
UMNAK I
ATKA I
ADAK I
Hayes 1103-05-
Spurr 04-
Redoubt 03-
Iliamna 02-
1103-01- Augustine
Fourpeaked 26- 1102-27-
25- Kaguyak
Snowy Mountain
Novarupta 18-
Martin 14-
Katmai
Trident
Ukinrek Maars 131
Ugashik-Peulik 13-
Chiginagak 11-
Yantarni 10-
Aniakchak 09-
Black Peak 08-
Veniaminof 07-
Kupreanof 06-
Dana 05-
Amak 1101-39-
Pavlof
Shishaldin 36-
Fisher 35-
Isanotski
Roundtop
34- Westdahl
Makushin 1101-31-
32- Akutan
Capital City
Selected City
Erupted 1500 to 2009
Erupted 0 to 1499 AD
< 10,000 BP (& undated AD)
Uncertain
1103-03- Subregion-Volcano
03- Volcano Number
0 km 200
0 km 500
1101-30- Bogoslof
Okmok
Vsevidof 27-
Carlisle 23-
Yunaska 21-
Kagamil
Cleveland
Amukta
Korovin
Atka
Seguam
Kasatochi 13-
Great Sitkin 12-
Kanaga 11-
Tanaga 08-
Takawangha 09-
Gareloi 07-
Semisopochnoi 06-
Little Sitkin 05-
Kiska 02-
1101-01-
167°
160°
150°
175°
180°
170°
168°
60°
54°
51°
A
B

The 2500-km-long Aleutian arc is a chain of large calc-alkaline stratovolcanoes and impressive calderas. This largely uninhabited arc, whose western end lies across the International Date Line and reaches within 900 km of Kamchatka, is responsible for nearly all the historical volcanism of Alaska. Alaska possesses more than half the Holocene volcanoes in the United States, but has produced nearly 70% of its historical eruptions, including many of its most explosive. The Wrangell Mountains, near the Canadian border to the east, include some of world's largest andesitic shield volcanoes, including Mount Wrangell itself, a glacier-covered caldera which has erupted in the past century, and the Mount Churchill-Bona complex, at 5005 m the highest volcano in the U.S. and the 4th highest in North America. Churchill was the source of the bilobate rhyodacitic White River Ash deposits, produced during two of the largest explosive eruptions in North America during the past 2000 years. Basaltic lava fields are scattered throughout the Bering Sea, the western interior, and the southeastern panhandle of Alaska.

Western record keeping began in 1741 when Vitus Bering (see introduction to Regions 09 & 10, above) landed in Alaska, but these commonly cloud-covered volcanoes were only occasionally documented in the following decades. Eruption reporting began with Kasatochi in 1760 (which also had a major eruption in 2008 that devastated the entire island and extended its shoreline); 4 more had erupted by 1768 and there has been a steady increase since. The first government of Russian America was set up near Sitka in 1799, and in 1867 the US bought Alaska from Russia for $7.2 million. Gold was discovered in 1896, and the population of this vast region had grown substantially by 1912, when the major eruption of Novarupta/Katmai, the world's largest in the 20th century, brought widespread attention to Alaska's many volcanoes. Recognition of their significance during WW-II led to a major USGS mapping program in the Aleutians during the early 1950s, bringing a quantum jump to understanding of these volcanoes. In 1959 Alaska entered the US as our 49th state, ranking first in area, 49th in population, and first in volcanism, with 42 of the nation's 65 historically active volcanoes.

Alaska has the world's largest proportion of stratovolcanoes (72%), several other regions have higher totals. Only Indonesia, Japan, and South America have had more volcanoes erupt during the past 100 years. Most volcanoes lie in sparsely populated areas, however, and only three Alaskan eruptions have caused fatalities. Weather in the Aleutian arc is notoriously bad, and eruptions take place even today without being observed. Only Antarctica has fewer people living within 100 km of volcanoes, but the Aleutian arc underlies the heavily traveled Great Circle commercial air corridor between the mainland U.S. and Asia, and several Alaskan eruptions have produced ash plumes that have damaged commercial aircraft. The Alaska Volcano Observatory has increased monitoring capability on many of these volcanoes to help anticipate and mitigate the impact of ash eruptions on aircraft.

Alaska is the latest region to be covered in the *CAVW* series. That catalog, published in the USGS Open-File Report format by Tom Miller and colleagues at the Alaska Volcano Observatory, and two other book-length treatments of Alaskan volcanoes (starred under REFERENCES - 1100) bring excellent modern coverage to this important volcanic group. These authors have not all followed the *CAVW* numbering of clockwise progression around the Pacific Rim, but naming has been reasonably consistent throughout. The Alaska Volcano Observatory, a collaborative program involving the USGS, the Geophysical Institute of the University of Alaska, and the Alaska Division of Geological & Geophysical Surveys, now posts detailed information about Alaska's present and past volcanism on the AVO website.

VOLCANO NAME (Subregion) / ERUPTION — Area of Activity	LAT	LONG	ELEV (m)	POPL (5 km 10 30 100)	ROCK TYPE	VOLC TYPE	NUMBER	STATUS	Start Year	Start M-Dy	Stop Year	Stop M-Dy	Central Flank vent Radial fiss Regional	Submarine New island Subglacial Crater lake	Explosive Pyro flow Phreatic Caldera	Lava flow Lava lake Dome Spine	Fatal Damage Mudflow Tsunami	VEI	Vol L/T
ALEUTIAN ISLANDS																			
Buldir (Aleutian Is)	**52.35 N**	**175.911 E**	**656**	0000	**BA**	**Stratovolcano**	**1101-01-**	Holocene?											
Kiska (Aleutian Is)	**52.103 N**	**177.602 E**	**1220**	0000	**ABd**	**Stratovolcano**	**1101-02-**	**Historical**											
									? *1907*	....	....	....	----	----	----	----	----	*2?*	
									? *1927*	....	....	....	----	----	----	----	----	*2?*	
North flank (Sirius Point)									**1962**	0124	....	....	-x--	----	x---	x---	----	3	
									1964	0318	....	....	----	----	----	x---	----	0	
									1969	0911	**1969**	0916	----	----	x---	x---	----	2?	
									? *1987*	*0415*	....	....	----	----	?---	----	----		
Upper NW? flank									**1990**	0601	**1990**	0601?	-x--	----	x-x-	----	----	2	
Segula (Aleutian Is)	**52.015 N**	**178.136 E**	**1160**	0000	**AB**	**Stratovolcano**	**1101-03-**	**Holocene**											
Davidof (Aleutian Is)	**51.97 N**	**178.33 E**	**328**	0000	**U**	**Stratovolcano**	**1101-04-**	Holocene?											
Little Sitkin (Aleutian Is)	**51.95 N**	**178.543 E**	**1174**	0000	**AD**	**Stratovolcano**	**1101-05-**	**Historical**											
									1776	....	....	....	----	----	x---	----	----	1?	
Summit and west flank									**1828**	....	? *1830*	....	x-x-	----	----	x---	----		
Semisopochnoi (Aleutian Is)	**51.93 N**	**179.58 E**	**1221**	0000	**BADY**	**Stratovolcano**	**1101-06-**	**Historical**											
Cerberus									? *1772*	....	....	....	x---	----	----	----	----		
Cerberus									? *1790*	....	....	....	x---	----	----	----	----		
Cerberus									? *1792*	....	....	....	x---	----	----	----	----		
Cerberus									? *1830*	....	....	....	x---	----	----	----	----		
Cerberus									**1873**	....	....	....	x---	----	----	----	----		
Sugarloaf ?									**1987**	0413	....	....	-?--	----	x---	----	----	2?	
Gareloi (Aleutian Is)	**51.790 N**	**178.794 W**	**1573**	0000	**BA**	**Stratovolcano**	**1101-07-**	**Historical**											
									? *1760*	....	....	....	----	----	----	----	----		
									1790	....	....	....	----	----	x---	----	----	2	
									1791	....	....	....	----	----	x---	----	----	2	
									1792	....	....	....	----	----	x---	x---	----	2	
									? *1828*	....	? *1829*	....	----	----	----	----	----	*2?*	
									1873	....	....	....	----	----	----	----	----	2?	
									1922	....	....	....	----	----	x---	----	----	3	
									? *1927*	....	....	....	----	----	----	----	----		
SE flank fissure (near summit to sea)									**1929**	04	**1930**	....	--x-	----	x-x-	x---	-x--	3	
									1950	....	**1951**	....	----	----	x-x-	----	----	1	
									1952	0117	....	....	----	----	x---	----	----	2?	
									1980	0807	**1980**	0917	x---	----	x---	----	----	3?	
									1982	0115	**1982**	0115	x---	----	x---	----	----	3	
									1987	0904	....	....	x---	----	-?--	x---	----	1?	
									1989	0817	....	....	x---	----	x---	----	----	1	
									? *1996*	*0927*	....	....	----	----	?---	----	----	*1?*	
Tanaga (Andreanof Is)	**51.885 N**	**178.146 W**	**1806**	0000	**BAd**	**Stratovolcanoes**	**1101-08-**	**Historical**											
Sajaka One									R-**1050***	....	....	....	----	----	----	x---	----	0	
Sajaka One									T-**0550***	....	....	....	x---	----	xx-A	----	----		
Tanaga									C **1050?**	....	....	....	x---	----	x---	----	----		
Tanaga, Sajaka Two									C **1550?**	....	....	....	x---	----	x---	----	----		
									? *1763*	....	? *1770*	....	----	----	----	----	----		

VOLCANO NAME (Subregion) / ERUPTION — Area of Activity	LAT	LONG	ELEV (m)	POPL 5 km 10 30 100	ROCK TYPE	VOLC TYPE / — Start — Year	NUMBER / M-Dy	STATUS / — Stop — Year	M-Dy	Central, Flank vent, Radial fiss, Regional	Submarine, New island, Subglacial, Crater lake	Explosive, Pyro flow, Phreatic, Caldera	Lava flow, Lava lake, Dome, Spine	Fatal, Damage, Mudflow, Tsunami	VEI	Vol L/T
Tanaga (Andreanof Is) *continued*						? 1791	0607	....	....	----	----	----	----	----		
						1829	....	....	....	----	----	x---	----	----		
						1914	....	....	....	----	----	----	x---	----	0	
Takawangha (Andreanof Is)	**51.873 N**	**178.006 W**	**1449**	0000	**BAd**	**Stratovolcano**	**1101-09-**	**Radiocarbon**								
						C **1550**?	....	....	....	x---	----	x---	----	----		
Bobrof (Andreanof Is)	**51.910 N**	**177.438 W**	**738**	0000	**BA**	**Stratovolcano**	**1101-10-**	Holocene?								
Kanaga (Andreanof Is)	**51.923 N**	**177.168 W**	**1307**	0000	**AYDB**	**Stratovolcano**	**1101-11-**	**Historical**								
(T2 tephra layer)						G-**7300**z	....	....	....	x---	----	x---	----	----		
(T3 tephra layer)						G-**4700**w	....	....	....	x---	----	x---	----	----		
(T4 tephra layer)						G-**2300**w	....	....	....	x---	----	x---	----	----		
(T5 tephra layer)						G-**2150**x	....	....	....	x---	----	x---	----	----		
(T6 tephra layer)						G-**1900**y	....	....	....	x---	----	x---	----	----		
(T7 tephra layer)						G-**1550**v	....	....	....	x---	----	x---	----	----		
(T8 tephra layer)						G **0200**w	....	....	....	x---	----	x---	----	----		
(T9 tephra layer)						G **0850**x	....	....	....	x---	----	x---	----	----		
(T10 tephra layer)						G **1150**v	....	....	....	x---	----	x---	----	----		
(T11 tephra layer)						G **1400**t	....	....	....	x---	----	x---	----	----		
						? 1763	....	....	....	----	----	----	----	----		
(steam emission)						X 1768	....	....	....	----	----	----	----	----		
						1783?	....	**1787**?	....	x---	----	x---	----	----		
(steam emission)						X 1790	....	X1791	....	----	----	----	----	----		
						? 1827	....	....	....	----	----	----	----	----		
						? 1829	....	....	....	----	----	----	----	----		
Upper south flank ?						**1904**	....	....	....	--x-	----	----	x---	----	0	
Summit, upper SW flank						**1906**	05	....	....	x-x-	----	----	x---	----		
(eruption from Great Sitkin, not Kanaga)						X 1933	....	....	....	----	----	----	----	----		
						1942	....	....	....	----	----	?---	----	----	1	
						1994	0105d	**1994**	1126d	x-x-	----	x---	x---	----	2	
						1995	0619?	**1995**	0623?	x---	----	x---	----	----	2?	
						? 1996	0611	....	....	x---	----	--?-	----	----	1?	
Moffett (Andreanof Is)	**51.944 N**	**176.747 W**	**1196**	0000	**AB**	**Stratovolcano**	**1101-111**	**Radiocarbon**								
(Main Ash deposit)						G-**7850**?	....	....	....	----	----	x---	----	----		
(Intermediate Ash deposit)						G-**3750**?	....	....	....	----	----	x---	----	----		
(Sandwich Ash deposit)						G-**1600**?	....	....	....	----	----	x---	----	----		
Great Sitkin (Andreanof Is)	**52.076 N**	**176.130 W**	**1740**	0000	**ABt**	**Stratovolcano**	**1101-12-**	**Historical**								
						? 1760	....	....	....	----	----	----	----	----		
						? 1784	....	....	....	----	----	----	----	----		
						1792	0526e	....	....	----	----	x---	----	----		
						? 1828	....	....	....	----	----	----	----	----		
						? 1829	....	....	....	----	----	----	----	----		
						? 1904	....	....	....	----	----	----	----	----		
						1933	11	....	....	----	----	x---	----	----	2	
						1945	03	....	....	x---	----	x---	x-x-	----	2	7/-
						? 1946	0814	....	....	x---	----	----	----	----		
						1949	1230	**1950**	0107	----	----	x---	----	----	1	-/4
						1950	1105	**1950**	1129	----	----	x---	----	----		
						X 1953	0511	X1953	0514	----	----	----	----	----		
						1974	0219	**1974**	09	x---	----	x---	x-x-	----	2	7/-
						? 1987	0318	....	....	?---	----	----	----	----		
Kasatochi (Andreanof Is)	**52.177 N**	**175.508 W**	**314**	0003	**BAD**	**Stratovolcano**	**1101-13-**	**Historical**								
						1760	....	....	....	----	----	----	?---	----	0	
						? 1827	....	....	....	----	----	----	----	----		
						? 1828	....	....	....	----	----	----	----	----		
						? 1899?	....	....	....	x---	----	?---	----	----		
						2008	0807	**2008**	0809?	x---	---x	xx--	----	-x--	4	
Koniuji (Andreanof Is)	**52.22 N**	**175.13 W**	**273**	0003	**AB**	**Stratovolcano**	**1101-14-**	**Ar/Ar**								
						R-**3850***	....	....	....	----	----	----	x---	----		
						R-**2650***	....	....	....	----	----	----	x---	----		
						R-**1150***	....	....	....	----	----	----	x-x-	----		
Sergief (Andreanof Is)	**52.05 N**	**174.95 W**	**560**	0003	**U**	**Stratovolcano**	**1101-15-**	Uncertain								
Atka (Atka I)	**52.332 N**	**174.137 W**	**1451**	0033	**BDA**	**Stratovolcanoes**	**1101-16-**	**Historical**								
Sarichef or more probably Kliuchef						**1812**	....	....	....	?---	----	x---	----	----	3?	
Kliuchef SW and WSW flanks						**1987**	0318	**1987**	0319?	-x--	----	x---	----	----	2	
						? 1995	0501	....	....	x---	----	--?-	----	----	1?	
Korovin (Atka I)	**52.381 N**	**174.154 W**	**1533**	0033	**BAD**	**Stratovolcanoes**	**1101-161**	**Historical**								
						? 1829	....	?1830	....	----	----	----	----	----		
						? 1844	....	....	....	----	----	----	----	----		
						1907	....	....	....	x---	----	x---	----	----		
						? 1951	....	....	....	----	----	----	----	----		
						? 1953	....	?1954	....	----	----	----	----	----		
						1973	0825b	....	....	x-x-	----	----	x---	----	0	
						? 1976	....	....	....	----	----	----	----	----		
						? 1986	0523	....	....	x---	----	x-x-	----	----	1	
						1987	0304?	**1987**	0319?	x---	----	x---	----	----	2	
(reported ash cloud meteorologic)						X 1996	0629	....	....	----	----	----	----	----		
						1998	0508a	**1998**	0708?	x---	---x	x-x-	----	----	3*	
						2002	07 <	....	....	x---	---x	x-x-	----	----	1?	
						2004	0704<	....	....	x---	---x	x-x-	----	----	1?	
						2005	0223	**2005**	0505d	x---	---x	x-x-	----	----	1	
						2006	1125e	**2007**	0303<	x---	----	x---	----	----	1	
Unnamed (Amlia-N of)	52.25 N	173.55 W					1101-17-	Not a Volcano								
(SOFAR eruption site not confirmed)						X 1966	07	X1967	08	----	----	----	----	----		
Seguam (Andreanof Is)	**52.315 N**	**172.510 W**	**1054**	0000	**ADBr**	**Stratovolcanoes**	**1101-18-**	**Historical**								
Wilcox volcano						R-**7300***	....	....	....	x---	----	xx--	----	----	**5?**	-/8
W flank of cone in eastern caldera						U-**5100***	....	....	....	-x--	----	----	x---	----	0	7/-
W flank of cone in eastern caldera						U-**4050***	....	....	....	-x--	----	----	x---	----	0	
West of Wilcox volcano						U **0250**z	....	....	....	-x--	----	----	--x-	----		
						1786	....	**1790**	....	----	----	----	----	----		
						? 1827	....	....	....	----	----	----	----	----		
						1891	12	....	....	----	----	x---	----	----	2	
						1892	0415q	....	....	----	----	x---	----	----	3	
						1902	....	....	....	----	----	x---	----	----	3	

VOLCANO NAME (Subregion) / **ERUPTION** — Area of Activity	**LAT**	**LONG**	**ELEV** (m)	**POPL** 5 km / 10 / 30 / 100	**ROCK TYPE**	**VOLC TYPE** / — Start — **Year**	M-Dy	**NUMBER** / — Stop — **Year**	**STATUS** / M-Dy	Central / Flank vent / Radial fiss / Regional	Submarine / New island / Subglacial / Crater lake	Explosive / Pyro flow / Phreatic / Caldera	Lava flow / Lava lake / Dome / Spine	Fatal / Damage / Mudflow / Tsunami	VEI	Vol L/T
Seguam (Andreanof Is) *continued*						? *1927*	....	....	....	----	----	----	----	----		
Pyre Peak (2.5 km SE of summit)						**1977**	0306	**1977**	0308?	--x-	----	x---	x---	----	1	7/-
Pyre Peak (1.5 km south of summit)						**1992**	1227	**1992**	1230	--x-	----	x---	----	----	2	
Near Pyre Peak						**1993**	0528	**1993**	0831>	-x--	----	x---	x---	----	2	
Amukta (Four Mountains)	**52.50 N**	**171.252 W**	**1066**	0000	**A**	**Stratovolcano**		**1101-19-**	**Historical**							
						? *1770*	....	....	....	----	----	----	----	----		
						1786	06	**1791**	....	----	----	x---	----	----	3↑	-/8
						? *1876*	....	....	....	----	----	----	----	----		
						1878	....	....	....	----	----	----	----	----		
						1963	0213	....	....	xxx-	----	x---	x---	----	3	
						1987	0904?	....	....	x---	----	x---	----	----	1	
						1996	0917	**1996**	0918	x---	----	x---	----	----	1	
						1997	0303	....	....	x---	----	x---	----	----	1	
Chagulak (Four Mountains)	**52.577 N**	**171.13 W**	**1142**	0000	**A**	**Stratovolcano**		**1101-20-**	**Holocene**							
Yunaska (Four Mountains)	**52.643 N**	**170.629 W**	**550**	0000	**ABD**	**Shield volcano**		**1101-21-**	**Historical**							
						? *1817*	....	....	....	----	----	----	----	----		
						1824	....	....	....	----	----	x---	----	----	3	
						1830	....	....	....	----	----	x---	----	----	2	
						? *1873*	....	....	....	----	----	----	----	----	*2?*	
						? *1929*	....	....	....	----	----	----	----	----		
						1937	1103	**1937**	1104	----	----	x---	?---	----	3	
Herbert (Four Mountains)	**52.742 N**	**170.111 W**	**1280**	0002	**A**	**Stratovolcano**		**1101-22-**	**Holocene**							
Carlisle (Four Mountains)	**52.894 N**	**170.054 W**	**1620**	0002	**A**	**Stratovolcano**		**1101-23-**	**Historical**							
						1774	....	....	....	----	----	----	----	----		
						1828	....	....	....	----	----	----	----	----		
						? *1838*	....	....	....	----	----	----	----	----		
						? *1987*	*1116*	....	....	x---	----	--?-	----	----		
Cleveland (Chuginadak I)	**52.825 N**	**169.944 W**	**1730**	0001	**AD**	**Stratovolcano**		**1101-24-**	**Historical**							
						1893	....	....	....	----	----	----	----	----		
						1897	....	....	....	----	----	----	----	----		
						? *1929*	*03*	....	....	----	----	----	----	----		
						1932	0101	....	....	----	----	x---	----	----		
						1938	....	....	....	----	----	----	----	----		
						1944	0610	**1944**	0612	x---	----	x---	x---	x-?-	3	
						? *1951*	*1101*	? *1951*	*12*	----	----	?---	----	----		
						? *1953*	*0625*	....	....	x---	----	x---	----	----		
						? *1975*	*09*	....	....	----	----	----	----	----		
						1984	0712	**1984**	0712	x---	----	x---	----	----	1	
						? *1985*	*1210*	....	....	x---	----	--?-	----	----	*1*	
						1986	0428	**1986**	0527>	x---	----	x---	x---	----	2	
						1987	0619	**1987**	0828	x---	----	x---	x---	----	3*	
						? *1989*	*1025*c	....	....	x---	----	----	?---	----	*0*	
						1994	0525	**1994**	0525	x---	----	x---	----	--x-	3	
						1994	1020	**1994**	1020	x---	----	x---	----	----	1?	
						1997	0505	**1997**	0505	x---	----	x---	----	----	2?	
						2001	0202<	**2001**	0415?	x---	----	x---	x---	--x-	3?	
						2005	0313?	**2005**	1127a	x---	----	x---	----	--x-	2*	
						2006	0206	**2006**	1028	x---	----	x---	----	----	3*	
						2007	0617?	**2008**	0812?	x---	----	x?--	x---	--?-	2?	
						2009	0102	? *2009*	*0121*	x---	----	x---	----	----		
						2009	0625	**2009**	0625	x---	----	x---	----	----	2	
						2009	1002	**2009**	1212?	x---	----	x---	----	----	2	
Tana (Chuginadak I)	**52.83 N**	**169.77 W**	**1170**	0001	**R**	**Stratovolcanoes**		**1101-241**	**Holocene**							
Uliaga (Four Mountains)	**53.065 N**	**169.77 W**	**888**	0002	**U**	**Stratovolcano**		**1101-25-**	**Holocene**							
Kagamil (Four Mountains)	**52.974 N**	**169.72 W**	**893**	0001	**U**	**Stratovolcano**		**1101-26-**	**Historical**							
						1929	12	....	....	----	----	----	----	----		
Vsevidof (Fox Is)	**53.130 N**	**168.693 W**	**2149**	0011	**AD**	**Stratovolcano**		**1101-27-**	**Historical**							
						? *1784*	....	....	....	x---	----	----	----	----		
						? *1790*	*0530*	....	....	x---	----	----	----	----		
						1817	....	....	....	----	----	----	----	----	3?	
SW end of Umnak Island						**1830**	....	....	....	----	----	----	----	----		
West flank fissure ?						**1878**	....	....	....	--?-	----	x---	?---	----	2	
						? *1880*	....	....	....	x---	----	----	----	----		
West flank fissure						? *1957*	*0311*	? *1957*	*0312*	--?-	----	x-x-	----	----	*2*	
Recheschnoi (Fox Is)	**53.157 N**	**168.539 W**	**1984**	0002	**ABR**	**Stratovolcano**		**1101-28-**	**Holocene**							
Okmok (Fox Is)	**53.43 N**	**168.13 W**	**1073**	0001	**BAdtr**	**Shield volcano**		**1101-29-**	**Historical**							
						C-**6310**z	....	....	....	x---	----	xx--	----	----	**P**	
(Okmok II caldera)						C-**0100**t	....	....	....	x---	----	xx-x	----	---x	**6**	-/10
						1805	....	....	....	x---	----	----	?---	----		
Cone E? or B?						**1817**	0301	**1820**	....	x---	----	x?--	----	-x--	3	
Cone B?						**1824**	....	**1830**	....	x-?-	----	x---	?---	----		
Cone A?						**1878**	....	....	....	x---	----	x---	----	---x	2?	
SW part of caldera (Cone A)						**1899**	....	....	....	x---	----	x---	----	----	3	
Cone A?						**1931**	0321	**1931**	0513>	x---	----	x---	?---	----	2	
SW part of caldera (Cone A)						? *1936*	....	....	....	x---	----	----	----	----		
SW part of caldera (Cone A)						**1938**	....	....	....	x---	----	----	?---	----		
SW part of caldera (Cone A)						**1943**	06	....	....	x---	----	x---	----	----	1	
SW part of caldera (Cone A)						**1945**	0604	**1945**	12	x---	----	x---	x---	----	2	7/-
SW part of caldera (Cone A)						**1958**	0814	**1958**	0825j	x---	----	x---	x---	----	3	8/-
SW part of caldera (Cone A)						**1960**	1015q	**1961**	0415q	x---	----	x---	----	----	3	-/7
SW part of caldera (Cone A)						**1981**	0324	**1981**	0324	x---	----	x---	----	----	3?	
SW part of caldera (Cone A)						**1983**	0708	**1983**	0708	x---	----	x---	----	----	2	
SW part of caldera (Cone A)						**1986**	1118	**1988**	0226	xx--	----	x---	----	----	2*	
SW part of caldera (Cone A)						**1997**	0211	**1997**	0519d	x---	----	x---	x---	----	3*	7/-
NE caldera floor						**2008**	0712	**2008**	0819	x---	----	x---	----	--x-	4?	
Bogoslof (Fox Is)	**53.93 N**	**168.03 W**	**150**	0004	**YBA**	**Submarine volc**		**1101-30-**	**Historical**							
Old Bogoslof (Castle Rock)						**1796**	05	**1804**	....	----	xx--	x---	x-x-	----	3?	7/8
Old Bogoslof (Castle Rock)						**1806**	....	**1823**	....	----	----	x---	x-x-	----	2*	7/-
New Bogoslof (Grewingk)						**1883**	0927<	**1895**b	....	----	xx--	x---	--x-	----	3*	7/-
Metcalf Peak, McCullough Peak						**1906**	0301p	**1907**	0901	----	xx--	x---	--xx	----	3*	6/8
Metcalf Peak						? *1908*	*0115*q	....	....	----	----	x---	----	----		

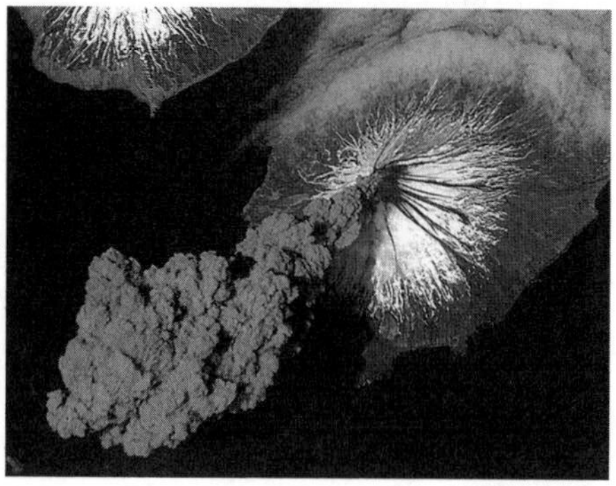

Jeffrey N. Williams (NASA)

2006 eruption

VOLCANO NAME (Subregion) / ERUPTION	Area of Activity	LAT	LONG	ELEV (m)	POPL (5 km, 10, 30, 100)	ROCK TYPE	VOLC TYPE / Start Year	Start M-Dy	NUMBER / Stop Year	STATUS / Stop M-Dy	Central / Flank vent / Radial fiss / Regional	Submarine / New island / Subglacial / Crater lake	Explosive / Pyro flow / Phreatic / Caldera	Lava flow / Lava lake / Dome / Spine	Fatal / Damage / Mudflow / Tsunami	VEI	Vol L/T
Bogoslof (Fox Is) *continued*	Tahoma Peak						**1909**	09	**1910**	0919	----	xx--	x---	--x-	----	2*	
	Tahoma Peak						? *1913*	*07*	....	....	----	----	----	----	----		
	Between New and Old Bogoslof						**1926**	07	**1928**	....	----	xx--	x---	--x-	----	2	6/-
	1926-1927 dome						**1931**	1031	....	....	----	----	x---	x---	----	1	
							? *1951*	*0921*	....	....	----	?---	----	----	----	*0*	
	North tip of island (NE of 1927 dome)						**1992**	0706	**1992**	0724	----	----	x---	--xx	----	3	6/-
Makushin (Fox Is)		**53.891 N**	**166.923 W**	**1800**	0044	**ABYDt**	**Stratovolcano**		**1101-31-**	**Historical**							
							C-**6650**x	....	....	....	x---	----	xx-A	----	----		
							C-**6100**t	....	....	....	x---	----	xx-x	----	----	**5**	-/9
							T-**3650***	....	....	....	----	----	x---	----	----	**P**	
							C-**1750**?	....	....	....	----	----	----	x---	--x-		
							T-**0550***	....	....	....	----	----	x---	----	----		
							T **1150**z	....	....	....	----	----	x---	----	----		
							1768	....	**1769**	....	----	----	x---	----	----	3↑	
							? *1790*	*0607*	....	....	----	----	----	----	----		
							? *1792*	*0214*	....	....	----	----	----	----	----		
							1802	....	....	....	----	----	x---	----	----	3	
							? *1818*	....	....	....	----	----	----	----	----		
							1826	06	....	....	----	----	x---	----	----	3	
							? *1827*	....	?*1838*	....	----	----	----	----	----	*2?*	
							? *1844*a	....	....	....	----	----	----	----	----		
							1865	....	....	....	----	----	----	----	----		
							? *1867*	....	....	....	----	----	----	----	----		
							1883	....	....	....	----	----	x---	----	----	2	
							1907	....	....	....	----	----	----	----	----		
							? *1912*	....	....	....	----	----	----	----	----		
							1926	1230	....	....	----	----	x---	----	----	2	
							1938	10	....	....	----	----	x---	----	----	2	
							1951	1220	....	....	----	----	x-x-	----	----	1	
							? *1952*	....	....	....	----	----	----	----	----		
	SE side of summit						**1980**	0501s	....	....	x---	----	x-x-	----	----	1	
	(strong steam plume: no ash detected)						X *1986*	*0428*	....	....	----	----	----	----	----		
							1987	0302	**1987**	0302	x---	----	x-?-	----	----	1	
							1993	08	**1994**	0119?	x---	----	x-x-	----	----	1	
							1995	0130	**1995**	0130	x---	----	xxx-	----	----	1	
Akutan (Fox Is)		**54.134 N**	**165.986 W**	**1303**	0234	**BAYtd**	**Stratovolcano**		**1101-32-**	**Historical**							
							G-**7620**y	....	....	....	x---	----	xx--	----	--x-		
							C-**4150**?	....	....	....	x---	----	x---	----	--x-		
	(formation of youngest caldera)						C **0340**?	....	....	....	x---	----	xx-x	----	----	**5**	-/9
							C **0550**?	....	....	....	x---	----	x---	----	----		
							G **1420**v	....	....	....	x---	----	x---	----	--x-		
							? *1790*	....	....	....	----	----	----	----	----		
							? *1828*	....	....	....	----	----	----	----	----		
							? *1838*	....	....	....	----	----	----	----	----		
							? *1845*	....	....	....	----	----	----	----	----		
							1848	0305d	....	....	----	----	x---	----	----	2	
	NW flank (Lava Point)						**1852**	....	....	....	-x--	----	x---	x---	----		
							? *1862*	....	....	....	----	----	----	----	----		
							1865	....	....	....	----	----	----	----	----		
							1867	....	....	....	----	----	----	----	----		
							1883	....	....	....	----	----	x---	----	----	2	
							1887	....	....	....	----	----	----	x---	----	0	
							1892	0923	....	....	----	----	x---	----	----	1	
							1896	....	....	....	----	----	----	----	----		
							1907	....	....	....	----	----	----	----	----		
							1908	0222	....	....	----	----	----	x---	----	0	
							1911	....	....	....	x---	----	x---	----	----	2	
							? *1912*	....	....	....	----	----	----	----	----		
							1927	....	**1928**	....	----	----	x---	----	----	2	
							1929	05 ?	....	....	x---	----	x---	x---	--x-	2	
							1931	05	**1931**	08	x---	----	x---	----	----	2	
							1946	12	**1947**	01	x---	----	x---	x---	----	2	
							1948	0429	**1948**	0807>	x---	----	x---	----	----	2	
							1951	10	....	....	----	----	x---	----	----	2	
							1953	....	....	....	----	----	x---	----	----	2	
							1962	1105d	....	....	x---	----	x---	----	----	2	
							? *1972*	*09* ?	....	....	x---	----	?---	----	----	*2?*	
							1973	03 ?	**1973**	05	x---	----	x---	----	----	2	
	West flank ?						**1974**	0211<	....	....	-?--	----	x---	x---	----	2	
							1976	1015q	**1977**	0509>	x---	----	x---	----	----	2	
							1978	0925e	**1978**	10	x---	----	x---	x---	----	2	
							1980	0703<	**1980**	0708?	x---	----	x---	?---	----	2	
							1982	1005d	**1983**	05	x---	----	x---	----	----	2	
							1986	0318	**1986**	0630	x---	----	x---	----	----	2	
							1987	0131	**1987**	0624	x---	----	x---	----	----	2	
							1988	0326	**1988**	0720	x---	----	x---	----	----	2	
							1989	0227	**1989**	0328<	x---	----	x---	----	----	2	
							1990	0126e	**1990**	0126e	x---	----	x---	----	----	2	
							1990	0906	**1990**	1001	x---	----	x---	----	----	2	
							1991	0915	**1991**	1029a	x---	----	x---	----	----	2	
							1992	0308	**1992**	0521	x---	----	x---	----	----	2	
							1992	1218	....	....	x---	----	x---	----	----	1	
Westdahl (Fox Is)		**54.518 N**	**164.65 W**	**1654**	0003	**BYAtd**	**Stratovolcano ?**		**1101-34-**	**Historical**							
	Pogromni or (more likely) Westdahl						**1795**	....	....	....	----	----	x---	----	--x-	4	-/9
	Pogromni or (more likely) Westdahl						**1796**	....	....	....	----	----	----	x---	--x-	0	
	Pogromni or (more likely) Westdahl						**1820**	....	....	....	----	----	x---	----	----	2	
	Pogromni or (more likely) Westdahl						**1827**	....	**1830**	....	----	----	x---	----	----	2	
							1964	0310	**1964**	0416	-x--	----	x---	x---	----	2	
	South of Westdahl Peak (1450 m)						**1978**	0204	**1978**	0209	x---	--x-	x---	----	-xx-	3	
							? *1979*	*0208*	?*1979*	*0209*	----	----	?---	----	----	*3?*	
	ENE flank (1560-760 m)						**1991**	1129	**1992**	0114	--x-	--x-	x---	x---	--x-	3	7/-

VOLCANO NAME (Subregion) / ERUPTION — Area of Activity	LAT	LONG	ELEV (m)	POPL (5 km, 10, 30, 100)	ROCK TYPE	VOLC TYPE	NUMBER	STATUS	Start Year	Start M-Dy	Stop Year	Stop M-Dy	Central / Flank vent / Radial fiss / Regional	Submarine / New island / Subglacial / Crater lake	Explosive / Pyro flow / Phreatic / Caldera	Lava flow / Lava lake / Dome / Spine	Fatal / Damage / Mudflow / Tsunami	VEI	Vol L/T
Fisher (Fox Is)	**54.65 N**	**164.43 W**	**1112**	0002	**ADBT**	**Stratovolcano**	**1101-35-**	**Historical**											
NE and SW parts of Fisher caldera									C-**7420**x	....	....	....	x---	----	xx-x	----	----	**6?**	-/10
Turquoise cone									C-**3170**u	....	....	....	x---	----	x---	----	----	**5**	-/9
Turquoise cone									C **0400**t	....	....	....	x---	----	xxx-	----	---x		
									1795<	....	....	....	----	----	?---	----	----		
Mount Finch									**1826**	1011	**1827**	01 ?	x---	----	x---	----	----	3	
Mount Finch									**1830**	08	....	....	x---	----	x---	----	----	2?	
Shishaldin (Fox Is)	**54.756 N**	**163.97 W**	**2857**	0023	**BAdtr**	**Stratovolcano**	**1101-36-**	**Historical**											
									C-**7550**?	....	....	....	x---	----	x--A	----	----		
									C-**7050**?	....	....	....	----	----	x---	----	----		
									C **0950**?	....	....	....	----	----	----	x---	----		
									? *1775*	....	?*1778*	....	----	----	----	----	----		
									? *1790*	....	....	....	----	----	----	----	----		
									1824	....	....	....	----	----	x---	x---	----	3	
NE flank (1300 m)									**1825**	....	....	....	-x--	----	x---	x---	--x-	2	
									1826	....	....	....	-x--	----	----	x---	----	0	
									1827	....	**1829**	....	----	----	----	----	----	2	
									1830	11	**1830**	12	----	----	x---	x---	----	3	
									1838	....	....	....	----	----	x---	----	----	2	
									1842	....	....	....	----	----	x---	x---	----	2	
									? *1865*	....	....	....	----	----	----	----	----		
									? *1880*	....	?*1881*	....	----	----	----	----	----		
									1883	....	....	....	----	----	x---	----	----	2	
									? *1897*	....	....	....	----	----	----	----	----		
									1898	....	....	....	----	----	x---	x---	----	2	
									? *1899*	....	....	....	----	----	----	----	----		
									1901	....	....	....	----	----	----	----	----		
									? *1912*	....	....	....	----	----	----	----	----		
									1922	1015q	....	....	----	----	x---	x---	--x-	2	
									1925	....	....	....	----	----	----	----	----		
									1927	....	....	....	----	----	----	----	----		
									1928	08	....	....	----	----	x---	----	----	2	
Summit and north flank									**1929**	0528	**1929**	0623>	xx--	----	x---	x---	----	2	
									1932	0201	**1932**	0521	x---	----	x---	x---	--x-	2	
									1946	08	**1947**	01	----	----	x---	----	----	2	
									1948	....	....	....	----	----	x---	----	----	2	
									1951	04	**1951**	1005d	x---	----	x---	----	----	2	
									1953	1004c	....	....	----	----	x---	----	----	2	
									1955	07	....	....	----	----	x---	----	----	2	
									1963	1228	....	....	----	----	x---	----	----	2	
									1967	0128	....	....	----	----	x-x-	----	----	2	
									1975	0913	**1975**	1026e	x---	----	x---	?---	--?-	2	
									1976	01	**1976**	0928	x---	----	x---	x---	--?-	2*	
									1978	0208	**1978**	0209?	x---	----	x---	----	----	2	
									1979	02	....	....	x---	----	x---	----	----	2	
									? *1981*	*0925*	....	....	----	----	?---	----	----		
									1986	0319	**1987**	0215?	x---	----	x-x-	----	----	2	
									1993	0904	**1993**	1029	x---	----	x---	----	----	2*	
									1995	1223	**1996**	0516<	x---	----	x---	----	----	3	
									1997	0602	**1997**	0602	x---	----	x---	----	----	1	
									1998	1104	**1998**	1104	x---	----	x-x-	----	----	1	
									1999	0313	**1999**	0527	x---	----	x---	----	--x-	3*	-/7
									? *1999*	*0925*e	?*2000*	*0204*?	x---	----	--?-	----	----		
									? *2000*	*0811*	....	....	x---	----	--?-	----	----		
									2004	0217	**2004**	07 >	x---	----	x---	----	----	2*	
									? *2008*	*0212*	?*2008*	*0212*	x---	----	?---	----	----	*1?*	
Isanotski (Fox Is)	**54.765 N**	**163.723 W**	**2446**	0023	**U**	**Stratovolcano**	**1101-37-**	Uncertain											
									? *1795*	....	....	....	----	----	x---	----	----	*3↑*	
									? *1825*	*0310*	....	....	----	----	x---	----	--x-	*4*	-/8
									? *1830*	*11*	....	....	----	----	?---	----	----	*2?*	
									? *1831*	*03*	?*1831*	*0506*a	----	----	----	x---	----		
									? *1845*	....	....	....	----	----	----	----	----		
Roundtop (Fox Is)	**54.80 N**	**163.589 W**	**1871**	0024	**R**	**Stratovolcano**	**1101-38-**	**Radiocarbon**											
									T-**7600**z	....	....	....	x---	----	xx-x	----	----	**5?**	
Amak (Fox Is)	**55.424 N**	**163.149 W**	**488**	0004	**A**	**Stratovolcano**	**1101-39-**	**Historical**											
									T-**2550**z	....	....	....	----	----	----	x---	----		
									1700	....	**1710**	....	x---	----	----	x---	----		
									1796	....	....	....	x---	----	----	x---	----		

David Johnson (USGS)

Shishaldin with flank cinder cones and Isanotski (left)

ALASKA - PENINSULA & SW

VOLCANO NAME (Subregion) / ERUPTION — Area of Activity	LAT	LONG	ELEV (m)	POPL	ROCK TYPE	VOLC TYPE	NUMBER	STATUS	Start Year	Start M-Dy	Stop Year	Stop M-Dy	Central / Flank vent / Radial fiss / Regional	Submarine / New island / Subglacial / Crater lake	Explosive / Pyro flow / Phreatic / Caldera	Lava flow / Lava lake / Dome / Spine	Fatal / Damage / Mudflow / Tsunami	VEI	Vol L/T
Frosty (Alaska Peninsula)	**55.082 N**	**162.814 W**	**2012**	0024	**AB**	**Stratovolcanoes**	**1102-01-**	**Holocene**											
Dutton (Alaska Peninsula)	**55.168 N**	**162.272 W**	**1506**	0334	**AD**	**Stratovolcano**	**1102-011**	**Holocene**											
Emmons Lake (Alaska Peninsula)	**55.341 N**	**162.079 W**	**1436**	0034	**ABR**	**Caldera**	**1102-02-**	**Holocene**											
Pavlof (Alaska Peninsula)	**55.42 N**	**161.887 W**	**2519**	0004	**AB**	**Stratovolcano**	**1102-03-**	**Historical**											
									@ **1762**	....	@**1786**	....	xx--	----	x---	----	----	4?	-/8
									1790	....	....	....	----	----	x---	----	----	2	
									1817	....	....	....	----	----	x---	----	----	2	
									1825	....	....	....	----	----	?---	----	----	2?	
									1838	....	....	....	----	----	x---	----	----	1	
(eruption in August 1845, not 1844)									**1845**	0812	....	....	----	----	x---	----	----	2	
									1846	08	**1846**	08	x?--	----	x---	x---	----	2	
Upper north flank									? *1852*	....	....	....	x---	----	----	----	----	*1?*	
									1866	0314	....	....	----	----	x---	----	----	2	
									1880	....	....	....	x---	----	----	----	----	1?	
									1886	....	....	....	x---	----	----	----	----	2?	
									1892	....	....	....	x---	----	x---	----	----	2?	
									1894	....	....	....	x---	----	x---	----	----	2?	
									1901	....	....	....	----	----	x---	----	----	2?	
Summit and north flank fissure									**1906**	....	**1911**	1207?	x-x-	----	x?--	x---	----	3*	
									1914	0706	....	....	----	----	x---	----	----	2	
									1917	10	....	....	----	----	x---	----	----	2	

VOLCANO NAME (Subregion) / **ERUPTION** — Area of Activity	**LAT**	**LONG**	**ELEV** (m)	**POPL** 5 km / 10 / 30 / 100	**ROCK TYPE**	**VOLC TYPE** / —Start— Year	M-Dy	**NUMBER** / —Stop— Year	M-Dy	**STATUS**	ERUPTIVE CHARACTERISTICS: Central / Flank vent / Radial fiss / Regional	Submarine / New island / Subglacial / Crater lake	Explosive / Pyro flow / Phreatic / Caldera	Lava flow / Lava lake / Dome / Spine	Fatal / Damage / Mudflow / Tsunami	**VEI**	**Vol L/T**
Pavlof (Alaska Peninsula) *continued*						**1922**	1224	**1923**	0228r		x---	----	x---	----	----	2	
						1924	0117	....	....		x---	----	x---	----	----	2	
						1929	03	**1931**	08		x---	----	x---	----	----	2*	
						1936	....	**1948**	05 ?		x---	----	x---	x---	----	3*	
Upper NE or NNE flank						**1950**	0731	**1951**	05		x---	----	x---	----	----	2	
Upper NE or NNE flank						**1951**	10	**1952**	02 ?		x---	----	x---	----	----	2	
Upper NE or NNE flank						**1953**	1125	**1954**	08		x---	----	----	----	----	1?	
Upper NNE flank						**1958**	0517	**1958**	0828		x---	----	x---	x---	----	2	
Upper NE or NNE flank						**1960**?	....	**1963**	06 ?		x---	----	x---	----	----	2	
Upper NE or NNE flank						**1966**	0315	....	....		x---	----	x---	x---	----	2	
Upper NE flank						**1973**	1112	**1973**	1113		x---	----	-?--	?---	----	2	-/6
						1974	0312	**1974**	0324?		x---	----	x---	----	----	1	
						1974	0901<	**1975**	0113		x---	----	x---	----	--?-	3*	
						1975	0913	**1977**	03 >		x---	----	xx--	?---	--?-	2*	-/7
						1980	0706a	....	....		x---	----	x---	----	----	1	
Upper NNE flank						**1980**	1108	**1980**	1113		x---	----	x---	x---	----	3*	-/6
						1981	0330<	**1981**	0528		x---	----	x---	----	----	1	
Upper NNE flank (100 m below summit)						**1981**	0925	**1981**	0927		x---	----	x---	x---	----	3	6/7
						? 1982	*0715q*	....	....		x---	----	--?-	----	----	*1?*	
						1983	0711	**1983**	0718		x---	----	x---	----	----	2?	
Upper NNE flank						**1983**	1111	**1983**	1218		x---	----	x---	x---	----	3*	-/7
NNE & SE summit vents, NE & SE flanks						**1986**	0416	**1988**	0813		xx--	----	xx--	x---	--x-	3*	6/-
						1990	0305	**1990**	0305		x---	----	?-?-	----	----	2?	
						1996	0911	**1997**	0103?		x---	----	x---	x---	--x-	2*	
						? 2001	*0605d*	....	....		x---	----	?---	----	----	*1?*	
						2007	0815	**2007**	0913		x---	----	x---	x---	--x-	2	
Pavlof Sister (Alaska Peninsula)	**55.453 N**	**161.843 W**	**2142**	0004	**B**	**Stratovolcano**		**1102-04-**		**Holocene**							
Dana (Alaska Peninsula)	**55.641 N**	**161.214 W**	**1354**	0004	**AD**	**Stratovolcano**		**1102-05-**		**Radiocarbon**							
						C-**1890**?	....	....	....		----	----	xx--	----	----	**5**	-/9
Stepovak Bay 2 (Alaska Peninsula)	**55.913 N**	**160.041 W**	**1323**	0004	**A**	**Cinder cone**		**1102-051**		**Holocene**							
Stepovak Bay 3 (Alaska Peninsula)	**55.929 N**	**160.002 W**	**1555**	0004	**AB**	**Cinder cone**		**1102-052**		Holocene?							
Stepovak Bay 4 (Alaska Peninsula)	**55.954 N**	**159.954 W**	**1557**	0024	**U**	**Stratovolcano**		**1102-053**		**Pleistocene**							
Kupreanof (Alaska Peninsula)	**56.011 N**	**159.797 W**	**1895**	0023	**AB**	**Stratovolcano**		**1102-06-**		**Historical**							
SSW flank (1575 m)						**1987**	0310	**1987**	0310		-x--	----	x-x-	----	----	1	
Veniaminof (Alaska Peninsula)	**56.17 N**	**159.38 W**	**2507**	0003	**ABD**	**Stratovolcano**		**1102-07-**		**Historical**							
						C-**1750**?	....	....	....		x---	----	xx-x	----	----	**6**	-/10
						? 1830	....	*?1838*	....		----	----	----	----	----	*2*	
Western intracaldera cone						**1838**	0804	**1839**	04		x---	----	x---	----	----	3	
Western intracaldera cone						*? 1852*	....	....	....		x---	----	----	----	----	*2?*	
Western intracaldera cone						**1874**	0715q	....	....		x---	----	x---	----	----	2?	
Western intracaldera cone						**1892**	0828	**1892**	0830		x---	----	x---	----	----	3	
Western intracaldera cone						**1930**	06	....	....		x---	----	x---	----	----	2	
Western intracaldera cone						**1939**	0523	**1939**	0626?		x---	----	x---	----	----	3	
Western intracaldera cone						**1939**	11	....	....		x---	----	x---	----	----	2	
Western intracaldera cone						**1944**	0328	....	....		x---	----	x---	----	----	2	
Western intracaldera cone						**1956**	03	**1956**	0523		x---	----	x---	----	----	3*	
Western intracaldera cone						**1983**	0602	**1984**	0417		x---	----	x---	x---	----	3	7/-
Western intracaldera cone						**1984**	1129	**1984**	1206?		x---	----	x---	----	----	2	
Western intracaldera cone						**1987**	0319	**1987**	0319		x---	----	x-x-	----	----	1	
Western cone and Half Cone						**1993**	0730	**1994**	0928?		xx--	--x-	x---	x---	----	2	7/-
Western intracaldera cone						**1995**	0417	**1995**	0417		x---	----	x---	----	----	1	
Western intracaldera cone						**1995**	1115	**1995**	1130?		x---	----	x---	----	----	1	
Western intracaldera cone						**2002**	0924	**2003**	0323		x---	----	x---	----	----	1	
Western intracaldera cone						**2004**	0216	**2004**	0905d		x---	----	x---	----	----	2*	
Western intracaldera cone						**2005**	0104	**2005**	0214c		x---	----	x---	----	----	2*	
Western intracaldera cone						**2005**	0907	**2005**	1104?		x---	----	x---	----	----	1	
Western intracaldera cone						**2006**	0303	**2006**	0907		x---	----	x---	----	----	1	
Western intracaldera cone						**2008**	0222	**2008**	0227?		x---	----	x---	----	----	1	
Black Peak (Alaska Peninsula)	**56.552 N**	**158.785 W**	**1032**	0003	**AD**	**Stratovolcano**		**1102-08-**		**Radiocarbon**							
						T-**1900**w	....	....	....		x---	----	xx-x	----	----	**6**	-/10
Aniakchak (Alaska Peninsula)	**56.88 N**	**158.17 W**	**1341**	0023	**ADbty**	**Caldera**		**1102-09-**		**Historical**							
						T-**5250***	....	....	....		x---	----	xx-?	----	----	**6?**	-/10
						T-**2550**z	....	....	....		x---	----	x---	----	----		
						I-**1645**j	....	....	....		x---	----	xx-x	----	---x	**6?**	-/10
						C-**0350**?	....	....	....		x---	----	x---	----	----		
Northern & western caldera floor						T **0200**	....	....	....		x---	---x	x---	--x-	----		
						C **0460**?	....	....	....		x---	---x	x---	x---	----		
S & NW caldera floor (Vent Mtn & Half Cone)						T **0700**y	....	....	....		x---	----	----	x---	----	0	
Vent Mtn and other vents?						T **1050**?	....	....	....		x---	----	x---	----	--x-		
NW caldera floor (Half Cone)						T **1220**w	....	....	....		x---	----	x---	x---	----		
NW caldera floor (Half Cone?)						C **1390**	....	....	....		x---	----	x---	----	----		
SE caldera floor (New Cone)						C **1550**?	....	....	....		x---	----	x---	----	----		
NW & S caldera floor (Half Cone, Vent Mtn)						C **1560**t	....	....	....		x---	----	xx--	x---	----	4+	-/8
West and SW caldera floor						**1931**	0501	**1931**	0613>		x-x-	----	xx--	x-x-	-x--	4*	-/8
						? 1942	....	....	....		----	----	----	----	----		
(resuspended ash)						*X 1951*	*0625*	*X1951*	*0625*		----	----	----	----	----		
Yantarni (Alaska Peninsula)	**57.019 N**	**157.185 W**	**1345**	0003	**AD**	**Stratovolcano**		**1102-10-**		**Tephrochronology**							
						T-**0800**z	....	....	....		x---	----	x?-A	--x-	----	**5**	8/9
Chiginagak (Alaska Peninsula)	**57.135 N**	**156.990 W**	**2221**	0002	**ADb**	**Stratovolcano**		**1102-11-**		**Historical**							
(likely fumarolic activity)						*X 1852*	....	....	....		----	----	----	----	----		
						? 1929	*12*	....	....		----	----	----	----	----		
						1971	07	**1971**	07		----	----	x---	----	----	2?	
						1998	0813	**1998**	0813?		x---	----	x---	----	----	1	
Kialagvik (Alaska Peninsula)	**57.203 N**	**156.745 W**	**1677**	0002	**AD**	**Stratovolcano**		**1102-12-**		**Holocene**							
Ugashik-Peulik (Alaska Peninsula)	**57.751 N**	**156.368 W**	**1474**	0003	**ABDR**	**Stratovolcano**		**1102-13-**		**Historical**							
Peulik						C-**6550**?	....	....	....		----	----	x---	----	----		
Peulik						C-**5850**?	....	....	....		----	----	x---	----	----		
Peulik						C **1050**v	....	....	....		----	----	x---	----	----		
Peulik						**1814**	....	....	....		x---	----	x---	----	----	3	
Peulik						*? 1852*	....	....	....		x---	----	----	----	----		

VOLCANO NAME (Subregion) / ERUPTION — Area of Activity	LAT	LONG	ELEV (m)	POPL (5 km, 10, 30, 100)	ROCK TYPE	VOLC TYPE / —Start— Year	NUMBER / M-Dy	STATUS / —Stop— Year	M-Dy	Central vent, Flank vent, Radial fiss, Regional	Submarine, New island, Subglacial, Crater lake	Explosive, Pyro flow, Phreatic, Caldera	Lava flow, Lava lake, Dome, Spine	Fatal, Damage, Mudflow, Tsunami	VEI	Vol L/T
Ukinrek Maars (Alaska Peninsula)	**57.832 N**	**156.510 W**	**91**	0003	**BD**	**Maars**	**1102-131**	**Historical**								
Gas Rocks						C-**0350**?	....	....	....	x---	---?	x-x-	----	----		
West and East Ukinrek Maars						**1977**	0330	**1977**	0409	---x	----	xxx-	-xx-	----	3	5/7
Unnamed (Alaska Peninsula)	**57.87 N**	**155.42 W**	**300**	0002	**U**	**Lava dome**	**1102-132**	**Holocene**								
Martin (Alaska Peninsula)	**58.172 N**	**155.361 W**	**1863**	0003	**DA**	**Stratovolcano**	**1102-14-**	**Historical**								
						C-**1750**?	....	....	....	x---	----	x---	x---	----		
						C-**0800**t	....	....	....	x---	----	x---	----	----		
(Kukak Bay ashfall probably from Martin)						@ **1951**	0722	....	....	----	----	x---	----	----		
(SW of Trident; probably Martin)						@ **1953**	0217	....	....	----	----	x---	----	----		
Mageik (Alaska Peninsula)	**58.195 N**	**155.253 W**	**2165**	0003	**AD**	**Stratovolcano**	**1102-15-**	**Radiocarbon**								
East Mageik						G-**8670**y	....	....	....	x---	----	x---	----	----		
East Mageik						G-**7380**w	....	....	....	x---	----	x---	----	----		
East Mageik						C-**4400**y	....	....	....	x---	----	x---	----	----		
East Mageik (ODLF tephra)						C-**1950**v	....	....	....	x---	----	x---	x---	----		
East Mageik						C-**1650**?	....	....	....	x---	----	x---	x---	----		
East Mageik						C-**0650**?	....	....	....	x---	----	x---	----	----		
East Mageik						C-**0550**?	....	....	....	x---	----	x---	----	----		
Between East and Central Mageik						C-**0500**t	....	....	....	x---	----	x-x-	----	----		
						? 1927	*0826*e	....	....	----	----	?---	----	----	*2*	
						? 1929	*0819*	*?1929*	*12*	----	----	?---	----	----	*2*	
						? 1936	*0704*	*?1936*	*0705*	----	----	?---	----	----	*2?*	
						? 1946	....	....	....	----	----	?---	----	----	*2?*	
Trident (Alaska Peninsula)	**58.236 N**	**155.10 W**	**1864**	0003	**AD**	**Stratovolcano**	**1102-16-**	**Historical**								
						1913	09	....	....	----	----	----	----	----	1	
						1949	06	....	....	----	----	----	----	----		
(ash eruption, attrib. to Trident)						@ **1950**	0702	**@1950**	0818	----	----	x---	----	----	2?	
SW flank (1100 m)						**1953**	0215	**1954**	1005?	-x--	----	x---	x-x-	----	3	8/7
(ash eruption, attrib. to Trident)						@ **1956**	0908	**@1956**	0909	----	----	x---	----	----	2	
SW flank						**1957**	....	**1960**	0810?	-x--	----	x---	x---	----	2	
SW flank (1100 m)						**1961**	0630?	....	....	-x--	----	x---	----	----	2	
SW flank						**1962**	0609	**1962**	0609	-x--	----	x---	----	----	3	
SW flank						**1963**	0401	**1963**	0403	-x--	----	x---	----	--x-	3	
SW flank						**1963**	1017	**1963**	1117?	-x--	----	x---	----	----	3	
SW flank						**1964**	0531	....	....	-x--	----	x---	----	----	3?	
SW flank						**1966**?	....	....	....	-x--	----	----	--x-	----		
SW flank						**1967**	0905	**1968**	0225	-x--	----	x---	--x-	----	3*	
SW flank						**1968**	1113	**1968**	1113	-x--	----	x---	--x-	----	3	
SW flank						**1974**	0715q	....	....	-x--	----	x---	--x-	----	3	
Katmai (Alaska Peninsula)	**58.280 N**	**154.963 W**	**2047**	0003	**ADbr**	**Stratovolcano**	**1102-17-**	**Historical**								
						1912	0606	**1912**	0721>	x---	----	x-xx	?---	----	3	-/7
(eruption report not valid: Hildreth)						*X 1914*	*07*	....	....	----	----	----	----	----		
(eruption report not valid: Hildreth)						*X 1920*	*0309*	....	....	----	----	----	----	----		
(eruption report not valid: Hildreth)						*X 1921*	*1127*	....	....	----	----	----	----	----		
(eruption report not valid: Hildreth)						*X 1929*	*12*	....	....	----	----	----	----	----		
(eruption report not valid: Hildreth)						*X 1931*	*0508*	*X1931*	*07*	----	----	----	----	----		
Novarupta (Alaska Peninsula)	**58.27 N**	**155.157 W**	**841**	0003	**RDa**	**Caldera**	**1102-18-**	**Historical**								
						1912	0606	**1912**	10 ?	x---	----	xxxx	----	xxx-	**6**	7/10
(eruption report not valid: Hildreth)						*X 1949*	*0519*	....	....	----	----	----	----	----		
(eruption report not valid: Hildreth)						*X 1950*	*0705*d	....	....	----	----	----	----	----		
Griggs (Alaska Peninsula)	**58.354 N**	**155.092 W**	**2317**	0003	**Ad**	**Stratovolcano**	**1102-19-**	**Radiocarbon**								
						G-**1790**s	....	....	....	x---	----	x---	----	----		
Snowy Mountain (Alaska Peninsula)	**58.336 N**	**154.682 W**	**2162**	0003	**AD**	**Stratovolcanoes**	**1102-20-**	**Radiocarbon**								
NE Snowy Mountain						G **1710**x	....	....	....	x---	----	x---	--x-	----		
Denison (Alaska Peninsula)	**58.418 N**	**154.449 W**	**2287**	0003	**AD**	**Stratovolcano**	**1102-21-**	Holocene?								
Steller (Alaska Peninsula)	**58.43 N**	**154.40 W**	**2272**	0003	**AD**	**Stratovolcano**	**1102-22-**	**Holocene**								
Kukak (Alaska Peninsula)	**58.453 N**	**154.355 W**	**2043**	0003	**AD**	**Stratovolcano**	**1102-23-**	**Fumarolic**								
Kaguyak (Alaska Peninsula)	**58.608 N**	**154.028 W**	**901**	0002	**DArb**	**Lava domes**	**1102-25-**	**Holocene**								
						C-**4060**w	....	....	....	x---	----	xx--	--x-	----		
Kaguyak caldera						C-**3850**?	....	....	....	x---	----	xx-x	----	----	**5**	-/9
Fourpeaked (Alaska Peninsula)	**58.770 N**	**153.672 W**	**2105**	0003	**A**	**Stratovolcano**	**1102-26-**	**Historical**								
Fissure trending N from summit						**2006**	0917	**2006**	0917	--x-	----	x-x-	----	----	2	
Douglas (Alaska Peninsula)	**58.855 N**	**153.542 W**	**2140**	0003	**A**	**Stratovolcano**	**1102-27-**	**Holocene**								
Augustine (Alaska-SW)	**59.363 N**	**153.43 W**	**1252**	0003	**ADrby**	**Lava domes**	**1103-01-**	**Historical**								
(tephra layer I)						C **0230**x	....	....	....	x---	----	x---	----	----		
(tephra layer H)						C **0510**x	....	....	....	x---	----	x---	----	----		
(tephra layer C)						C **0890**w	....	....	....	x---	----	x---	----	----		
(tephra layer M)						C **1200**u	....	....	....	x---	----	x---	----	----		
						G **1540**v	....	....	....	x---	----	xx-A	--?-	---x	4?	
						T **1650**v	....	....	....	x---	----	??-A	----	----		
						1812	....	....	....	x---	----	xx--	--x-	----	3?	
						1883	1006	**1884**?	....	x---	----	xx-A	?-x-	-xxx	4	8/8
(no 1902 eruption: Johnston 1979)						*X 1902*	....	....	....	----	----	----	----	----		
						? 1908	....	....	....	----	----	----	----	----		
						1935	0313	**1935**	0818	x---	----	xx--	--x-	--x-	3*	
						1963	1011	**1964**	0819	x---	----	xx--	--x-	--x-	2*	7/6
						1971	1007	**1971**	1008	x---	----	x---	----	----	1	
						1976	0122?	**1977**	0514?	x---	----	xx--	--x-	-xx-	4*	7/8
						1986	0327	**1986**	0831	x---	----	xx--	x-xx	-xx-	4?	-/8
						2005	1209?	**2006**	0427?	x---	----	xxx-	x-x-	--x-	3*	
Iliamna (Alaska-SW)	**60.032 N**	**153.090 W**	**3053**	0014	**Ab**	**Stratovolcano**	**1103-02-**	**Historical**								
						C-**5050**?	....	....	....	----	----	x---	----	----	**P**	
Upper NE flank						C-**2050**?	....	....	....	-x--	----	xx--	--x-	--x-	**P**	
						C-**0450**?	....	....	....	----	----	x---	----	--x-		
						C **1650**?	....	....	....	----	----	xx--	----	--x-		
						? 1768	....	....	....	----	----	----	----	----		
						1778	....	**1779**	....	----	----	x---	----	----		
						? 1786	....	....	....	----	----	----	----	----		
						? 1793	....	....	....	----	----	----	----	----		
						? 1843	....	....	....	----	----	x---	----	----		
						1867	....	....	....	----	----	x---	----	----	2	
						1876	....	....	....	----	----	x---	----	----	3	

VOLCANO NAME (Subregion) / ERUPTION	Area of Activity	LAT	LONG	ELEV (m)	POPL (5 km, 10, 30, 100)	ROCK TYPE	VOLC TYPE / Start Year	Start M-Dy	NUMBER / Stop Year	Stop M-Dy	STATUS	Central, Flank vent, Radial fiss, Regional	Submarine, New island, Subglacial, Crater lake	Explosive, Pyro flow, Phreatic, Caldera	Lava flow, Lava lake, Dome, Spine	Fatal, Damage, Mudflow, Tsunami	VEI	Vol L/T
Iliamna (Alaska-SW) *continued*							*? 1933*	*0505*	....	....		----	----	----	----	----		
							? 1947	*06*	....	....		----	----	----	----	----		
							? 1952	....	....	....		----	----	----	----	----		
							? 1953	*0301*	....	....		----	----	?---	----	----	*2?*	
	(steam plume, not eruption: Johnston)						*X 1978*	*1107*	*X1978*	*1107*		x---	----	----	----	----		
	(steam plumes, not an eruption)						*X 1987*	*0319*	*X1987*	*0502*		x---	----	----	----	----		
Redoubt (Alaska-SW)		**60.485 N**	**152.742 W**	**3108**	0015	**ABdyr**	**Stratovolcano**		**1103-03-**		**Historical**							
							C **-5780**w	....	....	....		----	----	**x**---	----	----		
							T **-4550**y	....	....	....		----	----	**x**---	----	----		
							C **-2890**u	....	....	....		----	----	**x**---	----	----		
							C **-1550**w	....	....	....		**x**---	----	**x**--A	----	--**xx**		
							T **-1080**w	....	....	....		----	----	**x**?--	----	--**x**-		
							T **-0210**x	....	....	....		----	----	**x**?--	----	--**x**-		
							C **0110**t	....	....	....		----	----	**x**?--	----	--**x**-		
							T **1550**t	....	....	....		----	----	**x**---	----	----		
							T **1600**t	....	....	....		----	----	**x**---	----	----		
	(steaming, no ash emission)						*X 1778*	....	....	....		----	----	----	----	----		
							? 1819	....	....	....		----	----	?---	----	----		
							1902	0118	....	....		**x**---	----	**x**---	----	----	3	
							? 1933	*0525*	....	....		----	----	?---	----	----		
	(water vapor emission)						*X 1965*	*0129*	*X1965*	*02*		**x**---	----	----	----	----		
	North end of summit crater (2300 m)						**1966**	0124	**1966**	0220		**x**---	----	**x**-**x**-	----	--J-	3*	
	North end of summit crater (2300 m)						**1966**	1007	**1967**	0115		**x**---	----	**x**---	----	----	3*	
	North end of summit crater (2300 m)						**1967**	1206	**1968**	0428>		**x**---	----	**x**---	--**x**-	----	3*	
	North end of summit crater (2470 m)						**1989**	1214	**1990**	0620?		**x**---	----	**xxx**-	--**x**-	-**xx**-	3*	7/8
	South of 1990 dome						**2009**	0315	**2009**	0701p		**x**---	----	**xxx**-	--**x**-	--**x**-	3*	7/7
Spurr (Alaska-SW)		**61.299 N**	**152.251 W**	**3374**	0005	**Adbr**	**Stratovolcano**		**1103-04-**		**Historical**							
	Mt. Spurr central dome/cone complex						C **-6050**?	....	....	....		**x**---	----	**x**---	----	----		
	Mt. Spurr central dome/cone complex						C **-5110**v	....	....	....		**x**---	----	**x**---	----	----		
	South flank (Crater Peak)						T **-4050**?	....	....	....		-**x**--	----	**x**---	----	----		
	Mt. Spurr central lava/cone complex						C **-3250**?	....	....	....		**x**---	----	**x**---	----	----		
	South flank (Crater Peak)						T **1650**t	....	....	....		-**x**--	----	**x**---	----	----		
	South flank (Crater Peak)						**1953**	0709	**1953**	0716		-**x**--	----	**x**-**x**-	----	--**x**-	4	
	(fumarolic activity only)						*X 1954*	....	....	....		----	----	----	----	----		
	South flank (Crater Peak)						**1992**	0627	**1992**	0917		-**x**--	---**x**	**xx**--	----	**xxx**-	4*	-/8
Hayes (Alaska-SW)		**61.640 N**	**152.411 W**	**3034**	0003	**D**	**Stratovolcano**		**1103-05-**		**Radiocarbon**							
							T **-1850**?	....	....	....		----	----	**x**---	----	----		
							T **-1550**?	....	....	....		----	----	**x**---	----	----	**5**	
							T **1200**y	....	....	....		----	----	**x**---	----	----		

ALASKA - W, E, & SE

VOLCANO NAME (Subregion) / ERUPTION	Area of Activity	LAT	LONG	ELEV (m)	POPL (5 km, 10, 30, 100)	ROCK TYPE	VOLC TYPE / Start Year	Start M-Dy	NUMBER / Stop Year	Stop M-Dy	STATUS	Central, Flank vent, Radial fiss, Regional	Submarine, New island, Subglacial, Crater lake	Explosive, Pyro flow, Phreatic, Caldera	Lava flow, Lava lake, Dome, Spine	Fatal, Damage, Mudflow, Tsunami	VEI	Vol L/T
St. Paul Island (Alaska-W)		**57.18 N***	**170.30 W**	**203**	3333	**XBr**	**Shield volcano**		**1104-01-**		**Radiocarbon**							
	West side (Fox Hill)						C **-1280**s	....	....	....		**x**---	----	**x**---	**x**---	----		7/-
	Several km SW of St. Paul						*? 1943*	....	....	....		-**x**--	?---	----	----	----		
Nunivak Island (Alaska-W)		**60.02 N***	**166.33 W**	**511**	0004	**BX**	**Shield volcano**		**1104-02-**		**Holocene**							
Ingakslugwat Hills (Alaska-W)		**61.43 N***	**164.47 W**	**190**	0004	**BXF**	**Cinder cones**		**1104-03-**		**Holocene**							
St. Michael (Alaska-W)		**63.45 N***	**162.12 W**	**715**	3334	**BX**	**Shield volcanoes**		**1104-04-**		**Anthropology**							
Kookooligit Mountains (Alaska-W)		**63.60 N***	**170.43 W**	**673**	0034	**BXf**	**Shield volcano**		**1104-05-**		**Holocene**							
Imuruk Lake (Alaska-W)		**65.60 N***	**163.92 W**	**610**	0000	**B**	**Shield volcanoes**		**1104-06-**		**Radiocarbon**							
	Lost Jim Cone						C **0300**?	....	....	....		**x**---	----	**x**---	**x**---	----		
Buzzard Creek (Alaska-E)		**64.07 N**	**148.42 W**	**830**	0025	**B**	**Tuff rings**		**1105-001**		**Radiocarbon**							
							C **-1050**?	....	....	....		**x**---	----	**x**---	----	----	2	-/6
Sanford (Alaska-E)		**62.22 N**	**144.13 W**	**4949**	0004	**Abdr**	**Shield volcano**		**1105-01-**		Holocene?							
Wrangell (Alaska-E)		**62.00 N**	**144.02 W**	**4317**	0004	**AD**	**Shield volcano**		**1105-02-**		**Historical**							
							C **0190**x	....	....	....		**x**---	----	**xx**-?	----	----	**C?**	
	(eruption possibly from Great Sitkin)						*? 1784*	*07*	....	....		**x**---	----	?---	----	----	*2?*	
							? 1819	....	....	....		**x**---	----	----	----	----	*2?*	
							? 1884	*1026*	*?1885*	*0204*		**x**---	----	--?-	----	----	*2?*	
							1899	0903	....	....		**x**---	----	**x**-**x**-	----	----	2?	
							1900	06 <	....	....		**x**---	----	**x**---	----	----	2?	
	West Crater						**1902**	0715q	....	....		**x**---	----	**x**-**x**-	----	----	2	
							? 1907	*0401<*	....	....		**x**---	----	?---	----	----		
							1911	0414	*?1912*	*0914?*		**x**---	----	**x**---	----	--?-	1	
	North flank?						*? 1921*	*0703*	*?1921*	*0703*		-?--	----	?---	----	----		
							? 1930	*0630*	....	....		**x**---	----	?---	----	----		
	West Crater						**1969**	08	....	....		**x**---	----	**x**-**x**-	----	----	1	
							1999	0514	**1999**	0514		**x**---	----	**x**-**x**-	----	----	1	
							2002	0801	**2002**	0802		**x**---	----	**x**-**x**-	----	----	1	
Gordon (Alaska-E)		**62.13 N**	**143.08 W**	**2755**	0003	**B**	**Cinder cones**		**1105-021**		Holocene?							
Churchill (Alaska-E)		**61.38 N**	**141.75 W**	**5005**	0002	**D**	**Stratovolcano**		**1105-03-**		**Radiocarbon**							
							C **0060**x	....	....	....		**x**---	----	**x**---	----	----	**6**	-/10
							G **0800**v	....	....	....		**x**---	----	**x**---	----	----	**6**	-/10
Edgecumbe (Alaska-SE)		**57.05 N**	**135.75 W**	**970**	0044	**ABRD**	**Stratovolcanoes**		**1105-04-**		**Radiocarbon**							
							C **-7220**w	....	....	....		----	----	**x**---	----	--**x**-		
							C **-3810**u	....	....	....		----	----	**x**---	----	----		
							C **-2220**v	....	....	....		----	----	**x**---	----	----		
Duncan Canal (Alaska-SE)		**56.50 N***	**133.10 W**	**15**	0024	**B**	**Volcanic field**		**1105-05-**		**Holocene**							
Tlevak Strait-Suemez Is. (Alaska)		**55.25 N***	**133.30 W**	**50**	0044	**B**	**Volcanic field**		**1105-06-**		**Holocene**							
Behm Canal-Rudyerd Bay (Alaska)		**55.32 N***	**131.05 W**	**500**	0015	**BAY**	**Cinder cones**		**1105-07-**		Holocene?							

Canada & Western USA (12)

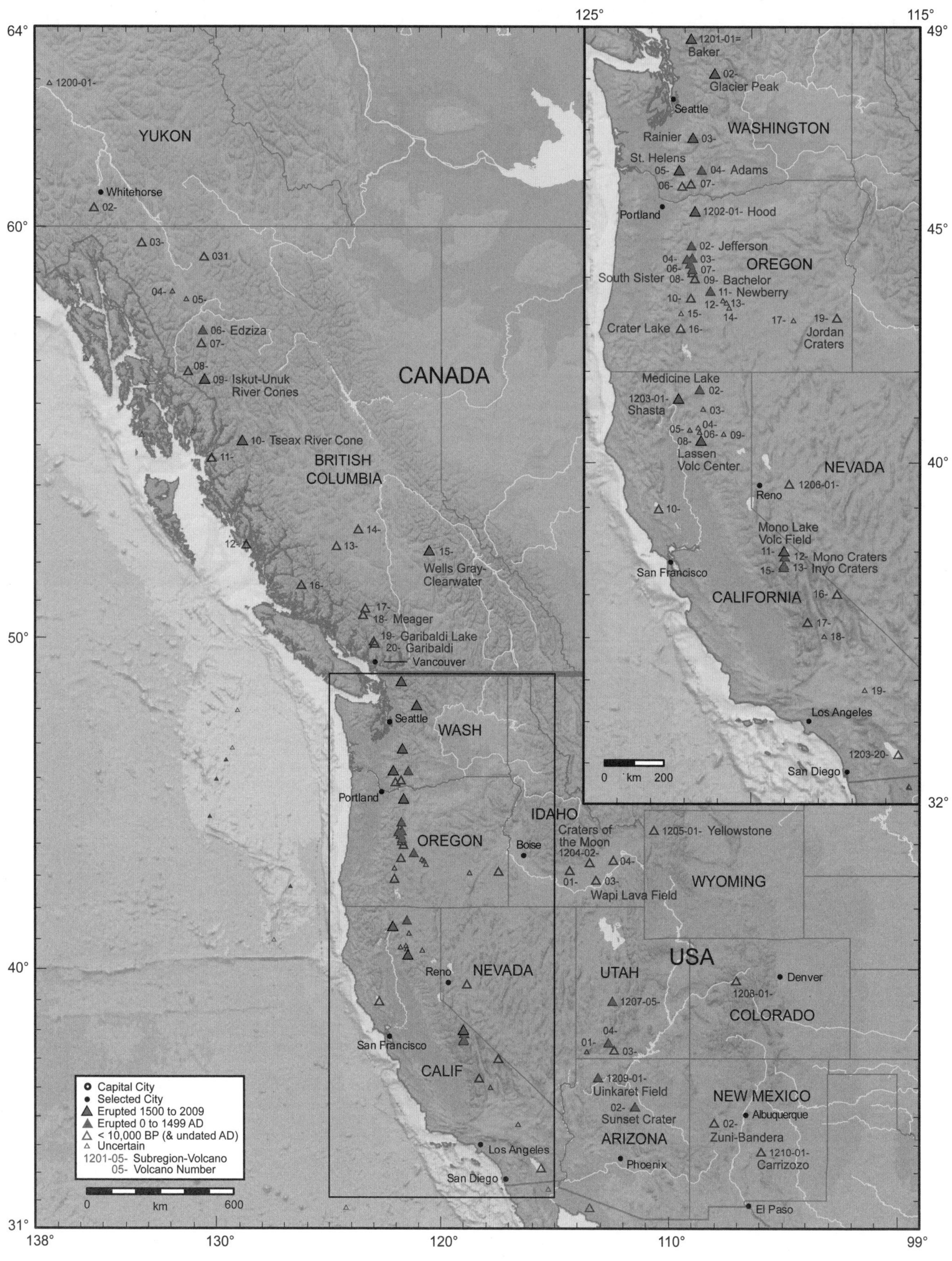

1200-01-
YUKON
Whitehorse
02-
03-
031
04-
05-
06- Edziza
07-
08-
09- Iskut-Unuk River Cones
CANADA
10- Tseax River Cone
11-
BRITISH COLUMBIA
14-
13-
12-
15- Wells Gray-Clearwater
16-
17-
18- Meager
19- Garibaldi Lake
20- Garibaldi
Vancouver
Seattle
WASH
Portland
OREGON
IDAHO
Boise
Craters of the Moon
1204-02-
04-
01-
03-
Wapi Lava Field
1205-01- Yellowstone
WYOMING
USA
UTAH
Reno
NEVADA
Denver
1208-01-
COLORADO
1207-05-
04-
01-
03-
San Francisco
CALIF
1209-01- Uinkaret Field
02- Sunset Crater
NEW MEXICO
Albuquerque
02- Zuni-Bandera
ARIZONA
1210-01- Carrizozo
Phoenix
Los Angeles
San Diego
El Paso
Capital City
Selected City
Erupted 1500 to 2009
Erupted 0 to 1499 AD
< 10,000 BP (& undated AD)
Uncertain
1201-05- Subregion-Volcano
05- Volcano Number
0 km 600
1201-01= Baker
02- Glacier Peak
Seattle
WASHINGTON
Rainier 03-
St. Helens
05-
04- Adams
06-
07-
Portland
1202-01- Hood
02- Jefferson
04- 03-
06- 07-
OREGON
South Sister 08- 09- Bachelor
11- Newberry
10-
12- 13-
15-
14-
17-
19- Jordan Craters
Crater Lake 16-
Medicine Lake
02-
1203-01- Shasta
03-
04-
05- 06- 09-
08-
Lassen Volc Center
NEVADA
Reno
1206-01-
10-
Mono Lake Volc Field
11- 12- Mono Craters
15- 13- Inyo Craters
San Francisco
CALIFORNIA
16-
17-
18-
19-
Los Angeles
1203-20-
San Diego
0 km 200
64°
60°
50°
40°
31°
138°
130°
120°
110°
99°
125°
115°
49°
45°
40°
32°

This region was originally restricted to the United States by the organizers of the *CAVW*, but we added Canada (as subregion 1200) in our first edition. If we add the US volcanoes here (subregions 1201-1210) to those of Alaska and Hawaii, we find 52 historically active volcanoes, tying the US for third with Russia (behind Indonesia with 78 and Japan with 66) in this national ranking. If volcanoes in the Commonwealth of the Northern Marianas Islands and American Samoa, and the North Gorda Ridge volcanic segment about 200 km off the coast of Oregon are included, the number of US historically active volcanoes rises to 64, approaching Japan's total of 66.

Volcanoes of region 12 occupy tectonic environments ranging from the subduction volcanism that dominates the Cascade Range to the extensional tectonics controlling vast regions of the western interior, giving region 12 the largest number (and percent) of volcanoes consisting primarily of cinder cone fields. Only Mount St. Helens and Lassen volcanoes in this region have had unequivocal eruptions in the past century, although eruptions have occurred since 1800 AD at glacier-clad Baker, Rainier, and Hood volcanoes in the Cascade Range, and radiocarbon dates document eruptions in the 18th-19th centuries from the Tseax River and Iskut-Unuk River cinder cones in British Columbia.

Native American legends describe eruptions of Sunset Crater, Arizona, for many years dated to 1064-65 AD by tree-ring counts, but this precise date is now considered unreliable, and the eruption has been dated by paleomagnetism to the 2nd half of the 11th century. After the historic voyages of Columbus, Spain dominated exploration of North America in the 16th century, with the Grand Canyon first viewed by western eyes in 1540 and the Oregon coast only 4 years later. Permanent inland settlement of Santa Fe came in 1609, only 2 years after the first settlement on the east coast by the British. The founding of the Massachusetts Bay Colony in 1630 started the great emigration to eastern North America. Exploration of the west was slow, though, and it was not until the 1770s that Captain Cook closed the gap between Spaniards working north along the coast and Russians moving toward them from the far northwest. Cook brought publicity to the Pacific coast, and by the end of the century ships from 6 nations were busily trading furs along seacoasts that 20 years earlier had not been seen by Europeans. The first documented eruption in the region was California's Shasta, in 1786. By that year every other region in the world, except Antarctica, had documented at least one historical eruption, and over half of region 01's current list of historical volcanism had been recorded.

In the latter half of the 18th century, while the US was gaining independence in the east, the Rocky Mountains were being explored by the British and French. In 1805 Lewis and Clark sighted the Pacific, and the first historical eruptions of Mount St. Helens were witnessed by settlers in the 1830s. In 1841 the first wagon train reached the Oregon Territories, and in 1848 gold was discovered in California. It was not until the end of the Civil War, though, that westward emigration exploded: the first transcontinental railroad was completed in 1869, and by 1890 the US Census Bureau Director declared that the American frontier was at an end. The US Geological Survey was founded in 1879 and from 1926 through 1931 operated a volcano observatory at Lassen, following that volcano's 1914-17 eruption. The second confirmed Cascade eruption of the century, at Mount St. Helens, brought the founding of the Cascades Volcano Observatory in 1980, and observatories followed documenting volcanic unrest at the major silicic calderas of Long Valley and Yellowstone.

VOLCANO NAME (Subregion) / **ERUPTION** — Area of Activity	**LAT**	**LONG**	**ELEV** (m)	**POPL** (5 km, 10, 30, 100)	**ROCK TYPE**	**VOLC TYPE**	**NUMBER**	**STATUS**	**Start Year**	Start M-Dy	**Stop Year**	Stop M-Dy	ERUPTIVE CHARACTERISTICS (Central, Flank vent, Radial fiss, Regional / Submarine, New island, Subglacial, Crater lake / Explosive, Pyro flow, Phreatic, Caldera / Lava flow, Lava lake, Dome, Spine / Fatal, Damage, Mudflow, Tsunami)	**VEI**	**Vol L/T**
CANADA															
Fort Selkirk (Canada-Yukon)	**62.93 N***	**137.38 W**	**1239**	1113	**XBF**	**Volcanic field**	**1200-01-**	Holocene?							
Alligator Lake (Canada-Yukon)	**60.42 N***	**135.42 W**	**2217**	0025	**BX**	**Volcanic field**	**1200-02-**	**Holocene**							
Atlin Volc Field (Canada-B.C.)	**59.68 N***	**133.32 W**	**1880**	0023	**XBf**	**Cinder cones**	**1200-03-**	**Holocene**							
									? 1898	*1108*	....	....	---- ---- ?--- ---- ----		
Tuya Volc Field (Canada-B.C.)	**59.37 N***	**130.58 W**	**2123**	0003	**BF**	**Volcanic field**	**1200-031**	**Holocene**							
Heart Peaks (Canada-B.C.)	**58.60 N**	**131.97 W**	**2012**	0003	**BXRt**	**Shield volcano**	**1200-04-**	Holocene?							
Level Mountain (Canada-B.C.)	**58.42 N**	**131.35 W**	**2190**	0003	**TRBXP**	**Shield volcano**	**1200-05-**	Holocene?							
Edziza (Canada-B.C.)	**57.72 N**	**130.63 W**	**2786**	0003	**TBXRy**	**Stratovolcano**	**1200-06-**	**Radiocarbon**							
North flank?									C-**6520**x	....	....	....	-?-- ---- ---- x--- ----		
									T-**0750**v	....	....	....	-x-- ---- ---- x--- ----		
NNE flank (Williams Cone)									C **0610**w	....	....	....	-x-- ---- x--- x--- ----		
SW flank of Ice Peak									F **0950***	....	....	....	-x-- ---- x--- x--- ----	3	-/7
Spectrum Range (Canada-B.C.)	**57.43 N**	**130.68 W**	**2430**	0003	**RTXB**	**Shield volcano**	**1200-07-**	**Holocene**							
Hoodoo Mountain (Canada-B.C.)	**56.78 N**	**131.28 W**	**1850**	0004	**PTb**	**Subglacial volc**	**1200-08-**	**Tephrochronology**							
									T-**7050**?	....	....	....	xx-- ---- ---- x--- ----	0	
Iskut-Unuk River Cones (B.C.)	**56.58 N***	**130.55 W**	**1880**	0003	**B**	**Cinder cones**	**1200-09-**	**Radiocarbon**							
Iskut River									C-**6830**w	....	....	....	x--- ---- x--- x--- ----		
Iskut River									C-**4700**y	....	....	....	x--- ---- ---- x--- ----		
Iskut River									C-**3450**w	....	....	....	x--- ---- ---- x--- ----		
Iskut River									C-**1830**y	....	....	....	x--- ---- ---- x--- ----		
Iskut River									C-**0620**w	....	....	....	x--- ---- x--- x--- ----		
Lava Fork									C **1590**t	....	....	....	x--- ---- ---- x--- ----		
Lava Fork									C **1800**?	....	....	....	x--- ---- ---- x--- ----		
Lava Fork									*? 1904*		....	....	x--- ---- ?--- ---- ----		
Tseax River Cone (Canada-B.C.)	**55.12 N**	**128.90 W**	**609**	0035	**B**	**Pyroclastic cone**	**1200-10-**	**Radiocarbon**							
									C **1330**u	....	....	....	x--- ---- x--- x--- ----		
									G **1690**w	....	....	....	x--- ---- x--- x--- xx--		8/-
Crow Lagoon (Canada-B.C.)	**54.70 N**	**130.23 W**	**335**	0035	**B**	**Pyroclastic cone**	**1200-11-**	**Holocene**							
Milbanke Sound Group (B.C.)	**52.50 N***	**128.73 W**	**335**	3334	**B**	**Cinder cones**	**1200-12-**	**Holocene**							
Satah Mountain (Canada-B.C.)	**52.47 N***	**124.70 W**	**1921**	2224	**XBRTy**	**Volcanic field**	**1200-13-**	**Holocene**							
Nazko (Canada-B.C.)	**52.90 N**	**123.73 W**	**1230**	1135	**XB**	**Cinder cones**	**1200-14-**	**Radiocarbon**							
									C-**5220**v	....	....	....	x--- ---- x--- x--- ----		
Wells Gray-Clearwater (B.C.)	**52.33 N***	**120.57 W**	**2015**	3335	**BX**	**Cinder cones**	**1200-15-**	**Dendrochronology**							
Dragon Cone									C-**5650**?	....	....	....	x--- ---- x--- x--- ----		
Kostal Cone									D **1550**?	....	....	....	x--- ---- x--- x--- ----		
Silverthrone (Canada-B.C.)	**51.43 N**	**126.30 W**	**3160**	1124	**ARD**	**Caldera**	**1200-16-**	**Holocene**							
Bridge River Cones (Canada-B.C)	**50.80 N***	**123.40 W**	**2500**	2235	**BX**	**Volcanic field**	**1200-17-**	**Holocene**							
Meager (Canada-B.C.)	**50.63 N**	**123.50 W**	**2680**	1335	**DAb**	**Complex volcano**	**1200-18-**	**Radiocarbon**							
NE flank of Plinth Peak									C-**0400**t	....	....	....	-x-- ---- xx-- x-x- --x-	**5?**	
Garibaldi Lake (Canada-B.C.)	**49.92 N***	**123.03 W**	**2316**	4457	**ABdy**	**Volcanic field**	**1200-19-**	**Holocene**							
Garibaldi (Canada-B.C.)	**49.85 N**	**123.00 W**	**2678**	0257	**DA**	**Stratovolcano**	**1200-20-**	**Radiocarbon**							
SE flank (Opal Cone)									C-**8060**z	....	....	....	-x-- ---- x--- x--- ----	3?	**9/7**

VOLCANO NAME (Subregion) / ERUPTION — Area of Activity	LAT	LONG	ELEV (m)	POPL (5 km, 10, 30, 100)	ROCK TYPE	VOLC TYPE / Start Year	Start M-Dy	NUMBER / Stop Year	Stop M-Dy	STATUS / Central, Flank vent, Radial fiss, Regional	Submarine, New island, Subglacial, Crater lake	Explosive, Pyro flow, Phreatic, Caldera	Lava flow, Lava lake, Dome, Spine	Fatal, Damage, Mudflow, Tsunami	VEI	Vol L/T
USA - W COAST STATES																
Baker (US-Washington)	**48.777 N**	**121.813 W**	**3285**	0247	**ADb**	**Stratovolcanoes**		**1201-01=**		**Historical**						
South flank (Schreibers Meadow Cone)						G-**7850**?	....	....	....	-x--	----	----	x---	--x-		8/-
Sherman Crater?						G-**4550**?	....	....	....	x---	----	xx--	x---	--x-	3?	-/7
(eruption possibly from Glacier Peak)						*? 1792*	*06*	....	....	----	----	?---	----	----	2	
						1820?	....	....	....	x---	----	x---	----	----	2	
Sherman Crater						**1843**	....	....	....	x---	----	x---	----	--x-	3?	
(possibly confused with 1843 eruption						*? 1846*	....	....	....	x---	----	?---	----	----		
Sherman Crater						*? 1850*	*03*	....	....	x---	----	----	----	----		
Sherman Crater						**1852**	1201p	**1853**	01 ?	x---	----	?---	----	--?-	2	
Sherman Crater						**1854**	....	....	....	x---	----	x---	----	----	2	
Sherman Crater						*? 1856*	....	....	....	x---	----	----	----	----		
Sherman Crater						**1858**	....	....	....	x---	----	x---	----	----	2	
Sherman Crater						**1859**	11	**1860**	0426?	x---	----	x---	----	----	2	
Sherman Crater						*? 1860*	*12*	....	....	x---	----	----	----	----		
Sherman Crater						**1863**	07	....	....	x---	----	x---	----	----	2	
Sherman Crater						*? 1865*	....	....	....	x---	----	----	----	----		
Sherman Crater						*? 1867*	*03*	....	....	x---	----	----	----	----		
Sherman Crater						*? 1869*	*06*	....	....	x---	----	----	----	----		
Sherman Crater						**1870**	....	....	....	x---	----	x---	----	----	2	
Sherman Crater						**1880**	0907	**1880**	1127	x---	----	x---	----	----	2	
Sherman Crater						*? 1884*	....	....	....	x---	----	----	----	----		
Glacier Peak (US-Washington)	**48.112 N**	**121.113 W**	**3213**	0027	**DAb**	**Stratovolcano**		**1201-02-**		**Tephrochronology**						
(White Chuck cone is Pleistocene)						*X-7350**	....	....	....	----	----	----	----	----		
						C-**3550**?	....	....	....	x---	----	xx--	--x-	--x-		
						C-**3150**?	....	....	....	x---	----	xx--	--x-	--x-		
						C-**0850**?	....	....	....	x---	----	x-?-	--?-	--x-		
						C **0200**t	....	....	....	x---	----	xx--	--x-	--x-	4+	-/8
						C **0900**t	....	....	....	x---	----	xx--	--x-	--x-	3?	-/8
						*? 1300*y	....	....	....	----	----	?---	----	--x-		
						T **1700**v	....	....	....	x---	----	x---	----	--x-	2	
Rainier (US-Washington)	**46.853 N**	**121.760 W**	**4392**	0347	**Ad**	**Stratovolcano**		**1201-03-**		**Historical**						
(tephra layer R)						G-**8050**?	....	....	....	x---	----	x---	----	----	3	-/7
						G-**7800**y	....	....	....	x---	----	x---	----	--x-		
(tephra layer A)						G-**5550**?	....	....	....	x---	----	xx--	----	----	2	-/6
(tephra layer L)						G-**5350**?	....	....	....	x---	----	x---	----	--x-	3	-/7
(tephra layer D)						G-**5050**?	....	....	....	x---	----	x---	----	----	3	-/7
(tephra layer N)						G-**4850**?	....	....	....	x---	----	xx--	----	--x-	2	-/6
						G-**3850**x	....	....	....	x---	----	x---	----	--x-		
(tephra layers S, F)						G-**3650**?	....	....	....	x---	----	x-xA	----	--x-	3	-/7
(tephra layer H)						C-**2750**?	....	....	....	x---	----	x---	----	----	2	-/6
(tephra layer B)						C-**2550**?	....	....	....	x---	----	x---	----	----	3	-/7
(tephra layer SL1)						T-**0700**t	....	....	....	x---	----	x?--	?---	--x-		
(tephra layer SL2)						T-**0650**t	....	....	....	x---	----	x?--	?---	----		
(tephra layers SL3 and SL4)						G-**0610**v	....	....	....	x---	----	xx--	x---	----		
(tephra layer SL5)						T-**0500**t	....	....	....	x---	----	x---	x---	----		
						T-**0400**t	....	....	....	x---	----	x-x-	----	----		
(tephra layer C)						G-**0250**x	....	....	....	x---	----	x---	----	--x-	4	-/8
(tephra layer SL8)						T-**0150**?	....	....	....	x---	----	x---	x---	----		
(tephra layers TC1 and TC2)						G **0440**v	....	....	....	x---	----	x---	----	--x-		
						G **0910**z	....	....	....	x---	----	xx--	----	--x-		
						G **1450**v	....	....	....	x---	----	?---	----	--x-		
(tephra layer X not a primary tephra)						*X 1825*?	....	....	....	----	----	----	----	----		
						? 1843	....	....	....	x---	----	?---	----	----	*2*	
						? 1854	....	....	....	x---	----	?---	----	----	*2*	
						? 1858	....	....	....	x---	----	?---	----	----	*2*	
						? 1870	....	....	....	x---	----	?---	----	----	*2*	
						? 1879	....	....	....	x---	----	?---	----	----	*2*	
						? 1882	....	....	....	x---	----	?---	----	----	*2*	
						1894	1121	**1894**	1224	x---	----	x-x-	----	----	1	
Adams (US-Washington)	**46.206 N**	**121.490 W**	**3742**	0246	**ABd**	**Stratovolcano**		**1201-04-**		**Tephrochronology**						
(tephra layers 1-4)						T-**7050***	....	....	....	----	----	x---	----	----	2	
(tephra layers 5-9)						T-**5150**z	....	....	....	----	----	x---	----	----	2	
NW flank (2200-2400 m), tephra layer 10						T-**4550**?	....	....	....	-x--	----	x---	x---	----	2	8/-
Upper SW flank? (tephra layers 11-13)						T-**4050**z	....	....	....	-x--	----	x-xA	----	--x-	2	
NNE flank (2100-2250 m)						T-**3800***	....	....	....	--x-	----	x---	x---	----	1?	8/-
(tephra layer 14)						T-**3550**?	....	....	....	x---	--x-	x---	----	----	2	
(tephra layer 15)						T-**3250**y	....	....	....	----	----	x-x-	----	----	2	
SSE flank (2600 m), tephra layer 16						T-**2950**v	....	....	....	-x--	----	x---	x---	----	1?	5/-
(tephra layers 17-18)						T-**2650**y	....	....	....	----	----	x-x-	----	----	2	
SSE flank (2100 m)						T-**1850**>	....	....	....	--x-	----	x---	x---	----	1?	7/-
(tephra layers 19-20)						T-**0550***	....	....	....	----	----	x-x-	----	----	2	
(tephra layer 21)						T-**0400**?	....	....	....	----	----	x---	----	----	2	
(tephra layer 22)						T-**0300**?	....	....	....	----	----	x-x-	----	----	2	
(tephra layer 23)						T **0200**?	....	....	....	----	----	x-x-	----	----	2	
East flank? (tephra layer 24)						T **0950**?	....	....	....	-?--	----	x---	?---	----	2	
St. Helens (US-Washington)	**46.20 N**	**122.18 W**	**2549**	2347	**DABXY**	**Stratovolcano**		**1201-05-**		**Historical**						
(Smith Creek eruptive period-layer Yb)						G-**2340**?	....	....	....	----	----	xx--	----	----	**5**	-/9
(tephra layer Yd)						T-**2100**y	....	....	....	----	----	x---	----	----		
(tephra layer Yn)						G-**1860**?	....	....	....	----	----	xx--	--x-	--x-	**6**	-/10
(tephra layer Ye)						T-**1770**v	....	....	....	----	----	xx--	--x-	----	**5**	-/9
(tephra layer ya)						G-**1680**?	....	....	....	----	----	xx--	----	----		
(Smith Creek eruptive period)						G-**1610**?	....	....	....	----	----	xx--	--x-	--x-		
(Pine Creek eruptive period-layer Pm)						G-**1180**?	....	....	....	----	----	xx--	--x-	--x-		
(Pine Creek eruptive period)						G-**1100**?	....	....	....	----	----	xx--	--x-	--x-		
(Pine Creek eruptive period)						G-**1010**?	....	....	....	----	----	xx--	--x-	--x-		
(Pine Creek eruptive period)						C-**0830**u	....	....	....	----	----	xx--	--x-	--x-		
(Pine Creek eruptive period)						G-**0800**?	....	....	....	----	----	xx--	--x-	--x-		
(Pine Creek tephra layers Ps and Pu)						G-**0530**?	....	....	....	----	----	xx--	--x-	--x-	**5**	-/9
(Castle Creek erupt. period--layer Bh)						G-**0280**?	....	....	....	----	----	xx--	x---	----		
(tephra layer Bo)						T-**0250**?	....	....	....	----	----	x---	x---	--x-		
NNE flank (Dogs Head, layer Bd)						G-**0220**?	....	....	....	-x--	----	xx--	--x-	----		

VOLCANO NAME (Subregion) / ERUPTION	Area of Activity	LAT	LONG	ELEV (m)	POPL (5 km, 10, 30, 100)	ROCK TYPE	VOLC TYPE	NUMBER	STATUS	Start Year	Start M-Dy	Stop Year	Stop M-Dy	Central, Flank vent, Radial fiss, Regional	Submarine, New island, Subglacial, Crater lake	Explosive, Pyro flow, Phreatic, Caldera	Lava flow, Lava lake, Dome, Spine	Fatal, Damage, Mudflow, Tsunami	VEI	Vol L/T
St. Helens (US-Washington) *continued*	(Castle Creek eruptive period)									G-0100?	....	....	....	----	----	xx--	----	----		
	SW flank (Cave basalts)									G 0100?	....	....	....	-x--	----	----	x---	----	0	
	Lower E flank (East Dome; layer Bi)									G 0190?	....	....	....	-x--	----	x---	--x-	----		
	(Castle Creek eruptive period)									T 0230?	....	....	....	----	----	----	x---	----	0	
	(tephra layer Bu)									G 0270?	....	....	....	----	----	x---	x---	----		
	(Castle Creek eruptive period)									G 0420?	....	....	....	x---	----	x---	----	--x-		
	NE flank (Sugar Bowl)									C 0780y	....	....	....	-x--	----	xx--	--x-	--x-		
	(Kalama eruptive period, tephra Wn)									D 1480	0115u	....	....	x---	----	xx--	--x-	--x-	5+	-/9
	(tephra layer We)									D 1482	0115u	....	....	x---	----	x---	----	----	5	-/9
	(Kalama eruptive period, tephra set X)									D 1525q	....	....	....	x---	----	xx--	x---	--x-		
	Pre-1980 summit dome (tephra layer z)									G 1610s	....	....	....	x---	----	xx--	--x-	--x-		8/-
	N flank--Goat Rocks area (layer T)									D 1800	0115u	....	....	-x--	----	x---	x---	x-x-	5	-/9
	North Flank (Goat Rocks area)									1831	08	....	....	-x--	----	x---	?-?-	----	3	
	North flank (Goat Rocks area)									1835	03 ?	....	....	-x--	----	x---	?-?-	----	2	
	North flank (Goat Rocks)									1842	1122	1845	0918?	-x--	----	xx--	--x-	----	3	-/7
	North flank (Goat Rocks)									1847	0326	1847	0330	-x--	----	x---	--?-	----	2	
										1848	0401<	....	....	----	----	?---	----	----	2?	
	North flank									? *1849*	....	....	....	-x--	----	?---	----	----	*2?*	
	North flank									1850	03	1850	05 ?	-x--	----	x---	----	----	2?	
	North flank									1853	0315e	1853	08 ?	-x--	----	x---	----	----	2?	
	North flank									1854	02	1854	04	-x--	----	x---	----	----	2	
										1857	04	....	....	----	----	x---	----	----	2	
										? *1898*	*0405*	....	....	----	----	----	----	----		
										? *1903*	*0915*	....	....	----	----	--?-	----	----		
										? *1921*	*0318*	....	....	----	----	----	----	----		
	Summit and north flank									1980	0327	1986	1028c	xx--	--x-	xxxA	--xx	xxx-	5*	7/9
	North side of lava dome									1989	1207	1990	0106	x---	----	x-x-	----	----	2*	
	North side of lava dome									1990	1105	1991	0214	x---	----	xxx-	----	--x-	3?	
	South of 1980-1986 lava dome									2004	1001	2008	0127j	xx--	----	x-x-	--xx	--x-	2	7/-
West Crater (US-Washington)		45.88 N*	122.08 W	1329	3357	AB	Volcanic field	1201-06-	Radiocarbon											
	West Crater, Hackamore Creek cone									C-6110?	....	....	....	---x	----	x---	x---	----	2?	
	Bare Mountain									C-5750?	....	....	....	x--x	----	x-x-	----	----	2?	
Indian Heaven (US-Washington)		45.93 N*	121.82 W	1806	3347	BA	Shield volcanoes	1201-07-	Radiocarbon											
	Big Lava Bed									C-6250v	....	....	....	---x	----	x---	x---	----		8/-
Hood (US-Oregon)		45.374N	121.695W	3426	0347	Ad	Stratovolcano	1202-01-	Historical											
	Lower NE flank (SSW of Parkdale)									C-4940w	....	....	....	-x--	----	x---	x---	----	2	
	Upper SW flank (Crater Rock)									C 0300x	....	....	....	-x--	----	xx--	----	--x-		
	Upper SW flank (Crater Rock)									C 0510w	....	....	....	-x--	----	xx--	----	----		
	Upper SW flank (Crater Rock)									C 1390w	....	....	....	-x--	----	x---	----	--x-		
	Upper SW flank (Crater Rock)									D 1765e	....	....	....	-x--	----	xx--	--x-	--x-		
	Upper SW flank (Crater Rock)									D 1795e	....	D1805e	....	-x--	----	xx--	--x-	--x-		
										? *1853*	....	....	....	----	----	?---	----	----		
										? *1854*	*08*	....	....	----	----	----	----	----		
										1859	0815	1859	0817	----	----	x---	----	----	2	
										1865	0921	1866	01 ?	----	----	x---	----	----	2	
										? *1869*	....	....	....	----	----	----	----	----		
	Upper SW flank (Crater Rock)									? *1907*	*0828*	....	....	-x--	----	--?-	----	----		
Jefferson (US-Oregon)		44.674N	121.800W	3199	0036	ADb	Stratovolcano	1202-02-	Varve Count											
	SSE of Jefferson (Forked Butte)									V-4500t	....	....	....	-x--	----	x---	x---	----		
	S of Jefferson (South Cinder Peak)									V 0950?	....	....	....	-x--	----	x---	x---	----		
Blue Lake Crater (US-Oregon)		44.411 N	121.774W	1230	2346	B	Maar	1202-03-	Radiocarbon											
										G 0680x	....	....	....	---x	----	x---	----	----		
Sand Mountain Field (US-Oregon)		44.38 N*	121.93 W	1664	2246	BA	Cinder cones	1202-04-	Radiocarbon											
	Nash Crater and other cones									G-2290y	....	....	....	---x	----	x---	x---	----	2?	
	North and south of Sand Mountain									G-1740y	....	....	....	---x	----	x---	----	----	2?	
	North Sand Mtn and other cones									G-0900v	....	....	....	---x	----	x---	x---	----	2?	
	Nash Crater									G-0800y	....	....	....	---x	----	x---	----	----	2?	
	Lost Lake cones									G 0070w	....	....	....	---x	----	x---	x---	----	2?	
Belknap (US-Oregon)		44.285N	121.841W	2095	0046	AB	Shield volcanoes	1202-06-	Radiocarbon											
	Little Belknap									G-1030y	....	....	....	-x--	----	----	x---	----	0	
	South Belknap and Twin Craters									G-0800y	....	....	....	---x	----	x---	x---	----	2?	
	Belknap Crater									G 0480?	....	....	....	xx--	----	x---	x---	----	2?	
North Sister Field (US-Oregon)		44.17 N	121.77 W	3074	0046	ABDR	Complex volcano	1202-07-	Radiocarbon											
	Sims Butte									T-7350*	....	....	....	-x--	----	x---	x---	----	2?	
	Yapoah Cone									T-0800?	....	....	....	---x	----	x---	x---	----	2?	
	Four-in-One Cone									G 0040x	....	....	....	---x	----	x---	x---	----	2?	
	Collier Cone									G 0440w	....	....	....	-x--	----	x---	x---	----	2?	8/-
South Sister (US-Oregon)		44.103 N	121.768W	3157	0046	ADbr	Complex volcano	1202-08-	Radiocarbon											
	SW flank (Rock Mesa)									C-0350?	....	....	....	-x--	----	xx--	x-x-	--x-	4	8/8
	North & south flanks (Devils Hill)									C-0050?	....	....	....	-x-x	----	xx--	x-x-	--x-	3	8/7
										? *1853*	*07*	....	....	x---	----	?---	----	----		
Bachelor (US-Oregon)		43.979N	121.688W	2763	2256	AB	Stratovolcano	1202-09-	Tephrochronology											
	North flank (Egan cone)									M-5800*	....	....	....	-x--	----	x---	x---	----		
Davis Lake (US-Oregon)		43.57 N*	121.82 W	2163	4446	A	Volcanic field	1202-10-	Radiocarbon											
	S flank of Hamner Butte (Black Rock)									C-2790?	....	....	....	-x--	----	x---	x---	----		
Newberry (US-Oregon)		43.722N	121.229W	2434	0056	ADBR	Shield volcano	1202-11-	Radiocarbon											
	South and east caldera rim									G-9210*	....	....	....	x---	----	x---	x-x-	----		
	NW rift zone (Lava Cast Forest)									G-5260w	....	....	....	--x-	----	----	x---	----	0	6/-
	Lower NW rift zone (Lava Butte)									G-5070w	....	....	....	--x-	----	x---	x---	----	3	8/7
	East Lake fissure, south flank									G-4960v	....	....	....	--x-	----	----	x---	----		5/-
	NW rift zone (Forest Road flow)									G-4860w	....	....	....	--x-	----	----	x---	----	0	6/-
	NW rift zone (Sugarpine Butte)									G-4770u	....	....	....	--x-	----	x---	x---	----		7/-
	NW rift zone (Lava Cascade flow)									G-4690w	....	....	....	--x-	----	----	x---	----	0	7/-
	Center, N & S caldera, upper SE flank									H-4450?	....	....	....	x---	----	x---	x---	----		7/-
	South of East Lake									H-1450?	....	....	....	x---	----	x---	x---	----		7/-
	South caldera wall									G 0490v	....	....	....	x---	----	x---	----	----	4	-/8
	S caldera wall (Big Obsidian Flow)									G 0690v	....	....	....	x---	----	xx--	x---	----	4	8/8
Devils Garden (US-Oregon)		43.512 N*	120.861 W	1698	2236	B	Volcanic field	1202-12-	Holocene?											
Squaw Ridge Lava Field (Oregon)		43.472N*	120.754W	1711	2236	B	Volcanic field	1202-13-	Holocene?											
Four Craters Lava Field (Oregon)		43.361 N*	120.669W	1501	3336	B	Volcanic field	1202-14-	Holocene?											
Cinnamon Butte (US-Oregon)		43.241 N*	122.108 W	1956	3335	B	Cinder cones	1202-15-	Holocene?											

VOLCANO NAME (Subregion) / ERUPTION — Area of Activity	LAT	LONG	ELEV (m)	POPL (5 km, 10, 30, 100)	ROCK TYPE	VOLC TYPE / —Start— Year	M-Dy	NUMBER / —Stop— Year	M-Dy	STATUS	Central, Flank vent, Radial fiss, Regional	Submarine, New island, Subglacial, Crater lake	Explosive, Pyro flow, Phreatic, Caldera	Lava flow, Lava lake, Dome, Spine	Fatal, Damage, Mudflow, Tsunami	VEI	Vol L/T
Crater Lake (US-Oregon)	**42.93** N	**122.12** W	**2487**	2236	**DAb**	**Caldera**		**1202-16-**		**Radiocarbon**							
North flank (Llao Rock)						G-**5900**t	....	....	....	-x--	----	x---	x---	----	**6**	8/**10**
Mt. Mazama summit and flank vents						I -**5677**w	1015q	....	....	xx--	----	xx-x	x---	----	**7**	8/**11**
Central Platform						T-**5550**?	....	....	....	x---	---x	----	x-x-	----	0	**9**/-
Wizard Island and Merriam Cone						T-**5250**?	....	....	....	x---	---x	x---	x---	----		
Lava dome ENE of Wizard Island						G-**2850**?	....	....	....	x---	---x	x---	--x-	----		7/-
Diamond Craters (US-Oregon)	**43.10** N*	**118.75** W	**1435**	2234	**B**	**Volcanic field**		**1202-17-**		Holocene?							
Jordan Craters (US-Oregon)	**43.147** N	**117.460** W	**1473**	0026	**BR**	**Volcanic field**		**1202-19-**		**Radiocarbon**							
Coffeepot Crater						C-**1250**?	....	....	....	x-x-	----	x-x-	xx--	----	2?	**9**/-
Shasta (US-California)	**41.409** N	**122.193** W	**4317**	0256	**ADb**	**Stratovolcano**		**1203-01-**		**Historical**							
						T-**8050**?	....	....	....	x---	----	xx--	----	----		
						C-**7750**?	....	....	....	x---	----	xx--	----	--x-		
Summit, S flank (Red Banks), and Shastina						C-**7650**v	....	....	....	xx--	----	xx--	x---	----	4	-/8
Shastina and Black Butte						C-**7420**y	....	....	....	-x--	----	xx--	--x-	----		
Summit, north and west flanks						T-**7350**?	....	....	....	xx--	----	----	x---	----	0	
						T-**7250**?	....	....	....	x---	----	x---	x---	----		
						T-**6650**?	....	....	....	x---	----	xx--	----	--x-		
						C-**6050**?	....	....	....	x---	----	x?--	----	--x-		
						C-**4050**?	....	....	....	x---	----	xx--	----	--x-		
						T-**3050***	....	....	....	x---	----	----	x---	----	0	
						C-**2550**?	....	....	....	x---	----	x---	----	--x-		
						C-**2050**?	....	....	....	x---	----	x---	----	--x-		
						C-**1150**?	....	....	....	x---	----	x---	----	--x-		
						C-**0850**?	....	....	....	x---	----	xx--	----	--x-		
						C-**0650***	....	....	....	x---	----	xx--	----	--x-		
						T-**0550**z	....	....	....	x---	----	xx--	x-x-	----		
						C-**0150**?	....	....	....	x---	----	xx--	----	----		
						T **0050**?	....	....	....	x---	----	----	x---	----	0	
						C **0150**?	....	....	....	x---	----	xx--	----	--?-		
						C **0850**?	....	....	....	x---	----	xx--	----	----		
						C **1200**?	....	....	....	x---	----	x---	----	--x-		
						C **1250**?	....	....	....	x---	----	xx--	----	----		
						1786	....	....	....	x---	----	xx--	----	--x-	3	
Medicine Lake (US-California)	**41.611** N	**121.554** W	**2412**	0036	**BARd**	**Shield volcano**		**1203-02-**		**Radiocarbon**							
SE caldera rim						C-**2410**v	....	....	....	x--x	----	x---	x---	----		7/-
Lower north flank (Black Crater)						C-**1080**t	....	....	....	-x-x	----	----	x---	----	0	6/-
SE flank (Burnt Lava flow)						C-**0780**v	....	....	....	-x-x	----	x---	x---	----		8/-
NW caldera floor (Medicine lava flow)						M-**0050**?	....	....	....	x---	----	----	x---	----	0	7/-
NE caldera rim (Mt. Hoffman area)						M **0720**?	....	....	....	x--x	----	x---	x---	----		8/-
North flank (Callahan lava flow)						M **0800**?	....	....	....	-x-x	----	x---	x---	----		8/-
SW flank (Paint Pot Crater)						T **0830**q	....	....	....	-x-x	----	x---	x---	----		7/-
SW flank (Little Glass Mountain)						C **0890**v	....	....	....	-x-x	----	x---	x-x-	----	3	8/7
Upper east flank (Glass Mountain)						M **1080**q	....	....	....	-x-x	----	x---	x-x-	----	3?	**9**/7
East flank (Glass Mountain ?)						*? 1910*	*01*	....	....	-?--	----	--?-	----	----	*1?*	
Brushy Butte (US-California)	**41.178** N	**121.443** W	**1174**	0345	**B**	**Shield volcano**		**1203-03-**		Holocene?							
Twin Buttes (US-California)	**40.777** N*	**121.591** W	**1631**	4446	**BD**	**Cinder cones**		**1203-04-**		Holocene?							
Silver Lake (US-California)	**40.731** N	**121.841** W	**1535**	0346	**B**	**Cinder cones**		**1203-05-**		Holocene?							
Tumble Buttes (US-California)	**40.68** N*	**121.55** W	**2191**	3346	**A**	**Cinder cones**		**1203-06-**		Holocene?							
Lassen Volc Center (California)	**40.492** N	**121.508** W	**3187**	0146	**ADRb**	**Stratovolcano**		**1203-08-**		**Historical**							
Chaos Crags						G **0800**y	....	....	....	-x--	----	xx--	--x-	----		
Chaos Crags						G **0880**y	....	....	....	-x--	----	xx--	--x-	----		
Chaos Crags						G **0980**y	....	....	....	-x--	----	xx--	--x-	----		
Chaos Crags						*? 1650*?	....	....	....	-x--	----	--?A	--?-	----		
Cinder Cone						D **1666**?	....	....	....	xx--	----	x---	x---	----	3?	
(Cinder Cone eruption predates 1850)						*X 1850*	*08*	X*1851*	....	----	----	----	----	----		
Lassen Peak						**1914**	0530	**1917**	0629	x---	----	xxx-	x-x-	-xx-	3*	
Eagle Lake Field (US-California)	**40.63** N*	**120.83** W	**1652**	3355	**BAr**	**Fissure vents**		**1203-09-**		Holocene?							
Clear Lake (US-California)	**38.97** N*	**122.77** W	**1439**	5557	**DARb**	**Volcanic field**		**1203-10-**		**Holocene**							
Mono Lake Volc Field (California)	**38.00** N*	**119.03** W	**2121**	4445	**DRB**	**Cinder cones**		**1203-11-**		**Tephrochronology**							
						T **0350**v	....	....	....	----	---x	----	x---	----		
Paoha Island						H **1150**x	....	....	....	----	----	----	--x-	----		
Negit Island						T **1550**y	....	....	....	----	----	----	x---	----		
Paoha Island						T **1790**u	....	....	....	----	----	----	--x-	----		
(South Mono Lake, uncorroborated)						*? 1890*	*0823*?	?*1890*	*0823*?	----	----	--?-	----	----		
Mono Craters (US-California)	**37.88** N	**119.00** W	**2796**	2345	**Rd**	**Lava domes**		**1203-12-**		**Radiocarbon**							
Punchbowl						H-**6750***	....	....	....	----	----	----	--x-	----		
Crater north of Punchbowl						H-**3850***	....	....	....	----	----	----	----	----		
Central Mono Craters						H-**0700***	....	....	....	----	----	----	--x-	----		
South Coulee?						G **0010**x	....	....	....	----	----	x---	----	----		
South Coulee?						G **0320**x	....	....	....	----	----	x---	----	----		
Southern Mono Craters						C **0440**v	....	....	....	----	----	xx--	----	----		
NW Coulee and Pumice Pit dome						C **0490**v	....	....	....	----	----	xx--	x-x-	----		
South Coulee						T **0700**?	....	....	....	----	----	xx--	x-x-	----		8/-
Northern Mono Craters?						G **0810**y	....	....	....	----	----	xx--	----	----	4	-/8
Dome on NW edge of NW Coulee						H **1000**x	....	....	....	----	----	x---	--x-	----		
Panum Crater and nearby vents						D **1350**p	....	....	....	----	----	xx--	x-x-	----	4	8/8
Inyo Craters (US-California)	**37.692** N	**119.02** W	**2629**	3445	**Rdxy**	**Lava domes**		**1203-13-**		**Radiocarbon**							
North of Deadman Creek						H-**4050**?	....	....	....	----	----	----	--x-	----		7/-
Wilson Butte						C **0600**u	....	....	....	----	----	xx--	--x-	----	4?	7/7
S Deadman, Obsidian Flow, Glass Creek						G **1380**t	....	....	....	---x	----	xxx-	x-x-	--x-	4	8/8
Mammoth Mountain (California)	**37.631** N	**119.032** W	**3369**	4445	**TXYbr**	**Lava domes**		**1203-15-**		**Radiocarbon**							
SSW of Mammoth Mtn (Red Cones)						C-**6990**u	....	....	....	x--x	----	x---	x---	----		
North flank of Mammoth Mountain						G **1260**s	....	....	....	---x	----	--x-	----	----		
Ubehebe Craters (US-California)	**37.02** N	**117.45** W	**752**	2235	**B**	**Maars**		**1203-16-**		**Anthropology**							
						A-**4050**?	....	....	....	x---	----	xx--	----	----		
Golden Trout Creek (California)	**36.358** N*	**118.32** W	**2886**	1136	**B**	**Volcanic field**		**1203-17-**		**Tephrochronology**							
Groundhog Crater						T-**5550***	....	....	....	x---	----	x---	x---	----		
Coso Volc Field (US-California)	**36.03** N*	**117.82** W	**2400**	3335	**RBDA**	**Lava domes**		**1203-18-**		Holocene?							
Lavic Lake (US-California)	**34.75** N*	**116.625** W	**1495**	4447	**B**	**Volcanic field**		**1203-19-**		Holocene?							

VOLCANO NAME (Subregion) / ERUPTION — Area of Activity	LAT	LONG	ELEV (m)	POPL (5 km, 10, 30, 100)	ROCK TYPE	VOLC TYPE / — Start — Year M-Dy	NUMBER	STATUS / — Stop — Year M-Dy	Central, Flank vent, Radial fiss, Regional	Submarine, New island, Subglacial, Crater lake	Explosive, Pyro flow, Phreatic, Caldera	Lava flow, Lava lake, Dome, Spine	Fatal, Damage, Mudflow, Tsunami	VEI	Vol L/T
Salton Buttes (US-California).....	**33.20 N**	**115.62 W**	**-40**	3357	**R**	**Lava domes**	**1203-20-**	**Hydration Rind**							
Obsidian Butte..................						H-**6450**?		....	x---	----	x---	--xx	----		
Unnamed (US-Calif-SW of).........	32.50 N	119.13 W					1203-21-	Not a Volcano							
(invalid submarine eruption report).......						*X 1853*?		....	----	----	----	----	----		

USA - WESTERN INTERIOR

VOLCANO NAME (Subregion) / ERUPTION — Area of Activity	LAT	LONG	ELEV (m)	POPL	ROCK TYPE	VOLC TYPE / Start Year M-Dy	NUMBER	STATUS / Stop Year M-Dy	Central, Flank vent, Radial fiss, Regional	Submarine, New island, Subglacial, Crater lake	Explosive, Pyro flow, Phreatic, Caldera	Lava flow, Lava lake, Dome, Spine	Fatal, Damage, Mudflow, Tsunami	VEI	Vol L/T
Shoshone Lava Field (US-Idaho) .	**43.18 N**	**114.35 W**	**1478**	3346	**B**	**Shield volcano**	**1204-01-**	**Holocene**							
						C-**8400**y		....	---x	----	----	x---	----	0	
Craters of the Moon (US-Idaho) . .	**43.42 N***	**113.50 W**	**2005**	2245	**BXY**	**Cinder cones**	**1204-02-**	**Radiocarbon**							
NW of Echo Crater..............						C-**5890**w		....	---x	----	----	x---	----	0	9/-
Grassy Cone..................						C-**5470**w		....	---x	----	----	x---	----	0	9/-
Silent Cone..................						C-**4600**v		....	---x	----	----	x---	----	0	9/-
Sentinel Cone..................						T-**4250**?		....	---x	----	----	x---	----	0	8/-
Big Cinder Butte and vents to the SE......						C-**4070**t		....	---x	----	----	x---	----	0	9/-
Black Top Butte..............						C-**2560**v		....	---x	----	----	x---	----	0	9/-
Vermillion Chasm to Minidoka-Larkspur....						C-**1680**w		....	---x	----	----	x---	----	0	9/-
North Crater..................						M-**0350**?		....	---x	----	----	x---	----	0	8/-
Big Craters, Trench Mortar Flat........						C-**0260**q		....	---x	----	----	x---	----	0	7/-
South of Big Craters, near Broken Top....						C-**0130**t		....	---x	----	----	x---	----	0	9/-
Wapi Lava Field (US-Idaho)......	**42.88 N***	**113.22 W**	**1604**	1146	**B**	**Shield volcano**	**1204-03-**	**Radiocarbon**							
Kings Bowl Rift, Wapi Lava Field........						T-**0300**?		....	---x	----	--x-	x---	----	2?	9/-
Hell's Half Acre (US-Idaho)......	**43.50 N**	**112.45 W**	**1631**	0356	**B**	**Shield volcano**	**1204-04-**	**Radiocarbon**							
						C-**3250**w		....	---x	----	----	x---	----	0	
Yellowstone (US-Wyoming).......	**44.43 N**	**110.67 W**	**2805**	0035	**Rb**	**Calderas**	**1205-01-**	**Tephrochronology**							
Turbid Lake (NE of Yellowstone Lake).....						G-**7400***		....	x---	----	--x-	----	----		
Elliott's Crater (Yellowstone Lake).......						T-**6050**?		....	x---	----	--x-	----	----		
Duck Lake, Evil Twin Craters (West Thumb) .						T-**3050**?		....	x---	----	--x-	----	----		
Indian Pond crater (N of Yellowstone Lake) . .						G-**1350**x		....	x---	----	--x-	----	----		
Soda Lakes (US-Nevada).........	**39.53 N**	**118.87 W**	**1251**	4556	**B**	**Maars**	**1206-01-**	**Holocene**							
Santa Clara (US-Utah)...........	**37.257 N***	**113.625 W**	**1465**	5566	**XA**	**Volcanic field**	**1207-01-**	Holocene?							
Bald Knoll (US-Utah)...........	**37.328 N**	**112.408 W**	**2135**	1246	**B**	**Cinder cones**	**1207-03-**	**Holocene**							
Markagunt Plateau (US-Utah)....	**37.58 N***	**112.67 W**	**2840**	3346	**BAtr**	**Volcanic field**	**1207-04-**	**Dendrochronology**							
						D **1050**<		....	----	----	----	x---	----		
Black Rock Desert (US-Utah)....	**38.97 N***	**112.50 W**	**1800**	4445	**BAr**	**Volcanic field**	**1207-05-**	**Radiocarbon**							
Ice Springs Craters..............						C **1290**w		....	x---	----	x---	x---	----		
Dotsero (US-Colorado)...........	**39.661 N**	**107.035 W**	**2230**	3456	**B**	**Maar**	**1208-01-**	**Radiocarbon**							
						C-**2200**y		....	x---	----	x---	x---	--x-	2?	
Uinkaret Field (US-Arizona)......	**36.38 N***	**113.13 W**	**1555**	2236	**Xb**	**Volcanic field**	**1209-01-**	**Anthropology**							
Little Springs..................						A **1100**u		....	---x	----	x---	x---	-x--	1	6/-
Sunset Crater (US-Arizona)......	**35.37 N***	**111.50 W**	**2447**	5556	**BYTDR**	**Cinder cone**	**1209-02-**	**Dendrochronology**							
Sunset Crater and SE-trending fissures....						M **1075**q		....	x--x	----	x---	x---	-x--	4?	8/-
Carrizozo (US-New Mexico).......	**33.78 N**	**105.93 W**	**1731**	1245	**B**	**Cinder cones**	**1210-01-**	**Surface Exposure**							
Little Black Peak................						E-**3250**z		....	x---	----	x---	x---	----		9/-
Zuni-Bandera (US-New Mexico) . . .	**34.80 N***	**108.00 W**	**2550**	2235	**B**	**Volcanic field**	**1210-02-**	**Anthropology**							
Bandera Crater................						G-**8710**y		....	----	----	x---	x---	----		
McCartys flow.................						G-**1170**y		....	----	----	x---	x---	----	0	9/-

Steve Schilling (USGS/CVO)

An aerial view of the Mount St. Helens crater and its new lava dome in February 2005 shows a smooth-textured "whaleback" feature formed by slow dome extrusion. This new episode of dome growth took place from 2004-2008, occasionally punctuated by minor explosive eruptions. The previous 1980-1986 lava dome is visible at the lower left.

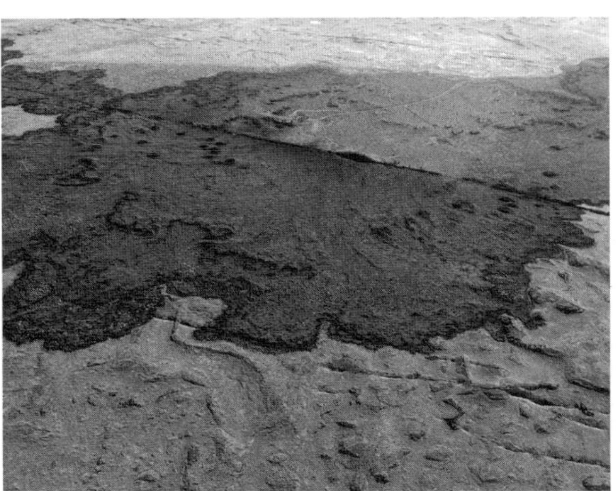
Susan Sakimoto (NASA)

The Kings Bowl rift cutting diagonally across the top of the photo produced a small 6 km^2 lava field about 2250 years ago immediately north of the much larger Wapi Lava Field in Idaho. Kings Bowl itself is the small elongated phreatic explosion crater on the right-center of the rift that produced the light-colored tephra at the upper right.

Pacific Ocean (13)

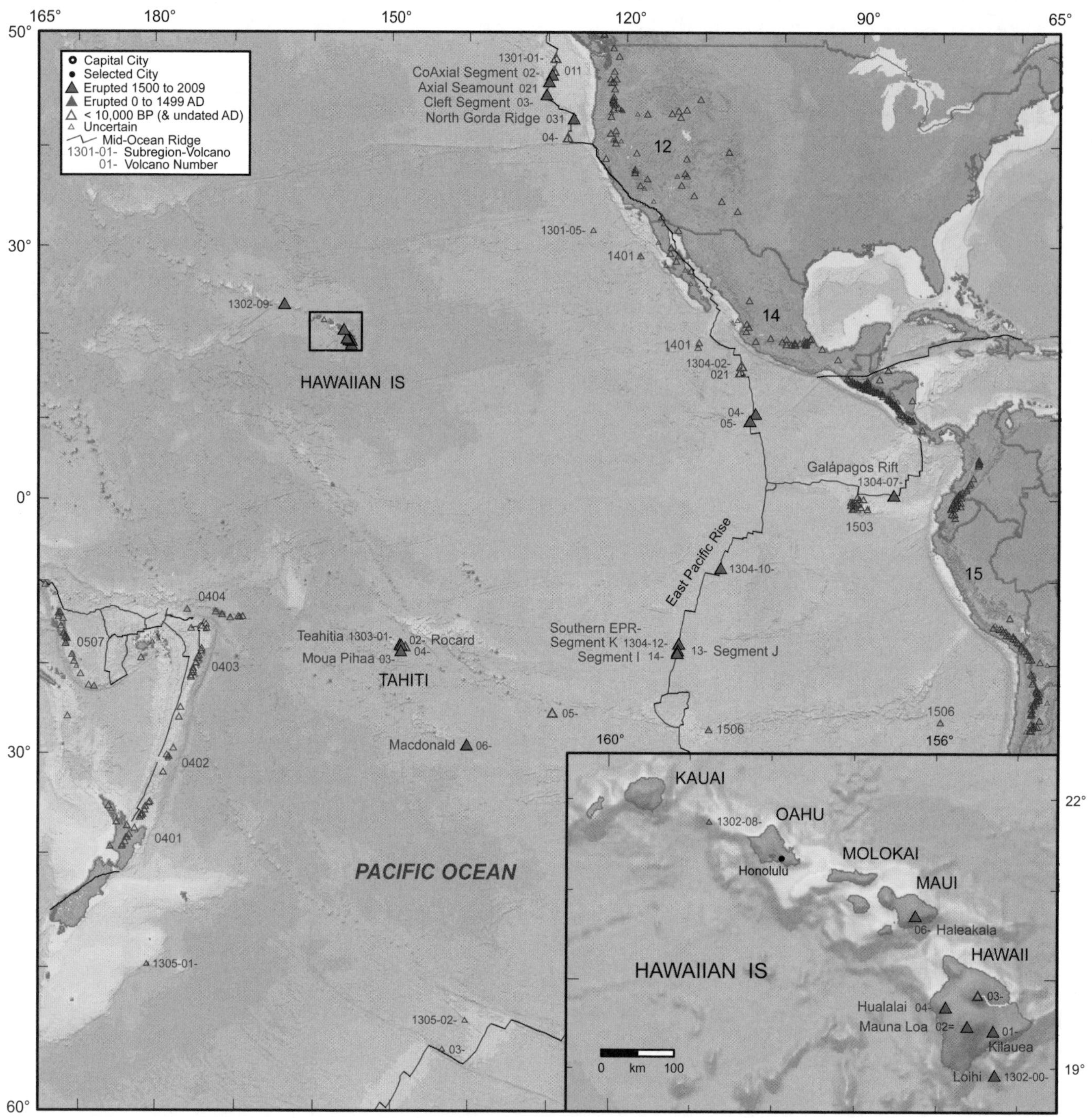

The Pacific Ocean forms the largest volcanic region in this book, but has the smallest total land area. Region 13 covered only "Hawaii" upon publication of the 1955 *CAVW* catalog. By the time of our 1981 book, it was clear that there was Holocene activity elsewhere in the Pacific and, in keeping with the original *CAVW* designations for both Atlantic and Indian oceans, we expanded this region to cover the full ocean basin not already covered by other catalogs (e.g. Galápagos, Chilean, and Mexican islands). Easter Island was included in this region in our 2nd edition, but has been moved since to be part of Chile's island volcanoes in subregion 1506.

Tahiti was discovered in 1767, 11 years before Captain Cook first sighted Hawaii, the most visibly volcanic part of the region. American missionaries arrived in Honolulu in 1820, and the Wilkes Expedition, with 27-yr-old J.D. Dana, arrived in Hawaii in 1840. In 1874, US troops landed in the islands, and in 1893 the Kingdom of Hawaii was overthrown by US Marines. Hawaii was annexed in 1898, ceded itself to the US as the Republic of Hawaii two years later, and became the 50th US state in 1959. In 1911, American volcanologists Perret & Shepherd started the first continuous monitoring of Kilauea, and the Hawaiian Volcano Observatory (HVO) was founded in the next year under the direction of the redoubtable Thomas Jaggar. In 1925 the Observatory came under the administration of the US Geological Survey, and the same year marked the first issue of *Volcano Letter*, an irregular periodical that carried news and volcano commentary from around the world until publication ceased in 1955. HVO has pioneered many approaches to monitoring of active volcanoes, and been instrumental in advancing understanding of ocean island volcanism.

Dominated by the fluid lavas of Hawaii, this region leads the world in eruptions producing lava flows, lava lakes, and radial fissure eruptions (in percentages of both its own total eruptions and those of each characteristic). The region is unusually homogeneous in its products, with virtually all eruptions consisting of basalt, from hotspot (Hawaii, Tahiti, Macdonald), ocean ridge crest, or fracture zone settings. Less than one-fifths of the eruptions in the Pacific Region display any explosive activity, and only 6% are strictly explosive, with no associated effusive activity; these are by far the lowest proportions of any region. This region has the highest proportion of submarine volcanoes (79%), and matches Africa and Arabia/Indian Ocean in having the fewest documented large explosive (VEI ≥4). The obvious focus on the dramatic effusive activity can be misleading, however, as Smithsonian and USGS volcanologists have recently documented a surprisingly high number of moderate-to-large explosive eruptions from Kilauea volcano.

A surge of interest in deep-sea volcanism has increased understanding of mid-ocean rift volcanism and documented several new eruptions. Evidence for a very recent, possibly ongoing eruption was detected during a series of dives in the submersible vessel *Alvin* in 1991 on the East Pacific Rise at about 9° 50' N. Hot-vent animal communities that had been documented during November to December 1989 imaging were observed to have been buried by fresh basaltic lava flows, and the scorched soft tissues of partially buried biota had not yet attracted bottom scavengers. Fresh black smoker chimneys were draped by new lava flows. This position was at a depth of about 2500 m south of the Clipperton fracture zone, about 1000 km SW of Acapulco, México. It coincided with a location where fresh lava flows previously estimated as less than roughly 50 years in age had been found; later Uranium-series dating extended the eruptive record here back 7000 years. Preliminary radiometric dating using ^{210}Pb techniques dated lava flows erupted along the East Pacific Rise at between late summer 2005 and January 2006, and a research expedition in April 2006 discovered that seismometers emplaced since 2003 had been buried by new lava flows. Further north, along the Juan de Fuca and North Gorda ridges off the coasts of Oregon and Washington, several eruptions were documented during the 1980s and 1990s by scientists of the NOAA Vents Program. These dramatic eruptions are evidence of the highly active mid-ocean ridge volcanism, but they only hint at the frequency of sea-floor volcanism. We have not included "zero-age" volcanoes unless they have specifically dated eruptions, and the volcanoes listed here are only a small fraction of the Holocene eruptive record in this active tectonic setting.

VOLCANO NAME (Subregion) / ERUPTION — Area of Activity	LAT	LONG	ELEV (m)	POPL (5 km, 10, 30, 100)	ROCK TYPE	VOLC TYPE	NUMBER	STATUS	Start Year	Start M-Dy	Stop Year	Stop M-Dy	Central / Flank vent / Radial fiss / Regional	Submarine / New island / Subglacial / Crater lake	Explosive / Pyro flow / Phreatic / Caldera	Lava flow / Lava lake / Dome / Spine	Fatal / Damage / Mudflow / Tsunami	VEI	Vol L/T
PACIFIC OCEAN - NE																			
Endeavour Ridge (Juan de Fuca)	**47.95 N**	**129.10 W**	**-2050**	0000	**B**	**Submarine volc**	**1301-01-**	**Uranium-series**											
									U-**6930**?	....	....	....	---**x**	**x**---	----	**x**---	----	0	
									U-**3490**?	....	....	....	---**x**	**x**---	----	**x**---	----	0	
Cobb Segment (Juan de Fuca)	**46.88 N**	**129.33 W**	**-2100**	0000	**B**	**Submarine volc**	**1301-011**	**Uranium-series**											
									U-**1180**?	....	....	....	---**x**	**x**---	----	**x**---	----		
CoAxial Segment (Juan de Fuca)	**46.52 N**	**129.58 W**	**-2400**	0000	**B**	**Submarine volc**	**1301-02-**	**Historical**											
CoAxial segment, Juan de Fuca Ridge									**1986**e	....	....	....	---**x**	**x**---	----	**x**---	----	0	7/-
N end CoAxial segment, Juan de Fuca Ridge.									**1993**	0626	**1993**	0704?	---**x**	**x**---	----	**x**---	----	0	6/-
Axial Seamount (Juan de Fuca)	**45.95 N**	**130.00 W**	**-1410**	0000	**B**	**Submarine volc**	**1301-021**	**Historical**											
South end of Axial caldera.									**1998**	0125	**1998**	0205?	---**x**	**x**---	----	**x**---	----	0	6/-
Cleft Segment (Juan de Fuca)	**44.83 N**	**130.30 W**	**-2140**	0000	**B**	**Submarine volc**	**1301-03-**	**Historical**											
S Cleft Segment, S Juan de Fuca Ridge									U-**0270**?	....	....	....	---**x**	**x**---	----	**x**---	----	0	
N Cleft Segment, S Juan de Fuca Ridge									**1982**<	....	....	....	---**x**	**x**---	----	**x**---	----	0	7/-
N Cleft Segment, S Juan de Fuca Ridge									**1986**	08 ?	....	....	---**x**	**x**---	----	**x**---	----	0	7/-
North Gorda Ridge (Gorda Ridge)	**42.67 N**	**126.78 W**	**-3000**	0000	**B**	**Submarine volc**	**1301-031**	**Historical**											
									U-**4840**?	....	....	....	---**x**	**x**---	----	**x**---	----	0	
									U-**3020**?	....	....	....	---**x**	**x**---	----	**x**---	----	0	
Near center of North Gorda Ridge segment.									**1996**	0228?	**1996**	0315?	---**x**	**x**---	----	**x**---	----	0	7/-
Escanaba Segment (Gorda Ridge)	**40.98 N**	**127.50 W**	**-1700**	0000	**B**	**Submarine volc**	**1301-04-**	**Uranium-series**											
40 deg 59 min North									U-**2260**?	....	....	....	---**x**	**x**---	----	**x**---	----	0	
Unnamed (Pacific-NE)	**31.75 N**	**124.25 W**	**-2533**	0000	**U**	**Submarine volc ?**	**1301-05-**	Uncertain											
400 km SW of Pt. Conception, Calif.									*? 1972*	*1007*	....	....	----	?---	----	----	----	*0*	
HAWAII																			
Loihi (Hawaii)	**18.92 N**	**155.27 W**	**-975**	0006	**Bx**	**Submarine volc**	**1302-00-**	**Historical**											
East flank?									K-**7050***	....	....	....	-?--	----	----	**x**---	----	0	
									K-**5050***	....	....	....	----	----	----	**x**---	----	0	
									K-**0050***	....	....	....	----	----	----	**x**---	----	0	
									? 1971	*0917*	*?1972*	*09*	----	?---	----	----	----	*0*	
									? 1975	*0824?*	*?1975*	*11*	----	?---	----	----	----	*0*	
									? 1984	*1111*	*?1985*	*0121*	----	?---	----	----	----	*0*	
									? 1986	*0920*	*?1986*	*0920*	----	?---	----	----	----	*0*	
									1996	0225p	**1996**	0809?	**x**---	**x**---	----	**x**---	----	0	
Kilauea (Hawaii)	**19.421 N**	**155.287 W**	**1222**	4446	**B**	**Shield volcano**	**1302-01-**	**Historical**											
SW rift zone									C-**4650**?	....	....	....	--**x**-	----	----	**x**---	----	0	
									G-**3300**?	....	....	....	**x**---	----	----	**x**---	----	0	
SW rift zone									C-**2850**?	....	....	....	--**x**-	----	----	**x**---	----	0	
									T-**2200**z	....	....	....	----	----	**x**---	----	----		
									G-**2080**?	....	....	....	**x**---	----	----	**x**---	----	0	
SW rift zone									C-**1650**?	....	....	....	--**x**-	----	----	**x**---	----	0	
SW rift zone									C-**1550**?	....	....	....	--**x**-	----	----	**x**---	----	0	
									G-**0800**?	....	....	....	**x**---	----	----	**x**---	----	0	
East rift zone.									C-**0410**v	....	....	....	--**x**-	----	----	**x**---	----	0	
(Kipuka Nene flows)									G-**0270**u	....	....	....	**x**---	----	----	**x**---	----	0	
Summit, East and SW rift zones.									G-**0200**w	....	....	....	**x**-**x**-	----	----	**x**---	----	0	
(Pre-Kulanaokuaiki tephra)									G-**0050**w	....	....	....	**x**---	----	**x**---	----	----		
Kilauea summit (Powers Caldera).									M **0150**y	....	....	....	**x**---	----	----	**x**---	----	0	
(Kulanaokuaiki 1 tephra).									T **0420**p	....	....	....	**x**---	----	**x**---	----	----		
Lower east rift zone									M **0450**<	....	....	....	--**x**-	----	----	**x**---	----	0	
(Kulanaokuaiki 2 tephra).									G **0540**x	....	....	....	**x**---	----	**x**---	**x**---	----		
East (near Kaipu) and SW rift zones									C **0680**u	....	....	....	--**x**-	----	**x**---	**x**---	----	1?	
(Kipuka Hornet flows)									G **0850**w	....	....	....	**x**---	----	----	**x**---	----	0	
(Upper Kulanaokuaiki tephra)									T **0900**t	....	....	....	**x**---	----	**x**---	----	----		
Lower east rift zone (NE of Iilewa).									C **1050**u	....	....	....	--**x**-	----	**x**---	**x**---	----	1?	
(Old Kalue flows)									G **1140**u	....	....	....	**x**---	----	----	**x**---	----	0	
Upper east rift zone (Kane Nui o Hamo)									A **1340**s	....	....	....	--**x**-	----	----	**x**---	----	0	

VOLCANO NAME (Subregion) / ERUPTION	LAT / LONG / ELEV (m) / POPL / ROCK TYPE / VOLC TYPE / NUMBER / STATUS — Area of Activity	Start Year	Start M-Dy	Stop Year	Stop M-Dy	Central / Flank vent / Radial fiss / Regional	Submarine / New island / Subglacial / Crater lake	Explosive / Pyro flow / Phreatic / Caldera	Lava flow / Lava lake / Dome / Spine	Fatal / Damage / Mudflow / Tsunami	VEI	Vol L/T
Kilauea (Hawaii) *continued*												
	Kilauea summit (Aila'au shield)	G **1410**?	....	G**1470**?	....	x---	----	----	x---	----	0	9/-
	Lower east rift zone (near Puu Kaliu)	C **1460**t	....	....	....	--x-	----	----	x---	----	0	
	Kilauea caldera	G **1490**n	....	....	....	x---	----	x--M	----	----	1?	
		G **1500**?	....	....	....	----	----	x---	----	----	1?	
	Lower east rift zone (near Kehena)	C **1510**t	....	....	....	--x-	----	----	x---	----	0	
	Lower east rift zone (Puu Honuaula)	C **1610**t	....	....	....	--x-	----	x---	x---	----	1?	
	Kilauea summit (Observatory vent)	T **1650**t	....	....	....	x---	----	----	x---	----	0	
	Upper east rift zone (Kokoolau)	M **1700**q	....	....	....	--x-	----	----	x---	----	0	
	East rift zone (Heiheiahulu, 520 m)	**1750**?	....	....	....	--x-	----	----	x---	----	0	7/-
	Lower east rift zone (230-375 m)	**1790**?	....	....	....	--x-	----	----	x---	----	0	7/-
	Kilauea Caldera (Keanakakoi ash)	**1790**	11 ?	....	....	x---	---x	xxx-	----	x---	4	-/8
	Kilauea Caldera	**1820**?	....	....	....	x---	----	x---	x---	----	2	
	SW rift zone (Great Crack, 75-580 m)	**1823**	02	**1823**	07	--x-	----	--x-	x---	xx--	0	7/-
	Halemaumau	**1823**	08 <	**1894**	1206	x---	----	----	xx--	----	0*	
	East rim of caldera (Byron's Ledge)	**1832**	0114	....	....	x---	----	----	x---	----	0	
	East rift zone (230-950 m)	**1840**	0530	**1840**	0625	--x-	----	----	xx--	-x--	0	8/-
	SW rift zone (775 m)	**1868**	0402?	....	....	--x-	----	x---	x---	----	1?	5/-
	East rift zone (-20? m)	**1884**	0122	**1884**	0122	--x-	x---	----	?---	----	0	
	Halemaumau	**1896**	0103	**1896**	0128	x---	----	----	-x--	----	0	
	Halemaumau	**1896**	0711	**1896**	0925e	x---	----	----	-x--	----	0	
	Halemaumau	**1897**	0624	**1897**	0627	x---	----	----	?---	----	0	
	Halemaumau	**1902**	0214<	**1902**	02	x---	----	----	x---	----	0	
	Halemaumau	**1902**	0603	**1903**	0305e	x---	----	----	-x--	----	0	
	Halemaumau	**1903**	1125	**1904**	0110	x---	----	----	-x--	----	0	
	Halemaumau	**1905**	0222	**1906**	04	x---	----	----	-x--	----	0	
	Halemaumau	**1906**	1202	**1924**	02	x---	----	----	-x--	----	0	
	Kilauea Caldera	**1918**	0223	**1918**	0309	x---	----	----	x---	----	0	5/-
	Kilauea Caldera	**1919**	0207	**1919**	1128	x---	----	----	x---	----	0	7/-
	SW rift zone (Mauna Iki, 915 m)	**1919**	1221	**1920**	0730	--x-	----	----	x---	----	0	7/-
	Kilauea Caldera	**1921**	0318	**1921**	0325	x---	----	----	x---	----	0	6/-
	East rift zone, Makaopuhi, Napau	**1922**	0528	**1922**	0530	-xx-	----	----	x---	----	0	6/-
	East rift zone (915 m)	**1923**	0825	**1923**	0825	--x-	----	----	x---	----	0	5/-
	Halemaumau	**1924**	0510	**1924**	0527	x---	----	x-x-	----	x---	2	-/5
	Halemaumau	**1924**	0719	**1924**	0729	x---	----	----	x---	----	0	5/-
	Halemaumau	**1927**	0707	**1927**	0720	x---	----	----	xx--	----	0	6/-
	(1927 lava squeezed out by rockfall)	*X 1928*	*0111*	*X1928*	*0111*	x---	----	----	----	----		
	Halemaumau	**1929**	0220	**1929**	0221	x---	----	----	xx--	----	0	6/-
	Halemaumau	**1929**	0725	**1929**	0728	x---	----	----	xx--	----	0	6/-
	Halemaumau	**1930**	1119	**1930**	1207	x---	----	----	xx--	----	0	6/-
	Halemaumau	**1931**	1223	**1932**	0105	x---	----	----	xx--	----	0	6/-
	Halemaumau	**1934**	0906	**1934**	1008	x---	----	----	xx--	----	0	6/-
	Halemaumau	**1952**	0627	**1952**	1110	x---	----	x---	xx--	----	0	7/-
	Halemaumau, Kilauea Caldera	**1954**	0531	**1954**	0603	x---	----	x---	xx--	----	0	6/-
	Lower east rift zone (50-400 m)	**1955**	0228	**1955**	0526	--x-	----	x-x-	x---	-x--	0	7/-
	Kilauea Iki	**1959**	1114	**1959**	1219	x---	----	x---	xx--	----	2	7/6
	East rift zone (near Kapoho, 30 m)	**1960**	0113	**1960**	0219	x-x-	----	x-x-	x---	-x--	2	8/-
	Halemaumau	**1961**	0224	**1961**	0224	x---	----	----	x---	----	1	5/-
	Halemaumau	**1961**	0303	**1961**	0325	x---	----	----	x---	----	1	5/-
	Halemaumau	**1961**	0710	**1961**	0717	x---	----	----	x---	----	1	7/-
	East rift zone (395-790 m)	**1961**	0922	**1961**	0924	--x-	----	----	x---	----	1	6/-
	East rift zone (945-990 m)	**1962**	1207	**1962**	1209	-xx-	----	----	xx--	----	0	5/-
	East rift zone (825-960 m)	**1963**	0821	**1963**	0823	-xx-	----	----	xx--	----	0	4/-
	East rift zone (700-840 m)	**1963**	1005	**1963**	1006	--x-	----	----	xx--	----	0	6/-
	East rift zone (700-915 m)	**1965**	0305	**1965**	0315	-xx-	----	----	xx--	----	0	7/-
	East rift zone (915-960 m)	**1965**	1224	**1965**	1225	--x-	----	----	x---	----	0	5/-
	Halemaumau	**1967**	1105	**1968**	0713	x-x-	----	----	xx--	----	0	7/-
	East rift zone (580-885 m)	**1968**	0822	**1968**	0826	--x-	----	----	xx--	----	0	4/-
	East rift zone (730-915 m)	**1968**	1007	**1968**	1022	--x-	----	----	x---	----	0	6/-
	East rift zone (885-945 m)	**1969**	0222	**1969**	0228	--x-	----	----	x---	-x--	0	7/-
	East rift zone (Mauna Ulu, 960 m)	**1969**	0524	**1974**	0722	-xx-	----	x---	xx--	-x--	0	8/-
	Kilauea Caldera	**1971**	0814	**1971**	0814	x---	----	----	x---	----	0	7/-
	Halemaumau and upper SW rift zone	**1971**	0924	**1971**	0929	x-x-	----	----	x---	-x--	0	6/-
	East rift zone, Pauahi, Hiiaka	**1973**	0505	**1973**	0505	--x-	----	----	x---	-x--	0	6/-
	East rift zone, Pauahi	**1973**	1110	**1973**	1209	-xx-	----	----	xx--	----	0	6/-
	Kilauea Caldera, Keanakakoi	**1974**	0719	**1974**	0722	xxx-	----	----	x---	-x--	0	6/-
	Kilauea Caldera (Halemaumau and to SW)	**1974**	0919	**1974**	0919	x-x-	----	----	x---	-x--	0	7/-
	SW rift zone (1095 m)	**1974**	1231	**1974**	1231	--x-	----	----	x---	----	0	6/-
	Kilauea Caldera, Halemaumau	**1975**	1129	**1975**	1129	x-x-	----	----	x---	----	0	5/-
	East rift zone (near Kalalua Crater)	**1977**	0913	**1977**	1001	--x-	----	----	x---	----	0	7/-
	East rift zone (Pauahi Crater)	**1979**	1116	**1979**	1117	--x-	----	----	x---	----	0	5/-
	East rift zone (near Mauna Ulu)	**1980**	0311	**1980**	0311	--x-	----	----	x---	----	0	0/-
	Kilauea Caldera (NE of Halemaumau)	**1982**	0430	**1982**	0501	x-x-	----	----	x---	----	0	5/-
	Kilauea Caldera (SSE of Halemaumau)	**1982**	0925	**1982**	0926	x---	----	----	x---	----	0	6/-
	East rift zone (Puu O'o), Halemaumau	**1983**	0103	**2010**>	....	--x-	----	x---	xx--	xx--	1*	9/-
Mauna Loa (Hawaii)	**19.475N** **155.608W** **4170** 2246 **B** **Shield volcano** **1302-02=** **Historical**											
	NE rift zone	C-**8050**?	....	....	....	--x-	----	----	x---	----	0	
	NE rift zone	C-**7850**?	....	....	....	--x-	----	----	x---	----	0	
	NE rift zone	C-**7550**?	....	....	....	--x-	----	----	x---	----	0	
	SW rift zone	C-**7350**?	....	....	....	--x-	----	----	x---	----	0	
	NE and SW rift zones	C-**7150**?	....	....	....	--x-	----	----	x---	----	0	
	NE rift zone	C-**6650**?	....	....	....	--x-	----	----	x---	----	0	
	Mokuaweoweo	C-**6550**?	....	....	....	x---	----	----	x---	----	0	
	NE rift zone	C-**6250**?	....	....	....	--x-	----	----	x---	----	0	
	NE and SW rift zones	C-**5850**?	....	....	....	--x-	----	----	x---	----	0	
	SW rift zone	C-**5650**?	....	....	....	--x-	----	----	x---	----	0	
	SW rift zone	C-**5350**?	....	....	....	--x-	----	----	x---	----	0	
	SW rift zone	C-**4250**?	....	....	....	--x-	----	----	x---	----	0	
	NE rift zone	C-**3750**?	....	....	....	--x-	----	----	x---	----	0	
	NE rift zone	C-**3350**?	....	....	....	--x-	----	----	x---	----	0	
	SW rift zone	C-**3250**?	....	....	....	--x-	----	----	x---	----	0	
	NE and SW rift zones	C-**2750**?	....	....	....	--x-	----	----	x---	----	0	
	Mokuaweoweo	C-**2350**?	....	....	....	x---	----	----	x---	----	0	
	NE rift zone	C-**2250**?	....	....	....	--x-	----	----	x---	----	0	
	NE rift zone	C-**2150**?	....	....	....	--x-	----	----	x---	----	0	

VOLCANO NAME (Subregion) ..... LAT / LONG / ELEV (m) / POPL (5 km, 10, 30, 100) / ROCK TYPE / VOLC TYPE / NUMBER / STATUS — ERUPTION — Area of Activity	Start Year	Start M-Dy	Stop Year	Stop M-Dy	Central / Flank vent / Radial fiss / Regional	Submarine / New island / Subglacial / Crater lake	Explosive / Pyro flow / Phreatic / Caldera	Lava flow / Lava lake / Dome / Spine	Fatal / Damage / Mudflow / Tsunami	VEI	Vol L/T
Mauna Loa (Hawaii) *continued*											
Mokuaweoweo	C-**2050**?	....	....	....	x---	----	----	x---	----	0	
SW rift zone	C-**2000**?	....	....	....	--x-	----	----	x---	----	0	
SW rift zone	C-**1900**?	....	....	....	--x-	----	----	x---	----	0	
NW and SW rift zones	C-**1800**?	....	....	....	--x-	----	----	x---	----	0	
NE rift zone	C-**1750**?	....	....	....	--x-	----	----	x---	----	0	
SW rift zone	C-**1700**?	....	....	....	--x-	----	----	x---	----	0	
NE and SW rift zones	C-**1650**?	....	....	....	--x-	----	----	x---	----	0	
Mokuaweoweo and NE rift zone	C-**1300**?	....	....	....	x-x-	----	----	x---	----	0	
Mokuaweoweo	C-**0950**?	....	....	....	x---	----	----	x---	----	0	
NE rift zone	C-**0600**?	....	....	....	--x-	----	----	x---	----	0	
SW rift zone	C-**0500**?	....	....	....	--x-	----	----	x---	----	0	
SW rift zone	C-**0400**?	....	....	....	--x-	----	----	x---	----	0	
NE rift zone	C-**0300**?	....	....	....	--x-	----	----	x---	----	0	
NE rift zone	C-**0200**?	....	....	....	--x-	----	----	x---	----	0	
SE rift zone	C-**0080**?	....	....	....	--x-	----	----	x---	----	0	
Mokuaweoweo	C-**0060**?	....	....	....	x---	----	----	x---	----	0	
NE and SW rift zones	C-**0030**?	....	....	....	--x-	----	----	x---	----	0	
NE rift zone	C **0050**?	....	....	....	--x-	----	----	x---	----	0	
SE rift zone	C **0100**?	....	....	....	--x-	----	----	x---	----	0	
SE rift zone	C **0150**?	....	....	....	--x-	----	----	x---	----	0	
Mokuaweoweo	C **0200**?	....	....	....	x---	----	----	x---	----	0	
NE rift zone	C **0300**?	....	....	....	--x-	----	----	x---	----	0	
Mokuaweoweo	C **0350**?	....	....	....	x---	----	----	x---	----	0	
NE rift zone	C **0450**?	....	....	....	--x-	----	----	x---	----	0	
Mokuaweoweo	C **0480**?	....	....	....	x---	----	----	x---	----	0	
Mokuaweoweo	C **0550**?	....	....	....	x---	----	----	x---	----	0	
Mokuaweoweo	C **0600**?	....	....	....	x---	----	----	x---	----	0	
NE rift zone	C **0630**?	....	....	....	--x-	----	----	x---	----	0	
Mokuaweoweo	C **0680**?	....	....	....	x---	----	----	x---	----	0	
Mokuaweoweo	C **0810**?	....	....	....	x---	----	----	x---	----	0	
Mokuaweoweo and NW flank	C **0830**?	....	....	....	x-x-	----	----	x---	----	0	
NE rift zone	C **0940**?	....	....	....	--x-	----	----	x---	----	0	
NE rift zone	C **1040**?	....	....	....	--x-	----	----	x---	----	0	
NE rift zone	C **1070**?	....	....	....	--x-	----	----	x---	----	0	
SW rift zone	C **1130**?	....	....	....	--x-	----	----	x---	----	0	
NE rift zone	C **1170**?	....	....	....	--x-	----	----	x---	----	0	
NE rift zone and Mokuaweoweo	C **1190**?	....	....	....	--x-	----	----	x---	----	0	
SW rift zone	C **1310**?	....	....	....	--x-	----	----	x---	----	0	
NE rift zone	C **1360**?	....	....	....	--x-	----	----	x---	----	0	
NE rift zone and Mokuaweoweo	C **1370**?	....	....	....	x-x-	----	----	x---	----	0	
NE rift zone	C **1390**?	....	....	....	--x-	----	----	x---	----	0	
NE rift zone and NW flank	C **1440**?	....	....	....	--x-	----	----	x---	----	0	
NE rift zone	C **1470**?	....	....	....	--x-	----	----	x---	----	0	
NE rift zone	C **1500**?	....	....	....	--x-	----	----	x---	----	0	
NE rift zone	C **1510**?	....	....	....	--x-	----	----	x---	----	0	
NE rift zone	C **1540**?	....	....	....	--x-	----	----	x---	----	0	
NE rift zone	C **1640**?	....	....	....	--x-	----	----	x---	----	0	
NE rift zone	C **1650**?	....	....	....	--x-	----	----	x---	----	0	
NW flank	C **1680**?	....	....	....	--x-	----	----	x---	----	0	
NE rift zone	C **1685**?	....	....	....	--x-	----	----	x---	----	0	
NE rift zone	C **1730**?	....	....	....	--x-	----	----	x---	----	0	
North flank (2380 m) and SW rift zone?	**1750**?	....	....	....	--x-	----	----	x---	----	0	
Mokuaweoweo and adjacent vents	**1832**	0620	**1832**	0715g	x-x-	----	----	x---	----	0	7/-
North flank, Mokuaweoweo and NE rift	**1843**	0109	**1843**	0410?	x-x-	----	----	x---	----	0	8/-
Mokuaweoweo	**1849**	05	....	....	x---	----	----	x---	----	0	7/-
Mokuaweoweo and SW rift zone	**1851**	0808	**1851**	0811a	x-x-	----	----	x---	----	0	7/-
NE rift zone (2560 m) and Mokuaweoweo	**1852**	0217	**1852**	0311?	x-x-	----	x---	x---	----	2	8/-
NE rift zone (3200 m) and Mokuaweoweo	**1855**	0811	**1856**	11	--x-	----	x---	x---	----	1	8/-
North flank (2800 m) and Mokuaweoweo	**1859**	0123	**1859**	1125	--x-	----	----	x---	-x--	1	8/-
Mokuaweoweo	**1865**	1230	**1866**	0429?	x---	----	----	x---	----	0	7/-
SW rift zone (1000 m) and Mokuaweoweo	**1868**	0327	**1868**	0422	x-x-	----	x---	x---	xx-x	2*	8/-
Mokuaweoweo	? *1870*	*0101*?	?*1870*	*0115*?	x---	----	----	?---	----	*0*	
Mokuaweoweo	**1871**	0810	**1871**	0830?	x---	----	----	x---	----	0	7/-
Mokuaweoweo	**1872**	0809	**1872**	09	x---	----	----	x---	----	1	
Mokuaweoweo	**1873**	0106	**1873**	0107?	x---	----	----	x---	----	0	
Mokuaweoweo	**1873**	0420	**1874**	1019?	x---	----	----	x---	----	1	
Mokuaweoweo	**1875**	0110	**1875**	0209?	x---	----	----	x---	----	0	
Mokuaweoweo	**1875**	0811	**1875**	0818?	x---	----	----	x---	----	0	
Mokuaweoweo	**1876**	0213	**1876**	0214?	x---	----	----	x---	----	0	
Mokuaweoweo, submarine west flank	**1877**	0214	**1877**	0224	x-x-	x---	----	x---	----	0	6/-
Mokuaweoweo	**1879**	0309	**1879**	0309?	x---	----	----	x---	----	0	6/-
Mokuaweoweo	**1880**	0501	**1880**	0506	x---	----	----	x---	----	1	7/-
NE rift zone (3170 m)	**1880**	1105	**1881**	0810	--x-	----	x---	x---	-x--	1	8/-
SW rift zone (1740 m) and Mokuaweoweo	**1887**	0116	**1887**	0128?	x-x-	----	----	x---	-x--	0	8/-
Mokuaweoweo	**1892**	1130	**1892**	1203	x---	----	----	x---	----	0	7/-
Mokuaweoweo	**1896**	0421	**1896**	0506	x---	----	----	x---	----	0	7/-
NE rift zone (3260 m) and Mokuaweoweo	**1899**	0701	**1899**	0723	x-x-	----	x---	x---	----	1	7/-
Mokuaweoweo	**1903**	0901	**1903**	1207?	x---	----	----	x---	----	0	7/-
SW rift zone (1890 m) and Mokuaweoweo	**1907**	0109	**1907**	0124>	x-x-	----	----	x---	-x--	0	7/-
Mokuaweoweo	**1914**	1125	**1915**	0111	x---	----	----	x---	----	0	7/-
SW rift zone (3000 and 2250 m)	**1916**	0519	**1916**	0530	--x-	----	----	x---	-x--	0	7/-
SW rift zone (3450 and 2350 m)	**1919**	0926	**1919**	1105?	--x-	----	----	x---	-x--	0	8/-
SW rift (2320 m)	**1926**	0410	**1926**	0428?	--x-	----	----	x---	-x--	0	8/-
Mokuaweoweo	**1933**	1202	**1933**	1218	x-x-	----	----	x---	----	0	8/-
NE rift zone (3690 m) and Mokuaweoweo	**1935**	1121	**1936**	0102	x-x-	----	----	x---	-x--	0	7/-
Mokuaweoweo and SW rift zone	**1940**	0407	**1940**	0818	x-x-	----	x---	x---	----	0	8/-
NE rift zone (2800 m) and Mokuaweoweo	**1942**	0426	**1942**	0510	x-x-	----	x---	x---	----	0	8/-
Mokuaweoweo and SW rift zone	**1949**	0106	**1949**	0531	x-x-	----	x---	x---	----	0	8/-
SW rift zone (2440 m)	**1950**	0601	**1950**	0623	--x-	----	x---	x---	-x--	0	8/-
Mokuaweoweo and NE and SW rift zones,	**1975**	0705	**1975**	0706	x-x-	----	----	x---	----	0	7/-
Mokuaweoweo, SW and NE rift zones	**1984**	0325	**1984**	0415	x-x-	----	----	x---	----	0	8/-
Mauna Kea (Hawaii) .... **19.82 N 155.47 W 4205** 3346 **BYX Shield volcano 1302-03- Radiocarbon**											
North flank (Puu Kole)	C-**5150**w	....	....	....	-x--	----	x---	x---	----		
South rift zone (Puu Kalaieha)	C-**3680**x	....	....	....	-xx-	----	x---	x---	----		

VOLCANO NAME (Subregion) / ERUPTION — Area of Activity	LAT	LONG	ELEV (m)	POPL (5 km, 10, 30, 100)	ROCK TYPE	VOLC TYPE	NUMBER	STATUS	Start Year	Start M-Dy	Stop Year	Stop M-Dy	ERUPTIVE CHARACTERISTICS (Central, Flank vent, Radial fiss, Regional / Submarine, New island, Subglacial, Crater lake / Explosive, Pyro flow, Phreatic, Caldera / Lava flow, Lava lake, Dome, Spine / Fatal, Damage, Mudflow, Tsunami)	VEI	Vol L/T
Mauna Kea (Hawaii) *continued*															
SE flank (near Hale Pohaku, 2740 m)									C -3370w	....	....	....	-xx- ---- x--- x--- ----		
NE flank (Puu Kanakaleonui, 2930 m)									C -2750x	....	....	....	-x-- ---- x--- x--- ----		
South rift zone (Puu Kole)									C -2540x	....	....	....	-xx- ---- x--- x--- ----		
NE flank (Puu Lehu, 3130 m)									C -2460v	....	....	....	-x-- ---- x--- x--- ----		
Hualalai (Hawaii)	19.692 N	155.87 W	2523	5556	Bxt	Shield volcano	1302-04-	Historical							
									C -7540x	....	....	....	---- ---- ---- x--- ----	0	
Cone 60 m north of Hainoa Crater									C -6820x	....	....	....	x--- ---- ---- x--- ----	0	
SE rift zone (1.6 km SE of Hainoa)									C -4410v	....	....	....	--x- ---- ---- x--- ----	0	
									C -2770u	....	....	....	---- ---- ---- x--- ----	0	
NW rift zone (1 km W of Hainoa Crater)									C -2440u	....	....	....	--x- ---- ---- x--- ----	0	
NW rift zone (0.3 km NW of Hainoa)									C -2040u	....	....	....	--x- ---- ---- x--- ----	0	
									C -1650x	....	....	....	---- ---- ---- x--- ----	0	
NW rift zone (0.7 km NW of Luamakami)									C -1150u	....	....	....	--x- ---- ---- x--- ----	0	
									C -1080x	....	....	....	---- ---- ---- x--- ----	0	
North rift zone (700 m ENE of Hainoa)									C -0720u	....	....	....	--x- ---- ---- x--- ----	0	
North rift zone (3 km NE of Hainoa)									C -0440t	....	....	....	--x- ---- ---- x--- ----	0	
NW rift zone (Luamakami)									C -0400u	....	....	....	--x- ---- ---- x--- ----	0	
SE flank (1 km west of Waha Pehe)									C -0350u	....	....	....	-x-- ---- ---- x--- ----	0	
North rift zone (1130-1830 m)									C -0080u	....	....	....	--x- ---- ---- x--- ----	0	8/-
SSE rift zone (4.5 km NW of Waha Pele									C 0770x	....	....	....	--x- ---- ---- x--- ----	1	8/-
NW rift zone (2 km NW of Luamakami)									C 0920t	....	....	....	--x- ---- ---- x--- ----	0	
SSE rift zone (3 km NE of Waha Pele)									C 1050v	....	....	....	--x- ---- ---- x--- ----	1	8/-
NW rift zone (Puu Alauawa, Nahaha)									T 1150?	....	....	....	--x- ---- ---- x--- ----	0	
SSE rift zone (Waha Pele)									C 1240w	....	....	....	--x- ---- --x- x--- ----	2	8/-
NW rift zone (Luamakami)									C 1650t	....	....	....	--x- ---- --x- x--- ----	1	
NW rift zone (1400-1900 m, Kaupulehu flow)									1784g	....	....	....	--x- ---- ---- x--- ?x--	0	8/-
NW rift zone (520 m, Huehue flow)									1800	....	1801	....	--x- ---- ---- x--- ?x--	0	7/-
Haleakala (Hawaii)	20.708 N	156.25 W	3055	5556	BX	Shield volcano	1302-06-	Anthropology							
SW rift zone (~1800 m)									G -7950x	....	....	....	--x- ---- x--- x--- ----		
East rift zone (Kuhiwa flow)									C -7570u	....	....	....	--x- ---- x--- x--- ----		
East rift zone									C -7450y	....	....	....	--x- ---- ---- x--- ----		
Upper SW rift zone									G -7210?	....	....	....	--x- ---- x--- x--- ----		
SW rift zone (W of Kanahau)									C -6760s	....	....	....	--x- ---- ---- x--- ----		
SW rift zone (Waiohuli flow)									C -6700v	....	....	....	--x- ---- ---- x--- ----		
SW rift zone (Kanahau flow)									C -6220t	....	....	....	--x- ---- ---- x--- ----		
East rift zone (Lo'alo'a flow)									C -6030s	....	....	....	--x- ---- ---- x--- ----		
East rift zone									C -5860s	....	....	....	--x- ---- ---- x--- ----		
									C -4760s	....	....	....	---- ---- x--- ---- ----		
East rift zone									C -3070s	....	....	....	--x- ---- x--- ---- ----		
									C -2580s	....	....	....	---- ---- x--- ---- ----		
SW rift zone (~2000 m)									G -2470t	....	....	....	--x- ---- x--- x--- ----		8/-
East rift zone (East Camp cone)									C -2260s	....	....	....	--x- ---- x--- ---- ----		
East rift zone									C -2210s	....	....	....	--x- ---- x--- ---- ----		
Haleakala crater (Puu Maile)									C -2120t	....	....	....	x-x- ---- x--- ---- ----		
SW rift zone									C -1940s	....	....	....	--x- ---- x--- ---- ----		
East rift zone (Wai'ele'ele flow)									C -1900t	....	....	....	--x- ---- ---- x--- ----		
SW rift zone (~1600 m)									G -1850?	....	....	....	--x- ---- x--- x--- ----		7/-
Haleakala crater									C -1800t	....	....	....	x-x- ---- x--- ---- ----		
Upper SW rift zone (~2600 m)									G -1310?	....	....	....	--x- ---- x--- x--- ----		7/-
Upper SW rift zone (~2800 m)									G -1240?	....	....	....	--x- ---- x--- x--- ----		6/-
SW rift zone (Auwahi flow)									C -1140r	....	....	....	--x- ---- ---- x--- ----		
Haleakala crater									C -0580t	....	....	....	x-x- ---- x--- ---- ----		
North crater wall									C -0390s	....	....	....	x-x- ---- ---- x--- ----		
SW rift zone (~2400 m)									G -0290?	....	....	....	--x- ---- x--- x--- ----		7/-
Haleakala crater									C 0080s	....	....	....	x-x- ---- x--- ---- ----		
Haleakala crater (Puu Nole)									C 0790t	....	....	....	x-x- ---- ---- x--- ----		
Haleakala crater (Kalua Awa flow)									C 0910s	....	....	....	x-x- ---- ---- x--- ----		
Haleakala crater (Puu o ka O'o)									C 0980t	....	....	....	x-x- ---- x--- x--- ----		
East rift zone (Puu Hina'i, Ka'eleku flows)									C 0990t	....	....	....	--x- ---- ---- x--- ----		
Haleakala crater (Halali'i)									C 1010s	....	....	....	x-x- ---- x--- x--- ----		
SW rift zone (Mauka flow)									C 1020t	....	....	....	--x- ---- ---- x--- ----		
North crater wall (Hanakauhi flow)									C 1080s	....	....	....	x-x- ---- ---- x--- ----		
SW rift zone (~1200 m)									G 1200u	....	....	....	--x- ---- x--- x--- ----		7/-
SW rift zone (Keonehunehune flow, ~1500 m)									G 1350w	....	....	....	--x- ---- x--- x--- ----		5/-
SW rift zone (Makua flow, ~1600 m)									G 1360v	....	....	....	--x- ---- x--- x--- ----		
SW rift zone									G 1420v	....	....	....	--x- ---- x--- x--- ----		
East rift zone (Kawaipapa lava flow)									C 1460u	....	....	....	--x- ---- ---- x--- ----		
SW rift zone (Kalua o Lapa flow, 180-360 m)									A 1750?	....	....	....	--x- ---- x--- x--- ----		8/-
Unnamed (Hawaii)	21.75 N	158.75 W	-3000	0006	U	Submarine volc ?	1302-08-	Uncertain							
									? 1956	*0522*	*?1956*	*0523*	---- ?--- ?--- ---- ----	*0*	
Unnamed (Hawaii)	23.58 N	163.83 W	-4000	0000	U	Submarine volc	1302-09-	Historical							
90 km NE of Necker Island									1955	0820	1955	0822?	---- x--- x--- ---- ---x	0	

PACIFIC OCEAN - E & S

VOLCANO NAME (Subregion) / ERUPTION — Area of Activity	LAT	LONG	ELEV (m)	POPL (5 km, 10, 30, 100)	ROCK TYPE	VOLC TYPE	NUMBER	STATUS	Start Year	Start M-Dy	Stop Year	Stop M-Dy	ERUPTIVE CHARACTERISTICS	VEI	Vol L/T
Teahitia (Society Is-C Pacific)	17.57 S	148.85 W	-1400	0006	XB	Submarine volc	1303-01-	Seismicity							
									S 1982	0316	S1982	0519	---- x--- ---- ---- ----	0	
									S 1983	0712	S1983	0726	---- x--- ---- ---- ----	0	
									S 1983	1218	S1984	0714	---- x--- ---- ---- ----	0	
									S 1985	0110	S1985	0125	---- x--- ---- ---- ----	0	
Rocard (Society Is-C Pacific)	17.642 S	148.60 W	-2100	0005	TB	Submarine volc	1303-02-	Seismicity							
									S 1966	0309	S1966	0320	---- x--- ---- ---- ----	0	
									S 1971	0906	....	....	---- x--- ---- ---- ----	0	
									S 1972	0704	S1972	0719	---- x--- ---- ---- ----	0	
Moua Pihaa (Society Is-C Pacific)	18.32 S	148.67 W	-160	0005	X	Submarine volc	1303-03-	Seismicity							
									S 1969	0422	S1969	0429	---- x--- ---- ---- ----	0	
									S 1970	0621	S1970	0623	---- x--- ---- ---- ----	0	
Mehetia (Society Is-C Pacific)	17.87 S	148.07 W	435	3333	XBz	Stratovolcano	1303-04-	Anthropology							
SE of Mehetia (-1700 m?)									*? 1981*	*0305*	*?1981*	*12*	---- ?--- ---- ---- ----	*0*	
Adams Seamount (Pacific-C)	25.37 S	129.27 W	-39	0002	BXTya	Submarine volc	1303-05-	Potassium-Argon							
									K -5050*	....	....	....	---- ---- ---- x--- ----	0	
									K -4050*	....	....	....	---- ---- ---- x--- ----	0	

VOLCANO NAME (Subregion) / **ERUPTION** — Area of Activity	LAT	LONG	ELEV (m)	POPL 5 km 10 30 100	ROCK TYPE	VOLC TYPE / — Start — Year	NUMBER / M-Dy	STATUS / — Stop — Year	M-Dy	Central Flank vent Radial fiss Regional	Submarine New island Subglacial Crater lake	Explosive Pyro flow Phreatic Caldera	Lava flow Lava lake Dome Spine	Fatal Damage Mudflow Tsunami	VEI	Vol L/T
Adams Seamount (Pacific-C) *continued*						K-1050*	....	....	....	----	----	----	x---	----	0	
						K-0050*	....	....	....	----	----	----	x---	----	0	
Macdonald (Austral Is-C Pacific)	28.98 S	140.25 W	-39	0000	BXy	**Submarine volc**	1303-06-	**Historical**								
(pumice rafts in South Pacific)						@ **1928**	....	....	....	----	x---	x---	----	----	0?	
(pumice rafts in South Pacific)						@ **1936**	....	....	....	----	x---	x---	----	----	0?	
						S **1967**	0529	S**1967**	0529	----	x---	----	----	----	0	
						S **1977**	1210	S**1977**	1215	----	x---	----	----	----	0	
						S **1979**	0930	S**1979**	0930	----	x---	----	----	----	0	
						S **1980**	0212	S**1980**	0213	----	x---	----	----	----	0	
						S **1980**	1110	S**1981**	0215	----	x---	----	----	----	0	
						S **1982**	0301	S**1982**	0606	----	x---	----	----	----	0	
						S **1983**	0314	S**1983**	0521	----	x---	----	----	----	0	
						S **1983**	1027	S**1984**	0103	----	x---	----	----	----	0	
						S **1986**	0516	S**1986**	0802	----	x---	----	----	----	0	
						1987	0604	**1989**	0128>	----	x---	x---	----	----	0	
Northern EPR-Segment RO2	16.55 N	105.32 W	-2700	0000	B	**Submarine volc**	1304-02-	**Magnetism**								
16.80 deg N						M-0050*	....	....	....	---x	x---	----	x---	----	0	
Northern EPR-Segment RO3	15.83 N	105.43 W	-2300	0000	B	**Submarine volc**	1304-021	**Magnetism**								
						M-0050*	....	....	....	---x	x---	----	x---	----	0	
Unnamed (East Pacific Rise)	10.73 N	103.58 W		0000	B	**Submarine volc**	1304-04-	**Historical**								
						2003	05 ?	**2003**	11	---x	x---	----	x---	----	0	
Unnamed (East Pacific Rise)	9.83 N	104.30 W	-2500	0000	B	**Submarine volc**	1304-05-	**Historical**								
EPR axis and East and West of axis						U-**5050***	....	....	....	---x	x---	----	x---	----	0	
East Pacific Rise (9.5 deg N)						U-**4050***	....	....	....	---x	x---	----	x---	----	0	
EPR axis and East of axis						U-**3050***	....	....	....	---x	x---	----	x---	----	0	
East Pacific Rise (9.5 deg N)						U-**2050***	....	....	....	---x	x---	----	x---	----	0	
East Pacific Rise (9.5 deg N)						U-**1050***	....	....	....	---x	x---	----	x---	----	0	
East Pacific Rise (9.5 deg N)						U-**0050***	....	....	....	---x	x---	----	x---	----	0	
East Pacific Rise (9.9 deg N)						U **0850**x	....	....	....	---x	x---	----	x---	----	0	
East Pacific Rise (9.5 deg N)						U **0950***	....	....	....	---x	x---	----	x---	----	0	
East Pacific Rise (9.8 deg N)						U **1200**y	....	....	....	---x	x---	----	x---	----	0	
East Pacific Rise (9.9 deg N)						U **1600**w	....	....	....	---x	x---	----	x---	----	0	
East Pacific Rise (9.8 deg N)						U **1650**v	....	....	....	---x	x---	----	x---	----	0	
East Pacific Rise (9.9 deg N)						M **1875**<	....	....	....	---x	x---	----	x---	----	0	
East Pacific Rise (9.9 deg N)						M **1950**?	....	....	....	---x	x---	----	x---	----	0	
East Pacific Rise (9.3 deg N)						**1988**a	....	....	....	---x	x---	----	x---	----	0	4/-
East Pacific Rise (9.8 deg N)						**1991**	03 ?	....	....	---x	x---	----	x---	----	0	6/-
East Pacific Rise (9.9 deg N)						**1991**	1201p	**1992**	0204p	---x	x---	----	x---	----	0	
East Pacific Rise (9.8 deg N)						**2005**	08 ?	**2006**	01 ?	---x	x---	----	x---	----	0	
Galápagos Rift (Pacific-E)	0.792 N	86.15 W	-2430	0000	B	**Submarine volc**	1304-07-	**Historical**								
Galápagos Rift (Clambake vent area)						**1972**	0629a	....	....	----	x---	----	x---	----		
						1996f	....	....	....	---x	x---	----	x---	----	0	
Unnamed (East Pacific Rise)	8.27 S	107.95 W	-2800	0000	B	**Submarine volc**	1304-10-	**Historical**								
East Pacific Rise (8.3 deg S)						**1964**?	....	**1969**?	....	?--?	x---	----	x---	----	0	**10/-**
Southern EPR-Segment K	17.436 S	113.206 W	-2566	0000	B	**Submarine volc**	1304-12-	**Historical**								
(South of Aldo-Kihi lava flow)						M **1625**?	....	....	....	---x	x---	----	x---	----	0	
(North of Aldo-Kiri lava flow)						M **1840**?	....	....	....	x--x	----	----	x---	----	0	
(North of Aldo-Kiri lava flow)						M **1930**?	....	....	....	x--x	----	----	x---	----	0	
(South of Aldo-Kihi lava flow)						M **1965**?	....	....	....	x--x	----	----	x---	----	0	
(Aldo-Kihi lava flow)						**1990**b	....	....	....	---x	x---	----	x---	----	0	8/-
Southern EPR-Segment J	18.175 S	113.35 W	-2650	0000	B	**Submarine volc**	1304-13-	**Magnetism**								
						M **1820**?	....	....	....	---x	x---	----	x---	----	0	
						M **1890**?	....	....	....	---x	x---	----	x---	----	0	
Southern EPR-Segment I	18.53 S	113.42 W	-2600	0000	B	**Submarine volc**	1304-14-	**Magnetism**								
(Northern South Hump lava flow)						M **1620**?	....	....	....	---x	x---	----	x---	----	0	
(Southern South Hump lava flow)						M **1860**?	....	....	....	---x	x---	----	x---	----	0	
(Animal Farm lava flow)						M **1915**s	....	....	....	---x	x---	----	x---	----	0	8/-
Antipodes Island (Pacific-S)	49.68 S	178.77 E	402	0000	BX	**Pyroclastic cones**	1305-01-	Holocene?								
Unnamed (Pacific-S)	53.90 S	140.30 W	-1000	0000	U	**Submarine volc**	1305-02-	Uncertain								
Seamount by Pacific-Antarctic Ridge?						*? 1991*	*0311*	*?1991*	*0319*	----	?---	----	----	----	*0*	
Unnamed (Pacific-S)	55.97 S	143.17 W		0000	U	**Submarine volc**	1305-03-	Uncertain								
Udinstev Fracture Zone						*? 1990*	*1029*	*?1990*	*1119*	----	?---	----	----	----	*0*	

Don Peterson (USGS/HVO)

This 1975 photo of the snow-covered summit of 4170-m-high Mauna Loa volcano on the island of Hawaii shows the 2.4 x 4.8 km Mokuaweoweo caldera in the center, with three circular pit craters and linear fissure vents in the foreground. Mauna Kea shield volcano rises across a broad saddle to a height of 4206 m in the distance.

Ridge2004 (NSF/WHOI)

Smoke pours from a "black smoker" vent chimney at 9 degrees North on the East Pacific Rise during a 2004 expedition. Hot-vent animal communities such as in the foreground that had been documented in 1989 were buried by fresh basaltic lava flows in 1991. A 2005-2006 eruption produced lava flows that entrapped previously emplaced seismometers.

México & Central America (14)

106°
100°
95°
117°
111°
22°
20°
14°
33°
30°
26°
1401-023
024
03= Ceboruco
Guadalajara
031
MEXICO
GULF of MEXICO
Michoacán-Guanajuato
06=
Zitácuaro-Valle de Bravo
062
México City
Cofre de Perote
093
094
095
096
097
098
10=
Colima
04=
061
081
082
091
092
Nevado de Toluca
07-
Chichinautzin
08=
09=
Puebla
Popocatépetl
Pico de Orizaba
San Martín 11=
1401-00-
001
Pinacate
002
003
004
005
007
008
BAJA
Tres Vírgenes 01=
011
0 km 200
012
110°
100°
91°
0 km 1000
30°
MEXICO
1401-022
Bárcena 02=
Socorro 021
20°
Acapulco
Villahermosa
12= El Chichón
PACIFIC OCEAN
0 km 300
Tacaná 13=
GUATEMALA

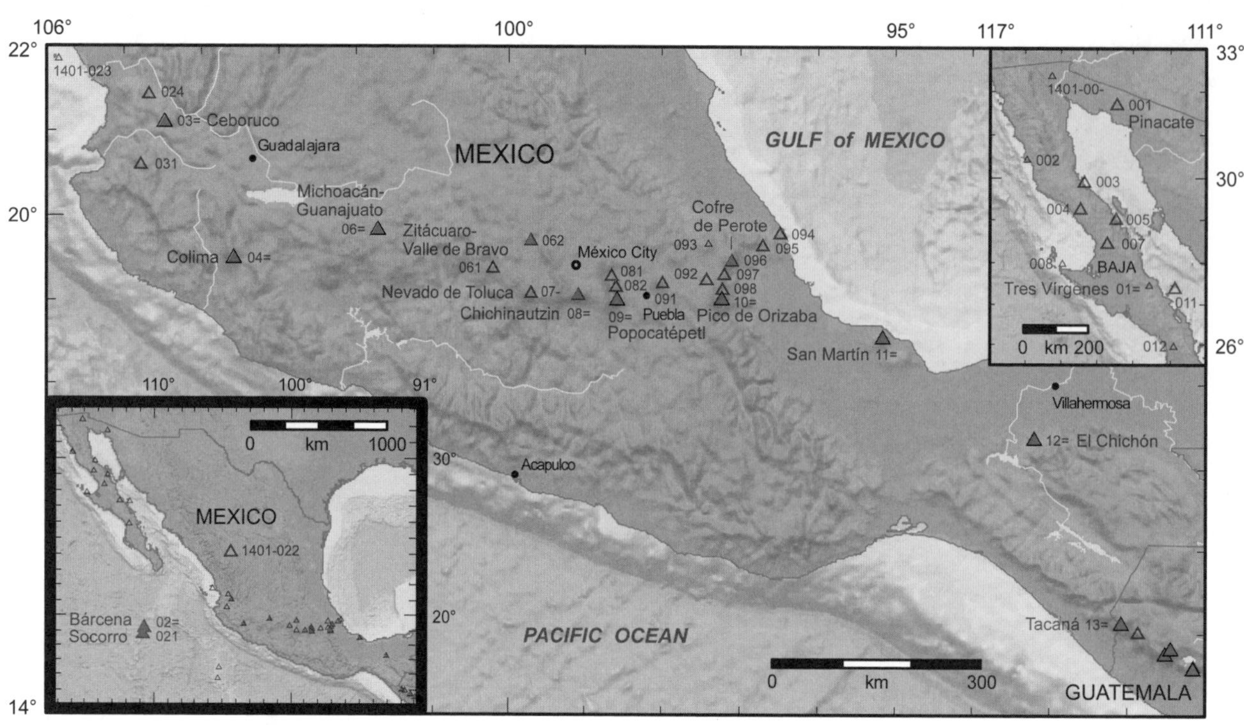

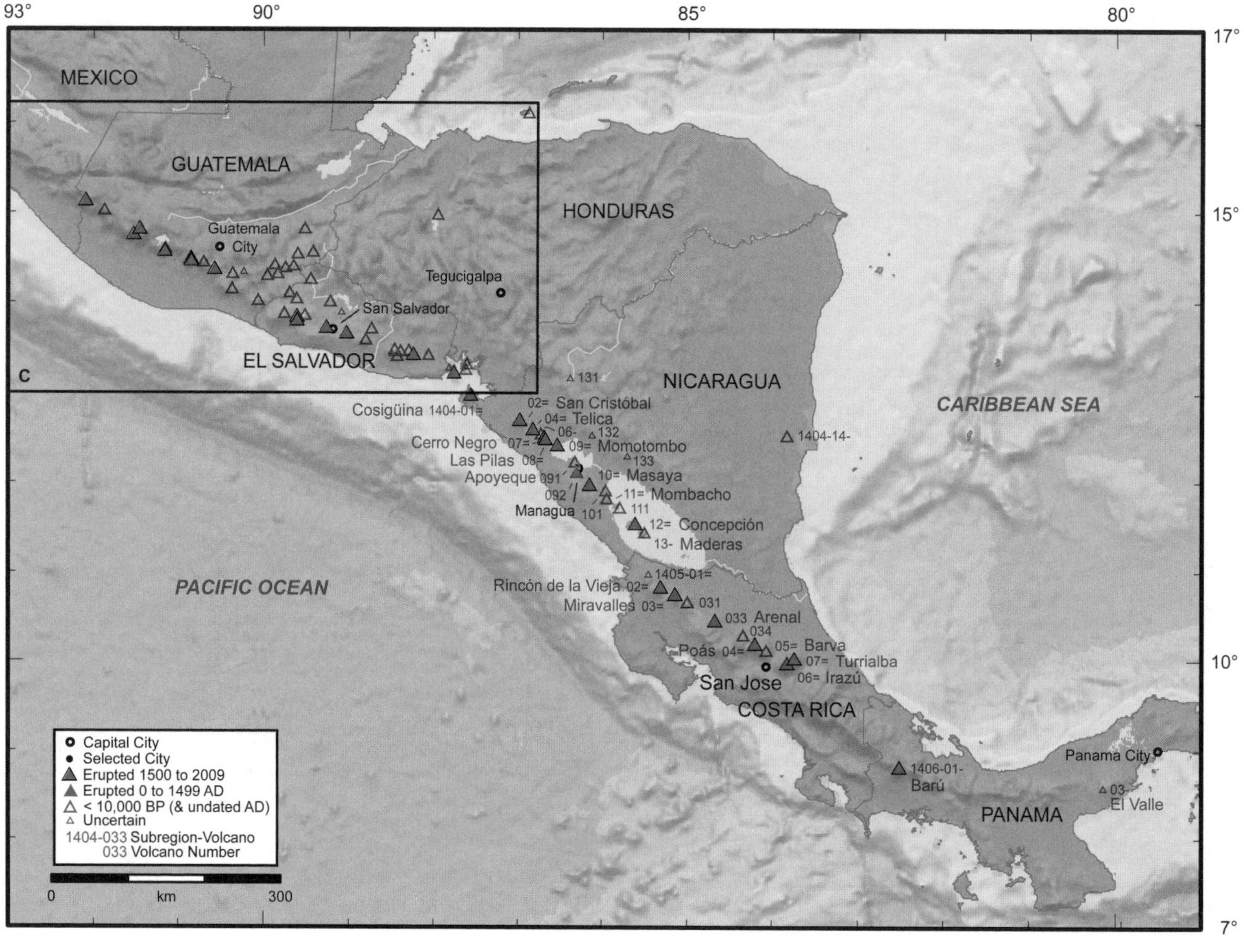

93°
90°
85°
80°
17°
15°
10°
7°
MEXICO
GUATEMALA
Guatemala City
HONDURAS
Tegucigalpa
San Salvador
EL SALVADOR
C
131
NICARAGUA
CARIBBEAN SEA
02= San Cristóbal
Cosigüina 1404-01=
04= Telica
06-
132
Cerro Negro 07=
09= Momotombo
Las Pilas 08=
133
1404-14-
Apoyeque 091
10= Masaya
092
11= Mombacho
Managua
101
111
12= Concepción
13- Maderas
PACIFIC OCEAN
1405-01=
Rincón de la Vieja 02=
Miravalles 03=
031
033 Arenal
034
Poás 04=
05= Barva
07= Turrialba
San Jose
06= Irazú
COSTA RICA
Capital City
Selected City
Erupted 1500 to 2009
Erupted 0 to 1499 AD
< 10,000 BP (& undated AD)
Uncertain
1404-033 Subregion-Volcano
033 Volcano Number
1406-01-
Barú
Panama City
03-
El Valle
PANAMA
0 km 300

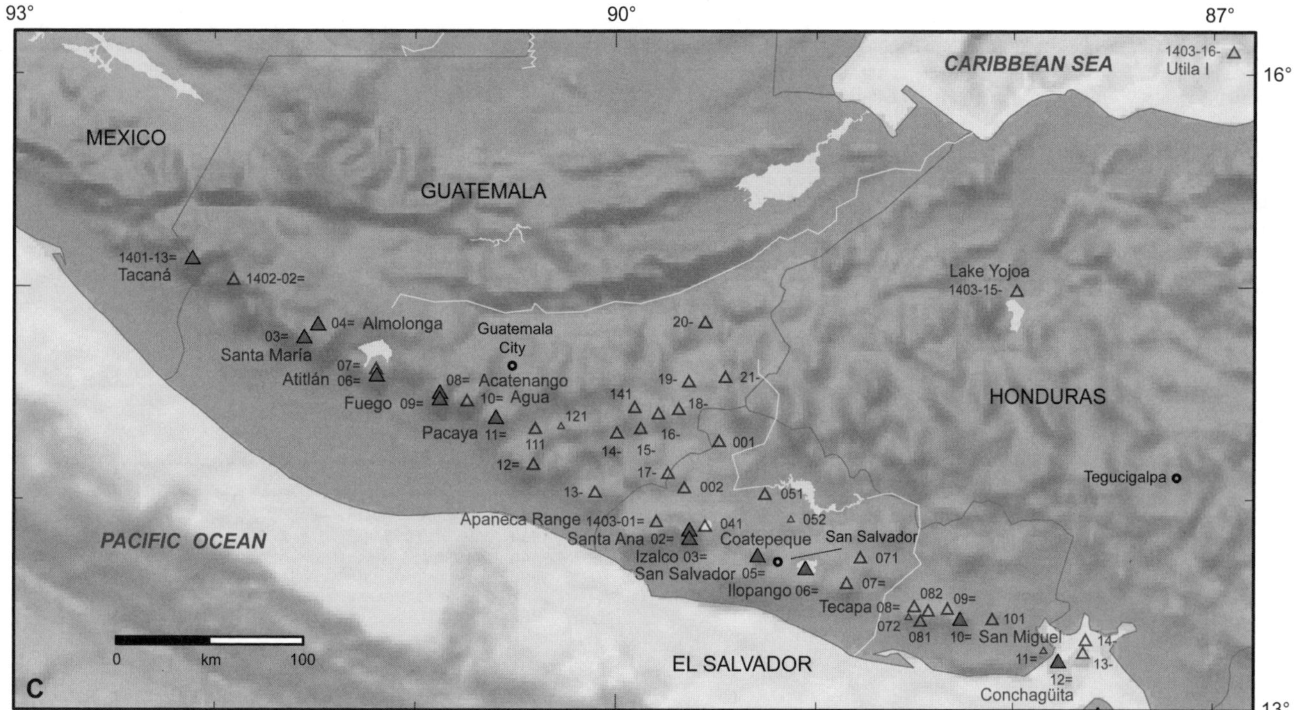

Originally designated "Central America" by *CAVW* organizers, this region also includes México. México dominates the region in both population (75%) and land area (80%), and the region's total population ranks it 5th among *CAVW* regions. The Holocene volcanoes of México and Central America, combined with those of South America and the Canary Islands, total 320, meaning that Spanish is spoken around more volcanoes than any other language.

México's early civilizations built the largest city in the Americas and pyramids larger than Egypt's in the second century AD. In 700 AD the Mayans were flourishing from Yucatan to the Pacific, but this civilization fell 200 years later. To the north, though, in the fertile central valley of México, the Toltecs were building the most highly developed pre-Columbian civilization in Latin America. From the mid-12th century the Aztecs dominated, and the first documented new world eruption (Popocatépetl, in 1345) was recorded in the Aztec codices. A population as large as 15 million was present in 1519, when Cortez and 600 conquistadores landed, but within two years the Spaniards had killed the Aztec king and captured their principal city. The spread of the Spanish empire over the region was swift, and most early documentation of volcanism was by Catholic priests.

To the south, Columbus had made the first European landfall on the Caribbean coast of Costa Rica in 1502, and Balboa first sighted the Pacific, at Panama, in 1513. The Kingdom of Guatemala (so known since 1549) was the political heart of Spanish rule in Central America, and had its largest population. Guatemala declared independence from Spain in 1821, along with the other Central American countries. The region has not been free of political unrest, and the quality of volcano reporting has varied in space and time.

Volcanism has had important impacts on the region. As was learned with the 1982 eruption of El Chichón (and the even larger ~450 AD eruption of Ilopango in El Salvador), the region produces large explosive eruptions. Only Japan and Kamchatka have higher numbers of volcanoes with average VEIs of 3 or larger, only Indonesia, South America and Japan have had more VEI $\geq$4 eruptions in the last 200 years, and only Indonesia has suffered more volcanic death tolls exceeding one thousand (see FATALITIES). El Chichón volcano, which last erupted in 1982, devastating adjacent towns and villages and producing ash and volcanic aerosols that circled the globe, has the 2nd highest average VEI (4.5) of any volcano in the world with 5 or more 5 VEI assignments.

Reflecting the strong archeological interest in México and Central America, this region trails only Region 01 for the largest number of eruptions dated archeologically (9 and 7 dates, respectively). Explosive eruptions and associated lahars from Popocatépetl volcano and lava flows from the Xitle cinder cone of the Sierra de Chichinautzin volcanic field have impacted pre-Columbian sites in the Valley of México, and archeologists have documented the impact of an eruption on villages of a 17th century NW-flank vent of San Salvador volcano. Two of the world's best examples of the formation of "new volcanoes" took place in central México, when the Jorullo and Parícutin cinder cones were added to the vast Michoacán-Guanajuato volcanic field in 1759 and 1943. The explosive eruption of Guatemala's Santa María volcano in 1902 was one of the world's largest 20th century eruptions, producing ashfall as far away as México City.

Most active volcanoes in region 14 occur in belts produced by subduction of Pacific oceanic crust beneath the southern edge of the North American Plate and the western edge of the Caribbean Plate. Large stratovolcanoes and silicic calderas are found here, but the region also contains many basaltic volcanic fields, particularly in the central valley of México and along the Guatemala-El Salvador border. A few other active volcanic fields in northern México are related to extensional tectonics of the Basin and Range Province, which split the Baja California peninsula from the mainland. Mafic behind-the-arc volcanic fields of Holocene and Pleistocene age also lie east of the volcanic front along the Caribbean Sea lowlands in Honduras, Nicaragua, and Costa Rica.

Honduras was not included in the *CAVW*, but Honduran volcanoes of Holocene age have since been recognized along the main volcanic front of Central America. Rather than break the geographic sequence, we have added the Honduran volcanoes at the end of subregion 1403, so that these volcanoes at the volcanic front in the Gulf of Fonseca area follow immediately after their Salvadorian neighbors. The Lake Yojoa volcanic field north of Honduras' largest lake and Utilia Island in the Caribbean Sea off the northern coast of Honduras then follow before resuming with subregion 1404 at the volcanic front on the Nicaraguan side of the Gulf of Fonseca.

MÉXICO - NW

VOLCANO NAME (Subregion) / ERUPTION — Area of Activity	LAT	LONG	ELEV (m)	POPL (5 km, 10, 30, 100)	ROCK TYPE	VOLC TYPE	NUMBER	STATUS	Start Year	Start M-Dy	Stop Year	Stop M-Dy	Central / Flank vent / Radial fiss / Regional	Submarine / New island / Subglacial / Crater lake	Explosive / Pyro flow / Phreatic / Caldera	Lava flow / Lava lake / Dome / Spine	Fatal / Damage / Mudflow / Tsunami	VEI	Vol L/T
Prieto, Cerro (México-NW)	32.418 N	115.305 W	223	4567	DBAR	Lava dome	1401-00-	Holocene?											
Pinacate (México-NW)	31.772 N*	113.498 W	1200	2235	BXYTa	Cinder cones	1401-001	Holocene											
									? 1928	*0609*	....	....	----	----	?---	----	----		
									? 1934	*1231*	*?1935*	*0102?*	----	----	?---	----	----		
San Quintín Volc Field (Baja)	30.468 N*	115.996 W	260	5555	XB	Cinder cones	1401-002	Holocene?											
San Luis, Isla (México-Baja)	29.97 N	114.40 W	180	0135	RDABy	Tuff cone	1401-003	Holocene											
Jaraguay Volc Field (México-Baja)	29.33 N*	114.50 W	960	4445	AY	Cinder cones	1401-004	Holocene											
Coronado (México-Baja)	29.08 N	113.513 W	440	1245	U	Stratovolcano	1401-005	Fumarolic											
Guadalupe (Baja-W of)	29.07 N	118.28 W	1100	0000	YXBT	Shield volcano	1401-006	Holocene											
San Borja Volc Field (Baja)	28.50 N*	113.75 W	1360	3345	AYb	Cinder cones	1401-007	Holocene											
Unnamed (México-Baja)	28.00 N	115.00 W		0035	U	Submarine volc ?	1401-008	Uncertain											
									? 1953	*0720*	....	....	----	?---	----	----	----	*0*	
Tres Vírgenes (México-Baja)	27.470 N	112.591 W	1940	0335	AD	Stratovolcanoes	1401-01=	Holocene?											
									? 1746	*0525*m	....	....	x---	----	?---	----	----		
									? 1857	....	....	....	?---	----	----	----	----		
Tortuga, Isla (México-Baja)	27.43 N	111.88 W	210	0035	Ba	Shield volcano	1401-011	Holocene											
Comondú-La Purísima (Baja)	26.00 N*	111.92 W	780	4445	YAB	Volcanic field	1401-012	Holocene?											

MÉXICO - ISLANDS

VOLCANO NAME (Subregion) / ERUPTION — Area of Activity	LAT	LONG	ELEV (m)	POPL (5 km, 10, 30, 100)	ROCK TYPE	VOLC TYPE	NUMBER	STATUS	Start Year	Start M-Dy	Stop Year	Stop M-Dy	Central / Flank vent / Radial fiss / Regional	Submarine / New island / Subglacial / Crater lake	Explosive / Pyro flow / Phreatic / Caldera	Lava flow / Lava lake / Dome / Spine	Fatal / Damage / Mudflow / Tsunami	VEI	Vol L/T
Bárcena (Revillagigedo Islands)	19.30 N	110.82 W	332	0000	TXYRb	Cinder cones	1401-02=	Historical											
South end of Isla San Benedicto									1952	0801	1953	0224d	x-x-	----	xx--	x-x-	----	3	7/8
Socorro (Revillagigedo Islands)	18.78 N	110.95 W	1050	0000	TRXBY	Shield volcano	1401-021	Historical											
Lower SW flank (near Bahia Braithwaite)									C-3090z	....	....	....	-x--	----	x---	x---	----		
									? 1848	....	....	....	----	----	----	----	----	*2?*	
									? 1896	....	....	....	----	----	----	----	----	*2?*	
									? 1905	*01*	....	....	----	----	--?-	----	----	*2?*	
SW flank (west of Lomas Coloradas)									1951	0522	1951	0522	-x--	----	--x-	----	----	2?	
Submarine vent 3 km W of Punta Tosca									1993	0129	1994	0224d	-x--	x---	----	----	----	0	

MÉXICO - CENTRAL BELT & DURANGO

VOLCANO NAME (Subregion) / ERUPTION — Area of Activity	LAT	LONG	ELEV (m)	POPL (5 km, 10, 30, 100)	ROCK TYPE	VOLC TYPE	NUMBER	STATUS	Start Year	Start M-Dy	Stop Year	Stop M-Dy	Central / Flank vent / Radial fiss / Regional	Submarine / New island / Subglacial / Crater lake	Explosive / Pyro flow / Phreatic / Caldera	Lava flow / Lava lake / Dome / Spine	Fatal / Damage / Mudflow / Tsunami	VEI	Vol L/T
Durango Volc Field (México)	24.15 N*	104.45 W	2075	6666	XB	Cinder cones	1401-022	Holocene											
Isabel, Isla (México)	21.848 N	105.886 W	95		BX	Tuff cones	1401-023	Holocene?											
Sangangüey (México)	21.45 N	104.73 W	2340	3466	ADBXT	Stratovolcano	1401-024	Holocene											
									? 1742	....	....	....	-?--	----	?---	----	----		
Ceboruco (México)	21.125 N	104.508 W	2280	3557	ADryt	Stratovolcano	1401-03=	Historical											
(Jala Pumice)									C 0930x	....	....	....	x---	----	xx-x	----	----	6	-/10
									1542	....	....	....	?---	----	----	?---	----		
									1567	....	....	....	?---	----	----	?---	----		
Upper west flank									1870	0221	1875	....	-x--	----	x?--	x-x-	-x--	3	9/8
Mascota Volc Field (México)	20.62 N*	104.83 W	2560	5557	AXY	Cinder cones	1401-031	Holocene											
Colima (México)	19.514 N	103.62 W	3850	2367	Adxyb	Stratovolcanoes	1401-04=	Historical											
									C-7690z	....	....	....	x---	----	x--A	----	----		
									C-7420z	....	....	....	x---	----	xx--	----	----		
									C-6320x	....	....	....	x---	----	x---	----	----		
(tephra unit P)									G-5880x	....	....	....	x---	----	xx--	----	----		
									C-4960x	....	....	....	x---	----	x---	----	----		
									C-4500x	....	....	....	x---	----	x---	----	----		
(tephra units S,R)									G-4430y	....	....	....	x---	----	xx--	----	----		
(tephra unit T)									G-4110v	....	....	....	x---	----	x---	----	----		
(tephra unit U)									G-3600x	....	....	....	x---	----	xx--	----	----		
									G-3510x	....	....	....	x---	----	x---	----	----		
(tephra unit V)									G-3350y	....	....	....	x---	----	xx--	----	----		
(tephra unit W)									T-3270?	....	....	....	x---	----	x---	----	----		
(tephra units X,Y)									G-3180v	....	....	....	x---	----	xx--	----	----		
									C-3030t	....	....	....	x---	----	xx--	----	----		
									G-2800v	....	....	....	x---	----	xx--	----	----		
									C-2370w	....	....	....	x---	----	xx--	----	--x-	4?	-/8
									G-1940y	....	....	....	x---	----	xx-A	----	--x-		
									C-1890u	....	....	....	x---	----	x---	----	----		
									C-1450v	....	....	....	x---	----	x---	----	----		
									C-1320?	....	....	....	x---	----	xx--	----	----		
									G-1170x	....	....	....	x---	----	xx--	----	----		
									C-1140?	....	....	....	x---	----	xx--	----	----		
									G-0650x	....	....	....	x---	----	xx-A	----	----		
									G 0540w	....	....	....	x---	----	xx--	----	----		
									C 0730v	....	....	....	x---	----	xx--	----	----		
									G 1110x	....	....	....	x---	----	xx--	----	----		
									1519	....	1523	....	x---	----	x---	----	----	3?	
									1560	....	....	....	----	----	?---	----	----	2	
									1576	....	....	....	x---	----	xx--	----	xx--	3	
									1585	0110	....	....	x---	----	xx--	----	-x--	4	
									1590	0114	1590	0115	x---	----	xx--	----	x---	3	
									? 1602	....	....	....	x---	----	?---	----	----	*2?*	
									1606	1125	1606	1213>	x---	----	xx--	----	-x--	4*	
									1611	0415	1613	....	x---	----	xx--	----	----	3	
									1622	0608	1622	0609	x---	----	xx--	----	----	4	
									1690	....	....	....	x---	----	xx--	----	----	3?	
									1711	....	....	....	x---	----	x---	----	----	3?	
									1743	1022	....	....	x---	----	x---	----	----	2?	
									1744	....	....	....	x---	----	x---	----	-xx-	2	
									? 1749	....	....	....	x---	----	?---	----	----	*2*	
									1769	....	....	....	x---	----	x---	----	----	2?	
									1770	0310	1770	0312	x---	----	xx--	x---	-x--	3	

Jamie Allan (NSF)

Fuego de Colima (L) and Nevado de Colima

VOLCANO NAME (Subregion) / ERUPTION — Area of Activity	LAT	LONG	ELEV (m)	POPL (5 km, 10, 30, 100)	ROCK TYPE	VOLC TYPE	NUMBER	STATUS	Start Year	Start M-Dy	Stop Year	Stop M-Dy	Central / Flank vent / Radial fiss / Regional	Submarine / New island / Subglacial / Crater lake	Explosive / Pyro flow / Phreatic / Caldera	Lava flow / Lava lake / Dome / Spine	Fatal / Damage / Mudflow / Tsunami	VEI	Vol L/T
Colima (México) *continued*									**1771**	....	....	....	x---	----	xx--	----	----	3	
									1780	1126	....	....	x---	----	x---	----	----	2	
									1794	08	....	....	x---	----	x---	----	----	2	
									1795	03	**1795**	09	x---	----	x---	x---	----	2	
									1804	....	....	....	----	----	x---	----	----	2	
									1806	....	**1809**	....	x---	----	xx--	x---	----	2?	
									1818	0215	**1818**	0216?	x---	----	xx--	----	xx--	4	
									1819	....	....	....	x---	----	x---	----	----	1	
(crater filling and overflow discounted)									X *1866*	*0304*	X*1868*	....	x---	----	----	----	----		
NE flank (El Volcancito)									**1869**	0612	**1869**	0824>	xx--	----	x-x-	x-x-	----	3	8/-
NE flank (El Volcancito)									**1870**	....	**1871**	....	-x--	----	----	x-x-	----	0	
El Volcancito and main crater									**1872**	0226	**1873**	0327	xx--	----	xx--	x-x-	-x--	3*	
NE flank (El Volcancito)									**1874**	0612	....	....	-x--	----	x---	x-x-	----	1	
NE flank (El Volcancito)									**1875**	....	**1878**	....	-x--	----	x---	x-x-	----	1	
Summit vent and SW flank									**1879**	1223	**1880**	0430	xx--	----	xx--	x---	----	1	
									1880	1201p	**1881**	0412	x---	----	xx--	x---	----	2*	
									1882	....	**1884**	....	x---	----	x---	----	----	1	
									1885	1226	**1886**	10	x---	----	xx--	x---	-x--	3?	
									1887	....	....	....	x---	----	----	--x-	----	0	
									1889	0809	**1890**	0216	x---	----	xx--	x---	----	4*	
									1890	1118	....	....	x---	----	xx--	----	----	2?	
									1891	07	**1892**	06	x---	----	xx--	----	----	2	
									1893	1204	**1902**	....	x---	----	xx--	x---	----	2*	
									1903	0215	**1903**	08	x---	----	xx--	x-x-	----	3	
									1904	....	**1906**	....	x---	----	?x--	x-x-	----	1?	
									1908	1218	**1909**	0701p	x---	----	xxx-	x---	----	3	
									1913	0117	**1913**	0124	x---	----	xx--	----	xxx-	**5***	-/**9**
									1926d	....	**1931**?	....	x---	----	?-x-	--x-	----	1?	
									? *1941*	*0415*	....	....	x---	----	??--	----	-x--	*3?*	
									1957	0514	**1960**	....	x---	----	--x-	--x-	----	1	
									1961	....	**1962**	1201p	x---	----	xx--	x-x-	----	1	6/-
									1963	....	**1970**	....	x---	----	xx--	x-x-	----	1	
									? *1973*	*0130*	....	....	x---	----	x---	--x-	----	*1*	
									1975	1211?	**1976**	0620	x---	----	-x--	x-x-	----	2	8/-
									1977	12	**1982**	06	x---	----	xx--	x-x-	----	1	5/-
(possibly confused with 1982 activity)									? *1983*	*0211*	?*1983*	*0215*	x---	----	x---	x-x-	----	*1?*	
									1985	....	**1986**	0105d	x---	----	x---	----	----	1	
East side of summit lava dome									**1987**	0702	**1987**	0702	x---	----	-xx-	----	----	1	
									? *1988*	*0615*w	....	....	x---	----	x---	----	----	*2?*	
									1991	0301	**1991**	10	x---	----	xx--	x-x-	-xx-	2	7/6
West of 1987 explosion crater									**1994**	0721	**1994**	0721	x---	----	xxx-	----	----	1	-/5
1994 crater									**1997**	1122	**2010>**	....	x---	----	xx--	x-x-	--x-	3*	7/6
Michoacán-Guanajuato (México)	**19.85**	**N* 101.75 W**	**3860**	7777	**AByxd**	**Cinder cones**	**1401-06=**	**Historical**											
Hoyo el Huanillo									C-**7350**y	....	....	....	x---	----	x---	x---	----	3	-/7
Cerro la Taza									C-**6480**y	....	....	....	x---	----	x---	x---	----	3	-/7
Cerro el Metate									C-**2750**x	....	....	....	x---	----	x---	x---	----	3	-/7
Valle de Santiago (La Alberca)									A-**2050**?	....	....	....	x---	----	xxx-	----	----		
Cerro el Jabalí									C-**1880**w	....	....	....	x---	----	x---	x---	----	3	
Valle de Santiago									? *1050*t	....	....	....	x---	----	?---	----	----		
Jorullo									**1759**	0929	**1774**	....	xx-x	----	xxx-	x---	-xx-	4*	8/**9**
Parícutin									**1943**	0220	**1952**	0225	xx-x	----	x---	x---	xx--	4	8/**9**
Zitácuaro-Valle de Bravo (México)	**19.40**	**N* 100.25 W**	**3500**	6667	**DAByx**	**Caldera**	**1401-061**	**Ar/Ar**											
West of Valle de Bravo									K-**3050***	....	....	....	----	----	----	x---	----	0	
Jocotitlán (México)	**19.73**	**N 99.758 W**	**3900**	4568	**DA**	**Stratovolcano**	**1401-062**	**Radiocarbon**											
									C-**7740**u	....	....	....	x---	----	xx-A	----	----		
									C **1270**u	....	....	....	x---	----	xx--	----	----		
Toluca, Nevado de (México)	**19.108**	**N 99.758 W**	**4680**	3478	**ADty**	**Stratovolcano**	**1401-07-**	**Radiocarbon**											
									C-**1350**?	....	....	....	----	----	xx--	--x-	----		
Chichinautzin (México)	**19.08**	**N* 99.13 W**	**3930**	6678	**AYDBx**	**Volcanic field**	**1401-08=**	**Radiocarbon**											
Volcán Pelado									C-**7930**z	....	....	....	x---	----	x---	x---	----	3	**9**/7
Tres Cruces									G-**7370**y	....	....	....	x---	----	x---	----	----	4	-/8
Cerro Tetepetl (Tenango lava flow)									G-**7290***	....	....	....	x---	----	----	x---	----	0	
Cuauhtzin									C-**5840**z	....	....	....	x---	----	x---	x-x-	--x-		8/-
Tláloc									C-**4250**u	....	....	....	x--x	----	x---	x---	----	3?	**9**/7
Guespalapa									G-**2240***	....	....	....	x--x	----	x---	x---	----	3	8/7
Chichinautzin									G **0200**v	....	....	....	x---	----	x---	x---	----	3	8/7
Xitle									G **0400**v	....	....	....	xx--	----	x---	x---	-x--	3?	**9**/-
Papayo (México)	**19.308**	**N 98.70 W**	**3600**	3478	**D**	**Lava dome**	**1401-081**	**Holocene**											
Iztaccíhuatl (México)	**19.179**	**N 98.642 W**	**5230**	2478	**ADrby**	**Stratovolcano**	**1401-082**	**Holocene**											
Popocatépetl (México)	**19.023**	**N 98.622 W**	**5426**	3468	**ADBy**	**Stratovolcanoes**	**1401-09=**	**Historical**											
Volcán El Fraile									C-**7150**?	....	....	....	x---	----	xx--	----	----	**P**	
Volcán El Fraile									T-**6250**z	....	....	....	x---	----	x---	----	----		
Volcán El Fraile									C-**5150**?	....	....	....	x---	----	xx--	----	----	**P**	
Volcán El Fraile									C-**3010**x	....	....	....	x---	----	xx--	----	-xx-	**P**	
Volcán El Fraile									C-**2370**u	....	....	....	x---	----	xx--	----	----		
Volcán El Fraile									C-**1890**u	....	....	....	x---	----	x---	----	----		
									C-**0200**y	....	....	....	x---	----	xx--	----	-xx-	**P**	
									C **0250**?	....	....	....	x---	----	xx--	x---	-xx-		
									I **0823**	0301t	....	....	x---	----	xx--	----	-xx-	**P**	
									1345	....	**1347**	....	x---	----	?---	----	----	2?	
									1354	....	....	....	x---	----	x---	----	----	2?	
									? *1363*	....	....	....	x---	----	?---	----	----	*2?*	
									1488	....	....	....	x---	----	?---	----	----	2?	
									1504	....	....	....	x---	----	?---	----	----	2?	
									? *1509*	....	....	....	x---	----	----	----	----		
									1512	....	....	....	x---	----	x---	----	----	2?	
									1518	....	....	....	x---	----	?---	----	----	2?	
									1519	09	**1523**?	....	x---	----	x---	----	----	3?	
									1528	....	....	....	x---	----	?---	----	----	2?	
									1530	....	....	....	x---	----	x---	----	----	2	
									1539	....	**1540**	....	x---	----	x---	----	----	2	
									1542	....	....	....	x---	----	?---	----	----	2	

VOLCANO NAME (Subregion) / ERUPTION — Area of Activity	LAT	LONG	ELEV (m)	POPL (5 km, 10, 30, 100)	ROCK TYPE	VOLC TYPE	Start Year	Start M-Dy	NUMBER	Stop Year	Stop M-Dy	STATUS	Central, Flank vent, Radial fiss, Regional	Submarine, New island, Subglacial, Crater lake	Explosive, Pyro flow, Phreatic, Caldera	Lava flow, Lava lake, Dome, Spine	Fatal, Damage, Mudflow, Tsunami	VEI	Vol L/T
Popocatépetl (México) *continued*							**1548**	....		....	....		x---	----	x---	----	----	2	
							1571	....		....	....		x---	----	x---	----	----	2	
							1580	....		....	....		x---	----	?---	----	----	2?	
							1590	....		....	....		x---	----	?---	----	----	2?	
							1592	....		**1594**	10		x---	----	x---	----	----	2	
							1642	....		....	....		x---	----	x---	----	----	2	
							1663	1013		**1665**	1019		x---	----	x---	----	----	3?	
							1666	....		**1667**	....		x---	----	?---	----	----	2?	
							1697	1020		....	....		x---	----	?---	----	----	1	
							1720	....		....	....		x---	----	?---	----	----	1	
							1802	....		**1804**	....		x---	----	?---	----	----	1	
							? *1827*	....		....	....		x---	----	?---	----	----	*1?*	
							? *1834*	....		....	....		x---	----	?---	----	----	*1?*	
							? *1852*	....		....	....		x---	----	?---	----	----	*1?*	
							1919	0219?		**1922**	....		x---	----	x-x-	--x-	x---	1	
							1923	1127		**1924**	0307		x---	----	x---	----	----	1	
							1925	....		**1927**?	....		x---	----	x---	----	----	2	
							1933	0123		....	....		x---	----	x---	----	----	1	
							1942	....		**1943**	....		x---	----	x-x-	----	----	1	
							1947	01		**1947**	02		x---	----	x-x-	----	----	1	
							1994	1221		**1995**	1005		x---	----	x-x-	----	----	2	
							1996	0305		**2003**	1122?		x---	----	xx--	x-x-	xxx-	3*	7/-
							2004	0526		**2004**	0526		x---	----	x---	----	----	2	
							2005	0109		**2010**>	....		x---	----	x-x-	--x-	----	2	
Malinche, La (México)	**19.231 N**	**98.032 W**	**4461**	2477	**AD**	**Stratovolcano**			**1401-091**			**Radiocarbon**							
							C-**6890**z	....		....	....		x---	----	xx--	----	----		
							C-**6710**x	....		....	....		x---	----	x---	----	--x-		
							C-**6310**u	....		....	....		x---	----	x---	----	--x-		
							C-**6120**v	....		....	....		x---	----	xx--	----	----		
							C-**5870**v	....		....	....		x---	----	xx--	----	----		
							C-**5580**y	....		....	....		x---	----	xx--	----	----		
							C-**1170**t	....		....	....		x---	----	xx--	--x-	-xx-		
Serdán-Oriental (México)	**19.27 N***	**97.47 W**	**3485**	5567	**RADyb**	**Tuff cones**			**1401-092**			**Holocene**							
Humeros, Los (México)	**19.68 N**	**97.45 W**	**3150**	4567	**RADBt**	**Calderas**			**1401-093**			Holocene?							
Atlixcos, Los (México)	**19.809 N**	**96.526 W**	**800**	4567	**BAd**	**Shield volcano**			**1401-094**			**Holocene**							
Naolinco Volc Field (México)	**19.67 N***	**96.75 W**	**2000**	6667	**BAXyt**	**Pyroclastic cones**			**1401-095**			**Radiocarbon**							
Rincón de Chapultepec							G-**1200**v	....		....	....		xx--	----	xx--	x---	----		8/-
Cofre de Perote (México)	**19.492 N**	**97.15 W**	**4282**	3567	**ADbxy**	**Shield volcanoes**			**1401-096**			**Radiocarbon**							
Lower NE flank (El Volcancillo)							G **1150**v	....		....	....		-x-x	----	x---	x---	----	2	9/-
Gloria, La (México)	**19.33 N***	**97.25 W**	**3500**	6667	**AYBd**	**Volcanic field**			**1401-097**			**Holocene**							
Cumbres, Las (México)	**19.15 N**	**97.27 W**	**3940**	3467	**ADR**	**Stratovolcano**			**1401-098**			**Radiocarbon**							
North flank (Yolotepec lava dome)							C-**3920**t	....		....	....		-x--	----	----	--x-	----		
Orizaba, Pico de (México)	**19.030 N**	**97.268 W**	**5675**	3467	**ADryt**	**Stratovolcano**			**1401-10=**			**Historical**							
							C-**7530**s	....		....	....		x---	----	xx--	----	----		
(lower Citlaltépetl ignimbrite)							C-**7030**t	....		....	....		x---	----	xxx-	--x-	----	4	-/8
(upper Citlaltépetl ignimbrite)							C-**6710**w	....		....	....		x---	----	xx--	--x-	----	**5?**	-/9
							C-**6220**u	....		....	....		x---	----	xx--	--x-	----	3	-/7
							C-**4690**y	....		....	....		x---	----	xx--	--x-	----	3	-/7
							C-**2780**u	....		....	....		x---	----	xx--	----	----	3	
							C-**2500**u	....		....	....		x---	----	xx--	----	----	3	
(La Perla unit)							C-**2300**u	....		....	....		x---	----	xx--	x-x-	--x-	4	-/8
							C-**2110**v	....		....	....		x---	----	x---	----	----	3	
							C-**1500**u	....		....	....		x---	----	x---	----	----	3	
							C-**0780**t	....		....	....		x---	----	xx--	----	----	3	
							C **0040**s	....		....	....		x---	----	xx--	----	----	3	
							C **0090**s	....		....	....		x---	----	x---	x-x-	-x--	3	7/7
							C **0140**t	....		....	....		x---	----	x---	----	----	3	
							C **0220**u	....		....	....		x---	----	xx--	----	----	3	
							? *1157*	....		....	....		x---	----	?---	----	----	*2*	
							A **1175**	....		....	....		x---	----	x---	----	----	3?	
							? *1187*	....		....	....		x---	----	?---	----	----	*2*	
							C **1260**t	....		....	....		x---	----	x---	----	----	3	
							? *1351*	....		....	....		x---	----	?---	----	----	*2*	
							? *1533*	....		?*1539*	....		x---	----	?---	?---	----	*2?*	
							1545	....		?*1555*j	....		x---	----	x---	x---	----	2	8/-
							1566	....		....	....		x---	----	x---	x---	----	2	
							1569	....		**1589**	....		x---	----	x---	----	----	2	
(eruption in 1613, not 1630)							**1613**	....		....	....		x---	----	----	x---	----	0	
							1687	....		....	....		x---	----	x---	----	----	2	
							1846	....		....	....		x---	----	x---	----	----	2	
San Martín (México)	**18.57 N**	**95.20 W**	**1650**	3467	**XB**	**Shield volcano**			**1401-11=**			**Historical**							
							C-**3440**t	....		....	....		----	----	x---	----	----		
							C-**2130**t	....		....	....		-?--	----	x---	----	----		
South flank (Cerro Mono Blanco)							C-**1320**y	....		....	....		-x--	----	x---	----	-x--		
							C-**0750**s	....		....	....		----	----	x---	----	----		
South flank							T-**0150**y	....		....	....		-x--	----	x---	----	----		
South flank (Cerro Puntiagudo)							C **0120**x	....		....	....		-x--	----	x---	x---	----		
South flank							T **0380**u	....		....	....		-x--	----	x---	----	----		
							C **0480**t	....		....	....		-?--	----	x---	----	----		
							C **0890**s	....		....	....		----	----	x---	----	----		
							? *1534?*	....		....	....		----	----	?---	----	-?--		
SE flank							**1664**	0115?		....	....		-x--	----	x---	x---	----	3	
Cinder cones in summit crater							**1793**	0302		**1793**	12		x---	----	x---	x---	-x--	4	7/8
							1794	05		**1796**	....		x---	----	x---	?---	----	2?	
							? *1797*	....		?*1805*	....		----	----	----	----	----	*2?*	
							? *1838*	....		....	....		----	----	----	----	----		
							? *1932*	*1231*y		....	....		----	----	----	----	----		

MÉXICO - S

VOLCANO NAME (Subregion) / ERUPTION — Area of Activity	LAT	LONG	ELEV (m)	POPL (5 km 10 30 100)	ROCK TYPE	VOLC TYPE / Start Year	Start M-Dy	NUMBER / Stop Year	Stop M-Dy	STATUS	Central / Flank vent / Radial fiss / Regional	Submarine / New island / Subglacial / Crater lake	Explosive / Pyro flow / Phreatic / Caldera	Lava flow / Lava lake / Dome / Spine	Fatal / Damage / Mudflow / Tsunami	VEI	Vol L/T
Chichón, El (México)	**17.360 N**	**93.228 W**	**1150**	4567	Yxa	**Lava domes**		**1401-12=**		**Historical**							
(tephra unit L)						G-**6510**u	....	....	....		x---	----	xx--	----	----		
(tephra unit K)						G-**2030**v	....	....	....		x---	----	xx--	----	----	**5**	-/9
(tephra unit J)						G-**1340**w	....	....	....		x---	----	xx--	----	----		
(tephra unit I)						G-**0700**x	....	....	....		x---	----	xx--	----	-x--		
(tephra unit H)						G-**0020**t	....	....	....		x---	----	xx--	----	----		
(tephra unit G)						G **0190**w	....	....	....		x---	----	xx--	----	----		
(tephra unit F)						G **0480**x	....	....	....		x---	----	xx--	----	----		
(tephra unit E)						G **0590**v	....	....	....		x---	----	xx--	----	----	3	-/7
(tephra unit D)						G **0780**v	....	....	....		x---	----	xx--	----	-x--	**5**	-/9
(tephra unit C)						G **1190**w	....	....	....		x---	----	xx--	----	----	4	-/8
(tephra unit B)						G **1360**v	....	....	....		x---	----	xx--	--?-	xxx-	**5**	-/9
						A **1850**?	....	....	....		x---	----	x---	----	----		
(tephra unit A)						**1982**	0328	**1982**	0911		x---	----	xxx-	----	xxx-	**5***	-/9
Tacaná (México/Guatemala)	**15.130 N**	**92.112 W**	**4060**	4567	ADby	**Stratovolcano**		**1401-13=**		**Historical**							
						G-**9450**w	....	....	....		----	----	xx--	----	----		
						C-**5940**z	....	....	....		----	----	xx--	----	----		
						G-**5720**x	....	....	....		----	----	xx--	----	----		
						G-**4740**x	....	....	....		----	----	xx--	----	----		
						G-**1080**w	....	....	....		----	----	xx--	----	----		
San Antonio (upper SW flank)						G **0070**v	....	....	....		-x--	----	xx--	x-x-	-xx-	4?	-/8
						C **1030**s	....	....	....		----	----	xx--	----	----		
SW side						*? 1855*	*0112*	....	....		--x-	----	?-?-	----	----	*1*	
SW side						**1878**	....	....	....		--x-	----	x-x-	----	----	1	
SW flank						**1949**	1222	**1950**	01		-x--	----	x-x-	----	----	1	
NE flank (ca. 3600 m)						**1986**	02	**1986**	06		-x--	----	--x-	----	----	1	

GUATEMALA

VOLCANO NAME (Subregion) / ERUPTION — Area of Activity	LAT	LONG	ELEV (m)	POPL (5 km 10 30 100)	ROCK TYPE	VOLC TYPE / Start Year	Start M-Dy	NUMBER / Stop Year	Stop M-Dy	STATUS	Central / Flank vent / Radial fiss / Regional	Submarine / New island / Subglacial / Crater lake	Explosive / Pyro flow / Phreatic / Caldera	Lava flow / Lava lake / Dome / Spine	Fatal / Damage / Mudflow / Tsunami	VEI	Vol L/T
Tajumulco (Guatemala)	**15.034 N**	**91.903 W**	**4220**	4567	DA	**Stratovolcano**		**1402-02=**		**Holocene**							
						? 1821	....	....	....		----	----	?---	----	----	*2*	
						? 1863	....	....	....		x---	----	?---	----	----	*2*	
Santa María (Guatemala)	**14.756 N**	**91.552 W**	**3772**	4677	DAb	**Stratovolcano**		**1402-03=**		**Historical**							
SW flank						**1902**	1024	**1902**	1112		-x--	----	x-x-	----	xxx-	**6?**	-/10
SW flank (east end of 1902 crater)						**1903**	....	**1913**	....		-x--	---x	x-x-	----	----	2	
SW flank (Santiaguito)						**1922**	0622	**2010>**	....		-x--	----	xxx-	x-xx	xxx-	3*	**9**/8
Almolonga (Guatemala)	**14.82 N**	**91.48 W**	**3197**	5677	DAb	**Stratovolcano**		**1402-04=**		**Historical**							
Cerro Quemado						G **0800**t	....	....	....		x---	----	xx-A	--x-	--x-	3	7/7
Cerro Quemado						**1765**	1024	**1765**	1025		-x--	----	x---	x---	-x--	2	
(1785 date refers to 1765 eruption)						*X 1785*	....	....	....		----	----	----	----	----		
East flank of Cerro Quemado						**1818**	0116	**1818**	0619>		-x--	----	x---	x---	-x--	2	
(fumarolic activity only: Sapper 1917)						*X 1823*	....	....	....		----	----	----	----	----		
(earthquake, not eruption: Sapper 1917)						*X 1891*	....	....	....		----	----	----	----	----		
Atitlán (Guatemala)	**14.583 N**	**91.186 W**	**3535**	4567	ARDb	**Stratovolcano**		**1402-06=**		**Historical**							
						C-**1020**w	....	....	....		----	----	xx--	x---	----		
						1469	....	....	....		----	----	x---	----	----	3↑	
						1505?	....	....	....		----	----	x---	----	--x-	3?	
						1579?	....	**1581**	1231p		----	----	x---	----	----	2	
						1663	....	....	....		----	----	x---	----	--x-	2	
(possibly eruption of Fuego volcano)						@ **1717**	0829	@**1721**	....		----	----	----	----	----		
						1826	11	....	....		----	----	x---	----	----	2	
						1827	0327	....	....		----	----	x---	----	----	2	
						1827	0901	**1828**	01 ?		----	----	x?--	x---	-x--	3	
						1833	....	....	....		----	----	x?--	----	-x--	2	
						1837	06	....	....		----	----	x---	----	----	2	
						1843	07	....	....		x---	----	x---	x---	----	2	
						? 1852	....	....	....		----	----	?---	----	----	*2?*	
						1853	0503	....	....		----	----	x?--	----	-xx-	3	
						? 1856	....	....	....		----	----	?---	----	----	*2*	
Tolimán (Guatemala)	**14.612 N**	**91.189 W**	**3158**	4567	A	**Stratovolcano**		**1402-07=**		**Holocene**							
Acatenango (Guatemala)	**14.501 N**	**90.876 W**	**3976**	4577	ADb	**Stratovolcano**		**1402-08=**		**Historical**							
Yepocapa						C-**2710**u	....	....	....		x---	----	xx--	?---	----		
Pico Central						C-**0370**x	....	....	....		x---	----	xx--	----	----		
Pico Central						C-**0260**u	....	....	....		x---	----	x---	----	----		
Pico Central						C **0090**v	....	....	....		x---	----	x---	----	----		
						A **1450**t	....	....	....		----	----	x---	----	----		
North slope of Pico Central						**1924**	1218	**1925**	0607		--x-	----	x---	----	----	3*	
Pico Central						**1926**	08	**1927**	0519		x---	----	x-x-	----	----	2*	
Pico Central-Yepocapa saddle						**1972**	1112	**1972**	12		-?x-	----	x-x-	----	----	1	
Fuego (Guatemala)	**14.473 N**	**90.880 W**	**3763**	4577	BAy	**Stratovolcano**		**1402-09=**		**Historical**							
						C-**1580**u	....	....	....		----	----	x---	----	----		
						C **0590**u	....	....	....		----	----	x---	----	----		
						C **0900**u	....	....	....		----	----	x---	----	----		
						C **0970**t	....	....	....		----	----	x---	----	----		
						1524	0430p	**1524**	0715q		----	----	x---	----	----	2	
(possibly only earthquakes)						*? 1526*	....	....	....		----	----	?---	----	----	*2*	
						1531	1231p	....	....		----	----	x---	----	----	2	
(possibly an eruption of Atitlán)						@ **1541**	....	....	....		----	----	?---	----	----		
						1542	0114	....	....		----	----	----	----	----		
						1551	....	**1552**	0331>		----	----	x---	----	----	2	
(possibly only an earthquake)						*? 1557*	*0115*	....	....		----	----	?---	----	----		
(possibly same as 1557 event)						*? 1559*	*0116*	....	....		----	----	?---	----	----		
(possibly only earthquakes)						*? 1565*	....	....	....		----	----	?---	----	----	*2*	
(possibly same as 1581 eruption)						*? 1571*	*1225*	....	....		----	----	x---	----	----		
(possibly only earthquakes)						*? 1575*	....	....	....		----	----	?---	----	----	*2*	
(possibly only an earthquake)						*? 1576*	....	....	....		----	----	?---	----	----	*2*	
(possibly only earthquakes)						*? 1577*	....	....	....		----	----	?---	----	----	*2*	
						1581	1205	**1582**	0115		x---	----	x---	x---	-x--	4?	-/8
						1585	0115	**1585**	07		----	----	x---	----	----	2	

VOLCANO NAME (Subregion) / ERUPTION — Area of Activity	LAT	LONG	ELEV (m)	POPL (5 km / 10 / 30 / 100)	ROCK TYPE	VOLC TYPE	NUMBER / Start Year	Start M-Dy	STATUS / Stop Year	Stop M-Dy	Central / Flank vent / Radial fiss / Regional	Submarine / New island / Subglacial / Crater lake	Explosive / Pyro flow / Phreatic / Caldera	Lava flow / Lava lake / Dome / Spine	Fatal / Damage / Mudflow / Tsunami	VEI	Vol L/T
Fuego (Guatemala) *continued*							**1586**	0603b	**1586**	12	x---	----	x---	x---	----	2	
							1587	0724	....	....	----	----	x---	----	----	2	
							1614	....	....	....	----	----	x---	----	----	2	
							1617	....	....	....	----	----	x---	----	-x--	3	
							1620	....	....	....	----	----	x---	----	----	2	
							1623	01	....	....	----	----	x---	----	----	2	
							1629	....	**1632**	....	----	----	x---	----	----	2	
(possibly only earthquakes)						?	*1679*	....	....	....	----	----	?---	----	----		
(pumice seen off Guatemala coast)						@	**1685**	09	....	....	----	----	x---	----	----	2	
							1686	....	....	....	----	----	x---	----	----	2	
(possibly only an earthquake)						?	*1689*	....	....	....	----	----	?---	----	----	*2*	
							1699	....	....	....	----	----	x---	----	----	2	
							1702	0804	....	....	----	----	x---	----	----	2	
							1705	0131	**1705**	0202	----	----	x---	----	--?-	2	
							1706	1004	....	....	----	----	x---	----	----	2	
(possibly same as 1710 eruption)						?	*1709*	*1014*	....	....	----	----	----	?---	----		
							1710	1014	....	....	----	----	x---	----	----	2	
							1717	0827	**1717**	1226e	----	----	x---	----	-x--	4?	-/8
							1730	09	....	....	----	----	x---	----	----	2	
							1732	05	....	....	----	----	x---	----	----	2	
							1737	0827	**1737**	0924	-x--	----	x---	----	----	4?	-/8
(possibly only an earthquake)						?	*1751*	....	....	....	----	----	?---	----	----	*2*	
(possibly only an earthquake)						?	*1765*	....	....	....	----	----	?---	----	----	*2*	
(possibly only earthquakes)						?	*1773*	....	....	....	----	----	?---	----	----	*2*	
							1799	....	....	....	----	----	x---	----	----	3	-/7
							1826	....	....	....	x---	----	x---	----	----	2	
							1829	....	....	....	----	----	x---	?---	----	2	
						?	*1850*	....	....	....	----	----	?---	----	----	*2*	
						?	*1852*	....	....	....	----	----	?---	?---	----	*2*	
							1855	0929	**1855**	0930	----	----	x---	----	----	2	
							1856	0109	**1856**	0307	----	----	x---	x---	----	2	
							1856	0929	**1856**	0930	----	----	x---	x---	----	2	
							1857	0115	**1857**	0217	x---	----	x---	x---	----	4?	-/8
							1857	0917	....	....	----	----	x---	x---	----	2	
							1860	0818	**1860**	0923	x---	----	x---	x---	-x--	2	
						?	*1861*	*1121*	....	....	----	----	?---	----	----	*2*	
						?	*1867*	....	....	....	----	----	?---	----	----	*2*	
							1880	0628	**1880**	0820	----	----	x---	x---	----	4?	-/8
							1896	0110	....	....	----	----	x---	----	----	2?	
							1932	0121	**1932**	0122	x---	----	xx--	----	x---	4	-/8
							1944	1201p	....	....	----	----	x---	----	----	2	
							1947	....	....	....	----	----	x---	----	----	2	
							1949	11	....	....	----	----	x---	----	----	2	
							1953	0409	**1953**	0413	x---	----	x---	x-x-	----	3	
							1955	0726e	....	....	x---	----	x---	x--x	----	1	
							1957	0219	**1957**	0221>	x---	----	xx--	----	----	3	-/7
							1962	0804	**1962**	1109	x---	----	x---	x---	--x-	3*	6/7
							1963	0928	**1963**	0930	x---	----	xx--	x---	xxx-	3	-/6
							1966	0207	**1966**	0501	x---	----	xx--	x---	----	3*	
							1966	0812	**1966**	0813	x---	----	x---	----	----	3	-/6
							1967	0422	**1967**	0424	x---	----	x---	----	----	2	-/6
							1971	0914	**1971**	0915	x---	----	xx--	----	xxx-	3	-/7
							1973	0223	**1973**	0323	x---	----	xx--	----	--x-	2	-/6
							1974	1010	**1974**	1204	x---	----	xx--	----	xx--	4*	-/8
							1975	0528	**1975**	1021	x---	----	xx--	----	----	1	-/5
							1977	0303	**1977**	0419	x---	----	x---	----	----	1	-/4
							1977	0911	**1979**	0808	x---	----	xx--	x-x-	----	2	-/6
							1987	0105d	**1987**	02 ?	x---	----	x---	----	----	1	
							1999	0521	**2000**	1209>	x---	----	xx--	x---	-xx-	2*	
							2002	0104	**2010>**	....	x---	----	xx--	x---	--x-	2	
Agua (Guatemala)	**14.465 N**	**90.743 W**	**3760**	4677	**Ad**	**Stratovolcano**	**1402-10=**		**Holocene**								
(mudflow, not eruption)						*X*	*1541*	*0911*	....	....	----	----	----	----	xxx-		
Pacaya (Guatemala)	**14.381 N**	**90.601 W**	**2552**	4577	**BDRAy**	**Complex volcano**	**1402-11=**		**Historical**								
(Pc-Pt 1 tephra)						C	**0400**t	....	....	....	x---	----	x---	----	----	2	
(Pc-Pt 5 tephra, Pacaya debris avalanche)						T	**0880**z	....	....	....	x---	----	xx-A	----	----	3?	
MacKenney Crater (Pc-Pt 10 tephra)						C	**1160**u	....	....	....	x---	----	x---	----	----	3?	
Cerro Chino (Pc-Pt 8 tephra)						C	**1360**u	....	....	....	-x--	----	x---	----	----	3?	
Cerro Chino (Pc-Pt 12 tephra)							**1565**	08 ?	....	....	-x--	----	x---	x---	-x--	3	
							1623?	....	....	....	----	----	x---	----	-x--	3	
							1651	0218	**1651**	0413	-x--	----	x---	x---	----	2	
							1655	07	....	....	----	----	x---	----	----	2	
							1664	....	....	....	----	----	x---	----	----	3	
							1668	08	**1669**	0629	----	----	x---	----	----	2	
							1671	08	....	....	----	----	x---	----	----	2	
							1674	07	....	....	----	----	x---	----	----	2	
(possibly same as 1674 eruption)						?	*1677*	*07*	....	....	----	----	?---	----	----		
							1678	08 ?	....	....	----	----	x---	----	----	2	
							1687	0326	**1687**	0327	----	----	x---	----	----	2	
							1690	....	....	....	----	----	x---	----	----	2?	
							1693	....	....	....	----	----	?---	----	----	2?	
							1699	0629	....	....	----	----	?---	----	----	2?	
						?	*1717*	....	....	....	----	----	?---	----	----		
						?	*1760*	....	....	....	----	----	?---	----	----		
Cerro Chino (SW flank and summit)							**1775**	0701	**1775**	0723>	-xx-	----	x---	x---	----	3	7/7
							1805	....	....	....	----	----	x---	----	----	2	
						?	*1830*	....	....	....	----	----	?---	----	----		
Cerro Chino							**1846**	02	....	....	-x--	----	x---	----	----	2	
							1885	12	....	....	----	----	x---	----	----	2	
Cachajinas vent (South flank, 1860 m)							**1961**	0311	**1961**	0415?	-xx-	----	x---	x---	-x--	2	6/-
MacKenney Crater and flank vents							**1965**	0704	**1989**	0310	xxx-	----	xx--	xx--	-x--	3*	
MacKenney Crater and flank vents							**1990**	0104?	**2000**	0301	x-x-	----	xx--	x---	xx--	3*	
MacKenney Crater							**2000**	08	**2001**	0705?	x---	----	x---	-x--	-x--	1	
MacKenney Crater							**2001**	1031	**2001**	1031	x---	----	x---	----	----	1	
MacKenney Crater							**2002**	0530	**2002**	0617?	x---	----	?---	----	----	1?	
MacKenney Crater							**2004**	0719?	**2010>**	....	x---	----	x---	x---	----	1	

Katia and Maurice Krafft

Fuego in eruption in 1974 and Acatenango (R) above Antigua Guatemala

VOLCANO NAME (Subregion) / ERUPTION — Area of Activity	LAT	LONG	ELEV (m)	POPL (5 km 10 30 100)	ROCK TYPE	VOLC TYPE	NUMBER	STATUS	Start Year	Start M-Dy	Stop Year	Stop M-Dy	ERUPTIVE CHARACTERISTICS (Central, Flank vent, Radial fiss, Regional / Submarine, New island, Subglacial, Crater lake / Explosive, Pyro flow, Phreatic, Caldera / Lava flow, Lava lake, Dome, Spine / Fatal, Damage, Mudflow, Tsunami)	VEI	Vol L/T
Cuilapa-Barbarena (Guatemala)	**14.33 N***	**90.40 W**	**1454**	6667	BA	**Volcanic field**	**1402-111**	**Holocene**							
Tecuamburro (Guatemala)	**14.156 N**	**90.407 W**	**1845**	4567	Ad	**Stratovolcano**	**1402-12=**	**Radiocarbon**							
NW flank (Ixpaco Crater)									C-0960u	....	....	....	-x-- ---- --x- ---- ----		
Jumaytepeque (Guatemala)	**14.336 N**	**90.269 W**	**1815**	5567	B	**Stratovolcano**	**1402-121**	Holocene?							
Moyuta (Guatemala)	**14.03 N**	**90.10 W**	**1662**	4567	Adb	**Stratovolcano**	**1402-13-**	**Hot Springs**							
Flores (Guatemala)	**14.308 N***	**89.992 W**	**1600**	6667	B	**Volcanic field**	**1402-14-**	**Holocene**							
Tahual (Guatemala)	**14.43 N**	**89.90 W**	**1716**	5567	BA	**Stratovolcano**	**1402-141**	**Holocene**							
Santiago, Cerro (Guatemala)	**14.33 N***	**89.87 W**	**1192**	6667	B	**Volcanic field**	**1402-15-**	**Holocene**							
Suchitán (Guatemala)	**14.40 N**	**89.78 W**	**2042**	4567	ABD	**Stratovolcanoes**	**1402-16-**	**Holocene**							
(probably Atitlán eruption)									*? 1469*	....	....	....	---- ---- ---- ---- ----		
Chingo (Guatemala)	**14.12 N***	**89.73 W**	**1775**	6667	AB	**Stratovolcano**	**1402-17-**	**Holocene**							
Ixtepeque (Guatemala)	**14.42 N***	**89.68 W**	**1292**	6667	RBA	**Lava domes**	**1402-18-**	**Holocene**							
Ipala (Guatemala)	**14.55 N**	**89.63 W**	**1650**	4567	B	**Stratovolcano**	**1402-19-**	**Holocene**							
Chiquimula Volc Field (Guat)	**14.83 N***	**89.55 W**	**1192**	6667	BA	**Cinder cones**	**1402-20-**	**Holocene**							
Quezaltepeque (Guatemala)	**14.57 N**	**89.45 W**	**1200**	4567	B	**Volcanic field**	**1402-21-**	**Holocene**							
EL SALVADOR & HONDURAS															
San Diego (El Salvador)	**14.27 N***	**89.48 W**	**781**	6667	B	**Volcanic field**	**1403-001**	**Holocene**							
Singüil, Cerro (El Salvador)	**14.05 N***	**89.65 W**	**957**	5667	B	**Cinder cones**	**1403-002**	**Holocene**							
Apaneca Range (El Salvador)	**13.891 N**	**89.786 W**	**2036**	5677	BAYDR	**Stratovolcanoes**	**1403-01=**	**Holocene**							
(small hydrothermal explosion)									*X 1990*	*1013*	....	....	---- ---- ---- ---- xx--		
Santa Ana (El Salvador)	**13.853 N**	**89.630 W**	**2381**	3577	AYBdr	**Stratovolcano**	**1403-02=**	**Historical**							
									? 1520	....	....	....	---- ---- ?--- ---- ----		
									1521	1231y	....	....	---- ---- x--- ---- -x--	3	
									1524	0430p	....	....	---- ---- x--- ---- ----	3	
									1570?	....	....	....	---- ---- x--- ---- ----		
									1576	....	....	....	---- ---- x--- ---- ----	3	
									? 1621	....	....	....	---- ---- ---- ---- ----		
(doubtful San Marcelino eruption)									*X 1650*t	....	....	....	--?- ---- ---- ?--- -?--		
SE flank (San Marcelino)									**1722**	0312	....	....	-xx- ---- x--- x--- -x--	2	
									1734	06 <	....	....	---- ---- x--- ---- -x--	2?	
									1874	....	....	....	---- ---- x--- ---- -x--	3	
									? 1878	....	....	....	---- ---- ?--- ---- ----	*2*	
									1879	0201p	....	....	---- ---- x--- ---- ----	2	
NW flank (Mala Cara)									**1880**	03	....	....	-x-- ---- x--- ---- -x--	3	
									? 1882	....	....	....	---- ---- ---- ---- ----		
									1884	0309	**1884**	0310	---- ---- x--- ---- ----	2	
									1904	0112	**1904**	0126?	x--- ---- x--- ---- ----	2	
									? 1920	*11*	....	....	---- ---- ?--- ---- ----	*2?*	
									2005	0616	**2005**	1001?	x--- ---x xxx- ---- xxx-	3*	
Izalco (El Salvador)	**13.813 N**	**89.633 W**	**1950**	3577	Ab	**Stratovolcano**	**1403-03=**	**Historical**							
(fumarolic activity prior to 1770)									*X 1636*	....	....	....	---- ---- ---- ---- ----		
									1770	0223	....	....	---- ---- x--- x--- ----	2	
									1772?	....	....	....	---- ---- x--- ---- ----	2	
									1783	07 ?	....	....	--?- ---- ---- x--- ----	0	
									1793	0329	**1793**	09	---- ---- x--- x--- ----	2	
									1798	04	....	....	x--- ---- x--- ?--- ----	2	
									1802	....	**1803**	....	---- ---- x--- x--- ----	2	
									1805	....	**1807**	....	---- ---- x--- ---- ----	2	
									1817	....	....	....	---- ---- x--- ---- ----	2	
									1825	....	....	....	---- ---- x--- x--- ----	2	
									1836	....	....	....	---- ---- x--- ---- ----	2	
									1838	....	**1840**	....	x--- ---- x--- x--- ----	2	
									1842	....	....	....	---- ---- x--- ---- ----	2	
									1844	06	**1844**	10	---- ---- x--- x--- ----	2	
									1850	....	....	....	x--- ---- x--- ---- ----	2	
									1854	0513	**1854**	0608	---- ---- x--- x--- ----	2	
Summit and south flank									**1856**	0524	**1856**	0901a	x-x- ---- x--- x--- -x--	2	
									1857	0215	**1857**	0219>	x--- ---- x--- x--- ----	2	
									1858	0206	**1859**	07	---- ---- x--- ?--- ----	2	
									1859	1208	**1860**	0122	---- ---- ---- x--- ----	0	
									1863	....	....	....	---- ---- ---- x--- ----	0	
Summit and NE flank									**1864**	0515b	**1865**	0615e	xx-- ---- x--- x--- ----	2	
									1866	0427	**1866**	0815e	---- ---- x--- ---- ----	2	
									1867	04	**1867**	08	---- ---- x--- ---- ----	2	
									1868	0216	**1868**	0217	---- ---- ?--- ---- ----	2	
Summit and east flank									**1869**	0301?	**1869**	0618>	xxx- ---- xx-- x--- -x--	2	
(possibly confused with May 19, 1869)									*? 1870*	*0519*	....	....	---- ---- ---- ?--- ----	*2?*	
									1872	12	**1873**	0319>	---- ---- x--- ---- ----	2	
									? 1874	....	?*1875*	....	---- ---- ---- ---- ----		
									1878	....	....	....	---- ---- ---- ---- ----		
									1879	1225	**1880**	03	---- ---- x--- ---- ----	2	
									1881	0101	....	....	---- ---- ---- x--- ----	0	
									1882	0712	....	....	---- ---- x--- ---- ----	2	
									1883	0905d	**1883**	1113	-x-- ---- x--- ---- ----	2	
									1884	0309	**1884**	0310	-x-- ---- x--- x--- ----	2	
									1885	....	....	....	-x-- ---- x--- x--- ----	2	
									1887	....	**1889**	....	---- ---- x--- ---- ----	2	
Summit and upper east flank									**1890**	0326e	**1890**	0420	xxx- ---- x--- x--- ----	0	
									1891	....	**1898**	07	---- ---- x--- x--- ----	2	
									1899	1231	**1900**	03	---- ---- x--- ---- ----	2	
Summit and NE flank									**1902**	0510	**1902**	1230	xxx- ---- x--- x--- ----	2	
Summit and east flank									**1903**	11	**1905**	03	xx-- ---- x--- ---- ----	2	
Summit and NE flank									**1912**	0116	**1916**	0126	xxx- ---- x--- x--- ----	2	
SE flank									**1920**	1029	**1921**	0410	-x-- ---- x--- x--- ----	2	
									1924	03	....	....	---- ---- x--- ---- ----	2	
									1925	1226	**1927**	01	---- ---- xx-- x--- xx--	3?	
									1927	....	**1928**?	....	---- ---- x--- ---- ----	2	

VOLCANO NAME (Subregion)	ERUPTION — Area of Activity	LAT	LONG	ELEV (m)	POPL (5 km, 10, 30, 100)	ROCK TYPE	VOLC TYPE	NUMBER	STATUS	Start Year	Start M-Dy	Stop Year	Stop M-Dy	Central / Flank vent / Radial fiss / Regional	Submarine / New island / Subglacial / Crater lake	Explosive / Pyro flow / Phreatic / Caldera	Lava flow / Lava lake / Dome / Spine	Fatal / Damage / Mudflow / Tsunami	VEI	Vol L/T
Izalco (El Salvador) *continued*	Outer slope of eastern summit crater									**1930**	04	....	....	--x-	----	----	x---	----	0	
										1931	0331t	....	....	----	----	x?--	----	----	2	
										1933	1130	**1934**	0112>	----	----	x---	x---	----	2	
										1937?	....	**1938**?	....	----	----	x---	x---	----	2?	
	Summit and SSE flank									**1939**	02	**1948**	02	xx--	----	x---	x---	----	2	
	Summit, SW and NE flanks									**1948**	1104	**1957**	1201p	xx--	----	xx--	x---	----	3*	
	SSE flank (550 m below summit)									**1966**	1028	**1966**	11	-x--	----	----	x---	----	0	5/-
Coatepeque Caldera (El Salvador)		**13.87 N**	**89.55 W**	**746**	6677	**RDAyb**	**Caldera**	**1403-041**	**Holocene**											
San Salvador (El Salvador)		**13.734 N**	**89.294 W**	**1893**	5677	**ABD**	**Stratovolcano**	**1403-05=**	**Historical**											
	(same as AD 260 Ilopango eruption)									*X-1040*y	....	....	....	----	----	----	----	----		
	NW flank (Loma Caldera)									G **0640**r	08	....	....	-xx-	----	xx--	----	?x--	3?	
	Boquerón (San Andrés Talpetate Tuff)									A **1200**?	....	....	....	x---	----	xx--	----	----	4	-/8
	North flank ?									**1572**b	....	....	....	-x--	----	x---	x---	----	3?	
	NW flank (El Playón)									**1658**	1103	....	....	-xx-	----	x---	x---	-x--	3	7/-
San Salvador (El Salvador) *continued*	NW flank (El Playón)									**1671**	08 ?	....	....	-x--	----	x---	----	----	2?	
	El Playón ?									? *1806*	....	....	....	-x--	----	----	?---	----	*0*	
	Boquerón summit and north flank									**1917**	0607	**1917**	11	xxx-	---x	x---	x---	xx--	3	7/-
Cinotepeque, Cerro (El Salvador)		**14.02 N**	**89.25 W**	**665**	4567	**U**	**Volcanic field**	**1403-051**	**Holocene**											
Guazapa (El Salvador)		**13.90 N**	**89.12 W**	**1438**	4577	**B**	**Stratovolcano**	**1403-052**	Holocene?											
Ilopango (El Salvador)		**13.672 N**	**89.053 W**	**450**	7777	**DABr**	**Caldera**	**1403-06=**	**Historical**											
	Ilopango									G **0450**r	....	....	....	x---	----	xx-x	----	xx--	**6+**	**-/10**
	Islas Quemadas									**1879**	1231	**1880**	0326e	x---	---x	x---	--x-	-x--	3*	8/-
San Vicente (El Salvador)		**13.595 N**	**88.837 W**	**2182**	4667	**ADBr**	**Stratovolcano**	**1403-07=**	**Holocene**											
Apastepeque Field (El Salvador)		**13.72 N***	**88.77 W**	**700**	6667	**DAB**	**Volcanic field**	**1403-071**	**Holocene**											
Taburete (El Salvador)		**13.435 N**	**88.532 W**	**1172**	5567	**BA**	**Stratovolcano**	**1403-072**	Holocene?											
Tecapa (El Salvador)		**13.494 N**	**88.502 W**	**1593**	5567	**ABD**	**Stratovolcano**	**1403-08=**	**Holocene**											
										? *1878*	*1002*	....	....	----	----	----	----	----		
Usulután (El Salvador)		**13.419 N**	**88.471 W**	**1449**	5667	**BA**	**Stratovolcano**	**1403-081**	**Holocene**											
Tigre, El (El Salvador)		**13.47 N**	**88.43 W**	**1640**	5667	**BA**	**Stratovolcano**	**1403-082**	**Holocene**											
Chinameca (El Salvador)		**13.478 N**	**88.330 W**	**1300**	5567	**A**	**Stratovolcano**	**1403-09=**	**Holocene**											
San Miguel (El Salvador)		**13.434 N**	**88.269 W**	**2130**	4567	**AB**	**Stratovolcano**	**1403-10=**	**Historical**											
	(eruption 70-80 years before 1586)									**1510**e	....	....	....	x---	----	x?--	?---	----		
	SE flank (400 m)									**1699**	....	....	....	-xx-	----	x---	x---	----	2	
	NE flank (400 m)									**1762**	....	....	....	--x-	----	?---	x---	----	2	
	East flank ?									**1769**	....	....	....	--?-	----	?---	x---	----	2	
	Summit, north and SE flanks									**1787**	0921	**1787**	0923	xxx-	----	x---	x---	-x--	2	
										? *1798*?	....	....	....	----	----	?---	----	----	*2*	
										? *1811*	....	....	....	----	----	?---	----	----	*2*	
	SSE flank (400 m; near Los Perolitos)									**1819**	0718	....	....	--x-	----	x---	x---	-x--	2	
	NNW (1120 m) and upper east flanks									**1844**	0725	**1848**	....	-xx-	----	x---	x---	----	2	
										? *1854*	....	....	....	----	----	?---	----	----	*2?*	
	SSE flank (800 m)									**1855**	12	....	....	-xx-	----	x---	x---	----	2	
										1857	11	....	....	----	----	x---	x---	----	2?	
										1862	01	....	....	----	----	x---	----	----	2	
	WSW flank (1000 m)									**1867**	1214	**1868**	0216>	-xx-	----	x---	x---	-x--	2	
										1882	1205d	....	....	----	----	x---	----	----	2	
	NE side of main crater									**1884**	0125	**1884**	0128a	x---	----	x---	x---	----	2	
										1890	....	**1891**	....	x---	----	x---	----	----	2	
										1919	1210	**1920**	01	----	----	x---	----	----	2	
										1920	0814	**1925**	....	----	----	x---	----	----	2	
										1929	08	....	....	x---	----	x---	----	----	2	
										1930	0126e	....	....	x---	----	x---	----	----	2	
										1931	03	**1931**	06	x---	----	x---	?---	----	2	
										? *1936*?	....	....	....	----	----	?---	----	----	*2*	
										1939	05	**1939**	07	----	----	x---	----	----	2	
										1954	1021	**1954**	1021	----	----	--x-	----	----	2	
										1964	1023	**1964**	11	x---	----	x---	----	-x--	2	
										1966	0222	....	....	----	----	x---	----	----	2	
										1966	07	....	....	----	----	x---	----	----	2	
										1967	0105	....	....	x---	----	x---	----	-?--	2	
										1970	0330	**1970**	0405	x---	----	x---	----	-x--	1	-/4
										1976	1202	**1977**	0301	x---	----	x---	x---	-x--	1	6/-
										1985	11	**1986**	02 >	x---	----	x-x-	----	----	1	
										1995	0112	**1995**	0419	x---	----	x-?-	----	-x--	1	
										1997	1231	....	....	x---	----	x-x-	----	----	1	
										2002	0116	**2002**	0116	x---	----	x---	----	----	1	
Aramuaca, Laguna (El Salvador)		**13.428 N**	**88.105 W**	**181**	5667	**U**	**Maar**	**1403-101**	**Holocene**											
Conchagua (El Salvador)		**13.275 N**	**87.845 W**	**1225**	4567	**BA**	**Stratovolcano**	**1403-11=**	Uncertain											
Conchagüita (El Salvador)		**13.229 N**	**87.767 W**	**505**	4467	**B**	**Stratovolcano**	**1403-12=**	**Historical**											
										1892	1012?	**1892**	1031?	x---	----	x---	----	----	1?	
Tigre, Isla el (Honduras)		**13.272 N**	**87.641 W**	**783**	4467	**B**	**Stratovolcano**	**1403-13-**	**Holocene**											
Zacate Grande, Isla (Honduras)		**13.33 N**	**87.63 W**	**640**	4567	**BA**	**Stratovolcano**	**1403-14-**	**Holocene**											
Yojoa, Lake (Honduras)		**14.98 N***	**87.98 W**	**1090**	6667	**XYTB**	**Volcanic field**	**1403-15-**	**Holocene**											
Utila Island (Honduras)		**16.10 N***	**86.90 W**	**74**	4446	**B**	**Pyroclastic cones**	**1403-16-**	**Holocene**											

NICARAGUA

VOLCANO NAME (Subregion)	ERUPTION — Area of Activity	LAT	LONG	ELEV (m)	POPL (5 km, 10, 30, 100)	ROCK TYPE	VOLC TYPE	NUMBER	STATUS	Start Year	Start M-Dy	Stop Year	Stop M-Dy	Central / Flank vent / Radial fiss / Regional	Submarine / New island / Subglacial / Crater lake	Explosive / Pyro flow / Phreatic / Caldera	Lava flow / Lava lake / Dome / Spine	Fatal / Damage / Mudflow / Tsunami	VEI	Vol L/T
Cosigüina (Nicaragua)		**12.98 N**	**87.57 W**	**872**	3457	**AB**	**Stratovolcano**	**1404-01=**	**Historical**											
										C **1500**?	....	....	....	----	----	xx--	----	--x-		
										? *1609*	....	....	....	----	----	?---	----	----		
										1709?	....	....	....	----	----	x?--	----	--?-		
	(confusion with 1709 eruption?)									? *1809*	*0328*	?*1809*	*0331*a	----	----	?---	----	----	*2?*	
										1835	0120	**1835**	0125?	x---	----	xx--	x---	xx--	**5**	-/9
										1852	12	....	....	x---	----	x---	----	----	2?	
										1859	0825	....	....	----	----	x---	----	----		
San Cristóbal (Nicaragua)		**12.702 N**	**87.004 W**	**1745**	3467	**BAD**	**Stratovolcano**	**1404-02=**	**Historical**											
										1528a	....	....	....	x---	----	x---	----	----	3	
										? *1613*	....	....	....	----	----	?---	----	----		
										1680	....	....	....	----	----	x---	----	----	2?	

VOLCANO NAME (Subregion) / ERUPTION — Area of Activity	LAT	LONG	ELEV (m)	POPL (5 km, 10, 30, 100)	ROCK TYPE	VOLC TYPE	NUMBER	STATUS		Start Year	Start M-Dy	Stop Year	Stop M-Dy	Central / Flank vent / Radial fiss / Regional	Submarine / New island / Subglacial / Crater lake	Explosive / Pyro flow / Phreatic / Caldera	Lava flow / Lava lake / Dome / Spine	Fatal / Damage / Mudflow / Tsunami	VEI	Vol L/T
San Cristóbal (Nicaragua) *continued*										1684	07	....	....	x---	----	x---	----	----	2	
										1685	08	....	....	x---	----	x---	----	----	2	
										1971	0503	1971	0705d	x---	----	x-x-	----	----	1	
										1976	0309	1976	0316	x---	----	x---	----	----	1	
										1976	0829	1976	0829	x---	----	x---	----	----	1	
										1977	1016	1977	1016	x---	----	x---	----	----	2	
									?	*1985*	*0902*	....	....	x---	----	--?-	----	----		
									?	*1987*	*11*	....	....	----	----	?---	----	----		
										1997	0519?	1997	0707>	x---	----	x---	----	----	1	
										1999	0501w	2000	06	x---	----	x-x-	----	--x-	2*	-/6
										2001	0511?	2001	1209?	x---	----	x---	----	----	1	
										2002	0529	2002	1216?	x---	----	x---	----	-x--	1	
										2003	0617	2004	0613	x---	----	x---	----	--x-	1?	
										2004	1203	2004	1207	x---	----	x---	----	----	1	
										2005	1113	2006	0525	x---	----	x---	----	----	2*	
										2008	0622	2008	0711	x---	----	x---	----	----	1	
										2008	1121	2008	1121	x---	----	x---	----	----	1	
										2009	0906	?*2009*	*1226?*	x---	----	x---	----	----	2?	
Telica (Nicaragua)	12.602 N	86.845 W	1061	4567	BA	Stratovolcanoes	1404-04=	Historical												
										1527?	....	....	....	----	----	x---	----	-x--	3?	
										1529	....	....	....	x---	----	x---	x---	----	4	8/8
										1613	....	....	....	----	----	x---	----	----	2?	
										1685	08	....	....	x---	----	x---	----	----	2	
									?	*1743*	*04*	....	....	----	----	?---	----	----	*2?*	
										1765	....	....	....	----	----	x---	----	----	2	
										1791	0124	....	....	----	----	----	----	----		
(confused with Cerro Negro eruption)									X	*1850*	....	....	....	----	----	----	----	----		
										1907	11	....	....	----	----	x---	----	----	2	
									?	*1918*	*01*	....	....	x---	----	?---	----	----	*2?*	
									?	*1919*	*1026*e	....	....	x---	----	?---	----	----	*2?*	
										1927	08	1927	11	x---	----	x---	----	----	2	
										1928	....	....	....	----	----	x---	----	----	2	
										1929	01	1929	01	x---	----	x---	----	----	1?	
										1934	01	....	....	x---	----	x---	----	----	2	
										1937	11	1938	08	x---	----	x---	----	-x--	2	
										1939	01	1939	06	x---	----	x---	----	----	2	
										1939	11	1939	11	x---	----	x---	----	----	2	
										1940	06	1940	10	x---	----	x---	----	----	2	
									?	*1941*	....	....	....	----	----	?---	----	----		
										1943	12	1944	04	x---	----	x---	----	-x--	2	
										1946	04	1946	08	x---	----	x---	----	-x--	2	
										1948	01	1948	01	x---	----	x---	----	----	2	
										1948	06	1949	11	x---	----	x---	----	-x--	2	
										1951	0715q	1951	1015e	x---	----	x---	----	----	2	
										1962	01	1962	01	x---	----	x---	----	----	1	
										1965	0116	1965	0128	x---	----	x---	----	-x--	1	
										1966	06	1966	06	x---	----	x---	----	----	1	
										1969	0211	1971	12 >	x---	----	x---	-x--	-x--	2	
										1975	05	1976	03	x---	----	----	-x--	----	0	
										1976	1103	1978	01 >	x---	----	x-x-	----	----	1	
										1981	02 ?	....	....	x---	----	x---	----	----	1	
										1981	1125e	1982	0302	x---	----	x---	----	-x--	2*	
Vent in NE corner of crater										1987	11	1987	11	x---	----	x---	----	----	1	
										1994	0731	1994	0812	x---	----	x-x-	----	----	2	
										1999	0521	2000	0906	x---	----	x-x-	-x--	-xx-	2*	
										2001	0117	2001	1219?	x---	----	x---	----	----	1	
										2002	1017	....	....	x---	----	----	-?--	----	0	
										2004	0331	2004	0331	x---	----	x---	----	----	1	
										2004	1105	2005	0129	x---	----	x---	----	----	1	
										2006	0804	2006	0806	x---	----	x---	----	----	1	
										2006	1211?	2007	0217	x---	----	x-x-	----	----	1	
									?	*2007*	*0612*	?*2007*	*0612*	x---	----	?---	----	----	*1*	
										2007	1028c	2008	0218	x---	----	x---	----	----	1?	
										2008	0705d	2008	0705d	x---	----	x---	----	----	1	
Rota (Nicaragua)	12.55 N	86.75 W	832	4567	AB	Stratovolcano	1404-06-	Holocene												
Negro, Cerro (Nicaragua)	12.506 N	86.702 W	728	4567	B	Cinder cones	1404-07=	Historical												
(formation of Cerro Negro)										1850	0413	1850	0527	x---	----	x---	x---	-x--	2	6/5
NE-SW-trending fissure										1867	1114	1867	1130	--x-	----	x---	?---	----	2	-/6
										1899	1122	1899	1129a	----	----	x---	----	-x--	2	-/6
										1914	1028	1914	1103	x---	----	x---	----	-xx-	2	-/6
										1919	0620	1919	0630	----	----	x---	----	----	2	
Summit and upper north flank										1923	1023	1923	1211	x-x-	----	x---	x---	----	3	7/7
										1929	0210	1929	03	-xx-	----	x---	x---	----	2	5/-
Summit and NE flank										1947	0709	1947	0802	xx--	----	x---	x---	-x--	3	6/7
										1948	0331	....	....	x---	----	x---	----	----	2	
										1949	06	1949	06	x---	----	x---	----	----	2	
										1950	1121	1950	1217	x---	----	x---	x---	----	3	5/7
										1954	02	1954	02	x---	----	x---	----	----	2?	
Summit and east flank										1957	0904	1957	0924	xx--	----	x---	x---	-x--	2	6/6
Summit and south flank										1960	0928	1960	1226e	x-x-	----	x---	x---	-x--	3	6/7
NE-flank fissure										1961	1025	....	....	--x-	----	x---	x---	----	1	
										1962	0321	1962	04 ?	x---	----	x---	x---	----	2	
										1963	03	....	....	x---	----	x---	----	----	1	
									?	*1964*	....	....	....	----	----	----	----	----	*2?*	
Summit and south flank										1968	1023	1968	1210	xx--	----	x---	x---	-x--	3	6/7
										1969	1219	1969	1229	x---	----	x---	----	----	1	
Summit and east flank										1971	0203	1971	0214	xx--	----	x---	----	-x--	3	-/7
										1992	0409	1992	0414	x---	----	x---	----	xx--	3	-/7
										1995	0529	1995	1206	x---	----	xxx-	x-x-	-x--	2*	6/6
South flank (near Cristo Rey crater)										1999	0805	1999	0807	-xx-	----	x-x-	x---	----	2	5/6
Pilas, Las (Nicaragua)	12.495 N	86.688 W	1088	3467	ABd	Complex volcano	1404-08=	Historical												
									@	1528	....	....	....	----	----	----	----	----		
El Hoyo										1952	1023	1952	12	---x	----	x-x-	----	----	1	
El Hoyo										1954	1029	1954	1031	x---	----	x-x-	----	----	2	

Paul Kimberly (Smithsonian)

Telica volcano; Las Pilas complex in background

VOLCANO NAME (Subregion) / ERUPTION — Area of Activity	LAT	LONG	ELEV (m)	POPL (5 km, 10, 30, 100)	ROCK TYPE	VOLC TYPE / —Start— Year	NUMBER / M-Dy	STATUS / —Stop— Year	M-Dy	Central, Flank vent, Radial fiss, Regional	Submarine, New island, Subglacial, Crater lake	Explosive, Pyro flow, Phreatic, Caldera	Lava flow, Lava lake, Dome, Spine	Fatal, Damage, Mudflow, Tsunami	VEI	Vol L/T
Momotombo (Nicaragua)	**12.422 N**	**86.540 W**	**1297**	3457	**BA**	**Stratovolcano**	**1404-09=**	**Historical**								
						C **-2550**y	....	....	....	x---	----	----	x---	----		
						C **-0800**t	....	....	....	x---	----	xx--	----	----	4+	-/8
						C **1100**t	....	....	....	x---	----	x---	----	----		
						1524	....	....	....	x---	----	x---	----	----	3	-/7
						1578	02	....	....	x---	----	x---	----	----	2	
						1605	....	**1606**	....	x---	----	x---	----	-xx-	4	-/8
(eruption more likely in 1605-1606)						? *1609*	....	....	....	----	----	?---	----	-??-		
						1736	....	....	....	x---	----	x---	----	----	2?	
						1764	....	....	....	x---	----	x---	----	----	2	
						1849	....	....	....	x---	----	x---	----	----	2	
						1852	....	....	....	x---	----	?---	----	----	2	
						1854	02	**1854**	03	x---	----	x---	----	----	2	
						1858	....	**1866**	....	x---	----	x---	----	----	2	
						1870	....	....	....	x---	----	x---	----	----	2?	
						1878	1014?	....	....	x---	----	x---	----	----	2	
						1882	0909	....	....	x---	----	x---	----	----	2?	
						? *1885*	*10*	....	....	x---	----	?---	----	----	*1?*	
						1886	0519?	**1887**?	....	x---	----	x---	x---	-x--	2	
						1902	0331p	....	....	x---	----	x---	----	----	2?	
						1905	0116	**1905**	0121	x---	----	x---	x---	----	2	-/6
						? *1918*	*04*	....	....	x---	----	?---	----	----	*1?*	
Apoyeque (Nicaragua)	**12.242 N**	**86.342 W**	**518**	4677	**DAB**	**Pyroclastic shield**	**1404-091**	**Radiocarbon**								
Laguna Xiloá						C **-4160**r	....	....	....	x---	----	xx--	----	----	**5**	-/9
W Chiltepe Peninsula (Mateare Tephra)						T **-2550***	....	....	....	-x--	---x	x---	----	---x	**5**	-/9
(Los Cedros Tephra)						T **-1050***	....	....	....	----	----	x---	----	----	4	-/8
Apoyeque (Chiltepe Tephra)						T **-0050**v	....	....	....	x---	----	xxx-	----	----	**6**	-/10
Nejapa-Miraflores (Nicaragua)	**12.12 N**	**86.32 W**	**360**	6677	**BAd**	**Fissure vents**	**1404-092**	**Tephrochronology**								
Refinería crater						C **-7430**y	....	....	....	---x	----	xx--	----	----		
(PM3 tephra)						T **-7300***	....	....	....	---x	----	x---	----	----		
Nejapa crater						C **-5350**x	....	....	....	---x	----	xx--	----	----		
(TC Tephra)						C **-5230**x	....	....	....	---x	----	x---	----	----		
El Hormigón						C **-4390**v	....	....	....	---x	----	x---	----	----		
(PM4 tephra)						T **-3050**z	....	....	....	---x	----	x---	----	----		
(PM5 tephra)						T **-0550**z	....	....	....	---	----	x---	----	----		
Asososco maar						C **0710**V	....	....	....	---x	----	xx--	----	----		
Masaya (Nicaragua)	**11.984 N**	**86.161 W**	**635**	6677	**BA**	**Caldera**	**1404-10=**	**Historical**								
NW of caldera (San Antonio Tephra)						T **-4050**?	....	....	....	-x--	----	xx--	----	----	**6**	-/10
(Masaya Triple Layer)						C **-0170**v	....	....	....	x---	----	xx--	----	----	**5**	-/9
(Masaya Tuff)						T **0150**?	....	....	....	x---	---x	x---	----	----	**5+**	-/9
Nindirí						**1524**	....	**1544**?	....	x---	----	----	-x--	----	0	
Nindirí						**1551**	....	....	....	x---	----	----	-x--	----	0	
Nindirí						**1570**	....	....	....	x---	----	----	-x--	----	0	
Nindirí						? *1586*	....	....	....	x---	----	----	-?--	----	*0*	
Nindirí						? *1613*	....	....	....	x---	----	----	-?--	----	*0*	
Nindirí						**1670**	....	....	....	x---	----	x---	xx--	----	3	7/-
North side of Old Masaya Crater						**1772**	0316	**1772**	0325?	x-x-	----	x---	x---	-x--	2	6/-
(confused with 1772 eruption)						*X* *1775*	....	....	....	----	----	----	----	----		
Between Masaya and Nindirí Craters						**1852**	06	**1852**	07	x-x-	----	x---	xx--	----	2	
Santiago						**1853**	0409?	**1853**	0915>	x---	----	x-x-	----	----	1?	
Santiago or San Pedro						**1856**	12	**1857**	01	x---	----	x---	----	----	2	
						? *1858*	*04*	....	....	x---	----	?---	----	----		
Santiago, San Pedro						**1858**	1110	**1859**	0327	x---	----	x---	----	----	2	
Santiago						**1902**	0715	**1903**	11	x---	----	x---	----	-x--	2	
Santiago						**1904**	05	**1904**	06	x---	----	x---	----	----	2	
Santiago and upper NE flank near El Pelón						**1906**	0102	**1906**	0109>	x-x-	----	x---	----	-x--	2	
Santiago						**1913**	0712	....	....	x---	----	?---	-x--	----	1?	
Santiago						**1918**	01	....	....	x---	----	x---	----	----	1	
Santiago						**1919**	....	**1924**	....	x---	----	x---	----	-x--	2	
Santiago						**1925**	04	....	....	x---	----	x---	----	----	2?	
Santiago						**1946**	06	**1947**	12 ?	x---	----	x---	-x--	----	1*	
Santiago						**1948**	09	**1948**	09	x---	----	x---	----	----	1	
Santiago						**1965**	1010?	**1985**	04 ?	x---	----	x---	xx--	-x--	1*	
Santiago						**1987**	0215	**1987**	0222>	x---	----	x-x-	----	----	1	
Santiago						**1989**	0220	**1989**	11	x---	----	x---	xx--	----	1	
Santiago						**1993**	0616	**1994**	11 >	x---	----	x---	-x--	----	1	
Santiago						**1996**	1205	**1996**	1205	x---	----	x---	----	----	1	
Santiago						**1997**	0603?	**1997**	1117	x---	----	x---	----	----	1	
Santiago						**1998**	0914	**1998**	0914	x---	----	x---	----	----	1	
Santiago						**1999**	1122	**2000**	0302?	x---	----	x-x-	----	----	1	
Santiago						**2001**	0423	**2001**	0425?	x---	----	x---	----	-x--	1	
Santiago						**2003**	0922<	**2003**	1212?	x---	----	x---	-x--	----	1*	
Santiago						? *2004*	*0704*	?*2004*	*0704*	x---	----	?---	----	----	*1?*	
Santiago						**2005**	0304?	**2005**	0330?	x---	----	x---	-?--	----	1	
Santiago						**2006**	0804	**2006**	1025?	x---	----	x---	-x--	----	1	
Santiago						**2008**	0618	?*2008*	*1217*	x---	----	x---	----	----	1	
Granada (Nicaragua)	**11.92 N**	**85.98 W**	**300**	6667	**Bd**	**Fissure vents**	**1404-101**	**Holocene**								
Mombacho (Nicaragua)	**11.826 N**	**85.968 W**	**1344**	3567	**AB**	**Stratovolcano**	**1404-11=**	**Holocene**								
(uncertain eruption in 1570, not 1560)						? *1570*	....	....	....	x---	----	?--A	----	xx--		
(confused with 1850 Cerro Negro eruption)						*X* *1850*	....	....	....	----	----	----	----	----		
Zapatera (Nicaragua)	**11.73 N**	**85.82 W**	**629**	3467	**ABd**	**Shield volcano**	**1404-111**	**Holocene**								
Concepción (Nicaragua)	**11.538 N**	**85.622 W**	**1700**	5557	**ABd**	**Stratovolcano**	**1404-12=**	**Historical**								
East flank (Las Pilas, Sintiope)						C **-0770**t	....	....	....	-x--	----	xx--	x-x-	----	**P**	
						? *1800*t	....	....	....	x---	----	?---	----	----	*2*	
						1883	0405d	**1883**	0630	x---	----	x---	x---	-x--	2	
						1884	....	**1886**	....	x---	----	x---	----	----	2	
						1891	04	**1891**	04	x---	----	x---	----	----	2	
						1902	....	....	....	x---	----	x---	x---	-x--	2	
						1907	09	**1910**	....	x-x-	----	x---	x---	----	2	
						1918	01	**1919**	07	x---	----	x---	----	----	2	
						1921	12	**1926**	05	x-x-	----	x---	x---	-x--	2	
						1928	0125	....	....	x---	----	x---	----	----	2	
						1929	08	**1929**	10	x---	----	x---	----	----	2	

VOLCANO NAME (Subregion) / ERUPTION — Area of Activity	LAT	LONG	ELEV (m)	POPL 5 km 10 30 100	ROCK TYPE	VOLC TYPE	NUMBER	STATUS	Start Year	Start M-Dy	Stop Year	Stop M-Dy	Central Flank vent Radial fiss Regional	Submarine New island Subglacial Crater lake	Explosive Pyro flow Phreatic Caldera	Lava flow Lava lake Dome Spine	Fatal Damage Mudflow Tsunami	VEI	Vol L/T
Concepción (Nicaragua) *continued*									**1935**	02	**1935**	02	x---	----	x---	----	-x--	2	
									1944	04	**1945**	12	x-x-	----	x---	x---	-x--	2	
									1948	....	**1950**	....	x---	----	x---	----	----	1	
									1951	07	**1955**	05	x---	----	x---	----	-x--	2	
									1957	0327	**1957**	07	x-x-	----	x---	x---	-x--	2	
									? *1961*	*1128*	?*1961*	*12*	x---	----	?---	----	----	*2?*	
									1962	06	**1962**	06	x---	----	x---	----	----	2	
									1963	0509	....	....	x---	----	x---	----	----	1	
									1973	1224	**1974**	0112	x---	----	x---	----	----	2	
									1977	0404	**1977**	0503	x---	----	x---	----	----	2	
									1978	0330<	**1978**	05 >	x---	----	x---	----	----	2	
									1982	0115e	**1982**	0214e	x---	----	x-x-	----	----	2	
									1983	0316	**1983**	0325	x---	----	x---	----	----	2	
									1984	12	**1985**	0102	x---	----	x-x-	----	-x--	2*	
									1985	1202a	**1986**	0420?	x---	----	x---	----	----	1	
									1988	06	....	....	x---	----	x---	----	----	2	
									1999	1227	**1999**	1229?	x---	----	x---	----	----	1	
									2005	0728	**2005**	1110	x---	----	x---	----	----	2	
									2006	0901	**2006**	0921	x---	----	x---	----	----	2*	
									2007	0209	**2007**	0710	x---	----	x---	----	-x--	1	
									2007	1124	**2007**	1220	x---	----	x---	----	----	2?	
									2008	0730	**2008**	0730	x---	----	x---	----	----	1	
									2009	1211	**2009**	1211	x---	----	x---	----	----	1	
Maderas (Nicaragua)	**11.446 N**	**85.515 W**	**1394**	4457	ABd	**Stratovolcano**	**1404-13-**	**Holocene**											
									? *1996*	*0927*	....	....	----	----	--?-	----	xxx-		
									? *1999*	*1227*	....	....	----	----	--?-	----	----		
Estelí (Nicaragua)	**13.17 N***	**86.40 W**	**899**	6667	B	**Fissure vents**	**1404-131**	Holocene?											
Ciguatepe, Cerro el (Nicaragua)	**12.53 N**	**86.142 W**	**603**	3457	B	**Stratovolcano**	**1404-132**	Holocene?											
Lajas, Las (Nicaragua)	**12.30 N**	**85.73 W**	**926**	4567	BAD	**Shield volcano**	**1404-133**	Holocene?											
Azul, Volcán (Nicaragua)	**12.53 N***	**83.87 W**	**201**	4456	B	**Cinder cones**	**1404-14-**	**Holocene**											

Jaime Incer

Concepción above Lake Nicaragua

COSTA RICA & PANAMA

VOLCANO NAME (Subregion) / ERUPTION — Area of Activity	LAT	LONG	ELEV (m)	POPL 5 km 10 30 100	ROCK TYPE	VOLC TYPE	NUMBER	STATUS	Start Year	Start M-Dy	Stop Year	Stop M-Dy	Central Flank vent Radial fiss Regional	Submarine New island Subglacial Crater lake	Explosive Pyro flow Phreatic Caldera	Lava flow Lava lake Dome Spine	Fatal Damage Mudflow Tsunami	VEI	Vol L/T
Orosí (Costa Rica)	**10.980 N**	**85.473 W**	**1659**	2456	AB	**Stratovolcanoes**	**1405-01=**	Holocene?											
Rincón de la Vieja (Costa Rica)	**10.830 N**	**85.324 W**	**1916**	3456	ARD	**Complex volcano**	**1405-02=**	**Historical**											
(Río Blanco tephra)									G-**1820** w	....	....	....	x---	----	xx--	----	----	4	-/8
									G **0430** v	....	....	....	x---	----	xx--	----	----		
									? *1529*	....	....	....	----	----	--?-	----	----		
									1765	....	....	....	x---	----	--?-	----	----	2?	
(more likely Rincón de la Vieja than Orosí)									@ **1844**	05	....	....	x---	----	x---	----	----	2	
(more likely Rincón de la Vieja than Orosí)									@ **1849**	....	....	....	x---	----	x---	----	----	2	
									? *1851*	....	....	....	----	----	--?-	----	----		
(more likely Rincón de la Vieja than Orosí)									**1853**	....	....	....	x---	----	x---	----	----	2	
									1854	....	**1863**	08	x---	----	x---	----	----	2*	
									? *1902*	*0622*	....	....	----	----	--?-	----	----	*2?*	
									1912	0614	....	....	x---	----	x---	----	----	3	
									? *1917*	....	....	....	----	----	--?-	----	----		
									1922	0411<	**1922**	0604	x---	---x	x---	----	----	2?	
									1966	1106?	**1967**	12	x---	---x	xxx-	----	-x--	3*	
									1969	0422	**1969**	05	x---	---x	x---	----	----	2	
									1969	0920	**1969**	1016	x---	---x	x---	----	----	2	
									1970	0814	**1970**	0815	x---	---x	x---	----	----	1	
									1983	0206	**1983**	0221	x---	---x	x-x-	----	--x-	1	
									1984	0331	**1984**	04	x---	---x	x-x-	----	--x-	2	
									1985	09	**1986**	04	x---	---x	x-x-	----	----	1	
									1986	1231	**1986**	1231	x---	---x	--x-	----	----	1	
									1987	0401	**1987**	0401	x---	---x	--x-	----	-xx-	1	
									1991	0507	**1992**	09	x---	---x	x-x-	----	-xx-	2	
									1995	1106	**1995**	1113	x---	---x	xxx-	----	--x-	2	
									1998	0215	**1998**	09	x---	---x	x-x-	----	--x-	2	
Miravalles (Costa Rica)	**10.748 N**	**85.153 W**	**2028**	2456	ARDB	**Stratovolcano**	**1405-03=**	**Historical**											
									T-**5050**?	....	....	....	----	----	x---	----	----		
SW flank (near Las Hornillas)									**1946**	0914	**1946**	0914	-x--	----	x-x-	----	----	1	
Tenorio (Costa Rica)	**10.673 N**	**85.015 W**	**1916**	3556	Ab	**Stratovolcanoes**	**1405-031**	**Holocene**											
Arenal (Costa Rica)	**10.463 N**	**84.703 W**	**1670**	4557	ABd	**Stratovolcano**	**1405-033**	**Historical**											
(tephra layer AR-1/SFB)									G-**5060** w	....	....	....	x---	----	xx--	----	----	4?	
(tephra layer AR-2/ET-16)									T-**4450**?	....	....	....	x---	----	x---	----	----		
(tephra layer AR-3/ET-15)									T-**3900**?	....	....	....	x---	----	x---	----	----	4	-/8
(tephra layer AR-4/ET-14)									T-**3350**?	....	....	....	x---	----	x---	----	----	4	-/8
Cerro Chato									C-**3190** v	....	....	....	x---	----	xx--	----	----		
(tephra layer AR-5/ET-13)									T-**2800**?	....	....	....	x---	----	x---	----	----	4	-/8
(tephra layer AR-6/ET-12)									T-**2250**?	....	....	....	x---	----	x---	----	----	4	-/8
Cerro Chato									G-**1770** v	....	....	....	x---	----	xx--	----	----		
(tephra layer AR-7/ET-11)									T-**1650**?	....	....	....	x---	----	x---	----	----	4	-/8
(tephra layer AR-8/ET-10)									T-**1450**?	....	....	....	x---	----	x---	----	----	4	-/8
(tephra layer AR-9/ET-9).									G-**1250** x	....	....	....	x---	----	xx--	----	----	4	-/8
(A4 lava flows).									T-**0830** z	....	....	....	x---	----	----	x---	----	0?	
(tephra layer AR-10/ET-9B)									G-**0380** x	....	....	....	-?--	----	x---	----	----	4	-/8
(tephra layer AR-11/ET-9A)									T-**0270**?	....	....	....	x---	----	x---	----	----	4	-/8
(tephra layer AR-12/ET-9N)									G-**0170** x	....	....	....	x---	----	x---	----	----	4	-/8
(tephra layer AR-13/ET-8B)									A **0400**?	....	....	....	x---	----	x---	----	-x--	4	-/8
(tephra layer AR-14/ET-8M)									T **0550**?	....	....	....	x---	----	x---	----	----	4	-/8
(tephra layer AR-15/ET-7; A3 lava flows)									G **0650** v	....	....	....	x---	----	xx--	x---	----	4	-/8
(tephra layer AR-16/ET-6)									T **0700**?	....	....	....	x---	----	x---	----	----	4	-/8
(tephra layer AR-17/ET-5)									A **0750** t	....	....	....	x---	----	xx--	----	----	4	-/8
(tephra layer AR-18/ET-4)									T **1020**?	....	....	....	x---	----	xx--	----	----	4	-/8
(tephra layer AR-19/ET-3)									T **1030**?	....	....	....	x---	----	xx--	----	----	4	-/8
(tephra layer AR-20/ET-2)									C **1400**?	....	....	....	x---	----	xx--	----	----	4	-/8
(tephra layer AR-21/UN-10)									C **1440**?	....	....	....	x---	----	xx--	x---	----	2?	7/-
Summit and NW flank (A2 lava flows)									T **1750** t	....	....	....	x-x-	----	----	x---	----	0?	
									? *1915*	*0205*	....	....	----	----	?---	----	----	*2?*	
									1922	1005?	**1922**	1023?	x---	----	x---	----	--x-	2	
W flank & summit (AR-22/ET-1 tephra)									**1968**	0729	**2010**>	....	xxx-	----	xxx-	x-x-	xxx-	3*	8/7

VOLCANO NAME (Subregion) / ERUPTION — Area of Activity	LAT	LONG	ELEV (m)	POPL (5 km, 10, 30, 100)	ROCK TYPE	VOLC TYPE	NUMBER	STATUS	Start Year	Start M-Dy	Stop Year	Stop M-Dy	Central, Flank vent, Radial fiss, Regional	Submarine, New island, Subglacial, Crater lake	Explosive, Pyro flow, Phreatic, Caldera	Lava flow, Lava lake, Dome, Spine	Fatal, Damage, Mudflow, Tsunami	VEI	Vol L/T
Platanar (Costa Rica)	10.30 N	84.366 W	2267	3567	ABDRy	Stratovolcanoes	1405-034	Holocene											
Poás (Costa Rica)	10.20 N	84.233 W	2708	4567	ABD	Stratovolcano	1405-04=	Historical											
									C-7920u	....	....	....	X---	----	XX--	----	----		
									C-7620v	....	....	....	X---	----	XX--	----	----		
Botos Cone									C-5590v	....	....	....	X---	----	X---	----	----		
North flank (Cerro Congo)									G-3950?	....	....	....	-X--	----	XX--	----	----		
North flank (Bosque Alegre)									G-0760x	....	....	....	-X--	----	XX--	----	----		
North flank (Bosque Alegre)									T 0210?	....	....	....	-X--	----	X---	----	----		
North flank (Bosque Alegre)									T 1280?	....	....	....	-X--	----	X---	----	----		
									1747	....	....	....	X---	----	?---	----	----	2?	
									1828	....	....	....	X---	---X	X-X-	----	----	1	
									1834	....	....	....	X---	---X	X-X-	----	-X--	2	
(possibly confused with 1834 eruption)									? *1838*	....	....	....	----	----	?---	----	----	*2?*	
									1860	....	....	....	X---	---X	--X-	----	----	1	
(possibly confused with 1880 eruption)									? *1879*	....	....	....	----	----	--?-	----	----	*1*	
									1880	....	....	....	X---	---X	X-X-	----	-X--	1	
									1888	01	1891	....	X---	---X	--X-	----	----	1	
									1895	....	....	....	X---	---X	--X-	----	----	1	
									1898	1229	1907	1231y	X---	---X	X-X-	----	----	1*	
									1910	0125	1910	02	X---	---X	X-X-	----	----	2	-/5
									1910	0912	1910	1014	X---	---X	--X-	----	----	1	
									1914	0530	....	....	X---	---X	X-X-	----	----	2	
									1914	1008	1915	0515>	X---	---X	X-X-	----	----	2	
									1916	....	....	....	X---	---X	X-X-	----	----	2	
									1925	....	....	....	X---	---X	--X-	----	----	1	
									1929	....	....	....	X---	---X	--X-	----	----	1	
									1932	....	1934	....	X---	---X	--X-	----	----	1?	
									1941	....	1946	....	X---	---X	--X-	----	----	1	
									1946	1104d	....	....	X---	---X	--X-	----	----	1	
									1948	....	1951	....	X---	---X	--X-	----	----	1	
									1952	0323	1957	1225	X---	---X	XXX-	X-X-	----	2*	
									1958	....	1961	0703?	X---	---X	X-X-	----	----	2*	
									1963	0523	1963	0702	X---	---X	X-X-	----	----	2	
									1964	1225	1965	03	X---	---X	X-X-	----	----	2	
									1967	0101	....	....	X---	---X	X-X-	----	----	1	
									1968	....	....	....	X---	---X	--X-	----	----	1	
									1969	0503	1969	0603	X---	---X	--X-	----	----	2	
									1970	07	....	....	X---	---X	--X-	----	----	1	
									1972	0209	1973	0908	X---	---X	X-X-	----	----	2*	
									1974	0911	1975	02	X---	---X	--X-	----	----	2	
									1976	0621	1976	11	X---	---X	X-X-	----	----	2	
									1977	05	1977	07 ?	X---	---X	X-X-	----	----	1	
									1977	1218	1978	0615	X---	---X	X-X-	----	----	2	
									1978	0922	1978	12	X---	---X	X-X-	----	----	1	
									1979	0908	1980	01	X---	---X	X-X-	----	----	1	
									1980	0912	1980	0912	X---	---X	X-X-	----	----	1	
									1980	1226	1980	1226	X---	---X	X-X-	----	----	1	
									1981	03	1981	05	X---	----	--X-	----	----	1	
									1987	06	1990	06	X---	---X	X-X-	----	-X--	2*	
									1991	0306	1991	09	X---	---X	--X-	----	----	1	
									1992	02	1992	03	X---	---X	--X-	----	-X--	1	
									1992	10	1993	09	X---	---X	--X-	----	----	0	
									1994	03 ?	1994	10 ?	X---	---X	X-X-	----	-X--	2*	
									1996	0408	1996	0408	X---	---X	X-X-	----	----	1	
									2006	0324	2006	0324?	X---	---X	--X-	----	----	1	
									2006	0925	2006	1216	X---	---X	X-X-	----	----	1	
									2008	0113	2008	0113	X---	---X	X-X-	----	----	1	
									2009	0112	2009	0112	X---	---X	--X-	----	----	1	
									2009	1225	2009	1225	X---	----	X---	----	----	1	
Barva (Costa Rica)	10.135 N	84.10 W	2906	3477	ABD	Complex volcano	1405-05=	Tephrochronology											
									T-6050*	....	....	....	----	----	X---	----	----	P	
									? *1867*	*03*	....	....	----	----	?---	----	----		
Irazú (Costa Rica)	9.979 N	83.852 W	3432	4577	AB	Stratovolcano	1405-06=	Historical											
									G-0640z	....	....	....	----	----	X---	----	----	3	
									G 0430z	....	....	....	----	----	X---	----	----	3	
									G 0690s	....	....	....	----	----	X---	----	----	3	
									G 1110v	....	....	....	----	----	X---	----	----	3	
									G 1560u	....	....	....	----	----	X---	----	----	3	
Diego de la Haya Crater									1723	0216	1724	02 ?	X---	----	XX--	----	-XX-	3	
Diego de la Haya Crater									1726	05	....	....	X---	----	X---	----	----	2	
									1775?	....	....	....	X---	----	X---	----	----	2?	
									? *1821*	*05*	....	....	X---	----	?---	----	----	*2*	
									1822	0507	....	....	X---	----	X---	----	----	2	
									1823	....	....	....	X---	----	X---	----	----	2?	
(possibly only steam emission)									? *1826*	....	....	....	X---	----	?---	----	----		
									1842	....	....	....	X---	----	X---	----	----	2	
									? *1844*	*05*	....	....	X---	----	X---	----	----	*2*	
									1847	0518	....	....	X---	----	X---	----	----	2	
									1864	0916	1864	0917	X---	----	X---	----	----	2	
									1875e	....	....	....	X---	----	X---	----	----	2	
(possibly only fumarolic activity)									? *1882*	....	....	....	X---	----	?---	----	----	*2*	
(fumarolic activity only)									X *1883*	*0103*	....	....	X---	----	----	----	----		
									1885	....	....	....	X---	----	X---	----	----	2?	
									1886	....	....	....	X---	----	X---	----	----	2?	
(fumarolic activity only)									X *1889*	*0228*	....	....	X---	----	----	----	----		
(no eruption this year)									X *1894*	....	....	....	----	----	----	----	----		
(fumarolic activity only)									X *1899*	....	....	....	----	----	----	----	----		
									? *1909*	....	....	....	X---	----	?---	----	----	*2*	
(fumarolic activity only)									X *1910*	....	....	....	X---	----	----	----	----		
									? *1914*	*0221*	....	....	X---	----	?---	----	----		
									1917	0927	1921	....	X---	----	XXX-	----	-X--	3*	
									1924	03	1924	04	X---	----	X---	----	----	2	
									1928	0214	1928	0526e	X---	----	X---	----	----	2	
									1930	10	....	....	X---	----	X---	----	----	2	

Jorge Barquero (Univ. Nac. Costa Rica)

Acidic Laguna Caliente summit crater lake

VOLCANO NAME (Subregion) / **ERUPTION** — Area of Activity	**LAT**	**LONG**	**ELEV** (m)	**POPL** 5 km 10 30 100	**ROCK TYPE**	**VOLC TYPE** — Start — Year	M-Dy	**NUMBER** — Stop — Year	M-Dy	**STATUS**	Central Flank vent Radial fiss Regional	Submarine New island Subglacial Crater lake	Explosive Pyro flow Phreatic Caldera	Lava flow Lava lake Dome Spine	Fatal Damage Mudflow Tsunami	VEI	Vol L/T
Irazú (Costa Rica) *continued*						**1933**	0322?	**1933**	0725		x---	----	x---	----	-x--	2*	-/6
						1939	0518	**1940**	02		x---	----	x---	----	-x--	2	
(fumarolic activity: no eruption)						*X 1962*	*0809*	....	....		x---	----	----	----	----		
						1963	0313	**1965**	0213		x---	----	xxx-	--x-	xxx-	3*	
(increased steaming: no eruption)						*X 1967*	*0807*	....	....		----	----	----	----	----		
(increased steaming: no eruption)						*X 1974*	*0302*	*X1974*	*0307*		----	----	----	----	----		
						1977	0303	....	....		x---	----	x---	----	----	1	
Upper NW flank						**1994**	1208	**1994**	1208		-x--	----	x-x-	----	--x-	2	
Turrialba (Costa Rica)	**10.025 N**	**83.767 W**	**3340**	4467	**ABD**	**Stratovolcano**		**1405-07=**		**Historical**							
NE summit crater						G-**7260**y	....	....	....		x---	----	xx--	x---	----		9/-
						G-**1420**y	....	....	....		x---	----	x-x-	----	----		
						T-**1120**x	....	....	....		x---	----	x-x-	----	----		
						G-**0830**w	....	....	....		x---	----	xx--	----	----		
Central summit crater						G **0040**t	....	....	....		x---	----	xx--	?-?-	----	4	-/8
						G **0640**s	....	....	....		x---	----	xxx-	----	----		
						C **1350**?	....	....	....		x---	----	x---	----	----		
						? 1723	....	....	....		x---	----	?---	----	----	*1*	
						? 1847	....	....	....		x---	----	----	----	----		
						1853	....	....	....		x---	----	x---	----	----	2	
						1855	05	....	....		x---	----	x---	----	----	2	
						? 1861	....	....	....		x---	----	----	----	----		
Central and SW summit craters						**1864**	0817	**1865**	03		x---	----	xxx-	----	----	2*	
Central and SW summit craters						**1866**	01	**1866**	0508		x---	----	xxx-	----	--x-	3	-/7
Barú (Panamá)	**8.808 N**	**82.543 W**	**3474**	3456	**Abdyt**	**Stratovolcano**		**1406-01-**		**Historical**							
						G-**9280**r	....	....	....		x---	----	x---	----	----		
						G-**7420**u	....	....	....		x---	----	x---	----	----		
						G-**1270**v	....	....	....		x---	----	x---	----	----		
						G **0260**w	....	....	....		x---	----	x---	----	----		
						G **0710**r	....	....	....		x---	----	xx--	----	-x--		
						G **1130**w	....	....	....		x---	----	xx--	----	----		
						T **1340**u	....	....	....		x---	----	xx--	----	----		
						1550j	....	....	....		x---	----	xx--	----	-x--		
Valle, El (Panamá)	**8.58 N**	**80.17 W**	**1185**	4467	**DA**	**Stratovolcano**		**1406-03-**		Holocene?							

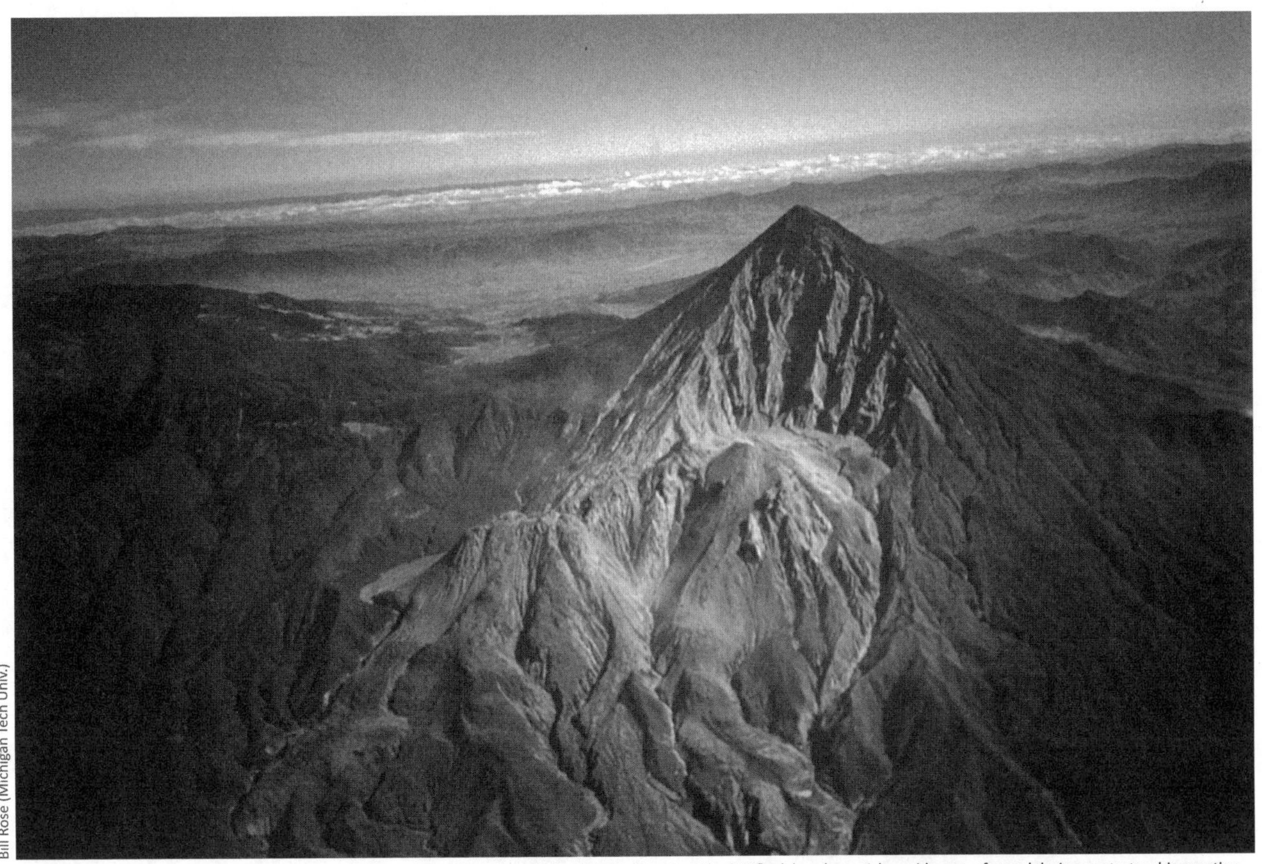

Bill Rose (Michigan Tech Univ.)

Santa María volcano, the most active in Guatemala, has a sharp-topped, conical profile that is cut on the SW flank by a large, 1-km-wide crater formed during a catastrophic eruption in 1902. The large dacitic Santiaguito lava-dome complex (center) has been growing at the base of the 1902 crater since 1922. Lava flows can be seen extending down the flank of the compound lava dome, whose growth is accompanied by a frequent minor explosions, along with periodic lava extrusion, larger explosions, pyroclastic flows, and lahars.

South America (15)

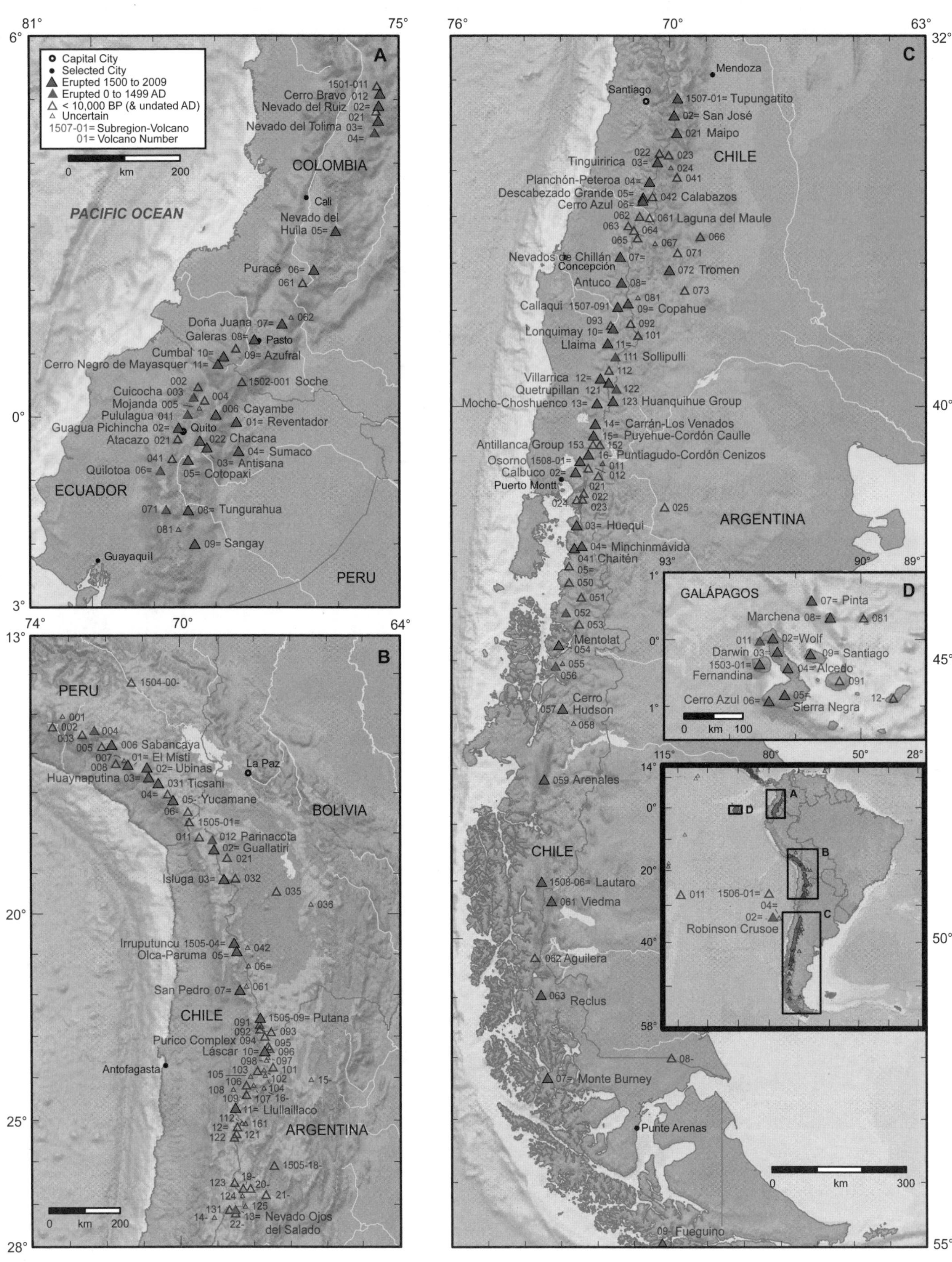

One of the largest of the *CAVW* regions, South America spans the greatest length of any continental volcanic region. Subduction of the eastern Pacific's Nazca Plate beneath South America has produced one of the Earth's highest mountain ranges, and its highest volcano, Nevados Ojos del Salado. Three distinct volcanic belts (see map) are separated by volcanically inactive gaps, where subduction is at such a shallow angle that magma is not generated by the process. South America's first *CAVW* covered the oceanic islands of Ecuador and Chile (in 1962). It was followed one year later by "The Chilean continent" and, in 1966, by "Colombia, Ecuador, & Peru."

South America leads all other regions in population of volcanoes, with 194: it also has the largest number of undated "Holocene" volcanoes (87). This number has dropped considerably from the 112 in the 2nd edition due to completion of more stratigraphic studies, and South America has now edged out Japan (Region 08) in the number of volcanoes with dated eruptions (109 to 108). Chile has the region's largest number of historically active volcanoes, with 41, ranking it 5th among nations, behind Russia's 52. Ecuador, the region's smallest in terms of population and area, is next with 16.

When South America was discovered by Columbus, on his 3rd voyage in 1498, the Inca civilization was large and highly developed, but no records survive of the Andean volcanism that they no doubt witnessed. In 1524, Pizarro started his first voyage along the Pacific coast and within 10 years Atahualpa was executed and the Inca conquered by Spain. Travel overland was slow and difficult, so the Spaniards sailed south, launching their exploration of the Andes from Peru and what is now Ecuador. A result of this pattern is that 27 16th century eruptions are known from Peru northward, while 3 are known south of Peru (and only 8 more in the 17th). In southern Chile, where the population is sparse and the mountains remote, only 3 (of 30) volcanoes have recorded eruptions before the early 1800s. Chaitén volcano sprang to life here in 2008 after more than 9000 years' quiescence, ejecting large amounts of rhyolitic tephra and forming a massive lava dome in the summit caldera, necessitating the evacuation of the coastal town of the same name.

The region's first historically documented eruption was at El Misti, sometime between 1438 and 1471, and the next two were from mainland Ecuador in the early 1530s. The Galápagos Islands were discovered in 1535, but their early visitors were largely pirates, and they were still uninhabited when the first scientific mission arrived in 1790. The first eruption was recorded near the end of that century and the first resident settled in 1807. The Chilean islands were discovered by Juan Fernandez in 1574, but no eruptions were recorded by their only early resident, Robinson Crusoe, during his 1704-09 visit: it remained for Charles Darwin to document the first (and only) certain eruption there in 1835.

South America is dominated by large, often glacier-clad, stratovolcanoes (119, more than any other region) and the world's highest Holocene volcano, the 6887-m-high Nevados Ojos del Salado along the Chile/Argentina border. South America contains 19 Holocene volcanoes in excess of 6000 m, but they are constructed on the high pedestal of the Andean Altiplano, and in terms of edifice heights do not exceed that of volcanoes in other regions. South America trails only Japan and Indonesia in having the most documented VEI ≥4 eruptions in the past 200 years. It has had 16% of the world's mudflow-producing eruptions, including the tragic one at Colombia's Ruiz volcano in 1985. Reflecting the many volcanoes remote from human observers, this region has the largest number of eruptions (24) prefixed by the commercial "at" symbol (@) indicating uncertainty about which of several neighboring volcanoes was actually erupting.

VOLCANO NAME (Subregion) / ERUPTION — Area of Activity	LAT	LONG	ELEV (m)	POPL (5 km, 10, 30, 100)	ROCK TYPE	VOLC TYPE / Start Year	NUMBER / Start M-Dy	Stop Year	STATUS / Stop M-Dy	Central, Flank vent, Radial fiss, Regional	Submarine, New island, Subglacial, Crater lake	Explosive, Pyro flow, Phreatic, Caldera	Lava flow, Lava lake, Dome, Spine	Fatal, Damage, Mudflow, Tsunami	VEI	Vol L/T
COLOMBIA																
Mesa Nevada de Herveo (Colombia)	5.30 N	75.47 W					1501-01=		Not a Volcano							
Romeral (Colombia)	**5.206 N**	**75.364 W**	**3858**	3467	AD	**Stratovolcano**	**1501-011**		**Radiocarbon**							
						C-**5950**z	....	....	....	----	----	x---	----	----	P	
Bravo, Cerro (Colombia)	**5.092 N**	**75.30 W**	**4000**	4467	DAY	**Stratovolcano**	**1501-012**		**Radiocarbon**							
(CB9 tephra)						C-**4280**w	....	....	....	x---	----	x---	----	----	4	-/9
(CB7 tephra)						C-**1310**w	....	....	....	x---	----	x---	----	----	4	-/9
(CB6 tephra)						T-**1050**x	....	....	....	x---	----	x---	----	----	4	-/8
(CB5 tephra)						C-**0730**u	....	....	....	x---	----	xx--	--x-	----	4+	-/8
(CB4 tephra)						C **0750**w	....	....	....	x---	----	xx--	--x-	----	4	-/8
(CB3 tephra)						C **1050**u	....	....	....	x---	----	xx--	--x-	----	4	-/8
(CB2 tephra)						C **1330**u	....	....	....	x---	----	x---	----	----	4	-/8
(CB1 tephra)						T **1720**w	....	....	....	x---	----	xx--	--x-	----	4	-/8
Ruiz, Nevado del (Colombia)	**4.895 N**	**75.322 W**	**5321**	4567	AD	**Stratovolcano**	**1501-02=**		**Historical**							
Arenas Crater (R9 tephra)						T-**6660**<	....	....	....	x---	----	xx--	----	--x-		
ENE flank ? (Alto la Piramide ?)						C-**1245**w	....	....	....	-?--	----	xxxA	--?-	--x-		
Arenas Crater (R8 tephra)						T-**0850**?	....	....	....	x---	----	xx--	----	--x-	4	-/8
Arenas Crater (R7 tephra)						C-**0200**v	....	....	....	x---	----	x---	----	----	4	-/8
West flank (La Olleta, R-6 tephra)						C **0350**y	....	....	....	-x--	----	x---	----	----	3	-/7
Arenas Crater (R5 tephra)						C **0675**t	....	....	....	x---	----	xx--	----	--x-	3	-/7
Arenas Crater (R4 tephra)						C **1350**?	....	....	....	x---	----	x---	----	--x-	4	-/8
						? *1541*	....	....	....	----	----	--?-	----	----		
Arenas Crater?						**1570**	....	....	....	x---	----	x---	----	----		
Arenas Crater (R2 tephra)						**1595**	0309<	....	....	x---	--x-	xx-A	----	xxx-	4*	-/8
Near Arenas Crater						**1623**	....	....	....	x---	----	?-?-	----	----	1?	
						1805	0314	....	....	??--	----	x-?-	----	----	2	
						? *1826*	....	....	....	----	----	--?-	----	----	*2?*	
						1828	06	....	....	??--	----	--x-	----	----	2	
						1829	0618	....	....	??--	----	x-?-	----	----	2	
						1831	....	....	....	??--	----	x-?-	----	----	2	
						? *1833*	....	....	....	??--	----	--?-	----	----	*2?*	
Arenas and La Olleta(?) craters (R1 tephra)						**1845**	0219	....	....	x?x-	--?-	xxx-	?---	xxx-	3	-/7
						1916	....	....	....	----	----	x-x-	----	----	2	
Arenas Crater						**1984**	1222	**1985**	0319?	x---	----	x-x-	----	----	1	
Arenas Crater						**1985**	0911	**1991**	0713	x---	----	xxx-	----	xxx-	3*	-/7
						? *1994*	*0423*	?*1994*	*0423*	x---	----	--?-	----	----		
Santa Isabel (Colombia)	**4.82 N**	**75.37 W**	**4950**	4567	A	**Shield volcano**	**1501-021**		**Radiocarbon**							
						G-**5500**?	....	....	....	----	----	----	x---	----		
						G-**4800**?	....	....	....	----	----	----	x---	----		
						G-**3550**?	....	....	....	----	----	----	x---	----		
						G-**0850**?	....	....	....	----	----	----	x---	----		
Tolima, Nevado del (Colombia)	**4.67 N**	**75.33 W**	**5200**	4467	AD	**Stratovolcano**	**1501-03=**		**Historical**							
(Canalones eruptive stage)						C-**7800**y	....	....	....	----	----	x---	----	----	P	
(Mesetas eruptive stage)						C-**5310**v	....	....	....	----	----	xx--	----	----		
(Mesetas eruptive stage)						G-**5160**x	....	....	....	----	----	x---	----	----		
(Mesetas eruptive stage)						G-**3500**y	....	....	....	----	----	xx--	----	----		
(Encanto eruptive stage)						G-**1990**x	....	....	....	----	----	xx--	----	----	**5?**	-/9

VOLCANO NAME (Subregion) / ERUPTION	LAT	LONG	ELEV (m)	POPL (5 km, 10, 30, 100)	ROCK TYPE	Area of Activity	VOLC TYPE / Start Year	Start M-Dy	NUMBER / Stop Year	STATUS / Stop M-Dy	Central, Flank vent, Radial fiss, Regional	Submarine, New island, Subglacial, Crater lake	Explosive, Pyro flow, Phreatic, Caldera	Lava flow, Lava lake, Dome, Spine	Fatal, Damage, Mudflow, Tsunami	VEI	Vol L/T
Tolima, Nevado del (Colombia) *continued*						(Encanto eruptive stage)	G-**0610**x	....	....	....	----	----	x---	----	----	3?	
						(Encanto eruptive stage)	G-**0200**x	....	....	....	----	----	x---	----	----	3?	
						(Encanto eruptive stage)	G **0260**w	....	....	....	----	----	x---	----	----	3?	
							1822	11 ?	....	....	----	----	x---	----	----	2	
							1825	0302?	....	....	----	----	x---	----	----	2	
							1826	05	**1826**	0617>	----	----	x---	----	----	2	
							1943	03	....	....	----	----	x---	----	----	2	
Machín (Colombia)	**4.48 N**	**75.392 W**	**2650**	4567	DA		**Stratovolcano**		**1501-04=**	**Radiocarbon**							
							G-**3800**w	....	....	....	----	----	xx--	----	----		
							C-**2650**?	....	....	....	----	----	x---	----	----		
							G-**2240**y	....	....	....	----	----	xx--	----	----		
							G-**2100**x	....	....	....	----	----	xx--	----	----		
							C-**0650**?	....	....	....	----	----	xx--	----	--x-		
							C **0750**?	....	....	....	----	----	x---	----	----		
							G **1180**w	....	....	....	x---	----	x---	----	----		
Huila, Nevado del (Colombia)	**2.93 N**	**76.03 W**	**5364**	3457	AD		**Stratovolcano**		**1501-05=**	**Historical**							
							1555e	....	....	....	----	----	x---	----	----		
							2007	0219	**2007**	0528?	x-x-	----	x---	----	-xx-	3?	
							2008	0102	**2008**	04 ?	x---	----	x---	----	----	2?	
						Upper SW side of Pico Central	**2008**	1026?	**2010>**	....	x-x-	----	x---	--x-	xxx-	3?	6/-
Puracé (Colombia)	**2.32 N**	**76.40 W**	**4650**	4467	AD		**Stratovolcanoes**		**1501-06=**	**Historical**							
							C-**0160**t	....	....	....	x---	----	xx--	----	----		
							1816	....	....	....	----	----	----	----	----		
							1827	1118	....	....	x---	----	x---	x---	----	2	
							1835	0123	....	....	x---	----	x---	----	----	2	
							1840	....	....	....	x---	----	x---	----	----	2	
							1847	1027	**1852**	....	x---	----	x---	----	-x--	3?	
							1860i	....	....	....	x---	----	x---	----	----	2?	
							1869	1004	**1869**	11	x---	----	xx--	----	--x-	3?	
							1870	10	....	....	x---	----	x---	----	----	2	
							1878	0831	....	....	x---	----	x---	----	----	2	
							1881	....	....	....	x---	----	x---	----	----	2	
							1885	0525	....	....	x---	----	x---	----	xx--	3	
							1899	....	....	....	x---	----	x---	----	----	2	
							1902?	....	....	....	x---	----	x---	----	----	2	
							1906	....	....	....	x---	----	x---	----	----	2	
							1924	....	....	....	x---	----	x---	----	----	2	
							1925	1012	**1925**	1105	x---	----	x---	----	----	2	
							1926	08	**1926**	09	x---	----	x---	----	----	2	
							1927	....	....	....	x---	----	x---	----	----	2	
							1946	03	**1946**	04	x---	----	x---	----	----	2	
							1947	0427	....	....	x---	----	x---	----	----	2	
							1949	0526	**1949**	0611	x---	----	x---	----	x---	2	
							1956<	....	....	....	x---	----	x---	----	----	2	
							1957	....	....	....	----	----	----	----	----	2?	
							1977	0319	**1977**	0328?	x---	----	x---	----	----	2	
Sotará (Colombia)	**2.108 N**	**76.592 W**	**4400**	4467	AD		**Stratovolcano**		**1501-061**	**Holocene**							
Petacas (Colombia)	**1.57 N**	**76.78 W**	**4054**	3457	U		**Lava dome**		**1501-062**	Holocene?							
Doña Juana (Colombia)	**1.47 N**	**76.92 W**	**4150**	4467	AD		**Stratovolcano**		**1501-07=**	**Historical**							
						Northeastern caldera	C-**2550**w	....	....	....	x---	----	xx-x	--x-	----	**C**	
							1897	1101	**1906**	....	x---	----	xx--	--x-	x-x-	4*	
Galeras (Colombia)	**1.22 N**	**77.37 W**	**4276**	3667	Ad		**Complex volcano**		**1501-08=**	**Historical**							
							T-**7050***	....	....	....	x---	----	xx--	----	----		
							G-**3150**x	....	....	....	x---	----	xx--	----	--x-	3	-/6
							G-**2580**z	....	....	....	x---	----	xx--	----	----	2	-/6
							G-**1160**y	....	....	....	x---	----	xx--	----	----	2	-/6
							G-**0490**v	....	....	....	x---	----	xx--	----	--x-	2	-/6
							G **0890**x	....	....	....	x---	----	xx--	----	--x-	2	-/6
							1535	....	....	....	x---	----	x---	----	----	3↑	
						(eruption December 7, 1580, not 1590)	**1580**	1207	**1580**	1207	x---	----	xx--	?---	----	3	
							1616	0704	**1616**	0704	x---	----	xx--	?---	----	3↑	
							1641	....	**1643**	....	x---	----	xx--	----	----	3	
							1670	....	**1736**	....	x---	----	x---	----	----	3*	
							1754	....	**1756**	....	x---	----	x---	----	----	2	
							1796	11	**1801**	....	x---	----	x---	?---	----	2	
							1823	0617	**1823**	0624	x---	----	x---	x---	----	2	
							1828	1024	**1834**	03	x---	----	x---	?-?-	----	3*	
							1834	....	....	....	x---	----	x---	x---	----	2	
							? *1836*	....	....	....	x---	----	x---	----	----	*2*	
							1865	1002	**1870**	....	x---	----	xx--	x-x-	--x-	3*	7/6
							1889	0703	....	....	x---	----	x---	?---	----	2	
							1891	....	....	....	x---	----	x---	?---	----	2	
							1923	1208	....	....	x---	----	x---	----	----	2	
							1924	10	**1927**	....	x---	----	x---	?-x-	----	3*	
							? *1930*	*0417*	....	....	x---	----	?---	----	----		
							1932	1010	....	....	x---	----	x---	----	----	2	
							? *1933*	....	....	....	x---	----	?---	----	----		
							1936	0209	**1936**	0827?	x---	----	xx--	?---	-x--	2	
							? *1947*	*0715*	....	....	x---	----	?---	----	----	*2?*	
							1950	0112	**1950**	0905	x---	----	x---	----	----	2	
							? *1973*	*05*	....	....	x---	----	x---	----	----	*2*	
							1974	....	**1983>**	....	x---	----	x---	----	----	1?	
						El Pinta vent	**1989**	0219	**1989**	0509	x---	----	xxx-	----	----	2	-/5
							1990	0107	**1992**	0716	x---	----	x?x-	--x-	-xx-	2*	5/5
						Summit crater, west, SW, & south rims	**1993**	0114	**1993**	0607	x-x-	----	x---	----	xx--	2	-/6
							2000	0321	**2000**	0518	x---	----	--?-	----	----	1	
						El Pinta vent	**2002**	0607	**2002**	0607?	x---	----	x-x-	----	----	1?	
						El Pinta vent	**2004**	0716	**2005**	0207?	x---	----	x---	----	-x--	3*	
							2005	1124	**2006**	0712	x---	----	x---	--x-	----	2	
							2007	1004	**2008**	0117	x---	----	x---	----	----	3?	
							2008	1021?	**2010>**	....	x---	----	x---	----	----	3*	

Norm Banks (USGS/CVO)

1989 eruption above Pasto

VOLCANO NAME (Subregion) / ERUPTION — Area of Activity	LAT	LONG	ELEV (m)	POPL (5 km 10 30 100)	ROCK TYPE	VOLC TYPE / Start Year	NUMBER / Start M-Dy	STATUS / Stop Year	Stop M-Dy	Central, Flank vent, Radial fiss, Regional	Submarine, New island, Subglacial, Crater lake	Explosive, Pyro flow, Phreatic, Caldera	Lava flow, Lava lake, Dome, Spine	Fatal, Damage, Mudflow, Tsunami	VEI	Vol L/T
Azufral (Colombia)	**1.08 N**	**77.68 W**	**4070**	4567	DA	**Stratovolcano**	**1501-09=**	**Radiocarbon**								
						C-**2095**v	....	....	....	x---	----	xx--	--x-	----		
						C-**1850**?	....	....	....	x---	----	x---	--x-	----		
						C-**1650**w	....	....	....	x---	----	xx--	--x-	----		
						C-**0930**?	....	....	....	x---	----	x---	----	----	**P**	
Cumbal (Colombia)	**0.95 N**	**77.87 W**	**4764**	4567	Ad	**Stratovolcano**	**1501-10=**	**Historical**								
						1877	12	....	....	x---	----	x---	----	----	2	
						1926	1220	**1926**	1221	x---	----	x---	----	----	2	
Negro de Mayasquer, Cerro (Col)	**0.828 N**	**77.964 W**	**4445**	3467	DA	**Stratovolcano**	**1501-11=**	Holocene?								
(eruption possibly from Reventador)						@ **1936**	0717	....	....	?---	----	?---	----	----	2	
ECUADOR																
Soche (Ecuador)	**0.552 N**	**77.580 W**	**3955**	3457	DA	**Stratovolcano**	**1502-001**	**Radiocarbon**								
						C-**6650**?	....	....	....	x---	----	xx--	--x-	----	**5?**	
Chachimbiro (Ecuador)	**0.468 N**	**78.287 W**	**4106**	3467	DA	**Stratovolcano**	**1502-002**	**Radiocarbon**								
NNE flank (Pitzantzi lava dome)						C-**3740**?	....	....	....	--x-	----	x---	--x-	----		
Cuicocha (Ecuador)	**0.308 N**	**78.364 W**	**3246**	6667	D	**Caldera**	**1502-003**	**Radiocarbon**								
						C-**2550**?	....	....	....	x---	----	x---	----	--x-		
						C-**1150**w	....	....	....	x---	----	xxxx	----	-x--	**5**	-/9
						C-**0950**?	....	....	....	x---	----	xx--	--x-	----		
						C **0650**?	....	....	....	x---	----	?---	----	----		
Imbabura (Ecuador)	**0.258 N**	**78.183 W**	**4609**	3567	AD	**Compound volc**	**1502-004**	**Radiocarbon**								
Huarmi Imbabura						C-**5550**z	....	....	....	x---	----	xx--	----	-x--		
Mojanda (Ecuador)	**0.13 N**	**78.27 W**	**4263**	3567	ADR	**Stratovolcanoes**	**1502-005**	Holocene?								
Cayambe (Ecuador)	**0.029 N**	**77.986 W**	**5790**	2467	ADr	**Compound volc**	**1502-006**	**Historical**								
						T-**1800**?	....	....	....	----	----	x---	----	----		
						T-**1650**?	....	....	....	----	----	x---	----	----		
						T-**1300**?	....	....	....	----	----	x---	----	----		
						T-**0560**?	....	....	....	----	----	x---	----	----		
						T-**0510**?	....	....	....	----	----	x---	----	----		
						T-**0460**?	....	....	....	----	----	x---	----	----		
						T-**0260**?	....	....	....	----	----	x---	----	----		
						T-**0230**?	....	....	....	----	----	x---	----	----		
						T-**0180**?	....	....	....	----	----	x---	----	----		
						T **0010**?	....	....	....	----	----	x---	----	----		
						T **0170**?	....	....	....	----	----	x---	----	----		
						T **0200**?	....	....	....	----	----	x---	----	----		
						T **0260**?	....	....	....	----	----	x---	----	----		
						T **0880**?	....	....	....	----	----	x---	----	----		
Lava dome near eastern summit						T **1040**?	....	....	....	-x--	----	xx--	--x-	----	4	8/-
						T **1270**?	....	....	....	----	----	x---	----	----		
Tarugo Corral lava dome (NE flank)						T **1290**?	....	....	....	-x--	----	xx--	--x-	--x-	4	8/-
						T **1440**?	....	....	....	----	----	x---	----	----		
North flank of main summit						T **1570**?	....	....	....	-x--	----	xx--	--x-	----	4	8/-
North flank of main summit						T **1590**?	....	....	....	-x--	----	xx--	----	----		
						T **1700**?	....	....	....	----	----	x---	----	----		
Upper SE flank						**1785**	02	**1786**	03	-x--	----	x---	?---	--?-	2?	
Reventador (Ecuador)	**0.077 S**	**77.656 W**	**3562**	3347	ABD	**Stratovolcano**	**1502-01=**	**Historical**								
						1541	04	....	....	x---	----	x---	----	----	3↑	
						1590	....	....	....	x---	----	x---	----	----	3↑	
						1691	....	....	....	x---	----	x---	----	----	3↑	
						@ **1748**<	....	....	....	x---	----	x---	----	----	2?	
						1797	01	....	....	x---	----	x---	----	----	3	
						@ **1802**	04 ?	@**1802**	05 ?	x---	----	x---	----	----	2	
						1843<	....	....	....	x---	----	x---	----	----	2?	
						1843	1207	....	....	x---	----	x---	----	----	3	
						1844	....	....	....	x---	----	x---	----	----	3	
						1856	1212	**1856**	1213	x---	----	x---	----	----	3	
						1871	0130	....	....	x---	----	x---	----	----	2	
						1894	....	....	....	x---	----	x---	----	----	3	
						1898	0408	**1906**	....	x---	----	xx--	----	----	3	
						1912	02	**1912**	03	x---	----	x---	----	----	3	
						1926	0105d	**1926**	05	x---	----	x---	----	----	3	
						1929	....	....	....	x---	----	x---	----	----	3	
						1936	0827	....	....	x---	----	x---	----	----	3	
						1944	0224	**1944**	0301	x---	----	x---	x---	--x-	3	
						1955	....	....	....	x---	----	x---	----	----	2	
						1958	11	....	....	x---	----	x---	----	----	3	
						1960	06	....	....	x---	----	x---	----	----	3	
						1972	07	**1972**	09	x---	----	x---	x---	--x-	2	7/-
						1973	11	**1974**	07	x---	----	x---	x---	--x-	3*	6/-
						1976	0104	**1976**	05	x---	----	xx--	x---	----	2	7/-
Summit and SE flank (2600 m)						**2002**	1103	**2003**	0110?	xx--	----	xx--	x---	xxx-	4	7/8
						2004	1107c	**2006**	03	x---	----	xx--	x-x-	--x-	2*	6/-
						2007	0315g	**2007**	1011?	x---	----	x---	x---	--x-	2*	
						2008	0727	**2010**>	....	x---	----	x---	x---	----	2	
Pululagua (Ecuador)	**0.038 N**	**78.463 W**	**3356**	6677	D	**Caldera**	**1502-011**	**Radiocarbon**								
						C-**4800**?	....	....	....	----	----	xx--	----	----		
						C-**0690**w	....	....	....	x---	----	xx-x	----	-x--	**5**	-/9
						C-**0450**w	....	....	....	x---	----	xx-x	--x-	-x--	**C**	
						C **0290**?	....	....	....	x---	----	xx--	x-x-	----		
Guagua Pichincha (Ecuador)	**0.171 S**	**78.598 W**	**4784**	3577	AD	**Stratovolcano**	**1502-02=**	**Historical**								
						C-**7000**?	....	....	....	x---	----	x---	--x-	----		
						C-**6650**?	....	....	....	x---	----	xx--	----	----		
						C-**6400**?	....	....	....	x---	----	xx--	--x-	----		
						C-**6300**?	....	....	....	x---	----	xx--	--x-	----		
						C-**6200**?	....	....	....	x---	----	xx--	----	----		
						T-**4850***	....	....	....	x---	----	x---	----	----		
						C-**3500**?	....	....	....	x---	----	x---	----	----		
						G-**2090**u	....	....	....	x---	----	xx--	--x-	--x-		
						G-**1860**v	....	....	....	x---	----	x---	--x-	----		

Patricio Ramon (Escuela Politecnica, Quito)

2005 eruption

VOLCANO NAME (Subregion) / ERUPTION — Area of Activity	LAT	LONG	ELEV (m)	POPL (5 km / 10 / 30 / 100)	ROCK TYPE	VOLC TYPE	NUMBER	STATUS	Start Year	Start M-Dy	Stop Year	Stop M-Dy	Central / Flank vent / Radial fiss / Regional	Submarine / New island / Subglacial / Crater lake	Explosive / Pyro flow / Phreatic / Caldera	Lava flow / Lava lake / Dome / Spine	Fatal / Damage / Mudflow / Tsunami	VEI	Vol L/T
Guagua Pichincha (Ecuador) *continued*									G-**1230**u	....	....	....	x---	----	x---	--x-	----		
									G **0070**u	....	....	....	x---	----	xx--	----	----	4	-/8
									G **0550**u	....	....	....	x---	----	xx--	--x-	----		
									G **0910**v	....	....	....	x---	----	xx--	----	----	**5**	-/9
									? *1533*	....	....	....	x---	----	x-?-	----	----	*2*	
									? *1534*	....	....	....	x---	----	x-?-	----	----	*2*	
									? *1535*	....	....	....	x---	----	x-?-	----	----	*2*	
									? *1538*	....	....	....	x---	----	x-?-	----	----	*3↑*	
									? *1539*	....	....	....	x---	----	x-?-	----	----	*2*	
									? *1560*	....	....	....	x---	----	x-?-	----	----	*2*	
									1566	1017	**1566**	1116	x---	----	xx--	----	-x--	3↑	
									1575	0908	....	....	x---	----	xx--	----	----	2	
(perhaps confused with 1575 eruption)									? *1577*	....	....	....	x---	----	?---	----	----	*2*	
									? *1580*	....	....	....	x---	----	x-?-	----	----	*2*	
									1582	0605	**1598**	....	x---	----	xx--	----	----	3*	
									1660	1027	**1660**	1128	x---	----	xx--	--x-	-xx-	4	-/8
									1830	....	....	....	x---	----	x-x-	----	----	2	
									1831	....	....	....	x---	----	x-x-	----	----	3	
									1868	0319	**1868**	0322	x---	----	x-x-	----	----	2	
									1868	08	....	....	x---	----	x-x-	----	----	2	
									1869	03	....	....	x---	----	x-x-	----	----	2	
									1869	0722	**1869**	0824	x---	----	x-x-	----	----	2	
									1881	0310	....	....	x---	----	x-x-	----	----	2	
NE side of 1660 lava dome									**1981**	0831e	**1982**	11 ?	x---	----	x-x-	----	----	1*	-/4
1981 crater									**1985**	05	**1985**	06	x---	----	--x-	----	----	1	
1981 crater									**1990**	0416	**1990**	0510	x---	----	--x-	----	----	1	
1981 crater									**1993**	0309	**1993**	0312	x---	----	x-x-	----	x---	1	
1981 crater									**1997**	03	**1997**	1018	x---	----	--x-	----	----	1	
West and SE of 1981 crater									**1998**	0807	**2001**	0525	x---	----	xxx-	--xx	xxx-	3*	6/-
North of 1981 crater									**2001**	1126	**2001**	1126	x---	----	--x-	----	----	1?	
									2002	04	**2004**	04	x---	----	--x-	----	----	1?	
									2002	1011	**2002**	1207	x---	----	--x-	----	----	1?	
									? *2003*	*0417*<	?*2003*	*0417*	x---	----	--x-	----	----	*1*	
									? *2008*	*0201*	?*2008*	*0201*	x---	----	--?-	----	----	*1?*	
									? *2009*	*0216*	?*2009*	*0217*	x---	----	--?-	----	----	*1?*	
Atacazo (Ecuador)	**0.353 S**	**78.617 W**	**4463**	3677	**AD**	**Stratovolcano**	**1502-021**	**Radiocarbon**											
La Cocha II dome (N3 tephra layer)									C-**6910**<	....	....	....	x---	----	x---	--x-	----	**P**	
Arenal II dome (N4 tephra layer)									C-**3490**v	....	....	....	x---	----	xx--	--x-	----	**P**	
Ninahuilca Chico I dome (N5 tephra layer)									C-**2490**s	....	....	....	x---	----	xx--	--x-	----	**5**	-/9
Ninahuilca Chico II dome (N6 tephra layer)									C-**0320**n	....	....	....	x---	----	xx--	--x-	----	**5**	-/9
Chacana (Ecuador)	**0.375 S**	**78.25 W**	**4643**	5567	**RDA**	**Caldera**	**1502-022**	**Historical**											
									T-**8050**?	....	....	....	x---	----	x---	x---	----		
									C-**1580**j	....	....	....	x---	----	x---	----	----		
									T-**0050**?	....	....	....	----	----	----	x---	----		
SW flank									**1760**	....	....	....	-x--	----	x---	x---	-x--	0	**9**/-
South part of caldera									**1773**	....	....	....	---x	----	----	x---	-x--	0	8/-
Antisana (Ecuador)	**0.481 S**	**78.141 W**	**5753**	3457	**AD**	**Stratovolcano**	**1502-03=**	**Historical**											
(eruption possibly from Reventador)									@ **1590**?	....	....	....	----	----	x---	----	----	2?	
									? *1728*	....	....	....	-x--	----	----	x---	----	*0*	
NNE side of summit									**1801**	....	**1802**	05 >	x---	--x-	x---	x-?-	----	2	
Sumaco (Ecuador)	**0.538 S**	**77.626 W**	**3990**	2346	**XZ**	**Stratovolcano**	**1502-04=**	**Historical**											
									? *1650*t	....	....	....	x---	----	x---	----	----	*3?*	
									1895r	....	....	....	x---	----	x---	----	----	2?	
									? *1933*	*02*	....	....	x---	----	x---	----	----	*2*	
Illiniza (Ecuador)	**0.659 S**	**78.714 W**	**5248**	3467	**ADr**	**Stratovolcano**	**1502-041**	**Holocene**											
Cotopaxi (Ecuador)	**0.677 S**	**78.436 W**	**5911**	3467	**ADR**	**Stratovolcano**	**1502-05=**	**Historical**											
(tephra set F-1)									C-**7690**u	....	....	....	x---	----	x?--	----	----	2	-/6
(tephra set F-2)									C-**5820**u	....	....	....	x---	----	xx--	----	----	**5+**	-/9
(tephra set F-3)									C-**4350**u	....	....	....	x---	----	xx--	----	----	**5**	-/9
(tephra set F-4)									C-**3880**u	....	....	....	x---	----	xx--	--x-	--x-	**5+**	-/9
(tephra set F-5)									T-**3280**z	....	....	....	x---	----	xx--	x---	--x-	**5**	8/9
(Colorado Canyon tephra set)									C-**2640**x	....	....	....	x---	----	xx-A	----	xxx-	**5**	-/9
									T-**2250**	....	....	....	x---	----	----	x---	----		8/-
(tephra set H)									C-**2220**v	....	....	....	x---	----	x---	----	--x-		
(tephra layers I1)									T-**2050**?	....	....	....	x---	----	x---	x---	----	**5**	7/**9**
									C-**1510**w	....	....	....	x---	----	x---	----	----		
(tephra layer I2)									T-**1050**?	....	....	....	x---	----	xx--	x---	----	4	**9**/8
(tephra layer J)									T-**0400**?	....	....	....	x---	----	x---	x---	----	4	7/8
(tephra layer JJ)									C-**0230**x	....	....	....	x---	----	x---	----	----	4	-/8
(tephra layer JK)									T-**0050**?	....	....	....	x---	----	x---	x---	----	3	7/7
(tephra layer Ka1)									C **0070**w	....	....	....	x---	----	xx--	----	----	4	-/8
(tephra layer Ka2)									T **0150**?	....	....	....	x---	----	x---	----	----	4	-/8
(tephra layer Kb2)									C **0180**v	....	....	....	x---	----	x---	x---	----	4	8/8
(tephra layer 11)									T **0370**x	....	....	....	x---	----	x---	----	----		
(tephra layer 10)									T **0550**x	....	....	....	x---	----	x---	----	----		
(tephra layer Kb2)									C **0740**u	....	....	....	x---	----	xx--	x---	----	4	7/8
(tephra layer L1)									C **0770**u	....	....	....	x---	----	xx--	x---	----	4	7/8
(tephra layer L2)									T **0950**?	....	....	....	x---	----	xx--	----	----	3	-/7
(tephra layer X)									C **1130**u	....	....	....	x---	----	xx--	----	----	**5**	-/9
									T **1260**w	....	....	....	x---	----	x---	?---	----		
(tephra layer Y4)									T **1350**?	....	....	....	x---	----	x---	?---	----	4+	-/8
									1532	1115	....	....	x---	----	x---	x---	-x?-	4	7/8
									1533	10	**1533**	11	x---	----	x---	----	--x-	2	
(tephra set MZ)									**1534**	06	**1534**	07	x---	----	xx--	----	-xx-	4	-/8
									1698	....	....	....	x---	----	xx--	----	xxx-	3?	
									1738	....	....	....	x---	----	xx--	----	--x-	2	
									1740	....	**1741**	....	x---	----	x---	----	----	2	
									1742	0615	**1742**	07	x---	----	xx--	----	xxx-	3?	
									1742	1209	....	....	x-x-	----	xx--	----	xxx-	3?	
									1743	04	....	....	x---	----	xx--	----	-xx-	3?	
									1743	0927	**1743**	1004	x---	----	xx--	----	--x-	2	
									1744	05	**1744**	12	x---	----	xx--	?---	-xx-	4*	7/8
									1746	02	....	....	x---	----	x---	----	----	2	

VOLCANO NAME (Subregion) / ERUPTION — Area of Activity	LAT	LONG	ELEV (m)	POPL (5 km, 10, 30, 100)	ROCK TYPE	VOLC TYPE	NUMBER	STATUS	Start Year	Start M-Dy	Stop Year	Stop M-Dy	Central, Flank vent, Radial fiss, Regional	Submarine, New island, Subglacial, Crater lake	Explosive, Pyro flow, Phreatic, Caldera	Lava flow, Lava lake, Dome, Spine	Fatal, Damage, Mudflow, Tsunami	VEI	Vol L/T
Cotopaxi (Ecuador) *continued*																			
									1747	....	**1749**	....	x---	----	x---	----	----	2	
									1750	0902a	**1750**	0904a	x---	----	x---	----	----	2	
									1766	0210	**1766**	12	x---	----	xx--	----	-xx-	3	
									1768	0404	....	....	x---	----	xx--	----	xxx-	4	7/8
									1803	0104	**1803**	0105	x---	----	xx--	----	-xx-	3	
									1844	....	....	....	x---	----	x---	----	----	2	
									1845	04	....	....	x---	----	x---	----	----	2	
									1850	....	....	....	x---	----	xx--	----	--x-	2	
									1851	06	....	....	x---	----	x---	----	----	2	
									1852	....	....	....	x---	----	x---	----	----	2	
									1853	0913	**1853**	0915	x---	----	xx--	x---	--x-	3	7/-
									1854	0403	....	....	x---	----	xx--	----	--x-	2	
									1854	0914	....	....	x---	----	xx--	----	--x-	2	
									1855	11	....	....	x---	----	xx--	----	--x-	2	
									1856	05	....	....	x---	----	xx--	----	--x-	2	
									1856	10	**1856**	12	x---	----	xx--	----	--x-	2	
									1857	....	....	....	x---	----	x---	----	----	2	
									1858	11	**1858**	12	x---	----	xx--	----	--x-	2	
									1859	....	....	....	x---	----	x---	----	----	2	
									1860	....	**1862**	....	x---	----	x---	----	----	2	
									1863	....	....	....	x---	----	xx--	----	--x-	2	
									1866	0921	**1866**	0926	x---	----	x---	----	----	2	
									1867	....	....	....	x---	----	x---	----	----	2	
									1868	0815	**1868**	0816	x---	----	x---	----	----	2	
									1869	07	**1869**	08	x---	----	x---	----	----	3	
									1870	....	**1876**	....	x---	----	x---	----	----	2	
									1877	01	**1877**	0902	x---	----	xx--	----	xxx-	4*	7/8
									1878	0823	**1878**	0824	x---	----	xx--	----	----	2	
									1879	0226	**1879**	0619	x---	----	x?--	----	----	2	
									1880	02	**1880**	07	x---	----	xx--	----	--x-	3*	
									1882	01	**1882**	03	x---	----	x---	----	----	2	
									1883	08	....	....	x---	----	xx--	----	--x-	2	
									1883	12	....	....	x---	----	xx--	----	--x-	2	
									1885	0723	....	....	x---	----	xx--	----	--x-	2	
									1886	01	....	....	x---	----	x---	----	----	2	
									1895	....	....	....	x---	----	x---	----	----	2	
									1903	0926	**1904**	12	x---	----	xx--	----	--x-	3*	
									1905	....	....	....	x---	----	x---	----	----	2	
									1906	0821	**1906**	0919	x---	----	x---	----	----	2	
									1907	06	....	....	x---	----	x---	----	----	2	
									1908	....	**1914**	....	x---	----	x---	----	----	1	
									1922	....	....	....	x---	----	x---	----	----	2	
									1926	....	....	....	x---	----	x---	----	----	2	
									1931	....	....	....	x---	----	x---	----	----	2	
									1939	0202	....	....	x---	----	x---	----	----	2	
									1940	....	....	....	x---	----	x---	----	----	2	
(press reports not confirmed)									*? 1942*	*0217*	*?1942*	*0219*	x---	----	x---	----	-x--	*3?*	
Quilotoa (Ecuador)	**0.85 S**	**78.90 W**	**3914**	5567	Da	**Caldera**	**1502-06=**	**Radiocarbon**											
									G **1280**?	....	....	....	x---	---x	xxxx	--x-	-xx-	**6**	-/10
(confused with 1660 Pichincha erupt)									*X 1660*	*1128*	....	....	----	----	----	----	----		
									? 1725	....	....	....	x---	---x	?---	----	----	*2*	
									? 1740	*12*	....	....	x---	---x	?---	----	-x--	*2*	
									? 1759	....	....	....	x---	---x	?---	----	----	*2*	
									? 1797	*0204*	....	....	x---	---x	----	----	----		
Llanganate (Ecuador)	1.22 S	78.25 W					1502-07=	Not a Volcano											
Chimborazo (Ecuador)	**1.464 S**	**78.815 W**	**6310**	3467	ADr	**Stratovolcano**	**1502-071**	**Radiocarbon**											
									T **-7500***	....	....	....	----	----	xx--	----	--x-		
									G **-5410**u	....	....	....	----	----	xx--	----	--x-		
									G **-4130**w	....	....	....	----	----	xx--	----	----		
									T **-2500***	....	....	....	----	----	xx--	----	----		
									G **0270**w	....	....	....	----	----	xx--	----	----		
									T **0550**w	....	....	....	----	----	xx--	----	----		
Tungurahua (Ecuador)	**1.467 S**	**78.442 W**	**5023**	3567	AD	**Stratovolcano**	**1502-08=**	**Historical**											
									C **-7750**?	....	....	....	x---	----	xx--	----	----	4	-/8
(collapse of Tungurahua II edifice)									C **-1010**v	....	....	....	x---	----	xx-A	x---	xxx-	**5**	-/9
									C **-0500**?	....	....	....	x---	----	xx--	----	----	3?	
									C **-0270**v	....	....	....	x---	----	xx--	x---	----		
									C **-0100**?	....	....	....	x---	----	xx--	x---	----	3?	
									C **-0050**?	....	....	....	x---	----	xx--	x---	----	3?	
									C **0100**?	....	....	....	x---	----	xx--	----	----	3?	
									C **0200**?	....	....	....	x---	----	xx--	----	----		
									C **0350**?	....	....	....	x---	----	xx--	----	----	3?	
									C **0480**u	....	....	....	x---	----	x---	----	----		8/-
									C **0600**?	....	....	....	x---	----	xx--	----	----	3?	
(P1 tephra unit)									C **0730**x	....	....	....	x---	----	xx--	----	----	4?	-/7
									C **0800**?	....	....	....	x---	----	xx--	----	----		
(tephra layer F)									C **1030**u	....	....	....	x---	----	xx--	----	----		
									G **1250**t	....	....	....	x---	----	xx--	----	----		
									G **1350**t	....	....	....	x---	----	xx--	----	----	3?	
									1557	....	....	....	x---	----	x---	----	----	2	
									1640	....	**1641**	....	x---	----	xx--	----	-x--	3?	
									1644	....	**1646**?	....	x---	----	x---	----	-x--	2	
									? 1757	....	....	....	x---	----	?---	----	----	*2*	
(P2 tephra; eruption began in 1773, not 1772)									**1773**	0204	**1773**	07 ?	x---	----	xx--	x---	-xx-	3*	8/-
									1776	0103	....	....	x---	----	x-x-	----	----	2	
									? 1777	....	....	....	x---	----	?---	?---	----	*2*	
									? 1781	....	....	....	x---	----	----	?---	----	*2*	
									1857	0910?	....	....	x---	----	x---	----	----	2?	
									1885	01 ?	**1885**	1016	x---	----	x---	----	----	2?	
									1886	0111	**1888**a	....	x---	----	xx--	x---	xxx-	4	7/-
									? 1900	....	....	....	x---	----	?---	----	----	*2?*	
									1916	0303	**1925**	1201p	x---	----	xxx-	x---	-xx-	4*	
									? 1944	....	....	....	x---	----	?---	----	----	*2*	

Tom Pierson (USGS/CVO)

Massive lahar boulder from 1877 eruption

VOLCANO NAME (Subregion) / ERUPTION — Area of Activity	LAT	LONG	ELEV (m)	POPL 5 km 10 30 100	ROCK TYPE	VOLC TYPE / Start Year	NUMBER / Start M-Dy	STATUS / Stop Year	Stop M-Dy	Central / Flank vent / Radial fiss / Regional	Submarine / New island / Subglacial / Crater lake	Explosive / Pyro flow / Phreatic / Caldera	Lava flow / Lava lake / Dome / Spine	Fatal / Damage / Mudflow / Tsunami	VEI	Vol L/T
Tungurahua (Ecuador) *continued*						*? 1993*	*0506*	*?1993*	*0506*	x---	----	--?-	----	----	*1?*	
						1999	1005	**2009**	0708g	x---	----	xx--	x?--	xxx-	3?	
Licto (Ecuador)	**1.780 S***	**78.613 W**	**3336**	6667	**A**	**Scoria cones**	**1502-081**	Holocene?								
Sangay (Ecuador)	**2.002 S**	**78.341 W**	**5230**	3457	**Adb**	**Stratovolcano**	**1502-09=**	**Historical**								
						1628	10	....	....	----	----	x---	----	-x--	3↑	
						1728	0930p	**1916<**	....	x---	----	xx--	x-x-	----	3*	
						1934	0808	**2010>**	....	xxx-	----	xx--	x-x-	x---	3*	
GALAPAGOS ISLANDS																
Fernandina (Galápagos)	**0.37 S**	**91.55 W**	**1476**	3334	**B**	**Shield volcano**	**1503-01=**	**Historical**								
						E **0950**z	....	....	....	----	----	----	x---	----	0	
						E **1150>**	....	....	....	----	----	----	x---	----	0	
						E **1550>**	....	....	....	----	----	----	x---	----	0	
South flank						**1813**	0714<	....	....	-x-?	----	--?-	----	----	2	
						1814	07	**1814**	08	-?-?	----	?---	?---	----	2	
(western Galápagos)						@ **1817<**	....	....	....	-?--	----	x---	x---	----	2	
						1819	....	....	....	-?--	----	x---	x---	----	2	
East summit and SE flank						**1825**	0214	**1825**	10 >	---x	----	?---	x---	----	3	
East flank						**1846**	11	....	....	-?-?	----	----	x---	----	0	
						1888	....	....	....	----	----	----	----	----	1	
						1926	....	....	....	----	----	----	----	----		
South flank near Punta Mangle						**1927**	1213<	....	....	-x--	----	----	x---	----	0	
						1937	03	**1937**	04	-?--	----	----	?---	----	0	
SE, SW and west caldera rim						**1958**	09 ?	**1958**	1230>	--x-	----	----	xx--	----	2	7/-
SE flank						**1961**	0321a	**1961**	09	x-x-	----	x---	x---	----	2	
ESE flank (600 m)						**1968**	0521	**1968**	0523a	-xx-	----	x---	x---	----	2	
West caldera wall						**1968**	0611	**1968**	0704<	x---	----	xxxM	x---	----	4	-/8
SE caldera bench						**1972**	0604q	....	....	x---	----	x---	x---	----	0	
ESE caldera wall						**1973**	1209	**1973**	1216a	x---	----	x---	x---	----	2	
SE caldera bench						**1977**	0323	**1977**	0327	x---	----	x---	x---	----	1	
NW caldera bench						**1978**	0808	**1978**	0826	x---	----	x---	x---	----	2	6/-
South caldera rim						**1981**	0801x	....	....	x---	----	----	x---	----	0	
NW corner of caldera						**1984**	0330	....	....	x---	----	x---	x---	----	1	
East caldera wall						**1988**	0914	**1988**	0916	x---	----	x-x-	x---	----	2?	6/-
Base of ESE and NW caldera wall						**1991**	0419	**1991**	0424	x---	----	x---	x---	----	2?	
SW flank						**1995**	0125	**1995**	0408?	--x-	----	x---	x---	----	2	7/-
South caldera rim						**2005**	0513	**2005**	0529?	x---	----	x---	x---	----	2	
SW flank (400 m)						**2009**	0410	**2009**	0428?	--x-	----	x---	x---	----	2	
Ecuador (Isabela I)	**0.02 S**	**91.546W**	**790**	3333	**B**	**Shield volcano**	**1503-011**	**Surface Exposure**								
						E **1150>**	....	....	....	----	----	----	x---	----	0	
Wolf (Isabela I)	**0.02 N**	**91.35 W**	**1710**	3334	**B**	**Shield volcano**	**1503-02=**	**Historical**								
Lower SW flank						E **0150***	....	....	....	--x-	----	----	x---	----	0	
Lower NE flank						E **0950>**	....	....	....	--x-	----	----	x---	----	0	
Lower NE and SE flanks						E **1450>**	....	....	....	--x-	----	----	x---	----	0	
						1797	08	....	....	----	----	----	----	----		
						1800	0821	**1800**	0821	?---	----	x---	----	----	2?	
ESE flank						**1925**	0411	**1926**	0326>	-x--	----	----	x---	----	1	
						1933	....	....	....	-x--	----	----	?---	----	0	
						1935	02	....	....	----	----	----	----	----		
						1938	....	....	....	-x--	----	----	----	----		
SE flank (1200 m)						**1948**	0124	**1948**	0131>	-x--	----	x---	?---	----	2	
SE flank (610 m)						**1963**	0304	**1963**	0316>	-x--	----	----	x---	----	0	
						? 1973	*1025*	*?1973*	*1029*	----	----	----	----	----		
Caldera and SE flank (875 m)						**1982**	0828	**1982**	0906?	x-x-	----	x---	x---	----	1	
Darwin (Isabela I)	**0.18 S**	**91.28 W**	**1330**	3334	**Ba**	**Shield volcano**	**1503-03=**	**Surface Exposure**								
						E **0210**z	....	....	....	----	----	----	x---	----	0	
						E **1150**y	....	....	....	----	----	----	x---	----	0	
(more likely Darwin than Wolf, Alcedo)						@ **1813**	0606	**@1813**	0607?	----	----	x---	----	----	2?	
Alcedo (Isabela I)	**0.43 S**	**91.12 W**	**1130**	3335	**Brda**	**Shield volcano**	**1503-04=**	**Historical**								
SE flank near Cartago Bay						**1953**g	....	....	....	-x--	----	----	x---	----	0	
(eruption more likely at Sierra Negra						*X 1954*	*1109*	....	....	----	----	----	----	----		
South caldera wall						**1993**	1205n	....	....	x---	----	x-x-	----	----	1	
Negra, Sierra (Isabela I)	**0.83 S**	**91.17 W**	**1124**	3334	**B**	**Shield volcano**	**1503-05=**	**Historical**								
						E **-8250***	....	....	....	----	----	----	x---	----	0	
SE flank						C **-1250**v	....	....	....	--x-	----	----	x---	----	0	
						E **0370***	....	....	....	----	----	----	x---	----	0	
						E **1060**z	....	....	....	----	----	----	x---	----	0	
						E **1350**z	....	....	....	----	----	----	x---	----	0	
(south end of Isabela Island)						@ **1813**	0713	....	....	----	----	x---	----	----	2?	
(Isabela Island)						@ **1817**	....	....	....	-x--	----	----	----	----		
(Isabela Island)						@ **1844**	....	....	....	----	----	----	x---	----	0	
(Isabela Island)						@ **1860**	....	....	....	----	----	x---	----	----	2	
						1911	1231y	....	....	----	----	----	----	----		
						1948	08	**1949**	02 ?	?---	----	x---	?---	----	2	
Volcán Chico area & NW caldera rim						**1953**	0827	**1954**	01	-x--	----	x---	x---	----	3?	
Upper NNE flank						@ **1954**	1109	....	....	-x--	----	x-x-	x---	----	2	
(Isabela Island)						@ **1957**	....	....	....	----	----	----	----	----		
Volcán Chico area & NW caldera rim						**1963**	0413	**1963**	05	-x--	----	x---	x---	----	2	
Upper NW and NE flanks (Volcán Chico)						**1979**	1113	**1980**	0114>	-xx-	----	x---	x---	-x--	3	8/-
North caldera rim						**2005**	1022	**2005**	1030	x-x-	----	x---	xx--	----	3	8/-
Azul, Cerro (Isabela I)	**0.92 S**	**91.408W**	**1640**	3334	**B**	**Shield volcano**	**1503-06=**	**Historical**								
						E **-0950***	....	....	....	----	----	----	x---	----	0	
						E **-0550***	....	....	....	----	----	----	x---	----	0	
						E **1250>**	....	....	....	----	----	----	x---	----	0	
						E **1850>**	....	....	....	----	----	----	x---	----		
						1932	....	....	....	----	----	----	----	----	1?	
East flank (Cerro de Las Animas)						**1940**	....	....	....	-x--	----	----	x---	----	0	
Caldera ring fracture						**1943**	0413b	**1943**	0511?	----	----	x---	x---	x---	3	
						1948	0630p	....	....	----	----	----	x---	----	0	
						1949?	....	....	....	x--x	----	----	x---	----	0	
						1951	....	....	....	----	----	----	----	----		

VOLCANO NAME (Subregion) / ERUPTION	LAT	LONG	ELEV (m)	POPL (5 km, 10, 30, 100)	ROCK TYPE	VOLC TYPE	NUMBER	STATUS	Area of Activity	Start Year	Start M-Dy	Stop Year	Stop M-Dy	Central / Flank vent / Radial fiss / Regional	Submarine / New island / Subglacial / Crater lake	Explosive / Pyro flow / Phreatic / Caldera	Lava flow / Lava lake / Dome / Spine	Fatal / Damage / Mudflow / Tsunami	VEI	Vol L/T
Azul, Cerro (Isabela I) *continued*									East flank	**1959**	0629	**1959**	0731?	---x	----	----	x---	----	2?	
									North flank?	*? 1968*	*0612*	....	....	----	----	?---	----	----		
									East flank (300 m) and summit	**1979**	0129	**1979**	0304>	xxx-	----	x---	x---	----	2?	
									N & W caldera floor, SE flank (630-680 m)	**1998**	0915	**1998**	1021	x-x-	----	x---	x---	----	1	8/-
									Summit and SE flank	**2008**	0529	**2008**	0617	x-x-	----	x---	x---	----	1?	
Pinta (Galápagos)	**0.58 N**	**90.75 W**	**780**	3334	B	**Shield volcano**	**1503-07=**	**Historical**												
										1928	....	....	....	?---	----	----	----	----		
Marchena (Galápagos)	**0.33 N**	**90.47 W**	**343**	3334	B	**Shield volcano**	**1503-08=**	**Historical**												
									West to SW caldera rim	**1991**	0925	**1991**	11 ?	x---	----	x---	x---	----	2	
Genovesa (Galápagos)	**0.32 N**	**89.958 W**	**64**	3334	B	**Shield volcano**	**1503-081**	**Holocene**												
Santiago (Galápagos)	**0.22 S**	**90.77 W**	**920**	2235	Baxyt	**Shield volcano**	**1503-09=**	**Historical**												
									West flank (James Bay)	A **1759**u	....	....	....	-?--	----	----	x---	----		
									SE flank (Sullivan Bay?)	**1897**	....	....	....	-?-?	----	----	x---	----	0	
									SE flank	**1904**	....	**1906**	1215q	-?--	----	----	?---	----	0	
Santa Cruz (Galápagos)	**0.62 S**	**90.33 W**	**864**	4445	BX	**Shield volcano**	**1503-091**	**Holocene**												
San Cristóbal (Galápagos)	**0.88 S**	**89.50 W**	**759**	4445	Bx	**Shield volcano**	**1503-12-**	**Holocene**												

PERU

VOLCANO NAME (Subregion) / ERUPTION	LAT	LONG	ELEV (m)	POPL (5 km, 10, 30, 100)	ROCK TYPE	VOLC TYPE	NUMBER	STATUS	Area of Activity	Start Year	Start M-Dy	Stop Year	Stop M-Dy	Central / Flank vent / Radial fiss / Regional	Submarine / New island / Subglacial / Crater lake	Explosive / Pyro flow / Phreatic / Caldera	Lava flow / Lava lake / Dome / Spine	Fatal / Damage / Mudflow / Tsunami	VEI	Vol L/T
Quimsachata (Perú)	**14.20 S**	**71.33 W**	**3923**	4456	RY	**Lava dome**	**1504-00-**	**Radiocarbon**												
									Oroscocha	C-**4450**?	....	....	....	---x	----	----	--x-	--x-		
Auquihuato, Cerro (Perú)	**15.07 S**	**73.18 W**	**4980**	3456	U	**Cinder cone**	**1504-001**	Holocene?												
Sara Sara (Perú)	**15.33 S**	**73.45 W**	**5522**	2356	A	**Stratovolcano**	**1504-002**	**Holocene**												
Coropuna (Perú)	**15.52 S**	**72.65 W**	**6377**	2356	AD	**Stratovolcano**	**1504-003**	**Holocene**												
Andahua-Orcopampa (Perú)	**15.42 S***	**72.33 W**	**4713**	5556	Yt	**Cinder cones**	**1504-004**	**Radiocarbon**												
									Cerro Tichsó	C-**2110**t	....	....	....	x---	----	x---	x---	----		
									Cerro Maurus I.	C-**0940**v	....	....	....	x---	----	x---	x---	----		
									Chilcayoc Grande	C **1490**s	....	....	....	x---	----	x---	x---	----		
										? 1913	*0306*	....	....	----	----	----	----	----		
Huambo (Perú)	**15.83 S**	**72.13 W**	**4550**	3447	Ya	**Volcanic field**	**1504-005**	**Radiocarbon**												
									Cerro Keyocc	C-**0700**t	....	....	....	x---	----	x---	x---	----		
Sabancaya (Perú)	**15.78 S**	**71.85 W**	**5967**	2357	AD	**Stratovolcanoes**	**1504-006**	**Historical**												
										T-**6600**?	....	....	....	----	----	x---	----	----		
										C-**3490**s	....	....	....	----	----	----	x---	----	0	
										T **1350**w	....	....	....	----	----	x---	----	----		
										1750	....	....	....	----	----	?---	----	----		
										1784	07	....	....	----	----	?---	----	-x--		
										1986	12	....	....	x---	----	x-?-	----	----	1	
										? 1987	*0807*	....	....	-x--	----	?---	----	----	*2?*	
										1988	0622	**1988**	10 ?	x---	----	x-x-	----	----	1	
										1990	0528	**1998**	09 ?	x---	----	x-x-	----	-xx-	3*	-/7
										2000	04 ?	**2000**	1029>	x---	----	x---	----	----	2	
										2003	0730a	....	....	x---	----	x---	----	----	2?	
Chachani, Nevado (Perú)	**16.191 S**	**71.530 W**	**6057**	2467	ADR	**Stratovolcano**	**1504-007**	Holocene?												
Nicholson, Cerro (Perú)	**16.258 S**	**71.753 W**	**2520**	3367	A	**Cinder cone**	**1504-008**	**Holocene**												
Misti, El (Perú)	**16.294 S**	**71.409 W**	**5822**	2467	ADr	**Stratovolcano**	**1504-01=**	**Historical**												
										G-**7190**w	....	....	....	x---	----	xx--	----	----		
										G-**5390**u	....	....	....	x---	----	xx--	----	----		
										G-**4020**x	....	....	....	x---	----	xx--	----	----		
										G-**3510**w	....	....	....	x---	----	xx--	----	----		
										G-**2230**x	....	....	....	x---	----	x---	----	----		
										G-**0310**v	....	....	....	x---	----	xx--	----	----		
										G-**0080**u	....	....	....	x---	----	xx--	----	--x-	4?	-/8
										G **0090**y	....	....	....	x---	----	x---	----	----		
										G **0760**v	....	....	....	x---	----	x---	----	----		
										G **1350**t	....	....	....	x---	----	xx--	----	----		
										1454n	....	....	....	x---	----	x---	----	-x--	2	-/6
										? 1542	....	....	....	x---	----	--?-	----	----	*1?*	
										? 1599	....	....	....	x---	----	--?-	----	----	*1?*	
										1677	0502	....	....	x---	----	--x-	----	----	2	
										1784	0709	....	....	x---	----	--x-	----	----	2	
										1787	0728	**1787**	1010	x---	----	--x-	----	----	1?	
										? 1826	*08*	....	....	x---	----	--?-	----	----	*1?*	
										? 1830	*08*	....	....	x---	----	--?-	----	----	*1?*	
										? 1831	*08*	....	....	x---	----	--?-	----	----	*1?*	
										? 1869	*09*	....	....	x---	----	?-?-	----	----	*1?*	
										? 1870	*03*	....	....	x---	----	--?-	----	----	*1?*	
										1985	....	....	....	x---	----	x-x-	----	----	1?	
Ubinas (Perú)	**16.355 S**	**70.903 W**	**5672**	3457	AYDR	**Stratovolcano**	**1504-02=**	**Historical**												
										G-**8560**y	....	....	....	x---	----	x---	----	----		
										G-**6850**w	....	....	....	x---	----	x---	----	----		
										G **1080**u	....	....	....	x---	----	x-x-	----	----	**5**	-/9
										1550t	....	....	....	x---	----	x---	----	----	3?	
										? 1600	....	....	....	----	----	----	----	----	*2?*	
										1662	....	....	....	x---	----	x---	----	----	3?	
									(eruption at Ubinas, not Huaynaputina)	**1667**	....	....	....	x---	----	x---	----	----	3	
										1677	....	....	....	x---	----	xx--	----	----	3?	
										1784	....	....	....	x---	----	x---	----	----	2	
										? 1826	....	....	....	----	----	----	----	----		
										1830	....	....	....	x---	----	x---	----	----	2	
										1862	....	....	....	x---	----	x---	----	----	2	
										1865	....	....	....	x---	----	x---	----	----	2	
										1867	0524	**1867**	0528	x---	----	x---	----	----	2	
										1869	10	....	....	x---	----	x---	----	----	2	
										1906	10	....	....	x---	----	x---	----	----	2	
										1907	....	....	....	x---	----	x---	----	----	2	
										1937	06	....	....	x---	----	x---	----	-x--	2	
										1951	0723h	....	....	x---	----	x---	----	----	2	
										1956	05	**1956**	1021	x---	----	x---	----	-x--	2	
										1969	06	....	....	----	----	x---	----	-x--	2?	
										2006	0325?	**2009**	0704?	x---	----	x-x-	--x-	-x--	2	

VOLCANO NAME (Subregion) / ERUPTION — Area of Activity	LAT	LONG	ELEV (m)	POPL (5 km, 10, 30, 100)	ROCK TYPE	VOLC TYPE	NUMBER / Start Year	Start M-Dy	STATUS / Stop Year	Stop M-Dy	Central, Flank vent, Radial fiss, Regional	Submarine, New island, Subglacial, Crater lake	Explosive, Pyro flow, Phreatic, Caldera	Lava flow, Lava lake, Dome, Spine	Fatal, Damage, Mudflow, Tsunami	VEI	Vol L/T
Huaynaputina (Perú)	**16.608 S**	**70.85 W**	**4850**	2347	**D**	**Stratovolcano**	**1504-03=**		**Historical**								
							C-**7750**x	....	....	....	x---	----	x---	----	----		
Summit and south flank							**1600**	0217a	**1600**	0306?	xx--	----	xx--	----	xxx-	**6***	-/10
Ticsani (Perú)	**16.755 S**	**70.595 W**	**5408**	2356	**DR**	**Lava domes**	**1504-031**		**Tephrochronology**								
							T **1800**x	....	....	....	--x-	----	x---	--x-	----		
Tutupaca (Perú)	**17.025 S**	**70.358 W**	**5815**	2456	**ART**	**Stratovolcano**	**1504-04=**		**Holocene**								
Yucamane (Perú)	**17.18 S**	**70.20 W**	**5550**	2356	**A**	**Stratovolcanoes**	**1504-05-**		**Historical**								
							C-**1320**?	....	....	....	x---	----	x---	----	----	**5**	-/9
							@ **1780**	....	....	....	----	----	x---	----	----	2	
							1787	....	....	....	----	----	----	----	----		
							@ **1802**	0330	@**1802**	07	----	----	x---	----	----	3	
							@ **1862**	04	@**1862**	05	----	----	x---	----	----	2	
							@ **1902**	06	@**1902**	11	----	----	x---	----	----	2	
Casiri, Nevados (Perú)	**17.47 S**	**69.813 W**	**5650**	3356	**TY**	**Stratovolcanoes**	**1504-06-**		**Holocene**								

CHILE - N, BOLIVIA, & ARGENTINA

VOLCANO NAME (Subregion) / ERUPTION — Area of Activity	LAT	LONG	ELEV (m)	POPL (5 km, 10, 30, 100)	ROCK TYPE	VOLC TYPE	NUMBER / Start Year	Start M-Dy	STATUS / Stop Year	Stop M-Dy	Central, Flank vent, Radial fiss, Regional	Submarine, New island, Subglacial, Crater lake	Explosive, Pyro flow, Phreatic, Caldera	Lava flow, Lava lake, Dome, Spine	Fatal, Damage, Mudflow, Tsunami	VEI	Vol L/T
Tacora (Chile-N)	**17.72 S**	**69.77 W**	**5980**	1346	**A**	**Stratovolcano**	**1505-01=**		**Fumarolic**								
							? 1930	....	....	....	----	----	----	----	----		
							? 1937	*0805*	....	....	----	----	?---	----	----		
Taapaca (Chile-N)	**18.10 S**	**69.50 W**	**5860**	1246	**DA**	**Complex volcano**	**1505-011**		**Radiocarbon**								
							C-**7900**u	....	....	....	----	----	x---	----	----		
							C-**5490**t	....	....	....	----	----	x---	----	----		
							C-**4620**u	....	....	....	----	----	x---	----	----		
							C-**2950**u	....	....	....	----	----	x---	----	----		
							C-**2400**u	....	....	....	----	----	x---	----	----		
							C-**1860**v	....	....	....	----	----	x---	----	----		
							C-**1580**u	....	....	....	----	----	x---	----	----		
							C-**0320**t	....	....	....	----	----	x---	----	----		
Parinacota (Chile/Bolivia)	**18.17 S**	**69.15 W**	**6348**	2345	**AYDR**	**Stratovolcano**	**1505-012**		**Surface Exposure**								
(Collapse of Parinacota 2 edifice)							C-**5840**t	....	....	....	x---	----	xx-A	----	----		
South flank (lower Volcanes de Ajata)							E-**4320***	....	....	....	-xx-	----	x---	x---	----		
South flank (lower Volcanes de Ajata)							E-**1100**z	....	....	....	-xx-	----	x---	x---	----		
South flank (upper Volcanes de Ajata)							A **0090**t	....	....	....	-xx-	----	x---	x---	----		
Parinacota 3 edifice							E **0290**y	....	....	....	----	----	----	x---	----	0	
Guallatiri (Chile-N)	**18.42 S**	**69.092 W**	**6071**	0245	**ADR**	**Stratovolcano**	**1505-02=**		**Historical**								
							1825q	....	....	....	x---	----	x---	----	----	2?	
							? 1908	....	....	....	----	----	----	----	----		
							1913	....	....	....	x---	----	x---	----	----	2	
							1959	0715e	....	....	x---	----	x---	----	----	2	
							1960	1202	....	....	----	--x-	x---	----	----	2	
							? 1985	*1201*	....	....	----	----	--?-	----	----		
Tambo Quemado (Bolivia)	**18.62 S**	**68.75 W**	**4215**	3345	**R**	**Pyroclastic shield**	**1505-021**		**Holocene**								
Isluga (Chile-N)	**19.15 S**	**68.83 W**	**5550**	1345	**AD**	**Stratovolcano**	**1505-03=**		**Historical**								
							1863	08	....	....	x---	----	----	----	----	1?	
							1868	....	....	....	----	----	----	----	----	2?	
							1869	08	....	....	x---	----	----	----	----	2	
							1877	....	....	....	----	----	----	----	----	2?	
							1878	02	....	....	x---	----	----	x---	-x--	2	
							1885	....	....	....	----	----	----	----	----	1?	
							1913	....	....	....	x---	----	x---	----	----	2	
							? 1960	....	....	....	----	----	----	----	----	*2?*	
Tata Sabaya (Bolivia)	**19.13 S**	**68.53 W**	**5430**	2345	**A**	**Stratovolcano**	**1505-032**		**Holocene**								
Jayu Khota, Laguna (Bolivia)	**19.45 S**	**67.42 W**	**3650**	3345	**B**	**Maars**	**1505-035**		**Holocene**								
Nuevo Mundo (Bolivia)	**19.78 S**	**66.48 W**	**5438**	2346	**D**	**Lava domes**	**1505-036**		Holocene?								
Irruputuncu (Chile/Bolivia)	**20.73 S**	**68.55 W**	**5163**	2345	**A**	**Stratovolcano**	**1505-04=**		**Historical**								
(unconfirmed press reports)							*? 1989*	*12*	....	....	----	----	----	----	----		
							1995	0901	**1995**	0926	x---	----	--x-	----	----	2	
Pampa Luxsar (Bolivia)	**20.85 S***	**68.20 W**	**5543**	3345	**A**	**Volcanic field**	**1505-042**		Holocene?								
Olca-Paruma (Chile/Bolivia)	**20.93 S**	**68.48 W**	**5407**	2345	**AD**	**Stratovolcanoes**	**1505-05=**		**Historical**								
							1865	....	**1867**	....	-x--	----	----	----	----		
Ollagüe (Chile/Bolivia)	**21.30 S**	**68.18 W**	**5868**	2345	**AD**	**Stratovolcano**	**1505-06=**		Holocene?								
							? 1903	*1208*	....	....	----	----	----	----	----		
Azufre, Cerro del (Chile-N)	**21.787 S**	**68.237 W**	**5846**	0245	**AD**	**Stratovolcano**	**1505-061**		Holocene?								
San Pedro (Chile-N)	**21.88 S**	**68.40 W**	**6145**	0346	**AD**	**Stratovolcanoes**	**1505-07=**		**Historical**								
							? 1870	....	....	....	----	----	----	----	----		
							1877?	....	....	....	x---	----	----	----	----	2	
							1891?	....	....	....	x---	----	----	----	----	2	
							1901	0525	**1901**	08	x---	----	----	----	-x--	2	
							1911	09	....	....	----	----	x---	----	----	2	
							? 1916	....	....	....	----	----	----	----	----		
							? 1917	....	....	....	----	----	----	----	----		
							? 1923	....	....	....	----	----	----	----	----		
							1938	02	....	....	----	----	x---	----	----	2	
							1960	1202	....	....	----	----	x---	----	----	2	
Putana (Chile-N)	**22.55 S**	**67.85 W**	**5890**	2245	**DA**	**Stratovolcano**	**1505-09=**		**Historical**								
							1810j	....	....	....	----	----	----	----	----		
							? 1972	....	....	....	----	----	----	----	----		
Sairecabur (Chile/Bolivia)	**22.72 S**	**67.892 W**	**5971**	2245	**AD**	**Stratovolcanoes**	**1505-091**		**Holocene**								
Licancabur (Chile/Bolivia)	**22.83 S**	**67.88 W**	**5916**	2245	**AD**	**Stratovolcano**	**1505-092**		**Holocene**								
Guayaques (Chile/Bolivia)	**22.895 S**	**67.566 W**	**5598**	1234	**Da**	**Lava domes**	**1505-093**		**Holocene**								
Purico Complex (Chile-N)	**23.00 S**	**67.75 W**	**5703**	0245	**DAR**	**Pyroclastic shield**	**1505-094**		**Holocene**								
Colachi (Chile-N)	**23.236 S**	**67.645 W**	**5631**	0134	**ADR**	**Stratovolcano**	**1505-095**		**Holocene**								
Acamarachi (Chile-N)	**23.30 S**	**67.62 W**	**6046**	0134	**DA**	**Stratovolcano**	**1505-096**		**Holocene**								
Overo, Cerro (Chile-N)	**23.52 S**	**67.67 W**	**4555**	1234	**A**	**Maar**	**1505-097**		Holocene?								
Chiliques (Chile-N)	**23.58 S**	**67.70 W**	**5778**	0134	**A**	**Stratovolcano**	**1505-098**		Holocene?								

VOLCANO NAME (Subregion)	ERUPTION — Area of Activity	LAT	LONG	ELEV (m)	POPL (5 km / 10 / 30 / 100)	ROCK TYPE	VOLC TYPE	NUMBER	STATUS	Start Year	Start M-Dy	Stop Year	Stop M-Dy	Central / Flank vent / Radial fiss / Regional	Submarine / New island / Subglacial / Crater lake	Explosive / Pyro flow / Phreatic / Caldera	Lava flow / Lava lake / Dome / Spine	Fatal / Damage / Mudflow / Tsunami	VEI	Vol L/T
Láscar (Chile-N)		23.37 S	67.73 W	5592	0234	AD	Stratovolcanoes	1505-10=	Historical											
	Lascar II (Tumbres scoria flow)									C-7250?	....	....	....	x---	----	xx--	----	----		
	Eastern crater (Tumbres-Talabre lava flow)									E-5150*	....	....	....	x---	----	----	x---	----	0	
	Lascar or Agua Calientes									1848	....	....	....	x---	----	x---	----	----	2	
										? 1853	....	....	....	----	----	----	----	----	2?	
	Lascar or Aguas Calientes									1854	0120	1854	0130	----	----	x---	----	----	1	
										1858	04	1858	12	----	----	x---	----	----	2?	
										1875	....	....	....	x---	----	x---	----	----	2	
										1883	....	1885	....	----	----	x-?-	----	----	2	
										1898	....	1900?	....	----	----	x---	----	----	2	
										1902	....	....	....	----	----	x---	----	----	2?	
										1933	1009	1933	12	x---	----	x---	----	----	2	
										1940	....	....	....	----	----	x---	----	----	2	
	East summit crater									1951	11	1952	0219	x---	----	x---	----	----	2?	
										1954	06	1954	07	----	----	----	----	----	2?	
										1959	11	1968	0131>	x---	----	x-x-	----	----	2*	
										1969	0516	....	....	----	----	----	----	----		
										? 1972	....	....	....	----	----	?---	----	----	2?	
										? 1974	07	?1974	09	x---	----	?---	----	----	1	
	Western crater of east summit cone									1984	12	1985	07	x---	----	----	--x-	----	0	5/-
	Western crater of east summit cone									1986	0914	1986	0916	x---	----	x---	----	----	3*	-/7
	Western crater of east summit cone									1987	11 <	1990	0406	x---	----	x-x-	--x-	----	3*	5/-
										1990	1124	1990	1124	x---	----	x---	----	----	1	
										1991	1021	1992	0523?	x---	----	x---	--x-	----	2	-/6
	Western crater of east summit cone									1993	0130	1993	08	x---	----	xxx-	--x-	-x--	4*	6/8
										1993	1217	1994	0227	x---	----	x---	----	----	2	
										1994	0720	1994	0726	x---	----	x---	----	----	2	
										1994	1113	1995	0720	x---	----	x-x-	----	----	2	
										1996	1018	1996	1018	x---	----	x---	----	----	2	
										2000	0720	?2001	0118?	x---	----	x---	----	----	2	
										? 2001	0517?	?2001	0705?	x---	----	----	----	----		
										2002	1026	2002	1027	x---	----	x---	----	----	2	
										? 2003	1209	?2003	1209	x---	----	?-?-	----	----	1	
										2005	0504	2005	0504	x---	----	x---	----	----	3?	
										2006	0418	2007	0718?	x---	----	x-x-	----	----	3	
Cordón de Puntas Negras (Chile)		23.743 S	67.534 W	5852	0034	AD	Stratovolcanoes	1505-101	Holocene											
Miñiques (Chile-N)		23.82 S	67.77 W	5910	1234	AD	Stratovolcanoes	1505-102	Holocene?											
Tujle, Cerro (Chile-N)		23.83 S	67.95 W	3550	1244	U	Maar	1505-103	Holocene											
Caichinque (Chile-N)		23.95 S	67.73 W	4450	0134	AD	Stratovolcanoes	1505-104	Holocene?											
Tilocalar (Chile-N)		23.97 S	68.13 W	3116	1134	A	Stratovolcanoes	1505-105	Holocene?											
Negrillar, El (Chile-N)		24.18 S*	68.25 W	3500	3334	A	Pyroclastic cones	1505-106	Holocene											
Pular (Chile-N)		24.188 S	68.054 W	6233	0024	AD	Stratovolcanoes	1505-107	Holocene?											
										? 1990	0424	?1990	0424	----	----	?---	----	----	1?	
Negrillar, La (Chile-N)		24.28 S	68.60 W	4109	2334	A	Pyroclastic cones	1505-108	Holocene?											
Socompa (Chile/Argentina)		24.40 S	68.25 W	6051	1334	DA	Stratovolcano	1505-109	Radiocarbon											
										C-5250?	....	....	....	x---	----	xx-A	----	----		
Llullaillaco (Chile/Argentina)		24.72 S	68.53 W	6739	0234	Dt	Stratovolcano	1505-11=	Historical											
										1854	0210	....	....	----	----	x---	----	----	2	
										1868	09	....	....	--x-	----	----	?---	----	0	
										1877	05	....	....	----	----	x---	----	----	2	
Escorial, Cerro (Chile/Argentina)		25.08 S	68.37 W	5447	1234	AD	Stratovolcano	1505-112	Holocene?											
Lastarria (Chile/Argentina)		25.17 S	68.50 W	5697	0234	AD	Stratovolcano	1505-12=	Holocene											
Cordón del Azufre (Chile/Argentina)		25.33 S	68.52 W	5463	0134	AD	Complex volcano	1505-121	Holocene											
Bayo, Cerro (Chile/Argentina)		25.42 S	68.58 W	5401	0234	AD	Complex volcano	1505-122	Holocene											
Nevada, Sierra (Chile/Argentina)		26.48 S*	68.58 W	6127	2234	U	Complex volcano	1505-123	Holocene											
Falso Azufre (Chile/Argentina)		26.80 S	68.37 W	5890	0234	U	Complex volcano	1505-124	Holocene?											
Incahuasi, Nevado de (Chile/Arg)		27.042 S	68.28 W	6621	1235	DA	Stratovolcanoes	1505-125	Holocene?											
Ojos del Salado, Nevados (Ch/Ar)		27.12 S	68.55 W	6887	0235	DAR	Stratovolcano	1505-13=	Tephrochronology											
										T 0700y	....	....	....	x---	----	xx--	----	----		
										? 1993	1114	?1993	1114	x---	----	?-x-	----	----	1?	
Solo, El (Chile/Argentina)		27.108 S	68.72 W	6190	0034	D	Stratovolcano	1505-131	Holocene											
Copiapó (Chile-N)		27.30 S	69.13 W	6052	0044	DA	Stratovolcano	1505-14-	Uncertain											
Tuzgle, Cerro (Argentina)		24.05 S	66.48 W	5500	2345	DA	Stratovolcano	1505-15-	Holocene?											
Aracar (Argentina)		24.25 S	67.77 W	6082	0024	AD	Stratovolcano	1505-16-	Uncertain											
										? 1993	0328	....	....	x---	----	?-?-	----	----	2?	
Unnamed (Argentina)		25.10 S	68.27 W		0234	A	Pyroclastic cone	1505-161	Holocene?											
Antofagasta de la Sierra (Argent)		26.08 S*	67.50 W	4000	3334	A	Scoria cones	1505-18-	Holocene											
Cóndor, Cerro el (Argentina)		26.62 S	68.35 W	6532	0024	U	Stratovolcano	1505-19-	Holocene											
Peinado (Argentina)		26.62 S	68.15 W	5740	0024	A	Stratovolcano	1505-20-	Holocene											
Robledo (Argentina)		26.77 S	67.72 W	4400	2225	R	Caldera	1505-21-	Holocene											
Tipas (Argentina)		27.20 S	68.55 W	6660	0135	U	Complex volcano	1505-22-	Holocene											

CHILE - ISLANDS

VOLCANO NAME (Subregion)	ERUPTION — Area of Activity	LAT	LONG	ELEV (m)	POPL (5 km / 10 / 30 / 100)	ROCK TYPE	VOLC TYPE	NUMBER	STATUS	Start Year	Start M-Dy	Stop Year	Stop M-Dy	Central / Flank vent / Radial fiss / Regional	Submarine / New island / Subglacial / Crater lake	Explosive / Pyro flow / Phreatic / Caldera	Lava flow / Lava lake / Dome / Spine	Fatal / Damage / Mudflow / Tsunami	VEI	Vol L/T
San Félix (Chile-Is)		26.28 S	80.12 W	193	0000	XBTf	Shield volcano	1506-01=	Holocene											
Easter Island (Chile-Is)		27.15 S	109.38 W	511	3444	BYXRt	Shield volcanoes	1506-011	Holocene											
Robinson Crusoe (Chile-Is)		33.658 S	78.85 W	922	0000	Bx	Shield volcanoes	1506-02=	Historical											
										? 1743	....	....	....	----	----	----	----	----		
	1.6 km north of Punta Bacalao									1835	0220	1835	0221	-x--	x---	x---	----	-x-x	1?	
Unnamed (Chile-Is)		33.62 S	76.83 W	-642	0000	U	Submarine volc	1506-04=	Uncertain											
										? 1839	0212	?1839	0213	----	??--	----	----	----		

CHILE - C & ARGENTINA

VOLCANO NAME (Subregion)	ERUPTION — Area of Activity	LAT	LONG	ELEV (m)	POPL (5 km / 10 / 30 / 100)	ROCK TYPE	VOLC TYPE	NUMBER	STATUS	Start Year	Start M-Dy	Stop Year	Stop M-Dy	Central / Flank vent / Radial fiss / Regional	Submarine / New island / Subglacial / Crater lake	Explosive / Pyro flow / Phreatic / Caldera	Lava flow / Lava lake / Dome / Spine	Fatal / Damage / Mudflow / Tsunami	VEI	Vol L/T
Tupungatito (Chile/Argentina)		33.40 S	69.80 W	6000	3347	AD	Stratovolcano	1507-01=	Historical											
										1829	....	....	....	x---	----	x---	----	----	2	
										? 1835	....	....	....	x---	----	?---	----	----	2	
										1861	....	....	....	x---	----	?---	----	----	2	

VOLCANO NAME (Subregion) / ERUPTION — Area of Activity	LAT	LONG	ELEV (m)	POPL (5 km, 10, 30, 100)	ROCK TYPE	VOLC TYPE	NUMBER	STATUS	Start Year	Start M-Dy	Stop Year	Stop M-Dy	Central / Flank vent / Radial fiss / Regional	Submarine / New island / Subglacial / Crater lake	Explosive / Pyro flow / Phreatic / Caldera	Lava flow / Lava lake / Dome / Spine	Fatal / Damage / Mudflow / Tsunami	VEI	Vol L/T
Tupungatito (Chile/Argentina) *continued*									? *1881*	....	....	....	----	----	----	----	----		
									1889	....	**1890**	....	x---	----	x---	----	----	2	
									1897	01	**1897**	0412>	x---	----	x---	----	----	2	
									1901	04	....	....	x---	----	x---	----	----	2	
									1907	0215	....	....	x---	----	x---	----	----	2	
									1925	....	....	....	x---	----	x---	----	----	2	
									1946	....	**1947**	....	x---	----	x---	----	----	2	
									1958	01	....	....	x---	----	----	----	----	2	
									1959	0326e	....	....	x---	----	x---	----	----	2	
									1959	1016	....	....	x---	----	x---	----	----	2	
									1960	0715e	....	....	x---	----	----	x---	----	2	
									1961	0505d	**1961**	08 >	x---	----	x---	----	----	2	
									1964	0803	**1964**	0919>	x---	----	x---	----	----	2	
									1968	....	....	....	x---	----	x---	----	----	2	
SW crater									**1980**	0110	**1980**	0111	x---	----	x---	----	----	2	
NW craters									**1986**	0120	**1986**	0120	x---	----	x-x-	----	----	1	
									1987	1128	**1987**	1130	x---	----	x---	----	----	2	
San José (Chile/Argentina)	**33.782 S**	**69.897 W**	**5856**	3357	**AD**	**Stratovolcano**	**1507-02=**	**Historical**											
									1822	1119	**1838**	....	x---	----	x---	----	----	2	
									1838	....	....	....	x---	----	x-x-	----	----	1	
									1881	....	....	....	x---	----	x---	----	----	2	
									1889	....	**1890**	....	x---	----	x---	----	----	2	
									1895	....	**1897**	....	x---	----	x---	----	----	2	
(fumarolic activity only)									X *1931*	....	....	....	x---	----	----	----	----		
(fumarolic activity only)									X *1941*	....	....	....	x---	----	----	----	----		
									1959	....	....	....	x---	----	x---	----	----	2	
									1960	....	....	....	x---	----	x---	----	----	2	
Maipo (Chile/Argentina)	**34.161 S**	**69.833 W**	**5264**	4447	**YDTAR**	**Caldera**	**1507-021**	**Historical**											
									? *1788*	....	....	....	----	----	----	----	----		
									? *1822*	....	....	....	----	----	----	----	----		
East flank (Riso Patrón)									**1826**	0301	....	....	-x--	----	x---	x---	----	2	
									1829	0926	....	....	----	----	x---	----	----	2?	
									? *1831*	*0216*	....	....	----	----	?---	----	--x-	*2?*	
									? *1833*	....	....	....	----	----	?---	----	----	*2?*	
									? *1835*	....	....	....	----	----	?---	----	----		
									? *1837*	....	....	....	----	----	?---	----	----		
									? *1869*	*0824*	....	....	----	----	?---	----	----	*2*	
									? *1881*	....	....	....	----	----	?---	----	----		
									1905	1028	**1905**	1030	----	----	x---	----	----	2	
									? *1908*	....	....	....	----	----	?---	----	----	*2*	
									1912	....	....	....	----	----	x---	----	----	2?	
Palomo (Chile-C)	**34.608 S**	**70.295 W**	**4860**	3346	**AD**	**Stratovolcano**	**1507-022**	**Holocene**											
Atuel, Caldera del (Argentina)	**34.65 S***	**70.05 W**	**5189**	3346	**ADB**	**Caldera**	**1507-023**	**Holocene**											
Risco Plateado (Argentina)	**34.93 S**	**70.00 W**	**4999**	0036	**ABD**	**Stratovolcano**	**1507-024**	Holocene?											
Tinguiririca (Chile-C)	**34.814 S**	**70.352 W**	**4280**	2246	**ADB**	**Stratovolcano**	**1507-03=**	**Historical**											
									1917	....	....	....	----	----	--?-	----	----	1?	
									? *1994*	*0115*	*?1994*	*0115*	x---	----	--?-	----	----	*2*	
Planchón-Peteroa (Chile/Argentina)	**35.240 S**	**70.570 W**	**4107**	1246	**ADb**	**Stratovolcanoes**	**1507-04=**	**Historical**											
(OPV tephra layer)									C-**5080**u	....	....	....	x---	--x-	xx--	----	----	3	-/7
(PLB tephra layer)									C **0900**v	....	....	....	x---	----	x---	----	----	3	-/7
Peteroa									**1660**	....	....	....	----	----	----	----	----	3↑	
									1751	11	**1751**	12	x---	----	x---	----	----	2	
Peteroa (2 km S of Planchón summit)									**1762**	1203	....	....	x---	----	x---	----	-xx-	4	
Peteroa									**1835**	....	....	....	x---	----	----	----	----	2	
Peteroa									**1837**	02	....	....	x---	----	x---	x---	-xx-	2	6/6
									? *1842*	....	....	....	----	----	----	----	----		
Peteroa									**1860**	....	....	....	x---	----	x---	----	----	2	
									? *1869*	....	....	....	----	----	----	----	----		
									? *1872*	....	....	....	----	----	----	----	----		
Peteroa									**1878**	....	....	....	x---	----	----	----	----	2	
Peteroa (SE of 1762 crater)									**1889**	09	**1894**?	....	x---	----	x---	----	----	2	
Petoroa (south of 1889-94 crater)									**1937**	04	**1937**	0505d	x---	----	x---	?---	----	2	
Peteroa									**1938**	09	**1938**	10	x---	----	?-x-	----	----	2	
Petoroa (1889-94 crater)									**1959**	1106	....	....	x---	----	x-x-	----	----	1	
Petoroa (1889-94 crater)									**1960**	0710?	....	....	x---	----	x-x-	----	----	1	
Peteroa									**1962**	01	....	....	x---	----	x---	----	----	1	
Peteroa (1889-94 crater)									? *1967*	*02*	....	....	x---	----	--?-	----	----	*1?*	
Peteroa									**1991**	0209	**1991**	0302b	x---	---x	x---	----	--x-	2	
									1998	1118	**1998**	1121	x---	----	x-x-	----	----	1	
Infiernillo (Argentina)	**35.142 S***	**69.83 W**		3345	**A**	**Volcanic field**	**1507-041**	**Radiocarbon**											
Volcán Hoyo Colorado									C-**6890**s	....	....	....	---x	----	----	x---	----		
Calabozos (Chile-C)	**35.558 S**	**70.496 W**	**3508**	3346	**DA**	**Caldera**	**1507-042**	**Holocene**											
Descabezado Grande (Chile-C)	**35.58 S**	**70.75 W**	**3953**	2346	**AD**	**Stratovolcanoes**	**1507-05=**	**Historical**											
Upper NNE slope									**1932**	0605e	**1933**	....	-x--	----	x-x-	----	----	3	
Azul, Cerro (Chile-C)	**35.653 S**	**70.761 W**	**3788**	1346	**DAb**	**Stratovolcano**	**1507-06=**	**Historical**											
Quizapu									**1846**	1126	**1853**?	....	--x-	----	x---	x---	----	2	9/-
Quizapu									? *1903*	*01*	....	....	-x--	----	--?-	----	----	*2?*	
Quizapu									**1906**	....	....	....	-x--	----	x-x-	----	----	2	
Quizapu									**1907**	0728	....	....	-x--	----	x-x-	----	----	2	
Quizapu									**1912**	02	....	....	-x--	----	x-x-	----	----	2	
Quizapu									? *1913*	*0115*q	....	....	-x--	----	--?-	----	----	*2?*	
Quizapu									**1914**	0908	....	....	-x--	----	x-x-	----	----	3	
Quizapu									**1916**	....	**1932**	0421	-x--	----	xxx-	----	-x--	**5+**	-/9
Quizapu									**1933**	....	**1938**	0725?	-x--	----	x---	----	----	2	
Quizapu									**1949**	0415e	....	....	-x--	----	x-x-	----	----	2?	
Quizapu									**1967**	0809	....	....	-x--	----	x-x-	----	----	2?	
Maule, Laguna del (Chile/Argentina)	**36.02 S***	**70.58 W**	**3092**	4446	**ARBD**	**Caldera**	**1507-061**	**Holocene**											
San Pedro-Pellado (Chile-C)	**35.989 S**	**70.849 W**	**3621**	2346	**ABDR**	**Stratovolcanoes**	**1507-062**	**Holocene**											
Longaví, Nevado de (Chile-C)	**36.193 S**	**71.161 W**	**3242**	2346	**Adb**	**Stratovolcano**	**1507-063**	**Radiocarbon**											
									C-**4890**u	....	....	....	----	----	x---	----	----		
Blancas, Lomas (Chile-C)	**36.286 S**	**71.009 W**	**2268**	3346	**BA**	**Stratovolcano**	**1507-064**	**Holocene**											

VOLCANO NAME (Subregion) / ERUPTION — Area of Activity	LAT	LONG	ELEV (m)	POPL (5 km, 10, 30, 100)	ROCK TYPE	VOLC TYPE / Start Year	Start M-Dy	NUMBER / Stop Year	STATUS / Stop M-Dy	Central, Flank vent, Radial fiss, Regional	Submarine, New island, Subglacial, Crater lake	Explosive, Pyro flow, Phreatic, Caldera	Lava flow, Lava lake, Dome, Spine	Fatal, Damage, Mudflow, Tsunami	VEI	Vol L/T
Resago (Chile-C)	36.45 S	70.92 W	1890	2346	A	Cinder cone		1507-065	Holocene							
Payún Matru (Argentina)	36.42 S	69.20 W	3680	0035	XBTYA	Shield volcano		1507-066	Holocene							
Domuyo (Argentina)	36.58 S	70.42 W	4709	1245	D	Stratovolcano		1507-067	Holocene?							
Chillán, Nevados de (Chile-C)	36.863 S	71.377 W	3212	2346	ADR	Stratovolcano		1507-07=	Historical							
Volcán Viejo						C-6890z	....	....	....	----	----	xx--	----	----		
Volcán Viejo						C-3660z	....	....	....	----	----	x---	----	----		
Volcán Viejo						C-1510t	....	....	....	----	----	xx--	----	----		
Volcán Viejo						C-0320u	....	....	....	----	----	xx--	----	----		
Volcán Viejo						1650t	....	....	....	----	----	x---	----	----	3?	
Volcán Viejo						1749?	....	1751	....	x---	----	x---	----	----	3↑	
Cerro Blanco and Volcán Viejo?						1752	0130	....	....	?---	----	?---	----	----	2?	
W flank of Volcán Viejo (Volcán Renegado)						1860	0725	....	....	-x--	----	?---	----	----	2?	
NW flank of Cerro Blanco (Santa Gertrudis)						1861	06	1863	....	-x--	----	x---	x---	--x-	2*	
NW flank of Cerro Blanco (Santa Gertrudis)						1864	1130	1865	0203a	-x--	----	x---	x---	--x-	3	
Volcán Chillán						1872	0722	....	....	----	----	x---	----	----	2	
Volcán Chillán						1877	0212?	....	....	----	----	x---	----	----	2	
Volcán Viejo (Volcán las Aguilas?)						? *1883*	*0121*	....	....	-?--	----	?---	----	--?-	*2?*	
Volcán Viejo						1891	02	....	....	----	----	x---	----	----	2	
Volcán Viejo						1893	0304	....	....	----	----	x---	----	-xx-	2	
Volcán Viejo						1898	....	....	....	----	----	x---	----	----	2	
Volcán Nuevo						1906	0806	1906	12	-x--	----	x---	x---	--x-	2	
Volcán Nuevo						1907	....	....	....	-x--	----	x---	----	----	1	
Volcán Nuevo						1914	....	....	....	----	----	x---	----	----	2	
Volcán Nuevo						? *1923*	....	....	....	-x--	----	?---	----	----	*2?*	
Volcán Nuevo						1927	0410	....	....	----	----	x---	----	----	2?	
Volcán Nuevo						1928	1130	1929	....	-x--	----	x---	----	----	2?	
Volcán Nuevo						1934	0117	....	....	----	----	x---	----	----	2?	
West flank of Volcán Viejo						1935	0702	....	....	-x--	----	?---	x---	--x-	2?	
Volcán Nuevo						? *1945*	....	....	....	-?--	----	?---	----	----		
Volcán Nuevo						1946	....	1947	....	-x--	----	x---	----	----	2?	
Volcán Nuevo						? *1965*	....	....	....	-x--	----	?---	----	----		
Volcán Nuevo						? *1972*	....	....	....	-x--	----	----	----	----		
Volcán Arrau (SE flank of Volcán Nuevo)						1973	07	1986	....	-x--	----	xx--	x-x-	----	2*	5/-
Saddle between Nuevo & Arrau volcanoes						2003	0829	2003	0915e	x-x-	----	x-x-	----	----	1	
						? *2009*	*0121*	?*2009*	*0122*	----	----	?---	----	----		
Cochiquito Volc Group (Argentina)	36.77 S	69.82 W	1435	2235	BA	Stratovolcanoes		1507-071	Holocene							
Tromen (Argentina)	37.142 S	70.03 W	3978	2345	ADBR	Stratovolcanoes		1507-072	Historical							
						1751	1231y	....	....	x---	----	x---	----	----	3?	
						1822	....	....	....	----	----	----	----	----		
Puesto Cortaderas (Argentina)	37.57 S	69.62 W	970	0035	B	Pyroclastic cone		1507-073	Holocene							
Antuco (Chile-C)	37.406 S	71.349 W	2979	3346	BA	Stratovolcano		1507-08=	Historical							
						C-7750?	....	....	....	x---	----	--xA	----	----		
						1750j	....	....	....	----	----	x---	----	----	2	
						1752	0131	1752	0201	x---	----	x---	x---	----	3?	
						1806?	05	....	....	x---	----	x---	----	----	2	
						1820	....	1821?	....	x---	----	x---	----	--x-	1	
						1828	1218	....	....	x---	----	x---	x---	----	2	
						? *1839*	....	....	....	x---	----	----	----	----	*2*	
						1845	0226	1845	0301>	x---	----	x---	x---	----	2	
						? *1848*	....	....	....	x---	----	x---	----	----	*2?*	
NE flank fissure and summit						1852	11	1853	01	xxx-	----	x---	x---	--x-	3*	7/-
						1861	02 ?	1861	08 ?	x---	----	----	x---	----	0	
						? *1862*	*01*	?*1862*	*0303*	----	----	----	----	----		
						1863	12	....	....	x---	----	x---	----	----	2	
						1869	....	....	....	x---	----	x---	----	----	2	
(fumarolic activity only)						X *1929*	....	....	....	----	----	----	----	----		
(fumarolic activity only)						X *1972*	....	....	....	----	----	----	----	----		
Trocon (Argentina)	37.73 S	70.90 W	2500	2345	DA	Lava domes		1507-081	Holocene?							
Copahue (Chile/Argentina)	37.85 S	71.17 W	2997	2346	XATR	Stratovolcano		1507-09=	Historical							
						C-6820?	....	....	....	----	----	xx--	----	----		
						C-0250?	....	....	....	----	----	xx--	----	----		
						1750?	....	....	....	----	----	x-x-	----	----	2	
						? *1759?*	....	....	....	----	----	?-?-	----	----		
						1867?	....	....	....	----	----	--?-	----	----	2?	
						1937	....	....	....	----	----	--?-	----	----	2?	
						1944	....	....	....	----	----	--?-	----	----		
						1960	....	....	....	----	----	--?-	----	----		
						1961	....	....	....	----	----	x-x-	----	----	2	
Del Agrio crater						1992	0722	1993	....	x---	---x	x-x-	----	--x-	2	
Del Agrio crater						1994	12	....	....	x---	---x	x---	----	----	2	
Del Agrio crater						1995	09	....	....	x---	---x	x-x-	----	----	2	
Del Agrio crater						2000	0701	2000	1018	x---	---x	xxx-	----	-xx-	2	
Callaqui (Chile-C)	37.92 S	71.45 W	3164	2346	ABd	Stratovolcano		1507-091	Historical							
						1751	1231	....	....	----	----	x---	----	----	2	
						? *1864*	*10*	....	....	----	----	?---	----	----		
(eruption from Quetrupillan)						X *1872*	....	....	....	----	----	----	----	----		
						? *1937*	*0918*	....	....	----	----	----	----	----		
						1980	10	1980	10	x---	----	x-x-	----	----	1	
						? *2009*	*0122*	....	....	----	----	?---	----	----		
Mariñaqui, Laguna (Chile-C)	38.27 S	71.10 W	2143	2345	A	Cinder cones		1507-092	Holocene							
Tolguaca (Chile-C)	38.310 S	71.645 W	2806	2356	AB	Stratovolcano		1507-093	Holocene							
Lonquimay (Chile-C)	38.377 S	71.58 W	2865	2356	ADB	Stratovolcano		1507-10=	Historical							
						1853	02	....	....	x---	----	x---	x---	----	3	
NE flank						1887	0602	1890	01	--x-	----	x---	x---	----	3*	8/-
						1933	0104	....	....	----	----	x---	x---	----	2	
						? *1940*	*02*	....	....	----	----	?---	----	----		
NE flank (Navidad Crater)						1988	1225	1990	0124a	-xx-	----	x---	xx--	xx--	3*	8/8
Tralihue (Argentina)	38.52 S	70.90 W		2345	YB	Stratovolcano		1507-101	Holocene							
Llaima (Chile-C)	38.692 S	71.729 W	3125	2356	BAd	Stratovolcano		1507-11=	Historical							
						C-7410y	....	....	....	----	----	x---	----	----		
						C-6880u	....	....	....	----	----	x---	----	----	**5**	-/9

VOLCANO NAME (Subregion) / **ERUPTION** — Area of Activity	**LAT**	**LONG**	**ELEV** (m)	**POPL** 5 km / 10 / 30 / 100	**ROCK TYPE**	**VOLC TYPE** — Start — Year	M-Dy	**NUMBER** — Stop — Year	**STATUS** M-Dy	ERUPTIVE CHARACTERISTICS: Central / Flank vent / Radial fiss / Regional	Submarine / New island / Subglacial / Crater lake	Explosive / Pyro flow / Phreatic / Caldera	Lava flow / Lava lake / Dome / Spine	Fatal / Damage / Mudflow / Tsunami	**VEI**	**Vol L/T**
Llaima (Chile-C) *continued*						C-**5290**x	....	....	....	----	----	**xx**--	----	----		
						1640	02	....	....	----	----	**x**---	?---	--**x**-	4	
						1751	1218	**1752**	....	**x**---	----	**x**---	**x**---	----	2	
						1759	12	....	....	----	----	**x**---	----	----	2	
						1822	....	....	....	----	----	**x**---	----	----	2	
						1852	....	**1853**	....	**x**---	----	**x**---	----	----	2	
						1862	....	....	....	**x**---	----	**x**---	----	----	3	
						1864	....	....	....	**x**---	----	**x**---	----	----	3	
						1866	....	....	....	**x**---	----	**x**---	----	----	2	
						1869	04	....	....	----	----	----	----	----	2?	
						1872	0606	....	....	**x**---	----	**x**---	**x**---	--**x**-	2	
						? *1874*	....	....	....	----	----	----	----	----		
						1875	....	**1876**	....	**x**---	----	**x**---	**x**---	-**xx**-	2	
						1877	0116	**1877**	0624	----	----	**x**---	**x**---	----	2	
						1883	....	....	....	**x**---	----	**x**---	----	----	2	
						1887	0116	**1887**	0624	**x**---	----	**x**---	**x**---	----	2	
						1889	0420	**1889**	07	----	----	**x**---	----	----	2	
						1892	....	....	....	----	----	**x**---	----	----	2	
						1893	12	**1894**	12	----	----	**x**---	----	----	2	
						1895	....	**1896**	....	**x**---	----	**x**---	**x**---	--**x**-	2	
						1903	0512	**1903**	0514	**xx**--	----	**x**---	**x**---	----	2	
						1907	....	**1908**	03	----	----	**x**---	**x**---	----	2	
						1912	....	....	....	**x**---	----	**x**---	**x**---	----	2	
						1914	0703	....	....	----	----	**x**---	**x**---	----	2	
						1917	0204	....	....	?---	----	**x**---	----	----	2	
						1922	1024	....	....	----	----	**x**---	----	----	2	
SE crater and summit crater.						**1927**	1005	**1927**	1205	**xxx**-	----	**x**---	**x**---	--**x**-	2	
						1929	12	....	....	**x**---	----	**x**---	**x**---	----	2	
						1930	0706	**1930**	0820	**x**---	----	**x**---	**x**---	----	2	
						1932	0302	**1932**	0302	**x**---	----	**x**---	?---	--?-	2?	
						1932	1231	**1933**	0105	**x**---	----	**x**---	**x**---	--**x**-	3	
						1937	0209?	**1937**	1102	**x**---	----	**x**---	**x**---	**xxx**-	2	
						1938	12	....	....	**x**---	----	**x**---	----	----	1	
						1941	0623	....	....	**x**---	----	**x**---	----	----	2	
						1942	0609	**1942**	11	----	----	**x**---	----	----	2	
						1944	....	....	....	----	----	**x**---	----	----	2	
						1945	0331	**1945**	0403	----	----	**x**?--	**x**---	--**x**-	3	
						1946	0723	....	....	----	----	**x**---	**x**---	--**x**-	2	
						1949	09	....	....	**x**---	----	**x**---	**x**---	----	2	
Summit and SE crater.						**1955**	1022	**1957**	11	**xx**--	----	**x**---	**x**---	-**xx**-	3*	
						? *1960*	....	....	....	----	----	----	----	----		
						1964	....	....	....	----	----	**x**---	**x**---	----	2	
						1971	1201p	**1972**	0312	----	----	**x**---	----	----	2	
						1979	1015	**1979**	1128	**x**---	----	**x**---	**x**---	--**x**-	2	
						1984	0420	**1984**	1126	**x**---	----	**x**---	----	--**x**-	2	
						1990	0225	**1990**	1125	**x**---	----	**x**---	----	--?-	1	
						1992	0823	**1992**	0902	**x**---	----	**x**-**x**-	----	----	1	
SE side summit crater, upper SW flank						**1994**	0517	**1994**	0830	**x**-**x**-	--**x**-	**x**---	**x**---	-**xx**-	2	
						1995	1013	**1995**	1022>	**x**---	----	**x**---	----	----	2?	
						1997	03 ?	**1997**	10 ?	**x**---	----	--**x**-	----	----	1	
						1998	0403	**1998**	0423?	**x**---	----	**x**---	----	----	2?	
						1998	1110c	....	....	**x**---	----	**x**---	----	----	2	
						2002	1013k	....	....	**x**---	----	**x**---	----	----	1	
						2003	0409	**2003**	0416>	**x**---	----	**x**---	----	----	2*	
						2007	0526	**2007**	0808?	**x**---	----	**x**---	----	----	2	
Summit and upper east flank						**2008**	0101	**2009**	0612d	**x**-**x**-	----	**xx**--	**xx**--	--**x**-	3	
Sollipulli (Chile-C).	**38.97** S	**71.52** W	**2282**	4446	**ADB**	**Caldera**		**1507-111**	**Radiocarbon**							
SW caldera rim (Alpehué crater)						C-**0920**u	....	....	....	-**x**--	----	**xx**--	----	--**x**-	**5+**	-/9
North flank (Redondo, Chufquén)						C **1240**t	....	....	....	-**x**--	----	**x**---	**x**---	----		
Caburgua-Huelemolle (Chile-C) . .	**39.25** S*	**71.70** W	**1496**	4456	**B**	**Cinder cones**		**1507-112**	**Tephrochronology**							
Huelemolle and Caburgua cones						T-**5050***	....	....	....	---**x**	----	**x**---	----	----		
Villarrica (Chile-C)	**39.42** S	**71.93** W	**2847**	3456	**BAR**	**Stratovolcano**		**1507-12=**	**Historical**							
						T-**7520***	....	....	....	----	----	----	**x**---	----	0	
(Voipir pyroclastic flow)						C-**6690**?	....	....	....	----	----	**xx**--	----	----	**P**	
(Candelaria pyroclastic flow)						C-**3730**?	....	....	....	----	----	**xx**--	----	----		
(El Pirao lava flows)						T-**2990**z	....	....	....	----	----	----	**x**---	----	0	
						C-**2240**?	....	....	....	----	----	**xx**--	----	----		
(Alfunalhue pyroclastic flow).						C-**2140**?	....	....	....	----	----	**xx**--	----	----		
(Zanjón Seco lava flows)						T-**1980**w	....	....	....	----	----	----	**x**---	----	0	
(Pucón Ignimbrite).						C-**1810**x	....	....	....	**x**---	----	**xx**-**x**	----	----	**5**	-/9
(FP-B unit; date out of strat. sequence)						C-**1080**?	....	....	....	----	----	**xx**--	----	----		
(Pedregoso pyroclastic surge).						C-**0670**?	....	....	....	----	----	**xx**--	----	----		
(Zanjón Seco pahoehoe lava flows).						C **0110**?	....	....	....	----	----	----	**x**---	----	0	
(Cónquil pyroclastic flow)						C **0330**?	....	....	....	----	----	**xx**--	----	----		
						1558	....	....	....	**x**---	----	**x**---	----	-**x**?-	2	
						1562	....	....	....	**x**---	----	**x**---	?---	----	2	
(earthquake, not eruption).						*X 1575*	....	....	....	----	----	----	----	**xx**--		
						1594	....	....	....	**x**---	----	**x**---	----	----	2	
(1640 eruption from Llaima volcano?).						? *1640*	*0203*	....	....	?---	----	?---	?---	--?-		
						1647	0513	....	....	**x**---	----	**x**---	?---	----	1?	
						1657	0315	....	....	**x**---	----	**x**---	----	----	1?	
						1688?	....	....	....	**x**---	----	**x**---	----	--?-	1	
						1716	....	....	....	**x**---	----	**x**---	----	----	1	
						1730	0708	....	....	**x**---	----	**x**---	----	----	2?	
						1737	1224	....	....	**x**---	----	**x**---	----	----	2?	
						1742	....	....	....	**x**---	----	**x**---	----	----	2?	
						1745	....	....	....	**x**---	----	**x**---	----	----	1?	
						1751	1214	....	....	**x**---	----	**x**---	?---	----	1?	
						1759	12	**1759**	12	**x**---	----	**x**---	----	----	1	
						? *1775*	....	....	....	**x**---	----	?---	?---	--?-	*2?*	
						1777	....	**1779**	....	**x**---	----	**x**---	----	----	1	
						1780	....	....	....	**x**---	----	**x**---	----	----	1	
						1787	....	....	....	**x**---	----	**x**---	**x**---	----	2	

OVDAS-SERNAGEOMIN

Lava flow and lahar, Llaima, July 2008

Villarrica (Chile-C) *continued*

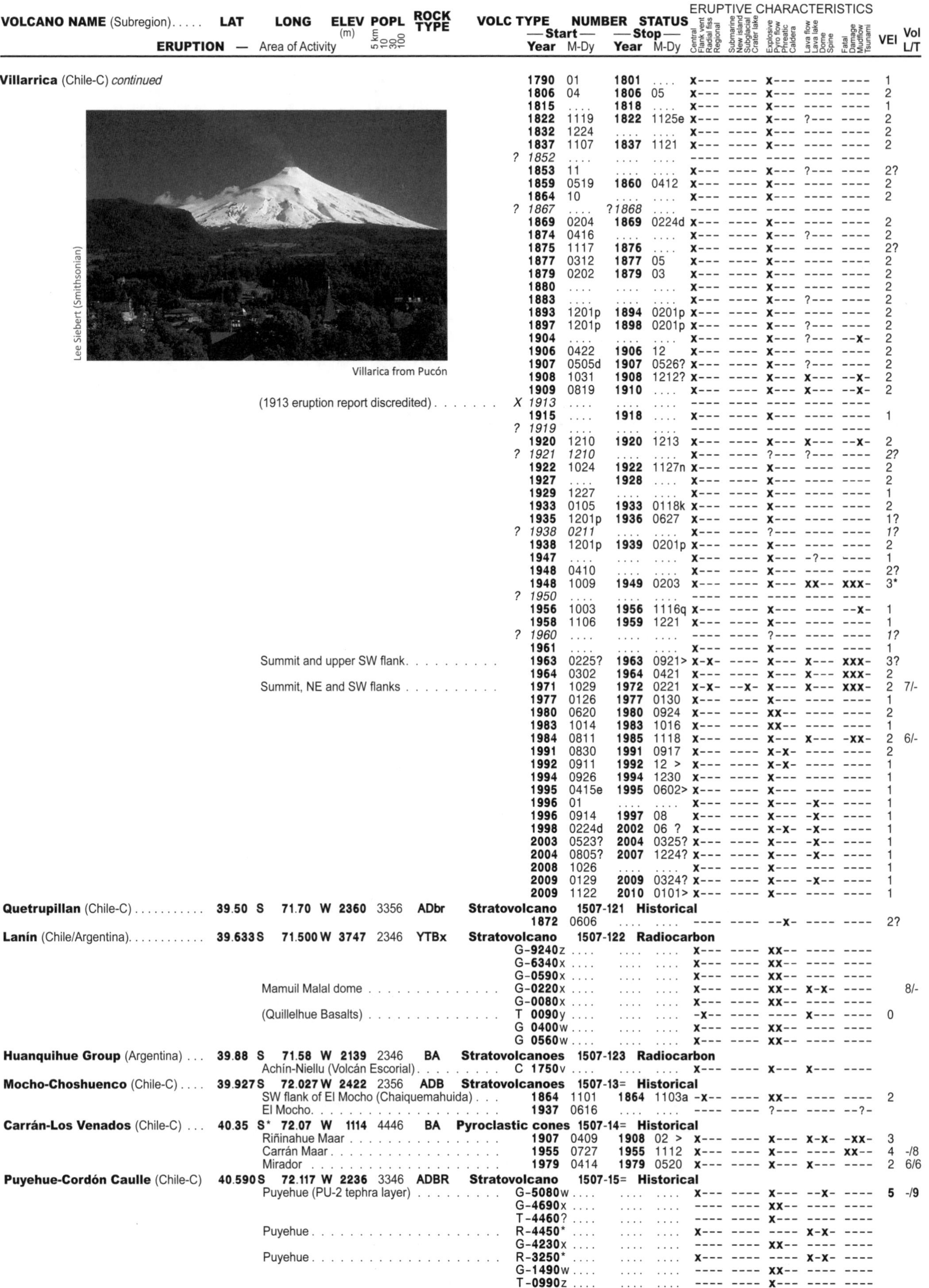

Lee Siebert (Smithsonian)

Villarica from Pucón

VOLCANO NAME (Subregion) / ERUPTION — Area of Activity	LAT	LONG	ELEV (m)	POPL (5 km, 10, 30, 100)	ROCK TYPE	VOLC TYPE	NUMBER	STATUS	Start Year	Start M-Dy	Stop Year	Stop M-Dy	Central / Flank vent / Radial fiss / Regional	Submarine / New island / Subglacial / Crater lake	Explosive / Pyro flow / Phreatic / Caldera	Lava flow / Lava lake / Dome / Spine	Fatal / Damage / Mudflow / Tsunami	VEI	Vol L/T
									1790	01	**1801**	....	x---	----	x---	----	----	1	
									1806	04	**1806**	05	x---	----	x---	----	----	2	
									1815	....	**1818**	....	x---	----	x---	----	----	1	
									1822	1119	**1822**	1125e	x---	----	x---	?---	----	2	
									1832	1224	....	....	x---	----	x---	----	----	2	
									1837	1107	**1837**	1121	x---	----	x---	----	----	2	
									? *1852*	....	....	....	----	----	----	----	----		
									1853	11	....	....	x---	----	x---	?---	----	2?	
									1859	0519	**1860**	0412	x---	----	x---	----	----	2	
									1864	10	....	....	x---	----	x---	----	----	2	
									? *1867*	....	? *1868*	....	----	----	----	----	----		
									1869	0204	**1869**	0224d	x---	----	x---	----	----	2	
									1874	0416	....	....	x---	----	x---	?---	----	2	
									1875	1117	**1876**	....	x---	----	x---	----	----	2?	
									1877	0312	**1877**	05	x---	----	x---	----	----	2	
									1879	0202	**1879**	03	x---	----	x---	----	----	2	
									1880	....	....	....	x---	----	x---	----	----	2	
									1883	....	....	....	x---	----	x---	?---	----	2	
									1893	1201p	**1894**	0201p	x---	----	x---	----	----	2	
									1897	1201p	**1898**	0201p	x---	----	x---	?---	----	2	
									1904	....	....	....	x---	----	x---	?---	--x-	2	
									1906	0422	**1906**	12	x---	----	x---	----	----	2	
									1907	0505d	**1907**	0526?	x---	----	x---	?---	----	2	
									1908	1031	**1908**	1212?	x---	----	x---	x---	--x-	2	
									1909	0819	**1910**	....	x---	----	x---	x---	--x-	2	
(1913 eruption report discredited)									X *1913*	....	....	....	----	----	----	----	----		
									1915	....	**1918**	....	x---	----	x---	----	----	1	
									? *1919*	....	....	....	----	----	----	----	----		
									1920	1210	**1920**	1213	x---	----	x---	x---	--x-	2	
									? *1921*	*1210*	....	....	x---	----	?---	?---	----	*2?*	
									1922	1024	**1922**	1127n	x---	----	x---	----	----	2	
									1927	....	**1928**	....	x---	----	x---	----	----	2	
									1929	1227	....	....	x---	----	x---	----	----	1	
									1933	0105	**1933**	0118k	x---	----	x---	----	----	2	
									1935	1201p	**1936**	0627	x---	----	x---	----	----	1?	
									? *1938*	*0211*	....	....	x---	----	?---	----	----	*1?*	
									1938	1201p	**1939**	0201p	x---	----	x---	----	----	2	
									1947	....	....	....	x---	----	x---	-?--	----	1	
									1948	0410	....	....	x---	----	x---	----	----	2?	
									1948	1009	**1949**	0203	x---	----	x---	xx--	xxx-	3*	
									? *1950*	....	....	....	----	----	----	----	----		
									1956	1003	**1956**	1116q	x---	----	x---	----	--x-	1	
									1958	1106	**1959**	1221	x---	----	x---	----	----	1	
									? *1960*	....	....	....	----	----	?---	----	----	*1?*	
									1961	....	....	....	x---	----	x---	----	----	1	
Summit and upper SW flank									**1963**	0225?	**1963**	0921>	x-x-	----	x---	x---	xxx-	3?	
									1964	0302	**1964**	0421	x---	----	x---	x---	xxx-	2	
Summit, NE and SW flanks									**1971**	1029	**1972**	0221	x-x-	--x-	x---	x---	xxx-	2	7/-
									1977	0126	**1977**	0130	x---	----	x---	----	----	1	
									1980	0620	**1980**	0924	x---	----	xx--	----	----	2	
									1983	1014	**1983**	1016	x---	----	xx--	----	----	1	
									1984	0811	**1985**	1118	x---	----	x---	x---	-xx-	2	6/-
									1991	0830	**1991**	0917	x---	----	x-x-	----	----	2	
									1992	0911	**1992**	12 >	x---	----	x-x-	----	----	1	
									1994	0926	**1994**	1230	x---	----	x---	----	----	1	
									1995	0415e	**1995**	0602>	x---	----	x---	----	----	1	
									1996	01	....	....	x---	----	x---	-x--	----	1	
									1996	0914	**1997**	08	x---	----	x---	-x--	----	1	
									1998	0224d	**2002**	06 ?	x---	----	x-x-	-x--	----	1	
									2003	0523?	**2004**	0325?	x---	----	x---	-x--	----	1	
									2004	0805?	**2007**	1224?	x---	----	x---	-x--	----	1	
									2008	1026	....	....	x---	----	x---	----	----	1	
									2009	0129	**2009**	0324?	x---	----	x---	-x--	----	1	
									2009	1122	**2010**	0101>	x---	----	x---	----	----	1	
Quetrupillan (Chile-C)	**39.50 S**	**71.70 W**	**2360**	3356	ADbr	**Stratovolcano**	**1507-121**	**Historical**											
									1872	0606	....	....	----	----	--x-	----	----	2?	
Lanín (Chile/Argentina)	**39.633 S**	**71.500 W**	**3747**	2346	YTBx	**Stratovolcano**	**1507-122**	**Radiocarbon**											
									G-**9240**z	....	....	....	x---	----	xx--	----	----		
									G-**6340**x	....	....	....	x---	----	xx--	----	----		
									G-**0590**x	....	....	....	x---	----	xx--	----	----		
Mamuil Malal dome									G-**0220**x	....	....	....	x---	----	xx--	x-x-	----		8/-
									G-**0080**x	....	....	....	x---	----	xx--	----	----		
(Quillelhue Basalts)									T **0090**y	....	....	....	-x--	----	----	x---	----	0	
									G **0400**w	....	....	....	x---	----	xx--	----	----		
									G **0560**w	....	....	....	x---	----	xx--	----	----		
Huanquihue Group (Argentina)	**39.88 S**	**71.58 W**	**2139**	2346	BA	**Stratovolcanoes**	**1507-123**	**Radiocarbon**											
Achín-Niellu (Volcán Escorial)									C **1750**v	....	....	....	x---	----	x---	x---	----		
Mocho-Choshuenco (Chile-C)	**39.927 S**	**72.027 W**	**2422**	2356	ADB	**Stratovolcanoes**	**1507-13=**	**Historical**											
SW flank of El Mocho (Chaiquemahuida)									**1864**	1101	**1864**	1103a	-x--	----	xx--	----	----	2	
El Mocho									**1937**	0616	....	....	----	----	?---	----	--?-		
Carrán-Los Venados (Chile-C)	**40.35 S***	**72.07 W**	**1114**	4446	BA	**Pyroclastic cones**	**1507-14=**	**Historical**											
Riñinahue Maar									**1907**	0409	**1908**	02 >	x---	----	x---	x-x-	-xx-	3	
Carrán Maar									**1955**	0727	**1955**	1112	x---	----	x---	----	xx--	4	-/8
Mirador									**1979**	0414	**1979**	0520	x---	----	x---	x---	----	2	6/6
Puyehue-Cordón Caulle (Chile-C)	**40.590 S**	**72.117 W**	**2236**	3346	ADBR	**Stratovolcano**	**1507-15=**	**Historical**											
Puyehue (PU-2 tephra layer)									G-**5080**w	....	....	....	x---	----	x---	--x-	----	**5**	-/9
									G-**4690**x	....	....	....	----	----	xx--	----	----		
									T-**4460**?	....	....	....	----	----	x---	----	----		
Puyehue									R-**4450***	....	....	....	x---	----	----	x-x-	----		
									G-**4230**x	....	....	....	----	----	xx--	----	----		
Puyehue									R-**3250***	....	....	....	x---	----	----	x-x-	----		
									G-**1490**w	....	....	....	----	----	xx--	----	----		
									T-**0990**z	....	....	....	----	----	x---	----	----		

VOLCANO NAME (Subregion) / ERUPTION — Area of Activity	LAT	LONG	ELEV (m)	POPL (5 km, 10, 30, 100)	ROCK TYPE	VOLC TYPE	NUMBER	STATUS	Start Year	Start M-Dy	Stop Year	Stop M-Dy	Central / Flank vent / Radial fiss / Regional	Submarine / New island / Subglacial / Crater lake	Explosive / Pyro flow / Phreatic / Caldera	Lava flow / Lava lake / Dome / Spine	Fatal / Damage / Mudflow / Tsunami	VEI	Vol L/T
Puyehue-Cordón Caulle (Chile-C) *continued*									G-0490y	....	....	....	----	----	xx--	----	----		
									G 0110x	....	....	....	----	----	xx--	----	----		
Puyehue?									T 0140y	....	....	....	?---	----	x---	----	----		
									G 0500v	....	....	....	----	----	xx--	----	----		
Puyehue (MH tephra)									G 0860u	....	....	....	x---	----	x---	----	----	**5**	-/9
									G 1140v	....	....	....	----	----	xx--	----	----		
									G 1220w	....	....	....	----	----	xx--	----	----		
Cordón Caulle									**1759**?	....	....	....	---x	----	xx--	----	----	2	
Cordón Caulle									**1893**?	....	....	....	---x	----	xx--	----	----	2	
Cordón Caulle									**1905**?	....	....	....	---x	----	x---	----	----	2	
Cordón Caulle									**1914**	0208	....	....	---x	----	x---	----	----	2	
Cordón Caulle									**1919**	....	**1920**	....	---x	----	x---	----	----	2	
Cordón Caulle-Cordillera Nevada									**1921**	1213	**1922**	0212	---x	----	x---	x---	----	3	8/-
Cordón Caulle									**1929**	0107	....	....	---x	----	x---	----	----	2	
Cordón Caulle									**1934**	0306	....	....	---x	----	x---	----	----	2	
Cordón Caulle									**1960**	0524	**1960**	0730	---x	----	x---	x---	----	3?	8/7
Cordón Caulle									**1990**	....	....	....	---x	----	x---	----	----	1	
Pantoja, Cerro (Chile-C)	**40.77 S**	**71.95 W**	**2024**	2346	**BA**	**Stratovolcano**	**1507-152**	**Holocene**											
Antillanca Group (Chile-C)	**40.771 S**	**72.153 W**	**1990**	2346	**BA**	**Stratovolcanoes**	**1507-153**	**Radiocarbon**											
									G-0960w	....	....	....	----	----	x---	----	----	**5**	-/9
Casablanca (Raihuén crater)									G-0230x	....	....	....	-x--	----	xx--	----	----	**5**	-/9
Puntiagudo-Cordón Cenizos (Ch)	**40.969 S**	**72.264 W**	**2493**	2346	**AB**	**Stratovolcano**	**1507-16-**	**Historical**											
Cordón Cenizos									**1850**	....	....	....	-x--	----	x---	----	----		
									? 1930	....	....	....	----	----	----	----	----		

CHILE - S & ARGENTINA

VOLCANO NAME (Subregion) / ERUPTION — Area of Activity	LAT	LONG	ELEV (m)	POPL (5 km, 10, 30, 100)	ROCK TYPE	VOLC TYPE	NUMBER	STATUS	Start Year	Start M-Dy	Stop Year	Stop M-Dy	Central / Flank vent / Radial fiss / Regional	Submarine / New island / Subglacial / Crater lake	Explosive / Pyro flow / Phreatic / Caldera	Lava flow / Lava lake / Dome / Spine	Fatal / Damage / Mudflow / Tsunami	VEI	Vol L/T
Osorno (Chile-S)	**41.10 S**	**72.493 W**	**2652**	2356	**BAd**	**Stratovolcano**	**1508-01=**	**Historical**											
									C-1710u	....	....	....	----	----	xx--	----	----		
									C-0210u	....	....	....	----	----	xx--	----	----		
									C 0420v	....	....	....	----	----	xx--	----	----	4?	
									C 0910v	....	....	....	----	----	xx--	----	----		
									C 1220v	....	....	....	----	----	xx--	----	----		
									C 1310u	....	....	....	----	----	xx--	----	----		
									1575	....	....	....	----	----	?---	----	----	2	
									1640	....	....	....	----	----	?---	----	----	2	
									1644	....	....	....	----	----	?---	----	----	2	
									1719	....	....	....	x---	----	----	----	----	2	
									1765m	....	....	....	x---	----	x---	----	----	1	
SE base									**1790**	0309	**1791**	1226e	-x--	----	x---	x---	--x-	2	
Summit & SSW side (Negrillar de Ensenada)									**1834**	1129	**1835**	0224d	xx--	----	x---	x---	----	3?	
									1837	1107	....	....	x---	----	x---	----	----	2	
(some sources list ca. 1850 date)									**1851**	....	....	....	----	----	x---	----	----	2?	
(fumarolic activity only)									*X 1852*	....	....	....	----	----	----	----	----		
									1855	....	....	....	x---	----	x---	----	----	2?	
									1869	....	....	....	x---	----	x---	----	----	2	
Tronador (Chile/Argentina)	**41.157 S**	**71.885 W**	**3491**	1346	**ABD**	**Stratovolcano**	**1508-011**	Holocene?											
Cayutué-La Viguería (Chile-S)	**41.25 S***	**72.27 W**	**506**	4446	**B**	**Pyroclastic cones**	**1508-012**	**Tephrochronology**											
La Viguería									T-1050?	....	....	....	---x	----	x---	x---	----		
Calbuco (Chile-S)	**41.326 S**	**72.614 W**	**2003**	2356	**A**	**Stratovolcano**	**1508-02=**	**Historical**											
									T-6050?	....	....	....	x---	----	x---	x---	----		
									C-5560s	....	....	....	x---	----	xx--	----	----		
									C-4300w	....	....	....	x---	----	xx--	----	----		
									C-1920t	....	....	....	x---	----	xx--	----	----		
									C-0330x	....	....	....	x---	----	xx--	----	----		
									C-0100v	....	....	....	x---	----	xx--	----	----		
									C 0040u	....	....	....	x---	----	xx--	----	----		
									C 0220u	....	....	....	x---	----	xx--	----	----		
									C 0520x	....	....	....	x---	----	xx--	----	----		
									C 1380t	....	....	....	x---	----	xx--	----	----		
									C 1600u	....	....	....	x---	----	xx--	----	----		
									1792?	....	....	....	x---	----	xx--	----	----		
(steam observed from Osorno: Moreno)									*X 1837*	....	*X1838*	....	----	----	----	----	----		
									1893	0107	**1894**	0116>	x---	----	x---	?---	-xx-	4*	
									1894	1116	**1895**?	....	x---	----	x---	----	--x-	2?	
									1906	....	....	....	----	----	x---	----	----	2	
									1907	0422	....	....	----	----	x---	----	----	2?	
									1909	03	....	....	----	----	x---	----	----	2	
									1911	....	**1912**	....	----	----	x---	----	----	2	
									1917	04	**1917**	05	x---	----	x---	x-x-	-xx-	3?	
									1929	0106	**1929**	0106	x---	----	xx--	x---	-xx-	3?	
									1961	0201	**1961**	0326>	x---	--x-	x-x-	x---	-xx-	3	
									1972	0826	**1972**	0826	x---	----	x---	----	----	2	
Cuernos del Diablo (Chile-S)	**41.40 S**	**72.00 W**	**1862**	2346	**B**	**Stratovolcano**	**1508-021**	**Holocene**											
Yate (Chile-S)	**41.755 S**	**72.396 W**	**2187**	2346	**A**	**Stratovolcano**	**1508-022**	**Holocene**											
Hornopirén (Chile-S)	**41.874 S**	**72.431 W**	**1572**	2346	**A**	**Stratovolcano**	**1508-023**	**Holocene**											
									? 1835	....	....	....	----	----	----	----	----		
Apagado (Chile-S)	**41.88 S**	**72.58 W**	**1210**	1246	**B**	**Pyroclastic cone**	**1508-024**	**Holocene**											
Crater Basalt Volc Field (Argenti)	**42.02 S***	**70.18 W**	**1359**	3345	**Xb**	**Cinder cones**	**1508-025**	**Holocene**											
Huequi (Chile-S)	**42.377 S**	**72.578 W**	**1318**	0146	**A**	**Stratovolcano**	**1508-03=**	**Historical**											
									1890	....	....	....	x---	----	x---	----	----	3?	
									1893	....	....	....	x---	----	x---	x---	----	2	
									1896	....	....	....	----	----	x---	----	----	2	
									1900	....	....	....	----	----	x---	----	----	2	
									1906	....	**1907**	....	----	----	x---	----	----	2	
									1920?	....	....	....	----	----	x---	----	----	2	
Minchinmávida (Chile-S)	**42.793 S**	**72.439 W**	**2404**	0145	**ABR**	**Stratovolcano**	**1508-04=**	**Historical**											
(MIC1 tephra)									T-3790z	....	....	....	----	----	x---	----	----		
(MIC2 tephra)									T-0880*	....	....	....	----	----	x---	----	----		
									*? 1650*t	....	....	....	----	----	----	----	----		
									1742	....	....	....	----	----	----	----	----	2	

VOLCANO NAME (Subregion) / ERUPTION — Area of Activity	LAT	LONG	ELEV (m)	POPL (5 km, 10, 30, 100)	ROCK TYPE	VOLC TYPE	NUMBER	STATUS	Start Year	Start M-Dy	Stop Year	Stop M-Dy	Central / Flank vent / Radial fiss / Regional	Submarine / New island / Subglacial / Crater lake	Explosive / Pyro flow / Phreatic / Caldera	Lava flow / Lava lake / Dome / Spine	Fatal / Damage / Mudflow / Tsunami	VEI	Vol L/T
Minchinmávida (Chile-S) *continued*									**1834**	1125	....	....	----	----	x---	?---	--x-	2	
									1835	0220	**1835**	0315e	-x--	----	----	x---	--x-	0?	
Chaitén (Chile-S)	**42.833 S**	**72.646 W**	**1122**	4445	**R**	**Caldera**	**1508-041**	**Historical**											
(CHA1 tephra)									**C-7420**u	....	....	....	x---	----	xx-x	----	----	**C**	
									2008	0502	**2010>**	....	x---	----	xx--	--x-	xxx-	4	-/8
Corcovado (Chile-S)	**43.18 S**	**72.80 W**	**2300**	1245	**AB**	**Stratovolcano**	**1508-05=**	**Historical**											
(COR1 tephra)									**T-6640***	....	....	....	----	----	x---	----	----		
(COR2 tephra)									**C-6030**v	....	....	....	----	----	x---	----	----		
(COR3 tephra)									**C-4920**v	....	....	....	----	----	x---	----	----		
(confused with Michinmavida eruption?)									*? 1834*	*11*	....	....	-?--	----	?---	----	----	*2*	
(confused with Michinmavida eruption?)									*? 1835*	*1111*	....	....	-?--	----	?---	----	----	*2*	
Yanteles (Chile-S)	**43.50 S**	**72.80 W**	**2042**	0245	**A**	**Stratovolcanoes**	**1508-050**	**Radiocarbon**											
(YAN1 tephra layer)									**C-7240**w	....	....	....	----	----	x---	----	----		
									T-6650?	....	....	....	----	----	x---	----	----		
									? 1835	*0220*	....	....	-x--	----	x---	----	----		
Palena Volc Group (Chile-S)	**43.78 S**	**72.47 W**		1245	**U**	**Cinder cones**	**1508-051**	**Holocene**											
Melimoyu (Chile-S)	**44.08 S**	**72.88 W**	**2400**	0135	**ADB**	**Stratovolcano**	**1508-052**	**Radiocarbon**											
(MEL1 tephra)									**C-0820**v	....	....	....	----	----	x---	----	----		
(MEL2 tephra)									**C 0200**u	....	....	....	----	----	x---	----	----		
Puyuhuapi (Chile-S)	**44.30 S**	**72.53 W**	**524**	3345	**Bxy**	**Cinder cones**	**1508-053**	**Holocene**											
Mentolat (Chile-S)	**44.70 S**	**73.08 W**	**1660**	0135	**AB**	**Stratovolcano**	**1508-054**	**Historical**											
									C-5010t	....	....	....	----	----	x---	----	----		
									1710e	....	....	....	x---	----	----	x---	----		
Cay (Chile-S)	**45.059 S**	**72.984 W**	**2090**	0235	**BD**	**Stratovolcano**	**1508-055**	Holocene?											
Maca (Chile-S)	**45.10 S**	**73.17 W**	**2960**	0035	**BAD**	**Stratovolcano**	**1508-056**	**Radiocarbon**											
(MAC1 tephra)									**C 0410**t	....	....	....	----	----	x---	----	----		
Hudson, Cerro (Chile-S)	**45.90 S**	**72.97 W**	**1905**	0225	**BYTXA**	**Stratovolcano**	**1508-057**	**Historical**											
									C-8010?	....	....	....	----	----	x---	----	----		
(tephra layer T1)									**C-4960**w	....	....	....	----	----	x---	----	----		
(tephra layer H1/T2)									**C-4750**?	....	....	....	x---	----	x---	----	----	**6**	**-/10**
(tephra layer T3)									**C-3890**z	....	....	....	----	----	x---	----	----		
(tephra layer T4)									**C-2250**<	....	....	....	----	----	x---	----	----		
(tephra layer H2/T5)									**G-1890**?	....	....	....	x---	----	x---	----	----	**6**	**-/10**
(tephra layer HW6)									**G-0790**u	....	....	....	----	----	x---	----	----		
(tephra layer T6)									**C-0120**x	....	....	....	----	----	x---	----	----		
(tephra layer HW7)									**G 0390**w	....	....	....	----	----	x---	----	----		
(tephra layer T7)									**C 0860**v	....	....	....	----	----	x---	----	----		
(tephra layer T8)									**C 1740**w	....	....	....	----	----	x---	----	----		
									1891	....	....	....	----	----	?---	----	----		
NW part of caldera (tephra layer T9)									**1971**	0812	**1971**	0918>	x---	--?-	x---	?---	xxx-	3	
NW caldera rim and SW caldera floor									**1991**	0808	**1991**	1027	x-x-	--x-	xx--	x---	-xx-	**5+**	-/9
Río Murta (Chile-S)	**46.17 S**	**72.67 W**		0035	**B**	**Pyroclastic cones**	**1508-058**	Holocene?											
Arenales (Chile-S)	**47.20 S**	**73.48 W**	**3437**	0004	**U**	**Stratovolcano**	**1508-059**	**Historical**											
									1979	0308<	....	....	----	----	x---	----	----	1?	
Lautaro (Chile-S)	**49.02 S**	**73.55 W**	**3607**	0024	**Da**	**Stratovolcano**	**1508-06=**	**Historical**											
									1876	10	....	....	----	----	x---	----	----	2?	
									? 1878	*0118*	....	....	----	----	?---	----	----	*1*	
(between lakes San Martín and Viedma)									**@ 1879**	....	....	....	----	----	----	----	----		
									1933	02	....	....	----	----	x---	----	----	2?	
									1945	0115q	....	....	----	----	x---	----	----	1	
									1959	1228	**1960**	0120	----	----	x---	x---	----	2	
(aerial observ., possibly Lautaro)									**@ 1961**	10	....	....	----	----	----	----	----	2	
									1972	....	....	....	----	----	?---	----	----		
									1978	06	....	....	----	----	?---	----	----		
									1979	0308<	....	....	----	----	x---	----	----	2?	
Viedma (Argentina)	**49.358 S**	**73.28 W**	**1500**	0024	**D**	**Subglacial volc**	**1508-061**	**Historical**											
Southernmost crater									**1988**	1115q	....	....	----	--x-	x---	----	--x-		
Aguilera (Chile-S)	**50.33 S**	**73.75 W**	**2546**	0034	**D**	**Stratovolcano**	**1508-062**	**Radiocarbon**											
									C-2610?	....	....	....	----	----	x---	----	----		
(A1 tephra)									**G-1250**w	....	....	....	----	----	x---	----	----	**5**	-/9
Reclus (Chile-S)	**50.964 S**	**73.585 W**	**1000**	0135	**D**	**Cinder cone**	**1508-063**	**Historical**											
									T-1830>	....	....	....	x---	----	x---	----	----		
									1869	....	....	....	x---	----	x---	----	----	2	
									1879	....	....	....	x---	----	x---	----	----	2	
									1908a	....	....	....	x---	----	x---	----	----	1?	
Burney, Monte (Chile-S)	**52.33 S**	**73.40 W**	**1758**	0004	**AD**	**Stratovolcano**	**1508-07=**	**Historical**											
(MB1 tephra layer)									**G-7450**z	....	....	....	----	----	x---	----	----	**5**	-/9
									T-7390x	....	....	....	----	----	x---	----	----		
									G-3740j	....	....	....	----	----	x---	----	----		
(MB2 tephra)									**G-2320**v	....	....	....	x---	----	x--?	----	----	**5**	-/9
									T-0800z	....	....	....	----	----	x---	----	----		
									G-0090v	....	....	....	----	----	x---	----	----		
									1910	03	....	....	----	----	?---	----	----	2	
Palei-Aike Volc Field (Chile/Argen)	**52.00 S***	**70.00 W**	**282**	3335	**BX**	**Cinder cones**	**1508-08-**	**Anthropology**											
									A-5550*	....	....	....	----	----	x---	x---	----		
Fueguino (Chile-S)	**54.95 S**	**70.25 W**	**150**	2234	**A**	**Lava domes**	**1508-09-**	**Historical**											
									? 1712	*1126*d	....	....	----	----	----	----	----		
									1820	1125	**1820**	1126>	----	----	x---	----	----	2?	

West Indies (16)

Of the broad region known as the West Indies, only the Lesser Antilles, an arc of small islands formed by subduction of oceanic crust moving westward from the Mid-Atlantic Ridge, are volcanically active, forming the smallest of the *CAVW* regions. The small size of the islands places its towns and cities in close proximity to volcanoes, however, and the West Indies exceeds four other regions in population residing within 100 km of a volcano

The northern islands were discovered by Columbus on his second voyage, in 1493, and other islands on his third in 1498, but they were passed over by settlers preferring the Greater Antilles to the west. It was not until the 1630s and the sugar trade that Europeans started to settle in the islands. On Saba they chose grassy flatlands that were apparently the newly vegetated tops of very recent valley-filling pyroclastic-flow deposits. And on Martinique settlers noticed that Mont Pelée was suspiciously bare of vegetation. The first historical eruption, though, was on Guadeloupe around 1690. Ownership of islands shifted among the French, British, and Dutch, with Carib Indians showing fierce resistance to colonization on some islands. Several islands retain formal ties to Europe, whereas others have achieved independence in recent decades. Monitoring of the volcanoes is by the Seismic Research Unit of the University of the West Indies, principally by seismic data telemetered to their base in Trinidad, and by French observatories in Guadeloupe and Martinique. For many years the Montserrat Volcano Observatory was operated by the British Geological Survey, but since April 2008, the Observatory has been managed through a partnership of the Eastern Caribbean's two major geo-hazard organizations, the UWI Seismic Research Centre (Trinidad and Tobago) and the Institut de Physique du Globe de Paris (France).

This region has the lowest number of volcanoes (18), and smallest area of affected nations. Stratovolcanoes dominate (67%) in the West Indies to a degree matched only by Alaska. More than 90% of its eruptions are explosive, and the West Indies has the highest proportion (87%) of any region with eruptions that are strictly explosive, with no accompanying lava flows or domes. No other region has had a lower proportion of its eruptions that produce lava flows (6 of 132, or 4.5%). However, a high proportion of its eruptions compared to other regions have produced lava domes (12%, second to Region 12's 20%). Dome growth is often accompanied by pyroclastic flows, and three West Indian volcanoes are in the top ten globally in percentage of eruptions (for volcanoes with at least 5 eruptions) producing pyroclastic flows. More than 90% of the 54 dated eruptions of Mont Pelée, including the devastating 1902 eruption, have produced these hazardous flows.

Many detailed tephra studies, largely by British and French volcanologists, have produced a regional high of 68% radiocarbon eruption dates. Only 28 historical dates have been recorded in the West Indies and, like the Western United States, a high percentage of its eruptions are dated by non-historical techniques. Two major eruptions in 1902 drew world-wide attention to volcanoes in this region. The eruption of Montagne Pelée destroyed the city of St. Pierre, causing 29,000 fatalities, but the comparably large eruption of Soufrière St. Vincent had lesser impact in a more sparsely populated island. Recent bathymetric studies have documented the widespread occurrence of massive submarine debris-avalanche deposits resulting from collapse of island volcanoes. This region has been relatively quiet in recent decades following the 1979 eruption of Soufrière St. Vincent volcano. The only eruption since then (aside from a small phreatic eruption at the Valley of Desolation on Dominica in 1997 and a submarine eruption from Kick-em-Jenney volcano north of Grenada in 2001) has been the long-term eruption at Soufrière Hills volcano on Montserrat. This eruption began with phreatic explosions in 1995, and soon intensified. Pyroclastic flows and mudflows accompanying growth and destruction of a new summit lava dome eventually entirely overran the capital city of Plymouth. The eruption continues at this writing, with long-term economic disruption resulting from evacuation of much of the southern half of the island.

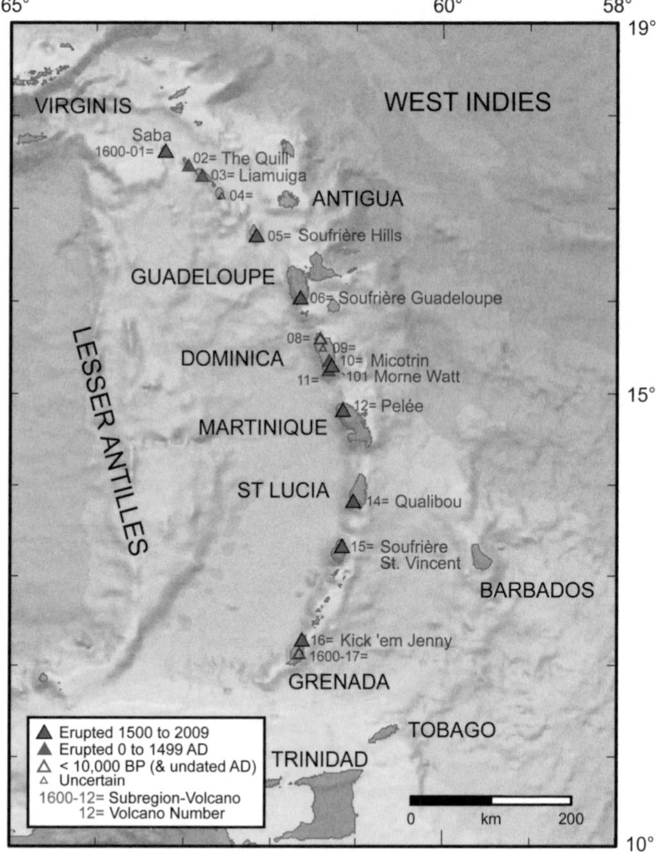

VOLCANO NAME (Subregion) / ERUPTION — Area of Activity	LAT	LONG	ELEV (m)	POPL (5 km, 10, 30, 100)	ROCK TYPE	VOLC TYPE / Start Year	Start M-Dy	NUMBER / Stop Year	Stop M-Dy	STATUS	Central, Flank vent, Radial fiss, Regional	Submarine, New island, Subglacial, Crater lake	Explosive, Pyro flow, Phreatic, Caldera	Lava flow, Lava lake, Dome, Spine	Fatal, Damage, Mudflow, Tsunami	VEI	Vol L/T
WEST INDIES																	
Saba (Saba)	**17.63 N**	**63.23 W**	**887**	4446	**ABd**	**Stratovolcano**		**1600-01=**		**Historical**							
SW flank						**1640**<	....	....	....		-x--	----	xx--	--??	----		
Quill, The (Statia)	**17.478 N**	**62.960 W**	**601**	4446	**Ardb**	**Stratovolcano**		**1600-02=**		**Radiocarbon**							
						C-**6140**x	....	....	....		x---	----	xx--	----	----	P	
						C-**0550**?	....	....	....		x---	----	xx--	----	----		
						C **0250**w	....	....	....		x---	----	xx--	----	----		
Liamuiga (St. Kitts)	**17.37 N**	**62.80 W**	**1156**	4456	**AB**	**Stratovolcano**		**1600-03=**		**Radiocarbon**							
(tephra unit D)						C-**2010**w	....	....	....		x---	----	xx--	----	--x-	P	
(tephra unit E)						C **0060**v	....	....	....		x---	----	xx--	----	----		
(tephra unit F)						C **0160**x	....	....	....		x---	----	xxx-	----	----	P	
						? 1692	....	....	....		x---	----	--?-	----	----		
						? 1843	*0208*	....	....		x---	----	--?-	----	----		
Nevis Peak (Nevis)	**17.15 N**	**62.58 W**	**985**	4456	**AD**	**Stratovolcano**		**1600-04=**		Holocene?							

VOLCANO NAME (Subregion) / ERUPTION — Area of Activity	LAT	LONG	ELEV (m)	POPL 5 km 10 30 100	ROCK TYPE	VOLC TYPE	NUMBER	STATUS	Start Year	Start M-Dy	Stop Year	Stop M-Dy	Central / Flank vent / Radial fiss / Regional	Submarine / New island / Subglacial / Crater lake	Explosive / Pyro flow / Phreatic / Caldera	Lava flow / Lava lake / Dome / Spine	Fatal / Damage / Mudflow / Tsunami	VEI	Vol L/T
Soufrière Hills (Montserrat)	16.72 N	62.18 W	915	4446	ADB	Stratovolcano	1600-05=	Historical											
English's crater									C-2000u	....	....	....	X---	----	XX-A	----	----		
Castle Peak									C 1630t	....	....	....	X---	----	XX--	--X-	----		7/-
									1995	0718	2003	1008	X---	----	XXXA	--XX	XXXX	3*	8/-
									2004	0303	2004	0502	X---	----	XX--	----	--X-	3?	
									2005	0415	2010>	....	X---	----	XX--	--XX	-XXX	3?	
Soufrière Guadeloupe (W Indies)	16.05 N	61.67 W	1467	4566	ADbr	Stratovolcano	1600-06=	Historical											
(formation of Amic Crater)									G-7490w	....	....	....	X---	----	XX-A	----	--X-		
									G-6450w	....	....	....	X---	----	XX-A	----	--X-		
South flank (Gros Fougas)									G-3310w	....	....	....	-X--	----	XX--	X-X-	----		
									? -2050?	....	....	....	----	----	?---	----	----		
									G-1810w	....	....	....	----	----	XXXA	----	--X-		
Morne Amic									G-1310w	....	....	....	X---	----	XX-A	--X-	----	3?	
									G-0980x	....	....	....	X---	----	X--A	----	--X-		
Morne Amic ?									G-0820v	....	....	....	X---	----	XXXA	--X-	--X-	3?	
South flank (Morne Lenglet)									C-0580>	....	....	....	-X--	----	X---	X---	----	2	
La Citerne and L'Eschelle cones									G 0370u	....	....	....	-X--	----	X-X-	X---	--X-		
									G 1340t	....	....	....	X---	----	XX--	----	----	3?	
									G 1370w	....	....	....	X---	----	XX--	----	--X-	P	
La Soufrière									G 1440v	....	....	....	X---	----	XX-A	--X-	----	P	7/-
									G 1600t	....	....	....	----	----	XX--	----	----		
Gouffre Dupuy, Gouffre Tarissan									1690	0405>	....	....	X-X-	----	X-X-	----	----	1	
North side of summit dome									1696	04	....	....	X---	----	X-X-	----	----	1	
NNW side of summit dome									1797	0929	1798	0426?	X-X-	----	XXX-	----	--X-	2	
E-W fissure on summit dome									1812	04	1812	0510	X-X-	----	X-X-	----	----	1	
SE to NW sides of summit dome									1836	1203	1837	0212	X-X-	----	XXX-	----	--X-	2	
SE side summit dome									*? 1903*	....	....	....	X---	----	--?-	----	----	*2*	
ESE side, Napoléon Crater									1956	1019	1956	1027	X-X-	----	XXX-	----	--X-	1	-/5
SE side of summit (Gouffre Tarissan)									1976	0708	1977	0301	X-X-	----	XXX-	----	-XX-	2	-/5
Unnamed (Guadeloupe-SE of)	15.97 N	61.43 W	-45				1600-07=	Not a Volcano											
(submarine geyser or karst collapse)									*X 1843*	*0217*	*X1843*	*0217*	----	----	----	----	----		
Diables, Morne aux (Dominica)	15.612 N	61.43 W	861	4556	AD	Stratovolcano	1600-08=	Holocene											
Diablotins, Morne (Dominica)	15.503 N	61.397 W	1430	3456	ADB	Stratovolcano	1600-09=	Holocene?											
Trois Pitons, Morne (Dominica)	15.37 N	61.33 W	1387	4556	A	Complex volcano	1600-10=	Radiocarbon											
Micotrin?									C 0790t	....	....	....	X---	----	XX--	--X-	----		
Micotrin?									C 0920t	....	....	....	X---	----	XX--	----	----		
Watt, Morne (Dominica)	15.307 N	61.305 W	1224	4556	AB	Stratovolcanoes	1600-101	Historical											
NE of Watt Mtn (Valley of Desolation)									C-1800v	....	....	....	-X--	----	X-X-	----	----		
NE of Watt Mtn (Valley of Desolation)									C-0950y	....	....	....	-X--	----	X-X-	----	----		
West flank of Morne Watt									C 0640w	....	....	....	-X--	----	XX--	----	--X-		
NE of Watt Mtn (Valley of Desolation)									1880	0104	1880	0104	-X--	----	X-X-	----	--X-	2?	
NE of Watt Mtn (Valley of Desolation)									1997	0715	1997	0715	-X--	----	X-X-	----	----	1	
Plat Pays, Morne (Dominica)	15.255 N	61.341 W	940	5556	DA	Stratovolcano	1600-11=	Radiocarbon											
Morne Plat Pays									C-4740?	....	....	....	----	----	XX--	----	----		
Morne Patates ?									C-0430?	....	....	....	?---	----	XX--	----	----		
Morne Patates									C 0390s	....	....	....	X---	----	XX--	--X-	----		
Morne Patates									C 1270t	....	....	....	X---	----	XX--	--X-	----		
Pelée (Martinique)	14.82 N	61.17 W	1397	3466	Adb	Stratovolcano	1600-12=	Historical											
(tephra layer P9)									G-8210x	....	....	....	X---	----	XX--	----	----	4?	-/8
ESE flank (Aileron lava dome)									U-7750z	....	....	....	-X--	----	----	--X-	----		
									G-7320*	....	....	....	X---	----	XX--	--X-	----		
ESE flank (Sans Nom lava dome)									U-7050*	....	....	....	-X--	----	----	--X-	----		
(tephra layer P8)									G-6610w	....	....	....	X---	----	XX--	----	----	4?	-/8
Vent slightly south of present summit									C-6450?	....	....	....	X---	----	XX--	--X-	----		
Vent slightly south of present summit									G-6220x	....	....	....	X---	----	XX--	----	----	P	
									C-5800?	....	....	....	X---	----	XX--	----	----		
									G-5500x	....	....	....	X---	----	XX--	----	----	P	
									G-4510z	....	....	....	X---	----	XX--	--X-	----		
(tephra layer NMR)									G-3930v	....	....	....	X---	----	XX--	--X-	----		
									C-3820?	....	....	....	X---	----	XX--	----	----	P	
									T-3500x	....	....	....	X---	----	XX--	----	----	P	
(tephra layer P6)									G-3430u	....	....	....	X---	----	XX--	----	----	4?	-/8
									C-3290?	....	....	....	X---	----	XX--	----	----		
									C-3250?	....	....	....	X---	----	XX--	--X-	----		
(NPM tephra layer)									G-3120x	....	....	....	X---	----	XX--	--X-	----		
									C-3020?	....	....	....	X---	----	XX--	--X-	----		
(tephra layer P5)									G-2660x	....	....	....	X---	----	XX--	----	----	4?	-/8
(tephra layer NRS1)									G-2460v	....	....	....	X---	----	XX--	--X-	----		
									C-2430?	....	....	....	X---	----	XX--	----	----	P	
									C-2360?	....	....	....	X---	----	XX--	--X-	----		
									C-2280?	....	....	....	X---	----	XX--	----	----		
(tephra layer NRS2)									G-2100x	....	....	....	X---	----	XX--	--X-	----		
(tephra layer NRS3)									G-1390w	....	....	....	X---	----	XX--	--X-	----		
(tephra layer NAB1)									G-0890t	....	....	....	X---	----	XX--	--X-	----		
									C-0730?	....	....	....	X---	----	XX--	----	----		
									C-0620?	....	....	....	X---	----	XX--	----	----		
									C-0600?	....	....	....	X---	----	XX--	----	----		
(tephra layers NAB2 and P4)									G-0590x	....	....	....	X---	----	XX--	--X-	----	4?	-/8
									C-0440?	....	....	....	X---	----	XX--	----	----	P	
									G-0300v	....	....	....	X---	----	XX--	--X-	----		
									C-0200?	....	....	....	X---	----	XX--	----	----	P	
(tephra layer P3)									G 0010t	....	....	....	X---	----	XX--	----	----	4	-/8
									C 0050?	....	....	....	X---	----	XX--	----	----	P	
									C 0130?	....	....	....	X---	----	XX--	----	----	P	
(NMP tephra layer)									C 0220u	....	....	....	X---	----	XX--	--X-	----		
									C 0300?	....	....	....	X---	----	XX--	----	----	P	
(tephra layer P2)									G 0350u	....	....	....	X---	----	XX--	----	----	4	-/8
									C 0450?	....	....	....	X---	----	XX--	----	----	P	
									C 0650?	....	....	....	X---	----	XX--	----	----		
									C 0720?	....	....	....	X---	----	XX--	----	----		
(NRC1 tephra layer)									G 0890v	....	....	....	X---	----	XX--	--X-	----	P	
									C 0910?	....	....	....	X---	----	XX--	----	----		
									C 1190?	....	....	....	X---	----	XX--	----	----		

VOLCANO NAME (Subregion) / ERUPTION	LAT	LONG	ELEV (m)	POPL (5 km, 10, 30, 100)	ROCK TYPE	Area of Activity	VOLC TYPE	NUMBER / Start Year	Start M-Dy	STATUS / Stop Year	Stop M-Dy	Central, Flank vent, Radial fiss, Regional	Submarine, New island, Subglacial, Crater lake	Explosive, Pyro flow, Phreatic, Caldera	Lava flow, Lava lake, Dome, Spine	Fatal, Damage, Mudflow, Tsunami	VEI	Vol L/T
Pelée (Martinique) *continued*						(NRC2 tephra layer)		C **1260**p	....	....	....	x---	----	xx--	----	----		
						(tephra layer P1)		G **1340**t	....	....	....	x---	----	xx--	----	----	4	-/8
						(tephra layer NRP1)		C **1370**?	....	....	....	x---	----	xx--	----	----		
						(tephra layer NRP2)		C **1460**p	....	....	....	x---	----	xx--	----	----		
						(tephra layer NRP3)		**1635**<	....	....	....	x---	----	xx--	--x-	----		
						Upper Rivière Claire valley		**1792**	0122	**1792**	04 ?	-x--	----	--x-	----	--x-	1	
						Upper Rivière Claire valley (900 m elevation)		**1851**	0805	**1852**	0201p	-x--	----	x-x-	----	--x-	2	
						Rivière Blanche and summit crater		**1902**	0423	**1905**	1005	xx--	---x	xxx-	--xx	xxxx	4*	8/8
								1929	0916	**1932**	1201p	x---	----	xx--	--xx	-xx-	3*	
Hodder's Volcano (W Indies)	14.03 N	61.07 W						1600-13=		Not a Volcano								
						(no volcano at this location)		*X 1902*	*0509*	....	....	----	----	----	----	----		
Qualibou (St. Lucia)	**13.83 N**	**61.05 W**	**777**	5566	ADb		**Caldera**	**1600-14=**		**Historical**								
						Sulphur Springs area		**1766**	....	....	....	x---	----	--x-	----	----	1	
Soufrière St. Vincent (St. Vincent)	**13.33 N**	**61.18 W**	**1220**	4566	AB		**Stratovolcano**	**1600-15=**		**Historical**								
								C-**2380**v	....	....	....	x---	----	xx--	x---	--x-		
								C-**2310**v	....	....	....	x---	----	xx--	----	----		
								C-**2200**w	....	....	....	x---	----	xx--	----	----		
								C-**2135**t	....	....	....	x---	----	xx--	----	--x-		
								C-**2020**u	....	....	....	x---	----	xx--	----	----		
								C-**1600**u	....	....	....	x---	----	xx--	----	----		
								C-**0750**v	....	....	....	x---	----	xx--	----	----		
								C-**0530**u	....	....	....	x---	----	xx--	----	----		
								C **0905**u	....	....	....	x---	----	xx--	----	----		
								C **1325**u	....	....	....	x---	----	xx--	----	----		
								C **1395**u	....	....	....	x---	----	xx--	----	----		
								C **1480**w	....	....	....	x---	----	xx--	----	----		
								C **1550**t	....	....	....	x---	----	xx--	----	----		
								C **1640**t	....	....	....	x---	----	xx--	----	----		
								1718	0326?	**1718**	0329	x---	----	x?--	----	----	3?	
								1784	03 <	....	....	x---	----	----	--?-	----	0	
						Old summit crater & new NE rim crater		**1812**	0427	**1812**	0609?	xx--	---x	xx--	----	xxx-	4	-/8
								1814	0109	**1814**	0109	x---	---x	--x-	----	----	1?	
								? 1880	....	....	....	x---	---x	----	?---	----	*0*	
								1902	0506	**1903**	0330	x---	---x	xxx-	----	xxxx	4?	-/8
								1971	1004f	**1972**	0320	x---	---x	----	x-x-	----	0	7/-
								1979	0413	**1979**	1026e	x---	---x	xxx-	--x-	?xx-	3	7/7
Kick 'em Jenny (Grenada-N of)	**12.300 N**	**61.640 W**	**-185**	0456	**Bad**		**Submarine volc**	**1600-16=**		**Historical**								
						Ile de Caille		A **1000**x	....	....	....	x---	----	----	x---	----		
								1939	0724	**1939**	0724	----	x---	x---	----	---?	1	
								S **1943**	1005	S**1943**	1006	----	x---	----	----	----	0	
								S **1953**	1030	S**1953**	1030	----	x---	----	----	----	0	
								S **1965**	1024	S**1965**	1024	x---	x---	----	----	----	0	
								S **1966**	0505	S**1966**	0806	x---	x---	----	----	----	0	
								S **1972**	0705	S**1972**	0705	x---	x---	----	----	----	0	
								1974	0905	**1974**	0906	x---	x---	x---	----	----	0	
								S **1977**	0114	S**1977**	0114	x---	x---	----	--x-	----	0?	
								S **1977**	1111	....	....	x---	x---	----	--x-	----	0	
								S **1988**	1229	S**1988**	1230	x---	x---	xx--	----	----	0	
								S **1990**	0326	S**1990**	0328	x---	x---	x---	----	----	0	
								S **2001**	1204	S**2001**	1206	x---	x---	----	----	----	0	
St. Catherine (Grenada)	**12.15 N**	**61.67 W**	**840**	4555	**AXBD**		**Stratovolcano**	**1600-17=**		**Holocene**								

Richard Fiske (Smithsonian)

A blocky lava dome, 130 m high and more than 840 m wide filled much of the crater floor of Soufrière St. Vincent volcano during the 1979 eruption. Dome growth began in May, after a series of powerful explosive eruptions April 13-15, and continued until October. Steam continues to rise from the dome in this 1983 photo from the SW crater rim.

Richard Herd (MVO)

A pyroclastic flow sweeps down the Tar River valley on the eastern flank of Soufrière Hills volcano on January 16, 1997. The January 16 pyroclastic flow was the largest to date during the eruption that had begun with phreatic explosions in 1995. Later pyroclastic flows overran populated areas and the capital city of Plymouth.

Iceland & Arctic Ocean (17)

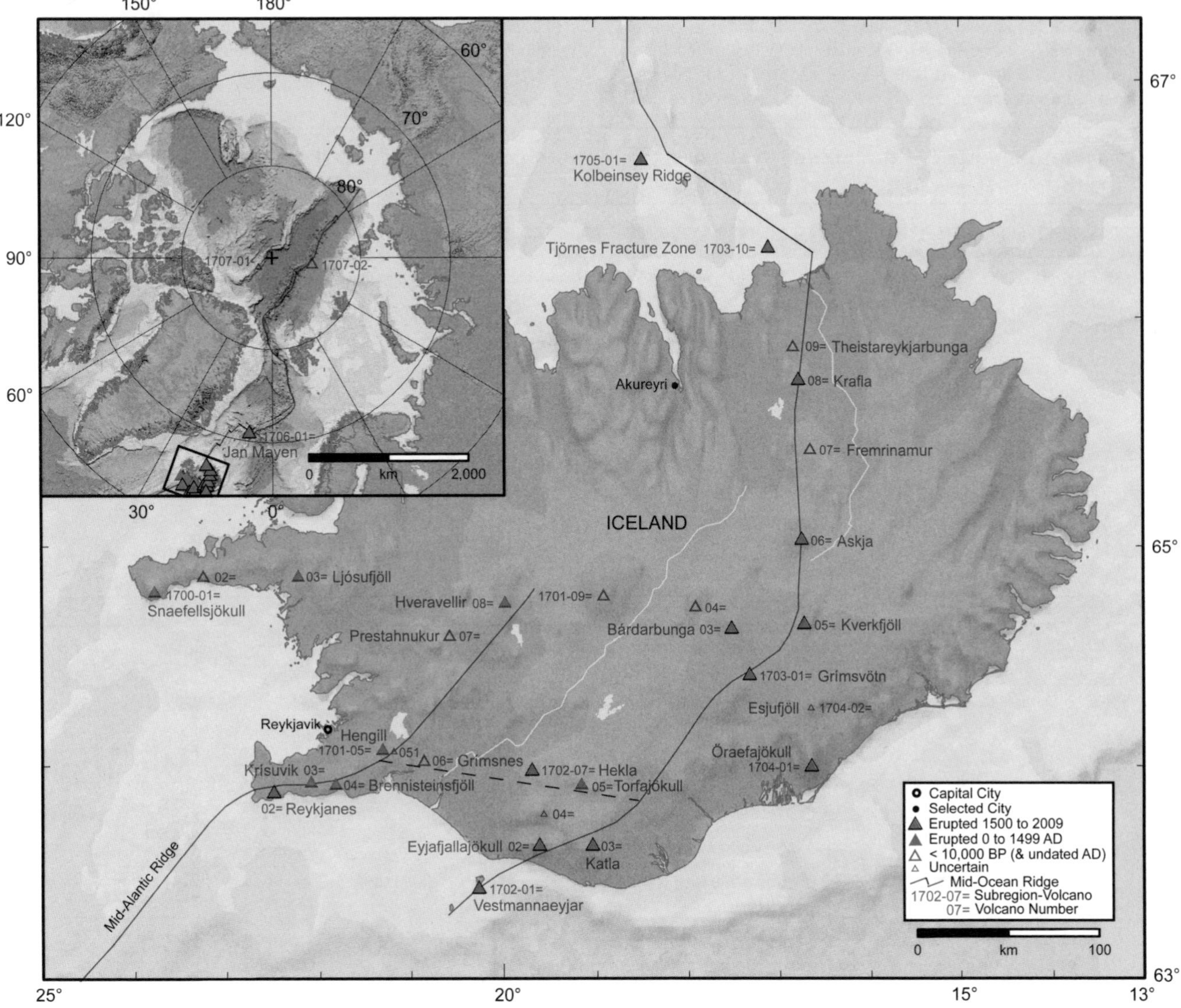

The volcano-rich island of Iceland has the land area of the state of Virginia with only 4% of its population. Iceland's population of 301,000 ranks it above only the Kurils and Antarctica, among *CAVW* regions, but it enjoys the highest literacy rate (100%) of any nation in the world, and its close interaction with volcanoes makes it indeed a nation of volcanologists. Iceland has the highest proportion of Holocene volcanoes that bear dated eruptions (86%), and this follows largely from work initiated by Iceland's pioneer of tephrochronology, Sigurdur Thorarinsson, who developed this stratigraphic dating technique and assigned its name. Iceland leads all regions with nearly half of its eruptions having been dated by this approach, and detailed studies of the products of Icelandic eruptions are ongoing and will modify the eruptive record shown here.

First settled by Vikings in the 9th century AD, Iceland established its own parliament in 930 and recorded its first historical eruption only a few years later. An eruption in 1000 AD played an important role in Icelandic history when it occurred during a debate over the national religion at a meeting of the Icelandic outdoor parliament at Thingvellier. After a golden age of literature in the 12th and 13th centuries, natural history reporting reached a low around the 15th century (only 5 historical eruptions recorded, as opposed to 12 each in the 12th and 13th centuries and 15 in the 17th century). In the years 1707-09 a third of the population died from smallpox, and the 1783-84 Laki eruption killed a fifth of the remaining population by famine. Iceland gained sovereignty from Denmark in 1918 and complete independence in 1944.

This land of fire and ice is noted for subglacial and regional fissure eruptions, having produced 89% and 43% (respectively) of the world's total for each type. Fissure eruptions dominate because Iceland combines a hotspot setting with one of the few places where the oceanic rift system emerges above sea level. This setting has brought widespread attention to the region's volcanoes from many geophysical sub-disciplines.

Following the 1974-84 fissure eruptions at Krafla caldera, Iceland has been relatively quiet, with eruptions from Hekla in 1991 and 2000 and subglacial eruptions from Grímsvötn caldera in 1996, 1998, and 2004. Further to the north, Jan Mayen erupted in 1986, and in 1999 a seismic swarm on the East Gakkel Ridge (near 86°N, 85°E) may have originated from submarine lava effusion, although this has not been confirmed.

Iceland's volcanoes have been organized by volcanic systems that provide meaningful grouping of genetically related surface features. We have followed the volcanic systems used in the tectonics sheet of the geological map of Iceland (Johannesson and Saemundsson, 1998). The *en echelon* distribution of volcanic systems along the subaerial component of the Mid-Atlantic Ridge has resulted in the construction of central volcanoes with long regional fissure systems, both of which are sometimes simultaneously active. The length of the fissures often exceeds the mid-point of the distance between adjacent central volcanoes, so that closely spaced eruptive fissures may actually be related to volcanic systems whose centers lie in opposite directions. Two of the largest recent eruptions in Iceland, the Eldgjá eruption about 934 AD and the 1783 Laki eruption, took place from fissures only about 5 km apart that parallel each other for several tens of kilometers, but are related to the Katla and Grímsvötn central volcanoes, respectively, whose summits lie 120 km apart.

The *CAVW* organizers did not recognize arctic volcanism and assigned no region numbers beyond 19, so we consequently have expanded region 17 beyond Jan Mayen to include the full Arctic Ocean and adjacent northern seas, thus including Pleistocene volcanism on Spitsbergen (north of Norway), and submarine rifts such as the East Gakkel Ridge.

ICELAND - W

VOLCANO NAME (Subregion) / **ERUPTION** — Area of Activity	**LAT**	**LONG**	**ELEV** (m)	**POPL** 5 km 10 30 100	**ROCK TYPE**	**VOLC TYPE**	**NUMBER**	**STATUS**	Start **Year**	Start M-Dy	Stop **Year**	Stop M-Dy	Central / Flank vent / Radial fiss / Regional	Submarine / New island / Subglacial / Crater lake	Explosive / Pyro flow / Phreatic / Caldera	Lava flow / Lava lake / Dome / Spine	Fatal / Damage / Mudflow / Tsunami	VEI	Vol L/T
Snaefellsjökull (Iceland-W)	**64.80 N**	**23.78 W**	**1448**	1345		**Stratovolcano**	**1700-01=**	**Radiocarbon**											
									G-**8460**x	....	....	....	----	----	x---	----	----		
(tephra layer Sn-3)									T-**6050***	....	....	....	x---	----	x---	----	----		
East of Snaefellsjökull (Budaklettur)									T-**4550***	....	....	....	---x	----	x---	x---	----	2	
West flank (Ondverdarnesholar)									T-**4050***	....	....	....	-x--	----	----	x---	----	0	
SE flank (Dagverdarahraun)									C-**2970**y	....	....	....	-x--	----	----	x---	----	0	
NE flank (800 m)									C-**2400**x	....	....	....	-x--	----	x---	x---	----	2?	8/-
South flank (Thufuhraun)									C-**2270**y	....	....	....	-x--	----	----	x---	----	0	
(tephra layer Sn-2)									C-**2010**v	....	....	....	x---	----	x---	----	----		
NW flank (Raudhólar)									C-**1000**z	....	....	....	-x--	----	x---	x---	----	2	8/-
(tephra layer Sn-1)									C **0200**w	....	....	....	x---	----	x---	?---	----		8/-
Helgrindur (Iceland-W)	**64.87 N***	**23.25 W**	**647**	3345	**B**	**Pyroclastic cones**	**1700-02=**	**Holocene**											
Ljósufjöll (Iceland-W)	**64.87 N***	**22.23 W**	**1063**	3346	**BRTYX**	**Fissure vents**	**1700-03=**	**Anthropology**											
Eldborg									T-**7050***	....	....	....	---x	----	x---	x---	----	2	**9/-**
Krothraunskula, Raudakúla, Graakula									T-**2050**?	....	....	....	---x	----	x---	x---	----	3?	
Grábrók									C-**1750**w	....	....	....	---x	----	x---	x---	----	2	
Ytri and Stóri Raudamelskula									C-**0665**v	....	....	....	---x	----	x---	x---	----	2	8/-
Raudhalsar									A **0960**j	....	....	....	---x	----	--x-	x---	-x--	2	8/7

ICELAND - SW

VOLCANO NAME (Subregion) / **ERUPTION** — Area of Activity	**LAT**	**LONG**	**ELEV** (m)	**POPL** 5 km 10 30 100	**ROCK TYPE**	**VOLC TYPE**	**NUMBER**	**STATUS**	Start **Year**	Start M-Dy	Stop **Year**	Stop M-Dy	Central / Flank vent / Radial fiss / Regional	Submarine / New island / Subglacial / Crater lake	Explosive / Pyro flow / Phreatic / Caldera	Lava flow / Lava lake / Dome / Spine	Fatal / Damage / Mudflow / Tsunami	VEI	Vol L/T
Reykjanes (Iceland-SW)	**63.88 N***	**22.50 W**	**230**	5556	**B**	**Crater rows**	**1701-02=**	**Historical**											
Thrainskjöldur									T-**8000**?	....	....	....	x---	----	----	xx--	----	0	**9/-**
Hopsnes									C-**5040**v	....	....	....	---x	----	----	x---	----	0	
Sandfellshaed									T-**4000**?	....	....	....	x---	----	----	xx--	----	0	**9/-**
Reykjaneshryggur (R-1 tephra layer)									T-**3800**y	....	....	....	----	x---	x---	----	----		
Reykjaneshryggur (R-2, R-3 tephras), Stampar									T-**1800**y	....	....	....	---x	x---	x---	x---	----	2	7/-
Sundhnukar									C-**0400**v	....	....	....	---x	----	x---	x---	----	2	8/-
Lambagjá									C-**0200**?	....	....	....	---x	----	----	x---	----	0	
Reykjaneshryggur (near Eldey; R-4 tephra)									T **0920**?	....	....	....	----	x---	x---	----	----		
Reykjaneshryggur, (R-5 and R-6 tephras)									**1179**<	....	....	....	----	x---	x---	----	----	2	
Vatnsfellsgigur									**1210**	....	....	....	---x	----	x---	----	----	3?	-/8
Stampar, Karlsgigur									**1211**	....	....	....	---x	----	x---	x---	----		7/-
Reykjaneshryggur (Karlsgigur; R-7 tephra)									**1211**	0831p	....	....	----	xx--	x---	----	----	4?	-/8
Reykjaneshryggur (R-8 tephra layer)									**1223**	....	....	....	----	x---	x---	----	----	3	-/7
Reykjaneshryggur (R-9 tephra layer)									**1226**	0715q	**1227**?	....	----	x---	x---	----	----	4	-/8
Reykjaneshryggur (R-10 tephra)									**1231**	....	....	....	----	xx--	x---	----	----	3	-/7
Reykjaneshryggur									**1238**	....	....	....	----	x---	----	----	----	0	
Reykjaneshryggur, Arnarsetur, Illahraun									**1240**	....	....	....	---x	x---	x---	x---	----	1	8/5
Reykjaneshryggur									**1340**?	....	....	....	----	x---	x---	----	----	3↑	
Reykjaneshryggur (Geirfuglasker-Eldey area)									**1422**	....	....	....	----	xx--	x---	----	----	2	
Reykjaneshryggur (near Eldeyjar Islands)									**1583**	0715q	....	....	----	x---	----	----	----	2?	
(no 1661 eruption at Grindavík)									*X 1661*	*12*	....	....	----	----	----	----	----		
Reykjaneshryggur (Nyey)									**1783**	0501<	**1783**	0815r	---x	xx--	x---	----	----	3↑	
Reykjaneshryggur (Eldeyjarbodi)									**1830**	0313?	**1831**	03 ?	---x	x?--	x---	----	----	3	
Reykjaneshryggur (Geirfugladrangur)									**1879**	0530?	**1879**	0615e	----	x---	x---	----	----	1	
Reykjaneshryggur (NW of Eldey)									*? 1884*	*0726*	....	....	----	??--	----	----	----	*2?*	
Reykjaneshryggur (NE of Eldey)									**1926**	0605d	....	....	----	x---	----	----	----	0	
Reykjaneshryggur (Eldeyjarbodi)									*? 1966*	....	....	....	----	x---	----	----	----	*0*	
Reykjaneshryggur (Eldeyjarbodi)									*? 1970?*	....	....	....	----	?---	----	----	----	*0*	
Krísuvík (Iceland-SW)	**63.93 N***	**22.10 W**	**379**	5566	**B**	**Crater rows**	**1701-03=**	**Historical**											
Hagafell									T-**8500**?	....	....	....	x---	----	----	xx--	----	0	**9/-**
Hrútagjár									T-**6000**?	....	....	....	x---	----	----	xx--	----	0	**9/-**
Burfell									C-**5290**w	....	....	....	---x	----	x---	x---	----	2	8/-
Sandfellskofagigir									C-**1060**u	....	....	....	---x	----	----	x---	----	0	7/-
Obrinnisholar									C-**0190**u	....	....	....	---x	----	x---	x---	----	2	8/-
Melholl, Afstapahraun									T **0900**?	....	....	....	---x	----	x---	x---	----	2	8/-
Gvendarselsgigar									C **1075**u	....	....	....	---x	----	----	x---	----	0	7/-
Ogmundargigar and other vents									**1151**	....	....	....	---x	----	x---	x---	-x--	1	8/5
Mavahlidargigir									**1188**	....	....	....	---x	----	x---	x---	----	1	7/5
Elborg vid Trolladyngju									T **1325**?	....	....	....	---x	----	x---	x---	----	1	8/5
Tradarfjöll									T **1340**?	....	....	....	---x	----	x---	x---	----	1	7/5
Brennisteinsfjöll (Iceland-SW)	**63.92 N***	**21.83 W**	**621**	5566	**B**	**Crater rows**	**1701-04=**	**Historical**											
Heidin Há									T-**9000**?	....	....	....	x---	----	----	xx--	----	0	**9/-**
Leitin									C-**2660**u	....	....	....	---x	----	----	x---	----	0	**9/-**
Eldborg at Brennisteinsfjöllum									C-**1040**u	....	....	....	---x	----	x---	x---	----	2	8/-
Tvibollar									C **0875**t	....	....	....	---x	----	x---	x---	----	2	8/-
Kista (Breiddalshraun)									C **0910**u	....	....	....	---x	----	x---	x---	----	2	7/-
Rjupnadyngjur									C **0950**?	....	....	....	---x	----	x---	x---	----	2	8/6
Eldborg at Lambafell									**1000**	0625d	....	....	---x	----	----	x---	----	0	8/-
Kongsfell									T **1200**?	....	....	....	---x	----	x---	x---	----	2	
Grafeldur (Selvogshraun)									**1341**a	....	....	....	---x	----	x---	x---	----	2	8/-
Hengill (Iceland-SW)	**64.08 N***	**21.32 W**	**803**	4466	**BAR**	**Crater rows**	**1701-05=**	**Historical**											
SSW of Hengill (Hellisheid-A)									G-**8350**?	....	....	....	x---	----	----	xx--	----	0	**9/-**
Thingvallahraun									G-**8250**?	....	....	....	x---	----	----	xx--	----	0	**10/-**
Hafnarhraun									T-**8200**?	....	....	....	x---	----	----	xx--	----	0	**9/-**
Selvogsheidi									T-**7550**?	....	....	....	x---	----	----	x---	----	0	8/-
Brunnar/Skogarkot									T-**7300**?	....	....	....	---x	----	----	x---	----		**9/-**

VOLCANO NAME (Subregion) / ERUPTION — Area of Activity	LAT	LONG	ELEV (m)	POPL (5 km, 10, 30, 100)	ROCK TYPE	VOLC TYPE / Start Year	Start M-Dy	NUMBER / Stop Year	Stop M-Dy	STATUS	Central, Flank vent, Radial fiss, Regional	Submarine, New island, Subglacial, Crater lake	Explosive, Pyro flow, Phreatic, Caldera	Lava flow, Lava lake, Dome, Spine	Fatal, Damage, Mudflow, Tsunami	VEI	Vol L/T
Hengill (Iceland-SW) *continued*																	
Gjabakkahraun						T-**7100**?	....	....	....		x---	----	----	xx--	----	0	9/-
Stangarhals						T-**5550**z	....	....	....		---x	----	----	x---	----	0	7/-
Eldborgir						T-**5000**?	....	....	....		---x	----	----	x---	----		9/-
Hagavikurhraun						G-**3750**?	....	....	....		---x	----	x---	x---	----	2	8/-
Leitahraun, Ellidaárhraun						G-**3250**?	....	....	....		x---	----	----	xx--	----	0	9/-
Thjófahraun						G-**1730**t	....	....	....		---x	----	----	x---	----	0	9/-
Eldborg undir Meitlum						C-**0080**u	....	....	....		---x	----	x---	x---	----	2	8/-
Nesjahraun, Reykjafellshraun						G **0150**u	....	....	....		---x	----	x-x-	x---	----	2	8/-
Hrómundartindur (Iceland-S)	**64.073** N*	**21.202** W	**540**	4456	**B**	**Stratovolcano**		**1701-051**		Holocene?							
Grímsnes (Iceland-SW)	**64.03** N*	**20.87** W	**214**	4456	**B**	**Crater rows**		**1701-06=**		**Tephrochronology**							
Seydisholar						G-**7750**?	....	....	....		---x	----	x---	x---	----	3	-/7
						G-**6250**?	....	....	....		----	----	x---	----	----		
Selholl South						T-**4500**?	....	....	....		---x	----	----	x---	----	0	
Selholl North						T-**4450**?	....	....	....		---x	----	x---	x---	----	2?	
Kerholar						C-**4270**w	....	....	....		---x	----	x---	x---	----	3	9/7
Borgaholl						T-**4050**?	....	....	....		---x	----	----	x---	----	0	
Alftarholl						T-**4000**?	....	....	....		---x	----	x---	x---	----	2?	
Kolgrafarholl						T-**3900**?	....	....	....		---x	----	----	x---	----	0	
Raudholar						T-**3750**?	....	....	....		---x	----	----	x---	----	0	
Borgarholar						T-**3650**?	....	....	....		---x	----	----	x---	----	0	
Kalfsholar						T-**3500**?	....	....	....		---x	----	x---	x---	----	2?	
Prestahnukur (Iceland-SW)	**64.60** N*	**20.58** W	**1400**	2236	**BR**	**Subglacial volc**		**1701-07=**		**Radiocarbon**							
Skjaldbreidur						C-**7550**z	....	....	....		x---	----	----	xx--	----	0	10/-
Geitlandshraun II						G-**6950**?	....	....	....		x---	----	----	xx--	----	0	9/-
Sköflungur						T-**3350**?	....	....	....		x---	----	----	x---	----	0	8/-
Hveravellir (Iceland-SW)	**64.75** N	**19.98** W	**1360**	0015	**BR**	**Subglacial volc**		**1701-08=**		**Radiocarbon**							
Leggjarbrjotur						T-**8600**?	....	....	....		x---	----	----	xx--	----	0	9/-
Kjalhraun						T-**5850**?	....	....	....		x---	----	x---	xx--	----	2?	10/-
Strytuhraun						T-**3550**?	....	....	....		x---	----	----	x---	----	0	8/-
Krákshraun						T-**2550**?	....	....	....		x---	----	----	x---	----	0	8/-
Lambahraun						G-**2050**?	....	....	....		x---	----	----	xx--	----	0	9/-
Hallmundahraun						T **0950**t	....	....	....		x---	----	x---	x---	----	2	9/6
Hofsjökull (Iceland-SW)	**64.78** N	**18.92** W	**1782**	0004	**BR**	**Subglacial volc**		**1701-09=**		**Holocene**							

ICELAND - S

VOLCANO NAME (Subregion) / ERUPTION — Area of Activity	LAT	LONG	ELEV (m)	POPL	ROCK TYPE	VOLC TYPE / Start Year	Start M-Dy	NUMBER / Stop Year	Stop M-Dy	STATUS	Central, Flank vent, Radial fiss, Regional	Submarine, New island, Subglacial, Crater lake	Explosive, Pyro flow, Phreatic, Caldera	Lava flow, Lava lake, Dome, Spine	Fatal, Damage, Mudflow, Tsunami	VEI	Vol L/T
Vestmannaeyjar (Iceland-S)	**63.43** N*	**20.28** W	**279**	4445	**Bxy**	**Submarine volcs**		**1702-01=**		**Historical**							
NW Heimaey (Háin tuff ring)						T-**8050**?	....	....	....		---x	x---	xx--	x---	----	4	-/8
NW Heimaey (Nordurklettar)						T-**7550**?	....	....	....		---x	x---	xx--	-x--	----	3?	
Alsey, Brandur, Sudurey, Hellisey						T-**6050**?	....	....	....		----	xx--	x---	----	----		
Heimaey (Stórhöfdi tuff cone)						T-**4550**z	....	....	....		----	x---	x---	x---	----		
Heimaey (Saefell tuff cone)						G-**4270**x	....	....	....		----	x---	xx--	x---	----	3	
Heimaey (Helgafell)						U-**3950**y	....	....	....		x---	----	x---	x---	----		8/-
SW of Heimaey ?						**1637**	10	**1638**	0228r		----	x---	x---	----	----		
South or SE of Hellisey						**1896**	09	....	....		----	x---	----	----	----		
Surtsey						**1963**	1108	**1967**	0605		---x	xx--	xx--	x---	----	3*	8/8
Heimaey (Eldfell)						**1973**	0123	**1973**	0628		---x	x---	x-x-	x---	xx--	3	8/7
Eyjafjallajökull (Iceland-S)	**63.63** N	**19.62** W	**1666**	0135	**BYXT**	**Stratovolcano**		**1702-02=**		**Historical**							
						T **0550**?	....	....	....		x---	--x-	----	----	----		
NW flank (Skerin ridge)						T **0920**?	....	....	....		--x-	--x-	x---	x---	--J-	3	7/7
						1612	....	....	....		x---	--x-	x---	----	----	2	-/6
						1821	1219	**1823**	0101		x---	--x-	x---	----	--J-	2*	-/6
Katla (Iceland-S)	**63.63** N	**19.05** W	**1512**	0035	**BRDa**	**Subglacial volc**		**1702-03=**		**Historical**							
						T-**6380**?	....	....	....		----	--x-	x---	----	----		
						T-**6230**?	....	....	....		----	--x-	x---	----	----		
						T-**6200**?	....	....	....		----	--x-	x---	----	----		
						T-**6170**?	....	....	....		----	--x-	x---	----	----		
						T-**6050**?	....	....	....		----	--x-	x---	----	----		
						T-**5960**?	....	....	....		----	--x-	x---	----	----		
						T-**5890**?	....	....	....		----	--x-	x---	----	----		
						T-**5850**?	....	....	....		----	--x-	x---	----	----		
						T-**5730**?	....	....	....		----	--x-	x---	----	----		
						T-**5720**?	....	....	....		----	--x-	x---	----	----		
						T-**5710**?	....	....	....		----	--x-	x---	----	----		
						T-**5630**?	....	....	....		----	--x-	x---	----	----		
(tephra layer A9)						T-**5560**?	....	....	....		x---	--x-	x---	----	--J-		
(Hólmsá Fires eruption; NE flank)						T-**5550**?	....	....	....		---x	--x-	x---	x---	----		9/-
						T-**5470**?	....	....	....		----	--x-	x---	----	----		
(tephra layer A8)						T-**5460**?	....	....	....		x---	--x-	x---	----	--J-		
						T-**5360**?	....	....	....		----	--x-	x---	----	----		
						T-**5230**?	....	....	....		----	--x-	x---	----	----		
(tephra layer A7)						T-**5180**?	....	....	....		x---	--x-	x---	----	--J-		
						T-**5070**?	....	....	....		----	--x-	x---	----	----		
						T-**5040**?	....	....	....		----	--x-	x---	----	----		
						T-**5020**?	....	....	....		----	--x-	x---	----	----		
						T-**4880**?	....	....	....		----	--x-	x---	----	----		
						T-**4810**?	....	....	....		----	--x-	x---	----	----		
						T-**4750**?	....	....	....		----	--x-	x---	----	----		
						T-**4660**?	....	....	....		----	--x-	x---	----	----		
						T-**4610**?	....	....	....		----	--x-	x---	----	----		
						T-**4430**?	....	....	....		----	--x-	x---	----	----		
						T-**4370**?	....	....	....		----	--x-	x---	----	----		
						T-**4280**?	....	....	....		----	--x-	x---	----	----		
						T-**4240**?	....	....	....		----	--x-	x---	----	----		
						T-**4210**?	....	....	....		----	--x-	x---	----	----		
						T-**4060**?	....	....	....		----	--x-	x---	----	----		
						T-**3930**?	....	....	....		----	--x-	x---	----	----		
(tephra layer A1)						T-**3810**?	....	....	....		x---	--x-	x---	----	--J-		
(tephra layer N1)						T-**3790**?	....	....	....		x---	--x-	x---	----	--J-		
						T-**3720**?	....	....	....		----	--x-	x---	----	----		
						T-**3670**?	....	....	....		----	--x-	x---	----	----		
						T-**3640**?	....	....	....		----	--x-	x---	----	----		

VOLCANO NAME (Subregion) / ERUPTION — Area of Activity	Start Year	Start M-Dy	Stop Year	Stop M-Dy	Central / Flank vent / Radial fiss / Regional	Submarine / New island / Subglacial / Crater lake	Explosive / Pyro flow / Phreatic / Caldera	Lava flow / Lava lake / Dome / Spine	Fatal / Damage / Mudflow / Tsunami	VEI	Vol L/T
Katla (Iceland-S) *continued*	T **-3510**?	....	....	....	----	--x-	x---	----	----		
	T **-3480**?	....	....	....	----	--x-	x---	----	----		
	T **-3390**?	....	....	....	----	--x-	x---	----	----		
	T **-3370**?	....	....	....	----	--x-	x---	----	----		
	T **-3280**?	....	....	....	----	--x-	x---	----	----		
	T **-3180**?	....	....	....	----	--x-	x---	----	----		
(tephra layer N2)	T **-2920**?	....	....	....	x---	--x-	x---	----	--J-	3	-/7
	T **-2850**?	....	....	....	----	--x-	x---	----	----		
	T **-2680**?	....	....	....	----	--x-	x---	----	----		
	T **-2540**?	....	....	....	----	--x-	x---	----	----		
	T **-2480**?	....	....	....	----	--x-	x---	----	----		
	T **-2420**?	....	....	....	----	--x-	x---	----	----		
	T **-2250**?	....	....	....	----	--x-	x---	----	----		
	T **-2220**?	....	....	....	----	--x-	x---	----	----		
	T **-2190**?	....	....	....	----	--x-	x---	----	----		
	T **-2160**?	....	....	....	----	--x-	x---	----	----		
	T **-2110**?	....	....	....	----	--x-	x---	----	----		
	T **-2050**?	....	....	....	----	--x-	x---	----	----		
	T **-2020**?	....	....	....	----	--x-	x---	----	----		
	T **-2000**?	....	....	....	----	--x-	x---	----	----		
	T **-1950**?	....	....	....	----	--x-	x---	----	----		
(tephra layer N4)	G **-1920**?	....	....	....	x---	--x-	x---	----	--J-	4	-/8
	T **-1910**?	....	....	....	----	--x-	x---	----	----		
	T **-1850**?	....	....	....	----	--x-	x---	----	----		
	T **-1700**?	....	....	....	----	--x-	x---	----	----		
	T **-1670**?	....	....	....	----	--x-	x---	----	----		
	T **-1640**?	....	....	....	----	--x-	x---	----	----		
	T **-1540**?	....	....	....	----	--x-	x---	----	----		
(tephra layer LN)	G **-1440**s	....	....	....	x---	--x-	x---	----	--J-	4	-/8
	T **-1290**?	....	....	....	----	--x-	x---	----	----		
	T **-1280**?	....	....	....	----	--x-	x---	----	----		
(tephra layer MN)	G **-1220**k	....	....	....	x---	--x-	x---	----	--J-	3	-/7
	T **-1190**?	....	....	....	----	--x-	x---	----	----		
	T **-1160**?	....	....	....	----	--x-	x---	----	----		
	T **-0990**?	....	....	....	----	--x-	x---	----	----		
	T **-0920**?	....	....	....	----	--x-	x---	----	----		
	T **-0860**?	....	....	....	----	--x-	x---	----	----		
(tephra layer UN)	G **-0850**t	....	....	....	x---	--x-	x---	----	--J-	4	-/8
	T **-0780**?	....	....	....	----	--x-	x---	----	----		
	T **-0740**?	....	....	....	----	--x-	x---	----	----		
	T **-0700**?	....	....	....	----	--x-	x---	----	----		
	T **-0650**?	....	....	....	----	--x-	x---	----	----		
	T **-0600**?	....	....	....	----	--x-	x---	----	----		
	T **-0560**?	....	....	....	----	--x-	x---	----	----		
	T **-0550**?	....	....	....	----	--x-	x---	----	----		
	T **-0530**?	....	....	....	----	--x-	x---	----	----		
	T **-0430**?	....	....	....	----	--x-	x---	----	----		
	T **-0370**?	....	....	....	----	--x-	x---	----	----		
	T **-0250**?	....	....	....	----	--x-	x---	----	----		
	T **-0080**?	....	....	....	----	--x-	x---	----	----		
	T **0030**?	....	....	....	----	--x-	x---	----	----		
	T **0130**?	....	....	....	----	--x-	x---	----	----		
	T **0200**?	....	....	....	----	--x-	x---	----	----		
	T **0260**?	....	....	....	----	--x-	x---	----	----		
(tephra layer YN)	C **0270**k	....	....	....	x---	--x-	x---	----	--J-	3	-/7
	T **0290**?	....	....	....	----	--x-	x---	----	----		
	T **0400**?	....	....	....	----	--x-	x---	----	----		
	T **0500**?	....	....	....	----	--x-	x---	----	----		
	T **0540**?	....	....	....	----	--x-	x---	----	----		
	T **0590**?	....	....	....	----	--x-	x---	----	----		
	T **0610**?	....	....	....	----	--x-	x---	----	----		
	T **0680**?	....	....	....	----	--x-	x---	----	----		
	T **0780**?	....	....	....	----	--x-	x---	----	----		
	T **0820**?	....	....	....	----	--x-	x---	----	----		
	? *0904*?	....	....	....	----	--?-	?---	----	----		
	0920	....	....	....	----	--x-	x---	----	-?J-	4	-/8
Eldgjá fissure system (NE flank)	I **0934**b	....	I **0940**?	....	---x	--x-	x---	x---	-xJ-	4?	**10/9**
	T **0950**?	....	....	....	----	--x-	----	x---	-xJ-		
	T **0960**?	....	....	....	----	--x-	x---	----	----	3	-/7
(tephra from 934 AD Eldgá eruption)	X *1000*?	....	....	....	----	----	----	----	----		
	T **1150**t	....	....	....	----	--x-	x---	----	--J-		
	1177b	....	....	....	----	--x-	x---	----	-xJ-	3	-/7
	T **1210**?	....	....	....	----	--x-	x---	----	----	4	-/8
	1245	....	....	....	----	--x-	x---	----	--J-	4	-/8
	1262	....	....	....	----	--x-	x---	----	?-J-	**5**	-/9
	1311	0118	....	....	----	--x-	x---	----	xxJ-		
SW of Kotlugja	**1357**c	....	....	....	----	--x-	x---	----	-xJ-	4+	-/8
	1416	....	....	....	----	--x-	x---	----	--J-	4?	-/8
	1440	....	....	....	----	--x-	x---	----	--J-	4	-/8
	T **1450**t	....	....	....	----	--x-	x---	----	--J-		
	T **1500**?	....	....	....	----	--x-	x---	----	-xJ-	4	-/8
	T **1550**?	....	....	....	----	--x-	x---	----	--J-	4	-/8
	1580	0811	....	....	----	--x-	x---	----	-xJ-	4	-/8
	1612	1012	....	....	----	--x-	x---	----	--J-	4	-/8
	1625	0902	**1625**	0914	----	--x-	x---	----	-xJ-	**5**	-/9
	1660	1103	**1661**	....	----	--x-	x---	----	-xJ-	4	-/8
	1721	0511	**1721**	1015q	----	--x-	x---	----	-xJ-	**5?**	-/9
E-W fissure in center of caldera	**1755**	1017	**1756**	0213	--x-	--x-	x---	----	xxJ-	**5?**	-/9
Arcuate fissure in south part of caldera	**1823**	0626	**1823**	0723	----	--x-	x---	----	--J-	3?	-/8
	1860	0508	**1860**	0527	----	--x-	x---	----	--J-	4	-/8
South side of caldera	**1918**	1012	**1918**	1104	----	--x-	x---	----	-xJ-	4+	-/8
East side of caldera	? *1955*	*0625*	....	....	----	--?-	----	----	--J-	*0*	
W, S, and E margins of caldera	? *1999*	*0717*?	?*1999*	*0815*e	----	--?-	----	----	--J-	*0*	
Tindfjallajökull (Iceland-S) **63.78 N 19.57 W 1463** 0035 **BYRA Stratovolcano**	**1702-04**=	Holocene?									

VOLCANO NAME (Subregion) / ERUPTION — Area of Activity	LAT	LONG	ELEV (m)	POPL (5 km, 10, 30, 100)	ROCK TYPE	VOLC TYPE / Start Year	NUMBER / Start M-Dy	STATUS / Stop Year	Stop M-Dy	Central, Flank vent, Radial fiss, Regional	Submarine, New island, Subglacial, Crater lake	Explosive, Pyro flow, Phreatic, Caldera	Lava flow, Lava lake, Dome, Spine	Fatal, Damage, Mudflow, Tsunami	VEI	Vol L/T
Torfajökull (Iceland-S)	**63.92 N**	**19.17 W**	**1259**	0015	**RBADy**	**Stratovolcano**	**1702-05=**	**Historical**								
W side of caldera (Slettahraun)						T **-6050***	....	....	....	---x	----	----	x---	----		7/-
Hrafntinnusker and Domadalshraun						T **-5050***	....	....	....	---x	----	----	x---	----		8/-
W of caldera (Laufafell domes)						T **-4850***	....	....	....	---x	----	----	x---	----		7/-
N of caldera (Haolduhraun)						T **-4550**z	....	....	....	---x	----	----	x---	----		7/-
W side of caldera (Markafljot domes)						T **-1550**z	....	....	....	---x	----	----	x---	----		7/-
N of caldera (Domadalshraun)						T **-1150**v	....	....	....	---x	----	----	x---	----		7/-
N of caldera (Domadalshraun)						T **0150**v	....	....	....	---x	----	x---	x---	----	3	7/7
W side of caldera (Hrafntinnuhraun)						T **0870**?	....	....	....	---x	----	x---	x---	----	3	8/7
W side of caldera (Hrafntinnuhraun)						T **1170**?	....	....	....	---x	----	x---	----	----		
N of caldera (Namshraun, Laugahraun)						**1477**	03	....	....	---x	----	x---	x---	----	2?	7/-
Hekla (Iceland-S)	**63.98 N**	**19.70 W**	**1491**	0035	**ABRD**	**Stratovolcano**	**1702-07=**	**Historical**								
Svinholdahraun						T **-5850***	....	....	....	----	----	----	x---	----		
(H5 tephra)						G **-5150**?	....	....	....	----	----	x---	----	----	**5**	-/9
Reydarvatnshraun lava flow, Vatnafjöll						T **-5050***	....	....	....	---x	----	----	x---	----		
Vatnafjöll (Raudölduhraun)						T **-4950***	....	....	....	---x	----	x---	x---	----		
Vatnafjöll (west of Laufafell)						T **-4750***	....	....	....	---x	----	----	x---	----		
Gunnarsholtshraun						T **-4650**z	....	....	....	----	----	----	x---	----		
Krokahraun, Vatnafjöll						T **-4550**z	....	....	....	---x	----	----	x---	----		
Vatnafjöll (Lambadalshraun)						T **-4350***	....	....	....	---x	----	x---	x---	----		
Knafaholdahraun						T **-4250**z	....	....	....	----	----	----	x---	----		
Vatnafjöll (Grasleysisfjallahraun)						T **-4150***	....	....	....	---x	----	x---	x---	----		
Baejarhraun						T **-4050**z	....	....	....	----	----	----	x---	----		
Axarhraun, Vatnafjöll						T **-3950**z	....	....	....	---x	----	----	x---	----		
Vatnafjöll						T **-3750***	....	....	....	---x	----	----	x---	----		
Vatnafjöll						T **-3450***	....	....	....	---x	----	x---	x---	----		
Raudkollar, Vatnafjöll (Grafellshraun)						T **-3350***	....	....	....	---x	----	----	x---	----		
Vatnafjöll (Tröllaskógahraun)						T **-2950**z	....	....	....	---x	----	----	x---	----		
Vatnafjöll						T **-2750***	....	....	....	---x	----	x---	x---	----		
Vatnafjöll (Reynnisfellshraun)						T **-2450***	....	....	....	---x	----	----	x---	----		
(H4 tephra)						G **-2310**p	....	....	....	----	----	xx--	----	--x-	**5**	-/9
NE flank (Krokagilsoduhraun), Vatnafjöll						T **-1850***	....	....	....	---x	----	x---	x---	----		
						T **-1750**z	....	....	....	---x	----	----	x---	----		
Vatnafjöll						T **-1650***	....	....	....	---x	----	x---	x---	----		
(Seslund pumice)						T **-1550**?	....	....	....	----	----	xx--	----	--x-	4	-/8
Vatnafjöll						T **-1350***	....	....	....	---x	----	x---	x---	----		
NE flank, Vatnafjöll						T **-1250***	....	....	....	---x	----	x---	x---	----		
Vatnafjöll (Hraunhalsshraun)						T **-1150***	....	....	....	---x	----	----	x---	----		
(H3 tephra)						G **-1100**t	....	....	....	----	----	xx--	----	--x-	**5+**	-/9
NE flank (Raudkembingahraun), Vatnafjöll						T **-0850***	....	....	....	---x	----	x---	x---	----		
NE flank, Vatnafjöll (Langviuhraun)						T **-0750**z	....	....	....	---x	----	----	x---	----		
Vatnafjöll (Svalaskardshraun)						T **-0650***	....	....	....	---x	----	x---	x---	----		
NE flank, Vatnafjöll (Langviuhraun)						T **-0250**z	....	....	....	---x	----	x---	x---	----		
Vatnafjöll (Kringluhraun)						T **-0150***	....	....	....	---x	----	x---	x---	----		
NE flank (Hestolduhraun), Vatnafjöll						T **0250***	....	....	....	---x	----	----	x---	----		
Vatnafjöll (Eskihlidarhraun)						T **0350***	....	....	....	---x	----	----	x---	----		
						T **0550***	....	....	....	----	----	----	x---	----		
NE flank (Helliskvislarhraun)						T **0650**z	....	....	....	---x	----	x---	x---	----		
Taglgigahraun, Solvahraun, Stakahraun						T **0750**?	....	....	....	---x	----	x---	x---	----		
Heklutaglahraun						T **0800**t	....	....	....	---x	----	----	x---	----		
Austurhraun						T **1050**z	....	....	....	----	----	----	x---	----		
(H1 tephra)						**1104**	1015q	....	....	---x	----	x---	----	xx--	**5**	-/**9**
						1158	0119	....	....	---x	----	x---	x---	-x--	4	8/8
						1206	1204	....	....	---x	----	x---	x---	-x--	3	-/7
						1222	....	....	....	---x	----	x---	x---	-x--	2	-/6
						1300	0711	**1301**	07	---x	----	x---	x---	xx--	4	8/8
						1341	0519	....	....	---x	----	x---	x---	-x--	3	-/7
Summit ridge, west flank (Raudoldur)						**1389**	1201p	**1390**	....	--xx	----	x---	x---	-x--	3	8/7
SE of Hekla						T **1440**?	....	....	....	---x	----	x---	----	-x--		
						1510	0725	....	....	---x	----	x---	x---	xx?-	4	-/8
SW of Hekla (Raudubjallar)						**1554**	05	**1554**	06 ?	---x	----	x---	x---	----	2?	8/-
						1597	0103	**1597**	06 >	---x	----	x---	x---	-xx-	4	-/8
						1636	0508	**1637**	06	---x	----	x---	x---	-xx-	3	-/7
						1693	0213	**1693**	0914?	---x	----	x---	x---	-xxx	4	-/8
SW, south and east of Hekla						**1725**	0402	....	....	---x	----	x---	x---	----	1?	
Bjallagigar						**1766**	0405	**1768**	05	---x	----	x---	x---	-xx-	4	**9**/8
Summit, SW and NE flanks						**1845**	0902	**1846**	0405?	---x	----	x---	x---	-xx-	4	8/8
East of Hekla (Krakagigar)						**1878**	0227	**1878**	04	---x	----	x---	x---	----	2	8/-
E & NE of Hekla (Mundafit, Lambafit)						**1913**	0425	**1913**	0518	---x	----	x---	x---	----	2	
Hraungigur, Axlargigur, Toppgigur						**1947**	0329	**1948**	0421	---x	----	xx--	x---	xxx-	4	8/8
Sudurgigar, Hlidargigar, Oldugigar						**1970**	0505	**1970**	0705	--x-	----	x---	x---	-x--	3	8/7
Summit, SW and NE flanks						**1980**	0817	**1980**	0820	---x	----	xx--	x---	-x--	3	8/7
Summit and north flank (900 and 740 m)						**1981**	0409	**1981**	0416	--x-	----	x---	x---	----	2	7/-
Summit, SW, SE & NE flank fissures						**1991**	0117	**1991**	0311	-xxx	----	x---	x---	----	3	8/7
SW flank						**2000**	0226	**2000**	0308	---x	----	xx--	x---	----	3	8/7

ICELAND - NE

VOLCANO NAME (Subregion) / ERUPTION — Area of Activity	LAT	LONG	ELEV (m)	POPL (5 km, 10, 30, 100)	ROCK TYPE	VOLC TYPE / Start Year	NUMBER / Start M-Dy	STATUS / Stop Year	Stop M-Dy	Central, Flank vent, Radial fiss, Regional	Submarine, New island, Subglacial, Crater lake	Explosive, Pyro flow, Phreatic, Caldera	Lava flow, Lava lake, Dome, Spine	Fatal, Damage, Mudflow, Tsunami	VEI	Vol L/T
Grímsvötn (Iceland-NE)	**64.42 N**	**17.33 W**	**1725**	0004	**B**	**Caldera**	**1703-01=**	**Historical**								
(Saksunarvatn tephra layer)						G **-8230**t	....	....	....	x---	--x-	x---	----	----	**6**	-/**10**
Laki (Botnahraun)						T **-4550**z	....	....	....	---x	----	----	x---	----	0	
S of Thordarhyrna (Bergvatnsarhraun)						T **-3550**z	....	....	....	---x	----	----	x---	----	0	8/-
Raudholar and Brunuholar						T **-1950**v	....	....	....	---x	----	x---	x---	----	2	**9**/-
Halsagigur						T **-0050**?	....	....	....	---x	----	x---	x---	----	2	
						T **0910**?	....	....	....	----	--x-	x---	----	----		
						I **0960**?	....	....	....	----	--x-	x---	----	----		
						I **1010**?	....	....	....	----	--x-	x---	----	----		
						T **1060**?	....	....	....	----	--x-	x---	----	----		
						I **1090**?	....	....	....	----	--x-	x---	----	----		
						I **1150**?	....	....	....	----	--x-	x---	----	----		
						I **1190**?	....	....	....	----	--x-	x---	----	----		
						I **1230**j	....	....	....	---x	--x-	x---	----	----		
						I **1270**j	....	....	....	---x	--x-	x---	----	----		
						I **1290**j	....	....	....	---x	--x-	x---	----	----		

VOLCANO NAME (Subregion) / ERUPTION	LAT	LONG	ELEV (m)	POPL (5 km, 10, 30, 100)	ROCK TYPE	VOLC TYPE / — Area of Activity	NUMBER / Start Year	Start M-Dy	STATUS / Stop Year	Stop M-Dy	Central, Flank vent, Radial fiss, Regional	Submarine, New island, Subglacial, Crater lake	Explosive, Pyro flow, Phreatic, Caldera	Lava flow, Lava lake, Dome, Spine	Fatal, Damage, Mudflow, Tsunami	VEI	Vol L/T
Grímsvötn (Iceland-NE) *continued*							I **1310**j	....	....	....	---x	--x-	x---	----	----		
							1332	11	....	....	----	--x-	x---	----	--?-	2	
							1341	05	....	....	----	--x-	x---	----	--?-	2	
							I **1350**?	....	....	....	----	--x-	x---	----	----		
							1354?	....	....	....	---x	--x-	x---	----	----		
							I **1369**?	....	....	....	----	--x-	x---	----	----		
							I **1370**j	....	....	....	---x	--x-	x---	----	----		
							I **1390**j	....	....	....	---x	--x-	x---	----	----		
							I **1430**j	....	....	....	---x	--x-	x---	----	----		
							I **1450**j	....	....	....	---x	--x-	x---	----	----		
							I **1469**?	....	....	....	----	--x-	x---	----	----		
							I **1470**j	....	....	....	---x	--x-	x---	----	----		
							I **1471**?	....	....	....	----	--x-	x---	----	----		
							I **1490**j	....	....	....	---x	--x-	x---	----	----		
							I **1500**?	....	....	....	----	--x-	x---	----	----		
							I **1509**?	....	....	....	----	--x-	x---	----	----		
							I **1510**j	....	....	....	---x	--x-	x---	----	----		
							I **1521**?	....	....	....	----	--x-	x---	----	----		
							I **1530**j	....	....	....	---x	--x-	x---	----	----		
							1598	1107	....	....	----	--x-	x---	----	--?-	3?	-/8
						(Vatnajökull, possibly Grímsvötn)	@ **1603**	1031	@**1603**	11	----	--x-	x---	----	--?-	2	
							I **1610**?	....	....	....	----	--x-	x---	----	----		
							1619	0729	....	....	----	--x-	x---	----	--?-	2	
							I **1622**?	....	....	....	----	--x-	x---	----	----		
							1629	....	....	....	----	--x-	x---	----	x-J-	2	
							I **1632**?	....	....	....	----	--x-	x---	----	----		
							1638	0224d	....	....	----	--x-	x---	----	--?-	2	
							1659	11	....	....	----	--x-	x---	----	--?-	2	
							1665	....	....	....	----	--x-	x---	----	----		
						(Vatnajökull)	@ **1681**	0410	....	....	----	--x-	----	----	----		
							1684	1105d	**1685**	01	----	--x-	x---	----	xxJ-	2	
							1697	....	....	....	----	--x-	x---	----	----		
							1706	1015q	....	....	----	--x-	x---	----	--?-	2	
							1716	1006	....	....	----	--x-	x---	----	--?-	2	
							1725	02	....	....	----	--x-	x---	----	--J-	2	
							1730	....	....	....	----	--x-	x---	----	----		
						NE of Palsfjall	**1753**	1015q	....	....	----	--x-	x---	----	-xJ-	2?	
						(Vatnajökull)	@ **1768**	....	....	....	----	--x-	x---	----	----	2	
							1774	02	....	....	----	--x-	x---	----	--J-	2	
						Lakagigar (Skaftar) and Grímsvötn	**1783**	05 ?	**1785**	0526?	---x	--x-	x---	x---	xxJ-	4+	**10**/8
						(W-Vatnajökull)	? *1794*	*0715*q	....	....	----	--?-	----	----	----		
						(jökulhlaup, probably no eruption)	*X 1796*	*06*	....	....	----	----	----	----	--J-		
							1816	05	**1816**	06 ?	----	--x-	x---	----	----	2	
						Grímsvötn-Thordarhyrna	**1823**	0204d	....	....	----	--x-	x---	----	----	2	
							1838	06	....	....	----	--x-	----	----	--J-	2	
							1854	....	....	....	----	--x-	x---	----	----	2	
							? *1861*	*05*	....	....	----	--?-	?---	----	-xJ-	*2*	
							1867	0829	....	....	----	--x-	x---	----	--J-	1	
							1873	0108	**1873**	08	----	--x-	x---	----	--J-	4	-/8
							1883	0115	**1883**	0415e	----	--x-	x---	----	--J-	2	
						Thordarhyrna	**1887**	0815	**1889**	....	----	--x-	x---	----	--J-	2	
							1891	11 ?	**1892**	0316	----	--x-	x---	----	--J-	2	
							@ **1897**	....	....	....	----	--x-	x---	----	----	2	
						Grímsvötn and Thordarhyrna	**1902**	12	**1904**	0112	----	--x-	x---	----	--J-	4*	8/-
							1910	....	....	....	----	--x-	x---	----	----		
							@ **1919**	....	....	....	----	--x-	x---	----	----	2?	
							1922	0929	**1922**	1023	----	--x-	x---	----	--J-	2	
						North of Grímsvötn caldera	**1933**	1129a	**1933**	1209a	---x	--x-	x---	----	----	1	
						Near south caldera wall	**1934**	0330	**1934**	0407	x---	--x-	x---	----	--J-	2	
						Vatnajökull	@ **1934**	1221	@**1934**	1226	----	--x-	----	----	----		
						8 km north of Svartibunki	**1938**	05	....	....	----	--x-	x---	----	--J-	1	
							? *1939*	*06*	....	....	----	--?-	----	----	--J-	*0*	
							? *1941*	*04*	?*1941*	*08*	----	--?-	----	----	--J-	*0*	
							? *1945*	*0925?*	....	....	----	--?-	?---	----	--J-	*1?*	
							? *1948*	*02*	....	....	----	--?-	----	----	--J-	*0*	
							1954	0115q	....	....	----	----	x-x-	----	----	1	
						North and south part of caldera	? *1954*	*07*	....	....	x---	--?-	--?-	----	--J-	*1?*	
							? *1972*	*03*	?*1972*	*04*	x---	--??	----	----	--J-	*0*	
						Near south caldera wall	**1983**	0528	**1983**	0602	x---	--xx	x---	----	----	2	
							? *1984*	*0820*<	....	....	x---	--?-	----	----	----	*0*	
						Gjálp (fissure N of caldera rim)	**1996**	0930	**1996**	1106	x--x	--xx	x-x-	x---	-xJ-	3?	8/-
						South caldera wall	**1998**	1218	**1998**	1228	x---	--xx	xx--	----	----	3	
						SW and east sides of caldera	**2004**	1101	**2004**	1104	x--x	--xx	x---	----	--J-	3	
Bárdarbunga (Iceland-NE)	**64.63 N**	**17.53 W**	**2009**	0004	**BR**	**Stratovolcano**	**1703-03=**		**Historical**								
						Trölladyngja (Bardarhalshraun)	T -**7100**?	....	....	....	---x	----	----	x---	----		**9**/-
						Veidivötn (Haahraun, Botnahraun)	T -**7050***	....	....	....	---x	----	----	x---	----		
						Veidivötn (Thjorsarhraun)	G -**6650**t	....	....	....	---x	----	----	x---	----		**10**/-
						Trölladyngja	T -**5000**?	....	....	....	x---	----	----	xx--	----		**10**/-
						Veidvötn (Tungnaárhraun THc)	T -**4800**?	....	....	....	---x	----	----	x---	----		**9**/-
						Veidvötn (Tungnaárhraun THd)	T -**4600**?	....	....	....	---x	----	----	x---	----		**9**/-
						Veidivötn (Sigolduhraun, Kalfahraun)	T -**4550**?	....	....	....	---x	----	----	x---	----		
						Veidvötn (Tungnaárhraun THe)	T -**4400**?	....	....	....	---x	----	----	x---	----		**9**/-
						Veidvötn (Sigolduhraun THf)	T -**4200**?	....	....	....	---x	----	----	x---	----		**9**/-
						Veidivötn (Burfellshraun, Drekahraun)	T -**1200**?	....	....	....	---x	----	----	x---	----		**9**/-
						Veidivötn (Tjorvahraun)	T **0150**v	....	....	....	---x	----	x---	x---	----	2?	8/-
						Vatnaöldur	T **0870**?	....	....	....	---x	----	xxx-	x---	----	4	7/**9**
							T **0880**?	....	....	....	----	--x-	x---	----	----		
							T **0940**?	....	....	....	----	--x-	----	----	----		
							T **1080**?	....	....	....	----	--x-	----	----	----		
							1159?	....	....	....	----	--x-	----	----	----		
							I **1210**j	....	....	....	---x	--x-	x---	----	----		
						Frambuni	T **1250**t	....	....	....	----	----	x---	x---	----	1	**9**/5
							I **1270**j	....	....	....	---x	--x-	x---	----	----		
							I **1290**j	....	....	....	---x	--x-	x---	----	----		

VOLCANO NAME (Subregion) / ERUPTION — Area of Activity	LAT	LONG	ELEV (m)	POPL 5 km 10 30 100	ROCK TYPE	VOLC TYPE	NUMBER	STATUS	Start Year	Start M-Dy	Stop Year	Stop M-Dy	ERUPTIVE CHARACTERISTICS (Central Flank vent Radial fiss Regional / Submarine New island Subglacial Crater lake / Explosive Pyro flow Phreatic Caldera / Lava flow Lava lake Dome Spine / Fatal Damage Mudflow Tsunami)	VEI	Vol L/T
Bárdarbunga (Iceland-NE) *continued*									I **1350**j				---x --x- x--- ---- ----		
									T **1410**?				---- --x- ---- ---- ----		
Veidivötn (Veidivatnahraun)									**1477**	02 ?			---x --x- xxx- x--- -x--	**6**	9/10
									I **1697**				---x --x- x--- ---- --J-	2	
Dyngjuhals ?									@ **1702**				---? --x- x--- ---- --?-	2	
									1706				---- --x- x--- ---- ----	2	
									1707				---- --x- x--- ---- ----	2	
(Bárdarbunga, not Kverkfjöll)									**1712**	0115q			---- --x- x--- ---- -xJ-	2	
(Bárdarbunga, not Kverkfjöll)									**1716**	1005d			---- --x- x--- ---- -xJ-	2	
(Bárdarbunga, not Kverkfjöll)									**1717**	0804	**1717**	0917>	---- --x- x--- ---- -xJ-	3?	
									I **1720**				---x --x- x--- ---- ----	2	
Dyngjujökull, Dyngjuhal ?									**1726**	0201p	**1726**	0501p	---- --x- ---- ---- -xJ-	1?	
Dyngjuhals ?									@ **1729**				---? --x- x--- ---- -xJ-	1	
									I **1739**				---x --x- x--- ---- ----	2	
									I **1750**j				---x --x- x--- ---- ----		
									1766	07			---- --x- x--- ---- --J-	2	
(Bárdarbunga, or Grímsvötn)									@ **1769**				---- --x- x--- ---- ----	2	
									1794				---- --x- x--- ---- ----		
									@ **1797**				---- ---- ---- ---- ----		
NW-Vatnajökull									*? 1807*				---- --?- ---- ---- ----		
Trollagigar									**1862**	0630	**1864**	1015q	---x ---- x--- x--- ----	2	8/5
Dyngjuhals ?									@ **1872**?				---? --?- ---- ---- ----		
Dyngjuhals ?									@ **1902**	12	@**1903**	06	---? --x- ---- ---- --J-	2?	
Loki-Fögrufjöll (East Loki cauldron)									**1910**	0618	**1910**	10	---x --x- x--- ---- ----	2	
Loki-Fögrufjöll (East Loki cauldron)									*? 1986*	*1129*	*?1986*	*1201*?	---? --?- ---- ---- --J-	*0*	
Loki-Fögrufjöll (East Loki cauldron)									*? 1991*	*0812*			---? --?- ---- ---- --J-	*0*	
Loki-Fögrufjöll (East Loki cauldron)									*? 1995*	*07*			---? --?- ---- ---- --J-	*0*	
Loki-Fögrufjöll (West Loki cauldron)									*? 1996*	*08*			---? --?- ---- ---- --J-	*0*	
Loki-Fögrufjöll (East Loki cauldron)									*? 1997*	*08*			---? --?- ---- ---- --J-	*0*	
Loki-Fögrufjöll (W and E Loki cauldron)									*? 2000*	*08*			---? --?- ---- ---- --J-	*0*	
Loki-Fögrufjöll (W and E Loki cauldron)									*? 2002*	*07*	*?2002*	*09*	---? --?- ---- ---- --J-	*0*	
Loki-Fögrufjöll (West Loki cauldron)									*? 2005*	*07*	*?2005*	*08*	---? --?- ---- ---- --J-	*0*	
Loki-Fögrufjöll (East Loki cauldron)									*? 2006*	*04*			---? --?- ---- ---- --J-	*0*	
Loki-Fögrufjöll (West Loki cauldron)									*? 2008*	*08*			---? --?- ---- ---- --J-	*0*	
Tungnafellsjökull (Iceland-NE)	**64.73** N	**17.92** W	**1535**	0003	**BR**	**Stratovolcano**	**1703-04=**	**Holocene**							
Kverkfjöll (Iceland-NE)	**64.65** N	**16.72** W	**1929**	0004	**BR**	**Stratovolcano**	**1703-05=**	**Historical**							
Arnadalsoldugjoska									T-**7050**?				---x ---- ?--- ---- ----		
Krepputunguhraun, Kverfjallahraun									T-**5000***				---x ---- ---- x--- ----		9/-
									1655	0415q			---- --x- ---- ---- --J-	0	
									1729	0215q			---- --x- ---- ---- --J-	1	
									1729	08			---- --x- ---- ---- --J-	1	
Hveradalur area									**1929**	01	**1929**	02	---- ---- x--- ---- ----	1	
									1959				---- --x- ---- ---- ----		
									1968	0523	**1968**	06	---- --x- ---- ---- ----		
Askja (Iceland-NE)	**65.03** N	**16.75** W	**1516**	0005	**Br**	**Stratovolcano**	**1703-06=**	**Historical**							
SE part of Askja caldera									G-**8910**x				x--- ---x xx-x ---- ----	**5**	-/9
Flatadyngja, other areas NE of Dyngjufjöll									T-**2050**z				x--x ---- ---- xx-- ----	0	9/-
Litladynga and Askja									T-**1250**y				x--x ---- ---- xx-- ----	0	9/-
South of Dyngjufjöll Ytri									T **1300**?				---x ---- --x- x--- ----	1	
Holuhraun									**1797**?				---x ---- ---- x--- ----	0	
Öskjuvatn Caldera, Viti, Sveinagja									**1875**	0101	**1875**	1017	x--x ---- xxxx x--- -x--	**5***	8/9
Dyngjufjöll									**1919**				---- ---- x--- ---- ----	2	
NE caldera wall, 0.6 km SE of Viti									**1921**	03			--x- ---- ---- x--- ----	0	
1 km SW of Öskjuvatn Caldera									**1922**	11			---- ---- ---- x--- ----	0	
SE corner of Öskjuvatn Caldera									**1923**	0115q			---x ---- ---- x--- ----	0	
South flank of Dyngjufjöll massif									**1924**?				---x ---- ---- x--- ----	0?	8/-
South end of Öskjuvatn lake									**1926**	0715q			x--- -x-x x--- x--- ----	2?	-/7
South shore of Öskjuvatn lake									**1938**	1219?			x--- ---- x--- x--- ----	2	
North of Öskjuvatn lake (Vikraborgir)									**1961**	1026	**1961**	1205d	--x- ---- x--- xx-- ----	2	8/6
Fremrinamur (Iceland-NE)	**65.43** N	**16.65** W	**939**	0035	**BR**	**Stratovolcano**	**1703-07=**	**Tephrochronology**							
Sveinar (Rauduborgir) fissure									T-**4050***				---x ---- x--- x--- ----		9/-
Kerlingardyngja									T-**4000**?				x--- ---- ---- xx-- ----	0	9/-
Ketildyngja									T-**2300**?				x--- ---- ---- xx-- ----	0	9/-
Kraeduborgir (Burfellshraun)									T-**1200**?				---x ---- ---- x--- ----		9/-
(no 1823 eruption at Lierhafnarskord)									*X 1823*				---- ---- ---- ---- ----		
Krafla (Iceland-NE)	**65.73** N	**16.78** W	**818**	3345	**BRAD**	**Caldera**	**1703-08=**	**Historical**							
Gjastykkisbunga									T-**8500**?				x--- ---- ---- xx-- ----	0	9/-
Ludent, Namafjall-Krofluhals									T-**7850**?				x--x ---- x-x- x--- ----		9/-
Heidarspordur									T-**7400**y				---x ---- ---- x--- ----	0	
Hraunbunga									T-**6950**?				x--- ---- ---- x--- ----	0	
Bondholshraun, Hveragil									T-**6850**?				x--- ---- x--- x--- ----	2?	
Hveragil									T-**6800**?				x--- ---- x--- ---- ----	2?	
Kröfluhalshraun									T-**6500**?				---x ---- ---- x--- ----		9/-
Drangagrundahraun									T-**6150**?				---x ---- ---- x--- ----	0	
Fjarborg									T-**5750**?				---x ---- ---- x--- ----	0	
Ludent crater rows									T-**4050**?				---x ---- ---- x--- ----	0	
Hvannstód									C-**3050**?				---x ---- ---- x--- ----	0	
Hverfjall, Jarbadsholar									T-**0650**?				x--- ---- x-x- x--- ----	4	-/8
North of Hverfjall									T-**0500**y				---x ---- ---- x--- ----	0	
Threngslaborgir-Ludentsborgir crater row									G-**0300**?				---x ---- x--- x--- ----	2	9/-
Holseldar									T-**0050**?				---x ---- x--- x--- ----	2	
Kerlingarholar									T **0250**y				---x ---- ---- x--- ----	0	
Daleldar, Svortuborgir									T **0850**?				---x ---- ---- x--- ----	0	7/-
Crater south of Víti									T **1300**x				x--- ---- x--- ---- ----	2?	
Víti (1.5 km east of Leirhnjúkur)									**1724**	0517	**1724**	0518	---x ---- x--- ---- ----	2	-/6
(solfataric activity, no eruption)									*X 1725*	*0111*			---- ---- ---- ---- ----		
North end of Leirhnjúkur									**1727**	0821			---x ---- ---- x--- ----	2	
Leirhnjúkur, Hrossadalur, Bjarnarflag									**1728**	0418			---x ---- ---- x--- ----	2	
Leirhnjúkur crater row									**1728**	1218			---x ---- ---- x--- ----	2	8/-
Leirhnjúkur crater row									**1729**	0630	**1729**	0925e	---x ---- ---- x--- -x--	2	
Leirhnjúkur crater row									**1746**	0710	**1746**	0710?	---x ---- x--- ---- ----	1	
1.5-2.5 km north of Leirhnjúkur									**1975**	1220	**1975**	1220	---x ---- ---- x--- ----	0	5/-
3 km north of Leirhnjúkur									**1977**	0427	**1977**	0908	---x ---- x-x- x--- -x--	1	6/1

VOLCANO NAME (Subregion) / ERUPTION — Area of Activity	LAT	LONG	ELEV (m)	POPL (5 km, 10, 30, 100)	ROCK TYPE	VOLC TYPE	NUMBER	STATUS	Start Year	Start M-Dy	Stop Year	Stop M-Dy	Central, Flank vent, Radial fiss, Regional	Submarine, New island, Subglacial, Crater lake	Explosive, Pyro flow, Phreatic, Caldera	Lava flow, Lava lake, Dome, Spine	Fatal, Damage, Mudflow, Tsunami	VEI	Vol L/T
Krafla (Iceland-NE) *continued*																			
Leirhnjúkur to 11 km north									**1980**	0316	**1980**	1023	---x	----	--x-	x---	----	0*	7/-
6-8 km north of Leirhnjúkur									**1981**	0130	**1981**	0204	---x	----	----	x---	----	0	7/-
Leirhnjúkur to 9 km north									**1981**	1118	**1981**	1123	---x	----	----	x---	----	0	7/-
Leirhnjúkur to 8.5 km north									**1984**	0904	**1984**	0918	---x	----	----	x---	----	0	8/-
Theistareykjarbunga (Iceland-NE)	**65.88** N	**16.83** W	**564**	0245	B	**Shield volcano**	**1703-09=**	**Tephrochronology**											
Theistareykjabunga shield volcano									T **-9500**?	....	....	....	x---	----	----	xx--	----	0	**10/-**
Borgarhraun and other flows									T **-6800**?	....	....	....	---x	----	----	x---	----	0	
Storihver (Theistareykjahraun)									T **-0900**v	....	....	....	---x	----	----	x---	----	0	
Tjörnes Fracture Zone (Iceland-N)	**66.30** N	**17.10** W		0035	B	**Submarine volc**	**1703-10=**	**Historical**											
Immediately north of Manareyjar Island									**1867**	12	**1868**	01	----	x---	----	----	----		
ICELAND - SE																			
Öraefajökull (Iceland-SE)	**64.00** N	**16.65** W	**2119**	0134	BRt	**Stratovolcano**	**1704-01=**	**Historical**											
									1362	0605d	**1362**	1015q	x---	--x-	xx--	--?-	xxJ-	**5**	-/9
Caldera, west flank (to 1100 m)									**1727**	0803	**1728**	0501p	x--x	--x-	x---	----	xxJ-	4	-/8
Esjufjöll (Iceland-SE)	**64.27** N	**16.65** W	**1760**	0004	Br	**Stratovolcano**	**1704-02=**	Uncertain											
									? 1927	*0905*d	....	....	?---	----	?---	----	x-J-	*1?*	
ICELAND - N OF																			
Kolbeinsey Ridge (Iceland-N of)	**66.67** N	**18.50** W	**5**	0034	B	**Submarine volc**	**1705-01=**	**Historical**											
NW of Grimsey Island									**1372**	....	....	....	----	xx--	----	----	----	2?	
(eruption north of Iceland)									@ **1755**	0918	....	....	----	?---	x---	----	----		
(no 1783 eruption north of Iceland)									*X 1783*	....	....	....	----	----	----	----	----		
(no 1838 eruption near Siglufjördur)									*X 1838*	*0611?*	....	....	----	----	----	----	----		
ARCTIC OCEAN																			
Jan Mayen (Atlantic-N-Jan Mayen)	**71.08** N	**8.17** W	**2277**	0000	BXT	**Stratovolcano**	**1706-01=**	**Historical**											
Beerenberg (Eggoya, SW flank)									T **1350**v	....	....	....	-x--	xx--	x-x-	----	----		
Beerenberg									*? 1558<*	....	....	....	----	----	----	----	----		
Beerenberg (Dagnyhaugen, SW flank)									**1732**	0517	**1732**	0518	-x--	----	x---	x---	----	3	
Beerenberg (Dagnyhaugen, SW flank)									**1818**	04	....	....	-x--	----	x---	x---	----	3?	
Beerenberg (Kokssletta, NE flank)									**1851**r	....	....	....	-x--	----	----	x---	----		
Beerenberg (NE & SW flanks, summit)									**1970**	0918	**1972**?	....	xx-x	--x-	x-x-	x---	--J-	3	8/7
Beerenberg (NE flank, Skrukkelia)									**1973**	0115q	....	....	-x--	----	x---	----	----	1	
Beerenberg (NE flank, 0-200 m)									**1985**	0106	**1985**	0109	-x-x	----	x---	x---	----	0	6/6
Unnamed (Lomonosov Ridge)	**88.27** N	**65.60** W	**-1500**		U	**Submarine volc ?**	**1707-01-**	Uncertain											
									*? 1475*q	....	....	....	----	?---	?---	----	----	*0*	
									*? 1725*q	....	....	....	----	?---	?---	----	----	*0*	
									? 1957	*1121*	*?1957*	*1124*	----	?---	----	----	----	*0*	
Unnamed (East Gakkel Ridge)	**85.58** N	**85.00** E	**-3800**	0000	U	**Submarine volc**	**1707-02-**	**Holocene**											
East Gakkel Ridge									*? 1999*	*01 ?*	*?1999*	*09 ?*	----	?---	----	?---	----	*0*	

Freysteinn Sigmundsson (Nordic Volc. Center)

An ash plume rises from a new crater near the southern margin of Grímsvötn caldera in November 2004. Grímsvötn, Iceland's most frequently active volcano in historical time, lies largely beneath the vast Vatnajökull icecap. The 6 x 8 km wide caldera is the source of frequent jökulhlaups (glacier outburst floods) produced when melting raises the water level high enough to lift its ice dam.

Atlantic Ocean (18)

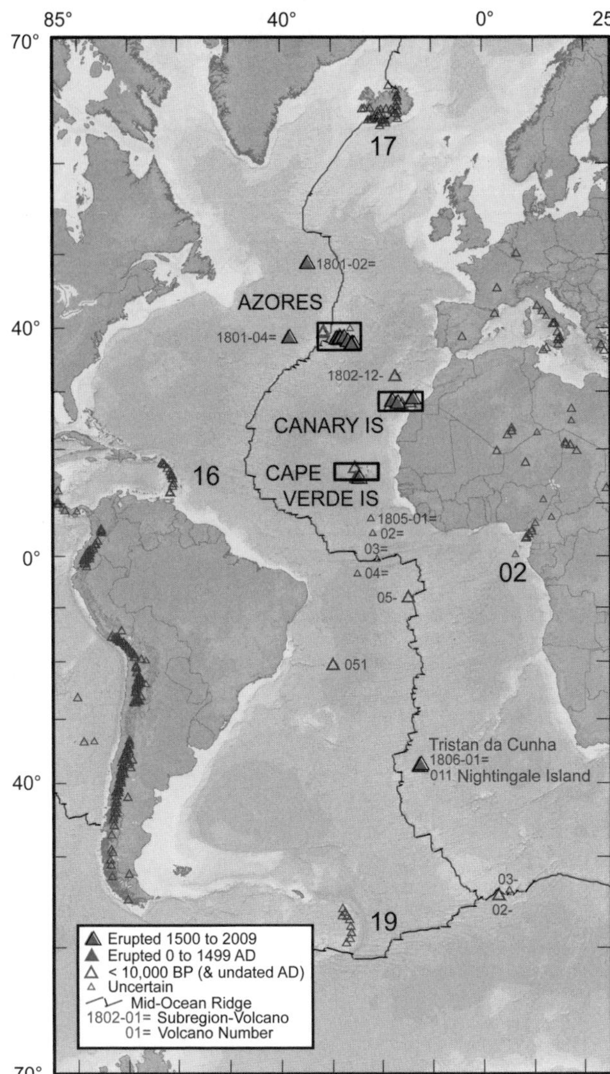

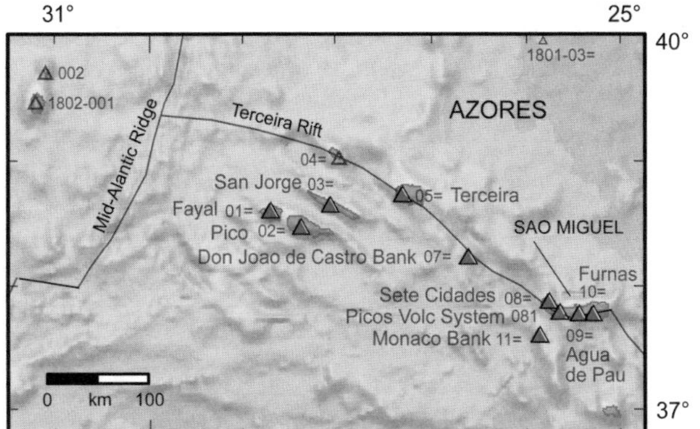

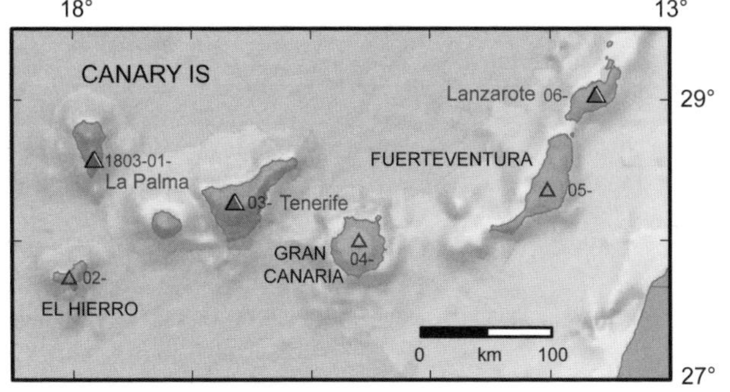

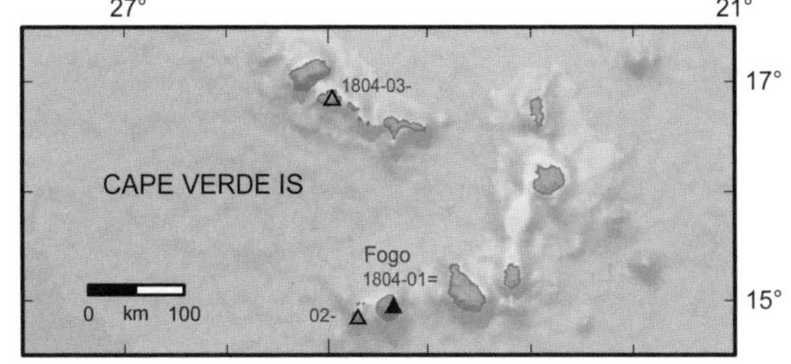

Despite the large size of this region, only 155 eruptions are known–only Antarctica has less–but its historical record is relatively long. The largest island group, the Canaries, is reached by favorable winds from Europe and was an important base for early voyages to the new world. In fact, Christopher Columbus recorded a 1492 eruption on Tenerife, just 7 weeks before that same logbook carried documentation of a more historic observation. The Azores were also well placed for sailors because of the predominant westerly winds used for return routes to Europe.

The Canaries were mentioned by Pliny around 40 AD, and were often rediscovered in the following centuries. They were claimed by Portugal in 1341, the year of the region's first historical eruption (a somewhat questionable report of activity somewhere on Tenerife), but were awarded to Spain by the Pope 3 years later. They were settled in 1402 and conquest of the indigenous Guanches population was complete by 1496. The Canaries now have the largest population (1.6 million) in the region and, as part of Spain, claim Pico de Teide as that nation's highest point.

A discovery date for the Azores is uncertain, but they appear on a map from 1351 AD. The Portuguese visited in 1427-31 and colonization began in 1445, a year after the first historical eruption. The 9 islands now support about 250,000 people, half of them on the island of Sao Miguel.

The Cape Verde islands were discovered by Portugal in 1456 and settled 6 years later. An eruption beginning in 1500 appears to have continued for about 260 years, with behavior similar to that of Italy's Stromboli. The islands were an important point in the trans-shipment of slaves until the 18th century. Independence from Portugal came in 1975.

Tristan da Cunha was discovered by the Portuguese in 1506 and the islands were much visited by whalers and sealers. They were first inhabited by St. Helenans in the 19th century and annexed by Britain in 1816. An eruption in 1961 broke out at the only inhabited area on the island, forcing residents to evacuate, but most elected to return within two years and the 1970 population was estimated at 280. In 2004 submarine eruptive activity was recorded near Nightingale Island at the southern end of the Tristan da Cunha island group. No previous Holocene activity was known from Nightingale Island, but an earthquake swarm lasting 6 hours beginning on July 29, 2004 was followed by observation of large blocks of floating phonolitic pumice that washed up on Tristan da Cunha. The event was considered to have originated from an eruption associated with an earthquake swarm 37-53 km SSE of Tristan da Cunha on the submarine SE flank of Nightingale Island. Aside from other submarine activity (most of it uncertain) the only other dated eruption in the South Atlantic region is from Norway's Bouvet Island, the most remote in the world. It was discovered in 1739, but it's only known eruption was 2000 years ago (by magnetic dating).

Volcanism in the region is largely caused by hotspots in oceanic crust, and the region has the highest proportion of fissure vent volcanoes (as primary features). Several known volcanoes lie along or near the Mid-Atlantic Ridge that separates the Eurasian and African plates from the North and South American plates, but the Canaries and Cape Verdes lie just west of the African continental margin. This region has been relatively quiet, with only 14 eruptions confirmed since 1900, including the two mentioned above in the Tristan da Cunha island group. No eruptions have occurred in the Canaries following small eruptions on La Palma in 1949 and 1971. The only confirmed eruption in the Azores since a 1907 submarine eruption at Monaco Bank took place along a fissure west of Terceira Island in 1998, when floating and steaming lava blocks were observed. Fogo volcano in the Cape Verde Islands erupted in 1951, but was quiet until 1995, when a new cinder cone produced lava flows that buried a village and croplands on the caldera floor.

VOLCANO NAME (Subregion) / **ERUPTION** — Area of Activity	**LAT**	**LONG**	**ELEV** (m)	**POPL** (5 km, 10, 30, 100)	**ROCK TYPE**	**VOLC TYPE** / — Start — **Year**	M-Dy	**NUMBER** / — Stop — **Year**	**STATUS** / M-Dy	ERUPTIVE CHARACTERISTICS: Central, Flank vent, Radial fiss, Regional	Submarine, New island, Subglacial, Crater lake	Explosive, Pyro flow, Phreatic, Caldera	Lava flow, Lava lake, Dome, Spine	Fatal, Damage, Mudflow, Tsunami	VEI	Vol L/T
ATLANTIC OCEAN - N																
Unnamed (Atlantic-N)	66.00 N*	27.75 W	-108					1801-01=	Not a Volcano							
(incorrect eruption report)						*X 1332*	....	....	....	----	----	----	----	----		
(incorrect eruption report)						*X 1456*	....	....	....	----	----	----	----	----		
(incorrect eruption report)						*X 1783*	....	....	....	----	----	----	----	----		
Unnamed (Atlantic-N)	**49.00 N**	**34.50 W**	**-1650**	0000	U	**Submarine volc**		**1801-02=**	**Historical**							
						1884	1229	....	....	----	x---	----	----	----	0	
Unnamed (Atlantic-N)	**39.95 N**	**25.83 W**	**-2835**	0000	U	**Submarine volc**		**1801-03=**	Uncertain							
						? 1856	*1125*	*?1856*	*1125*	----	x---	----	----	----	*0*	
Unnamed (Atlantic-N)	**38.75 N**	**38.08 W**	**-4200**	0000	U	**Submarine volc**		**1801-04=**	**Historical**							
						1865	0709	....	....	----	x---	----	----	----	0	
AZORES																
Flores (Azores)	**39.462N**	**31.216 W**	**914**	4444	**BXYTz**	**Stratovolcanoes**		**1802-001**	**Radiocarbon**							
Caldeira Funda de Lajes						C-**1200**v	....	....	....	x---	----	x---	x---	----		
Caldeira Comprida						C-**0950**v	....	....	....	x---	----	x---	x---	----		
Corvo (Azores)	**39.699N**	**31.111 W**	**718**	3344	**BA**	**Stratovolcano**		**1802-002**	**Holocene**							
Fayal (Azores)	**38.60 N**	**28.73 W**	**1043**	4555	**ABXTY**	**Stratovolcano**		**1802-01=**	**Historical**							
West flank						**1672**	0424	**1673**	0228	-x--	----	x---	x---	xx--	2	
West flank (Capelinhos) and summit						**1957**	0927	**1958**	1024	xxx-	xx--	xxx-	x---	-x--	2	7/7
Pico (Azores)	**38.47 N**	**28.40 W**	**2351**	3455	**BXy**	**Stratovolcano**		**1802-02=**	**Historical**							
East flank (800 m)						**1562**	0921?	**1564**?	....	-x--	----	x---	x---	-x--	2	
SE flank (200 m), NW flank (1200 m)						**1718**	0201	**1718**	1215e	-x--	?---	x---	x---	xx--	2	
SE flank (400 m)						**1720**	0710	**1720**	12 ?	-x--	----	x---	x---	-x--	2	
Off NW coast						*? 1963*	*1215<*	....	....	----	x---	----	----	----	*0*	
San Jorge (Azores)	**38.65 N**	**28.08 W**	**1053**	4455	**BAt**	**Fissure vent**		**1802-03=**	**Historical**							
Sao Jorge (SW side)						**1580**	0501	**1580**	0830?	---x	----	xx--	x---	xx--	3?	
Off south coast of Sao Jorge						**1757**	0709	**1757**	0710	----	xx--	----	----	----	0	
Subm. vent ca. 20 km SW of Terceira						**1800**	0624	**1800**	0625	----	x---	--x-	----	----	2	
Sao Jorge						**1808**	0501	**1808**	0610	---x	----	xx--	x---	xx--	1	
Subm. vent ca. 20 km SW of Terceira						**1902**	0507	**1902**	0508	----	x---	----	----	-x--	0	
						1907	....	....	....	----	x---	----	----	----	0	
Off SW coast						*? 1964*	*0218*	....	....	----	?---	----	----	----	*0*	
Graciosa (Azores)	**39.02 N**	**27.97 W**	**402**	4445	**BAT**	**Stratovolcano**		**1802-04=**	**Holocene**							
Terceira (Azores)	**38.73 N**	**27.32 W**	**1023**	4555	**BTXyr**	**Stratovolcanoes**		**1802-05=**	**Historical**							
Guilherme Moniz (Pico das Pardelas)						C-**6720**t	....	....	....	x---	----	xx--	----	----		
Fissure zone (east of Santa Barbara)						C-**2530**s	....	....	....	---x	----	x---	x---	----		
Santa Barbara NW flank (Lagoinha dome)						C-**0940**t	....	....	....	-x--	----	xx--	--x-	----		
Guilherme Moniz (Biscoito Rachado deposit)						C-**0670**y	....	....	....	x---	----	xx--	----	----		
Fissure zone (east of Santa Barbara)						C-**0090**v	....	....	....	---x	----	x---	----	----		
Fissure zone (south of Pico Alto)						C-**0060**?	....	....	....	---x	----	x---	x---	----		8/-
Fissure zone (east of Santa Barbara)						C **0070**s	....	....	....	---x	----	----	x---	----		
Guilherme Moniz (Pico Alto)						C **0190**s	....	....	....	x---	----	----	x---	----		
Santa Barbara						C **0820**s	....	....	....	?---	----	x---	----	----		
Guilherme Moniz (Quinta da Madalena)						C **0920**t	....	....	....	x---	----	x---	----	----		
Guilherme Moniz (Pico Alto)						T **1200**y	....	....	....	x---	----	----	--x-	----		
Farol I dome (Santa Barbara)						T **1400**t	....	....	....	-x--	----	----	--x-	----		
Fissure zone (east of Santa Barbara)						**1761**	0417	**1761**	0428?	---x	----	x---	x---	-x--	2	
Submarine vent 3-6 WNW of Terceira						**1867**	0601	**1867**	0608	---x	x---	x---	----	----	3	
Serreta Ridge (submarine vent W of Terceira)						**1998**	1125?	**2000**	03 ?	---x	x---	----	x---	----	0	
Don Joao de Castro Bank (Azores)	**38.23 N**	**26.63 W**	**-13**	0006	**B**	**Submarine volc**		**1802-07=**	**Historical**							
						1720	1208?	**1720**	1226e	x---	xx--	x---	----	----	3	
NW of Don Joao de Castro Bank						*? 1997*	*0627*	*?1997*	*07 ?*	-x--	?---	----	----	----	*0*	
Sete Cidades (Azores)	**37.87 N**	**25.78 W**	**856**	4566	**TXBY**	**Stratovolcano**		**1802-08=**	**Historical**							
Seara Cerrado da Ladeira						T-**3050**?	....	....	....	x---	---x	x---	----	----	4	-/8
Caldeira do Alfreres and NW flank						T-**2050***	....	....	....	xx--	xx--	x---	----	----		
SE flank (Eguas)						C-**0750**y	....	....	....	-x--	----	x---	x---	----		
SE caldera floor (Lagoa de Santiago)						C **0090**v	....	....	....	x---	----	xx--	----	----	4	-/8
SE caldera floor (Lagoa Rasa)						T **0380**y	....	....	....	x---	----	x---	----	--x-	4	-/8
SE flank (Carvao)						C **0670**w	....	....	....	-xx-	----	x---	x---	----	3	7/7
SE flank (Ferraria)						C **0950**v	....	....	....	-x--	----	x---	x---	----	2	7/6
West flank (Ponta de Ferraria)						C **1110**t	....	....	....	-x--	----	x---	x---	----	2	7/6
SW side of caldera (Caldeira Seca)						**1444**?	....	....	....	x---	---x	x---	?---	--x-	4	-/8
Submarine vent west of Sete Cidades						**1638**	0703	**1638**	0728	---x	xx--	x---	----	----	2	
Submarine vent west of Sete Cidades						**1682**	1213	....	....	---x	x---	x---	----	----	2	
West flank (Pico das Camarinhas)						**1713**	....	....	....	-x--	?---	x---	x---	----	2	7/6
Submarine vent west of Sete Cidades						**1811**	0201	**1811**	0208	---x	x---	x---	----	----	2?	
Submarine vent west of Sete Cidades						**1811**	0614	**1811**	0622	---x	xx--	x---	----	----	3	
Submarine vent off Sao Miguel						@ **1861**	....	....	....	----	x---	----	----	----	0	
Submarine vent off Sao Miguel						@ **1880**	....	....	....	----	x---	----	----	----	0	
Picos Volc System (Azores)	**37.78 N***	**25.67 W**	**350**	6666	**Xt**	**Pyroclastic cones**		**1802-081**	**Historical**							
						C-**4040**?	....	....	....	----	----	----	x---	----		
North-central part (Aflitos)						C-**0850**v	....	....	....	----	----	x---	x---	----		
North-central part (Furna)						C-**0510**x	....	....	....	----	----	x---	x---	----		
East-central part (Caldeirao)						C **0600**v	....	....	....	----	----	x---	x---	----		
East-central part (Cruz)						C **0850**w	....	....	....	----	----	xx--	x---	----		
Eastern part (Mata des Feiticeiras)						C **0940**v	....	....	....	----	----	x---	x---	----		
Eastern part (SW of Fogo 1 cone)						**1652**	1019	**1652**	1026	x---	----	x---	x---	----	2	6/6

VOLCANO NAME (Subregion) / ERUPTION — Area of Activity	LAT	LONG	ELEV (m)	POPL (5 km, 10, 30, 100)	ROCK TYPE	VOLC TYPE / Start Year	Start M-Dy	NUMBER / Stop Year	Stop M-Dy	STATUS	Central, Flank vent, Radial fiss, Regional	Submarine, New island, Subglacial, Crater lake	Explosive, Pyro flow, Phreatic, Caldera	Lava flow, Lava lake, Dome, Spine	Fatal, Damage, Mudflow, Tsunami	VEI	Vol L/T
Agua de Pau (Azores)	**37.77** N	**25.47** W	**947**	3566	**TXBY**	**Stratovolcano**		**1802-09=**		**Historical**							
West flank (Pico Joao Fernandes)						C-**6750**x	....	....	....		-x--	----	x---	x---	----		
SW flank (449 m)						C-**4550**v	....	....	....		-x--	----	x---	x---	----		
Lagoa do Fogo caldera and north flank						C-**2990**?	....	....	....		xx--	----	xx--	x---	--x-	**5**	-/9
East flank (East Congo maar)						C-**2210**w	....	....	....		-x--	----	xx--	----	----		
East flank (Lagoa do Congro)						C-**1850**z	....	....	....		-x--	----	xx--	--x-	----	3	6/7
Lagoa do Fogo caldera						C-**1290**?	....	....	....		x---	----	x---	----	----	4	-/8
NW flank (251 m)						C **0160**w	....	....	....		-x--	----	x---	x---	----		
WNW flank (Mos)						C **0700**w	....	....	....		-x--	----	x---	x---	----		
Caldera, NW flank (Cerro Queimado)						**1563**	0628	**1563**	0726e		xxx-	---x	x---	x---	-x--	**5?**	6/9
Lagoa do Fogo caldera						**1564**	0210	**1564**	0212		x---	----	x-?-	?---	----	2	
Furnas (Azores)	**37.77** N	**25.32** W	**805**	4456	**TBXY**	**Stratovolcano**		**1802-10=**		**Historical**							
East rim of caldera (Pico do Canário)						C-**4570**<	....	....	....		x---	----	xx--	----	----		
(tephra layer A)						T-**1670***	....	....	....		x---	----	x---	----	----		
(tephra layer B)						C-**0360**w	....	....	....		x---	----	x---	----	----		
N floor of younger caldera (tephra layer C)						C **0080**v	....	....	....		x---	----	xx--	----	--x-	**5**	-/9
Center of caldera (Gaspar; tephra F)						C **0840**v	....	....	....		x---	----	xx--	--x-	----	4	7/8
E caldera floor (Lake crater; tephra G)						C **1170**v	....	....	....		x---	----	x---	----	----	4	-/8
East caldera floor (tephra layer H)						C **1430**v	....	....	....		x---	----	x---	----	----	3	-/7
Center of caldera (Gaspar; tephra layer I)						**1441**b	....	....	....		x---	----	xx--	--x-	----	4	-/8
South end of caldera (Pico da Areia)						**1630**	0903	**1630**	1102		x---	----	xx--	--x-	xx--	**5**	7/9
Monaco Bank (Azores)	**37.60** N	**25.88** W	**-197**	0056	**U**	**Submarine volc**		**1802-11=**		**Historical**							
						1907	0401	....	....		---?	x---	----	----	----	0	
						1911	0307	....	....		---?	x---	--?-	----	----	1	
Madeira (Madeira)	**32.73** N	**16.97** W	**1862**	6666	**BXYta**	**Shield volcano**		**1802-12-**		**Radiocarbon**							
Paul da Serra						G-**4500**t	....	....	....		x---	----	x---	----	----		

CANARY ISLANDS

VOLCANO NAME (Subregion) / ERUPTION — Area of Activity	LAT	LONG	ELEV (m)	POPL (5 km, 10, 30, 100)	ROCK TYPE	VOLC TYPE / Start Year	Start M-Dy	NUMBER / Stop Year	Stop M-Dy	STATUS	Central, Flank vent, Radial fiss, Regional	Submarine, New island, Subglacial, Crater lake	Explosive, Pyro flow, Phreatic, Caldera	Lava flow, Lava lake, Dome, Spine	Fatal, Damage, Mudflow, Tsunami	VEI	Vol L/T
La Palma (Canary Is)	**28.57** N	**17.83** W	**2426**	3555	**XZPBT**	**Stratovolcanoes**		**1803-01-**		**Historical**							
						K-**6050***	....	....	....		---x	----	x---	x---	----		
						C-**4900**t	....	....	....		---x	----	?---	----	----		
L'Amendrita, Birigoyo						K-**4050***	....	....	....		---x	----	x---	x---	----		
La Fajana (Volcán Fuego)						C-**1320**v	....	....	....		---x	----	----	x---	----		
El Fraile						C-**0360**t	....	....	....		---x	----	x---	----	----		
Nambroque II-Malforada						C **0900**v	....	....	....		---x	----	x---	x---	----		
Tacande (Montaña Quemada)						**1480**j	....	....	....		-x-x	----	x---	----	-x--	2	7/6
Tahuya						**1585**	0519	**1585**	0810		-xxx	----	x---	x---	-x--	2	
South flank of San Martín (Tigalate)						**1646**	1002	**1646**	1221		-x-x	----	x---	x---	-x--	2	7/6
N & S flanks of San Antonio (Fuentecaliente)						**1677**	1117	**1678**	0121		-x-x	----	x---	x---	xx--	2	7/6
El Charco						**1712**	1009	**1712**	1203		--xx	----	x---	x---	-x--	2	7/-
San Juan, Llano del Banco, Hoyo Negro						**1949**	0624	**1949**	0730		-xxx	----	xx--	x---	-x--	2?	7/5
Teneguia						**1971**	1026	**1971**	1118		-xxx	----	x---	x-x-	xx--	2	7/-
Hierro (Canary Is)	**27.73** N	**18.03** W	**1500**	5555	**XBYtf**	**Shield volcano**		**1803-02-**		**Radiocarbon**							
						C-**4790**?	....	....	....		----	----	----	----	----		
East flank (Soliman)						C-**0950**w	....	....	....		-x--	----	x---	x---	----		
Montañas Chamuscada-Entremontañas						C-**0550**u	....	....	....		x---	----	----	x---	----		
						? 1677	....	....	....		----	----	----	----	----		
						? 1692	....	....	....		----	----	----	----	----		
NW rift (Volcán de Lomo Negro)?						*? 1793*	*05*	*?1793*	*06*		-xx-	----	----	?---	----	*0?*	
Tenerife (Canary Is)	**28.271** N	**16.641** W	**3715**	0366	**PXZTY**	**Stratovolcano**		**1803-03-**		**Historical**							
NW rift zone (Montañas Negras)						T-**7550**?	....	....	....		--x-	----	x---	x---	----		7/-
NE flank (Montaña Negra-Los Tomillos)						G-**7260**x	....	....	....		-x--	----	----	x-x-	----		
NW rift zone (Montaña de Abeque)						T-**6850**?	....	....	....		--x-	----	x---	x---	----		
Teide NNE flank (Montaña del Abrunco)						T-**6550**?	....	....	....		-x--	----	x---	x---	----		
NW rift zone (Montaña Liferfe)						G-**6200**u	....	....	....		--x-	----	----	x---	----		7/-
Teide NE flank (Montañas de los Conejos)						T-**5750**?	....	....	....		-x--	----	x---	x---	----		8/-
Teide N flank (Pico Cabras)						T-**5550***	....	....	....		--x-	----	x---	x---	----		
Teide E flank (Montaña de los Corrales)						T-**5250**?	....	....	....		-x--	----	x---	x---	----		7/-
Teide NE flank (Montañas de los Corrales)						T-**4650**?	....	....	....		--x-	----	x---	x---	----		
NW rift zone (Montaña Cueve de Ratón)						G-**4200**v	....	....	....		--x-	----	----	x---	----		7/-
Teide NE flank (upper Montaña Abejera)						G-**3960**y	....	....	....		-x--	----	----	x-x-	----		8/-
NW rift zone (Montaña del Estrucho)						T-**3750**?	....	....	....		--x-	----	x---	x---	----		
Teide NE flank (lower Montaña Abejera)						G-**3540**w	....	....	....		-x--	----	----	x-x-	----		8/-
NW rift zone (Montaña Cruz)						T-**3450**?	....	....	....		--x-	----	x---	x---	----		7/-
NW rift zone (Montaña Bilma)						T-**3050**?	....	....	....		--x-	----	x---	x---	----		7/-
Teide SE flank (Montaña de la Cruz)						T-**2850**?	....	....	....		-x--	----	x---	x---	----		8/-
NW rift zone (Las Montañetas Negras)						T-**2650**?	....	....	....		--x-	----	x---	x---	----		5/-
NW rift zone (Montaña Cruz de Tea)						T-**2300**?	....	....	....		--x-	----	x---	x---	----		
Teide SE flank (Montaña Majúa)						T-**2250**?	....	....	....		--x-	----	x---	x---	----		7/-
NW rift zone (Montaña de Chío)						G-**1980**x	....	....	....		--x-	----	----	x---	----		
NW rift zone (Montaña Botija)						T-**1700**?	....	....	....		--x-	----	x---	x---	----		7/-
Teide SW flank (La Mancha Ruana)						T-**1650**?	....	....	....		-x--	----	x---	x---	----		7/-
NW rift zone (Montaña Samara)						T-**1400**?	....	....	....		--x-	----	x---	x---	----		7/-
Teide SW flank (Los Gemelos)						T-**1150**?	....	....	....		-x--	----	----	x-x-	----		6/-
NW rift zone (Montaña de Cascajo)						T-**1050**?	....	....	....		--x-	----	x---	x---	----		8/-
NW rift zone (Volcán el Ciego)						G-**0670**x	....	....	....		--x-	----	x---	x---	----		7/-
NW flank of Teide (El Boquerón)						G-**0580**x	....	....	....		-x--	----	x---	----	----		7/-
Teide-Pico Viejo complex						C-**0520**?	....	....	....		----	----	----	x---	----		
Montaña Blanca, Pico Viejo						G-**0080**s	....	....	....		-xx-	----	x---	x-x-	----	4+	7/8
NW flank of Pico Viejo (Roques Blancos)						G **0030**w	....	....	....		-x--	----	x---	x---	----		**9**/-
Teide-Pico Viejo complex						C **0040**?	....	....	....		----	----	----	x---	----		
NW rift zone (Los Hornitos)						G **0090**u	....	....	....		--x-	----	----	x---	----		7/-
NW rift zone (Cuevas Negras)						T **0190**?	....	....	....		--x-	----	x---	x---	----		7/-
NW flank of Pico Viejo (Roques Blancos)						G **0240**w	....	....	....		-x--	----	----	x---	----		
NE rift zone (Volcán Negro)						T **0700**?	....	....	....		--x-	----	x---	x---	----		6/-
Pico de Tiede						G **0800**w	....	....	....		x---	----	----	x---	----	0	8/-
NW rift zone (Montaña Reventada)						G **1060**v	....	....	....		--x-	----	x---	x-x-	----		8/-
						? 1341	....	....	....		x---	----	----	----	----		
						*? 1396*c	....	....	....		x---	----	?---	x---	----		
Lower Orotava Valley						*? 1430*	....	....	....		-x--	----	x---	x---	----	*2*	
Pico del Teide						*? 1444*	....	....	....		x---	----	----	----	----		
NW rift zone (Montaña Boca Cangrejo)						**1492**	0824<	....	....		--x-	----	x---	x---	----		7/-

VOLCANO NAME (Subregion)	LAT	LONG	ELEV (m)	POPL 5 km 10 30 100	ROCK TYPE	ERUPTION — Area of Activity	VOLC TYPE	NUMBER / Start Year	Start M-Dy	STATUS / Stop Year	Stop M-Dy	Central Flank vent Radial fiss Regional	Submarine New island Subglacial Crater lake	Explosive Pyro flow Phreatic Caldera	Lava flow Lava lake Dome Spine	Fatal Damage Mudflow Tsunami	VEI	Vol L/T
Tenerife (Canary Is) *continued*						NW rift zone (Siete Fuentes, Fasnia, Güímar)		**1704**	1231	**1705**	0327	-xx-	----	x---	x---	-x--	2*	7/-
						NW rift zone (Garachico)		**1706**	0505	**1706**	0613	--x-	----	x---	x---	-x--	2	7/-
						SW flank of Pico Viejo (Chahorra)		**1798**	0609	**1798**	0914?	--x-	----	x---	x---	----	3	7/-
						NW rift zone (Chinyero)		**1909**	1118	**1909**	1127	--x-	----	x---	x---	-x--	2	7/-
Gran Canaria (Canary Is)	**28.00 N**	**15.58 W**	**1950**	4467	**XZPTB**		**Fissure vents**	**1803-04-**		**Radiocarbon**								
						Montañon Negro		C-**1125**t	....	....	....	x---	----	x---	----	----		
						Bandama		C-**0020**u	....	....	....	x---	----	x---	----	----		
Fuerteventura (Canary Is)	**28.358 N**	**14.02 W**	**529**	4456	**BXFY**		**Fissure vents**	**1803-05-**		**Holocene**								
Lanzarote (Canary Is)	**29.03 N**	**13.63 W**	**670**	5566	**BXYt**		**Fissure vents**	**1803-06-**		**Historical**								
						Montaña de Juan Perdomo		M **0500**t	....	....	....	-x-x	----	x---	x---	----		
						Mazo, Santa Catalina, Corazoncillo		M **0700**t	....	....	....	-x-x	----	x---	x---	----		
						Montañas del Fuego		**1730**	0901	**1736**	0416	-x-x	x---	x---	x---	?x--	3	**9/-**
						Tao, Nuevo del Fuego, Tinguatón		**1824**	0731	**1824**	1024	---x	----	x---	x---	----	2*	7/-

CAPE VERDE ISLANDS

VOLCANO NAME (Subregion)	LAT	LONG	ELEV (m)	POPL	ROCK TYPE	ERUPTION — Area of Activity	VOLC TYPE	NUMBER / Start Year	Start M-Dy	STATUS / Stop Year	Stop M-Dy	Central Flank vent Radial fiss Regional	Submarine New island Subglacial Crater lake	Explosive Pyro flow Phreatic Caldera	Lava flow Lava lake Dome Spine	Fatal Damage Mudflow Tsunami	VEI	Vol L/T
Fogo (Cape Verde Is)	**14.95 N**	**24.35 W**	**2829**	3556	**FXP**		**Stratovolcano**	**1804-01=**		**Historical**								
						Pico		**1500**	....	**1761**?	....	xx--	----	x---	x---	----	1	
						SW side		**1769**	04 >	....	....	-x--	----	x---	----	----		
						North caldera floor		**1785**	0124	**1785**	0225	?x--	----	--x-	x---	-x--	2	6/-
						North caldera floor		**1799**	0602	**1799**	0628	-x--	----	x---	x---	-x--	2	
								1816	1231y	....	....	----	----	----	----	----		
						North caldera floor		**1847**	0409	**1847**	0502?	-x--	----	x---	x---	xx--	2	
						NNW caldera floor		**1852**	0219	**1852**	0330?	-x--	----	x---	x---	----	2	
						SSE caldera floor		**1857**	0627	**1857**	1215	-x--	----	?---	x---	-x--	2	
								1909	....	....	....	----	----	----	----	----		
						Northwest and south caldera floor		**1951**	0612	**1951**	0821	-x--	----	x---	x---	-x--	2	7/-
						WSW flank of Pico		**1995**	0402	**1995**	0526	x-x-	----	x---	x---	-x--	2	6/-
Brava (Cape Verde Is)	**14.85 N**	**24.72 W**	**900**	4455	**FXP**		**Stratovolcano**	**1804-02-**		**Holocene**								
Sao Vicente (Cape Verde Is)	**16.85 N**	**24.97 W**	**725**	5556	**BFPXT**		**Stratovolcano**	**1804-03-**		**Holocene**								

ATLANTIC OCEAN - C & S

VOLCANO NAME (Subregion)	LAT	LONG	ELEV (m)	POPL	ROCK TYPE	ERUPTION — Area of Activity	VOLC TYPE	NUMBER / Start Year	Start M-Dy	STATUS / Stop Year	Stop M-Dy	Central Flank vent Radial fiss Regional	Submarine New island Subglacial Crater lake	Explosive Pyro flow Phreatic Caldera	Lava flow Lava lake Dome Spine	Fatal Damage Mudflow Tsunami	VEI	Vol L/T
Unnamed (Atlantic-C)	**7.00 N**	**21.83 W**	**-1415**	0000	**U**		**Submarine volc ?**	**1805-01=**		Uncertain								
								? 1824	*0501*	....	....	----	?---	----	----	----	*0*	
Unnamed (Atlantic-C)	**4.20 N**	**21.45 W**	**-2900**	0000	**U**		**Submarine volc**	**1805-02=**		Uncertain								
								? 1878	*0129*	....	....	----	?---	----	----	----	*0*	
Unnamed (Atlantic-C)	**0.72 S**	**20.53 W**	**-1528**	0000	**U**		**Submarine volc**	**1805-03=**		Uncertain								
						0.38 S, 19.17 W		*? 1761*	*0503*	....	....	----	?---	----	----	----	*0*	
						0.53 S 17.77 W		*? 1816*	*1208*	....	....	----	?---	----	----	----	*0*	
						0.58 S 15.83 W		*? 1836*	*11 <*	....	....	----	?---	----	----	----	*0*	
Unnamed (Atlantic-C)	**3.50 S**	**24.50 W**	**-5300**	0000	**U**		**Submarine volc**	**1805-04=**		Uncertain								
								? 1852	*0717*	....	....	----	x---	----	----	----	*0*	
Ascensión (Atlantic-C)	**7.95 S**	**14.37 W**	**858**	3444	**BXYTR**		**Stratovolcano**	**1805-05-**		**Holocene**								
Trindade (Atlantic-C)	**20.514 S**	**29.331 W**	**600**	0000	**FPXZT**		**Stratovolcano**	**1805-051**		**Holocene**								
Tristan da Cunha (Atlantic-S)	**37.092 S**	**12.28 W**	**2060**	2222	**XBYTp**		**Shield volcano**	**1806-01=**		**Historical**								
						South flank		T **1700**t	....	....	....	-x--	----	x---	--x-	----		
						North flank		**1961**	1010	**1962**	0315	-x--	----	x---	x-x-	-x--	2	
Nightingale Island (Atlantic-S)	**37.42 S**	**12.48 W**	**365**	0023	**TYXP**		**Stratovolcano**	**1806-011**		**Historical**								
						Submarine SE flank		**2004**	0729	**2004**	0730	-x--	x---	x---	----	----	0	
Bouvet (Atlantic-S)	**54.42 S**	**3.35 E**	**780**	0000	**BTRYx**		**Shield volcano**	**1806-02-**		**Magnetism**								
								M-**0050**?	....	....	....	----	----	----	x---	----		
						(landslide deposit, not eruption)		*X 1956*	*0715*z	....	....	----	----	----	----	----		
Thompson Island (Atlantic-S)	**53.93 S**	**5.50 E**		0000	**U**		**Submarine volc ?**	**1806-03-**		Uncertain								
								? 1895	*1231*y	....	....	----	----	?---	----	----		

Dick Moore (USGS)

An eruption plume rises from a vent on the flank of the central cone of Fogo volcano in the Cape Verde Islands in April 1995. The central cone was constructed with the large, 9-km-wide Cha caldera.

Antarctica & S Sandwich Islands (19)

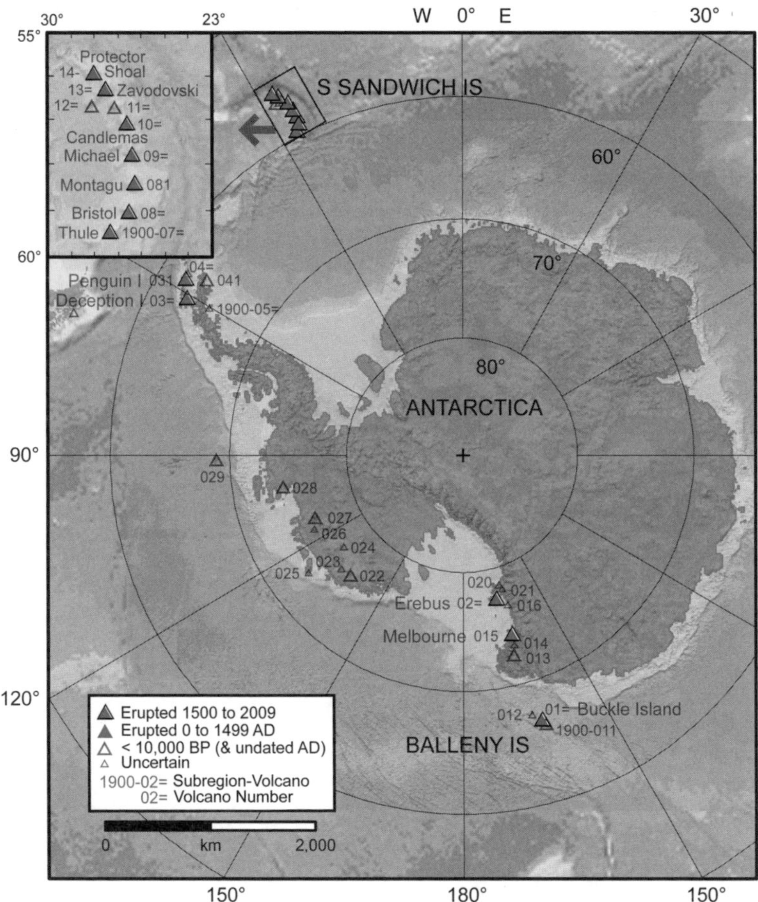

Antarctica, Earth's southernmost continent, is the largest *CAVW* region in land area and–with no permanent residents–easily the smallest in population. This region also includes the South Sandwich Islands and other island groups adjacent to Antarctica. It is the only region unblemished by a single fatal eruption; more a reflection on its low resident population than on its hazard mitigation efforts.

Although the continent of Antarctica was not discovered until 1840 (by the Wilkes expedition, 12 hours before the French), several nearby island groups now part of region 19 were recognized earlier. The northernmost of these, the South Sandwich Islands or Scotia Arc, was discovered on Captain Cook's 1772-75 voyages, and one of the group–Zavodovsky Island–was issuing a black ash cloud from its summit when discovered by Bellinghausen in 1819. Several other eruptions were reported from these islands in the following years, when fur sealing was at its peak in the region. Sometime between 1825 and 1828, sealers documented an eruption at Deception Island, a natural harbor formed by caldera collapse. And in 1839 an eruption was in progress in the Balleny Islands when they were first discovered by whalers. Two years later, Mount Erebus was erupting when this, the most active volcano in the region, was first sighted.

There followed nearly 60 years of little exploration, although whaling ships continued to work the region through the 19th century. Exploration resumed with a vengeance in 1895, with the next two decades known as the "heroic age" in Antarctica. Additional exploration between the World Wars, during the 1957-58 International Geophysical Year, and since the signing of the Antarctic Treaty in 1961 has contributed greatly to understanding this vast region, but it is clear that its historical record of volcanism is both short and very incomplete.

The Antarctic plate, largely aseismic and immobile, is broken internally by large rift structures which have produced one of the world's largest alkalic volcanic provinces. The 3200-km-long West Antarctic rift system is comparable in size to the better-known East African rift. Volcanic constructs range from large basaltic shields to small monogenetic vents; the presence of the continental icesheet has resulted in a larger volume of hyaloclastite rocks than perhaps any other subaerial volcanic region. The only subduction-related volcanoes within or adjacent to the Antarctic plate form the South Sandwich and South Shetland Islands.

Despite its large size, Antarctica ranks below all other regions in number of dated eruptions, and only the Pacific and Atlantic Ocean regions have fewer historically active volcanoes. The region has produced no known large Holocene eruptions (VEI ≥4 or lava ≥1 km^3) with the possible exception of a 0.19-0.31 km^3 subglacial tephra deposit from the Hudson Mountains estimated to have been erupted about 200 BC from ice thickness data. Antarctica contains one of the few volcanoes with long-term lava lake activity, which has attracted researchers to this 3794-m-high volcano overlooking the McMurdo Antarctic research station. Antarctica's historical record is brief, and nearly half of its known eruptions are from this century. Precise dating of past eruptions is difficult–much of the landscape is ice-covered, travel is daunting, and the wood needed for radiocarbon dating does not grow in this extreme climate–and the region has the highest proportion of volcanoes with uncertain status. Satellite imagery, however, has helped document recent activity that would otherwise go unnoticed. MODIS thermal alerts from NASA's first Earth Observing System (EOS) satellite 'Terra' have detected 21st century explosive and effusive eruptions on the glacier-covered surface of Montagu Island in the South Sandwich Islands. Antarctic ice sheets have proved a valuable resource for detailed dating of ice cores that contain ash and aerosol layers from both Antarctic and distant tropical and sub-tropical volcanoes and provide critical information regarding the impact of volcanism on global climate patterns during the Holocene.

VOLCANO NAME (Subregion) / ERUPTION — Area of Activity	LAT		LONG		ELEV (m)	POPL (5 km, 10, 30, 100)	ROCK TYPE	VOLC TYPE / —Start— Year	M-Dy	NUMBER / —Stop— Year	STATUS / M-Dy	ERUPTIVE CHARACTERISTICS: Central, Flank vent, Radial fiss, Regional	Submarine, New island, Subglacial, Crater lake	Explosive, Pyro flow, Phreatic, Caldera	Lava flow, Lava lake, Dome, Spine	Fatal, Damage, Mudflow, Tsunami	VEI	Vol L/T
ANTARCTICA																		
Buckle Island (Balleny Is)	**66.78**	**S**	**163.25**	**E**	**1239**	0000	X	**Stratovolcano**		**1900-01=**	**Historical**							
								1839	0209	....	....	x---	----	x---	----	----	2	
								1899	0112	....	....	----	----	x---	----	----	2	
Young Island (Balleny Is)	**66.42**	**S**	**162.47**	**E**	**1340**	0000	X	**Stratovolcano**		**1900-011**	**Fumarolic**							
Sturge Island (Balleny Is)	**67.40**	**S**	**164.83**	**E**	**1167**	0000	X	**Stratovolcano**		**1900-012**	Uncertain							
Pleiades, The (Antarctica)	**72.67**	**S**	**165.50**	**E**	**3040**	0000	YTZxp	**Stratovolcano**		**1900-013**	**Potassium-Argon**							
NE of Mount Pleiones (Taygete Cone)								K-**1050***	....	....	....	x---	----	----	--x-	----		
Unnamed (Antarctica)	**73.45**	**S***	**164.58**	**E**	**2987**	0000	X	**Scoria cones**		**1900-014**	Holocene?							
Melbourne (Antarctica)	**74.35**	**S**	**164.70**	**E**	**2732**	0000	TYBX	**Stratovolcano**		**1900-015**	**Tephrochronology**							
								T **1750**v	....	....	....	x---	----	x---	----	----		
Unnamed (Antarctica)	**76.83**	**S**	**163.00**	**E**	**-500**	0000	U	**Submarine volc**		**1900-016**	Holocene?							

VOLCANO NAME (Subregion) / ERUPTION — Area of Activity	LAT	LONG	ELEV (m)	POPL (5 km, 10, 30, 100)	ROCK TYPE	VOLC TYPE / Start Year	Start M-Dy	NUMBER / Stop Year	Stop M-Dy	STATUS	Central, Flank vent, Radial fiss, Regional	Submarine, New island, Subglacial, Crater lake	Explosive, Pyro flow, Phreatic, Caldera	Lava flow, Lava lake, Dome, Spine	Fatal, Damage, Mudflow, Tsunami	VEI	Vol L/T
Erebus (Antarctica)	77.53 S	167.17 E	3794	0000	PZXty	Stratovolcano		1900-02=		Historical							
NNW flank (Nausea Knob lava flow)						R-8050*	....	....	....		-x--	----	----	x---	----	0	
NW flank (Tramway lava flow)						R-7050*	....	....	....		-x--	----	----	x---	----	0	
NE flank						E-4550z	....	....	....		-x--	----	----	x---	----	0	
(Lower Ice Tower Ridge, S lava flows)						E-4050z	....	....	....		-x--	----	----	x---	----	0	
North flank (Lower Hut lava flow)						E-2950y	....	....	....		-x--	----	----	x---	----	0	
Western Crater (Upper Ice Tower flow)						R-2050*	....	....	....		-x--	----	----	x---	----	0	
(Northwest lava flow)						R 0950*	....	....	....		----	----	----	x---	----	0	
						1841	0128?	1841	02		x---	----	x---	?---	----	1	
						? *1900*	*02*	....	....		x---	----	?---	----	----	*2*	
						1903	0101*	....	....		x---	----	----	-?--	----	0	
						1908	03	1908	11		x---	----	x---	-?--	----	2	
						1911	04	1911	06		x---	----	x---	----	----	2	
						1911	10	....	....		x---	----	x---	----	----	2	
						1912	1212	....	....		x---	----	x---	----	----	2	
						1915	0322	....	....		x---	----	?---	-?--	----	2	
						1915	08	....	....		x---	----	x---	----	----	2	
						1947	02	....	....		x---	----	x---	?---	----	2	
						1955	....	....	....		x---	----	x---	----	----	2	
						? *1957*	....	?*1958*	....		x---	----	----	----	----		
						1963	11 <	....	....		x---	----	----	-x--	----	0	
						1972	0103?	....	....		x---	----	x---	----	----	1	
						1972	12 <	2010>	....		x---	----	x---	xx--	----	2*	
Morning, Mt. (Antarctica)	78.50 S	163.53 E	2723	0000	PXBYt	Shield volcano		1900-020		Holocene							
Royal Society Range (Antarctica)	78.25 S*	163.33 E	3000	0000	Yz	Cinder cones		1900-021		Holocene?							
Berlin (Antarctica)	76.05 S	136.00 W	3478	0000	TPYX	Shield volcanoes		1900-022		Ar/Ar							
						R-8350*	....	....	....		x---	----	----	x---	----	0	
Andrus (Antarctica)	75.80 S	132.33 W	2978	0000	TRY	Shield volcanoes		1900-023		Holocene?							
Waesche (Antarctica)	77.17 S	126.88 W	3292	0000	XYR	Shield volcanoes		1900-024		Holocene?							
Siple (Antarctica)	73.43 S	126.67 W	3110	0000	B	Shield volcano		1900-025		Holocene?							
Toney Mountain (Antarctica)	75.80 S	115.83 W	3595	0000	Xytr	Shield volcano		1900-026		Holocene?							
Takahe (Antarctica)	76.28 S	112.08 W	3460	0000	TX	Shield volcano		1900-027		Ice Core							
						I -7050?	....	....	....		----	----	x---	----	----		
						R-6250*	....	....	....		x---	----	x---	----	----		
						I -5550?	....	....	....		----	----	x---	----	----		
Hudson Mountains (Antarctica)	74.33 S*	99.42 W	749	0000	BX	Stratovolcanoes		1900-028		Ice Core							
Hudson Mts Subglacial Volcano						I -0210x	....	....	....		----	--x-	x---	----	----	4?	-/8
Webber Nunatak						? *1985*	....	....	....		x---	----	?---	----	----		
Peter I Island (Antarctica)	68.85 S	90.58 W	1640	0000	Bayt	Shield volcano		1900-029		Holocene							
Deception Island (Antarctica)	62.97 S	60.65 W	576	0000	BXYTd	Caldera		1900-03=		Historical							
						C-6750?	....	....	....		----	----	x---	----	----		
						C-3250?	....	....	....		----	----	x---	----	----		
(tephra layer AP-14)						C-2750?	....	....	....		----	----	x---	----	----		
(tephra layer AP-13)						C-1550?	....	....	....		----	----	x---	----	----		
(tephra layer AP-12)						C-0800?	....	....	....		----	----	x---	----	----		
(tephra layer AP-11)						C-0750?	....	....	....		----	----	x---	----	----		
(tephra layer AP-10)						C-0700?	....	....	....		----	----	x---	----	----		
(tephra layer AP-9)						C-0550?	....	....	....		----	----	x---	----	----		
(tephra layer AP-8)						C-0250?	....	....	....		----	----	x---	----	----		
(tephra layer AP-7)						C-0100?	....	....	....		----	----	x---	----	----		
(tephra layer AP-6)						C 0100?	....	....	....		----	----	x---	----	----		
(tephra layer AP-5)						C 0600?	....	....	....		----	----	x---	----	----		
(tephra layer AP-4)						C 0900?	....	....	....		----	----	x---	----	----		
(tephra layer AP-3)						C 1200?	....	....	....		----	----	x---	----	----		
(tephra layer AP-2)						C 1500?	....	....	....		----	----	x---	----	----		
(tephra layer AP-1)						I 1641c	....	....	....		----	----	x---	----	----		
N side caldera bay (near Telefon Bay)						1800<	....	....	....		x---	----	x---	----	----		
NE side caldera bay (Pendulum Cove)						1827b	....	....	....		x---	----	x---	----	----		
(vigorous steam emission only)						*X 1829*	....	....	....		----	----	----	----	----		
Crater Lake--Mt. Kirkwood area						*? 1839*<	....	....	....		----	----	?---	----	----		
S caldera rim (flanks of Mt Kirkwood)						1842	02	....	....		----	----	x---	x---	----	2	
SE side of caldera bay (Kroner Lake)						T 1871s	....	....	....		x---	----	x---	----	----		
(fumarolic activity only)						*X 1909*	....	....	....		----	----	----	----	----		
SW part of island						1912e	....	....	....		----	----	x---	----	----	3?	
(steam emission only)						*X 1927*	....	....	....		----	----	----	----	----		
North side (Telefon Bay, Yelcho I)						1967	1204	1967	1207		----	xx--	x-x-	----	-x?-	3	-/7
West side of Mount Pond						1969	0221	1969	03		----	--x-	x---	----	-xJ-	3	-/7
NE of Telefon Bay						1970	0812	....	....		----	x---	x-x-	----	--J-	3	
						? *1972*	*0929*	?*1972*	*0929*		----	----	----	----	----		
						? *1987*	*0723*	....	....		----	?---	?---	----	----		
Penguin Island (Antarctica)	62.10 S	57.93 W	180	0000	B	Stratovolcano		1900-031		Lichenometry							
Deacon Peak						L 1683?	....	....	....		x---	----	x---	----	----		
Deacon Peak						1850?	....	....	....		x---	----	----	x---	----		
NE flank (Petrel Crater)						L 1905?	....	....	....		-x--	----	x---	----	----		
Bridgeman Island (Antarctica)	62.05 S	56.75 W	240	0000	AB	Stratovolcano		1900-04=		Uncertain							
Paulet (Antarctica)	63.58 S	55.77 W	353	0000	BX	Cinder cone		1900-041		Holocene							
						? *1850*	....	....	....		----	----	----	----	----		
Seal Nunataks Group (Antarctica)	65.03 S*	60.05 W	368	0000	BX	Pyroclastic cones		1900-05=		Uncertain							
Lindenberg Island						? *1893*	*1211*	....	....		xx--	----	x---	----	----	*1*	
Dallman, Murdoch						? *1980*	*0615z*	....	....		x---	----	?---	?---	----		
Unnamed (Antarctica)	56.25 S	72.17 W	-4220					1900-051		Not a Volcano							

S SANDWICH ISLANDS

VOLCANO NAME (Subregion) / ERUPTION — Area of Activity	LAT	LONG	ELEV (m)	POPL	ROCK TYPE	VOLC TYPE / Start Year	Start M-Dy	NUMBER / Stop Year	Stop M-Dy	STATUS	Central, Flank vent, Radial fiss, Regional	Submarine, New island, Subglacial, Crater lake	Explosive, Pyro flow, Phreatic, Caldera	Lava flow, Lava lake, Dome, Spine	Fatal, Damage, Mudflow, Tsunami	VEI	Vol L/T
Thule Islands (S Sandwich Is)	59.45 S	27.37 W	1075	0000	ABD	Stratovolcanoes		1900-07=		Historical							
South flank of Bellinghausen Island						1975k	....	....	....		-x--	----	--x-	----	----	1?	
Bristol Island (S Sandwich Is)	59.03 S	26.58 W	1100	0000	BA	Stratovolcano		1900-08=		Historical							
						1823	....	....	....		----	----	?---	----	----	2	
						1935	1231	....	....		x---	----	x---	----	----	2	
						1936	1218	1937	0101?		x---	----	x---	x---	----	2	

VOLCANO NAME (Subregion) / ERUPTION — Area of Activity	LAT	LONG	ELEV (m)	POPL (5 km, 10, 30, 100)	ROCK TYPE	VOLC TYPE / Start Year	Start M-Dy	NUMBER / Stop Year	STATUS / Stop M-Dy	Central, Flank vent, Radial fiss, Regional	Submarine, New island, Subglacial, Crater lake	Explosive, Pyro flow, Phreatic, Caldera	Lava flow, Lava lake, Dome, Spine	Fatal, Damage, Mudflow, Tsunami	VEI	Vol L/T
Bristol Island (S Sandwich Is) *continued*						**1950**	0327	....	....	----	----	x---	----	----	2	
West flank						**1956**	0111	**1956**	0119?	-x--	----	x---	----	----	3	
Montagu Island (S Sandwich Is)	**58.42** S	**26.33** W	**1370**	0000	B	**Shield volcano**		**1900-081**	**Historical**							
						? 1996	*0901*w	....	....	x---	----	?---	----	----	*1?*	
NW of Mount Belinda						**2001**	1001n	**2007**	0920	x---	--x-	x---	xx--	----	1?	
Michael (S Sandwich Is)	**57.78** S	**26.45** W	**990**	0000	BA	**Stratovolcano**		**1900-09=**	**Historical**							
						1819	1229	....	....	x---	----	x---	----	----	2	
						? 1823	....	....	....	----	----	?---	----	----	*2?*	
North flank						T **1900**j	....	....	....	--x-	--x-	----	x---	----	0	
						1995	04 ?	**1996**	06	x---	----	----	-x--	----	0	
						1995	1005d	**1996**	04	x---	----	----	-x--	----	0	
						1996	10	....	....	x---	----	----	-x--	----	0	
						1997	05 ?	**1998**	02 >	x---	----	----	-x--	----	0	
						2000	08 ?	**2001**	01 ?	x---	----	----	-x--	----	0	
						2001	09 ?	**2001**	11 ?	x---	----	----	-x--	----	0	
						2002	07 ?	**2002**	11 ?	x---	----	----	-x--	----	0	
						2003	0506?	**2003**	0506?	x---	----	----	-x--	----	0	
						2005	1002?	**2006**	0120?	x---	----	----	-x--	----	0	
						2006	0609<	**2006**	1206?	x---	----	----	-x--	----	0	
Candlemas Island (S Sandwich Is)	**57.08** S	**26.67** W	**550**	0000	BAD	**Stratovolcano**		**1900-10=**	**Historical**							
S Sandwich Is (probably Candlemass)						I **-1250**?	....	....	....	----	----	x---	----	----		
NW flank (Lucifer Hill)						**1823**	....	....	....	-x--	----	?---	----	----	2	
NW flank (Lucifer Hill)						**1911**	1106	....	....	-x--	----	?---	----	----	2	
NW flank (Lucifer Hill)						*? 1953*	*1231*y	....	....	-x--	----	----	?---	----	*0*	
Hodson (S Sandwich Is)	**56.70** S	**27.15** W	**1005**	0000	BA	**Stratovolcano**		**1900-11=**	**Holocene**							
						? 1830	*0922*	....	....	----	----	?---	----	----		
						? 1930	....	....	....	x---	----	?---	----	----		
Leskov Island (S Sandwich Is)	**56.67** S	**28.13** W	**190**	0000	A	**Stratovolcano**		**1900-12=**	**Fumarolic**							
Zavodovski (S Sandwich Is)	**56.30** S	**27.57** W	**551**	0000	B	**Stratovolcano**		**1900-13=**	**Historical**							
						1819	12	....	....	x---	----	x---	----	----	2	
						? 1823	....	....	....	----	----	?---	----	----	*1*	
						? 1830	*09*	....	....	----	----	?---	----	----	*1*	
						? 1908	*11*	....	....	----	----	?---	----	----	*1*	
Protector Shoal (S Sandwich Is)	**55.92** S	**28.08** W	**-27**	0000	R	**Submarine volc**		**1900-14-**	**Historical**							
						1962	0305	....	....	----	x---	x---	----	----	0	-/8

Richard Waitt (USGS/CVO)

Mount Erebus, the world's southernmost historically active volcano, is viewed here from the SW, near the McMurdo research station on Ross Island. The 3794-m-high Erebus is capped by an elliptical 500 x 600 m wide, 110-m-deep summit crater that contains an active lava lake. The glacier-covered volcano was erupting when first sighted by Captain James Ross in 1841. Continuous lava-lake activity has been documented since 1972.

Chronology of Eruptions

Chronology of Eruptions: Context and Codes

This section arranges all 10,415 eruptions in a chronological sequence by **START** date **(YEAR M-Dy)**, displaying all volcanism known to have taken place in each year. For any given year, those eruptions known to be continuing from the previous year are listed first (sequenced by volcano number). These are followed by eruptions known only to have taken place sometime during the year (also sequenced by volcano number), and finally by eruptions starting in a known month or day. For non-historical eruptions, the dating method code is shown, and the date may be followed by a date uncertainty code (both discussed earlier on pages 19-24 and shown in the tables below). Attention must be paid, particularly with older dates, to the uncertainty code and to the uncorrected radiocarbon dates (p. 21-22); radiocarbon dates preceded by "C" may be as much as 900 years from the true calendar date during the early Holocene. An eruption listed simply as "seventeenth century" will be shown only *once* as "1650t" (1650 ± 50 years).

The **Duration** of an eruption, when known, is shown in days, but eruptions exceeding ~999 days are listed as "**>3yr**." **VOLCANO NUMBER** allows cross-reference to map or directory, for additional information, and both **VEI** and volume data (**Vol-L/T** as shown in the table below) indicate eruption size. When more than one **VEI** is assigned for an eruption, as for a paroxysmal explosion following the onset of the eruption, the two dates appear separately in chronologic sequence. Thus the catastrophic eruption of Tambora in Indonesia appears on April 5, 1815, but the eruption's start is also entered in 1812, and its continuing lower-level activity is noted for 1813 and 1814. The renowned 1980 eruption of Mount St. Helens is listed for its March 27 start, its May 18 paroxysmal eruption, and 5 subsequent events that produced ash cloud heights of 13 km or more.

CODE BEFORE DATE

A	=	Anthropology
C	=	Radiocarbon (uncorrected)
D	=	Dendrochronology (tree ring)
E	=	Surface Exposure
F	=	Fission Track
G	=	Radiocarbon (corrected)
H	=	Hydration Rind
I	=	Ice Core
K	=	Potassium-Argon (K-Ar)
L	=	Lichenometry
M	=	Magnetism
N	=	Thermoluminescence
R	=	Argon-Argon (Ar-Ar)
S	=	SOFAR (hydrophonic)
T	=	Tephrochronology
U	=	Uranium-Series
V	=	Varve Counts
-	=	BC date
?	=	Eruption uncertain
@	=	Eruption location uncertain
X	=	Discredited Eruption

VOLUME

L/T = volume of lava erupted (left column)
volume of tephra (right column)

7/- = 10^7 m^3 lava, no recorded tephra voume
-/**9** = 10^9 m^3 tephra, no recorded lava volume
7/8 = 10^7 m^3 lava, 10^8 m^3 tephra

CODE AFTER DATE (Uncertainty)

Code		±Years	±Days	Code		±Years	±Days	
a	=	1	1	o	=	18	25	
b	=	2	2	p	=	20	30	(1 mo)
c	=	3	3	q	=	25	45	
d	=	4	4	r	=	30	60	(2 mo)
e	=	5	5	s	=	40	75	
f	=	6	6	t	=	50	90	(3 mo)
g	=	7	7	u	=	75	120	
h	=	8	8	v	=	100	150	
i	=	9	9	w	=	150	180	(6 mo)
j	=	10	10	x	=	200	270	
k	=	12	12	y	=	300	365	(1 yr)
m	=	14	15	z	=	500	545	
n	=	16	20	*	=	1000	730	(2 yr)

> = eruption after date listed
< = eruption before date listed
? = date uncertain (no data)

EXAMPLES:

1731<	=	on or before 1731
1731a	=	between 1730 and 1732
1731 1105d	=	between Nov 1 & 9
1750t	=	18th century
1790j	=	late 18th century
1778 02?	=	February (?) 1778

START YEAR M-Dy	Duration	VOLCANO NAME (Subregion)	NUMBER	VEI	Vol L/T
V-9950w	?	**Nemrut Dagi** (Turkey)	0103-02=		
G-9850?	?	**Tongariro** (New Zealand)	0401-08=		
G-9850?	?	**Ruapehu** (New Zealand)	0401-10=		
T-9650?	?	**Tongariro** (New Zealand)	0401-08=	5	-/9
T-9650?	?	**Ruapehu** (New Zealand)	0401-10=		
G-9540z	?	**Nantai** (Honshu-Japan)	0803-141		
G-9520y	?	**Kuchinoerabu-jima** (Ryukyu Is)	0802-05=		
G-9500y	?	**Khangar** (Kamchatka)	1000-272	P	
T-9500?	?	**Theistareykjarbunga** (Iceland-NE)	1703-09=	0	10/-
G-9490?	?	**Towada** (Honshu-Japan)	0803-271	3	-/7
G-9460x	?	**Taupo** (New Zealand)	0401-07=	5	-/9
G-9450?	?	**Tongariro** (New Zealand)	0401-08=	5	-/9
G-9450w	?	**Tacaná** (México)	1401-13=		
T-9350?	?	**Tongariro** (New Zealand)	0401-08=	5	8/9
G-9280r	?	**Barú** (Panamá)	1406-01-		
G-9240u	?	**Taupo** (New Zealand)	0401-07=	5	-/9
G-9240z	?	**Lanín** (Chile-C)	1507-122		
T-9210*	?	**Taupo** (New Zealand)	0401-07=	4	7/8
G-9210*	?	**Newberry** (US-Oregon)	1202-11-		
G-9160*	?	**Kuju** (Kyushu-Japan)	0802-12=	4	8/8
T-9000?	?	**Brennisteinsfjöll** (Iceland-SW)	1701-04=	0	9/-
G-8910x	?	**Askja** (Iceland-NE)	1703-06=	5	-/9
T-8800y	?	**Akita-Komaga-take** (Honshu-Japan)	0803-23=	3?	-/8
G-8780w	?	**Merapi** (Java)	0603-25=		
G-8750?	?	**Ulreung** (Korea)	1006-03-	6	-/10
G-8740w	?	**West Eifel Volc Field** (Germany)	0100-01-		
G-8710y	?	**Zuni-Bandera** (US-New Mexico)	1210-02-		
G-8670y	?	**Mageik** (Alaska Peninsula)	1102-15-		
T-8600?	?	**Hveravellir** (Iceland-SW)	1701-08=	0	9/-
G-8560y	?	**Ubinas** (Perú)	1504-02=		
T-8550*	?	**Nasu** (Honshu-Japan)	0803-15=	2?	
C-8540>	?	**Fuji** (Honshu-Japan)	0803-03=		9/-
T-8500?	?	**Shiveluch** (Kamchatka)	1000-27=	3	-/7
T-8500?	?	**Krísuvík** (Iceland-SW)	1701-03=	0	9/-
T-8500?	?	**Krafla** (Iceland-NE)	1703-08=	0	9/-
G-8480v	?	**Campi Flegrei** (Italy)	0101-01=	4	
G-8460x	?	**Snaefellsjökull** (Iceland-W)	1700-01=		
T-8450?	?	**Oshima** (Izu Is-Japan)	0804-01=		
T-8450?	?	**Shiveluch** (Kamchatka)	1000-27=	3	-/7
C-8400y	?	**Shoshone Lava Field** (US-Idaho)	1204-01-	0	
T-8350?	?	**Shiveluch** (Kamchatka)	1000-27=	4	-/8
G-8350?	?	**Hengill** (Iceland-SW)	1701-05=	0	9/-
R-8350*	?	**Berlin** (Antarctica)	1900-022	0	
C-8300y	?	**West Eifel Volc Field** (Germany)	0100-01-		
T-8300y	?	**Akita-Komaga-take** (Honshu-Japan)	0803-23=	4	-/8
G-8250?	?	**Ngozi** (Africa-E)	0202-164	C	
G-8250?	?	**Towada** (Honshu-Japan)	0803-271	5	-/9
G-8250v	?	**Khangar** (Kamchatka)	1000-272		
E-8250*	?	**Negra, Sierra** (Galápagos)	1503-05=	0	
G-8250?	?	**Hengill** (Iceland-SW)	1701-05=	0	10/-
I-8232x	?	***Unknown Source*** *(GISP2, 148 ppb S)*	......		
G-8230t	?	**Grímsvötn** (Iceland-NE)	1703-01=	6	-/10
I-8230x	?	***Unknown Source*** *(GISP2, 150 ppb S)*	......		
G-8210x	?	**Pelée** (W Indies)	1600-12=	4?	-/8
T-8200?	?	**Shiveluch** (Kamchatka)	1000-27=	4	-/8
T-8200?	?	**Hengill** (Iceland-SW)	1701-05=	0	9/-
I-8169x	?	***Unknown Source*** *(GISP2, 142 ppb S)*	......		
I-8154x	?	***Unknown Source*** *(GISP2, 91 ppb sulfate)*	......		
G-8130x	?	**Taupo** (New Zealand)	0401-07=	5	-/9
I-8103x	?	***Unknown Source*** *(GISP2,109 ppb S)*	......		
T-8100?	?	**Shiveluch** (Kamchatka)	1000-27=	4	-/8
I-8098x	?	***Unknown Source*** *(GISP2, 94 ppb sulfate)*	......		
C-8060z	?	**Garibaldi** (Canada)	1200-20-	3?	9/7
T-8050?	?	**Süphan Dagi** (Turkey)	0103-021		
C-8050*	?	**Emuruangogolak** (Africa-E)	0202-051		
K-8050?	?	**Karisimbi** (Africa-C)	0203-04-		
T-8050?	?	**Okataina [Tarawera]** (New Zeal)	0401-05=		
C-8050?	?	**Inierie** (Lesser Sunda Is)	0604-08=		
T-8050*	?	**Aso** (Kyushu-Japan)	0802-11=	1	-/5
T-8050?	?	**Izu-Tobu** (Honshu-Japan)	0803-01=	3	6/7
T-8050?	?	**Adatara** (Honshu-Japan)	0803-17=	3	-/7
K-8050?	?	**Iwaki** (Honshu-Japan)	0803-27=		
T-8050z	?	**Oshima** (Izu Is-Japan)	0804-01=		
T-8050?	?	**Kozu-shima** (Izu Is-Japan)	0804-03=		
T-8050?	?	**Kuttara** (Hokkaido-Japan)	0805-034		7/-
T-8050?	?	**Vilyuchik** (Kamchatka)	1000-083	2?	
T-8050*	?	**Kostakan** (Kamchatka)	1000-122	3	-/7
C-8050?	?	**Krasheninnikov** (Kamchatka)	1000-19=		
T-8050?	?	**Kizimen** (Kamchatka)	1000-23=	5	-/9
G-8050?	?	**Rainier** (US-Washington)	1201-03-	3	-/7
T-8050?	?	**Shasta** (US-California)	1203-01-		
C-8050?	?	**Mauna Loa** (Hawaiian Is)	1302-02=	0	
T-8050?	?	**Chacana** (Ecuador)	1502-022		
T-8050?	?	**Vestmannaeyjar** (Iceland-S)	1702-01=	4	-/8
R-8050*	?	**Erebus** (Antarctica)	1900-02=	0	
G-8040v	?	**Palinuro** (Italy)	0101-031		
G-8040t	?	**Taveuni** (Fiji Is-SW Pacific)	0405-01-	2	

START YEAR M-Dy	Duration	VOLCANO NAME (Subregion)	NUMBER	VEI	Vol L/T
I-8031x	?	***Unknown Source*** *(GISP2, 109 ppb S)*	......		
I-8026x	?	***Unknown Source*** *(GISP2, 97 ppb sulfate)*	......		
C-8020t	?	**Tangkubanparahu** (Java)	0603-09=		
T-8020*	?	**Hachijo-jima** (Izu Is-Japan)	0804-05=	4	-/8
C-8010?	?	**Hudson, Cerro** (Chile-S)	1508-057		
T-8000?	?	**Reykjanes** (Iceland-SW)	1701-02=	0	9/-

-8000 (9950 BP)

START YEAR M-Dy	Duration	VOLCANO NAME (Subregion)	NUMBER	VEI	Vol L/T
T-7980z	?	**Campi Flegrei** (Italy)	0101-01=	3	-/7
I-7978x	?	***Unknown Source*** *(GISP2, 144 ppb S)*	......		
I-7953?	?	***Unknown Source*** *(Byrd Station 1968)*	......		
T-7950?	?	**Shiveluch** (Kamchatka)	1000-27=	4	-/8
G-7950x	?	**Haleakala** (Hawaiian Is)	1302-06-		
I-7943x	?	***Unknown Source*** *(GISP2, 199 ppb S)*	......		
C-7930z	?	**Chichinautzin [Pelado]** (México)	1401-08=	3	9/7
C-7920u	?	**Poás** (Costa Rica)	1405-04=		
G-7900w	?	**Hachimantai** (Honshu-Japan)	0803-25=		
G-7900?	?	**Ksudach** (Kamchatka)	1000-05=	5	-/9
C-7900u	?	**Taapaca** (Chile-N)	1505-011		
I-7870x	?	***Unknown Source*** *(GISP2, 111 ppb S)*	......		
G-7850?	?	**Nasu** (Honshu-Japan)	0803-15=	3	7/7
G-7850x	?	**Akita-Komaga-take** (Honshu-Japan)	0803-23=	4	-/8
T-7850?	?	**Shiveluch** (Kamchatka)	1000-27=	3	-/7
G-7850?	?	**Moffett** (Aleutian Is)	1101-111		
G-7850?	?	**Baker** (US-Washington)	1201-01=		8/-
C-7850?	?	**Mauna Loa** (Hawaiian Is)	1302-02=	0	
T-7850?	?	**Krafla** (Iceland-NE)	1703-08=		9/-
C-7840x	?	**Chaîne des Puys** (France)	0100-02-		
C-7840<	?	**Ruapehu** (New Zealand)	0401-10=	4	-/8
I-7837x	?	***Unknown Source*** *(GISP2, 120 ppb S)*	......		
C-7820x	?	**Fuji** (Honshu-Japan)	0803-03=		
C-7810?	?	**Acigöl-Nevsehir** (Turkey)	0103-004		
G-7800y	?	**Rainier** (US-Washington)	1201-03-		
C-7800y	?	**Tolima, Nevado del** (Colombia)	1501-03=	P	
V-7769?	?	**Nemrut Dagi** (Turkey)	0103-02=		
C-7750?	?	**Sakura-jima** (Kyushu-Japan)	0802-08=		
T-7750?	?	**Shiveluch** (Kamchatka)	1000-27=	3	
C-7750?	?	**Shasta** (US-California)	1203-01-		
C-7750?	?	**Tungurahua** (Ecuador)	1502-08=	4	-/8
C-7750x	?	**Huaynaputina** (Perú)	1504-03=		
C-7750?	?	**Antuco** (Chile-C)	1507-08=		
U-7750z	?	**Pelée** (W Indies)	1600-12=		
G-7750?	?	**Grímsnes** (Iceland-SW)	1701-06=	3	-/7
N-7740?	?	**Chaîne des Puys** (France)	0100-02-		
C-7740u	?	**Jocotitlán** (México)	1401-062		
I-7728?	?	***Unknown Source*** *(Byrd Station 1968)*	......		
T-7710x	?	**Barrier, The** (Africa-E)	0202-03=		
G-7700w	?	**Norikura** (Honshu-Japan)	0803-06=	3	-/7
T-7700?	?	**Shiveluch** (Kamchatka)	1000-27=	4	-/8
C-7690z	?	**Colima** (México)	1401-04=		
C-7690u	?	**Cotopaxi** (Ecuador)	1502-05=	2	-/6
I-7683x	?	***Unknown Source*** *(GISP2, 98 ppb sulfate)*	......		
C-7650?	?	**Taranaki [Egmont]** (New Zealand)	0401-03=		
T-7650?	?	**Oshima** (Izu Is-Japan)	0804-01=		
T-7650*	?	**Hachijo-jima** (Izu Is-Japan)	0804-05=		
C-7650v	?	**Shasta** (US-California)	1203-01-	4	-/8
T-7630?	?	**Shiveluch** (Kamchatka)	1000-27=	4	-/8
I-7629x	?	***Unknown Source*** *(GISP2, 114 ppb S)*	......		
I-7627x	?	***Unknown Source*** *(GISP2, 106 ppb S)*	......		
G-7620y	?	**Akutan** (Aleutian Is)	1101-32-		
C-7620v	?	**Poás** (Costa Rica)	1405-04=		
G-7600?	?	**Zao** (Honshu-Japan)	0803-19=		
G-7600	?	**Tolbachik** (Kamchatka)	1000-24=		
T-7600?	?	**Shiveluch** (Kamchatka)	1000-27=	4	-/8
T-7600z	?	**Roundtop** (Aleutian Is)	1101-38-	5?	
C-7590t	?	**Campi Flegrei** (Italy)	0101-01=		
C-7590v	?	**Ruapehu** (New Zealand)	0401-10=		
V-7579?	?	**Nemrut Dagi** (Turkey)	0103-02=		
C-7570u	?	**Haleakala** (Hawaiian Is)	1302-06-		
G-7560o	?	**Okataina [Haroharo]** (New Zeal)	0401-05=	5	9/9
K-7550*	?	**Ischia** (Italy)	0101-03=		
?-7550 t	?	*Hasan Dagi (Turkey)*	0103-002		
R-7550*	?	**Paka** (Africa-E)	0202-053	C	
G-7550t	?	**Haku-san** (Honshu-Japan)	0803-05=		
T-7550?	?	**Nemo Peak** (Kuril Is)	0900-32=		
T-7550z	?	**Kurile Lake** (Kamchatka)	1000-023		
T-7550?	?	**Mutnovsky** (Kamchatka)	1000-06=	2	-/6
T-7550z	?	**Bakening** (Kamchatka)	1000-123	2?	9/-
C-7550?	?	**Maly Semiachik** (Kamchatka)	1000-14=		
C-7550?	?	**Ushkovsky** (Kamchatka)	1000-261		
T-7550?	?	**Shiveluch** (Kamchatka)	1000-27=	3	-/7
T-7550z	?	**Elovsky** (Kamchatka)	1000-59-	4	9/8
C-7550?	?	**Shishaldin** (Aleutian Is)	1101-36-		
C-7550?	?	**Mauna Loa** (Hawaiian Is)	1302-02=	0	
T-7550?	?	**Hengill** (Iceland-SW)	1701-05=	0	8/-
C-7550z	?	**Prestahnukur** (Iceland-SW)	1701-07=	0	10/-

START YEAR M-Dy	Dura-tion	VOLCANO NAME (Subregion)	NUMBER	VEI	Vol L/T
T-7550?	?	**Vestmannaeyjar** (Iceland-S)	1702-01=	3?	
T-7550?	?	**Tenerife** (Canary Is).	1803-03-		7/-
C-7540x	?	**Hualalai** (Hawaiian Is).	1302-04-	0	
C-7530y	?	**Fuji** (Honshu-Japan)	0803-03=		
C-7530s	?	**Orizaba, Pico de** (México)	1401-10=		
T-7520*	?	**Villarrica** (Chile-C).	1507-12=	0	
C-7510w	?	**Pago** (New Britain-SW Pac)	0502-08=		
C-7500t	?	**Tangkubanparahu** (Java)	0603-09=		
T-7500?	?	**Shiveluch** (Kamchatka)	1000-27=	4+	-/8
T-7500*	?	**Chimborazo** (Ecuador)	1502-071		
G-7490w	?	**Soufrière Guadeloupe** (W Indies)	1600-06=		
C-7480t	?	**Lvinaya Past** (Kuril Is)	0900-041	6+	-/10
G-7460w	?	**Pinatubo** (Luzon-Philippines)	0703-083	6?	
T-7450?	?	**Yake-dake** (Honshu-Japan)	0803-07=	0	
T-7450?	?	**Bandai** (Honshu-Japan)	0803-16=		
C-7450t	?	**Ushishur** (Kuril Is)	0900-21=	C	
C-7450y	?	**Haleakala** (Hawaiian Is)	1302-06-		
G-7450z	?	**Burney, Monte** (Chile-S)	1508-07=	5	-/9
C-7430y	?	**Nejapa-Miraflores** (Nicaragua)	1404-092		
C-7420x	?	**Fisher** (Aleutian Is)	1101-35-	6?	-/10
C-7420y	?	**Shasta** (US-California).	1203-01-		
C-7420z	?	**Colima** (México).	1401-04=		
G-7420u	?	**Barú** (Panamá)	1406-01-		
C-7420u	?	**Chaitén** (Chile-S)	1508-041	C	
C-7410y	?	**Llaima** (Chile-C)	1507-11=		
T-7400w	?	**Gorely** (Kamchatka)	1000-07=	0	
G-7400w	?	**Shiveluch** (Kamchatka)	1000-27=	5	-/9
G-7400*	?	**Yellowstone** (US-Wyoming)	1205-01-		
T-7400y	?	**Krafla** (Iceland-NE)	1703-08=	0	
T-7390x	?	**Burney, Monte** (Chile-S)	1508-07=		
G-7380w	?	**Mageik** (Alaska Peninsula).	1102-15-		
G-7370y	?	**Chichinautzin [Tres Cruces]**	1401-08=	4	-/8
T-7350*	?	**Menengai** (Africa-E)	0202-06=		
T-7350*	?	**North Sister Field** (US-Oregon).	1202-07-	2?	
T-7350?	?	**Shasta** (US-California).	1203-01-	0	
C-7350?	?	**Mauna Loa** (Hawaiian Is)	1302-02=	0	
C-7350y	?	**Michoacán [El Huanillo]** (México).	1401-06=	3	-/7
T-7330?	?	**Taranaki [Egmont]** (New Zealand)	0401-03=		
G-7320*	?	**Pelée** (W Indies).	1600-12=		
G-7310y	?	**Merapi** (Java).	0603-25=		
C-7310z	?	**Fuji** (Honshu-Japan)	0803-03=		
T-7300*	?	**Tate-yama** (Honshu-Japan)	0803-08=		
T-7300?	?	**Shiveluch** (Kamchatka)	1000-27=	5	-/9
G-7300z	?	**Kanaga** (Aleutian Is)	1101-11-		
R-7300*	?	**Seguam** (Aleutian Is)	1101-18-	5?	-/8
T-7300*	?	**Nejapa-Miraflores** (Nicaragua)	1404-092		
T-7300?	?	**Hengill** (Iceland-SW)	1701-05=		9/-
C-7290v	?	**Udokan [Sini]** (Russia-SE).	1002-03-		
G-7290*	?	**Chichinautzin [Tetépetl]** (México)	1401-08=	0	
C-7270t	?	**Taranaki [Egmont]** (New Zealand)	0401-03=		
G-7260y	?	**Turrialba** (Costa Rica)	1405-07=		9/-
G-7260x	?	**Tenerife** (Canary Is).	1803-03-		
G-7250w	?	**Norikura** (Honshu-Japan)	0803-06=	3	8/7
G-7250?	?	**Towada** (Honshu-Japan).	0803-271	5?	-/9
T-7250?	?	**Gorely** (Kamchatka)	1000-07=	2	
C-7250?	?	**Krasheninnikov** (Kamchatka)	1000-19=		
T-7250?	?	**Shasta** (US-California).	1203-01-		
C-7250?	?	**Láscar** (Chile-N)	1505-10=		
C-7240w	?	**Yanteles** (Chile-S)	1508-050		
C-7220w	?	**Edgecumbe** (Alaska-E).	1105-04-		
G-7210?	?	**Haleakala** (Hawaiian Is)	1302-06-		
I-7210x	?	***Unknown Source*** *(GISP2, 146 ppb S)*	......		
C-7200v	?	**Longonot** (Africa-E).	0202-10=		
G-7200x	?	**Asama** (Honshu-Japan)	0803-11=		
G-7190w	?	**Misti, El** (Perú)	1504-01=		
T-7180*	?	**Kuju** (Kyushu-Japan).	0802-12=		8/-
T-7150z	?	**Oshima** (Izu Is-Japan).	0804-01=		
T-7150?	?	**Shiveluch** (Kamchatka).	1000-27=	5	-/9
C-7150?	?	**Mauna Loa** (Hawaiian Is)	1302-02=	0	
C-7150?	?	**Popocatépetl** (México)	1401-09=	P	
I-7148x	?	***Unknown Source*** *(GISP2, 116 ppb S)*	......		
C-7140w	?	**Karkar** (New Guinea-NE of)	0501-03=	C	
C-7130v	?	**Itasy Volc Field** (Madagascar).	0303-014		
T-7100*	?	**Akita-Komaga-take** (Honshu-Japan)	0803-23=		
G-7100v	?	**Khangar** (Kamchatka).	1000-272		
T-7100?	?	**Hengill** (Iceland-SW)	1701-05=	0	9/-
T-7100?	?	**Bárdarbunga** (Iceland-NE)	1703-03=		9/-
V-7087?	?	**Nemrut Dagi** (Turkey)	0103-02=		
K-7050?	?	**Pantelleria** (Italy)	0101-071		
R-7050*	?	**Silali** (Africa-E)	0202-052		
T-7050?	?	**Maroa [Orakeikorako]** (New Zeal).	0401-061		
T-7050*	?	**Kirishima** (Kyushu-Japan)	0802-09=	3	-/7
T-7050z	?	**Haku-san** (Honshu-Japan)	0803-05=		
T-7050?	?	**Megata** (Honshu-Japan).	0803-262		
G-7050?	?	**E-san** (Hokkaido-Japan)	0805-011	3	-/7
C-7050?	?	**Akan** (Hokkaido-Japan).	0805-07=	4	-/8
T-7050?	?	**Nemo Peak** (Kuril Is).	0900-32=		
T-7050*	?	**Zheltovsky** (Kamchatka)	1000-04=	5	-/9
T-7050*	?	**Bezymianny** (Kamchatka)	1000-25=		
C-7050*	?	**Sedankinsky** (Kamchatka).	1000-52-		
C-7050?	?	**Shishaldin** (Aleutian Is).	1101-36-		
T-7050?	?	**Hoodoo Mountain** (Canada)	1200-08-	0	
T-7050*	?	**Adams** (US-Washington).	1201-04-	2	
K-7050*	?	**Loihi** (Hawaiian Is).	1302-00-	0	
T-7050*	?	**Galeras** (Colombia)	1501-08=		
U-7050*	?	**Pelée** (W Indies).	1600-12=		
T-7050*	?	**Ljósufjöll** (Iceland-W).	1700-03=	2	9/-
T-7050*	?	**Bárdarbunga [Veidivötn]** (Iceland)	1703-03=		
T-7050?	?	**Kverkfjöll** (Iceland-NE)	1703-05=		
R-7050*	?	**Erebus** (Antarctica)	1900-02=	0	
I-7050?	?	**Takahe** (Antarctica).	1900-027		
G-7030y	?	**Pinatubo** (Luzon-Philippines)	0703-083		
C-7030t	?	**Orizaba, Pico de** (México)	1401-10=	4	-/8
C-7020v	?	**Chaîne des Puys** (France)	0100-02-		
C-7000v	?	**Taranaki [Egmont]** (New Zealand)	0401-03=		
T-7000?	?	**Shiveluch** (Kamchatka)	1000-27=	3	-/7
C-7000?	?	**Guagua Pichincha** (Ecuador).	1502-02=		
C-6990u	?	**Mammoth Mountain** (US-California)	1203-15-		
I-6955x	?	***Unknown Source*** *(GISP2, 236 ppb S)*	......		
C-6950?	?	**Loloru** (Bougainville-SW Pacific)	0505-03=		
C-6950?	?	**Shikotsu [Tarumai]** (Hokkaido).	0805-04=	5	-/9
C-6950?	?	**Maly Semiachik** (Kamchatka)	1000-14=		
T-6950?	?	**Ichinsky** (Kamchatka).	1000-28=		
G-6950?	?	**Prestahnukur** (Iceland-SW)	1701-07=	0	9/-
T-6950?	?	**Krafla** (Iceland-NE)	1703-08=	0	
G-6940v	?	**Vesuvius** (Italy).	0101-02=	5	-/9
U-6930?	?	**Endeavour Ridge** (Pacific-NE)	1301-01-	0	
C-6910<	?	**Atacazo** (Ecuador)	1502-021	P	
C-6890z	?	**Malinche, La** (México)	1401-091		
C-6890s	?	**Infiernillo** (Argentina).	1507-041		
C-6890z	?	**Chillán, Nevados de** (Chile-C)	1507-07=		
G-6880s	?	**Erciyes Dagi** (Turkey)	0103-01=		
C-6880u	?	**Llaima** (Chile-C)	1507-11=	5	-/9
N-6850?	?	**Abu** (Honshu-Japan)	0803-001		
G-6850w	?	**Ubinas** (Perú).	1504-02=		
T-6850?	?	**Krafla** (Iceland-NE)	1703-08=	2?	
T-6850?	?	**Tenerife** (Canary Is).	1803-03-		
C-6830w	?	**Iskut-Unuk River Cones** (Canada)	1200-09-		
C-6820x	?	**Hualalai** (Hawaiian Is).	1302-04-	0	
C-6820?	?	**Copahue** (Chile-C)	1507-09=		
C-6800y	?	**Bolshoi Semiachik** (Kamchatka)	1000-15=		
T-6800?	?	**Shiveluch** (Kamchatka).	1000-27=	5?	-/9
T-6800?	?	**Krafla** (Iceland-NE)	1703-08=	2?	
T-6800?	?	**Theistareykjarbunga** (Iceland-NE).	1703-09=	0	
I-6766x	?	***Unknown Source*** *(GISP2, 153 ppb S)*	......		
C-6760s	?	**Haleakala** (Hawaiian Is)	1302-06-		
?-6750 t	*?*	*Hasan Dagi (Turkey)*	*0103-002*		
G-6750t	?	**Kuchino-shima** (Ryukyu Is)	0802-043		
H-6750*	?	**Mono Craters** (US-California)	1203-12-		
C-6750x	?	**Agua de Pau** (Azores)	1802-09=		
C-6750?	?	**Deception Island** (Antarctica).	1900-03=		
I-6721x	?	***Unknown Source*** *(GISP2 572, 396 ppb S)*	......		
C-6720t	?	**Terceira** (Azores).	1802-05=		
C-6710x	?	**Malinche, La** (México)	1401-091		
C-6710w	?	**Orizaba, Pico de** (México)	1401-10=	5?	-/9
C-6700v	?	**Haleakala** (Hawaiian Is)	1302-06-		
C-6690?	?	**Villarrica** (Chile-C)	1507-12=	P	
C-6670w	?	**Ushkovsky** (Kamchatka)	1000-261		
T-6660<	?	**Ruiz, Nevado del** (Colombia)	1501-02=		
C-6650v	?	**Campi Flegrei** (Italy)	0101-01=	4	-/8
G-6650v	?	**Adatara** (Honshu-Japan)	0803-17=	3	-/7
T-6650?	?	**Oshima** (Izu Is-Japan).	0804-01=		
C-6650x	?	**Makushin** (Aleutian Is)	1101-31-		
T-6650?	?	**Shasta** (US-California).	1203-01-		
C-6650?	?	**Mauna Loa** (Hawaiian Is).	1302-02=	0	
C-6650?	?	**Soche** (Ecuador)	1502-001	5?	
C-6650?	?	**Guagua Pichincha** (Ecuador).	1502-02=		
T-6650?	?	**Yanteles** (Chile-S)	1508-050		
G-6650t	?	**Bárdarbunga [Veidivötn]** (Iceland)	1703-03=		10/-
T-6640*	?	**Corcovado** (Chile-S).	1508-05=		
I-6614w	?	***Unknown Source*** *(GISP2, 240 ppb S)*	......		
G-6610w	?	**Pelée** (W Indies).	1600-12=	4?	-/8
G-6600?	?	**Karymsky** (Kamchatka).	1000-13=	6	-/10
T-6600?	?	**Shiveluch** (Kamchatka).	1000-27=	4	-/8
T-6600?	?	**Sabancaya** (Perú)	1504-006		
C-6590w	?	**Dieng Volc Complex** (Java)	0603-20=	0	
C-6580<	?	**Fuji** (Honshu-Japan)	0803-03=		
G-6560u	?	**Taveuni** (Fiji Is-SW Pacific)	0405-01-	2	
I-6555w	?	***Unknown Source*** *(GISP2, 101 ppb S)*	......		
C-6550?	?	**Chaîne des Puys** (France)	0100-02-		
K-6550?	?	**Vulcano** (Italy)	0101-05=		
T-6550*	?	**Namarunu** (Africa-E)	0202-04-		
T-6550*	?	**Emuruangogolak** (Africa-E).	0202-051		
G-6550t	?	**Haku-san** (Honshu-Japan)	0803-05=		

START YEAR M-Dy	Duration	VOLCANO NAME (Subregion)	NUMBER	VEI	Vol L/T
G-6550?	?	**Kusatsu-Shirane** (Honshu-Japan)	0803-12=	3	7/7
T-6550?	?	**Oshima** (Izu Is-Japan)	0804-01=		
T-6550*	?	**Usu** (Hokkaido-Japan)	0805-03=		
T-6550z	?	**Kostakan** (Kamchatka)	1000-122	3	6/7
T-6550z	?	**Bakening** (Kamchatka)	1000-123	3	-/7
C-6550?	?	**Krasheninnikov** (Kamchatka)	1000-19=		
C-6550?	?	**Ugashik-Peulik** (Alaska Peninsula)	1102-13-		
C-6550?	?	**Mauna Loa** (Hawaiian Is)	1302-02=	0	
T-6550?	?	**Tenerife** (Canary Is)	1803-03-		
C-6520x	?	**Edziza** (Canada)	1200-06-		
G-6510u	?	**Chichón, El** (México)	1401-12=		
T-6500?	?	**Shiveluch** (Kamchatka)	1000-27=	3	-/7
T-6500?	?	**Krafla** (Iceland-NE)	1703-08=		**9**/-
T-6490?	?	**Campi Flegrei** (Italy)	0101-01=	3?	-/7
C-6480y	?	**Michoacán [La Taza]** (México)	1401-06=	3	-/7
I-6476w	?	***Unknown Source*** *(GISP2, 710 ppb S)*	......		
V-6471?	?	**Nemrut Dagi** (Turkey)	0103-02=		
I-6470w	?	***Unknown Source*** *(GISP2, 154 ppb S)*	......		
C-6450?	?	**Perbakti-Gagak** (Java)	0603-04=		
T-6450*	?	**Iwate** (Honshu-Japan)	0803-24=		
T-6450z	?	**Miyake-jima** (Izu Is-Japan)	0804-04=	4	-/8
G-6450?	?	**Ulreung** (Korea)	1006-03-		
H-6450?	?	**Salton Buttes** (US-California)	1203-20-		
G-6450w	?	**Soufrière Guadeloupe** (W Indies)	1600-06=		
C-6450?	?	**Pelée** (W Indies)	1600-12=		
G-6440q	?	**Kurile Lake** (Kamchatka)	1000-023	**7**	-/**11**
T-6400*	?	**Asama** (Honshu-Japan)	0803-11=		
C-6400t	?	**Kizimen** (Kamchatka)	1000-23=	**5**	-/**9**
G-6400w	?	**Shiveluch** (Kamchatka)	1000-27=	4	-/8
G-6400u	?	**Khangar** (Kamchatka)	1000-272		
C-6400?	?	**Guagua Pichincha** (Ecuador)	1502-02=		
I-6397w	?	***Unknown Source*** *(GISP2 424, 130 ppb S)*	......		
T-6380?	?	**Shiveluch** (Kamchatka)	1000-27=	4	-/8
T-6380?	?	**Katla** (Iceland-S)	1702-03=		
I-6360w	?	***Unknown Source*** *(GISP2, 92 ppb S)*	......		
K-6350*	?	**Vulcano** (Italy)	0101-05=		
C-6350?	?	**Sakura-jima** (Kyushu-Japan)	0802-08=		
T-6350?	?	**Bandai** (Honshu-Japan)	0803-16=		
G-6350x	?	**Akita-Komaga-take** (Honshu-Japan)	0803-23=	3	-/7
C-6350?	?	**Krasheninnikov** (Kamchatka)	1000-19=		
T-6350?	?	**Shiveluch** (Kamchatka)	1000-27=	4	-/8
G-6340x	?	**Lanín** (Chile-C)	1507-122		
I-6338w	?	***Unknown Source*** *(GISP2, 222 ppb S)*	......		
C-6320x	?	**Colima** (México)	1401-04=		
C-6310z	?	**Okmok** (Aleutian Is)	1101-29-	P	
C-6310u	?	**Malinche, La** (México)	1401-091		
C-6300t	?	**Campi Flegrei** (Italy)	0101-01=		
G-6300v	?	**Iwate** (Honshu-Japan)	0803-24=		
T-6300y	?	**Bakening** (Kamchatka)	1000-123		
C-6300?	?	**Guagua Pichincha** (Ecuador)	1502-02=		
I-6273w	?	***Unknown Source*** *(GISP2, 150 ppb S)*	......		
C-6270x	?	**Kusatsu-Shirane** (Honshu-Japan)	0803-12=		
N-6250?	?	**Chaîne des Puys** (France)	0100-02-		
T-6250?	?	**Sumiyoshi-ike** (Kyushu-Japan)	0802-081	2	-/6
G-6250?	?	**Towada** (Honshu-Japan)	0803-271	4	-/8
C-6250?	?	**Krasheninnikov** (Kamchatka)	1000-19=		
C-6250v	?	**Indian Heaven** (US-Washington)	1201-07-		8/-
C-6250?	?	**Mauna Loa** (Hawaiian Is)	1302-02=	0	
T-6250z	?	**Popocatépetl** (México)	1401-09=		
G-6250?	?	**Grímsnes** (Iceland-SW)	1701-06=		
R-6250*	?	**Takahe** (Antarctica)	1900-027		
C-6240y	?	**Fuji** (Honshu-Japan)	0803-03=		
C-6230?	?	**Acigöl-Nevsehir** (Turkey)	0103-004		
T-6230?	?	**Katla** (Iceland-S)	1702-03=		
C-6220t	?	**Haleakala** (Hawaiian Is)	1302-06-		
C-6220u	?	**Orizaba, Pico de** (México)	1401-10=	3	-/7
G-6220x	?	**Pelée** (W Indies)	1600-12=	P	
V-6213?	?	**Nemrut Dagi** (Turkey)	0103-02=		
C-6210v	?	**Udokan [Khangura]** (Russia-SE)	1002-03-		
C-6200*	?	**Sakura-jima** (Kyushu-Japan)	0802-08=	**6**	-/**10**
T-6200?	?	**Sumiyoshi-ike** (Kyushu-Japan)	0802-081	3	-/7
T-6200?	?	**Shiveluch** (Kamchatka)	1000-27=	3	-/7
C-6200?	?	**Guagua Pichincha** (Ecuador)	1502-02=		
T-6200?	?	**Katla** (Iceland-S)	1702-03=		
G-6200u	?	**Tenerife** (Canary Is)	1803-03-		7/-
C-6190x	?	**Etna** (Italy)	0101-06=		
T-6170?	?	**Katla** (Iceland-S)	1702-03=		
G-6150v	?	**Adatara** (Honshu-Japan)	0803-17=	3	-/7
T-6150y	?	**Akita-Komaga-take** (Honshu-Japan)	0803-23=		
G-6150?	?	**Maly Semiachik** (Kamchatka)	1000-14=		
G-6150t	?	**Ichinsky** (Kamchatka)	1000-28=		
T-6150?	?	**Krafla** (Iceland-NE)	1703-08=	0	
C-6140x	?	**Quill, The** (W Indies)	1600-02=	P	
C-6130u	?	**Pantelleria** (Italy)	0101-071		
C-6120v	?	**Malinche, La** (México)	1401-091		
C-6110?	?	**West Crater** (US-Washington)	1201-06-	2?	
T-6100?	?	**Avachinsky** (Kamchatka)	1000-10=		
T-6100?	?	**Shiveluch** (Kamchatka)	1000-27=	3	-/7
C-6100t	?	**Makushin** (Aleutian Is)	1101-31-	**5**	-/**9**
G-6060t	?	**Okataina [Haroharo]** (New Zeal)	0401-05=	**5**	**10/9**
M-6050?	?	**Stromboli** (Italy)	0101-04=	0	
R-6050*	?	**Silali** (Africa-E)	0202-052		
C-6050?	?	**Menengai** (Africa-E)	0202-06=	**6+**	-/**10**
T-6050?	?	**Olkaria** (Africa-E)	0202-09=		**9**/-
N-6050*	?	**Meidob Volc Field** (Africa-N)	0205-05-	P	
C-6050<	?	**Itasy Volc Field** (Madagascar)	0303-014		
C-6050u	?	**Mayor Island** (New Zealand)	0401-021		
T-6050?	?	**Taranaki [Egmont]** (New Zealand)	0401-03=		
C-6050?	?	**Sakura-jima** (Kyushu-Japan)	0802-08=	**5**	
T-6050?	?	**Fuji** (Honshu-Japan)	0803-03=		
T-6050?	?	**Hiuchi** (Honshu-Japan)	0803-131		
T-6050*	?	**Nasu** (Honshu-Japan)	0803-15=	2?	
T-6050z	?	**Oshima** (Izu Is-Japan)	0804-01=		
T-6050?	?	**Zheltovsky** (Kamchatka)	1000-04=		
T-6050?	?	**Gorely** (Kamchatka)	1000-07=	0	
C-6050?	?	**Tolbachik** (Kamchatka)	1000-24=		
C-6050?	?	**Spurr** (Alaska-SW)	1103-04-		
C-6050?	?	**Shasta** (US-California)	1203-01-		
T-6050?	?	**Yellowstone** (US-Wyoming)	1205-01-		
T-6050*	?	**Barva** (Costa Rica)	1405-05=	P	
T-6050?	?	**Calbuco** (Chile-S)	1508-02=		
T-6050*	?	**Snaefellsjökull** (Iceland-W)	1700-01=		
T-6050?	?	**Vestmannaeyjar** (Iceland-S)	1702-01=		
T-6050?	?	**Katla** (Iceland-S)	1702-03=		
T-6050*	?	**Torfajökull** (Iceland-S)	1702-05=		7/-
K-6050*	?	**La Palma** (Canary Is)	1803-01-		
C-6030s	?	**Haleakala** (Hawaiian Is)	1302-06-		
C-6030v	?	**Corcovado** (Chile-S)	1508-05=		
C-6020w	?	**Chaîne des Puys** (France)	0100-02-		
G-6000v	?	**Hakone** (Honshu-Japan)	0803-02=	3	-/7
T-6000?	?	**Mutnovsky** (Kamchatka)	1000-06=	2	-/6
C-6000t	?	**Krasheninnikov** (Kamchatka)	1000-19=	4	**9**/8
T-6000?	?	**Shiveluch** (Kamchatka)	1000-27=	3	-/7
T-6000?	?	**Krísuvík** (Iceland-SW)	1701-03=	0	**9**/-

-6000 (7950 BP)

START YEAR M-Dy	Duration	VOLCANO NAME (Subregion)	NUMBER	VEI	Vol L/T
I-5995w	?	***Unknown Source*** *(GISP2, 115 ppb S)*	......		
C-5990v	?	**Udokan Plateau** (Russia-SE)	1002-03-		
C-5980y	?	**Lamington** (New Guinea)	0503-01=		
G-5980v	?	**Avachinsky** (Kamchatka)	1000-10=	**5+**	-/**9**
T-5960?	?	**Katla** (Iceland-S)	1702-03=		
C-5950?	?	**Sakura-jima** (Kyushu-Japan)	0802-08=		
G-5950x	?	**Akita-Komaga-take** (Honshu-Japan)	0803-23=	3	-/7
T-5950?	?	**Nii-jima** (Izu Is-Japan)	0804-02=		
T-5950?	?	**Gorely** (Kamchatka)	1000-07=	3	-/7
C-5950z	?	**Romeral** (Colombia)	1501-011	P	
C-5940z	?	**Tacaná** (México)	1401-13=		
G-5920u	?	**Taveuni** (Fiji Is-SW Pacific)	0405-01-	2	
T-5900?	?	**Mutnovsky** (Kamchatka)	1000-06=	2	-/6
G-5900t	?	**Crater Lake** (US-Oregon)	1202-16-	**6**	8/**10**
C-5890w	?	**Craters of the Moon** (US-Idaho)	1204-02-	0	**9**/-
T-5890?	?	**Katla** (Iceland-S)	1702-03=		
I-5881?	?	***Unknown Source*** *(SP, 280 ppb S)*	......		
G-5880x	?	**Colima** (México)	1401-04=		
C-5870v	?	**Malinche, La** (México)	1401-091		
C-5860s	?	**Haleakala** (Hawaiian Is)	1302-06-		
C-5850?	?	**Meru** (Africa-E)	0202-16=	P	
C-5850?	?	**Newer Volcanics Prov** (Australia)	0509-01-		
G-5850?	?	**Maly Semiachik** (Kamchatka)	1000-14=		
T-5850?	?	**Ichinsky** (Kamchatka)	1000-28=		
C-5850?	?	**Ugashik-Peulik** (Alaska Peninsula)	1102-13-		
C-5850?	?	**Mauna Loa** (Hawaiian Is)	1302-02=	0	
T-5850?	?	**Hveravellir** (Iceland-SW)	1701-08=	2?	**10**/-
T-5850?	?	**Katla** (Iceland-S)	1702-03=		
T-5850*	?	**Hekla** (Iceland-S)	1702-07=		
C-5840z	?	**Chichinautzin [Cuauhtzin]** (Méx)	1401-08=		8/-
C-5840t	?	**Parinacota** (Chile-N)	1505-012		
C-5830y	?	**Rishiri** (Hokkaido-Japan)	0805-041		
G-5820u	?	**Lipari** (Italy)	0101-042		
C-5820u	?	**Cotopaxi** (Ecuador)	1502-05=	**5+**	-/**9**
M-5800y	?	**Stromboli** (Italy)	0101-04=	0	
T-5800*	?	**Kutcharo [Atosanupuri]** (Hokkaido)	0805-08=		
T-5800?	?	**Mutnovsky** (Kamchatka)	1000-06=	2	-/6
C-5800t	?	**Taunshits** (Kamchatka)	1000-16-		
C-5800t	?	**Krasheninnikov** (Kamchatka)	1000-19=	4	7/8
T-5800t	?	**Kizimen** (Kamchatka)	1000-23=		8/-
M-5800*	?	**Bachelor** (US-Oregon)	1202-09-		
C-5800?	?	**Pelée** (W Indies)	1600-12=		
C-5780w	?	**Redoubt** (Alaska-SW)	1103-03-		
N-5760?	?	**Chaîne des Puys** (France)	0100-02-		
U-5750*	?	**Tengchong** (SE Asia)	0705-11-		
G-5750?	?	**Maly Semiachik** (Kamchatka)	1000-14=		
T-5750?	?	**Uzon** (Kamchatka)	1000-17=		

START YEAR	M-Dy	Duration	VOLCANO NAME (Subregion)	NUMBER	VEI	Vol L/T
C-5750?		?	**West Crater** (US-Washington)	1201-06-	2?	
T-5750?		?	**Krafla** (Iceland-NE)	1703-08=	0	
T-5750?		?	**Tenerife** (Canary Is).	1803-03-		8/-
V-5745?		?	**Nemrut Dagi** (Turkey)	0103-02=		
T-5730?		?	**Katla** (Iceland-S)	1702-03=		
G-5720x		?	**Tacaná** (México)	1401-13=		
T-5720?		?	**Katla** (Iceland-S)	1702-03=		
T-5710?		?	**Katla** (Iceland-S)	1702-03=		
T-5700*		?	**Kirishima** (Kyushu-Japan)	0802-09=	3	-/7
G-5700t		?	**Azuma** (Honshu-Japan)	0803-18=	2	-/6
T-5700v		?	**Diky Greben** (Kamchatka)	1000-022		
T-5700t		?	**Ilyinsky** (Kamchatka)	1000-03=	**C**	
T-5700?		?	**Avachinsky** (Kamchatka)	1000-10=		
C-5700t		?	**Uzon** (Kamchatka)	1000-17=		
G-5700n		?	**Khangar** (Kamchatka)	1000-272	**6**	-/**10**
I-5677w	1015q	?	**Crater Lake** (US-Oregon)	1202-16-	**7**	8/**11**
G-5650t		?	**Iwate** (Honshu-Japan)	0803-24=		
T-5650?		?	**Gorely** (Kamchatka)	1000-07=	3	-/7
T-5650?		?	**Tolbachik** (Kamchatka)	1000-24=		
T-5650?		?	**Ichinsky** (Kamchatka)	1000-28=		
C-5650?		?	**Wells Gray-Clearwater** (Canada)	1200-15-		
C-5650?		?	**Mauna Loa** (Hawaiian Is)	1302-02=	0	
T-5630?		?	**Katla** (Iceland-S)	1702-03=		
C-5610v		?	**Pantelleria** (Italy)	0101-071		
G-5600?		?	**Zao** (Honshu-Japan)	0803-19=		
G-5600?		?	**Ksudach** (Kamchatka)	1000-05=		
T-5600?		?	**Avachinsky** (Kamchatka)	1000-10=		
T-5600?		?	**Tolbachik** (Kamchatka)	1000-24=		
C-5590v		?	**Poás** (Costa Rica)	1405-04=		
C-5580y		?	**Malinche, La** (México)	1401-091		
C-5560s		?	**Calbuco** (Chile-S)	1508-02=		
T-5560?		?	**Katla** (Iceland-S)	1702-03=		
M-5550?		?	**Stromboli** (Italy)	0101-04=	0	
T-5550?		?	**Okataina [Edgecumbe]** (New Zeal)	0401-05=	0	
T-5550*		?	**Ruapehu** (New Zealand)	0401-10=		
G-5550z		?	**Nasu** (Honshu-Japan)	0803-15=	3	7/7
G-5550?		?	**Towada** (Honshu-Japan)	0803-271	3?	-/8
T-5550?		?	**Oshima** (Izu Is-Japan)	0804-01=		
T-5550z		?	**Usu** (Hokkaido-Japan)	0805-03=		
G-5550v		?	**Mashu** (Hokkaido-Japan)	0805-081	**6**	-/0
C-5550u		?	**Tao-Rusyr Caldera** (Kuril Is)	0900-31=	**6**	-/**10**
T-5550?		?	**Nemo Peak** (Kuril Is)	0900-32=		
G-5550?		?	**Rainier** (US-Washington)	1201-03-	2	-/6
T-5550?		?	**Crater Lake** (US-Oregon)	1202-16-	0	**9**/-
T-5550*		?	**Golden Trout Creek** (US-California)	1203-17-		
C-5550z		?	**Imbabura** (Ecuador)	1502-004		
A-5550*		?	**Palei-Aike Volc Field** (Chile-S)	1508-08-		
T-5550z		?	**Hengill** (Iceland-SW)	1701-05=	0	7/-
T-5550?		?	**Katla** (Iceland-S)	1702-03=		**9**/-
T-5550*		?	**Tenerife** (Canary Is).	1803-03-		
I-5550?		?	**Takahe** (Antarctica)	1900-027		
C-5540x		?	**Fuji** (Honshu-Japan)	0803-03=		
I-5521w		?	***Unknown Source*** *(GISP2, 129 ppb S)*	......		
G-5500?		?	**Zao** (Honshu-Japan)	0803-19=		
T-5500?		?	**Gorely** (Kamchatka)	1000-07=	3	-/7
T-5500?		?	**Avachinsky** (Kamchatka)	1000-10=		
G-5500z		?	**Akademia Nauk** (Kamchatka)	1000-125	3?	
T-5500?		?	**Shiveluch** (Kamchatka)	1000-27=	**5**	-/**9**
G-5500q		?	**Khangar** (Kamchatka)	1000-272		
G-5500?		?	**Santa Isabel** (Colombia)	1501-021		
G-5500x		?	**Pelée** (W Indies)	1600-12=	**P**	
C-5490t		?	**Taapaca** (Chile-N)	1505-011		
C-5470w		?	**Craters of the Moon** (US-Idaho)	1204-02-	0	**9**/-
T-5470?		?	**Katla** (Iceland-S)	1702-03=		
T-5460?		?	**Katla** (Iceland-S)	1702-03=		
T-5450u		?	**Oshima** (Izu Is-Japan)	0804-01=		
T-5450?		?	**Mutnovsky** (Kamchatka)	1000-06=	2	-/6
T-5450?		?	**Gorely** (Kamchatka)	1000-07=	3	-/7
T-5450?		?	**Avachinsky** (Kamchatka)	1000-10=		
G-5450?		?	**Maly Semiachik** (Kamchatka)	1000-14=		
C-5450?		?	**Krasheninnikov** (Kamchatka)	1000-19=		
T-5450?		?	**Tolbachik** (Kamchatka)	1000-24=		
G-5410u		?	**Chimborazo** (Ecuador)	1502-071		
C-5400?		?	**Sakura-jima** (Kyushu-Japan)	0802-08=		
G-5400x		?	**Azuma** (Honshu-Japan)	0803-18=	1	-/5
T-5400?		?	**Shiveluch** (Kamchatka)	1000-27=	3	-/7
T-5400?		?	**Ichinsky** (Kamchatka)	1000-28=	**5**	**9/9**
G-5390u		?	**Misti, El** (Perú)	1504-01=		
T-5360?		?	**Katla** (Iceland-S)	1702-03=		
U-5350x		?	**Damavand** (Iran)	0302-01-	0	
T-5350?		?	**Hachimantai** (Honshu-Japan)	0803-25=		
T-5350?		?	**Mutnovsky** (Kamchatka)	1000-06=	2	-/6
G-5350?		?	**Rainier** (US-Washington)	1201-03-	3	-/7
C-5350?		?	**Mauna Loa** (Hawaiian Is)	1302-02=	0	
C-5350x		?	**Nejapa-Miraflores** (Nicaragua)	1404-092		
V-5320?		?	**Nemrut Dagi** (Turkey)	0103-02=		

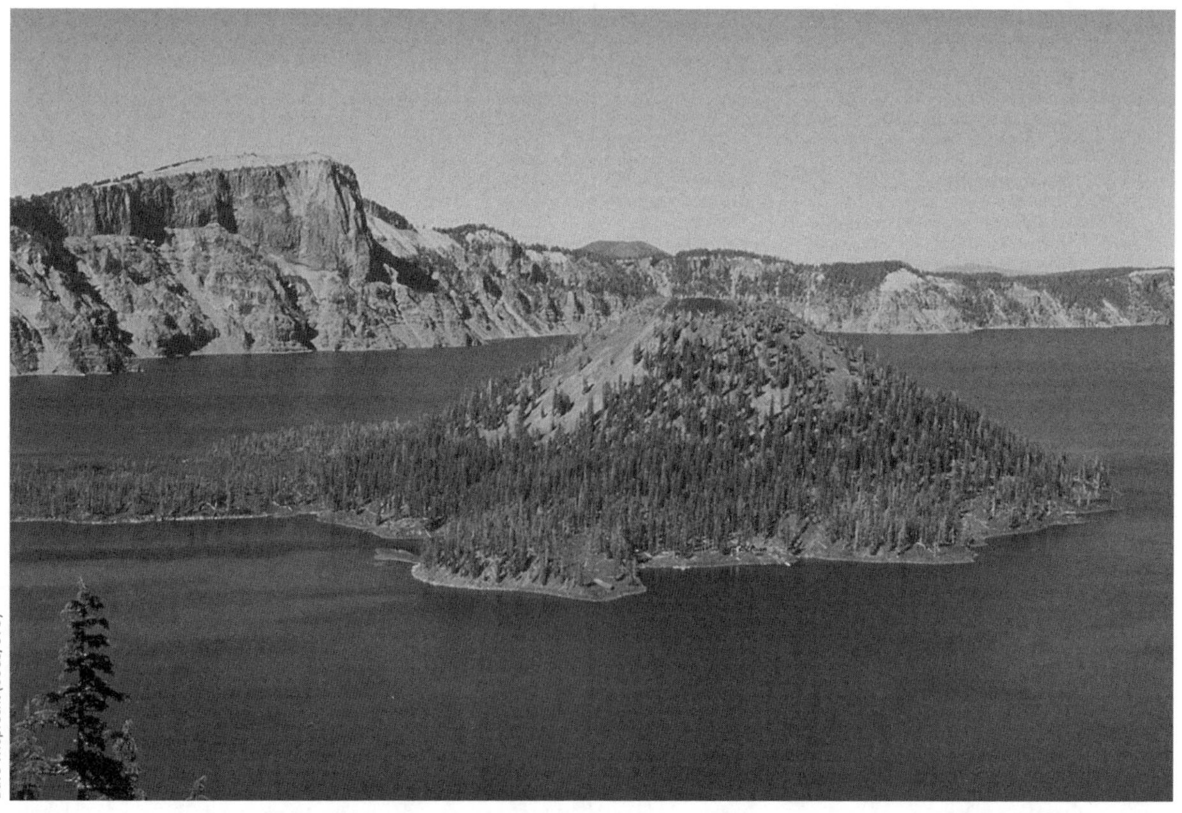
Dave Wieprecht (USGS/CVO)

Wizard Island, a post-caldera cone rising about 200 m above the surface of Crater Lake in the Oregon Cascade Range, erupted some 300 years after formation of the caldera about 6850 years ago. Llao Rock, the prominent peak on the caldera rim, is a massive, 350-m-thick lava flow erupted about 150 years prior to formation of Crater Lake caldera and is capped by light-colored deposits from the caldera-forming eruption.

START YEAR M-Dy	Duration	VOLCANO NAME (Subregion)	NUMBER	VEI	Vol L/T
C-5310 v	?	**Bolshoi-Kekuknaysky** (Kamchatka)	1000-36-	3	7/7
C-5310 v	?	**Tolima, Nevado del** (Colombia)	1501-03=		
T-5300 ?	?	**Gorely** (Kamchatka)	1000-07=	2	
C-5290 <	?	**Newer Volcanics Prov** (Australia)	0509-01-		
C-5290 x	?	**Llaima** (Chile-C)	1507-11=		
C-5290 w	?	**Krísuvík** (Iceland-SW)	1701-03=	2	8/-
I-5278 w	?	***Unknown Source*** *(GISP2 404, 667 ppb S)*	......		
C-5260 *	?	**Tengger Caldera** (Java)	0603-31=		
G-5260 w	?	**Newberry** (US-Oregon)	1202-11-	0	6/-
N-5250 z	?	**Meidob Volc Field** (Africa-N)	0205-05-		
T-5250 ?	?	**Mutnovsky** (Kamchatka)	1000-06=	2	-/6
G-5250 ?	?	**Krasheninnikov** (Kamchatka)	1000-19=		
T-5250 *	?	**Aniakchak** (Alaska Peninsula)	1102-09-	6?	-/10
T-5250 ?	?	**Crater Lake** (US-Oregon)	1202-16-		
C-5250 ?	?	**Socompa** (Chile-N)	1505-109		
T-5250 ?	?	**Tenerife** (Canary Is)	1803-03-		7/-
V-5242 u	?	**Nemrut Dagi** (Turkey)	0103-02=		
G-5230 v	?	**Taveuni** (Fiji Is-SW Pacific)	0405-01-	2	
C-5230 x	?	**Nejapa-Miraflores** (Nicaragua)	1404-092		
T-5230 ?	?	**Katla** (Iceland-S)	1702-03=		
C-5220 v	?	**Nazko** (Canada)	1200-14-		
G-5200 ?	?	**Ksudach** (Kamchatka)	1000-05=	5?	-/9
T-5180 ?	?	**Katla** (Iceland-S)	1702-03=		
G-5160 x	?	**Tolima, Nevado del** (Colombia)	1501-03=		
V-5152 ?	?	**Nemrut Dagi** (Turkey)	0103-02=		
C-5150 w	?	**Etna** (Italy)	0101-06=		
N-5150 *	?	**Tavui** (New Britain-SW Pac)	0502-15-	5	-/9
T-5150 ?	?	**Gorely** (Kamchatka)	1000-07=	3	-/7
T-5150 z	?	**Adams** (US-Washington)	1201-04-	2	
C-5150 w	?	**Mauna Kea** (Hawaiian Is)	1302-03-		
C-5150 ?	?	**Popocatépetl** (México)	1401-09=	P	
E-5150 *	?	**Láscar** (Chile-N)	1505-10=	0	
G-5150 ?	?	**Hekla** (Iceland-S)	1702-07=	5	-/9
C-5120 t	?	**Taranaki [Egmont]** (New Zealand)	0401-03=		
C-5110 v	?	**Spurr** (Alaska-SW)	1103-04-		
G-5100 ?	?	**Taupo** (New Zealand)	0401-07=	3	7/7
U-5100 *	?	**Seguam** (Aleutian Is)	1101-18-	0	7/-
V-5085 ?	?	**Nemrut Dagi** (Turkey)	0103-02=		
C-5080 u	?	**Planchón-Peteroa** (Chile-C)	1507-04=	3	-/7
G-5080 w	?	**Puyehue-Cordón Caulle** (Chile-C)	1507-15=	5	-/9
C-5070 x	?	**Fuji** (Honshu-Japan)	0803-03=		
G-5070 w	?	**Newberry** (US-Oregon)	1202-11-	3	8/7
T-5070 ?	?	**Katla** (Iceland-S)	1702-03=		
G-5060 x	?	**Mayor Island** (New Zealand)	0401-021	5	-/9
G-5060 w	?	**Arenal** (Costa Rica)	1405-033	4?	
M-5050 ?	?	**Stromboli** (Italy)	0101-04=	0	
R-5050 *	?	**Silali** (Africa-E)	0202-052		
C-5050 ?	?	**Hargy** (New Britain-SW Pac)	0502-10=		
T-5050 ?	?	**Ibusuki Volc Field** (Kyushu-Japan)	0802-07=		
T-5050 ?	?	**Bandai** (Honshu-Japan)	0803-16=		
T-5050 ?	?	**Mikura-jima** (Izu Is-Japan)	0804-041		
T-5050 ?	?	**Mutnovsky** (Kamchatka)	1000-06=	3	-/7
T-5050 ?	?	**Koryaksky** (Kamchatka)	1000-09=		
T-5050 ?	?	**Zhupanovsky** (Kamchatka)	1000-12=		
G-5050 ?	?	**Maly Semiachik** (Kamchatka)	1000-14=		
C-5050 ?	?	**Krasheninnikov** (Kamchatka)	1000-19=		
T-5050 ?	?	**Bezymianny** (Kamchatka)	1000-25=		
T-5050 ?	?	**Piip** (Kamchatka-E of)	1000-271		
C-5050 ?	?	**Iliamna** (Alaska-SW)	1103-02-	P	
G-5050 ?	?	**Rainier** (US-Washington)	1201-03-	3	-/7
K-5050 *	?	**Loihi** (Hawaiian Is)	1302-00-	0	
K-5050 *	?	**Adams Seamount** (Pacific-C)	1303-05-	0	
U-5050 *	?	**Unnamed [East Pacific Rise]**	1304-05-	0	
T-5050 ?	?	**Miravalles** (Costa Rica)	1405-03=		
T-5050 *	?	**Caburgua-Huelemolle** (Chile-C)	1507-112		
T-5050 *	?	**Torfajökull** (Iceland-S)	1702-05=		8/-
T-5050 *	?	**Hekla** (Iceland-S)	1702-07=		
C-5040 v	?	**Reykjanes** (Iceland-SW)	1701-02=	0	
T-5040 ?	?	**Katla** (Iceland-S)	1702-03=		
T-5020 *	?	**Hachijo-jima** (Izu Is-Japan)	0804-05=	3	-/7
T-5020 ?	?	**Katla** (Iceland-S)	1702-03=		
C-5010 t	?	**Mentolat** (Chile-S)	1508-054		
C-5000 ?	?	**Haku-san** (Honshu-Japan)	0803-05=		
T-5000 ?	?	**Mutnovsky** (Kamchatka)	1000-06=	2	-/6
T-5000 ?	?	**Hengill** (Iceland-SW)	1701-05=		9/-
T-5000 ?	?	**Bárdarbunga** (Iceland-NE)	1703-03=		10/-
T-5000 *	?	**Kverkfjöll** (Iceland-NE)	1703-05=		9/-
I-4988 w	?	***Unknown Source*** *(GISP2, 93 ppb S)*	......		
G-4960 v	?	**Newberry** (US-Oregon)	1202-11-		5/-
C-4960 x	?	**Colima** (México)	1401-04=		
C-4960 w	?	**Hudson, Cerro** (Chile-S)	1508-057		
T-4950 ?	?	**Gorely** (Kamchatka)	1000-07=	2	
T-4950 *	?	**Hekla** (Iceland-S)	1702-07=		
C-4940 w	?	**Hood** (US-Oregon)	1202-01-	2	
V-4938 u	?	**Nemrut Dagi** (Turkey)	0103-02=		
T-4920 z	?	**Oshima** (Izu Is-Japan)	0804-01=		
C-4920 v	?	**Corcovado** (Chile-S)	1508-05=		
G-4900 v	?	**Iwate** (Honshu-Japan)	0803-24=		
T-4900 ?	?	**Niseko** (Hokkaido-Japan)	0805-031		
G-4900 ?	?	**Ksudach** (Kamchatka)	1000-05=	5+	-/9
T-4900 ?	?	**Shiveluch** (Kamchatka)	1000-27=	3	-/7
C-4900 t	?	**La Palma** (Canary Is)	1803-01-		
C-4890 u	?	**Longaví, Nevado de** (Chile-C)	1507-063		
T-4880 ?	?	**Katla** (Iceland-S)	1702-03=		
G-4860 w	?	**Newberry** (US-Oregon)	1202-11-	0	6/-
C-4850 y	?	**Lamington** (New Guinea)	0503-01=		
G-4850 t	?	**Iwate** (Honshu-Japan)	0803-24=		
C-4850 ?	?	**Krasheninnikov** (Kamchatka)	1000-19=		
G-4850 ?	?	**Rainier** (US-Washington)	1201-03-	2	-/6
T-4850 *	?	**Guagua Pichincha** (Ecuador)	1502-02=		
T-4850 *	?	**Torfajökull** (Iceland-S)	1702-05=		7/-
V-4849 ?	?	**Nemrut Dagi** (Turkey)	0103-02=		
U-4840 ?	?	**North Gorda Ridge** (Pacific-NE)	1301-031	0	
T-4810 ?	?	**Katla** (Iceland-S)	1702-03=		
I-4803 w	?	***Unknown Source*** *(GISP2, 141 ppb S)*	......		
M-4800 y	?	**Stromboli** (Italy)	0101-04=	2?	
G-4800 v	?	**Taveuni** (Fiji Is-SW Pacific)	0405-01-	2	
C-4800 ?	?	**Sakura-jima** (Kyushu-Japan)	0802-08=		
G-4800 ?	?	**Santa Isabel** (Colombia)	1501-021		
C-4800 ?	?	**Pululagua** (Ecuador)	1502-011		
T-4800 ?	?	**Bárdarbunga** (Iceland-NE)	1703-03=		9/-
C-4790 ?	?	**Hierro** (Canary Is)	1803-02-		
G-4770 u	?	**Newberry** (US-Oregon)	1202-11-		7/-
C-4760 s	?	**Haleakala** (Hawaiian Is)	1302-06-		
G-4750 y	?	**Myoko** (Honshu-Japan)	0803-10=	5?	-/9
T-4750 ?	?	**Ksudach** (Kamchatka)	1000-05=		8/-
T-4750 ?	?	**Gorely** (Kamchatka)	1000-07=	3	-/7
C-4750 ?	?	**Hudson, Cerro** (Chile-S)	1508-057	6	-/10
T-4750 ?	?	**Katla** (Iceland-S)	1702-03=		
T-4750 *	?	**Hekla** (Iceland-S)	1702-07=		
G-4740 x	?	**Tacaná** (México)	1401-13=		
C-4740 ?	?	**Plat Pays, Morne** (W Indies)	1600-11=		
T-4730 z	?	**Fuji** (Honshu-Japan)	0803-03=		
G-4700 ?	?	**Taupo** (New Zealand)	0401-07=	4	-/8
T-4700 z	?	**Asama** (Honshu-Japan)	0803-11=		
T-4700 ?	?	**Mutnovsky** (Kamchatka)	1000-06=	2	-/6
T-4700 ?	?	**Gorely** (Kamchatka)	1000-07=	2	
G-4700 w	?	**Kanaga** (Aleutian Is)	1101-11-		
C-4700 y	?	**Iskut-Unuk River Cones** (Canada)	1200-09-		
G-4690 u	?	**Merapi** (Java)	0603-25=		
G-4690 w	?	**Newberry** (US-Oregon)	1202-11-	0	7/-
C-4690 y	?	**Orizaba, Pico de** (México)	1401-10=	3	-/7
G-4690 x	?	**Puyehue-Cordón Caulle** (Chile-C)	1507-15=		
I-4689 w	?	***Unknown Source*** *(GISP2, 310 ppb S)*	......		
T-4660 ?	?	**Katla** (Iceland-S)	1702-03=		
T-4650 ?	?	**Bandai** (Honshu-Japan)	0803-16=		
T-4650 ?	?	**Hachijo-jima** (Izu Is-Japan)	0804-05=	5	-/9
T-4650 ?	?	**Mutnovsky** (Kamchatka)	1000-06=	2	-/6
T-4650 ?	?	**Gorely** (Kamchatka)	1000-07=	3	-/7
G-4650 ?	?	**Maly Semiachik** (Kamchatka)	1000-14=		
C-4650 ?	?	**Kilauea** (Hawaiian Is)	1302-01-	0	
T-4650 z	?	**Hekla** (Iceland-S)	1702-07=		
T-4650 ?	?	**Tenerife** (Canary Is)	1803-03-		
C-4620 u	?	**Taapaca** (Chile-N)	1505-011		
V-4615 ?	?	**Nemrut Dagi** (Turkey)	0103-02=		
T-4610 ?	?	**Katla** (Iceland-S)	1702-03=		
G-4600 t	?	**Komaga-take** (Hokkaido-Japan)	0805-02=	5	-/9
T-4600 ?	?	**Gorely** (Kamchatka)	1000-07=	2	
C-4600 v	?	**Craters of the Moon** (US-Idaho)	1204-02-	0	9/-
T-4600 ?	?	**Bárdarbunga** (Iceland-NE)	1703-03=		9/-
I-4596 w	?	***Unknown Source*** *(GISP2, 257 ppb S)*	......		
G-4570 ?	?	**Takahara** (Honshu-Japan)	0803-143	4?	8/7
C-4570 <	?	**Furnas** (Azores)	1802-10=		
I-4564 w	?	***Unknown Source*** *(GISP2, 132 ppb S)*	......		
M-4550 ?	?	**Stromboli** (Italy)	0101-04=	0	
T-4550 *	?	**Azuma** (Honshu-Japan)	0803-18=		
T-4550 *	?	**To-shima** (Izu Is-Japan)	0804-011	0	
C-4550 z	?	**Akan** (Hokkaido-Japan)	0805-07=		
T-4550 ?	?	**Golovnin** (Kuril Is)	0900-01=		
C-4550 ?	?	**Koshelev** (Kamchatka)	1000-02=		
C-4550 ?	?	**Ilyinsky** (Kamchatka)	1000-03=		
T-4550 ?	?	**Ksudach** (Kamchatka)	1000-05=	3	
T-4550 ?	?	**Mutnovsky** (Kamchatka)	1000-06=	2	-/6
G-4550 x	?	**Avachinsky** (Kamchatka)	1000-10=	4	-/8
T-4550 ?	?	**Tolbachik** (Kamchatka)	1000-24=		
C-4550 ?	?	**Cherpuk Group** (Kamchatka)	1000-273		9/-
T-4550 y	?	**Redoubt** (Alaska-SW)	1103-03=		
G-4550 ?	?	**Baker** (US-Washington)	1201-01=	3?	-/7
T-4550 ?	?	**Adams** (US-Washington)	1201-04-	2	8/-
T-4550 *	?	**Snaefellsjökull** (Iceland-W)	1700-01=	2	
T-4550 z	?	**Vestmannaeyjar** (Iceland-S)	1702-01=		
T-4550 z	?	**Torfajökull** (Iceland-S)	1702-05=		7/-
T-4550 z	?	**Hekla** (Iceland-S)	1702-07=		
T-4550 z	?	**Grímsvötn** (Iceland-NE)	1703-01=	0	

START YEAR M-Dy	Duration	VOLCANO NAME (Subregion)	NUMBER	VEI	Vol L/T
T-4550?	?	**Bárdarbunga [Veidivötn]** (Iceland)	1703-03=		
C-4550v	?	**Agua de Pau** (Azores)	1802-09=		
E-4550z	?	**Erebus** (Antarctica)	1900-02=	0	
G-4530?	?	**Shiveluch** (Kamchatka)	1000-27=	3	-/7
T-4510y	?	**Porak** (Armenia)	0104-09-		
G-4510z	?	**Pelée** (W Indies)	1600-12=		
T-4500w	?	**Komaga-take** (Hokkaido-Japan)	0805-02=		
T-4500?	?	**Gorely** (Kamchatka)	1000-07=	2	
G-4500t	?	**Maly Semiachik** (Kamchatka)	1000-14=		
V-4500t	?	**Jefferson [Forked Butte]** (US-Ore)	1202-02-		
C-4500x	?	**Colima** (México)	1401-04=		
T-4500?	?	**Grímsnes** (Iceland-SW)	1701-06=	0	
G-4500t	?	**Madeira** (Azores)	1802-12-		
T-4490z	?	**Kuju** (Kyushu-Japan)	0802-12=		8/-
G-4460v	?	**Avachinsky** (Kamchatka)	1000-10=	4	-/8
T-4460?	?	**Puyehue-Cordón Caulle** (Chile-C)	1507-15=		
T-4450z	?	**Iwate** (Honshu-Japan)	0803-24=	0	
T-4450?	?	**Oshima** (Izu Is-Japan)	0804-01=		
T-4450?	?	**Gorely** (Kamchatka)	1000-07=	2	-/6
G-4450?	?	**Bolshoi Semiachik** (Kamchatka)	1000-15=		
G-4450?	?	**Krasheninnikov** (Kamchatka)	1000-19=		
T-4450?	?	**Kizimen** (Kamchatka)	1000-23=	4	-/8
H-4450?	?	**Newberry** (US-Oregon)	1202-11-		7/-
T-4450?	?	**Arenal** (Costa Rica)	1405-033		
C-4450?	?	**Quimsachata** (Perú)	1504-00-		
R-4450*	?	**Puyehue-Cordón Caulle** (Chile-C)	1507-15=		
T-4450?	?	**Grímsnes** (Iceland-SW)	1701-06=	2?	
I-4447w	?	***Unknown Source*** *(GISP2, 159 ppb S)*	......		
G-4430y	?	**Colima** (México)	1401-04=		
T-4430?	?	**Katla** (Iceland-S)	1702-03=		
I-4411w	?	***Unknown Source*** *(GISP2, 183 ppb S)*	......		
C-4410v	?	**Hualalai** (Hawaiian Is)	1302-04-	0	
G-4400>	?	**Narugo** (Honshu-Japan)	0803-20=		
T-4400?	?	**Avachinsky** (Kamchatka)	1000-10=		
G-4400?	?	**Shiveluch** (Kamchatka)	1000-27=	**5**	-/**9**
C-4400y	?	**Mageik** (Alaska Peninsula)	1102-15-		
T-4400?	?	**Bárdarbunga** (Iceland-NE)	1703-03=		**9**/-
C-4390v	?	**Nejapa-Miraflores** (Nicaragua)	1404-092		
D-4375?	?	***Unknown Source*** *(Belfast tree-ring)*	......		
T-4370?	?	**Katla** (Iceland-S)	1702-03=		
C-4360x	?	**Macauley Island** (Kermadec Is)	0402-021	**6**?	-/**10**
C-4350?	?	**Kikai** (Ryukyu Is)	0802-06=	**7**	-/**11**
C-4350?	?	**Kirishima** (Kyushu-Japan)	0802-09=	4	-/8
T-4350*	?	**Nasu** (Honshu-Japan)	0803-15=	2?	
T-4350z	?	**Iwate** (Honshu-Japan)	0803-24=		
T-4350?	?	**Nii-jima** (Izu Is-Japan)	0804-02=		
G-4350?	?	**Komaga-take** (Hokkaido-Japan)	0805-02=	**P**	
T-4350?	?	**Gorely** (Kamchatka)	1000-07=	3	-/7
G-4350?	?	**Shiveluch** (Kamchatka)	1000-27=	3	-/7
C-4350u	?	**Cotopaxi** (Ecuador)	1502-05=	**5**	-/**9**
T-4350*	?	**Hekla** (Iceland-S)	1702-07=		
G-4340u	?	**Avachinsky** (Kamchatka)	1000-10=	**5**	-/**9**
V-4321?	?	**Nemrut Dagi** (Turkey)	0103-02=		
E-4320*	?	**Parinacota** (Chile-N)	1505-012		
T-4300?	?	**Myoko** (Honshu-Japan)	0803-10=		
T-4300*	?	**Adatara** (Honshu-Japan)	0803-17=	3	-/7
T-4300w	?	**Gorely** (Kamchatka)	1000-07=	0	
C-4300w	?	**Calbuco** (Chile-S)	1508-02=		
C-4280w	?	**Bravo, Cerro** (Colombia)	1501-012	4	-/**9**
T-4280?	?	**Katla** (Iceland-S)	1702-03=		
C-4270w	?	**Grímsnes** (Iceland-SW)	1701-06=	3	**9**/7
G-4270x	?	**Vestmannaeyjar [Heimaey]**	1702-01=	3	
M-4250?	?	**Stromboli** (Italy)	0101-04=	2?	
T-4250?	?	**Oshima** (Izu Is-Japan)	0804-01=		
T-4250?	?	**Avachinsky** (Kamchatka)	1000-10=		
T-4250?	?	**Shiveluch** (Kamchatka)	1000-27=	3	-/7
C-4250?	?	**Gorny Institute** (Kamchatka)	1000-55-	0	
T-4250?	?	**Craters of the Moon** (US-Idaho)	1204-02-	0	8/-
C-4250?	?	**Mauna Loa** (Hawaiian Is)	1302-02=	0	
C-4250u	?	**Chichinautzin [Tláloc]** (México)	1401-08=	3?	**9**/7
T-4250z	?	**Hekla** (Iceland-S)	1702-07=		
T-4240?	?	**Katla** (Iceland-S)	1702-03=		
G-4230x	?	**Puyehue-Cordón Caulle** (Chile-C)	1507-15=		
T-4210?	?	**Katla** (Iceland-S)	1702-03=		
G-4200v	?	**Asama** (Honshu-Japan)	0803-11=		
T-4200?	?	**Avachinsky** (Kamchatka)	1000-10=		
T-4200?	?	**Bárdarbunga** (Iceland-NE)	1703-03=		**9**/-
G-4200v	?	**Tenerife** (Canary Is)	1803-03-		7/-
C-4160r	?	**Apoyeque** (Nicaragua)	1404-091	**5**	-/**9**
C-4150w	?	**Etna** (Italy)	0101-06=		
T-4150*	?	**Meidob Volc Field** (Africa-N)	0205-05-	**P**	
C-4150?	?	**Loloru** (Bougainville-SW Pacific)	0505-03=		
G-4150x	?	**Nikko-Shirane** (Honshu-Japan)	0803-14=		
G-4150z	?	**Azuma** (Honshu-Japan)	0803-18=	3	8/7
G-4150x	?	**Zao** (Honshu-Japan)	0803-19=		
G-4150?	?	**Towada** (Honshu-Japan)	0803-271	**5**+	-/**9**
T-4150?	?	**Gorely** (Kamchatka)	1000-07=	2	-/6
G-4150?	?	**Karymsky** (Kamchatka)	1000-13=		
C-4150?	?	**Akutan** (Aleutian Is)	1101-32-		
T-4150*	?	**Hekla** (Iceland-S)	1702-07=		
G-4130w	?	**Chimborazo** (Ecuador)	1502-071		
T-4120y	?	**Fuji** (Honshu-Japan)	0803-03=		
G-4110v	?	**Colima** (México)	1401-04=		
G-4100?	?	**Taupo** (New Zealand)	0401-07=	4	-/8
G-4100s	?	**Tatun Group** (Taiwan)	0801-032	1?	
G-4100v	?	**Mikura-jima** (Izu Is-Japan)	0804-041		7/-
T-4100?	?	**Ksudach** (Kamchatka)	1000-05=	3	
C-4090v	?	**Leonard Range** (Mindanao-Philippines)	0701-031		
C-4070t	?	**Craters of the Moon** (US-Idaho)	1204-02-	0	**9**/-
C-4060w	?	**Kaguyak** (Alaska Peninsula)	1102-25-		
T-4060?	?	**Katla** (Iceland-S)	1702-03=		
V-4055t	?	**Nemrut Dagi** (Turkey)	0103-02=		
C-4050?	?	**Stromboli** (Italy)	0101-04=	3?	
T-4050?	?	**Olkaria** (Africa-E)	0202-09=		
F-4050*	?	**Unzen** (Kyushu-Japan)	0802-10=		
T-4050?	?	**Iwaki** (Honshu-Japan)	0803-27=		
T-4050?	?	**Koshelev** (Kamchatka)	1000-02=		
T-4050?	?	**Yavinsky** (Kamchatka)	1000-021		
T-4050?	?	**Mutnovsky** (Kamchatka)	1000-06=	2	-/6
T-4050?	?	**Avachinsky** (Kamchatka)	1000-10=		
T-4050?	?	**Kizimen** (Kamchatka)	1000-23=	2	-/6
U-4050*	?	**Seguam** (Aleutian Is)	1101-18-	0	
T-4050?	?	**Spurr** (Alaska-SW)	1103-04-		
T-4050z	?	**Adams** (US-Washington)	1201-04-	2	
C-4050?	?	**Shasta** (US-California)	1203-01-		
H-4050?	?	**Inyo Craters** (US-California)	1203-13-		7/-
A-4050?	?	**Ubehebe Craters** (US-California)	1203-16-		
K-4050*	?	**Adams Seamount** (Pacific-C)	1303-05-	0	
U-4050*	?	**Unnamed [East Pacific Rise]**	1304-05-	0	
T-4050?	?	**Masaya** (Nicaragua)	1404-10=	**6**	-/**10**
T-4050*	?	**Snaefellsjökull** (Iceland-W)	1700-01=	0	
T-4050?	?	**Grímsnes** (Iceland-SW)	1701-06=	0	
T-4050z	?	**Hekla** (Iceland-S)	1702-07=		
T-4050*	?	**Fremrinamur** (Iceland-NE)	1703-07=		**9**/-
T-4050?	?	**Krafla** (Iceland-NE)	1703-08=	0	
K-4050*	?	**La Palma** (Canary Is)	1803-01-		
E-4050z	?	**Erebus** (Antarctica)	1900-02=	0	
C-4040w	?	**Chaîne des Puys** (France)	0100-02-		-/7
C-4040?	?	**Picos Volc System** (Azores)	1802-081		
I-4037v	?	***Unknown Source*** *(GISP2 148, 313 ppb S)*	......		
G-4020x	?	**Misti, El** (Perú)	1504-01=		
I-4010v	?	***Unknown Source*** *(GISP2, 133 ppb S)*	......		
C-4000t	?	**Kasbek** (Georgia)	0104-02-		
G-4000?	?	**Taupo** (New Zealand)	0401-07=	3	-/7
G-4000x	?	**Pago** (New Britain-SW Pac)	0502-08=	**6**?	-/**10**
T-4000?	?	**Myoko** (Honshu-Japan)	0803-10=		
T-4000y	?	**Oshima** (Izu Is-Japan)	0804-01=		
T-4000?	?	**Reykjanes** (Iceland-SW)	1701-02=	0	**9**/-
T-4000?	?	**Grímsnes** (Iceland-SW)	1701-06=	2?	
T-4000?	?	**Fremrinamur** (Iceland-NE)	1703-07=	0	**9**/-

-4000 (-5950 BP)

START YEAR M-Dy	Duration	VOLCANO NAME (Subregion)	NUMBER	VEI	Vol L/T
I-3977v	?	***Unknown Source*** *(GISP2, 137 ppb S)*	......		
G-3960y	?	**Tenerife** (Canary Is)	1803-03-		8/-
T-3950?	?	**Gorely** (Kamchatka)	1000-07=	2	-/6
C-3950?	?	**Kliuchevskoi** (Kamchatka)	1000-26=		
G-3950?	?	**Poás** (Costa Rica)	1405-04=		
U-3950y	?	**Vestmannaeyjar** (Iceland-S)	1702-01=		8/-
T-3950z	?	**Hekla** (Iceland-S)	1702-07=		
G-3930v	?	**Pelée** (W Indies)	1600-12=		
T-3930?	?	**Katla** (Iceland-S)	1702-03=		
C-3920t	?	**Cumbres, Las** (México)	1401-098		
C-3910x	?	**Tambora** (Lesser Sunda Is)	0604-04=		
I-3905v	?	***Unknown Source*** *(GISP2, 134 ppb S)*	......		
G-3900x	?	**Haku-san** (Honshu-Japan)	0803-05=		
G-3900v	?	**E-san** (Hokkaido-Japan)	0805-011		
T-3900?	?	**Gorely** (Kamchatka)	1000-07=	2	
T-3900?	?	**Arenal** (Costa Rica)	1405-033	4	-/8
T-3900?	?	**Grímsnes** (Iceland-SW)	1701-06=	0	
C-3890z	?	**Hudson, Cerro** (Chile-S)	1508-057		
M-3880x	?	**Ischia** (Italy)	0101-03=		
C-3880u	?	**Cotopaxi** (Ecuador)	1502-05=	**5**+	-/**9**
T-3850?	?	**Bandai** (Honshu-Japan)	0803-16=		
G-3850x	?	**Zao** (Honshu-Japan)	0803-19=		
G-3850?	?	**Akademia Nauk** (Kamchatka)	1000-125		
R-3850*	?	**Koniuji** (Aleutian Is)	1101-14-		
C-3850?	?	**Kaguyak** (Alaska Peninsula)	1102-25-	**5**	-/**9**
G-3850x	?	**Rainier** (US-Washington)	1201-03-		
H-3850*	?	**Mono Craters** (US-California)	1203-12-		
C-3820?	?	**Pelée** (W Indies)	1600-12=	**P**	
C-3810u	?	**Edgecumbe** (Alaska-E)	1105-04-		
T-3810?	?	**Katla** (Iceland-S)	1702-03=		
T-3800*	?	**Adams** (US-Washington)	1201-04-	1?	8/-

START YEAR M-Dy	Dura-tion	VOLCANO NAME (Subregion)	NUMBER	VEI	Vol L/T
G-**3800**w	?	**Machín** (Colombia)	1501-04=		
T-**3800**y	?	**Reykjanes** (Iceland-SW)	1701-02=		
G-**3790**v	?	**Avachinsky** (Kamchatka)	1000-10=	4	-/8
T-**3790**z	?	**Minchinmávida** (Chile-S)	1508-04=		
T-**3790**?	?	**Katla** (Iceland-S)	1702-03=		
G-**3780**z	?	**Kuju** (Kyushu-Japan)	0802-12=	4	8/8
G-**3750**?	?	**Kusatsu-Shirane** (Honshu-Japan)	0803-12=	2	-/6
T-**3750**v	?	**Iwate** (Honshu-Japan)	0803-24=		
T-**3750**?	?	**Oshima** (Izu Is-Japan)	0804-01=		
G-**3750**?	?	**Moffett** (Aleutian Is)	1101-111		
C-**3750**?	?	**Mauna Loa** (Hawaiian Is)	1302-02=	0	
G-**3750**?	?	**Hengill** (Iceland-SW)	1701-05=	2	8/-
T-**3750**?	?	**Grímsnes** (Iceland-SW)	1701-06=	0	
T-**3750***	?	**Hekla** (Iceland-S)	1702-07=		
T-**3750**?	?	**Tenerife** (Canary Is)	1803-03-		
C-**3740**?	?	**Chachimbiro** (Ecuador)	1502-002		
G-**3740**j	?	**Burney, Monte** (Chile-S)	1508-07=		
C-**3730**?	?	**Villarrica** (Chile-C)	1507-12=		
T-**3720**?	?	**Katla** (Iceland-S)	1702-03=		
G-**3700**v	?	**Hakone** (Honshu-Japan)	0803-02=	1	8/5
T-**3700**?	?	**Myoko** (Honshu-Japan)	0803-10=		
T-**3700**?	?	**Avachinsky** (Kamchatka)	1000-10=		
C-**3690**v	?	**Fuji** (Honshu-Japan)	0803-03=		
C-**3680**x	?	**Mauna Kea** (Hawaiian Is)	1302-03-		
T-**3670**?	?	**Katla** (Iceland-S)	1702-03=		
C-**3660**z	?	**Chillán, Nevados de** (Chile-C)	1507-07=		
T-**3650**?	?	**Oshima** (Izu Is-Japan)	0804-01=		
T-**3650**?	?	**Mutnovsky** (Kamchatka)	1000-06=	2	-/6
G-**3650**?	?	**Shiveluch** (Kamchatka)	1000-27=	**5**	-/**9**
T-**3650***	?	**Makushin** (Aleutian Is)	1101-31-	**P**	
G-**3650**?	?	**Rainier** (US-Washington)	1201-03-	3	-/7
T-**3650**?	?	**Grímsnes** (Iceland-SW)	1701-06=	0	
C-**3640**y	?	**Pantelleria** (Italy)	0101-071		
T-**3640**?	?	**Katla** (Iceland-S)	1702-03=		
C-**3610** t	?	**Aso** (Kyushu-Japan)	0802-11=		
G-**3600**z	?	**Calatrava Volc Field** (Spain)	0100-04-		
G-**3600**x	?	**Colima** (México)	1401-04=		
G-**3580**y	?	**Ischia** (Italy)	0101-03=		
G-**3580**t	?	**Okataina [Haroharo]** (New Zeal).	0401-05=	**5**	**9/9**
G-**3580**x	?	**Taveuni** (Fiji Is-SW Pacific)	0405-01-	2	
C-**3580**x	?	**Taal** (Luzon-Philippines)	0703-07=	**6**	-/**10**
C-**3580**v	?	**Gorely** (Kamchatka)	1000-07=	2?	
K-**3550***	?	**Vulcano** (Italy)	0101-05=	0	6/-
G-**3550**?	?	**Pinatubo** (Luzon-Philippines)	0703-083	**6**	-/**10**
T-**3550**?	?	**Kirishima** (Kyushu-Japan)	0802-09=	3	-/7
G-**3550**t	?	**Sanbe** (Honshu-Japan)	0803-002		
T-**3550**z	?	**Haku-san** (Honshu-Japan)	0803-05=		
T-**3550**?	?	**Yotei** (Hokkaido-Japan)	0805-032		
C-**3550**z	?	**Akan** (Hokkaido-Japan)	0805-07=	3	-/7
T-**3550**?	?	**Kutcharo [Atosanupuri]** (Hokkaido)	0805-08=		
G-**3550**s	?	**Mashu** (Hokkaido-Japan)	0805-081	4	-/8
T-**3550**?	?	**Gorely** (Kamchatka)	1000-07=	0	
T-**3550**>	?	**Barkhatnaya Sopka** (Kamchatka)	1000-084		
G-**3550**?	?	**Krasheninnikov** (Kamchatka)	1000-19=		
C-**3550**?	?	**Nylgimelkin** (Kamchatka)	1000-65-		
C-**3550**?	?	**Jingbo** (China-E)	1005-04-		
C-**3550**?	?	**Glacier Peak** (US-Washington)	1201-02-		
T-**3550**?	?	**Adams** (US-Washington)	1201-04-	2	
G-**3550**?	?	**Santa Isabel** (Colombia)	1501-021		
T-**3550**?	?	**Hveravellir** (Iceland-SW)	1701-08=	0	8/-
T-**3550**z	?	**Grímsvötn** (Iceland-NE)	1703-01=	0	8/-
I -**3541**v	?	***Unknown Source*** *(GISP2, 97 ppb S)*	......		
T-**3540***	?	**Kurikoma** (Honshu-Japan)	0803-21=		
G-**3540**w	?	**Tenerife** (Canary Is)	1803-03-		8/-
I -**3518**v	?	***Unknown Source*** *(GISP2, 174 ppb S)*	......		
C-**3510**w	?	**Etna** (Italy)	0101-06=		
G-**3510**x	?	**Colima** (México)	1401-04=		
G-**3510**w	?	**Misti, El** (Perú)	1504-01=		
T-**3510**?	?	**Katla** (Iceland-S)	1702-03=		
C-**3500**?	?	**Acigöl-Nevsehir** (Turkey)	0103-004		
T-**3500**?	?	**Opala** (Kamchatka)	1000-08=		
T-**3500**?	?	**Avachinsky** (Kamchatka)	1000-10=		
G-**3500**t	?	**Maly Semiachik** (Kamchatka)	1000-14=		
G-**3500**?	?	**Shiveluch** (Kamchatka)	1000-27=	**5**	-/**9**
G-**3500**y	?	**Tolima, Nevado del** (Colombia)	1501-03=		
C-**3500**?	?	**Guagua Pichincha** (Ecuador)	1502-02=		
T-**3500**x	?	**Pelée** (W Indies)	1600-12=	**P**	
T-**3500**?	?	**Grímsnes** (Iceland-SW)	1701-06=	2?	
U-**3490**?	?	**Endeavour Ridge** (Pacific-NE)	1301-01-	0	
C-**3490**v	?	**Atacazo** (Ecuador)	1502-021	**P**	
C-**3490**s	?	**Sabancaya** (Perú)	1504-006	0	
G-**3480**w	?	**Kuchinoerabu-jima** (Ryukyu Is)	0802-05=		
T-**3480**?	?	**Katla** (Iceland-S)	1702-03=		
T-**3450**?	?	**Myoko** (Honshu-Japan)	0803-10=		
C-**3450**?	?	**Asama** (Honshu-Japan)	0803-11=	3	
T-**3450**?	?	**Gorely** (Kamchatka)	1000-07=	3	-/7
G-**3450**?	?	**Karymsky** (Kamchatka)	1000-13=		8/-
C-**3450**?	?	**Spokoiny** (Kamchatka)	1000-671		
C-**3450**w	?	**Iskut-Unuk River Cones** (Canada)	1200-09-		
T-**3450***	?	**Hekla** (Iceland-S)	1702-07=		
T-**3450**?	?	**Tenerife** (Canary Is)	1803-03-		7/-
C-**3440** t	?	**San Martín** (México)	1401-11=		
G-**3430**u	?	**Pelée** (W Indies)	1600-12=	4?	-/8
G-**3420**?	?	**Taupo** (New Zealand)	0401-07=	3	-/7
G-**3400**?	?	**Numazawa** (Honshu-Japan)	0803-151	**5**	-/**9**
T-**3400**?	?	**Avachinsky** (Kamchatka)	1000-10=		
C-**3390** t	?	**Etna** (Italy)	0101-06=		
T-**3390**?	?	**Katla** (Iceland-S)	1702-03=		
C-**3370**w	?	**Mauna Kea** (Hawaiian Is)	1302-03-		
T-**3370**?	?	**Katla** (Iceland-S)	1702-03=		
G-**3350** t	?	**Zao** (Honshu-Japan)	0803-19=		
T-**3350***	?	**Hachijo-jima** (Izu Is-Japan)	0804-05=		
C-**3350**?	?	**Mauna Loa** (Hawaiian Is)	1302-02=	0	
G-**3350**y	?	**Colima** (México)	1401-04=		
T-**3350**?	?	**Arenal** (Costa Rica)	1405-033	4	-/8
T-**3350**?	?	**Prestahnukur** (Iceland-SW)	1701-07=	0	8/-
T-**3350***	?	**Hekla** (Iceland-S)	1702-07=		
G-**3310**w	?	**Soufrière Guadeloupe** (W Indies)	1600-06=		
G-**3300**?	?	**Kilauea** (Hawaiian Is)	1302-01-	0	
C-**3290**?	?	**Pelée** (W Indies)	1600-12=		
T-**3280**z	?	**Cotopaxi** (Ecuador)	1502-05=	**5**	8/**9**
T-**3280**?	?	**Katla** (Iceland-S)	1702-03=		
T-**3270**?	?	**Colima** (México)	1401-04=		
T-**3250**?	?	**Taranaki [Egmont]** (New Zealand)	0401-03=		
C-**3250**u	?	**Kikai** (Ryukyu Is)	0802-06=		
T-**3250**z	?	**Iwate** (Honshu-Japan)	0803-24=	0	
G-**3250**?	?	**Krasheninnikov** (Kamchatka)	1000-19=		
C-**3250**?	?	**Spurr** (Alaska-SW)	1103-04-		
T-**3250**y	?	**Adams** (US-Washington)	1201-04-	2	
C-**3250**w	?	**Hell's Half Acre** (US-Idaho)	1204-04-	0	
E-**3250**z	?	**Carrizozo** (US-New Mexico)	1210-01-		**9**/-
C-**3250**?	?	**Mauna Loa** (Hawaiian Is)	1302-02=	0	
R-**3250***	?	**Puyehue-Cordón Caulle** (Chile-C)	1507-15=		
C-**3250**?	?	**Pelée** (W Indies)	1600-12=		
G-**3250**?	?	**Hengill** (Iceland-SW)	1701-05=	0	**9**/-
C-**3250**?	?	**Deception Island** (Antarctica)	1900-03=		
I -**3201** v	?	***Unknown Source*** *(GISP2, 175 ppb S)*	......		
G-**3200**w	?	**Taveuni** (Fiji Is-SW Pacific)	0405-01-	2	
T-**3200***	?	**Tate-yama** (Honshu-Japan)	0803-08=		
G-**3200**u	?	**Daisetsu** (Hokkaido-Japan)	0805-06=		
G-**3200**w	?	**Avachinsky** (Kamchatka)	1000-10=	**5**	-/**9**
G-**3200**?	?	**Karymsky** (Kamchatka)	1000-13=	4	8/8
T-**3200**?	?	**Shiveluch** (Kamchatka)	1000-27=	4+	-/8
D-**3195**?	?	***Unknown Source*** *(Belfast tree-ring)*	......		
C-**3190** v	?	**Arenal** (Costa Rica)	1405-033		
G-**3180** v	?	**Colima** (México)	1401-04=		
T-**3180**?	?	**Katla** (Iceland-S)	1702-03=		
G-**3170** x	?	**Taupo** (New Zealand)	0401-07=	4	-/8
C-**3170** u	?	**Fisher** (Aleutian Is)	1101-35-	**5**	-/**9**
C-**3150**?	?	**Loloru** (Bougainville-SW Pacific)	0505-03=		
C-**3150**?	?	**Glacier Peak** (US-Washington)	1201-02-		
G-**3150** x	?	**Galeras** (Colombia)	1501-08=	3	-/6
T-**3120**?	?	**Taupo** (New Zealand)	0401-07=	3	-/7
G-**3120** x	?	**Pelée** (W Indies)	1600-12=		
T-**3110** z	?	**Kuju** (Kyushu-Japan)	0802-12=		8/-
C-**3100** y	?	**Mayon** (Luzon-Philippines)	0703-03=		
C-**3090** z	?	**Socorro** (México-Is)	1401-021		
G-**3070**?	?	**Taupo** (New Zealand)	0401-07=	4	-/8
C-**3070** s	?	**Haleakala** (Hawaiian Is)	1302-06-		
K-**3050***	?	**Ischia** (Italy)	0101-03=		
C-**3050**w	?	**Etna** (Italy)	0101-06=		
T-**3050**?	?	**Meidob Volc Field** (Africa-N)	0205-05-	**P**	
C-**3050**?	?	**Tambora** (Lesser Sunda Is)	0604-04=		
C-**3050**?	?	**Bulusan** (Luzon-Philippines)	0703-01=		
C-**3050**?	?	**Sakura-jima** (Kyushu-Japan)	0802-08=	4	
T-**3050**?	?	**Kirishima** (Kyushu-Japan)	0802-09=	3	-/7
C-**3050**?	?	**Fuji** (Honshu-Japan)	0803-03=		
C-**3050**?	?	**Omanago Group** (Honshu-Japan)	0803-142		
C-**3050**?	?	**Iwate** (Honshu-Japan)	0803-24=		
N-**3050**?	?	**Akita-Yake-yama** (Honshu-Japan)	0803-26=		
C-**3050**?	?	**Akan** (Hokkaido-Japan)	0805-07=		
T-**3050**?	?	**Nemo Peak** (Kuril Is)	0900-32=		
T-**3050**?	?	**Diky Greben** (Kamchatka)	1000-022		
C-**3050**?	?	**Zheltovsky** (Kamchatka)	1000-04=	**5**	-/**9**
T-**3050**?	?	**Zhupanovsky** (Kamchatka)	1000-12=		
T-**3050**?	?	**Shiveluch** (Kamchatka)	1000-27=	3	-/7
T-**3050***	?	**Shasta** (US-California)	1203-01-	0	
T-**3050**?	?	**Yellowstone** (US-Wyoming)	1205-01-		
U-**3050***	?	**Unnamed [East Pacific Rise]**	1304-05-	0	
K-**3050***	?	**Zitácuaro-Valle de Bravo** (México)	1401-061	0	
T-**3050**z	?	**Nejapa-Miraflores** (Nicaragua)	1404-092		
C-**3050**?	?	**Krafla** (Iceland-NE)	1703-08=	0	
T-**3050**?	?	**Sete Cidades** (Azores)	1802-08=	4	-/8
T-**3050**?	?	**Tenerife** (Canary Is)	1803-03-		7/-

START YEAR	M-Dy	Duration	VOLCANO NAME (Subregion)	NUMBER	VEI	Vol L/T
C-3030 t		?	Colima (México)	1401-04=		
U-3020 ?		?	North Gorda Ridge (Pacific-NE)	1301-031	0	
C-3020 ?		?	Pelée (W Indies)	1600-12=		
C-3010 x		?	Popocatépetl (México)	1401-09=	**P**	
T-3000 y		?	Tskhouk-Karckar (Armenia)	0104-10-		
T-3000 ?		?	Meidob Volc Field (Africa-N)	0205-05-	**P**	
F-3000 z		?	Newer Volcanics Prov (Australia)	0509-01-		
G-3000 t		?	Azuma (Honshu-Japan)	0803-18=	1	-/5
T-3000 ?		?	Ksudach (Kamchatka)	1000-05=	4	-/8
C-2990 s		?	Ulreung (Korea)	1006-03-		
T-2990 z		?	Villarrica (Chile-C)	1507-12=	0	
C-2990 ?		?	Agua de Pau (Azores)	1802-09=	**5**	**-/9**
C-2980 w		?	Taryatu-Chulutu (Mongolia)	1003-01-		
C-2970 y		?	Snaefellsjökull (Iceland-W)	1700-01=	0	
I -2958 v		?	*Unknown Source (GISP2, 124 ppb S)*	......		
N-2950 z		?	Meidob Volc Field (Africa-N)	0205-05-	0	
G-2950 t		?	Iwate (Honshu-Japan)	0803-24=		
T-2950 ?		?	Avachinsky (Kamchatka)	1000-10=		
G-2950 ?		?	Krasheninnikov (Kamchatka)	1000-19=		
T-2950 v		?	Adams (US-Washington)	1201-04-	1?	5/-
C-2950 u		?	Taapaca (Chile-N)	1505-011		
T-2950 z		?	Hekla (Iceland-S)	1702-07=		
E-2950 y		?	Erebus (Antarctica)	1900-02=	0	
T-2920 ?		?	Katla (Iceland-S)	1702-03=	3	-/7
G-2910 w		?	Merapi (Java)	0603-25=		
G-2900 ?		?	Taupo (New Zealand)	0401-07=	4	-/8
C-2900 w		?	Newer Volcanics Prov (Australia)	0509-01-		
C-2900 ?		?	Sakura-jima (Kyushu-Japan)	0802-08=	4	
T-2900 ?		?	Myoko (Honshu-Japan)	0803-10=		
T-2900 z		?	Miyake-jima (Izu Is-Japan)	0804-04=	4	7/8
T-2900 ?		?	Mutnovsky (Kamchatka)	1000-06=	2	-/6
T-2900 ?		?	Avachinsky (Kamchatka)	1000-10=		
T-2900 ?		?	Shiveluch (Kamchatka)	1000-27=	3	-/7
C-2890		?	Campi Flegrei (Italy)	0101-01=		
C-2890 u		?	Redoubt (Alaska-SW)	1103-03-		
T-2850 y		?	Taranaki [Egmont] (New Zealand)	0401-03=		
G-2850 ?		?	Taupo (New Zealand)	0401-07=	3	-/7
T-2850 ?		?	Aso (Kyushu-Japan)	0802-11=	0	
G-2850 ?		?	Hakkoda Group (Honshu-Japan)	0803-28=	2	-/6
C-2850 ?		?	Ilyinsky (Kamchatka)	1000-03=	**5**	**-/9**
G-2850 ?		?	Kikhpinych (Kamchatka)	1000-18=	3	-/7
G-2850 y		?	Ichinsky (Kamchatka)	1000-28=		
G-2850 ?		?	Crater Lake (US-Oregon)	1202-16-		7/-
C-2850 ?		?	Kilauea (Hawaiian Is)	1302-01-	0	
T-2850 ?		?	Katla (Iceland-S)	1702-03=		
T-2850 ?		?	Tenerife (Canary Is)	1803-03-		8/-
C-2830 t		?	Halla (Korea)	1006-04-		
C-2800 w		?	Fournaise, Piton de la (Indian O.)	0303-02=		
T-2800 ?		?	Taupo (New Zealand)	0401-07=	3	-/7
T-2800 y		?	Fuji (Honshu-Japan)	0803-03=		
G-2800 v		?	Daisetsu (Hokkaido-Japan)	0805-06=		
T-2800 *		?	Mashu (Hokkaido-Japan)	0805-081	3	-/7
G-2800 v		?	Colima (México)	1401-04=		
T-2800 ?		?	Arenal (Costa Rica)	1405-033	4	-/8
C-2790 ?		?	Davis Lake (US-Oregon)	1202-10-		
G-2780 q		?	Kikhpinych (Kamchatka)	1000-18=	4	8/8
C-2780 u		?	Orizaba, Pico de (México)	1401-10=	3	
C-2770 u		?	Hualalai (Hawaiian Is)	1302-04-	0	
C-2750 u		?	Fort Portal (Africa-C)	0203-001		
G-2750 v		?	Myoko (Honshu-Japan)	0803-10=	4	-/8
G-2750 x		?	Azuma (Honshu-Japan)	0803-18=		
T-2750 ?		?	Gorely (Kamchatka)	1000-07=	2	-/6
T-2750 z		?	Bezymianny (Kamchatka)	1000-25=		
T-2750 ?		?	Shiveluch (Kamchatka)	1000-27=	3	-/7
C-2750 ?		?	Rainier (US-Washington)	1201-03-	2	-/6
C-2750 ?		?	Mauna Loa (Hawaiian Is)	1302-02=	0	
C-2750 x		?	Mauna Kea (Hawaiian Is)	1302-03-		
C-2750 x		?	Michoacán [El Metate] (México)	1401-06=	3	-/7
T-2750 *		?	Hekla (Iceland-S)	1702-07=		
C-2750 ?		?	Deception Island (Antarctica)	1900-03=		
G-2720 y		?	Unzen (Kyushu-Japan)	0802-10=		
C-2710 u		?	Acatenango (Guatemala)	1402-08=		
T-2700 *		?	Ischia (Italy)	0101-03=		
G-2700 ?		?	Fournaise, Piton de la (Indian O.)	0303-02=	**5?**	**-/9**
T-2700 ?		?	Taranaki [Egmont] (New Zealand)	0401-03=		
T-2700 x		?	Iwate (Honshu-Japan)	0803-24=		
G-2700 v		?	Hachijo-jima (Izu Is-Japan)	0804-05=	3	-/7
G-2700 q		?	Khangar (Kamchatka)	1000-272		
C-2690 u		?	Ibusuki [Ikeda-ko] (Kyushu-Japan)	0802-07=	**5**	**-/9**
T-2680 ?		?	Katla (Iceland-S)	1702-03=		
G-2670 x		?	Unnamed (Syria)	0300-04-		
C-2670 v		?	Udokan [Aku] (Russia-SE)	1002-03-		
G-2660 x		?	Pelée (W Indies)	1600-12=	4?	-/8
C-2660 u		?	Brennisteinsfjöll (Iceland-SW)	1701-04=	0	**9/-**
K-2650 *		?	Vulcano (Italy)	0101-05=	3	6/7
C-2650 ?		?	Kirishima (Kyushu-Japan)	0802-09=	4	
G-2650 x		?	Tokachi (Hokkaido-Japan)	0805-05=		
C-2650 ?		?	Tolmachev Dol (Kamchatka)	1000-082	4+	-/8
T-2650 ?		?	Avachinsky (Kamchatka)	1000-10=		
R-2650 *		?	Koniuji (Aleutian Is)	1101-14-		
T-2650 y		?	Adams (US-Washington)	1201-04-	2	
C-2650 ?		?	Machín (Colombia)	1501-04=		
T-2650 ?		?	Tenerife (Canary Is)	1803-03-		5/-
G-2640 z		?	Unzen (Kyushu-Japan)	0802-10=		
C-2640 x		?	Cotopaxi (Ecuador)	1502-05=	**5**	**-/9**
G-2620 y		?	Shiveluch (Kamchatka)	1000-27=	**5**	**-/9**
C-2610 ?		?	Aguilera (Chile-S)	1508-062		
G-2600 ?		?	Taupo (New Zealand)	0401-07=	4	-/8
G-2600 t		?	Adatara (Honshu-Japan)	0803-17=	3	-/7
G-2600 x		?	Zao (Honshu-Japan)	0803-19=		
C-2580 t		?	Campi Flegrei (Italy)	0101-01=		
C-2580 s		?	Haleakala (Hawaiian Is)	1302-06-		
G-2580 z		?	Galeras (Colombia)	1501-08=	2	-/6
C-2560 v		?	Craters of the Moon (US-Idaho)	1204-02-	0	**9/-**
T-2550 ?		?	Aso (Kyushu-Japan)	0802-11=	1	-/5
T-2550 ?		?	Fuji (Honshu-Japan)	0803-03=		
G-2550 w		?	Haku-san (Honshu-Japan)	0803-05=		
T-2550 ?		?	Yake-dake (Honshu-Japan)	0803-07=	0	**9/-**
A-2550 z		?	Asama (Honshu-Japan)	0803-11=	4	
T-2550 ?		?	Oshima (Izu Is-Japan)	0804-01=		
T-2550 z		?	Hachijo-jima (Izu Is-Japan)	0804-05=	3	-/7
T-2550 z		?	Amak (Aleutian Is)	1101-39-		
T-2550 z		?	Aniakchak (Alaska Peninsula)	1102-09-		
C-2550 ?		?	Rainier (US-Washington)	1201-03-	3	-/7
C-2550 ?		?	Shasta (US-California)	1203-01-		
C-2550 y		?	Momotombo (Nicaragua)	1404-09=		
T-2550 *		?	Apoyeque (Nicaragua)	1404-091	**5**	**-/9**
C-2550 w		?	Doña Juana (Colombia)	1501-07=	**C**	
C-2550 ?		?	Cuicocha (Ecuador)	1502-003		
T-2550 ?		?	Hveravellir (Iceland-SW)	1701-08=	0	8/-
C-2540 x		?	Mauna Kea (Hawaiian Is)	1302-03-		
T-2540 ?		?	Katla (Iceland-S)	1702-03=		
G-2530 y		?	Avachinsky (Kamchatka)	1000-10=	4	-/8
T-2530 ?		?	Shiveluch (Kamchatka)	1000-27=	3	-/7
C-2530 s		?	Terceira (Azores)	1802-05=		
T-2500 ?		?	Campi Flegrei (Italy)	0101-01=	4	-/8
G-2500 ?		?	Taupo (New Zealand)	0401-07=	3	-/7
T-2500 ?		?	Avachinsky (Kamchatka)	1000-10=		
C-2500 u		?	Orizaba, Pico de (México)	1401-10=	3	
T-2500 *		?	Chimborazo (Ecuador)	1502-071		
G-2490 ?		?	Shiveluch (Kamchatka)	1000-27=	3	-/7
C-2490 s		?	Atacazo (Ecuador)	1502-021	**5**	**-/9**
T-2480 ?		?	Katla (Iceland-S)	1702-03=		
G-2470 t		?	Haleakala (Hawaiian Is)	1302-06-		8/-
C-2460 v		?	Mauna Kea (Hawaiian Is)	1302-03-		
G-2460 v		?	Pelée (W Indies)	1600-12=		
A-2450 t		?	Ararat (Turkey)	0103-04-		
T-2450 y		?	Taranaki [Egmont] (New Zealand)	0401-03=		
T-2450 *		?	Kikai (Ryukyu Is)	0802-06=		
C-2450 z		?	Fuji (Honshu-Japan)	0803-03=		
T-2450 z		?	Hachijo-jima (Izu Is-Japan)	0804-05=	4	-/8
T-2450 ?		?	Gorely (Kamchatka)	1000-07=	3	-/7
G-2450 ?		?	Maly Semiachik (Kamchatka)	1000-14=		
T-2450 *		?	Hekla (Iceland-S)	1702-07=		
C-2440 ?		?	Campi Flegrei (Italy)	0101-01=		
G-2440 y		?	Kuju (Kyushu-Japan)	0802-12=	4	7/8
C-2440 u		?	Hualalai (Hawaiian Is)	1302-04-	0	
C-2430 ?		?	Pelée (W Indies)	1600-12=	**P**	
G-2420 s		?	Vesuvius (Italy)	0101-02=	**5**	**-/9**
T-2420 ?		?	Katla (Iceland-S)	1702-03=		
C-2410 v		?	Medicine Lake (US-California)	1203-02-		7/-
G-2400 ?		?	Rungwe (Africa-E)	0202-166	**P**	
C-2400 s		?	Taranaki [Egmont] (New Zealand)	0401-03=		
C-2400 u		?	Taapaca (Chile-N)	1505-011		
C-2400 x		?	Snaefellsjökull (Iceland-W)	1700-01=	2?	8/-
C-2380 v		?	Soufrière St. Vincent (W Indies)	1600-15=		
C-2370 x		?	Acigöl-Nevsehir (Turkey)	0103-004		
C-2370 w		?	Colima (México)	1401-04=	4?	-/8
C-2370 u		?	Popocatépetl (México)	1401-09=		
C-2360 ?		?	Pelée (W Indies)	1600-12=		
K-2350 *		?	Ischia (Italy)	0101-03=		
C-2350 u		?	Aso (Kyushu-Japan)	0802-11=		
G-2350 ?		?	Karymsky (Kamchatka)	1000-13=	3	7/7
C-2350 ?		?	Mauna Loa (Hawaiian Is)	1302-02=	0	
G-2340 ?		?	St. Helens (US-Washington)	1201-05-	**5**	**-/9**
T-2330 w		?	Campi Flegrei (Italy)	0101-01=	3	
C-2330 v		?	Etna (Italy)	0101-06=		
G-2320 v		?	Burney, Monte (Chile-S)	1508-07=	**5**	**-/9**
C-2310 v		?	Soufrière St. Vincent (W Indies)	1600-15=		
G-2310 p		?	Hekla (Iceland-S)	1702-07=	**5**	**-/9**
G-2300 u		?	Zao (Honshu-Japan)	0803-19=		
T-2300 ?		?	Avachinsky (Kamchatka)	1000-10=		
G-2300 w		?	Kanaga (Aleutian Is)	1101-11-		
C-2300 u		?	Orizaba, Pico de (México)	1401-10=	4	-/8

START YEAR M-Dy	Duration	VOLCANO NAME (Subregion)	NUMBER	VEI	Vol L/T
T-2300?	?	**Fremrinamur** (Iceland-NE)	1703-07=	0	9/-
T-2300?	?	**Tenerife** (Canary Is)	1803-03-		
G-2290y	?	**Sand Mountain Field** (US-Oregon)	1202-04-	2?	
C-2280?	?	**Pelée** (W Indies)	1600-12=		
C-2270t	?	**Mendeleev** (Kuril Is)	0900-02=		
C-2270y	?	**Snaefellsjökull** (Iceland-W)	1700-01=	0	
U-2260?	?	**Escanaba Segment** (Pacific-NE)	1301-04-	0	
C-2260s	?	**Haleakala** (Hawaiian Is)	1302-06-		
C-2250w	?	**Galunggung** (Java)	0603-14=	5?	
G-2250?	?	**Hakkoda Group** (Honshu-Japan)	0803-28=	3	-/7
C-2250?	?	**Diky Greben** (Kamchatka)	1000-022		
T-2250?	?	**Gorely** (Kamchatka)	1000-07=	2	-/6
G-2250?	?	**Karymsky** (Kamchatka)	1000-13=	4	7/9
G-2250?	?	**Maly Semiachik** (Kamchatka)	1000-14=		
G-2250?	?	**Krasheninnikov** (Kamchatka)	1000-19=		
C-2250?	?	**Mauna Loa** (Hawaiian Is)	1302-02=	0	
T-2250?	?	**Arenal** (Costa Rica)	1405-033	4	-/8
T-2250	?	**Cotopaxi** (Ecuador)	1502-05=		8/-
C-2250<	?	**Hudson, Cerro** (Chile-S)	1508-057		
T-2250?	?	**Katla** (Iceland-S)	1702-03=		
T-2250?	?	**Tenerife** (Canary Is)	1803-03-		7/-
C-2240?	?	**Shisheika** (Kamchatka)	1000-511		8/-
G-2240*	?	**Chichinautzin [Guespalapa]** (Méx)	1401-08=	3	8/7
G-2240y	?	**Machín** (Colombia)	1501-04=		
C-2240?	?	**Villarrica** (Chile-C)	1507-12=		
G-2230x	?	**Misti, El** (Perú)	1504-01=		
C-2220t	?	**Campi Flegrei** (Italy)	0101-01=		
C-2220v	?	**Edgecumbe** (Alaska-E)	1105-04-		
C-2220v	?	**Cotopaxi** (Ecuador)	1502-05=		
T-2220?	?	**Katla** (Iceland-S)	1702-03=		
C-2210s	?	**Haleakala** (Hawaiian Is)	1302-06-		
C-2210w	?	**Agua de Pau** (Azores)	1802-09=		
T-2200?	?	**Gorely** (Kamchatka)	1000-07=	2	
T-2200?	?	**Shiveluch** (Kamchatka)	1000-27=	4+	-/8
C-2200y	?	**Dotsero** (US-Colorado)	1208-01-	2?	
T-2200z	?	**Kilauea** (Hawaiian Is)	1302-01-		
C-2200w	?	**Soufrière St. Vincent** (W Indies)	1600-15=		
T-2190?	?	**Katla** (Iceland-S)	1702-03=		
C-2160v	?	**Changbaishan** (China-E)	1005-06-	P	
T-2160?	?	**Katla** (Iceland-S)	1702-03=		
C-2150z	?	**Campi Flegrei** (Italy)	0101-01=	5	-/9
T-2150?	?	**Taranaki [Egmont]** (New Zealand)	0401-03=		
C-2150?	?	**Loloru** (Bougainville-SW Pacific)	0505-03=		
N-2150*	?	**Unzen** (Kyushu-Japan)	0802-10=		
T-2150?	?	**Mutnovsky** (Kamchatka)	1000-06=	3	-/7
T-2150?	?	**Shiveluch** (Kamchatka)	1000-27=	3	-/7
G-2150x	?	**Kanaga** (Aleutian Is)	1101-11-		
C-2150?	?	**Mauna Loa** (Hawaiian Is)	1302-02=	0	
C-2140?	?	**Villarrica** (Chile-C)	1507-12=		
C-2135t	?	**Soufrière St. Vincent** (W Indies)	1600-15=		
C-2130t	?	**San Martín** (México)	1401-11=		
C-2120v	?	**Fort Portal** (Africa-C)	0203-001		
C-2120t	?	**Haleakala** (Hawaiian Is)	1302-06-		
C-2110v	?	**Orizaba, Pico de** (México)	1401-10=	3	
C-2110t	?	**Andahua-Orcopampa** (Perú)	1504-004		
T-2110?	?	**Katla** (Iceland-S)	1702-03=		
G-2100v	?	**Izu-Tobu** (Honshu-Japan)	0803-01=	4	8/8
T-2100z	?	**Myoko** (Honshu-Japan)	0803-10=		
T-2100?	?	**Avachinsky** (Kamchatka)	1000-10=		
G-2100?	?	**Shiveluch** (Kamchatka)	1000-27=	5	-/9
T-2100y	?	**St. Helens** (US-Washington)	1201-05-		
G-2100x	?	**Machín** (Colombia)	1501-04=		
G-2100x	?	**Pelée** (W Indies)	1600-12=		
C-2095v	?	**Azufral** (Colombia)	1501-09=		
G-2090u	?	**Guagua Pichincha** (Ecuador)	1502-02=		
T-2080u	?	**Campi Flegrei** (Italy)	0101-01=	2	7/-
A-2080x	?	**Acigöl-Nevsehir** (Turkey)	0103-004		
G-2080?	?	**Kilauea** (Hawaiian Is)	1302-01-	0	
C-2050?	?	**Mariveles** (Luzon-Philippines)	0703-081		
M-2050?	?	**Sakura-jima** (Kyushu-Japan)	0802-08=		
C-2050?	?	**Kirishima** (Kyushu-Japan)	0802-09=	3	-/7
T-2050?	?	**Izu-Tobu** (Honshu-Japan)	0803-01=		6/-
C-2050?	?	**Fuji** (Honshu-Japan)	0803-03=		
G-2050x	?	**Iwate** (Honshu-Japan)	0803-24=		
T-2050?	?	**Megata** (Honshu-Japan)	0803-262		
T-2050?	?	**Hachijo-jima** (Izu Is-Japan)	0804-05=	5	-/9
C-2050?	?	**Akan** (Hokkaido-Japan)	0805-07=		
G-2050s	?	**Mashu** (Hokkaido-Japan)	0805-081	4	-/8
C-2050?	?	**Ilyinsky** (Kamchatka)	1000-03=		
T-2050?	?	**Mutnovsky** (Kamchatka)	1000-06=	2	-/6
T-2050?	?	**Gorely** (Kamchatka)	1000-07=	2	-/6
G-2050?	?	**Karymsky** (Kamchatka)	1000-13=		
T-2050?	?	**Tolbachik** (Kamchatka)	1000-24=	3	8/7
C-2050?	?	**Ostry** (Kamchatka)	1000-68-		
C-2050x	?	**Halla** (Korea)	1006-04-		
C-2050?	?	**Iliamna** (Alaska-SW)	1103-02-	P	
C-2050?	?	**Shasta** (US-California)	1203-01-		
C-2050?	?	**Mauna Loa** (Hawaiian Is)	1302-02=	0	
U-2050*	?	**Unnamed [East Pacific Rise]**	1304-05-	0	
A-2050?	?	**Michoacán [La Alberca]** (México)	1401-06=		
T-2050?	?	**Cotopaxi** (Ecuador)	1502-05=	5	7/9
?-2050?	*?*	*Soufrière Guadeloupe (W Indies)*	1600-06=		
T-2050?	?	**Ljósufjöll** (Iceland-W)	1700-03=	3?	
G-2050?	?	**Hveravellir** (Iceland-SW)	1701-08=	0	9/-
T-2050?	?	**Katla** (Iceland-S)	1702-03=		
T-2050z	?	**Askja** (Iceland-NE)	1703-06=	0	9/-
T-2050*	?	**Sete Cidades** (Azores)	1802-08=		
R-2050*	?	**Erebus** (Antarctica)	1900-02=	0	
T-2040?	?	**Campi Flegrei** (Italy)	0101-01=	3	-/7
C-2040v	?	**Long Island** (New Guinea-NE of)	0501-05=	6	-/10
C-2040u	?	**Hualalai** (Hawaiian Is)	1302-04-	0	
G-2030v	?	**Chichón, El** (México)	1401-12=	5	-/9
C-2020u	?	**Soufrière St. Vincent** (W Indies)	1600-15=		
T-2020?	?	**Katla** (Iceland-S)	1702-03=		
T-2010?	?	**Ibusuki [Kaimon]** (Kyushu-Japan)	0802-07=	4	-/8
C-2010w	?	**Liamuiga** (W Indies)	1600-03=	P	
C-2010v	?	**Snaefellsjökull** (Iceland-W)	1700-01=		
T-2000w	?	**Campi Flegrei** (Italy)	0101-01=	4	-/8
A-2000*	?	**Dar-Alages** (Armenia)	0104-08-		
G-2000?	?	**Marra, Jebel** (Africa-N)	0205-03-	C	
C-2000v	?	**Raoul Island** (Kermadec Is)	0402-03=	4	-/8
T-2000?	?	**Nikko-Shirane** (Honshu-Japan)	0803-14=		
T-2000*	?	**Nasu** (Honshu-Japan)	0803-15=	2?	
T-2000z	?	**Zao** (Honshu-Japan)	0803-19=		
G-2000?	?	**Iwate** (Honshu-Japan)	0803-24=		
G-2000v	?	**Miyake-jima** (Izu Is-Japan)	0804-04=	3	-/7
T-2000?	?	**Gorely** (Kamchatka)	1000-07=	2	-/6
G-2000?	?	**Shiveluch** (Kamchatka)	1000-27=	5	-/9
C-2000?	?	**Mauna Loa** (Hawaiian Is)	1302-02=	0	
C-2000u	?	**Soufrière Hills** (W Indies)	1600-05=		
T-2000?	?	**Katla** (Iceland-S)	1702-03=		

-2000 (3950 BP)

START YEAR M-Dy	Duration	VOLCANO NAME (Subregion)	NUMBER	VEI	Vol L/T
G-1990w	?	**Savai'i** (Samoa-SW Pacific)	0404-04=		
G-1990x	?	**Tolima, Nevado del** (Colombia)	1501-03=	5?	-/9
C-1980t	?	**Etna** (Italy)	0101-06=		
T-1980w	?	**Villarrica** (Chile-C)	1507-12=	0	
G-1980x	?	**Tenerife** (Canary Is)	1803-03-		
C-1950y	?	**Koryaksky** (Kamchatka)	1000-09=		
G-1950y	?	**Ichinsky** (Kamchatka)	1000-28=		
C-1950v	?	**Mageik** (Alaska Peninsula)	1102-15-		
T-1950?	?	**Katla** (Iceland-S)	1702-03=		
T-1950v	?	**Grímsvötn** (Iceland-NE)	1703-01=	2	9/-
C-1940s	?	**Haleakala** (Hawaiian Is)	1302-06-		
G-1940y	?	**Colima** (México)	1401-04=		
C-1920s	?	**Parker** (Mindanao-Philippines)	0701-011	P	
T-1920?	?	**Sanbe** (Honshu-Japan)	0803-002	4	9/8
C-1920t	?	**Calbuco** (Chile-S)	1508-02=		
G-1920?	?	**Katla** (Iceland-S)	1702-03=	4	-/8
T-1910?	?	**Katla** (Iceland-S)	1702-03=		
A-1900*	?	**Ghegam Ridge** (Armenia)	0104-07-	0	
T-1900*	?	**Niigata-Yake-yama** (Honshu-Japan)	0803-09=		
G-1900y	?	**Kanaga** (Aleutian Is)	1101-11-		
T-1900w	?	**Black Peak** (Alaska Peninsula)	1102-08-	6	-/10
C-1900?	?	**Mauna Loa** (Hawaiian Is)	1302-02=	0	
C-1900t	?	**Haleakala** (Hawaiian Is)	1302-06-		
G-1890	?	**Merapi** (Java)	0603-25=		
C-1890?	?	**Dana** (Alaska Peninsula)	1102-05-	5	-/9
C-1890u	?	**Colima** (México)	1401-04=		
C-1890u	?	**Popocatépetl** (México)	1401-09=		
G-1890?	?	**Hudson, Cerro** (Chile-S)	1508-057	6	-/10
C-1880w	?	**Michoacán [El Jabalí]** (México)	1401-06=	3	
C-1870t	?	**Campi Flegrei** (Italy)	0101-01=	4	-/9
G-1860?	?	**St. Helens** (US-Washington)	1201-05-	6	-/10
G-1860v	?	**Guagua Pichincha** (Ecuador)	1502-02=		
C-1860v	?	**Taapaca** (Chile-N)	1505-011		
C-1850w	?	**Fuji** (Honshu-Japan)	0803-03=		
T-1850?	?	**Nemo Peak** (Kuril Is)	0900-32=		
T-1850?	?	**Hayes** (Alaska-SW)	1103-05-		
T-1850>	?	**Adams** (US-Washington)	1201-04-	1?	7/-
G-1850?	?	**Haleakala** (Hawaiian Is)	1302-06-		7/-
C-1850?	?	**Azufral** (Colombia)	1501-09=		
T-1850?	?	**Katla** (Iceland-S)	1702-03=		
T-1850*	?	**Hekla** (Iceland-S)	1702-07=		
C-1850z	?	**Agua de Pau** (Azores)	1802-09=	3	6/7
C-1830u	?	**Kikai** (Ryukyu Is)	0802-06=		
C-1830u	?	**Aso** (Kyushu-Japan)	0802-11=		
C-1830y	?	**Iskut-Unuk River Cones** (Canada)	1200-09-		
T-1830>	?	**Reclus** (Chile-S)	1508-063		
G-1820w	?	**Rincón de la Vieja** (Costa Rica)	1405-02=	4	-/8
C-1810x	?	**Villarrica** (Chile-C)	1507-12=	5	-/9
G-1810w	?	**Soufrière Guadeloupe** (W Indies)	1600-06=		
T-1800*	?	**Bandai** (Honshu-Japan)	0803-16=		

START YEAR M-Dy	Duration	VOLCANO NAME (Subregion)	NUMBER	VEI	Vol L/T
G-**1800** t	?	**Azuma** (Honshu-Japan)	0803-18=		
T-**1800** t	?	**Miyake-jima** (Izu Is-Japan)	0804-04=	3	-/7
G-**1800** v	?	**Aoga-shima** (Izu Is-Japan)	0804-06=	2?	7/-
G-**1800** t	?	**Maly Semiachik** (Kamchatka)	1000-14=		
C-**1800** ?	?	**Mauna Loa** (Hawaiian Is)	1302-02=	0	
C-**1800** t	?	**Haleakala** (Hawaiian Is)	1302-06-		
T-**1800** ?	?	**Cayambe** (Ecuador)	1502-006		
C-**1800** v	?	**Watt, Morne** (W Indies)	1600-101		
T-**1800** y	?	**Reykjanes** (Iceland-SW)	1701-02=	2	7/-
C-**1790** v	?	**Fournaise, Piton de la** (Indian O.)	0303-02=		
G-**1790** s	?	**Griggs** (Alaska Peninsula)	1102-19-		
T-**1780** ?	?	**Ibusuki [Kaimon]** (Kyushu-Japan)	0802-07=	4	-/8
G-**1770** u	?	**Merapi** (Java)	0603-25=		
C-**1770** w	?	**Aso** (Kyushu-Japan)	0802-11=		
T-**1770** v	?	**St. Helens** (US-Washington)	1201-05-	**5**	-/**9**
G-**1770** v	?	**Arenal** (Costa Rica)	1405-033		
G-**1750** ?	?	**Okataina [Haroharo]** (New Zeal).	0401-05=	4+	8/8
G-**1750** ?	?	**Niigata-Yake-yama** (Honshu-Japan)	0803-09=		
G-**1750** t	?	**Tokachi** (Hokkaido-Japan)	0805-05=		
T-**1750** ?	?	**Tolbachik** (Kamchatka)	1000-24=	3	
C-**1750** ?	?	**Makushin** (Aleutian Is)	1101-31-		
C-**1750** ?	?	**Veniaminof** (Alaska Peninsula)	1102-07-	**6**	-/**10**
C-**1750** ?	?	**Martin** (Alaska Peninsula)	1102-14-		
C-**1750** ?	?	**Mauna Loa** (Hawaiian Is)	1302-02=	0	
C-**1750** w	?	**Ljósufjöll** (Iceland-W)	1700-03=	2	
T-**1750** z	?	**Hekla** (Iceland-S)	1702-07=		
G-**1740** y	?	**Sand Mountain Field** (US-Oregon)	1202-04-	2?	
G-**1730** t	?	**Hengill** (Iceland-SW)	1701-05=	0	**9**/-
T-**1720** y	?	**Kuju** (Kyushu-Japan)	0802-12=		8/-
C-**1710** u	?	**Osorno** (Chile-S)	1508-01=		
C-**1700** v	?	**Taranaki [Egmont]** (New Zealand)	0401-03=	**5**	-/**9**
T-**1700** ?	?	**Taveuni** (Fiji Is-SW Pacific)	0405-01-	2	
G-**1700** t	?	**Aso** (Kyushu-Japan)	0802-11=	**P**	
G-**1700** ?	?	**Nipesotsu-Maruyama** (Hokkaido)	0805-061	2	-/6
T-**1700** ?	?	**Avachinsky** (Kamchatka)	1000-10=		
T-**1700** ?	?	**Shiveluch** (Kamchatka)	1000-27=	4	-/8
C-**1700** ?	?	**Mauna Loa** (Hawaiian Is)	1302-02=	0	
T-**1700** ?	?	**Katla** (Iceland-S)	1702-03=		
T-**1700** ?	?	**Tenerife** (Canary Is)	1803-03-		7/-
I -**1695** u	?	***Unknown Source*** *(GISP2, 213 ppb S)*	......		
G-**1680** ?	?	**St. Helens** (US-Washington)	1201-05-		
C-**1680** w	?	**Craters of the Moon** (US-Idaho)	1204-02-	0	**9**/-
T-**1670** ?	?	**Katla** (Iceland-S)	1702-03=		
T-**1670** *	?	**Furnas** (Azores)	1802-10=		
V-**1662** ?	?	**Nemrut Dagi** (Turkey)	0103-02=		
T-**1650** ?	?	**Campi Flegrei** (Italy)	0101-01=	4	-/8
G-**1650** ?	?	**Iwate** (Honshu-Japan)	0803-24=		
G-**1650** ?	?	**Krasheninnikov** (Kamchatka)	1000-19=		
T-**1650** ?	?	**Gamchen** (Kamchatka)	1000-21=		
T-**1650** ?	?	**Tolbachik** (Kamchatka)	1000-24=		
T-**1650** ?	?	**Shiveluch** (Kamchatka)	1000-27=	3	-/7
C-**1650** ?	?	**Mageik** (Alaska Peninsula)	1102-15-		
C-**1650** ?	?	**Kilauea** (Hawaiian Is)	1302-01-	0	
C-**1650** ?	?	**Mauna Loa** (Hawaiian Is)	1302-02=	0	
C-**1650** x	?	**Hualalai** (Hawaiian Is)	1302-04-	0	
T-**1650** ?	?	**Arenal** (Costa Rica)	1405-033	4	-/8
C-**1650** w	?	**Azufral** (Colombia)	1501-09=		
T-**1650** ?	?	**Cayambe** (Ecuador)	1502-006		
T-**1650** *	?	**Hekla** (Iceland-S)	1702-07=		
T-**1650** ?	?	**Tenerife** (Canary Is)	1803-03-		7/-
I -**1645** j	?	**Aniakchak** (Alaska Peninsula)	1102-09-	**6**?	-/**10**
T-**1640** ?	?	**Katla** (Iceland-S)	1702-03=		
D-**1628** ?	?	***Unknown Source*** *(Belfast tree-ring)*	......		
I -**1623** u	?	***Unknown Source*** *(GISP2, 145 ppb S)*	......		
G-**1610** m	?	**Santorini** (Greece)	0102-04=	**7**?	-/**10**
T-**1610** ?	?	**Ibusuki [Kaimon]** (Kyushu-Japan)	0802-07=	3	-/7
G-**1610** ?	?	**St. Helens** (US-Washington)	1201-05-		
G-**1600** ?	?	**Zao** (Honshu-Japan)	0803-19=		
G-**1600** ?	?	**Moffett** (Aleutian Is)	1101-111		
C-**1600** u	?	**Soufrière St. Vincent** (W Indies)	1600-15=		
C-**1580** u	?	**Fuego** (Guatemala)	1402-09=		
C-**1580** j	?	**Chacana** (Ecuador)	1502-022		
C-**1580** u	?	**Taapaca** (Chile-N)	1505-011		
C-**1560** s	?	**Taranaki [Egmont]** (New Zealand)	0401-03=		
G-**1550** u	?	**Vesuvius** (Italy)	0101-02=	4	-/8
T-**1550** *	?	**Lengai, Ol Doinyo** (Africa-E)	0202-12=		
T-**1550** ?	?	**Ibusuki [Nabeshima-dake]** (Japan)	0802-07=		
T-**1550** *	?	**Adatara** (Honshu-Japan)	0803-17=		
T-**1550** *	?	**Kutcharo [Atosanupuri]** (Hokkaido)	0805-08=		
C-**1550** ?	?	**Opala** (Kamchatka)	1000-08=		
C-**1550** ?	?	**Koryaksky** (Kamchatka)	1000-09=		
T-**1550** ?	?	**Bakening** (Kamchatka)	1000-123		
T-**1550** ?	?	**Uzon** (Kamchatka)	1000-17=		
T-**1550** z	?	**Bezymianny** (Kamchatka)	1000-25=		
C-**1550** ?	?	**Severny** (Kamchatka)	1000-70-		
G-**1550** v	?	**Kanaga** (Aleutian Is)	1101-11-		
C-**1550** w	?	**Redoubt** (Alaska-SW)	1103-03-		
T-**1550** ?	?	**Hayes** (Alaska-SW)	1103-05-	**5**	
C-**1550** ?	?	**Kilauea** (Hawaiian Is)	1302-01-	0	
T-**1550** z	?	**Torfajökull** (Iceland-S)	1702-05=		7/-
T-**1550** ?	?	**Hekla** (Iceland-S)	1702-07=	4	-/8
C-**1550** ?	?	**Deception Island** (Antarctica)	1900-03=		
C-**1540** w	?	**Jingbo** (China-E)	1005-04-		
T-**1540** ?	?	**Katla** (Iceland-S)	1702-03=		
G-**1510** v	?	**Fuji** (Honshu-Japan)	0803-03=		
C-**1510** w	?	**Cotopaxi** (Ecuador)	1502-05=		
C-**1510** t	?	**Chillán, Nevados de** (Chile-C)	1507-07=		
-**1500** t	?	**Etna** (Italy)	0101-06=	**5**?	
T-**1500** ?	?	**Ibusuki [Kaimon]** (Kyushu-Japan)	0802-07=	4	-/8
T-**1500** y	?	**Iwate** (Honshu-Japan)	0803-24=		
G-**1500** ?	?	**Avachinsky** (Kamchatka)	1000-10=	**5**	-/**9**
T-**1500** ?	?	**Shiveluch** (Kamchatka)	1000-27=	3	-/7
C-**1500** u	?	**Orizaba, Pico de** (México)	1401-10=	3	
G-**1490** w	?	**Puyehue-Cordón Caulle** (Chile-C)	1507-15=		
M-**1480** y	?	**Ischia** (Italy)	0101-03=		
G-**1460** s	?	**Taupo** (New Zealand)	0401-07=	**6**	-/**10**
I -**1459** u	?	***Unknown Source*** *(GISP2, 104 ppb S)*	......		
I -**1454** u	?	***Unknown Source*** *(GISP2, 164 ppb S)*	......		
T-**1450** ?	?	**Taveuni** (Fiji Is-SW Pacific)	0405-01-	2	
G-**1450** u	?	**Kuchinoerabu-jima** (Ryukyu Is)	0802-05=		
T-**1450** ?	?	**Ibusuki Volc Field** (Kyushu-Japan)	0802-07=		
N-**1450** z	?	**Unzen** (Kyushu-Japan)	0802-10=		
T-**1450** v	?	**Fuji** (Honshu-Japan)	0803-03=		
G-**1450** t	?	**Akita-Komaga-take** (Honshu-Japan)	0803-23=		
T-**1450** ?	?	**Oshima** (Izu Is-Japan)	0804-01=		
T-**1450** z	?	**Miyake-jima** (Izu Is-Japan)	0804-04=		
G-**1450** t	?	**Daisetsu** (Hokkaido-Japan)	0805-06=		
H-**1450** ?	?	**Newberry** (US-Oregon)	1202-11-		7/-
C-**1450** v	?	**Colima** (México)	1401-04=		
T-**1450** ?	?	**Arenal** (Costa Rica)	1405-033	4	-/8

Lee Siebert (Smithsonian)

Lee Siebert (Smithsonian)

The youngest caldera at Santorini volcano in Greece was formed about 3500 years ago during the noted Minoan eruption. The steep inner walls of the caldera, capped by whitewashed villages, expose pyroclastic-flow deposits from four caldera-forming eruptions dating back to about 100,000 years ago. A nearby quarry (right photo) reveals light-colored airfall, pyroclastic-surge, and pyroclastic-flow deposits from the Minoan eruption that sequentally filled a valley cut in darker, bedded ashfall layers of Pleistocene age.

START YEAR M-Dy	Dura-tion	VOLCANO NAME (Subregion) . . .	NUMBER	VEI	Vol L/T
T-1440 z	?	**Nasu** (Honshu-Japan)	0803-15=	2?	
G-1440 s	?	**Katla** (Iceland-S)	1702-03=	4	-/8
G-1430 y	?	**Vesuvius** (Italy).	0101-02=	4	-/8
G-1420 u	?	**Etna** (Italy)	0101-06=		
G-1420 y	?	**Turrialba** (Costa Rica)	1405-07=		
G-1410 t	?	**Merapi** (Java).	0603-25=		
G-1400 v	?	**Hakone** (Honshu-Japan).	0803-02=		
T-1400 <	?	**Narugo** (Honshu-Japan).	0803-20=		
G-1400 ?	?	**Karymsky** (Kamchatka).	1000-13=	2?	7/6
T-1400 ?	?	**Tenerife** (Canary Is).	1803-03-		7/-
V-1396 ?	?	**Nemrut Dagi** (Turkey)	0103-02=		
G-1390 w	?	**Pelée** (W Indies).	1600-12=		
G-1370 v	?	**Pago** (New Britain-SW Pac).	0502-08=	**6**	**-/10**
T-1350 ?	?	**Fuji** (Honshu-Japan)	0803-03=	**5**	**-/9**
G-1350 t	?	**Narugo** (Honshu-Japan)	0803-20=		
G-1350 ?	?	**Tokachi** (Hokkaido-Japan).	0805-05=	3	-/7
C-1350 ?	?	**Koshelev** (Kamchatka)	1000-02=		
C-1350 ?	?	**Avachinsky** (Kamchatka).	1000-10=	**5**	**-/9**
G-1350 ?	?	**Krasheninnikov** (Kamchatka)	1000-19=	3	8/7
T-1350 ?	?	**Bezymianny** (Kamchatka)	1000-25=		
G-1350 x	?	**Yellowstone** (US-Wyoming)	1205-01-		
C-1350 ?	?	**Toluca, Nevado de** (México)	1401-07-		
T-1350 *	?	**Hekla** (Iceland-S)	1702-07=		
G-1340 w	?	**Chichón, El** (México).	1401-12=		
C-1330 v	?	**Longonot** (Africa-E).	0202-10=		
G-1330 u	?	**Okataina [Edgecumbe]** (New Zeal)	0401-05=		
G-1330 x	?	**Shiveluch** (Kamchatka).	1000-27=	3	-/7
C-1320 ?	?	**Colima** (México).	1401-04=		
C-1320 y	?	**San Martín** (México)	1401-11=		
C-1320 ?	?	**Yucamane** (Perú)	1504-05-	**5**	**-/9**
C-1320 v	?	**La Palma** (Canary Is).	1803-01-		
G-1310 ?	?	**Haleakala** (Hawaiian Is)	1302-06-		7/-
C-1310 w	?	**Bravo, Cerro** (Colombia).	1501-012	4	**-/9**
G-1310 w	?	**Soufrière Guadeloupe** (W Indies) .	1600-06=	3?	
T-1300 ?	?	**Vulcano** (Italy)	0101-05=	3	-/7
T-1300 ?	?	**Taveuni** (Fiji Is-SW Pacific)	0405-01-	2	
G-1300 w	?	**Fuji** (Honshu-Japan)	0803-03=		
C-1300 ?	?	**Mauna Loa** (Hawaiian Is)	1302-02=	0	
T-1300 ?	?	**Cayambe** (Ecuador)	1502-006		
T-1290 ?	?	**Katla** (Iceland-S)	1702-03=		
C-1290 ?	?	**Agua de Pau** (Azores)	1802-09=	4	-/8
C-1280 s	?	**St. Paul Island** (Alaska-W)	1104-01-		7/-
T-1280 ?	?	**Katla** (Iceland-S)	1702-03=		
C-1270 u	?	**Aso** (Kyushu-Japan)	0802-11=		
G-1270 v	?	**Barú** (Panamá)	1406-01-		
C-1260 y	?	**Loloru** (Bougainville-SW Pacific) . . .	0505-03=		
T-1250 ?	?	**Taranaki [Egmont]** (New Zealand) .	0401-03=		
G-1250 ?	?	**Taupo** (New Zealand)	0401-07=	3	-/7
G-1250 ?	?	**Iwate** (Honshu-Japan)	0803-24=	3	-/7
G-1250 x	?	**Akita-Yake-yama** (Honshu-Japan). .	0803-26=		
T-1250 ?	?	**Nii-jima** (Izu Is-Japan).	0804-02=		
T-1250 ?	?	**Miyake-jima** (Izu Is-Japan)	0804-04=	3	-/7
T-1250 *	?	**Hachijo-jima** (Izu Is-Japan).	0804-05=		
C-1250 ?	?	**Jordan Craters** (US-Oregon)	1202-19-	2?	**9**/-
G-1250 x	?	**Arenal** (Costa Rica)	1405-033	4	-/8
C-1250 v	?	**Negra, Sierra** (Galápagos).	1503-05=	0	
G-1250 w	?	**Aguilera** (Chile-S)	1508-062	**5**	**-/9**
T-1250 *	?	**Hekla** (Iceland-S)	1702-07=		
T-1250 y	?	**Askja** (Iceland-NE).	1703-06=	0	**9**/-
I -1250 ?	?	**Candlemas Island** (Antarctica) . . .	1900-10=		
C-1245 w	?	**Ruiz, Nevado del** (Colombia)	1501-02=		
G-1240 ?	?	**Haleakala** (Hawaiian Is)	1302-06-		6/-
G-1230 u	?	**Guagua Pichincha** (Ecuador). . . .	1502-02=		
G-1220 k	?	**Katla** (Iceland-S)	1702-03=	3	-/7
A-1200 >	?	**Haylan, Jabal** (Arabia-S)	0301-11-	0?	
C-1200 w	?	**Raoul Island** (Kermadec Is)	0402-03=	4	-/8
T-1200 ?	?	**Taveuni** (Fiji Is-SW Pacific)	0405-01-	2	
G-1200 ?	?	**Hakone** (Honshu-Japan).	0803-02=	2	8/6
T-1200 ?	?	**Myoko** (Honshu-Japan)	0803-10=		
T-1200 ?	?	**Oshima** (Izu Is-Japan).	0804-01=		
G-1200 t	?	**Aoga-shima** (Izu Is-Japan)	0804-06=		
T-1200 ?	?	**Ichinsky** (Kamchatka).	1000-28=		
G-1200 v	?	**Naolinco Volc Field** (México) . . .	1401-095		8/-
T-1200 ?	?	**Bárdarbunga [Veidivötn]** (Iceland)	1703-03=		**9**/-
T-1200 ?	?	**Fremrinamur** (Iceland-NE)	1703-07=		**9**/-
C-1200 v	?	**Flores** (Azores)	1802-001		
I -1192 u	?	***Unknown Source*** *(GISP2, 110 ppb S)* .	. . . . . .		
C-1190 s	?	**Taranaki [Egmont]** (New Zealand) .	0401-03=		
T-1190 ?	?	**Katla** (Iceland-S)	1702-03=		
C-1180 u	?	**Merapi** (Java).	0603-25=	**P**	
G-1180 ?	?	**St. Helens** (US-Washington)	1201-05-		
U-1180 ?	?	**Cobb Segment** (Pacific-NE)	1301-011		
G-1170 y	?	**Zuni-Bandera** (US-New Mexico) . . .	1210-02-	0	**9**/-
G-1170 x	?	**Colima** (México).	1401-04=		
C-1170 t	?	**Malinche, La** (México)	1401-091		
G-1160 y	?	**Galeras** (Colombia)	1501-08=	2	-/6
T-1160 ?	?	**Katla** (Iceland-S)	1702-03=		
G-1150 w	?	**Savai'i** (Samoa-SW Pacific)	0404-04=		
N-1150 z	?	**Unzen** (Kyushu-Japan).	0802-10=		
G-1150 t	?	**Izu-Tobu** (Honshu-Japan)	0803-01=	4+	8/8
C-1150 ?	?	**Iwate** (Honshu-Japan).	0803-24=		
G-1150 ?	?	**Hakkoda Group** (Honshu-Japan) . .	0803-28=	1	-/5
T-1150 *	?	**Hachijo-jima** (Izu Is-Japan).	0804-05=		
G-1150 ?	?	**Krasheninnikov** (Kamchatka)	1000-19=		
R-1150 *	?	**Koniuji** (Aleutian Is)	1101-14-		
C-1150 ?	?	**Shasta** (US-California).	1203-01-		
C-1150 u	?	**Hualalai** (Hawaiian Is).	1302-04-	0	
C-1150 w	?	**Cuicocha** (Ecuador)	1502-003	**5**	**-/9**
T-1150 v	?	**Torfajökull** (Iceland-S)	1702-05=		7/-
T-1150 *	?	**Hekla** (Iceland-S)	1702-07=		
T-1150 ?	?	**Tenerife** (Canary Is).	1803-03-		6/-
D-1150 ?	?	***Unknown Source*** *(Belfast tree-ring)* . .	. . . . . .		
G-1140 w	?	**Kuchinoerabu-jima** (Ryukyu Is) . .	0802-05=		
C-1140 r	?	**Haleakala** (Hawaiian Is)	1302-06-		
C-1140 ?	?	**Colima** (México).	1401-04=		
T-1130 x	?	**Taranaki [Egmont]** (New Zealand) .	0401-03=		
T-1130 *	?	**Asama** (Honshu-Japan)	0803-11=		
C-1125 t	?	**Gran Canaria** (Canary Is)	1803-04-		
C-1120 w	?	**Kusatsu-Shirane** (Honshu-Japan) . .	0803-12=	4	8/8
T-1120 x	?	**Turrialba** (Costa Rica)	1405-07=		
T-1100 ?	?	**Taveuni** (Fiji Is-SW Pacific)	0405-01-	2	
T-1100 y	?	**Aoga-shima** (Izu Is-Japan)	0804-06=		
G-1100 ?	?	**Karymsky** (Kamchatka).	1000-13=		7/-
G-1100 ?	?	**St. Helens** (US-Washington)	1201-05-		
E-1100 z	?	**Parinacota** (Chile-N).	1505-012		
G-1100 t	?	**Hekla** (Iceland-S)	1702-07=	**5+**	**-/9**
C-1090 v	?	**Kikai** (Ryukyu Is)	0802-06=	2	
I -1084 t	?	***Unknown Source*** *(GISP2, 129 ppb S)* .	. . . . . .		
C-1080 y	?	**Pantelleria** (Italy)	0101-071		
T-1080 w	?	**Redoubt** (Alaska-SW).	1103-03-		
C-1080 t	?	**Medicine Lake** (US-California). . . .	1203-02-	0	6/-
C-1080 x	?	**Hualalai** (Hawaiian Is).	1302-04-	0	
G-1080 w	?	**Tacaná** (México)	1401-13=		
C-1080 ?	?	**Villarrica** (Chile-C)	1507-12=		
C-1060 s	?	**Bliznetsy** (Kamchatka)	1000-552	1?	8/-
C-1060 u	?	**Krísuvík** (Iceland-SW).	1701-03=	0	7/-
C-1050 u	?	**Etna** (Italy)	0101-06=		
G-1050 ?	?	**Taupo** (New Zealand)	0401-07=	4	-/8
C-1050 ?	?	**Loloru** (Bougainville-SW Pacific) . . .	0505-03=		
C-1050 ?	?	**Tinakula** (Santa Cruz Is-SW Pacific) . .	0506-01=		
G-1050 z	?	**Pinatubo** (Luzon-Philippines)	0703-083	**6**	**-/10**
M-1050 ?	?	**Sakura-jima** (Kyushu-Japan)	0802-08=		
T-1050 ?	?	**Hakone** (Honshu-Japan).	0803-02=		
T-1050 ?	?	**Chokai** (Honshu-Japan)	0803-22=	0	8/-
T-1050 ?	?	**Iwaki** (Honshu-Japan)	0803-27=		
T-1050 x	?	**Oshima** (Izu Is-Japan).	0804-01=		
T-1050 ?	?	**E-san** (Hokkaido-Japan)	0805-011		
T-1050 ?	?	**Yotei** (Hokkaido-Japan)	0805-032		
T-1050 <	?	**Khodutka** (Kamchatka)	1000-053	4+	-/8
G-1050 ?	?	**Krasheninnikov** (Kamchatka)	1000-19=		
T-1050 ?	?	**Kliuchevskoi** (Kamchatka)	1000-26=		
R-1050 *	?	**Tanaga** (Aleutian Is).	1101-08-	0	
C-1050 ?	?	**Buzzard Creek** (Alaska-E).	1105-001	2	-/6
K-1050 *	?	**Adams Seamount** (Pacific-C).	1303-05-	0	
U-1050 *	?	**Unnamed [East Pacific Rise]** . .	1304-05-	0	
T-1050 *	?	**Apoyeque** (Nicaragua)	1404-091	4	-/8
T-1050 x	?	**Bravo, Cerro** (Colombia)	1501-012	4	-/8
T-1050 ?	?	**Cotopaxi** (Ecuador).	1502-05=	4	**9**/8
T-1050 ?	?	**Cayutué-La Viguería** (Chile-S). . . .	1508-012		
T-1050 ?	?	**Tenerife** (Canary Is).	1803-03-		8/-
K-1050 *	?	**Pleiades, The** (Antarctica)	1900-013		
C-1040 u	?	**Brennisteinsfjöll** (Iceland-SW) . . .	1701-04=	2	8/-
T-1030 ?	?	**Fuji** (Honshu-Japan)	0803-03=	4+	-/8
G-1030 y	?	**Belknap** (US-Oregon).	1202-06-	0	
T-1020 ?	?	**Taveuni** (Fiji Is-SW Pacific)	0405-01-	2	
C-1020 w	?	**Atitlán** (Guatemala)	1402-06=		
G-1010 x	?	**Taupo** (New Zealand)	0401-07=	4+	-/8
G-1010 x	?	**Merapi** (Java).	0603-25=		
G-1010 v	?	**Fuji** (Honshu-Japan)	0803-03=		
T-1010 ?	?	**Kizimen** (Kamchatka)	1000-23=		
T-1010 ?	?	**Shiveluch** (Kamchatka)	1000-27=	3	-/7
G-1010 ?	?	**St. Helens** (US-Washington)	1201-05-		
C-1010 v	?	**Tungurahua** (Ecuador).	1502-08=	**5**	**-/9**
G-1000 t	?	**Krasheninnikov** (Kamchatka)	1000-19=	3	-/7
A-1000 ?	?	**Changbaishan** (China-E)	1005-06-		
C-1000 z	?	**Snaefellsjökull** (Iceland-W)	1700-01=	2	8/-
G-0990 *	?	**Kuju** (Kyushu-Japan)	0802-12=	4	-/8
T-0990 z	?	**Puyehue-Cordón Caulle** (Chile-C).	1507-15=		
T-0990 ?	?	**Katla** (Iceland-S)	1702-03=		
G-0980 x	?	**Soufrière Guadeloupe** (W Indies) .	1600-06=		
C-0960 u	?	**Tecuamburro** (Guatemala).	1402-12=		
G-0960 w	?	**Antillanca Group** (Chile-C)	1507-153	**5**	**-/9**
U-0950 z	?	**Vulcano** (Italy)	0101-05=	0	
G-0950 ?	?	**Aso** (Kyushu-Japan)	0802-11=	**P**	

START YEAR	M-Dy	Duration	VOLCANO NAME (Subregion)	NUMBER	VEI	Vol L/T
G-0950 v	....	?	Azuma (Honshu-Japan)	0803-18=		
T-0950 x	....	?	Miyake-jima (Izu Is-Japan)	0804-04=	4+	-/8
G-0950 ?	....	?	Akademia Nauk (Kamchatka)	1000-125		
G-0950 ?	....	?	Shiveluch (Kamchatka)	1000-27=	5	-/9
C-0950 ?	....	?	Mauna Loa (Hawaiian Is)	1302-02=	0	
C-0950 ?	....	?	Cuicocha (Ecuador)	1502-003		
E-0950 *	....	?	Azul, Cerro (Galápagos)	1503-06=	0	
C-0950 y	....	?	Watt, Morne (W Indies)	1600-101		
C-0950 v	....	?	Flores (Azores)	1802-001		
C-0950 w	....	?	Hierro (Canary Is)	1803-02-		
C-0940 v	....	?	Andahua-Orcopampa (Perú)	1504-004		
C-0940 t	....	?	Terceira (Azores)	1802-05=		
G-0930 w	....	?	Ischia (Italy)	0101-03=		
C-0930 >	....	?	Fuji (Honshu-Japan)	0803-03=	5	-/9
G-0930 v	....	?	Khodutka (Kamchatka)	1000-053	5	7/9
C-0930 ?	....	?	Azufral (Colombia)	1501-09=	P	
C-0920 u	....	?	Sollipulli (Chile-C)	1507-111	5+	-/9
T-0920 ?	....	?	Katla (Iceland-S)	1702-03=		
C-0900 ?	....	?	Kuchino-shima (Ryukyu Is)	0802-043		
T-0900 ?	....	?	Tate-yama (Honshu-Japan)	0803-08=		
G-0900 v	....	?	Oshima (Izu Is-Japan)	0804-01=	2	5/6
T-0900 ?	....	?	Shiveluch (Kamchatka)	1000-27=	3	-/7
G-0900 v	....	?	Sand Mountain Field (US-Oregon)	1202-04-	2?	
T-0900 v	....	?	Theistareykjarbunga (Iceland-NE)	1703-09=	0	
G-0890 t	....	?	Pelée (W Indies)	1600-12=		
G-0880 t	....	?	Vesuvius (Italy)	0101-02=	4	-/8
T-0880 *	....	?	Minchinmávida (Chile-S)	1508-04=		
C-0870 u	....	?	Karkar (New Guinea-NE of)	0501-03=		
T-0860 ?	....	?	Katla (Iceland-S)	1702-03=		
T-0850 ?	....	?	Yake-dake (Honshu-Japan)	0803-07=		
G-0850 t	....	?	Ioto [Iwo-jima] (Volcano Is-Japan)	0804-12=		
C-0850 ?	....	?	Zavaritsky (Kamchatka)	1000-124	4+	7/8
G-0850 ?	....	?	Karymsky (Kamchatka)	1000-13=	3	7/7
G-0850 ?	....	?	Maly Semiachik (Kamchatka)	1000-14=		
G-0850 ?	....	?	Krasheninnikov (Kamchatka)	1000-19=		7/-
C-0850 ?	....	?	Glacier Peak (US-Washington)	1201-02-		
C-0850 ?	....	?	Shasta (US-California)	1203-01-		
T-0850 ?	....	?	Ruiz, Nevado del (Colombia)	1501-02=	4	-/8
G-0850 ?	....	?	Santa Isabel (Colombia)	1501-021		
G-0850 t	....	?	Katla (Iceland-S)	1702-03=	4	-/8
T-0850 *	....	?	Hekla (Iceland-S)	1702-07=		
C-0850 v	....	?	Picos Volc System (Azores)	1802-081		
C-0830 t	....	?	Tengger Caldera (Java)	0603-31=	P	
C-0830 u	....	?	St. Helens (US-Washington)	1201-05-		
T-0830 z	....	?	Arenal (Costa Rica)	1405-033	0?	
G-0830 w	....	?	Turrialba (Costa Rica)	1405-07=		
C-0820 v	....	?	Melimoyu (Chile-S)	1508-052		
G-0820 v	....	?	Soufrière Guadeloupe (W Indies)	1600-06=	3?	
T-0800 ?	....	?	Taupo (New Zealand)	0401-07=	2	7/6
G-0800 <	....	?	Narugo (Honshu-Japan)	0803-20=		
C-0800 v	....	?	Oshima-Oshima (Hokkaido-Japan)	0805-01=		
C-0800	....	?	Akan (Hokkaido-Japan)	0805-07=		
T-0800 z	....	?	Zavaritsky (Kamchatka)	1000-124	2	-/6
T-0800 ?	....	?	Tolbachik (Kamchatka)	1000-24=		
C-0800 y	....	?	Terpuk (Kamchatka)	1000-512		
T-0800 z	....	?	Yantarni (Alaska Peninsula)	1102-10-	5	8/9
C-0800 t	....	?	Martin (Alaska Peninsula)	1102-14-		
G-0800 ?	....	?	St. Helens (US-Washington)	1201-05-		
G-0800 y	....	?	Sand Mountain Field (US-Oregon)	1202-04-	2?	
G-0800 y	....	?	Belknap (US-Oregon)	1202-06-	2?	
T-0800 ?	....	?	North Sister Field (US-Oregon)	1202-07-	2?	
G-0800 ?	....	?	Kilauea (Hawaiian Is)	1302-01-	0	
C-0800 t	....	?	Momotombo (Nicaragua)	1404-09=	4+	-/8
T-0800 z	....	?	Burney, Monte (Chile-S)	1508-07=		
C-0800 ?	....	?	Deception Island (Antarctica)	1900-03=		
G-0790 u	....	?	Hudson, Cerro (Chile-S)	1508-057		
V-0787 q	....	?	Nemrut Dagi (Turkey)	0103-02=		
G-0780 z	....	?	Fuji (Honshu-Japan)	0803-03=		
G-0780 y	....	?	Shiveluch (Kamchatka)	1000-27=	4+	-/8
C-0780 v	....	?	Medicine Lake (US-California)	1203-02-		8/-
C-0780 t	....	?	Orizaba, Pico de (México)	1401-10=	3	
T-0780 ?	....	?	Katla (Iceland-S)	1702-03=		
A-0778 e	....	?	Porak (Armenia)	0104-09-		
C-0770 t	....	?	Concepción (Nicaragua)	1404-12=	P	
G-0760 x	....	?	Poás (Costa Rica)	1405-04=		
T-0750 t	....	?	Kasbek (Georgia)	0104-02-		
T-0750 ?	....	?	Izu-Tobu (Honshu-Japan)	0803-01=	3	8/7
T-0750	....	?	Myoko (Honshu-Japan)	0803-10=		
G-0750 ?	....	?	Towada (Honshu-Japan)	0803-271	4+	-/8
H-0750 *	....	?	Kozu-shima (Izu Is-Japan)	0804-03=		
T-0750 ?	....	?	Tolbachik (Kamchatka)	1000-24=		
T-0750 v	....	?	Edziza (Canada)	1200-06-		
C-0750 s	....	?	San Martín (México)	1401-11=		
C-0750 v	....	?	Soufrière St. Vincent (W Indies)	1600-15=		
T-0750 z	....	?	Hekla (Iceland-S)	1702-07=		
C-0750 y	....	?	Sete Cidades (Azores)	1802-08=		
C-0750 ?	....	?	Deception Island (Antarctica)	1900-03=		
?-0740 b	....	*?*	*Porak (Armenia)*	0104-09-		
T-0740 ?	....	?	Katla (Iceland-S)	1702-03=		
?-0735	....	*?*	*Etna (Italy)*	0101-06=		
C-0730 u	....	?	Bravo, Cerro (Colombia)	1501-012	4+	-/8
C-0730 ?	....	?	Pelée (W Indies)	1600-12=		
C-0720 u	....	?	Hualalai (Hawaiian Is)	1302-04-	0	
T-0700 u	....	?	Ischia (Italy)	0101-03=		
G-0700 w	....	?	Merapi (Java)	0603-25=		
T-0700 ?	....	?	Ibusuki [Kaimon] (Kyushu-Japan)	0802-07=	2	7/6
G-0700 v	....	?	Niigata-Yake-yama (Honshu-Japan)	0803-09=	3	
G-0700 x	....	?	Nasu (Honshu-Japan)	0803-15=	3	-/7
T-0700 *	....	?	Gorely (Kamchatka)	1000-07=	0	8/-
T-0700 ?	....	?	Tolbachik (Kamchatka)	1000-24=		
T-0700 t	....	?	Rainier (US-Washington)	1201-03-		
H-0700 *	....	?	Mono Craters (US-California)	1203-12-		
G-0700 x	....	?	Chichón, El (México)	1401-12=		
C-0700 t	....	?	Huambo (Perú)	1504-005		
T-0700 ?	....	?	Katla (Iceland-S)	1702-03=		
C-0700 ?	....	?	Deception Island (Antarctica)	1900-03=		
-0695 b	....	?	Etna (Italy)	0101-06=		
C-0690 w	....	?	Pululagua (Ecuador)	1502-011	5	-/9
T-0680 ?	....	?	Taveuni (Fiji Is-SW Pacific)	0405-01-	2	
C-0670 ?	....	?	Villarrica (Chile-C)	1507-12=		
C-0670 y	....	?	Terceira (Azores)	1802-05=		
G-0670 x	....	?	Tenerife (Canary Is)	1803-03-		7/-
C-0665 v	....	?	Ljósufjöll (Iceland-W)	1700-03=	2	8/-
C-0660 u	....	?	Alney-Chashakondzha (Kamchatka)	1000-45-	3	8/7
V-0657 q	....	?	Nemrut Dagi (Turkey)	0103-02=		
T-0650 ?	....	?	Ibusuki [Kaimon] (Kyushu-Japan)	0802-07=	4	-/8
C-0650 ?	....	?	Sakura-jima (Kyushu-Japan)	0802-08=		
C-0650 ?	....	?	Chokai (Honshu-Japan)	0803-22=		
G-0650 ?	....	?	Maly Semiachik (Kamchatka)	1000-14=		
G-0650 ?	....	?	Krasheninnikov (Kamchatka)	1000-19=		
T-0650 ?	....	?	Shiveluch (Kamchatka)	1000-27=	3	-/7
C-0650 u	....	?	Alney-Chashakondzha (Kamchatka)	1000-45-	3	8/7
C-0650 ?	....	?	Mageik (Alaska Peninsula)	1102-15-		
T-0650 t	....	?	Rainier (US-Washington)	1201-03-		
C-0650 *	....	?	Shasta (US-California)	1203-01-		
G-0650 x	....	?	Colima (México)	1401-04=		
C-0650 ?	....	?	Machín (Colombia)	1501-04=		
T-0650 ?	....	?	Katla (Iceland-S)	1702-03=		
T-0650 *	....	?	Hekla (Iceland-S)	1702-07=		
T-0650 ?	....	?	Krafla (Iceland-NE)	1703-08=	4	-/8
C-0640 y	....	?	Pago (New Britain-SW Pac)	0502-08=		
C-0640 t	....	?	Ijen (Java)	0603-35=		
G-0640 z	....	?	Irazú (Costa Rica)	1405-06=	3	
C-0630 t	....	?	Aso (Kyushu-Japan)	0802-11=		
C-0620 w	....	?	Iskut-Unuk River Cones (Canada)	1200-09-		
C-0620 ?	....	?	Pelée (W Indies)	1600-12=		
G-0610 v	....	?	Rainier (US-Washington)	1201-03-		
G-0610 x	....	?	Tolima, Nevado del (Colombia)	1501-03=	3?	
?-0600	....	*?*	*Alban Hills (Italy)*	0101-004		
A-0600 <	....	?	Vesuvius (Italy)	0101-02=	3	
T-0600 ?	....	?	Taveuni (Fiji Is-SW Pacific)	0405-01-	2	
T-0600 z	....	?	Oshima (Izu Is-Japan)	0804-01=	3	
T-0600 z	....	?	Miyake-jima (Izu Is-Japan)	0804-04=	3	-/7
C-0600 x	....	?	Aoga-shima (Izu Is-Japan)	0804-06=	4	8/8
T-0600 ?	....	?	Ichinsky (Kamchatka)	1000-28=		
C-0600 ?	....	?	Mauna Loa (Hawaiian Is)	1302-02=	0	
C-0600 ?	....	?	Pelée (W Indies)	1600-12=		
T-0600 ?	....	?	Katla (Iceland-S)	1702-03=		
T-0590 z	....	?	Taranaki [Egmont] (New Zealand)	0401-03=		
G-0590 x	....	?	Adatara (Honshu-Japan)	0803-17=	3	-/7
G-0590 x	....	?	Lanín (Chile-C)	1507-122		
G-0590 x	....	?	Pelée (W Indies)	1600-12=	4?	-/8
I-0585 t	....	?	*Unknown Source (GISP2, 132 ppb S)*	......		
G-0580 y	....	?	Nabukelevu (Fiji Is-SW Pacific)	0405-03-		
C-0580 t	....	?	Haleakala (Hawaiian Is)	1302-06-		
C-0580 >	....	?	Soufrière Guadeloupe (W Indies)	1600-06=	2	
G-0580 x	....	?	Tenerife (Canary Is)	1803-03-		7/-
?-0565		*?*	*Etna (Italy)*	0101-06=		
T-0560 ?	....	?	Cayambe (Ecuador)	1502-006		
T-0560 ?	....	?	Katla (Iceland-S)	1702-03=		
C-0550 ?	....	?	Tendürek Dagi (Turkey)	0103-03=		
A-0550		?	Ararat (Turkey)	0103-04-		
C-0550 x	....	?	Tongariro [Ngauruhoe] (New Zeal)	0401-08=	5	-/9
T-0550 ?	....	?	Kusatsu-Shirane (Honshu-Japan)	0803-12=	3	-/7
T-0550 ?	....	?	Bandai (Honshu-Japan)	0803-16=		
T-0550 z	....	?	Iwaki (Honshu-Japan)	0803-27=		
T-0550 ?	....	?	E-san (Hokkaido-Japan)	0805-011		
C-0550 ?	....	?	Shikotsu [Tarumai] (Hokkaido)	0805-04=	5	-/9
T-0550 z	....	?	Daisetsu (Hokkaido-Japan)	0805-06=		
T-0550 ?	....	?	Akan (Hokkaido-Japan)	0805-07=		
T-0550 v	....	?	Nemo Peak (Kuril Is)	0900-32=		
T-0550	....	?	Bakening (Kamchatka)	1000-123	2	-/6
G-0550 ?	....	?	Maly Semiachik (Kamchatka)	1000-14=		
C-0550 ?	....	?	Taunshits (Kamchatka)	1000-16-		

START YEAR	M-Dy	Duration	VOLCANO NAME (Subregion)	NUMBER	VEI	Vol L/T
T-0550 ?	....	?	**Gamchen** (Kamchatka)	1000-21=		
C-0550 ?	....	?	*Vysoky (Kamchatka)*	1000-221	*0*	
C-0550 ?	....	?	**Titila** (Kamchatka)	1000-56-		
T-0550 *	....	?	**Tanaga** (Aleutian Is)	1101-08-		
T-0550 *	....	?	**Makushin** (Aleutian Is)	1101-31-		
C-0550 ?	....	?	**Mageik** (Alaska Peninsula)	1102-15-		
T-0550 *	....	?	**Adams** (US-Washington)	1201-04-	2	
T-0550 z	....	?	**Shasta** (US-California)	1203-01-		
T-0550 z	....	?	**Nejapa-Miraflores** (Nicaragua)	1404-092		
E-0550 *	....	?	**Azul, Cerro** (Galápagos)	1503-06=	0	
C-0550 ?	....	?	**Quill, The** (W Indies)	1600-02=		
T-0550 ?	....	?	**Katla** (Iceland-S)	1702-03=		
C-0550 u	....	?	**Hierro** (Canary Is)	1803-02-		
C-0550 ?	....	?	**Deception Island** (Antarctica)	1900-03=		
V-0531 ?	....	?	**Nemrut Dagi** (Turkey)	0103-02=		
G-0530 ?	....	?	**St. Helens** (US-Washington)	1201-05-	**5**	**-/9**
C-0530 u	....	?	**Soufrière St. Vincent** (W Indies)	1600-15=		
T-0530 ?	....	?	**Katla** (Iceland-S)	1702-03=		
G-0520 y	....	?	**Fuji** (Honshu-Japan)	0803-03=		
C-0520 v	....	?	**Jingbo** (China-E)	1005-04-		
C-0520 ?	....	?	**Tenerife** (Canary Is)	1803-03-		
T-0510 ?	....	?	**Cayambe** (Ecuador)	1502-006		
C-0510 x	....	?	**Picos Volc System** (Azores)	1802-081		
C-0500 u	....	?	**Dieng Volc Complex** (Java)	0603-20=		
G-0500 ?	....	?	**Shiveluch** (Kamchatka)	1000-27=	4	-/8
C-0500 t	....	?	**Mageik** (Alaska Peninsula)	1102-15-		
T-0500 t	....	?	**Rainier** (US-Washington)	1201-03-		
C-0500 ?	....	?	**Mauna Loa** (Hawaiian Is)	1302-02=	0	
C-0500 ?	....	?	**Tungurahua** (Ecuador)	1502-08=	3?	
T-0500 y	....	?	**Krafla** (Iceland-NE)	1703-08=	0	
M-0490 w	....	?	**Ischia** (Italy)	0101-03=		
G-0490 v	....	?	**Galeras** (Colombia)	1501-08=	2	-/6
G-0490 y	....	?	**Puyehue-Cordón Caulle** (Chile-C)	1507-15=		
G-0480 y	....	?	**Savai'i** (Samoa-SW Pacific)	0404-04=		
-0479	08 ?	>3yr	**Etna** (Italy)	0101-06=		
-0478	*Cont*	....	*Etna (Italy)*	0101-06=		
-0477	*Cont*	....	*Etna (Italy)*	0101-06=		
-0476	*Cont*	....	*Etna (Italy)*	0101-06=		
-0475	*Cont*	....	*Etna (Italy)*	0101-06=		
-0475 ?	....	?	**Vulcano** (Italy)	0101-05=		
-0470 ?	....	?	**Ischia** (Italy)	0101-03=		
T-0460 ?	....	?	**Cayambe** (Ecuador)	1502-006		
-0450 t	....	?	**Cameroon** (Africa-W)	0204-01=	3	
T-0450 ?	....	?	**Chokai** (Honshu-Japan)	0803-22=		
G-0450 ?	....	?	**Iwate** (Honshu-Japan)	0803-24=		
T-0450 ?	....	?	**Mutnovsky** (Kamchatka)	1000-06=	2	-/6
G-0450 ?	....	?	**Bezymianny** (Kamchatka)	1000-25=	4	-/8
C-0450 ?	....	?	**Iliamna** (Alaska-SW)	1103-02-		
C-0450 w	....	?	**Pululagua** (Ecuador)	1502-011	**C**	
A-0442	....	?	**Popa** (SE Asia)	0705-08-		
C-0440 t	....	?	**Hualalai** (Hawaiian Is)	1302-04-	0	
C-0440 ?	....	?	**Pelée** (W Indies)	1600-12=	**P**	
I-0433 ?	....	?	***Unknown Source*** *(Byrd Station 1968)*	......		
C-0430 ?	....	?	**Plat Pays, Morne** (W Indies)	1600-11=		
T-0430 ?	....	?	**Katla** (Iceland-S)	1702-03=		
-0425	0315m	474w?	**Etna** (Italy)	0101-06=		
-0424	*Cont*	....	*Etna (Italy)*	0101-06=		
C-0420 r	....	?	**Taranaki [Egmont]** (New Zealand)	0401-03=		
G-0410 x	....	?	**Meager** (Canada)	1200-18-	**5**?	
C-0410 v	....	?	**Kilauea** (Hawaiian Is)	1302-01-	0	
G-0400 p	....	?	**Taveuni** (Fiji Is-SW Pacific)	0405-01-	2	
C-0400 t	....	?	**Matutum** (Mindanao-Philippines)	0701-02=		
G-0400 ?	....	?	**Fukue-jima** (Kyushu-Japan)	0802-091		
G-0400 >	....	?	**Kita Yatsuga-take** (Honshu-Japan)	0803-031		
T-0400 ?	....	?	**Yake-dake** (Honshu-Japan)	0803-07=		
T-0400 ?	....	?	**Nikko-Shirane** (Honshu-Japan)	0803-14=		
T-0400 ?	....	?	**Shiveluch** (Kamchatka)	1000-27=	3	-/7
T-0400 t	....	?	**Rainier** (US-Washington)	1201-03-		
T-0400 ?	....	?	**Adams** (US-Washington)	1201-04-	2	
C-0400 ?	....	?	**Mauna Loa** (Hawaiian Is)	1302-02=	0	
C-0400 u	....	?	**Hualalai** (Hawaiian Is)	1302-04-	0	
T-0400 ?	....	?	**Cotopaxi** (Ecuador)	1502-05=	4	7/8
C-0400 v	....	?	**Reykjanes** (Iceland-SW)	1701-02=	2	8/-
-0396 ?	0415q	?	**Etna** (Italy)	0101-06=		
C-0390 u	....	?	**Ebeko** (Kuril Is)	0900-38=		
C-0390 s	....	?	**Haleakala** (Hawaiian Is)	1302-06-		
G-0380 x	....	?	**Arenal** (Costa Rica)	1405-033	4	-/8
M-0370 w	....	?	**Ischia** (Italy)	0101-03=		
C-0370 x	....	?	**Acatenango** (Guatemala)	1402-08=		
T-0370 ?	....	?	**Katla** (Iceland-S)	1702-03=		
-0360 j	....	?	**Vulcano** (Italy)	0101-05=	2	
C-0360 w	....	?	**Furnas** (Azores)	1802-10=		
C-0360 t	....	?	**La Palma** (Canary Is)	1803-01-		
-0350 t	....	?	**Stromboli** (Italy)	0101-04=	2	
C-0350 u	....	?	**Bamus** (New Britain-SW Pac.)	0502-11=		
C-0350 v	....	?	**Ambitle** (New Ireland-SW Pacific)	0504-02=		
G-0350 ?	....	?	**Yake-dake** (Honshu-Japan)	0803-07=	4	8/8
G-0350 x	....	?	**Akita-Komaga-take** (Honshu-Japan)	0803-23=	3	-/7
C-0350 ?	....	?	**Iwate** (Honshu-Japan)	0803-24=		
T-0350 z	....	?	**Hachijo-jima** (Izu Is-Japan)	0804-05=	3	-/7
T-0350 ?	....	?	**Gorely** (Kamchatka)	1000-07=	3	-/7
G-0350 ?	....	?	**Krasheninnikov** (Kamchatka)	1000-19=		
G-0350 r	....	?	**Khangar** (Kamchatka)	1000-272		
C-0350 ?	....	?	**Aniakchak** (Alaska Peninsula)	1102-09-		
C-0350 ?	....	?	**Ukinrek Maars** (Alaska Peninsula)	1102-131		
C-0350 ?	....	?	**South Sister** (US-Oregon)	1202-08-	4	8/8
M-0350 ?	....	?	**Craters of the Moon** (US-Idaho)	1204-02-	0	8/-
C-0350 u	....	?	**Hualalai** (Hawaiian Is)	1302-04-	0	
I-0345 ?	....	?	***Unknown Source*** *(Byrd Station 1968)*	......		
G-0340 z	....	?	**Merapi** (Java)	0603-25=	3	-/7
G-0330 u	....	?	**Taveuni** (Fiji Is-SW Pacific)	0405-01-	2	
C-0330 x	....	?	**Calbuco** (Chile-S)	1508-02=		
I-0325 ?	....	?	***Unknown Source*** *(SP, 203 ppb S)*	......		
C-0320 n	....	?	**Atacazo** (Ecuador)	1502-021	**5**	**-/9**
C-0320 t	....	?	**Taapaca** (Chile-N)	1505-011		
C-0320 u	....	?	**Chillán, Nevados de** (Chile-C)	1507-07=		
G-0310 v	....	?	**Misti, El** (Perú)	1504-01=		
-0300	....	?	**Vulcano** (Italy)	0101-05=	2	
T-0300 ?	....	?	**Okataina [Edgecumbe]** (New Zeal)	0401-05=	0	**9/-**
T-0300 v	....	?	**Akan** (Hokkaido-Japan)	0805-07=		
T-0300 y	....	?	**Khodutka** (Kamchatka)	1000-053	0	
G-0300 ?	....	?	**Shiveluch** (Kamchatka)	1000-27=	4	-/8
T-0300 ?	....	?	**Adams** (US-Washington)	1201-04-	2	
T-0300 ?	....	?	**Wapi Lava Field** (US-Idaho)	1204-03-	2?	**9/-**
C-0300 ?	....	?	**Mauna Loa** (Hawaiian Is)	1302-02=	0	
G-0300 v	....	?	**Pelée** (W Indies)	1600-12=		
G-0300 ?	....	?	**Krafla** (Iceland-NE)	1703-08=	2	**9/-**
G-0290 ?	....	?	**Haleakala** (Hawaiian Is)	1302-06-		7/-
C-0280 u	....	?	**Kikai** (Ryukyu Is)	0802-06=		
G-0280 ?	....	?	**St. Helens** (US-Washington)	1201-05-		
C-0270 t	....	?	**Bamus** (New Britain-SW Pac)	0502-11=		
T-0270 ?	....	?	**Ibusuki [Kaimon]** (Kyushu-Japan)	0802-07=	4	-/8
G-0270 v	....	?	**Rausu** (Hokkaido-Japan)	0805-082		
U-0270 ?	....	?	**Cleft Segment** (Pacific-NE)	1301-03-	0	
G-0270 u	....	?	**Kilauea** (Hawaiian Is)	1302-01-	0	
T-0270 ?	....	?	**Arenal** (Costa Rica)	1405-033	4	-/8
C-0270 v	....	?	**Tungurahua** (Ecuador)	1502-08=		
C-0260 q	....	?	**Craters of the Moon** (US-Idaho)	1204-02-	0	7/-
C-0260 u	....	?	**Acatenango** (Guatemala)	1402-08=		
T-0260 ?	....	?	**Cayambe** (Ecuador)	1502-006		
-0258 o	....	?	**Methana** (Greece)	0102-02=	3	7/-
-0253 k	....	?	**Campi Flegrei Mar Sicilia** (Italy)	0101-07=		
C-0250 u	....	?	**Raoul Island** (Kermadec Is)	0402-03=	**6**	**-/10**
T-0250 ?	....	?	**Nasu** (Honshu-Japan)	0803-15=	2?	
G-0250 ?	....	?	**Krasheninnikov** (Kamchatka)	1000-19=		
G-0250 x	....	?	**Rainier** (US-Washington)	1201-03-	4	-/8
T-0250 ?	....	?	**St. Helens** (US-Washington)	1201-05-		
C-0250 ?	....	?	**Copahue** (Chile-C)	1507-09=		
T-0250 ?	....	?	**Katla** (Iceland-S)	1702-03=		
T-0250 z	....	?	**Hekla** (Iceland-S)	1702-07=		
C-0250 ?	....	?	**Deception Island** (Antarctica)	1900-03=		
C-0240 v	....	?	**St. Andrew Strait [Lou Is.]**	0500-01=		
C-0230 y	....	?	**Kelut** (Java)	0603-28=		
T-0230 ?	....	?	**Cayambe** (Ecuador)	1502-006		
C-0230 x	....	?	**Cotopaxi** (Ecuador)	1502-05=	4	-/8
G-0230 x	....	?	**Antillanca Group** (Chile-C)	1507-153	**5**	**-/9**
C-0220 t	....	?	**Zhupanovsky** (Kamchatka)	1000-12=		
C-0220 t	....	?	**Udokan [Chepe]** (Russia-SE)	1002-03-		
G-0220 ?	....	?	**St. Helens** (US-Washington)	1201-05-		
G-0220 x	....	?	**Lanín** (Chile-C)	1507-122		8/-
-0217	....	365y	**Vesuvius** (Italy)	0101-02=	3?	
-0216	*Cont*	....	*Vesuvius (Italy)*	0101-02=	*3?*	
-0215	....	?	**Vulcano** (Italy)	0101-05=		
-0210 j	....	?	**Stromboli** (Italy)	0101-04=	2	
T-0210 x	....	?	**Redoubt** (Alaska-SW)	1103-03-		
C-0210 u	....	?	**Osorno** (Chile-S)	1508-01=		
I-0210 x	....	?	**Hudson Mountains** (Antarctica)	1900-028	4?	-/8
D-0208 ?	....	?	***Unknown Source*** *(Belfast tree-ring)*	......		
M-0200 x	....	?	**Ischia** (Italy)	0101-03=		
G-0200 ?	....	?	**Taupo** (New Zealand)	0401-07=	4+	-/8
T-0200 ?	....	?	**Taveuni** (Fiji Is-SW Pacific)	0405-01-	2	
C-0200 t	....	?	**Tsurumi** (Kyushu-Japan)	0802-13=	4	
G-0200 ?	....	?	**Haku-san** (Honshu-Japan)	0803-05=	4	8/8
G-0200 x	....	?	**Akita-Komaga-take** (Honshu-Japan)	0803-23=		
T-0200 ?	....	?	**Ksudach** (Kamchatka)	1000-05=	3	-/7
T-0200 ?	....	?	**Mutnovsky** (Kamchatka)	1000-06=	2	-/6
T-0200 ?	....	?	**Tolbachik** (Kamchatka)	1000-24=		
G-0200 w	....	?	**Kilauea** (Hawaiian Is)	1302-01-	0	
C-0200 ?	....	?	**Mauna Loa** (Hawaiian Is)	1302-02=	0	
C-0200 y	....	?	**Popocatépetl** (México)	1401-09=	**P**	
C-0200 v	....	?	**Ruiz, Nevado del** (Colombia)	1501-02=	4	-/8
G-0200 x	....	?	**Tolima, Nevado del** (Colombia)	1501-03=	3?	
C-0200 ?	....	?	**Pelée** (W Indies)	1600-12=	**P**	
C-0200 ?	....	?	**Reykjanes** (Iceland-SW)	1701-02=	0	

START YEAR	M-Dy	Duration	VOLCANO NAME (Subregion)	NUMBER	VEI	Vol L/T
-0197	....	?	**Santorini** (Greece)	0102-04=	3	
T-**0190** v	....	?	**Fuji** (Honshu-Japan)	0803-03=		
C-**0190** u	....	?	**Krísuvík** (Iceland-SW)	1701-03=	2	8/-
-0183	....	?	**Vulcano** (Italy)	0101-05=	4	
C-**0180** u	....	?	**Changbaishan** (China-E)	1005-06-	**P**	
T-**0180** ?	....	?	**Cayambe** (Ecuador)	1502-006		
I-**0180** s	....	?	***Unknown Source*** *(GISP2, 93 ppb S)*	......		
I-**0171** ?	....	?	***Unknown Source*** *(Byrd Station 1968)*	......		
C-**0170** u	....	?	**Matutum** (Mindanao-Philippines)	0701-02=		
C-**0170** v	....	?	**Masaya** (Nicaragua)	1404-10=	**5**	-/**9**
G-**0170** x	....	?	**Arenal** (Costa Rica)	1405-033	4	-/8
C-**0160** y	....	?	**Muria** (Java)	0603-251		
C-**0160** t	....	?	**Puracé** (Colombia)	1501-06=		
U-**0150** y	....	?	**Vulcano** (Italy)	0101-05=		
C-**0150** r	....	?	**Taranaki [Egmont]** (New Zealand)	0401-03=		
G-**0150** x	....	?	**Azuma** (Honshu-Japan)	0803-18=		
T-**0150** ?	....	?	**Oshima** (Izu Is-Japan)	0804-01=	3	
G-**0150** t	....	?	**Hachijo-jima** (Izu Is-Japan)	0804-05=		
G-**0150** ?	....	?	**Krasheninnikov** (Kamchatka)	1000-19=	**C**	
T-**0150** ?	....	?	**Shiveluch** (Kamchatka)	1000-27=	3	-/7
T-**0150** ?	....	?	**Rainier** (US-Washington)	1201-03-		
C-**0150** ?	....	?	**Shasta** (US-California)	1203-01-		
T-**0150** y	....	?	**San Martín** (México)	1401-11=		
T-**0150** *	....	?	**Hekla** (Iceland-S)	1702-07=		
-0141	1231y	?	**Etna** (Italy)	0101-06=		
-0135	....	?	**Etna** (Italy)	0101-06=		
C-**0130** t	....	?	**Craters of the Moon** (US-Idaho)	1204-02-	0	**9**/-
-0126	06	?	**Vulcano** (Italy)	0101-05=		
-0126	06 <	?	**Etna** (Italy)	0101-06=		
-0122	....	?	**Etna** (Italy)	0101-06=	**5**	-/**9**
C-**0120** x	....	?	**Hudson, Cerro** (Chile-S)	1508-057		
-0104	....	?	**Vulsini** (Italy)	0101-003		
G-**0100** y	....	?	**Kuju** (Kyushu-Japan)	0802-12=	4	-/8
C-**0100** w	....	?	**Fuji** (Honshu-Japan)	0803-03=		
H-**0100** *	....	?	**Kozu-shima** (Izu Is-Japan)	0804-03=		
G-**0100** v	....	?	**Shikotsu [Eniwa]** (Hokkaido)	0805-04=	2	
T-**0100** ?	....	?	**Mutnovsky** (Kamchatka)	1000-06=	2	-/6
T-**0100** ?	....	?	**Tolbachik** (Kamchatka)	1000-24=		
C-**0100** t	....	?	**Okmok** (Aleutian Is)	1101-29-	**6**	-/**10**
G-**0100** ?	....	?	**St. Helens** (US-Washington)	1201-05-		
C-**0100** ?	....	?	**Tungurahua** (Ecuador)	1502-08=	3?	
C-**0100** v	....	?	**Calbuco** (Chile-S)	1508-02=		
C-**0100** ?	....	?	**Deception Island** (Antarctica)	1900-03=		
-0091	....	?	**Ischia** (Italy)	0101-03=		
-0091	....	?	**Vulcano** (Italy)	0101-05=	3?	
G-**0090** x	....	?	**Taveuni** (Fiji Is-SW Pacific)	0405-01-	2	
G-**0090** v	....	?	**Burney, Monte** (Chile-S)	1508-07=		
C-**0090** v	....	?	**Terceira** (Azores)	1802-05=		
C-**0080** t	....	?	**Leonard Range** (Mindanao-Philippines)	0701-031		
T-**0080** ?	....	?	**Ibusuki [Kaimon]** (Kyushu-Japan)	0802-07=	4	-/8
C-**0080** ?	....	?	**Mauna Loa** (Hawaiian Is)	1302-02=	0	
C-**0080** u	....	?	**Hualalai** (Hawaiian Is)	1302-04-	0	8/-
G-**0080** u	....	?	**Misti, El** (Perú)	1504-01=	4?	-/8
G-**0080** x	....	?	**Lanín** (Chile-C)	1507-122		
C-**0080** u	....	?	**Hengill** (Iceland-SW)	1701-05=	2	8/-
T-**0080** ?	....	?	**Katla** (Iceland-S)	1702-03=		
G-**0080** s	....	?	**Tenerife** (Canary Is)	1803-03-	4+	7/8
?-0061	....	*?*	*Etna (Italy)*	0101-06=		
C-**0060** ?	....	?	**Mauna Loa** (Hawaiian Is)	1302-02=	0	
C-**0060** ?	....	?	**Terceira** (Azores)	1802-05=		8/-
?-0056	....	*?*	*Etna (Italy)*	0101-06=		
I-**0054** s	....	?	***Unknown Source*** *(GISP2, 291 ppb S)*	......		
-0050 t	....	?	**Stromboli** (Italy)	0101-04=	2	
C-**0050** ?	....	?	**Alutu** (Ethiopia)	0201-27-		
T-**0050** ?	....	?	**Lengai, Ol Doinyo** (Africa-E)	0202-12=		
G-**0050** v	....	?	**Rungwe** (Africa-E)	0202-166		
T-**0050** ?	....	?	**Raoul Island** (Kermadec Is)	0402-03=	3?	-/7
C-**0050** v	....	?	**Dieng Volc Complex** (Java)	0603-20=	0	
T-**0050** ?	....	?	**Hakone** (Honshu-Japan)	0803-02=		
T-**0050** ?	....	?	**Norikura** (Honshu-Japan)	0803-06=	3	8/7
T-**0050** *	....	?	**Adatara** (Honshu-Japan)	0803-17=		
G-**0050** x	....	?	**Akita-Komaga-take** (Honshu-Japan)	0803-23=	2	-/6
G-**0050** ?	....	?	**Hakkoda Group** (Honshu-Japan)	0803-28=	1	-/5
G-**0050** t	....	?	**Miyake-jima** (Izu Is-Japan)	0804-04=	3	6/7
T-**0050** ?	....	?	**Shikotsu** (Hokkaido-Japan)	0805-04=	3	-/7
G-**0050** ?	....	?	**Akan** (Hokkaido-Japan)	0805-07=	**P**	
T-**0050** ?	....	?	**Medvezhia** (Kuril Is)	0900-10=		
T-**0050** ?	....	?	**Zhupanovsky** (Kamchatka)	1000-12=		
T-**0050** ?	....	?	**Kronotsky** (Kamchatka)	1000-20=		
C-**0050** ?	....	?	**South Sister** (US-Oregon)	1202-08-	3	8/7
M-**0050** ?	....	?	**Medicine Lake** (US-California)	1203-02-	0	7/-
K-**0050** *	....	?	**Loihi** (Hawaiian Is)	1302-00-	0	
G-**0050** w	....	?	**Kilauea** (Hawaiian Is)	1302-01-		
K-**0050** *	....	?	**Adams Seamount** (Pacific-C)	1303-05-	0	
M-**0050** *	....	?	**Northern EPR-Segment RO2**	1304-02-	0	
M-**0050** *	....	?	**Northern EPR-Segment RO3**	1304-021	0	
U-**0050** *	....	?	**Unnamed [East Pacific Rise]**	1304-05-	0	

START YEAR	M-Dy	Duration	VOLCANO NAME (Subregion)	NUMBER	VEI	Vol L/T
T-**0050** v	....	?	**Apoyeque** (Nicaragua)	1404-091	**6**	-/**10**
T-**0050** ?	....	?	**Chacana** (Ecuador)	1502-022		
T-**0050** ?	....	?	**Cotopaxi** (Ecuador)	1502-05=	3	7/7
C-**0050** ?	....	?	**Tungurahua** (Ecuador)	1502-08=	3?	
T-**0050** ?	....	?	**Grímsvötn** (Iceland-NE)	1703-01=	2	
T-**0050** ?	....	?	**Krafla** (Iceland-NE)	1703-08=	2	
M-**0050** ?	....	?	**Bouvet** (Atlantic-S)	1806-02-		
-0049	....	?	**Etna** (Italy)	0101-06=		
-0044	03 ?	?	**Etna** (Italy)	0101-06=	3?	
C-**0040** u	....	?	**Taranaki [Egmont]** (New Zealand)	0401-03=		
-0036	0715q	?	**Etna** (Italy)	0101-06=		
-0035	*Cont*	....	*Etna (Italy)*	0101-06=		
-0032	1231y	?	**Etna** (Italy)	0101-06=		
C-**0030** ?	....	?	**Mauna Loa** (Hawaiian Is)	1302-02=	0	
-0024 e	....	?	**Vulcano** (Italy)	0101-05=		
G-**0020** t	....	?	**Chichón, El** (México)	1401-12=		
C-**0020** u	....	?	**Gran Canaria** (Canary Is)	1803-04-		
?-0010 j	....	*?*	*Vulcano (Italy)*	0101-05=		
?-0010 ?	....	*?*	*Etna (Italy)*	0101-06=		
T-**0010** ?	....	?	**Shiveluch** (Kamchatka)	1000-27=	3	-/7
-0006 p	....	?	**Ischia** (Italy)	0101-03=		

BC / AD

START YEAR	M-Dy	Duration	VOLCANO NAME (Subregion)	NUMBER	VEI	Vol L/T
G **0000** t	....	?	**Tokachi** (Hokkaido-Japan)	0805-05=		
C **0000** w	....	?	**Arshan** (China-E)	1005-011		
0010 ?	....	>3yr	**Etna** (Italy)	0101-06=		
G **0010** x	....	?	**Mono Craters** (US-California)	1203-12-		
T **0010** ?	....	?	**Cayambe** (Ecuador)	1502-006		
G **0010** t	....	?	**Pelée** (W Indies)	1600-12=	4	-/8
0011	*Cont*	....	*Etna (Italy)*	0101-06=		
0012	*Cont*	....	*Etna (Italy)*	0101-06=		
0013	*Cont*	....	*Etna (Italy)*	0101-06=		
0014	*Cont*	....	*Etna (Italy)*	0101-06=		
0015	*Cont*	....	*Etna (Italy)*	0101-06=		
0016	*Cont*	....	*Etna (Italy)*	0101-06=		
0017	*Cont*	....	*Etna (Italy)*	0101-06=		
0018	*Cont*	....	*Etna (Italy)*	0101-06=		
0019	*Cont*	....	*Etna (Italy)*	0101-06=		
0020	*Cont*	....	*Etna (Italy)*	0101-06=		
G **0020** y	....	?	**Merapi** (Java)	0603-25=	**P**	
T **0030** ?	....	?	**Ibusuki [Kaimon]** (Kyushu-Japan)	0802-07=	3	-/7
T **0030** ?	....	?	**Katla** (Iceland-S)	1702-03=		
G **0030** w	....	?	**Tenerife** (Canary Is)	1803-03-		**9**/-
0039 a	....	?	**Etna** (Italy)	0101-06=		
G **0040** u	....	?	**Ischia** (Italy)	0101-03=	3	-/7
G **0040** x	....	?	**North Sister Field** (US-Oregon)	1202-07-	2?	
C **0040** s	....	?	**Orizaba, Pico de** (México)	1401-10=	3	
G **0040** t	....	?	**Turrialba** (Costa Rica)	1405-07=	4	-/8
C **0040** u	....	?	**Calbuco** (Chile-S)	1508-02=		
C **0040** ?	....	?	**Tenerife** (Canary Is)	1803-03-		
0046	1231	33*p*	**Santorini** (Greece)	0102-04=	3	
0047	*Cont*	....	*Santorini (Greece)*	0102-04=	*2*	
0050 t	....	?	**Stromboli** (Italy)	0101-04=	2	
0050 t	....	?	**Vulcano** (Italy)	0101-05=		
T **0050** t	....	?	**Elbrus** (Russia-SW)	0104-01-		
C **0050** v	....	?	**Ambrym** (Vanuatu-SW Pacific)	0507-04=	**6+**	-/**10**
T **0050** ?	....	?	**Fuji** (Honshu-Japan)	0803-03=	2	
T **0050** ?	....	?	**Kusatsu-Shirane** (Honshu-Japan)	0803-12=	2	-/6
C **0050** ?	....	?	**Ilyinsky** (Kamchatka)	1000-03=		
T **0050** ?	....	?	**Mutnovsky** (Kamchatka)	1000-06=	2	-/6
T **0050** ?	....	?	**Gorely** (Kamchatka)	1000-07=	3	-/7
T **0050** ?	....	?	**Tolbachik** (Kamchatka)	1000-24=	4+	8/8
T **0050** ?	....	?	**Bezymianny** (Kamchatka)	1000-25=		
G **0050** y	....	?	**Ichinsky** (Kamchatka)	1000-28=		
0050 t	....	?	**Tianshan Volc Group** (China-W)	1004-02-		
T **0050** ?	....	?	**Shasta** (US-California)	1203-01-	0	
C **0050** ?	....	?	**Mauna Loa** (Hawaiian Is)	1302-02=	0	
C **0050** ?	....	?	**Pelée** (W Indies)	1600-12=	**P**	
C **0060** x	....	?	**Churchill** (Alaska-E)	1105-03-	**6**	-/**10**
C **0060** v	....	?	**Liamuiga** (W Indies)	1600-03=		
? 0069	....	*?*	*Ischia (Italy)*	0101-03=		
G **0070** w	....	?	**Sand Mountain Field** (US-Oregon)	1202-04-	2?	
G **0070** v	....	?	**Tacaná** (México)	1401-13=	4?	-/8
G **0070** u	....	?	**Guagua Pichincha** (Ecuador)	1502-02=	4	-/8
C **0070** w	....	?	**Cotopaxi** (Ecuador)	1502-05=	4	-/8
C **0070** s	....	?	**Terceira** (Azores)	1802-05=		
0079	1024?	4*b*?	**Vesuvius** (Italy)	0101-02=	**5**?	-/**9**
0080 a	....	?	**Ischia** (Italy)	0101-03=		
? 0080 ?	....	*?*	*Etna (Italy)*	0101-06=		
G **0080** t	....	?	**Rausu** (Hokkaido-Japan)	0805-082	3	-/7
C **0080** s	....	?	**Haleakala** (Hawaiian Is)	1302-06-		
C **0080** v	....	?	**Furnas** (Azores)	1802-10=	**5**	-/**9**
C **0090** s	....	?	**Orizaba, Pico de** (México)	1401-10=	3	7/7
C **0090** v	....	?	**Acatenango** (Guatemala)	1402-08=		
G **0090** y	....	?	**Misti, El** (Perú)	1504-01=		
A **0090** t	....	?	**Parinacota** (Chile-N)	1505-012		

START YEAR M-Dy	Duration	VOLCANO NAME (Subregion)	NUMBER	VEI	Vol L/T
T **0090** y	?	**Lanín** (Chile-C)	1507-122	0	
C **0090** v	?	**Sete Cidades** (Azores)	1802-08=	4	-/8
G **0090** u	?	**Tenerife** (Canary Is)	1803-03-		7/-
T **0100** v	?	**Etna** (Italy)	0101-06=		
C **0100** s	?	**Taranaki [Egmont]** (New Zealand)	0401-03=		
T **0100** ?	?	**Raoul Island** (Kermadec Is)	0402-03=	4	-/8
T **0100** ?	?	**Fuji** (Honshu-Japan)	0803-03=	2	
T **0100** v	?	**Akan** (Hokkaido-Japan)	0805-07=		
T **0100** ?	?	**Avachinsky** (Kamchatka)	1000-10=		
T **0100** ?	?	**Shiveluch** (Kamchatka)	1000-27=	4	-/8
G **0100** ?	?	**St. Helens** (US-Washington)	1201-05-	0	
C **0100** ?	?	**Mauna Loa** (Hawaiian Is)	1302-02=	0	
C **0100** ?	?	**Tungurahua** (Ecuador)	1502-08=	3?	
C **0100** ?	?	**Deception Island** (Antarctica)	1900-03=		
C **0110** t	?	**Redoubt** (Alaska-SW)	1103-03-		
C **0110** ?	?	**Villarrica** (Chile-C)	1507-12=	0	
G **0110** x	?	**Puyehue-Cordón Caulle** (Chile-C)	1507-15=		
G **0120** ?	?	**Fournaise, Piton de la** (Indian O.-W)	0303-02=	0	
G **0120** u	?	**Merapi** (Java)	0603-25=		
C **0120** v	?	**Leonard Range** (Mindanao-Philippines)	0701-031		
G **0120** ?	?	**Shiveluch** (Kamchatka)	1000-27=	3	-/7
C **0120** x	?	**San Martín** (México)	1401-11=		
T **0130** ?	?	**Ibusuki [Kaimon]** (Kyushu-Japan)	0802-07=	4	7/8
C **0130** ?	?	**Pelée** (W Indies)	1600-12=	**P**	
T **0130** ?	?	**Katla** (Iceland-S)	1702-03=		
G **0140** y	?	**Mílos** (Greece)	0102-03=	1?	
C **0140** t	?	**Orizaba, Pico de** (México)	1401-10=	3	
T **0140** y	?	**Puyehue-Cordón Caulle** (Chile-C)	1507-15=		
0144	?	**Vulcano** (Italy)	0101-05=		
0145 ?	?	**Ischia** (Italy)	0101-03=		
0150 t	?	**Stromboli** (Italy)	0101-04=	2	
T **0150** ?	?	**Taranaki [Egmont]** (New Zealand)	0401-03=	3?	-/7
C **0150** ?	?	**Garbuna Group** (New Britain-SW Pac)	0502-07=		
T **0150** ?	?	**Ibusuki [Kaimon]** (Kyushu-Japan)	0802-07=	4	-/8
C **0150** ?	?	**Iwate** (Honshu-Japan)	0803-24=		
G **0150** t	?	**Oshima** (Izu Is-Japan)	0804-01=	3	
G **0150** v	?	**Mashu** (Hokkaido-Japan)	0805-081	4	-/8
T **0150** ?	?	**Tolbachik** (Kamchatka)	1000-24=		
T **0150** ?	?	**Bezymianny** (Kamchatka)	1000-25=		
C **0150** ?	?	**Shasta** (US-California)	1203-01-		
M **0150** y	?	**Kilauea** (Hawaiian Is)	1302-01-	0	
C **0150** ?	?	**Mauna Loa** (Hawaiian Is)	1302-02=	0	
T **0150** ?	?	**Masaya** (Nicaragua)	1404-10=	**5**+	-/**9**
T **0150** ?	?	**Cotopaxi** (Ecuador)	1502-05=	4	-/8
E **0150** *	?	**Wolf** (Galápagos)	1503-02=	0	
G **0150** u	?	**Hengill** (Iceland-SW)	1701-05=	2	8/-
T **0150** v	?	**Torfajökull** (Iceland-S)	1702-05=	3	7/7
T **0150** v	?	**Bárdarbunga [Veidivötn]** (Iceland)	1703-03=	2?	8/-
C **0160** x	?	**Liamuiga** (W Indies)	1600-03=	**P**	
C **0160** w	?	**Agua de Pau** (Azores)	1802-09=		
G **0170** v	?	**Savai'i** (Samoa-SW Pacific)	0404-04=		
G **0170** p	?	**Shiveluch** (Kamchatka)	1000-27=	3	-/7
T **0170** ?	?	**Cayambe** (Ecuador)	1502-006		
0172	?	**Vesuvius** (Italy)	0101-02=	3?	
T **0180** ?	?	**Okataina [Te Kopia]** (New Zeal)	0401-05=		
T **0180** ?	?	**Maroa [Orakeikorako]** (New Zeal)	0401-061		
C **0180** v	?	**Cotopaxi** (Ecuador)	1502-05=	4	8/8
G **0190** y	?	**Merapi** (Java)	0603-25=		
C **0190** t	?	**Tengger Caldera** (Java)	0603-31=	2	
C **0190** x	?	**Wrangell** (Alaska-E)	1105-02-	**C**?	
G **0190** ?	?	**St. Helens** (US-Washington)	1201-05-		
G **0190** w	?	**Chichón, El** (México)	1401-12=		
C **0190** s	?	**Terceira** (Azores)	1802-05=		
T **0190** ?	?	**Tenerife** (Canary Is)	1803-03-		7/-
A **0200** >	?	**Arhab, Harra of** (Arabia-S)	0301-09-	2?	
? 0200 ?	*?*	*Penanggungan (Java)*	0603-291		
T **0200** ?	?	**Fuji** (Honshu-Japan)	0803-03=	2	
T **0200** ?	?	**Haku-san** (Honshu-Japan)	0803-05=		
G **0200** u	?	**Kuttara** (Hokkaido-Japan)	0805-034		
T **0200** ?	?	**Gorely** (Kamchatka)	1000-07=	3	-/7
T **0200** y	?	**Uzon** (Kamchatka)	1000-17=		
G **0200** w	?	**Kanaga** (Aleutian Is)	1101-11-		
T **0200**	?	**Aniakchak** (Alaska Peninsula)	1102-09-		
C **0200** t	?	**Glacier Peak** (US-Washington)	1201-02-	4+	-/8
T **0200** ?	?	**Adams** (US-Washington)	1201-04-	2	
C **0200** ?	?	**Mauna Loa** (Hawaiian Is)	1302-02=	0	
G **0200** v	?	**Chichinautzin** (México)	1401-08=	3	8/7
T **0200** ?	?	**Cayambe** (Ecuador)	1502-006		
C **0200** ?	?	**Tungurahua** (Ecuador)	1502-08=		
C **0200** u	?	**Melimoyu** (Chile-S)	1508-052		
C **0200** w	?	**Snaefellsjökull** (Iceland-W)	1700-01=		8/-
T **0200** ?	?	**Katla** (Iceland-S)	1702-03=		
0203	?	**Vesuvius** (Italy)	0101-02=	**P**	
T **0210** ?	?	**Aso** (Kyushu-Japan)	0802-11=	3	

Yuri Doubik (Inst. Volc., Kamchatka)

The broad Krasheninnikov volcano in the foreground underwent caldera collapse about 2100 years ago. The 800-m-wide crater of the Northern Cone (lower center) formed during an explosive eruption about 1100 years ago; the latest eruption at Krasheninnikov formed the small lava cone in the Northern Cone crater about 400 years ago. Conical Kronotsky volcano in the background is largely of Pleistocene age, but had weak phreatic eruptions during the 20th century.

START YEAR M-Dy	Dura-tion	VOLCANO NAME (Subregion)	NUMBER	VEI	Vol L/T
T **0210** ?	?	**Poás** (Costa Rica)	1405-04=		
E **0210** z	?	**Darwin** (Galápagos)	1503-03=	0	
G **0220** v	?	**Taveuni** (Fiji Is-SW Pacific)	0405-01-	0	
T **0220** ?	?	**Fuji** (Honshu-Japan)	0803-03=	2	
C **0220** u	?	**Orizaba, Pico de** (México)	1401-10=	3	
C **0220** u	?	**Calbuco** (Chile-S)	1508-02=		
C **0220** u	?	**Pelée** (W Indies)	1600-12=		
0222	>3yr	**Vesuvius** (Italy)	0101-02=	2	
0223 Cont	....	*Vesuvius (Italy)*	0101-02=	*2*	
0224 Cont	....	*Vesuvius (Italy)*	0101-02=	*2*	
0225 Cont	....	*Vesuvius (Italy)*	0101-02=	*2*	
0226 Cont	....	*Vesuvius (Italy)*	0101-02=	*2*	
0227 Cont	....	*Vesuvius (Italy)*	0101-02=	*2*	
0228 Cont	....	*Vesuvius (Italy)*	0101-02=	*2*	
0229 Cont	....	*Vesuvius (Italy)*	0101-02=	*2*	
0230 Cont	....	*Vesuvius (Italy)*	0101-02=	*2*	
C **0230** ?	?	**Sundoro** (Java)	0603-21=		
T **0230** ?	?	**Shiveluch** (Kamchatka)	1000-27=	3	-/7
C **0230** x	?	**Augustine** (Alaska-SW)	1103-01-		
T **0230** ?	?	**St. Helens** (US-Washington)	1201-05-	0	
G **0230** n 0315n	?	**Taupo** (New Zealand)	0401-07=	**6**?	-/**10**
0231 Cont	....	*Vesuvius (Italy)*	0101-02=	*2*	
0232 Cont	....	*Vesuvius (Italy)*	0101-02=	*2*	
0233 Cont	....	*Vesuvius (Italy)*	0101-02=	*2*	
0234 Cont	....	*Vesuvius (Italy)*	0101-02=	*2*	
0235 Cont	....	*Vesuvius (Italy)*	0101-02=	*2*	
C **0240**w	?	**Fuji** (Honshu-Japan)	0803-03=		
G **0240** v	?	**Ksudach** (Kamchatka)	1000-05=	**6**	-/**10**
G **0240**w	?	**Tenerife** (Canary Is)	1803-03-		
0250 t	?	**Stromboli** (Italy)	0101-04=	2	
0250 t	?	**Krakatau** (Indonesia)	0602-00=		
C **0250** x	?	**Iraya** (Luzon-N of)	0704-06-		
T **0250** ?	?	**Fuji** (Honshu-Japan)	0803-03=	2	
G **0250** x	?	**Nasu** (Honshu-Japan)	0803-15=	3	-/7
T **0250** v	?	**Oshima** (Izu Is-Japan)	0804-01=	3	
C **0250**w	?	**Oshima-Oshima** (Hokkaido-Japan)	0805-01=		
G **0250** ?	?	**Akan** (Hokkaido-Japan)	0805-07=		
T **0250** ?	?	**Mutnovsky** (Kamchatka)	1000-06=	2	-/6
T **0250** ?	?	**Gorely** (Kamchatka)	1000-07=	3	-/7
T **0250** ?	?	**Tolbachik** (Kamchatka)	1000-24=		
T **0250** ?	?	**Bezymianny** (Kamchatka)	1000-25=		8/-
T **0250** ?	?	**Shiveluch** (Kamchatka)	1000-27=	4	-/8
U **0250** z	?	**Seguam** (Aleutian Is)	1101-18-		
C **0250** ?	?	**Popocatépetl** (México)	1401-09=		
C **0250**w	?	**Quill, The** (W Indies)	1600-02=		
T **0250** *	?	**Hekla** (Iceland-S)	1702-07=		
T **0250** y	?	**Krafla** (Iceland-NE)	1703-08=	0	
0252 0201	8*a*	**Etna** (Italy)	0101-06=	3?	
? 0253 <	*?*	*Erciyes Dagi (Turkey)*	0103-01=		
I **0256** ?	?	***Unknown Source*** *(Byrd Station 1968)*	......		
T **0260** ?	?	**Taupo** (New Zealand)	0401-07=	0	8/-
T **0260** z	?	**Miyake-jima** (Izu Is-Japan)	0804-04=	4	-/8
G **0260**w	?	**Barú** (Panamá)	1406-01-		
G **0260**w	?	**Tolima, Nevado del** (Colombia)	1501-03=	3?	
T **0260** ?	?	**Cayambe** (Ecuador)	1502-006		
T **0260** ?	?	**Katla** (Iceland-S)	1702-03=		
T **0270** ?	?	**Taveuni** (Fiji Is-SW Pacific)	0405-01-	1	
T **0270** ?	?	**Ibusuki [Kaimon]** (Kyushu-Japan)	0802-07=	3	-/7
G **0270** ?	?	**St. Helens** (US-Washington)	1201-05-		
G **0270**w	?	**Chimborazo** (Ecuador)	1502-071		
C **0270** k	?	**Katla** (Iceland-S)	1702-03=	3	-/7
G **0280**w	?	**Merapi** (Java)	0603-25=		
C **0290** ?	?	**Pululagua** (Ecuador)	1502-011		
E **0290** y	?	**Parinacota** (Chile-N)	1505-012	0	
T **0290** ?	?	**Katla** (Iceland-S)	1702-03=		
0295 j	?	**Ischia** (Italy)	0101-03=		
T **0300** ?	?	**Fuji** (Honshu-Japan)	0803-03=	1	
G **0300** x	?	**Zao** (Honshu-Japan)	0803-19=	4	-/8
T **0300**w	?	**Tolmachev Dol** (Kamchatka)	1000-082		
C **0300** ?	?	**Imuruk Lake** (Alaska-W)	1104-06-		
C **0300** x	?	**Hood** (US-Oregon)	1202-01-		
C **0300** ?	?	**Mauna Loa** (Hawaiian Is)	1302-02=	0	
C **0300** ?	?	**Pelée** (W Indies)	1600-12=	**P**	
? 0303	*?*	*Vesuvius (Italy)*	0101-02=	*2?*	
G **0310** v	?	**Pago** (New Britain-SW Pac)	0502-08=	**5**	-/**9**
G **0320** v	?	**Taveuni** (Fiji Is-SW Pacific)	0405-01-	2	
T **0320** z	?	**Miyake-jima** (Izu Is-Japan)	0804-04=	3?	5/7
G **0320** x	?	**Mono Craters** (US-California)	1203-12-		
C **0330** t	?	**Tengger Caldera** (Java)	0603-31=	3?	
G **0330** x	?	**Nasu** (Honshu-Japan)	0803-15=	2	
C **0330** ?	?	**Villarrica** (Chile-C)	1507-12=		
G **0340** ?	?	**Nabukelevu** (Fiji Is-SW Pacific)	0405-03-		
G **0340** x	?	**Oshima** (Izu Is-Japan)	0804-01=	4	7/8
C **0340** ?	?	**Akutan** (Aleutian Is)	1101-32-	**5**	-/**9**
T **0350** ?	?	**Taveuni** (Fiji Is-SW Pacific)	0405-01-	2	
C **0350** ?	?	**St. Andrew Strait [Lou Is.]**	0500-01=		

START YEAR M-Dy	Dura-tion	VOLCANO NAME (Subregion)	NUMBER	VEI	Vol L/T
C **0350** y	?	**Fuji** (Honshu-Japan)	0803-03=	3	
G **0350** v	?	**Tokachi** (Hokkaido-Japan)	0805-05=		
G **0350** v	?	**Mashu** (Hokkaido-Japan)	0805-081	2	-/6
T **0350** y	?	**Diky Greben** (Kamchatka)	1000-022		**10**/-
G **0350** ?	?	**Ksudach** (Kamchatka)	1000-05=	2	-/6
C **0350** u	?	**Kizimen** (Kamchatka)	1000-23=		
T **0350** ?	?	**Tolbachik** (Kamchatka)	1000-24=		
C **0350** ?	?	**Longgang Group** (China-E)	1005-05-		
T **0350** v	?	**Mono Lake Volc Field** (US-California	1203-11-		
C **0350** ?	?	**Mauna Loa** (Hawaiian Is)	1302-02=	0	
C **0350** y	?	**Ruiz, Nevado del** (Colombia)	1501-02=	3	-/7
C **0350** ?	?	**Tungurahua** (Ecuador)	1502-08=	3?	
G **0350** u	?	**Pelée** (W Indies)	1600-12=	4	-/8
T **0350** *	?	**Hekla** (Iceland-S)	1702-07=		
A **0350** j 1115m	?	**Asama** (Honshu-Japan)	0803-11=	4	8/8
G **0370** s	?	**Kuju** (Kyushu-Japan)	0802-12=	3	**9**/7
C **0370** x	?	**Fuji** (Honshu-Japan)	0803-03=		
T **0370** x	?	**Cotopaxi** (Ecuador)	1502-05=		
E **0370** *	?	**Negra, Sierra** (Galápagos)	1503-05=	0	
G **0370** u	?	**Soufrière Guadeloupe** (W Indies)	1600-06=		
0379	>3yr	**Vesuvius** (Italy)	0101-02=	2	
0380 Cont	....	*Vesuvius (Italy)*	0101-02=	*2*	
G **0380** ?	?	**Shiveluch** (Kamchatka)	1000-27=	3	-/7
T **0380** u	?	**San Martín** (México)	1401-11=		
T **0380** y	?	**Sete Cidades** (Azores)	1802-08=	4	-/8
0381 Cont	....	*Vesuvius (Italy)*	0101-02=	*2*	
0382 Cont	....	*Vesuvius (Italy)*	0101-02=	*2*	
0383 Cont	....	*Vesuvius (Italy)*	0101-02=	*2*	
0384 Cont	....	*Vesuvius (Italy)*	0101-02=	*2*	
0385 Cont	....	*Vesuvius (Italy)*	0101-02=	*2*	
0386 Cont	....	*Vesuvius (Italy)*	0101-02=	*2*	
0387 Cont	....	*Vesuvius (Italy)*	0101-02=	*2*	
0388 Cont	....	*Vesuvius (Italy)*	0101-02=	*2*	
0389 Cont	....	*Vesuvius (Italy)*	0101-02=	*2*	
0390 Cont	....	*Vesuvius (Italy)*	0101-02=	*2*	
C **0390** s	?	**Taranaki [Egmont]** (New Zealand)	0401-03=		
C **0390** v	?	**Kikai** (Ryukyu Is)	0802-06=	3	
T **0390** u	?	**Veer** (Kamchatka)	1000-121	2?	
G **0390**w	?	**Hudson, Cerro** (Chile-S)	1508-057		
C **0390** s	?	**Plat Pays, Morne** (W Indies)	1600-11=		
0391 Cont	....	*Vesuvius (Italy)*	0101-02=	*2*	
0392 Cont	....	*Vesuvius (Italy)*	0101-02=	*2*	
0393 Cont	....	*Vesuvius (Italy)*	0101-02=	*2*	
0394 Cont	....	*Vesuvius (Italy)*	0101-02=	*2*	
0395 Cont	....	*Vesuvius (Italy)*	0101-02=	*2*	
C **0400** y	?	**Kaikohe-Bay of Islands** (New Zeal)	0401-01=		
T **0400** ?	?	**Raoul Island** (Kermadec Is)	0402-03=	4	-/8
G **0400** t	?	**Taveuni** (Fiji Is-SW Pacific)	0405-01-	2	
T **0400** ?	?	**Fuji** (Honshu-Japan)	0803-03=	2	
T **0400** z	?	**Akita-Komaga-take** (Honshu-Japan)	0803-23=		
T **0400** ?	?	**Avachinsky** (Kamchatka)	1000-10=		
T **0400** ?	?	**Tolbachik** (Kamchatka)	1000-24=	4+	8/8
C **0400** t	?	**Fisher** (Aleutian Is)	1101-35-		
G **0400** v	?	**Chichinautzin [Xitle]** (México)	1401-08=	3?	**9**/-
C **0400** t	?	**Pacaya** (Guatemala)	1402-11=	2	
A **0400** ?	?	**Arenal** (Costa Rica)	1405-033	4	-/8
G **0400** w	?	**Lanín** (Chile-C)	1507-122		
T **0400** ?	?	**Katla** (Iceland-S)	1702-03=		
G **0410** w	?	**Merapi** (Java)	0603-25=	3	-/7
C **0410** t	?	**Maca** (Chile-S)	1508-056		
0416	?	**Krakatau** (Indonesia)	0602-00=	**C**	
0417 ?	?	**Etna** (Italy)	0101-06=		
G **0420** ?	?	**St. Helens** (US-Washington)	1201-05-		
T **0420** p	?	**Kilauea** (Hawaiian Is)	1302-01-		
C **0420** v	?	**Osorno** (Chile-S)	1508-01=	4?	
G **0430** v	?	**Rincón de la Vieja** (Costa Rica)	1405-02=		
G **0430** z	?	**Irazú** (Costa Rica)	1405-06=	3	
G **0440** u	?	**Aso** (Kyushu-Japan)	0802-11=		
G **0440** v	?	**Rainier** (US-Washington)	1201-03-		
G **0440**w	?	**North Sister Field** (US-Oregon)	1202-07-	2?	8/-
C **0440** v	?	**Mono Craters** (US-California)	1203-12-		
T **0450** t	?	**Haruna** (Honshu-Japan)	0803-122	3	-/7
G **0450** ?	?	**Hakkoda Group** (Honshu-Japan)	0803-28=	1	-/6
T **0450** ?	?	**Kutcharo [Atosanupuri]** (Hokkaido)	0805-08=		
C **0450** ?	?	**Komarov** (Kamchatka)	1000-22=	0	
T **0450** ?	?	**Tolbachik** (Kamchatka)	1000-24=	3	**9**/7
M **0450** <	?	**Kilauea** (Hawaiian Is)	1302-01=	0	
C **0450** ?	?	**Mauna Loa** (Hawaiian Is)	1302-02=	0	
G **0450** r	?	**Ilopango** (El Salvador)	1403-06=	**6**+	-/**10**
C **0450** ?	?	**Pelée** (W Indies)	1600-12=	**P**	
C **0460** ?	?	**Fournaise, Piton de la** (Indian O.)	0303-02=	0	
C **0460** ?	?	**Aniakchak** (Alaska Peninsula)	1102-09-		
C **0470** ?	?	**Sundoro** (Java)	0603-21=		
C **0470** u	?	**Mayon** (Luzon-Philippines)	0703-03=		
C **0470** t	?	**Iraya** (Luzon-N of)	0704-06-		
C **0470** v	?	**Fuji** (Honshu-Japan)	0803-03=	3?	

START YEAR	M-Dy	Duration	VOLCANO NAME (Subregion)	NUMBER	VEI	Vol L/T
0472	1105	1a?	**Vesuvius** (Italy)	0101-02=	**5**	-/**9**
G **0480** u	....	?	**Taveuni** (Fiji Is-SW Pacific)	0405-01-	2	
G **0480** u	....	?	**Merapi** (Java)	0603-25=		
G **0480** ?	....	?	**Belknap** (US-Oregon)	1202-06-	2?	
C **0480** ?	....	?	**Mauna Loa** (Hawaiian Is)	1302-02=	0	
C **0480** t	....	?	**San Martín** (México)	1401-11=		
G **0480** x	....	?	**Chichón, El** (México)	1401-12=		
C **0480** u	....	?	**Tungurahua** (Ecuador)	1502-08=		8/-
G **0490** v	....	?	**Newberry** (US-Oregon)	1202-11-	4	-/8
C **0490** v	....	?	**Mono Craters** (US-California)	1203-12-		

500

START YEAR	M-Dy	Duration	VOLCANO NAME (Subregion)	NUMBER	VEI	Vol L/T
0500 v	....	?	**Arhab, Harra of** (Arabia-S)	0301-09-	0	
G **0500** v	....	?	**Haku-san** (Honshu-Japan)	0803-05=		
G **0500** t	....	?	**Miyake-jima** (Izu Is-Japan)	0804-04=	3	-/7
G **0500** ?	....	?	**Shiveluch** (Kamchatka)	1000-27=	4+	-/8
G **0500** v	....	?	**Puyehue-Cordón Caulle** (Chile-C)	1507-15=		
T **0500** ?	....	?	**Katla** (Iceland-S)	1702-03=		
M **0500** t	....	?	**Lanzarote** (Canary Is)	1803-06-		
I **0505** ?	....	?	***Unknown Source*** *(Byrd Station 1968)*	......		
? 0505	*1109*	*?*	*Vesuvius (Italy)*	0101-02=	*2?*	
C **0510** x	....	?	**Augustine** (Alaska-SW)	1103-01-		
C **0510** w	....	?	**Hood** (US-Oregon)	1202-01-		
0512	0708	?	**Vesuvius** (Italy)	0101-02=	4?	
C **0520** w	....	?	**Taranaki [Egmont]** (New Zealand)	0401-03=		
G **0520** v	....	?	**Taveuni** (Fiji Is-SW Pacific)	0405-01-	2	
C **0520** v	....	?	**Karkar** (New Guinea-NE of)	0501-03=	**C**	
C **0520** v	....	?	**Fuji** (Honshu-Japan)	0803-03=	2	
C **0520** x	....	?	**Calbuco** (Chile-S)	1508-02=		
A **0520** j	0601p	?	**Haruna** (Honshu-Japan)	0803-122	4+	-/8
0526 ?	....	?	**Vulcano** (Italy)	0101-05=	3	
T **0530** ?	....	?	**Fuji** (Honshu-Japan)	0803-03=	3	
T **0530** ?	....	?	**Shiveluch** (Kamchatka)	1000-27=	3	-/7
0536	....	?	**Vesuvius** (Italy)	0101-02=		
G **0540** w	....	?	**Ischia** (Italy)	0101-03=		
C **0540** v	....	?	**Rabaul** (New Britain-SW Pac)	0502-14=	**6**	-/**10**
G **0540** t	....	?	**Merapi** (Java)	0603-25=		
C **0540** u	....	?	**Alamagan** (Mariana Is-C Pacific)	0804-18=		
G **0540** x	....	?	**Kilauea** (Hawaiian Is)	1302-01-		
G **0540** w	....	?	**Colima** (México)	1401-04=		
T **0540** ?	....	?	**Katla** (Iceland-S)	1702-03=		
0550 t	....	?	**Stromboli** (Italy)	0101-04=	3	
T **0550** ?	....	?	**Taranaki [Egmont]** (New Zealand)	0401-03=		
C **0550** ?	....	?	**Raoul Island** (Kermadec Is)	0402-03=	4	-/8
C **0550** ?	....	?	**Yasur** (Vanuatu-SW Pacific)	0507-10=		
T **0550** ?	....	?	**Ibusuki [Kaimon]** (Kyushu-Japan)	0802-07=	2	-/6
G **0550** v	....	?	**Rausu** (Hokkaido-Japan)	0805-082	4	-/8
T **0550** ?	....	?	**Gorely** (Kamchatka)	1000-07=	3	-/7
G **0550** ?	....	?	**Kikhpinych** (Kamchatka)	1000-18=	3	7/7
T **0550** ?	....	?	**Tolbachik** (Kamchatka)	1000-24=	3	**9**/7
C **0550** ?	....	?	**Kliuchevskoi** (Kamchatka)	1000-26=		
T **0550** ?	....	?	**Ichinsky** (Kamchatka)	1000-28=		
C **0550** ?	....	?	**Akutan** (Aleutian Is)	1101-32-		
C **0550** ?	....	?	**Mauna Loa** (Hawaiian Is)	1302-02=	0	
T **0550** ?	....	?	**Arenal** (Costa Rica)	1405-033	4	-/8
G **0550** u	....	?	**Guagua Pichincha** (Ecuador)	1502-02=		
T **0550** x	....	?	**Cotopaxi** (Ecuador)	1502-05=		
T **0550** w	....	?	**Chimborazo** (Ecuador)	1502-071		
T **0550** ?	....	?	**Eyjafjallajökull** (Iceland-S)	1702-02=		
T **0550** *	....	?	**Hekla** (Iceland-S)	1702-07=		
A **0550** j	0601p	?	**Haruna** (Honshu-Japan)	0803-122	**5**	8/**9**
? 0553	....	*?*	*Aso (Kyushu-Japan)*	0802-11=	*3↑*	
G **0560** w	....	?	**Lanín** (Chile-C)	1507-122		
T **0570** ?	....	?	**Akita-Yake-yama** (Honshu-Japan)	0803-26=		
? 0573	*03 ?*	*?*	*Chokai (Honshu-Japan)*	0803-22=		
? 0577	*1201p*	*226s*	*Chokai (Honshu-Japan)*	0803-22=		
? 0578	*Cont*	....	*Chokai (Honshu-Japan)*	0803-22=		
V **0580** ?	....	?	**Oshima** (Izu Is-Japan)	0804-01=	3	-/7
T **0580** ?	....	?	**Shiveluch** (Kamchatka)	1000-27=	4+	-/8
G **0590** v	....	?	**Chichón, El** (México)	1401-12=	3	-/7
C **0590** u	....	?	**Fuego** (Guatemala)	1402-09=		
T **0590** ?	....	?	**Katla** (Iceland-S)	1702-03=		
G **0600** ?	....	?	**Fournaise, Piton de la** (Indian O.-W)	0303-02=	0	
G **0600** u	....	?	**Kuchinoerabu-jima** (Ryukyu Is)	0802-05=		
T **0600** ?	....	?	**Ibusuki [Kaimon]** (Kyushu-Japan)	0802-07=	4	8/8
G **0600** x	....	?	**Azuma** (Honshu-Japan)	0803-18=		
V **0600** ?	....	?	**Oshima** (Izu Is-Japan)	0804-01=	3	-/7
T **0600** y	....	?	**Tokachi** (Hokkaido-Japan)	0805-05=		
T **0600** y	....	?	**Akan** (Hokkaido-Japan)	0805-07=		
T **0600** ?	....	?	**Bezymianny** (Kamchatka)	1000-25=		
G **0600** ?	....	?	**Shiveluch** (Kamchatka)	1000-27=	**5**	-/**9**
C **0600** u	....	?	**Inyo Craters** (US-California)	1203-13-	4?	7/7
C **0600** ?	....	?	**Mauna Loa** (Hawaiian Is)	1302-02=	0	
C **0600** ?	....	?	**Tungurahua** (Ecuador)	1502-08=	3?	
C **0600** v	....	?	**Picos Volc System** (Azores)	1802-081		
C **0600** ?	....	?	**Deception Island** (Antarctica)	1900-03=		
? 0610 o	....	*?*	*Chokai (Honshu-Japan)*	0803-22=		
G **0610** t	....	?	**Opala** (Kamchatka)	1000-08=	**5+**	8/**9**
C **0610** w	....	?	**Edziza** (Canada)	1200-06-		
T **0610** ?	....	?	**Katla** (Iceland-S)	1702-03=		
V **0625** ?	....	?	**Oshima** (Izu Is-Japan)	0804-01=	3	-/7
G **0630** r	....	?	**Merapi** (Java)	0603-25=		
T **0630** ?	....	?	**Yake-dake** (Honshu-Japan)	0803-07=	1	-/5
T **0630** ?	....	?	**Shiveluch** (Kamchatka)	1000-27=	3	-/7
C **0630** ?	....	?	**Mauna Loa** (Hawaiian Is)	1302-02=	0	
I **0639** q	....	?	***Unknown Source*** *(GISP2, 149 ppb S)*	......		
A **0640** ?	....	?	**'Uwayrid, Harrat** (Arabia-W)	0301-02=	2?	
G **0640** s	....	?	**Taveuni** (Fiji Is-SW Pacific)	0405-01-	2	
G **0640** s	....	?	**Turrialba** (Costa Rica)	1405-07=		
C **0640** w	....	?	**Watt, Morne** (W Indies)	1600-101		
G **0640** r	08	?	**San Salvador** (El Salvador)	1403-05=	3?	
0641	....	?	**Rahat, Harrat** (Arabia-W)	0301-07=	2	
? 0644	....	*?*	*Etna (Italy)*	0101-06=		
0650 t	....	?	**Khaybar, Harrat** (Arabia-W)	0301-06=	2?	
G **0650** t	....	?	**Sanbe** (Honshu-Japan)	0803-002		
C **0650** ?	....	?	**Kikhpinych** (Kamchatka)	1000-18=		
T **0650** ?	....	?	**Krasheninnikov** (Kamchatka)	1000-19=	2	-/6
G **0650** s	....	?	**Shiveluch** (Kamchatka)	1000-27=	**5**	-/**9**
0650 t	....	?	**Tianshan Volc Group** (China-W)	1004-02-		
G **0650** v	....	?	**Arenal** (Costa Rica)	1405-033	4	-/8
C **0650** v	....	?	**Cuicocha** (Ecuador)	1502-003		
C **0650** ?	....	?	**Pelée** (W Indies)	1600-12=		
T **0650** z	....	?	**Hekla** (Iceland-S)	1702-07=		
0654 ?	....	?	**Oshima** (Izu Is-Japan)	0804-01=	3	-/7
T **0660** ?	....	?	**Ibusuki [Kaimon]** (Kyushu-Japan)	0802-07=	4+	
C **0670** w	....	?	**Sete Cidades** (Azores)	1802-08=	3	7/7
C **0675** t	....	?	**Ruiz, Nevado del** (Colombia)	1501-02=	3	-/7
G **0680** x	....	?	**Merapi** (Java)	0603-25=		
0680 ?	....	268w>	**Oshima** (Izu Is-Japan)	0804-01=	4	-/8
G **0680** x	....	?	**Blue Lake Crater** (US-Oregon)	1202-03-		
C **0680** u	....	?	**Kilauea** (Hawaiian Is)	1302-01-	1?	
C **0680** ?	....	?	**Mauna Loa** (Hawaiian Is)	1302-02=	0	
T **0680** ?	....	?	**Katla** (Iceland-S)	1702-03=		
0681	*Cont*	....	*Oshima (Izu Is-Japan)*	0804-01=	*4*	*-/8*
0684 ?	1129	?	**Oshima** (Izu Is-Japan)	0804-01=		
0685	02	30p?	**Vesuvius** (Italy)	0101-02=	4	-/8
@ **0685**	04	?	**Asama** (Honshu-Japan)	0803-11=	3	
0686	....	?	**Yake-dake** (Honshu-Japan)	0803-07=	2	-/6
G **0690** v	....	?	**Pago** (New Britain-SW Pac)	0502-08=	**5**	-/**9**
G **0690** v	....	?	**Newberry** (US-Oregon)	1202-11-	4	8/8
G **0690** s	....	?	**Irazú** (Costa Rica)	1405-06=	3	
T **0700** ?	....	?	**Lengai, Ol Doinyo** (Africa-E)	0202-12=		
T **0700** ?	....	?	**Raoul Island** (Kermadec Is)	0402-03=	3	-/7
T **0700** ?	....	?	**Kirishima** (Kyushu-Japan)	0802-09=		
V **0700** ?	....	?	**Oshima** (Izu Is-Japan)	0804-01=	3	-/7
T **0700** ?	....	?	**Kutcharo [Atosanupuri]** (Hokkaido)	0805-08=		
T **0700** ?	....	?	**Ksudach** (Kamchatka)	1000-05=		
T **0700** ?	....	?	**Avachinsky** (Kamchatka)	1000-10=		
T **0700** t	....	?	**Kizimen** (Kamchatka)	1000-23=		
T **0700** t	....	?	**Bezymianny** (Kamchatka)	1000-25=	4?	-/8
T **0700** ?	....	?	**Shiveluch** (Kamchatka)	1000-27=	3	-/7
T **0700** y	....	?	**Aniakchak** (Alaska Peninsula)	1102-09-	0	
T **0700** ?	....	?	**Mono Craters** (US-California)	1203-12-		8/-
T **0700** ?	....	?	**Arenal** (Costa Rica)	1405-033	4	-/8
T **0700** y	....	?	**Ojos del Salado, Nevados** (Chile)	1505-13=		
C **0700** w	....	?	**Agua de Pau** (Azores)	1802-09=		
T **0700** ?	....	?	**Tenerife** (Canary Is)	1803-03-		6/-
M **0700** t	....	?	**Lanzarote** (Canary Is)	1803-06-		
? 0704	....	*?*	*Tate-yama (Honshu-Japan)*	0803-08=		
0706	09 ?	?	**Haku-san** (Honshu-Japan)	0803-05=		
0708	....	?	**Sakura-jima** (Kyushu-Japan)	0802-08=	3↑	
C **0710** u	....	?	**Pago** (New Britain-SW Pac)	0502-08=	**6**	-/**10**
G **0710** r	....	?	**Barú** (Panamá)	1406-01-		
0711 c	....	?	**Chokai** (Honshu-Japan)	0803-22=		
? 0712	....	*?*	*Sakura-jima (Kyushu-Japan)*	0802-08=	*3?*	
V **0713** ?	....	?	**Oshima** (Izu Is-Japan)	0804-01=	3	-/7
0716	....	730y	**Sakura-jima** (Kyushu-Japan)	0802-08=	3↑	
0717	*Cont*	....	*Sakura-jima (Kyushu-Japan)*	0802-08=	*3↑*	
? 0717	*07*	*?*	*Chokai (Honshu-Japan)*	0803-22=		
0718	*Cont*	....	*Sakura-jima (Kyushu-Japan)*	0802-08=	*3↑*	
T **0720** ?	....	?	**Ibusuki [Kaimon]** (Kyushu-Japan)	0802-07=	4	-/8
C **0720** v	....	?	**Fuji** (Honshu-Japan)	0803-03=	2	
M **0720** ?	....	?	**Medicine Lake** (US-California)	1203-02-		8/-
C **0720** ?	....	?	**Pelée** (W Indies)	1600-12=		
0726	0715q	?	**Santorini** (Greece)	0102-04=	4?	7/-
0729	....	?	**Vulcano** (Italy)	0101-05=		
C **0730** ?	....	?	**Karkar** (New Guinea-NE of)	0501-03=	**P**	
C **0730** v	....	?	**Colima** (México)	1401-04=		
C **0730** x	....	?	**Tungurahua** (Ecuador)	1502-08=	4?	-/7
C **0740** w	....	?	**Tambora** (Lesser Sunda Is)	0604-04=		
C **0740** u	....	?	**Cotopaxi** (Ecuador)	1502-05=	4	7/8

Ingibjörg Kaldal (Icelandic Nat. Energy Auth.)

The Vatnaöldur crater row, extending diagonally across the center of the photo SW from Iceland's Bárdarbunga volcano, which lies beneath the Vatnajökull icecap, was the source of a large, dominantly explosive eruption at about 870 AD. The Vatnaöldur eruption originated from a 42-km-long fissure and produced 3.3 km^3 of tephra at the time of the settlement of Iceland, forming the the Landnam (Settlement) tephra layer, which extends over much of southern Iceland.

START YEAR	M-Dy	Duration	VOLCANO NAME (Subregion) . . .	NUMBER	VEI	Vol L/T
0742	1228	?	**Kirishima** (Kyushu-Japan)	0802-09=	3	
G **0750** t	....	?	**Kuchino-shima** (Ryukyu Is)	0802-043		
T **0750** ?	....	?	**Kikai** (Ryukyu Is)	0802-06=	3	
G **0750** t	....	?	**Miyake-jima** (Izu Is-Japan)	0804-04=	3	-/7
T **0750** ?	....	?	**Nemo Peak** (Kuril Is)	0900-32=		
T **0750** ?	....	?	**Mutnovsky** (Kamchatka)	1000-06=	3	-/7
G **0750** ?	....	?	**Krasheninnikov** (Kamchatka)	1000-19=	3	-/7
T **0750** ?	....	?	**Shiveluch** (Kamchatka)	1000-27=	3	-/7
A **0750** t	....	?	**Arenal** (Costa Rica)	1405-033	4	-/8
C **0750** w	....	?	**Bravo, Cerro** (Colombia)	1501-012	4	-/8
C **0750** ?	....	?	**Machín** (Colombia)	1501-04=		
T **0750** ?	....	?	**Hekla** (Iceland-S)	1702-07=		
? 0753	....	*?*	*Dar-Alages (Armenia)*	0104-08-		
G **0760** v	....	?	**Misti, El** (Perú)	1504-01=		
0764	01	?	**Sakura-jima** (Kyushu-Japan)	0802-08=	4	
0766	0720	?	**Sakura-jima** (Kyushu-Japan)	0802-08=	3↑	
T **0770** ?	....	?	**Taveuni** (Fiji Is-SW Pacific)	0405-01-	2	
T **0770** ?	....	?	**Ibusuki [Kaimon]** (Kyushu-Japan)	0802-07=	4	-/8
C **0770** x	....	?	**Hualalai** (Hawaiian Is)	1302-04-	1	8/-
C **0770** u	....	?	**Cotopaxi** (Ecuador)	1502-05=	4	7/8
0771	....	?	**Tsurumi** (Kyushu-Japan)	0802-13=	0	
? 0773	*11 ?*	*?*	*Zao (Honshu-Japan)*	0803-19=		
? 0774	....	*?*	*On-take (Honshu-Japan)*	0803-04=		
0778	....	?	**Sakura-jima** (Kyushu-Japan)	0802-08=	0?	
G **0780** v	....	?	**Lipari** (Italy)	0101-042		
C **0780** y	....	?	**St. Helens** (US-Washington)	1201-05-		
G **0780** v	....	?	**Chichón, El** (México)	1401-12=	**5**	-/**9**
T **0780** ?	....	?	**Katla** (Iceland-S)	1702-03=		
0781	07	16*m*	**Fuji** (Honshu-Japan)	0803-03=	3	
0787	1015q	92*v*	**Vesuvius** (Italy)	0101-02=	3	
0788	*Cont*	....	*Vesuvius (Italy)*	0101-02=	*3*	
0788	0418	?	**Kirishima** (Kyushu-Japan)	0802-09=	4	-/8
C **0790** t	....	?	**Haleakala** (Hawaiian Is)	1302-06-		
C **0790** t	....	?	**Trois Pitons, Morne** (W Indies)	1600-10=		
? 0796	*08*	*?*	*Aso (Kyushu-Japan)*	0802-11=	*0?*	
C **0800** t	....	?	**Dakataua** (New Britain-SW Pac)	0502-04=	**6**?	-/**10**
T **0800** ?	....	?	**Nikko-Shirane** (Honshu-Japan)	0803-14=		
T **0800** t	....	?	**Kostakan** (Kamchatka)	1000-122	3	7/7
G **0800** y	....	?	**Ichinsky** (Kamchatka)	1000-28=		
G **0800** V	....	?	**Churchill** (Alaska-E)	1105-03-	**6**	
M **0800** ?	....	?	**Medicine Lake** (US-California)	1203-02-		8/-
G **0800** y	....	?	**Lassen [Chaos Crags]** (US-Calif)	1203-08-		
G **0800** t	....	?	**Almolonga [C. Quemado]** (Guat)	1402-04=	3	7/7
C **0800** ?	....	?	**Tungurahua** (Ecuador)	1502-08=		
T **0800** t	....	?	**Hekla** (Iceland-S)	1702-07=		
G **0800** w	....	?	**Tenerife** (Canary Is)	1803-03-	0	8/-
0800	0411	674*m*>	**Fuji** (Honshu-Japan)	0803-03=	4	
0801	*Cont*	....	*Fuji (Honshu-Japan)*	0803-03=	*2*	
0802	*Cont*	....	*Fuji (Honshu-Japan)*	0803-03=	*2*	
? 0804	....	*730y*	*Chokai (Honshu-Japan)*	0803-22=		
? 0805	*Cont*	....	*Chokai (Honshu-Japan)*	0803-22=		
? 0806	*Cont*	....	*Chokai (Honshu-Japan)*	0803-22=		
0806	....	?	**Bandai** (Honshu-Japan)	0803-16=	3	
0807 ?	....	?	**Akita-Komaga-take** (Honshu-Japan)	0803-23=	3	-/7
? 0807	*1101*	*?*	*Akita-Yake-yama (Honshu-Japan)*	0803-26=		
G **0810** y	....	?	**Mono Craters** (US-California)	1203-12-	4	-/8
C **0810** ?	....	?	**Mauna Loa** (Hawaiian Is)	1302-02=	0	
? 0812 ?	....	*?*	*Etna (Italy)*	0101-06=		*8/5*
0813 ?	....	?	**Niigata-Yake-yama** (Honshu-Japan)	0803-09=		
? 0814	....	*?*	*Etna (Italy)*	0101-06=		
0817 g	....	?	**Chokai** (Honshu-Japan)	0803-22=		
G **0820** y	....	?	**Ischia** (Italy)	0101-03=		
C **0820** r	....	?	**Taranaki [Egmont]** (New Zealand)	0401-03=		
T **0820** ?	....	?	**Katla** (Iceland-S)	1702-03=		
C **0820** s	....	?	**Terceira** (Azores)	1802-05=		
V **0822** ?	....	?	**Oshima** (Izu Is-Japan)	0804-01=	3	-/7
I **0823**	0301t	?	**Popocatépetl** (México)	1401-09=	**P**	
0826	1231p	?	**Fuji** (Honshu-Japan)	0803-03=	2?	
C **0830** s	....	?	**Kikai** (Ryukyu Is)	0802-06=		
0830	....	?	**Fuji** (Honshu-Japan)	0803-03=	2	
T **0830** q	....	?	**Kikhpinych** (Kamchatka)	1000-18=		
T **0830** q	....	?	**Medicine Lake** (US-California)	1203-02-		7/-
C **0830** ?	....	?	**Mauna Loa** (Hawaiian Is)	1302-02=	0	
0830	01	?	**Chokai** (Honshu-Japan)	0803-22=		
? 0832	....	*?*	*Kozu-shima (Izu Is-Japan)*	0804-03=		
0832	0623	?	**Miyake-jima** (Izu Is-Japan)	0804-04=	3	-/7
0837	....	730*y?*	**Kirishima** (Kyushu-Japan)	0802-09=	3	
0837	0527	?	**Narugo** (Honshu-Japan)	0803-20=	1	
0838	*Cont*	....	*Kirishima (Kyushu-Japan)*	0802-09=	*2*	
0838 ?	08 ?	?	**Oshima** (Izu Is-Japan)	0804-01=	3	-/7
0838	0802?	?	**Kozu-shima** (Izu Is-Japan)	0804-03=	4	8/8
0839	*Cont*	....	*Kirishima (Kyushu-Japan)*	0802-09=	*2*	
? 0839	*1014*	*?*	*Chokai (Honshu-Japan)*	0803-22=		
C **0840** v	....	?	**Furnas** (Azores)	1802-10=	4	7/8
0843	....	>3yr	**Kirishima** (Kyushu-Japan)	0802-09=	2?	

	START YEAR	M-Dy	Duration	VOLCANO NAME (Subregion)	NUMBER	VEI	Vol L/T
	0844	*Cont*	....	*Kirishima (Kyushu-Japan)*	0802-09=	*2?*	
	0845	*Cont*	....	*Kirishima (Kyushu-Japan)*	0802-09=	*2?*	
	0846	*Cont*	....	*Kirishima (Kyushu-Japan)*	0802-09=	*2?*	
	0847	*Cont*	....	*Kirishima (Kyushu-Japan)*	0802-09=	*2?*	
	0848	*Cont*	....	*Kirishima (Kyushu-Japan)*	0802-09=	*2?*	
C	**0850** t	....	?	**Bayuda Volc Field** (Africa-N)	0205-06-		
T	**0850** ?	....	?	**Raoul Island** (Kermadec Is)	0402-03=	4	-/8
C	**0850** y	....	?	**Yasur** (Vanuatu-SW Pacific)	0507-10=		
	0850 t	....	?	**Krakatau** (Indonesia)	0602-00=		
?	*0850 t*	....	*?*	*Galunggung (Java)*	0603-14=		
	0850 ?	....	?	**Miyake-jima** (Izu Is-Japan)	0804-04=	4	7/8
G	**0850** x	....	?	**Hachijo-jima** (Izu Is-Japan)	0804-05=		
T	**0850** z	....	?	**Shiretoko-Iwo-zan** (Hokkaido-Japan)	0805-09=		
G	**0850** ?	....	?	**Krasheninnikov** (Kamchatka)	1000-19=		
T	**0850** ?	....	?	**Kizimen** (Kamchatka)	1000-23=	3	7/7
T	**0850** ?	....	?	**Bezymianny** (Kamchatka)	1000-25=		
C	**0850** t	....	?	**Kinenin** (Kamchatka)	1000-551	4	-/8
G	**0850** x	....	?	**Kanaga** (Aleutian Is)	1101-11-		
C	**0850** ?	....	?	**Shasta** (US-California)	1203-01-		
G	**0850** w	....	?	**Kilauea** (Hawaiian Is)	1302-01-	0	
U	**0850** x	....	?	**Unnamed [East Pacific Rise]**	1304-05-	0	
T	**0850** ?	....	?	**Krafla** (Iceland-NE)	1703-08=	0	7/-
C	**0850** w	....	?	**Picos Volc System** (Azores)	1802-081		
?	*0853*	....	*?*	*Haku-san (Honshu-Japan)*	0803-05=		
	0854 ?	0914?	656*w*?	**Oshima** (Izu Is-Japan)	0804-01=	4	-/8
	0855	*Cont*	....	*Oshima (Izu Is-Japan)*	0804-01=	*4*	*-/8*
	0856	*Cont*	....	*Oshima (Izu Is-Japan)*	0804-01=	*4*	*-/8*
?	*0856*	....	*?*	*Chokai (Honshu-Japan)*	0803-22=		
	0856 ?	....	365*w*?	**Nii-jima** (Izu Is-Japan)	0804-02=	2	7/6
	0857	*Cont*	....	*Nii-jima (Izu Is-Japan)*	0804-02=	*2*	*7/6*
	0857	....	?	**Kirishima** (Kyushu-Japan)	0802-09=	2?	
?	*0857*	*05*	*?*	*Chokai (Honshu-Japan)*	0803-22=		
	0858	....	?	**Kirishima** (Kyushu-Japan)	0802-09=	2?	
?	*0859*	....	*?*	*Etna (Italy)*	0101-06=		
?	*0859*	....	*?*	*Haku-san (Honshu-Japan)*	0803-05=		
M	**0860** t	....	?	**Vesuvius** (Italy)	0101-02=	0?	
?	*0860*	....	*?*	*Unzen (Kyushu-Japan)*	0802-10=		
G	**0860** u	....	?	**Puyehue-Cordón Caulle** (Chile-C)	1507-15=	**5**	-/**9**
C	**0860** v	....	?	**Hudson, Cerro** (Chile-S)	1508-057		
D	**0860** p	....	?	***Unknown Source*** *(Irish peat tephra)*	......		
?	*0860*	*04*	*?*	*Ibusuki [Kaimon] (Kyushu-Japan)*	0802-07=	*2?*	
?	*0861*	*05*	*?*	*Chokai (Honshu-Japan)*	0803-22=	*3*	
	0864	0612?	599*p*?	**Fuji** (Honshu-Japan)	0803-03=	3	**9**/-
	0864	1109	?	**Aso** (Kyushu-Japan)	0802-11=	3?	
	0865	*Cont*	....	*Fuji (Honshu-Japan)*	0803-03=	*2*	
	0866	*Cont*	....	*Fuji (Honshu-Japan)*	0803-03=	*2*	
?	*0866*	*05*	*?*	*Ibusuki [Kaimon] (Kyushu-Japan)*	0802-07=	*2?*	
	0867	0304	61*m*	**Tsurumi** (Kyushu-Japan)	0802-13=	3	
	0867	0620?	?	**Aso** (Kyushu-Japan)	0802-11=	2	
G	**0870** v	....	?	**Merapi** (Java)	0603-25=		
C	**0870** v	....	?	**Alamagan** (Mariana Is-C Pacific)	0804-18=	4	-/8
T	**0870** ?	....	?	**Torfajökull** (Iceland-S)	1702-05=	3	8/7
T	**0870** ?	....	?	**Bárdarbunga [Vatnaöldur]**	1703-03=	4	7/**9**
	0870	08	?	**Fuji** (Honshu-Japan)	0803-03=	2?	
	0871	0505	?	**Chokai** (Honshu-Japan)	0803-22=	2	7/6
	0874	0329	110*m*?	**Ibusuki [Kaimon]** (Kyushu-Japan)	0802-07=	4	
C	**0875** t	....	?	**Brennisteinsfjöll** (Iceland-SW)	1701-04=	2	8/-
T	**0880** ?	....	?	**Taveuni** (Fiji Is-SW Pacific)	0405-01-	2	
G	**0880** y	....	?	**Lassen [Chaos Crags]** (US-Calif)	1203-08-		
T	**0880** z	....	?	**Pacaya** (Guatemala)	1402-11=	3?	
T	**0880** ?	....	?	**Cayambe** (Ecuador)	1502-006		
T	**0880** ?	....	?	**Bárdarbunga** (Iceland-NE)	1703-03=		
?	*0882*	*11*	*?*	*Ibusuki [Kaimon] (Kyushu-Japan)*	0802-07=	*2?*	
?	*0884*	....	*?*	*Haku-san (Honshu-Japan)*	0803-05=		
	0884 ?	....	?	**Zao** (Honshu-Japan)	0803-19=	3	-/7
?	*0884*	*0726*	*20m*	*Chokai (Honshu-Japan)*	0803-22=		
	0885	0829	30*a*	**Ibusuki [Kaimon]** (Kyushu-Japan)	0802-07=	4	
	0886 ?	0629?	?	**Oshima** (Izu Is-Japan)	0804-01=	4	4/8
	0886	0629	?	**Nii-jima** (Izu Is-Japan)	0804-02=	4+	8/8
	0887	....	?	**Niigata-Yake-yama** (Honshu-Japan)	0803-09=	4	-/8
C	**0890** w	....	?	**Augustine** (Alaska-SW)	1103-01-		
C	**0890** v	....	?	**Medicine Lake** (US-California)	1203-02-	3	8/7
C	**0890** s	....	?	**San Martín** (México)	1401-11=		
G	**0890** x	....	?	**Galeras** (Colombia)	1501-08=	2	-/6
G	**0890** v	....	?	**Pelée** (W Indies)	1600-12=	**P**	
M	**0900** s	....	?	**Vesuvius** (Italy)	0101-02=	0?	
?	*0900 ?*	....	*?*	*Haku-san (Honshu-Japan)*	0803-05=		
T	**0900** ?	....	?	**Avachinsky** (Kamchatka)	1000-10=		
C	**0900** t	....	?	**Kikhpinych** (Kamchatka)	1000-18=	3?	-/8
T	**0900** ?	....	?	**Tolbachik** (Kamchatka)	1000-24=	4	**9/9**
C	**0900** t	....	?	**Glacier Peak** (US-Washington)	1201-02-	3?	-/8
T	**0900** t	....	?	**Kilauea** (Hawaiian Is)	1302-01-		
C	**0900** u	....	?	**Fuego** (Guatemala)	1402-09=		
C	**0900** v	....	?	**Planchón-Peteroa** (Chile-C)	1507-04=	3	-/7
T	**0900** ?	....	?	**Krísuvík** (Iceland-SW)	1701-03=	2	8/-
C	**0900** v	....	?	**La Palma** (Canary Is)	1803-01-		
C	**0900** ?	....	?	**Deception Island** (Antarctica)	1900-03=		
?	*0904 ?*	....	*?*	*Katla (Iceland-S)*	1702-03=		
C	**0905** u	....	?	**Soufrière St. Vincent** (W Indies)	1600-15=		
G	**0910** z	....	?	**Rainier** (US-Washington)	1201-03-		
C	**0910** s	....	?	**Haleakala** (Hawaiian Is)	1302-06-		
G	**0910** v	....	?	**Guagua Pichincha** (Ecuador)	1502-02=	**5**	-/**9**
C	**0910** v	....	?	**Osorno** (Chile-S)	1508-01=		
C	**0910** ?	....	?	**Pelée** (W Indies)	1600-12=		
C	**0910** u	....	?	**Brennisteinsfjöll** (Iceland-SW)	1701-04=	2	7/-
T	**0910** ?	....	?	**Grímsvötn** (Iceland-NE)	1703-01=		
?	*0911*	....	*?*	*Etna (Italy)*	0101-06=		
	0915	0817	?	**Towada** (Honshu-Japan)	0803-271	**5**	8/**9**
C	**0920** t	....	?	**Hualalai** (Hawaiian Is)	1302-04-	0	
C	**0920** t	....	?	**Trois Pitons, Morne** (W Indies)	1600-10=		
T	**0920** ?	....	?	**Reykjanes** (Iceland-SW)	1701-02=		
T	**0920** ?	....	?	**Eyjafjallajökull** (Iceland-S)	1702-02=	3	7/7
	0920	....	?	**Katla** (Iceland-S)	1702-03=	4	-/8
C	**0920** t	....	?	**Terceira** (Azores)	1802-05=		
	0925 q	....	?	**Vulcano** (Italy)	0101-05=	3?	
C	**0930** x	....	?	**Ceboruco** (México)	1401-03=	**6**	-/**10**
	0932	1119	?	**Fuji** (Honshu-Japan)	0803-03=	2?	
I	**0934** b	....	>3yr	**Katla [Eldgja]**	1702-03=	4?	**10/9**
I	*0935*	*Cont*	....	*Katla [Eldgja]*	1702-03=	*4?*	
I	*0936*	*Cont*	....	*Katla [Eldgja]*	1702-03=	*4?*	
?	*0936*	....	*?*	*Oshima (Izu Is-Japan)*	0804-01=		
I	*0937*	*Cont*	....	*Katla [Eldgja]*	1702-03=	*4?*	
	0937	1218	?	**Fuji** (Honshu-Japan)	0803-03=	2	
I	*0938*	*Cont*	....	*Katla [Eldgja]*	1702-03=	*4?*	
I	*0939*	*Cont*	....	*Katla [Eldgja]*	1702-03=	*4?*	
	0939	0515	?	**Chokai** (Honshu-Japan)	0803-22=		
I	*0940*	*Cont*	....	*Katla [Eldgja]*	1702-03=	*4?*	
G	**0940** v	....	?	**Merapi** (Java)	0603-25=	3	-/7
C	**0940** ?	....	?	**Mauna Loa** (Hawaiian Is)	1302-03=	0	
T	**0940** ?	....	?	**Bárdarbunga** (Iceland-NE)	1703-03=		
C	**0940** v	....	?	**Picos Volc System** (Azores)	1802-081		
	0945	....	?	**Kirishima** (Kyushu-Japan)	0802-09=	2?	
?	*0948*	*1231y*	*?*	*Chokai (Honshu-Japan)*	0803-22=		
	0950 t	....	?	**Stromboli** (Italy)	0101-04=	2	
?	*0950 ?*	....	*?*	*Bir Borhut (Arabia-S)*	0301-18-		
T	**0950** ?	....	?	**Pago** (New Britain-SW Pac)	0502-08=		
C	**0950** ?	....	?	**Hargy** (New Britain-SW Pac)	0502-10=		
	0950 t	....	?	**Krakatau** (Indonesia)	0602-00=		
C	**0950** ?	....	?	**Bulusan** (Luzon-Philippines)	0703-01=		
T	**0950** t	....	?	**Adatara** (Honshu-Japan)	0803-17=		
G	**0950** t	....	?	**Tokachi** (Hokkaido-Japan)	0805-05=		
T	**0950** ?	....	?	**Akan** (Hokkaido-Japan)	0805-07=		
T	**0950** ?	....	?	**Mutnovsky** (Kamchatka)	1000-06=	2	-/6
G	**0950** ?	....	?	**Karymsky** (Kamchatka)	1000-13=		
C	**0950** >	....	?	**Komarov** (Kamchatka)	1000-22=		
T	**0950** ?	....	?	**Tolbachik** (Kamchatka)	1000-24=	4+	8/8
T	**0950** ?	....	?	**Bezymianny** (Kamchatka)	1000-25=	4?	-/8
C	**0950** ?	....	?	**Shishaldin** (Aleutian Is)	1101-36-		
F	**0950** *	....	?	**Edziza** (Canada)	1200-06-	3	-/7
T	**0950** ?	....	?	**Adams** (US-Washington)	1201-04-	2	
V	**0950** ?	....	?	**Jefferson [S Cinder Peak]** (US)	1202-02-		
U	**0950** *	....	?	**Unnamed [East Pacific Rise]**	1304-05-	0	
T	**0950** ?	....	?	**Cotopaxi** (Ecuador)	1502-05=	3	-/7
E	**0950** z	....	?	**Fernandina** (Galápagos)	1503-01=	0	
E	**0950** >	....	?	**Wolf** (Galápagos)	1503-02=	0	
C	**0950** ?	....	?	**Brennisteinsfjöll** (Iceland-SW)	1701-04=	2	8/6
T	**0950** t	....	?	**Hveravellir** (Iceland-SW)	1701-08=	2	**9**/6
T	**0950** ?	....	?	**Katla** (Iceland-S)	1702-03=		
C	**0950** v	....	?	**Sete Cidades** (Azores)	1802-08=	2	7/6
R	**0950** *	....	?	**Erebus** (Antarctica)	1900-02=	0	
?	*0952*	*03 ?*	*?*	*Fuji (Honshu-Japan)*	0803-03=		
G	**0960** ?	....	?	**Fournaise, Piton de la** (Indian O.)	0303-02=	0	
A	*0960 j*	....	*?*	*Ljósufjöll (Iceland-W)*	1700-03=	*3*	*8/7*
T	**0960** ?	....	?	**Katla** (Iceland-S)	1702-03=	3	-/7
I	**0960** ?	....	?	**Grímsvötn** (Iceland-NE)	1703-01=		
	0968	1201p	?	**Vesuvius** (Italy)	0101-02=	4	-/8
C	**0970** r	....	?	**Taranaki [Egmont]** (New Zealand)	0401-03=		
G	**0970** u	....	?	**Kuchinoerabu-jima** (Ryukyu Is)	0802-05=		
G	**0970** ?	....	?	**Shiveluch** (Kamchatka)	1000-27=	4	-/8
C	**0970** t	....	?	**Fuego** (Guatemala)	1402-09=		
G	**0980** y	....	?	**Lassen [Chaos Crags]** (US-Calif)	1203-08-		
C	**0980** t	....	?	**Haleakala** (Hawaiian Is)	1302-06-		
?	*0986*	*0902*	*?*	*Aso (Kyushu-Japan)*	0802-11=	*2?*	
	0989	....	?	**Niigata-Yake-yama** (Honshu-Japan)	0803-09=		
C	**0990** t	....	?	**Haleakala** (Hawaiian Is)	1302-06-		
	0991	....	?	**Vesuvius** (Italy)	0101-02=	3	
?	*0993*	*0901p*	*?*	*Fuji (Honshu-Japan)*	0803-03=		
	0999	....	?	**Vesuvius** (Italy)	0101-02=	3	
?	*0999*	....	*?*	*Chokai (Honshu-Japan)*	0803-22=		
	0999	03	?	**Fuji** (Honshu-Japan)	0803-03=	2?	

1000

START YEAR	M-Dy	Duration	VOLCANO NAME (Subregion)	NUMBER	VEI	Vol L/T
1000 <	....	?	**Lunayyir, Harrat** (Arabia-W)	0301-04-		
1000	....	?	**Kelut** (Java)	0603-28=	3	
T **1000** ?	....	?	**Kirishima** (Kyushu-Japan)	0802-09=		
G **1000** t	....	?	**Ksudach** (Kamchatka)	1000-05=	4+	-/8
T **1000** z	....	?	**Zhupanovsky** (Kamchatka)	1000-12=		
T **1000** t	....	?	**Kostakan** (Kamchatka)	1000-122	3	7/7
T **1000** ?	....	?	**Tolbachik** (Kamchatka)	1000-24=	4+	**9**/8
T **1000** ?	....	?	**Shiveluch** (Kamchatka)	1000-27=	3	-/8
G **1000** n	....	?	**Khangar** (Kamchatka)	1000-272		
C **1000** ?	....	?	**Gorny Institute** (Kamchatka)	1000-55-		
G **1000** s	....	?	**Changbaishan** (China-E)	1005-06-	**7**?	-/**10**
H **1000** x	....	?	**Mono Craters** (US-California)	1203-12-		
A **1000** x	....	?	**Kick 'em Jenny** (W Indies)	1600-16=		
1000	0625d	?	**Brennisteinsfjöll** (Iceland-SW)	1701-04=	0	8/-
1002	....	?	**Halla** (Korea)	1006-04-		
? 1004	....	*?*	*Etna (Italy)*	0101-06=		
1006	1231y	?	**Vesuvius** (Italy)	0101-02=	3	
1007	....	?	**Halla** (Korea)	1006-04-		
G **1010** q	....	?	**Merapi** (Java)	0603-25=		
C **1010** s	....	?	**Kikai** (Ryukyu Is)	0802-06=		
C **1010** s	....	?	**Haleakala** (Hawaiian Is)	1302-06-		
I **1010** ?	....	?	**Grímsvötn** (Iceland-NE)	1703-01=		
? 1017	*1001p*	*?*	*Fuji (Honshu-Japan)*	0803-03=		
T **1020** ?	....	?	**Taveuni** (Fiji Is-SW Pacific)	0405-01-	2	
C **1020** t	....	?	**Haleakala** (Hawaiian Is)	1302-06-		
T **1020** ?	....	?	**Arenal** (Costa Rica)	1405-033	4	-/8
M **1030** w	....	?	**Barrier, The** (Africa-E)	0202-03=	0	
C **1030** q	....	?	**Billy Mitchell** (Bougainville-SW Pacific)	0505-011	**5**+	-/**9**
C **1030** s	....	?	**Kikai** (Ryukyu Is)	0802-06=		
T **1030** q	....	?	**Gorely** (Kamchatka)	1000-07=	3	-/7
G **1030** v	....	?	**Shiveluch** (Kamchatka)	1000-27=	**5**	-/**9**
C **1030** s	....	?	**Tacaná** (México)	1401-13=		
T **1030** ?	....	?	**Arenal** (Costa Rica)	1405-033	4	-/8
C **1030** u	....	?	**Tungurahua** (Ecuador)	1502-08=		
1033	0119?	?	**Fuji** (Honshu-Japan)	0803-03=	2	
1037	0127	6*a*	**Vesuvius** (Italy)	0101-02=	3	
M **1040** u	....	?	**Vulcano** (Italy)	0101-05=	2?	
G **1040** w	....	?	**Savai'i** (Samoa-SW Pacific)	0404-04=		
C **1040** ?	....	?	**Mauna Loa** (Hawaiian Is)	1302-02=	0	
T **1040** ?	....	?	**Cayambe** (Ecuador)	1502-006	4	8/-
1042	....	?	**Haku-san** (Honshu-Japan)	0803-05=	3?	
? 1044	....	*?*	*Etna (Italy)*	0101-06=		
? 1049	....	*?*	*Vesuvius (Italy)*	0101-02=	*1*	
M **1050** w	....	?	**Barrier, The** (Africa-E)	0202-03=	0	
1050 w	....	?	**Karthala** (Indian O.-W)	0303-01=		
T **1050** v	....	?	**Pago** (New Britain-SW Pac)	0502-08=		
1050 t	....	?	**Krakatau** (Indonesia)	0602-00=		
T **1050** x	....	?	**Tokachi** (Hokkaido-Japan)	0805-05=		
G **1050** ?	....	?	**Karymsky** (Kamchatka)	1000-13=		
T **1050** ?	....	?	**Tolbachik** (Kamchatka)	1000-24=	3	**9**/7
C **1050** ?	....	?	**Tanaga** (Aleutian Is)	1101-08-		
T **1050** ?	....	?	**Aniakchak** (Alaska Peninsula)	1102-09-		
C **1050** v	....	?	**Ugashik-Peulik** (Alaska Peninsula)	1102-13-		
D **1050** <	....	?	**Markagunt Plateau** (US-Utah)	1207-04-		
C **1050** u	....	?	**Kilauea** (Hawaiian Is)	1302-01-	1?	
C **1050** v	....	?	**Hualalai** (Hawaiian Is)	1302-04-	1	8/-
? 1050 t	....	*?*	*Michoacán [V. Santiago] (México)*	1401-06=		
C **1050** u	....	?	**Bravo, Cerro** (Colombia)	1501-012	4	-/8
T **1050** z	....	?	**Hekla** (Iceland-S)	1702-07=		
T **1060**	....	?	**Nejapa-Miraflores** (Nicaragua)	1404-092	3?	
E **1060** z	....	?	**Negra, Sierra** (Galápagos)	1503-05=	0	
T **1060** ?	....	?	**Grímsvötn** (Iceland-NE)	1703-01=		
G **1060** v	....	?	**Tenerife** (Canary Is)	1803-03-		8/-
1063 a	....	?	**Etna** (Italy)	0101-06=		
C **1070** s	....	?	**Taranaki [Egmont]** (New Zealand)	0401-03=		
C **1070** x	....	?	**Karkar** (New Guinea-NE of)	0501-03=		
C **1070** ?	....	?	**Mauna Loa** (Hawaiian Is)	1302-02=	0	
? 1073 e	....	*?*	*Vesuvius (Italy)*	0101-02=	*3*	
M **1075** q	....	?	**Sunset Crater** (US-Arizona)	1209-02-	4?	8/-
C **1075** u	....	?	**Krísuvík** (Iceland-SW)	1701-03=	0	7/-
G **1080** v	....	?	**Mashu** (Hokkaido-Japan)	0805-081	**5**	-/**9**
M **1080** q	....	?	**Medicine Lake** (US-California)	1203-02-	3?	**9**/7
C **1080** s	....	?	**Haleakala** (Hawaiian Is)	1302-06-		
G **1080** u	....	?	**Ubinas** (Perú)	1504-02=	**5**	-/**9**
T **1080** ?	....	?	**Bárdarbunga** (Iceland-NE)	1703-03=		
1083	0417	?	**Fuji** (Honshu-Japan)	0803-03=	2?	
1085	....	?	**Miyake-jima** (Izu Is-Japan)	0804-04=	2	6/-
M **1090** t	....	?	**Barrier, The** (Africa-E)	0202-03=	0	
G **1090** v	....	?	**Merapi** (Java)	0603-25=		
I **1090** ?	....	?	**Grímsvötn** (Iceland-NE)	1703-01=		
C **1100** r	....	?	**Lolobau** (New Britain-SW Pac)	0502-13=	4	-/8
G **1100** v	....	?	**Kuchinoerabu-jima** (Ryukyu Is)	0802-05=		
T **1100** ?	....	?	**Akita-Komaga-take** (Honshu-Japan)	0803-23=	2	
T **1100** ?	....	?	**Avachinsky** (Kamchatka)	1000-10=		
A **1100** u	....	?	**Uinkaret Field** (US-Arizona)	1209-01-	1	6/-
C **1100** t	....	?	**Momotombo** (Nicaragua)	1404-09=		
1104	1015q	?	**Hekla** (Iceland-S)	1702-07=	**5**	-/**9**
1108	0829	41*m*	**Asama** (Honshu-Japan)	0803-11=	**5**	8/**9**
G **1110** u	....	?	**Kuchinoerabu-jima** (Ryukyu Is)	0802-05=		
G **1110** x	....	?	**Colima** (México)	1401-04=		
G **1110** v	....	?	**Irazú** (Costa Rica)	1405-06=	3	
C **1110** t	....	?	**Sete Cidades** (Azores)	1802-08=	2	7/6
1111	....	?	**Nemrut Dagi** (Turkey)	0103-02=		
1112	0309	?	**Kirishima** (Kyushu-Japan)	0802-09=	2?	
? 1112	*1118*	*38e*	*Oshima (Izu Is-Japan)*	0804-01=		
1113	0227	?	**Kirishima** (Kyushu-Japan)	0802-09=	2?	
M **1120** w	....	?	**Emuruangogolak** (Africa-E)	0202-051	0	
1120 w	....	?	**Turfan** (China-W)	1004-01-		
? 1128		*?*	*Asama (Honshu-Japan)*	0803-11=		
C **1130** ?	....	?	**Mauna Loa** (Hawaiian Is)	1302-02=	0	
G **1130** w	....	?	**Barú** (Panamá)	1406-01-		
C **1130** u	....	?	**Cotopaxi** (Ecuador)	1502-05=	**5**	-/**9**
1139	0601	8*a*	**Vesuvius** (Italy)	0101-02=	3	
G **1140** w	....	?	**Merapi** (Java)	0603-25=		
G **1140** u	....	?	**Kilauea** (Hawaiian Is)	1302-01-	0	
G **1140** v	....	?	**Puyehue-Cordón Caulle** (Chile-C)	1507-15=		
1150	....	?	**Vesuvius** (Italy)	0101-02=	3?	
C **1150** ?	....	?	**Yasur** (Vanuatu-SW Pacific)	0507-10=	2	
1150 t	....	?	**Krakatau** (Indonesia)	0602-00=		
G **1150** ?	....	?	**Karymsky** (Kamchatka)	1000-13=	2	-/6
T **1150** ?	....	?	**Shiveluch** (Kamchatka)	1000-27=	3	-/7
G **1150** v	....	?	**Kanaga** (Aleutian Is)	1101-11-		
T **1150** z	....	?	**Makushin** (Aleutian Is)	1101-31-		
H **1150** x	....	?	**Mono Lake Volc Field** (US-California	1203-11-		
T **1150** ?	....	?	**Hualalai** (Hawaiian Is)	1302-04-	0	
G **1150** v	....	?	**Cofre de Perote** (México)	1401-096	2	**9**/-
E **1150** >	....	?	**Fernandina** (Galápagos)	1503-01=	0	
E **1150** >	....	?	**Ecuador** (Galápagos)	1503-011	0	
E **1150** y	....	?	**Darwin** (Galápagos)	1503-03=	0	
T **1150** t	....	?	**Katla** (Iceland-S)	1702-03=		
I **1150** ?	....	?	**Grímsvötn** (Iceland-NE)	1703-01=		
1151	....	?	**Krísuvík** (Iceland-SW)	1701-03=	1	8/5
1154	11	?	**Miyake-jima** (Izu Is-Japan)	0804-04=	3	-/7
1157	....	?	**Etna** (Italy)	0101-06=	2?	
? 1157	....	*?*	*Orizaba, Pico de (México)*	1401-10=	*2*	
1158	0119	?	**Hekla** (Iceland-S)	1702-07=	4	8/8
1159 ?	....	?	**Bárdarbunga** (Iceland-NE)	1703-03=		
1160	....	?	**Etna** (Italy)	0101-06=	2?	
M **1160** w	....	?	**Emuruangogolak** (Africa-E)	0202-051	0	
G **1160** w	....	?	**Taveuni** (Fiji Is-SW Pacific)	0405-01-	2	
C **1160** u	....	?	**Pacaya** (Guatemala)	1402-11=	3?	
1164 ?	....	?	**Etna** (Italy)	0101-06=	2?	
1167	....	?	**Kirishima** (Kyushu-Japan)	0802-09=	2?	
I **1168** ?	....	?	***Unknown Source*** *(Byrd Station 68)*	......		
? 1169	*0204*	*?*	*Etna (Italy)*	0101-06=		
G **1170** v	....	?	**Hakone** (Honshu-Japan)	0803-02=		
C **1170** ?	....	?	**Mauna Loa** (Hawaiian Is)	1302-02=	0	
T **1170** ?	....	?	**Torfajökull** (Iceland-S)	1702-05=		
C **1170** v	....	?	**Furnas** (Azores)	1802-10=	4	-/8
A **1175**	....	?	**Orizaba, Pico de** (México)	1401-10=	3?	
? 1175	*01 ?*	*?*	*Kirishima (Kyushu-Japan)*	0802-09=	*2?*	
I **1176** n	....	?	***Unknown Source*** *(GISP2, 148; SP, 293)*	......		
1177 b	....	?	**Katla** (Iceland-S)	1702-03=	3	-/7
? 1177	*0518*	*?*	*Haku-san (Honshu-Japan)*	0803-05=	*3?*	
1179 <	....	?	**Reykjanes** (Iceland-SW)	1701-02=	2	
T **1180** ?	....	?	**Reporoa [Waiotapu]** (New Zealand)	0401-06-		
C **1180** v	....	?	**Dieng Volc Complex** (Java)	0603-20=		
G **1180** w	....	?	**Machín** (Colombia)	1501-04=		
V **1183** ?	....	?	**Oshima** (Izu Is-Japan)	0804-01=	4	-/8
1183	0528?	?	**Zao** (Honshu-Japan)	0803-19=	2?	
1184	0207	?	**Kirishima** (Kyushu-Japan)	0802-09=	2?	
? 1187	....	*?*	*Orizaba, Pico de (México)*	1401-10=	*2*	
1188	....	?	**Krísuvík** (Iceland-SW)	1701-03=	1	7/5
G **1190** r	....	?	**Merapi** (Java)	0603-25=		
G **1190** s	....	?	**Kuchino-shima** (Ryukyu Is)	0802-043		
C **1190** ?	....	?	**Mauna Loa** (Hawaiian Is)	1302-02=	0	
G **1190** w	....	?	**Chichón, El** (México)	1401-12=	4	-/8
C **1190** ?	....	?	**Pelée** (W Indies)	1600-12=		
I **1190** ?	....	?	**Grímsvötn** (Iceland-NE)	1703-01=		
1194	....	?	**Etna** (Italy)	0101-06=	2?	
1198	....	?	**Campi Flegrei** (Italy)	0101-01=	1	
M **1200** u	....	?	**Vulcano** (Italy)	0101-05=	2?	
G **1200** v	....	?	**Kita Yatsuga-take** (Honshu-Japan)	0803-031		6/-
T **1200** ?	....	?	**Avachinsky** (Kamchatka)	1000-10=		
T **1200** t	....	?	**Kostakan** (Kamchatka)	1000-122	2	7/6
C **1200** u	....	?	**Augustine** (Alaska-SW)	1103-01-		
T **1200** y	....	?	**Hayes** (Alaska-SW)	1103-05-		
C **1200** ?	....	?	**Shasta** (US-California)	1203-01-		
G **1200** u	....	?	**Haleakala** (Hawaiian Is)	1302-06-		7/-

	START YEAR	M-Dy	Duration	VOLCANO NAME (Subregion)	NUMBER	VEI	Vol L/T
U	**1200**	y	?	**Unnamed [East Pacific Rise]**	1304-05-	0	
A	**1200**	?	?	**San Salvador** (El Salvador)	1403-05=	4	-/8
T	**1200**	?	?	**Brennisteinsfjöll** (Iceland-SW)	1701-04=	2	
T	**1200**	y	?	**Terceira** (Azores)	1802-05=		
C	**1200**	?	?	**Deception Island** (Antarctica)	1900-03=		
	1206	1204	?	**Hekla** (Iceland-S)	1702-07=	3	-/7
C	**1210**	w	?	**Ruapehu** (New Zealand)	0401-10=	3	-/7
	1210	....	?	**Reykjanes** (Iceland-SW)	1701-02=	3?	-/8
T	**1210**	?	?	**Katla** (Iceland-S)	1702-03=	4	-/8
I	**1210**	j	?	**Bárdarbunga** (Iceland-NE)	1703-03=		
	1211	....	?	**Reykjanes** (Iceland-SW)	1701-02=		7/-
	1211	0831p	?	**Reykjanes** (Iceland-SW)	1701-02=	4?	-/8
T	**1220**	w	?	**Aniakchak** (Alaska Peninsula)	1102-09-		
G	**1220**	w	?	**Puyehue-Cordón Caulle** (Chile-C)	1507-15=		
C	**1220**	v	?	**Osorno** (Chile-S)	1508-01=		
	1222	....	?	**Unnamed** (Syria)	0300-02-	0?	
	1222	....	?	**Hekla** (Iceland-S)	1702-07=	2	-/6
	1223	....	?	**Reykjanes** (Iceland-SW)	1701-02=	3	-/7
	1224	08 ?	?	**Etna** (Italy)	0101-06=		
	1226	0715q	352*w?*	**Reykjanes** (Iceland-SW)	1701-02=	4	-/8
	1227	*Cont*	....	*Reykjanes (Iceland-SW)*	1701-02=	*4*	*-/8*
	1227	10 ?	?	**Zao** (Honshu-Japan)	0803-19=	3	
?	*1229*	*1231y*	?	*Aso (Kyushu-Japan)*	0802-11=	*2?*	
M	**1230**	s	?	**Lipari** (Italy)	0101-042		
M	**1230**	p	?	**Vulcano** (Italy)	0101-05=	0	
M	**1230**	w	?	**Emuruangogolak** (Africa-E)	0202-051	0	
G	**1230**	x	?	**Merapi** (Java)	0603-25=		
I	**1230**	j	?	**Grímsvötn** (Iceland-NE)	1703-01=		
	1230	1129?	?	**Zao** (Honshu-Japan)	0803-19=	2?	
	1231	....	?	**Reykjanes** (Iceland-SW)	1701-02=	3	-/7
	1235	0125	?	**Kirishima** (Kyushu-Japan)	0802-09=	**P**	
	1238	....	?	**Reykjanes** (Iceland-SW)	1701-02=	0	
	1239	?	?	**Haku-san** (Honshu-Japan)	0803-05=	3	-/7
	1239	0208	?	**Aso** (Kyushu-Japan)	0802-11=	2	
G	**1240**	r	?	**Savai'i** (Samoa-SW Pacific)	0404-04=		
	1240	....	?	**Aso** (Kyushu-Japan)	0802-11=	2	
C	**1240**	w	?	**Hualalai** (Hawaiian Is)	1302-04-	2	8/-
C	**1240**	t	?	**Sollipulli** (Chile-C)	1507-111		
	1240	....	?	**Reykjanes** (Iceland-SW)	1701-02=	1	8/5
V	**1245**	?	?	**Oshima** (Izu Is-Japan)	0804-01=	1	-/5
	1245	....	?	**Katla** (Iceland-S)	1702-03=	4	-/8
	1250	....	?	**Etna** (Italy)	0101-06=	2?	
	1250	t	?	**Fentale** (Ethiopia)	0201-19=		
G	**1250**	?	?	**Tokachi** (Hokkaido-Japan)	0805-05=	3	-/7
T	**1250**	y	?	**Akan** (Hokkaido-Japan)	0805-07=		
C	**1250**	?	?	**Gorny Institute** (Kamchatka)	1000-55-		
C	**1250**	?	?	**Shasta** (US-California)	1203-01-		
G	**1250**	t	?	**Tungurahua** (Ecuador)	1502-08=		
E	**1250**	>	?	**Azul, Cerro** (Galápagos)	1503-06=	0	
T	**1250**	t	?	**Bárdarbunga** (Iceland-NE)	1703-03=	1	**9**/5
?	*1251*	*0518*	?	*Akagi (Honshu-Japan)*	0803-13=		
	1253	....	?	**Sawâd, Harra es-** (Arabia-S)	0301-16-	3	
	1256	0605	52*a?*	**Rahat, Harrat** (Arabia-W)	0301-07=	3	8/-
I	**1259**	j	?	***Unknown Source*** *(GISP2, 349; SP 1220)*	......		
G	**1260**	s	?	**Mammoth Mountain** (US-California)	1203-15-		
C	**1260**	t	?	**Orizaba, Pico de** (México)	1401-10=	3	
T	**1260**	w	?	**Cotopaxi** (Ecuador)	1502-05=		
C	**1260**	p	?	**Pelée** (W Indies)	1600-12=		
	1262	....	?	**Katla** (Iceland-S)	1702-03=	**5**	-/**9**
	1265	1201?	?	**Aso** (Kyushu-Japan)	0802-11=	2	
I	**1269**	j	?	***Unknown Source*** *(SP, 242 ppb sulfate)*	......		
	1269	08	?	**Aso** (Kyushu-Japan)	0802-11=	2	
?	*1270*	....	?	*Vesuvius (Italy)*	0101-02=	*2?*	
T	**1270**	?	?	**Yake-dake** (Honshu-Japan)	0803-07=		
C	**1270**	u	?	**Jocotitlán** (México)	1401-062		
T	**1270**	?	?	**Cayambe** (Ecuador)	1502-006		
C	**1270**	t	?	**Plat Pays, Morne** (W Indies)	1600-11=		
I	**1270**	j	?	**Grímsvötn** (Iceland-NE)	1703-01=		
I	**1270**	j	?	**Bárdarbunga** (Iceland-NE)	1703-03=		
	1271	0105	?	**Aso** (Kyushu-Japan)	0802-11=	2	
	1272	0416	?	**Aso** (Kyushu-Japan)	0802-11=	2	
	1272	1129	?	**Aso** (Kyushu-Japan)	0802-11=	2	
	1273	08	?	**Aso** (Kyushu-Japan)	0802-11=	2	
	1274	....	?	**Aso** (Kyushu-Japan)	0802-11=	2	
I	**1279**	j	?	***Unknown Source*** *(SP, 818 ppb sulfate)*	......		
T	**1280**	?	?	**Poás** (Costa Rica)	1405-04=		
G	**1280**	?	?	**Quilotoa** (Ecuador)	1502-06=	**6**	-/**10**
	1281	07	31*p*	**Aso** (Kyushu-Japan)	0802-11=	2	
?	*1281*	*0703*	?	*Asama (Honshu-Japan)*	0803-11=	*3*	
	1282	<	7*a*	**Larderello** (Italy)	0101-001	3?	
	1284	....	198*w?*	**Etna** (Italy)	0101-06=		
	1285	*Cont*	....	*Etna (Italy)*	0101-06=		
	1286	0830	?	**Aso** (Kyushu-Japan)	0802-11=	2	
G	**1290**	?	?	**Ischia** (Italy)	0101-03=		
C	**1290**	s	?	**Matutum** (Mindanao-Philippines)	0701-02=		
T	**1290**	P	?	**Golovnin** (Kuril Is)	0900-01=		

Minard Hall (Escuela Politecnica, Quito)

Quilotoa volcano in Ecuador contains a steep-walled, 3-km-wide caldera filled by a 250-m-deep lake. Its most recent large eruption about 700 years ago produced voluminous pyroclastic flows, lahars that reached the Pacific Ocean, and one of the largest Holocene airfall-tephra deposits of the northern Andes.

START YEAR	M-Dy	Dura-tion	VOLCANO NAME (Subregion)	NUMBER	VEI	Vol L/T
C **1290** w	....	?	**Black Rock Desert** (US-Utah)	1207-05-		
T **1290** ?	....	?	**Cayambe** (Ecuador)	1502-006	4	8/-
I **1290** j	....	?	**Grímsvötn** (Iceland-NE)	1703-01=		
I **1290** j	....	?	**Bárdarbunga** (Iceland-NE)	1703-03=		
? 1292	....	*?*	*Rahat, Harrat (Arabia-W)*	0301-07=		
M **1300** w	....	?	**Emuruangogolak** (Africa-E)	0202-051	0	
C **1300** t	....	?	**Taranaki [Egmont]** (New Zealand)	0401-03=		
G **1300** u	....	?	**Merapi** (Java)	0603-25=		
T **1300** t	....	?	**Iwate** (Honshu-Japan)	0803-24=	3	-/7
T **1300** ?	....	?	**Mutnovsky** (Kamchatka)	1000-06=	2	-/6
G **1300** x	....	?	**Ichinsky** (Kamchatka)	1000-28=		
? 1300 y	....	*?*	*Glacier Peak (US-Washington)*	1201-02-		
T **1300** ?	....	?	**Askja** (Iceland-NE)	1703-06=	1	
T **1300** x	....	?	**Krafla** (Iceland-NE)	1703-08=	2?	
1300	0711	369*m*?	**Hekla** (Iceland-S)	1702-07=	4	8/8
1301	*Cont*	....	*Hekla (Iceland-S)*	1702-07=	*2*	*8/8*
1302	0118	59*m*	**Ischia** (Italy)	0101-03=		
1305	0502	?	**Aso** (Kyushu-Japan)	0802-11=	2	
V **1307** ?	....	?	**Oshima** (Izu Is-Japan)	0804-01=	3	6/7
G **1310** k	....	>3yr	**Okataina [Tarawera]** (New Zeal)	0401-05=	**5**	**9/9**
G **1310** t	....	?	**Savai'i** (Samoa-SW Pacific)	0404-04=		
C **1310** ?	....	?	**Mauna Loa** (Hawaiian Is)	1302-02=	0	
C **1310** u	....	?	**Osorno** (Chile-S)	1508-01=		
I **1310** j	....	?	**Grímsvötn** (Iceland-NE)	1703-01=		
G 1311	*Cont*	....	*Okataina [Tarawera] (New Zeal)*	0401-05=	***5***	
1311	....	?	**Kelut** (Java)	0603-28=	3	
1311	0118	?	**Katla** (Iceland-S)	1702-03=		
G 1312	*Cont*	....	*Okataina [Tarawera] (New Zeal)*	0401-05=	***5***	
G 1313	*Cont*	....	*Okataina [Tarawera] (New Zeal)*	0401-05=	***5***	
G 1314	*Cont*	....	*Okataina [Tarawera] (New Zeal)*	0401-05=	***5***	
G 1315	*Cont*	....	*Okataina [Tarawera] (New Zeal)*	0401-05=	***5***	
1320 ?	....	?	**Krakatau** (Indonesia)	0602-00=		
T **1320** y	....	?	**Kutcharo [Atosanupuri]** (Hokkaido)	0805-08=		
1324	0907	?	**Aso** (Kyushu-Japan)	0802-11=	2	
C **1325** u	....	?	**Soufrière St. Vincent** (W Indies)	1600-15=		
T **1325** ?	....	?	**Krísuvík** (Iceland-SW)	1701-03=	1	8/5
1329	0628	37*d*?	**Etna** (Italy)	0101-06=	3?	7/6
T **1330** q	....	?	**Gorely** (Kamchatka)	1000-07=	2?	
C **1330** u	....	?	**Tseax River Cone** (Canada)	1200-10-		
C **1330** u	....	?	**Bravo, Cerro** (Colombia)	1501-012	4	-/8
1331	....	?	**Azuma** (Honshu-Japan)	0803-18=	1	-/5
? 1331	....	*731y*	*Zao (Honshu-Japan)*	0803-19=	*2?*	
1331	04	15*m*	**Aso** (Kyushu-Japan)	0802-11=	2	
1331	12	548*p*	**Aso** (Kyushu-Japan)	0802-11=	2	
1332	*Cont*	....	*Aso (Kyushu-Japan)*	0802-11=	*2*	
? 1332	*Cont*	....	*Zao (Honshu-Japan)*	0803-19=	*2?*	
1332	11	?	**Grímsvötn** (Iceland-NE)	1703-01=	2	
1333	*Cont*	....	*Aso (Kyushu-Japan)*	0802-11=	*2*	
? 1333	*Cont*	....	*Zao (Honshu-Japan)*	0803-19=	*2?*	
1333	....	?	**Etna** (Italy)	0101-06=	2	
1334	....	?	**Kelut** (Java)	0603-28=	3	
1335	0207	47*a*	**Aso** (Kyushu-Japan)	0802-11=	2	
1338	0915e	61*j*	**Oshima** (Izu Is-Japan)	0804-01=	3	-/7
G **1340** ?	....	?	**Fournaise, Piton de la** (Indian O.-W)	0303-02=	0	
C **1340** s	....	?	**Taranaki [Egmont]** (New Zealand)	0401-03=		
C **1340** r	....	?	**Kikai** (Ryukyu Is)	0802-06=		
G **1340** u	....	?	**Hakkoda Group** (Honshu-Japan)	0803-28=	1	
G **1340** v	....	?	**Pagan** (Mariana Is-C Pacific)	0804-17=		
A **1340** s	....	?	**Kilauea** (Hawaiian Is)	1302-01-	0	
T **1340** u	....	?	**Barú** (Panamá)	1406-01-		
G **1340** t	....	?	**Soufrière Guadeloupe** (W Indies)	1600-06=	3?	
G **1340** t	....	?	**Pelée** (W Indies)	1600-12=	4	-/8
1340 ?	....	?	**Reykjanes** (Iceland-SW)	1701-02=	3↑	
T **1340** ?	....	?	**Krísuvík** (Iceland-SW)	1701-03=	1	7/5
1340	0203	22*a*	**Aso** (Kyushu-Japan)	0802-11=	2	
1341 a	....	?	**Brennisteinsfjöll** (Iceland-SW)	1701-04=	2	8/-
? 1341	....	*?*	*Tenerife (Canary Is)*	1803-03-		
1341	05	?	**Grímsvötn** (Iceland-NE)	1703-01=	2	
1341	0519	?	**Hekla** (Iceland-S)	1702-07=	3	-/7
1343	....	?	**Aso** (Kyushu-Japan)	0802-11=	2	
1345	....	730*y*	**Popocatépetl** (México)	1401-09=	2?	
1346	*Cont*	....	*Popocatépetl (México)*	1401-09=	*2?*	
? 1346	....	*?*	*Aso (Kyushu-Japan)*	0802-11=	*2*	
1347	*Cont*	....	*Popocatépetl (México)*	1401-09=	*2?*	
? 1347	....	*?*	*Vesuvius (Italy)*	0101-02=	*2?*	
1350	....	?	**Etna** (Italy)	0101-06=	2	
T **1350** ?	....	?	**Lengai, Ol Doinyo** (Africa-E)	0202-12=		
G **1350** s	....	?	**Rungwe** (Africa-E)	0202-166		
C **1350** ?	....	?	**Auckland Field** (New Zealand)	0401-02=		**9/-**
G **1350** t	....	?	**Savai'i** (Samoa-SW Pacific)	0404-04=		
T **1350** u	....	?	**Taveuni** (Fiji Is-SW Pacific)	0405-01=	2	
H **1350** ?	....	?	**Dawson Strait Group** (D'Entrecast)	0503-06=		
A **1350** v	....	?	**San Pablo Volc Field** (Philippines)	0703-06=		
? 1350 ?	....	*?*	*Zao (Honshu-Japan)*	0803-19=	*2?*	
T **1350** ?	....	?	**E-san** (Hokkaido-Japan)	0805-011		
G **1350** v	....	?	**Rausu** (Hokkaido-Japan)	0805-082	3	-/7
T **1350** ?	....	?	**Nemo Peak** (Kuril Is)	0900-32=		
C **1350** ?	....	?	**Kambalny** (Kamchatka)	1000-01=		
T **1350** ?	....	?	**Kostakan** (Kamchatka)	1000-122	1?	
C **1350** ?	....	?	**Kikhpinych** (Kamchatka)	1000-18=	4	8/8
T **1350** ?	....	?	**Krasheninnikov** (Kamchatka)	1000-19=	0	7/-
D **1350** p	....	?	**Mono Craters** (US-California)	1203-12-	4	8/8
G **1350** w	....	?	**Haleakala** (Hawaiian Is)	1302-06-		5/-
C **1350** ?	....	?	**Turrialba** (Costa Rica)	1405-07=		
C **1350** ?	....	?	**Ruiz, Nevado del** (Colombia)	1501-02=	4	-/8
T **1350** ?	....	?	**Cotopaxi** (Ecuador)	1502-05=	4+	-/8
G **1350** t	....	?	**Tungurahua** (Ecuador)	1502-08=	3?	
E **1350** z	....	?	**Negra, Sierra** (Galápagos)	1503-05=	0	
T **1350** w	....	?	**Sabancaya** (Perú)	1504-006		
G **1350** t	....	?	**Misti, El** (Perú)	1504-01=		
I **1350** ?	....	?	**Grímsvötn** (Iceland-NE)	1703-01=		
I **1350** j	....	?	**Bárdarbunga** (Iceland-NE)	1703-03=		
T **1350** v	....	?	**Jan Mayen** (Atlantic-N-Jan Mayen)	1706-01=		
? 1351	....	*?*	*Orizaba, Pico de (México)*	1401-10=	*2*	
1354	....	?	**Popocatépetl** (México)	1401-09=	2?	
1354 ?	....	?	**Grímsvötn** (Iceland-NE)	1703-01=		
1357 c	....	?	**Katla** (Iceland-S)	1702-03=	4+	-/8
G **1360** u	....	?	**Healy** (New Zealand)	0401-14-		
C **1360** ?	....	?	**Mauna Loa** (Hawaiian Is)	1302-02=	0	
G **1360** v	....	?	**Haleakala** (Hawaiian Is)	1302-06-		
G **1360** v	....	?	**Chichón, El** (México)	1401-12=	**5**	**-/9**
C **1360** u	....	?	**Pacaya** (Guatemala)	1402-11=	3?	
1361	....	?	**Niigata-Yake-yama** (Honshu-Japan)	0803-09=	3	8/7
1362	0605d	133*q*	**Öraefajökull** (Iceland-SE)	1704-01=	**5**	**-/9**
? 1363	....	*?*	*Popocatépetl (México)*	1401-09=	*2?*	
? 1369	....	*?*	*Aso (Kyushu-Japan)*	0802-11=	*2*	
I **1369** ?	....	?	**Grímsvötn** (Iceland-NE)	1703-01=		
C **1370** ?	....	?	**Mauna Loa** (Hawaiian Is)	1302-02=	0	
G **1370** w	....	?	**Soufrière Guadeloupe** (W Indies)	1600-06=	**P**	
C **1370** ?	....	?	**Pelée** (W Indies)	1600-12=		
I **1370** j	....	?	**Grímsvötn** (Iceland-NE)	1703-01=		
1372	....	?	**Kolbeinsey Ridge** (Iceland-N of)	1705-01=	2?	
1375 u	....	?	**Dieng Volc Complex** (Java)	0603-20=	3↑	
1375 q	....	?	**Lokon-Empung** (Sulawesi-Indonesia)	0606-10=	3↑	
1375	1220	42*a*	**Aso** (Kyushu-Japan)	0802-11=	2	
1376	....	?	**Kelut** (Java)	0603-28=	3↑	
1376	0620	?	**Aso** (Kyushu-Japan)	0802-11=	2	
1377	0506	?	**Aso** (Kyushu-Japan)	0802-11=	2	
G **1380** y	....	?	**Merapi** (Java)	0603-25=		
G **1380** u	....	?	**Parker** (Mindanao-Philippines)	0701-011	**P**	
G **1380** t	....	?	**Inyo Craters** (US-California)	1203-13-	4	8/8
C **1380** t	....	?	**Calbuco** (Chile-S)	1508-02=		
? 1381	....	*?*	*Kirishima (Kyushu-Japan)*	0802-09=	*2?*	
1381 ?	0806?	?	**Etna** (Italy)	0101-06=	2	7/6
1385	....	?	**Kelut** (Java)	0603-28=	3↑	
1387	0619	?	**Aso** (Kyushu-Japan)	0802-11=	2	
? 1388	*1016*	*?*	*Aso (Kyushu-Japan)*	0802-11=	*2*	
1389	1201p	213*w*	**Hekla** (Iceland-S)	1702-07=	3	8/7
1390	*Cont*	....	*Hekla (Iceland-S)*	1702-07=	*2*	*8/7*
? 1390	....	*?*	*Aso (Kyushu-Japan)*	0802-11=	*2?*	
G **1390** u	....	?	**Akita-Yake-yama** (Honshu-Japan)	0803-26=		
C **1390**	....	?	**Aniakchak** (Alaska Peninsula)	1102-09-		
C **1390** w	....	?	**Hood** (US-Oregon)	1202-01-		
C **1390** ?	....	?	**Mauna Loa** (Hawaiian Is)	1302-02=	0	
I **1390** j	....	?	**Grímsvötn** (Iceland-NE)	1703-01=		
1395	....	?	**Kelut** (Java)	0603-28=	3↑	
C **1395** u	....	?	**Soufrière St. Vincent** (W Indies)	1600-15=		
? 1396 c	....	*?*	*Tenerife (Canary Is)*	1803-03-		
1397	0217	?	**Nasu** (Honshu-Japan)	0803-15=	3	
C **1400** t	....	?	**Taranaki [Egmont]** (New Zealand)	0401-03=		
G **1400** v	....	?	**Zao** (Honshu-Japan)	0803-19=	3	-/7
C **1400** ?	....	?	**Avachinsky** (Kamchatka)	1000-10=		
G **1400** t	....	?	**Maly Semiachik** (Kamchatka)	1000-14=		
G **1400** t	....	?	**Kanaga** (Aleutian Is)	1101-11-		
C **1400** ?	....	?	**Arenal** (Costa Rica)	1405-033	4	-/8
T **1400** t	....	?	**Terceira** (Azores)	1802-05=		
1400	0715q	7*a*>	**Dubbi** (Ethiopia)	0201-10=	2?	
V **1402** ?	....	?	**Nemrut Dagi** (Turkey)	0103-02=		
1404	0211	?	**Nasu** (Honshu-Japan)	0803-15=	3	
1408	0224	?	**Nasu** (Honshu-Japan)	0803-15=	3	
1408	1108	17*a*?	**Etna** (Italy)	0101-06=	3	
G **1410** ?	....	>3yr	**Kilauea** (Hawaiian Is)	1302-01-	0	**9/-**
T **1410** ?	....	?	**Bárdarbunga** (Iceland-NE)	1703-03=		
1410	0305	?	**Nasu** (Honshu-Japan)	0803-15=	3	6/7
G 1411	*Cont*	....	*Kilauea (Hawaiian Is)*	1302-01-	*0*	
1411	....	?	**Kelut** (Java)	0603-28=	3↑	
G 1412	*Cont*	....	*Kilauea (Hawaiian Is)*	1302-01-	*0*	
G 1413	*Cont*	....	*Kilauea (Hawaiian Is)*	1302-01-	*0*	
? 1413	....	*?*	*Changbaishan (China-E)*	1005-06-		
G 1414	*Cont*	....	*Kilauea (Hawaiian Is)*	1302-01-	*0*	
G 1415	*Cont*	....	*Kilauea (Hawaiian Is)*	1302-01-	*0*	
1415	0521	?	**Oshima** (Izu Is-Japan)	0804-01=		

START YEAR	M-Dy	Duration	VOLCANO NAME (Subregion) . . . NUMBER		VEI	Vol L/T
G 1416	*Cont*	....	*Kilauea (Hawaiian Is)*	1302-01-	*0*	
1416	....	?	**Katla** (Iceland-S)	1702-03=	4?	-/8
1416	0902	303*w*?	**Oshima** (Izu Is-Japan)	0804-01=	2	-/6
1417	*Cont*	....	*Oshima (Izu Is-Japan)*	0804-01=	*2*	*-/6*
G 1417	*Cont*	....	*Kilauea (Hawaiian Is)*	1302-01-	*0*	
G 1418	*Cont*	....	*Kilauea (Hawaiian Is)*	1302-01-	*0*	
G 1419	*Cont*	....	*Kilauea (Hawaiian Is)*	1302-01-	*0*	
G 1420	*Cont*	....	*Kilauea (Hawaiian Is)*	1302-01-	*0*	
G **1420** p	....	?	**Taveuni** (Fiji Is-SW Pacific)	0405-01-	0	
G **1420** v	....	?	**Akutan** (Aleutian Is)	1101-32-		
G **1420** v	....	?	**Haleakala** (Hawaiian Is)	1302-06-		
G 1421	*Cont*	....	*Kilauea (Hawaiian Is)*	1302-01-	*0*	
1421	0514	?	**Oshima** (Izu Is-Japan)	0804-01=	4	8/8
G 1422	*Cont*	....	*Kilauea (Hawaiian Is)*	1302-01-	*0*	
1422	....	?	**Nisyros** (Greece)	0102-05=	2	
1422	....	?	**Reykjanes** (Iceland-SW)	1701-02=	2	
G 1423	*Cont*	....	*Kilauea (Hawaiian Is)*	1302-01-	*0*	
G 1424	*Cont*	....	*Kilauea (Hawaiian Is)*	1302-01-	*0*	
G 1425	*Cont*	....	*Kilauea (Hawaiian Is)*	1302-01-	*0*	
G 1426	*Cont*	....	*Kilauea (Hawaiian Is)*	1302-01-	*0*	
G 1427	*Cont*	....	*Kilauea (Hawaiian Is)*	1302-01-	*0*	
? 1427	*0628*	*?*	*Fuji (Honshu-Japan)*	0803-03=		
? 1427	*0707*	*?*	*Asama (Honshu-Japan)*	0803-11=		
G 1428	*Cont*	....	*Kilauea (Hawaiian Is)*	1302-01-	*0*	
G 1429	*Cont*	....	*Kilauea (Hawaiian Is)*	1302-01-	*0*	
G 1430	*Cont*	....	*Kilauea (Hawaiian Is)*	1302-01-	*0*	
G **1430** ?	....	?	**Kuwae** (Vanuatu-SW Pacific)	0507-07=		
C **1430** u	....	?	**Kikai** (Ryukyu Is)	0802-06=		
G **1430** ?	....	?	**Shiveluch** (Kamchatka)	1000-27=	4	-/8
I **1430** j	....	?	**Grímsvötn** (Iceland-NE)	1703-01=		
C **1430** v	....	?	**Furnas** (Azores)	1802-10=	3	-/7
? 1430	....	*?*	*Tenerife (Canary Is)*	1803-03-	*2*	
G 1431	*Cont*	....	*Kilauea (Hawaiian Is)*	1302-01-	*0*	
G 1432	*Cont*	....	*Kilauea (Hawaiian Is)*	1302-01-	*0*	
G 1433	*Cont*	....	*Kilauea (Hawaiian Is)*	1302-01-	*0*	
G 1434	*Cont*	....	*Kilauea (Hawaiian Is)*	1302-01-	*0*	
1434	0510	8*a*	**Aso** (Kyushu-Japan)	0802-11=	2	
G 1435	*Cont*	....	*Kilauea (Hawaiian Is)*	1302-01-	*0*	
1435	1231r	?	**Fuji** (Honshu-Japan)	0803-03=	2?	
G 1436	*Cont*	....	*Kilauea (Hawaiian Is)*	1302-01-	*0*	
G 1437	*Cont*	....	*Kilauea (Hawaiian Is)*	1302-01-	*0*	
G 1438	*Cont*	....	*Kilauea (Hawaiian Is)*	1302-01-	*0*	
1438	0109	40*a*	**Aso** (Kyushu-Japan)	0802-11=	2	
G 1439	*Cont*	....	*Kilauea (Hawaiian Is)*	1302-01-	*0*	
G 1440	*Cont*	....	*Kilauea (Hawaiian Is)*	1302-01-	*0*	
G **1440** ?	....	?	**Fournaise, Piton de la** (Indian O.-W)	0303-02=	0	
G **1440** v	....	?	**Merapi** (Java)	0603-25=		
G **1440** t	....	?	**Kuchinoerabu-jima** (Ryukyu Is)	0802-05=		
T **1440** ?	....	?	**Yake-dake** (Honshu-Japan)	0803-07=		
C **1440** ?	....	?	**Mauna Loa** (Hawaiian Is)	1302-02=	0	
C **1440** ?	....	?	**Arenal** (Costa Rica)	1405-033	2?	7/-
T **1440** ?	....	?	**Cayambe** (Ecuador)	1502-006		
G **1440** v	....	?	**Soufrière Guadeloupe** (W Indies)	1600-06=	**P**	7/-
1440	....	?	**Katla** (Iceland-S)	1702-03=	4	-/8
T **1440** ?	....	?	**Hekla** (Iceland-S)	1702-07=		
G 1441	*Cont*	....	*Kilauea (Hawaiian Is)*	1302-01-	*0*	
1441	....	?	**Nemrut Dagi** (Turkey)	0103-02=		
1441 b	....	?	**Furnas** (Azores)	1802-10=	4	-/8
G 1442	*Cont*	....	*Kilauea (Hawaiian Is)*	1302-01-	*0*	
1442	08	320*w*	**Oshima** (Izu Is-Japan)	0804-01=		
1443	*Cont*	....	*Oshima (Izu Is-Japan)*	0804-01=		
G 1443	*Cont*	....	*Kilauea (Hawaiian Is)*	1302-01-	*0*	
G 1444	*Cont*	....	*Kilauea (Hawaiian Is)*	1302-01-	*0*	
1444	....	?	**Etna** (Italy)	0101-06=	2	
1444 ?	....	?	**Sete Cidades** (Azores)	1802-08=	4	-/8
? 1444	....	*?*	*Tenerife (Canary Is)*	1803-03-		
1444	0204	?	**Vulcano** (Italy)	0101-05=	3	
G 1445	*Cont*	....	*Kilauea (Hawaiian Is)*	1302-01-	*0*	
G 1446	*Cont*	....	*Kilauea (Hawaiian Is)*	1302-01-	*0*	
1446	0925	?	**Etna** (Italy)	0101-06=	1	
G 1447	*Cont*	....	*Kilauea (Hawaiian Is)*	1302-01-	*0*	
1447	0921	?	**Etna** (Italy)	0101-06=	1	
G 1448	*Cont*	....	*Kilauea (Hawaiian Is)*	1302-01-	*0*	
G 1449	*Cont*	....	*Kilauea (Hawaiian Is)*	1302-01-	*0*	
G 1450	*Cont*	....	*Kilauea (Hawaiian Is)*	1302-01-	*0*	
? 1450	....	*?*	*Ararat (Turkey)*	0103-04-		
? 1450 t	....	*?*	*Kars Plateau (Turkey)*	0103-05-	*2?*	
G **1450** s	....	?	**Ngozi** (Africa-E)	0202-164		
T **1450** ?	....	?	**Raoul Island** (Kermadec Is)	0402-03=		
T **1450** ?	....	?	**Pago** (New Britain-SW Pac)	0502-08=		
T **1450** w	....	?	**Rabaul** (New Britain-SW Pac)	0502-14=		
1450	....	?	**Kelut** (Java)	0603-28=	3↑	
1450 j	....	?	**Soputan** (Sulawesi-Indonesia)	0606-03=	3↑	
G **1450** t	....	?	**Pinatubo** (Luzon-Philippines)	0703-083	**5**?	
T **1450** t	....	?	**Kurikoma** (Honshu-Japan)	0803-21=	1	-/5
C **1450** v	....	?	**Iwate** (Honshu-Japan)	0803-24=		
G **1450** ?	....	?	**Karymsky** (Kamchatka)	1000-13=		

START YEAR	M-Dy	Duration	VOLCANO NAME (Subregion) . . . NUMBER		VEI	Vol L/T
G **1450** v	....	?	**Rainier** (US-Washington)	1201-03-		
A **1450** t	....	?	**Acatenango** (Guatemala)	1402-08=		
E **1450** >	....	?	**Wolf** (Galápagos)	1503-02=	0	
T **1450** t	....	?	**Katla** (Iceland-S)	1702-03=		
I **1450** j	....	?	**Grímsvötn** (Iceland-NE)	1703-01=		
G 1451	*Cont*	....	*Kilauea (Hawaiian Is)*	1302-01-	*0*	
1451	....	?	**Kelut** (Java)	0603-28=	3↑	
G 1452	*Cont*	....	*Kilauea (Hawaiian Is)*	1302-01-	*0*	
I **1452** b	....	?	***Unknown Source*** *(SP sulfate peak)*	......		
G 1453	*Cont*	....	*Kilauea (Hawaiian Is)*	1302-01-	*0*	
G 1454	*Cont*	....	*Kilauea (Hawaiian Is)*	1302-01-	*0*	
1454 ?	....	?	**Iraya** (Luzon-N of)	0704-06-		
1454 n	....	14*g*	**Misti, El** (Perú)	1504-01=	2	-/6
G 1455	*Cont*	....	*Kilauea (Hawaiian Is)*	1302-01-	*0*	
G 1456	*Cont*	....	*Kilauea (Hawaiian Is)*	1302-01-	*0*	
G 1457	*Cont*	....	*Kilauea (Hawaiian Is)*	1302-01-	*0*	
G 1458	*Cont*	....	*Kilauea (Hawaiian Is)*	1302-01-	*0*	
G 1459	*Cont*	....	*Kilauea (Hawaiian Is)*	1302-01-	*0*	
T **1460** ?	....	?	**Yake-dake** (Honshu-Japan)	0803-07=	2	-/6
C **1460** r	....	?	**Baransky** (Kuril Is)	0900-08=		
C **1460** t	....	?	**Kilauea** (Hawaiian Is)	1302-01-	0	
C **1460** u	....	?	**Haleakala** (Hawaiian Is)	1302-06-		
C **1460** p	....	?	**Pelée** (W Indies)	1600-12=		
G 1461	*Cont*	....	*Kilauea (Hawaiian Is)*	1302-01-	*0*	
G 1462	*Cont*	....	*Kilauea (Hawaiian Is)*	1302-01-	*0*	
1462	....	?	**Kelut** (Java)	0603-28=	3↑	
G 1463	*Cont*	....	*Kilauea (Hawaiian Is)*	1302-01-	*0*	
G 1464	*Cont*	....	*Kilauea (Hawaiian Is)*	1302-01-	*0*	
G 1465	*Cont*	....	*Kilauea (Hawaiian Is)*	1302-01-	*0*	
G 1466	*Cont*	....	*Kilauea (Hawaiian Is)*	1302-01-	*0*	
G 1467	*Cont*	....	*Kilauea (Hawaiian Is)*	1302-01-	*0*	
G 1468	*Cont*	....	*Kilauea (Hawaiian Is)*	1302-01-	*0*	
1468	....	?	**Sakura-jima** (Kyushu-Japan)	0802-08=	2	
G 1469	*Cont*	....	*Kilauea (Hawaiian Is)*	1302-01-	*0*	
1469	....	?	**Atitlán** (Guatemala)	1402-06=	3↑	
? 1469	....	*?*	*Suchitán (Guatemala)*	1402-16-		
I **1469** ?	....	?	**Grímsvötn** (Iceland-NE)	1703-01=		
1469	1224	?	**Miyake-jima** (Izu Is-Japan)	0804-04=	3	6/-
G 1470	*Cont*	....	*Kilauea (Hawaiian Is)*	1302-01-	*0*	
C **1470** x	....	?	**Chyulu Hills** (Africa-E)	0202-13=		
G **1470** t	....	?	**Kuchinoerabu-jima** (Ryukyu Is)	0802-05=		
C **1470** w	....	?	**Kusatsu-Shirane** (Honshu-Japan)	0803-12=		
C **1470** ?	....	?	**Mauna Loa** (Hawaiian Is)	1302-02=	0	
I **1470** j	....	?	**Grímsvötn** (Iceland-NE)	1703-01=		
V **1471** ?	....	?	**Oshima** (Izu Is-Japan)	0804-01=	2	-/6
I **1471** ?	....	?	**Grímsvötn** (Iceland-NE)	1703-01=		
1471	1103	>3yr	**Sakura-jima** (Kyushu-Japan)	0802-08=	**5**?	8/**9**
1472	*Cont*	....	*Sakura-jima (Kyushu-Japan)*	0802-08=	*2*	
1473	*03*	....	*Sakura-jima (Kyushu-Japan)*	0802-08=	*2*	
1473	0516	334*q*	**Aso** (Kyushu-Japan)	0802-11=	2	
1474	*Cont*	....	*Sakura-jima (Kyushu-Japan)*	0802-08=	*2*	
1474	*Cont*	....	*Aso (Kyushu-Japan)*	0802-11=	*2*	
? 1475 q	....	*?*	*Unnamed [Lomonosov Ridge] (Arctic)*	1707-01-	*0*	
1475	*0924*	....	*Sakura-jima (Kyushu-Japan)*	0802-08=	*2*	
1476	*1008*	....	*Sakura-jima (Kyushu-Japan)*	0802-08=	*3*	
? 1477	....	*?*	*Chokai (Honshu-Japan)*	0803-22=		
1477	02 ?	?	**Bárdarbunga [Veidivötn]** (Iceland)	1703-03=	**6**	**9**/**10**
1477	03	?	**Torfajökull** (Iceland-S)	1702-05=	2?	7/-
1478	0923	?	**Sakura-jima** (Kyushu-Japan)	0802-08=	2?	
C **1480** t	....	?	**Taranaki [Egmont]** (New Zealand)	0401-03=		
G **1480** y	....	?	**Merapi** (Java)	0603-25=		
C **1480** w	....	?	**Soufrière St. Vincent** (W Indies)	1600-15=		
1480 j	....	?	**La Palma** (Canary Is)	1803-01-	2	7/6
D **1480**	0115u	?	**St. Helens** (US-Washington)	1201-05-	**5+**	-/**9**
1481	....	?	**Kelut** (Java)	0603-28=	3↑	
D **1482**	0115u	?	**St. Helens** (US-Washington)	1201-05-	**5**	-/**9**
1485	0105	?	**Aso** (Kyushu-Japan)	0802-11=	2	
1487	1207	?	**Hachijo-jima** (Izu Is-Japan)	0804-05=	2	
1488	....	?	**Popocatépetl** (México)	1401-09=	2?	
G **1490** n	....	?	**Kilauea** (Hawaiian Is)	1302-01-	1?	
C **1490** s	....	?	**Andahua-Orcopampa** (Perú)	1504-004		
I **1490** j	....	?	**Grímsvötn** (Iceland-NE)	1703-01=		
1492	0824<	?	**Tenerife** (Canary Is)	1803-03-		7/-
1493 ?	....	>3yr	**Etna** (Italy)	0101-06=	1	
1494	*Cont*	....	*Etna (Italy)*	0101-06=	*1*	
1495	*Cont*	....	*Etna (Italy)*	0101-06=	*1*	
1496	*Cont*	....	*Etna (Italy)*	0101-06=	*1*	
1497	*Cont*	....	*Etna (Italy)*	0101-06=	*1*	
1498	*Cont*	....	*Etna (Italy)*	0101-06=	*1*	
1499	*Cont*	....	*Etna (Italy)*	0101-06=	*1*	

1500

START YEAR	M-Dy	Duration	VOLCANO NAME (Subregion) . . . NUMBER		VEI	Vol L/T
1500	*Cont*	....	*Etna (Italy)*	0101-06=	*1*	
1500	....	?	**Vesuvius** (Italy)	0101-02=	2?	
C **1500** r	....	?	**Taranaki [Egmont]** (New Zealand)	0401-03=		
T **1500** t	....	?	**Tongariro** (New Zealand)	0401-08=		

START YEAR	M-Dy	Duration	VOLCANO NAME (Subregion)	NUMBER	VEI	Vol L/T
? 1500 ?	....	?	Kelut (Java)	0603-28=		
G **1500** w	....	?	**Shikotsu [Eniwa]** (Hokkaido)	0805-04=	2	
G **1500** s	....	?	**Khangar** (Kamchatka)	1000-272		
G **1500** ?	....	?	**Kilauea** (Hawaiian Is)	1302-01-	1?	
C **1500** ?	....	?	**Mauna Loa** (Hawaiian Is)	1302-02=	0	
C **1500** ?	....	?	**Cosigüina** (Nicaragua)	1404-01=		
T **1500** ?	....	?	**Katla** (Iceland-S)	1702-03=	4	-/8
I **1500** ?	....	?	**Grímsvötn** (Iceland-NE)	1703-01=		
1500	....	>3yr	**Fogo** (Cape Verde Is)	1804-01=	1	
C **1500** ?	....	?	**Deception Island** (Antarctica)	1900-03=		
1501	Cont	....	Fogo (Cape Verde Is)	1804-01=	1	
1502	Cont	....	Fogo (Cape Verde Is)	1804-01=	1	
1503	Cont	....	Fogo (Cape Verde Is)	1804-01=	1	
1504	Cont	....	Fogo (Cape Verde Is)	1804-01=	1	
1504	....	?	**Popocatépetl** (México)	1401-09=	2?	
1505	Cont	....	Fogo (Cape Verde Is)	1804-01=	1	
1505 ?	....	?	**Atitlán** (Guatemala)	1402-06=	3?	
1505	02	?	**Aso** (Kyushu-Japan)	0802-11=	2	
1506	Cont	....	Fogo (Cape Verde Is)	1804-01=	1	
1506	0406	?	**Aso** (Kyushu-Japan)	0802-11=	2	
1507	Cont	....	Fogo (Cape Verde Is)	1804-01=	1	
1508	Cont	....	Fogo (Cape Verde Is)	1804-01=	1	
1509	Cont	....	Fogo (Cape Verde Is)	1804-01=	1	
? 1509	....	?	Popocatépetl (México)	1401-09=		
I **1509** ?	....	?	**Grímsvötn** (Iceland-NE)	1703-01=		
1510	Cont	....	Fogo (Cape Verde Is)	1804-01=	1	
1510 j	....	?	**Seulawah Agam** (Sumatra)	0601-02=	2	
1510 j	....	?	**Gamalama** (Halmahera-Indonesia)	0608-06=	3↑	
C **1510** t	....	?	**Kilauea** (Hawaiian Is)	1302-01-	0	
C **1510** ?	....	?	**Mauna Loa** (Hawaiian Is)	1302-02=	0	
1510 e	....	?	**San Miguel** (El Salvador)	1403-10=		
I **1510** j	....	?	**Grímsvötn** (Iceland-NE)	1703-01=		
1510	0725	?	**Hekla** (Iceland-S)	1702-07=	4	-/8
1511	Cont	....	Fogo (Cape Verde Is)	1804-01=	1	
1511	0901p	?	**Fuji** (Honshu-Japan)	0803-03=	2?	
1512	Cont	....	Fogo (Cape Verde Is)	1804-01=	1	
1512	....	?	**Sangeang Api** (Lesser Sunda Is)	0604-05=	3↑	
1512	....	?	**Gunungapi Wetar** (Banda Sea)	0605-03=	3↑	
1512	....	?	**Popocatépetl** (México)	1401-09=	2?	
1513	Cont	....	Fogo (Cape Verde Is)	1804-01=	1	
1514	Cont	....	Fogo (Cape Verde Is)	1804-01=	1	
1515	Cont	....	Fogo (Cape Verde Is)	1804-01=	1	
1516	Cont	....	Fogo (Cape Verde Is)	1804-01=	1	
1517	Cont	....	Fogo (Cape Verde Is)	1804-01=	1	
1518	Cont	....	Fogo (Cape Verde Is)	1804-01=	1	
? 1518	....	?	Asama (Honshu-Japan)	0803-11=		
1518	....	?	**Popocatépetl** (México)	1401-09=	2?	
1518	02	>3yr	**Hachijo-jima** (Izu Is-Japan)	0804-05=	2	
1519	Cont	....	Hachijo-jima (Izu Is-Japan)	0804-05=	2	
1519	Cont	....	Fogo (Cape Verde Is)	1804-01=	1	
1519	....	>3yr	**Colima** (México)	1401-04=	3?	
1519	09	>3yr	**Popocatépetl** (México)	1401-09=	3?	
1520	Cont	....	Hachijo-jima (Izu Is-Japan)	0804-05=	2	
1520	Cont	....	Colima (México)	1401-04=	2	
1520	Cont	....	Popocatépetl (México)	1401-09=	2	
1520	Cont	....	Fogo (Cape Verde Is)	1804-01=	1	
? 1520	....	?	Santa Ana (El Salvador)	1403-02=		
1521	Cont	....	Hachijo-jima (Izu Is-Japan)	0804-05=	2	
1521	Cont	....	Colima (México)	1401-04=	2	
1521	Cont	....	Popocatépetl (México)	1401-09=	2	
1521	Cont	....	Fogo (Cape Verde Is)	1804-01=	1	
I **1521** ?	....	?	**Grímsvötn** (Iceland-NE)	1703-01=		
1521	1231y	?	**Santa Ana** (El Salvador)	1403-02=	3	
1522	Cont	....	Hachijo-jima (Izu Is-Japan)	0804-05=	2	
1522	Cont	....	Colima (México)	1401-04=	2	
1522	Cont	....	Popocatépetl (México)	1401-09=	2	
1522	Cont	....	Fogo (Cape Verde Is)	1804-01=	1	
1522	0215	?	**Aso** (Kyushu-Japan)	0802-11=	2	
1523	Cont	....	Hachijo-jima (Izu Is-Japan)	0804-05=	2	
1523	Cont	....	Colima (México)	1401-04=	2	
1523	Cont	....	Popocatépetl (México)	1401-09=	2	
1523	Cont	....	Fogo (Cape Verde Is)	1804-01=	1	
1524	Cont	....	Fogo (Cape Verde Is)	1804-01=	1	
1524	....	?	**Kirishima** (Kyushu-Japan)	0802-09=	2?	
1524	....	?	**Momotombo** (Nicaragua)	1404-09=	3	-/7
1524	....	>3yr	**Masaya** (Nicaragua)	1404-10=	0	
1524	0430p	77s	**Fuego** (Guatemala)	1402-09=	2	
1524	0430p	?	**Santa Ana** (El Salvador)	1403-02=	3	
1525	Cont	....	Masaya (Nicaragua)	1404-10=	0	
1525	Cont	....	Fogo (Cape Verde Is)	1804-01=	1	
D **1525** q	....	?	**St. Helens** (US-Washington)	1201-05-		
1526	Cont	....	Masaya (Nicaragua)	1404-10=	0	
1526	Cont	....	Fogo (Cape Verde Is)	1804-01=	1	
? 1526	....	?	Fuego (Guatemala)	1402-09=	2	
1527	Cont	....	Masaya (Nicaragua)	1404-10=	0	
1527	Cont	....	Fogo (Cape Verde Is)	1804-01=	1	
1527 ?	....	?	**Telica** (Nicaragua)	1404-04=	3?	
1527	05	?	**Asama** (Honshu-Japan)	0803-11=	2	
1528	Cont	....	Masaya (Nicaragua)	1404-10=	0	
1528	Cont	....	Fogo (Cape Verde Is)	1804-01=	1	
1528	....	?	**Asama** (Honshu-Japan)	0803-11=	2	
1528	....	?	**Popocatépetl** (México)	1401-09=	2?	
1528 a	....	?	**San Cristóbal** (Nicaragua)	1404-02=	3	
@ **1528**	....	?	**Pilas, Las** (Nicaragua)	1404-08=		
1529	Cont	....	Masaya (Nicaragua)	1404-10=	0	
1529	Cont	....	Fogo (Cape Verde Is)	1804-01=	1	
1529	....	?	**Telica** (Nicaragua)	1404-04=	4	8/8
? 1529	....	?	Rincón de la Vieja (Costa Rica)	1405-02=		
1530	Cont	....	Masaya (Nicaragua)	1404-10=	0	
1530	Cont	....	Fogo (Cape Verde Is)	1804-01=	1	
C **1530** ?	....	?	**Aoba** (Vanuatu-SW Pacific)	0507-03=		
1530	....	?	**Krakatau** (Indonesia)	0602-00=		
1530	....	?	**Popocatépetl** (México)	1401-09=	2	
I **1530** j	....	?	**Grímsvötn** (Iceland-NE)	1703-01=		
1531	Cont	....	Masaya (Nicaragua)	1404-10=	0	
1531	Cont	....	Fogo (Cape Verde Is)	1804-01=	1	
1531	1231p	?	**Fuego** (Guatemala)	1402-09=	2	
1532	Cont	....	Masaya (Nicaragua)	1404-10=	0	
1532	Cont	....	Fogo (Cape Verde Is)	1804-01=	1	
? 1532	0114	?	Asama (Honshu-Japan)	0803-11=		-/6
1532	1115	?	**Cotopaxi** (Ecuador)	1502-05=	4	7/8
1533	Cont	....	Masaya (Nicaragua)	1404-10=	0	
1533	Cont	....	Fogo (Cape Verde Is)	1804-01=	1	
? 1533	....	>3yr	Orizaba, Pico de (México)	1401-10=	2?	
? 1533	....	?	Guagua Pichincha (Ecuador)	1502-02=	2	
1533	0717	?	**Aso** (Kyushu-Japan)	0802-11=	2	
1533	10	30p	**Cotopaxi** (Ecuador)	1502-05=	2	
? 1534	Cont	....	Orizaba, Pico de (México)	1401-10=	2?	
1534	Cont	....	Masaya (Nicaragua)	1404-10=	0	
1534	Cont	....	Fogo (Cape Verde Is)	1804-01=	1	
? 1534	....	?	Asama (Honshu-Japan)	0803-11=		
? 1534 ?	....	?	San Martín (México)	1401-11=		
? 1534	....	?	Guagua Pichincha (Ecuador)	1502-02=	2	
1534	06	30p	**Cotopaxi** (Ecuador)	1502-05=	4	-/8
? 1535	Cont	....	Orizaba, Pico de (México)	1401-10=	2?	
1535	Cont	....	Masaya (Nicaragua)	1404-10=	0	
1535	Cont	....	Fogo (Cape Verde Is)	1804-01=	1	
1535	....	?	**Galeras** (Colombia)	1501-08=	3↑	
? 1535	....	?	Guagua Pichincha (Ecuador)	1502-02=	2	
1535	03	?	**Miyake-jima** (Izu Is-Japan)	0804-04=	2	6/-
? 1536	Cont	....	Orizaba, Pico de (México)	1401-10=	2?	
1536	Cont	....	Masaya (Nicaragua)	1404-10=	0	
1536	Cont	....	Fogo (Cape Verde Is)	1804-01=	1	
1536	0322	238a?	**Etna** (Italy)	0101-06=	3	7/5
? 1537	Cont	....	Orizaba, Pico de (México)	1401-10=	2?	
1537	Cont	....	Masaya (Nicaragua)	1404-10=	0	
1537	Cont	....	Fogo (Cape Verde Is)	1804-01=	1	
1537	03 ?	121p	**Etna** (Italy)	0101-06=	2	7/6
? 1538	Cont	....	Orizaba, Pico de (México)	1401-10=	2?	
1538	Cont	....	Masaya (Nicaragua)	1404-10=	0	
1538	Cont	....	Fogo (Cape Verde Is)	1804-01=	1	
1538	....	?	**Gamalama** (Halmahera-Indonesia)	0608-06=	3↑	
? 1538	....	?	Guagua Pichincha (Ecuador)	1502-02=	3↑	
1538	0929	7	**Campi Flegrei** (Italy)	0101-01=	3	-/7
? 1539	Cont	....	Orizaba, Pico de (México)	1401-10=	2?	
1539	Cont	....	Masaya (Nicaragua)	1404-10=	0	
1539	Cont	....	Fogo (Cape Verde Is)	1804-01=	1	
1539	....	365y	**Popocatépetl** (México)	1401-09=	2	
? 1539	....	?	Guagua Pichincha (Ecuador)	1502-02=	2	
1540	Cont	....	Popocatépetl (México)	1401-09=	2	
1540	Cont	....	Masaya (Nicaragua)	1404-10=	0	
1540	Cont	....	Fogo (Cape Verde Is)	1804-01=	1	
G **1540** v	....	?	**Augustine** (Alaska-SW)	1103-01-	4?	
C **1540** ?	....	?	**Mauna Loa** (Hawaiian Is)	1302-02=	0	
1540	07	?	**Etna** (Italy)	0101-06=	1	
1541	Cont	....	Masaya (Nicaragua)	1404-10=	0	
1541	Cont	....	Fogo (Cape Verde Is)	1804-01=	1	
@ **1541**	....	?	**Fuego** (Guatemala)	1402-09=		
? 1541	....	?	Ruiz, Nevado del (Colombia)	1501-02=		
1541	04	?	**Reventador** (Ecuador)	1502-01=	3↑	
1541	07 ?	?	**Etna** (Italy)	0101-06=	2	
1542	Cont	....	Masaya (Nicaragua)	1404-10=	0	
1542	Cont	....	Fogo (Cape Verde Is)	1804-01=	1	
1542	....	?	**Ceboruco** (México)	1401-03=		
1542	....	?	**Popocatépetl** (México)	1401-09=	2	
? 1542	....	?	Misti, El (Perú)	1504-01=	1?	
1542	0114	?	**Fuego** (Guatemala)	1402-09=		
1542	0429	?	**Aso** (Kyushu-Japan)	0802-11=	2	
1543	Cont	....	Masaya (Nicaragua)	1404-10=	0	
1543	Cont	....	Fogo (Cape Verde Is)	1804-01=	1	
1543	....	?	**Kaitoku Seamount** (Volcano Is-Japan)	0804-10=	0	
1544	Cont	....	Masaya (Nicaragua)	1404-10=	0	
1544	Cont	....	Fogo (Cape Verde Is)	1804-01=	1	
1544	0728	?	**Hiuchi** (Honshu-Japan)	0803-131	2	-/6

START YEAR	M-Dy	Duration	VOLCANO NAME (Subregion)	NUMBER	VEI	Vol L/T
1545	Cont	....	Fogo (Cape Verde Is)	1804-01=	1	
1545	....	>3yr	**Orizaba, Pico de** (México)	1401-10=	2	8/-
1546	Cont	....	Orizaba, Pico de (México)	1401-10=	2	8/-
1546	Cont	....	Fogo (Cape Verde Is)	1804-01=	1	
1547	Cont	....	Orizaba, Pico de (México)	1401-10=	2	8/-
1547	Cont	....	Fogo (Cape Verde Is)	1804-01=	1	
1547	0304	225m?	**Haku-san** (Honshu-Japan)	0803-05=	3	
1548	Cont	....	Orizaba, Pico de (México)	1401-10=	2	8/-
1548	Cont	....	Fogo (Cape Verde Is)	1804-01=	1	
1548	....	?	**Merapi** (Java)	0603-25=	3↑	
1548	....	?	**Kelut** (Java)	0603-28=	3↑	
1548	....	?	**Haku-san** (Honshu-Japan)	0803-05=	3?	
1548	....	?	**Popocatépetl** (México)	1401-09=	2	
1549	Cont	....	Orizaba, Pico de (México)	1401-10=	2	8/-
1549	Cont	....	Fogo (Cape Verde Is)	1804-01=	1	
1550	Cont	....	Orizaba, Pico de (México)	1401-10=	2	8/-
1550	Cont	....	Fogo (Cape Verde Is)	1804-01=	1	
1550	....	?	**Vulcano** (Italy)	0101-05=	3	
G **1550** v	....	?	**Nyamuragira** (Africa-C)	0203-02=		
? 1550 v	....	?	Oku Volc Field [L. Nyos] (Africa-W)	0204-03-	3	-/7
C **1550** s	....	?	**Taranaki [Egmont]** (New Zealand)	0401-03=		
G **1550** v	....	?	**Taveuni** (Fiji Is-SW Pacific)	0405-01-	0	
T **1550** ?	....	?	**Pago** (New Britain-SW Pac)	0502-08=	P	
1550 <	....	?	**Makian** (Halmahera-Indonesia)	0608-07=	3↑	
G **1550** v	....	?	**Hakkoda Group** (Honshu-Japan)	0803-28=	1	-/2
G **1550** u	....	?	**Shikotsu [Eniwa]** (Hokkaido)	0805-04=	2	
T **1550** ?	....	?	**Akan** (Hokkaido-Japan)	0805-07=		
C **1550** ?	....	?	**Avachinsky** (Kamchatka)	1000-10=		
G **1550** ?	....	?	**Karymsky** (Kamchatka)	1000-13=		8/-
G **1550** ?	....	?	**Maly Semiachik** (Kamchatka)	1000-14=	4	-/8
T **1550** ?	....	?	**Kikhpinych** (Kamchatka)	1000-18=		7/-
T **1550** ?	....	?	**Krasheninnikov** (Kamchatka)	1000-19=		7/-
T **1550** ?	....	?	**Tolbachik** (Kamchatka)	1000-24=	2	8/6
T **1550** ?	....	?	**Shiveluch** (Kamchatka)	1000-27=	3	-/7
C **1550** ?	....	?	**Tanaga** (Aleutian Is)	1101-08-		
C **1550** ?	....	?	**Takawangha** (Aleutian Is)	1101-09-		
C **1550** ?	....	?	**Aniakchak** (Alaska Peninsula)	1102-09-		
T **1550** t	....	?	**Redoubt** (Alaska-SW)	1103-03-		
D **1550** ?	....	?	**Wells Gray-Clearwater** (Canada)	1200-15-		
T **1550** y	....	?	**Mono Lake Volc Field** (US-California	1203-11-		
1550 j	....	?	**Barú** (Panamá)	1406-01-		
E **1550** >	....	?	**Fernandina** (Galápagos)	1503-01=	0	
1550 t	....	?	**Ubinas** (Perú)	1504-02=	3?	
C **1550** t	....	?	**Soufrière St. Vincent** (W Indies)	1600-15=		
T **1550** ?	....	?	**Katla** (Iceland-S)	1702-03=	4	-/8
1550	1120n	?	**Dukono** (Halmahera-Indonesia)	0608-01=	3	-/8
1551	Cont	....	Orizaba, Pico de (México)	1401-10=	2	8/-
1551	Cont	....	Fogo (Cape Verde Is)	1804-01=	1	
1551	....	273w>	**Fuego** (Guatemala)	1402-09=	2	
1551	....	?	**Masaya** (Nicaragua)	1404-10=	0	
1552	Cont	....	Orizaba, Pico de (México)	1401-10=	2	8/-
1552	Cont	....	Fuego (Guatemala)	1402-09=	2	
1552	Cont	....	Fogo (Cape Verde Is)	1804-01=	1	
1552	1007	8a	**Oshima** (Izu Is-Japan)	0804-01=	3	8/7
1553	Cont	....	Orizaba, Pico de (México)	1401-10=	2	8/-
1553	Cont	....	Fogo (Cape Verde Is)	1804-01=	1	
1554	Cont	....	Orizaba, Pico de (México)	1401-10=	2	8/-
1554	Cont	....	Fogo (Cape Verde Is)	1804-01=	1	
? 1554	....	?	Etna (Italy)	0101-06=	2	
1554	....	?	**Merapi** (Java)	0603-25=	3↑	
1554	....	?	**Kirishima** (Kyushu-Japan)	0802-09=	2?	
1554	05	787w	**Haku-san** (Honshu-Japan)	0803-05=	3	
1554	05	40b	**Hekla [Raudubjallar]** (Iceland-S)	1702-07=	2?	8/-
1555	Cont	....	Haku-san (Honshu-Japan)	0803-05=	2	
1555	Cont	....	Orizaba, Pico de (México)	1401-10=	2	8/-
1555	Cont	....	Fogo (Cape Verde Is)	1804-01=	1	
1555 e	....	?	**Huila, Nevado del** (Colombia)	1501-05=		
1556	Cont	....	Haku-san (Honshu-Japan)	0803-05=	2	
1556	Cont	....	Fogo (Cape Verde Is)	1804-01=	1	
1557	Cont	....	Fogo (Cape Verde Is)	1804-01=	1	
1557	....	?	**Tungurahua** (Ecuador)	1502-08=	2	
? 1557	0115	?	Fuego (Guatemala)	1402-09=		
1558	Cont	....	Fogo (Cape Verde Is)	1804-01=	1	
1558 <	....	>3yr	Stromboli (Italy)	0101-04=	2	
1558	....	365y	**Aso** (Kyushu-Japan)	0802-11=	2	
1558	....	?	**Villarrica** (Chile-C)	1507-12=	2	
? 1558 <	....	?	Jan Mayen (Atlantic-N-Jan Mayen)	1706-01=		
1559	Cont	....	Stromboli (Italy)	0101-04=	1	
1559	Cont	....	Aso (Kyushu-Japan)	0802-11=	2	
1559	Cont	....	Fogo (Cape Verde Is)	1804-01=	1	
? 1559	....	?	Iya (Lesser Sunda Is)	0604-11=		
? 1559	0116	?	Fuego (Guatemala)	1402-09=		
1560	Cont	....	Stromboli (Italy)	0101-04=	1	
1560	Cont	....	Fogo (Cape Verde Is)	1804-01=	1	
C **1560** s	....	?	**Taranaki [Egmont]** (New Zealand)	0401-03=		
1560	....	?	**Merbabu** (Java)	0603-24=		
1560	....	?	**Merapi** (Java)	0603-25=	3↑	
G **1560** v	....	?	**Kuchinoerabu-jima** (Ryukyu Is)	0802-05=		
? 1560	....	?	Chokai (Honshu-Japan)	0803-22=		
C **1560** t	....	?	**Aniakchak** (Alaska Peninsula)	1102-09-	4+	-/8
1560	....	?	**Colima** (México)	1401-04=	2	
G **1560** u	....	?	**Irazú** (Costa Rica)	1405-06=	3	
? 1560	....	?	Guagua Pichincha (Ecuador)	1502-02=	2	
? 1560	0104	?	Fuji (Honshu-Japan)	0803-03=		
1561	Cont	....	Stromboli (Italy)	0101-04=	1	
1561	Cont	....	Fogo (Cape Verde Is)	1804-01=	1	
1561	1231y	2a	**Gamalama** (Halmahera-Indonesia)	0608-06=	2	
1562	Cont	....	Stromboli (Italy)	0101-04=	1	
1562	Cont	....	Fogo (Cape Verde Is)	1804-01=	1	
1562	....	?	**Villarrica** (Chile-C)	1507-12=	2	
1562	03	?	**Aso** (Kyushu-Japan)	0802-11=	2	
1562	0921?	648w?	**Pico** (Azores)	1802-02=	2	
1563	Cont	....	Stromboli (Italy)	0101-04=	1	
1563	Cont	....	Pico (Azores)	1802-02=	2	
1563	Cont	....	Fogo (Cape Verde Is)	1804-01=	1	
? 1563	0503	?	Aso (Kyushu-Japan)	0802-11=	2?	
1563	0628	28e	**Agua de Pau** (Azores)	1802-09=	**5**?	6/**9**
1564	Cont	....	Stromboli (Italy)	0101-04=	1	
1564	Cont	....	Pico (Azores)	1802-02=	2	
1564	Cont	....	Fogo (Cape Verde Is)	1804-01=	1	
1564	0210	2a	**Agua de Pau** (Azores)	1802-09=	2	
1564	12	?	**Aso** (Kyushu-Japan)	0802-11=	2	
1564	1231y	?	**Gamkonora** (Halmahera-Indonesia)	0608-04=	3↑	
1565	Cont	....	Stromboli (Italy)	0101-04=	1	
1565	Cont	....	Fogo (Cape Verde Is)	1804-01=	1	
? 1565	....	?	Fuego (Guatemala)	1402-09=	2	
1565	08 ?	?	**Pacaya** (Guatemala)	1402-11=	3	
1566	Cont	....	Stromboli (Italy)	0101-04=	1	
1566	Cont	....	Fogo (Cape Verde Is)	1804-01=	1	
1566	....	?	**Orizaba, Pico de** (México)	1401-10=	2	
1566	0506	?	**Kirishima** (Kyushu-Japan)	0802-09=	2?	
1566	1017	30a	**Guagua Pichincha** (Ecuador)	1502-02=	3↑	
1566	1031	?	**Kirishima** (Kyushu-Japan)	0802-09=	3	
1566	1101?	45m?	**Etna** (Italy)	0101-06=	2	7/5
1567	Cont	....	Stromboli (Italy)	0101-04=	1	
1567	Cont	....	Fogo (Cape Verde Is)	1804-01=	1	
1567	....	?	**Ceboruco** (México)	1401-03=		
1568	Cont	....	Stromboli (Italy)	0101-04=	1	
1568	Cont	....	Fogo (Cape Verde Is)	1804-01=	1	
1568 <	....	?	**Savo** (Solomon Is-SW Pacific)	0505-07=	3	
1569	Cont	....	Stromboli (Italy)	0101-04=	1	
1569	Cont	....	Fogo (Cape Verde Is)	1804-01=	1	
1569	....	>3yr	**Orizaba, Pico de** (México)	1401-10=	2	
1570	Cont	....	Stromboli (Italy)	0101-04=	1	
1570	Cont	....	Orizaba, Pico de (México)	1401-10=	2	
1570	Cont	....	Fogo (Cape Verde Is)	1804-01=	1	
1570 <	....	730x<	**Vesuvius** (Italy)	0101-02=	1?	
1570	....	>3yr	**Santorini** (Greece)	0102-04=	3	6/-
C **1570** s	....	?	**Taranaki [Egmont]** (New Zealand)	0401-03=		
? 1570	....	?	Merbabu (Java)	0603-24=		
G **1570** v	....	?	**Tokachi** (Hokkaido-Japan)	0805-05=	2?	7/-
C **1570** r	....	?	**Baransky** (Kuril Is)	0900-08=		
1570 ?	....	?	**Santa Ana** (El Salvador)	1403-02=		
1570	....	?	**Masaya** (Nicaragua)	1404-10=	0	
? 1570	....	?	Mombacho (Nicaragua)	1404-11=		
1570	....	?	**Ruiz, Nevado del** (Colombia)	1501-02=		
T **1570** ?	....	?	**Cayambe** (Ecuador)	1502-006	4	8/-
1571	Cont	....	Vesuvius (Italy)	0101-02=	1?	
1571	Cont	....	Stromboli (Italy)	0101-04=	1	
1571	Cont	....	Santorini (Greece)	0102-04=	2	6/-
1571	Cont	....	Orizaba, Pico de (México)	1401-10=	2	
1571	Cont	....	Fogo (Cape Verde Is)	1804-01=	1	
1571	....	?	**Popocatépetl** (México)	1401-09=	2	
? 1571	1225	?	Fuego (Guatemala)	1402-09=		
1572	Cont	....	Vesuvius (Italy)	0101-02=	1?	
1572	Cont	....	Stromboli (Italy)	0101-04=	1	
1572	Cont	....	Santorini (Greece)	0102-04=	2	6/-
1572	Cont	....	Orizaba, Pico de (México)	1401-10=	2	
1572	Cont	....	Fogo (Cape Verde Is)	1804-01=	1	
1572	....	?	**Taal** (Luzon-Philippines)	0703-07=	3	
1572 b	....	?	**San Salvador** (El Salvador)	1403-05=	3?	
1573	Cont	....	Stromboli (Italy)	0101-04=	1	
1573	Cont	....	Santorini (Greece)	0102-04=	2	6/-
1573	Cont	....	Orizaba, Pico de (México)	1401-10=	2	
1573	Cont	....	Fogo (Cape Verde Is)	1804-01=	1	
1573	....	?	**Aso** (Kyushu-Japan)	0802-11=	2	
1574	Cont	....	Stromboli (Italy)	0101-04=	1	
1574	Cont	....	Orizaba, Pico de (México)	1401-10=	2	
1574	Cont	....	Fogo (Cape Verde Is)	1804-01=	1	
1574	....	?	**Aso** (Kyushu-Japan)	0802-11=	2	
1574	02	?	**Kirishima** (Kyushu-Japan)	0802-09=	2?	
1575	Cont	....	Stromboli (Italy)	0101-04=	1	
1575	Cont	....	Orizaba, Pico de (México)	1401-10=	2	

START YEAR	M-Dy	Duration	VOLCANO NAME (Subregion)	NUMBER	VEI	Vol L/T
1575	Cont	....	Fogo (Cape Verde Is)	1804-01=	1	
? 1575	....	?	Fuego (Guatemala)	1402-09=	2	
1575	....	?	**Osorno** (Chile-S)	1508-01=	2	
1575	0908	?	**Guagua Pichincha** (Ecuador)	1502-02=	2	
1576	Cont	....	Stromboli (Italy)	0101-04=	1	
1576	Cont	....	Orizaba, Pico de (México)	1401-10=	2	
1576	Cont	....	Fogo (Cape Verde Is)	1804-01=	1	
1576	....	730y	**Kirishima** (Kyushu-Japan)	0802-09=	2?	
1576	....	?	**Colima** (México)	1401-04=	3	
? 1576	....	?	Fuego (Guatemala)	1402-09=	2	
1576	....	?	**Santa Ana** (El Salvador)	1403-02=	3	
1576	1115	?	**Aso** (Kyushu-Japan)	0802-11=	2	
1577	Cont	....	Stromboli (Italy)	0101-04=	1	
1577	Cont	....	Kirishima (Kyushu-Japan)	0802-09=	2	
1577	Cont	....	Orizaba, Pico de (México)	1401-10=	2	
1577	Cont	....	Fogo (Cape Verde Is)	1804-01=	1	
? 1577	....	?	Fuego (Guatemala)	1402-09=	2	
? 1577	....	?	Guagua Pichincha (Ecuador)	1502-02=	2	
1578	Cont	....	Stromboli (Italy)	0101-04=	1	
1578	Cont	....	Kirishima (Kyushu-Japan)	0802-09=	2	
1578	Cont	....	Orizaba, Pico de (México)	1401-10=	2	
1578	Cont	....	Fogo (Cape Verde Is)	1804-01=	1	
? 1578	....	?	Etna (Italy)	0101-06=		
1578	02	?	**Momotombo** (Nicaragua)	1404-09=	2	
1579	Cont	....	Stromboli (Italy)	0101-04=	1	
1579	Cont	....	Orizaba, Pico de (México)	1401-10=	2	
1579	Cont	....	Fogo (Cape Verde Is)	1804-01=	1	
1579 ?	....	913w?	**Atitlán** (Guatemala)	1402-06=	2	
1579	0909?	296w?	**Etna** (Italy)	0101-06=		
1579	0927a	?	**Haku-san** (Honshu-Japan)	0803-05=	3	
1580	Cont	....	Stromboli (Italy)	0101-04=	1	
1580	Cont	....	Etna (Italy)	0101-06=		
1580	Cont	....	Orizaba, Pico de (México)	1401-10=	2	
1580	Cont	....	Atitlán (Guatemala)	1402-06=	2	
1580	Cont	....	Fogo (Cape Verde Is)	1804-01=	1	
C **1580** p	....	?	**Billy Mitchell** (Bougainville-SW Pacific)	0505-011	**6**	**-/10**
1580	....	?	**Popocatépetl** (México)	1401-09=	2?	
? 1580	....	?	Guagua Pichincha (Ecuador)	1502-02=	2	
1580	0501	121a?	**San Jorge** (Azores)	1802-03=	3?	
1580	0811	?	**Katla** (Iceland-S)	1702-03=	4	-/8
1580	1207	<1	**Galeras** (Colombia)	1501-08=	3	
1581	Cont	....	Stromboli (Italy)	0101-04=	1	
1581	Cont	....	Orizaba, Pico de (México)	1401-10=	2	
1581	Cont	....	Atitlán (Guatemala)	1402-06=	2	
1581	Cont	....	Fogo (Cape Verde Is)	1804-01=	1	
1581	1205	41a	Fuego (Guatemala)	1402-09=	2	-/8
1581	1226	....	**Fuego** (Guatemala)	1402-09=	4?	-/8
1582	Cont	....	Stromboli (Italy)	0101-04=	1	
1582	Cont	....	Orizaba, Pico de (México)	1401-10=	2	
1582	Cont	....	Fogo (Cape Verde Is)	1804-01=	1	
1582	....	?	**Haku-san** (Honshu-Japan)	0803-05=	2	
1582	0114	....	Fuego (Guatemala)	1402-09=	4?	-/8
1582	0216	?	**Asama** (Honshu-Japan)	0803-11=	2	
1582	0217	?	**Aso** (Kyushu-Japan)	0802-11=	2	
1582	0605	>3yr	Guagua Pichincha (Ecuador)	1502-02=	2	
1582	0703	?	**Asama** (Honshu-Japan)	0803-11=	2	
1583	Cont	....	Stromboli (Italy)	0101-04=	1	
1583	Cont	....	Orizaba, Pico de (México)	1401-10=	2	
1583	Cont	....	Guagua Pichincha (Ecuador)	1502-02=	2	
1583	Cont	....	Fogo (Cape Verde Is)	1804-01=	1	
1583	0715q	?	**Reykjanes** (Iceland-SW)	1701-02=	2?	
1583	1214	?	**Aso** (Kyushu-Japan)	0802-11=	2	
1584	Cont	....	Stromboli (Italy)	0101-04=	1	
1584	Cont	....	Orizaba, Pico de (México)	1401-10=	2	
1584	Cont	....	Guagua Pichincha (Ecuador)	1502-02=	2	
1584	Cont	....	Fogo (Cape Verde Is)	1804-01=	1	
1584	....	?	**Merapi** (Java)	0603-25=	3↑	
1584	08	?	**Aso** (Kyushu-Japan)	0802-11=	2	
1585	Cont	....	Stromboli (Italy)	0101-04=	1	
1585	Cont	....	Orizaba, Pico de (México)	1401-10=	2	
1585	Cont	....	Guagua Pichincha (Ecuador)	1502-02=	2	
1585	Cont	....	Fogo (Cape Verde Is)	1804-01=	1	
1585	0110	?	**Colima** (México)	1401-04=	4	
1585	0115	181m	**Fuego** (Guatemala)	1402-09=	2	
1585	0519	83a	**La Palma** (Canary Is)	1803-01-	2	
1585	11 ?	?	**Kirishima** (Kyushu-Japan)	0802-09=	2?	
1585	12 ?	?	**Yake-dake** (Honshu-Japan)	0803-07=	3↑	
1586	Cont	....	Stromboli (Italy)	0101-04=	1	
1586	Cont	....	Orizaba, Pico de (México)	1401-10=	2	
1586	Cont	....	Guagua Pichincha (Ecuador)	1502-02=	2	
1586	Cont	....	Fogo (Cape Verde Is)	1804-01=	1	
? 1586	....	?	Merapi (Java)	0603-25=		
1586	....	?	**Kelut** (Java)	0603-28=	**5**?	**-/9**
? 1586	....	?	Raung (Java)	0603-34=	3	
? 1586	....	?	Masaya (Nicaragua)	1404-10=	0	
1586	0417	?	**Banda Api** (Banda Sea)	0605-09=	3↑	

Wally Johnson ((Australian Bur. Min. Resour.)

The beautiful caldera lake of Billy Mitchell provides a dramatic setting for unvegetated Bagana volcano, one of the most active in Papua New Guinea. Two major explosive eruptions from Billy Mitchell, one about 900 and the other about 370 years ago, produced pyroclastic-fall deposits that cover most of the northern half of Bougainville Island and pyroclastic-flow and -surge deposits that extend 25 km to the eastern coast. The younger eruption may have been responsible for formation of the summit caldera.

	START YEAR	M-Dy	Duration	VOLCANO NAME (Subregion)	NUMBER	VEI	Vol L/T
	1586	0603b	196m	Fuego (Guatemala)	1402-09=	2	
	1587	Cont	....	Stromboli (Italy)	0101-04=	1	
	1587	Cont	....	Orizaba, Pico de (México)	1401-10=	2	
	1587	Cont	....	Fogo (Cape Verde Is)	1804-01=	1	
	1587	....	?	Merapi (Java)	0603-25=	3↑	
	1587	....	?	Aso (Kyushu-Japan)	0802-11=	2	
	1587	0524	?	Kirishima (Kyushu-Japan)	0802-09=	2?	
	1587	0724	?	Fuego (Guatemala)	1402-09=	2	
	1587	0903	....	Guagua Pichincha (Ecuador)	1502-02=	3	
	1588	Cont	....	Stromboli (Italy)	0101-04=	1	
	1588	Cont	....	Orizaba, Pico de (México)	1401-10=	2	
	1588	Cont	....	Guagua Pichincha (Ecuador)	1502-02=	2	
	1588	Cont	....	Fogo (Cape Verde Is)	1804-01=	1	
	1588	0407	?	Kirishima (Kyushu-Japan)	0802-09=	2?	
	1589	Cont	....	Stromboli (Italy)	0101-04=	1	
	1589	Cont	....	Orizaba, Pico de (México)	1401-10=	2	
	1589	Cont	....	Guagua Pichincha (Ecuador)	1502-02=	2	
	1589	Cont	....	Fogo (Cape Verde Is)	1804-01=	1	
	1590	Cont	....	Stromboli (Italy)	0101-04=	1	
	1590	Cont	....	Guagua Pichincha (Ecuador)	1502-02=	2	
	1590	Cont	....	Fogo (Cape Verde Is)	1804-01=	1	
C	1590 s	....	?	Taranaki [Egmont] (New Zealand)	0401-03=		
C	1590 t	....	?	Tengger Caldera (Java)	0603-31=	2	
C	1590 t	....	?	Iskut-Unuk River Cones (Canada)	1200-09-		
	1590	....	?	Popocatépetl (México)	1401-09=	2?	
T	1590 ?	....	?	Cayambe (Ecuador)	1502-006		
	1590	....	?	Reventador (Ecuador)	1502-01=	3↑	
@	1590 ?	....	?	Antisana (Ecuador)	1502-03=	2?	
	1590	0114	<1	Colima (México)	1401-04=	3	
	1590	0415q	?	Asama (Honshu-Japan)	0803-11=	2?	
	1591	Cont	....	Stromboli (Italy)	0101-04=	1	
	1591	Cont	....	Guagua Pichincha (Ecuador)	1502-02=	2	
	1591	Cont	....	Fogo (Cape Verde Is)	1804-01=	1	
	1591	....	?	Taal (Luzon-Philippines)	0703-07=	3↑	
	1591	0415q	?	Asama (Honshu-Japan)	0803-11=	2?	
	1591	1129	?	Asama (Honshu-Japan)	0803-11=	3?	
	1592	Cont	....	Stromboli (Italy)	0101-04=	1	
	1592	Cont	....	Guagua Pichincha (Ecuador)	1502-02=	2	
	1592	Cont	....	Fogo (Cape Verde Is)	1804-01=	1	
	1592	....	?	Aso (Kyushu-Japan)	0802-11=	2	
	1592	....	835x	Popocatépetl (México)	1401-09=	2	
	1593	Cont	....	Stromboli (Italy)	0101-04=	1	
	1593	Cont	....	Popocatépetl (México)	1401-09=	2	
	1593	Cont	....	Guagua Pichincha (Ecuador)	1502-02=	2	
	1593	Cont	....	Fogo (Cape Verde Is)	1804-01=	1	
	1593	....	?	Raung (Java)	0603-34=	5?	-/9
	1594	Cont	....	Stromboli (Italy)	0101-04=	1	
	1594	Cont	....	Popocatépetl (México)	1401-09=	2	
	1594	Cont	....	Guagua Pichincha (Ecuador)	1502-02=	2	
	1594	Cont	....	Fogo (Cape Verde Is)	1804-01=	1	
	1594	....	?	Villarrica (Chile-C)	1507-12=	2	
	1595	Cont	....	Stromboli (Italy)	0101-04=	1	
	1595	Cont	....	Guagua Pichincha (Ecuador)	1502-02=	2	
	1595	Cont	....	Fogo (Cape Verde Is)	1804-01=	1	
	1595	....	?	Tinakula (Santa Cruz Is-SW Pacific)	0506-01=	3↑	
	1595	....	?	Kirishima (Kyushu-Japan)	0802-09=	2?	
	1595	0309<	?	Ruiz, Nevado del (Colombia)	1501-02=	2?	-/8
	1595	0312	....	Ruiz, Nevado del (Colombia)	1501-02=	4	-/8
	1595	0601	?	Asama (Honshu-Japan)	0803-11=	2?	
	1595	1122	?	Miyake-jima (Izu Is-Japan)	0804-04=	2	5/-
	1596	Cont	....	Stromboli (Italy)	0101-04=	1	
	1596	Cont	....	Guagua Pichincha (Ecuador)	1502-02=	2	
	1596	Cont	....	Fogo (Cape Verde Is)	1804-01=	1	
?	1596	....	?	Kirishima (Kyushu-Japan)	0802-09=	2?	
	1596	0501	137m	Asama (Honshu-Japan)	0803-11=	3	-/7
	1597	Cont	....	Stromboli (Italy)	0101-04=	1	
	1597	Cont	....	Guagua Pichincha (Ecuador)	1502-02=	2	
	1597	Cont	....	Fogo (Cape Verde Is)	1804-01=	1	
	1597 <	....	?	Nemrut Dagi (Turkey)	0103-02=		
?	1597	....	?	Iyang-Argapura (Java)	0603-33=		
?	1597	01	?	Iwaki (Honshu-Japan)	0803-27=	2	
	1597	0103	164m>	Hekla (Iceland-S)	1702-07=	4	-/8
	1597	0117	16a>	Raung (Java)	0603-34=	3	
	1597	0417	?	Asama (Honshu-Japan)	0803-11=	2	
?	1597	0613	?	Iwaki (Honshu-Japan)	0803-27=	2	
?	1597	1006	?	Changbaishan (China-E)	1005-06-		
?	1597	1008	?	Xianjindao (Korea)	1006-01-		
	1598	Cont	....	Stromboli (Italy)	0101-04=	1	
	1598	Cont	....	Guagua Pichincha (Ecuador)	1502-02=	2	
	1598	Cont	....	Fogo (Cape Verde Is)	1804-01=	1	
	1598	....	>3yr	Banda Api (Banda Sea)	0605-09=	3	
	1598	....	730y	Kirishima (Kyushu-Japan)	0802-09=	2?	
	1598	0513	?	Asama (Honshu-Japan)	0803-11=	2	
	1598	1107	?	Grímsvötn (Iceland-NE)	1703-01=	3?	-/8
	1598	12	199w	Aso (Kyushu-Japan)	0802-11=	2	
	1599	Cont	....	Stromboli (Italy)	0101-04=	1	
	1599	Cont	....	Banda Api (Banda Sea)	0605-09=	2	
	1599	Cont	....	Kirishima (Kyushu-Japan)	0802-09=	2	
	1599	Cont	....	Aso (Kyushu-Japan)	0802-11=	2	
	1599	Cont	....	Fogo (Cape Verde Is)	1804-01=	1	
?	1599	....	?	Misti, El (Perú)	1504-01=	1?	
	1600						
	1600	Cont	....	Stromboli (Italy)	0101-04=	1	
	1600	Cont	....	Banda Api (Banda Sea)	0605-09=	2	
	1600	Cont	....	Kirishima (Kyushu-Japan)	0802-09=	2	
	1600	Cont	....	Fogo (Cape Verde Is)	1804-01=	1	
G	1600 ?	....	?	Fournaise, Piton de la (Indian O.-W)	0303-02=	0	
T	1600 ?	....	?	Suwanose-jima (Ryukyu Is)	0802-03=	4+	
T	1600 t	....	?	Akan (Hokkaido-Japan)	0805-07=		
C	1600 ?	....	?	Ebeko (Kuril Is)	0900-38=		
C	1600 ?	....	?	Alney-Chashakondzha (Kamchatka)	1000-45-		
T	1600 t	....	?	Redoubt (Alaska-SW)	1103-03-		
U	1600 w	....	?	Unnamed [East Pacific Rise]	1304-05-	0	
?	1600	....	?	Ubinas (Perú)	1504-02=	2?	
C	1600 u	....	?	Calbuco (Chile-S)	1508-02=		
G	1600 t	....	?	Soufrière Guadeloupe (W Indies)	1600-06=		
	1600	0114	14a	Asama (Honshu-Japan)	0803-11=	3?	
	1600	0217a	18a?	Huaynaputina (Perú)	1504-03=	1?	
	1600	0219	....	Huaynaputina (Perú)	1504-03=	6	-/10
	1600	0222	?	Iwaki (Honshu-Japan)	0803-27=	2	
	1600	0723	2a	Iwaki (Honshu-Japan)	0803-27=	2	
	1600	10 w	?	Oshima (Izu Is-Japan)	0804-01=		
	1601	Cont	....	Stromboli (Italy)	0101-04=	1	
	1601	Cont	....	Banda Api (Banda Sea)	0605-09=	2	
	1601	Cont	....	Fogo (Cape Verde Is)	1804-01=	1	
	1602	Cont	....	Stromboli (Italy)	0101-04=	1	
	1602	Cont	....	Banda Api (Banda Sea)	0605-09=	2	
	1602	Cont	....	Fogo (Cape Verde Is)	1804-01=	1	
?	1602	....	?	Colima (México)	1401-04=	2?	
	1603	Cont	....	Stromboli (Italy)	0101-04=	1	
	1603	Cont	....	Fogo (Cape Verde Is)	1804-01=	1	
	1603	07	>3yr	Etna (Italy)	0101-06=	2	6/-
@	1603	1031	15m	Grímsvötn (Iceland-NE)	1703-01=	2	
	1604	Cont	....	Stromboli (Italy)	0101-04=	1	
	1604	Cont	....	Etna (Italy)	0101-06=	2	6/-
	1604	Cont	....	Fogo (Cape Verde Is)	1804-01=	1	
?	1604	....	?	Asama (Honshu-Japan)	0803-11=	2	
	1604	0207	?	Iwaki (Honshu-Japan)	0803-27=	3?	
	1605	Cont	....	Stromboli (Italy)	0101-04=	1	
	1605	Cont	....	Etna (Italy)	0101-06=	2	6/-
	1605	Cont	....	Fogo (Cape Verde Is)	1804-01=	1	
	1605	....	365y	Momotombo (Nicaragua)	1404-09=	4	-/8
?	1605	0410	?	Iwaki (Honshu-Japan)	0803-27=	2?	
	1605	05	?	Gamalama (Halmahera-Indonesia)	0608-06=	2	
	1605	1027	?	Hachijo-jima (Izu Is-Japan)	0804-05=	2	6/6
	1605	12	61a	Asama (Honshu-Japan)	0803-11=	2	
	1606	Cont	....	Stromboli (Italy)	0101-04=	1	
	1606	Cont	....	Etna (Italy)	0101-06=	2	6/-
	1606	Cont	....	Asama (Honshu-Japan)	0803-11=	2	
	1606	Cont	....	Momotombo (Nicaragua)	1404-09=	3	-/8
	1606	Cont	....	Fogo (Cape Verde Is)	1804-01=	1	
?	1606	....	?	Mere Lava (Vanuatu-SW Pacific)	0507-021		
	1606	0123	?	Hachijo-jima (Izu Is-Japan)	0804-05=	2	
	1606	1125	18a>	Colima (México)	1401-04=	4	
	1606	1213	....	Colima (México)	1401-04=	4	
	1607	Cont	....	Stromboli (Italy)	0101-04=	1	
	1607	Cont	....	Fogo (Cape Verde Is)	1804-01=	1	
	1607	0628	368w?	Etna (Italy)	0101-06=	2	8/6
	1608	Cont	....	Stromboli (Italy)	0101-04=	1	
	1608	Cont	....	Etna (Italy)	0101-06=	1	8/6
	1608	Cont	....	Fogo (Cape Verde Is)	1804-01=	1	
	1608 c	....	?	Taal (Luzon-Philippines)	0703-07=	2?	
	1608	0718	1a	Gamalama (Halmahera-Indonesia)	0608-06=	3	
	1609	Cont	....	Stromboli (Italy)	0101-04=	1	
	1609	Cont	....	Etna (Italy)	0101-06=	2	6/-
	1609	Cont	....	Fogo (Cape Verde Is)	1804-01=	1	
	1609	....	?	Banda Api (Banda Sea)	0605-09=	3↑	
?	1609	....	?	Tengchong (SE Asia)	0705-11-		
?	1609	....	?	Cosigüina (Nicaragua)	1404-01=		
?	1609	....	?	Momotombo (Nicaragua)	1404-09=		
	1609	0405	?	Asama (Honshu-Japan)	0803-11=	2	
	1610	Cont	....	Stromboli (Italy)	0101-04=	1	
	1610	Cont	....	Fogo (Cape Verde Is)	1804-01=	1	
G	1610 x	....	?	Savai'i (Samoa-SW Pacific)	0404-04=		
G	1610 s	....	?	St. Helens (US-Washington)	1201-05-		8/-
C	1610 t	....	?	Kilauea (Hawaiian Is)	1302-01-	1?	
I	1610 ?	....	?	Grímsvötn (Iceland-NE)	1703-01=		
	1610	0206	190a	Etna (Italy)	0101-06=	2	8/6
	1611	Cont	....	Stromboli (Italy)	0101-04=	1	
	1611	Cont	....	Fogo (Cape Verde Is)	1804-01=	1	
	1611	....	?	Aso (Kyushu-Japan)	0802-11=	2	
?	1611	....	?	Bandai (Honshu-Japan)	0803-16=		

START YEAR	M-Dy	Duration	VOLCANO NAME (Subregion)	NUMBER	VEI	Vol L/T
1611	0415	808w	Colima (México)	1401-04=	3	
? 1611	10	?	Usu (Hokkaido-Japan)	0805-03=		
1612	Cont	....	Stromboli (Italy)	0101-04=	1	
1612	Cont	....	Colima (México)	1401-04=	2	
1612	Cont	....	Fogo (Cape Verde Is)	1804-01=	1	
1612	....	?	Eyjafjallajökull (Iceland-S)	1702-02=	2	-/6
1612	0812	?	Aso (Kyushu-Japan)	0802-11=	2	
1612	1012	?	Katla (Iceland-S)	1702-03=	4	-/8
1612	1015w	?	Oshima (Izu Is-Japan)	0804-01=		
1613	Cont	....	Stromboli (Italy)	0101-04=	1	
1613	Cont	....	Colima (México)	1401-04=	2	
1613	Cont	....	Fogo (Cape Verde Is)	1804-01=	1	
1613	....	365y	Kirishima (Kyushu-Japan)	0802-09=	2?	
1613	....	?	Orizaba, Pico de (México)	1401-10=	0	
? 1613	....	?	San Cristóbal (Nicaragua)	1404-02=		
1613	....	?	Telica (Nicaragua)	1404-04=	2?	
? 1613	....	?	Masaya (Nicaragua)	1404-10=	0	
1613	0808	?	Aso (Kyushu-Japan)	0802-11=	2	
1614	Cont	....	Stromboli (Italy)	0101-04=	1	
1614	Cont	....	Kirishima (Kyushu-Japan)	0802-09=	2	
1614	Cont	....	Fogo (Cape Verde Is)	1804-01=	1	
? 1614	....	?	Banda Api (Banda Sea)	0605-09=		
1614	....	?	Fuego (Guatemala)	1402-09=	2	
1614	0701?	>3yr	Etna (Italy)	0101-06=	2	9/6
1615	Cont	....	Stromboli (Italy)	0101-04=	1	
1615	Cont	....	Etna (Italy)	0101-06=	2	
1615	Cont	....	Fogo (Cape Verde Is)	1804-01=	1	
1615	....	>3yr	Kirishima (Kyushu-Japan)	0802-09=	2?	
1615	0316	30m?	Banda Api (Banda Sea)	0605-09=	3	
? 1615	0807?	?	Ibusuki [Kaimon] (Kyushu-Japan)	0802-07=		
1616	Cont	....	Stromboli (Italy)	0101-04=	1	
1616	Cont	....	Etna (Italy)	0101-06=	2	
1616	Cont	....	Kirishima (Kyushu-Japan)	0802-09=	2	
1616	Cont	....	Fogo (Cape Verde Is)	1804-01=	1	
1616	0219	4a	Mayon (Luzon-Philippines)	0703-03=	3	
1616	0704	<1	Galeras (Colombia)	1501-08=	3↑	
1616	0706	?	Manam (New Guinea-NE of)	0501-02=	2?	
1617	Cont	....	Stromboli (Italy)	0101-04=	1	
1617	Cont	....	Etna (Italy)	0101-06=	2	
1617	Cont	....	Kirishima (Kyushu-Japan)	0802-09=	2	
1617	Cont	....	Fogo (Cape Verde Is)	1804-01=	1	
1617	....	3a	Fuego (Guatemala)	1402-09=	3	
1618	Cont	....	Stromboli (Italy)	0101-04=	1	
1618	Cont	....	Etna (Italy)	0101-06=	2	
1618	Cont	....	Kirishima (Kyushu-Japan)	0802-09=	2	
1618	Cont	....	Fogo (Cape Verde Is)	1804-01=	1	
1618	....	?	Vulcano (Italy)	0101-05=		
1618	0131	?	Iwaki (Honshu-Japan)	0803-27=	2	
1619	Cont	....	Etna (Italy)	0101-06=	2	
1619	Cont	....	Fogo (Cape Verde Is)	1804-01=	1	
1619	....	....	Stromboli (Italy)	0101-04=	2?	
1619	0729	?	Grímsvötn (Iceland-NE)	1703-01=	2	
1620	Cont	....	Stromboli (Italy)	0101-04=	1	
1620	Cont	....	Etna (Italy)	0101-06=	2	
1620	Cont	....	Fogo (Cape Verde Is)	1804-01=	1	
1620	....	?	Kirishima (Kyushu-Japan)	0802-09=	2?	
1620	....	?	Zao (Honshu-Japan)	0803-19=	2?	
M 1620 ?	....	?	Southern EPR-Segment I (Pacific)	1304-14-	0	
1620	....	?	Fuego (Guatemala)	1402-09=	2	
1620	0603	?	Aso (Kyushu-Japan)	0802-11=	2	
1621	Cont	....	Stromboli (Italy)	0101-04=	1	
1621	Cont	....	Etna (Italy)	0101-06=	2	
1621	Cont	....	Fogo (Cape Verde Is)	1804-01=	1	
? 1621	....	?	Santa Ana (El Salvador)	1403-02=		
1622	Cont	....	Stromboli (Italy)	0101-04=	1	
1622	Cont	....	Etna (Italy)	0101-06=	2	
1622	Cont	....	Fogo (Cape Verde Is)	1804-01=	1	
1622	....	?	Zao (Honshu-Japan)	0803-19=	2?	
I 1622 ?	....	?	Grímsvötn (Iceland-NE)	1703-01=		
1622	0608	1a	Colima (México)	1401-04=	4	
1623	Cont	....	Stromboli (Italy)	0101-04=	1	
1623	Cont	....	Etna (Italy)	0101-06=	2	
1623	Cont	....	Fogo (Cape Verde Is)	1804-01=	1	
1623	....	?	Oshima (Izu Is-Japan)	0804-01=		
1623 ?	....	?	Pacaya (Guatemala)	1402-11=	3	
1623	....	?	Ruiz, Nevado del (Colombia)	1501-02=	1?	
1623	01	?	Fuego (Guatemala)	1402-09=	2	
1623	0515?	549m?	Zao (Honshu-Japan)	0803-19=	3	
1624	Cont	....	Stromboli (Italy)	0101-04=	1	
1624	Cont	....	Etna (Italy)	0101-06=	2	
1624	Cont	....	Fogo (Cape Verde Is)	1804-01=	1	
1624	0206	....	Zao (Honshu-Japan)	0803-19=	2?	
1625	Cont	....	Stromboli (Italy)	0101-04=	1	
1625	Cont	....	Fogo (Cape Verde Is)	1804-01=	1	
1625	....	?	Nikko-Shirane (Honshu-Japan)	0803-14=	3	
M 1625 ?	....	?	Southern EPR-Segment K (Pacific)	1304-12-	0	
1625	0902	12a	Katla (Iceland-S)	1702-03=	5	-/9
1626	Cont	....	Stromboli (Italy)	0101-04=	1	
1626	Cont	....	Fogo (Cape Verde Is)	1804-01=	1	
1626	03	15m	Vulcano (Italy)	0101-05=	3	
1626	0519	57m?	Usu (Hokkaido-Japan)	0805-03=		
1627	Cont	....	Stromboli (Italy)	0101-04=	1	
1627	Cont	....	Fogo (Cape Verde Is)	1804-01=	1	
? 1627	....	?	Fuji (Honshu-Japan)	0803-03=		
1628	Cont	....	Stromboli (Italy)	0101-04=	1	
1628	Cont	....	Fogo (Cape Verde Is)	1804-01=	1	
1628	10	?	Sangay (Ecuador)	1502-09=	3↑	
1628	1026	?	Kirishima (Kyushu-Japan)	0802-09=	2?	
1629	Cont	....	Stromboli (Italy)	0101-04=	1	
1629	Cont	....	Fogo (Cape Verde Is)	1804-01=	1	
1629	....	>3yr	Fuego (Guatemala)	1402-09=	2	
1629	....	?	Grímsvötn (Iceland-NE)	1703-01=	2	
1630	Cont	....	Stromboli (Italy)	0101-04=	1	
1630	Cont	....	Fuego (Guatemala)	1402-09=	2	
1630	Cont	....	Fogo (Cape Verde Is)	1804-01=	1	
C 1630 t	....	?	Raoul Island (Kermadec Is)	0402-03=	4	-/8
1630	....	?	Zao (Honshu-Japan)	0803-19=	2?	
C 1630 t	....	?	Soufrière Hills (W Indies)	1600-05=		7/-
1630	0903	60a	Furnas (Azores)	1802-10=	5	7/9
1631	Cont	....	Stromboli (Italy)	0101-04=	1	
1631	Cont	....	Fuego (Guatemala)	1402-09=	2	
1631	Cont	....	Fogo (Cape Verde Is)	1804-01=	1	
1631	....	?	Vulcano (Italy)	0101-05=		
@ 1631	0214?	?	Dama Ali (Ethiopia)	0201-141		
1631	12	?	Aso (Kyushu-Japan)	0802-11=	2	
1631	1216	45a?	Vesuvius (Italy)	0101-02=	5?	-/9
1632	Cont	....	Vesuvius (Italy)	0101-02=	5?	-/9
1632	Cont	....	Stromboli (Italy)	0101-04=	1	
1632	Cont	....	Fuego (Guatemala)	1402-09=	2	
1632	Cont	....	Fogo (Cape Verde Is)	1804-01=	1	
1632	....	?	Campi Flegrei Mar Sicilia (Italy)	0101-07=	0	
I 1632 ?	....	?	Grímsvötn (Iceland-NE)	1703-01=		
1632	1216	?	Banda Api (Banda Sea)	0605-09=	3↑	
1633	Cont	....	Stromboli (Italy)	0101-04=	1	
1633	Cont	....	Fogo (Cape Verde Is)	1804-01=	1	
? 1633	0221	?	Etna (Italy)	0101-06=		
1634	Cont	....	Stromboli (Italy)	0101-04=	1	
1634	Cont	....	Fogo (Cape Verde Is)	1804-01=	1	
1634	....	?	Taal (Luzon-Philippines)	0703-07=	3↑	
1634	....	?	Oshima (Izu Is-Japan)	0804-01=		
1634	1219?	>3yr	Etna (Italy)	0101-06=	1	8/5
1635	Cont	....	Stromboli (Italy)	0101-04=	1	
1635	Cont	....	Etna (Italy)	0101-06=	1	8/5
1635	Cont	....	Fogo (Cape Verde Is)	1804-01=	1	
1635	....	?	Taal (Luzon-Philippines)	0703-07=	3↑	
1635 <	....	?	Pelée (W Indies)	1600-12=		
1635	0329	?	Gamalama (Halmahera-Indonesia)	0608-06=	2	
1635	1118	?	Banda Api (Banda Sea)	0605-09=	1?	
1636	Cont	....	Stromboli (Italy)	0101-04=	1	
1636	Cont	....	Etna (Italy)	0101-06=	1	8/5
1636	Cont	....	Fogo (Cape Verde Is)	1804-01=	1	
1636	0508	390m	Hekla (Iceland-S)	1702-07=	3	-/7
1637	Cont	....	Stromboli (Italy)	0101-04=	1	
1637	Cont	....	Etna (Italy)	0101-06=	1	8/5
1637	Cont	....	Hekla (Iceland-S)	1702-07=	2	-/7
1637	Cont	....	Fogo (Cape Verde Is)	1804-01=	1	
1637	....	365y	Kirishima (Kyushu-Japan)	0802-09=	2?	
1637	0701	>3yr	Vesuvius (Italy)	0101-02=	2	
1637	0826	232m	Oshima (Izu Is-Japan)	0804-01=		
1637	0929	6a	Aso (Kyushu-Japan)	0802-11=	2	
1637	10	136s	Vestmannaeyjar (Iceland-S)	1702-01=		
1638	Cont	....	Vesuvius (Italy)	0101-02=	2	
1638	Cont	....	Etna (Italy)	0101-06=	1	8/5
1638	Cont	....	Kirishima (Kyushu-Japan)	0802-09=	2	
1638	Cont	....	Oshima (Izu Is-Japan)	0804-01=		
1638	Cont	....	Vestmannaeyjar (Iceland-S)	1702-01=		
1638	Cont	....	Fogo (Cape Verde Is)	1804-01=	1	
1638	....	?	Raung (Java)	0603-34=	4?	-/8
1638	0224d	?	Grímsvötn (Iceland-NE)	1703-01=	2	
1638	0327	....	Stromboli (Italy)	0101-04=	2	
1638	0703	25a	Sete Cidades (Azores)	1802-08=	2	
1638	0725	?	Usu (Hokkaido-Japan)	0805-03=		
1639	Cont	....	Vesuvius (Italy)	0101-02=	2	
1639	Cont	....	Stromboli (Italy)	0101-04=	1	
1639	Cont	....	Fogo (Cape Verde Is)	1804-01=	1	
1640	Cont	....	Vesuvius (Italy)	0101-02=	2	
1640	Cont	....	Stromboli (Italy)	0101-04=	1	
1640	Cont	....	Fogo (Cape Verde Is)	1804-01=	1	
1640	....	?	Fournaise, Piton de la (Indian O.)	0303-02=	2	
C 1640 ?	....	?	Mauna Loa (Hawaiian Is)	1302-02=	0	
1640	....	365y	Tungurahua (Ecuador)	1502-08=	3?	
1640	....	?	Osorno (Chile-S)	1508-01=	2	
1640 <	....	?	Saba (W Indies)	1600-01=		
C 1640 t	....	?	Soufrière St. Vincent (W Indies)	1600-15=		

START YEAR	M-Dy	Duration	VOLCANO NAME (Subregion)	NUMBER	VEI	Vol L/T
1640	02	?	**Llaima** (Chile-C)	1507-11=	4	
? 1640	0203	?	*Villarrica (Chile-C)*	1507-12=		
1640	0731	70a	**Komaga-take** (Hokkaido-Japan)	0805-02=	5	-/9
? 1640	12	20m	*Awu (Sangihe Is-Indonesia)*	0607-04=	3↑	
1640	1226e	9e	*Parker (Mindanao-Philippines)*	0701-011	2?	-/9
1641	Cont	....	*Vesuvius (Italy)*	0101-02=	2	
1641	Cont	....	*Stromboli (Italy)*	0101-04=	1	
? 1641	Cont	....	*Awu (Sangihe Is-Indonesia)*	0607-04=	3↑	
1641	Cont	....	*Tungurahua (Ecuador)*	1502-08=	3?	
1641	Cont	....	*Fogo (Cape Verde Is)*	1804-01=	1	
? 1641	....	?	*Wilis (Java)*	0603-27=		
1641	....	?	**Kelut** (Java)	0603-28=	4?	-/8
1641	....	?	**Taal** (Luzon-Philippines)	0703-07=	3	
1641	....	?	**Zao** (Honshu-Japan)	0803-19=	2?	
1641	....	730y	**Galeras** (Colombia)	1501-08=	3	
I 1641 c	....	?	**Deception Island** (Antarctica)	1900-03=		
1641	0104	....	**Parker** (Mindanao-Philippines)	0701-011	5?	-/9
1642	Cont	....	*Vesuvius (Italy)*	0101-02=	2	
1642	Cont	....	*Stromboli (Italy)*	0101-04=	1	
1642	Cont	....	*Galeras (Colombia)*	1501-08=	3	
1642	Cont	....	*Fogo (Cape Verde Is)*	1804-01=	1	
1642	....	?	**Popocatépetl** (México)	1401-09=	2	
1642	0406	?	**Sakura-jima** (Kyushu-Japan)	0802-08=	2?	
1643	Cont	....	*Vesuvius (Italy)*	0101-02=	2	
1643	Cont	....	*Stromboli (Italy)*	0101-04=	1	
1643	Cont	....	*Galeras (Colombia)*	1501-08=	3	
1643	Cont	....	*Fogo (Cape Verde Is)*	1804-01=	1	
1643	0220	8a	**Etna** (Italy)	0101-06=	1	6/5
1643	0331	15m	**Miyake-jima** (Izu Is-Japan)	0804-04=	3	6/7
1643	0420	?	**Karkar** (New Guinea-NE of)	0501-03=	3↑	
1643	0421	?	**Manam** (New Guinea-NE of)	0501-02=	2	
? 1643	0615	?	*Gamalama (Halmahera-Indonesia)*	0608-06=	2?	
1644	Cont	....	*Vesuvius (Italy)*	0101-02=	2	
1644	Cont	....	*Stromboli (Italy)*	0101-04=	1	
1644	Cont	....	*Fogo (Cape Verde Is)*	1804-01=	1	
1644	....	730y?	**Tungurahua** (Ecuador)	1502-08=	2	
1644	....	?	**Osorno** (Chile-S)	1508-01=	2	
1644	0220	?	**Asama** (Honshu-Japan)	0803-11=	2	
1645	Cont	....	*Vesuvius (Italy)*	0101-02=	2	
1645	Cont	....	*Stromboli (Italy)*	0101-04=	1	
1645	Cont	....	*Tungurahua (Ecuador)*	1502-08=	2	
1645	Cont	....	*Fogo (Cape Verde Is)*	1804-01=	1	
1645	....	?	**Taal** (Luzon-Philippines)	0703-07=	3↑	
1645	0224?	86a?	**Asama** (Honshu-Japan)	0803-11=	2	
1646	Cont	....	*Vesuvius (Italy)*	0101-02=	2	
1646	Cont	....	*Stromboli (Italy)*	0101-04=	1	
1646	Cont	....	*Tungurahua (Ecuador)*	1502-08=	2	
1646	Cont	....	*Fogo (Cape Verde Is)*	1804-01=	1	
1646 e	....	?	**Awu** (Sangihe Is-Indonesia)	0607-04=	2?	
1646	0719	2a	**Makian** (Halmahera-Indonesia)	0608-07=	4?	-/8
1646	1002	80a	**La Palma** (Canary Is)	1803-01-	2	7/6
1646	1120	58a	**Etna** (Italy)	0101-06=	2	8/6
1647	Cont	....	*Vesuvius (Italy)*	0101-02=	2	
1647	Cont	....	*Stromboli (Italy)*	0101-04=	1	
1647	Cont	....	*Etna (Italy)*	0101-06=	2	8/6
1647	Cont	....	*Fogo (Cape Verde Is)*	1804-01=	1	
1647	0218	35a	**Asama** (Honshu-Japan)	0803-11=	2	
1647	0513	?	**Villarrica** (Chile-C)	1507-12=	1?	
1648	Cont	....	*Vesuvius (Italy)*	0101-02=	2	
1648	Cont	....	*Stromboli (Italy)*	0101-04=	1	
1648	Cont	....	*Fogo (Cape Verde Is)*	1804-01=	1	
1648	0320?	?	**Asama** (Honshu-Japan)	0803-11=	2	
1648	0615	3a	**Gamalama** (Halmahera-Indonesia)	0608-06=	2	
1648	0830?	?	**Asama** (Honshu-Japan)	0803-11=	2	
1649	Cont	....	*Stromboli (Italy)*	0101-04=	1	
1649	Cont	....	*Fogo (Cape Verde Is)*	1804-01=	1	
1649	....	?	**Fournaise, Piton de la** (Indian O.)	0303-02=	2	
1649	02	?	**Nikko-Shirane** (Honshu-Japan)	0803-14=	2	-/6
1649	07	31p	**Aso** (Kyushu-Japan)	0802-11=	2	
1649	0817?	1a?	**Asama** (Honshu-Japan)	0803-11=	2	
1649	1128	....	*Vesuvius (Italy)*	0101-02=	2	
1650	Cont	....	*Vesuvius (Italy)*	0101-02=	2	
1650	Cont	....	*Stromboli (Italy)*	0101-04=	1	
1650	Cont	....	*Fogo (Cape Verde Is)*	1804-01=	1	
1650 t	....	?	**Cameroon** (Africa-W)	0204-01=	3↑	
C 1650 t	....	?	**Bamus** (New Britain-SW Pac)	0502-11=		
G 1650 p	....	?	**Savo** (Solomon Is-SW Pacific)	0505-07=		
1650 t	....	?	**Paluweh** (Lesser Sunda Is)	0604-15=	3	
C 1650 ?	....	?	**Ebeko** (Kuril Is)	0900-38=		
1650 t	....	?	**Mutnovsky** (Kamchatka)	1000-06=	2	
G 1650 j	....	?	**Shiveluch** (Kamchatka)	1000-27=	5	-/9
T 1650 v	....	?	**Augustine** (Alaska-SW)	1103-01-		
C 1650 ?	....	?	**Iliamna** (Alaska-SW)	1103-02-		
T 1650 t	....	?	**Spurr** (Alaska-SW)	1103-04-		
? 1650 ?	....	?	*Lassen [Chaos Crags] (US-Calif)*	1203-08-		
T 1650 t	....	?	**Kilauea** (Hawaiian Is)	1302-01-	0	

START YEAR	M-Dy	Duration	VOLCANO NAME (Subregion)	NUMBER	VEI	Vol L/T
C 1650 ?	....	?	**Mauna Loa** (Hawaiian Is)	1302-02=	0	
C 1650 t	....	?	**Hualalai** (Hawaiian Is)	1302-04-	1	
U 1650 v	....	?	**Unnamed [East Pacific Rise]**	1304-05-	0	
? 1650 t	....	?	*Sumaco (Ecuador)*	1502-04=	3?	
1650 t	....	?	**Chillán, Nevados de** (Chile-C)	1507-07=	3?	
? 1650 t	....	?	*Minchinmávida (Chile-S)*	1508-04=		
? 1650	0702?	?	*Asama (Honshu-Japan)*	0803-11=	2?	
1650	0927	70a	**Santorini** (Greece)	0102-04=	4?	-/8
1650	1027	?	**Nemrut Dagi** (Turkey)	0103-02=		
1651	Cont	....	*Vesuvius (Italy)*	0101-02=	2	
1651	Cont	....	*Stromboli (Italy)*	0101-04=	1	
1651	Cont	....	*Fogo (Cape Verde Is)*	1804-01=	1	
1651	....	?	**Vulcano** (Italy)	0101-05=		
1651	0117	914m?	**Etna** (Italy)	0101-06=	1	8/5
1651	0218	54a	**Pacaya** (Guatemala)	1402-11=	2	
1651	0412	?	**Asama** (Honshu-Japan)	0803-11=	2	
1652	Cont	....	*Vesuvius (Italy)*	0101-02=	2	
1652	Cont	....	*Stromboli (Italy)*	0101-04=	1	
1652	Cont	....	*Etna (Italy)*	0101-06=	1	8/5
1652	Cont	....	*Fogo (Cape Verde Is)*	1804-01=	1	
1652	....	?	**Babuyan Claro** (Luzon-N of)	0704-03=	3↑	
1652	....	?	**Aoga-shima** (Izu Is-Japan)	0804-06=	3	
1652	0412	?	**Asama** (Honshu-Japan)	0803-11=	2	
1652	1019	7a	**Picos Volc System** (Azores)	1802-081	2	6/6
1653	Cont	....	*Stromboli (Italy)*	0101-04=	1	
1653	Cont	....	*Etna (Italy)*	0101-06=	1	8/5
1653	Cont	....	*Fogo (Cape Verde Is)*	1804-01=	1	
? 1653	....	365y	*Asama (Honshu-Japan)*	0803-11=	2?	
1653	1231y	?	**Gamalama** (Halmahera-Indonesia)	0608-06=	3↑	
1654	Cont	....	*Stromboli (Italy)*	0101-04=	1	
? 1654	Cont	....	*Asama (Honshu-Japan)*	0803-11=	2?	
1654	Cont	....	*Fogo (Cape Verde Is)*	1804-01=	1	
1654	0101	912w?	**Etna** (Italy)	0101-06=	1	
1654	0225	>3yr	*Vesuvius (Italy)*	0101-02=	2?	
1655	Cont	....	*Vesuvius (Italy)*	0101-02=	2?	
1655	Cont	....	*Stromboli (Italy)*	0101-04=	1	
1655	Cont	....	*Etna (Italy)*	0101-06=	1	
1655	Cont	....	*Fogo (Cape Verde Is)*	1804-01=	1	
D 1655 ?	....	?	**Taranaki [Egmont]** (New Zealand)	0401-03=	4	-/8
1655	0415q	?	**Kverkfjöll** (Iceland-NE)	1703-05=	0	
1655	07	?	**Pacaya** (Guatemala)	1402-11=	2	
1655	1125	?	**Asama** (Honshu-Japan)	0803-11=	2	
1656	Cont	....	*Vesuvius (Italy)*	0101-02=	2?	
1656	Cont	....	*Stromboli (Italy)*	0101-04=	1	
1656	Cont	....	*Etna (Italy)*	0101-06=	1	
1656	Cont	....	*Fogo (Cape Verde Is)*	1804-01=	1	
1656	1210	?	**Asama** (Honshu-Japan)	0803-11=	2	
1657	Cont	....	*Vesuvius (Italy)*	0101-02=	2?	
1657	Cont	....	*Stromboli (Italy)*	0101-04=	1	
1657	Cont	....	*Fogo (Cape Verde Is)*	1804-01=	1	
1657	0315	?	**Villarrica** (Chile-C)	1507-12=	1?	
1657	1125	?	**Asama** (Honshu-Japan)	0803-11=	2	
1658	Cont	....	*Vesuvius (Italy)*	0101-02=	2?	
1658	Cont	....	*Stromboli (Italy)*	0101-04=	1	
1658	Cont	....	*Fogo (Cape Verde Is)*	1804-01=	1	
1658	....	?	**Merapi** (Java)	0603-25=	3↑	
1658	0724	?	**Asama** (Honshu-Japan)	0803-11=	2	
1658	10 ?	?	**Haku-san** (Honshu-Japan)	0803-05=	2?	
1658	1103	?	**San Salvador** (El Salvador)	1403-05=	3	7/-
1659	Cont	....	*Vesuvius (Italy)*	0101-02=	2?	
1659	Cont	....	*Stromboli (Italy)*	0101-04=	1	
1659	Cont	....	*Fogo (Cape Verde Is)*	1804-01=	1	
1659	02	868w	**Kirishima** (Kyushu-Japan)	0802-09=	2?	
1659	04	>3yr	**Chokai** (Honshu-Japan)	0803-22=		
1659	0421	109a	**Haku-san** (Honshu-Japan)	0803-05=	2?	
1659	06	?	**Gamalama** (Halmahera-Indonesia)	0608-06=	2	
1659	0724	?	**Asama** (Honshu-Japan)	0803-11=	2	
1659	11	?	**Grímsvötn** (Iceland-NE)	1703-01=	2	
1659	1111	?	**Teon** (Banda Sea)	0605-05=	3↑	
1660	Cont	....	*Stromboli (Italy)*	0101-04=	1	
1660	Cont	....	*Kirishima (Kyushu-Japan)*	0802-09=	2?	
1660	Cont	....	*Chokai (Honshu-Japan)*	0803-22=		
1660	Cont	....	*Fogo (Cape Verde Is)*	1804-01=	1	
G 1660 r	....	?	**Nabukelevu** (Fiji Is-SW Pacific)	0405-03-		
C 1660 p	....	?	**Long Island** (New Guinea-NE of)	0501-05=	6	-/10
1660	....	?	**Lewotolo** (Lesser Sunda Is)	0604-23=	3↑	
? 1660	....	?	*Makian (Halmahera-Indonesia)*	0608-07=		
1660	....	?	**Planchón-Peteroa** (Chile-C)	1507-04=	3↑	
1660	02	?	**Teon** (Banda Sea)	0605-05=	4?	-/8
1660	0408?	?	**Asama** (Honshu-Japan)	0803-11=	2	
1660	0703	....	**Vesuvius** (Italy)	0101-02=	3	
1660	1027	32a	**Guagua Pichincha** (Ecuador)	1502-02=	4	-/8
1660	1103	240w	**Katla** (Iceland-S)	1702-03=	4	-/8
1661	Cont	....	*Vesuvius (Italy)*	0101-02=	2?	
1661	Cont	....	*Stromboli (Italy)*	0101-04=	1	
1661	Cont	....	*Kirishima (Kyushu-Japan)*	0802-09=	2?	
1661	Cont	....	*Chokai (Honshu-Japan)*	0803-22=		

	START YEAR	M-Dy	Duration	VOLCANO NAME (Subregion)	NUMBER	VEI	Vol L/T
	1661	Cont	....	Katla (Iceland-S)	1702-03=	2	-/8
	1661	Cont	....	Fogo (Cape Verde Is)	1804-01=	1	
	1661	0414	13a	Asama (Honshu-Japan)	0803-11=	2	
	1661	1021	?	Asama (Honshu-Japan)	0803-11=	2	
	1662	Cont	....	Vesuvius (Italy)	0101-02=	2?	
	1662	Cont	....	Stromboli (Italy)	0101-04=	1	
	1662	Cont	....	Chokai (Honshu-Japan)	0803-22=		
	1662	Cont	....	Fogo (Cape Verde Is)	1804-01=	1	
	1662	....	?	Ubinas (Perú)	1504-02=	3?	
	1662	0126?	?	Kuju (Kyushu-Japan)	0802-12=	2?	
	1662	09	655w	Kirishima (Kyushu-Japan)	0802-09=	2?	
	1663	Cont	....	Vesuvius (Italy)	0101-02=	2?	
	1663	Cont	....	Stromboli (Italy)	0101-04=	1	
	1663	Cont	....	Kirishima (Kyushu-Japan)	0802-09=	2	
	1663	Cont	....	Chokai (Honshu-Japan)	0803-22=		
	1663	Cont	....	Fogo (Cape Verde Is)	1804-01=	1	
	1663	....	?	Atitlán (Guatemala)	1402-06=	2	
	1663	0118	?	Teon (Banda Sea)	0605-05=	3↑	
	1663	04	25a	Unzen (Kyushu-Japan)	0802-10=	2?	
	1663	0816	20d	Usu (Hokkaido-Japan)	0805-03=	5	-/9
	1663	1013	737a	Popocatépetl (México)	1401-09=	3?	
	1663	1211	16a>	Unzen (Kyushu-Japan)	0802-10=	2?	6/-
	1663	1231y	?	Merapi (Java)	0603-25=	3↑	
	1664	Cont	....	Vesuvius (Italy)	0101-02=	2?	
	1664	Cont	....	Stromboli (Italy)	0101-04=	1	
	1664	Cont	....	Kirishima (Kyushu-Japan)	0802-09=	2	
	1664	Cont	....	Popocatépetl (México)	1401-09=	2	
	1664	Cont	....	Fogo (Cape Verde Is)	1804-01=	1	
	1664	....	?	Iwo-Tori-shima (Ryukyu Is)	0802-02=		
	1664	....	7a?	Pacaya (Guatemala)	1402-11=	3	
	1664	0115?	?	San Martín (México)	1401-11=	3	
	1665	Cont	....	Vesuvius (Italy)	0101-02=	2?	
	1665	Cont	....	Stromboli (Italy)	0101-04=	1	
	1665	Cont	....	Popocatépetl (México)	1401-09=	2	
	1665	Cont	....	Fogo (Cape Verde Is)	1804-01=	1	
	1665	....	?	Grímsvötn (Iceland-NE)	1703-01=		
	1666	Cont	....	Vesuvius (Italy)	0101-02=	2?	
	1666	Cont	....	Stromboli (Italy)	0101-04=	1	
	1666	Cont	....	Fogo (Cape Verde Is)	1804-01=	1	
D	1666 ?	....	?	Lassen [Cinder Cone] (US-Calif)	1203-08-	3?	
	1666	....	730y	Popocatépetl (México)	1401-09=	2?	
	1667	Cont	....	Vesuvius (Italy)	0101-02=	2?	
	1667	Cont	....	Stromboli (Italy)	0101-04=	1	
	1667	Cont	....	Popocatépetl (México)	1401-09=	2?	
	1667	Cont	....	Fogo (Cape Verde Is)	1804-01=	1	
?	1667	....	?	Kirishima (Kyushu-Japan)	0802-09=		
	1667	....	?	Ubinas (Perú)	1504-02=	3	
	1667	0923	3a?	Shikotsu [Tarumai] (Hokkaido)	0805-04=	5	-/9
	1668	Cont	....	Vesuvius (Italy)	0101-02=	2?	
	1668	Cont	....	Stromboli (Italy)	0101-04=	1	
	1668	Cont	....	Fogo (Cape Verde Is)	1804-01=	1	
	1668	02	?	Aso (Kyushu-Japan)	0802-11=	2	
	1668	06	?	Changbaishan (China-E)	1005-06-		
	1668	08	321w	Aso (Kyushu-Japan)	0802-11=	2	
	1668	08	?	Zao (Honshu-Japan)	0803-19=	2?	
	1668	08	317m	Pacaya (Guatemala)	1402-11=	2	
	1669	Cont	....	Vesuvius (Italy)	0101-02=	2?	
	1669	Cont	....	Stromboli (Italy)	0101-04=	1	
	1669	Cont	....	Aso (Kyushu-Japan)	0802-11=	2	
	1669	Cont	....	Pacaya (Guatemala)	1402-11=	2	
	1669	Cont	....	Fogo (Cape Verde Is)	1804-01=	1	
	1669	....	?	Fournaise, Piton de la (Indian O.)	0303-02=	2	
	1669	....	?	Zao (Honshu-Japan)	0803-19=	3	
	1669	....	?	Pagan (Mariana Is-C Pacific)	0804-17=		
	1669	0311	122a?	Etna (Italy)	0101-06=	3?	9/8
	1669	0405	10a	Asama (Honshu-Japan)	0803-11=	2	
	1670	Cont	....	Vesuvius (Italy)	0101-02=	2?	
	1670	Cont	....	Stromboli (Italy)	0101-04=	1	
	1670	Cont	....	Fogo (Cape Verde Is)	1804-01=	1	
A	1670 ?	....	?	Aoba (Vanuatu-SW Pacific)	0507-03=	2?	
	1670	....	>3yr	Aoga-shima (Izu Is-Japan)	0804-06=	2	
C	1670 ?	....	?	Ebeko (Kuril Is)	0900-38=		
	1670	....	?	Masaya (Nicaragua)	1404-10=	3	7/-
	1670	....	>3yr	Galeras (Colombia)	1501-08=	2	
	1670	0426	153a	Zao (Honshu-Japan)	0803-19=	2	
?	1670	0601	?	Sakura-jima (Kyushu-Japan)	0802-08=	2?	
	1670	0813	....	Zao (Honshu-Japan)	0803-19=	2?	
	1671	Cont	....	Vesuvius (Italy)	0101-02=	2?	
	1671	Cont	....	Stromboli (Italy)	0101-04=	1	
	1671	Cont	....	Aoga-shima (Izu Is-Japan)	0804-06=	2	
	1671	Cont	....	Galeras (Colombia)	1501-08=	2	
	1671	Cont	....	Fogo (Cape Verde Is)	1804-01=	1	
	1671	....	?	Fournaise, Piton de la (Indian O.)	0303-02=	2	
	1671 ?	....	?	Iya (Lesser Sunda Is)	0604-11=	3↑	
?	1671	....	?	Aso (Kyushu-Japan)	0802-11=	2	
	1671	08	?	Pacaya (Guatemala)	1402-11=	2	
	1671	08 ?	?	San Salvador (El Salvador)	1403-05=	2?	
	1672	Cont	....	Vesuvius (Italy)	0101-02=	2?	
	1672	Cont	....	Stromboli (Italy)	0101-04=	1	
	1672	Cont	....	Aoga-shima (Izu Is-Japan)	0804-06=	2	
	1672	Cont	....	Galeras (Colombia)	1501-08=	2	
	1672	Cont	....	Fogo (Cape Verde Is)	1804-01=	1	
	1672	....	?	Fournaise, Piton de la (Indian O.)	0303-02=	2	
?	1672 ?	....	?	Smith Rock (Izu Is-Japan)	0804-08=	0	
	1672	0424	340a	Fayal (Azores)	1802-01=	2	
?	1672	0712	16a	Iwaki (Honshu-Japan)	0803-27=	2?	
	1672	0804	?	Merapi (Java)	0603-25=	3	
	1673	Cont	....	Vesuvius (Italy)	0101-02=	2?	
	1673	Cont	....	Stromboli (Italy)	0101-04=	1	
	1673	Cont	....	Aoga-shima (Izu Is-Japan)	0804-06=	2	
	1673	Cont	....	Galeras (Colombia)	1501-08=	2	
	1673	Cont	....	Fayal (Azores)	1802-01=	2	
	1673	Cont	....	Fogo (Cape Verde Is)	1804-01=	1	
	1673	0520	?	Gamkonora (Halmahera-Indonesia)	0608-04=	5?	-/9
	1674	Cont	....	Vesuvius (Italy)	0101-02=	2?	
	1674	Cont	....	Stromboli (Italy)	0101-04=	1	
	1674	Cont	....	Aoga-shima (Izu Is-Japan)	0804-06=	2	
	1674	Cont	....	Galeras (Colombia)	1501-08=	2	
	1674	Cont	....	Fogo (Cape Verde Is)	1804-01=	1	
	1674	07	?	Pacaya (Guatemala)	1402-11=	2	
	1675	Cont	....	Vesuvius (Italy)	0101-02=	2?	
	1675	Cont	....	Stromboli (Italy)	0101-04=	1	
	1675	Cont	....	Aoga-shima (Izu Is-Japan)	0804-06=	2	
	1675	Cont	....	Galeras (Colombia)	1501-08=	2	
	1675	Cont	....	Fogo (Cape Verde Is)	1804-01=	1	
	1675 q	....	?	Lewotobi (Lesser Sunda Is)	0604-18=	3↑	
	1675	....	?	Karangetang [Api Siau] (Sangihe Is	0607-02=	3↑	
	1675	0216	?	Aso (Kyushu-Japan)	0802-11=	2	
	1675	06 ?	?	Kuju (Kyushu-Japan)	0802-12=	2?	
	1676	Cont	....	Vesuvius (Italy)	0101-02=	2?	
	1676	Cont	....	Stromboli (Italy)	0101-04=	1	
	1676	Cont	....	Aoga-shima (Izu Is-Japan)	0804-06=	2	
	1676	Cont	....	Galeras (Colombia)	1501-08=	2	
	1676	Cont	....	Fogo (Cape Verde Is)	1804-01=	1	
	1676	1231y	?	Gamalama (Halmahera-Indonesia)	0608-06=	2	
	1677	Cont	....	Vesuvius (Italy)	0101-02=	2?	
	1677	Cont	....	Stromboli (Italy)	0101-04=	1	
	1677	Cont	....	Aoga-shima (Izu Is-Japan)	0804-06=	2	
	1677	Cont	....	Galeras (Colombia)	1501-08=	2	
	1677	Cont	....	Fogo (Cape Verde Is)	1804-01=	1	
	1677	....	?	Merapi (Java)	0603-25=	3↑	
	1677	....	?	Kirishima (Kyushu-Japan)	0802-09=	2?	
	1677	....	?	Ubinas (Perú)	1504-02=	3?	
?	1677	....	?	Hierro (Canary Is)	1803-02-		
	1677	0502	?	Misti, El (Perú)	1504-01=	2	
?	1677	07	?	Pacaya (Guatemala)	1402-11=		
	1677	1117	65a	La Palma (Canary Is)	1803-01-	2	7/6
	1678	Cont	....	Vesuvius (Italy)	0101-02=	2?	
	1678	Cont	....	Stromboli (Italy)	0101-04=	1	
	1678	Cont	....	Aoga-shima (Izu Is-Japan)	0804-06=	2	
	1678	Cont	....	Galeras (Colombia)	1501-08=	2	
	1678	Cont	....	La Palma (Canary Is)	1803-01-	2	7/6
	1678	Cont	....	Fogo (Cape Verde Is)	1804-01=	1	
	1678	0222?	?	Akita-Yake-yama (Honshu-Japan)	0803-26=	2	-/6
	1678	0229	?	Kirishima (Kyushu-Japan)	0802-09=	2?	
	1678	0301	?	Sakura-jima (Kyushu-Japan)	0802-08=	2?	
	1678	08 ?	3a?	Pacaya (Guatemala)	1402-11=	2	
	1678	0819	?	Merapi (Java)	0603-25=	3↑	
	1679	Cont	....	Vesuvius (Italy)	0101-02=	2?	
	1679	Cont	....	Stromboli (Italy)	0101-04=	1	
	1679	Cont	....	Aoga-shima (Izu Is-Japan)	0804-06=	2	
	1679	Cont	....	Galeras (Colombia)	1501-08=	2	
	1679	Cont	....	Fogo (Cape Verde Is)	1804-01=	1	
?	1679	....	?	Fuego (Guatemala)	1402-09=		
	1680	Cont	....	Vesuvius (Italy)	0101-02=	2?	
	1680	Cont	....	Stromboli (Italy)	0101-04=	1	
	1680	Cont	....	Aoga-shima (Izu Is-Japan)	0804-06=	2	
	1680	Cont	....	Galeras (Colombia)	1501-08=	2	
	1680	Cont	....	Fogo (Cape Verde Is)	1804-01=	1	
	1680	....	?	Tongkoko (Sulawesi-Indonesia)	0606-13=	5?	-/9
C	1680 ?	....	?	Mauna Loa (Hawaiian Is)	1302-02=	0	
	1680	....	?	San Cristóbal (Nicaragua)	1404-02=	2?	
	1680	05	552m>	Krakatau (Indonesia)	0602-00=	3	-/8
	1681	Cont	....	Stromboli (Italy)	0101-04=	1	
	1681	Cont	....	Krakatau (Indonesia)	0602-00=	2	-/8
	1681	Cont	....	Galeras (Colombia)	1501-08=	2	
	1681	Cont	....	Fogo (Cape Verde Is)	1804-01=	1	
@	1681	0410	?	Grímsvötn (Iceland-NE)	1703-01=		
	1682	Cont	....	Stromboli (Italy)	0101-04=	1	
	1682	Cont	....	Galeras (Colombia)	1501-08=	2	
	1682	Cont	....	Fogo (Cape Verde Is)	1804-01=	1	
	1682	0812	10a	Vesuvius (Italy)	0101-02=	3	-/6
	1682	0901	45m?	Etna (Italy)	0101-06=	2	
	1682	1213	?	Sete Cidades (Azores)	1802-08=	2	

	START YEAR	M-Dy	Duration	VOLCANO NAME (Subregion)	NUMBER	VEI	Vol L/T
	1683	Cont	....	Stromboli (Italy)	0101-04=	1	
	1683	Cont	....	Galeras (Colombia)	1501-08=	2	
	1683	Cont	....	Fogo (Cape Verde Is)	1804-01=	1	
	1683	....	?	**Serua** (Banda Sea)	0605-07=	3↑	
	1683	....	?	**Banda Api** (Banda Sea)	0605-09=	3	
	1683	....	?	**Tongkoko** (Sulawesi-Indonesia)	0606-13=	3↑	
L	**1683** ?	....	?	**Penguin Island** (Antarctica)	1900-031		
	1683	06	?	**Aso** (Kyushu-Japan)	0802-11=	2	
	1684	Cont	....	Stromboli (Italy)	0101-04=	1	
	1684	Cont	....	Galeras (Colombia)	1501-08=	2	
	1684	Cont	....	Fogo (Cape Verde Is)	1804-01=	1	
	1684	0201	?	**Krakatau** (Indonesia)	0602-00=	3↑	
	1684	0214	>3yr	**Oshima** (Izu Is-Japan)	0804-01=	3	7/8
	1684	07	?	**San Cristóbal** (Nicaragua)	1404-02=	2	
	1684	1105d	72m	**Grímsvötn** (Iceland-NE)	1703-01=	2	
	1685	Cont	....	Stromboli (Italy)	0101-04=	1	
	1685	Cont	....	Oshima (Izu Is-Japan)	0804-01=	2	7/8
	1685	Cont	....	Galeras (Colombia)	1501-08=	2	
	1685	Cont	....	Grímsvötn (Iceland-NE)	1703-01=	2	
	1685	Cont	....	Fogo (Cape Verde Is)	1804-01=	1	
C	**1685** ?	....	?	**Mauna Loa** (Hawaiian Is)	1302-02=	0	
	1685	08	?	**San Cristóbal** (Nicaragua)	1404-02=	2	
	1685	08	?	**Telica** (Nicaragua)	1404-04=	2	
@	**1685**	09	?	**Fuego** (Guatemala)	1402-09=	2	
	1685	1003	>3yr	Vesuvius (Italy)	0101-02=	2?	
	1686	Cont	....	Vesuvius (Italy)	0101-02=	2?	
	1686	Cont	....	Stromboli (Italy)	0101-04=	1	
	1686	Cont	....	Oshima (Izu Is-Japan)	0804-01=	2	7/8
	1686	Cont	....	Galeras (Colombia)	1501-08=	2	
	1686	Cont	....	Fogo (Cape Verde Is)	1804-01=	1	
	1686	....	?	**Fuego** (Guatemala)	1402-09=	2	
	1686	0326	<1	**Iwate** (Honshu-Japan)	0803-24=	3	-/7
	1686	09 ?	28m?	**Gamalama** (Halmahera-Indonesia)	0608-06=	2	
	1687	Cont	....	Vesuvius (Italy)	0101-02=	2?	
	1687	Cont	....	Stromboli (Italy)	0101-04=	1	
	1687	Cont	....	Oshima (Izu Is-Japan)	0804-01=	2	7/8
	1687	Cont	....	Fogo (Cape Verde Is)	1804-01=	1	
	1687	....	?	**Orizaba, Pico de** (México)	1401-10=	2	
	1687	....	....	Galeras (Colombia)	1501-08=	2	
	1687	0326	2a	**Pacaya** (Guatemala)	1402-11=	2	
?	1687	0414	92m	Iwate (Honshu-Japan)	0803-24=	2?	
	1687	0510	1a	**Gamalama** (Halmahera-Indonesia)	0608-06=	3↑	
	1687	0615	?	**Serua** (Banda Sea)	0605-07=	3↑	
	1688	Cont	....	Vesuvius (Italy)	0101-02=	2?	
	1688	Cont	....	Oshima (Izu Is-Japan)	0804-01=	2	7/8
	1688	Cont	....	Galeras (Colombia)	1501-08=	2	
	1688	Cont	....	Fogo (Cape Verde Is)	1804-01=	1	
	1688	....	?	**Vulcano** (Italy)	0101-05=		
	1688	....	?	**Etna** (Italy)	0101-06=	1	
	1688 ?	....	?	**Villarrica** (Chile-C)	1507-12=	1	
	1688	0605	....	Stromboli (Italy)	0101-04=	2	
	1689	Cont	....	Vesuvius (Italy)	0101-02=	2?	
	1689	Cont	....	Stromboli (Italy)	0101-04=	1	
	1689	Cont	....	Oshima (Izu Is-Japan)	0804-01=	2	7/8
	1689	Cont	....	Galeras (Colombia)	1501-08=	2	
	1689	Cont	....	Fogo (Cape Verde Is)	1804-01=	1	
?	1689	....	?	Fuego (Guatemala)	1402-09=	2	
	1689	0314	?	**Etna** (Italy)	0101-06=	1	7/-
?	1689	0622	?	Iwate (Honshu-Japan)	0803-24=	2?	
	1690	Cont	....	Vesuvius (Italy)	0101-02=	2?	
	1690	Cont	....	Stromboli (Italy)	0101-04=	1	
	1690	Cont	....	Oshima (Izu Is-Japan)	0804-01=	2	7/8
	1690	Cont	....	Fogo (Cape Verde Is)	1804-01=	1	
	1690	....	?	**Guntur** (Java)	0603-13=	3	
	1690	....	>3yr	**Banda Api** (Banda Sea)	0605-09=	3↑	
	1690	....	?	**Kirishima** (Kyushu-Japan)	0802-09=	2?	
?	1690	....	730y	Unzen (Kyushu-Japan)	0802-10=		
?	1690 j	....	?	Asuncion (Mariana Is-C Pacific)	0804-15=		
T	**1690** j	....	?	**Usu** (Hokkaido-Japan)	0805-03=		
T	**1690** j	....	?	**Chikurachki** (Kuril Is)	0900-36=	4	
	1690 j	....	?	**Koshelev** (Kamchatka)	1000-02=	3↑	
G	**1690** w	....	?	**Tseax River Cone** (Canada)	1200-10=		8/-
	1690	....	?	**Colima** (México)	1401-04=	3?	
	1690	....	?	**Pacaya** (Guatemala)	1402-11=	2?	
	1690	....	....	Galeras (Colombia)	1501-08=	2	
	1690	0405>	?	**Soufrière Guadeloupe** (W Indies)	1600-06=	1	
	1691	Cont	....	Vesuvius (Italy)	0101-02=	2?	
	1691	Cont	....	Stromboli (Italy)	0101-04=	1	
	1691	Cont	....	Banda Api (Banda Sea)	0605-09=	2	
?	1691	Cont	....	Unzen (Kyushu-Japan)	0802-10=		
	1691	Cont	....	Galeras (Colombia)	1501-08=	2	
	1691	Cont	....	Fogo (Cape Verde Is)	1804-01=	1	
	1691	....	?	**Reventador** (Ecuador)	1502-01=	3↑	
	1691	04	121p	**Aso** (Kyushu-Japan)	0802-11=	2	
	1692	Cont	....	Vesuvius (Italy)	0101-02=	2?	
	1692	Cont	....	Stromboli (Italy)	0101-04=	1	
	1692	Cont	....	Banda Api (Banda Sea)	0605-09=	2	
?	1692	Cont	....	Unzen (Kyushu-Japan)	0802-10=		
	1692	Cont	....	Galeras (Colombia)	1501-08=	2	
	1692	Cont	....	Fogo (Cape Verde Is)	1804-01=	1	
?	1692	....	?	Liamuiga (W Indies)	1600-03=		
?	1692	....	42c	Hierro (Canary Is)	1803-02-		
?	1692	0413	?	Nemrut Dagi (Turkey)	0103-02=		
?	1692	0604?	?	Serua (Banda Sea)	0605-07=		
	1693	Cont	....	Vesuvius (Italy)	0101-02=	2?	
	1693	Cont	....	Banda Api (Banda Sea)	0605-09=	2	
	1693	Cont	....	Galeras (Colombia)	1501-08=	2	
	1693	Cont	....	Fogo (Cape Verde Is)	1804-01=	1	
	1693	....	?	**Teon** (Banda Sea)	0605-05=	3↑	
	1693	....	?	**Pacaya** (Guatemala)	1402-11=	2?	
?	1693	0109	?	Etna (Italy)	0101-06=		
	1693	0213	214a?	**Hekla** (Iceland-S)	1702-07=	4	-/8
	1693	0604	41m	**Serua** (Banda Sea)	0605-07=	4?	-/8
	1693	0901	....	Stromboli (Italy)	0101-04=	2	
	1693	12	334p?	Etna (Italy)	0101-06=	2	
	1694	Cont	....	Stromboli (Italy)	0101-04=	1	
	1694	Cont	....	Galeras (Colombia)	1501-08=	2	
	1694	Cont	....	Fogo (Cape Verde Is)	1804-01=	1	
	1694	....	?	**Serua** (Banda Sea)	0605-07=	3↑	
	1694	....	?	**Tongkoko** (Sulawesi-Indonesia)	0606-13=	3?	
	1694	03	....	**Etna** (Italy)	0101-06=	3?	
	1694	0413	....	**Vesuvius** (Italy)	0101-02=	3	
	1694	0529	93a?	**Zao** (Honshu-Japan)	0803-19=	2	
?	1694	0619	?	Iwaki (Honshu-Japan)	0803-27=	2?	
	1694	0704	2a	**Komaga-take** (Hokkaido-Japan)	0805-02=	4	-/8
	1694	1130	....	Banda Api (Banda Sea)	0605-09=	3	
	1695	Cont	....	Stromboli (Italy)	0101-04=	1	
	1695	Cont	....	Banda Api (Banda Sea)	0605-09=	2	
	1695	Cont	....	Galeras (Colombia)	1501-08=	2	
	1695	Cont	....	Fogo (Cape Verde Is)	1804-01=	1	
	1695	0412?	?	**Oshima** (Izu Is-Japan)	0804-01=		
	1695	0623	?	**Asama** (Honshu-Japan)	0803-11=	2	
	1696	Cont	....	Stromboli (Italy)	0101-04=	1	
	1696	Cont	....	Banda Api (Banda Sea)	0605-09=	2	
	1696	Cont	....	Fogo (Cape Verde Is)	1804-01=	1	
	1696	....	....	Galeras (Colombia)	1501-08=	2	
	1696	04	?	**Soufrière Guadeloupe** (W Indies)	1600-06=	1	
	1696	0731	14a?	**Vesuvius** (Italy)	0101-02=	2	
	1697	Cont	....	Stromboli (Italy)	0101-04=	1	
	1697	Cont	....	Galeras (Colombia)	1501-08=	2	
	1697	Cont	....	Fogo (Cape Verde Is)	1804-01=	1	
	1697	....	365y	**Kliuchevskoi** (Kamchatka)	1000-26=	3↑	
	1697	....	?	**Grímsvötn** (Iceland-NE)	1703-01=		
I	**1697**	....	?	**Bárdarbunga** (Iceland-NE)	1703-03=	2	
	1697	0915	303m	Vesuvius (Italy)	0101-02=	2	
	1697	1020	?	**Popocatépetl** (México)	1401-09=	1	
	1698	Cont	....	Stromboli (Italy)	0101-04=	1	
	1698	Cont	....	Kliuchevskoi (Kamchatka)	1000-26=	3	
	1698	Cont	....	Galeras (Colombia)	1501-08=	2	
	1698	Cont	....	Fogo (Cape Verde Is)	1804-01=	1	
	1698	....	?	**Cotopaxi** (Ecuador)	1502-05=	3?	
	1698	0203	?	**Cereme** (Java)	0603-17=	3	
	1698	0525	....	**Vesuvius** (Italy)	0101-02=	3	
	1699	Cont	....	Stromboli (Italy)	0101-04=	1	
	1699	Cont	....	Galeras (Colombia)	1501-08=	2	
	1699	Cont	....	Fogo (Cape Verde Is)	1804-01=	1	
	1699	....	?	**Gunungapi Wetar** (Banda Sea)	0605-03=	3↑	
?	1699	....	?	Awu (Sangihe Is-Indonesia)	0607-04=		
?	1699 a	....	?	Tolbachik (Kamchatka)	1000-24=	2?	
	1699	....	?	**Fuego** (Guatemala)	1402-09=	2	
	1699	....	?	**San Miguel** (El Salvador)	1403-10=	2	
?	1699	0105	?	Salak (Java)	0603-05=		
	1699	0629	?	**Pacaya** (Guatemala)	1402-11=	2?	

1700

	START YEAR	M-Dy	Duration	VOLCANO NAME (Subregion)	NUMBER	VEI	Vol L/T
	1700	Cont	....	Stromboli (Italy)	0101-04=	1	
	1700	Cont	....	Galeras (Colombia)	1501-08=	2	
	1700	Cont	....	Fogo (Cape Verde Is)	1804-01=	1	
C	**1700** v	....	?	**Emuruangogolak** (Africa-E)	0202-051	0	
C	**1700** t	....	?	**Taranaki [Egmont]** (New Zealand)	0401-03=		
	1700	....	?	**Fuji** (Honshu-Japan)	0803-03=	2?	
T	**1700** ?	....	?	**Shiveluch** (Kamchatka)	1000-27=	3	-/7
	1700	....	>3yr	**Amak** (Aleutian Is)	1101-39-		
T	**1700** v	....	?	**Glacier Peak** (US-Washington)	1201-02-	2	
M	**1700** q	....	?	**Kilauea** (Hawaiian Is)	1302-01-	0	
T	**1700** ?	....	?	**Cayambe** (Ecuador)	1502-006		
T	**1700** t	....	?	**Tristan da Cunha** (Atlantic-S)	1806-01=		
	1700	0311	?	**Ulawun** (New Britain-SW Pac)	0502-12=	2	
	1700	0324	?	**Ritter Island** (New Guinea-NE of)	0501-07=	3↑	
?	1700	04	?	Kadovar (New Guinea-NE of)	0501-002		
	1700	0402	?	**Manam** (New Guinea-NE of)	0501-02=		
	1701	Cont	....	Stromboli (Italy)	0101-04=	1	
	1701	Cont	....	Amak (Aleutian Is)	1101-39-		

START YEAR	M-Dy	Duration	VOLCANO NAME (Subregion)	NUMBER	VEI	Vol L/T
1701	*Cont*	....	*Galeras (Colombia)*	1501-08=	*2*	
1701	*Cont*	....	*Fogo (Cape Verde Is)*	1804-01=	*1*	
? *1701*	....	?	*Campi Flegrei Mar Sicilia (Italy)*	0101-07=	*2*	
1701	*0701*	*398a*	*Vesuvius (Italy)*	0101-02=	*1*	*-/6*
1702	*Cont*	....	*Vesuvius (Italy)*	0101-02=	*1*	*-/6*
1702	*Cont*	....	*Stromboli (Italy)*	0101-04=	*1*	
1702	*Cont*	....	*Amak (Aleutian Is)*	1101-39-		
1702	*Cont*	....	*Galeras (Colombia)*	1501-08=	*2*	
1702	*Cont*	....	*Fogo (Cape Verde Is)*	1804-01=	*1*	
@ **1702**	....	?	**Bárdarbunga** (Iceland-NE)	1703-03=	2	
1702	0308	61*a*	**Etna** (Italy)	0101-06=	1	7/-
1702	0609	?	**Changbaishan** (China-E)	1005-06-		
1702	0804	?	**Fuego** (Guatemala)	1402-09=	2	
1703	*Cont*	....	*Vesuvius (Italy)*	0101-02=	*1*	*-/6*
1703	*Cont*	....	*Stromboli (Italy)*	0101-04=	*1*	
1703	*Cont*	....	*Amak (Aleutian Is)*	1101-39-		
1703	*Cont*	....	*Galeras (Colombia)*	1501-08=	*2*	
1703	*Cont*	....	*Fogo (Cape Verde Is)*	1804-01=	*1*	
1703 <	....	730*y*>	**Fournaise, Piton de la** (Indian O.)	0303-02=	0	
1703	....	?	**Asama** (Honshu-Japan)	0803-11=	2	
1704	*Cont*	....	*Vesuvius (Italy)*	0101-02=	*1*	*-/6*
1704	*Cont*	....	*Stromboli (Italy)*	0101-04=	*1*	
1704	*Cont*	....	*Fournaise, Piton de la (Indian O.)*	0303-02=	*0*	
1704	*Cont*	....	*Amak (Aleutian Is)*	1101-39-		
1704	*Cont*	....	*Galeras (Colombia)*	1501-08=	*2*	
1704	*Cont*	....	*Fogo (Cape Verde Is)*	1804-01=	*1*	
1704	0205	4*a*	**Asama** (Honshu-Japan)	0803-11=	2	
1704	1231	87*a*	**Tenerife** (Canary Is)	1803-03-	2	7/-
1705	*Cont*	....	*Vesuvius (Italy)*	0101-02=	*1*	*-/6*
1705	*Cont*	....	*Stromboli (Italy)*	0101-04=	*1*	
1705	*Cont*	....	*Fournaise, Piton de la (Indian O.)*	0303-02=	*0*	
1705	*Cont*	....	*Amak (Aleutian Is)*	1101-39-		
1705	*Cont*	....	*Galeras (Colombia)*	1501-08=	*2*	
1705	*Cont*	....	*Fogo (Cape Verde Is)*	1804-01=	*1*	
1705	*0105*	....	*Tenerife (Canary Is)*	1803-03-	*2*	*7/-*
1705	0131	2*a*	**Fuego** (Guatemala)	1402-09=	2	
1706	*Cont*	....	*Stromboli (Italy)*	0101-04=	*1*	
1706	*Cont*	....	*Amak (Aleutian Is)*	1101-39-		
1706	*Cont*	....	*Galeras (Colombia)*	1501-08=	*2*	
1706	*Cont*	....	*Fogo (Cape Verde Is)*	1804-01=	*1*	
1706	....	?	**Bárdarbunga** (Iceland-NE)	1703-03=	2	
1706	01	?	**Sakura-jima** (Kyushu-Japan)	0802-08=	2?	
1706	0128	?	**Kirishima** (Kyushu-Japan)	0802-09=	2	
1706	0505	39*a*	**Tenerife** (Canary Is)	1803-03-	2	7/-
1706	*0720*	....	*Vesuvius (Italy)*	0101-02=	*2?*	*-/6*
1706	1004	?	**Fuego** (Guatemala)	1402-09=	2	
1706	1015q	?	**Grímsvötn** (Iceland-NE)	1703-01=	2	
1706	1120	?	**Asama** (Honshu-Japan)	0803-11=	2	
1707	*Cont*	....	*Stromboli (Italy)*	0101-04=	*1*	
1707	*Cont*	....	*Amak (Aleutian Is)*	1101-39-		
1707	*Cont*	....	*Galeras (Colombia)*	1501-08=	*2*	
1707	*Cont*	....	*Fogo (Cape Verde Is)*	1804-01=	*1*	
1707	....	?	**Taal** (Luzon-Philippines)	0703-07=	2	
? *1707*	....	?	*Hachijo-jima (Izu Is-Japan)*	0804-05=	*2*	
T **1707** r	....	?	**Shikotsu [Eniwa]** (Hokkaido)	0805-04=	2	
1707	....	?	**Bárdarbunga** (Iceland-NE)	1703-03=	2	
1707	0523	>3yr	**Santorini** (Greece)	0102-04=	3	7/-
1707	0729	....	**Vesuvius** (Italy)	0101-02=	3	-/6
1707	1216	39*a*?	**Fuji** (Honshu-Japan)	0803-03=	**5**	-/**9**
1708	*Cont*	....	*Stromboli (Italy)*	0101-04=	*1*	
1708	*Cont*	....	*Santorini (Greece)*	0102-04=	*3*	*7/-*
1708	*Cont*	....	*Amak (Aleutian Is)*	1101-39-		
1708	*Cont*	....	*Galeras (Colombia)*	1501-08=	*2*	
1708	*Cont*	....	*Fogo (Cape Verde Is)*	1804-01=	*1*	
1708	04	15*m*	**Fournaise, Piton de la** (Indian O.)	0303-02=	0	7/-
1708	*0814*	*>3yr*	*Vesuvius (Italy)*	0101-02=	*1*	*-/6*
? *1708*	*0917*	?	*Aso (Kyushu-Japan)*	0802-11=	*2*	
? *1708*	*12*	*32m?*	*Fuji (Honshu-Japan)*	0803-03=		
1708	1229	10*a*	**Asama** (Honshu-Japan)	0803-11=	2	
1709	*Cont*	....	*Vesuvius (Italy)*	0101-02=	*1*	*-/6*
1709	*Cont*	....	*Stromboli (Italy)*	0101-04=	*1*	
1709	*Cont*	....	*Santorini (Greece)*	0102-04=	*3*	*7/-*
? *1709*	*Cont*	....	*Fuji (Honshu-Japan)*	0803-03=		
1709	*Cont*	....	*Asama (Honshu-Japan)*	0803-11=	*2*	
1709	*Cont*	....	*Amak (Aleutian Is)*	1101-39-		
1709	*Cont*	....	*Galeras (Colombia)*	1501-08=	*2*	
1709	*Cont*	....	*Fogo (Cape Verde Is)*	1804-01=	*1*	
1709	....	?	**Fournaise, Piton de la** (Indian O.)	0303-02=	2	
1709	....	?	**Taal** (Luzon-Philippines)	0703-07=	2	
1709 ?	....	?	**Cosigüina** (Nicaragua)	1404-01=		
1709	0213	?	**Aso** (Kyushu-Japan)	0802-11=	2	
? *1709*	*0423*	?	*Iwaki (Honshu-Japan)*	0803-27=	*2?*	
? *1709*	*0423*	?	*Miyake-jima (Izu Is-Japan)*	0804-04=		
? *1709*	*1014*	?	*Fuego (Guatemala)*	1402-09=		
1710	*Cont*	....	*Vesuvius (Italy)*	0101-02=	*1*	*-/6*
1710	*Cont*	....	*Stromboli (Italy)*	0101-04=	*1*	
1710	*Cont*	....	*Santorini (Greece)*	0102-04=	*3*	*7/-*
1710	*Cont*	....	*Amak (Aleutian Is)*	1101-39-		
1710	*Cont*	....	*Fogo (Cape Verde Is)*	1804-01=	*1*	
1710 j	....	?	**Ushishur** (Kuril Is)	0900-21=	1	

Chip Clark (Smithsonian)

A contemporary folding screen by Ogata Korin correctly depicts the last major eruption of Mount Fuji, in 1707, as originating from Hoei crater on the SE flank (far left panel). Ashfall from this eruption, the largest from Fuji-san in historical time, reached the capital city of Edo (present-day Tokyo).

START YEAR	M-Dy	Duration	VOLCANO NAME (Subregion)	NUMBER	VEI	Vol L/T
1710 j	....	?	**Nemo Peak** (Kuril Is)	0900-32=	2	
G 1710 x	....	?	**Snowy Mountain** (Alaska Peninsula)	1102-20-		
1710	....	....	*Galeras (Colombia)*	1501-08=	2	
1710 e	....	?	**Mentolat** (Chile-S)	1508-054		
1710	0325	19a	**Asama** (Honshu-Japan)	0803-11=	2	
? 1710	0627	?	*Komaga-take (Hokkaido-Japan)*	0805-02=		
1710	1014	?	**Fuego** (Guatemala)	1402-09=	2	
1711	Cont	....	*Vesuvius (Italy)*	0101-02=	1	-/6
1711	Cont	....	*Stromboli (Italy)*	0101-04=	1	
1711	Cont	....	*Santorini (Greece)*	0102-04=	3	7/-
1711	Cont	....	*Galeras (Colombia)*	1501-08=	2	
1711	Cont	....	*Fogo (Cape Verde Is)*	1804-01=	1	
1711 ?	....	?	**Azuma** (Honshu-Japan)	0803-18=	1	-/5
1711	....	3a	**Colima** (México)	1401-04=	3?	
1711	0413	?	**Asama** (Honshu-Japan)	0803-11=	2	
1711	1210	6a	**Awu** (Sangihe Is-Indonesia)	0607-04=	3	
1712	Cont	....	*Stromboli (Italy)*	0101-04=	1	
1712	Cont	....	*Galeras (Colombia)*	1501-08=	2	
1712	Cont	....	*Fogo (Cape Verde Is)*	1804-01=	1	
1712	0115q	?	**Bárdarbunga** (Iceland-NE)	1703-03=	2	
1712	0116	?	**Karangetang [Api Siau]** (Sangihe Is	0607-02=	2	
1712	0204	878w	**Miyake-jima** (Izu Is-Japan)	0804-04=	3?	5/8
1712	0205	....	*Vesuvius (Italy)*	0101-02=	1	-/6
1712	05	214p	**Banda Api** (Banda Sea)	0605-09=	2	
1712	1009	55a	**La Palma** (Canary Is)	1803-01-	2	7/-
? 1712	1126d	?	*Fueguino (Chile-S)*	1508-09-		
1712	1231y	?	**Chirpoi** (Kuril Is)	0900-15=	4?	
1713	Cont	....	*Stromboli (Italy)*	0101-04=	1	
1713	Cont	....	*Miyake-jima (Izu Is-Japan)*	0804-04=	1	5/8
1713	Cont	....	*Galeras (Colombia)*	1501-08=	2	
1713	Cont	....	*Fogo (Cape Verde Is)*	1804-01=	1	
1713	....	?	**Kharimkotan** (Kuril Is)	0900-30=	3↑	
1713	....	?	**Sete Cidades** (Azores)	1802-08=	2	7/6
1713	0417	....	*Vesuvius (Italy)*	0101-02=	2	-/6
1713	0629	?	**Asama** (Honshu-Japan)	0803-11=	2	
1714	Cont	....	*Stromboli (Italy)*	0101-04=	1	
1714	Cont	....	*Miyake-jima (Izu Is-Japan)*	0804-04=	1	5/8
1714	Cont	....	*Galeras (Colombia)*	1501-08=	2	
1714	Cont	....	*Fogo (Cape Verde Is)*	1804-01=	1	
1714	0615	....	*Vesuvius (Italy)*	0101-02=	2	-/6
1715	Cont	....	*Vesuvius (Italy)*	0101-02=	1	-/6
1715	Cont	....	*Stromboli (Italy)*	0101-04=	1	
1715	Cont	....	*Galeras (Colombia)*	1501-08=	2	
1715	Cont	....	*Fogo (Cape Verde Is)*	1804-01=	1	
1715	....	?	**Sangeang Api** (Lesser Sunda Is)	0604-05=	2	
1715	....	?	**Taal** (Luzon-Philippines)	0703-07=	2	
1716	Cont	....	*Vesuvius (Italy)*	0101-02=	1	-/6
1716	Cont	....	*Stromboli (Italy)*	0101-04=	1	
1716	Cont	....	*Galeras (Colombia)*	1501-08=	2	
1716	Cont	....	*Fogo (Cape Verde Is)*	1804-01=	1	
1716	....	?	**Villarrica** (Chile-C)	1507-12=	1	
1716	0311	?	**Kirishima** (Kyushu-Japan)	0802-09=	3	-/7
1716	0720	?	**Kelut** (Java)	0603-28=	2	
1716	0924	3a	**Taal** (Luzon-Philippines)	0703-07=	4?	
1716	1005d	?	**Bárdarbunga** (Iceland-NE)	1703-03=	2	
1716	1006	?	**Grímsvötn** (Iceland-NE)	1703-01=	2	
1716	1109	96a	**Kirishima** (Kyushu-Japan)	0802-09=	3	-/8
1717	Cont	....	*Stromboli (Italy)*	0101-04=	1	
1717	Cont	....	*Fogo (Cape Verde Is)*	1804-01=	1	
? 1717	....	?	*Pacaya (Guatemala)*	1402-11=		
1717	....	....	**Galeras** (Colombia)	1501-08=	3	
1717	0207	....	*Kirishima (Kyushu-Japan)*	0802-09=	3	-/8
1717	0606	....	*Vesuvius (Italy)*	0101-02=	2	-/6
1717	0804	44a>	**Bárdarbunga** (Iceland-NE)	1703-03=	3?	
1717	0827	121e	**Fuego** (Guatemala)	1402-09=	4?	-/8
@ 1717	0829	>3yr	**Atitlán** (Guatemala)	1402-06=		
1717	0919	?	**Kirishima** (Kyushu-Japan)	0802-09=	3	-/7
1717	0923	?	**Asama** (Honshu-Japan)	0803-11=	2	
1718	Cont	....	*Vesuvius (Italy)*	0101-02=	1	-/6
1718	Cont	....	*Stromboli (Italy)*	0101-04=	1	
@ 1718	Cont	....	*Atitlán (Guatemala)*	1402-06=		
1718	Cont	....	*Galeras (Colombia)*	1501-08=	2	
1718	Cont	....	*Fogo (Cape Verde Is)*	1804-01=	1	
1718	0201	318e	**Pico** (Azores)	1802-02=	2	
1718	0326?	3a	**Soufrière St. Vincent** (W Indies)	1600-15=	3?	
1718	0926	?	**Asama** (Honshu-Japan)	0803-11=	2	
1719	Cont	....	*Vesuvius (Italy)*	0101-02=	1	-/6
1719	Cont	....	*Stromboli (Italy)*	0101-04=	1	
@ 1719	Cont	....	*Atitlán (Guatemala)*	1402-06=		
1719	Cont	....	*Galeras (Colombia)*	1501-08=	2	
1719	Cont	....	*Fogo (Cape Verde Is)*	1804-01=	1	
1719 w	....	?	**Dukono** (Halmahera-Indonesia)	0608-01=		
1719	....	?	**Kirishima** (Kyushu-Japan)	0802-09=	2	
? 1719 <	....	?	*Bandai (Honshu-Japan)*	0803-16=		
1719	....	?	**Osorno** (Chile-S)	1508-01=	2	
@ 1719	0610	1a	**Asama** (Honshu-Japan)	0803-11=		
1720	Cont	....	*Vesuvius (Italy)*	0101-02=	1	-/6
1720	Cont	....	*Stromboli (Italy)*	0101-04=	1	
@ 1720	Cont	....	*Atitlán (Guatemala)*	1402-06=		
1720	Cont	....	*Galeras (Colombia)*	1501-08=	2	
1720	Cont	....	*Fogo (Cape Verde Is)*	1804-01=	1	
C 1720 t	....	?	**Raoul Island** (Kermadec Is)	0402-03=	4	-/8
1720	....	365y	**Kliuchevskoi** (Kamchatka)	1000-26=	2	
1720	....	?	**Popocatépetl** (México)	1401-09=	1	
T 1720 w	....	?	**Bravo, Cerro** (Colombia)	1501-012	4	-/8
I 1720	....	?	**Bárdarbunga** (Iceland-NE)	1703-03=	2	
1720	0114	514m	**Wudalianchi** (China-E)	1005-03-	3	**9**/8
1720	0606	?	**Asama** (Honshu-Japan)	0803-11=	2	
1720	0710	159m?	**Pico** (Azores)	1802-02=	2	
1720	1208?	22e?	**Don Joao de Castro Bank** (Azores)	1802-07=	3	
1721	Cont	....	*Vesuvius (Italy)*	0101-02=	1	-/6
1721	Cont	....	*Stromboli (Italy)*	0101-04=	1	
1721	Cont	....	*Kliuchevskoi (Kamchatka)*	1000-26=	2	
1721	Cont	....	*Wudalianchi (China-E)*	1005-03-	2	**9**/8
@ 1721	Cont	....	*Atitlán (Guatemala)*	1402-06=		
1721	Cont	....	*Galeras (Colombia)*	1501-08=	2	
1721	Cont	....	*Fogo (Cape Verde Is)*	1804-01=	1	
1721	0511	157q	**Katla** (Iceland-S)	1702-03=	**5**?	-/**9**
1721	06	?	**Fournaise, Piton de la** (Indian O.)	0303-02=	2	
1721	0622	?	**Asama** (Honshu-Japan)	0803-11=	1	-/5
1722	Cont	....	*Vesuvius (Italy)*	0101-02=	1	-/6
1722	Cont	....	*Stromboli (Italy)*	0101-04=	1	
1722	Cont	....	*Galeras (Colombia)*	1501-08=	2	
1722	Cont	....	*Fogo (Cape Verde Is)*	1804-01=	1	
1722	....	?	**Banda Api** (Banda Sea)	0605-09=	2	
1722	0312	?	**Santa Ana [San Marecelino]**	1403-02=	2	
1722	1118	79a	**Asama** (Honshu-Japan)	0803-11=	2	
1723	Cont	....	*Stromboli (Italy)*	0101-04=	1	
1723	Cont	....	*Galeras (Colombia)*	1501-08=	2	
1723	Cont	....	*Fogo (Cape Verde Is)*	1804-01=	1	
? 1723	....	?	*Turrialba (Costa Rica)*	1405-07=	1	
1723	0216	363m?	**Irazú** (Costa Rica)	1405-06=	3	
1723	0420	....	**Vesuvius** (Italy)	0101-02=	3	-/6
1723	0820	?	**Asama** (Honshu-Japan)	0803-11=	2	
? 1723	1122	175m?	*Etna (Italy)*	0101-06=	2	
1724	Cont	....	*Stromboli (Italy)*	0101-04=	1	
? 1724	Cont	....	*Etna (Italy)*	0101-06=	2	
1724	Cont	....	*Irazú (Costa Rica)*	1405-06=	3	
1724	Cont	....	*Galeras (Colombia)*	1501-08=	2	
1724	Cont	....	*Fogo (Cape Verde Is)*	1804-01=	1	
? 1724	....	?	*Xianjindao (Korea)*	1006-01-		
1724	0517	1a	**Krafla** (Iceland-NE)	1703-08=	2	-/6
1724	0904	>3yr	*Vesuvius (Italy)*	0101-02=	2	-/6
1725	Cont	....	*Vesuvius (Italy)*	0101-02=	2	-/6
1725	Cont	....	*Stromboli (Italy)*	0101-04=	1	
1725	Cont	....	*Galeras (Colombia)*	1501-08=	2	
1725	Cont	....	*Fogo (Cape Verde Is)*	1804-01=	1	
1725 q	....	?	**Sinarka** (Kuril Is)	0900-29=	2?	
? 1725	....	?	*Quilotoa (Ecuador)*	1502-06=	2	
? 1725 q	....	?	*Unnamed [Lomonosov Ridge] (Arctic)*	1707-01-	0	
1725	02	?	**Grímsvötn** (Iceland-NE)	1703-01=	2	
1725	0402	?	**Hekla** (Iceland-S)	1702-07=	1?	
1726	Cont	....	*Vesuvius (Italy)*	0101-02=	2	-/6
1726	Cont	....	*Stromboli (Italy)*	0101-04=	1	
1726	Cont	....	*Galeras (Colombia)*	1501-08=	2	
1726	Cont	....	*Fogo (Cape Verde Is)*	1804-01=	1	
1726 j	....	?	**Kurikoma** (Honshu-Japan)	0803-21=	1?	
1726	0201p	90r	**Bárdarbunga** (Iceland-NE)	1703-03=	1?	
1726	05	?	**Irazú** (Costa Rica)	1405-06=	2	
1727	Cont	....	*Vesuvius (Italy)*	0101-02=	2	-/6
1727	Cont	....	*Stromboli (Italy)*	0101-04=	1	
1727	Cont	....	*Fogo (Cape Verde Is)*	1804-01=	1	
1727	....	?	**Vulcano** (Italy)	0101-05=	3	
1727	....	>3yr	**Kliuchevskoi** (Kamchatka)	1000-26=	2	
1727	....	....	*Galeras (Colombia)*	1501-08=	3	
1727	0803	268p	**Öraefajökull** (Iceland-SE)	1704-01=	4	-/8
1727	0821	?	**Krafla** (Iceland-NE)	1703-08=	2	
1727	1122	169a?	**Etna** (Italy)	0101-06=	2?	
1728	Cont	....	*Vesuvius (Italy)*	0101-02=	2	-/6
1728	Cont	....	*Stromboli (Italy)*	0101-04=	1	
1728	Cont	....	*Etna (Italy)*	0101-06=	2?	
1728	Cont	....	*Kliuchevskoi (Kamchatka)*	1000-26=	2	
1728	Cont	....	*Galeras (Colombia)*	1501-08=	2	
1728	Cont	....	*Öraefajökull (Iceland-SE)*	1704-01=	2	-/8
1728	Cont	....	*Fogo (Cape Verde Is)*	1804-01=	1	
? 1728	....	?	*Antisana (Ecuador)*	1502-03=	0	
1728	0418	?	**Krafla** (Iceland-NE)	1703-08=	2	
1728	0930p	>3yr	**Sangay** (Ecuador)	1502-09=	3	
1728	1110	?	**Asama** (Honshu-Japan)	0803-11=	2	
1728	1218	?	**Krafla** (Iceland-NE)	1703-08=	2	8/-
1729	Cont	....	*Vesuvius (Italy)*	0101-02=	2	-/6
1729	Cont	....	*Stromboli (Italy)*	0101-04=	1	
1729	Cont	....	*Kliuchevskoi (Kamchatka)*	1000-26=	2	
1729	Cont	....	*Galeras (Colombia)*	1501-08=	2	

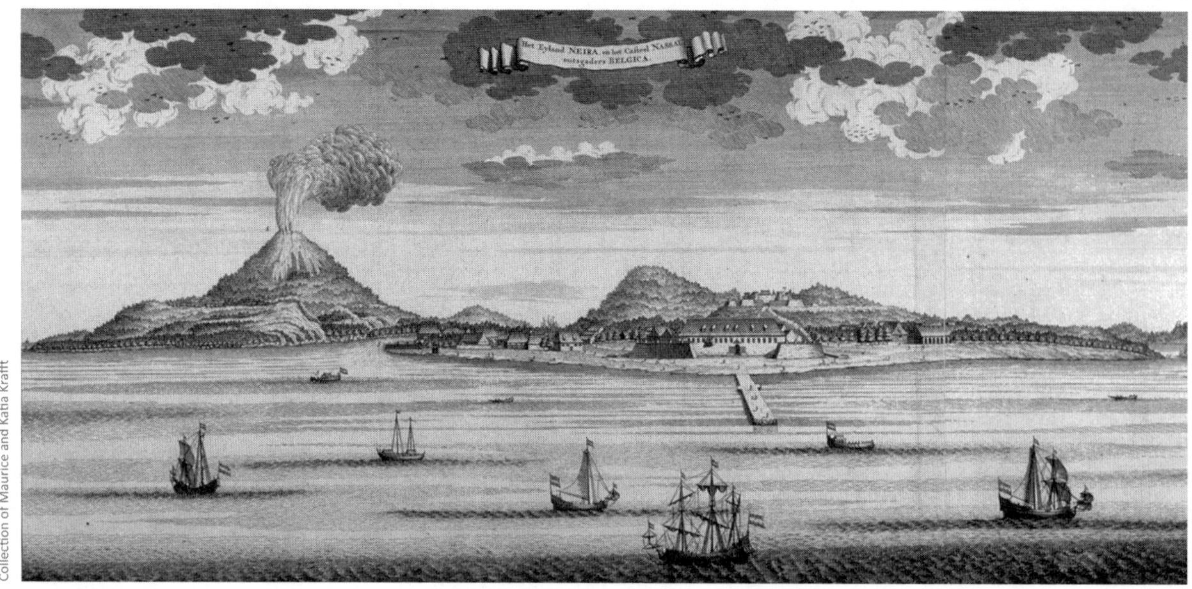

Collection of Maurice and Katia Krafft

This 1726 lithograph shows an eruption plume from the summit of Banda Api, possibly from the last previous eruption, which took place in 1722. This sketch shows sailing ships plying the strait between the islands of Lonthur and Neira in the historic Banda Islands, the original Spice Islands of the Dutch East Indies.

	START YEAR	M-Dy	Duration	VOLCANO NAME (Subregion)	NUMBER	VEI	Vol L/T
	1729	Cont	....	Sangay (Ecuador)	1502-09=	2	
	1729	Cont	....	Fogo (Cape Verde Is)	1804-01=	1	
	1729	....	?	**Taal** (Luzon-Philippines)	0703-07=	2	
@	**1729**	....	?	**Bárdarbunga** (Iceland-NE)	1703-03=	1	
	1729	02	?	**Asama** (Honshu-Japan)	0803-11=	2	
	1729	0215q	?	**Kverkfjöll** (Iceland-NE)	1703-05=	1	
	1729	0630	87e	**Krafla** (Iceland-NE)	1703-08=	2	
	1729	08	?	**Kverkfjöll** (Iceland-NE)	1703-05=	1	
	1729	11	31p	**Asama** (Honshu-Japan)	0803-11=	2	
	1730	Cont	....	Stromboli (Italy)	0101-04=	1	
	1730	Cont	....	Kliuchevskoi (Kamchatka)	1000-26=	2	
	1730	Cont	....	Galeras (Colombia)	1501-08=	2	
	1730	Cont	....	Sangay (Ecuador)	1502-09=	2	
	1730	Cont	....	Fogo (Cape Verde Is)	1804-01=	1	
T	**1730** q	....	?	**Pago** (New Britain-SW Pac)	0502-08=		
	1730 ?	....	?	**Sumbing** (Java)	0603-22=	1	
	1730	....	?	**Raung** (Java)	0603-34=	3?	-/8
?	1730	....	?	Banahaw (Luzon-Philippines)	0703-05=		
G	**1730** q	....	?	**Karymsky** (Kamchatka)	1000-13=		8/-
C	**1730** ?	....	?	**Mauna Loa** (Hawaiian Is)	1302-02=	0	
	1730	....	?	**Grímsvötn** (Iceland-NE)	1703-01=		
	1730	0227	....	**Vesuvius** (Italy)	0101-02=	3	-/6
	1730	0708	?	**Villarrica** (Chile-C)	1507-12=	2?	
	1730	09	?	**Fuego** (Guatemala)	1402-09=	2	
	1730	0901	>3yr	**Lanzarote** (Canary Is)	1803-06-	3	**9**/-
	1731	Cont	....	Stromboli (Italy)	0101-04=	1	
	1731	Cont	....	Kliuchevskoi (Kamchatka)	1000-26=	2	
	1731	Cont	....	Galeras (Colombia)	1501-08=	2	
	1731	Cont	....	Sangay (Ecuador)	1502-09=	2	
	1731	Cont	....	Lanzarote (Canary Is)	1803-06-	3	**9**/-
	1731	Cont	....	Fogo (Cape Verde Is)	1804-01=	1	
	1731	....	>3yr	Vulcano (Italy)	0101-05=	2?	6/7
	1731	....	?	**Taal** (Luzon-Philippines)	0703-07=	2	
	1731	....	?	**Asama** (Honshu-Japan)	0803-11=	2	
	1732	Cont	....	Stromboli (Italy)	0101-04=	1	
	1732	Cont	....	Vulcano (Italy)	0101-05=	2?	6/7
	1732	Cont	....	Galeras (Colombia)	1501-08=	2	
	1732	Cont	....	Sangay (Ecuador)	1502-09=	2	
	1732	Cont	....	Lanzarote (Canary Is)	1803-06-	3	**9**/-
	1732	Cont	....	Fogo (Cape Verde Is)	1804-01=	1	
	1732	0122	267m?	**Iwate** (Honshu-Japan)	0803-24=	2	
	1732	05	?	**Fuego** (Guatemala)	1402-09=	2	
	1732	0517	1a	**Jan Mayen** (Atlantic-N-Jan Mayen)	1706-01=	3	
	1732	0730	?	**Asama** (Honshu-Japan)	0803-11=	2	
	1732	1209	>3yr	**Etna** (Italy)	0101-06=	2	7/-
	1732	1225	>3yr	Vesuvius (Italy)	0101-02=	2	7/-
	1733	Cont	....	Vesuvius (Italy)	0101-02=	2	7/-
	1733	Cont	....	Stromboli (Italy)	0101-04=	1	
	1733	Cont	....	Vulcano (Italy)	0101-05=	2?	6/7
	1733	Cont	....	Etna (Italy)	0101-06=	2	7/-
	1733	Cont	....	Galeras (Colombia)	1501-08=	2	
	1733	Cont	....	Sangay (Ecuador)	1502-09=	2	
	1733	Cont	....	Lanzarote (Canary Is)	1803-06-	3	**9**/-
	1733	Cont	....	Fogo (Cape Verde Is)	1804-01=	1	
	1733 ?	....	?	**Fournaise, Piton de la** (Indian O.)	0303-02=	0	
	1733	0730	?	**Asama** (Honshu-Japan)	0803-11=	2	
	1734	Cont	....	Vesuvius (Italy)	0101-02=	2	7/-
	1734	Cont	....	Stromboli (Italy)	0101-04=	1	
	1734	Cont	....	Vulcano (Italy)	0101-05=	2?	6/7
	1734	Cont	....	Etna (Italy)	0101-06=	2	7/-
	1734	Cont	....	Galeras (Colombia)	1501-08=	2	
	1734	Cont	....	Sangay (Ecuador)	1502-09=	2	
	1734	Cont	....	Lanzarote (Canary Is)	1803-06-	3	**9**/-
	1734	Cont	....	Fogo (Cape Verde Is)	1804-01=	1	
	1734	0101	64a	**Fournaise, Piton de la** (Indian O.)	0303-02=	2	
	1734	06 <	?	**Santa Ana** (El Salvador)	1403-02=	2?	
	1734	12	16m	**Fournaise, Piton de la** (Indian O.)	0303-02=	2	
	1735	Cont	....	Vesuvius (Italy)	0101-02=	2	7/-
	1735	Cont	....	Stromboli (Italy)	0101-04=	1	
	1735	Cont	....	Vulcano (Italy)	0101-05=	2?	6/7
	1735	Cont	....	Galeras (Colombia)	1501-08=	2	
	1735	Cont	....	Sangay (Ecuador)	1502-09=	2	
	1735	Cont	....	Lanzarote (Canary Is)	1803-06-	3	**9**/-
	1735	Cont	....	Fogo (Cape Verde Is)	1804-01=	1	
?	1735	....	?	Chokai (Honshu-Japan)	0803-22=	2	
	1735	1004	....	Etna (Italy)	0101-06=	2	7/-
	1736	Cont	....	Vesuvius (Italy)	0101-02=	2	7/-
	1736	Cont	....	Stromboli (Italy)	0101-04=	1	
	1736	Cont	....	Vulcano (Italy)	0101-05=	2?	6/7
	1736	Cont	....	Etna (Italy)	0101-06=	2	7/-
	1736	Cont	....	Sangay (Ecuador)	1502-09=	2	
	1736	Cont	....	Lanzarote (Canary Is)	1803-06-	3	**9**/-
	1736	Cont	....	Fogo (Cape Verde Is)	1804-01=	1	
	1736	....	?	**Momotombo** (Nicaragua)	1404-09=	2?	
	1736	....	....	Galeras (Colombia)	1501-08=	2	
	1737	Cont	....	Stromboli (Italy)	0101-04=	1	
	1737	Cont	....	Vulcano (Italy)	0101-05=	2?	6/7
	1737	Cont	....	Etna (Italy)	0101-06=	2	7/-
	1737	Cont	....	Sangay (Ecuador)	1502-09=	2	
	1737	Cont	....	Fogo (Cape Verde Is)	1804-01=	1	
	1737	0310	3a	**Gamalama** (Halmahera-Indonesia)	0608-06=	2	
	1737	0514	....	**Vesuvius** (Italy)	0101-02=	3?	7/-
	1737	08	1a?	**Avachinsky** (Kamchatka)	1000-10=	3	-/7
	1737	0827	28a	**Fuego** (Guatemala)	1402-09=	4?	-/8
	1737	0925?	40a?	**Kliuchevskoi** (Kamchatka)	1000-26=	2	
	1737	1224	?	**Villarrica** (Chile-C)	1507-12=	2?	
	1738	Cont	....	Stromboli (Italy)	0101-04=	1	
	1738	Cont	....	Vulcano (Italy)	0101-05=	2?	6/7
	1738	Cont	....	Etna (Italy)	0101-06=	2	7/-
	1738	Cont	....	Fogo (Cape Verde Is)	1804-01=	1	
	1738	....	?	**Cotopaxi** (Ecuador)	1502-05=	2	
	1738	03	....	Sangay (Ecuador)	1502-09=	2	
?	1738	0813	?	Kuju (Kyushu-Japan)	0802-12=	2?	
?	1738	1231y	183m	Chokai (Honshu-Japan)	0803-22=	2	
	1739	Cont	....	Stromboli (Italy)	0101-04=	1	
	1739	Cont	....	Etna (Italy)	0101-06=	2	7/-
	1739	Cont	....	Fogo (Cape Verde Is)	1804-01=	1	
	1739	....	....	**Vulcano** (Italy)	0101-05=	3	6/7
	1739	....	?	**Gamalama** (Halmahera-Indonesia)	0608-06=	2	
T	**1739** >	....	?	**Daisetsu** (Hokkaido-Japan)	0805-06=		

	START YEAR	M-Dy	Duration	VOLCANO NAME (Subregion)	NUMBER	VEI	Vol L/T
	1739	....	?	**Shiveluch** (Kamchatka)	1000-27=	3	-/7
	1739	....	....	Sangay (Ecuador)	1502-09=	3	
I	**1739**	....	?	**Bárdarbunga** (Iceland-NE)	1703-03=	2	
	1739	0201p	?	**Tolbachik** (Kamchatka)	1000-24=	2?	
	1739	0819	12a	**Shikotsu [Tarumai]** (Hokkaido)	0805-04=	**5**	**-/9**
	1740	Cont	....	Stromboli (Italy)	0101-04=	1	
	1740	Cont	....	Etna (Italy)	0101-06=	2	7/-
	1740	Cont	....	Sangay (Ecuador)	1502-09=	2	
	1740	Cont	....	Fogo (Cape Verde Is)	1804-01=	1	
	1740	....	?	**Kliuchevskoi** (Kamchatka)	1000-26=		
	1740	....	?	**Ichinsky** (Kamchatka)	1000-28=	0?	
	1740	....	365y	**Cotopaxi** (Ecuador)	1502-05=	2	
C	**1740** w	....	?	**Hudson, Cerro** (Chile-S)	1508-057		
	1740	06 ?	>3yr	**Chokai** (Honshu-Japan)	0803-22=	2?	
	1740	12	?	**Tolbachik** (Kamchatka)	1000-24=	2	
?	1740	12	?	Quilotoa (Ecuador)	1502-06=	2	
	1741	Cont	....	Stromboli (Italy)	0101-04=	1	
	1741	Cont	....	Etna (Italy)	0101-06=	2	7/-
	1741	Cont	....	Chokai (Honshu-Japan)	0803-22=	2?	
	1741	Cont	....	Cotopaxi (Ecuador)	1502-05=	2	
	1741	Cont	....	Sangay (Ecuador)	1502-09=	2	
	1741	Cont	....	Fogo (Cape Verde Is)	1804-01=	1	
?	1741	....	?	Koshelev (Kamchatka)	1000-02=		
	1741	0818?	270p	Oshima-Oshima (Hokkaido-Japan)	0805-01=	3	-/8
	1741	0829	....	**Oshima-Oshima** (Hokkaido-Japan)	0805-01=	4	-/8
	1742	Cont	....	Stromboli (Italy)	0101-04=	1	
	1742	Cont	....	Etna (Italy)	0101-06=	2	7/-
	1742	Cont	....	Chokai (Honshu-Japan)	0803-22=	2?	
	1742	Cont	....	Oshima-Oshima (Hokkaido-Japan)	0805-01=	3	-/8
	1742	Cont	....	Sangay (Ecuador)	1502-09=	2	
	1742	Cont	....	Fogo (Cape Verde Is)	1804-01=	1	
	1742	....	365y	**Vesuvius** (Italy)	0101-02=	1	
?	1742	....	?	Fuss Peak (Kuril Is)	0900-34=		
?	1742	....	?	Sangangüey (México)	1401-024		
	1742	....	?	**Villarrica** (Chile-C)	1507-12=	2?	
	1742	....	?	**Minchinmávida** (Chile-S)	1508-04=	2	
	1742	0406	?	**Sakura-jima** (Kyushu-Japan)	0802-08=	2?	
	1742	0615	31m	**Cotopaxi** (Ecuador)	1502-05=	3?	
	1742	1209	?	**Cotopaxi** (Ecuador)	1502-05=	3?	
	1743	Cont	....	Vesuvius (Italy)	0101-02=	1	
	1743	Cont	....	Stromboli (Italy)	0101-04=	1	
	1743	Cont	....	Etna (Italy)	0101-06=	2	7/-
	1743	Cont	....	Chokai (Honshu-Japan)	0803-22=	2?	
	1743	Cont	....	Sangay (Ecuador)	1502-09=	2	
	1743	Cont	....	Fogo (Cape Verde Is)	1804-01=	1	
?	1743 ?	....	?	Banahaw (Luzon-Philippines)	0703-05=		
?	1743	....	?	Robinson Crusoe (Chile-Is)	1506-02=		
?	1743	04	?	Telica (Nicaragua)	1404-04=	2?	
	1743	04	?	**Cotopaxi** (Ecuador)	1502-05=	3?	
	1743	0927	8a	**Cotopaxi** (Ecuador)	1502-05=	2	
	1743	1022	?	**Colima** (México)	1401-04=	2?	
	1744	Cont	....	Stromboli (Italy)	0101-04=	1	
	1744	Cont	....	Chokai (Honshu-Japan)	0803-22=	2?	
	1744	Cont	....	Sangay (Ecuador)	1502-09=	2	
	1744	Cont	....	Fogo (Cape Verde Is)	1804-01=	1	
	1744	....	?	**Colima** (México)	1401-04=	2	
	1744	0203	?	**Kurikoma** (Honshu-Japan)	0803-21=	2	
	1744	04 ?	....	Etna (Italy)	0101-06=	2	7/-
	1744	05	214p	Cotopaxi (Ecuador)	1502-05=	2	7/8
	1744	11 ?	>3yr	Vesuvius (Italy)	0101-02=	2	6/-
	1744	1130	....	**Cotopaxi** (Ecuador)	1502-05=	4	7/8
	1745	Cont	....	Vesuvius (Italy)	0101-02=	2	6/-
	1745	Cont	....	Stromboli (Italy)	0101-04=	1	
	1745	Cont	....	Etna (Italy)	0101-06=	2	7/-
	1745	Cont	....	Chokai (Honshu-Japan)	0803-22=	2?	
	1745	Cont	....	Sangay (Ecuador)	1502-09=	2	
	1745	Cont	....	Fogo (Cape Verde Is)	1804-01=	1	
	1745	....	?	**Merapi** (Java)	0603-25=	2	
	1745	....	?	**Villarrica** (Chile-C)	1507-12=	1?	
	1746	Cont	....	Vesuvius (Italy)	0101-02=	2	6/-
	1746	Cont	....	Stromboli (Italy)	0101-04=	1	
	1746	Cont	....	Etna (Italy)	0101-06=	2	7/-
	1746	Cont	....	Chokai (Honshu-Japan)	0803-22=	2?	
	1746	Cont	....	Sangay (Ecuador)	1502-09=	2	
	1746	Cont	....	Fogo (Cape Verde Is)	1804-01=	1	
	1746	02	?	**Cotopaxi** (Ecuador)	1502-05=	2	
	1746	0418	1a	**Yake-dake** (Honshu-Japan)	0803-07=	2	-/6
?	1746	0525m	?	Tres Vírgenes (México)	1401-01=		
	1746	0710	<1 ?	**Krafla** (Iceland-NE)	1703-08=	1	
	1747	Cont	....	Vesuvius (Italy)	0101-02=	2	6/-
	1747	Cont	....	Stromboli (Italy)	0101-04=	1	
	1747	Cont	....	Chokai (Honshu-Japan)	0803-22=	2?	
	1747	Cont	....	Sangay (Ecuador)	1502-09=	2	
	1747	Cont	....	Fogo (Cape Verde Is)	1804-01=	1	
	1747	....	365y	**Gede** (Java)	0603-06=	3	
	1747	....	?	**Poás** (Costa Rica)	1405-04=	2?	
	1747	....	731y	**Cotopaxi** (Ecuador)	1502-05=	2	
	1747	09	....	Etna (Italy)	0101-06=	2	7/-
	1748	Cont	....	Vesuvius (Italy)	0101-02=	2	6/-
	1748	Cont	....	Stromboli (Italy)	0101-04=	1	
	1748	Cont	....	Etna (Italy)	0101-06=	2	7/-
	1748	Cont	....	Gede (Java)	0603-06=	2	
	1748	Cont	....	Cotopaxi (Ecuador)	1502-05=	2	
	1748	Cont	....	Sangay (Ecuador)	1502-09=	2	
	1748	Cont	....	Fogo (Cape Verde Is)	1804-01=	1	
@	**1748** <	....	?	**Reventador** (Ecuador)	1502-01=	2?	
	1749	Cont	....	Vesuvius (Italy)	0101-02=	2	6/-
	1749	Cont	....	Stromboli (Italy)	0101-04=	1	
	1749	Cont	....	Etna (Italy)	0101-06=	2	7/-
	1749	Cont	....	Cotopaxi (Ecuador)	1502-05=	2	
	1749	Cont	....	Sangay (Ecuador)	1502-09=	2	
	1749	Cont	....	Fogo (Cape Verde Is)	1804-01=	1	
	1749	....	?	**Banda Api** (Banda Sea)	0605-09=	2	
?	1749	....	?	Colima (México)	1401-04=	2	
	1749 ?	....	730y?	**Chillán, Nevados de** (Chile-C)	1507-07=	3↑	
	1749	0811?	35m?	**Taal** (Luzon-Philippines)	0703-07=	4	-/8
	1749	09	?	**Sakura-jima** (Kyushu-Japan)	0802-08=	2	
	1750	Cont	....	Vesuvius (Italy)	0101-02=	2	6/-
	1750	Cont	....	Stromboli (Italy)	0101-04=	1	
	1750	Cont	....	Etna (Italy)	0101-06=	2	7/-
	1750	Cont	....	Sangay (Ecuador)	1502-09=	2	
	1750	Cont	....	Chillán, Nevados de (Chile-C)	1507-07=	2	
	1750	Cont	....	Fogo (Cape Verde Is)	1804-01=	1	
	1750 t	....	?	**Tair, Jebel at** (Red Sea)	0201-01=	2	
G	**1750** ?	....	?	**Ksudach** (Kamchatka)	1000-05=	4	-/8
	1750 t	....	?	**Mutnovsky** (Kamchatka)	1000-06=	2	
T	**1750** t	....	?	**Gorely** (Kamchatka)	1000-07=	2?	
	1750 ?	....	?	**Kilauea** (Hawaiian Is)	1302-01-	0	7/-
	1750 ?	....	?	**Mauna Loa** (Hawaiian Is)	1302-02=	0	
A	**1750** ?	....	?	**Haleakala** (Hawaiian Is)	1302-06-		8/-
T	**1750** t	....	?	**Arenal** (Costa Rica)	1405-033	0?	
	1750	....	?	**Sabancaya** (Perú)	1504-006		
	1750 j	....	?	**Antuco** (Chile-C)	1507-08=	2	
	1750 ?	....	?	**Copahue** (Chile-C)	1507-09=	2	
C	**1750** v	....	?	**Huanquihue Group** (Argentina)	1507-123		
I	**1750** j	....	?	**Bárdarbunga** (Iceland-NE)	1703-03=		
T	**1750** v	....	?	**Melbourne** (Antarctica)	1900-015		
	1750	0902a	2a	**Cotopaxi** (Ecuador)	1502-05=	2	
	1751	Cont	....	Stromboli (Italy)	0101-04=	1	
	1751	Cont	....	Etna (Italy)	0101-06=	2	7/-
	1751	Cont	....	Sangay (Ecuador)	1502-09=	2	
	1751	Cont	....	Chillán, Nevados de (Chile-C)	1507-07=	2	
	1751	Cont	....	Fogo (Cape Verde Is)	1804-01=	1	
?	1751	....	?	Fuego (Guatemala)	1402-09=	2	
	1751	06	15m	**Fournaise, Piton de la** (Indian O.)	0303-02=	2	
	1751	1025	....	Vesuvius (Italy)	0101-02=	2	6/-
	1751	11	31p	**Planchón-Peteroa** (Chile-C)	1507-04=	2	
	1751	1214	?	**Villarrica** (Chile-C)	1507-12=	1?	
	1751	1218	195w	**Llaima** (Chile-C)	1507-11=	2	
	1751	1231y	?	**Tromen** (Argentina)	1507-072	3?	
	1751	1231	?	**Callaqui** (Chile-C)	1507-091	2	
	1752	Cont	....	Vesuvius (Italy)	0101-02=	2	6/-
	1752	Cont	....	Stromboli (Italy)	0101-04=	1	
	1752	Cont	....	Sangay (Ecuador)	1502-09=	2	
	1752	Cont	....	Llaima (Chile-C)	1507-11=	2	
	1752	Cont	....	Fogo (Cape Verde Is)	1804-01=	1	
	1752	....	....	Etna (Italy)	0101-06=	2	7/-
	1752	....	?	**Merapi** (Java)	0603-25=	2	
	1752	0130	?	**Chillán, Nevados de** (Chile-C)	1507-07=	2?	
	1752	0131	1a	**Antuco** (Chile-C)	1507-08=	3?	
	1752	0501	?	**Kelut** (Java)	0603-28=	2	
	1752	09	31p	**Asama** (Honshu-Japan)	0803-11=	2?	
	1753	Cont	....	Vesuvius (Italy)	0101-02=	2	6/-
	1753	Cont	....	Stromboli (Italy)	0101-04=	1	
	1753	Cont	....	Etna (Italy)	0101-06=	2	7/-
	1753	Cont	....	Sangay (Ecuador)	1502-09=	2	
	1753	Cont	....	Fogo (Cape Verde Is)	1804-01=	1	
	1753	....	?	**Fournaise, Piton de la** (Indian O.)	0303-02=	2	
?	1753	....	365y	Aso (Kyushu-Japan)	0802-11=	2?	
	1753	1015q	?	**Grímsvötn [NE of Palsfjall]** (Icelan	1703-01=	2?	
	1754	Cont	....	Stromboli (Italy)	0101-04=	1	
	1754	Cont	....	Etna (Italy)	0101-06=	2	7/-
?	1754	Cont	....	Aso (Kyushu-Japan)	0802-11=	2?	
	1754	Cont	....	Sangay (Ecuador)	1502-09=	2	
	1754	Cont	....	Fogo (Cape Verde Is)	1804-01=	1	
	1754	....	730y	**Galeras** (Colombia)	1501-08=	2	
	1754	0515	203a	Taal (Luzon-Philippines)	0703-07=	3	-/8
	1754	0807	12a	**Asama** (Honshu-Japan)	0803-11=	2	
	1754	1128	....	**Taal** (Luzon-Philippines)	0703-07=	4	-/8
	1754	1202	....	Vesuvius (Italy)	0101-02=	2	6/-
	1755	Cont	....	Vesuvius (Italy)	0101-02=	2	6/-
	1755	Cont	....	Stromboli (Italy)	0101-04=	1	
	1755	Cont	....	Galeras (Colombia)	1501-08=	2	

	START YEAR	M-Dy	Duration	VOLCANO NAME (Subregion)	NUMBER	VEI	Vol L/T
	1755	Cont	....	Sangay (Ecuador)	1502-09=	2	
	1755	Cont	....	Fogo (Cape Verde Is)	1804-01=	1	
D	**1755** ?	....	?	**Taranaki [Egmont]** (New Zealand)	0401-03=		
	1755	....	?	**Merapi** (Java)	0603-25=	2	
	1755	0302	....	Etna (Italy)	0101-06=	2	7/-
	1755	0309	6a	**Etna** (Italy)	0101-06=	3	6/-
	1755	0705	32a	**Asama** (Honshu-Japan)	0803-11=	2	
@	**1755**	0918	?	**Kolbeinsey Ridge** (Iceland-N of)	1705-01=		
	1755	1017	119a	**Katla** (Iceland-S)	1702-03=	5?	-/9
	1756	Cont	....	Vesuvius (Italy)	0101-02=	2	6/-
	1756	Cont	....	Stromboli (Italy)	0101-04=	1	
	1756	Cont	....	Etna (Italy)	0101-06=	2	7/-
	1756	Cont	....	Galeras (Colombia)	1501-08=	2	
	1756	Cont	....	Sangay (Ecuador)	1502-09=	2	
	1756	Cont	....	Katla (Iceland-S)	1702-03=	2	-/9
	1756	Cont	....	Fogo (Cape Verde Is)	1804-01=	1	
?	1756	....	?	Kelut (Java)	0603-28=		
	1756	0909	?	**Sakura-jima** (Kyushu-Japan)	0802-08=	2	
	1757	Cont	....	Vesuvius (Italy)	0101-02=	2	6/-
	1757	Cont	....	Stromboli (Italy)	0101-04=	1	
	1757	Cont	....	Etna (Italy)	0101-06=	2	7/-
	1757	Cont	....	Sangay (Ecuador)	1502-09=	2	
	1757	Cont	....	Fogo (Cape Verde Is)	1804-01=	1	
?	1757	....	?	Unnamed (Indian O.-E)	0305-01=	0	
?	1757	....	?	Tungurahua (Ecuador)	1502-08=	2	
	1757	0709	1a	**San Jorge** (Azores)	1802-03=	0	
	1758	Cont	....	Vesuvius (Italy)	0101-02=	2	6/-
	1758	Cont	....	Stromboli (Italy)	0101-04=	1	
	1758	Cont	....	Sangay (Ecuador)	1502-09=	2	
	1758	Cont	....	Fogo (Cape Verde Is)	1804-01=	1	
	1758	10	....	Etna (Italy)	0101-06=	2	7/-
	1758	1103?	271a?	**Etna** (Italy)	0101-06=	2	
	1759	Cont	....	Vesuvius (Italy)	0101-02=	2	6/-
	1759	Cont	....	Stromboli (Italy)	0101-04=	1	
	1759	Cont	....	Sangay (Ecuador)	1502-09=	2	
	1759	Cont	....	Fogo (Cape Verde Is)	1804-01=	1	
	1759	....	?	**Fournaise, Piton de la** (Indian O.)	0303-02=		
?	1759	....	?	Quilotoa (Ecuador)	1502-06=	2	
A	**1759** u	....	?	**Santiago** (Galápagos)	1503-09=		
?	1759 ?	....	?	Copahue (Chile-C)	1507-09=		
	1759 ?	....	?	**Puyehue-Cordón Caulle** (Chile-C)	1507-15=	2	
	1759	0414	....	Etna (Italy)	0101-06=	2	7/-
	1759	0419	....	Etna (Italy)	0101-06=	2	
	1759	0819	?	**Oshima-Oshima** (Hokkaido-Japan)	0805-01=	2	-/6
	1759	0929	>3yr	**Michoacán [Jorullo]** (México)	1401-06=	4	8/9
	1759	12	?	**Llaima** (Chile-C)	1507-11=	2	
	1759	12	16m	**Villarrica** (Chile-C)	1507-12=	1	
	1760	Cont	....	Stromboli (Italy)	0101-04=	1	
	1760	Cont	....	Etna (Italy)	0101-06=	2	7/-
	1760	Cont	....	Michoacán [Jorullo] (México)	1401-06=	2	8/9
	1760	Cont	....	Sangay (Ecuador)	1502-09=	2	
	1760	Cont	....	Fogo (Cape Verde Is)	1804-01=	1	
	1760	....	?	**Savai'i** (Samoa-SW Pacific)	0404-04=	2	9/-
?	1760 ?	....	?	Chirinkotan (Kuril Is)	0900-26=	2	
?	1760	....	?	Gareloi (Aleutian Is)	1101-07-		
?	1760	....	?	Great Sitkin (Aleutian Is)	1101-12-		
	1760	....	?	**Kasatochi** (Aleutian Is)	1101-13-	0	
?	1760	....	15a	Pacaya (Guatemala)	1402-11=		
	1760	....	?	**Chacana** (Ecuador)	1502-022	0	9/-
	1760	0922	220a>	**Makian** (Halmahera-Indonesia)	0608-07=	4?	-/8
	1760	1215	14a	**Fournaise, Piton de la** (Indian O.)	0303-02=	2	
	1760	1223	....	**Vesuvius** (Italy)	0101-02=	3	6/-
	1761	Cont	....	Vesuvius (Italy)	0101-02=	2	6/-
	1761	Cont	....	Stromboli (Italy)	0101-04=	1	
	1761	Cont	....	Etna (Italy)	0101-06=	2	7/-
	1761	Cont	....	Makian (Halmahera-Indonesia)	0608-07=	4?	-/8
	1761	Cont	....	Michoacán [Jorullo] (México)	1401-06=	2	8/9
	1761	Cont	....	Sangay (Ecuador)	1502-09=	2	
	1761	Cont	....	Fogo (Cape Verde Is)	1804-01=	1	
	1761	....	?	**Gede** (Java)	0603-06=	2	
	1761	0417	11a?	**Terceira** (Azores)	1802-05=	2	
?	1761	0503	?	Unnamed (Atlantic-C)	1805-03=	0	
	1762	Cont	....	Stromboli (Italy)	0101-04=	1	
	1762	Cont	....	Etna (Italy)	0101-06=	2	7/-
	1762	Cont	....	Michoacán [Jorullo] (México)	1401-06=	2	8/9
	1762	Cont	....	Sangay (Ecuador)	1502-09=	2	
	1762	....	?	**Banda Api** (Banda Sea)	0605-09=	2	
	1762	....	?	**Kliuchevskoi** (Kamchatka)	1000-26=	2	
@	1762	....	>3yr	Pavlof (Alaska Peninsula)	1102-03-		-/8
	1762	....	?	**San Miguel** (El Salvador)	1403-10=	2	
	1762	04	?	**Asama** (Honshu-Japan)	0803-11=	2	
	1762	1203	?	**Planchón-Peteroa** (Chile-C)	1507-04=	4	
	1763	Cont	....	Stromboli (Italy)	0101-04=	1	
@	1763	Cont	....	Pavlof (Alaska Peninsula)	1102-03-		-/8
	1763	Cont	....	Michoacán [Jorullo] (México)	1401-06=	2	8/9
	1763	Cont	....	Sangay (Ecuador)	1502-09=	2	
	1763	....	?	**Gamalama** (Halmahera-Indonesia)	0608-06=	2	7/-
?	1763	....	>3yr	Tanaga (Aleutian Is)	1101-08-		
?	1763	....	?	Kanaga (Aleutian Is)	1101-11-		
	1763	0206	32a?	**Etna** (Italy)	0101-06=	2	7/6
	1763	0618	84a	**Etna** (Italy)	0101-06=	3	8/7
	1763	0817	>3yr	**Miyake-jima** (Izu Is-Japan)	0804-04=	4	5/8
	1764	Cont	....	Stromboli (Italy)	0101-04=	1	
	1764	Cont	....	Miyake-jima (Izu Is-Japan)	0804-04=	2	5/8
?	1764	Cont	....	Tanaga (Aleutian Is)	1101-08-		
@	1764	Cont	....	Pavlof (Alaska Peninsula)	1102-03-		-/8
	1764	Cont	....	Sangay (Ecuador)	1502-09=	2	
	1764	....	>3yr	Vesuvius (Italy)	0101-02=	2	7/6
	1764	....	548m?	**Etna** (Italy)	0101-06=	1	8/5
?	1764	....	?	Chokai (Honshu-Japan)	0803-22=	2	
	1764	....	....	Michoacán [Jorullo] (México)	1401-06=	4	8/9
	1764	....	?	**Momotombo** (Nicaragua)	1404-09=	2	
	1765	Cont	....	Vesuvius (Italy)	0101-02=	2	7/6
	1765	Cont	....	Stromboli (Italy)	0101-04=	1	
	1765	Cont	....	Etna (Italy)	0101-06=	1	8/5
	1765	Cont	....	Miyake-jima (Izu Is-Japan)	0804-04=	2	5/8
?	1765	Cont	....	Tanaga (Aleutian Is)	1101-08-		
@	1765	Cont	....	Pavlof (Alaska Peninsula)	1102-03-		-/8
	1765	Cont	....	Michoacán [Jorullo] (México)	1401-06=	2	8/9
	1765	Cont	....	Sangay (Ecuador)	1502-09=	2	
	1765	....	?	**Ragang** (Mindanao-Philippines)	0701-06=	2	
?	1765	....	?	Komaga-take (Hokkaido-Japan)	0805-02=	2	
	1765 e	....	?	**Prevo Peak** (Kuril Is)	0900-19=	3↑	
	1765 e	....	?	**Sarychev Peak** (Kuril Is)	0900-24=	2?	
	1765 e	....	?	**Raikoke** (Kuril Is)	0900-25=	2	
D	**1765** e	....	?	**Hood** (US-Oregon)	1202-01-		
?	1765	....	?	Fuego (Guatemala)	1402-09=	2	
	1765	....	?	**Telica** (Nicaragua)	1404-04=	2	
	1765	....	?	**Rincón de la Vieja** (Costa Rica)	1405-02=	2?	
	1765 m	....	?	**Osorno** (Chile-S)	1508-01=	1	
	1765	01	? 274p?	Aso (Kyushu-Japan)	0802-11=	2?	
	1765	0419	545m	**Banda Api** (Banda Sea)	0605-09=	2	
	1765	0615	....	**Aso** (Kyushu-Japan)	0802-11=	3?	
	1765	1024	1a	**Almolonga [C. Quemado]** (Guat)	1402-04=	2	
	1766	Cont	....	Stromboli (Italy)	0101-04=	1	
	1766	Cont	....	Banda Api (Banda Sea)	0605-09=	2	
	1766	Cont	....	Miyake-jima (Izu Is-Japan)	0804-04=	2	5/8
?	1766	Cont	....	Tanaga (Aleutian Is)	1101-08-		
@	1766	Cont	....	Pavlof (Alaska Peninsula)	1102-03-		-/8
	1766	Cont	....	Michoacán [Jorullo] (México)	1401-06=	2	8/9
	1766	Cont	....	Sangay (Ecuador)	1502-09=	2	
?	1766	....	?	Dieng Volc Complex (Java)	0603-20=		
	1766	....	?	**Qualibou** (W Indies)	1600-14=	1	
	1766	0210	309m	**Cotopaxi** (Ecuador)	1502-05=	3	
	1766	03	72n	**Fournaise, Piton de la** (Indian O.)	0303-02=	2	
	1766	0328	....	Vesuvius (Italy)	0101-02=	2	7/6
	1766	0405	770m	**Hekla [Bjallagigar]** (Iceland-S)	1702-07=	4	9/8
	1766	0427	193a	**Etna** (Italy)	0101-06=	2	8/6
	1766	07	?	**Bárdarbunga** (Iceland-NE)	1703-03=	2	
	1766	0720	5a	**Mayon** (Luzon-Philippines)	0703-03=	3	
	1767	Cont	....	Stromboli (Italy)	0101-04=	1	
	1767	Cont	....	Miyake-jima (Izu Is-Japan)	0804-04=	2	5/8
?	1767	Cont	....	Tanaga (Aleutian Is)	1101-08-		
@	1767	Cont	....	Pavlof (Alaska Peninsula)	1102-03-		-/8
	1767	Cont	....	Michoacán [Jorullo] (México)	1401-06=	2	8/9
	1767	Cont	....	Sangay (Ecuador)	1502-09=	2	
	1767	Cont	....	Hekla [Bjallagigar] (Iceland-S)	1702-07=	2	9/8
?	1767	....	?	Tengger Caldera [Bromo] (Java)	0603-31=		
?	1767 n	....	?	Bandai (Honshu-Japan)	0803-16=		
	1767	....	731y	**Ekarma** (Kuril Is)	0900-27=	2	
	1767	....	?	**Kliuchevskoi** (Kamchatka)	1000-26=	2	
	1767	0502	?	**Etna** (Italy)	0101-06=		
	1767	0910	?	**Rabaul** (New Britain-SW Pac)	0502-14=	2	
	1767	1019	....	**Vesuvius** (Italy)	0101-02=	3	7/6
	1768	Cont	....	Miyake-jima (Izu Is-Japan)	0804-04=	2	5/8
	1768	Cont	....	Ekarma (Kuril Is)	0900-27=	2	
?	1768	Cont	....	Tanaga (Aleutian Is)	1101-08-		
@	1768	Cont	....	Pavlof (Alaska Peninsula)	1102-03-		-/8
	1768	Cont	....	Michoacán [Jorullo] (México)	1401-06=	2	8/9
	1768	Cont	....	Sangay (Ecuador)	1502-09=	2	
	1768	Cont	....	Hekla [Bjallagigar] (Iceland-S)	1702-07=	2	9/8
	1768	....	?	**Fournaise, Piton de la** (Indian O.)	0303-02=	2	
	1768	....	?	**Kirishima** (Kyushu-Japan)	0802-09=	0	
	1768	....	365y	Makushin (Aleutian Is)	1101-31-	2	
?	1768	....	?	Iliamna (Alaska-SW)	1103-02-		
@	**1768**	....	?	**Grímsvötn** (Iceland-NE)	1703-01=	2	
	1768	0404	?	**Cotopaxi** (Ecuador)	1502-05=	4	7/8
	1768	08	?	**Tinakula** (Santa Cruz Is-SW Pacific)	0506-01=	2	
	1768	0819	?	**Merapi** (Java)	0603-25=	2?	
	1768	10	....	Stromboli (Italy)	0101-04=	2	
	1769	Cont	....	Stromboli (Italy)	0101-04=	1	
	1769	Cont	....	Miyake-jima (Izu Is-Japan)	0804-04=	2	5/8
	1769	Cont	....	Ekarma (Kuril Is)	0900-27=	2	

START YEAR	M-Dy	Duration	VOLCANO NAME (Subregion)	NUMBER	VEI	Vol L/T
? *1769*	*Cont*	....	*Tanaga (Aleutian Is)*	1101-08-		
@ *1769*	*Cont*	....	*Pavlof (Alaska Peninsula)*	1102-03-		*-/8*
1769	*Cont*	....	*Michoacán [Jorullo] (México)*	1401-06=	*2*	*8/9*
1769	*Cont*	....	*Sangay (Ecuador)*	1502-09=	*2*	
1769	....	?	**Kirishima** (Kyushu-Japan)	0802-09=	2	
? *1769*	....	?	*Iwaki (Honshu-Japan)*	0803-27=	*2*	
1769 >	....	?	**Ushishur** (Kuril Is)	0900-21=		7/-
1769	....	....	**Makushin** (Aleutian Is)	1101-31-	3↑	
1769	....	?	**Colima** (México)	1401-04=	2?	
1769	....	?	**San Miguel** (El Salvador)	1403-10=	2	
@ **1769**	....	?	**Bárdarbunga** (Iceland-NE)	1703-03=	2	
1769	0123	?	**Usu** (Hokkaido-Japan)	0805-03=	4	7/8
1769	0215q	243*t*	**Tolbachik** (Kamchatka)	1000-24=	2	
1769	04 >	?	**Fogo** (Cape Verde Is)	1804-01=		
@ **1769**	0806	?	**Asama** (Honshu-Japan)	0803-11=		
? *1770*	*Cont*	....	*Tanaga (Aleutian Is)*	1101-08-		
@ *1770*	*Cont*	....	*Pavlof (Alaska Peninsula)*	1102-03-		*-/8*
1770	*Cont*	....	*Michoacán [Jorullo] (México)*	1401-06=	*2*	*8/9*
1770	*Cont*	....	*Sangay (Ecuador)*	1502-09=	*2*	
1770	....	....	*Stromboli (Italy)*	0101-04=	*2?*	
C **1770** t	....	?	**Olkaria** (Africa-E)	0202-09=		
1770	....	?	**Marapi** (Sumatra)	0601-14=	2	
? *1770*	....	?	*Amukta (Aleutian Is)*	1101-19-		
1770	*0215*	*>3yr*	*Vesuvius (Italy)*	0101-02=	*2*	*7/6*
1770	0223	?	**Izalco** (El Salvador)	1403-03=	2	
1770	0310	1	**Colima** (México)	1401-04=	3	
1770	05	?	**Kliuchevskoi** (Kamchatka)	1000-26=	2	
? *1770*	*0528a*	?	*Etna (Italy)*	0101-06=		
1770	0706	156*a*	**Gamalama** (Halmahera-Indonesia)	0608-06=	3	
? *1770*	*0916*	?	*Fuji (Honshu-Japan)*	0803-03=		
1771	*Cont*	....	*Stromboli (Italy)*	0101-04=	*1*	
@ *1771*	*Cont*	....	*Pavlof (Alaska Peninsula)*	1102-03-		*-/8*
1771	*Cont*	....	*Michoacán [Jorullo] (México)*	1401-06=	*2*	*8/9*
1771	*Cont*	....	*Sangay (Ecuador)*	1502-09=	*2*	
1771	....	?	**Fournaise, Piton de la** (Indian O.)	0303-02=		
1771	....	365*y*	**Kirishima** (Kyushu-Japan)	0802-09=	2	-/6
1771	....	?	**Karymsky** (Kamchatka)	1000-13=	2	
1771	....	?	**Colima** (México)	1401-04=	3	
1771	0110	?	**Kelut** (Java)	0603-28=	2	
1771	0217	87*m*	**Vulcano** (Italy)	0101-05=	3	
1771	*0501*	....	*Vesuvius (Italy)*	0101-02=	*2*	*7/6*
1771	0828	407*a*	**Gamalama** (Halmahera-Indonesia)	0608-06=	3	
1772	*Cont*	....	*Vesuvius (Italy)*	0101-02=	*2*	*7/6*
1772	*Cont*	....	*Stromboli (Italy)*	0101-04=	*1*	
1772	*Cont*	....	*Gamalama (Halmahera-Indonesia)*	0608-06=	*3*	
1772	*Cont*	....	*Kirishima (Kyushu-Japan)*	0802-09=	*2*	*-/6*
@ *1772*	*Cont*	....	*Pavlof (Alaska Peninsula)*	1102-03-		*-/8*
1772	*Cont*	....	*Michoacán [Jorullo] (México)*	1401-06=	*2*	*8/9*
1772	*Cont*	....	*Sangay (Ecuador)*	1502-09=	*2*	
1772	....	>3yr	**Aso** (Kyushu-Japan)	0802-11=	2	
1772	....	?	**Avachinsky** (Kamchatka)	1000-10=	2	
1772	....	?	**Kliuchevskoi** (Kamchatka)	1000-26=	2	
? *1772*	....	?	*Semisopochnoi (Aleutian Is)*	1101-06-		
1772 ?	....	?	**Izalco** (El Salvador)	1403-03=	2	
1772	02	?	**Fournaise, Piton de la** (Indian O.)	0303-02=	2	
1772	0316	9*a*?	**Masaya** (Nicaragua)	1404-10=	2	6/-
1772	0811	1*a*	**Cereme** (Java)	0603-17=	2	
1772	0811	1*a*	**Slamet** (Java)	0603-18=	2	
1772	0812	<1	**Papandayan** (Java)	0603-10=	3	
1772	1118	?	**Fournaise, Piton de la** (Indian O.)	0303-02=	2	
1773	*Cont*	....	*Vesuvius (Italy)*	0101-02=	*2*	*7/6*
1773	*Cont*	....	*Stromboli (Italy)*	0101-04=	*1*	
1773	*Cont*	....	*Aso (Kyushu-Japan)*	0802-11=	*2*	
@ *1773*	*Cont*	....	*Pavlof (Alaska Peninsula)*	1102-03-		*-/8*
1773	*Cont*	....	*Michoacán [Jorullo] (México)*	1401-06=	*2*	*8/9*
1773	*Cont*	....	*Sangay (Ecuador)*	1502-09=	*2*	
1773	....	?	**Niigata-Yake-yama** (Honshu-Japan)	0803-09=	3	-/7
? *1773*	....	?	*Fuego (Guatemala)*	1402-09=	*2*	
1773	....	?	**Chacana** (Ecuador)	1502-022	0	8/-
1773	0202	5*a*	**Gamalama** (Halmahera-Indonesia)	0608-06=	2	
1773	*0204*	*127m?*	*Tungurahua (Ecuador)*	1502-08=	*2*	*8/-*
1773	0206	?	**Banda Api** (Banda Sea)	0605-09=	2	
1773	0423	....	**Tungurahua** (Ecuador)	1502-08=	3	8/-
1773	10	?	**Didicas** (Luzon-N of)	0704-02=	1?	
1773	10	?	**Unnamed** (Luzon-N of)	0704-05=	0	
1773	1021	92*a*	**Gamalama** (Halmahera-Indonesia)	0608-06=	2	
1774	*Cont*	....	*Vesuvius (Italy)*	0101-02=	*2*	*7/6*
1774	*Cont*	....	*Stromboli (Italy)*	0101-04=	*1*	
1774	*Cont*	....	*Gamalama (Halmahera-Indonesia)*	0608-06=	*2*	
1774	*Cont*	....	*Aso (Kyushu-Japan)*	0802-11=	*2*	
@ *1774*	*Cont*	....	*Pavlof (Alaska Peninsula)*	1102-03-		*-/8*
1774	*Cont*	....	*Michoacán [Jorullo] (México)*	1401-06=	*2*	*8/9*
1774	*Cont*	....	*Sangay (Ecuador)*	1502-09=	*2*	
1774	....	?	**Fournaise, Piton de la** (Indian O.)	0303-02=	0	7/-
1774	....	?	**Ambrym** (Vanuatu-SW Pacific)	0507-04=	2	
1774 <	....	*>3yr*	*Yasur (Vanuatu-SW Pacific)*	0507-10=	*2*	
1774	....	?	**Carlisle** (Aleutian Is)	1101-23-		
1774	02	?	**Grímsvötn** (Iceland-NE)	1703-01=	2	
1774	06	?	**Tofua** (Tonga-SW Pacific)	0403-06=	2	
1775	*Cont*	....	*Vesuvius (Italy)*	0101-02=	*2*	*7/6*
1775	*Cont*	....	*Stromboli (Italy)*	0101-04=	*1*	
1775	*Cont*	....	*Yasur (Vanuatu-SW Pacific)*	0507-10=	*2*	
1775	*Cont*	....	*Aso (Kyushu-Japan)*	0802-11=	*2*	
@ *1775*	*Cont*	....	*Pavlof (Alaska Peninsula)*	1102-03-		*-/8*
1775	*Cont*	....	*Sangay (Ecuador)*	1502-09=	*2*	
? *1775*	....	?	*Vulcano (Italy)*	0101-05=		
A **1775** q	....	?	**Tullu Moje** (Ethiopia)	0201-25-		
1775	....	?	**Fournaise, Piton de la** (Indian O.)	0303-02=	2	
? *1775*	....	?	*Tengger Caldera [Bromo] (Java)*	0603-31=		
1775	....	?	**Banda Api** (Banda Sea)	0605-09=	2	
1775 q	....	?	**Lokon-Empung** (Sulawesi-Indonesia)	0606-10=	3	
? *1775 j*	....	?	*Asuncion (Mariana Is-C Pacific)*	0804-15=	*2*	
? *1775*	....	*>3yr*	*Shishaldin (Aleutian Is)*	1101-36-		
1775 ?	....	?	**Irazú** (Costa Rica)	1405-06=	2?	
? *1775*	....	?	*Villarrica (Chile-C)*	1507-12=	*2?*	
1775	0104	?	**Cereme** (Java)	0603-17=	2	
1775	0701	22*a*>	**Pacaya** (Guatemala)	1402-11=	3	7/7
1775	*0820*	*78a*	*Gamalama (Halmahera-Indonesia)*	0608-06=	*2*	
1775	0906	....	**Gamalama** (Halmahera-Indonesia)	0608-06=	3	
1776	*Cont*	....	*Stromboli (Italy)*	0101-04=	*1*	
1776	*Cont*	....	*Yasur (Vanuatu-SW Pacific)*	0507-10=	*2*	
1776	*Cont*	....	*Aso (Kyushu-Japan)*	0802-11=	*2*	
? *1776*	*Cont*	....	*Shishaldin (Aleutian Is)*	1101-36-		
@ *1776*	*Cont*	....	*Pavlof (Alaska Peninsula)*	1102-03-		*-/8*
1776	*Cont*	....	*Sangay (Ecuador)*	1502-09=	*2*	
1776	....	?	**Etna** (Italy)	0101-06=		
1776	....	?	**Fournaise, Piton de la** (Indian O.)	0303-02=	0	6/-
? *1776*	....	?	*Dieng Volc Complex (Java)*	0603-20=		
1776	....	?	**Kelut** (Java)	0603-28=	2	
1776	....	?	**Wudalianchi** (China-E)	1005-03-	2?	
1776	....	?	**Little Sitkin** (Aleutian Is)	1101-05-	1?	
1776	0103	?	**Tungurahua** (Ecuador)	1502-08=	2	
1776	*0328*	....	*Vesuvius (Italy)*	0101-02=	*2*	*7/6*
1776	0905	?	**Asama** (Honshu-Japan)	0803-11=	2	
1776	10	?	**Zhupanovsky** (Kamchatka)	1000-12=	2	
1776	1023	?	**Opala** (Kamchatka)	1000-08=	2?	
1777	*Cont*	....	*Vesuvius (Italy)*	0101-02=	*2*	*7/6*
1777	*Cont*	....	*Stromboli (Italy)*	0101-04=	*1*	
1777	*Cont*	....	*Yasur (Vanuatu-SW Pacific)*	0507-10=	*2*	
1777	*Cont*	....	*Aso (Kyushu-Japan)*	0802-11=	*2*	
? *1777*	*Cont*	....	*Shishaldin (Aleutian Is)*	1101-36-		
@ *1777*	*Cont*	....	*Pavlof (Alaska Peninsula)*	1102-03-		*-/8*
1777	*Cont*	....	*Sangay (Ecuador)*	1502-09=	*2*	
1777	....	?	**Guntur** (Java)	0603-13=	2?	
1777	....	?	**Asama** (Honshu-Japan)	0803-11=	2	
? *1777*	....	?	*Tungurahua (Ecuador)*	1502-08=	*2*	
1777	....	730*y*	**Villarrica** (Chile-C)	1507-12=	1	
1777	0831	670*w*	**Oshima** (Izu Is-Japan)	0804-01=	3	8/8
1778	*Cont*	....	*Vesuvius (Italy)*	0101-02=	*2*	*7/6*
1778	*Cont*	....	*Yasur (Vanuatu-SW Pacific)*	0507-10=	*2*	
1778	*Cont*	....	*Aso (Kyushu-Japan)*	0802-11=	*2*	
1778	*Cont*	....	*Oshima (Izu Is-Japan)*	0804-01=	*2*	*8/8*
? *1778*	*Cont*	....	*Shishaldin (Aleutian Is)*	1101-36-		
@ *1778*	*Cont*	....	*Pavlof (Alaska Peninsula)*	1102-03-		*-/8*
1778	*Cont*	....	*Sangay (Ecuador)*	1502-09=	*2*	
1778	*Cont*	....	*Villarrica (Chile-C)*	1507-12=	*1*	
1778	....	?	**Banda Api** (Banda Sea)	0605-09=	2	
1778	....	?	**Raikoke** (Kuril Is)	0900-25=	4↑	
1778	....	365*y*	**Iliamna** (Alaska-SW)	1103-02-		
1778	*0301*	....	*Stromboli (Italy)*	0101-04=	*2*	
1778	1231y	?	**Medvezhia** (Kuril Is)	0900-10=	2	
1779	*Cont*	....	*Stromboli (Italy)*	0101-04=	*1*	
1779	*Cont*	....	*Yasur (Vanuatu-SW Pacific)*	0507-10=	*2*	
1779	*Cont*	....	*Aso (Kyushu-Japan)*	0802-11=	*2*	
@ *1779*	*Cont*	....	*Pavlof (Alaska Peninsula)*	1102-03-		*-/8*
1779	*Cont*	....	*Iliamna (Alaska-SW)*	1103-02-		
1779	*Cont*	....	*Sangay (Ecuador)*	1502-09=	*2*	
1779	*Cont*	....	*Villarrica (Chile-C)*	1507-12=	*1*	
1779	*0104*	....	*Oshima (Izu Is-Japan)*	0804-01=	*3*	*8/8*
1779	0615	1*a*	**Avachinsky** (Kamchatka)	1000-10=	3	-/7
1779	0808	....	**Vesuvius** (Italy)	0101-02=	3?	7/6
? *1779*	*09 ?*	?	*Asama (Honshu-Japan)*	0803-11=		
1779	1108	554*m*	**Sakura-jima** (Kyushu-Japan)	0802-08=	4	**9**/8
1780	*Cont*	....	*Stromboli (Italy)*	0101-04=	*1*	
1780	*Cont*	....	*Yasur (Vanuatu-SW Pacific)*	0507-10=	*2*	
1780	*Cont*	....	*Aso (Kyushu-Japan)*	0802-11=	*2*	
@ *1780*	*Cont*	....	*Pavlof (Alaska Peninsula)*	1102-03-		*-/8*
1780	*Cont*	....	*Sangay (Ecuador)*	1502-09=	*2*	
1780	....	?	**Vulcano** (Italy)	0101-05=	2	
? *1780* <	....	?	*Fonualei (Tonga-SW Pacific)*	0403-01=		
1780	....	?	**Salak** (Java)	0603-05=	2	
1780	....	?	**Guntur** (Java)	0603-13=	2	

START YEAR	M-Dy	Dura-tion	VOLCANO NAME (Subregion)	NUMBER	VEI	Vol L/T
1780	....	?	**Kita-Iwo-jima** (Volcano Is-Japan)	0804-11=	0	
1780 u	....	?	**Akan** (Hokkaido-Japan)	0805-07=	1	
1780 j	....	?	**Kolokol Group** (Kuril Is)	0900-12=	2?	
@ **1780**	....	?	**Yucamane** (Perú)	1504-05-	2	
1780	....	?	**Villarrica** (Chile-C)	1507-12=	1	
1780	0420?	86*m*?	**Etna** (Italy)	0101-06=	2	7/4
1780	*0518*	....	*Etna (Italy)*	0101-06=	*1*	*7/4*
1780	*0727*	*>3yr*	*Aoga-shima (Izu Is-Japan)*	0804-06=	*2*	*6/7*
1780	*09*	....	*Sakura-jima (Kyushu-Japan)*	0802-08=	*2?*	***9**/8*
1780	1126	?	**Colima** (México)	1401-04=	2	
1781	*Cont*	....	*Stromboli (Italy)*	0101-04=	*1*	
1781	*Cont*	....	*Yasur (Vanuatu-SW Pacific)*	0507-10=	*2*	
1781	*Cont*	....	*Aoga-shima (Izu Is-Japan)*	0804-06=	*2*	*6/7*
@ *1781*	*Cont*	....	*Pavlof (Alaska Peninsula)*	1102-03-		*-/8*
1781	*Cont*	....	*Sangay (Ecuador)*	1502-09=	*2*	
? *1781*	....	*?*	*Falcon Island (Tonga-SW Pacific)*	0403-05=	*0*	
1781 <	....	?	**Metis Shoal** (Tonga-SW Pacific)	0403-07=	2?	
? *1781*	....	*?*	*Gamalama (Halmahera-Indonesia)*	0608-06=		
1781	....	>3yr	**Aso** (Kyushu-Japan)	0802-11=	1	
? *1781*	....	*?*	*Tungurahua (Ecuador)*	1502-08=	*2*	
1781	03	55*m*	**Etna** (Italy)	0101-06=	2	
1781	*04*	....	*Sakura-jima (Kyushu-Japan)*	0802-08=	*2*	***9**/8*
1782	*Cont*	....	*Stromboli (Italy)*	0101-04=	*1*	
1782	*Cont*	....	*Yasur (Vanuatu-SW Pacific)*	0507-10=	*2*	
1782	*Cont*	....	*Aso (Kyushu-Japan)*	0802-11=	*1*	
1782	*Cont*	....	*Aoga-shima (Izu Is-Japan)*	0804-06=	*2*	*6/7*
@ *1782*	*Cont*	....	*Pavlof (Alaska Peninsula)*	1102-03-		*-/8*
1782	*Cont*	....	*Sangay (Ecuador)*	1502-09=	*2*	
1782	0118	?	**Sakura-jima** (Kyushu-Japan)	0802-08=	2?	
? *1782*	*0412*	*?*	*Iwaki (Honshu-Japan)*	0803-27=	*2*	
1782	1201p	101*p*	**Iwaki** (Honshu-Japan)	0803-27=	2	

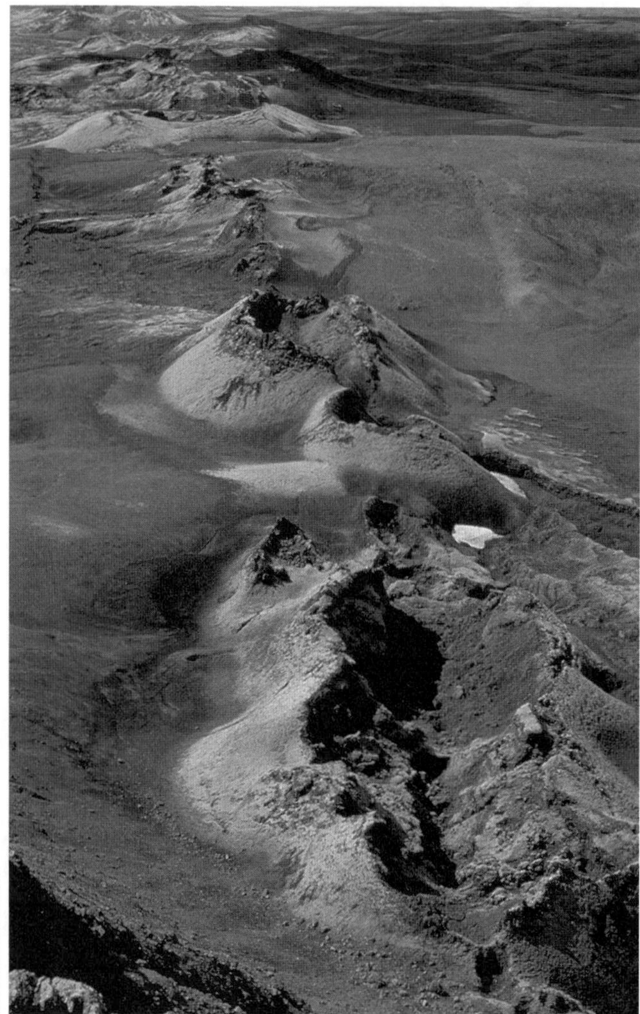

Katia and Maurice Krafft

The noted Laki (Skaftár) fissure of Grímsvötn central volcano in Iceland produced the world's largest known historical lava flow during an eruption in 1783. The 15 km³ Laki lavas were erupted over a 7-month period from a 27-km-long fissure system. Extensive crop damage and livestock losses caused a severe famine that resulted in the decimation of 22% of the population of Iceland.

START YEAR	M-Dy	Dura-tion	VOLCANO NAME (Subregion)	NUMBER	VEI	Vol L/T
1783	*Cont*	....	*Yasur (Vanuatu-SW Pacific)*	0507-10=	*2*	
1783	*Cont*	....	*Aso (Kyushu-Japan)*	0802-11=	*1*	
@ *1783*	*Cont*	....	*Pavlof (Alaska Peninsula)*	1102-03-		*-/8*
1783	*Cont*	....	*Sangay (Ecuador)*	1502-09=	*2*	
? *1783*	....	*?*	*Ararat (Turkey)*	0103-04-		
? *1783*	....	*?*	*Kurikoma (Honshu-Japan)*	0803-21=		
1783	....	1096*y*	**Oshima** (Izu Is-Japan)	0804-01=	2	
1783 ?	....	>3yr	**Kanaga** (Aleutian Is)	1101-11-		
1783	*0205*	....	*Stromboli (Italy)*	0101-04=	*2?*	
1783	0410	....	**Aoga-shima** (Izu Is-Japan)	0804-06=	3	6/7
1783	*05*	*? 741m?*	*Grímsvötn [Lakagigar] (Iceland)*	1703-01=	*2*	
1783	0501<	106*r*	**Reykjanes** (Iceland-SW)	1701-02=	3↑	
1783	*0509*	*88a*	*Asama (Honshu-Japan)*	0803-11=	*2*	*8/8*
1783	0608	....	**Grímsvötn [Lakagigar]** (Iceland)	1703-01=	4+	**10**/8
1783	07 ?	?	**Izalco** (El Salvador)	1403-03=	0	
1783	0803	....	**Asama** (Honshu-Japan)	0803-11=	4	8/8
1783	*0818*	*>3yr*	*Vesuvius (Italy)*	0101-02=	*2*	*7/8*
1783	0903	?	**Sakura-jima** (Kyushu-Japan)	0802-08=	3	
? *1783*	*1203*	*?*	*Iwaki (Honshu-Japan)*	0803-27=	*2?*	
1784	*Cont*	....	*Vesuvius (Italy)*	0101-02=	*2*	*7/8*
1784	*Cont*	....	*Stromboli (Italy)*	0101-04=	*1*	
1784	*Cont*	....	*Yasur (Vanuatu-SW Pacific)*	0507-10=	*2*	
1784	*Cont*	....	*Aso (Kyushu-Japan)*	0802-11=	*1*	
1784	*Cont*	....	*Oshima (Izu Is-Japan)*	0804-01=	*2*	
1784	*Cont*	....	*Aoga-shima (Izu Is-Japan)*	0804-06=	*2*	*6/7*
1784	*Cont*	....	*Kanaga (Aleutian Is)*	1101-11-		
@ *1784*	*Cont*	....	*Pavlof (Alaska Peninsula)*	1102-03-		*-/8*
1784	*Cont*	....	*Sangay (Ecuador)*	1502-09=	*2*	
1784	*Cont*	....	*Grímsvötn [Lakagigar] (Iceland)*	1703-01=	*2*	***10**/8*
1784	....	365*y*	**Fournaise, Piton de la** (Indian O.)	0303-02=	2	
? *1784*	....	*?*	*Great Sitkin (Aleutian Is)*	1101-12-		
? *1784*	....	*?*	*Vsevidof (Aleutian Is)*	1101-27-		
1784 g	....	?	**Hualalai** (Hawaiian Is)	1302-04-	0	8/-
1784	....	?	**Ubinas** (Perú)	1504-02=	2	
? *1784*	*0208*	*?*	*Komaga-take (Hokkaido-Japan)*	0805-02=	*2*	
1784	03 <	?	**Soufrière St. Vincent** (W Indies)	1600-15=	0	
? *1784*	*07*	*?*	*Wrangell (Alaska-E)*	1105-02-	*2?*	
1784	07	?	**Sabancaya** (Perú)	1504-006		
1784	0709	?	**Misti, El** (Perú)	1504-01=	2	
1785	*Cont*	....	*Stromboli (Italy)*	0101-04=	*1*	
1785	*Cont*	....	*Fournaise, Piton de la (Indian O.)*	0303-02=	*2*	
1785	*Cont*	....	*Yasur (Vanuatu-SW Pacific)*	0507-10=	*2*	
1785	*Cont*	....	*Aso (Kyushu-Japan)*	0802-11=	*1*	
1785	*Cont*	....	*Oshima (Izu Is-Japan)*	0804-01=	*2*	
1785	*Cont*	....	*Kanaga (Aleutian Is)*	1101-11-		
@ *1785*	*Cont*	....	*Pavlof (Alaska Peninsula)*	1102-03-		*-/8*
1785	*Cont*	....	*Sangay (Ecuador)*	1502-09=	*2*	
1785	*Cont*	....	*Grímsvötn [Lakagigar] (Iceland)*	1703-01=	*2*	
1785	....	?	**Kelut** (Java)	0603-28=	2	
1785 j	....	?	**Kueishantao** (Taiwan-E of)	0801-031	0	
1785	0124	32*a*	**Fogo** (Cape Verde Is)	1804-01=	2	6/-
1785	02	394*p*	**Cayambe** (Ecuador)	1502-006	2?	
1785	*0418*	....	*Aoga-shima (Izu Is-Japan)*	0804-06=	*3*	*6/7*
1785	*0701*	....	*Vesuvius (Italy)*	0101-02=	*1*	*7/8*
1785	11	?	**Kliuchevskoi** (Kamchatka)	1000-26=	2	
1785	1120	?	**Sakura-jima** (Kyushu-Japan)	0802-08=	2	
1785	1231y	?	**Soputan** (Sulawesi-Indonesia)	0606-03=	2	
1786	*Cont*	....	*Vesuvius (Italy)*	0101-02=	*2*	*7/8*
1786	*Cont*	....	*Stromboli (Italy)*	0101-04=	*1*	
1786	*Cont*	....	*Yasur (Vanuatu-SW Pacific)*	0507-10=	*2*	
1786	*Cont*	....	*Aso (Kyushu-Japan)*	0802-11=	*1*	
1786	*Cont*	....	*Oshima (Izu Is-Japan)*	0804-01=	*2*	
1786	*Cont*	....	*Kanaga (Aleutian Is)*	1101-11-		
1786	*Cont*	....	*Cayambe (Ecuador)*	1502-006	*2?*	
1786	*Cont*	....	*Sangay (Ecuador)*	1502-09=	*2*	
? *1786*	....	*15a*	*Vulcano (Italy)*	0101-05=	*3*	
1786	....	120*p*	**Dieng Volc Complex** (Java)	0603-20=	2	
? *1786*	....	*?*	*Oshima-Oshima (Hokkaido-Japan)*	0805-01=	*2?*	
1786	....	>3yr	**Seguam** (Aleutian Is)	1101-18-		
@ **1786**	....	....	**Pavlof** (Alaska Peninsula)	1102-03-	4?	-/8
? *1786*	....	*?*	*Iliamna (Alaska-SW)*	1103-02-		
1786	....	?	**Shasta** (US-California)	1203-01-	3	
1786	06	>3yr	**Amukta** (Aleutian Is)	1101-19-	3↑	-/8
1786	0605?	60*a*>	**Fournaise, Piton de la** (Indian O.)	0303-02=	2	
1786	0717	?	**Merapi** (Java)	0603-25=	1?	
1787	*Cont*	....	*Vesuvius (Italy)*	0101-02=	*2*	*7/8*
1787	*Cont*	....	*Stromboli (Italy)*	0101-04=	*1*	
1787	*Cont*	....	*Yasur (Vanuatu-SW Pacific)*	0507-10=	*2*	
1787	*Cont*	....	*Aso (Kyushu-Japan)*	0802-11=	*1*	
1787	*Cont*	....	*Kanaga (Aleutian Is)*	1101-11-		
1787	*Cont*	....	*Seguam (Aleutian Is)*	1101-18-		
1787	*Cont*	....	*Amukta (Aleutian Is)*	1101-19-	*2*	*-/8*
1787	*Cont*	....	*Sangay (Ecuador)*	1502-09=	*2*	
1787 <	....	?	**Bandai** (Honshu-Japan)	0803-16=	2?	
1787 <	....	?	**Osore-yama** (Honshu-Japan)	0803-29=		
1787	....	?	**Yucamane** (Perú)	1504-05-		
1787	....	?	**Villarrica** (Chile-C)	1507-12=	2	

START YEAR	M-Dy	Duration	VOLCANO NAME (Subregion)	NUMBER	VEI	Vol L/T
1787	0512	?	Barren Island (Andaman Is-Indian O)	0600-01=	2	
1787	0604d	68e	Etna (Italy)	0101-06=	2	6/-
1787	0614	48a	Fournaise, Piton de la (Indian O.)	0303-02=	2	7/-
1787	0718	....	Etna (Italy)	0101-06=	4	6/-
1787	0728	74a	Misti, El (Perú)	1504-01=	1?	
1787	09	?	Kliuchevskoi (Kamchatka)	1000-26=	2?	
1787	0921	2a	San Miguel (El Salvador)	1403-10=	2	
1788	Cont	....	Vesuvius (Italy)	0101-02=	2	7/8
1788	Cont	....	Yasur (Vanuatu-SW Pacific)	0507-10=	2	
1788	Cont	....	Aso (Kyushu-Japan)	0802-11=	1	
1788	Cont	....	Seguam (Aleutian Is)	1101-18-		
1788	Cont	....	Amukta (Aleutian Is)	1101-19-	2	-/8
1788	Cont	....	Sangay (Ecuador)	1502-09=	2	
1788	....	....	Stromboli (Italy)	0101-04=	2	
1788 <	....	?	Mahawu (Sulawesi-Indonesia)	0606-11=		
1788	....	?	Tolbachik (Kamchatka)	1000-24=	2	
? 1788	....	?	Maipo (Chile-C)	1507-021		
1788	02	?	Kliuchevskoi (Kamchatka)	1000-26=	2	
1788	08	?	Kliuchevskoi (Kamchatka)	1000-26=	2	
1789	Cont	....	Vesuvius (Italy)	0101-02=	2	7/8
1789	Cont	....	Stromboli (Italy)	0101-04=	1	
1789	Cont	....	Yasur (Vanuatu-SW Pacific)	0507-10=	2	
1789	Cont	....	Seguam (Aleutian Is)	1101-18-		
1789	Cont	....	Amukta (Aleutian Is)	1101-19-	2	-/8
1789	Cont	....	Sangay (Ecuador)	1502-09=	2	
1789	....	?	Oshima (Izu Is-Japan)	0804-01=	2	
? 1789	....	?	Avachinsky (Kamchatka)	1000-10=		
1789	....	?	Tolbachik (Kamchatka)	1000-24=	2	
1789	0324	?	Barren Island (Andaman Is-Indian O)	0600-01=	2	
1789	06	31p	Fournaise, Piton de la (Indian O.)	0303-02=	2	
1789	1201	76m	Kliuchevskoi (Kamchatka)	1000-26=	2	
1789	1231y	?	Mahawu (Sulawesi-Indonesia)	0606-11=	2	
1790	Cont	....	Stromboli (Italy)	0101-04=	1	
1790	Cont	....	Yasur (Vanuatu-SW Pacific)	0507-10=	2	
1790	Cont	....	Kliuchevskoi (Kamchatka)	1000-26=	2	
1790	Cont	....	Seguam (Aleutian Is)	1101-18-		
1790	Cont	....	Amukta (Aleutian Is)	1101-19-	2	-/8
1790	Cont	....	Sangay (Ecuador)	1502-09=	2	
1790	....	?	Late (Tonga-SW Pacific)	0403-09=	2	
1790	....	?	Taal (Luzon-Philippines)	0703-07=	2	
1790 p	....	?	Chirpoi (Kuril Is)	0900-15=		
1790	....	>3yr	Alaid (Kuril Is)	0900-39=	2	
1790	....	?	Tolbachik (Kamchatka)	1000-24=	2	
? 1790	....	?	Semisopochnoi (Aleutian Is)	1101-06-		
1790	....	?	Gareloi (Aleutian Is)	1101-07-	2	
? 1790	....	?	Akutan (Aleutian Is)	1101-32-		
? 1790	....	?	Shishaldin (Aleutian Is)	1101-36-		
1790	....	?	Pavlof (Alaska Peninsula)	1102-03-	2	
T 1790 u	....	?	Mono Lake Volc Field (US-California	1203-11-		
1790 ?	....	?	Kilauea (Hawaiian Is)	1302-01-	0	7/-
1790	01 ?	?	Oshima-Oshima (Hokkaido-Japan)	0805-01=	2	
1790	01	>3yr	Villarrica (Chile-C)	1507-12=	1	
1790	0309	657e	Osorno (Chile-S)	1508-01=	2	
1790	05	....	Vesuvius (Italy)	0101-02=	1	7/8
? 1790	0530	?	Vsevidof (Aleutian Is)	1101-27-		
? 1790	0607	?	Makushin (Aleutian Is)	1101-31-		
1790	0729	?	Sakura-jima (Kyushu-Japan)	0802-08=	2	
1790	1009	?	Iwaki (Honshu-Japan)	0803-27=	2	
1790	11 ?	2a?	Kilauea (Hawaiian Is)	1302-01-	4	-/8
1791	Cont	....	Vesuvius (Italy)	0101-02=	2	7/8
1791	Cont	....	Stromboli (Italy)	0101-04=	1	
1791	Cont	....	Yasur (Vanuatu-SW Pacific)	0507-10=	2	
1791	Cont	....	Alaid (Kuril Is)	0900-39=	2	
1791	Cont	....	Amukta (Aleutian Is)	1101-19-	2	-/8
1791	Cont	....	Sangay (Ecuador)	1502-09=	2	
1791	Cont	....	Villarrica (Chile-C)	1507-12=	1	
1791	Cont	....	Osorno (Chile-S)	1508-01=	2	
1791	....	?	Fonualei (Tonga-SW Pacific)	0403-10=	2	
1791 <	....	?	Merapi (Java)	0603-25=	2	
1791	....	?	Gareloi (Aleutian Is)	1101-07-	2	
1791	0124	?	Telica (Nicaragua)	1404-04=		
1791	02	213p	Etna (Italy)	0101-06=	2	
1791	04	?	Kliuchevskoi (Kamchatka)	1000-26=	2	
1791	0522	?	Rabaul (New Britain-SW Pac)	0502-14=	2?	
1791	0605d	52d?	Fournaise, Piton de la (Indian O.)	0303-02=	0	7/-
? 1791	0607	?	Tanaga (Aleutian Is)	1101-08-		
1791	0717	....	Fournaise, Piton de la (Indian O.)	0303-02=	2	7/-
1791	08	?	Kliuchevskoi (Kamchatka)	1000-26=	2	
1791	0911	?	Sakura-jima (Kyushu-Japan)	0802-08=	2	
1792	Cont	....	Vesuvius (Italy)	0101-02=	2	7/8
1792	Cont	....	Stromboli (Italy)	0101-04=	1	
1792	Cont	....	Yasur (Vanuatu-SW Pacific)	0507-10=	2	
1792	Cont	....	Alaid (Kuril Is)	0900-39=	2	
1792	Cont	....	Sangay (Ecuador)	1502-09=	2	
1792	Cont	....	Villarrica (Chile-C)	1507-12=	1	
1792	....	?	Tofua (Tonga-SW Pacific)	0403-06=	0	
? 1792	....	?	Sakura-jima (Kyushu-Japan)	0802-08=	2?	
1792	....	?	Oshima (Izu Is-Japan)	0804-01=	2	
? 1792	....	?	Semisopochnoi (Aleutian Is)	1101-06-		
1792	....	?	Gareloi (Aleutian Is)	1101-07-	2	
1792 ?	....	?	Calbuco (Chile-S)	1508-02=		
1792	0122	84m?	Pelée (W Indies)	1600-12=	1	
1792	0210	163a	Unzen (Kyushu-Japan)	0802-10=	2	7/-
? 1792	0214	?	Makushin (Aleutian Is)	1101-31-		
1792	03	69m	Etna (Italy)	0101-06=	2	6/-
1792	0525	367e	Etna (Italy)	0101-06=	3	7/5
1792	0526e	?	Great Sitkin (Aleutian Is)	1101-12-		
? 1792	06	?	Baker (US-Washington)	1201-01=		
1792	1219?	?	Fournaise, Piton de la (Indian O.)	0303-02=	0	
1793	Cont	....	Vesuvius (Italy)	0101-02=	2	7/8
1793	Cont	....	Stromboli (Italy)	0101-04=	1	
1793	Cont	....	Yasur (Vanuatu-SW Pacific)	0507-10=	2	
1793	Cont	....	Sangay (Ecuador)	1502-09=	2	
1793	Cont	....	Villarrica (Chile-C)	1507-12=	1	
1793 ?	....	>3yr	Etna (Italy)	0101-06=	2	
1793	....	?	St. Paul (Indian O.-S)	0304-002	2	
1793 f	....	?	Raung (Java)	0603-34=	2	
1793	....	?	Ebeko (Kuril Is)	0900-38=	2	-/5
1793	....	?	Tolbachik (Kamchatka)	1000-24=	2	
? 1793	....	?	Iliamna (Alaska-SW)	1103-02-		
1793	02	....	Alaid (Kuril Is)	0900-39=	4↑	
1793	0302	289m	San Martín (México)	1401-11=	4	7/8
1793	0329	170m	Izalco (El Salvador)	1403-03=	2	
? 1793	0402	?	Iwaki (Honshu-Japan)	0803-27=	2	
? 1793	05	31p	Hierro (Canary Is)	1803-02-	0?	
1793	0629	?	Ritter Island (New Guinea-NE of)	0501-07=	2	
1794	Cont	....	Stromboli (Italy)	0101-04=	1	
1794	Cont	....	Etna (Italy)	0101-06=	2	
1794	Cont	....	Yasur (Vanuatu-SW Pacific)	0507-10=	2	
1794	Cont	....	Sangay (Ecuador)	1502-09=	2	
1794	Cont	....	Villarrica (Chile-C)	1507-12=	1	
1794	....	?	Sakura-jima (Kyushu-Japan)	0802-08=	2	
1794	....	?	Bárdarbunga (Iceland-NE)	1703-03=		
1794	01	16m	Fournaise, Piton de la (Indian O.)	0303-02=	0	
? 1794	0403	?	Iwaki (Honshu-Japan)	0803-27=	2	
1794	05	765w	San Martín (México)	1401-11=	2?	
1794	0616	....	Vesuvius (Italy)	0101-02=	3?	7/8
? 1794	0715q	?	Grímsvötn (Iceland-NE)	1703-01=		
1794	08	?	Colima (México)	1401-04=	2	
1794	0922	84m>	Zao (Honshu-Japan)	0803-19=	2	
1795	Cont	....	Stromboli (Italy)	0101-04=	1	
1795	Cont	....	Etna (Italy)	0101-06=	2	
1795	Cont	....	Yasur (Vanuatu-SW Pacific)	0507-10=	2	
1795	Cont	....	San Martín (México)	1401-11=	2	
1795	Cont	....	Sangay (Ecuador)	1502-09=	2	
1795	Cont	....	Villarrica (Chile-C)	1507-12=	1	
1795	....	7a>	Fournaise, Piton de la (Indian O.)	0303-02=		
1795	....	?	Westdahl [Pogromni ?] (Aleutian Is)	1101-34-	4	-/9
1795 <	....	?	Fisher (Aleutian Is)	1101-35-		
? 1795	....	?	Isanotski (Aleutian Is)	1101-37-	3↑	
D 1795 e	....	>3yr	Hood (US-Oregon)	1202-01-		
1795	03	183p	Colima (México)	1401-04=	2	
1795	1220	1a>	Barren Island (Andaman Is-Indian O)	0600-01=	2	
1796	Cont	....	Stromboli (Italy)	0101-04=	1	
1796	Cont	....	Etna (Italy)	0101-06=	2	
1796	Cont	....	Yasur (Vanuatu-SW Pacific)	0507-10=	2	
D 1796	Cont	....	Hood (US-Oregon)	1202-01-		
1796	Cont	....	San Martín (México)	1401-11=	2	
1796	Cont	....	Sangay (Ecuador)	1502-09=	2	
1796	Cont	....	Villarrica (Chile-C)	1507-12=	1	
1796	....	?	Ijen (Java)	0603-35=	2	
1796	....	?	Westdahl [Pogromni ?] (Aleutian Is)	1101-34-	0	
1796	....	?	Amak (Aleutian Is)	1101-39-		
1796	01	>3yr	Vesuvius (Italy)	0101-02=	1	6/7
1796	0324	?	Zao (Honshu-Japan)	0803-19=	2	
1796	05	>3yr	Bogoslof (Aleutian Is)	1101-30-	3?	7/8
1796	10	31p	Iwo-Tori-shima (Ryukyu Is)	0802-02=	2	
1796	11	>3yr	Galeras (Colombia)	1501-08=	2	
1797	Cont	....	Vesuvius (Italy)	0101-02=	2	6/7
1797	Cont	....	Stromboli (Italy)	0101-04=	1	
1797	Cont	....	Yasur (Vanuatu-SW Pacific)	0507-10=	2	
1797	Cont	....	Bogoslof (Aleutian Is)	1101-30-	0	7/8
D 1797	Cont	....	Hood (US-Oregon)	1202-01-		
1797	Cont	....	Galeras (Colombia)	1501-08=	2	
1797	Cont	....	Sangay (Ecuador)	1502-09=	2	
1797	Cont	....	Villarrica (Chile-C)	1507-12=	1	
1797 ?	....	7a	Fournaise, Piton de la (Indian O.)	0303-02=	0	
1797	....	<1	Tinakula (Santa Cruz Is-SW Pacific)	0506-01=	1?	
? 1797	....	?	Hunter Island (SW Pacific)	0508-02=		
1797	....	?	Merbabu (Java)	0603-24=	2	
1797	....	?	Merapi (Java)	0603-25=	1	
1797	....	?	Sakura-jima (Kyushu-Japan)	0802-08=	2	
? 1797	....	>3yr	San Martín (México)	1401-11=	2?	

START YEAR	M-Dy	Duration	VOLCANO NAME (Subregion)	NUMBER	VEI	Vol L/T
@ 1797	....	?	**Bárdarbunga** (Iceland-NE)	1703-03=		
1797 ?	....	?	**Askja** (Iceland-NE)	1703-06=	0	
1797	01	....	*Etna (Italy)*	0101-06=	2	
1797	01	?	**Reventador** (Ecuador)	1502-01=	3	
? 1797	0204	?	*Quilotoa (Ecuador)*	1502-06=		
1797	08	?	**Wolf** (Galápagos)	1503-02=		
1797	0929	209a?	**Soufrière Guadeloupe** (W Indies)	1600-06=	2	
1798	Cont	....	*Vesuvius (Italy)*	0101-02=	2	6/7
1798	Cont	....	*Stromboli (Italy)*	0101-04=	1	
1798	Cont	....	*Etna (Italy)*	0101-06=	2	
1798	Cont	....	*Yasur (Vanuatu-SW Pacific)*	0507-10=	2	
1798	Cont	....	*Bogoslof (Aleutian Is)*	1101-30-	0	7/8
D 1798	Cont	....	*Hood (US-Oregon)*	1202-01-		
? 1798	Cont	....	*San Martín (México)*	1401-11=	2	
1798	Cont	....	*Galeras (Colombia)*	1501-08=	2	
1798	Cont	....	*Sangay (Ecuador)*	1502-09=	2	
1798	Cont	....	*Villarrica (Chile-C)*	1507-12=	1	
1798	Cont	....	*Soufrière Guadeloupe (W Indies)*	1600-06=	2	
? 1798 ?	....	?	*San Miguel (El Salvador)*	1403-10=	2	
1798	04	?	**Izalco** (El Salvador)	1403-03=	2	
1798	0609	97a	**Tenerife** (Canary Is)	1803-03-	3	7/-
? 1798	1113	33m	*Unzen (Kyushu-Japan)*	0802-10=		
1799	Cont	....	*Vesuvius (Italy)*	0101-02=	2	6/7
1799	Cont	....	*Stromboli (Italy)*	0101-04=	1	
1799	Cont	....	*Etna (Italy)*	0101-06=	2	
1799	Cont	....	*Yasur (Vanuatu-SW Pacific)*	0507-10=	2	
1799	Cont	....	*Bogoslof (Aleutian Is)*	1101-30-	0	7/8
D 1799	Cont	....	*Hood (US-Oregon)*	1202-01-		
? 1799	Cont	....	*San Martín (México)*	1401-11=	2	
1799	Cont	....	*Galeras (Colombia)*	1501-08=	2	
1799	Cont	....	*Sangay (Ecuador)*	1502-09=	2	
1799	Cont	....	*Villarrica (Chile-C)*	1507-12=	1	
1799	....	?	**Lamongan** (Java)	0603-32=	2	
1799	....	3a	**Fuego** (Guatemala)	1402-09=	3	-/7
1799	0327	?	**Sakura-jima** (Kyushu-Japan)	0802-08=	2	
1799	0602	26a	**Fogo** (Cape Verde Is)	1804-01=	2	
			1800			
1800	Cont	....	*Vesuvius (Italy)*	0101-02=	2	6/7
1800	Cont	....	*Stromboli (Italy)*	0101-04=	1	
1800	Cont	....	*Yasur (Vanuatu-SW Pacific)*	0507-10=	2	
1800	Cont	....	*Bogoslof (Aleutian Is)*	1101-30-	0	7/8
D 1800	Cont	....	*Hood (US-Oregon)*	1202-01-		
? 1800	Cont	....	*San Martín (México)*	1401-11=	2	
1800	Cont	....	*Galeras (Colombia)*	1501-08=	2	
1800	Cont	....	*Sangay (Ecuador)*	1502-09=	2	
1800	Cont	....	*Villarrica (Chile-C)*	1507-12=	1	
1800 ?	....	3a	**Kieyo** (Africa-E)	0202-17=	2	
T 1800 ?	....	?	**Taranaki [Egmont]** (New Zealand)	0401-03=		
T 1800 ?	....	?	**Pago** (New Britain-SW Pac)	0502-08=	P	
1800	....	?	**Guntur** (Java)	0603-13=		
1800 ?	....	?	**Azuma** (Honshu-Japan)	0803-18=		
C 1800 t	....	?	**Pagan** (Mariana Is-C Pacific)	0804-17=		
T 1800 t	....	?	**Rausu** (Hokkaido-Japan)	0805-082	3	
? 1800 j	....	?	*Shiveluch (Kamchatka)*	1000-27=	3	-/7
C 1800 ?	....	?	**Iskut-Unuk River Cones** (Canada)	1200-09-		
1800	....	365y	**Hualalai** (Hawaiian Is)	1302-04-	0	7/-
? 1800 t	....	?	*Concepción (Nicaragua)*	1404-12=	2	
T 1800 x	....	?	**Ticsani** (Perú)	1504-031		
1800 <	....	?	**Deception Island** (Antarctica)	1900-03=		
D 1800	0115u	?	**St. Helens** (US-Washington)	1201-05-	**5**	**-/9**
1800	0304	....	**Etna** (Italy)	0101-06=	3?	
? 1800	0511	?	*Iwaki (Honshu-Japan)*	0803-27=	2	
1800	0624	1a	**San Jorge** (Azores)	1802-03=	2	
1800	0821	<1	**Wolf** (Galápagos)	1503-02=	2?	
1800	1030	1a	**Mayon** (Luzon-Philippines)	0703-03=	2	
1800	1102	6a	**Fournaise, Piton de la** (Indian O.)	0303-02=	0	7/-
1800	12	>3yr	*Chokai (Honshu-Japan)*	0803-22=	1?	6/-
1801	Cont	....	*Vesuvius (Italy)*	0101-02=	2	6/7
1801	Cont	....	*Stromboli (Italy)*	0101-04=	1	
1801	Cont	....	*Etna (Italy)*	0101-06=	2	
1801	Cont	....	*Yasur (Vanuatu-SW Pacific)*	0507-10=	2	
1801	Cont	....	*Bogoslof (Aleutian Is)*	1101-30-	0	7/8
D 1801	Cont	....	*Hood (US-Oregon)*	1202-01-		
1801	Cont	....	*Hualalai (Hawaiian Is)*	1302-04-	0	7/-
? 1801	Cont	....	*San Martín (México)*	1401-11=	2	
1801	Cont	....	*Galeras (Colombia)*	1501-08=	2	
1801	Cont	....	*Sangay (Ecuador)*	1502-09=	2	
1801	Cont	....	*Villarrica (Chile-C)*	1507-12=	1	
1801	....	?	**Tongkoko** (Sulawesi-Indonesia)	0606-13=	2	6/-
1801	....	318w>	**Antisana** (Ecuador)	1502-03=	2	
1801	0810	....	**Chokai** (Honshu-Japan)	0803-22=	2	6/-
1801	1027	153g	**Fournaise, Piton de la** (Indian O.)	0303-02=	2	
1802	Cont	....	*Vesuvius (Italy)*	0101-02=	2	6/7
1802	Cont	....	*Stromboli (Italy)*	0101-04=	1	
1802	Cont	....	*Yasur (Vanuatu-SW Pacific)*	0507-10=	2	
1802	Cont	....	*Chokai (Honshu-Japan)*	0803-22=	1?	6/-
1802	Cont	....	*Bogoslof (Aleutian Is)*	1101-30-	0	7/8
D 1802	Cont	....	*Hood (US-Oregon)*	1202-01-		
? 1802	Cont	....	*San Martín (México)*	1401-11=	2	
1802	Cont	....	*Antisana (Ecuador)*	1502-03=	2	
1802	Cont	....	*Sangay (Ecuador)*	1502-09=	2	
1802	....	?	**Makushin** (Aleutian Is)	1101-31-	3	
1802	....	730y	**Popocatépetl** (México)	1401-09=	1	
1802	....	365y	**Izalco** (El Salvador)	1403-03=	2	
@ 1802	0330	108m	**Yucamane** (Perú)	1504-05-	3	
@ 1802	04 ?	31p?	**Reventador** (Ecuador)	1502-01=	2	
1802	1115	3a	**Etna** (Italy)	0101-06=	2	7/-
1802	12	?	**Fournaise, Piton de la** (Indian O.)	0303-02=	2	
1803	Cont	....	*Vesuvius (Italy)*	0101-02=	2	6/7
1803	Cont	....	*Stromboli (Italy)*	0101-04=	1	
1803	Cont	....	*Yasur (Vanuatu-SW Pacific)*	0507-10=	2	
1803	Cont	....	*Chokai (Honshu-Japan)*	0803-22=	1?	6/-
1803	Cont	....	*Bogoslof (Aleutian Is)*	1101-30-	0	7/8
D 1803	Cont	....	*Hood (US-Oregon)*	1202-01-		
1803	Cont	....	*Popocatépetl (México)*	1401-09=	1	
? 1803	Cont	....	*San Martín (México)*	1401-11=	2	
1803	Cont	....	*Izalco (El Salvador)*	1403-03=	2	
1803	Cont	....	*Sangay (Ecuador)*	1502-09=	2	
1803	0101	>3yr	**Etna** (Italy)	0101-06=	2	
1803	0104	1a	**Cotopaxi** (Ecuador)	1502-05=	3	
1803	0403	12a	**Guntur** (Java)	0603-13=	2	
1803	0704	?	**Asama** (Honshu-Japan)	0803-11=	2	
1803	0926?	49a?	**Oshima** (Izu Is-Japan)	0804-01=	2	
1803	11	77a>	**Barren Island** (Andaman Is-Indian O)	0600-01=	2	
1803	1107	14a	**Asama** (Honshu-Japan)	0803-11=	2	
1804	Cont	....	*Stromboli (Italy)*	0101-04=	1	
1804	Cont	....	*Etna (Italy)*	0101-06=	2	
1804	Cont	....	*Yasur (Vanuatu-SW Pacific)*	0507-10=	2	
1804	Cont	....	*Barren Island (Andaman Is-Indian O)*	0600-01=	2	
1804	Cont	....	*Chokai (Honshu-Japan)*	0803-22=	1?	6/-
D 1804	Cont	....	*Hood (US-Oregon)*	1202-01-		
1804	Cont	....	*Popocatépetl (México)*	1401-09=	1	
? 1804	Cont	....	*San Martín (México)*	1401-11=	2	
1804	Cont	....	*Sangay (Ecuador)*	1502-09=	2	
1804 d	....	?	**Raung** (Java)	0603-34=	2	
1804	....	?	**Batur** (Lesser Sunda Is)	0604-01=	2	
1804	....	>3yr	**Shikotsu [Tarumai]** (Hokkaido)	0805-04=	3	-/7
1804	....	?	**Maly Semiachik** (Kamchatka)	1000-14=	3	
1804	....	....	*Bogoslof (Aleutian Is)*	1101-30-	2	7/8
1804	....	?	**Colima** (México)	1401-04=	2	
1804	05 ?	?	**Zao** (Honshu-Japan)	0803-19=	2	
1804	0812	....	*Vesuvius (Italy)*	0101-02=	2	6/7
1804	09	?	**Tengger Caldera [Bromo]** (Java)	0603-31=	2	
1804	0905	?	**Aso** (Kyushu-Japan)	0802-11=	2	
1805	Cont	....	*Stromboli (Italy)*	0101-04=	1	
1805	Cont	....	*Yasur (Vanuatu-SW Pacific)*	0507-10=	2	
1805	Cont	....	*Shikotsu [Tarumai] (Hokkaido)*	0805-04=	2	-/7
D 1805	Cont	....	*Hood (US-Oregon)*	1202-01-		
? 1805	Cont	....	*San Martín (México)*	1401-11=	2	
1805	Cont	....	*Sangay (Ecuador)*	1502-09=	2	
1805	....	?	**Kusatsu-Shirane** (Honshu-Japan)	0803-12=	2	
1805	....	?	**Sarychev Peak** (Kuril Is)	0900-24=		
1805	....	?	**Okmok** (Aleutian Is)	1101-29-		
1805	....	?	**Pacaya** (Guatemala)	1402-11=	2	
1805	....	730y	**Izalco** (El Salvador)	1403-03=	2	
1805	0311	....	*Etna (Italy)*	0101-06=	2	
1805	0314	?	**Ruiz, Nevado del** (Colombia)	1501-02=	2	
1805	04	?	**Cereme** (Java)	0603-17=	2	
1805	0711	....	*Etna (Italy)*	0101-06=	2	
1805	0812	....	*Vesuvius (Italy)*	0101-02=	2	6/7
1806	Cont	....	*Stromboli (Italy)*	0101-04=	1	
1806	Cont	....	*Etna (Italy)*	0101-06=	2	
1806	Cont	....	*Yasur (Vanuatu-SW Pacific)*	0507-10=	2	
1806	Cont	....	*Shikotsu [Tarumai] (Hokkaido)*	0805-04=	2	-/7
1806	Cont	....	*Izalco (El Salvador)*	1403-03=	2	
1806	Cont	....	*Sangay (Ecuador)*	1502-09=	2	
1806 ?	....	?	**Sundoro** (Java)	0603-21=	2	
1806	....	>3yr	*Bogoslof (Aleutian Is)*	1101-30-	1	7/-
1806	....	>3yr	**Colima** (México)	1401-04=	2?	
? 1806	....	?	*San Salvador (El Salvador)*	1403-05=	0	
1806	04	31m	**Villarrica** (Chile-C)	1507-12=	2	
1806	05	?	**Lamongan** (Java)	0603-32=	2	
1806 ?	05	?	**Antuco** (Chile-C)	1507-08=	2	
1806	0531	....	*Vesuvius (Italy)*	0101-02=	2	6/7
1806	06 ?	123p?	**Aso** (Kyushu-Japan)	0802-11=	2	
1806	0712	?	**Zao** (Honshu-Japan)	0803-19=	2	
1807	Cont	....	*Vesuvius (Italy)*	0101-02=	2	6/7
1807	Cont	....	*Stromboli (Italy)*	0101-04=	1	
1807	Cont	....	*Yasur (Vanuatu-SW Pacific)*	0507-10=	2	
1807	Cont	....	*Shikotsu [Tarumai] (Hokkaido)*	0805-04=	2	-/7
1807	Cont	....	*Bogoslof (Aleutian Is)*	1101-30-	1	7/-
1807	Cont	....	*Colima (México)*	1401-04=	1	

	START YEAR	M-Dy	Dura-tion	VOLCANO NAME (Subregion)	NUMBER	VEI	Vol L/T
	1807	*Cont*	....	*Izalco (El Salvador)*	1403-03=	*2*	
	1807	*Cont*	....	*Sangay (Ecuador)*	1502-09=	*2*	
	1807 h	....	?	**Cameroon** (Africa-W)	0204-01=	3	
	1807	....	?	**Marapi** (Sumatra)	0601-14=	2	
	1807	....	?	**Merapi** (Java)	0603-25=	1?	
?	*1807*	....	?	*Bárdarbunga (Iceland-NE)*	1703-03=		
	1807	*0112*	....	*Etna (Italy)*	0101-06=	*2*	
	1807	0201p	?	**Kliuchevskoi** (Kamchatka)	1000-26=	2	
	1807	0323	82*a*	**Fournaise, Piton de la** (Indian O.)	0303-02=	2	
?	*1807*	*0331*	?	*Iwaki (Honshu-Japan)*	0803-27=	*2*	
	1807	0901	5*a*	**Guntur** (Java)	0603-13=	2	
	1808	*Cont*	....	*Vesuvius (Italy)*	0101-02=	*2*	*6/7*
	1808	*Cont*	....	*Stromboli (Italy)*	0101-04=	*1*	
	1808	*Cont*	....	*Yasur (Vanuatu-SW Pacific)*	0507-10=	*2*	
	1808	*Cont*	....	*Shikotsu [Tarumai] (Hokkaido)*	0805-04=	*2*	*-/7*
	1808	*Cont*	....	*Bogoslof (Aleutian Is)*	1101-30-	*1*	*7/-*
	1808	*Cont*	....	*Colima (México)*	1401-04=	*1*	
	1808	*Cont*	....	*Sangay (Ecuador)*	1502-09=	*2*	
	1808	....	?	**Karthala** (Indian O.-W)	0303-01=		
	1808	....	?	**Agung** (Lesser Sunda Is)	0604-02=	2	
	1808	....	?	**Ruang** (Sangihe Is-Indonesia)	0607-01=	2	
	1808 ?	....	?	**Bandai** (Honshu-Japan)	0803-16=	2	
	1808 ?	....	?	**Akan** (Hokkaido-Japan)	0805-07=		
	1808	02	59*p*	**Taal** (Luzon-Philippines)	0703-07=	2	
	1808	0501	40*a*	**San Jorge** (Azores)	1802-03=	1	
	1808	*07*	....	*Etna (Italy)*	0101-06=	*2*	
	1808	1208	?	**Lamongan** (Java)	0603-32=	2	
	1809	*Cont*	....	*Vesuvius (Italy)*	0101-02=	*2*	*6/7*
	1809	*Cont*	....	*Stromboli (Italy)*	0101-04=	*1*	
	1809	*Cont*	....	*Yasur (Vanuatu-SW Pacific)*	0507-10=	*2*	
	1809	*Cont*	....	*Shikotsu [Tarumai] (Hokkaido)*	0805-04=	*2*	*-/7*
	1809	*Cont*	....	*Bogoslof (Aleutian Is)*	1101-30-	*1*	*7/-*
	1809	*Cont*	....	*Colima (México)*	1401-04=	*1*	
	1809	*Cont*	....	*Sangay (Ecuador)*	1502-09=	*2*	
I	**1809** b	....	?	***Unknown Source*** *(SP, 818 ppb sulfate)*	......		
	1809	0327	13*a*	**Etna** (Italy)	0101-06=	2	7/6
?	*1809*	*0328*	*3a*	*Cosigüina (Nicaragua)*	1404-01=	*2?*	
	1809	0509	?	**Guntur** (Java)	0603-13=	2	
	1809	0612	200*a*	**Zao** (Honshu-Japan)	0803-19=	2	
	1809	0717	22*a*	**Fournaise, Piton de la** (Indian O.)	0303-02=	2	
	1810	*Cont*	....	*Stromboli (Italy)*	0101-04=	*1*	
	1810	*Cont*	....	*Yasur (Vanuatu-SW Pacific)*	0507-10=	*2*	
	1810	*Cont*	....	*Shikotsu [Tarumai] (Hokkaido)*	0805-04=	*2*	*-/7*
	1810	*Cont*	....	*Bogoslof (Aleutian Is)*	1101-30-	*1*	*7/-*
	1810	*Cont*	....	*Sangay (Ecuador)*	1502-09=	*2*	
	1810 j	....	?	**Yar, Jabal** (Arabia-W)	0301-08-	2	
?	*1810 j*	....	?	*Victory (New Guinea)*	0503-03=	*2?*	
	1810	....	?	**Merapi** (Java)	0603-25=	1	
	1810 j	....	?	**Putana** (Chile-N)	1505-09=		
	1810	*0911*	....	*Vesuvius (Italy)*	0101-02=	*1*	*6/7*
	1810	1120	8*a*	**Fournaise, Piton de la** (Indian O.)	0303-02=	2	
	1810	*1226e*	....	*Etna (Italy)*	0101-06=	*2*	
	1811	*Cont*	....	*Vesuvius (Italy)*	0101-02=	*2*	*6/7*
	1811	*Cont*	....	*Stromboli (Italy)*	0101-04=	*1*	
	1811	*Cont*	....	*Yasur (Vanuatu-SW Pacific)*	0507-10=	*2*	
	1811	*Cont*	....	*Shikotsu [Tarumai] (Hokkaido)*	0805-04=	*2*	*-/7*
	1811	*Cont*	....	*Bogoslof (Aleutian Is)*	1101-30-	*1*	*7/-*
	1811	*Cont*	....	*Sangay (Ecuador)*	1502-09=	*2*	
?	*1811*	....	?	*San Miguel (El Salvador)*	1403-10=	*2*	
	1811	0127	1*a*	**Miyake-jima** (Izu Is-Japan)	0804-04=	2	-/6
	1811	0201	104*m*	**Gamalama** (Halmahera-Indonesia)	0608-06=	2	
	1811	0201	7*a*	**Sete Cidades** (Azores)	1802-08=	2?	
	1811	0605	?	**Kelut** (Java)	0603-28=	2	
	1811	0611	?	**Chirpoi** (Kuril Is)	0900-15=	2	
	1811	0614	8*a*	**Sete Cidades** (Azores)	1802-08=	3	
?	*1811*	*1005*	*1a?*	*Mayon (Luzon-Philippines)*	0703-03=	*2*	
	1811	1027	200*m*?	**Etna** (Italy)	0101-06=	2	7/6
	1811	*1031*	....	*Etna (Italy)*	0101-06=	*2*	*7/6*
	1812	*Cont*	....	*Stromboli (Italy)*	0101-04=	*1*	
	1812	*Cont*	....	*Etna (Italy)*	0101-06=	*2*	*7/6*
	1812	*Cont*	....	*Yasur (Vanuatu-SW Pacific)*	0507-10=	*2*	
	1812	*Cont*	....	*Shikotsu [Tarumai] (Hokkaido)*	0805-04=	*2*	*-/7*
	1812	*Cont*	....	*Bogoslof (Aleutian Is)*	1101-30-	*1*	*7/-*
	1812	*Cont*	....	*Sangay (Ecuador)*	1502-09=	*2*	
?	*1812*	....	?	*Vulcano (Italy)*	0101-05=	*1?*	
	1812	....	>3yr	**Merapi** (Java)	0603-25=	1	
	1812	....	730*y*?	**Raung** (Java)	0603-34=	2	
	1812	....	*>3yr*	*Tambora (Lesser Sunda Is)*	0604-04=	*2*	
?	*1812*	....	?	*Berutarube (Kuril Is)*	0900-04=	*1*	
	1812	....	?	**Atka [Kliuchef]** (Aleutian Is)	1101-16-	3?	
	1812	....	?	**Augustine** (Alaska-SW)	1103-01-	3?	
	1812	*0101*	....	*Vesuvius (Italy)*	0101-02=	*1*	*6/7*
	1812	04	25*m*	**Soufrière Guadeloupe** (W Indies)	1600-06=	1	
	1812	0427	43*a*?	**Soufrière St. Vincent** (W Indies)	1600-15=	4	-/8
	1812	08	?	**Tiatia** (Kuril Is)	0900-03=	2	
	1812	0805d	132*n*	**Fournaise, Piton de la** (Indian O.)	0303-02=	2	
	1812	0806	2*a*	**Awu** (Sangihe Is-Indonesia)	0607-04=	4?	-/8
	1812	09	?	**Kliuchevskoi** (Kamchatka)	1000-26=	2	
	1812	0905d	?	**Atsonupuri** (Kuril Is)	0900-05=	1	
	1812	0907	<1	**Gamalama** (Halmahera-Indonesia)	0608-06=	2	
	1813	*Cont*	....	*Stromboli (Italy)*	0101-04=	*1*	
	1813	*Cont*	....	*Etna (Italy)*	0101-06=	*2*	
	1813	*Cont*	....	*Yasur (Vanuatu-SW Pacific)*	0507-10=	*2*	
	1813	*Cont*	....	*Merapi (Java)*	0603-25=	*1*	
	1813	*Cont*	....	*Raung (Java)*	0603-34=	*2*	
	1813	*Cont*	....	*Tambora (Lesser Sunda Is)*	0604-04=	*2*	
	1813	*Cont*	....	*Shikotsu [Tarumai] (Hokkaido)*	0805-04=	*2*	*-/7*
	1813	*Cont*	....	*Bogoslof (Aleutian Is)*	1101-30-	*1*	*7/-*
	1813	*Cont*	....	*Sangay (Ecuador)*	1502-09=	*2*	
	1813	....	365*y*	**Suwanose-jima** (Ryukyu Is)	0802-03=	4	
?	*1813*	*0110*	?	*Adatara (Honshu-Japan)*	0803-17=	*1?*	
	1813	02	?	**Kliuchevskoi** (Kamchatka)	1000-26=	2	
@	**1813**	0606	1*a*	**Darwin** (Galápagos)	1503-03=	2?	
@	**1813**	0713	?	**Negra, Sierra** (Galápagos)	1503-05=	2?	
	1813	0714<	?	**Fernandina** (Galápagos)	1503-01=	2	
	1813	0926	61*a*	**Fournaise, Piton de la** (Indian O.)	0303-02=	2	
	1813	*1029*	....	*Vesuvius (Italy)*	0101-02=	*2*	*6/7*
	1814	*Cont*	....	*Vesuvius (Italy)*	0101-02=	*2*	*6/7*
	1814	*Cont*	....	*Stromboli (Italy)*	0101-04=	*1*	
	1814	*Cont*	....	*Etna (Italy)*	0101-06=	*2*	
	1814	*Cont*	....	*Yasur (Vanuatu-SW Pacific)*	0507-10=	*2*	
	1814	*Cont*	....	*Merapi (Java)*	0603-25=	*1*	
	1814	*Cont*	....	*Raung (Java)*	0603-34=	*2*	
	1814	*Cont*	....	*Tambora (Lesser Sunda Is)*	0604-04=	*2*	
	1814	*Cont*	....	*Suwanose-jima (Ryukyu Is)*	0802-03=	*4*	
	1814	*Cont*	....	*Shikotsu [Tarumai] (Hokkaido)*	0805-04=	*2*	*-/7*
	1814	*Cont*	....	*Sangay (Ecuador)*	1502-09=	*2*	
	1814	....	?	**Niuafo'ou** (Tonga-SW Pacific)	0403-11=	2	
	1814	....	?	**Aso** (Kyushu-Japan)	0802-11=	2	
	1814	....	....	**Bogoslof** (Aleutian Is)	1101-30-	2	7/-
	1814	....	?	**Ugashik-Peulik** (Alaska Peninsula)	1102-13-	3	
	1814	0109	<1	**Soufrière St. Vincent** (W Indies)	1600-15=	1?	
	1814	0201	14*a*>	**Mayon** (Luzon-Philippines)	0703-03=	4	-/8
	1814	0309	?	**Raoul Island** (Kermadec Is)	0402-03=	3	-/7
	1814	07	31*p*	**Fernandina** (Galápagos)	1503-01=	2	
	1814	0910	33*a*	**Fournaise, Piton de la** (Indian O.)	0303-02=	2	
	1814	1127	<1	**Gamalama** (Halmahera-Indonesia)	0608-06=	2	
	1814	1231y	?	**Karthala** (Indian O.-W)	0303-01=		
	1815	*Cont*	....	*Vesuvius (Italy)*	0101-02=	*2*	*6/7*
	1815	*Cont*	....	*Stromboli (Italy)*	0101-04=	*1*	
	1815	*Cont*	....	*Etna (Italy)*	0101-06=	*2*	
	1815	*Cont*	....	*Yasur (Vanuatu-SW Pacific)*	0507-10=	*2*	
	1815	*Cont*	....	*Merapi (Java)*	0603-25=	*1*	
	1815	*Cont*	....	*Shikotsu [Tarumai] (Hokkaido)*	0805-04=	*2*	*-/7*
	1815	*Cont*	....	*Bogoslof (Aleutian Is)*	1101-30-	*1*	*7/-*
	1815	*Cont*	....	*Sangay (Ecuador)*	1502-09=	*2*	
	1815	....	>3yr	**Villarrica** (Chile-C)	1507-12=	1	
	1815	0121	6*a*	**Fournaise, Piton de la** (Indian O.)	0303-02=	2	
	1815	0210	247*m*	**Aso** (Kyushu-Japan)	0802-11=	2	
	1815	0228	?	**Asama** (Honshu-Japan)	0803-11=	3	
	1815	0405	12*a*>	**Tengger Caldera [Bromo]** (Java)	0603-31=	2	
	1815	0410	....	**Tambora** (Lesser Sunda Is)	0604-04=	**7**	**-/11**
	1815	0815	1*a*	**Fournaise, Piton de la** (Indian O.)	0303-02=	2	
	1815	0815	?	**Guntur** (Java)	0603-13=	2	
	1815	1231y	?	**Raung** (Java)	0603-34=	2	
	1816	*Cont*	....	*Vesuvius (Italy)*	0101-02=	*2*	*6/7*
	1816	*Cont*	....	*Stromboli (Italy)*	0101-04=	*1*	
	1816	*Cont*	....	*Yasur (Vanuatu-SW Pacific)*	0507-10=	*2*	
	1816	*Cont*	....	*Merapi (Java)*	0603-25=	*1*	
	1816	*Cont*	....	*Shikotsu [Tarumai] (Hokkaido)*	0805-04=	*2*	*-/7*
	1816	*Cont*	....	*Bogoslof (Aleutian Is)*	1101-30-	*1*	*7/-*
	1816	*Cont*	....	*Sangay (Ecuador)*	1502-09=	*2*	
	1816	*Cont*	....	*Villarrica (Chile-C)*	1507-12=	*1*	
	1816	....	?	**Puracé** (Colombia)	1501-06=		
?	*1816*	*0306*	?	*Etna (Italy)*	0101-06=	*0*	
	1816	05	30*p*?	**Grímsvötn** (Iceland-NE)	1703-01=	2	
	1816	0609	27*a*	**Aso** (Kyushu-Japan)	0802-11=	2	
	1816	0921	?	**Guntur** (Java)	0603-13=	2	
	1816	1011	65*m*	**Banda Api** (Banda Sea)	0605-09=	2	
?	*1816*	*1208*	?	*Unnamed (Atlantic-C)*	1805-03=	*0*	
	1816	1215	?	**Fournaise, Piton de la** (Indian O.)	0303-02=	0	
	1816	1231y	?	**Fogo** (Cape Verde Is)	1804-01=		
	1817	*Cont*	....	*Stromboli (Italy)*	0101-04=	*1*	
	1817	*Cont*	....	*Etna (Italy)*	0101-06=	*2*	
	1817	*Cont*	....	*Yasur (Vanuatu-SW Pacific)*	0507-10=	*2*	
	1817	*Cont*	....	*Merapi (Java)*	0603-25=	*1*	
	1817	*Cont*	....	*Shikotsu [Tarumai] (Hokkaido)*	0805-04=	*2*	*-/7*
	1817	*Cont*	....	*Bogoslof (Aleutian Is)*	1101-30-	*1*	*7/-*
	1817	*Cont*	....	*Sangay (Ecuador)*	1502-09=	*2*	
	1817	*Cont*	....	*Villarrica (Chile-C)*	1507-12=	*1*	
	1817	....	?	**Lamongan** (Java)	0603-32=	2	
?	*1817*	....	?	*Yunaska (Aleutian Is)*	1101-21-		
	1817	....	?	**Vsevidof** (Aleutian Is)	1101-27-	3?	

	START YEAR	M-Dy	Dura-tion	VOLCANO NAME (Subregion)	NUMBER	VEI	Vol L/T
	1817	....	?	Pavlof (Alaska Peninsula)	1102-03-	2	
	1817	....	?	Izalco (El Salvador)	1403-03=	2	
@	1817 <	....	?	Fernandina (Galápagos)	1503-01=	2	
@	1817	....	?	Negra, Sierra (Galápagos)	1503-05=		
	1817	01	89p	Fournaise, Piton de la (Indian O.)	0303-02=	0	
	1817	0115	34e?	Ijen (Java)	0603-35=	1?	
	1817	0116	25a?	Raung (Java)	0603-34=	4?	-/8
	1817	0124	....	Ijen (Java)	0603-35=	2	
	1817	0301	>3yr	Okmok (Aleutian Is)	1101-29-	3	
	1817	1222	....	Vesuvius (Italy)	0101-02=	1	6/7
	1817	1231y	?	Dempo (Sumatra)	0601-23=	2	
	1818	Cont	....	Vesuvius (Italy)	0101-02=	2	6/7
	1818	Cont	....	Stromboli (Italy)	0101-04=	1	
	1818	Cont	....	Etna (Italy)	0101-06=	2	
	1818	Cont	....	Yasur (Vanuatu-SW Pacific)	0507-10=	2	
	1818	Cont	....	Merapi (Java)	0603-25=	1	
	1818	Cont	....	Okmok (Aleutian Is)	1101-29-	2	
	1818	Cont	....	Bogoslof (Aleutian Is)	1101-30-	1	7/-
	1818	Cont	....	Sangay (Ecuador)	1502-09=	2	
	1818	Cont	....	Villarrica (Chile-C)	1507-12=	1	
	1818	....	?	Sundoro (Java)	0603-21=	2	
?	1818	....	?	Makushin (Aleutian Is)	1101-31-		
	1818	0116	154a>	Almolonga [C. Quemado] (Guat)	1402-04=	2	
	1818	0215	<1?	Colima (México)	1401-04=	4	
	1818	04	?	Jan Mayen (Atlantic-N-Jan Mayen)	1706-01=	3?	
	1818	1008	?	Lamongan (Java)	0603-32=	2	
	1818	1021	2	Guntur (Java)	0603-13=	2	
	1818	1108	?	Semeru (Java)	0603-30=	2	
	1819	Cont	....	Vesuvius (Italy)	0101-02=	2	6/7
	1819	Cont	....	Stromboli (Italy)	0101-04=	1	
	1819	Cont	....	Yasur (Vanuatu-SW Pacific)	0507-10=	2	
	1819	Cont	....	Merapi (Java)	0603-25=	1	
	1819	Cont	....	Okmok (Aleutian Is)	1101-29-	2	
	1819	Cont	....	Bogoslof (Aleutian Is)	1101-30-	1	7/-
	1819	Cont	....	Sangay (Ecuador)	1502-09=	2	
	1819	....	?	Lewotolo (Lesser Sunda Is)	0604-23=	2	
	1819	....	?	Soputan (Sulawesi-Indonesia)	0606-03=	2	
?	1819	....	?	Sempu (Sulawesi-Indonesia)	0606-04=		
	1819	....	1096y	Kliuchevskoi (Kamchatka)	1000-26=	2	
?	1819	....	?	Redoubt (Alaska-SW)	1103-03-		
?	1819	....	?	Wrangell (Alaska-E)	1105-02-	2?	
	1819	....	?	Colima (México)	1401-04=	1	
	1819	....	?	Fernandina (Galápagos)	1503-01=	2	
	1819	0527	70a	Etna (Italy)	0101-06=	2?	7/5
	1819	0613	....	Etna (Italy)	0101-06=	2?	7/5
	1819	0718	?	San Miguel (El Salvador)	1403-10=	2	
	1819	08	?	Tambora (Lesser Sunda Is)	0604-04=	2	
	1819	12	?	Zavodovski (Antarctica)	1900-13=	2	
	1819	1229	?	Michael (Antarctica)	1900-09=	2	
	1820	Cont	....	Stromboli (Italy)	0101-04=	1	
	1820	Cont	....	Yasur (Vanuatu-SW Pacific)	0507-10=	2	
	1820	Cont	....	Merapi (Java)	0603-25=	1	
	1820	Cont	....	Kliuchevskoi (Kamchatka)	1000-26=	2	
	1820	Cont	....	Okmok (Aleutian Is)	1101-29-	2	
	1820	Cont	....	Bogoslof (Aleutian Is)	1101-30-	1	7/-
	1820	Cont	....	Sangay (Ecuador)	1502-09=	2	
	1820 ?	....	?	Fentale (Ethiopia)	0201-19=	0	7/-
	1820 j	....	?	Kone (Ethiopia)	0201-20-	1	
	1820 ?	....	?	Ambrym (Vanuatu-SW Pacific)	0507-04=		
	1820	....	?	Tengger Caldera [Bromo] (Java)	0603-31=	2	
C	1820 r	....	?	Cabalían (Philippines-C)	0702-05=		
T	1820 v	....	?	Kuttara (Hokkaido-Japan)	0805-034	1	-/5
	1820	....	?	Westdahl [Pogromni ?] (Aleutian Is)	1101-34-	2	
	1820 ?	....	?	Baker (US-Washington)	1201-01=	2	
	1820 ?	....	?	Kilauea (Hawaiian Is)	1302-01-	2	
M	1820 ?	....	?	Southern EPR-Segment J (Pacific)	1304-13-	0	
	1820	....	183w?	Antuco (Chile-C)	1507-08=	1	
	1820	01	....	Vesuvius (Italy)	0101-02=	1	6/7
	1820	01	30p	Fournaise, Piton de la (Indian O.)	0303-02=	2	
	1820	0611	58a	Banda Api (Banda Sea)	0605-09=	2	
	1820	1125	1a>	Fueguino (Chile-S)	1508-09-	2?	
	1820	12 ?	>3yr	Etna (Italy)	0101-06=	1	
	1821	Cont	....	Vesuvius (Italy)	0101-02=	2	6/7
	1821	Cont	....	Stromboli (Italy)	0101-04=	1	
	1821	Cont	....	Etna (Italy)	0101-06=	1	
	1821	Cont	....	Yasur (Vanuatu-SW Pacific)	0507-10=	2	
	1821	Cont	....	Merapi (Java)	0603-25=	1	
	1821	Cont	....	Bogoslof (Aleutian Is)	1101-30-	1	7/-
	1821	Cont	....	Sangay (Ecuador)	1502-09=	2	
	1821	Cont	....	Antuco (Chile-C)	1507-08=	1	
	1821	....	?	Tongkoko (Sulawesi-Indonesia)	0606-13=	0	
V	1821 ?	....	?	Oshima (Izu Is-Japan)	0804-01=	3	-/7
?	1821	....	?	Gorely (Kamchatka)	1000-07=		
?	1821	....	?	Tajumulco (Guatemala)	1402-02=	2	
	1821	0127	94a	Zao (Honshu-Japan)	0803-19=	2	
	1821	02	....	Kliuchevskoi (Kamchatka)	1000-26=	2	
	1821	0227	42a	Fournaise, Piton de la (Indian O.)	0303-02=	2	
	1821	0316	?	Batur (Lesser Sunda Is)	0604-01=	2	
?	1821	0316	?	Agung (Lesser Sunda Is)	0604-02=	2	
	1821	0323	?	Sangeang Api (Lesser Sunda Is)	0604-05=	2	
?	1821	05	?	Irazú (Costa Rica)	1405-06=	2	
	1821	0501	....	Zao (Honshu-Japan)	0803-19=	2	
	1821	0523	?	Chokai (Honshu-Japan)	0803-22=	2?	
?	1821	0822	?	Gamalama (Halmahera-Indonesia)	0608-06=	1	
	1821	1215e	21e	Lamongan (Java)	0603-32=	2	
	1821	1219	378a	Eyjafjallajökull (Iceland-S)	1702-02=	2	-/6
	1821	1231y	?	Karthala (Indian O.-W)	0303-01=		
	1822	Cont	....	Yasur (Vanuatu-SW Pacific)	0507-10=	2	
	1822	Cont	....	Lamongan (Java)	0603-32=	2	
	1822	Cont	....	Kliuchevskoi (Kamchatka)	1000-26=	2	
	1822	Cont	....	Bogoslof (Aleutian Is)	1101-30-	1	7/-
	1822	Cont	....	Sangay (Ecuador)	1502-09=	2	
?	1822	....	365y	Vulcano (Italy)	0101-05=	2?	
	1822	....	730y	Oshima (Izu Is-Japan)	0804-01=	2	
?	1822	....	?	Maipo (Chile-C)	1507-021		
	1822	....	?	Tromen (Argentina)	1507-072		
	1822	....	?	Llaima (Chile-C)	1507-11=	2	
	1822	0112	?	Kirishima (Kyushu-Japan)	0802-09=	2	-/6
	1822	0228	....	Eyjafjallajökull (Iceland-S)	1702-02=	1	-/6
	1822	0312	187m	Usu (Hokkaido-Japan)	0805-03=	4	-/8
	1822	0501	?	Zao (Honshu-Japan)	0803-19=		
	1822	0507	?	Irazú (Costa Rica)	1405-06=	2	
	1822	0621	....	Etna (Italy)	0101-06=	1?	
	1822	0723	8a	Marapi (Sumatra)	0601-14=	2	
	1822	1008	54p	Galunggung (Java)	0603-14=	5	-/9
	1822	1022	....	Vesuvius (Italy)	0101-02=	3?	6/7
	1822	1022	....	Stromboli (Italy)	0101-04=	3	
	1822	11 ?	?	Tolima, Nevado del (Colombia)	1501-03=	2	
	1822	1119	>3yr	San José (Chile-C)	1507-02=	2	
	1822	1119	6e	Villarrica (Chile-C)	1507-12=	2	
	1822	1227	100a	Merapi (Java)	0603-25=	3?	8/7
	1822	1228	8d	Tengger Caldera [Bromo] (Java)	0603-31=	2	
	1823	Cont	....	Stromboli (Italy)	0101-04=	1	
?	1823	Cont	....	Vulcano (Italy)	0101-05=	2?	
	1823	Cont	....	Yasur (Vanuatu-SW Pacific)	0507-10=	2	
	1823	Cont	....	Merapi (Java)	0603-25=	2	8/7
	1823	Cont	....	Tengger Caldera [Bromo] (Java)	0603-31=	2	
	1823	Cont	....	Oshima (Izu Is-Japan)	0804-01=	2	
	1823	Cont	....	Bogoslof (Aleutian Is)	1101-30-	1	7/-
	1823	Cont	....	Sangay (Ecuador)	1502-09=	2	
	1823	Cont	....	San José (Chile-C)	1507-02=	2	
	1823	Cont	....	Eyjafjallajökull (Iceland-S)	1702-02=	1	-/6
?	1823 e	....	?	Zheltovsky (Kamchatka)	1000-04=		
	1823	....	?	Irazú (Costa Rica)	1405-06=	2?	
	1823	....	?	Bristol Island (Antarctica)	1900-08=	2	
?	1823	....	?	Michael (Antarctica)	1900-09=	2?	
	1823	....	?	Candlemas Island (Antarctica)	1900-10=	2	
?	1823	....	?	Zavodovski (Antarctica)	1900-13=	1	
	1823	02	151p	Kilauea (Hawaiian Is)	1302-01-	0	7/-
	1823	0204d	?	Grímsvötn [Thordarhyrna] (Iceland	1703-01=	2	
	1823	0617	7a	Galeras (Colombia)	1501-08=	2	
	1823	0626	27a	Katla (Iceland-S)	1702-03=	3?	-/8
	1823	08 <	>3yr	Kilauea (Hawaiian Is)	1302-01-	0	
	1823	1227	....	Etna (Italy)	0101-06=	2	
	1824	Cont	....	Stromboli (Italy)	0101-04=	1	
	1824	Cont	....	Etna (Italy)	0101-06=	1	
	1824	Cont	....	Yasur (Vanuatu-SW Pacific)	0507-10=	2	
	1824	Cont	....	Oshima (Izu Is-Japan)	0804-01=	2	
	1824	Cont	....	Kilauea (Hawaiian Is)	1302-01-	0	
	1824	Cont	....	Sangay (Ecuador)	1502-09=	2	
	1824	Cont	....	San José (Chile-C)	1507-02=	2	
	1824	....	?	Zubair, Jebel (Red Sea)	0201-02=	2	
	1824	....	?	Yunaska (Aleutian Is)	1101-21-	3	
	1824	....	>3yr	Okmok (Aleutian Is)	1101-29-		
	1824	....	?	Shishaldin (Aleutian Is)	1101-36-	3	
	1824	0101?	30a?	Lamongan (Java)	0603-32=	2	
	1824	02	?	Fournaise, Piton de la (Indian O.)	0303-02=	0	
	1824	0422	67a	Banda Api (Banda Sea)	0605-09=	2	
?	1824	0501	?	Unnamed (Atlantic-C)	1805-01=	0	
	1824	0702	>3yr	Vesuvius (Italy)	0101-02=	2	7/-
	1824	0731	85a	Lanzarote (Canary Is)	1803-06-	1	7/-
	1824	0929	....	Lanzarote (Canary Is)	1803-06-	2	7/-
	1824	1016	....	Lanzarote (Canary Is)	1803-06-	2	7/-
	1824	12	?	Fournaise, Piton de la (Indian O.)	0303-02=	0	
	1825	Cont	....	Vesuvius (Italy)	0101-02=	2	7/-
	1825	Cont	....	Stromboli (Italy)	0101-04=	1	
	1825	Cont	....	Etna (Italy)	0101-06=	1	
	1825	Cont	....	Yasur (Vanuatu-SW Pacific)	0507-10=	2	
	1825	Cont	....	Okmok (Aleutian Is)	1101-29-		
	1825	Cont	....	Kilauea (Hawaiian Is)	1302-01-	0	
	1825	Cont	....	Sangay (Ecuador)	1502-09=	2	
	1825	Cont	....	San José (Chile-C)	1507-02=	2	
	1825 j	....	?	Cameroon (Africa-W)	0204-01=	2	

START YEAR	M-Dy	Duration	VOLCANO NAME (Subregion)	NUMBER	VEI	Vol L/T
? 1825 q	....	?	*Balbi (Bougainville-SW Pacific)*	0505-01=		
1825	....	?	**Dieng Volc Complex** (Java)	0603-20=	2	
1825	....	?	**Kelut** (Java)	0603-28=	2	
1825 ?	....	>3yr	**Banda Api** (Banda Sea)	0605-09=	1	
1825	....	?	**Karangetang [Api Siau]** (Sangihe Is	0607-02=	2	
1825	....	?	**Taal** (Luzon-Philippines)	0703-07=	2	
1825 e	....	?	**Pagan** (Mariana Is-C Pacific)	0804-17=	2?	
1825 q	....	?	**Prevo Peak** (Kuril Is)	0900-19=	2	
1825	....	?	**Shishaldin** (Aleutian Is)	1101-36-	2	
1825	....	?	**Pavlof** (Alaska Peninsula)	1102-03-	2?	
1825	....	?	**Izalco** (El Salvador)	1403-03=	2	
1825 q	....	?	**Guallatiri** (Chile-N)	1505-02=	2?	
1825	0214	244*m*>	**Fernandina** (Galápagos)	1503-01=	3	
1825	0302?	?	**Tolima, Nevado del** (Colombia)	1501-03=	2	
? 1825	*0310*	?	*Isanotski (Aleutian Is)*	1101-37-	*4*	*-/8*
1825	0614	<1	**Guntur** (Java)	0603-13=	2	
? 1825	*0906*	?	*Macauley Island (Kermadec Is)*	0402-021	*0*	
1825	10	?	**Slamet** (Java)	0603-18=	2	
1825	1105	3*a*	**Tengger Caldera [Bromo]** (Java)	0603-31=	2	
1826	*Cont*	....	*Vesuvius (Italy)*	0101-02=	*2*	*7/-*
1826	*Cont*	....	*Stromboli (Italy)*	0101-04=	*1*	
1826	*Cont*	....	*Etna (Italy)*	0101-06=	*1*	
1826	*Cont*	....	*Yasur (Vanuatu-SW Pacific)*	0507-10=	*2*	
1826	*Cont*	....	*Banda Api (Banda Sea)*	0605-09=	*1*	
1826	*Cont*	....	*Okmok (Aleutian Is)*	1101-29-		
1826	*Cont*	....	*Kilauea (Hawaiian Is)*	1302-01-	*0*	
1826	*Cont*	....	*Sangay (Ecuador)*	1502-09=	*2*	
1826	*Cont*	....	*San José (Chile-C)*	1507-02=	*2*	
1826	....	?	**Lamongan** (Java)	0603-32=	2	
1826	....	?	**Shishaldin** (Aleutian Is)	1101-36-	0	
1826	....	?	**Fuego** (Guatemala)	1402-09=	2	
? 1826	....	?	*Irazú (Costa Rica)*	1405-06=		
? 1826	....	?	*Ruiz, Nevado del (Colombia)*	1501-02=	*2?*	
? 1826	....	?	*Ubinas (Perú)*	1504-02=		
1826	0301	?	**Maipo** (Chile-C)	1507-021	2	
1826	05	32*m*>	**Tolima, Nevado del** (Colombia)	1501-03=	2	
1826	06	?	**Makushin** (Aleutian Is)	1101-31-	3	
? 1826	*08*	?	*Misti, El (Perú)*	1504-01=	*1?*	
1826	1003	50*a*	**Aso** (Kyushu-Japan)	0802-11=	2	
1826	1011	<1	**Tangkubanparahu** (Java)	0603-09=	2	
1826	1011	4*a*	**Dieng Volc Complex** (Java)	0603-20=	2	
1826	1011	14*a*	**Kelut** (Java)	0603-28=	4?	-/8
1826	1011	96*m*?	**Fisher** (Aleutian Is)	1101-35-	3	
1826	11	?	**Atitlán** (Guatemala)	1402-06=	2	
1826	1201	?	**White Island** (New Zealand)	0401-04=	2	
1827	*Cont*	....	*Vesuvius (Italy)*	0101-02=	*2*	*7/-*
1827	*Cont*	....	*Stromboli (Italy)*	0101-04=	*1*	
1827	*Cont*	....	*Yasur (Vanuatu-SW Pacific)*	0507-10=	*2*	
1827	*Cont*	....	*Banda Api (Banda Sea)*	0605-09=	*1*	
1827	*Cont*	....	*Okmok (Aleutian Is)*	1101-29-		
1827	*Cont*	....	*Fisher (Aleutian Is)*	1101-35-	*2*	
1827	*Cont*	....	*Kilauea (Hawaiian Is)*	1302-01-	*0*	
1827	*Cont*	....	*Sangay (Ecuador)*	1502-09=	*2*	
1827	*Cont*	....	*San José (Chile-C)*	1507-02=	*2*	
1827	....	?	**Camiguin [Hibok-Hibok]** (Philippine	0701-08=	2	
? 1827	....	?	*Oshima (Izu Is-Japan)*	0804-01=		
? 1827	....	?	*Opala (Kamchatka)*	1000-08=		
? 1827	....	?	*Kanaga (Aleutian Is)*	1101-11-		
? 1827	....	?	*Kasatochi (Aleutian Is)*	1101-13-		
? 1827	....	?	*Seguam (Aleutian Is)*	1101-18-		
? 1827	....	*>3yr*	*Makushin (Aleutian Is)*	1101-31-	*2?*	
1827	....	>3yr	**Westdahl [Pogromni ?]** (Aleutian Is)	1101-34-	2	
1827	....	731y	**Shishaldin** (Aleutian Is)	1101-36-	2	
? 1827	....	?	*Popocatépetl (México)*	1401-09=	*1?*	
1827 b	....	?	**Deception Island** (Antarctica)	1900-03=		
1827	0327	?	**Atitlán** (Guatemala)	1402-06=	2	
1827	05	?	**Aso** (Kyushu-Japan)	0802-11=	2	
1827	0513	?	**Guntur** (Java)	0603-13=	2	
1827	0627	246*a*	**Mayon** (Luzon-Philippines)	0703-03=	2	
1827	0627	2*a*	**Avachinsky** (Kamchatka)	1000-10=	4	-/8
1827	0901	141*m*?	**Atitlán** (Guatemala)	1402-06=	3	
1827	*1010*	....	*Etna (Italy)*	0101-06=	*1?*	
1827	1112	65*m*	**Aso** (Kyushu-Japan)	0802-11=	2	
1827	1118	?	**Puracé** (Colombia)	1501-06=	2	
1828	*Cont*	....	*Vesuvius (Italy)*	0101-02=	*2*	*7/-*
1828	*Cont*	....	*Stromboli (Italy)*	0101-04=	*1*	
1828	*Cont*	....	*Yasur (Vanuatu-SW Pacific)*	0507-10=	*2*	
1828	*Cont*	....	*Banda Api (Banda Sea)*	0605-09=	*1*	
1828	*Cont*	....	*Mayon (Luzon-Philippines)*	0703-03=	*2*	
1828	*Cont*	....	*Okmok (Aleutian Is)*	1101-29-		
? 1828	*Cont*	....	*Makushin (Aleutian Is)*	1101-31-	*2?*	
1828	*Cont*	....	*Westdahl [Pogromni ?] (Aleutian Is)*	1101-34-	*2*	
1828	*Cont*	....	*Shishaldin (Aleutian Is)*	1101-36-	*2*	
1828	*Cont*	....	*Kilauea (Hawaiian Is)*	1302-01-	*0*	
1828	*Cont*	....	*Atitlán (Guatemala)*	1402-06=	*3*	
1828	*Cont*	....	*Sangay (Ecuador)*	1502-09=	*2*	
1828	*Cont*	....	*San José (Chile-C)*	1507-02=	*2*	
? 1828	....	?	*Adwa (Ethiopia)*	0201-17=	*2*	
1828	....	730*y*	**Little Sitkin** (Aleutian Is)	1101-05-		
? 1828	....	*365y?*	*Gareloi (Aleutian Is)*	1101-07-	*2?*	
? 1828	....	?	*Great Sitkin (Aleutian Is)*	1101-12-		
? 1828	....	?	*Kasatochi (Aleutian Is)*	1101-13-		
1828	....	?	**Carlisle** (Aleutian Is)	1101-23-		
? 1828	....	?	*Akutan (Aleutian Is)*	1101-32-		
1828	....	?	**Poás** (Costa Rica)	1405-04=	1	
? 1828	*01*	?	*Matthew Island (SW Pacific)*	0508-01=		
1828	0417	?	**Avachinsky** (Kamchatka)	1000-10=	2	
1828	05	?	**Karthala** (Indian O.-W)	0303-01=	2?	
1828	0514	55*a*	**Guntur** (Java)	0603-13=	2	
1828	06	?	**Aso** (Kyushu-Japan)	0802-11=	2	
1828	06	?	**Gorely** (Kamchatka)	1000-07=	3	-/7
1828	06	?	**Ruiz, Nevado del** (Colombia)	1501-02=	2	
1828	*0823*	....	*Etna (Italy)*	0101-06=	*1?*	
1828	*1024*	*>3yr*	*Galeras (Colombia)*	1501-08=	*2*	
1828	1218	1*a*	**Merapi** (Java)	0603-25=	2	
1828	1218	?	**Antuco** (Chile-C)	1507-08=	2	
1829	*Cont*	....	*Vesuvius (Italy)*	0101-02=	*2*	*7/-*
1829	*Cont*	....	*Stromboli (Italy)*	0101-04=	*1*	
1829	*Cont*	....	*Yasur (Vanuatu-SW Pacific)*	0507-10=	*2*	
1829	*Cont*	....	*Banda Api (Banda Sea)*	0605-09=	*1*	
1829	*Cont*	....	*Little Sitkin (Aleutian Is)*	1101-05-		
? 1829	*Cont*	....	*Gareloi (Aleutian Is)*	1101-07-	*2?*	
1829	*Cont*	....	*Okmok (Aleutian Is)*	1101-29-		
? 1829	*Cont*	....	*Makushin (Aleutian Is)*	1101-31-	*2?*	
1829	*Cont*	....	*Westdahl [Pogromni ?] (Aleutian Is)*	1101-34-	*2*	
1829	*Cont*	....	*Shishaldin (Aleutian Is)*	1101-36-	*2*	
1829	*Cont*	....	*Kilauea (Hawaiian Is)*	1302-01-	*0*	
1829	*Cont*	....	*Galeras (Colombia)*	1501-08=	*2*	
1829	*Cont*	....	*Sangay (Ecuador)*	1502-09=	*2*	
1829	*Cont*	....	*San José (Chile-C)*	1507-02=	*2*	
1829 ?	....	?	**Sorikmarapi** (Sumatra)	0601-12=	2	
1829	....	?	**Guntur** (Java)	0603-13=	2	
1829	....	?	**Tanaga** (Aleutian Is)	1101-08-		
? 1829	....	?	*Kanaga (Aleutian Is)*	1101-11-		
? 1829	....	?	*Great Sitkin (Aleutian Is)*	1101-12-		
? 1829	....	*365y*	*Korovin (Aleutian Is)*	1101-161		
1829	....	?	**Fuego** (Guatemala)	1402-09=	2	
1829	....	?	**Tupungatito** (Chile-C)	1507-01=	2	
1829	01	30*p*	**Lamongan** (Java)	0603-32=	2	
1829	02	?	**Semeru** (Java)	0603-30=	2	
1829	03	?	**Lokon-Empung** (Sulawesi-Indonesia)	0606-10=	2	
1829	0401	3*a*?	**Tangkubanparahu** (Java)	0603-09=	2	
1829	06	?	**Aso** (Kyushu-Japan)	0802-11=	2	
1829	0618	?	**Ruiz, Nevado del** (Colombia)	1501-02=	2	
1829	0909	?	**Kliuchevskoi** (Kamchatka)	1000-26=	4?	7/8
1829	0926	?	**Maipo** (Chile-C)	1507-021	2?	
1829	1105	6*a*	**Tengger Caldera [Bromo]** (Java)	0603-31=	2	
1829	*1111*	....	*Etna (Italy)*	0101-06=	*1?*	
1829	1201	15*a*	**Iwo-Tori-shima** (Ryukyu Is)	0802-02=	1?	
1830	*Cont*	....	*Vesuvius (Italy)*	0101-02=	*2*	*7/-*
1830	*Cont*	....	*Stromboli (Italy)*	0101-04=	*1*	
1830	*Cont*	....	*Yasur (Vanuatu-SW Pacific)*	0507-10=	*2*	
1830	*Cont*	....	*Banda Api (Banda Sea)*	0605-09=	*1*	
? 1830	*Cont*	....	*Korovin (Aleutian Is)*	1101-161		
1830	*Cont*	....	*Okmok (Aleutian Is)*	1101-29-		
? 1830	*Cont*	....	*Makushin (Aleutian Is)*	1101-31-	*2?*	
1830	*Cont*	....	*Westdahl [Pogromni ?] (Aleutian Is)*	1101-34-	*2*	
1830	*Cont*	....	*Kilauea (Hawaiian Is)*	1302-01-	*0*	
1830	*Cont*	....	*Galeras (Colombia)*	1501-08=	*2*	
1830	*Cont*	....	*Sangay (Ecuador)*	1502-09=	*2*	
1830	*Cont*	....	*San José (Chile-C)*	1507-02=	*2*	
1830	....	?	**Karthala** (Indian O.-W)	0303-01=	2?	
1830	....	?	**Manam** (New Guinea-NE of)	0501-02=	2	
? 1830	....	?	*Karkar (New Guinea-NE of)*	0501-03=		
1830	....	?	**Ebulobo** (Lesser Sunda Is)	0604-10=	2	
? 1830	....	?	*Gamalama (Halmahera-Indonesia)*	0608-06=		
1830	....	?	**Zao** (Honshu-Japan)	0803-19=	2	
1830	....	?	**Karymsky** (Kamchatka)	1000-13=	2	
? 1830	....	?	*Semisopochnoi (Aleutian Is)*	1101-06-		
1830	....	?	**Yunaska** (Aleutian Is)	1101-21-	2	
1830	....	?	**Vsevidof** (Aleutian Is)	1101-27-		
? 1830	....	*>3yr*	*Veniaminof (Alaska Peninsula)*	1102-07-	*2*	
? 1830	....	?	*Pacaya (Guatemala)*	1402-11=		
1830	....	?	**Guagua Pichincha** (Ecuador)	1502-02=	2	
1830	....	?	**Ubinas** (Perú)	1504-02=	2	
1830	02	30*p*	**Lamongan** (Java)	0603-32=	2	
1830	0216	28*m*	**Aso** (Kyushu-Japan)	0802-11=	2	
1830	*03*	....	*Etna (Italy)*	0101-06=	*1?*	
1830	0303	?	**Tengger Caldera [Bromo]** (Java)	0603-31=	2	
1830	0313?	365*p*?	**Reykjanes** (Iceland-SW)	1701-02=	3	
1830	08	?	**Fisher** (Aleutian Is)	1101-35-	2?	
? 1830	*08*	?	*Misti, El (Perú)*	1504-01=	*1?*	
1830	0811	735*m*	**Aso** (Kyushu-Japan)	0802-11=	2	

START YEAR	M-Dy	Duration	VOLCANO NAME (Subregion)	NUMBER	VEI	Vol L/T
? *1830*	*09*	?	*Zavodovski (Antarctica)*	1900-13=	*1*	
? *1830*	*0922*	?	*Hodson (Antarctica)*	1900-11=		
1830	10	?	**Fournaise, Piton de la** (Indian O.)	0303-02=	0	
1830	11	31*p*	**Shishaldin** (Aleutian Is)	1101-36-	3	
? *1830*	*11*	?	*Isanotski (Aleutian Is)*	1101-37-	*2?*	
1830	1215	1*a*	**Semeru** (Java)	0603-30=	2	
1830	1215	1*a*	**Tengger Caldera [Bromo]** (Java)	0603-31=	2	
1831	*Cont*	....	*Stromboli (Italy)*	0101-04=	*1*	
1831	*Cont*	....	*Yasur (Vanuatu-SW Pacific)*	0507-10=	*2*	
1831	*Cont*	....	*Banda Api (Banda Sea)*	0605-09=	*1*	
1831	*Cont*	....	*Aso (Kyushu-Japan)*	0802-11=	*2*	
? *1831*	*Cont*	....	*Makushin (Aleutian Is)*	1101-31-	*2?*	
? *1831*	*Cont*	....	*Veniaminof (Alaska Peninsula)*	1102-07-	*2*	
1831	*Cont*	....	*Kilauea (Hawaiian Is)*	1302-01-	*0*	
1831	*Cont*	....	*Sangay (Ecuador)*	1502-09=	*2*	
1831	*Cont*	....	*San José (Chile-C)*	1507-02=	*2*	
1831	*Cont*	....	*Reykjanes (Iceland-SW)*	1701-02=	*2*	
? *1831*	....	?	*Vulcano (Italy)*	0101-05=	*1?*	
? *1831*	....	?	*Pantelleria (Italy)*	0101-071		
? *1831*	....	?	*Paluweh (Lesser Sunda Is)*	0604-15=		
1831	....	?	**Babuyan Claro** (Luzon-N of)	0704-03=	4?	-/8
1831	....	?	**Ruiz, Nevado del** (Colombia)	1501-02=	2	
1831	....	?	**Guagua Pichincha** (Ecuador)	1502-02=	3	
? *1831*	*0216*	?	*Maipo (Chile-C)*	1507-021	*2?*	
? *1831*	*03*	*51m*	*Isanotski (Aleutian Is)*	1101-37-		
1831	*0304*	....	*Etna (Italy)*	0101-06=	*2*	
1831	05	....	**Galeras** (Colombia)	1501-08=	3	
1831	0527	31*a*	**Gamalama** (Halmahera-Indonesia)	0608-06=	2	
1831	*0628>*	*44d<*	*Campi Flegrei Mar Sicilia (Italy)*	0101-07=	*0*	*-/8*
1831	0710	....	**Campi Flegrei Mar Sicilia** (Italy)	0101-07=	3	-/8
1831	08	?	**St. Helens** (US-Washington)	1201-05-	3	
? *1831*	*08*	?	*Misti, El (Perú)*	1504-01=	*1?*	
1831	*0814*	....	*Vesuvius (Italy)*	0101-02=	*1*	*7/-*
1831	1122	?	**Zao** (Honshu-Japan)	0803-19=	2	
1832	*Cont*	....	*Vesuvius (Italy)*	0101-02=	*2*	*7/-*
1832	*Cont*	....	*Stromboli (Italy)*	0101-04=	*1*	
1832	*Cont*	....	*Yasur (Vanuatu-SW Pacific)*	0507-10=	*2*	
1832	*Cont*	....	*Aso (Kyushu-Japan)*	0802-11=	*2*	
? *1832*	*Cont*	....	*Makushin (Aleutian Is)*	1101-31-	*2?*	
? *1832*	*Cont*	....	*Veniaminof (Alaska Peninsula)*	1102-07-	*2*	
1832	*Cont*	....	*Galeras (Colombia)*	1501-08=	*2*	
1832	*Cont*	....	*Sangay (Ecuador)*	1502-09=	*2*	
1832	*Cont*	....	*San José (Chile-C)*	1507-02=	*2*	
1832	0114	?	**Kilauea** (Hawaiian Is)	1302-01-	0	
1832	0116	?	**Guntur** (Java)	0603-13=	2	
1832	02	?	**Gorely** (Kamchatka)	1000-07=	3	-/7
1832	03	21*m*	**Fournaise, Piton de la** (Indian O.)	0303-02=	0	
1832	03	?	**Barren Island** (Andaman Is-Indian O)	0600-01=	2?	
1832	0418	?	**Semeru** (Java)	0603-30=	2	
1832	0420	?	**Kirishima** (Kyushu-Japan)	0802-09=	2	
1832	0620	25*g*	**Mauna Loa** (Hawaiian Is)	1302-02=	0	7/-
1832	0808	5*a*	**Guntur** (Java)	0603-13=	2	
1832	0829	<1	**Gede** (Java)	0603-06=	3	
1832	1031	22*a*	**Etna** (Italy)	0101-06=	2	7/6
1832	1224	?	**Villarrica** (Chile-C)	1507-12=	2	
1832	1225	919*w*	**Merapi** (Java)	0603-25=	2?	7/7
1833	*Cont*	....	*Vesuvius (Italy)*	0101-02=	*2*	*7/-*
1833	*Cont*	....	*Etna (Italy)*	0101-06=	*1*	
1833	*Cont*	....	*Yasur (Vanuatu-SW Pacific)*	0507-10=	*2*	
1833	*Cont*	....	*Merapi (Java)*	0603-25=	*2*	*7/7*
? *1833*	*Cont*	....	*Makushin (Aleutian Is)*	1101-31-	*2?*	
? *1833*	*Cont*	....	*Veniaminof (Alaska Peninsula)*	1102-07-	*2*	
1833	*Cont*	....	*Kilauea (Hawaiian Is)*	1302-01-	*0*	
1833	*Cont*	....	*Galeras (Colombia)*	1501-08=	*2*	
1833	*Cont*	....	*Sangay (Ecuador)*	1502-09=	*2*	
1833	*Cont*	....	*San José (Chile-C)*	1507-02=	*2*	
1833	....	....	*Stromboli (Italy)*	0101-04=	*2*	
1833	....	?	**Karthala** (Indian O.-W)	0303-01=		
1833	....	365*y*	**Marapi** (Sumatra)	0601-14=	2?	
1833 ?	....	?	**Soputan** (Sulawesi-Indonesia)	0606-03=	2	
1833	....	?	**Zao** (Honshu-Japan)	0803-19=	2	
1833	....	?	**Atitlán** (Guatemala)	1402-06=	2	
? *1833*	....	?	*Ruiz, Nevado del (Colombia)*	1501-02=	*2?*	
? *1833*	....	?	*Maipo (Chile-C)*	1507-021	*2?*	
? *1833*	*0411*	?	*Iwaki (Honshu-Japan)*	0803-27=	*2*	
1833	0615	?	**Gamalama** (Halmahera-Indonesia)	0608-06=	2	
1833	0901	?	**Guntur** (Java)	0603-13=	2	
1833	10	?	**Talang** (Sumatra)	0601-16=	2	
1833	1124	1*a*	**Kaba** (Sumatra)	0601-22=	2	
1833	1231y	?	**Tair, Jebel at** (Red Sea)	0201-01=	2	
1833	1231y	?	**Ebeko** (Kuril Is)	0900-38=	2	
1834	*Cont*	....	*Yasur (Vanuatu-SW Pacific)*	0507-10=	*2*	
1834	*Cont*	....	*Marapi (Sumatra)*	0601-14=	*2?*	
1834	*Cont*	....	*Merapi (Java)*	0603-25=	*2*	*7/7*
? *1834*	*Cont*	....	*Makushin (Aleutian Is)*	1101-31-	*2?*	
? *1834*	*Cont*	....	*Veniaminof (Alaska Peninsula)*	1102-07-	*2*	
1834	*Cont*	....	*Kilauea (Hawaiian Is)*	1302-01-	*0*	
1834	*Cont*	....	*Sangay (Ecuador)*	1502-09=	*2*	
1834	*Cont*	....	*San José (Chile-C)*	1507-02=	*2*	
1834	....	?	**Ragang** (Mindanao-Philippines)	0701-06=	2	
1834	....	*317w*	*Mayon (Luzon-Philippines)*	0703-03=	*2*	
? *1834*	....	?	*Popocatépetl (México)*	1401-09=	*1?*	
1834	....	?	**Poás** (Costa Rica)	1405-04=	2	
1834	....	?	**Galeras** (Colombia)	1501-08=	2	
1834	*0301*	....	*Galeras (Colombia)*	1501-08=	*3*	
1834	0709	11*k*	**Chokai** (Honshu-Japan)	0803-22=	2?	
1834	0822	....	**Vesuvius** (Italy)	0101-02=	3	7/-
1834	*09*	....	*Stromboli (Italy)*	0101-04=	*2*	
1834	11	?	**Kaba** (Sumatra)	0601-22=	2	
? *1834*	*11*	?	*Corcovado (Chile-S)*	1508-05=	*2*	
1834	1125	?	**Minchinmávida** (Chile-S)	1508-04=	2	
1834	1129	86*d*	**Osorno** (Chile-S)	1508-01=	3?	
1834	12	31*p*	**Guntur** (Java)	0603-13=	2	
1835	*Cont*	....	*Stromboli (Italy)*	0101-04=	*1*	
1835	*Cont*	....	*Yasur (Vanuatu-SW Pacific)*	0507-10=	*2*	
1835	*Cont*	....	*Guntur (Java)*	0603-13=	*2*	
1835	*Cont*	....	*Merapi (Java)*	0603-25=	*2*	*7/7*
? *1835*	*Cont*	....	*Makushin (Aleutian Is)*	1101-31-	*2?*	
? *1835*	*Cont*	....	*Veniaminof (Alaska Peninsula)*	1102-07-	*2*	
1835	*Cont*	....	*Kilauea (Hawaiian Is)*	1302-01-	*0*	
1835	*Cont*	....	*Sangay (Ecuador)*	1502-09=	*2*	
1835	*Cont*	....	*San José (Chile-C)*	1507-02=	*2*	
1835	*Cont*	....	*Osorno (Chile-S)*	1508-01=	*0*	
1835 e	....	>3yr	**Savo** (Solomon Is-SW Pacific)	0505-07=	3?	
1835	....	?	**Hunter Island** (SW Pacific)	0508-02=		
1835	....	?	**Kelut** (Java)	0603-28=	2	
1835	....	?	**Tengger Caldera [Bromo]** (Java)	0603-31=	2	
1835 r	....	?	**Yokoate-jima** (Ryukyu Is)	0802-021	2?	
? *1835*	....	?	*Tupungatito (Chile-C)*	1507-01=	*2*	
? *1835*	....	?	*Maipo (Chile-C)*	1507-021		
1835	....	?	**Planchón-Peteroa** (Chile-C)	1507-04=	2	
? *1835*	....	?	*Hornopirén (Chile-S)*	1508-023		
1835	*01*	*>3yr*	*Vesuvius (Italy)*	0101-02=	*1*	*7/-*
1835	0104	?	**Gamalama** (Halmahera-Indonesia)	0608-06=	2	
1835	0120	5*a*?	**Cosigüina** (Nicaragua)	1404-01=	**5**	**-/9**
1835	0123	?	**Puracé** (Colombia)	1501-06=	2	
1835	0220	1*a*	**Robinson Crusoe** (Chile-Is)	1506-02=	1?	
1835	0220	23*e*	**Minchinmávida** (Chile-S)	1508-04=	0?	
? *1835*	*0220*	?	*Yanteles (Chile-S)*	1508-050		
1835	03 ?	?	**St. Helens** (US-Washington)	1201-05-	2	
1835	0423	3*a*	**Banua Wuhu** (Sangihe Is-Indonesia)	0607-03=	2	6/-
1835	05	....	**Mayon** (Luzon-Philippines)	0703-03=	3	
1835	0501	?	**Aso** (Kyushu-Japan)	0802-11=	2	
1835	09	2*a*	**Slamet** (Java)	0603-18=	2	
? *1835*	*10*	?	*Banda Api (Banda Sea)*	0605-09=		
1835	1111 ?	?	**Miyake-jima** (Izu Is-Japan)	0804-04=	2	5/-
? *1835*	*1111*	?	*Corcovado (Chile-S)*	1508-05=	*2*	
1836	*Cont*	....	*Vesuvius (Italy)*	0101-02=	*1*	*7/-*
1836	*Cont*	....	*Stromboli (Italy)*	0101-04=	*1*	
1836	*Cont*	....	*Savo (Solomon Is-SW Pacific)*	0505-07=	*2*	
1836	*Cont*	....	*Yasur (Vanuatu-SW Pacific)*	0507-10=	*2*	
1836	*Cont*	....	*Merapi (Java)*	0603-25=	*2*	*7/7*
? *1836*	*Cont*	....	*Makushin (Aleutian Is)*	1101-31-	*2?*	
? *1836*	*Cont*	....	*Veniaminof (Alaska Peninsula)*	1102-07-	*2*	
1836	*Cont*	....	*Kilauea (Hawaiian Is)*	1302-01-	*0*	
1836	*Cont*	....	*Sangay (Ecuador)*	1502-09=	*2*	
1836	*Cont*	....	*San José (Chile-C)*	1507-02=	*2*	
1836 b	....	?	**White Island** (New Zealand)	0401-04=	2	
1836	....	?	**Izalco** (El Salvador)	1403-03=	2	
? *1836*	....	?	*Galeras (Colombia)*	1501-08=	*2*	
1836 ?	0422	2*a*	**Ruang** (Sangihe Is-Indonesia)	0607-01=	2	
1836	0709	?	**Tate-yama** (Honshu-Japan)	0803-08=	1	-/5
1836	0803	2*a*	**Semeru** (Java)	0603-30=	2	
1836	1011	?	**Guntur** (Java)	0603-13=	2	
? *1836*	*11* <	?	*Unnamed (Atlantic-C)*	1805-03=	*0*	
1836	1203	71*a*	**Soufrière Guadeloupe** (W Indies)	1600-06=	2	
1837	*Cont*	....	*Vesuvius (Italy)*	0101-02=	*1*	*7/-*
1837	*Cont*	....	*Stromboli (Italy)*	0101-04=	*1*	
1837	*Cont*	....	*Savo (Solomon Is-SW Pacific)*	0505-07=	*2*	
1837	*Cont*	....	*Yasur (Vanuatu-SW Pacific)*	0507-10=	*2*	
? *1837*	*Cont*	....	*Makushin (Aleutian Is)*	1101-31-	*2?*	
? *1837*	*Cont*	....	*Veniaminof (Alaska Peninsula)*	1102-07-	*2*	
1837	*Cont*	....	*Kilauea (Hawaiian Is)*	1302-01-	*0*	
1837	*Cont*	....	*Sangay (Ecuador)*	1502-09=	*2*	
1837	*Cont*	....	*San José (Chile-C)*	1507-02=	*2*	
1837	*Cont*	....	*Soufrière Guadeloupe (W Indies)*	1600-06=	*2*	
? *1837*	....	*365y*	*Oshima (Izu Is-Japan)*	0804-01=	*2*	
? *1837*	....	?	*Avachinsky (Kamchatka)*	1000-10=		
? *1837*	....	?	*Maipo (Chile-C)*	1507-021		
1837	02	?	**Planchón-Peteroa** (Chile-C)	1507-04=	2	6/6
1837	06	?	**Atitlán** (Guatemala)	1402-06=	2	
1837	0810	309*m*	**Merapi** (Java)	0603-25=	2?	7/7
1837	0925e	?	**Telong, Bur ni** (Sumatra)	0601-05=	2	
1837	1008	?	**Aso** (Kyushu-Japan)	0802-11=	2	

START YEAR	M-Dy	Duration	VOLCANO NAME (Subregion)	NUMBER	VEI	Vol L/T
1837	1107	14*a*	**Villarrica** (Chile-C)	1507-12=	2	
1837	1107	?	**Osorno** (Chile-S)	1508-01=	2	
1838	*Cont*	....	*Vesuvius (Italy)*	0101-02=	*1*	*7/-*
1838	*Cont*	....	*Stromboli (Italy)*	0101-04=	*1*	
1838	*Cont*	....	*Savo (Solomon Is-SW Pacific)*	0505-07=	*2*	
1838	*Cont*	....	*Yasur (Vanuatu-SW Pacific)*	0507-10=	*2*	
1838	*Cont*	....	*Merapi (Java)*	0603-25=	*2*	*7/7*
? 1838	*Cont*	....	*Oshima (Izu Is-Japan)*	0804-01=	*2*	
? 1838	*Cont*	....	*Makushin (Aleutian Is)*	1101-31-	*2?*	
1838	*Cont*	....	*Kilauea (Hawaiian Is)*	1302-01-	*0*	
1838	*Cont*	....	*Sangay (Ecuador)*	1502-09=	*2*	
1838	....	?	**Kerinci** (Sumatra)	0601-17=	2	
? 1838	....	?	*Kaba (Sumatra)*	0601-22=		
1838	....	?	**Raung** (Java)	0603-34=	2	
? 1838	....	?	*Carlisle (Aleutian Is)*	1101-23-		
? 1838	....	?	*Akutan (Aleutian Is)*	1101-32-		
1838	....	?	**Shishaldin** (Aleutian Is)	1101-36-	2	
1838	....	?	**Pavlof** (Alaska Peninsula)	1102-03-	1	
? 1838	....	?	*San Martín (México)*	1401-11=		
1838	....	730*y*	**Izalco** (El Salvador)	1403-03=	2	
? 1838	....	?	*Poás (Costa Rica)*	1405-04=	*2?*	
1838	....	?	**San José** (Chile-C)	1507-02=	1	
1838	0226	79*m*	**Gamalama** (Halmahera-Indonesia)	0608-06=	2	
1838	0304	?	**Aso** (Kyushu-Japan)	0802-11=	2	
1838	06	?	**Grímsvötn** (Iceland-NE)	1703-01=	2	
1838	07	94*m*	**Semeru** (Java)	0603-30=	2	
1838	0704	2*a*	**Lamongan** (Java)	0603-32=	2	
1838	0708	221*m*	**Etna** (Italy)	0101-06=	2	7/-
1838	0804	254*m*	**Veniaminof** (Alaska Peninsula)	1102-07-	3	
1838	1018	?	**Lamongan** (Java)	0603-32=	2	
1838	1231y	?	**Cameroon** (Africa-W)	0204-01=	2	
1839	*Cont*	....	*Stromboli (Italy)*	0101-04=	*1*	
1839	*Cont*	....	*Etna (Italy)*	0101-06=	*2*	*7/-*
1839	*Cont*	....	*Savo (Solomon Is-SW Pacific)*	0505-07=	*2*	
1839	*Cont*	....	*Yasur (Vanuatu-SW Pacific)*	0507-10=	*2*	
1839	*Cont*	....	*Veniaminof (Alaska Peninsula)*	1102-07-	*2*	
1839	*Cont*	....	*Kilauea (Hawaiian Is)*	1302-01-	*0*	
1839	*Cont*	....	*Izalco (El Salvador)*	1403-03=	*2*	
1839	*Cont*	....	*Sangay (Ecuador)*	1502-09=	*2*	
1839 ?	....	?	**Dempo** (Sumatra)	0601-23=	2	
? 1839	....	?	*Gede (Java)*	0603-06=		
1839	....	?	**Mayon** (Luzon-Philippines)	0703-03=	2	
? 1839	....	?	*Antuco (Chile-C)*	1507-08=	*2*	
? 1839 <	....	?	*Deception Island (Antarctica)*	1900-03=		
1839	0101	....	**Vesuvius** (Italy)	0101-02=	3	7/-
1839	0112	1*a*	**Seulawah Agam** (Sumatra)	0601-02=	2	
1839	0112	1*a*	**Telong, Bur ni** (Sumatra)	0601-05=	2	
1839	*0129*	*56a*	*Gamalama (Halmahera-Indonesia)*	0608-06=	*1*	
1839	02	30*p*	**Tongariro [Ngauruhoe]** (New Zeal)	0401-08=	1?	
1839	0209	?	**Buckle Island** (Antarctica)	1900-01=	2	
? 1839	*0212*	*1a?*	*Unnamed (Chile-Is)*	1506-04=		
1839	0325	....	**Gamalama** (Halmahera-Indonesia)	0608-06=	2	
1839	0610	?	**Tate-yama** (Honshu-Japan)	0803-08=	2	
1840	*Cont*	....	*Stromboli (Italy)*	0101-04=	*1*	
1840	*Cont*	....	*Savo (Solomon Is-SW Pacific)*	0505-07=	*2*	
1840	*Cont*	....	*Yasur (Vanuatu-SW Pacific)*	0507-10=	*2*	
1840	*Cont*	....	*Izalco (El Salvador)*	1403-03=	*2*	
1840	*Cont*	....	*Sangay (Ecuador)*	1502-09=	*2*	
1840 ?	....	?	**Tinakula** (Santa Cruz Is-SW Pacific)	0506-01=	3?	
1840	....	?	**Ruang** (Sangihe Is-Indonesia)	0607-01=	2	
1840 <	....	?	**Kuchinoerabu-jima** (Ryukyu Is)	0802-05=	2?	
1840	....	?	**Kliuchevskoi** (Kamchatka)	1000-26=	2	
M **1840** ?	....	?	**Southern EPR-Segment K** (Pacific)	1304-12-	0	
1840	....	?	**Puracé** (Colombia)	1501-06=	2	
1840	0104	?	**Merapi** (Java)	0603-25=	1	
1840	0120	76*a*	**Ragang** (Mindanao-Philippines)	0701-06=	2	
1840	0202	240*a*	**Gamalama** (Halmahera-Indonesia)	0608-06=	3	
1840	0520	4*a*	**Guntur** (Java)	0603-13=	2	
1840	0530	26*a*	**Kilauea** (Hawaiian Is)	1302-01-	0	8/-
1840	0702	?	**Ararat** (Turkey)	0103-04-	3?	
1840	*1112*	*29a*	*Gede (Java)*	0603-06=	*2*	
1840	1201	....	**Gede** (Java)	0603-06=	3	
1841	*Cont*	....	*Stromboli (Italy)*	0101-04=	*1*	
1841	*Cont*	....	*Savo (Solomon Is-SW Pacific)*	0505-07=	*2*	
1841	*Cont*	....	*Yasur (Vanuatu-SW Pacific)*	0507-10=	*2*	
1841	*Cont*	....	*Kilauea (Hawaiian Is)*	1302-01-	*0*	
1841	*Cont*	....	*Sangay (Ecuador)*	1502-09=	*2*	
1841	....	?	**Tongariro [Ngauruhoe]** (New Zeal)	0401-08=	2	
? 1841	....	?	*Suretamatai (Vanuatu-SW Pacific)*	0507-01=		

Collection of Maurice and Katia Krafft

An eruption from 1866 to 1870 at Nea Kameni Island in the center of Santorini caldera in Greece's Agean Sea began with quiet submarine effusion of lava that built a dome above sea level. Explosive eruptions, such as shown here, accompanied lava effusion that produced flows that underlie more than half of the island of Nea Kameni. Palea Kameni Island, which formed in 46-47 AD, is visible at the right.

START YEAR	M-Dy	Duration	VOLCANO NAME (Subregion)	NUMBER	VEI	Vol L/T
1841	0128?	17m?	**Erebus** (Antarctica)	1900-02=	1	
1841	0315	?	**Hunter Island** (SW Pacific)	0508-02=		
? 1841	0330	235a	*Gamalama (Halmahera-Indonesia)*	0608-06=	1	
1841	0523	100a	**Kuchinoerabu-jima** (Ryukyu Is)	0802-05=	2	
1841	0716	396m	**Lamongan** (Java)	0603-32=	2	
1841	0801	....	*Kuchinoerabu-jima (Ryukyu Is)*	0802-05=	2	
1841	0920	>3yr	**Vesuvius** (Italy)	0101-02=	2	7/-
1841	1114	<1	**Guntur** (Java)	0603-13=	2	
1842	Cont	....	*Vesuvius (Italy)*	0101-02=	2	7/-
1842	Cont	....	*Stromboli (Italy)*	0101-04=	1	
1842	Cont	....	*Savo (Solomon Is-SW Pacific)*	0505-07=	2	
1842	Cont	....	*Yasur (Vanuatu-SW Pacific)*	0507-10=	2	
1842	Cont	....	*Lamongan (Java)*	0603-32=	2	
1842	Cont	....	*Kilauea (Hawaiian Is)*	1302-01-	0	
1842	....	?	**Kerinci** (Sumatra)	0601-17=	2	
1842	....	?	**Tangkubanparahu** (Java)	0603-09=		
1842	....	?	**Taal** (Luzon-Philippines)	0703-07=	2	
1842	....	?	**Shishaldin** (Aleutian Is)	1101-36-	2	
1842	....	?	**Izalco** (El Salvador)	1403-03=	2	
1842	....	?	**Irazú** (Costa Rica)	1405-06=	2	
1842	....	....	*Sangay (Ecuador)*	1502-09=	3	
? 1842	....	?	*Planchón-Peteroa (Chile-C)*	1507-04=		
1842	01	59p	**Semeru** (Java)	0603-30=	2	
1842	0124	142m	**Tengger Caldera [Bromo]** (Java)	0603-31=	2	
1842	02	?	**Deception Island** (Antarctica)	1900-03=	2	
1842	0315	?	**Bagana** (Bougainville-SW Pacific)	0505-02=	1	
1842	04	?	**Fournaise, Piton de la** (Indian O.)	0303-02=	0	
1842	06	?	**Goriaschaia Sopka** (Kuril Is)	0900-17=	3?	
1842	1006	87	**Gamalama** (Halmahera-Indonesia)	0608-06=	1	
1842	1118	41a?	**Etna** (Italy)	0101-06=	2	6/-
1842	1122	>3yr	**St. Helens** (US-Washington)	1201-05-	3	-/7
1843	Cont	....	*Vesuvius (Italy)*	0101-02=	2	7/-
1843	Cont	....	*Stromboli (Italy)*	0101-04=	1	
1843	Cont	....	*Savo (Solomon Is-SW Pacific)*	0505-07=	2	
1843	Cont	....	*Yasur (Vanuatu-SW Pacific)*	0507-10=	2	
1843	Cont	....	*St. Helens (US-Washington)*	1201-05-	2	-/7
1843	Cont	....	*Kilauea (Hawaiian Is)*	1302-01-	0	
1843	....	?	**Fournaise, Piton de la** (Indian O.)	0303-02=	0	
1843	....	?	**Agung** (Lesser Sunda Is)	0604-02=	2	
1843	....	>3yr	**Tongkoko** (Sulawesi-Indonesia)	0606-13=	2	
? 1843	....	?	*Banahaw (Luzon-Philippines)*	0703-05=		
1843	....	?	**Chirip** (Kuril Is)	0900-09=	2?	
? 1843	....	?	*Iliamna (Alaska-SW)*	1103-02-		
1843	....	?	**Baker** (US-Washington)	1201-01=	3?	
? 1843	....	?	*Rainier (US-Washington)*	1201-03-	2	
1843 <	....	?	**Reventador** (Ecuador)	1502-01=	2?	
1843	....	....	*Sangay (Ecuador)*	1502-09=	3	
1843	01	?	**Tengger Caldera [Bromo]** (Java)	0603-31=	2	
1843	0104	<1	**Guntur** (Java)	0603-13=	3	-/6
1843	0109	90a?	**Mauna Loa** (Hawaiian Is)	1302-02=	0	8/-
? 1843	0208	?	*Liamuiga (W Indies)*	1600-03=		
1843	0410	47a	**Gamalama** (Halmahera-Indonesia)	0608-06=	2	
1843	07	>3yr	**Ketoi** (Kuril Is)	0900-20=	2	
1843	07	?	**Atitlán** (Guatemala)	1402-06=	2	
1843	0728	?	**Gede** (Java)	0603-06=	2	
1843	08	411p	**Lamongan** (Java)	0603-32=	2	
1843	1021	?	**Talang** (Sumatra)	0601-16=	2	
1843	1117	29a?	**Etna** (Italy)	0101-06=	2	7/6
1843	1126	<1	**Guntur** (Java)	0603-13=	2?	
1843	1207	?	**Reventador** (Ecuador)	1502-01=	3	
1844	Cont	....	*Vesuvius (Italy)*	0101-02=	2	7/-
1844	Cont	....	*Stromboli (Italy)*	0101-04=	1	
1844	Cont	....	*Savo (Solomon Is-SW Pacific)*	0505-07=	2	
1844	Cont	....	*Yasur (Vanuatu-SW Pacific)*	0507-10=	2	
1844	Cont	....	*Lamongan (Java)*	0603-32=	2	
1844	Cont	....	*Tongkoko (Sulawesi-Indonesia)*	0606-13=	2	
1844	Cont	....	*Ketoi (Kuril Is)*	0900-20=	2	
1844	Cont	....	*St. Helens (US-Washington)*	1201-05-	2	-/7
1844	Cont	....	*Kilauea (Hawaiian Is)*	1302-01-	0	
1844	Cont	....	*Sangay (Ecuador)*	1502-09=	2	
? 1844	....	?	*Azuma (Honshu-Japan)*	0803-18=	1?	
? 1844	....	?	*Korovin (Aleutian Is)*	1101-161		
? 1844 a	....	?	*Makushin (Aleutian Is)*	1101-31-		
1844	....	?	**Reventador** (Ecuador)	1502-01=	3	
1844	....	?	**Cotopaxi** (Ecuador)	1502-05=	2	
@ 1844	....	?	**Negra, Sierra** (Galápagos)	1503-05=	0	
1844	0319	53a	**Fournaise, Piton de la** (Indian O.)	0303-02=	2	
? 1844	0324	235a	*Gamalama (Halmahera-Indonesia)*	0608-06=	1	
1844	0407	?	**Iwaki** (Honshu-Japan)	0803-27=	2	
1844	05	?	**Iya** (Lesser Sunda Is)	0604-11=	2	
@ 1844	05	?	**Rincón de la Vieja** (Costa Rica)	1405-02=	2	
? 1844	05	?	*Irazú (Costa Rica)*	1405-06=	2	
1844	06	122p	**Izalco** (El Salvador)	1403-03=	2	
1844	0725	>3yr	**San Miguel** (El Salvador)	1403-10=	2	
1844	08	31p	**Serua** (Banda Sea)	0605-07=	2	
1844	0925	2a	**Semeru** (Java)	0603-30=	2	
1844	10	92p	**Tongariro [Ngauruhoe]** (New Zeal)	0401-08=	2	
1844	1109	?	**Tengger Caldera [Bromo]** (Java)	0603-31=	2	
1844	12	?	**Fournaise, Piton de la** (Indian O.)	0303-02=	2	
1845	Cont	....	*Vesuvius (Italy)*	0101-02=	2	7/-
1845	Cont	....	*Stromboli (Italy)*	0101-04=	1	
1845	Cont	....	*Tongariro [Ngauruhoe] (New Zeal)*	0401-08=	2	
1845	Cont	....	*Savo (Solomon Is-SW Pacific)*	0505-07=	2	
1845	Cont	....	*Yasur (Vanuatu-SW Pacific)*	0507-10=	2	
1845	Cont	....	*Tongkoko (Sulawesi-Indonesia)*	0606-13=	2	
1845	Cont	....	*Ketoi (Kuril Is)*	0900-20=	2	
1845	Cont	....	*St. Helens (US-Washington)*	1201-05-	2	-/7
1845	Cont	....	*Kilauea (Hawaiian Is)*	1302-01-	0	
1845	Cont	....	*San Miguel (El Salvador)*	1403-10=	2	
1845	Cont	....	*Sangay (Ecuador)*	1502-09=	2	
1845	....	?	**Fournaise, Piton de la** (Indian O.)	0303-02=	0	
? 1845	....	?	*Serua (Banda Sea)*	0605-07=	2	
1845 e	....	?	**Ambang** (Sulawesi-Indonesia)	0606-02=		
1845	....	365y	**Kolokol Group** (Kuril Is)	0900-12=	2	
? 1845	....	?	*Akutan (Aleutian Is)*	1101-32-		
? 1845	....	?	*Isanotski (Aleutian Is)*	1101-37-		
1845	01	184p	**Semeru** (Java)	0603-30=	2	
1845	0120a	10b	**Mayon** (Luzon-Philippines)	0703-03=	3	
1845	0123	41a	**Gede** (Java)	0603-06=	2	
1845	0208	?	**Soputan** (Sulawesi-Indonesia)	0606-03=	2	
1845	0219	?	**Ruiz, Nevado del** (Colombia)	1501-02=	3	-/7
1845	0226	6a>	**Antuco** (Chile-C)	1507-08=	2	
1845	04	?	**Cotopaxi** (Ecuador)	1502-05=	2	
1845	0404	?	**Iwaki** (Honshu-Japan)	0803-27=	2	
1845	0422	?	**Talang** (Sumatra)	0601-16=	2	
? 1845	0423	133a	*Gamalama (Halmahera-Indonesia)*	0608-06=	1	
1845	0812	?	**Pavlof** (Alaska Peninsula)	1102-03-	2	
1845	0902	215a?	**Hekla** (Iceland-S)	1702-07=	4	8/8
1845	1116	2a	**Marapi** (Sumatra)	0601-14=	2?	
1846	Cont	....	*Vesuvius (Italy)*	0101-02=	2	7/-
1846	Cont	....	*Stromboli (Italy)*	0101-04=	1	
1846	Cont	....	*Savo (Solomon Is-SW Pacific)*	0505-07=	2	
1846	Cont	....	*Yasur (Vanuatu-SW Pacific)*	0507-10=	2	
1846	Cont	....	*Tongkoko (Sulawesi-Indonesia)*	0606-13=	2	
1846	Cont	....	*Kolokol Group (Kuril Is)*	0900-12=	2	
1846	Cont	....	*Ketoi (Kuril Is)*	0900-20=	2	
1846	Cont	....	*Kilauea (Hawaiian Is)*	1302-01-	0	
1846	Cont	....	*San Miguel (El Salvador)*	1403-10=	2	
1846	Cont	....	*Sangay (Ecuador)*	1502-09=	2	
1846	Cont	....	*Hekla (Iceland-S)*	1702-07=	3	8/8
1846	....	?	**Fournaise, Piton de la** (Indian O.)	0303-02=	0	
1846	....	?	**Mahawu** (Sulawesi-Indonesia)	0606-11=	2	
1846	....	4a?	**Oshima** (Izu Is-Japan)	0804-01=	2	
1846	....	?	**Rasshua** (Kuril Is)	0900-22=	3	
1846	....	?	**Sinarka** (Kuril Is)	0900-29=	3	
1846	....	?	**Kharimkotan** (Kuril Is)	0900-30=	2	
? 1846	....	?	*Baker (US-Washington)*	1201-01=		
1846	....	?	**Orizaba, Pico de** (México)	1401-10=	2	
1846	02	?	**Pacaya** (Guatemala)	1402-11=	2	
1846	0406	?	**Merapi** (Java)	0603-25=	2	
1846	0511	<1	**Mayon** (Luzon-Philippines)	0703-03=	3	
1846	0519	<1	**Gamalama** (Halmahera-Indonesia)	0608-06=	2	
1846	0527	?	**Tangkubanparahu** (Java)	0603-09=	2	
1846	0611?	121a>	**Fonualei** (Tonga-SW Pacific)	0403-10=	4?	7/8
1846	08	?	**Nasu** (Honshu-Japan)	0803-15=	1	-/5
1846	08	1a	**Pavlof** (Alaska Peninsula)	1102-03-	2	
? 1846	0814	?	*Zubair, Jebel (Red Sea)*	0201-02=	2	
1846	09 ?	?	**Serua** (Banda Sea)	0605-07=	2	
1846	0902	409m	**Merapi** (Java)	0603-25=	3	
1846	1004	1a	**Campi Flegrei Mar Sicilia** (Italy)	0101-07=	2	
1846	11	?	**Fernandina** (Galápagos)	1503-01=	0	
1846	1118	?	**E-san** (Hokkaido-Japan)	0805-011	1	
1846	1126	>3yr	**Azul, Cerro** (Chile-C)	1507-06=	2	**9**/-
1847	Cont	....	*Vesuvius (Italy)*	0101-02=	2	7/-
1847	Cont	....	*Stromboli (Italy)*	0101-04=	1	
1847	Cont	....	*Savo (Solomon Is-SW Pacific)*	0505-07=	2	
1847	Cont	....	*Yasur (Vanuatu-SW Pacific)*	0507-10=	2	
1847	Cont	....	*Merapi (Java)*	0603-25=	2	
1847	Cont	....	*Kilauea (Hawaiian Is)*	1302-01-	0	
1847	Cont	....	*San Miguel (El Salvador)*	1403-10=	2	
1847	Cont	....	*Sangay (Ecuador)*	1502-09=	2	
1847	Cont	....	*Azul, Cerro (Chile-C)*	1507-06=	0	
1847	....	?	**Fournaise, Piton de la** (Indian O.)	0303-02=	0	
? 1847	....	?	*Batur (Lesser Sunda Is)*	0604-01=		
1847	....	>3yr	**Tara, Batu** (Lesser Sunda Is)	0604-26=	2	
? 1847	....	?	*Turrialba (Costa Rica)*	1405-07=		
1847	0207	<1	**Gamalama** (Halmahera-Indonesia)	0608-06=	2	
1847	0320	?	**Slamet** (Java)	0603-18=	2	
1847	0326	92a	**Lamongan** (Java)	0603-32=	2	
1847	0326	4a	**St. Helens** (US-Washington)	1201-05-	2	
1847	0409	23a?	**Fogo** (Cape Verde Is)	1804-01=	2	
1847	0518	?	**Irazú** (Costa Rica)	1405-06=	2	
1847	0907	<1	**Gamalama** (Halmahera-Indonesia)	0608-06=		
1847	0910	2a	**Rinjani** (Lesser Sunda Is)	0604-03=	2	

	START YEAR	M-Dy	Duration	VOLCANO NAME (Subregion)	NUMBER	VEI	Vol L/T
	1847	0925	?	**Lamongan** (Java)	0603-32=	2	
	1847	1016	12a	**Guntur** (Java)	0603-13=	2	
	1847	1017	1a	**Gede** (Java)	0603-06=	2	
	1847	1027	>3yr	Puracé (Colombia)	1501-06=	2	
	1847	1204	?	**Dieng Volc Complex** (Java)	0603-20=	2	
	1848	Cont	....	Vesuvius (Italy)	0101-02=	2	7/-
	1848	Cont	....	Stromboli (Italy)	0101-04=	1	
	1848	Cont	....	Yasur (Vanuatu-SW Pacific)	0507-10=	2	
	1848	Cont	....	Tara, Batu (Lesser Sunda Is)	0604-26=	2	
	1848	Cont	....	Kilauea (Hawaiian Is)	1302-01-	0	
	1848	Cont	....	San Miguel (El Salvador)	1403-10=	2	
	1848	Cont	....	Puracé (Colombia)	1501-06=	2	
	1848	Cont	....	Sangay (Ecuador)	1502-09=	2	
	1848	Cont	....	Azul, Cerro (Chile-C)	1507-06=	0	
	1848	....	?	**Karthala** (Indian O.-W)	0303-01=	0	
	1848	....	?	**Fournaise, Piton de la** (Indian O.)	0303-02=	0	
	1848	....	?	**Golovnin** (Kuril Is)	0900-01=	1	
	1848	....	?	**Kharimkotan** (Kuril Is)	0900-30=	2	
	1848	....	?	**Mutnovsky** (Kamchatka)	1000-06=	3	-/7
	1848	....	?	**Kliuchevskoi** (Kamchatka)	1000-26=	2	
?	1848	....	?	Socorro (México-Is)	1401-021	2?	
	1848	....	?	**Láscar** (Chile-N)	1505-10=	2	
?	1848	....	?	Antuco (Chile-C)	1507-08=	2?	
?	1848	0108	?	Merapi (Java)	0603-25=		
?	1848	0118	?	Iwaki (Honshu-Japan)	0803-27=	2	
	1848	02	?	**Semeru** (Java)	0603-30=	2	
	1848	0305d	?	**Akutan** (Aleutian Is)	1101-32-	2	
	1848	0401<	?	**St. Helens** (US-Washington)	1201-05-	2?	
?	1848	0413	88a?	Ritter Island (New Guinea-NE of)	0501-07=		
	1848	0508	?	**Gede** (Java)	0603-06=	2	
	1848	0516	1a	**Kelut** (Java)	0603-28=	3	
	1848	0804	?	**Semeru** (Java)	0603-30=	2	
	1849	Cont	....	Vesuvius (Italy)	0101-02=	2	7/-
	1849	Cont	....	Stromboli (Italy)	0101-04=	1	
	1849	Cont	....	Yasur (Vanuatu-SW Pacific)	0507-10=	2	
	1849	Cont	....	Tara, Batu (Lesser Sunda Is)	0604-26=	2	
	1849	Cont	....	Kilauea (Hawaiian Is)	1302-01-	0	
	1849	Cont	....	Azul, Cerro (Chile-C)	1507-06=	0	
	1849	....	?	**Fournaise, Piton de la** (Indian O.)	0303-02=	0	
?	1849	....	?	Kelut (Java)	0603-28=		
?	1849	....	?	Semeru (Java)	0603-30=		
	1849	....	?	**Batur** (Lesser Sunda Is)	0604-01=	2	
	1849	....	?	**Goriaschaia Sopka** (Kuril Is)	0900-17=	2	
?	1849	....	?	St. Helens (US-Washington)	1201-05-	2?	
	1849	....	?	**Momotombo** (Nicaragua)	1404-09=	2	
@	1849	....	?	**Rincón de la Vieja** (Costa Rica)	1405-02=	2	
	1849	0426	<1	**Merapi** (Java)	0603-25=	2	-/6
	1849	05	18e	**Mauna Loa** (Hawaiian Is)	1302-02=	0	7/-
	1849	06	92p	**Lamongan** (Java)	0603-32=	2	
	1849	0914	10a	**Merapi** (Java)	0603-25=	3	-/7
	1849	1006	?	**Lewotolo** (Lesser Sunda Is)	0604-23=	2	
	1849	1127	357a	**Gamalama** (Halmahera-Indonesia)	0608-06=	2	
	1849	12	....	**Puracé** (Colombia)	1501-06=	3?	
	1849	12	....	Sangay (Ecuador)	1502-09=	3	
	1849	1201	?	**Slamet** (Java)	0603-18=	2	
	1849	1201p	?	**Raung** (Java)	0603-34=		
	1850	Cont	....	Yasur (Vanuatu-SW Pacific)	0507-10=	2	
	1850	Cont	....	Tara, Batu (Lesser Sunda Is)	0604-26=	2	
	1850	Cont	....	Gamalama (Halmahera-Indonesia)	0608-06=	2	
	1850	Cont	....	Kilauea (Hawaiian Is)	1302-01-	0	
	1850	Cont	....	Puracé (Colombia)	1501-06=	2	
	1850	Cont	....	Sangay (Ecuador)	1502-09=	2	
	1850	Cont	....	Azul, Cerro (Chile-C)	1507-06=	0	
	1850	....	....	Stromboli (Italy)	0101-04=	2?	
	1850 j	....	?	**Es Safa** (Syria)	0300-05-	0	
	1850 ?	....	?	**Karthala** (Indian O.-W)	0303-01=	0	
	1850 ?	....	?	**Rabaul** (New Britain-SW Pac)	0502-14=	2	
	1850	....	?	**Unnamed** (Luzon-N of)	0704-05=	0	
?	1850	....	?	Unnamed (Taiwan-E of)	0801-01=	0	
?	1850 t	....	?	Kunlun Volc Group (China-W)	1004-03-		
A	1850 ?	....	?	**Chichón, El** (México)	1401-12=		
?	1850	....	?	Fuego (Guatemala)	1402-09=	2	
	1850	....	?	**Izalco** (El Salvador)	1403-03=	2	
	1850	....	?	**Cotopaxi** (Ecuador)	1502-05=	2	
E	1850 >	....	?	**Azul, Cerro** (Galápagos)	1503-06=		
	1850	....	?	**Puntiagudo-Cordón Cenizos**	1507-16-		
	1850 ?	....	?	**Penguin Island** (Antarctica)	1900-031		
?	1850	....	?	Paulet (Antarctica)	1900-041		
	1850	0205	....	Vesuvius (Italy)	0101-02=	2	7/-
?	1850	03	?	Baker (US-Washington)	1201-01=		
	1850	03	61p?	**St. Helens** (US-Washington)	1201-05-	2?	
	1850	0413	44a	**Negro, Cerro** (Nicaragua)	1404-07=	2	6/5
	1850	1103	9a	**Fournaise, Piton de la** (Indian O.)	0303-02=	0	
	1851	Cont	....	Stromboli (Italy)	0101-04=	1	
	1851	Cont	....	Yasur (Vanuatu-SW Pacific)	0507-10=	2	
	1851	Cont	....	Tara, Batu (Lesser Sunda Is)	0604-26=	2	
	1851	Cont	....	Puracé (Colombia)	1501-06=	2	
	1851	Cont	....	Sangay (Ecuador)	1502-09=	2	
	1851	Cont	....	Azul, Cerro (Chile-C)	1507-06=	0	
	1851	....	?	**Fournaise, Piton de la** (Indian O.)	0303-02=	0	
	1851	....	?	**Metis Shoal** (Tonga-SW Pacific)	0403-07=	0	
?	1851	....	?	Rincón de la Vieja (Costa Rica)	1405-02=		
	1851	....	?	**Osorno** (Chile-S)	1508-01=	2?	
	1851 r	....	?	**Jan Mayen** (Atlantic-N-Jan Mayen)	1706-01=		
	1851	01	?	**Semeru** (Java)	0603-30=	2	
	1851	01	....	Kilauea (Hawaiian Is)	1302-01-	0	
	1851	0124	?	**Kelut** (Java)	0603-28=	2	
	1851	0526	20m	**Mayon** (Luzon-Philippines)	0703-03=	1	
	1851	06	?	**Cotopaxi** (Ecuador)	1502-05=	2	
	1851	0805	193p	**Pelée** (W Indies)	1600-12=	2	
	1851	0808	3a	**Mauna Loa** (Hawaiian Is)	1302-02=	0	7/-
	1851	09	?	**Maly Semiachik** (Kamchatka)	1000-14=	2	
	1851	1126	80d	**Avachinsky** (Kamchatka)	1000-10=	2	
	1852	Cont	....	Stromboli (Italy)	0101-04=	1	
	1852	Cont	....	Yasur (Vanuatu-SW Pacific)	0507-10=	2	
	1852	Cont	....	Tara, Batu (Lesser Sunda Is)	0604-26=	2	
	1852	Cont	....	Avachinsky (Kamchatka)	1000-10=	2	
	1852	Cont	....	Kilauea (Hawaiian Is)	1302-01-	0	
	1852	Cont	....	Puracé (Colombia)	1501-06=	2	
	1852	Cont	....	Sangay (Ecuador)	1502-09=	2	
	1852	Cont	....	Azul, Cerro (Chile-C)	1507-06=	0	
	1852	Cont	....	Pelée (W Indies)	1600-12=	2	
	1852	....	?	**Cameroon** (Africa-W)	0204-01=	2	
	1852	....	?	**Fournaise, Piton de la** (Indian O.)	0303-02=	0	
?	1852	....	?	Metis Shoal (Tonga-SW Pacific)	0403-07=	0	
	1852	....	?	**Home Reef** (Tonga-SW Pacific)	0403-08=	2	
?	1852	....	?	Barren Island (Andaman Is-Indian O)	0600-01=	2	
?	1852	....	?	Sirung (Lesser Sunda Is)	0604-27=	2	
?	1852	....	?	Bulusan (Luzon-Philippines)	0703-01=		
	1852	....	?	**Karymsky** (Kamchatka)	1000-13=	2	
	1852	....	?	**Akutan** (Aleutian Is)	1101-32-		
?	1852	....	?	Pavlof (Alaska Peninsula)	1102-03-	1?	
?	1852	....	?	Veniaminof (Alaska Peninsula)	1102-07-	2?	
?	1852	....	?	Ugashik-Peulik (Alaska Peninsula)	1102-13-		
?	1852	....	?	Popocatépetl (México)	1401-09=	1?	
?	1852	....	?	Atitlán (Guatemala)	1402-06=	2?	
?	1852	....	?	Fuego (Guatemala)	1402-09=	2	
	1852	....	?	**Momotombo** (Nicaragua)	1404-09=	2	
	1852	....	?	**Cotopaxi** (Ecuador)	1502-05=	2	
	1852	....	365y	**Llaima** (Chile-C)	1507-11=	2	
?	1852	....	?	Villarrica (Chile-C)	1507-12=		
	1852	02	30p	**Kliuchevskoi** (Kamchatka)	1000-26=	2	
	1852	0217	23a?	**Mauna Loa** (Hawaiian Is)	1302-02=	2	8/-
	1852	0219	40a?	**Fogo** (Cape Verde Is)	1804-01=	2	
	1852	03	?	**Mutnovsky** (Kamchatka)	1000-06=	2	
	1852	0415q	91r	**Maly Semiachik** (Kamchatka)	1000-14=	2	
	1852	0528	<1	**Gede** (Java)	0603-06=	2	
	1852	06	31p	**Masaya** (Nicaragua)	1404-10=	2	
?	1852	0717	?	Unnamed (Atlantic-C)	1805-04=	0	
	1852	08	?	**Kliuchevskoi** (Kamchatka)	1000-26=	2	
	1852	0820	290a	**Etna** (Italy)	0101-06=	2	8/6
	1852	1005	1a	**Lewotolo** (Lesser Sunda Is)	0604-23=	2	
	1852	11	62p	Antuco (Chile-C)	1507-08=	0	7/-
	1852	1101	196m?	**Niigata-Yake-yama** (Honshu-Japan)	0803-09=	2	
	1852	12	?	**Cosigüina** (Nicaragua)	1404-01=	2?	
	1852	1201p	45q?	**Baker** (US-Washington)	1201-01=	2	
	1853	Cont	....	Stromboli (Italy)	0101-04=	1	
	1853	Cont	....	Etna (Italy)	0101-06=	2	8/6
	1853	Cont	....	Yasur (Vanuatu-SW Pacific)	0507-10=	2	
	1853	Cont	....	Niigata-Yake-yama (Honshu-Japan)	0803-09=	2	
	1853	Cont	....	Baker (US-Washington)	1201-01=	2	
	1853	Cont	....	Kilauea (Hawaiian Is)	1302-01-	0	
	1853	Cont	....	Sangay (Ecuador)	1502-09=	2	
	1853	Cont	....	Azul, Cerro (Chile-C)	1507-06=	0	
	1853	Cont	....	Llaima (Chile-C)	1507-11=	2	
?	1853	....	?	Hood (US-Oregon)	1202-01-		
	1853	....	?	**Rincón de la Vieja** (Costa Rica)	1405-02=	2	
	1853	....	?	**Turrialba** (Costa Rica)	1405-07=	2	
?	1853	....	?	Láscar (Chile-N)	1505-10=	2?	
	1853	01	?	**Mutnovsky** (Kamchatka)	1000-06=	2	
	1853	01	....	**Antuco** (Chile-C)	1507-08=	3	7/-
	1853	0101	?	**Dempo** (Sumatra)	0601-23=	2	
	1853	02	?	**Lonquimay** (Chile-C)	1507-10=	3	
	1853	0314	<1	**Gede** (Java)	0603-06=	3?	
	1853	0315e	153n?	**St. Helens** (US-Washington)	1201-05-	2?	
	1853	0409?	159a>	**Masaya** (Nicaragua)	1404-10=	1?	
	1853	0422	146m	**Usu** (Hokkaido-Japan)	0805-03=	4	8/8
	1853	0503	?	**Atitlán** (Guatemala)	1402-06=	3	
	1853	0624	<1	**Niuafo'ou** (Tonga-SW Pacific)	0403-11=	0	
?	1853	07	?	South Sister (US-Oregon)	1202-08-		
	1853	0713	44	**Mayon** (Luzon-Philippines)	0703-03=	3	
	1853	0913	2a	**Cotopaxi** (Ecuador)	1502-05=	3	7/-
	1853	10	124m	**Kliuchevskoi** (Kamchatka)	1000-26=	2	

START YEAR	M-Dy	Duration	VOLCANO NAME (Subregion) . . .	NUMBER	VEI	Vol L/T
1853	1029	17m?	Unnamed (Taiwan-E of)	0801-03=	2?	
1853	11	?	Kaba (Sumatra)	0601-22=	2	
1853	11	?	Villarrica (Chile-C)	1507-12=	2?	
1853	12	>3yr	Chikurachki (Kuril Is)	0900-36=	3?	-/7
1853	1218	87m	Mutnovsky (Kamchatka)	1000-06=	2	
1853	1221	83a?	Avachinsky (Kamchatka)	1000-10=	2	
1854	Cont	....	Stromboli (Italy)	0101-04=	1	
1854	Cont	....	Yasur (Vanuatu-SW Pacific)	0507-10=	2	
1854	Cont	....	Chikurachki (Kuril Is)	0900-36=	2	-/7
1854	Cont	....	Mutnovsky (Kamchatka)	1000-06=	2	
1854	Cont	....	Kliuchevskoi (Kamchatka)	1000-26=	2	
1854	Cont	....	Kilauea (Hawaiian Is)	1302-01-	0	
1854	....	?	Taranaki [Egmont] (New Zealand)	0401-03=		
1854	....	?	Tofua (Tonga-SW Pacific)	0403-06=	2	
1854	....	?	Late (Tonga-SW Pacific)	0403-09=	2	
1854	....	?	Niigata-Yake-yama (Honshu-Japan)	0803-09=		
? 1854	....	?	Opala (Kamchatka)	1000-08=		
1854	....	?	Baker (US-Washington)	1201-01=	2	
? 1854	....	?	Rainier (US-Washington)	1201-03-	2	
? 1854	....	?	San Miguel (El Salvador)	1403-10=	2?	
1854	....	>3yr	Rincón de la Vieja (Costa Rica)	1405-02=	2	
1854	....	?	Grímsvötn (Iceland-NE)	1703-01=	2	
1854	0115	?	Unnamed (Luzon-N of)	0704-05=	0	
? 1854	0115	?	Unnamed (Taiwan-E of)	0801-03=	0	
1854	0120	10a	Láscar (Chile-N)	1505-10=	1	
1854	02	61p	St. Helens (US-Washington)	1201-05-	2	
1854	02	30p	Momotombo (Nicaragua)	1404-09=	2	
1854	0210	?	Llullaillaco (Chile-N)	1505-11=	2	
1854	0218	?	Shiveluch (Kamchatka)	1000-27=	5	-/9
1854	0226	?	Aso (Kyushu-Japan)	0802-11=	2	
1854	0403	?	Cotopaxi (Ecuador)	1502-05=	2	
1854	0428	?	Batur (Lesser Sunda Is)	0604-01=	1?	
1854	0513	26a	Izalco (El Salvador)	1403-03=	2	
? 1854	0618	<1	Makian (Halmahera-Indonesia)	0608-07=	1	
1854	0624	?	Chirpoi (Kuril Is)	0900-15=	2	
1854	0627	?	Alaid (Kuril Is)	0900-39=	3	
1854	0705	?	Fuss Peak (Kuril Is)	0900-34=	3	
? 1854	08	?	Hood (US-Oregon)	1202-01-		
1854	08	....	Sangay (Ecuador)	1502-09=	2	
1854	0813	?	Avachinsky (Kamchatka)	1000-10=	2	
1854	0829>	?	Marapi (Sumatra)	0601-14=	2	
? 1854	09	?	Merapi (Java)	0603-25=		
1854	09	?	Karymsky (Kamchatka)	1000-13=	2	
1854	0914	?	Cotopaxi (Ecuador)	1502-05=	2	
1854	1214	164a	Vesuvius (Italy)	0101-02=	2	7/-
? 1854	1223	17a	Fuji (Honshu-Japan)	0803-03=		
1855	Cont	....	Yasur (Vanuatu-SW Pacific)	0507-10=	2	
? 1855	Cont	....	Fuji (Honshu-Japan)	0803-03=		
1855	Cont	....	Chikurachki (Kuril Is)	0900-36=	2	-/7
1855	Cont	....	Kilauea (Hawaiian Is)	1302-01-	0	
1855	Cont	....	Rincón de la Vieja (Costa Rica)	1405-02=	2	
1855	Cont	....	Sangay (Ecuador)	1502-09=	2	
1855	....	?	Tendürek Dagi (Turkey)	0103-03=		
A 1855 e	....	?	Chyulu Hills (Africa-E)	0202-13=	2	
1855	....	?	Tongariro (New Zealand)	0401-08=	2	
1855	....	?	Sinarka (Kuril Is)	0900-29=	2	
1855	....	?	Osorno (Chile-S)	1508-01=	2?	
? 1855	0112	?	Tacaná (México)	1401-13=	1	
1855	03	61p	Iwo-Tori-shima (Ryukyu Is)	0802-02=	2	
1855	0322	?	Mayon (Luzon-Philippines)	0703-03=	2	
? 1855	04	?	Gorely (Kamchatka)	1000-07=	2?	
1855	05	?	Turrialba (Costa Rica)	1405-07=	2	
1855	0501	....	Vesuvius (Italy)	0101-02=	3	7/-
1855	0528	98n	Avachinsky (Kamchatka)	1000-10=	2	
1855	0701p	?	Karthala (Indian O.-W)	0303-01=	2	
1855	08	?	Tinakula (Santa Cruz Is-SW Pacific)	0506-01=	2	
1855	0811	462m	Mauna Loa (Hawaiian Is)	1302-02=	1	8/-
1855	0929	1a	Fuego (Guatemala)	1402-09=	2	
1855	1002	105m	Marapi (Sumatra)	0601-14=	2	
1855	1003	....	Stromboli (Italy)	0101-04=	2	
1855	11	?	Cotopaxi (Ecuador)	1502-05=	2	
1855	12	?	San Miguel (El Salvador)	1403-10=	2	
1855	1219	>3yr	Vesuvius (Italy)	0101-02=	2	8/-
? 1855	1229	1a	Banda Api (Banda Sea)	0605-09=		
1856	Cont	....	Vesuvius (Italy)	0101-02=	2	8/-
1856	Cont	....	Yasur (Vanuatu-SW Pacific)	0507-10=	2	
1856	Cont	....	Marapi (Sumatra)	0601-14=	1	
1856	Cont	....	Chikurachki (Kuril Is)	0900-36=	2	-/7
1856	Cont	....	Kilauea (Hawaiian Is)	1302-01-	0	
1856	Cont	....	Mauna Loa (Hawaiian Is)	1302-02=	1	8/-
1856	Cont	....	Rincón de la Vieja (Costa Rica)	1405-02=	2	
? 1856 h	....	?	White Island (New Zealand)	0401-04=	2	
1856 ?	....	?	Suretamatai (Vanuatu-SW Pacific)	0507-01=	2?	
? 1856	....	?	Makaturing (Mindanao-Philippines)	0701-04=		
? 1856	....	?	Baker (US-Washington)	1201-01=		
? 1856	....	?	Atitlán (Guatemala)	1402-06=	2	
1856	0109	57a	Fuego (Guatemala)	1402-09=	2	
1856	0212	....	Sangay (Ecuador)	1502-09=	3	
1856	0301	105a	Lamongan (Java)	0603-32=	2	
1856	0302	15a	Awu (Sangihe Is-Indonesia)	0607-04=	3?	-/8
1856	0318	97a	Aso (Kyushu-Japan)	0802-11=	2	
1856	0414	?	Telong, Bur ni (Sumatra)	0601-05=	2	
1856	05	?	Cotopaxi (Ecuador)	1502-05=	2	
? 1856	0520	?	Iwaki (Honshu-Japan)	0803-27=	2	
1856	0524	100a	Izalco (El Salvador)	1403-03=	2	
1856	07	....	Stromboli (Italy)	0101-04=	2	
1856	09	?	Ruang (Sangihe Is-Indonesia)	0607-01=	1	
1856	0910	?	Semeru (Java)	0603-30=	2	
@ 1856	0910	?	Tengger Caldera [Bromo] (Java)	0603-31=	2	
1856	0925	?	Komaga-take (Hokkaido-Japan)	0805-02=	4	-/8
1856	0929	1a	Fuego (Guatemala)	1402-09=	2	
1856	0930p	>3yr	Didicas (Luzon-N of)	0704-02=	0	8/-
1856	10	61p	Cotopaxi (Ecuador)	1502-05=	2	
1856	1101	?	Ragang (Mindanao-Philippines)	0701-06=	2	
? 1856	1125	<1 ?	Unnamed (Atlantic-N)	1801-03=	0	
1856	12	31p	Masaya (Nicaragua)	1404-10=	2	
1856	1212	1a	Reventador (Ecuador)	1502-01=	3	
1857	Cont	....	Vesuvius (Italy)	0101-02=	2	8/-
1857	Cont	....	Yasur (Vanuatu-SW Pacific)	0507-10=	2	
1857	Cont	....	Didicas (Luzon-N of)	0704-02=	0	8/-
1857	Cont	....	Chikurachki (Kuril Is)	0900-36=	2	-/7
1857	Cont	....	Kilauea (Hawaiian Is)	1302-01-	0	
1857	Cont	....	Masaya (Nicaragua)	1404-10=	2	
1857	Cont	....	Rincón de la Vieja (Costa Rica)	1405-02=	2	
1857	Cont	....	Sangay (Ecuador)	1502-09=	2	
1857	....	>3yr	Stromboli (Italy)	0101-04=	1	4/-
1857	....	?	Karthala (Indian O.-W)	0303-01=	2	
? 1857	....	?	Home Reef (Tonga-SW Pacific)	0403-08=	2	
1857	....	?	Tengger Caldera [Bromo] (Java)	0603-31=	2	
1857	....	?	Mayon (Luzon-Philippines)	0703-03=	2	
1857 <	....	?	Camiguin de Babuyanes (Luzon-N)	0704-01=	2	
1857	....	?	Tokachi (Hokkaido-Japan)	0805-05=	2	
1857	....	365y	Shiretoko-Iwo-zan (Hokkaido-Japan)	0805-09=		
? 1857	....	?	Tres Vírgenes (México)	1401-01=		
1857	....	?	Cotopaxi (Ecuador)	1502-05=	2	
1857	0115	33a	Fuego (Guatemala)	1402-09=	4?	-/8
1857	02	18c	Tongariro [Ngauruhoe] (New Zeal)	0401-08=	2	
1857	0215	4a>	Izalco (El Salvador)	1403-03=	2	
1857	04	?	St. Helens (US-Washington)	1201-05-	2	
1857	0627	171a	Fogo (Cape Verde Is)	1804-01=	2	
1857	07	?	Chirpoi (Kuril Is)	0900-15=	3	
1857	08	?	Tinakula (Santa Cruz Is-SW Pacific)	0506-01=	2	
1857	0813	33m	Semeru (Java)	0603-30=	2	
? 1857	0906	?	Etna (Italy)	0101-06=	1?	
1857	0910?	?	Tungurahua (Ecuador)	1502-08=	2?	
1857	0917	?	Fuego (Guatemala)	1402-09=	2	
1857	11	?	San Miguel (El Salvador)	1403-10=	2?	
1858	Cont	....	Stromboli (Italy)	0101-04=	1	4/-
1858	Cont	....	Yasur (Vanuatu-SW Pacific)	0507-10=	2	
1858	Cont	....	Didicas (Luzon-N of)	0704-02=	0	8/-
1858	Cont	....	Shiretoko-Iwo-zan (Hokkaido-Japan)	0805-09=		
1858	Cont	....	Chikurachki (Kuril Is)	0900-36=	2	-/7
1858	Cont	....	Kilauea (Hawaiian Is)	1302-01-	0	
1858	Cont	....	Rincón de la Vieja (Costa Rica)	1405-02=	2	
1858	....	?	Karthala (Indian O.-W)	0303-01=	2	
1858	....	?	Metis Shoal (Tonga-SW Pacific)	0403-07=	2	
1858	....	?	Serua (Banda Sea)	0605-07=	2	
? 1858	....	?	Makaturing (Mindanao-Philippines)	0701-04=		
1858	....	?	Baker (US-Washington)	1201-01=	2	
? 1858	....	?	Rainier (US-Washington)	1201-03-	2	
1858	....	>3yr	Momotombo (Nicaragua)	1404-09=	2	
1858	01	334p	Mayon (Luzon-Philippines)	0703-03=	2	
1858	0206	524m	Izalco (El Salvador)	1403-03=	2	
1858	0218	?	Ragang (Mindanao-Philippines)	0701-06=	2	
1858	0304	?	Tengger Caldera [Bromo] (Java)	0603-31=	2	
? 1858	04	?	Masaya (Nicaragua)	1404-10=		
1858	04	245p	Láscar (Chile-N)	1505-10=	2?	
1858	0527	....	Vesuvius (Italy)	0101-02=	2	8/-
1858	1018	?	Tengger Caldera [Bromo] (Java)	0603-31=	2	
? 1858	11	302p	Gamalama (Halmahera-Indonesia)	0608-06=	1	
1858	11	30p	Cotopaxi (Ecuador)	1502-05=	2	
1858	1103	74m	Fournaise, Piton de la (Indian O.)	0303-02=	2	7/-
1858	1110	137a	Masaya (Nicaragua)	1404-10=	2	
1858	12	....	Sangay (Ecuador)	1502-09=	2	
1859	Cont	....	Vesuvius (Italy)	0101-02=	2	8/-
1859	Cont	....	Stromboli (Italy)	0101-04=	1	4/-
1859	Cont	....	Yasur (Vanuatu-SW Pacific)	0507-10=	2	
? 1859	Cont	....	Gamalama (Halmahera-Indonesia)	0608-06=	1	
1859	Cont	....	Didicas (Luzon-N of)	0704-02=	0	8/-
1859	Cont	....	Chikurachki (Kuril Is)	0900-36=	2	-/7
1859	Cont	....	Kilauea (Hawaiian Is)	1302-01-	0	
1859	Cont	....	Momotombo (Nicaragua)	1404-09=	2	
1859	Cont	....	Masaya (Nicaragua)	1404-10=	2	
1859	Cont	....	Rincón de la Vieja (Costa Rica)	1405-02=	2	

	START YEAR	M-Dy	Duration	VOLCANO NAME (Subregion)	NUMBER	VEI	Vol L/T
	1859	....	?	Karthala (Indian O.-W)	0303-01=	2	
	1859	....	?	Serua (Banda Sea)	0605-07=	2	
	1859	....	?	Mayon (Luzon-Philippines)	0703-03=		
	1859	....	?	Cotopaxi (Ecuador)	1502-05=	2	
	1859	0123	306a	Mauna Loa (Hawaiian Is)	1302-02=	1	8/-
	1859	0130	33d	Tengger Caldera [Bromo] (Java)	0603-31=	2	
	1859	0227	16m	Lamongan (Java)	0603-32=	2	
	1859	0421	?	Tongariro (New Zealand)	0401-08=	1?	
	1859	05	....	Sangay (Ecuador)	1502-09=	2	
	1859	0508	15a>	Fournaise, Piton de la (Indian O.)	0303-02=	2	
	1859	0519	327a	Villarrica (Chile-C)	1507-12=	2	
?	1859	07	?	Lewotobi (Lesser Sunda Is)	0604-18=		
	1859	0815	2a	Hood (US-Oregon)	1202-01-	2	
	1859	0825	?	Cosigüina (Nicaragua)	1404-01=		
	1859	0927	?	Ebeko (Kuril Is)	0900-38=	2	
	1859	11	163m?	Baker (US-Washington)	1201-01=	2	
	1859	1208	45a	Izalco (El Salvador)	1403-03=	0	
	1859	1214	?	Raung (Java)	0603-34=	2	
	1860	Cont	....	Vesuvius (Italy)	0101-02=	2	8/-
	1860	Cont	....	Stromboli (Italy)	0101-04=	1	4/-
	1860	Cont	....	Yasur (Vanuatu-SW Pacific)	0507-10=	2	
	1860	Cont	....	Kilauea (Hawaiian Is)	1302-01-	0	
	1860	Cont	....	Izalco (El Salvador)	1403-03=	0	
	1860	Cont	....	Momotombo (Nicaragua)	1404-09=	2	
	1860	Cont	....	Sangay (Ecuador)	1502-09=	2	
	1860	Cont	....	Villarrica (Chile-C)	1507-12=	2	
?	1860	....	?	Makian (Halmahera-Indonesia)	0608-07=	1	
	1860	....	?	Mayon (Luzon-Philippines)	0703-03=		
	1860	....	....	Didicas (Luzon-N of)	0704-02=	2	8/-
	1860	....	?	Babuyan Claro (Luzon-N of)	0704-03=	2	
	1860	....	?	Sakura-jima (Kyushu-Japan)	0802-08=	1	
	1860 ?	....	?	Chirip (Kuril Is)	0900-09=	1	
M	1860 ?	....	?	Southern EPR-Segment I (Pacific)	1304-14-	0	
	1860	....	....	Rincón de la Vieja (Costa Rica)	1405-02=	2	
	1860	....	?	Poás (Costa Rica)	1405-04=	1	
	1860 i	....	?	Puracé (Colombia)	1501-06=	2?	
	1860	....	730y	Cotopaxi (Ecuador)	1502-05=	2	
@	1860	....	?	Negra, Sierra (Galápagos)	1503-05=	2	
	1860	....	?	Planchón-Peteroa (Chile-C)	1507-04=	2	
	1860	0122	58a	Fournaise, Piton de la (Indian O.)	0303-02=	2	-/5
	1860	0319	23a	Slamet (Java)	0603-18=	2	
	1860	04	60p?	Semeru (Java)	0603-30=	2	
	1860	0508	19a	Katla (Iceland-S)	1702-03=	4	-/8
?	1860	06	?	Gamalama (Halmahera-Indonesia)	0608-06=	1	
	1860	0612	2a	Tengger Caldera [Bromo] (Java)	0603-31=	2	
	1860	0707	2a	Alaid (Kuril Is)	0900-39=	3	
	1860	0725	?	Chillán, Nevados de (Chile-C)	1507-07=	2?	
	1860	0818	36a	Fuego (Guatemala)	1402-09=	2	
	1860	09 <	?	Raung (Java)	0603-34=	2	
	1860	0911	34m	Sangeang Api (Lesser Sunda Is)	0604-05=	2	
	1860	10	?	Cagua (Luzon-Philippines)	0703-09=	2	
?	1860	12	?	Baker (US-Washington)	1201-01=		
	1860	1229	?	Karthala (Indian O.-W)	0303-01=	0	
	1861	Cont	....	Stromboli (Italy)	0101-04=	1	4/-
	1861	Cont	....	Yasur (Vanuatu-SW Pacific)	0507-10=	2	
	1861	Cont	....	Kilauea (Hawaiian Is)	1302-01-	0	
	1861	Cont	....	Momotombo (Nicaragua)	1404-09=	2	
	1861	Cont	....	Rincón de la Vieja (Costa Rica)	1405-02=	2	
	1861	Cont	....	Cotopaxi (Ecuador)	1502-05=	2	
	1861	Cont	....	Sangay (Ecuador)	1502-09=	2	
	1861 ?	....	?	Suretamatai (Vanuatu-SW Pacific)	0507-01=	2	
	1861	....	?	Merapi (Java)	0603-25=	2	
	1861	....	?	Lamongan (Java)	0603-32=	2	
	1861	....	?	Mayon (Luzon-Philippines)	0703-03=	1	
?	1861	....	?	Turrialba (Costa Rica)	1405-07=		
	1861	....	?	Tupungatito (Chile-C)	1507-01=	2	
@	1861	....	?	Sete Cidades (Azores)	1802-08=	0	
	1861	02 ?	183p?	Antuco (Chile-C)	1507-08=	0	
	1861	0213	92a>	Ruapehu (New Zealand)	0401-10=	2	
	1861	0319	<1	Fournaise, Piton de la (Indian O.)	0303-02=	2	
	1861	04	?	Marapi (Sumatra)	0601-14=	2?	
?	1861	05	?	Karaha, Kawah (Java)	0603-16=		
?	1861	05	?	Grimsvötn (Iceland-NE)	1703-01=	2	
	1861	0504	14a	Lewotobi (Lesser Sunda Is)	0604-18=	2	
	1861	0508	161m?	Dubbi (Ethiopia)	0201-10=	3?	9/-
	1861	06	747w	Chillán, Nevados de (Chile-C)	1507-07=	1	
	1861	0802	....	Chillán, Nevados de (Chile-C)	1507-07=	2	
?	1861	1121	?	Fuego (Guatemala)	1402-09=	2	
	1861	1208	....	Vesuvius (Italy)	0101-02=	3	8/-
	1861	1228	292m	Makian (Halmahera-Indonesia)	0608-07=	4?	-/8
	1862	Cont	....	Stromboli (Italy)	0101-04=	1	4/-
	1862	Cont	....	Yasur (Vanuatu-SW Pacific)	0507-10=	2	
	1862	Cont	....	Makian (Halmahera-Indonesia)	0608-07=	4?	-/8
	1862	Cont	....	Kilauea (Hawaiian Is)	1302-01-	0	
	1862	Cont	....	Momotombo (Nicaragua)	1404-09=	2	
	1862	Cont	....	Rincón de la Vieja (Costa Rica)	1405-02=	2	
	1862	Cont	....	Cotopaxi (Ecuador)	1502-05=	2	
	1862	Cont	....	Sangay (Ecuador)	1502-09=	2	
	1862	Cont	....	Chillán, Nevados de (Chile-C)	1507-07=	1	
?	1862	....	?	Karthala (Indian O.-W)	0303-01=	2	
	1862	....	?	Camiguin [Hibok-Hibok] (Philippine	0701-08=	2	
	1862	....	?	Mayon (Luzon-Philippines)	0703-03=	2	
?	1862	....	?	Akutan (Aleutian Is)	1101-32-		
	1862	....	?	Ubinas (Perú)	1504-02=	2	
	1862	....	?	Llaima (Chile-C)	1507-11=	3	
	1862	01	?	Tongariro [Ngauruhoe] (New Zeal)	0401-08=	2	
	1862	01	?	San Miguel (El Salvador)	1403-10=	2	
?	1862	01	47m	Antuco (Chile-C)	1507-08=		
@	1862	04	31p	Yucamane (Perú)	1504-05-	2	
	1862	0526	693w	Merapi (Java)	0603-25=	2	7/6
	1862	0630	837q	Bárdarbunga [Trollagigar] (Iceland	1703-03=	2	8/5
	1862	0715	91m	Gamalama (Halmahera-Indonesia)	0608-06=	2	
	1863	Cont	....	Stromboli (Italy)	0101-04=	1	4/-
	1863	Cont	....	Yasur (Vanuatu-SW Pacific)	0507-10=	2	
	1863	Cont	....	Kilauea (Hawaiian Is)	1302-01-	0	
	1863	Cont	....	Momotombo (Nicaragua)	1404-09=	2	
	1863	Cont	....	Sangay (Ecuador)	1502-09=	2	
	1863	Cont	....	Chillán, Nevados de (Chile-C)	1507-07=	1	
	1863	Cont	....	Bárdarbunga [Trollagigar] (Iceland	1703-03=	2	8/5
	1863	....	?	Tair, Jebel at (Red Sea)	0201-01=	2	
?	1863	....	?	Dubbi (Ethiopia)	0201-10=	2	
A	1863 e	....	?	Longonot (Africa-E)	0202-10=	0	7/-
	1863	....	303w	Tongariro [Ngauruhoe] (New Zeal)	0401-08=	2	
	1863	....	365y	Ambrym (Vanuatu-SW Pacific)	0507-04=	2	
	1863	....	?	Lopevi (Vanuatu-SW Pacific)	0507-05=	2	
?	1863	....	?	Tajumulco (Guatemala)	1402-02=	2	
	1863	....	?	Izalco (El Salvador)	1403-03=	0	
	1863	....	?	Cotopaxi (Ecuador)	1502-05=	2	
	1863	0323	?	Iwaki (Honshu-Japan)	0803-27=	1	
	1863	0501	85a?	Etna (Italy)	0101-06=	2	
?	1863	0501?	45m?	Gamalama (Halmahera-Indonesia)	0608-06=	2	
	1863	0523	?	Marapi (Sumatra)	0601-14=	2?	
?	1863	0530	?	Mayon (Luzon-Philippines)	0703-03=		
	1863	07	?	Baker (US-Washington)	1201-01=	2	
	1863	0707	....	Etna (Italy)	0101-06=	3?	
	1863	0728		Merapi (Java)	0603-25=	2	7/6
	1863	08	....	Rincón de la Vieja (Costa Rica)	1405-02=	2	
	1863	08	?	Isluga (Chile-N)	1505-03=	1?	
	1863	0812	?	Campi Flegrei Mar Sicilia (Italy)	0101-07=	2	
	1863	0825	6a	Makian (Halmahera-Indonesia)	0608-07=	1	
	1863	12	?	Antuco (Chile-C)	1507-08=	2	
	1863	1220	40a	Fournaise, Piton de la (Indian O.)	0303-02=	0	
	1864	Cont	....	Stromboli (Italy)	0101-04=	1	4/-
	1864	Cont	....	Fournaise, Piton de la (Indian O.)	0303-02=	0	
	1864	Cont	....	Ambrym (Vanuatu-SW Pacific)	0507-04=	2	
	1864	Cont	....	Yasur (Vanuatu-SW Pacific)	0507-10=	2	
	1864	Cont	....	Merapi (Java)	0603-25=	2	7/6
	1864	Cont	....	Kilauea (Hawaiian Is)	1302-01-	0	
	1864	Cont	....	Momotombo (Nicaragua)	1404-09=	2	
	1864	Cont	....	Sangay (Ecuador)	1502-09=	2	
	1864	Cont	....	Bárdarbunga [Trollagigar] (Iceland	1703-03=	2	8/5
	1864	....	?	Lewotolo (Lesser Sunda Is)	0604-23=	2	
	1864	....	?	Pagan (Mariana Is-C Pacific)	0804-17=	1?	
	1864	....	?	Llaima (Chile-C)	1507-11=	3	
?	1864	01	?	Alamagan (Mariana Is-C Pacific)	0804-18=		
	1864	0104?	<1	Kelut (Java)	0603-28=	2	
	1864	0107	?	Farallon de Pajaros (Mariana Is-Pac)	0804-14=	2	
	1864	0120	28a	Gamalama (Halmahera-Indonesia)	0608-06=	2	
	1864	0210	>3yr	Vesuvius (Italy)	0101-02=	2	6/-
	1864	0515b	396g	Izalco (El Salvador)	1403-03=	2	
?	1864	0604d	21d	Gamalama (Halmahera-Indonesia)	0608-06=	1	
	1864	0606	?	Karangetang [Api Siau] (Sangihe Is	0607-02=	2	
	1864	0609	?	Lopevi (Vanuatu-SW Pacific)	0507-05=	3	
	1864	0609	36m	Lamongan (Java)	0603-32=	2	
	1864	0702	166m	Raung (Java)	0603-34=	2	
	1864	0805d	45d	Etna (Italy)	0101-06=	2	
	1864	0817	210m	Turrialba (Costa Rica)	1405-07=	1?	
	1864	0916	1a	Irazú (Costa Rica)	1405-06=	2	
	1864	0916	....	Turrialba (Costa Rica)	1405-07=	2	
	1864	10	16m	Makian (Halmahera-Indonesia)	0608-07=	1	
?	1864	10	?	Callaqui (Chile-C)	1507-091		
	1864	10	?	Villarrica (Chile-C)	1507-12=	2	
	1864	1101	2a	Mocho-Choshuenco (Chile-C)	1507-13=	2	
	1864	1130	66a	Chillán, Nevados de (Chile-C)	1507-07=	3	
	1864	12	31p	Tongariro [Ngauruhoe] (New Zeal)	0401-08=	2	
	1864	1227	6a	Gamalama (Halmahera-Indonesia)	0608-06=	2	
	1865	Cont	....	Vesuvius (Italy)	0101-02=	2	6/-
	1865	Cont	....	Tongariro [Ngauruhoe] (New Zeal)	0401-08=	2	
	1865	Cont	....	Yasur (Vanuatu-SW Pacific)	0507-10=	2	
	1865	Cont	....	Gamalama (Halmahera-Indonesia)	0608-06=	2	
	1865	Cont	....	Kilauea (Hawaiian Is)	1302-01-	0	
	1865	Cont	....	Izalco (El Salvador)	1403-03=	2	
	1865	Cont	....	Momotombo (Nicaragua)	1404-09=	2	

START YEAR	M-Dy	Duration	VOLCANO NAME (Subregion)	NUMBER	VEI	Vol L/T
1865	Cont	....	Sangay (Ecuador)	1502-09=	2	
1865	Cont	....	Chillán, Nevados de (Chile-C)	1507-07=	2	
1865	....	?	Nyamuragira (Africa-C)	0203-02=		
1865	....	?	Cameroon (Africa-W)	0204-01=	2	
1865	....	?	Karthala (Indian O.-W)	0303-01=	2?	
? 1865	....	?	Falcon Island (Tonga-SW Pacific)	0403-05=	0	
1865 c	....	>3yr	Bagana (Bougainville-SW Pacific)	0505-02=	2	
? 1865 p	....	?	Savo (Solomon Is-SW Pacific)	0505-07=		
1865 e	....	?	Kelimutu (Lesser Sunda Is)	0604-14=	2	
1865	....	?	Makaturing (Mindanao-Philippines)	0701-04=	2	
1865	....	?	Makushin (Aleutian Is)	1101-31-		
1865	....	?	Akutan (Aleutian Is)	1101-32-		
? 1865	....	?	Shishaldin (Aleutian Is)	1101-36-		
? 1865	....	?	Baker (US-Washington)	1201-01=		
1865	....	?	Ubinas (Perú)	1504-02=	2	
1865	....	730y	Olca-Paruma (Chile-N)	1505-05=		
1865	0124	....	Turrialba (Costa Rica)	1405-07=	2	
1865	0126e	....	Stromboli (Italy)	0101-04=	2	4/-
1865	0130	149a	Etna (Italy)	0101-06=	2	7/6
1865	0205	5a	Fournaise, Piton de la (Indian O.)	0303-02=	2	
1865	04	31p	Tengger Caldera [Bromo] (Java)	0603-31=	2	
1865	0415e	?	Semeru (Java)	0603-30=	2	
1865	0504	?	Lewotobi (Lesser Sunda Is)	0604-18=	2	
1865	0709	?	Unnamed (Atlantic-N)	1801-04=	0	
1865	09	....	Stromboli (Italy)	0101-04=	2	4/-
1865	09	?	Kliuchevskoi (Kamchatka)	1000-26=	2	
1865	0921	117m?	Hood (US-Oregon)	1202-01-	2	
1865	1002	>3yr	Galeras (Colombia)	1501-08=	3	7/6
1865	1024	>3yr	Merapi (Java)	0603-25=	2	7/7
1865	1201	17a	Tengger Caldera [Bromo] (Java)	0603-31=	2	
1865	1230	120a?	Mauna Loa (Hawaiian Is)	1302-02=	0	7/-
1866	Cont	....	Vesuvius (Italy)	0101-02=	2	6/-
1866	Cont	....	Stromboli (Italy)	0101-04=	1	4/-
1866	Cont	....	Bagana (Bougainville-SW Pacific)	0505-02=	2	
1866	Cont	....	Yasur (Vanuatu-SW Pacific)	0507-10=	2	
1866	Cont	....	Merapi (Java)	0603-25=	2	7/7
1866	Cont	....	Hood (US-Oregon)	1202-01-	2	
1866	Cont	....	Mauna Loa (Hawaiian Is)	1302-02=	0	7/-
1866	Cont	....	Momotombo (Nicaragua)	1404-09=	2	
1866	Cont	....	Galeras (Colombia)	1501-08=	2	7/6
1866	Cont	....	Sangay (Ecuador)	1502-09=	2	
1866	Cont	....	Olca-Paruma (Chile-N)	1505-05=		
? 1866	....	?	Sorikmarapi (Sumatra)	0601-12=		
? 1866	....	?	Semeru (Java)	0603-30=	2?	
1866	....	?	Kanlaon (Philippines-C)	0702-02=	2	
1866 ?	....	....	Kilauea (Hawaiian Is)	1302-01-	0	
1866	....	?	Llaima (Chile-C)	1507-11=	2	
1866	01 ?	?	Cameroon (Africa-W)	0204-01=	2	
1866	01	113m	Turrialba (Costa Rica)	1405-07=	3	-/7
1866	0126	>3yr	Santorini (Greece)	0102-04=	2	8/-
1866	0314	?	Pavlof (Alaska Peninsula)	1102-03-	2	
1866	0427	110e	Izalco (El Salvador)	1403-03=	2	
1866	07	?	Tengger Caldera [Bromo] (Java)	0603-31=	2	
1866	0912	64e	Ofu-Olosega (Samoa-SW Pacific)	0404-01=	2	
1866	0918	?	Gede (Java)	0603-06=	2	
1866	0921	5a	Cotopaxi (Ecuador)	1502-05=	2	
1867	Cont	....	Stromboli (Italy)	0101-04=	1	4/-
1867	Cont	....	Santorini (Greece)	0102-04=	2	8/-
1867	Cont	....	Bagana (Bougainville-SW Pacific)	0505-02=	2	
1867	Cont	....	Yasur (Vanuatu-SW Pacific)	0507-10=	2	
1867	Cont	....	Merapi (Java)	0603-25=	2	7/7
1867	Cont	....	Kilauea (Hawaiian Is)	1302-01-	0	
1867	Cont	....	Galeras (Colombia)	1501-08=	2	7/6
1867	Cont	....	Sangay (Ecuador)	1502-09=	2	
1867	Cont	....	Olca-Paruma (Chile-N)	1505-05=		
1867	....	?	Campi Flegrei Mar Sicilia (Italy)	0101-07=	0	
? 1867	....	?	Unnamed (Taiwan-N of)	0801-04=	0	
1867	....	?	Akita-Yake-yama (Honshu-Japan)	0803-26=		
? 1867	....	?	Makushin (Aleutian Is)	1101-31-		
1867	....	?	Akutan (Aleutian Is)	1101-32-		
1867	....	?	Iliamna (Alaska-SW)	1103-02-	2	
? 1867	....	?	Fuego (Guatemala)	1402-09=	2	
1867	....	?	Cotopaxi (Ecuador)	1502-05=	2	
1867 ?	....	?	Copahue (Chile-C)	1507-09=	2?	
? 1867	....	365y	Villarrica (Chile-C)	1507-12=		
1867	01	?	Iya (Lesser Sunda Is)	0604-11=	2	
? 1867	03	?	Baker (US-Washington)	1201-01=		
? 1867	03	?	Barva (Costa Rica)	1405-05=		
1867	04	138m	Izalco (El Salvador)	1403-03=	2	
1867	0412	?	Niuafo'ou (Tonga-SW Pacific)	0403-11=	1	
1867	0415e	30m	Semeru (Java)	0603-30=	2	
1867	0524	4a	Ubinas (Perú)	1504-02=	2	
1867	0601	7a	Terceira (Azores)	1802-05=	3	
1867	0829	?	Grímsvötn (Iceland-NE)	1703-01=	1	
1867	0908	?	Shikotsu [Tarumai] (Hokkaido)	0805-04=	2	
1867	1021	?	Zao (Honshu-Japan)	0803-19=	2	
1867	1114	16a	Negro, Cerro (Nicaragua)	1404-07=	2	-/6
1867	1115	....	Vesuvius (Italy)	0101-02=	1	6/-
1867	12	31p	Tjornes [Manareyjar]	1703-10=		
1867	1213	30a	Tengger Caldera [Bromo] (Java)	0603-31=	2	
1867	1214	64a>	San Miguel (El Salvador)	1403-10=	2	
1868	Cont	....	Stromboli (Italy)	0101-04=	1	4/-
1868	Cont	....	Santorini (Greece)	0102-04=	2	8/-
1868	Cont	....	Bagana (Bougainville-SW Pacific)	0505-02=	2	
1868	Cont	....	Yasur (Vanuatu-SW Pacific)	0507-10=	2	
1868	Cont	....	Merapi (Java)	0603-25=	2	7/7
1868	Cont	....	Tengger Caldera [Bromo] (Java)	0603-31=	2	
1868	Cont	....	San Miguel (El Salvador)	1403-10=	2	
1868	Cont	....	Galeras (Colombia)	1501-08=	2	7/6
1868	Cont	....	Sangay (Ecuador)	1502-09=	2	
? 1868	Cont	....	Villarrica (Chile-C)	1507-12=		
1868	Cont	....	Tjornes [Manareyjar]	1703-10=		
1868	....	?	Cameroon (Africa-W)	0204-01=	2	
? 1868 c	....	?	Talang (Sumatra)	0601-16=		
1868 ?	....	?	Dukono (Halmahera-Indonesia)	0608-01=	2	
1868	....	?	Isluga (Chile-N)	1505-03=	2?	
1868	02	45p	Iwo-Tori-shima (Ryukyu Is)	0802-02=	1	
1868	0216	1a	Izalco (El Salvador)	1403-03=	2	
1868	03	30m	Fournaise, Piton de la (Indian O.)	0303-02=	0	
1868	0313	<1	Gamalama (Halmahera-Indonesia)	0608-06=	1	
1868	0319	3a	Guagua Pichincha (Ecuador)	1502-02=	2	
1868	0327	26a	Mauna Loa (Hawaiian Is)	1302-02=	0	8/-
1868	0402?	?	Kilauea (Hawaiian Is)	1302-01-	1?	5/-
1868	0407	....	Mauna Loa (Hawaiian Is)	1302-02=	2	8/-
1868	0504	?	Iya (Lesser Sunda Is)	0604-11=	2	
1868	0713<	?	Lewotobi (Lesser Sunda Is)	0604-18=	2	
1868	08	?	Guagua Pichincha (Ecuador)	1502-02=	2	
1868	0815	3a	Cotopaxi (Ecuador)	1502-05=	2	
1868	09	?	Llullaillaco (Chile-N)	1505-11=	0	
1868	10	260w	Kaba (Sumatra)	0601-22=	2	
1868	1113	90a	Gamalama (Halmahera-Indonesia)	0608-06=	2	
1868	1115	....	Vesuvius (Italy)	0101-02=	2	6/-
1868	1126?	12a?	Etna (Italy)	0101-06=	3	
1868	1215	?	Lewotobi (Lesser Sunda Is)	0604-18=	2	
1868	1217	?	Mayon (Luzon-Philippines)	0703-03=	2	
? 1868	1231y	4a	Oshima (Izu Is-Japan)	0804-01=		
1869	Cont	....	Stromboli (Italy)	0101-04=	1	4/-
1869	Cont	....	Santorini (Greece)	0102-04=	2	8/-
1869	Cont	....	Bagana (Bougainville-SW Pacific)	0505-02=	2	
1869	Cont	....	Yasur (Vanuatu-SW Pacific)	0507-10=	2	
1869	Cont	....	Kaba (Sumatra)	0601-22=	2	
1869	Cont	....	Gamalama (Halmahera-Indonesia)	0608-06=	2	
1869	Cont	....	Kilauea (Hawaiian Is)	1302-01-	0	
1869 ?	....	?	Fournaise, Piton de la (Indian O.)	0303-02=	2?	
1869	....	?	Tongariro (New Zealand)	0401-08=	2	
1869	....	?	Gorely (Kamchatka)	1000-07=	2	
? 1869	....	?	Hood (US-Oregon)	1202-01-		
1869	....	....	Sangay (Ecuador)	1502-09=	3	
? 1869	....	?	Planchón-Peteroa (Chile-C)	1507-04=		
1869	....	?	Antuco (Chile-C)	1507-08=	2	
1869	....	?	Osorno (Chile-S)	1508-01=	2	
1869	....	?	Reclus (Chile-S)	1508-063	2	
1869	0204	20d	Villarrica (Chile-C)	1507-12=	2	
1869	03	?	Tinakula (Santa Cruz Is-SW Pacific)	0506-01=	2	
1869	03	?	Guagua Pichincha (Ecuador)	1502-02=	2	
1869	0301?	109a>	Izalco (El Salvador)	1403-03=	2	
1869	04	?	Llaima (Chile-C)	1507-11=	2?	
1869	0406	28a	Lamongan (Java)	0603-32=	2	
1869	05	160m	Asama (Honshu-Japan)	0803-11=	2	
@ 1869	0506	?	Bayonnaise Rocks (Izu Is-Japan)	0804-07=	0	
1869	0528	....	Merapi (Java)	0603-25=	2	7/7
? 1869	06	?	Baker (US-Washington)	1201-01=		
1869	0612	73a>	Colima (México)	1401-04=	3	8/-
1869	0615	....	Galeras (Colombia)	1501-08=	3	7/6
1869	07	31p	Cotopaxi (Ecuador)	1502-05=	3	
1869	0707	20a	Lewotobi (Lesser Sunda Is)	0604-18=	2	
1869	0722	33a	Guagua Pichincha (Ecuador)	1502-02=	2	
1869	08	?	Tongariro [Ngauruhoe] (New Zeal)	0401-08=	2	
1869	08	?	Isluga (Chile-N)	1505-03=	2	
? 1869	0824	?	Maipo (Chile-C)	1507-021	2	
? 1869	09	?	Misti, El (Perú)	1504-01=	1?	
1869	0912	?	Lamongan (Java)	0603-32=	2	
1869	0926	<1	Etna (Italy)	0101-06=	0	6/-
1869	10	?	Ubinas (Perú)	1504-02=	2	
1869	1004	43m	Puracé (Colombia)	1501-06=	3?	
1870	Cont	....	Stromboli (Italy)	0101-04=	1	4/-
1870	Cont	....	Santorini (Greece)	0102-04=	2	8/-
1870	Cont	....	Bagana (Bougainville-SW Pacific)	0505-02=	2	
1870	Cont	....	Yasur (Vanuatu-SW Pacific)	0507-10=	2	
1870	Cont	....	Merapi (Java)	0603-25=	2	7/7
1870	Cont	....	Kilauea (Hawaiian Is)	1302-01-	0	
1870	Cont	....	Galeras (Colombia)	1501-08=	2	7/6
1870	Cont	....	Sangay (Ecuador)	1502-09=	2	

START YEAR	M-Dy	Duration	VOLCANO NAME (Subregion)	NUMBER	VEI	Vol L/T
1870 ?	....	?	**Aoba** (Vanuatu-SW Pacific)	0507-03=	2?	
? 1870	....	?	Ambrym (Vanuatu-SW Pacific)	0507-04=		
1870	....	?	**Iliwerung** (Lesser Sunda Is)	0604-25=	3	
1870	....	?	**Oshima** (Izu Is-Japan)	0804-01=	2	
1870	....	?	**Baker** (US-Washington)	1201-01=	2	
? 1870	....	?	Rainier (US-Washington)	1201-03-	2	
1870	....	365y	**Colima** (México)	1401-04=	0	
1870	....	?	**Momotombo** (Nicaragua)	1404-09=	2?	
1870	....	>3yr	**Cotopaxi** (Ecuador)	1502-05=	2	
? 1870	....	?	San Pedro (Chile-N)	1505-07=		
? 1870	0101?	14a	Mauna Loa (Hawaiian Is)	1302-02=	0	
? 1870	0201p	?	Fournaise, Piton de la (Indian O.)	0303-02=	0	
1870	0221	>3yr	**Ceboruco** (México)	1401-03=	3	**9**/8
? 1870	03	?	Misti, El (Perú)	1504-01=	1?	
1870	0302	3a	**Lamongan** (Java)	0603-32=	2	
1870	04	123m	**Tongariro [Ngauruhoe]** (New Zeal)	0401-08=	2	5/-
1870	05	?	**Smith Rock** (Izu Is-Japan)	0804-08=	2	
? 1870	0519	?	Izalco (El Salvador)	1403-03=	2?	
1870	0620d	105d	**Raoul Island** (Kermadec Is)	0402-03=	3	-/7
1870	08	48m	**Gede** (Java)	0603-06=	2	
1870	0818	171b	**Lamongan** (Java)	0603-32=	2	
1870	0827	1a	**Ruang** (Sangihe Is-Indonesia)	0607-01=	3?	
1870	10	?	**Puracé** (Colombia)	1501-06=	2	
1870	12	501m	Vesuvius (Italy)	0101-02=	2	7/7
1871	Cont	....	Vesuvius (Italy)	0101-02=	2	7/7
1871	Cont	....	Stromboli (Italy)	0101-04=	1	4/-
1871	Cont	....	Bagana (Bougainville-SW Pacific)	0505-02=	2	
1871	Cont	....	Yasur (Vanuatu-SW Pacific)	0507-10=	2	
1871	Cont	....	Merapi (Java)	0603-25=	2	7/7
1871	Cont	....	Lamongan (Java)	0603-32=	2	
1871	Cont	....	Kilauea (Hawaiian Is)	1302-01-	0	
1871	Cont	....	Colima (México)	1401-04=	0	
1871	Cont	....	Cotopaxi (Ecuador)	1502-05=	2	
1871	Cont	....	Sangay (Ecuador)	1502-09=	2	
1871	....	?	**Nisyros** (Greece)	0102-05=	2	
1871 c	....	?	**Barrier, The** (Africa-E)	0202-03=	2	
1871	....	?	**Cameroon** (Africa-W)	0204-01=	2	
1871	....	?	**Tinakula** (Santa Cruz Is-SW Pacific)	0506-01=	2?	
1871	....	?	**Ambrym** (Vanuatu-SW Pacific)	0507-04=	2	
@ 1871	....	?	**Bayonnaise Rocks** (Izu Is-Japan)	0804-07=	0	
T 1871 s	....	?	**Deception Island** (Antarctica)	1900-03=		
1871	0130	?	**Reventador** (Ecuador)	1502-01=	2	
1871	0302	12a	**Ruang** (Sangihe Is-Indonesia)	0607-01=	2	
? 1871	04	?	Nikko-Shirane (Honshu-Japan)	0803-14=		
1871	04	?	**Tori-shima** (Izu Is-Japan)	0804-09=	0	
1871	0424	?	**Marapi** (Sumatra)	0601-14=	2?	
1871	0430	>3yr	**Camiguin [Hibok-Hibok]** (Philippine	0701-08=	2	8/-
1871	0621	14a	**Fournaise, Piton de la** (Indian O.)	0303-02=	0	
1871	0807	49a	**Gamalama** (Halmahera-Indonesia)	0608-06=	2	
1871	0810	20a?	**Mauna Loa** (Hawaiian Is)	1302-02=	0	7/-
1871	0901	?	**Iya** (Lesser Sunda Is)	0604-11=	2	
1871	0924	?	**Marapi** (Sumatra)	0601-14=	2?	
1871	1208<	?	**Ragang** (Mindanao-Philippines)	0701-06=	2	
1871	1208	39m	**Mayon** (Luzon-Philippines)	0703-03=	3	
? 1871	1225	3a	Shikotsu [Tarumai] (Hokkaido)	0805-04=	2	
1872	Cont	....	Stromboli (Italy)	0101-04=	1	4/-
1872	Cont	....	Bagana (Bougainville-SW Pacific)	0505-02=	2	
1872	Cont	....	Yasur (Vanuatu-SW Pacific)	0507-10=	2	
1872	Cont	....	Camiguin [Hibok-Hibok] (Philippine	0701-08=	2	8/-
1872	Cont	....	Kilauea (Hawaiian Is)	1302-01-	0	
1872	Cont	....	Cotopaxi (Ecuador)	1502-05=	2	
1872	....	?	**Karthala** (Indian O.-W)	0303-01=	2	
1872 d	....	?	**Bam** (New Guinea-NE of)	0501-01=	3	
1872	....	>3yr	**Sinarka** (Kuril Is)	0900-29=	4	7/-
? 1872	....	?	Planchón-Peteroa (Chile-C)	1507-04=		
@ 1872 ?	....	?	**Bárdarbunga** (Iceland-NE)	1703-03=		
? 1872	0201p	?	Fournaise, Piton de la (Indian O.)	0303-02=	0	
1872	0226	395a	**Colima** (México)	1401-04=	3	
1872	0415	5	**Merapi** (Java)	0603-25=	4	-/8
1872	0424	....	**Vesuvius** (Italy)	0101-02=	3	7/7
1872	05	....	Sangay (Ecuador)	1502-09=	2	
1872	0514	?	**Nikko-Shirane** (Honshu-Japan)	0803-14=	2	
1872	0606	?	**Llaima** (Chile-C)	1507-11=	2	
1872	0606	?	**Quetrupillan** (Chile-C)	1507-121	2?	
1872	0722	?	**Chillán, Nevados de** (Chile-C)	1507-07=	2	
1872	0809	37m?	**Mauna Loa** (Hawaiian Is)	1302-02=	1	
1872	0813	....	Colima (México)	1401-04=	3	
1872	0815	34a	**Lamongan** (Java)	0603-32=	2	
1872	0905	4a	**Mayon** (Luzon-Philippines)	0703-03=	1	
1872	1023	<1	**Semeru** (Java)	0603-30=	2	
1872	1103	74m?	**Merapi** (Java)	0603-25=	2	
1872	12	92m>	**Izalco** (El Salvador)	1403-03=	2	
1872	12	....	Sangay (Ecuador)	1502-09=	2	
1872	1201	189a	Aso (Kyushu-Japan)	0802-11=	2	
1873	Cont	....	Stromboli (Italy)	0101-04=	1	4/-
1873	Cont	....	Bagana (Bougainville-SW Pacific)	0505-02=	2	
1873	Cont	....	Yasur (Vanuatu-SW Pacific)	0507-10=	2	
1873	Cont	....	Merapi (Java)	0603-25=	2	
1873	Cont	....	Camiguin [Hibok-Hibok] (Philippine	0701-08=	2	8/-
1873	Cont	....	Sinarka (Kuril Is)	0900-29=	1	7/-
1873	Cont	....	Kilauea (Hawaiian Is)	1302-01-	0	
1873	Cont	....	Izalco (El Salvador)	1403-03=	2	
1873	Cont	....	Cotopaxi (Ecuador)	1502-05=	2	
? 1873	....	?	Erta Ale (Ethiopia)	0201-08=	2	
1873	....	>3yr	**Kaba** (Sumatra)	0601-22=	2	
1873	....	?	**Leroboleng** (Lesser Sunda Is)	0604-20=	2	
1873	....	?	**Taal** (Luzon-Philippines)	0703-07=	2	
? 1873	....	?	Smith Rock (Izu Is-Japan)	0804-08=	0	
1873 ?	....	?	**Pagan** (Mariana Is-C Pacific)	0804-17=	3?	
1873	....	?	**Semisopochnoi** (Aleutian Is)	1101-06-		
1873	....	?	**Gareloi** (Aleutian Is)	1101-07-	2?	
? 1873	....	?	Yunaska (Aleutian Is)	1101-21-	2?	
1873	0106	1a?	**Mauna Loa** (Hawaiian Is)	1302-02=	0	
1873	0108	219m	**Grímsvötn** (Iceland-NE)	1703-01=	4	-/8
1873	0110	....	Colima (México)	1401-04=	2?	
1873	0116	89m	**Ragang** (Mindanao-Philippines)	0701-06=	2	
1873	0301	....	**Aso** (Kyushu-Japan)	0802-11=	3	
1873	0312	?	**Nikko-Shirane** (Honshu-Japan)	0803-14=	1	
1873	0420	547a?	**Mauna Loa** (Hawaiian Is)	1302-02=	1	
1873	06	193m	**Nisyros** (Greece)	0102-05=	2	
1873	0620	32a	**Mayon** (Luzon-Philippines)	0703-03=	2	
1873	08	30p	**Zao** (Honshu-Japan)	0803-19=	1?	
1873	09	>3yr	**Vulcano** (Italy)	0101-05=	3	
1873	11	....	Sangay (Ecuador)	1502-09=	2	
1874	Cont	....	Vulcano (Italy)	0101-05=	2	
1874	Cont	....	Bagana (Bougainville-SW Pacific)	0505-02=	2	
1874	Cont	....	Yasur (Vanuatu-SW Pacific)	0507-10=	2	
1874	Cont	....	Kaba (Sumatra)	0601-22=	2	
1874	Cont	....	Camiguin [Hibok-Hibok] (Philippine	0701-08=	2	8/-
1874	Cont	....	Sinarka (Kuril Is)	0900-29=	1	7/-
1874	Cont	....	Kilauea (Hawaiian Is)	1302-01-	0	
1874	Cont	....	Mauna Loa (Hawaiian Is)	1302-02=	1	
1874	Cont	....	Cotopaxi (Ecuador)	1502-05=	2	
1874	Cont	....	Sangay (Ecuador)	1502-09=	2	
1874	....	?	**Lopevi** (Vanuatu-SW Pacific)	0507-05=	2	
1874 ?	....	?	**Kerinci** (Sumatra)	0601-17=	2?	
1874 ?	....	551w?	**Farallon de Pajaros** (Mariana Is-Pac)	0804-14=	2	
1874	....	?	**Santa Ana** (El Salvador)	1403-02=	3	
? 1874	....	365y	Izalco (El Salvador)	1403-03=		
? 1874	....	?	Llaima (Chile-C)	1507-11=		
? 1874	01	?	Vesuvius (Italy)	0101-02=	1	
1874	0201p	1a?	**Fournaise, Piton de la** (Indian O.)	0303-02=		
1874	0207	?	**Aso** (Kyushu-Japan)	0802-11=	2	
1874	0208	8a	Shikotsu [Tarumai] (Hokkaido)	0805-04=	2	-/7
1874	0216	....	**Shikotsu [Tarumai]** (Hokkaido)	0805-04=	3	-/7
1874	0416	?	**Villarrica** (Chile-C)	1507-12=	2	
1874	05	?	**Etna** (Italy)	0101-06=	2	
1874	0520	?	**Bam** (New Guinea-NE of)	0501-01=	2	
1874	0520	93a	**Lamongan** (Java)	0603-32=	2	
1874	06	....	Stromboli (Italy)	0101-04=	2?	4/-
1874	0608	?	**E-san** (Hokkaido-Japan)	0805-011	1	-/5
1874	0612	?	**Colima** (México)	1401-04=	1	
1874	0629	131a>	**Fournaise, Piton de la** (Indian O.)	0303-02=	2	
1874	0703	14a?	**Miyake-jima** (Izu Is-Japan)	0804-04=	3	
1874	0715q	?	**Veniaminof** (Alaska Peninsula)	1102-07-	2?	
1874	0719	?	**Taal** (Luzon-Philippines)	0703-07=	2	
1874	0829	2a	**Etna** (Italy)	0101-06=	2	6/6
1874	0901	....	Stromboli (Italy)	0101-04=	2	4/-
1874	1115	?	**Ruang** (Sangihe Is-Indonesia)	0607-01=	2	
1875	Cont	....	Stromboli (Italy)	0101-04=	1	4/-
1875	Cont	....	Vulcano (Italy)	0101-05=	2	
1875	Cont	....	Bagana (Bougainville-SW Pacific)	0505-02=	2	
1875	Cont	....	Yasur (Vanuatu-SW Pacific)	0507-10=	2	
1875	Cont	....	Kaba (Sumatra)	0601-22=	2	
1875	Cont	....	Camiguin [Hibok-Hibok] (Philippine	0701-08=	2	8/-
1875	Cont	....	Farallon de Pajaros (Mariana Is-Pac)	0804-14=	2	
1875	Cont	....	Sinarka (Kuril Is)	0900-29=	1	7/-
1875	Cont	....	Kilauea (Hawaiian Is)	1302-01-	0	
? 1875	Cont	....	Izalco (El Salvador)	1403-03=		
1875	Cont	....	Cotopaxi (Ecuador)	1502-05=	2	
1875	Cont	....	Sangay (Ecuador)	1502-09=	2	
M 1875 <	....	?	**Unnamed [East Pacific Rise]**	1304-05-	0	
1875	....	>3yr	**Colima** (México)	1401-04=	1	
1875 e	....	?	**Irazú** (Costa Rica)	1405-06=	2	
1875	....	?	**Láscar** (Chile-N)	1505-10=	2	
1875	....	365y	**Llaima** (Chile-C)	1507-11=	2	
1875	0101	289a	Askja (Iceland-NE)	1703-06=	2	
1875	0110	30a?	**Mauna Loa** (Hawaiian Is)	1302-02=	0	
1875	0329	....	**Askja** (Iceland-NE)	1703-06=	**5**	8/**9**
1875	0529<	6d>	**Slamet** (Java)	0603-18=	2	
1875	0614	?	**Asama** (Honshu-Japan)	0803-11=	2	
1875	08	16m	**Awu** (Sangihe Is-Indonesia)	0607-04=	2	
1875	0811	7a?	**Mauna Loa** (Hawaiian Is)	1302-02=	0	
? 1875	1001t	?	Tongariro [Ngauruhoe] (New Zeal)	0401-08=	2	

START YEAR	M-Dy	Duration	VOLCANO NAME (Subregion)	NUMBER	VEI	Vol L/T
1875	1102b	54*f*	**Slamet** (Java)	0603-18=	2	
1875	1117	365*y*	**Villarrica** (Chile-C)	1507-12=	2?	
1875	1126	15*a*	**Fournaise, Piton de la** (Indian O.)	0303-02=	0	
1875	*1218*	*>3yr*	*Vesuvius (Italy)*	0101-02=	*2*	*8/8*
1876	*Cont*	....	*Vesuvius (Italy)*	0101-02=	*2*	*8/8*
1876	*Cont*	....	*Stromboli (Italy)*	0101-04=	*1*	*4/-*
1876	*Cont*	....	*Bagana (Bougainville-SW Pacific)*	0505-02=	*2*	
1876	*Cont*	....	*Yasur (Vanuatu-SW Pacific)*	0507-10=	*2*	
1876	*Cont*	....	*Kaba (Sumatra)*	0601-22=	*2*	
1876	*Cont*	....	*Farallon de Pajaros (Mariana Is-Pac)*	0804-14=	*2*	
1876	*Cont*	....	*Sinarka (Kuril Is)*	0900-29=	*1*	*7/-*
1876	*Cont*	....	*Kilauea (Hawaiian Is)*	1302-01-	*0*	
1876	*Cont*	....	*Colima (México)*	1401-04=	*1*	
1876	*Cont*	....	*Cotopaxi (Ecuador)*	1502-05=	*2*	
1876	*Cont*	....	*Sangay (Ecuador)*	1502-09=	*2*	
1876	*Cont*	....	*Llaima (Chile-C)*	1507-11=	*2*	
1876	*Cont*	....	*Villarrica (Chile-C)*	1507-12=	*2?*	
1876	....	....	*Vulcano (Italy)*	0101-05=	*3*	
1876	....	?	**Karthala** (Indian O.-W)	0303-01=	0	
1876 ?	....	?	**Talang** (Sumatra)	0601-16=	2	
1876	....	?	**Leroboleng** (Lesser Sunda Is)	0604-20=	2	
? 1876	....	*?*	*Amukta (Aleutian Is)*	1101-19-		
1876	....	?	**Iliamna** (Alaska-SW)	1103-02-	3	
1876	0213	1*a*	**Mauna Loa** (Hawaiian Is)	1302-02=	0	
1876	04	?	**Mayon** (Luzon-Philippines)	0703-03=	1	
1876	0404	?	**Marapi** (Sumatra)	0601-14=	2?	
1876	08	303*p*	**Marapi** (Sumatra)	0601-14=	2?	
1876	0923	3*a*	**Shiretoko-Iwo-zan** (Hokkaido-Japan)	0805-09=	2	
1876	10	?	**Lautaro** (Chile-S)	1508-06=	2?	
1876	1126	<1	**Mayon** (Luzon-Philippines)	0703-03=	1	
1876	1211	<1	**Fournaise, Piton de la** (Indian O.)	0303-02=		
1876	1227	40*a*	**Oshima** (Izu Is-Japan)	0804-01=	2	6/6
1877	*Cont*	....	*Vesuvius (Italy)*	0101-02=	*2*	*8/8*
1877	*Cont*	....	*Stromboli (Italy)*	0101-04=	*1*	*4/-*
1877	*Cont*	....	*Vulcano (Italy)*	0101-05=	*2*	
1877	*Cont*	....	*Bagana (Bougainville-SW Pacific)*	0505-02=	*2*	
1877	*Cont*	....	*Yasur (Vanuatu-SW Pacific)*	0507-10=	*2*	
1877	*Cont*	....	*Marapi (Sumatra)*	0601-14=	*2*	
1877	*Cont*	....	*Kaba (Sumatra)*	0601-22=	*2*	
1877	*Cont*	....	*Oshima (Izu Is-Japan)*	0804-01=	*2*	*6/6*
1877	*Cont*	....	*Sinarka (Kuril Is)*	0900-29=	*1*	*7/-*
1877	*Cont*	....	*Kilauea (Hawaiian Is)*	1302-01-	*0*	
1877	*Cont*	....	*Colima (México)*	1401-04=	*1*	
1877	*Cont*	....	*Sangay (Ecuador)*	1502-09=	*2*	
1877	....	?	**Falcon Island** (Tonga-SW Pacific)	0403-05=	2	
1877	....	?	**Suwanose-jima** (Ryukyu Is)	0802-03=	4?	
1877	....	?	**Kliuchevskoi** (Kamchatka)	1000-26=	2	
1877	....	?	**Isluga** (Chile-N)	1505-03=	2?	
1877 ?	....	?	**San Pedro** (Chile-N)	1505-07=	2	
1877	*01*	*230m*	*Cotopaxi (Ecuador)*	1502-05=	*2*	*7/8*
1877	0116	159*a*	**Llaima** (Chile-C)	1507-11=	2	
1877	0212?	?	**Chillán, Nevados de** (Chile-C)	1507-07=	2	
1877	0214	10*a*	**Mauna Loa** (Hawaiian Is)	1302-02=	0	6/-
1877	0312	64*m*	**Villarrica** (Chile-C)	1507-12=	2	
1877	04	?	**Semeru** (Java)	0603-30=	2	
1877	0424?	?	**Tengger Caldera [Bromo]** (Java)	0603-31=	2	
1877	*0424?*	*18a?*	*Lamongan (Java)*	0603-32=	*2*	
1877	05	?	**Llullaillaco** (Chile-N)	1505-11=	2	
1877	0511	....	**Lamongan** (Java)	0603-32=	3?	
1877	*0511*	....	*Cotopaxi (Ecuador)*	1502-05=	*2*	*7/8*
1877	*0531*	....	*Cotopaxi (Ecuador)*	1502-05=	*2*	*7/8*
1877	0626	....	**Cotopaxi** (Ecuador)	1502-05=	4	7/8
1877	09	?	**Semeru** (Java)	0603-30=	2	
1877	1029	15*a*>	**Manam** (New Guinea-NE of)	0501-02=	2	
1877	1113	?	**Bam** (New Guinea-NE of)	0501-01=	3	
1877	12	?	**Cumbal** (Colombia)	1501-10=	2	
1878	*Cont*	....	*Vesuvius (Italy)*	0101-02=	*2*	*8/8*
1878	*Cont*	....	*Stromboli (Italy)*	0101-04=	*1*	*4/-*
1878	*Cont*	....	*Vulcano (Italy)*	0101-05=	*2*	
1878	*Cont*	....	*Bagana (Bougainville-SW Pacific)*	0505-02=	*2*	
1878	*Cont*	....	*Kaba (Sumatra)*	0601-22=	*2*	
1878	*Cont*	....	*Sinarka (Kuril Is)*	0900-29=	*1*	*7/-*
1878	*Cont*	....	*Kilauea (Hawaiian Is)*	1302-01-	*0*	
1878	*Cont*	....	*Colima (México)*	1401-04=	*1*	
1878	*Cont*	....	*Sangay (Ecuador)*	1502-09=	*2*	
1878 a	....	?	**Meru** (Africa-E)	0202-16=	2	
1878	....	?	**Langila** (New Britain-SW Pac)	0502-01=	2	
1878	....	?	**Ulawun** (New Britain-SW Pac)	0502-12=	2	
1878	....	....	**Yasur** (Vanuatu-SW Pacific)	0507-10=	3	
1878	....	355*w*	**Merapi** (Java)	0603-25=	2	
1878	....	?	**Semeru** (Java)	0603-30=	2	
? 1878	....	*?*	*Asama (Honshu-Japan)*	0803-11=	*2*	
1878	....	?	**Avachinsky** (Kamchatka)	1000-10=	2	
1878	....	?	**Amukta** (Aleutian Is)	1101-19-		
1878	....	?	**Vsevidof** (Aleutian Is)	1101-27-	2	
1878	....	?	**Okmok** (Aleutian Is)	1101-29-	2?	
1878	....	?	**Tacaná** (México)	1401-13=	1	

START YEAR	M-Dy	Duration	VOLCANO NAME (Subregion)	NUMBER	VEI	Vol L/T
? 1878	....	*?*	*Santa Ana (El Salvador)*	1403-02=	*2*	
1878	....	?	**Izalco** (El Salvador)	1403-03=		
1878	....	?	**Planchón-Peteroa** (Chile-C)	1507-04=	2	
? 1878	*0118*	*?*	*Lautaro (Chile-S)*	1508-06=	*1*	
? 1878	*0129*	*?*	*Unnamed (Atlantic-C)*	1805-02=	*0*	
1878	0130?	27*b*?	**Rabaul** (New Britain-SW Pac)	0502-14=	3	-/8
1878	02	?	**Isluga** (Chile-N)	1505-03=	2	
1878	0227	47*m*	**Hekla [Krakagigar]** (Iceland-S)	1702-07=	2	8/-
1878	0314	16*a*	**Fournaise, Piton de la** (Indian O.)	0303-02=	0	
1878	04 <	?	**Metis Shoal** (Tonga-SW Pacific)	0403-07=	2	
1878	0823	1*a*	**Cotopaxi** (Ecuador)	1502-05=	2	
1878	0831	?	**Puracé** (Colombia)	1501-06=	2	
1878	09	?	**Kliuchevskoi** (Kamchatka)	1000-26=	2	
1878	0901u	?	**Tongariro [Ngauruhoe]** (New Zeal)	0401-08=	2	
? 1878	*1002*	*?*	*Tecapa (El Salvador)*	1403-08=		
1878	1014?	?	**Momotombo** (Nicaragua)	1404-09=	2	
1878	1112	3*a*	**Taal** (Luzon-Philippines)	0703-07=	2	
? 1878	*12*	*?*	*Marapi (Sumatra)*	0601-14=	*2?*	
1878	1211	?	**Kerinci** (Sumatra)	0601-17=	2	
1878	1223	>3yr	**Etna** (Italy)	0101-06=	2	
? 1878	*1231p*	*?*	*Ritter Island (New Guinea-NE of)*	0501-07=		
1879	*Cont*	....	*Vesuvius (Italy)*	0101-02=	*2*	*8/8*
1879	*Cont*	....	*Vulcano (Italy)*	0101-05=	*2*	
1879	*Cont*	....	*Bagana (Bougainville-SW Pacific)*	0505-02=	*2*	
1879	*Cont*	....	*Yasur (Vanuatu-SW Pacific)*	0507-10=	*2*	
1879	*Cont*	....	*Kaba (Sumatra)*	0601-22=	*2*	
1879	*Cont*	....	*Merapi (Java)*	0603-25=	*2*	
1879	....	?	**Sorikmarapi** (Sumatra)	0601-12=	2	
1879	....	?	**Semeru** (Java)	0603-30=	2	
1879	....	?	**Kliuchevskoi** (Kamchatka)	1000-26=	2	
1879	....	>3yr	**Shiveluch** (Kamchatka)	1000-27=	3	
? 1879	....	*?*	*Rainier (US-Washington)*	1201-03-	*2*	
? 1879	....	*?*	*Poás (Costa Rica)*	1405-04=	*1*	
@ **1879**	....	?	**Lautaro** (Chile-S)	1508-06=		
1879	....	?	**Reclus** (Chile-S)	1508-063	2	
1879	0115q	?	**Sarychev Peak** (Kuril Is)	0900-24=	0	
1879	0201p	?	**Santa Ana** (El Salvador)	1403-02=	2	
1879	0202	44*m*	**Villarrica** (Chile-C)	1507-12=	2	
1879	*0204*	....	*Stromboli (Italy)*	0101-04=	*2?*	*4/-*
1879	0226	113*a*	**Cotopaxi** (Ecuador)	1502-05=	2	
1879	0309	<1	**Mauna Loa** (Hawaiian Is)	1302-02=	0	6/-
1879	05	31*p*	**Chirpoi** (Kuril Is)	0900-15=	2	
1879	0518	?	**Dempo** (Sumatra)	0601-23=	2	
1879	0526	12*a*	**Etna** (Italy)	0101-06=	3	7/7
1879	0530?	16*e*?	**Reykjanes** (Iceland-SW)	1701-02=	1	
1879	*0603*	....	*Stromboli (Italy)*	0101-04=	*2?*	*4/-*
1879	*0714*	....	*Kilauea (Hawaiian Is)*	1302-01-	*0*	
1879	0927	1*a*	**Asama** (Honshu-Japan)	0803-11=	2	
1879	*12*	....	*Sangay (Ecuador)*	1502-09=	*2*	
1879	1223	129*a*	**Colima** (México)	1401-04=	1	
1879	1225	80*m*	**Izalco** (El Salvador)	1403-03=	2	
1879	*1231*	*87e*	*Ilopango (El Salvador)*	1403-06=	*0*	*8/-*
1880	*Cont*	....	*Vesuvius (Italy)*	0101-02=	*2*	*8/8*
1880	*Cont*	....	*Stromboli (Italy)*	0101-04=	*1*	*4/-*
1880	*Cont*	....	*Etna (Italy)*	0101-06=	*2*	
1880	*Cont*	....	*Bagana (Bougainville-SW Pacific)*	0505-02=	*2*	
1880	*Cont*	....	*Yasur (Vanuatu-SW Pacific)*	0507-10=	*2*	
1880	*Cont*	....	*Kaba (Sumatra)*	0601-22=	*2*	
1880	*Cont*	....	*Shiveluch (Kamchatka)*	1000-27=	*2*	
1880	*Cont*	....	*Kilauea (Hawaiian Is)*	1302-01-	*0*	
1880	*Cont*	....	*Izalco (El Salvador)*	1403-03=	*2*	
1880	....	?	**Karthala** (Indian O.-W)	0303-01=	2	
1880 r	....	?	**Tambora** (Lesser Sunda Is)	0604-04=	2	
1880	....	?	**Tongkoko** (Sulawesi-Indonesia)	0606-13=	1	
? 1880 ?	....	*?*	*Veteran (SE Asia)*	0705-07-	*0*	
1880	....	>3yr	**Kita-Iwo-jima** (Volcano Is-Japan)	0804-11=	0	
1880	....	?	**Mendeleev** (Kuril Is)	0900-02=	1	
? 1880	....	*?*	*Vsevidof (Aleutian Is)*	1101-27-		
? 1880	....	*365y*	*Shishaldin (Aleutian Is)*	1101-36-		
1880	....	?	**Pavlof** (Alaska Peninsula)	1102-03-	1?	
1880	....	?	**Poás** (Costa Rica)	1405-04=	1	
1880	....	?	**Villarrica** (Chile-C)	1507-12=	2	
? 1880	....	*?*	*Soufrière St. Vincent (W Indies)*	1600-15=	*0*	
@ **1880**	....	?	**Sete Cidades** (Azores)	1802-08=	0	
1880	*01*	....	*Sangay (Ecuador)*	1502-09=	*3*	
1880	0104	<1	**Watt, Morne** (W Indies)	1600-101	2?	
1880	0120	....	**Ilopango** (El Salvador)	1403-06=	3	8/-
1880	*02*	*151p*	*Cotopaxi (Ecuador)*	1502-05=	*2*	
1880	03	?	**Sta. Ana [Mala Cara]** (El Salvador)	1403-02=	3	
1880	05	?	**Dempo** (Sumatra)	0601-23=	2	
1880	0501	5*a*	**Mauna Loa** (Hawaiian Is)	1302-02=	1	7/-
1880	0628	53*a*	**Fuego** (Guatemala)	1402-09=	4?	-/8
1880	0703	....	**Cotopaxi** (Ecuador)	1502-05=	3	
? 1880 ?	*0712*	*<1*	*Srednii (Kuril Is)*	0900-211	*0*	
1880	09	?	**Kirishima** (Kyushu-Japan)	0802-09=	2	
1880	0907	81*a*	**Baker** (US-Washington)	1201-01=	2	

START YEAR	M-Dy	Duration	VOLCANO NAME (Subregion)	NUMBER	VEI	Vol L/T
1880	1105	278a	**Mauna Loa** (Hawaiian Is)	1302-02=	1	8/-
? 1880	1124	2a	Shiretoko-Iwo-zan (Hokkaido-Japan)	0805-09=		
1880	12	?	**Lengai, Ol Doinyo** (Africa-E)	0202-12=	2	
1880	1201p	20a?	**Colima** (México)	1401-04=	2	
1881	Cont	....	Etna (Italy)	0101-06=	2	
1881	Cont	....	Bagana (Bougainville-SW Pacific)	0505-02=	2	
1881	Cont	....	Yasur (Vanuatu-SW Pacific)	0507-10=	2	
1881	Cont	....	Kaba (Sumatra)	0601-22=	2	
1881	Cont	....	Kita-Iwo-jima (Volcano Is-Japan)	0804-11=	0	
1881	Cont	....	Shiveluch (Kamchatka)	1000-27=	2	
? 1881	Cont	....	Shishaldin (Aleutian Is)	1101-36-		
1881	Cont	....	Kilauea (Hawaiian Is)	1302-01-	0	
1881	Cont	....	Mauna Loa (Hawaiian Is)	1302-02=	0	8/-
1881	Cont	....	Sangay (Ecuador)	1502-09=	2	
1881	....	?	**Traitor's Head** (Vanuatu-SW Pacific)	0507-09=	0	
1881	....	?	**Sibayak** (Sumatra)	0601-07=		
? 1881	....	?	Sinabung (Sumatra)	0601-08=		
1881	....	?	**Raung** (Java)	0603-34=		
1881	....	?	**Avachinsky** (Kamchatka)	1000-10=	2	
1881	....	?	**Puracé** (Colombia)	1501-06=	2	
? 1881	....	?	Tupungatito (Chile-C)	1507-01=		
1881	....	?	**San José** (Chile-C)	1507-02=	2	
? 1881	....	?	Maipo (Chile-C)	1507-021		
1881	0101	?	**Izalco** (El Salvador)	1403-03=	0	
1881	0216	?	**Dempo** (Sumatra)	0601-23=	2	
1881	0310	?	**Guagua Pichincha** (Ecuador)	1502-02=	2	
1881	0316	?	**Leroboleng** (Lesser Sunda Is)	0604-20=	2	
1881	0323?	....	Colima (México)	1401-04=	2	
? 1881	0602	?	Heard (Indian O.-S)	0304-01=	2	
1881	0701	?	**Nasu** (Honshu-Japan)	0803-15=	1?	-/5
1881	0706	?	**Tongariro [Ngauruhoe]** (New Zeal)	0401-08=	2	
1881	0706	406m	**Mayon** (Luzon-Philippines)	0703-03=	3	
1881	09	?	**Goriaschaia Sopka** (Kuril Is)	0900-17=	2	
1881	1015	....	Stromboli (Italy)	0101-04=	2	4/-
1881	12	16m	**Dempo** (Sumatra)	0601-23=	2	
1881	1216	....	Vesuvius (Italy)	0101-02=	1	8/8
1882	Cont	....	Vesuvius (Italy)	0101-02=	2	8/8
1882	Cont	....	Etna (Italy)	0101-06=	2	
1882	Cont	....	Bagana (Bougainville-SW Pacific)	0505-02=	2	
1882	Cont	....	Yasur (Vanuatu-SW Pacific)	0507-10=	2	
1882	Cont	....	Kaba (Sumatra)	0601-22=	2	
1882	Cont	....	Mayon (Luzon-Philippines)	0703-03=	3	
1882	Cont	....	Kita-Iwo-jima (Volcano Is-Japan)	0804-11=	0	
1882	Cont	....	Shiveluch (Kamchatka)	1000-27=	2	
1882	Cont	....	Sangay (Ecuador)	1502-09=	2	
1882	....	365y	**Lengai, Ol Doinyo** (Africa-E)	0202-12=	2	
1882	....	?	**Nyamuragira** (Africa-C)	0203-02=		
? 1882	....	?	Fournaise, Piton de la (Indian O.)	0303-02=	0	
1882	....	?	**Iya** (Lesser Sunda Is)	0604-11=	2	
1882	....	?	**Makaturing** (Mindanao-Philippines)	0701-04=		
1882	....	?	**Zhupanovsky** (Kamchatka)	1000-12=	2	
? 1882	....	?	Rainier (US-Washington)	1201-03-	2	
1882	....	730y	**Colima** (México)	1401-04=	1	
? 1882	....	?	Santa Ana (El Salvador)	1403-02=		
? 1882	....	?	Irazú (Costa Rica)	1405-06=	2	
1882	01	59p	**Cotopaxi** (Ecuador)	1502-05=	2	
1882	0130	....	Stromboli (Italy)	0101-04=	2	4/-
1882	0401	6a	**Sundoro** (Java)	0603-21=	2	
1882	0425	....	Stromboli (Italy)	0101-04=	2	4/-
1882	0712	?	**Izalco** (El Salvador)	1403-03=	2	
1882	0806	10a>	**Kusatsu-Shirane** (Honshu-Japan)	0803-12=	2	-/6
1882	09	?	**Kliuchevskoi** (Kamchatka)	1000-26=	2	
1882	09	....	Kilauea (Hawaiian Is)	1302-01-	0	
1882	0909	?	**Momotombo** (Nicaragua)	1404-09=	2?	
1882	1117	....	**Stromboli** (Italy)	0101-04=	3	4/-
1882	1205d	?	**San Miguel** (El Salvador)	1403-10=	2	
1883	Cont	....	Vesuvius (Italy)	0101-02=	2	8/8
1883	Cont	....	Lengai, Ol Doinyo (Africa-E)	0202-12=	2	
1883	Cont	....	Yasur (Vanuatu-SW Pacific)	0507-10=	2	
1883	Cont	....	Kaba (Sumatra)	0601-22=	2	
1883	Cont	....	Kita-Iwo-jima (Volcano Is-Japan)	0804-11=	0	
1883	Cont	....	Shiveluch (Kamchatka)	1000-27=	2	
1883	Cont	....	Kilauea (Hawaiian Is)	1302-01-	0	
1883	Cont	....	Colima (México)	1401-04=	1	
1883	Cont	....	Sangay (Ecuador)	1502-09=	2	
1883	....	?	**Tair, Jebel at** (Red Sea)	0201-01=	2	
1883	....	?	**Ambrym** (Vanuatu-SW Pacific)	0507-04=	2	
1883	....	365y	**Lopevi** (Vanuatu-SW Pacific)	0507-05=		
1883	....	?	**Hainan Dao** (SE Asia)	0705-001		
1883 a	....	?	**Guguan** (Mariana Is-C Pacific)	0804-19=	2?	
1883	....	?	**Kharimkotan** (Kuril Is)	0900-30=	3	
1883	....	?	**Makushin** (Aleutian Is)	1101-31-	2	
1883	....	?	**Akutan** (Aleutian Is)	1101-32-	2	
1883	....	?	**Shishaldin** (Aleutian Is)	1101-36-	2	
1883	....	731y	**Láscar** (Chile-N)	1505-10=	2	
1883	....	?	**Llaima** (Chile-C)	1507-11=	2	
1883	....	?	**Villarrica** (Chile-C)	1507-12=	2	
1883	01 ?	668p	**Merapi** (Java)	0603-25=	1	7/-
1883	0115	90e	**Grímsvötn** (Iceland-NE)	1703-01=	2	
? 1883	0121	?	Chillán, Nevados de (Chile-C)	1507-07=	2?	
1883	0208	....	Stromboli (Italy)	0101-04=	2	4/-
1883	03	473w	**Karthala** (Indian O.-W)	0303-01=	2	
? 1883	03	?	Bam (New Guinea-NE of)	0501-01=		
1883	0316	....	Stromboli (Italy)	0101-04=	2	4/-
1883	0322	2a	**Etna** (Italy)	0101-06=	2	4/5
1883	0328	?	**St. Andrew Strait [Tuluman]**	0500-01=	2	
1883	0405d	86d	**Concepción** (Nicaragua)	1404-12=	2	
1883	0413	21a	**Lamongan** (Java)	0603-32=	2	7/-
1883	0415q	?	**Goriaschaia Sopka** (Kuril Is)	0900-17=	1	7/-
1883	0425e	?	**Tongariro [Ngauruhoe]** (New Zeal)	0401-08=	2	
1883	05	31p	**Medvezhia** (Kuril Is)	0900-10=	2	
1883	0520	154a?	Krakatau (Indonesia)	0602-00=	3	
1883	0625	63a	**Marapi** (Sumatra)	0601-14=	1	
? 1883	07	?	Kanlaon (Philippines-C)	0702-02=	2	
1883	07	31p	**Kliuchevskoi** (Kamchatka)	1000-26=	2	
1883	08 ?	?	**Sundoro** (Java)	0603-21=	2	
1883	08	?	**Cotopaxi** (Ecuador)	1502-05=	2	
1883	0825	1a	**Karangetang [Api Siau]** (Sangihe Is	0607-02=	2	
1883	0825	1a	**Awu** (Sangihe Is-Indonesia)	0607-04=	2	
1883	0827	....	**Krakatau** (Indonesia)	0602-00=	**6**	-/**10**
1883	0905d	69n	**Izalco** (El Salvador)	1403-03=	2	
1883	0927<	>3yr	Bogoslof (Aleutian Is)	1101-30-	1	7/-
1883	1006	269w?	**Augustine** (Alaska-SW)	1103-01-	4	8/8
1883	1007	29a	**Shikotsu [Tarumai]** (Hokkaido)	0805-04=	2	
1883	1020	....	Bogoslof (Aleutian Is)	1101-30-	2?	7/-
1883	12	15m	**Marapi** (Sumatra)	0601-14=	1	
1883	12	?	**Cotopaxi** (Ecuador)	1502-05=	2	
1883	1226e	83e	**Dieng Volc Complex** (Java)	0603-20=	1	
1883	1231p	?	**Bagana** (Bougainville-SW Pacific)	0505-02=	3	
1884	Cont	....	Vesuvius (Italy)	0101-02=	2	8/8
1884	Cont	....	Stromboli (Italy)	0101-04=	1	4/-

Family of R. Breon (Simkin and Fiske, 1983)

One week after the onset of an eruption of Krakatau volcano in Indonesia in May 1883, an eruption column rises above Perboewatan vent on Krakatau Island. Three months later one of history's most renowned eruptions created a large caldera, accompanied by pyroclastic flows and devastating tsunamis that swept the coasts of Sumatra and Java.

START YEAR	M-Dy	Duration	VOLCANO NAME (Subregion)	NUMBER	VEI	Vol L/T
1884	Cont	....	Karthala (Indian O.-W)	0303-01=	2	
1884	Cont	....	Lopevi (Vanuatu-SW Pacific)	0507-05=		
1884	Cont	....	Yasur (Vanuatu-SW Pacific)	0507-10=	2	
1884	Cont	....	Kaba (Sumatra)	0601-22=	2	
1884	Cont	....	Merapi (Java)	0603-25=	1	7/-
1884	Cont	....	Kita-Iwo-jima (Volcano Is-Japan)	0804-11=	0	
1884	Cont	....	Bogoslof (Aleutian Is)	1101-30-	1	7/-
1884	Cont	....	Augustine (Alaska-SW)	1103-01-	2	8/8
1884	Cont	....	Colima (México)	1401-04=	1	
1884	Cont	....	Sangay (Ecuador)	1502-09=	2	
1884	Cont	....	Láscar (Chile-N)	1505-10=	2	
1884	....	653w	Etna (Italy)	0101-06=	1	
1884	....	?	Nyiragongo (Africa-C)	0203-03=	1	
? 1884	....	?	Manam (New Guinea-NE of)	0501-02=		
1884	....	?	Langila (New Britain-SW Pac)	0502-01=	2	
1884	....	?	Ambrym (Vanuatu-SW Pacific)	0507-04=	2?	
1884	....	?	Suwanose-jima (Ryukyu Is)	0802-03=	1	
1884 f	....	?	Chirinkotan (Kuril Is)	0900-26=	0	
? 1884	....	?	Baker (US-Washington)	1201-01=		
1884	....	730y	Concepción (Nicaragua)	1404-12=	2	
1884	0106	168a	Lamongan (Java)	0603-32=	2	
1884	0122	<1	Kilauea (Hawaiian Is)	1302-01-	0	
1884	0125	3a	San Miguel (El Salvador)	1403-10=	2	
1884	0204	1a	Fournaise, Piton de la (Indian O.)	0303-02=	0	
1884	0309	1a	Santa Ana (El Salvador)	1403-02=	2	
1884	0309	1a	Izalco (El Salvador)	1403-03=	2	
1884	0311	....	Dieng Volc Complex (Java)	0603-20=	1	
1884	0321	86m	Aso (Kyushu-Japan)	0802-11=	2	
1884	05	15m	Gamalama (Halmahera-Indonesia)	0608-06=	2	
? 1884	05	31m	Kanlaon (Philippines-C)	0702-02=	2	
1884	06	31p	Dempo (Sumatra)	0601-23=	2	
1884	07	?	Ushishur (Kuril Is)	0900-21=	1	
? 1884	0726	?	Reykjanes (Iceland-SW)	1701-02=	2?	
1884	0808	2a	Rinjani (Lesser Sunda Is)	0604-03=	2	
? 1884	1026	71a	Wrangell (Alaska-E)	1105-02-	2?	
? 1884	1208	<1	Gamalama (Halmahera-Indonesia)	0608-06=	1	
1884	1210?	279m?	Semeru (Java)	0603-30=	2	
1884	1229	?	Unnamed (Atlantic-N)	1801-02=	0	
1885	Cont	....	Etna (Italy)	0101-06=	1	
1885	Cont	....	Yasur (Vanuatu-SW Pacific)	0507-10=	2	
1885	Cont	....	Kaba (Sumatra)	0601-22=	2	
1885	Cont	....	Semeru (Java)	0603-30=	2	
1885	Cont	....	Kita-Iwo-jima (Volcano Is-Japan)	0804-11=	0	
1885	Cont	....	Bogoslof (Aleutian Is)	1101-30-	1	7/-
? 1885	Cont	....	Wrangell (Alaska-E)	1105-02-	2?	
1885	Cont	....	Concepción (Nicaragua)	1404-12=	2	
1885	Cont	....	Sangay (Ecuador)	1502-09=	2	
1885	Cont	....	Láscar (Chile-N)	1505-10=	2	
1885 a	....	730y	Tongariro (New Zealand)	0401-08=	1	
1885	....	?	Karkar (New Guinea-NE of)	0501-03=	2?	
1885 e	....	?	Gamkonora (Halmahera-Indonesia)	0608-04=	2	
? 1885	....	?	Taal (Luzon-Philippines)	0703-07=		
1885	....	?	Izalco (El Salvador)	1403-03=	2	
1885	....	?	Irazú (Costa Rica)	1405-06=	2?	
1885	....	?	Isluga (Chile-N)	1505-03=	1?	
? 1885	01	?	White Island (New Zealand)	0401-04=	2	
? 1885	01	30m	Gede (Java)	0603-06=	2?	
1885	01	130p	Suwanose-jima (Ryukyu Is)	0802-03=	2?	
1885	01 ?	274m	Tungurahua (Ecuador)	1502-08=	2?	
1885	0104	71m	Shikotsu [Tarumai] (Hokkaido)	0805-04=	2	
? 1885	0113?	?	Ritter Island (New Guinea-NE of)	0501-07=		
? 1885	0118	?	Guntur (Java)	0603-13=		
1885	0224d	858w	Merapi (Java)	0603-25=	1	
1885	03	....	Kilauea (Hawaiian Is)	1302-01-	0	
1885	0301	....	Stromboli (Italy)	0101-04=	2	4/-
1885	0311	583e	Lamongan (Java)	0603-32=	2	
1885	0321	9a	Slamet (Java)	0603-18=	2	
1885	05	?	Manam (New Guinea-NE of)	0501-02=		
1885	0502	....	Vesuvius (Italy)	0101-02=	1	8/8
? 1885	0520	?	Bam (New Guinea-NE of)	0501-01=		
1885	0525	?	Puracé (Colombia)	1501-06=	3	
1885	06 ?	?	Tengger Caldera [Bromo] (Java)	0603-31=	2	
1885	0621	1a	Raung (Java)	0603-34=	2	
1885	0723	?	Cotopaxi (Ecuador)	1502-05=	2	
1885	0818	?	Awu (Sangihe Is-Indonesia)	0607-04=	2	
1885	09	31m	Iliboleng (Lesser Sunda Is)	0604-22=	2	
1885	10	?	White Island (New Zealand)	0401-04=	2	
1885	10 <	?	Tofua (Tonga-SW Pacific)	0403-06=	2	
? 1885	10	?	Momotombo (Nicaragua)	1404-09=	1?	
1885	1012?	251w	Falcon Island (Tonga-SW Pacific)	0403-05=	3	-/8
1885	1031	71a	Tengger Caldera [Bromo] (Java)	0603-31=	2	
1885	1112	?	Marapi (Sumatra)	0601-14=	2?	
1885	1121	11a	Mayon (Luzon-Philippines)	0703-03=	2	
1885	1128	<1	Lawu (Java)	0603-26=	1	
1885	12	?	Pacaya (Guatemala)	1402-11=	2	
1885	1226	293m	Colima (México)	1401-04=	2	
1886	Cont	....	Vesuvius (Italy)	0101-02=	2	8/8
1886	Cont	....	Falcon Island (Tonga-SW Pacific)	0403-05=	2	-/8
1886	Cont	....	Yasur (Vanuatu-SW Pacific)	0507-10=	2	
1886	Cont	....	Kaba (Sumatra)	0601-22=	2	
1886	Cont	....	Merapi (Java)	0603-25=	1	
1886	Cont	....	Lamongan (Java)	0603-32=	2	
1886	Cont	....	Kita-Iwo-jima (Volcano Is-Japan)	0804-11=	0	
1886	Cont	....	Bogoslof (Aleutian Is)	1101-30-	1	7/-
1886	Cont	....	Kilauea (Hawaiian Is)	1302-01-	0	
1886	Cont	....	Concepción (Nicaragua)	1404-12=	2	
1886	Cont	....	Sangay (Ecuador)	1502-09=	2	
1886 ?	....	?	Meru (Africa-E)	0202-16=	0	
1886	....	?	Metis Shoal (Tonga-SW Pacific)	0403-07=	2	
1886 h	....	?	Bamus (New Britain-SW Pac)	0502-11=	3?	
1886	....	?	Tinakula (Santa Cruz Is-SW Pacific)	0506-01=		
1886	....	?	Bulusan (Luzon-Philippines)	0703-01=	2	
1886	....	?	Pavlof (Alaska Peninsula)	1102-03-	2?	
1886	....	?	Irazú (Costa Rica)	1405-06=	2?	
1886	01	?	Cotopaxi (Ecuador)	1502-05=	2	
1886	0105d	?	Vulcano (Italy)	0101-05=	3	
1886	0111	902y?	Tungurahua (Ecuador)	1502-08=	4	7/-
1886	0122	....	Stromboli (Italy)	0101-04=	2	4/-
1886	0125	213e	Semeru (Java)	0603-30=	2	
1886	03	?	Raoul Island (Kermadec Is)	0402-03=	0	
1886	0331	33a	Marapi (Sumatra)	0601-14=	2	
1886	0413	15a	Shikotsu [Tarumai] (Hokkaido)	0805-04=	2	
1886	0415	11a	Tengger Caldera [Bromo] (Java)	0603-31=	2	
1886	0425	51a>	Karangetang [Api Siau] (Sangihe Is	0607-02=	2	
1886	0518	20a	Etna (Italy)	0101-06=	3	7/6
1886	0519?	409w?	Momotombo (Nicaragua)	1404-09=	2	
1886	06	?	Tongariro (New Zealand)	0401-08=	2	
? 1886	0610	5a?	White Island (New Zealand)	0401-04=	2	
1886	0610	65m	Okataina [Tarawera] (New Zeal)	0401-05=	5	-/9
1886	0610	67a	Gede (Java)	0603-06=	2	
1886	07	?	Ambrym (Vanuatu-SW Pacific)	0507-04=	2	
1886	0708	246a	Mayon (Luzon-Philippines)	0703-03=	2	
1886	0826	....	Colima (México)	1401-04=	3?	
1886	0831	18a?	Niuafo'ou (Tonga-SW Pacific)	0403-11=	4?	-/8
1886	0916	91m?	White Island (New Zealand)	0401-04=	2	
1886	1016	....	Tungurahua (Ecuador)	1502-08=	2?	
1886	1111	76a	Tengger Caldera [Bromo] (Java)	0603-31=	2	
1886	1231y	?	Musuan (Mindanao-Philippines)	0701-07=	2	
1887	Cont	....	Vesuvius (Italy)	0101-02=	2	8/8
1887	Cont	....	Tongariro (New Zealand)	0401-08=	1	
1887	Cont	....	Yasur (Vanuatu-SW Pacific)	0507-10=	2	
1887	Cont	....	Kaba (Sumatra)	0601-22=	2	
1887	Cont	....	Merapi (Java)	0603-25=	1	
1887	Cont	....	Tengger Caldera [Bromo] (Java)	0603-31=	2	
1887	Cont	....	Kita-Iwo-jima (Volcano Is-Japan)	0804-11=	0	
1887	Cont	....	Bogoslof (Aleutian Is)	1101-30-	1	7/-
1887	Cont	....	Kilauea (Hawaiian Is)	1302-01-	0	
1887	Cont	....	Momotombo (Nicaragua)	1404-09=	2	
1887	Cont	....	Tungurahua (Ecuador)	1502-08=	2	7/-
1887	Cont	....	Sangay (Ecuador)	1502-09=	2	
1887	....	?	Niuafo'ou (Tonga-SW Pacific)	0403-11=	2	
? 1887	....	?	Guntur (Java)	0603-13=		
1887	....	?	Akita-Yake-yama (Honshu-Japan)	0803-26=	2	
1887	....	?	Akutan (Aleutian Is)	1101-32-	0	
1887	....	?	Colima (México)	1401-04=	0	
1887	....	731y	Izalco (El Salvador)	1403-03=	2	
1887	0116	12a?	Mauna Loa (Hawaiian Is)	1302-02=	0	8/-
1887	0116	159a	Llaima (Chile-C)	1507-11=	2	
1887	0131	....	Stromboli (Italy)	0101-04=	2	4/-
1887	02	30p	Semeru (Java)	0603-30=	2	
@ 1887	0202	3a	Ritter Island (New Guinea-NE of)	0501-07=	2	
1887	0309	....	Mayon (Luzon-Philippines)	0703-03=	3	
1887	0323	7a	Kerinci (Sumatra)	0601-17=	2?	
1887	0331	....	Stromboli (Italy)	0101-04=	2?	4/-
1887	05	?	Kirishima (Kyushu-Japan)	0802-09=	2?	
1887	0527	<1	Karangetang [Api Siau] (Sangihe Is	0607-02=	2	
1887	0531	77m	Etna (Italy)	0101-06=	1	
1887	06	>3yr	Manam (New Guinea-NE of)	0501-02=	2	
1887	06	?	Tokachi (Hokkaido-Japan)	0805-05=	2	
1887	0602	958m	Lonquimay (Chile-C)	1507-10=	2	8/-
1887	0703a	6a	Lamongan (Java)	0603-32=	2	
1887	08 ?	57m?	Semeru (Java)	0603-30=	0	
1887	0815	686w	Grímsvötn [Thordarhyrna] (Iceland	1703-01=	2	
1887	0903	35a	Shikotsu [Tarumai] (Hokkaido)	0805-04=	2	
1887	0910	....	Semeru (Java)	0603-30=	2	
? 1887	1007	105a	Ranau (Sumatra)	0601-251		
1887	1022	<1	Gede (Java)	0603-06=	2	
1887	11	103m	Lamongan (Java)	0603-32=	2	
1887	1113	1a	Sundoro (Java)	0603-21=	2	
1887	1118	....	Stromboli (Italy)	0101-04=	2	4/-
? 1887	1129	?	Alamagan (Mariana Is-C Pacific)	0804-18=		
? 1887	1201	?	Macauley Island (Kermadec Is)	0402-021	0	
1888	Cont	....	Vesuvius (Italy)	0101-02=	2	8/8
1888	Cont	....	Manam (New Guinea-NE of)	0501-02=	2	

	START YEAR	M-Dy	Duration	VOLCANO NAME (Subregion)	NUMBER	VEI	Vol L/T
	1888	Cont	....	Yasur (Vanuatu-SW Pacific)	0507-10=	2	
	1888	Cont	....	Kaba (Sumatra)	0601-22=	2	
?	1888	Cont	....	Ranau (Sumatra)	0601-251		
	1888	Cont	....	Kita-Iwo-jima (Volcano Is-Japan)	0804-11=	0	
	1888	Cont	....	Bogoslof (Aleutian Is)	1101-30-	1	7/-
	1888	Cont	....	Izalco (El Salvador)	1403-03=	2	
	1888	Cont	....	Tungurahua (Ecuador)	1502-08=	2	7/-
	1888	Cont	....	Sangay (Ecuador)	1502-09=	2	
	1888	Cont	....	Lonquimay (Chile-C)	1507-10=	2	8/-
	1888	Cont	....	Grímsvötn [Thordarhyrna] (Iceland...	1703-01=	2	
	1888	....	?	**South Island** (Africa-E)	0202-02=	1	
	1888	....	?	**Barrier, The** (Africa-E)	0202-03=	0	
?	1888	....	?	Bam (New Guinea-NE of)	0501-01=		
	1888	....	?	**Gede** (Java)	0603-06=	2?	
	1888	....	?	**Ebulobo** (Lesser Sunda Is)	0604-10=	2	
?	1888	....	>3yr	Egon (Lesser Sunda Is)	0604-16=	2	
	1888	....	?	**Iliboleng** (Lesser Sunda Is)	0604-22=	2	
	1888	....	?	**Fernandina** (Galápagos)	1503-01=	1	
	1888	01	>3yr	**Poás** (Costa Rica)	1405-04=	1	
?	1888	02	?	Sorikmarapi (Sumatra)	0601-12=		
	1888	02	243p	**Semeru** (Java)	0603-30=	2	
	1888	0219	29a	**Marapi** (Sumatra)	0601-14=	2?	
	1888	0221	78a	**Kirishima** (Kyushu-Japan)	0802-09=	2	
	1888	0224d	50m?	**Ambrym** (Vanuatu-SW Pacific)	0507-04=	2	
?	1888	0227	?	Tengger Caldera [Bromo] (Java)	0603-31=	2	
	1888	0313	<1	**Ritter Island** (New Guinea-NE of)	0501-07=	2?	
	1888	0413<	490m>	**Etna** (Italy)	0101-06=	2	
	1888	0414	?	**Komaga-take** (Hokkaido-Japan)	0805-02=	2	
	1888	0530	1a	**Batur** (Lesser Sunda Is)	0604-01=	2	
	1888	0715	<1	**Bandai** (Honshu-Japan)	0803-16=	4	-/8
	1888	08	....	Kilauea (Hawaiian Is)	1302-01-	0	
	1888	0802	806d	**Vulcano** (Italy)	0101-05=	3	
	1888	0818	124a	**Merapi** (Java)	0603-25=	2	
	1888	09	21m	**Lamongan** (Java)	0603-32=	2	
	1888	0925d	?	**Nisyros** (Greece)	0102-05=	2	
	1888	1024	....	Stromboli (Italy)	0101-04=	2	4/-
?	1888	12	?	Iya (Lesser Sunda Is)	0604-11=		
	1888	1215	?	**Mayon** (Luzon-Philippines)	0703-03=	1	
	1889	Cont	....	Vesuvius (Italy)	0101-02=	2	8/8
	1889	Cont	....	Stromboli (Italy)	0101-04=	1	4/-
	1889	Cont	....	Etna (Italy)	0101-06=	2	
	1889	Cont	....	Manam (New Guinea-NE of)	0501-02=	2	
	1889	Cont	....	Yasur (Vanuatu-SW Pacific)	0507-10=	2	
	1889	Cont	....	Kaba (Sumatra)	0601-22=	2	
?	1889	Cont	....	Egon (Lesser Sunda Is)	0604-16=	2	
	1889	Cont	....	Kita-Iwo-jima (Volcano Is-Japan)	0804-11=	0	
	1889	Cont	....	Bogoslof (Aleutian Is)	1101-30-	1	7/-
	1889	Cont	....	Kilauea (Hawaiian Is)	1302-01-	0	
	1889	Cont	....	Izalco (El Salvador)	1403-03=	2	
	1889	Cont	....	Poás (Costa Rica)	1405-04=	1	
	1889	Cont	....	Sangay (Ecuador)	1502-09=	2	
	1889	Cont	....	Grímsvötn [Thordarhyrna] (Iceland...	1703-01=	2	
	1889	....	?	**Lewotobi** (Lesser Sunda Is)	0604-18=	2	
	1889	....	?	**Bulusan** (Luzon-Philippines)	0703-01=		
	1889	....	?	**Tokachi** (Hokkaido-Japan)	0805-05=	2	
	1889	....	365y	**Tupungatito** (Chile-C)	1507-01=	2	
	1889	....	365y	**San José** (Chile-C)	1507-02=	2	
	1889	01	869m>	**Semeru** (Java)	0603-30=	2	
	1889	0219	288a	**Tandikat** (Sumatra)	0601-15=	1	
	1889	0327	21a?	**Marapi** (Sumatra)	0601-14=	2?	
	1889	0420	96m	**Llaima** (Chile-C)	1507-11=	2	
	1889	0501	?	**Ruapehu** (New Zealand)	0401-10=	2	
?	1889	0508<	?	Gede (Java)	0603-06=	1	
	1889	06	57m>	**Fournaise, Piton de la** (Indian O.)	0303-02=	2	
	1889	06	?	**Ruang** (Sangihe Is-Indonesia)	0607-01=	1	
	1889	07	?	**Merapi** (Java)	0603-25=	1	
	1889	0703	?	**Galeras** (Colombia)	1501-08=	2	
	1889	0809	14a	**Shiretoko-Iwo-zan** (Hokkaido-Japan)	0805-09=	2?	
	1889	0809	191a	Colima (México)	1401-04=	2?	
	1889	09	>3yr	**Planchón-Peteroa** (Chile-C)	1507-04=	2	
	1889	0906	3a	**Banua Wuhu** (Sangihe Is-Indonesia)	0607-03=	2	
	1889	0907	69m	**Lamongan** (Java)	0603-32=	2	
	1889	1002	11a	**Suwanose-jima** (Ryukyu Is)	0802-03=	4	
	1889	1026	....	Colima (México)	1401-04=	3	
	1889	1204	?	**Nikko-Shirane** (Honshu-Japan)	0803-14=	1	
	1889	1210	8a	**Kirishima** (Kyushu-Japan)	0802-09=	2	
	1889	1222	....	**Lonquimay** (Chile-C)	1507-10=	3	8/-
	1889	1224	?	**Asama** (Honshu-Japan)	0803-11=	2	
	1889	1226	....	Vulcano (Italy)	0101-05=	3	
	1889	1231y	?	**Ioto [Iwo-jima]** (Volcano Is-Japan)	0804-12=	1	
	1890	Cont	....	Vesuvius (Italy)	0101-02=	2	8/8
	1890	Cont	....	Manam (New Guinea-NE of)	0501-02=	2	
	1890	Cont	....	Yasur (Vanuatu-SW Pacific)	0507-10=	2	
	1890	Cont	....	Kaba (Sumatra)	0601-22=	2	
	1890	Cont	....	Semeru (Java)	0603-30=	2	
?	1890	Cont	....	Egon (Lesser Sunda Is)	0604-16=	2	
	1890	Cont	....	Kilauea (Hawaiian Is)	1302-01-	0	
	1890	Cont	....	Poás (Costa Rica)	1405-04=	1	
	1890	Cont	....	Sangay (Ecuador)	1502-09=	2	
	1890	Cont	....	Tupungatito (Chile-C)	1507-01=	2	
	1890	Cont	....	San José (Chile-C)	1507-02=	2	
	1890	Cont	....	Planchón-Peteroa (Chile-C)	1507-04=	2	
	1890	Cont	....	Lonquimay (Chile-C)	1507-10=	2	8/-
	1890	....	>3yr	Stromboli (Italy)	0101-04=	1	4/-
	1890	....	?	**Langila** (New Britain-SW Pac)	0502-01=	0	
	1890 ?	....	>3yr	**Victory** (New Guinea)	0503-03=	2	
	1890	....	?	**Soputan** (Sulawesi-Indonesia)	0606-03=	2	
?	1890	....	?	Zao (Honshu-Japan)	0803-19=	1?	
	1890 c	....	?	**Koryaksky** (Kamchatka)	1000-09=	1?	
M	**1890 ?**	....	?	**Southern EPR-Segment J** (Pacific)	1304-13-	0	
	1890	....	365y	**San Miguel** (El Salvador)	1403-10=	2	
	1890	....	?	**Huequi** (Chile-S)	1508-03=	3?	
	1890	02	355m	**Fournaise, Piton de la** (Indian O.)	0303-02=	2	
	1890	02	....	Bogoslof (Aleutian Is)	1101-30-	2	7/-
	1890	0216	....	**Colima** (México)	1401-04=	4	
?	1890	03	?	Tongariro (New Zealand)	0401-08=	1	
	1890	0315	....	Vulcano (Italy)	0101-05=	3	
	1890	0323h	53o	**Lamongan** (Java)	0603-32=	2	
	1890	0326e	25e	**Izalco** (El Salvador)	1403-03=	0	
	1890	04	?	**Kliuchevskoi** (Kamchatka)	1000-26=	2	
	1890	04	?	**Ushkovsky** (Kamchatka)	1000-261	2?	
	1890	05	155m?	Etna (Italy)	0101-06=	1	
	1890	05	123p	**Tengger Caldera [Bromo]** (Java)	0603-31=	2	
	1890	0615	?	**Shiretoko-Iwo-zan** (Hokkaido-Japan)	0805-09=	1	
	1890	0620	10a	**Makian** (Halmahera-Indonesia)	0608-07=	2	
	1890	07	61m	**Raung** (Java)	0603-34=	2	
	1890	0806	23a	**Slamet** (Java)	0603-18=	2	
	1890	0822	?	**Nikko-Shirane** (Honshu-Japan)	0803-14=	1	
?	1890	0823?	<1	Mono Lake Volc Field (US-California	1203-11-		
	1890	0905d	132o>	**Lamongan** (Java)	0603-32=	2	
	1890	0910	20a	**Mayon** (Luzon-Philippines)	0703-03=	2	
	1890	0923	?	**Akita-Yake-yama** (Honshu-Japan)	0803-26=	2	
	1890	1017	....	**Etna** (Italy)	0101-06=	2	
	1890	1118	?	**Colima** (México)	1401-04=	2?	
	1890	1123	<1	**Banda Api** (Banda Sea)	0605-09=	2	
	1890	12	30p	**Akita-Komaga-take** (Honshu-Japan)	0803-23=	2	
	1891	Cont	....	Fournaise, Piton de la (Indian O.)	0303-02=	2	
	1891	Cont	....	Manam (New Guinea-NE of)	0501-02=	2	
	1891	Cont	....	Victory (New Guinea)	0503-03=	1	
	1891	Cont	....	Yasur (Vanuatu-SW Pacific)	0507-10=	2	
	1891	Cont	....	Kaba (Sumatra)	0601-22=	2	
?	1891	Cont	....	Egon (Lesser Sunda Is)	0604-16=	2	
	1891	Cont	....	Akita-Komaga-take (Honshu-Japan)	0803-23=	2	
	1891	Cont	....	Kilauea (Hawaiian Is)	1302-01-	0	
	1891	Cont	....	San Miguel (El Salvador)	1403-10=	2	
	1891	Cont	....	Poás (Costa Rica)	1405-04=	1	
	1891	Cont	....	Sangay (Ecuador)	1502-09=	2	
	1891	Cont	....	Planchón-Peteroa (Chile-C)	1507-04=	2	
@	**1891** <	....	?	**Nyiragongo** (Africa-C)	0203-03=		
@	**1891**	....	?	**Visoke** (Africa-C)	0203-05-		
	1891	....	?	**Gede** (Java)	0603-06=	2	
	1891	....	....	**Bogoslof** (Aleutian Is)	1101-30-	3	7/-
	1891	....	>3yr	**Izalco** (El Salvador)	1403-03=	2	
	1891	....	?	**Galeras** (Colombia)	1501-08=	2	
	1891 ?	....	?	**San Pedro** (Chile-N)	1505-07=	2	
	1891	....	?	**Hudson, Cerro** (Chile-S)	1508-057		
	1891	02	....	Semeru (Java)	0603-30=	2	
	1891	02	?	**Chillán, Nevados de** (Chile-C)	1507-07=	2	
	1891	0220	298m	**Etna** (Italy)	0101-06=	2	
	1891	04	15m	**Concepción** (Nicaragua)	1404-12=	2	
	1891	0607	....	Vesuvius (Italy)	0101-02=	2	8/8
	1891	0619?	?	**Kirishima** (Kyushu-Japan)	0802-09=	2?	
	1891	0624	....	**Stromboli** (Italy)	0101-04=	3	4/-
	1891	07	334p	**Colima** (México)	1401-04=	2	
	1891	0825	311w	**Merapi** (Java)	0603-25=	2?	
	1891	0831	....	Stromboli (Italy)	0101-04=	2?	4/-
	1891	0925e	10i	**Lamongan** (Java)	0603-32=	2	
	1891	10 ?	31p?	**Asama** (Honshu-Japan)	0803-11=		
	1891	1003	149a	**Mayon** (Luzon-Philippines)	0703-03=	2	
	1891	1017	8a	**Pantelleria** (Italy)	0101-071	1	
	1891	11 ?	121m?	**Grímsvötn** (Iceland-NE)	1703-01=	2	
	1891	1110	10a?	**Kirishima** (Kyushu-Japan)	0802-09=	2	
?	1891	12	?	Pantelleria (Italy)	0101-071		
	1891	12	7b	**Seguam** (Aleutian Is)	1101-18-	2	
	1891	1208	....	Etna (Italy)	0101-06=	2	
	1892	Cont	....	Vesuvius (Italy)	0101-02=	2	8/8
	1892	Cont	....	Manam (New Guinea-NE of)	0501-02=	2	
	1892	Cont	....	Victory (New Guinea)	0503-03=	1	
	1892	Cont	....	Yasur (Vanuatu-SW Pacific)	0507-10=	2	
	1892	Cont	....	Kaba (Sumatra)	0601-22=	2	
	1892	Cont	....	Merapi (Java)	0603-25=	2?	
?	1892	Cont	....	Egon (Lesser Sunda Is)	0604-16=	2	
	1892	Cont	....	Mayon (Luzon-Philippines)	0703-03=	2	

	START YEAR	M-Dy	Duration	VOLCANO NAME (Subregion)	NUMBER	VEI	Vol L/T
	1892	Cont	....	Bogoslof (Aleutian Is)	1101-30-	1	7/-
	1892	Cont	....	Colima (México)	1401-04=	2	
	1892	Cont	....	Izalco (El Salvador)	1403-03=	2	
	1892	Cont	....	Sangay (Ecuador)	1502-09=	2	
	1892	Cont	....	Planchón-Peteroa (Chile-C)	1507-04=	2	
	1892	Cont	....	Grímsvötn (Iceland-NE)	1703-01=	2	
?	1892	....	?	Hunter Island (SW Pacific)	0508-02=		
?	1892	....	?	Tandikat (Sumatra)	0601-15=		
	1892	....	?	**Bulusan** (Luzon-Philippines)	0703-01=	2	
?	1892	....	?	Asama (Honshu-Japan)	0803-11=		
	1892	....	?	**Pavlof** (Alaska Peninsula)	1102-03-	2?	
	1892	....	....	Kilauea (Hawaiian Is)	1302-01-	0	
	1892	....	?	**Llaima** (Chile-C)	1507-11=	2	
	1892	02	30p	**Tongariro [Ngauruhoe]** (New Zeal)	0401-08=	2	
	1892	03	30p	**Semeru** (Java)	0603-30=	2	
	1892	0415q	?	**Seguam** (Aleutian Is)	1101-18-	3	
	1892	0521	?	**Sorikmarapi** (Sumatra)	0601-12=	2	
	1892	0603	2a	**Wurlali** (Banda Sea)	0605-04=	2	
	1892	0607	5a?	**Awu** (Sangihe Is-Indonesia)	0607-04=	3	
	1892	0614?	?	**Karangetang [Api Siau]** (Sangihe Is	0607-02=	2	
	1892	0620	18a?	Etna (Italy)	0101-06=	1	
	1892	0708	....	**Etna** (Italy)	0101-06=	2	
	1892	0709	173a	**Etna** (Italy)	0101-06=	2	8/6
	1892	0828	2	**Veniaminof** (Alaska Peninsula)	1102-07-	3	
	1892	0923	?	**Akutan** (Aleutian Is)	1101-32-	1	
	1892	10	259w	**Lopevi** (Vanuatu-SW Pacific)	0507-05=	2?	
	1892	1012?	19a?	**Conchagüita** (El Salvador)	1403-12=	1?	
	1892	11	31p	**Tongariro [Ngauruhoe]** (New Zeal)	0401-08=	2	
	1892	1105	....	Stromboli (Italy)	0101-04=	2	4/-
	1892	1130	?	**Tongariro** (New Zealand)	0401-08=	2	
	1892	1130	3a	**Mauna Loa** (Hawaiian Is)	1302-02=	0	7/-
?	1892	1214	?	Vulcano (Italy)	0101-05=	0	
	1893	Cont	....	Vesuvius (Italy)	0101-02=	2	8/8
	1893	Cont	....	Manam (New Guinea-NE of)	0501-02=	2	
	1893	Cont	....	Victory (New Guinea)	0503-03=	1	
	1893	Cont	....	Lopevi (Vanuatu-SW Pacific)	0507-05=	2?	
	1893	Cont	....	Yasur (Vanuatu-SW Pacific)	0507-10=	2	
	1893	Cont	....	Bogoslof (Aleutian Is)	1101-30-	1	7/-
	1893	Cont	....	Kilauea (Hawaiian Is)	1302-01-	0	
	1893	Cont	....	Izalco (El Salvador)	1403-03=	2	
	1893	Cont	....	Sangay (Ecuador)	1502-09=	2	
	1893	Cont	....	Planchón-Peteroa (Chile-C)	1507-04=	2	
?	1893 <	....	?	Emperor of China (Banda Sea)	0605-01=	1?	
?	1893 <	....	?	Nieuwerkerk (Banda Sea)	0605-02=	1?	
	1893	....	?	**Awu** (Sangihe Is-Indonesia)	0607-04=	2	
	1893	....	?	**Cleveland** (Aleutian Is)	1101-24-		
	1893 ?	....	?	**Puyehue-Cordón Caulle** (Chile-C)	1507-15=	2	
	1893	....	?	**Huequi** (Chile-S)	1508-03=	2	
	1893	01	120p	**Semeru** (Java)	0603-30=	2	
	1893	0104	<1	**Sorikmarapi** (Sumatra)	0601-12=	2	
	1893	0107	374a>	Calbuco (Chile-S)	1508-02=	2	
	1893	0110	....	**Calbuco** (Chile-S)	1508-02=	4	
	1893	0113	73a	**Tengger Caldera [Bromo]** (Java)	0603-31=	2	
	1893	0130	....	Stromboli (Italy)	0101-04=	2	4/-
	1893	0304	?	**Chillán, Nevados de** (Chile-C)	1507-07=	2	
	1893	0329	503a>	**Lokon-Empung** (Sulawesi-Indonesia)	0606-10=	2	
	1893	0426	>3yr	**Etna** (Italy)	0101-06=	1	
	1893	0519	55a	**Azuma** (Honshu-Japan)	0803-18=	1	
	1893	07	?	**Kanlaon** (Philippines-C)	0702-02=	2	
	1893	0811	....	Stromboli (Italy)	0101-04=	2	4/-
	1893	10	?	**Merapi** (Java)	0603-25=	1	
	1893	1003?	28a	**Mayon** (Luzon-Philippines)	0703-03=	1	
	1893	1109	1a	**Azuma** (Honshu-Japan)	0803-18=	1	
	1893	1118	?	**Lamongan** (Java)	0603-32=	2	
	1893	12	365y	**Llaima** (Chile-C)	1507-11=	2	
	1893	1201p	62r	**Villarrica** (Chile-C)	1507-12=	2	
	1893	1204	>3yr	**Colima** (México)	1401-04=	2	
	1893	1211	64m	**Semeru** (Java)	0603-30=	2	
?	1893	1211	?	Seal Nunataks Group (Antarctica)	1900-05=	1	
	1894	Cont	....	Stromboli (Italy)	0101-04=	1	4/-
	1894	Cont	....	Etna (Italy)	0101-06=	1	
	1894	Cont	....	Manam (New Guinea-NE of)	0501-02=	2	
	1894	Cont	....	Victory (New Guinea)	0503-03=	1	
	1894	Cont	....	Yasur (Vanuatu-SW Pacific)	0507-10=	2	
	1894	Cont	....	Lokon-Empung (Sulawesi-Indonesia)	0606-10=	2	
	1894	Cont	....	Bogoslof (Aleutian Is)	1101-30-	1	7/-
	1894	Cont	....	Colima (México)	1401-04=	2	
	1894	Cont	....	Izalco (El Salvador)	1403-03=	2	
	1894	Cont	....	Sangay (Ecuador)	1502-09=	2	
	1894	Cont	....	Planchón-Peteroa (Chile-C)	1507-04=	2	
	1894	Cont	....	Llaima (Chile-C)	1507-11=	2	
	1894	Cont	....	Villarrica (Chile-C)	1507-12=	2	
	1894	....	....	Vesuvius (Italy)	0101-02=	1	8/8
	1894	....	?	**Nyiragongo** (Africa-C)	0203-03=	1	
?	1894 <	....	?	Metis Shoal (Tonga-SW Pacific)	0403-07=	2	
	1894	....	365y	**Bagana** (Bougainville-SW Pacific)	0505-02=	2	
	1894	....	?	**Bulusan** (Luzon-Philippines)	0703-01=	2	
	1894	....	?	**Alaid** (Kuril Is)	0900-39=	2	
	1894	....	?	**Pavlof** (Alaska Peninsula)	1102-03-	2?	
	1894	....	?	**Reventador** (Ecuador)	1502-01=	3	
	1894	0127	6a	**Merapi** (Java)	0603-25=	2?	-/6
	1894	02	....	Semeru (Java)	0603-30=	1	
	1894	0208	<1	**Shikotsu [Tarumai]** (Hokkaido)	0805-04=	2	
	1894	0225	3a?	**Kirishima** (Kyushu-Japan)	0802-09=	2	
	1894	0306	177a	**Aso** (Kyushu-Japan)	0802-11=	2	
	1894	0316	27a	**Azuma** (Honshu-Japan)	0803-18=	1	
	1894	0321	....	Kilauea (Hawaiian Is)	1302-01-	0	
	1894	0406	69a	**Asama** (Honshu-Japan)	0803-11=	2	
	1894	05	31p	**Kanlaon** (Philippines-C)	0702-02=	2	
	1894	06	?	**Nyamuragira** (Africa-C)	0203-02=	2	
	1894	0703	<1	**Zao** (Honshu-Japan)	0803-19=	2?	
	1894	0707	....	Kilauea (Hawaiian Is)	1302-01-	0	
	1894	0725	1a	**Kolokol Group** (Kuril Is)	0900-12=	2	
	1894	08	?	**Fournaise, Piton de la** (Indian O.)	0303-02=	2	
	1894	0817	<1	**Shikotsu [Tarumai]** (Hokkaido)	0805-04=	2	
	1894	10	?	**Merapi** (Java)	0603-25=	1?	
	1894	10	121p	**Avachinsky** (Kamchatka)	1000-10=	2	7/6
	1894	1015	118a>	**Ambrym** (Vanuatu-SW Pacific)	0507-04=	3	
	1894	1017	59m	**Galunggung** (Java)	0603-14=	3	-/7
	1894	1116	228w?	**Calbuco** (Chile-S)	1508-02=	2?	
	1894	1121	33a	**Rainier** (US-Washington)	1201-03-	1	
?	1894	12	?	Falcon Island (Tonga-SW Pacific)	0403-05=	0?	
	1895	Cont	....	Etna (Italy)	0101-06=	1	
	1895	Cont	....	Manam (New Guinea-NE of)	0501-02=	2	
	1895	Cont	....	Victory (New Guinea)	0503-03=	1	
	1895	Cont	....	Bagana (Bougainville-SW Pacific)	0505-02=	2	
	1895	Cont	....	Ambrym (Vanuatu-SW Pacific)	0507-04=	2	
	1895	Cont	....	Yasur (Vanuatu-SW Pacific)	0507-10=	2	
	1895	Cont	....	Avachinsky (Kamchatka)	1000-10=	2	7/6
	1895	Cont	....	Bogoslof (Aleutian Is)	1101-30-	1	7/-
	1895	Cont	....	Colima (México)	1401-04=	2	
	1895	Cont	....	Izalco (El Salvador)	1403-03=	2	
	1895	Cont	....	Sangay (Ecuador)	1502-09=	2	
	1895	Cont	....	Calbuco (Chile-S)	1508-02=	2?	
	1895	....	?	**Barrier, The** (Africa-E)	0202-03=	2	
A	1895 e	....	?	**Dakatau [Mt. Makalia]** (New Britain)	0502-04=	2	
?	1895	....	?	Mahagnao (Philippines-C)	0702-07=		
	1895	....	?	**Poás** (Costa Rica)	1405-04=	1	
	1895 r	....	?	**Sumaco** (Ecuador)	1502-04=	2?	
	1895	....	?	**Cotopaxi** (Ecuador)	1502-05=	2	
	1895	....	731y	**San José** (Chile-C)	1507-02=	2	
	1895	....	365y	**Llaima** (Chile-C)	1507-11=	2	
	1895	0215	35a	**Zao** (Honshu-Japan)	0803-19=	1	-/5
	1895	0308	189a	**Azuma** (Honshu-Japan)	0803-18=	1	
	1895	0310	4a>	**Ruapehu** (New Zealand)	0401-10=	2	
	1895	0329	....	Stromboli (Italy)	0101-04=	2	4/-
	1895	0522	132a>	**Semeru** (Java)	0603-30=	2	
	1895	0617	59m	**Karkar** (New Guinea-NE of)	0501-03=	2	7/-
	1895	07	164n	**Banua Wuhu** (Sangihe Is-Indonesia)	0607-03=	2	
	1895	0702	90a	**Dempo** (Sumatra)	0601-23=	2	
	1895	0703	....	Vesuvius (Italy)	0101-02=	2	8/8
	1895	0716	345a	**Kirishima** (Kyushu-Japan)	0802-09=	2	
	1895	0720	129a	**Mayon** (Luzon-Philippines)	0703-03=	2	
	1895	0822	37a	**Zao** (Honshu-Japan)	0803-19=	2	
	1895	1124	?	**Hunter Island** (SW Pacific)	0508-02=		
	1895	1219	<1	**Gamalama** (Halmahera-Indonesia)	0608-06=	1	
?	1895	1231y	?	Thompson Island (Atlantic-S)	1806-03-		
	1896	Cont	....	Vesuvius (Italy)	0101-02=	2	8/8
	1896	Cont	....	Etna (Italy)	0101-06=	1	
	1896	Cont	....	Victory (New Guinea)	0503-03=	1	
	1896	Cont	....	Yasur (Vanuatu-SW Pacific)	0507-10=	2	
	1896	Cont	....	Colima (México)	1401-04=	2	
	1896	Cont	....	Izalco (El Salvador)	1403-03=	2	
	1896	Cont	....	Sangay (Ecuador)	1502-09=	2	
	1896	Cont	....	San José (Chile-C)	1507-02=	2	
	1896	Cont	....	Llaima (Chile-C)	1507-11=	2	
	1896	....	?	**Nyamuragira** (Africa-C)	0203-02=	1	
	1896	....	?	**Okataina [Waimangu]** (New Zeal)	0401-05=	1?	
	1896	....	?	**Tengger Caldera [Bromo]** (Java)	0603-31=	2	
	1896	....	?	**Bayonnaise Rocks** (Izu Is-Japan)	0804-07=	2	
	1896	....	?	**Akutan** (Aleutian Is)	1101-32-		
?	1896	....	?	Socorro (México-Is)	1401-021	2?	
	1896	....	?	**Huequi** (Chile-S)	1508-03=	2	
	1896	0103	25	**Kilauea** (Hawaiian Is)	1302-01-	0	
	1896	0110	?	**Fuego** (Guatemala)	1402-09=	2?	
	1896	0308	<1	**Zao** (Honshu-Japan)	0803-19=	1	
	1896	0421	15a	**Mauna Loa** (Hawaiian Is)	1302-02=	0	7/-
	1896	05	31p	**Semeru** (Java)	0603-30=	2	
	1896	0522	<1	**Tangkubanparahu** (Java)	0603-09=	2	
	1896	0711	76e	**Kilauea** (Hawaiian Is)	1302-01-	0	
	1896	0713	....	Stromboli (Italy)	0101-04=	2	4/-
	1896	08	?	**Raung** (Java)	0603-34=	2	
?	1896	0803	1a?	Gamalama (Halmahera-Indonesia)	0608-06=	1	
	1896	0831	27a	**Mayon** (Luzon-Philippines)	0703-03=	2	

	START YEAR	M-Dy	Duration	VOLCANO NAME (Subregion)	NUMBER	VEI	Vol L/T
	1896	09	?	**Vestmannaeyjar** (Iceland-S)	1702-01=		
?	*1896*	*0901?*	*?*	*Zao (Honshu-Japan)*	0803-19=	*1?*	
	1896	0905	14*a*>	**Lamongan** (Java)	0603-32=	2	
?	*1896*	*0905*	*14a*	*Azuma (Honshu-Japan)*	0803-18=	*1*	
	1896	11	44*m*	**Tongariro** (New Zealand)	0401-08=	2	
	1896	12	334*p*	**Kliuchevskoi** (Kamchatka)	1000-26=	2	
	1896	1221	?	**Kirishima** (Kyushu-Japan)	0802-09=	2	
	1897	*Cont*	....	*Vesuvius (Italy)*	0101-02=	*2*	*8/8*
	1897	*Cont*	....	*Stromboli (Italy)*	0101-04=	*1*	*4/-*
	1897	*Cont*	....	*Etna (Italy)*	0101-06=	*1*	
	1897	*Cont*	....	*Victory (New Guinea)*	0503-03=	*1*	
	1897	*Cont*	....	*Yasur (Vanuatu-SW Pacific)*	0507-10=	*2*	
	1897	*Cont*	....	*Kliuchevskoi (Kamchatka)*	1000-26=	*2*	
	1897	*Cont*	....	*Colima (México)*	1401-04=	*2*	
	1897	*Cont*	....	*Izalco (El Salvador)*	1403-03=	*2*	
	1897	*Cont*	....	*Sangay (Ecuador)*	1502-09=	*2*	
	1897	*Cont*	....	*San José (Chile-C)*	1507-02=	*2*	
	1897	....	?	**Tongariro [Ngauruhoe]** (New Zeal)	0401-08=	2	
?	*1897*	....	*365y*	*Bam (New Guinea-NE of)*	0501-01=		
	1897	....	?	**Merapi** (Java)	0603-25=	2?	
	1897	....	?	**Batur** (Lesser Sunda Is)	0604-01=	2	
	1897	....	365*y*	**Shiveluch** (Kamchatka)	1000-27=	2	
	1897	....	?	**Cleveland** (Aleutian Is)	1101-24-		
?	*1897*	....	*?*	*Shishaldin (Aleutian Is)*	1101-36-		
	1897	....	?	**Santiago** (Galápagos)	1503-09=	0	
@	**1897**	....	?	**Grímsvötn** (Iceland-NE)	1703-01=	2	
	1897	01	86*m*>	**Tupungatito** (Chile-C)	1507-01=	2	
	1897	0101	2*a*	**Semeru** (Java)	0603-30=	2	
	1897	0105d	19*d*	**Fournaise, Piton de la** (Indian O.)	0303-02=	0	
?	*1897*	*0114*	*<1*	*Zao (Honshu-Japan)*	0803-19=	*1?*	
	1897	0224d	?	**Aso** (Kyushu-Japan)	0802-11=	2	
	1897	0326e	?	**Tinakula** (Santa Cruz Is-SW Pacific)	0506-01=	2?	
	1897	04	?	**Raung** (Java)	0603-34=	2	
	1897	05 <	?	**Barrier, The** (Africa-E)	0202-03=	2?	
	1897	0503	124*a*	**Kirishima** (Kyushu-Japan)	0802-09=	2	
	1897	0516?	?	**Bagana** (Bougainville-SW Pacific)	0505-02=	2	
	1897	*0523<*	*61a>*	*Mayon (Luzon-Philippines)*	0703-03=	*0*	*-/7*
	1897	0525?	>3yr	**Kuwae [Karua]** (Vanuatu-SW Pac)	0507-07=	2	
	1897	*0604*	....	*Mayon (Luzon-Philippines)*	0703-03=	*2*	*-/7*
	1897	0624	3*a*	**Kilauea** (Hawaiian Is)	1302-01-	0	
	1897	0625	....	**Mayon** (Luzon-Philippines)	0703-03=	4?	-/7
	1897	0708	39*a*	**Kusatsu-Shirane** (Honshu-Japan)	0803-12=	2	
	1897	0907	17*a*	**Gamalama** (Halmahera-Indonesia)	0608-06=	1	
	1897	0921	?	**Jolo** (Sulu Is-Philippines)	0700-01=	0	
	1897	*1101*	*>3yr*	*Doña Juana (Colombia)*	1501-07=	*2*	
	1897	1201p	64*r*	**Villarrica** (Chile-C)	1507-12=	2	
	1898	*Cont*	....	*Vesuvius (Italy)*	0101-02=	*2*	*8/8*
	1898	*Cont*	....	*Etna (Italy)*	0101-06=	*1*	
?	*1898*	*Cont*	....	*Bam (New Guinea-NE of)*	0501-01=		
	1898	*Cont*	....	*Victory (New Guinea)*	0503-03=	*1*	
	1898	*Cont*	....	*Kuwae [Karua] (Vanuatu-SW Pac)*	0507-07=	*2*	
	1898	*Cont*	....	*Yasur (Vanuatu-SW Pacific)*	0507-10=	*2*	
	1898	*Cont*	....	*Shiveluch (Kamchatka)*	1000-27=	*2*	
	1898	*Cont*	....	*Colima (México)*	1401-04=	*2*	
	1898	*Cont*	....	*Izalco (El Salvador)*	1403-03=	*2*	
	1898	*Cont*	....	*Sangay (Ecuador)*	1502-09=	*2*	
	1898	*Cont*	....	*Villarrica (Chile-C)*	1507-12=	*2*	
	1898	....	?	**Nyiragongo** (Africa-C)	0203-03=	1	
	1898 ?	....	?	**Santa Isabel** (Africa-W)	0204-004		
	1898	....	?	**Ulawun** (New Britain-SW Pac)	0502-12=	3	
	1898	....	?	**Changbaishan** (China-E)	1005-06-	2?	
?	*1898*	....	*?*	*Xianjindao (Korea)*	1006-01-		
	1898	....	?	**Shishaldin** (Aleutian Is)	1101-36-	2	
	1898	....	196*y*?	**Láscar** (Chile-N)	1505-10=	2	
	1898	....	?	**Chillán, Nevados de** (Chile-C)	1507-07=	2	
	1898	01	?	**Tongariro [Ngauruhoe]** (New Zeal)	0401-08=	2	
	1898	0114	6*a*	**Fournaise, Piton de la** (Indian O.)	0303-02=	2	
	1898	0205	10*a*	**Lamongan** (Java)	0603-32=	2	
	1898	0208	31	**Kirishima** (Kyushu-Japan)	0802-09=	2	
	1898	0220	?	**Kliuchevskoi** (Kamchatka)	1000-26=	2	
	1898	0223	?	**Semeru** (Java)	0603-30=	2	
	1898	0326	?	**Ambrym** (Vanuatu-SW Pacific)	0507-04=	1?	
	1898	04	91*q*	**Mutnovsky** (Kamchatka)	1000-06=	2	-/6
?	*1898*	*0405*	*?*	*St. Helens (US-Washington)*	1201-05-		
	1898	0408	>3yr	**Reventador** (Ecuador)	1502-01=	3	
	1898	0502	791*w*?	**Colo [Una Una]** (Sulawesi-Indonesia)	0606-01=	3?	-/7
	1898	0514	14*a*?	**Gamalama** (Halmahera-Indonesia)	0608-06=	2	
	1898	0603	51*a*?	**Lopevi** (Vanuatu-SW Pacific)	0507-05=	2?	
	1898	08 ?	243*p*>	**Aso** (Kyushu-Japan)	0802-11=	2	
	1898	*0824*	....	*Stromboli (Italy)*	0101-04=	*2*	*4/-*
	1898	*0906*	....	*Doña Juana (Colombia)*	1501-07=	*2*	
?	*1898*	*1108*	*?*	*Atlin Volc Field (Canada)*	1200-03-		
	1898	1126	?	**Fournaise, Piton de la** (Indian O.)	0303-02=	2	
	1898	1203?	3*a*?	**Nipesotsu-Maruyama** (Hokkaido)	0805-061	2	-/6
	1898	1226	4*a*	**Kirishima** (Kyushu-Japan)	0802-09=	2	
	1898	1229	>3yr	**Poás** (Costa Rica)	1405-04=	1	
	1899	*Cont*	....	*Vesuvius (Italy)*	0101-02=	*2*	*8/8*
	1899	*Cont*	....	*Stromboli (Italy)*	0101-04=	*1*	*4/-*
	1899	*Cont*	....	*Victory (New Guinea)*	0503-03=	*1*	
	1899	*Cont*	....	*Kuwae [Karua] (Vanuatu-SW Pac)*	0507-07=	*2*	
	1899	*Cont*	....	*Yasur (Vanuatu-SW Pacific)*	0507-10=	*2*	
	1899	*Cont*	....	*Colo [Una Una] (Sulawesi-Indonesia)*	0606-01=	*2*	*-/7*
	1899	*Cont*	....	*Aso (Kyushu-Japan)*	0802-11=	*2*	
	1899	*Cont*	....	*Colima (México)*	1401-04=	*2*	
	1899	*Cont*	....	*Poás (Costa Rica)*	1405-04=	*1*	
	1899	*Cont*	....	*Reventador (Ecuador)*	1502-01=	*2*	
	1899	*Cont*	....	*Sangay (Ecuador)*	1502-09=	*2*	
	1899	*Cont*	....	*Láscar (Chile-N)*	1505-10=	*2*	
	1899	....	?	**Nyiragongo** (Africa-C)	0203-03=	1	
	1899 a	....	?	**Manam** (New Guinea-NE of)	0501-02=	2?	
	1899	....	?	**Bagana** (Bougainville-SW Pacific)	0505-02=		
	1899	....	?	**Karangetang [Api Siau]** (Sangihe Is	0607-02=	2	
?	*1899 ?*	....	*?*	*Kasatochi (Aleutian Is)*	1101-13-		
	1899	....	?	**Okmok** (Aleutian Is)	1101-29-	3	
?	*1899*	....	*?*	*Shishaldin (Aleutian Is)*	1101-36-		
	1899	....	?	**Puracé** (Colombia)	1501-06=	2	
	1899	0112	?	**Buckle Island** (Antarctica)	1900-01=	2	
	1899	0117	73*a*?	**Semeru** (Java)	0603-30=	2	
	1899	02	?	**Nyamuragira** (Africa-C)	0203-02=	1	
	1899	0213	155*a*>	**Fournaise, Piton de la** (Indian O.)	0303-02=	2	
?	*1899*	*03*	*30p*	*Sirung (Lesser Sunda Is)*	0604-27=	*2*	
	1899	0311	?	**Asama** (Honshu-Japan)	0803-11=	2	
	1899	0501	13*a*	**Gede** (Java)	0603-06=	2	
	1899	0602	?	**Lewotolo** (Lesser Sunda Is)	0604-23=	2	
	1899	0701	22*a*	**Mauna Loa** (Hawaiian Is)	1302-02=	1	7/-
	1899	0710	28*a*	**Asama** (Honshu-Japan)	0803-11=	2	
	1899	0719	17	**Etna** (Italy)	0101-06=	3	
	1899	0728	203*a*	**Kirishima** (Kyushu-Japan)	0802-09=	2	
	1899	0811	?	**Semeru** (Java)	0603-30=	2	
	1899	0824	80*a*	**Adatara** (Honshu-Japan)	0803-17=	2	
	1899	0903	?	**Wrangell** (Alaska-E)	1105-02-	2?	
?	*1899*	*0924*	*1a*	*Sakura-jima (Kyushu-Japan)*	0802-08=	*1?*	
	1899	1113	....	**Doña Juana** (Colombia)	1501-07=	4	
	1899	*1115*	*>3yr*	*Etna (Italy)*	0101-06=	*1*	
	1899	1122	7*a*	**Negro, Cerro** (Nicaragua)	1404-07=	2	-/6
	1899	12	?	**Semeru** (Java)	0603-30=	2	
	1899	1231	75*m*	**Izalco** (El Salvador)	1403-03=	2	

1900

START YEAR	M-Dy	Duration	VOLCANO NAME (Subregion)	NUMBER	VEI	Vol L/T
1900	*Cont*	....	*Etna (Italy)*	0101-06=	*1*	
1900	*Cont*	....	*Victory (New Guinea)*	0503-03=	*1*	
1900	*Cont*	....	*Kuwae [Karua] (Vanuatu-SW Pac)*	0507-07=	*2*	
1900	*Cont*	....	*Yasur (Vanuatu-SW Pacific)*	0507-10=	*2*	
1900	*Cont*	....	*Colo [Una Una] (Sulawesi-Indonesia)*	0606-01=	*2*	*-/7*
1900	*Cont*	....	*Kirishima (Kyushu-Japan)*	0802-09=	*2*	
1900	*Cont*	....	*Colima (México)*	1401-04=	*2*	
1900	*Cont*	....	*Izalco (El Salvador)*	1403-03=	*2*	

A. Lacroix (Museum of Natural History, Paris)

A pyroclastic flow, smaller but similiar to the one that destroyed the city of St. Pierre on Martinique on May 8, 1902, sweeps down the flanks of Mount Pelée volcano on December 16, 1902. A towering column of ash and steam rises above the advancing pyroclastic flow, which was formed by collapse of gas-rich rocks on a growing lava dome in the summit crater.

START YEAR	M-Dy	Duration	VOLCANO NAME (Subregion)	NUMBER	VEI	Vol L/T
1900	Cont	....	Poás (Costa Rica)	1405-04=	1	
1900	Cont	....	Doña Juana (Colombia)	1501-07=	2	
1900	Cont	....	Reventador (Ecuador)	1502-01=	2	
1900	Cont	....	Sangay (Ecuador)	1502-09=	2	
1900	Cont	....	Láscar (Chile-N)	1505-10=	2	
? 1900 ?	....	?	Dubbi (Ethiopia)	0201-10=		
1900 ?	....	?	**Tullu Moje** (Ethiopia)	0201-25-		
1900	....	?	**Nyiragongo** (Africa-C)	0203-03=	1	
1900	....	?	**Langila** (New Britain-SW Pac)	0502-01=	2	
1900	....	?	**Karangetang [Api Siau]** (Sangihe Is	0607-02=	2	
1900	....	?	**Didicas** (Luzon-N of)	0704-02=	0?	
1900 ?	....	325w?	**Farallon de Pajaros** (Mariana Is-Pac)	0804-14=	2	
? 1900	....	?	Mendeleev (Kuril Is)	0900-02=	2?	
1900 j	....	?	**Chirinkotan** (Kuril Is)	0900-26=		
? 1900	....	?	Tungurahua (Ecuador)	1502-08=	2?	
1900	....	?	**Huequi** (Chile-S)	1508-03=	2	
T 1900 j	....	?	**Michael** (Antarctica)	1900-09=	0	
1900	01	>3yr	**Okataina [Waimangu]** (New Zeal)	0401-05=	1	
1900	0122	631m	**Asama** (Honshu-Japan)	0803-11=	2	
? 1900	02	?	Erebus (Antarctica)	1900-02=	2	
1900	0301	5a	**Mayon** (Luzon-Philippines)	0703-03=	2	
1900	0329	13a>	**Semeru** (Java)	0603-30=	2	
1900	0410	....	Stromboli (Italy)	0101-04=	2	4/-
? 1900	05	20m	Gamalama (Halmahera-Indonesia)	0608-06=	1	
1900	0509	....	Vesuvius (Italy)	0101-02=	2	8/8
1900	0511	19a	**Fournaise, Piton de la** (Indian O.)	0303-02=	0	
1900	06 <	?	**Wrangell** (Alaska-E)	1105-02-	2?	
1900	0604	<1	**Dempo** (Sumatra)	0601-23=	2	
1900	0717	<1	**Adatara** (Honshu-Japan)	0803-17=	2	-/6
1900	1001	<1	**Kusatsu-Shirane** (Honshu-Japan)	0803-12=	1	
1900	1026	1a	**Dempo** (Sumatra)	0601-23=	2	
1900	1130	1	**Rinjani** (Lesser Sunda Is)	0604-03=	2	
1901	Cont	....	Vesuvius (Italy)	0101-02=	2	8/8
1901	Cont	....	Etna (Italy)	0101-06=	1	
1901	Cont	....	Okataina [Waimangu] (New Zeal)	0401-05=	2	
1901	Cont	....	Victory (New Guinea)	0503-03=	1	
1901	Cont	....	Kuwae [Karua] (Vanuatu-SW Pac)	0507-07=	2	
1901	Cont	....	Yasur (Vanuatu-SW Pacific)	0507-10=	2	
1901	Cont	....	Asama (Honshu-Japan)	0803-11=	2	
1901	Cont	....	Farallon de Pajaros (Mariana Is-Pac)	0804-14=	2	
1901	Cont	....	Poás (Costa Rica)	1405-04=	1	
1901	Cont	....	Doña Juana (Colombia)	1501-07=	2	
1901	Cont	....	Reventador (Ecuador)	1502-01=	2	
1901	Cont	....	Sangay (Ecuador)	1502-09=	2	
1901	....	?	**Nyamuragira** (Africa-C)	0203-02=	2	7/6
1901	....	?	**Nyiragongo** (Africa-C)	0203-03=	1	
? 1901	....	365y?	Manam (New Guinea-NE of)	0501-02=		
1901	....	?	**Dukono** (Halmahera-Indonesia)	0608-01=	2	
1901	....	?	**Ilyinsky** (Kamchatka)	1000-03=	3	
1901	....	?	**Shishaldin** (Aleutian Is)	1101-36-		
1901	....	?	**Pavlof** (Alaska Peninsula)	1102-03-	2?	
1901	....	....	Colima (México)	1401-04=	1	
1901	0129	1a>	**Semeru** (Java)	0603-30=	2	
1901	0204	?	**Soputan** (Sulawesi-Indonesia)	0606-03=	2	
1901	0221	4a	**Fournaise, Piton de la** (Indian O.)	0303-02=	2	
1901	0308	....	Stromboli (Italy)	0101-04=	2	4/-
1901	04	?	**Tupungatito** (Chile-C)	1507-01=	2	
1901	0518	?	**Banda Api** (Banda Sea)	0605-09=	2	
1901	0522	1a	**Kelut** (Java)	0603-28=	3	-/6
1901	0525	114m	**San Pedro** (Chile-N)	1505-07=	2	
1901	0601	<1	**Rinjani** (Lesser Sunda Is)	0604-03=	2	
1901	0704	2a	**Fournaise, Piton de la** (Indian O.)	0303-02=	2	
1901	0707	6a	**Avachinsky** (Kamchatka)	1000-10=	2	-/6
1901	1229	....	Stromboli (Italy)	0101-04=	2	4/-
1902	Cont	....	Vesuvius (Italy)	0101-02=	2	8/8
1902	Cont	....	Stromboli (Italy)	0101-04=	1	4/-
1902	Cont	....	Etna (Italy)	0101-06=	1	
1902	Cont	....	Okataina [Waimangu] (New Zeal)	0401-05=	2	
? 1902	Cont	....	Manam (New Guinea-NE of)	0501-02=		
1902	Cont	....	Victory (New Guinea)	0503-03=	1	
1902	Cont	....	Yasur (Vanuatu-SW Pacific)	0507-10=	2	
1902	Cont	....	Poás (Costa Rica)	1405-04=	1	
1902	Cont	....	Doña Juana (Colombia)	1501-07=	2	
1902	Cont	....	Reventador (Ecuador)	1502-01=	2	
1902	Cont	....	Sangay (Ecuador)	1502-09=	2	
1902	....	?	**Nyiragongo** (Africa-C)	0203-03=	1	
1902	....	365y	**Salak** (Java)	0603-05=	2	
1902	....	?	**Mayon** (Luzon-Philippines)	0703-03=	1	
1902	....	?	**Akita-Komaga-take** (Honshu-Japan)	0803-23=	1?	
1902	....	?	**Seguam** (Aleutian Is)	1101-18-	3	
1902	....	....	Colima (México)	1401-04=	1	
1902	....	?	**Concepción** (Nicaragua)	1404-12=	2	
1902 ?	....	?	**Puracé** (Colombia)	1501-06=	2	
1902	....	?	**Láscar** (Chile-N)	1505-10=	2?	
? 1902	01	?	Taftan (Iran)	0302-05-		
1902	0118	?	**Redoubt** (Alaska-SW)	1103-03-	3	
1902	0131	?	**Kanlaon** (Philippines-C)	0702-02=	2	
1902	0203	<1	**Merapi** (Java)	0603-25=	1	
1902	0207	<1	**Asama** (Honshu-Japan)	0803-11=	2	
1902	0214<	7g?	**Kilauea** (Hawaiian Is)	1302-01-	0	
1902	0216	11a>	**Raung** (Java)	0603-34=	2	
? 1902	0320	?	Banda Api (Banda Sea)	0605-09=		
1902	0331p	?	**Momotombo** (Nicaragua)	1404-09=	2?	
1902	0422?	?	**Nyamuragira** (Africa-C)	0203-02=	0	
1902	0423	>3yr	Pelée (W Indies)	1600-12=	2	
1902	0501	24a	**Sundoro** (Java)	0603-21=	1	
1902	0502	....	**Pelée** (W Indies)	1600-12=	4	8/8
1902	0506	298a	**Soufrière St. Vincent** (W Indies)	1600-15=	4?	-/8
1902	0507	1a	**San Jorge** (Azores)	1802-03=	0	
1902	0508	....	Pelée (W Indies)	1600-12=	4	
1902	0510	233a	**Izalco** (El Salvador)	1403-03=	2	
@ 1902	06	153p	**Yucamane** (Perú)	1504-05-	2	
1902	0603	275e	**Kilauea** (Hawaiian Is)	1302-01-	0	
? 1902	0622	?	Rincón de la Vieja (Costa Rica)	1405-02=	2?	
1902	0715	71a	**Kusatsu-Shirane** (Honshu-Japan)	0803-12=	1	-/5
1902	0715q	?	**Wrangell** (Alaska-E)	1105-02-	2	
1902	0715	488m	**Masaya** (Nicaragua)	1404-10=	2	
1902	0805	15a?	**Asama** (Honshu-Japan)	0803-11=	2	
1902	0807	14a	**Tori-shima** (Izu Is-Japan)	0804-09=	3	-/7
1902	0813	5a	**Fournaise, Piton de la** (Indian O.)	0303-02=	2	
1902	1013	....	Soufrière St. Vincent (W Indies)	1600-15=	3?	-/8
1902	1024	19a	**Santa María** (Guatemala)	1402-03=	**6**?	-/**10**
1902	1030	18d	**Savai'i** (Samoa-SW Pacific)	0404-04=	1	
1902	12	551n	**Merapi** (Java)	0603-25=	2	6/6
1902	12	393m	Grímsvötn [Thordarhyrna] (Iceland.	1703-01=	2?	8/-
@ 1902	12	182p	**Bárdarbunga** (Iceland-NE)	1703-03=	2?	
1903	Cont	....	Etna (Italy)	0101-06=	1	
1903	Cont	....	Okataina [Waimangu] (New Zeal)	0401-05=	2	
1903	Cont	....	Victory (New Guinea)	0503-03=	1	
1903	Cont	....	Yasur (Vanuatu-SW Pacific)	0507-10=	2	
1903	Cont	....	Salak (Java)	0603-05=	2	
1903	Cont	....	Merapi (Java)	0603-25=	2	6/6
1903	Cont	....	Masaya (Nicaragua)	1404-10=	2	
1903	Cont	....	Poás (Costa Rica)	1405-04=	1	
1903	Cont	....	Doña Juana (Colombia)	1501-07=	2	
1903	Cont	....	Reventador (Ecuador)	1502-01=	2	
1903	Cont	....	Pelée (W Indies)	1600-12=	2	
@ 1903	Cont	....	Bárdarbunga (Iceland-NE)	1703-03=	2?	
? 1903	....	?	Erta Ale (Ethiopia)	0201-08=	2	
1903	....	?	**Santa Isabel** (Africa-W)	0204-004		
1903 ?	....	?	**Fournaise, Piton de la** (Indian O.)	0303-02=	0	
1903	....	?	**Ruapehu** (New Zealand)	0401-10=	2	
1903	....	?	**Hunter Island** (SW Pacific)	0508-02=	0	
? 1903	....	?	Kusatsu-Shirane (Honshu-Japan)	0803-12=		
1903	....	>3yr	**Santa María** (Guatemala)	1402-03=	2	
? 1903	....	?	Soufrière Guadeloupe (W Indies)	1600-06=	2	
? 1903	01	?	Azul, Cerro (Chile-C)	1507-06=	2?	
1903	0101	....	Stromboli (Italy)	0101-04=	2	4/-
1903	0101*	?	**Erebus** (Antarctica)	1900-02=	0	
1903	0215	181m	**Colima** (México)	1401-04=	3	
1903	0315e	164j?	**Iwo-Tori-shima** (Ryukyu Is)	0802-02=	2	
1903	0321	....	Soufrière St. Vincent (W Indies)	1600-15=	3?	-/8
1903	0326	81m	**Semeru** (Java)	0603-30=	2	
1903	04	?	**Taal** (Luzon-Philippines)	0703-07=	2	
1903	0415q	?	**Changbaishan** (China-E)	1005-06-		
1903	0512	2a	**Llaima** (Chile-C)	1507-11=	2	
? 1903	0528	33a	Asama (Honshu-Japan)	0803-11=	2	
1903	0528	....	**Grímsvötn [Thordarhyrna]** (Iceland	1703-01=	4	8/-
1903	06	....	Sangay (Ecuador)	1502-09=	3	
1903	0713	....	Sangay (Ecuador)	1502-09=	3	
1903	0827	....	Vesuvius (Italy)	0101-02=	2	8/8
1903	0829	88a	**Kirishima** (Kyushu-Japan)	0802-09=	2	
1903	0901	97a?	**Mauna Loa** (Hawaiian Is)	1302-02=	0	7/-
? 1903	0915	?	St. Helens (US-Washington)	1201-05-		
1903	0926	446m	Cotopaxi (Ecuador)	1502-05=	2	
1903	1017	4a	**Sundoro** (Java)	0603-21=	2	
1903	11	475m	**Izalco** (El Salvador)	1403-03=	2	
1903	1111	....	Stromboli (Italy)	0101-04=	2	4/-
1903	1125	46a	**Kilauea** (Hawaiian Is)	1302-01-	0	
1903	1128	48m	**Raung** (Java)	0603-34=	2	
1903	1208	?	**Nila** (Banda Sea)	0605-06=	2	
? 1903	1208	?	Ollagüe (Chile-N)	1505-06=		
? 1903	1209	<1	Ranau (Sumatra)	0601-251		
1904	Cont	....	Vesuvius (Italy)	0101-02=	2	8/8
1904	Cont	....	Etna (Italy)	0101-06=	1	
1904	Cont	....	Okataina [Waimangu] (New Zeal)	0401-05=	2	
1904	Cont	....	Victory (New Guinea)	0503-03=	1	
1904	Cont	....	Yasur (Vanuatu-SW Pacific)	0507-10=	2	
1904	Cont	....	Raung (Java)	0603-34=	2	
1904	Cont	....	Kilauea (Hawaiian Is)	1302-01-	0	
1904	Cont	....	Santa María (Guatemala)	1402-03=	2	
1904	Cont	....	Izalco (El Salvador)	1403-03=	2	
1904	Cont	....	Doña Juana (Colombia)	1501-07=	2	
1904	Cont	....	Reventador (Ecuador)	1502-01=	2	

START YEAR	M-Dy	Duration	VOLCANO NAME (Subregion)	NUMBER	VEI	Vol L/T
1904	Cont	....	*Sangay (Ecuador)*	1502-09=	2	
1904	Cont	....	*Pelée (W Indies)*	1600-12=	2	
1904	Cont	....	*Grímsvötn [Thordarhyrna] (Iceland*	1703-01=	2	8/-
1904	....	?	**Lengai, Ol Doinyo** (Africa-E)	0202-12=	0	
1904	....	?	**Batur** (Lesser Sunda Is)	0604-01=	2	
1904	....	?	**Iliboleng** (Lesser Sunda Is)	0604-22=	2	
1904	....	?	**Kanlaon** (Philippines-C)	0702-02=	2	
1904	....	?	**Tolbachik** (Kamchatka)	1000-24=	2	
1904	....	?	**Kanaga** (Aleutian Is)	1101-11-	0	
? 1904	....	?	*Great Sitkin (Aleutian Is)*	1101-12-		
? 1904	....	?	*Iskut-Unuk River Cones (Canada)*	1200-09-		
1904	....	730y	**Colima** (México)	1401-04=	1?	
1904	....	881w	**Santiago** (Galápagos)	1503-09=	0	
1904	....	?	**Villarrica** (Chile-C)	1507-12=	2	
1904	0102	14a	**Semeru** (Java)	0603-30=	2	
1904	0112	14a?	**Santa Ana** (El Salvador)	1403-02=	2	
1904	0130	....	*Merapi (Java)*	0603-25=	2	6/6
1904	0131p	134p>	**Kliuchevskoi** (Kamchatka)	1000-26=	2	
1904	0225	50m	**Karthala** (Indian O.-W)	0303-01=	2	
1904	0319	....	*Stromboli (Italy)*	0101-04=	2	4/-
1904	04	31m?	**Nyamuragira** (Africa-C)	0203-02=	2	7/7
1904	04	91n	**Taal** (Luzon-Philippines)	0703-07=	1	
1904	0402	85a>	**Mutnovsky** (Kamchatka)	1000-06=	2	
1904	0417	<1	**Banua Wuhu** (Sangihe Is-Indonesia)	0607-03=	2	
1904	0418	<1	**Marapi** (Sumatra)	0601-14=	1	
1904	0422	395a	**Ruang** (Sangihe Is-Indonesia)	0607-01=	3?	6/-
1904	0430p	?	**Manam** (New Guinea-NE of)	0501-02=		
1904	05	31p	**Masaya** (Nicaragua)	1404-10=	2	
1904	0603	?	**Teon** (Banda Sea)	0605-05=	2	
1904	07	....	*Poás (Costa Rica)*	1405-04=	1	
1904	0714	26a	**Slamet** (Java)	0603-18=	2	
1904	0804	<1	**Asama** (Honshu-Japan)	0803-11=	2	
1904	0809	435a>	*Lolobau (New Britain-SW Pac)*	0502-13=	2	
1904	0819	59a	**Fournaise, Piton de la** (Indian O.)	0303-02=	2	
1904	0822	....	*Stromboli (Italy)*	0101-04=	2	4/-
1904	0827	?	**Banua Wuhu** (Sangihe Is-Indonesia)	0607-03=	2	
1904	1004<	?	**Mahawu** (Sulawesi-Indonesia)	0606-11=	2	
1904	1026	<1	**Manam** (New Guinea-NE of)	0501-02=	3?	
? 1904	1101r	?	*Erta Ale (Ethiopia)*	0201-08=	2	
1904	1114	183a?	**Fukutoku-Okanoba** (Volcano Is-Japan	0804-13=	3	8/8
1904	1114	....	**Cotopaxi** (Ecuador)	1502-05=	3	
1904	1122	?	**Tongariro [Ngauruhoe]** (New Zeal)	0401-08=	2	
1905	Cont	....	*Vesuvius (Italy)*	0101-02=	2	8/8
1905	Cont	....	*Etna (Italy)*	0101-06=	1	
1905	Cont	....	*Victory (New Guinea)*	0503-03=	1	
1905	Cont	....	*Yasur (Vanuatu-SW Pacific)*	0507-10=	2	
1905	Cont	....	*Ruang (Sangihe Is-Indonesia)*	0607-01=	2	6/-
1905	Cont	....	*Fukutoku-Okanoba (Volcano Is-Japan*	0804-13=	2	8/8
1905	Cont	....	*Colima (México)*	1401-04=	1	
1905	Cont	....	*Santa María (Guatemala)*	1402-03=	2	
1905	Cont	....	*Izalco (El Salvador)*	1403-03=	2	
1905	Cont	....	*Doña Juana (Colombia)*	1501-07=	2	
1905	Cont	....	*Reventador (Ecuador)*	1502-01=	2	
1905	Cont	....	*Sangay (Ecuador)*	1502-09=	2	
1905	Cont	....	*Santiago (Galápagos)*	1503-09=	0	
1905	Cont	....	*Pelée (W Indies)*	1600-12=	2	
1905	....	?	**Nyiragongo** (Africa-C)	0203-03=	1	
1905	....	?	**Tongariro [Ngauruhoe]** (New Zeal)	0401-08=	2	
1905	....	....	**Lolobau** (New Britain-SW Pac)	0502-13=	**P**	
1905	....	?	**Dempo** (Sumatra)	0601-23=	0	
1905	....	?	**Batur** (Lesser Sunda Is)	0604-01=	2	
? 1905	....	?	*Asama (Honshu-Japan)*	0803-11=		
1905	....	?	**Zao** (Honshu-Japan)	0803-19=	1?	
1905	....	?	**Shiveluch** (Kamchatka)	1000-27=		
1905	....	?	**Cotopaxi** (Ecuador)	1502-05=	2	
1905 ?	....	?	**Puyehue-Cordón Caulle** (Chile-C)	1507-15=	2	
L 1905 ?	....	?	**Penguin Island** (Antarctica)	1900-031		
1905	01	137m	**Merapi** (Java)	0603-25=	2	-/6
? 1905	01	?	*Socorro (México-Is)*	1401-021	2?	
1905	0116	5a	**Momotombo** (Nicaragua)	1404-09=	2	-/6
1905	0215	1a	**Fournaise, Piton de la** (Indian O.)	0303-02=	2	
1905	0218	5a	**Okataina [Waimangu]** (New Zeal)	0401-05=	1	
1905	0222	417m	**Kilauea** (Hawaiian Is)	1302-01-	0	
1905	0225	....	*Stromboli (Italy)*	0101-04=	2	4/-
1905	0521	<1	**Karangetang [Api Siau]** (Sangihe Is	0607-02=	2	
1905	0608	....	*Poás (Costa Rica)*	1405-04=	1	
1905	0617	<1	**Okataina [Waimangu]** (New Zeal)	0401-05=	1	
1905	0722	65a>	**Nyamuragira** (Africa-C)	0203-02=	2	7/7
1905	0804	>3yr	**Savai'i** (Samoa-SW Pacific)	0404-04=	2	**9**/6
1905	0804	?	**Semeru** (Java)	0603-30=	2	
1905	0819	13a?	**Komaga-take** (Hokkaido-Japan)	0805-02=	2	
1905	0927	....	*Stromboli (Italy)*	0101-04=	2	4/-
1905	10	16m	**Kusatsu-Shirane** (Honshu-Japan)	0803-12=	2	
1905	1028	2a	**Maipo** (Chile-C)	1507-021	2	
1905	11	<1	**Inielika** (Lesser Sunda Is)	0604-09=	2	
1905	1101	?	**Marapi** (Sumatra)	0601-14=	2?	
1905	1106	71a>	**Kanlaon** (Philippines-C)	0702-02=	2	
1906	Cont	....	*Savai'i (Samoa-SW Pacific)*	0404-04=	1	**9**/6
1906	Cont	....	*Victory (New Guinea)*	0503-03=	1	
1906	Cont	....	*Yasur (Vanuatu-SW Pacific)*	0507-10=	2	
1906	Cont	....	*Kanlaon (Philippines-C)*	0702-02=	2	
1906	Cont	....	*Colima (México)*	1401-04=	1	
1906	Cont	....	*Santa María (Guatemala)*	1402-03=	2	
1906	Cont	....	*Poás (Costa Rica)*	1405-04=	1	
1906	Cont	....	*Doña Juana (Colombia)*	1501-07=	2	
1906	Cont	....	*Reventador (Ecuador)*	1502-01=	2	
1906	Cont	....	*Sangay (Ecuador)*	1502-09=	2	
1906	Cont	....	*Santiago (Galápagos)*	1503-09=	0	
? 1906	....	?	*Barrier, The (Africa-E)*	0202-03=		
? 1906	....	?	*Nyamuragira (Africa-C)*	0203-02=	1	
1906	....	?	**Nyiragongo** (Africa-C)	0203-03=	1	
? 1906	....	365y	*Kuchinoerabu-jima (Ryukyu Is)*	0802-05=		
1906	....	?	**Asuncion** (Mariana Is-C Pacific)	0804-15=	2	
1906	....	?	**Nemo Peak** (Kuril Is)	0900-32=	2	
1906	....	>3yr	*Pavlof (Alaska Peninsula)*	1102-03-	2?	
1906	....	?	**Puracé** (Colombia)	1501-06=	2	
1906	....	?	**Azul, Cerro** (Chile-C)	1507-06=	2	
1906	....	?	**Calbuco** (Chile-S)	1508-02=	2	
1906	....	365y	**Huequi** (Chile-S)	1508-03=	2	
1906	01	30p	**Tofua** (Tonga-SW Pacific)	0403-06=	2	
1906	0102	7a>	**Masaya** (Nicaragua)	1404-10=	2	
1906	0105	....	**Etna** (Italy)	0101-06=	2	
1906	0119	....	*Stromboli (Italy)*	0101-04=	2	4/-
1906	0126e	387e	*Merapi (Java)*	0603-25=	1	7/6
1906	0221	<1	**Okataina [Waimangu]** (New Zeal)	0401-05=	1	
1906	0228	....	**Merapi** (Java)	0603-25=	2	7/6
1906	03	?	**Tongariro [Ngauruhoe]** (New Zeal)	0401-08=	2	
1906	03	?	**Fonualei** (Tonga-SW Pacific)	0403-10=		
1906	0301p	550p	*Bogoslof (Aleutian Is)*	1101-30-	1	6/8
1906	0315	?	**Ruapehu** (New Zealand)	0401-10=	2	
1906	0406	<1	**Asama** (Honshu-Japan)	0803-11=	2	
1906	0407	7a	**Bayonnaise Rocks** (Izu Is-Japan)	0804-07=	1	
1906	0408	....	**Vesuvius** (Italy)	0101-02=	4?	8/8
1906	0422	245m	**Villarrica** (Chile-C)	1507-12=	2	
1906	0429	?	**Rinjani** (Lesser Sunda Is)	0604-03=	1?	
1906	05	?	**Erta Ale** (Ethiopia)	0201-08=	0	
1906	05	?	**Kanaga** (Aleutian Is)	1101-11-		
1906	0607	?	**Aso** (Kyushu-Japan)	0802-11=	3	
1906	0617	90m	**Soputan** (Sulawesi-Indonesia)	0606-03=	2	
1906	0711	....	*Stromboli (Italy)*	0101-04=	2	4/-
1906	0806	131m	**Chillán, Nevados de** (Chile-C)	1507-07=	2	
1906	0821	29a	**Cotopaxi** (Ecuador)	1502-05=	2	
1906	0922	89a	**Sundoro** (Java)	0603-21=	2	
1906	0925	235a	**Tengger Caldera [Bromo]** (Java)	0603-31=	2	
1906	10	?	**Ubinas** (Perú)	1504-02=	2	
1906	12	?	**Tofua** (Tonga-SW Pacific)	0403-06=	2	
1906	1202	>3yr	**Kilauea** (Hawaiian Is)	1302-01-	0	
1907	Cont	....	*Etna (Italy)*	0101-06=	1	
1907	Cont	....	*Savai'i (Samoa-SW Pacific)*	0404-04=	1	**9**/6
1907	Cont	....	*Victory (New Guinea)*	0503-03=	1	
1907	Cont	....	*Yasur (Vanuatu-SW Pacific)*	0507-10=	2	
1907	Cont	....	*Merapi (Java)*	0603-25=	2	7/6
? 1907	Cont	....	*Kuchinoerabu-jima (Ryukyu Is)*	0802-05=		
1907	Cont	....	*Pavlof (Alaska Peninsula)*	1102-03-	2?	
1907	Cont	....	*Kilauea (Hawaiian Is)*	1302-01-	0	
1907	Cont	....	*Santa María (Guatemala)*	1402-03=	2	
1907	Cont	....	*Poás (Costa Rica)*	1405-04=	1	
1907	Cont	....	*Sangay (Ecuador)*	1502-09=	2	
1907	Cont	....	*Huequi (Chile-S)*	1508-03=	2	
1907 c	....	>3yr	**Lengai, Ol Doinyo** (Africa-E)	0202-12=	0	
? 1907	....	?	*Manam (New Guinea-NE of)*	0501-02=		
1907	....	?	**Langila** (New Britain-SW Pac)	0502-01=	2	
1907	....	?	**Kaba** (Sumatra)	0601-22=	2	
1907	....	?	**Babuyan Claro** (Luzon-N of)	0704-03=	2	
? 1907	....	?	*Kiska (Aleutian Is)*	1101-02-	2?	
1907	....	?	**Korovin** (Aleutian Is)	1101-161		
1907	....	?	**Makushin** (Aleutian Is)	1101-31-		
1907	....	?	**Akutan** (Aleutian Is)	1101-32-		
1907	....	?	**Ubinas** (Perú)	1504-02=	2	
1907	....	?	**Chillán, Nevados de** (Chile-C)	1507-07=	1	
1907	....	257m	**Llaima** (Chile-C)	1507-11=	2	
1907	....	?	**San Jorge** (Azores)	1802-03=	0	
1907	0107	3a	**Semeru** (Java)	0603-30=	2	
1907	0109	15a>	**Mauna Loa** (Hawaiian Is)	1302-02=	0	7/-
1907	0111	....	*Stromboli (Italy)*	0101-04=	2	4/-
1907	0118	69a	**Asama** (Honshu-Japan)	0803-11=	2	
1907	02	91p	**Tongariro [Ngauruhoe]** (New Zeal)	0401-08=	2	
1907	0215	?	**Tupungatito** (Chile-C)	1507-01=	2	
1907	0328?	?	**Ksudach** (Kamchatka)	1000-05=	**5**	-/**9**
1907	04	31m	**Nyamuragira** (Africa-C)	0203-02=	1	
? 1907	0401<	?	*Wrangell (Alaska-E)*	1105-02-		
1907	0401	?	**Monaco Bank** (Azores)	1802-11=	0	
1907	0409	311m>	**Carrán-Los Venados** (Chile-C)	1507-14=	3	
1907	0422	?	**Calbuco** (Chile-S)	1508-02=	2?	

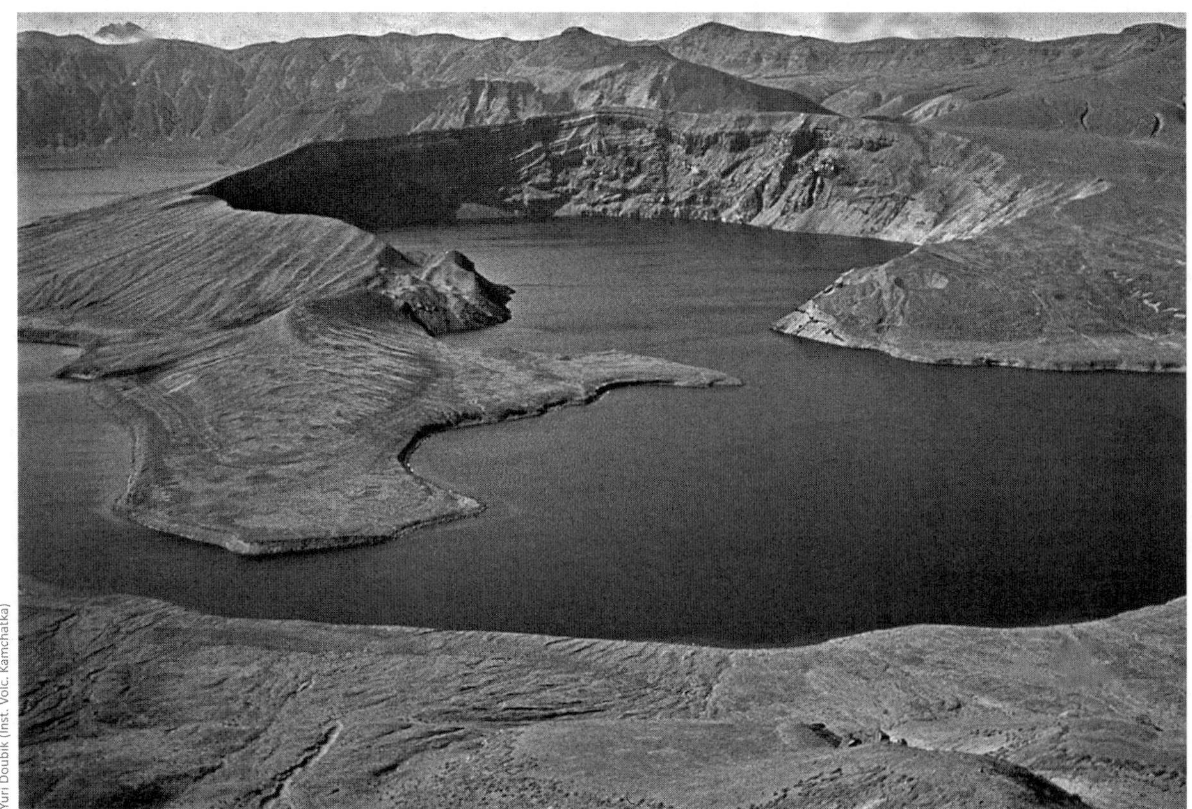

Yuri Doubik (Inst. Volc. Kamchatka)

One of the largest 20th-century eruptions in Kamchatka took place in March 1907 from Stubel Crater (center) within the Ksudach caldera. Plinian explosions depositing 1.5 km³ of ash as far as 1000 km to the NNE were followed by a laterally directed explosion accompanying destruction of the Stubel cone. The eruption formed a chain of three craters and lowered the height of Stubel cone by about 650 m.

START YEAR	M-Dy	Duration	VOLCANO NAME (Subregion)	NUMBER	VEI	Vol L/T
1907	*0427*	....	*Stromboli (Italy)*	0101-04=	*3*	*4/-*
1907	0505d	21*d?*	**Villarrica** (Chile-C)	1507-12=	2	
1907	06	50*m>*	**Alayta** (Ethiopia)	0201-112	2	
1907	06	?	**Cotopaxi** (Ecuador)	1502-05=	2	
1907	0605	20*a?*	**Soputan** (Sulawesi-Indonesia)	0606-03=	2	
1907	07	?	**Unnamed** (Tonga-SW Pacific)	0403-01=	0	
1907	0709<	?	**Semeru** (Java)	0603-30=	2	
1907	0728	?	**Azul, Cerro** (Chile-C)	1507-06=	2	
1907	08	?	**Kliuchevskoi** (Kamchatka)	1000-26=	2	
1907	0824	<1	**Asama** (Honshu-Japan)	0803-11=	2	
1907	0828	?	**Tengger Caldera [Bromo]** (Java)	0603-31=	2	
? 1907	*0828*	*?*	*Hood (US-Oregon)*	1202-01-		
1907	09	>3yr	**Concepción** (Nicaragua)	1404-12=	2	
1907	0901	....	**Bogoslof** (Aleutian Is)	1101-30-	3	6/8
1907	0928	32*a*	**Lewotobi** (Lesser Sunda Is)	0604-18=	3	
1907	11	?	**Tongariro [Ngauruhoe]** (New Zeal)	0401-08=	2	
1907	11	?	**Bam** (New Guinea-NE of)	0501-01=	2	
1907	11	?	**Telica** (Nicaragua)	1404-04=	2	
1907	1107	28*a*	**Nyamuragira** (Africa-C)	0203-02=	3	
1907	1117	3*a*	**Gamalama** (Halmahera-Indonesia)	0608-06=	2	
1907	1129	6*d*	**Fournaise, Piton de la** (Indian O.)	0303-02=	0	
1907	1208	541*a*	**Yake-dake** (Honshu-Japan)	0803-07=	2	
1907	1212	?	**Aso** (Kyushu-Japan)	0802-11=	2	
1907	1214	61*a*	**Tengger Caldera [Bromo]** (Java)	0603-31=	2	
1907	1217	272*m*	**Marapi** (Sumatra)	0601-14=	2?	
1908	*Cont*	....	*Lengai, Ol Doinyo (Africa-E)*	0202-12=	*0*	
1908	*Cont*	....	*Savai'i (Samoa-SW Pacific)*	0404-04=	*1*	***9/6***
1908	*Cont*	....	*Victory (New Guinea)*	0503-03=	*1*	
1908	*Cont*	....	*Yasur (Vanuatu-SW Pacific)*	0507-10=	*2*	
1908	*Cont*	....	*Marapi (Sumatra)*	0601-14=	*2*	
1908	*Cont*	....	*Tengger Caldera [Bromo] (Java)*	0603-31=	*2*	
1908	*Cont*	....	*Yake-dake (Honshu-Japan)*	0803-07=	*2*	
1908	*Cont*	....	*Pavlof (Alaska Peninsula)*	1102-03-	*2?*	
1908	*Cont*	....	*Kilauea (Hawaiian Is)*	1302-01-	*0*	
1908	*Cont*	....	*Santa María (Guatemala)*	1402-03=	*2*	
1908	*Cont*	....	*Concepción (Nicaragua)*	1404-12=	*2*	
1908	*Cont*	....	*Sangay (Ecuador)*	1502-09=	*2*	
1908	*Cont*	....	*Llaima (Chile-C)*	1507-11=	*2*	
1908	*Cont*	....	*Carrán-Los Venados (Chile-C)*	1507-14=	*3*	
1908	....	?	**Nyamuragira** (Africa-C)	0203-02=		
? 1908	....	*?*	*Fournaise, Piton de la (Indian O.)*	0303-02=	*0*	
? 1908	....	*?*	*Lolobau (New Britain-SW Pac)*	0502-13=		
1908	....	?	**Ambrym** (Vanuatu-SW Pacific)	0507-04=	2?	
1908	....	?	**Lopevi** (Vanuatu-SW Pacific)	0507-05=	2	
1908	....	?	**Merapi** (Java)	0603-25=	1?	
1908	....	?	**Karymsky** (Kamchatka)	1000-13=	2	
? 1908	....	*?*	*Augustine (Alaska-SW)*	1103-01-		
1908	....	>3yr	**Cotopaxi** (Ecuador)	1502-05=	1	
? 1908	....	*?*	*Guallatiri (Chile-N)*	1505-02=		
? 1908	....	*?*	*Maipo (Chile-C)*	1507-021	*2*	
1908 a	....	?	**Reclus** (Chile-S)	1508-063	1?	
1908	01	335*p*	**Semeru** (Java)	0603-30=	2	
? 1908	*0115q*	*?*	*Bogoslof (Aleutian Is)*	1101-30-		
1908	0117	12*a?*	**Aso** (Kyushu-Japan)	0802-11=	2	
1908	0213?	6*a?*	**Asama** (Honshu-Japan)	0803-11=	2	
1908	0216	1*a*	**Dempo** (Sumatra)	0601-23=	2	
1908	0222	?	**Akutan** (Aleutian Is)	1101-32-	0	
1908	03	245*p*	**Erebus** (Antarctica)	1900-02=	2	
1908	0429	2*a*	**Etna** (Italy)	0101-06=	2	6/5
1908	0520	496*a*	**Etna** (Italy)	0101-06=	2	
1908	06	365*p*	**Soputan** (Sulawesi-Indonesia)	0606-03=	2	
1908	0712	?	**Bam** (New Guinea-NE of)	0501-01=	2	
1908	0715	?	**Bagana** (Bougainville-SW Pacific)	0505-02=	2?	
1908	0805	49*a*	**Asama** (Honshu-Japan)	0803-11=	2	
1908	10	259*w?*	**Kerinci** (Sumatra)	0601-17=	2	
1908	1001	<1	**Okataina [Waimangu]** (New Zealand)	0401-05=	1	
1908	1031	42*a?*	**Villarrica** (Chile-C)	1507-12=	2	
? 1908	*11*	*?*	*Zavodovski (Antarctica)*	1900-13=	*1*	
? 1908	*1128*	*8a?*	*White Island (New Zealand)*	0401-04=	*2*	
? 1908	*1201p*	*?*	*Nyiragongo (Africa-C)*	0203-03=		
1908	1218	195*p*	**Colima** (México)	1401-04=	3	
1909	*Cont*	....	*Etna (Italy)*	0101-06=	*2*	
1909	*Cont*	....	*Lengai, Ol Doinyo (Africa-E)*	0202-12=	*0*	
1909	*Cont*	....	*Savai'i (Samoa-SW Pacific)*	0404-04=	*1*	***9/6***
1909	*Cont*	....	*Victory (New Guinea)*	0503-03=	*1*	
1909	*Cont*	....	*Yasur (Vanuatu-SW Pacific)*	0507-10=	*2*	
1909	*Cont*	....	*Kerinci (Sumatra)*	0601-17=	*2*	
1909	*Cont*	....	*Soputan (Sulawesi-Indonesia)*	0606-03=	*2*	
1909	*Cont*	....	*Yake-dake (Honshu-Japan)*	0803-07=	*2*	
1909	*Cont*	....	*Pavlof (Alaska Peninsula)*	1102-03-	*2?*	
1909	*Cont*	....	*Kilauea (Hawaiian Is)*	1302-01-	*0*	
1909	*Cont*	....	*Colima (México)*	1401-04=	*2*	
1909	*Cont*	....	*Santa María (Guatemala)*	1402-03=	*2*	
1909	*Cont*	....	*Concepción (Nicaragua)*	1404-12=	*2*	
1909	*Cont*	....	*Cotopaxi (Ecuador)*	1502-05=	*1*	
1909	*Cont*	....	*Sangay (Ecuador)*	1502-09=	*2*	

START YEAR	M-Dy	Duration	VOLCANO NAME (Subregion)	NUMBER	VEI	Vol L/T
1909	....	>3yr	**Manam** (New Guinea-NE of)	0501-02=	2	
? 1909	....	?	Banahaw (Luzon-Philippines)	0703-05=		
1909	....	?	**Pagan** (Mariana Is-C Pacific)	0804-17=	2	
? 1909	....	?	Irazú (Costa Rica)	1405-06=	2	
1909	....	?	**Fogo** (Cape Verde Is)	1804-01=		
1909	0108	503a	**Lewotobi** (Lesser Sunda Is)	0604-18=	2	
1909	0111	101a	Shikotsu [Tarumai] (Hokkaido)	0805-04=	2	7/-
1909	0112	2a	**Tengger Caldera [Bromo]** (Java)	0603-31=	2	
1909	0129	>3yr	**Asama** (Honshu-Japan)	0803-11=	1	-/5
1909	0201	>3yr	**Merapi** (Java)	0603-25=	1	6/-
1909	03	123p	**Tongariro [Ngauruhoe]** (New Zeal)	0401-08=	2	
1909	03	?	**Calbuco** (Chile-S)	1508-02=	2	
1909	0330	....	**Shikotsu [Tarumai]** (Hokkaido)	0805-04=	3	7/-
1909	04	?	**Fournaise, Piton de la** (Indian O.)	0303-02=	2	
1909	04	?	**Aso** (Kyushu-Japan)	0802-11=	2	
1909	0412	....	Shikotsu [Tarumai] (Hokkaido)	0805-04=	3	7/-
1909	0419	147a	**Bam** (New Guinea-NE of)	0501-01=	2	
1909	0428	48m?	**Cameroon** (Africa-W)	0204-01=	2	6/-
1909	05	15a	**Nyamuragira** (Africa-C)	0203-02=	1?	
1909	0502	<1	**Gede** (Java)	0603-06=	1	
1909	0513	?	**White Island** (New Zealand)	0401-04=	2	
1909	06	?	**Kliuchevskoi** (Kamchatka)	1000-26=	2	
1909	0603	43m	**Sumbing** (Sumatra)	0601-18=	2	
? 1909	0628	?	Ambrym (Vanuatu-SW Pacific)	0507-04=		
? 1909	07	?	Bagana (Bougainville-SW Pacific)	0505-02=		
1909	08	?	**Tinakula** (Santa Cruz Is-SW Pacific)	0506-01=	2	
1909	08	?	**Avachinsky** (Kamchatka)	1000-10=	2	-/6
1909	0819	317w	**Villarrica** (Chile-C)	1507-12=	2	
1909	09	187m	**Semeru** (Java)	0603-30=	2	
1909	09	369m	Bogoslof (Aleutian Is)	1101-30-	1	
1909	1109	?	**Iliboleng** (Lesser Sunda Is)	0604-22=	2	
1909	1118	9a	**Tenerife** (Canary Is)	1803-03-	2	7/-
1909	1130	2a	**Rinjani** (Lesser Sunda Is)	0604-03=	2	
1910	Cont	....	Lengai, Ol Doinyo (Africa-E)	0202-12=	0	
1910	Cont	....	Savai'i (Samoa-SW Pacific)	0404-04=	1	9/6
1910	Cont	....	Manam (New Guinea-NE of)	0501-02=	2	
1910	Cont	....	Victory (New Guinea)	0503-03=	1	
1910	Cont	....	Yasur (Vanuatu-SW Pacific)	0507-10=	2	
1910	Cont	....	Merapi (Java)	0603-25=	1	6/-
1910	Cont	....	Lewotobi (Lesser Sunda Is)	0604-18=	2	
1910	Cont	....	Asama (Honshu-Japan)	0803-11=	1	-/5
1910	Cont	....	Pavlof (Alaska Peninsula)	1102-03-	2?	
1910	Cont	....	Kilauea (Hawaiian Is)	1302-01-	0	
1910	Cont	....	Santa María (Guatemala)	1402-03=	2	
1910	Cont	....	Concepción (Nicaragua)	1404-12=	2	
1910	Cont	....	Cotopaxi (Ecuador)	1502-05=	1	
1910	Cont	....	Sangay (Ecuador)	1502-09=	2	
1910	Cont	....	Villarrica (Chile-C)	1507-12=	2	
M 1910	t	?	**Emuruangogolak** (Africa-E)	0202-051	0	
A 1910	j	?	**Simbo** (Solomon Is-SW Pacific)	0505-05=		
1910	....	?	**Ambrym** (Vanuatu-SW Pacific)	0507-04=	0?	
1910	....	?	**Marapi** (Sumatra)	0601-14=	2?	
1910	....	?	**Iliwerung** (Lesser Sunda Is)	0604-25=	2	
? 1910	....	?	Avachinsky (Kamchatka)	1000-10=		
1910	....	?	**Grímsvötn** (Iceland-NE)	1703-01=		
1910	01	?	**Tongariro [Ngauruhoe]** (New Zeal)	0401-08=	2	
? 1910	01	?	Medicine Lake (US-California)	1203-02-	1?	
1910	0118	3a	**Tengger Caldera [Bromo]** (Java)	0603-31=	2	
1910	0120	....	Semeru (Java)	0603-30=	2	
1910	0125	20m	**Poás** (Costa Rica)	1405-04=	2	-/5
1910	0221	<1	**Etna** (Italy)	0101-06=	1	
1910	03	16m	**Karthala** (Indian O.-W)	0303-01=	1	
1910	03	16m	**Heard** (Indian O.-S)	0304-01=	2	
1910	03	?	**Burney, Monte** (Chile-S)	1508-07=	2	
1910	0323	26a	**Etna** (Italy)	0101-06=	2	7/5
1910	0403	?	**Aso** (Kyushu-Japan)	0802-11=	2	
1910	0407	39m	**Tangkubanparahu** (Java)	0603-09=	2	
1910	0410	?	**Ebulobo** (Lesser Sunda Is)	0604-10=	2	
1910	05	>3yr	Stromboli (Italy)	0101-04=	1	5/-
1910	0618	120m	**Bárdarbunga** (Iceland-NE)	1703-03=	2	
1910	0724	1a	**Okataina [Waimangu]** (New Zeal)	0401-05=	1	
1910	0725	113m	**Usu** (Hokkaido-Japan)	0805-03=	2	-/6
1910	08	?	**Kliuchevskoi** (Kamchatka)	1000-26=	2	
1910	0912	32a	**Poás** (Costa Rica)	1405-04=	1	
1910	0918	....	**Bogoslof** (Aleutian Is)	1101-30-	2	
1910	10	91p	**Tongariro [Ngauruhoe]** (New Zeal)	0401-08=	2	
1910	1026	57a	**Meru** (Africa-E)	0202-16=	2	
1910	1111	19a	**Yake-dake** (Honshu-Japan)	0803-07=	2	
1910	1115 q	?	**Soputan** (Sulawesi-Indonesia)	0606-03=	2	
1910	1116	26a	**Fournaise, Piton de la** (Indian O.)	0303-02=	2	
1910	1116	90m	**Semeru** (Java)	0603-30=	2	
1910	12	10a?	**Oshima** (Izu Is-Japan)	0804-01=	1	-/4
1910	1227	52a	**Etna** (Italy)	0101-06=	2	
1911	Cont	....	Stromboli (Italy)	0101-04=	1	5/-
1911	Cont	....	Tongariro [Ngauruhoe] (New Zeal)	0401-08=	2	
1911	Cont	....	Savai'i (Samoa-SW Pacific)	0404-04=	1	9/6
1911	Cont	....	Manam (New Guinea-NE of)	0501-02=	2	
1911	Cont	....	Victory (New Guinea)	0503-03=	1	
1911	Cont	....	Yasur (Vanuatu-SW Pacific)	0507-10=	2	
1911	Cont	....	Merapi (Java)	0603-25=	1	6/-
1911	Cont	....	Asama (Honshu-Japan)	0803-11=	1	-/5
1911	Cont	....	Kilauea (Hawaiian Is)	1302-01-	0	
1911	Cont	....	Santa María (Guatemala)	1402-03=	2	
1911	Cont	....	Cotopaxi (Ecuador)	1502-05=	1	
1911	Cont	....	Sangay (Ecuador)	1502-09=	2	
1911	....	>3yr	**Pago** (New Britain-SW Pac)	0502-08=	3	
1911	....	365y	**Lolobau** (New Britain-SW Pac)	0502-13=	4	8/8
1911	....	?	**Gamkonora** (Halmahera-Indonesia)	0608-04=	2?	
1911	....	365y	**Aso** (Kyushu-Japan)	0802-11=	2	
1911	....	?	**Karymsky** (Kamchatka)	1000-13=	2	
1911	....	?	**Akutan** (Aleutian Is)	1101-32-	2	
1911	....	365y	**Calbuco** (Chile-S)	1508-02=	2	
1911	0127	12a	Taal (Luzon-Philippines)	0703-07=	2	-/7
1911	0130	....	**Taal** (Luzon-Philippines)	0703-07=	3	-/7
1911	0213	17a	**Sangeang Api** (Lesser Sunda Is)	0604-05=	2	
? 1911	0307	?	Matutum (Mindanao-Philippines)	0701-02=		
1911	0307	?	**Monaco Bank** (Azores)	1802-11=	1	
1911	04	60p	**Erebus** (Antarctica)	1900-02=	2	
1911	0414	518a?	**Wrangell** (Alaska-E)	1105-02-	1	
1911	0506	109a?	**Yake-dake** (Honshu-Japan)	0803-07=	2	
1911	08	42d	**Etna** (Italy)	0101-06=	2	
1911	08	61p	**Nyiragongo** (Africa-C)	0203-03=	1	
1911	08	?	**Unnamed** (Tonga-SW Pacific)	0403-03=	0	
1911	0830	2a	**Ibu** (Halmahera-Indonesia)	0608-03=	2	
1911	09	?	**San Pedro** (Chile-N)	1505-07=	2	
1911	0902	4a	**Gamalama** (Halmahera-Indonesia)	0608-06=	1	
1911	0910	12a	**Etna** (Italy)	0101-06=	1	7/6
? 1911	0930	?	Campi Flegrei Mar Sicilia (Italy)	0101-07=	1?	
1911	10	?	**Erebus** (Antarctica)	1900-02=	2	
1911	11	166p	**Soputan** (Sulawesi-Indonesia)	0606-03=	2	
1911	11	?	**Kliuchevskoi** (Kamchatka)	1000-26=	2	
1911	1102	?	**Marapi** (Sumatra)	0601-14=	2?	
1911	1106	?	**Candlemas Island** (Antarctica)	1900-10=	2	
1911	1108	37m	Semeru (Java)	0603-30=	2	
1911	1115	....	**Semeru** (Java)	0603-30=	3	
1911	1206	....	**Pavlof** (Alaska Peninsula)	1102-03-	3	
1911	1231y	?	**Negra, Sierra** (Galápagos)	1503-05=		
1912	Cont	....	Manam (New Guinea-NE of)	0501-02=	2	
1912	Cont	....	Pago (New Britain-SW Pac)	0502-08=	2	
1912	Cont	....	Lolobau (New Britain-SW Pac)	0502-13=	4	8/8
1912	Cont	....	Victory (New Guinea)	0503-03=	1	
1912	Cont	....	Yasur (Vanuatu-SW Pacific)	0507-10=	2	
1912	Cont	....	Merapi (Java)	0603-25=	1	6/-
1912	Cont	....	Soputan (Sulawesi-Indonesia)	0606-03=	2	
1912	Cont	....	Aso (Kyushu-Japan)	0802-11=	2	
1912	Cont	....	Asama (Honshu-Japan)	0803-11=	1	-/5
1912	Cont	....	Wrangell (Alaska-E)	1105-02-	1	
1912	Cont	....	Kilauea (Hawaiian Is)	1302-01-	0	
1912	Cont	....	Santa María (Guatemala)	1402-03=	2	
1912	Cont	....	Cotopaxi (Ecuador)	1502-05=	1	
1912	Cont	....	Sangay (Ecuador)	1502-09=	2	
1912	Cont	....	Calbuco (Chile-S)	1508-02=	2	
1912	....	?	**Ambrym** (Vanuatu-SW Pacific)	0507-04=		
1912	....	?	**Farallon de Pajaros** (Mariana Is-Pac)	0804-14=	2	
? 1912	....	?	Makushin (Aleutian Is)	1101-31-		
? 1912	....	?	Akutan (Aleutian Is)	1101-32-		
? 1912	....	?	Shishaldin (Aleutian Is)	1101-36-		
1912	....	?	**Maipo** (Chile-C)	1507-021	2?	
1912	....	?	**Llaima** (Chile-C)	1507-11=	2	
1912 e	....	?	**Deception Island** (Antarctica)	1900-03=	3?	
1912	01	?	**Karymsky** (Kamchatka)	1000-13=	2	
1912	0116	>3yr	**Izalco** (El Salvador)	1403-03=	2	
1912	02	30p	**Reventador** (Ecuador)	1502-01=	3	
1912	02	?	**Azul, Cerro** (Chile-C)	1507-06=	2	
1912	0211	217m?	**Yake-dake** (Honshu-Japan)	0803-07=	2	
1912	0223	340a	**Oshima** (Izu Is-Japan)	0804-01=	1	7/5
1912	04	?	**Okataina [Waimangu]** (New Zeal)	0401-05=	1	
1912	04	?	**Sangeang Api** (Lesser Sunda Is)	0604-05=	2	
1912	0429	?	**Hunga Tonga-Hunga Ha'apai**	0403-04=	2	
1912	0606	45a>	**Katmai** (Alaska Peninsula)	1102-17-	3	-/7
1912	0606	131m?	**Novarupta** (Alaska Peninsula)	1102-18-	**6**	**7/10**
1912	0614	?	**Rincón de la Vieja** (Costa Rica)	1405-02=	3	
1912	0722	....	Stromboli (Italy)	0101-04=	2	5/-
1912	0804	14k	**Etna** (Italy)	0101-06=	3	
1912	0828	?	**Semeru** (Java)	0603-30=	2	
1912	1015e	3a	**Niuafo'ou** (Tonga-SW Pacific)	0403-11=	2	
1912	1025	....	Stromboli (Italy)	0101-04=	2	5/-
1912	1203	132m	**Nyamuragira** (Africa-C)	0203-02=	3	7/7
1912	1212	?	**Erebus** (Antarctica)	1900-02=	2	
1913	Cont	....	Stromboli (Italy)	0101-04=	1	5/-
1913	Cont	....	Nyamuragira (Africa-C)	0203-02=	2	7/7
1913	Cont	....	Manam (New Guinea-NE of)	0501-02=	2	
1913	Cont	....	Pago (New Britain-SW Pac)	0502-08=	2	

	START YEAR	M-Dy	Duration	VOLCANO NAME (Subregion)	NUMBER	VEI	Vol L/T
	1913	Cont	....	Victory (New Guinea)	0503-03=	1	
	1913	Cont	....	Yasur (Vanuatu-SW Pacific)	0507-10=	2	
	1913	Cont	....	Asama (Honshu-Japan)	0803-11=	1	-/5
	1913	Cont	....	Oshima (Izu Is-Japan)	0804-01=	1	7/5
	1913	Cont	....	Kilauea (Hawaiian Is)	1302-01-	0	
	1913	Cont	....	Santa María (Guatemala)	1402-03=	2	
	1913	Cont	....	Izalco (El Salvador)	1403-03=	2	
	1913	Cont	....	Cotopaxi (Ecuador)	1502-05=	1	
	1913	Cont	....	Sangay (Ecuador)	1502-09=	2	
	1913	....	?	Bam (New Guinea-NE of)	0501-01=		
	1913	....	....	Merapi (Java)	0603-25=	0	6/-
?	1913	....	?	Babuyan Claro (Luzon-N of)	0704-03=	2	
	1913	....	?	Guallatiri (Chile-N)	1505-02=	2	
	1913	....	?	Isluga (Chile-N)	1505-03=	2	
	1913	01	?	Tongariro [Ngauruhoe] (New Zeal)	0401-08=	2	
	1913	01	?	Kliuchevskoi (Kamchatka)	1000-26=	2	
?	1913	0115q	?	Azul, Cerro (Chile-C)	1507-06=	2?	
	1913	0117	7a	Colima (México)	1401-04=	2?	
	1913	0120	....	Colima (México)	1401-04=	5	-/9
	1913	0127	<1	Okataina [Waimangu] (New Zeal)	0401-05=	1	
?	1913	0306	?	Andahua-Orcopampa (Perú)	1504-004		
	1913	0314	<1	Awu (Sangihe Is-Indonesia)	0607-04=	2	
	1913	04	107p	Soputan (Sulawesi-Indonesia)	0606-03=	2	
	1913	0425	23a	Hekla [Mundafit, Lambafit] (Icel.)	1702-07=	2	
	1913	05	?	Tongariro [Ngauruhoe] (New Zeal)	0401-08=	2	
	1913	0510	219m	Raung (Java)	0603-34=	2	
	1913	0623	38a	Marapi (Sumatra)	0601-14=	2?	
	1913	0623	3a?	Semeru (Java)	0603-30=	2	
?	1913	07	?	Bogoslof (Aleutian Is)	1101-30-		
	1913	0705	>3yr	Vesuvius (Italy)	0101-02=	2	8/7
	1913	0710	24a	Fournaise, Piton de la (Indian O.)	0303-02=	2	
	1913	0712	?	Masaya (Nicaragua)	1404-10=	1?	
	1913	09	?	Trident (Alaska Peninsula)	1102-16-	1	
	1913	0901?	134a?	Yake-dake (Honshu-Japan)	0803-07=	2	
	1913	1014	261w	Ambrym (Vanuatu-SW Pacific)	0507-04=	2	
	1913	1108	61a	Kirishima (Kyushu-Japan)	0802-09=	2	
	1913	1113	>3yr	Etna (Italy)	0101-06=	2	
	1913	1206	....	Ambrym (Vanuatu-SW Pacific)	0507-04=	3	
	1914	Cont	....	Vesuvius (Italy)	0101-02=	2	8/7
	1914	Cont	....	Stromboli (Italy)	0101-04=	1	5/-
	1914	Cont	....	Etna (Italy)	0101-06=	2	
	1914	Cont	....	Manam (New Guinea-NE of)	0501-02=	2	
	1914	Cont	....	Pago (New Britain-SW Pac)	0502-08=	2	
	1914	Cont	....	Victory (New Guinea)	0503-03=	1	
	1914	Cont	....	Ambrym (Vanuatu-SW Pacific)	0507-04=	2	
	1914	Cont	....	Yasur (Vanuatu-SW Pacific)	0507-10=	2	
	1914	Cont	....	Yake-dake (Honshu-Japan)	0803-07=	2	
	1914	Cont	....	Kilauea (Hawaiian Is)	1302-01-	0	
	1914	Cont	....	Izalco (El Salvador)	1403-03=	2	
	1914	Cont	....	Cotopaxi (Ecuador)	1502-05=	1	
	1914	Cont	....	Sangay (Ecuador)	1502-09=	2	
	1914	....	?	Tanaga (Aleutian Is)	1101-08-	0	
	1914	....	?	Chillán, Nevados de (Chile-C)	1507-07=	2	
	1914	01	?	Nakano-shima (Ryukyu Is)	0802-04=	1	
	1914	0105	?	Kuchinoerabu-jima (Ryukyu Is)	0802-05=	2?	
	1914	0112	488m	Sakura-jima (Kyushu-Japan)	0802-08=	4	9/8
	1914	0113	?	Aso (Kyushu-Japan)	0802-11=	2	
	1914	0113	220a>	Fukutoku-Okanoba (Volcano Is-Japan	0804-13=	3	-/9
	1914	0128	17m	Okataina [Waimangu] (New Zeal)	0401-05=	1	
	1914	0208	?	Puyehue-Cordón Caulle (Chile-C)	1507-15=	2	
?	1914	0213	?	Kikai (Ryukyu Is)	0802-06=		
?	1914	0221	?	Irazú (Costa Rica)	1405-06=		
?	1914	0321	?	Suwanose-jima (Ryukyu Is)	0802-03=		
	1914	0515	11a	Oshima (Izu Is-Japan)	0804-01=	2	7/6
	1914	0529	255p	Ruang (Sangihe Is-Indonesia)	0607-01=	2	
	1914	0530	>3yr	Lassen Volc Center (US-California)	1203-08-	2	
	1914	0530	?	Poás (Costa Rica)	1405-04=	2	
	1914	0531	?	Tandikat (Sumatra)	0601-15=	1	
	1914	0604	<1	Goriaschaia Sopka (Kuril Is)	0900-17=	2	
	1914	0629	?	Lewotobi (Lesser Sunda Is)	0604-18=	2	
	1914	0701	?	Marapi (Sumatra)	0601-14=	2?	
	1914	0703	?	Llaima (Chile-C)	1507-11=	2	
	1914	0706	?	Pavlof (Alaska Peninsula)	1102-03-	2	
	1914	0815x	319x	Lengai, Ol Doinyo (Africa-E)	0202-12=	0	
	1914	09	31p	Tongariro [Ngauruhoe] (New Zeal)	0401-08=	2	
	1914	0908	?	Azul, Cerro (Chile-C)	1507-06=	3	
	1914	1008	219a>	Poás (Costa Rica)	1405-04=	2	
	1914	1028	6a	Negro, Cerro (Nicaragua)	1404-07=	2	-/6
	1914	1108	?	Kirishima (Kyushu-Japan)	0802-09=		
	1914	1112	34a	Asama (Honshu-Japan)	0803-11=	2	
?	1914	1112	2a	Azuma (Honshu-Japan)	0803-18=	1	
	1914	1125	47a	Mauna Loa (Hawaiian Is)	1302-02=	0	7/-
	1915	Cont	....	Vesuvius (Italy)	0101-02=	2	8/7
	1915	Cont	....	Etna (Italy)	0101-06=	2	
	1915	Cont	....	Lengai, Ol Doinyo (Africa-E)	0202-12=	0	
	1915	Cont	....	Pago (New Britain-SW Pac)	0502-08=	2	
	1915	Cont	....	Victory (New Guinea)	0503-03=	1	
	1915	Cont	....	Yasur (Vanuatu-SW Pacific)	0507-10=	2	
	1915	Cont	....	Ruang (Sangihe Is-Indonesia)	0607-01=	2	
	1915	Cont	....	Sakura-jima (Kyushu-Japan)	0802-08=	2	9/8
	1915	Cont	....	Kilauea (Hawaiian Is)	1302-01-	0	
	1915	Cont	....	Mauna Loa (Hawaiian Is)	1302-02=	0	7/-
	1915	Cont	....	Izalco (El Salvador)	1403-03=	2	
	1915	Cont	....	Poás (Costa Rica)	1405-04=	2	
	1915	Cont	....	Sangay (Ecuador)	1502-09=	2	
	1915	....	?	Alayta (Ethiopia)	0201-112	2	
?	1915 a	....	?	Aoba (Vanuatu-SW Pacific)	0507-03=		
	1915 a	....	?	Semeru (Java)	0603-30=	2?	
?	1915	....	?	Ragang (Mindanao-Philippines)	0701-06=	2?	
	1915	....	?	Karymsky (Kamchatka)	1000-13=	2	
M	1915 s	....	?	Southern EPR-Segment I (Pacific)	1304-14-	0	8/-
	1915	....	>3yr	Villarrica (Chile-C)	1507-12=	1	
	1915	01	?	Kliuchevskoi (Kamchatka)	1000-26=	2	
	1915	02	14m	Yake-dake (Honshu-Japan)	0803-07=	2?	
	1915	02	151p	Bayonnaise Rocks (Izu Is-Japan)	0804-07=	0	
	1915	0204	68a	Okataina [Waimangu] (New Zeal)	0401-05=	1	
?	1915	0205	?	Arenal (Costa Rica)	1405-033	2?	
	1915	0322	?	Erebus (Antarctica)	1900-02=	2	
	1915	0328	48a	Merapi (Java)	0603-25=	1	
	1915	04	?	Ulawun (New Britain-SW Pac)	0502-12=	3	
	1915	04	76p	Soputan (Sulawesi-Indonesia)	0606-03=	2	6/-
	1915	05	?	Raung (Java)	0603-34=	2	
	1915	0513?	106a?	Asama (Honshu-Japan)	0803-11=	1	
	1915	0522	....	Lassen Volc Center (US-California)	1203-08-	3	
	1915	0606	40a	Yake-dake (Honshu-Japan)	0803-07=	2	-/6
?	1915	07	61p	Suwanose-jima (Ryukyu Is)	0802-03=	2?	
	1915	0722	122a	Fournaise, Piton de la (Indian O.)	0303-02=	2	
	1915	08	?	Erebus (Antarctica)	1900-02=	2	
	1915	1010	15a?	Oshima (Izu Is-Japan)	0804-01=	2	
	1915	1020	?	Ambrym (Vanuatu-SW Pacific)	0507-04=	2	
	1915	11	212p	Tengger Caldera [Bromo] (Java)	0603-31=	3	
	1915	1104	?	Rinjani (Lesser Sunda Is)	0604-03=	2	
	1915	1105	4a	Okataina [Waimangu] (New Zeal)	0401-05=	1	
	1915	12	?	Marapi (Sumatra)	0601-14=	2?	
	1915	1225	....	Stromboli (Italy)	0101-04=	2	5/-
	1916	Cont	....	Vesuvius (Italy)	0101-02=	2	8/7
	1916	Cont	....	Etna (Italy)	0101-06=	2	
	1916	Cont	....	Pago (New Britain-SW Pac)	0502-08=	2	
	1916	Cont	....	Victory (New Guinea)	0503-03=	1	
	1916	Cont	....	Yasur (Vanuatu-SW Pacific)	0507-10=	2	
	1916	Cont	....	Tengger Caldera [Bromo] (Java)	0603-31=	2	
	1916	Cont	....	Lassen Volc Center (US-California)	1203-08-	2	
	1916	Cont	....	Kilauea (Hawaiian Is)	1302-01-	0	
	1916	Cont	....	Izalco (El Salvador)	1403-03=	2	
	1916	Cont	....	Sangay (Ecuador)	1502-09=	2	
	1916	Cont	....	Villarrica (Chile-C)	1507-12=	1	
	1916	....	?	Poás (Costa Rica)	1405-04=	2	
	1916	....	?	Ruiz, Nevado del (Colombia)	1501-02=	2	
?	1916	....	?	San Pedro (Chile-N)	1505-07=		
	1916	....	>3yr	Azul, Cerro (Chile-C)	1507-06=	2	
	1916	0118	4a	Bulusan (Luzon-Philippines)	0703-01=	2	
	1916	0303	>3yr	Tungurahua (Ecuador)	1502-08=	2	
	1916	0317	26a?	Yake-dake (Honshu-Japan)	0803-07=	2	
	1916	0413	....	Tungurahua (Ecuador)	1502-08=	3	
?	1916	0418	?	Zengyu (Taiwan-N of)	0801-05=	0	
	1916	0419	?	Aso (Kyushu-Japan)	0802-11=	2	
	1916	0505	63a	Marapi (Sumatra)	0601-14=	1	
	1916	0512?	143a	Asama (Honshu-Japan)	0803-11=	1	
	1916	0519	11a	Mauna Loa (Hawaiian Is)	1302-02=	0	7/-
	1916	0621	?	Smith Rock (Izu Is-Japan)	0804-08=	0	
?	1916	07	?	Ragang (Mindanao-Philippines)	0701-06=		
	1916	0702	....	Stromboli (Italy)	0101-04=	2?	5/-
	1916	0715e	?	Mutnovsky (Kamchatka)	1000-06=	2	
	1916	11	31p	Raung (Java)	0603-34=	2	
	1916	12	?	Mutnovsky (Kamchatka)	1000-06=	2	
	1916	1201p	182p	Lengai, Ol Doinyo (Africa-E)	0202-12=	2?	
	1917	Cont	....	Vesuvius (Italy)	0101-02=	2	8/7
	1917	Cont	....	Stromboli (Italy)	0101-04=	1	5/-
	1917	Cont	....	Pago (New Britain-SW Pac)	0502-08=	2	
	1917	Cont	....	Victory (New Guinea)	0503-03=	1	
	1917	Cont	....	Yasur (Vanuatu-SW Pacific)	0507-10=	2	
	1917	Cont	....	Lassen Volc Center (US-California)	1203-08-	2	
	1917	Cont	....	Kilauea (Hawaiian Is)	1302-01-	0	
	1917	Cont	....	Tungurahua (Ecuador)	1502-08=	2	
	1917	Cont	....	Azul, Cerro (Chile-C)	1507-06=	2	
	1917	Cont	....	Villarrica (Chile-C)	1507-12=	1	
	1917	....	?	Barrier, The (Africa-E)	0202-03=	2	
	1917	....	?	Manam (New Guinea-NE of)	0501-02=	2	
	1917	....	?	Babuyan Claro (Luzon-N of)	0704-03=	2	
	1917	....	?	Yake-dake (Honshu-Japan)	0803-07=	1	
	1917	....	?	Pagan (Mariana Is-C Pacific)	0804-17=	2	
?	1917	....	?	Rincón de la Vieja (Costa Rica)	1405-02=		
?	1917	....	?	San Pedro (Chile-N)	1505-07=		
	1917	....	?	Tinguiririca (Chile-C)	1507-03=	1?	

	START YEAR	M-Dy	Dura-tion	VOLCANO NAME (Subregion)	NUMBER	VEI	Vol L/T
	1917	01	....	**Lengai, Ol Doinyo** (Africa-E)	0202-12=	3	
	1917	0204	?	**Llaima** (Chile-C)	1507-11=	2	
	1917	0222	?	**Raung** (Java)	0603-34=	2	
	1917	0225	17*a*	**Ijen** (Java)	0603-35=	1	
	1917	0324	11*a*	**Okataina [Waimangu]** (New Zeal)	0401-05=	1	
	1917	04	31*m*	**Calbuco** (Chile-S)	1508-02=	3?	
	1917	0409	?	**Agrigan** (Mariana Is-C Pacific)	0804-16=	4	
	1917	0429	<1	**Fournaise, Piton de la** (Indian O.)	0303-02=	0	
	1917	0430	12*a*	**Shikotsu [Tarumai]** (Hokkaido)	0805-04=	2	
	1917	0503?	89*a*?	**Asama** (Honshu-Japan)	0803-11=	1	
	1917	0520	<1	**Sorikmarapi** (Sumatra)	0601-12=	2	
	1917	0607	161*m*	**San Salvador** (El Salvador)	1403-05=	3	7/-
	1917	0616	92*a*	**Marapi** (Sumatra)	0601-14=	2?	
	1917	0624	9*d*	**Etna** (Italy)	0101-06=	2	
	1917	0705d	?	**Mutnovsky** (Kamchatka)	1000-06=	3?	
	1917	*0927*	*>3yr*	*Irazú (Costa Rica)*	1405-06=	*2*	
	1917	10	31*p*	**Tongariro [Ngauruhoe]** (New Zeal)	0401-08=	2	
	1917	10	?	**Pavlof** (Alaska Peninsula)	1102-03-	2	
	1917	1018	<1	**Gamkonora** (Halmahera-Indonesia)	0608-04=	2	
	1917	11	?	**Soputan** (Sulawesi-Indonesia)	0606-03=	2	
	1918	*Cont*	....	*Vesuvius (Italy)*	0101-02=	*2*	*8/7*
	1918	*Cont*	....	*Stromboli (Italy)*	0101-04=	*1*	*5/-*
	1918	*Cont*	....	*Pago (New Britain-SW Pac)*	0502-08=	*2*	
	1918	*Cont*	....	*Victory (New Guinea)*	0503-03=	*1*	
	1918	*Cont*	....	*Yasur (Vanuatu-SW Pacific)*	0507-10=	*2*	
	1918	*Cont*	....	*Azul, Cerro (Chile-C)*	1507-06=	*2*	
	1918	*Cont*	....	*Villarrica (Chile-C)*	1507-12=	*1*	
	1918	....	?	**Nyiragongo** (Africa-C)	0203-03=	1	
	1918	....	730*y*	**Okataina [Waimangu]** (New Zeal)	0401-05=	1	
	1918	....	>3yr	**Peuet Sague** (Sumatra)	0601-03=	2	
	1918	....	?	**Yake-dake** (Honshu-Japan)	0803-07=	1	
?	*1918*	....	*?*	*Asama (Honshu-Japan)*	0803-11=		
	1918	01	?	**Merapi** (Java)	0603-25=	1	
?	*1918*	*01*	*?*	*Telica (Nicaragua)*	1404-04=	*2?*	
	1918	01	?	**Masaya** (Nicaragua)	1404-10=	1	
	1918	01	546*p*	**Concepción** (Nicaragua)	1404-12=	2	
	1918	*0105*	....	*Tungurahua (Ecuador)*	1502-08=	*3*	
	1918	0116	?	**Aso** (Kyushu-Japan)	0802-11=	2	
	1918	0120	....	**Irazú** (Costa Rica)	1405-06=	3	
	1918	0223	14*a*	**Kilauea** (Hawaiian Is)	1302-01-	0	5/-
	1918	*03*	*244p*	*Etna (Italy)*	0101-06=	*1*	
	1918	0308	2*a*	**Marapi** (Sumatra)	0601-14=	2?	
?	*1918*	*04*	*?*	*Momotombo (Nicaragua)*	1404-09=	*1?*	
	1918	0405	....	**Tungurahua** (Ecuador)	1502-08=	4	
	1918	0517	2*a*	**Babuyan Claro** (Luzon-N of)	0704-03=	2	
	1918	0613	48*a*	**Shikotsu [Tarumai]** (Hokkaido)	0805-04=	1	
	1918	0629	?	**Ruapehu** (New Zealand)	0401-10=	2	
	1918	0717	13*a*	**Galunggung** (Java)	0603-14=	1	7/-
	1918	*0718*	*500p*	*Banua Wuhu (Sangihe Is-Indonesia)*	0607-03=	*2*	
	1918	0721?	?	**Ulawun** (New Britain-SW Pac)	0502-12=	2	
	1918	08	19*m*	**Gamalama** (Halmahera-Indonesia)	0608-06=	1	
?	*1918*	*0809*	*?*	*Kaba (Sumatra)*	0601-22=	*2?*	
	1918	*0811*	*14*	*Karthala (Indian O.-W)*	0303-01=	*2*	
	1918	0815e	<1	**Marapi** (Sumatra)	0601-14=	2?	
	1918	0825	....	**Karthala** (Indian O.-W)	0303-01=	3	
	1918	10	>3yr	**Bulusan** (Luzon-Philippines)	0703-01=	2	
	1918	1007	....	**Etna** (Italy)	0101-06=	2	
	1918	1012	23*a*	**Katla** (Iceland-S)	1702-03=	4+	-/8
	1918	*1116*	....	*Tungurahua (Ecuador)*	1502-08=	*3?*	
	1918	1130?	1*a*	**Etna** (Italy)	0101-06=	1?	6/-
	1918	*1130*	....	*Irazú (Costa Rica)*	1405-06=	*3*	
	1919	*Cont*	....	*Vesuvius (Italy)*	0101-02=	*2*	*8/7*
	1919	*Cont*	....	*Okataina [Waimangu] (New Zeal)*	0401-05=	*1*	
	1919	*Cont*	....	*Victory (New Guinea)*	0503-03=	*1*	
	1919	*Cont*	....	*Yasur (Vanuatu-SW Pacific)*	0507-10=	*2*	
	1919	*Cont*	....	*Peuet Sague (Sumatra)*	0601-03=	*2*	
	1919	*Cont*	....	*Bulusan (Luzon-Philippines)*	0703-01=	*2*	
	1919	*Cont*	....	*Concepción (Nicaragua)*	1404-12=	*2*	
	1919	*Cont*	....	*Irazú (Costa Rica)*	1405-06=	*2*	
	1919	*Cont*	....	*Tungurahua (Ecuador)*	1502-08=	*2*	
	1919	*Cont*	....	*Azul, Cerro (Chile-C)*	1507-06=	*2*	
	1919	....	?	**Salak** (Java)	0603-05=	2	
	1919	....	>3yr	**Masaya** (Nicaragua)	1404-10=	2	
?	*1919*	....	*?*	*Villarrica (Chile-C)*	1507-12=		
	1919	....	?	**Puyehue-Cordón Caulle** (Chile-C)	1507-15=	2	
@	**1919**	....	?	**Grímsvötn** (Iceland-NE)	1703-01=	2?	
	1919	....	?	**Askja** (Iceland-NE)	1703-06=	2	
	1919	0207	294*a*	**Kilauea** (Hawaiian Is)	1302-01-	0	7/-
	1919	0219?	832*w*?	**Popocatépetl** (México)	1401-09=	1	
	1919	0228	1*a*	**Marapi** (Sumatra)	0601-14=	2?	
	1919	0314	166*a*?	**Asama** (Honshu-Japan)	0803-11=	2	
	1919	0315	>3yr	**Etna** (Italy)	0101-06=	2	6/-
	1919	04	....	**Banua Wuhu** (Sangihe Is-Indonesia)	0607-03=	3	
	1919	04	31*p*	**Aso** (Kyushu-Japan)	0802-11=	2	
	1919	05	?	**Babuyan Claro** (Luzon-N of)	0704-03=	2	
	1919	0504	<1	**Shikotsu [Tarumai]** (Hokkaido)	0805-04=	2	

Tom Miller (USGS/AVO)

A 65-m-high, 380-m-wide lava dome within a circular ejecta ring caps the 1912 vent of Alaska's Novarupta volcano. A 60-hour-long eruption beginning on June 6, 1912, the Earth's largest eruption during the 20th century, produced The Valley of Ten Thousand Smokes ashflow deposit, which forms the flat ground at the right. The face of Falling Mountain, behind Novarupta dome, was sheared off by a 2-km-wide collapse around the Novarupta vent. Snow-capped Mageik volcano lies in the background.

?	START YEAR	M-Dy	Dura-tion	VOLCANO NAME (Subregion)	NUMBER	VEI	Vol L/T
	1919	0518	219a	Oshima (Izu Is-Japan)	0804-01=	0	
	1919	0519	1a	Kelut (Java)	0603-28=	4	-/8
	1919	0522	....	Stromboli (Italy)	0101-04=	3	5/-
	1919	0528?	?	Ulawun (New Britain-SW Pac)	0502-12=	2	
	1919	0617	39a	Komaga-take (Hokkaido-Japan)	0805-02=	2	
	1919	0620	10a	Negro, Cerro (Nicaragua)	1404-07=	2	
	1919	0715?	<1?	Iwate (Honshu-Japan)	0803-24=	1	-/5
	1919	0811	?	Manam (New Guinea-NE of)	0501-02=	4	
	1919	0926	40a?	Mauna Loa (Hawaiian Is)	1302-02=	0	8/-
?	1919	1026e	?	Telica (Nicaragua)	1404-04=	2?	
	1919	11	?	Serua (Banda Sea)	0605-07=	2	
	1919	1101	<1	Yake-dake (Honshu-Japan)	0803-07=	2	
	1919	12	?	Telong, Bur ni (Sumatra)	0601-05=	2	
	1919	1210	37m	San Miguel (El Salvador)	1403-10=	2	
	1919	1221	221a	Kilauea (Hawaiian Is)	1302-01-	0	7/-
	1920	Cont	....	Vesuvius (Italy)	0101-02=	2	8/7
	1920	Cont	....	Stromboli (Italy)	0101-04=	1	5/-
	1920	Cont	....	Etna (Italy)	0101-06=	2	6/-
	1920	Cont	....	Okataina [Waimangu] (New Zeal)	0401-05=	1	
	1920	Cont	....	Victory (New Guinea)	0503-03=	1	
	1920	Cont	....	Yasur (Vanuatu-SW Pacific)	0507-10=	2	
	1920	Cont	....	Peuet Sague (Sumatra)	0601-03=	2	
	1920	Cont	....	Bulusan (Luzon-Philippines)	0703-01=	2	
	1920	Cont	....	Kilauea (Hawaiian Is)	1302-01-	0	7/-
	1920	Cont	....	Popocatépetl (México)	1401-09=	1	
	1920	Cont	....	Masaya (Nicaragua)	1404-10=	2	
	1920	Cont	....	Irazú (Costa Rica)	1405-06=	2	
	1920	Cont	....	Tungurahua (Ecuador)	1502-08=	2	
	1920	Cont	....	Azul, Cerro (Chile-C)	1507-06=	2	
	1920	Cont	....	Puyehue-Cordón Caulle (Chile-C)	1507-15=	2	
?	1920 c	....	?	Barrier, The (Africa-E)	0202-03=		
	1920	....	?	Nyamuragira (Africa-C)	0203-02=	0	
	1920	....	365y	Nyiragongo (Africa-C)	0203-03=	1	
?	1920 b	....	?	Bam (New Guinea-NE of)	0501-01=		
	1920 b	....	?	Pago (New Britain-SW Pac)	0502-08=	0	8/-
	1920	....	?	Lewotolo (Lesser Sunda Is)	0604-23=	2	
	1920	....	?	Aso (Kyushu-Japan)	0802-11=	2	
	1920	....	?	Yake-dake (Honshu-Japan)	0803-07=		
?	1920	....	?	Oshima (Izu Is-Japan)	0804-01=		
	1920 ?	....	?	Huequi (Chile-S)	1508-03=	2	
	1920	0122	?	Epi (Vanuatu-SW Pacific)	0507-06=	2	
	1920	0628	112a	Fournaise, Piton de la (Indian O.)	0303-02=	0	
	1920	0717	5	Shikotsu [Tarumai] (Hokkaido)	0805-04=	1	
	1920	0725	204m	Merapi (Java)	0603-25=	2	-/6
	1920	0814	>3yr	San Miguel (El Salvador)	1403-10=	2	
	1920	1029	163a	Izalco (El Salvador)	1403-03=	2	
?	1920	11	?	Santa Ana (El Salvador)	1403-02=	2?	
	1920	1205?	103m?	Manam (New Guinea-NE of)	0501-02=	2	
	1920	1206	6a	Kelut (Java)	0603-28=	2	5/-
	1920	1206	505a	Asama (Honshu-Japan)	0803-11=	2	
	1920	1210	3a	Villarrica (Chile-C)	1507-12=	2	
	1921	Cont	....	Vesuvius (Italy)	0101-02=	2	8/7
	1921	Cont	....	Etna (Italy)	0101-06=	2	6/-
	1921	Cont	....	Nyiragongo (Africa-C)	0203-03=	1	
	1921	Cont	....	Manam (New Guinea-NE of)	0501-02=	2	
	1921	Cont	....	Victory (New Guinea)	0503-03=	1	
	1921	Cont	....	Yasur (Vanuatu-SW Pacific)	0507-10=	2	
	1921	Cont	....	Peuet Sague (Sumatra)	0601-03=	2	
	1921	Cont	....	Merapi (Java)	0603-25=	2	-/6
	1921	Cont	....	Bulusan (Luzon-Philippines)	0703-01=	2	
	1921	Cont	....	Asama (Honshu-Japan)	0803-11=	2	
	1921	Cont	....	Popocatépetl (México)	1401-09=	1	
	1921	Cont	....	Izalco (El Salvador)	1403-03=	2	
	1921	Cont	....	San Miguel (El Salvador)	1403-10=	2	
	1921	Cont	....	Masaya (Nicaragua)	1404-10=	2	
	1921	Cont	....	Irazú (Costa Rica)	1405-06=	2	
	1921	Cont	....	Tungurahua (Ecuador)	1502-08=	2	
	1921	Cont	....	Azul, Cerro (Chile-C)	1507-06=	2	
	1921	....	>3yr	Nyamuragira (Africa-C)	0203-02=	0	8/-
	1921	....	?	Yake-dake (Honshu-Japan)	0803-07=		
	1921	0101	354a	Lewotobi (Lesser Sunda Is)	0604-18=	2	5/-
	1921	0129	78a	Batur (Lesser Sunda Is)	0604-01=	2	
	1921	02	?	Lengai, Ol Doinyo (Africa-E)	0202-12=	2	
	1921	02	229t	Awu (Sangihe Is-Indonesia)	0607-04=	0	
	1921	0214d	60p	Raung (Java)	0603-34=	2	
	1921	03	92m>	Karangetang [Api Siau] (Sangihe Is	0607-02=	2	
	1921	03	?	Askja (Iceland-NE)	1703-06=	0	
?	1921	0318	?	St. Helens (US-Washington)	1201-05-		
	1921	0318	7a	Kilauea (Hawaiian Is)	1302-01-	0	6/-
	1921	04	15m	Dempo (Sumatra)	0601-23=	1	
	1921	05	31p	Kerinci (Sumatra)	0601-17=	2	
	1921	0523	11a	Sumbing (Sumatra)	0601-18=	2	
	1921	06	124m	Tengger Caldera [Bromo] (Java)	0603-31=	2	
	1921	0616	....	Stromboli (Italy)	0101-04=	2	5/-
?	1921	0703	<1	Wrangell (Alaska-E)	1105-02-		
	1921	0706	<1	Shikotsu [Tarumai] (Hokkaido)	0805-04=	1	
	1921	09	?	Karymsky (Kamchatka)	1000-13=	2	
	1921	0918	?	Serua (Banda Sea)	0605-07=	2	
	1921	10	?	Ruapehu (New Zealand)	0401-10=	2	
?	1921	11	?	Falcon Island (Tonga-SW Pacific)	0403-05=	0?	
	1921	1127	6a	Fournaise, Piton de la (Indian O.)	0303-02=	2	
	1921	12	>3yr	Concepción (Nicaragua)	1404-12=	2	
	1921	1208	49a	Suwanose-jima (Ryukyu Is)	0802-03=	2?	
?	1921	1210	?	Villarrica (Chile-C)	1507-12=	2?	
	1921	1213	62a	Puyehue-Cordón Caulle (Chile-C)	1507-15=	3	8/-
	1921	1231y	?	Barrier, The (Africa-E)	0202-03=	2	
	1922	Cont	....	Vesuvius (Italy)	0101-02=	2	8/7
	1922	Cont	....	Etna (Italy)	0101-06=	2	6/-
	1922	Cont	....	Nyamuragira (Africa-C)	0203-02=	0	8/-
	1922	Cont	....	Victory (New Guinea)	0503-03=	1	
	1922	Cont	....	Yasur (Vanuatu-SW Pacific)	0507-10=	2	
	1922	Cont	....	Bulusan (Luzon-Philippines)	0703-01=	2	
	1922	Cont	....	Suwanose-jima (Ryukyu Is)	0802-03=	2?	
	1922	Cont	....	Asama (Honshu-Japan)	0803-11=	2	
	1922	Cont	....	Popocatépetl (México)	1401-09=	1	
	1922	Cont	....	San Miguel (El Salvador)	1403-10=	2	
	1922	Cont	....	Masaya (Nicaragua)	1404-10=	2	
	1922	Cont	....	Concepción (Nicaragua)	1404-12=	2	
	1922	Cont	....	Tungurahua (Ecuador)	1502-08=	2	
	1922	Cont	....	Azul, Cerro (Chile-C)	1507-06=	2	
	1922	Cont	....	Puyehue-Cordón Caulle (Chile-C)	1507-15=	3	8/-
	1922	....	?	White Island (New Zealand)	0401-04=	2	
	1922	....	?	Manam (New Guinea-NE of)	0501-02=	3?	
	1922	....	?	Gareloi (Aleutian Is)	1101-07-	3	
	1922	....	?	Cotopaxi (Ecuador)	1502-05=	2	
?	1922	0201p	?	Unnamed (Sangihe Is-Indonesia)	0607-05=	0	
	1922	0203	202a	Cameroon (Africa-W)	0204-01=	2	7/-
	1922	0205	135a	Tengger Caldera [Bromo] (Java)	0603-31=	2	
	1922	0218	171a	Merapi (Java)	0603-25=	1	6/-
	1922	0310	9a	Yake-dake (Honshu-Japan)	0803-07=	1?	
	1922	0411<	54a>	Rincón de la Vieja (Costa Rica)	1405-02=	2?	
	1922	05	?	Kliuchevskoi (Kamchatka)	1000-26=	2	
	1922	0504	222a	Karangetang [Api Siau] (Sangihe Is	0607-02=	2	
	1922	0522	?	Komaga-take (Hokkaido-Japan)	0805-02=	2	
	1922	0528	2a	Kilauea (Hawaiian Is)	1302-01-	0	6/-
	1922	0620	97m	Awu (Sangihe Is-Indonesia)	0607-04=	0	
	1922	0622	>3yr	Santa María (Guatemala)	1402-03=	3	9/8
	1922	0628	3a	Lopevi (Vanuatu-SW Pacific)	0507-05=	2	
	1922	07	?	Ioto [Iwo-jima] (Volcano Is-Japan)	0804-12=	1	
?	1922	08	?	Methana (Greece)	0102-02=		
	1922	0820	....	Stromboli (Italy)	0101-04=	2	5/-
	1922	0830	?	Batur (Lesser Sunda Is)	0604-01=	2	
	1922	0929	24a	Grímsvötn (Iceland-NE)	1703-01=	2	
	1922	1005?	18a?	Arenal (Costa Rica)	1405-033	2	
	1922	1015q	?	Shishaldin (Aleutian Is)	1101-36-	2	
	1922	1024	?	Llaima (Chile-C)	1507-11=	2	
	1922	1024	34n	Villarrica (Chile-C)	1507-12=	2	
	1922	11	?	Kronotsky (Kamchatka)	1000-20=	2	
	1922	11	?	Askja (Iceland-NE)	1703-06=	0	
	1922	1208	53a	Oshima (Izu Is-Japan)	0804-01=	1	6/5
	1922	1224	66r	Pavlof (Alaska Peninsula)	1102-03-	2	
	1923	Cont	....	Vesuvius (Italy)	0101-02=	2	8/7
	1923	Cont	....	Nyamuragira (Africa-C)	0203-02=	0	8/-
	1923	Cont	....	Victory (New Guinea)	0503-03=	1	
	1923	Cont	....	Yasur (Vanuatu-SW Pacific)	0507-10=	2	
	1923	Cont	....	Oshima (Izu Is-Japan)	0804-01=	1	6/5
	1923	Cont	....	Pavlof (Alaska Peninsula)	1102-03-	2	
	1923	Cont	....	San Miguel (El Salvador)	1403-10=	2	
	1923	Cont	....	Masaya (Nicaragua)	1404-10=	2	
	1923	Cont	....	Concepción (Nicaragua)	1404-12=	2	
	1923	Cont	....	Tungurahua (Ecuador)	1502-08=	2	
	1923	Cont	....	Azul, Cerro (Chile-C)	1507-06=	2	
	1923	....	?	Santa Isabel (Africa-W)	0204-004		
?	1923	....	?	Manam (New Guinea-NE of)	0501-02=	2?	
	1923	....	730y	Kuwae [Karua] (Vanuatu-SW Pac)	0507-07=	2?	
	1923	....	2a	Batur (Lesser Sunda Is)	0604-01=	2	
	1923 h	....	?	Zavaritzki Caldera (Kuril Is)	0900-18=	1	
	1923	....	....	Santa María (Guatemala)	1402-03=	2	9/8
?	1923	....	?	San Pedro (Chile-N)	1505-07=		
?	1923	....	?	Chillán, Nevados de (Chile-C)	1507-07=	2?	
	1923	01	244m	Aso (Kyushu-Japan)	0802-11=	2	
	1923	0115q	?	Askja (Iceland-NE)	1703-06=	0	
	1923	0117	5a	Sarychev Peak (Kuril Is)	0900-24=	2	
	1923	02	? 840m?	Pagan (Mariana Is-C Pacific)	0804-17=	2	
	1923	02	190m	Shikotsu [Tarumai] (Hokkaido)	0805-04=	1	
	1923	02	?	Karymsky (Kamchatka)	1000-13=	2	
	1923	02	?	Kronotsky (Kamchatka)	1000-20=	2	
	1923	0211	63m	Zheltovsky (Kamchatka)	1000-04=	3	
	1923	0227	16a	Komaga-take (Hokkaido-Japan)	0805-02=	2	
	1923	0302	72a	Cendres, Ile des (SE Asia)	0705-06-	2	-/8
	1923	0303	....	Pagan (Mariana Is-C Pacific)	0804-17=	3	
	1923	0311	728a	Papandayan (Java)	0603-10=	1	
	1923	0413	23a	Gamalama (Halmahera-Indonesia)	0608-06=	2	

START YEAR	M-Dy	Duration	VOLCANO NAME (Subregion)	NUMBER	VEI	Vol L/T
1923	0519?	<1	**Dempo** (Sumatra)	0601-23=	1	
1923	06	?	**Perbakti-Gagak** (Java)	0603-04=	1	
1923	0602	<1	**Slamet** (Java)	0603-18=	2	
1923	0617	31a	**Etna** (Italy)	0101-06=	2	7/5
1923	0626	37a	**Yake-dake** (Honshu-Japan)	0803-07=	2	
1923	07	16m	**Kirishima** (Kyushu-Japan)	0802-09=	2	
1923	0701	?	**Unnamed** (Tonga-SW Pacific)	0403-03=	0	
1923	08	30p	**Kliuchevskoi** (Kamchatka)	1000-26=	2	
1923	0825	<1	**Kilauea** (Hawaiian Is)	1302-01-	0	5/-
1923	09	<1	**Kerinci** (Sumatra)	0601-17=	1	
? 1923	09	61p	*Merapi (Java)*	0603-25=		
1923	1009	266w	**Etna** (Italy)	0101-06=	1	
1923	1023	49m	**Negro, Cerro** (Nicaragua)	1404-07=	3	7/7
1923	1127	53a	**Soputan** (Sulawesi-Indonesia)	0606-03=	2	7/-
1923	1127	121p	**Popocatépetl** (México)	1401-09=	1	
1923	12	....	*Stromboli (Italy)*	0101-04=	2	5/-
1923	1208	?	**Galeras** (Colombia)	1501-08=	2	
1924	Cont	....	*Vesuvius (Italy)*	0101-02=	2	8/7
1924	Cont	....	*Stromboli (Italy)*	0101-04=	1	5/-
1924	Cont	....	*Etna (Italy)*	0101-06=	1	
1924	Cont	....	*Nyamuragira (Africa-C)*	0203-02=	0	8/-
1924	Cont	....	*Victory (New Guinea)*	0503-03=	1	
1924	Cont	....	*Kuwae [Karua] (Vanuatu-SW Pac)*	0507-07=	2?	
1924	Cont	....	*Yasur (Vanuatu-SW Pacific)*	0507-10=	2	
1924	Cont	....	*Papandayan (Java)*	0603-10=	1	
1924	Cont	....	*Popocatépetl (México)*	1401-09=	1	
1924	Cont	....	*San Miguel (El Salvador)*	1403-10=	2	
1924	Cont	....	*Masaya (Nicaragua)*	1404-10=	2	
1924	Cont	....	*Concepción (Nicaragua)*	1404-12=	2	
1924	Cont	....	*Tungurahua (Ecuador)*	1502-08=	2	
1924	Cont	....	*Azul, Cerro (Chile-C)*	1507-06=	2	
1924	....	?	**White Island** (New Zealand)	0401-04=	2	
1924	....	?	**Okataina [Waimangu]** (New Zeal)	0401-05=	1	
1924	....	5a	**Bam** (New Guinea-NE of)	0501-01=	2	
? 1924	....	?	*Manam (New Guinea-NE of)*	0501-02=	2?	
1924	....	?	**Babuyan Claro** (Luzon-N of)	0704-03=	2	
? 1924	....	?	*Asuncion (Mariana Is-C Pacific)*	0804-15=	2?	
1924	....	?	**Ketoi** (Kuril Is)	0900-20=	2	
1924	....	....	*Santa María (Guatemala)*	1402-03=	2	**9/8**
1924	....	?	**Puracé** (Colombia)	1501-06=	2	
1924 ?	....	?	**Askja** (Iceland-NE)	1703-06=	0?	8/-
1924	0109	21a	**Tongariro [Ngauruhoe]** (New Zeal)	0401-08=	2	
1924	0114	....	*Soputan (Sulawesi-Indonesia)*	0606-03=	2	7/-
1924	0117	?	**Pavlof** (Alaska Peninsula)	1102-03-	2	
1924	02 <	?	**Raung** (Java)	0603-34=	2	
1924	0215	?	**Unnamed** (Kuril Is)	0900-23=	0	
1924	0215	?	**Raikoke** (Kuril Is)	0900-25=	4	
1924	03	2a	**Batur** (Lesser Sunda Is)	0604-01=	2	
1924	03	?	**Izalco** (El Salvador)	1403-03=	2	
1924	03	30m	**Irazú** (Costa Rica)	1405-06=	2	
1924	0313	?	**Kolokol Group** (Kuril Is)	0900-12=	2?	
1924	04	15m?	**Tandikat** (Sumatra)	0601-15=	1	
1924	05	?	**Karangetang [Api Siau]** (Sangihe Is	0607-02=	2	
1924	0510	17	**Kilauea** (Hawaiian Is)	1302-01-	2	-/5
1924	0519	4a>	**Fournaise, Piton de la** (Indian O.)	0303-02=	0	
1924	0522	?	**Tongariro [Ngauruhoe]** (New Zeal)	0401-08=	2	
1924	0719	10a	**Kilauea** (Hawaiian Is)	1302-01-	0	5/-
1924	0731	?	**Komaga-take** (Hokkaido-Japan)	0805-02=	2	
? 1924	0820	?	*Raung (Java)*	0603-34=	2?	
1924	0903	10a	**Fournaise, Piton de la** (Indian O.)	0303-02=	2	
1924	0907	22a	**Asama** (Honshu-Japan)	0803-11=	2	
1924	0910	2a	**Merapi** (Java)	0603-25=	1	
1924	10	31p	**Tongariro [Ngauruhoe]** (New Zeal)	0401-08=	2	
1924	10	988w	*Galeras (Colombia)*	1501-08=	2	
1924	1031	?	**Iriomote-jima** (Ryukyu Is)	0802-01=	4?	-/**9**
1924	11	?	**Ebulobo** (Lesser Sunda Is)	0604-10=	2	
1924	1116	739a	**Yake-dake** (Honshu-Japan)	0803-07=	2	
? 1924	1207	?	*Telong, Bur ni (Sumatra)*	0601-05=	2	
1924	1218	171a	*Acatenango (Guatemala)*	1402-08=	2	
1925	Cont	....	*Vesuvius (Italy)*	0101-02=	2	8/7
1925	Cont	....	*Stromboli (Italy)*	0101-04=	1	5/-
1925	Cont	....	*Etna (Italy)*	0101-06=	1	
1925	Cont	....	*Nyamuragira (Africa-C)*	0203-02=	0	8/-
1925	Cont	....	*Victory (New Guinea)*	0503-03=	1	
1925	Cont	....	*Kuwae [Karua] (Vanuatu-SW Pac)*	0507-07=	2?	
1925	Cont	....	*Yasur (Vanuatu-SW Pacific)*	0507-10=	2	
1925	Cont	....	*Papandayan (Java)*	0603-10=	1	
1925	Cont	....	*Yake-dake (Honshu-Japan)*	0803-07=	2	
1925	Cont	....	*San Miguel (El Salvador)*	1403-10=	2	
1925	Cont	....	*Concepción (Nicaragua)*	1404-12=	2	
1925	Cont	....	*Tungurahua (Ecuador)*	1502-08=	2	
1925	Cont	....	*Azul, Cerro (Chile-C)*	1507-06=	2	
1925	....	?	**Cameroon** (Africa-W)	0204-01=		
1925	....	?	**Manam** (New Guinea-NE of)	0501-02=	2?	
1925	....	?	**Iliboleng** (Lesser Sunda Is)	0604-22=	2	
1925	....	?	**Farallon de Pajaros** (Mariana Is-Pac)	0804-14=	2	
1925	....	?	**Zhupanovsky** (Kamchatka)	1000-12=	2	
1925	....	?	**Shishaldin** (Aleutian Is)	1101-36-		
1925	....	730y?	**Popocatépetl** (México)	1401-09=	2	
1925	....	....	*Santa María (Guatemala)*	1402-03=	2	**9/8**
1925	....	....	**Acatenango** (Guatemala)	1402-08=	3	
1925	....	?	**Poás** (Costa Rica)	1405-04=	1	
1925	....	?	**Tupungatito** (Chile-C)	1507-01=	2	
1925	0105d	<1	**Batur** (Lesser Sunda Is)	0604-01=	2	
1925	0106	?	**Aso** (Kyushu-Japan)	0802-11=	2	
1925	0122	?	**Ruapehu** (New Zealand)	0401-10=	2	
1925	0122?	8a?	**Kusatsu-Shirane** (Honshu-Japan)	0803-12=	2	-/6
1925	02	80m	**Pagan** (Mariana Is-C Pacific)	0804-17=	2	
1925	0215	....	**Galeras** (Colombia)	1501-08=	3	
1925	04 ?	?	**Marapi** (Sumatra)	0601-14=	0	
1925	04	?	**Masaya** (Nicaragua)	1404-10=	2?	
1925	0404	189a	**Kliuchevskoi** (Kamchatka)	1000-26=	2	
1925	0411	349a>	**Wolf** (Galápagos)	1503-02=	1	
1925	0513	?	**Suwanose-jima** (Ryukyu Is)	0802-03=	2?	
1925	0525	....	*Galeras (Colombia)*	1501-08=	3	
1925	07	?	**Karymsky** (Kamchatka)	1000-13=	2	
1925	0701	....	*Galeras (Colombia)*	1501-08=	3	
1925	0811	277m	**Santorini** (Greece)	0102-04=	2	8/-
? 1925	0924	?	*Nieuwerkerk (Banda Sea)*	0605-02=	2	
1925	1012	24a	**Puracé** (Colombia)	1501-06=	2	
1925	11	31p	**Tongariro [Ngauruhoe]** (New Zeal)	0401-08=	2	
1925	1120	664m	*Tokachi (Hokkaido-Japan)*	0805-05=	2	
1925	1226	371m	*Izalco (El Salvador)*	1403-03=	2	
1925	1230	111a	**Fournaise, Piton de la** (Indian O.)	0303-02=	2	
1926	Cont	....	*Vesuvius (Italy)*	0101-02=	2	8/7
1926	Cont	....	*Stromboli (Italy)*	0101-04=	1	5/-
1926	Cont	....	*Nyamuragira (Africa-C)*	0203-02=	0	8/-
1926	Cont	....	*Victory (New Guinea)*	0503-03=	1	
1926	Cont	....	*Yasur (Vanuatu-SW Pacific)*	0507-10=	2	
1926	Cont	....	*Yake-dake (Honshu-Japan)*	0803-07=	2	
1926	Cont	....	*Popocatépetl (México)*	1401-09=	2	
1926	Cont	....	*Santa María (Guatemala)*	1402-03=	1	**9/8**
1926	Cont	....	*Concepción (Nicaragua)*	1404-12=	2	
1926	Cont	....	*Galeras (Colombia)*	1501-08=	2	
1926	Cont	....	*Wolf (Galápagos)*	1503-02=	1	
1926	Cont	....	*Azul, Cerro (Chile-C)*	1507-06=	2	
1926	....	?	**Dallol** (Ethiopia)	0201-041	1	
1926	....	21m	**Lengai, Ol Doinyo** (Africa-E)	0202-12=	2	
1926 d	....	>3yr	*Colima (México)*	1401-04=	0	
1926	....	?	**Cotopaxi** (Ecuador)	1502-05=	2	
1926	....	?	**Fernandina** (Galápagos)	1503-01=		
1926	0102	164a	**Etna** (Italy)	0101-06=	1	
1926	0105d	120p	**Reventador** (Ecuador)	1502-01=	3	
1926	0203	?	**White Island** (New Zealand)	0401-04=	2	
1926	03	714q	**Manam** (New Guinea-NE of)	0501-02=	2	
1926	0301	130a	**Tangkubanparahu** (Java)	0603-09=	1?	
1926	0323	15a	**Kliuchevskoi** (Kamchatka)	1000-26=	2	
1926	0327	352a?	*Avachinsky (Kamchatka)*	1000-10=	2	6/8
1926	0405	....	**Avachinsky** (Kamchatka)	1000-10=	4	6/8
1926	0410	18a?	**Mauna Loa** (Hawaiian Is)	1302-02=	0	8/-
1926	0416	61m	**Tongariro [Ngauruhoe]** (New Zeal)	0401-08=	2	
1926	0422	2a	**Dempo** (Sumatra)	0601-23=	2	
1926	05	....	*Santorini (Greece)*	0102-04=	2	8/-
1926	0524	....	**Tokachi** (Hokkaido-Japan)	0805-05=	3	
1926	06	?	**Gamkonora** (Halmahera-Indonesia)	0608-04=	1?	
1926	0605d	?	**Reykjanes** (Iceland-SW)	1701-02=	0	
1926	07	715w	**Bogoslof** (Aleutian Is)	1101-30-	2	6/-
1926	0715q	?	**Askja** (Iceland-NE)	1703-06=	2?	-/7
1926	08	276m	**Acatenango** (Guatemala)	1402-08=	2	
1926	08	31p	**Puracé** (Colombia)	1501-06=	2	
1926	0802	50a	**Batur** (Lesser Sunda Is)	0604-01=	2	7/6
1926	0918	270a	**Fournaise, Piton de la** (Indian O.)	0303-02=	2	
1926	0921	479a	**Aso** (Kyushu-Japan)	0802-11=	2	
1926	10	?	**Karangetang [Api Siau]** (Sangihe Is	0607-02=	2	
1926	1019	11a	**Shikotsu [Tarumai]** (Hokkaido)	0805-04=	2	
1926	1105	....	**Izalco** (El Salvador)	1403-03=	3?	
1926	1117	1a	**Okataina [Waimangu]** (New Zeal)	0401-05=	1	
1926	1123a	7b	**Slamet** (Java)	0603-18=	2	
1926	1220	1a	**Cumbal** (Colombia)	1501-10=	2	
1926	1221	9a?	**Tongariro [Ngauruhoe]** (New Zeal)	0401-08=	2	
1926	1222	<1	**Koryaksky** (Kamchatka)	1000-09=	1?	
1926	1230	?	**Makushin** (Aleutian Is)	1101-31-	2	
1927	Cont	....	*Vesuvius (Italy)*	0101-02=	2	8/7
1927	Cont	....	*Stromboli (Italy)*	0101-04=	1	5/-
1927	Cont	....	*Nyamuragira (Africa-C)*	0203-02=	0	8/-
1927	Cont	....	*Fournaise, Piton de la (Indian O.)*	0303-02=	0	
1927	Cont	....	*Manam (New Guinea-NE of)*	0501-02=	2	
1927	Cont	....	*Victory (New Guinea)*	0503-03=	1	
1927	Cont	....	*Yasur (Vanuatu-SW Pacific)*	0507-10=	2	
1927	Cont	....	*Aso (Kyushu-Japan)*	0802-11=	2	
1927	Cont	....	*Tokachi (Hokkaido-Japan)*	0805-05=	2	
1927	Cont	....	*Avachinsky (Kamchatka)*	1000-10=	2	6/8
1927	Cont	....	*Bogoslof (Aleutian Is)*	1101-30-	1	6/-
1927	Cont	....	*Colima (México)*	1401-04=	0	

	START YEAR	M-Dy	Duration	VOLCANO NAME (Subregion)	NUMBER	VEI	Vol L/T
	1927	Cont	....	Popocatépetl (México)	1401-09=	2	
	1927	Cont	....	Santa María (Guatemala)	1402-03=	1	9/8
	1927	Cont	....	Galeras (Colombia)	1501-08=	2	
	1927	Cont	....	Azul, Cerro (Chile-C)	1507-06=	2	
?	1927	....	?	Tongariro (New Zealand)	0401-08=	1?	
	1927	....	?	**Sangeang Api** (Lesser Sunda Is)	0604-05=	2	
	1927	....	?	**Iliboleng** (Lesser Sunda Is)	0604-22=	2	
?	1927	....	?	Sirung (Lesser Sunda Is)	0604-27=	2	
?	1927	....	?	Zao (Honshu-Japan)	0803-19=	1?	
	1927	....	?	**Sarychev Peak** (Kuril Is)	0900-24=	2?	
?	1927	....	?	Kiska (Aleutian Is)	1101-02-	2?	
?	1927	....	?	Gareloi (Aleutian Is)	1101-07-		
?	1927	....	?	Seguam (Aleutian Is)	1101-18-		
	1927	....	365y	**Akutan** (Aleutian Is)	1101-32-	2	
	1927	....	?	**Shishaldin** (Aleutian Is)	1101-36-		
	1927	....	365y?	**Izalco** (El Salvador)	1403-03=	2	
	1927	....	?	**Puracé** (Colombia)	1501-06=	2	
	1927	....	365y	**Villarrica** (Chile-C)	1507-12=	2	
	1927	01	30p	**Mutnovsky** (Kamchatka)	1000-06=	2	
	1927	0123	96	**Yake-dake** (Honshu-Japan)	0803-07=	2	
	1927	0205	179m	**Marapi** (Sumatra)	0601-14=	2	
	1927	0227	<1	**Slamet** (Java)	0603-18=	2	
	1927	03	>3yr	**Nyiragongo** (Africa-C)	0203-03=	1	
	1927	03 ?	497m?	**Asama** (Honshu-Japan)	0803-11=	2	
?	1927	0301p	?	Emperor of China (Banda Sea)	0605-01=	2	
?	1927	0301p	?	Nieuwerkerk (Banda Sea)	0605-02=	2	
	1927	0320	?	**Kanlaon** (Philippines-C)	0702-02=	2	
	1927	0330	....	Acatenango (Guatemala)	1402-08=	2	
?	1927	04	30p	Akan (Hokkaido-Japan)	0805-07=	1	
	1927	0410	?	**Chillán, Nevados de** (Chile-C)	1507-07=	2?	
	1927	07	63m>	**Ulawun** (New Britain-SW Pac)	0502-12=	2	
	1927	0707	13a	**Kilauea** (Hawaiian Is)	1302-01-	0	6/-
	1927	08	91p	**Telica** (Nicaragua)	1404-04=	2	
	1927	0802	225m?	**Raung** (Java)	0603-34=	2	
?	1927	0826e	5a?	Mageik (Alaska Peninsula)	1102-15-	2	
?	1927	0905d	?	Esjufjöll (Iceland-SE)	1704-02=	1?	
	1927	1004	346m>	**Falcon Island** (Tonga-SW Pacific)	0403-05=	2	-/7
	1927	1005	61a	**Llaima** (Chile-C)	1507-11=	2	
	1927	12	31p	**Kizimen** (Kamchatka)	1000-23=	2	
	1927	1213<	?	**Fernandina** (Galápagos)	1503-01=	0	
	1927	1215	<1	**Yake-dake** (Honshu-Japan)	0803-07=	2	
	1927	1229	960a	**Krakatau** (Indonesia)	0602-00=	2	
	1927	1229	2a	**Kusatsu-Shirane** (Honshu-Japan)	0803-12=	2	
	1928	Cont	....	Vesuvius (Italy)	0101-02=	2	8/7
	1928	Cont	....	Stromboli (Italy)	0101-04=	1	5/-
	1928	Cont	....	Nyamuragira (Africa-C)	0203-02=	0	8/-
	1928	Cont	....	Nyiragongo (Africa-C)	0203-03=	0	
	1928	Cont	....	Falcon Island (Tonga-SW Pacific)	0403-05=	2	-/7
	1928	Cont	....	Manam (New Guinea-NE of)	0501-02=	2	
	1928	Cont	....	Victory (New Guinea)	0503-03=	1	
	1928	Cont	....	Yasur (Vanuatu-SW Pacific)	0507-10=	2	
	1928	Cont	....	Asama (Honshu-Japan)	0803-11=	2	
	1928	Cont	....	Kizimen (Kamchatka)	1000-23=	2	
	1928	Cont	....	Bogoslof (Aleutian Is)	1101-30-	1	6/-
	1928	Cont	....	Akutan (Aleutian Is)	1101-32-	2	
	1928	Cont	....	Colima (México)	1401-04=	0	
	1928	Cont	....	Izalco (El Salvador)	1403-03=	2	
	1928	Cont	....	Azul, Cerro (Chile-C)	1507-06=	2	
	1928	Cont	....	Villarrica (Chile-C)	1507-12=	2	
?	1928	....	?	Ayelu (Ethiopia)	0201-16=	2	
?	1928	....	?	Adwa (Ethiopia)	0201-17=	2	
	1928 b	....	?	**Karthala** (Indian O.-W)	0303-01=	1?	
	1928	....	?	**Iliwerung** (Lesser Sunda Is)	0604-25=	2	7/-
?	1928	....	?	Veteran (SE Asia)	0705-07-	0	
@	1928	....	?	**Macdonald** (Austral Is-C Pacific)	1303-06-	0?	
	1928	....	....	Santa María (Guatemala)	1402-03=	2	9/8
	1928	....	?	**Telica** (Nicaragua)	1404-04=	2	
	1928	....	?	**Pinta** (Galápagos)	1503-07=		
	1928	01 ?	212m?	Mayon (Luzon-Philippines)	0703-03=	2	7/7
	1928	01	127m	**Tokachi** (Hokkaido-Japan)	0805-05=	1	
	1928	0107	<1	**Shikotsu [Tarumai]** (Hokkaido)	0805-04=	2	
	1928	0123	54a	**Santorini** (Greece)	0102-04=	2	4/-
	1928	0125	40m	**Mutnovsky** (Kamchatka)	1000-06=	2	
	1928	0125	?	**Concepción** (Nicaragua)	1404-12=	2	
	1928	0127	443q	**Shiveluch** (Kamchatka)	1000-27=	1	
	1928	0205	....	Krakatau (Indonesia)	0602-00=	2	
	1928	0214	?	**Sarychev Peak** (Kuril Is)	0900-24=	2	
	1928	0214	102e	**Irazú** (Costa Rica)	1405-06=	2	
	1928	0303	?	**Tongariro [Ngauruhoe]** (New Zeal)	0401-08=	2	
	1928	0315e	122m	**Tengger Caldera [Bromo]** (Java)	0603-31=	2	
	1928	0320	49a	**Slamet** (Java)	0603-18=	2	
	1928	0328	?	**Komaga-take** (Hokkaido-Japan)	0805-02=	1	
	1928	0513	?	**Dieng Volc Complex** (Java)	0603-20=	2	
	1928	06	?	**Bulusan** (Luzon-Philippines)	0703-01=	2	
?	1928	0609	?	Pinacate (México)	1401-001		
	1928	0625	....	**Mayon** (Luzon-Philippines)	0703-03=	3	7/7
	1928	07	?	**Tongariro [Ngauruhoe]** (New Zeal)	0401-08=	2	
	1928	0731	21a	**Etna** (Italy)	0101-06=	1	
	1928	08	?	**Shishaldin** (Aleutian Is)	1101-36-	2	
	1928	0804	52a	**Paluweh** (Lesser Sunda Is)	0604-15=	3	6/7
	1928	0807	1a	**Oshima** (Izu Is-Japan)	0804-01=	2	
	1928	0901	3a	**White Island** (New Zealand)	0401-04=	1	
	1928	0906	413a	**Aso** (Kyushu-Japan)	0802-11=	2	
	1928	0906	157a	**Shikotsu [Tarumai]** (Hokkaido)	0805-04=	1	
	1928	11	?	**Raung** (Java)	0603-34=	2	
	1928	1102	16a	**Etna** (Italy)	0101-06=	1	7/6
	1928	1130	214w	**Chillán, Nevados de** (Chile-C)	1507-07=	2?	
	1928	1204	21a	**Tokachi** (Hokkaido-Japan)	0805-05=	1	
	1928	1215e	?	**Farallon de Pajaros** (Mariana Is-Pac)	0804-14=	2?	
	1928	1216	?	**Tengger Caldera [Bromo]** (Java)	0603-31=	2	
	1928	1231y	?	**Manda-Inakir** (Ethiopia)	0201-122	2?	
	1929	Cont	....	Stromboli (Italy)	0101-04=	1	5/-
	1929	Cont	....	Nyamuragira (Africa-C)	0203-02=	0	8/-
	1929	Cont	....	Nyiragongo (Africa-C)	0203-03=	0	
	1929	Cont	....	Victory (New Guinea)	0503-03=	1	
	1929	Cont	....	Yasur (Vanuatu-SW Pacific)	0507-10=	2	
	1929	Cont	....	Aso (Kyushu-Japan)	0802-11=	2	
	1929	Cont	....	Shikotsu [Tarumai] (Hokkaido)	0805-04=	1	
	1929	Cont	....	Shiveluch (Kamchatka)	1000-27=	1	
	1929	Cont	....	Colima (México)	1401-04=	0	
	1929	Cont	....	Azul, Cerro (Chile-C)	1507-06=	2	
	1929	Cont	....	Chillán, Nevados de (Chile-C)	1507-07=	2?	
	1929	....	?	**Perbakti-Gagak** (Java)	0603-04=	1	
?	1929	....	365y?	Pagan (Mariana Is-C Pacific)	0804-17=		
	1929	....	?	**Zhupanovsky** (Kamchatka)	1000-12=	2	
	1929	....	?	**Karymsky** (Kamchatka)	1000-13=	2	
?	1929	....	?	Yunaska (Aleutian Is)	1101-21-		
	1929	....	?	**Poás** (Costa Rica)	1405-04=	1	
	1929	....	?	**Reventador** (Ecuador)	1502-01=	3	
	1929	01	15m	**Telica** (Nicaragua)	1404-04=	1?	
	1929	01	30p	**Kverkfjöll** (Iceland-NE)	1703-05=	1	
	1929	0106	<1	**Calbuco** (Chile-S)	1508-02=	3?	
	1929	0107	?	**Puyehue-Cordón Caulle** (Chile-C)	1507-15=	2	
	1929	0112	....	Krakatau (Indonesia)	0602-00=	2	
	1929	0122	73a	**Asama** (Honshu-Japan)	0803-11=	2	
	1929	02	?	**Mutnovsky** (Kamchatka)	1000-06=	2	
	1929	0210	33m	**Negro, Cerro** (Nicaragua)	1404-07=	2	5/-
	1929	0220	1	**Kilauea** (Hawaiian Is)	1302-01-	0	6/-
?	1929	03	?	Cleveland (Aleutian Is)	1101-24-		
	1929	03	883p	**Pavlof** (Alaska Peninsula)	1102-03-	2	
	1929	04	443w	**Gareloi** (Aleutian Is)	1101-07-	3	
	1929	0417	2a	**Yake-dake** (Honshu-Japan)	0803-07=	2	
	1929	0427r	?	**Raung** (Java)	0603-34=	2	
	1929	05 ?	?	**Akutan** (Aleutian Is)	1101-32-	2	
	1929	0520	<1	**Tangkubanparahu** (Java)	0603-09=	0	
	1929	0528	26a>	**Shishaldin** (Aleutian Is)	1101-36-	2	
	1929	06	61p	**Kliuchevskoi** (Kamchatka)	1000-26=	2	
	1929	0603	....	Vesuvius (Italy)	0101-02=	2	8/7
	1929	0606	9a	**Slamet** (Java)	0603-18=	2	
	1929	0617	81a	**Komaga-take** (Hokkaido-Japan)	0805-02=	4	-/8
	1929	0622	<1	**Marapi** (Sumatra)	0601-14=	2	
	1929	0628	3a	**Ambrym** (Vanuatu-SW Pacific)	0507-04=	2	
	1929	0725	1a	**Niuafo'ou** (Tonga-SW Pacific)	0403-11=	2	
	1929	0725	3	**Kilauea** (Hawaiian Is)	1302-01-	0	6/-
	1929	08	?	**San Miguel** (El Salvador)	1403-10=	2	
	1929	08	61p	**Concepción** (Nicaragua)	1404-12=	2	
	1929	0802	?	**Etna** (Italy)	0101-06=	1	
	1929	0807	32a	**Tengger Caldera [Bromo]** (Java)	0603-31=	2	
?	1929	0819	118m	Mageik (Alaska Peninsula)	1102-15-	2	
	1929	09	?	**Akita-Yake-yama** (Honshu-Japan)	0803-26=	2	
	1929	0901	226m	**Gorely** (Kamchatka)	1000-07=	3	-/7
	1929	0916	>3yr	Pelée (W Indies)	1600-12=	2	
	1929	0918	58a	**Asama** (Honshu-Japan)	0803-11=	2	
	1929	1102	....	Santa María (Guatemala)	1402-03=	3	9/8
	1929	12	?	**Kagamil** (Aleutian Is)	1101-26-		
?	1929	12	?	Chiginagak (Alaska Peninsula)	1102-11-		
	1929	12	?	**Llaima** (Chile-C)	1507-11=	2	
	1929	1215e	....	**Pelée** (W Indies)	1600-12=	3	
	1929	1223	8a	**Fournaise, Piton de la** (Indian O.)	0303-02=	2	
	1929	1227	?	**Villarrica** (Chile-C)	1507-12=	1	
	1930	Cont	....	Vesuvius (Italy)	0101-02=	2	8/7
	1930	Cont	....	Nyamuragira (Africa-C)	0203-02=	0	8/-
	1930	Cont	....	Nyiragongo (Africa-C)	0203-03=	0	
	1930	Cont	....	Victory (New Guinea)	0503-03=	1	
	1930	Cont	....	Yasur (Vanuatu-SW Pacific)	0507-10=	2	
?	1930	Cont	....	Pagan (Mariana Is-C Pacific)	0804-17=		
	1930	Cont	....	Gareloi (Aleutian Is)	1101-07-	3	
	1930	Cont	....	Azul, Cerro (Chile-C)	1507-06=	2	
	1930	....	>3yr	**Kita-Iwo-jima** (Volcano Is-Japan)	0804-11=	2?	
	1930 ?	....	?	**Ioto [Iwo-jima]** (Volcano Is-Japan)	0804-12=	1	
M	1930 ?	....	?	**Southern EPR-Segment K** (Pacific)	1304-12-	0	
	1930	....	....	Santa María (Guatemala)	1402-03=	2	9/8
?	1930	....	?	Tacora (Chile-N)	1505-01=		

START YEAR	M-Dy	Duration	VOLCANO NAME (Subregion)	NUMBER	VEI	Vol L/T
? 1930	....	?	Puntiagudo-Cordón Cenizos (Chile	1507-16-		
? 1930	....	?	Hodson (Antarctica)	1900-11=		
1930	0114	....	Krakatau (Indonesia)	0602-00=	2	
1930	0126e	?	**San Miguel** (El Salvador)	1403-10=	2	
1930	0201p	?	**Shiveluch** (Kamchatka)	1000-27=	1	
1930	0203	....	Stromboli (Italy)	0101-04=	2	5/-
1930	0203	....	Pelée (W Indies)	1600-12=	2	
1930	0204	2a	**Karangetang [Api Siau]** (Sangihe Is	0607-02=	2	
1930	0213	<1	**Sarychev Peak** (Kuril Is)	0900-24=	3	
? 1930	0301p	?	Izu-Tobu (Honshu-Japan)	0803-01=		
1930	0313	59a?	**Yake-dake** (Honshu-Japan)	0803-07=	2	
1930	0316	?	**White Island** (New Zealand)	0401-04=	2	
1930	0330	....	Pavlof (Alaska Peninsula)	1102-03-	2	
1930	04	?	**Izalco** (El Salvador)	1403-03=	0	
1930	0402	11a	**Slamet** (Java)	0603-18=	2	
1930	0409<	242a>	Marapi (Sumatra)	0601-14=	0	
? 1930	0417	?	Galeras (Colombia)	1501-08=		
1930	0418	183a	**Asama** (Honshu-Japan)	0803-11=	2	
1930	05	....	**Marapi** (Sumatra)	0601-14=	2?	
1930	0523	1a	**Fournaise, Piton de la** (Indian O.)	0303-02=	0	
1930	0530	45m	**Tengger Caldera [Bromo]** (Java)	0603-31=	2	
1930	06	?	**Veniaminof** (Alaska Peninsula)	1102-07-	2	
? 1930	0630	?	Wrangell (Alaska-E)	1105-02-		
1930	0706	45a	**Llaima** (Chile-C)	1507-11=	2	
1930	08	?	**Lokon-Empung** (Sulawesi-Indonesia)	0606-10=	2	
1930	09	124m	**Gorely** (Kamchatka)	1000-07=	3	-/7
1930	0903	3a	**Aso** (Kyushu-Japan)	0802-11=	2	
1930	0911	....	Stromboli (Italy)	0101-04=	3?	5/-
1930	10	....	**Colima** (México)	1401-04=	1?	
1930	10	?	**Irazú** (Costa Rica)	1405-06=	2	
1930	11 ?	?	**Karangetang [Api Siau]** (Sangihe Is	0607-02=	2	
1930	1101	?	**Etna** (Italy)	0101-06=	1	
1930	1119	18a	**Kilauea** (Hawaiian Is)	1302-01-	0	6/-
1930	1125	295m	Merapi (Java)	0603-25=	2	7/6
1930	12	365p	Awu (Sangihe Is-Indonesia)	0607-04=	0	6/-
1930	1219	....	**Merapi** (Java)	0603-25=	3	7/6
1931	Cont	....	Vesuvius (Italy)	0101-02=	2	8/7
1931	Cont	....	Nyamuragira (Africa-C)	0203-02=	0	8/-
1931	Cont	....	Nyiragongo (Africa-C)	0203-03=	0	
1931	Cont	....	Victory (New Guinea)	0503-03=	1	
1931	Cont	....	Yasur (Vanuatu-SW Pacific)	0507-10=	2	
1931	Cont	....	Merapi (Java)	0603-25=	2	7/6
1931	Cont	....	Kita-Iwo-jima (Volcano Is-Japan)	0804-11=	0	
1931	Cont	....	Pavlof (Alaska Peninsula)	1102-03-	2	
1931	Cont	....	Colima (México)	1401-04=	0	
1931	Cont	....	Azul, Cerro (Chile-C)	1507-06=	2	
1931	Cont	....	Pelée (W Indies)	1600-12=	2	
? 1931	....	?	Baluan (Admiralty Is-SW Pacific)	0500-02-	0	
1931	....	?	**Cotopaxi** (Ecuador)	1502-05=	2	
1931	0122	216e	**Fournaise, Piton de la** (Indian O.)	0303-02=	2	8/-
1931	02	90p	**Tongariro [Ngauruhoe]** (New Zeal)	0401-08=	2	
1931	03	....	Santa María (Guatemala)	1402-03=	2	**9**/8
1931	03	92p	**San Miguel** (El Salvador)	1403-10=	2	
1931	0304	485w	**Tolbachik** (Kamchatka)	1000-24=	2	
1931	0315	....	**Awu** (Sangihe Is-Indonesia)	0607-04=	2	6/-
1931	0321	53a>	**Okmok** (Aleutian Is)	1101-29-	2	
1931	0325	2a	**Kliuchevskoi** (Kamchatka)	1000-26=	4	
1931	0326	90a	**Yake-dake** (Honshu-Japan)	0803-07=	2	
1931	0331	5028a	Asama (Honshu-Japan)	0803-11=	2	
1931	0331t	?	**Izalco** (El Salvador)	1403-03=	2	
1931	0402	81a	**Kuchinoerabu-jima** (Ryukyu Is)	0802-05=	3?	
1931	0403	....	Stromboli (Italy)	0101-04=	2	5/-
1931	05	60r	**Gorely** (Kamchatka)	1000-07=	2	
1931	05	91p	**Akutan** (Aleutian Is)	1101-32-	2	
1931	0501	43a>	Aniakchak (Alaska Peninsula)	1102-09-	3?	
1931	0511	....	**Aniakchak** (Alaska Peninsula)	1102-09-	4	-/8
1931	0516	<1	**Tokachi** (Hokkaido-Japan)	0805-05=	1	
1931	0520	....	Aniakchak (Alaska Peninsula)	1102-09-	3?	-/8
1931	0707	....	Stromboli (Italy)	0101-04=	2	5/-
1931	0726e	781n	**Etna** (Italy)	0101-06=	2	
1931	08	31p	**Kliuchevskoi** (Kamchatka)	1000-26=	2	
1931	0820	....	**Asama** (Honshu-Japan)	0803-11=	3	
1931	09	?	**Kharimkotan** (Kuril Is)	0900-30=	1	
1931	0923	147a	**Krakatau** (Indonesia)	0602-00=	2	
1931	1011	13a	**Shikotsu [Tarumai]** (Hokkaido)	0805-04=	1	
? 1931	1018	?	Aso (Kyushu-Japan)	0802-11=	1?	
1931	1031	?	**Bogoslof** (Aleutian Is)	1101-30-	1	
1931	1208	....	Asama (Honshu-Japan)	0803-11=	3	
1931	1223	13a	**Kilauea** (Hawaiian Is)	1302-01-	0	6/-
1932	Cont	....	Vesuvius (Italy)	0101-02=	2	8/7
1932	Cont	....	Etna (Italy)	0101-06=	2	
1932	Cont	....	Nyamuragira (Africa-C)	0203-02=	0	8/-
1932	Cont	....	Nyiragongo (Africa-C)	0203-03=	0	
1932	Cont	....	Victory (New Guinea)	0503-03=	1	
1932	Cont	....	Yasur (Vanuatu-SW Pacific)	0507-10=	2	
1932	Cont	....	Asama (Honshu-Japan)	0803-11=	2	
1932	Cont	....	Kita-Iwo-jima (Volcano Is-Japan)	0804-11=	0	
1932	Cont	....	Tolbachik (Kamchatka)	1000-24=	2	
1932	Cont	....	Kilauea (Hawaiian Is)	1302-01-	0	6/-
1932	Cont	....	Pelée (W Indies)	1600-12=	2	
1932	....	730y	**Manam** (New Guinea-NE of)	0501-02=	2	
1932	....	?	**Marapi** (Sumatra)	0601-14=	2?	
1932	....	?	**Atsonupuri** (Kuril Is)	0900-05=	2	
? 1932 ?	....	?	Sarychev Peak (Kuril Is)	0900-24=		
? 1932 ?	....	?	Nemo Peak (Kuril Is)	0900-32=		
? 1932	....	?	Gorely (Kamchatka)	1000-07=		
1932	....	730y	**Poás** (Costa Rica)	1405-04=	1?	
1932	....	?	**Azul, Cerro** (Galápagos)	1503-06=	1?	
1932	0101	?	**Cleveland** (Aleutian Is)	1101-24-		
1932	0121	1a	**Fuego** (Guatemala)	1402-09=	4	-/8
1932	0125	335e	**Kliuchevskoi** (Kamchatka)	1000-26=	2	7/6
1932	0201	110a	**Shishaldin** (Aleutian Is)	1101-36-	2	
1932	0206	<1	**Yake-dake** (Honshu-Japan)	0803-07=	2	
1932	0302	<1	**Llaima** (Chile-C)	1507-11=	2?	
1932	0313	?	**Nila** (Banda Sea)	0605-06=	2	
1932	0410	....	**Azul, Cerro** (Chile-C)	1507-06=	**5**+	-/**9**
1932	0523	583f	**Lewotobi** (Lesser Sunda Is)	0604-18=	3	5/-
1932	06	470m	**Aso** (Kyushu-Japan)	0802-11=	2	
1932	06	?	**Karymsky** (Kamchatka)	1000-13=	2	
1932	0603	<1	**Stromboli** (Italy)	0101-04=	2	
1932	0605e	392w	**Descabezado Grande** (Chile-C)	1507-05=	3	
1932	0701	71a	**Slamet** (Java)	0603-18=	2	
1932	0721	22a	**Akita-Komaga-take** (Honshu-Japan)	0803-23=	2	
? 1932	0723	<1	Kuchinoerabu-jima (Ryukyu Is)	0802-05=	1?	
1932	0907	30a	**Farallon de Pajaros** (Mariana Is-Pac)	0804-14=	2	
1932	1001	45m	Kusatsu-Shirane (Honshu-Japan)	0803-12=	2	-/4
1932	1010	?	**Galeras** (Colombia)	1501-08=	2	
1932	1023	....	**Kusatsu-Shirane** (Honshu-Japan)	0803-12=	3	-/4
1932	11	2a	**Fournaise, Piton de la** (Indian O.)	0303-02=		
1932	11	?	**Merapi** (Java)	0603-25=	1	
1932	1110	3a	**Gamalama** (Halmahera-Indonesia)	0608-06=	2	
1932	1114	572a	Krakatau (Indonesia)	0602-00=	2	
1932	12	31p	**Kanlaon** (Philippines-C)	0702-02=	2	
1932	12	....	Santa María (Guatemala)	1402-03=	2	**9**/8
1932	1201p	?	**Unnamed** (Tonga-SW Pacific)	0403-01=	0	
? 1932	1231y	?	San Martín (México)	1401-11=		
1932	1231	6a	**Llaima** (Chile-C)	1507-11=	3	
1933	Cont	....	Vesuvius (Italy)	0101-02=	2	8/7
1933	Cont	....	Etna (Italy)	0101-06=	2	
1933	Cont	....	Nyamuragira (Africa-C)	0203-02=	0	8/-
1933	Cont	....	Nyiragongo (Africa-C)	0203-03=	0	
1933	Cont	....	Manam (New Guinea-NE of)	0501-02=	2	
1933	Cont	....	Victory (New Guinea)	0503-03=	1	
1933	Cont	....	Yasur (Vanuatu-SW Pacific)	0507-10=	2	
1933	Cont	....	Lewotobi (Lesser Sunda Is)	0604-18=	3	5/-
1933	Cont	....	Kanlaon (Philippines-C)	0702-02=	2	
1933	Cont	....	Aso (Kyushu-Japan)	0802-11=	2	
1933	Cont	....	Kita-Iwo-jima (Volcano Is-Japan)	0804-11=	0	
1933	Cont	....	Santa María (Guatemala)	1402-03=	1	**9**/8
1933	Cont	....	Poás (Costa Rica)	1405-04=	1?	
1933	Cont	....	Descabezado Grande (Chile-C)	1507-05=	2	
1933	Cont	....	Llaima (Chile-C)	1507-11=	2	
1933	....	?	**Long Island** (New Guinea-NE of)	0501-05=		
1933	....	?	**Lopevi** (Vanuatu-SW Pacific)	0507-05=		
? 1933	....	?	Kusatsu-Shirane (Honshu-Japan)	0803-12=		
? 1933	....	?	Fuss Peak (Kuril Is)	0900-34=		
? 1933	....	?	Galeras (Colombia)	1501-08=		
1933	....	?	**Wolf** (Galápagos)	1503-02=	0	
1933	....	>3yr	**Azul, Cerro** (Chile-C)	1507-06=	2	
1933	0104	?	**Lonquimay** (Chile-C)	1507-10=	2	
1933	0105	13k	**Villarrica** (Chile-C)	1507-12=	2	
1933	0108	96a>	**Kharimkotan** (Kuril Is)	0900-30=	**5**	8/**9**
1933	0109	206a	**Asama** (Honshu-Japan)	0803-11=	2	
1933	0123	?	**Popocatépetl** (México)	1401-09=	1	
? 1933	02	?	Sumaco (Ecuador)	1502-04=	2	
1933	02	?	**Lautaro** (Chile-S)	1508-06=	2?	
1933	0322?	125a?	Irazú (Costa Rica)	1405-06=	1	-/6
1933	04	?	**Falcon Island** (Tonga-SW Pacific)	0403-05=	2	
1933	0402	?	**White Island** (New Zealand)	0401-04=	3	
? 1933	0415q	?	Chikurachki (Kuril Is)	0900-36=		
1933	0501	....	**Krakatau** (Indonesia)	0602-00=	3	
? 1933	0505	?	Iliamna (Alaska-SW)	1103-02-		
1933	0512	<1	**Slamet** (Java)	0603-18=	1?	
? 1933	0525	?	Redoubt (Alaska-SW)	1103-03-		
1933	0607	298a	**Fournaise, Piton de la** (Indian O.)	0303-02=	2	
1933	0615?	....	**Irazú** (Costa Rica)	1405-06=	2	-/6
1933	0626d	12d>	**Hainan Dao** (SE Asia)	0705-001		
1933	07 ?	31p?	**Pago** (New Britain-SW Pac)	0502-08=	2	
1933	0710	26a	**Suoh [Pematang Bata]** (Sumatra)	0601-27=	4	-/8
1933	0813	>3yr	Dukono (Halmahera-Indonesia)	0608-01=	2	
1933	09	31p	**Karymsky** (Kamchatka)	1000-13=	2	
1933	1001	561m	**Merapi** (Java)	0603-25=	2	6/6
1933	1009	67a	**Láscar** (Chile-N)	1505-10=	2	
1933	1014	47m	**Oshima** (Izu Is-Japan)	0804-01=	0	5/-

	START YEAR	M-Dy	Duration	VOLCANO NAME (Subregion)	NUMBER	VEI	Vol L/T
	1933	11	?	**Great Sitkin** (Aleutian Is)	1101-12-	2	
	1933	1112	?	**Gamalama** (Halmahera-Indonesia)	0608-06=	2	
	1933	1113	214*m*	**Alaid** (Kuril Is)	0900-39=	2	
	1933	1121	15*a*	**Raung** (Java)	0603-34=	2	
	1933	1129a	10*b*	**Grímsvötn** (Iceland-NE)	1703-01=	1	
	1933	1130	43*a*>	**Izalco** (El Salvador)	1403-03=	2	
	1933	12	....	**Dukono** (Halmahera-Indonesia)	0608-01=	3	
	1933	1201	13*a*	**Shikotsu [Tarumai]** (Hokkaido)	0805-04=	2	
	1933	1202	16*a*	**Mauna Loa** (Hawaiian Is)	1302-02=	0	8/-
	1933	*1223*	*20a*	*Kuchinoerabu-jima (Ryukyu Is)*	0802-05=	*2*	
	1933	1224	....	**Kuchinoerabu-jima** (Ryukyu Is)	0802-05=	4?	
	1933	1225	?	**Bulusan** (Luzon-Philippines)	0703-01=	2	
	1934	*Cont*	....	*Vesuvius (Italy)*	0101-02=	*2*	*8/7*
	1934	*Cont*	....	*Nyamuragira (Africa-C)*	0203-02=	*0*	*8/-*
	1934	*Cont*	....	*Nyiragongo (Africa-C)*	0203-03=	*0*	
	1934	*Cont*	....	*Fournaise, Piton de la (Indian O.)*	0303-02=	*2*	
	1934	*Cont*	....	*Manam (New Guinea-NE of)*	0501-02=	*2*	
	1934	*Cont*	....	*Victory (New Guinea)*	0503-03=	*1*	
	1934	*Cont*	....	*Yasur (Vanuatu-SW Pacific)*	0507-10=	*2*	
	1934	*Cont*	....	*Dukono (Halmahera-Indonesia)*	0608-01=	*2*	
	1934	*Cont*	....	*Kita-Iwo-jima (Volcano Is-Japan)*	0804-11=	*0*	
	1934	*Cont*	....	*Alaid (Kuril Is)*	0900-39=	*2*	
	1934	*Cont*	....	*Izalco (El Salvador)*	1403-03=	*2*	
	1934	*Cont*	....	*Poás (Costa Rica)*	1405-04=	*1?*	
	1934	*Cont*	....	*Azul, Cerro (Chile-C)*	1507-06=	*2*	
?	*1934*	....	*?*	*Slamet (Java)*	0603-18=		
	1934	....	?	**Kusatsu-Shirane** (Honshu-Japan)	0803-12=	2	
	1934	01	?	**Telica** (Nicaragua)	1404-04=	2	
	1934	0105	70*m*	**Etna** (Italy)	0101-06=	1	
	1934	*0106*	....	*Krakatau (Indonesia)*	0602-00=	*2*	
	1934	0109	33	**Asama** (Honshu-Japan)	0803-11=	1	
?	*1934*	*0111*	*?*	*Suwanose-jima (Ryukyu Is)*	0802-03=	*2?*	
	1934	*0111*	....	*Kuchinoerabu-jima (Ryukyu Is)*	0802-05=	*2*	
	1934	0117	?	**Chillán, Nevados de** (Chile-C)	1507-07=	2?	
	1934	0124	91*a*	**Dempo** (Sumatra)	0601-23=	2	
	1934	0202	>3yr	**Stromboli** (Italy)	0101-04=	2?	7/-
	1934	0306	?	**Puyehue-Cordón Caulle** (Chile-C)	1507-15=	2	
	1934	0330	8*a*	**Grímsvötn** (Iceland-NE)	1703-01=	2	
	1934	0415	10*a?*	**Oshima** (Izu Is-Japan)	0804-01=	0	
	1934	*0421*	....	*Merapi (Java)*	0603-25=	*2*	*6/6*
	1934	05	?	**Bayonnaise Rocks** (Izu Is-Japan)	0804-07=	0	
	1934	06	?	**Tongariro [Ngauruhoe]** (New Zeal)	0401-08=	2	
	1934	06	15*m*	**Asama** (Honshu-Japan)	0803-11=	1	
	1934	0614	32*e*	**Sirung** (Lesser Sunda Is)	0604-27=	2	
?	*1934*	*07*	*350m*	*Iwate (Honshu-Japan)*	0803-24=		
	1934	0715q	?	**Farallon de Pajaros** (Mariana Is-Pac)	0804-14=	0	
	1934	0716	?	**Aso** (Kyushu-Japan)	0802-11=	2	
	1934	0808	>3yr	**Sangay** (Ecuador)	1502-09=	3	
	1934	0811	?	**Ruapehu** (New Zealand)	0401-10=	2	
	1934	*0821*	....	*Stromboli (Italy)*	0101-04=	*2*	*7/-*
?	*1934*	*09*	*?*	*Oshima (Izu Is-Japan)*	0804-01=		
	1934	0906	32*a*	**Kilauea** (Hawaiian Is)	1302-01-	0	6/-
	1934	0919	331*m?*	**Kikai** (Ryukyu Is)	0802-06=	2	6/-
	1934	1004	376*q*	**Ebeko** (Kuril Is)	0900-38=	2	-/5
	1934	11	120*p*	**Karymsky** (Kamchatka)	1000-13=	2	8/-
	1934	*1113*	*959p*	*Asama (Honshu-Japan)*	0803-11=	*2*	
	1934	12	90*p*	**Tongariro [Ngauruhoe]** (New Zeal)	0401-08=	2	
	1934	12	90*p*	**Ruapehu** (New Zealand)	0401-10=	2	
	1934	*1214*	....	*Santa María (Guatemala)*	1402-03=	*2*	***9/8***
@	**1934**	1221	5*a*	**Grímsvötn** (Iceland-NE)	1703-01=		
?	*1934*	*1231*	*2a?*	*Pinacate (México)*	1401-001		
	1935	*Cont*	....	*Vesuvius (Italy)*	0101-02=	*2*	*8/7*
	1935	*Cont*	....	*Stromboli (Italy)*	0101-04=	*1*	*7/-*
	1935	*Cont*	....	*Nyamuragira (Africa-C)*	0203-02=	*0*	*8/-*
	1935	*Cont*	....	*Nyiragongo (Africa-C)*	0203-03=	*0*	
	1935	*Cont*	....	*Tongariro [Ngauruhoe] (New Zeal)*	0401-08=	*2*	
	1935	*Cont*	....	*Ruapehu (New Zealand)*	0401-10=	*2*	
	1935	*Cont*	....	*Victory (New Guinea)*	0503-03=	*1*	
	1935	*Cont*	....	*Yasur (Vanuatu-SW Pacific)*	0507-10=	*2*	
	1935	*Cont*	....	*Merapi (Java)*	0603-25=	*2*	*6/6*
	1935	*Cont*	....	*Dukono (Halmahera-Indonesia)*	0608-01=	*2*	
?	*1935*	*Cont*	....	*Iwate (Honshu-Japan)*	0803-24=		
	1935	*Cont*	....	*Kita-Iwo-jima (Volcano Is-Japan)*	0804-11=	*0*	
	1935	*Cont*	....	*Ebeko (Kuril Is)*	0900-38=	*2*	*-/5*
	1935	*Cont*	....	*Karymsky (Kamchatka)*	1000-13=	*2*	*8/-*
?	*1935*	*Cont*	....	*Pinacate (México)*	1401-001		
	1935	*Cont*	....	*Azul, Cerro (Chile-C)*	1507-06=	*2*	
	1935 ?	....	?	**Fournaise, Piton de la** (Indian O.)	0303-02=	2	
	1935	....	?	**Ioto [Iwo-jima]** (Volcano Is-Japan)	0804-12=	1	
	1935	0104	189*a*	**Krakatau** (Indonesia)	0602-00=	2	
	1935	0107	274*a*	**Aso** (Kyushu-Japan)	0802-11=	2	
	1935	*0108*	....	*Kikai (Ryukyu Is)*	0802-06=	*2*	*6/-*
	1935	02	?	**Salak** (Java)	0603-05=	2	
	1935	02	14*m*	**Concepción** (Nicaragua)	1404-12=	2	
	1935	02	?	**Wolf** (Galápagos)	1503-02=		
	1935	*03*	....	*Santa María (Guatemala)*	1402-03=	*2*	***9/8***
	1935	*0313*	*158a*	*Augustine (Alaska-SW)*	1103-01-	*2*	
	1935	0420	....	**Asama** (Honshu-Japan)	0803-11=	3	
	1935	*0421*	*563a>*	*Kliuchevskoi (Kamchatka)*	1000-26=	*2*	
	1935	0426	10*a?*	**Oshima** (Izu Is-Japan)	0804-01=	0	
	1935	0531p	?	**Perbakti-Gagak** (Java)	0603-04=	1	
	1935	0618	....	**Augustine** (Alaska-SW)	1103-01-	3	
	1935	07	?	**Tengger Caldera [Bromo]** (Java)	0603-31=	2	
	1935	*07*	....	*Sangay (Ecuador)*	1502-09=	*3*	
	1935	0702	?	**Chillán, Nevados de** (Chile-C)	1507-07=	2?	
	1935	*0707*	*>3yr*	*Etna (Italy)*	0101-06=	*2*	
	1935	0831	?	**Karangetang [Api Siau]** (Sangihe Is	0607-02=	2	
	1935	09	123*p*	**Ambrym** (Vanuatu-SW Pacific)	0507-04=	2	
	1935	0911	62*a*	**Yake-dake** (Honshu-Japan)	0803-07=	2	
	1935	0920	4*a*	**Sakura-jima** (Kyushu-Japan)	0802-08=	1	
?	*1935*	*1015*	*<1*	*Komaga-take (Hokkaido-Japan)*	0805-02=		
	1935	1121	42*a*	**Mauna Loa** (Hawaiian Is)	1302-02=	0	7/-
	1935	12	15*m*	**Lewotobi** (Lesser Sunda Is)	0604-18=	2	
	1935	12	306*p*	**Shiretoko-Iwo-zan** (Hokkaido-Japan)	0805-09=	1	
	1935	*1201p*	*208p*	*Villarrica (Chile-C)*	1507-12=	*2*	
	1935	1207	69*m?*	**Niuafo'ou** (Tonga-SW Pacific)	0403-11=	2	
	1935	1231	?	**Bristol Island** (Antarctica)	1900-08=	2	
	1936	*Cont*	....	*Vesuvius (Italy)*	0101-02=	*2*	*8/7*
	1936	*Cont*	....	*Etna (Italy)*	0101-06=	*2*	
	1936	*Cont*	....	*Nyamuragira (Africa-C)*	0203-02=	*0*	*8/-*
	1936	*Cont*	....	*Nyiragongo (Africa-C)*	0203-03=	*0*	
	1936	*Cont*	....	*Niuafo'ou (Tonga-SW Pacific)*	0403-11=	*2*	
	1936	*Cont*	....	*Ambrym (Vanuatu-SW Pacific)*	0507-04=	*2*	
	1936	*Cont*	....	*Yasur (Vanuatu-SW Pacific)*	0507-10=	*2*	
	1936	*Cont*	....	*Dukono (Halmahera-Indonesia)*	0608-01=	*2*	
	1936	*Cont*	....	*Kita-Iwo-jima (Volcano Is-Japan)*	0804-11=	*0*	
	1936	*Cont*	....	*Shiretoko-Iwo-zan (Hokkaido-Japan)*	0805-09=	*1*	
	1936	*Cont*	....	*Mauna Loa (Hawaiian Is)*	1302-02=	*0*	*7/-*
	1936	*Cont*	....	*Santa María (Guatemala)*	1402-03=	*1*	***9/8***
	1936	*Cont*	....	*Azul, Cerro (Chile-C)*	1507-06=	*2*	
	1936	*Cont*	....	*Villarrica (Chile-C)*	1507-12=	*2*	
?	*1936*	....	*?*	*Okmok (Aleutian Is)*	1101-29-		
	1936	....	*>3yr*	*Pavlof (Alaska Peninsula)*	1102-03-	*2*	
@	**1936**	....	?	**Macdonald** (Austral Is-C Pacific)	1303-06-	0?	
?	*1936 ?*	....	*?*	*San Miguel (El Salvador)*	1403-10=	*2*	
	1936	*0131*	....	*Stromboli (Italy)*	0101-04=	*2?*	*7/-*
	1936	*02*	....	*Asama (Honshu-Japan)*	0803-11=	*3*	
	1936	0205	<1	**Aso** (Kyushu-Japan)	0802-11=	2	
	1936	0209	200*a?*	**Galeras** (Colombia)	1501-08=	2	
	1936	0218	....	**Kliuchevskoi** (Kamchatka)	1000-26=	3	
	1936	0415q	?	**Farallon de Pajaros** (Mariana Is-Pac)	0804-14=	2	
	1936	0419	<1	**Shikotsu [Tarumai]** (Hokkaido)	0805-04=	1	
	1936	0429	<1	**Kerinci** (Sumatra)	0601-17=	2	
	1936	0509?	4*a?*	**Ruapehu** (New Zealand)	0401-10=	2	
	1936	*0512*	....	*Stromboli (Italy)*	0101-04=	*2*	*7/-*
	1936	06	?	**Falcon Island** (Tonga-SW Pacific)	0403-05=	2	
?	*1936*	*0618*	*180m*	*Curtis Island (Kermadec Is)*	0402-01=		
?	*1936*	*07*	*>3yr*	*Bam (New Guinea-NE of)*	0501-01=		
?	*1936*	*0704*	*1a*	*Mageik (Alaska Peninsula)*	1102-15-	*2?*	
@	**1936**	0717	?	**Negro de Mayasquer, Cerro** (Col.)	1501-11=	2	
	1936	*08*	....	*Sangay (Ecuador)*	1502-09=	*2*	
	1936	0808	6*a*	**Aso** (Kyushu-Japan)	0802-11=	2	
	1936	0813<	201*a*>	**Tolbachik** (Kamchatka)	1000-24=	2	
	1936	*0822*	....	*Stromboli (Italy)*	0101-04=	*2*	*7/-*
	1936	0822	111*a*	**Raung** (Java)	0603-34=	2	
	1936	0827	?	**Reventador** (Ecuador)	1502-01=	3	
	1936	0830	<1	**Kerinci** (Sumatra)	0601-17=	2	
	1936	09	?	**Fournaise, Piton de la** (Indian O.)	0303-02=	0	
	1936	09	>3yr	**Manam** (New Guinea-NE of)	0501-02=	3	
	1936	1013	34*m*	**Krakatau** (Indonesia)	0602-00=	1	
	1936	*1026*	....	*Stromboli (Italy)*	0101-04=	*2?*	*7/-*
	1936	1026	2*a*	**Perbakti-Gagak** (Java)	0603-04=	1	
	1936	1105	20*a*	**Ijen** (Java)	0603-35=	2	
	1936	1115	11*a*	**Shikotsu [Tarumai]** (Hokkaido)	0805-04=	1	
	1936	1126	1*a*	**Dempo** (Sumatra)	0601-23=	2	
	1936	1218	14*a?*	**Bristol Island** (Antarctica)	1900-08=	2	
	1937	*Cont*	....	*Vesuvius (Italy)*	0101-02=	*2*	*8/7*
	1937	*Cont*	....	*Etna (Italy)*	0101-06=	*2*	
	1937	*Cont*	....	*Nyamuragira (Africa-C)*	0203-02=	*0*	*8/-*
	1937	*Cont*	....	*Nyiragongo (Africa-C)*	0203-03=	*0*	
?	*1937*	*Cont*	....	*Bam (New Guinea-NE of)*	0501-01=		
	1937	*Cont*	....	*Yasur (Vanuatu-SW Pacific)*	0507-10=	*2*	
	1937	*Cont*	....	*Dukono (Halmahera-Indonesia)*	0608-01=	*2*	
	1937	*Cont*	....	*Asama (Honshu-Japan)*	0803-11=	*2*	
	1937	*Cont*	....	*Kita-Iwo-jima (Volcano Is-Japan)*	0804-11=	*0*	
	1937	*Cont*	....	*Santa María (Guatemala)*	1402-03=	*1*	***9/8***
	1937	*Cont*	....	*Azul, Cerro (Chile-C)*	1507-06=	*2*	
	1937	*Cont*	....	*Bristol Island (Antarctica)*	1900-08=	*2*	
	1937	....	?	**Dhamar, Harras of** (Arabia-S)	0301-12-	2	
	1937	....	?	**Hunga Tonga-Hunga Ha'apai**	0403-04=	2	
	1937	....	?	**Telong, Bur ni** (Sumatra)	0601-05=		
	1937	....	?	**Slamet** (Java)	0603-18=		
?	*1937*	....	*?*	*Kita-Fukutokutai (Volcano Is-Japan)*	0804-121	*0*	
	1937 ?	....	365*y?*	**Izalco** (El Salvador)	1403-03=	2?	

	START YEAR	M-Dy	Duration	VOLCANO NAME (Subregion)	NUMBER	VEI	Vol L/T
	1937	....	?	**Copahue** (Chile-C)	1507-09=	2?	
	1937	01	?	**Tongariro [Ngauruhoe]** (New Zeal)	0401-08=	2	
	1937	*0106*	....	*Stromboli (Italy)*	0101-04=	*2*	*7/-*
	1937	*0110*	....	*Tolbachik (Kamchatka)*	1000-24=	*2*	
	1937	0113	<1	**Aso** (Kyushu-Japan)	0802-11=	2	
	1937	0209?	266*a*?	**Llaima** (Chile-C)	1507-11=	2	
	1937	03	31*p*	**Fernandina** (Galápagos)	1503-01=	0	
	1937	*0315*	....	*Manam (New Guinea-NE of)*	0501-02=	*3*	
	1937	0317	2*a*	**Komaga-take** (Hokkaido-Japan)	0805-02=	1	
	1937	0327	19*m*	**Ambrym** (Vanuatu-SW Pacific)	0507-04=	2	
	1937	*04*	....	*Sangay (Ecuador)*	1502-09=	*3*	
	1937	04	20*m*	**Planchón-Peteroa** (Chile-C)	1507-04=	2	
	1937	0403	712*m*	**Kliuchevskoi** (Kamchatka)	1000-26=	3	8/7
?	*1937*	*05*	?	*Ulawun (New Britain-SW Pac)*	0502-12=		
	1937	0507	6*a*	**Aso** (Kyushu-Japan)	0802-11=	2	
	1937	0529	4*a*	**Rabaul** (New Britain-SW Pac)	0502-14=	4?	-/8
	1937	06	?	**Ubinas** (Perú)	1504-02=	2	
	1937	0616	?	**Mocho-Choshuenco** (Chile-C)	1507-13=		
	1937	0624	197*a*	**Cereme** (Java)	0603-17=	2	
	1937	*07*	....	*Pavlof (Alaska Peninsula)*	1102-03-	*2*	
	1937	0717	30*m*	**Oshima** (Izu Is-Japan)	0804-01=	0	
?	*1937*	*0805*	?	*Tacora (Chile-N)*	1505-01=		
	1937	0806	109*a*	**Krakatau** (Indonesia)	0602-00=	2	
	1937	0813	104*a*	**Fournaise, Piton de la** (Indian O.)	0303-02=	2	6/-
	1937	0907	?	**Bagana** (Bougainville-SW Pacific)	0505-02=	3	
?	*1937*	*0908*	?	*Talakmau (Sumatra)*	0601-13=	*1*	
	1937	0908	?	**Kerinci** (Sumatra)	0601-17=	2	
?	*1937*	*0918*	?	*Callaqui (Chile-C)*	1507-091		
	1937	1027	31*a*	**Raung** (Java)	0603-34=	2	
	1937	11	274*p*	**Telica** (Nicaragua)	1404-04=	2	
	1937	1103	1*a*	**Yunaska** (Aleutian Is)	1101-21-	3	
	1937	*1114?*	....	*Stromboli (Italy)*	0101-04=	*2*	*7/-*
	1937	1127	82*a*?	**Kusatsu-Shirane** (Honshu-Japan)	0803-12=	1	
	1938	*Cont*	....	*Vesuvius (Italy)*	0101-02=	*2*	*8/7*
	1938	*Cont*	....	*Stromboli (Italy)*	0101-04=	*1*	*7/-*
	1938	*Cont*	....	*Etna (Italy)*	0101-06=	*2*	
	1938	*Cont*	....	*Nyiragongo (Africa-C)*	0203-03=	*0*	
?	*1938*	*Cont*	....	*Bam (New Guinea-NE of)*	0501-01=		
	1938	*Cont*	....	*Manam (New Guinea-NE of)*	0501-02=	*0*	
	1938	*Cont*	....	*Yasur (Vanuatu-SW Pacific)*	0507-10=	*2*	
	1938	*Cont*	....	*Cereme (Java)*	0603-17=	*2*	
	1938	*Cont*	....	*Dukono (Halmahera-Indonesia)*	0608-01=	*2*	
	1938	*Cont*	....	*Kita-Iwo-jima (Volcano Is-Japan)*	0804-11=	*0*	
	1938	*Cont*	....	*Pavlof (Alaska Peninsula)*	1102-03-	*2*	
	1938	*Cont*	....	*Santa María (Guatemala)*	1402-03=	*1*	***9**/8*
	1938	*Cont*	....	*Izalco (El Salvador)*	1403-03=	*2?*	
	1938	*Cont*	....	*Telica (Nicaragua)*	1404-04=	*2*	
	1938	*Cont*	....	*Azul, Cerro (Chile-C)*	1507-06=	*2*	
	1938	....	?	**Long Island** (New Guinea-NE of)	0501-05=		
	1938	....	?	**Ambrym** (Vanuatu-SW Pacific)	0507-04=	2	
	1938 j	....	?	**Colo [Una Una]** (Sulawesi-Indonesia)	0606-01=	1	
	1938	....	406*w*	**Aso** (Kyushu-Japan)	0802-11=	2	
	1938	....	?	**Cleveland** (Aleutian Is)	1101-24-		
	1938	....	?	**Okmok** (Aleutian Is)	1101-29-		
	1938	....	?	**Wolf** (Galápagos)	1503-02=		
	1938	0119	58*a*	**Kerinci** (Sumatra)	0601-17=	2	
	1938	0128	878*e*	**Nyamuragira** (Africa-C)	0203-02=	1	8/-
	1938	0131e	?	**Salak** (Java)	0603-05=	2	
	1938	02	?	**San Pedro** (Chile-N)	1505-07=	2	
	1938	*0207*	....	*Kliuchevskoi (Kamchatka)*	1000-26=	*3*	*8/7*
?	*1938*	*0211*	?	*Villarrica (Chile-C)*	1507-12=	*1?*	
	1938	0225	33	**Sakura-jima** (Kyushu-Japan)	0802-08=	2	
	1938	0306	243*a*>	**Avachinsky** (Kamchatka)	1000-10=	3	-/7
	1938	0311	<1	**Suwanose-jima** (Ryukyu Is)	0802-03=	2?	
	1938	0325	>3yr	**Asama** (Honshu-Japan)	0803-11=	1	-/5
	1938	05	31*p*	**Ebulobo** (Lesser Sunda Is)	0604-10=		
	1938	05	31*p*	**Kelimutu** (Lesser Sunda Is)	0604-14=	2	
	1938	05	?	**Grímsvötn** (Iceland-NE)	1703-01=	1	
	1938	0515	?	**Bagana** (Bougainville-SW Pacific)	0505-02=	3	
	1938	0605	?	**Mayon** (Luzon-Philippines)	0703-03=	2	-/6
	1938	*0704*	*729a*	*Krakatau (Indonesia)*	0602-00=	*2*	
?	*1938*	*0716<*	?	*Akagi (Honshu-Japan)*	0803-13=		
	1938	0717?	80*a*?	**Kusatsu-Shirane** (Honshu-Japan)	0803-12=	1	
	1938	0725	4*a*	**Fournaise, Piton de la** (Indian O.)	0303-02=	1	
	1938	0811	<1	**Oshima** (Izu Is-Japan)	0804-01=	1	5/5
	1938	0812	?	**Nemo Peak** (Kuril Is)	0900-32=	2	
	1938	0813	110*a*>	**Raung** (Java)	0603-34=	2	
	1938	*09*	....	*Sangay (Ecuador)*	1502-09=	*2*	
	1938	09	31*p*	**Planchón-Peteroa** (Chile-C)	1507-04=	2	
	1938	0908	<1	**Gamalama** (Halmahera-Indonesia)	0608-06=	2	
	1938	10	?	**Karymsky** (Kamchatka)	1000-13=	2	
	1938	10	?	**Makushin** (Aleutian Is)	1101-31-	2	
	1938	11	?	**Mutnovsky** (Kamchatka)	1000-06=	2	
	1938	12	?	**Perbakti-Gagak** (Java)	0603-04=	1	
	1938	12	?	**Llaima** (Chile-C)	1507-11=	1	
	1938	1201p	62*r*	**Villarrica** (Chile-C)	1507-12=	2	
	1938	1207	39*a*	**Fournaise, Piton de la** (Indian O.)	0303-02=	2	7/-
	1938	1219?	?	**Askja** (Iceland-NE)	1703-06=	2	
	1939	*Cont*	....	*Vesuvius (Italy)*	0101-02=	*2*	*8/7*
	1939	*Cont*	....	*Stromboli (Italy)*	0101-04=	*1*	*7/-*
	1939	*Cont*	....	*Etna (Italy)*	0101-06=	*2*	
	1939	*Cont*	....	*Nyamuragira (Africa-C)*	0203-02=	*1*	*8/-*
	1939	*Cont*	....	*Nyiragongo (Africa-C)*	0203-03=	*0*	
	1939	*Cont*	....	*Fournaise, Piton de la (Indian O.)*	0303-02=	*2*	*7/-*
?	*1939*	*Cont*	....	*Bam (New Guinea-NE of)*	0501-01=		
	1939	*Cont*	....	*Manam (New Guinea-NE of)*	0501-02=	*0*	
	1939	*Cont*	....	*Yasur (Vanuatu-SW Pacific)*	0507-10=	*2*	
	1939	*Cont*	....	*Raung (Java)*	0603-34=	*2*	
	1939	*Cont*	....	*Dukono (Halmahera-Indonesia)*	0608-01=	*2*	
	1939	*Cont*	....	*Aso (Kyushu-Japan)*	0802-11=	*2*	
	1939	*Cont*	....	*Asama (Honshu-Japan)*	0803-11=	*1*	*-/5*
	1939	*Cont*	....	*Kita-Iwo-jima (Volcano Is-Japan)*	0804-11=	*0*	
	1939	*Cont*	....	*Kliuchevskoi (Kamchatka)*	1000-26=	*2*	*8/7*
	1939	*Cont*	....	*Pavlof (Alaska Peninsula)*	1102-03-	*2*	
	1939	*Cont*	....	*Santa María (Guatemala)*	1402-03=	*1*	***9**/8*
	1939	*Cont*	....	*Sangay (Ecuador)*	1502-09=	*2*	
	1939	*Cont*	....	*Villarrica (Chile-C)*	1507-12=	*2*	
	1939	....	?	**Farallon de Pajaros** (Mariana Is-Pac)	0804-14=	2	
	1939	01	151*p*	**Telica** (Nicaragua)	1404-04=	2	
	1939	0130?	?	**Bagana** (Bougainville-SW Pacific)	0505-02=	2	
	1939	02	? 195*m*?	**Kusatsu-Shirane** (Honshu-Japan)	0803-12=	1	
	1939	02	14*m*	**Oshima** (Izu Is-Japan)	0804-01=	1?	
	1939	02	>3yr	**Izalco** (El Salvador)	1403-03=	2	
	1939	0202	?	**Lopevi** (Vanuatu-SW Pacific)	0507-05=	2	
	1939	0202	?	**Cotopaxi** (Ecuador)	1502-05=	2	
	1939	0329	108*a*	**Slamet** (Java)	0603-18=	2	
	1939	0406<	?	**Perbakti-Gagak** (Java)	0603-04=	1	
	1939	0430?	?	**Kavachi** (Solomon Is-SW Pacific)	0505-06=	2	
	1939	05	?	**Mutnovsky** (Kamchatka)	1000-06=	2	
	1939	05	61*p*	**San Miguel** (El Salvador)	1403-10=	2	
	1939	0518	272*m*	**Irazú** (Costa Rica)	1405-06=	2	
	1939	0523	34*a*?	**Veniaminof** (Alaska Peninsula)	1102-07-	3	
	1939	06	?	**Fonualei** (Tonga-SW Pacific)	0403-10=	2	
?	*1939*	*06*	?	*Grímsvötn (Iceland-NE)*	1703-01=	*0*	
	1939	0604	<1	**Yake-dake** (Honshu-Japan)	0803-07=	2	
	1939	0617	....	**Krakatau** (Indonesia)	0602-00=	3	
	1939	0624	25*m*	**Tengger Caldera [Bromo]** (Java)	0603-31=	2	
?	*1939*	*07*	?	*Zaò (Honshu-Japan)*	0803-19=	*1?*	
	1939	0718	12*a*	**Dempo** (Sumatra)	0601-23=	2	
	1939	0724	<1	**Kick 'em Jenny** (W Indies)	1600-16=	1	
	1939	08	?	**Tongariro [Ngauruhoe]** (New Zeal)	0401-08=	2	
	1939	0817	131*e*	**Tori-shima** (Izu Is-Japan)	0804-09=	3	7/7
	1939	0820	682*b*	**Santorini** (Greece)	0102-04=	2	7/-
	1939	0821	?	**Mayon** (Luzon-Philippines)	0703-03=	1	
	1939	0901	15*a*	**Oshima** (Izu Is-Japan)	0804-01=	1	5/-
	1939	0925	2*a*	**Tolbachik** (Kamchatka)	1000-24=	2	
	1939	0926	?	**Biliran** (Philippines-C)	0702-08=	1?	
	1939	1013	2*a*	**Dieng Volc Complex** (Java)	0603-20=	1?	
	1939	1026	17*a*?	**Sakura-jima** (Kyushu-Japan)	0802-08=	2	-/5
	1939	11	?	**Veniaminof** (Alaska Peninsula)	1102-07-	2	
	1939	11	15*m*	**Telica** (Nicaragua)	1404-04=	2	
	1939	1101	?	**Lopevi** (Vanuatu-SW Pacific)	0507-05=	2	
	1939	1119	481*a*	**Kaba** (Sumatra)	0601-22=	2	
	1939	1204	<1	**Slamet** (Java)	0603-18=	2	
	1939	1213	276*m*	**Merapi** (Java)	0603-25=	2	6/-
	1939	1217	125*a*	**Lewotobi** (Lesser Sunda Is)	0604-18=	2	
	1939	1219	64*a*	**Dempo** (Sumatra)	0601-23=	2	
	1940	*Cont*	....	*Vesuvius (Italy)*	0101-02=	*2*	*8/7*
	1940	*Cont*	....	*Stromboli (Italy)*	0101-04=	*1*	*7/-*
	1940	*Cont*	....	*Santorini (Greece)*	0102-04=	*2*	*7/-*
	1940	*Cont*	....	*Nyamuragira (Africa-C)*	0203-02=	*1*	*8/-*
	1940	*Cont*	....	*Nyiragongo (Africa-C)*	0203-03=	*0*	
	1940	*Cont*	....	*Yasur (Vanuatu-SW Pacific)*	0507-10=	*2*	
	1940	*Cont*	....	*Kaba (Sumatra)*	0601-22=	*2*	
	1940	*Cont*	....	*Krakatau (Indonesia)*	0602-00=	*2*	
	1940	*Cont*	....	*Lewotobi (Lesser Sunda Is)*	0604-18=	*2*	
	1940	*Cont*	....	*Dukono (Halmahera-Indonesia)*	0608-01=	*2*	
	1940	*Cont*	....	*Asama (Honshu-Japan)*	0803-11=	*1*	*-/5*
	1940	*Cont*	....	*Kita-Iwo-jima (Volcano Is-Japan)*	0804-11=	*0*	
	1940	*Cont*	....	*Pavlof (Alaska Peninsula)*	1102-03-	*2*	
	1940	*Cont*	....	*Santa María (Guatemala)*	1402-03=	*1*	***9**/8*
	1940	*Cont*	....	*Izalco (El Salvador)*	1403-03=	*2*	
	1940	*Cont*	....	*Irazú (Costa Rica)*	1405-06=	*2*	
	1940	*Cont*	....	*Sangay (Ecuador)*	1502-09=	*2*	
	1940	....	?	**Erta Ale** (Ethiopia)	0201-08=	0	
	1940	....	?	**Raung** (Java)	0603-34=	2	
	1940 f	....	?	**Kolokol Group** (Kuril Is)	0900-12=		7/-
	1940	....	?	**Karymsky** (Kamchatka)	1000-13=	2	
	1940	....	?	**Cotopaxi** (Ecuador)	1502-05=	2	
	1940	....	?	**Azul, Cerro** (Galápagos)	1503-06=	0	
	1940	....	?	**Láscar** (Chile-N)	1505-10=	2	
	1940	01	30*p*	**Zhupanovsky** (Kamchatka)	1000-12=	2	
	1940	*0124*	....	*Merapi (Java)*	0603-25=	*2*	*6/-*

	START YEAR	M-Dy	Duration	VOLCANO NAME (Subregion)	NUMBER	VEI	Vol L/T
	1940	*0130*	....	*Dempo (Sumatra)*	0601-23=	*2*	
	1940	02	60*p*	**Tolbachik** (Kamchatka)	1000-24=	2	
?	*1940*	*02*	*?*	*Lonquimay (Chile-C)*	1507-10=		
	1940	0204d	103*d*	**Rabaul** (New Britain-SW Pac)	0502-14=	1	
	1940	0301	8*a*	**Karangetang [Api Siau]** (Sangihe Is	0607-02=	2	
	1940	0315	31*a*	**Slamet** (Java)	0603-18=	2	
	1940	0316	....	**Etna** (Italy)	0101-06=	3	
	1940	04	?	**Ruapehu** (New Zealand)	0401-10=	2	
	1940	04	?	**Besar** (Sumatra)	0601-25=	1	
	1940	0407	159*a*	**Kusatsu-Shirane** (Honshu-Japan)	0803-12=	1?	
	1940	0407	133*a*	**Mauna Loa** (Hawaiian Is)	1302-02=	0	8/-
	1940	0420	110*a*	**Aso** (Kyushu-Japan)	0802-11=	2	
	1940	0424	76*a*	**Sakura-jima** (Kyushu-Japan)	0802-08=	2	
	1940	0425	69*a*>	**Tengger Caldera [Bromo]** (Java)	0603-31=	2	
	1940	0518	<1	**Zao** (Honshu-Japan)	0803-19=	1	-/5
	1940	06	123*p*	**Telica** (Nicaragua)	1404-04=	2	
	1940	0620	64*a*	**Karangetang [Api Siau]** (Sangihe Is	0607-02=	2	
	1940	07	?	**Dempo** (Sumatra)	0601-23=	2	
	1940	0712	24*a*	**Miyake-jima** (Izu Is-Japan)	0804-04=	3	6/7
	1940	*0724*	*205m*	*Lengai, Ol Doinyo (Africa-E)*	0202-12=	*2*	
	1940	0731	....	**Lengai, Ol Doinyo** (Africa-E)	0202-12=	3	
	1940	0818	1*a*	**Oshima** (Izu Is-Japan)	0804-01=	1	5/5
	1940	09	31*p*	**Tongariro [Ngauruhoe]** (New Zeal)	0401-08=	2	
	1940	*11*	*242q*	*Tolbachik (Kamchatka)*	1000-24=	*2*	*7/7*
	1940	1129	?	**Suwanose-jima** (Ryukyu Is)	0802-03=	2?	
	1941	*Cont*	....	*Santorini (Greece)*	0102-04=	*2*	*7/-*
	1941	*Cont*	....	*Lengai, Ol Doinyo (Africa-E)*	0202-12=	*2*	
	1941	*Cont*	....	*Nyiragongo (Africa-C)*	0203-03=	*0*	
	1941	*Cont*	....	*Yasur (Vanuatu-SW Pacific)*	0507-10=	*2*	
	1941	*Cont*	....	*Kaba (Sumatra)*	0601-22=	*2*	
	1941	*Cont*	....	*Dukono (Halmahera-Indonesia)*	0608-01=	*2*	
	1941	*Cont*	....	*Aso (Kyushu-Japan)*	0802-11=	*2*	
	1941	*Cont*	....	*Asama (Honshu-Japan)*	0803-11=	*1*	*-/5*
	1941	*Cont*	....	*Kita-Iwo-jima (Volcano Is-Japan)*	0804-11=	*0*	
	1941	*Cont*	....	*Pavlof (Alaska Peninsula)*	1102-03-	*2*	
	1941	*Cont*	....	*Santa María (Guatemala)*	1402-03=	*1*	***9***/*8*
	1941	*Cont*	....	*Izalco (El Salvador)*	1403-03=	*2*	
	1941	*Cont*	....	*Sangay (Ecuador)*	1502-09=	*2*	
	1941 ?	....	?	**Fournaise, Piton de la** (Indian O.)	0303-02=	1	
?	*1941*	....	*?*	*Telica (Nicaragua)*	1404-04=		
	1941	....	>3yr	**Poás** (Costa Rica)	1405-04=	1	
	1941	0119	<1	**Kusatsu-Shirane** (Honshu-Japan)	0803-12=	1?	
	1941	0126	<1	**Ulawun** (New Britain-SW Pac)	0502-12=	2	
	1941	0128	15*a*	**Krakatau** (Indonesia)	0602-00=	2	
	1941	0328	?	**Farallon de Pajaros** (Mariana Is-Pac)	0804-14=		
?	*1941*	*04*	*122p*	*Grímsvötn (Iceland-NE)*	1703-01=	*0*	
?	*1941*	*0415*	*?*	*Colima (México)*	1401-04=	*3?*	
	1941	0428	120*a*	**Sakura-jima** (Kyushu-Japan)	0802-08=	2	
	1941	0507	....	**Tolbachik** (Kamchatka)	1000-24=	3	7/7
?	*1941*	*0530*	*?*	*Rinjani (Lesser Sunda Is)*	0604-03=		
?	*1941*	*0605*	*?*	*Iliwerung (Lesser Sunda Is)*	0604-25=		
	1941	0606	298*p*	**Rabaul** (New Britain-SW Pac)	0502-14=	2	
	1941	0623	?	**Llaima** (Chile-C)	1507-11=	2	
	1941	*0822*	....	*Stromboli (Italy)*	0101-04=	*2*	*7/-*
	1941	0823h	?	**Ebulobo** (Lesser Sunda Is)	0604-10=	0?	
	1941	0913	?	**Mayon** (Luzon-Philippines)	0703-03=	1	
	1941	0921	145*m*	**Semeru** (Java)	0603-30=	2	7/-
	1941	10	? 923*m*?	**Etna** (Italy)	0101-06=	2	
	1941	*1022*	....	*Vesuvius (Italy)*	0101-02=	*2*	*8/7*
	1941	1030	<1	**Karangetang [Api Siau]** (Sangihe Is	0607-02=	2	
	1941	1213	?	**Raung** (Java)	0603-34=	2	
	1942	*Cont*	....	*Vesuvius (Italy)*	0101-02=	*2*	*8/7*
	1942	*Cont*	....	*Stromboli (Italy)*	0101-04=	*1*	*7/-*
	1942	*Cont*	....	*Nyiragongo (Africa-C)*	0203-03=	*0*	
	1942	*Cont*	....	*Rabaul (New Britain-SW Pac)*	0502-14=	*2*	
	1942	*Cont*	....	*Yasur (Vanuatu-SW Pacific)*	0507-10=	*2*	
	1942	*Cont*	....	*Semeru (Java)*	0603-30=	*2*	*7/-*
	1942	*Cont*	....	*Dukono (Halmahera-Indonesia)*	0608-01=	*2*	
	1942	*Cont*	....	*Asama (Honshu-Japan)*	0803-11=	*1*	*-/5*
	1942	*Cont*	....	*Kita-Iwo-jima (Volcano Is-Japan)*	0804-11=	*0*	
	1942	*Cont*	....	*Santa María (Guatemala)*	1402-03=	*1*	***9***/*8*
	1942	*Cont*	....	*Izalco (El Salvador)*	1403-03=	*2*	
	1942	*Cont*	....	*Poás (Costa Rica)*	1405-04=	*1*	
	1942	*Cont*	....	*Sangay (Ecuador)*	1502-09=	*2*	
?	*1942 e*	....	*?*	*Langila (New Britain-SW Pac)*	0502-01=	*1?*	
	1942 ?	....	?	**Kavachi** (Solomon Is-SW Pacific)	0505-06=	1	
	1942	....	?	**Kanaga** (Aleutian Is)	1101-11-	1	
	1942	....	?	**Pavlof** (Alaska Peninsula)	1102-03-	3	
?	*1942*	....	*?*	*Aniakchak (Alaska Peninsula)*	1102-09-		
	1942	....	365*y*	**Popocatépetl** (México)	1401-09=	1	
	1942	0129	1*a*	**Krakatau** (Indonesia)	0602-00=	2	
	1942	0202	?	**Kusatsu-Shirane** (Honshu-Japan)	0803-12=	1	
?	*1942*	*0217*	*2a*	*Cotopaxi (Ecuador)*	1502-05=	*3?*	
	1942	0426	14*a*	**Mauna Loa** (Hawaiian Is)	1302-02=	0	8/-
	1942	0530	>3yr	**Merapi** (Java)	0603-25=	2	6/6
	1942	0606	?	**Ambrym** (Vanuatu-SW Pacific)	0507-04=	2	
?	*1942*	*0608*	*14a*	*Aso (Kyushu-Japan)*	0802-11=	*1?*	
	1942	0609	159*m*	**Llaima** (Chile-C)	1507-11=	2	
	1942	0630	1*a*	**Etna** (Italy)	0101-06=	2	6/5
	1942	0716	<1	**Sakura-jima** (Kyushu-Japan)	0802-08=	1	
	1942	0810	?	**Ruapehu** (New Zealand)	0401-10=	2	
	1942	0815	1*a*	**Papandayan** (Java)	0603-10=	1?	
	1942	0903	?	**Lokon-Empung** (Sulawesi-Indonesia)	0606-10=	2	
	1942	1005	20*a*	**Fournaise, Piton de la** (Indian O.)	0303-02=	2	6/-
	1942	1116	2	**Komaga-take** (Hokkaido-Japan)	0805-02=	3	-/6
	1943	*Cont*	....	*Vesuvius (Italy)*	0101-02=	*2*	*8/7*
	1943	*Cont*	....	*Etna (Italy)*	0101-06=	*2*	
	1943	*Cont*	....	*Nyiragongo (Africa-C)*	0203-03=	*0*	
	1943	*Cont*	....	*Yasur (Vanuatu-SW Pacific)*	0507-10=	*2*	
	1943	*Cont*	....	*Dukono (Halmahera-Indonesia)*	0608-01=	*2*	
	1943	*Cont*	....	*Kita-Iwo-jima (Volcano Is-Japan)*	0804-11=	*0*	
	1943	*Cont*	....	*Pavlof (Alaska Peninsula)*	1102-03-	*2*	
	1943	*Cont*	....	*Popocatépetl (México)*	1401-09=	*1*	
	1943	*Cont*	....	*Santa María (Guatemala)*	1402-03=	*1*	***9***/*8*
	1943	*Cont*	....	*Izalco (El Salvador)*	1403-03=	*2*	
	1943	*Cont*	....	*Poás (Costa Rica)*	1405-04=	*1*	
	1943	*Cont*	....	*Sangay (Ecuador)*	1502-09=	*2*	
	1943	....	?	**Long Island** (New Guinea-NE of)	0501-05=		
	1943 e	....	?	**Marapi** (Sumatra)	0601-14=		
	1943	....	?	**Krakatau** (Indonesia)	0602-00=	2	
	1943	....	?	**Mayon** (Luzon-Philippines)	0703-03=	1	
	1943	....	?	**Farallon de Pajaros** (Mariana Is-Pac)	0804-14=	2	
?	*1943*	....	*?*	*St. Paul Island (Alaska-W)*	1104-01-		
	1943	0201p	?	**Karymsky** (Kamchatka)	1000-13=	2	
	1943	0220	>3yr	**Michoacán [Parícutin]** (México)	1401-06=	4	8/**9**
	1943	03	?	**Tolima, Nevado del** (Colombia)	1501-03=	2	
	1943	0317	93*a*	**Raung** (Java)	0603-34=	2	
?	*1943*	*0318*	*?*	*Slamet (Java)*	0603-18=		
	1943	*0320*	....	*Merapi (Java)*	0603-25=	*2*	*6/6*
	1943	0330?	56*e*?	**Fournaise, Piton de la** (Indian O.)	0303-02=	2	7/-
	1943	0407<	?	**Bagana** (Bougainville-SW Pacific)	0505-02=	1	
	1943	0413b	28*c*?	**Azul, Cerro** (Galápagos)	1503-06=	3	
	1943	06	?	**Okmok** (Aleutian Is)	1101-29-	1	
	1943	0621	3*a*	**Aso** (Kyushu-Japan)	0802-11=	2	
	1943	*0918*	*347a*	*Waiowa (New Guinea)*	0503-04=	*2*	
	1943	0926	20*p*	**Niuafo'ou** (Tonga-SW Pacific)	0403-11=	2	
	1943	1002	95*a*	**Slamet** (Java)	0603-18=	2	
S	1943	1005	1*a*	**Kick 'em Jenny** (W Indies)	1600-16=	0	
	1943	1103	?	**Dieng Volc Complex** (Java)	0603-20=	1	
	1943	1124	29*a*>	**Rabaul** (New Britain-SW Pac)	0502-14=	2	
	1943	12	121*p*	**Telica** (Nicaragua)	1404-04=	2	
	1943	*1203*	....	*Stromboli (Italy)*	0101-04=	*2?*	*7/-*
	1943	1209	67*m*	**Aso** (Kyushu-Japan)	0802-11=	2	
	1943	1227	....	**Waiowa** (New Guinea)	0503-04=	3	
	1944	*Cont*	....	*Etna (Italy)*	0101-06=	*2*	
	1944	*Cont*	....	*Nyiragongo (Africa-C)*	0203-03=	*0*	
	1944	*Cont*	....	*Yasur (Vanuatu-SW Pacific)*	0507-10=	*2*	
	1944	*Cont*	....	*Merapi (Java)*	0603-25=	*2*	*6/6*
	1944	*Cont*	....	*Dukono (Halmahera-Indonesia)*	0608-01=	*2*	
	1944	*Cont*	....	*Aso (Kyushu-Japan)*	0802-11=	*2*	
	1944	*Cont*	....	*Kita-Iwo-jima (Volcano Is-Japan)*	0804-11=	*0*	
	1944	*Cont*	....	*Pavlof (Alaska Peninsula)*	1102-03-	*2*	
	1944	*Cont*	....	*Michoacán [Parícutin] (México)*	1401-06=	*3*	*8/*__*9*__
	1944	*Cont*	....	*Santa María (Guatemala)*	1402-03=	*1*	***9***/*8*
	1944	*Cont*	....	*Izalco (El Salvador)*	1403-03=	*2*	
	1944	*Cont*	....	*Telica (Nicaragua)*	1404-04=	*2*	
	1944	*Cont*	....	*Poás (Costa Rica)*	1405-04=	*1*	
	1944	*Cont*	....	*Sangay (Ecuador)*	1502-09=	*2*	
?	*1944*	....	*?*	*Monowai Seamount (Kermadec Is)*	0402-05-	*0*	
	1944	....	?	**Bam** (New Guinea-NE of)	0501-01=	2	
?	*1944*	....	*?*	*Unnamed (New Guinea-NE of)*	0501-04=	*0*	
	1944	....	?	**Krakatau** (Indonesia)	0602-00=	2	
?	*1944*	....	*?*	*Goriaschaia Sopka (Kuril Is)*	0900-17=	*2*	
?	*1944*	....	*?*	*Tungurahua (Ecuador)*	1502-08=	*2*	
	1944	....	?	**Copahue** (Chile-C)	1507-09=		
	1944	....	?	**Llaima** (Chile-C)	1507-11=	2	
	1944	01	? 668*p*?	**Asama** (Honshu-Japan)	0803-11=	2	
	1944	0224	6*a*	**Reventador** (Ecuador)	1502-01=	3	
	1944	0318	....	**Vesuvius** (Italy)	0101-02=	3	8/7
	1944	0328	?	**Veniaminof** (Alaska Peninsula)	1102-07-	2	
	1944	04	611*p*	**Concepción** (Nicaragua)	1404-12=	2	
	1944	0411	20*a*	**Fournaise, Piton de la** (Indian O.)	0303-02=	2	
	1944	0509	173*a*	**Slamet** (Java)	0603-18=	2	
	1944	0610	2*a*	**Cleveland** (Aleutian Is)	1101-24-	3	
	1944	0623	452*a*	**Usu** (Hokkaido-Japan)	0805-03=	2	7/6
	1944	0630	292*a*	**Raung** (Java)	0603-34=	2	
	1944	0702	<1	**Shikotsu [Tarumai]** (Hokkaido)	0805-04=	1	
	1944	*0723*	....	*Waiowa (New Guinea)*	0503-04=	*3*	
	1944	08	61*p*	**Iliboleng** (Lesser Sunda Is)	0604-22=	2	
	1944	*0820*	....	*Stromboli (Italy)*	0101-04=	*2*	*7/-*
?	*1944*	*0820j*	*?*	*Esmeralda Bank (Mariana Is-C Pacific)*	0804-21=	*0*	
	1944	10	?	**Ruapehu** (New Zealand)	0401-10=	2	
	1944	1105	>3yr	**Shiveluch** (Kamchatka)	1000-27=	2	8/-
	1944	1120	26*m*	**Kurikoma** (Honshu-Japan)	0803-21=	1	-/4

The first lava flow from Parícutin, the renowned volcano born in a Mexican cornfield in 1943, moves northward over fields prepared for planting. The flows eventually buried the town of San Juan Parangaricutiro. An ash-rich plume rises from the new cone, which by this 5th day of the eruption, was already more than 150 m high.

Instituto de Geología, México (Luhr and Simkin, 1993)

START YEAR	M-Dy	Duration	VOLCANO NAME (Subregion)	NUMBER	VEI	Vol L/T
? 1944	1125	<1	*Shikotsu [Tarumai] (Hokkaido)*	0805-04=	1?	
1944	12	?	**Ioto [Iwo-jima]** (Volcano Is-Japan)	0804-12=	1	
1944	1201p	<1	**Fuego** (Guatemala)	1402-09=	2	
1944	1204	?	**Dieng Volc Complex** (Java)	0603-20=	2	
1944	1209	41a>	*Kliuchevskoi (Kamchatka)*	1000-26=	2	-/7
1944	1225	7a?	**Rinjani** (Lesser Sunda Is)	0604-03=	2	7/-
1945	Cont	....	*Stromboli (Italy)*	0101-04=	1	7/-
1945	Cont	....	*Nyiragongo (Africa-C)*	0203-03=	0	
1945	Cont	....	*Yasur (Vanuatu-SW Pacific)*	0507-10=	2	
1945	Cont	....	*Merapi (Java)*	0603-25=	2	6/6
1945	Cont	....	*Raung (Java)*	0603-34=	2	
1945	Cont	....	*Rinjani (Lesser Sunda Is)*	0604-03=	2	7/-
1945	Cont	....	*Dukono (Halmahera-Indonesia)*	0608-01=	2	
1945	Cont	....	*Asama (Honshu-Japan)*	0803-11=	2	
1945	Cont	....	*Kita-Iwo-jima (Volcano Is-Japan)*	0804-11=	0	
1945	Cont	....	*Usu (Hokkaido-Japan)*	0805-03=	1	7/6
1945	Cont	....	*Shiveluch (Kamchatka)*	1000-27=	2	8/-
1945	Cont	....	*Pavlof (Alaska Peninsula)*	1102-03-	2	
1945	Cont	....	*Michoacán [Parícutin] (México)*	1401-06=	3	8/**9**
1945	Cont	....	*Santa María (Guatemala)*	1402-03=	1	**9**/8
1945	Cont	....	*Izalco (El Salvador)*	1403-03=	2	
1945	Cont	....	*Concepción (Nicaragua)*	1404-12=	2	
1945	Cont	....	*Poás (Costa Rica)*	1405-04=	1	
1945	Cont	....	*Sangay (Ecuador)*	1502-09=	2	
1945	....	730y	**Bagana** (Bougainville-SW Pacific)	0505-02=	2	
1945	....	?	**Krakatau** (Indonesia)	0602-00=	2	
? 1945	....	?	*Chillán, Nevados de (Chile-C)*	1507-07=		
1945	0101	....	**Kliuchevskoi** (Kamchatka)	1000-26=	3?	-/7
1945	0115q	?	**Lautaro** (Chile-S)	1508-06=	1	
1945	0225	<1	**Avachinsky** (Kamchatka)	1000-10=	4	-/8
1945	03	?	**Great Sitkin** (Aleutian Is)	1101-12-	2	7/-
1945	0308	313m	*Ruapehu (New Zealand)*	0401-10=	2	7/-
1945	0331	4a	**Llaima** (Chile-C)	1507-11=	3	
1945	0415	21a	**Fournaise, Piton de la** (Indian O.)	0303-02=	2	6/-
1945	0604	210m	**Okmok** (Aleutian Is)	1101-29-	2	7/-
1945	0605d	132m	**Etna** (Italy)	0101-06=	1	
1945	0612	6a	**Semeru** (Java)	0603-30=	2	
1945	0619	18a	**Kliuchevskoi** (Kamchatka)	1000-26=	3	7/7
1945	0623	?	**Mutnovsky** (Kamchatka)	1000-06=	2	
1945	0822	....	**Ruapehu** (New Zealand)	0401-10=	3	7/-
1945	09	?	**Karymsky** (Kamchatka)	1000-13=	2	
1945	09 ?	212t	**Maly Semiachik** (Kamchatka)	1000-14=	2	
1945	0916	3a	**Aso** (Kyushu-Japan)	0802-11=	2	
? 1945	0925?	?	*Grímsvötn (Iceland-NE)*	1703-01=	1?	
1945	1103	<1	**Kuchinoerabu-jima** (Ryukyu Is)	0802-05=	2	
1946	Cont	....	*Stromboli (Italy)*	0101-04=	1	7/-
1946	Cont	....	*Nyiragongo (Africa-C)*	0203-03=	0	
1946	Cont	....	*Bagana (Bougainville-SW Pacific)*	0505-02=	2	
1946	Cont	....	*Yasur (Vanuatu-SW Pacific)*	0507-10=	2	
1946	Cont	....	*Dukono (Halmahera-Indonesia)*	0608-01=	2	
1946	Cont	....	*Maly Semiachik (Kamchatka)*	1000-14=	2	
1946	Cont	....	*Shiveluch (Kamchatka)*	1000-27=	2	8/-
1946	Cont	....	*Pavlof (Alaska Peninsula)*	1102-03-	2	
1946	Cont	....	*Michoacán [Parícutin] (México)*	1401-06=	3	8/**9**
1946	Cont	....	*Santa María (Guatemala)*	1402-03=	1	**9**/8
1946	Cont	....	*Izalco (El Salvador)*	1403-03=	2	
? 1946	....	?	*Medvezhia (Kuril Is)*	0900-10=	2	
? 1946	....	?	*Mageik (Alaska Peninsula)*	1102-15-	2?	
1946	....	365y	**Tupungatito** (Chile-C)	1507-01=	2	
1946	....	365y	**Chillán, Nevados de** (Chile-C)	1507-07=	2?	
1946	01	304p	**Sakura-jima** (Kyushu-Japan)	0802-08=	2	8/7
1946	02	243p	**Etna** (Italy)	0101-06=	1	
1946	02	91p	**Semeru** (Java)	0603-30=	2	
1946	0204d	?	**Bayonnaise Rocks** (Izu Is-Japan)	0804-07=	2	7/-
1946	03	31p	**Puracé** (Colombia)	1501-06=	2	
1946	04	91p	**Ruapehu** (New Zealand)	0401-10=	2	
? 1946	04	?	*Kirishima (Kyushu-Japan)*	0802-09=	2	
1946	04	?	**Karymsky** (Kamchatka)	1000-13=	2	
1946	04	123p	**Telica** (Nicaragua)	1404-04=	2	
1946	0415q	?	**Kolokol Group** (Kuril Is)	0900-12=	2	
1946	0429	56a	**Aso** (Kyushu-Japan)	0802-11=	2	
1946	06	563p?	*Masaya (Nicaragua)*	1404-10=	0	
1946	0618	17a	**Fournaise, Piton de la** (Indian O.)	0303-02=	2	6/-
1946	0723	?	**Llaima** (Chile-C)	1507-11=	2	
1946	0725	<1	**Krakatau** (Indonesia)	0602-00=	1	
1946	08	152p	**Shishaldin** (Aleutian Is)	1101-36-	2	
? 1946	0814	?	*Great Sitkin (Aleutian Is)*	1101-12-		
1946	09	31p	**Karymsky** (Kamchatka)	1000-13=	2	
1946	09	....	*Sangay (Ecuador)*	1502-09=	2	
1946	0909	8a	**Niuafo'ou** (Tonga-SW Pacific)	0403-11=	2	
1946	0914	<1	**Miravalles** (Costa Rica)	1405-03=	1	
1946	1023	31a?	**Kliuchevskoi** (Kamchatka)	1000-26=	2	7/5
1946	1029	228m	**Semeru** (Java)	0603-30=	2	
1946	1029	1a	**Asama** (Honshu-Japan)	0803-11=	2	
1946	1104d	?	**Poás** (Costa Rica)	1405-04=	1	
1946	1109	2a	**Sarychev Peak** (Kuril Is)	0900-24=	4	
1946	1121	192a	**Ruapehu** (New Zealand)	0401-10=	1	
1946	1124	?	**Kurikoma** (Honshu-Japan)	0803-21=	2	
1946	12	31p	**Akutan** (Aleutian Is)	1101-32-	2	
1946	1201p	289q	**Manam** (New Guinea-NE of)	0501-02=	3	7/-

START YEAR	M-Dy	Dura-tion	VOLCANO NAME (Subregion)	NUMBER	VEI	Vol L/T
1946	1226e	224j>	**Krakatau** (Indonesia)	0602-00=	2	
1946	1230	<1	**Aso** (Kyushu-Japan)	0802-11=	2	
1947	*Cont*	....	*Stromboli (Italy)*	0101-04=	*1*	*7/-*
1947	*Cont*	....	*Nyiragongo (Africa-C)*	0203-03=	*0*	
1947	*Cont*	....	*Ruapehu (New Zealand)*	0401-10=	*1*	
1947	*Cont*	....	*Manam (New Guinea-NE of)*	0501-02=	*2*	*7/-*
1947	*Cont*	....	*Bagana (Bougainville-SW Pacific)*	0505-02=	*2*	
1947	*Cont*	....	*Yasur (Vanuatu-SW Pacific)*	0507-10=	*2*	
1947	*Cont*	....	*Krakatau (Indonesia)*	0602-00=	*2*	
1947	*Cont*	....	*Semeru (Java)*	0603-30=	*2*	
1947	*Cont*	....	*Dukono (Halmahera-Indonesia)*	0608-01=	*2*	
1947	*Cont*	....	*Shiveluch (Kamchatka)*	1000-27=	*2*	*8/-*
1947	*Cont*	....	*Akutan (Aleutian Is)*	1101-32-	*2*	
1947	*Cont*	....	*Shishaldin (Aleutian Is)*	1101-36-	*2*	
1947	*Cont*	....	*Pavlof (Alaska Peninsula)*	1102-03-	*2*	
1947	*Cont*	....	*Michoacán [Paricutin] (México)*	1401-06=	*3*	*8/**9***
1947	*Cont*	....	*Santa María (Guatemala)*	1402-03=	*1*	***9**/8*
1947	*Cont*	....	*Izalco (El Salvador)*	1403-03=	*2*	
1947	*Cont*	....	*Sangay (Ecuador)*	1502-09=	*2*	
1947	*Cont*	....	*Tupungatito (Chile-C)*	1507-01=	*2*	
1947	*Cont*	....	*Chillán, Nevados de (Chile-C)*	1507-07=	*2?*	
1947 ?	....	?	**Fournaise, Piton de la** (Indian O.)	0303-02=	2	
? *1947*	....	?	*Kita-Fukutokutai (Volcano Is-Japan)*	0804-121	*0*	
1947	....	?	**Fuego** (Guatemala)	1402-09=	2	
1947	....	?	**Villarrica** (Chile-C)	1507-12=	1	
1947	01 <	?	**White Island** (New Zealand)	0401-04=	2	
? *1947*	*01*	*?*	*Niuafo'ou (Tonga-SW Pacific)*	0403-11=		
1947	01 ?	?	**Farallon de Pajaros** (Mariana Is-Pac)	0804-14=	0?	
1947	01	?	**Tolbachik** (Kamchatka)	1000-24=	2?	
1947	01	30p	**Popocatépetl** (México)	1401-09=	1	
1947	0108	37m	**Mayon** (Luzon-Philippines)	0703-03=	2	
1947	*0129*	*26a*	*Etna (Italy)*	0101-06=	*2*	
1947	02	?	**Erebus** (Antarctica)	1900-02=	2	
1947	0205	....	**Etna** (Italy)	0101-06=	3?	
1947	0209	<1	**Karangetang [Api Siau]** (Sangihe Is	0607-02=	2	
1947	0224	17a	**Etna** (Italy)	0101-06=	1	7/4
1947	0313s	1a	**Bam** (New Guinea-NE of)	0501-01=	2	
1947	0329	388a	**Hekla** (Iceland-S)	1702-07=	4	8/8
1947	04	31p	**Sirung** (Lesser Sunda Is)	0604-27=	2	
1947	04	?	**Karymsky** (Kamchatka)	1000-13=	2	
1947	0427	?	**Puracé** (Colombia)	1501-06=	2	
1947	0526	112m	**Aso** (Kyushu-Japan)	0802-11=	2	
1947	06	39a	**Asama** (Honshu-Japan)	0803-11=	1	-/5
? *1947*	*06*	*?*	*Iliamna (Alaska-SW)*	1103-02-		
1947	07	....	**Masaya** (Nicaragua)	1404-10=	1	
1947	0709	24a	**Negro, Cerro** (Nicaragua)	1404-07=	3	6/7
? *1947*	*0715*	*?*	*Galeras (Colombia)*	1501-08=	*2?*	
1947	0822	5a	**Soputan** (Sulawesi-Indonesia)	0606-03=	2	
1947	0902	148a	**Gede** (Java)	0603-06=	2	-/5
1947	12	?	**Gorely** (Kamchatka)	1000-07=	2	
1947	1201	20a	**Karangetang [Api Siau]** (Sangihe Is	0607-02=	2	
1948	*Cont*	....	*Stromboli (Italy)*	0101-04=	*1*	*7/-*
1948	*Cont*	....	*Nyiragongo (Africa-C)*	0203-03=	*0*	
1948	*Cont*	....	*Yasur (Vanuatu-SW Pacific)*	0507-10=	*2*	
1948	*Cont*	....	*Dukono (Halmahera-Indonesia)*	0608-01=	*2*	
1948	*Cont*	....	*Shiveluch (Kamchatka)*	1000-27=	*2*	*8/-*
1948	*Cont*	....	*Michoacán [Paricutin] (México)*	1401-06=	*3*	*8/**9***
1948	*Cont*	....	*Santa María (Guatemala)*	1402-03=	*1*	***9**/8*
1948	*Cont*	....	*Sangay (Ecuador)*	1502-09=	*2*	
1948	*Cont*	....	*Hekla (Iceland-S)*	1702-07=	*0*	*8/8*
1948	....	?	**Akita-Yake-yama** (Honshu-Japan)	0803-26=	1?	
1948	....	?	**Shishaldin** (Aleutian Is)	1101-36-	2	
1948	....	730y	**Concepción** (Nicaragua)	1404-12=	1	
1948	....	>3yr	**Poás** (Costa Rica)	1405-04=	1	
1948	01	16m	**Telica** (Nicaragua)	1404-04=	2	
1948	0124	7a>	**Wolf** (Galápagos)	1503-02=	2	
? *1948*	*02*	*?*	*Grímsvötn (Iceland-NE)*	1703-01=	*0*	
1948	0214	23a	**Fournaise, Piton de la** (Indian O.)	0303-02=	2	6/-
1948	0215	69a	**Tengger Caldera [Bromo]** (Java)	0603-31=	3	
1948	0301	137e	**Nyamuragira** (Africa-C)	0203-02=	2	7/7
1948	0331	?	**Negro, Cerro** (Nicaragua)	1404-07=	2	
1948	0407	233a	**Iliwerung** (Lesser Sunda Is)	0604-25=	2	6/6
1948	0409	251m	**Aso** (Kyushu-Japan)	0802-11=	1	
1948	0410	?	**Villarrica** (Chile-C)	1507-12=	2?	
1948	0422	55a	**Karthala** (Indian O.-W)	0303-01=	2	
1948	0429	?	**Iliboleng** (Lesser Sunda Is)	0604-22=	2	
1948	0429	100a>	**Akutan** (Aleutian Is)	1101-32-	2	
1948	0430	16m	**Tongariro [Ngauruhoe]** (New Zeal)	0401-08=	2	
1948	*05*	....	*Pavlof (Alaska Peninsula)*	1102-03-	*2*	
1948	0501	?	**Ruapehu** (New Zealand)	0401-10=	1	
1948	06	502w	**Telica** (Nicaragua)	1404-04=	2	
1948	0630p	?	**Azul, Cerro** (Galápagos)	1503-06=	0	
1948	0727	<1	**Sakura-jima** (Kyushu-Japan)	0802-08=	1	
1948	08	?	**Kliuchevskoi** (Kamchatka)	1000-26=	2?	
1948	08	182p?	**Negra, Sierra** (Galápagos)	1503-05=	2	
1948	09	?	**Tongariro [Ngauruhoe]** (New Zeal)	0401-08=	2	

U.S. Navy

An ash-rich eruption column rises above the summit of Vesuvius volcano in Italy in 1944, near the end of a long-duration eruption that began in 1913. The March 18 to April 4, 1944 paroxysmal phase included the emission of voluminous lava flows and vigorous explosions that left a 300-m-deep crater at the summit.

	START YEAR	M-Dy	Duration	VOLCANO NAME (Subregion)	NUMBER	VEI	Vol L/T
	1948	09	15m	**Masaya** (Nicaragua)	1404-10=	1	
	1948	*0901*	*>3yr*	*Camiguin [Hibok-Hibok] (Philippine*	0701-08=	*2*	
	1948	0922	7a	**Kuwae [Karua]** (Vanuatu-SW Pac)	0507-07=	2	
	1948	0929	77m	**Merapi** (Java)	0603-25=	2	6/-
	1948	*1009*	*117a*	*Villarrica (Chile-C)*	1507-12=	*2*	
	1948	*1018*	....	*Villarrica (Chile-C)*	1507-12=	*2*	
	1948	*1104*	*>3yr*	*Izalco (El Salvador)*	1403-03=	*2*	
	1948	1114	31a	**Slamet** (Java)	0603-18=	2	
	1948	1115	82a	**Gede** (Java)	0603-06=	2	-/5
	1948	12	?	**Karangetang [Api Siau]** (Sangihe Is	0607-02=	2	
	1948	*1201p*	*>3yr*	*Bagana (Bougainville-SW Pacific)*	0505-02=	*2*	
	1949	*Cont*	....	*Nyiragongo (Africa-C)*	0203-03=	*0*	
	1949	*Cont*	....	*Bagana (Bougainville-SW Pacific)*	0505-02=	*2*	
	1949	*Cont*	....	*Yasur (Vanuatu-SW Pacific)*	0507-10=	*2*	
	1949	*Cont*	....	*Gede (Java)*	0603-06=	*2*	*-/5*
	1949	*Cont*	....	*Dukono (Halmahera-Indonesia)*	0608-01=	*2*	
	1949	*Cont*	....	*Camiguin [Hibok-Hibok] (Philippine*	0701-08=	*2*	
	1949	*Cont*	....	*Shiveluch (Kamchatka)*	1000-27=	*2*	*8/-*
	1949	*Cont*	....	*Michoacán [Parícutin] (México)*	1401-06=	*3*	*8/**9***
	1949	*Cont*	....	*Santa María (Guatemala)*	1402-03=	*1*	***9**/8*
	1949	*Cont*	....	*Izalco (El Salvador)*	1403-03=	*2*	
	1949	*Cont*	....	*Telica (Nicaragua)*	1404-04=	*2*	
	1949	*Cont*	....	*Concepción (Nicaragua)*	1404-12=	*1*	
	1949	*Cont*	....	*Poás (Costa Rica)*	1405-04=	*1*	
	1949	*Cont*	....	*Sangay (Ecuador)*	1502-09=	*2*	
	1949	*Cont*	....	*Negra, Sierra (Galápagos)*	1503-05=	*2*	
	1949 <	....	?	**Matthew Island** (SW Pacific)	0508-01=	2	
	1949	....	365y	**Rinjani** (Lesser Sunda Is)	0604-03=	0	
	1949	....	?	**Gamkonora** (Halmahera-Indonesia)	0608-04=	2	
	1949 ?	....	?	**Azul, Cerro** (Galápagos)	1503-06=	0	
	1949	0101	....	**Villarrica** (Chile-C)	1507-12=	3	
	1949	0105	14a>	**Ruang** (Sangihe Is-Indonesia)	0607-01=	2	
	1949	0106	145a	**Mauna Loa** (Hawaiian Is)	1302-02=	0	8/-
	1949	0204	?	**Iliboleng** (Lesser Sunda Is)	0604-22=	2	
	1949	0205	220	**Niigata-Yake-yama** (Honshu-Japan)	0803-09=	2	
	1949	0209	22a	**Tongariro [Ngauruhoe]** (New Zeal)	0401-08=	2	5/-
	1949	0310	228a	**Asama** (Honshu-Japan)	0803-11=	2	
	1949	04	?	**Kuwae [Karua]** (Vanuatu-SW Pac)	0507-07=	3	
	1949	0409	20a	**Iliwerung** (Lesser Sunda Is)	0604-25=	2	
	1949	0415e	?	**Azul, Cerro** (Chile-C)	1507-06=	2?	
	1949	0429	1a	**Marapi** (Sumatra)	0601-14=	2	
	1949	05	?	**Kliuchevskoi** (Kamchatka)	1000-26=	2	
	1949	0512	?	**Krakatau** (Indonesia)	0602-00=	2	
	1949	0526	16a	**Puracé** (Colombia)	1501-06=	2	
	1949	06	?	**Trident** (Alaska Peninsula)	1102-16-		
	1949	06	15m	**Negro, Cerro** (Nicaragua)	1404-07=	2	
	1949	*0606*	....	*Stromboli (Italy)*	0101-04=	*2*	*7/-*
	1949	0612	?	**Iliboleng** (Lesser Sunda Is)	0604-22=	2	
	1949	0624	36	**La Palma** (Canary Is)	1803-01-	2?	7/5
	1949	0830	2a	**Akita-Yake-yama** (Honshu-Japan)	0803-26=	1	-/5
	1949	09	?	**Llaima** (Chile-C)	1507-11=	2	
	1949	0914	?	**Lokon-Empung** (Sulawesi-Indonesia)	0606-10=	1	
	1949	0914	?	**Karangetang [Api Siau]** (Sangihe Is	0607-02=	2	
?	*1949*	*10*	*?*	*Fournaise, Piton de la (Indian O.)*	0303-02=	*2*	
	1949	10	61p	**Kuwae [Karua]** (Vanuatu-SW Pac)	0507-07=	3	
	1949	10	>3yr	**Suwanose-jima** (Ryukyu Is)	0802-03=	2	
?	*1949*	*10*	*?*	*Nakano-shima (Ryukyu Is)*	0802-04=	*1?*	
	1949	1015e	7c	**Marapi** (Sumatra)	0601-14=	2	
	1949	11	?	**Fuego** (Guatemala)	1402-09=	2	
	1949	1202	3a	**Etna** (Italy)	0101-06=	2	7/5
	1949	1203	347m	**Etna** (Italy)	0101-06=	1	
	1949	1222	24m	**Tacaná** (México)	1401-13=	1	
	1949	1226	110a	**Aso** (Kyushu-Japan)	0802-11=	2	
	1949	1230	8a	**Great Sitkin** (Aleutian Is)	1101-12-	1	-/4
	1950	*Cont*	....	*Nyiragongo (Africa-C)*	0203-03=	*0*	
	1950	*Cont*	....	*Yasur (Vanuatu-SW Pacific)*	0507-10=	*2*	
	1950	*Cont*	....	*Rinjani (Lesser Sunda Is)*	0604-03=	*0*	
	1950	*Cont*	....	*Dukono (Halmahera-Indonesia)*	0608-01=	*2*	
	1950	*Cont*	....	*Suwanose-jima (Ryukyu Is)*	0802-03=	*2*	
	1950	*Cont*	....	*Shiveluch (Kamchatka)*	1000-27=	*2*	*8/-*
	1950	*Cont*	....	*Michoacán [Parícutin] (México)*	1401-06=	*3*	*8/**9***
	1950	*Cont*	....	*Tacaná (México)*	1401-13=	*1*	
	1950	*Cont*	....	*Santa María (Guatemala)*	1402-03=	*1*	***9**/8*
	1950	*Cont*	....	*Izalco (El Salvador)*	1403-03=	*2*	
	1950	*Cont*	....	*Concepción (Nicaragua)*	1404-12=	*1*	
	1950	*Cont*	....	*Poás (Costa Rica)*	1405-04=	*1*	
	1950	*Cont*	....	*Sangay (Ecuador)*	1502-09=	*2*	
	1950	....	?	**Akita-Yake-yama** (Honshu-Japan)	0803-26=	1	
	1950	....	365y	**Gareloi** (Aleutian Is)	1101-07-	1	
M	**1950** ?	....	?	**Unnamed [East Pacific Rise]**	1304-05-	0	
?	*1950*	....	*?*	*Villarrica (Chile-C)*	1507-12=		
	1950	0110	23a	**Santorini** (Greece)	0102-04=	2	4/-
	1950	0112	236a	**Galeras** (Colombia)	1501-08=	2	
	1950	0115	?	**Kurikoma** (Honshu-Japan)	0803-21=	2	
	1950	0124	777a?	**Heard** (Indian O.-S)	0304-01=	2	
?	*1950*	*0201*	*<1*	*Fukutoku-Okanoba (Volcano Is-Japan*	0804-13=	*0*	
	1950	0210	9a	**Azuma** (Honshu-Japan)	0803-18=	1	
	1950	0225	36a	**Fournaise, Piton de la** (Indian O.)	0303-02=	2	6/-
	1950	03	395p	**Kaba** (Sumatra)	0601-22=	1	
	1950	03	153p?	**Iliboleng** (Lesser Sunda Is)	0604-22=	2	
	1950	0327	?	**Bristol Island** (Antarctica)	1900-08=	2	
	1950	0527	80m	**Tengger Caldera [Bromo]** (Java)	0603-31=	2	
	1950	0601	22a	**Mauna Loa** (Hawaiian Is)	1302-02=	0	8/-
	1950	0616	?	**Tongariro [Ngauruhoe]** (New Zeal)	0401-08=	2	
	1950	0626	<1	**Ruapehu** (New Zealand)	0401-10=	1	
	1950	0629	72a	**Sakura-jima** (Kyushu-Japan)	0802-08=	1	
@	**1950**	0702	47a?	**Trident** (Alaska Peninsula)	1102-16-	2?	
	1950	0703	4a	**Krakatau** (Indonesia)	0602-00=	2	
	1950	0716	347a	**Oshima** (Izu Is-Japan)	0804-01=	2	7/6
	1950	*0723*	*>3yr*	*Semeru (Java)*	0603-30=	*1*	
	1950	0731	289m	**Pavlof** (Alaska Peninsula)	1102-03-	2	
	1950	0830	6a	**Fournaise, Piton de la** (Indian O.)	0303-02=	2	
	1950	0910	21	**Iliwerung** (Lesser Sunda Is)	0604-25=	2	
	1950	*0915*	....	*Camiguin [Hibok-Hibok] (Philippine*	0701-08=	*2*	
	1950	0923	267a	**Asama** (Honshu-Japan)	0803-11=	1	-/5
	1950	0926e	....	**Bagana** (Bougainville-SW Pacific)	0505-02=	3	
	1950	0927	626a	**Marapi** (Sumatra)	0601-14=	2?	
	1950	10	?	**Gamkonora** (Halmahera-Indonesia)	0608-04=	2	
	1950	*1020*	....	*Stromboli (Italy)*	0101-04=	*2?*	*7/-*
	1950	1030	?	**Arjuno-Welirang** (Java)	0603-29=	2	
	1950	11	61p	**Aso** (Kyushu-Japan)	0802-11=	2	
	1950	1105	24a	**Great Sitkin** (Aleutian Is)	1101-12-		
	1950	1121	26a	**Negro, Cerro** (Nicaragua)	1404-07=	3	5/7
	1950	1125	373a	**Etna** (Italy)	0101-06=	2	8/6
	1950	1201p	?	**Kavachi** (Solomon Is-SW Pacific)	0505-06=	2	
	1950	*1206*	*354e*	*Ambrym (Vanuatu-SW Pacific)*	0507-04=	*3*	*-/8*
	1951	*Cont*	....	*Stromboli (Italy)*	0101-04=	*1*	*7/-*
	1951	*Cont*	....	*Nyiragongo (Africa-C)*	0203-03=	*0*	
	1951	*Cont*	....	*Heard (Indian O.-S)*	0304-01=	*2*	
	1951	*Cont*	....	*Bagana (Bougainville-SW Pacific)*	0505-02=	*2*	
	1951	*Cont*	....	*Yasur (Vanuatu-SW Pacific)*	0507-10=	*2*	
	1951	*Cont*	....	*Marapi (Sumatra)*	0601-14=	*2*	
	1951	*Cont*	....	*Semeru (Java)*	0603-30=	*1*	
	1951	*Cont*	....	*Dukono (Halmahera-Indonesia)*	0608-01=	*2*	
	1951	*Cont*	....	*Suwanose-jima (Ryukyu Is)*	0802-03=	*2*	
	1951	*Cont*	....	*Asama (Honshu-Japan)*	0803-11=	*1*	*-/5*
	1951	*Cont*	....	*Oshima (Izu Is-Japan)*	0804-01=	*2*	*7/6*
	1951	*Cont*	....	*Gareloi (Aleutian Is)*	1101-07-	*1*	
	1951	*Cont*	....	*Michoacán [Parícutin] (México)*	1401-06=	*3*	*8/**9***
	1951	*Cont*	....	*Santa María (Guatemala)*	1402-03=	*1*	***9**/8*
	1951	*Cont*	....	*Izalco (El Salvador)*	1403-03=	*2*	
	1951	*Cont*	....	*Poás (Costa Rica)*	1405-04=	*1*	
	1951	*Cont*	....	*Sangay (Ecuador)*	1502-09=	*2*	
?	*1951*	....	*?*	*Ulawun (New Britain-SW Pac)*	0502-12=		
?	*1951*	....	*?*	*Unnamed (New Britain-SW Pac)*	0502-131	*0*	
	1951	....	....	**Ambrym** (Vanuatu-SW Pacific)	0507-04=	4+	-/8
	1951	....	?	**Iliboleng** (Lesser Sunda Is)	0604-22=	2?	
	1951	....	?	**Gamkonora** (Halmahera-Indonesia)	0608-04=	2	
?	*1951*	....	*?*	*Korovin (Aleutian Is)*	1101-161		
	1951	....	?	**Azul, Cerro** (Galápagos)	1503-06=		
	1951	*0117*	*>3yr*	*Lamington (New Guinea)*	0503-01=	*3*	*8/-*
	1951	0121	....	**Lamington** (New Guinea)	0503-01=	4	8/-
	1951	0129	<1	**Shikotsu [Tarumai]** (Hokkaido)	0805-04=	2	
	1951	02	?	**Akita-Yake-yama** (Honshu-Japan)	0803-26=	1	
	1951	0211	?	**Slamet** (Java)	0603-18=	2	
	1951	0301	<1	**Cereme** (Java)	0603-17=	2?	
	1951	*0307*	....	*Kaba (Sumatra)*	0601-22=	*1*	
	1951	0319	?	**Ruapehu** (New Zealand)	0401-10=	1	
	1951	04	173d	**Shishaldin** (Aleutian Is)	1101-36-	2	
	1951	05	?	**Tongariro [Ngauruhoe]** (New Zeal)	0401-08=	2	
	1951	0504	92p?	**Aso** (Kyushu-Japan)	0802-11=	2	
	1951	0522	<1	**Socorro** (México-Is)	1401-021	2?	
	1951	0527	?	**Kunlun Volc Group** (China-W)	1004-03-	2	
?	*1951*	*06*	*?*	*Fournaise, Piton de la (Indian O.)*	0303-02=	*0*	
	1951	06	?	**Okataina [Rotomahana]** (New Zeal)	0401-05=	1	
	1951	0612	70a	**Fogo** (Cape Verde Is)	1804-01=	2	7/-
	1951	0626	185a	**Slamet** (Java)	0603-18=	2	
	1951	07	>3yr	**Concepción** (Nicaragua)	1404-12=	2	
	1951	*0702*	*623m*	*Lokon-Empung (Sulawesi-Indonesia)*	0606-10=	*2*	
	1951	0715q	91q	**Fukujin** (Volcano Is-Japan)	0804-133	0	
	1951	0715q	?	**Baransky** (Kuril Is)	0900-08=	1	
	1951	0715q	92q	**Telica** (Nicaragua)	1404-04=	2	
@	**1951**	0722	?	**Martin** (Alaska Peninsula)	1102-14-		
	1951	0723h	8h	**Ubinas** (Perú)	1504-02=	2	
	1951	0725	3a	**Nyamuragira** (Africa-C)	0203-02=	1	-/4
	1951	0728	<1	**Shikotsu [Tarumai]** (Hokkaido)	0805-04=	2	
?	*1951*	*0731*	*227m*	*Akan (Hokkaido-Japan)*	0805-07=	*1*	
	1951	08	?	**Farallon de Pajaros** (Mariana Is-Pac)	0804-14=	2	
	1951	0821	?	**Fonualei** (Tonga-SW Pacific)	0403-10=	2	
	1951	0831	<1	**Kelut** (Java)	0603-28=	4	-/8
	1951	0910	10a	**Fournaise, Piton de la** (Indian O.)	0303-02=	1	
	1951	0921	251a	**Etna** (Italy)	0101-06=	1	
?	*1951*	*0921*	*?*	*Bogoslof (Aleutian Is)*	1101-30-	*0*	

START YEAR	M-Dy	Dura-tion	VOLCANO NAME (Subregion)	NUMBER	VEI	Vol L/T
1951	10	?	Akutan (Aleutian Is)	1101-32-	2	
1951	10	135p?	Pavlof (Alaska Peninsula)	1102-03-	2	
1951	1023	34p	Tinakula (Santa Cruz Is-SW Pacific)	0506-01=	3	
1951	11	96m	Láscar (Chile-N)	1505-10=	2?	
? 1951	1101	45m?	Cleveland (Aleutian Is)	1101-24-		
1951	1112	4a	Iliwerung (Lesser Sunda Is)	0604-25=	2	
1951	1116	61a	Nyamuragira (Africa-C)	0203-02=	2	7/5
1951	1119	11a	Kliuchevskoi (Kamchatka)	1000-26=	2	7/6
? 1951	1124	?	Unnamed (New Guinea-NE of)	0501-04=	0	
1951	1201p	?	Kavachi (Solomon Is-SW Pacific)	0505-06=	2	
1951	1204	....	Camiguin [Hibok-Hibok] (Philippine	0701-08=	3	
1951	1215	?	Lewotolo (Lesser Sunda Is)	0604-23=	2	
1951	1220	?	Makushin (Aleutian Is)	1101-31-	1	
1952	Cont	....	Etna (Italy)	0101-06=	1	
1952	Cont	....	Nyamuragira (Africa-C)	0203-02=	2	7/5
1952	Cont	....	Nyiragongo (Africa-C)	0203-03=	0	
1952	Cont	....	Heard (Indian O.-S)	0304-01=	2	
1952	Cont	....	Lamington (New Guinea)	0503-01=	3	8/-
1952	Cont	....	Yasur (Vanuatu-SW Pacific)	0507-10=	2	
1952	Cont	....	Slamet (Java)	0603-18=	2	
1952	Cont	....	Semeru (Java)	0603-30=	1	
1952	Cont	....	Dukono (Halmahera-Indonesia)	0608-01=	2	
1952	Cont	....	Camiguin [Hibok-Hibok] (Philippine	0701-08=	2	
1952	Cont	....	Suwanose-jima (Ryukyu Is)	0802-03=	2	
? 1952	Cont	....	Akan (Hokkaido-Japan)	0805-07=	1	
1952	Cont	....	Pavlof (Alaska Peninsula)	1102-03-	2	
1952	Cont	....	Michoacán [Parícutin] (México)	1401-06=	3	8/9
1952	Cont	....	Santa María (Guatemala)	1402-03=	1	9/8
1952	Cont	....	Izalco (El Salvador)	1403-03=	2	
1952	Cont	....	Concepción (Nicaragua)	1404-12=	2	
1952	Cont	....	Sangay (Ecuador)	1502-09=	2	
1952	Cont	....	Láscar (Chile-N)	1505-10=	2?	
1952	....	?	Mahawu (Sulawesi-Indonesia)	0606-11=	2?	
? 1952	....	?	Ambalatungan Group (Luzon-Philippines)	0703-088	1?	
? 1952	....	?	Aso (Kyushu-Japan)	0802-11=		
? 1952	....	?	Fukujin (Volcano Is-Japan)	0804-133	0	
? 1952	....	?	Makushin (Aleutian Is)	1101-31-		
? 1952	....	?	Iliamna (Alaska-SW)	1103-02-		
1952	01	151p	Kerinci (Sumatra)	0601-17=	2	
? 1952	01	16m	Asama (Honshu-Japan)	0803-11=	1?	
1952	0115q	?	Kolokol Group (Kuril Is)	0900-12=	2	
1952	0117	?	Gareloi (Aleutian Is)	1101-07-	2?	
1952	02	137m	Karangetang [Api Siau] (Sangihe Is	0607-02=	2	
1952	0210?	2a?	Karthala (Indian O.-W)	0303-01=	2	
1952	0229	229m	Bagana (Bougainville-SW Pacific)	0505-02=	4	
1952	0316<	472w>	Didicas (Luzon-N of)	0704-02=	2	8/-
1952	0323	>3yr	Poás (Costa Rica)	1405-04=	1	
1952	0324	?	Iliwerung (Lesser Sunda Is)	0604-25=	1	
1952	0401	27a	Kaba (Sumatra)	0601-22=	2	
1952	0416	290a?	Kavachi (Solomon Is-SW Pacific)	0505-06=	2	
1952	0422	2a	Ijen (Java)	0603-35=	1	
1952	0519	62a	Fournaise, Piton de la (Indian O.)	0303-02=	2	6/-
1952	0529	....	Marapi (Sumatra)	0601-14=	2	
1952	0607	....	Stromboli (Italy)	0101-04=	2	7/-
1952	0607	7a	Asama (Honshu-Japan)	0803-11=	2	
? 1952	0618	?	Azuma (Honshu-Japan)	0803-18=	1	
? 1952	0620	<1	Fukutoku-Okanoba (Volcano Is-Japan.	0804-13=	0	
1952	0626	....	Lokon-Empung (Sulawesi-Indonesia)	0606-10=	3	
1952	0627	136a	Kilauea (Hawaiian Is)	1302-01-	0	7/-
1952	07	?	Ruapehu (New Zealand)	0401-10=	1	
? 1952	07	?	Dieng Volc Complex (Java)	0603-20=	1?	
1952	07	61p	Nikko-Shirane (Honshu-Japan)	0803-14=	2	
1952	0704?	7a?	Tangkubanparahu (Java)	0603-09=	1	
1952	0716	51e	Gamkonora (Halmahera-Indonesia)	0608-04=	2	
1952	0801	207d	Bárcena (México-Is)	1401-02=	3	7/8
1952	0810	138e	Ambrym (Vanuatu-SW Pacific)	0507-04=	2	
1952	0815e	?	Arjuno-Welirang (Java)	0603-29=	0	
1952	0817	?	Tokachi (Hokkaido-Japan)	0805-05=		
1952	0916	395m	Bayonnaise Rocks (Izu Is-Japan)	0804-07=	2	7/-
1952	1003	?	Kuwae [Karua] (Vanuatu-SW Pac)	0507-07=	1	
1952	1010	1a	Krakatau (Indonesia)	0602-00=	2	
1952	1023	54m	Pilas, Las (Nicaragua)	1404-08=	1	
1952	1026e	171e	Farallon de Pajaros (Mariana Is-Pac)	0804-14=	2	
1952	11	?	Karymsky (Kamchatka)	1000-13=	2	
1952	1105	?	Karpinsky Group (Kuril Is)	0900-35=	1	
1952	1112	7a	Tao-Rusyr Caldera (Kuril Is)	0900-31=	3	7/-
1952	1129	228m	Tongariro [Ngauruhoe] (New Zeal)	0401-08=	2	
1952	1205d	?	Maly Semiachik (Kamchatka)	1000-14=	2	
1953	Cont	....	Nyiragongo (Africa-C)	0203-03=	0	
1953	Cont	....	Lamington (New Guinea)	0503-01=	3	8/-
1953	Cont	....	Kavachi (Solomon Is-SW Pacific)	0505-06=	2	
1953	Cont	....	Yasur (Vanuatu-SW Pacific)	0507-10=	2	
1953	Cont	....	Semeru (Java)	0603-30=	1	
1953	Cont	....	Lokon-Empung (Sulawesi-Indonesia)	0606-10=	2	
1953	Cont	....	Dukono (Halmahera-Indonesia)	0608-01=	2	
1953	Cont	....	Camiguin [Hibok-Hibok] (Philippine	0701-08=	2	
1953	Cont	....	Didicas (Luzon-N of)	0704-02=	2	8/-
1953	Cont	....	Suwanose-jima (Ryukyu Is)	0802-03=	2	
1953	Cont	....	Bayonnaise Rocks (Izu Is-Japan)	0804-07=	2	7/-
1953	Cont	....	Farallon de Pajaros (Mariana Is-Pac)	0804-14=	2	
1953	Cont	....	Bárcena (México-Is)	1401-02=	2	7/8
1953	Cont	....	Santa María (Guatemala)	1402-03=	1	9/8
1953	Cont	....	Izalco (El Salvador)	1403-03=	2	
1953	Cont	....	Concepción (Nicaragua)	1404-12=	2	
1953	Cont	....	Sangay (Ecuador)	1502-09=	2	
1953	....	?	Karangetang [Api Siau] (Sangihe Is	0607-02=	2	
1953	....	365y	Kita-Fukutokutai (Volcano Is-Japan)	0804-121	0	
1953	....	?	Karymsky (Kamchatka)	1000-13=	2	
? 1953	....	365y	Korovin (Aleutian Is)	1101-161		
1953	....	?	Akutan (Aleutian Is)	1101-32-	2	
1953 g	....	?	Alcedo (Galápagos)	1503-04=	0	
1953	0131	75e	Raung (Java)	0603-34=	3	8/-
1953	0212	7a	Epi (Vanuatu-SW Pacific)	0507-06=	3	
1953	0212	?	Kuwae [Karua] (Vanuatu-SW Pac)	0507-07=	1?	
1953	0215	597a?	Trident (Alaska Peninsula)	1102-16-	3	8/7
@ 1953	0217	?	Martin (Alaska Peninsula)	1102-14-		
? 1953	0301	?	Iliamna (Alaska-SW)	1103-02-	2?	
1953	0302	>3yr	Merapi (Java)	0603-25=	1	6/7
1953	0313	117a	Fournaise, Piton de la (Indian O.)	0303-02=	2	7/-
1953	0317	48a?	Krakatau (Indonesia)	0602-00=	2	
1953	0319	57a>	Sangeang Api (Lesser Sunda Is)	0604-05=	3	
1953	0324	1a	Dieng Volc Complex (Java)	0603-20=	2	
1953	04	121p	Manam (New Guinea-NE of)	0501-02=	2	
? 1953	0404	72m	Lamongan (Java)	0603-32=	2?	
1953	0409	4a	Fuego (Guatemala)	1402-09=	3	
1953	0427	95a	Aso (Kyushu-Japan)	0802-11=	2	
1953	05	151m?	Ambrym (Vanuatu-SW Pacific)	0507-04=	2	
? 1953	05	16m	Kita-Iwo-jima (Volcano Is-Japan)	0804-11=	0	
1953	05	....	Poás (Costa Rica)	1405-04=	2	
1953	0508	244a	Long Island (New Guinea-NE of)	0501-05=	3	
1953	06	92p	Bagana (Bougainville-SW Pacific)	0505-02=	2	
1953	06	?	Sirung (Lesser Sunda Is)	0604-27=		
1953	0607	18a	Kliuchevskoi (Kamchatka)	1000-26=	2	7/6
? 1953	0625	?	Cleveland (Aleutian Is)	1101-24-		
1953	0627	>3yr	St. Andrew Strait [Tuluman]	0500-01=	0	8/-
1953	0709	7a	Spurr (Alaska-SW)	1103-04-	4	
1953	0710	....	Bagana (Bougainville-SW Pacific)	0505-02=	3	
? 1953	0720	?	Unnamed (México)	1401-008	0	
? 1953	0730	?	Etna (Italy)	0101-06=	2	
1953	08	61p	Slamet (Java)	0603-18=	2	
1953	0820	90a	Heard (Indian O.-S)	0304-01=	2	
1953	0827	142m	Negra, Sierra (Galápagos)	1503-05=	3?	
1953	0904	1a	Iya (Lesser Sunda Is)	0604-11=	2?	
1953	0914?	<1	Shikotsu [Tarumai] (Hokkaido)	0805-04=	1	
1953	0921	65a	Krakatau (Indonesia)	0602-00=	2	
1953	1004c	?	Shishaldin (Aleutian Is)	1101-36-	2	
1953	1005	126a	Oshima (Izu Is-Japan)	0804-01=	1	5/4
1953	1015q	?	Rinjani (Lesser Sunda Is)	0604-03=	0?	
1953	1024	5a	Nasu (Honshu-Japan)	0803-15=	1	
S 1953	1030	<1	Kick 'em Jenny (W Indies)	1600-16=	0	
? 1953	11	?	Epi (Vanuatu-SW Pacific)	0507-06=	0	
1953	11	?	Soputan (Sulawesi-Indonesia)	0606-03=	2	
1953	1125	....	Stromboli (Italy)	0101-04=	2	7/-
1953	1125	264m	Pavlof (Alaska Peninsula)	1102-03-	1?	
1953	12	16m	Aso (Kyushu-Japan)	0802-11=	1	
? 1953	1201	<1	Fukutoku-Okanoba (Volcano Is-Japan.	0804-13=	0	
1953	1227	583a	Asama (Honshu-Japan)	0803-11=	2	
1953	1228<	?	Tongariro [Ngauruhoe] (New Zeal)	0401-08=	0	
? 1953	1231y	?	Candlemas Island (Antarctica)	1900-10=	0	
1954	Cont	....	Nyiragongo (Africa-C)	0203-03=	0	
1954	Cont	....	Long Island (New Guinea-NE of)	0501-05=	2	
1954	Cont	....	Lamington (New Guinea)	0503-01=	3	8/-
1954	Cont	....	Yasur (Vanuatu-SW Pacific)	0507-10=	2	
1954	Cont	....	Semeru (Java)	0603-30=	1	
1954	Cont	....	Dukono (Halmahera-Indonesia)	0608-01=	2	
1954	Cont	....	Asama (Honshu-Japan)	0803-11=	2	
1954	Cont	....	Oshima (Izu Is-Japan)	0804-01=	1	5/4
1954	Cont	....	Kita-Fukutokutai (Volcano Is-Japan)	0804-121	0	
? 1954	Cont	....	Korovin (Aleutian Is)	1101-161		
1954	Cont	....	Pavlof (Alaska Peninsula)	1102-03-	1?	
1954	Cont	....	Trident (Alaska Peninsula)	1102-16-	2	8/7
1954	Cont	....	Santa María (Guatemala)	1402-03=	1	9/8
1954	Cont	....	Izalco (El Salvador)	1403-03=	2	
1954	Cont	....	Concepción (Nicaragua)	1404-12=	2	
1954	Cont	....	Poás (Costa Rica)	1405-04=	2	
1954	Cont	....	Sangay (Ecuador)	1502-09=	2	
1954	....	?	Ambrym (Vanuatu-SW Pacific)	0507-04=	2	
1954 ?	....	?	Suwanose-jima (Ryukyu Is)	0802-03=	0	
1954	01	334p	Fournaise, Piton de la (Indian O.)	0303-02=		
1954	0107?	87m	Akan (Hokkaido-Japan)	0805-07=	1?	
1954	0115q	?	Grímsvötn (Iceland-NE)	1703-01=	1	
1954	0118	....	Merapi (Java)	0603-25=	2?	6/7
1954	02	14m	Negro, Cerro (Nicaragua)	1404-07=	2?	
1954	0201	....	Stromboli (Italy)	0101-04=	2?	7/-

	START YEAR	M-Dy	Duration	VOLCANO NAME (Subregion)	NUMBER	VEI	Vol L/T
?	*1954*	*0204d*	*?*	*Fukutoku-Okanoba (Volcano Is-Japan*	0804-13=	*0*	
	1954	0218	....	**St. Andrew Strait [Tuluman]**	0500-01=	2	8/-
	1954	0221	96	**Nyamuragira** (Africa-C)	0203-02=	1	7/6
	1954	0221	112a	**Tolbachik** (Kamchatka)	1000-24=	2	
	1954	*0408*	....	*Akan (Hokkaido-Japan)*	0805-07=	*1*	
	1954	0413?	61a?	**Heard** (Indian O.-S)	0304-01=	2	
	1954	0426	?	**Sangeang Api** (Lesser Sunda Is)	0604-05=	2	
	1954	05	30p	**Manam** (New Guinea-NE of)	0501-02=	2	
	1954	0502	<1	**Shikotsu [Tarumai]** (Hokkaido)	0805-04=	1	
	1954	0513	408a	**Tongariro [Ngauruhoe]** (New Zeal)	0401-08=	3	6/-
	1954	0518	179a	**Langila** (New Britain-SW Pac)	0502-01=	3	
	1954	0526	<1	**Aso** (Kyushu-Japan)	0802-11=	1	
	1954	0528	110m	**Kliuchevskoi** (Kamchatka)	1000-26=	2	
	1954	0531	3a	**Kilauea** (Hawaiian Is)	1302-01-	0	6/-
	1954	06	31p	**Láscar** (Chile-N)	1505-10=	2?	
	1954	0628	28a	**Cameroon** (Africa-W)	0204-01=	2	
?	*1954*	*07*	*?*	*Grímsvötn (Iceland-NE)*	1703-01=	*1?*	
	1954	0726e	51n	**Lengai, Ol Doinyo** (Africa-E)	0202-12=	2	
	1954	08	>3yr	**Marapi** (Sumatra)	0601-14=	2?	
	1954	08	61p	**Sarychev Peak** (Kuril Is)	0900-24=	2	
	1954	0803	883a	**Bam** (New Guinea-NE of)	0501-01=	2	
	1954	09	15m	**Tokachi** (Hokkaido-Japan)	0805-05=	1	
	1954	10 ?	?	**Matthew Island** (SW Pacific)	0508-01=	2	
	1954	1021	<1	**San Miguel** (El Salvador)	1403-10=	2	
	1954	1029	2a	**Pilas, Las** (Nicaragua)	1404-08=	2	
?	*1954*	*11*	*31p*	*Sakura-jima (Kyushu-Japan)*	0802-08=	*1?*	
	1954	1104	?	**Sangeang Api** (Lesser Sunda Is)	0604-05=	2	
	1954	1104	1a	**Bayonnaise Rocks** (Izu Is-Japan)	0804-07=	0	
@	**1954**	1109	?	**Negra, Sierra** (Galápagos)	1503-05=	2	
	1954	1119	86	**Shikotsu [Tarumai]** (Hokkaido)	0805-04=	1	
	1954	1206	<1	**Dieng Volc Complex** (Java)	0603-20=	0	
	1955	*Cont*	....	*Stromboli (Italy)*	0101-04=	*1*	*7/-*
	1955	*Cont*	....	*Nyiragongo (Africa-C)*	0203-03=	*0*	
	1955	*Cont*	....	*Tongariro [Ngauruhoe] (New Zeal)*	0401-08=	*2*	*6/-*
	1955	*Cont*	....	*Lamington (New Guinea)*	0503-01=	*3*	*8/-*
	1955	*Cont*	....	*Yasur (Vanuatu-SW Pacific)*	0507-10=	*2*	
	1955	*Cont*	....	*Marapi (Sumatra)*	0601-14=	*2*	
	1955	*Cont*	....	*Merapi (Java)*	0603-25=	*1*	*6/7*
	1955	*Cont*	....	*Semeru (Java)*	0603-30=	*1*	
	1955	*Cont*	....	*Dukono (Halmahera-Indonesia)*	0608-01=	*2*	
	1955	*Cont*	....	*Shikotsu [Tarumai] (Hokkaido)*	0805-04=	*1*	
	1955	*Cont*	....	*Santa María (Guatemala)*	1402-03=	*1*	***9**/8*
	1955	*Cont*	....	*Concepción (Nicaragua)*	1404-12=	*2*	
	1955	*Cont*	....	*Poás (Costa Rica)*	1405-04=	*2*	
	1955	*Cont*	....	*Sangay (Ecuador)*	1502-09=	*2*	
	1955	....	319m	**Ambrym** (Vanuatu-SW Pacific)	0507-04=	2	
	1955	....	?	**Sangeang Api** (Lesser Sunda Is)	0604-05=	1	
	1955 ?	....	?	**Chirinkotan** (Kuril Is)	0900-26=	2?	
	1955	....	?	**Karymsky** (Kamchatka)	1000-13=	2	
	1955	....	?	**Reventador** (Ecuador)	1502-01=	2	
	1955	....	?	**Erebus** (Antarctica)	1900-02=	2	
	1955	01	?	**White Island** (New Zealand)	0401-04=	2	
	1955	0107	33a	**Tolbachik** (Kamchatka)	1000-24=	2	
	1955	0118	<1	**Raung** (Java)	0603-34=	2?	
	1955	0119	1a	**Lengai, Ol Doinyo** (Africa-E)	0202-12=	2	
	1955	*0210*	....	*St. Andrew Strait [Tuluman]*	0500-01=	*2*	*8/-*
	1955	0211	?	**Krakatau** (Indonesia)	0602-00=	2	
?	*1955*	*0213*	*?*	*Unnamed (Sangihe Is-Indonesia)*	0607-05=	*0*	
	1955	0215	2a	**Langila** (New Britain-SW Pac)	0502-01=	2	
	1955	0228	87	**Kilauea** (Hawaiian Is)	1302-01-	0	7/-
	1955	0228	....	**Izalco** (El Salvador)	1403-03=	3	
?	*1955*	*0401*	*<1*	*Fukutoku-Okanoba (Volcano Is-Japan*	0804-13=	*0*	
	1955	*0405*	*366*	*Etna (Italy)*	0101-06=	*1*	*6/6*
	1955	0601	15a	**Langila** (New Britain-SW Pac)	0502-01=	2	
	1955	*0603*	....	*Bam (New Guinea-NE of)*	0501-01=	*2*	
	1955	0605	8a	**Long Island** (New Guinea-NE of)	0501-05=	3	
	1955	0611	....	**Asama** (Honshu-Japan)	0803-11=	3	
	1955	0625	?	**Bayonnaise Rocks** (Izu Is-Japan)	0804-07=	0	
?	*1955*	*0625*	*?*	*Katla (Iceland-S)*	1702-03=	*0*	
	1955	07	?	**Shishaldin** (Aleutian Is)	1101-36-	2	
	1955	0706	618a	**Fournaise, Piton de la** (Indian O.)	0303-02=	2	7/-
?	*1955*	*0721*	*12a*	*Gede (Java)*	0603-06=	*1*	
	1955	0725	3a	**Aso** (Kyushu-Japan)	0802-11=	1	
	1955	0726e	4a	**Fuego** (Guatemala)	1402-09=	1	
	1955	0727	108a	**Carrán-Los Venados** (Chile-C)	1507-14=	4	-/8
?	*1955*	*08*	*61t*	*Tinakula (Santa Cruz Is-SW Pacific)*	0506-01=	*2?*	
	1955	0820	2a?	**Unnamed** (Hawaiian Is)	1302-09-	0	
?	*1955*	*10*	*?*	*Unnamed (Taiwan-E of)*	0801-011	*0*	
	1955	1006	63a	**Tolbachik** (Kamchatka)	1000-24=	2	
	1955	*1013*	*>3yr*	*Sakura-jima (Kyushu-Japan)*	0802-08=	*2*	
	1955	*1022*	*496a*	*Bezymianny (Kamchatka)*	1000-25=	*3*	*-/**9***
	1955	*1022*	*755m*	*Llaima (Chile-C)*	1507-11=	*2*	
	1955	1112	38a?	**Slamet** (Java)	0603-18=	2	
	1955	1119	<1	**Akan** (Hokkaido-Japan)	0805-07=	1	-/4
	1955	1229	1a	**Tengger Caldera [Bromo]** (Java)	0603-31=	2	
	1956	*Cont*	....	*Stromboli (Italy)*	0101-04=	*1*	*7/-*
	1956	*Cont*	....	*Nyiragongo (Africa-C)*	0203-03=	*0*	
	1956	*Cont*	....	*Bam (New Guinea-NE of)*	0501-01=	*2*	
	1956	*Cont*	....	*Lamington (New Guinea)*	0503-01=	*3*	*8/-*
	1956	*Cont*	....	*Yasur (Vanuatu-SW Pacific)*	0507-10=	*2*	
	1956	*Cont*	....	*Marapi (Sumatra)*	0601-14=	*2*	
	1956	*Cont*	....	*Semeru (Java)*	0603-30=	*1*	
	1956	*Cont*	....	*Dukono (Halmahera-Indonesia)*	0608-01=	*2*	
	1956	*Cont*	....	*Sakura-jima (Kyushu-Japan)*	0802-08=	*2*	
	1956	*Cont*	....	*Izalco (El Salvador)*	1403-03=	*2*	
	1956	*Cont*	....	*Poás (Costa Rica)*	1405-04=	*2*	
	1956	*Cont*	....	*Sangay (Ecuador)*	1502-09=	*2*	
	1956	*Cont*	....	*Llaima (Chile-C)*	1507-11=	*2*	
	1956	....	?	**Bagana** (Bougainville-SW Pacific)	0505-02=	2	
	1956 b	....	?	**Matthew Island** (SW Pacific)	0508-01=	0?	
	1956 <	....	?	**Puracé** (Colombia)	1501-06=	2	
	1956	01	199m	**Kliuchevskoi** (Kamchatka)	1000-26=	2	6/-
	1956	*0103*	....	*Merapi (Java)*	0603-25=	*2*	*6/7*
	1956	0103?	10a?	**Aso** (Kyushu-Japan)	0802-11=	2	
	1956	0103	2	**Oshima** (Izu Is-Japan)	0804-01=	1	
	1956	0111	32a	**Tongariro [Ngauruhoe]** (New Zeal)	0401-08=	2	
	1956	0111	8a?	**Bristol Island** (Antarctica)	1900-08=	3	
	1956	*0213*	*40a*	*Raung (Java)*	0603-34=	*2*	
	1956	0219	....	**Raung** (Java)	0603-34=	3	
	1956	0228	....	**Etna** (Italy)	0101-06=	2	6/6
	1956	03	335p	**Karymsky** (Kamchatka)	1000-13=	1	
	1956	*03*	*69m*	*Veniaminof (Alaska Peninsula)*	1102-07-	*2*	
	1956	0318	226a	**Akan** (Hokkaido-Japan)	0805-07=	1	-/5
	1956	0322	6	**Kaba** (Sumatra)	0601-22=	2	
	1956	0325	6a	**Langila** (New Britain-SW Pac)	0502-01=	2	
	1956	*0329*	....	*St. Andrew Strait [Tuluman]*	0500-01=	*2*	*8/-*
	1956	0330	....	**Bezymianny** (Kamchatka)	1000-25=	**5**	-/**9**
?	*1956*	*0401*	*30a*	*Fukutoku-Okanoba (Volcano Is-Japan*	0804-13=	*0*	
	1956	*0414*	....	*Santa María (Guatemala)*	1402-03=	*3*	***9**/8*
	1956	0428	<1	**Gede** (Java)	0603-06=	2?	
	1956	05	158m	**Ubinas** (Perú)	1504-02=	2	
	1956	0519	....	**Veniaminof** (Alaska Peninsula)	1102-07-	3	
?	*1956*	*0522*	*1a*	*Unnamed (Hawaiian Is)*	1302-08-	*0*	
	1956	06	31p?	**Tengger Caldera [Bromo]** (Java)	0603-31=	2	
	1956	06	15m	**Tokachi** (Hokkaido-Japan)	0805-05=	1	
	1956	0601?	?	**Karthala** (Indian O.-W)	0303-01=	2?	
	1956	0602	<1	**Dieng Volc Complex** (Java)	0603-20=	1	
	1956	*0727*	....	*Kliuchevskoi (Kamchatka)*	1000-26=	*2*	*6/-*
	1956	08	?	**Aso** (Kyushu-Japan)	0802-11=	2	
?	*1956*	*0825*	*1a*	*Oshima (Izu Is-Japan)*	0804-01=	*1?*	
@	**1956**	0908	1a	**Trident** (Alaska Peninsula)	1102-16-	2	
	1956	0928	428a	**Tolbachik** (Kamchatka)	1000-24=	2	
	1956	1003	45q	**Villarrica** (Chile-C)	1507-12=	1	
	1956	1019	8a	**Soufrière Guadeloupe** (W Indies)	1600-06=	1	-/5
	1956	11	>3yr	**Suwanose-jima** (Ryukyu Is)	0802-03=	2	
	1956	1117	1a	**Nyamuragira** (Africa-C)	0203-02=	1	5/4
	1956	1118	<1	**Ruapehu** (New Zealand)	0401-10=	1	
	1956	12	?	**Sangeang Api** (Lesser Sunda Is)	0604-05=	1	
	1956	*12*	*180p*	*Koryaksky (Kamchatka)*	1000-09=	*2*	
	1956	*1208*	*615m*	*Manam (New Guinea-NE of)*	0501-02=	*2*	*7/7*
	1956	1221	<1	**Aso** (Kyushu-Japan)	0802-11=	1	
	1956	1227	170m	**Zhupanovsky** (Kamchatka)	1000-12=	2	
	1956	*1230*	....	*Fournaise, Piton de la (Indian O.)*	0303-02=	*2*	*7/-*
	1957	*Cont*	....	*Stromboli (Italy)*	0101-04=	*1*	*7/-*
	1957	*Cont*	....	*Nyiragongo (Africa-C)*	0203-03=	*0*	
	1957	*Cont*	....	*Yasur (Vanuatu-SW Pacific)*	0507-10=	*2*	
	1957	*Cont*	....	*Marapi (Sumatra)*	0601-14=	*2*	
	1957	*Cont*	....	*Merapi (Java)*	0603-25=	*1*	*6/7*
	1957	*Cont*	....	*Semeru (Java)*	0603-30=	*1*	
	1957	*Cont*	....	*Dukono (Halmahera-Indonesia)*	0608-01=	*2*	
	1957	*Cont*	....	*Suwanose-jima (Ryukyu Is)*	0802-03=	*2*	
	1957	*Cont*	....	*Sakura-jima (Kyushu-Japan)*	0802-08=	*2*	
	1957	*Cont*	....	*Zhupanovsky (Kamchatka)*	1000-12=	*2*	
	1957	*Cont*	....	*Karymsky (Kamchatka)*	1000-13=	*1*	
	1957	*Cont*	....	*Tolbachik (Kamchatka)*	1000-24=	*2*	
	1957	*Cont*	....	*Poás (Costa Rica)*	1405-04=	*2*	
	1957	*Cont*	....	*Sangay (Ecuador)*	1502-09=	*2*	
	1957	....	?	**Sangeang Api** (Lesser Sunda Is)	0604-05=	1	
	1957	....	?	**Akita-Yake-yama** (Honshu-Japan)	0803-26=	1	
	1957	....	?	**Kliuchevskoi** (Kamchatka)	1000-26=	1	
	1957	....	>3yr	**Trident** (Alaska Peninsula)	1102-16-	2	
	1957	....	....	*Santa María (Guatemala)*	1402-03=	*2*	***9**/8*
	1957	....	?	**Puracé** (Colombia)	1501-06=	2?	
@	**1957**	....	?	**Negra, Sierra** (Galápagos)	1503-05=		
?	*1957*	....	*365y*	*Erebus (Antarctica)*	1900-02=		
	1957	*01*	....	*St. Andrew Strait [Tuluman]*	0500-01=	*2*	*8/-*
	1957	01	16m	**Tangkubanparahu** (Java)	0603-09=	1	
	1957	0117	....	**Koryaksky** (Kamchatka)	1000-09=	3	
	1957	*0118?*	....	*Izalco (El Salvador)*	1403-03=	*3*	
	1957	0205	91a	**Etna** (Italy)	0101-06=	2	6/7
	1957	0208	?	**Kavachi** (Solomon Is-SW Pacific)	0505-06=	0	
	1957	0208	<1	**Slamet** (Java)	0603-18=	2	
	1957	0219	2a>	**Fuego** (Guatemala)	1402-09=	3	-/7
	1957	0219	....	**Llaima** (Chile-C)	1507-11=	3	

	START YEAR	M-Dy	Duration	VOLCANO NAME (Subregion)	NUMBER	VEI	Vol L/T
	1957	0226	203*a*	**Akan** (Hokkaido-Japan)	0805-07=	1	
?	*1957*	*0311*	*1a*	*Vsevidof (Aleutian Is)*	1101-27-	*2*	
	1957	0313	<1	**Gede** (Java)	0603-06=	2	
	1957	0327	111*m*	**Concepción** (Nicaragua)	1404-12=	2	
	1957	0328	<1	**Ioto [Iwo-jima]** (Volcano Is-Japan)	0804-12=	1	-/3
	1957	0412	<1	**Aso** (Kyushu-Japan)	0802-11=	1	
	1957	05	?	**Chikurachki** (Kuril Is)	0900-36=	2	
	1957	0502	?	**Bayonnaise Rocks** (Izu Is-Japan)	0804-07=	0	
	1957	0514	>3yr	**Colima** (México)	1401-04=	1	
	1957	06	?	**Fonualei** (Tonga-SW Pacific)	0403-10=		
	1957	0731	<1	**Bezymianny** (Kamchatka)	1000-25=	2	
	1957	08	122*p*	**Oshima** (Izu Is-Japan)	0804-01=	1	-/4
	1957	0801	1	**Visoke** (Africa-C)	0203-05-	1	5/5
?	*1957*	*0820*	*<1*	*Tokachi (Hokkaido-Japan)*	0805-05=	*1*	
	1957	0825	251*a*	**Etna** (Italy)	0101-06=	2	
	1957	0826e	50*n*	**Ambrym** (Vanuatu-SW Pacific)	0507-04=	1?	
	1957	0902	75*a*	**Fournaise, Piton de la** (Indian O.)	0303-02=	2	6/-
	1957	0904	20*a*	**Negro, Cerro** (Nicaragua)	1404-07=	2	6/6
	1957	0927	392*a*	**Fayal** (Azores)	1802-01=	2	7/7
	1957	*10*	*425p*	*Aso (Kyushu-Japan)*	0802-11=	*1*	*-/5*
	1957	10	?	**Rasshua** (Kuril Is)	0900-22=	1	
	1957	1026	<1	**Bam** (New Guinea-NE of)	0501-01=	1	
	1957	*1112*	*19a*	*Zavaritzki Caldera (Kuril Is)*	0900-18=	*2*	
?	*1957*	*1121*	*3a*	*Unnamed [Lomonosov Ridge] (Arctic)*	1707-01-	*0*	
	1957	1128	....	**Zavaritzki Caldera** (Kuril Is)	0900-18=	3	
	1957	1210	....	**Manam** (New Guinea-NE of)	0501-02=	3	7/7
	1957	1211	?	**White Island** (New Zealand)	0401-04=	2	
	1957	1228	?	**Nyamuragira** (Africa-C)	0203-02=	0	6/-
	1958	*Cont*	....	*Stromboli (Italy)*	0101-04=	*1*	*7/-*
	1958	*Cont*	....	*Nyiragongo (Africa-C)*	0203-03=	*0*	
	1958	*Cont*	....	*Yasur (Vanuatu-SW Pacific)*	0507-10=	*2*	
	1958	*Cont*	....	*Merapi (Java)*	0603-25=	*1*	*6/7*
	1958	*Cont*	....	*Semeru (Java)*	0603-30=	*1*	
	1958	*Cont*	....	*Dukono (Halmahera-Indonesia)*	0608-01=	*2*	
	1958	*Cont*	....	*Suwanose-jima (Ryukyu Is)*	0802-03=	*2*	
	1958	*Cont*	....	*Sakura-jima (Kyushu-Japan)*	0802-08=	*2*	

A column of ash and steam towers above a new submarine vent off the western coast of Fayal Island in October 1957. Horizontally traveling base surges form a ring at the base of the eruption column. Explosive eruptions formed a small island that eventually was joined to the main island, partially burying the Capelinhos lighthouse, visible on the center shoreline.

U.S. Air Force

	START YEAR	M-Dy	Duration	VOLCANO NAME (Subregion)	NUMBER	VEI	Vol L/T
	1958	*Cont*	....	*Trident (Alaska Peninsula)*	1102-16-	*2*	
	1958	*Cont*	....	*Colima (México)*	1401-04=	*1*	
	1958	*Cont*	....	*Sangay (Ecuador)*	1502-09=	*2*	
	1958	*Cont*	....	*Fayal (Azores)*	1802-01=	*2*	*7/7*
?	*1958*	*Cont*	....	*Erebus (Antarctica)*	1900-02=		
	1958	....	?	**Sangeang Api** (Lesser Sunda Is)	0604-05=	1?	
	1958	....	?	**Bayonnaise Rocks** (Izu Is-Japan)	0804-07=	0	
	1958	....	?	**Medvezhia** (Kuril Is)	0900-10=	1	
	1958	....	....	*Santa María (Guatemala)*	1402-03=	*2*	***9**/8*
	1958	....	*>3yr*	*Poás (Costa Rica)*	1405-04=	*1*	
	1958	01	29*m*	**Bezymianny** (Kamchatka)	1000-25=	1	
	1958	01	?	**Tupungatito** (Chile-C)	1507-01=	2	
	1958	*0110*	....	*Manam (New Guinea-NE of)*	0501-02=	*3*	*7/7*
	1958	0201r	?	**Ulawun** (New Britain-SW Pac)	0502-12=	2	
	1958	0206<	?	**Lengai, Ol Doinyo** (Africa-E)	0202-12=	1	
	1958	0219	672*a*	**Lokon-Empung** (Sulawesi-Indonesia)	0606-10=	2	
	1958	0223	<1	**Akan** (Hokkaido-Japan)	0805-07=	1	
	1958	0311j	39*j?*	**Bam** (New Guinea-NE of)	0501-01=	2	
	1958	0417	20*a*	**Slamet** (Java)	0603-18=	2	
	1958	0417	57*a*	**Oshima** (Izu Is-Japan)	0804-01=	1	-/4
	1958	0421	44*d*	**Langila** (New Britain-SW Pac)	0502-01=	2	
	1958	0517	103*a*	**Pavlof** (Alaska Peninsula)	1102-03-	2	
	1958	0518	92*a*>	**Kliuchevskoi** (Kamchatka)	1000-26=	1	
	1958	0521	?	**Bezymianny** (Kamchatka)	1000-25=	1	
	1958	0526	1*a*	**Chikurachki** (Kuril Is)	0900-36=	2	
	1958	0530	113*a*	**Fournaise, Piton de la** (Indian O.)	0303-02=	2	
	1958	0623	<1*?*	**Marapi** (Sumatra)	0601-14=	1	
	1958	0624	....	**Aso** (Kyushu-Japan)	0802-11=	2	-/5
?	*1958*	*0701*	*92a*	*Fukutoku-Okanoba (Volcano Is-Japan*	0804-13=	*0*	
S	1958	0709	>3yr	**Rumble III** (New Zealand)	0401-13-	0	
	1958	0712	17*a*	**Mahawu** (Sulawesi-Indonesia)	0606-11=	2?	
	1958	0713<	?	**Tolbachik** (Kamchatka)	1000-24=	2?	
?	*1958*	*08*	*31p*	*Fukujin (Volcano Is-Japan)*	0804-133	*0*	
	1958	0807	107*a*	**Nyamuragira** (Africa-C)	0203-02=	2	7/6
	1958	0814	12*j*	**Okmok** (Aleutian Is)	1101-29-	3	8/-
	1958	09 ?	61*p?*	**Epi** (Vanuatu-SW Pacific)	0507-06=	2?	
	1958	09 ?	106*m*>	**Fernandina** (Galápagos)	1503-01=	2	7/-
	1958	0905	5*a*	**Bam** (New Guinea-NE of)	0501-01=	2	
	1958	0913	53*d*	**Slamet** (Java)	0603-18=	2	
	1958	1002	266*d*	**Krakatau** (Indonesia)	0602-00=	2	
	1958	*1003*	*327e*	*Asama (Honshu-Japan)*	0803-11=	*1*	*-/5*
	1958	1004	<1	**Tokachi** (Hokkaido-Japan)	0805-05=	1	
	1958	*1007?*	*72a?*	*Kuwae [Karua] (Vanuatu-SW Pac)*	0507-07=	*0*	
	1958	1017	8*a*	**Marapi** (Sumatra)	0601-14=	1	
	1958	11	31*p*	**Etna** (Italy)	0101-06=	1	
	1958	11	?	**Reventador** (Ecuador)	1502-01=	3	
	1958	1105	13*a?*	**Tongariro [Ngauruhoe]** (New Zeal)	0401-08=	2	
	1958	1106	410*a*	**Villarrica** (Chile-C)	1507-12=	1	
	1958	1110	....	**Asama** (Honshu-Japan)	0803-11=	2	-/5
	1958	1118	?	**Ambrym** (Vanuatu-SW Pacific)	0507-04=	2?	
	1958	1121	11*a?*	**Kavachi** (Solomon Is-SW Pacific)	0505-06=	0	
	1958	12	?	**White Island** (New Zealand)	0401-04=	1	
	1958	1218	....	**Kuwae [Karua]** (Vanuatu-SW Pac)	0507-07=	2?	
	1958	*1228*	*92a*	*Bezymianny (Kamchatka)*	1000-25=	*1*	
	1958	1231u	549*u?*	**Tofua** (Tonga-SW Pacific)	0403-06=	2	
	1958	1231y	?	**Kusatsu-Shirane** (Honshu-Japan)	0803-12=	1	
	1959	*Cont*	....	*Nyiragongo (Africa-C)*	0203-03=	*0*	
S	*1959*	*Cont*	....	*Rumble III (New Zealand)*	0401-13-	*0*	
	1959	*Cont*	....	*Tofua (Tonga-SW Pacific)*	0403-06=	*2*	
	1959	*Cont*	....	*Yasur (Vanuatu-SW Pacific)*	0507-10=	*2*	
	1959	*Cont*	....	*Semeru (Java)*	0603-30=	*1*	
	1959	*Cont*	....	*Lokon-Empung (Sulawesi-Indonesia)*	0606-10=	*2*	
	1959	*Cont*	....	*Dukono (Halmahera-Indonesia)*	0608-01=	*2*	
	1959	*Cont*	....	*Suwanose-jima (Ryukyu Is)*	0802-03=	*2*	
	1959	*Cont*	....	*Sakura-jima (Kyushu-Japan)*	0802-08=	*2*	
	1959	*Cont*	....	*Trident (Alaska Peninsula)*	1102-16-	*2*	
	1959	*Cont*	....	*Colima (México)*	1401-04=	*1*	
	1959	*Cont*	....	*Poás (Costa Rica)*	1405-04=	*1*	
	1959	*Cont*	....	*Villarrica (Chile-C)*	1507-12=	*1*	
?	*1959*	....	*?*	*Niuafo'ou (Tonga-SW Pacific)*	0403-11=		
	1959 ?	....	318*w?*	**Bagana** (Bougainville-SW Pacific)	0505-02=	2	
?	*1959*	....	*?*	*Traitor's Head (Vanuatu-SW Pacific)*	0507-09=		
	1959	....	?	**Bayonnaise Rocks** (Izu Is-Japan)	0804-07=	0	
?	*1959*	....	*?*	*Kita-Fukutokutai (Volcano Is-Japan)*	0804-121	*0*	
	1959	....	?	**Zhupanovsky** (Kamchatka)	1000-12=	2	
	1959	....	365*y*	**Tolbachik** (Kamchatka)	1000-24=	2	
	1959	....	....	*Santa María (Guatemala)*	1402-03=	*2*	***9**/8*
	1959	....	?	**San José** (Chile-C)	1507-02=	2	
	1959	....	?	**Kverkfjöll** (Iceland-NE)	1703-05=		
	1959	01	16*m*	**Oshima** (Izu Is-Japan)	0804-01=	1	
	1959	0103	?	**Kliuchevskoi** (Kamchatka)	1000-26=	1	
	1959	0123	55*a*	**Cameroon** (Africa-W)	0204-01=	2	6/-
	1959	0213	4*a*	**Kirishima** (Kyushu-Japan)	0802-09=	2	-/6
	1959	0228	....	**Bezymianny** (Kamchatka)	1000-25=	2	
	1959	0311	148*a*	**Fournaise, Piton de la** (Indian O.)	0303-02=	2	6/-
	1959	0323	33*e*	**Etna** (Italy)	0101-06=	1	
	1959	0326e	?	**Tupungatito** (Chile-C)	1507-01=	2	

	START YEAR	M-Dy	Duration	VOLCANO NAME (Subregion)	NUMBER	VEI	Vol L/T
	1959	04	?	**Ambrym** (Vanuatu-SW Pacific)	0507-04=	2	
	1959	0402	212*a*	**Bam** (New Guinea-NE of)	0501-01=	2	
	1959	*0414*	....	*Asama (Honshu-Japan)*	0803-11=	*2*	*-/5*
	1959	0515e	153*m*	**Akan** (Hokkaido-Japan)	0805-07=	1	
	1959	*0519*	....	*Stromboli (Italy)*	0101-04=	*2*	*7/-*
	1959	0521	72*a*	**Ruapehu** (New Zealand)	0401-10=	1	
	1959	06	30*p*	**Manam** (New Guinea-NE of)	0501-02=	2	
	1959	0601	?	**Tongariro [Ngauruhoe]** (New Zeal)	0401-08=	2	
	1959	0608	37*m*	**Iwo-Tori-shima** (Ryukyu Is)	0802-02=	2	
	1959	0629	32*a*?	**Azul, Cerro** (Galápagos)	1503-06=	2?	
?	*1959*	*07*	?	*Kars Plateau (Turkey)*	0103-05-	*2*	
	1959	07	79*m*	**Aso** (Kyushu-Japan)	0802-11=	1	
?	*1959*	*0701*	*92a*	*Fukutoku-Okanoba (Volcano Is-Japan.*	0804-13=	*0*	
	1959	0715q	?	**Kasuga** (Volcano Is-Japan)	0804-134	0	
	1959	0715e	?	**Guallatiri** (Chile-N)	1505-02=	2	
?	*1959*	*08*	*61p*	*Fukujin (Volcano Is-Japan)*	0804-133	*0*	
	1959	0815e	102*e*	**Tokachi** (Hokkaido-Japan)	0805-05=	1	
	1959	0918?	3*a*	**Kuwae [Karua]** (Vanuatu-SW Pac)	0507-07=	2	
	1959	10	396*p*	**Oshima** (Izu Is-Japan)	0804-01=	1	
	1959	1015	20*a*?	**Bezymianny** (Kamchatka)	1000-25=	1	-/4
	1959	1016	?	**Tupungatito** (Chile-C)	1507-01=	2	
	1959	*1017*	*>3yr*	*Etna (Italy)*	0101-06=	*1*	*7/-*
	1959	11	>3yr	**Láscar** (Chile-N)	1505-10=	2	
	1959	1106	?	**Planchón-Peteroa** (Chile-C)	1507-04=	1	
	1959	1114	36*a*	**Kilauea** (Hawaiian Is)	1302-01-	2	7/6
	1959	12	365*p*>	**Manam** (New Guinea-NE of)	0501-02=	2	6/-
	1959	12	>3yr	**Krakatau** (Indonesia)	0602-00=	2	6/-
	1959	*12*	....	*Sangay (Ecuador)*	1502-09=	*3*	
	1959	1214	6*a*	**White Island** (New Zealand)	0401-04=	2	
	1959	1228	23*a*	**Lautaro** (Chile-S)	1508-06=	2	
	1960	*Cont*	....	*Stromboli (Italy)*	0101-04=	*1*	*7/-*
	1960	*Cont*	....	*Nyiragongo (Africa-C)*	0203-03=	*0*	
S	*1960*	*Cont*	....	*Rumble III (New Zealand)*	0401-13-	*0*	
	1960	*Cont*	....	*Tofua (Tonga-SW Pacific)*	0403-06=	*2*	
	1960	*Cont*	....	*Manam (New Guinea-NE of)*	0501-02=	*2*	*6/-*
	1960	*Cont*	....	*Bagana (Bougainville-SW Pacific)*	0505-02=	*2*	
	1960	*Cont*	....	*Yasur (Vanuatu-SW Pacific)*	0507-10=	*2*	
	1960	*Cont*	....	*Krakatau (Indonesia)*	0602-00=	*2*	*6/-*
	1960	*Cont*	....	*Semeru (Java)*	0603-30=	*1*	
	1960	*Cont*	....	*Dukono (Halmahera-Indonesia)*	0608-01=	*2*	
	1960	*Cont*	....	*Sakura-jima (Kyushu-Japan)*	0802-08=	*2*	
	1960	*Cont*	....	*Oshima (Izu Is-Japan)*	0804-01=	*1*	
	1960	*Cont*	....	*Tolbachik (Kamchatka)*	1000-24=	*2*	
	1960	*Cont*	....	*Trident (Alaska Peninsula)*	1102-16-	*2*	
	1960	*Cont*	....	*Colima (México)*	1401-04=	*1*	
	1960	*Cont*	....	*Poás (Costa Rica)*	1405-04=	*1*	
	1960	*Cont*	....	*Sangay (Ecuador)*	1502-09=	*2*	
	1960	*Cont*	....	*Lautaro (Chile-S)*	1508-06=	*2*	
	1960 ?	....	?	**Suwanose-jima** (Ryukyu Is)	0802-03=	0	
	1960 ?	....	>3yr	**Pavlof** (Alaska Peninsula)	1102-03-	2	
	1960	....	....	*Santa María (Guatemala)*	1402-03=	*2*	***9**/8*
?	*1960*	....	?	*Isluga (Chile-N)*	1505-03=	*2?*	
	1960	....	?	**San José** (Chile-C)	1507-02=	2	
	1960	....	?	**Copahue** (Chile-C)	1507-09=		
?	*1960*	....	?	*Llaima (Chile-C)*	1507-11=		
?	*1960*	....	?	*Villarrica (Chile-C)*	1507-12=	*1?*	
	1960	01	?	**Erta Ale** (Ethiopia)	0201-08=	0	
	1960	01	84*m*	**Aso** (Kyushu-Japan)	0802-11=	2	
	1960	0111	59*a*	**Fournaise, Piton de la** (Indian O.)	0303-02=	2	6/-
	1960	0113	37*a*	**Kilauea** (Hawaiian Is)	1302-01-	2	8/-
	1960	*03* <	*>3yr*	*Lengai, Ol Doinyo (Africa-E)*	0202-12=	*1*	
	1960	0313	?	**Sirung** (Lesser Sunda Is)	0604-27=	2?	
	1960	*0328*	....	*Láscar (Chile-N)*	1505-10=	*2?*	
	1960	*04*	*>3yr*	*Karymsky (Kamchatka)*	1000-13=	*2*	*6/7*
	1960	0413	1	**Bezymianny** (Kamchatka)	1000-25=	2	-/6
	1960	0428	69*a*	**Bam** (New Guinea-NE of)	0501-01=	2	
	1960	0524	67*a*	**Puyehue-Cordón Caulle** (Chile-C)	1507-15=	3?	8/7
	1960	06	?	**Reventador** (Ecuador)	1502-01=	3	
	1960	07 ?	?	**Epi** (Vanuatu-SW Pacific)	0507-06=	0	
	1960	07	?	**Kerinci** (Sumatra)	0601-17=	2	
?	*1960*	*0701*	*61a*	*Fukutoku-Okanoba (Volcano Is-Japan.*	0804-13=	*0*	
	1960	0710	67*m*	**Lopevi** (Vanuatu-SW Pacific)	0507-05=	3	
	1960	0710?	?	**Planchón-Peteroa** (Chile-C)	1507-04=	1	
	1960	0715e	?	**Tupungatito** (Chile-C)	1507-01=	2	
	1960	0717	....	**Etna** (Italy)	0101-06=	3	7/-
	1960	0721	?	**Bayonnaise Rocks** (Izu Is-Japan)	0804-07=	2	
	1960	0729c	838*m*	**Ulawun** (New Britain-SW Pac)	0502-12=	2	
	1960	0830	<1	**Sarychev Peak** (Kuril Is)	0900-24=	3	
	1960	09	791*p*	**Aso** (Kyushu-Japan)	0802-11=	1	
	1960	09	15*m*	**Akan** (Hokkaido-Japan)	0805-07=	1	
	1960	0917	?	**Ambrym** (Vanuatu-SW Pacific)	0507-04=	1?	
	1960	0927	?	**Ketoi** (Kuril Is)	0900-20=	2	
	1960	0928	89*e*?	**Negro, Cerro** (Nicaragua)	1404-07=	3	6/7
	1960	1010?	?	**Nasu** (Honshu-Japan)	0803-15=	1	
	1960	1015q	183*w*	**Okmok** (Aleutian Is)	1101-29-	3	-/7
	1960	1020	?	**Chirpoi** (Kuril Is)	0900-15=	2?	
	1960	12	31*p*	**Slamet** (Java)	0603-18=	2	
	1960	12	31*p*	**Mutnovsky** (Kamchatka)	1000-06=	2	-/6
	1960	*12*	*826m>*	*Kliuchevskoi (Kamchatka)*	1000-26=	*2*	*-/6*
	1960	1202	?	**Guallatiri** (Chile-N)	1505-02=	2	
	1960	1202	?	**San Pedro** (Chile-N)	1505-07=	2	
	1960	1219	279*e*	**Langila** (New Britain-SW Pac)	0502-01=	2	4/-
	1961	*Cont*	....	*Stromboli (Italy)*	0101-04=	*1*	*7/-*
	1961	*Cont*	....	*Etna (Italy)*	0101-06=	*2*	*7/-*
	1961	*Cont*	....	*Lengai, Ol Doinyo (Africa-E)*	0202-12=	*1*	
	1961	*Cont*	....	*Nyiragongo (Africa-C)*	0203-03=	*0*	
S	*1961*	*Cont*	....	*Rumble III (New Zealand)*	0401-13-	*0*	
	1961	*Cont*	....	*Langila (New Britain-SW Pac)*	0502-01=	*2*	*4/-*
	1961	*Cont*	....	*Ulawun (New Britain-SW Pac)*	0502-12=	*2*	
	1961	*Cont*	....	*Yasur (Vanuatu-SW Pacific)*	0507-10=	*2*	
	1961	*Cont*	....	*Krakatau (Indonesia)*	0602-00=	*2*	*6/-*
	1961	*Cont*	....	*Slamet (Java)*	0603-18=	*2*	
	1961	*Cont*	....	*Semeru (Java)*	0603-30=	*1*	
	1961	*Cont*	....	*Dukono (Halmahera-Indonesia)*	0608-01=	*2*	
	1961	*Cont*	....	*Suwanose-jima (Ryukyu Is)*	0802-03=	*2*	
	1961	*Cont*	....	*Aso (Kyushu-Japan)*	0802-11=	*1*	
	1961	*Cont*	....	*Mutnovsky (Kamchatka)*	1000-06=	*2*	*-/6*
	1961	*Cont*	....	*Karymsky (Kamchatka)*	1000-13=	*2*	*6/7*
	1961	*Cont*	....	*Kliuchevskoi (Kamchatka)*	1000-26=	*2*	*-/6*
	1961	*Cont*	....	*Okmok (Aleutian Is)*	1101-29-	*2*	*-/7*
	1961	*Cont*	....	*Pavlof (Alaska Peninsula)*	1102-03-	*2*	
	1961	*Cont*	....	*Santa María (Guatemala)*	1402-03=	*1*	***9**/8*
	1961	*Cont*	....	*Sangay (Ecuador)*	1502-09=	*2*	
	1961	*Cont*	....	*Láscar (Chile-N)*	1505-10=	*2*	
?	*1961*	....	?	*Long Island (New Guinea-NE of)*	0501-05=		
?	*1961*	....	?	*Oshima (Izu Is-Japan)*	0804-01=		
	1961	....	700*p*	**Colima** (México)	1401-04=	1	6/-
	1961	....	?	**Copahue** (Chile-C)	1507-09=	2	
	1961	....	?	**Villarrica** (Chile-C)	1507-12=	1	
	1961	01	?	**Gorely** (Kamchatka)	1000-07=	2	
	1961	0201	53*a*>	**Calbuco** (Chile-S)	1508-02=	3	
	1961	0224	<1	**Kilauea** (Hawaiian Is)	1302-01-	1	5/-
	1961	0228	18*m*	**Karangetang [Api Siau]** (Sangihe Is	0607-02=	2	-/6
	1961	0303	22*a*	**Kilauea** (Hawaiian Is)	1302-01-	1	5/-
	1961	0311	35*a*?	**Pacaya** (Guatemala)	1402-11=	2	6/-
	1961	0321a	193*m*	**Fernandina** (Galápagos)	1503-01=	2	
	1961	0324	269*a*>	**Tolbachik** (Kamchatka)	1000-24=	2	
	1961	0325	1*a*	**Bezymianny** (Kamchatka)	1000-25=	3	-/6
	1961	0328<	?	**Kavachi** (Solomon Is-SW Pacific)	0505-06=	2	
	1961	0405	20*a*	**Fournaise, Piton de la** (Indian O.)	0303-02=	0	7/-
	1961	0411	231*a*	**Merapi** (Java)	0603-25=	3	7/7
	1961	0502	99*a*	**Chikurachki** (Kuril Is)	0900-36=	1	
	1961	0505d	101*n*>	**Tupungatito** (Chile-C)	1507-01=	2	
	1961	*0508*	....	*Merapi (Java)*	0603-25=	*3*	*7/7*
	1961	0519	210*m*	**Lokon-Empung** (Sulawesi-Indonesia)	0606-10=	2	
	1961	0521	16*a*	**Bezymianny** (Kamchatka)	1000-25=	2	
	1961	0625e	....	**Poás** (Costa Rica)	1405-04=	2	
	1961	0630?	?	**Trident** (Alaska Peninsula)	1102-16-	2	
	1961	07	61*p*	**Manam** (New Guinea-NE of)	0501-02=	2	
	1961	0710	7*a*	**Kilauea** (Hawaiian Is)	1302-01-	1	7/-
	1961	0716	16*a*	**Tangkubanparahu** (Java)	0603-09=	1	
	1961	0726	?	**Bagana** (Bougainville-SW Pacific)	0505-02=	2	
	1961	0814	<1	**Tokachi** (Hokkaido-Japan)	0805-05=	1	
	1961	*0815*	*596a*	*Ambrym (Vanuatu-SW Pacific)*	0507-04=	*1*	
	1961	0818	89*a*	**Asama** (Honshu-Japan)	0803-11=	2	-/4
	1961	0922	1	**Kilauea** (Hawaiian Is)	1302-01-	1	6/-
@	**1961**	10	?	**Lautaro** (Chile-S)	1508-06=	2	
	1961	1009	10*a*>	**Karangetang [Api Siau]** (Sangihe Is	0607-02=	2	-/6
	1961	1010	156*a*	**Tristan da Cunha** (Atlantic-S)	1806-01=	2	
	1961	1018	58*a*	**Bezymianny** (Kamchatka)	1000-25=	3	
	1961	1025	?	**Negro, Cerro** (Nicaragua)	1404-07=	1	
	1961	1026	40*d*	**Askja** (Iceland-NE)	1703-06=	2	8/6
	1961	*1127*	....	*Merapi (Java)*	0603-25=	*3*	*7/7*
?	*1961*	*1128*	*18m*	*Concepción (Nicaragua)*	1404-12=	*2?*	
	1961	12	....	**Sakura-jima** (Kyushu-Japan)	0802-08=	3	
	1962	*Cont*	....	*Stromboli (Italy)*	0101-04=	*1*	*7/-*
	1962	*Cont*	....	*Etna (Italy)*	0101-06=	*2*	*7/-*
	1962	*Cont*	....	*Lengai, Ol Doinyo (Africa-E)*	0202-12=	*1*	
	1962	*Cont*	....	*Nyiragongo (Africa-C)*	0203-03=	*0*	
S	*1962*	*Cont*	....	*Rumble III (New Zealand)*	0401-13-	*0*	
	1962	*Cont*	....	*Ulawun (New Britain-SW Pac)*	0502-12=	*2*	
	1962	*Cont*	....	*Yasur (Vanuatu-SW Pacific)*	0507-10=	*2*	
	1962	*Cont*	....	*Krakatau (Indonesia)*	0602-00=	*2*	*6/-*
	1962	*Cont*	....	*Semeru (Java)*	0603-30=	*1*	
	1962	*Cont*	....	*Dukono (Halmahera-Indonesia)*	0608-01=	*2*	
	1962	*Cont*	....	*Suwanose-jima (Ryukyu Is)*	0802-03=	*2*	
	1962	*Cont*	....	*Sakura-jima (Kyushu-Japan)*	0802-08=	*2*	
	1962	*Cont*	....	*Aso (Kyushu-Japan)*	0802-11=	*1*	
	1962	*Cont*	....	*Pavlof (Alaska Peninsula)*	1102-03-	*2*	
	1962	*Cont*	....	*Colima (México)*	1401-04=	*1*	*6/-*
	1962	*Cont*	....	*Santa María (Guatemala)*	1402-03=	*1*	***9**/8*
	1962	*Cont*	....	*Sangay (Ecuador)*	1502-09=	*2*	
	1962	*Cont*	....	*Láscar (Chile-N)*	1505-10=	*2*	

	START YEAR	M-Dy	Duration	VOLCANO NAME (Subregion)	NUMBER	VEI	Vol L/T
	1962	Cont	....	Tristan da Cunha (Atlantic-S)	1806-01=	2	
?	1962 ?	....	?	Karkar (New Guinea-NE of)	0501-03=	2?	
	1962	01	30p	Kavachi (Solomon Is-SW Pacific)	0505-06=	2	
	1962	01	>3yr	Oshima (Izu Is-Japan)	0804-01=	1	
	1962	01	16m	Telica (Nicaragua)	1404-04=	1	
	1962	01	?	Planchón-Peteroa (Chile-C)	1507-04=	1	
	1962	0109	....	Ambrym (Vanuatu-SW Pacific)	0507-04=	3	
	1962	0124	?	Kiska (Aleutian Is)	1101-02-	3	
	1962	0129	701m	Karangetang [Api Siau] (Sangihe Is	0607-02=	2	
	1962	0215	502w	Bagana (Bougainville-SW Pacific)	0505-02=	2	
	1962	03	513m	Langila (New Britain-SW Pac)	0502-01=	2	
	1962	0305	?	Protector Shoal (Antarctica)	1900-14-	0	-/8
	1962	0314	<1	Niigata-Yake-yama (Honshu-Japan)	0803-09=	1	
	1962	0321	24m?	Negro, Cerro (Nicaragua)	1404-07=	2	
	1962	04	?	Manam (New Guinea-NE of)	0501-02=	2	
	1962	04	214p	Lokon-Empung (Sulawesi-Indonesia)	0606-10=	1	
	1962	0428	<1	Akan (Hokkaido-Japan)	0805-07=	1	
	1962	0524	?	Tongariro [Ngauruhoe] (New Zeal)	0401-08=	2	
	1962	06	15m	Concepción (Nicaragua)	1404-12=	2	
	1962	0609	<1	Trident (Alaska Peninsula)	1102-16-	3	
	1962	0617	377a	Yake-dake (Honshu-Japan)	0803-07=	2	-/6
	1962	0629	78m	Tokachi (Hokkaido-Japan)	0805-05=	3	-/7
	1962	07 <	?	Gaua (Vanuatu-SW Pacific)	0507-02=	2?	
	1962	07	16m?	Lopevi (Vanuatu-SW Pacific)	0507-05=	0	
?	1962	0701	92a	Fukutoku-Okanoba (Volcano Is-Japan	0804-13=	0	
	1962	08	320w	Tolbachik (Kamchatka)	1000-24=	1	
	1962	0804	97a	Fuego (Guatemala)	1402-09=	2	6/7
	1962	0824	2 ?	Miyake-jima (Izu Is-Japan)	0804-04=	2	6/6
	1962	1017	....	Karymsky (Kamchatka)	1000-13=	3	6/7
	1962	1021	16a	Bezymianny (Kamchatka)	1000-25=	2	
	1962	1105d	?	Akutan (Aleutian Is)	1101-32-	2	
	1962	1107	....	Ambrym (Vanuatu-SW Pacific)	0507-04=	3	
	1962	1109	....	Fuego (Guatemala)	1402-09=	3	6/7
	1962	1113	....	Kliuchevskoi (Kamchatka)	1000-26=	3	-/6
	1962	1207	2	Kilauea (Hawaiian Is)	1302-01-	0	5/-
	1962	1215	?	White Island (New Zealand)	0401-04=	3	
	1962	1231	2a?	Gamalama (Halmahera-Indonesia)	0608-06=	2	
	1963	Cont	....	Stromboli (Italy)	0101-04=	1	7/-
	1963	Cont	....	Etna (Italy)	0101-06=	2	7/-
	1963	Cont	....	Lengai, Ol Doinyo (Africa-E)	0202-12=	1	
	1963	Cont	....	Nyiragongo (Africa-C)	0203-03=	0	
	1963	Cont	....	Langila (New Britain-SW Pac)	0502-01=	2	
	1963	Cont	....	Bagana (Bougainville-SW Pacific)	0505-02=	2	
	1963	Cont	....	Yasur (Vanuatu-SW Pacific)	0507-10=	2	
	1963	Cont	....	Krakatau (Indonesia)	0602-00=	2	6/-
	1963	Cont	....	Karangetang [Api Siau] (Sangihe Is	0607-02=	2	
	1963	Cont	....	Dukono (Halmahera-Indonesia)	0608-01=	2	
	1963	Cont	....	Gamalama (Halmahera-Indonesia)	0608-06=	2	
	1963	Cont	....	Suwanose-jima (Ryukyu Is)	0802-03=	2	
	1963	Cont	....	Sakura-jima (Kyushu-Japan)	0802-08=	2	
	1963	Cont	....	Yake-dake (Honshu-Japan)	0803-07=	2	-/6
	1963	Cont	....	Oshima (Izu Is-Japan)	0804-01=	1	
	1963	Cont	....	Tolbachik (Kamchatka)	1000-24=	1	
	1963	Cont	....	Pavlof (Alaska Peninsula)	1102-03-	2	
	1963	Cont	....	Santa María (Guatemala)	1402-03=	1	9/8
	1963	Cont	....	Sangay (Ecuador)	1502-09=	2	
	1963	Cont	....	Láscar (Chile-N)	1505-10=	2	
	1963	....	?	Talang (Sumatra)	0601-16=	2	
	1963	....	>3yr	Colima (México)	1401-04=	1	
S	1963	01	>3yr	Rumble III (New Zealand)	0401-13-	0	
	1963	02	91p>	Manam (New Guinea-NE of)	0501-02=	2	
	1963	0213	?	Amukta (Aleutian Is)	1101-19-	3	
	1963	0214	?	Niigata-Yake-yama (Honshu-Japan)	0803-09=	1	
	1963	0218	344a	Agung (Lesser Sunda Is)	0604-02=	3	8/9
	1963	0225?	208a>	Villarrica (Chile-C)	1507-12=	2	
	1963	03	?	Negro, Cerro (Nicaragua)	1404-07=	1	
	1963	0304	12a>	Wolf (Galápagos)	1503-02=	0	
	1963	0308	481w	Ebeko (Kuril Is)	0900-38=	1	-/3
	1963	0313	702a	Irazú (Costa Rica)	1405-06=	3	
	1963	0317	49a?	Ulawun (New Britain-SW Pac)	0502-12=	2	
	1963	0317	....	Agung (Lesser Sunda Is)	0604-02=	5	8/9
	1963	0322	....	Kliuchevskoi (Kamchatka)	1000-26=	2	-/6
	1963	0401	2a>	Trident (Alaska Peninsula)	1102-16-	3	
	1963	0413	30c?	Negra, Sierra (Galápagos)	1503-05=	2	
	1963	0421	86m	Aso (Kyushu-Japan)	0802-11=	1	
	1963	05	122p?	Bezymianny (Kamchatka)	1000-25=	1	
	1963	0502	....	Villarrica (Chile-C)	1507-12=	3?	
	1963	0505	....	Semeru (Java)	0603-30=	2	
	1963	0509	?	Concepción (Nicaragua)	1404-12=	1	
	1963	0511	....	Karymsky (Kamchatka)	1000-13=	3	6/7
	1963	0516	....	Agung (Lesser Sunda Is)	0604-02=	4	8/9
	1963	0523	40a	Poás (Costa Rica)	1405-04=	2	
	1963	07	?	Kerinci (Sumatra)	0601-17=	2	
	1963	0703	....	Irazú (Costa Rica)	1405-06=	3	
	1963	0707	724w	Lopevi (Vanuatu-SW Pacific)	0507-05=	2	
	1963	0710	82a	Niigata-Yake-yama (Honshu-Japan)	0803-09=	1	
?	1963	0710	1a	Nasu (Honshu-Japan)	0803-15=	1	
	1963	0821	1	Kilauea (Hawaiian Is)	1302-01-	0	4/-
	1963	0830	24a>	Ambrym (Vanuatu-SW Pacific)	0507-04=	2	
	1963	0905	247a	Batur (Lesser Sunda Is)	0604-01=	2	7/5
S	1963	0911	294w	Unnamed (SW Pacific)	0508-03-	0	
	1963	0915e	55e>	Gaua (Vanuatu-SW Pacific)	0507-02=	2	
	1963	0928	3a	Fuego (Guatemala)	1402-09=	3	-/6
	1963	1005	1	Kilauea (Hawaiian Is)	1302-01-	0	6/-
	1963	1011	313a	Augustine (Alaska-SW)	1103-01-	2	7/6
	1963	1017	31a?	Trident (Alaska Peninsula)	1102-16-	3	
?	1963	1027	?	Fukutoku-Okanoba (Volcano Is-Japan	0804-13=	0	
	1963	11 <	?	Erebus (Antarctica)	1900-02=	0	
	1963	1107	14a	Fournaise, Piton de la (Indian O.)	0303-02=	2	-/7
	1963	1108	>3yr	Vestmannaeyjar [Surtsey]	1702-01=	0	8/8
	1963	1110	66m?	Aso (Kyushu-Japan)	0802-11=	2	
	1963	1113	397m?	Kliuchevskoi (Kamchatka)	1000-26=	1	
	1963	1114	....	Vestmannaeyjar [Surtsey]	1702-01=	3	8/8
	1963	1120	1a	Nasu (Honshu-Japan)	0803-15=	1	
	1963	1126	142m	Manam (New Guinea-NE of)	0501-02=	2	6/-
	1963	1214	48a?	Kavachi (Solomon Is-SW Pacific)	0505-06=	0	
?	1963	1215<	?	Pico (Azores)	1802-02=	0	
	1963	1217	120m	Lokon-Empung (Sulawesi-Indonesia)	0606-10=	2	
	1963	1228	?	Shishaldin (Aleutian Is)	1101-36-	2	
	1963	1231	807a	Paluweh (Lesser Sunda Is)	0604-15=	2	7/-
	1964	Cont	....	Stromboli (Italy)	0101-04=	1	7/-
	1964	Cont	....	Lengai, Ol Doinyo (Africa-E)	0202-12=	1	
	1964	Cont	....	Nyiragongo (Africa-C)	0203-03=	0	
S	1964	Cont	....	Rumble III (New Zealand)	0401-13-	0	
	1964	Cont	....	Yasur (Vanuatu-SW Pacific)	0507-10=	2	
S	1964	Cont	....	Unnamed (SW Pacific)	0508-03-	0	
	1964	Cont	....	Semeru (Java)	0603-30=	1	
	1964	Cont	....	Batur (Lesser Sunda Is)	0604-01=	2	7/5
	1964	Cont	....	Agung (Lesser Sunda Is)	0604-02=	2	8/9
	1964	Cont	....	Lokon-Empung (Sulawesi-Indonesia)	0606-10=	2	
	1964	Cont	....	Dukono (Halmahera-Indonesia)	0608-01=	2	
	1964	Cont	....	Suwanose-jima (Ryukyu Is)	0802-03=	2	
	1964	Cont	....	Sakura-jima (Kyushu-Japan)	0802-08=	2	
	1964	Cont	....	Oshima (Izu Is-Japan)	0804-01=	1	
	1964	Cont	....	Ebeko (Kuril Is)	0900-38=	1	-/3
	1964	Cont	....	Karymsky (Kamchatka)	1000-13=	2	6/7
	1964	Cont	....	Kliuchevskoi (Kamchatka)	1000-26=	1	
	1964	Cont	....	Colima (México)	1401-04=	1	
	1964	Cont	....	Santa María (Guatemala)	1402-03=	1	9/8
	1964	Cont	....	Sangay (Ecuador)	1502-09=	2	
	1964	Cont	....	Vestmannaeyjar [Surtsey]	1702-01=	2	8/8
	1964 ?	....	>3yr	Unnamed (Pacific-E)	1304-10-	0	10/-
?	1964	....	?	Negro, Cerro (Nicaragua)	1404-07=	2?	
	1964	....	?	Llaima (Chile-C)	1507-11=	2	
	1964	01	....	Manam (New Guinea-NE of)	0501-02=	2	6/-
	1964	0102	....	Kavachi (Solomon Is-SW Pacific)	0505-06=	2	
	1964	0114	....	Irazú (Costa Rica)	1405-06=	3	
	1964	0129	670p?	Sangeang Api (Lesser Sunda Is)	0604-05=	2	6/-
	1964	02 ?	943p>	Ambrym (Vanuatu-SW Pacific)	0507-04=	2	
	1964	02	....	Paluweh (Lesser Sunda Is)	0604-15=	2	7/-
	1964	0201	....	Etna (Italy)	0101-06=	2	7/-
	1964	0201	12k	Chikurachki (Kuril Is)	0900-36=	2	
	1964	0208	240a>	Sirung (Lesser Sunda Is)	0604-27=	1	
	1964	0214	<1	Dempo (Sumatra)	0601-23=	2	
?	1964	0218	?	San Jorge (Azores)	1802-03=	0	
	1964	03	16m	Nila (Banda Sea)	0605-06=	1?	
	1964	03	39m>	Tolbachik (Kamchatka)	1000-24=	2	
	1964	0302	50a	Villarrica (Chile-C)	1507-12=	2	
	1964	0310	37a	Westdahl (Aleutian Is)	1101-34-	2	
	1964	0318	?	Kiska (Aleutian Is)	1101-02-	0	
	1964	0408	....	Lopevi (Vanuatu-SW Pacific)	0507-05=	3	
?	1964	0414	?	Esmeralda Bank (Mariana Is-C Pacific)	0804-21=	2	
	1964	0414	....	Irazú (Costa Rica)	1405-06=	3	
	1964	0424	434w	Bagana (Bougainville-SW Pacific)	0505-02=	2	
	1964	0430	8a	Fournaise, Piton de la (Indian O.)	0303-02=	2	
	1964	0514	<1	Aso (Kyushu-Japan)	0802-11=	1	
	1964	0531	?	Trident (Alaska Peninsula)	1102-16-	3?	
	1964	0618	16a?	Akan (Hokkaido-Japan)	0805-07=	1	
	1964	0625	87a	Bezymianny (Kamchatka)	1000-25=	2	6/-
	1964	0706	....	Irazú (Costa Rica)	1405-06=	3	
	1964	0708	<1 ?	Kerinci (Sumatra)	0601-17=	2	
	1964	0803	47a>	Tupungatito (Chile-C)	1507-01=	2	
	1964	0819	....	Augustine (Alaska-SW)	1103-01-	1	7/6
	1964	0917	....	Láscar (Chile-N)	1505-10=	2	
	1964	10	792m	Aso (Kyushu-Japan)	0802-11=	2	
	1964	1023	24m	San Miguel (El Salvador)	1403-10=	2	
	1964	1112	<1	Shiveluch (Kamchatka)	1000-27=	4+	-/8
	1964	1119	157a?	Raoul Island (Kermadec Is)	0402-03=	0	
	1964	1121	....	Raoul Island (Kermadec Is)	0402-03=	2	
	1964	1204d	658g	Langila (New Britain-SW Pac)	0502-01=	2	
	1964	1213	<1	Dieng Volc Complex (Java)	0603-20=	1	
	1964	1221	56a	Fournaise, Piton de la (Indian O.)	0303-02=	2?	7/-
	1964	1225	1a	Bezymianny (Kamchatka)	1000-25=	1	
	1964	1225	80m	Poás (Costa Rica)	1405-04=	2	

	START YEAR	M-Dy	Duration	VOLCANO NAME (Subregion)	NUMBER	VEI	Vol L/T
	1965	*Cont*	....	*Stromboli (Italy)*	0101-04=	*1*	*7/-*
	1965	*Cont*	....	*Lengai, Ol Doinyo (Africa-E)*	0202-12=	*1*	
	1965	*Cont*	....	*Nyiragongo (Africa-C)*	0203-03=	*0*	
	1965	*Cont*	....	*Fournaise, Piton de la (Indian O.)*	0303-02=	*2*	*7/-*
S	*1965*	*Cont*	....	*Rumble III (New Zealand)*	0401-13-	*0*	
	1965	*Cont*	....	*Raoul Island (Kermadec Is)*	0402-03=	*1*	
	1965	*Cont*	....	*Langila (New Britain-SW Pac)*	0502-01=	*2*	
	1965	*Cont*	....	*Bagana (Bougainville-SW Pacific)*	0505-02=	*2*	
	1965	*Cont*	....	*Ambrym (Vanuatu-SW Pacific)*	0507-04=	*2*	
	1965	*Cont*	....	*Lopevi (Vanuatu-SW Pacific)*	0507-05=	*2*	
	1965	*Cont*	....	*Yasur (Vanuatu-SW Pacific)*	0507-10=	*2*	
	1965	*Cont*	....	*Sangeang Api (Lesser Sunda Is)*	0604-05=	*2*	*6/-*
	1965	*Cont*	....	*Dukono (Halmahera-Indonesia)*	0608-01=	*2*	
	1965	*Cont*	....	*Suwanose-jima (Ryukyu Is)*	0802-03=	*2*	
	1965	*Cont*	....	*Sakura-jima (Kyushu-Japan)*	0802-08=	*2*	
	1965	*Cont*	....	*Colima (México)*	1401-04=	*1*	
	1965	*Cont*	....	*Santa María (Guatemala)*	1402-03=	*1*	***9/8***
	1965	*Cont*	....	*Poás (Costa Rica)*	1405-04=	*2*	
	1965	*Cont*	....	*Sangay (Ecuador)*	1502-09=	*2*	
	1965	*Cont*	....	*Láscar (Chile-N)*	1505-10=	*2*	
	1965	*Cont*	....	*Vestmannaeyjar [Surtsey]*	1702-01=	*2*	*8/8*
	1965	....	208*w*>	**Manam** (New Guinea-NE of)	0501-02=	2	6/-
	1965 ?	....	?	**Krakatau** (Indonesia)	0602-00=	1?	
	1965	....	?	**Tolbachik** (Kamchatka)	1000-24=	1	
M	**1965** ?	....	?	**Southern EPR-Segment K** (Pacific)	1304-12-	0	
?	*1965*	....	?	*Chillán, Nevados de (Chile-C)*	1507-07=		
	1965	0116	12*a*	**Telica** (Nicaragua)	1404-04=	1	
	1965	*0131*	....	*Irazú (Costa Rica)*	1405-06=	*3*	
	1965	02	30*m*	**Tangkubanparahu** (Java)	0603-09=	1	
	1965	*0211*	....	*Paluweh (Lesser Sunda Is)*	0604-15=	*2*	*7/-*
	1965	0305	10	**Kilauea** (Hawaiian Is)	1302-01-	0	7/-
	1965	0309	>3yr	**Bezymianny** (Kamchatka)	1000-25=	3	7/7
	1965	0405d	801*n*	**Karangetang [Api Siau]** (Sangihe Is	0607-02=	2	
	1965	0507	11*a*	**Sirung** (Lesser Sunda Is)	0604-27=	1	
	1965	0515e	<1	**Akan** (Hokkaido-Japan)	0805-07=	1	
	1965	0515e	639*n*	**Karymsky** (Kamchatka)	1000-13=	3	
	1965	0523	<1	**Asama** (Honshu-Japan)	0803-11=	2	
	1965	*0704*	*>3yr*	*Pacaya (Guatemala)*	1402-11=	*2*	
	1965	0710	<1	**Lokon-Empung** (Sulawesi-Indonesia)	0606-10=	1	
	1965	0712	<1	**Karthala** (Indian O.-W)	0303-01=	2?	5/-
	1965	08 ?	16*m*?	**Ebeko** (Kuril Is)	0900-38=	1	
	1965	*08*	*498m*	*Kliuchevskoi (Kamchatka)*	1000-26=	*2*	*8/7*
	1965	0809	327*w*	**Suretamatai** (Vanuatu-SW Pacific)	0507-01=	2	
	1965	0818	119*m*	**Batur** (Lesser Sunda Is)	0604-01=	1	
	1965	09	?	**Rinjani** (Lesser Sunda Is)	0604-03=	0	
	1965	0927	3*a*>	**Gaua** (Vanuatu-SW Pacific)	0507-02=	3	
	1965	0928	2	**Taal** (Luzon-Philippines)	0703-07=	4	-/7
	1965	10	16*m*	**Tangkubanparahu** (Java)	0603-09=	1	
	1965	*1010?*	*>3yr*	*Masaya (Nicaragua)*	1404-10=	*0*	
	1965	1019	....	**Pacaya** (Guatemala)	1402-11=	3	
	1965	*1021*	....	*Aso (Kyushu-Japan)*	0802-11=	*2*	
S	**1965**	1024	<1	**Kick 'em Jenny** (W Indies)	1600-16=	0	
	1965	1102	<1	**Sirung** (Lesser Sunda Is)	0604-27=	1	
S	**1965**	1113	22*d*	**Tori-shima** (Izu Is-Japan)	0804-09=	0	
	1965	1123	200*a*	**Tinakula** (Santa Cruz Is-SW Pacific)	0506-01=	3	
	1965	1125	201*a*	**Oshima** (Izu Is-Japan)	0804-01=	1	
	1965	1209	<1	**Sarychev Peak** (Kuril Is)	0900-24=	2	
	1965	*1209*	....	*Pacaya (Guatemala)*	1402-11=	*3*	
	1965	1211	2*a*	**Kavachi** (Solomon Is-SW Pacific)	0505-06=	2	
	1965	1224	<1	**Kilauea** (Hawaiian Is)	1302-01-	0	5/-
	1966	*Cont*	....	*Stromboli (Italy)*	0101-04=	*1*	*7/-*
	1966	*Cont*	....	*Nyiragongo (Africa-C)*	0203-03=	*0*	
S	*1966*	*Cont*	....	*Rumble III (New Zealand)*	0401-13-	*0*	
	1966	*Cont*	....	*Manam (New Guinea-NE of)*	0501-02=	*2*	*6/-*
	1966	*Cont*	....	*Langila (New Britain-SW Pac)*	0502-01=	*2*	
	1966	*Cont*	....	*Suretamatai (Vanuatu-SW Pacific)*	0507-01=	*2*	
	1966	*Cont*	....	*Ambrym (Vanuatu-SW Pacific)*	0507-04=	*2*	
	1966	*Cont*	....	*Yasur (Vanuatu-SW Pacific)*	0507-10=	*2*	
	1966	*Cont*	....	*Karangetang [Api Siau] (Sangihe Is*	0607-02=	*2*	
	1966	*Cont*	....	*Dukono (Halmahera-Indonesia)*	0608-01=	*2*	
	1966	*Cont*	....	*Suwanose-jima (Ryukyu Is)*	0802-03=	*2*	
	1966	*Cont*	....	*Sakura-jima (Kyushu-Japan)*	0802-08=	*2*	
	1966	*Cont*	....	*Aso (Kyushu-Japan)*	0802-11=	*2*	
	1966	*Cont*	....	*Oshima (Izu Is-Japan)*	0804-01=	*1*	
	1966	*Cont*	....	*Karymsky (Kamchatka)*	1000-13=	*1*	
	1966	*Cont*	....	*Bezymianny (Kamchatka)*	1000-25=	*1*	*7/7*
	1966	*Cont*	....	*Unnamed (Pacific-E)*	1304-10-	*0*	
	1966	*Cont*	....	*Colima (México)*	1401-04=	*1*	
	1966	*Cont*	....	*Santa María (Guatemala)*	1402-03=	*1*	***9/8***
	1966	*Cont*	....	*Pacaya (Guatemala)*	1402-11=	*1*	
	1966	*Cont*	....	*Masaya (Nicaragua)*	1404-10=	*0*	
	1966	*Cont*	....	*Sangay (Ecuador)*	1502-09=	*2*	
	1966	*Cont*	....	*Láscar (Chile-N)*	1505-10=	*2*	
	1966	*Cont*	....	*Vestmannaeyjar [Surtsey]*	1702-01=	*2*	*8/8*
	1966	....	?	**Gaua** (Vanuatu-SW Pacific)	0507-02=	2	
	1966	....	?	**Slamet** (Java)	0603-18=	2	
	1966 ?	....	?	**Trident** (Alaska Peninsula)	1102-16-		
?	*1966*	....	?	*Reykjanes (Iceland-SW)*	1701-02=	*0*	
	1966	0110	>3yr	**Etna** (Italy)	0101-06=	2	7/-
	1966	*0113*	....	*Tinakula (Santa Cruz Is-SW Pacific)*	0506-01=	*2*	
	1966	0124	27*a*	**Redoubt** (Alaska-SW)	1103-03-	3	
	1966	02	....	**Kliuchevskoi** (Kamchatka)	1000-26=	3	8/7
	1966	*0204*	....	*Redoubt (Alaska-SW)*	1103-03-	*3*	
	1966	*0207*	*72a*	*Fuego (Guatemala)*	1402-09=	*2*	
	1966	*0211*	....	*Redoubt (Alaska-SW)*	1103-03-	*3*	
	1966	0222	?	**San Miguel** (El Salvador)	1403-10=	2	
	1966	0228	260*m*	**Sangeang Api** (Lesser Sunda Is)	0604-05=	2	
	1966	03	92*p*	**Marapi** (Sumatra)	0601-14=	1	
S	**1966**	0309	11*a*?	**Rocard** (Society Is-C Pacific)	1303-02-	0	
	1966	*0310*	....	*Paluweh (Lesser Sunda Is)*	0604-15=	*2*	*7/-*
	1966	0315	61*a*	**Fournaise, Piton de la** (Indian O.)	0303-02=	2?	7/-
	1966	0315	?	**Pavlof** (Alaska Peninsula)	1102-03-	2	
	1966	0319	3*a*>	**Kavachi** (Solomon Is-SW Pacific)	0505-06=	2	
	1966	*0320*	*619a*	*Bagana (Bougainville-SW Pacific)*	0505-02=	*1*	
	1966	0328	133*a*	**Rinjani** (Lesser Sunda Is)	0604-03=	1	6/4
	1966	0404	176*a*	**Ruapehu** (New Zealand)	0401-10=	1	
	1966	0415q	?	**Tolbachik** (Kamchatka)	1000-24=	2	
	1966	0420	....	**Fuego** (Guatemala)	1402-09=	3	
S	**1966**	0421g	23*n*	**Ruby** (Mariana Is-C Pacific)	0804-202	0	
	1966	0426	<1	**Kelut** (Java)	0603-28=	4	-/7
	1966	0428	?	**Batur** (Lesser Sunda Is)	0604-01=	1	
?	*1966*	*05*	*92p*	*Azuma (Honshu-Japan)*	0803-18=	*1*	
S	**1966**	0505	93*a*	**Kick 'em Jenny** (W Indies)	1600-16=	0	
	1966	0521	543*m*	**Soputan** (Sulawesi-Indonesia)	0606-03=	3	7/-
	1966	0530	....	**Bagana** (Bougainville-SW Pacific)	0505-02=	3	
	1966	06	15*m*	**Telica** (Nicaragua)	1404-04=	1	
	1966	0609	21*a*>	**Kerinci** (Sumatra)	0601-17=	2	
	1966	0615e	<1	**Akan** (Hokkaido-Japan)	0805-07=	1	
	1966	07	?	**San Miguel** (El Salvador)	1403-10=	2	
	1966	*0705*	*30*	*Taal (Luzon-Philippines)*	0703-07=	*2*	
?	*1966*	*08*	?	*Matthew Island (SW Pacific)*	0508-01=		
	1966	0804	....	**Taal** (Luzon-Philippines)	0703-07=	3	
	1966	0812	64*m*	**Awu** (Sangihe Is-Indonesia)	0607-04=	4	
	1966	0812	1*a*	**Fuego** (Guatemala)	1402-09=	3	-/6
	1966	0822	....	**Lengai, Ol Doinyo** (Africa-E)	0202-12=	3	
	1966	0924	6*a*?	**Lokon-Empung** (Sulawesi-Indonesia)	0606-10=	2	
	1966	*1006*	....	*Kliuchevskoi (Kamchatka)*	1000-26=	*2*	*8/7*
	1966	1007	100*a*	**Redoubt** (Alaska-SW)	1103-03-	3	
	1966	1028	18*m*	**Izalco** (El Salvador)	1403-03=	0	5/-
	1966	*1106?*	*405m?*	*Rincón de la Vieja (Costa Rica)*	1405-02=	*2*	
	1966	1113	122*m*	**White Island** (New Zealand)	0401-04=	3	
	1966	1122	<1	**Kuchinoerabu-jima** (Ryukyu Is)	0802-05=	2	
	1967	*Cont*	....	*Stromboli (Italy)*	0101-04=	*1*	*7/-*
	1967	*Cont*	....	*Etna (Italy)*	0101-06=	*2*	*7/-*
	1967	*Cont*	....	*Nyiragongo (Africa-C)*	0203-03=	*0*	
	1967	*Cont*	....	*White Island (New Zealand)*	0401-04=	*2*	
	1967	*Cont*	....	*Bagana (Bougainville-SW Pacific)*	0505-02=	*2*	
	1967	*Cont*	....	*Yasur (Vanuatu-SW Pacific)*	0507-10=	*2*	
	1967	*Cont*	....	*Dukono (Halmahera-Indonesia)*	0608-01=	*2*	
	1967	*Cont*	....	*Suwanose-jima (Ryukyu Is)*	0802-03=	*2*	
	1967	*Cont*	....	*Sakura-jima (Kyushu-Japan)*	0802-08=	*2*	
	1967	*Cont*	....	*Bezymianny (Kamchatka)*	1000-25=	*1*	*7/7*
	1967	*Cont*	....	*Unnamed (Pacific-E)*	1304-10-	*0*	
	1967	*Cont*	....	*Colima (México)*	1401-04=	*1*	
	1967	*Cont*	....	*Santa María (Guatemala)*	1402-03=	*1*	***9/8***
	1967	*Cont*	....	*Pacaya (Guatemala)*	1402-11=	*1*	
	1967	*Cont*	....	*Masaya (Nicaragua)*	1404-10=	*0*	
	1967	*Cont*	....	*Sangay (Ecuador)*	1502-09=	*2*	
	1967	*Cont*	....	*Láscar (Chile-N)*	1505-10=	*2*	
	1967	*Cont*	....	*Vestmannaeyjar [Surtsey]*	1702-01=	*2*	*8/8*
	1967 <	....	>3yr	**Erta Ale** (Ethiopia)	0201-08=	0	
	1967 p	....	?	**Tambora** (Lesser Sunda Is)	0604-04=	0	
	1967	....	?	**Kliuchevskoi** (Kamchatka)	1000-26=	1	
	1967	01	90*p*?	**Ebeko** (Kuril Is)	0900-38=	1	-/4
	1967	*0101*	....	*Redoubt (Alaska-SW)*	1103-03-	*2*	
	1967	0101	....	**Rincón de la Vieja** (Costa Rica)	1405-02=	3	
	1967	0101	?	**Poás** (Costa Rica)	1405-04=	1	
	1967	0105	?	**San Miguel** (El Salvador)	1403-10=	2	
	1967	0112	>3yr	**Merapi** (Java)	0603-25=	2	7/7
	1967	0119	512*m*	**Langila** (New Britain-SW Pac)	0502-01=	2	4/-
	1967	0122	340*a*	**Ulawun** (New Britain-SW Pac)	0502-12=	2	
	1967	*0127*	*794a*	*Lopevi (Vanuatu-SW Pacific)*	0507-05=	*2*	
	1967	0128	?	**Shishaldin** (Aleutian Is)	1101-36-	2	
?	*1967*	*02*	?	*Planchón-Peteroa (Chile-C)*	1507-04=	*1?*	
	1967	0218	<1	**Kelut** (Java)	0603-28=	1	
	1967	03	61*p*	**Tolbachik** (Kamchatka)	1000-24=	2	
	1967	0301	....	**Lopevi** (Vanuatu-SW Pacific)	0507-05=	3	
	1967	*0311*	....	*Soputan (Sulawesi-Indonesia)*	0606-03=	*3*	*7/-*
S	**1967**	0327	13	**Farallon de Pajaros** (Mariana Is-Pac)	0804-14=	0	
	1967	04	92*p*	**Marapi** (Sumatra)	0601-14=	1	
	1967	0422	2*a*	**Fuego** (Guatemala)	1402-09=	2	-/6
	1967	0423	16*a*	**Nyamuragira** (Africa-C)	0203-02=	2	7/7
?	*1967*	*0426*	?	*Unnamed (Kuril Is)*	0900-061		
	1967	05	944*p*	**Aso** (Kyushu-Japan)	0802-11=	1	

	START YEAR	M-Dy	Dura-tion	VOLCANO NAME (Subregion)	NUMBER	VEI	Vol L/T
	1967	05	92p	**Oshima** (Izu Is-Japan)	0804-01=	1	
	1967	0507	70m	**Slamet** (Java)	0603-18=	2	
S	1967	0529	<1	**Macdonald** (Austral Is-C Pacific)	1303-06-	0	
	1967	*0610*	....	*Rincón de la Vieja (Costa Rica)*	1405-02=	*3*	
	1967	07	?	**Gaua** (Vanuatu-SW Pacific)	0507-02=	2	
	1967	07	>3yr	**Ambrym** (Vanuatu-SW Pacific)	0507-04=	2	
	1967	07	16m	**Tangkubanparahu** (Java)	0603-09=	1	
?	*1967*	*0701*	<1	*Fukutoku-Okanoba (Volcano Is-Japan.*	0804-13=	*0*	
	1967	0708	58a	**Lengai, Ol Doinyo** (Africa-E)	0202-12=	3	
	1967	0722	74a?	**Ruapehu** (New Zealand)	0401-10=	1	
	1967	0809	?	**Azul, Cerro** (Chile-C)	1507-06=	2?	
	1967	0816	2	**Taal** (Luzon-Philippines)	0703-07=	1	
	1967	*0831*	>3yr	*Semeru (Java)*	0603-30=	*2*	
	1967	*0905*	172a	*Trident (Alaska Peninsula)*	1102-16-	*2*	
	1967	0906	14a	**Chikurachki** (Kuril Is)	0900-36=	2	
	1967	10	30p	**Tolbachik** (Kamchatka)	1000-24=	2	
	1967	1010	<1	**Talang** (Sumatra)	0601-16=	1	
	1967	11	15m	**Karymsky** (Kamchatka)	1000-13=	1	
	1967	1102	?	**Kerinci** (Sumatra)	0601-17=	2	
	1967	1105	250a	**Kilauea** (Hawaiian Is)	1302-01-	0	7/-
	1967	1125e	?	**Iwo-Tori-shima** (Ryukyu Is)	0802-02=	1	
	1967	1129	3a	**Karangetang [Api Siau]** (Sangihe Is	0607-02=	2	
	1967	1204	3a	**Deception Island** (Antarctica)	1900-03=	3	-/7
	1967	*1206*	144a>	*Redoubt (Alaska-SW)*	1103-03-	*2*	
	1967	1211<	24d>	**Metis Shoal** (Tonga-SW Pacific)	0403-07=	2	
	1967	1211	<1	**Kelut** (Java)	0603-28=	1	
	1967	1218	....	**Trident** (Alaska Peninsula)	1102-16-	3	
	1967	1223	<1	**Ioto [Iwo-jima]** (Volcano Is-Japan)	0804-12=	1	-/5
	1968	*Cont*	....	*Stromboli (Italy)*	0101-04=	*1*	*7/-*
	1968	*Cont*	....	*Erta Ale (Ethiopia)*	0201-08=	*0*	
	1968	*Cont*	....	*Nyiragongo (Africa-C)*	0203-03=	*0*	
	1968	*Cont*	....	*Metis Shoal (Tonga-SW Pacific)*	0403-07=	*2*	
	1968	*Cont*	....	*Langila (New Britain-SW Pac)*	0502-01=	*2*	*4/-*
	1968	*Cont*	....	*Ambrym (Vanuatu-SW Pacific)*	0507-04=	*2*	
	1968	*Cont*	....	*Lopevi (Vanuatu-SW Pacific)*	0507-05=	*2*	
	1968	*Cont*	....	*Yasur (Vanuatu-SW Pacific)*	0507-10=	*2*	
	1968	*Cont*	....	*Dukono (Halmahera-Indonesia)*	0608-01=	*2*	
	1968	*Cont*	....	*Suwanose-jima (Ryukyu Is)*	0802-03=	*2*	
	1968	*Cont*	....	*Sakura-jima (Kyushu-Japan)*	0802-08=	*2*	
	1968	*Cont*	....	*Aso (Kyushu-Japan)*	0802-11=	*1*	
	1968	*Cont*	....	*Bezymianny (Kamchatka)*	1000-25=	*1*	*7/7*
	1968	*Cont*	....	*Unnamed (Pacific-E)*	1304-10-	*0*	
	1968	*Cont*	....	*Colima (México)*	1401-04=	*1*	
	1968	*Cont*	....	*Santa María (Guatemala)*	1402-03=	*1*	**9**/8
	1968	*Cont*	....	*Masaya (Nicaragua)*	1404-10=	*0*	
	1968	*Cont*	....	*Sangay (Ecuador)*	1502-09=	*2*	
	1968	....	152u	**Gaua** (Vanuatu-SW Pacific)	0507-02=	2	
	1968	....	365y	**Tolbachik** (Kamchatka)	1000-24=	1	
	1968	....	?	**Poás** (Costa Rica)	1405-04=	1	
	1968	....	?	**Tupungatito** (Chile-C)	1507-01=	2	
	1968	*01*	....	*Semeru (Java)*	0603-30=	*2*	
	1968	*0103*	....	*Pacaya (Guatemala)*	1402-11=	*2*	
	1968	0107	118a	**Etna** (Italy)	0101-06=	0	6/-
	1968	0114	<1 ?	**Talang** (Sumatra)	0601-16=	1	
	1968	0119	<1	**Oshima** (Izu Is-Japan)	0804-01=	1	
	1968	0123	23	**Batur** (Lesser Sunda Is)	0604-01=	2	6/-
	1968	*0127*	382m	*White Island (New Zealand)*	0401-04=	*2*	
	1968	0131	61a	**Taal** (Luzon-Philippines)	0703-07=	2	
	1968	*0131*	....	*Láscar (Chile-N)*	1505-10=	*2*	
	1968	02	14m	**Grozny Group** (Kuril Is)	0900-07=	1	
	1968	0203	44a	**Kerinci** (Sumatra)	0601-17=	2	
?	*1968*	*0209*	<1	*Fukutoku-Okanoba (Volcano Is-Japan.*	0804-13=	*0*	
	1968	0214	....	**Redoubt** (Alaska-SW)	1103-03-	3	
	1968	0225d	....	**White Island** (New Zealand)	0401-04=	3	
	1968	0316	88a	**Long Island** (New Guinea-NE of)	0501-05=	2	
	1968	*0406*	65a	*Ruapehu (New Zealand)*	0401-10=	*1*	
	1968	0421	29a	**Mayon** (Luzon-Philippines)	0703-03=	3	7/7
	1968	0426	....	**Ruapehu** (New Zealand)	0401-10=	2	
	1968	0507	39m	**Nila** (Banda Sea)	0605-06=	1	
	1968	0521	2a?	**Fernandina** (Galápagos)	1503-01=	2	
	1968	0523	23m	**Kverkfjöll** (Iceland-NE)	1703-05=		
	1968	0603	55	**Kelimutu** (Lesser Sunda Is)	0604-14=	1	
	1968	0611	23a<	**Fernandina** (Galápagos)	1503-01=	4	-/8
?	*1968*	*0612*	?	*Azul, Cerro (Galápagos)*	1503-06=		
	1968	07	31p	**Soputan** (Sulawesi-Indonesia)	0606-03=	1	
	1968	0703	<1	**Kliuchevskoi** (Kamchatka)	1000-26=	3	
	1968	0718	<1	**Iwo-Tori-shima** (Ryukyu Is)	0802-02=	1	
	1968	0728	<1	**Oshima** (Izu Is-Japan)	0804-01=	1	
	1968	0729	>3yr	**Arenal** (Costa Rica)	1405-033	3	8/7
	1968	08	16m	**Bagana** (Bougainville-SW Pacific)	0505-02=	2	
?	*1968*	*08*	31p	*Awu (Sangihe Is-Indonesia)*	0607-04=	*2*	
?	*1968*	*08*	16m	*Kita-Iwo-jima (Volcano Is-Japan)*	0804-11=	*0*	
?	*1968*	*0814*	6a	*Fukutoku-Okanoba (Volcano Is-Japan.*	0804-13=	*0*	
	1968	0818	?	**Tongariro [Ngauruhoe]** (New Zeal)	0401-08=	2	
	1968	0822	4a	**Kilauea** (Hawaiian Is)	1302-01-	0	4/-
	1968	09	31p	**Talang** (Sumatra)	0601-16=	2	
	1968	09	?	**Fukujin** (Volcano Is-Japan)	0804-133	0	
?	*1968*	*0905*	4d	*Banua Wuhu (Sangihe Is-Indonesia)*	0607-03=	*0*	
	1968	1007	15a	**Kilauea** (Hawaiian Is)	1302-01-	0	6/-
	1968	*1008*	....	*Merapi (Java)*	0603-25=	*2*	*7/7*
	1968	1023	56a	**Negro, Cerro** (Nicaragua)	1404-07=	3	6/7
	1968	1113	<1	**Trident** (Alaska Peninsula)	1102-16-	3	
	1968	1128	65	**Lewotobi** (Lesser Sunda Is)	0604-18=	2	
?	*1968*	*12*	16m	*Marapi (Sumatra)*	0601-14=	*1*	
	1968	*1221*	79a	*Kuchinoerabu-jima (Ryukyu Is)*	0802-05=	*2*	
	1968	1229	....	**Kuchinoerabu-jima** (Ryukyu Is)	0802-05=	3	
	1969	*Cont*	....	*Stromboli (Italy)*	0101-04=	*1*	*7/-*
	1969	*Cont*	....	*Etna (Italy)*	0101-06=	*2*	*7/-*
	1969	*Cont*	....	*Erta Ale (Ethiopia)*	0201-08=	*0*	
	1969	*Cont*	....	*Nyiragongo (Africa-C)*	0203-03=	*0*	
	1969	*Cont*	....	*Ambrym (Vanuatu-SW Pacific)*	0507-04=	*2*	
	1969	*Cont*	....	*Lopevi (Vanuatu-SW Pacific)*	0507-05=	*2*	
	1969	*Cont*	....	*Yasur (Vanuatu-SW Pacific)*	0507-10=	*2*	
	1969	*Cont*	....	*Semeru (Java)*	0603-30=	*2*	
	1969	*Cont*	....	*Lewotobi (Lesser Sunda Is)*	0604-18=	*2*	
	1969	*Cont*	....	*Dukono (Halmahera-Indonesia)*	0608-01=	*2*	
	1969	*Cont*	....	*Suwanose-jima (Ryukyu Is)*	0802-03=	*2*	
	1969	*Cont*	....	*Sakura-jima (Kyushu-Japan)*	0802-08=	*2*	
	1969	*Cont*	....	*Aso (Kyushu-Japan)*	0802-11=	*1*	
	1969	*Cont*	....	*Tolbachik (Kamchatka)*	1000-24=	*1*	
	1969	*Cont*	....	*Unnamed (Pacific-E)*	1304-10-	*0*	
	1969	*Cont*	....	*Colima (México)*	1401-04=	*1*	
	1969	*Cont*	....	*Santa María (Guatemala)*	1402-03=	*1*	**9**/8
	1969	*Cont*	....	*Masaya (Nicaragua)*	1404-10=	*0*	
	1969	*Cont*	....	*Sangay (Ecuador)*	1502-09=	*2*	
	1969	....	365y	**Kerinci** (Sumatra)	0601-17=	2	
?	*1969*	....	?	*Krakatau (Indonesia)*	0602-00=	*2?*	
	1969	*0107*	....	*Merapi (Java)*	0603-25=	*2*	*7/7*
	1969	0112?	9a?	**Ioto [Iwo-jima]** (Volcano Is-Japan)	0804-12=	1	
	1969	0119	177m	**Oshima** (Izu Is-Japan)	0804-01=	1	
	1969	0121	?	**Tongariro [Ngauruhoe]** (New Zeal)	0401-08=	2	
	1969	0127	3a	**Iya** (Lesser Sunda Is)	0604-11=	3	
	1969	02	14m?	**Ebeko** (Kuril Is)	0900-38=	1	
	1969	*0205*	....	*Kuchinoerabu-jima (Ryukyu Is)*	0802-05=	*2*	
	1969	0211	>3yr	**Telica** (Nicaragua)	1404-04=	2	
	1969	0221	23m	**Deception Island** (Antarctica)	1900-03=	3	-/7
	1969	0222	6a	**Kilauea** (Hawaiian Is)	1302-01-	0	7/-
	1969	0227	?	**Ebulobo** (Lesser Sunda Is)	0604-10=	2?	
S	1969	0311	1	**Supply Reef** (Mariana Is-C Pacific)	0804-142	0	
	1969	0321	86m	**Didicas** (Luzon-N of)	0704-02=	2	
S	1969	0422	7a?	**Moua Pihaa** (Society Is-C Pacific)	1303-03-	0	
	1969	0422	23m	**Rincón de la Vieja** (Costa Rica)	1405-02=	2	
	1969	*0503*	....	*Arenal (Costa Rica)*	1405-033	*3*	*8/7*
	1969	0503	31	**Poás** (Costa Rica)	1405-04=	2	
	1969	0516	?	**Láscar** (Chile-N)	1505-10=		
	1969	0524	>3yr	**Kilauea** (Hawaiian Is)	1302-01-	0	8/-
	1969	06	?	**Ubinas** (Perú)	1504-02=	2?	
	1969	*0607*	....	*Pacaya (Guatemala)*	1402-11=	*2*	
	1969	0622	1a	**Ruapehu** (New Zealand)	0401-10=	2	
	1969	0623	53m	**Slamet** (Java)	0603-18=	2	
?	*1969*	*07 ?*	?	*Lengai, Ol Doinyo (Africa-E)*	0202-12=		
	1969	0720	93a	**Tangkubanparahu** (Java)	0603-09=	1	
	1969	08	30p	**White Island** (New Zealand)	0401-04=	2	
	1969	08	?	**Wrangell** (Alaska-E)	1105-02-	1	
	1969	09	91p	**Kliuchevskoi** (Kamchatka)	1000-26=	2	
	1969	0911	4a	**Kiska** (Aleutian Is)	1101-02-	2?	
	1969	0920	26a	**Rincón de la Vieja** (Costa Rica)	1405-02=	2	
	1969	0922	?	**Gaua** (Vanuatu-SW Pacific)	0507-02=	2	
	1969	0929	<1	**Langila** (New Britain-SW Pac)	0502-01=	2	
	1969	1010	18	**Kanlaon** (Philippines-C)	0702-02=	2	
	1969	*1011*	....	*Bezymianny (Kamchatka)*	1000-25=	*2*	*7/7*
	1969	1028	101a	**Kavachi** (Solomon Is-SW Pacific)	0505-06=	2	
	1969	1029	43a	**Taal** (Luzon-Philippines)	0703-07=	2	6/6
	1969	1127	394e	**Lokon-Empung** (Sulawesi-Indonesia)	0606-10=	2	
	1969	1201p	<1	**Ioto [Iwo-jima]** (Volcano Is-Japan)	0804-12=	1	
	1969	1219	10a	**Negro, Cerro** (Nicaragua)	1404-07=	1	
	1970	*Cont*	....	*Stromboli (Italy)*	0101-04=	*1*	*7/-*
	1970	*Cont*	....	*Etna (Italy)*	0101-06=	*2*	*7/-*
	1970	*Cont*	....	*Erta Ale (Ethiopia)*	0201-08=	*0*	
	1970	*Cont*	....	*Nyiragongo (Africa-C)*	0203-03=	*0*	
	1970	*Cont*	....	*Kavachi (Solomon Is-SW Pacific)*	0505-06=	*2*	
	1970	*Cont*	....	*Ambrym (Vanuatu-SW Pacific)*	0507-04=	*2*	
	1970	*Cont*	....	*Yasur (Vanuatu-SW Pacific)*	0507-10=	*2*	
	1970	*Cont*	....	*Kerinci (Sumatra)*	0601-17=	*2*	
	1970	*Cont*	....	*Merapi (Java)*	0603-25=	*2*	*7/7*
	1970	*Cont*	....	*Semeru (Java)*	0603-30=	*2*	
	1970	*Cont*	....	*Lokon-Empung (Sulawesi-Indonesia)*	0606-10=	*2*	
	1970	*Cont*	....	*Dukono (Halmahera-Indonesia)*	0608-01=	*2*	
	1970	*Cont*	....	*Suwanose-jima (Ryukyu Is)*	0802-03=	*2*	
	1970	*Cont*	....	*Sakura-jima (Kyushu-Japan)*	0802-08=	*2*	
	1970	*Cont*	....	*Kilauea (Hawaiian Is)*	1302-01-	*0*	*8/-*
	1970	*Cont*	....	*Colima (México)*	1401-04=	*1*	
	1970	*Cont*	....	*Telica (Nicaragua)*	1404-04=	*2*	

START YEAR	M-Dy	Duration	VOLCANO NAME (Subregion)	NUMBER	VEI	Vol L/T
1970	Cont	....	*Sangay (Ecuador)*	1502-09=	2	
S 1970	....	?	**Rumble III** (New Zealand)	0401-13-	0	
1970	....	?	**Sorikmarapi** (Sumatra)	0601-12=	2	
1970	....	?	**Lewotobi** (Lesser Sunda Is)	0604-18=	2	
1970	....	?	**Sirung** (Lesser Sunda Is)	0604-27=	2?	
? 1970 a	....	?	*Esmeralda Bank (Mariana Is-C Pacific)*	0804-21=	0	
1970	....	?	**Grozny Group** (Kuril Is)	0900-07=	1	
1970	....	....	*Santa María (Guatemala)*	1402-03=	2	**9**/8
1970	....	....	*Arenal (Costa Rica)*	1405-033	2	8/7
? 1970 ?	....	?	*Reykjanes (Iceland-SW)*	1701-02=	0	
1970	01	89p	**Tolbachik** (Kamchatka)	1000-24=	1	
? 1970	0103	?	*Falcon Island (Tonga-SW Pacific)*	0403-05=	0	
1970	0105d	10d	**Batur** (Lesser Sunda Is)	0604-01=	1	
1970	0115	27a	**Ulawun** (New Britain-SW Pac)	0502-12=	3	6/6
1970	0126	5a	**Oshima** (Izu Is-Japan)	0804-01=	1	
1970	0129	137m	**Bayonnaise Rocks** (Izu Is-Japan)	0804-07=	2	
1970	02	101n	**Soputan** (Sulawesi-Indonesia)	0606-03=	2	
1970	02	29p	**Kolokol Group** (Kuril Is)	0900-12=	3	
1970	02	....	*Bezymianny (Kamchatka)*	1000-25=	2	7/7
1970	0330	6a	**San Miguel** (El Salvador)	1403-10=	1	-/4
1970	0404	....	**Masaya** (Nicaragua)	1404-10=	1	
1970	0421	877m	**Aso** (Kyushu-Japan)	0802-11=	2	
1970	0505	61a	**Hekla** (Iceland-S)	1702-07=	3	8/7
1970	0509	821a	**Lopevi** (Vanuatu-SW Pacific)	0507-05=	2	
1970	0511	>3yr	**Karymsky** (Kamchatka)	1000-13=	3	7/7
1970	0520	125a	**Langila** (New Britain-SW Pac)	0502-01=	2	
1970	0521m	451p>	**Bagana** (Bougainville-SW Pacific)	0505-02=	2	
1970	0526	215a	**Kliuchevskoi** (Kamchatka)	1000-26=	2	
? 1970	0602	11a	*Unnamed (New Britain-SW Pac)*	0502-131	0	
1970	0605	79	**Kanlaon** (Philippines-C)	0702-02=	1?	
S 1970	0621	2a?	**Moua Pihaa** (Society Is-C Pacific)	1303-03-	0	
1970	0630p	?	**White Island** (New Zealand)	0401-04=	2	
1970	0630	132a	**Oshima** (Izu Is-Japan)	0804-01=	1	
1970	07	?	**Poás** (Costa Rica)	1405-04=	1	
1970	0726e	390e	**Marapi** (Sumatra)	0601-14=	2	
1970	0812	?	**Deception Island** (Antarctica)	1900-03=	3	
1970	0814	1a	**Rincón de la Vieja** (Costa Rica)	1405-02=	1	
1970	09	92p	*Tolbachik (Kamchatka)*	1000-24=	1	
? 1970	0912	8a	*Kuwae [Karua] (Vanuatu-SW Pac)*	0507-07=	0	
1970	0916	1a	**Ruapehu** (New Zealand)	0401-10=	1	
1970	0918	130a	**Akita-Komaga-take** (Honshu-Japan)	0803-23=	2	7/6
1970	0918	652w?	**Jan Mayen** (Atlantic-N-Jan Mayen)	1706-01=	3	8/7
1970	1109	4a	**Taal** (Luzon-Philippines)	0703-07=	1	
1970	1127	78m	**Karangetang [Api Siau]** (Sangihe Is	0607-02=	2	
1970	1201p	....	**Tolbachik** (Kamchatka)	1000-24=	2	
1970	1212	....	*Pacaya (Guatemala)*	1402-11=	2	
1971	Cont	....	*Stromboli (Italy)*	0101-04=	1	7/-
1971	Cont	....	*Erta Ale (Ethiopia)*	0201-08=	0	
1971	Cont	....	*Nyiragongo (Africa-C)*	0203-03=	0	
1971	Cont	....	*Bagana (Bougainville-SW Pacific)*	0505-02=	2	
1971	Cont	....	*Yasur (Vanuatu-SW Pacific)*	0507-10=	2	
1971	Cont	....	*Marapi (Sumatra)*	0601-14=	2	
1971	Cont	....	*Semeru (Java)*	0603-30=	2	
1971	Cont	....	*Karangetang [Api Siau] (Sangihe Is*	0607-02=	2	
1971	Cont	....	*Dukono (Halmahera-Indonesia)*	0608-01=	2	
1971	Cont	....	*Suwanose-jima (Ryukyu Is)*	0802-03=	2	
1971	Cont	....	*Sakura-jima (Kyushu-Japan)*	0802-08=	2	
1971	Cont	....	*Aso (Kyushu-Japan)*	0802-11=	2	
1971	Cont	....	*Akita-Komaga-take (Honshu-Japan)*	0803-23=	2	7/6
1971	Cont	....	*Karymsky (Kamchatka)*	1000-13=	2	7/7
1971	Cont	....	*Santa María (Guatemala)*	1402-03=	1	**9**/8
1971	Cont	....	*Pacaya (Guatemala)*	1402-11=	1	
1971	Cont	....	*Telica (Nicaragua)*	1404-04=	2	
1971	Cont	....	*Masaya (Nicaragua)*	1404-10=	0	
1971	Cont	....	*Sangay (Ecuador)*	1502-09=	2	
1971	Cont	....	*Jan Mayen (Atlantic-N-Jan Mayen)*	1706-01=	1	8/7
? 1971	....	?	*Ebeko (Kuril Is)*	0900-38=	1	
? 1971	01	195m	*Merapi (Java)*	0603-25=	1?	
1971	01	?	**Lewotobi** (Lesser Sunda Is)	0604-18=	2	
1971	0126e	525j	**Langila** (New Britain-SW Pac)	0502-01=	2	
1971	0203	275a	**Ambrym** (Vanuatu-SW Pacific)	0507-04=	2	
1971	0203	11a	**Negro, Cerro** (Nicaragua)	1404-07=	3	-/7
1971	0222	<1	**Kuwae [Karua]** (Vanuatu-SW Pac)	0507-07=	2	
1971	03	....	*Lopevi (Vanuatu-SW Pacific)*	0507-05=	2	
1971	03	>3yr	*Bezymianny (Kamchatka)*	1000-25=	2?	
1971	0311	167a>	**Batur** (Lesser Sunda Is)	0604-01=	1	
? 1971	0318	?	*Bayonnaise Rocks (Izu Is-Japan)*	0804-07=	0	
1971	0324	42d	**Nyamuragira** (Africa-C)	0203-02=	3	7/7
1971	04	....	*Arenal (Costa Rica)*	1405-033	2	8/7
1971	0403	212a	*Ruapehu (New Zealand)*	0401-10=	1	-/6
1971	0405	68a	**Etna** (Italy)	0101-06=	2	7/6
1971	0405	<1	**Oshima** (Izu Is-Japan)	0804-01=	1	
1971	0409c	?	**White Island** (New Zealand)	0401-04=	2	
1971	0503	63e	**San Cristóbal** (Nicaragua)	1404-02=	1	
1971	0508	....	**Ruapehu** (New Zealand)	0401-10=	2	-/6
1971	0511	168e	**Lokon-Empung** (Sulawesi-Indonesia)	0606-10=	2	2/-
1971	0512	1a	**Gaua** (Vanuatu-SW Pacific)	0507-02=	2	
1971	0519	<1	**Soputan** (Sulawesi-Indonesia)	0606-03=	1	
? 1971	06	15m	*Kerinci (Sumatra)*	0601-17=	1?	
? 1971	06	15m	*Iya (Lesser Sunda Is)*	0604-11=	1	
1971	06	31p	**Kliuchevskoi** (Kamchatka)	1000-26=	1	
1971	07	<1	**Chiginagak** (Alaska Peninsula)	1102-11-	2?	
1971	0719	1a	**White Island** (New Zealand)	0401-04=	2	
1971	0805	<1	**Kirishima** (Kyushu-Japan)	0802-09=	1	
1971	0812	37a>	**Hudson, Cerro** (Chile-S)	1508-057	3	
1971	0814	<1	**Kilauea** (Hawaiian Is)	1302-01-	0	7/-
1971	0906	96a	**Tinakula** (Santa Cruz Is-SW Pacific)	0506-01=	2	
S 1971	0906	?	**Rocard** (Society Is-C Pacific)	1303-02-	0	
1971	0914	<1	**Raung** (Java)	0603-34=	1	
1971	0914	<1	**Fuego** (Guatemala)	1402-09=	3	-/7
? 1971	0917	363m	*Loihi (Hawaiian Is)*	1302-00-	0	
1971	0919	>3yr	**Etna** (Italy)	0101-06=	2	6/-
1971	0924	5a	**Kilauea** (Hawaiian Is)	1302-01-	0	6/-
1971	1004f	168f	**Soufrière St. Vincent** (W Indies)	1600-15=	0	7/-
1971	1007	<1	**Augustine** (Alaska-SW)	1103-01-	1	
1971	1026	22	**La Palma** (Canary Is)	1803-01-	2	7/-
? 1971	1028	18a?	*Epi (Vanuatu-SW Pacific)*	0507-06=	0	
1971	1029	11a	**Sundoro** (Java)	0603-21=	2	
1971	1029	115a	**Villarrica** (Chile-C)	1507-12=	2	7/-
1971	11	761p	**Kliuchevskoi** (Kamchatka)	1000-26=	1	
1971	1201p	101m	**Llaima** (Chile-C)	1507-11=	2	
1972	Cont	....	*Etna (Italy)*	0101-06=	2	6/-
1972	Cont	....	*Erta Ale (Ethiopia)*	0201-08=	0	
1972	Cont	....	*Nyiragongo (Africa-C)*	0203-03=	0	
1972	Cont	....	*Langila (New Britain-SW Pac)*	0502-01=	2	
1972	Cont	....	*Semeru (Java)*	0603-30=	2	
1972	Cont	....	*Dukono (Halmahera-Indonesia)*	0608-01=	2	
1972	Cont	....	*Suwanose-jima (Ryukyu Is)*	0802-03=	2	
1972	Cont	....	*Sakura-jima (Kyushu-Japan)*	0802-08=	2	
1972	Cont	....	*Aso (Kyushu-Japan)*	0802-11=	2	
1972	Cont	....	*Karymsky (Kamchatka)*	1000-13=	2	7/7
1972	Cont	....	*Kliuchevskoi (Kamchatka)*	1000-26=	2	
? 1972	Cont	....	*Loihi (Hawaiian Is)*	1302-00-	0	
1972	Cont	....	*Kilauea (Hawaiian Is)*	1302-01-	0	8/-
1972	Cont	....	*Santa María (Guatemala)*	1402-03=	1	**9**/8
1972	Cont	....	*Masaya (Nicaragua)*	1404-10=	0	
1972	Cont	....	*Arenal (Costa Rica)*	1405-033	1	8/7
1972	Cont	....	*Sangay (Ecuador)*	1502-09=	2	
1972	Cont	....	*Llaima (Chile-C)*	1507-11=	2	
1972	Cont	....	*Villarrica (Chile-C)*	1507-12=	2	7/-
1972	Cont	....	*Soufrière St. Vincent (W Indies)*	1600-15=	0	7/-
1972	Cont	....	*Jan Mayen (Atlantic-N-Jan Mayen)*	1706-01=	1	8/7
1972	....	>3yr	*Bagana (Bougainville-SW Pacific)*	0505-02=	1	6/-
? 1972	....	?	*Putana (Chile-N)*	1505-09=		
? 1972	....	?	*Láscar (Chile-N)*	1505-10=	2?	
? 1972	....	?	*Chillán, Nevados de (Chile-C)*	1507-07=		
1972	....	?	**Lautaro** (Chile-S)	1508-06=		
1972	01	>3yr	*Karangetang [Api Siau] (Sangihe Is*	0607-02=	2	
1972	0103?	?	**Erebus** (Antarctica)	1900-02=	1	
S 1972	0108	4a	**Unnamed** (Admiralty Is-SW Pacific)	0500-03-	0	
1972	0119	55m	**Batur** (Lesser Sunda Is)	0604-01=	2	
1972	0126	49m	**Tengger Caldera [Bromo]** (Java)	0603-31=	2	
1972	0202	....	*Pacaya (Guatemala)*	1402-11=	2	
1972	0209	577a	*Poás (Costa Rica)*	1405-04=	1	
? 1972	03	?	*Zheltovsky (Kamchatka)*	1000-04=	1?	
1972	03	....	**Bezymianny** (Kamchatka)	1000-25=	3	
? 1972	03	31p	*Grímsvötn (Iceland-NE)*	1703-01=	0	
? 1972	0305e	71j?	*Kuwae [Karua] (Vanuatu-SW Pac)*	0507-07=	0	
1972	0319	79a	**Tongariro [Ngauruhoe]** (New Zeal)	0401-08=	2	
1972	04	....	*Yasur (Vanuatu-SW Pacific)*	0507-10=	3	
1972	0415	122a	*Ambrym (Vanuatu-SW Pacific)*	0507-04=	2	
1972	0424	....	*Lopevi (Vanuatu-SW Pacific)*	0507-05=	1	
S 1972	0429	<1	**Unnamed** (Kuril Is)	0900-16-	0	
? 1972	0515e	55j?	*Epi (Vanuatu-SW Pacific)*	0507-06=	0	
1972	0604q	?	**Fernandina** (Galápagos)	1503-01=	0	
1972	0609?	221a?	**Fournaise, Piton de la** (Indian O.)	0303-02=	2	7/5
1972	0610c	386p	**Krakatau** (Indonesia)	0602-00=	2	6/-
1972	0618	85a	**Alaid** (Kuril Is)	0900-39=	3	7/8
1972	0629a	?	**Galápagos Rift** (Pacific-E)	1304-07-		
1972	07	61p	**Reventador** (Ecuador)	1502-01=	2	7/-
S 1972	0704	15a?	**Rocard** (Society Is-C Pacific)	1303-02-	0	
S 1972	0705	<1	**Kick 'em Jenny** (W Indies)	1600-16=	0	
1972	0728f	....	**Ambrym** (Vanuatu-SW Pacific)	0507-04=	3	
1972	0826	<1	**Calbuco** (Chile-S)	1508-02=	2	
? 1972	09 ?	?	*Akutan (Aleutian Is)*	1101-32-	2?	
1972	0902	<1	**Kuchinoerabu-jima** (Ryukyu Is)	0802-05=	2	
1972	0908	27a	**Karthala** (Indian O.-W)	0303-01=	1	6/-
? 1972	0929	<1	*Deception Island (Antarctica)*	1900-03=		
? 1972	1001	<1	*Fukutoku-Okanoba (Volcano Is-Japan*	0804-13=	0	
1972	1006	>3yr	**Merapi** (Java)	0603-25=	2	7/7
? 1972	1007	?	*Unnamed (Pacific-NE)*	1301-05-	0	
1972	1009	<1 ?	**Ritter Island** (New Guinea-NE of)	0501-07=	1	
1972	1022	80a	**Ruapehu** (New Zealand)	0401-10=	1	
1972	1022	86a	*Paluweh (Lesser Sunda Is)*	0604-15=	2?	

	START YEAR	START M-Dy	Duration	VOLCANO NAME (Subregion)	NUMBER	VEI	Vol L/T
	1972	1024	?	Kavachi (Solomon Is-SW Pacific)	0505-06=	0	
	1972	1112	33m	Acatenango (Guatemala)	1402-08=	1	
	1972	1122	635a	Tongariro [Ngauruhoe] (New Zeal)	0401-08=	2	
	1972	12	....	Stromboli (Italy)	0101-04=	2	7/-
	1972	12 <	>3yr	Erebus (Antarctica)	1900-02=	2	
	1973	Cont	....	Etna (Italy)	0101-06=	2	6/-
	1973	Cont	....	Erta Ale (Ethiopia)	0201-08=	0	
	1973	Cont	....	Nyiragongo (Africa-C)	0203-03=	0	
	1973	Cont	....	Bagana (Bougainville-SW Pacific)	0505-02=	1	6/-
	1973	Cont	....	Yasur (Vanuatu-SW Pacific)	0507-10=	2	
	1973	Cont	....	Krakatau (Indonesia)	0602-00=	2	6/-
	1973	Cont	....	Karangetang [Api Siau] (Sangihe Is	0607-02=	2	
	1973	Cont	....	Dukono (Halmahera-Indonesia)	0608-01=	2	
	1973	Cont	....	Suwanose-jima (Ryukyu Is)	0802-03=	2	
	1973	Cont	....	Karymsky (Kamchatka)	1000-13=	2	7/7
	1973	Cont	....	Bezymianny (Kamchatka)	1000-25=	2?	
	1973	Cont	....	Kliuchevskoi (Kamchatka)	1000-26=	2	
	1973	Cont	....	Pacaya (Guatemala)	1402-11=	1	
	1973	Cont	....	Masaya (Nicaragua)	1404-10=	0	
	1973	Cont	....	Arenal (Costa Rica)	1405-033	1	8/7
	1973	Cont	....	Sangay (Ecuador)	1502-09=	2	
	1973	....	?	Batur (Lesser Sunda Is)	0604-01=		
?	1973	....	?	Alaid (Kuril Is)	0900-39=		
	1973	....	....	Santa María (Guatemala)	1402-03=	2	9/8
	1973	01	....	Semeru (Java)	0603-30=	3	
	1973	01	881p	Aso (Kyushu-Japan)	0802-11=	2	
	1973	01	<1	Grozny Group (Kuril Is)	0900-07=	1	
	1973	0102	....	Tongariro [Ngauruhoe] (New Zeal)	0401-08=	3	
	1973	0106	141a	Soputan (Sulawesi-Indonesia)	0606-03=	2	
	1973	0109	....	Paluweh (Lesser Sunda Is)	0604-15=	3	
	1973	0115q	?	Jan Mayen (Atlantic-N-Jan Mayen)	1706-01=	1	
	1973	0123	156a	Vestmannaeyjar [Heimaey]	1702-01=	3	8/7
	1973	0124	1a	Dempo (Sumatra)	0601-23=	2	
	1973	0125	....	Poás (Costa Rica)	1405-04=	2	
?	1973	0130	?	Colima (México)	1401-04=	1	
	1973	0201	111a	Asama (Honshu-Japan)	0803-11=	2	
	1973	0222	<1	Okataina [Waimangu] (New Zeal)	0401-05=	1	-/3
	1973	0223	40a	Fuego (Guatemala)	1402-09=	2	-/6
	1973	0224d	>3yr	Langila (New Britain-SW Pac)	0502-01=	2	7/-
	1973	0228	....	Merapi (Java)	0603-25=	2	7/7
	1973	03 ?	62p	Akutan (Aleutian Is)	1101-32-	2	
	1973	04	319m	Long Island (New Guinea-NE of)	0501-05=	2	3/-
	1973	04	365p	Iliboleng (Lesser Sunda Is)	0604-22=	2	
	1973	0412	388d	Nishino-shima (Volcano Is-Japan)	0804-096	2	
	1973	0415e	>3yr	Ambrym (Vanuatu-SW Pacific)	0507-04=	2	
	1973	05	....	Stromboli (Italy)	0101-04=	2	7/-
	1973	05	153p	Raung (Java)	0603-34=	1	
?	1973	05	?	Galeras (Colombia)	1501-08=	2	
?	1973	0505d	173i?	Epi (Vanuatu-SW Pacific)	0507-06=	0	
?	1973	0505d	163m	Kuwae [Karua] (Vanuatu-SW Pac)	0507-07=	0	
	1973	0505	<1	Kilauea (Hawaiian Is)	1302-01-	0	6/-
	1973	0510	118a?	Fournaise, Piton de la (Indian O.)	0303-02=	2	6/-
	1973	0516	1a	Grozny Group (Kuril Is)	0900-07=	2?	
	1973	0601	....	Sakura-jima (Kyushu-Japan)	0802-08=	3	
	1973	07	>3yr	Chillán, Nevados de (Chile-C)	1507-07=	2	5/-
S	1973	0710	<1	Vailulu'u (Samoa-SW Pacific)	0404-00-	0	
	1973	0711	5a	Curacoa (Tonga-SW Pacific)	0403-102	3	
	1973	0714	14a	Tiatia (Kuril Is)	0900-03=	4	-/8
	1973	0724	<1	Marapi (Sumatra)	0601-14=	2	
	1973	0725	1a	Kolokol Group (Kuril Is)	0900-12=	1	
	1973	08	?	Slamet (Java)	0603-18=	1?	
	1973	0810	49a	Chikurachki (Kuril Is)	0900-36=	2	-/6
	1973	0825b	?	Korovin (Aleutian Is)	1101-161	0	
	1973	0915	456m	Lokon-Empung (Sulawesi-Indonesia)	0606-10=	1	
	1973	0927	148a	Fukujin (Volcano Is-Japan)	0804-133	1	
?	1973	10	410p	Tolbachik (Kamchatka)	1000-24=	1?	
	1973	1004	15a	Ulawun (New Britain-SW Pac)	0502-12=	2	7/6
	1973	1009	104a	Gaua (Vanuatu-SW Pacific)	0507-02=	2	
S	1973	1015	1	Rumble III (New Zealand)	0401-13-	0	
?	1973	1025	4a?	Wolf (Galápagos)	1503-02=		
	1973	1027	1a	Paluweh (Lesser Sunda Is)	0604-15=	2	
	1973	1031	360a	Ruapehu (New Zealand)	0401-10=	1	
	1973	11	242p	Reventador (Ecuador)	1502-01=	3	6/-
	1973	1105	14	Kuchinoerabu-jima (Ryukyu Is)	0802-05=	2	
	1973	1110	29a	Kilauea (Hawaiian Is)	1302-01-	0	6/-
	1973	1111	....	Erebus (Antarctica)	1900-02=	1	
	1973	1112	1a	Pavlof (Alaska Peninsula)	1102-03-	2	-/6
	1973	12	....	Ambrym (Vanuatu-SW Pacific)	0507-04=	3	
	1973	1205	260a	Iliwerung (Lesser Sunda Is)	0604-25=	0	
	1973	1207	....	Tongariro [Ngauruhoe] (New Zeal)	0401-08=	2	
	1973	1209	6a	Fernandina (Galápagos)	1503-01=	2	
	1973	1218	60a	Fukutoku-Okanoba (Volcano Is-Japan.	0804-13=	0	
	1973	1224	19a	Concepción (Nicaragua)	1404-12=	2	
	1974	Cont	....	Erta Ale (Ethiopia)	0201-08=	0	
	1974	Cont	....	Nyiragongo (Africa-C)	0203-03=	0	
	1974	Cont	....	Ruapehu (New Zealand)	0401-10=	1	
	1974	Cont	....	Long Island (New Guinea-NE of)	0501-05=	2	3/-
	1974	Cont	....	Bagana (Bougainville-SW Pacific)	0505-02=	1	6/-
	1974	Cont	....	Yasur (Vanuatu-SW Pacific)	0507-10=	2	
	1974	Cont	....	Merapi (Java)	0603-25=	1	7/7
	1974	Cont	....	Iliboleng (Lesser Sunda Is)	0604-22=	2	
	1974	Cont	....	Lokon-Empung (Sulawesi-Indonesia)	0606-10=	1	
	1974	Cont	....	Dukono (Halmahera-Indonesia)	0608-01=	2	
	1974	Cont	....	Suwanose-jima (Ryukyu Is)	0802-03=	2	
	1974	Cont	....	Sakura-jima (Kyushu-Japan)	0802-08=	2	
	1974	Cont	....	Aso (Kyushu-Japan)	0802-11=	2	
	1974	Cont	....	Nishino-shima (Volcano Is-Japan)	0804-096	2	
	1974	Cont	....	Fukujin (Volcano Is-Japan)	0804-133	1	
	1974	Cont	....	Karymsky (Kamchatka)	1000-13=	2	7/7
?	1974	Cont	....	Tolbachik (Kamchatka)	1000-24=	1?	
	1974	Cont	....	Bezymianny (Kamchatka)	1000-25=	2?	
	1974	Cont	....	Santa María (Guatemala)	1402-03=	1	9/8
	1974	Cont	....	Pacaya (Guatemala)	1402-11=	1	
	1974	Cont	....	Masaya (Nicaragua)	1404-10=	0	
	1974	Cont	....	Concepción (Nicaragua)	1404-12=	2	
	1974	Cont	....	Sangay (Ecuador)	1502-09=	2	
	1974	....	....	Langila (New Britain-SW Pac)	0502-01=	2	7/-
	1974	....	....	Semeru (Java)	0603-30=	3	
	1974	....	>3yr	Galeras (Colombia)	1501-08=	1?	
	1974	01	264m	Lopevi (Vanuatu-SW Pacific)	0507-05=	2	
?	1974	01	18m	Ioto [Iwo-jima] (Volcano Is-Japan)	0804-12=	0	
	1974	0111	....	Gaua (Vanuatu-SW Pacific)	0507-02=	2	
	1974	0122	....	Tongariro [Ngauruhoe] (New Zeal)	0401-08=	3	
	1974	0130	58a	Etna (Italy)	0101-06=	2	6/6
	1974	0204d	223m?	Kuwae [Karua] (Vanuatu-SW Pac)	0507-07=	0	
	1974	0211	....	Karangetang [Api Siau] (Sangihe Is	0607-02=	3	
	1974	0211<	?	Akutan (Aleutian Is)	1101-32-	2	
	1974	0214	175a	Karkar (New Guinea-NE of)	0501-03=	2	7/-
?	1974	0216	?	Fonualei (Tonga-SW Pacific)	0403-10=	1	
	1974	0216	....	Fukutoku-Okanoba (Volcano Is-Japan	0804-13=	2	
	1974	0219	208m	Great Sitkin (Aleutian Is)	1101-12-	2	7/-
	1974	0226	236a	Dempo (Sumatra)	0601-23=	2	
	1974	0228	114a	Oshima (Izu Is-Japan)	0804-01=	1	
?	1974	03	?	Unnamed (Volcano Is-Japan)	0804-101	0	
	1974	0301	60a	Chokai (Honshu-Japan)	0803-22=	1	-/5
	1974	0303	....	Chillán, Nevados de (Chile-C)	1507-07=	2	5/-
	1974	0304?	>3yr	Manam (New Guinea-NE of)	0501-02=	3	7/7
	1974	0312	34m	Batur (Lesser Sunda Is)	0604-01=	2	
	1974	0312	12a?	Pavlof (Alaska Peninsula)	1102-03-	1	
	1974	0328	....	Tongariro [Ngauruhoe] (New Zeal)	0401-08=	3	
	1974	0401	....	Arenal (Costa Rica)	1405-033	2	8/7
	1974	0408	251m?	Kliuchevskoi (Kamchatka)	1000-26=	3	7/6
?	1974	0529	<1	Slamet (Java)	0603-18=	2	
	1974	0603	<1	Kuchinoerabu-jima (Ryukyu Is)	0802-05=	1	
	1974	0615	32a?	Raung (Java)	0603-34=	2	
	1974	07	....	Iliwerung (Lesser Sunda Is)	0604-25=	2	
	1974	07	....	Reventador (Ecuador)	1502-01=	2	6/-
?	1974	07	61p	Láscar (Chile-N)	1505-10=	1	
?	1974	0706	<1	Smith Rock (Izu Is-Japan)	0804-08=	0	
	1974	0715q	?	Trident (Alaska Peninsula)	1102-16-	3	
	1974	0719	2	Kilauea (Hawaiian Is)	1302-01-	0	6/-
?	1974	0722?	5a?	Central Island (Africa-E)	0202-01=	1	
	1974	0728	<1	Niigata-Yake-yama (Honshu-Japan)	0803-09=	2	-/5
	1974	0823	....	Kliuchevskoi (Kamchatka)	1000-26=	2	7/6
	1974	0901<	76a>	Pavlof (Alaska Peninsula)	1102-03-	2?	
	1974	0905	<1	Kick 'em Jenny (W Indies)	1600-16=	0	
	1974	0908j	1a	White Island (New Zealand)	0401-04=	2	
	1974	0909	....	Stromboli (Italy)	0101-04=	2	7/-
	1974	0911	156m	Poás (Costa Rica)	1405-04=	2	
	1974	0919	<1	Kilauea (Hawaiian Is)	1302-01-	0	7/-
	1974	0929?	>3yr	Etna (Italy)	0101-06=	2	7/-
	1974	1010	55a	Fuego (Guatemala)	1402-09=	1	-/8
	1974	1014	....	Fuego (Guatemala)	1402-09=	3	-/8
	1974	1017	<1	Ritter Island (New Guinea-NE of)	0501-07=	1	
	1974	1017	....	Fuego (Guatemala)	1402-09=	4	-/8
	1974	1029	....	Pavlof (Alaska Peninsula)	1102-03-	3	
?	1974	11	15m?	Epi (Vanuatu-SW Pacific)	0507-06=	0	
	1974	11	....	Erebus (Antarctica)	1900-02=	1	
	1974	1112	30a?	Kavachi (Solomon Is-SW Pacific)	0505-06=	1	
	1974	1220	....	Ambrym (Vanuatu-SW Pacific)	0507-04=	2	
	1974	1224	324a	Fukutoku-Okanoba (Volcano Is-Japan	0804-13=	2	
	1974	1230?	188a?	Karkar (New Guinea-NE of)	0501-03=	2	6/-
	1974	1231	<1	Kilauea (Hawaiian Is)	1302-01-	0	6/-
	1975	Cont	....	Erta Ale (Ethiopia)	0201-08=	0	
	1975	Cont	....	Nyiragongo (Africa-C)	0203-03=	0	
	1975	Cont	....	Manam (New Guinea-NE of)	0501-02=	2	7/7
	1975	Cont	....	Karkar (New Guinea-NE of)	0501-03=	2	6/-
	1975	Cont	....	Langila (New Britain-SW Pac)	0502-01=	2	7/-
	1975	Cont	....	Ambrym (Vanuatu-SW Pacific)	0507-04=	2	
	1975	Cont	....	Yasur (Vanuatu-SW Pacific)	0507-10=	2	
	1975	Cont	....	Merapi (Java)	0603-25=	1	7/7
	1975	Cont	....	Semeru (Java)	0603-30=	2	
	1975	Cont	....	Karangetang [Api Siau] (Sangihe Is	0607-02=	2	
	1975	Cont	....	Dukono (Halmahera-Indonesia)	0608-01=	2	

START YEAR	M-Dy	Duration	VOLCANO NAME (Subregion)	NUMBER	VEI	Vol L/T
1975	*Cont*	....	*Suwanose-jima (Ryukyu Is)*	0802-03=	*2*	
1975	*Cont*	....	*Sakura-jima (Kyushu-Japan)*	0802-08=	*2*	
1975	*Cont*	....	*Fukutoku-Okanoba (Volcano Is-Japan*	0804-13=	*2*	
1975	*Cont*	....	*Karymsky (Kamchatka)*	1000-13=	*2*	*7/7*
1975	*Cont*	....	*Pacaya (Guatemala)*	1402-11=	*1*	
1975	*Cont*	....	*Masaya (Nicaragua)*	1404-10=	*0*	
1975	*Cont*	....	*Poás (Costa Rica)*	1405-04=	*2*	
1975	*Cont*	....	*Galeras (Colombia)*	1501-08=	*1?*	
1975	*Cont*	....	*Sangay (Ecuador)*	1502-09=	*2*	
1975	*Cont*	....	*Chillán, Nevados de (Chile-C)*	1507-07=	*2*	*5/-*
? *1975*	....	*?*	*Sofugan (Izu Is-Japan)*	0804-091	*0*	
? *1975*	....	*730y*	*Nishino-shima (Volcano Is-Japan)*	0804-096	*0*	
1975	....	....	*Erebus (Antarctica)*	1900-02=	*2*	
1975 k	....	?	**Thule Islands** (Antarctica)	1900-07=	1?	
1975	01	>3yr	**Marapi** (Sumatra)	0601-14=	2	
1975	0212	11*a*	**Tongariro [Ngauruhoe]** (New Zeal)	0401-08=	3	-/6
1975	0224	186*a*	**Etna** (Italy)	0101-06=	1	6/-
1975	03	60*p*	**Raung** (Java)	0603-34=	1	
1975	0306c	109*c*	**Lopevi** (Vanuatu-SW Pacific)	0507-05=	2	
1975	0327	213*e*	**Krakatau** (Indonesia)	0602-00=	2	6/-
1975	04	....	**Bagana** (Bougainville-SW Pacific)	0505-02=	2	6/-
1975	*04*	....	*Santa María (Guatemala)*	1402-03=	*2*	***9**/8*
1975	0424	3	**Ruapehu** (New Zealand)	0401-10=	2	
? *1975*	*0426*	*3a*	*Esmeralda Bank (Mariana Is-C Pacific)*	0804-21=	*0*	
1975	05	304*p*	**Telica** (Nicaragua)	1404-04=	0	
1975	0528	166*a*	**Fuego** (Guatemala)	1402-09=	1	-/5
1975	*0617*	....	*Arenal (Costa Rica)*	1405-033	*2*	*8/7*
1975	*0628*	*530a*	*Tolbachik (Kamchatka)*	1000-24=	*1*	
1975	0705	<1	**Mauna Loa** (Hawaiian Is)	1302-02=	0	7/-
1975	0706	....	**Tolbachik** (Kamchatka)	1000-24=	4+	**9**/8
1975	08	14*c*	**Kavachi** (Solomon Is-SW Pacific)	0505-06=	1	
? *1975*	*0813*	*44a*	*Smith Rock (Izu Is-Japan)*	0804-08=	*0*	
? *1975*	*0824?*	*83m*	*Loihi (Hawaiian Is)*	1302-00-	*0*	
1975	0825	?	**Minami-Hiyoshi** (Volcano Is-Japan)	0804-131	0	
? *1975*	*09*	*?*	*Cleveland (Aleutian Is)*	1101-24-		
? *1975*	*0910*	*?*	*Unnamed (Mariana Is-C Pacific)*	0804-138	*0*	
? *1975*	*0910*	*?*	*Unnamed (Mariana Is-C Pacific)*	0804-139	*0*	
1975	0913	43*e*	**Shishaldin** (Aleutian Is)	1101-36-	2	
1975	0913	549*m*>	**Pavlof** (Alaska Peninsula)	1102-03-	2	-/7
1975	10	89*m*	**Aso** (Kyushu-Japan)	0802-11=	1	
1975	1002	?	**Tori-shima** (Izu Is-Japan)	0804-09=	2	
1975	1017<	<1	**Ruapehu** (New Zealand)	0401-10=	1	
1975	*11 <*	*>3yr*	*Lokon-Empung (Sulawesi-Indonesia)*	0606-10=	*1*	*4/-*
? *1975*	*11*	*?*	*Kasuga (Volcano Is-Japan)*	0804-134	*0*	
1975	*1104*	....	*Stromboli (Italy)*	0101-04=	*2*	*7/-*
1975	1104	154*a*	**Fournaise, Piton de la** (Indian O.)	0303-02=	1	7/5
1975	1129	<1	**Kilauea** (Hawaiian Is)	1302-01-	0	5/-
1975	1211?	191*a?*	**Colima** (México)	1401-04=	2	8/-
1975	1220	<1	**Krafla** (Iceland-NE)	1703-08=	0	5/-
1976	*Cont*	....	*Stromboli (Italy)*	0101-04=	*1*	*7/-*
1976	*Cont*	....	*Etna (Italy)*	0101-06=	*2*	*7/-*
1976	*Cont*	....	*Erta Ale (Ethiopia)*	0201-08=	*0*	
1976	*Cont*	....	*Nyiragongo (Africa-C)*	0203-03=	*0*	
1976	*Cont*	....	*Manam (New Guinea-NE of)*	0501-02=	*2*	*7/7*
1976	*Cont*	....	*Langila (New Britain-SW Pac)*	0502-01=	*2*	*7/-*
1976	*Cont*	....	*Bagana (Bougainville-SW Pacific)*	0505-02=	*1*	*6/-*
1976	*Cont*	....	*Yasur (Vanuatu-SW Pacific)*	0507-10=	*2*	
1976	*Cont*	....	*Marapi (Sumatra)*	0601-14=	*1*	
1976	*Cont*	....	*Lokon-Empung (Sulawesi-Indonesia)*	0606-10=	*1*	*4/-*
1976	*Cont*	....	*Dukono (Halmahera-Indonesia)*	0608-01=	*2*	
1976	*Cont*	....	*Suwanose-jima (Ryukyu Is)*	0802-03=	*2*	
1976	*Cont*	....	*Sakura-jima (Kyushu-Japan)*	0802-08=	*2*	
1976	*Cont*	....	*Aso (Kyushu-Japan)*	0802-11=	*1*	
? *1976*	*Cont*	....	*Nishino-shima (Volcano Is-Japan)*	0804-096	*0*	
1976	*Cont*	....	*Karymsky (Kamchatka)*	1000-13=	*2*	*7/7*
1976	*Cont*	....	*Colima (México)*	1401-04=	*2*	*8/-*
1976	*Cont*	....	*Pacaya (Guatemala)*	1402-11=	*1*	
1976	*Cont*	....	*Masaya (Nicaragua)*	1404-10=	*0*	
1976	*Cont*	....	*Galeras (Colombia)*	1501-08=	*1?*	
1976	*Cont*	....	*Sangay (Ecuador)*	1502-09=	*2*	
1976	*Cont*	....	*Chillán, Nevados de (Chile-C)*	1507-07=	*2*	*5/-*
1976	*Cont*	....	*Erebus (Antarctica)*	1900-02=	*1*	
? *1976*	....	*?*	*Korovin (Aleutian Is)*	1101-161		
1976	01	?	**Ioto [Iwo-jima]** (Volcano Is-Japan)	0804-12=	1	
1976	01	257*m*	**Shishaldin** (Aleutian Is)	1101-36-	2	
1976	0102u	?	**Long Island** (New Guinea-NE of)	0501-05=	1	
1976	0104	133*m*	**Reventador** (Ecuador)	1502-01=	2	7/-
1976	0115e	?	**Gaua** (Vanuatu-SW Pacific)	0507-02=	2	
1976	0122?	477*a?*	**Augustine** (Alaska-SW)	1103-01-	4	7/8
? *1976*	*02*	*?*	*Minami-Hiyoshi (Volcano Is-Japan)*	0804-131	*0*	
1976	*0204*	....	*Merapi (Java)*	0603-25=	*2*	*7/7*
1976	0302	<1	**Kusatsu-Shirane** (Honshu-Japan)	0803-12=	1	-/4
1976	0306	<1	**Ruapehu** (New Zealand)	0401-10=	1	
? *1976*	*0308*	*?*	*Iliwerung (Lesser Sunda Is)*	0604-25=	*0*	

Juergen Kienle (Univ. Alaska Fairbanks)

An ash column rises from a phreatomagmatic eruption forming the Ukinrek maars in the Alaska Peninsula. Lighter-colored ashfall and pyroclastic-surge deposits surround the vent, and the snow-covered shores of Becharof Lake are in the background. Two maars, East Maar, erupting in this photo and later filled by a smal dome, and West Maar (bottom center), were formed during a 10-day eruption in March and April of 1977.

	START YEAR	M-Dy	Duration	VOLCANO NAME (Subregion)	NUMBER	VEI	Vol L/T
	1976	0309	7a	**San Cristóbal** (Nicaragua)	1404-02=	1	
	1976	0325	?	**Bezymianny** (Kamchatka)	1000-25=	2	
?	1976	0326	<1	*Batur (Lesser Sunda Is)*	0604-01=	1?	
	1976	0402	<1	**Kuchinoerabu-jima** (Ryukyu Is)	0802-05=	2	
	1976	0406	....	*Shishaldin (Aleutian Is)*	1101-36-	2	
	1976	0501	126a	**Lopevi** (Vanuatu-SW Pacific)	0507-05=	1	
	1976	0507	....	*Santa María (Guatemala)*	1402-03=	3	9/8
	1976	0524	....	*Ambrym (Vanuatu-SW Pacific)*	0507-04=	2	
	1976	0607	167a	**Raung** (Java)	0603-34=	2	
	1976	0621	147m	**Poás** (Costa Rica)	1405-04=	2	
	1976	0708	236a	**Soufrière Guadeloupe** (W Indies)	1600-06=	2	-/5
?	1976	08	16m	*Smith Rock (Izu Is-Japan)*	0804-08=	0	
?	1976	0802	>3yr	*Fukutoku-Okanoba (Volcano Is-Japan.*	0804-13=	0	
?	1976	0802	262a	*Fukujin (Volcano Is-Japan)*	0804-133	0	
	1976	0823	5a	**Tongariro [Ngauruhoe]** (New Zeal)	0401-08=	1	
	1976	0824	50a?	**Kavachi** (Solomon Is-SW Pacific)	0505-06=	1	
	1976	0829	<1	**San Cristóbal** (Nicaragua)	1404-02=	1	
	1976	0831	....	*Semeru (Java)*	0603-30=	2	
	1976	0903	44a	**Taal** (Luzon-Philippines)	0703-07=	2	-/6
	1976	0912<	71a?	**Ruapehu** (New Zealand)	0401-10=	1	
	1976	0915	365m	**Karangetang [Api Siau]** (Sangihe Is	0607-02=	2	7/-
	1976	0923	9a	**Sarychev Peak** (Kuril Is)	0900-24=	2	6/-
	1976	0927	....	*Shishaldin (Aleutian Is)*	1101-36-	2	
	1976	1012	....	*Arenal (Costa Rica)*	1405-033	2	8/7
	1976	1015q	205q>	**Akutan** (Aleutian Is)	1101-32-	2	
	1976	1102	2a?	**Fournaise, Piton de la** (Indian O.)	0303-02=	1	5/4
	1976	1103	438m>	**Telica** (Nicaragua)	1404-04=	1	
	1976	1110	....	*Pavlof (Alaska Peninsula)*	1102-03-	2	-/7
?	1976	1127	?	*Matthew Island (SW Pacific)*	0508-01=	1?	
	1976	1202	77a	**San Miguel** (El Salvador)	1403-10=	1	6/-
	1976	1218	>3yr	*White Island (New Zealand)*	0401-04=	2	-/7
?	1976	1220	98a	*Minami-Hiyoshi (Volcano Is-Japan)*	0804-131	0	
	1976	1223	174e	**Nyamuragira** (Africa-C)	0203-02=	1	7/7
	1977	Cont	....	*Stromboli (Italy)*	0101-04=	1	7/-
	1977	Cont	....	*Etna (Italy)*	0101-06=	2	7/-
	1977	Cont	....	*Erta Ale (Ethiopia)*	0201-08=	0	
	1977	Cont	....	*Nyamuragira (Africa-C)*	0203-02=	1	7/7
	1977	Cont	....	*Manam (New Guinea-NE of)*	0501-02=	2	7/7
	1977	Cont	....	*Langila (New Britain-SW Pac)*	0502-01=	2	7/-
	1977	Cont	....	*Bagana (Bougainville-SW Pacific)*	0505-02=	1	6/-
	1977	Cont	....	*Marapi (Sumatra)*	0601-14=	1	
	1977	Cont	....	*Merapi (Java)*	0603-25=	1	7/7
	1977	Cont	....	*Semeru (Java)*	0603-30=	2	
	1977	Cont	....	*Karangetang [Api Siau] (Sangihe Is*	0607-02=	1	7/-
	1977	Cont	....	*Dukono (Halmahera-Indonesia)*	0608-01=	2	
	1977	Cont	....	*Suwanose-jima (Ryukyu Is)*	0802-03=	2	
	1977	Cont	....	*Sakura-jima (Kyushu-Japan)*	0802-08=	2	
?	1977	Cont	....	*Nishino-shima (Volcano Is-Japan)*	0804-096	0	
?	1977	Cont	....	*Fukutoku-Okanoba (Volcano Is-Japan.*	0804-13=	0	
?	1977	Cont	....	*Minami-Hiyoshi (Volcano Is-Japan)*	0804-131	0	
	1977	Cont	....	*Karymsky (Kamchatka)*	1000-13=	2	7/7
	1977	Cont	....	*Akutan (Aleutian Is)*	1101-32-	2	
	1977	Cont	....	*Pavlof (Alaska Peninsula)*	1102-03-	2	-/7
	1977	Cont	....	*San Miguel (El Salvador)*	1403-10=	1	6/-
	1977	Cont	....	*Telica (Nicaragua)*	1404-04=	1	
	1977	Cont	....	*Masaya (Nicaragua)*	1404-10=	0	
	1977	Cont	....	*Arenal (Costa Rica)*	1405-033	1	8/7
	1977	Cont	....	*Galeras (Colombia)*	1501-08=	1?	
	1977	Cont	....	*Sangay (Ecuador)*	1502-09=	2	
	1977	Cont	....	*Chillán, Nevados de (Chile-C)*	1507-07=	2	5/-
	1977	Cont	....	*Soufrière Guadeloupe (W Indies)*	1600-06=	1	-/5
	1977	Cont	....	*Erebus (Antarctica)*	1900-02=	1	
	1977	0110	<1	**Nyiragongo** (Africa-C)	0203-03=	1	7/4
S	1977	0114	<1	**Kick 'em Jenny** (W Indies)	1600-16=	0?	
	1977	0120e	8e?	**Ambrym** (Vanuatu-SW Pacific)	0507-04=	2	
	1977	0126	4a	**Villarrica** (Chile-C)	1507-12=	1	
?	1977	0201	?	*Kuwae [Karua] (Vanuatu-SW Pac)*	0507-07=	0	
	1977	0209	....	*Santa María (Guatemala)*	1402-03=	3	9/8
	1977	0222	?	**Kavachi** (Solomon Is-SW Pacific)	0505-06=	1	
	1977	0303	47a	**Fuego** (Guatemala)	1402-09=	1	-/4
	1977	0303	?	**Irazú** (Costa Rica)	1405-06=	1	
	1977	0306	2a?	**Seguam** (Aleutian Is)	1101-18-	1	7/-
	1977	0311	....	*White Island (New Zealand)*	0401-04=	2	-/7
	1977	0319	9a?	**Puracé** (Colombia)	1501-06=	2	
	1977	0323	4a	**Fernandina** (Galápagos)	1503-01=	1	
	1977	0324	23a	**Fournaise, Piton de la** (Indian O.)	0303-02=	0	7/-
	1977	0325	?	**Bezymianny** (Kamchatka)	1000-25=	3	5/7
	1977	0328	....	**Lokon-Empung** (Sulawesi-Indonesia)	0606-10=	2	4/-
	1977	0330	10a	**Ukinrek Maars** (Alaska Peninsula)	1102-131	3	5/7
S	1977	04	15m	**Monowai Seamount** (Kermadec Is)	0402-05-	0	
	1977	0404	29a	**Concepción** (Nicaragua)	1404-12=	2	
	1977	0405	5a	**Karthala** (Indian O.-W)	0303-01=	1	6/5
	1977	0411	492m	**Aso** (Kyushu-Japan)	0802-11=	2	
	1977	0411	....	*Augustine (Alaska-SW)*	1103-01-	1	7/8
	1977	0413	<1	**Gaua** (Vanuatu-SW Pacific)	0507-02=	2	
	1977	0427	134	**Krafla** (Iceland-NE)	1703-08=	1	6/1
	1977	05	60p?	**Poás** (Costa Rica)	1405-04=	1	
	1977	0609	21a	**Raung** (Java)	0603-34=	2	
	1977	0704	<1	**Tongariro [Ngauruhoe]** (New Zeal)	0401-08=	1	
	1977	0716	550m	*Ruapehu (New Zealand)*	0401-10=	1	-/5
	1977	0717?	5a?	**Kavachi** (Solomon Is-SW Pacific)	0505-06=	1	
	1977	08	45m	**Ambrym** (Vanuatu-SW Pacific)	0507-04=	2	
	1977	0802	952a	*Kliuchevskoi (Kamchatka)*	1000-26=	2	5/7
	1977	0807	>3yr	**Usu** (Hokkaido-Japan)	0805-03=	3	-/8
	1977	0819	....	*Pacaya (Guatemala)*	1402-11=	2	
	1977	0825	....	**White Island** (New Zealand)	0401-04=	3	-/7
	1977	0911	696a	**Fuego** (Guatemala)	1402-09=	2	-/6
	1977	0913	17	**Kilauea** (Hawaiian Is)	1302-01-	0	7/-
	1977	10	....	*Yasur (Vanuatu-SW Pacific)*	0507-10=	3	
?	1977	10	16m	*Smith Rock (Izu Is-Japan)*	0804-08=	0	
	1977	1003	39a?	**Taal** (Luzon-Philippines)	0703-07=	2	
?	1977	1014	161a	*Fukujin (Volcano Is-Japan)*	0804-133	0	
	1977	1016	<1	**San Cristóbal** (Nicaragua)	1404-02=	2	
	1977	1017	10a?	**Monowai Seamount** (Kermadec Is)	0402-05-	0	
	1977	1024	24	**Fournaise, Piton de la** (Indian O.)	0303-02=	1	7/-
	1977	1102	....	**Ruapehu** (New Zealand)	0401-10=	2	-/5
S	1977	1111	?	**Kick 'em Jenny** (W Indies)	1600-16=	0	
	1977	1116	?	**Mahawu** (Sulawesi-Indonesia)	0606-11=	0	
	1977	12	>3yr	**Colima** (México)	1401-04=	1	5/-
	1977	1207	<1	**Azuma** (Honshu-Japan)	0803-18=	1	
S	1977	1210	5	**Macdonald** (Austral Is-C Pacific)	1303-06-	0	
	1977	1218	179a	**Poás** (Costa Rica)	1405-04=	2	
	1978	Cont	....	*Stromboli (Italy)*	0101-04=	1	7/-
	1978	Cont	....	*Erta Ale (Ethiopia)*	0201-08=	0	
	1978	Cont	....	*White Island (New Zealand)*	0401-04=	2	-/7
	1978	Cont	....	*Ruapehu (New Zealand)*	0401-10=	1	-/5
	1978	Cont	....	*Manam (New Guinea-NE of)*	0501-02=	2	7/7
	1978	Cont	....	*Langila (New Britain-SW Pac)*	0502-01=	2	7/-
	1978	Cont	....	*Bagana (Bougainville-SW Pacific)*	0505-02=	1	6/-
	1978	Cont	....	*Yasur (Vanuatu-SW Pacific)*	0507-10=	2	
	1978	Cont	....	*Merapi (Java)*	0603-25=	1	7/7
	1978	Cont	....	*Suwanose-jima (Ryukyu Is)*	0802-03=	2	
	1978	Cont	....	*Sakura-jima (Kyushu-Japan)*	0802-08=	2	
	1978	Cont	....	*Aso (Kyushu-Japan)*	0802-11=	1	
?	1978	Cont	....	*Fukutoku-Okanoba (Volcano Is-Japan.*	0804-13=	0	
	1978	Cont	....	*Karymsky (Kamchatka)*	1000-13=	2	7/7
	1978	Cont	....	*Kliuchevskoi (Kamchatka)*	1000-26=	2	5/7
	1978	Cont	....	*Colima (México)*	1401-04=	1	5/-
	1978	Cont	....	*Santa María (Guatemala)*	1402-03=	1	9/8
	1978	Cont	....	*Fuego (Guatemala)*	1402-09=	2	-/6
	1978	Cont	....	*Pacaya (Guatemala)*	1402-11=	1	
	1978	Cont	....	*Telica (Nicaragua)*	1404-04=	1	
	1978	Cont	....	*Masaya (Nicaragua)*	1404-10=	0	
	1978	Cont	....	*Arenal (Costa Rica)*	1405-033	1	8/7
	1978	Cont	....	*Galeras (Colombia)*	1501-08=	1?	
	1978	Cont	....	*Sangay (Ecuador)*	1502-09=	2	
	1978	Cont	....	*Chillán, Nevados de (Chile-C)*	1507-07=	2	5/-
	1978	Cont	....	*Erebus (Antarctica)*	1900-02=	1	
	1978	01	....	*Semeru (Java)*	0603-30=	1	
	1978	01	700p>	**Raung** (Java)	0603-34=	1	
	1978	01	....	*Lokon-Empung (Sulawesi-Indonesia)*	0606-10=	1	4/-
	1978	0106	3a	**Didicas** (Luzon-N of)	0704-02=	2	
	1978	0113	....	*Usu (Hokkaido-Japan)*	0805-03=	2	-/8
?	1978	0126?	57a?	*Minami-Hiyoshi (Volcano Is-Japan)*	0804-131	0	
S	1978	02	152p	**Monowai Seamount** (Kermadec Is)	0402-05-	0	
	1978	0204	5a	**Westdahl** (Aleutian Is)	1101-34-	3	
	1978	0208	<1 ?	**Shishaldin** (Aleutian Is)	1101-36-	2	
	1978	0222	299a	**Karangetang [Api Siau]** (Sangihe Is	0607-02=	1	
	1978	0223	<1	**Okataina** (New Zealand)	0401-05=	1	
	1978	0307	193m?	*Mayon (Luzon-Philippines)*	0703-03=	1	7/-
	1978	0330<	35d>	**Concepción** (Nicaragua)	1404-12=	2	
?	1978	0331	?	*Unnamed (Kuril Is)*	0900-13-	0	
	1978	0429	215a	**Etna** (Italy)	0101-06=	2	7/-
	1978	0507	7a	**Ulawun** (New Britain-SW Pac)	0502-12=	3	6/7
	1978	0507	....	**Mayon** (Luzon-Philippines)	0703-03=	2	7/-
	1978	0514	3a	**Shikotsu [Tarumai]** (Hokkaido)	0805-04=	1	-/4
	1978	06	?	**Lautaro** (Chile-S)	1508-06=		
	1978	0621	31f	**Kavachi** (Solomon Is-SW Pacific)	0505-06=	2	
	1978	0627	67a	**Kanlaon** (Philippines-C)	0702-02=	2	
	1978	07	....	*Dukono (Halmahera-Indonesia)*	0608-01=	3	
	1978	0710	127m	**Krakatau** (Indonesia)	0602-00=	1	-/4
	1978	0720	?	**Tiatia** (Kuril Is)	0900-03=	2	
	1978	0729	16a	**Bulusan** (Luzon-Philippines)	0703-01=	2	-/5
	1978	0808	18a	**Fernandina** (Galápagos)	1503-01=	2	6/-
	1978	0822	....	*Etna (Italy)*	0101-06=	2	7/-
?	1978	0824	1a	*Fukujin (Volcano Is-Japan)*	0804-133	0	
	1978	0908	....	*Marapi (Sumatra)*	0601-14=	2	
	1978	0908p	?	**Bezymianny** (Kamchatka)	1000-25=	2	
	1978	0922	84m	**Poás** (Costa Rica)	1405-04=	1	
	1978	0925e	21m	**Akutan** (Aleutian Is)	1101-32-	2	
	1978	1107	7a	**Ardoukôba** (Djibouti)	0201-126	1	7/-
?	1978	1116	228w?	*Nishino-shima (Volcano Is-Japan)*	0804-096	0	
	1978	1118	....	*Etna (Italy)*	0101-06=	2	7/-
	1978	1122	113m	*Lopevi (Vanuatu-SW Pacific)*	0507-05=	0	

	START YEAR	M-Dy	Duration	VOLCANO NAME (Subregion)	NUMBER	VEI	Vol L/T
	1978	1211	<1	**Ioto [Iwo-jima]** (Volcano Is-Japan)	0804-12=	1	
	1978	1212	150*a*	**Shikotsu [Tarumai]** (Hokkaido)	0805-04=	1	
	1979	*Cont*	....	*Stromboli (Italy)*	0101-04=	*1*	*7/-*
	1979	*Cont*	....	*Erta Ale (Ethiopia)*	0201-08=	*0*	
	1979	*Cont*	....	*White Island (New Zealand)*	0401-04=	*2*	*-/7*
	1979	*Cont*	....	*Manam (New Guinea-NE of)*	0501-02=	*2*	*7/7*
	1979	*Cont*	....	*Langila (New Britain-SW Pac)*	0502-01=	*2*	*7/-*
	1979	*Cont*	....	*Bagana (Bougainville-SW Pacific)*	0505-02=	*1*	*6/-*
	1979	*Cont*	....	*Yasur (Vanuatu-SW Pacific)*	0507-10=	*2*	
	1979	*Cont*	....	*Marapi (Sumatra)*	0601-14=	*1*	
	1979	*Cont*	....	*Merapi (Java)*	0603-25=	*1*	*7/7*
	1979	*Cont*	....	*Semeru (Java)*	0603-30=	*2*	
	1979	*Cont*	....	*Raung (Java)*	0603-34=	*1*	
	1979	*Cont*	....	*Lokon-Empung (Sulawesi-Indonesia)*	0606-10=	*1*	*4/-*
	1979	*Cont*	....	*Dukono (Halmahera-Indonesia)*	0608-01=	*2*	
	1979	*Cont*	....	*Suwanose-jima (Ryukyu Is)*	0802-03=	*2*	
	1979	*Cont*	....	*Sakura-jima (Kyushu-Japan)*	0802-08=	*2*	
?	*1979*	*Cont*	....	*Nishino-shima (Volcano Is-Japan)*	0804-096	*0*	
?	*1979*	*Cont*	....	*Fukutoku-Okanoba (Volcano Is-Japan.*	0804-13=	*0*	
	1979	*Cont*	....	*Usu (Hokkaido-Japan)*	0805-03=	*0*	*-/8*
	1979	*Cont*	....	*Shikotsu [Tarumai] (Hokkaido)*	0805-04=	*1*	
	1979	*Cont*	....	*Karymsky (Kamchatka)*	1000-13=	*2*	*7/7*
	1979	*Cont*	....	*Kliuchevskoi (Kamchatka)*	1000-26=	*2*	*5/7*
	1979	*Cont*	....	*Colima (México)*	1401-04=	*1*	*5/-*
	1979	*Cont*	....	*Fuego (Guatemala)*	1402-09=	*2*	*-/6*
	1979	*Cont*	....	*Pacaya (Guatemala)*	1402-11=	*1*	
	1979	*Cont*	....	*Masaya (Nicaragua)*	1404-10=	*0*	
	1979	*Cont*	....	*Arenal (Costa Rica)*	1405-033	*1*	*8/7*
	1979	*Cont*	....	*Galeras (Colombia)*	1501-08=	*1?*	
	1979	*Cont*	....	*Sangay (Ecuador)*	1502-09=	*2*	
	1979	*Cont*	....	*Chillán, Nevados de (Chile-C)*	1507-07=	*2*	*5/-*
	1979	*Cont*	....	*Erebus (Antarctica)*	1900-02=	*1*	
	1979 e	....	?	**Epi** (Vanuatu-SW Pacific)	0507-06=	0	
	1979	....	?	**Peuet Sague** (Sumatra)	0601-03=	2	
	1979	0112?	209*a*?	**Karkar** (New Guinea-NE of)	0501-03=	2	-/7
	1979	0126e	23*e*?	**Ambrym** (Vanuatu-SW Pacific)	0507-04=	2	
	1979	0129	36*a*>	**Azul, Cerro** (Galápagos)	1503-06=	2?	
S	**1979**	02 ?	64*m*?	**Monowai Seamount** (Kermadec Is)	0402-05-		
	1979	02	?	**Shishaldin** (Aleutian Is)	1101-36-	2	
?	*1979*	*0208*	*1*	*Westdahl (Aleutian Is)*	1101-34-	*3?*	
	1979	0211	?	**Bezymianny** (Kamchatka)	1000-25=	3	5/7
	1979	0216r	?	**Kirishima** (Kyushu-Japan)	0802-09=	1	
	1979	0220	<1	**Dieng Volc Complex** (Java)	0603-20=	1	-/5
	1979	0224d	....	**Lopevi** (Vanuatu-SW Pacific)	0507-05=	2	
	1979	*0308*	....	*Karkar (New Guinea-NE of)*	0501-03=	*2?*	*-/7*
	1979	0308<	?	**Arenales** (Chile-S)	1508-059	1?	
	1979	0308<	?	**Lautaro** (Chile-S)	1508-06=	2?	
	1979	04	543*m*	**Chirinkotan** (Kuril Is)	0900-26=	2	
	1979	0413	196*e*	**Soufrière St. Vincent** (W Indies)	1600-15=	3	7/7
	1979	0414	36*a*	**Carrán-Los Venados** (Chile-C)	1507-14=	2	6/6
?	*1979*	*0426*	*382a*	*Fukujin (Volcano Is-Japan)*	0804-133	*0*	
	1979	0510<	72*a*>	**Metis Shoal** (Tonga-SW Pacific)	0403-07=	2	
	1979	0514	?	**Curacoa** (Tonga-SW Pacific)	0403-102	1	
	1979	0528	47*a*	**Fournaise, Piton de la** (Indian O.)	0303-02=	1	5/-
	1979	0531	<1	**Karangetang [Api Siau]** (Sangihe Is	0607-02=	1	
	1979	*0605d*	*276d*	*Aso (Kyushu-Japan)*	0802-11=	*1*	
	1979	0606	101*m*?	**Ambrym** (Vanuatu-SW Pacific)	0507-04=	2	
	1979	0613	....	**Aso** (Kyushu-Japan)	0802-11=	2	
	1979	0630	15*a*	**Ruapehu** (New Zealand)	0401-10=	1	
	1979	0702	72*a*	**Lopevi** (Vanuatu-SW Pacific)	0507-05=	2	
	1979	*0703*	*>3yr*	*Etna (Italy)*	0101-06=	*1*	
?	*1979*	*0712*	*?*	*Nikko (Volcano Is-Japan)*	0804-132	*0*	
?	*1979*	*0713*	*?*	*Bayonnaise Rocks (Izu Is-Japan)*	0804-07=	*0*	
	1979	0715e	111*m*	**Krakatau** (Indonesia)	0602-00=	2	4/-
	1979	*0716*	*413e*	*Etna (Italy)*	0101-06=	*2*	*6/-*
	1979	0803	....	**Etna** (Italy)	0101-06=	3?	6/-
	1979	*0823*	....	*Santa María (Guatemala)*	1402-03=	*2*	***9**/8*
?	*1979*	*09*	*?*	*Kuwae [Karua] (Vanuatu-SW Pac)*	0507-07=	*0*	
	1979	0908	129*m*	**Poás** (Costa Rica)	1405-04=	1	
	1979	0912	....	**Etna** (Italy)	0101-06=	2	
	1979	0918	?	**Bezymianny** (Kamchatka)	1000-25=	2	5/6
S	**1979**	0930	<1	**Macdonald** (Austral Is-C Pacific)	1303-06-	0	
	1979	1015	44*a*	**Llaima** (Chile-C)	1507-11=	2	
	1979	1028	179*a*	**On-take** (Honshu-Japan)	0803-04=	1	
	1979	1113	62*a*>	**Negra, Sierra** (Galápagos)	1503-05=	3	8/-
?	*1979*	*1115*	*?*	*Ahyi (Mariana Is-C Pacific)*	0804-141	*0*	
	1979	1116	<1	**Kilauea** (Hawaiian Is)	1302-01-	0	5/-
	1979	*1227*	*275a*	*Bulusan (Luzon-Philippines)*	0703-01=	*2*	
	1980	*Cont*	....	*Stromboli (Italy)*	0101-04=	*1*	*7/-*
	1980	*Cont*	....	*Erta Ale (Ethiopia)*	0201-08=	*0*	
	1980	*Cont*	....	*White Island (New Zealand)*	0401-04=	*2*	*-/7*
	1980	*Cont*	....	*Manam (New Guinea-NE of)*	0501-02=	*2*	*7/7*
	1980	*Cont*	....	*Bagana (Bougainville-SW Pacific)*	0505-02=	*1*	*6/-*
	1980	*Cont*	....	*Yasur (Vanuatu-SW Pacific)*	0507-10=	*2*	
	1980	*Cont*	....	*Merapi (Java)*	0603-25=	*1*	*7/7*
	1980	*Cont*	....	*Semeru (Java)*	0603-30=	*2*	
	1980	*Cont*	....	*Lokon-Empung (Sulawesi-Indonesia)*	0606-10=	*1*	*4/-*
	1980	*Cont*	....	*Dukono (Halmahera-Indonesia)*	0608-01=	*2*	
	1980	*Cont*	....	*Suwanose-jima (Ryukyu Is)*	0802-03=	*2*	
	1980	*Cont*	....	*Sakura-jima (Kyushu-Japan)*	0802-08=	*2*	
	1980	*Cont*	....	*On-take (Honshu-Japan)*	0803-04=	*1*	
?	*1980*	*Cont*	....	*Fukutoku-Okanoba (Volcano Is-Japan.*	0804-13=	*0*	
?	*1980*	*Cont*	....	*Fukujin (Volcano Is-Japan)*	0804-133	*0*	
	1980	*Cont*	....	*Usu (Hokkaido-Japan)*	0805-03=	*0*	*-/8*
	1980	*Cont*	....	*Chirinkotan (Kuril Is)*	0900-26=	*2*	
	1980	*Cont*	....	*Karymsky (Kamchatka)*	1000-13=	*2*	*7/7*
	1980	*Cont*	....	*Colima (México)*	1401-04=	*1*	*5/-*
	1980	*Cont*	....	*Pacaya (Guatemala)*	1402-11=	*1*	
	1980	*Cont*	....	*Masaya (Nicaragua)*	1404-10=	*0*	
	1980	*Cont*	....	*Arenal (Costa Rica)*	1405-033	*1*	*8/7*
	1980	*Cont*	....	*Galeras (Colombia)*	1501-08=	*1?*	
	1980	*Cont*	....	*Sangay (Ecuador)*	1502-09=	*2*	
	1980	*Cont*	....	*Negra, Sierra (Galápagos)*	1503-05=	*0*	*8/-*
	1980	*Cont*	....	*Chillán, Nevados de (Chile-C)*	1507-07=	*2*	*5/-*
	1980	*Cont*	....	*Erebus (Antarctica)*	1900-02=	*1*	
	1980	....	....	**Langila** (New Britain-SW Pac)	0502-01=	3	7/-
	1980	....	?	**Gaua** (Vanuatu-SW Pacific)	0507-02=	1?	
S	**1980**	01	16*m*	**Monowai Seamount** (Kermadec Is)	0402-05-	0	
	1980	01	....	**Kliuchevskoi** (Kamchatka)	1000-26=	3	5/7
?	*1980*	*0107*	*10a?*	*Karkar (New Guinea-NE of)*	0501-03=	*1*	
	1980	0110	1*a*	**Tupungatito** (Chile-C)	1507-01=	2	
	1980	0115?	72*a*?	**Ruapehu** (New Zealand)	0401-10=	1	
	1980	*0122*	....	*Santa María (Guatemala)*	1402-03=	*2*	***9**/8*
	1980	0130	25	**Nyamuragira** (Africa-C)	0203-02=	3	7/7
	1980	0207	....	**Bulusan** (Luzon-Philippines)	0703-01=	3	
S	**1980**	0212	<1	**Macdonald** (Austral Is-C Pacific)	1303-06-	0	
	1980	0311	<1	**Kilauea** (Hawaiian Is)	1302-01-	0	0/-
	1980	0313	<1	**Ioto [Iwo-jima]** (Volcano Is-Japan)	0804-12=	1	
	1980	0315e	276*e*	**Krakatau** (Indonesia)	0602-00=	2	5/-
	1980	0316	221	**Krafla** (Iceland-NE)	1703-08=	0	7/-
	1980	0324	173*a*	**Karangetang [Api Siau]** (Sangihe Is	0607-02=	1	
	1980	*0327*	*>3yr*	*St. Helens (US-Washington)*	1201-05-	*2*	
	1980	0329	?	**Marapi** (Sumatra)	0601-14=	1	
	1980	0415	127*a*	**Lopevi** (Vanuatu-SW Pacific)	0507-05=	3	
	1980	0418	1*a*	**Bezymianny** (Kamchatka)	1000-25=	3	5/7
	1980	0501s	?	**Makushin** (Aleutian Is)	1101-31-	1	
	1980	*0516*	*94a*	*Ambrym (Vanuatu-SW Pacific)*	0507-04=	*2*	
	1980	0518	....	**St. Helens** (US-Washington)	1201-05-	**5**	7/**9**
	1980	0524	?	**Ekarma** (Kuril Is)	0900-27=	1	
	1980	*0525*	....	*St. Helens (US-Washington)*	1201-05-	*3*	*-/7*
	1980	0605a	107*b*	**Tengger Caldera [Bromo]** (Java)	0603-31=	2	
	1980	*0612*	....	*St. Helens (US-Washington)*	1201-05-	*3*	*6/7*
	1980	*0615e*	*383e*	*Gorely (Kamchatka)*	1000-07=	*2*	*-/7*
?	*1980*	*0615z*	*?*	*Seal Nunataks Group (Antarctica)*	1900-05=		
	1980	0620	96*a*>	**Villarrica** (Chile-C)	1507-12=	2	
	1980	0703<	5*a*?	**Akutan** (Aleutian Is)	1101-32-	2	
	1980	0706a	?	**Pavlof** (Alaska Peninsula)	1102-03-	1	
?	*1980*	*0707*	*360y?*	*Nishino-shima (Volcano Is-Japan)*	0804-096	*0*	
	1980	*0708*	*80a*	*Etna (Italy)*	0101-06=	*2*	*6/-*
	1980	*0710*	....	*Krafla (Iceland-NE)*	1703-08=	*0*	*7/-*
	1980	*0722*	....	*St. Helens (US-Washington)*	1201-05-	*3*	*-/7*
	1980	0723	....	**Ambrym** (Vanuatu-SW Pacific)	0507-04=	3	
	1980	0731	....	**Gorely** (Kamchatka)	1000-07=	3	-/7
	1980	0807	41*a*	**Gareloi** (Aleutian Is)	1101-07-	3?	
	1980	*0807*	....	*St. Helens (US-Washington)*	1201-05-	*3*	*6/6*
	1980	0808	?	**Kanlaon** (Philippines-C)	0702-02=	2	
	1980	0817	3*a*	**Hekla** (Iceland-S)	1702-07=	3	8/7
?	*1980*	*0820*	*?*	*Kuwae [Karua] (Vanuatu-SW Pac)*	0507-07=	*0*	
	1980	0821	5*d*	**Bezymianny** (Kamchatka)	1000-25=	2	5/-
	1980	0823	465*p*	**Shiveluch** (Kamchatka)	1000-27=	1	7/-
	1980	09 ?	?	**Marion Island** (Indian O.-S)	0304-07-	1	6/-
	1980	0901	....	**Etna** (Italy)	0101-06=	3	6/-
	1980	0904	19*a*	**Gamalama** (Halmahera-Indonesia)	0608-06=	2	-/6
	1980	0912	<1	**Poás** (Costa Rica)	1405-04=	1	
	1980	0924	<1	**Aso** (Kyushu-Japan)	0802-11=	1	
	1980	0928	<1	**Kuchinoerabu-jima** (Ryukyu Is)	0802-05=	2	-/6
	1980	10	<1	**Callaqui** (Chile-C)	1507-091	1	
	1980	1006	<1	**Ulawun** (New Britain-SW Pac)	0502-12=	3	-/7
	1980	1007	141*a*	**Kavachi** (Solomon Is-SW Pacific)	0505-06=	1	
	1980	*1016*	....	*St. Helens (US-Washington)*	1201-05-	*3*	*6/6*
	1980	1018	15*a*	**Ruapehu** (New Zealand)	0401-10=	1	
	1980	*1018*	....	*Krafla (Iceland-NE)*	1703-08=	*0*	*7/-*
	1980	1105	314*m*	**Paluweh** (Lesser Sunda Is)	0604-15=	2	6/-
	1980	*1108*	*4*	*Pavlof (Alaska Peninsula)*	1102-03-	*1*	*-/6*
S	**1980**	1110	97	**Macdonald** (Austral Is-C Pacific)	1303-06-	0	
	1980	1111	....	**Pavlof** (Alaska Peninsula)	1102-03-	3	-/6
?	*1980*	*1115*	*38a>*	*Bayonnaise Rocks (Izu Is-Japan)*	0804-07=	*0*	
	1980	1226	<1	**Poás** (Costa Rica)	1405-04=	1	
	1981	*Cont*	....	*Stromboli (Italy)*	0101-04=	*1*	*7/-*
	1981	*Cont*	....	*Erta Ale (Ethiopia)*	0201-08=	*0*	
	1981	*Cont*	....	*White Island (New Zealand)*	0401-04=	*2*	*-/7*
	1981	*Cont*	....	*Manam (New Guinea-NE of)*	0501-02=	*2*	*7/7*
	1981	*Cont*	....	*Langila (New Britain-SW Pac)*	0502-01=	*2*	*7/-*

START YEAR	M-Dy	Dura-tion	VOLCANO NAME (Subregion)	NUMBER	VEI	Vol L/T
1981	Cont	....	*Bagana (Bougainville-SW Pacific)*	0505-02=	1	6/-
1981	Cont	....	*Yasur (Vanuatu-SW Pacific)*	0507-10=	2	
1981	Cont	....	*Merapi (Java)*	0603-25=	1	7/7
1981	Cont	....	*Semeru (Java)*	0603-30=	2	
1981	Cont	....	*Paluweh (Lesser Sunda Is)*	0604-15=	2	6/-
1981	Cont	....	*Dukono (Halmahera-Indonesia)*	0608-01=	2	
1981	Cont	....	*Suwanose-jima (Ryukyu Is)*	0802-03=	2	
1981	Cont	....	*Sakura-jima (Kyushu-Japan)*	0802-08=	2	
? 1981	Cont	....	*Nishino-shima (Volcano Is-Japan)*	0804-096	0	
? 1981	Cont	....	*Fukutoku-Okanoba (Volcano Is-Japan.*	0804-13=	0	
1981	Cont	....	*Usu (Hokkaido-Japan)*	0805-03=	0	-/8
1981	Cont	....	*Gorely (Kamchatka)*	1000-07=	2	-/7
1981	Cont	....	*Karymsky (Kamchatka)*	1000-13=	2	7/7
1981	Cont	....	*Shiveluch (Kamchatka)*	1000-27=	1	7/-
1981	Cont	....	*St. Helens (US-Washington)*	1201-05-	1	
S 1981	Cont	....	*Macdonald (Austral Is-C Pacific)*	1303-06-	0	
1981	Cont	....	*Colima (México)*	1401-04=	1	5/-
1981	Cont	....	*Pacaya (Guatemala)*	1402-11=	1	
1981	Cont	....	*Arenal (Costa Rica)*	1405-033	1	8/7
1981	Cont	....	*Galeras (Colombia)*	1501-08=	1?	
1981	Cont	....	*Sangay (Ecuador)*	1502-09=	2	
1981	Cont	....	*Chillán, Nevados de (Chile-C)*	1507-07=	2	5/-
1981	Cont	....	*Erebus (Antarctica)*	1900-02=	1	
1981	....	?	**Dieng Volc Complex** (Java)	0603-20=	1?	
? 1981	0107	1a	*Fukujin (Volcano Is-Japan)*	0804-133	0	
1981	0125	187a?	**Kliuchevskoi** (Kamchatka)	1000-26=	1	
1981	0126e	41j	**Etna** (Italy)	0101-06=	2	6/-
1981	0130	4	**Krafla** (Iceland-NE)	1703-08=	0	7/-
1981	02	....	*Santa María (Guatemala)*	1402-03=	2	**9**/8
1981	02 ?	?	**Telica** (Nicaragua)	1404-04=	1	
1981	0203	91a	**Fournaise, Piton de la** (Indian O.)	0303-02=	2	7/-
1981	0220	222a	**Ambrym** (Vanuatu-SW Pacific)	0507-04=	2	
1981	0227<	?	**Shikotsu [Tarumai]** (Hokkaido)	0805-04=	0	-/2
1981	03	61p	**Poás** (Costa Rica)	1405-04=	1	
1981	0304	143a	**Gamkonora** (Halmahera-Indonesia)	0608-04=	1	-/5
? 1981	0305	286m	*Mehetia (Society Is-C Pacific)*	1303-04-	0	
1981	0317	6	**Etna** (Italy)	0101-06=	2	7/6
1981	0324	<1	**Okmok** (Aleutian Is)	1101-29-	3?	
1981	0330<	59a	**Pavlof** (Alaska Peninsula)	1102-03-	1	
1981	0409	18a	**Bulusan** (Luzon-Philippines)	0703-01=	3	
1981	0409	7	**Hekla** (Iceland-S)	1702-07=	2	7/-
1981	0424	178	**Krakatau** (Indonesia)	0602-00=	1	
1981	0427	39a	*Alaid (Kuril Is)*	0900-39=	3	-/8
1981	0430	....	**Alaid** (Kuril Is)	0900-39=	4	-/8
1981	05	16m	**Okataina** (New Zealand)	0401-05=	1	
1981	0515	>3yr	**Pagan** (Mariana Is-C Pacific)	0804-17=	4	7/8
1981	0610	15a	**Tiatia** (Kuril Is)	0900-03=	2?	
1981	0612	724a	**Bezymianny** (Kamchatka)	1000-25=	3	6/7
1981	0615	<1	**Aso** (Kyushu-Japan)	0802-11=	1	
1981	0709	<1	**Gaua** (Vanuatu-SW Pacific)	0507-02=	1?	
1981	0801x	?	**Fernandina** (Galápagos)	1503-01=	0	
1981	0831e	442n?	**Guagua Pichincha** (Ecuador)	1502-02=	1	-/4
? 1981	0915e	?	*Kavachi (Solomon Is-SW Pacific)*	0505-06=	0	
? 1981	0925	?	*Shishaldin (Aleutian Is)*	1101-36-		
1981	0925	2a	**Pavlof** (Alaska Peninsula)	1102-03-	3	6/7
1981	1025?	171m	**Ruapehu** (New Zealand)	0401-10=	1	
1981	1118	5	**Krafla** (Iceland-NE)	1703-08=	0	7/-
1981	1125	?	**Alaid** (Kuril Is)	0900-39=	2	
1981	1125e	97e	*Telica (Nicaragua)*	1404-04=	1	
1981	1126	<1	**Etna** (Italy)	0101-06=	2	
1981	1216	....	*Masaya (Nicaragua)*	1404-10=	1	
? 1981	1221	?	*Kliuchevskoi (Kamchatka)*	1000-26=		
1981	1225	20a	**Nyamuragira** (Africa-C)	0203-02=	3	7/7
1982	Cont	....	*Stromboli (Italy)*	0101-04=	1	7/-
1982	Cont	....	*Etna (Italy)*	0101-06=	1	
1982	Cont	....	*Erta Ale (Ethiopia)*	0201-08=	0	
1982	Cont	....	*Nyamuragira (Africa-C)*	0203-02=	3	7/7
1982	Cont	....	*White Island (New Zealand)*	0401-04=	2	-/7
1982	Cont	....	*Ruapehu (New Zealand)*	0401-10=	1	
1982	Cont	....	*Bagana (Bougainville-SW Pacific)*	0505-02=	1	6/-
1982	Cont	....	*Yasur (Vanuatu-SW Pacific)*	0507-10=	2	
1982	Cont	....	*Merapi (Java)*	0603-25=	1	7/7
1982	Cont	....	*Semeru (Java)*	0603-30=	2	
1982	Cont	....	*Dukono (Halmahera-Indonesia)*	0608-01=	2	
1982	Cont	....	*Suwanose-jima (Ryukyu Is)*	0802-03=	2	
1982	Cont	....	*Sakura-jima (Kyushu-Japan)*	0802-08=	2	
? 1982	Cont	....	*Fukutoku-Okanoba (Volcano Is-Japan.*	0804-13=	0	
1982	Cont	....	*Usu (Hokkaido-Japan)*	0805-03=	0	-/8
1982	Cont	....	*Karymsky (Kamchatka)*	1000-13=	2	7/7
1982	Cont	....	*Colima (México)*	1401-04=	1	5/-
1982	Cont	....	*Santa María (Guatemala)*	1402-03=	1	**9**/8
1982	Cont	....	*Pacaya (Guatemala)*	1402-11=	1	
1982	Cont	....	*Arenal (Costa Rica)*	1405-033	1	8/7
1982	Cont	....	*Galeras (Colombia)*	1501-08=	1?	
1982	Cont	....	*Sangay (Ecuador)*	1502-09=	2	
1982	Cont	....	*Chillán, Nevados de (Chile-C)*	1507-07=	2	5/-
1982	Cont	....	*Erebus (Antarctica)*	1900-02=	1	
1982	....	?	**Karangetang [Api Siau]** (Sangihe Is	0607-02=	1	
1982 <	....	?	**Cleft Segment** (Pacific-NE)	1301-03-	0	7/-
? 1982	0112	64a	*Fukujin (Volcano Is-Japan)*	0804-133	0	
1982	0115	<1	**Gareloi** (Aleutian Is)	1101-07-	3	
1982	0115e	30j	**Concepción** (Nicaragua)	1404-12=	2	
? 1982	0210	4a	*Tiatia (Kuril Is)*	0900-03=	1	
1982	0212	....	**Telica** (Nicaragua)	1404-04=	2	
1982	0213	....	*Langila (New Britain-SW Pac)*	0502-01=	3	7/-
S **1982**	0301	84	**Macdonald** (Austral Is-C Pacific)	1303-06-	0	
1982	0309	1	**Ioto [Iwo-jima]** (Volcano Is-Japan)	0804-12=	1	
1982	0310<	66m>	**Marapi** (Sumatra)	0601-14=	1	
S **1982**	0316	64a	**Teahitia** (Society Is-C Pacific)	1303-01-	0	
1982	0319	....	*St. Helens (US-Washington)*	1201-05-	3	6/-
1982	0324	39a	**Kliuchevskoi** (Kamchatka)	1000-26=	1	
1982	0327	....	*Manam (New Guinea-NE of)*	0501-02=	3	7/7
1982	0328	167a	*Chichón, El (México)*	1401-12=	4+	-/**9**
1982	0329	<1	**Alaid** (Kuril Is)	0900-39=	2	
? 1982	04	15m	*Nishino-shima (Volcano Is-Japan)*	0804-096	0	
1982	0403	....	**Chichón, El** (México)	1401-12=	**5**	**-/9**
1982	0405	278a	*Galunggung (Java)*	0603-14=	3	-/8
? 1982	0406	?	*Esmeralda Bank (Mariana Is-C Pacific)*	0804-21=	0	
1982	0407	56b	**Kavachi** (Solomon Is-SW Pacific)	0505-06=	2	
1982	0418	<1	**Gaua** (Vanuatu-SW Pacific)	0507-02=	2	
1982	0426	<1	**Asama** (Honshu-Japan)	0803-11=	2	
1982	0430	<1	**Kilauea** (Hawaiian Is)	1302-01-	0	5/-
S **1982**	05	16m	**Monowai Seamount** (Kermadec Is)	0402-05-	0	
1982	0517	....	**Galunggung** (Java)	0603-14=	4	-/8
1982	0528k	....	*Guagua Pichincha (Ecuador)*	1502-02=	1	-/4
? 1982	06	15m	*Kita-Iwo-jima (Volcano Is-Japan)*	0804-11=	0	
1982	0610	....	*Bezymianny (Kamchatka)*	1000-25=	2	6/7
1982	0621	118m	**Nyiragongo** (Africa-C)	0203-03=	1	7/-
? 1982	0715q	?	*Pavlof (Alaska Peninsula)*	1102-03-	1?	
1982	0718	2a	**Raung** (Java)	0603-34=	3	
? 1982	0810	?	*Bayonnaise Rocks (Izu Is-Japan)*	0804-07=	0	
1982	0826	76a	**Soputan** (Sulawesi-Indonesia)	0606-03=	3	-/6
1982	0828	9a?	**Wolf** (Galápagos)	1503-02=	1	
1982	0925	<1	**Kilauea** (Hawaiian Is)	1302-01-	0	6/-
1982	0930j	....	*Pagan (Mariana Is-C Pacific)*	0804-17=	3?	7/8
1982	1002	<1	**Asama** (Honshu-Japan)	0803-11=	1	
1982	1005d	221n	**Akutan** (Aleutian Is)	1101-32-	2	
1982	1007	263a	**Kliuchevskoi** (Kamchatka)	1000-26=	2	7/-
1982	1007	....	*Masaya (Nicaragua)*	1404-10=	1	
1982	1016	27a	**Cameroon** (Africa-W)	0204-01=	2	7/5
1982	1024	1a	**Lopevi** (Vanuatu-SW Pacific)	0507-05=	2	
1982	1026	64	**Kusatsu-Shirane** (Honshu-Japan)	0803-12=	1	-/4
1982	1117	<1	**Iliboleng** (Lesser Sunda Is)	0604-22=	2	
1982	1122	?	**Chirpoi** (Kuril Is)	0900-15=	2	
1982	1128	18m?	**Ioto [Iwo-jima]** (Volcano Is-Japan)	0804-12=	1	
1982	12	15m	**Marapi** (Sumatra)	0601-14=	1	
? 1982	1215	?	*Fukujin (Volcano Is-Japan)*	0804-133	0	
1983	Cont	....	*Stromboli (Italy)*	0101-04=	1	7/-
1983	Cont	....	*Erta Ale (Ethiopia)*	0201-08=	0	
1983	Cont	....	*Manam (New Guinea-NE of)*	0501-02=	2	7/7
1983	Cont	....	*Bagana (Bougainville-SW Pacific)*	0505-02=	1	6/-
1983	Cont	....	*Yasur (Vanuatu-SW Pacific)*	0507-10=	2	
1983	Cont	....	*Galunggung (Java)*	0603-14=	1	-/8
1983	Cont	....	*Merapi (Java)*	0603-25=	1	7/7
1983	Cont	....	*Semeru (Java)*	0603-30=	2	
1983	Cont	....	*Dukono (Halmahera-Indonesia)*	0608-01=	2	
1983	Cont	....	*Suwanose-jima (Ryukyu Is)*	0802-03=	2	
1983	Cont	....	*Sakura-jima (Kyushu-Japan)*	0802-08=	2	
? 1983	Cont	....	*Fukutoku-Okanoba (Volcano Is-Japan.*	0804-13=	0	
1983	Cont	....	*Pagan (Mariana Is-C Pacific)*	0804-17=	2	7/8
1983	Cont	....	*Akutan (Aleutian Is)*	1101-32-	2	
1983	Cont	....	*Pacaya (Guatemala)*	1402-11=	1	
1983	Cont	....	*Masaya (Nicaragua)*	1404-10=	0	
1983	Cont	....	*Arenal (Costa Rica)*	1405-033	1	8/7
1983	Cont	....	*Galeras (Colombia)*	1501-08=	1?	
1983	Cont	....	*Sangay (Ecuador)*	1502-09=	2	
1983	Cont	....	*Chillán, Nevados de (Chile-C)*	1507-07=	2	5/-
1983	Cont	....	*Erebus (Antarctica)*	1900-02=	1	
1983	....	?	**Ambrym** (Vanuatu-SW Pacific)	0507-04=	2	
1983	....	?	**Marapi** (Sumatra)	0601-14=	1	
? 1983	....	365y	*Nishino-shima (Volcano Is-Japan)*	0804-096	0	
1983	0101	>3yr	**Lengai, Ol Doinyo** (Africa-E)	0202-12=	2	7/-
1983	0103	>3yr	*Kilauea (Hawaiian Is)*	1302-01-	0	**9**/-
1983	0129	....	*Santa María (Guatemala)*	1402-03=	2	**9**/8
1983	0202	....	*St. Helens (US-Washington)*	1201-05-	2	7/-
1983	0206	15a	**Rincón de la Vieja** (Costa Rica)	1405-02=	1	
? 1983	0211	4a	*Colima (México)*	1401-04=	1?	
1983	0308	....	*Kliuchevskoi (Kamchatka)*	1000-26=	1	7/-
S **1983**	0314	68a	**Macdonald** (Austral Is-C Pacific)	1303-06-	0	
1983	0316	9a	**Concepción** (Nicaragua)	1404-12=	2	
1983	0328	131a	**Etna** (Italy)	0101-06=	1	7/5
1983	0408	<1	**Asama** (Honshu-Japan)	0803-11=	2	
1983	0414?	<1	**Niigata-Yake-yama** (Honshu-Japan)	0803-09=	1	
? 1983	0415e	74f	*Tengger Caldera [Bromo] (Java)*	0603-31=	1	

Steam rises from the intracaldera cinder cone at Veniaminof volcano in the Alaska Peninsula in the waning stages of the 1983 to 1984 eruption. Cooling lava flows fill a pit about 2.3 x 1.0 km wide that has been melted in the ice cap filling the broad summit caldera, whose rim is visible in the background.

Betsy Yount (USGS/AVO)

START YEAR	M-Dy	Duration	VOLCANO NAME (Subregion)	NUMBER	VEI	Vol L/T
1983	*0418*	....	*Langila (New Britain-SW Pac)*	0502-01=	*3*	*7/-*
1983	*05*	*>3yr*	*Karangetang [Api Siau] (Sangihe Is*	0607-02=	*1*	*4/-*
1983	*0511*	*337a*	*Iliboleng (Lesser Sunda Is)*	0604-22=	*1*	
? *1983*	*0512*	*?*	*Bayonnaise Rocks (Izu Is-Japan)*	0804-07=	*0*	
1983	*0517*	....	*Langila (New Britain-SW Pac)*	0502-01=	*3*	*7/-*
1983	*0522*	....	*Bezymianny (Kamchatka)*	1000-25=	*3*	*6/7*
1983	0528	4	**Grímsvötn** (Iceland-NE)	1703-01=	2	
1983	0602	319*a*	**Veniaminof** (Alaska Peninsula)	1102-07-	3	7/-
? *1983*	*0615*	*1a*	*Unnamed (New Britain-SW Pac)*	0502-001		
1983	0625	4	**Bulusan** (Luzon-Philippines)	0703-01=	2	
1983	07	92*p*	**Aso** (Kyushu-Japan)	0802-11=	1	
? *1983*	*07*	*16m*	*Kita-Iwo-jima (Volcano Is-Japan)*	0804-11=	*0*	
1983	0708	<1	**Okmok** (Aleutian Is)	1101-29-	2	
1983	0711	7*a*	**Pavlof** (Alaska Peninsula)	1102-03-	2?	
S **1983**	0712	14*a*	**Teahitia** (Society Is-C Pacific)	1303-01-	0	
1983	*0718*	*150m*	*Colo [Una Una] (Sulawesi-Indonesia)*	0606-01=	*2*	
1983	0723	....	**Colo [Una Una]** (Sulawesi-Indonesia)	0606-01=	4	
1983	0726	147	**Kusatsu-Shirane** (Honshu-Japan)	0803-12=	1	
1983	0809	2	**Gamalama** (Halmahera-Indonesia)	0608-06=	3	
1983	0817	<1	**Iliwerung** (Lesser Sunda Is)	0604-25=	1	
1983	0914	?	**Tangkubanparahu** (Java)	0603-09=	1	
1983	1003	<1	**Miyake-jima** (Izu Is-Japan)	0804-04=	3	6/7
1983	1014	2*a*	**Villarrica** (Chile-C)	1507-12=	1	
S **1983**	1027	68*a*	**Macdonald** (Austral Is-C Pacific)	1303-06-	0	
1983	1106	128*a*	**Ulawun** (New Britain-SW Pac)	0502-12=	1	
1983	*1111*	*37a*	*Pavlof (Alaska Peninsula)*	1102-03-	*2*	*-/7*
1983	1114	....	**Pavlof** (Alaska Peninsula)	1102-03-	3	-/7
1983	1204	76*a*	**Fournaise, Piton de la** (Indian O.)	0303-02=	2	7/-
S **1983**	1218	208*a*	**Teahitia** (Society Is-C Pacific)	1303-01-	0	
1983	1221	<1	**Tengger Caldera [Bromo]** (Java)	0603-31=	1	
1983	1226e	48*e*	**White Island** (New Zealand)	0401-04=	2	
1984	*Cont*	....	*Stromboli (Italy)*	0101-04=	*1*	*7/-*
1984	*Cont*	....	*Erta Ale (Ethiopia)*	0201-08=	*0*	
1984	*Cont*	....	*Lengai, Ol Doinyo (Africa-E)*	0202-12=	*1*	*7/-*
1984	*Cont*	....	*Fournaise, Piton de la (Indian O.)*	0303-02=	*2*	*7/-*
1984	*Cont*	....	*White Island (New Zealand)*	0401-04=	*2*	
1984	*Cont*	....	*Bagana (Bougainville-SW Pacific)*	0505-02=	*1*	*6/-*
1984	*Cont*	....	*Yasur (Vanuatu-SW Pacific)*	0507-10=	*2*	
1984	*Cont*	....	*Semeru (Java)*	0603-30=	*2*	
1984	*Cont*	....	*Dukono (Halmahera-Indonesia)*	0608-01=	*2*	
1984	*Cont*	....	*Sakura-jima (Kyushu-Japan)*	0802-08=	*2*	
? *1984*	*Cont*	....	*Nishino-shima (Volcano Is-Japan)*	0804-096	*0*	
? *1984*	*Cont*	....	*Fukutoku-Okanoba (Volcano Is-Japan.*	0804-13=	*0*	
1984	*Cont*	....	*Pagan (Mariana Is-C Pacific)*	0804-17=	*2*	*7/8*
1984	*Cont*	....	*St. Helens (US-Washington)*	1201-05-	*1*	
S *1984*	*Cont*	....	*Teahitia (Society Is-C Pacific)*	1303-01-	*0*	
S *1984*	*Cont*	....	*Macdonald (Austral Is-C Pacific)*	1303-06-	*0*	
1984	*Cont*	....	*Santa María (Guatemala)*	1402-03=	*1*	***9**/8*
1984	*Cont*	....	*Sangay (Ecuador)*	1502-09=	*2*	
1984	*Cont*	....	*Chillán, Nevados de (Chile-C)*	1507-07=	*2*	*5/-*
1984	....	616*w*>	**Ambrym** (Vanuatu-SW Pacific)	0507-04=	2	
1984	0103	....	**Iliboleng** (Lesser Sunda Is)	0604-22=	2	
1984	*0107*	....	*Langila (New Britain-SW Pac)*	0502-01=	*3*	*7/-*
1984	0109	22*a*?	**Galunggung** (Java)	0603-14=	1	
1984	*02*	....	*Manam (New Guinea-NE of)*	0501-02=	*3*	*7/7*
1984	*0205*	*313m*	*Bezymianny (Kamchatka)*	1000-25=	*2*	*-/7*
1984	0223	20*a*	**Nyamuragira** (Africa-C)	0203-02=	2	7/7
1984	0301	4*a*	**Home Reef** (Tonga-SW Pacific)	0403-08=	3?	
1984	0308	18*a*?	**Kaitoku Seamount** (Volcano Is-Japan)	0804-10=	0	
1984	*0310*	*324a*	*Kliuchevskoi (Kamchatka)*	1000-26=	*1*	
1984	0317	173*a*	**Shiveluch** (Kamchatka)	1000-27=	2?	
1984	0325	21*a*	**Mauna Loa** (Hawaiian Is)	1302-02=	0	8/-
1984	0330	?	**Fernandina** (Galápagos)	1503-01=	1	
1984	0331	16*m*	**Rincón de la Vieja** (Costa Rica)	1405-02=	2	
1984	0402	?	**Ruapehu** (New Zealand)	0401-10=	1	
1984	*0405d*	....	*Masaya (Nicaragua)*	1404-10=	*1*	
1984	0413c	437*d*	**Aso** (Kyushu-Japan)	0802-11=	1	
1984	0420	220*a*	**Llaima** (Chile-C)	1507-11=	2	
1984	0428	174	**Etna** (Italy)	0101-06=	1	7/5
1984	0501	<1	**Akan** (Hokkaido-Japan)	0805-07=	1	
1984	0509	12*a*	**Paluweh** (Lesser Sunda Is)	0604-15=	2	
1984	0512	19*a*	**Tengger Caldera [Bromo]** (Java)	0603-31=	1	
1984	*0515*	....	*Pacaya (Guatemala)*	1402-11=	*2*	
1984	0524	99	**Soputan** (Sulawesi-Indonesia)	0606-03=	3	-/7
1984	0603<	375*a*>	**Tinakula** (Santa Cruz Is-SW Pacific)	0506-01=	2	
1984	*0603c*	....	*Arenal (Costa Rica)*	1405-033	*2*	*8/7*
? *1984*	*0605d*	*163n*	*Lokon-Empung (Sulawesi-Indonesia)*	0606-10=	*1*	
1984	*0615*	....	*Merapi (Java)*	0603-25=	*2*	*7/7*
1984	0712	<1	**Cleveland** (Aleutian Is)	1101-24-	1	
1984	*0720*	*796*	*Etna (Italy)*	0101-06=	*2*	*5/6*
1984	0804	779*a*?	**Gorely** (Kamchatka)	1000-07=	2	
1984	0811	464*a*	**Villarrica** (Chile-C)	1507-12=	2	6/-
? *1984*	*0820<*	*?*	*Grímsvötn (Iceland-NE)*	1703-01=	*0*	
1984	0823	19*a*	**Ulawun** (New Britain-SW Pac)	0502-12=	1	
1984	*0831*	....	*Soputan (Sulawesi-Indonesia)*	0606-03=	*3*	*-/7*
1984	0904	14	**Krafla** (Iceland-NE)	1703-08=	0	8/-

START YEAR	M-Dy	Duration	VOLCANO NAME (Subregion)	NUMBER	VEI	Vol L/T
1984	0905	....	**Karangetang [Api Siau]** (Sangihe Is	0607-02=	3	4/-
1984	0909	27	**Mayon** (Luzon-Philippines)	0703-03=	3	7/7
1984	*0913*	....	*Mayon (Luzon-Philippines)*	0703-03=	*3?*	*7/7*
1984	*0913*	....	*Erebus (Antarctica)*	1900-02=	*2*	
1984	0919	....	**Kilauea** (Hawaiian Is)	1302-01-	1	**9**/-
1984	10	16*m*	**Suwanose-jima** (Ryukyu Is)	0802-03=	2	
1984	1013	....	**Bezymianny** (Kamchatka)	1000-25=	3	-/7
1984	1025?	51*m*?	**Ruapehu** (New Zealand)	0401-10=	1	
? *1984*	*1111*	*71a*	*Loihi (Hawaiian Is)*	1302-00-	*0*	
1984	1113	....	**Kliuchevskoi** (Kamchatka)	1000-26=	3	
1984	1115	<1	**Marapi** (Sumatra)	0601-14=	1	
1984	1129	7*a*?	**Veniaminof** (Alaska Peninsula)	1102-07-	2	
1984	*12*	*17m*	*Concepción (Nicaragua)*	1404-12=	*1*	
1984	12	212*p*	**Láscar** (Chile-N)	1505-10=	0	5/-
1984	1222	87*a*?	**Ruiz, Nevado del** (Colombia)	1501-02=	1	
? *1984*	*1223*	*<1*	*Kaitoku Seamount (Volcano Is-Japan)*	0804-10=	*0*	
1984	1230	28*a*	**Ulawun** (New Britain-SW Pac)	0502-12=	1	5/-
1985	*Cont*	....	*Erta Ale (Ethiopia)*	0201-08=	*0*	
1985	*Cont*	....	*Lengai, Ol Doinyo (Africa-E)*	0202-12=	*1*	*7/-*
1985	*Cont*	....	*Manam (New Guinea-NE of)*	0501-02=	*2*	*7/7*
1985	*Cont*	....	*Bagana (Bougainville-SW Pacific)*	0505-02=	*1*	*6/-*
1985	*Cont*	....	*Tinakula (Santa Cruz Is-SW Pacific)*	0506-01=	*2*	
1985	*Cont*	....	*Ambrym (Vanuatu-SW Pacific)*	0507-04=	*2*	
1985	*Cont*	....	*Yasur (Vanuatu-SW Pacific)*	0507-10=	*2*	
1985	*Cont*	....	*Merapi (Java)*	0603-25=	*1*	*7/7*
1985	*Cont*	....	*Semeru (Java)*	0603-30=	*2*	
1985	*Cont*	....	*Karangetang [Api Siau] (Sangihe Is*	0607-02=	*2*	*4/-*
1985	*Cont*	....	*Dukono (Halmahera-Indonesia)*	0608-01=	*2*	
1985	*Cont*	....	*Sakura-jima (Kyushu-Japan)*	0802-08=	*2*	
1985	*Cont*	....	*Aso (Kyushu-Japan)*	0802-11=	*1*	
? *1985*	*Cont*	....	*Fukutoku-Okanoba (Volcano Is-Japan.*	0804-13=	*0*	
1985	*Cont*	....	*Pagan (Mariana Is-C Pacific)*	0804-17=	*2*	*7/8*
1985	*Cont*	....	*Gorely (Kamchatka)*	1000-07=	*2*	
1985	*Cont*	....	*St. Helens (US-Washington)*	1201-05-	*1*	
? *1985*	*Cont*	....	*Loihi (Hawaiian Is)*	1302-00-	*0*	
1985	*Cont*	....	*Pacaya (Guatemala)*	1402-11=	*1*	
1985	*Cont*	....	*Sangay (Ecuador)*	1502-09=	*2*	
1985	*Cont*	....	*Láscar (Chile-N)*	1505-10=	*0*	*5/-*
1985	*Cont*	....	*Chillán, Nevados de (Chile-C)*	1507-07=	*2*	*5/-*
1985	*Cont*	....	*Villarrica (Chile-C)*	1507-12=	*2*	*6/-*
1985	*Cont*	....	*Erebus (Antarctica)*	1900-02=	*1*	
1985	....	188*w*	**Colima** (México)	1401-04=	1	
1985	....	....	*Arenal (Costa Rica)*	1405-033	*2*	*8/7*
1985	....	?	**Misti, El** (Perú)	1504-01=	1?	
? *1985*	....	*?*	*Hudson Mountains (Antarctica)*	1900-028		
1985	0102	....	**Concepción** (Nicaragua)	1404-12=	2	
1985	*0103*	....	*Kilauea (Hawaiian Is)*	1302-01-	*1*	***9**/-*
1985	*0106*	*3a*	*Jan Mayen (Atlantic-N-Jan Mayen)*	1706-01=	*2*	*6/6*
S **1985**	0110	15*a*	**Teahitia** (Society Is-C Pacific)	1303-01=	0	
1985	0114	732*m*?	**Heard** (Indian O.-S)	0304-01=	2?	
1985	*0124*	....	*Santa María (Guatemala)*	1402-03=	*2*	***9**/8*
1985	*0129*	....	*Langila (New Britain-SW Pac)*	0502-01=	*3*	*7/-*
1985	0203	<1	**Paluweh** (Lesser Sunda Is)	0604-15=	1	
1985	0308	127*a*	**Etna** (Italy)	0101-06=	1	7/4
1985	0313	<1	**Kanlaon** (Philippines-C)	0702-02=	1	
1985	0321	<1	**Niuafo'ou** (Tonga-SW Pacific)	0403-11=	0	-/2
1985	*04*	....	*Masaya (Nicaragua)*	1404-10=	*1*	
1985	05	31*p*	**Guagua Pichincha** (Ecuador)	1502-02=	1	
1985	0519	<1	**Soputan** (Sulawesi-Indonesia)	0606-03=	2	-/6
1985	0521<	19*a*>	**Ruapehu** (New Zealand)	0401-10=	1	
1985	0526	152*a*	**Shiveluch** (Kamchatka)	1000-27=	2	
1985	*0612*	*185a*	*Bezymianny (Kamchatka)*	1000-25=	*1*	*-/7*
1985	0614	>3yr	**Fournaise, Piton de la** (Indian O.)	0303-02=	1	8/-
1985	0619	3*a*	**Tokachi** (Hokkaido-Japan)	0805-05=	1	
1985	0629	....	**Bezymianny** (Kamchatka)	1000-25=	3	-/7
1985	0730	929*a*	**Sangeang Api** (Lesser Sunda Is)	0604-05=	3	7/-
1985	*0816*	*158a*	*Kliuchevskoi (Kamchatka)*	1000-26=	*2*	
1985	0823	189*a*	**Raung** (Java)	0603-34=	2	
1985	09	638*p*	**Suwanose-jima** (Ryukyu Is)	0802-03=	2	
1985	09	212*p*	**Rincón de la Vieja** (Costa Rica)	1405-02=	1	
? *1985*	*0902*	*?*	*Supply Reef (Mariana Is-C Pacific)*	0804-142	*0*	
? *1985*	*0902*	*?*	*San Cristóbal (Nicaragua)*	1404-02=		
1985	*0911*	*>3yr*	*Ruiz, Nevado del (Colombia)*	1501-02=	*2*	*-/7*
1985	1005	63*a*	**Kanlaon** (Philippines-C)	0702-02=	1	
1985	11	91*p*>	**San Miguel** (El Salvador)	1403-10=	1	
1985	1113	....	**Ruiz, Nevado del** (Colombia)	1501-02=	3	-/7
1985	1115	<1	**Ruapehu** (New Zealand)	0401-10=	1	
? *1985*	*1115*	*<1*	*Tangkubanparahu (Java)*	0603-09=	*1*	
1985	*1117*	*4*	*Ulawun (New Britain-SW Pac)*	0502-12=	*2*	*6/6*
1985	1120	....	**Ulawun** (New Britain-SW Pac)	0502-12=	3	6/6
? *1985*	*1201*	*?*	*Guallatiri (Chile-N)*	1505-02=		
? *1985*	*1202*	*<1*	*Nishino-shima (Volcano Is-Japan)*	0804-096	*0*	
1985	1202	....	**Kliuchevskoi** (Kamchatka)	1000-26=	3?	
1985	1202a	139*b*?	**Concepción** (Nicaragua)	1404-12=	1	
1985	*1206*	....	*Stromboli (Italy)*	0101-04=	*2*	*7/-*
1985	1209	81*c*	**Kavachi** (Solomon Is-SW Pacific)	0505-06=	1	
? *1985*	*1210*	*?*	*Cleveland (Aleutian Is)*	1101-24-	*1*	
1985	1219	13*a*	**Etna** (Italy)	0101-06=	1	5/4
1986	*Cont*	....	*Stromboli (Italy)*	0101-04=	*1*	*7/-*
1986	*Cont*	....	*Erta Ale (Ethiopia)*	0201-08=	*0*	
1986	*Cont*	....	*Lengai, Ol Doinyo (Africa-E)*	0202-12=	*1*	*7/-*
1986	*Cont*	....	*Fournaise, Piton de la (Indian O.)*	0303-02=	*1*	*8/-*
1986	*Cont*	....	*Heard (Indian O.-S)*	0304-01=	*1*	
1986	*Cont*	....	*Manam (New Guinea-NE of)*	0501-02=	*2*	*7/7*
1986	*Cont*	....	*Langila (New Britain-SW Pac)*	0502-01=	*2*	*7/-*
1986	*Cont*	....	*Bagana (Bougainville-SW Pacific)*	0505-02=	*1*	*6/-*
1986	*Cont*	....	*Yasur (Vanuatu-SW Pacific)*	0507-10=	*2*	
1986	*Cont*	....	*Semeru (Java)*	0603-30=	*2*	
1986	*Cont*	....	*Raung (Java)*	0603-34=	*2*	
1986	*Cont*	....	*Sangeang Api (Lesser Sunda Is)*	0604-05=	*3*	*7/-*
1986	*Cont*	....	*Karangetang [Api Siau] (Sangihe Is*	0607-02=	*2*	*4/-*
1986	*Cont*	....	*Dukono (Halmahera-Indonesia)*	0608-01=	*2*	
1986	*Cont*	....	*Suwanose-jima (Ryukyu Is)*	0802-03=	*2*	
1986	*Cont*	....	*Sakura-jima (Kyushu-Japan)*	0802-08=	*2*	
1986	*Cont*	....	*Gorely (Kamchatka)*	1000-07=	*2*	
1986	*Cont*	....	*Kilauea (Hawaiian Is)*	1302-01-	*0*	***9**/-*
1986	*Cont*	....	*Colima (México)*	1401-04=	*1*	
1986	*Cont*	....	*Santa María (Guatemala)*	1402-03=	*1*	***9**/8*
1986	*Cont*	....	*Pacaya (Guatemala)*	1402-11=	*1*	
1986	*Cont*	....	*San Miguel (El Salvador)*	1403-10=	*1*	
1986	*Cont*	....	*Concepción (Nicaragua)*	1404-12=	*1*	
1986	*Cont*	....	*Arenal (Costa Rica)*	1405-033	*1*	*8/7*
1986	*Cont*	....	*Ruiz, Nevado del (Colombia)*	1501-02=	*2*	*-/7*
1986	*Cont*	....	*Sangay (Ecuador)*	1502-09=	*2*	
1986	*Cont*	....	*Chillán, Nevados de (Chile-C)*	1507-07=	*2*	*5/-*
1986	*Cont*	....	*Erebus (Antarctica)*	1900-02=	*1*	
1986	....	?	**Peuet Sague** (Sumatra)	0601-03=	2	
? *1986*	....	*>3yr*	*Nishino-shima (Volcano Is-Japan)*	0804-096	*0*	
1986 e	....	?	**CoAxial Segment** (Pacific-NE)	1301-02-	0	7/-
1986	0118	69*a*?	**Fukutoku-Okanoba** (Volcano Is-Japan	0804-13=	2	
1986	0120	<1	**Tupungatito** (Chile-C)	1507-01=	1	
1986	02	121*p*	**Tacaná** (México)	1401-13=	1	
1986	*0201?*	*>3yr*	*White Island (New Zealand)*	0401-04=	*1*	
1986	0208	1*a*?	**Ruapehu** (New Zealand)	0401-10=	1	
1986	*03*	*230m?*	*Etna (Italy)*	0101-06=	*1*	
1986	0318	104*a*	**Akutan** (Aleutian Is)	1101-32-	2	
1986	0319	333*a*?	**Shishaldin** (Aleutian Is)	1101-36-	2	
1986	0322	417*a*	**Lokon-Empung** (Sulawesi-Indonesia)	0606-10=	2	
1986	*0326e*	*95e*	*Bezymianny (Kamchatka)*	1000-25=	*1*	*6/5*
1986	0327	157*a*	**Augustine** (Alaska-SW)	1103-01-	4?	-/8
1986	*0328*	*702a*	*Shiveluch (Kamchatka)*	1000-27=	*2*	
? *1986*	*0407*	*445a*	*Fukutoku-Okanoba (Volcano Is-Japan)*	0804-13=	*0*	
1986	*0416*	*850a*	*Pavlof (Alaska Peninsula)*	1102-03-	*2*	*6/-*
1986	*0416*	....	*St. Helens (US-Washington)*	1201-05-	*2*	*6/-*
1986	0418	....	**Pavlof** (Alaska Peninsula)	1102-03-	3	6/-
1986	0428	29*a*>	**Cleveland** (Aleutian Is)	1101-24-	2	
S **1986**	0516	78*a*	**Macdonald** (Austral Is-C Pacific)	1303-06-	0	
? *1986*	*0523*	*?*	*Korovin (Aleutian Is)*	1101-161	*1*	
1986	0525	3*c*	**Alaid** (Kuril Is)	0900-39=	2?	
1986	0528	179	**Iliboleng** (Lesser Sunda Is)	0604-22=	1	
S **1986**	06	15*m*	**Monowai Seamount** (Kermadec Is)	0402-05-	0	
1986	0603	76*a*	**Kanlaon** (Philippines-C)	0702-02=	2	-/5
1986	0608	33*a*	**Kliuchevskoi** (Kamchatka)	1000-26=	2	
S **1986**	0615	51*a*?	**Rumble III** (New Zealand)	0401-13-	0	
? *1986*	*0618*	*<1*	*Kaitoku Seamount (Volcano Is-Japan)*	0804-10=	*0*	
1986	0622	....	**Bezymianny** (Kamchatka)	1000-25=	2	6/5
1986	0705	18*a*	**Kavachi** (Solomon Is-SW Pacific)	0505-06=	1	
1986	0705	9*a*	**Sorikmarapi** (Sumatra)	0601-12=	1	-/2
1986	0716	35*a*	**Nyamuragira** (Africa-C)	0203-02=	2	7/7
? *1986*	*0716*	*89a*	*Talang (Sumatra)*	0601-16=	*1*	
1986	08 ?	?	**Cleft Segment** (Pacific-NE)	1301-03-	0	7/-
1986	0804	....	**Shiveluch** (Kamchatka)	1000-27=	3	
1986	0806	<1	**Dieng Volc Complex** (Java)	0603-20=	1	
? *1986*	*0821*	*131a?*	*Oku Volc Field [L. Nyos] (Africa-W)*	0204-03-		
1986	09 ?	?	**Sarychev Peak** (Kuril Is)	0900-24=		
1986	*0914*	*2a*	*Láscar (Chile-N)*	1505-10=	*1*	*-/7*
1986	0916	....	**Láscar** (Chile-N)	1505-10=	3	-/7
? *1986*	*0920*	*<1*	*Loihi (Hawaiian Is)*	1302-00-	*0*	
1986	0924	....	**Etna** (Italy)	0101-06=	3	5/6
1986	1010	>3yr	**Merapi** (Java)	0603-25=	2	6/-
1986	1011	1*a*	**Chirinkotan** (Kuril Is)	0900-26=	1	
? *1986*	*1024*	*<1*	*Bayonnaise Rocks (Izu Is-Japan)*	0804-07=	*0*	
1986	1030	122*a*	**Etna** (Italy)	0101-06=	2	7/6
1986	1031	....	**Etna** (Italy)	0101-06=	2?	
1986	1113	6*a*?	**Ambrym** (Vanuatu-SW Pacific)	0507-04=	2	
1986	*1115*	*32*	*Oshima (Izu Is-Japan)*	0804-01=	*2*	*7/7*
1986	*1118*	*19a*	*Chikurachki (Kuril Is)*	0900-36=	*2*	*7/8*
1986	*1118*	*467a*	*Okmok (Aleutian Is)*	1101-29-	*1*	
1986	1120	....	**Chikurachki** (Kuril Is)	0900-36=	4	7/8
1986	1121	....	**Oshima** (Izu Is-Japan)	0804-01=	3	7/7
1986	*1127*	*>3yr*	*Kliuchevskoi (Kamchatka)*	1000-26=	*2*	*7/8*
? *1986*	*1129*	*2a?*	*Bárdarbunga (Iceland-NE)*	1703-03=	*0*	
1986	12	?	**Sabancaya** (Perú)	1504-006	1	
1986	*1205d*	*598i*	*Bezymianny (Kamchatka)*	1000-25=	*0*	

START YEAR	M-Dy	Duration	VOLCANO NAME (Subregion)	NUMBER	VEI	Vol L/T
1986	1216	....	**Bezymianny** (Kamchatka)	1000-25=	3	
1986	1231	<1	**Rincón de la Vieja** (Costa Rica)	1405-02=	1	
1987	Cont	....	Stromboli (Italy)	0101-04=	1	7/-
1987	Cont	....	Erta Ale (Ethiopia)	0201-08=	0	
1987	Cont	....	Lengai, Ol Doinyo (Africa-E)	0202-12=	1	7/-
1987	Cont	....	Fournaise, Piton de la (Indian O.)	0303-02=	1	8/-
1987	Cont	....	Heard (Indian O.-S)	0304-01=	1	
1987	Cont	....	Manam (New Guinea-NE of)	0501-02=	2	7/7
1987	Cont	....	Langila (New Britain-SW Pac)	0502-01=	2	7/-
1987	Cont	....	Bagana (Bougainville-SW Pacific)	0505-02=	1	6/-
1987	Cont	....	Yasur (Vanuatu-SW Pacific)	0507-10=	2	
1987	Cont	....	Merapi (Java)	0603-25=	1	6/-
1987	Cont	....	Semeru (Java)	0603-30=	2	
1987	Cont	....	Lokon-Empung (Sulawesi-Indonesia)	0606-10=	2	
1987	Cont	....	Dukono (Halmahera-Indonesia)	0608-01=	2	
1987	Cont	....	Suwanose-jima (Ryukyu Is)	0802-03=	2	
1987	Cont	....	Sakura-jima (Kyushu-Japan)	0802-08=	2	
? 1987	Cont	....	Nishino-shima (Volcano Is-Japan)	0804-096	0	
1987	Cont	....	Shishaldin (Aleutian Is)	1101-36-	2	
1987	Cont	....	Pavlof (Alaska Peninsula)	1102-03-	2	6/-
1987	Cont	....	Kilauea (Hawaiian Is)	1302-01-	0	**9**/-
1987	Cont	....	Santa María (Guatemala)	1402-03=	1	**9**/8
1987	Cont	....	Ruiz, Nevado del (Colombia)	1501-02=	2	-/7
1987	Cont	....	Sangay (Ecuador)	1502-09=	2	
1987	Cont	....	Erebus (Antarctica)	1900-02=	1	
1987	01	....	Sangeang Api (Lesser Sunda Is)	0604-05=	1	7/-
1987	0105d	41m?	**Fuego** (Guatemala)	1402-09=	1	
1987	0115	>3yr	**Marapi** (Sumatra)	0601-14=	2	
1987	0125	....	White Island (New Zealand)	0401-04=	2	
1987	0125	....	Pacaya (Guatemala)	1402-11=	3	
1987	0131	....	**Okmok** (Aleutian Is)	1101-29-	2	
1987	0131	144a	**Akutan** (Aleutian Is)	1101-32-	2	
1987	0206	....	Karangetang [Api Siau] (Sangihe Is	0607-02=	3	4/-
1987	0215	7a>	**Masaya** (Nicaragua)	1404-10=	1	
1987	0219	....	Kliuchevskoi (Kamchatka)	1000-26=	3	7/8
1987	0302	<1	**Makushin** (Aleutian Is)	1101-31-	1	
1987	0304?	15a?	**Korovin** (Aleutian Is)	1101-161	2	
1987	0308h	69h	Etna (Italy)	0101-06=	1	
1987	0310	<1	**Kupreanof** (Alaska Peninsula)	1102-06-	1	
? 1987	0318	?	Great Sitkin (Aleutian Is)	1101-12-		
1987	0318	1a?	**Atka [Kliuchef]** (Aleutian Is)	1101-16-	2	
1987	0318	....	Arenal (Costa Rica)	1405-033	2	8/7
1987	0319	<1	**Veniaminof** (Alaska Peninsula)	1102-07-	1	
? 1987	0325	<1	Raoul Island (Kermadec Is)	0402-03=	0	
1987	0330?	94a?	**Kanlaon** (Philippines-C)	0702-02=	1	
1987	0401	<1	**Rincón de la Vieja** (Costa Rica)	1405-02=	1	
1987	0413	13a	**Gamkonora** (Halmahera-Indonesia)	0608-04=	1	
1987	0413	?	**Semisopochnoi** (Aleutian Is)	1101-06-	2?	
? 1987	0415	?	Kiska (Aleutian Is)	1101-02-		
1987	0417	....	**Etna** (Italy)	0101-06=	2	
1987	0425e	?	**Niigata-Yake-yama** (Honshu-Japan)	0803-09=	1	
1987	05	756w	**Raung** (Java)	0603-34=	1	
? 1987	0526	?	Esmeralda Bank (Mariana Is-C Pacific)	0804-21=	0	
1987	06	>3yr	Poás (Costa Rica)	1405-04=	1	
1987	0604	603a>	**Macdonald** (Austral Is-C Pacific)	1303-06-	0	
1987	0619	70a	Cleveland (Aleutian Is)	1101-24-	2	
1987	0702	<1	**Colima** (México)	1401-04=	1	
1987	0714	47a?	**Fukutoku-Okanoba** (Volcano Is-Japan	0804-13=	0	
1987	0719	....	Shiveluch (Kamchatka)	1000-27=	3	
? 1987	0723	?	Deception Island (Antarctica)	1900-03=		
? 1987	08	16m	Kita-Iwo-jima (Volcano Is-Japan)	0804-11=	0	
? 1987	0807	?	Sabancaya (Perú)	1504-006	2?	
1987	0824	6a	**Ruapehu** (New Zealand)	0401-10=	1	
1987	0828	....	**Cleveland** (Aleutian Is)	1101-24-	3	
? 1987	0904	>3yr	Fukutoku-Okanoba (Volcano Is-Japan.	0804-13=	0	
1987	0904	<1	**Pagan** (Mariana Is-C Pacific)	0804-17=	1	
1987	0904	?	**Gareloi** (Aleutian Is)	1101-07-	1?	
1987	0904?	?	**Amukta** (Aleutian Is)	1101-19-	1	
1987	1002	<1	**Iliboleng** (Lesser Sunda Is)	0604-22=	2	
1987	1011	....	Bezymianny (Kamchatka)	1000-25=	1	
1987	1014	93m	**Ebeko** (Kuril Is)	0900-38=	1	-/4
? 1987	1021	40a	Bayonnaise Rocks (Izu Is-Japan)	0804-07=	0	
? 1987	11	?	San Cristóbal (Nicaragua)	1404-02=		
1987	11	15m	**Telica** (Nicaragua)	1404-04=	1	
1987	11	< 869m>	Láscar (Chile-N)	1505-10=	0	5/-
1987	1116	72	**Oshima** (Izu Is-Japan)	0804-01=	2	-/4
? 1987	1116	?	Carlisle (Aleutian Is)	1101-23-		
1987	1128	2a	**Tupungatito** (Chile-C)	1507-01=	2	
1987	1228	473m>	Ranakah (Lesser Sunda Is)	0604-071	2	7/6
1987	1230	4	**Nyamuragira** (Africa-C)	0203-02=	1	6/6
1988	Cont	....	Erta Ale (Ethiopia)	0201-08=	0	
1988	Cont	....	Lengai, Ol Doinyo (Africa-E)	0202-12=	1	7/-
1988	Cont	....	Nyamuragira (Africa-C)	0203-02=	1	6/6
1988	Cont	....	Fournaise, Piton de la (Indian O.)	0303-02=	1	8/-
1988	Cont	....	Manam (New Guinea-NE of)	0501-02=	2	7/7
1988	Cont	....	Langila (New Britain-SW Pac)	0502-01=	2	7/-
1988	Cont	....	Bagana (Bougainville-SW Pacific)	0505-02=	1	6/-
1988	Cont	....	Yasur (Vanuatu-SW Pacific)	0507-10=	2	
1988	Cont	....	Marapi (Sumatra)	0601-14=	2	
1988	Cont	....	Merapi (Java)	0603-25=	1	6/-
1988	Cont	....	Semeru (Java)	0603-30=	2	
1988	Cont	....	Raung (Java)	0603-34=	1	
1988	Cont	....	Sangeang Api (Lesser Sunda Is)	0604-05=	3	7/-
1988	Cont	....	Karangetang [Api Siau] (Sangihe Is	0607-02=	2	4/-
1988	Cont	....	Dukono (Halmahera-Indonesia)	0608-01=	2	
1988	Cont	....	Sakura-jima (Kyushu-Japan)	0802-08=	2	
? 1988	Cont	....	Nishino-shima (Volcano Is-Japan)	0804-096	0	
? 1988	Cont	....	Fukutoku-Okanoba (Volcano Is-Japan.	0804-13=	0	
1988	Cont	....	Ebeko (Kuril Is)	0900-38=	1	-/4
1988	Cont	....	Bezymianny (Kamchatka)	1000-25=	0	
1988	Cont	....	Kliuchevskoi (Kamchatka)	1000-26=	2	7/8
1988	Cont	....	Okmok (Aleutian Is)	1101-29-	2	
1988	Cont	....	Pavlof (Alaska Peninsula)	1102-03-	2	6/-
1988	Cont	....	Kilauea (Hawaiian Is)	1302-01-	0	**9**/-
1988	Cont	....	Macdonald (Austral Is-C Pacific)	1303-06-	0	
1988	Cont	....	Santa María (Guatemala)	1402-03=	1	**9**/8
1988	Cont	....	Pacaya (Guatemala)	1402-11=	1	
1988	Cont	....	Ruiz, Nevado del (Colombia)	1501-02=	2	-/7
1988	Cont	....	Sangay (Ecuador)	1502-09=	2	
1988	Cont	....	Erebus (Antarctica)	1900-02=	1	
1988	a	?	**Unnamed [East Pacific Rise]**	1304-05-	0	4/-
1988	01	668p	**Suwanose-jima** (Ryukyu Is)	0802-03=	2	
1988	01	?	Láscar (Chile-N)	1505-10=	2	5/-
1988	0103	....	**Ranakah** (Lesser Sunda Is)	0604-071	3	7/6
1988	0105	44a	**Akan** (Hokkaido-Japan)	0805-07=	1	
1988	0118	<1	**Kikai** (Ryukyu Is)	0802-06=	1	
1988	0125	....	Oshima (Izu Is-Japan)	0804-01=	1	-/4
? 1988	0127	?	Kita-Fukutokutai (Volcano Is-Japan)	0804-121	1?	
1988	02	....	Arenal (Costa Rica)	1405-033	2	8/7
1988	0212?	192a?	**Ambrym** (Vanuatu-SW Pacific)	0507-04=	3	6/-
1988	0212	33m?	**Gamalama** (Halmahera-Indonesia)	0608-06=	2	
1988	0214e	60n?	**Krakatau** (Indonesia)	0602-00=	2	5/-
? 1988	0216	?	Pagan (Mariana Is-C Pacific)	0804-17=		
1988	0220	16	**Bulusan** (Luzon-Philippines)	0703-01=	2	-/4
1988	0314	....	White Island (New Zealand)	0401-04=	2	
? 1988	0318	1a	Bayonnaise Rocks (Izu Is-Japan)	0804-07=	0	
1988	0320	66c	**Ruapehu** (New Zealand)	0401-10=	1	
1988	0326	116a	**Akutan** (Aleutian Is)	1101-32-	2	
1988	0409	....	**Poás** (Costa Rica)	1405-04=	2	
1988	0421	10a	**Lokon-Empung** (Sulawesi-Indonesia)	0606-10=	1	
1988	0509	8a	**Banda Api** (Banda Sea)	0605-09=	3?	6/-
1988	0526e	235e	**Aso** (Kyushu-Japan)	0802-11=	1	
1988	06	?	**Concepción** (Nicaragua)	1404-12=	2	
1988	0601	2a>	**Hunga Tonga-Hunga Ha'apai**	0403-04=	0	
? 1988	0615w	?	Colima (México)	1401-04=	2?	
1988	0621	10	**Kanlaon** (Philippines-C)	0702-02=	1	
1988	0622	116m?	**Sabancaya** (Perú)	1504-006	1	
1988	0712	<1	**Slamet** (Java)	0603-18=	1	
1988	0729	7a	**Makian** (Halmahera-Indonesia)	0608-07=	3	
? 1988	08	?	Epi (Vanuatu-SW Pacific)	0507-06=	0	
1988	0824	49a	**Pagan** (Mariana Is-C Pacific)	0804-17=	2	
1988	0830	....	Stromboli (Italy)	0101-04=	2	7/-
S **1988**	0908	<1	**Monowai Seamount** (Kermadec Is)	0402-05-	0	
1988	0914	2	**Fernandina** (Galápagos)	1503-01=	2?	6/-
1988	1002	269a	**Etna** (Italy)	0101-06=	1	
1988	1115 q	?	**Viedma** (Argentina)	1508-061		
1988	1207	<1	**Shiveluch** (Kamchatka)	1000-27=	2?	
1988	1208	87a?	**Ruapehu** (New Zealand)	0401-10=	1	
1988	1210?	156m?	Tokachi (Hokkaido-Japan)	0805-05=	1?	-/5
1988	1216	....	**Tokachi** (Hokkaido-Japan)	0805-05=	2	-/5
1988	1225	395b	Lonquimay (Chile-C)	1507-10=	2	
1988	1227	....	**Lonquimay** (Chile-C)	1507-10=	3	8/8
S **1988**	1229	<1	**Kick 'em Jenny** (W Indies)	1600-16=	0	
1989	Cont	....	Erta Ale (Ethiopia)	0201-08=	0	
1989	Cont	....	Lengai, Ol Doinyo (Africa-E)	0202-12=	1	7/-
1989	Cont	....	Manam (New Guinea-NE of)	0501-02=	2	7/7
1989	Cont	....	Langila (New Britain-SW Pac)	0502-01=	2	7/-
1989	Cont	....	Bagana (Bougainville-SW Pacific)	0505-02=	1	6/-
1989	Cont	....	Yasur (Vanuatu-SW Pacific)	0507-10=	2	
1989	Cont	....	Marapi (Sumatra)	0601-14=	2	
1989	Cont	....	Merapi (Java)	0603-25=	1	6/-
1989	Cont	....	Semeru (Java)	0603-30=	2	
1989	Cont	....	Raung (Java)	0603-34=	1	
1989	Cont	....	Ranakah (Lesser Sunda Is)	0604-071	0	7/6
1989	Cont	....	Dukono (Halmahera-Indonesia)	0608-01=	2	
1989	Cont	....	Suwanose-jima (Ryukyu Is)	0802-03=	2	
1989	Cont	....	Sakura-jima (Kyushu-Japan)	0802-08=	2	
? 1989	Cont	....	Nishino-shima (Volcano Is-Japan)	0804-096	0	
? 1989	Cont	....	Fukutoku-Okanoba (Volcano Is-Japan.	0804-13=	0	
1989	Cont	....	Tokachi (Hokkaido-Japan)	0805-05=	1?	-/5
1989	Cont	....	Kliuchevskoi (Kamchatka)	1000-26=	2	7/8
1989	Cont	....	Kilauea (Hawaiian Is)	1302-01-	0	**9**/-
1989	Cont	....	Macdonald (Austral Is-C Pacific)	1303-06-	0	
1989	Cont	....	Ruiz, Nevado del (Colombia)	1501-02=	2	-/7

	START YEAR	M-Dy	Dura-tion	VOLCANO NAME (Subregion)	NUMBER	VEI	Vol L/T
	1989	*Cont*	....	*Sangay (Ecuador)*	1502-09=	*2*	
	1989	*Cont*	....	*Láscar (Chile-N)*	1505-10=	*0*	*5/-*
	1989	*Cont*	....	*Lonquimay (Chile-C)*	1507-10=	*2*	*8/8*
	1989	*Cont*	....	*Erebus (Antarctica)*	1900-02=	*1*	
	1989	....	....	*Arenal (Costa Rica)*	1405-033	*2*	*8/7*
	1989	0101	349*m*?	**Ulawun** (New Britain-SW Pac)	0502-12=	2	
?	*1989*	*0106*	*<1*	*Kusatsu-Shirane (Honshu-Japan)*	0803-12=	*1*	
	1989	0113	1*a*	**Sarychev Peak** (Kuril Is)	0900-24=	1?	
?	*1989*	*0118*	*<1*	*Smith Rock (Izu Is-Japan)*	0804-08=	*0*	
	1989	0202	232*a*?	**Ebeko** (Kuril Is)	0900-38=	2	-/6
	1989	0219	79*a*	**Galeras** (Colombia)	1501-08=	2	-/5
	1989	0220	268*m*	**Masaya** (Nicaragua)	1404-10=	1	
	1989	0227	29*a*<	**Akutan** (Aleutian Is)	1101-32-	2	
	1989	*0307*	....	*Pacaya (Guatemala)*	1402-11=	*3*	
	1989	*0314*	....	*White Island (New Zealand)*	0401-04=	*2*	
	1989	*0325*	....	*Stromboli (Italy)*	0101-04=	*2*	*7/-*
	1989	*0405*	*675a*	*Aso (Kyushu-Japan)*	0802-11=	*0*	
	1989	0407	80	**Shiveluch** (Kamchatka)	1000-27=	2	
	1989	0419	7*a*	**Niigata-Yake-yama** (Honshu-Japan)	0803-09=	1	
	1989	0422	<1	**Soputan** (Sulawesi-Indonesia)	0606-03=	2	
	1989	0424	113*e*	**Nyamuragira** (Africa-C)	0203-02=	3	7/7
	1989	0424	243*a*	**Ambrym** (Vanuatu-SW Pacific)	0507-04=	2	
	1989	*05*	....	*Poás (Costa Rica)*	1405-04=	*2*	
	1989	0503	95*d*	**Grozny Group** (Kuril Is)	0900-07=	2	
	1989	0529	<1	**Cameroon** (Africa-W)	0204-01=	1?	
	1989	07	16*m*	**Karangetang [Api Siau]** (Sangihe Is	0607-02=	1	
?	*1989*	*07*	*16m*	*Kita-Iwo-jima (Volcano Is-Japan)*	0804-11=	*0*	
	1989	0701	81*a*?	**Ruapehu** (New Zealand)	0401-10=	1	
	1989	0713	<1	**Izu-Tobu** (Honshu-Japan)	0803-01=	1	-/5
	1989	0716	....	**Aso** (Kyushu-Japan)	0802-11=	2	
?	*1989*	*0718*	*<1*	*Smith Rock (Izu Is-Japan)*	0804-08=	*0*	

Hugo Moreno (Univ. Chile)

A billowing ash-rich eruption column rises above a cinder cone on the NE flank of Chile's Lonquimay volcano in January 1989. During the course of an eruption that lasted from December 1988 until January 1990, heavy ashfall blanketed the countryside, causing severe disruption to agricultural areas near the volcano. The ash was high in fluorine, and fluorine poisoning from ash on ingested grass caused the deaths of hundreds of cattle and horses, producing severe economic hardship.

	START YEAR	M-Dy	Dura-tion	VOLCANO NAME (Subregion)	NUMBER	VEI	Vol L/T
	1989	*0719*	....	*Santa María (Guatemala)*	1402-03=	*3*	***9**/8*
	1989	08	< 183*p*>	**Tinakula** (Santa Cruz Is-SW Pacific)	0506-01=	1	
	1989	0801	3*a*	**Bezymianny** (Kamchatka)	1000-25=	2	
	1989	0817	?	**Gareloi** (Aleutian Is)	1101-07-	1	
	1989	0911	28*a*	**Etna** (Italy)	0101-06=	2	7/-
@	**1989**	0921	97	**Supply Reef** (Mariana Is-C Pacific)	0804-142	0	
	1989	1025	49*a*>	**Kanlaon** (Philippines-C)	0702-02=	2	
?	*1989*	*1025c*	*?*	*Cleveland (Aleutian Is)*	1101-24-	*0*	
?	*1989*	*12*	*?*	*Irruputuncu (Chile-N)*	1505-04=		
	1989	*1207*	*30a*	*St. Helens (US-Washington)*	1201-05-	*1*	
	1989	1214	188*a*?	**Redoubt** (Alaska-SW)	1103-03-	3	7/8
	1989	*1216*	*939a*	*Etna (Italy)*	0101-06=	*1*	*6/7*
	1990	*Cont*	....	*Erta Ale (Ethiopia)*	0201-08=	*0*	
	1990	*Cont*	....	*Lengai, Ol Doinyo (Africa-E)*	0202-12=	*1*	*7/-*
	1990	*Cont*	....	*White Island (New Zealand)*	0401-04=	*1*	
	1990	*Cont*	....	*Manam (New Guinea-NE of)*	0501-02=	*2*	*7/7*
	1990	*Cont*	....	*Langila (New Britain-SW Pac)*	0502-01=	*2*	*7/-*
	1990	*Cont*	....	*Bagana (Bougainville-SW Pacific)*	0505-02=	*1*	*6/-*
	1990	*Cont*	....	*Tinakula (Santa Cruz Is-SW Pacific)*	0506-01=	*1*	
	1990	*Cont*	....	*Yasur (Vanuatu-SW Pacific)*	0507-10=	*2*	
	1990	*Cont*	....	*Marapi (Sumatra)*	0601-14=	*2*	
	1990	*Cont*	....	*Merapi (Java)*	0603-25=	*1*	*6/-*
	1990	*Cont*	....	*Semeru (Java)*	0603-30=	*2*	
	1990	*Cont*	....	*Dukono (Halmahera-Indonesia)*	0608-01=	*2*	
	1990	*Cont*	....	*Sakura-jima (Kyushu-Japan)*	0802-08=	*2*	
	1990	*Cont*	....	*Aso (Kyushu-Japan)*	0802-11=	*0*	
?	*1990*	*Cont*	....	*Nishino-shima (Volcano Is-Japan)*	0804-096	*0*	
?	*1990*	*Cont*	....	*Fukutoku-Okanoba (Volcano Is-Japan.*	0804-13=	*0*	
	1990	*Cont*	....	*Ebeko (Kuril Is)*	0900-38=	*2*	*-/6*
	1990	*Cont*	....	*Kilauea (Hawaiian Is)*	1302-01-	*0*	***9**/-*
	1990	*Cont*	....	*Poás (Costa Rica)*	1405-04=	*1*	
	1990	*Cont*	....	*Ruiz, Nevado del (Colombia)*	1501-02=	*2*	*-/7*
	1990	*Cont*	....	*Sangay (Ecuador)*	1502-09=	*2*	
	1990	*Cont*	....	*Lonquimay (Chile-C)*	1507-10=	*2*	*8/8*
	1990	*Cont*	....	*Erebus (Antarctica)*	1900-02=	*1*	
	1990 b	....	?	**Southern EPR-Segment K** (Pacific)	1304-12-	0	8/-
	1990	....	....	*Arenal (Costa Rica)*	1405-033	*2*	*8/7*
	1990	....	?	**Puyehue-Cordón Caulle** (Chile-C)	1507-15=	1	
	1990	*0102*	....	*Redoubt (Alaska-SW)*	1103-03-	*3*	*7/8*
	1990	0104	....	**Etna** (Italy)	0101-06=	3	6/7
	1990	*0104?*	*>3yr*	*Pacaya (Guatemala)*	1402-11=	*1*	
	1990	0106	....	**St. Helens** (US-Washington)	1201-05-	2	
	1990	0107	19*a*	**Ruapehu** (New Zealand)	0401-10=	1	
	1990	*0107*	*921a*	*Galeras (Colombia)*	1501-08=	*1*	*5/5*
	1990	*0110*	*>3yr*	*Shiveluch (Kamchatka)*	1000-27=	*2*	*8/6*
	1990	0116	< 334*m*>	**Raung** (Java)	0603-34=	2	
	1990	0118	110*a*	**Fournaise, Piton de la** (Indian O.)	0303-02=	0	6/-
	1990	0126e	3*a*	**Akutan** (Aleutian Is)	1101-32-	2	
	1990	0128	138*m*	**Lewotobi** (Lesser Sunda Is)	0604-18=	1	
	1990	*0129*	*667a*	*Bezymianny (Kamchatka)*	1000-25=	*2*	
	1990	0130	....	**Kliuchevskoi** (Kamchatka)	1000-26=	4	7/8
	1990	0210	32*q*	**Kelut** (Java)	0603-28=	4	-/8
	1990	0220	....	**Láscar** (Chile-N)	1505-10=	3	5/-
	1990	0225	273*a*	**Llaima** (Chile-C)	1507-11=	1	
	1990	0305	<1	**Pavlof** (Alaska Peninsula)	1102-03-	2?	
	1990	0310	....	**Bezymianny** (Kamchatka)	1000-25=	3	
S	**1990**	0326	1	**Kick 'em Jenny** (W Indies)	1600-16=	0	
	1990	04	>3yr	**Suwanose-jima** (Ryukyu Is)	0802-03=	2	
	1990	*0415*	....	*Stromboli (Italy)*	0101-04=	*2*	*7/-*
	1990	0416	24*a*	**Guagua Pichincha** (Ecuador)	1502-02=	1	
?	*1990*	*0424*	*<1*	*Pular (Chile-N)*	1505-107	*1?*	
	1990	0425	1*a*	**Gamalama** (Halmahera-Indonesia)	0608-06=	3?	
	1990	*0528*	*>3yr*	*Sabancaya (Perú)*	1504-006	*2*	*-/7*
S	**1990**	0530	299*a*	**Monowai Seamount** (Kermadec Is)	0402-05-	0	
	1990	0601	<1?	**Kiska** (Aleutian Is)	1101-02-	2	
	1990	0605	....	**Sabancaya** (Perú)	1504-006	3	-/7
	1990	0617	83*a*<	**Ruapehu** (New Zealand)	0401-10=	0	
	1990	*0713*	....	*Santa María (Guatemala)*	1402-03=	*3*	***9**/8*
	1990	*0714*	....	*Pacaya (Guatemala)*	1402-11=	*2*	
	1990	0720	<1	**Asama** (Honshu-Japan)	0803-11=	2	-/3
	1990	0804	....	**Shiveluch** (Kamchatka)	1000-27=	3	8/6
	1990	09	< 304*p*>	**Ambrym** (Vanuatu-SW Pacific)	0507-04=	2	
	1990	0906	25*a*	**Akutan** (Aleutian Is)	1101-32-	2	
	1990	1004	<1	**Oshima** (Izu Is-Japan)	0804-01=	2	
?	*1990*	*1029*	*21a*	*Unnamed (Pacific-S)*	1305-03-	*0*	
	1990	1105	101*a*	**St. Helens** (US-Washington)	1201-05-	3?	
	1990	1117	>3yr	**Unzen** (Kyushu-Japan)	0802-10=	1	8/6
	1990	1124	<1	**Láscar** (Chile-N)	1505-10=	1	
	1990	1231y	?	**Kerinci** (Sumatra)	0601-17=	2	
	1991	*Cont*	....	*Stromboli (Italy)*	0101-04=	*1*	*7/-*
	1991	*Cont*	....	*Erta Ale (Ethiopia)*	0201-08=	*0*	
	1991	*Cont*	....	*Lengai, Ol Doinyo (Africa-E)*	0202-12=	*1*	*7/-*
S	*1991*	*Cont*	....	*Monowai Seamount (Kermadec Is)*	0402-05-	*0*	
	1991	*Cont*	....	*Manam (New Guinea-NE of)*	0501-02=	*2*	*7/7*
	1991	*Cont*	....	*Langila (New Britain-SW Pac)*	0502-01=	*2*	*7/-*
	1991	*Cont*	....	*Bagana (Bougainville-SW Pacific)*	0505-02=	*1*	*6/-*

	START YEAR	M-Dy	Duration	VOLCANO NAME (Subregion)	NUMBER	VEI	Vol L/T
	1991	Cont	....	Ambrym (Vanuatu-SW Pacific)	0507-04=	2	
	1991	Cont	....	Yasur (Vanuatu-SW Pacific)	0507-10=	2	
	1991	Cont	....	Marapi (Sumatra)	0601-14=	2	
	1991	Cont	....	Semeru (Java)	0603-30=	2	
	1991	Cont	....	Dukono (Halmahera-Indonesia)	0608-01=	2	
	1991	Cont	....	Suwanose-jima (Ryukyu Is)	0802-03=	2	
	1991	Cont	....	Sakura-jima (Kyushu-Japan)	0802-08=	2	
	1991	Cont	....	Unzen (Kyushu-Japan)	0802-10=	2	8/6
	1991	Cont	....	Aso (Kyushu-Japan)	0802-11=	0	
	1991	Cont	....	Bezymianny (Kamchatka)	1000-25=	2	
	1991	Cont	....	St. Helens (US-Washington)	1201-05-	3?	
	1991	Cont	....	Kilauea (Hawaiian Is)	1302-01-	0	9/-
	1991	Cont	....	Ruiz, Nevado del (Colombia)	1501-02=	2	-/7
	1991	Cont	....	Galeras (Colombia)	1501-08=	1	5/5
	1991	Cont	....	Sangay (Ecuador)	1502-09=	2	
	1991	Cont	....	Sabancaya (Perú)	1504-006	2	-/7
	1991	Cont	....	Erebus (Antarctica)	1900-02=	1	
	1991	....	?	**Peuet Sague** (Sumatra)	0601-03=	2	
	1991	....	....	Arenal (Costa Rica)	1405-033	2	8/7
	1991	01	3a	**Ebeko** (Kuril Is)	0900-38=	1	
	1991	0113	17a	**Avachinsky** (Kamchatka)	1000-10=	2	7/5
	1991	0117	52	**Hekla** (Iceland-S)	1702-07=	3	8/7
	1991	0209	21b	**Planchón-Peteroa** (Chile-C)	1507-04=	2	
	1991	0214	<1	**Kanlaon** (Philippines-C)	0702-02=	2	
	1991	03 <	?	**Ranakah** (Lesser Sunda Is)	0604-071	1	
	1991	03 ?	<1	**Unnamed [East Pacific Rise]**	1304-05-	0	6/-
	1991	0301	228m	**Colima** (México)	1401-04=	2	7/6
	1991	0306	193m	**Poás** (Costa Rica)	1405-04=	1	
?	1991	0311	8a	Unnamed (Pacific-S)	1305-02-	0	
	1991	0329	216g>	**Barren Island** (Andaman Is-Indian O)	0600-01=	2	6/6
	1991	0402	153a	Pinatubo (Luzon-Philippines)	0703-083	2?	
	1991	0408	77a?	**Kliuchevskoi** (Kamchatka)	1000-26=	2	
	1991	0408	....	Shiveluch (Kamchatka)	1000-27=	2	8/6
	1991	0410	....	Santa María (Guatemala)	1402-03=	2	9/8
	1991	0419	4	**Fernandina** (Galápagos)	1503-01=	2?	
	1991	0504<	134m>	**Kavachi** (Solomon Is-SW Pacific)	0505-06=	2	
	1991	0507	496m	**Rincón de la Vieja** (Costa Rica)	1405-02=	2	
	1991	0508	53a>	**Iliboleng** (Lesser Sunda Is)	0604-22=	1	
	1991	0511	599a>	**Lewotobi** (Lesser Sunda Is)	0604-18=	1	
	1991	0517	243m	Lokon-Empung (Sulawesi-Indonesia)	0606-10=	1	5/7
	1991	0522	>3yr	Soputan (Sulawesi-Indonesia)	0606-03=	1	7/-
?	1991	0615	<1	Gamalama (Halmahera-Indonesia)	0608-06=	1?	
	1991	0615	....	**Pinatubo** (Luzon-Philippines)	0703-083	**6**	**-/10**
	1991	0624<	?	**Metis Shoal** (Tonga-SW Pacific)	0403-07=	0	
	1991	0702<	912a>	Karangetang [Api Siau] (Sangihe Is	0607-02=	1	6/6
	1991	0705?	9a?	**Ruapehu** (New Zealand)	0401-10=	1	
	1991	0711	<1	**Karthala** (Indian O.-W)	0303-01=	2	-/6
	1991	0719	1	**Fournaise, Piton de la** (Indian O.)	0303-02=	0	6/-
?	1991	0719	91a	Fukutoku-Okanoba (Volcano Is-Japan.	0804-13=	0	
	1991	0727	....	**Pacaya** (Guatemala)	1402-11=	3	
	1991	0808	80	Hudson, Cerro (Chile-S)	1508-057	3	-/9
	1991	0812	....	**Hudson, Cerro** (Chile-S)	1508-057	**5+**	**-/9**
?	1991	0812	?	Bárdarbunga (Iceland-NE)	1703-03=	0	
	1991	0830	18a	**Villarrica** (Chile-C)	1507-12=	2	
	1991	0910	63a?	**Raung** (Java)	0603-34=	2	
?	1991	0913	?	Arjuno-Welirang (Java)	0603-29=		
	1991	0915	44a	**Akutan** (Aleutian Is)	1101-32-	2	
	1991	0916	....	**White Island** (New Zealand)	0401-04=	3	
	1991	0920	507a	Nyamuragira (Africa-C)	0203-02=	2	-/7
	1991	0925	51m?	**Marchena** (Galápagos)	1503-08=	2	
	1991	1015	....	**Nyamuragira** (Africa-C)	0203-02=	3	-/7
	1991	1021	215a?	**Láscar** (Chile-N)	1505-10=	2	-/6
	1991	1025	....	**Lokon-Empung** (Sulawesi-Indonesia)	0606-10=	3	5/7
	1991	1103	12a	**Iliboleng** (Lesser Sunda Is)	0604-22=	1	
?	1991	1105	<1	Smith Rock (Izu Is-Japan)	0804-08=	0	
	1991	1129	46a	**Westdahl** (Aleutian Is)	1101-34-	3	7/-
	1991	1201	131a	**Kirishima** (Kyushu-Japan)	0802-09=	1	-/3
	1991	1201p	65r	**Unnamed [East Pacific Rise]**	1304-05-	0	
	1991	1214	472a	**Etna** (Italy)	0101-06=	2	8/-
	1992	Cont	....	Stromboli (Italy)	0101-04=	1	7/-
	1992	Cont	....	Etna (Italy)	0101-06=	2	8/-
	1992	Cont	....	Erta Ale (Ethiopia)	0201-08=	0	
	1992	Cont	....	Lengai, Ol Doinyo (Africa-E)	0202-12=	1	7/-
	1992	Cont	....	Nyamuragira (Africa-C)	0203-02=	2	-/7
	1992	Cont	....	White Island (New Zealand)	0401-04=	1	
	1992	Cont	....	Langila (New Britain-SW Pac)	0502-01=	2	7/-
	1992	Cont	....	Bagana (Bougainville-SW Pacific)	0505-02=	1	6/-
	1992	Cont	....	Yasur (Vanuatu-SW Pacific)	0507-10=	2	
	1992	Cont	....	Marapi (Sumatra)	0601-14=	2	
	1992	Cont	....	Semeru (Java)	0603-30=	2	
	1992	Cont	....	Lewotobi (Lesser Sunda Is)	0604-18=	1	
	1992	Cont	....	Soputan (Sulawesi-Indonesia)	0606-03=	1	7/-
	1992	Cont	....	Lokon-Empung (Sulawesi-Indonesia)	0606-10=	1	5/7
	1992	Cont	....	Dukono (Halmahera-Indonesia)	0608-01=	2	
	1992	Cont	....	Suwanose-jima (Ryukyu Is)	0802-03=	2	
	1992	Cont	....	Sakura-jima (Kyushu-Japan)	0802-08=	2	
	1992	Cont	....	Kirishima (Kyushu-Japan)	0802-09=	1	-/3
	1992	Cont	....	Unzen (Kyushu-Japan)	0802-10=	2	8/6
	1992	Cont	....	Westdahl (Aleutian Is)	1101-34-	3	7/-
	1992	Cont	....	Kilauea (Hawaiian Is)	1302-01-	0	9/-
	1992	Cont	....	Unnamed [East Pacific Rise]	1304-05-	0	
	1992	Cont	....	Santa María (Guatemala)	1402-03=	1	9/8
	1992	Cont	....	Pacaya (Guatemala)	1402-11=	1	
	1992	Cont	....	Rincón de la Vieja (Costa Rica)	1405-02=	1	
	1992	Cont	....	Sangay (Ecuador)	1502-09=	2	
	1992	Cont	....	Sabancaya (Perú)	1504-006	2	-/7
	1992	Cont	....	Láscar (Chile-N)	1505-10=	2	-/6
	1992	Cont	....	Erebus (Antarctica)	1900-02=	1	
	1992	....	....	Arenal (Costa Rica)	1405-033	2	8/7
	1992	0108	<1	**Kanlaon** (Philippines-C)	0702-02=	1	
?	1992	0117	1a	Heard (Indian O.-S)	0304-01=		
	1992	0120	>3yr	**Merapi** (Java)	0603-25=	2	7/-
	1992	0125	119a?	**Kliuchevskoi** (Kamchatka)	1000-26=	2	
	1992	02	31p	**Poás** (Costa Rica)	1405-04=	1	
	1992	0205	....	**Karangetang [Api Siau]** (Sangihe Is	0607-02=	2	6/6
	1992	0208	27a	**Ruapehu** (New Zealand)	0401-10=	1	
?	1992	0212	21a	Minami-Hiyoshi (Volcano Is-Japan)	0804-131	0	
	1992	0308	74a	**Akutan** (Aleutian Is)	1101-32-	2	
	1992	0312	92a	**Bezymianny** (Kamchatka)	1000-25=	2	
	1992	0407i	?	**Awu** (Sangihe Is-Indonesia)	0607-04=	1	
	1992	0409	5a	**Negro, Cerro** (Nicaragua)	1404-07=	3	-/7
	1992	0411	....	Shiveluch (Kamchatka)	1000-27=	2	8/6
	1992	0413	<1	**Pagan** (Mariana Is-C Pacific)	0804-17=	1?	
	1992	0423	413a?	Aso (Kyushu-Japan)	0802-11=	0	
	1992	0529?	?	**Heard** (Indian O.-S)	0304-01=	0	
	1992	0610	<1	**Kanlaon** (Philippines-C)	0702-02=	2	
	1992	0627	81	**Spurr** (Alaska-SW)	1103-04-	4	-/8
	1992	0706	18a	**Bogoslof** (Aleutian Is)	1101-30-	3	6/-
	1992	0709<	113a	**Pinatubo** (Luzon-Philippines)	0703-083	1	6/-
	1992	0716	....	**Galeras** (Colombia)	1501-08=	2	5/5
	1992	0722	314w	**Copahue** (Chile-C)	1507-09=	2	
?	1992	0805	63a	Smith Rock (Izu Is-Japan)	0804-08=	0	
	1992	0818	....	Spurr (Alaska-SW)	1103-04-	3	-/8
	1992	0823	10a	**Llaima** (Chile-C)	1507-11=	1	
	1992	0827	27a	**Fournaise, Piton de la** (Indian O.)	0303-02=	1	6/-
	1992	0831	....	Manam (New Guinea-NE of)	0501-02=	3	7/7
	1992	0911	96m>	**Villarrica** (Chile-C)	1507-12=	1	
	1992	0912	366a?	**Kliuchevskoi** (Kamchatka)	1000-26=	2	
	1992	0917	....	Spurr (Alaska-SW)	1103-04-	3	-/8
	1992	10	365p	**Poás** (Costa Rica)	1405-04=	0	
	1992	1026	....	**Aso** (Kyushu-Japan)	0802-11=	2	
	1992	1107	341m	**Krakatau** (Indonesia)	0602-00=	1	6/-
	1992	1110	303a?	**Fukutoku-Okanoba** (Volcano Is-Japan	0804-13=	1	-/5
	1992	12	?	**McDonald Islands** (Indian O.-S)	0304-011	0	
	1992	1218	?	**Akutan** (Aleutian Is)	1101-32-	1	
	1992	1227	3a	**Seguam** (Aleutian Is)	1101-18-	2	
	1993	Cont	....	Erta Ale (Ethiopia)	0201-08=	0	
	1993	Cont	....	Nyamuragira (Africa-C)	0203-02=	2	-/7
	1993	Cont	....	White Island (New Zealand)	0401-04=	1	
	1993	Cont	....	Langila (New Britain-SW Pac)	0502-01=	2	7/-
	1993	Cont	....	Bagana (Bougainville-SW Pacific)	0505-02=	1	6/-
	1993	Cont	....	Yasur (Vanuatu-SW Pacific)	0507-10=	2	
	1993	Cont	....	Marapi (Sumatra)	0601-14=	2	
	1993	Cont	....	Krakatau (Indonesia)	0602-00=	1	6/-
	1993	Cont	....	Merapi (Java)	0603-25=	2	7/-
	1993	Cont	....	Semeru (Java)	0603-30=	2	
	1993	Cont	....	Soputan (Sulawesi-Indonesia)	0606-03=	1	7/-
	1993	Cont	....	Karangetang [Api Siau] (Sangihe Is	0607-02=	1	6/6
	1993	Cont	....	Dukono (Halmahera-Indonesia)	0608-01=	2	
	1993	Cont	....	Suwanose-jima (Ryukyu Is)	0802-03=	2	
	1993	Cont	....	Sakura-jima (Kyushu-Japan)	0802-08=	2	
	1993	Cont	....	Unzen (Kyushu-Japan)	0802-10=	2	8/6
	1993	Cont	....	Aso (Kyushu-Japan)	0802-11=	0	
	1993	Cont	....	Fukutoku-Okanoba (Volcano Is-Japan.	0804-13=	0	-/5
	1993	Cont	....	Kilauea (Hawaiian Is)	1302-01-	0	9/-
	1993	Cont	....	Santa María (Guatemala)	1402-03=	1	9/8
	1993	Cont	....	Poás (Costa Rica)	1405-04=	0	
	1993	Cont	....	Sangay (Ecuador)	1502-09=	2	
	1993	Cont	....	Sabancaya (Perú)	1504-006	2	-/7
	1993	Cont	....	Copahue (Chile-C)	1507-09=	2	
	1993	Cont	....	Erebus (Antarctica)	1900-02=	1	
	1993	....	....	Arenal (Costa Rica)	1405-033	2	8/7
	1993	0102m	?	**Heard** (Indian O.-S)	0304-01=	2?	
	1993	0110	....	Pacaya (Guatemala)	1402-11=	2	
	1993	0112	19a?	**Ulawun** (New Britain-SW Pac)	0502-12=	2	
	1993	0114	144	**Galeras** (Colombia)	1501-08=	2	-/6
	1993	0115e	304m>	**Pagan** (Mariana Is-C Pacific)	0804-17=	2	
	1993	0123	<1?	**Dieng Volc Complex** (Java)	0603-20=	1	
	1993	0129	391d?	**Socorro** (México-Is)	1401-021	0	
	1993	0130	197m	Láscar (Chile-N)	1505-10=	2	6/8
	1993	02	151p?	**Pinatubo** (Luzon-Philippines)	0703-083	1	
	1993	0202	61a	**Mayon** (Luzon-Philippines)	0703-03=	2?	7/6
	1993	0203	<1	**Etna** (Italy)	0101-06=	1	
	1993	0210	....	Stromboli (Italy)	0101-04=	2	7/-

START YEAR	M-Dy	Duration	VOLCANO NAME (Subregion)	NUMBER	VEI	Vol L/T
1993	0309	3*a*	**Guagua Pichincha** (Ecuador)	1502-02=	1	
1993	*0318*	....	*Shiveluch (Kamchatka)*	1000-27=	*2*	*8/6*
1993	*0320*	....	*Kliuchevskoi (Kamchatka)*	1000-26=	*2*	
? *1993*	*0328*	?	*Aracar (Argentina)*	1505-16-	*2?*	
1993	0401t	?	**Raung** (Java)	0603-34=	1	
1993	0419	....	**Láscar** (Chile-N)	1505-10=	4	6/8
1993	*0422*	....	*Shiveluch (Kamchatka)*	1000-27=	*3*	*8/6*
? *1993*	*0425*	?	*Taftan (Iran)*	0302-05-		
? *1993*	*0429*	?	*Tofua (Tonga-SW Pacific)*	0403-06=	*0*	
1993	0506	25*a*	**Gamalama** (Halmahera-Indonesia)	0608-06=	2	
? *1993*	*0506*	<1	*Tungurahua (Ecuador)*	1502-08=	*1?*	
1993	0528	95*a*>	**Seguam** (Aleutian Is)	1101-18-	2	
1993	06 ?	31*p?*	**Iliboleng** (Lesser Sunda Is)	0604-22=	1?	
1993	*0614*	....	*Lengai, Ol Doinyo (Africa-E)*	0202-12=	*2*	*7/-*
1993	0616	517*w*>	**Masaya** (Nicaragua)	1404-10=	1	
1993	0626	8*a?*	**CoAxial Segment** (Pacific-NE)	1301-02-	0	6/-
1993	0703	29*a*	**Ijen** (Java)	0603-35=	1	
1993	*0714*	....	*Manam (New Guinea-NE of)*	0501-02=	*3*	*7/7*
1993	0730	426*a?*	**Veniaminof** (Alaska Peninsula)	1102-07-	2	7/-
1993	08	156*m?*	**Makushin** (Aleutian Is)	1101-31-	1	
1993	0803	71*a*	**Etna** (Italy)	0101-06=	1	
1993	0825	9	**Kanlaon** (Philippines-C)	0702-02=	2	
1993	*0904*	*55a*	*Shishaldin (Aleutian Is)*	1101-36-	*1*	
? *1993*	*0908*	*2a*	*Smith Rock (Izu Is-Japan)*	0804-08=	*0*	
1993	0915	3	**Iliwerung** (Lesser Sunda Is)	0604-25=	2	
1993	1021	106*d*	**Bezymianny** (Kamchatka)	1000-25=	3	-/7
? *1993*	*1027?*	*20a?*	*Ioto [Iwo-jima] (Volcano Is-Japan)*	0804-12=	*1?*	
1993	1028	....	**Shishaldin** (Aleutian Is)	1101-36-	2	
1993	1103?	22*e?*	**Long Island** (New Guinea-NE of)	0501-05=	1	
? *1993*	*1114*	*<1*	*Ojos del Salado, Nevados (Chile)*	1505-13=	*1?*	
1993	1205n	?	**Alcedo** (Galápagos)	1503-04=	1	
1993	1217	72*a*	**Láscar** (Chile-N)	1505-10=	2	
1994	*Cont*	....	*Stromboli (Italy)*	0101-04=	*1*	*7/-*
1994	*Cont*	....	*Erta Ale (Ethiopia)*	0201-08=	*0*	
1994	*Cont*	....	*White Island (New Zealand)*	0401-04=	*1*	
1994	*Cont*	....	*Langila (New Britain-SW Pac)*	0502-01=	*2*	*7/-*
1994	*Cont*	....	*Bagana (Bougainville-SW Pacific)*	0505-02=	*1*	*6/-*
1994	*Cont*	....	*Yasur (Vanuatu-SW Pacific)*	0507-10=	*2*	
1994	*Cont*	....	*Marapi (Sumatra)*	0601-14=	*2*	
1994	*Cont*	....	*Semeru (Java)*	0603-30=	*2*	
1994	*Cont*	....	*Soputan (Sulawesi-Indonesia)*	0606-03=	*1*	*7/-*
1994	*Cont*	....	*Dukono (Halmahera-Indonesia)*	0608-01=	*2*	
1994	*Cont*	....	*Suwanose-jima (Ryukyu Is)*	0802-03=	*2*	
1994	*Cont*	....	*Sakura-jima (Kyushu-Japan)*	0802-08=	*2*	
1994	*Cont*	....	*Unzen (Kyushu-Japan)*	0802-10=	*2*	*8/6*
1994	*Cont*	....	*Shiveluch (Kamchatka)*	1000-27=	*2*	*8/6*
1994	*Cont*	....	*Makushin (Aleutian Is)*	1101-31-	*1*	
1994	*Cont*	....	*Veniaminof (Alaska Peninsula)*	1102-07-	*2*	*7/-*
1994	*Cont*	....	*Kilauea (Hawaiian Is)*	1302-01-	*0*	***9**/-*
1994	*Cont*	....	*Socorro (México-Is)*	1401-021	*0*	
1994	*Cont*	....	*Santa María (Guatemala)*	1402-03=	*1*	***9**/8*
1994	*Cont*	....	*Masaya (Nicaragua)*	1404-10=	*1*	
1994	*Cont*	....	*Arenal (Costa Rica)*	1405-033	*1*	*8/7*
1994	*Cont*	....	*Sangay (Ecuador)*	1502-09=	*2*	
1994	*Cont*	....	*Sabancaya (Perú)*	1504-006	*2*	*-/7*
1994	*Cont*	....	*Erebus (Antarctica)*	1900-02=	*1*	
1994	01	272*m*>	**Gamalama** (Halmahera-Indonesia)	0608-06=	2	
1994	0105d	325*h*	**Kanaga** (Aleutian Is)	1101-11-	2	
? *1994*	*0115*	*<1*	*Tinguiririca (Chile-C)*	1507-03=	*2*	
? *1994*	*0117*	*<1*	*Smith Rock (Izu Is-Japan)*	0804-08=	*0*	
1994	0203	<1	**Ijen** (Java)	0603-35=	1	
? *1994*	*0212*	*48a*	*Ruapehu (New Zealand)*	0401-10=	*1*	
1994	*03 ?*	*214p?*	*Poás (Costa Rica)*	1405-04=	*1*	
1994	0319	454*m*>	**Krakatau** (Indonesia)	0602-00=	2	
1994	0419?	57*m?*	**Ulawun** (New Britain-SW Pac)	0502-12=	1	
? *1994*	*0423*	*<1*	*Ruiz, Nevado del (Colombia)*	1501-02=		
1994	*0502*	*562m*	*Aso (Kyushu-Japan)*	0802-11=	*1*	
1994	0517	105	**Llaima** (Chile-C)	1507-11=	2	
1994	0525	<1	**Cleveland** (Aleutian Is)	1101-24-	3	
1994	0603	171*a*	**Rinjani** (Lesser Sunda Is)	0604-03=	3?	
1994	0603	....	**Poás** (Costa Rica)	1405-04=	2	
1994	*0617*	*>3yr*	*Etna (Italy)*	0101-06=	*1*	*7/8*
1994	0623	631*m?*	**Nyiragongo** (Africa-C)	0203-03=	1	7/-
1994	0704	52*a*>	**Nyamuragira** (Africa-C)	0203-02=	2?	
1994	*0707*	*90d*	*Bezymianny (Kamchatka)*	1000-25=	*1*	
1994	0714	<1	**Raung** (Java)	0603-34=	1	
1994	0720	5	**Láscar** (Chile-N)	1505-10=	2	
1994	0721	<1	**Colima** (México)	1401-04=	1	-/5
? *1994*	*0727*	*<1*	*Smith Rock (Izu Is-Japan)*	0804-08=	*0*	
? *1994*	*0728*	*<1*	*Fukutoku-Okanoba (Volcano Is-Japan)*	0804-13=	*0*	
1994	0731	12*a*	**Telica** (Nicaragua)	1404-04=	2	
1994	0807	7*a*>	**Batur** (Lesser Sunda Is)	0604-01=	1	
1994	0822	<1	**Ioto [Iwo-jima]** (Volcano Is-Japan)	0804-12=	1	
1994	0902	....	**Bezymianny** (Kamchatka)	1000-25=	2	
1994	*0908*	*128a>*	*Kliuchevskoi (Kamchatka)*	1000-26=	*2*	*7/7*
1994	0912	....	**Aso** (Kyushu-Japan)	0802-11=	2	

Peter Francis (Open Univ.)

This large delta, photographed here in 1997, formed by the accumulation of pyroclastic-flow deposits on the southern flank of Soufrière Hills volcano in Montserrat. The pyroclastic flows accompanied long-term growth and collapse of a summit lava dome in an eruptive episode that begin in 1995 and was continuing in 2010. Accumulated pyroclastic-flow deposits buried the evacuated town of O'Garra's here on the coast and the capital city of Plymouth out of view to the left.

	START YEAR	M-Dy	Duration	VOLCANO NAME (Subregion)	NUMBER	VEI	Vol L/T
	1994	0918	>3yr	**Lengai, Ol Doinyo** (Africa-E)	0202-12=	1	5/-
	1994	0919	208	**Rabaul** (New Britain-SW Pac)	0502-14=	4?	5/-
	1994	0926	95a	**Villarrica** (Chile-C)	1507-12=	1	
	1994	10	<1	**Dempo** (Sumatra)	0601-23=	1	
	1994	1001	....	**Kliuchevskoi** (Kamchatka)	1000-26=	3	7/7
	1994	1012	....	*Pacaya (Guatemala)*	1402-11=	2	
	1994	1017	....	*Manam (New Guinea-NE of)*	0501-02=	3	7/7
	1994	1020	<1	**Cleveland** (Aleutian Is)	1101-24-	1?	
	1994	1113	249a	**Láscar** (Chile-N)	1505-10=	2	
	1994	1122	....	*Merapi (Java)*	0603-25=	2	7/-
	1994	1127	63a>	**Bulusan** (Luzon-Philippines)	0703-01=	2	
	1994	12 <	?	**Ambrym** (Vanuatu-SW Pacific)	0507-04=	1?	
	1994	12	?	**Copahue** (Chile-C)	1507-09=	2	
	1994	1208	<1	**Irazú** (Costa Rica)	1405-06=	2	
	1994	1220<	166h	**Barren Island** (Andaman Is-Indian O)	0600-01=	2	6/6
	1994	1221	287a	**Popocatépetl** (México)	1401-09=	2	
	1995	Cont	....	*Stromboli (Italy)*	0101-04=	1	7/-
	1995	Cont	....	*Erta Ale (Ethiopia)*	0201-08=	0	
	1995	Cont	....	*Lengai, Ol Doinyo (Africa-E)*	0202-12=	1	5/-
	1995	Cont	....	*Nyiragongo (Africa-C)*	0203-03=	1	7/-
	1995	Cont	....	*Manam (New Guinea-NE of)*	0501-02=	2	7/7
	1995	Cont	....	*Langila (New Britain-SW Pac)*	0502-01=	2	7/-
	1995	Cont	....	*Bagana (Bougainville-SW Pacific)*	0505-02=	1	6/-
	1995	Cont	....	*Yasur (Vanuatu-SW Pacific)*	0507-10=	2	
	1995	Cont	....	*Barren Island (Andaman Is-Indian O)*	0600-01=	2	6/6
	1995	Cont	....	*Krakatau (Indonesia)*	0602-00=	2	
	1995	Cont	....	*Merapi (Java)*	0603-25=	2	7/-
	1995	Cont	....	*Semeru (Java)*	0603-30=	2	
	1995	Cont	....	*Dukono (Halmahera-Indonesia)*	0608-01=	2	
	1995	Cont	....	*Bulusan (Luzon-Philippines)*	0703-01=	2	
	1995	Cont	....	*Suwanose-jima (Ryukyu Is)*	0802-03=	2	
	1995	Cont	....	*Sakura-jima (Kyushu-Japan)*	0802-08=	2	
	1995	Cont	....	*Unzen (Kyushu-Japan)*	0802-10=	2	8/6
	1995	Cont	....	*Kliuchevskoi (Kamchatka)*	1000-26=	2	7/7
	1995	Cont	....	*Shiveluch (Kamchatka)*	1000-27=	2	8/6
	1995	Cont	....	*Kilauea (Hawaiian Is)*	1302-01-	0	**9**/-
	1995	Cont	....	*Popocatépetl (México)*	1401-09=	2	
	1995	Cont	....	*Santa María (Guatemala)*	1402-03=	1	**9**/8
	1995	Cont	....	*Arenal (Costa Rica)*	1405-033	1	8/7
	1995	Cont	....	*Sangay (Ecuador)*	1502-09=	2	
	1995	Cont	....	*Sabancaya (Perú)*	1504-006	2	-/7
	1995	Cont	....	*Láscar (Chile-N)*	1505-10=	2	
	1995	Cont	....	*Erebus (Antarctica)*	1900-02=	1	
	1995	....	?	**Tinakula** (Santa Cruz Is-SW Pacific)	0506-01=	1?	
S	**1995**	0109	20a	**Vailulu'u** (Samoa-SW Pacific)	0404-00-	0	
	1995	0111?	302a?	*Ruapehu (New Zealand)*	0401-10=	0	-/7
	1995	0112	97a	**San Miguel** (El Salvador)	1403-10=	1	
	1995	0125	73a?	**Fernandina** (Galápagos)	1503-01=	2	7/-
	1995	0130	<1	**Makushin** (Aleutian Is)	1101-31-	1	
	1995	0211	<1	**Yake-dake** (Honshu-Japan)	0803-07=	1	-/3
	1995	03	16m	**Raung** (Java)	0603-34=	1	
	1995	0302	1a?	**Aoba** (Vanuatu-SW Pacific)	0507-03=	2	
	1995	0303	84e	**Tengger Caldera [Bromo]** (Java)	0603-31=	1	
	1995	0317	....	*Aso (Kyushu-Japan)*	0802-11=	2	
	1995	04 ?	61p	**Michael** (Antarctica)	1900-09=	0	
	1995	0402	54a	**Fogo** (Cape Verde Is)	1804-01=	2	6/-
	1995	0415e	48e>	**Villarrica** (Chile-C)	1507-12=	1	
	1995	0417	<1	**Veniaminof** (Alaska Peninsula)	1102-07-	1	
?	*1995*	0501	?	*Atka (Aleutian Is)*	1101-16-	1?	
	1995	0529	191a	**Negro, Cerro** (Nicaragua)	1404-07=	2	6/6
	1995	0601	....	*Pacaya (Guatemala)*	1402-11=	3	
	1995	0606	17b	**Metis Shoal** (Tonga-SW Pacific)	0403-07=	2	6/-
	1995	0619?	4a?	**Kanaga** (Aleutian Is)	1101-11-	2?	
	1995	0628?	<1	**White Island** (New Zealand)	0401-04=	1	
	1995	0629	....	*Ruapehu (New Zealand)*	0401-10=	2	-/7
?	*1995*	07	?	*Bárdarbunga (Iceland-NE)*	1703-03=	0	
?	*1995*	0705	2a	*Smith Rock (Izu Is-Japan)*	0804-08=	0	
	1995	0718	>3yr	*Soufrière Hills (W Indies)*	1600-05=	2	8/-
?	*1995*	0815	?	*Raung (Java)*	0603-34=	2?	
	1995	09 <	23m>	*Bezymianny (Kamchatka)*	1000-25=	0	
	1995	09	?	**Copahue** (Chile-C)	1507-09=	2	
	1995	0901	25a	**Irruputuncu** (Chile-N)	1505-04=	2	
	1995	0909	97m	**Tengger Caldera [Bromo]** (Java)	0603-31=	1	
?	*1995*	0912	?	*Rinjani (Lesser Sunda Is)*	0604-03=		
	1995	0923	....	**Ruapehu** (New Zealand)	0401-10=	3	-/7
	1995	1005	....	**Bezymianny** (Kamchatka)	1000-25=	3?	
	1995	1005d	193m	**Michael** (Antarctica)	1900-09=	0	
	1995	1011	164a	**Kuju** (Kyushu-Japan)	0802-12=	1	-/5
	1995	1011?	14a?	**Ruby** (Mariana Is-C Pacific)	0804-202	0	
	1995	1013	9a>	**Llaima** (Chile-C)	1507-11=	2?	
	1995	1106	7a	**Rincón de la Vieja** (Costa Rica)	1405-02=	2	
	1995	1107	....	**Soputan** (Sulawesi-Indonesia)	0606-03=	2	7/-
	1995	1109	38a	**Karangetang [Api Siau]** (Sangihe Is	0607-02=	1	
	1995	1115	15a?	**Veniaminof** (Alaska Peninsula)	1102-07-	1	
	1995	1119	....	*Negro, Cerro (Nicaragua)*	1404-07=	2	6/6
?	*1995*	1121	614a	*Fukutoku-Okanoba (Volcano Is-Japan.*	0804-13=	0	
S	**1995**	1127	3	**Monowai Seamount** (Kermadec Is)	0402-05-	0	
	1995	1128	>3yr	**Rabaul** (New Britain-SW Pac)	0502-14=	2	6/-
U	**1995**	1201p	?	**Boomerang Seamount** (Indian O.-S)	0304-00-	0	
	1995	1223	....	*Etna (Italy)*	0101-06=	2	7/8
	1995	1223	144a<	**Shishaldin** (Aleutian Is)	1101-36-	3	
	1996	Cont	....	*Stromboli (Italy)*	0101-04=	1	7/-
	1996	Cont	....	*Erta Ale (Ethiopia)*	0201-08=	0	
	1996	Cont	....	*Lengai, Ol Doinyo (Africa-E)*	0202-12=	1	5/-
	1996	Cont	....	*Nyiragongo (Africa-C)*	0203-03=	1	7/-
	1996	Cont	....	*Langila (New Britain-SW Pac)*	0502-01=	2	7/-
	1996	Cont	....	*Rabaul (New Britain-SW Pac)*	0502-14=	2	6/-
	1996	Cont	....	*Merapi (Java)*	0603-25=	2	7/-
	1996	Cont	....	*Dukono (Halmahera-Indonesia)*	0608-01=	2	
	1996	Cont	....	*Sakura-jima (Kyushu-Japan)*	0802-08=	2	
	1996	Cont	....	*Kuju (Kyushu-Japan)*	0802-12=	1	-/5
?	*1996*	Cont	....	*Fukutoku-Okanoba (Volcano Is-Japan.*	0804-13=	0	
	1996	Cont	....	*Shishaldin (Aleutian Is)*	1101-36-	3	
	1996	Cont	....	*Kilauea (Hawaiian Is)*	1302-01-	0	**9**/-
	1996	Cont	....	*Santa María (Guatemala)*	1402-03=	1	**9**/8
	1996	Cont	....	*Pacaya (Guatemala)*	1402-11=	1	
	1996	Cont	....	*Arenal (Costa Rica)*	1405-033	1	8/7
	1996	Cont	....	*Sangay (Ecuador)*	1502-09=	2	
	1996	Cont	....	*Sabancaya (Perú)*	1504-006	2	-/7
	1996	Cont	....	*Erebus (Antarctica)*	1900-02=	1	
	1996	....	?	**Gamalama** (Halmahera-Indonesia)	0608-06=	2?	
	1996	....	?	**Pagan** (Mariana Is-C Pacific)	0804-17=	1	
	1996 f	....	?	**Galápagos Rift** (Pacific-E)	1304-07-	0	
	1996	01	?	**Villarrica** (Chile-C)	1507-12=	1	
	1996	0102	<1	**Akademia Nauk** (Kamchatka)	1000-125	3	-/7
	1996	0102	>3yr	*Karymsky (Kamchatka)*	1000-13=	2	7/-
?	*1996*	0111	1a	*Minami-Hiyoshi (Volcano Is-Japan)*	0804-131	0	
?	*1996*	0122	<1	*Smith Rock (Izu Is-Japan)*	0804-08=	0	
	1996	0210	81a	**Unzen** (Kyushu-Japan)	0802-10=	2	
	1996	0218	4a>	**Eastern Gemini Seamount** (S Pac)	0508-001	1	
	1996	0225p	165p?	**Loihi** (Hawaiian Is)	1302-00-	0	
	1996	0228?	16a?	**North Gorda Ridge** (Pacific-NE)	1301-031	0	7/-
	1996	0305	7a?	**Komaga-take** (Hokkaido-Japan)	0805-02=	1	
	1996	0305	>3yr	*Popocatépetl (México)*	1401-09=	2	7/-
	1996	0315	....	*Soputan (Sulawesi-Indonesia)*	0606-03=	2	7/-
?	*1996*	0321<	?	*Ruapehu (New Zealand)*	0401-10=	0	
	1996	0408	<1	**Poás** (Costa Rica)	1405-04=	1	
?	*1996*	0505	?	*Sorikmarapi (Sumatra)*	0601-12=		
	1996	0505	....	*Semeru (Java)*	0603-30=	3	
	1996	06 <	>3yr	**Ambrym** (Vanuatu-SW Pacific)	0507-04=	1	
?	*1996*	0611	?	*Kanaga (Aleutian Is)*	1101-11-	1?	
	1996	0616	77a	*Ruapehu (New Zealand)*	0401-10=	2	-/6
	1996	0625	....	*Etna (Italy)*	0101-06=	2	7/8
?	*1996*	0627	?	*Ruang (Sangihe Is-Indonesia)*	0607-01=		
	1996	07 <	92p>	**Krakatau** (Indonesia)	0602-00=	2	
	1996	0720	....	**Ruapehu** (New Zealand)	0401-10=	3	-/6
	1996	0723?	40a?	**Bezymianny** (Kamchatka)	1000-25=	0	
	1996	08	61p	**Kerinci** (Sumatra)	0601-17=	1	
?	*1996*	08	?	*Bárdarbunga (Iceland-NE)*	1703-03=	0	
	1996	0810	<1	**Kanlaon** (Philippines-C)	0702-02=	2	
	1996	0901	<1	**Adatara** (Honshu-Japan)	0803-17=	1	
?	*1996*	0901w	?	*Montagu Island (Antarctica)*	1900-081	1?	
	1996	0911	115a?	*Pavlof (Alaska Peninsula)*	1102-03-	1	
	1996	0914	336m	**Villarrica** (Chile-C)	1507-12=	1	
	1996	0917	1a	**Amukta** (Aleutian Is)	1101-19-	1	
	1996	0917	....	**Soufrière Hills** (W Indies)	1600-05=	3	8/-
S	**1996**	0920	2	**Monowai Seamount** (Kermadec Is)	0402-05-	0	
?	*1996*	0927	?	*Gareloi (Aleutian Is)*	1101-07-	1?	
?	*1996*	0927	?	*Maderas (Nicaragua)*	1404-13-		
	1996	0930	36	*Grímsvötn (Iceland-NE)*	1703-01=	0	8/-
	1996	10	?	**Michael** (Antarctica)	1900-09=	0	
	1996	1001<	257m>	**Karangetang [Api Siau]** (Sangihe Is	0607-02=	1	
	1996	1003	....	**Grímsvötn** (Iceland-NE)	1703-01=	3?	8/-
	1996	1018	....	**Pavlof** (Alaska Peninsula)	1102-03-	2	
	1996	1018	<1	**Láscar** (Chile-N)	1505-10=	2	
	1996	1114	126k>	**Kliuchevskoi** (Kamchatka)	1000-26=	2	
	1996	1121	<1	**Akan** (Hokkaido-Japan)	0805-07=	1	
	1996	12	57t	**McDonald Islands** (Indian O.-S)	0304-011	1?	
	1996	1201	4a>	**Nyamuragira** (Africa-C)	0203-02=	3	
	1996	1203	....	*Manam (New Guinea-NE of)*	0501-02=	3	7/7
	1996	1203	?	**Alaid** (Kuril Is)	0900-39=	2	
	1996	1205	<1	**Masaya** (Nicaragua)	1404-10=	1	
	1996	1226	112a	**Suwanose-jima** (Ryukyu Is)	0802-03=	1	
	1996	1231	<1	**Dieng Volc Complex** (Java)	0603-20=	1	
	1997	Cont	....	*Stromboli (Italy)*	0101-04=	1	7/-
	1997	Cont	....	*Etna (Italy)*	0101-06=	1	7/8
	1997	Cont	....	*Erta Ale (Ethiopia)*	0201-08=	0	
	1997	Cont	....	*Lengai, Ol Doinyo (Africa-E)*	0202-12=	1	5/-
	1997	Cont	....	*McDonald Islands (Indian O.-S)*	0304-011	1?	
	1997	Cont	....	*Manam (New Guinea-NE of)*	0501-02=	2	7/7
	1997	Cont	....	*Rabaul (New Britain-SW Pac)*	0502-14=	2	6/-
	1997	Cont	....	*Ambrym (Vanuatu-SW Pacific)*	0507-04=	1	
	1997	Cont	....	*Yasur (Vanuatu-SW Pacific)*	0507-10=	2	
	1997	Cont	....	*Merapi (Java)*	0603-25=	2	7/-

	START YEAR	M-Dy	Duration	VOLCANO NAME (Subregion)	NUMBER	VEI	Vol L/T
	1997	Cont	....	Semeru (Java)	0603-30=	2	
	1997	Cont	....	Karangetang [Api Siau] (Sangihe Is	0607-02=	1	
	1997	Cont	....	Dukono (Halmahera-Indonesia)	0608-01=	2	
	1997	Cont	....	Suwanose-jima (Ryukyu Is)	0802-03=	1	
	1997	Cont	....	Sakura-jima (Kyushu-Japan)	0802-08=	2	
	1997	Cont	....	Karymsky (Kamchatka)	1000-13=	2	7/-
	1997	Cont	....	Pavlof (Alaska Peninsula)	1102-03-	1	
	1997	Cont	....	Kilauea (Hawaiian Is)	1302-01-	0	9/-
	1997	Cont	....	Santa María (Guatemala)	1402-03=	1	9/8
	1997	Cont	....	Pacaya (Guatemala)	1402-11=	1	
	1997	Cont	....	Arenal (Costa Rica)	1405-033	1	8/7
	1997	Cont	....	Sangay (Ecuador)	1502-09=	2	
	1997	Cont	....	Villarrica (Chile-C)	1507-12=	1	
	1997	Cont	....	Erebus (Antarctica)	1900-02=	1	
	1997	....	730y	Sangeang Api (Lesser Sunda Is)	0604-05=	2?	
	1997	....	?	Kikai (Ryukyu Is)	0802-06=	1?	
	1997	0107	....	Kliuchevskoi (Kamchatka)	1000-26=	2	
	1997	0116	1a>	Kavachi (Solomon Is-SW Pacific)	0505-06=	1	
	1997	0211	....	Langila (New Britain-SW Pac)	0502-01=	3	7/-
	1997	0211	98d	Okmok (Aleutian Is)	1101-29-	2	7/-
	1997	03 <	60p>	Krakatau (Indonesia)	0602-00=	2	
	1997	03	217m	Guagua Pichincha (Ecuador)	1502-02=	1	
	1997	03 ?	214p?	Llaima (Chile-C)	1507-11=	1	
	1997	0303	?	Amukta (Aleutian Is)	1101-19-	1	
	1997	0308	27a	Shiveluch (Kamchatka)	1000-27=	2	
?	1997	0310	<1	Kita-Iwo-jima (Volcano Is-Japan)	0804-11=	0	
	1997	0311	....	Okmok (Aleutian Is)	1101-29-	3	7/-
	1997	04 <	?	Raung (Java)	0603-34=	2	
S	1997	0418	3	Monowai Seamount (Kermadec Is)	0402-05-	0	
	1997	05 ?	245p>	Michael (Antarctica)	1900-09=	0	
	1997	0501	....	Sabancaya (Perú)	1504-006	3	-/7
	1997	0505	<1	Cleveland (Aleutian Is)	1101-24-	2?	
	1997	0508	8a?	Bezymianny (Kamchatka)	1000-25=	0	-/7
	1997	0509	....	Bezymianny (Kamchatka)	1000-25=	3	-/7
	1997	0511	<1	Akita-Yake-yama (Honshu-Japan)	0803-26=	1	-/3
	1997	0519?	49a>	San Cristóbal (Nicaragua)	1404-02=	1	
	1997	0602	<1	Shishaldin (Aleutian Is)	1101-36-	1	
	1997	0603?	167a?	Masaya (Nicaragua)	1404-10=	1	
?	1997	0627	19m?	Don Joao de Castro Bank (Azores)	1802-07=	0	
	1997	0630	....	Popocatépetl (México)	1401-09=	3	7/-
	1997	0715	<1	Watt, Morne (W Indies)	1600-101	1	
?	1997	08	?	Bárdarbunga (Iceland-NE)	1703-03=	0	
	1997	0816	<1	Akita-Yake-yama (Honshu-Japan)	0803-26=	1	-/3
?	1997	0823	<1	Alaid (Kuril Is)	0900-39=		
	1997	0907	19a	Kliuchevskoi (Kamchatka)	1000-26=	1	
	1997	1009	9a	Ruapehu (New Zealand)	0401-10=	1	
	1997	1029	42a	Niigata-Yake-yama (Honshu-Japan)	0803-09=	1	
?	1997	1118	549a	Fukutoku-Okanoba (Volcano Is-Japan)	0804-13=	0	
?	1997	1121	<1	Smith Rock (Izu Is-Japan)	0804-08=	0	
	1997	1122	>3yr	Colima (México)	1401-04=	1	7/6
	1997	1205	1a	Bezymianny (Kamchatka)	1000-25=	3	
S	1997	1215	50a?	Monowai Seamount (Kermadec Is)	0402-05-	0	
	1997	1226	....	Soufrière Hills (W Indies)	1600-05=	3	8/-
	1997	1231	?	San Miguel (El Salvador)	1403-10=	1	
	1998	Cont	....	Stromboli (Italy)	0101-04=	1	7/-
	1998	Cont	....	Erta Ale (Ethiopia)	0201-08=	0	
	1998	Cont	....	Lengai, Ol Doinyo (Africa-E)	0202-12=	1	5/-
S	1998	Cont	....	Monowai Seamount (Kermadec Is)	0402-05-	0	
	1998	Cont	....	Manam (New Guinea-NE of)	0501-02=	2	7/7
	1998	Cont	....	Langila (New Britain-SW Pac)	0502-01=	2	7/-
	1998	Cont	....	Rabaul (New Britain-SW Pac)	0502-14=	2	6/-
	1998	Cont	....	Ambrym (Vanuatu-SW Pacific)	0507-04=	1	
	1998	Cont	....	Yasur (Vanuatu-SW Pacific)	0507-10=	2	
	1998	Cont	....	Merapi (Java)	0603-25=	2	7/-
	1998	Cont	....	Semeru (Java)	0603-30=	2	
	1998	Cont	....	Sangeang Api (Lesser Sunda Is)	0604-05=	2?	
	1998	Cont	....	Sakura-jima (Kyushu-Japan)	0802-08=	2	
	1998	Cont	....	Kilauea (Hawaiian Is)	1302-01-	0	9/-
	1998	Cont	....	Popocatépetl (México)	1401-09=	2	7/-
	1998	Cont	....	Santa María (Guatemala)	1402-03=	1	9/8
	1998	Cont	....	Sangay (Ecuador)	1502-09=	2	
	1998	Cont	....	Sabancaya (Perú)	1504-006	2	-/7
	1998	Cont	....	Soufrière Hills (W Indies)	1600-05=	2	8/-
	1998	Cont	....	Erebus (Antarctica)	1900-02=	1	
	1998	Cont	....	Michael (Antarctica)	1900-09=	0	
?	1998	....	?	Kavachi (Solomon Is-SW Pacific)	0505-06=	0	
	1998	0125	11a?	Axial Seamount (Pacific-NE)	1301-021	0	6/-
	1998	0215	181m	Rincón de la Vieja (Costa Rica)	1405-02=	2	
	1998	0224d	>3yr	Villarrica (Chile-C)	1507-12=	1	
	1998	0309	195a?	Fournaise, Piton de la (Indian O.)	0303-02=	1	7/-
	1998	0328	1a	White Island (New Zealand)	0401-04=	1	
	1998	0330	?	Niigata-Yake-yama (Honshu-Japan)	0803-09=	1	
	1998	0403	20a?	Llaima (Chile-C)	1507-11=	2?	
	1998	0419	7a?	Peuet Sague (Sumatra)	0601-03=	1	
	1998	0425	477m	Kikai (Ryukyu Is)	0802-06=	2	
	1998	0505	....	Arenal (Costa Rica)	1405-033	2	8/7
	1998	0508a	61b?	Korovin (Aleutian Is)	1101-161	2	
	1998	0520	....	Pacaya (Guatemala)	1402-11=	2	
?	1998	0521	<1	Kita-Iwo-jima (Volcano Is-Japan)	0804-11=	0	
	1998	0530	66a	Shiveluch (Kamchatka)	1000-27=	2	
	1998	0620?	2a?	Bezymianny (Kamchatka)	1000-25=	0	
	1998	0630	....	Korovin (Aleutian Is)	1101-161	3	
	1998	07	649m?	Lopevi (Vanuatu-SW Pacific)	0507-05=	2	3/-
	1998	0704	<1	Kerinci (Sumatra)	0601-17=	2	
	1998	0704c	?	Batur (Lesser Sunda Is)	0604-01=	1	
	1998	0705d	?	Karangetang [Api Siau] (Sangihe Is	0607-02=	1	
	1998	0722	....	Etna (Italy)	0101-06=	3	7/8
	1998	0723	41a?	Kliuchevskoi (Kamchatka)	1000-26=	1	
	1998	0807	>3yr	Guagua Pichincha (Ecuador)	1502-02=	2	6/-
	1998	0813	<1	Chiginagak (Alaska Peninsula)	1102-11-	1	
	1998	0822	359m	White Island (New Zealand)	0401-04=	2	
	1998	0902	....	Kliuchevskoi (Kamchatka)	1000-26=	2	
	1998	0903	....	Shiveluch (Kamchatka)	1000-27=	3	
	1998	0914	<1	Masaya (Nicaragua)	1404-10=	1	
	1998	0915	....	Etna (Italy)	0101-06=	2	7/8
	1998	0915	35	Azul, Cerro (Galápagos)	1503-06=	1	8/-
	1998	0918	....	Pacaya (Guatemala)	1402-11=	2	
?	1998	1016	88a	Fukutoku-Okanoba (Volcano Is-Japan)	0804-13=	0	
	1998	1017	8a>	Nyamuragira (Africa-C)	0203-02=	2?	
	1998	1025	<1	Komaga-take (Hokkaido-Japan)	0805-02=	2	
?	1998	1027	78a	Smith Rock (Izu Is-Japan)	0804-08=	0	
?	1998	1027	<1	Kita-Iwo-jima (Volcano Is-Japan)	0804-11=	0	
	1998	1103	?	Kerinci (Sumatra)	0601-17=	2?	
	1998	1104	<1	Shishaldin (Aleutian Is)	1101-36-	1	
	1998	1109	<1	Akan (Hokkaido-Japan)	0805-07=	1	
	1998	1110 c	?	Llaima (Chile-C)	1507-11=	2	
	1998	1118	3a	Planchón-Peteroa (Chile-C)	1507-04=	1	
	1998	1120	....	Colima (México)	1401-04=	0	7/6
	1998	1124	....	Karymsky (Kamchatka)	1000-13=	3	7/-
	1998	1125?	475m?	Terceira (Azores)	1802-05=	0	
	1998	1218	271m>	Ibu (Halmahera-Indonesia)	0608-03=	1	
	1998	1218	10	Grímsvötn (Iceland-NE)	1703-01=	3	
	1999	Cont	....	Stromboli (Italy)	0101-04=	1	7/-
	1999	Cont	....	Erta Ale (Ethiopia)	0201-08=	0	
	1999	Cont	....	Lengai, Ol Doinyo (Africa-E)	0202-12=	1	5/-
	1999	Cont	....	White Island (New Zealand)	0401-04=	2	
	1999	Cont	....	Manam (New Guinea-NE of)	0501-02=	2	7/7
	1999	Cont	....	Langila (New Britain-SW Pac)	0502-01=	2	7/-
	1999	Cont	....	Rabaul (New Britain-SW Pac)	0502-14=	2	6/-
	1999	Cont	....	Ambrym (Vanuatu-SW Pacific)	0507-04=	1	
	1999	Cont	....	Lopevi (Vanuatu-SW Pacific)	0507-05=	2	3/-
	1999	Cont	....	Yasur (Vanuatu-SW Pacific)	0507-10=	2	
	1999	Cont	....	Merapi (Java)	0603-25=	2	7/-
	1999	Cont	....	Semeru (Java)	0603-30=	2	
	1999	Cont	....	Sangeang Api (Lesser Sunda Is)	0604-05=	2?	
	1999	Cont	....	Kikai (Ryukyu Is)	0802-06=	2	
	1999	Cont	....	Sakura-jima (Kyushu-Japan)	0802-08=	2	
?	1999	Cont	....	Smith Rock (Izu Is-Japan)	0804-08=	0	
	1999	Cont	....	Karymsky (Kamchatka)	1000-13=	2	7/-
	1999	Cont	....	Kilauea (Hawaiian Is)	1302-01-	0	9/-
	1999	Cont	....	Popocatépetl (México)	1401-09=	2	7/-
	1999	Cont	....	Santa María (Guatemala)	1402-03=	1	9/8
	1999	Cont	....	Pacaya (Guatemala)	1402-11=	1	
	1999	Cont	....	Arenal (Costa Rica)	1405-033	1	8/7
	1999	Cont	....	Sangay (Ecuador)	1502-09=	2	
	1999	Cont	....	Villarrica (Chile-C)	1507-12=	1	
	1999	Cont	....	Soufrière Hills (W Indies)	1600-05=	2	8/-
	1999	Cont	....	Terceira (Azores)	1802-05=	0	
	1999	Cont	....	Erebus (Antarctica)	1900-02=	1	
?	1999	01 ?	242p?	Unnamed [E Gakkel Ridge] (Arctic)	1707-02-	0	
	1999	0102	....	Ibu (Halmahera-Indonesia)	0608-03=	2	
	1999	0105e	16m?	Suwanose-jima (Ryukyu Is)	0802-03=	1?	
	1999	0108<	6a?	Unnamed [NW of Tongatapu]	0403-03=	1	
	1999	02	90n	Kavachi (Solomon Is-SW Pacific)	0505-06=	1	
	1999 ?	0201p	?	Epi (Vanuatu-SW Pacific)	0507-06=	1?	
	1999	0204	....	Etna (Italy)	0101-06=	2	7/8
	1999	0205	222m>	Krakatau (Indonesia)	0602-00=	2	
	1999	0205	157a	Kliuchevskoi (Kamchatka)	1000-26=	2	
	1999	0210	....	Colima (México)	1401-04=	2	7/6
	1999	0225	<1	Bezymianny (Kamchatka)	1000-25=	2	
	1999	03 <	183p>	Kerinci (Sumatra)	0601-17=	2	
	1999	03 <	>3yr	Karangetang [Api Siau] (Sangihe Is	0607-02=	1	
	1999	0309?	51c?	Peuet Sague (Sumatra)	0601-03=	1	
	1999	0313	75a	Shishaldin (Aleutian Is)	1101-36-	1	-/7
	1999	0315	442m?	Batur (Lesser Sunda Is)	0604-01=	1	
	1999	0328	20a	Cameroon (Africa-W)	0204-01=	2	7/6
	1999	0331	92a?	Lewotobi (Lesser Sunda Is)	0604-18=	1	
	1999	04 <	153p>	Marapi (Sumatra)	0601-14=	2	
	1999	0403	9	Shiveluch (Kamchatka)	1000-27=	2	
	1999	0419	....	Shishaldin (Aleutian Is)	1101-36-	3	-/7
	1999	05	?	Tinakula (Santa Cruz Is-SW Pacific)	0506-01=	1?	
	1999	0501?	137m?	Slamet (Java)	0603-18=	1	
	1999	0501w	410m>	San Cristóbal (Nicaragua)	1404-02=	1	-/6
	1999	0510	....	Colima (México)	1401-04=	3	7/6

	START YEAR	M-Dy	Duration	VOLCANO NAME (Subregion)	NUMBER	VEI	Vol L/T
	1999	0514	<1	**Wrangell** (Alaska-E)	1105-02-	1	
	1999	0521	568a>	*Fuego (Guatemala)*	1402-09=	1	
	1999	0521	473a	*Telica (Nicaragua)*	1404-04=	1	
	1999	0522	116m>	**Iliwerung** (Lesser Sunda Is)	0604-25=	0	
S	1999	0606	5a	**Monowai Seamount** (Kermadec Is)	0402-05-	0	
	1999	0615e	15i	**Suwanose-jima** (Ryukyu Is)	0802-03=	1?	
	1999	0622	271a	**Mayon** (Luzon-Philippines)	0703-03=	3	
	1999	0628	<1	**Ijen** (Java)	0603-35=	1?	
	1999	0701	....	**Lewotobi** (Lesser Sunda Is)	0604-18=	2	
	1999	0717	....	*Colima (México)*	1401-04=	3	7/6
?	1999	0717?	28e?	*Katla (Iceland-S)*	1702-03=	0	
	1999	0719	96a	**Fournaise, Piton de la** (Indian O.)	0303-02=	1	6/-
	1999	0730	?	**Raung** (Java)	0603-34=	2	
	1999	0805	2a	**Negro, Cerro** (Nicaragua)	1404-07=	2	5/6
	1999	0815	>3yr	*Shiveluch (Kamchatka)*	1000-27=	1	8/-
	1999	0821	....	**Guagua Pichincha** (Ecuador)	1502-02=	3	6/-
	1999	0904	....	*Etna (Italy)*	0101-06=	2	7/8
?	1999	0907	9a	*Kita-Iwo-jima (Volcano Is-Japan)*	0804-11=	0	
?	1999	0908	163a	*Fukutoku-Okanoba (Volcano Is-Japan)*	0804-13=	0	
	1999	0910	<1	**Ioto [Iwo-jima]** (Volcano Is-Japan)	0804-12=	1	
?	1999	0925e	132e?	*Shishaldin (Aleutian Is)*	1101-36-		
	1999	1005	>3yr	*Tungurahua (Ecuador)*	1502-08=	2	
	1999	1007	6a	**Medvezhia** (Kuril Is)	0900-10=	1	
	1999	1017	....	*Guagua Pichincha (Ecuador)*	1502-02=	3?	6/-
	1999	1020	<1	**Ulawun** (New Britain-SW Pac)	0502-12=	1	
	1999	11 ?	>3yr	**Kavachi** (Solomon Is-SW Pacific)	0505-06=	1	
	1999	11	....	*Shiveluch (Kamchatka)*	1000-27=	2	8/-
	1999	1120	....	**San Cristóbal** (Nicaragua)	1404-02=	2	-/6
	1999	1122	101a?	**Masaya** (Nicaragua)	1404-10=	1	
	1999	1227	2a?	**Concepción** (Nicaragua)	1404-12=	1	
?	1999	1227	?	*Maderas (Nicaragua)*	1404-13-		
	1999	1229	....	**Telica** (Nicaragua)	1404-04=	2	

2000

	START YEAR	M-Dy	Duration	VOLCANO NAME (Subregion)	NUMBER	VEI	Vol L/T
	2000	Cont	....	*Stromboli (Italy)*	0101-04=	1	7/-
	2000	Cont	....	*Etna (Italy)*	0101-06=	1	7/8
	2000	Cont	....	*Erta Ale (Ethiopia)*	0201-08=	0	
	2000	Cont	....	*Lengai, Ol Doinyo (Africa-E)*	0202-12=	1	5/-
	2000	Cont	....	*Langila (New Britain-SW Pac)*	0502-01=	2	7/-
	2000	Cont	....	*Rabaul (New Britain-SW Pac)*	0502-14=	2	6/-
	2000	Cont	....	*Kavachi (Solomon Is-SW Pacific)*	0505-06=	1	
	2000	Cont	....	*Ambrym (Vanuatu-SW Pacific)*	0507-04=	1	
	2000	Cont	....	*Yasur (Vanuatu-SW Pacific)*	0507-10=	2	
	2000	Cont	....	*Merapi (Java)*	0603-25=	2	7/-
	2000	Cont	....	*Batur (Lesser Sunda Is)*	0604-01=	1	
	2000	Cont	....	*Dukono (Halmahera-Indonesia)*	0608-01=	2	
	2000	Cont	....	*Sakura-jima (Kyushu-Japan)*	0802-08=	2	
	2000	Cont	....	*Karymsky (Kamchatka)*	1000-13=	2	7/-
	2000	Cont	....	*Kilauea (Hawaiian Is)*	1302-01-	0	**9**/-
	2000	Cont	....	*Colima (México)*	1401-04=	1	7/6
	2000	Cont	....	*Santa María (Guatemala)*	1402-03=	1	**9**/8
	2000	Cont	....	*San Cristóbal (Nicaragua)*	1404-02=	1	-/6
	2000	Cont	....	*Telica (Nicaragua)*	1404-04=	1	
	2000	Cont	....	*Masaya (Nicaragua)*	1404-10=	1	
	2000	Cont	....	*Guagua Pichincha (Ecuador)*	1502-02=	2	6/-
	2000	Cont	....	*Tungurahua (Ecuador)*	1502-08=	2	
	2000	Cont	....	*Sangay (Ecuador)*	1502-09=	2	
	2000	Cont	....	*Villarrica (Chile-C)*	1507-12=	1	
	2000	Cont	....	*Terceira (Azores)*	1802-05=	0	
?	2000	01	?	*Barren Island (Andaman Is-Indian O)*	0600-01=	1?	
	2000	01	60p	**Kikai** (Ryukyu Is)	0802-06=	2?	
	2000	0116	....	*Pacaya (Guatemala)*	1402-11=	3	
?	2000	0125	1a	*Kita-Iwo-jima (Volcano Is-Japan)*	0804-11=	0	
	2000	0127	14a>	**Nyamuragira** (Africa-C)	0203-02=	2?	
	2000	0203	5a?	**Kliuchevskoi** (Kamchatka)	1000-26=	2	
	2000	0214	19	**Fournaise, Piton de la** (Indian O.)	0303-02=	1	6/-
	2000	0218	....	**Lopevi** (Vanuatu-SW Pacific)	0507-05=	3	3/-
	2000	0224d	1?	**Suwanose-jima** (Ryukyu Is)	0802-03=	2?	
	2000	0226	12	**Hekla** (Iceland-S)	1702-07=	3	8/7
	2000	0228	....	*Mayon (Luzon-Philippines)*	0703-03=	3	
	2000	0307?	344m?	*Heard (Indian O.-S)*	0304-01=	1	
	2000	0307	182d	*White Island (New Zealand)*	0401-04=	1	
	2000	0311	23a>	**Marapi** (Sumatra)	0601-14=	2	
	2000	0314	12a	**Bezymianny** (Kamchatka)	1000-25=	2	
	2000	0317	<1	**Mutnovsky** (Kamchatka)	1000-06=	2	
	2000	0320	....	*Soufrière Hills (W Indies)*	1600-05=	3	8/-
	2000	0321	58a	**Galeras** (Colombia)	1501-08=	1	
	2000	0331	533e	**Usu** (Hokkaido-Japan)	0805-03=	2	
	2000	04 ?	197m?	**Sabancaya** (Perú)	1504-006	2	
	2000	0418	....	*White Island (New Zealand)*	0401-04=	2	
	2000	0510c	465c	**Lokon-Empung** (Sulawesi-Indonesia)	0606-10=	2	
	2000	0513	>3yr	**Soputan** (Sulawesi-Indonesia)	0606-03=	2	7/-
	2000	0528	110e	**Cameroon** (Africa-W)	0204-01=	2?	6/-
	2000	0529	154a?	**Krakatau** (Indonesia)	0602-00=	1	
	2000	0603	<1	**Manam** (New Guinea-NE of)	0501-02=	2	
	2000	0623	143	**Fournaise, Piton de la** (Indian O.)	0303-02=	1	7/-
	2000	0627	93a	*Miyake-jima (Izu Is-Japan)*	0804-04=	0	-/7
S	2000	0630	<1	**Mutnovsky** (Kamchatka)	1000-06=	1?	
?	2000	07 ?	92p?	*Slamet (Java)*	0603-18=	1?	
	2000	0701	109a	**Copahue** (Chile-C)	1507-09=	2	
	2000	0708	....	*Miyake-jima (Izu Is-Japan)*	0804-04=	2	-/7
	2000	0709	?	**Raung** (Java)	0603-34=	2?	
	2000	0716	46	**Mayon** (Luzon-Philippines)	0703-03=	2	
	2000	0718	109a>	*Bezymianny (Kamchatka)*	1000-25=	1	
	2000	0720	182a?	**Láscar** (Chile-N)	1505-10=	2	
?	2000	0726	322a	*Fukutoku-Okanoba (Volcano Is-Japan)*	0804-13=	0	
	2000	0727	....	**White Island** (New Zealand)	0401-04=	3?	
	2000	0728	56a	**Kliuchevskoi** (Kamchatka)	1000-26=	2	
	2000	08	323m?	**Pacaya** (Guatemala)	1402-11=	1	
?	2000	08	?	*Bárdarbunga (Iceland-NE)*	1703-03=	0	
	2000	08 ?	153p	**Michael** (Antarctica)	1900-09=	0	
?	2000	0811	?	*Shishaldin (Aleutian Is)*	1101-36-		
	2000	0818	....	**Miyake-jima** (Izu Is-Japan)	0804-04=	3	-/7
	2000	0822?	5a?	**Kaba** (Sumatra)	0601-22=	1	
	2000	0823	....	*Arenal (Costa Rica)*	1405-033	2	8/7
	2000	0829	....	*Shiveluch (Kamchatka)*	1000-27=	3	8/-
	2000	0829	....	**Fuego** (Guatemala)	1402-09=	2	
?	2000	0901e	9e	*Ijen (Java)*	0603-35=	1	
	2000	0904	64	**Komaga-take** (Hokkaido-Japan)	0805-02=	1	
	2000	0916	>3yr	**Bagana** (Bougainville-SW Pacific)	0505-02=	2	
	2000	0928	34	*Ulawun (New Britain-SW Pac)*	0502-12=	1	
	2000	0929	....	**Ulawun** (New Britain-SW Pac)	0502-12=	4	
	2000	10	457p	**Kikai** (Ryukyu Is)	0802-06=	1	
	2000	1027	....	*Karangetang [Api Siau] (Sangihe Is*	0607-02=	2	
?	2000	1030	<1	*Smith Rock (Izu Is-Japan)*	0804-08=	0	
?	2000	1030	<1	*Kita-Iwo-jima (Volcano Is-Japan)*	0804-11=	0	
	2000	1031	....	**Bezymianny** (Kamchatka)	1000-25=	2	
	2000	1102?	165a?	**Tinakula** (Santa Cruz Is-SW Pacific)	0506-01=	1?	
	2000	1129	47a>	**Tengger Caldera [Bromo]** (Java)	0603-31=	2	
	2000	12	....	*Erebus (Antarctica)*	1900-02=	2	
	2000	1212	....	*Popocatépetl (México)*	1401-09=	3	7/-
	2000	1219	>3yr	*Suwanose-jima (Ryukyu Is)*	0802-03=	2?	
	2000	1225	1a>	**Peuet Sague** (Sumatra)	0601-03=	2	
	2001	Cont	....	*Stromboli (Italy)*	0101-04=	1	7/-
	2001	Cont	....	*Erta Ale (Ethiopia)*	0201-08=	0	
	2001	Cont	....	*Lengai, Ol Doinyo (Africa-E)*	0202-12=	1	5/-
	2001	Cont	....	*Rabaul (New Britain-SW Pac)*	0502-14=	2	6/-
	2001	Cont	....	*Bagana (Bougainville-SW Pacific)*	0505-02=	2	
	2001	Cont	....	*Kavachi (Solomon Is-SW Pacific)*	0505-06=	1	
	2001	Cont	....	*Tinakula (Santa Cruz Is-SW Pacific)*	0506-01=	1?	
	2001	Cont	....	*Ambrym (Vanuatu-SW Pacific)*	0507-04=	1	
	2001	Cont	....	*Yasur (Vanuatu-SW Pacific)*	0507-10=	2	
	2001	Cont	....	*Merapi (Java)*	0603-25=	2	7/-
	2001	Cont	....	*Tengger Caldera [Bromo] (Java)*	0603-31=	2	
	2001	Cont	....	*Soputan (Sulawesi-Indonesia)*	0606-03=	0	7/-
	2001	Cont	....	*Lokon-Empung (Sulawesi-Indonesia)*	0606-10=	2	
	2001	Cont	....	*Karangetang [Api Siau] (Sangihe Is*	0607-02=	1	
	2001	Cont	....	*Kikai (Ryukyu Is)*	0802-06=	1	
	2001	Cont	....	*Sakura-jima (Kyushu-Japan)*	0802-08=	2	
	2001	Cont	....	*Usu (Hokkaido-Japan)*	0805-03=	2	
	2001	Cont	....	*Kilauea (Hawaiian Is)*	1302-01-	0	**9**/-
	2001	Cont	....	*Colima (México)*	1401-04=	1	7/6
	2001	Cont	....	*Santa María (Guatemala)*	1402-03=	1	**9**/8
	2001	Cont	....	*Arenal (Costa Rica)*	1405-033	1	8/7
	2001	Cont	....	*Tungurahua (Ecuador)*	1502-08=	2	
	2001	Cont	....	*Sangay (Ecuador)*	1502-09=	2	
	2001	Cont	....	*Villarrica (Chile-C)*	1507-12=	1	
	2001	Cont	....	*Soufrière Hills (W Indies)*	1600-05=	2	8/-
	2001	Cont	....	*Erebus (Antarctica)*	1900-02=	1	
?	2001	01	?	*Nishino-shima (Volcano Is-Japan)*	0804-096	0	
	2001	0108	212a	*Mayon (Luzon-Philippines)*	0703-03=	0	7/7
	2001	0111	53m?	**Inielika** (Lesser Sunda Is)	0604-09=	2	
	2001	0111	682a	*Miyake-jima (Izu Is-Japan)*	0804-04=	1	
	2001	0116?	107a?	**Ulawun** (New Britain-SW Pac)	0502-12=	3?	
	2001	0117	336a?	**Telica** (Nicaragua)	1404-04=	1	
	2001	0122	....	*Mayon (Luzon-Philippines)*	0703-03=	1	7/7
	2001	0122	....	*Popocatépetl (México)*	1401-09=	3	7/-
	2001	0202	....	**Heard** (Indian O.-S)	0304-01=	2	
	2001	0202	....	*Ulawun (New Britain-SW Pac)*	0502-12=	2	
	2001	0202<	71a?	*Cleveland (Aleutian Is)*	1101-24-	0	
	2001	0206	58d	**Nyamuragira** (Africa-C)	0203-02=	2?	
	2001	0219	<1?	**White Island** (New Zealand)	0401-04=	2	
	2001	0219	....	**Cleveland** (Aleutian Is)	1101-24-	3?	
	2001	0307	....	*Shiveluch (Kamchatka)*	1000-27=	3	8/-
	2001	0327	7	**Fournaise, Piton de la** (Indian O.)	0303-02=	1	6/-
	2001	0413	53a	**Marapi** (Sumatra)	0601-14=	2	
	2001	0423	2a?	**Masaya** (Nicaragua)	1404-10=	1	
S	2001	0424	<1	**Ahyi** (Mariana Is-C Pacific)	0804-141	0	
	2001	0429	....	*Ulawun (New Britain-SW Pac)*	0502-12=	3	
	2001	0503v	?	**McDonald Islands** (Indian O.-S)	0304-011	1?	
	2001	0511	....	**Suwanose-jima** (Ryukyu Is)	0802-03=	3?	
	2001	0511?	212a?	**San Cristóbal** (Nicaragua)	1404-02=	1	
	2001	0512	471a?	**Kerinci** (Sumatra)	0601-17=	2	

	START YEAR	M-Dy	Duration	VOLCANO NAME (Subregion)	NUMBER	VEI	Vol L/T
?	2001	0517?	49a?	*Láscar (Chile-N)*	1505-10=		
	2001	0522	....	**Shiveluch** (Kamchatka)	1000-27=	4?	8/-
	2001	0527	....	**Miyake-jima** (Izu Is-Japan)	0804-04=	2	
	2001	0528?	128a?	**Ibu** (Halmahera-Indonesia)	0608-03=	0	
?	2001	0605d	?	*Pavlof (Alaska Peninsula)*	1102-03-	1?	
	2001	0608	11a>	**Lopevi** (Vanuatu-SW Pacific)	0507-05=	3	
	2001	0611	26a	**Fournaise, Piton de la** (Indian O.)	0303-02=	1	6/-
	2001	0614	9a?	**Manam** (New Guinea-NE of)	0501-02=	2	
	2001	0624	....	**Mayon** (Luzon-Philippines)	0703-03=	3	7/7
	2001	0717	24	*Etna (Italy)*	0101-06=	1	7/6
	2001	0721	....	**Etna** (Italy)	0101-06=	2	7/6
	2001	0721	58a?	**Krakatau** (Indonesia)	0602-00=	1	
	2001	0723?	18a?	*Bezymianny (Kamchatka)*	1000-25=	0	
	2001	0726	....	*Mayon (Luzon-Philippines)*	0703-03=	3	7/7
	2001	0807	....	**Bezymianny** (Kamchatka)	1000-25=	3	
	2001	0828	<1	**Ulawun** (New Britain-SW Pac)	0502-12=	2	
	2001	09 ?	61p?	**Michael** (Antarctica)	1900-09=	0	
	2001	0921	32a	**Ioto [Iwo-jima]** (Volcano Is-Japan)	0804-12=	1	
	2001	0925	51c	**Talang** (Sumatra)	0601-16=	1	
	2001	0927	1a?	**Unnamed [NW of Vavau]** (Tonga)	0403-091	2	
	2001	0930	....	*Shiveluch (Kamchatka)*	1000-27=	3	8/-
	2001	1001n	>3yr	**Montagu Island** (Antarctica)	1900-081	1?	
	2001	1005	<1	**Avachinsky** (Kamchatka)	1000-10=	1	
	2001	1016	....	*Miyake-jima (Izu Is-Japan)*	0804-04=	2	
?	2001	1029	<1	*Kita-Iwo-jima (Volcano Is-Japan)*	0804-11=	0	
?	2001	1030	<1	*Kita-Fukutokutai (Volcano Is-Japan)*	0804-121	0	
?	2001	1030	232a	*Fukutoku-Okanoba (Volcano Is-Japan)*	0804-13=	0	
?	2001	1031	120a	*Smith Rock (Izu Is-Japan)*	0804-08=	0	
	2001	1031	<1	**Pacaya** (Guatemala)	1402-11=	1	
	2001	1115	>3yr	*Karymsky (Kamchatka)*	1000-13=	2	
	2001	1126	<1	**Guagua Pichincha** (Ecuador)	1502-02=	1?	
	2001	12 ?	319m?	**Etna** (Italy)	0101-06=	1	
S	2001	1204	2a	**Kick 'em Jenny** (W Indies)	1600-16=	0	
	2001	1210	27a?	**Bezymianny** (Kamchatka)	1000-25=	2	
	2002	Cont	....	*Erta Ale (Ethiopia)*	0201-08=	0	
	2002	Cont	....	*Lengai, Ol Doinyo (Africa-E)*	0202-12=	1	5/-
	2002	Cont	....	*Bagana (Bougainville-SW Pacific)*	0505-02=	2	
	2002	Cont	....	*Kavachi (Solomon Is-SW Pacific)*	0505-06=	1	
	2002	Cont	....	*Ambrym (Vanuatu-SW Pacific)*	0507-04=	1	
	2002	Cont	....	*Yasur (Vanuatu-SW Pacific)*	0507-10=	2	
	2002	Cont	....	*Kerinci (Sumatra)*	0601-17=	2	
	2002	Cont	....	*Merapi (Java)*	0603-25=	2	7/-
	2002	Cont	....	*Semeru (Java)*	0603-30=	2	
	2002	Cont	....	*Soputan (Sulawesi-Indonesia)*	0606-03=	0	7/-
	2002	Cont	....	*Karangetang [Api Siau] (Sangihe Is*	0607-02=	1	
	2002	Cont	....	*Dukono (Halmahera-Indonesia)*	0608-01=	2	
	2002	Cont	....	*Suwanose-jima (Ryukyu Is)*	0802-03=	2?	
	2002	Cont	....	*Sakura-jima (Kyushu-Japan)*	0802-08=	2	
	2002	Cont	....	*Miyake-jima (Izu Is-Japan)*	0804-04=	1	
	2002	Cont	....	*Shiveluch (Kamchatka)*	1000-27=	1	8/-
	2002	Cont	....	*Kilauea (Hawaiian Is)*	1302-01-	0	**9**/-
	2002	Cont	....	*Colima (México)*	1401-04=	1	7/6
	2002	Cont	....	*Popocatépetl (México)*	1401-09=	2	7/-
	2002	Cont	....	*Santa María (Guatemala)*	1402-03=	1	**9**/8
	2002	Cont	....	*Arenal (Costa Rica)*	1405-033	1	8/7
	2002	Cont	....	*Tungurahua (Ecuador)*	1502-08=	2	
	2002	Cont	....	*Sangay (Ecuador)*	1502-09=	2	
	2002	Cont	....	*Villarrica (Chile-C)*	1507-12=	1	
	2002	Cont	....	*Soufrière Hills (W Indies)*	1600-05=	2	8/-
	2002	Cont	....	*Erebus (Antarctica)*	1900-02=	1	
	2002	Cont	....	*Montagu Island (Antarctica)*	1900-081	1?	
	2002	0104	>3yr	**Fuego** (Guatemala)	1402-09=	2	
	2002	0105	10	**Fournaise, Piton de la** (Indian O.)	0303-02=	1	7/-
	2002	0113	128a	*Manam (New Guinea-NE of)*	0501-02=	1	
	2002	0116	<1	**San Miguel** (El Salvador)	1403-10=	1	
	2002	0117	17a>	**Nyiragongo** (Africa-C)	0203-03=	1	7/-
	2002	0125	87a?	**Chikurachki** (Kuril Is)	0900-36=	2	
	2002	0201	....	**Karymsky** (Kamchatka)	1000-13=	3	
	2002	0209	96m?	**Lokon-Empung** (Sulawesi-Indonesia)	0606-10=	2	
?	2002	0228	<1	*Kita-Iwo-jima (Volcano Is-Japan)*	0804-11=	0	
	2002	03	16m	**Epi** (Vanuatu-SW Pacific)	0507-06=	1?	
	2002	04	?	**Tinakula** (Santa Cruz Is-SW Pacific)	0506-01=	1	
	2002	04	15m	**Guagua Pichincha** (Ecuador)	1502-02=	1?	
	2002	0409	61a<	**Kliuchevskoi** (Kamchatka)	1000-26=	2	
	2002	0511	65m	**Kikai** (Ryukyu Is)	0802-06=	2	
	2002	0517?	>3yr	*Nyiragongo (Africa-C)*	0203-03=	1	
	2002	0520	....	**Manam** (New Guinea-NE of)	0501-02=	3?	
S	2002	0524	<1	**Monowai Seamount** (Kermadec Is)	0402-05-	0	
	2002	0525?	339a?	**Langila** (New Britain-SW Pac)	0502-01=	2	
	2002	0529	201a?	**San Cristóbal** (Nicaragua)	1404-02=	1	
	2002	0530	18a?	**Pacaya** (Guatemala)	1402-11=	1?	
	2002	06 <	71m>	**Raung** (Java)	0603-34=	2	
	2002	0607	<1?	**Galeras** (Colombia)	1501-08=	1?	
	2002	07 <	?	**Korovin** (Aleutian Is)	1101-161	1?	
?	2002	07	61m	*Bárdarbunga (Iceland-NE)*	1703-03=	0	
	2002	07 ?	123p?	**Michael** (Antarctica)	1900-09=	0	
	2002	0725	52m?	**Nyamuragira** (Africa-C)	0203-02=	2?	
?	2002	0729	17c	*Ijen (Java)*	0603-35=	1	
	2002	0801	1a	**Wrangell** (Alaska-E)	1105-02-	1	
?	2002	0802	<1	*Ritter Island (New Guinea-NE of)*	0501-07=	2?	
	2002	0803	177o>	**Pago** (New Britain-SW Pac)	0502-08=	3	8/-
	2002	0812	8a	**Tori-shima** (Izu Is-Japan)	0804-09=	2	

Jean-Claude Tanguy (Univ. Paris)

The 2001 south-flank eruption of Italy's Etna volcano ejected a dark ash plume from the upper vent and a smaller series of plumes from lower vents that also produced a lava flow. The flows destroyed buildings, cable car facilities, and overran a highway in two places. Heavy tephra fall disrupted air traffic.

	START YEAR	M-Dy	Dura-tion	VOLCANO NAME (Subregion)	NUMBER	VEI	Vol L/T
	2002	0822?	73*a*?	**Ulawun** (New Britain-SW Pac)	0502-12=	2	
?	*2002*	*0904*	*<1*	*Smith Rock (Izu Is-Japan)*	0804-08=	*0*	
	2002	0924	180*a*	**Veniaminof** (Alaska Peninsula)	1102-07-	1	
	2002	0925	4*a*?	**Ruang** (Sangihe Is-Indonesia)	0607-01=	4?	
	2002	*1006?*	*499a?*	*Rabaul (New Britain-SW Pac)*	0502-14=	*1*	
	2002	1011	<1	**Mayon** (Luzon-Philippines)	0703-03=	1	
	2002	1011	57*a*	**Guagua Pichincha** (Ecuador)	1502-02=	1?	
	2002	1012	<1?	**Lewotobi** (Lesser Sunda Is)	0604-18=	1	
	2002	1013k	?	**Llaima** (Chile-C)	1507-11=	1	
	2002	1017	?	**Telica** (Nicaragua)	1404-04=	0	
	2002	1020?	....	**Rabaul** (New Britain-SW Pac)	0502-14=	2	
	2002	*1021*	....	*Ulawun (New Britain-SW Pac)*	0502-12=	*2*	
	2002	1026	93	**Etna** (Italy)	0101-06=	3	7/7
	2002	1026	1	**Láscar** (Chile-N)	1505-10=	2	
	2002	1031	?	**Manam** (New Guinea-NE of)	0501-02=	2	
?	*2002*	*11*	*?*	*Tinakula (Santa Cruz Is-SW Pacific)*	0506-01=	*1?*	
S	**2002**	1101	23*a*	**Monowai Seamount** (Kermadec Is)	0402-05-	0	
	2002	1103	68*a*?	**Reventador** (Ecuador)	1502-01=	4	7/8
	2002	*1111*	*38c*	*Papandayan (Java)*	0603-10=	*1*	
	2002	1115	....	**Papandayan** (Java)	0603-10=	2	
	2002	1116	17*a*	**Fournaise, Piton de la** (Indian O.)	0303-02=	2	6/-
	2002	*1124*	*501a*	*Kliuchevskoi (Kamchatka)*	1000-26=	*1*	
	2002	1128	<1	**Kanlaon** (Philippines-C)	0702-02=	1	
?	*2002*	*1219*	*82a*	*Fukutoku-Okanoba (Volcano Is-Japan)*	0804-13=	*0*	
	2002	*1223*	*97a*	*Lokon-Empung (Sulawesi-Indonesia)*	0606-10=	*1*	
	2002	1224	....	**Kliuchevskoi** (Kamchatka)	1000-26=	2	
	2002	1225	3*a*?	**Bezymianny** (Kamchatka)	1000-25=	2	
	2002	*1228*	....	*Stromboli (Italy)*	0101-04=	*1*	*7/-*
	2003	*Cont*	....	*Erta Ale (Ethiopia)*	0201-08=	*0*	
	2003	*Cont*	....	*Lengai, Ol Doinyo (Africa-E)*	0202-12=	*1*	*5/-*
	2003	*Cont*	....	*Nyiragongo (Africa-C)*	0203-03=	*1*	
	2003	*Cont*	....	*Langila (New Britain-SW Pac)*	0502-01=	*2*	
	2003	*Cont*	....	*Pago (New Britain-SW Pac)*	0502-08=	*0*	*8/-*
	2003	*Cont*	....	*Rabaul (New Britain-SW Pac)*	0502-14=	*1*	
	2003	*Cont*	....	*Bagana (Bougainville-SW Pacific)*	0505-02=	*2*	
	2003	*Cont*	....	*Kavachi (Solomon Is-SW Pacific)*	0505-06=	*1*	
	2003	*Cont*	....	*Ambrym (Vanuatu-SW Pacific)*	0507-04=	*1*	
	2003	*Cont*	....	*Yasur (Vanuatu-SW Pacific)*	0507-10=	*2*	
	2003	*Cont*	....	*Semeru (Java)*	0603-30=	*2*	
	2003	*Cont*	....	*Dukono (Halmahera-Indonesia)*	0608-01=	*2*	
	2003	*Cont*	....	*Suwanose-jima (Ryukyu Is)*	0802-03=	*2?*	
	2003	*Cont*	....	*Sakura-jima (Kyushu-Japan)*	0802-08=	*2*	
?	*2003*	*Cont*	....	*Fukutoku-Okanoba (Volcano Is-Japan)*	0804-13=	*0*	
	2003	*Cont*	....	*Karymsky (Kamchatka)*	1000-13=	*2*	
	2003	*Cont*	....	*Kliuchevskoi (Kamchatka)*	1000-26=	*1*	
	2003	*Cont*	....	*Shiveluch (Kamchatka)*	1000-27=	*1*	*8/-*
	2003	*Cont*	....	*Veniaminof (Alaska Peninsula)*	1102-07-	*1*	
	2003	*Cont*	....	*Kilauea (Hawaiian Is)*	1302-01-	*0*	***9**/-*
	2003	*Cont*	....	*Colima (México)*	1401-04=	*1*	*7/6*
	2003	*Cont*	....	*Popocatépetl (México)*	1401-09=	*2*	*7/-*
	2003	*Cont*	....	*Santa María (Guatemala)*	1402-03=	*1*	***9**/8*
	2003	*Cont*	....	*Fuego (Guatemala)*	1402-09=	*2*	
	2003	*Cont*	....	*Arenal (Costa Rica)*	1405-033	*1*	*8/7*
	2003	*Cont*	....	*Reventador (Ecuador)*	1502-01=	*2*	*7/8*
	2003	*Cont*	....	*Tungurahua (Ecuador)*	1502-08=	*2*	
	2003	*Cont*	....	*Sangay (Ecuador)*	1502-09=	*2*	
	2003	*Cont*	....	*Erebus (Antarctica)*	1900-02=	*1*	
	2003	*Cont*	....	*Montagu Island (Antarctica)*	1900-081	*1?*	
	2003 ?	....	>3yr	**NW Rota-1** (Mariana Is-C Pacific)	0804-211	0	
	2003	02 ?	244*p*	**Kikai** (Ryukyu Is)	0802-06=	2	
	2003	0206	71*a*	**Asama** (Honshu-Japan)	0803-11=	1	-/2
	2003	0208	....	**Lokon-Empung** (Sulawesi-Indonesia)	0606-10=	2	
	2003	0307	138	**Kanlaon** (Philippines-C)	0702-02=	1	
	2003	0308c	215*c*	**Etna** (Italy)	0101-06=	1	
?	*2003*	*0310*	*<1*	*Kita-Iwo-jima (Volcano Is-Japan)*	0804-11=	*0*	
	2003	0317	58*a*	**Mayon** (Luzon-Philippines)	0703-03=	2	
	2003 b	04	?	**Vailulu'u** (Samoa-SW Pacific)	0404-00-	0	
	2003	*0405*	....	*Stromboli (Italy)*	0101-04=	*2*	*7/-*
	2003	*0409*	*7a>*	*Llaima (Chile-C)*	1507-11=	*1*	
S	**2003**	0410	524*m*	**Monowai Seamount** (Kermadec Is)	0402-05-	0	
	2003	0411	....	**Llaima** (Chile-C)	1507-11=	2	
	2003	0414?	179*a*?	**Ulawun** (New Britain-SW Pac)	0502-12=	2	
	2003	0417	77*a*?	**Chikurachki** (Kuril Is)	0900-36=	2	
?	*2003*	*0417<*	*<1?*	*Guagua Pichincha (Ecuador)*	1502-02=	*1*	
	2003	05 ?	184*p*?	**Unnamed** (Pacific-E)	1304-04-	0	
	2003	0506?	<1?	**Michael** (Antarctica)	1900-09=	0	
	2003	0510	63*c*	**Anatahan** (Mariana Is-C Pacific)	0804-20=	3	-/7
	2003	0517	6*a*	**Manam** (New Guinea-NE of)	0501-02=	1	
	2003	0523?	307*a*?	**Villarrica** (Chile-C)	1507-12=	1	
	2003	0530	225*a*	**Fournaise, Piton de la** (Indian O.)	0303-02=	1	7/-
	2003	*0530*	*94a>*	*Lewotobi (Lesser Sunda Is)*	0604-18=	*1*	
	2003	0608	8*a*?	**Lopevi** (Vanuatu-SW Pacific)	0507-05=	3	
	2003	0609	371*a*	**Heard** (Indian O.-S)	0304-01=	0	
	2003	0617	361*a*	**San Cristóbal** (Nicaragua)	1404-02=	1?	
	2003	*0626*	*32*	*Leroboleng (Lesser Sunda Is)*	0604-20=	*1*	
	2003	07	<1	**Dieng Volc Complex** (Java)	0603-20=	1?	
	2003	*0702*	....	*Ulawun (New Britain-SW Pac)*	0502-12=	*2*	
	2003	0710	4*a*	**Aso** (Kyushu-Japan)	0802-11=	1	
	2003	*0712*	....	*Soufrière Hills (W Indies)*	1600-05=	*3*	*8/-*
	2003	*0714*	....	*Leroboleng (Lesser Sunda Is)*	0604-20=	*2*	
	2003	*0718*	....	*Soputan (Sulawesi-Indonesia)*	0606-03=	*2*	*7/-*
	2003	0719c	....	**Karangetang [Api Siau]** (Sangihe Is	0607-02=	3?	
	2003	0726	6*a*?	**Bezymianny** (Kamchatka)	1000-25=	3	
	2003	0729	....	**Leroboleng** (Lesser Sunda Is)	0604-20=	3	
	2003	0730a	?	**Sabancaya** (Perú)	1504-006	2?	
	2003	0731	64*c*	**Gamalama** (Halmahera-Indonesia)	0608-06=	2	
	2003	0829	17*e*	**Chillán, Nevados de** (Chile-C)	1507-07=	1	
	2003	0901	....	**Lewotobi** (Lesser Sunda Is)	0604-18=	2	
	2003	0912	<1	**Lokon-Empung** (Sulawesi-Indonesia)	0606-10=	3	
	2003	*0922<*	*81a?*	*Masaya (Nicaragua)*	1404-10=	*0*	
?	*2003*	*1008*	*3a?*	*Mayon (Luzon-Philippines)*	0703-03=	*0*	
	2003	1026e	154*e*	**Manam** (New Guinea-NE of)	0501-02=	1	
?	*2003*	*1104*	*<1*	*Kita-Iwo-jima (Volcano Is-Japan)*	0804-11=	*0*	
?	*2003*	*1106*	*<1*	*Smith Rock (Izu Is-Japan)*	0804-08=	*0*	
	2003	1129	....	**Masaya** (Nicaragua)	1404-10=	1	
?	*2003*	*1209*	*<1*	*Láscar (Chile-N)*	1505-10=	*1*	
	2004	*Cont*	....	*Stromboli (Italy)*	0101-04=	*1*	*7/-*
	2004	*Cont*	....	*Erta Ale (Ethiopia)*	0201-08=	*0*	
	2004	*Cont*	....	*Lengai, Ol Doinyo (Africa-E)*	0202-12=	*1*	*5/-*
	2004	*Cont*	....	*Heard (Indian O.-S)*	0304-01=	*0*	
S	*2004*	*Cont*	....	*Monowai Seamount (Kermadec Is)*	0402-05-	*0*	
	2004	*Cont*	....	*Rabaul (New Britain-SW Pac)*	0502-14=	*1*	
	2004	*Cont*	....	*Bagana (Bougainville-SW Pacific)*	0505-02=	*2*	
	2004	*Cont*	....	*Ambrym (Vanuatu-SW Pacific)*	0507-04=	*1*	
	2004	*Cont*	....	*Yasur (Vanuatu-SW Pacific)*	0507-10=	*2*	
	2004	*Cont*	....	*Sakura-jima (Kyushu-Japan)*	0802-08=	*2*	
	2004	*Cont*	....	*NW Rota-1 (Mariana Is-C Pacific)*	0804-211	*0*	
	2004	*Cont*	....	*Kilauea (Hawaiian Is)*	1302-01-	*0*	***9**/-*
	2004	*Cont*	....	*Colima (México)*	1401-04=	*1*	*7/6*
	2004	*Cont*	....	*Fuego (Guatemala)*	1402-09=	*2*	
	2004	*Cont*	....	*Arenal (Costa Rica)*	1405-033	*1*	*8/7*
	2004	*Cont*	....	*Guagua Pichincha (Ecuador)*	1502-02=	*1?*	
	2004	*Cont*	....	*Tungurahua (Ecuador)*	1502-08=	*2*	
	2004	*Cont*	....	*Sangay (Ecuador)*	1502-09=	*2*	
	2004	*Cont*	....	*Erebus (Antarctica)*	1900-02=	*1*	
	2004	*Cont*	....	*Montagu Island (Antarctica)*	1900-081	*1?*	
	2004	0114	<1	**Aso** (Kyushu-Japan)	0802-11=	1	
	2004	*0114*	*397m>*	*Bezymianny (Kamchatka)*	1000-25=	*2*	
	2004	0120?	7*a*?	**Langila** (New Britain-SW Pac)	0502-01=	2?	
	2004	0129	7*a*?	**Egon** (Lesser Sunda Is)	0604-16=	1	
	2004	0212	2*a*	**Etna** (Italy)	0101-06=	1?	
	2004	0216	8*a*	**Epi** (Vanuatu-SW Pacific)	0507-06=	2	
	2004	*0216*	*202m*	*Veniaminof (Alaska Peninsula)*	1102-07-	*1*	
	2004	*0217*	*150m>*	*Shishaldin (Aleutian Is)*	1101-36-	*1*	
	2004	0220	....	**Shishaldin** (Aleutian Is)	1101-36-	2	
?	*2004*	*0224*	*<1*	*Pago (New Britain-SW Pac)*	0502-08=	*1?*	
	2004	0225	54*a*	**Tokachi** (Hokkaido-Japan)	0805-05=	1?	
	2004	0303	59	**Soufrière Hills** (W Indies)	1600-05=	3?	
	2004	0305	255*m*	**Kikai** (Ryukyu Is)	0802-06=	2	
	2004	0315	?	**Kavachi** (Solomon Is-SW Pacific)	0505-06=	1	
?	*2004*	*0319*	*71a*	*Tofua (Tonga-SW Pacific)*	0403-06=	*1?*	
	2004	0331	<1	**Telica** (Nicaragua)	1404-04=	1	
	2004	*0402?*	*274a>*	*Karangetang [Api Siau] (Sangihe Is*	0607-02=	*0*	
	2004	0412	2*a*	**Ulawun** (New Britain-SW Pac)	0502-12=	2	
	2004	*0412<*	*509a>*	*Anatahan (Mariana Is-C Pacific)*	0804-20=	*2*	
?	*2004*	*0415?*	*176a?*	*Raung (Java)*	0603-34=	*2?*	
	2004	05 ?	283*m*?	**Ibu** (Halmahera-Indonesia)	0608-03=	0?	
	2004	0502	167*a*	**Fournaise, Piton de la** (Indian O.)	0303-02=	0	7/-
	2004	0508	21*c*	**Nyamuragira** (Africa-C)	0203-02=	2?	
	2004	*0509*	....	*Shiveluch (Kamchatka)*	1000-27=	*3*	*8/-*
	2004	0526	<1	**Popocatépetl** (México)	1401-09=	2	
	2004	*0602<*	*75m?*	*Awu (Sangihe Is-Indonesia)*	0607-04=	*0*	
	2004	0603	101*a*?	**Mayon** (Luzon-Philippines)	0703-03=	1	
	2004	0604	....	**Nyiragongo** (Africa-C)	0203-03=	2	
?	*2004*	*0606*	*2a*	*Ioto [Iwo-jima] (Volcano Is-Japan)*	0804-12=	*1*	
	2004	0608	16*c*	**Tengger Caldera [Bromo]** (Java)	0603-31=	2	
	2004	0610	....	**Awu** (Sangihe Is-Indonesia)	0607-04=	2	
	2004	0619	....	**Bezymianny** (Kamchatka)	1000-25=	3	
	2004	*0622?*	*124a?*	*Kerinci (Sumatra)*	0601-17=	*1*	
	2004	0624	<1?	**Marion Island** (Indian O.-S)	0304-07-	1	
	2004	*0703*	*75a?*	*Egon (Lesser Sunda Is)*	0604-16=	*1*	
	2004	0704<	?	**Korovin** (Aleutian Is)	1101-161	1?	
?	*2004*	*0704*	*<1*	*Masaya (Nicaragua)*	1404-10=	*1?*	
	2004	*0716*	*206a?*	*Galeras (Colombia)*	1501-08=	*1*	
	2004	0717c	....	**Veniaminof** (Alaska Peninsula)	1102-07-	2	
	2004	0719?	>3yr	**Pacaya** (Guatemala)	1402-11=	1	
	2004	0720	<1	**Chirinkotan** (Kuril Is)	0900-26=	2	
	2004	0725	....	**Egon** (Lesser Sunda Is)	0604-16=	2	
	2004	*0728*	....	*Galeras (Colombia)*	1501-08=	*2*	
	2004	0729	<1	**Nightingale Island** (Atlantic-S)	1806-011	0	
	2004	0805	<1?	**Marapi** (Sumatra)	0601-14=	2	
	2004	0805?	>3yr	**Villarrica** (Chile-C)	1507-12=	1	
	2004	0811	....	**Galeras** (Colombia)	1501-08=	3	
	2004	09	15*m*	**Lopevi** (Vanuatu-SW Pacific)	0507-05=	2	

	START YEAR	M-Dy	Duration	VOLCANO NAME (Subregion)	NUMBER	VEI	Vol L/T
	2004	0901	99a	Asama (Honshu-Japan)	0803-11=	2	6/5
	2004	0907	174a	Etna (Italy)	0101-06=	0	7/-
	2004	0915	<1	Kliuchevskoi (Kamchatka)	1000-26=	1	
	2004	0927	....	Kerinci (Sumatra)	0601-17=	2	
	2004	10	?	Tofua (Tonga-SW Pacific)	0403-06=	1	
	2004	1001	4a>	Rinjani (Lesser Sunda Is)	0604-03=	2	
	2004	1001	>3yr	St. Helens (US-Washington)	1201-05-	2	7/-
	2004	1014	....	Santa María (Guatemala)	1402-03=	3	9/8
	2004	1018	74a?	Soputan (Sulawesi-Indonesia)	0606-03=	1	
	2004	1023	>3yr	Suwanose-jima (Ryukyu Is)	0802-03=	2	
	2004	1024	>3yr	Manam (New Guinea-NE of)	0501-02=	3?	
	2004	1101	2	Grímsvötn (Iceland-NE)	1703-01=	3	
	2004	1105	85a	Telica (Nicaragua)	1404-04=	1	
	2004	1107c	494m	Reventador (Ecuador)	1502-01=	0	6/-
?	2004	1114	<1	McDonald Islands (Indian O.-S)	0304-011	1?	
	2004	1121	....	Galeras (Colombia)	1501-08=	3	
	2004	1123	....	Manam (New Guinea-NE of)	0501-02=	3?	
	2004	1124?	31a?	Langila (New Britain-SW Pac)	0502-01=	2?	
	2004	1130	9	Miyake-jima (Izu Is-Japan)	0804-04=	1	
	2004	1202	....	Reventador (Ecuador)	1502-01=	2	6/-
	2004	1203	4a?	San Cristóbal (Nicaragua)	1404-02=	1	
	2004	1212	....	Soputan (Sulawesi-Indonesia)	0606-03=	3?	
	2004	1219	....	Manam (New Guinea-NE of)	0501-02=	3?	
	2004	1230	....	Karymsky (Kamchatka)	1000-13=	3	
	2005	Cont	....	Stromboli (Italy)	0101-04=	1	7/-
	2005	Cont	....	Erta Ale (Ethiopia)	0201-08=	0	
	2005	Cont	....	Lengai, Ol Doinyo (Africa-E)	0202-12=	1	5/-
	2005	Cont	....	Nyiragongo (Africa-C)	0203-03=	1	
	2005	Cont	....	Bagana (Bougainville-SW Pacific)	0505-02=	2	
	2005	Cont	....	Ambrym (Vanuatu-SW Pacific)	0507-04=	1	
	2005	Cont	....	Yasur (Vanuatu-SW Pacific)	0507-10=	2	
	2005	Cont	....	Semeru (Java)	0603-30=	2	
	2005	Cont	....	Ibu (Halmahera-Indonesia)	0608-03=	0?	
	2005	Cont	....	Suwanose-jima (Ryukyu Is)	0802-03=	2	
	2005	Cont	....	Sakura-jima (Kyushu-Japan)	0802-08=	2	
	2005	Cont	....	NW Rota-1 (Mariana Is-C Pacific)	0804-211	0	
	2005	Cont	....	Karymsky (Kamchatka)	1000-13=	2	
	2005	Cont	....	Shiveluch (Kamchatka)	1000-27=	1	8/-
	2005	Cont	....	St. Helens (US-Washington)	1201-05-	1	7/-
	2005	Cont	....	Kilauea (Hawaiian Is)	1302-01-	0	9/-
	2005	Cont	....	Santa María (Guatemala)	1402-03=	1	9/8
	2005	Cont	....	Fuego (Guatemala)	1402-09=	2	
	2005	Cont	....	Pacaya (Guatemala)	1402-11=	1	
	2005	Cont	....	Telica (Nicaragua)	1404-04=	1	
	2005	Cont	....	Arenal (Costa Rica)	1405-033	1	8/7
	2005	Cont	....	Tungurahua (Ecuador)	1502-08=	2	
	2005	Cont	....	Sangay (Ecuador)	1502-09=	2	
	2005	Cont	....	Villarrica (Chile-C)	1507-12=	1	
	2005	Cont	....	Erebus (Antarctica)	1900-02=	1	
	2005	Cont	....	Montagu Island (Antarctica)	1900-081	1?	
?	2005	....	?	Kolokol Group (Kuril Is)	0900-12=	1?	
	2005	0104	41c	Veniaminof (Alaska Peninsula)	1102-07-	1	
	2005	0108	....	Etna (Italy)	0101-06=	1	7/-
	2005	0108	....	Veniaminof (Alaska Peninsula)	1102-07-	2	
	2005	0109	>3yr	Popocatépetl (México)	1401-09=	2	
	2005	0111	....	Bezymianny (Kamchatka)	1000-25=	3	
	2005	0120<	78a>	Kliuchevskoi (Kamchatka)	1000-26=	2	
	2005	0125	387a	Rabaul (New Britain-SW Pac)	0502-14=	1	
	2005	0125	120a	Kanlaon (Philippines-C)	0702-02=	1	
	2005	0127	....	Manam (New Guinea-NE of)	0501-02=	4?	
	2005	0129	18a	Ebeko (Kuril Is)	0900-38=	1	
	2005	0130	....	Rabaul (New Britain-SW Pac)	0502-14=	2	
	2005	0130	60a?	Lopevi (Vanuatu-SW Pacific)	0507-05=	2	
	2005	0206	21a	Egon (Lesser Sunda Is)	0604-16=	1	
	2005	0207	....	Ebeko (Kuril Is)	0900-38=	2	
	2005	0212	....	Kliuchevskoi (Kamchatka)	1000-26=	2	
	2005	0217	8a	Fournaise, Piton de la (Indian O.)	0303-02=	0	7/-
	2005	0223	74d	Korovin (Aleutian Is)	1101-161	1	
S	2005	0302	482a	Monowai Seamount (Kermadec Is)	0402-05-	0	
	2005	0304?	26a?	Masaya (Nicaragua)	1404-10=	1	
?	2005	0308	<1	Smith Rock (Izu Is-Japan)	0804-08=	0	
	2005	0312	26a	Chikurachki (Kuril Is)	0900-36=	1	
	2005	0313?	259a?	Cleveland (Aleutian Is)	1101-24-	1?	
	2005	0327?	136a?	Ulawun (New Britain-SW Pac)	0502-12=	1	
	2005	0405	....	Anatahan (Mariana Is-C Pacific)	0804-20=	3?	
	2005	0412?	127a?	Talang (Sumatra)	0601-16=	2	
	2005	0412	36a	Miyake-jima (Izu Is-Japan)	0804-04=	1	
	2005	0414	124m	Aso (Kyushu-Japan)	0802-11=	1	
	2005	0415	....	Kanlaon (Philippines-C)	0702-02=	2	
	2005	0415	>3yr	Soufrière Hills (W Indies)	1600-05=	2	
	2005	0416	2a	Karthala (Indian O.-W)	0303-01=	2?	
	2005	0419?	347a?	Langila (New Britain-SW Pac)	0502-01=	2	
	2005	0419	80a?	Soputan (Sulawesi-Indonesia)	0606-03=	2	
	2005	0424	....	Colima (México)	1401-04=	3	7/6
	2005	0427	....	Cleveland (Aleutian Is)	1101-24-	2	
	2005	0504	<1	Láscar (Chile-N)	1505-10=	3?	
	2005	0513	16a?	Fernandina (Galápagos)	1503-01=	2	
	2005	0526	942a?	Barren Island (Andaman Is-Indian O)	0600-01=	2	
	2005	0530	....	Karangetang [Api Siau] (Sangihe Is	0607-02=	2	
	2005	0611	....	Anatahan (Mariana Is-C Pacific)	0804-20=	3?	
	2005	0616	107a?	Santa Ana (El Salvador)	1403-02=	1	
	2005	0619	....	Anatahan (Mariana Is-C Pacific)	0804-20=	3?	
	2005	0621	....	Ulawun (New Britain-SW Pac)	0502-12=	2	
?	2005	07	31m	Bárdarbunga (Iceland-NE)	1703-03=	0	
	2005	0702	19a?	Fukutoku-Okanoba (Volcano Is-Japan	0804-13=	1	
	2005	0703	....	Anatahan (Mariana Is-C Pacific)	0804-20=	3?	
	2005	0706	....	Anatahan (Mariana Is-C Pacific)	0804-20=	3?	
	2005	0712<	?	McDonald Islands (Indian O.-S)	0304-011	0	
?	2005	0723?	23a?	Raung (Java)	0603-34=	2?	
	2005	0728	105a	Concepción (Nicaragua)	1404-12=	2	
	2005	08 ?	153r?	Unnamed [East Pacific Rise]	1304-05-	0	
	2005	0817<	?	Mayon (Luzon-Philippines)	0703-03=	0	
	2005	0907	58a?	Veniaminof (Alaska Peninsula)	1102-07-	1	
?	2005	0911	521m>	Fukutoku-Okanoba (Volcano Is-Japan.	0804-13=	0	
	2005	0912	....	Reventador (Ecuador)	1502-01=	2	6/-
	2005	0926	3a	Dabbahu (Ethiopia)	0201-113	3?	
	2005	1001	....	Santa Ana (El Salvador)	1403-02=	3	
	2005	1002?	110a?	Michael (Antarctica)	1900-09=	0	
	2005	1004	106a	Fournaise, Piton de la (Indian O.)	0303-02=	0	7/-
	2005	1007	....	Cleveland (Aleutian Is)	1101-24-	2	
	2005	1016	32a>	Garbuna Group (New Britain-SW Pac)	0502-07=	2	
	2005	1022	8	Negra, Sierra (Galápagos)	1503-05=	3	8/-
	2005	1027?	278a?	Lopevi (Vanuatu-SW Pacific)	0507-05=	2	
	2005	1113	193a	San Cristóbal (Nicaragua)	1404-02=	1	
	2005	1124	14a	Karthala (Indian O.-W)	0303-01=	3	
	2005	1124	196a	Galeras (Colombia)	1501-08=	2	
	2005	1127	79m	Aoba (Vanuatu-SW Pacific)	0507-03=	2	
	2005	1129?	2a>	Bezymianny (Kamchatka)	1000-25=	0	
	2005	1130	....	Bezymianny (Kamchatka)	1000-25=	2	
	2005	1209?	139a?	Augustine (Alaska-SW)	1103-01-	1	
	2005	1216	6a	Etna (Italy)	0101-06=	1	
	2005	1226	29a?	Soputan (Sulawesi-Indonesia)	0606-03=	1	
	2006	Cont	....	Stromboli (Italy)	0101-04=	1	7/-
	2006	Cont	....	Erta Ale (Ethiopia)	0201-08=	0	
	2006	Cont	....	Lengai, Ol Doinyo (Africa-E)	0202-12=	1	5/-
	2006	Cont	....	Nyiragongo (Africa-C)	0203-03=	1	
	2006	Cont	....	Bagana (Bougainville-SW Pacific)	0505-02=	2	
	2006	Cont	....	Lopevi (Vanuatu-SW Pacific)	0507-05=	2	
	2006	Cont	....	Yasur (Vanuatu-SW Pacific)	0507-10=	2	
	2006	Cont	....	Barren Island (Andaman Is-Indian O)	0600-01=	2	
	2006	Cont	....	Semeru (Java)	0603-30=	2	
	2006	Cont	....	Dukono (Halmahera-Indonesia)	0608-01=	2	
	2006	Cont	....	Suwanose-jima (Ryukyu Is)	0802-03=	2	
	2006	Cont	....	Sakura-jima (Kyushu-Japan)	0802-08=	2	
?	2006	Cont	....	Fukutoku-Okanoba (Volcano Is-Japan.	0804-13=	0	
	2006	Cont	....	NW Rota-1 (Mariana Is-C Pacific)	0804-211	0	
	2006	Cont	....	Karymsky (Kamchatka)	1000-13=	2	
	2006	Cont	....	Shiveluch (Kamchatka)	1000-27=	1	8/-
	2006	Cont	....	St. Helens (US-Washington)	1201-05-	1	7/-
	2006	Cont	....	Kilauea (Hawaiian Is)	1302-01-	0	9/-
	2006	Cont	....	Unnamed [East Pacific Rise]	1304-05-	0	
	2006	Cont	....	Colima (México)	1401-04=	1	7/6
	2006	Cont	....	Popocatépetl (México)	1401-09=	2	
	2006	Cont	....	Santa María (Guatemala)	1402-03=	1	9/8
	2006	Cont	....	Fuego (Guatemala)	1402-09=	2	
	2006	Cont	....	Pacaya (Guatemala)	1402-11=	1	
	2006	Cont	....	Arenal (Costa Rica)	1405-033	1	8/7
	2006	Cont	....	Galeras (Colombia)	1501-08=	2	
	2006	Cont	....	Reventador (Ecuador)	1502-01=	0	6/-
	2006	Cont	....	Sangay (Ecuador)	1502-09=	2	
	2006	Cont	....	Villarrica (Chile-C)	1507-12=	1	
	2006	Cont	....	Erebus (Antarctica)	1900-02=	1	
	2006	Cont	....	Montagu Island (Antarctica)	1900-081	1?	
	2006	0111	....	Augustine (Alaska-SW)	1103-01-	3	
	2006	02	< 638p>	Tinakula (Santa Cruz Is-SW Pacific)	0506-01=	2	
	2006	0206	264a	Cleveland (Aleutian Is)	1101-24-	3	
	2006	0217	<1	Miyake-jima (Izu Is-Japan)	0804-04=	1	
	2006	0221	2a	Mayon (Luzon-Philippines)	0703-03=	1	
	2006	0227	....	Manam (New Guinea-NE of)	0501-02=	3?	
	2006	03	526m?	Merapi (Java)	0603-25=	1	6/-
	2006	0301	323a	Ulawun (New Britain-SW Pac)	0502-12=	1	
	2006	0303	188a	Veniaminof (Alaska Peninsula)	1102-07-	1	
	2006	0311	722a	Heard (Indian O.-S)	0304-01=	0	
	2006	0317	<1	Raoul Island (Kermadec Is)	0402-03=	1?	
	2006	0320?	100a?	Anatahan (Mariana Is-C Pacific)	0804-20=	1	
	2006	0321	99a	Bulusan (Luzon-Philippines)	0703-01=	2	
	2006	0321	<1	Akan (Hokkaido-Japan)	0805-07=	1	
	2006	0324	<1?	Poás (Costa Rica)	1405-04=	1	
	2006	0325?	>3yr	Ubinas (Perú)	1504-02=	2	
	2006	04	< 258m?	Bezymianny (Kamchatka)	1000-25=	0	
?	2006	04	?	Bárdarbunga (Iceland-NE)	1703-03=	0	
	2006	0418	456a?	Láscar (Chile-N)	1505-10=	3	
	2006	05	31p	Tofua (Tonga-SW Pacific)	0403-06=	0	
	2006	0509	....	Bezymianny (Kamchatka)	1000-25=	3	

courtesy Brad Scott (New Zealand IGNS)

A phreatic eruption from Ruapehu volcano in New Zealand on September 25, 2007 ejected material from Crater Lake (left center) onto the summit area, including at the right, the North Crater basin. A large lahar formed the strikingly linear stripe down the Whangaehu Glacier (left).

	START YEAR	M-Dy	Dura-tion	VOLCANO NAME (Subregion) . . .	NUMBER	VEI	Vol L/T
	2006	0520	....	**Soufrière Hills** (W Indies)	1600-05=	3?	
	2006	*0523*	....	*Cleveland (Aleutian Is)*	1101-24-	*3*	
	2006	0525	....	**San Cristóbal** (Nicaragua)	1404-02=	2	
	2006	0528	5*a*?	**Karthala** (Indian O.-W)	0303-01=	0	
	2006	0529	....	**Anatahan** (Mariana Is-C Pacific)	0804-20=	2	
	2006	0603	52*a*	**Kanlaon** (Philippines-C)	0702-02=	2	
	2006	0609<	180*a*?	**Michael** (Antarctica)	1900-09=	0	
?	*2006*	*0701*	*<1*	*Tara, Batu (Lesser Sunda Is)*	0604-26=	*1?*	
	2006	0703	470*m*>	**Karangetang [Api Siau]** (Sangihe Is	0607-02=	1	
	2006	0713	80*a*	**Mayon** (Luzon-Philippines)	0703-03=	1	7/-
	2006	*0714*	*154a*	*Etna (Italy)*	0101-06=	*1*	*7/-*
	2006	0714	....	**Tungurahua** (Ecuador)	1502-08=	3?	
	2006	0720	285*a*	**Fournaise, Piton de la** (Indian O.)	0303-02=	1?	8/-
	2006	0804	2*a*	**Telica** (Nicaragua)	1404-04=	1	
	2006	0804	82*a*?	**Masaya** (Nicaragua)	1404-10=	1	
	2006	0807	9*a*?	**Home Reef** (Tonga-SW Pacific)	0403-08=	2?	
	2006	0809	698*a*?	**Langila** (New Britain-SW Pac)	0502-01=	2	
	2006	*0811*	*>3yr*	*Rabaul (New Britain-SW Pac)*	0502-14=	*1*	
	2006	0815	....	**Ulawun** (New Britain-SW Pac)	0502-12=	2	
	2006	*0816*	....	*Tungurahua (Ecuador)*	1502-08=	*3?*	
	2006	0823	<1	**Miyake-jima** (Izu Is-Japan)	0804-04=	1	
	2006	*0824*	....	*Cleveland (Aleutian Is)*	1101-24-	*2*	
	2006	0831	....	**Etna** (Italy)	0101-06=	2	7/-
	2006	*0901*	*20a*	*Concepción (Nicaragua)*	1404-12=	*1*	
	2006	0910	<1	**Talang** (Sumatra)	0601-16=	1	
	2006	0917	<1	**Fourpeaked** (Alaska Peninsula)	1102-26-	2	
	2006	0921	....	**Concepción** (Nicaragua)	1404-12=	2	
	2006	0925	<1	**Dempo** (Sumatra)	0601-23=	1	
	2006	0925	81	**Poás** (Costa Rica)	1405-04=	1	
	2006	1004	<1	**Ruapehu** (New Zealand)	0401-10=	1	
	2006	1007	....	**Rabaul** (New Britain-SW Pac)	0502-14=	4?	
	2006	1010	359*a*	**Bulusan** (Luzon-Philippines)	0703-01=	2	
	2006	1017	<1?	**Ritter Island** (New Guinea-NE of)	0501-07=	1?	
	2006	*1028*	....	*Cleveland (Aleutian Is)*	1101-24-	*3*	
	2006	*1108*	*414a>*	*Ambrym (Vanuatu-SW Pacific)*	0507-04=	*1*	
	2006	1125e	98*e*<	**Korovin** (Aleutian Is)	1101-161	1	
	2006	1127	8*a*?	**Nyamuragira** (Africa-C)	0203-02=	2	
	2006	1204	4*a*	**Pagan** (Mariana Is-C Pacific)	0804-17=	1	
	2006	1211?	68*a*?	**Telica** (Nicaragua)	1404-04=	1	
S	**2006**	1212	19*a*?	**Monowai Seamount** (Kermadec Is)	0402-05-	0	
	2006	1214	12*a*?	**Soputan** (Sulawesi-Indonesia)	0606-03=	1	
	2006	*1224*	....	*Bezymianny (Kamchatka)*	1000-25=	*3*	
	2007	*Cont*	....	*Erta Ale (Ethiopia)*	0201-08=	*0*	
	2007	*Cont*	....	*Nyiragongo (Africa-C)*	0203-03=	*1*	
	2007	*Cont*	....	*Fournaise, Piton de la (Indian O.)*	0303-02=	*1?*	*8/-*
	2007	*Cont*	....	*Heard (Indian O.-S)*	0304-01=	*0*	
	2007	*Cont*	....	*Manam (New Guinea-NE of)*	0501-02=	*2*	
	2007	*Cont*	....	*Langila (New Britain-SW Pac)*	0502-01=	*2*	
	2007	*Cont*	....	*Rabaul (New Britain-SW Pac)*	0502-14=	*1*	
	2007	*Cont*	....	*Bagana (Bougainville-SW Pacific)*	0505-02=	*2*	
	2007	*Cont*	....	*Tinakula (Santa Cruz Is-SW Pacific)*	0506-01=	*2*	
	2007	*Cont*	....	*Yasur (Vanuatu-SW Pacific)*	0507-10=	*2*	
	2007	*Cont*	....	*Barren Island (Andaman Is-Indian O)*	0600-01=	*2*	
	2007	*Cont*	....	*Merapi (Java)*	0603-25=	*1*	*6/-*
	2007	*Cont*	....	*Semeru (Java)*	0603-30=	*2*	
	2007	*Cont*	....	*Karangetang [Api Siau] (Sangihe Is*	0607-02=	*1*	
	2007	*Cont*	....	*Dukono (Halmahera-Indonesia)*	0608-01=	*2*	
	2007	*Cont*	....	*Suwanose-jima (Ryukyu Is)*	0802-03=	*2*	
	2007	*Cont*	....	*Sakura-jima (Kyushu-Japan)*	0802-08=	*2*	
?	*2007*	*Cont*	....	*Fukutoku-Okanoba (Volcano Is-Japan*	0804-13=	*0*	
	2007	*Cont*	....	*NW Rota-1 (Mariana Is-C Pacific)*	0804-211	*0*	
	2007	*Cont*	....	*Karymsky (Kamchatka)*	1000-13=	*2*	
	2007	*Cont*	....	*Shiveluch (Kamchatka)*	1000-27=	*1*	*8/-*
	2007	*Cont*	....	*Korovin (Aleutian Is)*	1101-161	*1*	
	2007	*Cont*	....	*St. Helens (US-Washington)*	1201-05-	*1*	*7/-*
	2007	*Cont*	....	*Kilauea (Hawaiian Is)*	1302-01-	*0*	***9**/-*
	2007	*Cont*	....	*Colima (México)*	1401-04=	*1*	*7/6*
	2007	*Cont*	....	*Popocatépetl (México)*	1401-09=	*2*	
	2007	*Cont*	....	*Santa María (Guatemala)*	1402-03=	*1*	***9**/8*
	2007	*Cont*	....	*Fuego (Guatemala)*	1402-09=	*2*	
	2007	*Cont*	....	*Pacaya (Guatemala)*	1402-11=	*1*	
	2007	*Cont*	....	*Arenal (Costa Rica)*	1405-033	*1*	*8/7*
	2007	*Cont*	....	*Tungurahua (Ecuador)*	1502-08=	*2*	
	2007	*Cont*	....	*Sangay (Ecuador)*	1502-09=	*2*	
	2007	*Cont*	....	*Ubinas (Perú)*	1504-02=	*2*	
	2007	*Cont*	....	*Láscar (Chile-N)*	1505-10=	*2*	
	2007	*Cont*	....	*Villarrica (Chile-C)*	1507-12=	*1*	
	2007	*Cont*	....	*Soufrière Hills (W Indies)*	1600-05=	*2*	
	2007	*Cont*	....	*Erebus (Antarctica)*	1900-02=	*1*	
	2007	*Cont*	....	*Montagu Island (Antarctica)*	1900-081	*1?*	
	2007	0112	3*a*?	**Karthala** (Indian O.-W)	0303-01=	2	
	2007	0117?	>3yr	**Tara, Batu** (Lesser Sunda Is)	0604-26=	2	
	2007	0209	151*a*	**Concepción** (Nicaragua)	1404-12=	1	
	2007	*0215*	*150a*	*Kliuchevskoi (Kamchatka)*	1000-26=	*1*	
	2007	*0219*	*98a?*	*Huila, Nevado del (Colombia)*	1501-05=	*1*	
	2007	*0227*	....	*Stromboli (Italy)*	0101-04=	*2*	*7/-*
	2007	0304	45*a*	**Chikurachki** (Kuril Is)	0900-36=	2	
	2007	*0315g*	*210g?*	*Reventador (Ecuador)*	1502-01=	*1*	

START YEAR	M-Dy	Dura-tion	VOLCANO NAME (Subregion)	NUMBER	VEI	Vol L/T
2007	0319	422m?	*Etna (Italy)*	0101-06=	1	
2007	0319	96c?	**Talang** (Sumatra)	0601-16=	2	
2007	0324	....	**Reventador** (Ecuador)	1502-01=	2	
2007	0402?	4a>	**Kavachi** (Solomon Is-SW Pacific)	0505-06=	1	
2007	0417	....	**Huila, Nevado del** (Colombia)	1501-05=	3?	
2007	0421	23a?	**Lopevi** (Vanuatu-SW Pacific)	0507-05=	2	
2007	0422	....	**Kliuchevskoi** (Kamchatka)	1000-26=	2	
2007	0429	....	**Etna** (Italy)	0101-06=	2	
2007	0501	<1	**Ulawun** (New Britain-SW Pac)	0502-12=	2	
2007	0501	....	**Ambrym** (Vanuatu-SW Pacific)	0507-04=	2	
2007	0510?	228a?	*Bezymianny (Kamchatka)*	1000-25=	1?	
2007	0512	....	*Bezymianny (Kamchatka)*	1000-25=	2	
2007	0519	2a?	**Ritter Island** (New Guinea-NE of)	0501-07=	1?	
2007	0526	74a?	**Llaima** (Chile-C)	1507-11=	2	
2007	0527	....	*Kliuchevskoi (Kamchatka)*	1000-26=	2	
2007	06	>3yr	*Lengai, Ol Doinyo (Africa-E)*	0202-12=	1	
2007	06 ?	147m?	*Soputan (Sulawesi-Indonesia)*	0606-03=	1	
? 2007	0612	<1	*Telica (Nicaragua)*	1404-04=	1	
2007	0617?	452a?	*Cleveland (Aleutian Is)*	1101-24-	1	
2007	0708	8a?	*Gamkonora (Halmahera-Indonesia)*	0608-04=	1	
2007	0710	....	**Gamkonora** (Halmahera-Indonesia)	0608-04=	2	
2007	0713	....	*Bulusan (Luzon-Philippines)*	0703-01=	2?	
2007	0720	....	**Cleveland** (Aleutian Is)	1101-24-	2?	
2007	0726	31a	**Raung** (Java)	0603-34=	2	
2007	0812	36a?	**Manda Hararo** (Ethiopia)	0201-115	2	
2007	0815	29a	**Pavlof** (Alaska Peninsula)	1102-03-	2	
2007	0819	74g	**Chikurachki** (Kuril Is)	0900-36=	2	
? 2007	0823	?	*Gamalama (Halmahera-Indonesia)*	0608-06=	1?	
2007	0828	<1	**Pago** (New Britain-SW Pac)	0502-08=	1?	
2007	0904	....	*Etna (Italy)*	0101-06=	2	
2007	0904	....	**Lengai, Ol Doinyo** (Africa-E)	0202-12=	3	
2007	0909	<1	**Kerinci** (Sumatra)	0601-17=	1	
2007	0925	<1	**Ruapehu** (New Zealand)	0401-10=	1?	
2007	0930	258m?	**Tair, Jebel at** (Red Sea)	0201-01=	3?	
2007	10 ?	182p?	*Kelut (Java)*	0603-28=	0	7/-
2007	1004	105a	*Galeras (Colombia)*	1501-08=	2	
2007	1023	342a?	**Krakatau** (Indonesia)	0602-00=	2	
2007	1025	....	**Soputan** (Sulawesi-Indonesia)	0606-03=	3	
2007	1028c	123c	**Telica** (Nicaragua)	1404-04=	1?	
2007	1111	....	**Kelut** (Java)	0603-28=	2	7/-
2007	1123	....	*Etna (Italy)*	0101-06=	2	
2007	1124	26a	**Concepción** (Nicaragua)	1404-12=	2?	
2007	1127	19m?	**Talang** (Sumatra)	0601-16=	2	
2007	1127 c	287c?	*Anatahan (Mariana Is-C Pacific)*	0804-20=	1?	
2007	1224	....	**Bezymianny** (Kamchatka)	1000-25=	3?	
? 2007	1225	?	*Ulawun (New Britain-SW Pac)*	0502-12=	1?	
2008	Cont	....	*Stromboli (Italy)*	0101-04=	1	7/-
2008	Cont	....	*Tair, Jebel at (Red Sea)*	0201-01=	1	
2008	Cont	....	*Erta Ale (Ethiopia)*	0201-08=	0	
2008	Cont	....	*Lengai, Ol Doinyo (Africa-E)*	0202-12=	1	
2008	Cont	....	*Nyiragongo (Africa-C)*	0203-03=	1	
2008	Cont	....	*Heard (Indian O.-S)*	0304-01=	0	
2008	Cont	....	*Manam (New Guinea-NE of)*	0501-02=	2	
2008	Cont	....	*Langila (New Britain-SW Pac)*	0502-01=	2	
2008	Cont	....	*Rabaul (New Britain-SW Pac)*	0502-14=	1	
2008	Cont	....	*Bagana (Bougainville-SW Pacific)*	0505-02=	2	
2008	Cont	....	*Yasur (Vanuatu-SW Pacific)*	0507-10=	2	
2008	Cont	....	*Krakatau (Indonesia)*	0602-00=	2	
2008	Cont	....	*Kelut (Java)*	0603-28=	0	7/-
2008	Cont	....	*Semeru (Java)*	0603-30=	2	
2008	Cont	....	*Tara, Batu (Lesser Sunda Is)*	0604-26=	2	
2008	Cont	....	*Suwanose-jima (Ryukyu Is)*	0802-03=	2	
2008	Cont	....	*Sakura-jima (Kyushu-Japan)*	0802-08=	2	
? 2008	Cont	....	*Fukutoku-Okanoba (Volcano Is-Japan*	0804-13=	0	
2008	Cont	....	*NW Rota-1 (Mariana Is-C Pacific)*	0804-211	0	
2008	Cont	....	*Karymsky (Kamchatka)*	1000-13=	2	
2008	Cont	....	*Shiveluch (Kamchatka)*	1000-27=	1	8/-
2008	Cont	....	*Cleveland (Aleutian Is)*	1101-24-	1	
2008	Cont	....	*St. Helens (US-Washington)*	1201-05-	1	7/-
2008	Cont	....	*Kilauea (Hawaiian Is)*	1302-01-	0	**9**/-
2008	Cont	....	*Colima (México)*	1401-04=	1	7/6
2008	Cont	....	*Popocatépetl (México)*	1401-09=	2	
2008	Cont	....	*Santa María (Guatemala)*	1402-03=	1	**9**/8
2008	Cont	....	*Fuego (Guatemala)*	1402-09=	2	
2008	Cont	....	*Pacaya (Guatemala)*	1402-11=	1	
2008	Cont	....	*Arenal (Costa Rica)*	1405-033	1	8/7
2008	Cont	....	*Tungurahua (Ecuador)*	1502-08=	2	
2008	Cont	....	*Sangay (Ecuador)*	1502-09=	2	
2008	Cont	....	*Ubinas (Perú)*	1504-02=	2	
2008	Cont	....	*Erebus (Antarctica)*	1900-02=	1	
2008 a	....	?	**Rumble III** (New Zealand)	0401-13-	0	
2008	0101	565d	**Llaima** (Chile-C)	1507-11=	3	
2008	0102	103m?	**Huila, Nevado del** (Colombia)	1501-05=	2?	
2008	0107	<1	**Miyake-jima** (Izu Is-Japan)	0804-04=	1	
2008	0113	<1	**Poás** (Costa Rica)	1405-04=	1	
2008	0117	....	**Galeras** (Colombia)	1501-08=	3?	
? 2008	0201	<1	*Guagua Pichincha (Ecuador)*	1502-02=	1?	
2008	0203	....	**Anatahan** (Mariana Is-C Pacific)	0804-20=	2	
S 2008	0208?	?	**Monowai Seamount** (Kermadec Is)	0402-05-	0	
? 2008	0212	<1	*Shishaldin (Aleutian Is)*	1101-36-	1?	
2008	0217	<1	**Aso** (Kyushu-Japan)	0802-11=	1	
2008	0222	5a?	**Veniaminof** (Alaska Peninsula)	1102-07-	1	
? 2008	0224	<1?	*Lopevi (Vanuatu-SW Pacific)*	0507-05=	2	
? 2008	0307	259a	*Tofua (Tonga-SW Pacific)*	0403-06=	1?	
2008	0311	2a	**Garbuna Group** (New Britain-SW Pac)	0502-07=	1	
? 2008	0312	?	*Karangetang [Api Siau] (Sangihe Is*	0607-02=	1?	
2008	0324	?	**Kerinci** (Sumatra)	0601-17=	1	
2008	0405	824w>	**Ibu** (Halmahera-Indonesia)	0608-03=	1	
2008	0415	13a?	**Egon** (Lesser Sunda Is)	0604-16=	2	
2008	0502	781w>	**Chaitén** (Chile-S)	1508-041	4	-/8
2008	0508	<1	**Miyake-jima** (Izu Is-Japan)	0804-04=	1	
? 2008	0510	?	*Gamalama (Halmahera-Indonesia)*	0608-06=	1	
2008	0513	417a	**Etna** (Italy)	0101-06=	1	
2008	0513	779w>	**Barren Island** (Andaman Is-Indian O)	0600-01=	2	
? 2008	0519	?	*Merapi (Java)*	0603-25=		
2008	0523	770w>	**Ambrym** (Vanuatu-SW Pacific)	0507-04=	1	
2008	0529	19a	**Azul, Cerro** (Galápagos)	1503-06=	1?	
2008	0606	149a?	**Soputan** (Sulawesi-Indonesia)	0606-03=	3?	
2008	0612	5a?	**Raung** (Java)	0603-34=	2	
2008	0618	182a?	**Masaya** (Nicaragua)	1404-10=	1	
2008	0622	19a	**San Cristóbal** (Nicaragua)	1404-02=	1	
2008	0705d	5d	**Telica** (Nicaragua)	1404-04=	1	
2008	0711	43a?	*Bezymianny (Kamchatka)*	1000-25=	0	
2008	0712	38a	**Okmok** (Aleutian Is)	1101-29-	4?	
2008	0713	83a	**Garbuna Group** (New Britain-SW Pac)	0502-07=	2	
2008	0727	705w>	**Reventador** (Ecuador)	1502-01=	2	
2008	0728	....	*Soufrière Hills (W Indies)*	1600-05=	3?	
2008	0729	10a?	**Chikurachki** (Kuril Is)	0900-36=	2	
2008	0730	<1	**Concepción** (Nicaragua)	1404-12=	1	
? 2008	08	?	*Bárdarbunga (Iceland-NE)*	1703-03=	0	
2008	0807	2a?	**Kasatochi** (Aleutian Is)	1101-13-	4	
2008	0810	<1	**Mayon** (Luzon-Philippines)	0703-03=	1	
2008	0810	4	**Asama** (Honshu-Japan)	0803-11=	1	
2008	0819	....	**Bezymianny** (Kamchatka)	1000-25=	3?	
2008	0822	<1	**Kirishima** (Kyushu-Japan)	0802-09=	1	
2008	0919?	651w>	**Tinakula** (Santa Cruz Is-SW Pacific)	0506-01=	1?	
2008	0921	136a	**Fournaise, Piton de la** (Indian O.-W)	0303-02=	1	6/-
2008	1008	190a?	**Kliuchevskoi** (Kamchatka)	1000-26=	1	
2008	1021?	619w>	*Galeras (Colombia)*	1501-08=	1?	
2008	1026?	614w>	*Huila, Nevado del (Colombia)*	1501-05=	2	6/-
2008	1026	?	**Villarrica** (Chile-C)	1507-12=	1	
2008	11 ?	15m?	**Tafu-Maka** (Tonga-SW Pacific)	0403-12-	0	
2008	11	< 182m>	*West Mata (Tonga-SW Pacific)*	0403-13-	0	
2008	1103	42m?	**Dalaffilla** (Ethiopia)	0201-07=	3?	
2008	1118	10a	**Akan** (Hokkaido-Japan)	0805-07=	1	
2008	1120	....	**Huila, Nevado del** (Colombia)	1501-05=	3?	6/-
2008	1121	<1	**San Cristóbal** (Nicaragua)	1404-02=	1	
2008	1129?	580w>	**Karangetang [Api Siau]** (Sangihe Is	0607-02=	2	
2008	1223?	247a?	*Koryaksky (Kamchatka)*	1000-09=	1	
2009	Cont	....	*Stromboli (Italy)*	0101-04=	1	7/-
2009	Cont	....	*Etna (Italy)*	0101-06=	1	
2009	Cont	....	*Erta Ale (Ethiopia)*	0201-08=	0	
2009	Cont	....	*Lengai, Ol Doinyo (Africa-E)*	0202-12=	1	
2009	Cont	....	*Nyiragongo (Africa-C)*	0203-03=	1	
2009	Cont	....	*West Mata (Tonga-SW Pacific)*	0403-13-	0	
2009	Cont	....	*Rabaul (New Britain-SW Pac)*	0502-14=	1	
2009	Cont	....	*Bagana (Bougainville-SW Pacific)*	0505-02=	2	
2009	Cont	....	*Tinakula (Santa Cruz Is-SW Pacific)*	0506-01=	1?	
2009	Cont	....	*Ambrym (Vanuatu-SW Pacific)*	0507-04=	1	
2009	Cont	....	*Yasur (Vanuatu-SW Pacific)*	0507-10=	2	
2009	Cont	....	*Barren Island (Andaman Is-Indian O)*	0600-01=	2	
2009	Cont	....	*Semeru (Java)*	0603-30=	2	
2009	Cont	....	*Tara, Batu (Lesser Sunda Is)*	0604-26=	2	
2009	Cont	....	*Karangetang [Api Siau] (Sangihe Is*	0607-02=	2	
2009	Cont	....	*Dukono (Halmahera-Indonesia)*	0608-01=	2	
2009	Cont	....	*Ibu (Halmahera-Indonesia)*	0608-03=	1	
2009	Cont	....	*Suwanose-jima (Ryukyu Is)*	0802-03=	2	
2009	Cont	....	*Sakura-jima (Kyushu-Japan)*	0802-08=	2	
? 2009	Cont	....	*Fukutoku-Okanoba (Volcano Is-Japan*	0804-13=	0	
2009	Cont	....	*NW Rota-1 (Mariana Is-C Pacific)*	0804-211	0	
2009	Cont	....	*Karymsky (Kamchatka)*	1000-13=	2	
2009	Cont	....	*Shiveluch (Kamchatka)*	1000-27=	1	8/-
2009	Cont	....	*Kilauea (Hawaiian Is)*	1302-01-	0	**9**/-
2009	Cont	....	*Colima (México)*	1401-04=	1	7/6
2009	Cont	....	*Popocatépetl (México)*	1401-09=	2	
2009	Cont	....	*Santa María (Guatemala)*	1402-03=	1	**9**/8
2009	Cont	....	*Fuego (Guatemala)*	1402-09=	2	
2009	Cont	....	*Pacaya (Guatemala)*	1402-11=	1	
2009	Cont	....	*Arenal (Costa Rica)*	1405-033	1	8/7
2009	Cont	....	*Huila, Nevado del (Colombia)*	1501-05=	1	6/-
2009	Cont	....	*Reventador (Ecuador)*	1502-01=	2	
2009	Cont	....	*Tungurahua (Ecuador)*	1502-08=	2	
2009	Cont	....	*Sangay (Ecuador)*	1502-09=	2	
2009	Cont	....	*Ubinas (Perú)*	1504-02=	2	

START YEAR	M-Dy	Duration	VOLCANO NAME (Subregion)	NUMBER	VEI	Vol L/T
2009	Cont	....	*Llaima (Chile-C)*	1507-11=	2	
2009	Cont	....	*Chaitén (Chile-S)*	1508-041	2	-/8
2009	Cont	....	*Soufrière Hills (W Indies)*	1600-05=	2	
2009	Cont	....	*Erebus (Antarctica)*	1900-02=	1	
2009	0101	<1	**Dempo** (Sumatra)	0601-23=	1?	
2009	0102	19a	*Cleveland (Aleutian Is)*	1101-24-	2	
2009	0112	<1	**Poás** (Costa Rica)	1405-04=	1	
2009	0115	<1	**Dieng Volc Complex** (Java)	0603-20=	1	
? 2009	0118	1a?	*Curtis Island (Kermadec Is)*	0402-01=	0	
2009	0121	101a	*Asama (Honshu-Japan)*	0803-11=	1	
? 2009	0121	1a	*Chillán, Nevados de (Chile-C)*	1507-07=		
? 2009	0122	?	*Callaqui (Chile-C)*	1507-091		
2009	0129	54a?	**Villarrica** (Chile-C)	1507-12=	1	
2009	0202	....	**Asama** (Honshu-Japan)	0803-11=	2	
2009	0211	152a?	**Ebeko** (Kuril Is)	0900-38=	1	
? 2009	0216	1a	*Guagua Pichincha (Ecuador)*	1502-02=	1?	
2009	0220	....	**Galeras** (Colombia)	1501-08=	3	
2009	03	16m	**Tofua** (Tonga-SW Pacific)	0403-06=	1	
2009	0311	....	**Koryaksky** (Kamchatka)	1000-09=	2	
2009	0315	108p	*Redoubt (Alaska-SW)*	1103-03-	2?	
2009	0317?	5a?	**Hunga Tonga-Hunga Ha'apai**	0403-04=	2	
2009	0322	....	**Redoubt** (Alaska-SW)	1103-03-	3	7/7
2009	0325?	174m?	**Krakatau** (Indonesia)	0602-00=	2	
2009	0401?	69a?	**Kerinci** (Sumatra)	0601-17=	1	
2009	0401	<1	**Miyake-jima** (Izu Is-Japan)	0804-04=	1	
2009	0410	18a?	**Fernandina** (Galápagos)	1503-01=	2	
? 2009	0415	?	*Pagan (Mariana Is-C Pacific)*	0804-17=	2	
2009	0421	62a?	**Slamet** (Java)	0603-18=	1	
? 2009	0501p	?	*Karkar (New Guinea-NE of)*	0501-03=		
? 2009	0501	?	*Sangeang Api (Lesser Sunda Is)*	0604-05=		
2009	0502	232a?	**Rinjani** (Lesser Sunda Is)	0604-03=	2	
2009	0611	10e	**Sarychev Peak** (Kuril Is)	0900-24=	4	-/8
2009	0625	?	**Cleveland** (Aleutian Is)	1101-24-	2	
2009	0628	3a?	**Manda Hararo** (Ethiopia)	0201-115	2?	
2009	0801?	153a>	**Kliuchevskoi** (Kamchatka)	1000-26=	1	
? 2009	0826	?	*Kolokol Group (Kuril Is)*	0900-12=	2	
2009	09	< 60m?	**Langila** (New Britain-SW Pac)	0502-01=	2	
2009	0906	111a?	**San Cristóbal** (Nicaragua)	1404-02=	2?	
2009	0915	108a>	*Mayon (Luzon-Philippines)*	0703-03=	1	
2009	0927	96a>	**Gaua** (Vanuatu-SW Pacific)	0507-02=	2	
2009	0927	<1	**Dieng Volc Complex** (Java)	0603-20=	1	
2009	1002	71a?	**Cleveland** (Aleutian Is)	1101-24-	2	
2009	1105	57a>	**Fournaise, Piton de la** (Indian O.-W)	0303-02=	1?	
2009	1122	40a>	**Villarrica** (Chile-C)	1507-12=	1	
2009	1211	?	**Concepción** (Nicaragua)	1404-12=	1	
2009	1214	....	**Mayon** (Luzon-Philippines)	0703-03=	2	
2009	1217	15a>	**Bezymianny** (Kamchatka)	1000-25=	3?	
2009	1225	<1	**Poás** (Costa Rica)	1405-04=	1	

Jeff Marso (USGS/CVO)

An eruption plume on May 26, 2008 rises from the lava-dome complex in the caldera of Chaitén volcano in southern Chile. A major explosive eruption at Chaitén began on May 2, marking the first historical eruption of the volcano. Mudflows destroyed much of the town of Chaitén. The elliptical, 2.5 x 4 km wide summit caldera was formed during an eruption dated at about 9400 years ago. A rhyolitic, 962-m-high obsidian lava dome occupied much of the caldera floor prior to the 2008 eruption, which was continuing in 2010 and produced a new compound lava dome.

Large-Volume Holocene Eruptions

Large-Volume Holocene Eruptions: Context

There is substantial interest in the larger-volume eruptions that have affected our planet, and this section highlights those eruptions, both explosive and effusive, in separate tables. The **Explosive Eruptions** table includes all Holocene explosive eruptions with a **VEI** of 4 or larger (≥0.1 km^3 of tephra). Data are shown in the same format as in the **CHRONOLOGY** tables, except that only dates of eruptive events of VEI 4 or larger are displayed, whenever they may occur during the course of an eruption. The start date of an eruption is displayed only when there is only one VEI assignment for the full eruption. The associated data for the eruption duration and the lava volume, however, are for the full eruption, giving context for the eruption as a whole, while noting the magnitude (VEI and tephra volume) of the sometimes more specifically dated explosive event. Thus the **VEI** 7 eruption of Tambora volcano, the largest in historical time, appears only under its April 10, 1815 date, but the **Duration** column indicates that the eruption lasted for more than three years. As with the **DIRECTORY** and **CHRONOLOGY** tables, explosive eruptions without tephra volumes that are described as "plinian" or caldera-forming are shown with a "P" or "C," respectively, in the **VEI** column.

The ensuing **Effusive Eruptions** table includes all eruptions producing ≥0.1 km^3 (or 10^8 m^3) of lava. In contrast to the **Explosive Eruptions** table, all data in the **Effusive Eruptions** table, including the eruption duration, VEI, and lava and tephra volumes, provide context for the eruption as a whole and are listed under the start date of the eruption. This means that the lava volume, even for long-duration eruptions, is applied to the first year of the eruption. The compound Santiaguito lava dome at Santa María volcano in Guatemala, for example, still in eruption after almost 90 years, has now produced more than 1 km^3 of lava, but its lava volume of 9 (10^9 m^3) appears only with its 1922 start date.

As with the **CHRONOLOGY** listing discussed above, it must be emphasized that these "Large Eruption" tables include dates with large dating uncertainties and incorporate both corrected and uncorrected radiocarbon dates (discussed in more detail later under **Dating Technique**). Consequently events do not always appear in strict chronological sequence. It must also be noted that these tables are clearly substantially incomplete, as deposits of many Holocene eruptions have not been studied in sufficient detail to determine their volumes.

Explosive Eruptions

START YEAR	M-Dy	Duration	VOLCANO NAME (Subregion)	NUMBER	VEI	Vol L/T
T-9650?	....	?	**Tongariro** (New Zealand)	0401-08=	5	-/9
G-9500y	....	?	**Khangar** (Kamchatka)	1000-272	P	-/-
G-9460x	....	?	**Taupo** (New Zealand)	0401-07=	5	-/9
G-9450?	....	?	**Tongariro** (New Zealand)	0401-08=	5	-/9
T-9350?	....	?	**Tongariro** (New Zealand)	0401-08=	5	8/9
G-9240u	....	?	**Taupo** (New Zealand)	0401-07=	5	-/9
T-9210?	....	?	**Taupo** (New Zealand)	0401-07=	4	7/8
G-9160*	....	?	**Kuju** (Kyushu-Japan)	0802-12=	4	8/8
G-8910x	....	?	**Askja** (Iceland-NE)	1703-06=	5	-/9
G-8750?	....	?	**Ulreung** (Korea)	1006-03-	6	-/10
G-8480v	....	?	**Campi Flegrei** (Italy)	0101-01=	4	-/-
T-8350?	....	?	**Shiveluch** (Kamchatka)	1000-27=	4	-/8
T-8300y	....	?	**Akita-Komaga-take** (Honshu-Japan)	0803-23=	4	-/8
G-8250?	....	?	**Ngozi** (Africa-E)	0202-164	C	-/-
G-8250?	....	?	**Towada** (Honshu-Japan)	0803-271	5	-/9
G-8230t	....	?	**Grímsvötn** (Iceland-NE)	1703-01=	6	-/10
G-8210x	....	?	**Pelée** (W Indies)	1600-12=	4?	-/8
T-8200?	....	?	**Shiveluch** (Kamchatka)	1000-27=	4	-/8
G-8130x	....	?	**Taupo** (New Zealand)	0401-07=	5	-/9
T-8100?	....	?	**Shiveluch** (Kamchatka)	1000-27=	4	-/8
T-8050?	....	?	**Kizimen** (Kamchatka)	1000-23=	5	-/9
T-8050?	....	?	**Vestmannaeyjar** (Iceland-S)	1702-01=	4	-/8
T-8020*	....	?	**Hachijo-jima** (Izu Is-Japan)	0804-05=	4	-/8
T-7950?	....	?	**Shiveluch** (Kamchatka)	1000-27=	4	-/8
G-7900?	....	?	**Ksudach** (Kamchatka)	1000-05=	5	-/9
G-7850x	....	?	**Akita-Komaga-take** (Honshu-Japan)	0803-23=	4	-/8
C-7840<	....	?	**Ruapehu** (New Zealand)	0401-10=	4	-/8
C-7800y	....	?	**Tolima, Nevado del** (Colombia)	1501-03=	P	-/-
C-7750?	....	?	**Tungurahua** (Ecuador)	1502-08=	4	-/8
T-7700?	....	?	**Shiveluch** (Kamchatka)	1000-27=	4	-/8
C-7650v	....	?	**Shasta** (US-California)	1203-01-	4	-/8
T-7630?	....	?	**Shiveluch** (Kamchatka)	1000-27=	4	-/8
T-7600?	....	?	**Shiveluch** (Kamchatka)	1000-27=	4	-/8
T-7600z	....	?	**Roundtop** (Aleutian Is)	1101-38-	5?	-/-
G-7560o	....	?	**Okataina** (New Zealand)	0401-05=	5	9/9
R-7550*	....	?	**Paka** (Africa-E)	0202-053	C	-/-
T-7550z	....	?	**Elovsky** (Kamchatka)	1000-59-	4	9/8
T-7500?	....	?	**Shiveluch** (Kamchatka)	1000-27=	4+	-/8
C-7480t	....	?	**Lvinaya Past** (Kuril Is)	0900-041	6+	-/10
G-7460w	....	?	**Pinatubo** (Luzon-Philippines)	0703-083	6?	-/-
C-7450t	....	?	**Ushishur** (Kuril Is)	0900-21=	C	-/-
G-7450z	....	?	**Burney, Monte** (Chile-S)	1508-07=	5	-/9
C-7420x	....	?	**Fisher** (Aleutian Is)	1101-35-	6?	-/10
C-7420u	....	?	**Chaitén** (Chile-S)	1508-041	C	-/-
G-7400w	....	?	**Shiveluch** (Kamchatka)	1000-27=	5	-/9
G-7370y	....	?	**Chichinautzin** (México)	1401-08=	4	-/8
T-7300?	....	?	**Shiveluch** (Kamchatka)	1000-27=	5	-/9
R-7300*	....	?	**Seguam** (Aleutian Is)	1101-18-	5?	-/8
G-7250?	....	?	**Towada** (Honshu-Japan)	0803-271	5?	-/9
T-7150?	....	?	**Shiveluch** (Kamchatka)	1000-27=	5	-/9
C-7150?	....	?	**Popocatépetl** (México)	1401-09=	P	-/-
C-7140w	....	?	**Karkar** (New Guinea-NE of)	0501-03=	C	-/-
C-7050?	....	?	**Akan** (Hokkaido-Japan)	0805-07=	4	-/8
T-7050*	....	?	**Zheltovsky** (Kamchatka)	1000-04=	5	-/9
C-7030t	....	?	**Orizaba, Pico de** (México)	1401-10=	4	-/8
C-6950?	....	?	**Shikotsu** (Hokkaido-Japan)	0805-04=	5	-/9
G-6940v	....	?	**Vesuvius** (Italy)	0101-02=	5	-/9
C-6910<	....	?	**Atacazo** (Ecuador)	1502-021	P	-/-
C-6880u	....	?	**Llaima** (Chile-C)	1507-11=	5	-/9
T-6800?	....	?	**Shiveluch** (Kamchatka)	1000-27=	5?	-/9
C-6710w	....	?	**Orizaba, Pico de** (México)	1401-10=	5?	-/9
C-6690?	....	?	**Villarrica** (Chile-C)	1507-12=	P	-/-
C-6650v	....	?	**Campi Flegrei** (Italy)	0101-01=	4	-/8
C-6650?	....	?	**Soche** (Ecuador)	1502-001	5?	-/-
G-6610w	....	?	**Pelée** (W Indies)	1600-12=	4?	-/8
G-6600?	....	?	**Karymsky** (Kamchatka)	1000-13=	6	-/10
T-6600?	....	?	**Shiveluch** (Kamchatka)	1000-27=	4	-/8
T-6450z	....	?	**Miyake-jima** (Izu Is-Japan)	0804-04=	4	-/8
G-6440q	....	?	**Kurile Lake** (Kamchatka)	1000-023	7	-/11
C-6400t	....	?	**Kizimen** (Kamchatka)	1000-23=	5	-/9
G-6400w	....	?	**Shiveluch** (Kamchatka)	1000-27=	4	-/8
T-6380?	....	?	**Shiveluch** (Kamchatka)	1000-27=	4	-/8
T-6350?	....	?	**Shiveluch** (Kamchatka)	1000-27=	4	-/8
C-6310z	....	?	**Okmok** (Aleutian Is)	1101-29-	P	-/-
G-6250?	....	?	**Towada** (Honshu-Japan)	0803-271	4	-/8
G-6220x	....	?	**Pelée** (W Indies)	1600-12=	P	-/-
C-6200*	....	?	**Sakura-jima** (Kyushu-Japan)	0802-08=	6	-/10
C-6140x	....	?	**Quill, The** (W Indies)	1600-02=	P	-/-
C-6100t	....	?	**Makushin** (Aleutian Is)	1101-31-	5	-/9
G-6060t	....	?	**Okataina** (New Zealand)	0401-05=	5	10/9
C-6050?	....	?	**Menengai** (Africa-E)	0202-06=	6+	-/10
N-6050*	....	?	**Meidob Volc Field** (Africa-N)	0205-05-	P	-/-
C-6050?	....	?	**Sakura-jima** (Kyushu-Japan)	0802-08=	5	-/-
T-6050*	....	?	**Barva** (Costa Rica)	1405-05=	P	-/-
C-6000t	....	?	**Krasheninnikov** (Kamchatka)	1000-19=	4	9/8
G-5980v	....	?	**Avachinsky** (Kamchatka)	1000-10=	5+	-/9
C-5950z	....	?	**Romeral** (Colombia)	1501-011	P	-/-
G-5900t	....	?	**Crater Lake** (US-Oregon)	1202-16-	6	8/10
C-5850?	....	?	**Meru** (Africa-E)	0202-16=	P	-/-
C-5820u	....	?	**Cotopaxi** (Ecuador)	1502-05=	5+	-/9
C-5800t	....	?	**Krasheninnikov** (Kamchatka)	1000-19=	4	7/8
T-5700t	....	?	**Ilyinsky** (Kamchatka)	1000-03=	C	-/-
G-5700n	....	?	**Khangar** (Kamchatka)	1000-272	6	-/10
I-5677w	1015q	?	**Crater Lake** (US-Oregon)	1202-16-	7	8/11
G-5550v	....	?	**Mashu** (Hokkaido-Japan)	0805-081	6	-/-
C-5550u	....	?	**Tao-Rusyr Caldera** (Kuril Is)	0900-31=	6	-/10
T-5500?	....	?	**Shiveluch** (Kamchatka)	1000-27=	5	-/9
G-5500x	....	?	**Pelée** (W Indies)	1600-12=	P	-/-
T-5400?	....	?	**Ichinsky** (Kamchatka)	1000-28=	5	9/9
T-5250*	....	?	**Aniakchak** (Alaska Peninsula)	1102-09-	6?	-/10
G-5200?	....	?	**Ksudach** (Kamchatka)	1000-05=	5?	-/9
N-5150*	....	?	**Tavui** (New Britain-SW Pac)	0502-15-	5	-/9
C-5150?	....	?	**Popocatépetl** (México)	1401-09=	P	-/-
G-5150?	....	?	**Hekla** (Iceland-S)	1702-07=	5	-/9
G-5080w	....	?	**Puyehue-Cordón Caulle** (Chile-C)	1507-15=	5	-/9
G-5060x	....	?	**Mayor Island** (New Zealand)	0401-021	5	-/9
G-5060w	....	?	**Arenal** (Costa Rica)	1405-033	4?	-/-
C-5050?	....	?	**Iliamna** (Alaska-SW)	1103-02-	P	-/-
-5000 (6950 BP)						
G-4900?	....	?	**Ksudach** (Kamchatka)	1000-05=	5+	-/9
G-4750y	....	?	**Myoko** (Honshu-Japan)	0803-10=	5?	-/9
C-4750?	....	?	**Hudson, Cerro** (Chile-S)	1508-057	6	-/10
G-4700?	....	?	**Taupo** (New Zealand)	0401-07=	4	-/8
T-4650?	....	?	**Hachijo-jima** (Izu Is-Japan)	0804-05=	5	-/9
G-4600t	....	?	**Komaga-take** (Hokkaido-Japan)	0805-02=	5	-/9
G-4570?	....	?	**Takahara** (Honshu-Japan)	0803-143	4?	8/7
G-4550x	....	?	**Avachinsky** (Kamchatka)	1000-10=	4	-/8
G-4460v	....	?	**Avachinsky** (Kamchatka)	1000-10=	4	-/8
T-4450?	....	?	**Kizimen** (Kamchatka)	1000-23=	4	-/8
G-4400?	....	?	**Shiveluch** (Kamchatka)	1000-27=	5	-/9
C-4360x	....	?	**Macauley Island** (Kermadec Is)	0402-021	6?	-/10
C-4350?	....	?	**Kikai** (Ryukyu Is)	0802-06=	7	-/11
C-4350?	....	?	**Kirishima** (Kyushu-Japan)	0802-09=	4	-/8
G-4350?	....	?	**Komaga-take** (Hokkaido-Japan)	0805-02=	P	-/-
C-4350u	....	?	**Cotopaxi** (Ecuador)	1502-05=	5	-/9
G-4340u	....	?	**Avachinsky** (Kamchatka)	1000-10=	5	-/9
C-4280w	....	?	**Bravo, Cerro** (Colombia)	1501-012	4	-/9
C-4160r	....	?	**Apoyeque** (Nicaragua)	1404-091	5	-/9
T-4150*	....	?	**Meidob Volc Field** (Africa-N)	0205-05-	P	-/-
G-4150?	....	?	**Towada** (Honshu-Japan)	0803-271	5+	-/9
G-4100?	....	?	**Taupo** (New Zealand)	0401-07=	4	-/8
T-4050?	....	?	**Masaya** (Nicaragua)	1404-10=	6	-/10
G-4000x	....	?	**Pago** (New Britain-SW Pac)	0502-08=	6?	-/10
T-3900?	....	?	**Arenal** (Costa Rica)	1405-033	4	-/8
C-3880u	....	?	**Cotopaxi** (Ecuador)	1502-05=	5+	-/9
C-3850?	....	?	**Kaguyak** (Alaska Peninsula)	1102-25-	5	-/9
C-3820?	....	?	**Pelée** (W Indies)	1600-12=	P	-/-
G-3790v	....	?	**Avachinsky** (Kamchatka)	1000-10=	4	-/8
G-3780z	....	?	**Kuju** (Kyushu-Japan)	0802-12=	4	8/8
G-3650?	....	?	**Shiveluch** (Kamchatka)	1000-27=	5	-/9
T-3650*	....	?	**Makushin** (Aleutian Is)	1101-31-	P	-/-
G-3580t	....	?	**Okataina** (New Zealand)	0401-05=	5	9/9
C-3580x	....	?	**Taal** (Luzon-Philippines)	0703-07=	6	-/10
G-3550?	....	?	**Pinatubo** (Luzon-Philippines)	0703-083	6	-/10
G-3550s	....	?	**Mashu** (Hokkaido-Japan)	0805-081	4	-/8
G-3500?	....	?	**Shiveluch** (Kamchatka)	1000-27=	5	-/9
T-3500x	....	?	**Pelée** (W Indies)	1600-12=	P	-/-
C-3490v	....	?	**Atacazo** (Ecuador)	1502-021	P	-/-

START YEAR	M-Dy	Dura-tion	VOLCANO NAME (Subregion)	NUMBER	VEI	Vol L/T
G-3430u	....	?	**Pelée** (W Indies)	1600-12=	4?	-/8
G-3400?	....	?	**Numazawa** (Honshu-Japan)	0803-151	5	-/9
T-3350?	....	?	**Arenal** (Costa Rica)	1405-033	4	-/8
T-3280z	....	?	**Cotopaxi** (Ecuador)	1502-05=	5	8/9
G-3200w	....	?	**Avachinsky** (Kamchatka)	1000-10=	5	-/9
G-3200?	....	?	**Karymsky** (Kamchatka)	1000-13=	4	8/8
T-3200?	....	?	**Shiveluch** (Kamchatka)	1000-27=	4+	-/8
G-3170x	....	?	**Taupo** (New Zealand)	0401-07=	4	-/8
C-3170u	....	?	**Fisher** (Aleutian Is)	1101-35-	5	-/9
G-3070?	....	?	**Taupo** (New Zealand)	0401-07=	4	-/8
T-3050?	....	?	**Meidob Volc Field** (Africa-N)	0205-05-	P	-/-
C-3050?	....	?	**Sakura-jima** (Kyushu-Japan)	0802-08=	4	-/-
C-3050?	....	?	**Zheltovsky** (Kamchatka)	1000-04=	5	-/9
T-3050?	....	?	**Sete Cidades** (Azores)	1802-08=	4	-/8
C-3010x	....	?	**Popocatépetl** (México)	1401-09=	P	-/-
T-3000?	....	?	**Meidob Volc Field** (Africa-N)	0205-05-	P	-/-
T-3000?	....	?	**Ksudach** (Kamchatka)	1000-05=	4	-/8
C-2990?	....	?	**Agua de Pau** (Azores)	1802-09=	5	-/9
G-2900?	....	?	**Taupo** (New Zealand)	0401-07=	4	-/8
C-2900?	....	?	**Sakura-jima** (Kyushu-Japan)	0802-08=	4	-/-
T-2900z	....	?	**Miyake-jima** (Izu Is-Japan)	0804-04=	4	7/8
C-2850?	....	?	**Ilyinsky** (Kamchatka)	1000-03=	5	-/9
T-2800?	....	?	**Arenal** (Costa Rica)	1405-033	4	-/8
G-2780q	....	?	**Kikhpinych** (Kamchatka)	1000-18=	4	8/8
G-2750v	....	?	**Myoko** (Honshu-Japan)	0803-10=	4	-/8
G-2700?	....	?	**Fournaise, Piton de la** (Indian O.-W)	0303-02=	5?	-/9
C-2690u	....	?	**Ibusuki Volc Field** (Kyushu-Japan)	0802-07=	5	-/9
G-2660x	....	?	**Pelée** (W Indies)	1600-12=	4?	-/8
C-2650?	....	?	**Kirishima** (Kyushu-Japan)	0802-09=	4	-/-
C-2650?	....	?	**Tolmachev Dol** (Kamchatka)	1000-082	4+	-/8
C-2640x	....	?	**Cotopaxi** (Ecuador)	1502-05=	5	-/9
G-2620y	....	?	**Shiveluch** (Kamchatka)	1000-27=	5	-/9
G-2600?	....	?	**Taupo** (New Zealand)	0401-07=	4	-/8
A-2550z	....	?	**Asama** (Honshu-Japan)	0803-11=	4	-/-
T-2550*	....	?	**Apoyeque** (Nicaragua)	1404-091	5	-/9
C-2550w	....	?	**Doña Juana** (Colombia)	1501-07=	C	-/-
G-2530y	....	?	**Avachinsky** (Kamchatka)	1000-10=	4	-/8
T-2500?	....	?	**Campi Flegrei** (Italy)	0101-01=	4	-/8
C-2490s	....	?	**Atacazo** (Ecuador)	1502-021	5	-/9
T-2450z	....	?	**Hachijo-jima** (Izu Is-Japan)	0804-05=	4	-/8
G-2440y	....	?	**Kuju** (Kyushu-Japan)	0802-12=	4	7/8
C-2430?	....	?	**Pelée** (W Indies)	1600-12=	P	-/-
G-2420s	....	?	**Vesuvius** (Italy)	0101-02=	5	-/9
G-2400?	....	?	**Rungwe** (Africa-E)	0202-166	P	-/-
C-2370w	....	?	**Colima** (México)	1401-04=	4?	-/8
G-2340?	....	?	**St. Helens** (US-Washington)	1201-05-	5	-/9
G-2320v	....	?	**Burney, Monte** (Chile-S)	1508-07=	5	-/9
G-2310p	....	?	**Hekla** (Iceland-S)	1702-07=	5	-/9
C-2300u	....	?	**Orizaba, Pico de** (México)	1401-10=	4	-/8
C-2250w	....	?	**Galunggung** (Java)	0603-14=	5?	-/-
G-2250?	....	?	**Karymsky** (Kamchatka)	1000-13=	4	7/9
T-2250?	....	?	**Arenal** (Costa Rica)	1405-033	4	-/8
T-2200?	....	?	**Shiveluch** (Kamchatka)	1000-27=	4+	-/8
C-2160v	....	?	**Changbaishan** (China-E)	1005-06-	P	-/-
C-2150z	....	?	**Campi Flegrei** (Italy)	0101-01=	5	-/9
G-2100v	....	?	**Izu-Tobu** (Honshu-Japan)	0803-01=	4	8/8
G-2100?	....	?	**Shiveluch** (Kamchatka)	1000-27=	5	-/9
T-2050?	....	?	**Hachijo-jima** (Izu Is-Japan)	0804-05=	5	-/9
G-2050s	....	?	**Mashu** (Hokkaido-Japan)	0805-081	4	-/8
C-2050?	....	?	**Iliamna** (Alaska-SW)	1103-02-	P	-/-
T-2050?	....	?	**Cotopaxi** (Ecuador)	1502-05=	5	7/9
C-2040v	....	?	**Long Island** (New Guinea-NE of)	0501-05=	6	-/10
G-2030v	....	?	**Chichón, El** (México)	1401-12=	5	-/9
T-2010?	....	?	**Ibusuki Volc Field** (Kyushu-Japan)	0802-07=	4	-/8
C-2010w	....	?	**Liamuiga** (W Indies)	1600-03=	P	-/-
T-2000w	....	?	**Campi Flegrei** (Italy)	0101-01=	4	-/8
G-2000?	....	?	**Marra, Jebel** (Africa-N)	0205-03-	C	-/-
C-2000v	....	?	**Raoul Island** (Kermadec Is)	0402-03=	4	-/8
G-2000?	....	?	**Shiveluch** (Kamchatka)	1000-27=	5	-/9
G-1990x	....	?	**Tolima, Nevado del** (Colombia)	1501-03=	5?	-/9
C-1920s	....	?	**Parker** (Mindanao-Philippines)	0701-011	P	-/-
T-1920?	....	?	**Sanbe** (Honshu-Japan)	0803-002	4	9/8
G-1920?	....	?	**Katla** (Iceland-S)	1702-03=	4	-/8
T-1900w	....	?	**Black Peak** (Alaska Peninsula)	1102-08-	6	-/10
C-1890?	....	?	**Dana** (Alaska Peninsula)	1102-05-	5	-/9
G-1890?	....	?	**Hudson, Cerro** (Chile-S)	1508-057	6	-/10
C-1870t	....	?	**Campi Flegrei** (Italy)	0101-01=	4	-/9
G-1860?	....	?	**St. Helens** (US-Washington)	1201-05-	6	-/10
G-1820w	....	?	**Rincón de la Vieja** (Costa Rica)	1405-02=	4	-/8
C-1810x	....	?	**Villarrica** (Chile-C)	1507-12=	5	-/9
T-1780?	....	?	**Ibusuki Volc Field** (Kyushu-Japan)	0802-07=	4	-/8
T-1770v	....	?	**St. Helens** (US-Washington)	1201-05-	5	-/9
G-1750?	....	?	**Okataina** (New Zealand)	0401-05=	4+	8/8
C-1750?	....	?	**Veniaminof** (Alaska Peninsula)	1102-07-	6	-/10
C-1700v	....	?	**Taranaki [Egmont]** (New Zealand)	0401-03=	5	-/9
G-1700t	....	?	**Aso** (Kyushu-Japan)	0802-11=	P	-/-
T-1700?	....	?	**Shiveluch** (Kamchatka)	1000-27=	4	-/8
T-1650?	....	?	**Campi Flegrei** (Italy)	0101-01=	4	-/8
T-1650?	....	?	**Arenal** (Costa Rica)	1405-033	4	-/8
I-1645j	....	?	**Aniakchak** (Alaska Peninsula)	1102-09-	6?	-/10
G-1610m	....	?	**Santorini** (Greece)	0102-04=	7?	-/10
G-1550u	....	?	**Vesuvius** (Italy)	0101-02=	4	-/8
T-1550?	....	?	**Hayes** (Alaska-SW)	1103-05-	5	-/-
T-1550?	....	?	**Hekla** (Iceland-S)	1702-07=	4	-/8
-1500t	....	?	**Etna** (Italy)	0101-06=	5?	-/-
T-1500?	....	?	**Ibusuki Volc Field** (Kyushu-Japan)	0802-07=	4	-/8
G-1500?	....	?	**Avachinsky** (Kamchatka)	1000-10=	5	-/9
G-1460s	....	?	**Taupo** (New Zealand)	0401-07=	6	-/10
T-1450?	....	?	**Arenal** (Costa Rica)	1405-033	4	-/8
G-1440s	....	?	**Katla** (Iceland-S)	1702-03=	4	-/8
G-1430y	....	?	**Vesuvius** (Italy)	0101-02=	4	-/8
G-1370v	....	?	**Pago** (New Britain-SW Pac)	0502-08=	6	-/10
T-1350?	....	?	**Fuji** (Honshu-Japan)	0803-03=	5	-/9
C-1350?	....	?	**Avachinsky** (Kamchatka)	1000-10=	5	-/9
C-1320?	....	?	**Yucamane** (Perú)	1504-05-	5	-/9
C-1310w	....	?	**Bravo, Cerro** (Colombia)	1501-012	4	-/9
C-1290?	....	?	**Agua de Pau** (Azores)	1802-09=	4	-/8
G-1250x	....	?	**Arenal** (Costa Rica)	1405-033	4	-/8
G-1250w	....	?	**Aguilera** (Chile-S)	1508-062	5	-/9
C-1200w	....	?	**Raoul Island** (Kermadec Is)	0402-03=	4	-/8
C-1180u	....	?	**Merapi** (Java)	0603-25=	P	-/-
G-1150t	....	?	**Izu-Tobu** (Honshu-Japan)	0803-01=	4+	8/8
C-1150w	....	?	**Cuicocha** (Ecuador)	1502-003	5	-/9
C-1120w	....	?	**Kusatsu-Shirane** (Honshu-Japan)	0803-12=	4	8/8
G-1100t	....	?	**Hekla** (Iceland-S)	1702-07=	5+	-/9
G-1050?	....	?	**Taupo** (New Zealand)	0401-07=	4	-/8
G-1050z	....	?	**Pinatubo** (Luzon-Philippines)	0703-083	6	-/10
T-1050<	....	?	**Khodutka** (Kamchatka)	1000-053	4+	-/8
T-1050*	....	?	**Apoyeque** (Nicaragua)	1404-091	4	-/8
T-1050x	....	?	**Bravo, Cerro** (Colombia)	1501-012	4	-/8
T-1050?	....	?	**Cotopaxi** (Ecuador)	1502-05=	4	9/8
T-1030?	....	?	**Fuji** (Honshu-Japan)	0803-03=	4+	-/8
G-1010x	....	?	**Taupo** (New Zealand)	0401-07=	4+	-/8
C-1010v	....	?	**Tungurahua** (Ecuador)	1502-08=	5	-/9
G-0990*	....	?	**Kuju** (Kyushu-Japan)	0802-12=	4	-/8
G-0960w	....	?	**Antillanca Group** (Chile-C)	1507-153	5	-/9
G-0950?	....	?	**Aso** (Kyushu-Japan)	0802-11=	P	-/-
T-0950x	....	?	**Miyake-jima** (Izu Is-Japan)	0804-04=	4+	-/8
G-0950?	....	?	**Shiveluch** (Kamchatka)	1000-27=	5	-/9
C-0930>	....	?	**Fuji** (Honshu-Japan)	0803-03=	5	-/9
G-0930v	....	?	**Khodutka** (Kamchatka)	1000-053	5	7/9
C-0930?	....	?	**Azufral** (Colombia)	1501-09=	P	-/-
C-0920u	....	?	**Sollipulli** (Chile-C)	1507-111	5+	-/9
G-0880t	....	?	**Vesuvius** (Italy)	0101-02=	4	-/8
C-0850?	....	?	**Zavaritsky** (Kamchatka)	1000-124	4+	7/8
T-0850?	....	?	**Ruiz, Nevado del** (Colombia)	1501-02=	4	-/8
G-0850t	....	?	**Katla** (Iceland-S)	1702-03=	4	-/8
C-0830t	....	?	**Tengger Caldera** (Java)	0603-31=	P	-/-
T-0800z	....	?	**Yantarni** (Alaska Peninsula)	1102-10-	5	8/9
C-0800t	....	?	**Momotombo** (Nicaragua)	1404-09=	4+	-/8
G-0780y	....	?	**Shiveluch** (Kamchatka)	1000-27=	4+	-/8
C-0770t	....	?	**Concepción** (Nicaragua)	1404-12=	P	-/-
G-0750?	....	?	**Towada** (Honshu-Japan)	0803-271	4+	-/8
C-0730u	....	?	**Bravo, Cerro** (Colombia)	1501-012	4+	-/8
C-0690w	....	?	**Pululagua** (Ecuador)	1502-011	5	-/9
T-0650?	....	?	**Ibusuki Volc Field** (Kyushu-Japan)	0802-07=	4	-/8
T-0650?	....	?	**Krafla** (Iceland-NE)	1703-08=	4	-/8
C-0600x	....	?	**Aoga-shima** (Izu Is-Japan)	0804-06=	4	8/8
G-0590x	....	?	**Pelée** (W Indies)	1600-12=	4?	-/8
C-0550x	....	?	**Tongariro** (New Zealand)	0401-08=	5	-/9
C-0550?	....	?	**Shikotsu** (Hokkaido-Japan)	0805-04=	5	-/9
G-0530?	....	?	**St. Helens** (US-Washington)	1201-05-	5	-/9
G-0500?	....	?	**Shiveluch** (Kamchatka)	1000-27=	4	-/8
G-0450?	....	?	**Bezymianny** (Kamchatka)	1000-25=	4	-/8
C-0450w	....	?	**Pululagua** (Ecuador)	1502-011	C	-/-
C-0440?	....	?	**Pelée** (W Indies)	1600-12=	P	-/-
G-0410x	....	?	**Meager** (Canada)	1200-18-	5?	-/-
T-0400?	....	?	**Cotopaxi** (Ecuador)	1502-05=	4	7/8
G-0380x	....	?	**Arenal** (Costa Rica)	1405-033	4	-/8
G-0350?	....	?	**Yake-dake** (Honshu-Japan)	0803-07=	4	8/8

START YEAR	M-Dy	Duration	VOLCANO NAME (Subregion)	NUMBER	VEI	Vol L/T
C-**0350**?	....	?	**South Sister** (US-Oregon)	1202-08-	4	8/8
C-**0320**n	....	?	**Atacazo** (Ecuador)	1502-021	**5**	-/**9**
G-**0300**?	....	?	**Shiveluch** (Kamchatka)	1000-27=	4	-/8
T-**0270**?	....	?	**Ibusuki Volc Field** (Kyushu-Japan)	0802-07=	4	-/8
T-**0270**?	....	?	**Arenal** (Costa Rica)	1405-033	4	-/8
C-**0250**u	....	?	**Raoul Island** (Kermadec Is)	0402-03=	**6**	-/**10**
G-**0250**x	....	?	**Rainier** (US-Washington)	1201-03-	4	-/8
C-**0230**x	....	?	**Cotopaxi** (Ecuador)	1502-05=	4	-/8
G-**0230**x	....	?	**Antillanca Group** (Chile-C)	1507-153	**5**	-/**9**
I -**0210**x	....	?	**Hudson Mountains** (Antarctica)	1900-028	4?	-/8
G-**0200**?	....	?	**Taupo** (New Zealand)	0401-07=	4+	-/8
C-**0200**t	....	?	**Tsurumi** (Kyushu-Japan)	0802-13=	4	-/-
G-**0200**?	....	?	**Haku-san** (Honshu-Japan)	0803-05=	4	8/8
C-**0200**y	....	?	**Popocatépetl** (México)	1401-09=	**P**	-/-
C-**0200**v	....	?	**Ruiz, Nevado del** (Colombia)	1501-02=	4	-/8
C-**0200**?	....	?	**Pelée** (W Indies)	1600-12=	**P**	-/-
-0183	....	?	**Vulcano** (Italy)	0101-05=	4	-/-
C-**0180**u	....	?	**Changbaishan** (China-E)	1005-06-	**P**	-/-
C-**0170**v	....	?	**Masaya** (Nicaragua)	1404-10=	**5**	-/**9**
G-**0170**x	....	?	**Arenal** (Costa Rica)	1405-033	4	-/8
G-**0150**?	....	?	**Krasheninnikov** (Kamchatka)	1000-19=	**C**	-/-
-0122	....	?	**Etna** (Italy)	0101-06=	**5**	-/**9**
G-**0100**y	....	?	**Kuju** (Kyushu-Japan)	0802-12=	4	-/8
C-**0100**t	....	?	**Okmok** (Aleutian Is)	1101-29-	**6**	-/**10**
T-**0080**?	....	?	**Ibusuki Volc Field** (Kyushu-Japan)	0802-07=	4	-/8
G-**0080**u	....	?	**Misti, El** (Perú)	1504-01=	4?	-/8
G-**0080**s	....	?	**Tenerife** (Canary Is)	1803-03-	4+	7/8
G-**0050**?	....	?	**Akan** (Hokkaido-Japan)	0805-07=	**P**	-/-
T-**0050**v	....	?	**Apoyeque** (Nicaragua)	1404-091	**6**	-/**10**
BC / AD						
G **0010** t	....	?	**Pelée** (W Indies)	1600-12=	4	-/8
G **0020**y	....	?	**Merapi** (Java)	0603-25=	**P**	-/-
G **0040**t	....	?	**Turrialba** (Costa Rica)	1405-07=	4	-/8
C **0050**v	....	?	**Ambrym** (Vanuatu-SW Pacific)	0507-04=	**6**+	-/**10**
T **0050**?	....	?	**Tolbachik** (Kamchatka)	1000-24=	4+	8/8
C **0050**?	....	?	**Pelée** (W Indies)	1600-12=	**P**	-/-
C **0060**x	....	?	**Churchill** (Alaska-E)	1105-03-	**6**	-/**10**
G **0070**v	....	?	**Tacaná** (México)	1401-13=	4?	-/8
G **0070**u	....	?	**Guagua Pichincha** (Ecuador)	1502-02=	4	-/8
C **0070**w	....	?	**Cotopaxi** (Ecuador)	1502-05=	4	-/8
0079	1024?	4b?	**Vesuvius** (Italy)	0101-02=	**5**?	-/**9**
C **0080**v	....	?	**Furnas** (Azores)	1802-10=	**5**	-/**9**
C **0090**v	....	?	**Sete Cidades** (Azores)	1802-08=	4	-/8
T **0100**?	....	?	**Raoul Island** (Kermadec Is)	0402-03=	4	-/8
T **0100**?	....	?	**Shiveluch** (Kamchatka)	1000-27=	4	-/8
T **0130**?	....	?	**Ibusuki Volc Field** (Kyushu-Japan)	0802-07=	4	7/8
C **0130**?	....	?	**Pelée** (W Indies)	1600-12=	**P**	-/-
T **0150**?	....	?	**Ibusuki Volc Field** (Kyushu-Japan)	0802-07=	4	-/8
G **0150**v	....	?	**Mashu** (Hokkaido-Japan)	0805-081	4	-/8
T **0150**?	....	?	**Masaya** (Nicaragua)	1404-10=	**5**+	-/**9**
T **0150**?	....	?	**Cotopaxi** (Ecuador)	1502-05=	4	-/8
C **0160**x	....	?	**Liamuiga** (W Indies)	1600-03=	**P**	-/-
C **0180**v	....	?	**Cotopaxi** (Ecuador)	1502-05=	4	8/8
C **0190**x	....	?	**Wrangell** (Alaska-E)	1105-02-	**C**?	-/-
C **0200**t	....	?	**Glacier Peak** (US-Washington)	1201-02-	4+	-/8
0203	....	?	**Vesuvius** (Italy)	0101-02=	**P**	-/-
G **0230**n	0315n	?	**Taupo** (New Zealand)	0401-07=	**6**?	-/**10**
G **0240**v	....	?	**Ksudach** (Kamchatka)	1000-05=	**6**	-/**10**
T **0250**?	....	?	**Shiveluch** (Kamchatka)	1000-27=	4	-/8
T **0260**z	....	?	**Miyake-jima** (Izu Is-Japan)	0804-04=	4	-/8
G **0300**x	....	?	**Zao** (Honshu-Japan)	0803-19=	4	-/8
C **0300**?	....	?	**Pelée** (W Indies)	1600-12=	**P**	-/-
G **0310**v	....	?	**Pago** (New Britain-SW Pac)	0502-08=	**5**	-/**9**
G **0340**x	....	?	**Oshima** (Izu Is-Japan)	0804-01=	4	7/8
C **0340**?	....	?	**Akutan** (Aleutian Is)	1101-32-	**5**	-/**9**
G **0350**u	....	?	**Pelée** (W Indies)	1600-12=	4	-/8
A **0350**j	1115m	?	**Asama** (Honshu-Japan)	0803-11=	4	8/8
T **0380**y	....	?	**Sete Cidades** (Azores)	1802-08=	4	-/8
T **0400**?	....	?	**Raoul Island** (Kermadec Is)	0402-03=	4	-/8
T **0400**?	....	?	**Tolbachik** (Kamchatka)	1000-24=	4+	8/8
A **0400**?	....	?	**Arenal** (Costa Rica)	1405-033	4	-/8
0416	....	?	**Krakatau** (Indonesia)	0602-00=	**C**	-/-
C **0420**v	....	?	**Osorno** (Chile-S)	1508-01=	4?	-/-
G **0450**r	....	?	**Ilopango** (El Salvador)	1403-06=	**6**+	-/**10**
C **0450**?	....	?	**Pelée** (W Indies)	1600-12=	**P**	-/-
0472	1105	1a?	**Vesuvius** (Italy)	0101-02=	**5**	-/**9**
G **0490**v	....	?	**Newberry** (US-Oregon)	1202-11-	4	-/8
G **0500**?	....	?	**Shiveluch** (Kamchatka)	1000-27=	4+	-/8
0512	0708	?	**Vesuvius** (Italy)	0101-02=	4?	-/-
C **0520**v	....	?	**Karkar** (New Guinea-NE of)	0501-03=	**C**	-/-
A **0520**j	0601p	?	**Haruna** (Honshu-Japan)	0803-122	4+	-/8
C **0540**v	....	?	**Rabaul** (New Britain-SW Pac)	0502-14=	**6**	-/**10**
C **0550**?	....	?	**Raoul Island** (Kermadec Is)	0402-03=	4	-/8
G **0550**v	....	?	**Rausu** (Hokkaido-Japan)	0805-082	4	-/8
T **0550**?	....	?	**Arenal** (Costa Rica)	1405-033	4	-/8
A **0550**j	0601p	?	**Haruna** (Honshu-Japan)	0803-122	**5**	8/**9**
T **0580**?	....	?	**Shiveluch** (Kamchatka)	1000-27=	4+	-/8
T **0600**?	....	?	**Ibusuki Volc Field** (Kyushu-Japan)	0802-07=	4	8/8
G **0600**?	....	?	**Shiveluch** (Kamchatka)	1000-27=	**5**	-/**9**
C **0600**u	....	?	**Inyo Craters** (US-California)	1203-13-	4?	7/7
G **0610** t	....	?	**Opala** (Kamchatka)	1000-08=	**5**+	8/**9**
G **0650**s	....	?	**Shiveluch** (Kamchatka)	1000-27=	**5**	-/**9**
G **0650**v	....	?	**Arenal** (Costa Rica)	1405-033	4	-/8
T **0660**?	....	?	**Ibusuki Volc Field** (Kyushu-Japan)	0802-07=	4+	-/-
0680?	....	268w>	**Oshima** (Izu Is-Japan)	0804-01=	4	-/8
0685	02	30p?	**Vesuvius** (Italy)	0101-02=	4	-/8
G **0690**v	....	?	**Pago** (New Britain-SW Pac)	0502-08=	**5**	-/**9**
G **0690**v	....	?	**Newberry** (US-Oregon)	1202-11-	4	8/8
T **0700** t	....	?	**Bezymianny** (Kamchatka)	1000-25=	4?	-/8
T **0700**?	....	?	**Arenal** (Costa Rica)	1405-033	4	-/8
C **0710** u	....	?	**Pago** (New Britain-SW Pac)	0502-08=	**6**	-/**10**
T **0720**?	....	?	**Ibusuki Volc Field** (Kyushu-Japan)	0802-07=	4	-/8
0726	0715q	?	**Santorini** (Greece)	0102-04=	4?	-/-
C **0730**?	....	?	**Karkar** (New Guinea-NE of)	0501-03=	**P**	-/-
C **0730**x	....	?	**Tungurahua** (Ecuador)	1502-08=	4?	-/-
C **0740**u	....	?	**Cotopaxi** (Ecuador)	1502-05=	4	7/8
A **0750** t	....	?	**Arenal** (Costa Rica)	1405-033	4	-/8
C **0750**w	....	?	**Bravo, Cerro** (Colombia)	1501-012	4	-/8
0764	01	?	**Sakura-jima** (Kyushu-Japan)	0802-08=	4	-/-
T **0770**?	....	?	**Ibusuki Volc Field** (Kyushu-Japan)	0802-07=	4	-/8
C **0770**u	....	?	**Cotopaxi** (Ecuador)	1502-05=	4	7/8
G **0780**v	....	?	**Chichón, El** (México)	1401-12=	**5**	-/**9**
0788	0418	?	**Kirishima** (Kyushu-Japan)	0802-09=	4	-/8
C **0800** t	....	?	**Dakataua** (New Britain-SW Pac)	0502-04=	**6**?	-/**10**
G **0800**V	....	?	**Churchill** (Alaska-E)	1105-03-	**6**	-/-
0800	0411	674m>	**Fuji** (Honshu-Japan)	0803-03=	4	-/-
G **0810** y	....	?	**Mono Craters** (US-California)	1203-12-	4	-/8
I **0823**	0301t	?	**Popocatépetl** (México)	1401-09=	**P**	-/-
0838	0802?	?	**Kozu-shima** (Izu Is-Japan)	0804-03=	4	8/8
C **0840**v	....	?	**Furnas** (Azores)	1802-10=	4	7/8
T **0850**?	....	?	**Raoul Island** (Kermadec Is)	0402-03=	4	-/8
0850?	....	?	**Miyake-jima** (Izu Is-Japan)	0804-04=	4	7/8
C **0850** t	....	?	**Kinenin** (Kamchatka)	1000-551	4	-/8
0854?	0914?	656w?	**Oshima** (Izu Is-Japan)	0804-01=	4	-/8
G **0860**u	....	?	**Puyehue-Cordón Caulle** (Chile-C)	1507-15=	**5**	-/**9**
C **0870**v	....	?	**Alamagan** (Mariana Is-C Pacific)	0804-18=	4	-/8
T **0870**?	....	?	**Bárdarbunga** (Iceland-NE)	1703-03=	4	7/**9**
0874	0329	110m?	**Ibusuki Volc Field** (Kyushu-Japan)	0802-07=	4	-/-
0885	0829	30a	**Ibusuki Volc Field** (Kyushu-Japan)	0802-07=	4	-/-
0886?	0629?	?	**Oshima** (Izu Is-Japan)	0804-01=	4	4/8
0886	0629	?	**Nii-jima** (Izu Is-Japan)	0804-02=	4+	8/8
0887	....	?	**Niigata-Yake-yama** (Honshu-Japan)	0803-09=	4	-/8
G **0890**v	....	?	**Pelée** (W Indies)	1600-12=	**P**	-/-
T **0900**?	....	?	**Tolbachik** (Kamchatka)	1000-24=	4	**9**/**9**
G **0910** v	....	?	**Guagua Pichincha** (Ecuador)	1502-02=	**5**	-/**9**
0915	0817	?	**Towada** (Honshu-Japan)	0803-271	**5**	8/**9**
0920	....	?	**Katla** (Iceland-S)	1702-03=	4	-/8
C **0930**x	....	?	**Ceboruco** (México)	1401-03=	**6**	-/**10**
I **0934**b	....	>3yr	**Katla** (Iceland-S)	1702-03=	4?	**10**/**9**
T **0950**?	....	?	**Tolbachik** (Kamchatka)	1000-24=	4+	8/8
T **0950**?	....	?	**Bezymianny** (Kamchatka)	1000-25=	4?	-/8
0968	1201p	?	**Vesuvius** (Italy)	0101-02=	4	-/8
G **0970**?	....	?	**Shiveluch** (Kamchatka)	1000-27=	4	-/8
G **1000** t	....	?	**Ksudach** (Kamchatka)	1000-05=	4+	-/8
T **1000**?	....	?	**Tolbachik** (Kamchatka)	1000-24=	4+	**9**/8
G **1000** s	....	?	**Changbaishan** (China-E)	1005-06-	**7**?	-/**10**
T **1020**?	....	?	**Arenal** (Costa Rica)	1405-033	4	-/8
C **1030** q	....	?	**Billy Mitchell** (Bougainville-SW Pacific)	0505-011	**5**+	-/**9**
G **1030** v	....	?	**Shiveluch** (Kamchatka)	1000-27=	**5**	-/**9**
T **1030**?	....	?	**Arenal** (Costa Rica)	1405-033	4	-/8
T **1040**?	....	?	**Cayambe** (Ecuador)	1502-006	4	8/-
C **1050** u	....	?	**Bravo, Cerro** (Colombia)	1501-012	4	-/8
M **1075** q	....	?	**Sunset Crater** (US-Arizona)	1209-02-	4?	8/-
G **1080** v	....	?	**Mashu** (Hokkaido-Japan)	0805-081	**5**	-/**9**
G **1080** u	....	?	**Ubinas** (Perú)	1504-02=	**5**	-/**9**
C **1100** r	....	?	**Lolobau** (New Britain-SW Pac)	0502-13=	4	-/8
1104	1015q	?	**Hekla** (Iceland-S)	1702-07=	**5**	-/**9**
1108	0829	41m	**Asama** (Honshu-Japan)	0803-11=	**5**	8/**9**

	START YEAR	M-Dy	Duration	VOLCANO NAME (Subregion)	NUMBER	VEI	Vol L/T
C	1130 u	....	?	**Cotopaxi** (Ecuador)	1502-05=	5	-/9
	1158	0119	?	**Hekla** (Iceland-S)	1702-07=	4	8/8
C	1170 v	....	?	**Furnas** (Azores)	1802-10=	4	-/8
V	1183 ?	....	?	**Oshima** (Izu Is-Japan)	0804-01=	4	-/8
G	1190 w	....	?	**Chichón, El** (México)	1401-12=	4	-/8
A	1200 ?	....	?	**San Salvador** (El Salvador)	1403-05=	4	-/8
T	1210 ?	....	?	**Katla** (Iceland-S)	1702-03=	4	-/8
	1211	0831p	?	**Reykjanes** (Iceland-SW)	1701-02=	4?	-/8
	1226	0715q	352w?	**Reykjanes** (Iceland-SW)	1701-02=	4	-/8
	1235	0125	?	**Kirishima** (Kyushu-Japan)	0802-09=	P	-/-
	1245	....	?	**Katla** (Iceland-S)	1702-03=	4	-/8
	1262	....	?	**Katla** (Iceland-S)	1702-03=	5	-/9
G	1280 ?	....	?	**Quilotoa** (Ecuador)	1502-06=	6	-/10
T	1290 ?	....	?	**Cayambe** (Ecuador)	1502-006	4	8/-
	1300	0711	369m?	**Hekla** (Iceland-S)	1702-07=	4	8/8
G	1310 k	....	>3yr	**Okataina** (New Zealand)	0401-05=	5	9/9
C	1330 u	....	?	**Bravo, Cerro** (Colombia)	1501-012	4	-/8
G	1340 t	....	?	**Pelée** (W Indies)	1600-12=	4	-/8
C	1350 ?	....	?	**Kikhpinych** (Kamchatka)	1000-18=	4	8/8
D	1350 p	....	?	**Mono Craters** (US-California)	1203-12-	4	8/8
C	1350 ?	....	?	**Ruiz, Nevado del** (Colombia)	1501-02=	4	-/8
T	1350 ?	....	?	**Cotopaxi** (Ecuador)	1502-05=	4+	-/8
	1357 c	....	?	**Katla** (Iceland-S)	1702-03=	4+	-/8
G	1360 v	....	?	**Chichón, El** (México)	1401-12=	5	-/9
	1362	0605d	133q	**Öraefajökull** (Iceland-SE)	1704-01=	5	-/9
G	1370 w	....	?	**Soufrière Guadeloupe** (W Indies)	1600-06=	P	-/-
G	1380 u	....	?	**Parker** (Mindanao-Philippines)	0701-011	P	-/-
G	1380 t	....	?	**Inyo Craters** (US-California)	1203-13-	4	8/8
C	1400 ?	....	?	**Arenal** (Costa Rica)	1405-033	4	-/8
	1416	....	?	**Katla** (Iceland-S)	1702-03=	4?	-/8
	1421	0514	?	**Oshima** (Izu Is-Japan)	0804-01=	4	8/8
G	1430 ?	....	?	**Shiveluch** (Kamchatka)	1000-27=	4	-/8
G	1440 v	....	?	**Soufrière Guadeloupe** (W Indies)	1600-06=	P	-/-
	1440	....	?	**Katla** (Iceland-S)	1702-03=	4	-/8
	1441 b	....	?	**Furnas** (Azores)	1802-10=	4	-/8
	1444 ?	....	?	**Sete Cidades** (Azores)	1802-08=	4	-/8
G	1450 t	....	?	**Pinatubo** (Luzon-Philippines)	0703-083	5?	-/-
	1471	1103	>3yr	**Sakura-jima** (Kyushu-Japan)	0802-08=	5?	8/9
	1477	02 ?	?	**Bárdarbunga** (Iceland-NE)	1703-03=	6	9/10
D	1480	0115u	?	**St. Helens** (US-Washington)	1201-05-	5+	-/9
D	1482	0115u	?	**St. Helens** (US-Washington)	1201-05-	5	-/9

1500

	START YEAR	M-Dy	Duration	VOLCANO NAME (Subregion)	NUMBER	VEI	Vol L/T
T	1500 ?	....	?	**Katla** (Iceland-S)	1702-03=	4	-/8
	1510	0725	?	**Hekla** (Iceland-S)	1702-07=	4	-/8
	1529	....	?	**Telica** (Nicaragua)	1404-04=	4	8/8
	1532	1115	?	**Cotopaxi** (Ecuador)	1502-05=	4	7/8
	1534	06	30p	**Cotopaxi** (Ecuador)	1502-05=	4	-/8
G	1540 v	....	?	**Augustine** (Alaska-SW)	1103-01-	4?	-/-
T	1550 ?	....	?	**Pago** (New Britain-SW Pac)	0502-08=	P	-/-
G	1550 ?	....	?	**Maly Semiachik** (Kamchatka)	1000-14=	4	-/8
T	1550 ?	....	?	**Katla** (Iceland-S)	1702-03=	4	-/8
C	1560 t	....	?	**Aniakchak** (Alaska Peninsula)	1102-09-	4+	-/8
	1563	0628	28e	**Agua de Pau** (Azores)	1802-09=	5?	6/9
T	1570 ?	....	?	**Cayambe** (Ecuador)	1502-006	4	8/-
C	1580 p	....	?	**Billy Mitchell** (Bougainville-SW Pacific)	0505-011	6	-/10
	1580	0811	?	**Katla** (Iceland-S)	1702-03=	4	-/8
	1581	1226	41a	**Fuego** (Guatemala)	1402-09=	4?	-/8
	1582	0114	41a	**Fuego** (Guatemala)	1402-09=	4?	-/8
	1585	0110	?	**Colima** (México)	1401-04=	4	-/-
	1586	....	?	**Kelut** (Java)	0603-28=	5?	-/9
	1593	....	?	**Raung** (Java)	0603-34=	5?	-/9
	1595	0312	?	**Ruiz, Nevado del** (Colombia)	1501-02=	4	-/8
	1597	0103	164m>	**Hekla** (Iceland-S)	1702-07=	4	-/8
T	1600 ?	....	?	**Suwanose-jima** (Ryukyu Is)	0802-03=	4+	-/-
	1600	0219	18a?	**Huaynaputina** (Perú)	1504-03=	6	-/10
	1605	....	365y	**Momotombo** (Nicaragua)	1404-09=	4	-/8
	1606	1125	18a>	**Colima** (México)	1401-04=	4	-/-
	1606	1213	18a>	**Colima** (México)	1401-04=	4	-/-
	1612	1012	?	**Katla** (Iceland-S)	1702-03=	4	-/8
	1622	0608	1a	**Colima** (México)	1401-04=	4	-/-
	1625	0902	12a	**Katla** (Iceland-S)	1702-03=	5	-/9
C	1630 t	....	?	**Raoul Island** (Kermadec Is)	0402-03=	4	-/8
	1630	0903	60a	**Furnas** (Azores)	1802-10=	5	7/9
	1631	1216	45a?	**Vesuvius** (Italy)	0101-02=	5?	-/9
	1638	....	?	**Raung** (Java)	0603-34=	4?	-/8
	1640	02	?	**Llaima** (Chile-C)	1507-11=	4	-/-
	1640	0731	70a	**Komaga-take** (Hokkaido-Japan)	0805-02=	5	-/9
	1641	....	?	**Kelut** (Java)	0603-28=	4?	-/8
	1641	0104	9e	**Parker** (Mindanao-Philippines)	0701-011	5?	-/9
	1646	0719	2a	**Makian** (Halmahera-Indonesia)	0608-07=	4?	-/8
G	1650 j	....	?	**Shiveluch** (Kamchatka)	1000-27=	5	-/9
	1650	0927	70a	**Santorini** (Greece)	0102-04=	4?	-/8
D	1655 ?	....	?	**Taranaki [Egmont]** (New Zealand)	0401-03=	4	-/8
C	1660 p	....	?	**Long Island** (New Guinea-NE of)	0501-05=	6	-/10
	1660	02	?	**Teon** (Banda Sea)	0605-05=	4?	-/8
	1660	1027	32a	**Guagua Pichincha** (Ecuador)	1502-02=	4	-/8
	1660	1103	240w	**Katla** (Iceland-S)	1702-03=	4	-/8
	1663	0816	20d	**Usu** (Hokkaido-Japan)	0805-03=	5	-/9
	1667	0923	3a?	**Shikotsu** (Hokkaido-Japan)	0805-04=	5	-/9
	1673	0520	?	**Gamkonora** (Halmahera-Indonesia)	0608-04=	5?	-/9
	1680	....	?	**Tongkoko** (Sulawesi-Indonesia)	0606-13=	5?	-/9
T	1690 j	....	?	**Chikurachki** (Kuril Is)	0900-36=	4	-/-
	1693	0213	214a?	**Hekla** (Iceland-S)	1702-07=	4	-/8
	1693	0604	41m	**Serua** (Banda Sea)	0605-07=	4?	-/8
	1694	0704	2a	**Komaga-take** (Hokkaido-Japan)	0805-02=	4	-/8
	1707	1216	39a?	**Fuji** (Honshu-Japan)	0803-03=	5	-/9
	1712	1231y	?	**Chirpoi** (Kuril Is)	0900-15=	4?	-/-
	1716	0924	3a	**Taal** (Luzon-Philippines)	0703-07=	4?	-/-
	1717	0827	121e	**Fuego** (Guatemala)	1402-09=	4?	-/8
C	1720 t	....	?	**Raoul Island** (Kermadec Is)	0402-03=	4	-/8
T	1720 w	....	?	**Bravo, Cerro** (Colombia)	1501-012	4	-/8
	1721	0511	157q	**Katla** (Iceland-S)	1702-03=	5?	-/9
	1727	0803	268p	**Öraefajökull** (Iceland-SE)	1704-01=	4	-/8
	1737	0827	28a	**Fuego** (Guatemala)	1402-09=	4?	-/8
	1739	0819	12a	**Shikotsu** (Hokkaido-Japan)	0805-04=	5	-/9
	1741	0829	270p	**Oshima-Oshima** (Hokkaido-Japan)	0805-01=	4	-/8
	1744	1130	214p	**Cotopaxi** (Ecuador)	1502-05=	4	7/8
	1749	0811 ?	35m?	**Taal** (Luzon-Philippines)	0703-07=	4	-/8
G	1750 ?	....	?	**Ksudach** (Kamchatka)	1000-05=	4	-/8
	1754	1128	203a	**Taal** (Luzon-Philippines)	0703-07=	4	-/8
	1755	1017	119a	**Katla** (Iceland-S)	1702-03=	5?	-/9
	1759	0929	>3yr	**Michoacán-Guanajuato** (México)	1401-06=	4	8/9
	1760	0922	220a>	**Makian** (Halmahera-Indonesia)	0608-07=	4?	-/8
	1762	1203	?	**Planchón-Peteroa** (Chile-C)	1507-04=	4	-/-
	1763	0817	>3yr	**Miyake-jima** (Izu Is-Japan)	0804-04=	4	5/8
	1764	....	>3yr	**Michoacán-Guanajuato** (México)	1401-06=	4	8/9
	1766	0405	770m	**Hekla** (Iceland-S)	1702-07=	4	9/8
	1768	0404	?	**Cotopaxi** (Ecuador)	1502-05=	4	7/8
	1769	0123	?	**Usu** (Hokkaido-Japan)	0805-03=	4	7/8
	1778	....	?	**Raikoke** (Kuril Is)	0900-25=	4↑	-/-
	1779	1108	554m	**Sakura-jima** (Kyushu-Japan)	0802-08=	4	9/8
	1783	0608	741m?	**Grímsvötn** (Iceland-NE)	1703-01=	4+	10/8
	1783	0803	88a	**Asama** (Honshu-Japan)	0803-11=	4	8/8
@	1786	....	>3yr	**Pavlof** (Alaska Peninsula)	1102-03-	4?	-/8
	1787	0718	68e	**Etna** (Italy)	0101-06=	4	-/-
	1790	11 ?	2a?	**Kilauea** (Hawaiian Is)	1302-01-	4	-/8
	1793	02	>3yr	**Alaid** (Kuril Is)	0900-39=	4↑	-/-
	1793	0302	289m	**San Martín** (México)	1401-11=	4	7/8
	1795	....	?	**Westdahl** (Aleutian Is)	1101-34-	4	-/9
T	1800 ?	....	?	**Pago** (New Britain-SW Pac)	0502-08=	P	-/-
D	1800	0115u	?	**St. Helens** (US-Washington)	1201-05-	5	-/9
	1812	0427	43a?	**Soufrière St. Vincent** (W Indies)	1600-15=	4	-/8
	1812	0806	2a	**Awu** (Sangihe Is-Indonesia)	0607-04=	4?	-/8
	1813	....	365y	**Suwanose-jima** (Ryukyu Is)	0802-03=	4	-/-
	1814	0201	14a>	**Mayon** (Luzon-Philippines)	0703-03=	4	-/8
	1815	0410	>3yr	**Tambora** (Lesser Sunda Is)	0604-04=	7	-/11
	1817	0116	25a?	**Raung** (Java)	0603-34=	4?	-/8
	1818	0215	<1?	**Colima** (México)	1401-04=	4	-/-
	1822	0312	187m	**Usu** (Hokkaido-Japan)	0805-03=	4	-/8
	1822	1008	54p	**Galunggung** (Java)	0603-14=	5	-/9
?	1825	0310	?	**Isanotski** (Aleutian Is)	1101-37-	4	-/8
	1826	1011	14a	**Kelut** (Java)	0603-28=	4?	-/8
	1827	0627	2a	**Avachinsky** (Kamchatka)	1000-10=	4	-/8
	1829	0909	?	**Kliuchevskoi** (Kamchatka)	1000-26=	4?	7/8
	1831	....	?	**Babuyan Claro** (Luzon-N of)	0704-03=	4?	-/8
	1835	0120	5a?	**Cosigüina** (Nicaragua)	1404-01=	5	-/9
	1845	0902	215a?	**Hekla** (Iceland-S)	1702-07=	4	8/8
	1846	0611 ?	121a>	**Fonualei** (Tonga-SW Pacific)	0403-10=	4?	7/8
	1853	0422	146m	**Usu** (Hokkaido-Japan)	0805-03=	4	8/8
	1854	0218	?	**Shiveluch** (Kamchatka)	1000-27=	5	-/9
	1856	0925	?	**Komaga-take** (Hokkaido-Japan)	0805-02=	4	-/8
	1857	0115	33a	**Fuego** (Guatemala)	1402-09=	4?	-/8
	1860	0508	19a	**Katla** (Iceland-S)	1702-03=	4	-/8
	1861	1228	292m	**Makian** (Halmahera-Indonesia)	0608-07=	4?	-/8
	1872	....	>3yr	**Sinarka** (Kuril Is)	0900-29=	4	-/-
	1872	0415	5	**Merapi** (Java)	0603-25=	4	-/8
	1873	0108	219m	**Grímsvötn** (Iceland-NE)	1703-01=	4	-/8
	1875	0329	289a	**Askja** (Iceland-NE)	1703-06=	5	8/9

START YEAR	M-Dy	Duration	VOLCANO NAME (Subregion)	NUMBER	VEI	Vol L/T
1877	....	?	**Suwanose-jima** (Ryukyu Is)	0802-03=	4?	-/-
1877	0626	230m	**Cotopaxi** (Ecuador)	1502-05=	4	7/8
1880	0628	53a	**Fuego** (Guatemala)	1402-09=	4?	-/8
1883	0827	154a?	**Krakatau** (Indonesia)	0602-00=	**6**	-/**10**
1883	1006	269w?	**Augustine** (Alaska-SW)	1103-01-	4	8/8
1886	0111	902y?	**Tungurahua** (Ecuador)	1502-08=	4	-/-
1886	0610	65m	**Okataina** (New Zealand)	0401-05=	**5**	-/**9**
1886	0831	18a?	**Niuafo'ou** (Tonga-SW Pacific)	0403-11=	4?	-/8
1888	0715	<1	**Bandai** (Honshu-Japan)	0803-16=	4	-/8
1889	1002	11a	**Suwanose-jima** (Ryukyu Is)	0802-03=	4	-/-
1890	0216	191a	**Colima** (México)	1401-04=	4	-/-
1893	0110	374a>	**Calbuco** (Chile-S)	1508-02=	4	-/-
1897	0625	61a>	**Mayon** (Luzon-Philippines)	0703-03=	4?	-/-
1899	1113	>3yr	**Doña Juana** (Colombia)	1501-07=	4	-/-
1902	0502	>3yr	**Pelée** (W Indies)	1600-12=	4	8/8
1902	0506	298a	**Soufrière St. Vincent** (W Indies)	1600-15=	4?	-/8
1902	0508	>3yr	**Pelée** (W Indies)	1600-12=	4	8/8
1902	1024	19a	**Santa María** (Guatemala)	1402-03=	**6**?	-/**10**
1903	0528	393m	**Grímsvötn** (Iceland-NE)	1703-01=	4	8/-
1905	....	435a>	**Lolobau** (New Britain-SW Pac)	0502-13=	**P**	-/-
1906	0408	>3yr	**Vesuvius** (Italy)	0101-02=	4?	8/8
1907	0328?	?	**Ksudach** (Kamchatka)	1000-05=	**5**	-/**9**
1911	....	365y	**Lolobau** (New Britain-SW Pac)	0502-13=	4	8/8
1912	0606	131m?	**Novarupta** (Alaska Peninsula)	1102-18-	**6**	7/**10**
1913	0120	7a	**Colima** (México)	1401-04=	**5**	-/**9**
1914	0112	488m	**Sakura-jima** (Kyushu-Japan)	0802-08=	4	**9**/8
1917	0409	?	**Agrigan** (Mariana Is-C Pacific)	0804-16=	4	-/-
1918	0405	>3yr	**Tungurahua** (Ecuador)	1502-08=	4	-/-
1918	1012	23a	**Katla** (Iceland-S)	1702-03=	4+	-/8
1919	0519	1a	**Kelut** (Java)	0603-28=	4	-/8
1919	0811	?	**Manam** (New Guinea-NE of)	0501-02=	4	-/-
1924	0215	?	**Raikoke** (Kuril Is)	0900-25=	4	-/-
1924	1031	?	**Iriomote-jima** (Ryukyu Is)	0802-01=	4?	-/**9**
1926	0405	352a?	**Avachinsky** (Kamchatka)	1000-10=	4	6/8
1929	0617	81a	**Komaga-take** (Hokkaido-Japan)	0805-02=	4	-/8
1931	0325	2a	**Kliuchevskoi** (Kamchatka)	1000-26=	4	-/-
1931	0501	43a>	**Aniakchak** (Alaska Peninsula)	1102-09-	4	-/8
1931	0511	43a>	**Aniakchak** (Alaska Peninsula)	1102-09-	4?	-/8
1932	0121	1a	**Fuego** (Guatemala)	1402-09=	4	-/8
1932	0410	>3yr	**Azul, Cerro** (Chile-C)	1507-06=	**5+**	-/**9**
1933	0108	96a>	**Kharimkotan** (Kuril Is)	0900-30=	**5**	8/**9**
1933	0710	26a	**Suoh** (Sumatra)	0601-27=	4	-/8
1933	1224	20a	**Kuchinoerabu-jima** (Ryukyu Is)	0802-05=	4?	-/-
1937	0529	4a	**Rabaul** (New Britain-SW Pac)	0502-14=	4?	-/8
1943	0220	>3yr	**Michoacán-Guanajuato** (México)	1401-06=	4	8/**9**
1945	0225	<1	**Avachinsky** (Kamchatka)	1000-10=	4	-/8
1946	1109	2a	**Sarychev Peak** (Kuril Is)	0900-24=	4	-/-
1947	0329	388a	**Hekla** (Iceland-S)	1702-07=	4	8/8
1951	....	354e	**Ambrym** (Vanuatu-SW Pacific)	0507-04=	4+	-/8
1951	0121	>3yr	**Lamington** (New Guinea)	0503-01=	4	8/-
1951	0831	<1	**Kelut** (Java)	0603-28=	4	-/8
1952	0229	229m	**Bagana** (Bougainville-SW Pacific)	0505-02=	4	-/-
1953	0709	7a	**Spurr** (Alaska-SW)	1103-04-	4	-/-
1955	0727	108a	**Carrán-Los Venados** (Chile-C)	1507-14=	4	-/8
1956	0330	496a	**Bezymianny** (Kamchatka)	1000-25=	**5**	-/**9**
1963	0317	344a	**Agung** (Lesser Sunda Is)	0604-02=	**5**	8/**9**
1963	0516	344a	**Agung** (Lesser Sunda Is)	0604-02=	4	8/**9**
1964	1112	<1	**Shiveluch** (Kamchatka)	1000-27=	4+	-/8
1965	0928	2	**Taal** (Luzon-Philippines)	0703-07=	4	-/-
1966	0426	<1	**Kelut** (Java)	0603-28=	4	-/-
1966	0812	64m	**Awu** (Sangihe Is-Indonesia)	0607-04=	4	-/-
1968	0611	23a<	**Fernandina** (Galápagos)	1503-01=	4	-/8
1973	0714	14a	**Tiatia** (Kuril Is)	0900-03=	4	-/8
1974	1017	55a	**Fuego** (Guatemala)	1402-09=	4	-/8
1975	0706	530a	**Tolbachik** (Kamchatka)	1000-24=	4+	**9**/8
1976	0122?	477a?	**Augustine** (Alaska-SW)	1103-01-	4	7/8
1980	0518	>3yr	**St. Helens** (US-Washington)	1201-05-	**5**	7/**9**
1981	0430	39a	**Alaid** (Kuril Is)	0900-39=	4	-/8
1981	0515	>3yr	**Pagan** (Mariana Is-C Pacific)	0804-17=	4	7/8
1982	0328	167a	**Chichón, El** (México)	1401-12=	4+	-/8
1982	0403	167a	**Chichón, El** (México)	1401-12=	**5**	-/**9**
1982	0517	278a	**Galunggung** (Java)	0603-14=	4	-/8
1983	0723	150m	**Colo [Una Una]** (Sulawesi-Indonesia)	0606-01=	4	-/-
1986	0327	157a	**Augustine** (Alaska-SW)	1103-01-	4?	-/8
1986	1120	19a	**Chikurachki** (Kuril Is)	0900-36=	4	7/8
1990	0130	>3yr	**Kliuchevskoi** (Kamchatka)	1000-26=	4	7/8
1990	0210	32q	**Kelut** (Java)	0603-28=	4	-/8
1991	0615	153a	**Pinatubo** (Luzon-Philippines)	0703-083	**6**	-/**10**
1991	0812	80	**Hudson, Cerro** (Chile-S)	1508-057	**5+**	-/**9**
1992	0627	81	**Spurr** (Alaska-SW)	1103-04-	4	-/8
1993	0419	197m	**Láscar** (Chile-N)	1505-10=	4	6/8
1994	0919	208	**Rabaul** (New Britain-SW Pac)	0502-14=	4?	-/-
2000	0929	34	**Ulawun** (New Britain-SW Pac)	0502-12=	4	-/-
2001	0522	>3yr	**Shiveluch** (Kamchatka)	1000-27=	4?	8/-
2002	0925	4a?	**Ruang** (Sangihe Is-Indonesia)	0607-01=	4?	-/-
2002	1103	68a?	**Reventador** (Ecuador)	1502-01=	4	7/8
2005	0127	>3yr	**Manam** (New Guinea-NE of)	0501-02=	4?	-/-
2006	1007	>3yr	**Rabaul** (New Britain-SW Pac)	0502-14=	4?	-/-
2008	0502	781w>	**Chaitén** (Chile-S)	1508-041	4	-/8
2008	0712	38a	**Okmok** (Aleutian Is)	1101-29-	4?	-/-
2008	0807	2a?	**Kasatochi** (Aleutian Is)	1101-13-	4	-/-
2009	0611	10e	**Sarychev Peak** (Kuril Is)	0900-24=	4	-/8

Effusive Eruptions

START YEAR	M-Dy	Duration	VOLCANO NAME (Subregion)	NUMBER	VEI	Vol L/T
T-9500?	....	?	**Theistareykjarbunga** (Iceland-NE)	1703-09=	0	**10**/-
T-9350?	....	?	**Tongariro** (New Zealand)	0401-08=	**5**	8/**9**
G-9160*	....	?	**Kuju** (Kyushu-Japan)	0802-12=	4	8/8
T-9000?	....	?	**Brennisteinsfjöll** (Iceland-SW)	1701-04=	0	**9**/-
T-8600?	....	?	**Hveravellir** (Iceland-SW)	1701-08=	0	**9**/-
C-8540>	....	?	**Fuji** (Honshu-Japan)	0803-03=		**9**/-
T-8500?	....	?	**Krísuvík** (Iceland-SW)	1701-03=	0	**9**/-
T-8500?	....	?	**Krafla** (Iceland-NE)	1703-08=	0	**9**/-
G-8350?	....	?	**Hengill** (Iceland-SW)	1701-05=	0	**9**/-
G-8250?	....	?	**Hengill** (Iceland-SW)	1701-05=	0	**10**/-
T-8200?	....	?	**Hengill** (Iceland-SW)	1701-05=	0	**9**/-
C-8060z	....	?	**Garibaldi** (Canada)	1200-20-	3?	**9**/7
T-8000?	....	?	**Reykjanes** (Iceland-SW)	1701-02=	0	**9**/-
C-7930z	....	?	**Chichinautzin** (México)	1401-08=	3	**9**/7
G-7850?	....	?	**Baker** (US-Washington)	1201-01=		8/-
T-7850?	....	?	**Krafla** (Iceland-NE)	1703-08=		**9**/-
G-7560o	....	?	**Okataina** (New Zealand)	0401-05=	**5**	**9**/**9**
T-7550z	....	?	**Bakening** (Kamchatka)	1000-123	2?	**9**/-
T-7550z	....	?	**Elovsky** (Kamchatka)	1000-59-	4	**9**/8
T-7550?	....	?	**Hengill** (Iceland-SW)	1701-05=	0	8/-
C-7550z	....	?	**Prestahnukur** (Iceland-SW)	1701-07=	0	**10**/-
T-7300?	....	?	**Hengill** (Iceland-SW)	1701-05=		**9**/-
G-7260y	....	?	**Turrialba** (Costa Rica)	1405-07=		**9**/-
G-7250w	....	?	**Norikura** (Honshu-Japan)	0803-06=	3	8/7
T-7180*	....	?	**Kuju** (Kyushu-Japan)	0802-12=		8/-
T-7100?	....	?	**Hengill** (Iceland-SW)	1701-05=	0	**9**/-
T-7100?	....	?	**Bárdarbunga** (Iceland-NE)	1703-03=		**9**/-
T-7050*	....	?	**Ljósufjöll** (Iceland-W)	1700-03=	2	**9**/-
G-6950?	....	?	**Prestahnukur** (Iceland-SW)	1701-07=	0	**9**/-
G-6650t	....	?	**Bárdarbunga** (Iceland-NE)	1703-03=		**10**/-
T-6500?	....	?	**Krafla** (Iceland-NE)	1703-08=		**9**/-
C-6250v	....	?	**Indian Heaven** (US-Washington)	1201-07-		8/-
G-6060t	....	?	**Okataina** (New Zealand)	0401-05=	**5**	**10**/**9**
T-6050?	....	?	**Olkaria** (Africa-E)	0202-09=		**9**/-
C-6000t	....	?	**Krasheninnikov** (Kamchatka)	1000-19=	4	**9**/8
T-6000?	....	?	**Krísuvík** (Iceland-SW)	1701-03=	0	**9**/-
G-5900t	....	?	**Crater Lake** (US-Oregon)	1202-16-	**6**	8/**10**
C-5890w	....	?	**Craters of the Moon** (US-Idaho)	1204-02-	0	**9**/-
T-5850?	....	?	**Hveravellir** (Iceland-SW)	1701-08=	2?	**10**/-
C-5840z	....	?	**Chichinautzin** (México)	1401-08=		8/-
T-5800t	....	?	**Kizimen** (Kamchatka)	1000-23=		8/-
T-5750?	....	?	**Tenerife** (Canary Is)	1803-03-		8/-
I-5677w	1015q	?	**Crater Lake** (US-Oregon)	1202-16-	**7**	8/**11**
T-5550?	....	?	**Crater Lake** (US-Oregon)	1202-16-	0	**9**/-
T-5550?	....	?	**Katla** (Iceland-S)	1702-03=		**9**/-
C-5470w	....	?	**Craters of the Moon** (US-Idaho)	1204-02-	0	**9**/-
T-5400?	....	?	**Ichinsky** (Kamchatka)	1000-28=	**5**	**9**/**9**
C-5290w	....	?	**Krísuvík** (Iceland-SW)	1701-03=	2	8/-
G-5070w	....	?	**Newberry** (US-Oregon)	1202-11-	3	8/7
T-5050*	....	?	**Torfajökull** (Iceland-S)	1702-05=		8/-
T-5000?	....	?	**Hengill** (Iceland-SW)	1701-05=		**9**/-
T-5000?	....	?	**Bárdarbunga** (Iceland-NE)	1703-03=		**10**/-
T-5000*	....	?	**Kverkfjöll** (Iceland-NE)	1703-05=		**9**/-

-5000 (6950 BP)

START YEAR	M-Dy	Duration	VOLCANO NAME (Subregion)	NUMBER	VEI	Vol L/T
T-4800?	....	?	**Bárdarbunga** (Iceland-NE)	1703-03=		9/-
T-4750?	....	?	**Ksudach** (Kamchatka)	1000-05=		8/-
C-4600v	....	?	**Craters of the Moon** (US-Idaho)	1204-02-	0	9/-
T-4600?	....	?	**Bárdarbunga** (Iceland-NE)	1703-03=		9/-
G-4570?	....	?	**Takahara** (Honshu-Japan)	0803-143	4?	8/7
C-4550?	....	?	**Cherpuk Group** (Kamchatka)	1000-273		9/-
T-4550?	....	?	**Adams** (US-Washington)	1201-04-	2	8/-
T-4490z	....	?	**Kuju** (Kyushu-Japan)	0802-12=		8/-
T-4400?	....	?	**Bárdarbunga** (Iceland-NE)	1703-03=		9/-
C-4270w	....	?	**Grímsnes** (Iceland-SW)	1701-06=	3	9/7
T-4250?	....	?	**Craters of the Moon** (US-Idaho)	1204-02-	0	8/-
C-4250u	....	?	**Chichinautzin** (México)	1401-08=	3?	9/7
T-4200?	....	?	**Bárdarbunga** (Iceland-NE)	1703-03=		9/-
G-4150z	....	?	**Azuma** (Honshu-Japan)	0803-18=	3	8/7
C-4070t	....	?	**Craters of the Moon** (US-Idaho)	1204-02-	0	9/-
T-4050*	....	?	**Fremrinamur** (Iceland-NE)	1703-07=		9/-
T-4000?	....	?	**Reykjanes** (Iceland-SW)	1701-02=	0	9/-
T-4000?	....	?	**Fremrinamur** (Iceland-NE)	1703-07=	0	9/-
G-3960y	....	?	**Tenerife** (Canary Is)	1803-03-		8/-
U-3950y	....	?	**Vestmannaeyjar** (Iceland-S)	1702-01=		8/-
T-3800*	....	?	**Adams** (US-Washington)	1201-04-	1?	8/-
G-3780z	....	?	**Kuju** (Kyushu-Japan)	0802-12=	4	8/8
G-3750?	....	?	**Hengill** (Iceland-SW)	1701-05=	2	8/-
G-3700v	....	?	**Hakone** (Honshu-Japan)	0803-02=	1	8/5
G-3580t	....	?	**Okataina** (New Zealand)	0401-05=	**5**	**9/9**
T-3550?	....	?	**Hveravellir** (Iceland-SW)	1701-08=	0	8/-
T-3550z	....	?	**Grímsvötn** (Iceland-NE)	1703-01=	0	8/-
G-3540w	....	?	**Tenerife** (Canary Is)	1803-03-		8/-
G-3450?	....	?	**Karymsky** (Kamchatka)	1000-13=		8/-
T-3350?	....	?	**Prestahnukur** (Iceland-SW)	1701-07=	0	8/-
T-3280z	....	?	**Cotopaxi** (Ecuador)	1502-05=	**5**	8/9
E-3250z	....	?	**Carrizozo** (US-New Mexico)	1210-01-		9/-
G-3250?	....	?	**Hengill** (Iceland-SW)	1701-05=	0	9/-
G-3200?	....	?	**Karymsky** (Kamchatka)	1000-13=	4	8/8
T-3110 z	....	?	**Kuju** (Kyushu-Japan)	0802-12=		8/-
T-2850?	....	?	**Tenerife** (Canary Is)	1803-03-		8/-
G-2780q	....	?	**Kikhpinych** (Kamchatka)	1000-18=	4	8/8
C-2660u	....	?	**Brennisteinsfjöll** (Iceland-SW)	1701-04=	0	9/-
C-2560v	....	?	**Craters of the Moon** (US-Idaho)	1204-02-	0	9/-
T-2550?	....	?	**Yake-dake** (Honshu-Japan)	0803-07=	0	9/-
T-2550?	....	?	**Hveravellir** (Iceland-SW)	1701-08=	0	8/-
G-2470t	....	?	**Haleakala** (Hawaiian Is)	1302-06-		8/-
C-2400x	....	?	**Snaefellsjökull** (Iceland-W)	1700-01=	2?	8/-
T-2300?	....	?	**Fremrinamur** (Iceland-NE)	1703-07=	0	9/-
T-2250	....	?	**Cotopaxi** (Ecuador)	1502-05=		8/-
C-2240?	....	?	**Shisheika** (Kamchatka)	1000-511		8/-
G-2240*	....	?	**Chichinautzin** (México)	1401-08=	3	8/7
G-2100v	....	?	**Izu-Tobu** (Honshu-Japan)	0803-01=	4	8/8
T-2050?	....	?	**Tolbachik** (Kamchatka)	1000-24=	3	8/7
G-2050?	....	?	**Hveravellir** (Iceland-SW)	1701-08=	0	9/-
T-2050z	....	?	**Askja** (Iceland-NE)	1703-06=	0	9/-
T-1950v	....	?	**Grímsvötn** (Iceland-NE)	1703-01=	2	9/-
T-1920?	....	?	**Sanbe** (Honshu-Japan)	0803-002	4	9/8
G-1750?	....	?	**Okataina** (New Zealand)	0401-05=	4+	8/8
G-1730t	....	?	**Hengill** (Iceland-SW)	1701-05=	0	9/-
T-1720y	....	?	**Kuju** (Kyushu-Japan)	0802-12=		8/-
C-1680w	....	?	**Craters of the Moon** (US-Idaho)	1204-02-	0	9/-
G-1350?	....	?	**Krasheninnikov** (Kamchatka)	1000-19=	3	8/7
C-1250?	....	?	**Jordan Craters** (US-Oregon)	1202-19-	2?	9/-
T-1250y	....	?	**Askja** (Iceland-NE)	1703-06=	0	9/-
G-1200?	....	?	**Hakone** (Honshu-Japan)	0803-02=	2	8/6
G-1200v	....	?	**Naolinco Volc Field** (México)	1401-095		8/-
T-1200?	....	?	**Bárdarbunga** (Iceland-NE)	1703-03=		9/-
T-1200?	....	?	**Fremrinamur** (Iceland-NE)	1703-07=		9/-
G-1170 y	....	?	**Zuni-Bandera** (US-New Mexico)	1210-02-	0	9/-
G-1150 t	....	?	**Izu-Tobu** (Honshu-Japan)	0803-01=	4+	8/8
C-1120 w	....	?	**Kusatsu-Shirane** (Honshu-Japan)	0803-12=	4	8/8
C-1060s	....	?	**Bliznetsy** (Kamchatka)	1000-552	1?	8/-
T-1050?	....	?	**Chokai** (Honshu-Japan)	0803-22=	0	8/-
T-1050?	....	?	**Cotopaxi** (Ecuador)	1502-05=	4	9/8
T-1050?	....	?	**Tenerife** (Canary Is)	1803-03-		8/-
C-1040u	....	?	**Brennisteinsfjöll** (Iceland-SW)	1701-04=	2	8/-
C-1000z	....	?	**Snaefellsjökull** (Iceland-W)	1700-01=	2	8/-
T-0800z	....	?	**Yantarni** (Alaska Peninsula)	1102-10-	**5**	8/9
C-0780v	....	?	**Medicine Lake** (US-California)	1203-02-		8/-
T-0750?	....	?	**Izu-Tobu** (Honshu-Japan)	0803-01=	3	8/7
T-0700*	....	?	**Gorely** (Kamchatka)	1000-07=	0	8/-
C-0665v	....	?	**Ljósufjöll** (Iceland-W)	1700-03=	2	8/-
C-0660u	....	?	**Alney-Chashakondzha** (Kamchatka)	1000-45-	3	8/7
C-0650u	....	?	**Alney-Chashakondzha** (Kamchatka)	1000-45-	3	8/7
C-0600x	....	?	**Aoga-shima** (Izu Is-Japan)	0804-06=	4	8/8
C-0400v	....	?	**Reykjanes** (Iceland-SW)	1701-02=	2	8/-
G-0350?	....	?	**Yake-dake** (Honshu-Japan)	0803-07=	4	8/8
C-0350?	....	?	**South Sister** (US-Oregon)	1202-08-	4	8/8
M-0350?	....	?	**Craters of the Moon** (US-Idaho)	1204-02-	0	8/-
T-0300?	....	?	**Okataina** (New Zealand)	0401-05=	0	9/-
T-0300?	....	?	**Wapi Lava Field** (US-Idaho)	1204-03-	2?	9/-
G-0300?	....	?	**Krafla** (Iceland-NE)	1703-08=	2	9/-
G-0220x	....	?	**Lanín** (Chile-C)	1507-122		8/-
G-0200?	....	?	**Haku-san** (Honshu-Japan)	0803-05=	4	8/8
C-0190u	....	?	**Krísuvík** (Iceland-SW)	1701-03=	2	8/-
C-0130 t	....	?	**Craters of the Moon** (US-Idaho)	1204-02-	0	9/-
C-0080u	....	?	**Hualalai** (Hawaiian Is)	1302-04-	0	8/-
C-0080u	....	?	**Hengill** (Iceland-SW)	1701-05=	2	8/-
C-0060?	....	?	**Terceira** (Azores)	1802-05=		8/-
T-0050?	....	?	**Norikura** (Honshu-Japan)	0803-06=	3	8/7
C-0050?	....	?	**South Sister** (US-Oregon)	1202-08-	3	8/7

BC / AD

START YEAR	M-Dy	Duration	VOLCANO NAME (Subregion)	NUMBER	VEI	Vol L/T
G 0030w	....	?	**Tenerife** (Canary Is)	1803-03-		9/-
T 0050?	....	?	**Tolbachik** (Kamchatka)	1000-24=	4+	8/8
G 0150u	....	?	**Hengill** (Iceland-SW)	1701-05=	2	8/-
T 0150v	....	?	**Bárdarbunga** (Iceland-NE)	1703-03=	2?	8/-
C 0180v	....	?	**Cotopaxi** (Ecuador)	1502-05=	4	8/8
G 0200v	....	?	**Chichinautzin** (México)	1401-08=	3	8/7
C 0200w	....	?	**Snaefellsjökull** (Iceland-W)	1700-01=		8/-
T 0250?	....	?	**Bezymianny** (Kamchatka)	1000-25=		8/-
T 0260?	....	?	**Taupo** (New Zealand)	0401-07=	0	8/-
T 0350y	....	?	**Diky Greben** (Kamchatka)	1000-022		**10/-**
A 0350j	1115m	?	**Asama** (Honshu-Japan)	0803-11=	4	8/8
G 0370s	....	?	**Kuju** (Kyushu-Japan)	0802-12=	3	9/7
T 0400?	....	?	**Tolbachik** (Kamchatka)	1000-24=	4+	8/8
G 0400v	....	?	**Chichinautzin** (México)	1401-08=	3?	9/-
G 0440w	....	?	**North Sister Field** (US-Oregon)	1202-07-	2?	8/-
T 0450?	....	?	**Tolbachik** (Kamchatka)	1000-24=	3	9/7
C 0480u	....	?	**Tungurahua** (Ecuador)	1502-08=		8/-
T 0550?	....	?	**Tolbachik** (Kamchatka)	1000-24=	3	9/7
A 0550j	0601p	?	**Haruna** (Honshu-Japan)	0803-122	**5**	8/9
T 0600?	....	?	**Ibusuki Volc Field** (Kyushu-Japan)	0802-07=	4	8/8
G 0610 t	....	?	**Opala** (Kamchatka)	1000-08=	**5+**	8/9
G 0690v	....	?	**Newberry** (US-Oregon)	1202-11-	4	8/8
T 0700?	....	?	**Mono Craters** (US-California)	1203-12-		8/-
M 0720?	....	?	**Medicine Lake** (US-California)	1203-02-		8/-
C 0770x	....	?	**Hualalai** (Hawaiian Is)	1302-04-	1	8/-
M 0800?	....	?	**Medicine Lake** (US-California)	1203-02-		8/-
G 0800w	....	?	**Tenerife** (Canary Is)	1803-03-	0	8/-
? 0812?	....	?	**Etna** (Italy)	0101-06=		8/5
0838	0802?	?	**Kozu-shima** (Izu Is-Japan)	0804-03=	4	8/8
0864	0612?	599p?	**Fuji** (Honshu-Japan)	0803-03=	3	9/-
T 0870?	....	?	**Torfajökull** (Iceland-S)	1702-05=	3	8/7
C 0875t	....	?	**Brennisteinsfjöll** (Iceland-SW)	1701-04=	2	8/-
0886	0629	?	**Nii-jima** (Izu Is-Japan)	0804-02=	4+	8/8
C 0890v	....	?	**Medicine Lake** (US-California)	1203-02-	3	8/7
T 0900?	....	?	**Tolbachik** (Kamchatka)	1000-24=	4	9/9
T 0900?	....	?	**Krísuvík** (Iceland-SW)	1701-03=	2	8/-
0915	0817	?	**Towada** (Honshu-Japan)	0803-271	**5**	8/9
I 0934b	....	>3yr	**Katla** (Iceland-S)	1702-03=	4?	**10/9**
T 0950?	....	?	**Tolbachik** (Kamchatka)	1000-24=	4+	8/8
C 0950?	....	?	**Brennisteinsfjöll** (Iceland-SW)	1701-04=	2	8/6
T 0950t	....	?	**Hveravellir** (Iceland-SW)	1701-08=	2	9/6
A 0960j	....	?	**Ljósufjöll** (Iceland-W)	1700-03=	2	8/7
T 1000?	....	?	**Tolbachik** (Kamchatka)	1000-24=	4+	9/8
1000	0625d	?	**Brennisteinsfjöll** (Iceland-SW)	1701-04=	0	8/-
T 1040?	....	?	**Cayambe** (Ecuador)	1502-006	4	8/-
T 1050?	....	?	**Tolbachik** (Kamchatka)	1000-24=	3	9/7
C 1050v	....	?	**Hualalai** (Hawaiian Is)	1302-04-	1	8/-
G 1060v	....	?	**Tenerife** (Canary Is)	1803-03-		8/-
M 1075q	....	?	**Sunset Crater** (US-Arizona)	1209-02-	4?	8/-
M 1080q	....	?	**Medicine Lake** (US-California)	1203-02-	3?	9/7
1108	0829	41m	**Asama** (Honshu-Japan)	0803-11=	**5**	8/9
G 1150v	....	?	**Cofre de Perote** (México)	1401-096	2	9/-
1151	....	?	**Krísuvík** (Iceland-SW)	1701-03=	1	8/5
1158	0119	?	**Hekla** (Iceland-S)	1702-07=	4	8/8
C 1240w	....	?	**Hualalai** (Hawaiian Is)	1302-04-	2	8/-
1240	....	?	**Reykjanes** (Iceland-SW)	1701-02=	1	8/5
T 1250t	....	?	**Bárdarbunga** (Iceland-NE)	1703-03=	1	9/5

	START YEAR	M-Dy	Duration	VOLCANO NAME (Subregion)	NUMBER	VEI	Vol L/T
	1256	0605	52a?	**Rahat, Harrat** (Arabia-W)	0301-07=	3	8/-
T	1290?	....	?	**Cayambe** (Ecuador)	1502-006	4	8/-
	1300	0711	369m?	**Hekla** (Iceland-S)	1702-07=	4	8/8
G	1310 k	....	>3yr	**Okataina** (New Zealand)	0401-05=	5	9/9
T	1325?	....	?	**Krísuvík** (Iceland-SW)	1701-03=	1	8/5
	1341 a	....	?	**Brennisteinsfjöll** (Iceland-SW)	1701-04=	2	8/-
C	1350?	....	?	**Auckland Field** (New Zealand)	0401-02=		9/-
C	1350?	....	?	**Kikhpinych** (Kamchatka)	1000-18=	4	8/8
D	1350 p	....	?	**Mono Craters** (US-California)	1203-12-	4	8/8
	1361	....	?	**Niigata-Yake-yama** (Honshu-Japan)	0803-09=	3	8/7
G	1380 t	....	?	**Inyo Craters** (US-California)	1203-13-	4	8/8
	1389	1201p	213w	**Hekla** (Iceland-S)	1702-07=	3	8/7
G	1410?	....	>3yr	**Kilauea** (Hawaiian Is)	1302-01-	0	9/-
	1421	0514	?	**Oshima** (Izu Is-Japan)	0804-01=	4	8/8
	1471	1103	>3yr	**Sakura-jima** (Kyushu-Japan)	0802-08=	5?	8/9
	1477	02 ?	?	**Bárdarbunga** (Iceland-NE)	1703-03=	6	9/10
	1500						
	1529	....	?	**Telica** (Nicaragua)	1404-04=	4	8/8
	1545	....	>3yr	**Orizaba, Pico de** (México)	1401-10=	2	8/-
G	1550?	....	?	**Karymsky** (Kamchatka)	1000-13=		8/-
T	1550?	....	?	**Tolbachik** (Kamchatka)	1000-24=	2	8/6
	1552	1007	8a	**Oshima** (Izu Is-Japan)	0804-01=	3	8/7
	1554	05	40b	**Hekla** (Iceland-S)	1702-07=	2?	8/-
T	1570?	....	?	**Cayambe** (Ecuador)	1502-006	4	8/-
	1607	0628	368w?	**Etna** (Italy)	0101-06=	2	8/6
G	1610 s	....	?	**St. Helens** (US-Washington)	1201-05-		8/-
	1610	0206	190a	**Etna** (Italy)	0101-06=	2	8/6
	1614	0701?	>3yr	**Etna** (Italy)	0101-06=	2	9/6
	1634	1219?	>3yr	**Etna** (Italy)	0101-06=	1	8/5
	1646	1120	58a	**Etna** (Italy)	0101-06=	2	8/6
	1651	0117	914m?	**Etna** (Italy)	0101-06=	1	8/5
	1669	0311	122a?	**Etna** (Italy)	0101-06=	3?	9/8
G	1690w	....	?	**Tseax River Cone** (Canada)	1200-10-		8/-
	1720	0114	514m	**Wudalianchi** (China-E)	1005-03-	3	9/8
	1728	1218	?	**Krafla** (Iceland-NE)	1703-08=	2	8/-
G	1730q	....	?	**Karymsky** (Kamchatka)	1000-13=		8/-
	1730	0901	>3yr	**Lanzarote** (Canary Is)	1803-06-	3	9/-
A	1750?	....	?	**Haleakala** (Hawaiian Is)	1302-06-		8/-
	1759	0929	>3yr	**Michoacán-Guanajuato** (México)	1401-06=	4	8/9
	1760	....	?	**Savai'i** (Samoa-SW Pacific)	0404-04=	2	9/-
	1760	....	?	**Chacana** (Ecuador)	1502-022	0	9/-
	1763	0618	84a	**Etna** (Italy)	0101-06=	3	8/7
	1764	....	548m?	**Etna** (Italy)	0101-06=	1	8/5
	1766	0405	770m	**Hekla** (Iceland-S)	1702-07=	4	9/8
	1766	0427	193a	**Etna** (Italy)	0101-06=	2	8/6
	1773	....	?	**Chacana** (Ecuador)	1502-022	0	8/-
	1773	0204	127m?	**Tungurahua** (Ecuador)	1502-08=	3	8/-
	1777	0831	670w	**Oshima** (Izu Is-Japan)	0804-01=	3	8/8
	1779	1108	554m	**Sakura-jima** (Kyushu-Japan)	0802-08=	4	9/8
	1783	05 ?	741m?	**Grímsvötn** (Iceland-NE)	1703-01=	4+	10/8
	1783	0509	88a	**Asama** (Honshu-Japan)	0803-11=	4	8/8
	1784 g	....	?	**Hualalai** (Hawaiian Is)	1302-04-	0	8/-
	1822	1227	100a	**Merapi** (Java)	0603-25=	3?	8/7
	1840	0530	26a	**Kilauea** (Hawaiian Is)	1302-01-	0	8/-
	1843	0109	90a?	**Mauna Loa** (Hawaiian Is)	1302-02=	0	8/-
	1845	0902	215a?	**Hekla** (Iceland-S)	1702-07=	4	8/8
	1846	1126	>3yr	**Azul, Cerro** (Chile-C)	1507-06=	2	9/-
	1852	0217	23a?	**Mauna Loa** (Hawaiian Is)	1302-02=	2	8/-
	1852	0820	290a	**Etna** (Italy)	0101-06=	2	8/6
	1853	0422	146m	**Usu** (Hokkaido-Japan)	0805-03=	4	8/8
	1855	0811	462m	**Mauna Loa** (Hawaiian Is)	1302-02=	1	8/-
	1855	1219	>3yr	**Vesuvius** (Italy)	0101-02=	3	8/-
	1856	0930p	>3yr	**Didicas** (Luzon-N of)	0704-02=	2	8/-
	1859	0123	306a	**Mauna Loa** (Hawaiian Is)	1302-02=	1	8/-
	1861	0508	161m?	**Dubbi** (Ethiopia)	0201-10=	3?	9/-
	1862	0630	837q	**Bárdarbunga** (Iceland-NE)	1703-03=	2	8/5
	1866	0126	>3yr	**Santorini** (Greece)	0102-04=	2	8/-
	1868	0327	26a	**Mauna Loa** (Hawaiian Is)	1302-02=	2	8/-
	1869	0612	73a>	**Colima** (México)	1401-04=	3	8/-
	1870	0221	>3yr	**Ceboruco** (México)	1401-03=	3	9/8
	1871	0430	>3yr	**Camiguin** (Mindanao-Philippines)	0701-08=	2	8/-
	1875	0101	289a	**Askja** (Iceland-NE)	1703-06=	5	8/9
	1875	1218	>3yr	**Vesuvius** (Italy)	0101-02=	4?	8/8
	1878	0227	47m	**Hekla** (Iceland-S)	1702-07=	2	8/-
	1879	1231	87e	**Ilopango** (El Salvador)	1403-06=	3	8/-
	1880	1105	278a	**Mauna Loa** (Hawaiian Is)	1302-02=	1	8/-
	1883	1006	269w?	**Augustine** (Alaska-SW)	1103-01-	4	8/8
	1887	0116	12a?	**Mauna Loa** (Hawaiian Is)	1302-02=	0	8/-
	1887	0602	958m	**Lonquimay** (Chile-C)	1507-10=	3	8/-
	1892	0709	173a	**Etna** (Italy)	0101-06=	2	8/6
	1902	12	393m	**Grímsvötn** (Iceland-NE)	1703-01=	4	8/-
	1902	0423	>3yr	**Pelée** (W Indies)	1600-12=	4	8/8
	1904	1114	183a?	**Fukutoku-Okanoba** (Japan)	0804-13=	3	8/8
	1905	0804	>3yr	**Savai'i** (Samoa-SW Pacific)	0404-04=	2	9/6
	1911	....	365y	**Lolobau** (New Britain-SW Pac)	0502-13=	4	8/8
	1913	0705	>3yr	**Vesuvius** (Italy)	0101-02=	3	8/7
	1914	0112	488m	**Sakura-jima** (Kyushu-Japan)	0802-08=	4	9/8
M	1915 s	....	?	**Southern EPR-Segment I** (Pacific-E)	1304-14-	0	8/-
	1919	0926	40a?	**Mauna Loa** (Hawaiian Is)	1302-02=	0	8/-
	1920 b	....	?	**Pago** (New Britain-SW Pac)	0502-08=	0	8/-
	1921	....	>3yr	**Nyamuragira** (Africa-C)	0203-02=	0	8/-
	1921	1213	62a	**Puyehue-Cordón Caulle** (Chile-C)	1507-15=	3	8/-
	1922	0622	>3yr	**Santa María** (Guatemala)	1402-03=	3	9/8
	1924?	....	?	**Askja** (Iceland-NE)	1703-06=	0?	8/-
	1925	0811	277m	**Santorini** (Greece)	0102-04=	2	8/-
	1926	0410	18a?	**Mauna Loa** (Hawaiian Is)	1302-02=	0	8/-
	1931	0122	216e	**Fournaise, Piton de la** (Indian O.-W)	0303-02=	2	8/-
	1933	0108	96a>	**Kharimkotan** (Kuril Is)	0900-30=	5	8/9
	1933	1202	16a	**Mauna Loa** (Hawaiian Is)	1302-02=	0	8/-
	1934	11	120p	**Karymsky** (Kamchatka)	1000-13=	2	8/-
	1937	0403	712m	**Kliuchevskoi** (Kamchatka)	1000-26=	3	8/7
	1938	0128	878e	**Nyamuragira** (Africa-C)	0203-02=	1	8/-
	1940	0407	133a	**Mauna Loa** (Hawaiian Is)	1302-02=	0	8/-
	1942	0426	14a	**Mauna Loa** (Hawaiian Is)	1302-02=	0	8/-
	1943	0220	>3yr	**Michoacán-Guanajuato** (México)	1401-06=	4	8/9
	1944	1105	>3yr	**Shiveluch** (Kamchatka)	1000-27=	2	8/-
	1946	01	304p	**Sakura-jima** (Kyushu-Japan)	0802-08=	2	8/7
	1947	0329	388a	**Hekla** (Iceland-S)	1702-07=	4	8/8
	1949	0106	145a	**Mauna Loa** (Hawaiian Is)	1302-02=	0	8/-
	1950	0601	22a	**Mauna Loa** (Hawaiian Is)	1302-02=	0	8/-
	1950	1125	373a	**Etna** (Italy)	0101-06=	2	8/6
	1951	0117	>3yr	**Lamington** (New Guinea)	0503-01=	4	8/-
	1952	0316<	472w>	**Didicas** (Luzon-N of)	0704-02=	2	8/-
	1953	0131	75e	**Raung** (Java)	0603-34=	3	8/-
	1953	0215	597a?	**Trident** (Alaska Peninsula)	1102-16-	3	8/7
	1953	0627	>3yr	**St. Andrew Strait** (SW Pacific)	0500-01=	2	8/-
	1958	0814	12j	**Okmok** (Aleutian Is)	1101-29-	3	8/-
	1960	0113	37a	**Kilauea** (Hawaiian Is)	1302-01-	2	8/-
	1960	0524	67a	**Puyehue-Cordón Caulle** (Chile-C)	1507-15=	3?	8/7
	1961	1026	40d	**Askja** (Iceland-NE)	1703-06=	2	8/6
	1963	0218	344a	**Agung** (Lesser Sunda Is)	0604-02=	5	8/9
	1963	1108	>3yr	**Vestmannaeyjar** (Iceland-S)	1702-01=	3	8/8
	1964?	....	>3yr	**Unnamed** (Pacific-E)	1304-10-	0	10/-
	1965	08	498m	**Kliuchevskoi** (Kamchatka)	1000-26=	3	8/7
	1968	0729	>3yr	**Arenal** (Costa Rica)	1405-033	3	8/7
	1969	0524	>3yr	**Kilauea** (Hawaiian Is)	1302-01-	0	8/-
	1970	0505	61a	**Hekla** (Iceland-S)	1702-07=	3	8/7
	1970	0918	652w?	**Jan Mayen** (Atlantic-N-Jan Mayen)	1706-01=	3	8/7
	1973	0123	156a	**Vestmannaeyjar** (Iceland-S)	1702-01=	3	8/7
	1975	0628	530a	**Tolbachik** (Kamchatka)	1000-24=	4+	9/8
	1975	1211?	191a?	**Colima** (México)	1401-04=	2	8/-
	1979	1113	62a>	**Negra, Sierra** (Galápagos)	1503-05=	3	8/-
	1980	0817	3a	**Hekla** (Iceland-S)	1702-07=	3	8/7
	1983	0103	>3yr	**Kilauea** (Hawaiian Is)	1302-01-	1	9/-
	1984	0325	21a	**Mauna Loa** (Hawaiian Is)	1302-02=	0	8/-
	1984	0904	14	**Krafla** (Iceland-NE)	1703-08=	0	8/-
	1985	0614	>3yr	**Fournaise, Piton de la** (Indian O.-W)	0303-02=	1	8/-
	1988	1225	395b	**Lonquimay** (Chile-C)	1507-10=	3	8/8
	1990 b	....	?	**Southern EPR-Segment K** (Pacific)	1304-12-	0	8/-
	1990	0110	>3yr	**Shiveluch** (Kamchatka)	1000-27=	3	8/6
	1990	1117	>3yr	**Unzen** (Kyushu-Japan)	0802-10=	1	8/6
	1991	0117	52	**Hekla** (Iceland-S)	1702-07=	3	8/7
	1991	1214	472a	**Etna** (Italy)	0101-06=	2	8/-
	1995	0718	>3yr	**Soufrière Hills** (W Indies)	1600-05=	3	8/-
	1996	0930	36	**Grímsvötn** (Iceland-NE)	1703-01=	3?	8/-
	1998	0915	35	**Azul, Cerro** (Galápagos)	1503-06=	1	8/-
	1999	0815	>3yr	**Shiveluch** (Kamchatka)	1000-27=	4?	8/-
	2000	0226	12	**Hekla** (Iceland-S)	1702-07=	3	8/7
	2002	0803	177o>	**Pago** (New Britain-SW Pac)	0502-08=	3	8/-
	2005	1022	8	**Negra, Sierra** (Galápagos)	1503-05=	3	8/-
	2006	0720	285a	**Fournaise, Piton de la** (Indian O.-W)	0303-02=	1?	8/-

Fatalities and Evacuations

Fatalities and Evacuations: Context and Codes

The **agent** code is a single **bolded** letter to simplify the coded information and make it easy to find all fatalities caused by each agent. We have not attempted a more detailed breakdown because the data often do not permit it, but we have included more detailed information in the **remarks** where possible. It should be easy to find all fatal eruptions with pyroclastic flows (sensu lato), for example, but readers interested in pyroclastic surge deaths as distinct from directed blasts deaths must find them in the remarks. The code is at genus rather than species level. Descriptions of the various agents causing eruptive fatalities have already been described (p. 20-22). The following table identifies the code:

A = **A**valanche (debris and landslides)
E = **E**lectrical (lighting)
F = **F**loods (and Jökulhlaups)
G = **G**as (emission from eruptive craters as well as fumarolic/solfataric activity)
I = **I**ndirect deaths (disease, starvation, exposure, desolation)
L = **L**ava flows
M = **M**udflows/Lahars
m = Secondary (post-eruption) **m**udflows
P = **P**yroclastic flows, surges, & directed blasts
S = **S**eismic, or volcanic earthquake (tectonic earthquake deaths excluded)
T = **T**ephra (ash, bombs, lapilli, steam blasts). Killing either by ballistic impact, or, with finer-grained ash, by suffocation, collapse of ash-covered roofs, etc.
W = **W**aves, or Tsunami

Agents have a subscripted number indicating what percentage of the total deaths were by that cause. Those with uncertain percentages are followed by a question mark. A double question mark is used when the percentages are crudely estimated from the nature of the reported eruption alone. An agent code without a percentage indicates that the agent, but not percent, of fatalities is known. An agent code followed by a question mark denotes uncertainty about the agent.

Accurate **death** tolls are often difficult to obtain, even today, and the historical record often fails to provide numbers. Many accounts use words like “many,” “several,” or “thousands,” and we have not attempted to quantify the usage of the original account. In the Evacuation table that follows, a dash in the “Evacuees” column indicates an eruption with fatalities but no evacuations. A question mark in this column indicates an eruption with an unknown number of evacuees.

Non-volcanic earthquake fatalities are not listed in the **deaths** column, but may be mentioned in the **remarks**. These have often been confused with volcanic fatalities, particularly on a notorious volcano like Etna, but unless we have a firm “x” in the fatality column of the main DIRECTORY (p. 37-161), we have resisted entering a number in the **deaths** column here.

Eruption-related injuries span a huge spectrum of severity, and their historical data are even less reliable than those for fatalities. We have not included entries that describe injuries without evidence of clear fatalities.

The **start date** of each eruption is included in curly brackets at the end of each eruption’s remarks, using an equal sign {=} if it is the same as the date of known fatalities. This both facilitates cross-reference to other parts of the book and alerts the reader to the rather different hazard conditions that surround an eruption’s first day and its second or third year.

The following abbreviations have been used. See REFERENCES for citations.

BVE = Bulletin of Volcanic Eruptions (Volcanological Society of Japan)
CAVW = Catalog of Active Volcanoes of the World (IAVCEI)
IAVCEI = International Association of Volcanology and Chemistry of Earth’s Interior
JMA = Japan Meteorological Agency
VL = Volcano Letter (Hawaii Research Association, 1925-55)
CSLP/SEAN/GVN = Smithsonian publications of: Center for Short-Lived Phenomena (1968-75); Scientific Event Alert Network (1975-89); Global Volcanism Network (1990-present)

The prime instigator of, and contributor to, early versions of this table was Russell Blong, formerly of Macquarie University in Australia. His interest in the impact of volcanic eruptions led to the incorporation of fatality information in our database from a wide variety of sources. We particularly acknowledge the compilations of Tanguy et al. (1998) and Witham (2005).

Fatalities

EUROPE (01)

Campi Flegrei (0101-01=)

Year M-Dy	Deaths	Agent	Remarks	{Start Date}
1538 1006	24	$T_{100?}$	Phreatic explosion at 2200 on Monte Nuovo eruption's 8th day. Many people climbing the cone lost their footing in the dark, sliding to their deaths on loose stones.	{1538 0929}
1970 0302	3	S_{100}	Volcanogenic earthquake: 3 killed by falling masonry and rocks in the collapse of houses.	{No eruption}

Vesuvius (0101-02=)

Year M-Dy	Deaths	Agent	Remarks	{Start Date}
~2420 BC	?	P T	Avellino eruption.	{=}
0079 0825	>2,100?	$P_{70?}$ $T_{30?}$	Luongo et al. (2003) indicate about 1150 identified victims in Pompeii and a total of about 1600, including estimates for unexcavated areas. Within the city 62% were killed by pyroclastic surges and 38% mainly by roof and wall collapse from plinian pumice-fall. Another 236 victims were identified outside the city walls. About 300 persons were killed by pyroclastic surges in shoreline boathouses at Herculaneum as well as an unknown number of others within the mostly evacuated city.	{0079 0824}
0787 1015q	?	?	Possible damage and fatalities.	{=}
1631 1216	>4,000	$P_{95?}$ $E_{?}$ $M_{?}$	Most of >4,000 fatalities caused by pyroclastic surges. Earlier accounts ascribe deaths to lava flows, mudflows and tephra falls, but lava flows are uncertain. One estimate of the total death toll reached 18,000. Hamilton reported men and beasts struck dead by lightning. 30 cm tephra in Naples.	{1631 1215}
1682 0812?	4	?	One fatality in Torre Annunziata, 3 in Castellammare during Aug 12-22 eruption.	{1682 0812}
1737 05	2	$T_{100?}$	Serious damage from tephra fall near end of 5-year eruption.	{1732 1225}
1779 0808	Few	?		{1770 0215}
1794	400	$M_{?}$ $L_{?}$ $T_{?}$ $G_{?}$	60 fatalities at Torre del Greco, with 80% of the town destroyed by lava flows. Several people died from CO_2. Sapper reported 26 killed, possibly by lava flows. Hoffer described 15 deaths by lava flows and explosions when the lava reached the bay. Scandone et al. reported a total of 400 fatalities, and complete destruction (by mudflows and ashfall?) of S. Guiseppe, Ottaviano, and Somma.	{1783 0818}
1805	4	?		{1796 01}
1872	>9	$L_{80?}$ $G_{20?}$	Young people in Valle del Inferno failed to notice retreat cut off by lava which trapped them between precipice of Monte Somma and active flow. Nazzaro reported 9 killed and 11 injured, plus some fatalities from CO_2.	{1870 12}
1873 Spring	9	G_{78} T_{22}	Date probably mistaken for 1872 (Vesuvius not in eruption in 1873) but Fisher reported that 2 tourists fell while fleeing a slight eruption at the summit and were covered with lava; 7 others died of suffocation.	{1870 12}
1905 0310	1	T_{100}	One guide killed on rim and another injured by explosion.	{1875 1218}
1906 0406	350?	$T_{99?}$ L_{1}	Nazarro suggests a total of 216 fatalities. Delme-Radcliffe indicates ~300 killed and 300 injured: 105 killed and 90 injured in fall of church roof in San Giuseppe, ~90 killed in collapse of house roofs thereabouts, ~90 killed in Ottaviano, ~20 killed in San Gennaro, and about 50 others elsewhere including 14 killed in the collapse of the Monte Oliveto Market in Naples. Lacroix indicates 3 deaths in a lava flow. Witham lists 218-700 fatalities.	{1875 1218}
1944 03	27	$T_{88?}$ $L_{8?}$ $I_{4?}$	Roof collapses under tephra loads caused 12 deaths at Nocera and 9 at Pagani. Trees falling under tephra load or falling fragments at Terzigno killed 3. Two small boys were killed at San Sebastiano when lava exploded upon reaching a water tank. One elderly man killed himself, in sorrow at the desolation of San Sabastiano.	{1913 0705}

Ischia (0101-03=)

Year M-Dy	Deaths	Agent	Remarks	{Start Date}
1302	?	?	People and animals reportedly killed. Many persons fled to neighboring islands and the mainland.	{1302 0118}

Stromboli (0101-04=)

Year M-Dy	Deaths	Agent	Remarks	{Start Date}
1919 0522	4	T_{100}	Blocks of 30-60 tons fell on houses in S. Vicenzo (8 destroyed) & Ginostra (2 destroyed); 4 killed, several injured.	{1910 05}
1930 0911	6	P_{67} T_{18} W_{18}	Three people killed by pyroclastic flows, and a fourth died after being scalded in the sea near the point where the flows reached the coast. One person died from a tsunami and another from a falling block.	{1910 05}
1986 0724	1	T_{100}	A biologist was hit on the head by a falling block and died instantly ~15 m from W edge of crater rim.	{1934 0202}
2001 1020	1	T_{100}	Ejecta from a stronger than normal explosion impacted a tourist group at Pizzo Sopra la Fossa. One seriously injured woman fell into a coma and died two days later after being hospitalized.	{1934 0202}

Etna (0101-06=)

Year M-Dy	Deaths	Agent	Remarks	{Start Date}
1169 02	?	S W	Violent earthquake about dawn buried many people in Catania during vigil of feast of St. Agatha, and tsunami swept away people who had gathered on shore at Messina. Earthquake (probably tectonic) occurred on 4/11/1169. Romano & Sturiale uncertain about an eruption at this time. Hyde reports 15,000 deaths during eruption in 1185 but gives no details and it is likely that this is a spurious account and/or confused with the 1169 event.	{1169 0204}
1329 0715?	Many?	I	Many persons said to have died from terror. Multitudes of animals and birds perished and the fields were burned up by hot sand and ashes.	{=}
1536 0326	1	T_{100}	A physician of Lentini approached too closely (to a newly active crater?) and was killed by a volley of red-hot stones.	{1536 0322}
1669	?	?	Coleman indicates that 20,000 perished in this eruption, but this seems unlikely. Neither Rittmann nor Romano & Sturiale mention deaths in their accounts. Detailed report by Winchilsea mentions only a few deaths as a result of murders and executions amidst widespread destruction of towns and croplands. The Coleman account is perhaps confused with a 1693 tectonic earthquake that killed 60,000-100,000 in 50 towns in Sicily and 18,000 in Catania. Rodwell reported a 1693 eruption, but Sapper and Tanguy consider the eruption doubtful, and most others ignore it.	{1669 0311}
1669 0319	2	L_{100}	A lava flow killed two persons and injured 5 on March 19 in the forest close to Mt. Cagliato.	{1669 0314}
1832	Several	$L_{100?}$	Explosion at front of lava flow moving over ice killed several people.	{1832 1031}
1843 1125	59	$L_{100?}$	Near the end of the year, while many of the inhabitants of Bronte were watching the lava's progress, the flow front was suddenly blown out by an explosion (the lava may have entered a cistern). 36 were killed on the spot and 20 survived but a few hours. Branca and Carlo list 59 fatalities and a November 25 rather than November 24 date.	{1843 1117}
1928 1108	5?	L_{100}	Three men who had returned to their homes in Mascali to rescue household goods were surrounded by lava flows and killed. On the same day in the same town an aged couple were also engulfed in their home.	{1928 1102}
1929 0802	2	T_{100}	An explosion from the NE Crater killed two persons.	{=}
1979 0912	9	T_{100}	Nine killed and 20 or 23 seriously injured by non-juvenile bombs ejected by violent phreatic explosion of Bocca Nuova vent. 150-200 tourists in area at time. A vehicle used for emergency accommodation was hit by a bomb, causing a gas cylinder to explode, destroying vehicle and burning several nearby tourists.	{1979 0705}

Year M-Dy	Deaths	Agent	Remarks	{Start Date}
1984 1016	1	S_{100}		{1984 0720}
1985 1219<	1	S_{100}	A strong earthquake and fracturing of the ground caused one death at Piano Provenzana	{=}
1987 0417	2	T_{100}	Phreatic explosion killed 2 tourists and injured 7 out of about 30 gathered ~500 m SSE of SE crater.	{1987 0308h}
Santorini			(0102-04=)	
~1610 BC	?	?	Deaths probably occurred here, and, as a result of tsunamis, in ports and seaside villages on Crete and elsewhere. However, no direct evidence of deaths has been found.	{=}
1650	>120?	$G_{40?}$ $W_{40?}$ $T_{20?}$	Some died of opthalmias caused by sulfurous vapor; others (~50?) were suffocated by vapors on Sept 30. The crew of a ship passing too near the volcano was suffocated on Oct 2. Others (~20 laborers) were killed by a shower of black dust on Nov 4. Fytikas attributes 50 deaths to a tsunami, and does not mention other fatalities.	{1650 0927}
1866 0220	1	T_{100}	The captain of a ship loading materials at a dock on Micra Kameni island was killed by an ejected block, and others were injured.	{1826 0126}
1926	48	$S_{100?}$	Deaths more likely due to an earthquake than an eruption. CAVW lists no fatalities.	{1925 0811}
Ararat			(0103-04-)	
1840 0702	1,900	P_{100}	A pyroclastic flow at the time of a phreatic eruption and landslide on July 2, 1840 swept over the village of Akory, killing 1900 persons. Four days later, failure of a landslide-dammed lake destroyed the town of Aralik; fatalities were not explicitly mentioned.	{=}

AFRICA, MID-EAST, & INDIAN OCEAN (02 & 03)

Year M-Dy	Deaths	Agent	Remarks	{Start Date}
Tair, Jebel at			(0201-01=)	
2007 0930	4	?	Bodies of 4 Yemini Coast Guard personnel were recovered offshore	{=}
Dubbi			(0201-10=)	
1861	106	$P_{100?}$	Fatalities occurred during initial explosive phase of eruption. Two villages were destroyed and large herds of cattle were killed. The agent of fatalities is not clear, but may have been pyroclastic flows.	{1861 0508}
Alayta			(0201-112)	
1907	?	?	CAVW reports fatalities from Afdera, but eruption now thought to be from Alayta.	{1907 06}
Dama Ali			(0201-141)	
1631	50	$S_{100?}$	Believed 50 deaths occurred when village of Waraba was destroyed by earthquake. Site of this eruption uncertain.	{1631 0214}
Kieyo			(0202-17=)	
1800?	?	$L_{100?}$	Oral history records an eruption about 1800 AD in which lava engulfed villages whose inhabitants were still asleep.	{=}
Nyamuragira			(0203-02=)	
1912 12	20	L_{100}	20 villagers were killed when a lava flow changed directions.	{1912 1203}
Nyiragongo			(0203-03=)	
1977 0110	100?	$L_{100?}$	Extremely fluid, fast-moving lava flows draining from lava lake killed numbers variously estimated at none to 2,000 persons. Best estimate seems to be 50 to 100. Several villages destroyed.	{=}
1990 1121	1	S_{100}		{No eruption}
2002 0117	100	L_{100}	About 100 persons, mostly children from the villages on the volcano flank, were killed by very high velocity lava flows, which entered the city of Goma; 20 persons died when hot lava flows ignited gas-station tanks on January 21.	{=}
Oku Volc Field			(0204-03-)	
1984 0815	37	G_{100}	Lake Monoun. A white cloud in the vicinity of the lake at daybreak looked like typical fog, but contained CO_2. Victims suffered vomiting, paralysis, and very rapid death.	{No eruption}
1986 0821	1,700	G_{100}	Lake Nyos. Deaths caused by release of large volume of CO_2 from lake. More than 300 survivors hospitalized.	{=}
'Uwayrid, Harrat			(0301-02=)	
0640?	?	$T_{100?}$	Bedouin describe fire & stones killing herdsmen, cattle, and sheep. Location & date uncertain.	{=}
Karthala			(0303-01=)	
1883 03	?	L_{100}	Voluminous lava flows destroyed a village and its inhabitants.	{=}
1903	17	G_{100}	In the summer of 1903 the emanation of suffocating gases was so strong that 17 people, who stayed near the solfataras at an elevation of 1,600 m, were killed.	{No eruption}
1904	1	L_{100}	A lava flow destroyed cultivated land and killed one person.	{1904 0225}
1977 0405	1?	?	One possible fatality from lava flow.	{=}
2005 1125	1	$T_{100?}$	One infant died, apparently as a result of ashfall, during the eruption.	{=}
Fournaise, Piton de la			(0303-02=)	
1972 08	3	$I_{100?}$	Three visitors died after 48 hours in cold mists on the rugged lava fields during the second phase of the eruption.	{1972 0609}

NEW ZEALAND TO FIJI (04)

Year M-Dy	Deaths	Agent	Remarks	{Start Date}
White Island			(0401-04=)	
1914 0910	11	A_{100}	Debris avalanche from SW corner of crater wall overwhelmed party of 11 sulfur workers and two buildings.	{No eruption.}
Okataina			(0401-05=)	
1886 0610	153	$T_{98?}$	Almost all died as a result of burial by tephra. 147 Maoris and 6 Europeans. Villages affected included: Te Ariki (52 killed), Moura (39), Te Wairo (14), Rotomahana (11).	{=}
1903 0830	4	T_{100}	4 killed by eruption of Waimangu geyser.	{1900 01}
1917 0401	2	T_{100}	Steam blast at Frying Pan Flat lifted roof off Waimangu accommodation 800 m away. 3 occupants scalded by searing steam blast. Wife and child of resident guide died later.	{1917 0324}
Taupo			(0401-07=)	
1846 0507	63	m_{100}	A lahar (mudflow) or debris avalanche of hydrothermally altered rocks along the Waihi fault destroyed fortified village of Te Heu Heu, a famous Maori chieftain. An earlier event may have occurred in 1836 but is unclear.	{No eruption}
1910 0320	1	m_{100}	Lahar from collapse of hydrothermally-altered rocks at the SW end of Lake Taupo.	{No eruption}
Ruapehu			(0401-10=)	
1953 1224	151	m_{100}	Summit crater lake drained when crevassing glacier caused ash barrier holding it in to collapse. The resulting mudflow swept away one of the piers of the Tangiwai bridge just before the arrival of the Wellington-Auckland express. Locomotive, tender and 5 carriages plunged into the river.	{No eruption}
Raoul Island			(0402-03=)	
2006 0317	1	T_{100}	One person making water-temperature measurements at Green Lake was killed by sudden explosion.	{=}
Niuafo'ou			(0403-11=)	
1853 0624	25?	$L_{100?}$	Lava flows from fissure cutting directly through village of Ahau killed 25 persons. Chief of Selusalema and 7 subjects were killed by lava flows. Estimates of fatalities range from 8 to 70-80.	{=}
1886	11?	?	None known to have been killed during eruption, but several missing. Several older men, including chiefs of rank, died of shock; total of dead and missing is 11.	{1886 0831}

MELANESIA (05)

Year M-Dy	Deaths	Agent	Remarks	{Start Date}
St. Andrew Strait			(0500-01=)	
~0350 AD	?	T	Eruption of the Rei tephra about 1600 years ago must have killed many people on the island. Tephra covered all villages.	{=}

Year M-Dy	Deaths	Agent	Remarks	{Start Date}
Bam			(0501-01=)	
1954	25	$I_{100?}$	The population of Bam was evacuated to Bogia on the mainland for 6 months. For a number of reasons, the people could not adapt to their new environment. 25 died while at Bogia and many more suffered from illness.	{1954 0803}
Manam			(0501-02=)	
1898-1900?	2	?	Taylor writes that during "the eruption of 1902," Father Aerni was informed that two natives from Bokure village were killed. 1902 was publication date of book which may pertain to events from 1898-1900 eruption.	{=}
1996 1203	13	P_{100}	Pyroclastic flows overran the village of Budua Old on the SW flank, resulting in 13 deaths. Witham lists range of 4-13 fatalities and 29 injured.	{1974 0304?}
2004 1024	5	T_{100}	Two elderly women and three children died from respiratory complications from ash inhalation.	{=}
2005 0127	1	$T_{100?}$	14 injured and one killed at Warisi village, apparently due to heavy ashfall.	{=}
2007 03	4	$M_{100?}$	Four people were killed and one injured from an "ash-and-mud avalanche" in a valley on the northern part of the island.	{=}
Karkar			(0501-03=)	
1895	21?	$I_{95?}$ $M_{5?}$	Island covered with falls of ash and lapilli. At least one person died in a mud flow. Gardens were affected and many (20?) children and old people died of starvation. It is possible that some of these deaths resulted from smallpox.	{1895 0617}
1979 0308	2	P_{100}	Two volcanologists killed by hot high-velocity directed gas-and-ejecta blast at observation camp 800 m away on caldera rim.	{1979 0112}
Long Island			(0501-05=)	
1660?	2,000?	$T_{30??}$ $P_{15??}$ $W_{5??}$ $I_{50?}$	Impossible to give accurate estimate of deaths. Legends on Long Island report deaths in pyroclastic flows and tsunamis. On Papua New Guinea mainland widespread legends report deaths as a result of house collapse and starvation.	{=}
Ritter Island			(0501-07=)	
1888 0313	3,000?	W_{100}	Hundreds of people were killed on the coasts of neighboring islands (including Umboi & New Britain) by a tsunami created by the debris avalanche. Tsunami reached 12-15 m above normal sea level. Latter believes ~3,000 killed.	{=}
Dakataua			(0502-04=)	
1895e	?	?	Eruption "some years" before 1923 killed people and destroyed property on E coast. Last known eruption was in 1890s.	{=}
Pago			(0502-08=)	
-3680	?	$T_{?}$		{=}
1914?	?	$I_{100?}$	People on NE coast ~13 km from volcano faced with starvation and perhaps died from it.	{1911}
Rabaul			(0502-14=)	
1850?	Many	$T_{100?}$	Many deaths caused by fall of huge blocks of pumice. Several other outbursts in ~12 years before 1877 report.	{=}
1878 0204	1	T_{100}	Woman supposedly killed by the first shower of stones from Tavurvur. This is the only fatality recorded, the Matupi people having fled to higher lands for safety.	{1878 0130?}
1937 0529	507	$P_{50?}$ $T_{40?}$ $W_{5?}$ $I_{5?}$	Official death toll: 505 New Guineans and 2 Europeans. Territory of Papua New Guinea medical officer at time gives 440 New Guineans killed by suffocation and/or burial with only a few dying later from exposure or shock. Subsequent investigations indicate importance of pyroclastic flows in area around Vulcan cone.	{=}
1990 0624>	6	G_{100}	An adult and two children died of suffocation in a vent on the east side of Tavurvur while hunting for wildfowl eggs. 3 friends and relatives died the following day trying to retrieve the bodies.	{No eruption}
1994 0919?	5	T_{80} E_{20}	The official death toll from the eruption and associated events was 5; four due to house roofs collapsing and one due to lightning. Witham lists range of 2-10 fatalities.	{1994 0919}
Lamington			(0503-01=)	
1951 0121	2,942	P_{100}	All killed in pyroclastic flows at N-flank villages. Of 40 survivors from inner zone of devastation who reached hospital, 22 died within 24 hours.	{1951 0117}
Victory			(0503-03=)	
1890j	Many	$P_{100?}$	Deaths reported by local people in 1880-1890 AD eruption.	{=}
Balbi			(0505-01=)	
1825?	Many	$P_{100?}$	Last major eruption occurred between 1800 and 1825 and produced nuees ardentes.	{1825q}
Bagana			(0505-02=)	
1883 1231p	Several	$T_{?}$	"Great explosion" Dec 1883 or Jan 1884 killed several people.	{=}
Savo			(0505-07=)	
1568?	>1000	P T M	Legends recall an eruption in which almost everyone on the island was killed by processes that include pyroclastic flows, ballistic impacts, and mudflows. The event was termed the "toghavitu eruption," which can be translated as either 1007 or 7000, referring to the number of fatalities. Only a few survived by escaping to neighboring islands.	{=}
1840j	100?	$P_{100?}$	Between about 1830-1850 AD, ash and stones killed many people. Petterson et al. (2003) estimated tens to hundreds of fatalities.	{1835e}
Tinakula			(0506-01=)	
1840?	Many	P_{100}	Nuees ardentes swept all sides of the island, killing all inhabitants. Heavy seas prevented escape.	{=}
Aoba			(0507-03=)	
1670?	Many	$L_{100?}$	Legend of lava flow with many fatalities about 300 years ago.	{=}
1870?	>100?	M_{100}	Lahars annihilated villages on SE flank about 1870, causing >100? fatalities.	{=}
1914	100	L_{100}	Lahars in about 1916 (some sources say 1914) caused by a possible eruption or a landslide killed 100 persons.	{=}
Ambrym			(0507-04=)	
1894 1015?	10	T_{60} L_{40}	Six persons were killed by volcanic bombs, 4 were overtaken by lava flows.	{1894 1015}
1913 1205	21	T_{100}	Several villages were destroyed; explosions destroyed the mission hospital at Dip Point, killing 21 persons.	{1913 1014}
Kuwae			(0507-07=)	
1430?	Many	$P_{100?}$	Pyroclastic-flow deposits on southern Tongoa contain human remains.	{=}
Yasur			(0507-10=)	
1994 0115e	1	T_{100}		{1774<}
1995 0204d	2	T_{100}	Two visitors on the crater rim died when they were struck by a 15 kg bomb ejected from the vent.	{1774<}

INDONESIA (06)

Year M-Dy	Deaths	Agent	Remarks	{Start Date}
Sorikmarapi			(0601-12=)	
1892 0521	180	M_{100}	Deaths at Sibangor village, 7 km NNE of summit.	{=}
Marapi			(0601-14=)	
1979 0430	80	M_{100}	About 300 mm of rainfall mobilized old lahar deposit and other volcanic material on N and E flanks. Landslides traveled as much as 20 km downslope and damaged 5 villages and farmland.	{1975 01}
1992 0705	1	T_{100}	One person was killed and 5 injured by volcanic bombs during climb to summit.	{1987 0115}
Kaba			(0601-22=)	
1833 1124	126	M_{100}	Water ejected from crater lake. Lahars killed 36 at Talang, 90 at Klingi and Bliti villages.	{=}

Year M-Dy	Deaths	Agent	Remarks	{Start Date}
Krakatau			(0602-00=)	
1883 0826>	36,417	$W_{<95}$ $P_{>5}$ $I_{<1}$	Although all recorded deaths have commonly been attributed to the devastating tsunamis, an estimated 2,000 were killed on southern Sumatra by "hot ashes" and there is clear evidence that pyroclastic flows reached that far. All 3,150 people in the path of these flows, on islands between Krakatau and Sumatra were killed; probably most by early tsunami but surely none survived the culminating eruption at 1000 on Aug 27. Various indirect causes killed a small number elsewhere. Unknown number of injured. 165 villages completely destroyed, 132 partly destroyed.	{1883 0520}
1993 0613	1	T_{100}	One tourist killed and 5 injured by an explosion while they were climbing on the old crater rim of Anak Krakatau.	{1992 1107}
Salak			(0603-05=)	
2007 0707	6	G_{100}	Six of 50 teenagers camping on the volcano died from suspected sulfur gas inhalation and several others were hospitalized.	{No eruption}
Tangkubanparahu			(0603-09=)	
1846 0527	?	?		{=}
1923 06	3	G_{100}	End of June, 3 high school boys killed by asphyxiating gas. Carbonic acid and H_2S involved.	{No eruption}
Papandayan			(0603-10=)	
1772 0812	2,957	A_{100}	Debris avalanche from collapse of NE part of mountain completely destroyed 40 villages.	{=}
1924 1218	1	G_{100}	Gas emission, believed to be H_2S, caused suffocation of a volcanological observer. Date from Jaggar.	{1923 0311}
Guntur			(0603-13=)	
1690	?	?	Fatality details unknown.	{=}
1800 1008>	Many	$M_{100?}$	The river became charged with white, acid, sulfurous mud, that poured down the valley carrying carcasses of men and sundry animals, and covered the countryside with a thick coat of mud. The same occurred with greater violence on the 12th.	{1800}
1829	Many?	?	Many killed, several wounded.	{=}
Galunggung			(0603-14=)	
1822 1008	4,011	$P_{90?}$ $M_{10?}$	114 villages destroyed. Katili & Sudrajat consider most of the fatalities to result from nuees ardentes, which extended 10 km.	{=}
1982	68?	$I_{96?}$ $T_{4?}$	Death toll estimates vary from "a few" to 72. Washington Post reported 3 killed by falling rocks. Koesman Aboeng reported 58 deaths at Tasikmalaya due to traffic accidents, old age, infant deaths, cold, ash, and lack of food. SEAN reported total of 27 fatalities as of late May (including deaths in refugee camps). Press reports 2 fatalities April 5, 8 on April 8. 22 villages rendered uninhabitable; damage estimates exceeded 15 million dollars. Witham gives range of 23-188.	{1982 0405}
Cereme			(0603-17=)	
1698	?	?	Fatality details unknown.	{1698 0203}
Dieng Volc Complex			(0603-20=)	
1786	38	$A_{100?}$	Ground fissuring occurred and 38 persons died from a collapse that destroyed Jampang village.	{=}
1826	Several	?	Fatalities "low."	{1826 1011}
1847 1204	Several	?	Fatalities "low."	{=}
1928 0513	40?	$T_{3?}$	One person was killed by a falling rock at Simbar, 750 m from the vent near Timbang. Verstappen does not specify cause of death but reports 39 people killed at Butak. The Volcanological Survey of Indonesia (VSI) plaque near Sinila crater lists 39 fatalities in 1928.	{=}
1939 1013	10	$T_{100?}$	Lahars destroyed 50 ha of land and steam explosions caused 10 deaths and damage. Verstappen reports deaths were at Timbang.	{=}
1944 1204	117	$T_{50?}$ $T_{50?}$	VSI plaque notes 117 fatalities and 250 injuries from 1944 eruption. Van Bemmelen lists 59 dead; 55 missing; 38 hurt. Coarse gray-white ashes and blocks of old volcanic material rained on 7 villages evidently all within ~1 km of vent. Blocks reached as far as Bitingan, ~1 km from vent, where 11 people were killed and 7 hurt. Ash mud here up to 20 cm thick. At Djawera 300 m N of crater 29 were killed and 19 hurt - ash mud layer 1.5-2.0 m thick. 18 killed at Kepakisan and 1 at Pagerkandang. Wounds caused by boiling hot mud.	{=}
1964 1213	114	?	VSI plaque: 114 fatalities from this eruption.	{=}
1978 late	3	I_{100}	SEAN report mentions geothermal well blowout.	{No eruption}
1979 0220	149?	G_{100}	Inhabitants of Kaputjukan, frightened by phreatic eruptions at Sinila and Sigludung Craters, fled toward Batur along trail. 149 (variously reported as 142 to 182) later found dead on the track, seeming to be asleep, in a single file as when they were walking. Killed by emission of poisonous gases from Timbang Crater; either CO_2 or CO_2 and H_2S (hydrogen sulfide).	{=}
1992 0318	1	G_{100}	One person was killed and two persons hospitalized by a gas emission on March 18, 1992 not associated with an eruption.	{No eruption}
Merapi			(0603-25=)	
1587	?	?	Fatality details unknown.	{=}
1672 0804	3,000?	$P_{100?}$	Hadikisumo, Thouret et al. give total of 3,000 fatalities, Kusumadinata 300. Only evidence of agent is that this was a major eruption producing pyroclastic flows.	{=}
1822 1227?	100?	?	100 killed, many wounded, 4 villages completely destroyed, and 4 villages partly devastated. Sapper gives death toll as 20 and indicates villages were on W side. Hadikusumo gives 16 villages destroyed.	{1822 1227}
1832 1225?	32	?	1 village completely destroyed.	{1832 1225}
1872 0415	30	T_{100}	The ejection of incandescent lapilli caused 30 fatalities and wounded many others in Selo, at the saddle between Merapi and Merbabu, burning about 50 houses.	{=}
1872 0417>	170	P_{100}	The paroxysmal phase April 17-20 produced many pyroclastic flows; 3 villages completely destroyed, 8 villages partly destroyed, many cattle killed.	{1872 0415}
1904 0130	16	P_{100}	16 killed, 45 injured & 3 small villages destroyed when pyroclastic flows swept down Woro ravine.	{1902 12}
1920 1012	35	P_{100}	Pyroclastic surge on October 12 killed 35 persons in ravine on SW flank. Most were immediately killed, but some sucumbed a few days later.	{1920 0725}
1930 1218	1,369	P_{100} M	13 villages totally and 29 partially destroyed, 1,109 houses destroyed, 2,140 cattle killed. Van Bemmelen notes that deaths were caused by nuees and the volcano observer died of burns. Thouret et al. also note lahar fatalities.	{1930 1125}
1932 02	?	m_{100}	Secondary lahars caused unknown number of fatalities.	{No eruption}
1954 0118	64	P_{100}	57 wounded, 1 village totally destroyed, 2 partly destroyed, 144 houses destroyed. Pyroclastic flows reached villages of Pentjarngisor and Pentjarduwar; 30 were killed at the time of the eruption and 34 died in hospital from burns. Witham lists range of 37-68.	{1953 0302}
1961 0508	6	P_{100}	Pyroclastic flows destroyed 8 villages totally and 2 partially; six persons killed, another 6 seriously injured.	{1961 0411}
1962 10	2	m	Secondary lahar swept through villages, killing 2 persons and injuring 5.	{No eruption}
1969 0107	1-3	$P_{100?}$	Pyroclastic flows swept as far as 13.5 km, but villages had been evacuated as a result of a seismic swarm, and only one fatality occurred (some sources list 3 fatalities).	{1967 0112}
1974 1022	9	M_{100}	There were 9 fatalities from lahars; 6 houses were damaged.	{1972 1006}
1976 1125	29	M_{100}	There were 29 fatalities from lahars in the Krasak valley on the SW flank; 306 houses were damaged.	{1972 1006}
1986 1231	1	M_{100}	Driver of stalled truck swept away by rain-induced lahar.	{1986 1010}
1994 1122	66	P_{100}	Pyroclastic flows killed 66 villagers (and an additional 100 were hospitalized in serious condition)	

Year M-Dy	Deaths	Agent	Remarks	{Start Date}
			living or working on the southwest flank, most from the two villages of Desa Purobingangun and Desa Hargobinangun. Witham lists range of 41-66 fatalities.	{1992 0120}
1997 0114	6	?	Six persons missing, several injured. Witham lists 1-6 fatalities and a date of November 17.	{1992 0120}
2000 11	1	$\mathbf{A}_{100}$	High rainfall during the second week in November caused a landslide at the source of the Boyong River near Kaliurang, causing one death.	{1992 0120}
2001 0805d	2?	$\mathbf{P}_{100}$	Unconfirmed reports from volcano guides encountered at Babadan Observatory stated that two tourists were killed by dome collapse phenomena in early August after walking into the S-flank danger zone.	{1992 0120}
2006 0614	2	$\mathbf{P}_{100}$	Two rescuers died when taking shelter in an underground bunker during a pyroclastic flow.	{2006 03}
Kelut			(0603-28=)	
1311	?	?	Only Kusumadinata (1979) lists fatalities.	{=}
1334	?	?	Fatalities occurred - number not known.	{=}
1376	?	?	Fatality details unknown.	{=}
1385	?	?	Fatalities occurred - number not known.	{=}
1586	10,000?	?	10,000 reported killed, cause not known. Original accounts describe violent eruption of "flaming sulfur," ejection of large stones into a city, and large amounts of ash that obscured the sun for 3 days.	{=}
1716 0720	?	$\mathbf{M}_{?}$	Fatalities occurred - number not known.	{=}
1826 1013	?	$\mathbf{M}_{?}$	Unknown number killed, 65 villages destroyed Kusumadinata (1979) gives this as 65 wounded.	{1826 1011}
1848 0516	22	$\mathbf{M}_{?}$	22 killed, 11 villages, & 800 houses destroyed.	{=}
1864 0104	54	$\mathbf{M}_{100}$	Death toll from Natuurkundig Tijdschrift voor Nederlendisch-Indie. Kusumadinata (1979) gives many killed, hundreds of houses destroyed, many cattle killed (& 0103 date).	{=}
1875 0129	?	**m**	Failure of W crater wall freed lakewater producing lahar that killed an unknown number and destroyed 30 villages. Kusumadinata (1979) gives this as 30 wounded.	{No eruption}
1901 0522	Many?	?		{=}
1919 0519	5,110	$\mathbf{M}_{100?}$	5,110 killed, 9,000 houses destroyed, 104 villages destroyed. Pyroclastic flows were produced but inference is that deaths resulted from lahars. VL and some other sources give death total as 5,500. Kusumadinata (1979) gives 0519-20 date.	{=}
1951 0831	7?	?	Volcano observer & 2 assistants killed at the crater observatory along with 4 bamboo cutters within the devastated zone.	{=}
1966 0426	215	$\mathbf{M}_{98}\,\mathbf{m}_{2}\,\mathbf{P}$	Main lahar entered R Badak attaining maximum height of 25 m and maximum distance of 31 km in SW direction. Initial reports listed 208 killed, 78 missing, 86 wounded; later official reports list 211 primary lahar, 3 secondary lahar, and 1 pyroclastic flow fatality. Other sources give death tolls ranging from 210 to 288.	{=}
1990 0210	35	$\mathbf{T}_{80?}\,\mathbf{P}_{20?}$	30 deaths on 10 Feb with most of the damage and casualties attributed to heavy tephra falls causing house roofs to collapse. By 20 Feb official death toll had risen to 32, and VSI internal reports listed a total of 35 fatalities.	{=}
1990 1125	4	$\mathbf{m}_{100}$	Lahars killed 4 about 30 km S of the volcano.	{No eruption}
1998 07	10	$\mathbf{m}_{100}$		{No eruption}
Semeru			(0603-30=)	
1885 0418	74	$\mathbf{A}_{100}$	A debris avalanche covering 6.7 km^2 buried the Kali Bening estate with 4 administrators and some 70 Madurese workers and family members early in the morning. Another estimate lists 70-85 fatalities.	{1884 1210}
1895	80?	$\mathbf{M}_{100?}$	80(?) fatalities, presumably from lahars; devastated arable land.	{1895 0522}
1909 0829	221	$\mathbf{m}_{100}$	Major, & fatal lahar was not attributed to eruptive activity, although ash & block eruptions and pyroclastic flows caused damage from Sept through Dec.	{1909 09}
1946 0507	6	**F**	Heavy rains caused floods in valleys below Semeru. Kusumadinata (1979) gives 0304-30 dates - 6 killed, 81 houses destroyed, 8 ha rice, 1000 ha arable land destroyed (& agents T? M?).	{1946 02}
1968 0308	5	$\mathbf{M}_{100}$	3 killed by mudflows, 10 ha arable land destroyed, 1,000 evacuated.	{1967 0831}
1976 1113	133	$\mathbf{M}_{100}$	BVE gives only 40 deaths, & Nov 11 date; Siswowidjoyo et al. (1995) listed 119 fatalities, Thouret et al. (2007) 133 fatalities.	{1967 0831}
1978 0919	12	$\mathbf{M}_{100}$		{1967 0831}
1981 0329	1	$\mathbf{P}_{100}$	One person killed during series of pyroclastic flows down S flank.	{1967 0831}
1981 0514	372?	$\mathbf{m}_{100}$	Secondary lahar due to heavy rainfall dislodged pyroclastic debris down Tunggeng and Sat rivers, killing 252 plus 120 missing, and injuring 152. Siswowidjoyo listed 275 fatalities, Witham a range of 192-378.	{1967 0831}
1985 0510?	70?	$\mathbf{A}_{100?}$	About 70 fatalities near Pronojiwo	{1967 0831}
1988 0730	1	$\mathbf{T}_{100}$	Climber killed by ballistic block at summit.	{1967 0831}
1992	3	$\mathbf{T}_{100}$	Three killed in vent area.	{1967 0831}
1994 0203	6	$\mathbf{P}_{100}$	Pyroclastic flows reached Sumbersari village, killing 4 and injuring 3, of whom 2 later died.	{1967 0831}
1997 0902	2	$\mathbf{T}_{100}$	Two climbers were killed by ballistic ejecta near the summit crater.	{1967 0831}
2000 0727	2	$\mathbf{T}_{100}$	Two volcanologists were killed and 5 others injured by ballistic ejecta near the summit crater.	{1967 0831}
2002	3	$\mathbf{T}_{100}$	Three filmmakers were killed at the summit at a time it was closed to access.	{1967 0831}
Tengger Caldera			(0603-31=)	
2004 0608	2	$\mathbf{T}_{100}$	Two tourists were killed and 5 injured by ejecta from a sudden explosive eruption at Bromo crater.	{=}
Lamongan			(0603-32=)	
1843 1005	4	?		{1843 08}
1869 0912	8	$\mathbf{T}_{?}\,\mathbf{A}_{?}$	Ashfall and volcanic bombs killed 8, Neumann van Padang cites rock avalanches.	{=}
Raung			(0603-34=)	
1593	?	?	A major reported eruption of Raung in 1586 that produced 10,000 fatalities is thought to have occurred in 1593, and the 10,000 fatalities in 1586 to have been from Kelut volcano.	{=}
1597 0117?	?	$\mathbf{T}_{?}$		{1597 0117}
1638	>1,000	$\mathbf{M}_{100}$	Great flood and lahar between Stail and Klatak Rivers caused thousands of fatalities.	{=}
1730	>100?	$\mathbf{M}_{60??}\,\mathbf{T}_{40??}$	Explosive eruption with lahars caused damage and >100? fatalities.	{=}
1817	?	?	Fatality details unknown.	{1817 0116}
Ijen			(0603-35=)	
1817 01	Many	$\mathbf{M}_{100?}$	CAVW mentions casualties but provides no further information. Kusumadinata (1979) mentions 3 villages completely destroyed, 90 houses destroyed ,and about 400 cattle killed, but gives no human fatalities. Neall notes many casualties from lahars produced by collapse of crater lake.	{1817 0115e}
Batur			(0604-01=)	
1963 09	2?	?	2 reported killed, 3 villages partly destroyed, 18 houses destroyed, 1,600 ha arable land destroyed. VSI says there were no fatalities from this eruption.	{1963 0905}
Agung			(0604-02=)	
1963 0317>	1,148	$\mathbf{P}_{71}\,\mathbf{T}_{14}\,\mathbf{M}_{14}\,\mathbf{A}_{1?}$	Surjo gives: 820 killed, 59 injured by pyroclastic flows, 163 and 201 by pyroclastic fall, 165 and 36 by lahars. Bodies of about half victims never found. Perhaps 140 killed at Subagan village by lahar plus others swept to sea and killed crossing lahar fields during rainy season. Also, 8 killed by landslides on Batur caldera rim. 1,148 represents most recent official figure, presumably including 120 pyroclastic flow fatalities on May 16. Perhaps 200 of the lahar deaths occurred after the eruption. Keesings suggests 1,584 killed in the March eruption and 106 in the May eruption.	{1963 0218}

Year M-Dy	Deaths	Agent	Remarks	{Start Date}
Rinjani			(0604-03=)	
1994 1103	31	$\mathbf{m}_{100}$	A cold lahar from the summit area killed 30 residents of the village of Aikmel who were collecting water from the Kokok Jenggak River. One other person remained missing on November 9.	{1994 0603}
Tambora			(0604-04=)	
1815 0410	11,000?	$\mathbf{P}_{90?}$ $\mathbf{A}_{5?}$ $\mathbf{W}_{5}$	Approximately 11,000 direct deaths from bomb impacts, tephra falls, and tsunamis; recent work indicates pyroclastic flows reached all but W coast and probably caused most direct fatalities on Sumbawa.	{1812}
Indirect	49,000?	$\mathbf{I}_{100}$	An estimated 49,000 persons died of famine and disease on Sumbawa and Lombok islands following the eruption. This replaces an earlier estimate of 82,000.	{1812}
Iya			(0604-11=)	
1969 0127	2	$\mathbf{T}_{50}$ $\mathbf{m}_{50}$	2 killed, 10 wounded, 1 village totally and 7 partly destroyed, 287 houses destroyed. VSI report houses were damaged on the island of Ende and one person was killed. Secondary lahars later caused another fatality.	{=}
Kelimutu			(0604-14=)	
1995 0515	1	?	Tourist fell into crater lake.	{No eruption}
Paluweh			(0604-15=)	
1928 0804	226	$\mathbf{W}_{70?}$ $\mathbf{T}_{30?}$	Tsunami generated by a large landslide at two places on S and E coast of island during explosive eruption during night of Aug 4-5 killed 128 out of total 226 who perished. Latter says tsunami, consisting of 3 waves of 5-10 m in height, killed at least 160 people. 200 injured & 5 villages totally destroyed.	{=}
1964 0101	1	?	1 killed, 3 wounded.	{1963 1231}
Egon			(0604-16=)	
2004 0129	1	$\mathbf{T}_{100}$	One person was killed by smoke and ash inhalation; another fatality from unknown causes may have occurred.	{=}
Lewotobi			(0604-18=)	
1869 0727	2	?		{1869 0707}
1907 1016?	1	?	1 killed, several wounded.	{1907 0928}
Iliwerung			(0604-25=)	
1870	?	?	Fatality details unknown.	{=}
1948 0407	?	?	Van Bemmelen mentions no human deaths but notes nuees down E coast killed 300 cattle & destroyed 100 gardens.	{=}
1973 12?	2	$\mathbf{W}_{100}$	A tsunami 50 m high generated by submarine activity swept away 2 fishermen.	{1973 1205}
1979 0718	539?	$\mathbf{W}_{100}$	Massive landslide 7 km N of Iliwerung caused tsunami up to 9 m high, and devastated 4 villages. Death toll on Lomblen Island listed as 539 (175 bodies recovered and 364 missing).	{No eruption}
1983 0817	?	$\mathbf{W}_{100?}$	Some people disappeared because of tsunami associated with submarine eruption.	{=}
Sirung			(0604-27=)	
1953 06	5	?	5 killed, 1 injured.	{=}
Wurlali			(0605-04=)	
1993 0121	1	$\mathbf{m}_{100?}$	One killed and 12 injured by debris flow or avalanche.	{No eruption}
Teon			(0605-05=)	
1660 02	3	$\mathbf{G}_{?}$ $\mathbf{T}_{?}$	2 or 3 choked and died.	{=}
Serua			(0605-07=)	
1693 0604	Many?	$\mathbf{L}_{100?}$	Many killed at Hislo on W part of the island by a stream of "burning brimstone."	{=}
Banda Api			(0605-09=)	
1598-1602?	?	?	Fatality details unknown.	{=}
1615	?	?	Sapper notes all settlements destroyed.	{1615 0316}
1694 1130?	Many?	?	The whole population at the foot of the volcano was destroyed. Neumann van Padang reports an enormous outburst on this day destroyed vegetation on the island. Some sources do not list fatalities.	{1690}
1820	?	?	Kusumadinata (1979): unknown number killed.	{1820 0611}
1988 0509	4	**T L**	A lava flow overran the mosque in Batu Angus village, killing an elderly man who had sought refuge rather than flee with the evacuees. Two young men drowned when their canoe was hit by a block. SEAN gives 3 killed.	{=}
Lokon-Empung			(0606-10=)	
1750-1800?	?	?	Fatality details unknown.	{1775}
1991 1024	1	$\mathbf{T}_{?}$ $\mathbf{P}_{?}$	An amateur Swiss volcanologist was killed while observing the eruption.	{1991 0517}
Mahawu			(0606-11=)	
1958 0712	1	$\mathbf{M}_{100?}$	1 killed by hot mud, 10 injured.	{=}
Ruang			(0607-01=)	
1870 0827	?	?	Unknown number of deaths, 1 village completely destroyed, 40 houses destroyed.	{=}
1871 0303	400?	**W**	300-400 killed, 1 village completely destroyed, 75 houses destroyed at Bahhuas on Tagulandang Island by tsunami associated with partial collapse of lava dome.	{1871 0302}
Karangetang [Api Siau]			(0607-02=)	
1940 0823?	1	?	1 killed, 2 wounded. Date is variably given as Aug 23 or March in same source.	{1940 0620}
1974 0427	4	$\mathbf{A}_{100}$	Earthquakes caused landslides.	{1972 01}
1976 1015	1	$\mathbf{P}_{100}$	1 killed and 1 injured by small pyroclastic flow from collapse of lava flow front when evacuees returned at night to witness incandescent lava. 24 houses destroyed by lava. Witham lists September 19 date.	{1976 0915}
1992 0121	2?	$\mathbf{M}_{100}$		{1991 0702<}
1992 0511	6	$\mathbf{P}_{100}$	7 farmers were burned by pyroclastic flows from collapsing lava flow front; 6 later died in hospitals.	{1991 0702<}
1997 0608	3	$\mathbf{P}_{100}$	Three persons were killed as a result of pyroclastic flows on June 8, 1997.	{1996 1001<}
Awu			(0607-04=)	
1711 1211	~3,000	$\mathbf{P}_{100?}$	About 3,000 killed. Sapper gives death toll as about 2030. Pyroclastic flows before morning of Dec 12 took around 3,000 lives, 2,030 of which were in the Kendhar area, 408 from Taruna, 70 from Kolongan, and the remainder from Talawid and Motane.	{1711 1210}
1812 0806?	~953	$\mathbf{P}_{75??}$ $\mathbf{M}_{25??}$	From the number of fatalities and the amount of damage it can be concluded that the eruption also included lahars and glowing clouds. Sapper gives death toll as 953. Kusumadinata (1979) gives toll as hundreds killed, 3 wounded.	{1812 0806}
1856 0302>	2,806	$\mathbf{P}_{100?}$	8 villages partly destroyed.	{=}
1892 0607	1,532	$\mathbf{P}_{75??}$ $\mathbf{M}_{25??}$	Fatalities all on N coast attributed to pyroclastic flows and lahars; 10-12 villages totally destroyed. Sapper gives death toll as 1,000-1,500.	{=}
1966 0812	39	$\mathbf{P}_{72??}$ $\mathbf{M}_{25??}$ $\mathbf{I}_{3}$	38 killed by pyroclastic flows and lahars, one person drowned while swimming to ship. Only 1 body was found, most were covered with rocks and hot pumice flows. 1,000 were injured by the impact of ejected fragments from the lava plug. 2 villages totally destroyed, 3 partly destroyed. Witham lists range of 39-88.	{=}
Dukono			(0608-01=)	
1550	?	?	Fatality details unknown.	{1550 1120}
Gamkonora			(0608-04=)	
1564?	?	?	1564 or 1565	{1564 1231y}
1673 0520	Many?	$\mathbf{W}_{100}$	Tsunami inundated villages.	{=}
Gamalama			(0608-06=)	
1772 0509	35	$\mathbf{T}_{100?}$	30-40 slaves working at NW foot of the volcano were killed by glowing ash and rock.	{1771 0828}
1773 1025	Several	$\mathbf{I}_{?}$	Drownings on overloaded boats fleeing eruption.	{1773 1021}
1775	1,300?	$\mathbf{P}_{100?}$ $\mathbf{I}_{?}$	Maar-forming eruption on N coast, with widespread base surge deposition killing 141. Some drowned while escaping by boat. Bronto et al. give 1,300 fatalities.	{1775 0820}
1838 0226	4	$\mathbf{T}_{100}$	Javanese sulfur collectors killed in crater.	{=}

Year M-Dy	Deaths	Agent	Remarks	{Start Date}
1871 0907	1	T_{100}	1 killed & another injured by block ejection.	{1871 0807}
1962 1231	5	?	5 dead, 5 wounded.	{=}

Makian (0608-07=)

Year M-Dy	Deaths	Agent	Remarks	{Start Date}
1646 0719?	Many	?	Many died. Not listed in Kusumadinata (1979). VSI comments that major explosive eruption devastated villages on flanks.	{1646 0719}
1760	~2,000	$M_{100?}$	Major explosive eruption. IAVCEI attributes deaths to a lahar.	{1760 0922}
1861 1229	326	$P_{100?}$ $I_{0?}$	326 deaths, 47 injuries. Ashflows reached the coast. Some drowned while fleeing by boat. Kusumadinata (1979) gives 309 killed and 15 villages totally destroyed. Wallace also mentions this eruption but places it on the same day in 1862.	{1861 1228}
1890 0629	?	?	Kusumadinata (1979) makes no mention of human fatalities but records several villages destroyed completely, many houses destroyed, many cattle killed.	{1890 0620}

PHILIPPINES (07)

Parker (0701-011)

Year M-Dy	Deaths	Agent	Remarks	{Start Date}
1995 0906	<100	?	Nearly 100 persons killed by flood from breach of caldera wall either due to natural causes or man-made blasting; 300 homes were destroyed and 50,000 persons displaced.	{No eruption}

Ragang (0701-06=)

Year M-Dy	Deaths	Agent	Remarks	{Start Date}
1873	?	?		{1873 0116}

Camiguin (0701-08=)

Year M-Dy	Deaths	Agent	Remarks	{Start Date}
1870 0430	Some?	?	One account says nearby townspeople fled during premonitory quake activity, so there were very few victims even though destruction reached Cartaman. Another says very considerable number of victims.	{=}
1949 06	2	$P_{100?}$	Witham lists 2 fatalities, possibly from pyroclastic flows.	{1948 0901}
1950 0915	68	P_{100}	Macdonald and Alcaraz note only several killed (Time 12/17/51, p36 gives 68) by pyroclastic flow and that clothing was not burned. Witham lists range of 66-84 fatalities.	{1948 0901}
1951 1204	>500?	P_{100}	Time (see above) gives 500 killed, 266 bodies found and maybe 1,500 unaccounted for. Alcaraz gives 500 killed, & 3 more on 12/06.	{1948 0901}
1954 early	2	m_{100}	2 killed by mudflows caused by typhoon rains.	{1948 0901}

Kanlaon (0702-02=)

Year M-Dy	Deaths	Agent	Remarks	{Start Date}
1996 0810	3	T_{100}	Three members of a large climbing group at the summit of Canlaon were killed during a brief explosive eruption on August 10. Eighteen other members were hospitalized because of injuries from falling ejecta.	{=}

Bulusan (0703-01=)

Year M-Dy	Deaths	Agent	Remarks	{Start Date}
2006 0610	1	T_{100}	One person died from asthma condition aggravated by exposure to ash.	{2006 0321}

Mayon (0703-03=)

Year M-Dy	Deaths	Agent	Remarks	{Start Date}
1766 1023	49	m_{100}	Deaths caused by mudflows from typhoon rains some months after July eruption. 30 deaths in Malinao, 16 in Albay. Death total 49 from Ramos-Vallarta.	{1766 0720}
1800 10	?	?		{1800 1030}
1814 0201	1,200	$P_{90?}$ $M_{10?}$ $E_{?}$	COMVOL regarded most deaths as due to lahars but more recent work at Casagua suggests pyroclastic flows were dominant cause of fatalities. Town of Budiao destroyed; town of Camalig also destroyed and burned; towns of Albay, Guinobatan and Balusan partly destroyed. Some deaths from electrical discharges.	{=}
1853 0713	34?	P_{100}	33 fatalities (Sapper, Faustino) or 35 (Saderra Maso). Deaths caused by incandescent rocks rolling down from the summit, destroying many houses and their occupants (Faustino).	{=}
1858	?	$P_{?}$	Incandescent materials rolled downslope, destroying forests and plantations. Cause of fatalities not stated.	{1858 01}
1871 1208	3	P_{100}	Deaths by nuees ardentes. In the "vista" of Boctong, two persons were suffocated and in Buyuhan, one was burned.	{=}
1875	~1,500	m_{100}	Deaths due to rain-triggered lahars. Not in eruption since July 1873.	{1873 0620}
1887 0309	15	T_{100}	20-hour ash eruption at end of 9-month eruption deposited 8 cm of ash on roofs in Guinobatan and Libog. Collapse of roofs killed 15.	{1886 0708}
1897 0625	350	$P_{90?}$ $T_{10?}$ $M_{1?}$	Large nuees burned victims or they suffocated by ash. 350 total from Maso & Sapper. Other estimates vary 250-400. 1 death at Bulwan R caused by lahar. Latter indicates 400 deaths in town of Libog. All but 56 of the 261 dead died during event - the rest during the following week.	{1897 0523}
1928 0625>	>1	P_{100}	Pyroclastic flows between June 25 and Aug 7 killed at least one (Ramos-Villarta).	{1928 01}
1938	?	?	Fatality details unknown.	{1938 0605}
1947	?	?	Fatality details unknown.	{1947 0107}
1968	6?	$M_{80?}$ $P_{20?}$	One death by lahar in Aug or Oct, the others during the eruption. One man who was caught in a blast of hot gas died of burns to his whole body. BVE lists mudflows in SE sector; probably 3 killed.	{1968 0421}
1981 0630	>200	m_{100}	At least 200 fatalities caused by lahars initiated by typhoon. BVE gives 40 confirmed dead and 7 missing.	{No eruption}
1984	1	M_{100}	1 killed by lahar. Other reports say only that unsanitary conditions led to deaths of children in evacuation centers.	{1984 0909}
1993 0202	77	P_{100}	77 killed and 100 injured by a pyroclastic flow on the SE flank; most were farmers tending crops within the 6-km-wide permanent danger zone. Witham listed range of 70-79 fatalities.	{=}
2006 1130	1,266	m_{100}	1,266 persons were dead or missing from post-eruptive lahars down the slopes of Mayon produced during a November 30 typhoon.	{2006 0713}

Taal (0703-07=)

Year M-Dy	Deaths	Agent	Remarks	{Start Date}
1716	?	?	Fatality details unknown.	{1716 0924}
1749	?	?	CAVW lists possible fatalities. Arboleda et al. note casualties mentioned but it is not clear that these are deaths. Maso believes there were no deaths.	{1749 0811}
1754 1128	12	$W_{50?}$ $T_{50?}$	12 villagers killed at Taal village, some by tsunami and others by collapsing houses. As Saderra Maso refers to 4 villages around lake being completely destroyed, these fatalities may refer only to those in Taal village. Permanent abandonment of several villages on lake shore.	{1754 0515}
1874 0719	?	?	Fatality details unknown.	{=}
1911 0130	>1,335	$P_{80?}$ $W_{20?}$	~1,335 killed chiefly by pyroclastic flows. Only 732 bodies found. 12 or 13 on island survived but all badly injured. Heiser, medical officer in area at time, estimates deaths at about 2,000.	{1911 0127}
1965 0928	>250	$P_{60?}$ $W_{40?}$	Estimates range 150 to 355 including those drowned and several murdered. Witham lists range of 190-355. Many of the fatalities occurred when tsunami capsized boats filled with fleeing residents. Newspaper and other reports suggesting 3,000-5,000 deaths are very unreliable.	{=}

Pinatubo (0703-083)

Year M-Dy	Deaths	Agent	Remarks	{Start Date}
1991 0615	350?	P_{70} m_{30}	4 were killed and 4 injured prior to the catastrophic June 15-16 eruptions that killed several hundred. By Aug 20, mudflows had killed more than 100.	{1991 0402}
1991 0615>	450?	I_{100}	Disease at evacuation camps had (by Sept 20) brought the total fatalities to about 800.	{1991 0402}
1992 0712	6?	m_{100}	Secondary lahars from 1991 deposits killed 2 on July 12, 1992. Total fatalities during the 1992 rainy season were reported by one source to be 60, but the official figure was listed as 6.	{1992 0709}
1993 0626	4	m_{100}		{1993 02}
1993 1004	14	m_{100}		{1993 02}

Ambalatungan Group (0703-088)

Year M-Dy	Deaths	Agent	Remarks	{Start Date}
1952	12	$M_{100?}$	May have been a steam eruption because sulfur melted and flowed downhill, mixing with debris and killing about a dozen people.	{=}

Year M-Dy	Deaths	Agent	Remarks	{Start Date}
Didicas			(0704-02=)	
1969 0326	3	W_{100}	3 drowned while fishing: tsunami generated by a submarine explosion at Didicas, 70 km away.	{1969 0321}
Tengchong			(0705-11-)	
1609	?	E_{100}	Some shepherds and 500-600 sheep were struck by lightning.	{=}

JAPAN (08)

Year M-Dy	Deaths	Agent	Remarks	{Start Date}
Iwo-Tori-shima			(0802-02=)	
1664	1	A	Landslide swept over a village, killing a woman.	{=}
Kuchinoerabu-jima			(0802-05=)	
1841 0801	?	$T_{?}$	JMA reports large explosion devastating villages at volcano's foot.	{1841 0523}
1933 1224	8	T_{100}	An explosion ejected tephra to the SSE, killing 8 and injuring 26. Nanakama village, 1.5 km from the crater was burned by fire from glowing blocks. CAVW gives date as 12/23.	{1933 1223}
Kikai			(0802-06=)	
~4350 BC	?	?	Major ash eruption & pyroclastic flows, from Japan's largest Holocene eruption, devastated S Kyushu. Fatalities likely large, but not estimated. S Kyushu not resettled for 300-800 years.	{=}
Sakura-jima			(0802-08=)	
0764 01	80	$T_{?}$ $L_{?}$	Deaths possibly by phreatomagmatic eruption or lava flow.	{=}
0766	Many	?		{0766 0720}
1471+1476	Many	$P_{?}$	Sakurajima's largest historical eruption caused fatalities in its first and last years. Deaths possibly resulted from pyroclastic flows.	{1471 1103}
1779 1109	153	$T_{70??}$ $W_{28??}$ $I_{2??}$	Official report dated 1780 0115 gives 79 men, 74 women killed. Kamo attributes deaths to tsunami, lava and burial of villages by tephra. One person drowned while attempting to cross the Seto Channel which was filled with pumice. Inscription on stone monument erected in 1779 notes 148 killed and gives villages. Sapper gives 140 killed and notes that some sources say 16-17,000! Koto notes 141 killed + 1,576 horses, 135 oxen, and that some sources report 9,600 humans killed.	{1779 1108}
1780 0209	Many	F_{100}	Water gushed out from the summit and many people drowned. This account, by Milne, does not appear in other sources, and may be suspect.	{1779 1108}
1781 0411	38?	W_{100}	Tsunami upset 3 boats, drowning 14 men and 1 woman. Koto reports 23 sightseers killed in 1781 by paroxysmal outburst.	{1779 1108}
1914 0112	63?	$I_{37?}$ $S_{34?}$ $A_{19?}$ $T_{10?}$	Half or more of the deaths resulted from collapse of stone walls and cliffs, mainly in Kagoshima during the earthquake. Few (6?) deaths on island because of effective evacuation; another 12 buried in landslide that was probably earthquake-induced. Uncertain number were killed in building collapses during earthquake. Two people buried by pumice at Fumato. 23 drowned attempting to swim from island. Other estimates of deaths range 23 to 140. Injuries probably totalled 121 but estimates range from 87 to 127.	{=}
1946	1	?		{1946 01}
1955 1013	1	?		{=}
1974 0617	3	M_{100}	Rain-induced mudflows killed 3.	{1955 1013}
1974 0809	5	M_{100}	Rain-induced mudflows killed 5.	{1955 1013}
Kirishima			(0802-09=)	
1566 1031	Many	?	JMA mentions fatalities, Murayama says many.	{=}
1716 1109	1	?	1 dead and 31 injured. One source lists 6 fatalities for the 1716-1717 eruption.	{=}
1717 0207	1	?	1 killed and 30 injured.	{1716 1109}
1895 1016>	4	T_{100}		{1895 0716}
1896 0315	1	$T?_{100}$	One climber killed and another injured.	{1895 0716}
1900 0216	2	?	2 killed, 3 injured.	{1899 0728}
1923 07	1	?		{=}
1989 0826	2	G_{100}		{No eruption}
Unzen			(0802-10=)	
1664 0415q	>30	m_{100}	In the spring of 1664 water poured out of Tsukumo-jima pond at the summit of Fugen-dake, producing floods that killed >30 in the Mizunashi river valley.	{1663 1211}
1792 0521	14,524	$W_{95?}$ $A_{5?}$	Figures from Katayama indicate 9,528 fatalities along the Shimabara peninsula and an additional 4,996 fatalities in Higo and Amakusa provinces across Ariake Sea. The vast majority were killed by the tsunami, the avalanche reaching only the southern outskirts of Shimabara city.	{1792 0210}
1957 07	13	m_{100}	Heavy rains produced debris flows on the NW flank of Mayu-yama; 13 dead or missing.	{No eruption}
1991 0603	43	P_{100}	A pyroclastic flow and surge killed 43, including 3 volcanologists.	{1990 1117}
1993 0623	1	P_{100}	A homeowner who had entered the evacuation zone to watch his house being burned by a pyroclastic flow was killed by a second pyroclastic flow.	{1990 1117}
Aso			(0802-11=)	
1331+	?	?	Milne says all the people of Hojo were destroyed in 19-month eruption, but other compilers list no fatalities.	{1331 12}
1485 01	1	?		{1485 0105}
1816 0705	1	T_{100}		{1816 0609}
1827 1127	Many	$T_{100?}$	Sapper states that many people who had come to pray 2,200 m S of the crater lake died from ash suffocation. Fatalities are not mentioned in Japanese compilations.	{1827 1112}
1854 0226	3	?	Sapper mentions thunder, earthquakes, and eruption of muddy water but cause of deaths not known. These were 3 pilgrims who came to crater to pray.	{=}
1872 1201	4	T?	4 sulfur miners in crater killed by explosion.	{=}
1953 0427	6	T_{100}	6 tourists killed near crater rim. Witham lists range of 5-11 fatalities.	{=}
1958 0624	12	T_{100}	12 ropeway workers killed, 20 (JMA says 28) injured by nighttime explosion. Witham lists 5-11 fatalities	{1957 10}
1979 0906	3	T_{100}	Block ejection killed 3 tourists & injured 11, near ropeway station ~850 m NNE of crater.	{1979 02}
1989 0212	1	G_{100}	A tourist died from gas inhalation.	{No eruption}
1990 0326	1	G_{100}	A tourist died from gas inhalation.	{1989 0405}
1990 0418	1	G_{100}	A tourist died from gas inhalation.	{1989 0405}
1990 1019	1	G_{100}	A tourist died from gas inhalation.	{1989 0405}
1994 0529	1	G_{100}	A tourist died from gas inhalation.	{1994 0502}
1997 1123	2	G_{100}	Two men were killed by gas inhalation about 100 m south of the rim of crater #1 on November 23, 1997. No eruptive activity occurred.	{No eruption}
Hakone			(0803-02=)	
1933 0510	1	$G_{100?}$	One killed during fumarolic activity.	{No eruption}
1951 1105	2	G_{100}		{No eruption}
1952 0327	1	G_{100}		{No eruption}
1953 0726	10	A_{100}	Landslide killed 10.	{No eruption}
1972 1002	2	?		{No eruption}
On-take			(0803-04=)	
1984 0914	29	A_{100}	An earthquake caused the S flank of the volcano to collapse, creating a debris avalanche which killed 10 people in a hot spa. Some deaths may be from other landslides caused by quake. First historical eruption ended in April 1980, after 6 months.	{No eruption}
Yake-dake			(0803-07=)	
1995 0211	4	T_{100}	Four persons killed at highway construction site by hydrothermal explosions.	{=}
Tate-yama			(0803-08=)	
1858 0423	Many	m_{100}	Mudflows following earthquake-generated landslide killed many; eruption uncertain	{No eruption}

Year M-Dy	Deaths	Agent	Remarks	{Start Date}
1858 0703	Many	m_{100}	Mudflows following earthquake-generated landslide killed many; no eruption	{No eruption}
1954 0721	1	G_{100}		{No eruption}
1961 0423	1	G_{100}		{No eruption}
1967 1104	2	?		{No eruption}
1970 0430	1	?		{No eruption}
1972 1125	1	?		{No eruption}
1975 0812	1	?		{No eruption}
1985 0722	1	?		{No eruption}
Niigata-Yake-yama			(0803-09=)	
1974 0728	3	T_{100}	Mountain climbing students of Chiba University killed by ejecta while camped near fissure crater.	{=}
Asama			(0803-11=)	
1596 0501	Many	T_{100}	Many killed by tephra on May 1. One source also lists many fatalities for 8/19 eruption of same year.	{=}
1598 0513	800?	T_{100}	Religious pilgrims who had climbed the volcano were killed at the summit (where they were staying because it was not a religiously auspicious day to descend). Hayakawa and Nakajima (1998) question this report.	{=}
1721 0622	15	T_{100}	Fifteen climbers killed, some sources say 5.	{=}
1783 0805	1,491	$F_{70?}$ $P_{30?}$ I?	466 killed by Kamabara pyroclastic flow. 93 people who were able to climb up steps of small temple survived. Hot mudflows from the Kamabara nuee flowed into the Agatsuma R, causing a temporary dam. Flood downstream over a distance of 100 km washed away 1,300 houses and up to 1,400 people. Suspended ash and dust decreased sunlight, and resulting cold and rainy weather caused a famine in the Kanto region. Approximately 300,000 people died in northern Japan from the Tenmei famine, which lasted from 1783-1787. Some estimates suggest up to 1 million deaths, then about 3% of Japan's population, but the eruption is considered only a contributing factor.	{1783 0509}
1803 0704/1107	?	?	CAVW lists fatalities but does not specify which 1803 eruption. JMA (1975) and Murayama mention no fatalities for either.	{1803 0704}
1911 0508	1	T_{100}	1 climber killed & ~60 houses destroyed.	{1909 0129}
1911 0815	>2	T_{100}	Two or more climbers killed and 36 injured.	{1909 0129}
1913 0529	1	T_{100}	One climber killed and another injured.	{1909 0129}
1930 0820	6	T_{100}	6 killed by projectiles near crater rim.	{1930 0418}
1931 0820	3?	?		{1931 03}
1936 0729>	2	$P_{50?}$ $T_{50?}$	Single climbers killed on 7/29 & 10/29: the first possibly by small pyroclastic flow.	{1934 1113}
1938 0716	Few	T_{100}	There were a few fatalities on July 16, 1938.	{1938 0325}
1941 0713	1	$T_{100?}$	Death (& 1 injury) assumed to be from ballistics because of number of explosions. Near end of >4-year eruption.	{1938 0325}
1947 0814	11	?	Eleven persons climbing volcano were killed.	{1947 06}
1950 0923	1	T_{100}	One climber killed, one injured from lithic ejecta. Air shock damaged houses.	{=}
1961 0818	1	$T_{100?}$	A climber at the summit at the time of an eruption was killed.	{=}
Kusatsu-Shirane			(0803-12=)	
1932 1001	2	$M_{100?}$	2 killed, 7 injured in lahar generated by eruption while 20 were mining native sulfur from the crater lake bottom.	{=}
1971 1227	6	G_{100}	Six skiers were killed by hydrogen sulfide inhalation.	{No eruption}
1976 0803	3	G_{100}	Three school trip hikers were killed by hydrogen sulfide inhalation.	{No eruption}
Akagi			(0803-13=)	
1947 0916	699	m_{100}	A non-eruptive lahar due to a typhoon caused 699 fatalities, mostly on the Aratogawa river, originating from the summit crater of Akagi.	{No eruption}

Year M-Dy	Deaths	Agent	Remarks	{Start Date}
Nasu			(0803-15=)	
1410 0305	180	?	180 persons and many cattle killed.	{=}
1919 0706	2	G_{100}		{No eruption}
1921 1126	1?	G_{100}		{No eruption}
Bandai			(0803-16=)	
1888 0715	461	$A_{80??}$ $P_{20??}$	Debris avalanche buried several villages. Only ~116 bodies recovered; 70 injured, mostly burned and scarred by pyroclastic surge.	{=}
1938 0509	2	m_{100}	Secondary lahars on May 9 and 15 caused two fatalities	{No eruption}
Adatara			(0803-17=)	
1900 0717	72	T_{100}	72 sulfur miners in crater killed, 10 injured in explosive eruption.	{=}
1997 0915	4	G_{100}	Four hikers died from inhalation of volcanic gases after being exposed to fumes on the floor of Numano-taira crater on September 15, 1997, a year after the last eruption of Adatara. The hikers were part of a group of 14 who became disoriented in foggy conditions and departed from a trail where warning signs were posted.	{No eruption}
Azuma			(0803-18=)	
1893 0607	2	T_{100}	2 geologists were killed on the crater rim by falling stones.	{1893 0519}
Zao			(0803-19=)	
1867 1021	3	M_{100}	Overflow of muddy water from Okama crater lake killed 3 hot springs bathers at E foot of Goshiki-dake.	{=}
Narugo			(0803-20=)	
1969 0826	1	G_{100}		{No eruption}
Chokai			(0803-22=)	
1801 0814	8	T_{100}	Climbers killed by volcanic ejecta.	{1800 12}
Akita-Yake-yama			(0803-26=)	
1986 0508	1	G_{100}		{No eruption}
1988	3?	I_{100}	3? non-eruptive fatalities of unknown cause.	{No eruption}
Hakkoda Group			(0803-28=)	
1997 0712	3	G_{100}	Three Japanese Army soldiers were killed by carbon dioxide inhalation during a training mission.	{No eruption}
Oshima			(0804-01=)	
1789	?	T_{100}	Heavy ashfall buried Shimotaka village, including people and animals.	{=}
1953 1013	1	?		{1953 1005}
1957 1013	1	T_{100}	One tourist killed and 53 injured by explosion.	{1957 08}
1986 1115	1	I_{100}	A 74-year-old man died of a heart attack while being evacuated by ship from the island, on eruption's first day.	{=}
Miyake-jima			(0804-04=)	
1874 07	1?	$T_{?}$	A person near the crater was missing and presumed dead.	{1874 0703}
1940 0808	11	?	11 killed, 20 injured.	{1940 0712}
Aoga-shima			(0804-06=)	
1783 04	7?	?	Eruption and earthquake; 7 persons (one source says 14) and all houses at foot of cone burned.	{1780 0727}
1785 0418	~135	?	130-140 killed by explosion in last month of 5-year eruption after rescue boats from Hachijo-jima did not have room for all residents. Island abandoned for 50 years.	{1780 0727}
Bayonnaise Rocks			(0804-07=)	
1952 0924	31	$P_{100?}$	Research ship Kaiyo-maru, while over central submarine dome Myojin-sho, sunk by explosion; all 31 on board killed. Witham lists 29-31 fatalities.	{1952 0916}
Tori-shima			(0804-09=)	
1902 0809	125	?	All islanders killed; no bodies recovered.	{1902 0807}
1939	2	?		{1939 0817}

Year M-Dy	Deaths	Agent	Remarks	{Start Date}
Oshima-Oshima			(0805-01=)	
1741 0823	1,475	W_{100}	1467 killed on W coast of Oshima Peninsula, 729 houses washed away by tsunami following tectonic earthquake & debris avalanche from N flank of Nishi-yama. 8 more people killed & 82 houses destroyed by tsunami on coast of N Honshu.	{1741 0818}
E-san			(0805-011)	
1846	Many	M_{100}	Many killed by mudflows.	{1846 1118}
Komaga-take			(0805-02=)	
1640 0731	700	W_{100}	Debris avalanche caused tsunami which killed 700; many ships also destroyed.	{=}
1856 0925	25?	$P_{92?}$ $T_{8?}$	Nearly all houses at Honbetsu near Shikabe were burned from ash and pumice fall; 2 fatalities. 19-27 fatalities produced by pumice flow.	{=}
1929	2	T_{100}	2 killed and 4 injured by pyroclastic fall; VL 372 (1932) reports 1 death, probably as a result of pumice flows.	{1929 0617}
Usu			(0805-03=)	
1663 0816	5	$T_{60??}$ $P_{40??}$	Deaths by ashfall (& base surge?).	{=}
1822	50	P_{100}	50 killed & 53 injured (= CAVW total of 103), all in old village of Abuta (S side of volcano). 1,437 horses also killed and old Abuta destroyed.	{1822 0312}
1910	1	M_{100}	Death in lahar.	{1910 0725}
1944 0826	1	G_{100}	One fatality from gas inhalation.	{1944 0623}
1944 1228	1	T_{100}	Child suffocated by ash fall.	{1944 0623}
1977 0807	3	I_{100}	Three non-eruptive fatalities occurred during evacuation.	{=}
1978 1024	3	m_{100}	Deaths at Toyako-onsen resulted from mudflows derived from newly deposited tephra. 2 injuries also reported.	{1977 0807}
Shikotsu			(0805-04=)	
1804-1817	Many?	?	Some sources report many fatalities, but Jaggar thinks report doubtful and Katsui does not list fatalities.	{1804}
Tokachi			(0805-05=)	
1926 0504	144	$M_{98?}$ $T_{2?}$	Initial explosion destroyed hot spring bath house killing 3. Second explosion 4 hours later produced avalanche from cone and hot mudflows which swept down Hurano valley mixed with snowmelt reaching town 20 km W of crater in 26 minutes. 137 killed, 207 or more injured, and 5,080 houses destroyed in Hurano Valley. Finch cites newspaper reports as suggesting 400 lives lost - lava flows, floods and explosions each taking a share - with 144 bodies recovered in 2 days. Witham lists range of 144-207.	{1925 1120}
1926 0908	2	?		{1925 1120}
1962 0629	5	T_{100}	5 killed, 11 injured by falling blocks.	{=}
Daisetsu			(0805-06=)	
1958 0721	2	G_{100}		{No eruption}
1961 0618	2	G_{100}		{No eruption}

RUSSIA & MAINLAND ASIA (09 & 10)

Year M-Dy	Deaths	Agent	Remarks	{Start Date}
Raikoke			(0900-25=)	
1778	15	T_{100}	15 persons under the command of Cpt. Cherny were killed by volcanic bombs, prompting the first volcanological investigation in the Kurile Islands.	{=}
Sinarka			(0900-29=)	
1872	?	$P_{?}$	Ainu village destroyed, possibly by incandescent avalanches; Gorshkov considers this eruption to be from Sinarka, not Kuntomintar.	{=}
Kharimkotan			(0900-30=)	
1933 0108	2	W_{100}	A tsunami from the collapse of Severgin volcano reached as far as Onekotan and Paramushir Islands, where two persons were killed. Tsunami reported to be 20-m high.	{=}
Mutnovsky			(1000-06=)	
1991 06	1	I_{100}	A geology student was killed when he fell through a snowfield crust into a thermal area mudpot.	{No eruption}
Vilyuchik			(1000-083)	
1981	several	A_{100}	Landslides caused by heavy rains during a typhoon swept down the flanks and killed several persons on a road below the volcano.	{No eruption}
Kliuchevskoi			(1000-26=)	
1762	?	?	Doubik writes that it is difficult to estimate the number of casualties because of lack of exact information.	{=}
1978	1	T_{100}	A glaciologist camped near the summit was killed by a single bomb from a strombolian eruption.	{1977 0802}
1983	1	T_{100}	A geophysicist was killed by a volcanic bomb 3.5-4 km from the summit.	{1982 1007}

USA & CANADA (11, 12, & 13)

Year M-Dy	Deaths	Agent	Remarks	{Start Date}
Cleveland			(1101-24-)	
1944 0610	1	T_{100}	Large blocks ejected over island; newspaper reported one man crushed by falling rocks and later covered by lava.	{=}
Novarupta			(1102-18-)	
1912 0606	2	$T_{100?}$	An elderly, tuburcular Indian woman died in Kodiak during the tephra fall. One man died some weeks later after being buried for 3 hours up to his arms in wet ash.	{=}
Spurr			(1103-04-)	
1992 08	1	I_{100}	One person in Anchorage died from a heart attack while shoveling ash from the eruption.	{1992 0627}
Tseax River Cone			(1200-10-)	
1730w	Several	G_{100}	Lava flow overran village. Several people who had dug pits for shelter died of "poison smoke."	{=}
St. Helens			(1201-05-)	
1800	?	I_{100}	Oral tradition of NE Washington tribes noted many people starved to death the winter following the eruption.	{1800 0115?}
1980 0518	57	P_{96} M_2 T_2	All known direct deaths were attributable to the lateral blast, ashfall, and lahars of the May 18 eruption. Among the 25 victims who were autopsied, asphyxiation by airway construction with ash was the cause of death in 17 and contributory in 2 others with thermal injuries. Thermal injuries alone accounted for 3 deaths; three victims died of trauma.	{1980 0327}
1980 0518>	4	I_{100}	A pilot of a crop duster was killed when his plane hit powerlines in central Washington State during tephra fall. In Yakima, a traffic accident, attributed to poor visibility, resulted in 1 death and 2 elderly people with heart conditions died while shovelling tephra from their property. Almost certainly, other indirect deaths also occurred.	{1980 0327}
Hood			(1202-01-)	
1934	1	G_{100}		{No eruption}
1980 1225	1	m_{100}	A debris flow from Polallie Creek canyon on the NE flank of Mount Hood as a result of heavy rainfall killed one person.	{No eruption}
Mammoth Mountain			(1203-15-)	
1998 0524	1	G_{100}	Cross country skier asphyxiated May 24, 1998 by carbon dioxide gas in a snow well.	{No eruption}
Kilauea			(1302-01-)	
1790 11	5,405?	P_{100}	Recent papers have increased the number of estimated deaths from about 80 to near 400, to near 800, and lastly 5,405 from an 1834 interview of botanist David Douglas with the last of the Priests of Pele, who witnessed the catastrophe. Deaths probably due to a hot, relatively ash-free base surge.	{=}
1823 02	Few	$L_{100?}$	Macdonald indicates that the flow advanced so rapidly on a coastal village that a few older persons and children were killed. Stearns does not mention fatalities, but quotes the report of Ellis that the sudden inundation burned one canoe and carried others out to sea.	{=}
1924 0518	1	T_{100}	Photographer hit by falling stones died that night from internal hemorrhage.	{1924 0510}
1975 1129	2	W_{100}	M 7.2 earthquake created tsunami 2 hours before beginning of eruption. Extensive damage, sub-	

Year M-Dy	Deaths	Agent	Remarks {Start Date}
			sidence and 2 deaths in Halape Park area when sea inundated acres of land. {=}
1993 0419	1	$A?_{100}$	Man watching lava enter sea was swept away when new lava bench collapsed, sliding into the ocean near Kalapana. At the same time, steam explosions threw incandescent blocks on the lava delta, injuring 22 other spectators. {1983 0103}
1998 0428	1	L_{100}	{1983 0103}
2000 1103	2	$G?_{100}$	Two hikers died above lava bench after possibly inhaling hot gases or being scalded by hot water. {1983 0103}

Mauna Loa (1302-02=)

Year M-Dy	Deaths	Agent	Remarks {Start Date}
1868 0402	77	W_{60} M_{40}	Earthquake during eruption generated tsunamis; heavy rains produced mudflows. 46 killed by tsunami, 31 by mudflows. {1868 0327}

Hualalai (1302-04-)

Year M-Dy	Deaths	Agent	Remarks {Start Date}
1784g	Some?	L_{100}	A number of lives were said to be lost as a result of the Kaupulehu lava flow, although this report first appeared in 1844 after earlier reports mentioned no fatalities. {=}
1800	2?	L_{100}	A mother and her child were reported to be killed when lava flows surrounded their hut at night. This report did not appear until 1844, after other reports noting no fatalities. {=}

MÈXICO AND CENTRAL AMERICA (14)

Colima (1401-04=)

Year M-Dy	Deaths	Agent	Remarks {Start Date}
1576	?	?	Strong explosive eruption, great destruction of land. Deaths reported - number unknown. {=}
1590 0115>	Many	I_{100}	An explosive eruption was followed by a plague that killed many native residents. {1590 0115>}
1818 0215?	?	?	Medina lists fatalities and property damage. Servando de la Cruz suggests deaths could be due to starvation and disease after the eruption. {1818 0215}
1913 0120>	>13?	$P_{92?}$ $m_{8?}$	At least 8 persons died following the January 20 plinian eruption from burns produced when they walked and collapsed in hot pyroclastic-flow deposits or were buried by collapsing walls of hot deposits in river valleys. Four or five persons died from an explosion when hot pyroclastic-flow debris forming a dam collapsed into the water. One person was killed by secondary lahars. {1913 0118?}

Michoacán-Guanajuato (1401-06=)

Year M-Dy	Deaths	Agent	Remarks {Start Date}
1943	3	E_{100}	Lightning associated with eruptive activity. {1943 0220}
1943	>100	I	Deaths included killings of refugees by new neighbors, murders in land disputes after the eruption, and deaths in the refugee communities from disease and lack of will to live. {1943 0220}

Popocatépetl (1401-09=)

Year M-Dy	Deaths	Agent	Remarks {Start Date}
1919 0219	Some	A_{100}	{=}
1996 0430	5	T_{100}	Five climbers, who had disregarded restrictions against climbing the volcano, were killed by an explosion on April 30. {1996 0305}
1997 0630	?	?	Fatality details unknown. {1996 0305}

Chichón, El (1401-12=)

Year M-Dy	Deaths	Agent	Remarks {Start Date}
1375u	?	M_{100}	Hot flood produced by drainage of pyroclastic-flow-dammed lake caused fatalities. {1375u}
1982 0329	1,879?	$P_{90??}$ $T_{6??}$ $M_{2??}$ $S_{2??}$	1,755 missing and 124 dead mostly in pyroclastic flows. Other estimates range up to 2,000. Two caretakers at dam construction killed by lahar, 11 killed when dam created by pyroclastic flow broke. Government sources list 187 fatalities (including 4/04), but do not include missing persons. Most of casualties on N side were due to fires started by incandescent tephra and building collapse due to earthquakes. {1982 0328}
1982 0404	33	P_{100}	32 soldiers and 1 geologist killed by pyroclastic flow that overran Francisco Leon, 5 km SW of summit. {1982 0328}
1982 0527	1	m_{100}	Failure of pumice dam from pyroclastic flow caused rapid drainage of lake at Francisco Leon. One worker at hydroelectric plant downstream killed. {1982 0328}

Santa María (1402-03=)

Year M-Dy	Deaths	Agent	Remarks {Start Date}
1902 1025	2,500?	$T_{80?}$ $G_{20?}$	Sapper says that hundreds of people were killed in collapsing houses. One source says 10 villages of 50-5,000 inhabitants each were buried beneath tons of volcanic debris. At one plantation 11 km from the volcano, 105 of 112 laborers died. At a village over 350 died, suffocated by deadly fumes. {=}
Indirect	7,500?	?	Anderson suggested 2-3,000 killed and many more (i.e. >2,000) died in subsequent malaria outbreak because ashfall killed birds but not mosquitoes. Both Coleman and Wilcoxson give estimates of 6,000 killed; Witham estimates 5,000-10,000 deaths from disease. {1902 1024}
1929 1102	>200	$P_{90??}$ $M_{10??}$	CAVW lists 23 fatalities for pyroclastic flow. VL gives 45 deaths, with 21 bodies found at El Palmar, 10 km from the crater but later VL details 26 more killed by hot mud at a plantation on the Rio Tambor. This source also implies that loss of life approached that in the 1902 eruption. Mercado et al. suggest 11/02 dome collapse pyroclastic flow killed from several hundred to as many as 5,000 persons. {1922 0622}
1978 0902	1	M_{100}	Mudflow from breakup of ash & block dams on rivers killed 1. {1922 0622}
1990 0719	4	T_{100}	Four hikers on a government-sponsored filming expedition were killed by explosions while on the E rim of the 1902 crater. {1922 0622}
1991 01	25	A_{100}	{1922 0622}

Fuego (1402-09=)

Year M-Dy	Deaths	Agent	Remarks {Start Date}
1963 0930	7	$M_{100?}$	Renewed ashfall triggered a lahar in which 7 persons perished. {1963 0928}
1971 0914	10	$M_?$ $T_?$	BVE gives 10 killed of unstated causes. CSLP gives 2 killed in San Pedro Yepocapa by about 30 cm ashfall. {=}
1974 1014?	?	$T_?$ $M_?$	Deaths caused by a shower of bombs. 2-3 killed by "hot water and mud." Although there were few casualties, thousands abandoned their houses, many of which were destroyed by the weight of ash. {=}

Agua (1402-10=)

Year M-Dy	Deaths	Agent	Remarks {Start Date}
1541 0911	>1,300	m_{100}	Draining of crater lake evidently created mudflows which destroyed former Guatemalan capital of Cuidad Vieja. Gobernadora Donna Beatrix, the first woman head of government in the American continent, was one of the dead. {No eruption}

Pacaya (1402-11=)

Year M-Dy	Deaths	Agent	Remarks {Start Date}
1995 0407	1	M_{100}	A lahar completely buried a house in Los Rios and killed a small girl. {1990 0104?}

Apaneca Range (1403-01=)

Year M-Dy	Deaths	Agent	Remarks {Start Date}
1990 1013	26	T_{100}	A minor hydrothermal directed explosion from a thermal area in the village of El Barro caused 13 fatalities; another 13 persons later died in hospitals. {No eruption}

Santa Ana (1403-02=)

Year M-Dy	Deaths	Agent	Remarks {Start Date}
2005 1001	2	$A_{100?}$	Two persons were killed at the settlement of Palo de Campana, on the NE flank, possibly due to landslides associated with heavy rainfall. {=}

Izalco (1403-03=)

Year M-Dy	Deaths	Agent	Remarks {Start Date}
1926 1105	?	P	Deaths probably occurred in pyroclastic flow. {1925 1226}

San Salvador (1403-05=)

Year M-Dy	Deaths	Agent	Remarks {Start Date}
0640r 08	?	?	Sheets (1979) noted unverified reports from lay sources of bodies found on the floor of a house beneath the Cerén tephra during the initial bulldozer excavation. No bodies were subsequently found by archaeologists. {=}
1917 0606	325?	$S_{92?}$ $L_{8?}$	CAVW and Roy make no mention of fatalities in this eruption, but Jagger reports some people caught and killed in lava flow; several hundred were killed and many wounded when 15 towns including capital destroyed by volcanogenic(?) earthquake on same day. {1917 0607}

Ilopango (1403-06=)

Year M-Dy	Deaths	Agent	Remarks {Start Date}
0450r	30,000	?	Major plinian eruption associated with caldera formation destroyed early Mayan cities. Sheets

Year M-Dy | Deaths | Agent | Remarks | {Start Date}

estimates 30,000 fatalities in the area swept by pyroclastic flows. {=}

Cosigüina (1404-01=)

1835 0120 Several? ? Despite the magnitude of the eruption there were few fatalities in this sparsely populated region; a few cattle ranchers near the base of the volcano and some fishermen in a boat offshore. Johnston-Lavis reports deaths from "mephitic vapors." Galindo reports the death of a 7 year old girl at Union with sore throat believed to be caused by dust, and the death of 7 people in Leon on Jan 23. {=}

San Cristóbal (1404-02=)

1998 1030 1,620? m_{100} Collapse of a ridge near the summit of Casita volcano during heavy rains accompanying Hurricane Mitch produced a debris avalanche that transformed into a lahar that destroyed the towns of El Porvenir and Rolando Rodriguez, killing an estimated 1560-1680 persons. {No eruption}

Negro, Cerro (1404-07=)

1992 04 9 T_{100} 9 persons died from building collapse due to heavy ashfall {1992 0409}

1992 0410 2? I_{100} 1 or 2 persons died from falls while shoveling tephra from roofs {1992 0409}

Mombacho (1404-11=)

1570 ~400 A_{100} Avalanche on S flank destroyed an Indian village of 400 persons. {=}

Maderas (1404-13-)

1996 0927 6 m_{100} A lahar triggered by unusually heavy rainfalls on the E flank of Maderas destroyed the village of El Corozal (~3 km from the volcano) and other settlements. Five children and an adult were killed, and several more people injured. A report of a possible eruption was not confirmed. {No eruption?}

Arenal (1405-033)

1968 0729 ~80 $P_{50?}$ $T_{50?}$ 80 (+/-5) killed in first 3 days; many by pyroclastic flows, but perhaps half by ballistic blocks. Village of Tabacon nearly obliterated by impact craters. One source reports 78 killed in pyroclastic flows. Other sources give totals ranging 76 to >100. {=}

1975 0617 2? ? 2 killed, many injured. Alvarado lists 1 injury, no fatalities. {1968 0729}

1988 0706 1 T_{100} A climber was struck on the head by tephra from an explosion while 3 m from crater rim. {1968 0729}

2000 0823 2 P_{100} A guide and two tourists were engulfed in a pyroclastic flow 2.3 km from the summit; the guide died that night, and one of the tourists, a young girl, died of burns about two weeks later. {1968 0729}

Irazú (1405-06=)

1963 0317 ~15 T_{100} Witham lists 15 fatalities, with range of 5-15. {1963 0313}

1963 1210> ~40 M_{95} $T_{5?}$ Waldron gives number killed in mudflows as >20. Other estimates range from "only a few" to 30. 2 killed & 10 injured by a shower of ash and stones on the crater rim in mid-April. 5 died and many wounded in April & Aug 1964. Stine & Banks report that mudflows killing 20 persons and destroying many structures along the Rio Chiquito were secondary. Over a 2-year period 46 mudflows occurred along the Rio Reventado valley; one killed at least 20 persons & destroyed 400 houses and some factories. {1963 0313}

SOUTH AMERICA (15)

Ruiz, Nevado del (1501-02=)

1595 0312 636 M_{100} Lahars in the Lagunillas and Guali river valleys killed 636 persons, mostly Guali Indians.{1595 0309}

1845 0219 ~1,000 M_{100} Mudflows, again caused by eruption melting of snow cover, buried the entire population along the Lagunillas valley. {=}

1985 1113 23,080 M_{100} Death tolls uncertain with most estimates in the range 23-26,000. This figure from Pierson et al., quoting office of Colombian President. Katsui et al. indicate 24,470 including 21,000 of the 29,000 inhabitants of Armero. Naranjo et al. suggest approximately 1,000 died in Chinchina. About 10,000 injured, 5,200 requiring medical attention. {1985 0911}

Huila, Nevado del (1501-05=)

1994 0606 650? m_{100} {No eruption}

2008 1120 20? M_{100} There may have been as many as 10 fatalities and 10 others were missing due to destructive lahars on November 20. {2008 1026}

Puracé (1501-06=)

1885 0525 Many ? A catastrophic explosion accompanied by an earthquake killed many people and destroyed many houses. {=}

1949 0526 17 $T_{100?}$ University students killed by block ejection as they attempted to reach the summit. {=}

Doña Juana (1501-07=)

1899 1113 55 $P_{100?}$ 50-60 killed by burns from blocks and ash from hot avalanches. 200-300 animals also killed. {1897 1101}

Galeras (1501-08=)

1993 0114 9 T_{100} A sudden explosion killed 9 persons, including 6 volcanologists who were in (and on the rim of) the inner crater. {=}

Reventador (1502-01=)

2001 1103 ? I_{100} Widespread ashfall to the W and SW caused visibility problems, respiratory ailments, some roof collapses, and an undisclosed number of deaths and injuries to people attempting to clean their roofs of ash. {=}

Guagua Pichincha (1502-02=)

1993 0312 2 T_{100} Volcanologists visiting the lava dome to investigate an eruption 3 days earlier were killed by second phreatic eruption. {1993 0309}

1999 1005 2 $T_{100?}$ One person died because of respiratory problems from ashfall (GVN). Witham lists 2 fatalities. {1998 0807}

Cotopaxi (1502-05=)

-0455w BC ? M Giant lahar - deaths assumed? {=}

1698 ? M Latacunga and 3/4 of its inhabitants destroyed by lahars. Coleman also mentions other settlements destroyed. {=}

1742 0615? ? M Lahars caused much destruction and probable loss of life {=}

1742 1209 Many $M_{100?}$ A major eruption on December 9, 1742 produced ashfall and lahars that caused much destruction of property in the Rio Cutuchi valley. Hundreds of people and animals were killed {=}

1768 0404 ? M Lahars devastated the Los Chillos, Tumbaco and Cutuchi valleys. Latacunga was destroyed again. {=}

1877 0626 400 M_{100} Wolf reported the priest at Mullao observed 20 people swept away by the lahar. The Latacunga district had 300 fatalities, not including outsiders and 20 Indians were killed by lahars at Napo. Tanguy attributed 400 fatalities to Wolf and Von Rath (1877). Coleman gives the death toll at 1,000 but the basis for this is not clear. {1877 01}

Tungurahua (1502-08=)

~1010 BC Many ? The lateral blast cloud contains pottery shards and the eruption likely impacted settled areas and killed hundreds to thousands. {=}

1640? 5,000 $P_{100?}$ Destruction of the village of Cacha and its 5000 inhabitants was attributed to the 1640 eruption of Tungurahua. {=}

1886 0112 2 P_{100} {1886 0111}

1999 1016? 1 T_{100} Witham (2005) reported one fatality and four injuries on October 16, 1999. {1999 1005}

2006 0714 5? P_{100} At least 5 persons were dead or missing as a result of the July 14, 2006 pyroclastic flows. {1999 1005}

Year M-Dy	Deaths	Agent	Remarks	{Start Date}
2008 0822	2	m_{100}	Two children were killed when a secondary lahar from failure of a dam swept away two homes in Baños.	{1999 1005}
Sangay			(1502-09=)	
1976 0812	2	T_{100}	2 killed and 4 seriously injured as British Vulcan Expedition neared summit of perennially active cone.	{1934 0808}
Azul, Cerro			(1503-06=)	
1943 0413b	1	$T_{100?}$	P-39 fighter pilot from WW-II Galapagos air base crashed when flying over eruption.	{=}
Huaynaputina			(1504-03=)	
1600 0219	1,500?	?	About 1,500 persons were killed, excluding fatalities from lahars down the Rio Tambo or earthquakes in Arequipa.	{1600 0217a}
Lonquimay			(1507-10=)	
1989 06	1	T_{100}	Autopsy of a 64-year-old wood cutter exposed to ash for 8 hours daily, revealed lung and nervous system problems similar to that causing many livestock deaths.	{1988 1225}
Llaima			(1507-11=)	
1937 0209+	3	F_{100}	Castroen River swelled with ash, destroying a house and killing 1. The next day, summit lava flows melted snow to produce floods of hot water down the same river killing 2 and destroying 2 bridges.	{=}
Villarrica			(1507-12=)	
1575	350?	S_{100}	Destruction of Villarica village during tectonic earthquake: reports of eruption are in error.	{No eruption}
1949 0101	54	M_{100}	Lahars caused great damage and killed 23 persons, with an additional 31 missing. Witham lists a range of 40-100 fatalities	{1948 1009}
1963 0521>	?	M_{100}	Snowmelt from lava and super-heated steam May 21-24 caused mudflows with fatalities.	{1963 0225}
1964 0303	25	M_{100}	Mudflows swept over 50% of Conripe village, 25 killed or missing.	{1964 0302}
1971 11	15	M_{100}	Lahars down N, W, and S sides of volcano caused by lava flows melting ice killed 15 in Chaillupen and Turbio valleys, destroying many houses and agricultural installations. Concrete bridges across major rivers cut.	{1971 1029}
Carrán-Los Venados			(1507-14=)	
1955 0727?	2	G_{100}	Two persons killed by gases.	{1955 0727}
Chaitén			(1508-041)	
2008 0502	1	I_{100}	One elderly person died during evacuation efforts.	{=}
Hudson, Cerro			(1508-057)	
1971 0818	5	M_{100}	Lahar mobilized by melting ice down Rio de Los Huemules. Adult and 2 children reported missing; houses remained intact, filling to ceiling with mud and clasts. Witham lists range of 3-5 fatalities, accepts 5 figure.	{1971 0812}
1973 0405	2	m_{100}		{No eruption}

WEST INDIES (16)

Year M-Dy	Deaths	Agent	Remarks	{Start Date}
Soufrière Hills			(1600-05=)	
1997 0625	22?	P_{100}	Pyroclastic flows within a restricted zone on the NE flank on June 25 caused 19 confirmed fatalities; 3 others were missing and presumed dead.	{1995 0718}
1997 0801e	2	P_{100}	Two local residents who had often entered the restricted area were killed by pyroclastic flows in Plymouth in late July or early August 1997.	{1995 0718}
Pelée			(1600-12=)	
1902 0505	23	M_{100}	Draining of crater lake upon failure of crater rim produced mudflows that destroyed a rum distillery, killing 23.	{1902 0423}
1902 0508	28,000	P_{100}	CAVW gives death toll as 28,000 but accounts published at time give 30,000. More recent workers argue that normal population of 26,000 had been swollen by a few thousand refugees from outlying areas, despite the many evacuees. 28,000 is compromise figure.	{1902 0423}
1902 0830	1,500	P_{100}	CAVW gives estimate of 1,000, but Heilprin reports that at Morne Rouge 1,200-1,500 died, and that fatalities also occurred in Ajoupa-Bouillon, Morne Capot, Moine Balar, and Bourden.	{1902 0423}
Soufrière St. Vincent			(1600-15=)	
1812 0430	56	$T_{100?}$	Most fatalities were workers killed by falling hot stones and hut collapses.	{1812 0427}
Indirect	Some	$m_{100?}$	Some killed in a lake burst a few months after the eruption.	{1812 0427}
1902 0507	1,680	P_{100}	Estimate of fatalities is that given in official documents, though most accounts give 1,565 with others ranging from 1,351 to >2,000. Of 224 in hospital after May 7, ~80 died; 221 with burns and 3 children with fractured skulls. Hovey reports only 1 killed on leeward side and 1,350 dead on windward side.	{1902 0506}
1979 0413	2?	$T_?$ $P_?$	Uncertain report of 2 fatalities.	{=}

ICELAND (17)

Year M-Dy	Deaths	Agent	Remarks	{Start Date}
Vestmannaeyjar			(1702-01=)	
1973 0127	1	G_{100}	Sleeping man killed by pooling of CO_2 in house basement. Witham (2005) lists January 23 date.	{1973 0123}
Katla			(1702-03=)	
1262	?	F?	Probably some casualties.	{=}
1311 0118	Many	F	Many farms destroyed by jökulhlaups and probably many people drowned.	{=}
1755	2	E_{100}	2 killed by lightning during tephra fall.	{1755 1017}
Hekla			(1702-07=)	
1510 1015q	?	I_{100}	No confirmed fatalities, but likely cause of famine in northern Iceland.	{=}
Indirect	~600	I_{100}	Tephra fall associated with eruption caused famine, killing 600 in the winter following the eruption.	{1300 0711}
1510 0725	1	T_{100}	Man killed by block 20 km from volcano	{=}
1947 1102	1	L_{100}	A scientist filming the eruption was killed by a glowing block which rolled off the front of a lava flow, killing him instantly.	{1947 0329}
Grímsvötn			(1703-01=)	
1629	4?	F_{100}	Jökulhlaup killed a couple with children.	{=}
1684 11	1	F_{100}	Drowned during a jökulhlaup in the Jokulsa River.	{1684 1105d}
Indirect	9,350	$I_{100?}$	Widespread famine resulted from destruction of summer crops and poisoning of livestock. The human population was reduced by 10,521 from 48,884 in 1783 to 38,363 in 1786, a loss of 22%. When natural birth and death rates are taken into account the best estimate of the death toll becomes 9,350. Fine dust in Scotland also destroyed crops, and volcanic gas and aerosols in England may have contributed to mortality spikes in 1783 and 1784. The combined effects of the Lakagigar and Asama eruptions may have contributed to the Tenmei famine in N Japan and elsewhere.	{1783 05}
1860	1	m_{100}	One fatality from drowning in water-filled kettle hole following a jökulhlaup in 1860.	{no eruption}
Öraefajökull			(1704-01=)	
1362	>220	$T_?$ $F_?$	Some deaths were from floods, but most were from tephra falls.	{1362 0605d}
1727 0804	3	F_{100}	3 drowned when jökulhlaup swept chalet away. Many sheep and horses were also drowned and many horses killed by bomb fall.	{1727 0803}
Esjufjöll			(1704-02=)	
1927 0905d	1	M_{100}	One person died as a result of the jökulhlaup.	{=}

ATLANTIC (18)

Year M-Dy	Deaths	Agent	Remarks	{Start Date}
Fayal			(1802-01=)	
1672	3?	?		{1672 0424}
Pico			(1802-02=)	
1718	2?	?		{1718 0201}
San Jorge			(1802-03=)	
1580	15	P_{100}	15 men burned by a pyroclastic flow.	{1580 0501}
1757	Hundreds	S_{100}	The submarine eruption of 1757 coincided with history's most violent earthquake in the Azores, centered in the E part of the island and causing several hundred deaths.	{1757 0709}
1808	>10	L_{100}	People attempting to save furniture remained too long in vicinity of advancing lava. About 60 were scalded by flashes of steam. 8-10 (?) died on the spot or a few days later. Another source stated that many who fled to safety in the Urzelina church were engulfed in lava and killed.	{1808 0501}
Furnas			(1802-10=)	
1630 0903	195	**P T M**	On September 3, 1630 about 30 people were killed during the first explosions, and in Ponta Garca 80-115 people died from pyroclastic surges and building collapse; at most 195 persons were killed.	{=}
La Palma			(1803-01-)	
1677	1	G_{100}	Gas killed one man and many animals. Johnston-Lavis gives date as 1678 and deaths from "mephitic vapours."	{1677 1117}
1971 1028	?	?	Casualties occurred but very little damage reported.	{1971 1026}
Fogo			(1804-01=)	
1847	?	S_{100}	Fatalities caused by earthquake.	{1847 0409}

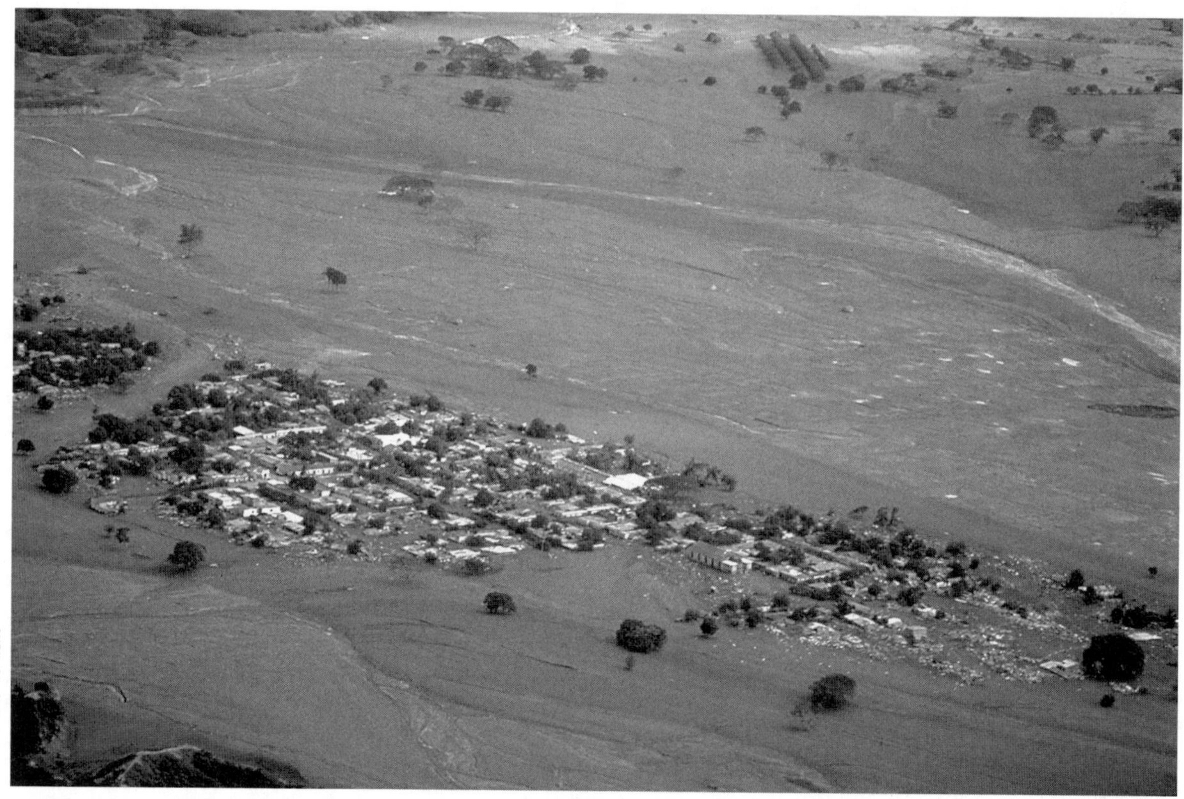

Katia and Maurice Krafft

The 1985 eruption of Colombia's Nevado del Ruiz volcano produced the deadliest lahars (volcanic mudflows) in recorded history. A relatively moderate explosive eruption melted parts of the summit icecap and sent lahars down four major drainages. The town of Armero, shown here, was destroyed by a lahar that had traveled 74 km east of the summit and exited a narrow canyon above the town in a 40-m-high wave, killing three-quarters of the 28,000 inhabitants of Armero.

Evacuations

A complementary positive side to the lengthy preceding listing of fatal eruptions is the strong record of recent evacuations that have saved many thousands of lives from the eruptions that followed. That record is shown here for the interval since 1976, the years covered by our monthly SEAN and then GVN Bulletins, and includes all evacuations known to us. Although this time period has not been without eruptions with high volcano fatalities, the rising number of successful evacuations reflects both the hard work of the many volcanologists and public officials evaluating volcanic hazards on the front lines and subsequent educational efforts that have enhanced the understanding and recognition of volcanic risks by those living in proximity to active volcanoes.

Year M-Dy	Volcano	Evacuees	Deaths	Causes
1976				
0708	Soufrière (Guadeloupe)	72,000	0	phreatic explosions
0803	Kusatsu-Shirane (Japan)	—	3	gas
0812	Sangay (Ecuador)	—	2	explosions
0831	Taal (Luzon-Philippines)	2,000?	0	explosions
0915	Karangetang (Indonesia)	1,800	0	pyroclastic flow
0923	Sarychev Peak (Kuril Is)	?	0	explosions, lahars
1015	Karangetang (Indonesia)	—	1	pyroclastic flows
11	Kadovar (New Guinea)	1,000?	0	thermal activity, seismicity
1113	Semeru (Java)	—	133	mudflows
1125	Merapi (Java)	—	29	mudflows
1202	San Miguel (El Salvador)	a few	0	explosions
1977				
0110	Nyiragongo (Africa-C)	50,000?	100?	earthquakes, lava flows
0405	Karthala (Indian O.-W)	4,000	1?	lava flows
0408	Fournaise, Piton de la	2,500	0	lava flows
0807	Usu (Hokkaido-Japan)	27,000	3	lahars, indirect
0913	Kilauea (Hawaiian Is)	?	0	lava flows
1003	Taal (Luzon-Philippines)	?	0	explosions
1978				
....	Kliuchevskoi (Kamchatka)	—	1	explosions
0204	Westdahl (Aleutian Is)	?	0	tephra fall
0307	Mayon (Luzon-Philippines)	23,000	0	explosions, lava flows
0902	Santa María (Guatemala)	—	1	mudflows
0919	Semeru (Java)	—	12	mudflows
1024	Usu (Hokkaido-Japan)	—	3	secondary mudflows
late	Dieng Volc Complex (Java)	—	3	indirect
1979				
0220	Dieng Volc Complex (Java)	15,000	149?	CO_2
0308	Karkar (New Guinea-NE of)	—	2	pyroclastic flows
0413	Soufrière (St. Vincent)	15,000	2?	pyroclastic flows, explosions
0414	Carrán-Los Venados (Chile-C)	125	0	explosions
0430	Marapi (Sumatra)	—	80	mudflows
0615	Aso (Kyushu-Japan)	some	0	phreatic explosions
0718	Iliwerung (Lesser Sunda Is)	—	539?	tsunami
0906	Aso (Kyushu-Japan)	—	3	explosions
0912	Etna (Italy)	—	9	explosions
1015	Llaima (Chile-C)	?	0	explosions
1113	Negra, Sierra (Galápagos)	?	0	explosions, lava flows
1980				
0207	Bulusan (Luzon-Philippines)	?	0	explosions, earthquakes
0327	St. Helens (US-Washington)	360?	0	directed blast, lahars
0518>	St. Helens (US-Washington)	—	4	indirect
0518	St. Helens (US-Washington)	—	57	pyroclastic flows
0904	Gamalama (Indonesia)	40,000	0	hot tephra, forest fires
0924	Aso (Kyushu-Japan)	?	0	phreatic explosions
1225	Hood (US-Oregon)	—	1	secondary mudflows
1981				
....	Vilyuchik (Kamchatka)	—	several	avalanche
0118	Paluweh (Lesser Sunda Is)	1,850	0	pyroclastic flows
0317	Etna (Italy)	250	0	lava flow
0329	Semeru (Java)	—	1	pyroclastic flows
0514	Semeru (Java)	—	372?	secondary mudflows
0515	Pagan (Mariana Is-C Pacific)	53	0	explosions, lava flows
0615	Aso (Kyushu-Japan)	?	0	phreatic explosions
0630	Mayon (Luzon-Philippines)	—	200>	secondary mudflows
0719	Gamkonora (Indonesia)	3,500>	0	explosions
1225	Nyamuragira (Africa-C)	?	0	lava flows
1982				
....	Galunggung (Java)	—	68?	lexplosions, explosions
0212	Telica (Nicaragua)	50>	0	explosions
0328	Chichón, El (México)	20,000>	0	pyroclastic flows
0329	Chichón, El (México)	—	1,879?	pyroclastic flows
0404	Chichón, El (México)	—	33	pyroclastic flows
0405	Galunggung (Java)	40,000	0	lahars
0527	Chichón, El (México)	—	1	secondary mudflows
0826	Soputan (Sulawesi-Indonesia)	850	0	explosions
1983				
....	Kliuchevskoi (Kamchatka)	—	1	explosions
0718	Colo [Una Una] (Indonesia)	7,000	0	pyroclastic flows
0809	Gamalama (Indonesia)	5,000>	0	explosions
0817	Iliwerung (Lesser Sunda Is)	—	?	tsunami
1003	Miyake-jima (Izu Is-Japan)	1,500	0	explosions, lava flows
1984				
....	Mayon (Luzon-Philippines)	—	1	mudflows
0413	Aso (Kyushu-Japan)	?	0	phreatic explosions
0420	Llaima (Chile-C)	?	0	explosions
0524	Soputan (Sulawesi-Indonesia)	350	0	explosions
0815	Oku Volc Field (Africa-W)	—	37	gas
0905	Karangetang (Indonesia)	20,000	0	explosions, pyroclastic flows
0909	Mayon (Luzon-Philippines)	73,000	0	explosions, lahars
0914	On-take (Honshu-Japan)	—	29	avalanche
1016	Etna (Italy)	—	1	earthquakes
1985				
01	Kilauea (Hawaiian Is)	300>	0	lava flows
0510?	Semeru (Java)	—	70?	avalanche
0722	Tate-yama (Honshu-Japan)	—	1	?
0730	Sangeang Api (Indonesia)	1,242	0	lava flow, explosions
0911	Ruiz, Nevado del (Colombia)	?	0	lahars
1005	Kanlaon (Philippines-C)	?	0	explosions
1113	Ruiz, Nevado del (Colombia)	—	23,080	mudflows
1219<	Etna (Italy)	—	1	earthquakes
1986				
0104	Ruiz, Nevado del (Colombia)	15,000	0	explosions
02	Tacaná (México)	17,000	0	seismicity, explosion
0320	Fournaise, Piton de la	250	0	lava flows
0508	Akita-Yake-yama (Japan)	—	1	gas
0528	Iliboleng (Lesser Sunda Is)	571	0	hot tephra, grass fires
0724	Stromboli (Italy)	—	1	explosions
0821	Oku Volc Field (Africa-W)	2,000?	1,700	CO_2
1115	Oshima (Izu Is-Japan)	—	1	indirect
1121	Oshima (Izu Is-Japan)	12,250	0	explosions, lava flows
1231	Merapi (Java)	—	1	mudflows
1987				
0417	Etna (Italy)	—	2	explosions
06	Poás (Costa Rica)	?	0	phreatic explosions
1116	Oshima (Izu Is-Japan)	150	0	explosions
1228	Ranakah (Lesser Sunda Is)	4,200	0	explosions, pyroclastic flows
1988				
....	Akita-Yake-yama (Japan)	—	3?	indirect
0212	Gamalama (Indonesia)	3,500	0	explosions
0322	Ruiz, Nevado del (Colombia)	300?	0	explosions
0509	Banda Api (Banda Sea)	10,000	4	ballistics and lava flow
0706	Arenal (Costa Rica)	—	1	explosions
0718	Makian (Indonesia)	15,000	0	explosions
0730	Semeru (Java)	—	1	explosions
1224	Tokachi (Hokkaido-Japan)	?	0	explosion, lahar hazard
1989				
01	Lonquimay (Chile-C)	2,000	0	explosions, lava flow
0212	Aso (Kyushu-Japan)	—	1	gas
0405	Aso (Kyushu-Japan)	?	0	phreatic explosions
0422	Soputan (Sulawesi-Indonesia)	500	0	tephra fall
06	Lonquimay (Chile-C)	4,600?	1	tephra fall, flourine gas
0713	Izu-Tobu (Honshu-Japan)	300	0	submarine eruption
0826	Kirishima (Kyushu-Japan)	—	2	gas
0901	Ruiz, Nevado del (Colombia)	5,000<	0	explosions
1214	Redoubt (Alaska-SW)	15?	0	explosions, lahars

Year M-Dy	Volcano	Evacuees	Deaths	Causes
1990				
0210	Kelut (Java)	60,000	35	explosions, lahars
0326	Aso (Kyushu-Japan)	—	1	gas
0418	Aso (Kyushu-Japan)	—	1	gas
0605	Sabancaya (Perú)	?	0	gas, ashfall
0624>	Rabaul (New Britain-SW Pac)	—	6	gas
0719	Santa María (Guatemala)	—	4	explosions
1013	Apaneca Range (El Salvador)	—	26	explosions
1019	Aso (Kyushu-Japan)	—	1	gas
1121	Nyiragongo (Africa-C)	—	1	earthquakes
1125	Kelut (Java)	—	4	secondary mudflows
1991				
01	Santa María (Guatemala)	—	25	avalanche
0402	Pinatubo (Luzon-Philippines)	7,000	0	explosions, gas emission
06	Mutnovsky (Kamchatka)	—	1	indirect
0603	Unzen (Kyushu-Japan)	12,395	43	pyroclastic flows, lahars
0615	Pinatubo (Philippines)	250,000	450?	explosions, lahars, disease
0711	Karthala (Indian O.-W)	1,000	0	quakes, pyroclastic flows
0719	Lewotobi (Lesser Sunda Is)	?	0	ashfall
0727	Pacaya (Guatemala)	1,500	0	explosions, earthquakes
0808	Hudson, Cerro (Chile-S)	600>	0	explosions
1024	Lokon-Empung (Indonesia)	11,000	1	explosions, pyroclastic flows
1992				
....	Semeru (Java)	—	3	explosions
0121	Karangetang (Indonesia)	—	2?	mudflows
0318	Dieng Volc Complex (Java)	—	1	gas
04	Negro, Cerro (Nicaragua)	—	9	explosions
0409	Negro, Cerro (Nicaragua)	28,000	0	ashfall, accidents
0410	Negro, Cerro (Nicaragua)	—	2?	indirect
0505d	Pacaya (Guatemala)	villages	0	explosions
0511	Karangetang (Indonesia)	—	6	pyroclastic flows
0624	Aso (Kyushu-Japan)	?	0	phreatic explosions
0705	Marapi (Sumatra)	—	1	explosions
0712	Pinatubo (Luzon-Philippines)	—	6?	secondary mudflows
0722	Copahue (Chile-C)	?	0	explosions
08	Spurr (Alaska-SW)	—	1	indirect
07-08	Pinatubo (Philippines)	2,000?	0	secondary mudflows
02<	Sabancaya (Perú)	?	0	gas, ashfall
1993				
0110	Pacaya (Guatemala)	2 villages	0	explosions, avalanche
0114	Galeras (Colombia)	—	9	explosions
0121	Karangetang (Indonesia)	452	0	pyroclastic flows
0121	Wurlali (Banda Sea)	—	1	secondary mudflows
0202	Mayon (Philippines)	57,000>	77	explosion, pyroclastic flows
0312	Guagua Pichincha (Ecuador)	—	2	explosions
0419	Láscar (Chile-N)	70	0	explosions, pyroclastic flows
0419	Kilauea (Hawaiian Is)	—	1	avalanche?
0613	Krakatau (Indonesia)	—	1	explosions
0623	Unzen (Kyushu-Japan)	—	1	pyroclastic flows
0626	Pinatubo (Luzon-Philippines)	?	4	secondary mudflows
07	Unzen (Kyushu-Japan)	3,600	0	pyroclastic flows
1004	Pinatubo (Luzon-Philippines)	—	14	secondary mudflows
1994				
0115e	Yasur (Vanuatu-SW Pacific)	—	1	explosions
02	Yasur (Vanuatu-SW Pacific)	—	2	explosions
0203	Semeru (Java)	—	6	pyroclastic flows
0517	Llaima (Chile-C)	100?	0	explosion, lahars
0529	Aso (Kyushu-Japan)	—	1	gas
0606	Huila, Nevado del (Colombia)	—	650?	secondary mudflows
0721	Colima (México)	?	0	phreatic explosion
0919	Rabaul (New Britain)	53,000	5	explosions, ashfall
1012	Pacaya (Guatemala)	142	0	explosions
1103	Rinjani (Lesser Sunda Is)	—	31	secondary mudflows
1122	Merapi (Java)	6,026	66	pyroclastic flows
1221	Popocatépetl (México)	50,000	0	explosions
1995				
0204d	Yasur (Vanuatu-SW Pacific)	—	2	explosions
0211	Yake-dake (Honshu-Japan)	—	4	explosions
0402	Fogo (Cape Verde Is)	1,300	0	explosions, lava flow
0407	Pacaya (Guatemala)	2 villages	1	explosions, lahar, mudflows
0515	Kelimutu (Lesser Sunda Is)	—	1	gas
0529	Negro, Cerro (Nicaragua)	6,000	0	ashfall
0718	Soufrière Hills (W Indies)	6,000	0	explosions
0906	Parker (Mindanao-Philippines)	—	100<	?
1106	Rincón de la Vieja	1,000?	0	lahars
1996				
0305	Komaga-take (Hokkaido-Japan)	?	0	phreatic explosions
0430	Popocatépetl (México)	—	5	explosions
0810	Kanlaon (Philippines-C)	—	3	explosions
0927	Maderas (Nicaragua)	250	0	lahar
1010	Pacaya (Guatemala)	3 villages	0	explosions, pyroclastic flows
1203	Manam (New Guinea-NE of)	—	13	pyroclastic flows
1997				
0114	Merapi (Java)	—	6	?
0127	Merapi (Java)	5,000	0	pyroclastic flows
0511	Akita-Yake-yama (Japan)	?	0	landslide, lahar
0608	Karangetang (Indonesia)	400	3	pyroclastic flows
0625	Soufrière Hills (W Indies)	—	22?	pyroclastic flows
0630	Popocatépetl (México)	1,500	?	explosions
0712	Hakkoda Group (Japan)	—	3	gas
0801e	Soufrière Hills (W Indies)	—	2	pyroclastic flows
0902	Semeru (Java)	—	2	explosions
0915	Adatara (Honshu-Japan)	—	4	gas
1123	Aso (Kyushu-Japan)	—	2	gas
1998				
0428	Kilauea (Hawaiian Is)	—	1	lava flows
0520	Pacaya (Guatemala)	3 villages	0	explosions
0524	Mammoth Mountain (US-Calif.)	—	1	gas
07	Kelut (Java)	—	10	secondary mudflows
1009	Guagua Pichincha (Ecuador)	20	0	landslide
1030	San Cristóbal (Nicaragua)	—	1,620?	secondary mudflows
1118	Colima (México)	300	0	dome, pyroclastic flows
1999				
0214	Colima (México)	?	0	explosions
0411	Cameroon (Africa-W)	600	0	lava flows, ashfall
0521	Telica (Nicaragua)	6,000	0	explosions
1005	Tungurahua (Ecuador)	22,000?	0	explosions
1005	Guagua Pichincha (Ecuador)	—	2	explosions
1016?	Tungurahua (Ecuador)	—	1	explosions
2000				
0116	Pacaya (Guatemala)	1,500	0	explosions
0223	Mayon (Luzon-Philippines)	?	0	explosions
0329	Usu (Hokkaido-Japan)	16,000	0	explosions
0627	Miyake-jima (Izu Is-Japan)	4,000	0	explosions, pyroclastic flows
0701	Copahue (Chile-C)	200	0	explosions
0727	Semeru (Java)	—	2	explosions
0823	Arenal (Costa Rica)	—	2	pyroclastic flows
11	Merapi (Java)	—	1	avalanche
1103	Kilauea (Hawaiian Is)	—	2	gas?
1215	Popocatépetl (México)	41,000	0	explosions
2001				
0608	Lopevi (Vanuatu-SW Pacific)	105	0	ashfall
0727	Mayon (Luzon-Philippines)	?	0	explosions
0805d	Merapi (Java)	—	2?	pyroclastic flows
1020	Stromboli (Italy)	—	1	explosions
1103	Reventador (Ecuador)	—	?	indirect
2002				
....	Semeru (Java)	—	3	explosions
0117	Nyiragongo (Africa-C)	350,000	100	lava flows, lava flows
0205	Colima (México)	?	0	lava flows, pyroclastic flows
0803	Pago (New Britain-SW Pac)	13,000	0	explosions
1026	Etna (Italy)	50	0	explosions, lava flows
1103	Reventador (Ecuador)	?	0	explosions, pyroclastic flows
2003				
0108	Fuego (Guatemala)	Several	0	explosions
0530	Lewotobi (Indonesia)	Hundreds	0	explosions
0731	Gamalama (Indonesia)	?	0	ashfall, pyroclastic flows
2004				
0129	Egon (Lesser Sunda Is)	5,000	1	ashfall, explosions
0608	Tengger Caldera (Java)	—	2	explosions
0703	Egon (Lesser Sunda Is)	1,888	0	ashfall
0716	Galeras (Colombia)	500?	0	explosions
1024	Manam (New Guinea-NE of)	—	5	explosions
1201	Manam (New Guinea-NE of)	9,000	0	explosions, pyroclastic flows
2005				
0127	Manam (New Guinea-NE of)	2,000	1	explosions, explosions
0217	Egon (Lesser Sunda Is)	300?	0	ashfall
0412	Talang (Sumatra)	25,150	0	ashfall
0416	Karthala (Indian O.-W)	10,000	0	explosions
0616	Santa Ana (El Salvador)	Many	0	explosions
0926	Dabbahu (Ethiopia)	6,384	0	explosions
1001	Santa Ana (El Salvador)	—	2	avalanche

Year M-Dy	Volcano	Evacuees	Deaths	Causes
1124	Galeras (Colombia)	3,000?	0	explosions
1125	Karthala (Indian O.-W)	—	1	explosions
1127	Aoba (Vanuatu-SW Pacific)	5,000	0	explosions
2006				
0317	Raoul Island (Kermadec Is)	—	1	explosions
0401	Lengai, Ol Doinyo (Africa-E)	3,000	0	lava flows
0516	Merapi (Java)	22,000	0	pyroclastic flows
0610	Ubinas (Perú)	?	0	explosions
0610	Bulusan (Luzon-Philippines)	—	1	explosions
0614	Merapi (Java)	—	2	pyroclastic flows
0712	Galeras (Colombia)	10,000	0	explosions
0713	Mayon (Luzon-Philippines)	50,000	0	pyroclastic flows
0714	Tungurahua (Ecuador)	4,000	5?	explosions, pyroclastic flows
0810	Karangetang (Indonesia)	500	0	lava flows, pyroclastic flows
1007	Rabaul (New Britain-SW Pac)	?	0	explosions
1130	Mayon (Luzon-Philippines)	—	1266	secondary mudflows
2007				
03	Manam (New Guinea-NE of)	—	4	mudflows
0418	Huila, Nevado del (Colombia)	5,000	0	explosions, lahars
0519	Ritter Island (New Guinea)	2,000	0	explosions
0707	Salak (Java)	—	6	gas
0708	Gamkonora (Indonesia)	8,400	0	explosions
0719	Lengai, Ol Doinyo (Africa)	1,500>	0	earthquakes, explosions
0925	Ruapehu (New Zealand)	?	0	phreatic explosion, lahars
0930	Tair, Jebel at (Red Sea)	50?	4	explosions, lava flows
10	Kelut (Java)	117,000	0	dome growth
1226e	Tungurahua (Ecuador)	1,200	0	explosions, pyroclastic flows
2008				
0101	Llaima (Chile-C)	700	0	explosions
0113	Poás (Costa Rica)	20	0	phreatic explosions
0117	Galeras (Colombia)	100	0	explosions
02	Tungurahua (Ecuador)	2,000?	0	explosions
03	Lengai, Ol Doinyo (Africa-E)	5,000	0	explosions
04	Huila, Nevado del	15,000?	0	ashfall
0415	Egon (Lesser Sunda Is)	600	0	phreatic eruption
0502	Chaitén (Chile-S)	4,500?	1	explosions, indirect
0712	Okmok (Aleutian Is)	?	0	explosions, ashfall
0807	Kasatochi (Aleutian Is)	2	0	explosions, pyroclastic flows
0822	Tungurahua (Ecuador)	—	2	secondary mudflows
1120	Huila, Nevado del (Colombia)	300?	20?	explosions, mudflows
2009				
0315	Redoubt (Alaska-SW)	11	0	explosions, lahars
04	Kilauea (Hawaiian Is)	2,000	0	SO_2 emission
04	Krakatau (Indonesia)	Some	0	explosions
05	Karangetang (Indonesia)	Hundreds	0	explosions
0617	Arenal (Costa Rica)	50	0	rock avalanches
0915	Mayon (Luzon-Philippines)	47,000	0	explosions
1120	Galeras (Colombia)	1,000?	0	explosions
1126	Gaua (Vanuatu-SW Pacific)	300>	0	explosions

Tom Casadevall (USGS)

Evacuees on the island of Neira in the Banda Islands board an Indonesian Navy ship on May 20, 1988, bound for the island of Sulawesi. About 10,000 persons of a population of 16,000 living in the Banda Islands were evacuated during the 1988 eruption. The eruption plume reached a maximum height of 16.5 km, and lava flows reached the north, northwest, and south coasts of Banda Api Island, destroying two villages.

Preliminary List of Pleistocene Volcanoes

Pleistocene Volcano List: Context and Codes

Detailed field studies of volcanoes have shown that they can remain dormant for very long periods of time before resuming eruptive activity. We have thus begun the long process of expanding the time span covered in our data to include the Pleistocene (from 10,000 years to 1.81 million years). Obtaining representative global coverage for the entire Pleistocene will be a long-term project, and we have emphasized the very preliminary nature of these data in the title of this section. The coverage is regionally quite variable. For some regions, such as Japan (Nakano et al., 2001-), and the West Indies (Lindsay et al., 2005), volcanologists have compiled comprehensive lists of Quaternary volcanoes, but in many other regions only a small percentage of Pleistocene volcanoes are shown here.

In the first two editions of this book, we included some Pleistocene volcanoes with continuing vigorous thermal activity (such as Long Valley and Valles calderas) in the Holocene list, but here they appear in the Pleistocene list with their thermal activity noted in the Status (below). The Pleistocene list also includes volcanoes from the *Post-Miocene Volcanoes of the World* compilation (IAVCEI, 1973-80) for which a specific age date is not listed. The latest eruptive activity fromthese volcanoes could range from Pliocene to Holocene age, and they appear below with a "PM" status. Detailed field studies since the 2nd edition have also demonstrated that some volcanoes thought to have erupted during the Holocene actually ceased eruption during the late Pleistocene. Volcanoes that would otherwise have disappeared from this edition can now be found in this Pleistocene volcano listing and also appear in the **GAZETTEER**.

Status Codes

P = Pleistocene
P? = Uncertain Pleistocene
Q = Quaternary (Pleistocene or Holocene)
PT = Pleistocene-thermal
PM = Post-Miocene

MEDITERRANEAN & W ASIA

Volcano Name (Subregion)	LAT	LONG	ELEV	TYPE	STATUS
Calimani (Romania)	47.15 N	25.25 E	2100	Stratovolcano	P
Ciomadul (Romania)	46.13 N	25.88 E	1289	Lava domes	P
Persani Mountains (Romania)	46.00 N	25.33 E	-	Volcanic field	P
Beritia (Romania)	45.93 N	22.88 E	353	Volcanic field	P
Unnamed (Romania)	45.83 N	21.67 E	-	Volcanic field	P
Unnamed (Hungary)	46.03 N	18.75 E	-	Volcanic field	PM
Balaton Highland (Hungary)	46.92 N*	17.63 E	600	Volcanic field	P
Kemenesalja (Hungary)	47.19 N*	17.20 E	433	Volcanic field	P
Nográd (Hungary)	48.12 N*	19.80 E	671	Volcanic field	P
Filakovo-Salgotarjan (Slovakia)	48.22 N*	19.83 E	608	Volcanic field	P
Central Slovakia (Slovakia)	48.42 N*	18.93 E	737	Volcanic field	P
Unnamed (Czech)	49.88 N*	17.48 E	780	Volcanic field	P
Cheb Basin (Czech)	49.97 N*	12.39 E	585	Volcanic field	P
East Eifel Volc Field (Germany)	50.42 N	7.27 E	588	Maars	P
Rodderberg (Germany)	50.62 N	7.20 E	150	Cinder cone	P
Cofrentes (Spain)	39.24 N*	1.06 W	514	Volcanic field	P
Columbretes, Islas (Spain)	40.87 N*	0.67 E	-	Volcanic field	Q
Amiata (Italy)	42.90 N	11.63 E	1738	Lava domes	PT
Radicofani (Italy)	42.87 N	11.77 E	-	Volcanic neck	P
Torre Alfina (Italy)	42.78 N	11.92 E	-	Volcanic neck	P
San Venanzo (Italy)	42.85 N	12.28 E	466	Maar	P
Acquasparta (Italy)	42.65 N*	12.30 E	-	Volcanic field	P
Polino (Italy)	42.57 N	12.82 E	-	Explosion craters	P
Cupaello (Italy)	42.43 N	12.93 E	650	Pyroclastic cone	P
Oricola-Carsoli (Italy)	42.15 N*	13.08 E	-	Pyroclastic cones	P
Vico-Cimino Complex (Italy)	42.33 N	12.17 E	1053	Stratovolcanoes	P
Sabatini Complex (Italy)	42.17 N	12.22 E	612	Stratovolcanoes	P
Ernici, Monti (Italy)	41.58 N*	13.33 E	-	Volcanic field	P
Roccamonfina (Italy)	41.30 N	13.93 E	1066	Stratovolcano	P
Vulture, Monte (Italy)	40.92 N	15.67 E	1330	Stratovolcano	P
Ventotene (Italy)	40.80 N	13.42 E	139	Stratovolcanoes	P
Pontine Islands (Italy)	40.90 N	12.95 E	283	Lava domes	P
Logudoro (Italy)	40.58 N	8.67 E	-	Volcanic field	P
Salina (Italy)	38.58 N	14.85 E	962	Stratovolcanoes	P
Filicudi (Italy)	38.58 N	14.55 E	773	Stratovolcanoes	P
Alicudi (Italy)	38.55 N	14.33 E	675	Stratovolcano	P
Ustica (Italy)	38.72 N	13.18 E	248	Stratovolcanoes	P
Iblei (Italy)	37.17 N	14.83 E	-	Shield volcano?	P
Linosa (Italy)	35.87 N	12.87 E	195	Cinder cones	P
Sporades (Greece)	39.48 N	24.17 E	-	Lava dome	P
Volos-Atalanti (Greece)	38.85 N	22.82 E	-	Volcanic field	P
Aegina (Greece)	37.75 N	23.50 E	530	Volcanic field	P
Poros (Greece)	37.48 N	23.43 E	80	Fissure vent	P
Antiparos (Greece)	36.93 N	24.98 E	300	Pyroclastic cones	P
Kos (Greece)	36.85 N	27.25 E	430	Calderas	PT
Balikesir-Bigadic (Turkey)	39.50 N	28.00 E	-	Volcanic field	Q
Selendi (Turkey)	38.75 N	28.88 E	-	Unknown	Q
Gölcük (Turkey)	37.72 N	30.49 E	-	Caldera	P
Pasinler (Turkey)	39.90 N	41.67 E	-	Unknown	P
Arpacay (Turkey)	40.87 N	43.33 E	-	Volcanic field	P
Kisir Dagi (Turkey)	40.97 N	43.07 E	3192	Unknown	P
Kirtik (Russia-SW)	43.25 N	42.58 E	3500	Unknown	Q
Kanjal (Russia-SW)	43.57 N	42.83 E	2000	Fissure vent	Q
Unnamed (Russia-SW)	43.38 N*	43.02 E	3630	Volcanic field	P
Unnamed (Georgia)	41.35 N*	43.85 E	3100	Shield volcano	P
Unnamed (Armenia)	41.09 N*	43.80 E	3157	Volcanic field	P
Unnamed (Armenia)	40.46 N*	44.02 E	3300	Volcanic field	P
Unnamed (Armenia)	40.06 N*	45.61 E	3047	Volcanic field	P
Unnamed (Armenia)	39.67 N*	46.07 E	3548	Volcanic field	P

AFRICA & RED SEA

Volcano Name (Subregion)	LAT	LONG	ELEV	TYPE	STATUS
Oyma (Ethiopia)	12.88 N	41.62 E	1041	Stratovolcano	P
Didolli (Ethiopia)	12.70 N	41.58 E	1191	Caldera	P
As-Ali (Ethiopia)	12.37 N	41.68 E	1322	Shield volcano	PM
Katahelu (Ethiopia)	12.58 N	41.45 E	1175	Cone	P
Alimelali (Ethiopia)	12.73 N	41.38 E	-	Cone	P
Dawa Ale-Quarry (Ethiopia)	12.75 N	41.00 E	-	Stratovolcano	P
Badi (Ethiopia)	12.38 N	40.35 E	-	Stratovolcano	P
Gad Elu (Ethiopia)	12.43 N	41.03 E	-	Stratovolcano	P
Ela (Ethiopia)	12.53 N	41.20 E	-	Stratovolcano	P
Asgura (Ethiopia)	11.75 N	40.90 E	-	Stratovolcano	P
Finini (Ethiopia)	11.98 N	41.35 E	-	Stratovolcano	P
Dalaha'ale (Ethiopia)	12.20 N	42.02 E	-	Stratovolcano	P
Data Gabalti (Ethiopia)	12.17 N	42.12 E	-	Stratovolcano	P
Egersuwa (Ethiopia)	12.47 N	42.18 E	-	Lava domes	P
Tiho (Djibouti)	11.53 N	42.05 E	500	Fumarole field	P
Garbes (Djibouti)	11.42 N	42.20 E	1000	Fumarole field	PT
Boina (Djibouti)	11.25 N	41.83 E	300	Fumarole field	PT
Zikwala (Ethiopia)	8.53 N	38.85 E	2989	Stratovolcano	P
Ch'llalo (Ethiopia)	7.92 N	39.27 E	4005	Stratovolcano	P
Gademota Caldera (Ethiopia)	7.88 N	38.60 E	2090	Caldera	P
Duguna (Ethiopia)	6.95 N	38.07 E	2205	Stratovolcano	P
Chew Bahir (Ethiopia)	4.47 N	36.87 E	600	Pyroclastic cones	Q
Porr (Africa-E)	2.90 N	36.55 E	-	Pyroclastic cone	Q
Kulal (Africa-E)	2.75 N	36.93 E	2285	Shield volcano	P
Asie (Africa-E)	2.97 N	37.10 E	1074	Shield volcano	P
Huri (Africa-E)	3.50 N	37.75 E	1300	Shield volcano	P
Bogoria (Africa-E)	0.25 N	36.08 E	-	Shield volcano	PT
Kilombe Caldera (Africa-E)	0.08 S	35.83 E	2550	Caldera	P?
Nyokie, Ol Doinyo (Africa-E)	1.80 S	36.38 E	1169	Tuff cone	P
Mosonik (Africa-E)	2.57 S	35.83 E	1770	Stratovolcano	P
Gelai (Africa-E)	2.60 S	36.10 E	2942	Shield volcano	P
Ketumbeine (Africa-E)	2.88 S	36.22 E	2942	Shield volcano	P
Kerimasi (Africa-E)	2.87 S	35.95 E	2600	Stratovolcano	P
Embagai (Africa-E)	2.92 S	35.83 E	3220	Caldera	Q
Loolmalasin (Africa-E)	3.00 S	35.83 E	3684	Unknown	P?
Olmoti (Africa-E)	3.00 S	35.65 E	3099	Caldera	Q
Lemagarut (Africa-E)	3.17 S	35.37 E	3132	Stratovolcano	PM
Sadiman (Africa-E)	3.18 S	35.42 E	2865	Stratovolcano	P?
Oldeani (Africa-E)	3.30 S	35.45 E	3215	Stratovolcano	PM
Ngorongoro (Africa-E)	3.17 S	35.57 E	2376	Caldera	P
Sultan Hamud-Simba (Africa-E)	2.12 S*	37.40 E	-	Volcanic field	P
Ngurdoto (Africa-E)	3.30 S	36.92 E	1835	Caldera	PM
Tarosero (Africa-E)	3.20 S	36.35 E	2106	Stratovolcano	PM
Burko (Africa-E)	3.30 S	36.22 E	2136	Stratovolcano	P
Essimingor (Africa-E)	3.38 S	36.08 E	2300	Stratovolcano	P
Kwaraha (Africa-E)	4.23 S	35.82 E	2415	Stratovolcano	P
Hanang (Africa-E)	4.43 S	35.40 E	3418	Stratovolcano	Q
Tukuyu (Africa-E)	9.25 S	33.63 E	1370	Shield volcano	PM
Katete (Africa-E)	9.10 S	33.75 E	2590	Stratovolcano	PM
Mikeno (Africa-C)	1.47 S	29.42 E	4437	Stratovolcano	P
Sabinyo (Africa-C)	1.38 S	29.58 E	3634	Stratovolcano	P
Unnamed (Africa-C)	2.67 S*	28.62 E	1460	Fissure vents	PM
Zoutpan (Africa-S)	25.42 S	28.08 E	1062	Pyroclastic cone	PM
Tin Taralle Volc Field (Africa-N)	18.27 N*	9.33 E	-	Volcanic field	P
Cap-Vert (Africa-N)	14.77 N	17.40 W	-	Volcanic field	P
In Teria Volc Field (Africa-N)	22.67 N*	8.95 E	-	Tuff rings	Q
Oulmès Volc Field (Africa-N)	33.33 N*	6.00 W	-	Volcanic field	P
Azrou Volc Field (Africa-N)	33.67 N*	5.17 W	1785	Volcanic field	Q
Rekkame Volc Field (Africa-N)	33.17 N*	3.33 W	1500	Explosion craters	P
Oujda Volc Field (Africa-N)	34.53 N*	3.30 W	700	Volcanic field	Q
Mrit-Ment Volc Field (Africa-N)	33.47 N*	2.97 W	700	Volcanic field	Q
Berguent Volc Field (Africa-N)	33.75 N*	2.40 W	1200	Lava domes	Q
Chott Tigri Volc Field (Africa-N)	32.92 N*	1.85 W	1388	Volcanic field	Q
Nemours-Nedroma (Africa-N)	35.07 N*	2.00 W	444	Volcanic field	P
Tafna Beni Saf (Africa-N)	35.28 N*	1.45 W	480	Volcanic field	P
Gharyan Volc Field (Africa-N)	31.70 N*	13.30 E	-	Stratovolcanoes	P
Chi, Tarso Emi (Africa-N)	21.22 N	18.52 E	2650	Volcanic field	Q
Ahon, Tarso (Africa-N)	21.40 N	18.30 E	3325	Volcanic field	Q
Gurgei (Africa-N)	13.83 N*	24.33 E	-	Volcanic field	PM
Tebel Umm Arafibia (Africa-N)	18.15 N	33.83 E	500	Stratovolcano	PM

MIDDLE EAST & INDIAN OCEAN

Volcano Name (Subregion)	LAT	LONG	ELEV	TYPE	STATUS
Unnamed (Syria)	37.13 N	41.85 E	693	Cone	P
Unnamed (Syria)	35.63 N*	40.33 E	404	Cones	P
Unnamed (Syria)	35.82 N*	39.47 E	473	Cones	P
Unnamed (Syria)	36.67 N	38.33 E	-	Cone	Q
Unnamed (Israel)	33.13 N*	35.52 E	965	Cone	PM
Unnamed (Israel)	32.73 N*	35.32 E	300	Cone	PM
Unnamed (Syria)	34.02 N*	38.68 E	775	Cones	P
Unnamed (Syria)	33.75 N*	38.68 E	781	Cones	P
Unnamed (Jordan)	32.50 N*	37.50 E	1078	Volcanic field	P
Unnamed (Jordan)	31.37 N*	35.73 E	-	Volcanic field	PM
Unnamed (Jordan)	30.73 N*	35.75 E	-	Volcanic field	PM
Jabel-Jubeiq (Jordan)	29.55 N*	37.33 E	-	Volcanic field	PM
Unnamed (Jordan)	29.73 N*	37.97 E	-	Volcanic field	PM
Shamah (Arabia)	31.05 N*	38.42 E	813	Volcanic field	PM
Unnamed (Arabia)	26.02 N*	37.80 E	-	Cones	PM
Unnamed (Arabia)	26.05 N	38.67 E	-	Cones	PM
Hutaymah, Harrat (Arabia)	26.98 N*	42.40 E	-	Volcanic field	Q
Nawasif, Harrat (Arabia)	21.17 N*	42.00 E	-	Volcanic field	PM
Al-Hayloh, Jibal (Arabia)	18.52 N	42.03 E	-	Cone	Q
Hayil, Jibal (Arabia)	18.43 N*	41.63 E	381	Cones	Q
Akwah, Jibal (Arabia)	17.17 N*	42.82 E	-	Cones	Q
Unnamed (Iran)	39.37 N	44.58 E	-	Unknown	Q
Unnamed (Iran)	37.50 N	47.15 E	-	Unknown	Q
Bijar Volc Field (Iran)	36.58 N	47.75 E	-	Cinder cones	P

Volcano Name (Subregion)	LAT	LONG	ELEV	TYPE	STATUS
Unnamed (Iran)	32.50 N	57.50 E	-	Unknown	Q
Unnamed (Iran)	31.15 N	57.50 E	-	Unknown	Q
Unnamed (Iran)	30.50 N	59.13 E	880	Unknown	PM
Dehaj-Meduk (Iran)	30.33 N	55.50 E	-	Volcanic field	Q
Shahsavaran (Iran)	28.17 N	59.10 E	-	Volcanic field	Q
Sultan (Pakistan)	29.10 N	62.80 E	2333	Volcanic field	P
Zardolou Group (Afghanistan)	33.25 N	67.92 E	3000	Lava domes	Q
Loman Volcano Group (Afghan.)	33.33 N	67.85 E	4559	Lava domes	Q
Wacht-i-Navar Group (Afghanistan)	33.78 N	67.83 E	3560	Lava domes	Q
Moheli Island (Indian O.-W)	12.30 S	43.72 E	790	Shield volcano	P
Anjouan Island (Indian O.-W)	12.20 S	44.45 E	1595	Shield volcano	P
Mayotte Island (Indian O.-W)	12.83 S	45.05 E	660	Shield volcano	P
Nieges, Piton des (Indian O.-W)	21.08 S	55.48 E	3070	Shield volcano	P
Mauritius (Indian O.-W)	20.32 S	57.65 E	826	Shield volcano	P
Rodriguez Island (Indian O.-W)	19.70 S	63.42 E	396	Shield volcano	P

NEW ZEALAND TO FIJI

Volcano Name (Subregion)	LAT	LONG	ELEV	TYPE	STATUS
Hautere (New Zealand)	46.55 S	166.90 E	330	Stratovolcano	P
South Auckland (New Zealand)	37.37 S	*174.92 E	314	Shield volcanoes	P
Mokohinau Islands (New Zealand)	35.90 S	175.12 E	134	Volcanic field	P
Little Barrier (New Zealand)	36.20 S	175.12 E	722	Stratovolcano	P
Mercury Islands (New Zealand)	36.62 S	175.82 E	230	Volcanic field	P
Alderman Islands (New Zealand)	36.97 S	176.08 E	-	Lava domes	P?
South Coromandel Peninsula	37.25 S	175.78 E	795	Volcanic field	P
Kaimai (New Zealand)	37.80 S	176.22 E	564	Volcanic field	P?
Karioi (New Zealand)	37.87 S	174.80 E	756	Stratovolcano	P
Pirongia (New Zealand)	38.00 S	175.10 E	959	Stratovolcano	P
Kakepuku (New Zealand)	38.07 S	175.25 E	450	Lava cones	P
Kaitake (New Zealand)	39.17 S	173.97 E	684	Stratovolcano	P
Pouakai (New Zealand)	39.23 S	174.02 E	1399	Stratovolcano	P
Solander Island (New Zealand)	46.55 S	166.87 E	300	Stratovolcano	P
Rungapapa Knoll (New Zealand)	37.55 S	176.98 E	-	Submarine volc	Q
Whale Island (New Zealand)	37.86 S	176.98 E	354	Complex volcano	PT
Rotorua (New Zealand)	38.08 S	176.27 E	757	Caldera	PT
Kapenga (New Zealand)	38.27 S	176.27 E	840	Calderas	P
Mangakino (New Zealand)	38.35 S	175.75 E	1165	Caldera	P
Northern Tongariro Group (N. Z.)	38.98 S	175.70 E	1327	Stratovolcanoes	P
Rumble I (New Zealand)	35.50 S	178.88 E	-1100	Submarine volc	Q
Rose Island (Samoa-SW Pacific)	14.50 S	168.17 W	3	Shield volcano	P
Nairai (Fiji Is-SW Pacific)	17.80 S	179.42 E	335	Complex volcano	P
Waikama (Fiji Is-SW Pacific)	18.02 S	179.30 E	760	Complex volcano	P
Mago (Fiji Is-SW Pacific)	17.45 S	179.15 W	-	Scoria cones	P
Katafaga (Fiji Is-SW Pacific)	17.52 S	178.72 W	-	Unknown	P
Kabara (Fiji Is-SW Pacific)	18.95 S	178.95 W	-	Unknown	P

MELANESIA & AUSTRALIA

Volcano Name (Subregion)	LAT	LONG	ELEV	TYPE	STATUS
Vokeo (New Guinea-NE of)	3.20 S	144.10 E	609	Stratovolcano	P
Viai (New Guinea-NE of)	3.35 S	144.37 E	160	Stratovolcano	Q
Bagabag (New Guinea-NE of)	4.78 S	146.23 E	692	Stratovolcano	Q
Crown Island (New Guinea-NE of)	5.12 S	146.97 E	566	Stratovolcano	Q
Tolokiwa (New Guinea-NE of)	5.32 S	147.58 E	1372	Stratovolcano	Q
Tangi (New Britain-SW Pac)	5.67 S	148.40 E	1524	Stratovolcano	P
Unea (New Britain-SW Pac)	4.90 S	149.15 E	597	Caldera	Q
Narage (New Britain-SW Pac)	4.55 S	149.13 E	307	Stratovolcano	PT
Lotomgan Group (New Britain)	5.22 S	150.07 E	555	Pyroclastic cones	Q
Bangum (New Britain-SW Pac)	5.35 S	149.93 E	990	Stratovolcano	P
Du Faure (New Britain-SW Pac)	5.58 S	150.12 E	728	Stratovolcano	PM
Kimbe (New Britain-SW Pac)	5.21 S	150.38 E	80	Stratovolcano	PM
Wulai (New Britain-SW Pac)	5.36 S	150.48 E	20	Stratovolcano	PM
Oto Group (New Britain-SW Pac)	5.57 S	150.40 E	1314	Stratovolcanoes	P
Saddle Mount (New Britain-SW Pac)	5.47 S	150.76 E	200	Lava dome	PM
Likuruanga (New Britain-SW Pac)	4.95 S	151.38 E	922	Stratovolcano	P
Banban (New Britain-SW Pac)	4.90 S	151.05 E	1092	Stratovolcano	PM
Tavui (New Britain-SW Pac)	4.12 S	152.20 E	-18	Submarine volc	Q
Watom (New Britain-SW Pac)	4.12 S	152.07 E	341	Stratovolcano	PM
Kerewa (New Guinea)	6.02 S	143.15 E	3700	Stratovolcano	P
Sisa (New Guinea)	6.13 S	142.73 E	2650	Stratovolcano	P
Bosavi (New Guinea)	6.58 S	142.82 E	2397	Stratovolcano	P
Darai Hills (New Guinea)	6.80 S	143.08 E	500	Volcanic field	P
Biwau Hills (New Guinea)	7.32 S	143.28 E	400	Pyroclastic cones	P
Sugarloaf (New Guinea)	5.78 S	143.75 E	3900	Volcanic field	P
Hagen, Mt. (New Guinea)	5.77 S	144.03 E	3765	Stratovolcanoes	P
Giluwe, Mt. (New Guinea)	6.05 S	143.88 E	4368	Shield volcano	P
Ialibu, Mt. (New Guinea)	6.23 S	144.03 E	3465	Stratovolcano	P
Murray, Mt. (New Guinea)	6.75 S	144.02 E	2254	Stratovolcano	P
Suaru, Mt. (New Guinea)	6.25 S	144.83 E	2667	Stratovolcano	P
Karimui, Mt. (New Guinea)	6.57 S	144.77 E	2561	Stratovolcano	P
Duau, Mt. (New Guinea)	6.92 S	144.58 E	1850	Stratovolcano	P
Favenc, Mt. (New Guinea)	6.97 S	144.68 E	1583	Stratovolcano	P
Aird Hills (New Guinea)	7.45 S	144.35 E	328	Lava domes	P
Trafalgar (New Guinea)	9.17 S	149.17 E	1726	Stratovolcano	P
Tabar (New Ireland-SW Pacific)	2.90 S	152.03 E	600	Stratovolcano	P
Tanga (New Ireland-SW Pacific)	3.50 S	153.22 E	472	Stratovolcano	PT
Emperor Range (Bougainville)	5.70 S	154.95 E	2040	Calderas	P
Numa Numa (Bougainville-SW Pac.)	6.02 S	155.19 E	1567	Stratovolcano	P
Bakanovi (Bougainville-SW Pacific)	6.15 S	155.35 E	600	Stratovolcano	P?
Nonda (Solomon Is-SW Pacific)	7.67 S	156.60 E	760	Stratovolcano	PT
Maetambe (Solomon Is-SW Pacific)	7.08 S	157.03 E	960	Unknown	P?
Kömboro (Solomon Is-SW Pacific)	7.33 S	157.53 E	610	Stratovolcano	PM
Laena (Solomon Is-SW Pacific)	7.33 S	157.60 E	-	Unknown	PM
Kolombangara (Solomon Is)	7.97 S	157.08 E	1760	Stratovolcano	P
Rendova (Solomon Is-SW Pacific)	8.47 S	157.33 E	1050	Stratovolcano	P
Mbaniata (Solomon Is-SW Pacific)	8.55 S	157.25 E	750	Stratovolcano	PM
Mase (Solomon Is-SW Pacific)	8.12 S	157.50 E	-	Unknown	PM
Raveti (Solomon Is-SW Pacific)	8.25 S	157.65 E	-	Unknown	PM
Kanekolo, Mt. (Solomon Is-SW Pac)	8.45 S	157.70 E	800	Unknown	PM
Mbareke (Solomon Is-SW Pacific)	8.55 S	158.07 E	500	Stratovolcano	P
Vangunu, Mt. (Solomon Is-SW Pac.)	8.67 S	158.00 E	1040	Stratovolcano	P
Nggatokae (Solomon Is-SW Pacific)	8.78 S	158.18 E	840	Stratovolcano	P
Mborokua (Solomon Is-SW Pacific)	9.03 S	158.75 E	360	Stratovolcano	PM
Utupua (Santa Cruz Is-SW Pacific)	11.30 S	166.53 E	-	Unknown	PM
Vanikolo (Santa Cruz Is-SW Pacific)	11.63 S	166.83 E	1000	Unknown	PM
Ureparapara (Vanuatu-SW Pacific)	13.53 S	167.32 E	764	Stratovolcano	P
Mota (Vanuatu-SW Pacific)	13.85 S	167.68 E	411	Stratovolcano	P
Merig (Vanuatu-SW Pacific)	14.32 S	167.80 E	-	Stratovolcano	P
Paama Island (Vanuatu-SW Pacific)	16.47 S	168.23 E	544	Complex volcano	P
Emae (Vanuatu-SW Pacific)	17.05 S	168.40 E	549	Complex volcano	P
Unnamed (Vanuatu-SW Pacific)	17.30 S	168.62 E	-	Submarine volc	Q
Fatmalapa (Vanuatu-SW Pacific)	17.57 S	168.37 E	500	Stratovolcanoes	P
William, Mt. (Vanuatu-SW Pacific)	18.70 S	169.08 E	886	Stratovolcano	P
Pumpan, Mt. (Vanuatu-SW Pacific)	18.85 S	169.12 E	802	Stratovolcano	P
Melkum, Mt. (Vanuatu-SW Pacific)	18.85 S	169.05 E	758	Stratovolcanoes	P
East Tanna Volcano (Vanuatu)	19.42 S	169.45 E	552	Stratovolcano	P
Maer Volc Province (Australia)	9.92 S	144.03 E	225	Pyroclastic cones	P
Piebald Volc Province (Australia)	15.23 S	*145.03 E	420	Shield volcanoes	P
Mclean Volc Province (Australia)	15.87 S	*144.83 E	610	Scoria cones	P
Atherton Volc Province (Australia)	17.30 S	*145.72 E	1160	Shield volcanoes	P
McBride Volc Province (Australia)	18.33 S	*144.55 E	1020	Shield volcanoes	P
Fox, Mt. (Australia)	18.85 S	145.80 E	840	Pyroclastic cone	P
Chudleigh Volc Province (Austr.)	19.73 S	*144.20 E	1000	Shield volcanoes	P
Nulla Volc Province (Australia)	19.82 S	*145.08 E	840	Shield volcanoes	P
Sturgeon Volc Province (Australia)	20.35 S	144.25 E	-	Shield volcanoes	P
Bundaberg-Boyne Province (Aus)	25.58 S	151.87 E	330	Pyroclastic cones	P

INDONESIA

Volcano Name (Subregion)	LAT	LONG	ELEV	TYPE	STATUS
Pulau Weh (Sumatra)	5.82 N	95.28 E	617	Stratovolcano	PT
Seulawah Inong (Sumatra)	5.43 N	95.77 E	730	Unknown	Q
Olim (Sumatra)	5.20 N	96.18 E	-	Fissure vents	P
Teu Minas (Sumatra)	5.17 N	96.43 E	-	Stratovolcano	P
Geureugoh (Sumatra)	5.15 N	96.67 E	-	Fissure vents	P
Meugeurinceng (Sumatra)	4.75 N	96.27 E	-	Fissure vents	P
Tudeuk, Gunung (Sumatra)	5.00 N	96.57 E	-	Lava dome	P
Nama Salah (Sumatra)	4.65 N	96.78 E	-	Unknown	P
Telago, Gunung (Sumatra)	4.47 N	96.82 E	1930	Unknown	P
Sembuang, Gunung (Sumatra)	4.62 N	97.42 E	-	Explosion crater	P
Geureudong (Sumatra)	4.81 N	96.82 E	2885	Stratovolcano	PT
Kembar (Sumatra)	3.85 N	97.66 E	2245	Shield volcano	PT
Bekulap (Sumatra)	3.28 N	98.37 E	-	Lava domes?	P
Siasar (Sumatra)	3.33 N	98.22 E	1610	Unknown	PM
Merubai (Sumatra)	3.33 N	98.40 E	1720	Unknown	PM
Takur-Takur (Sumatra)	3.25 N	98.63 E	-	Unknown	P
Tenaroh, Bukit (Sumatra)	3.12 N	98.63 E	-	Unknown	P
Simbolon (Sumatra)	3.02 N	98.90 E	1509	Stratovolcano	P
Panindi (Sumatra)	2.22 N	98.90 E	1627	Unknown	PM
Tolong (Sumatra)	1.97 N	98.80 E	1524	Unknown	PM
Helatoba-Tarutung (Sumatra)	2.03 N	98.93 E	1100	Fumarole field	PT
Sitarinda (Sumatra)	1.82 N	98.70 E	1617	Unknown	PM
Martimbang (Sumatra)	1.97 N	98.97 E	1680	Stratovolcano	P
Saut-Nagodang (Sumatra)	1.70 N	98.82 E	1804	Unknown	PM
Daung (Sumatra)	0.60 N	99.10 E	1784	Unknown	PM
Talu (Sumatra)	0.18 N	99.58 E	-	Unknown	PM
Gadang, Bukit (Sumatra)	0.05 N	99.80 E	2270	Stratovolcano	PM
Atar (Sumatra)	0.45 S	100.67 E	-	Unknown	PM
Melintang (Sumatra)	0.32 S	100.67 E	2262	Stratovolcano	Q
Maninjau (Sumatra)	0.35 S	100.20 E	1724	Caldera	P
Melalo, Bukit (Sumatra)	0.50 S	100.43 E	1375	Unknown	PM
Lantik (Sumatra)	0.67 S	100.47 E	1707	Unknown	PM
Gadut-Bungsu (Sumatra)	0.90 S	100.53 E	1859	Unknown	Q
Telor, Bukit (Sumatra)	1.23 S	103.62 E	38	Pyroclastic cone	P

Volcano Name (Subregion)	LAT	LONG	ELEV	TYPE	STATUS
Butak, Bukit (Sumatra)	1.48 S	101.15 E	1250	Unknown	PM
Tujuh (Sumatra)	1.70 S	101.42 E	2732	Stratovolcano	Q
Runcing (Sumatra)	1.75 S	101.63 E	1835	Unknown	Q
Patah Sembilan-Pandan (Sumatra)	1.70 S	101.07 E	2591	Unknown	PM
Raja-Sabanda (Sumatra)	2.02 S	101.32 E	2550	Unknown	PM
Mesurai-Ulu Nino (Sumatra)	2.23 S	101.72 E	2900	Unknown	PM
Tungkat, Bukit (Sumatra)	2.22 S	101.82 E	1550	Unknown	PM
Kumbang (Sumatra)	2.50 S	101.87 E	2935	Stratovolcano	P
Pabus, Bukit (Sumatra)	2.87 S	102.42 E	1006	Unknown	PM
Ulu Palik, Bukit (Sumatra)	3.08 S	102.17 E	2493	Unknown	PM
Basak, Bukit (Sumatra)	3.13 S	102.28 E	1077	Unknown	PM
Cundung Kelam, Bukit (Sumatra)	3.05 S	102.45 E	-	Unknown	PM
Dingin, Bukit (Sumatra)	4.17 S	102.72 E	2020	Unknown	PM
Bepagut (Sumatra)	4.33 S	103.47 E	2550	Unknown	PM
Jambul, Bukit (Sumatra)	4.13 S	103.55 E	1856	Unknown	PM
Isau-Isau (Sumatra)	4.15 S	103.35 E	1431	Unknown	Q
Sumur Tinggi, Bukit (Sumatra)	4.00 S	103.60 E	1394	Unknown	PM
Nanti, Bukit (Sumatra)	4.20 S	103.85 E	1619	Unknown	Q
Ringgit, Bukit (Sumatra)	4.30 S	103.62 E	2129	Unknown	PM
Garanggarag, Bukit (Sumatra)	4.38 S	103.52 E	2406	Unknown	PM
Pandan I, Bukit (Sumatra)	4.58 S	103.52 E	1811	Unknown	PM
Pandan Ii, Bukit (Sumatra)	4.80 S	103.77 E	1678	Unknown	PM
Pugung (Sumatra)	4.98 S	103.85 E	1964	Unknown	PM
Raja (Sumatra)	4.83 S	104.08 E	1643	Unknown	P
Kukusan (Sumatra)	4.90 S	104.05 E	1402	Unknown	PM
Pesagi (Sumatra)	4.92 S	104.15 E	2232	Unknown	P
Punggur, Bukit (Sumatra)	4.82 S	104.37 E	1877	Unknown	PM
Benatan, Bukit (Sumatra)	4.95 S	104.45 E	1688	Unknown	PM
Rantai-Betung (Sumatra)	5.55 S	104.27 E	1602	Unknown	PM
Tanggamus (Sumatra)	5.42 S	104.67 E	2102	Stratovolcano	Q
Sukadana (Sumatra)	5.25 S	*105.65 E	300	Shield volcano	P
Gede (Java)	5.93 S	106.07 E	595	Unknown	Q
Cibugis (Java)	6.50 S	106.57 E	613	Stratovolcano	Q
Kendeng (Java)	6.72 S	106.57 E	1370	Stratovolcano	Q
Endut (Java)	6.62 S	106.37 E	1297	Stratovolcano	P
Halimun (Java)	6.72 S	106.45 E	1929	Stratovolcano	P
Halimun (Java)	6.82 S	106.55 E	1750	Stratovolcano	P
Sanggabuana (Java)	6.58 S	107.22 E	1291	Stratovolcano	Q
Kancana (Java)	6.88 S	107.05 E	1233	Stratovolcano	P
Tilu (Java)	7.18 S	107.53 E	2040	Stratovolcano	P
Kancana (Java)	7.32 S	107.63 E	2182	Stratovolcano	Q
Mandalagiri (Java)	7.40 S	107.78 E	1831	Stratovolcano	Q
Cikuray (Java)	7.33 S	107.87 E	2821	Stratovolcano	Q
Kamojang, Kawah (Java)	7.13 S	107.80 E	1730	Stratovolcanoes	PT
Mandalawangi-Haruman (Java)	7.05 S	107.87 E	1663	Stratovolcano	Q
Kaledong-Haruman (Java)	7.05 S	107.92 E	1249	Lava domes	PM
Canlancang (Java)	6.97 S	107.95 E	1667	Unknown	Q
Sedakeling (Java)	7.12 S	108.03 E	1676	Stratovolcano	Q
Cakrabuana (Java)	7.03 S	108.13 E	1721	Stratovolcano	P
Sawal (Java)	7.18 S	108.27 E	1764	Stratovolcano	Q
Lasem (Java)	6.68 S	111.52 E	806	Stratovolcano	P
Selokaki (Java)	7.83 S	112.35 E	1083	Stratovolcano	Q
Argowayang (Java)	7.77 S	112.43 E	2198	Stratovolcano	Q
Ringgit (Java)	7.72 S	113.85 E	1250	Stratovolcano	P
Merbuk (Lesser Sunda Is)	8.25 S	114.65 E	1386	Unknown	Q
Patas (Lesser Sunda Is)	8.28 S	114.75 E	1414	Unknown	Q
Tambanan (Lesser Sunda Is)	8.33 S	114.95 E	2276	Unknown	Q
Seraja (Lesser Sunda Is)	8.37 S	115.67 E	1058	Unknown	Q
Punikan (Lesser Sunda Is)	8.47 S	116.13 E	1490	Unknown	Q
Lanteh, Batu (Lesser Sunda Is)	8.58 S	117.27 E	1276	Unknown	Q
Olet Takan (Lesser Sunda Is)	8.88 S	117.52 E	1400	Unknown	PM
Ramu, Doro (Lesser Sunda Is)	8.38 S	118.22 E	1128	Unknown	PM
Lambuwu, Doro (Lesser Sunda Is)	8.40 S	118.53 E	1678	Stratovolcano	Q
Maria, Doro (Lesser Sunda Is)	8.48 S	118.90 E	1484	Unknown	Q
Saboke, Doro (Lesser Sunda Is)	8.68 S	119.12 E	1000	Unknown	Q
Gilibanta (Lesser Sunda Is)	8.42 S	119.32 E	363	Stratovolcano?	Q
Otota, Doro (Lesser Sunda Is)	8.72 S	119.42 E	518	Unknown	Q
Ora, Doro (Lesser Sunda Is)	8.75 S	119.67 E	668	Unknown	Q
Beliling, Gunung (Lesser Sunda Is)	8.62 S	119.97 E	1153	Unknown	Q
Unnamed (Lesser Sunda Is)	8.72 S	120.35 E	2010	Unknown	PM
Unnamed (Lesser Sunda Is)	8.40 S	120.50 E	1084	Unknown	PM
Mere, Wai (Lesser Sunda Is)	8.63 S	120.95 E	1700	Unknown	PM
Lambo (Lesser Sunda Is)	8.67 S	121.30 E	2361	Unknown	PM
Delaki (Lesser Sunda Is)	8.50 S	122.12 E	1365	Unknown	PM
Mapi Group (Lesser Sunda Is)	8.60 S	122.35 E	1472	Unknown	PM
Wodong-Glaak (Lesser Sunda Is)	8.65 S	122.50 E	1492	Unknown	PM
Lewolaga (Lesser Sunda Is)	8.42 S	122.68 E	880	Unknown	PM
Iliberapun (Lesser Sunda Is)	8.53 S	122.92 E	705	Unknown	PM
Iliwaitami (Lesser Sunda Is)	8.47 S	122.98 E	890	Unknown	PM
Unnamed (Lesser Sunda Is)	8.45 S	123.02 E	880	Unknown	PM
Ilikedeka (Lesser Sunda Is)	8.30 S	122.90 E	871	Stratovolcano	PT
Lewobunga (Lesser Sunda Is)	8.15 S	122.92 E	811	Unknown	PM
Ilipasengdaeng (Lesser Sunda Is)	8.38 S	123.05 E	663	Unknown	PM
Ililawuung (Lesser Sunda Is)	8.45 S	123.12 E	880	Unknown	PM
Iliseburi (Lesser Sunda Is)	8.37 S	123.13 E	990	Unknown	PM
Unnamed (Lesser Sunda Is)	8.42 S	123.30 E	813	Unknown	PM
Iliminggar (Lesser Sunda Is)	8.50 S	123.32 E	1020	Stratovolcano	PM
Unnamed (Lesser Sunda Is)	8.37 S	123.75 E	738	Unknown	PM
Ilikedang (Lesser Sunda Is)	8.22 S	123.80 E	1533	Unknown	PM
Telagapui (Lesser Sunda Is)	8.22 S	125.02 E	1765	Unknown	PM
Tenagatu Humun (Lesser Sunda Is)	7.82 S	126.03 E	1396	Unknown	PM
Unnamed (Lesser Sunda Is)	7.70 S	126.58 E	1418	Unknown	PM
Lompobatang (Sulawesi-Indonesia)	5.35 S	119.92 E	2871	Stratovolcano	Q
Laposo (Sulawesi-Indonesia)	4.37 S	119.80 E	1395	Stratovolcano	Q
Rantemario-Latimojong (Sulawesi)	3.37 S	120.08 E	3440	Stratovolcanoes	Q
Ogoamas (Sulawesi-Indonesia)	0.67 S	120.20 E	2565	Unknown	Q
Sidole (Sulawesi-Indonesia)	0.48 S	119.88 E	2195	Unknown	Q
Maling (Sulawesi-Indonesia)	0.25 N	120.80 E	2707	Unknown	Q
Tentolomatinan (Sulawesi)	0.93 N	121.75 E	2207	Unknown	Q
Nunuka (Sulawesi-Indonesia)	0.38 N	123.77 E	1606	Unknown	Q
Hamiding (Halmahera-Indonesia)	1.62 N	127.82 E	1204	Unknown	Q
Mostyn (New Guinea-W)	4.60 N	*118.18 E	-	Fissure vents?	Q
Quoin Hill (New Guinea-W)	4.40 N	118.03 E	539	Cone	Q
Usun Apau Plateau (New Guinea)	2.75 N	114.67 E	-	Unknown	Q
Linau-Balui Plateau (New Guinea)	2.35 N	114.10 E	-	Unknown	Q
Kajang Plateau, Bukit (N Guinea)	2.33 N	113.67 E	-	Unknown	Q
Nuit, Mt. (New Guinea-W)	1.02 N	109.93 E	1701	Unknown	Q

PHILIPPINES & SE ASIA

Volcano Name (Subregion)	LAT	LONG	ELEV	TYPE	STATUS
Blit (Mindanao-Philippines)	6.96 N	124.23 E	1198	Unknown	P
Quezon (Mindanao-Philippines)	6.58 N	124.62 E	652	Lava domes	P
Kitabud (Mindanao-Philippines)	7.29 N	124.66 E	1167	Unknown	P
Imbing (Mindanao-Philippines)	7.68 N	123.23 E	700	Stratovolcanoes	P
Kaladis (Mindanao-Philippines)	7.58 N	122.97 E	-	Stratovolcano	P
Ampiro (Mindanao-Philippines)	8.39 N	123.63 E	1532	Stratovolcano?	Q
Pana-on (Philippines-C)	9.95 N	125.27 E	-	Unknown	P
Silago (Philippines-C)	10.50 N	125.17 E	-	Unknown	P
Cancajanag (Philippines-C)	11.07 N	124.78 E	900	Lava domes	Q
Alto (Philippines-C)	11.11 N	124.75 E	1350	Compound volc	P
Maripipi (Philippines-C)	11.80 N	124.33 E	924	Unknown	Q
Gate Mountains (Luzon-Philippines)	12.60 N	124.00 E	559	Unknown	P
Malinao (Luzon-Philippines)	13.42 N	123.61 E	1548	Stratovolcano	PT
Sangay (Luzon-Philippines)	13.52 N	123.53 E	-	Unknown	P
Cone-Culasi (Luzon-Philippines)	13.92 N	*123.02 E	959	Volcanic field	P
Labo (Luzon-Philippines)	14.02 N	122.79 E	1544	Compound volc	PT
Dagit-Dagitan (Luzon-Philippines)	13.53 N	121.08 E	364	Stratovolcano	P
Panay (Luzon-Philippines)	13.72 N	120.89 E	501	Stratovolcano	PT
Malepunyo (Luzon-Philippines)	14.95 N	121.23 E	963	Stratovolcano	P
Anilao Hill (Luzon-Philippines)	13.90 N	121.18 E	358	Scoria cone	P
Cariliao (Luzon-Philippines)	14.13 N	120.75 E	656	Stratovolcano	P
Corregidor (Luzon-Philippines)	14.40 N	120.58 E	173	Caldera	P
Matarem (Luzon-N of)	20.38 N	121.93 E	459	Compound volc	P
Gaojianshi (SE Asia)	17.00 N	112.50 E	-	Unknown	Q
Weizhoudao (SE Asia)	21.05 N	109.13 E	-	Shield volcano	P?
Unnamed (SE Asia)	19.45 N	*105.53 E	-	Cone	P
Unnamed (SE Asia)	19.32 N	*105.53 E	-	Cone	P
Vinkh-Linkh (SE Asia)	17.08 N	107.05 E	-	Cone	P
Ban Chay (SE Asia)	14.00 N	107.50 E	-	Unknown	P
Pleiku-Bantour Volc Field	13.85 N	*108.10 E	1028	Cones	P
Darlac Volc Field (SE Asia)	12.88 N	*108.20 E	-	Cones	P
Bas Song Be (SE Asia)	11.67 N	106.67 E	-	Volcanic field	P
Pailin (SE Asia)	12.90 N	102.60 E	-	Unknown	P
Cham (SE Asia)	12.10 N	105.60 E	-	Unknown	P
Chup (SE Asia)	11.90 N	105.82 E	-	Unknown	P
Snoul (SE Asia)	12.10 N	106.40 E	-	Unknown	P
Haut Song Be (SE Asia)	12.05 N	*107.25 E	-	Volcanic field	P
Bokeo Volc Field (SE Asia)	13.50 N	107.20 E	500	Scoria cones	Q
Plateau des Bolovens (SE Asia)	15.00 N	106.30 E	-	Fissure vents	P
Buriram (SE Asia)	15.00 N	103.00 E	-	Unknown	P
Chanthaburi (SE Asia)	12.50 N	102.20 E	-	Unknown	P
Lampang (SE Asia)	18.30 N	99.60 E	-	Unknown	P
Ban Chiang Khian (SE Asia)	19.80 N	100.00 E	-	Unknown	P
Ban Hui Sai (SE Asia)	20.30 N	100.30 E	-	Unknown	P
Kuantan (SE Asia)	3.90 N	103.40 E	-	Volcanic field	P
Medaw Island (SE Asia)	11.72 N	98.67 E	115	Fissure vents	P
Thaton (SE Asia)	17.42 N	96.95 E	30	Fissure vents	P?
Sonetaung (SE Asia)	21.53 N	95.10 E	270	Unknown	PM
Loi Han Hun (SE Asia)	22.48 N	97.98 E	1100	Lava dome	P
Wuntho (SE Asia)	23.83 N	95.50 E	-	Unknown	PM
Namyong (SE Asia)	25.68 N	96.43 E	508	Fissure vents	P
Loiyme, Mt. (SE Asia)	26.00 N	96.50 E	1561	Lava dome	PM

JAPAN, TAIWAN, MARIANAS

Volcano Name (Subregion)	LAT	LONG	ELEV	TYPE	STATUS
Chi-Mei (Taiwan)	23.50 N	121.43 E	815	Lava dome	PM
Tsaolingshan (Taiwan)	24.83 N	121.28 E	347	Shield volcano	P
Chilung Group (Taiwan)	25.08 N	121.85 E	729	Lava domes	P
Huapinghsü (Taiwan)	25.42 N	121.92 E	51	Stratovolcano	P
Mienhuayu (Taiwan)	25.48 N	122.12 E	61	Stratovolcano	P
Pengchiahsu (Taiwan-N of)	25.63 N	122.07 E	129	Stratovolcano	PT
Kobi-sho (Ryukyu Is)	25.92 N	123.68 E	117	Stratovolcano	P
Gaja-jima (Ryukyu Is)	29.90 N	129.54 E	497	Stratovolcano	P
Tokara Hirase (Ryukyu Is)	30.04 N	130.06 E	27	Unknown	Q
Kuro-shima (Ryukyu Is)	30.83 N	129.94 E	622	Stratovolcano	P
Ata Caldera (Kyushu-Japan)	31.33 N	130.67 E	-	Caldera	P
Sendai (Kyushu-Japan)	31.73 N	130.45 E	677	Pyroclastic cone	P
Satsuma Maru-yama (Kyushu)	31.80 N	130.41 E	218	Lava dome	P
Imuta (Kyushu-Japan)	31.82 N	130.46 E	509	Lava domes	P
Hokusatsu (Kyushu-Japan)	31.87 N	130.61 E	703	Pyroclastic cone	P
Kakuto (Kyushu-Japan)	32.04 N	130.77 E	-	Caldera	P
Sone (Kyushu-Japan)	33.21 N	129.09 E	143	Pyroclastic cone	P
Ojika-jima (Kyushu-Japan)	33.21 N	129.09 E	126	Shield volcanoes	P
Tara-dake (Kyushu-Japan)	32.98 N	130.08 E	1076	Stratovolcano	P
Kinpo (Kyushu-Japan)	32.81 N	130.64 E	665	Stratovolcano	P
Yabakei (Kyushu-Japan)	33.17 N	131.22 E	800	Caldera	P
Hane-yama (Kyushu-Japan)	33.23 N	131.13 E	1140	Shield volcano	P
Hohi (Kyushu-Japan)	33.28 N	131.32 E	1236	Stratovolcanoes	P
Futago (Kyushu-Japan)	33.58 N	131.60 E	720	Lava domes	P
Hime-shima Volc Group (Kyushu)	33.72 N	131.67 E	267	Lava domes	P
Kurose (Kyushu-Japan)	33.70 N	130.23 E	8	Volcanic neck	P
Iki Volc Group (Kyushu-Japan)	33.74 N	129.71 E	213	Pyroclastic cones	P
Mutsure-jima (Honshu-Japan)	33.97 N	130.87 E	104	Cinder cones	P
Shikuma (Honshu-Japan)	34.10 N	131.76 E	504	Lava domes	P
Tokuyama-Mitake (Honshu-Japan)	34.19 N	131.84 E	790	Lava dome	P
Sengoku (Honshu-Japan)	34.19 N	131.76 E	661	Lava domes	P
Chojagahara (Honshu-Japan)	34.27 N	131.67 E	390	Pyroclastic cone	P
Aono-yama (Honshu-Japan)	34.46 N	131.80 E	908	Lava domes	P
Oetaka-yama (Honshu-Japan)	35.06 N	132.43 E	808	Lava domes	P
Yokote (Honshu-Japan)	35.20 N	133.27 E	967	Scoria cones	P
Noro (Honshu-Japan)	35.41 N	133.18 E	180	Pyroclastic cone	P
Daikon-jima (Honshu-Japan)	35.49 N	133.17 E	42	Pyroclastic cone	P
Tsuruta (Honshu-Japan)	35.34 N	133.42 E	301	Scoria cones	P
Daisen (Honshu-Japan)	35.37 N	133.55 E	1729	Stratovolcano	P
Ogino-Sen (Honshu-Japan)	35.44 N	134.44 E	1310	Scoria cones	P
Kannabe (Honshu-Japan)	35.50 N	134.68 E	460	Shield volcano	Q
Takara (Honshu-Japan)	35.34 N	134.92 E	350	Shield volcano	P
Nanzaki (Honshu-Japan)	34.60 N	138.83 E	106	Pyroclastic cone	P
Jaishi (Honshu-Japan)	34.71 N	138.79 E	520	Shield volcano	P
Tanaba (Honshu-Japan)	34.91 N	138.85 E	1035	Stratovolcano	P
Daruma (Honshu-Japan)	34.95 N	138.84 E	982	Stratovolcano	P
Tenshi (Honshu-Japan)	34.92 N	138.97 E	608	Stratovolcano	P
Usami (Honshu-Japan)	34.97 N	139.06 E	592	Stratovolcano	P
Taga (Honshu-Japan)	35.08 N	139.03 E	798	Stratovolcano	P
Yugawara (Honshu-Japan)	35.17 N	139.03 E	1004	Stratovolcano	P
Ashitaka (Honshu-Japan)	35.24 N	138.80 E	1504	Stratovolcano	P
Kurofuji (Honshu-Japan)	35.80 N	138.51 E	1764	Stratovolcanoes	P
Yatsuga-take (Honshu-Japan)	35.97 N	138.37 E	2899	Stratovolcanoes	P
Kirigamine (Honshu-Japan)	36.10 N	138.20 E	1925	Shield volcano	P
Utsukushigahara (Honshu-Japan)	36.22 N	138.11 E	2034	Shield volcano	P
Ueno (Honshu-Japan)	35.59 N	137.51 E	606	Shield volcano	P
Yuga-mine (Honshu-Japan)	35.80 N	137.28 E	1067	Lava dome	P
Eboshi-Washigatake (Honshu)	35.94 N	136.97 E	1672	Stratovolcano	P
Bishamon-dake (Honshu-Japan)	35.94 N	136.80 E	1386	Stratovolcano	P
Dainichiga-take (Honshu-Japan)	36.00 N	136.84 E	1709	Stratovolcano	P
Ryohaku Maru-yama (Honshu)	36.05 N	136.80 E	1786	Stratovolcano	P
Gankyoji (Honshu-Japan)	36.05 N	136.74 E	1691	Stratovolcano	P
Kyoga-take (Honshu-Japan)	36.04 N	136.63 E	1671	Stratovolcanoes	P
Dainichi-yama (Honshu-Japan)	36.15 N	136.50 E	1369	Stratovolcano	P
Tomuro (Honshu-Japan)	36.53 N	136.75 E	548	Lava domes	P
Kamitakara (Honshu-Japan)	36.20 N	137.50 E	1831	Unknown	P
Hodaka-dake (Honshu-Japan)	36.29 N	137.65 E	3190	Caldera	P
Momisawa-dake (Honshu-Japan)	36.36 N	137.61 E	2755	Unknown	P
Kaminoroka (Honshu-Japan)	36.47 N	137.60 E	2465	Unknown	P
Shirouma-Oike (Honshu-Japan)	36.79 N	137.80 E	2469	Stratovolcanoes	P
Madarao (Honshu-Japan)	36.83 N	138.28 E	1382	Stratovolcano	P
Kurohime (Honshu-Japan)	36.81 N	138.13 E	2053	Stratovolcano	P
Iizuna (Honshu-Japan)	36.74 N	138.14 E	1917	Stratovolcano	P
Motodori (Honshu-Japan)	36.72 N	138.25 E	745	Lava dome	P
Minakami (Honshu-Japan)	36.55 N	138.23 E	659	Lava dome	P
Eboshi (Honshu-Japan)	36.43 N	138.39 E	2227	Stratovolcano	P
Hanamagari (Honshu-Japan)	36.41 N	138.65 E	1757	Stratovolcanoes	P
Azumaya (Honshu-Japan)	36.54 N	138.42 E	2354	Stratovolcano	P
Omeshi-dake (Honshu-Japan)	36.63 N	138.46 E	2160	Stratovolcano	P
Takayashiro (Honshu-Japan)	36.80 N	138.41 E	1351	Stratovolcano	P
Sekita (Honshu-Japan)	36.97 N	138.39 E	1289	Stratovolcano?	P
Kenashi (Honshu-Japan)	36.90 N	138.49 E	1650	Stratovolcano	P
Torikabuto (Honshu-Japan)	36.84 N	138.59 E	2038	Stratovolcano	P
Naeba (Honshu-Japan)	36.84 N	138.69 E	2145	Stratovolcano	P
Iiji (Honshu-Japan)	36.95 N	138.84 E	1112	Stratovolcano	P
Masugata (Honshu-Japan)	37.08 N	138.83	749	Pyroclastic cone	P
Komochi-Onoko (Honshu-Japan)	36.59 N	139.00 E	1296	Stratovolcanoes	P
Sukai-Kesemaru (Honshu-Japan)	36.69 N	139.34 E	2144	Stratovolcanoes	P
Numanokami (Honshu-Japan)	36.77 N	139.28 E	1541	Stratovolcano	P
Hotaka (Honshu-Japan)	36.80 N	139.14 E	2158	Stratovolcano	P
Ayame-daira (Honshu-Japan)	36.90 N	139.24 E	1969	Stratovolcanoes	P
Kinunuma-Nenakusa (Honshu)	36.88 N	139.38 E	2141	Lava domes	P
Nyoho-Akanagi (Honshu-Japan)	36.81 N	139.54 E	2483	Stratovolcano	P
Futamata (Honshu-Japan)	37.24 N	139.97 E	1544	Stratovolcano	P
Aizu Nunobiki (Honshu-Japan)	37.32 N	140.02 E	1108	Stratovolcano	P
Asakusa (Honshu-Japan)	37.34 N	139.24 E	1585	Stratovolcano	P
Sumon (Honshu-Japan)	37.40 N	139.14 E	1537	Stratovolcano	P
Sunagohara (Honshu-Japan)	37.45 N	139.69 E	729	Caldera	P
Nekoma (Honshu-Japan)	37.61 N	140.03 E	1404	Stratovolcano	P
Aoso (Honshu-Japan)	38.08 N	140.61 E	820	Stratovolcano	P
Shirataka (Honshu-Japan)	38.22 N	140.18 E	994	Stratovolcano	P
Ganto-Kamuro (Honshu-Japan)	38.20 N	140.48 E	1485	Stratovolcanoes	P
Adachi (Honshu-Japan)	38.22 N	140.65 E	-	Pumice cone	P
Daito (Honshu-Japan)	38.30 N	140.53 E	1366	Stratovolcano	P
Funagata (Honshu-Japan)	38.45 N	140.62 E	1500	Stratovolcanoes	P
Gassan (Honshu-Japan)	38.55 N	140.03 E	1984	Stratovolcano	P
Mukaimachi (Honshu-Japan)	38.75 N	140.52 E	657	Caldera	P
Onikobe (Honshu-Japan)	38.83 N	140.70 E	769	Caldera	PT
Takamatsu (Honshu-Japan)	38.97 N	140.61 E	1348	Stratovolcano	P
Kobinai (Honshu-Japan)	39.02 N	140.52 E	1004	Stratovolcano	P
Yakeishi (Honshu-Japan)	39.16 N	140.83 E	1548	Stratovolcano	P
Tazawa (Honshu-Japan)	39.72 N	140.67 E	249	Caldera?	P?
Kayo (Honshu-Japan)	39.80 N	140.73 E	1254	Stratovolcano	P
Nyuto-Takakura (Honshu-Japan)	39.80 N	140.84 E	1478	Stratovolcanoes	P
Tamagawa (Honshu-Japan)	39.90 N	140.78 E	1300	Caldera	P
Moriyoshi (Honshu-Japan)	39.97 N	140.55 E	1454	Stratovolcano	P
Kanpu (Honshu-Japan)	39.93 N	139.88 E	355	Stratovolcano	P
Nanashigure (Honshu-Japan)	40.07 N	141.11 E	1063	Lava dome	P
Daira-Komaga-take (Honshu)	40.41 N	140.26 E	1158	Stratovolcano	Q
Tashiro (Honshu-Japan)	40.43 N	140.41 E	1178	Stratovolcano	P
Okiura (Honshu-Japan)	40.57 N	140.73 E	985	Caldera	P
Mutsu-Hiuchi-dake (Honshu-Japan)	41.44 N	141.06 E	781	Stratovolcano	PT
Udone-Jima (Izu Is-Japan)	34.47 N	139.30 E	209	Stratovolcano	P
Onohara-jima (Izu Is-Japan)	34.05 N	139.39 E	114	Lava dome	P
Inamba-jima (Izu Is-Japan)	33.65 N	139.30 E	74	Lava dome	P
Tracey Seamount (Mariana Is)	13.65 N	144.42 E	-900	Submarine volc	Q
Oshima-Ko-jima (Hokkaido-Japan)	41.36 N	139.81 E	282	Stratovolcano	Q
Oshima Maru-yama (Hokkaido)	41.54 N	140.38 E	855	Stratovolcano	P
Hakodate-yama (Hokkaido-Japan)	41.76 N	140.71 E	333	Stratovolcano	P
Zenikame (Hokkaido-Japan)	41.74 N	140.86 E	-30	Submarine volc	P
E-san Maru-yama (Hokkaido-Japan)	41.85 N	141.10 E	691	Stratovolcano	P
Yokotsu (Hokkaido-Japan)	41.94 N	140.78 E	1167	Stratovolcano	P
Nigorigawa (Hokkaido-Japan)	42.12 N	140.45 E	356	Hydrothermal field	PT
Okushiri-Katsuma-yama (Japan)	42.19 N	139.47 E	428	Shield volcano	P
Kariba (Hokkaido-Japan)	42.61 N	139.94 E	1520	Stratovolcano	P
Washibetsu (Hokkaido-Japan)	42.43 N	141.01 E	911	Stratovolcano	P
Raiden (Hokkaido-Japan)	42.90 N	140.47 E	1212	Stratovolcanoes	P
Akaigawa (Hokkaido-Japan)	43.08 N	140.82 E	725	Stratovolcano	P
Shiribetsu (Hokkaido-Japan)	42.77 N	140.92 E	1107	Stratovolcano	P
Orofure-Raiba (Hokkaido-Japan)	42.56 N	141.09 E	1231	Stratovolcanoes	P
Horohoro-Tokushumbetsu	42.63 N	141.15 E	1322	Stratovolcanoes	P
Soranuma (Hokkaido-Japan)	42.86 N	141.26 E	1251	Shield volcano	P
Sapporo (Hokkaido-Japan)	42.90 N	141.20 E	1294	Shield volcano	P
Tomuraushi Volc Group (Japan)	43.53 N	142.85 E	2141	Stratovolcanoes	P
Chubetsu (Hokkaido-Japan)	43.59 N	142.90 E	1963	Stratovolcano	P
Niseikaushuppe (Hokkaido-Japan)	43.78 N	142.99 E	1883	Stratovolcano	P
Tengu-Hirayama (Hokkaido-Japan)	43.78 N	143.02 E	1796	Stratovolcanoes	P
Shiitokoro (Hokkaido-Japan)	43.61 N	143.18 E	1336	Lava dome	P
Kumaneshiri (Hokkaido-Japan)	43.52 N	143.24 E	1635	Stratovolcanoes	P
Tokachi-Mitsumata (Hokkaido)	43.52 N	143.15 E	700	Caldera	P
Tokachi-Eboshi (Hokkaido-Japan)	43.38 N	143.13 E	1291	Lava domes	P
Birao (Hokkaido-Japan)	43.50 N	144.41 E	554	Stratovolcanoes	P
Samakkenupuri (Hokkaido-Japan)	43.68 N	144.74 E	1063	Stratovolcano	P
Musa (Hokkaido-Japan)	43.68 N	144.89 E	1006	Stratovolcanoes	P
Shari (Hokkaido-Japan)	43.76 N	144.72 E	1545	Stratovolcano	P
Unabetsu (Hokkaido-Japan)	43.87 N	144.88 E	1419	Stratovolcano	P
Onnebetsu (Hokkaido-Japan)	43.99 N	145.02 E	1331	Stratovolcano	P
Shiretoko (Hokkaido-Japan)	44.23 N	145.28 E	1254	Stratovolcano	P

KURIL ISLANDS & KAMCHATKA

Volcano Name (Subregion)	LAT	LONG	ELEV	TYPE	STATUS
Urbich Caldera (Kuril Is)	44.58 N	147.17 E	907	Calderas	P
Vetrovoi Isthmus Caldera (Kurils)	45.22 N	148.35 E	264	Caldera	P
Tsirk (Kuril Is)	45.40 N	148.58 E	853	Caldera	P
Petr Shmidt Ridge (Kuril Is)	45.90 N	150.08 E	1031	Unknown	P
Antipin (Kuril Is)	46.15 N	150.23 E	1120	Stratovolcano	P
Desantnaya Mountain (Kuril Is)	46.15 N	150.40 E	867	Stratovolcano	P
Brontona Island (Kuril Is)	46.67 N	150.72 E	-	Unknown	P
Ikanmikot (Kuril Is)	46.97 N	152.03 E	645	Stratovolcano	P
Kuntomintar (Kuril Is)	48.75 N	154.02 E	828	Hydrothermal field	PT
Shestakov, Mt. (Kuril Is)	49.75 N	154.75 E	-	Stratovolcano	P
Avos' Rocks (Kuril Is)	49.72 N	154.12 E	35	Unknown	P
Makanru Island (Kuril Is)	49.83 N	154.43 E	-	Stratovolcano	P
Vysokii (Kamchatka)	51.12 N	156.88 E	703	Stratovolcano	P
Tumanniy (Kamchatka)	51.18 N	156.93 E	711	Shield volcano	P
Ded i Baba (Kamchatka)	51.30 N	156.58 E	1032	Shield volcano	P
Tretya Rechka (Kamchatka)	51.40 N	156.57 E	754	Shield volcano	P
Koshegochek (Kamchatka)	51.62 N	156.80 E	1175	Shield volcano	P
Sredniy Koshegochek	51.68 N	156.90 E	-	Shield volcano	P
Unnamed (Kamchatka)	51.77 N	156.87 E	560	Shield volcano	P
Leviy Koshegochek (Kamchatka)	51.78 N	156.93 E	987	Shield volcano	P
Kuzheten (Kamchatka)	51.82 N	157.22 E	925	Shield volcano	P
Vostochnaya Khodutka	51.93 N	157.73 E	-	Shield volcanoes	P
Zheltiy (Kamchatka)	51.93 N	157.60 E	792	Stratovolcano	P
Kuzanek (Kamchatka)	51.93 N	157.18 E	968	Shield volcano	P
Unnamed (Kamchatka)	51.95 N	157.02 E	740	Shield volcano	P
Igolki (Kamchatka)	52.02 N	156.88 E	707	Shield volcanoes	P
Skalistiy (Kamchatka)	52.02 N	157.18 E	1005	Shield volcano	P
Perevalny (Kamchatka)	52.13 N	157.78 E	-	Shield volcano	P
Krugliy (Kamchatka)	51.13 N	157.62 E	984	Shield volcano	P
Savan (Kamchatka)	52.22 N	157.28 E	911	Shield volcano	P
Malaya Ipelka (Kamchatka)	52.28 N	156.73 E	-	Complex volcano	P
Kamen (Kamchatka)	52.28 N	157.65 E	866	Stratovolcano	P
Ploskiy (Kamchatka)	52.37 N	157.62 E	877	Stratovolcano	P
Udochka (Kamchatka)	52.50 N	157.20 E	891	Shield volcano	P
Bolshaya Ipelka (Kamchatka)	52.63 N	156.97 E	1194	Shield volcano	P
Tolmachev (Kamchatka)	52.55 N	157.73 E	1118	Stratovolcanoes	P
Unnamed (Kamchatka)	52.78 N	158.28 E	-	Shield volcano	P
Unnamed (Kamchatka)	52.80 N	158.37 E	-	Lava domes	P
Unnamed (Kamchatka)	52.90 N	158.37 E	-	Shield volcanoes	P
Unnamed (Kamchatka)	52.75 N	157.97 E	-	Lava domes	P
Shemodogan (Kamchatka)	52.92 N	157.72 E	1446	Shield volcano	P
Khalzan-Shapochka (Kamchatka)	53.12 N	157.60 E	-	Shield volcano	P
Aak (Kamchatka)	53.38 N	158.67 E	2319	Stratovolcanoes	P
Kupol (Kamchatka)	53.50 N	158.65 E	-	Stratovolcano	P
Kitkhoysky (Kamchatka)	53.55 N	158.58 E	-	Shield volcanoes	P
Vershinsky (Kamchatka)	53.60 N	158.70 E	1812	Stratovolcano	P
Skalistiy (Kamchatka)	53.72 N	159.22 E	-	Unknown	P
Pik (Kamchatka)	53.80 N	158.87 E	-	Unknown	P
Vodorazdelny (Kamchatka)	53.80 N	158.80 E	-	Unknown	P
Kurgannaya (Kamchatka)	54.02 N	158.57 E	-	Unknown	P
Kavychinsky (Kamchatka)	54.13 N	158.45 E	-	Unknown	P
Baraniy (Kamchatka)	54.25 N	158.48 E	-	Unknown	P
Zhupanovskiye Vostriyaky	53.80 N	159.28 E	1684	Stratovolcano	P
Ditmara (Kamchatka)	53.87 N	159.53 E	1389	Stratovolcano	P
Krainy (Kamchatka)	53.95 N	159.33 E	1199	Stratovolcano	P
Razlaty (Kamchatka)	54.02 N	159.38 E	-	Stratovolcano	P
Pribrezhny (Kamchatka)	54.07 N	159.77 E	-	Stratovolcano	P
Unnamed (Kamchatka)	54.37 N	159.43 E	-	Stratovolcano	P
Unana (Kamchatka)	54.63 N	159.72 E	2131	Stratovolcano	P
Adamozhets (Kamchatka)	54.75 N	159.40 E	-	Unknown	P
Bogachensky (Kamchatka)	55.13 N	160.90 E	-	Shield volcano	P
Piip (Kamchatka)	55.30 N	160.93 E	-	Shield volcano	P
Konechnaya (Kamchatka)	55.23 N	160.97 E	-	Shield volcano	P
Konradi (Kamchatka)	55.08 N	160.53 E	1912	Stratovolcano	P
Sokol (Kamchatka)	55.20 N	160.52 E	1711	Stratovolcano	P
Tumrok (Kamchatka)	55.37 N	160.87 E	2197	Shield volcano	P
Uspensky (Kamchatka)	55.53 N	160.78 E	1893	Unknown	P
Shish (Kamchatka)	55.75 N	161.18 E	2399	Cone	P
Iult (Kamchatka)	55.23 N	160.59 E	1857	Stratovolcano	P
Nikolka (Kamchatka)	55.33 N	159.95 E	1591	Unknown	P
Gorny Zub (Kamchatka)	56.83 N	160.68 E	2241	Unknown	P
Zarechny (Kamchatka)	56.38 N	160.83 E	760	Somma volcano	P
Kharchinsky (Kamchatka)	56.43 N	160.83 E	1410	Stratovolcano	P
Unnamed (Kamchatka)	56.53 N*	160.87 E	200	Cinder cones	P
Unnamed (Kamchatka)	56.70 N	161.75 E	-	Lava domes	P
Lyzyk (Kamchatka)	57.23 N	161.52 E	-	Unknown	P
Uchkoren (Kamchatka)	57.27 N	161.35 E	-	Unknown	P
Nachikinsky (Kamchatka)	57.83 N	162.68 E	1211	Unknown	P
Khailyulya (Kamchatka)	58.03 N	161.62 E	-	Unknown	P
Lauchachan (Kamchatka)	55.35 N	157.10 E	1018	Shield volcano	P
Prodolny (Kamchatka)	55.45 N	157.25 E	1505	Shield volcanoes	P
Kobalan (Kamchatka)	55.43 N	157.37 E	1174	Stratovolcano	P
Unnamed (Kamchatka)	55.73 N	157.22 E	-	Shield volcano	Q
Tynua (Kamchatka)	55.85 N	157.87 E	1727	Shield volcanoes	P
Etopan (Kamchatka)	55.97 N	157.63 E	1264	Shield volcano	P
Kimitina (Kamchatka)	55.25 N	158.18 E	1438	Stratovolcano	P
Unnamed (Kamchatka)	55.52 N	158.43 E	2140	Shield volcano	P
Ochchamo (Kamchatka)	55.62 N	158.15 E	2136	Shield volcano	P
Bolshoy Kozyrevsky (Kamchatka)	55.60 N	158.52 E	1672	Shield volcano	P
Bolshaya Romanovka (Kamchatka)	55.73 N	158.77 E	1821	Shield volcano	P
Unnamed (Kamchatka)	55.88 N	158.83 E	1821	Stratovolcanoes	P
Bongabti (Kamchatka)	55.83 N	158.32 E	1790	Shield volcano	P
Nosichan (Kamchatka)	56.08 N	157.75 E	1105	Shield volcano	P
Buduli (Kamchatka)	56.40 N	158.70 E	1477	Shield volcano	P
Kopkan (Kamchatka)	56.48 N	158.83 E	1120	Shield volcanoes	P
Yanpat (Kamchatka)	56.53 N	158.80 E	1205	Shield volcanoes	P
Chavycha (Kamchatka)	56.55 N	158.65 E	1190	Shield volcanoes	P
Malaya Ketepana (Kamchatka)	56.68 N	158.47 E	1230	Shield volcano	P
Bolshoy Ketepana (Kamchatka)	57.05 N	158.37 E	1521	Shield volcano	P
Unnamed (Kamchatka)	56.97 N	158.75 E	-	Shield volcano	P
Ovalny (Kamchatka)	56.98 N	158.98 E	732	Shield volcano	P
Tigilsky (Kamchatka)	56.82 N	159.13 E	1495	Shield volcano	P
Perevalovyi (Kamchatka)	56.57 N	159.35 E	1328	Shield volcano	P
Maly Alney (Kamchatka)	56.47 N	159.77 E	1858	Stratovolcanoes	P
Maly Chekchebonay (Kamchatka)	56.80 N	159.45 E	1247	Shield volcano	P
Bolshoy Chekchebonay	56.92 N	159.42 E	1391	Shield volcano	P
Kireunsky (Kamchatka)	56.78 N	159.75 E	1925	Shield volcano	P
Dvukhyurtochny (Kamchatka)	56.82 N	159.88 E	1631	Shield volcano	P
Unnamed (Kamchatka)	56.93 N	159.95 E	-	Lava domes	P
Kalgauch (Kamchatka)	56.93 N	159.73 E	1206	Stratovolcano	P
Kunkhilok (Kamchatka)	57.32 N	160.50 E	1325	Stratovolcano	P
Shlen (Kamchatka)	57.48 N	159.57 E	1001	Shield volcano	P
Pirozhnikova (Kamchatka)	57.47 N	160.25 E	1665	Stratovolcano	P
Kamenisty (Kamchatka)	57.65 N	160.43 E	1762	Stratovolcano	P
Tekletunup (Kamchatka)	57.75 N	160.23 E	1395	Shield volcano	P
Ulvaney (Kamchatka)	57.78 N	160.62 E	1445	Shield volcano	P
Mutny (Kamchatka)	57.72 N	160.37 E	1345	Shield volcano	P
Khuvkhoitun (Kamchatka)	57.92 N	160.65 E	2618	Complex volcano	P
Keveney (Kamchatka)	58.05 N	160.73 E	1887	Shield volcano	P
Langtutkin (Kamchatka)	58.23 N	161.10 E	1545	Shield volcano	P
Unnamed (Kamchatka)	58.50 N	160.93 E	-	Shield volcanoes	P
Kikhiikhylkhangei (Kamchatka)	59.25 N	162.50 E	-	Cone	P

MAINLAND ASIA

Volcano Name (Subregion)	LAT	LONG	ELEV	TYPE	STATUS
Unnamed (Russia-NE)	62.10 N	162.70 E	-	Unknown	Q
Aluchin Group (Russia-NE)	66.12 N*	165.63 E	1000	Pyroclastic cones	P
Anjuisky (Russia-NE)	67.17 N*	165.20 E	1050	Pyroclastic cones	P
Unnamed (Russia-NE)	67.48 N	170.28 E	-	Unknown	P
Unnamed (Russia-NE)	68.17 N	167.45 E	-	Unknown	P
Unnamed (Russia-NE)	68.60 N*	170.95 E	-	Explosion craters	Q
Unnamed (Russia-NE)	69.40 N*	167.75 E	-	Explosion craters	Q
Unnamed (Russia-NE)	68.35 N	163.70 E	-	Unknown	Q
Unnamed (Russia-NE)	69.15 N*	161.00 E	-	Explosion craters	Q
Unnamed (Russia-NE)	64.20 N	148.80 E	-	Unknown	Q
Unnamed (Russia-NE)	69.17 N	147.15 E	-	Unknown	P
Balagan-Tas (Russia-NE)	65.96 N	145.89 E	993	Cinder cones	P
Unnamed (Russia-NE)	60.00 N	150.00 E	-	Fissure vents	Q
Khamar-Daban (Russia-SE)	51.40 N	102.50 E	2369	Volcanic field	Q
Dgida Basin (Russia-SE)	50.52 N*	103.25 E	1500	Cinder cones	P
Khulugayshi (Russia-SE)	52.00 N	102.50 E	-	Explosion crater	Q
Unnamed (Russia-SE)	51.25 N*	96.50 E	1300	Fissure vent	Q
Unnamed (Mongolia)	51.33 N	99.33 E	1922	Cone	P
Khubsugal Region (Mongolia)	51.00 N*	101.00 E	-	Volcanic field	Q
Ika-Togo-Ula (Mongolia)	47.88 N	103.08 E	1619	Pyroclastic cones	Q
Orkhon Gol (Mongolia)	48.65 N*	103.50 E	-	Volcanic field	P
Unnamed (Mongolia)	48.17 N	109.83 E	-	Cones	P
Tabun Urtu-Ula (Mongolia)	44.85 N	107.63 E	1167	Unknown	P
Khutza-Ula (Mongolia)	42.58 N*	107.50 E	1162	Unknown	P?
Unnamed (Mongolia)	42.33 N*	105.98 E	1217	Volcanic field	P
Unnamed (Mongolia)	43.40 N*	104.02 E	1752	Volcanic field	P
Unnamed (Mongolia)	44.25 N*	103.53 E	1527	Volcanic field	P
Durbulzhi-Ula (Mongolia)	42.80 N	102.08 E	1445	Unknown	P
Ubur-Khangay (Mongolia)	44.38 N*	101.98 E	1640	Volcanic field	P
Unnamed (China-W)	35.47 N	82.92 E	6900	Unknown	Q
Unnamed (China-W)	30.50 N*	85.00 E	-	Unknown	PM
Unnamed (China-W)	36.50 N*	86.50 E	7000	Volcanic field	PM
Unnamed (China-W)	36.50 N	88.60 E	-	Unknown	PM
Unnamed (China-E)	23.30 N	116.15 E	-	Unknown	Q

Volcano Name (Subregion)	LAT	LONG	ELEV	TYPE	STATUS
Longhai (China-E)	24.50 N	117.50 E	-	Unknown	Q
Jianghui Group (China-E)	31.95 N	118.95 E	-	Cinder cone	P
Nushan (China-E)	33.12 N	118.75 E	-	Cone	P
Yichuan (China-E)	34.00 N	113.00 E	-	Volcanic field	Q
Tangy'n (China-E)	35.25 N	114.50 E	-	Unknown	Q
Huixian (China-E)	36.00 N	115.25 E	-	Unknown	Q
Taian (China-E)	36.50 N	119.00 E	-	Unknown	Q
Linqu (China-E)	26.50 N	120.00 E	-	Unknown	Q
Jimo (China-E)	36.75 N	121.00 E	-	Unknown	Q
Penglai (China-E)	37.75 N	120.75 E	-	Unknown	Q
Heibei Plain (China-E)	38.00 N	117.50 E	-	Unknown	Q
Unnamed (China-E)	37.00 N	114.50 E	-	Unknown	Q
Taihangshanlu (China-E)	38.00 N	113.75 E	-	Unknown	Q
Unnamed (China-E)	38.75 N	115.00 E	-	Unknown	Q
Unnamed (China-E)	39.25 N	113.52 E	-	Unknown	Q
Datong-Fengzen (China-E)	40.00 N*	113.28 E	1882	Volcanic field	P
Unnamed (China-E)	40.75 N	112.67 E	-	Cones	P
Unnamed (China-E)	40.75 N	113.12 E	-	Cinder cones	P
Chifeng (China-E)	42.25 N	118.50 E	-	Unknown	Q
Dalainuoer (China-E)	44.00 N*	115.50 E	-	Cinder cones	P
Motianling Group (China-E)	47.58 N*	121.28 E	300	Volcanic field	Q
Baerqian (China-E)	48.00 N	119.80 E	-	Stratovolcano?	P
Shatu (China-E)	49.08 N*	123.67 E	845	Cinder cones	Q
Gankui Group (China-E)	49.63 N*	124.58 E	450	Volcanic field	Q
Jiacong (China-E)	49.83 N	126.83 E	750	Shield volcano	P
Yijiashan (China-E)	49.70 N	127.67 E	350	Cone	PM
Jianshan (China-E)	48.45 N	125.67 E	400	Shield volcano	Q
Erkeshan (China-E)	48.08 N	126.30 E	450	Shield volcano	P
Sung-Hua-Chiang (China-E)	47.00 N	131.00 E	-	Lava domes	Q
Unnamed (China-E)	45.00 N	130.50 E	-	Volcanic field	PM
Unnamed (China-E)	44.00 N*	131.00 E	-	Volcanic field	Q
Dabingshan (China-E)	44.33 N	129.83 E	1145	Shield volcano	PM
Unnamed (China-E)	43.58 N	131.08 E	800	Shield volcanoes	PM
Unnamed (China-E)	43.50 N*	129.50 E	-	Volcanic field	PM
Dunhua (China-E)	43.25 N	128.00 E	-	Unknown	Q
Yitong Group (China-E)	43.33 N	125.25 E	389	Lava domes	Q
Fanjiatung Group (China-E)	43.75 N	125.17 E	283	Cones	Q
Kuandian (China-E)	40.75 N	124.67 E	513	Pyroclastic cones	Q
Wantianfeng (China-E)	41.75 N	127.83 E	2260	Shield volcano	PM
Unnamed (China-E)	42.25 N	127.92 E	1500	Cinder cones	PM
Kilchu-Myongch'on (Korea)	41.00 N*	129.70 E	-	Volcanic field	P
Koksan-Singye (Korea)	38.67 N	127.42 E	680	Shield volcano	P

ALASKA

Volcano Name (Subregion)	LAT	LONG	ELEV	TYPE	STATUS
Adagdak (Aleutian Is)	51.99 N	176.59 W	610	Stratovolcano	PT
Table Top (Aleutian Is)	53.97 N	166.68 W	792	Cinder cone	P
Wide Bay (Aleutian Is)	53.96 N	166.62 W	640	Cinder cone	P
Gilbert, Mt. (Aleutian Is)	54.25 N	165.65 W	818	Stratovolcano	P
Morzhovoi (Alaska Peninsula)	55.00 N	162.82 W	893	Stratovolcano	P
Trader Mountain (Alaska Peninsula)	55.54 N	161.95 W	802	Stratovolcano	P
Stepovak Bay 1 (Alaska Peninsula)	55.87 N	160.10 W	1320	Stratovolcano	P
Blue Mountain (Alaska Peninsula)	57.72 N	157.83 W	541	Lava domes	P
Gertrude Creek (Alaska Peninsula)	58.04 N	156.14 W	437	Scoria cone	P
Devils Desk (Alaska Peninsula)	58.47 N	154.31 W	1955	Stratovolcano	P
Savonovski River Cluster (Alaska)	58.55 N*	154.50 W	1298	Stratovolcanoes	P
Double Glacier (Alaska-SW)	60.68 N	152.62 W	1239	Lava domes	P
St. George (Alaska-W)	56.58 N	169.58 W	288	Volcanic field	P
Otter Island (Alaska-W)	57.05 N	170.40 W	87	Unknown	P
Walrus Island (Alaska-W)	57.18 N	169.93 W	0	Unknown	P
Togiak Valley (Alaska-W)	59.20 N*	160.08 W	300	Volcanic field	P
Kinia River (Alaska-W)	60.15 N*	164.27 W	500	Cinder cones	PM
Ingrichuak Hills (Alaska-W)	62.22 N*	164.30 W	188	Cinder cones	P
Selawik Hills (Alaska-W)	66.03 N*	161.18 W	365	Cinder cones	P
Espenberg (Alaska-W)	66.35 N*	164.33 W	243	Volcanic field	P
Jumbo Dome (Alaska-W)	63.97 N	148.69 W	1369	Lava dome	P
Prindle (Alaska-E)	63.72 N	141.62 W	1250	Cinder cone	P
Capital (Alaska-E)	62.43 N	144.12 W	2356	Shield volcano	P
Drum (Alaska-E)	62.12 N	144.63 W	3661	Stratovolcano	P
Tanada (Alaska-E)	62.30 N	143.52 W	2816	Shield volcano	P
Jarvis (Alaska-E)	62.03 N	143.62 W	4091	Unknown	P
Basalt Knob (Alaska-E)	58.03 N	136.33 W	100	Cone	Q

CANADA & WESTERN USA

Volcano Name (Subregion)	LAT	LONG	ELEV	TYPE	STATUS
Rabbit Mountain (Canada)	61.88 N	140.97 W	1990	Unknown	P
Kawdy Metah (Canada)	59.02 N*	131.15 W	1950	Volcanic field	P
Dark Mountain (Canada)	58.52 N*	129.60 W	1972	Volcanic field	P
Klastline Group (Canada)	57.88 N*	130.20 W	1980	Cinder cones	P
Hogum Range (Canada)	56.15 N	126.70 W	2020	Volcanic field	P
Alice Arm (Canada)	55.43 N*	129.37 W	-	Volcanic field	P
Itcha Range (Canada)	52.70 N	124.85 W	2368	Shield volcano	P
Quesnel Cone Group (Canada)	52.50 N	121.17 W	900	Pyroclastic cones	Q
Chilcotin Group-North (Canada)	51.45 N*	122.33 W	1800	Volcanic field	P
Cayley, Mt. (Canada)	50.12 N	123.28 W	2375	Stratovolcano	P
Squamish (Canada)	49.65 N	123.22 W	790	Volcanic field	P
Chilcotin Group-South (Canada)	50.15 N*	119.62 W	2100	Volcanic field	P
Tumac Mountain (US-Washington)	46.71 N	121.35 W	1932	Cinder cone	P
Goat Rocks (US-Washington)	46.50 N	121.40 W	2494	Stratovolcano	P
Marble Mountain (US-Washington)	46.11 N	122.13 W	1255	Shield volcano	P
Simcoe (US-Washington)	46.10 N	120.90 W	1775	Volcanic field	P
Boring Lava (US-Oregon)	45.30 N*	122.50 W	1236	Volcanic field	P
Defiance (US-Oregon)	45.65 N	121.72 W	1512	Shield volcano	P
Lost Lake Butte (US-Oregon)	45.50 N	121.80 W	1362	Shield volcano	P
Wilson (US-Oregon)	45.07 N	121.66 W	1707	Shield volcanoes	P
Olallie Butte (US-Oregon)	44.82 N	121.75 W	2199	Shield volcanoes	P
Three Fingered Jack (US-Oregon)	44.48 N	121.84 W	2390	Shield volcanoes	P
Black Butte (US-Oregon)	44.40 N	121.63 W	1962	Stratovolcano	P
Washington (US-Oregon)	44.33 N	121.84 W	2376	Shield volcano	P
Black Crater (US-Oregon)	44.27 N	121.75 W	2210	Shield volcanoes	P
Scott Mountain (US-Oregon)	44.24 N	121.92 W	1864	Shield volcano	P
Tumalo (US-Oregon)	44.10 N	121.54 W	1955	Lava domes	P
Broken Top (US-Oregon)	44.08 N	121.70 W	2797	Stratovolcano	P
Williamson Mountain (US-Oregon)	43.92 N	121.83 W	1921	Shield volcanoes	P
Irish Mountain (US-Oregon)	43.85 N	121.98 W	2101	Shield volcano	P
Taylor Butte (US-Oregon)	43.81 N	122.02 W	1775	Shield volcano	P
Cultus Mountain (US-Oregon)	43.82 N	121.87 W	2060	Shield volcano	P
Wuksi Butte-Twin Lakes	43.77 N	121.77 W	1590	Volcanic field	P
Cupit Mary Mountain (US-Oregon)	43.73 N	122.11 W	1879	Shield volcano	P
Fuji Mountain (US-Oregon)	43.66 N	122.10 W	2177	Shield volcanoes	P
Maiden Peak (US-Oregon)	43.63 N	121.97 W	2383	Shield volcanoes	P
Red Top Mountain (US-Oregon)	43.51 N	122.03 W	2118	Shield volcanoes	P
Cowhorn Mountain (US-Oregon)	43.40 N	122.05 E	2336	Shield volcanoes	P
Cappy Mountain (US-Oregon)	43.31 N	121.98 W	2253	Stratovolcano	P
China Hat-East Butte (US-Oregon)	43.68 N	121.03 W	2004	Lava domes	P
Quartz Mountain (US-Oregon)	43.63 N	120.90 W	1885	Lava dome	P
Fort Rock Volc Field (US-Oregon)	43.32 N*	120.83 W	1431	Maars	P
Diamond Peak (US-Oregon)	43.52 N	122.15 W	2665	Shield volcano	P
Thielsen (US-Oregon)	43.15 N	122.07 W	2799	Shield volcano	P
Bailey (US-Oregon)	43.16 N	122.22 W	2551	Shield volcano	P
Goosenest (US-Oregon)	42.79 N	122.15 W	2213	Shield volcano	P
Big Bunchgrass (US-Oregon)	42.70 N	122.19 W	2024	Pyroclastic cone	P
Imagination Peak (US-Oregon)	42.55 N	122.20 W	1986	Pyroclastic cone	P
Sprague River Valley (US-Oregon)	42.50 N*	121.50 W	1300	Shield volcanoes	P
Pelican Butte (US-Oregon)	42.52 N	122.13 W	2449	Shield volcano	P
McLoughlin (US-Oregon)	42.45 N	122.32 W	2894	Stratovolcano	P
Brown Mountain (US-Oregon)	42.37 N	122.27 W	2228	Shield volcano	P
Mountain Lakes (US-Oregon)	42.32 N*	122.08 W	2502	Volcanic field	Q
Silver Creek (US-Oregon)	43.40 N*	119.50 W	1375	Volcanic field	P?
Saddle Butte (US-Oregon)	43.00 N*	117.80 W	1700	Volcanic field	P
Lava Butte (US-Oregon)	43.00 N	117.42 W	1447	Shield volcanoes	P
Jackies Butte (US-Oregon)	42.61 N*	117.59 W	1418	Volcanic field	Q
Copco Lake (US-California)	41.97 N	122.33 W	975	Cinder cones	P
Goosenest (US-California)	41.72 N	122.22 W	2528	Shield volcano	P
Whaleback (US-California)	41.53 N	122.14 W	2605	Shield volcano	P
Rainbow Mountain (US-California)	41.47 N	121.96 W	2323	Stratovolcano	P
Hackamore (US-California)	41.67 N*	121.17 E	-	Volcanic field	P
Big Cave (US-California)	40.96 N	121.37 W	1259	Shield volcano	P
Cinder Butte (US-California)	40.87 N	121.49 W	1337	Shield volcano	P
Burney Mountain (US-California)	40.81 N	121.63 W	2397	Lava domes	P
Snow Mountain (US-California)	40.76 N	121.80 W	2077	Stratovolcano	P
Magee Peak (US-California)	40.70 N	121.62 W	2647	Stratovolcano	P
Blacks Mountain (US-California)	40.78 N	121.19 W	2220	Shield volcano	P
Potato Butte (US-California)	40.63 N*	121.43 W	1532	Shield volcanoes	P
Latour Butte (US-California)	40.61 N	121.71 W	2054	Lava cone	P
Caribou (US-California)	40.60 N*	121.15 W	2309	Volcanic field	P
Red Lake Mountain (US-California)	40.57 N	121.59 E	2036	Cinder cone	P
Table Mountain (US-California)	40.56 N	121.55 W	2097	Stratovolcano	P
Black Butte (US-California)	40.45 N	122.00 W	813	Pyroclastic cone	P
Dittmar (US-California)	40.45 N	121.35 W	2328	Stratovolcano	P
Sifford Mountain (US-California)	40.42 N	121.41 W	2149	Shield volcano	P
Maidu (US-California)	40.30 N	121.62 W	2123	Stratovolcano	P
Inskip Hill (US-California)	40.34 N	121.94 W	945	Pyroclastic cones	P
Sutter Buttes (US-California)	39.21 N	121.82 E	645	Lava domes	P
Long Valley (US-California)	37.70 N	118.87 W	3390	Caldera	PT
Big Pine Volc Field (US-California)	37.05 N	118.25 W	1950	Cinder cones	P
Lava Mountains Volc Field (Calif.)	35.50 N	117.50 W	1510	Lava domes	P?
Cima Lava Field (US-California)	35.27 N*	115.75 W	1509	Volcanic field	P
Amboy (US-California)	34.55 N	115.78 W	288	Cinder cone	P
Pinto Basin-Salton Creek (Calif.)	33.90 N	115.63 W	600	Volcanic field	P
Sinker Butte (US-Idaho)	43.25 N	116.62 W	-	Shield volcano	P
Kuna Butte (US-Idaho)	43.20 N	115.98 W	1040	Cinder cones	P

Volcano Name (Subregion)	LAT	LONG	ELEV	TYPE	STATUS
Grande, Cerro (US-Idaho)	43.45 N	112.83 W	-	Fissure vents	P
Blackfoot Lava Field (US-Idaho)	42.85 N*	111.75 W	2185	Cinder cones	P
Menan Buttes (US-Idaho)	43.78 N	111.97 W	1713	Tuff cones	P
Red Rock Valley (US-Montana)	44.80 N	112.70 W	-	Stratovolcano	P
Emigrant Valley (US-Montana)	45.40 N	110.70 W	-	Unknown	P
Leucite Hills (US-Wyoming)	41.80 N	108.90 W	-	Volcanic field	P
Sheldon-Antelope (US-Nevada)	41.80 N*	119.10 W	-	Volcanic field	Q
Buffalo Valley (US-Nevada)	40.35 N*	117.30 W	1750	Volcanic field	P
Steamboat Springs (US-Nevada)	39.38 N	119.72 W	1415	Lava domes	PT
Aurora-Bodie (US-Nevada)	38.32 N*	118.88 W	2365	Volcanic field	P
Lunar Crater Field (US-Nevada)	38.48 N*	115.97 W	2255	Cinder cones	P
Clayton Valley (US-Nevada)	37.82 N	117.62 W	1490	Cinder cone	P
Crater Flat (US-Nevada)	36.77 N*	116.55 W	1128	Volcanic field	P
Erie (US-Nevada)	35.90 N	115.20 W	-	Cinder cones	P?
Kolob (US-Utah)	37.33 N*	113.12 W	2727	Volcanic field	P
Mineral Mts-Cove Fort (US-Utah)	38.58 N	112.67 W	2770	Volcanic field	P
Smelter Knolls (US-Utah)	39.43 N	112.86 W	1555	Lava domes	P
Fumarole Butte (US-Utah)	39.62 N	112.80 W	1609	Shield volcano	P
Willow Peak (US-Colorado)	39.67 N	107.17 W	3054	Cinder cone	Q
McCoy (US-Colorado)	39.97 N	106.70 W	2402	Scoria cones	P
San Francisco Volc Field (Ariz.)	35.30 N*	111.72 W	3846	Stratovolcanoes	P
Sentinel Plain (US-Arizona)	32.80 N	113.20 W	160	Volcanic field	P
Springerville (US-Arizona)	33.88 N*	109.75 W	3100	Volcanic field	P
San Carlos (US-Arizona)	33.25 N	110.25 W	1000	Volcanic field	P
Geronimo (US-Arizona)	32.50 N	109.25 W	1300	Volcanic field	P
Potrillo Volc Field (New Mexico)	31.98 N*	107.13 W	1695	Cinder cones	P
Jornada del Muerto (New Mexico)	33.53 N	106.87 W	1555	Shield volcano	P
Red Hill (US-New Mexico)	34.25 N	108.83 W	2300	Volcanic field	P
Lucero (US-New Mexico)	34.42 N	107.20 W	2395	Volcanic field	P
Taylor Volc Field (US-New Mexico)	35.33 N*	107.45 W	3460	Stratovolcano	P
Cat Hills (US-New Mexico)	34.83 N	106.83 W	1750	Volcanic field	P
Albuquerque (US-New Mexico)	35.12 N	106.75 W	1800	Volcanic field	P
Valles Caldera (US-New Mexico)	35.87 N	106.57 W	3430	Caldera	PT
Taos Plateau (US-New Mexico)	36.83 N*	105.83 W	3087	Volcanic field	P
Ocate (US-New Mexico)	36.12 N	104.75 W	3000	Volcanic field	P
Raton-Clayton (US-New Mexico)	36.42 N*	104.08 W	3350	Volcanic field	P

HAWAII & PACIFIC OCEAN

Volcano Name (Subregion)	LAT	LONG	ELEV	TYPE	STATUS
Kohala (Hawaiian Is)	20.08 N	155.72 W	1668	Shield volcano	P
Kahoolawe (Hawaiian Is)	20.57 N	156.57 W	450	Shield volcano	P
Mahukona (Hawaiian Is)	20.17 N	156.42 E	-1080	Submarine volc	P
West Maui (Hawaiian Is)	20.88 N	156.60 W	1764	Shield volcano	P
Lanai (Hawaiian Is)	20.82 N	156.85 W	1021	Shield volcano	P
East Molokai (Hawaiian Is)	21.12 N	156.87 W	1506	Shield volcano	P
West Molokai (Hawaiian Is)	21.15 N	157.17 W	418	Shield volcano	P
Koolau (Hawaiian Is)	21.37 N	157.80 W	941	Shield volcano	P
Waianae (Hawaiian Is)	21.52 N	158.15 W	1220	Shield volcano	P
Kauai (Hawaiian Is)	22.07 N	159.50 W	1668	Shield volcano	P
Niihau (Hawaiian Is)	21.95 N	160.08 W	390	Shield volcano	P
Kaula (Hawaiian Is)	21.67 N	160.55 W	194	Shield volcano	P
Hiva Oa (Pacific-C)	9.78 S	139.03 W	1067	Shield volcano	P
Fatu Hiva (Pacific-C)	10.47 S	138.65 W	955	Shield volcano	P
Moorea (Pacific-C)	17.50 S	149.83 W	1207	Shield volcano	P
Tahiti-Nui (Pacific-C)	17.63 S	149.48 W	2241	Shield volcano	P
Tahiti-Iti (Pacific-C)	17.82 S	149.22 W	1306	Shield volcano	P
Aitutaki (Pacific-C)	18.90 S	159.77 W	124	Shield volcano	P
Rarotonga (Pacific-C)	21.23 S	159.75 W	639	Shield volcano	P
Rurutu (Pacific-C)	22.45 S	151.35 W	394	Shield volcano	P
Pitcairn (Pacific-C)	24.07 S	130.12 W	347	Shield volcano	P
Clipperton Island (Pacific-E)	10.33 N	109.22 W	29	Lava dome	PM

MÉXICO & CENTRAL AMERICA

Volcano Name (Subregion)	LAT	LONG	ELEV	TYPE	STATUS
León, Cerro (México)	30.23 N	114.66 W	280	Cone	P
San Ignacio Volc Field (México)	27.60 N	113.17 W	-	Volcanic field	P
Aguajito, El (México)	27.60 N	112.53 W	1300	Caldera	PT
Reforma, La (México)	27.51 N	112.39 W	1300	Caldera	P
Púlpito, Punta (México)	26.52 N	111.48 W	-	Lava dome	PT
Mencenares, Cerro (México)	26.28 N	111.47 W	790	Lava domes	P
Moctezuma Volc Field (México)	29.63 N*	109.52 W	-	Volcanic field	P
Camargo Volc Field (México)	27.75 N*	104.42 W	1900	Cinder cones	P
Aldama Volc Field (México)	23.20 N*	98.02 W	600	Volcanic field	Q
Flores, Los (México)	22.58 N*	99.38 W	520	Volcanic field	Q
Santo Domingo Volc Field (Méx.)	22.83 N*	100.08 W	1550	Maars	P
Ventura Volc Field (México)	22.35 N*	100.70 W	2035	Maars	P
San Juan (México)	21.47 N	104.97 W	2240	Stratovolcanoes	P
Navajas, Las (México)	21.53 N	104.73 W	1680	Shield volcano	P
Santa María del Oro (México)	21.37 N	104.57 W	1120	Maar	P
Tepetiltic (México)	21.27 N	104.70 W	2020	Stratovolcano	P
San Pedro (México)	21.17 N	104.73 W	2000	Caldera	P
San Sebastián Volc Field (México)	20.83 N*	104.82 W	1780	Cinder cones	P
Volcanes, Los (México)	20.33 N*	104.50 W	2080	Volcanic field	P
Northern Atenguillo (México)	20.75 N*	104.50 W	1700	Shield volcanoes	P
Tequila (México)	20.79 N	103.85 W	2920	Stratovolcano	P
Northern Guadalajara Mesa	20.88 N*	103.40 W	1820	Lava domes	P
Primavera, Sierra la (México)	20.62 N	103.52 W	2270	Caldera	PT
Southern Guadalajara (México)	20.53 N*	103.24 W	2160	Volcanic field	P
Acatlán Volc Field (México)	20.45 N*	103.57 W	1990	Caldera	P
Cántaro, Volcán el (México)	19.72 N	103.63 W	2920	Stratovolcano	P
Azufres, Los (México)	19.85 N	100.63 W	3400	Caldera	PT
Apan-Tezontepec (México)	19.75 N*	98.50 W	3100	Volcanic field	Q
Tláloc (México)	19.41 N	98.71 W	4120	Stratovolcano	P
Telapón (México)	19.37 N	98.72 W	4080	Stratovolcano	P
Acoculco (México)	19.97 N	98.20 W	3020	Caldera	P
Grande, Cerro (México)	19.62 N*	97.93 W	3050	Volcanic field	P
Poza Rica (México)	20.42 N*	97.83 E	2250	Volcanic field	P
San Martín Pajapan (México)	18.30 N	94.73 W	1250	Stratovolcanoes	P
Apas-Navenchauc (México)	16.72 N	92.79 W	-	Calderas	P
Huitepec (México)	16.76 N	92.69 W	-	Lava dome	P
Mispía (México)	16.45 N	92.54 W	1750	Lava domes	P
Siete Orejas (Guatemala)	14.82 N	91.62 W	3370	Stratovolcano	Q
Santo Tomás (Guatemala)	14.71 N	91.48 W	3542	Stratovolcanoes	PT
Cuxliquel (Guatemala)	14.88 N	91.40 W	3004	Lava domes	P
San Pedro (Guatemala)	14.66 N	91.27 W	3020	Stratovolcano	Q
Barahona (Guatemala)	14.55 N	90.78 W	2282	Calderas	P
Pueblo Nuevo Viñas (Guatemala)	14.20 N	90.50 W	1955	Stratovolcano	P
Piedra Grande (Guatemala)	14.25 N	90.40 W	1640	Stratovolcanoes	P
Ixhuatán (Guatemala)	14.17 N	90.23 W	1718	Complex volcano	P
Ayarza (Guatemala)	14.42 N	90.12 W	1409	Calderas	P
Alutate, Cerro (Guatemala)	14.65 N	90.14 W	2116	Stratovolcano	P
Jumay Volc Field (Guatemala)	14.70 N	90.00 W	2176	Stratovolcano	Q
Ananopa, Cerro (Guatemala)	14.90 N*	89.93 W	386	Volcanic field	Q
Güistepeque Volc Field (Guate.)	14.57 N	89.78 W	1358	Cinder cones	P
Redondo, Cerro (Guatemala)	14.27 N	89.62 W	768	Shield volcanoes	Q
Masahuat Volc Field (El Salvador)	14.20 N	89.40 W	1005	Stratovolcano	P
Tablas, Cerro las (El Salvador)	14.07 N	89.40 W	782	Stratovolcanoes	P
Limones Volc Field, Los (El Salv.)	14.05 N	89.13 W	420	Cinder cones	P
Lolotique, Cerro (El Salvador)	13.55 N	88.37 W	826	Unknown	Q
Cacahuatique, Cerro (El Salvador)	13.75 N	88.20 W	1500	Stratovolcano	P
Buena Vista, Cerro (El Salvador)	13.25 N	88.15 W	750	Stratovolcano	P
Yayantique, Cerro (El Salvador)	13.43 N	88.00 W	616	Volcanic field	P
Unnamed (El Salvador)	13.67 N	87.82 W	377	Volcanic field	P
Zacatillo, Isla (El Salvador)	13.30 N	87.75 W	160	Cinder cones	P
Meanguera, Isla (El Salvador)	13.20 N	87.70 W	493	Stratovolcanoes	Q
Izopo, Montaña de (Honduras)	13.92 N	87.15 W	2020	Shield volcanoes	Q
Hule, Cerro de (Honduras)	13.95 N	87.23 W	1725	Shield volcano	Q
Gavilantepeque, Cerro (Honduras)	14.00 N	87.18 W	1280	Shield volcano	Q
Pedregal, El (Honduras)	14.10 N	87.27 W	1593	Shield volcano	Q
Calanterique, Cerro (Honduras)	14.60 N	87.87 W	-	Lava cone	Q
Malpaisillo (Nicaragua)	12.58 N	86.60 W	181	Pyroclastic shield	P
Apoyo (Nicaragua)	11.92 N	86.03 W	600	Caldera	P
San Jacinto, Cerro (Nicaragua)	12.37 N	86.02 W	300	Stratovolcano	P?
Tambor Grande (Nicaragua)	10.97 N*	84.08 W	648	Caldera	Q
Chopo, Cerro (Costa Rica)	10.47 N	85.07 W	402	Pyroclastic cone	P
Tilarán, Cerro (Costa Rica)	10.45 N	84.98 W	634	Shield volcano	P
Perdidos, Los (Costa Rica)	10.40 N	84.68 W	1370	Caldera	P
Poco Sol, Laguna (Costa Rica)	10.35 N	84.67 W	789	Explosion crater?	P
San Miguel, Cerro (Costa Rica)	10.02 N	84.71 W	414	Lava dome	P
Mercedes, Cerro las (Costa Rica)	10.97 N	84.35 W	190	Cinder cone	P
Negro, Cerro (Costa Rica)	10.46 N	83.86 W	136	Shield volcano	P
Colorado, Lomas de (Costa Rica)	10.66 N*	83.72 W	229	Shield volcanoes	P
Tortuguero (Costa Rica)	10.59 N	83.53 W	119	Pyroclastic cone	P
Sierpe, Lomas de (Costa Rica)	10.38 N*	83.55 W	311	Shield volcanoes	P
Dúrika (Costa Rica)	9.37 N*	83.22 W	2330	Lava domes	P
Coco, Isla del (Costa Rica)	5.53 N	87.08 W	575	Shield volcano	P
Tisingal (Panamá)	8.88 N	82.67 W	2986	Stratovolcano	P
Yeguada, La (Panamá)	8.47 N	80.82 W	1297	Stratovolcano	PT

SOUTH AMERICA

Volcano Name (Subregion)	LAT	LONG	ELEV	TYPE	STATUS
Santa Rosa (Colombia)	4.80 N	75.47 W	4600	Shield volcano	P
Quindío, Nevado del (Colombia)	4.71 N	75.38 W	4800	Stratovolcano	P
Páramo de Miraflores (Colombia)	3.93 N	75.73 W	3500	Unknown	Q
Unnamed (Colombia)	2.20 N*	76.03 W	2500	Volcanic field	Q
San Augustín-Isnos (Colombia)	1.92 N*	76.23 W	1900	Volcanic field	Q
Cutanga (Colombia)	1.83 N	76.45 W	4300	Unknown	Q
Animas (Colombia)	1.67 N	77.03 W	4242	Stratovolcano	Q
Potosí (Colombia)	1.43 N	76.82 W	3800	Unknown	PM
Tajumbina (Colombia)	1.35 N	76.85 W	4125	Unknown	PM
Juanoy (Colombia)	1.28 N	76.95 W	4125	Unknown	PM
Bordoncillo (Colombia)	1.22 N	77.13 W	3699	Unknown	PM

Volcano Name (Subregion)	**LAT**	**LONG**	**ELEV**	**TYPE**	**STATUS**
Chalpatan (Ecuador)	0.71 N	77.78 W	3624	Caldera	P
Chiltazón (Ecuador)	0.69 N	78.02 W	3967	Stratovolcano	P
Iguan (Ecuador)	0.62 N	78.01 W	3870	Stratovolcano	P
Yanaurcu de Piñán (Ecuador)	0.48 N	78.33 W	4535	Stratovolcano	P
Pilavo (Ecuador)	0.53 N	78.37 W	4254	Stratovolcano	P
Cotacachi (Ecuador)	0.36 N	78.35 W	4939	Stratovolcano	P
Cusín (Ecuador)	0.13 N	78.15 W	3989	Stratovolcano	P
Pambamarca (Ecuador)	0.08 S	78.21 W	4076	Stratovolcano	P
Casitagua (Ecuador)	0.13 S	78.48 W	3515	Stratovolcano	P
Puntas, Cerro (Ecuador)	0.17 S	78.20 W	4348	Stratovolcano	P
Ilaló (Ecuador)	0.26 S	78.42 W	3185	Stratovolcano	P
Pasochoa (Ecuador)	0.46 S	78.48 W	4199	Stratovolcano	P
Pan de Azúcar (Ecuador)	0.43 S	77.72 W	3482	Stratovolcano	P
Sincholagua (Ecuador)	0.53 S	78.37 W	4893	Stratovolcano	P
Rumiñahui (Ecuador)	0.58 S	78.50 W	4712	Stratovolcano	P?
Corazón (Ecuador)	0.53 S	78.66 W	4786	Stratovolcano	P
Santa Cruz (Ecuador)	0.65 S	78.63 W	3945	Stratovolcano	P
Chalupas (Ecuador)	0.80 S	78.39 W	4780	Caldera	Q
Putzalagua (Ecuador)	0.96 S	78.56 W	3512	Lava dome	P
Sagoatoa (Ecuador)	1.15 S	78.67 W	4153	Stratovolcano	P
Llimpi (Ecuador)	1.38 S	78.57 W	3732	Stratovolcano	P
Puyo (Ecuador)	1.38 S	77.91 W	-	Scoria cones	P
Carihuairazo (Ecuador)	1.40 S	78.75 W	5102	Stratovolcano	P
Igualata (Ecuador)	1.49 S	78.64 W	4430	Stratovolcano	P
Calpi (Ecuador)	1.63 S	78.73 W	3215	Tuff cones	P
Altar (Ecuador)	1.67 S	78.42 W	5321	Stratovolcano	P
Roca Redonda (Galápagos)	0.27 N	91.63 W	67	Shield volcano	Q
Culpepper (Galápagos)	1.62 N	92.00 W	168	Shield volcano	P
Wenman (Galápagos)	1.37 N	91.80 W	253	Shield volcano	P
Rábida (Galápagos)	0.37 S	90.70 W	367	Lava domes	P
Pinzón (Galápagos)	0.60 S	90.68 W	458	Shield volcano	P
Santa Fe (Galápagos)	0.81 S	90.07 W	200	Shield volcano	PT
Floreana (Galápagos)	1.30 S	90.45 W	640	Shield volcano	P
Española (Galápagos)	1.38 S	89.70 W	205	Shield volcano	PM
Huambutillo-Rumicola (Perú)	13.58 S	71.72 W	-	Unknown	P
Solimana (Perú)	15.40 S	72.90 W	6093	Stratovolcano	P
Firura, Nevados (Perú)	15.23 S	72.63 W	5498	Stratovolcanoes	P
Purupuruni, Cerros (Perú)	17.32 S	69.90 W	5315	Lava domes	P
Lexone (Chile-N)	17.87 S	69.48 W	5340	Lava domes	P
Anallajsi, Nevado (Bolivia)	17.92 S	68.92 W	5750	Stratovolcano	P
Larur Kouy (Chile-N)	17.92 S	69.25 W	4800	Stratovolcano	PM
Pucara, Cerro (Bolivia)	17.87 S	68.50 W	4080	Volcanic field	P
Sillota (Bolivia)	17.83 S	67.33 W	4373	Stratovolcano	PM
Patilla Pata (Bolivia)	18.05 S	69.03 W	5300	Stratovolcano	P
Sajama, Nevado del (Bolivia)	18.10 S	68.88 W	6542	Stratovolcano	P
Larancagua (Chile-N)	18.02 S	69.08 W	5580	Stratovolcano	P?
Pichagas (Bolivia)	18.03 S	66.87 W	4950	Stratovolcano	PM
Ujansi (Bolivia)	18.47 S	68.67 W	4298	Unknown	PM
Caquena (Chile-N)	18.07 S	69.22 W	-	Lava domes	P
Vilacollo (Chile-N)	18.23 S	69.30 W	-	Cinder cones	P
Acotango (Chile-N)	18.37 S	69.05 W	6052	Stratovolcanoes	P
Arintica (Chile-N)	18.75 S	69.05 W	5597	Stratovolcanoes	P
Rochaculla-Inca Camacha (Boliv.)	18.80 S	68.30 W	5300	Stratovolcanoes	P?
Pumire, Cerro (Chile-N)	19.08 S	69.02 W	5470	Unknown	PM
Gloria Pata, Cerro (Bolivia)	18.88 S	67.13 W	3800	Stratovolcano	PM
Azanaques (Bolivia)	18.97 S	66.72 W	5050	Unknown	PM
Condoriquiña (Bolivia)	19.00 S	66.00 W	4600	Unknown	PM
Latarana, Cerro (Chile-N)	19.32 S	69.00 W	5210	Unknown	PM
Puchuldiza (Chile-N)	19.42 S	68.97 W	4500	Hydrothermal field	PT
Tatajachura, Cerro (Chile-N)	19.50 S	69.12 W	5240	Stratovolcano	P
Cariquima, Cerro (Chile-N)	19.55 S	68.68 W	5365	Stratovolcano	P?
Sillajguai, Cerro (Chile-N)	19.75 S	68.70 W	5995	Stratovolcano	PM
Quimsachata, Cerro (Chile-N)	19.70 S	68.82 W	5400	Unknown	PM
Guantija, Cerro (Chile-N)	19.85 S	68.78 W	4780	Unknown	PM
Porquesa (Chile-N)	19.96 S	68.73 W	5190	Lava domes	P
Sapajos, Cerro (Bolivia)	19.83 S	68.32 W	5900	Stratovolcano	PM
Chinchillaguay, Cerro (Bolivia)	19.75 S	68.33 W	5950	Stratovolcano	PM
Guachacollo (Bolivia)	19.62 S	68.05 W	5010	Stratovolcano	PM
Tupua (Bolivia)	19.83 S	67.67 W	5321	Stratovolcano	PM
Coracora, Cerro (Bolivia)	19.55 S	67.67 W	4800	Stratovolcano	PM
Tollocci, Cerro (Bolivia)	19.67 S	65.85 W	4600	Stratovolcano	PM
Piga, Cerro (Chile-N)	20.08 S	68.78 W	5022	Unknown	PM
Bonito, Cerro (Chile-N)	20.17 S	68.70 W	4940	Unknown	PM
Laqueca, Cerro (Bolivia)	20.17 S	68.50 W	5500	Stratovolcano	PM
Laguna-Pulacayo, Cerro (Chile-N)	20.33 S	68.67 W	4929	Unknown	PM
Pichicollo, Cerro (Bolivia)	20.30 S	68.58 W	4290	Unknown	PM
Ubina, Cerro (Bolivia)	20.37 S	68.42 W	5300	Stratovolcano	PM
Pulucha, Cerro (Bolivia)	20.47 S	68.42 W	5070	Stratovolcano	PM
Napa, Cerro (Chile-N)	20.52 S	68.68 W	5145	Stratovolcano	P
Ocaña (Bolivia)	20.58 S	68.45 W	-	Stratovolcano	P

Volcano Name (Subregion)	**LAT**	**LONG**	**ELEV**	**TYPE**	**STATUS**
Copa, Cerro (Chile-N)	20.63 S	68.45 W	5330	Stratovolcanoes	P
Ajencha, Cerro (Bolivia)	20.67 S	67.42 W	5100	Stratovolcano	PM
Serrania (Bolivia)	20.75 S	67.33 W	5900	Stratovolcano	PM
Uguilla, Cerro (Bolivia)	20.87 S	68.33 W	4500	Stratovolcano	PM
Talapaca, Cerro (Bolivia)	20.98 S	68.07 W	5459	Stratovolcano	PM
Aucanquilcha (Chile-N)	21.22 S	68.47 W	6176	Stratovolcano	PT
Abra Chica, Cerro (Bolivia)	21.25 S	68.00 W	4200	Cone	PM
San Agustín, Cerro (Bolivia)	21.25 S	67.75 W	4980	Stratovolcano	PM
Tapaquilcha, Volcano (Bolivia)	21.48 S	67.97 W	5800	Stratovolcano	PM
Callejón, Cerro (Bolivia)	21.45 S	68.07 W	5880	Stratovolcano	PM
Cañapa (Chile-N)	21.50 S	68.12 W	5630	Stratovolcano	P
Ascotán, Cerro (Chile-N)	21.68 S	68.12 W	5473	Stratovolcano	P
Escala (Bolivia)	21.60 S	66.88 W	4000	Lava dome	P
Moiro, Cerro (Bolivia)	21.68 S	67.47 W	4250	Scoria cone	P?
Galera (Bolivia)	21.03 S	66.18 W	-	Cone	PM
Galán, Cerro (Bolivia)	21.67 S	66.33 W	5200	Stratovolcano	PM
Bonete, Cerro (Bolivia)	21.75 S	66.37 W	5150	Stratovolcano	PM
San Roque, Cerro (Bolivia)	21.73 S	67.20 W	4750	Cone	PM
Chascon, Cerro (Bolivia)	21.88 S	67.90 W	5125	Lava dome	P
Apagado (Chile-N)	22.05 S	67.97 W	5680	Stratovolcano	P
Paniri (Chile-N)	22.08 S	68.25 W	5946	Stratovolcano	P?
Leon, Cerro del (Chile-N)	22.18 S	68.12 W	5760	Stratovolcanoes	P
Deslinde (Chile-N)	22.27 S	67.97 W	5651	Stratovolcano	P
Linzor (Chile-N)	22.18 S	67.95 W	5680	Stratovolcano	P
Jorcada (Bolivia)	22.08 S	67.77 W	5750	Stratovolcano	P
Quetena (Bolivia)	22.25 S	67.42 W	5730	Fissure vent	P?
Sunequera (Bolivia)	21.98 S	67.23 W	5899	Shield volcano	P
Uturuncu (Bolivia)	22.27 S	67.18 W	6008	Stratovolcano	PT
Tatio, El (Chile-N)	22.35 S	68.03 W	4280	Hydrothermal field	PT
Tatio, Volcán (Chile-N)	22.42 S	68.02 W	5314	Stratovolcano	P
Volcán, El (Chile-N)	22.33 S	67.97 W	5100	Stratovolcano	P
Volcanes, Cerro (Bolivia)	22.43 S	67.80 W	5440	Unknown	PM
Tocorpuri, Cerros de (Chile-N)	22.44 S	67.89 W	5808	Stratovolcano	P
Zapaleri, Cerro (Chile-N)	22.82 S	67.18 W	5643	Stratovolcano	P?
Poquis (Chile-N)	23.02 S	67.05 W	5770	Stratovolcano	P
Curutú (Chile-N)	23.17 S	67.07 W	5394	Stratovolcano	P
Losloyo (Chile-N)	23.13 S	67.37 W	5343	Stratovolcano	P
Potor (Chile-N)	23.20 S	67.67 W	5318	Stratovolcano	P
Hécar (Chile-N)	23.23 S	67.75 W	5029	Stratovolcano	P
Verde, Laguna (Chile-N)	23.25 S	67.71 W	5464	Stratovolcano	P
Río Negro, Cerro de (Chile-N)	23.38 S	67.58 W	5071	Stratovolcano	P
Abra (Chile-N)	23.43 S	67.75 W	5266	Stratovolcano	P
Tumisa (Chile-N)	23.45 S	67.82 W	5671	Stratovolcano	P
Lejía (Chile-N)	23.55 S	67.77 W	5790	Stratovolcano	P
Miscanti (Chile-N)	23.67 S	67.72 W	5613	Stratovolcano	P
Laco (Chile-N)	23.80 S	67.50 W	5472	Lava dome	P?
Incaguasi (Chile-N)	24.03 S	67.53 W	5689	Unknown	P
Cápur (Chile-N)	24.02 S	67.85 W	5216	Stratovolcano	P
Aguas Delgadas (Chile-N)	24.45 S	68.40 W	-	Stratovolcano	P
Niebla, Cerro de la (Chile-N)	25.25 S	68.63 W	4500	Compound volc	P?
Azufre, El (Chile-N)	25.37 S	68.88 W	5480	Unknown	P?
Piedra Parada (Chile-N)	26.40 S	68.75 W	5920	Stratovolcano	P
San Francisco (Chile-N)	26.90 S	68.27 W	6018	Stratovolcano	P
Tres Cruces (Chile-N)	27.08 S	68.80 W	6620	Stratovolcano	P
Patos, Los (Chile-N)	27.27 S	69.00 W	6250	Stratovolcano	P?
Queva, Nevado (Argentina)	24.20 S	66.57 W	-	Unknown	P
Tocomar (Argentina)	24.17 S	66.57 W	-	Unknown	P
Gemelos-Saladillo (Argentina)	24.75 S	66.17 W	-	Scoria cones	P
Antofalla (Argentina)	25.55 S	67.92 W	6409	Stratovolcanoes	P
Galán, Cerro (Argentina)	25.93 S	66.92 W	6000	Caldera	P
Colorado, Cerro (Argentina)	26.18 S	68.37 W	6049	Stratovolcano	P?
Incapillo (Argentina)	27.90 S	68.80 W	5750	Caldera	P
Sala y Gómez (Chile-Is)	26.47 S	105.47 W	15	Shield volcano?	P
Alexander Selkirk (Chile-Is)	33.87 S	80.90 W	1615	Shield volcano	P
Tupungato (Chile-C)	33.35 S	69.77 W	6550	Stratovolcano	P
Piuquenes, Nevado de los (Chile)	33.52 S	69.83 W	6019	Stratovolcano	P
Northern Mendoza Field (Argent.)	34.67 S *	69.00 W	-	Volcanic field	P
Llancanelo Volc Field (Chile-C)	35.75 S *	69.25 W	1876	Scoria cones	P
Puelche Volc Field (Chile-C)	35.78 S *	70.48 W	3140	Volcanic field	P
Sordo Lucas (Chile-C)	34.99 S	70.46 W	3349	Stratovolcano	P
Unnamed (Argentina)	36.70 S *	68.32 W	-	Volcanic field	P
Puente-Chapúa Field (Argentina)	36.75 S *	68.33 W	-	Volcanic field	P
Nevada, Sierra (Chile-C)	38.58 S	71.58 W	2554	Stratovolcano	P
Pino Hachado (Argentina)	38.68 S	70.82 W	-	Caldera	P
Trautrén, Cerro (Chile-C)	39.17 S	71.40 W	1846	Stratovolcanoes	P
Caburgua, Nevados de (Chile-C)	39.17 S	70.53 W	1862	Stratovolcanoes	P
Maichín, Cerro (Chile-C)	39.35 S	71.55 W	-	Stratovolcano	P
Quinchilca (Chile-C)	39.68 S	72.01 W	1632	Stratovolcanoes	P
Pequeño Cono Glacier H.P.N.I.	47.15 S	73.87 W	-	Cone	PM
Silueta, Cerro La (Chile-S)	52.35 S	72.20 W	1285	Unknown	PM

WEST INDIES & HISPANOLIA

Volcano Name (Subregion)	LAT	LONG	ELEV	TYPE	STATUS
Vigie, Morne la (Hispaniola)	18.78 N	72.28 W	831	Scoria cone	P
Thomazeau (Hispaniola)	18.68 N	72.08 W	-	Pyroclastic cones	P
San Juan (Hispaniola)	18.87 N	71.33 W	-	Cinder cones	P
Dos Hermanos (Hispaniola)	18.75 N	70.92 W	-	Volcanic field	P
Valle Nuevo (Hispaniola)	18.83 N	70.67 W	-	Volcanic field	P
South East Range (W Indies)	17.33 N	62.77 W	900	Stratovolcano	P
Northern Centres (W Indies)	17.51 N	62.99 W	-	Stratovolcanoes	P
Silver Hills (W Indies)	16.81 N	62.19 W	403	Lava domes	P
Centre Hills (W Indies)	16.76 N	62.20 W	741	Lava domes	P
Northern Chain (W Indies)	16.23 N	61.72 W	744	Lava domes	P
Axial Chain (W Indies)	16.12 N	61.70 W	1354	Stratovolcanoes	P
Bouillante Chain (W Indies)	16.12 N	61.75 W	-	Maars	PT
Caraïbes, Monts (W Indies)	15.97 N	61.68 W	687	Stratovolcano	P
Terre de Bas (W Indies)	15.87 N	61.63 W	274	Stratovolcanoes	P
Foundland (W Indies)	15.27 N	61.28 W	960	Stratovolcano	P
Carbets, Pitons de (W Indies)	14.70 N	61.12 W	1196	Stratovolcano	P
Unnamed (W Indies)	14.65 N	61.08 W	-	Volcanic field	P
Garu, Morne (W Indies)	13.29 N	61.20 W	1074	Stratovolcano	P
Grand Bonhomme (W Indies)	13.22 N	61.21 W	1021	Stratovolcano	P

ICELAND & ARCTIC OCEAN

Volcano Name (Subregion)	LAT	LONG	ELEV	TYPE	STATUS
Fagradalsfjall (Iceland-SW)	63.90 N	22.27 W	385	Tuya	P
Grensdalur (Iceland-S)	64.02 N*	21.17 W	497	Stratovolcano	PT
Lyngdalsheidi (Iceland-SW)	64.15 N	20.90 W	404	Shield volcano	P
Geysir (Iceland-SW)	64.32 N	20.30 W	700	Stratovolcano	PT
Hlödufell (Iceland-SW)	64.93 N	20.53 W	1188	Tuya	P
Thorisjökull (Iceland-SW)	64.53 N	20.70 W	1350	Subglacial volc	P
Ok (Iceland-SW)	64.62 N	20.88 W	1141	Shield volcano	P
Eríksjökull (Iceland-SW)	64.77 N	20.40 W	1675	Tuya	P
Hrútfell (Iceland-SW)	64.73 N	19.72 W	1396	Tuya	P
Bláfell (Iceland-SW)	64.49 N	19.87 W	1204	Tuya	P
Hreppar (Iceland-SW)	64.42 N	19.50 W	-	Fissure vents	P
Strútur (Iceland-S)	63.85 N	18.93 W	968	Tuya	P
Tungnaárfjöll (Iceland-NE)	64.17 N	18.50 W	-	Fissure vents	P
Kistufell (Iceland-NE)	64.78 N	17.20 W	1444	Tuya	P
Valdalda (Iceland-NE)	64.97 N	16.48 W	941	Shield volcano	P
Herdubreid (Iceland-NE)	65.18 N	16.35 W	1682	Tuya	P
Sellandafjall (Iceland-NE)	65.42 N	17.03 W	988	Tuya	P
Bláfjall (Iceland-NE)	65.43 N	16.85 W	1222	Tuya	P
Burfell (Iceland-NE)	65.55 N	16.65 W	953	Tuya	P
Fjallgardar Ridge (Iceland-NE)	65.50 N	15.67 W	1035	Fissure vents	P
Gaesafjöll (Iceland-NE)	65.78 N	16.88 W	882	Tuya	P
Lambafjöll (Iceland-NE)	65.83 N	17.13 W	-	Fissure vents	P
Breidabunga (Iceland-SE)	64.42 N	16.08 W	1520	Subglacial volc	P
Snaefell (Iceland-SE)	64.80 N	15.57 W	1833	Stratovolcano	P
Sigurd (Spitsbergen)	79.17 N	13.50 E	1100	Explosion crater	P
Halvdan (Spitsbergen)	79.33 N	13.50 E	834	Explosion crater	P
Sverrefjell (Spitsbergen)	79.43 N	13.30 E	506	Cinder cone	P

ATLANTIC OCEAN & ANTARCTICA

Volcano Name (Subregion)	LAT	LONG	ELEV	TYPE	STATUS
Santo Antao (Cape Verde Is)	17.07 N	25.17 W	1979	Stratovolcano	P
Sao Nicolau (Cape Verde Is)	16.62 N	24.35 W	1270	Stratovolcano	P
Martin Vaz (Atlantic-C)	20.47 S	28.85 W	-	Stratovolcano	P
Inaccessible Island (Atlantic-S)	37.32 S	12.73 W	449	Stratovolcano	P
Gough Island (Atlantic-S)	40.32 S	9.93 W	910	Shield volcano	P
Gaussberg (Antarctica)	66.78 S	89.30 E	370	Cone	P
Adare Peninsula (Antarctica)	71.70 S	170.60 E	2083	Shield volcanoes	PM
Hallett Peninsula (Antarctica)	72.53 S	169.92 E	1770	Shield volcanoes	PM
Daniell Peninsula (Antarctica)	72.95 S	169.37 E	2026	Shield volcanoes	PM
Coulman Island (Antarctica)	73.55 S	169.67 E	1998	Shield volcano	PM
Franklin Island (Antarctica)	76.17 S	168.38 E	247	Shield volcano	Q
Beaufort Island (Antarctica)	76.98 S	167.02 E	740	Stratovolcano	Q
Terror, Mt. (Antarctica)	77.52 S	168.55 E	3262	Shield volcano	P
Hut Point Peninsula (Antarctica)	77.75 S*	166.75 E	431	Scoria cones	P
White Island (Antarctica)	78.17 S	167.50 E	762	Shield volcanoes	P
Mason Spurr (Antarctica)	78.58 S*	164.37 E	-	Lava domes	P
Unnamed (Antarctica)	86.90 S	153.00 W	-	Unknown	Q
Taylor Valley (Antarctica)	77.67 S	162.17 E	1400	Cinder cones	P
Fosdick Mountains (Antarctica)	76.50 S	145.00 E	-	Scoria cones	PM
Bursey, Mt. (Antarctica)	76.00 S	132.67 W	2787	Shield volcanoes	P
Obiglio, Mt. (Antarctica)	74.47 S	131.83 W	510	Cinder cone	P
Shepard Island (Antarctica)	74.42 S	132.67 W	-	Tuff cones	P
Crary Group (Antarctica)	76.80 S	117.70 W	3654	Shield volcanoes	P
Murphy, Mt. (Antarctica)	75.37 S	110.67 W	2703	Shield volcano	P
Beethoven Peninsula (Antarctica)	71.55 S*	73.42 W	1050	Volcanic field	P
Brabant Island (Antarctica)	64.28 S	62.33 W	2522	Volcanic field	P
Livingston-Greenwich Islands	62.52 S	60.02 W	530	Tuff cones	P
Melville (Antarctica)	62.02 S	57.67 W	549	Stratovolcano	Q
Tabarin Peninsula (Antarctica)	63.60 S	57.00 W	730	Shield volcano?	P
James Ross Island (Antarctica)	64.15 S	57.75 W	1470	Shield volcano	P
Argo Point (Antarctica)	66.25 S	60.92 W	360	Scoria cone	P

Bill Rose (Michigan Tech Univ)

Ayarza volcano is a scenic 5 x 7 km wide double caldera in Guatemala filled by Laguna de Ayarza. Both calderas, whose steep walls rise nearly 600 m above the lake surface, were formed within several thousand years of each other during major rhyolitic explosive eruptions between about 27,000 and 23,100 years ago.

Preliminary List of Large-Volume Pleistocene Eruptions

Large-Volume Pleistocene Eruptions: Context and Codes

The recognition of potential global-scale impacts of large-volume eruptions has promoted interest in expanding documentation of these eruptions into the Pleistocene. Data are listed here chronologically, first in thousands of years (ka) Before Present and then in millions of years (Ma) Before Present. Thus 22.6 ka = 22,600 years BP, and 0.58 Ma = 580,000 years BP. We have included all Pleistocene eruptions (1.81 million years or younger) known to us that meet the criteria of being dated, either explicitly or within a stratigraphic range (the latter are flagged by an "*"), and have an estimated volume for either bulk tephra ejection or lava effusion in excess of 1 km^3.

There are two exceptions. One is that explosive eruptions known to have resulted in caldera formation, but without a volume calculation, are included with a "C" in the VEI field. We have also included some eruptions without volume calculations where a VEI value has been assigned by our data source. Radiocarbon dates appear as uncorrected dates, unless only a corrected date is known (flagged by an apostrophe after the "ka"). Effusive eruptions are classified as VEI 0 to distinguish from explosive eruptions, but many may have also had an explosive component. References are listed regionally at the end of the list; full citations can be found in the pertinent regional section of the **REFERENCES** at the end of this book.

Volume calculations can vary significantly depending on the density of thickness measurements and the calculation technique used; we display published volumes, but users should be aware of their considerable uncertainties. As the table title indicates, this is a preliminary list, and both volumes and dates are subject to change as more detailed studies are conducted. Compilation of these data was begun independently at the Smithsonian and has continued as a collaborative "Volcano Global Risk Identification and Analysis" project (VOGRIPA) with Steve Sparks and colleagues of Bristol University to assess the impact of large-volume eruptions. We are pleased to acknowledge the important contributions to this preliminary list by Laura Hobbs and Natalie Oritz of the VOGRIPA project and Yukio Hayakawa of Gunma University, who provided data and VEI assignments for Japanese eruptions.

ka = Thousand years Before Present (uncorrected radiocarbon date)
Ma = Million years Before Present
***** = Dated within a stratigraphic range
' = Corrected radiocarbon date

DRE = Dense Rock Equivalent
LF = Lava Flow
T = Tephra
VEI = Volcanic Explosivity Index
C in VEI column = caldera-forming eruption without known tephra volume

Large-Volume Pleistocene Eruptions

DATE	VOLCANO NAME (Subregion)	UNIT	VEI	VOLUME (km^3)
10.3 ka	**Hijiori** (Japan-Honshu)	Obanazawa Ignimbrite (Hj Tephra)	**5**	2.3
10.5 ka	**Toluca** (México)	Upper Toluca Pumice (UTP)	**6**	18
10.6 ka	**Krafla** (Iceland)	Krofluhals	**0**	1 LF
10.6 ka	**Medicine Lake** (US-California)	Giant Crater	**0**	4.35 LF
10.7 ka	**Ulreung** (Korea)	Ulreung-Oki Tephra (U-Oki)	**6**	>10
11.0 ka	**East Eifel** (Germany)	Laacher See	**6**	20
11.0 ka	**Shasta** (US-California)	Red Banks Pumice	**5**	>1 DRE
11.2 ka	**Tolima** (Colombia)	Canalones stage	**5**	>1 DRE
11.3 ka	**St. Helens** (US-Washington)	Jy Tephra	**5**	~1 DRE
11.4 ka	**Campi Flegrei** (Italy)	Lagno Amendolare Pumice	**5**	....
11.6 ka	**Glacier Peak** (US-Washington)	B Tephra	**5**	6.5
11.6 ka	**Glacier Peak** (US-Washington)	M Tephra	**5**	1.1
11.6 ka	**Glacier Peak** (US-Washington)	G Tephra	**5**	6
11.9 ka	**Mashu** (Japan-Hokkaido)	Ma-I Ash	**5**+	6.6
11.9 ka	**Okataina** (New Zealand)	Waiohau Tephra	**6**	15 T; 4 LF
12.0 ka	**Campi Flegrei** (Italy)	Neopolitan Yellow Tuff (NYT)	**6**+	79
12.0 ka	**Furnas** (Azores)	Furnas caldera	**6**?	>>7
12.0 ka	**Katla** (Iceland)	Sólheimar Ignimbrite/Zedde/Ash Zone 1	**6**	>10
12.0 ka*'	**Kuchinoerabu-jima** (Japan-Ryukyus)	Furutake-Megasaki Tephra	**5**	0.8 DRE
12.0 ka	**Okmok** (Aleutian Is-Alaska)	Okmok I caldera	**6**+	>21-31 DRE
12.1 ka	**Toluca** (México)	Middle Toluca Pumice (MTP)	**5**	3.9
12.2 ka'	**Theistareykjarbunga** (Iceland)	Skildingahraun lava shield	**0**	10 LF
12.4 ka	**Apoyeque** (Nicaragua)	Upper Apoyeque Pumice	**5**	4.3
12.5 ka*	**El Misti** (Peru)	Summit caldera	**5**	>1.5?
12.5 ka*	**Nantai** (Japan-Honshu)	Imaichi (Nt-IP), Shichihonzakura (Nt-SP)	**5**	6.3
12.5 ka	**Reykjanes** (Iceland)	Sandfellshaed	**0**	4.8 LF
12.5 ka*	**Towada** (Japan-Honshu)	Towada Hachinohe Ash (To-HP, To-HPf)	**6**	>50
12.7 ka	**Reclus** (Chile-S)	R1 Tephra	**6**	>10
12.8 ka	**Sakura-jima** (Japan-Kyushu)	Sz-14 (Satsuma; Sz-S) Tephra	**5**?	....
12.9 ka	**St. Helens** (US-Washington)	Sg Tephra	**5**	~1 DRE
13.0 ka*'	**Akan** (Japan-Hokkaido)	Me-Akan (Nakamachineshiri) Pumice	**5**	....
13.0 ka	**Nulla** (Australia)	Toomba	**0**	12 LF
13.0 ka*	**Shikotsu (Eniwa)** (Japan-Hokkaido)	Eniwa En-a Pumice	**5**+	8.9
13.0 ka	**Tolima** (Colombia)	Romerales stage Unit 7	**5**	>1 DRE
13.1 ka	**Okataina** (New Zealand)	Rotorua Tephra	**5**+	7 T; 1 LF
13.2 ka	**Llaima** (Chile-C)	Curacautin Ignimbrite	**6**	24
13.4 ka	**Cerro Grande** (US-Idaho)	Cerro Grande lava field	**0**	2.3 LF
13.5 ka*	**Asama** (Japan-Honshu)	As-YP, YPk (Tsumagoi, Kusatsu)	**5**	>4.4
13.5 ka*	**Garibaldi Lake** (Canada)	Clinker Peak LF	**0**	4 LF
13.8 ka	**Villarica** (Chile-C)	Licán Ignimbrite	**6**	10
14.0 ka	**Popocatépetl** (México)	Tutti Frutti Pumice	**6**	....
14.6 ka*	**Reclus** (Chile-S)	Pre-R1 Reclus tephra	**5**?	....
14.7 ka	**Okataina** (New Zealand)	Rerewhakaaitu Tephra	**6**	17 T; 2 LF
14.7 ka	**Rabaul** (New Britain)	Vunabug	**5**	5?
14.8 ka	**Quilotoa** (Ecuador)	Q-2 Tephra	**6**	11.5
14.8 ka	**San Juan** (México)	Tepic Pumice	**5**	5.6
15.0 ka	**Alid** (Eritrea)	Alid crater	**5**	1-5
15.0 ka'	**Kuchinoerabu-jima** (Japan-Ryukyus)	Yumugi Tephra	**5**	....
15.0 ka	**Maly Semiachik** (Kamchatka)	Maly Semiachik caldera	**6**	15-20
15.0 ka	**Nigorigawa** (Japan-Hokkaido)	Ng Tephra	**6**?	....
15.0 ka*	**Rishiri** (Japan-Hokkaido)	Rishiri Wankonosawa Pumice (Rs-Wn)	**5**	....
15.2 ka	**Agua de Pau** (Azores)	Inner caldera	**5**?	>>1.5
15.5 ka	**Etna** (Italy)	Biancavilla Ignimbrite (Y-1 Tephra)	**C**	....
16.0 ka*'	**Kirishima** (Japan-Kyushu)	Karakunidake-Kobayashi Tephra (Kr-Kb)	**5**	....
16.0 ka	**Long Island** (Papua New Guinea)	Kiau Ignimbrite	**C**	....
16.0 ka	**Rabaul** (New Britain)	Namale	**5**	5?
16.0 ka	**Vesuvius** (Italy)	Green Pumice (Pomici Verdoline)	**5**	1.6
16.5 ka*	**Bachelor** (US-Oregon)	Sheridan Mtn LF	**0**	<7 LF
17.0 ka	**Apoyeque** (Nicaragua)	Lower Apoyeque Pumice	**5**	3.9
17.0 ka*'	**Yotei** (Japan-Hokkaido)	Y-1 Scoria	**5**	....
18.0 ka*'	**Komaga-take** (Japan-Hokkaido)	Ko-P5 Pumice	**5**?	....
18.2 ka*'	**Asama** (Japan-Honshu)	Okubozawa Pumice (OkP2)	**5**?	....
18.3 ka	**Vesuvius** (Italy)	Basal Pumice (Pomici di Base)	**5**	>4.4
18.5 ka	**Santorini** (Greece)	Cape Riva	**5/6**	....
18.7 ka*'	**Kusatsu-Shirane** (Japan-Honshu)	Heibei-ike lava	**0**	1 LF
19.0 ka*	**Concepción** (Nicaragua)	Upper Ometepe Tephra	**5**	5.2
19.1 ka	**Okataina** (New Zealand)	Okareka Tephra	**6**	12 T; 5 LF
19.2 ka	**Katmai** (Alaska Peninsula)	LPFI Ignimbrite	**6**?	....
19.6 ka*'	**Asama** (Japan-Honshu)	Okubozawa Pumice (OkP1)	**5**?	....
19.8 ka*'	**Shiga** (Japan-Honshu)	Maru-ike lava	**0**	1 LF
19.8 ka	**St. Helens** (US-Washington)	M Tephra	**5**	~0.8 DRE
19.9 ka*	**Ubinas** (Peru)	Pumice-fall layer	**5**	1-2
20.0 ka*'	**Komaga-take** (Japan-Hokkaido)	Ko-h Pumice	**5**?	....
20.0 ka	**Las Cumbres** (México)	Quetzalapa Pumice	**5**+	>8.4
20.0 ka	**McBride Volc Prov** (Australia)	Kinrara	**0**	1 LF
20.0 ka	**Nantai** (Japan-Honshu)	Ogawa Scoria (OgS)	**5**	1.2
20.0 ka*'	**Nikko-Shirane** (Japan-Honshu)	Marunuma lava	**0**	1 LF
20.0 ka*	**Olkaria** (Kenya)	Njorowa Pantellerite Formation	**C**	....
20.0 ka	**Rabaul** (New Britain)	Kulua	**6**?	>10?
20.0 ka	**Towada** (Japan-Honshu)	Towada-Bisuketo 2 Pumices (To-BP2)	**5**	....
20.2 ka	**Batur** (Indonesia-Bali)	Gunungkawi Ignimbrite (Gki)	**6**?	7-13
20.5 ka*	**Sanbe** (Japan-Honshu)	Sanbe (SUk) Tephra	**5**	....
20.8 ka*'	**Asama** (Japan-Honshu)	Shiraito Pumice As-SP (As-Sr)	**5**	2.6

DATE	VOLCANO NAME (Subregion)	UNIT	VEI	VOLUME (km³)
21.0 ka	**Daisen** (Japan-Honshu)	Daisen-Misen (DMs)	5	....
21.1 ka	**Okataina** (New Zealand)	Te Rere	6	43 T; 8 LF
21.2 ka	**Terceira** (Azores)	Lajes Ignimbrite (Guilherme Moniz)	C	....
21.8 ka	**Toluca** (México)	Lower Toluca Pumice (LTP)	5	2.1
22.0 ka*	**Cosigüina** (Nicaragua)	MCO Tephra	5	6
22.0 ka	**Sete Cidades** (Azores)	Sete Cidades caldera	5	>>1
22.5 ka*	**Campi Flegrei** (Italy)	TAU-e Tephra	5?	>2.4-11.5
22.6 ka	**Taupo** (New Zealand)	Kawakawa (Oruanui)	8	1170
22.8 ka	**Apoyo** (Nicaragua)	Upper Apoyo Tephra	6	43
23.1 ka	**Ayarza** (Guatemala)	Piños Altos Tephra (PAT)	5	2 DRE
23.1 ka	**Ayarza** (Guatemala)	Mixta Tephra (MFT)	5+	9
23.2 ka	**Mazama** (US-Oregon)	Trego Hot Springs Tephra	5	1.6 DRE
23.3 ka	**Apoyo** (Nicaragua)	Lower Apoyo Tephra, Apoyo Ignimbrite	6	14.5
23.3 ka*'	**Asama** (Japan-Honshu)	Itahana BP3 Pumice	5?	....
23.5 ka	**Taupo** (New Zealand)	Poihipi Tephra	5	2.5
24.0 ka	**Potato Butte** (US-California)	Hat Creek	0	5 LF
24.3 ka*'	**Asama** (Japan-Honshu)	Itahana BP2 Pumice	5	....
24.5 ka*	**Daisen** (Japan-Honshu)	Daisen Sasaganaru (DSs) Tephra	5	....
24.5 ka	**Nemo Peak** (Kuril Islands)	Nemo III caldera	6?	9-11
25.0 ka*'	**Asama** (Japan-Honshu)	Itahana BP1 Pumice	5	....
25.0 ka	**Ilyinsky** (Kamchatka)	Ilyinsky caldera	C	....
25.0 ka*	**Los Humeros** (México)	El Xalapaxco caldera	5	1 DRE
25.1 ka	**Taupo** (New Zealand)	Okaia Tephra	5+	7
25.8 ka	**Emmons Lake** (Alaska Peninsula)	Dawson Tephra	6?	>50
26.0 ka	**Sakura-jima** (Japan-Kyushu)	Sz-17 (Sz-Tk6) Tephra	5	....
26.5 ka*'	**Asama** (Japan-Honshu)	Itahana BP0 Pumice	5	....
26.5 ka	**Láscar** (Chile-N)	Soncor Unit	6	15
26.5 ka	**Okataina** (New Zealand)	Mangaone-L Tephra	5+	8.1
26.7 ka	**Okataina** (New Zealand)	Omataroa Tephra	6	16
27.0 ka*'	**Kutcharo (Nishibetsu)** (Japan-Hokkaido)	Higashi Kayano Pumice	5	....
28.0 ka'	**Hachijo-jima** (Japan-Izu Is)	Mihara caldera, Sueyoshi Tephra	5	....
28.0 ka*	**Laguna Caldera** (Luzon-Philippines)	Teresa Scoria Flow	C	....
28.0 ka	**Okataina** (New Zealand)	Mangaone-I Tephra	6	19.9
28.0 ka'	**Sakura-jima** (Japan-Kyushu)	Aira-Tanzawa Tephra (AT)	7/8	>450; 2000
28.0 ka*	**Shikotsu (Eniwa)** (Japan-Hokkaido)	Eniwa En-b Tephra	5	4.5
28.0 ka*	**Terceira** (Azores)	Outer Santa Barbara caldera	C	....
28.0 ka	**Toluca** (México)	28 ka block-and-ash flow unit	5	3
29.0 ka*	**Ksudach** (Kamchatka)	Ksudach II caldera	6	25
29.0 ka	**Menengai** (Kenya)	First Menengai caldera	6	20 DRE
29.0 ka	**Okataina** (New Zealand)	Awakeri Tephra	5	2
29.3 ka	**Batur** (Indonesia-Bali)	Ubud Ignimbrite (Ubi)	7?	18-36; >108
29.9 ka	**Avachinsky** (Kamchatka)	Avachinsky caldera	C	....
30.0 ka*'	**Kutcharo (Nishibetsu)** (Japan-Hokkaido)	Tokotan-1 Tephra	5	....
30.0 ka	**Micotrin** (West Indies)	Roseau Ash	6	58
30.0 ka'	**Sakura-jima** (Japan-Kyushu)	Aira Fukaminato (A-Fm)	5	....
30.0 ka*'	**Towada** (Japan-Honshu)	Towado-Ofudo (To-Of), To-BP1 Pumices	6	50
30.0 ka*	**Yasur** (Vanuatu-SW Pacific)	Siwi Group	5	>1
30.0 ka*'	**Yotei** (Japan-Hokkaido)	Y-3 Scoria	5	....
30.2 ka	**Shiveluch** (Kamchatka)	Molodoy Shiveluch caldera	6	15-20
31.0 ka	**Aso** (Japan-Kyushu)	Kusasenrigahama Pumice (Kpfa, Aso-K)	5	2.4
31.0 ka	**Zitácuaro** (México)	La Dieta Pumice	5	1.5
31.9 ka'	**Okataina** (New Zealand)	Mangaone-K Tephra	6	16.2
32.0 ka*'	**Daisetsu** (Japan-Hokkaido)	Sounkyo Ignimbrite	6?	....
32.0 ka*	**Komaga-take** (Japan-Hokkaido)	Ko-i Pumice	5?	....
32.3 ka*	**El Misti** (Peru)	Group 3-1 ashflow deposits	5	>1.5
33.0 ka*	**Akademia Nauk** (Kamchatka)	Akademia Nauk (Karymsky Lake) caldera	C	....
33.0 ka	**Tengger** (Indonesia-Java)	Sand Sea caldera	C	....
33.6 ka	**Agua de Pau** (Azores)	Older caldera	5?	>>5
33.7 ka	**Quilotoa** (Ecuador)	Q-3 Tephra	5?	>4
34.0 ka*'	**Kutcharo (Nishibetsu)** (Japan-Hokkaido)	Tokotan-2 Tephra	5	....
34.2 ka'	**Okataina** (New Zealand)	Mangaone-G Tephra	5	2.5
35.0 ka*	**Medicine Lake** (US-California)	Mammoth Crater	0	4-5? LF
35.1 ka'	**Okataina** (New Zealand)	Mangaone-F Tephra	6	15.2
35.2 ka*'	**Akagi** (Japan-Honshu)	Akagi Kanuma Pumice (Ag-KP)	5?	26; 5
35.9 ka	**Bulusan** (Luzon-Philippines)	Irosin Ignimbrite	6	>10
35.9 ka	**Okataina** (New Zealand)	Hauparu Tephra	6	10
36.0 ka*	**Galeras** (Colombia)	Jenoy caldera	5	2
36.0 ka	**Tres Vírgenes** (México)	La Vírgen Tephra	5	>1.1
36.3 ka	**Los Azufres** (México)	Acambaro (AC) Ignimbrite	5	1 DRE
36.5 ka*	**Krashenninokov** (Kamchatka)	Krashenninokov caldera	6	50
37.0 ka	**Campi Flegrei** (Italy)	Campanian Ignimbrite (CI; Y-5 Tephra)	7	620
37.0 ka	**Rabual** (New Britain)	Latlat Tephra	5	5
37.0 ka*	**Sanbe** (Japan-Honshu)	Sanbe Ikeda (SI)	6?	....
37.0 ka	**Santorini** (Greece)	US2 Tephra	5	....
37.0 ka	**Toluca** (México)	37 ka block-and-ash flow unit	5	3
37.1 ka'	**Okataina** (New Zealand)	Mangaone-D Tephra	6	11
37.5 ka	**Nevados de Chillán** (Chile-C)	Nev2 Ignimbrite	C	....
38.0 ka*'	**Ata** (Japan-Kyushu)	Ata-Karayama	5?	....
38.0 ka*'	**Kutcharo (Nishibetsu)** (Japan-Hokkaido)	Tokotan-3 Tephra	5	....
38.0 ka	**Rabaul** (New Britain)	Malaguna	6	....
38.8 ka	**Golovnin** (Kuril Islands)	Kn III-5 Tephra	5+	7-8
39.0 ka	**Erebus** (Antactica)	Mt. Dewitt Tephra	C?	....
39.0 ka	**Gorely** (Kamchatka)	Gorely Khrebet caldera	7	120
39.0 ka*	**Ksudach** (Kamchatka)	Ksudach I caldera	6	40
39.0 ka	**Qualibou** (West Indies)	Choiseul Pumice	6?	>11?
39.1 ka*	**Opala** (Kamchatka)	Opala caldera	7	150
39.3 ka*	**Khangar** (Kamchatka)	Khangar II caldera	C	....
39.6 ka	**Uzon** (Kamchatka)	Uzon-Geizerny caldera	7	150

DATE	VOLCANO NAME (Subregion)	UNIT	VEI	VOLUME (km^3)
39.8 ka	**Mendeleev** (Kuril Islands)	Mendeleev caldera	C	....
40.0 ka	**Bandai** (Japan-Honshu)	Hayama-1 Pumice (HP1)	5?	....
40.0 ka	**Changbaishan** (China/Korea)	Outer Changbaishan caldera	C	....
40.0 ka*	**Emmons Lake** (Alaska Peninsula)	Unnamed tephra	C	....
40.0 ka*'	**Iwate** (Japan-Honshu)	Yukiura Pumice (Iw-Y)	5?	....
40.0 ka*	**Kutcharo** (Japan-Hokkaido)	Kutcharo-Shoro Ash (Kc-Sr), Kc-1 Ignimbrite	7	100
40.0 ka*	**Kutcharo (Nishibetsu)** (Japan-Hokkaido)	Nishibetsu Yambetsu Pumice (Ns-Ym)	6?	....
40.0 ka*	**Nemo Peak** (Kuril Islands)	Nemo II caldera	6	10-15 DRE
40.0 ka	**Rabaul** (New Britain)	Barge T.	5	5
40.0 ka*	**Ugashik-Peulik** (Alaska Peninsula)	Ugashik caldera	6?	5-10 DRE
41.0 ka*	**Okataina** (New Zealand)	Maketu Tephra	6	15
41.0 ka*	**Shikotsu** (Japan-Hokkaido)	Shikotsu-Spfa1 Pumice	7	200
41.0 ka*	**Towada** (Japan-Honshu)	Towada-Godo Pumice (To-G)	5	....
41.5 ka*	**Kurile Lake** (Kamchatka)	Old Kurile Lake caldera	C	....
42.0 ka*	**Kuttara** (Japan-Hokkaido)	Kuttara-1 (Kt-1)	6	....
42.0 ka'	**Okataina** (New Zealand)	Mangaone-B Tephra	5	4.6
42.0 ka	**Soufrière Guadeloupe** (West Indies)	Pintade Pumice	5	1-3
42.0 ka*	**Towada** (Japan-Honshu)	Towada-Kibidango Tephra (To-Kb)	5	....
42.2 ka*	**Haruna** (Japan-Honshu)	Haruna Hassaki Pumice (Hr-HP)	5	2.6
42.5 ka*	**St. Helens** (US-Washington)	C Tephra	5?	>4 DRE
43.0 ka*	**Okataina** (New Zealand)	Tahuna Tephra	5	2?
43.0 ka*'	**Sakura-jima** (Japan-Kyushu)	Aira Otsuka (A-Ot)	5	....
43.0 ka	**Tambora** (Indonesia-Lesser Sunda)	Pre-1815 caldera	C	....
43.0 ka*	**Taupo** (New Zealand)	Tahuna Tephra	5	4
43.0 ka*	**Towada** (Japan-Honshu)	Towada-Okuse Tephra (To-Os)	6?	....
43.5 ka*	**El Misti** (Peru)	Summit caldera	5	4-6.5
45.0 ka*	**Mazama** (US-Oregon)	Devils Backbone	0	1.4 LF
45.0 ka*	**Nemo Peak** (Kuril Islands)	Nemo I caldera	6?	>50 DRE
45.0 ka*	**Numazawa** (Japan-Honshu)	Numazawa-Mizunuma (Nm-MZ)	5	1.0 DRE
45.0 ka*	**Okataina** (New Zealand)	Ngamotu Tephra	5	2
45.0 ka*	**Smith Rock** (Japan-Volcano Is)	Sumisu (Smith) caldera	6	48-50
45.7 ka	**Zitácuaro** (México)	La Soledad	5+	9
46.0 ka*	**Sanbe** (Japan-Honshu)	Sanbe Oda, Unan (SOd, Sun)	6?	5-20
46.0 ka*	**Taupo** (New Zealand)	Tihoi Tephra	5	5
46.2 ka*	**Akagi** (Japan-Honshu)	Akagi-Yunoguchi Pumice (Ag-UP)	5	5.1
47.0 ka*	**Hakone** (Japan-Honshu)	Central Cone-1 Tephra (Hk-CC1)	5?	....
47.0 ka*	**Taupo** (New Zealand)	Waihora Tephra	5	1
47.5 ka*	**Pantelleria** (Italy)	Green Tuff (Y-6 Ash)	5	>2.75 DRE
48.0 ka*	**Akagi** (Japan-Honshu)	Akagi Namegawa-1 (Ag-Nm1)	5	2
48.0 ka*	**Taupo** (New Zealand)	Otake Tephra	5	2
49.0 ka*	**Akagi** (Japan-Honshu)	Akagi Namegawa-2 (Ag-Nm2)	5	2.9
50,000 years BP (50 ka)				
50.0 ka*	**Daisen** (Japan-Honshu)	Daisen-Kurayoshi Pumice (DKP)	6	>20
50.0 ka*	**Hakone** (Japan-Honshu)	Sanshokuki Tephra (Hk-S)	5?	....
50.0 ka*	**Towada** (Japan-Honshu)	Towada SP Pumice (To-SP)	5?	....
50.0 ka*	**Usu (Toya)** (Japan-Hokkaido)	Osarugawa Pumice	5	....
51.0 ka'	**Campi Flegrei** (Italy)	Santa Lucia Tephra	6?	>4.2-22
51.0 ka*	**Coatepeque** (El Salvador)	Conacaste Tephra (CCT)	6	12
51.0 ka*	**Pacaya (Amatitlán)** (Guatemala)	Amatitlán-E Tephra	6	45
51.9 ka*	**Hakone** (Japan-Honshu)	Hakone-Tokyo, Tokyo Pumice (Hk-T, Hk-TP)	6	>30
52.0 ka*'	**Kirishima** (Japan-Kyushu)	Hinamori (Awaokoshi Tephra) (Kr-Aw)	6?	....
53.0 ka	**Mazama** (US-Oregon)	Scoria Cone	0	1.6 LF
53.0 ka*	**Zenikame** (Japan-Hokkaido)	Zenikame-Menagawa (Z-M)	6	28
54.5 ka	**Tindfjallajökull** (Iceland)	Thórsmörk Ignimbrite/Ash Zone 2	5+	8
55.0 ka*	**Akagi** (Japan-Honshu)	Akagi-Mizunuma Pumice-1 (Ag-MzP-1)	5	2.6
55.0 ka*	**Kuttara** (Japan-Hokkaido)	Kuttara-2 (Kt-2)	6?	....
55.0 ka*	**Taupo** (New Zealand)	Unnamed Tephra	5	3.5
55.0 ka*	**Valles** (US-New Mexico)	El Cajete-Battleship Rock	5	1.8 DRE
56.0 ka	**El Valle** (Panamá)	El Hato Ignimbrite	C	....
56.0 ka*	**Hakone** (Japan-Honshu)	Hakone-Miura Pumice (Hk-MP)	5?	....
56.0 ka	**Ischia** (Italy)	Green Tuff (Ischia Tephra, Y-7 Tephra)	C	....
56.9 ka	**Coatepeque** (El Salvador)	Congo Tephra (CGT)	5	23
57.0 ka*	**Kuju** (Japan-Kyushu)	Kuju-1 (Kj-P1) Tephra	5	....
58.0 ka*	**Kuttara** (Japan-Hokkaido)	Kuttara Takeura Scoria (K-Tk)	5?	....
58.1 ka*	**Kuttara** (Japan-Hokkaido)	Kuttara-3 (Kt-3)	6	....
58.3 ka*	**Shikotsu** (Japan-Hokkaido)	Spfa5 Pumice	5	....
58.5 ka*	**Kuttara** (Japan-Hokkaido)	Kuttara Hayakita Tephra (K-Hy)	5?	....
60.0 ka*'	**Ata** (Japan-Kyushu)	Ata-Hananoki Tephra	5?	....
60.0 ka*	**Daisen** (Japan-Honshu)	Daisen Sekigane Pumice (DSP)	5	....
60.0 ka*	**Kirishima** (Japan-Kyushu)	Kirishima-Iwaokoshi (Kr-Iw)	6?	....
60.0 ka*	**Los Humeros** (México)	Xoxoctic Tuff	5	2.2
60.0 ka*	**Masaya** (Nicaragua)	Fontana Tephra	5	2.9-3.8
60.0 ka*	**Shikotsu** (Japan-Hokkaido)	Spfa6 Pumice	5	....
60.0 ka*	**Tecapa** (El Salvador)	Twins/A Tephra (TT-AT)	6	10.4
60.0 ka*	**Towada** (Japan-Honshu)	Towada-Okoshi Tephra (To-Ok2)	5?	....
60.1 ka*	**Shikotsu** (Japan-Hokkaido)	Spfa7-10 Scoria	6	....
61.0 ka*	**Hakone** (Japan-Honshu)	Hakone-Anjin Pumice (Hk-AP)	5?	....
61.0 ka*	**Okataina** (New Zealand)	Earthquake Flat Tephra	6	15.5
62.0 ka*	**Kuttara** (Japan-Hokkaido)	Kuttara-4 (Kt-4)	6	....
64.0 ka	**Okataina** (New Zealand)	Rotoiti Tephra	7	241
64.5 ka*	**Campi Flegrei** (Italy)	CA1-a Tephra	6?	>4.2-20.5
65.0 ka*	**Sakura-jima** (Japan-Kyushu)	Aira-Iwato Tephra (A-Iw)	6?	5-20
65.3 ka*	**Akagi** (Japan-Honshu)	Akagi Okkai Pumice (Ag-Ok)	5	3.9
69.0 ka	**Akademia Nauk** (Kamchatka)	Second Odnoboky caldera	6	10-15
70.0 ka*	**Towada** (Japan-Honshu)	Towada-QP Pumice (To-QP)	5?	....
71.0 ka*	**Mazama** (US-Oregon)	Summer Lake tephra bed 8	5	>1 DRE
71.0 ka	**Mazama** (US-Oregon)	Pumice Castle	5	2 DRE, 1.8 LF

DATE	VOLCANO NAME (Subregion)	UNIT	VEI	VOLUME (km³)
72.0 ka	**Coatepeque** (El Salvador)	Arce Tephra (ACT)	**6**	26?
72.0 ka*	**Yakeishi** (Japan-Honshu)	Yamagata Pumcie (Yk-Y)	**5**?	....
72.0 ka*	**Yakeishi** (Japan-Honshu)	Murasakino Pumice (Yk-M)	**5**?	....
73.0 ka*	**On-take** (Japan-Honshu)	Ontake-Mitake Pumice (On-Mt)	**5**	....
74.0 ka	**Toba** (Indonesia-Sumatra)	Youngest Toba Tuff (YTT)	**8**	2500-3000 DRE
75.0 ka*	**Bandai** (Japan-Honshu)	Hayama 2 Pumice (HP2)	**5**?	....
75.0 ka*	**Jefferson** (US-Oregon)	Jefferson E Tephra	**5**	~1 DRE
75.0 ka*	**Kuju** (Japan-Kyushu)	Kuju-Handa (Kj-Hd) Tephra	**5/6**	....
75.0 ka	**Newberry** (US-Oregon)	Paulina Creek/Olema Tephra	**6**?	>5? DRE
75.0 ka*	**Tecapa** (El Salvador)	Blanca Rosa Tephra (BRT)	**5**	4.6
75.0 ka	**Yellowstone** (US-Wyoming)	Central Plateau	**0**	30-60 LF
75.3 ka*	**Tateyama** (Japan-Honshu)	Tateyama-E (Tt-E Pumice)	**5**	....
76.0 ka	**Ilopango** (El Salvador)	Tierra Blanca 4 (TB4)	**6**	36
77.0 ka	**Coatepeque** (El Salvador)	Bellavista	**5**	1
77.3 ka*	**On-take** (Japan-Honshu)	Ontake-Senbonmatsu Pumice (On-Sn)	**5**?	....
78.0 ka*	**Fuji** (Japan-Honshu)	Fuji-Yoshioka Pumice (F-YP)	**5**	....
79.0 ka	**Santorini** (Greece)	Upper Scoriae 2 (US2)	**5**	....
79.0 ka	**Yellowstone** (US-Wyoming)	Pitchstone Plateau	**0**	70 LF
80.0 ka	**Bolshoi Semiachik** (Kamchatka)	Bolshoi Semiachik II caldera	**6**	20-30
80.0 ka*	**Hakone** (Japan-Honshu)	Hakone-Obaradai (Hk-OP)	**5**	....
80.0 ka*	**Los Humeros** (México)	Zaragoza	**6**	30
80.0 ka*	**Narugo** (Japan-Honshu)	Narugo-Yanagizawa PF (Nr-Y Tephra)	**6**?	....
80.0 ka*	**Towada** (Japan-Honshu)	Towada-T17 Tephra (To-T17)	**5**?	....
81.0 ka	**Pinatubo** (Luzon-Philippines)	Inararo Tuff	**7**?	....
83.0 ka*	**Daisen** (Japan-Honshu)	Daisen-Namatake Pumice (DNP)	**6**	....
83.0 ka*	**Kuttara** (Japan-Hokkaido)	Kuttara-5 (Kt-5)	**5**	....
84.0 ka	**Atitlán** (Guatemala)	H Tephra, Los Chocoyos (LCY)	**7**	620
84.0 ka*	**Towada** (Japan-Honshu)	Towada-Kawaguchi Pumice	**5**	....
84.9 ka*	**On-take** (Japan-Honshu)	Ontake-Nagawa Pumice (On-Ng)	**5**	....
85.0 ka	**Medicine Lake** (US-California)	Yellowjacket Butte	**0**	4-5 LF
85.0 ka*	**Rishiri** (Japan-Hokkaido)	Rishiri Kabutonuma-1 Tephra (Rs-KB1)	**5**?	....
85.3 ka	**Nevados de Chillán** (Chile-C)	Nev1a lava flow	**0**	>1 LF
86.0 ka*	**Kuttara** (Japan-Hokkaido)	Kuttara-6 (Kt-6)	**6**	....
86.0 ka*	**Nyoho** (Japan-Honshu)	Higashiakata-1 (Hg-1)	**5**	>1
86.9 ka*	**Kutcharo** (Japan-Hokkaido)	Kc-2-3 Ignimbrite	**7**?	5-20; 100
87.0 ka	**Aso** (Japan-Kyushu)	Aso-4 Tephra	**7/8**	>600; 3000
87.0 ka*	**Nyoho** (Japan-Honshu)	Higashiakata-2 (Hg-2)	**5**	>1
88.0 ka*	**Hakone** (Japan-Honshu)	Hakone-Daruma 5 (Hk-Da5)	**5**	....
88.0 ka*	**Kuttara** (Japan-Hokkaido)	Kuttara-7 (Kt-7)	**6**	....
90.0 ka	**Sakura-jima** (Japan-Kyushu)	Aira-Fukuyama (A-Fk)	**6**	....
90.0 ka*	**Santorini** (Greece)	Upper Scoriae 1 (US1)	**5**	....
90.0 ka*	**Tolima** (Colombia)	Combeima caldera, Río Totare Ignimbrite	**5**	>5
92.0 ka	**Barrier** (Kenya)	Inner caldera	**C**	....
93.0 ka*	**Chascón** (Chile-C)	Chascón dome	**0**	4.8
93.0 ka*	**Towada** (Japan-Honshu)	Towada-Aosuji Pumice (To-AP)	**5**	....
93.7 ka*	**On-take** (Japan-Kyushu)	Ontake-Ina Pumice(On-In)	**6**?	....
95.0 ka	**Kikai** (Japan-Ryukyus)	Nagase (K-Ns), Tozurahara (K-Tz)	**7**	150
95.0 ka*	**Kuttara** (Japan-Hokkaido)	Kuttara-8 (Kt-8)	**6**	....
95.0 ka	**La Primavera** (México)	Tala Tuff	**6**+	90
95.0 ka*	**Santorini** (Greece)	Vourvoulos	**5**	....
95.9 ka*	**On-take** (Japan-Kyushu)	Ontake Katamachi Pumice (On-Kt)	**5**	....
99.0 ka*	**Ata** (Japan-Kyushu)	Ata-Tashiro (Ts) Tephra	**6**?	....
99.0 ka*	**Towada** (Japan-Honshu)	Towada-Kasutera Pumice (To-CP)	**5**	....

ka / Ma

DATE	VOLCANO NAME (Subregion)	UNIT	VEI	VOLUME (km³)
0.10 Ma	**Akagi** (Japan-Honshu)	Akagi-Mizunuma-6 (Ag-Mz6)	**5**	3.1
0.10 Ma*	**Alcedo** (Galápagos)	Alcedo-A,-B Tephra	**5**	>3.4
0.10 Ma*	**Aso** (Japan-Kyushu)	Aso-ABCD Tephra	**5**	....
0.10 Ma*	**Ata** (Japan-Kyushu)	Ata Tephra	**7**	>300
0.10 Ma	**Emmons Lake** (Alaska Peninsula)	Gap Welded Tuff	**C**	....
0.10 Ma*	**Hakone** (Japan-Honshu)	KmP10 Pumice	**5**?	....
0.10 Ma*	**Hakone** (Japan-Honshu)	Hakone-Daruma 4 (Hk-Da4)	**5**?	....
0.10 Ma	**Krafla** (Iceland)	Krafla Welded Layer	**5**?	2.4 DRE
0.10 Ma*	**Narugo** (Japan-Honshu)	Narugo-Nisaka PF (Nr-N)	**5**	....
0.10 Ma	**Nyoho** (Japan-Honshu)	Mamiana Scoria (MaS)	**5**	5.5
0.10 Ma	**On-take** (Japan-Honshu)	Ontake-Daiichi Pumice (On-Pm1)	**6**	50
0.10 Ma	**Rabaul** (New Britain)	Malaguna	**6**?	10?
0.10 Ma	**Rabaul** (New Britain)	Boroi	**6**?	10?
0.10 Ma*	**Rishiri** (Japan-Hokkaido)	Rishiri Kabutonuma-2 Tephra (Rs-KB2)	**5**?	....
0.10 Ma	**Santorini** (Greece)	Middle Pumice (MP)	**6**?	....
0.10 Ma	**Tacaná** (México)	Chanjalé	**C**	....
0.10 Ma*	**Tateyama** (Japan-Honshu)	Tateyama-D (Tt-D Pumice)	**6**	....
0.10 Ma	**Yellowstone** (US-Wyoming)	Solfatara Plateau	**0**	7 LF
0.10 Ma	**Yellowstone** (US-Wyoming)	Hayden Valley	**0**	2 LF
0.11 Ma*	**Acigöl-Nevishir** (Turkey)	Upper Acigöl Tuff	**6**	>15
0.11 Ma*	**Adachi** (Japan-Honshu)	Medeshima Pumice (Ac-Md)	**5**	....
0.11 Ma	**Akademia Nauk** (Kamchatka)	Stena-Soboliny Ignimbrite	**7**	100
0.11 Ma*	**Akagi** (Japan-Honshu)	Akagi-Mizunuma 9,10 (Ag-Mz9,10)	**5**	2
0.11 Ma*	**Akita-Yake-yama** (Japan-Honshu)	Bunamori-bokujo Welded Tuff	**6**	50
0.11 Ma*	**Aso** (Japan-Kyushu)	Aso-K Tephra	**5**	....
0.11 Ma*	**Hakkoda** (Japan-Honshu)	Hakkoda-Ottomo Pumice	**6**?	....
0.11 Ma*	**Hakone** (Japan-Honshu)	Kissawa Middle Pumice-7 (KmP7)	**5**	....
0.11 Ma*	**Hakone** (Japan-Honshu)	Kissawa Middle Pumice-6 (KmP6)	**5**	....
0.11 Ma*	**Hakone** (Japan-Honshu)	Kissawa Middle Pumice-3 (KmP3)	**5**?	....
0.11 Ma*	**Hakone** (Japan-Honshu)	Kissawa Middle Pumice-2 (KmP2)	**5**?	....
0.11 Ma*	**Hakone** (Japan-Honshu)	Kissawa Middle Pumice-1 (KmP1)	**5**	....
0.11 Ma	**Hudson** (Chile-S)	Late-stage caldera	**C**	....
0.11 Ma	**Numazawa** (Japan-Honshu)	Numazawa-Shibahara (Nm-SB)	**5**	0.7 DRE

DATE	VOLCANO NAME (Subregion)	UNIT	VEI	VOLUME (km³)
0.11 Ma*	**Nyoho** (Japan-Honshu)	Namegawa Tephra (Nm)	5	2.4
0.11 Ma	**Pantelleria** (Italy)	La Vecchia caldera	C	....
0.11 Ma*	**Rishiri** (Japan-Hokkaido)	Rishiri Acharu Tephra (Rs-Ac)	5	....
0.11 Ma	**Sanbe** (Japan-Honshu)	Sanbe Kisuki (SK Tephra)	6	20
0.11 Ma	**Soufrière Guadeloupe** (West Indies)	Montval	C	....
0.11 Ma*	**Towada** (Japan-Honshu)	Towado Zarume-1 Pumice (To-ZP1)	5?	....
0.11 Ma	**Usu (Toya)** (Japan-Hokkaido)	Toya Ash (Tpfl-I to Tpfl-IV)	7	>170
0.11 Ma	**Yellowstone** (US-Wyoming)	West Yellowstone	0	41 LF
0.12 Ma	**Aso** (Japan-Kyushu)	Aso-3 Tephra	7	>150
0.12 Ma	**Ata** (Japan-Kyushu)	Ata-Marumine (Ata-Mr)	6?	....
0.12 Ma*	**Cordón Caulle** (Chile-S)	San Pablo Ignimbrite	6	20
0.12 Ma	**Emmons Lake** (Alaska Peninsula)	Unnamed tephra	C	....
0.12 Ma*	**Hakone** (Japan-Honshu)	Kissawa Lower Pumice-13 (KIP13)	5	....
0.12 Ma*	**Hakone** (Japan-Honshu)	Kissawa Lower Pumice-11 (KIP11)	5?	....
0.12 Ma*	**Kutcharo** (Japan-Hokkaido)	Kutcharo Haboro (Kc-Hb) Ash, Kc-4 Ignimbrite	7	>150
0.12 Ma*	**Mazama** (US-Oregon)	NW of Pumice Flat	0	1.5 LF
0.12 Ma*	**Nyoho** (Japan-Honshu)	Ogikubo (Ok) Tephra	5	1.2
0.12 Ma*	**Nyoho** (Japan-Honshu)	Sotome Tephra (So)	5	3
0.12 Ma*	**Nyoho** (Japan-Honshu)	Yaita Tephra (Yt)	5	2.3
0.12 Ma	**Pacaya (Amatitlán)** (Guatemala)	Amatitlán-T Tephra	6	34
0.12 Ma*	**Yatsuga-take** (Japan-Honshu)	Kawakami Pumice (KwP)	5	....
0.12 Ma	**Yellowstone** (US-Wyoming)	Bechler River	0	8 LF
0.13 Ma*	**Adatara** (Japan-Honshu)	Adatara-Dake Pumice (Ad-DK), PF	5	>2 DRE
0.13 Ma*	**Ashitaka?** (Japan-Honshu)	Kissawa Lower Pumice-4 (KIP4)	5?	....
0.13 Ma*	**Aso** (Japan-Kyushu)	Aso-P/Q Tephras	6?	....
0.13 Ma*	**Aso** (Japan-Kyushu)	Aso-R Tephra	5?	....
0.13 Ma*	**Daisen** (Japan-Honshu)	Daisen-Hiruzenbara Pumice (DHP)	6?	....
0.13 Ma*	**Daisen** (Japan-Honshu)	Daisen-Matsue Pumice (DMP)	6?	5-20
0.13 Ma*	**Hakkoda** (Japan-Honshu)	Hakkoda-Katchi Pumice	6?	....
0.13 Ma*	**Hakone** (Japan-Honshu)	Kissawa Lower Pumice-10 (KIP10)	5?	....
0.13 Ma*	**Hakone** (Japan-Honshu)	Hakone-Daruma 1 (Hk-Da1; KIP9)	6?	....
0.13 Ma*	**Hakone** (Japan-Honshu)	Kissawa Lower Pumice-8 (KIP8)	5	....
0.13 Ma*	**Hakone** (Japan-Honshu)	Kissawa Lower Pumice-7 (KIP7)	5	....
0.13 Ma*	**Hakone** (Japan-Honshu)	Kissawa Lower Pumice-6 (KIP6)	5?	....
0.13 Ma*	**Hakone** (Japan-Honshu)	Kissawa Lower Pumice-5 (KIP5)	5?	....
0.13 Ma*	**Hakone** (Japan-Honshu)	Kissawa Lower Pumice-3 (KIP3)	5?	....
0.13 Ma*	**Narugo** (Japan-Honshu)	Narugo-Ichihazama (Nr-It)	5	....
0.13 Ma	**Numazawa?** (Japan-Honshu)	Tagashira Pumice (TgP)	5?	....
0.13 Ma*	**Nyoho** (Japan-Honshu)	Yumihari-7 Tephra (Ym-7)	5	1.2
0.13 Ma*	**Takahara** (Japan-Honshu)	Takahara-KitaAkata (Kt) Tephra	5	3.7
0.14 Ma*	**Aso** (Japan-Kyushu)	Aso-S Tephra	5	....
0.14 Ma	**Aso** (Japan-Kyushu)	Aso-2 Tephra	6	50
0.14 Ma*	**Iizuna** (Japan-Honshu)	Kamitaru Pumice	6?	....
0.14 Ma	**Kikai** (Japan-Ryukyus)	Koabi (K-ab) Tephra	C	....
0.14 Ma*	**Nyoho** (Japan-Honshu)	Yumihari-10 Tephra (Ym-10)	5	1.3
0.14 Ma*	**Santorini** (Greece)	Cape Thera	5	....
0.14 Ma	**Soufrière Guadeloupe** (West Indies)	Anse des Pères	C	....
0.14 Ma	**Yellowstone** (US-Wyoming)	Cold Mountain Creek Tuff	6	10? DRE
0.15 Ma	**Calabozos** (Chile-C)	Loma Seca Tuff-Unit S	7	200
0.15 Ma*	**Hakone** (Japan-Honshu)	Tama A Upper-12 (TAu12) Tephra	5?	....
0.15 Ma	**Nisyros-Kos** (Greece)	Kos Plateau Tuff (KPT)	7	>100
0.15 Ma*	**Takahara** (Japan-Honshu)	Ubazawakita Tephra (Ub)	5	2.4
0.15 Ma	**Tengger** (Indonesia-Java)	Sukapura Ignimbrite	C	....
0.15 Ma	**Vico-Cimino** (Italy)	Sutri Formation/Ignimbrite C	6	10
0.15 Ma	**Yellowstone** (US-Wyoming)	Nez Perce Creek	0	6 LF
0.15 Ma	**Yellowstone** (US-Wyoming)	Elephant Back	0	25 LF
0.15 Ma*	**Yellowstone** (US-Wyoming)	Spring Creek	0	7 LF
0.15 Ma*	**Yellowstone** (US-Wyoming)	Spruce Creek	0	7 LF
0.16 Ma	**Atitlán** (Guatemala)	W Tephra	6	26
0.16 Ma*	**Hakone** (Japan-Honshu)	Tama A Upper-2 (TAu2) Tephra	5?	....
0.16 Ma*	**Iizuna** (Japan-Honshu)	Nishiyama Pumice	6?	....
0.16 Ma	**Ksudach** (Kamchatka)	Earliest Ksudach caldera	6?	>>10
0.16 Ma	**Long Valley** (US-California)	West Moat Coulee	0	4 LF
0.16 Ma	**Yellowstone** (US-Wyoming)	Aster Creek	0	10 LF
0.16 Ma	**Yellowstone** (US-Wyoming)	Buffalo Lake	0	54 LF
0.16 Ma	**Yellowstone** (US-Wyoming)	Mallard Lake	0	13 LF
0.17 Ma*	**Akan** (Japan-Hokkaido)	Ak1 Pumice	6?	....
0.17 Ma*	**Chacana** (Ecuador)	Chacana caldera	C	....
0.17 Ma*	**Hakone** (Japan-Honshu)	Tama A middle-7 (TAm7) Tephra	5?	....
0.17 Ma*	**Hakone** (Japan-Honshu)	Tama A middle-6 (TAm6) Tephra	5?	....
0.17 Ma*	**Nasu** (Japan-Honshu)	Shirakawa-7 Tephra (Sr-7)	5?	2
0.17 Ma*	**Nasu** (Japan-Honshu)	Shirakawa-8 Tephra (Sr-8)	5	1.1
0.17 Ma*	**Nasu** (Japan-Honshu)	Shirakawa-9 Tephra (Sr-9)	5	2
0.17 Ma*	**Nasu** (Japan-Honshu)	Shirakawa-10 Tephra (Sr-10)	5	1.9
0.17 Ma*	**Nyoho** (Japan-Honshu)	Shiobara-1 Tephra (Si-1)	5	1.6
0.17 Ma*	**Nyoho** (Japan-Honshu)	Shiobara-3 Tephra (Si-3)	5?	1.0
0.17 Ma*	**Payún Matru** (Argentina)	Caldera-forming ignimbrite	C	....
0.17 Ma	**Santorini** (Greece)	Lower Pumice 2 (LP2)	5	....
0.17 Ma	**Vulsini (Latera)** (Italy)	Grotte di Castro	5	1-10
0.17 Ma	**Yellowstone** (US-Wyoming)	Mary Lake	0	2 LF
0.17 Ma	**Yellowstone** (US-Wyoming)	West Thumb	0	11 LF
0.17 Ma	**Yellowstone** (US-Wyoming)	Bluff Point Tuff	7?	50? DRE
0.17 Ma	**Yellowstone** (US-Wyoming)	Dry Creek	0	9 LF
0.18 Ma*	**Acigöl-Nevishir** (Turkey)	Lower Acigöl Tuff	6	>13
0.18 Ma*	**Hakone** (Japan-Honshu)	Tama A middle-5 (TAm5) Tephra	6?	....
0.18 Ma*	**Hakone** (Japan-Honshu)	Tama A middle-4 (TAm4) Tephra	6?	....
0.18 Ma*	**Hiuchi** (Japan-Honshu)	Hiuchigatake-Takaku (Nanairi) Pumice	5+	8
0.18 Ma	**Medicine Lake** (US-California)	Antelope Well Tuff	6	10

DATE	VOLCANO NAME (Subregion)	UNIT	VEI	VOLUME (km³)
0.18 Ma*	**Vulsini (Latera)** (Italy)	Sorano eruptive unit	**5**	1-10
0.19 Ma*	**Hakone** (Japan-Honshu)	Tama A middle-1 (TAm1) Tephra	**6**?	....
0.19 Ma*	**Hakone** (Japan-Honshu)	Tama B-13 (TB-13) Tephra	**6**?	....
0.19 Ma*	**Iiji** (Japan-Honshu)	Moka Pumice (MoP)	**5**+	7.3
0.19 Ma*	**Kinunuma** (Japan-Honshu)	Kinunuma-Kurodahara Tephra	**5**	<6
0.19 Ma	**McBride Volc Prov** (Australia)	Undara	**0**	30 LF
0.19 Ma	**Pacaya (Amatitlán)** (Guatemala)	Amatitlán-L Tephra	**6**+	75
0.19 Ma	**Rainier** (US-Washington)	White pumice fall	**5**	>1 DRE
0.19 Ma	**Tangkubanparahu** (Indonesia-Java)	Sunda caldera	**C**	....
0.19 Ma	**Vulsini (Latera)** (Italy)	Sovana (Piansano PF)	**5**	1-10
0.20 Ma*	**Akan** (Japan-Hokkaido)	Ak2 Pumice	**5**?	....
0.20 Ma	**Chudleigh Volc Prov** (Australia)	Barker	**0**	3-4 LF
0.20 Ma	**Gedemsa** (Ethiopia)	Younger caldera	**C**	....
0.20 Ma	**Las Navajas** (México)	Las Cuevas Ash	**5**	>3
0.20 Ma	**Mojanda** (Ecuador)	Mojanda-2 caldera	**C**	....
0.20 Ma	**Ruiz, Nevado del** (Colombia)	Rio Claro	**5**	5-6?
0.20 Ma	**Santo Antao** (Cape Verde Islands)	Cao Grande Pumice	**5**	1.7-2.7 DRE
0.20 Ma	**Santorini** (Greece)	Lower Pumice 1 (LP1)	**5**	....
0.20 Ma	**Tenerife** (Canary Islands)	Abrigo Member	**7**	20 DRE
0.20 Ma*	**Tenerife** (Canary Islands)	Cruz Sequence	**6**	25
0.20 Ma	**Tolima** (Colombia)	El Rancho stage	**0**	>1 LF
0.21 Ma	**Chalupas** (Ecuador)	Chalupas Ashflow	**6**+	80-100
0.21 Ma*	**Haruna** (Japan-Honshu)	Miyazawa Ignimbrite	**5**?	....
0.21 Ma*	**Maroa** (New Zealand)	Pukeahua Tephra	**5**?	1?
0.21 Ma	**Puelche Volc Field** (Chile-C)	Arroyo San Francisco	**0**	8.6 LF
0.21 Ma*	**Tenerife** (Canary Islands)	Benijos Member	**5**	5?
0.21 Ma*	**Tenerife** (Canary Islands)	Hidalga Member	**5**	5?
0.21 Ma*	**Tenerife** (Canary Islands)	Socorro Member	**5**	4.9
0.22 Ma*	**Iiji** (Japan-Honshu)	Takatsue Tephra	**5**	....
0.22 Ma*	**Onikobe** (Japan-Honshu)	Onikobe-Shimonakazato Tephra	**6**?	....
0.22 Ma	**Piton des Nieges** (Indian Ocean)	Dalle Soudée Formation	**6**	20
0.22 Ma	**Sunagohara** (Japan-Honshu)	Sunagohara-Kubota Tephra	**5**+	>6
0.22 Ma	**Tenerife** (Canary Islands)	Batista Member	**6**	10.1
0.22 Ma	**Tenerife** (Canary Islands)	Caleta Member	**6**	10.1
0.23 Ma	**Emmons Lake** (Alaska Peninsula)	Cathedral Welded Tuff	**6**?	>50
0.23 Ma*	**Hakone** (Japan-Honshu)	Tama B-7 (TB-7) Tephra	**5**?	....
0.23 Ma	**Los Humeros** (México)	Faby Tuff	**6**	40
0.23 Ma	**Maroa** (New Zealand)	Atiamuri Tephra	**5**?	1?
0.23 Ma	**Puelche Volc Field** (Chile-C)	Río Invernada	**0**	1.0 LF
0.23 Ma	**Reporoa** (New Zealand)	Kaingaroa Ignimbrites	**7**	100 DRE
0.23 Ma	**Roccamonfina** (Italy)	Upper White Trachytic Tuff (UWTT)	**5**	1-2 DRE
0.23 Ma	**Roccamonfina** (Italy)	Yellow Trachytic Tuff (YTT)	**5**	1 DRE
0.23 Ma	**Tepetiltic** (México)	Tepetiltic caldera	**C**	....
0.24 Ma*	**Hakone** (Japan-Honshu)	Tama B-1 (TB-1) Tephra	**5**	....
0.24 Ma	**Kapenga** (New Zealand)	Ohakuri	**7**	100 DRE
0.24 Ma*	**O'a** (Ethiopia)	Qi3 Pumice	**7**	120
0.24 Ma*	**Ososre-yama** (Japan-Honshu)	Tanabu-A Tephra	**5**	....
0.24 Ma	**Rotorua** (New Zealand)	Mamaku Ignimbrite	**7**	145
0.24 Ma*	**Suswa** (Kenya)	Caldera 1 (Esinoni Pumice)	**6**	>14
0.24 Ma*	**Vulsini (Latera)** (Italy)	Farnese (Arlena de Castro PF)	**5**	1-10
0.25 Ma*	**Ata** (Japan-Kyushu)	Ata-Torihama (Ata-Th)	**7**	>150
0.25 Ma	**Azumaya** (Japan-Honshu)	Minohara Pumice (MiP)	**5**	3.5
0.25 Ma*	**Minakami (Matsushiro)** (Japan-Honshu)	Karasawa Pumice	**6**?	....
0.25 Ma*	**Onikobe** (Japan-Honshu)	Onikobe-Ikezuki PF	**6**	>18
0.25 Ma*	**Santorini** (Greece)	Cape Therma 3 (CTM3)	**5**	....
0.25 Ma*	**Tenerife** (Canary Islands)	Arafo Member	**7**	18.6
0.25 Ma	**Vulsini (Bolsena)** (Italy)	Ospedaletto Pumice (P4)	**5**	1.2
0.26 Ma*	**Hakone** (Japan-Honshu)	Tama C Upper-1 (TCu1) Tephra	**6**?	....
0.26 Ma	**Maroa** (New Zealand)	Orakonui Tephra	**5**	2
0.26 Ma*	**Puelche Volc Field** (Chile-C)	Cajón Grande	**0**	7.8 LF
0.26 Ma	**Tumalo** (US-Oregon)	Shevlin Park Tuff	**5**?	>5 DRE
0.27 Ma	**Aso** (Japan-Kyushu)	Aso-1 Tephra	**7/8**	>>50; 1000
0.27 Ma	**Maroa** (New Zealand)	Putauaki Tephra	**5**	2
0.27 Ma	**Nemrut** (Turkey)	Ash flow, caldera formation?	**C**	....
0.27 Ma	**Tenerife** (Canary Islands)	Poris Member	**6**	12.4
0.28 Ma	**Damavand** (Iran)	Ask Ignimbrite	**5**	2-3?
0.28 Ma	**Kapenga** (New Zealand)	Pokai	**7**	100 DRE
0.28 Ma	**Maninjau** (Indonesia-Sumatra)	Maninjau caldera	**7**	100-250
0.28 Ma	**Maroa** (New Zealand)	Korotai Tephra	**5**?	1?
0.28 Ma	**Mazama** (US-Oregon)	W of Fumarole Bay	**0**	1.5 LF
0.28 Ma	**Okataina (Haroharo)** (New Zealand)	Matahina Ignimbrite	**7**	150
0.28 Ma	**Uzon** (Kamchatka)	Uzon-Geizerny caldera	**6**	46
0.28 Ma	**Vulsini (Latera)** (Italy)	Canino (Pianiano PF)	**5**	1-10
0.29 Ma	**Emmons Lake** (Alaska Peninsula)	Leontovich Welded Tuff	**C**	....
0.29 Ma	**Long Valley** (US-California)	Hot Creek	**0**	<1.5 LF
0.29 Ma*	**Mazama** (US-Oregon)	Cloudcap Bay	**0**	1.2 LF
0.29 Ma*	**Newberry** (US-Oregon)	Tepee Draw Tuff	**6**?	~10? DRE
0.29 Ma	**Sunagohara** (Japan-Honshu)	Sunagohara-Sakasegawa Tephra	**6**	>10 DRE
0.29 Ma*	**Tateyama** (Japan-Honshu)	Tateyama-C (Omachi-C) Pumice	**5**?	....
0.30 Ma	**Calabozos** (Chile-C)	Loma Seca Tuff-Unit V	**7**	>350
0.30 Ma*	**Kapenga** (New Zealand)	Chimpanzee	**7**?	50 DRE
0.30 Ma*	**Ososre-yama** (Japan-Honshu)	Tanabu-B Tephra	**5**	....
0.30 Ma*	**Santorini** (Greece)	Cape Therma 2 (CTM2)	**5**	....
0.30 Ma*	**St. Helens** (US-Washington)	Summer Lake tephra bed OO	**5**	>1 DRE
0.30 Ma*	**Tateyama** (Japan-Honshu)	Tateyama-B (Omachi-B) Pumice	**5**?	....
0.30 Ma	**Vico-Cimino** (Italy)	Ignimbrite A	**5**	1 DRE
0.30 Ma*	**Yatsuga-take** (Japan-Honshu)	Yatsugatake-BBP (Yt-BBP)	**6**?	5-20
0.31 Ma	**Roccamonfina** (Italy)	Lower White Trachytic Tuff (LWTT)	**6**?	6 DRE

DATE	VOLCANO NAME (Subregion)	UNIT	VEI	VOLUME (km³)
0.31 Ma	**Tenerife** (Canary Islands)	Fasnia Member	**6**	62
0.32 Ma	**Barva** (Costa Rica)	Tibirí Tuff	**6**+	78
0.32 Ma	**Tenerife** (Canary Islands)	Aldea Member	**6**	13.5?
0.33 Ma	**Maroa** (New Zealand)	Whakamaru 2 Tephra	**8**?	500 DRE
0.33 Ma*	**Momisawa (Suiendani)** (Japan-Honshu)	Takayama-Ng1 (Tky-Ng1)	**5**?	50; 1
0.33 Ma*	**Puelche Volc Field** (Chile-C)	Campo la Hora	**0**	1.8 LF
0.34 Ma	**Kakuto** (Japan-Kyushu)	Kakuto Ash (Kkt)	**7**	>100
0.34 Ma	**Maroa** (New Zealand)	Whakamaru 1 Tephra	**8**	1500 DRE
0.34 Ma*	**Momisawa (Suiendani)** (Japan-Honshu)	Suiendani A4 (Omachi-Apm4)	**5**?	....
0.34 Ma	**Okataina** (New Zealand)	Bonisch Tephra	**6**	>25
0.35 Ma*	**Mojanda** (Ecuador)	Mojanda-1 caldera	**C**	....
0.35 Ma*	**Momisawa (Suiendani)** (Japan-Honshu)	Suiendani A3 (Omachi-Apm3)	**6**?	....
0.35 Ma	**Puelche Volc Field** (Chile-C)	Arroyo Saavedra	**0**	1.5 LF
0.35 Ma	**Puelche Volc Field** (Chile-C)	Río Invernada	**0**	1.0 LF
0.35 Ma	**Roccamonfina** (Italy)	Brown Leucitic Tuff (BLT)	**5**	4-5
0.35 Ma*	**Takahara** (Japan-Honshu)	Otawara Ignimbrite (Shiobara caldera)	**6**?	2.4
0.35 Ma	**Tenerife** (Canary Islands)	Roque Member	**6**	13.6
0.35 Ma	**Vulsini (Bolsena)** (Italy)	Ponticello Pumice (P2)	**5**	1.1
0.35 Ma*	**Yatsuga-take** (Japan-Honshu)	Hirose Pumice	**5**?	....
0.36 Ma	**Gorely** (Kamchatka)	Older Gorely Khrebet caldera	**C**	....
0.36 Ma*	**Haruna** (Japan-Honshu)	Nakamura Pumice	**5**?	....
0.36 Ma*	**Momisawa (Suiendani)** (Japan-Honshu)	Suiendani A2 (Omachi-Apm2)	**6**?	....
0.36 Ma	**Santorini** (Greece)	Cape Therma 1 (CTM1)	**5**	....
0.37 Ma	**Alban Hills** (Italy)	Villa Senni Ignimbrite (VSN)	**6**	>50
0.37 Ma*	**Kusatsu-Shirane** (Japan-Honshu)	Oshi Ignimbrite	**6**	....
0.37 Ma*	**Momisawa (Suiendani)** (Japan-Honshu)	Suiendani A1 (Omachi-Apm1, TE5)	**7**?	....
0.37 Ma*	**Nyoho** (Japan-Honshu)	Yaguchi Tephra (Yg)	**6**?	1.0
0.37 Ma*	**Ososre-yama** (Japan-Honshu)	Tanabu-C Tephra	**5**?	....
0.37 Ma	**Sabatini** (Italy)	Morphi Tephra	**7**	>200
0.37 Ma*	**San Pedro** (México)	Cuastecomate Pumice	**C**	....
0.37 Ma*	**Socorro** (México)	Tephra E	**C**	....
0.38 Ma	**Rainier** (US-Washington)	Biotite-bearing pumice fall	**5**	>1 DRE
0.38 Ma	**Ubinas** (Peru)	Ubi-127 Pumice Flows	**5**	1.8
0.40 Ma*	**Apeneca Range** (El Salvador)	Concepción de Ataco caldera	**6**+	63
0.40 Ma*	**Atka** (Aleutian Is-Alaska)	Atka caldera	**C**	....
0.40 Ma	**Emmons Lake** (Alaska Peninsula)	Unnamed tephra	**C**	....
0.40 Ma	**Khangar** (Kamchatka)	Older Khangar caldera	**C**	....
0.41 Ma	**Alban Hills** (Italy)	Pozzolane Nere Ignimbrite (PN)	**6**	9 DRE
0.41 Ma	**Medvezhia** (Kuril Islands)	Medvezhia Ignimbrite	**7**+	80-100
0.41 Ma*	**Onikobe** (Japan-Honshu)	Onikobe-Takamori-16 Tephra	**5**?	....
0.42 Ma	**Torre** (Bougainville)	Torre Ignimbrite	**5**+	5-10
0.43 Ma	**Akademia Nauk** (Kamchatka)	Polovinka caldera	**6**	>42
0.43 Ma	**Leon (Chao)** (Chile-N)	Chao	**5**	>1.5 DRE; 22 LF
0.43 Ma	**Sabatini** (Italy)	SRTBS	**6**?	10?
0.44 Ma*	**Onikobe** (Japan-Honshu)	Onikobe-Takamori-12 Tephra	**5**?	....
0.44 Ma	**Pauzhetka** (Kamchatka)	Golygin Ignimbrite	**7**	300-450
0.44 Ma	**Roccamonfina** (Italy)	Rio Rava Pumice	**C**	....
0.44 Ma	**Tumalo** (US-Oregon)	Bend Pumice/Tumalo Tuff/Loleta Ash	**6**?	>5 DRE
0.45 Ma	**Maipo** (Chile-C)	Diamante Tuff	**7**	270-350
0.45 Ma*	**Togawan** (Japan-Honshu)	Jizodaira Ash	**6**?	....
0.46 Ma	**Alban Hills** (Italy)	Pozzolane Rosse Ignimbrite (PR)	**6**	>34
0.46 Ma	**Los Humeros** (México)	Xaltipan	**7**	230
0.46 Ma	**Malpaisillo** (Nicaragua)	Malpaisillo Ignimbrite	**C**	....
0.46 Ma*	**Onikobe** (Japan-Honshu)	Onikobe-Takamori-8 Tephra	**5**?	....
0.46 Ma*	**Sakura-jima** (Japan-Kyushu)	Aira Ksm-5 Tephra, Oda Ignimbrite	**7**	>100
0.47 Ma*	**Hakkoda** (Japan-Honshu)	Hakkoda Hkd-Ku (Hkd-2) Ignimbrite	**7**?	....
0.48 Ma	**Medicine Lake** (US-California)	Rhyolite LF E of Glass Mtn	**0**	4.8 LF

500,000 years BP (0.50 Ma)

DATE	VOLCANO NAME (Subregion)	UNIT	VEI	VOLUME (km³)
0.50 Ma*	**Akan** (Japan-Hokkaido)	Ak3 Pumice	**5**?	....
0.50 Ma*	**Alban Hills** (Italy)	Genazzano Ignimbrite	**5**	>1
0.50 Ma*	**Copahue** (Chile-C)	Copahue caldera	**C**	....
0.50 Ma*	**Mazama** (US-Oregon)	S of Crater Peak	**0**	1.4 LF
0.50 Ma	**Sturgeon Volc Prov** (Australia)	Twins	**0**	2 LF
0.50 Ma*	**Tateyama** (Japan-Honshu)	Yaguchi Ignimbrite	**6**?	....
0.50 Ma	**Toba** (Indonesia-Sumatra)	Middle Toba Tuff (MTT)	**6**	60
0.51 Ma	**Incapillo** (Chile-N)	Incapillo Ignimbrite	**6**	32
0.52 Ma*	**Alban Hills** (Italy)	Casale del Cavaliere Ignimbrite	**6**?	10?
0.52 Ma	**Bolshoi Semiachik** (Kamchatka)	Upper Bolshoi Semiachik ignimbrite	**6**	42
0.52 Ma	**Kakuto (Kobayashi)** (Japan-Kyushu)	Kobayashi-Ks (Kb-Ks)	**7/8**	>100; 1000
0.53 Ma	**Alban Hills** (Italy)	Palatino Ignimbrite (TP)	**6**?	10?
0.54 Ma*	**Tolima** (Colombia)	El Boqueron caldera	**6**?	15?
0.54 Ma	**Yellowstone** (US-Wyoming)	Biscuit Basin	**0**	2.5-25 LF
0.55 Ma	**Ranau** (Indonesia-Sumatra)	Ranau Tuff	**C**	....
0.55 Ma	**Uinkaret** (US-Arizona)	Black Ledge lava dam	**0**	2.1 LF
0.56 Ma	**Alban Hills** (Italy)	Tor de Cenci Ignimbrite	**6**	10
0.56 Ma	**Alban Hills** (Italy)	Trigoria Ignimbrite (TPT)	**5**	>1
0.56 Ma	**Bolshoi Semiachik** (Kamchatka)	Lower Bolshoi Semiachik ignimbrite	**6**	42
0.56 Ma	**Galeras** (Colombia)	Coba Negra caldera	**6**	16
0.56 Ma*	**Yellowstone** (US-Wyoming)	Falls River Basalt	**0**	20 LF
0.58 Ma	**Kakuto?** (Japan-Kyushu)	Hiwaki Tephra (Hwk)	**7**	>100
0.58 Ma	**Kikai** (Japan-Ryukyus)	Koseda Ignimbrite (Ksd Tephra)	**C**	....
0.59 Ma	**Vulsini (Bolsena)** (Italy)	Basal Pumice (P1)	**5**	9
0.60 Ma*	**Akan** (Japan-Hokkaido)	Ak4 Pumice	**5**?	....
0.60 Ma	**Tenerife** (Canary Islands)	Granadillo Pumice	**6**	45
0.60 Ma	**Tenerife** (Canary Islands)	Abades Member	**5**	>1.6
0.60 Ma*	**Uinkaret** (US-Arizona)	Lava Falls lava dam	**0**	1.2 LF
0.61 Ma*	**Kamitakara (Kaisho)** (Japan-Honshu)	Kamitakara Ignimbrite (Kmt)	**7**?	>>50

DATE	VOLCANO NAME (Subregion)	UNIT	VEI	VOLUME (km³)
0.61 Ma	**Lassen** (US-California)	Rockland Ash and Ignimbrite	**7**	>75 DRE
0.61 Ma	**Uinkaret** (US-Arizona)	Ponderosa lava dam	**0**	2.5 LF
0.63 Ma*	**Hohi** (Japan-Kyushu)	Seiganji-Toga (Se-Tg)	**7**?	>>50
0.64 Ma	**Yellowstone** (US-Wyoming)	Lava Creek Tuff	**8**	>1000
0.65 Ma*	**Akan** (Japan-Hokkaido)	Ak5 Pumice	**5**?	....
0.65 Ma*	**Tumalo** (US-Oregon)	Rye Patch Dam Ash	**5**	2?
0.65 Ma<	**Acatlán Volc Field** (México)	Acatlán Ignimbrite	**7**	150
0.67 Ma	**Azumaya** (Japan-Honshu)	Ochiaibashi Ignimbrite	**6**?	....
0.67 Ma	**Tenerife** (Canary Islands)	Arico Member/Saltadero Ignimbrite	**5**	>2
0.68 Ma	**Kapenga** (New Zealand)	Matahana A	**6/7**	30-100 DRE
0.71 Ma	**Kapenga** (New Zealand)	Waiotapu	**7**	100 DRE
0.75 Ma*	**Akan** (Japan-Hokkaido)	Ak6 Pumice	**5**	....
0.76 Ma	**El Aguajito** (México)	El Aguajito caldera	**C**	....
0.76 Ma	**Hakkoda** (Japan-Honshu)	Hakkoda Hkd-Ku (Hkd-1) Ignimbrite	**7**	253
0.76 Ma	**Jornada del Muerto** (US-New Mexico)	Jornada del Muerto shield	**0**	13 LF
0.76 Ma	**Long Valley** (US-California)	Bishop Tuff	**7**	600
0.77 Ma	**Kapenga?** (New Zealand)	Rahopaka	**6**	30 DRE
0.80 Ma*	**Akan** (Japan-Hokkaido)	Ak7 Pumice	**5**	....
0.80 Ma*	**Shirataka** (Japan-Honshu)	Numata Pumice-Flow	**5**	>1.1
0.81 Ma	**Calabozos** (Chile-C)	Cerro del Medio	**5**	1-2
0.83 Ma	**Kapenga** (New Zealand)	Matahana B	**6/7**	30-100 DRE
0.84 Ma	**Calabozos** (Chile-C)	Loma Seca Tuff-Unit L	**7**	>500
0.84 Ma	**Toba** (Indonesia-Sumatra)	Oldest Toba Tuff (OTT)	**7**	500
0.86 Ma*	**Yabakei (Shishimuta)** (Japan-Kyushu)	Shishimuta-Azuki (Ss-Az)	**7/8**	>>100; 1000
0.89 Ma	**Kapenga?** (New Zealand)	Tikorangi	**6**	30 DRE
0.90 Ma*	**Akan** (Japan-Hokkaido)	Ak8 Pumice	**5**?	....
0.90 Ma*	**Ruiz, Nevado del** (Colombia)	Post Líbano caldera	**C**	....
0.95 Ma*	**Akan** (Japan-Hokkaido)	Ak9 Pumice	**5**?	....
0.95 Ma*	**Aoso** (Japan-Honshu)	Aoso caldera	**C**	....
0.95 Ma	**Mangakino?** (New Zealand)	Marshall	**7**?	50 DRE
0.97 Ma	**Mangakino** (New Zealand)	Unit E	**7**	100-300 DRE

1 million years BP (1.00 Ma)

DATE	VOLCANO NAME (Subregion)	UNIT	VEI	VOLUME (km³)
1.00 Ma	**Chacana** (Ecuador)	Chacana caldera	**C**	....
1.00 Ma	**Futamata (Ono)** (Japan-Honshu)	Ono caldera (Kumado PF)	**7**?	....
1.00 Ma	**Gassan** (Japan-Honshu)	Chobohzan Breccia	**C**	....
1.00 Ma	**Mangakino** (New Zealand)	Rocky Hill	**7**	200 DRE
1.00 Ma	**Medicine Lake** (US-California)	Box Canyon Tuff	**5**	>1? DRE
1.00 Ma*	**North Vate** (Vanuatu-SW Pacific)	Efeté Pumice Formation	**7**?	>85
1.00 Ma*	**Tokachimitsumata** (Japan-Hokkaido)	HR-4 Ash, Tokachi-Mitsumata PF	**7**?	....
1.01 Ma*	**Akan** (Japan-Hokkaido)	Ak11 Pumice	**5**	....
1.01 Ma	**Mangakino** (New Zealand)	Kidnappers Ignimbrite	**8**	1200 DRE
1.02 Ma	**Chachani** (Peru)	Yura	**5**	1.5
1.02 Ma	**Yabakei (Shishimuta)** (Japan-Kyushu)	Shishimuta-Pink (Ss-Pk)	**7/8**	>>100; 1000
1.05 Ma*	**Akan** (Japan-Hokkaido)	Ak10 Pumice	**5**?	....
1.10 Ma	**Laguna del Maule** (Chile-C)	Bobadilla caldera	**C**	....
1.11 Ma*	**Haruna** (Japan-Honshu)	Joetsu Pumice	**6**	....
1.12 Ma	**Baker (Kulshan)** (US-Washington)	Lake Tapps Tephra	**7**?	>50 DRE
1.15 Ma*	**Akan** (Japan-Hokkaido)	Ak12 Pumice	**5**?	....
1.18 Ma	**Mangakino** (New Zealand)	Ahuroa Ignimbrite	**7**	100 DRE
1.18 Ma	**Tenerife** (Canary Islands)	Ucanca Formation	**C**	....
1.20 Ma*	**Akan** (Japan-Hokkaido)	Ak13 Pumice	**5**?	....
1.20 Ma	**Futamata (Tonohetsuri)** (Japan-Honshu)	Tonohetsuri caldera (Ashino PF)	**C**	....
1.20 Ma	**Mangakino?** (New Zealand)	Unit D Ignimbrite	**7**	100 DRE
1.20 Ma	**Toba** (Indonesia-Sumatra)	Haranggoal Dacite Tuff (HDT)	**6**	35 DRE
1.20 Ma	**Yabakei (Shishimuta?)** (Japan-Kyushu)	Shikito (Skt)	**7**?	100?
1.21 Ma	**Mangakino** (New Zealand)	Ongatiti	**8**?	400 DRE
1.22 Ma	**Valles** (US-New Mexico)	Upper Bandelier Tuff (Tshirege)	**8**	600 DRE
1.25 Ma*	**Akan** (Japan-Hokkaido)	Ak14 Pumice	**5**?	....
1.25 Ma*	**Tokachi** (Japan-Hokkaido)	HR-5 Ash	**6**?	....
1.25 Ma*	**Tokachi** (Japan-Hokkaido)	HR-6 Ash	**7**?	....
1.29 Ma	**Yellowstone** (US-Wyoming)	Mesa Falls Tuff	**7**	>280
1.30 Ma*	**Akan** (Japan-Hokkaido)	Ak15 Pumice	**5**?	....
1.30 Ma	**Nulla** (Australia)	Birdbush	**0**	5 LF
1.30 Ma	**Nulla** (Australia)	Hann Creek	**0**	5 LF
1.30 Ma	**Purico Complex** (Chile-N)	Purico (Cajón) Ignimbrite	**7**	100 DRE
1.30 Ma	**Tolima** (Colombia)	Porfias-Honduras stage	**0**	>1 LF
1.31 Ma	**Rincón de la Vieja** (Costa Rica)	Buena Vista Tuff	**5**	4.9
1.35 Ma*	**Akan** (Japan-Hokkaido)	Ak16 Pumice	**5**?	....
1.36 Ma	**Rincón de la Vieja** (Costa Rica)	Salitral Tuff	**5**	5.6
1.40 Ma*	**Akan** (Japan-Hokkaido)	Ak17 Pumice	**5**?	....
1.40 Ma	**Emi Koussi** (Chad)	Koussi III	**C**	....
1.40 Ma	**Futamata (Narioka)** (Japan-Honshu)	Narioka caldera (Nishigo PF)	**C**	....
1.40 Ma*	**Mangakino** (New Zealand)	Unit C	**7**?	50 DRE
1.46 Ma	**Miravalles** (Costa Rica)	Guayabo caldera	**6**	30
1.47 Ma	**Rincón de la Vieja** (Costa Rica)	Liberia Tuff	**6**	25
1.50 Ma*	**La Reforma** (México)	La Reforma caldera	**C**	....
1.53 Ma	**Mangakino?** (New Zealand)	Unit B	**7**	100 DRE
1.55 Ma	**Mangakino?** (New Zealand)	Ngaroma (Unit A?)	**7**	100 DRE
1.60 Ma*	**Smith Rock** (Japan-Volcano Is)	Sumisu (Smith) caldera	**C**	....
1.61 Ma	**Valles** (US-New Mexico)	Lower Bandelier Tuff (Otowi)	**8**	474 DRE
1.62 Ma	**Bolshe-Bannaye** (Kamchatka)	Younger Karymshina caldera?	**C**	....
1.63 Ma	**Chachani** (Peru)	Arequipa Airport Ignimbrite	**6**	18
1.63 Ma*	**Hodaka-dake** (Japan-Honshu)	Omine Ignimbrite (Omn)	**7/8**	50; 1000
1.75 Ma	**Hodaka-dake** (Japan-Honshu)	Chayano-Ebisutoge Tephra (Ebs-Fkd)	**7/8**	380-490; 2000
1.76 Ma	**Hodaka-dake** (Japan-Honshu)	Nyukawa Pyroclastic Flow Deposit	**8**?	1000
1.78 Ma	**Bolshe-Bannaye** (Kamchatka)	Karymshina caldera	**7**?	800

Data Sources

Mediterranean to Indian Ocean: Ayalew et al., 2003; Baales et al., 2002; Calanchi and Dinelli, 2008; Cioni et al., 1999, 2003; Civetta et al., 1988; Cole et al., 1992; Coltelli et al. 2000; Davidson et al., 2004; De Rita et al., 1996, 1997, 2002; Di Vito et al., 2008; Druitt, 1985; Druitt et al., 1989, 1995, 1999; Duffield et al., 1997; Dunkley, 1993 p.c.; Fedele et al., 2008; Fisher et al., 1993; Fretzdorff et al., 2000; Gertisser et al., 2009; Gillot et al., 1982; Giannetti and Luhr, 1983; Giannetti and De Casa, 2000; Giordano et al., 2006; Gourgaud and Vincent 2004; Keller et al., 1990; Leat et al., 1984; Lucchi et al., 2008; Luhr and Giannetti, 1987; Machida, 2002; Mahood and Hildreth, 1986; Marra et al., 2009; Marshall et al. (2009); Mohr et al., 1980; Nappi et al., 1994; Orsi et al. 1996; Palladino and Simei, 2005; Palladino and Valentine, 1995; Palladino et al. 2008; Perini et al. 2004; Pyle et al., 1998; Rouchon et al., 2008; Santacroce, 1983; Santacroce et al., 2008; Scarpeti et al., 1993; Schmincke et al., 1999; Siani et al., 2004; Skilling, 1993; Sollevanti, 1983; Ulusoy et al., 2008; Williams et al., 1984.

SW Pacific (New Zealand to Philippines): Allen, 2004; Alloway et al., 2005; Bailey and Carr, 1994; Bellier et al., 1999; Beresford and Cole, 2000; Carter et al., 1995; Catane et al., 2005; Chesner and Rose, 1991; Froggatt and Lowe, 1990; Houghton et al. 1995; Jurado-Chichay and Walker, 2001; Knight et al., 1986; Ku et al., 2008; Lowe and Hogg, 1995; Lowe et al., 2008; Machida, 2002; Machida and Arai, 1992; Manning, 1996; McKee et al., 1990; Milner et al., 2003; Mirabueno et al., 2007; Mulyadi, 2000; Nairn et al., 1995; Nasution et al., 2004; Newhall et al., 1996, 2006 p.c.; Pain et al., 1981; Reubi and Anicholls, 2004; Raos and McPhie, 2003; Shane et al., 2006; Sigurdsson and Carey, 1992; Spinks et al., 2004, 2005; Stephenson et al., 1998; Stephenson and Griffin, 1976; Sutawidjadja 2000; Sutton et al., 2005; Wilson, 1993; Wilson et al., 1995, 2006, 2009.

Japan: Aoki, 2008; Ban et al., 2005, 2007; Cole et al., 2002; Fujii et al., 2001; Geishi and Kobayashi, 2006; Hasegawa et al., 2008; Hasegawa and Nakagawa, 2007; Hayakawa, 2000, 2008- and 2009 p.c.; Hayashida et al., 1996; Hirotani and Ban, 2006; Ishii et al., 2008; Ishikawa et al., 1969; Kaneko et al., 2007; Kano and Ohguchi, 2004; Kataoka et al., 2001, 2006; Kimura and Nagahashi, 2007; Kishimoto et al., 2009; Koyama et al., 1995; Kuwahara and Yamazaki, 2001; Machida, 1990, 2002; Machida and Arai, 2003; Maeno and Taniguchi, 2005; Miyabuchi et al., 2003; Miyagi, 2004, 2008; Moriwaki et al., 2005; Nakagawa, 1993; Nakagawa et al., 2003; Nakano et al., 2001-; Nappi et al., 1994; Shakuno et al., 2006; Sollevanti, 1983; Suzuki, 1996, 2001; Suzuki and Nakayama, 2007; Suzuki et al., 1998; Takai et al., 2002; Tani et al., 2008; Tsukui et al., 1991; Yamagata and Furai, 1989; Yamamoto, 1999, 2007; Yamamoto and Sakaguchi, 2000; Yamamoto and Suto, 1996; Yoshimoto et al., 2008.

Kuriles to Mainland Asia: Bindeman et al., 2010; Braitseva et al., 1995; Erlich, 1986; Ermkov and Shteinberg, 1999; Fedotov et al., 1991; Leonov and Grib, 2005; Machida, 2002; Machida and Arai, 2003; Melekestsev et al., 1988, 1990, 1997; Ponomareva, 1990; Ponomareva et al., 2007; Raszhigaeva et al., 1999; Sakno, 2007; Selyangin and Ponomareva, 1999.

North America: Arce et al., 2003; Bacon, 2008; Bacon and Lanphere, 2006; Beget et al., 2005; Beget and Motyka, 1998; Blatter et al., 2001; Bohrson et al., 1996; Bohrson and Reid, 1997; Capra et al., 1998, 2006, 2008; Chiesa et al., 1992; Christiansen, 1984; Christiansen et al., 2007; Clynne, 1990; Cook et al., 2006; Costantini et al., 2009; Crumpler and Aubele, 1990; Dalrymple and Hamblin, 1998; Defant et al., 1991; Donnelly-Nolan et al., 1989, 2007, 2008; Ferrari et al., 1997; Ferriz and Mahood, 1984; Fierstein, 2007; Gardner et al., 1998; Garduno-Monroy et al., 2003; Gonzalez-Partida et al., 1997; Hamblin, 1994; Hannah et al., 2002; Hidalgo, 2007; Hildreth, 1996, 2004, 2007; Hildreth et al., 1984; Izett and Obradovich, 1994; Kuehn and Foit, 2006; Kuehn et al., 2009; Kunz et al., 1992; Kutterolf et al., 2008; Larsen et al., 2007; Luhr, 2000; Macias, 2005; Mahood, 1981; Machida, 1992; Miller, 2004; Miller et al., 1998; Mullineaux, 1986; Nelson and Hegre, 1990; Newhall, 1987; Petrone et al., 2006; Pradal and Robin, 1994; Pullinger, 1998; Reihle et al., 1992; Rodriguez et al., 2002; Rose et al., 1999; Schmitt et al., 2006; Self and Wolff, 2005; Self et al. 1991; Sherrod et al., 2004; Siebe and Macias, 2005; Siebe 2008 p.c.; Sussman, 1985; Waythomas et al., 2006; Wunderman and Rose, 1984; Viramonte et al., 1997; Vogel et al., 2004.

South America: Calvache et al., 1997; de Silva et al., 1994; de Silva and Gosnold, 2007; Dixon et al., 1999; Gardeweg et al., 1998; Geist et al., 1994; Germa et al., 2007; Goss et al., 2009; Grunder and Mahood, 1988; Hall and Mothes, 2008; Hall et al., 2008; Hildreth et al., 1984, 1991, 1999; Lara et al., 2006; Moreno and Sparks, 2004; Moreno et al., 1991; Naranjo and Moreno, 1991; Naranjo and Polanco, 2004; Orihashi et al., 2004; Paquereau et al., 2006; Sruoga et al., 2005; Stern, 1990, 2008; Stern et al., 1984; Thouret et al., 1990, 1995, 2001, 2005; Watts et al.,1999.

West Indies, Iceland, Atlantic to Antarctica: Boudon et al., 1989; Brown et al., 2003; Brown and Branney, 2004; Bryan, 2006; Calderone et al., 1990; Calvert et al., 2006; Carey and Sigurdsson, 1980; Cas et al., 2005; Edgar et al., 2007; Harpel et al., 2008; Jonasson, 1994; Lindsay 2005; Marti et al., 1994; Moore, 1990; Mortensen et al., 2009; Newhall and Dzurisin, 1988; Komorowski et al., 2005; Lacasse and Garbe-Schonberg, 2001; Thordarson and Hoskuldsson, 2008; Thordarson et al., 2008; Wohletz et al., 1986.

(worldwind.arc.nasa.gov)

Toba, the Earth's largest Quaternary caldera, is seen here in a NASA Landsat satellite image. The 35 x 100 km caldera on the Indonesian island of Sumatra was formed during four major ignimbrite-producing eruptions in the Pleistocene. The latest of these took place about 74,000 years ago and produced the Younger Toba Tuff (YTT). Lake Toba surrounds Samosir, a massive uplifted resurgent block.

Katia and Maurice Krafft

A. Three 5000-m-high stratovolcanoes in Ecuador have undergone varying degrees of erosion. Tungurahua volcano in the foreground rises more than 3000 m above its northern base and has produced some of Ecuador's most powerful explosive eruptions during historical time. Altar (center) is an extensively eroded volcano of Pleistocene age. Symmetrical, undissected Sangay volcano in the background is Ecuador's most active and has been in nearly continuous eruption since 1934.

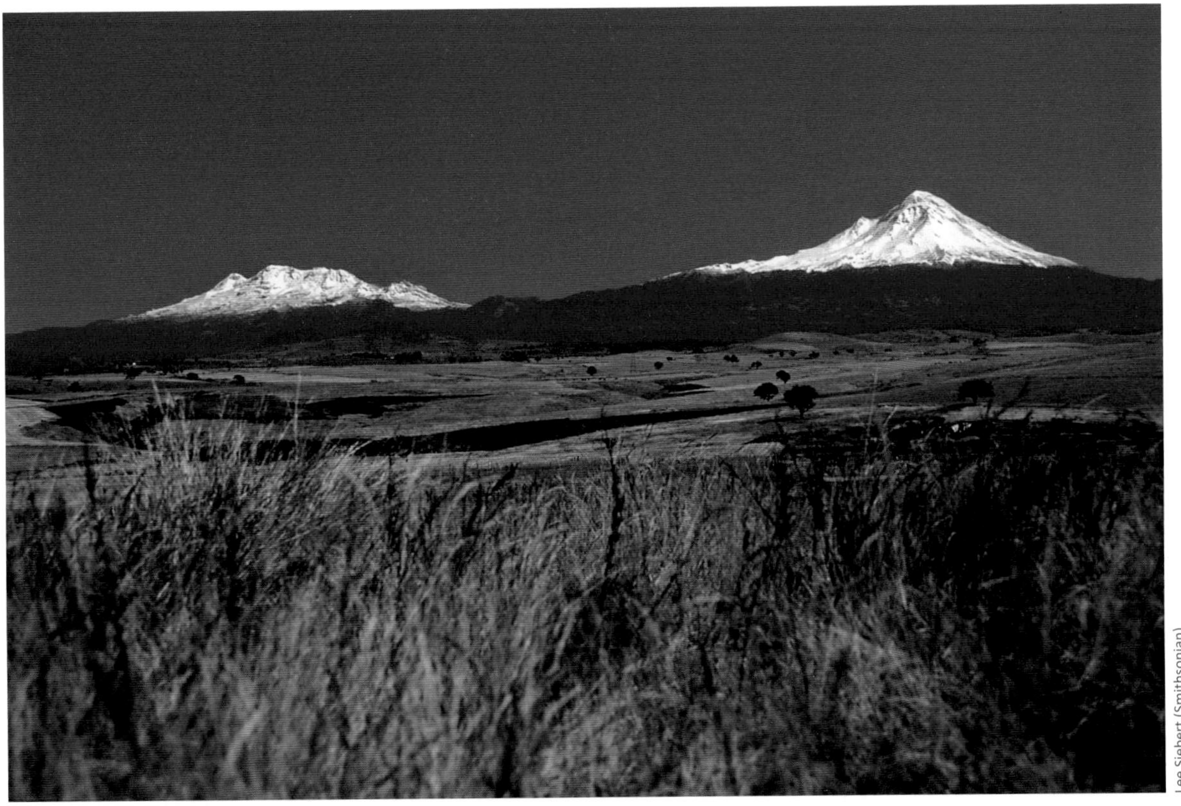

Lee Siebert (Smithsonian)

B. Iztaccíhuatl (left) and Popocatépetl (right), mantled by fresh snow, are seen on a rare cloud and smog-free day. Multiple vents forming Iztaccíhuatl give the volcano the elongated profile often compared to that of a sleeping woman. Repeated late-stage eruptions from the central conduit of Popocatépetl give it a more conical profile.

Plate 2

Lee Siebert (Smithsonian)

Clockwise from top: **A.** Strombolian eruption and lava flow (right) in 1988 from Pacaya volcano, Guatemala. **B.** Pyroclastic flow from 1984 eruption of Mayon volcano, Philippines. **C.** Ash plume rises above a lava dome in 1999 at the summit of Colima volcano, México. **D.** Plinian eruption column from Pintatubo volcano, Philppines in 1991.

Robert LaPointe (U.S. Air Force)

Olimpio Pena (PHIVOLCS)

Jim Luhr (Smithsonian)

A. Incandescent blocks from the growing lava dome at Kelut volcano in Java form traces extending into a crater lake (lower left). The slowly extruding lava dome first rose above the surface of the crater lake in November 2007 and soon reached a visible radius of 250 m and a height of 120 m.

Tom Pfeiffer (Volcano Discovery)

Michael Ryan (USGS)

B. Lava fountains rise along an eruptive fissure at Krafla volcano in northern Iceland near the end of a decade-long series of eruptions beginning in 1975 that accompanied an episode of crustal spreading along the Mid-Atlantic Rift.

C. Lava fountains bubble through the partially solidified crust of a lava lake in Halemaumau crater at Hawaii's Kilauea volcano in January 1968. Incandescent streams of lava at the bottom overflow the rim of the lava lake.

Richard Fiske (Smithsonian)

Plate 4

Lee Siebert (Smithsonian)

A. The broad, low-angle slopes of Hawaii's basasltic Mauna Loa shield volcano are seen here from the summit of neighboring Mauna Kea shield volcano. Dark-colored, unvegetated lava flows, many of historical age, descend the flanks of Mauna Loa. The symmetrical cone in the right foreground is one of many late-stage cinder cones capping the summit of Mauna Kea.

B. The glacier-capped summit of Ecuador's 5911-m-high Cotopaxi volcano is truncated by two nested craters. The outer crater, seen here from the SE, is 800 x 550 m wide. Frequent explosive eruptions during historical time have modified the shape of the summit crater.

Tom Simkin (Smithsonian)

Jim Luhr (Smithsonian)

C. Parícutin, the renowned volcano born in a Mexican cornfield in 1943, is the best-known feature of the Michoacán-Guanajuato volcanic field. Cinder cones are the dominant volcanic landform of this huge volcanic field containing over 1400 vents. The flank vent of Nueva Juatita in the foreground was the main source of extensive lava flows from Parícutin erupted from 1943-52.

NASA Space Shuttle Image ISS005E15296

A. The 6 x 8.5 km wide Segara Anak caldera of Rinjani volcano on the island of Lombok, Indonesia contains a crescent-shaped caldera lake. The post-caldera cone of Baru Jani (New Mountain) has been the source of lava flows that have entered the lake.

Tom Simkin (Smithsonian)

B. The summit of the massive Cerro Azul shield volcano at the SW end of Isabella Island in the Galápagos Islands is cut by a 4 x 5 km wide caldera. Flat benches near the top of the 650-m-deep caldera mark remants of former caldera floors. The large tuff cone in the foreground was formed by explosive eruptions from this basaltic shield volcano.

Plate 6

Jim Luhr (Smithsonian)

A. The course of the block-lava flow in the foreground, which was emplaced during the 1975-76 eruption of Mexico's Colima volcano, can be seen descending from the summit through the vegetation at the center.

B. An a'a lava flow, with a characteristic hackly surface, advances across an earlier smooth-textured pahoehoe lava flow at Hawaii's Kilauea volcano in 1994. A'a flows are produced by eruptions with high lava fountains of gas-rich magma. Eruptions producing a'a lava commonly evolve into sustained eruptions of gas-poor pahoehoe.

Paul Kimberly (Smithsonian)

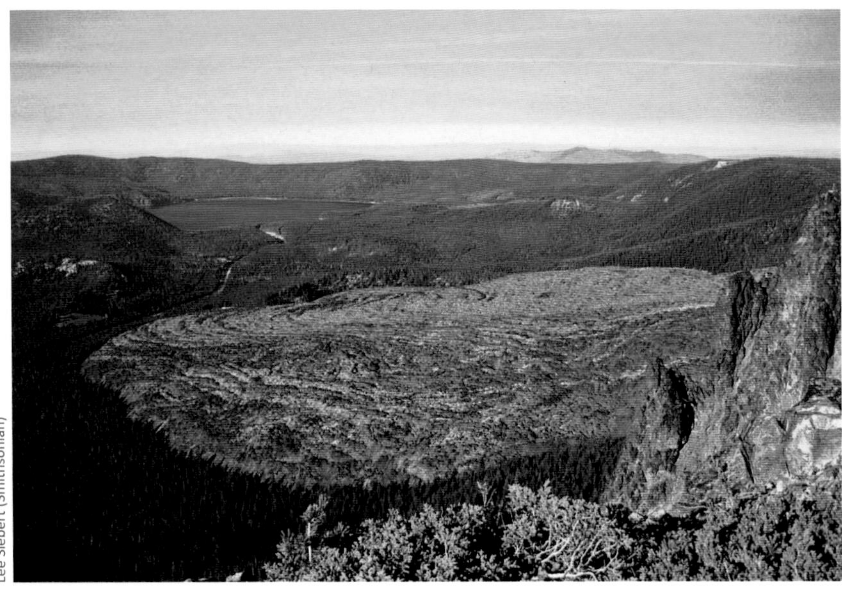

Lee Siebert (Smithsonian)

C. Prominent flow ridges mark the surface of a broad glass-rich, rhyolitic obsidian lava flow on the caldera floor of Oregon's Newberry volcano. The obsidian flow was emplaced about 1300 years ago following large explosive eruptions producing rhyolitic pumice fall and pyroclastic flows.

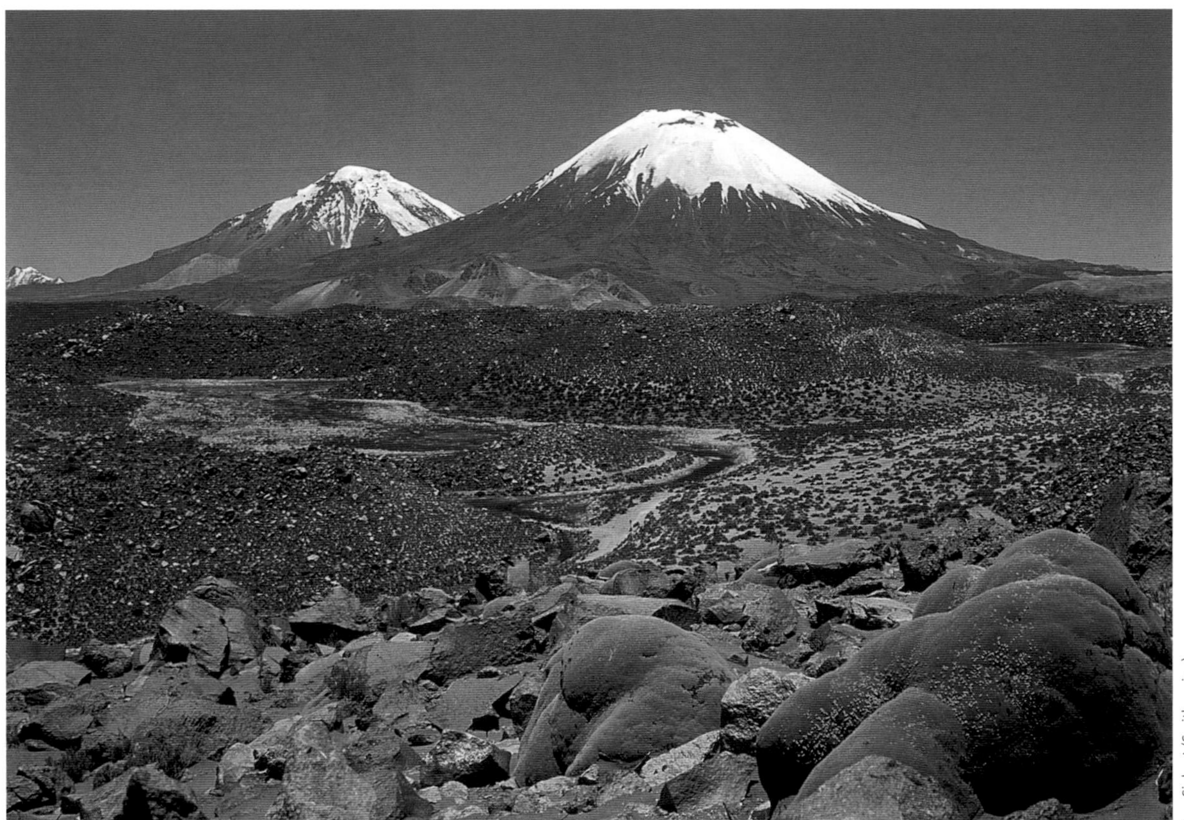

Lee Siebert (Smithsonian)

A. The extensive hummocky terrain in the foreground was formed by collapse of Parinacota volcano (right) in northern Chile, forming a massive 6 km^3 debris avalanche. Subsequent eruptions filled in the collapse scarp and constructed the symmetrical, 6348-m-high Parinacota adjacent to its older Pleistocene twin, 6222-m-high Pomerape.

Tokiwa Museum of Historical Materials, Shimabara

B. This 18th century water-color map of Japan's Unzen volcano shows the extent of the catastrophic landslide (bottom center) from Mayu-yama in 1792 that swept into the Ariake Sea. The irregular, yellow-colored area along the coast delineates the extent of runup of the resulting tsunami that scoured 77 km of the Shimabara Peninsula and neighboring coastlines, causing nearly 15,000 fatalities. An ash plume rises from erupting Fugen-dake (top-center), and a lava flow descends its right flank.

Plate 8

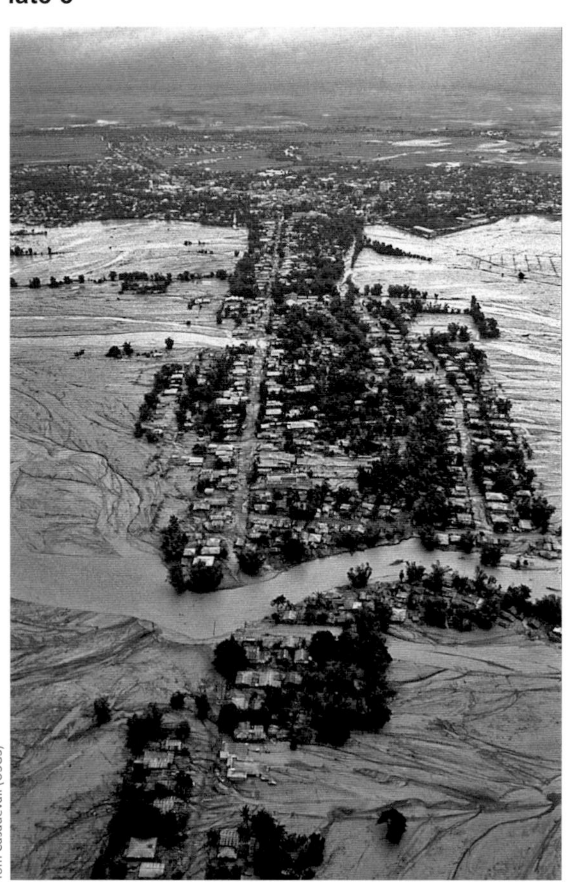

Tom Casadevall (USGS)

A. Secondary mudflows (lahars) following the major June 1991 explosive eruption of Mount Pinatubo, Philippines, caused stream diversion and overbank lahar deposits producing extensive damage to towns and villages downstream.

Peter Francis (Open Univ.)

B. Pyroclastic flows and surges from Soufrière Hills volcano swept through the abandoned capital city of Plymouth on the West Indies island of Montserrat beginning in 1997, eventually burying much of the town. The eruptive episode that began in 1995 was continuing in 2010.

Lee Siebert (Smithsonian)

C. Volcanoes also create some of Earth's most spectacular topography, drawing visitors to these scenic landscapes and enhancing local economies. Japan's snow-capped Mount Fuji rises above the Ashinoko caldera lake of neighboring Hakone volcano in the Fuji-Hakone-Izu National Park, one of the country's premier tourist destinations.

Gazetteer

Gazetteer: Context

The gazetteer lists volcano names, synonyms, and subsidiary feature names (with their synonyms). For each volcano, we also list type, number of Holocene eruptions, and date of the last eruption (these eruptions do *not* include uncertain events, and neither dating method codes nor uncertainties are listed). Some frequently encountered spelling variations of names have been eliminated from the gazetteer for reasons of space and redundancy.

- The Japanese word for island is transliterated shima or jima in the officially-approved style; the older Hepburn-style transliterated of sima or zima is often not listed. Chokai is simply preferred over Tyokai, and Fuji over Huzi. However, synonyms with distinct spelling differences are listed separately in the gazetteer.

- The Dutch “oe” spelling of the Indonesian “u” (Keloed, Kelud) is not listed where it would have resulted in adjacent entries in the gazetteer. However, other spelling variations, such as the Dutch “Tj” for the Indonesian “C”, and “Dj” for “J” appear separately in the gazetteer; both Cereme and its synonym Tjereme are listed.

- Variations of Cyrillic transliterations such as Karymsky, Karymskiy, Karymiskii, Karymskaya, and Karymskaia, are not listed separately.

A synonym of a volcano name is sometimes followed by one or more additional synonyms that would otherwise have appeared in an adjacent line. When synonyms of a volcano subsidiary feature name are so similar as to result in adjacent entries in the gazetteer, one of the entries has been removed, and the preferred name is shown in brackets following the synonym.

A

Name (Subregion)	Type (Eruptions, Most Recent) Status / Relation to Named Volcano	Volcano Number
Aabida (Ethiopia)	Synonym of Adwa	0201-17=
Aag (Kamchatka)	Synonym of Aak	....
Aaga (Kamchatka)	Synonym of Aak	....
Aak (Kamchatka)	Stratovolcanoes (None) Pleistocene	....
Ab E Garm (Iran)	Thermal feature of Damavand	0302-01-
Abang, Gunung (Lesser Sunda Is)	Stratovolcano of Batur	0604-01=
Abaro (Ethiopia)	Cone of Corbetti Caldera	0201-29-
Abas Tepe (Turkey)	Cone of Erciyes Dagi	0103-01=
Abbott Peak (Antarctica)	Cone of Erebus	1900-02=
Abejera, Montaña (Canary Is)	Dome of Tenerife	1803-03-
Abeque, Montaña de (Canary Is)	Cinder cone of Tenerife	1803-03-
Aberdeen Volc Field (US-California)	Synonym of Big Pine Volc Field	....
Abida (Ethiopia)	Synonym of Adwa	0201-17=
Abili Agituk [Wargess] (Africa-E)	Tuff cone of Barrier, The	0202-03=
Abingdon (Galápagos)	Synonym of Pinta	1503-07=
Aboa (Vanuatu-SW Pacific)	Synonym of Aoba	0507-03=
Abour, Jebel El (Africa-N)	Cone of Bayuda Volc Field	0205-06-
Abra (Chile-N)	Stratovolcano (None) Pliocene	....
Abra Chica, Cerro (Bolivia)	Cone (None) Post-Miocene	....
Abra, Cerro el (México)	Synonym of Atlixcos, Los	1401-094
Abraham Hot Springs (US-Utah)	Thermal feature of Fumarole Butte	....
Abrigo, Cerro Del (US-New Mexico)	Dome of Valles Caldera	....
Abrunco (Canary Is)	Dome of Tenerife	1803-03-
Abu (Honshu-Japan)	Shield volcanoes (1, -6850) Thermolum	**0803-001**
Abu Ail Island (Red Sea)	Cone of Zukur	0201-021
Abu Haris, Jabal (Arabia-W)	Dome of Kishb, Harrat	0301-071
Abyad, Jabal (Arabia-W)	Dome of Khaybar, Harrat	0301-06=
Academii Nauk (Kamchatka)	Synonym of Akademia Nauk	1000-125
Acamarachi (Chile-N)	Stratovolcano (None) Holocene	**1505-096**
Acantilados Mayor (México)	Tuff cone of Isabel, Isla	1401-023
Acantilados Rabijuncos (México)	Tuff cone of Isabel, Isla	1401-023
Acatenango (Guatemala)	Stratovolcano (8, 1972) Historical	**1402-08=**
Acatlán Volc Field (México)	Caldera (None) Pleistocene	....
Acatlán, Cerro (México)	Cinder cone of Naolinco Volc Field	1401-095
Accademia (Italy)	Dome of Campi Flegrei	0101-01=
Achacara, Loma (Perú)	Cinder cone of Andahua-Orcopampa	1504-004
Achelone (Greece)	Vent of Nisyros	0102-05=
Acheolus (Greece)	Vent of Nisyros	0102-05=
Achillion (Greece)	Dome of Volos-Atalanti	....
Achin-Niellu (Argentina)	Synonym of Huanquihue Group	1507-123
Achin-Niellu (Argentina)	Cone of Huanquihue Group	1507-123
Achiotes, Cerro los (Guatemala)	Dome of Ixhuatán	....
Achiotillal (Costa Rica)	Stratovolcano of Barva	1405-05=
Achi-yama (Izu Is-Japan)	Dome of Nii-jima	0804-02=
Achlan (Kamchatka)	Synonym of Ichinsky	1000-28=
Acigol (Turkey)	Crater of Karapinar Field	0103-001
Acigöl-Nevsehir (Turkey)	Caldera (5, -2080) Anthropology	**0103-004**
Acigol-Neysehir (Turkey)	Synonym of Acigöl-Nevsehir	0103-004
Acoculco (México)	Caldera (None) Pleistocene	....
Acotango (Chile-N)	Stratovolcanoes (None) Pleistocene	....
Acouma, Morne (W Indies)	Dome of Plat Pays, Morne	1600-11=
Acquarium (Mariana Is-C Pacific)	Thermal feature of East Diamante	0804-201
Acquasparta (Italy)	Volcanic field (None) Pleistocene	....
Acque Calde (Italy)	Thermal feature of Vulcano	0101-05=
Acropoli (Italy)	Cone of Pantelleria	0101-071
Active Crater (Costa Rica)	Crater of Rincón de la Vieja	1405-02=
Adachi (Honshu-Japan)	Pumice cone (None) Pleistocene	....
Adagdak (Aleutian Is)	Stratovolcano (None) Pleist.-Hot Springs	....
Adamozhets (Kamchatka)	Unknown (None) Pleistocene	....
Adams (US-Washington)	Stratovolcano (15, 950) Tephrochron	**1201-04-**
Adams Seamount (Pacific-C)	Submarine volcano (4, -50) K-Ar	**1303-05-**
Adare Peninsula (Antarctica)	Shield volcanoes (None) Post-Miocene	....
Adas Tepe [Abas Tepe] (Turkey)	Cone of Erciyes Dagi	0103-01=
Adatara (Honshu-Japan)	Stratovolcanoes (12, 1996) Historical	**0803-17=**
Adatara-yama (Honshu-Japan)	Dome of Adatara	0803-17=
Aden (US-New Mexico)	Shield volcano of Potrillo Volc Field	....
Adhamas (Greece)	Thermal feature of Mílos	0102-03=
Adika-wilis (Java)	Synonym of Wilis	0603-27=
Adler Hill (Australia)	Cone of Atherton Volc Province	....
Ado Ale (Ethiopia)	Synonym of Assab Volc Field	0201-125
Ado Wadjung [Ado Wajung] (Lesser Sunda Is)	Crater of Iliwerung	0604-25=
Ado Wajung (Lesser Sunda Is)	Crater of Iliwerung	0604-25=
Adwa (Ethiopia)	Stratovolcano (Uncertain) Holocene	**0201-17=**
Aegina (Greece)	Volcanic field (None) Pleistocene	....
Aek Madurana (Sumatra)	Thermal feature of Sibualbuali	0601-11=
Aek Waliran (Sumatra)	Thermal feature of Sibualbuali	0601-11=
Aer Panas (Sumatra)	Thermal feature of Kembar	....
A-Ershan (China-E)	Cone of Motianling Group	....
Aeseput (Sulawesi-Indonesia)	Cone of Soputan	0606-03=
Aeseput Wero (Sulawesi-Indonesia)	Dome of Soputan	0606-03=
Aetna (Italy)	Synonym of Etna	0101-06=
Afana (SW Pacific)	Crater of Wallis Islands	0404-05-
Afate, Cerro (El Salvador)	Dome of Coatepeque Caldera	1403-041
Afderà (Ethiopia)	Stratovolcano (None) Holocene?	**0201-11=**
Aflitos (Azores)	Cone of Picos Volc System	1802-081
Afolau (Samoa-SW Pacific)	Cone of Upolu	0404-03-
Afono (Samoa-SW Pacific)	Dome of Tutuila	0404-02-
Afosa, Montaña de (Canary Is)	Cinder cone of Hierro	1803-02-
Afrera (Ethiopia)	Synonym of Afderà	0201-11=
Afton Craters [Hunt's Hole] (US-New Mexico)	Maar of Potrillo Volc Field	....
Afutina (Samoa-SW Pacific)	Cone of Savai'i	0404-04=
Agajedan (Aleutian Is)	Synonym of Shishaldin	1101-36-
Agarteto (Hungary)	Shield volcano of Balaton Highland	....
Agaschagoch (Aleutian Is)	Synonym of Bogoslof	1101-30-
Agelu (Ethiopia)	Synonym of Ayelu	0201-16=
Aghie [Pechan] (China-W)	Cone of Tianshan Volc Group	1004-02-
Agincourt (Taiwan-N of)	Synonym of Pengchiahsu	....
Agios Joannis (Greece)	Vent of Nisyros	0102-05=
Agios Nikolaos (Greece)	Thermal feature of Methana	0102-02=
Agmagan-Karadag (Armenia)	Synonym of Ghegam Ridge	0104-07-
Agnano (Italy)	Caldera of Campi Flegrei	0101-01=
Agnano Monte Spina (Italy)	Crater of Campi Flegrei	0101-01=
Agoeng (Lesser Sunda Is)	Synonym of Agung	0604-02=
Agonia, Puig S' (Spain)	Cone of Olot Volc Field	0100-03-
Agotu Valley (New Guinea)	Cone of Crater Mountain	0503-001
Agri Dagi (Turkey)	Synonym of Ararat	0103-04-
Agrigan (Mariana Is-C Pacific)	Stratovolcano (1, 1917) Historical	**0804-16=**
Agrihan (Mariana Is-C Pacific)	Synonym of Agrigan	0804-16=
Agrio, del [Caviahue] (Chile-C)	Caldera of Copahue	1507-09=
Agritas, Volcán las (México)	Dome of Mascota Volc Field	1401-031
Agua (Guatemala)	Stratovolcano (None) Holocene	**1402-10=**
Agua Agria (México)	Thermal feature of Aguajito, El	....
Agua Agria, Ausoles de (El Salvador)	Thermal feature of San Vicente	1403-07=
Agua Amarga, Cerro (Chile-N)	Dome of Purico Complex	1505-094
Agua Bendita, Cerro (México)	Cone of Zitácuaro-Valle de Bravo	1401-061
Agua Caliente (México)	Thermal feature of Chichón, El	1401-12=
Agua Caliente del Tuzgle (Argentina)	Thermal feature of Tuzgle, Cerro	1505-15-
Agua Caliente Hot Springs (US-Washington)	Thermal feature of St. Helens	1201-05-
Agua de Pau (Azores)	Stratovolcano (10, 1564) Historical	**1802-09=**
Agua de Torres (Argentina)	Cinder cone of Unnamed	....
Agua Fría, Laguna de (Costa Rica)	Synonym of Poás	1405-04=
Agua Grande, Cerro (México)	Cinder cone of Comondú-La Purísima	1401-012
Agua Helada, Cerro (El Salvador)	Stratovolcano of Tablas, Cerro las	....
Agua Shuca (El Salvador)	Thermal feature of Apaneca Range	1403-01=
Agua Tibia, Cerro (México)	Dome of San Pedro	....
Agua, Cerro (Galápagos)	Pyroclastic cone of Negra, Sierra	1503-05=
Agua, Cerro del (México)	Cinder cone of Chichinautzin	1401-08=
Agua, Laguna de (Nicaragua)	Crater of San Cristóbal	1404-02=
Aguada, Cerro de la (Argentina)	Stratovolcano of Antofalla	....
Aguajito, El (México)	Caldera (None) Pleistocene-Hot Springs	....
Agualva (Azores)	Dome of Terceira	1802-05=
Aguas Amargas (Guatemala)	Thermal feature of Santo Tomás	....
Aguas Calientes (Chile-N)	Synonym of Incaguasi	....
Aguas Calientes (Chile-N)	Stratovolcano of Láscar	1505-10=
Aguas Delgadas (Chile-N)	Stratovolcano (None) Pleistocene	....
Aguas Perdidas (Chile-N)	Synonym of Negrillar, La	1505-108
Aguas Termales (Costa Rica)	Thermal feature of Rincón de la Vieja	1405-02=
Aguas Zarcas (Costa Rica)	Cinder cone of Platanar	1405-034
Aguero, Cerro de (Nicaragua)	Cone of Telica	1404-04=
Aguila, Cerro el (El Salvador)	Stratovolcano of Apaneca Range	1403-01=
Aguila, Cerro la (México)	Stratovolc of Michoacán-Guanajuato	1401-06=
Aguila, Cerro Pico de (México)	Stratovolcano of San Martín Pajapan	....
Aguila, El (Argentina)	Cinder cone of Unnamed	....
Aguila, El [San Antonio] (México)	Stratovolcano of Tacaná	1401-13=
Aguila, Pico del (México)	Dome of Toluca, Nevado de	1401-07-
Aguilas, Las (México)	Dome of Humeros, Los	1401-093
Aguilas, Volcán las (Chile-C)	Cone of Chillán, Nevados de	1507-07=
Aguilera (Chile-S)	Stratovolcano (2, -1250) Radiocarbon	**1508-062**
Aguilillas, Cerro (México)	Cinder cone of Comondú-La Purísima	1401-012
Aguirre (Argentina)	Pyrocl. cone Northern Mendoza Field	....
Agung (Lesser Sunda Is)	Stratovolcano (3, 1964) Historical	**0604-02=**
Agung (Java)	Crater of Guntur	0603-13=
Aguroshi-yama (Honshu-Japan)	Cone of Kurikoma	0803-21=
Ahalapam Cinder Field (US-Oregon)	Synonym of North Sister Field	1202-07-
Ahalapan Cinder Field (US-Oregon)	Cinder cone of North Sister Field	1202-07-
Ahding Ingrid Mountain (Alaska-W)	Cone of Nunivak Island	1104-02-
Ahkiwiksnuk (Alaska-W)	Maar of Nunivak Island	1104-02-
Aholo, Volcán (México)	Cone of Chichinautzin	1401-08=
Ahon, Tarso (Africa-N)	Volcanic field (None) Quaternary	....
Ahrup (New Guinea-NE of)	Synonym of Long Island	0501-05=
Ahuacatlán, Volcán de (México)	Synonym of Ceboruco	1401-03=
Ahuachapán (El Salvador)	Synonym of Apaneca Range	1403-01=
Ahuatepec, Cerro (México)	Cone of Serdán-Oriental	1401-092
Ahuazatépetl, Volcán (México)	Cinder cone of Chichinautzin	1401-08=
Ahumoa (Hawaiian Is)	Cone of Mauna Kea	1302-03-
Ahyi (Mariana Is-C Pacific)	Submarine volcano (1, 2001) Seismicity	**0804-141**
Aielu (Ethiopia)	Synonym of Ayelu	0201-16=
Aigagin (Aleutian Is)	Synonym of Makushin	1101-31-
Aigina (Greece)	Synonym of Aegina	....
Aiguanegra, Volcà (Spain)	Cone of Olot Volc Field	0100-03-
Aiguille Noire (Indian O.-S)	Cone of Kerguelen Islands	0304-02=
Ai-Laau (Hawaiian Is)	Shield volcano of Kilauea	1302-01-
Aileron (W Indies)	Dome of Pelée	1600-12=
Aïn Temouchent (Africa-N)	Cone of Tafna Beni Saf	....
Aino-mine (Honshu-Japan)	Cone of Kusatsu-Shirane	0803-12=
Ainu Tukap [Tukap] (Kuril Is)	Stratovolcano of Medvezhia	0900-10=
Aira (Kyushu-Japan)	Pleistocene caldera of Sakura-jima	0802-08=
Aird Hills (New Guinea)	Lava domes (None) Pleistocene	....
Aire, Cerro del (México)	Cinder cone of Michoacán-Guanajuato	1401-06=
Aisepoet [Aeseput] (Sulawesi-Indonesia)	Cone of Soputan	0606-03=
Aitutaki (Pacific-C)	Shield volcano (None) Pleistocene	....
Aiyansh Volcano (Canada)	Synonym of Tseax River Cone	1200-10-
Aiyina (Greece)	Synonym of Aegina	....
Aizu Nunobiki (Honshu-Japan)	Stratovolcano (None) Pleistocene	....
Aizu-Fuji (Aizu-yama) (Honshu-Japan)	Synonym of Bandai	0803-16=

Name (Subregion)	Type (Eruptions, Most Recent) Status Relation to Named Volcano	Volcano Number
Ajagin (Ajagisch) (Aleutian Is)	Synonym of Makushin	1101-31-
Ajakan [Ayakan] (Java)	Crater of Guntur	0603-13=
Ajata, Volcanes de (Chile-N)	Cinder cone of Parinacota	1505-012
Ajek-Ajek (Java)	Caldera of Semeru	0603-30=
Ajel (Ethiopia)	Synonym of Ayelu	0201-16=
Ajelou (Ethiopia)	Synonym of Ayelu	0201-16=
Ajencha, Cerro (Bolivia)	Stratovolcano (None) Post-Miocene	....
Ajer Panas [Ayer Panas] (Sumatra)	Thermal feature of Lumut Balai, Bukit	0601-24=
Ajusco, Volcán (México)	Dome of Chichinautzin	1401-08=
Aka-dake (Hokkaido-Japan)	Stratovolcano of Daisetsu	0805-06=
Aka-dake (Kuril Is)	Synonym of Sinarka	0900-29=
Aka-dake (Honshu-Japan)	Stratovolcano of Yatsuga-take	....
Akademia Nauk (Kamchatka)	Stratovolcanoes (4, 1996) Historical	**1000-125**
Akademia Nauk (Kamchatka)	Fissure vent of Kliuchevskoi	1000-26=
Akademia Nauk Springs (Kamchatka)	Thermal feature of Akademia Nauk	1000-125
Akagi (Honshu-Japan)	Stratovolcano (Uncertain) Holocene?	**0803-13=**
Akahani-yama (Honshu-Japan)	Stratovolcano of Bandai	0803-16=
Akai (Kyushu-Japan)	Cinder cone of Aso	0802-11=
Akaigawa (Hokkaido-Japan)	Stratovolcano (None) Pleistocene	....
Aka-jima (Kyushu-Japan)	Cone of Fukue-jima	0802-091
Akakubo (Honshu-Japan)	Cone of Izu-Tobu	0803-01=
Akakura (Honshu-Japan)	Thermal feature of Myoko	0803-10=
Akakura-dake (Honshu-Japan)	Cone of Hakkoda Group	0803-28=
Akamizu (Kyushu-Japan)	Thermal feature of Aso	0802-11=
Akan (Hokkaido-Japan)	Caldera (35, 2008) Historical	**0805-07=**
Akanagure (Honshu-Japan)	Dome of Hiuchi	0803-131
Akandana-yama (Honshu-Japan)	Stratovolcano of Yake-dake	0803-07=
Akan-Fuji (Hokkaido-Japan)	Stratovolcano of Akan	0805-07=
Akan-Huzi [Akan-Fuji] (Hokkaido-Japan)	Stratovolcano of Akan	0805-07=
Akan-Kohan (Hokkaido-Japan)	Thermal feature of Akan	0805-07=
Akasaka-Minami (Honshu-Japan)	Cone of Izu-Tobu	0803-01=
Akatsuka (Honshu-Japan)	Cone of Fuji	0803-03=
Akausagi-yama (Honshu-Japan)	Stratovolcano of Kyoga-take	....
Akazaki-no-mine (Izu Is-Japan)	Dome of Nii-jima	0804-02=
Akazawa-kaikyu (Honshu-Japan)	Submarine vent of Izu-Tobu	0803-01=
Akerlundh (Antarctica)	Cone of Seal Nunataks Group	1900-05=
Akhat (Mongolia)	Cone of Dariganga Volc Field	1003-04-
Akhlan (Kamchatka)	Synonym of Ichinsky	1000-28=
Akhomten (Kamchatka)	Cone of Mutnovsky	1000-06=
Akhtang (Kamchatka)	Shield volcano (None) Holocene?	**1000-32-**
Akhuachapán [Playón de Ahuachapán]	Thermal feature of Apaneca Range	1403-01=
Aki [Menshoi Brat] (Kuril Is)	Dome of Medvezhia	0900-10=
Akiloset Springs (Africa-E)	Thermal feature of Silali	0202-052
Akimoana (Hawaiian Is)	Submarine vent of Mauna Loa	1302-02=
Akita-Fuji (Honshu-Japan)	Synonym of Chokai	0803-22=
Akita-Komaga-take (Honshu-Japan)	Stratovolcanoes (18, 1971) Historical	**0803-23=**
Akita-Yake-yama (Honshu-Japan)	Stratovolcano (16, 1997) Historical	**0803-26=**
Akkktivnaya Voronka (Kamchatka)	Crater of Mutnovsky	1000-06=
Akmoan (Mindanao-Philippines)	Thermal feature of Matutum	0701-02=
Akoma, Tavani (Vanuatu-SW Pacific)	Cone of Kuwae	0507-07=
Aku (Russia-SE)	Cone of Udokan Plateau	1002-03-

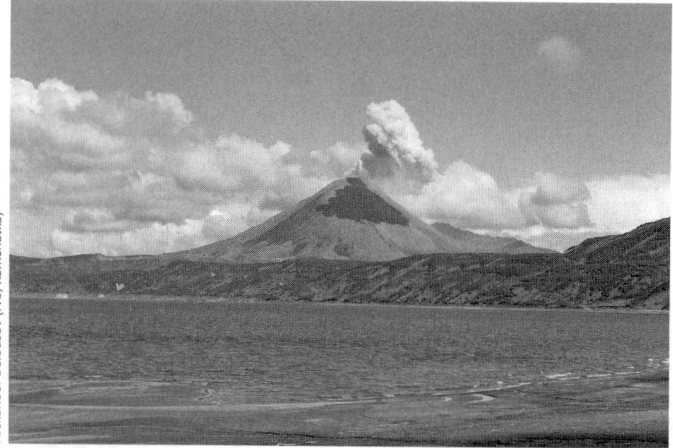

Alexander Belousov (IVS, Kamchatka)

Karymsky Lake fills the 3 x 5 km **Akademia Nauk** caldera in Kamchatka, with erupting Karymsky volcano in the background. Akademia Nauk had its first historical eruption in 1996.

Name (Subregion)	Type (Eruptions, Most Recent) Status Relation to Named Volcano	Volcano Number
Akun (Aleutian Is)	Synonym of Gilbert, Mt.	....
Akuseki-jima (Ryukyu Is)	Stratovolcanoes (None) Holocene?	**0802-022**
Akutan (Aleutian Is)	Stratovolcano (39, 1992) Historical	**1101-32-**
Akwah, Jibal (Arabia)	Cones (None) Quaternary	....
Al Harrah (Arabia)	Synonym of Shamah	....
Al Wahbah (Arabia-W)	Maar of Kishb, Harrat	0301-071
Ala Dag (Turkey)	Cone of Kars Plateau	0103-05-
Alae (Hawaiian Is)	Former pit crater of Kilauea	1302-01-
Alaembakeo, Vuti (Vanuatu-SW Pacific)	Cone of Aoba	0507-03=
Alagey (Armenia)	Synonym of Aragats	0104-06-
Alagogshak (Alaska Peninsula)	Stratovolcano of Martin	1102-14-
Alaid (Kuril Is)	Stratovolcano (11, 1996) Historical	**0900-39=**
Alaid (Kamchatka)	Cinder cone of Tolbachik	1000-24=
Alamagan (Mariana Is-C Pacific)	Stratovolcano (2, 870) Radiocarbon	**0804-18=**
Alang (Java)	Stratovolcano of Dieng Volc Complex	0603-20=
Alapars (Armenia)	Dome of Ghegam Ridge	0104-07-
Al-Arab, Djebel (Syria)	Synonym of Druze, Jabal ad	0300-06-
Alauawa, Puu (Hawaiian Is)	Cone of Hualalai	1302-04-
Alayta (Ethiopia)	Shield volcano (2, 1915) Historical	**0201-112**
Albains, Monts (Italy)	Synonym of Alban Hills	0101-004
Alban Hills (Italy)	Caldera (Uncertain) Holocene?	**0101-004**
Alban Hills (Italy)	Synonym of Alban Hills	0101-004
Albano (Italy)	Maar of Alban Hills	0101-004
Albano, Monte (Italy)	Cinder cone of Etna	0101-06=
Albany Island (Galápagos)	Cone of Santiago	1503-09=
Albatross Point (Pacific-S)	Tuff cone of Antipodes Island	1305-01-
Albay Volcano (Luzon-Philippines)	Synonym of Mayon	0703-03=
Alberca, Cerro de la [Cerro de Pario] (México)	Cinder cone of Michoacán-Guanajuato	1401-06=
Alberca, La (México)	Maar of Michoacán-Guanajuato	1401-06=
Albert Park (New Zealand)	Cone of Auckland Field	0401-02=
Albert, Mt. (New Zealand)	Cone of Auckland Field	0401-02=
Albine-Boldok (Russia-SE)	Cone of Azas Plateau	1002-07-
Albit Hut (Arabia-S)	Synonym of Bir Borhut	0301-18-
Albulhek (Mindanao-Philippines)	Cone of Matutum	0701-02=
Albuquerque (US-New Mexico)	Volcanic field (None) Pleistocene	....
Alcedo (Galápagos)	Shield volcano (2, 1993) Historical	**1503-04=**
Alchichica (México)	Tuff ring of Serdán-Oriental	1401-092
Aldama Volc Field (México)	Volcanic field (None) Quaternary	....
Alder Creek (US-California)	Vent of Whaleback	....
Alderman Islands (New Zealand)	Lava domes (None) Pleistocene?	....
Al-djabal Al-aswad (Arabia-S)	Synonym of Sawâd, Harra es-	0301-16-
Ale Bagu (Ethiopia)	Stratovolcano (None) Holocene	**0201-09=**
Alebbagu (Ethiopia)	Synonym of Ale Bagu	0201-09=
Alegría, Ausoles de la Laguna de (El Salv.)	Thermal feature of Tecapa	1403-08=
Alegría, Cerro (El Salvador)	Cone of Tecapa	1403-08=
Alessi, Djebel [Jabal el-Esi] (Arabia-S)	Stratovolcano of Dhamar, Harras of	0301-12-
Alexander Selkirk (Chile-Is)	Shield volcano (None) Pleistocene	....
Alexander, Mt. (W Indies)	Dome of St. Catherine	1600-17=
Alexandros (Greece)	Vent of Nisyros	0102-05=
Aleyone (Antarctica)	Cone of Pleiades, The	1900-013
Alferes, Caldeira do (Azores)	Cone of Sete Cidades	1802-08=
Alferes, Caldeira do (Azores)	Pumice ring of Sete Cidades	1802-08=
Alfred Picard, Cratere (Indian O.-W)	Crater of Fournaise, Piton de la	0303-02=
Alftakvislarhraun (Iceland-S)	Fissure vent of Katla	1702-03=
Alftarholl (Iceland-SW)	Crater of Grímsnes	1701-06=
Al-Haruj al Aswad (Africa-N)	Synonym of Haruj	0205-007
Al-Hayloh, Jibal (Arabia)	Cone (None) Quaternary	....
Ali Bogo (Ethiopia)	Synonym of Erta Ale	0201-08=
Ali Dag (Turkey)	Dome of Erciyes Dagi	0103-01=
Alianngei (Kamchatka)	Synonym of Ichinsky	1000-28=
Aliante (Chile-C)	Synonym of Llaima	1507-11=
Alice Arm (Canada)	Volcanic field (None) Pleistocene	....
Alicudi (Italy)	Stratovolcano (None) Pleistocene	....
Alid (Ethiopia)	Stratovolcano (None) Holocene	**0201-04=**
Alimelali (Ethiopia)	Cone (None) Pleistocene	....
Alit (Ethiopia)	Synonym of Alid	0201-04=
Alitar (Chile-N)	Maar of Purico Complex	1505-094
Aljanngej (Kamchatka)	Synonym of Ichinsky	1000-28=
Aljojuca (México)	Maar of Serdán-Oriental	1401-092
Al-khurdj Bal Djild [Khurdj El-Aisar] (Arabia-S)	Tuff cone of Haylan, Jabal	0301-11-
Alligator Lake (Canada)	Volcanic field (None) Holocene	**1200-02-**
Alligator Lake (Luzon-Philippines)	Maar of San Pablo Volc Field	0703-06=
Alma, Piton l' (W Indies)	Dome of Carbets, Pitons de	....
Almarchiga [Volcán de Fasnia] (Canary Is)	Cinder cone of Tenerife	1803-03-
Almasigahan (Luzon-Philippines)	Dome of Labo	....
Almenningahraun (Iceland-S)	Fissure vent of Katla	1702-03=
Almolonga (Guatemala)	Stratovolcano (3, 1818) Historical	**1402-04=**
Almolonga, Baños (Guatemala)	Thermal feature of Almolonga	1402-04=
Almonza (Italy)	Vent of Pantelleria	0101-071
Alnei (Kamchatka)	Synonym of Ichinsky	1000-28=
Alnei [Alney] (Kamchatka)	Stratovolc. of Alney-Chashakondzha	1000-45-
Alney (Kamchatka)	Stratovolc. of Alney-Chashakondzha	1000-45-
Alney-Chashakondzha (Kamchatka)	Stratovolcano (3, 1600) Radiocarbon	**1000-45-**
Alngei (Kamchatka)	Synonym of Alngey	1000-60-
Alngey (Kamchatka)	Stratovolcano (None) Holocene?	**1000-60-**
Alofau (Samoa-SW Pacific)	Pleistocene caldera of Tutuila	0404-02-
Aloi (Hawaiian Is)	Former pit crater of Kilauea	1302-01-
Alon, Mt. (Halmahera-Indonesia)	Cone of Gamkonora	0608-04=
Alpehue (Chile-C)	Crater of Sollipulli	1507-111
Alpha (Russia-NE)	Cinder cone of Aluchin Group	....
Alsey (Iceland-S)	Cone of Vestmannaeyjar	1702-01=
Alta Gracia (Nicaragua)	Cinder cone of Concepción	1404-12=
Alta, Montana (Canary Is)	Cone of Gran Canaria	1803-04-
Altar (Ecuador)	Stratovolcano (None) Pleistocene	....
Alter Voss (Germany)	Cone of West Eifel Volc Field	0100-01-
Altinetes, Pico (Azores)	Dome of Agua de Pau	1802-09=
Alto (Philippines-C)	Compound volcano (None) Pleistocene	....
Alto (Spanish for Peak) see proper name (e.g. Santano, Alto de)		
Alto del Padre, Cerro (Chile-C)	Synonym of Sordo Lucas	....
Alto Grande, Cerro (Costa Rica)	Cone of Irazú	1405-06=
Alto la China (Colombia)	Pyrocl. cone of San Augustín-Isnos	....
Alto, Cerro (El Salvador)	Cinder cone of Coatepeque Caldera	1403-041
Alto, Cerro (Guatemala)	Cinder cone of Cuilapa-Barbarena	1402-111
Alto, Cerro (México)	Shield volc. of Michoacán-Guanajuato	1401-06=
Alto, Cerro (México)	Dome of Primavera, Sierra la	....
Alto, Cerro (México)	Stratovolcano of San Juan	....
Alto, Pico (Azores)	Stratovolcano of Terceira	1802-05=
Alu (Ethiopia)	Fissure vents (None) Holocene	**0201-06=**
Aluchin Group (Russia-NE)	Pyroclastic cones (None) Pleistocene	....
Alunalun (Java)	Crater of Papandayan	0603-10=

Name (Subregion)	Type (Eruptions, Most Recent) Status / Relation to Named Volcano	Volcano Number
Alutate, Cerro (Guatemala)	Stratovolcano (None) Pleistocene	....
Alutu (Ethiopia)	Stratovolcano (1, -50) Radiocarbon	**0201-27-**
Alvarez (México)	Maar of Michoacán-Guanajuato	1401-06=
Alzatate, Volcán (Guatemala)	Cone of Jumay Volc Field	....
Amacan-Gopod (Mindanao-Philippines)	Thermal feature of Leonard Range	0701-031
Amado (Ethiopia)	Dome of Borawli	0201-121
Amado Nervo (México)	Shield volcano of San Pedro	....
Amagase (Kyushu-Japan)	Thermal feature of Kuju	0802-12=
Amagi (Honshu-Japan)	Stratovolcano of Izu-Tobu	0803-01=
Amahuitz (México)	Dome of Mispía	....
Amajaque, Cerro (Guatemala)	Cinder cone of Redondo, Cerro	....
Amak (Aleutian Is)	Stratovolcano (3, 1796) Historical	**1101-39-**
'Am'am, Jabal (Arabia-W)	Dome of Khaybar, Harrat	0301-06=
Amani (Africa-C)	Cone of Nyamuragira	0203-02=
Amarchta (Aleutian Is)	Synonym of Amukta	1101-19-
Amargura (Tonga-SW Pacific)	Synonym of Fonualei	0403-10=
Amarilla, Montana (Canary Is)	Cone of Lanzarote	1803-06-
Amarillo (Argentina)	Cinder cone of Unnamed	....
Amarillo, Cerro (Chile-Is)	Tuff cone of San Félix	1506-01=
Amarti (Ethiopia)	Synonym of Borawli	0201-107
Amas, Mt (Sumatra)	Cone of Gadang, Bukit	....
Amasing (Halmahera-Indonesia)	Stratovolcanoes (None) Holocene	**0608-072**
Amate, El (El Salvador)	Synonym of Tablas, Cerro las	....
Amate, El [Cerro las Tablas] (El Salvador)	Stratovolcano of Tablas, Cerro las	....
Amatepeque [El Jabalí] (El Salvador)	Stratovolcano of San Salvador	1403-05=
Amatillo, Cerro (Guatemala)	Cinder cone of Güistepeque Volc Field	....
Amatitlán (Guatemala)	Pleistocene caldera of Pacaya	1402-11=
Amatofua (Tonga-SW Pacific)	Synonym of Tofua	0403-06=
Amaya, Ausoles de (El Salvador)	Thermal feature of Apaneca Range	1403-01=
Amayo, Volcán (Guatemala)	Synonym of Flores	1402-14-
Amaytoli (Ethiopia)	Synonym of Ale Bagu	0201-09=
Ambae (Vanuatu-SW Pacific)	Synonym of Aoba	0507-03=
Ambalatungan Group (Philippines)	Compound volc. (Uncertain) Fumarolic	**0703-088**
Ambang (Sulawesi-Indonesia)	Complex volcano (1, 1845) Historical	**0606-02=**
Ambato [Ampato] (Perú)	Stratovolcano of Sabancaya	1504-006
Ambitle (New Ireland-SW Pacific)	Stratovolcano (1, -350) Radiocarbon	**0504-02=**
Amboelombo (Lesser Sunda Is)	Synonym of Ebulobo	0604-10=
Ambohibe (Madagascar)	Dome of Itasy Volc Field	0303-014
Ambohimalala (Madagascar)	Cone of Itasy Volc Field	0303-014
Ambohitritainerina (Madagascar)	Cone of Itasy Volc Field	0303-014
Ambohitrondry (Madagascar)	Cone of Itasy Volc Field	0303-014
Amboy (US-California)	Cinder cone (None) Pleistocene	....
Ambre-Bobaomby (Madagascar)	Volcanic field (None) Holocene	**0303-011**
Ambrim (Vanuatu-SW Pacific)	Synonym of Ambrym	0507-04=
Ambrym (Vanuatu-SW Pacific)	Pyroclastic shield (53, 2010) Historical	**0507-04=**
Amburembu (Amburombu) (Lesser Sunda Is)	Synonym of Ebulobo	0604-10=
Ameba (Kuril Is)	Dome of Medvezhia	0900-10=
Ames Range (Antarctica)	Synonym of Andrus	1900-023
Amgai Highlands-Higashi (Honshu-Japan)	Vent of Izu-Tobu	0803-01=
Amiak (Aleutian Is)	Synonym of Amak	1101-39-
Amiata (Italy)	Lava domes (None) Pleist.-Fumarolic	....
Amiata, Monte (Italy)	Dome of Amiata	....
Amic (W Indies)	Crater of Soufrière Guadeloupe	1600-06=
Amic, Morne (W Indies)	Dome of Soufrière Guadeloupe	1600-06=
Amida-dake (Honshu-Japan)	Stratovolcano of Yatsuga-take	....
Amigasa-yama (Honshu-Japan)	Stratovolcano of Yatsuga-take	....
Amikake Spa (Honshu-Japan)	Thermal feature of Iwate	0803-24=
Amka-Usyr (Kuril Is)	Synonym of Nemo Peak	0900-32=
Amoissa (Ethiopia)	Synonym of Adwa	0201-17=
Amoles, Cerro los (México)	Cinder cone of Camargo Volc Field	....
Amoloc, Volcán (México)	Cinder cone of Chichinautzin	1401-08=
Amor (Vanuatu-SW Pacific)	Stratovolcano of Suretamatai	0507-01=
Amorong (Luzon-Philippines)	Lava domes (None) Fumarolic	**0703-085**
Ampary (Madagascar)	Dome of Itasy Volc Field	0303-014
Ampato (Perú)	Stratovolcano of Sabancaya	1504-006
Ampiro (Mindanao-Philippines)	Stratovolcano? (None) Quaternary	....
Amsterdam Island (Indian O.-S)	Stratovolcano (None) Holocene	**0304-001**
Amuchta (Aleutian Is)	Synonym of Amukta	1101-19-
Amud, Jabal al (Arabia-W)	Cone of Harrah, Al	0301-001
Amukta (Aleutian Is)	Stratovolcano (6, 1997) Historical	**1101-19-**
Amutychi (Russia-SE)	Cinder cone of Udokan Plateau	1002-03-
Anagi-yama [Anano-yama] (Izu Is-Japan)	Dome of Kozu-shima	0804-03=
Anagona (Vanuatu-SW Pacific)	Cone of Aoba	0507-03=
Anak Krakatau (Indonesia)	Cone of Krakatau	0602-00=
Anak Ranakah (Lesser Sunda Is)	Dome of Ranakah	0604-071
Anakena, Volcán (Chile-Is)	Pyroclastic cone of Easter Island	1506-011
Anallajsi, Nevado (Bolivia)	Stratovolcano (None) Pleistocene	....
Anamarama, Maunga (Chile-Is)	Pyroclastic cone of Easter Island	1506-011
Anangusik (Aleutian Is)	Synonym of Gareloi	1101-07-
Ananokubo (Honshu-Japan)	Tuff ring of Izu-Tobu	0803-01=
Ananopa, Cerro (Guatemala)	Volcanic field (None) Quaternary	....
Anano-yama (Honshu-Japan)	Dome of Izu-Tobu	0803-01=
Anano-yama (Izu Is-Japan)	Dome of Kozu-shima	0804-03=
Anaota (Samoa-SW Pacific)	Cone of Savai'i	0404-04=
Anas (Philippines-C)	Thermal feature of Biliran	0702-08=
Anatahan (Mariana Is-C Pacific)	Stratovolcano (4, 2008) Historical	**0804-20=**
Anatom (Vanuatu-SW Pacific)	Synonym of Aneityum	0507-11-
Anaun (Kamchatka)	Stratovolcano (None) Holocene?	**1000-39-**
Anburo (Ecuador)	Dome of Chachimbiro	1502-002
Anchal, Maar d' (France)	Maar of Chaîne des Puys	0100-02-
Ancho (Argentina)	Pyrocl. cone Northern Mendoza Field	....
Andabi Gabalti (Ethiopia)	Cone of Manda-Inakir	0201-122
Andagua Valley [Andahua Valley] (Perú)	Synonym of Andahua-Orcopampa	1504-004
Andahua-Orcopampa (Perú)	Cinder cones (3, 1490) Radiocarbon	**1504-004**

An ash-bearing eruption column rises from the east crater of **Anatahan** volcano in the Northern Mariana Islands on June 16, 2003. The column reached a maximum height of about 2.5 km in less than 40 seconds.

Name (Subregion)	Type (Eruptions, Most Recent) Status / Relation to Named Volcano	Volcano Number
Andersson Island (Antarctica)	Cone of Tabarin Peninsula	....
Andes, Cerro los (Perú)	Cone of Chachani, Nevado	1504-007
Andikli Tepe (Turkey)	Cone of Karapinar Field	0103-001
Andikli-Ayirtmeke Tepe (Turkey)	Cone of Karapinar Field	0103-001
Andjasmoro (Java)	Stratovolcano of Arjuno-Welirang	0603-29=
Andraikiba (Madagascar)	Crater of Ankaratra Field	0303-015
Andranojavatra (Madagascar)	Cone of Itasy Volc Field	0303-014
Andranoratsy (Madagascar)	Crater of Itasy Volc Field	0303-014
Andranotoraha (Madagascar)	Crater of Itasy Volc Field	0303-014
Andreas (Greece)	Vent of Nisyros	0102-05=
Andres (Chile-C)	Stratovolcano of Palomo	1507-022
Andrew Bay (Aleutian Is)	Caldera of Adagdak	....
Andrew Bay Hot Springs (Aleutian Is)	Thermal feature of Adagdak	....
Andrew's Cone (Africa-E)	Stratovolcano of Barrier, The	0202-03=
Andromeda Cone (Alaska-W)	Cone of Imuruk Lake	1104-06-
Andrus (Antarctica)	Shield volcanoes (None) Holocene?	**1900-023**
Aneityum (Vanuatu-SW Pacific)	Stratovolcanoes (None) Holocene?	**0507-11-**
Anetchom (Vanuatu-SW Pacific)	Synonym of Aneityum	0507-11-
Anfitrite (Italy)	Submarine vent C. Flegrei Mar Sicilia	0101-07=
Angalafib (Africa-N)	Cone of Bayuda Volc Field	0205-06-
Angar, Gof (Africa-E)	Maar of Marsabit	0202-021
Angavo (Madagascar)	Dome of Itasy Volc Field	0303-014
Anget (Sumatra)	Crater of Lumut Balai, Bukit	0601-24=
Angila (New Britain-SW Pac)	Cone of Langila	0502-01=
Anglais, Morne (W Indies)	Stratovolcano of Watt, Morne	1600-101
Angnjioman [Angnyioman] (Lesser Sunda Is)	Thermal feature of Ilimuda	0604-17=
Angnyioman (Lesser Sunda Is)	Thermal feature of Ilimuda	0604-17=
Angoes, Batoe [Batu Angus] (Indonesia)	Dome of Tongkoko	0606-13=
Angostura, La (Argentina)	Tuff ring of Huanquihue Group	1507-123
Angostura, Montaña de la (Canary Is)	Cinder cone of Tenerife	1803-03-
Angudi (Ethiopia)	Synonym of Yangudi	0201-151
Angureal (Ecuador)	Stratovolcano of Cayambe	1502-006
Angus Baru, Batu (Sulawesi-Indonesia)	Dome of Tongkoko	0606-13=
Angus, Batu (Banda Sea)	Crater of Banda Api	0605-09=
Angus, Batu (Sulawesi-Indonesia)	Dome of Tongkoko	0606-13=
Aniakchak (Alaska Peninsula)	Caldera (13, 1931) Historical	**1102-09-**
Anilao Hill (Luzon-Philippines)	Scoria cone (None) Pleistocene	....
Anillo, Cerro del (México)	Cinder cone of Michoacán-Guanajuato	1401-06=
Animas (Colombia)	Stratovolcano (None) Quaternary	....
Animas, Cerro de las (Galápagos)	Cone of Azul, Cerro	1503-06=
Anir (New Ireland-SW Pacific)	Synonym of Ambitle	0504-02=
Aniusk (Russia-NE)	Cinder cone of Anjuisky	....
Anjar, Gunung (Java)	Cone of Ijen	0603-35=
Anjar, Kawah (Java)	Thermal feature of Kamojang, Kawah	....
Anjouan Island (Indian O.-W)	Shield volcano (None) Pleistocene	....

Name (Subregion)	Type (Eruptions, Most Recent) Status Relation to Named Volcano	Volcano Number
Anjuisky (Russia-NE)	Pyroclastic cones (None) Pleistocene	....
Ankaizina Field (Madagascar)	Cinder cones (None) Holocene	**0303-013**
Ankaratra Field (Madagascar)	Cinder cones (None) Holocene	**0303-015**
Annexation (Kermadec Is)	Shield volcano of Macauley Island	0402-021
Anoengola [Anunggola] (Lesser Sunda Is)	Crater of Sirung	0604-27=
Anonimo (Chile-C)	Synonym of Llaima	1507-11=
Ansei (Hokkaido-Japan)	Crater of Komaga-take	0805-02=
Antaymarca, Volcán (Perú)	Cinder cone of Andahua-Orcopampa	1504-004
Anteojos, Los (El Salvador)	Dome of Coatepeque Caldera	1403-041
Anti, Gunung (Lesser Sunda Is)	Cone of Batur	0604-01=
Anticura (Chile-C)	Cone of Antillanca Group	1507-153
Anticura (Chile-C)	Pyrocl. cone Puyehue-Cordón Caulle	1507-15=
Antillanca Group (Chile-C)	Stratovolcanoes (2, -230) Radiocarbon	**1507-153**
Antimilos (Greece)	Cone of Mílos	0102-03=
Antiparos (Greece)	Pyroclastic cones (None) Pleistocene	....
Antipin (Kuril Is)	Stratovolcano (None) Pleistocene	....
Antipodes Island (Pacific-S)	Pyroclastic cones (None) Holocene?	**1305-01-**
Antisana (Ecuador)	Stratovolcano (2, 1802) Historical	**1502-03=**
Antitruz, Cerro (Chile-S/Argentina)	Cinder cone of Crater Basalt Field	1508-025

Glaciers mantle massive, 5753-m-high **Antisana** stratovolcano in the Ecuadorian Andes.

Name (Subregion)	Type (Eruptions, Most Recent) Status Relation to Named Volcano	Volcano Number
Antizana (Ecuador)	Synonym of Antisana	1502-03=
Antoco (Chile-C)	Synonym of Antuco	1507-08=
Antofagasta de la Sierra (Argentina)	Scoria cones (None) Holocene	**1505-18-**
Antofalla (Argentina)	Stratovolcanoes (None) Pleistocene	....
Antoine, Lake (W Indies)	Crater of St. Catherine	1600-17=
Antojo (Chile-C)	Synonym of Antuco	1507-08=
Antombran (Guatemala)	Lava cone of Ananopa, Cerro	....
Antonelli (Indian O.-S)	Cone of Amsterdam Island	0304-001
Antonia Peak (Kuril Is)	Synonym of Tiatia	0900-03=
Antsiferova (Kuril Is)	Synonym of Shirinki	0900-331
Antsirabe (Madagascar)	Cone of Ankaratra Field	0303-015
Antsirable (Madagascar)	Synonym of Ankaratra Field	0303-015
Antuco (Chile-C)	Stratovolcano (11, 1869) Historical	**1507-08=**
Anunciación, Cerro (Costa Rica)	Synonym of Chopo, Cerro	....
Anunggola (Lesser Sunda Is)	Crater of Sirung	0604-27=
Anvil Peak (Aleutian Is)	Cone of Semisopochnoi	1101-06-
Anvil, The [El Yunque] (Chile-Is)	Stratovolcano of Robinson Crusoe	1506-02=
Anyuy Group (Russia-NE)	Synonym of Anjuisky	....
Aoba (Vanuatu-SW Pacific)	Shield volcano (5, 2006) Historical	**0507-03=**
Aobuna (Honshu-Japan)	Stratovolcano of Towada	0803-271
A'ofa (Samoa-SW Pacific)	Shield volcano of Ofu-Olosega	0404-01=
Aoga-shima (Izu Is-Japan)	Stratovolcano (7, 1785) Historical	**0804-06=**
Aone Spa (Honshu-Japan)	Thermal feature of Zao	0803-19=
Aono-yama (Honshu-Japan)	Lava domes (None) Pleistocene	....
Aopo [Mauga Mu] (Samoa-SW Pacific)	Cinder cone of Savai'i	0404-04=
Aoso (Honshu-Japan)	Stratovolcano (None) Radiocarbon	....
Apacagua (Guatemala)	Synonym of Pacaya	1402-11=
Apache Volc Field (US-Arizona)	Synonym of Springerville	....
Apacheta, Cerro (Chile-N)	Dome of Azufre, Cerro del	1505-061
Apachinskaia Sopka (Kamchatka)	Synonym of Opala	1000-08=
Apagado (Chile-N)	Stratovolcano (None) Pleistocene	....
Apagado (Chile-S)	Pyroclastic cone (None) Holocene	**1508-024**
Apagado, El [Escalante] (Chile-N)	Stratovolcano of Sairecabur	1505-091
Apakhonchich (Kamchatka)	Fissure vent of Kliuchevskoi	1000-26=
Apale [Cerro Afate] (El Salvador)	Dome of Coatepeque Caldera	1403-041
Apalong (New Guinea-NE of)	Crater of Umboi	0501-06=
Apalskaia Sopka (Kamchatka)	Synonym of Opala	1000-08=
Apaneca Range (El Salvador)	Stratovolcanoes (None) Holocene	**1403-01=**
Apaneca, Cerro de (El Salvador)	Stratovolcano of Apaneca Range	1403-01=
Apantes, Cerro de (Guatemala)	Cinder cone of Santiago, Cerro	1402-15-
Apan-Tezontepec (México)	Volcanic field (None) Quaternary	....
Apas-Navenchauc (México)	Calderas (None) Pleistocene	....
Apaste, El (México)	Cinder cone of Santo Domingo Field	....
Apastepe, Loma (Nicaragua)	Cinder cone of San Cristóbal	1404-02=
Apastepeque Field (El Salvador)	Volcanic field (None) Holocene	**1403-071**
Apastepeque, Cerro de (El Salvador)	Dome of Apastepeque Field	1403-071
Apastepeque, Laguna (El Salvador)	Pit crater of Apastepeque Field	1403-071
Apatihegy (Hungary)	Cone of Balaton Highland	....
Apaxtepec (México)	Cinder cone of Colima	1401-04=
Api (Banda Sea)	Synonym of Gunungapi Wetar	0605-03=
Api Siau (Sangihe Is-Indonesia)	Synonym of Karangetang [Api Siau]	0607-02=
Apo (Mindanao-Philippines)	Stratovolcano (None) Fumarolic	**0701-03=**
Apo Spring (Mindanao-Philippines)	Thermal feature of Apo	0701-03=
Apolima (Samoa-SW Pacific)	Tuff cone of Upolu	0404-03-
Apoyeque (Nicaragua)	Pyroclastic shield (4, -50) Radiocarbon	**1404-091**
Apoyo (Nicaragua)	Caldera (None) Pleistocene	....
Apoyo (Africa-E)	Cone of Homa Mountain	0202-07=
Apoyoito (Nicaragua)	Dome of Apoyo	....
Ap-san (Korea)	Shield volcano of Ch'uga-ryong	1006-02-
Apsian (Luzon-Philippines)	Cone of Natib	0703-082
Apuahoe [Rolles Peak] (New Zealand)	Stratovolcano of Maroa	0401-061
Aracar (Argentina)	Stratovolcano (Uncertain)	**1505-16-**
Aradas, Cerro las (Guatemala)	Cinder cone of Santiago, Cerro	1402-15-
Arafo, Volcan de [Volcán de Güimar]	Cinder cone of Tenerife	1803-03-
Aragats (Armenia)	Stratovolcano (None) Holocene	**0104-06-**
Aragatz (Armenia)	Synonym of Aragats	0104-06-
Aragay (Armenia)	Synonym of Aragats	0104-06-
Araisa (Kuril Is)	Synonym of Atsonupuri	0900-05=
Araito (Kuril Is)	Synonym of Alaid	0900-39=
Araito-Fuji (Kuril Is)	Synonym of Alaid	0900-39=
Ara-Khangay Volc Field (Mongolia)	Synonym of Taryatu-Chulutu	1003-01-
Aramuaca, Laguna (El Salvador)	Maar (None) Holocene	**1403-101**
Aranguadi (Ethiopia)	Tuff ring of Bishoftu Volc Field	0201-22-
Ararat (Turkey)	Stratovolcano (3, 1840) Historical	**0103-04-**
Araumakutan (Kuril Is)	Synonym of Kharimkotan	0900-30=
Ara-yama (Honshu-Japan)	Cone of Izu-Tobu	0803-01=
Ara-yama (Honshu-Japan)	Synonym of Nikko-Shirane	0803-14=
Arayat (Luzon-Philippines)	Stratovolcano (None) Holocene?	**0703-084**
Arayu Hot Spring (Honshu-Japan)	Thermal feature of Takahara	0803-143
Arbre (Africa-C)	Cone of Karisimbi	0203-04-
Archiaverno (Italy)	Tuff cone of Campi Flegrei	0101-01=
Arco Rift Zone (US-Idaho)	Fissure vent of Grande, Cerro	....
Arcotango (Chile-N)	Synonym of Acotango	....
Arctowsky (Antarctica)	Cone of Seal Nunataks Group	1900-05=
Arcturus Lake (Galápagos)	Crater of Genovesa	1503-081
Ardjoeno [Arjuno] (Java)	Stratovolcano of Arjuno-Welirang	0603-29=
Ardoukôba (Djibouti)	Fissure vents (1, 1978) Historical	**0201-126**
Ardschich Dagh (Turkey)	Synonym of Erciyes Dagi	0103-01=
Areia, Pico Da (Azores)	Dome of Furnas	1802-10=
Arekikapakapa (New Zealand)	Thermal feature of Rotorua	....
Arena, Montana de la (Canary Is)	Cone of Fuerteventura	1803-05-
Arenal (Costa Rica)	Stratovolcano (27, 2010) Historical	**1405-033**
Arenal I (Ecuador)	Dome of Atacazo	1502-021
Arenal II (Ecuador)	Dome of Atacazo	1502-021
Arenal, Cerro (Nicaragua)	Cinder cone of Masaya	1404-10=
Arenal, Volcán (Chile-C)	Tuff ring of Lanín	1507-122
Arenales (Chile-S)	Stratovolcano (1, 1979) Historical	**1508-059**
Arenas (Colombia)	Crater of Ruiz, Nevado del	1501-02=
Arenas, Cerro (México)	Cone of Humeros, Los	1401-093
Arenas, Montaña de Las [Volcán de Güimar]	Cinder cone of Tenerife	1803-03-
Arequipa, Volcan de (Perú)	Synonym of Misti, El	1504-01=
'Ares, Djebel el- [Jabal 'Urais] (Arabia-S)	Cone of Sawâd, Harra es-	0301-16-
Arfat (Halmahera-Indonesia)	Synonym of Gamalama	0608-06=
Argaeus Mons (Argaios) (Turkey)	Synonym of Erciyes Dagi	0103-01=
Argapura (Java)	Stratovolcano of Iyang-Argapura	0603-33=
Argelia, Cerro de (Guatemala)	Cone of Flores	1402-14-
Argo Point (Antarctica)	Scoria cone (None) Pleistocene	....
Argopeoro [Argapura] (Java)	Stratovolcano of Iyang-Argapura	0603-33=
Argowajang (Java)	Synonym of Argowayang	....
Argowayang (Java)	Stratovolcano (None) Quaternary	....
Arhab, Harra of (Arabia-S)	Volcanic field (2, 500) Historical	**0301-09-**
Ariccia (Italy)	Maar of Alban Hills	0101-004
Arig [Arik] (Kamchatka)	Stratovolcano of Aak	....
Arik (Kamchatka)	Stratovolcano of Aak	....
Arika [Arik] (Kamchatka)	Stratovolcano of Aak	....
Arintica (Chile-N)	Stratovolcanoes (None) Pleistocene	....
Aris Island (New Guinea-NE of)	Synonym of Boisa	0501-011
Arjuno-Welirang (Java)	Stratovolcano (2, 1952) Historical	**0603-29=**
Arkathio (Greece)	Dome of Mílos	0102-03=
Arlington (US-Arizona)	Cone of Sentinel Plain	....
Armadillo Peak (Canada)	Stratovolcano of Edziza	1200-06-
Armado, El (Costa Rica)	Cone of Turrialba	1405-07=
Armado, Isla el (Nicaragua)	Tuff ring of Zapatera	1404-111
Armagan (Armenia)	Cone of Ghegam Ridge	0104-07-
Armarelo, Monte (Cape Verde Is)	Cone of Fogo	1804-01=
Arnardalsoldugjoska Yngri (Iceland-NE)	Crater Row of Kverkfjöll	1703-05=
Arnarsetur (Iceland-SW)	Crater Row of Reykjanes	1701-02=
Arooma (Ethiopia)	Crater of Dubbi	0201-10=
Arop (New Guinea-NE of)	Synonym of Long Island	0501-05=
Arpacay (Turkey)	Volcanic field (None) Pleistocene	....
Arpong (Korea)	Cone of Ulreung	1006-03-
Arrabales, Caldera de los (Canary Is)	Cinder cone of Fuerteventura	1803-05-
Arrau, Volcán (Chile-C)	Dome of Chillán, Nevados de	1507-07=
Arrayanes (Chile-C)	Cone of Antillanca Group	1507-153
Arroyo Colorado (México)	Dome of Primavera, Sierra la	....
Arroyo Ixtahuatonte (México)	Dome of Primavera, Sierra la	....
Arroyo La Cuartilla (México)	Dome of Primavera, Sierra la	....

Name (Subregion)	Type (Eruptions, Most Recent) Status / Relation to Named Volcano	Volcano Number
Arroyo las Animas (México)	Dome of Primavera, Sierra la	....
Arroyo los Pilas (México)	Dome of Primavera, Sierra la	....
Arroyo San José (México)	Synonym of Jaraguay Volc Field	1401-004
Arroyo Saucillo (México)	Vent of Primavera, Sierra la	....
Arshan (China-E)	Cinder cones (1, 0) Radiocarbon	**1005-011**
Arso (Italy)	Cone of Ischia	0101-03=
Arso, Monte (Italy)	Cinder cone of Etna	0101-06=
Artali (Ethiopia)	Synonym of Erta Ale	0201-08=
Artemisio (Italy)	Synonym of Alban Hills	0101-004
Artemisio-Tuscolana [Tuscolana-Artemisio]	Pleistocene caldera of Alban Hills	0101-004
Aruba Rock (Africa-E)	Tuff cone of Namarunu	0202-04-
Arucas, Montana de (Canary Is)	Cone of Gran Canaria	1803-04-
Arufat (Halmahera-Indonesia)	Synonym of Gamalama	0608-06=
Arufta (Ethiopia)	Stratovolcano of Gabillema	0201-15=
Aruicas, Montana (Canary Is)	Cone of Gran Canaria	1803-04-
Arum, Gunung (Java)	Cone of Sundoro	0603-21=
Arusi (Ethiopia)	Cone of Mega Basalt Field	0201-33-
As Safa (Syria)	Synonym of Es Safa	0300-05-
as Sumth [Et-Tadawin] (Arabia-S)	Tuff cone of Haylan, Jabal	0301-11-
Asa Ale (Ethiopia)	Pleistocene caldera of Dalaha'ale	....
Asacha (Kamchatka)	Complex volcano (None) Holocene	**1000-058**
Asacha (Kamchatka)	Synonym of Gorely	1000-07=
Asacha (Kamchatka)	Synonym of Mutnovsky	1000-06=
Asahi-dake (Hokkaido-Japan)	Stratovolcano of Daisetsu	0805-06=
Asahi-dake (Honshu-Japan)	Stratovolcano of Nasu	0803-15=
Asahina-dake (Honshu-Japan)	Dome of Osore-yama	0803-29=
Asakizuka (Honshu-Japan)	Cone of Fuji	0803-03=
Asakusa (Honshu-Japan)	Stratovolcano (None) Pleistocene	....
As-Ali (Ethiopia)	Shield volcano (None) Post-Miocene	....
Asam, Wai (Sumatra)	Thermal feature of Hulubelu	0601-28=
Asama (Honshu-Japan)	Complex volcano (127, 2009) Historical	**0803-11=**
Asamakakushi-yama (Honshu-Japan)	Stratovolcano of Hanamagari	....
Asar (Iceland-SW)	Shield volcano of Hengill	1701-05=
Asase (Ryukyu Is)	Cone of Kikai	0802-06=
Asavio (Ethiopia)	Synonym of Asavyo	0201-104
Asavyo (Ethiopia)	Shield volcano (None) Holocene	**0201-104**
Asay Knoll (US-Utah)	Cone of Markagunt Plateau	1207-04-
Asboru (Ethiopia)	Stratovolcano of Gabillema	0201-15=
Ascensión (Atlantic-C)	Stratovolcano (None) Holocene	**1805-05-**
Ascotán, Cerro (Chile-N)	Stratovolcano (None) Pleistocene	....
Asdaga (Ethiopia)	Synonym of Sork Ale	0201-103
Aseba, Ol Doinyo (Africa-E)	Cone of Chyulu Hills	0202-13=
Asgura (Ethiopia)	Stratovolcano (None) Pleistocene	....
Ash Cone (Africa-E)	Cone of Meru	0202-16=
Ash Hill (New Zealand)	Tuff cone of Auckland Field	0401-02=
Ash Mountain (Canada)	Tuya of Tuya Volc Field	1200-031
Ash Pit, the (Canada)	Cone of Spectrum Range	1200-07-
Ashen Hills (Antarctica)	Cone of Michael	1900-09=
Ashes Vent Field (Pacific-NE)	Thermal feature of Axial Seamount	1301-021
Ashi Shan (China-W)	Cinder cone of Kunlun Volc Group	1004-03-
Ashitaka (Honshu-Japan)	Stratovolcano (None) Pleistocene	....
Ashtarak (Armenia)	Pyroclastic cone of Aragats	0104-06-
'Asi, Hala-'l- (Arabia-W)	Tuff cone of 'Uwayrid, Harrat	0301-02=
Asi, Mt. (Samoa-SW Pacific)	Cone of Savai'i	0404-04=
Asie (Africa-E)	Shield volcano (None) Pleistocene	....
Asin (Luzon-Philippines)	Thermal feature of Pinatubo	0703-083
Asin Hot Spring (Luzon-Philippines)	Thermal feature of Natib	0703-082
Asitaka (Honshu-Japan)	Synonym of Ashitaka	....
Ask (Iran)	Thermal feature of Damavand	0302-01-
Askahraun (Iceland-NE)	Fissure vent of Bárdarbunga	1703-03=
Askedna Hot Spring (Luzon-N of)	Thermal feature of Babuyan Claro	0704-03=
Askja (Iceland-NE)	Stratovolcano (14, 1961) Historical	**1703-06=**
Aslaj, Jabal (Arabia-W)	Cinder cone of Kishb, Harrat	0301-071
Asmara (Ethiopia)	Pyroclastic cone of Dama Ali	0201-141
Aso (Kyushu-Japan)	Caldera (166, 2008) Historical	**0802-11=**
Asobenomori (Honshu-Japan)	Synonym of Iwaki	0803-27=
Asog (Luzon-Philippines)	Synonym of Iriga	0703-041
Asomada, Montaña de (Canary Is)	Cinder cone of Hierro	1803-02-
Asomadas Negras, Montaña (Canary Is)	Cinder cone of Hierro	1803-02-
Aso-san (Kyushu-Japan)	Synonym of Aso	0802-11=
Asososca, Cerro (Nicaragua)	Stratovolcano of Pilas, Las	1404-08=
Asososca, Laguna de (Nicaragua)	Maar of Nejapa-Miraflores	1404-092
Asososca, Laguna de (Nicaragua)	Maar of Pilas, Las	1404-08=
Aso-Uchinomaki (Kyushu-Japan)	Thermal feature of Aso	0802-11=
Aspen Butte (US-Oregon)	Cone of Mountain Lakes	....
Aspero, Cerro (Chile-N)	Dome of Purico Complex	1505-094
Aspronisi (Greece)	Tuff ring of Santorini	0102-04=
Assab Volc Field (Ethiopia)	Volcanic field (None) Holocene	**0201-125**
Assalo (Ethiopia)	Synonym of Ayelu	0201-16=
Assirmatsky (Kuril Is)	Synonym of Ebeko	0900-38=
Assongsong (Mariana Is-C Pacific)	Synonym of Asuncion	0804-15=
Astillero, Cerrito el (Guatemala)	Lava cone of Chiquimula Volc Field	1402-20-
Astillero, Cerro el (México)	Cinder cone of Michoacán-Guanajuato	1401-06=
Astillero, Cerro el (El Salvador)	Cinder cone of Santa Ana	1403-02=
Astrol, Puig (Spain)	Cone of Olot Volc Field	0100-03-
Astroni (Italy)	Tuff ring of Campi Flegrei	0101-01=
Asuncion (Mariana Is-C Pacific)	Stratovolcano (1, 1906) Historical	**0804-15=**
Asunción (Costa Rica)	Synonym of Chopo, Cerro	....
Asunción, La (Guatemala)	Cone of Suchitán	1402-16-
Asur (Vanuatu-SW Pacific)	Synonym of Yasur	0507-10=
Asyrmintar (Kuril Is)	(None) Not a Volcano	0900-33=
Ata Caldera (Kyushu-Japan)	Caldera (None) Pleistocene	....
Atacama, Volcan de (Chile-N)	Synonym of Licancabur	1505-092
Atacama, Volcán de (Chile-N)	Synonym of Lastarria	1505-12=
Atacazo (Ecuador)	Stratovolcano (4, -320) Radiocarbon	**1502-021**
Atagawa-kaikyu (Honshu-Japan)	Submarine vent of Izu-Tobu	0803-01=
Atakor Volc Field (Africa-N)	Scoria cones (None) Holocene	**0205-005**
Atalanti-Volos (Greece)	Synonym of Volos-Atalanti	....
Atalaya, La (Canary Is)	Cone of Tenerife	1803-03-
Atapijuk, Bukit (Sumatra)	Cone of Hutapanjang	0601-172
Atar (Sumatra)	Unknown (None) Post-Miocene	....
Atarjea de Tescalame (México)	Dome of San Pedro	....
Atchi-yama [Achi-yama] (Izu Is-Japan)	Dome of Nii-jima	0804-02=
Atexcac, Laguna (México)	Maar of Serdán-Oriental	1401-092
Atherton Volc Province (Australia)	Shield volcanoes (None) Pleistocene	....
Atiamuri (New Zealand)	Thermal feature of Maroa	0401-061
Atimbia, Mt. (Luzon-Philippines)	Cone of San Pablo Volc Field	0703-06=
Atitlán (Guatemala)	Stratovolcano (13, 1853) Historical	**1402-06=**
Atka (Aleutian Is)	Stratovolcanoes (2, 1987) Historical	**1101-16-**
Atlacorra, Volcán (México)	Cinder cone of Chichinautzin	1401-08=
Atlas, Mount [Mount Pleiones] (Antarctica)	Stratovolcano of Pleiades, The	1900-013
Atlasov (Kamchatka)	Fissure vent of Kliuchevskoi	1000-26=
Atlasov (Atlasova) (Kamchatka)	Synonym of Nylgimelkin	1000-65-
Atlin Volc Field (Canada)	Cinder cones (Uncertain) Holocene	**1200-03-**
Atlixcos, Los (México)	Shield volcano (None) Holocene	**1401-094**
Atosa (Atosanobori) (Kuril Is)	Synonym of Atsonupuri	0900-05=
Atosanupuri (Kuril Is)	Synonym of Atsonupuri	0900-05=
Atosanupuri (Hokkaido-Japan)	Dome of Kutcharo	0805-08=
Atsonupuri (Kuril Is)	Stratovolcano (2, 1932) Historical	**0900-05=**
At-Tabâb (Arabia-S)	Tuff cone of Bal Haf, Harra of	0301-17-
Attalora, Cuddia (Italy)	Cone of Pantelleria	0101-071
Attis (Armenia)	Dome of Ghegam Ridge	0104-07-
Atti-yama [Achi-yama] (Izu Is-Japan)	Dome of Nii-jima	0804-02=
Atuel, Caldera del (Argentina)	Caldera (None) Holocene	**1507-023**
Atug (Vanuatu-SW Pacific)	Cone of Motlav	0507-001
Atuk Mountain (Alaska-W)	Cone of Kookooligit Mountains	1104-05-
Atunapara (D'Entrecasteaux Is)	Therm. feature of Dawson Strait Group	0503-06=
Atuputih (Sumatra)	Cone of Kembar	....
Atwell Peak (Canada)	Dome of Garibaldi	1200-20-
Auau, Puu (Hawaiian Is)	Cone of Kauai	....
Aucanquilcha (Chile-N)	Stratovolcano (None) Pleist.-Fumarolic	....
Auckland Field (New Zealand)	Volcanic field (1, 1350) Radiocarbon	**0401-02=**
Auel (Germany)	Maar of West Eifel Volc Field	0100-01-
Augustine (Alaska-SW)	Lava domes (14, 2006) Historical	**1103-01-**
Aunuu Island (Samoa-SW Pacific)	Tuff cone of Tutuila	0404-02-
Auquihuato, Cerro (Perú)	Cinder cone (None) Holocene?	**1504-001**
Aurora-Bodie (US-Nevada)	Volcanic field (None) Pleistocene	....
Auruhoe [Ngauruhoe] (New Zealand)	Stratovolcano of Tongariro	0401-08=

Ausoles (Spanish for Fumarole Field) see proper name (e.g. San Vicente, Ausoles de)

Name (Subregion)	Type (Eruptions, Most Recent) Status / Relation to Named Volcano	Volcano Number
Austurhraun (Iceland-S)	Fissure vent of Hekla	1702-07=
Auvergne, Monts d' (France)	Synonym of Chaîne des Puys	0100-02-

Bill Rose (Michigan Tech. Univ.)

Conical Volcán **Atitlán** in Guatemala directly overlies the inferred southern margin of the Pleistocene Atitlán III caldera, whose northern rim lies in the background across Lake Atitlán.

Name (Subregion)	Type (Eruptions, Most Recent) Status / Relation to Named Volcano	Volcano Number
Avacha (Kamchatka)	Synonym of Avachinsky	1000-10=
Avachi (Kamchatka)	Cone of Avachinsky	1000-10=
Avachinskaia, Sopka (Kamchatka)	Synonym of Avachinsky	1000-10=
Avachinsky (Kamchatka)	Stratovolcano (55, 2001) Historical	**1000-10=**
Avazan (Armenia)	Dome of Ghegam Ridge	0104-07-
Avdalsmoya (Atlantic-N-Jan Mayen)	Dome of Jan Mayen	1706-01=
Averno (Italy)	Tuff ring of Campi Flegrei	0101-01=
Avlhaugene (Atlantic-N-Jan Mayen)	Tuff ring of Jan Mayen	1706-01=
Avos' Rocks (Kuril Is)	Unknown (None) Pleistocene	....
Awaatua Bay (New Zealand)	Crater of Okataina	0401-05=
Awaru River (New Guinea)	Synonym of Musa River	0503-02=
Awasa (Ethiopia)	Pleist. caldera of Corbetti Caldera	0201-29-
Awatscha (Awatschinskij) (Kamchatka)	Synonym of Avachinsky	1000-10=
'Awayridh, Harrat el- (Arabia-W)	Synonym of 'Uwayrid, Harrat	0301-02=
Awibengkok (Java)	Thermal feature of Perbakti-Gagak	0603-04=
Awoe (Sangihe Is-Indonesia)	Synonym of Awu	0607-04=
Awoeh (Sangihe Is-Indonesia)	Synonym of Karangetang [Api Siau]	0607-02=

Name (Subregion)	Type (Eruptions, Most Recent) Status / Relation to Named Volcano	Volcano Number
Awu (Sangihe Is-Indonesia)	Stratovolcano (16, 2004) Historical	**0607-04=**
Axial Chain (W Indies)	Stratovolcanoes (None) Pleistocene	....
Axial Gardens Vent Field (Pacific-NE)	Thermal feature of Axial Seamount	1301-021
Axial Seamount (Pacific-NE)	Submarine volcano (1, 1998) Historical	**1301-021**
Axlargigur (Iceland-S)	Fissure vent of Hekla	1702-07=
Axusco [Laguna de Asososca] (Nicaragua)	Maar of Pilas, Las	1404-08=
Ayagsh (Aleutian Is)	Synonym of Makushin	1101-31-
Ayakan (Java)	Crater of Guntur	0603-13=
Ayaktas Tepe (Turkey)	Cone of Acigöl-Nevsehir	0103-004
Ayalu (Ethiopia)	Synonym of Ayelu	0201-16=
Ay-alu (Ethiopia)	Synonym of Ayelu	0201-16=
Ayame-daira (Honshu-Japan)	Stratovolcanoes (None) Pleistocene	....

Augustine volcano, forming an island in Cook Inlet, Alaska, has repeatedly collapsed during the past 2000 years, producing debris avalanches whose deposits ring the island, such the one about 400 years ago that formed the hummocks in the foreground.

Name (Subregion)	Type (Eruptions, Most Recent) Status / Relation to Named Volcano	Volcano Number
Ayaqueme, Cerro (México)	Cone of Chichinautzin	1401-08=
Ayarza (Guatemala)	Calderas (None) Pleistocene	....
Ayeco [Malacara] (El Salvador)	Stratovolcano of Santa Ana	1403-02=
Ayelu (Ethiopia)	Stratovolcano (Uncertain) Holocene	**0201-16=**
Ayer Panas (Sumatra)	Thermal feature of Lumut Balai, Bukit	0601-24=
Aygirgolu (Turkey)	Maar of Süphan Dagi	0103-021
Aymond (Chile-S)	Cinder cone of Palei-Aike Volc Field	1508-08-
Ayyalu (Ethiopia)	Synonym of Adwa	0201-17=
Azafatudo, Cerro (Colombia)	Synonym of Sotará	1501-061
Azanaques (Bolivia)	Unknown (None) Post-Miocene	....
Azas Plateau (Russia-SE)	Volcanic field (None) Holocene	**1002-07-**
Azeitona, Pico da (Azores)	Cone of Furnas	1802-10=
Azhdahak (Armenia)	Cone of Ghegam Ridge	0104-07-
Azrou Volc Field (Africa-N)	Volcanic field (None) Quaternary	....
Azucar, Piton de [Pico del Teide] (Canary Is)	Stratovolcano of Tenerife	1803-03-
Azufrado (Costa Rica)	Stratovolcano of Platanar	1405-034
Azufrados, Baños (Guatemala)	Thermal feature of Almolonga	1402-04=
Azufral (Colombia)	Stratovolcano (4, -930) Radiocarbon	**1501-09=**
Azufral (Guatemala)	Thermal feature of Tecuamburro	1402-12=
Azufral De Tuquerres (Colombia)	Synonym of Azufral	1501-09=
Azufral, El (Chile-C)	Crater of Puyehue-Cordón Caulle	1507-15=
Azufrales (Costa Rica)	Thermal feature of Rincón de la Vieja	1405-02=
Azufre (Chile-C)	Caldera of Planchón-Peteroa	1507-04=
Azufre, Baños (Chile-C)	Thermal feature of Planchón-Peteroa	1507-04=
Azufre, Cerro de (Chile-N)	Synonym of Copiapó	1505-14-
Azufre, Cerro de (Chile-N)	Synonym of Lastarria	1505-12=
Azufre, Cerro del (Chile-N)	Stratovolcano (None) Holocene?	**1505-061**
Azufre, El (Chile-N)	Unknown (None) Pleistocene?	....
Azufre, Mt. (Philippines-C)	Thermal feature of Mandalagan	0702-03=
Azufre, Volcán de (Galápagos)	Thermal feature of Negra, Sierra	1503-05=
Azufre, Volcán el (México)	Stratovolcano of Tres Vírgenes	1401-01=
Azufreas, Volcán (Chile-C)	Stratovolcano of Tinguiririca	1507-03=
Azufre-Plachón-Peteroa (Chile-C)	Synonym of Planchón-Peteroa	1507-04=
Azufrera Aguas Calientes, Cerro (Chile-N)	Cone of Cordón de Puntas Negras	1505-101
Azufrera Perro Muerto, Cerro (Chile-N)	Cone of Cordón de Puntas Negras	1505-101
Azufrera Yacimiento, Cerro (Chile-N)	Cone of Cordón de Puntas Negras	1505-101
Azufreras Tuyajto (Chile-N)	Cone of Cordón de Puntas Negras	1505-101
Azufreres, Las [Los Azufres] (Chile-C)	Therm. feature Puyehue-Cordón Caulle	1507-15=
Azufres, Los (México)	Caldera (None) Pleist.-Fumarolic	....
Azufres, Los (Chile-C)	Therm. feature Puyehue-Cordón Caulle	1507-15=
Azul, Cerro (Chile-C)	Stratovolcano (9, 1967) Historical	**1507-06=**
Azul, Cerro (Galápagos)	Shield volcano (14, 2008) Historical	**1503-06=**
Azul, Cerro (Galápagos)	Cone of San Cristóbal	1503-12-
Azul, Cerro (México)	Dome of Zitácuaro-Valle de Bravo	1401-061
Azul, Volcán (Nicaragua)	Cinder cones (None) Holocene	**1404-14-**
Azules, Cerro las Lomas (Costa Rica)	Synonym of Sierpe, Lomas de	....
Azuma (Honshu-Japan)	Stratovolcanoes (19, 1977) Historical	**0803-18=**
Azuma-Kofuji (Honshu-Japan)	Cone of Azuma	0803-18=
Azuma-Kohuzi [Azuma-Kofuji] (Japan)	Cone of Azuma	0803-18=
Azumaya (Honshu-Japan)	Stratovolcano (None) Pleistocene	....
Azuma-yama (Honshu-Japan)	Synonym of Fuji	0803-03=
Azuma-yama (Kyushu-Japan)	Dome of Unzen	0802-10=

B

Name (Subregion)	Type (Eruptions, Most Recent) Status / Relation to Named Volcano	Volcano Number
Ba, Jabal [Jabal Ba'a] (Arabia-W)	Cone of Birk, Harrat al	0301-072
Ba'a, Jabal (Arabia-W)	Cone of Birk, Harrat al	0301-072
Baarley (Germany)	Cinder cone of West Eifel Volc Field	0100-01-
Babase (New Ireland-SW Pacific)	Stratovolcano of Ambitle	0504-02=
Babbingtons Hill (Australia)	Dome of Newer Volcanics Prov	0509-01-
Babilonia, Cerro (Honduras)	Stratovolcano of Yojoa, Lake	1403-15-
Babiy Kamen (Kamchatka)	Dome of Barkhatnaya Sopka	1000-084
Babuyan Claro (Luzon-N of)	Stratovolcanoes (8, 1924) Historical	**0704-03=**
Babuyan, Mt. [Smith Volcano] (Luzon-N of)	Cinder cone of Babuyan Claro	0704-03=
Baby Capulin (US-New Mexico)	Cone of Raton-Clayton	....
Bacauan (Mindanao-Philippines)	Cone of Imbing	....
Baccano (Italy)	Caldera of Sabatini Complex	....
Bachelor (US-Oregon)	Stratovolcano (1, -5800) Tephrochron	**1202-09-**
Bachelor Butte (US-Oregon)	Synonym of Bachelor	1202-09-
Backlockdam (Korea)	Crater of Halla	1006-04-
Bacoli (Italy)	Crater of Campi Flegrei	0101-01=
Bacon-Manito Complex (Luzon-Philippines)	Synonym of Pocdol Mountains	0703-02=
Badak (Java)	Crater of Kelut	0603-28=
Badak, Kawah (Java)	Crater of Tangkubanparahu	0603-09=
Badascony (Hungary)	Shield volcano of Balaton Highland	....
Baddi Koma (Djibouti)	Tuff cone of Ardoukôba	0201-126
Badger Peak (US-California)	Cone of Medicine Lake	1203-02-
Badi (Ethiopia)	Stratovolcano (None) Pleistocene	....
Badillo Crater (México)	Maar of Pinacate	1401-001
Badjini (Indian O.-W)	Cone of Karthala	0303-01=
Badlands (Africa-E)	Synonym of Elmenteita Badlands	0202-071
Badsvallagigir (Iceland-SW)	Crater Row of Reykjanes	1701-02=
Baegdu (China-E)	Synonym of Changbaishan	1005-06-
Baejarhraun (Iceland-S)	Fissure vent of Hekla	1702-07=
Baekdoosan (China-E)	Synonym of Changbaishan	1005-06-
Baerqian (China-E)	Stratovolcano? (None) Pleistocene	....
Baga Togo Uul (Mongolia)	Cinder cone of Khanuy Gol	1003-02-
Bagabag (New Guinea-NE of)	Stratovolcano (None) Quaternary	....
Bagagaure (D'Entrecasteaux Is)	Therm. feature of Dawson Strait Group	0503-06=
Bagana (Bougainville-SW Pacific)	Lava cone (25, 2010) Historical	**0505-02=**
Bagiai (New Guinea-NE of)	Cone of Karkar	0501-03=
Bagum (New Britain-SW Pac)	Synonym of Bangum	....
Bagusa (Africa-C)	Crater of Bunyaruguru	0203-004
Baia (Italy)	Tuff ring of Campi Flegrei	0101-01=
Baia di Levante (Italy)	Thermal feature of Vulcano	0101-05=
Baidjan (Iran)	Thermal feature of Damavand	0302-01-
Bailey (US-Oregon)	Shield volcano (None) Pleistocene	....
Baille-Argent, Plton (W Indies)	Dome of Northern Chain	....
Baishan [Pechan] (China-W)	Cone of Tianshan Volc Group	1004-02-
Baitoushan (China-E)	Synonym of Changbaishan	1005-06-
Baiyuda Volc Field (Africa-N)	Synonym of Bayuda Volc Field	0205-06-
Bajawa (Lesser Sunda Is)	Thermal feature of Inierie	0604-08=
Bakal (Java)	Cone of Arjuno-Welirang	0603-29=
Bakang (Bakangin) (Kamchatka)	Synonym of Bakening	1000-123
Bakanovi (Bougainville-SW Pacific)	Stratovolcano (None) Pleistocene?	....
Bakenin (Kamchatka)	Synonym of Bakening	1000-123
Bakening (Kamchatka)	Stratovolcano (5, -550) Tephrochron	**1000-123**
Baker (US-Washington)	Stratovolcanoes (12, 1880) Historical	**1201-01=**
Baker Hot Springs (US-Washington)	Thermal feature of Baker	1201-01=
Baker Hot Springs [Crater Springs] (US-Utah)	Thermal feature of Fumarole Butte	....
Bakia Warm Springs (Luzon-Philippines)	Thermal feature of Banahaw	0703-05=
Bakkenin (Kamchatka)	Synonym of Bakening	1000-123
Bal Haf, Harra of (Arabia-S)	Volcanic field (None) Holocene	**0301-17-**
Balagan-Tas (Russia-NE)	Cinder cones (None) Pleistocene	....
Balai, Bukit (Sumatra)	Stratovolcano of Lumut Balai, Bukit	0601-24=
Balak (Sumatra)	Caldera of Sekincau Belirang	0601-26=
Balantok (Luzon-Philippines)	Cone of Taal	0703-07=
Balastrera, El Cerrito [Cerro el Cerrito]	Cinder cone of San Salvador	1403-05=
Balatocan (Mindanao-Philippines)	Synonym of Balatukan	0701-072
Balaton Highland (Hungary)	Volcanic field (None) Pleistocene	....
Balatukan (Mindanao-Philippines)	Compound volcano (None) Uncertain	**0701-072**
Balbi (Bougainville-SW Pacific)	Stratovolcano (Uncertain) Holocene	**0505-01=**
Bald Crater (US-Oregon)	Cinder cone of Crater Lake	1202-16-
Bald Knoll (US-Utah)	Cinder cones (None) Holocene	**1207-03-**
Baleng (Africa-W)	Maar of Oku Volc Field	0204-03-
Bali Island (New Britain-SW Pac)	Synonym of Unea	....
Bali, Peak of (Lesser Sunda Is)	Synonym of Agung	0604-02=
Balikesir-Bigadic (Turkey)	Volcanic field (None) Quaternary	....
Balile (Lesser Sunda Is)	Cone of Iliboleng	0604-22=
Balingoan (Mindanao-Philippines)	Synonym of Balatukan	0701-072
Bali-vitu (New Britain-SW Pac)	Synonym of Unea	....
Bali-witu (New Britain-SW Pac)	Synonym of Unea	....
Baljane (Atlantic-N-Jan Mayen)	Cone of Jan Mayen	1706-01=
Ball Butte (US-Oregon)	Cone of Broken Top	....
Ballena, Cerro (Galápagos)	Tuff cone of Negra, Sierra	1503-05=
Balmann, Piton de (Indian O.-W)	Cinder cone of Fournaise, Piton de la	0303-02=
Balmet, Puy (France)	Cone of Chaîne des Puys	0100-02-
Balong Anito (Luzon-Philippines)	Thermal feature of Mariveles	0703-081
Baluan (Admiralty Is-SW Pacific)	Stratovolcano (Uncertain) Holocene?	**0500-02-**
Baluran (Java)	Stratovolcano (None) Holocene?	**0603-351**
Balusan (Luzon-Philippines)	Synonym of Bulusan	0703-01=
Balut (Mindanao-Philippines)	Stratovolcano (None) Fumarolic	**0701-01=**
Bam (New Guinea-NE of)	Stratovolcano (16, 1960) Historical	**0501-01=**
Bamaoqiongzhong (China-W)	Shield volcano of Unnamed	1004-04-
Bambang, Gunung (Java)	Maar of Muria	0603-251

Name (Subregion)	Type (Eruptions, Most Recent) Status / Relation to Named Volcano	Volcano Number
Bambuluwe, Lake (Africa-W)	Maar of Oku Volc Field	0204-03-
Bamni (Armenia)	Synonym of Porak	0104-09-
Bamus (New Britain-SW Pac)	Stratovolcano (4, 1886) Anthropology	**0502-11=**
Ban Chay (SE Asia)	Unknown (None) Pleistocene	....
Ban Chiang Khian (SE Asia)	Unknown (None) Pleistocene	....
Ban Hui Sai (SE Asia)	Unknown (None) Pleistocene	....
Banahao (Luzon-Philippines)	Synonym of Banahaw	0703-05=
Banahaw (Luzon-Philippines)	Complex volcano (Uncertain) Holocene	**0703-05=**
Banahaw de Lucban (Luzon-Philippines)	Stratovolcano of Banahaw	0703-05=
Banajao (Luzon-Philippines)	Synonym of Banahaw	0703-05=
Banban (New Britain-SW Pac)	Stratovolcano (None) Post-Miocene	....
Banbanlongwan (China-E)	Crater of Longgang Group	1005-05-
Bancah Caldera (Sumatra)	Caldera of Marapi	0601-14=
Bancen (Java)	Thermal feature of Merbabu	0603-24=
Banco Di Nisida (Italy)	Tuff cone of Campi Flegrei	0101-01=
Banco Miseno (Italy)	Cone of Campi Flegrei	0101-01=
Banco, El (México)	Maar of Santo Domingo Volc Field	....
Banda Api (Banda Sea)	Caldera (23, 1988) Historical	**0605-09=**
Bandai (Honshu-Japan)	Stratovolcano (11, 1888) Historical	**0803-16=**
Bandaiko Hot Springs (Honshu-Japan)	Thermal feature of Kusatsu-Shirane	0803-12=
Bandai-san (Honshu-Japan)	Synonym of Bandai	0803-16=
Bandama, Caldera de (Canary Is)	Maar of Gran Canaria	1803-04-
Bandera Crater (US-New Mexico)	Cone of Zuni-Bandera	1210-02-
Bandera Lava Field (US-New Mexico)	Synonym of Zuni-Bandera	1210-02-
Bandera, Cerro (US-New Mexico)	Cinder cone of Zuni-Bandera	1210-02-
Bandera, Cerro de la (El Salvador)	Synonym of Conchagua	1403-11=
Banderas, Cerro las (Nicaragua)	Dome of Zapatera	1404-111
Banga-banga (Luzon-Philippines)	Dome of Labo	....
Bangeshan (SE Asia)	Cone of Tengchong	0705-11-
Bango (New Britain-SW Pac)	Synonym of Pago	0502-08=
Bangum (New Britain-SW Pac)	Stratovolcano (None) Pleistocene	....
Bani Abdullah, Harrat (Arabia-W)	Volcanic field of Rahat, Harrat	0301-07=
Bannieres, Puy des (France)	Cone of Chaîne des Puys	0100-02-
Bannoe Lake (Kamchatka)	Maar of Uzon	1000-17=
Banoea Woehoe (Sangihe Is-Indonesia)	Synonym of Banua Wuhu	0607-03=
Baños (Spanish for Spa) see proper name (e.g. Azufrados, Baños)		
Baños, Crateres de los (Chile-C)	Dome of Maule, Laguna del	1507-061
Baños, Los (Argentina)	Thermal feature of Tromen	1507-072
Banos, Nevado de los (Chile-C)	Synonym of Planchón-Peteroa	1507-04=
Bantjah Caldera [Bancah Caldera] (Sumatra)	Caldera of Marapi	0601-14=
Banua Bauja (Banua Bauya) (Indonesia)	Synonym of Banua Wuhu	0607-03=
Banua Wuhu (Sangihe Is-Indonesia)	Submarine volcano (6, 1919) Historical	**0607-03=**
Ban-yagamine (Ryukyu Is)	Stratovolcano of Kuchinoerabu-jima	0802-05=
Banyudeng Hot Spring (Lesser Sunda Is)	Thermal feature of Bratan	0604-001
Barachuma, Gof (Africa-E)	Maar of Marsabit	0202-021
Barahona (Guatemala)	Calderas (None) Pleistocene	....
Barahona, Cerro (Galápagos)	Pyroclastic cone of Negra, Sierra	1503-05=
Bar-Ali (Ethiopia)	Synonym of Dabbayra	0201-114
Bar-Ali (Ethiopia)	Cone of Dabbayra	0201-114
Baranii [Barany] (Kamchatka)	Stratovolcano of Gamchen	1000-21=
Baranii Amphitheater [Barany Amphitheater]	Crater of Opala	1000-08=
Baraniy (Kamchatka)	Unknown (None) Pleistocene	....
Baranskii (Kuril Is)	Synonym of Baransky	0900-08=
Baransky (Kuril Is)	Stratovolcano (3, 1951) Historical	**0900-08=**
Barany (Kamchatka)	Stratovolcano of Gamchen	1000-21=
Barany Amphitheater (Kamchatka)	Crater of Opala	1000-08=
Bararumbo (Africa-N)	Cone of Bayuda Volc Field	0205-06-
Barba (Costa Rica)	Synonym of Barva	1405-05=
Barberena, Cerrito de (Guatemala)	Cinder cone of Cuilapa-Barbarena	1402-111
Barca, Monte (Italy)	Cinder cone of Etna	0101-06=
Bárcena (México-Is)	Cinder cones (1, 1953) Historical	**1401-02=**
Bárdarbunga (Iceland-NE)	Stratovolcano (43, 1910) Historical	**1703-03=**
Bardarlaug (Iceland-W)	Cone of Snaefellsjökull	1700-01=
Bare Mountain (US-Washington)	Cone of West Crater	1201-06-
Bariccia [Bericha] (Ethiopia)	Stratovolcano of Boset-Bericha	0201-21-
Baricha [Bericha] (Ethiopia)	Stratovolcano of Boset-Bericha	0201-21-
Barik (New Guinea-NE of)	Stratovolcano of Umboi	0501-06=
Barker Crater (Australia)	Crater of Chudleigh Volc Province	....
Barker Crater (Australia)	Crater of McBride Volc Province	....
Barkhatnaya (Kamchatka)	Cone of Vilyuchik	1000-083
Barkhatnaya Sopka (Kamchatka)	Lava domes (1, -3550) Tephrochron	**1000-084**
Barme, Puy de (France)	Cone of Chaîne des Puys	0100-02-
Barnabe, Pico (Azores)	Dome of Agua de Pau	1802-09=
Barnaborg (Iceland-W)	Cone of Ljósufjöll	1700-03=
Barombe Koto, Lake (Africa-W)	Maar of Tombel Graben	0204-011
Barombe Mbo, Lake (Africa-W)	Maar of Tombel Graben	0204-011
Baros (Sumatra)	Cone of Sibayak	0601-07=
Barrancas, Cerro (Chile-C)	Cone of Maule, Laguna del	1507-061
Barrancas, Volcán (Chile-C)	Dome of Maule, Laguna del	1507-061
Barranco Negro, Cerro (El Salvador)	Cinder cone of Cinotepeque, Cerro	1403-051
Barranco, El (Nicaragua)	Maar of Cosigüina	1404-01=
Barranes Colorado (Chile-S)	Cone of Huequi	1508-03=
Barrantes, Loma (Costa Rica)	Cinder cone of Platanar	1405-034
Barren Island (Andaman Is-Indian O)	Stratovolcano (9, 2010) Historical	**0600-01=**
Barrera, Cerro (Costa Rica)	Cone of Tenorio	1405-031
Barrier, The (Africa-E)	Shield volcano (10, 1921) Historical	**0202-03=**
Barril, Cerro el (México)	Cinder cone of Moctezuma Volc Field	....
Barrine, Lake (Australia)	Maar of Atherton Volc Province	....
Barrington Island (Galápagos)	Synonym of Santa Fe	....
Bartholome, Pic (Africa-C)	Stratovolcano of Karisimbi	0203-04-
Bartholomew Island (Galápagos)	Crater of Santiago	1503-09=
Bartoi Group (Russia-SE)	Cinder cone of Dgida Basin	....
Bartolinas, Cerro (México)	Dome of San Pedro	....
Baru (Java)	Crater of Gede	0603-06=
Barú (Panamá)	Stratovolcano (8, 1550) Historical	**1406-01-**
Baru [Gunung Barujari] (Lesser Sunda Is)	Cone of Rinjani	0604-03=
Baru, Kaba (Sumatra)	Crater of Kaba	0601-22=
Baru, Kawah (Java)	Crater of Papandayan	0603-10=
Baru, Kawah (Java)	Crater of Tangkubanparahu	0603-09=
Barujari, Gunung (Lesser Sunda Is)	Cone of Rinjani	0604-03=
Baruku (Solomon Is-SW Pacific)	Synonym of Mborokua	....
Barun Khobol (Russia-SE)	Stratovolcano of Dgida Basin	....
Barun-Nerte-Ula (Mongolia)	Cone of Dariganga Volc Field	1003-04-
Barus, Bukit (Sumatra)	Cone of Sibayak	0601-07=
Baruta (Africa-C)	Stratovolcano of Nyiragongo	0203-03=
Barva (Costa Rica)	Complex volcano (1, -6050) Tephrochron	**1405-05=**
Bas Dong Nai (SE Asia)	Volcanic field (None) Holocene?	**0705-05-**
Bas Song Be (SE Asia)	Volcanic field (None) Pleistocene	....
Basak, Bukit (Sumatra)	Unknown (None) Post-Miocene	....
Basalt Knob (Alaska-E)	Cone (None) Quaternary	....
Basanjo (Africa-E)	Synonym of Lengai, Ol Doinyo	0202-12=
Basar (Sumatra)	Synonym of Besar	0601-25=
Basen (Atlantic-N-Jan Mayen)	Cone of Jan Mayen	1706-01=
Basile, Pico de (Africa-W)	Synonym of Santa Isabel	0204-004
Basiluzzo (Italy)	Dome of Panarea	0101-041
Bass Marle (Africa-E)	Synonym of Central Island	0202-01=
Basso Narok (Africa-E)	Synonym of Central Island	0202-01=
Bastioni Hill (Africa-E)	Dome of Meru	0202-16=
Baston (Colombia)	Crater of Galeras	1501-08=
Basu (México)	Cinder cone of San Quintín Volc Field	1401-002
Batang (Java)	Dome of Merapi	0603-25=
Batapona Mountain (Admiralty Is-SW Pacific)	Cone of Baluan	0500-02-
Batchelors Crater (Australia)	Crater of Chudleigh Volc Province	....
Batea, La (México)	Cone of Michoacán-Guanajuato	1401-06=
Bathhouse Spring (US-New Mexico)	Thermal feature of Valles Caldera	....
Batidoras, Las (Nicaragua)	Thermal feature of Cosigüina	1404-01=

Conical debris-avalanche hummocks in the foreground orignated from the 1888 collapse of **Bandai** volcano in Japan. Steam plumes rise from fissures in the large horseshoe-shaped crater in the background created by the collapse. The 1.5 km³ debris avalanche dammed river drainages, forming five new lakes.

Name (Subregion)	Type (Eruptions, Most Recent) Status Relation to Named Volcano	Volcano Number
Batoe, Batu (Dutch spelling of, and Indonesian word for Mt.) see proper name (e.g. Angus, Batu)		
Batoer (Lesser Sunda Is)	Synonym of Batur	0604-01=
Batok (Java)	Cinder cone of Tengger Caldera	0603-31=
Bator (Lesser Sunda Is)	Synonym of Batur	0604-01=
Batshraun (Iceland-NE)	Fissure vent of Askja	1703-06=
Batu Field (Sumatra)	Thermal feature of Kembar	....
Batuan, Mt. (Luzon-Philippines)	Cone of Bulusan	0703-01=
Batuharang, Dolok (Sumatra)	Cone of Toba	0601-09=
Batukau (Lesser Sunda Is)	Stratovolcano of Bratan	0604-001
Batukau (Lesser Sunda Is)	Synonym of Tambanan	....
Batukolok (Sulawesi-Indonesia)	Thermal feature of Tondano Caldera	0606-07-
Batulao, Mt. (Luzon-Philippines)	Stratovolcano of Taal	0703-07=
Batur (Lesser Sunda Is)	Caldera (26, 2000) Historical	**0604-01=**
Baturiti Hot Spring (Lesser Sunda Is)	Thermal feature of Bratan	0604-001
Batuwalang Merapi (Java)	Stratovolcano of Merapi	0603-25=
Baúl, El [Cerro Tecún Umán] (Guatemala)	Dome of Almolonga	1402-04=
Bay of Islands (New Zealand)	Synonym of Kaikohe-Bay of Islands	0401-01=
Bayabes (Luzon-Philippines)	Dome of Labo	....

A lava flow at the right issues from a fissure in 1952 on the flank of **Bárcena** volcano in the Revillagigedo Islands west of México, forming a peninsula about 300 m wide that extends about 230 m out to sea. A dark-colored lava dome was also emplaced in the summit crater.

Name (Subregion)	Type (Eruptions, Most Recent) Status Relation to Named Volcano	Volcano Number
Ba-yan (Taiwan)	Thermal feature of Tatun Group	0801-032
Bayan-Darkhoo-Ula (Mongolia)	Cone of Ika-Togo-Ula	....
Bayan-Tsagan (Mongolia)	Cone of Dariganga Volc Field	1003-04-
Bayan-Tsagan-Dzurikhe (Mongolia)	Crater of Orkhon Gol	....
Bayaquitos, Mt. (Luzon-Philippines)	Cone of San Pablo Volc Field	0703-06=
Bayda, Jabal (Arabia-W)	Tuff cone of Khaybar, Harrat	0301-06=
Bayo (Chile-N)	Synonym of Aguas Delgadas	....
Bayo, Cerro (Argentina)	Stratovolcano of Antofalla	....
Bayo, Cerro (Chile-N)	Complex volcano (None) Holocene	**1505-122**
Bayo, Cerro (Argentina)	Cone of Tromen	1507-072
Bayo, Cerro (Argentina)	Dome of Tromen	1507-072
Bayonesu-Gansho (Izu Is-Japan)	Synonym of Bayonnaise Rocks	0804-07=
Bayonnaise Reef (Izu Is-Japan)	Synonym of Bayonnaise Rocks	0804-07=
Bayonnaise Rocks (Izu Is-Japan)	Submarine volcano (15, 1970) Historical	**0804-07=**
Bayuda Volc Field (Africa-N)	Cinder cones (1, 850) Radiocarbon	**0205-06-**
Bayuyo (Canary Is)	Vent of Fuerteventura	1803-05-
Bazman (Iran)	Stratovolcano (None) Fumarolic	**0302-03-**
Beacon Hill [Ndughore] (Solomon Is)	Dome of Kolombangara	....
Beagle (Galápagos)	Tuff cone of Darwin	1503-03=
Bear Butte (US-Oregon)	Cone of Crater Lake	1202-16-
Bear Wallow Butte (US-California)	Cinder cone of Tumble Buttes	1203-06-
Bearhead Peak (US-New Mexico)	Dome of Valles Caldera	....
Bearpaw Butte (US-California)	Cone of Medicine Lake	1203-02-
Beaufort Island (Antarctica)	Stratovolcano (None) Quaternary	....
Beauloup, Maar de (France)	Maar of Chaîne des Puys	0100-02-
Beaunit, Cratere de (France)	Maar of Chaîne des Puys	0100-02-
Beaver Ridge (US-Utah)	Vent of Black Rock Desert	1207-05-
Becco, Mt. (Italy)	Cone of Vulsini	0101-003
Bedali, Ranu (Java)	Maar of Lamongan	0603-32=
Bedr, Hala-'l- (Arabia-W)	Cone of 'Uwayrid, Harrat	0301-02=
Bedul (Admiralty Is-SW Pacific)	Cone of St. Andrew Strait	0500-01=
Beehives, the (New Zealand)	Dome of Taranaki [Egmont]	0401-03=
Beehives, the [Davapia Rocks] (New Britain)	Cone of Rabaul	0502-14=
Beerenberg (Atlantic-N-Jan Mayen)	Stratovolcano of Jan Mayen	1706-01=
Beethoven Peninsula (Antarctica)	Volcanic field (None) Pleistocene	....
Begour (Africa-N)	Maar of Tôh, Tarso	0205-009
Behm Canal-Rudyerd Bay (Alaska-E)	Cinder cones (None) Holocene?	**1105-07-**
Beigelaqiushan (China-E)	Cone of Wudalianchi	1005-03-
Beihuokou (China-W)	Cinder cone of Kunlun Volc Group	1004-03-
Bejenado (Canary Is)	Stratovolcano of La Palma	1803-01-
Bekel, Gunung (Java)	Dome of Penanggungan	0603-291
Bekulap (Sumatra)	Lava domes? (None) Pleistocene	....
Belaia Sopka (Kamchatka)	Synonym of Ichinsky	1000-28=
Belaya (Aleutian Is)	Synonym of Great Sitkin	1101-12-
Belenkaya (Kamchatka)	Stratovolcano (None) Holocene	**1000-042**
Belerang, Gunung (Sulawesi-Indonesia)	Synonym of Colo [Una Una]	0606-01=
Belesme (Turkey)	Cone of Erciyes Dagi	0103-01=

Name (Subregion)	Type (Eruptions, Most Recent) Status Relation to Named Volcano	Volcano Number
Belfond (W Indies)	Dome of Qualibou	1600-14=
Beliankin (Kamchatka)	Stratovolcano of Akademia Nauk	1000-125
Beliankin [Belyankin] (Kamchatka)	Fissure vent of Kliuchevskoi	1000-26=
Beliling, Gunung (Lesser Sunda Is)	Unknown (None) Quaternary	....
Belinda, Mount (Antarctica)	Cone of Montagu Island	1900-081
Belirang (Sumatra)	Thermal feature of Hulubelu	0601-28=
Belirang (Sumatra)	Caldera of Sekincau Belirang	0601-26=
Belirang (Sumatra)	Crater of Sumbing	0601-18=
Belirang, Gunung (Sumatra)	Synonym of Kunyit	0601-171
Belirang-Beriti (Sumatra)	Compound volcano (None) Fumarolic	**0601-20=**
Belknap (US-Oregon)	Shield volcanoes (3, 480) Radiocarbon	**1202-06-**
Bellaire, Volcà (Spain)	Cone of Olot Volc Field	0100-03-
Bellavista (Italy)	Crater of Campi Flegrei	0101-01=
Bellavista, Cerro (Chile-C)	Cinder cone of Carrán-Los Venados	1507-14=
Bellavista, Loma (Ecuador)	Cinder cone of Licto	1502-081
Bellevue Mountain (W Indies)	Dome of Diables, Morne aux	1600-08=
Bellingshausen Island (Antarctica)	Submarine vent of Thule Islands	1900-07=
Bellisle Mountain (US-New Mexico)	Cone of Raton-Clayton	....
Bellizzi, Cuddie (Italy)	Vent of Pantelleria	0101-071
Below, Mount [Mount Talawe] (New Britain)	Stratovolcano of Langila	0502-01=
Belu (Lesser Sunda Is)	Cone of Inierie	0604-08=
Belu, Wai (Sumatra)	Thermal feature of Hulubelu	0601-28=
Belvedere (Italy)	Crater of Campi Flegrei	0101-01=
Belvedere (México)	Cone of Zitácuaro-Valle de Bravo	1401-061
Bely (Kamchatka)	Shield volcanoes (None) Holocene?	**1000-64-**
Belyankin (Kamchatka)	Fissure vent of Kliuchevskoi	1000-26=
Belyi (Kamchatka)	Synonym of Bely	1000-64-
Ben Lomond (New Zealand)	Dome of Maroa	0401-061
Ben Lomond (New Zealand)	Dome of Taupo	0401-07=
Benatan, Bukit (Sumatra)	Unknown (None) Post-Miocene	....
Benbow (Vanuatu-SW Pacific)	Crater of Ambrym	0507-04=
Benda (New Britain-SW Pac)	Synonym of Dakataua	0502-04=
Bengo, Cerro (El Salvador)	Cinder cone of Apastepeque Field	1403-071
Beni Hilal, Harra (Arabia-W)	Synonym of Birk, Harrat al	0301-072
Beni Maimun (Arabia-S)	Crater of Arhab, Harra of	0301-09-
Beni Zubeir (Arabia-S)	Crater of Arhab, Harra of	0301-09-
Bepagut (Sumatra)	Unknown (None) Post-Miocene	....
Beppu (Kyushu-Japan)	Thermal feature of Tsurumi	0802-13=
Berapi (Sumatra)	Synonym of Kerinci	0601-17=
Berapi (Sumatra)	Synonym of Marapi	0601-14=
Berapi-Elok (Sumatra)	Crater of Kerinci	0601-17=
Bercek, Kawah (Java)	Thermal feature of Kamojang, Kawah	....
Beresowskaja (Kamchatka)	Synonym of Karymsky	1000-13=
Berezovaia Sopka (Kamchatka)	Synonym of Karymsky	1000-13=
Berezovy (Kamchatka)	Stratovolcano of Maly Semiachik	1000-14=
Berezovy (Kamchatka)	Cinder cone of Zavaritsky	1000-124
Berg (Kuril Is)	Somma volcano of Kolokol Group	0900-12=
Berg Isi [Jabal el-Esi] (Arabia-S)	Stratovolcano of Dhamar, Harras of	0301-12-
Bergholl (Iceland-SW)	Shield volcano of Reykjanes	1701-02=
Bergje (W Indies)	Dome of Northern Centres	....
Bergje (W Indies)	Dome of Quill, The	1600-02=
Berguent Volc Field (Africa-N)	Lava domes (None) Quaternary	....
Bergvatnsarhraun (Iceland-NE)	Crater Row of Grímsvötn	1703-01=
Bericcio (Ethiopia)	Pumice cone of Bora-Bericcio	0201-24-
Bericha (Ethiopia)	Synonym of Bora-Bericcio	0201-24-
Bericha (Ethiopia)	Stratovolcano of Boset-Bericha	0201-21-
Bering (Kamchatka)	Fissure vent of Kliuchevskoi	1000-26=
Beritaribi (Kuril Is)	Synonym of Berutarube	0900-04=
Beritia (Romania)	Volcanic field (None) Pleistocene	....
Berlin (Antarctica)	Shield volcanoes (1, -8350) Ar/Ar	**1900-022**
Berlín (El Salvador)	Pleistocene caldera of Tecapa	1403-08=
Berlín-Tecapa (El Salvador)	Synonym of Tecapa	1403-08=
Bermeja, Montana (Canary Is)	Cone of Fuerteventura	1803-05-
Bermeja, Montana (Canary Is)	Cone of Lanzarote	1803-06-
Berna (Atlantic-N-Jan Mayen)	Cone of Jan Mayen	1706-01=
Bernadskogo [Vernadskiy] (Kamchatka)	Fissure vent of Kliuchevskoi	1000-26=
Berrazales (Canary Is)	Thermal feature of Gran Canaria	1803-04-
Berritarabenobori (Kuril Is)	Synonym of Berutarube	0900-04=
Berti Hills (Africa-N)	Synonym of Kutum Volc Field	0205-04-
Bertjek, Kawah [Kawah Bercek] (Java)	Thermal feature of Kamojang, Kawah	....
Beru (Ethiopia)	Volcanic field (None) Holocene	**0201-191**
Berutarube (Kuril Is)	Stratovolcano (Uncertain) Holocene	**0900-04=**
Besar (Sumatra)	Stratovolcano? (1, 1940) Historical	**0601-25=**
Besar, Kaba [Lama, Kaba] (Sumatra)	Crater of Kaba	0601-22=
Beser (Java)	Stratovolcano of Sumbing	0603-22=
Bessie Butte (US-Oregon)	Cone of Newberry	1202-11-
Besymyannaya (Kamchatka)	Synonym of Bezymianny	1000-25=
Beta (Russia-NE)	Cinder cone of Aluchin Group	....
Betafo (Madagascar)	Cone of Ankaratra Field	0303-015
Betung (Sumatra)	Cone of Rantai-Betung	....
Beyonesu-Retugan (Izu Is-Japan)	Synonym of Bayonnaise Rocks	0804-07=
Bezymianny (Kamchatka)	Stratovolcano (64, 2010) Historical	**1000-25=**
Bezymjannaja Sopka (Kamchatka)	Synonym of Bezymianny	1000-25=
Bezymyannaya (Kamchatka)	Dome of Uzon	1000-17=
Bezymyannyi (Kamchatka)	Synonym of Bezymianny	1000-25=
Biam (New Guinea-NE of)	Synonym of Bam	0501-01=
Biao, Pico (Africa-W)	Synonym of San Joaquin	0204-003
Bibi, Gunung (Java)	Cone of Merapi	0603-25=
Bibinoi (Halmahera-Indonesia)	Stratovolcanoes (None) Holocene	**0608-073**
Bichbalick [Pechan] (China-W)	Cone of Tianshan Volc Group	1004-02-
Biei-dake (Hokkaido-Japan)	Stratovolcano of Tokachi	0805-05=
Biei-Fuji (Hokkaido-Japan)	Stratovolcano of Tokachi	0805-05=
Biem (New Guinea-NE of)	Synonym of Bam	0501-01=
Biete Mengest (Ethiopia)	Tuff ring of Bishoftu Volc Field	0201-22-

Name (Subregion)	Type (Eruptions, Most Recent) Status Relation to Named Volcano	Volcano Number
Big Ben (Indian O.-S)	Stratovolcano of Heard	0304-01=
Big Bomb Crater (US-Oregon)	Cinder cone of Diamond Craters	1202-17-
Big Bunchgrass (US-Oregon)	Pyroclastic cone (None) Pleistocene	....
Big Cave (US-California)	Shield volcano (None) Pleistocene	....
Big Cinder Butte (US-Idaho)	Cinder cone of Craters of the Moon	1204-02-
Big Craters (US-Idaho)	Cone of Craters of the Moon	1204-02-
Big Glass Mountain [Glass Mountain] (US)	Dome of Medicine Lake	1203-02-
Big Green Hill (Atlantic-S)	Cinder cone of Tristan da Cunha	1806-01=
Big Hill (Australia)	Cone of Newer Volcanics Prov	0509-01-
Big Hole (US-Oregon)	Maar of Fort Rock Volc Field	....
Big John (New Zealand)	Former crater of White Island	0401-04=
Big Lava Bed Cone (US-Washington)	Cinder cone of Indian Heaven	1201-07-
Big Mt. Gulu [Mt. Gulu] (New Britain-SW Pac)	Cone of Lotomgan Group	....
Big Mt. Worri (New Britain-SW Pac)	Cone of Garua Harbour	0502-06=
Big Obsidian Flow (US-Oregon)	Vent of Newberry	1202-11-
Big Pine Volc Field (US-California)	Cinder cones (None) Pleistocene	....
Big Sand Butte (US-California)	Cone of Medicine Lake	1203-02-
Bihadi (Africa-N)	Crater of Bayuda Volc Field	0205-06-
Bihiram (Africa-C)	Cone of Karisimbi	0203-04-
Bihunde (Africa-C)	Cone of Nyamuragira	0203-02=
Bijagua (Costa Rica)	Dome of Tenorio	1405-031
Bijar Volc Field (Iran)	Cinder cones (None) Pleistocene	....
Bijiashan (China-E)	Cone of Wudalianchi	1005-03-
Bikin Plateau Volc Field (Russia-SE)	Fissure vent of Sikhote-Alin	1002-01-
Bil Tepe (Turkey)	Dome of Erciyes Dagi	0103-01=
Bilate River Field (Ethiopia)	Maars (None) Holocene	**0201-291**
Bilibin (Kuril Is)	Cone of Vernadskii Ridge	0900-37-
Biliran (Philippines-C)	Compound volcano (1, 1939) Historical	**0702-08=**
Biliukaya [Bilyukai] (Kamchatka)	Fissure vent of Kliuchevskoi	1000-26=
Bill Williams Mt. (US-Arizona)	Cone of San Francisco Volc Field	....
Billy Mitchell (Bougainville-SW Pacific)	Pyroclastic shield (2, 1580) Radiocarbon	**0505-011**
Bilma, Montaña (Canary Is)	Cinder cone of Tenerife	1803-03-
Bilyukai (Kamchatka)	Fissure vent of Kliuchevskoi	1000-26=
Bilyukai (Kamchatka)	Fissure vent of Kliuchevskoi	1000-26=
Binalik (Alaska-W)	Maar of Nunivak Island	1104-02-
Binangunan, Mt. (Sulawesi-Indonesia)	Stratovolcano of Ambang	0606-02=
Bindloe (Galápagos)	Synonym of Marchena	1503-08=
Binem (Java)	Cone of Dieng Volc Complex	0603-20=
Binga (Mindanao-Philippines)	Dome of Paco	0701-09-
Binintiang Malaki (Luzon-Philippines)	Cone of Taal	0703-07=
Binintiang Malaqui [Binintiang Malaki] (Luzon)	Cone of Taal	0703-07=
Binintiang Munti (Luzon-Philippines)	Cone of Taal	0703-07=
Binna (Atlantic-N-Jan Mayen)	Dome of Jan Mayen	1706-01=
Binone (Mindanao-Philippines)	Cinder cone of Camiguin	0701-08=
Bintacan, Mt. (Luzon-Philippines)	Stratovolcano of Bulusan	0703-01=
Binuluan (Luzon-Philippines)	Stratovolcano of Ambalatungan Group	0703-088
Biokos' (Kamchatka)	Fissure vent of Kliuchevskoi	1000-26=
Bir Ali (Arabia-S)	Synonym of Bal Haf, Harra of	0301-17-
Bir Bahrahut (Bir Bahut) (Arabia-S)	Synonym of Bir Borhut	0301-18-
Bir Barhout (Bir Barhut) (Arabia-S)	Synonym of Bir Borhut	0301-18-
Bir Borhut (Arabia-S)	Volcanic field (Uncertain) Holocene?	**0301-18-**
Birao (Hokkaido-Japan)	Stratovolcanoes (None) Pleistocene	....
Birap (New Guinea)	Cone of Sugarloaf	....
Bird Mountain (US-Washington)	Shield volcano of Indian Heaven	1201-07-
Bird Nest Island (Africa-E)	Crater of Central Island	0202-01=
Birk, Harrat al (Arabia-W)	Volcanic field (None) Holocene	**0301-072**
Biro-yama (Ryukyu Is)	Stratovolcano of Akuseki-jima	0802-022
Birua (Africa-C)	Cone of Visoke	0203-05-
Bisaroques, Volcà les (Spain)	Cone of Olot Volc Field	0100-03-
Bisati Ndubi (Africa-C)	Cone of Visoke	0203-05-
Bisentina, Isola (Italy)	Cone of Vulsini	0101-003
Bishamon-dake (Honshu-Japan)	Stratovolcano (None) Pleistocene	....
Bishan Waka (Ethiopia)	Pit crater of Tepi	0201-292
Bishoftu Hayk (Ethiopia)	Tuff ring of Bishoftu Volc Field	0201-22-
Bishoftu Volc Field (Ethiopia)	Fissure vents (None) Holocene	**0201-22-**
Bishusha (Africa-C)	Cone of Nyamuragira	0203-02=
Bisma (Java)	Cone of Dieng Volc Complex	0603-20=
Bismarck, Lago (Chile-S)	Maar of Palei-Aike Volc Field	1508-08-
Bismo [Bisma] (Java)	Cone of Dieng Volc Complex	0603-20=
Bisoke (Bisoko) (Africa-C)	Synonym of Visoke	0203-05-
Bitgood, Mt. (Antarctica)	Cone of Fosdick Mountains	....
Bitingan, Kawah (Java)	Crater of Dieng Volc Complex	0603-20=
Bitivogala (Solomon Is-SW Pacific)	Crater of Savo	0505-07=
Bitjara, Lake (Halmahera-Indonesia)	Maar of Ibu	0608-03=
Bituin (Luzon-Philippines)	Dome of Pinatubo	0703-083
Biu Plateau (Africa-W)	Volcanic field (None) Holocene?	**0204-05-**
Biwai Hills (New Guinea)	Synonym of Biwau Hills	....
Biwa-ike (Kyushu-Japan)	Crater of Kirishima	0802-09=
Biwanokuba (Kyushu-Japan)	Vent of Unzen	0802-10=
Biwau Hills (New Guinea)	Pyroclastic cones (None) Pleistocene	....
Bjallagigar (Iceland-S)	Fissure vent of Hekla	1702-07=
Bjarnarey (Iceland-S)	Cone of Vestmannaeyjar	1702-01=
Bjarnarfell (Iceland-SW)	Cone of Geysir	....
Bjarnarflag (Iceland-NE)	Crater Row of Krafla	1703-08=
Bjarnargigar [Bjarnarflag] (Iceland-NE)	Crater Row of Krafla	1703-08=
Black Bluffs (Alaska-W)	Tuff cone of St. Paul Island	1104-01-
Black Butte (US-California)	Pyroclastic cone (None) Pleistocene	....
Black Butte (US-Oregon)	Stratovolcano (None) Pleistocene	....
Black Butte (US-California)	Dome of Shasta	1203-01-
Black Butte [Cinder Cone] (US-California)	Cinder cone of Lassen Volc Center	1203-08-
Black Butte Crater (US-Idaho)	Shield volc. of Shoshone Lava Field	1204-01-
Black Buttes (US-Washington)	Stratovolcano of Baker	1201-01=
Black Cone (US-Nevada)	Cone of Crater Flat	....
Black Crater (US-Oregon)	Shield volcanoes (None) Pleistocene	....

Name (Subregion)	Type (Eruptions, Most Recent) Status Relation to Named Volcano	Volcano Number
Black Crater (El Salvador)	Dome of Tecapa	1403-08=
Black Crater (US-California)	Synonym of Whaleback	....
Black Forest (Mariana Is-C Pacific)	Thermal feature of East Diamante	0804-201
Black Hill (Australia)	Cone of Newer Volcanics Prov	0509-01-
Black Hill (Australia)	Cone of Nulla Volc Province	....
Black Hump (US-Oregon)	Dome of North Sister Field	1202-07-
Black Knob (Antarctica)	Cone of Hut Point Peninsula	....
Black Knoll (US-Utah)	Cinder cone of Bald Knoll	1207-03-
Black Mountain (US-California)	Cone of Medicine Lake	1203-02-
Black Mountain (Africa-E)	Synonym of Meru	0202-16=
Black Peak (Alaska Peninsula)	Stratovolcano (1, -1900) Radiocarbon	**1102-08-**
Black Peak (Alaska Peninsula)	Synonym of Veniaminof	1102-07-
Black Point (Hawaiian Is)	Cone of Koolau	....
Black Point (US-California)	Cone of Mono Lake Volc Field	1203-11-
Black Rock Desert (US-Utah)	Volcanic field (1, 1290) Radiocarbon	**1207-05-**
Black Rock Volcano (US-Utah)	Cone of Black Rock Desert	1207-05-
Black Tank (US-California)	Cone of Cima Lava Field	....
Black Top Butte (US-Idaho)	Cone of Craters of the Moon	1204-02-
Black Tusk, the (Canada)	Stratovolcano of Garibaldi Lake	1200-19-
Blackfly Tuya (Canada)	Tuya of Tuya Volc Field	1200-031
Blackfoot Lava Field (US-Idaho)	Cinder cones (None) Pleistocene	....
Blacks Mountain (US-California)	Shield volcano (None) Pleistocene	....
Blacktop (Australia)	Cone of McBride Volc Province	....
Blacktop, Mt. (Australia)	Cone of McBride Volc Province	....
Blackwood, Mt. (Australia)	Cone of Newer Volcanics Prov	0509-01-
Bláfell (Iceland-SW)	Tuya (None) Pleistocene	....
Bláfjall (Iceland-NE)	Tuya (None) Pleistocene	....
Bláhnúkur (Iceland-S)	Tuya of Torfajökull	1702-05=
Blakiston (Kuril Is)	Synonym of Tao-Rusyr Caldera	0900-31=
Blanca (México)	Maar of Michoacán-Guanajuato	1401-06=
Blanca, Caldera (Canary Is)	Crater of Lanzarote	1803-06-
Blanca, La (Argentina)	Cinder cone of Unnamed	....
Blanca, Montana (Canary Is)	Cone of Lanzarote	1803-06-
Blanca, Montaña (Canary Is)	Fissure vent of Tenerife	1803-03-
Blancas, Calderas (Canary Is)	Cone of Fuerteventura	1803-05-
Blancas, Lomas (Chile-C)	Stratovolcano (None) Holocene	**1507-064**
Blanche Bay (New Britain-SW Pac)	Synonym of Rabaul	0502-14=
Blanche Crater (US-Idaho)	Cinder cone of Shoshone Lava Field	1204-01-
Blanco del Robledo, Cerro (Argentina)	Dome of Robledo	1505-21-
Blanco, Cerro (El Salvador)	Thermal feature of Apaneca Range	1403-01=
Blanco, Cerro (Chile-C)	Stratovolcano of Chillán, Nevados de	1507-07=
Blanco, Cerro (México)	Shield volc. of Michoacán-Guanajuato	1401-06=
Blanco, Cerro (México)	Cinder cone of Moctezuma Volc Field	....
Blaufdel [Burfell I Olfusi] (Iceland-SW)	Shield volcano of Hengill	1701-05=
Blerang-beriti (Sumatra)	Synonym of Belirang-Beriti	0601-20=
Bligh Island (Vanuatu-SW Pacific)	Synonym of Ureparapara	....
Blik (Mindanao-Philippines)	Synonym of Blit	....
Blit (Mindanao-Philippines)	Unknown (None) Pleistocene	....
Blizhnaya Ploskaya [Krestovsky]	Stratovolcano of Ushkovsky	1000-261
Blizhny Ploski [Krestovsky] (Kamchatka)	Stratovolcano of Ushkovsky	1000-261

Katia and Maurice Krafft

A pristine satellitic tuff cone of **The Barrier** volcano rises 180 m above Lake Turkana in northern Kenya adjacent to a lava flow (top) from The Barrier.

Name (Subregion)	Type (Eruptions, Most Recent) Status Relation to Named Volcano	Volcano Number
Bliznets (Kamchatka)	Stratovolcano (None) Holocene?	**1000-49-**
Bliznetsy (Kamchatka)	Lava cone (1, -1060) Radiocarbon	**1000-552**
Blocky Cone (Alaska Peninsula)	Cone of Aniakchak	1102-09-
Blosseville Island (New Guinea-NE of)	Synonym of Kadovar	0501-002
Blowouts, the (US-Oregon)	Vent of Devils Garden	1202-12-
Blue Lake (Australia)	Tuff ring of Newer Volcanics Prov.	0509-01-
Blue Lake (Kermadec Is)	Crater of Raoul Island	0402-03=
Blue Lake (New Zealand)	Crater of Tongariro	0401-08=
Blue Lake Crater (US-Oregon)	Maar (1, 680) Radiocarbon	**1202-03-**
Blue Mountain (Alaska Peninsula)	Lava domes (None) Pleistocene	....
Blue Mountain (Australia)	Dome of Newer Volcanics Prov	0509-01-
Blue, Volcán (Nicaragua)	Synonym of Azul, Volcán	1404-14-
Bluff, the (Australia)	Cone of Newer Volcanics Prov	0509-01-
Blumbang (Java)	Dome of Muria	0603-251
Blup Blup (New Guinea-NE of)	Stratovolcano (None) Holocene	**0501-001**
Bm-caldera (Greece)	Pleistocene caldera of Santorini	0102-04=

Name (Subregion)	Type (Eruptions, Most Recent) Status Relation to Named Volcano	Volcano Number
Bo Kham (SE Asia)	Cone of Bokeo Volc Field	....
Boat Cove (Kermadec Is)	Synonym of Raoul Island	0402-03=
Bobadilla, Crater (Chile-C)	Cone of Maule, Laguna del	1507-061
Bobaomby (Madagascar)	Cone of Ambre-Bobaomby	0303-011
Bobo (Lesser Sunda Is)	Thermal feature of Inierie	0604-08=
Bobopajo (Halmahera-Indonesia)	Caldera of Jailolo	0608-051
Bobrof (Aleutian Is)	Stratovolcano (None) Holocene?	**1101-10-**
Bobs Hill (US-Oregon)	Cone of Boring Lava	....
Boca Cangrejo (Canary Is)	Cinder cone of Tenerife	1803-03-
Boca Tronadora (El Salvador)	Fissure vent of San Salvador	1403-05=
Bocas de Fogo (Azores)	Vent of Pico	1802-02=
Bocas Marie (Canary Is)	Crater of Tenerife	1803-03-
Bocca del Viulo (Italy)	Vent of Vesuvius	0101-02=
Bocca Grande (Colombia)	Crater of Cumbal	1501-10=
Bocca Nuova (Italy)	Crater of Etna	0101-06=
Bocharova ? (Alaska Peninsula)	Synonym of Ugashik-Peulik	1102-13-
Bode Ameda Hayk (Ethiopia)	Crater of Bilate River Field	0201-291
Boeal Boeali (Sumatra)	Synonym of Sibualbuali	0601-11=
Boedoegasoe, Gunung [Gunung Budugasu]	Cone of Arjuno-Welirang	0603-29=
Boekit, Boer (Dutch: of Indonesian word for Hill, Mt.) see proper name (e.g. Moetelong, Boer)		
Boekitdaoen (Sumatra)	Synonym of Daun, Bukit	0601-21=
Boeliran, Kawah [Kawah Buliran] (Java)	Thermal feature of Kamojang, Kawah	....
Boender [Bunder] (Lesser Sunda Is)	Cone of Batur	0604-01=
Boetak [Butak] (Java)	Cone of Dieng Volc Complex	0603-20=
Boetak Petarangan [Butak Petarangan]	Cone of Dieng Volc Complex	0603-20=
Boetak, Gunung [Gunung Butak] (Java)	Cone of Arjuno-Welirang	0603-29=
Bogachensky (Kamchatka)	Shield volcano (None) Pleistocene	....
Bogana (Bougainville-SW Pacific)	Synonym of Bagana	0505-02=
Bogatyr Ridge (Kuril Is)	Stratovolcano (None) Holocene	**0900-06-**
Bogdan Khmelnitskii (Kuril Is)	Stratovolcano of Chirip	0900-09=
Bogdanovich (Kuril Is)	Crater of Vernadskii Ridge	0900-37-
Bogdanovich (Kamchatka)	Shield volcano of Vysoky	1000-221
Boggel (Indian O.)	Cone of Prince Edward Island	0304-06-
Boglari Varteto (Hungary)	Cone of Balaton Highland	....
Bogoria (Africa-E)	Shield volcano (None) Pleist.-Geysers	....
Bogoslof (Aleutian Is)	Submarine volcano (8, 1992) Historical	**1101-30-**
Bogoslof Hill (Alaska-W)	Shield volcano of St. Paul Island	1104-01-
Bogo-Togo-Ula (Mongolia)	Cone of Ika-Togo-Ula	....

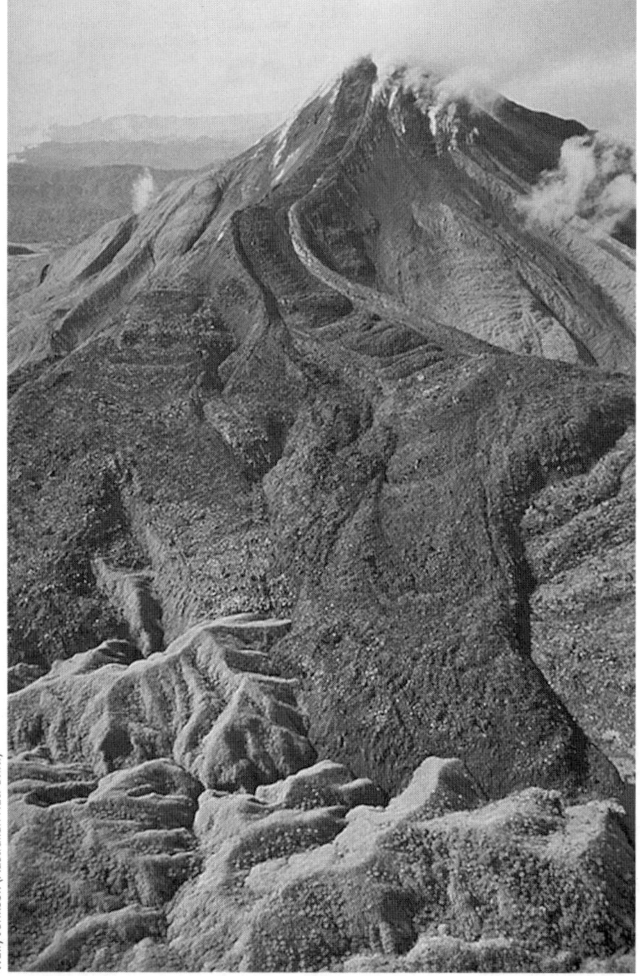

Bagana volcano, on Papua New Guinea's Bougainville Island, is characterized by the extrusion of thick, viscous andesitic lava flows with prominent lateral levees.

Name (Subregion)	Type (Eruptions, Most Recent) Status Relation to Named Volcano	Volcano Number
Bogo-Togo-Ula [Baga Togo Uul] (Mongolia)	Cinder cone of Khanuy Gol	1003-02-
Bogousar (Armenia)	Pyroclastic cone of Ghegam Ridge	0104-07-
Bogueroncitos (El Salvador)	Fissure vent of San Salvador	1403-05=
Boi (Africa-E)	Synonym of Central Island	0202-01=
Boi, Pico do (Azores)	Cone of Sete Cidades	1802-08=
Boiling Lake (W Indies)	Thermal feature of Watt, Morne	1600-101
Boiling Springs Lake (US-California)	Thermal feature of Lassen Volc Center	1203-08-
Boina (Djibouti)	Fumarole field (None) Pleist.-Fumarolic	....
Boina (Ethiopia)	Synonym of Dabbahu	0201-113
Boina (Ethiopia)	Cone of Dabbahu	0201-113
Bois d'Inde (W Indies)	Dome of Plat Pays, Morne	1600-11=
Bois d'Inde Franciou (W Indies)	Dome of Qualibou	1600-14=
Boisa (New Guinea-NE of)	Stratovolcano (None) Holocene?	**0501-011**
Bokeo Volc Field (SE Asia)	Scoria cones (None) Quaternary	....
Boki, Wolo (Lesser Sunda Is)	Crater of Inielika	0604-09=
Bokki (Iceland-NE)	Crater Row of Tungnafellsjökull	1703-04=
Bokluca (Turkey)	Cone of Erciyes Dagi	0103-01=
Bokovoi (Kamchatka)	Fissure vent of Kliuchevskoi	1000-26=
Bola (New Britain-SW Pac)	Stratovolcano (None) Holocene	**0502-05=**
Bolas, Las (Argentina)	Pyrocl. cone Northern Mendoza Field	....
Boletas, Cerro (US-New Mexico)	Dome of Valles Caldera	....
Boliche (Ecuador)	Dome of Chacana	1502-022
Bolin (Lesser Sunda Is)	Synonym of Iliboleng	0604-22=
Boljshaia Udina [Bolshaya Udina]	Stratovolcano of Udina	1000-241
Boljshaya Katepana (Kamchatka)	Synonym of Bolshoy Ketepana	....
Boljshoy [Bolshoi] (Kamchatka)	Shield volcano Bolshoi-Kekuknaysky	1000-36-
Bollons Island (Pacific-S)	Cone of Antipodes Island	1305-01-
Bolsa, Cerro la (México)	Cinder cone of Naolinco Volc Field	1401-095
Bolsa, Cerro la (México)	Cinder cone Zitácuaro-Valle de Bravo	1401-061
Bolsena (Italy)	Pleistocene caldera of Vulsini	0101-003
Bolshaya Ipelka (Kamchatka)	Shield volcano (None) Pleistocene	....
Bolshaya Plosky [Daljny Plosky] (Kamchatka)	Shield volcano of Ushkovsky	1000-261
Bolshaya Romanovka (Kamchatka)	Shield volcano (None) Pleistocene	....
Bolshaya Udina (Kamchatka)	Stratovolcano of Udina	1000-241
Bolshe-Bannaya (Kamchatka)	Lava domes (None) Holocene	**1000-087**
Bolshe-Banny (Kamchatka)	Thermal feature of Bolshe-Bannaya	1000-087
Bol'shiye Igolki (Kamchatka)	Shield volcano of Igolki	....
Bolshoi (Kamchatka)	Shield volcano Bolshoi-Kekuknaysky	1000-36-
Bolshoi Dome (Alaska Peninsula)	Dome of Aniakchak	1102-09-
Bolshoi Payalpan (Kamchatka)	Shield volcanoes (None) Holocene?	**1000-30-**
Bolshoi Semiachik (Kamchatka)	Stratovolcanoes (2, -4450) Radiocarbon	**1000-15=**
Bolshoi Semiachik (Kamchatka)	Synonym of Maly Semiachik	1000-14=
Bolshoi Sitkin (Aleutian Is)	Synonym of Great Sitkin	1101-12-
Bolshoi-Kekuknaysky (Kamchatka)	Shield volcanoes (1, -5310) Radiocarbon	**1000-36-**
Bolshoy Chekchebonay (Kamchatka)	Shield volcano (None) Pleistocene	....
Bolshoy Ketepana (Kamchatka)	Shield volcano (None) Pleistocene	....
Bolshoy Kozyrevsky (Kamchatka)	Shield volcano (None) Pleistocene	....
Bolshoy Payalpan (Kamchatka)	Synonym of Bolshoi Payalpan	1000-30-
Bol'shoy Semyachik (Kamchatka)	Synonym of Bolshoi Semiachik	1000-15=
Bolshoy-Kekuknaysky (Kamchatka)	Synonym of Bolshoi-Kekuknaysky	1000-36-
Boludo (México)	Cinder cone of Chichinautzin	1401-08=
Bomb Peak (Antarctica)	Cone of Erebus	1900-02=
Bombalai (Borneo)	Pyroclastic cone (None) Holocene?	**0610-01-**
Bombarda (Greece)	Pumice cone of Mílos	0102-03=
Bombay Hill (New Zealand)	Shield volcano of South Auckland	....
Bombellestoppen (Atlantic-N-Jan Mayen)	Dome of Jan Mayen	1706-01=
Bomboli, Cerro (Ecuador)	Cone of Corazón	....
Bombon, Lake (Luzon-Philippines)	Synonym of Taal	0703-07=
Bonaccorsi-Montarello (Italy)	Cinder cone of Etna	0101-06=
Bona-Churchill (Alaska-E)	Synonym of Churchill	1105-03-
Bonde (Africa-C)	Cone of Karisimbi	0203-04-
Bondholshraun (Iceland-NE)	Shield volcano of Krafla	1703-08=
Bondoro [Agarteto] (Hungary)	Shield volcano of Balaton Highland	....
Bones Knob (Australia)	Cone of Atherton Volc Province	....
Bonete de Carrao (Nicaragua)	Cone of Estelí	1404-131
Bonete, Cerro (Bolivia)	Stratovolcano (None) Post-Miocene	....
Bonete, Cerro el (Guatemala)	Stratovolcano of Moyuta	1402-13-
Bongabti (Kamchatka)	Shield volcano (None) Pleistocene	....
Bongapti (Kamchatka)	Synonym of Bongabti	....
Bongkok, Bukit (Lesser Sunda Is)	Cone of Batur	0604-01=
Bongole, Gof (Africa-E)	Maar of Marsabit	0202-021
Bongsu, Kepundan (Sumatra)	Crater of Marapi	0601-14=
Bonin, Morne (W Indies)	Dome of Qualibou	1600-14=
Bonita Butte (US-California)	Cone of Medicine Lake	1203-02-
Bonita, Loma (México)	Dome of Zitácuaro-Valle de Bravo	1401-061
Bonito, Cerro (Chile-N)	Unknown (None) Post-Miocene	....
Bonnet, Le (Indian O.-W)	Crater of Fournaise, Piton de la	0303-02=
Bono (New Guinea-NE of)	Crater of Umboi	0501-06=
Bonsulton, Cuddie (Italy)	Vent of Pantelleria	0101-071
Booby Hill (W Indies)	Dome of Saba	1600-01=
Boomerang Seamount (Indian O.-S)	Submarine volcano (1, 1995) Historical	**0304-00-**
Booser (Germany)	Maar of West Eifel Volc Field	0100-01-
Boot Rock (Indian O.-S)	Tuff cone of Marion Island	0304-07-
Boquerón, Ausoles el (El Salvador)	Thermal feature of Chinameca	1403-09=
Boquerón, El (México-Is)	Synonym of Bárcena	1401-02=
Boquerón, El (El Salvador)	Stratovolcano of San Salvador	1403-05=
Boquerón, El (Canary Is)	Dome of Tenerife	1803-03-
Boqueroncito (El Salvador)	Cinder cone of San Salvador	1403-05=
Bor Gheleba (Africa-E)	Synonym of Central Island	0202-01=
Bora (Ethiopia)	Pumice cone of Bora-Bericcio	0201-24-
Bora-Bericcio (Ethiopia)	Pumice cones (None) Holocene	**0201-24-**
Borale Ale (Ethiopia)	Stratovolcano (None) Holocene	**0201-071**
Boraule (Ethiopia)	Synonym of Borawli	0201-121
Borawli (Ethiopia)	Lava domes (None) Holocene	**0201-121**

Name (Subregion)	Type (Eruptions, Most Recent) Status Relation to Named Volcano	Volcano Number
Borawli (Ethiopia)	Stratovolcano (None) Holocene	**0201-107**
Border Mountain (US-California)	Cone of Medicine Lake	1203-02-
Bordoncillo (Colombia)	Unknown (None) Post-Miocene	....
Borele-ali (Ethiopia)	Synonym of Borale Ale	0201-071
Bor-eli (Ethiopia)	Synonym of Borale Ale	0201-071
Borgahraun (Iceland-NE)	Fissure vent of Theistareykjarbunga	1703-09=
Borgarholar (Iceland-SW)	Cone of Grímsnes	1701-06=
Borgarhraun (Iceland-SW)	Crater Row of Reykjanes	1701-02=
Borghetto (Italy)	Pyroclastic cone of Ernici, Monti	....
Boriatiko Vouno (Greece)	Dome of Nisyros	0102-05=
Boring Lava (US-Oregon)	Volcanic field (None) Pleistocene	....
Boriquén (Costa Rica)	Thermal feature of Rincón de la Vieja	1405-02=
Borisyak, Mt. (Kuril Is)	Cone of Lomonosov Group	0900-351
Boro, Gof (Africa-E)	Maar of Marsabit	0202-021
Borokua (Solomon Is-SW Pacific)	Synonym of Mborokua	....
Borrego, Cerro el (México)	Cinder cone of Michoacán-Guanajuato	1401-06=
Bort (Kamchatka)	Stratovolcano of Bolshoi Semiachik	1000-15=
Bortovaya (Kamchatka)	Dome of Uzon	1000-17=
Bory (Indian O.-W)	Crater of Fournaise, Piton de la	0303-02=
Borzov (Kuril Is)	Cone of Kolokol Group	0900-12=
Bosavi (New Guinea)	Stratovolcano (None) Pleistocene	....
Boschan [Pechan] (China-W)	Cone of Tianshan Volc Group	1004-02-
Bosco dei Conti (Italy)	Cone of Ischia	0101-03=
Bosco Della Maddalena (Italy)	Stratovolcano of Ischia	0101-03=
Boset (Ethiopia)	Stratovolcano of Boset-Bericha	0201-21-
Boset-Bericha (Ethiopia)	Stratovolcanoes (None) Holocene	**0201-21-**
Boseti-Bariccia (Ethiopia)	Synonym of Boset-Bericha	0201-21-
Boseti-Bericcia [Bericha] (Ethiopia)	Stratovolcano of Boset-Bericha	0201-21-
Boseti-Gudda [Boset] (Ethiopia)	Stratovolcano of Boset-Bericha	0201-21-
Bo-shan (China-E)	Synonym of Wudalianchi	1005-03-
Bosotlán (El Salvador)	Synonym of San Miguel	1403-10=
Bosque Alegre (Costa Rica)	Maar of Poás	1405-04=
Bosque, El (Nicaragua)	Dome of Rota	1404-06-
Boss Mountain (Canada)	Cone of Quesnel Cone Group	....
Botija, Montaña la (Canary Is)	Cinder cone of Tenerife	1803-03-
Botijuela, Cerro la (Argentina)	Dome of Antofalla	....
Botnahraun (Iceland-NE)	Fissure vent of Askja	1703-06=
Botnahraun (Iceland-NE)	Fissure vent of Grímsvötn	1703-01=
Botna-Skyrtunna (Iceland-W)	Cone of Ljósufjöll	1700-03=
Botos (Costa Rica)	Stratovolcano of Poás	1405-04=
Botos, Los (Costa Rica)	Synonym of Poás	1405-04=
Bottom Hill (W Indies)	Dome of Saba	1600-01=
Boucher, Piton (W Indies)	Dome of Carbets, Pitons de	....
Bouillante Chain (W Indies)	Maars (None) Pleistocene-Hot Springs	....
Bouillante, Pitons de (W Indies)	Stratovolcano of Axial Chain	....
Boulder Cones (Antarctica)	Cone of Hut Point Peninsula	....
Bouvet (Atlantic-S)	Shield volcano (1, -50) Magnetism	**1806-02-**
Bouvetoya (Atlantic-S)	Synonym of Bouvet	1806-02-
Bove, Valle del (Italy)	Caldera of Etna	0101-06=
Boven (W Indies)	Cone of Northern Centres	....
Boven (W Indies)	Stratovolcano of Quill, The	1600-02=
Bowden Crater (US-Oregon)	Synonym of Jackies Butte	....
Bowers Knoll (US-Utah)	Cone of Markagunt Plateau	1207-04-
Bowman Hill (Australia)	Cone of McBride Volc Province	....
Boyd Ridge (Antarctica)	Cone of Crary Group	....
Boyna (Ethiopia)	Synonym of Dabbahu	0201-113
Boz Dag (Turkey)	Cone of Erciyes Dagi	0103-01=
Boz Dag (Turkey)	Dome of Erciyes Dagi	0103-01=
Bozu-jigoku (Kyushu-Japan)	Thermal feature of Tsurumi	0802-13=
Brabant Island (Antarctica)	Volcanic field (None) Pleistocene	....
Bradleys Hill (Australia)	Cone of Atherton Volc Province	....
Brama [Bromo] (Java)	Cinder cone of Tengger Caldera	0603-31=
Branca, Caldeira (Azores)	Maar of Flores	1802-001
Branca, Caldera (Africa-C)	Pleistocene caldera of Karisimbi	0203-04-
Branca, Mont (Indian O.-S)	Cone of Possession, Ile de la	0304-04-
Branco, Pico (Atlantic-C)	Dome of Trindade	1805-051
Brandur (Iceland-S)	Cone of Vestmannaeyjar	1702-01=
Brasil, Cerro (Guatemala)	Cinder cone of Cuilapa-Barbarena	1402-111
Brasil, Monte (Azores)	Cone of Terceira	1802-05=
Brat Chirpoev (Kuril Is)	Stratovolcano of Chirpoi	0900-15=
Bratan (Lesser Sunda Is)	Caldera (None) Holocene	**0604-001**
Braun [Von Seebach] (Costa Rica)	Cone of Rincón de la Vieja	1405-02=
Brava (Cape Verde Is)	Stratovolcano (None) Holocene	**1804-02-**
Bravard (Chile-C)	Synonym of Tupungatito	1507-01=
Bravas, Lagunas (Chile-N)	Synonym of Nevada, Sierra	1505-123
Bravo, Cerro (Colombia)	Stratovolcano (8, 1720) Radiocarbon	**1501-012**
Breached Cone (Antarctica)	Cone of Hut Point Peninsula	....
Bredes, Piton (Indian O.-W)	Cinder cone of Fournaise, Piton de la	0303-02=
Breidabunga (Iceland-SE)	Subglacial volcano (None) Pleistocene	....
Breña, La (México)	Maar of Durango Volc Field	1401-022
Brenal (México)	Synonym of Durango Volc Field	1401-022
Brennisteinsfjöll (Iceland-SW)	Crater rows (9, 1341) Historical	**1701-04=**
Brennisteinsgigar (Iceland-SW)	Synonym of Brennisteinsfjöll	1701-04=
Brew, Mount (Canada)	Vent of Garibaldi Lake	1200-19-
Brewster, Mount (Antarctica)	Shield volcano of Daniell Peninsula	....
Bridge River Cones (Canada)	Volcanic field (None) Holocene	**1200-17-**
Bridge River Vent (Canada)	Vent of Meager	1200-18-
Bridgeman Island (Antarctica)	Stratovolcano (None) Uncertain	**1900-04=**
Bridgman Island (Antarctica)	Synonym of Bridgeman Island	1900-04=
Bridlicna (Czech)	Cone of Unnamed	....
Brighton (W Indies)	Cinder cone of Grand Bonhomme	....
Brillantes, Montagnas (Alaska-SW)	Synonym of Iliamna	1103-02-
Brimstone Hill (W Indies)	Dome of Liamuiga	1600-03=
Brimstone Island (Kermadec Is)	(None) Not a Volcano	0402-02=
Brimstone Pit (Mariana Is-C Pacific)	Crater of NW Rota-1	0804-211
Brinco del Diablo, Cerro (México)	Shield volc. of Michoacán-Guanajuato	1401-06=
Bristol Island (Antarctica)	Stratovolcano (5, 1956) Historical	**1900-08=**
Brito, Cerro de (Guatemala)	Cinder cone of Cuilapa-Barbarena	1402-111
Broad Acres (Africa-E)	Dome of Olkaria	0202-09=
Broadlands (New Zealand)	Thermal feature of Reporoa	0401-06-
Brockman Flat (US-California)	Synonym of Eagle Lake Field	1203-09-
Broken Back (US-New Mexico)	Crater of Carrizozo	1210-01-
Broken Island (Africa-E)	Crater of Central Island	0202-01=
Broken Top (US-Oregon)	Stratovolcano (None) Pleistocene	....
Broken Top (US-Idaho)	Cone of Craters of the Moon	1204-02-
Brokeoff Mountain (US-California)	Stratovolcano of Lassen Volc Center	1203-08-
Bromfield Swamp (Australia)	Crater of Atherton Volc Province	....
Bromo (Java)	Cinder cone of Tengger Caldera	0603-31=
Bromo-Tengger Caldera (Java)	Synonym of Tengger Caldera	0603-31=

Lava dome remnants from three historical eruptions can be seen in this aerial view of **Bogoslof** Island in the Aleutians. The dome in the center foreground was formed during the most recent eruption of Bogoslof in 1992. The steep-sided pinnacle behind it is Castle Rock (also referred to as Old Bogoslof), a remnant of a 1796 lava dome. The circular, flat-topped area to the right is a remnant of a 1927 lava dome.

USGS (AVO)

Name (Subregion)	Type (Eruptions, Most Recent) Status Relation to Named Volcano	Volcano Number
Brontona Island (Kuril Is)	Unknown (None) Pleistocene	....
Brothers (New Zealand)	Submarine volcano (None) Fumarolic	**0401-15-**
Brothers, the (Australia)	Cone of Mclean Volc Province	....
Broughton Island (Kuril Is)	Synonym of Brontona Island	....
Brouton Caldera (Kuril Is)	Caldera of Urataman	0900-191
Broutona (Kuril Is)	Synonym of Brontona Island	....
Brown Mountain (US-Oregon)	Shield volcano (None) Pleistocene	....
Brown Peak (Antarctica)	Synonym of Sturge Island	1900-012
Brown's Island [Motukorea] (New Zealand)	Cone of Auckland Field	0401-02=
Bruce (Antarctica)	Cone of Seal Nunataks Group	1900-05=
Bruciata, Cuddia (Italy)	Cone of Pantelleria	0101-071
Brück (Germany)	Crater of West Eifel Volc Field	0100-01-
Bruja, Loma la (Nicaragua)	Dome of San Cristóbal	1404-02=
Brujillo, Cerro (Guatemala)	Lava cone of Ixtepeque	1402-18-
Brujo, Cerro (Galápagos)	Tuff cone of San Cristóbal	1503-12-
Brujo, Cerro el (México)	Shield volcano of Serdán-Oriental	1401-092
Brujo, El (Guatemala)	Vent of Santa María	1402-03=
Brulant (Indian O.-W)	Crater of Fournaise, Piton de la	0303-02=
Brulé du Baril (Indian O.-W)	Crater of Fournaise, Piton de la	0303-02=
Brulés, Morne (W Indies)	Dome of Diables, Morne aux	1600-08=
Brulot (Indian O.-S)	Cone of Amsterdam Island	0304-001
Brunaborg [Hrossadaliur] (Iceland-NE)	Crater Row of Krafla	1703-08=
Brunagigir (Iceland-SW)	Crater Row of Brennisteinsfjöll	1701-04=
Brushy Butte (US-California)	Shield volcano (None) Holocene?	**1203-03-**
Bryant Beach (New Zealand)	Cone of Karioi	....
Brydjuhraun (Iceland-NE)	Fissure vent of Bárdarbunga	1703-03=
Brytalaekir (Iceland-S)	Fissure vent of Katla	1702-03=
Bu Jerman (SE Asia)	Shield volcano of Haut Dong Nai	0705-04-
Bu Kong Rong (SE Asia)	Caldera of Haut Dong Nai	0705-04-
Bual Buali (Sumatra)	Synonym of Sibualbuali	0601-11=
Bubay, Mt. (Luzon-Philippines)	Cone of San Pablo Volc Field	0703-06=
Bubochka (Kamchatka)	Cinder cone of Tolbachik	1000-24=
Bu-caldera (Greece)	Pleistocene caldera of Santorini	0102-04=
Buck Butte (US-California)	Cone of Medicine Lake	1203-02-
Buck Hill (Canada)	Cone of Wells Gray-Clearwater	1200-15-
Buck Knoll (US-Utah)	Cinder cone of Bald Knoll	1207-03-
Buckhorn Lake (US-California)	Cinder cone of Silver Lake	1203-05-
Buckle Island (Antarctica)	Stratovolcano (2, 1899) Historical	**1900-01=**
Bucu, Gunung (Java)	Cone of Dieng Volc Complex	0603-20=
Bud Dajo (Sulu Is-Philippines)	Cinder cone of Jolo	0700-01=
Budaklettur (Iceland-W)	Cone of Snaefellsjökull	1700-01=
Budamado Hayk (Ethiopia)	Crater of Bilate River Field	0201-291
Buddajo [Bud Dajo] (Sulu Is-Philippines)	Cinder cone of Jolo	0700-01=
Budugasu, Gunung (Java)	Cone of Arjuno-Welirang	0603-29=
Buduli (Kamchatka)	Shield volcano (None) Pleistocene	....
Buena Vista, Cerro (El Salvador)	Stratovolcano (None) Pleistocene	....
Buena Vista, Cerro (El Salvador)	Dome of Ilopango	1403-06=
Buena Vista, Cerro (Guatemala)	Cinder cone of Moyuta	1402-13-
Buenavista (Ecuador)	Dome of Chalupas	....

Name (Subregion)	Type (Eruptions, Most Recent) Status Relation to Named Volcano	Volcano Number
Buenavista (México)	Vent of Iztaccíhuatl	1401-082
Buenavista Tomatlan, Cerro (México)	Shield volc. of Michoacán-Guanajuato	1401-06=
Buenos Aires (Costa Rica)	Cinder cone of Platanar	1405-034
Buenventura Spring (Luzon-Philippines)	Thermal feature of Banahaw	0703-05=
Buey, Crater del (Chile-C)	Crater of Mocho-Choshuenco	1507-13=
Buey, Laguna la (Colombia)	Crater of Puracé	1501-06=
Bueyes, Cerro de los (Guatemala)	Cinder cone of Cuilapa-Barbarena	1402-111
Buffalo Valley (US-Nevada)	Volcanic field (None) Pleistocene	....
Bufumbira (Africa-C)	Cinder cones (None) Holocene?	**0203-07-**
Bug Island (Africa-E)	Crater of Central Island	0202-01=
Buga (Mindanao-Philippines)	Cone of Imbing	....
Bugeshi (Africa-C)	Cone of Karisimbi	0203-04-
Bugogo (Africa-C)	Cone of Nyiragongo	0203-03=
Bugumba (Africa-C)	Tuff cone of Fort Portal	0203-001
Bugwaye (Africa-C)	Crater of Bunyaruguru	0203-004
Buhangin (Mindanao-Philippines)	Dome of Paco	0701-09-

Chris Newhall (USGS)

Bulusan volcano in southern Luzon, Philippines, rises above the flat floor of the 11-km-wide Pleistocene Irosin caldera and was constructed over its northern rim.

Name (Subregion)	Type (Eruptions, Most Recent) Status Relation to Named Volcano	Volcano Number
Buhara (Africa-C)	Tuff cone of Fort Portal	0203-001
Buhi (Luzon-Philippines)	Synonym of Malinao	....
Buho (Luzon-Philippines)	Dome of Banahaw	0703-05=
Buhubie (Africa-C)	Cone of Nyamuragira	0203-02=
Buhuma (Africa-C)	Cone of Nyiragongo	0203-03=
Bujishan (China-E)	Cone of Datong-Fengzen	....
Bukit, Bur (Indonesian for Hill, Mt.) see proper name (e.g. Daun, Bukit)		
Bukoli (Africa-C)	Cone of Nyamuragira	0203-02=
Bula (New Britain-SW Pac)	Synonym of Bola	0502-05=
Bulal Volc Field (Ethiopia)	Synonym of Mega Basalt Field	0201-33-
Bulalo, Mt. (Luzon-Philippines)	Cone of San Pablo Volc Field	0703-06=
Buldir (Aleutian Is)	Stratovolcano (None) Holocene?	**1101-01-**
Bulengira (Africa-C)	Cone of Karisimbi	0203-04-
Bulengo (Africa-C)	Cone of Nyiragongo	0203-03=
Bulgan Volc Field (Mongolia)	Synonym of Khanuy Gol	1003-02-
Bulienmerri, Lake (Australia)	Tuff ring of Newer Volcanics Prov	0509-01-
Buliran, Kawah (Java)	Thermal feature of Kamojang, Kawah	....
Bulka (Kamchatka)	Dome of Avachinsky	1000-10=
Bull (Antarctica)	Cone of Seal Nunataks Group	1900-05=
Bullarook Hill (Australia)	Cone of Newer Volcanics Prov	0509-01-
Bullengarook, Mt. (Australia)	Cone of Newer Volcanics Prov	0509-01-
Bulochka (Kamchatka)	Fissure vent of Kliuchevskoi	1000-26=
Bulu (New Britain-SW Pac)	Synonym of Bola	0502-05=
Bulu [Gulu] (New Britain-SW Pac)	Cone of Langila	0502-01=
Bulumorsum (Admiralty Is-SW Pacific)	Cone of St. Andrew Strait	0500-01=
Bulusan (Luzon-Philippines)	Stratovolcanoes (18, 2007) Historical	**0703-01=**
Bumabag (Luzon-Philippines)	Stratovolcano of Ambalatungan Group	0703-088
Bumpass Hell (US-California)	Thermal feature of Lassen Volc Center	1203-08-
Bumpass Mountain (US-California)	Dome of Lassen Volc Center	1203-08-
Bunaga [Cerisy Peak] (New Guinea-NE of)	Stratovolcano of Long Island	0501-05=
Bunanya (Kamchatka)	Shield volcano of Kekurny	1000-41-
Bunanya (Kamchatka)	Shield volcano of Uksichan	1000-35-
Bunbulan (Lesser Sunda Is)	Crater of Batur	0604-01=
Bunbulan, Gunung (Lesser Sunda Is)	Dome of Batur	0604-01=
Bundaberg-Boyne Province (Austr.)	Pyroclastic cones (None) Pleistocene	....
Bunder (Lesser Sunda Is)	Cone of Batur	0604-01=
Bundjuli (Africa-C)	Cone of Karisimbi	0203-04-
Bungbrung (Java)	Crater of Papandayan	0603-10=
Bungsu (Sumatra)	Cone of Gadut-Bungsu	....
Bungsu, Kapundan [Kepundan Bungsu]	Crater of Marapi	0601-14=
Buninyong, Mt. (Australia)	Cone of Newer Volcanics Prov	0509-01-
Bunker Hill (W Indies)	Dome of Saba	1600-01=
Bunnell Butte (US-Washington)	Cinder cone of Adams	1201-04-
Bunot, Lake (Luzon-Philippines)	Maar of San Pablo Volc Field	0703-06=
Buntak, Bukit (Sumatra)	Cone of Kerinci	0601-17=
Buntuk Gede, Gunung (Java)	Vent of Sundoro	0603-21=
Bunuholar (Iceland-NE)	Fissure vent of Grímsvötn	1703-01=
Bunyampaka [Kasenyi] (Africa-C)	Tuff cone of Katwe-Kikorongo	0203-003
Bunyaro (Africa-C)	Cone of Visoke	0203-05-
Bunyaruguru (Africa-C)	Maars (None) Holocene	**0203-004**
Bunyogwe (Africa-C)	Cone of Karisimbi	0203-04-
Bunyoke (Africa-C)	Cone of Visoke	0203-05-
Buqum, Harrat al (Arabia)	Volcanic field of Nawasif, Harrat	....
Buraco, Pico do (Azores)	Dome of Furnas	1802-10=
Burak (Lesser Sunda Is)	Crater of Leroboleng	0604-20=
Burauen (Philippines-C)	Synonym of Mahagnao	0702-07=
Buraya (Kamchatka)	Cinder cone of Tolbachik	1000-24=
Burevestnik (Kuril Is)	Cone of Bogatyr Ridge	0900-06-
Burfell (Iceland-NE)	Tuya (None) Pleistocene	....
Burfell (Iceland-SW)	Crater Row of Krísuvík	1701-03=
Burfell I Olfusi (Iceland-SW)	Shield volcano of Hengill	1701-05=
Burfellshraun (Iceland-NE)	Fissure vent of Bárdarbunga	1703-03=
Burgess Island (New Zealand)	Cone of Mokohinau Islands	....
Burilan (Vanuatu-SW Pacific)	Cone of Gaua	0507-02=
Buriram (SE Asia)	Unknown (None) Pleistocene	....
Burko (Africa-E)	Stratovolcano (None) Pleistocene	....
Burliastchy [Burlyashchy] (Kamchatka)	Stratovolcano of Bolshoi Semiachik	1000-15=
Burlich (Germany)	Tuff cone of West Eifel Volc Field	0100-01-
Burlow Hill (Africa-E)	Dome of Meru	0202-16=
Burlyashchy (Kamchatka)	Stratovolcano of Bolshoi Semiachik	1000-15=
Burn Butte (US-Oregon)	Cone of Cappy Mountain	....
Burney Mountain (US-California)	Lava domes (None) Pleistocene	....
Burney, Monte (Chile-S)	Stratovolcano (7, 1910) Historical	**1508-07=**
Burning Mountain (Alaska-SW)	Synonym of Iliamna	1103-02-
Burning Volcano (Aleutian Is)	Synonym of Gareloi	1101-07-
Burnt Lava Flow (US-California)	Cone of Medicine Lake	1203-02-
Burnt Mountain (Alaska-SW)	Synonym of Redoubt	1103-03-
Burnthill (Atlantic-S)	Cinder cone of Tristan da Cunha	1806-01=
Burr, Mt. (Australia)	Cone of Newer Volcanics Prov	0509-01-
Burro, Cerro el (México)	Dome of Michoacán-Guanajuato	1401-06=
Burru, Doinyo (Africa-E)	Synonym of Eburru, Ol Doinyo	0202-08=
Bursey, Mt. (Antarctica)	Shield volcanoes (None) Pleistocene	....
Buru (New Britain-SW Pac)	Caldera of Pago	0502-08=
Buru, Doinyo (Africa-E)	Synonym of Eburru, Ol Doinyo	0202-08=
Bushenye (Africa-C)	Cone of Nyiragongo	0203-03=
Bushwaga (Africa-C)	Cone of Nyiragongo	0203-03=
Bus-Obo (Mongolia)	Cinder cone (None) Holocene?	**1003-03-**
Busui (New Britain-SW Pac)	Caldera of Oto Group	....
Butajiri-Silti Field (Ethiopia)	Fissure vents (None) Holocene	**0201-26-**
Butak (Java)	Cone of Dieng Volc Complex	0603-20=
Butak Petarangan (Java)	Cone of Dieng Volc Complex	0603-20=
Butak, Bukit (Sumatra)	Unknown (None) Post-Miocene	....
Butak, Gunung (Java)	Cone of Arjuno-Welirang	0603-29=
Butaka (Africa-C)	Cone of Karisimbi	0203-04-
Butay, Mt. (Mindanao-Philippines)	Stratovolcano of Camiguin	0701-08=
Butler's Mountain (W Indies)	Dome of Nevis Peak	1600-04=
Butte Creek (US-California)	Vent of Whaleback	....
Button Hill (Africa-E)	Dome of Meru	0202-16=
Butubut, Mt. (Vanuatu-SW Pacific)	Cone of Kuwae	0507-07=
Butus, Gunung (Lesser Sunda Is)	Cone of Batur	0604-01=
Buyan-Bratan (Lesser Sunda Is)	Synonym of Bratan	0604-001
Buyuk Agri Dagi (Turkey)	Synonym of Ararat	0103-04-
Buyuk Kizil Tepe (Turkey)	Cone of Erciyes Dagi	0103-01=
Buyukkale Tepe (Turkey)	Dome of Erciyes Dagi	0103-01=
Buzz (Africa-E)	Synonym of Central Island	0202-01=
Buzzard Creek (Alaska-E)	Tuff rings (1, -1050) Radiocarbon	**1105-001**
Bwanika (Africa-C)	Tuff cone of Fort Portal	0203-001
Bwasi-lai-lai (D'Entrecasteaux Is)	Therm. feature of Dawson Strait Group	0503-06=
Byakushi-ike (Kyushu-Japan)	Crater of Kirishima	0802-09=
Byakusi-ike [Byakushi-ike] (Kyushu-Japan)	Crater of Kirishima	0802-09=
Bylandt Rheyt (Atlantic-N-Jan Mayen)	Cone of Jan Mayen	1706-01=
Bylinkina (Kamchatka)	Fissure vent of Kliuchevskoi	1000-26=
Bylinkinoy [Bylinkina] (Kamchatka)	Fissure vent of Kliuchevskoi	1000-26=
Byobu-dake (Honshu-Japan)	Stratovolcano of Zao	0803-19=
Byobu-yama (Hokkaido-Japan)	Dome of Tokachi-Eboshi	....

C

Name (Subregion)	Type (Eruptions, Most Recent) Status Relation to Named Volcano	Volcano Number
Caanoan (Luzon-N of)	Cone of Camiguin de Babuyanes	0704-01=
Cabalían (Philippines-C)	Stratovolcano (1, 1820) Radiocarbon	**0702-05=**
Caballito (México)	Cinder cone of Chichinautzin	1401-08=
Cabana (Chile-N)	Synonym of Apagado	....
Cabeza de Vaca (Chile-S)	Cone of Cayutué-La Viguería	1508-012
Cabeza de Vaca, Cerro (Costa Rica)	Stratovolcano of Irazú	1405-06=
Cabeza de Vaca, Cerro (Nicaragua)	Cinder cone of Pilas, Las	1404-08=
Cabeza, La (México)	Stratovolcano of Iztaccíhuatl	1401-082
Cabezuelo, Volcán de el (Spain)	Maar of Calatrava Volc Field	0100-04-
Cabo Cowan (Galápagos)	Tuff cone of Santiago	1503-09=
Cabra, Isla de [Cerro Grande] (El Salvador)	Dome of Coatepeque Caldera	1403-041
Cabras, Cerro las (México)	Cinder cone of Michoacán-Guanajuato	1401-06=
Cabras, Montana de las [San Antonio]	Cinder cone of La Palma	1803-01-
Cabras, Picos (Canary Is)	Dome of Tenerife	1803-03-
Cabret, Djebel (Red Sea)	Synonym of Tair, Jebel at	0201-01=
Cabrioler, Volcáns de (Spain)	Cone of Olot Volc Field	0100-03-
Cabris, Piton des (Indian O.-W)	Cinder cone of Fournaise, Piton de la	0303-02=
Cabrits, Morne (W Indies)	Dome of Plat Pays, Morne	1600-11=
Cabro Muco-La Giganta (Costa Rica)	Stratovolcano of Miravalles	1405-03=
Caburgua, Nevados de (Chile-C)	Stratovolcanoes (None) Pleistocene	....
Caburgua, Volcanes de (Chile-C)	Cone of Caburgua-Huelemolle	1507-112
Caburgua-Huelemolle (Chile-C)	Cinder cones (1, -5050) Tephrochron	**1507-112**
Cabut, Bukit (Sumatra)	Cone of Besar	0601-25=
Cacaguatique, Cerro (El Salvador)	Synonym of Cacahuatique, Cerro	....
Cacahuatique, Cerro (El Salvador)	Stratovolcano (None) Pleistocene	....

Name (Subregion)	Type (Eruptions, Most Recent) Status / Relation to Named Volcano	Volcano Number
Cacao (Costa Rica)	Stratovolcano of Orosí	1405-01=
Cachani (Perú)	Synonym of Chachani, Nevado	1504-007
Cache Hill (Canada)	Shield volcano of Edziza	1200-06-
Cache Mountain (US-Oregon)	Cinder cone of Washington	....
Cachio, Cerro (El Salvador)	Stratovolcano of Apaneca Range	1403-01=
Cacho Negro, Volcán (Costa Rica)	Stratovolcano of Barva	1405-05=
Cacique, Cerro (México)	Dome of Zitácuaro-Valle de Bravo	1401-061
Cactus Peak (US-California)	Dome of Coso Volc Field	1203-18-
Cadenita (México)	Cinder cone of Chichinautzin	1401-08=
Cades Bay (W Indies)	Dome of Nevis Peak	1600-04=
Cafieri (Italy)	Crater of Ischia	0101-03=
Cage volcano (Pacific-NE)	Shield volcano of CoAxial Segment	1301-02-
Cagsiay Hot Springs (Luzon-Philippines)	Thermal feature of Banahaw	0703-05=
Cagua (Luzon-Philippines)	Stratovolcano (1, 1860) Historical	**0703-09=**
Caichinque (Chile-N)	Stratovolcanoes (None) Holocene?	**1505-104**
Caille, Ile de (W Indies)	Tuff ring of Kick 'em Jenny	1600-16=
Caiman, Montana (Canary Is)	Cone of Fuerteventura	1803-05-
Cairat, Volcà (Spain)	Cone of Olot Volc Field	0100-03-
Cajeros, Cerro (Argentina)	Stratovolcano of Antofalla	....
Cajete, El (US-New Mexico)	Crater of Valles Caldera	....
Cajon los Calabozos (Chile-C)	Thermal feature of Calabozos	1507-042
Cakasuanggi (Halmahera-Indonesia)	Stratovolcano of Amasing	0608-072
Cakrabuana (Java)	Stratovolcano (None) Pleistocene	....
Cala Bianca (Italy)	Crater of Panarea	0101-041
Cala dell'Alca (Italy)	Cone of Pantelleria	0101-071
Cala dell'Altura (Italy)	Shield volcano of Pantelleria	0101-071
Cala di Tramontana (Italy)	Cone of Pantelleria	0101-071
Cala Fico (Italy)	Submarine vent of Lipari	0101-042
Calabozos (Chile-C)	Caldera (None) Holocene	**1507-042**
Calajata (Chile-N)	Dome of Arintica	....
Calajata, Cerro (Chile-N)	Stratovolcano of Arintica	....
Calanterique, Cerro (Honduras)	Lava cone (None) Quaternary	....
Calatrava Volc Field (Spain)	Pyroclastic cones (1, -3600) Radiocarbon	**0100-04-**
Calayo (Mindanao-Philippines)	Synonym of Musuan	0701-07=
Calbuco (Chile-S)	Stratovolcano (22, 1972) Historical	**1508-02=**
Calcara, La (Italy)	Thermal feature of Panarea	0101-041
Calcarazzi, Monte (Italy)	Cinder cone of Etna	0101-06=
Caldeira (Azores)	Crater of Picos Volc System	1802-081
Caldera, Calderas, Caldiera, Caldeira see proper name (e.g. Cuervo, Caldera de los)		
Caldera, Cerro de la (México)	Cone of Chichinautzin	1401-08=
Caldera, La (Canary Is)	Crater of Lanzarote	1803-06-
Caldera, Laguna (El Salvador)	Cinder cone of San Salvador	1403-05=
Caldera, Loma (El Salvador)	Tuff ring of San Salvador	1403-05=
Calderas, Las (Canary Is)	Cinder cone of Fuerteventura	1803-05-
Caldereta, La (Canary Is)	Crater of Tenerife	1803-03-
Caldereta, Montana de la (Canary Is)	Cone of Fuerteventura	1803-05-
Calderita, La (Canary Is)	Vent of Fuerteventura	1803-05-
Calderon, El (US-New Mexico)	Crater of Zuni-Bandera	1210-02-
Calderon, Volcan (Galápagos)	Synonym of Alcedo	1503-04=
Caldiera (Azores)	Caldera of Corvo	1802-002
Caldiera (Azores)	Caldera of Fayal	1802-01=
Caldieras (Azores)	Thermal feature of Furnas	1802-10=
Caldwell Butte (US-California)	Cone of Medicine Lake	1203-02-
Caldwell Island (Galápagos)	Tuff cone of Floreana	....
Calebasse, Morne (W Indies)	Dome of Pelée	1600-12=
Calibato, Lake (Luzon-Philippines)	Maar of San Pablo Volc Field	0703-06=
Caliente (Guatemala)	Vent of Santa María	1402-03=
Caliente, Cerro (Perú)	Twin volcano of Yucamane	1504-05-
Caliente, Laguna (Costa Rica)	Crater of Poás	1405-04=
Calimani (Romania)	Stratovolcano (None) Pleistocene	....
Calimani-Cerbuc (Romania)	Dome of Calimani	....
Callaquen (Chile-C)	Synonym of Callaqui	1507-091
Callaqui (Chile-C)	Stratovolcano (2, 1980) Historical	**1507-091**
Callejón, Cerro (Bolivia)	Stratovolcano (None) Post-Miocene	....
Callo, Cerrito del (Ecuador)	Cone of Cotopaxi	1502-05=
Callvuco (Calluneto) (Chile-S)	Synonym of Osorno	1508-01=
Caloa (Ecuador)	Cone of Sagoatoa	....
Calomets, Piton (Indian O.-W)	Cinder cone of Fournaise, Piton de la	0303-02=
Calpi (Ecuador)	Tuff cones (None) Pleistocene	....
Calunan, Mt. (Luzon-Philippines)	Stratovolcano of Bulusan	0703-01=
Calungalan, Mt. (Luzon-Philippines)	Cone of Bulusan	0703-01=
Calvario, El (México)	Cone of Chichinautzin	1401-08=
Cam Tiem Mount (SE Asia)	Cone of Bas Dong Nai	0705-05-
Camaldoli della Torre (Italy)	Cone of Vesuvius	0101-02=
Camargo Volc Field (México)	Cinder cones (None) Pleistocene	....
Camarinhas, Pico das (Azores)	Cone of Sete Cidades	1802-08=
Camataran, Cerro (México)	Shield volc. of Michoacán-Guanajuato	1401-06=
Cambado, Pico do (Azores)	Cone of Picos Volc System	1802-081
Cambria, Mt. (New Zealand)	Cone of Auckland Field	0401-02=
Camels Hump, the (Australia)	Dome of Newer Volcanics Prov	0509-01-
Camercia (Italy)	Cinder cone of Etna	0101-06=
Cameron, Mt. (Australia)	Cone of Newer Volcanics Prov	0509-01-
Cameroon (Africa-W)	Stratovolcano (19, 2000) Historical	**0204-01=**
Cameroun, Mont (Africa-W)	Synonym of Cameroon	0204-01=
Camiguin (Mindanao-Philippines)	Stratovolcanoes (4, 1953) Historical	**0701-08=**
Camiguin de Babuyanes (Luzon-N of)	Stratovolcano (1, 1857) Historical	**0704-01=**
Camiguin de Mindanao [Mt. Vulcan]	Dome of Camiguin	0701-08=
Camiguin de Misamis [Mt. Vulcan]	Dome of Camiguin	0701-08=
Camiguin del Sur [Mt. Vulcan] (Philippines)	Dome of Camiguin	0701-08=
Camiguin Tanda (Mindanao-Philippines)	Stratovolcano of Camiguin	0701-08=
Camiguin, Mt. (Luzon-N of)	Stratovolc. of Camiguin de Babuyanes	0704-01=
Camille Cone (Alaska-W)	Cone of Imuruk Lake	1104-06-
Camogon (Mindanao-Philippines)	Dome of Leonard Range	0701-031
Camp Hill (Canada)	Shield volcano of Edziza	1200-06-
Campagnano, Mt. (Italy)	Crater of Ischia	0101-03=
Campana Hill (Mindanao-Philippines)	Dome of Camiguin	0701-08=
Campanario, El (Canary Is)	Cinder cone of Hierro	1803-02-
Campanian Ignimbrite (Italy)	Pleistocene caldera of Campi Flegrei	0101-01=
Campi Flegrei (Italy)	Caldera (20, 1538) Historical	**0101-01=**
Campi Flegrei Mar Sicilia (Italy)	Submarine volcs. (6, 1867) Historical	**0101-07=**
Campi Fleigrei Canale de Sicilia (Italy)	Synonym of Campi Flegrei Mar Sicilia	0101-07=
Camposanto, Cerro (Guatemala)	Cone of Ixtepeque	1402-18-
Campotese (Italy)	Crater of Ischia	0101-03=
Camprida, Caldeira (Azores)	Tuff ring of Flores	1802-001
Camps Ridge [Madden's Mount] (W Indies)	Dome of Nevis Peak	1600-04=
Can Simo, Volcà (Spain)	Cone of Olot Volc Field	0100-03-
Can Tia, Volcà (Spain)	Cone of Olot Volc Field	0100-03-
Canacuaran [Metate, Cerro el] (México)	Shield volc. of Michoacán-Guanajuato	1401-06=
Cañada Obscura, Cerro (México)	Dome of Zitácuaro-Valle de Bravo	1401-061
Cañadas, Las (Canary Is)	Pleistocene caldera of Tenerife	1803-03-
Canalaon (Philippines-C)	Synonym of Kanlaon	0702-02=
Cañapa (Chile-N)	Stratovolcano (None) Pleistocene	....
Canar (Java)	Crater of Talagabodas	0603-15=
Canario, Lagoa do (Azores)	Maar of Sete Cidades	1802-08=
Canario, Pico de (Azores)	Pumice cone of Furnas	1802-10=
Cañas Dulces (Costa Rica)	Dome of Rincón de la Vieja	1405-02=
Canaste (Costa Rica)	Synonym of Arenal	1405-033
Canasto (Chile-C)	Crater of Lonquimay	1507-10=
Canastos Mondeyal (Colombia)	Pyroclastic cone of San Augustín-Isnos	....
Cancajanag (Philippines-C)	Lava domes (None) Quaternary	....
Candado, El (Chile-C)	Cone of Maule, Laguna del	1507-061
Candelero (México)	Dome of Zitácuaro-Valle de Bravo	1401-061
Candlemas Island (Antarctica)	Stratovolcano (3, 1911) Historical	**1900-10=**
Cangkuang (Java)	Crater of Salak	0603-05=
Cañitas, Cerro (El Salvador)	Cinder cone of Coatepeque Caldera	1403-041
Canlancang (Java)	Unknown (None) Quaternary	....
Canlaon (Philippines-C)	Synonym of Kanlaon	0702-02=
Canneto Dentro (Italy)	Stratovolcano of Lipari	0101-042
Cañón de las Flores (México)	Vent of Primavera, Sierra la	....
Canot, Morne (W Indies)	Dome of Plat Pays, Morne	1600-11=
Cantariello (Italy)	Cone of Ischia	0101-03=
Cántaro, Volcán el (México)	Stratovolcano (None) Pleistocene	....
Cantarranas, Cerro (México)	Cone of Zitácuaro-Valle de Bravo	1401-061
Cantera, Cerro la (México)	Dome of Michoacán-Guanajuato	1401-06=
Canto, Cabeco do (Azores)	Cone of Fayal	1802-01=
Cantocloc [Cantoloc] (Philippines-C)	Stratovolcano of Cabalían	0702-05=
Cantoloc (Philippines-C)	Stratovolcano of Cabalían	0702-05=
Cantone (Italy)	Cinder cone of Etna	0101-06=
Canya, Volcà la (Spain)	Cone of Olot Volc Field	0100-03-
Canyon Creek [Second Canyon] (Canada)	Cone of Iskut-Unuk River Cones	1200-09-
Caolangojan [Kasiboi] (Philippines-C)	Cone of Mahagnao	0702-07=
Caopo (SE Asia)	Cone of Tengchong	0705-11-
Capac Urcu (Ecuador)	Synonym of Altar	....
Capacuaro, Cerros de (México)	Shield volc. of Michoacán-Guanajuato	1401-06=
Caparina (Ecuador)	Dome of Chacana	1502-022

Daniel Kergomard (courtesy J.G. Fitton, BRGM, France)

Steam rises from a crater and a lava flow in 1982 near the summit of 4095-m-high Mount **Cameroon**, one of Africa's largest volcanoes.

Name (Subregion)	Type (Eruptions, Most Recent) Status / Relation to Named Volcano	Volcano Number
Caparra, Loma (Nicaragua)	Dome of San Cristóbal	1404-02=
Capatacutiro, Cerro de (México)	Cinder cone of Michoacán-Guanajuato	1401-06=
Capaxtiro, Cerro (México)	Shield volc. of Michoacán-Guanajuato	1401-06=
Cape Balos (Greece)	Cinder cone of Santorini	0102-04=
Cape Berkeley Volcano (Galápagos)	Synonym of Ecuador	1503-011
Cape Bidlingmaier (Indian O.-S)	Cone of Heard	0304-01=
Cape Bridgewater (Australia)	Cone of Newer Volcanics Prov	0509-01-
Cape Cartwright (Indian O.-S)	Cone of Heard	0304-01=
Cape Columbos (Greece)	Tuff ring of Santorini	0102-04=
Cape Deschamp (New Britain-SW Pac)	Cone of Likuruanga	....
Cape Espenberg (Alaska-W)	Synonym of Espenberg	....
Cape Kokkinopetra (Greece)	Cinder cone of Santorini	0102-04=
Cape Mavrorachidi (Greece)	Cinder cone of Santorini	0102-04=
Cape Melville (Antarctica)	Synonym of Melville	....
Cape Reilnitz (New Britain-SW Pac)	Synonym of Saddle Mount	....

Name (Subregion)	Type (Eruptions, Most Recent) Status Relation to Named Volcano	Volcano Number
Cape Valdivia (Atlantic-S)	Dome of Bouvet	1806-02-
Capelas (Azores)	Tuff cone of Picos Volc System	1802-081
Capelinhos (Azores)	Cone of Fayal	1802-01=
Capesterre, Montagne de (W Indies)	Stratovolcano of Axial Chain	....
Capilla, La (México)	Crater of Cumbres, Las	1401-098
Capital (Alaska-E)	Shield volcano (None) Pleistocene	....
Capitolo, Monte (Italy)	Cone of Roccamonfina	....
Capo (Italy)	Stratovolcano of Salina	....
Capo Grosso (Italy)	Submarine vent of Lipari	0101-042
Cappy Mountain (US-Oregon)	Stratovolcano (None) Pleistocene	....
Caprara (Italy)	Dome of Campi Flegrei	0101-01=
Capricorn, Mt. (Canada)	Cone of Meager	1200-18-
Capulín (México)	Cinder cone of Chichinautzin	1401-08=
Capulin Mountain (US-New Mexico)	Cone of Raton-Clayton	....
Capullo (El Salvador)	Cone of Masahuat Volc Field	....
Cápur (Chile-N)	Stratovolcano (None) Pleistocene	....
Capurata (Chile-N)	Stratovolcano of Acotango	....
Cap-Vert (Africa-N)	Volcanic field (None) Pleistocene	....
Caquena (Chile-N)	Lava domes (None) Pleistocene	....
Carabao Killer (Philippines-C)	Thermal feature of Kanlaon	0702-02=
Caracha, La (Ecuador)	Stratovolcano of Atacazo	1502-021
Caracol (Chile-C)	Crater of Azul, Cerro	1507-06=
Caracol, Volcán (Chile-C)	Cone of Tolguaca	1507-093
Caracoral, Cerro (Panamá)	Dome of Valle, El	1406-03-
Caraïbes, Monts (W Indies)	Stratovolcano (None) Pleistocene	....
Carang Assam (Lesser Sunda Is)	Synonym of Agung	0604-02=
Carapacho (Chile-C)	Tuff ring of Llancanelo Volc Field	....
Caravajales Crater (México)	Crater of Pinacate	1401-001
Carbet, Fumerolles du (W Indies)	Therm. feature of Soufrière Guadeloupe	1600-06=
Carbets, Pitons de (W Indies)	Stratovolcano (None) Pleistocene	....
Carbonera, La (El Salvador)	Pleistocene caldera of San Vicente	1403-07=
Carbonilla, La (Argentina)	Pyrocl. cone Northern Mendoza Field	....
Carcabullo o Pedregal [Caldera Colorada]	Cinder cone of Lanzarote	1803-06-
Cardakh (Turkey)	Crater of Erciyes Dagi	0103-01=
Cardamomes (SE Asia)	Synonym of Pailin	....
Cardos, Los (México)	Cinder cone of Chichinautzin	1401-08=
Careme (Java)	Synonym of Cereme	0603-17=
Caribald Hill [Garibaldi Hill] (W Indies)	Stratovolcano of Soufrière Hills	1600-05=
Cariblanco [Cerro Congo] (Costa Rica)	Stratovolcano of Poás	1405-04=
Caribou (US-California)	Volcanic field (None) Pleistocene	....
Caribou Tuya (Canada)	Tuya of Tuya Volc Field	1200-031
Caricias (Costa Rica)	Stratovolcano of Barva	1405-05=
Carihuairazo (Ecuador)	Stratovolcano (None) Pleistocene	....
Carik Tepe (Turkey)	Dome of Erciyes Dagi	0103-01=
Cari-Launa, Volcanes (Chile-C)	Dome of Maule, Laguna del	1507-061
Cariliao (Luzon-Philippines)	Stratovolcano (None) Pleistocene	....
Cariquima, Cerro (Chile-N)	Stratovolcano (None) Pleistocene?	....
Caririñe (Argentina)	Stratovolcano of Huanquihue Group	1507-123
Carling Hill (Mindanao-Philippines)	Dome of Camiguin	0701-08=
Carlisle (Aleutian Is)	Stratovolcano (2, 1828) Historical	**1101-23-**
Carmelo Crater (US-Washington)	Crater of Baker	1201-01=

Lee Siebert (Smithsonian)

A period of glacial erosion separates tephra layers from two late-Pleistocene eruptive episodes at **Chimborazo** volcano, Ecuador.

Name (Subregion)	Type (Eruptions, Most Recent) Status Relation to Named Volcano	Volcano Number
Carmelo, la montana del (US-Washington)	Synonym of Baker	1201-01=
Carmichaël (W Indies)	Stratovolcano of Soufrière Guadeloupe	1600-06=
Carnegie Volcano (México)	Cinder cone of Pinacate	1401-001
Carneiro, Monte (Azores)	Cone of Fayal	1802-01=
Carnero, Cerro el (Guatemala)	Cone of Flores	1402-14-
Caroli ? (Aleutian Is)	Synonym of Shishaldin	1101-36-
Carpintero Norte, El (México)	Cinder cone of Colima	1401-04=
Carpintero Sur, El (México)	Cinder cone of Colima	1401-04=
Carr Mountain (US-New Mexico)	Cone of Raton-Clayton	....
Carrán (Chile-C)	Maar of Carrán-Los Venados	1507-14=
Carrán, Cerro [Los Guindos] (Chile-C)	Stratovolcano of Carrán-Los Venados	1507-14=
Carrán-Los Venados (Chile-C)	Pyroclastic cones (3, 1979) Historical	**1507-14=**
Carrizal I, Cerro del (Guatemala)	Cinder cone of Güistepeque Volc Field	....
Carrizozo (US-New Mexico)	Cinder cones (1, -3250) Surface Exposure	**1210-01-**
Cartago, Volcán de (Costa Rica)	Synonym of Irazú	1405-06=

Name (Subregion)	Type (Eruptions, Most Recent) Status Relation to Named Volcano	Volcano Number
Carvao (Azores)	Cone of Sete Cidades	1802-08=
Casa Diablo Hot Springs (US-California)	Thermal feature of Long Valley	....
Casablanca (Chile-C)	Stratovolcano of Antillanca Group	1507-153
Casas, Las (Costa Rica)	Thermal feature of Tenorio	1405-031
Cascajo, Montaña (Canary Is)	Cinder cone of Tenerife	1803-03-
Case Zacame (Italy)	Crater of Ustica	....
Casiboy [Kasiboi] (Philippines-C)	Cone of Mahagnao	0702-07=
Casiri, Nevados (Perú)	Stratovolcanoes (None) Holocene	**1504-06-**
Casita (Nicaragua)	Stratovolcano of San Cristóbal	1404-02=
Casitagua (Ecuador)	Stratovolcano (None) Pleistocene	....
Casitas, Cerros las (México)	Cinder cone of Camargo Volc Field	....
Casitas, Volcán (Chile-C)	Fissure vent of Azul, Cerro	1507-06=
CASM Vent Field (Pacific-NE)	Thermal feature of Axial Seamount	1301-021
Casma, Cerro (Costa Rica)	Dome of Dúrika	....
Cassien, Cratere (Indian O.-W)	Crater of Fournaise, Piton de la	0303-02=
Cassiope Cone (Alaska-W)	Cone of Imuruk Lake	1104-06-
Casteihano, Pico do (Azores)	Cone of Picos Volc System	1802-081
Castelgandolfo [Albano] (Italy)	Maar of Alban Hills	0101-004
Castellaro (Italy)	Pleistocene caldera of Lipari	0101-042
Castello (Italy)	Dome of Panarea	0101-041
Castello D'ischia (Italy)	Dome of Ischia	0101-03=
Castelo Branco (Azores)	Dome of Fayal	1802-01=
Castiglione (Italy)	Crater of Alban Hills	0101-004
Castiglione (Italy)	Dome of Ischia	0101-03=
Castillo, Cerro de los (Guatemala)	Cinder cone of Chingo	1402-17-
Castillo, Cerro el (Nicaragua)	Cone of Lajas, Las	1404-133
Castillo, El (Panamá)	Dome of Yeguada, La	....
Castle of Ischia [Castello D'ischia] (Italy)	Dome of Ischia	0101-03=
Castle Peak (W Indies)	Dome of Soufrière Hills	1600-05=
Castle Rock (Aleutian Is)	Dome of Bogoslof	1101-30-
Castle Rock (Antarctica)	Cone of Hut Point Peninsula	....
Castle Rock (Canada)	Cone of Klastline Group	....
Castle, the (Canada)	Cone of Squamish	....
Castor (Antarctica)	Cone of Seal Nunataks Group	1900-05=
Castrino (Argentina)	Pyrocl. cone Northern Mendoza Field	....
Castro Bank (Azores)	Synonym of Don Joao de Castro Bank	1802-07=
Casuela Juyu (Guatemala)	Synonym of Tolimán	1402-07=
Cat Hills (US-New Mexico)	Volcanic field (None) Pleistocene	....
Catacu, Cerro (México)	Cinder cone of Michoacán-Guanajuato	1401-06=
Catania, Monte di (Italy)	Synonym of Etna	0101-06=
Catarman (Mindanao-Philippines)	Synonym of Camiguin	0701-08=
Catarman [Hibok-Hibok] (Philippines)	Stratovolcano of Camiguin	0701-08=
Catatungan (Mindanao-Philippines)	Synonym of Kalatungan	0701-061
Cateratte, Monte (Italy)	Cinder cone of Etna	0101-06=
Cathedral Rock [Naperito] (Africa-E)	Tuff cone of Barrier, The	0202-03=
Catherine (Ethiopia)	Tuff ring of Gada Ale	0201-05=
Catinocjuyup [Cerro Quemado] (Guatemala)	Dome of Almolonga	1402-04=
Catu (Lesser Sunda Is)	Crater of Batur	0604-01=
Catur Caldera (Lesser Sunda Is)	Synonym of Bratan	0604-001
Caua (Luzon-Philippines)	Synonym of Cagua	0703-09=
Caubet, Cratere (Indian O.-W)	Crater of Fournaise, Piton de la	0303-02=
Cauldron Dome (Canada)	Tuya of Cayley, Mt.	....
Caulle Chico [Pichi Caulle] (Chile-C)	Cone of Puyehue-Cordón Caulle	1507-15=
Caulle Grande (Chile-C)	Synonym of Puyehue-Cordón Caulle	1507-15=
Cava Nocelle (Italy)	Crater of Ischia	0101-03=
Cava Petrella (Italy)	Cone of Ischia	0101-03=
Cavagnaro (Galápagos)	Crater of Santa Cruz	1503-091
Cavalo, Pico do (Azores)	Cone of Sete Cidades	1802-08=
Cave Gulch Hill (Atlantic-S)	Cinder cone of Tristan da Cunha	1806-01=
Caverne Pomme de Terre, Piton (Indian O.)	Cinder cone of Fournaise, Piton de la	0303-02=
Caverne, Ile de la (Indian O.)	Synonym of Prince Edward Island	0304-06-
Caviahue (Chile-C)	Caldera of Copahue	1507-09=
Cavo, Monte (Italy)	Synonym of Alban Hills	0101-004
Cavo, Mt. (Italy)	Cinder cone of Alban Hills	0101-004
Cavoni (Italy)	Submarine vent of Stromboli	0101-04=
Cawalo (Lesser Sunda Is)	Thermal feature of Paluweh	0604-15=
Caws Road (New Zealand)	Dome of Maroa	0401-061
Cay (Chile-S)	Stratovolcano (None) Holocene?	**1508-055**
Cayambe (Ecuador)	Compound volcano (22, 1786) Historical	**1502-006**
Cayapiren (Chile-S)	Synonym of Minchinmávida	1508-04=
Cayley, Mt. (Canada)	Stratovolcano (None) Pleistocene	....
Cayonan (Luzon-N of)	Cone of Babuyan Claro	0704-03=
Cayuse Cone (US-Oregon)	Cone of Broken Top	....
Cayuse Cone (US-Oregon)	Cinder cone of South Sister	1202-08-
Cayute, Volcán (Chile-S)	Cone of Cayutué-La Viguería	1508-012
Cayutué-La Viguería (Chile-S)	Pyroclastic cones (1, -1050) Tephrochron	**1508-012**
Cazuel, Cerro (Galápagos)	Pyroclastic cone of Negra, Sierra	1503-05=
Cebollas, Las (México)	Dome of Zitácuaro-Valle de Bravo	1401-061
Ceboroquito (México)	Cinder cone of Ceboruco	1401-03=
Ceboruco (México)	Stratovolcano (4, 1875) Historical	**1401-03=**
Cedar Grove (US-Utah)	Cone of Mineral Mts-Cove Fort	....
Cedar Hill (Africa-E)	Dome of Eburru, Ol Doinyo	0202-08=
Cedro, Pico do (Azores)	Cone of Sete Cidades	1802-08=
Cehennem Tepe (Turkey)	Crater of Tendürek Dagi	0103-03=
Ceiba Chacha, Cerro (El Salvador)	Cinder cone of Coatepeque Caldera	1403-041
Ceille, Piton (Indian O.-W)	Cinder cone of Fournaise, Piton de la	0303-02=
Cekok, Kawah (Java)	Thermal feature of Galunggung	0603-14=
Celaya Crater (México)	Maar of Pinacate	1401-001
Celle (Italy)	Crater of Campi Flegrei	0101-01=
Celletta (Italy)	Pyroclastic cone of Ernici, Monti	....
Celosa, Cerro la (Chile-N)	Cone of Ollagüe	1505-06=
Cemara Lawang (Java)	Stratovolcano of Tengger Caldera	0603-31=
Cemara, Gunung (Java)	Cone of Ijen	0603-35=
Cemel Tepe (Turkey)	Maar of Kula	0103-00-

Name (Subregion)	Type (Eruptions, Most Recent) Status / Relation to Named Volcano	Volcano Number
Cementerio Brito, Cerro del (Guatemala)	Cinder cone of Cuilapa-Barbarena	1402-111
Cementerio Cerro Redondo, Cerro (Guat.)	Cinder cone of Cuilapa-Barbarena	1402-111
Cemetary Crater (New Zealand)	Maar of Auckland Field	0401-02=
Cemorolawang [Cemara Lawang] (Java)	Stratovolcano of Tengger Caldera	0603-31=
Cemrkopru Baraj Golu (Turkey)	Cone of Kula	0103-00-
Cendres, Ile des (SE Asia)	Submarine volcanoes (1, 1923) Historical	**0705-06-**
Cengyu (Taiwan-N of)	Synonym of Zengyu	0801-05=
Ceniza, Volcán (México)	Cinder cone of San Quintín Volc Field	1401-002
Cenizas, Cerro (Chile-N)	Cone of Cordón de Puntas Negras	1505-101
Cenizas, Cerro (Chile-C)	Synonym Puntiagudo-Cordón Cenizos	1507-16-
Ceno-Semiachik (Kamchatka)	Stratovolcano of Maly Semiachik	1000-14=
Centenari, Monte (Italy)	Cinder cone of Etna	0101-06=
Central Atitlán (Guatemala)	Cone of Tolimán	1402-07=
Central Cone (New Zealand)	Stratovolcano of White Island	0401-04=
Central Cone Group (México)	Cinder cone of Cofre de Perote	1401-096
Central Crater Complex (US-Oregon)	Caldera of Diamond Craters	1202-17-
Central Dome (New Zealand)	Dome of Whale Island	....
Central Group (US-Oregon)	Cinder cone of Sand Mountain Field	1202-04-
Central Island (Africa-E)	Tuff cones (Uncertain) Holocene	**0202-01=**
Central Pumice Cone (US-Oregon)	Pumice cone of Newberry	1202-11-
Central Reefs (Italy)	Crater of Panarea	0101-041
Central Slovakia (Slovakia)	Volcanic field (None) Pleistocene	....
Central, Pico (Guatemala)	Synonym of Acatenango	1402-08=
Centralny (Kamchatka)	Shield volcano of Pogranychny	1000-47-
Centre Hills (W Indies)	Lava domes (None) Pleistocene	....
Centre Peak (Red Sea)	Cone of Zubair, Jebel	0201-02=
Centro, El (México)	Dome of Ceboruco	1401-03=
Cerberus (Aleutian Is)	Stratovolcano of Semisopochnoi	1101-06-
Cerberus, Mt. (Alaska Peninsula)	Dome of Trident	1102-16-
Cereme (Java)	Stratovolcano (6, 1951) Historical	**0603-17=**
Cerimai (Java)	Synonym of Cereme	0603-17=
Cerisy Peak (New Guinea-NE of)	Stratovolcano of Long Island	0501-05=
Cerme (Java)	Synonym of Cereme	0603-17=
Cerra, La (Guatemala)	Cone of Pacaya	1402-11=
Cerrado Novo (Azores)	Dome of Agua de Pau	1802-09=
Cerrillo, Cerro el [Cerro Chajnantor] (Chile-N)	Dome of Purico Complex	1505-094
Cerritito (Nicaragua)	Dome of Apoyo	....
Cerrito, Cerro el (México)	Cinder cone of Naolinco Volc Field	1401-095
Cerrito, Cerro el (El Salvador)	Cinder cone of San Salvador	1403-05=
Cerrito, El (El Salvador)	Cinder cone of Apaneca Range	1403-01=
Cerrito, El (Nicaragua)	Dome of Apoyo	....
Cerritos, Los (Guatemala)	Cone of Santiago, Cerro	1402-15-
Cerro de Agrás (Spain)	Cone of Cofrentes	....
Cerro, Cerrito (Spanish for Peak, Hill) see proper name (e.g. Mesa, Cerro de La)		
Cerrón, Cerro (El Salvador)	Dome of Apastepeque Field	1403-071
Cerrón, Cerro el (Guatemala)	Cone of Ixtepeque	1402-18-
Cerrón, El (El Salvador)	Synonym of Singüil, Cerro	1403-002
Cerute (Chile-N)	Synonym of Curutú	....
Cervena Hora [Cerveny Kopec] (Czech)	Cone of Unnamed	....
Cerveny Kopec (Czech)	Cone of Unnamed	....
Ceyssat, Maar de (France)	Maar of Chaîne des Puys	0100-02-
Cha (Cape Verde Is)	Caldera of Fogo	1804-01=
Chabbi [Chebbi] (Ethiopia)	Stratovolcano of Corbetti Caldera	0201-29-
Chacana (Ecuador)	Caldera (5, 1773) Historical	**1502-022**
Chacha (Kuril Is)	Synonym of Tiatia	0900-03=
Chachacaste, Cerro (El Salvador)	Dome of Ilopango	1403-06=
Chachani, Nevado (Perú)	Stratovolcano (None) Holocene?	**1504-007**
Chachanobori (Chachanupuri) (Kuril Is)	Synonym of Tiatia	0900-03=
Chachanupuri (Kuril Is)	Synonym of Alaid	0900-39=
Chachimbiro (Ecuador)	Stratovolcano (1, -3740) Radiocarbon	**1502-002**
Chac-Inca, Cerro (Chile-N)	Dome of Azufre, Cerro del	1505-061
Chadutka (Kamchatka)	Synonym of Khodutka	1000-053
Chaguitillo, Cerro (Guatemala)	Dome of Ixtepeque	1402-18-
Chagulak (Aleutian Is)	Stratovolcano (None) Holocene	**1101-20-**
Chahalé (Indian O.-W)	Pit crater of Karthala	0303-01=
Chaholo (Africa-E)	Dome of SW Usangu Basin	0202-163
Chahorra (Canary Is)	Cinder cone of Tenerife	1803-03-
Chaikutes (Greece)	Thermal feature of Kos	....
Chaimu (Africa-E)	Cone of Chyulu Hills	0202-13=
Chain of Craters (Africa-E)	Crater of Central Island	0202-01=
Chaîne des Puys (France)	Cinder cones (8, -4040) Radiocarbon	**0100-02-**
Chaiquemahuida, Volcán (Chile-C)	Cinder cone of Mocho-Choshuenco	1507-13=
Chaisanduku (Africa-C)	Crater of Bunyaruguru	0203-004
Chaitén (Chile-S)	Caldera (2, 2010) Historical	**1508-041**
Chajnantor, Cerro (Chile-N)	Dome of Purico Complex	1505-094
Chakatah Creek Peak (Canada)	Cone of Kawdy Metah	....
Chakunage (Hokkaido-Japan)	Cone of Niseko	0805-031
Chala (Africa-E)	Cone of Kilimanjaro	0202-15=
Chalard, Puy (France)	Cone of Chaîne des Puys	0100-02-
Chalchihuites (México)	Cinder cone of Chichinautzin	1401-08=
Chalchuapa, Cerrito de (El Salvador)	Cinder cone of Apastepeque Field	1403-071
Chalchuapa, Laguna de	Pit crater of Apastepeque Field	1403-071
Chalchuapán, Laguna de (El Salvador)	Pit crater of Apastepeque Field	1403-071
Challapiren (Chile-S)	Synonym of Minchinmávida	1508-04=
Challhue Mauras, Volcán (Perú)	Cinder cone of Andahua-Orcopampa	1504-004
Chalpatan (Ecuador)	Caldera (None) Pleistocene	....
Chaluhangi (Africa-E)	Cone of Katete	....
Chalupas (Ecuador)	Caldera (None) Quaternary	....
Cham (SE Asia)	Unknown (None) Pleistocene	....
Chamar Daban (Russia-SE)	Synonym of Khamar-Daban	....
Chambagunguru (Africa-E)	Cone of Kieyo	0202-17=
Chambaji (Africa-E)	Dome of SW Usangu Basin	0202-163
Chambasegera (Africa-E)	Cone of Kieyo	0202-17=
Chambuga [Mbuga] (Africa-C)	Maar of Katwe-Kikorongo	0203-003
Chamengo (Africa-C)	Crater of Bunyaruguru	0203-004
Chamongera (Africa-E)	Dome of SW Usangu Basin	0202-163
Champagne (Volcano Is-Japan)	Thermal feature of NW Eifuku	0804-136
Champagne (W Indies)	Thermal feature of Plat Pays, Morne	1600-11=
Champalala (Africa-E)	Dome of SW Usangu Basin	0202-163
Champes Phlegrais (Italy)	Synonym of Campi Flegrei	0101-01=
Champion Island (Galápagos)	Tuff cone of Floreana	....
Chamuscada, Montaña (Canary Is)	Cinder cone of Hierro	1803-02-
Chana (Chile-S)	Synonym of Minchinmávida	1508-04=
Chanal, Cerro el (Nicaragua)	Cinder cone of Granada	1404-101
Chance's Mountain (W Indies)	Synonym of Soufrière Hills	1600-05=
Chance's Peak (W Indies)	Dome of Soufrière Hills	1600-05=
Chanchani (Perú)	Synonym of Chachani, Nevado	1504-007
Chancho, Volcán (Chile-C)	Cinder cone of Carrán-Los Venados	1507-14=

Lee Siebert (Smithsonian)

The 7 x 10 km **Coatepeque** caldera in El Salvador was formed by collapse of a group of stratovolcanoes immediately east of Santa Ana volcano during a series of major explosive eruptions between about 70,000 and 57,000 years ago.

Name (Subregion)	Type (Eruptions, Most Recent) Status / Relation to Named Volcano	Volcano Number
Chanchoco, Termas de (Chile-C)	Thermal feature of Copahue	1507-09=
Chanchos, de los (Argentina)	Pyrocl. cone Northern Mendoza Field	....
Chanchos, Los (Nicaragua)	Dome of Cosigüina	1404-01=
Chanduini (Africa-E)	Cone of Sultan Hamud-Simba	....
Chanel (Chile-C)	Synonym of Llaima	1507-11=
Chang Peak (Antarctica)	Shield volcano of Waesche	1900-024
Changar (Kamchatka)	Synonym of Khangar	1000-272
Changbaishan (China-E)	Stratovolcano (8, 1903) Historical	**1005-06-**
Changomeni [Choungou-Chagnoumeni]	Pit crater of Karthala	0303-01=
Changou-Chahale [Choungou-Chahale]	Pit crater of Karthala	0303-01=
Chang-Pai (China-E)	Thermal feature of Changbaishan	1005-06-
Chang-Pai-shan (China-E)	Synonym of Changbaishan	1005-06-
Changpo (SE Asia)	Cone of Tengchong	0705-11-
Chanjale (México)	Caldera of Tacaná	1401-13=
Chanka (Chile-N)	Dome of Azufre, Cerro del	1505-061
Chankorogo (Africa-E)	Dome of SW Usangu Basin	0202-163
Chanmico, Laguna de (El Salvador)	Maar of San Salvador	1403-05=
Chanque-Mallin (Argentina)	Stratovolcano of Domuyo	1507-067
Chanthaburi (SE Asia)	Unknown (None) Pleistocene	....
Chanuj Gol (Mongolia)	Synonym of Khanuy Gol	1003-02-
Chao (Chile-N)	Dome of Leon, Cerro del	....
Chaokhch (Kamchatka)	Synonym of Koshelev	1000-02=
Chaos Crags (US-California)	Dome of Lassen Volc Center	1203-08-
Chaparrastique (El Salvador)	Synonym of San Miguel	1403-10=
Chapchap (Africa-W)	Cone of Oku Volc Field	0204-03-
Chapulín, Cerro el (México)	Dome of Primavera, Sierra la	....
Chapultepec (México)	Lava cone of Chichinautzin	1401-08=
Chapulul, Cerro (Chile-C)	Cinder cone of Mariñaqui, Laguna	1507-092
Charash-Dag (Russia-SE)	Shield volcano of Azas Plateau	1002-07-
Charco Muerto (Nicaragua)	Tuff ring of Zapatera	1404-111
Charco, El (Canary Is)	Cinder cone of La Palma	1803-01-
Charles (Galápagos)	Synonym of Floreana	....
Charlton Butte (US-Oregon)	Shield volcano of Maiden Peak	....
Charmont, Puy de (France)	Cone of Chaîne des Puys	0100-02-
Charos (Greece)	Thermal feature of Milos	0102-03=
Chascón de Purico [Cerro el Chascón] (Chile)	Dome of Purico Complex	1505-094
Chascon Norte, Cerro (Chile-C)	Cinder cone of Carrán-Los Venados	1507-14=
Chascon Sur, Cerro (Chile-C)	Cinder cone of Carrán-Los Venados	1507-14=
Chascon, Cerro (Bolivia)	Lava dome (None) Pleistocene	....
Chascon, Cerro (Chile-N)	Dome of Guayaques	1505-093
Chascón, Cerro el (Chile-N)	Dome of Purico Complex	1505-094
Chashakondzha (Kamchatka)	Stratovolcano of Alney-Chashakondzha	1000-45-
Chasm, The [La Voragine] (Italy)	Crater of Etna	0101-06=
Chasm, The [Wahanga-Waimangu]	Fissure vent of Okataina	0401-05=
Chat, Piton de (Indian O.-W)	Cinder cone of Fournaise, Piton de la	0303-02=
Chata, Cerro la (El Salvador)	Lava cone of San Diego	1403-001
Chateau Fort, Le (Indian O.-W)	Crater of Fournaise, Piton de la	0303-02=
Chatham (Galápagos)	Synonym of San Cristóbal	1503-12-
Chatito (Costa Rica)	Dome of Arenal	1405-033
Chato (Argentina)	Pyrocl. cone Northern Mendoza Field	....
Chato (Argentina)	Cinder cone of Unnamed	....

Name (Subregion)	Type (Eruptions, Most Recent) Status. Relation to Named Volcano	Volcano Number
Chato (México)	Dome of Zitácuaro-Valle de Bravo	1401-061
Chato Segundo (Argentina)	Cinder cone of Unnamed	
Chato, Cerrito (US-New Mexico)	Dome of Valles Caldera	
Chato, Cerro (Costa Rica)	Stratovolcano of Arenal	1405-033
Chato, Cerro (México)	Dome of Primavera, Sierra la	
Chato, Cerro (Costa Rica)	Cone of Rincón de la Vieja	1405-02=
Chaudieres, Les (W Indies)	Thermal feature Soufrière Guadeloupe	1600-06=
Chaudron (Indian O.-S)	Cone of Amsterdam Island	0304-001
Chaumont, Puy de (France)	Cone of Chaîne des Puys	0100-02-
Chaupi Loma (Ecuador)	Cone of Santa Cruz	
Chaupi, Cerros de (Ecuador)	Synonym of Santa Cruz	
Chausu-dake (Honshu-Japan)	Dome of Nasu	0803-15=
Chausu-yama (Honshu-Japan)	Dome of Kita Yatsuga-take	0803-031
Chausu-yama (Honshu-Japan)	Synonym of Niigata-Yake-yama	0803-09=
Chavas (Colombia)	Crater of Galeras	1501-08=

The 6377-m-high Nevado **Coropuna**, Perú's highest and largest volcano, is a massive ice-covered volcanic complex with at least a half dozen summit cones.

Name (Subregion)	Type (Eruptions, Most Recent) Status. Relation to Named Volcano	Volcano Number
Chavycha (Kamchatka)	Shield volcanoes (None) Pleistocene	
Chayachii (Kamchatka)	Dome of Kurile Lake	1000-023
Chayll (Chile-C)	Synonym of Llaima	1507-11=
Cheakamus Valley (Canada)	Vent of Cayley, Mt.	
Cheb Basin (Czech)	Volcanic field (None) Pleistocene	
Chebbi (Ethiopia)	Stratovolcano of Corbetti Caldera	0201-29-
Chebrit Ale (Ethiopia)	Synonym of Gada Ale	0201-05=
Chechitno Peak (Alaska-E)	Synonym of Wrangell	1105-02-
Cheimu [Chaimu] (Africa-E)	Cone of Chyulu Hills	0202-13=
Cheju-do (Korea)	Synonym of Halla	1006-04-
Cheli Mine, Piton (Indian O.-W)	Cinder cone of Fournaise, Piton de la	0303-02=
Cheminee Nord [Changomeni] (Indian O.-W)	Pit crater of Karthala	0303-01=
Cheminee Sud [Chahale] (Indian O.-W)	Pit crater of Karthala	0303-01=
Chengzilou (SE Asia)	Cone of Tengchong	0705-11-
Chenque, El (Argentina)	Pyrocl. cone Northern Mendoza Field	
Chepe (Russia-SE)	Cinder cone of Udokan Plateau	1002-03-
Cheptomas (Africa-E)	Dome of Paka	0202-053
Chequepuquina (Perú)	Synonym of Huaynaputina	1504-03=
Cheringerán, Cerro de (México)	Cinder cone of Michoacán-Guanajuato	1401-06=
Cherinkutan (Kuril Is)	Synonym of Chirinkotan	0900-26=
Chernabura (Alaska-SW)	Synonym of Augustine	1103-01-
Chernoye Lake (Kamchatka)	Thermal feature of Bolshoi Semiachik	1000-15=
Cherny (Kamchatka)	Dome of Bolshoi Semiachik	1000-15=
Cherny (Kamchatka)	Stratovolcano (None) Holocene?	**1000-46-**
Cherny (Kuril Is)	Stratovolcano of Chirpoi	0900-15=
Chernyi Utes (Kamchatka)	Dome of Ksudach	1000-05=
Cherpuk Group (Kamchatka)	Pyroclastic cones (1, -4550) Radiocarbon	**1000-273**
Chesoro (Africa-E)	Vent of Korosi	0202-054
Chetkin (Aleutian Is)	Synonym of Great Sitkin	1101-12-
Chew Bahir (Ethiopia)	Pyroclastic cones (None) Quaternary	
Cheyu (Africa-E)	Dome of SW Usangu Basin	0202-163
Chfealin (Kamchatka)	Synonym of Ichinsky	1000-28=
Chi, Tarso Emi (Africa-N)	Volcanic field (None) Quaternary	
Chiapa (México)	Shield volcano of Humeros, Los	1401-093
Chiar Kkollu (Bolivia)	Cinder cone of Jayu Khota, Laguna	1505-035
Chia-Ts'sung (China-E)	Synonym of Jiacong	
Chiaus (Banda Sea)	Synonym of Teon	0605-05=
Chibuzú (Costa Rica)	Synonym of Poás	1405-04=
Chicabal, Volcán (Guatemala)	Stratovolcano of Siete Orejas	
Chicaval [Volcán Chicabal] (Guatemala)	Stratovolcano of Siete Orejas	
Chichaldinskoi (Aleutian Is)	Synonym of Shishaldin	1101-36-
Chicharrón, Cerro El (México)	Dome of Northern Guadalajara Mesa	
Chichicastepec [Cerro de Apaneca] (El Salv.)	Stratovolcano of Apaneca Range	1403-01=
Chichigalpa [Casita] (Nicaragua)	Stratovolcano of San Cristóbal	1404-02=
Chichihuale (México)	Dome of Cumbres, Las	1401-098
Chichimeco (México)	Dome of Orizaba, Pico de	1401-10=
Chichinautzin (México)	Volcanic field (8, 400) Radiocarbon	**1401-08=**
Chichinautzin, Cerro (México)	Shield volcano of Chichinautzin	1401-08=
Chichintor, Cerrito (Guatemala)	Cone of Ipala	1402-19-
Chichón, El (México)	Lava domes (13, 1982) Historical	**1401-12=**
Chichonal, El (México)	Synonym of Chichón, El	1401-12=
Chichontepec (El Salvador)	Synonym of San Vicente	1403-07=
Chichontepeque (El Salvador)	Synonym of San Vicente	1403-07=
Chichuj (México)	Stratovolcano of Tacaná	1401-13=
Chicken Killer (Philippines-C)	Thermal feature of Kanlaon	0702-02=
Chico (Argentina)	Stratovolcano Northern Mendoza Field	
Chico Volc Field (US-New Mexico)	Synonym of Raton-Clayton	
Chico, Pico [Yepocapa] (Guatemala)	Stratovolcano of Acatenango	1402-08=
Chico, Volcán (Galápagos)	Fissure vent of Negra, Sierra	1503-05=
Chiconautla (México)	Cone of Apan-Tezontepec	
Chien-shan (China-E)	Synonym of Jianshan	
Chien-Shui-Ting-Tzu [Jianshuidingzi] (China)	Cone of Longgang Group	1005-05-
Chiesa Vecchia (Italy)	Stratovolcano of Lipari	0101-042
Chiewo (Africa-E)	Cone of Homa Mountain	0202-07=
Chifeng (China-E)	Unknown (None) Quaternary	
Chigignagak (Alaska Peninsula)	Synonym of Chiginagak	1102-11-
Chiginagak (Alaska Peninsula)	Stratovolcano (2, 1998) Historical	**1102-11-**
Chigowe (Africa-E)	Dome of SW Usangu Basin	0202-163
Chi-Haedrong (SE Asia)	Crater of Pleiku-Bantour Volc Field	
Chi-Hodron Mount [Chi-haedrong] (SE Asia)	Crater of Pleiku-Bantour Volc Field	
Chi-Holam Mount (SE Asia)	Cone of Pleiku-Bantour Volc Field	
Chihsingshan [Cising] (Taiwan)	Dome of Tatun Group	0801-032
Chihuido (Argentina)	Pyrocl. cone Northern Mendoza Field	
Chihuio (Argentina)	Stratovolcano of Huanquihue Group	1507-123
Chikoida Mountain (Canada)	Cone of Atlin Volc Field	1200-03-
Chikose (Africa-E)	Dome of SW Usangu Basin	0202-163
Chikubo (Honshu-Japan)	Cone of Izu-Tobu	0803-01=
Chikurachki (Kuril Is)	Stratovolcanoes (15, 2008) Historical	**0900-36=**
Chikura-dake (Kuril Is)	Synonym of Chikurachki	0900-36=
Chilacayote, Cerro el (México)	Shield volc. of Zitácuaro-Valle de Bravo	1401-061
Ch'Ilalo (Ethiopia)	Stratovolcano (None) Pleistocene	
Chilcapugro (Ecuador)	Dome of Casitagua	
Chilcas, Cerro las (Perú)	Dome of Huaynaputina	1504-03=
Chilcayoc Grande, Volcán (Perú)	Cinder cone of Andahua-Orcopampa	1504-004
Chilcayoc, Volcánes (Perú)	Cinder cone of Andahua-Orcopampa	1504-004
Chilcotin Creek (Canada)	Cinder cone of Satah Mountain	1200-13-
Chilcotin Group-North (Canada)	Volcanic field (None) Pleistocene	
Chilcotin Group-South (Canada)	Volcanic field (None) Pleistocene	
Chilena, La (Argentina)	Pyrocl. cone Northern Mendoza Field	
Chiles (Colombia)	Stratovolcano C. Negro de Mayasquer	1501-11=
Chiles, Los (Costa Rica)	Cinder cone of Platanar	1405-034
Chilesdo (México)	Dome of Zitácuaro-Valle de Bravo	1401-061
Chiliques (Chile-N)	Stratovolcano (None) Holocene?	**1505-098**
Chillahuita, Cerro (Chile-N)	Dome of Leon, Cerro del	
Chillan Viejo [Volcán Viejo] (Chile-C)	Stratovolcano of Chillán, Nevados de.	1507-07=
Chillán, Nevados de (Chile-C)	Stratovolcano (25, 2003) Historical	**1507-07=**
Chilling Island [Silenge Island] (New Britain)	Cone of Mundua	0502-021
Chiloe, Volcan de? (Chile-S)	Synonym of Corcovado	1508-05=
Chiltazón (Ecuador)	Stratovolcano (None) Pleistocene	
Chiltepe (Nicaragua)	Synonym of Apoyeque	1404-091
Chiltepe, Volcán (Nicaragua)	Dome of Apoyeque	1404-091
Chilung Group (Taiwan)	Lava domes (None) Pleistocene	
Chimaltepeque, Cerro (Guatemala)	Cinder cone of Redondo, Cerro	
Chimborazo (Ecuador)	Stratovolcano (6, 550) Radiocarbon	**1502-071**
Chi-Mei (Taiwan)	Lava dome (None) Post-Miocene	
Chimney Crater (New Britain-SW Pac)	Crater of Langila	0502-01=
Chimney Mountain (Galápagos)	Cone of Santa Cruz	1503-091
China Hat (US-Oregon)	Dome of China Hat-East Butte	
China Hat-East Butte (US-Oregon)	Lava domes (None) Pleistocene	
Chinabora, Mt. (Alaska-SW)	Synonym of Augustine	1103-01-
Chinal (Chile-C)	Synonym of Llaima	1507-11=
Chinameca (El Salvador)	Stratovolcano (None) Holocene	**1403-09=**
Chinandega (Nicaragua)	Synonym of San Cristóbal	1404-02=
Chinapo, Cerro (México)	Dome of Azufres, Los	
Chinchillaguay, Cerro (Bolivia)	Stratovolcano (None) Post-Miocene	
Chincillas, Cerro las (Chile-N)	Cone of Cordón de Puntas Negras	1505-101
Chinconquiat, Cerro (México)	Cinder cone of Chichinautzin	1401-08=
Chinendega (Nicaragua)	Synonym of San Cristóbal	1404-02=
Chingana, Cerro la (Perú)	Dome of Chachani, Nevado	1504-007
Chingeingein (Kamchatka)	Shield volcano of Uksichan	1000-35-
Ching-i-shan [Jingyishan] (China-E)	Cone of Kuandian	
Chingo (Guatemala)	Stratovolcano (None) Holocene	**1402-17-**
Chingo, Volcán (Guatemala)	Stratovolcano of Chingo	1402-17-
Ching-pe (China-E)	Synonym of Jingbo	1005-04-
Chingpohu (China-E)	Synonym of Jingbo	1005-04-
Chingyu (China-E)	Synonym of Longgang Group	1005-05-
Chinitos, Los (El Salvador)	Fissure vent of San Salvador	1403-05=
Chino el Pital, Cerro (Guatemala)	Dome of Ixhuatán	
Chino, Cerro (Guatemala)	Cinder cone of Pacaya	1402-11=
Chino, Cerro [Olla, Cerro la] (El Salvador)	Cinder cone of Santa Ana	1403-02=
Chino, Cerro del (México)	Cinder cone of Michoacán-Guanajuato	1401-06=
Chino, Cerro el (México)	Dome of Acatlán Volc Field	
Chino, Cerro el (México)	Dome of Azufres, Los	
Chinoike-jigoku (Kyushu-Japan)	Thermal feature of Tsurumi	0802-13=
Chinyero (Canary Is)	Cinder cone of Tenerife	1803-03-
Chío, Montaña (Canary Is)	Fissure vent of Tenerife	1803-03-
Chipilapa (El Salvador)	Thermal feature of Apaneca Range	1403-01=
Chiquimula Volc Field (Guatemala)	Cinder cones (None) Holocene	**1402-20-**
Chiquiomate (Perú)	Synonym of Huaynaputina	1504-03=
Chiquito, Cerro (Guatemala)	Dome of Pacaya	1402-11=
Chiracha (Ethiopia)	Stratovolcano (None) Holocene?	**0201-30-**
Chirica (Italy)	Stratovolcano of Lipari	0101-042
Chirihoi [Brat Chirpoev] (Kuril Is)	Stratovolcano of Chirpoi	0900-15=
Chirihoigaku [Brat Chirpoev] (Kuril Is)	Stratovolcano of Chirpoi	0900-15=
Chirinkotan (Kuril Is)	Stratovolcano (6, 2004) Historical	**0900-26=**

Name (Subregion)	Type (Eruptions, Most Recent) Status Relation to Named Volcano	Volcano Number
Chirinkutan (Kuril Is)	Synonym of Chirinkotan	0900-26=
Chirip (Kuril Is)	Stratovolcanoes (2, 1860) Historical	**0900-09=**
Chiripnupui (Chiripnupuri) (Kuril Is)	Synonym of Chirip	0900-09=
Chiriporupuri (Chirippu-dake) (Kuril Is)	Synonym of Chirip	0900-09=
Chiriqui, Volcán de (Panamá)	Synonym of Barú	1406-01-
Chiri-yama (Honshu-Japan)	Synonym of Fuji	0803-03=
Chirpoi (Kuril Is)	Caldera (8, 1982) Historical	**0900-15=**
Chirripó Atlántico (Costa Rica)	Shield volcano of Colorado, Lomas de	....
Chirriqui (Panamá)	Synonym of Barú	1406-01-
Chisenupuri (Hokkaido-Japan)	Dome of Niseko	0805-031
Chishima-iwo-zan (Kuril Is)	Synonym of Ebeko	0900-38=
Chisny, Piton (Indian O.-W)	Cinder cone of Fournaise, Piton de la	0303-02=
Chi-Ten Mount (SE Asia)	Crater of Pleiku-Bantour Volc Field	....
Chitra-Calobre (Panamá)	Synonym of Yeguada, La	....
Chitu (Ethiopia)	Maar of O'a Caldera	0201-28-
Chiucham, Cerro (Guatemala)	Dome of Santo Tomás	....
Chivato, Volcán (Chile-C)	Cone of Descabezado Grande	1507-05=
Chivo, Cerro (Galápagos)	Cone of San Cristóbal	1503-12-
Chivo, Cerro el (México)	Cone of Pinacate	1401-001
Chivo, del (Argentina)	Cinder cone of Unnamed	....
Chivo, Loma el (Ecuador)	Dome of Pululagua	1502-011
Choaschen (Kamchatka)	Synonym of Ichinsky	1000-28=
Chocolate, Cerro [Cerro Colorado] (El Salv.)	Dome of Ilopango	1403-06=
Chocosuela (Costa Rica)	Pleistocene caldera of Platanar	1405-034
Chodueco (Choduanpire) (Chile-S)	Synonym of Osorno	1508-01=
Chojagahara (Honshu-Japan)	Pyroclastic cone (None) Pleistocene	....
Chojochongen (Kamchatka)	Synonym of Khodutka	1000-053
Chokai (Honshu-Japan)	Stratovolcanoes (14, 1974) Historical	**0803-22=**
Chokai-san (Honshu-Japan)	Synonym of Chokai	0803-22=
Cholomdyk (Cholomdik) (Russia-SE)	Cinder cone of Udokan Plateau	1002-03-
Chome (Chile-C)	Crater of Llaima	1507-11=
Chompipe, Cerro (Costa Rica)	Stratovolcano of Barva	1405-05=
Chonajtajuyub, Cerro (Guatemala)	Dome of Santo Tomás	....
Chonce, El [Volcán el Chonco] (Nicaragua)	Stratovolcano of San Cristóbal	1404-02=
Choncle [Volcán el Chonco] (Nicaragua)	Stratovolcano of San Cristóbal	1404-02=
Chonco, Volcán el (Nicaragua)	Stratovolcano of San Cristóbal	1404-02=
Choni (Greece)	Dome of Methana	0102-02=
Ch'on-ji [Tianchi] (China-E)	Caldera of Changbaishan	1005-06-
Choogaryong (Korea)	Synonym of Ch'uga-ryong	1006-02-
Chopine, Puy (France)	Dome of Chaîne des Puys	0100-02-
Chopo, Cerro (Costa Rica)	Pyroclastic cone (None) Pleistocene	....
Chorny (Kamchatka)	Synonym of Cherny	1000-46-
Choshichiro-yama (Honshu-Japan)	Dome of Akagi	0803-13=
Choshuenco (Chile-C)	Stratovolcano of Mocho-Choshuenco	1507-13=
Choshuenco-El Mocho (Chile-C)	Synonym of Mocho-Choshuenco	1507-13=
Choshuenco-Pillan (Chile-C)	Synonym of Mocho-Choshuenco	1507-13=
Chott Tigri Volc Field (Africa-N)	Volcanic field (None) Quaternary	....
Choungou-Chagnoumeni (Indian O.-W)	Pit crater of Karthala	0303-01=
Choungou-Chahale (Indian O.-W)	Pit crater of Karthala	0303-01=
Choungou-Chamadji (Indian O.-W)	Crater of Karthala	0303-01=
Choupanov (Kamchatka)	Synonym of Zhupanovsky	1000-12=
Chovsgol (Mongolia)	Synonym of Khubsugal Region	....
Chowder Ridge (US-Washington)	Stratovolcano of Baker	1201-01=
Christensen Nunatak (Antarctica)	Cone of Seal Nunataks Group	1900-05=
Christie Hill (US-California)	Dome of Maidu	....
Christmas (New Zealand)	Former crater of White Island	0401-04=
Chubbe, Jabal (Arabia-S)	Crater of Arhab, Harra of	0301-09-
Chubbers Hill (Australia)	Cone of McBride Volc Province	....
Chubetsu (Hokkaido-Japan)	Stratovolcano (None) Pleistocene	....
Chucamitepeque [Loma los Siete Cerros]	Cone of Chingo	1402-17-
Chúcaro, Cerro el (Nicaragua)	Synonym of Malpaisillo	....
Chudleigh Volc Province (Australia)	Shield volcanoes (None) Pleistocene	....
Chufquen, Volcán (Chile-C)	Cone of Sollipulli	1507-111
Ch'uga-ryong (Korea)	Shield volcano (None) Holocene?	**1006-02-**
Chuginadak (Aleutian Is)	Synonym of Cleveland	1101-24-
Chugul (Aleutian Is)	Synonym of Segula	1101-03-
Chuichumil, Cerro (Guatemala)	Cone of San Pedro	....
Chuicinivit, Cerro (Guatemala)	Cone of San Pedro	....
Chuluut (Mongolia)	Synonym of Taryatu-Chulutu	1003-01-
Chungururu (Africa-E)	Maar of Kieyo	0202-17=
Chun-po (SE Asia)	Synonym of Tengchong	0705-11-
Chuo-Kakokyu (Hokkaido-Japan)	Cone of Tokachi	0805-05=
Chuo-Zao (Honshu-Japan)	Stratovolcano of Zao	0803-19=
Chup (SE Asia)	Unknown (None) Pleistocene	....
Chupadero (Guatemala)	Crater of Tecuamburro	1402-12=
Chupiquiña, Nevado (Chile-N)	Stratovolcano of Tacora	1505-01=
Churchill (Alaska-E)	Stratovolcano (2, 700) Radiocarbon	**1105-03-**
Chuwera (Africa-C)	Crater of Bunyaruguru	0203-004
Chyornogo (Kuril Is)	Synonym of Chirpoi	0900-15=
Chyulu Hills (Africa-E)	Volcanic field (2, 1855) Anthropology	**0202-13=**
Ciampino (Italy)	Crater of Alban Hills	0101-004
Ciatur (Java)	Thermal feature of Tangkubanparahu	0603-09=
Cibeureum (Java)	Thermal feature of Kamojang, Kawah	....
Cibeureum (Java)	Thermal feature of Perbakti-Gagak	0603-04=
Cibeureum Palasari (Java)	Thermal feature of Perbakti-Gagak	0603-04=
Cibodas, Cipanas (Java)	Thermal feature of Perbakti-Gagak	0603-04=
Cibodas, Kawah (Java)	Thermal feature of Perbakti-Gagak	0603-04=
Cibodas, Kawah (Java)	Thermal feature of Salak	0603-05=
Cibolang, Kawah (Java)	Thermal feature of Wayang-Windu	0603-08=
Cibugis (Java)	Stratovolcano (None) Quaternary	....
Cibuni, Kawah (Java)	Thermal feature of Patuha	0603-07=
Ciburial (Java)	Thermal feature of Kamojang, Kawah	....
Ciega, Laguna (El Salvador)	Vent of San Salvador	1403-05=
Ciega, Laguna (El Salvador)	Stratovolcano of Tecapa	1403-08=

Name (Subregion)	Type (Eruptions, Most Recent) Status Relation to Named Volcano	Volcano Number
Ciego, Montaña (Canary Is)	Cinder cone of Tenerife	1803-03-
Cigamea, Kawah (Java)	Thermal feature of Salak	0603-05=
Cigliano (Italy)	Crater of Campi Flegrei	0101-01=
Ciglio (Italy)	Cone of Ischia	0101-03=
Ciguatepe, Cerro el (Nicaragua)	Stratovolcano (None) Holocene?	**1404-132**
Cigupakan (Java)	Thermal feature of Kendang	0603-11=
Cigushan (Taiwan)	Dome of Tatun Group	0801-032
Ciharus (Java)	Stratovolcano of Kamojang, Kawah	....
Cihideung, Cipanas (Java)	Thermal feature of Salak	0603-05=
Cikaluwung Putri, Kawah (Java)	Thermal feature of Salak	0603-05=
Cikaluwung, Cipanas (Java)	Thermal feature of Perbakti-Gagak	0603-04=
Cikaluwungherang, Kawah (Java)	Thermal feature of Perbakti-Gagak	0603-04=
Cikuray (Java)	Stratovolcano (None) Quaternary	....
Cilallo (Ethiopia)	Synonym of Ch'Ilalo	....
Cilekatan, Gunung (Java)	Cone of Slamet	0603-18=
Ciliano (Italy)	Dome of Vico-Cimino Complex	....
Cilik, Gunung (Java)	Cone of Ijen	0603-35=
Cilik, Gunung (Java)	Cone of Slamet	0603-18=
Cima Lava Field (US-California)	Volcanic field (None) Pleistocene	....
Cimini, Monti (Italy)	Dome of Vico-Cimino Complex	....
Cimino (Italy)	Stratovolcano of Vico-Cimino Complex	....
Cimotoe (Italy)	Submarine vent C. Flegrei Mar Sicilia	0101-07=
Cinco Picos (Azores)	Shield volcano of Terceira	1802-05=
Cinder Butte (US-California)	Shield volcano (None) Pleistocene	....
Cinder Butte (US-California)	Cone of Medicine Lake	1203-02-
Cinder Cliff (Canada)	Cone of Edziza	1200-06-
Cinder Cone (US-California)	Cinder cone of Lassen Volc Center	1203-08-
Cinder Cone (US-California)	Cinder cone of Medicine Lake	1203-02-
Cinder Cone (US-California)	Cinder cone of Shasta	1203-01-
Cinder Cone, the (Canada)	Cone of Garibaldi Lake	1200-19-
Cinder Hill (US-Oregon)	Cone of Newberry	1202-11-
Cinder Hills (Hawaiian Is)	Cone of Kilauea	1302-01-
Cinder Mountain (Canada)	Cone of Iskut-Unuk River Cones	1200-09-
Cinnamon Butte (US-Oregon)	Cinder cones (None) Holocene?	**1202-15-**
Cinotepec, Cerro (El Salvador)	Synonym of Cinotepeque, Cerro	1403-051
Cinotepeque, Cerro (El Salvador)	Volcanic field (None) Holocene	**1403-051**
Cinotepeque, Cerro (El Salvador)	Cinder cone of Cinotepeque, Cerro	1403-051
Cinque Denti (Italy)	Pleistocene caldera of Pantelleria	0101-071
Cintepec, Cerro [Cerro Pico de Aguila] (Méx.)	Stratovolcano of San Martín Pajapan	....
Cintrao (Azores)	Dome of Agua de Pau	1802-09=
Ciomadul (Romania)	Lava domes (None) Pleistocene	....
Ciothirai (Africa-E)	Cone of Nyambeni Hills	0202-056
Cipamatutan (Java)	Thermal feature of Perbakti-Gagak	0603-04=
Cipanas (Indonesian for Hot Springs) see proper name (e.g. Cibodas, Cipanas)		
Cipanas, Kawah (Java)	Thermal feature of Salak	0603-05=
Cipengasahan, Kawah (Java)	Thermal feature of Kamojang, Kawah	....
Ciremai (Java)	Synonym of Cereme	0603-17=
Cis, Mount (Antarctica)	Cone of Erebus	1900-02=
Cisalada, Cipanas (Java)	Thermal feature of Salak	0603-05=
Cisalada, Kawah (Java)	Thermal feature of Salak	0603-05=
Cisekati, Cipanas (Java)	Thermal feature of Perbakti-Gagak	0603-04=
Ciseupan, Cipanas (Java)	Thermal feature of Perbakti-Gagak	0603-04=

Lake-filled **Cosigüina** caldera at the NW tip of Nicaragua along the Gulf of Fonseca was the source of a major explosive eruption in 1835.

Name (Subregion)	Type (Eruptions, Most Recent) Status Relation to Named Volcano	Volcano Number
Cising (Taiwan)	Dome of Tatun Group	0801-032
Cisne, Nevado el (Colombia)	Dome of Ruiz, Nevado del	1501-02=
Cisternazza (Italy)	Crater of Etna	0101-06=
Citerne, Cratere (Indian O.-W)	Crater of Karthala	0303-01=
Citerne, La (W Indies)	Cinder cone of Soufrière Guadeloupe	1600-06=
Citlaltepec (México)	Synonym of Orizaba, Pico de	1401-10=
Citlaltépetl (México)	Synonym of Orizaba, Pico de	1401-10=
Citrons Galets, Piton (Indian O.-W)	Cinder cone of Fournaise, Piton de la	0303-02=
Ciwidei, Kawah (Java)	Thermal feature of Patuha	0603-07=
Clambake (Pacific-E)	Thermal feature of Galápagos Rift	1304-07-
Claperols, Volcà (Spain)	Cone of Olot Volc Field	0100-03-
Clara Peak (US-New Mexico)	Shield volcano of Valles Caldera	....
Clara, Laguneta (El Salvador)	Cinder cone of San Diego	1403-001
Clara, Montana (Canary Is)	Cone of Lanzarote	1803-06-
Clark (New Zealand)	Submarine volcano (None) Fumarolic	**0401-101**

Name (Subregion)	Type (Eruptions, Most Recent) Status Relation to Named Volcano	Volcano Number
Clarks Butte (US-Oregon)	Shield volcano of Lava Butte	
Clay, Mt. (Australia)	Cone of Newer Volcanics Prov	0509-01-
Clayton Valley (US-Nevada)	Cinder cone (None) Pleistocene	
Clear Lake (US-California)	Volcanic field (None) Holocene	**1203-10-**
Clear Lake Butte (US-Oregon)	Shield volcano of Wilson	
Clearwater Cone Group (Canada)	Synonym of Wells Gray-Clearwater	1200-15-
Cleetwood (US-Oregon)	Vent of Crater Lake	1202-16-
Cleft Segment (Pacific-NE)	Submarine volcano (3, 1986) Historical	**1301-03-**
Clerigo Duarte, Montana del [Volcán Tao]	Cone of Lanzarote	1803-06-
Clermont Chamalieres (France)	Maar of Chaîne des Puys	0100-02-
Cleveland (Aleutian Is)	Stratovolcano (18, 2009) Historical	**1101-24-**
Clierzou (France)	Dome of Chaîne des Puys	0100-02-
Clinker Peak (Canada)	Stratovolcano of Garibaldi Lake	1200-19-
Clipperton Island (Pacific-E)	Lava dome (None) Post-Miocene	
Clover Butte (US-Oregon)	Cone of Cappy Mountain	
Coatepeque Caldera (El Salvador)	Caldera (None) Holocene	**1403-041**
Coats Caldera (Aleutian Is)	Caldera of Yunaska	1101-21-
CoAxial Segment (Pacific-NE)	Submarine volcano (2, 1993) Historical	**1301-02-**
Coaxusco (México)	Cinder cone of Chichinautzin	1401-08=
Coba Negra (Colombia)	Pleistocene caldera of Galeras	1501-08=
Cobb Mountain (US-California)	Cone of Clear Lake	1203-10-
Cobb Segment (Pacific-NE)	Submarine volcano (1, -1180) U-series	**1301-011**
Cocha I, La (Ecuador)	Dome of Atacazo	1502-021
Cocha II, La (Ecuador)	Dome of Atacazo	1502-021
Cochague (El Salvador)	Synonym of Conchagua	1403-11=
Cochapampa, Cerro (Perú)	Cinder cone of Andahua-Orcopampa	1504-004
Cochapata (Ecuador)	Dome of Chachimbiro	1502-002
Cochiquito Volc Group (Argentina)	Stratovolcanoes (None) Holocene	**1507-071**
Cochiquito, Volcán (Argentina)	Stratovolcano Cochiquito Volc Group	1507-071
Cochons, Ile aux (Indian O.-S)	Stratovolcano (None) Holocene	**0304-05-**
Cochons, Piton des (Indian O.-W)	Cinder cone of Fournaise, Piton de la	0303-02=
Coco, Isla del (Costa Rica)	Shield volcano (None) Pleistocene	
Coco, Piton de (Indian O.-W)	Cinder cone of Fournaise, Piton de la	0303-02=
Cocoa (Canada)	Crater of Edziza	1200-06-
Coconucos, Los (Colombia)	Cone of Puracé	1501-06=
Coconuscos-Aguas Herviendo (Colombia)	Thermal feature of Puracé	1501-06=
Coconuscos-Aguas Tibias (Colombia)	Thermal feature of Puracé	1501-06=
Cocorí, Cerro (Costa Rica)	Shield volcano of Colorado, Lomas de	
Cocorí, Cerro (Costa Rica)	Cone of Tortuguero	
Cocos Island (Costa Rica)	Synonym of Coco, Isla del	
Coffee (Canada)	Crater of Edziza	1200-06-
Coffeepot Crater (US-Oregon)	Crater of Jordan Craters	1202-19-
Cofre de Perote (México)	Shield volcanoes (1, 1150) Radiocarbon	**1401-096**
Cofrentes (Spain)	Volcanic field (None) Pleistocene	
Cofrentes (Spain)	Cone of Cofrentes	
Cogon (Luzon-Philippines)	Dome of Labo	
Cohuazalo, Volcán (México)	Cone of Chichinautzin	1401-08=
Coigue (Chile-C)	Crater of Llaima	1507-11=
Cojutepeque (El Salvador)	Synonym of Ilopango	1403-06=
Colachi (Chile-N)	Stratovolcano (None) Holocene	**1505-095**
Colada Dendriforme [Crateres de los Baños]	Dome of Maule, Laguna del	1507-061
Colada las Nieblas (Chile-C)	Dome of Maule, Laguna del	1507-061
Colada Occidental (Chile-C)	Dome of Maule, Laguna del	1507-061
Colangal, Cerro (Ecuador)	Dome of Mojanda	1502-005
Colardeau, Fumerolles (W Indies)	Thermal feature Soufrière Guadeloupe	1600-06=
Colburn, Mount (Antarctica)	Dome of Shepard Island	
Cold Bay Volc Center (Alaska Peninsula)	Synonym of Frosty	1102-01-
Cold Creek Butte (US-California)	Cinder cone of Maidu	
Coleman Seamount (Solomon Is)	Submarine volcano (None) Holocene	**0505-053**
Colima (México)	Stratovolcanoes (77, 2010) Historical	**1401-04=**
Colima, Nevado de (México)	Stratovolcano of Colima	1401-04=
Collanes (Ecuador)	Synonym of Altar	
Collaqui (Chile-C)	Synonym of Callaqui	1507-091
Colle Castellone (Italy)	Pyroclastic cone of Ernici, Monti	
Colle Iano (Italy)	Cinder cone of Alban Hills	0101-004
Colle Margherita (Italy)	Dome of Vesuvius	0101-02=
Colle Rotondella (Italy)	Dome of Campi Flegrei	0101-01=
Colle Umberto (Italy)	Dome of Vesuvius	0101-02=
Collero, Loma (Ecuador)	Dome of Pambamarca	
Colli Albani (Italy)	Synonym of Alban Hills	0101-004
Colli Euganei Group (Italy)	(None) Not a Volcano	0101-00-
Colli Laziale (Italy)	Synonym of Alban Hills	0101-004
Colli, Cerro El (México)	Dome of Primavera, Sierra la	
Collier Cone (US-Oregon)	Cinder cone of North Sister Field	1202-07-
Collins Point (Antarctica)	Tuff cone of Deception Island	1900-03=
Colo [Una Una] (Sulawesi-Indonesia)	Stratovolcano (3, 1983) Historical	**0606-01=**
Coloci [Taulevu] (Fiji Is-SW Pacific)	Cone of Taveuni	0405-01-
Colombo Bank (Greece)	Maar of Santorini	0102-04=
Colombo, Mount (Antarctica)	Cone of Fosdick Mountains	
Colón (Costa Rica)	Shield volcano of Sierpe, Lomas de	
Coloot (Java)	Synonym of Kelut	0603-28=
Colorada, Caldera (Canary Is)	Cinder cone of Lanzarote	1803-06-
Colorada, Montaña [Montaña Rodeos]	Cinder cone of Lanzarote	1803-06-
Coloradas, Lomas (México-Is)	Cinder cone of Socorro	1401-021
Colorado (Chile-C)	Cone of Antillanca Group	1507-153
Colorado (Chile-C)	Crater of Llaima	1507-11=
Colorado (Chile-S)	Cinder cone of Palei-Aike Volc Field	1508-08-
Colorado (Panamá)	Synonym of Tisingal	
Colorado, Cerro (México)	Cone of Acatlán Volc Field	
Colorado, Cerro (Chile-C)	Cone of Calabozos	1507-042
Colorado, Cerro (Chile-C)	Cone of Chillán, Nevados de	1507-07=
Colorado, Cerro (México)	Cinder cone of Cofre de Perote	1401-096
Colorado, Cerro (Argentina)	Stratovolcano (None) Pleistocene?	
Colorado, Cerro (El Salvador)	Dome of Ilopango	1403-06=
Colorado, Cerro (Nicaragua)	Stratovolcano of Momotombo	1404-09=
Colorado, Cerro (México)	Tuff ring of Pinacate	1401-001
Colorado, Cerro (Chile-N)	Cone of Sairecabur	1505-091
Colorado, Cerro (US-New Mexico)	Cone of Zuni-Bandera	1210-02-
Colorado, Lomas de (Costa Rica)	Shield volcanoes (None) Pleistocene	
Colorados (Argentina)	Synonym of Colorado, Cerro	
Colorados, Cerro los (México)	Cinder cone of Camargo Volc Field	
Colton Crater (US-Arizona)	Cone of San Francisco Volc Field	
Columba, Volcán (Spain)	Cone of Calatrava Volc Field	0100-04-
Columbia Crest (US-Washington)	Crater of Rainier	1201-03-
Columbo Bank [Colombo Bank] (Greece)	Maar of Santorini	0102-04=
Columbretes, Islas (Spain)	Volcanic field (None) Quaternary	
Columnar Peak (Canada)	Dome of Garibaldi	1200-20-
Comal Chico (México)	Cinder cone of Colima	1401-04=
Comal Grande (México)	Cinder cone of Colima	1401-04=
Comalito (Nicaragua)	Cinder cone of Masaya	1404-10=
Combegrasse, Puy de (France)	Cone of Chaîne des Puys	0100-02-
Come, Puy de (France)	Cone of Chaîne des Puys	0100-02-
Commerson, Cratere (Indian O.-W)	Cinder cone of Fournaise, Piton de la	0303-02=
Commissioners Cap (Australia)	Cone of McBride Volc Province	
Comondú-La Purísima (México)	Volcanic field (None) Holocene?	**1401-012**
Compana, Cerro la (México)	Cone of Zitácuaro-Valle de Bravo	1401-061
Compañía, Cerro (Guatemala)	Cinder cone of Chingo	1402-17-
Company Butte (US-Oregon)	Cone of Newberry	1202-11-
Competri, Monte (Italy)	Cone of Alban Hills	0101-004
Comunidad (México)	Cone of Zitácuaro-Valle de Bravo	1401-061
Conacaste, Cerro [Cerro Chachacaste]	Dome of Ilopango	1403-06=
Concepción (Costa Rica)	Cone of Barva	1405-05=
Concepción (Nicaragua)	Stratovolcano (32, 2009) Historical	**1404-12=**
Concepción de Ataco (El Salvador)	Pit crater of Apaneca Range	1403-01=
Concha, La (Nicaragua)	Fissure vent of Concepción	1404-12=
Conchagua (El Salvador)	Stratovolcano (None) Uncertain	**1403-11=**
Conchagua Island (El Salvador)	Synonym of Conchagüita	1403-12=
Conchagüita (El Salvador)	Stratovolcano (1, 1892) Historical	**1403-12=**
Concola (Italy)	Crater of Campi Flegrei	0101-01=
Concordia, Cerro la [Guarazí] (Costa Rica)	Cinder cone of Barva	1405-05=
Condon Butte (US-Oregon)	Cinder cone of North Sister Field	1202-07-
Condor, Cerro (Chile-C)	Stratovolcano of Antuco	1507-08=
Cóndor, Cerro el (Argentina)	Stratovolcano (None) Holocene	**1505-19-**
Condoriquiña (Bolivia)	Unknown (None) Post-Miocene	
Condrodimuko (Java)	Thermal feature Dieng Volc Complex	0603-20=
Condrodimuko, Kawah (Java)	Thermal feature of Merbabu	0603-24=
Cone Crater (Hawaiian Is)	Cone of Kilauea	1302-01-
Cone Glacier (Canada)	Cone of Iskut-Unuk River Cones	1200-09-
Cone Hill (Alaska-W)	Fissure vent of St. Paul Island	1104-01-
Cone Peak (Hawaiian Is)	Cone of Kilauea	1302-01-
Cone Place (Africa-E)	Cone of Kilimanjaro	0202-15=
Cone, the (New Zealand)	Cone of Pirongia	
Cone-Culasi (Luzon-Philippines)	Volcanic field (None) Pleistocene	
Conejal, Cerro el (El Salvador)	Cinder cone of Santa Ana	1403-02=
Conejo, Loma el (Guatemala)	Dome of Redondo, Cerro	
Conejos, Montañas de los (Canary Is)	Vent of Tenerife	1803-03-
Congo, Cerro (Costa Rica)	Stratovolcano of Poás	1405-04=
Congo, Volcán (Costa Rica)	Synonym of Platanar	1405-034
Congress (New Zealand)	Former crater of White Island	0401-04=
Congro, Lagoa do (Azores)	Maar of Agua de Pau	1802-09=
Conguaco, Cerro (Guatemala)	Crater of Moyuta	1402-13-
Conguillio Group (Chile-C)	Crater of Llaima	1507-11=
Conical Hill (Antarctica)	Cone of Terror, Mt.	
Conil, Mont (W Indies)	Stratovolcano of Pelée	1600-12=
Conito de Anotfalla (Argentina)	Stratovolcano of Antofalla	
Connected Island (Red Sea)	Cone of Zubair, Jebel	0201-02=
Conte Vidua Solfatara Field (Indonesia)	Thermal feature of Tondano Caldera	0606-07-
Conte, Le (US-Oregon)	Cinder cone of South Sister	1202-08-
Contodoc [Cantoloc] (Philippines-C)	Stratovolcano of Cabalían	0702-05=
Contrada Caffefi, Cuddioli Di (Italy)	Vent of Pantelleria	0101-071
Contrada Murera (Italy)	Crater of Campi Flegrei	0101-01=
Contreras, Cerro (Chile-S/Argentina)	Cinder cone Crater Basalt Volc Field	1508-025
Conventilio, Cerro (El Salvador)	Cone of San Diego	1403-001
Cook (Solomon Is-SW Pacific)	(None) Not a Volcano	0505-051
Cook Island (Antarctica)	Submarine vent of Thule Islands	1900-07=
Cook, Volcán (Chile-S)	Synonym of Fueguino	1508-09-
Cooper Knoll (US-Utah)	Cone of Markagunt Plateau	1207-04-
Copa, Cerro (Chile-N)	Stratovolcanoes (None) Pleistocene	
Copacoya, Geisers de (Chile-N)	Synonym of Tatio, El	
Copahue (Chile-C)	Stratovolcano (12, 2000) Historical	**1507-09=**
Copahue, Baños (Chile-C)	Thermal feature of Copahue	1507-09=
Copahues, Los (Chile-C)	Synonym of Copahue	1507-09=
Copco Lake (US-California)	Cinder cones (None) Pleistocene	
Copete, El (Ecuador)	Dome of Reventador	1502-01=
Copiapó (Chile-N)	Stratovolcano (None) Uncertain	**1505-14-**
Cópitiro, Cerro de (México)	Cinder cone of Michoacán-Guanajuato	1401-06=
Coporito, Cerro el (México)	Cone of Zitácuaro-Valle de Bravo	1401-061
Coques, Ile de (Costa Rica)	Synonym of Coco, Isla del	
Coquille, Puy de la (France)	Cone of Chaîne des Puys	0100-02-
Cora (Turkey)	Maar of Erciyes Dagi	0103-01=
Coracora, Cerro (Bolivia)	Stratovolcano (None) Post-Miocene	
Coragulac, Lake (Australia)	Tuff ring of Newer Volcanics Prov	0509-01-
Corazón (Ecuador)	Stratovolcano (None) Pleistocene	
Corazoncillo, Caldera del (Canary Is)	Crater of Lanzarote	1803-06-
Corbetti Caldera (Ethiopia)	Caldera (None) Holocene	**0201-29-**
Corcobado (Chile-S)	Synonym of Corcovado	1508-05=
Corcovado (Chile-S)	Stratovolcano (3, -4920) Historical	**1508-05=**
Cordemoy, Cratere de (Indian O.-W)	Crater of Fournaise, Piton de la	0303-02=

Name (Subregion)	Type (Eruptions, Most Recent) Status / Relation to Named Volcano	Volcano Number
Cordillera Blanca (Chile-C)	Synonym of Callaqui	1507-091
Cordillera del Pedregal [Cordón Caulle]	Fissure vent Puyehue-Cordón Caulle	1507-15=
Cordillera Dorsal (Canary Is)	Fissure vent of Tenerife	1803-03-
Cordillera Nevada (Chile-C)	Caldera of Puyehue-Cordón Caulle	1507-15=
Cordillera Pelada [Cordón Caulle] (Chile-C)	Fissure vent Puyehue-Cordón Caulle	1507-15=
Cordón Caulle (Chile-C)	Fissure vent Puyehue-Cordón Caulle	1507-15=
Cordon Cenizos (Chile-C)	Cone of Puntiagudo-Cordón Cenizos	1507-16-
Cordon de Alvarez (Chile-C)	Cone of Antillanca Group	1507-153
Cordón de Puntas Negras (Chile-N)	Stratovolcanoes (None) Holocene	**1505-101**
Cordón del Azufre (Chile-N)	Complex volcano (None) Holocene	**1505-121**
Cordon el Cauye (Chile-C)	Synonym Puntiagudo-Cordón Cenizos	1507-16-
Cordón Pelón (México)	Stratovolcano of San Martín Pajapan	....
Corero de la Charca, Cerro (Panamá)	Dome of Yeguada, La	....
Corinth Head (Indian O.-S)	Cone of Heard	0304-01=
Cormorant Point (Galápagos)	Tuff cone of Floreana	....
Corno de Bellaria (Italy)	Dome of Amiata	....
Corona, La [La Caldereta] (Canary Is)	Crater of Tenerife	1803-03-
Corona, Monte (Canary Is)	Cone of Lanzarote	1803-06-
Coronación (Costa Rica)	Synonym of Chopo, Cerro	....
Coronado (México)	Stratovolcano (None) Fumarolic	**1401-005**
Coronel I (Costa Rica)	Shield volcano of Colorado, Lomas de	....
Coronel II (Costa Rica)	Shield volcano of Colorado, Lomas de	....
Coronel III (Costa Rica)	Shield volcano of Colorado, Lomas de	....
Coronel, Cerro (Costa Rica)	Cone of Tortuguero	....
Coronilla, Cerro la (México)	Dome of Acatlán Volc Field	....
Coropuna (Perú)	Stratovolcano (None) Holocene	**1504-003**
Corozal Viejo, El (Nicaragua)	Cone of Maderas	1404-13-
Corral Knoll [Black Knoll] (US-Utah)	Cinder cone of Bald Knoll	1207-03-
Corral Quemado [Riñinahue] (Chile-C)	Maar of Carrán-Los Venados	1507-14=
Corrales, Los (Argentina)	Cinder cone of Unnamed	....
Corrales, Montaña (Canary Is)	Cone of Tenerife	1803-03-
Corrao [Giulia-Ferdinandeo] (Italy)	Submarine vent C. Flegrei Mar Sicilia	0101-07=
Corregidor (Luzon-Philippines)	Caldera (None) Pleistocene	....
Cortaderal, Cerro el (Perú)	Fissure vent of Chachani, Nevado	1504-007
Cortaderas, Las [Pampa de Palacio] (Perú)	Shield volcano of Chachani, Nevado	1504-007
Corvo (Azores)	Stratovolcano (None) Holocene	**1802-002**
Corvo (Italy)	Stratovolcano of Salina	....
Cos (Greece)	Synonym of Kos	....
Coseguina (Nicaragua)	Synonym of Cosigüina	1404-01=
Cosigüina (Nicaragua)	Stratovolcano (5, 1859) Historical	**1404-01=**
Coso Hot Springs (US-California)	Thermal feature of Coso Volc Field	1203-18-
Coso Range (US-California)	Synonym of Coso Volc Field	1203-18-
Coso Volc Field (US-California)	Lava domes (None) Holocene?	**1203-18-**
Costa d'Agosto (Italy)	Stratovolcano of Lipari	0101-042
Costa De Lenzuola (Italy)	Crater of Ischia	0101-03=
Costa Del Fallo, Monte (Italy)	Cone of Ustica	....
Costa Rica, Volcán (Costa Rica)	Synonym of Arenal	1405-033
Costa Sparaina (Italy)	Dome of Ischia	0101-03=
Costa, Puig de la (Spain)	Cone of Olot Volc Field	0100-03-
Coste San Domenico (Italy)	Crater of Campi Flegrei	0101-01=
Costo Maar (México)	Maar of Michoacán-Guanajuato	1401-06=
Cotacachi (Ecuador)	Stratovolcano (None) Pleistocene	....
Cotji, Cerro (Costo Maar) (México)	Maar of Michoacán-Guanajuato	1401-06=
Cotopaxi (Ecuador)	Stratovolcano (83, 1940) Historical	**1502-05=**
Cotteril, Mt. (Australia)	Cone of Newer Volcanics Prov	0509-01-
Cotto Barano, Mt. (Italy)	Cone of Ischia	0101-03=
Cotto, Monte (Italy)	Cone of Ischia	0101-03=
Cotton Volcano (New Zealand)	Stratovolcano of Healy	0401-14-
Cottonwood Peak (Canada)	Cone of Tuya Volc Field	1200-031
Cougar Butte (US-California)	Cone of Medicine Lake	1203-02-
Coulman Island (Antarctica)	Shield volcano (None) Post-Miocene	....
Courtney, Mt. (Australia)	Cone of Nulla Volc Province	....
Cova Da Burra [Pico da Areia] (Azores)	Dome of Furnas	1802-10=
Cova, Pico do (Azores)	Cone of Picos Volc System	1802-081
Cove Fort (US-Utah)	Cone of Mineral Mts-Cove Fort	....
Cow Hill Soufriere [Tar River Soufriere]	Thermal feature of Soufrière Hills	1600-05=
Cow Lakes Lava Field (US-Oregon)	Synonym of Jordan Craters	1202-19-
Cowhorn Mountain (US-Oregon)	Shield volcanoes (None) Pleistocene	....
Cowley Island (Galápagos)	Fissure vent of Alcedo	1503-04=
Coyoltepec (México)	Cinder cone of Chichinautzin	1401-08=
Coyote Butte (US-Idaho)	Cone of Craters of the Moon	1204-02-
Coyotepe, Cerro el (Nicaragua)	Cinder cone of Masaya	1404-10=
Coyotes, Cerro los (El Salvador)	Cone of San Diego	1403-001
Crabier, Morne (W Indies)	Dome of Plat Pays, Morne	1600-11=
Crac, Piton de (Indian O.-W)	Cinder cone of Fournaise, Piton de la	0303-02=
Cracatoa (Indonesia)	Synonym of Krakatau	0602-00=
Cracker Creek Cone (Canada)	Cone of Atlin Volc Field	1200-03-
Crary Group (Antarctica)	Shield volcanoes (None) Pleistocene	....
Crater Basalt Volc Field (Chile/Arg.)	Cinder cones (None) Holocene	**1508-025**
Crater Butte (US-Oregon)	Cone of Diamond Peak	....
Crater Buttes (US-Oregon)	Cone of Newberry	1202-11-
Crater Dome (New Zealand)	Dome of Okataina	0401-05=
Crater Flat (US-Nevada)	Volcanic field (None) Pleistocene	....
Crater Forest (China-E)	Cinder cone of Jingbo	1005-04-
Crater Hill (New Zealand)	Tuff cone of Auckland Field	0401-02=
Crater Hill (Antarctica)	Cone of Hut Point Peninsula	....
Crater Hill (US-Utah)	Cinder cone of Kolob	....
Crater Hill (Alaska-W)	Cinder cone of St. Paul Island	1104-01-
Crater Knoll (US-Utah)	Cone of Mineral Mts-Cove Fort	....
Crater Lake (US-Oregon)	Caldera (5, -2850) Radiocarbon	**1202-16-**
Crater Lake (Antarctica)	Maar of Deception Island	1900-03=
Crater Lake (New Zealand)	Crater of Ruapehu	0401-10=
Crater Mountain (New Guinea)	Stratovolcano (None) Holocene?	**0503-001**
Crater Mountain (US-California)	Dome of Mono Craters	1203-12-
Crater Mountain (Alaska-W)	Cone of St. Michael	1104-04-
Crater Peak (US-Oregon)	Cone of Crater Lake	1202-16-
Crater Peak (Alaska-SW)	Stratovolcano of Spurr	1103-04-
Crater Ridge (Alaska-E)	Dome of Edgecumbe	1105-04-
Crater Rock (US-Oregon)	Dome of Hood	1202-01-
Crater SE Springs (Luzon-Philippines)	Thermal feature of Pinatubo	0703-083
Crater Springs (US-Utah)	Thermal feature of Fumarole Butte	....
Crater Top (Kamchatka)	Dome of Shiveluch	1000-27=
Crater, Cratere see proper name (e.g. Citeme, Cratere)		
Cratered Dome (US-California)	Dome of Mono Craters	1203-12-

Post-caldera lava domes form islands in **Cuicocha** caldera lake at the foot of Pleistocene **Cotacachi** stratovolcano north of Quito, Ecuador. The 3-km-wide, steep-walled caldera was created during a major explosive eruption about 3100 years ago that produced nearly 5 km³ of pyroclastic-flow and airfall deposits.

Patricio Ramon (Escuela Politecnica, Quito)

Name (Subregion)	Type (Eruptions, Most Recent) Status Relation to Named Volcano	Volcano Number
Crateres, Monte De (Indian O.-S)	Cone of Possession, Ile de la	0304-04-
Craters of the Moon (US-Idaho)	Cinder cones (10, -130) Radiocarbon	**1204-02-**
Craters of the Moon (New Zealand)	Thermal feature of Maroa	0401-061
Craven, Mt. (W Indies)	Dome of St. Catherine	1600-17=
Crawford Bay (Indian O.-S)	Tuff cone of Marion Island	0304-07-
Crescent (US-Utah)	Crater of Black Rock Desert	1207-05-
Crescent Butte (US-Idaho)	Cinder cone of Craters of the Moon	1204-02-
Crescent Butte (US-California)	Cone of Medicine Lake	1203-02-
Crescent Crater (US-California)	Crater of Lassen Volc Center	1203-08-
Crescent, the (Africa-E)	Tuff ring of Namarunu	0202-04-
Crespo, Cerro [Cerro Quemado] (Guatemala)	Dome of Almolonga	1402-04=
Crimson Hill Cones (Antarctica)	Tuff cone of Deception Island	1900-03=
Cristal (Ecuador)	Dome of Guagua Pichincha	1502-02=
Cristi (Chile-N)	Stratovolcano of Tres Cruces	....
Cristo Rey (Nicaragua)	Cinder cone of Negro, Cerro	1404-07=
Crocker, Mt. (Galápagos)	Cone of Santa Cruz	1503-091
Crocodile Island (Africa-E)	Synonym of Central Island	0202-01=
Crocodile Lake (Africa-E)	Crater of Central Island	0202-01=
Crocodrilos, Laguna (México)	Maar of San Martín	1401-11=
Crommyonia (Greece)	Synonym of Susaki	0102-01=
Croscat, Volcà (Spain)	Cone of Olot Volc Field	0100-03-
Cross Hill (Antarctica)	Tuff cone of Deception Island	1900-03=
Crow Lagoon (Canada)	Pyroclastic cone (None) Holocene	**1200-11-**
Crown Island (New Guinea-NE of)	Stratovolcano (None) Quaternary	....
Cruces, Cerro las (El Salvador)	Cinder cone of Santa Ana	1403-02=
Crucible Dome (Canada)	Tuya of Cayley, Mt.	....
Cruz de Tea, Montaña la (Canary Is)	Cone of Tenerife	1803-03-
Cruz, Cerro de la (Honduras)	Cone of Pedregal, El	....
Cruz, Cerro la (Perú)	Cinder cone of Andahua-Orcopampa	1504-004
Cruz, Cerro la (México)	Cone of Southern Guadalajara	....
Cruz, Cerro la (México)	Cinder cone Zitácuaro-Valle de Bravo	1401-061
Cruz, Montaña de la (Canary Is)	Dome of Tenerife	1803-03-
Cruz, Montaña la (Canary Is)	Cinder cone of Tenerife	1803-03-
Cruz, Monte de la (Costa Rica)	Cinder cone of Barva	1405-05=
Cruz, Pico da (Azores)	Cone of Sete Cidades	1802-08=
Cruz, Pico do (Azores)	Cone of Picos Volc System	1802-081
Cryder Butte (US-Oregon)	Shield volcano of Davis Lake	1202-10-
Csobanc (Hungary)	Cone of Balaton Highland	....
Cuadrado, Mount (Luzon-Philippines)	Dome of Pinatubo	0703-083
Cualta, La (México)	Dome of Zitácuaro-Valle de Bravo	1401-061
Cuatépetl, Volcán (México)	Cinder cone of Chichinautzin	1401-08=
Cuates, Cerro los (México)	Crater of Pinacate	1401-001
Cuates, Cerros (México)	Shield volc. of Michoacán-Guanajuato	1401-06=
Cuatro, El (México)	Stratovolcano of Southern Guadalajara	....
Cuauatl (México)	Cinder cone of Chichinautzin	1401-08=
Cuauhtemoc (México)	Cinder cone of Colima	1401-04=
Cuautzin (México)	Shield volcano of Chichinautzin	1401-08=
Cubilche, Loma (Ecuador)	Dome of Imbabura	1502-004
Cucco, Monte (Italy)	Cone of Sabatini Complex	....
Cuchucavi (Chile-S)	Synonym of Minchinmávida	1508-04=
Cucundicata, Cerro (México)	Cinder cone of Michoacán-Guanajuato	1401-06=
Cuddia, Cuddie (Itilian for Hill) see proper name (e.g. Rosse, Cuddia)		
Cuernos de Negros (Philippines-C)	Complex volcano (None) Fumarolic	**0702-01=**
Cuernos del Diablo (Chile-S)	Stratovolcano (None) Holocene	**1508-021**
Cuerrizí [Guararí] (Costa Rica)	Cinder cone of Barva	1405-05=
Cuervo, the [Caldera de los Lapas]	Cinder cone of Lanzarote	1803-06-
Cuervos, Caldera de los [Caldera Lapas]	Cinder cone of Lanzarote	1803-06-
Cuervos, Los (Chile-C)	Cinder cone of Chillán, Nevados de	1507-07=
Cuervos, Montaña de los [Caldera Lapas]	Cinder cone of Lanzarote	1803-06-
Cuesta del Guayabo (Guatemala)	Cinder cone of Suchitán	1402-16-
Cuesta, Cerro La (México)	Dome of Primavera, Sierra la	....
Cuevas Negras, Montaña (Canary Is)	Fissure vent of Tenerife	1803-03-
Cuevas, Cerro las (México)	Dome of San Pedro	....
Cuevas, Montaña de las (Canary Is)	Cinder cone of Hierro	1803-02-
Cuevas, Volcán las (Spain)	Maar of Calatrava Volc Field	0100-04-
Cuevos del Ratón, Volcan (Canary Is)	Fissure vent of Tenerife	1803-03-
Cugno di Mandra (Italy)	Stratovolcano of Lipari	0101-042
Cuicocha (Ecuador)	Caldera (4, 650) Radiocarbon	**1502-003**
Cuidad Arce, Cerrito (El Salvador)	Dome of Coatepeque Caldera	1403-041
Cuidad Guzmán, Volcán de [Nevado de Colima]	Stratovolcano of Colima	1401-04=
Cuilapa Sur, Cerro (Guatemala)	Cinder cone of Cuilapa-Barbarena	1402-111
Cuilapa, Volcán (Guatemala)	Cinder cone of Cuilapa-Barbarena	1402-111
Cuilapa-Barbarena (Guatemala)	Volcanic field (None) Holocene	**1402-111**
Cuipilapa (Costa Rica)	Synonym of Miravalles	1405-03=
Cu-Lao Bo Bai (SE Asia)	Cone of Cù-Lao Ré Group	0705-02-
Cù-Lao Ré Group (SE Asia)	Volcanic field (None) Holocene	**0705-02-**
Culasi (Luzon-Philippines)	Stratovolcano of Cone-Culasi	....
Culebra, Loma la (El Salvador)	Cinder cone of San Diego	1403-001
Culebras Bank ? (Tonga-SW Pacific)	Synonym of Falcon Island	0403-05=
Culebreado, Cerro el (México)	Dome of Primavera, Sierra la	....
Culiacán (México)	Maar of Michoacán-Guanajuato	1401-06=
Culiacán, Cerro (México)	Shield volc. of Michoacán-Guanajuato	1401-06=
Culma, Volcán (Guatemala)	Cinder cone of Santiago, Cerro	1402-15-
Culpepper (Galápagos)	Shield volcano (None) Pleistocene	....
Cultus Mountain (US-Oregon)	Shield volcano (None) Pleistocene	....
Cuma (Italy)	Dome of Campi Flegrei	0101-01=
Cumbal (Colombia)	Stratovolcano (2, 1926) Historical	**1501-10=**
Cumbal, Nevado de (Colombia)	Synonym of Cumbal	1501-10=
Cumbicata (Ecuador)	Synonym of Calpi	....
Cumbre de la Linea (Chile-N)	Cone of Falso Azufre	1505-124
Cumbre del Laudo (Chile-N)	Stratovolcano of Nevada, Sierra	1505-123
Cumbre Grande, El (México)	Dome of Cumbres, Las	1401-098
Cumbre Vieja (Canary Is)	Stratovolcano of La Palma	1803-01-
Cumbre, Cerro la (El Salvador)	Cinder cone of Apaneca Range	1403-01=
Cumbre, La (Galápagos)	Synonym of Fernandina	1503-01=
Cumbres, Las (México)	Stratovolcano (1, -3920) Radiocarbon	**1401-098**
Cundung Kelam, Bukit (Sumatra)	Unknown (None) Post-Miocene	....
Cunistepeque, Cerro (Guatemala)	Cinder cone of Chingo	1402-17-
Cunru (Ecuador)	Dome of Imbabura	1502-004
Cupaello (Italy)	Pyroclastic cone (None) Pleistocene	....
Cupahue (Chile-C)	Synonym of Copahue	1507-09=
Cupit Mary Mountain (US-Oregon)	Shield volcano (None) Pleistocene	....
Cupu, Gunung (Java)	Cone of Lamongan	0603-32=
Cura, Baños del (Guatemala)	Thermal feature of Almolonga	1402-04=
Curacoa (Tonga-SW Pacific)	Submarine volcano (2, 1979) Historical	**0403-102**
Curiquinca, Cerro (Chile-N)	Stratovolcano of Sairecabur	1505-091
Curitzerán, Cerro de (México)	Cinder cone of Michoacán-Guanajuato	1401-06=
Curry, Mount (Antarctica)	Submarine vent of Zavodovski	1900-13=
Curtis Island (Kermadec Is)	Submarine volcano (Uncertain)	**0402-01=**
Curub (Ethiopia)	Synonym of Kurub	0201-12=
Curungueo (México)	Cone of Zitácuaro-Valle de Bravo	1401-061
Curutú (Chile-N)	Stratovolcano (None) Pleistocene	....
Cuscachapa, Laguna de (El Salvador)	Pit crater of Santa Ana	1403-02=
Cuscungo (Ecuador)	Dome of Atacazo	1502-021
Cushnirumi (Ecuador)	Stratovolcano of Mojanda	1502-005
Cusín (Ecuador)	Stratovolcano (None) Pleistocene	....
Cutanga (Colombia)	Unknown (None) Quaternary	....
Cutzato, Cerro de (México)	Cinder cone of Michoacán-Guanajuato	1401-06=
Cuvigghiuni (Italy)	Cinder cone of Etna	0101-06=
Cuxliquel (Guatemala)	Lava domes (None) Pleistocene	....
Cuyanausul (El Salvador)	Synonym of Apaneca Range	1403-01=
Cuyanausul, Ausoles de (El Salvador)	Thermal feature of Apaneca Range	1403-01=
Cuyotepe (El Salvador)	Cone of Apaneca Range	1403-01=
Cuyucut (Luzon-Philippines)	Thermal feature of Pinatubo	0703-083
Cuyufa (Ecuador)	Synonym of Sumaco	1502-04=
Cweajain (Kamchatka)	Synonym of Ichinsky	1000-28=

D

Name (Subregion)	Type (Eruptions, Most Recent) Status Relation to Named Volcano	Volcano Number
D.D. Cone (Pacific-NE)	Lava cone of Axial Seamount	1301-021
Da Ore (Ethiopia)	Tuff ring of Manda Hararo	0201-115
Daam (Banda Sea)	Synonym of Wurlali	0605-04=
Dabayra (Ethiopia)	Synonym of Dabbayra	0201-114
Dabbahu (Ethiopia)	Stratovolcano (1, 2005) Historical	**0201-113**
Dabbaira [Boina] (Ethiopia)	Cone of Dabbahu	0201-113
Dabbayra (Ethiopia)	Shield volcano (None) Holocene	**0201-114**
Dabingshan (China-E)	Shield volcano (None) Post-Miocene	....
Dabita (Ethiopia)	Synonym of Adwa	0201-17=
Dabita Ale (Ethiopia)	Synonym of Hertali	0201-171
Dacht-i-Navar Group (Afghanistan)	Lava domes (None) Holocene?	**0302-06-**
Dacht-i-Nawar (Afghanistan)	Synonym of Dacht-i-Navar Group	0302-06-
Dadongbinglingshan (China-E)	Dome of Fanjiatung Group	....
Da'enkei (Hokkaido-Japan)	Crater of Komaga-take	0805-02=
Dafni (Greece)	Dome of Santorini	0102-04=
Daftan (Iran)	Synonym of Taftan	0302-05-
Dagan, Jabal (Arabia-S)	Crater of Arhab, Harra of	0301-09-
Daganpao (China-E)	Cinder cone of Jingbo	1005-04-
Dagatan, Lake (Luzon-Philippines)	Maar of Banahaw	0703-05=
Dagelet (Korea)	Synonym of Ulreung	1006-03-
Dagit-Dagitan (Luzon-Philippines)	Stratovolcano (None) Pleistocene	....
Dagnyhaugen (Atlantic-N-Jan Mayen)	Cone of Jan Mayen	1706-01=
Dagongjie (SE Asia)	Cone of Tengchong	0705-11-
Dagsa (Luzon-Philippines)	Thermal feature of Pinatubo	0703-083
Dagushan (China-E)	Dome of Yitong Group	....
Dagushanzi [Dayishan] (China-E)	Cone of Longgang Group	1005-05-
Dahei Shan (China-W)	Cinder cone of Kunlun Volc Group	1004-03-
Dahei Shan (China-W)	Cinder cone of Kunlun Volc Group	1004-03-
Daichigamori (Honshu-Japan)	Dome of Kurikoma	0803-21=
Daihannya-yama (Izu Is-Japan)	Fissure vent of Miyake-jima	0804-04=
Dai-lo-san [Tatarinov] (Kuril Is)	Stratovolcano of Chikurachki	0900-36=
Daikoku (Volcano Is-Japan)	Submarine volcano (None) Fumarolic	**0804-137**
Daikoku-yama (Hokkaido-Japan)	Cone of Akigawa	....
Daikon-jima (Honshu-Japan)	Pyroclastic cone (None) Pleistocene	....
Dainichi-dake (Honshu-Japan)	Synonym of Dainichiga-take	....
Dainichi-dake (Honshu-Japan)	Synonym of Kurikoma	0803-21=
Dainichiga-take (Honshu-Japan)	Stratovolcano (None) Pleistocene	....
Dainichi-yama (Honshu-Japan)	Stratovolcano (None) Pleistocene	....
Dainiti-yama (Honshu-Japan)	Synonym of Dainichi-yama	....
Daino-yama (Honshu-Japan)	Dome of Izu-Tobu	0803-01=
Daintrees Lookout (Australia)	Cone of Nulla Volc Province	....
Daira-Komaga-take (Honshu-Japan)	Stratovolcano (None) Quaternary	....
Daisen (Honshu-Japan)	Stratovolcano (None) Pleistocene	....
Daisetsu (Hokkaido-Japan)	Stratovolcanoes (5, 1739) Tephrochron	**0805-06=**
Daisetu-zan (Hokkaido-Japan)	Synonym of Daisetsu	0805-06=
Daitimori [Daichigamori] (Honshu-Japan)	Dome of Kurikoma	0803-21=
Daito (Honshu-Japan)	Stratovolcano (None) Pleistocene	....
Daiton Geothermal Area (Taiwan)	Thermal feature of Tatun Group	0801-032
Dajianhoushan (Taiwan)	Dome of Tatun Group	0801-032
Dajianshan (Taiwan)	Dome of Tatun Group	0801-032
Dakara, Gof (Africa-E)	Maar of Marsabit	0202-021
Dakataua (New Britain-SW Pac)	Caldera (2, 1895) Anthropology	**0502-04=**
Dakelabai (Dakelabalai) (Luzon-N of)	Synonym of Camiguin de Babuyanes	0704-01=
Dake-yama (Honshu-Japan)	Dome of Shikuma	....
Dakongshan (SE Asia)	Cone of Tengchong	0705-11-
Dakula, Mt. (Sulu Is-Philippines)	Cinder cone of Jolo	0700-01=
Dakut (Sulu Is-Philippines)	Cone of Jolo	0700-01=
Dala Filla (Ethiopia)	Synonym of Dalaffilla	0201-07=

Name (Subregion)	Type (Eruptions, Most Recent) Status / Relation to Named Volcano	Volcano Number
Dalaffilla (Ethiopia)	Stratovolcano (1, 2008) Historical	**0201-07=**
Dalaha'ale (Ethiopia)	Stratovolcano (None) Pleistocene	....
Dalahraun (Iceland-SW)	Crater Row of Reykjanes	1701-02=
Dalahum (Vanuatu-SW Pacific)	Cone of Ambrym	0507-04=
Dalainuoer (China-E)	Cinder cones (None) Pleistocene	....
Daleldar (Iceland-NE)	Crater Row of Krafla	1703-08=
Dalfjall (Iceland-NE)	Fissure vent of Krafla	1703-08=
Dalibo (China-E)	Synonym of Dalainuoer	....
Dalinor (China-E)	Synonym of Dalainuoer	....
Daliuchong (SE Asia)	Cone of Tengchong	0705-11-
Daljny Plosky (Kamchatka)	Shield volcano of Ushkovsky	1000-261
Dallol (Ethiopia)	Explosion craters (1, 1926) Historical	**0201-041**
Dalman (Antarctica)	Cone of Seal Nunataks Group	1900-05=
Dal'nee, Lake [Lake Dalny] (Kamchatka)	Maar of Uzon	1000-17=
Dal'nii Plosky [Daljny Plosky] (Kamchatka)	Shield volcano of Ushkovsky	1000-261
Dalny (Kamchatka)	Cone of Bolshoi Semiachik	1000-15=
Dalny (Kamchatka)	Cinder cone of Tolbachik	1000-24=
Dalny, Lake (Kamchatka)	Maar of Uzon	1000-17=
Dalnyaya Plosky [Daljny Plosky] (Kamchatka)	Shield volcano of Ushkovsky	1000-261
Dal'nyeye, Lake [Lake Dalny] (Kamchatka)	Maar of Uzon	1000-17=
Dalongwan (China-E)	Maar of Longgang Group	1005-05-
Dalton Dome (Canada)	Dome of Garibaldi	1200-20-
Daly-Tapa (Armenia)	Synonym of Dar-Alages	0104-08-
Dama Ale (Ethiopia)	Synonym of Dama Ali	0201-141
Dama Ali (Ethiopia)	Shield volcano (1, 1631) Historical	**0201-141**
Dama Hali (Damahale) (Ethiopia)	Synonym of Dama Ali	0201-141
Damar (Banda Sea)	Synonym of Wurlali	0605-04=
Damavand (Iran)	Stratovolcano (1, -5350) Uranium-series	**0302-01-**
Dammer (Banda Sea)	Synonym of Wurlali	0605-04=
Dampier Island (New Guinea-NE of)	Synonym of Karkar	0501-03=
Dana (Alaska Peninsula)	Stratovolcano (1, -1890) Radiocarbon	**1102-05-**
Danan (Philippines-C)	Thermal feature of Mahagnao	0702-07=
Danao, Lake (Philippines-C)	Crater of Mahagnao	0702-07=
Danau (Java)	Pleistocene caldera of Karang	0603-02=
Danau (Indonesian for Lake) see proper name (e.g. Talang, Danau)		
Danbaru (Kyushu-Japan)	Crater of Kuju	0802-12=
Danger Bay (US-Oregon)	Stratovolcano of Crater Lake	1202-16-
Dangey (Luzon-Philippines)	Thermal feature of Pinatubo	0703-083
D'ango, Piton (Indian O.-W)	Cinder cone of Fournaise, Piton de la	0303-02=
Dangsanbong (Korea)	Tuff cone of Halla	1006-04-
Daniell Peninsula (Antarctica)	Shield volcanoes (None) Post-Miocene	....
Dankole (Ethiopia)	Cone of Bishoftu Volc Field	0201-22-
Dansan (Korea)	Tuff cone of Halla	1006-04-
Da-pu (Taiwan)	Thermal feature of Tatun Group	0801-032
Darai Hills (New Guinea)	Volcanic field (None) Pleistocene	....
Darajat (Java)	Thermal feature of Kendang	0603-11=
Dar-Alages (Armenia)	Pyroclastic cones (1, -2000) Anthropology	**0104-08-**
Daralages Kette (Armenia)	Synonym of Dar-Alages	0104-08-
Daralagezskiy Khrebet (Armenia)	Synonym of Dar-Alages	0104-08-
Dargo (Java)	Crater of Kelut	0603-28=
Dariganga Volc Field (Mongolia)	Cinder cones (None) Holocene	**1003-04-**
Dark Mountain (Canada)	Volcanic field (None) Pleistocene	....
Dark Mountain North (Canada)	Cone of Dark Mountain	....
Dark Mountain South (Canada)	Cone of Dark Mountain	....
Dark Mountain West (Canada)	Cone of Dark Mountain	....
Darlac Volc Field (SE Asia)	Cones (None) Pleistocene	....
Darnley Island (Australia)	Cone of Maer Volc Province	....
Darnley, Mount (Antarctica)	Cone of Bristol Island	1900-08=
Daroegan, Ranoe [Ranu Darungan] (Java)	Maar of Semeru	0603-30=
Daruma (Honshu-Japan)	Stratovolcano (None) Pleistocene	....
Darungan, Ranu (Java)	Maar of Semeru	0603-30=
Darwin (Galápagos)	Shield volc. (3, 1813) Surface Exposure	**1503-03=**
Darwin Bay (Galápagos)	Caldera of Genovesa	1503-081
Darwin Island (Galápagos)	Synonym of Culpepper	....
Data Gabalti (Ethiopia)	Stratovolcano (None) Pleistocene	....
Datil, Cerro el (México)	Cinder cone of Comondú-La Purísima	1401-012
Datong-Fengzen (China-E)	Volcanic field (None) Pleistocene	....
Datun (China-E)	Synonym of Fanjiatung Group	....
Datun Volcano Group (Taiwan)	Synonym of Tatun Group	0801-032
Datundongshan (China-E)	Dome of Fanjiatung Group	....
Datunshan (Taiwan)	Dome of Tatun Group	0801-032
Dauar Island (Australia)	Cone of Maer Volc Province	....
Daun, Bukit (Sumatra)	Stratovolcanoes (None) Fumarolic	**0601-21=**
Dauner (Germany)	Maar of West Eifel Volc Field	0100-01-
Daung (Sumatra)	Unknown (None) Post-Miocene	....
Dauphine Estate, La (W Indies)	Crater of Qualibou	1600-14=
Da'Ure (Ethiopia)	Fissure vent of Dabbahu	0201-113
Davao Volcano (Mindanao-Philippines)	Synonym of Apo	0701-03=
Davapia Rocks (New Britain-SW Pac)	Cone of Rabaul	0502-14=
Davey Peak (Antarctica)	Cone of Toney Mountain	1900-026
Davidof (Aleutian Is)	Stratovolcano (None) Holocene?	**1101-04-**
Davis Lake (US-Oregon)	Volcanic field (1, -2790) Radiocarbon	**1202-10-**
Davis Mountain (US-Oregon)	Shield volcano of Davis Lake	1202-10-
Dawa Ale (Ethiopia)	Stratovolcano of Dawa Ale-Quarry	....
Dawa Ale-Quarry (Ethiopia)	Stratovolcano (None) Pleistocene	....
Dawon, Boekit (Sumatra)	Synonym of Daun, Bukit	0601-21=
Dawson Strait Group	Volcanic field (1, 1350) Hydration Rind	**0503-06=**
Dayanzhifeng (China-E)	Cone of Changbaishan	1005-06-
Dayingshan (SE Asia)	Stratovolcano of Tengchong	0705-11-
Dayishan (China-E)	Cone of Longgang Group	1005-05-
Da-you-keng (Taiwan)	Thermal feature of Tatun Group	0801-032
Deacon Peak (Antarctica)	Cone of Penguin Island	1900-031
Dead Man's Hill (W Indies)	Dome of St. Catherine	1600-17=
Deadea [Deidei] (D'Entrecasteaux Is)	Thermal feature of Dawson Strait Group	0503-06=
Deadman Creek (US-California)	Dome of Inyo Craters	1203-13-
Debado Gera Hayk (Ethiopia)	Maar of Liado Hayk	0201-172
Debawala (D'Entrecasteaux Is)	Synonym of Iamalele	0503-05=
Debawala (D'Entrecasteaux Is)	Thermal feature of Iamalele	0503-05=
Debre Zeit (Ethiopia)	Synonym of Bishoftu Volc Field	0201-22-
Debunscha (Africa-W)	Cone of Cameroon	0204-01=
Deception Island (Antarctica)	Caldera (24, 1970) Historical	**1900-03=**
Ded i Baba (Kamchatka)	Shield volcano (None) Pleistocene	....
Dedica (Dedicas) (Luzon-N of)	Synonym of Didicas	0704-02=
Deep Crater (US-California)	Crater of Medicine Lake	1203-02-
Deep Crater (Galápagos)	Crater of Santa Cruz	1503-091
Deer Hill (New Zealand)	Dome of Reporoa	0401-06-
Deer Mountain (US-California)	Dome of Long Valley	....
Deer Mountain [Cerro Hueco] (US)	Shield volcano of Zuni-Bandera	1210-02-
Defiance (US-Oregon)	Shield volcano (None) Pleistocene	....
Deformes (Colombia)	Thermal feature of Galeras	1501-08=
Dehaj-Meduk (Iran)	Volcanic field (None) Quaternary	....
Deidei (D'Entrecasteaux Is)	Thermal feature of Dawson Strait Group	0503-06=
Delaire, Volcán (México)	Cone of Chichinautzin	1401-08=
Delaki (Lesser Sunda Is)	Unknown (None) Post-Miocene	....
Delaki, Gunung (Lesser Sunda Is)	Synonym of Sirung	0604-27=
Delicias, Cerro las (El Salvador)	Dome of Apastepeque Field	1403-071
Delicias, Cerro las (El Salvador)	Dome of Ilopango	1403-06=
Delirio, El (Nicaragua)	Cone of Maderas	1404-13-
Dema Ali (Ethiopia)	Synonym of Dama Ali	0201-141
Demavend (Demawend) (Iran)	Synonym of Damavand	0302-01-
Democrático (Chile-C)	Stratovolcano of Chillán, Nevados de	1507-07=
Demon (Kuril Is)	Stratovolcano (None) Holocene	**0900-11-**
Dempo (Sumatra)	Stratovolcanoes (27, 2009) Historical	**0601-23=**
Denham Bay (Kermadec Is)	Caldera of Raoul Island	0402-03=
Denison (Alaska Peninsula)	Stratovolcano (None) Holocene?	**1102-21-**
Dent Bicorne (Indian O.-S)	Cone of Kerguelen Islands	0304-02=
Dent Blanches (Indian O.-S)	Cone of Kerguelen Islands	0304-02=
Depresión de San Lorenzo (Guatemala)	Maar of Chingo	1402-17-
Derbi-Taiga [Derbi-Tayga] (Russia-SE)	Shield volcano of Azas Plateau	1002-07-
Derbi-Tayga (Russia-SE)	Shield volcano of Azas Plateau	1002-07-
Deriba (Africa-N)	Caldera of Marra, Jebel	0205-03-
Derrumbadas, Las (México)	Dome of Serdán-Oriental	1401-092
Des Voeux Peak (Fiji Is-SW Pacific)	Cone of Taveuni	0405-01-
Desantnaya Mountain (Kuril Is)	Stratovolcano (None) Pleistocene	....
Descabezado Chico (Chile-C)	Cone of Calabozos	1507-042
Descabezado del Maule (Chile-C)	Synonym of Descabezado Grande	1507-05=
Descabezado Grande (Chile-C)	Stratovolcanoes (1, 1933) Historical	**1507-05=**
Desconocido-Tecomales (México)	Synonym of Gloria, La	1401-097
Desejado, Pico (Atlantic-C)	Dome of Trindade	1805-051
Deseret (US-Utah)	Vent of Black Rock Desert	1207-05-
Desert Cone (US-Oregon)	Cone of Crater Lake	1202-16-
Deslacs Island (New Britain-SW Pac)	Synonym of Garove	0502-03=

Asfawossen Asrat (Addis Ababa Univ.)

An explosive eruption on September 26, 2005, the first in historical time from **Dabbahu** in Ethiopia, took place from a 500-m-long, N-S-trending fissure vent; a small 30-m-wide pumice dome (upper left) was formed at the northern end of the fissure.

Name (Subregion)	Type (Eruptions, Most Recent) Status / Relation to Named Volcano	Volcano Number
Deslinde (Chile-N)	Stratovolcano (None) Pleistocene	....
Desmonte, Volcán (México)	Dome of Mascota Volc Field	1401-031
Desolation Lava Field (Canada)	Vent of Edziza	1200-06-
Desolation, Valley of (W Indies)	Thermal feature of Watt, Morne	1600-101
Destinée, Morne (W Indies)	Dome of Diables, Morne aux	1600-08=
Deuxieme Formica Leo (Indian O.-W)	Crater of Fournaise, Piton de la	0303-02=
Devastation (Canada)	Vent of Meager	1200-18-
Devastation Volcano [Pogromni] (Aleutian Is)	Stratovolcano of Westdahl	1101-34-
Devastator, the (Canada)	Cone of Meager	1200-18-
Devil Mountain (Alaska-W)	Shield volcano of Espenberg	....
Devil Rock [Ngwala Rock] (Vanuatu)	Tuff cone of Aoba	0507-03=
Devils Cauldron (US-Idaho)	Cone of Craters of the Moon	1204-02-
Devils Desk (Alaska Peninsula)	Stratovolcano (None) Pleistocene	....
Devils Garden (US-Oregon)	Volcanic field (None) Holocene?	**1202-12-**

Name (Subregion)	Type (Eruptions, Most Recent) Status Relation to Named Volcano	Volcano Number
Devils Hill (US-Oregon)	Dome of South Sister	1202-08-
Devils Kitchen (US-California)	Thermal feature of Lassen Volc Center	1203-08-
Devil's Needle (Africa-E)	Vent of Lengai, Ol Doinyo	0202-12=
Devils Throat (Hawaiian Is)	Pit crater of Kilauea	1302-01-
Dewa-Fuji (Honshu-Japan)	Synonym of Chokai	0803-22=
Dgida Basin (Russia-SE)	Cinder cones (None) Pleistocene	....
Dhamar, Harras of (Arabia-S)	Volcanic field (1, 1937) Historical	**0301-12-**
Dhemeneghaki (Greece)	Pumice cone of Mílos	0102-03=
Dhin, Jabal (Arabia-S)	Crater of Arhab, Harra of	0301-09-
Dhu Rakham, Jabal (Arabia-S)	Cone of Dhamar, Harras of	0301-12-
Di Baruh, Danau (Sumatra)	Crater of Talang	0601-16=
Diables, Morne aux (W Indies)	Stratovolcano (None) Holocene	**1600-08=**
Diablo, Cerro del (Chile-S)	Cinder cone of Palei-Aike Volc Field	1508-08-
Diablotins, Morne (W Indies)	Stratovolcano (None) Holocene?	**1600-09=**
Diamante (Chile-C)	Pleistocene caldera of Maipo	1507-021

Patricio Ramon (Escuela Politecnica, Quito)

The 5-km-wide caldera of **Darwin** volcano in the Galápagos Islands, named after the renowned naturalist, displays terraces of former caldera floor lava flows. Volcán Wolf (right) and the tip of Volcán Ecuador (far left) are in the background.

Name (Subregion)	Type (Eruptions, Most Recent) Status Relation to Named Volcano	Volcano Number
Diamante (Argentina)	Stratovolc. of Northern Mendoza Field	....
Diamond Craters (US-Oregon)	Volcanic field (None) Holocene?	**1202-17-**
Diamond Peak (US-Oregon)	Shield volcano (None) Pleistocene	....
Diamond Rock (W Indies)	Dome of Kick 'em Jenny	1600-16=
Diamond Rockpile (US-Oregon)	Cone of Diamond Peak	....
Diau [Mt. Oiau] (D'Entrecasteaux Is)	Stratovolcano of Dawson Strait Group	0503-06=
Diaz, De (Argentina)	Cinder cone of Unnamed	....
Diba' Al Hurus, Jibal (Arabia-W)	Dome of Rahat, Harrat	0301-07=
Dickah Hill (Australia)	Cone of Atherton Volc Province	....
Didica (Didicas) (Luzon-N of)	Synonym of Didicas	0704-02=
Didicas (Luzon-N of)	Compound volcano (6, 1978) Historical	**0704-02=**
Didikas Rocks (Luzon-N of)	Synonym of Didicas	0704-02=
Didimtu (Ethiopia)	Cone of Mega Basalt Field	0201-33-
Didolli (Ethiopia)	Caldera (None) Pleistocene	....
Diego Alvarez (Atlantic-S)	Synonym of Gough Island	....
Diego de la Haya (Costa Rica)	Crater of Irazú	1405-06=
Diego de la Haya Fernández	Crater of Irazú	1405-06=
Diego Hernandez (Canary Is)	Pleistocene caldera of Tenerife	1803-03-
Dieng Volc Complex (Java)	Complex volcano (26, 2009) Historical	**0603-20=**
Dietro Isola, Cuddioli di (Italy)	Shield volcano of Pantelleria	0101-071
Difeso, Monte (Italy)	Cinder cone of Etna	0101-06=
Diguillin (Chile-C)	Pleist. caldera of Chillán, Nevados de	1507-07=
Dikii Greben' [Dikiy Greben] (Kamchatka)	Synonym of Diky Greben	1000-022
Dikkartin Dag (Turkey)	Dome of Erciyes Dagi	0103-01=
Dikkartini (Turkey)	Dome of Erciyes Dagi	0103-01=
Diky Greben (Kamchatka)	Lava domes (4, 350) Radiocarbon	**1000-022**
Diky Khrebet [Dikye Greben] (Kamchatka)	Synonym of Diky Greben	1000-022
Dilekene (Halmahera-Indonesia)	Crater of Dukono	0608-01=
Dilham, Jabal (Arabia)	Tuff ring of Hutaymah, Harrat	....
Diller Cone [Maklaks Crater] (US-Oregon)	Cinder cone of Crater Lake	1202-16-
Dima (Kamchatka)	Lava cone of Krasheninnikov	1000-19=
Dimmadalshaedh (Iceland-SW)	Shield volcano of Hengill	1701-05=
Dinero (Chile-S)	Cinder cone of Palei-Aike Volc Field	1508-08-
Dingin, Bukit (Sumatra)	Unknown (None) Post-Miocene	....
Diodio (D'Entrecasteaux Is)	Maar of Goodenough	0503-041
Diogeneas, Mt. [Hanging Rock] (Australia)	Dome of Newer Volcanics Prov	0509-01-
Dionisio (Luzon-N of)	Stratovolcano of Babuyan Claro	0704-03=
Dirdo Koma (Ethiopia)	Crater of Manda-Inakir	0201-122
Disappointment Cleaver (US-Washington)	Thermal feature of Rainier	1201-03-
Disappointment Peak (US-Washington)	Dome of Glacier Peak	1201-02-
Dishpan Gap (US-Washington)	Cinder cone of Glacier Peak	1201-02-
Ditmara (Kamchatka)	Stratovolcano (None) Pleistocene	....
Ditmar-Taushits-Sosed (Kamchatka)	Fissure vent of Kliuchevskoi	1000-26=
Dittmar (US-California)	Stratovolcano (None) Pleistocene	....
Dives, Mont De La (Indian O.-S)	Stratovolcano of Amsterdam Island	0304-001
Divisadero, Cerro el (México)	Cone of Camargo Volc Field	....

Name (Subregion)	Type (Eruptions, Most Recent) Status Relation to Named Volcano	Volcano Number
Dixon, Mt. (Indian O.-S)	Stratovolcano of Heard	0304-01=
Djabi (Ethiopia)	Synonym of Corbetti Caldera	0201-29-
Djailolo (Halmahera-Indonesia)	Synonym of Jailolo	0608-051
Djambangan [Jambangan] (Java)	Crater of Iyang-Argapura	0603-33=
Djambull, Bukit (Sumatra)	Synonym of Jambul, Bukit	....
Djapati [Japati] (Java)	Crater of Guntur	0603-13=
Djar'a, Djebel (Arabia-W)	Synonym of Yar, Jabal	0301-08-
Djar'atain, Harra of [Jar'atain] (Arabia-W)	Cone of Yar, Jabal	0301-08-
Djarian, Kawah [Kawah Jarian] (Java)	Crater of Tangkubanparahu	0603-09=
Djarra (Arabia-W)	Synonym of Yar, Jabal	0301-08-
Djawalo [Jawalo] (Lesser Sunda Is)	Crater of Paluweh	0604-15=
Djebel (French: of Arabic word for Mt.) see proper name (e.g. Doukkhan, Djebel)		
Djembangan [Jambangan] (Java)	Caldera of Semeru	0603-30=
Djembangan [Jambangan] (Java)	Caldera of Semeru	0603-30=
Djerban (Arabia-S)	Crater of Arhab, Harra of	0301-09-
Djero [Jero] (Java)	Crater of Arjuno-Welirang	0603-29=
Djinggo, Kapundan [Kepundan Jinggo]	Crater of Marapi	0601-14=
Djiring Plateau (SE Asia)	Synonym of Haut Dong Nai	0705-04-
Djonggring Seloko [Jonggring Seloko] (Java)	Crater of Semeru	0603-30=
Djougoudja Dsaha (Indian O.-W)	Crater of Karthala	0303-01=
Djungo, Le (Africa-W)	Cone of Tombel Graben	0204-011
Djurig, Kawah [Kawah Jurig] (Java)	Crater of Tangkubanparahu	0603-09=
Dobu (D'Entrecasteaux Is)	Stratovolcano of Dawson Strait Group	0503-06=
Dodoekko (Halmahera-Indonesia)	Synonym of Dukono	0608-01=
Doe Mountain (US-California)	Dome of Maidu	....
Doe Peak (US-California)	Cone of Medicine Lake	1203-02-
Doeang (Sangihe Is-Indonesia)	Synonym of Ruang	0607-01=
Doekono (Halmahera-Indonesia)	Synonym of Dukono	0608-01=
Doewang (Sangihe Is-Indonesia)	Synonym of Ruang	0607-01=
Dofan (Dofane, Dofani) (Ethiopia)	Synonym of Dofen	0201-18=
Dofen (Ethiopia)	Stratovolcano (None) Holocene	**0201-18=**
Dogana, La (Italy)	Cone of Vulsini	0101-003
Dogs Head (US-Washington)	Dome of St. Helens	1201-05-
Döhmberg (Germany)	Cone of West Eifel Volc Field	0100-01-
Doinyo, Donyo (Masai for Mt.) see proper name (e.g. Buru, Doinyo)		
Dolinnyi (Russia-SE)	Cinder cone of Udokan Plateau	1002-03-
Dolok (Indonesian for Mountain) see proper name (e.g. Singgalang, Dolok)		
Dolomieu (Indian O.-W)	Crater of Fournaise, Piton de la	0303-02=
Dolon Nor (China-E)	Synonym of Dalainuoer	....
Dom Joao de Castro Bank (Azores)	Synonym of Don Joao de Castro Bank	1802-07=
Doma Ale (Ethiopia)	Synonym of Dama Ali	0201-141
Dôma Carva (Indian O.-S)	Pleist. caldera of Kerguelen Islands	0304-02=
Doma Peaks (New Guinea)	Stratovolcano (None) Holocene?	**0503-00-**
Domadalshraun (Iceland-S)	Fissure vent of Torfajökull	1702-05=
Domain (New Zealand)	Tuff ring of Auckland Field	0401-02=
Domas, Kawah (Java)	Crater of Tangkubanparahu	0603-09=
Domashnii (Kamchatka)	Cinder cone of Kostakan	1000-122
Dombrovskiy (Russia-SE)	Cone of Vitim Plateau	1002-04-
Dome Mountain (Canada)	Cone of Dark Mountain	....
Dome, Puy de (France)	Dome of Chaîne des Puys	0100-02-
Dome, The (US-Oregon)	Cinder cone of Newberry	1202-11-
Dome, the (New Zealand)	Dome of Taranaki [Egmont]	0401-03=
Domeshnyaya (Kamchatka)	Dome of Ksudach	1000-05=
Domingo Spring (US-California)	Thermal feature of Lassen Volc Center	1203-08-
Domo del Azufre (Chile-C)	Dome of Puyehue-Cordón Caulle	1507-15=
Domuyo (Argentina)	Stratovolcano (None) Holocene?	**1507-067**
Don Casimiro, Volcán (Chile-C)	Cinder cone of Maipo	1507-021
Don Chana, Cerro (Guatemala)	Cinder cone of Cuilapa-Barbarena	1402-111
Don Chuco (Chile-C)	Stratovolcano of Tinguiririca	1507-03=
Don Gregorio [Cerro Don Chana] (Guat.)	Cinder cone of Cuilapa-Barbarena	1402-111
Don Joao de Castro Bank (Azores)	Submarine volcano (1, 1720) Historical	**1802-07=**
Don Pedro, Cerro (México)	Cinder cone of Camargo Volc Field	....
Doña Juana (Colombia)	Stratovolcano (2, 1906) Historical	**1501-07=**
Donald (Antarctica)	Cone of Seal Nunataks Group	1900-05=
Donald Duck (New Zealand)	Crater of White Island	0401-04=
Dong Shan (China-W)	Cinder cone of Kunlun Volc Group	1004-03-
Dongdapotou (SE Asia)	Cone of Tengchong	0705-11-
Donghengdaoshan (China-E)	Cone of Longgang Group	1005-05-
Donghuokou (China-W)	Cinder cone of Kunlun Volc Group	1004-03-
Dongjianshan (China-E)	Dome of Yitong Group	....
Dongjiaodebushan (China-E)	Cone of Wudalianchi	1005-03-
Donglongmenshan (China-E)	Cone of Wudalianchi	1005-03-
Donglongwan (China-E)	Maar of Longgang Group	1005-05-
Dongo, Morne (W Indies)	Dome of Soufrière Guadeloupe	1600-06=
Dongshan (China-E)	Cone of Erkeshan	....
Donkoro-yama (Hokkaido-Japan)	Cone of Usu	0805-03=
Donnoye (Kamchatka)	Thermal feature of Mutnovsky	1000-06=
Doon [Trou au Natron] (Africa-N)	Pleistocene caldera of Toussidé, Tarso	0205-01=
Doon Kidimi (Africa-N)	Crater of Toussidé, Tarso	0205-01=
Doon Kinimi [Doon Kidimi] (Africa-N)	Crater of Toussidé, Tarso	0205-01=
Doon Orei [Trou au Natron] (Africa-N)	Pleistocene caldera of Toussidé, Tarso	0205-01=
Dora, Mount (US-New Mexico)	Shield volcano of Raton-Clayton	....
Doro Afi Toi (Lesser Sunda Is)	Dome of Tambora	0604-04=
Doro Api (Lesser Sunda Is)	Cone of Sangeang Api	0604-05=
Doro Mantai (Lesser Sunda Is)	Cone of Sangeang Api	0604-05=
Doro Mantoi [Doro Mantai] (Lesser Sunda Is)	Cone of Sangeang Api	0604-05=
Dorr Fumarole Field (US-Washington)	Thermal feature of Baker	1201-01=
Dos Cerros (México)	Shield volcano of Chichinautzin	1401-08=
Dos Coyotes (México)	Dome of Primavera, Sierra la	....
Dos Equis (México)	Dome of Ceboruco	1401-03=
Dos Hermanos (Hispaniola)	Volcanic field (None) Pleistocene	....
Dos Novillos, Volcán (Costa Rica)	Stratovolcano of Turrialba	1405-07=
Dos Trinta, Cabeco (Azores)	Cone of Fayal	1802-01=
Dotsero (US-Colorado)	Maar (1, -2200) Radiocarbon	**1208-01-**

Name (Subregion)	Type (Eruptions, Most Recent) Status Relation to Named Volcano	Volcano Number
Double Crater (Alaska Peninsula)	Stratovolcano of Emmons Lake	1102-02-
Double Glacier (Alaska-SW)	Lava domes (None) Pleistocene	....
Double Head Mountain (US-California)	Cone of Hackamore	....
Double Hole Crater (US-California)	Crater of Medicine Lake	1203-02-
Douglas (Alaska Peninsula)	Stratovolcano (None) Holocene	**1102-27-**
Doukkhan, Djebel [Jebel Duchan] (Red Sea)	Cone of Tair, Jebel at	0201-01=
Doussaints (Costa Rica)	Cone of Irazú	1405-06=
Dowi [Mt. Reaumur] (New Guinea-NE of)	Stratovolcano of Long Island	0501-05=
Downs Cone (Antarctica)	Cone of Toney Mountain	1900-026
Downton (Canada)	Cone of Itcha Range	....
Doyo Seamount (Izu Is-Japan)	Submarine volcano (None) Fumarolic	**0804-095**
Dr. Ferreira, Pico (Azores)	Cone of Picos Volc System	1802-081
Dragon (Canada)	Cone of Wells Gray-Clearwater	1200-15-
Drakesbad (US-California)	Thermal feature of Lassen Volc Center	1203-08-
Drakon (Kuril Is)	Dome of Grozny Group	0900-07=
Drangagrundir (Iceland-NE)	Fissure vent of Krafla	1703-08=
Dreiser Weiher (Germany)	Maar of West Eifel Volc Field	0100-01-
Drekagigarod (Iceland-NE)	Fissure vent of Bárdarbunga	1703-03=
Dringo (Java)	Crater of Dieng Volc Complex	0603-20=
Drouz, Djebel ed (Syria)	Synonym of Druze, Jabal ad	0300-06-
Drum (Alaska-E)	Stratovolcano (None) Pleistocene	....
Druse, Jabal (Syria)	Cone of Es Safa	0300-05-
Druz, Jabal al (Syria)	Synonym of Druze, Jabal ad	0300-06-
Druze, Jabal ad (Syria)	Volcanic field (None) Holocene	**0300-06-**
Dry Butte (US-Oregon)	Cinder cone of Bachelor	1202-09-
Dry Crater (Africa-E)	Crater of Central Island	0202-01=
Dry Creek Dome (US-California)	Dome of Long Valley	....
Dry Maar (US-Oregon)	Maar of Diamond Craters	1202-17-
Dryden's Rock [Hanging Rock] (Australia)	Dome of Newer Volcanics Prov	0509-01-
Drygalski, Mt. (Indian O.-S)	Cone of Heard	0304-01=
Du Faure (New Britain-SW Pac)	Stratovolcano (None) Post-Miocene	....
Dua Saudara (Halmahera-Indonesia)	Cone of Amasing	0608-072
Dua Saudara (Sulawesi-Indonesia)	Stratovolcano of Tongkoko	0606-13=
Duang (Sangihe Is-Indonesia)	Synonym of Ruang	0607-01=
Duani (Africa-E)	Cone of Chyulu Hills	0202-13=
Duanzishan [Tuanzishan] (China-E)	Cinder cone of Keluo Group	1005-02-
Duau, Mt. (New Guinea)	Stratovolcano (None) Pleistocene	....
Dubbeh, Djebel (Ethiopia)	Synonym of Dubbi	0201-10=
Dubbey, Gebel (Ethiopia)	Synonym of Dubbi	0201-10=
Dubbi (Ethiopia)	Stratovolcano (2, 1861) Historical	**0201-10=**
Duchan, Jebel (Red Sea)	Cone of Tair, Jebel at	0201-01=
Duck Lake (US-Wyoming)	Crater of Yellowstone	1205-01-
Ducrot (Indian O.-W)	Crater of Fournaise, Piton de la	0303-02=
Duders Hill (New Zealand)	Cone of Auckland Field	0401-02=
Duenjo (Masai for Mt.) see proper name (e.g. Ngai, Duenjo)		
Dufferinbreen (Atlantic-N-Jan Mayen)	Cone of Jan Mayen	1706-01=
Duffrin Island (Canada)	Cone of Milbanke Sound Group	1200-12-
Duffy Butte (US-Oregon)	Cone of Three Fingered Jack	....
Duga (Kamchatka)	Cinder cone of Krasheninnikov	1000-19=
Duguna (Ethiopia)	Stratovolcano (None) Pleistocene	....
Dujianshan (China-W)	Cinder cone of Kunlun Volc Group	1004-03-
Dukana Volc Field (Ethiopia)	Synonym of Mega Basalt Field	0201-33-
Duko Ma Tala (Halmahera-Indonesia)	Synonym of Dukono	0608-01=
Dukono (Halmahera-Indonesia)	Complex volcano (5, 2010) Historical	**0608-01=**
Dulan-Khara (Mongolia)	Cone of Orkhon Gol	....
Dumas (Indian O.-S)	Cone of Amsterdam Island	0304-001
Dumauzé, Piton (W Indies)	Dome of Carbets, Pitons de	....
Dumilah (Java)	Crater of Lawu	0603-26=
Dumpel (Germany)	Maar of East Eifel Volc Field	....
Duncan (Galápagos)	Synonym of Pinzón	....
Duncan Canal (Alaska-E)	Volcanic field (None) Holocene	**1105-05-**
Dundee Island (Antarctica)	Cone of Tabarin Peninsula	....
Dundoli (Africa-E)	Cone of Ngozi	0202-164
Dunhua (China-E)	Unknown (None) Quaternary	....
Duniva Hora (Slovakia)	Vent of Filakovo-Salgotarjan	....
Duportail (New Britain-SW Pac)	Synonym of Lolobau	0502-13=
Duppacher Weiher (Germany)	Maar of West Eifel Volc Field	0100-01-
Dupungan (Mindanao-Philippines)	Cone of Imbing	....
Durandal (Indian O.-W)	Cinder cone of Fournaise, Piton de la	0303-02=
Durango Volc Field (México)	Cinder cones (None) Holocene	**1401-022**
Duraz, Jebel (Syria)	Synonym of Druze, Jabal ad	0300-06-
Duraznero [San Juan] (Canary Is)	Fissure vent of La Palma	1803-01-
Duraznillo, Cerro (El Salvador)	Stratovolcano of Santa Ana	1403-02=
Durbulzhi-Ula (Mongolia)	Unknown (None) Pleistocene	....
Dúrika (Costa Rica)	Lava domes (None) Pleistocene	....
Dürres (Germany)	Maar of West Eifel Volc Field	0100-01-
Duruz, Jabal ed (Syria)	Synonym of Druze, Jabal ad	0300-06-
Dusy (Mongolia)	Cone of Dariganga Volc Field	1003-04-
Dutton (Alaska Peninsula)	Stratovolcano (None) Holocene	**1102-011**
Dutton Cliff (US-Oregon)	Stratovolcano of Crater Lake	1202-16-
Duwang (Sangihe Is-Indonesia)	Synonym of Ruang	0607-01=
Dveggar (Iceland-NE)	Crater Row of Tungnafellsjökull	1703-04=
Dvergahraun (Iceland-NE)	Crater Row of Bárdarbunga	1703-03=
Dvoinoi (Russia-SE)	Dome of Udokan Plateau	1002-03-
Dvoinoy (Kamchatka)	Cinder cone of Tolbachik	1000-24=
Dvor (Kamchatka)	Stratovolcano of Karymsky	1000-13=
Dvukhglavy (Kamchatka)	Dome of Bezymianny	1000-25=
Dvukhyurtochny (Kamchatka)	Shield volcano (None) Pleistocene	....
D'yakhtardakh (Russia-NE)	Cone of Unnamed	....
Dyngjufjallahraun (Iceland-NE)	Crater Row of Askja	1703-06=
Dyngjufjöll (Iceland-NE)	Crater Row of Askja	1703-06=
Dyngjuhals (Iceland-NE)	Fissure vent of Bárdarbunga	1703-03=
Dyngnahraun (Iceland-SW)	Crater Row of Krísuvík	1701-03=
Dynjufjöll (Dyngjufjall) (Iceland-NE)	Synonym of Askja	1703-06=
Dzan Tologai (Mongolia)	Cone of Taryatu-Chulutu	1003-01-
Dzenzurskaia, Sopka (Kamchatka)	Synonym of Dzenzursky	1000-11=
Dzenzursky (Kamchatka)	Compound volcano (None) Holocene	**1000-11=**
Dzhanga-Tapa (Armenia)	Cone of Aragats	0104-06-
Dzhida Basin (Russia-SE)	Synonym of Dgida Basin	....
Dzigoku [Trezubetz] (Kuril Is)	Somma volcano of Kolokol Group	0900-12=
Dzun-Nerette (Mongolia)	Cone of Dariganga Volc Field	1003-04-

E

Name (Subregion)	Type (Eruptions, Most Recent) Status Relation to Named Volcano	Volcano Number
Eacham, Lake (Australia)	Maar of Atherton Volc Province	....
Eagle Lake Field (US-California)	Fissure vents (None) Holocene?	**1203-09-**
Eagle Peak (US-California)	Dome of Lassen Volc Center	1203-08-
Eagle Tail Mountain (US-New Mexico)	Cone of Raton-Clayton	....
Eaglehawk Hill (Australia)	Cone of McBride Volc Province	....
Eanastick Meadow (Canada)	Vent of Garibaldi	1200-20-
Earthquake Dome (US-California)	Dome of Mammoth Mountain	1203-15-
Earthquake Flat (New Zealand)	Crater of Kapenga	....
East Butte (US-Oregon)	Dome of China Hat-East Butte	....
East Cabrit (W Indies)	Dome of Diables, Morne aux	1600-08=
East Cape Volcano (Aleutian Is)	Stratovolcano of Buldir	1101-01-
East Crater (US-Washington)	Shield volcano of Indian Heaven	1201-07-
East Crater (US-Washington)	Crater of Rainier	1201-03-
East Crater (New Zealand)	Crater of Ruapehu	0401-10=
East Crater (New Zealand)	Crater of White Island	0401-04=
East Crater (Alaska-E)	Crater of Wrangell	1105-02-
East Diamante (Mariana Is-C Pacific)	Submarine volcano (None) Fumarolic	**0804-201**
East Dome (US-Washington)	Dome of St. Helens	1201-05-
East Dome (New Zealand)	Dome of Whale Island	....
East Eifel Volc Field (Germany)	Maars (None) Pleistocene	....
East Epi (Vanuatu-SW Pacific)	Caldera of Epi	0507-06=
East Island (Indian O.-S)	Synonym of Est, Ile de l'	0304-03-
East Lake Fissure (US-Oregon)	Fissure vent of Newberry	1202-11-
East Lava Field (US-Oregon)	Synonym of Squaw Ridge Lava Field	1202-13-
East Maar (Alaska Peninsula)	Maar of Ukinrek Maars	1102-131
East Maui Volcano (Hawaiian Is)	Synonym of Haleakala	1302-06-
East Molokai (Hawaiian Is)	Shield volcano (None) Pleistocene	....
East Rift Zone (Hawaiian Is)	Fissure vent of Kilauea	1302-01-
East Sand Butte (US-California)	Cone of Medicine Lake	1203-02-
East Sayan Volc Field (Russia-SE)	Synonym of Oka Plateau	1002-06-
East Sikhote-Alin (Russia-SE)	Synonym of Sikhote-Alin	1002-01-
East Tanaka (Aleutian Is)	Stratovolcano of Tanaga	1101-08-
East Tanna Volcano (Vanuatu)	Stratovolcano (None) Pleistocene	....
East Trident (Alaska Peninsula)	Stratovolcano of Trident	1102-16-
East Tuva Plateau (Russia-SE)	Synonym of Azas Plateau	1002-07-
East Twin Crater (US-Oregon)	Maar of Diamond Craters	1202-17-
East Zeway (Ethiopia)	Synonym of East Zway	0201-252
East Ziway (Ethiopia)	Synonym of East Zway	0201-252
East Zwai (Ethiopia)	Synonym of East Zway	0201-252

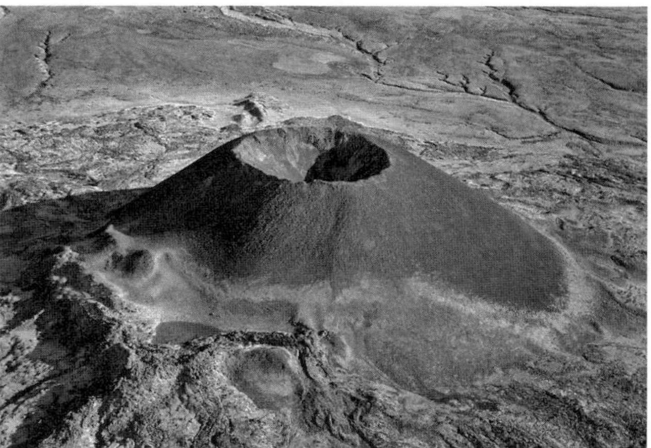
Ben Edwards (Dickinson College)

Eve Cone is one of many pyroclastic cones at **Edziza** volcano in northern British Columbia.

Name (Subregion)	Type (Eruptions, Most Recent) Status Relation to Named Volcano	Volcano Number
East Zway (Ethiopia)	Fissure vents (None) Holocene	**0201-252**
Easter Island (Chile-Is)	Shield volcanoes (None) Holocene	**1506-011**
Eastern Dome (New Zealand)	Dome of Okataina	0401-05=
Eastern Gemini Seamount (SW Pac.)	Submarine volcano (1, 1996) Historical	**0508-001**
Eastern Hill (Australia)	Cone of Newer Volcanics Prov	0509-01-
Eastern Mound (Aleutian Is)	Stratovolcano of Fisher	1101-35-
East-Matthew (SW Pacific)	Cone of Matthew Island	0508-01=
Ebeko (Kuril Is)	Somma volcano (17, 2009) Historical	**0900-38=**
Ebino-dake (Kyushu-Japan)	Stratovolcano of Kirishima	0802-09=
Ebo Lobo (Eboeloba) (Lesser Sunda Is)	Synonym of Ebulobo	0604-10=
Eboga (Africa-W)	Pleistocene caldera of Manengouba	0204-02-
Eboshi (Honshu-Japan)	Stratovolcano (None) Pleistocene	....
Eboshi-dake (Kyushu-Japan)	Stratovolcano of Aso	0802-11=
Eboshi-dake (Hokkaido-Japan)	Stratovolcano of Daisetsu	0805-06=
Eboshi-dake (Kyushu-Japan)	Cone of Kirishima	0802-09=
Eboshi-dake (Honshu-Japan)	Cone of Norikura	0803-06=

Name (Subregion)	Type (Eruptions, Most Recent) Status / Relation to Named Volcano	Volcano Number
Eboshi-dake (Nyuto-san) (Honshu-Japan)	Stratovolcano of Nyuto-Takakura	....
Eboshi-Washigatake (Honshu-Japan)	Stratovolcano (None) Pleistocene	....
Eboshi-yama (Honshu-Japan)	Stratovolcano of Eboshi	....
Eboshi-yama (Hokkaido-Japan)	Dome of Tokachi-Eboshi	....
Ebosi-dake [Eboshi-dake] (Hokkaido-Japan)	Stratovolcano of Daisetsu	0805-06=
Ebosi-dake [Eboshi-dake] (Kyushu-Japan)	Cone of Kirishima	0802-09=
Ebu Lobo (Lesser Sunda Is)	Synonym of Ebulobo	0604-10=
Ebulobo (Lesser Sunda Is)	Stratovolcano (7, 1969) Historical	**0604-10=**
Eburru (Africa-E)	Synonym of Eburru, Ol Doinyo	0202-08=
Eburru, Ol Doinyo (Africa-E)	Complex volcano (None) Holocene	**0202-08=**
Ecatzingo Cones (México)	Cinder cone of Popocatépetl	1401-09=
Eccles, Mt. (Australia)	Cone of Newer Volcanics Prov	0509-01-
Echado (Cerro Chillahuita) (Chile-N)	Dome of Leon, Cerro del	....
Echo Crater Butte (US-Idaho)	Cinder cone of Craters of the Moon	1204-02-
Eckersley, Mt. (Australia)	Cone of Newer Volcanics Prov	0509-01-
Ecoma, Kawah (Java)	Crater of Tangkubanparahu	0603-09=
Ecuador (Galápagos)	Shield volc. (1, 1150) Surface Exposure	**1503-011**
Edd Lava Field (Ethiopia)	Volcanic field of Dubbi	0201-10=
Edd, Volcano of (Ethiopia)	Synonym of Dubbi	0201-10=
Eddystone Island (Solomon Is-SW Pacific)	Synonym of Simbo	0505-05=
Eden, Mt. (New Zealand)	Cone of Auckland Field	0401-02=
Edgecumbe (Alaska-E)	Stratovolcanoes (3, -2220) Radiocarbon	**1105-04-**
Edgecumbe, Mt. (New Zealand)	Dome of Okataina	0401-05=
Edziza (Canada)	Stratovolcano (4, 950) Radiocarbon	**1200-06-**
Eek (Alaska Peninsula)	Synonym of Veniaminof	1102-07-

Jürg Alean (Stromboli Online)

The summit of **Erta Ale** volcano, the most active in Ethiopia, contains a dramatic 0.7 x 1.6 km, elliptical caldera housing steep-sided pit craters that have hosted long-term active lava lakes.

Name (Subregion)	Type (Eruptions, Most Recent) Status / Relation to Named Volcano	Volcano Number
Egan (US-Oregon)	Cinder cone of Bachelor	1202-09-
Egersuwa (Ethiopia)	Lava domes (None) Pleistocene	....
Eggella (Kamchatka)	Shield volcano (None) Holocene?	**1000-42-**
Eggoya (Atlantic-N-Jan Mayen)	Tuff cone of Jan Mayen	1706-01=
Egmont (New Zealand)	Synonym of Taranaki [Egmont]	0401-03=
Egon (Lesser Sunda Is)	Stratovolcano (4, 2008) Historical	**0604-16=**
Eguas (Azores)	Cone of Sete Cidades	1802-08=
Ehi (Chad term for Mountain) see proper name (e.g. Sosso, Ehi)		
Eickelberg Peak (Aleutian Is)	Stratovolcano of Fisher	1101-35-
Eifel Volc Field (Germany)	Synonym of West Eifel Volc Field	0100-01-
Eigo-zan (Honshu-Japan)	Synonym of Fuji	0803-03=
Eiler Butte (US-California)	Cinder cone of Tumble Buttes	1203-06-
Eimnakh (Russia-SE)	Cinder cone of Udokan Plateau	1002-03-
Einindrangur (Iceland-S)	Submarine vent of Vestmannaeyjar	1702-01=
Eisenbuhl [Zelezna Hurka] (Czech)	Cinder cone of Cheb Basin	....
Ekarma (Kuril Is)	Stratovolcano (2, 1980) Historical	**0900-27=**
Ekaruma (Kuril Is)	Synonym of Ekarma	0900-27=
Ekstrusivny Greben (Kamchatka)	Dome of Bezymianny	1000-25=
Ekundo (Africa-W)	Cone of Cameroon	0204-01=
El see proper name (e.g. Nuevo, El)		
El Fraile (Spain)	Cone of Cofrentes	....
Ela (Ethiopia)	Stratovolcano (None) Pleistocene	....
Elaho Valley (Canada)	Vent of Meager	1200-18-
Elanairobi (Africa-E)	Synonym of Embagai	....
Elbrus (Russia-SW)	Stratovolcano (1, 50) Tephrochronology	**0104-01-**
Eldborg (Iceland-W)	Cone of Ljósufjöll	1700-03=
Eldborg a Brennisteinsfjollum (Iceland-SW)	Crater Row of Brennisteinsfjöll	1701-04=
Eldborg Nyrdri at Lambafell (Iceland-SW)	Crater Row of Brennisteinsfjöll	1701-04=
Eldborg Sydri at Lambafell (Iceland-SW)	Crater Row of Brennisteinsfjöll	1701-04=
Eldborg undir Meitlum (Iceland-SW)	Crater Row of Hengill	1701-05=
Eldborg-Drottningu (Iceland-SW)	Crater Row of Brennisteinsfjöll	1701-04=
Eldborgir (Iceland-SW)	Crater Row of Hengill	1701-05=
Eldborgir-Tindaskaga (Iceland-SW)	Crater Row of Hengill	1701-05=
Eldborg-Thingvallavatn (Iceland-SW)	Crater Row of Hengill	1701-05=
Eldborg-Trolladyngja (Iceland-SW)	Crater Row of Krísuvík	1701-03=
Eldey (Iceland-SW)	Submarine vent of Reykjanes	1701-02=
Eldeyjar (Iceland-SW)	Submarine vent of Reykjanes	1701-02=
Eldeyjarbodi (Iceland-SW)	Submarine vent of Reykjanes	1701-02=
Eldfell (Iceland-S)	Fissure vent of Vestmannaeyjar	1702-01=
Eldgigur (Iceland-NE)	Fissure vent of Grímsvötn	1703-01=
Eldgjá (Iceland-S)	Fissure vent of Katla	1702-03=
Eldividarhraun (Iceland-S)	Fissure vent of Hekla	1702-07=
Eldoerne [Eldeyjar] (Iceland-SW)	Submarine vent of Reykjanes	1701-02=
Eldvorp (Iceland-SW)	Crater Row of Reykjanes	1701-02=
Electra, Mt. (Antarctica)	Synonym of Pleiades, The	1900-013
Elegante, Volcán el (México)	Maar of Pinacate	1401-001
Eleitoga (Samoa-SW Pacific)	Cone of Savai'i	0404-04=
Elelau (Ethiopia)	Synonym of Jalua	0201-03=
Elena Capurata [Capurata] (Chile-N)	Stratovolcano of Acotango	....
Elena, Cráter (México)	Crater of Pinacate	1401-001
Elengoum (Africa-W)	Pleistocene caldera of Manengouba	0204-02-
Elephant, Mt. (Australia)	Cone of Newer Volcanics Prov	0509-01-
Eliane Cone (Indian O.-W)	Submarine vent Fournaise, Piton de la	0303-02=
Eliza, Mt. (Australia)	Dome of Newer Volcanics Prov	0509-01-
Elk Butte (US-Wyoming)	Dome of Yellowstone	1205-01-
Elk Mountain (US-Oregon)	Cone of Williamson Mountain	....
Ellidaey (Iceland-S)	Cone of Vestmannaeyjar	1702-01=
Elliott's Crater (US-Wyoming)	Crater of Yellowstone	1205-01-
Ellis Cone (Antarctica)	Cone of Toney Mountain	1900-026
Ellittico (Italy)	Pleistocene caldera of Etna	0101-06=
Elmau (Africa-E)	Cone of Chyulu Hills	0202-13=
Elmenteita Badlands (Africa-E)	Pyroclastic cones (None) Holocene	**0202-071**
Eloi, Morne (W Indies)	Dome of Plat Pays, Morne	1600-11=
Elovsky (Kamchatka)	Shield volcanoes (1, -7550) Tephrochron	**1000-59-**
Elwyn Hot Springs (Canada)	Thermal feature of Edziza	1200-06-
Emae (Vanuatu-SW Pacific)	Complex volcano (None) Pleistocene	....
Emao [Loboa] (Vanuatu-SW Pacific)	Stratovolcano of North Vate	0507-081
Embagai (Africa-E)	Caldera (None) Quaternary	....
Embajada, Cerro de la (Nicaragua)	Cinder cone of Nejapa-Miraflores	1404-092
Embanques, Los (Argentina)	Pyrocl. cone Northern Mendoza Field	....
Ember Ridge (Canada)	Dome of Cayley, Mt.	....
Embocadero, Volcán (México)	Cinder cone of Mascota Volc Field	1401-031
Emborio (Greece)	Thermal feature of Nisyros	0102-05=
Emi (Chad term for Mountain) see proper name (e.g. Koussi, Emi)		
Emigrant Valley (US-Montana)	Unknown (None) Pleistocene	....
Emma, Mt. (US-Arizona)	Cinder cone of Uinkaret Field	1209-01-
Emmons Lake (Alaska Peninsula)	Caldera (None) Holocene	**1102-02-**
Emmons, Mount (Alaska Peninsula)	Stratovolcano of Emmons Lake	1102-02-
Empaakai (Africa-E)	Synonym of Embagai	....
Empajada, La (Nicaragua)	Cinder cone of Nejapa-Miraflores	1404-092
Empedrado, El (Honduras)	Cone of Pedregal, El	....
Emperor Cone (Antarctica)	Cinder cone of Morning, Mt.	1900-020
Emperor of China (Banda Sea)	Submarine volcano? (Uncertain)	**0605-01=**
Emperor Range (Bougainville)	Calderas (None) Pleistocene	....
Empoeng (Sulawesi-Indonesia)	Synonym of Lokon-Empung	0606-10=
Empong [Empung] (Sulawesi-Indonesia)	Crater of Lokon-Empung	0606-10=
Empung (Sulawesi-Indonesia)	Crater of Lokon-Empung	0606-10=
Emstruhruan (Iceland-S)	Fissure vent of Katla	1702-03=
Emu Hill (Australia)	Cone of McBride Volc Province	....
Emuruangogolak (Africa-E)	Shield volcano (8, 1910) Radiocarbon	**0202-051**
Emuruepoli (Africa-E)	Cone of Emuruangogolak	0202-051
Enambaba (Africa-E)	Cone of Emuruangogolak	0202-051
'Enaz, Hala-'l- (Arabia-W)	Cone of 'Uwayrid, Harrat	0301-02=
Encantada Mayor, La (México)	Synonym of San Luis, Isla	1401-003
Encantada, Caldera (Canary Is)	Cinder cone of Fuerteventura	1803-05-
Encantada, Laguna (México)	Maar of San Martín	1401-11=
Encierro, Cerro (US-New Mexico)	Vent of Zuni-Bandera	1210-02-
Enclos Velain [Velain] (Indian O.-W)	Crater of Fournaise, Piton de la	0303-02=
Endeavour Ridge (Pacific-NE)	Submarine volcano (2, -3490) U-series	**1301-01-**
Endeh Api (Lesser Sunda Is)	Synonym of Iya	0604-11=
Enderby Island (Galápagos)	Tuff cone of Floreana	....
Endut (Java)	Stratovolcano (None) Pleistocene	....
Endut, Gunung (Java)	Stratovolcano of Perbakti-Gagak	0603-04=
Enforcado, Pico do (Azores)	Cone of Sete Cidades	1802-08=
Engare Sukuta [Suguta-Logkipi] (Africa-E)	Thermal feature of Barrier, The	0202-03=
Engeloreti, Ol Doinyo (Africa-E)	Cone of Chyulu Hills	0202-13=
English's Crater (W Indies)	Crater of Soufrière Hills	1600-05=
Engorda, Volcán la (Chile-C)	Stratovolcano of San José	1507-02=
Enid Creek (Canada)	Cone of Dark Mountain	....
Eniwa (Hokkaido-Japan)	Stratovolcano of Shikotsu	0805-04=
Enko-dake (Honshu-Japan)	Cone of Norikura	0803-06=
Enkorika (Africa-E)	Fissure vent of Suswa	0202-11=
Enostuck Meadow [Eanastick Meadow]	Vent of Garibaldi	1200-20-
Ensenada el Viejo (Nicaragua)	Tuff ring of Zapatera	1404-111
Ensenada los Chiqueros (Nicaragua)	Lava cone of Zapatera	1404-111
Ensenadas de Punta Gorda (Nicaragua)	Cone of Zapatera	1404-111
Entremontanas, Montaña (Canary Is)	Cinder cone of Hierro	1803-02-
Enval, Maar d' (France)	Maar of Chaîne des Puys	0100-02-
Eonostuck Meadow [Eanastick Meadow]	Vent of Garibaldi	1200-20-
Epi (Vanuatu-SW Pacific)	Stratovolcanoes (8, 2004) Historical	**0507-06=**
Epi A (Vanuatu-SW Pacific)	Submarine vent of Epi	0507-06=
Epi B (Vanuatu-SW Pacific)	Submarine vent of Epi	0507-06=
Epi C (Vanuatu-SW Pacific)	Submarine vent of Epi	0507-06=
Epomeo (Italy)	Synonym of Ischia	0101-03=
Eppelsberg (Germany)	Cone of East Eifel Volc Field	....
Epsom Avenue (New Zealand)	Cone of Auckland Field	0401-02=
Epun (Chile-C)	Crater of Callaqui	1507-091
Era Kohor (Africa-N)	Caldera of Koussi, Emi	0205-021
Er-Bal Haf (Arabia-S)	Synonym of Bal Haf, Harra of	0301-17-
Erbenschell (Germany)	Cone of West Eifel Volc Field	0100-01-
Erciyas Dagi (Turkey)	Synonym of Erciyes Dagi	0103-01=
Erciyes Dagi (Turkey)	Stratovolcano (1, -6880) Radiocarbon	**0103-01=**
Erdjas (Erdschias, Erdzhias) (Turkey)	Synonym of Erciyes Dagi	0103-01=

Name (Subregion)	Type (Eruptions, Most Recent) Status / Relation to Named Volcano	Volcano Number
Erebus (Antarctica)	Stratovolcano (20, 2010) Historical	**1900-02=**
Erebus (Indian O.-S)	Cone of Kerguelen Islands	0304-02=
Erh-Ko-shan (China-E)	Synonym of Erkeshan	....
Erh-Lung-wan [Erlongwan] (China-E)	Maar of Longgang Group	1005-05-
Erie (US-Nevada)	Cinder cones (None) Pleistocene?	....
Eríksjökull (Iceland-SW)	Tuya (None) Pleistocene.	....
Erita, La (México)	Cinder cone of Colima	1401-04=
Erkeshan (China-E)	Shield volcano (None) Pleistocene	....
Erk-Keh-shan (China-E)	Synonym of Erkeshan	....
Erlongwan (China-E)	Maar of Longgang Group	1005-05-
Ermak (Kuril Is)	Dome of Grozny Group	0900-07=
Ernici, Monti (Italy)	Volcanic field (None) Pleistocene	....
Erpingdingshan (Taiwan)	Dome of Tatun Group	0801-032
Errant Cone (Nicaragua)	Cinder cone of Masaya	1404-10=
Erta Ale (Ethiopia)	Shield volcano (4, 2010) Historical	**0201-08=**
Erta Ali (Ertahale, Erto Ale) (Ethiopia)	Synonym of Erta Ale	0201-08=
Es Safa (Syria)	Volcanic field (1, 1850) Historical	**0300-05-**
Esa 'Ala (D'Entrecasteaux Is)	Synonym of Dawson Strait Group	0503-06=
Esan (Hokkaido-Japan)	Synonym of E-san	0805-011
E-san (Hokkaido-Japan)	Stratovolcano (7, 1874) Historical	**0805-011**
E-san Maru-yama (Hokkaido-Japan)	Stratovolcano (None) Pleistocene	....
Escala (Bolivia)	Lava dome (None) Pleistocene	....
Escalante (Chile-N)	Stratovolcano of Sairecabur	1505-091
Escanaba Segment (Pacific-NE)	Submarine volcano (1, -2260) U-series	**1301-04-**
Escangraga, Montana de (Canary Is)	Cone of Fuerteventura	1803-05-
Eschelle (W Indies)	Cinder cone of Soufrière Guadeloupe	1600-06=
Esclavos, Cerrito los (Guatemala)	Cinder cone of Cuilapa-Barbarena	1402-111
Escobeta, Cerro (México)	Cone of Chichinautzin	1401-08=
Escondida, Cerro Laguna (Chile-N)	Cone of Cordón de Puntas Negras	1505-101
Escondida, Laguna (Argentina)	Synonym of Cóndor, Cerro el	1505-19-
Escondido, Cerro (México)	Cone of Southern Guadalajara	....
Escorial (Argentina)	Cinder cone of Unnamed	....
Escorial, Cerro (Chile-N)	Stratovolcano (None) Holocene?	**1505-112**
Escorial, Cerro (Achin-Niuellu) (Argentina)	Cone of Huanquihue Group	1507-123
Escorias, Crater de las (Chile-C)	Crater of Calabozos	1507-042
Escuro, Monte (Azores)	Cone of Agua de Pau	1802-09=
Eshougedashan (China-E)	Cone of Datong-Fengzen	....
Esh-Shamit, Djebel (Arabia-W)	Cone of Khaybar, Harrat	0301-06=
Esi, Jabal el- (Arabia-S)	Stratovolcano of Dhamar, Harras of	0301-12-
Esjufjöll (Iceland-SE)	Stratovolcano (Uncertain)	**1704-02=**
Eski Acigöl (Turkey)	Maar of Acigöl-Nevsehir	0103-004
Eskihlidarfjöll (Iceland-S)	Crater Row of Hekla	1702-07=
Eskimo Hill (US-California)	Cinder cone of Table Mountain	....
Eskkrateret (Atlantic-N-Jan Mayen)	Cone of Jan Mayen	1706-01=
Esmeralda Bank (Mariana Is-C Pacific)	Submarine volc. (Uncertain) Fumarolic	**0804-21=**
Espagnol, Morne (W Indies)	Dome of Diablotins, Morne	1600-09=
Espana, Cerro (Colombia)	Dome of Santa Isabel	1501-021
Española (Galápagos)	Shield volcano (None) Post-Miocene	....
Espárrago, El (Canary Is)	Cone of Tenerife	1803-03-
Espazote, Cerro el (México)	Cone of Zitácuaro-Valle de Bravo	1401-061
Espejos, Loma de los (Chile-C)	Dome of Maule, Laguna del	1507-061
Espenberg (Alaska-W)	Volcanic field (None) Pleistocene	....
Esperance, Mt. (Solomon Is-SW Pacific)	Cone of Gallego	0505-062
Espiiritu Santo (Chile-C)	Stratovolcano of San José	1507-02=
Espina (Costa Rica)	Dome of Arenal	1405-033
Espinasse, Puy d' (France)	Cone of Chaîne des Puys	0100-02-
Espino, Cerrito el (El Salvador)	Dome of Ilopango	1403-06=
Espíritu Santo (Costa Rica)	Stratovolcano of Miravalles	1405-03=
Essa (Atlantic-N-Jan Mayen)	Cone of Jan Mayen	1706-01=
Es-Sawad, Djebel (Arabia-S)	Synonym of Marha, Jabal el-	0301-10-
Essi, Djebel al [Jabal el-Esi] (Arabia-S)	Stratovolcano of Dhamar, Harras of	0301-12-
Essimingor (Africa-E)	Stratovolcano (None) Pliocene	....
Essingen (Germany)	Maar of West Eifel Volc Field	0100-01-
Essino (Greece)	Thermal feature of Kos	....
Est, Ile de l' (Indian O.-S)	Stratovolcano (None) Holocene?	**0304-03-**
Estancia, Cerro la (México)	Dome of Zitácuaro-Valle de Bravo	1401-061
Estany, Volca l' (Spain)	Cone of Olot Volc Field	0100-03-
Estelí (Nicaragua)	Fissure vents (None) Holocene?	**1404-131**
Estivadoux, Maar d' (France)	Maar of Chaîne des Puys	0100-02-
Estrada (México)	Maar of Michoacán-Guanajuato	1401-06=
Estrecho, Montaña del (Canary Is)	Cinder cone of Tenerife	1803-03-
Estrella, Cerro de la (México)	Cone of Chichinautzin	1401-08=
Etapan (Kamchatka)	Synonym of Etopan	....
Ethnein, Hala-'l- (Arabia-W)	Synonym of Ithnayn, Harrat	0301-05=
Etinde (Africa-W)	Stratovolcano of Cameroon	0204-01=
Etna (Italy)	Stratovolcanoes (193, 2009) Historical	**0101-06=**
Etnea (Italy)	Synonym of Etna	0101-06=
Etoile, Pic de l' (Vanuatu-SW Pacific)	Synonym of Mere Lava	0507-021
Etopan (Kamchatka)	Shield volcano (None) Pleistocene	....
Etorofu-Atosa-dake (Kuril Is)	Synonym of Atsonupuri	0900-05=
Etorofu-Yake-yama [Ivan Grozny] (Kuril Is)	Somma volcano of Grozny Group	0900-07=
Et-Tadawin (Arabia-S)	Tuff cone of Haylan, Jabal	0301-11-
Euramoo, Lake (Australia)	Crater of Atherton Volc Province	....
Eurh, Jabal El (Arabia-S)	Cone of Dhamar, Harras of	0301-12-
Evangelista, Mt. (Italy)	Cone of Vulsini	0101-003
Evans Knoll (Antarctica)	Cone of Hudson Mountains	1900-028
Eve (Canada)	Cinder cone of Edziza	1200-06-
Eve [Galloseulo] (New Britain-SW Pac)	Stratovolcano of Hargy	0502-10=
Evensen (Antarctica)	Cone of Seal Nunataks Group	1900-05=
Everitt Hill (US-California)	Shield volcano of Shasta	1203-01-
Evermann, Cerro (México-Is)	Stratovolcano of Socorro	1401-021
Evliya Tepe (Turkey)	Dome of Erciyes Dagi	0103-01=
Ewen, Mt. (Australia)	Cone of Newer Volcanics Prov	0509-01-

Name (Subregion)	Type (Eruptions, Most Recent) Status / Relation to Named Volcano	Volcano Number
Exile Hill (Canada)	Cone of Spectrum Range	1200-07-
Expedition Crater (Kermadec Is)	Crater of Raoul Island	0402-03=
Expeditsii (Kamchatka)	Dome of Bezymianny	1000-25=
Eyafjalla (Iceland-S)	Synonym of Eyjafjallajökull	1702-02=
Eyjafjallajökull (Iceland-S)	Stratovolcano (3, 1823) Historical	**1702-02=**
Eyjafjöll (Iceland-S)	Synonym of Eyjafjallajökull	1702-02=
Eyra (Iceland-SW)	Fissure vent of Brennisteinsfjöll	1701-04=
Ezh [Yezh] (Kamchatka)	Dome of Bolshoi Semiachik	1000-15=

F

Name (Subregion)	Type (Eruptions, Most Recent) Status / Relation to Named Volcano	Volcano Number
Fa'afafine Seamount (Samoa-SW Pacific)	Synonym of Vailulu'u	0404-00-
Faamotu (Tonga-SW Pacific)	Cone of Niuafo'ou	0403-11=
Fa'ani (Samoa-SW Pacific)	Cone of Savai'i	0404-04=
Fa'asemene (Samoa-SW Pacific)	Tuff cone of Ta'u	0404-001
Faete, Monte della (Italy)	Stratovolcano of Alban Hills	0101-004
Fagalo (Samoa-SW Pacific)	Cone of Savai'i	0404-04=
Fagamaa (Samoa-SW Pacific)	Tuff cone of Tutuila	0404-02-
Fagatele (Samoa-SW Pacific)	Tuff cone of Tutuila	0404-02-
Fagradalsfjall (Iceland-SW)	Tuya (None) Pleistocene.	....
Fagradalshraun (Iceland-SW)	Shield volcano of Krísuvík	1701-03=
Fagululu (D'Entrecasteaux Is)	Synonym of Iamalele	0503-05=
Faial (Azores)	Synonym of Fayal	1802-01=
Faina (Kamchatka)	Fissure vent of Kliuchevskoi	1000-26=
Fako (Africa-W)	Crater of Cameroon	0204-01=
Falaise, La (W Indies)	Dome of Plat Pays, Morne	1600-11=
Falcon Island (Tonga-SW Pacific)	Submarine volcano (5, 1936) Historical	**0403-05=**
Falconiera (Italy)	Cone of Ustica	....
Faleasao (Samoa-SW Pacific)	Tuff cone of Ta'u	0404-001
Falen (Mindanao-Philippines)	Synonym of Parker	0701-011
Falling Mountain (Alaska Peninsula)	Dome of Trident	1102-16-
Falls Creek [Dragon Cone] (Canada)	Cone of Wells Gray-Clearwater	1200-15-
Falso Azufre (Chile-N)	Complex volcano (None) Holocene?	**1505-124**
Fanal Island (New Zealand)	Dome of Mokohinau Islands	....
Fan-Chia-Tung (China-E)	Synonym of Fanjiatung Group	....
Fang (Antarctica)	Stratovolcano of Erebus	1900-02=
Fangshan (China-E)	Synonym of Jianghui Group	....
Fanjiatung Group (China-E)	Cones (None) Quaternary	....
Fantale (Fantali, Fantalle) (Ethiopia)	Synonym of Fentale	0201-19=
Fanthams Peak (New Zealand)	Cone of Taranaki [Egmont]	0401-03=
Fanua Lai (Tonga-SW Pacific)	Synonym of Fonualei	0403-10=
Fanuatapu (Samoa-SW Pacific)	Tuff ring of Upolu	0404-03-
Faraglione (Italy)	Cone of Vulcano	0101-05=
Farallon a Fortuna (Volcano Is-Japan)	Synonym of Ioto [Iwo-jima]	0804-12=
Farallon de Pajaros (Mariana Is)	Stratovolcano (16, 1967) Historical	**0804-14=**
Faris Peak (Aleutian Is)	Cone of Westdahl	1101-34-
Farm Flat (W Indies)	Dome of Liamuiga	1600-03=
Faro, Cerro el (México)	Tuff cone of Isabel, Isla	1401-023
Faro, El (El Salvador)	Synonym of Izalco	1403-03=

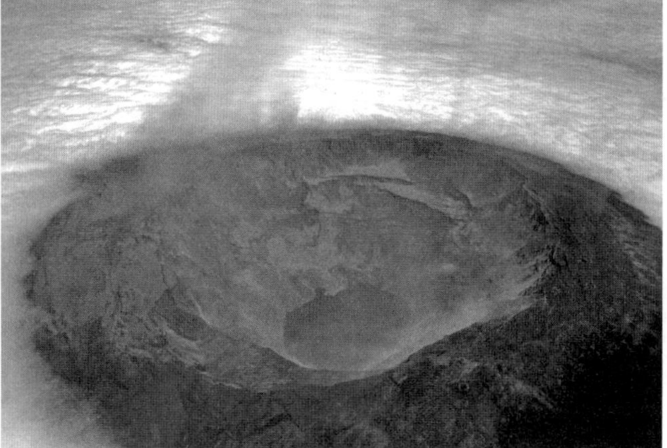

Dust clouds rise from **Fernandina** caldera in the Galápagos Islands on July 4, 1968, about three weeks after a major explosive eruption that was followed by asymmetrical collapse up to 350 m of the floor of the 4 x 6.5 km wide caldera.

Name (Subregion)	Type (Eruptions, Most Recent) Status / Relation to Named Volcano	Volcano Number
Farol (Azores)	Dome of Terceira	1802-05=
Fasnia, Volcán de (Canary Is)	Cinder cone of Tenerife	1803-03-
Father Clancy, Mt. (Australia)	Cone of Atherton Volc Province	....
Father, the (New Britain-SW Pac)	Synonym of Ulawun	0502-12=
Fatmalapa (Vanuatu-SW Pacific)	Stratovolcanoes (None) Pleistocene	....
Fatouleo-Kakoulo (Vanuatu-SW Pacific)	Stratovolcano of North Vate	0507-081
Fatu Hiva (Pacific-C)	Shield volcano (None) Pleistocene	....
Fatuaga Point (Samoa-SW Pacific)	Cone of Ofu-Olosega	0404-01=
Faujas, Cratere (Indian O.-W)	Crater of Fournaise, Piton de la	0303-02=
Favare (Italy)	Thermal feature of Pantelleria	0101-071
Favenc, Mt. (New Guinea)	Stratovolcano (None) Pleistocene	....
Fayal (Azores)	Stratovolcano (2, 1958) Historical	**1802-01=**
Fearn Island (SW Pacific)	Synonym of Hunter Island	0508-02=
Fedon's Camp (W Indies)	Stratovolcano of St. Catherine	1600-17=

Name (Subregion)	Type (Eruptions, Most Recent) Status / Relation to Named Volcano	Volcano Number
Fedotych (Kamchatka)	Shield volcano (None) Holocene?	**1000-51-**
Fee, Mount (Canada)	Cone of Cayley, Mt.	....
Fefina (Tonga-SW Pacific)	Synonym of Falcon Island	0403-05=
Felci [Fossa delle Felci] (Italy)	Stratovolcano of Salina	....
Fell (Chile-S)	Cinder cone of Palei-Aike Volc Field	1508-08-
Fellshraun (Iceland-SW)	Crater Row of Reykjanes	1701-02=
Feni (New Ireland-SW Pacific)	Synonym of Ambitle	0504-02=
Fentale (Ethiopia)	Stratovolcano (2, 1820) Historical	**0201-19=**
Fente du Nord, Fumerolle de la (W Indies)	Therm. feature Soufrière Guadeloupe	1600-06=
Ferdinandea Bank [Guila-Ferdinandeo] (Italy)	Submarine vent C. Flegrei Mar Sicilia	0101-07=
Ferle (Italy)	Cone of Pantelleria	0101-071
Fermin, Cerro (Chile-S/Argentina)	Cinder cone Crater Basalt Volc Field	1508-025
Fern Lake (US-Wyoming)	Crater of Yellowstone	1205-01-
Fernand (Indian O.-S)	Stratovolcano of Amsterdam Island	0304-001
Fernandez, Volcano de (Aleutian Is)	Synonym of Shishaldin	1101-36-

Tom Pierson (USGS/CVO)

Winter snows cover the slopes of Mount **Fuji**, Japan's highest and most renowned volcano. A 700-m-wide crater caps the 3776-m-high stratovolcano. Historical eruptions have been recorded from summit and flank vents since the 8th century.

Name (Subregion)	Type (Eruptions, Most Recent) Status / Relation to Named Volcano	Volcano Number
Fernandina (Galápagos)	Shield volcano (28, 2009) Historical	**1503-01=**
Ferranto, Mount (Antarctica)	Cone of Fosdick Mountains	....
Ferrarias (Azores)	Cone of Sete Cidades	1802-08=
Ferro (Canary Is)	Synonym of Hierro	1803-02-
Ferro, Pico do (Azores)	Dome of Furnas	1802-10=
Feuerberg (Germany)	Cone of West Eifel Volc Field	0100-01-
Fiamoe (Samoa-SW Pacific)	Cone of Upolu	0404-03-
Ficoreto, Monte (Italy)	Cone of Sabatini Complex	....
Fierros, Cerro los (México)	Cinder cone of Moctezuma Volc Field	....
Fiftytwo Ridge (Canada)	Tuya of Wells Gray-Clearwater	1200-15-
Filakopi (Greece)	Pumice cone of Milos	0102-03=
Filakovo-Salgotarjan (Slovakia)	Volcanic field (None) Pleistocene	....
Filete Cresta Montosa (Nicaragua)	Caldera of Cosigüina	1404-01=
Filete el Yankee (Nicaragua)	Cone of Cosigüina	1404-01=
Filete la Salvia (Nicaragua)	Cone of Cosigüina	1404-01=
Filicudi (Italy)	Stratovolcanoes (None) Pleistocene	....
Filicudi Seamount (Italy)	Submarine vent of Filicudi	....
Filines, Cerrito los (Guatemala)	Dome of Redondo, Cerro	....
Filo dello Zolfo (Italy)	Vent of Stromboli	0101-04=
Fimerich (Germany)	Cone of West Eifel Volc Field	0100-01-
Finca Liebres, Volcán (Costa Rica)	Stratovolcano of Turrialba	1405-07=
Finch, Mt. (Aleutian Is)	Stratovolcano of Fisher	1101-35-
Finini (Ethiopia)	Stratovolcano (None) Pleistocene	....
Finley Butte (US-Oregon)	Cone of Newberry	1202-11-
Fire Island (Aleutian Is)	Dome of Bogoslof	1101-30-
Firepit Knoll (US-Utah)	Cinder cone of Kolob	....
Firestone Butte (US-Oregon)	Cone of Newberry	1202-11-
Firgas, Montana de (Canary Is)	Cone of Gran Canaria	1803-04-
First (Kamchatka)	Dome of Uzon	1000-17=
First Crater (Antarctica)	Crater of Hut Point Peninsula	....
First Red Hill (Indian O.-S)	Cinder cone of Marion Island	0304-07-
Firura, Nevados (Perú)	Stratovolcanoes (None) Pleistocene	....
Fischbach (Germany)	Cone of West Eifel Volc Field	0100-01-
Fischer, Mt. (Australia)	Cone of Atherton Volc Province	....
Fisher (Aleutian Is)	Stratovolcano (6, 1830) Historical	**1101-35-**
Fissure Butte (US-Idaho)	Cinder cone of Craters of the Moon	1204-02-
Fissure Cone (Pacific-NE)	Lava cone of Axial Seamount	1301-021
Fissure Crater (New Britain-SW Pac)	Crater of Langila	0502-01=
Fiteko (Africa-E)	Cone of Kieyo	0202-17=
Fito (Samoa-SW Pacific)	Cinder cone of Upolu	0404-03-
Fiuchá (Chile-C)	Stratovolcano of Antillanca Group	1507-153
Fiumicello (Italy)	Tuff ring of Campi Flegrei	0101-01=
Fjallgardar Ridge (Iceland-NE)	Fissure vents (None) Pleistocene	....
Fjarborg (Iceland-NE)	Fissure vent of Krafla	1703-08=
Fjarholadyngja (Iceland-NE)	Shield volcano of Askja	1703-06=
Flagdahraun (Iceland-NE)	Fissure vent of Bárdarbunga	1703-03=
Flamingo Lake (Africa-E)	Crater of Central Island	0202-01=
Flat Top (US-Oregon)	Tuff ring of Fort Rock Volc Field	....

Name (Subregion)	Type (Eruptions, Most Recent) Status / Relation to Named Volcano	Volcano Number
Flatadyngja (Iceland-NE)	Shield volcano of Askja	1703-06=
Flatiron (Canada)	Cone of Wells Gray-Clearwater	1200-15-
Flealiin (Kamchatka)	Synonym of Ichinsky	1000-28=
Fleri (Italy)	Cinder cone of Etna	0101-06=
Fljotahraun (Iceland-S)	Fissure vent of Katla	1702-03=
Fljotsoddahraun (Iceland-NE)	Crater Row of Grímsvötn	1703-01=
Flor, Cerro de la (Nicaragua)	Dome of Lajas, Las	1404-133
Floreana (Galápagos)	Shield volcano (None) Pleistocene	....
Florencia (Colombia)	Crater of Galeras	1501-08=
Flores (Azores)	Stratovolcanoes (2, -950) Radiocarbon	**1802-001**
Flores (Guatemala)	Volcanic field (None) Holocene	**1402-14-**
Flores, Cerro las (Nicaragua)	Cinder cone of Negro, Cerro	1404-07=
Flores, Cerro las (México)	Dome of Zitácuaro-Valle de Bravo	1401-061
Flores, Las (México)	Dome of Zitácuaro-Valle de Bravo	1401-061
Flores, Los (México)	Volcanic field (None) Quaternary	....
Flotudyngjuhraun (Iceland-NE)	Shield volcano of Askja	1703-06=
Flourmill (Canada)	Cone of Wells Gray-Clearwater	1200-15-
Foerstner (Italy)	Submarine vent of Pantelleria	0101-071
Fogalepulu (Samoa-SW Pacific)	Cone of Upolu	0404-03-
Fogapoa (Samoa-SW Pacific)	Cone of Savai'i	0404-04=
Fogo (Azores)	Synonym of Agua de Pau	1802-09=
Fogo (Cape Verde Is)	Stratovolcano (11, 1995) Historical	**1804-01=**
Fogo, Cabeco do (Azores)	Cone of Fayal	1802-01=
Fogo, Lagoa do (Azores)	Pleistocene caldera of Agua de Pau	1802-09=
Fogrufjöll (Iceland-NE)	Fissure vent of Bárdarbunga	1703-03=
Fonck (Chile-S)	Cinder cone of Tronador	1508-011
Fond Doux (W Indies)	Cone of Qualibou	1600-14=
Fondi di Baia (Italy)	Tuff ring of Campi Flegrei	0101-01=
Fondo Ferraro (Italy)	Dome of Ischia	0101-03=
Fondo Riccio (Italy)	Cone of Campi Flegrei	0101-01=
Fontaipe, Cratere (Indian O.-W)	Crater of Fournaise, Piton de la	0303-02=
Fontan (Armenia)	Dome of Ghegam Ridge	0104-07-
Fontpobra, Volcà (Spain)	Cone of Olot Volc Field	0100-03-
Fontur (Iceland-NE)	Fissure vent of Bárdarbunga	1703-03=
Fonua Fo'ou (Tonga-SW Pacific)	Synonym of Falcon Island	0403-05=
Fonuafooa (Tonga-SW Pacific)	Synonym of Metis Shoal	0403-07=
Fonualei (Tonga-SW Pacific)	Stratovolcano (6, 1957) Historical	**0403-10=**
Forecast Seamount (Mariana Is)	Submarine volcano (None) Fumarolic	**0804-22-**
Forest Hill (Australia)	Cone of Newer Volcanics Prov	0509-01-
Forgia Vecchia (Italy)	Vent of Lipari	0101-042
Forgia Vecchia (Italy)	Crater of Vulcano	0101-05=
Forgotten Cone (US-Oregon)	Cinder cone of Crater Lake	1202-16-
Forgotten Crater [Williams Crater] (US)	Crater of Crater Lake	1202-16-
Forked Butte (US-Oregon)	Cinder cone of Jefferson	1202-02-
Formica Leo (Indian O.-W)	Crater of Fournaise, Piton de la	0303-02=
Forneau (Indian O.-S)	Cone of Amsterdam Island	0304-001
Fort Butte (US-Oregon)	Cinder cone of Olallie Butte	....
Fort De Kock (Sumatra)	Synonym of Marapi	0601-14=
Fort Portal (Africa-C)	Tuff cones (2, -2120) Radiocarbon	**0203-001**
Fort Rock (US-Oregon)	Tuff ring of Fort Rock Volc Field	....
Fort Rock Volc Field (US-Oregon)	Maars (None) Pleistocene	....
Fort Selkirk (Canada)	Volcanic field (None) Holocene?	**1200-01-**
Fortuna, Cerro (Guatemala)	Cinder cone of Güistepeque Volc Field	....
Fortuna, Cerro (Costa Rica)	Dome of Rincón de la Vieja	1405-02=
Fosdick Mountains (Antarctica)	Scoria cones (None) Post-Miocene	....
Fossa (Italy)	Crater of Stromboli	0101-04=
Fossa Carbonara (Italy)	Dome of Pantelleria	0101-071
Fossa del Russo (Italy)	Dome of Pantelleria	0101-071
Fossa delle Felci (Italy)	Stratovolcano of Salina	....
Fossa Grande (Italy)	Thermal feature of Vulcano	0101-05=
Fossa Lupara (Italy)	Crater of Campi Flegrei	0101-01=
Fossa Pagani (Italy)	Cinder cone of Etna	0101-06=
Fossa, Caldera della (Italy)	Caldera of Vulcano	0101-05=
Fossa, La (Italy)	Tuff cone of Vulcano	0101-05=
Fossamonaca (Italy)	Vent of Vesuvius	0101-02=
Fossetta (Italy)	Crater of Stromboli	0101-04=
Foster Crater (Antarctica)	Cone of Royal Society Range	1900-021
Foumbot Volc Field (Africa-W)	Synonym of Oku Volc Field	0204-03-
Foundland (W Indies)	Stratovolcano (None) Pleistocene	....
Fountain Vent (Pacific-NE)	Thermal feature of Cleft Segment	1301-03-
Fouque (Greece)	Dome of Santorini	0102-04=
Four Craters Lava Field (US-Oregon)	Volcanic field (None) Holocene?	**1202-14-**
Four Peaks, Island of the (Alaska Peninsula)	Synonym of Fourpeaked	1102-26-
Fourche, Piton de (Indian O.-W)	Cinder cone of Fournaise, Piton de la	0303-02=
Four-in-One Cone (US-Oregon)	Cinder cone of North Sister Field	1202-07-
Fourmile Hill (US-California)	Cone of Medicine Lake	1203-02-
Fournaise, Piton de la (Indian O.-W)	Shield volcano (177, 2010) Historical	**0303-02=**
Fourpeaked (Alaska Peninsula)	Stratovolcano (1, 2006) Historical	**1102-26-**
Fourth Top (Kamchatka)	Dome of Shiveluch	1000-27=
Fous, Morne (W Indies)	Dome of Plat Pays, Morne	1600-11=
Fox Hill (Alaska-W)	Cinder cone of St. Paul Island	1104-01-
Fox, Mt. (Australia)	Pyroclastic cone (None) Pleistocene	....
Fragatas, Lagunas (México)	Maar of Isabel, Isla	1401-023
Fraile, Montaña (Canary Is)	Cone of Tenerife	1803-03-
Fraile, Pico del (México)	Dome of Toluca, Nevado de	1401-07-
Fraile, Volcán el (México)	Stratovolcano of Popocatépetl	1401-09=
Frailes, Cerro los (Hispaniola)	Cone of Dos Hermanos	....
Frailes, Los [Cerro Nocarne] (Perú)	Dome of Chachani, Nevado	1504-007
Frailes, Montaña de los (Canary Is)	Cinder cone of Hierro	1803-02-
Fraisse, Puy de (France)	Cone of Chaîne des Puys	0100-02-
Frakes, Mount (Antarctica)	Shield volcano of Crary Group	....
Franklin Island (Antarctica)	Shield volcano (None) Quaternary	....
Franklin, Mt. (Australia)	Cone of Newer Volcanics Prov	0509-01-

Name (Subregion)	Type (Eruptions, Most Recent) Status / Relation to Named Volcano	Volcano Number
Frascati (Italy)	Crater of Alban Hills	0101-004
Frawley, Cerro (Nicaragua)	Cinder cone of Nejapa-Miraflores	1404-092
Fray Carlos, Cerro (Chile-C)	Stratovolcano of Tinguiririca	1507-03=
Frazer, Mt. (Australia)	Cone of Newer Volcanics Prov	0509-01-
Freaner Peak (US-California)	Shield volcano of Magee Peak	....
Fred Hudson Crater (Indian O.-W)	Crater of Fournaise, Piton de la	0303-02=
Fred's Hill (Indian O.-S)	Cone of Marion Island	0304-07-
Freeman Peak (Antarctica)	Synonym of Young Island	1900-011
Fremrinamur (Iceland-NE)	Stratovolcano (4, -1200) Tephrochron	**1703-07=**
Frenchmen's Solfatara (Vanuatu-SW Pacific)	Thermal feature of Suretamatai	0507-01=
Fresno, Cerro (México)	Shield volc. of Michoacán-Guanajuato	1401-06=
Frosty (Alaska Peninsula)	Stratovolcanoes (None) Holocene	**1102-01-**
Frumento della Concazze, Monte (Italy)	Cinder cone of Etna	0101-06=
Frumento Supino, Monte (Italy)	Cinder cone of Etna	0101-06=
Frumento, Monte (Italy)	Cinder cone of Etna	0101-06=
Frutilla, Cerro (Chile-C)	Cone of Antillanca Group	1507-153
Fualua (Samoa-SW Pacific)	Cone of Savai'i	0404-04=
Fubo-san (Honshu-Japan)	Stratovolcano of Zao	0803-19=
Fuchich (Africa-E)	Synonym of Central Island	0202-01=
Fudeshima (Izu Is-Japan)	Stratovolcano of Oshima	0804-01=
Fudo-ike (Kyushu-Japan)	Crater of Kirishima	0802-09=
Fuego (Guatemala)	Stratovolcano (61, 2010) Historical	**1402-09=**
Fuego de Colima (México)	Synonym of Colima	1401-04=
Fuego de Timanfaya, Montañas del	Crater of Lanzarote	1803-06-
Fuego, Montanas del (Canary Is)	Cone of Lanzarote	1803-06-
Fuego, Volcán de (México)	Synonym of Colima	1401-04=
Fueguino (Chile-S)	Lava domes (1, 1820) Historical	**1508-09-**
Fueguino, Volcán (Chile-S)	Synonym of Fueguino	1508-09-
Fuencaliente, Caldera de [Corazoncillo]	Crater of Lanzarote	1803-06-
Fuencalietne [San Antonio] (Canary Is)	Cinder cone of La Palma	1803-01-
Fuerteventura (Canary Is)	Fissure vents (None) Holocene	**1803-05-**
Fue-san (Kuril Is)	Synonym of Sarychev Peak	0900-24=
Fugen-dake (Kyushu-Japan)	Stratovolcano of Unzen	0802-10=
Fugendake-sancho (Kyushu-Japan)	Dome of Unzen	0802-10=
Fui, Volcanes de (Chile-C)	Cinder cone of Mocho-Choshuenco	1507-13=
Fui'avea (Samoa-SW Pacific)	Lava cone of Savai'i	0404-04=
Fuji (Honshu-Japan)	Stratovolcano (58, 1708) Historical	**0803-03=**
Fuji Mountain (US-Oregon)	Shield volcanoes (None) Pleistocene	....
Fujiga-dake (Honshu-Japan)	Synonym of Fuji	0803-03=
Fujimikubo (Honshu-Japan)	Tuff ring of Izu-Tobu	0803-01=
Fuji-san (Honshu-Japan)	Synonym of Fuji	0803-03=
Fuji-san (Honshu-Japan)	Dome of Takahara	0803-143
Fukeno-yu (Honshu-Japan)	Thermal feature of Hachimantai	0803-25=
Fukiage-Onsen (Honshu-Japan)	Thermal feature of Onikobe	....
Fukue-jima (Kyushu-Japan)	Shield volcanoes (1, -400) Tephrochron	**0802-091**
Fukujin (Volcano Is-Japan)	Submarine volcano (3, 1974) Historical	**0804-133**
Fukujin-kaizan (Volcano Is-Japan)	Synonym of Fukujin	0804-133
Fukujin-Nakanoba (Volcano Is-Japan)	Synonym of Minami Kasuga	0804-135
Fukujin-okanoba (Volcano Is-Japan)	Synonym of Fukujin	0804-133
Fukukazeana-yama (Honshu-Japan)	Synonym of Fuji	0803-03=
Fukutoku-Okanoba (Volcano Is-Japan)	Submarine volcano (8, 2005) Historical	**0804-13=**
Fumarole Butte (US-Utah)	Shield volcano (None) Pleistocene	....
Fumarole Valley (US-California)	Thermal feature of Long Valley	....
Fumarole, Fumarolle see proper name (e.g. Gambouli, Fumarole Field of)		
Fumaroles, Las (Costa Rica)	Thermal feature of Irazú	1405-06=
Fumarolles, Mont des (Indian O.-S)	Thermal feature of Kerguelen Islands	0304-02=
Funabara (Honshu-Japan)	Cinder cone of Izu-Tobu	0803-01=
Funagata (Honshu-Japan)	Stratovolcanoes (None) Pleistocene	....
Funda da Caldiera (Azores)	Cone of Fayal	1802-01=
Funda de Lajes, Caldeira (Azores)	Tuff ring of Flores	1802-001
Funda, Lagoa (Azores)	Stratovolcano of Flores	1802-001
Fundera (Italy)	Crater of Ischia	0101-03=
Funka-Asane (Volcano Is-Japan)	Crater of Kita-Iwo-jima	0804-11=
Fuppushi (Hokkaido-Japan)	Stratovolcano of Akan	0805-07=
Fuppushi-dake (Hokkaido-Japan)	Stratovolcano of Shikotsu	0805-04=
Furebetsu (Hokkaido-Japan)	Stratovolcano of Akan	0805-07=
Furihata-yama (Kyushu-Japan)	Dome of Sakura-jima	0802-08=
Furna (Azores)	Cone of Picos Volc System	1802-081
Furnas (Azores)	Stratovolcano (9, 1630) Historical	**1802-10=**
Furo-sen (Kyushu-Japan)	Thermal feature of Tsurumi	0802-13=
Furumio (Izu Is-Japan)	Maar of Miyake-jima	0804-04=
Furu-take (Ryukyu Is)	Stratovolcano of Kuchinoerabu-jima	0802-05=
Fuss Peak (Kuril Is)	Stratovolcano (1, 1854) Historical	**0900-34=**
Futago (Kyushu-Japan)	Lava domes (None) Pleistocene	....
Futagoishi (Kyushu-Japan)	Stratovolcano of Kirishima	0802-09=
Futagomine (Kyushu-Japan)	Cone of Kita Yatsuga-take	0803-031
Futago-san (Kyushu-Japan)	Dome of Futago	....
Futago-yama (Honshu-Japan)	Cone of Fuji	0803-03=
Futago-yama (Honshu-Japan)	Dome of Hakone	0803-02=
Futago-yama (Honshu-Japan)	Dome of Kusatsu-Shirane	0803-12=
Futago-yama (Izu Is-Japan)	Cone of Oshima	0804-01=
Futamata (Honshu-Japan)	Stratovolcano (None) Pleistocene	....
Futamata (Hokkaido-Japan)	Cone of Tomuraushi Volc Group	....
Futamata-yama (Honshu-Japan)	Stratovolcano of Nasu	0803-15=
Futatsu-dake (Hokkaido-Japan)	Pyroclastic cone of Akan	0805-07=
Futatsu-dake (Honshu-Japan)	Dome of Haruna	0803-122
Futatsu-ishi (Kyushu-Japan)	Stratovolcano of Kirishima	0802-09=
Futatsu-yama (Honshu-Japan)	Cone of Fuji	0803-03=
Futatsuzuka (Honshu-Japan)	Cone of Fuji	0803-03=
Futiga (Samoa-SW Pacific)	Cone of Tutuila	0404-02-
Fuya Fuya (Ecuador)	Stratovolcano of Mojanda	1502-005
Fuyoga-mine (Honshu-Japan)	Synonym of Fuji	0803-03=
Fuzztail Butte (US-Oregon)	Cone of Newberry	1202-11-
Fyriplaka (Greece)	Tuff ring of Mílos	0102-03=

G

Name (Subregion)	Type (Eruptions, Most Recent) Status / Relation to Named Volcano	Volcano Number
Gabellotto-Fiume Bianco (Italy)	Stratovolcano of Lipari	0101-042
Gabia, Cerro la (Guatemala)	Synonym of Pueblo Nuevo Viñas	....
Gabii [Castiglione] (Italy)	Crater of Alban Hills	0101-004
Gabillema (Ethiopia)	Stratovolcano (None) Holocene	**0201-15=**
Gablaytu (Ethiopia)	Shield volcano of Manda Hararo	0201-115
Gabriel, Mt. (New Zealand)	Cone of Auckland Field	0401-02=
Gabrielse Cone (Canada)	Cinder cone of Tuya Volc Field	1200-031
Gabuli (Ethiopia)	Synonym of Dalaffilla	0201-07=
Gachupín, El (México)	Cone of Southern Guadalajara	....
Gacong (China-E)	Synonym of Jiacong	....
Gad Elu (Ethiopia)	Stratovolcano (None) Pleistocene	....
Gada Ale (Ethiopia)	Stratovolcano (None) Holocene	**0201-05=**
Gadamsa Caldera (Ethiopia)	Synonym of Gedamsa	0201-23-
Gadang, Bukit (Sumatra)	Stratovolcano (None) Post-Miocene	....
Gadang, Gunung (Sumatra)	Synonym of Kerinci	0601-17=
Gademota Caldera (Ethiopia)	Caldera (None) Pleistocene	....
Gadir, Cuddia del (Italy)	Shield volcano of Pantelleria	0101-071
Gadjah [Gajah] (Java)	Crater of Guntur	0603-13=
Gadjahmoengkoer [Gajamunkur] (Java)	Dome of Kelut	0603-28=
Gadut-Bungsu (Sumatra)	Unknown (None) Quaternary	....
Gaesafjallarani (Iceland-NE)	Fissure vent of Krafla	1703-08=
Gaesafjöll (Iceland-NE)	Tuya (None) Pleistocene	....
Gafanhoto (Azores)	Cone of Furnas	1802-10=
Gafuranindi (Africa-C)	Cone of Nyamuragira	0203-02=
Gaga Spa (Honshu-Japan)	Thermal feature of Zao	0803-19=
Gagak, Gunung (Java)	Stratovolcano of Perbakti-Gagak	0603-04=
Gage Hill (Canada)	Tuya of Wells Gray-Clearwater	1200-15-
Gages Lower Soufriere (W Indies)	Thermal feature of Soufrière Hills	1600-05=
Gage's Mountain (W Indies)	Dome of Soufrière Hills	1600-05=
Gages Upper Soufriere (W Indies)	Thermal feature of Soufrière Hills	1600-05=
Gagua (Luzon-Philippines)	Synonym of Cagua	0703-09=
Gagxanul (Guatemala)	Synonym of Santa María	1402-03=
Gahi (SW Pacific)	Tuff cone of Wallis Islands	0404-05-
Gahinga (Africa-C)	Cone of Muhavura	0203-06-
Gaia [Tavurvur] (New Britain-SW Pac)	Stratovolcano of Rabaul	0502-14=
Gairia, Caldera de (Canary Is)	Cinder cone of Fuerteventura	1803-05-
Gaital, Cerro (Panamá)	Dome of Valle, El	1406-03-
Gajah (Java)	Crater of Guntur	0603-13=
Gajah (Sumatra)	Cone of Sarik-Gajah	0601-131
Gaja-jima (Ryukyu Is)	Stratovolcano (None) Pleistocene	....
Gajamungkur (Java)	Dome of Kelut	0603-28=
Gajolesten (Sumatra)	Synonym of Kembar	....
Gakararanga (Africa-C)	Cone of Nyamuragira	0203-02=
Gakurokuji (Kyushu-Japan)	Dome of Kuju	0802-12=
Galán, Cerro (Argentina)	Caldera (None) Pleistocene	....
Galán, Cerro (Bolivia)	Stratovolcano (None) Post-Miocene	....
Galán, Monte (Nicaragua)	Caldera of Momotombo	1404-09=
Galápago, Cerro [Las Majadas] (Guatemala)	Stratovolcano of Santa María	1402-03=
Galápagos Rift (Pacific-E)	Submarine volcano (2, 1996) Historical	**1304-07-**

Lee Siebert (Smithsonian)

Glacier Peak, the most isolated of the Cascade Range volcanoes, rises to 3213 m above the forested slopes of the Suiattle River valley. Glacier Peak resembles Mount St. Helens in its production of frequent powerful explosive eruptions with associated pyroclastic flows and lahars that traveled long distances from the volcano.

Name (Subregion)	Type (Eruptions, Most Recent) Status / Relation to Named Volcano	Volcano Number
Galatea (Italy)	Submarine vent C. Flegrei Mar Sicilia	0101-07=
Galera (Bolivia)	Cone (None) Post-Miocene	....
Galera, La (Colombia)	Synonym of Galeras	1501-08=
Galeras (Colombia)	Complex volcano (34, 2010) Historical	**1501-08=**
Galion (W Indies)	Thermal feature of Plat Pays, Morne	1600-11=
Gallego (Solomon Is-SW Pacific)	Volcanic field (None) Holocene?	**0505-062**
Gallo (Italy)	Vent of Pantelleria	0101-071
Gallo Cantano (Ecuador)	Dome of Atacazo	1502-021
Gallo, Cerro (Costa Rica)	Dome of Rincón de la Vieja	1405-02=
Gallo, Cerro el (México)	Dome of Azufres, Los	....
Gallo, Cerro el (Guatemala)	Cinder cone of Güistepeque Volc Field	....
Gallo, Cuddia del (Italy)	Dome of Pantelleria	0101-071
Gallop (Africa-E)	Synonym of Central Island	0202-01=
Galloseulo (New Britain-SW Pac)	Stratovolcano of Hargy	0502-10=

Name (Subregion)	Type (Eruptions, Most Recent) Status Relation to Named Volcano	Volcano Number
Galloway, Mt. (Pacific-S)	Cone of Antipodes Island	1305-01-
Galoenggoeng (Java)	Synonym of Galunggung	0603-14=
Galunggung (Java)	Stratovolcano (6, 1984) Historical	**0603-14=**
Galway's Mountain (W Indies)	Dome of Soufrière Hills	1600-05=
Galway's Soufriere (W Indies)	Thermal feature of Soufrière Hills	1600-05=
Gam Itji, Lake (Halmahera-Indonesia)	Maar of Ibu	0608-03=
Gamalama (Halmahera-Indonesia)	Stratovolcanoes (61, 2003) Historical	**0608-06=**
Gambia, Volcán la (Guatemala)	Synonym of Pueblo Nuevo Viñas	....
Gambier, Mt. (Australia)	Maar of Newer Volcanics Prov	0509-01-
Gambouli, Fumarole Field of (Djibouti)	Synonym of Boina	....
Gamchen (Kamchatka)	Complex volcano (2, -550) Tephrochron	**1000-21=**
Gamchensky (Kamchatka)	Synonym of Gamchen	1000-21=
Gamkanora (Halmahera-Indonesia)	Synonym of Gamkonora	0608-04=
Gamkonora (Halmahera-Indonesia)	Stratovolcano (13, 2007) Historical	**0608-04=**
Gamkunora (Halmahera-Indonesia)	Synonym of Gamkonora	0608-04=
Gamma (Russia-NE)	Cinder cone of Aluchin Group	....
Gamma Hot Springs (US-Washington)	Thermal feature of Glacier Peak	1201-02-
Gammacanore (Halmahera-Indonesia)	Synonym of Gamkonora	0608-04=
Gammakunowa (Halmahera-Indonesia)	Synonym of Gamkonora	0608-04=
Gamping (Java)	Crater of Lawu	0603-26=
Gamtschen (Kamchatka)	Synonym of Gamchen	1000-21=
Gan-ana (Honshu-Japan)	Vent of Fuji	0803-03=
Gananias, Montaña (Canary Is)	Cone of Tenerife	1803-03-
Ganaya (Africa-C)	Cone of Nyiragongo	0203-03=
Gandapura (Java)	Stratovolcano of Kamojang, Kawah	....
Gando (Honshu-Japan)	Synonym of Ganto-Kamuro	....
Gando-san (Honshu-Japan)	Stratovolcano of Zao	0803-19=
Ganju-san (Ganzyu-san) (Honshu-Japan)	Synonym of Iwate	0803-24=
Gan-Kui (China-E)	Cone of Gankui Group	....
Gankui Group (China-E)	Volcanic field (None) Quaternary	....
Gankyoji (Honshu-Japan)	Stratovolcano (None) Pleistocene	....
Ganto-Kamuro (Honshu-Japan)	Stratovolcanoes (None) Pleistocene	....
Gaojianshi (SE Asia)	Unknown (None) Quaternary	....
Gaolule (Ethiopia)	Synonym of Dalaffilla	0201-07=
Gaoshan (China-E)	Cinder cone of Arshan	1005-011
Gaoshanling (SE Asia)	Pyroclastic cone of Hainan Dao	0705-001
Gaozhi (SE Asia)	Cone of Tengchong	0705-11-
Garachico, Volcán de (Canary Is)	Cinder cone of Tenerife	1803-03-
Garafía (Canary Is)	Shield volcano of La Palma	1803-01-
Garan-dake (Kyushu-Japan)	Dome of Tsurumi	0802-13=
Garang, Bukit (Sumatra)	Synonym of Garanggarag, Bukit	....
Garanggarag, Bukit (Sumatra)	Unknown (None) Post-Miocene	....
Garat, Mt. (Vanuatu-SW Pacific)	Cone of Gaua	0507-02=
Garbes (Djibouti)	Fumarole field (None) Pleist.-Fumarolic	....
Garbuna Group (New Britain-SW Pac)	Stratovolcanoes (4, 2008) Historical	**0502-07=**
Garca, Puig de la (Spain)	Cone of Olot Volc Field	0100-03-
Garda, Montaña (Canary Is)	Cone of Tenerife	1803-03-
Gardners Island (Tonga-SW Pacific)	Synonym of Fonualei	0403-10=
Gareloi (Aleutian Is)	Stratovolcano (12, 1989) Historical	**1101-07-**
Garet Chalfalla (Africa-N)	Cone of Haruj	0205-007
Garet El Graabia (Africa-N)	Cone of Haruj	0205-007
Garet, Mt. [Mt. Garat] (Vanuatu-SW Pacific)	Cone of Gaua	0507-02=
Garian Volc Field (Africa-N)	Synonym of Gharyan Volc Field	....
Garibaldi (Canada)	Stratovolcano (1, -8060) Radiocarbon	**1200-20-**
Garibaldi Hill (W Indies)	Stratovolcano of Soufrière Hills	1600-05=
Garibaldi Lake (Canada)	Volcanic field (None) Holocene	**1200-19-**
Gariboldi (Ethiopia)	Synonym of Kone	0201-20-
Gariboldi caldera (Ethiopia)	Caldera of Kone	0201-20-
Garnot Island (New Guinea-NE of)	Synonym of Blup Blup	0501-001
Garok Spring (Mindanao-Philippines)	Thermal feature of Apo	0701-03=
Garou, Morne (W Indies)	Synonym of Soufrière St. Vincent	1600-15=
Garove (New Britain-SW Pac)	Stratovolcano (None) Holocene	**0502-03=**
Garrinada, Volcà la (Spain)	Cone of Olot Volc Field	0100-03-
Garrotxa Volc Field (Spain)	Synonym of Olot Volc Field	0100-03-
Garu, Morne (W Indies)	Stratovolcano (None) Pleistocene	....
Garu, Morne (W Indies)	Synonym of Soufrière St. Vincent	1600-15=
Garua Harbour (New Britain-SW Pac)	Volcanic field (None) Holocene?	**0502-06=**
Gar-uli (Ethiopia)	Synonym of Ma Alalta	0201-111
Gas Rocks, The (Alaska Peninsula)	Dome of Ukinrek Maars	1102-131
Gasenyi (Africa-C)	Cone of Nyamuragira	0203-02=
Gashovu (Africa-C)	Cone of Nyamuragira	0203-02=
Gaspar (Argentina)	Pyrocl. cone Northern Mendoza Field	....
Gaspar, Pico Do (Azores)	Dome of Furnas	1802-10=
Gassan (Honshu-Japan)	Stratovolcano (None) Pleistocene	....
Gate Mountains (Luzon-Philippines)	Unknown (None) Pleistocene	....
Gaua (Vanuatu-SW Pacific)	Stratovolcano (15, 2010) Historical	**0507-02=**
Gaudal, Volcán (Chile-C)	Stratovolcano of San Pedro-Pellado	1507-062
Gauro (Italy)	Tuff cone of Campi Flegrei	0101-01=
Gauss, Mt. (Antarctica)	Synonym of Gaussberg	....
Gaussberg (Antarctica)	Cone (None) Pleistocene	....
Gavilantepeque, Cerro (Honduras)	Shield volcano (None) Quaternary	....
Gavrilova (Kamchatka)	Stratovolcano of Vysoky	1000-221
Gayolesten (Sumatra)	Synonym of Kembar	....
Gebala, (Ethiopia)	Synonym of Katahelu	....
Gebel (Italian: of Arabic word for Mt.) see proper name (e.g. Teer, Gebel)		
Geboeg, Gunung [Gunung Gebug] (Java)	Cone of Arjuno-Welirang	0603-29=
Gebug, Gunung (Java)	Cone of Arjuno-Welirang	0603-29=
Gedamsa (Ethiopia)	Caldera (None) Holocene	**0201-23-**
Gede (Java)	Stratovolcano (22, 1957) Historical	**0603-06=**
Gede (Java)	Unknown (None) Quaternary	....
Gedeh (Java)	Synonym of Gede	0603-06=
Gedemsa Caldera (Ethiopia)	Synonym of Gedamsa	0201-23-
Gedroits, Mount (Kuril Is)	Dome of Smirnov	0900-021
Gegamsk Upland (Armenia)	Synonym of Ghegam Ridge	0104-07-

Name (Subregion)	Type (Eruptions, Most Recent) Status Relation to Named Volcano	Volcano Number
Geger Halang (Java)	Pleistocene caldera of Cereme	0603-17=
Geirfugladrangur (Iceland-SW)	Submarine vent of Reykjanes	1701-02=
Geirfuglasker (Iceland-S)	Cone of Vestmannaeyjar	1702-01=
Geisers, Geysers see proper name (e.g. Copacoya, Geisers de)		
Geitlandshraun (Iceland-SW)	Fissure vent of Prestahnukur	1701-07=
Geizernaya (Kamchatka)	Dome of Uzon	1000-17=
Gelai (Africa-E)	Shield volcano (None) Pleistocene	....
Gelaman, Gunung (Java)	Cone of Ijen	0603-35=
Gelfiser, Monte (Italy)	Cone of Pantelleria	0101-071
Geli Mutu (Geli Moetoe) (Lesser Sunda Is)	Synonym of Kelimutu	0604-14=
Gelimoen [Gelimun] (Lesser Sunda Is)	Crater of Leroboleng	0604-20=
Gelimun (Lesser Sunda Is)	Crater of Leroboleng	0604-20=
Gelkhamar, Monte (Italy)	Cone of Pantelleria	0101-071
Gellibrand, Mt. (Australia)	Cone of Newer Volcanics Prov	0509-01-
Gelso (Italy)	Thermal feature of Vulcano	0101-05=
Gembong, Gunung (Java)	Maar of Muria	0603-251
Gembudo (Honshu-Japan)	Shield volcano of Kannabe	....
Gemelkeret (Vanuatu-SW Pacific)	Crater of Suretamatai	0507-01=
Gemellaro, Monte (Italy)	Cinder cone of Etna	0101-06=
Gemelos, Cerro de los (Galápagos)	Cone of Floreana	....
Gemelos-Saladillo (Argentina)	Scoria cones (None) Pleistocene	....
Gemolong (Java)	Crater of Lawu	0603-26=
Gemündener (Germany)	Maar of West Eifel Volc Field	0100-01-
Gemurah Badas (Sumatra)	Thermal feature of Besar	0601-25=
Gemurah Bubur (Sumatra)	Thermal feature of Besar	0601-25=
Gemurah Ilahan (Sumatra)	Thermal feature of Besar	0601-25=
Gemurah Keniningan (Sumatra)	Thermal feature of Besar	0601-25=
Genbodo [Gembudo] (Honshu-Japan)	Shield volcano of Kannabe	....
Genbudo [Gembudo] (Honshu-Japan)	Shield volcano of Kannabe	....
Gendal, Kawah (Java)	Thermal feature of Merapi	0603-25=
Gendingwaluh, Gunung (Java)	Cone of Ijen	0603-35=
Gendol, Kawah (Java)	Thermal feature of Merbabu	0603-24=
Gengi, Volcà (Spain)	Cone of Olot Volc Field	0100-03-
Geng-zi-ping (Taiwan)	Thermal feature of Tatun Group	0801-032
Geni, Gunung (Java)	Cone of Lamongan	0603-32=
Genovesa (Galápagos)	Shield volcano (None) Holocene	**1503-081**
Genpuku-yama (Hokkaido-Japan)	Cone of Akaigawa	....
Genta-ana (Hokkaido-Japan)	Crater of Usu	0805-03=
Genteng, Gunung (Java)	Cone of Ijen	0603-35=
Genuk (Java)	Dome of Muria	0603-251
Geodesistoy (Kamchatka)	Shield volcano (None) Holocene?	**1000-38-**
Georgios (Greece)	Dome of Santorini	0102-04=
Geraldino (Galápagos)	Synonym of Pinta	1503-07=
Gerente, Le (Indian O.-W)	Crater of Fournaise, Piton de la	0303-02=
German Hill (New Zealand)	Cone of Pouakai	....
Germav Tepe (Turkey)	Dome of Nemrut Dagi	0103-02=
Gerokgak Hot Spring (Lesser Sunda Is)	Thermal feature of Bratan	0604-001
Geronimo (US-Arizona)	Volcanic field (None) Pleistocene	....
Gertrude Creek (Alaska Peninsula)	Scoria cone (None) Pleistocene	....
Gervasi, Monte (Italy)	Cinder cone of Etna	0101-06=
Gesi (Java)	Crater of Lawu	0603-26=
Geststadavatn (Iceland-SW)	Maar of Krísuvík	1701-03=
Getang (Africa-E)	Crater of Korosi	0202-054
Getlandshraun [Geitlandshraun] (Iceland-SW)	Fissure vent of Prestahnukur	1701-07=
Geulis (Java)	Crater of Guntur	0603-13=
Geureudong (Sumatra)	Stratovolcano (None) Pleist.-Fumarolic	....
Geureugoh (Sumatra)	Fissure vents (None) Pleistocene	....
Geyser Bight (Aleutian Is)	Thermal feature of Recheschnoi	1101-28-
Geyser Valley (New Zealand)	Thermal feature of Maroa	0401-061
Geysernaya (Kamchatka)	Pleistocene caldera of Uzon	1000-17=
Geysers, The (US-California)	Thermal feature of Clear Lake	1203-10-
Geysers, Valley of (Kamchatka)	Thermal feature of Uzon	1000-17=
Geysir (Iceland-SW)	Stratovolc. (None) Pleistocene-Geysers	....
Geysir (Iceland-SW)	Thermal feature of Hveravellir	1701-08=
Geyzernaya [Geysernaya] (Kamchatka)	Pleistocene caldera of Uzon	1000-17=
Ghaie [Tavurvur] (New Britain-SW Pac)	Stratovolcano of Rabaul	0502-14=
Gharat, Mt. [Mt. Garat] (Vanuatu-SW Pacific)	Cone of Gaua	0507-02=
Gharyan Volc Field (Africa-N)	Stratovolcanoes (None) Pleistocene	....
Ghegam Ridge (Armenia)	Volcanic field (1, -1900) Anthropology	**0104-07-**
Gheghassar (Armenia)	Dome of Ghegam Ridge	0104-07-
Ghentolug (Vanuatu-SW Pacific)	Stratovolcano of Suretamatai	0507-01=
Gheraki (Greece)	Tuff ring of Milos	0102-03=
Ghost (SW Pacific)	Crater of Wallis Islands	0404-05-
Giano (Ethiopia)	Dome of Tullu Moje	0201-25-
Giant Crater (US-California)	Crater of Medicine Lake	1203-02-
Gianti (Java)	Stratovolcano of Sumbing	0603-22=
Giardina, Monte (Italy)	Dome of Lipari	0101-042
Gibbon Hill (US-Wyoming)	Dome of Yellowstone	1205-01-
Gibele, Monte (Italy)	Thermal feature of Pantelleria	0101-071
Gibille, Monti (Italy)	Dome of Pantelleria	0101-071
Gibrus (New Zealand)	Crater of White Island	0401-04=
Gifford Peak (US-Washington)	Shield volcano of Indian Heaven	1201-07-
Gigante, Cerro (Guatemala)	Cinder cone of Moyuta	1402-13-
Giggenbach (Kermadec Is)	Submarine vent (None) Fumarolic	**0402-022**
Gigir at Storkonugja (Iceland-SW)	Crater Row of Brennisteinsfjöll	1701-04=
Gigoldugjoska (Iceland-NE)	Crater Row of Askja	1703-06=
Giguan (Aleutian Is)	Synonym of Seguam	1101-18-
Gil (Galápagos)	Synonym of Santiago	1503-09=
Gilbert Dome (US-California)	Dome of Long Valley	....
Gilbert, Mt. (Aleutian Is)	Stratovolcano (None) Pleistocene	....
Gilboa Hill (W Indies)	Cone of Northern Centres	....
Gilboa Hill (W Indies)	Stratovolcano of Quill, The	1600-02=
Gilibanta (Lesser Sunda Is)	Stratovolcano? (None) Quaternary	....
Gillett Nunataks (Antarctica)	Cone of Toney Mountain	1900-026

Name (Subregion)	Type (Eruptions, Most Recent) Status / Relation to Named Volcano	Volcano Number
Gillies Crater (Australia)	Crater of Atherton Volc Province	....
Gilliver (New Zealand)	Former crater of White Island	0401-04=
Gilolo (Halmahera-Indonesia)	Synonym of Jailolo	0608-051
Giluwe, Mt. (New Guinea)	Shield volcano (None) Pleistocene	....
Gimbala, Jebel (Africa-N)	Synonym of Marra, Jebel	0205-03-
Gimie, Mt. (W Indies)	Stratovolcano of Qualibou	1600-14=
Ginna Ale (Ethiopia)	Synonym of Erta Ale	0201-08=
Gin-numa (Hokkaido-Japan)	Crater of Usu	0805-03=
Ginsiliban, Mt. (Mindanao-Philippines)	Stratovolcano of Camiguin	0701-08=
Gipps Island (New Britain-SW Pac)	Synonym of Narage	....
Gira-le-Koma (Djibouti)	Cone of Ardoukôba	0201-126
Girdlestone (New Zealand)	Crater of Ruapehu	0401-10=
Girekol Tepe (Turkey)	Shield volcano (None) Holocene	**0103-022**
Girian Volc Field (Africa-N)	Synonym of Gharyan Volc Field	....
Girungo-Namlagira (Africa-C)	Synonym of Nyamuragira	0203-02=
Gisborne, Mt. (Australia)	Cone of Newer Volcanics Prov	0509-01-
Gisi (Africa-C)	Cone of Nyiragongo	0203-03=
Gitebe (Africa-C)	Cone of Nyamuragira	0203-02=
Gituro (Africa-C)	Cone of Nyamuragira	0203-02=
Giulia-Ferdinandeo (Italy)	Submarine vent C. Flegrei Mar Sicilia	0101-07=
Giuliano di Roma (Italy)	Pyroclastic cone of Ernici, Monti	....
Giumoush (Armenia)	Dome of Ghegam Ridge	0104-07-
Giuturna (Italy)	Crater of Alban Hills	0101-004
Giwu Peak (New Britain-SW Pac)	Cone of Lolobau	0502-13=
Gjabakkahraun (Iceland-SW)	Shield volcano of Hengill	1701-05=
Gjálp (Iceland-NE)	Fissure vent of Grímsvötn	1703-01=
Gjastykkisbunga (Iceland-NE)	Shield volcano of Krafla	1703-08=
Glaa, El (Africa-N)	Cone of Haruj	0205-007
Glaak (Lesser Sunda Is)	Cone of Wodong-Glaak	....
Glace, Piton (Indian O.-W)	Cinder cone of Fournaise, Piton de la	0303-02=
Glacier (Canada)	Dome of Edziza	1200-06-
Glacier Peak (US-Washington)	Stratovolcano (6, 1700) Tephrochron	**1201-02-**
Glacier Pikes (Canada)	Dome of Garibaldi	1200-20-
Gladky (Kamchatka)	Dome of Bezymianny	1000-25=
Glanvillia Hot Springs (W Indies)	Thermal feature of Diablotins, Morne	1600-09=
Glass Creek (US-California)	Dome of Inyo Craters	1203-13-
Glass Mountain (US-California)	Dome of Long Valley	....
Glass Mountain (US-California)	Dome of Medicine Lake	1203-02-
Glavny (Kamchatka)	Cinder cone of Kostakan	1000-122
Glen Allyn (Australia)	Cone of Atherton Volc Province	....
Glenbervie [Maruata] (New Zealand)	Cone of Whangarei	0401-011
Glenbrook (New Zealand)	Shield volcano of South Auckland	....
Gli Moetoe (Lesser Sunda Is)	Synonym of Kelimutu	0604-14=
Glindo (Italy)	Vent of Pantelleria	0101-071
Gloria Pata, Cerro (Bolivia)	Stratovolcano (None) Post-Miocene	....
Gloria, Cerro el (El Salvador)	Synonym of Tablas, Cerro las	....
Gloria, Cerro la (El Salvador)	Dome of Coatepeque Caldera	1403-041
Gloria, Cerro la (México)	Cinder cone Zitácuaro-Valle de Bravo	1401-061
Gloria, Cerro la [Cerro las Tablas] (El Salv.)	Stratovolcano of Tablas, Cerro las	....
Gloria, La (México)	Volcanic field (None) Holocene	**1401-097**
Goan (Africa-N)	Cone of Bayuda Volc Field	0205-06-
Goat Butte (US-Washington)	Cinder cone of Adams	1201-04-
Goat Rocks (US-Washington)	Stratovolcano (None) Pleistocene	....
Goat Rocks (US-Washington)	Former dome of St. Helens	1201-05-
Goat's Peak (US-Oregon)	Dome of Jefferson	1202-02-
God, Mountain of (Africa-E)	Synonym of Lengai, Ol Doinyo	0202-12=
Godagi (New Guinea-NE of)	Cone of Manam	0501-02=
Goeha Songgadikit (Lesser Sunda Is)	Crater of Batur	0604-01=
Goentoer (Java)	Synonym of Guntur	0603-13=
Gof (Kenyan term for Hill) see proper name (e.g. Dakara, Gof)		
Gof Dukana (Ethiopia)	Maar of Mega Basalt Field	0201-33-
Gog (Vanuatu-SW Pacific)	Synonym of Gaua	0507-02=
Gogdag (Turkey)	Dome of Erciyes Dagi	0103-01=
Gogodom, Gunung (Halmahera-Indonesia)	Crater of Dukono	0608-01=
Gok Dag (Turkey)	Dome of Erciyes Dagi	0103-01=
Golan (Ethiopia)	Cone of Mega Basalt Field	0201-33-
Golan Heights (Syria)	Volcanic field (None) Holocene	**0300-03-**
Golaya (Kamchatka)	Stratovolcano (None) Holocene	**1000-057**
Gölcük (Turkey)	Caldera (None) Pleistocene	....
Golden Gate (Indian O.)	Tuff cone of Prince Edward Island	0304-06-
Golden Trout Creek (US-California)	Volcanic field (1, -5550) Tephrochron	**1203-17-**
Golets-Tornyi Group (Kuril Is)	Pyroclastic cones (None) Holocene?	**0900-091**
Golfo, El (Canary Is)	Shield volcano of Hierro	1803-02-
Golgat (Armenia)	Cone of Aragats	0104-06-
Golgol (Chile-C)	Pyrocl. cone Puyehue-Cordón Caulle	1507-15=
Göllü Dag (Turkey)	Lava dome (None) Holocene?	**0103-003**
Golovnin (Kuril Is)	Caldera (3, 1848) Historical	**0900-01=**
Goltepe (Turkey)	Cone of Nemrut Dagi	0103-02=
Goluboe Ozero Hot Spring (Kuril Is)	Thermal feature of Baransky	0900-08=
Golygina (Golyginski) (Kamchatka)	Synonym of Khodutka	1000-053
Golyi (Kamchatka)	Shield volcano of Visokiy	1000-059
Goma, Mont (Africa-C)	Cone of Nyiragongo	0203-03=
Goma, Monte (Italy)	Cinder cone of Etna	0101-06=
Gomon-ishi (Honshu-Japan)	Dome of Towada	0803-271
Gomulion [Komolion] (Africa-E)	Vent of Korosi	0202-054
Gomwa Bay-Salamo Area	Thermal feature Dawson Strait Group	0503-06=
Gondang (Java)	Dome of Tengger Caldera	0603-31=
Gongen-ike (Honshu-Japan)	Crater of Norikura	0803-06=
Gongen-yama (Kyushu-Japan)	Dome of Sakura-jima	0802-08=
Gongora (Costa Rica)	Cone of Orosí	1405-01=
Gongora, Cerro (Costa Rica)	Dome of Rincón de la Vieja	1405-02=
Gonnard, Puy (France)	Cone of Chaîne des Puys	0100-02-
Gono-ike (Honshu-Japan)	Crater of Norikura	0803-06=
Gono-ike (Honshu-Japan)	Crater of On-take	0803-04=
Gonzales, Islota (Chile-Is)	Tuff cone of San Félix	1506-01=
Good Hope Island (Tonga-SW Pacific)	Synonym of Niuafo'ou	0403-11=

Mount **Garibaldi**, rising above scenic Garibaldi Lake in southern British Columbia, Canada, is a largely Pleistocene stratovolcano capped by a lava-dome complex. "The Table," the dark, flat-topped ridge below Garibaldi, is a "tuya" formed when lava flows filled a pit melted through the Cordilleran ice sheet. The lake was formed as a result of lava flows from the Clinker Peak cinder cone of the of the Pleistocene-to-Holocene **Garibaldi Lake** volcanic field.

Name (Subregion)	Type (Eruptions, Most Recent) Status / Relation to Named Volcano	Volcano Number
Goodenough (D'Entrecasteaux Is)	Volcanic field (None) Holocene	**0503-041**
Goodhope Bay (Indian O.-S)	Tuff cone of Marion Island	0304-07-
Goose Creek Knoll (US-Utah)	Cinder cone of Kolob	
Goosenest (US-California)	Shield volcano (None) Pleistocene	
Goosenest (US-Oregon)	Shield volcano (None) Pleistocene	
Gora Chetierek Glavaia (Alaska Peninsula)	Synonym of Fourpeaked	1102-26-
Gora Edgkom (Alaska-E)	Synonym of Edgecumbe	1105-04-
Gorda (Nicaragua)	Cone of Maderas	1404-13-
Gordo de Jutiapa, Cerro (Guatemala)	Cinder cone of Flores	1402-14-
Gordo, Cerrito (Guatemala)	Cinder cone of Cuilapa-Barbarena	1402-111
Gordo, Cerro (México)	Cone of Apan-Tezontepec	
Gordo, Cerro (México)	Dome of Cumbres, Las	1401-098
Gordo, Cerro (Guatemala)	Cinder cone of Moyuta	1402-13-
Gordo, Cerro (México)	Cinder cone of Naolinco Volc Field	1401-095
Gordo, Cerro (México)	Cinder cone of Naolinco Volc Field	1401-095
Gordo, Cerro (Guatemala)	Cinder cone of Redondo, Cerro	
Gordo, Cerro (México)	Dome of Toluca, Nevado de	1401-07-
Gordo, Cerro (México)	Cone of Zitácuaro-Valle de Bravo	1401-061
Gordo, Cerro (México)	Dome of Zitácuaro-Valle de Bravo	1401-061
Gordo, Monte (Cape Verde Is)	Cinder cone of Sao Nicolau	
Gordo, Volcán (México)	Cone of Zitácuaro-Valle de Bravo	1401-061
Gordon (Alaska-E)	Cinder cones (None) Holocene?	**1105-021**
Gordon's Hill (Indian O.-S)	Cone of Marion Island	0304-07-
Gordon's Hill (Australia)	Cone of Newer Volcanics Prov	0509-01-
Gorelaia Sopka (Kamchatka)	Synonym of Avachinsky	1000-10=
Gorelaia Sopka (Kamchatka)	Synonym of Gorely	1000-07=
Goreli (Aleutian Is)	Synonym of Seguam	1101-18-
Goreloi (Alaska-SW)	Synonym of Redoubt	1103-03-
Gorely (Kamchatka)	Caldera (49, 1986) Historical	**1000-07=**
Gorely (Kamchatka)	Cinder cone of Koshelev	1000-02=
Gorely Khrebet (Gorely Kurebet)	Synonym of Gorely	1000-07=
Gorge Farm (Africa-E)	Dome of Olkaria	0202-09=
Goriachy Pliazh (Kuril Is)	Thermal feature of Mendeleev	0900-02=
Goriaschaia Sopka (Kuril Is)	Stratovolcano (5, 1914) Historical	**0900-17=**
Goriaschi Dol (Kamchatka)	Synonym of Uzon	1000-17=
Gorna, Monte (Italy)	Cinder cone of Etna	0101-06=
Gornoe Plateau (Kamchatka)	Dome of Uzon	1000-17=
Gornogo Instituta (Kamchatka)	Synonym of Gorny Institute	1000-55-
Gorny Institute (Kamchatka)	Stratovolcano (3, 1250) Radiocarbon	**1000-55-**
Gorny Zub (Kamchatka)	Unknown (None) Pleistocene	
Gornyi Institute (Kamchatka)	Synonym of Gorny Institute	1000-55-
Goropu (New Guinea)	Synonym of Waiowa	0503-04=
Gorra (Sulu Is-Philippines)	Cone of Jolo	0700-01=
Gorshkov (Kamchatka)	Cone of Ushkovsky	1000-261
Gorshok (Kamchatka)	Fissure vent of Kliuchevskoi	1000-26=
Goru (New Britain-SW Pac)	Crater of Mundua	0502-021
Gorupu (New Guinea)	Synonym of Waiowa	0503-04=
Goryachy (Kamchatka)	Dome of Bolshoi Semiachik	1000-15=
Goryashchaya Sopka (Kuril Is)	Synonym of Goriaschaia Sopka	0900-17=

A small pond fills the bottom of the Kerid crater of the **Grímsnes** volcanic system, with other cinder cones of the Holocene Grímsnes volcanic field in the distance.

Name (Subregion)	Type (Eruptions, Most Recent) Status / Relation to Named Volcano	Volcano Number
Goryashchiy Dol (Kamchatka)	Synonym of Uzon	1000-17=
Gosei-dake (Honshu-Japan)	Synonym of Zao	0803-19=
Goshiki-dake (Honshu-Japan)	Tuff cone of Zao	0803-19=
Goshikigahara (Hokkaido-Japan)	Cone of Tomuraushi Volc Group	
Goshikiiwa (Honshu-Japan)	Stratovolcano of Towada	0803-271
Goshiki-numa (Honshu-Japan)	Crater of Azuma	0803-18=
Goshiki-numa [Okama] (Honshu-Japan)	Crater of Zao	0803-19=
Goshogake (Honshu-Japan)	Thermal feature of Akita-Yake-yama	0803-26=
Gosiki-dake [Goshiki-dake] (Honshu-Japan)	Tuff cone of Zao	0803-19=
Gosiki-numa [Goshiki-numa] (Honshu-Japan)	Crater of Azuma	0803-18=
Gosling Cone (Alaska-W)	Cone of Imuruk Lake	1104-06-
Gosyogake [Goshogake] (Honshu-Japan)	Thermal feature of Akita-Yake-yama	0803-26=
Got Ojawa (Africa-E)	Cone of Homa Mountain	0202-07=
Got Oloo (Africa-E)	Cone of Homa Mountain	0202-07=

Name (Subregion)	Type (Eruptions, Most Recent) Status / Relation to Named Volcano	Volcano Number
Gotterberg (Africa-W)	Synonym of Cameroon	0204-01=
Goudberg (Sumatra)	Synonym of Seulawah Agam	0601-02=
Gouffre Dupuis (W Indies)	Crater of Soufrière Guadeloupe	1600-06=
Gouffre Tarissan (W Indies)	Crater of Soufrière Guadeloupe	1600-06=
Gough Island (Atlantic-S)	Shield volcano (None) Pleistocene	
Goules, Puy de (France)	Cone of Chaîne des Puys	0100-02-
Goulie, Puy de la (France)	Cone of Chaîne des Puys	0100-02-
Goulvain [Dobu] (D'Entrecasteaux Is)	Stratovolcano of Dawson Strait Group	0503-06=
Goutansar (Armenia)	Dome of Ghegam Ridge	0104-07-
Gouttes, Puy de (France)	Cone of Chaîne des Puys	0100-02-
Government Gardens (New Zealand)	Thermal feature of Rotorua	
Gozyachaya Sopka (Kamchatka)	Dome of Barkhatnaya Sopka	1000-084
Graakula (Iceland-W)	Cone of Ljósufjöll	1700-03=
Graciosa (Azores)	Stratovolcano (None) Holocene	**1802-04=**
Graenavatn (Iceland-SW)	Maar of Krísuvík	1701-03=
Graf Gotzen Krater (Africa-C)	Synonym of Nyiragongo	0203-03=
Grafeldur (Iceland-SW)	Crater Row of Brennisteinsfjöll	1701-04=
Grafellshraun (Iceland-S)	Crater Row of Hekla	1702-07=
Grahahraun (Iceland-NE)	Fissure vent of Bárdarbunga	1703-03=
Graham Bank [Guila-Ferdinandeo] (Italy)	Submarine vent C. Flegrei Mar Sicilia	0101-07=
Graham Island [Giulia-Ferdinandeo] (Italy)	Submarine vent C. Flegrei Mar Sicilia	0101-07=
Graham, Mt. (Australia)	Cone of Newer Volcanics Prov	0509-01-
Grakolluhraun (Iceland-S)	Fissure vent of Torfajökull	1702-05=
Gramelur (Iceland-SW)	Crater Row of Hengill	1701-05=
Gran Canaria (Canary Is)	Fissure vents (2, -20) Radiocarbon	**1803-04-**
Gran Cono (Italy)	Stratovolcano of Vesuvius	0101-02=
Gran Cratere (Italy)	Crater of Vulcano	0101-05=
Granada (Nicaragua)	Fissure vents (None) Holocene	**1404-101**
Granada, Cerro (Guatemala)	Cinder cone of Redondo, Cerro	
Granadito (Nicaragua)	Cinder cone of Granada	1404-101
Granby, Mount (W Indies)	Stratovolcano of St. Catherine	1600-17=
Grand Bonhomme (W Indies)	Stratovolcano (None) Pleistocene	
Grand Botoum (Africa-N)	Cone of Toussidé, Tarso	0205-01=
Grand Dadoi (Africa-N)	Cone of Toussidé, Tarso	0205-01=
Grand Etang (W Indies)	Crater of St. Catherine	1600-17=
Grand Pays Brule (Indian O.-W)	Synonym of Fournaise, Piton de la	0303-02=
Grand Sarcoui (France)	Dome of Chaîne des Puys	0100-02-
Grand Soufrière [Valley of Desolation]	Thermal feature of Watt, Morne	1600-101
Grand Suchet, Le (France)	Cone of Chaîne des Puys	0100-02-
Grande de Güímar, Montaña (Canary Is)	Cone of Tenerife	1803-03-
Grande Découverte, La (W Indies)	Stratovolcano Soufrière Guadeloupe	1600-06=
Grande la Piedad, Cerro (México)	Shield volc. of Michoacán-Guanajuato	1401-06=
Grande Marmite (Indian O.-S)	Crater of Amsterdam Island	0304-001
Grande Soufrière Hills (W Indies)	Stratovolcano of Watt, Morne	1600-101
Grande, Cerro (El Salvador)	Dome of Apastepeque Field	1403-071
Grande, Cerro (El Salvador)	Dome of Coatepeque Caldera	1403-041
Grande, Cerro (Galápagos)	Tuff cone of Ecuador	1503-011
Grande, Cerro (México)	Volcanic field (None) Pleistocene	
Grande, Cerro (US-Idaho)	Fissure vents (None) Pleistocene	
Grande, Cerro (México)	Shield volc. of Michoacán-Guanajuato	1401-06=
Grande, Cerro (Guatemala)	Dome of Pacaya	1402-11=
Grande, Cerro (Nicaragua)	Cone of Pilas, Las	1404-08=
Grande, Cerro (México)	Shield volcano of San Pedro	
Grande, Cerro (México)	Cone of Zitácuaro-Valle de Bravo	1401-061
Grande, Pico (Cape Verde Is)	Synonym of Fogo	1804-01=
Grande, Pico (Azores)	Cone of Picos Volc System	1802-081
Grande, Sierra (US-New Mexico)	Shield volcano of Raton-Clayton	
Grande, Volcan (Galápagos)	Synonym of Negra, Sierra	1503-05=
Grande, Volcán (México)	Stratovolc. of Michoacán-Guanajuato	1401-06=
Grandes Pentes (Indian O.-W)	Synonym of Fournaise, Piton de la	0303-02=
Grandfather's Chair (US-Nevada)	Maar of Lunar Crater Field	
Grands Bois, Piton des (Indian O.-W)	Cinder cone of Fournaise, Piton de la	0303-02=
Grange Kop, La (Indian O.-S)	Tuff cone of Marion Island	0304-07-
Grants Malpais (US-New Mexico)	Synonym of Zuni-Bandera	1210-02-
Grants Ridge (US-New Mexico)	Cone of Taylor Volc Field	
Grasleysufjöll (Iceland-S)	Crater Row of Hekla	1702-07=
Grassy (US-Idaho)	Cinder cone of Craters of the Moon	1204-02-
Grati (Java)	Maar of Tengger Caldera	0603-31=
Gray (Antarctica)	Cone of Seal Nunataks Group	1900-05=
Gray Butte (US-California)	Dome of Shasta	1203-01-
Grazinas, Pico (Atlantic-C)	Dome of Trindade	1805-051
Great Crack (Hawaiian Is)	Fissure vent of Kilauea	1302-01-
Great Crater (Iran)	Maar of Qal'eh Hasan Ali	0302-02-
Great Domberg Hill (Africa-E)	Cone of Meru	0202-16=
Great Hanish Island (Red Sea)	Shield volcano of Hanish	0201-022
Great Hill (W Indies)	Dome of Saba	1600-01=
Great Rift Zone (US-Idaho)	Fissure vent of Craters of the Moon	1204-02-
Great Sitchin (Aleutian Is)	Synonym of Great Sitkin	1101-12-
Great Sitkin (Aleutian Is)	Stratovolcano (6, 1974) Historical	**1101-12-**
Greben' (Kamchatka)	Dome of Uzon	1000-17=
Grechishkina (Kamchatka)	Shield volcano of Snezhniy	1000-66-
Green Butte (US-Oregon)	Cone of Newberry	1202-11-
Green Hill (Australia)	Cone of Atherton Volc Province	
Green Hill (New Zealand)	Cone of Auckland Field	0401-02=
Green Hill (Vanuatu-SW Pacific)	Stratovolcano of East Tanna Volcano	
Green Island (W Indies)	Dome of St. Catherine	1600-17=
Green Lake Plug (New Zealand)	Dome of Okataina	0401-05=
Green Lake Pumice Crater (Kermadec Is)	Crater of Raoul Island	0402-03=
Greenock, Mt. (Australia)	Cone of Newer Volcanics Prov	0509-01-
Grensdalur (Iceland-S)	Stratovolcano (None) Pleist.-Fumarolic	
Grewingk [Castle Rock] (Aleutian Is)	Former dome of Bogoslof	1101-30-
Griggs (Alaska Peninsula)	Stratovolcano (1, -1790) Radiocarbon	**1102-19-**
Grille, La (Indian O.-W)	Shield volcano (None) Holocene	**0303-001**
Grímsnes (Iceland-SW)	Crater rows (11, -3500) Tephrochron	**1701-06=**

Name (Subregion)	Type (Eruptions, Most Recent) Status Relation to Named Volcano	Volcano Number
Grímsvötn (Iceland-NE)	Caldera (78, 2004) Historical	**1703-01=**
Gris (Chile-C)	Crater of Puyehue-Cordón Caulle	1507-15=
Gris, Crater (Chile-C)	Cinder cone of Mocho-Choshuenco	1507-13=
Grizzly Butte (Canada)	Shield volcano of Tuya Volc Field	1200-031
Grjothryggur (Iceland-SW)	Submarine vent of Reykjanes	1701-02=
Groppo (Ethiopia)	Stratovolcano (None) Holocene	**0201-116**
Gros Benard, Le (Indian O.-W)	Crater of Fournaise, Piton de la	0303-02=
Gros Fougas (W Indies)	Cinder cone of Soufrière Guadeloupe	1600-06=
Gros Hasan Dagi (Turkey)	Dome of Hasan Dagi	0103-002
Gros Morne (W Indies)	Dome of Northern Chain	....
Gros Piton (Indian O.-W)	Cinder cone of Fournaise, Piton de la	0303-02=
Gros Piton (W Indies)	Dome of Qualibou	1600-14=
Grosse Ssemjatschik (Kamchatka)	Synonym of Maly Semiachik	1000-14=
Grotta del Cane (Italy)	Crater of Campi Flegrei	0101-01=
Ground Crater (Hokkaido-Japan)	Crater of Tokachi	0805-05=
Groundhog (US-California)	Cinder cone of Golden Trout Creek	1203-17-
Grouse Hill (US-Oregon)	Dome of Crater Lake	1202-16-
Growler Hot Springs (US-California)	Thermal feature of Lassen Volc Center	1203-08-
Grozny (Kuril Is)	Dome of Grozny Group	0900-07=
Grozny Group (Kuril Is)	Complex volcanoes (5, 1989) Historical	**0900-07=**
Gua Waled [Gua Walet] (Java)	Crater of Cereme	0603-17=
Gua Walet (Java)	Crater of Cereme	0603-17=
Guaca, La (Colombia)	Cone of Galeras	1501-08=
Guaca, La (Colombia)	Pyroclastic cone of San Augustín-Isnos	....
Guacamaya, Cerro la (México)	Cone of Zitácuaro-Valle de Bravo	1401-061
Guacamayas, Cerro de las (Guatemala)	Cinder cone of Chingo	1402-17-
Guacamayero, Cerro (El Salvador)	Cinder cone of Coatepeque Caldera	1403-041
Guacamayo (Ecuador)	Synonym of Sumaco	1502-04=
Guacha, Loma (Chile-S/Argentina)	Cinder cone of Crater Basalt Volc Field	1508-025
Guachacollo (Bolivia)	Stratovolcano (None) Post-Miocene	....
Guachipelín (Costa Rica)	Pleist. caldera of Rincón de la Vieja	1405-02=
Guaco, Cerro el (México)	Dome of Michoacán-Guanajuato	1401-06=
Guadal (Argentina)	Pyrocl. cone Northern Mendoza Field	....
Guadaloso (Argentina)	Pyrocl. cone Northern Mendoza Field	....
Guadalupe (México)	Shield volcano (None) Holocene	**1401-006**
Guadalupe, Cerro de (El Salvador)	Cinder cone of San Vicente	1403-07=
Guagua Pichincha (Ecuador)	Stratovolcano (33, 2002) Historical	**1502-02=**
Guagua Sumaco (Ecuador)	Cone of Sumaco	1502-04=
Guagua-Putina (Perú)	Synonym of Misti, El	1504-01=
Guaillane, Cerro (Chile-N)	Stratovolcano of Puchuldiza	....
Guajara (Canary Is)	Pleistocene caldera of Tenerife	1803-03-
Guallatiri (Chile-N)	Stratovolcano (4, 1960) Historical	**1505-02=**
Guanaqueros, Volcán (Argentina)	Cinder cone of Atuel, Caldera del	1507-023
Guangoche, Cerro el (México)	Dome of Azufres, Los	....
Guantija, Cerro (Chile-N)	Unknown (None) Post-Miocene	....
Guanyin, Piton (Indian O.-W)	Cinder cone of Fournaise, Piton de la	0303-02=
Guararí (Costa Rica)	Cinder cone of Barva	1405-05=
Guarda, Cerro el (México)	Cone of Chichinautzin	1401-08=
Guardia Dei Turchi, Monte (Italy)	Dome of Ustica	....
Guardia, Monte (Italy)	Dome of Lipari	0101-042
Guardián, Cerro (Costa Rica)	Cinder cone of Irazú	1405-06=
Guardiola, La (Italy)	Cone of Ischia	0101-03=
Guatisea, Montana (Canary Is)	Cone of Lanzarote	1803-06-
Guatojón, Cerro (Guatemala)	Cinder cone of Chiquimula Volc Field	1402-20-
Guatusa, Loma la (Nicaragua)	Dome of Momotombo	1404-09=
Guatusos Peak (Costa Rica)	Synonym of Arenal	1405-033
Guayabál, El (México)	Tuff cone of Chichón, El	1401-12=
Guayabo (Costa Rica)	Pleistocene caldera of Miravalles	1405-03=
Guayaques (Chile-N)	Lava domes (None) Holocene	**1505-093**
Guayta (Perú)	Synonym of Huaynaputina	1504-03=
Guazapa (El Salvador)	Stratovolcano (None) Holocene?	**1403-052**
Guberabia (Africa-C)	Cone of Nyiragongo	0203-03=
Gudda [Boset] (Ethiopia)	Stratovolcano of Boset-Bericha	0201-21-
Guduack (Korea)	Cone of Halla	1006-04-
Gueguensi, Isla (Honduras)	Cone of Zacate Grande, Isla	1403-14-
Gueuie Ronde, Piton (Indian O.-W)	Cinder cone of Fournaise, Piton de la	0303-02=
Gufa (Ethiopia)	Volcanic field (None) Holocene	**0201-124**
Guguan (Mariana Is-C Pacific)	Stratovolcano (1, 1883) Historical	**0804-19=**
Guia, Monte de (Azores)	Tuff cone of Fayal	1802-01=
Guianason, Mt. (Philippines-C)	Thermal feature of Biliran	0702-08=
Guieshan (Guishan) (Taiwan-E of)	Synonym of Kueishantao	0801-031
Güija I, Cerro (Guatemala)	Cinder cone of Redondo, Cerro	....
Güija II, Cerro (Guatemala)	Dome of Redondo, Cerro	....
Güija III, Cerro (Guatemala)	Dome of Redondo, Cerro	....
Güija Volc Field (El Salvador)	Synonym of San Diego	1403-001
Guilherme Moniz (Azores)	Stratovolcano of Terceira	1802-05=
Güímar, Volcán de (Canary Is)	Cinder cone of Tenerife	1803-03-
Guimba (Sulu Is-Philippines)	Cinder cone of Jolo	0700-01=
Guindos, Los (Chile-C)	Stratovolcano of Carrán-Los Venados	1507-14=
Guinea, La (Nicaragua)	Dome of Zapatera	1404-111
Guineo, Cerro el (Guatemala)	Cinder cone of Güistepeque Volc Field	....
Guinsayawan, Mt. (Philippines-C)	Cone of Cuernos de Negros	0702-01=
Guinsiliban, Mt. [Mt. Ginsiliban] (Philippines)	Stratovolcano of Camiguin	0701-08=
Guintabon Dome (Philippines-C)	Dome of Cuernos de Negros	0702-01=
Guiso del Monte Panámao (Philippines-C)	Thermal feature of Biliran	0702-08=
Güistepeque Volc Field (Guatemala)	Cinder cones (None) Pleistocene	....
Gulacs (Hungary)	Cone of Balaton Highland	....
Gulizar (Turkey)	Crater of Tendürek Dagi	0103-03=
Gullborg (Iceland-W)	Cone of Ljósufjöll	1700-03=
Gullholl (Iceland-SW)	Submarine vent of Reykjanes	1701-02=
Gulu (New Britain-SW Pac)	Cone of Langila	0502-01=
Gulu, Mt. (New Britain-SW Pac)	Cone of Lotomgan Group	....
Gumansan (Philippines-C)	Dome of Biliran	0702-08=
Gumatmali (Ethiopia)	Fissure vent of Manda Hararo	0201-115

Name (Subregion)	Type (Eruptions, Most Recent) Status Relation to Named Volcano	Volcano Number
Gumawang (Java)	Crater of Lawu	0603-26=
Gumuruh (Java)	Crater of Gede	0603-06=
Gun Creek (Canada)	Synonym of Bridge River Cones	1200-17-
Güneydag (Turkey)	Dome of Acigöl-Nevsehir	0103-004
Gungpo (SE Asia)	Synonym of Tengchong	0705-11-
Gunkan-yama (Hokkaido-Japan)	Dome of Nipesotsu-Maruyama	0805-061
Gunnarsholtshraun (Iceland-S)	Fissure vent of Hekla	1702-07=
Guntur (Java)	Crater of Galunggung	0603-14=
Guntur (Java)	Complex volcano (24, 1847) Historical	**0603-13=**
Gunturan (Java)	Dome of Tengger Caldera	0603-31=
Gunung (Indonesian for Mt.) see proper name (e.g. Tudeuk, Gunung)		
Gunung Api North of Wetar (Banda Sea)	Synonym of Gunungapi Wetar	0605-03=
Gunungapi (Lesser Sunda Is)	Synonym of Agung	0604-02=
Gunungapi (Lesser Sunda Is)	Synonym of Iya	0604-11=
Gunungapi (Lesser Sunda Is)	Synonym of Lewotolo	0604-23=

A large breached caldera formed by edifice collapse during the Pleistocene truncates the summit of 4784-m-high **Guagua Pichincha** volcano, which overlooks Ecuador's capital city, Quito. A lava dome was constructed within the active crater at the head of the collapse scarp.

Patricio Ramon (Escuela Politecnica, Quito)

Name (Subregion)	Type (Eruptions, Most Recent) Status Relation to Named Volcano	Volcano Number
Gunungapi Bima (Lesser Sunda Is)	Synonym of Sangeang Api	0604-05=
Gunungapi Wetar (Banda Sea)	Stratovolcano (2, 1699) Historical	**0605-03=**
Gupit (Java)	Crater of Kelut	0603-28=
Guraundo-kako [Ground Crater] (Japan)	Crater of Tokachi	0805-05=
Gurgei (Africa-N)	Volcanic field (None) Post-Miocene	....
Gushan (China-E)	Cinder cone of Keluo Group	1005-02-
Guynemer, Massif (Indian O.-S)	Stratovolcano of Kerguelen Islands	0304-02=
Guzmanes, Los (Chile-C)	Stratovolcano of Tinguiririca	1507-03=
Guznayal, Cerro el (Guatemala)	Cinder cone of Pueblo Nuevo Viñas	....
Gvendarhyran (Iceland-S)	Tuya of Torfajökull	1702-05=
Gvendarselsgigar (Iceland-SW)	Crater Row of Krísuvík	1701-03=
Gwanguoa (Africa-C)	Cone of Karisimbi	0203-04-
Gyojanoiwaya (Izu Is-Japan)	Stratovolcano of Oshima	0804-01=
Gyoko (Ryukyu Is)	Stratovolcano of Kuchinoerabu-jima	0802-05=
Gyp (US-Arizona)	Crater of Sunset Crater	1209-02-

H

Name (Subregion)	Type (Eruptions, Most Recent) Status Relation to Named Volcano	Volcano Number
Haabunga (Iceland-NE)	Cone of Grímsvötn	1703-01=
Haahraun (Iceland-NE)	Fissure vent of Bárdarbunga	1703-03=
Haahraun (Iceland-S)	Fissure vent of Hekla	1702-07=
Habuminato (Izu Is-Japan)	Crater of Oshima	0804-01=
Haccho-rindo (Honshu-Japan)	Vent of Izu-Tobu	0803-01=
Hachigakubo Group (Honshu-Japan)	Cone of Izu-Tobu	0803-01=
Hachijo-Fuji (Izu Is-Japan)	Synonym of Hachijo-jima	0804-05=
Hachijo-jima (Izu Is-Japan)	Stratovolcanoes (18, 1606) Historical	**0804-05=**
Hachijo-jima Nishi-yama (Izu Is-Japan)	Synonym of Hachijo-jima	0804-05=
Hachikubo (Ryukyu Is)	Stratovolcano of Kuchinoerabu-jima	0802-05=
Hachikubo-yama (Honshu-Japan)	Cone of Izu-Tobu	0803-01=
Hachimaki-yama (Kyushu-Japan)	Dome of Unzen	0802-10=
Hachiman-jigoku (Kyushu-Japan)	Thermal feature of Tsurumi	0802-13=
Hachimantai (Honshu-Japan)	Stratovolcano (2, -5350) Radiocarbon	**0803-25=**
Hachiman-yama (Izu Is-Japan)	Cone of Hachijo-jima	0804-05=
Hachinokubo (Kyushu-Japan)	Vent of Unzen	0802-10=
Hachi-yama (Honshu-Japan)	Cone of Izu-Tobu	0803-01=
Hachi-yama (Honshu-Japan)	Cinder cone of Shiga	0803-121
Hachiyama-Higashioku (Honshu-Japan)	Cone of Izu-Tobu	0803-01=
Hachiyo-take (Honshu-Japan)	Synonym of Fuji	0803-03=
Hacienda de Jarideo Group (México)	Therm. feature Michoacán-Guanajuato	1401-06=
Hacienda del Agua Fría Group (México)	Therm. feature Michoacán-Guanajuato	1401-06=
Hackamore (US-California)	Volcanic field (None) Pleistocene	....
Hackamore Creek (US-Washington)	Cone of West Crater	1201-06-
Hackett, Mt. (Australia)	Cone of Nulla Volc Province	....
Haddington (Antarctica)	Shield volcano of James Ross Island	....
Hades (Tonga-SW Pacific)	Vent of West Mata	0403-13-

Name (Subregion)	Type (Eruptions, Most Recent) Status / Relation to Named Volcano	Volcano Number
Hadji, Kawah [Kawah Haji] (Java)	Crater of Karang	0603-02=
Hagafell (Iceland-SW)	Shield volcano of Hveravellir	1701-08=
Hagafell (Iceland-SW)	Shield volcano of Krísuvík	1701-03=
Hagavikurhraun (Iceland-SW)	Fissure vent of Hengill	1701-05=
Hagen, Mt. (New Guinea)	Stratovolcanoes (None) Pleistocene	....
Hagley (W Indies)	Dome of Plat Pays, Morne	1600-11=
Hágöng (Iceland-NE)	Dome of Krafla	1703-08=
Hagonguhraun (Iceland-NE)	Fissure vent of Bárdarbunga	1703-03=
Hágöngur (Iceland-NE)	Stratovolcano of Tungnafellsjökull	1703-04=
Hagoromo-yama (Honshu-Japan)	Synonym of Fuji	0803-03=
Hague (Alaska Peninsula)	Stratovolcano of Emmons Lake	1102-02-
Haid al-Isi [Jabal el-Esi] (Arabia-S)	Stratovolcano of Dhamar, Harras of	0301-12-
Haid el-'Arqub (Arabia-S)	Cone of Sawâd, Harra es-	0301-16-
Haid El-esi [Jabal el-Esi] (Arabia-S)	Stratovolcano of Dhamar, Harras of	0301-12-
Haight Mountain (US-California)	Synonym of Rainbow Mountain	....
Haimon-dake [Kaimon] (Kyushu-Japan)	Stratovolcano of Ibusuki Volc Field	0802-07=

Oddur Sigurdsson (Icelandic National Energy Authority)

The elongated profile of snow-covered **Hekla**, one of Iceland's most prominent and active volcanoes, results from repeated eruptions along an ENE-WSW-trending rift. Lava flows from Hekla's historical eruptions, which date back to 1104 AD, cover much of the volcano's flanks.

Name (Subregion)	Type (Eruptions, Most Recent) Status / Relation to Named Volcano	Volcano Number
Háin (Iceland-S)	Tuff ring of Vestmannaeyjar	1702-01=
Hainan Dao (SE Asia)	Pyroclastic cones (2, 1933) Historical	**0705-001**
Hainini (New Zealand)	Dome of Okataina	0401-05=
Hainoa Crater (Hawaiian Is)	Crater of Hualalai	1302-04-
Haique (Chile-C)	Cone of Antillanca Group	1507-153
Haiwahine, Puu (Hawaiian Is)	Cone of Mauna Kea	1302-03-
Haji, Kawah (Java)	Crater of Karang	0603-02=
Hajnacka (Slovakia)	Vent of Filakovo-Salgotarjan	....
Hakka (Honshu-Japan)	Stratovolcano of Towada	0803-271
Hakken-yama (Honshu-Japan)	Cone of Fuji	0803-03=
Hakkoda Group (Honshu-Japan)	Stratovolcanoes (7, 1550) Radiocarbon	**0803-28=**
Hakkoda-odake (Honshu-Japan)	Stratovolcano of Hakkoda Group	0803-28=
Hakodate-yama (Hokkaido-Japan)	Stratovolcano (None) Pleistocene	....
Hakone (Honshu-Japan)	Complex volcano (7, 1170) Radiocarbon	**0803-02=**
Hakudairyuo (Honshu-Japan)	Cone of Fuji	0803-03=
Hakuen (Hakuen-zan) (Kuril Is)	Synonym of Karpinsky Group	0900-35=
Haku-san (Honshu-Japan)	Stratovolcano (20, 1659) Historical	**0803-05=**
Hakuto (China-E)	Synonym of Changbaishan	1005-06-
Hakuun-dake (Hokkaido-Japan)	Dome of Daisetsu	0805-06=
Hakuun-zan (Hokkaido-Japan)	Dome of Shikaribetsu Group	0805-062
Hala- (Arabic for Volcanic Cone) see proper name (e.g. 'Asi, Hala- 'l-)		
Halalii (Hawaiian Is)	Cone of Haleakala	1302-06-
Halap (Hungary)	Cone of Balaton Highland	....
Haleakala (Hawaiian Is)	Shield volcano (40, 1750) Anthropology	**1302-06-**
Haleakala (Hawaiian Is)	Synonym of Kauai	....
Halekamahina (Hawaiian Is)	Cone of Kilauea	1302-01-
Halemaumau (Hawaiian Is)	Pit crater of Kilauea	1302-01-
Halepa (Greece)	Dome of Mílos	0102-03=
Haleyjabunga (Iceland-SW)	Shield volcano of Reykjanes	1701-02=
Half Cone (Alaska Peninsula)	Cone of Aniakchak	1102-09-
Half Cone (US-Idaho)	Cone of Craters of the Moon	1204-02-
Half Cone (Indian O.)	Tuff cone of Prince Edward Island	0304-06-
Half Moon Crater (Antarctica)	Crater of Hut Point Peninsula	....
Halimun (Java)	Stratovolcano (None) Pleistocene	....
Halimun (Java)	Stratovolcano (None) Pleistocene	....
Hall Butte (US-California)	Cinder cone of Tumble Buttes	1203-06-
Halla (Korea)	Shield volcano (4, 1007) Historical	**1006-04-**
Hallett Peninsula (Antarctica)	Shield volcanoes (None) Post-Miocene	....
Hallmundarhraun (Iceland-SW)	Shield volcano of Hveravellir	1701-08=
Halsagigir (Iceland-NE)	Fissure vent of Grímsvötn	1703-01=
Ha-Lun-Erh-shan (China-E)	Thermal feature of Baerqian	....
Halvdan (Spitsbergen)	Explosion crater (None) Pleistocene	....
Halvdanpiggen (Spitsbergen)	Synonym of Halvdan	....
Halyagos (Hungary)	Cone of Balaton Highland	....
Halyki (Greece)	Thermal feature of Mílos	0102-03=
Hamarinn (Iceland-NE)	Stratovolcano of Bárdarbunga	1703-03=
Hamatang (China-E)	Cinder cone of Jingbo	1005-04-
Hambariana (Armenia)	Cone of Ghegam Ridge	0104-07-
Hamiding (Halmahera-Indonesia)	Unknown (None) Quaternary	....

Name (Subregion)	Type (Eruptions, Most Recent) Status / Relation to Named Volcano	Volcano Number
Hamilton, Mt. (Australia)	Cone of Newer Volcanics Prov	0509-01-
Hamma al-hamdani [Jabal el-Esi] (Arabia-S)	Stratovolcano of Dhamar, Harras of	0301-12-
Hammam Damt (Arabia-S)	Synonym of Hamman Demt, Jabal	0301-13-
Hammam el-Zebib (Arabia-S)	Thermal feature of Dhamar, Harras of	0301-12-
Hamman Alessi, Djebel [Jabal el-Esi] (Arabia)	Stratovolcano of Dhamar, Harras of	0301-12-
Hamman Demt, Jabal (Arabia-S)	(None) Not a Volcano	0301-13-
Hammat Es-Sa'tar (Arabia-S)	Cone of Dhamar, Harras of	0301-12-
Hamner Butte (US-Oregon)	Shield volcano of Davis Lake	1202-10-
Hamragardarhraun (Iceland-S)	Fissure vent of Eyjafjallajökull	1702-02=
Hamudi, Jabal al (Arabia-S)	Stratovolcano of Arhab, Harra of	0301-09-
Hamugoma (Africa-C)	Tuff cone of Fort Portal	0203-001
Hana Ridge (Hawaiian Is)	Fissure vent of Haleakala	1302-06-
Hanahanapuni (Hawaiian Is)	Cone of Kauai	....
Hanamagari (Honshu-Japan)	Stratovolcanoes (None) Pleistocene	....
Hanang (Africa-E)	Stratovolcano (None) Quaternary	....
Hanare-yama (Honshu-Japan)	Dome of Asama	0803-11=
Hanatate (Izu Is-Japan)	Dome of Kozu-shima	0804-03=
Hanauma Bay (Hawaiian Is)	Tuff cone of Koolau	....
Hando-iwa (Kyushu-Japan)	Vent of Unzen	0802-10=
Hane-yama (Kyushu-Japan)	Shield volcano (None) Pleistocene	....
Hanga o Tea (Chile-Is)	Crater of Easter Island	1506-011
Hangar (Kamchatka)	Synonym of Khangar	1000-272
Hangayn Volc Field (Mongolia)	Synonym of Taryatu-Chulutu	1003-01-
Hangelberg (Germany)	Cone of West Eifel Volc Field	0100-01-
Hangetsu-ko (Hokkaido-Japan)	Tuff cone of Yotei	0805-032
Hanging Rock (Australia)	Dome of Newer Volcanics Prov	0509-01-
Hangura [Khangura] (Russia-SE)	Cone of Udokan Plateau	1002-03-
Hani-Hani (Chile-Is)	Pyroclastic cone of Easter Island	1506-011
Hanish (Red Sea)	Shield volcano (None) Holocene	**0201-022**
Hanjale, Gof (Africa-E)	Maar of Marsabit	0202-021
Hankow Reef (New Guinea-NE of)	Synonym of Yomba	0501-041
Hannah, Mt. (US-California)	Dome of Clear Lake	1203-10-
Hannington (Africa-E)	Synonym of Bogoria	....
Hans Meyer Crater [Muntango] (Africa-C)	Pit crater of Karisimbi	0203-04-
Hansa Island (New Guinea-NE of)	Synonym of Manam	0501-02=
Hantsongoma (Indian O.-W)	Crater of Karthala	0303-01=
Hanui (Hanuy) Gol (Mongolia)	Synonym of Khanuy Gol	1003-02-
Hao, Maunga [Maunga Vao] (Chile-Is)	Pyroclastic cone of Easter Island	1506-011
Haofa (SW Pacific)	Tuff cone of Wallis Islands	0404-05-
Haolduhraun (Iceland-SW)	Fissure vent of Hofsjökull	1701-09=
Haolduhraun (Iceland-S)	Fissure vent of Torfajökull	1702-05=
Haotiansi (China-E)	Cone of Datong-Fengzen	....
Haparangi (New Zealand)	Dome of Kapenga	....
Hapberg [Kapberg] (New Britain-SW Pac)	Stratovolcano of Lolo	0502-071
Harai (Honshu-Japan)	Cinder cone of Izu-Tobu	0803-01=
Harai (Honshu-Japan)	Vent of Izu-Tobu	0803-01=
Harakandi (Africa-C)	Cone of Nyamuragira	0203-02=
Haranggaol (Sumatra)	Caldera of Toba	0601-09=
Hararo Manda (Ethiopia)	Synonym of Manda Hararo	0201-115
Hararu (Ethiopia)	Synonym of Manda Hararo	0201-115
Harasztos (Hungary)	Cone of Balaton Highland	....
Harcourt, Mount (Antarctica)	Stratovolcano of Hallett Peninsula	....
Hardin Butte (US-California)	Cone of Medicine Lake	1203-02-
Hardt-Maar (Germany)	Maar of West Eifel Volc Field	0100-01-
Hargy (New Britain-SW Pac)	Stratovolcano (2, 950) Radiocarbon	**0502-10=**
Ha-r-Hin-Tun (China-E)	Synonym of Baerqian	....
Harimkotan (Kuril Is)	Synonym of Kharimkotan	0900-30=
Harkness, Mount (US-California)	Stratovolcano of Dittmar	....
Haro Maja (Ethiopia)	Tuff ring of Bishoftu Volc Field	0201-22-
Haro Maja (Ethiopia)	Maar of Butajiri-Silti Field	0201-26-
Haroharo (New Zealand)	Fissure vent of Okataina	0401-05=
Harosu (Izu Is-Japan)	Synonym of Bayonnaise Rocks	0804-07=
Haroto Bay (New Zealand)	Cone of Karioi	....
Harotsiatsianopori (Kuril Is)	Synonym of Rasshua	0900-22=
Haroudj, Djebel (Africa-N)	Synonym of Haruj	0205-007
Harra, Harras, Harrat, Harret (Arabic for Lava Field) see proper name (e.g. Birk, Harrat al)		
Harrah, Al (Arabia-W)	Volcanic field (None) Holocene	**0301-001**
Harruj, Jabal um (Arabia)	Tuff ring of Hutaymah, Harrat	....
Harry's Spa Hot Springs (US-Washington)	Thermal feature of St. Helens	1201-05-
Haruj (Africa-N)	Volcanic field (None) Holocene	**0205-007**
Haruki (Honshu-Japan)	Cinder cone of Ogino-Sen	....
Haruman (Java)	Dome of Kaledong-Haruman	....
Harumukotan (Kuril Is)	Synonym of Kharimkotan	0900-30=
Haruna (Honshu-Japan)	Stratovolcano (3, 550) Anthropology	**0803-122**
Haruna-Fuji (Honshu-Japan)	Cone of Haruna	0803-122
Haruta-yama (Kyushu-Japan)	Dome of Sakura-jima	0802-08=
Harvey's Knob (Australia)	Cone of Bundaberg-Boyne Province	....
Hasan Dagi (Turkey)	Cone of Erciyes Dagi	0103-01=
Hasan Dagi (Turkey)	Stratovolcano (Uncertain) Holocene	**0103-002**
Haszard, Mt. (Kermadec Is)	Cone of Macauley Island	0402-021
Hat Creek (US-California)	Fissure vent of Potato Butte	....
Hat Mountain (US-California)	Cone of Lassen Volc Center	1203-08-
Hatachi-yama (Honshu-Japan)	Synonym of Fuji	0803-03=
Hatchobaru (Kyushu-Japan)	Thermal feature of Kuju	0802-12=
Hatchodaira (Izu Is-Japan)	Caldera of Miyake-jima	0804-04=
Hatenji (Africa-E)	Cone of Ngozi	0202-164
Hatimaki-yama [Hachimaki-yama] (Japan)	Dome of Unzen	0802-10=
Hatimantai (Honshu-Japan)	Synonym of Hachimantai	0803-25=
Hati-yama [Hachi-yama] (Honshu-Japan)	Cinder cone of Shiga	0803-121
Hatizyo-Huzi (Izu Is-Japan)	Synonym of Hachijo-jima	0804-05=
Hatizyo-zima Nisi-yama (Izu Is-Japan)	Synonym of Hachijo-jima	0804-05=
Hattab, Jabal [Kaulet Hattab] (Arabia-S)	Tuff cone of Arhab, Harra of	0301-09-
Hattur (Iceland-NE)	Fissure vent of Bárdarbunga	1703-03=
Ha'u Epa, Maunga (Chile-Is)	Pyroclastic cone of Easter Island	1506-011

Name (Subregion)	Type (Eruptions, Most Recent) Status / Relation to Named Volcano	Volcano Number
Haug, Cratere (Indian O.-W)	Crater of Fournaise, Piton de la	0303-02=
Haugur (Iceland-SW)	Crater Row of Reykjanes	1701-02=
Hauhungatahi (New Zealand)	Cone of Ruapehu	0401-10=
Haukadalur (Iceland-SW)	Thermal feature of Hveravellir	1701-08=
Haulucani, Cerro (Chile-N)	Cone of Copa, Cerro	
Haussez, Iles d' (New Zealand)	Synonym of Mercury Islands	
Haut Chhlong (SE Asia)	Synonym of Haut Song Be	
Haut Dong Nai (SE Asia)	Volcanic field (None) Holocene?	**0705-04-**
Haut Song Be (SE Asia)	Volcanic field (None) Pleistocene	
Hautere (New Zealand)	Stratovolcano (None) Pleistocene	
Hauy, Piton (Indian O.-W)	Cinder cone of Fournaise, Piton de la	0303-02=
Havfuen Peak (Antarctica)	Cone of Bristol Island	1900-08=
Hawkes Heights (Antarctica)	Synonym of Coulman Island	
Hawshuenshan [Maanshan] (SE Asia)	Cinder cone of Tengchong	0705-11-
Haycock Island (Red Sea)	Cone of Hanish	0201-022
Haycock Island (Red Sea)	Cone of Zubair, Jebel	0201-02=
Hayes (Alaska-SW)	Stratovolcano (3, 1200) Radiocarbon	**1103-05-**
Hayil, Harrat (Arabia-W)	Synonym of Birk, Harrat al	0301-072
Hayil, Jibal (Arabia-W)	Cone of Birk, Harrat al	0301-072
Hayil, Jibal (Arabia)	Cones (None) Quaternary	
Haylah, Jabal al (Arabia-W)	Cone of Birk, Harrat al	0301-072
Haylan, Jabal (Arabia-S)	Volcanic field (1, -1200) Anthropology	**0301-11-**
Hayli Gub (Ethiopia)	Synonym of Hayli Gubbi	0201-091
Hayli Gubbi (Ethiopia)	Shield volcano (None) Holocene	**0201-091**
Hayrick Butte (US-Oregon)	Cinder cone of Washington	
Hazam Khadra', Jabal (Arabia-W)	Cone of Ithnayn, Harrat	0301-05=
Healy (New Zealand)	Submarine volcano (1, 1360) Radiocarbon	**0401-14-**
Heard (Indian O.-S)	Stratovolcano (10, 2008) Historical	**0304-01=**
Heart Lake (US-Wyoming)	Thermal feature of Yellowstone	1205-01-
Heart of Alaid [Serdtze Alaida] (Kamchatka)	Dome of Kurile Lake	1000-023
Heart Peaks (Canada)	Shield volcano (None) Holocene?	**1200-04-**
Heath Island [Kakolan Island] (New Britain)	Cone of Likuruanga	
Hebert (Indian O.-S)	Cone of Amsterdam Island	0304-001
Hebri, Jebel (Africa-N)	Cone of Azrou Volc Field	
Hécar (Chile-N)	Stratovolcano (None) Pleistocene	
Hegyesd (Hungary)	Cone of Balaton Highland	
Hegyesteto (Hungary)	Cone of Nográd	
Hehu (Africa-C)	Cone of Karisimbi	0203-04-
Heibei Plain (China-E)	Unknown (None) Quaternary	
Heidarspordur (Iceland-NE)	Fissure vent of Krafla	1703-08=
Heidin Há (Iceland-SW)	Shield volcano of Brennisteinsfjöll	1701-04=
Heienliglar [Marumliglar] (Vanuatu)	Crater of Ambrym	0507-04=
Heiguotou (China-W)	Cone of Unnamed	1004-04-
Heiheiahulu (Hawaiian Is)	Shield volcano of Kilauea	1302-01-
Heiji-dake (Kyushu-Japan)	Stratovolcano of Kuju	0802-12=
Heikongshan (SE Asia)	Cinder cone of Tengchong	0705-11-
Heikongshan (SE Asia)	Cone of Tengchong	0705-11-
Heilong Shan (China-W)	Cinder cone of Kunlun Volc Group	1004-03-
Heimaey (Iceland-S)	Cinder cone of Vestmannaeyjar	1702-01=
Heishan (China-E)	Cone of Datong-Fengzen	
Heishan (China-E)	Cinder cone of Keluo Group	1005-02-
Heishan (SE Asia)	Cone of Tengchong	0705-11-
Heishibeihu (China-W)	Cinder cone of Kunlun Volc Group	1004-03-
Heizi-dake [Heiji-dake] (Kyushu-Japan)	Stratovolcano of Kuju	0802-12=
Hejo, Kawah (Java)	Thermal feature of Galunggung	0603-14=
Hekla (Iceland-S)	Stratovolcano (63, 2000) Historical	**1702-07=**
Heklufell (Heklufjall) (Iceland-S)	Synonym of Hekla	1702-07=
Heklugja (Iceland-S)	Fissure vent of Hekla	1702-07=
Helatoba-Taroetoeng (Sumatra)	Synonym of Helatoba-Tarutung	
Helatoba-Tarutung (Sumatra)	Fumarole field (None) Pleist.-Fumarolic	
Helechos, Los (Canary Is)	Cone of Lanzarote	1803-06-
Helen, Mount (US-California)	Dome of Lassen Volc Center	1203-08-
Helena (Africa-W)	Cone of Cameroon	0204-01=
Helgadalshraun (Iceland-SW)	Crater Row of Brennisteinsfjöll	1701-04=
Helgafell (Iceland-S)	Cinder cone of Vestmannaeyjar	1702-01=
Helgafellsgigir (Iceland-SW)	Crater Row of Krísuvík	1701-03=
Helgrindur (Iceland-W)	Pyroclastic cones (None) Holocene	**1700-02=**
Hellisey (Iceland-S)	Cone of Vestmannaeyjar	1702-01=
Hellisheidi (Iceland-SW)	Thermal feature of Hengill	1701-05=
Helliskvislarhraun (Iceland-S)	Fissure vent of Hekla	1702-07=
Hell's Gate (New Zealand)	Thermal feature of Rotorua	
Hell's Gate (Vanuatu-SW Pacific)	Thermal feature of Suretamatai	0507-01=
Hell's Half Acre (US-Idaho)	Shield volcano (1, -3250) Radiocarbon	**1204-04-**
Helmet Peak (Canada)	Cone of Milbanke Sound Group	1200-12-
Heltagi (Ethiopia)	Cone of Assab Volc Field	0201-125
Helvellyn (W Indies)	Dome of St. Catherine	1600-17=
Helviti [Viti] (Iceland-NE)	Maar of Krafla	1703-08=
Hembe (Africa-C)	Cone of Nyamuragira	0203-02=
Hemlock Butte (US-Oregon)	Cone of Bailey	
Hemlock Butte (US-Oregon)	Cone of Cappy Mountain	
Hendrik Fisher Kop (Indian O.-S)	Cinder cone of Marion Island	0304-07-
Henedura, La (Chile-C)	Crater of Antuco	1507-08=
Heneowara (Halmahera-Indonesia)	Crater of Dukono	0608-01=
Hengill (Iceland-SW)	Crater rows (13, 150) Historical	**1701-05=**
Hengstweiler (Germany)	Maar of West Eifel Volc Field	0100-01-
Henri Rallier du Baty, Mont (Indian O.-S)	Cone of Kerguelen Islands	0304-02=
Henrie Knolls (US-Utah)	Cone of Markagunt Plateau	1207-04-
Henrys Fork (US-Wyoming)	Pleistocene caldera of Yellowstone	1205-01-
Henwoshan (China-E)	Cone of Datong-Fengzen	
Herai-dake (Honshu-Japan)	Stratovolcano of Towada	0803-271
Herald Islets (Kermadec Is)	Crater of Raoul Island	0402-03=
Herbert (Aleutian Is)	Stratovolcano (None) Holocene	**1101-22-**
Herdisarvikurhraun (Iceland-SW)	Shield volcano of Brennisteinsfjöll	1701-04=
Herdubreid (Iceland-NE)	Tuya (None) Pleistocene	
Herdubreidartaglagjoska (Iceland-NE)	Crater of Askja	1703-06=
Herivderos, Los (Costa Rica)	Thermal feature of Tenorio	1405-031
Hermoso, Valle (Costa Rica)	Cinder cone of Platanar	1405-034
Herradura (México)	Cone of Chichinautzin	1401-08=
Herradura, Cerro la (México)	Cinder cone Zitácuaro-Valle de Bravo	1401-061
Herrera, Crater (México-Is)	Dome of Bárcena	1401-02=
Hertale (Ethiopia)	Synonym of Erta Ale	0201-08=
Hertali (Ethiopia)	Fissure vent (None) Holocene	**0201-171**
Hertha (Antarctica)	Cone of Seal Nunataks Group	1900-05=
Hervideros (Spanish for Hot Springs) see proper name (e.g. San Jacinto, Hervideros de)		
Herz (Kamchatka)	Cone of Ushkovsky	1000-261
Hestolduhraun (Iceland-S)	Fissure vent of Hekla	1702-07=
Heuco, Cerro (US-Arizona)	Maar of Springerville	
Hfealin (Kamchatka)	Synonym of Ichinsky	1000-28=
Hi, Puu (Hawaiian Is)	Cone of Kauai	
Hibok-Hibok (Mindanao-Philippines)	Stratovolcano of Camiguin	0701-08=
Hibran, Jabal (Arabia-W)	Crater of Ithnayn, Harrat	0301-05=
Hierro (Canary Is)	Shield volcano (3, -550) Radiocarbon	**1803-02-**
Higashi-Azuma (Honshu-Japan)	Cone of Azuma	0803-18=
Higashi-Chokai (Honshu-Japan)	Stratovolcano of Chokai	0803-22=
Higashi-Daiten (Honshu-Japan)	Cone of Azuma	0803-18=
Higashi-dake (Hokkaido-Japan)	Cone of Akan	0805-07=
Higashi-hakuunzan (Izu Is-Japan)	Cone of Hachijo-jima	0804-05=
Higashi-Iwate (Honshu-Japan)	Stratovolcano of Iwate	0803-24=
Higashi-Izu Volcano Group (Honshu-Japan)	Synonym of Izu-Tobu	0803-01=
Higashi-Izu-Oki Group (Honshu-Japan)	Synonym of Izu-Tobu	0803-01=
Higashi-Kagonoto-yama (Honshu-Japan)	Stratovolcano of Eboshi	
Higashi-Kaitokuba (Volcano Is-Japan)	Cone of Kaitoku Seamount	0804-10=
Higashi-Kurikoma (Honshu-Japan)	Stratovolcano of Kurikoma	0803-21=
Higashi-Maruyama (Hokkaido-Japan)	Dome of Usu	0805-03=
Higashimine (Ryukyu Is)	Cone of Yokoate-jima	0802-021
Higashi-Nupukaushinupuri (Hokkaido-Japan)	Dome of Shikaribetsu Group	0805-062
Higashi-oike (Honshu-Japan)	Maar of Izu-Tobu	0803-01=
Higashi-onsen (Kyushu-Japan)	Thermal feature of Tsurumi	0802-13=
Higashi-Tokachi-Maruyama [Maru-yama]	Dome of Nipesotsu-Maruyama	0805-061
Higashi-Tsurugi (Honshu-Japan)	Cone of Fuji	0803-03=
Higashi-Usuzuka (Honshu-Japan)	Cone of Fuji	0803-03=
Higashi-yama (Izu Is-Japan)	Stratovolcano of Hachijo-jima	0804-05=
Higashi-yama (Hokkaido-Japan)	Stratovolcano of Oshima-Oshima	0805-01=
Higasi-dake [Higashi-dake] (Hokkaido-Japan)	Cone of Akan	0805-07=
Higasi-yama [Higashi-yama] (Izu Is-Japan)	Stratovolcano of Hachijo-jima	0804-05=
Higaturu (New Guinea)	Synonym of Lamington	0503-01=
High Hole Crater (US-California)	Crater of Medicine Lake	1203-02-
High Island (Red Sea)	Cone of Zukur	0201-021
High Rise (Pacific-NE)	Thermal feature of Endeavour Ridge	1301-01-
High Tuya Lake Volc Field (Canada)	Volcanic field of Tuya Volc Field	1200-031
Highland Butte (US-Oregon)	Shield volcano of Boring Lava	
Hiiaka (Hawaiian Is)	Pit crater of Kilauea	1302-01-
Hijang (Java)	Synonym of Iyang-Argapura	0603-33=

An eruption of **Home Reef** in the Tonga Islands in March 1984 produced an island with an estimated size of 500 x 1500 m and a height of 30-50 m. A plume to 12 km height was reported during the March 1-5 eruption, and large amounts of floating pumice were later encountered by passing ships. Discolored water surrounds the ephemeral island.

Name (Subregion)	Type (Eruptions, Most Recent) Status / Relation to Named Volcano	Volcano Number
Hijiori (Honshu-Japan)	Caldera (None) Holocene	**0803-191**
Hijiri-yu (Kyushu-Japan)	Thermal feature of Tsurumi	0802-13=
Hijo del Cuauhtzin (México)	Cinder cone of Chichinautzin	1401-08=
Hijo del Volcán [Santiaguito] (Guatemala)	Dome of Santa María	1402-03=
Hikinohira (Kyushu-Japan)	Dome of Sakura-jima	0802-08=
Hikubo (Izu Is-Japan)	Crater of Oshima	0804-01=
Hikutemotu (Tonga-SW Pacific)	Cone of Niuafo'ou	0403-11=
Hil, Jabal (Arabia-W)	Cinder cone of Kishb, Harrat	0301-071
Hilas, Cerro de las (Guatemala)	Cinder cone of Moyuta	1402-13-
Hildarhraun (Iceland-SW)	Shield volcano of Hengill	1701-05=
Hill 32 (Australia)	Cone of McBride Volc Province	
Hill 404 (Alaska-W)	Cinder cone of St. Paul Island	1104-01-
Hill Piece (Atlantic-S)	Tuff cone of Tristan da Cunha	1806-01=
Hilla Ethnan (Arabia-W)	Synonym of Ithnayn, Harrat	0301-05=
Hillman Peak (US-Oregon)	Stratovolcano of Crater Lake	1202-16-

Name (Subregion)	Type (Eruptions, Most Recent) Status Relation to Named Volcano	Volcano Number
Hillview (Australia)	Cone of Atherton Volc Province	....
Himaicagan [Kasiboi] (Philippines-C)	Cone of Mahagnao	0702-07=
Himalaya, Cerro (El Salvador)	Dome of Apaneca Range	1403-01=
Hime-shima Volc Group (Japan)	Lava domes (None) Pleistocene	....
Himo (Africa-E)	Cone of Kilimanjaro	0202-15=
Hinamori-dake (Kyushu-Japan)	Stratovolcano of Kirishima	0802-09=
Hinemoa Point (New Zealand)	Dome of Rotorua	....
Hinkelsmaar (Germany)	Maar of West Eifel Volc Field	0100-01-
Hinokizuka (Honshu-Japan)	Cone of Fuji	0803-03=
Hino-take (Kyushu-Japan)	Cone of Fukue-jima	0802-091
Hinoyama-toge (Izu Is-Japan)	Fissure vent of Miyake-jima	0804-04=
Hipaua (New Zealand)	Thermal feature of Taupo	0401-07=
Hippersbach (Germany)	Tuff ring of West Eifel Volc Field	0100-01-
Hippo Butte (US-California)	Cone of Medicine Lake	1203-02-
Hirabe-yama (Izu Is-Japan)	Crater of Miyake-jima	0804-04=
Hiragakura-yama (Honshu-Japan)	Cone of Nyuto-Takakura	....
Hirakiki-dake [Kaimon] (Kyushu-Japan)	Stratovolcano of Ibusuki Volc Field	0802-07=
Hirase (Kyushu-Japan)	Cone of Sakura-jima	0802-08=
Hiratsuka (Honshu-Japan)	Cone of Fuji	0803-03=
Hira-yama (Hokkaido-Japan)	Stratovolcano of Tengu-Hirayama	....
Hiri (Halmahera-Indonesia)	Stratovolcano (None) Holocene	**0608-052**
Hiro (Lesser Sunda Is)	Synonym of Iliwerung	0604-25=
Hiroyiyama-Oyunuma-Urajigoku (Japan)	Fissure vent of Kuttara	0805-034
Hirup, Kawah (Java)	Thermal feature of Salak	0603-05=
Hiruzen (Honshu-Japan)	Cone of Daisen	....
Hisagogata (Hokkaido-Japan)	Crater of Komaga-take	0805-02=
Histum Yani (US-California)	Synonym of Sutter Buttes	....
Hitim (Sumatra)	Stratovolcano of Kaba	0601-22=
Hitokappu Volcano Group (Kuril Is)	Synonym of Bogatyr Ridge	0900-06-
Hitokappu-yama (Kuril Is)	Stratovolcano of Bogatyr Ridge	0900-06-
Hiuchi (Honshu-Japan)	Stratovolcano (2, 1544) Historical	**0803-131**
Hiuchiga-take (Honshu-Japan)	Synonym of Hiuchi	0803-131
Hiukau, Puu (Hawaiian Is)	Cone of Mauna Kea	1302-03-
Hiva Hiva, Maunga (Chile-Is)	Pyroclastic cone of Easter Island	1506-011
Hiva Hoa (Pacific-C)	Synonym of Hiva Oa	....
Hiva Oa (Pacific-C)	Shield volcano (None) Pleistocene	....
Hiwaish Abu Siba (Africa-N)	Cone of Bayuda Volc Field	0205-06-
Hiyang (Java)	Synonym of Iyang-Argapura	0603-33=
Hiyori-yama (Hokkaido-Japan)	Dome of Kuttara	0805-034
Hiyoshi-okinoba (Volcano Is-Japan)	Synonym of Minami-Hiyoshi	0804-131
Hiyosi-okinoba (Volcano Is-Japan)	Synonym of Minami-Hiyoshi	0804-131
Hizengajo (Kyushu-Japan)	Dome of Kuju	0802-12=
Hiziori (Honshu-Japan)	Synonym of Hijiori	0803-191
Hlascar (Chile-N)	Synonym of Láscar	1505-10=
Hlídarfjall (Iceland-NE)	Dome of Krafla	1703-08=
Hlidargigar (Iceland-S)	Fissure vent of Hekla	1702-07=
Hlidarhraun (Iceland-SW)	Shield volcano of Brennisteinsfjöll	1701-04=
Hlidarsel [Dalfjall] (Iceland-NE)	Fissure vent of Krafla	1703-08=
Hlödufell (Iceland-SW)	Tuya (None) Pleistocene	....
Hnappafellsjokull (Iceland-SE)	Synonym of Öraefajökull	1704-01=

Lee Siebert (Smithsonian)

Sharp-topped Mount **Hood**, Oregon's highest peak, rises above Lost Lake and is a prominent landmark on both sides of the Columbia River. At least four major eruptive periods have occurred during the past 15,000 years, the last of which was only about 170-220 years ago.

Name (Subregion)	Type (Eruptions, Most Recent) Status Relation to Named Volcano	Volcano Number
Hnausagigarod (Iceland-NE)	Fissure vent of Bárdarbunga	1703-03=
Hnausapollur (Iceland-NE)	Crater of Bárdarbunga	1703-03=
Hoashen (Kamchatka)	Synonym of Ichinsky	1000-28=
Hobicha Caldera (Ethiopia)	Caldera (None) Holocene?	**0201-293**
Hobley Volcano (Africa-E)	Synonym of Olkaria	0202-09=
Hobson, Mt. (New Zealand)	Cone of Auckland Field	0401-02=
Hochan [Pechan] (China-W)	Cone of Tianshan Volc Group	1004-02-
Hochsetter (Atlantic-N-Jan Mayen)	Cone of Jan Mayen	1706-01=
Hodaka Graben (Honshu-Japan)	Synonym of Hodaka-dake	....
Hodaka-dake (Honshu-Japan)	Caldera (None) Pleistocene	....
Hodder's Volcano (W Indies)	(None) Not a Volcano	1600-13=
Hodgson Nunatak (Antarctica)	Cone of Hudson Mountains	1900-028
Hodo (Korea)	Dome of Halla	1006-04-
Hodson (Antarctica)	Stratovolcano (Uncertain) Holocene	**1900-11=**
Hoedberg (Indian O.)	Cone of Prince Edward Island	0304-06-
Hoefdhajokull (Iceland-S)	Synonym of Katla	1702-03=
Hoei Craters (Honshu-Japan)	Crater of Fuji	0803-03=
Hoeloebeloe (Sumatra)	Synonym of Hulubelu	0601-28=
Hofdahraun (Iceland-S)	Fissure vent of Eyjafjallajökull	1702-02=
Hofdarhraun (Iceland-SW)	Crater Row of Krísuvík	1701-03=
Hofenfels (Germany)	Maar of West Eifel Volc Field	0100-01-
Hoffman, Mt. (US-California)	Dome of Medicine Lake	1203-02-
Hofsfjall (Iceland-SE)	Cone of Öraefajökull	1704-01=
Hofsjökull (Iceland-SW)	Subglacial volcano (None) Holocene	**1701-09=**
Hog Killer (Philippines-C)	Thermal feature of Kanlaon	0702-02=
Hogback Mountain (US-Washington)	Shield volcano of Goat Rocks	....
Hogg Rock (US-Oregon)	Cone of Three Fingered Jack	....
Hogum Range (Canada)	Volcanic field (None) Pleistocene	....
Hohen List (Germany)	Maar of West Eifel Volc Field	0100-01-
Hohenlohoe (Atlantic-N-Jan Mayen)	Cone of Jan Mayen	1706-01=
Hohi (Kyushu-Japan)	Stratovolcanoes (None) Pleistocene	....
Hohnel Island (Africa-E)	Synonym of South Island	0202-02=
Hohonu, Lua (Hawaiian Is)	Pit crater of Mauna Loa	1302-02=
Hokibara-Higashi (Honshu-Japan)	Maar of Izu-Tobu	0803-01=
Hokkaido-Komagatake (Hokkaido-Japan)	Synonym of Komaga-take	0805-02=
Hokuchin-dake (Hokkaido-Japan)	Dome of Daisetsu	0805-06=
Hokusatsu (Kyushu-Japan)	Pyroclastic cone (None) Pleistocene	....
Hokutin-dake [Hokuchin-dake] (Japan)	Dome of Daisetsu	0805-06=
Holaholar (Iceland-W)	Cone of Snaefellsjökull	1700-01=
Holandesa, Volcán la (Chile-C)	Cinder cone of Lonquimay	1507-10=
Holandesa, Volcán la (Chile-C)	Cone of Tolguaca	1507-093
Holantindur (Iceland-W)	Cone of Snaefellsjökull	1700-01=
Hole-in-the-Ground (US-Oregon)	Maar of Fort Rock Volc Field	....
Holin [Kopan] (Slovakia)	Cone of Filakovo-Salgotarjan	....
Hollowback, Mt. (Australia)	Cone of Newer Volcanics Prov	0509-01-
Holm (Kamchatka)	Fissure vent of Kliuchevskoi	1000-26=
Holmshraun (Iceland-SW)	Crater Row of Brennisteinsfjöll	1701-04=
Holotepec, Volcán (México)	Cinder cone of Chichinautzin	1401-08=
Holseldar (Iceland-NE)	Crater Row of Krafla	1703-08=
Holte Creek (Canada)	Cinder cone of Satah Mountain	1200-13-
Holuhraun (Iceland-NE)	Crater Row of Askja	1703-06=
Holzmaar (Germany)	Maar of West Eifel Volc Field	0100-01-
Homa Mountain (Africa-E)	Complex volcano (None) Holocene	**0202-07=**
Homahan, Mt. (Luzon-Philippines)	Cone of Bulusan	0703-01=
Hombre Muerto, Montaña del (Canary Is)	Cinder cone of Hierro	1803-02-
Home Reef (Tonga-SW Pacific)	Submarine volcano (3, 2006) Historical	**0403-08=**
Home Valley Knoll (US-Utah)	Cinder cone of Kolob	....
Hondo, Calderon (Canary Is)	Cinder cone of Fuerteventura	1803-05-
Hondura (Costa Rica)	Stratovolcano of Barva	1405-05=
Honggeertu (China-E)	Cinder cones (None) Holocene?	**1005-01-**
Honokahua (Hawaiian Is)	Cone of Haleakala	1302-06-
Honor, Mt. (Halmahera-Indonesia)	Cone of Todoko-Ranu	0608-05=
Hontanigawa-Shiryu (Honshu-Japan)	Vent of Izu-Tobu	0803-01=
Hontsuka (Kyushu-Japan)	Cone of Aso	0802-11=
Hood (Galápagos)	Synonym of Española	....
Hood (US-Oregon)	Stratovolcano (8, 1866) Historical	**1202-01-**
Hoodoo Butte (US-Oregon)	Tuya of Washington	....
Hoodoo Mountain (Canada)	Subglacial volcano (1, -7050) Tephrochron	**1200-08-**
Hookomo, Puu (Hawaiian Is)	Cone of Mauna Kea	1302-03-
Hooper Crags (Antarctica)	Cone of Royal Society Range	1900-021
Hoopers Shoulder (Antarctica)	Cone of Erebus	1900-02=
Hopua (New Zealand)	Tuff ring of Auckland Field	0401-02=
Hora Arsedi Hayk (Ethiopia)	Tuff ring of Bishoftu Volc Field	0201-22-
Horace Mesa (US-New Mexico)	Cone of Taylor Volc Field	....
Horaro Hayk (Ethiopia)	Tuff ring of Bishoftu Volc Field	0201-22-
Horcones, Cerro de (Guatemala)	Cone of Suchitán	1402-16-
Hormigón, El (Nicaragua)	Cinder cone of Nejapa-Miraflores	1404-092
Hornillas, Las (Costa Rica)	Thermal feature of Miravalles	1405-03=
Hornitos, Los (Chile-C)	Cone of Azul, Cerro	1507-06=
Hornitos, Los (Canary Is)	Fissure vent of Tenerife	1803-03-
Hornopirén (Chile-S)	Stratovolcano (Uncertain) Holocene	**1508-023**
Horog [Khorog] (Mongolia)	Cinder cone of Taryatu-Chulutu	1003-01-
Horohoro (New Zealand)	Dome of Kapenga	....
Horohoro-Tokushumbetsu (Japan)	Stratovolcanoes (None) Pleistocene	....
Horohoro-yama (Hokkaido-Japan)	Stratovolc. Horohoro-Tokushumbetsu	....
Horoka (Hokkaido-Japan)	Thermal feature Nipesotsu-Maruyama	0805-061
Horomatangi Reef (New Zealand)	Vent of Taupo	0401-07=
Horonai-gawa (Hokkaido-Japan)	Pleist. caldera Okushiri-Katsuma-yama	....
Horossadal [Hrossadaliur] (Iceland-NE)	Crater Row of Krafla	1703-08=
Horqueta, Cerro (Perú)	Cone of Chachani, Nevado	1504-007
Horqueta, La (Colombia)	Pyrocl. cone of San Augustín-Isnos	....
Horse Butte (US-Oregon)	Cone of Newberry	1202-11-
Horseshoe Cone (US-Oregon)	Cinder cone of Jefferson	1202-02-
Horseshoe Crater (US-New Mexico)	Cone of Raton-Clayton	....
Horseshoe Island (Alaska Peninsula)	Dome of Katmai	1102-17-
Hosh Ed Dalan (Africa-N)	Crater of Bayuda Volc Field	0205-06-
Hosh Es Siddig (Africa-N)	Crater of Bayuda Volc Field	0205-06-
Hosh Umm Araysh, Jebel (Africa-N)	Cone of Bayuda Volc Field	0205-06-
Hosho-zan (Kyushu-Japan)	Dome of Kuju	0802-12=
Hosyo-zan [Hosho-zan] (Kyushu-Japan)	Dome of Kuju	0802-12=
Hot Creek (US-California)	Thermal feature of Long Valley	....
Hot Lagoon (Solomon Is-SW Pacific)	Thermal feature of Simbo	0505-05=
Hot Springs Bay (Aleutian Is)	Thermal feature of Akutan	1101-32-
Hot Springs Cone (Aleutian Is)	Thermal feature of Okmok	1101-29-
Hot Springs Cove (Aleutian Is)	Thermal feature of Recheschnoi	1101-28-
Hotaka (Honshu-Japan)	Synonym of Hodaka-dake	....
Hotaka (Honshu-Japan)	Stratovolcano (None) Pleistocene	....
Hotcheou (China-W)	Synonym of Turfan	1004-01-
Hotham [Giulia-Ferdinandeo] (Italy)	Submarine vent C. Flegrei Mar Sicilia	0101-07=

Name (Subregion)	Type (Eruptions, Most Recent) Status Relation to Named Volcano	Volcano Number
Hotokeiwa (Honshu-Japan)	Shield volcano of Asama	0803-11=
Hotta (Kyushu-Japan)	Thermal feature of Tsurumi	0802-13=
Hou, Lua (Hawaiian Is)	Pit crater of Mauna Loa	1302-02=
Houchens Hill (New Zealand)	Cone of Karioi	
Houonji-yama (Honshu-Japan)	Stratovolcano of Kyoga-take	
Hovsgol (Mongolia)	Synonym of Khubsugal Region	
Howlock Mountain (US-Oregon)	Shield volcano of Thielsen	
Hoya de Cintora (México)	Maar of Michoacán-Guanajuato	1401-06=
Hoya de Fileba (Canary Is)	Crater of Hierro	1803-02-
Hoya Honda [La Joya Honda] (México)	Maar of Ventura Volc Field	
Hoya, La (Nicaragua)	Crater of San Cristóbal	1404-02=
Hoyada de los Geisers del Tatio (Chile-N)	Synonym of Tatio, El	
Hoyada, La (Nicaragua)	Crater of San Cristóbal	1404-02=
Hoyadas, Las (Argentina)	Vent of Infiernillo	1507-041
Hoyberg (Atlantic-N-Jan Mayen)	Cone of Jan Mayen	1706-01=
Hoyo Cedro (Canary Is)	Crater of Tenerife	1803-03-
Hoyo Colorado, Volcán (Argentina)	Vent of Infiernillo	1507-041
Hoyo de Calderas (El Salvador)	Crater of Apastepeque Field	1403-071
Hoyo de Cibola (US-New Mexico)	Vent of Zuni-Bandera	1210-02-
Hoyo de Cuajuste (El Salvador)	Crater of Apaneca Range	1403-01=
Hoyo el Huanillo (México)	Cinder cone of Michoacán-Guanajuato	1401-06=
Hoyo Negro (Canary Is)	Crater of La Palma	1803-01-
Hoyo, Cerro el (México)	Cinder cone of Naolinco Volc Field	1401-095
Hoyo, Cerro el (Honduras)	Cinder cone of Yojoa, Lake	1403-15-
Hoyo, El (Nicaragua)	Synonym of Pilas, Las	1404-08=
Hoyo, El (Colombia)	Crater of Tolima, Nevado del	1501-03=
Hoyo, Laguna de (Guatemala)	Maar of Suchitán	1402-16-
Hoyo, Laguna de (Guatemala)	Crater of Tahual	1402-141
Hoyo, Volcán el (Nicaragua)	Stratovolcano of Pilas, Las	1404-08=
Hoyos, Cerro los (México)	Cone of Zitácuaro-Valle de Bravo	1401-061
Hrafnshildargigir (Iceland-SW)	Crater Row of Krísuvík	1701-03=
Hrafntinnuhryggur (Iceland-NE)	Fissure vent of Krafla	1703-08=
Hraftinnuhraun (Iceland-S)	Crater Row of Torfajökull	1702-05=
Hraftinnusker (Iceland-S)	Dome of Torfajökull	1702-05=
Hraunbunga (Iceland-NE)	Shield volcano of Krafla	1703-08=
Hraungigur (Iceland-S)	Fissure vent of Hekla	1702-07=
Hraunhalshraun (Iceland-S)	Crater Row of Hekla	1702-07=
Hraunholl (Iceland-SW)	Crater Row of Krísuvík	1701-03=
Hraunsels-Vatnsfell (Iceland-SW)	Shield volcano of Krísuvík	1701-03=
Hreidhur (Iceland-SW)	Crater Row of Reykjanes	1701-02=
Hreppar (Iceland-SW)	Fissure vents (None) Pleistocene	
Hrolfsvikurhraun (Iceland-SW)	Shield volcano of Reykjanes	1701-02=
Hrómundartindur (Iceland-S)	Stratovolcano (None) Holocene?	**1701-051**
Hronarassar [Khronarassar] (Armenia)	Cone of Porak	0104-09-
Hrossaborg (Iceland-NE)	Tuff ring of Askja	1703-06=
Hrossadaliur (Iceland-NE)	Crater Row of Krafla	1703-08=
Hrossagigar [Hrossadaliur] (Iceland-NE)	Crater Row of Krafla	1703-08=
Hrútagjár (Iceland-SW)	Shield volcano of Krísuvík	1701-03=
Hrútagjárdyngja [Hrutagja] (Iceland-SW)	Shield volcano of Krísuvík	1701-03=
Hrútfell (Iceland-SW)	Tuya (None) Pleistocene	
Hrutshalsar (Iceland-NE)	Fissure vent of Askja	1703-06=
Hsiao-i-shan [Xiaoyishan] (China-E)	Cone of Longgang Group	1005-05-
Hsiao-ko-shan [Xiaokeshan] (China-E)	Cone of Erkeshan	
Hsiao-ku-shan [Xiaokushan] (China-E)	Cone of Longgang Group	1005-05-
Hsiao-Lung-wan [Xiaolongwan] (China-E)	Crater of Longgang Group	1005-05-
Hsiao-Weng-Chuan [Xiaowengjuan] (China)	Cone of Longgang Group	1005-05-
Hsiao-Yen-Chih-Feng [Xiaoyanzhifeng]	Cone of Changbaishan	1005-06-
Hsi-Chiao-te-Pu-shan [Xijiaodebushan]	Cone of Wudalianchi	1005-03-
Hsi-Heng-Tao-shan [Xihengdaoshan] (China)	Cone of Longgang Group	1005-05-
Hsing-an (China-E)	Synonym of Dalainuoer	
Hsing-an-Nan-shan [Xingannanshan] (China)	Cone of Longgang Group	1005-05-
Hsi-Pai-Tzu-Lung-wan [Xibaizilongwan]	Crater of Longgang Group	1005-05-
Hsi-shan [Xishan] (China-E)	Cone of Erkeshan	
Huacha, Loma (Chile-S/Argentina)	Cinder cone Crater Basalt Volc Field	1508-025
Huahui (Ecuador)	Vent of Chalupas	
Hualalai (Hawaiian Is)	Shield volcano (22, 1801) Historical	**1302-04-**
Hualalai, Puu (Hawaiian Is)	Synonym of Hualalai	1302-04-
Hualca Hualca (Perú)	Stratovolcano of Sabancaya	1504-006
Hualiaque (Chile-S)	Synonym of Apagado	1508-024
Huallatire (Huallatiri) (Chile-N)	Synonym of Guallatiri	1505-02=
Huambo (Perú)	Volcanic field (1, -700) Radiocarbon	**1504-005**
Huambutillo-Rumicola (Perú)	Unknown (None) Pleistocene	
Huanchángueran, Cerro de (México)	Cinder cone of Michoacán-Guanajuato	1401-06=
Huang-i-shan (China-E)	Synonym of Kuandian	
Huanguillaro (Ecuador)	Stratovolcano of Chachimbiro	1502-002
Huangyangling (China-W)	Cinder cone of Kunlun Volc Group	1004-03-
Huangyishan (China-E)	Synonym of Kuandian	
Huangzo (SE Asia)	Pyroclastic cone of Hainan Dao	0705-001
Huangzueishan (Taiwan)	Dome of Tatun Group	0801-032
Huanquihue Group (Argentina)	Stratovolcanoes (1, 1750) Radiocarbon	**1507-123**
Huanul (Argentina)	Vent of Unnamed	
Huapinghsü (Taiwan)	Stratovolcano (None) Pleistocene	
Huapo (SE Asia)	Cone of Tengchong	0705-11-
Huarmi Imbabura (Ecuador)	Dome of Imbabura	1502-004
Huaynaputina (Perú)	Stratovolcano (2, 1600) Historical	**1504-03=**
Huaypuna [Ampato] (Perú)	Stratovolcano of Sabancaya	1504-006
Hubert, Piton (Indian O.-W)	Cinder cone of Fournaise, Piton de la	0303-02=
Hubhub al Sheikh (Arabia-W)	Synonym of Birk, Harrat al	0301-072
Huckack (Korea)	Cone of Halla	1006-04-
Hudo-ike [Fudo-ike] (Kyushu-Japan)	Crater of Kirishima	0802-09=
Hudson Mountains (Antarctica)	Stratovolcanoes (1, -210) Ice Core	**1900-028**
Hudson, Cerro (Chile-S)	Stratovolcano (14, 1991) Historical	**1508-057**
Huechulepun, Volcán (Chile-C)	Cone of Sollipulli	1507-111
Hueco, Cerro (US-New Mexico)	Shield volcano of Zuni-Bandera	1210-02-

Name (Subregion)	Type (Eruptions, Most Recent) Status Relation to Named Volcano	Volcano Number
Huehuel, Volcán (México)	Cone of Chichinautzin	1401-08=
Huehuelcón, Volcán (México)	Cone of Chichinautzin	1401-08=
Huelemolle, Volcán (Chile-C)	Cone of Caburgua-Huelemolle	1507-112
Huenuauca (Chile-S)	Synonym of Osorno	1508-01=
Huenú-Huenú (Chile-S)	Stratovolcano of Calbuco	1508-02=
Hueque (Huequen) (Chile-S)	Synonym of Huequi	1508-03=
Huequi (Chile-S)	Stratovolcano (6, 1920) Historical	**1508-03=**
Hugá (Ecuador)	Dome of Chachimbiro	1502-002
Hugen-dake [Fugen-dake] (Kyushu-Japan)	Stratovolcano of Unzen	0802-10=
Hugolin, Crateres (Indian O.-W)	Crater of Fournaise, Piton de la	0303-02=
Huihuilanco, Lomas (México)	Cone of Chichinautzin	1401-08=
Huila, Nevado del (Colombia)	Stratovolcano (4, 2010) Historical	**1501-05=**
Huililco (Chile-C)	Cinder cone of Quetrupillan	1507-121
Huilote (México)	Cinder cone of Chichinautzin	1401-08=
Huilotito (México)	Cinder cone of Chichinautzin	1401-08=

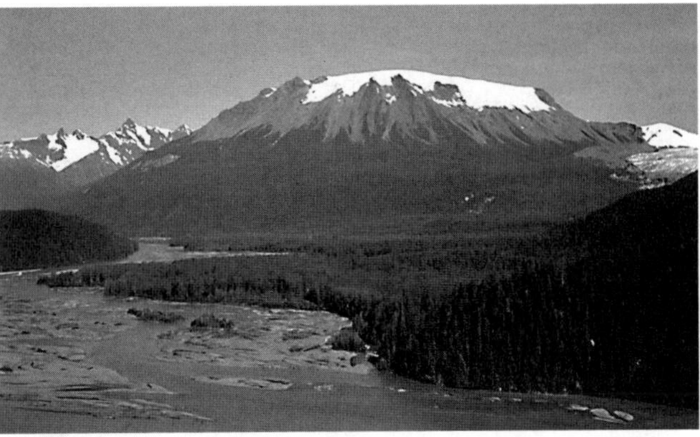

Hoodoo Mountain rises above the Iskut River in NW British Columbia. This flat-topped stratovolcano has an ice cap 3 km in diameter and has had several periods of subglacial eruptions, most recently about 9000 years ago.

Ben Edwards (Dickinson College)

Name (Subregion)	Type (Eruptions, Most Recent) Status Relation to Named Volcano	Volcano Number
Huinfiuca (Chile-C)	Fissure vent of Lanín	1507-122
Huipilo, Volcán (México)	Cone of Chichinautzin	1401-08=
Huitán, Cerro (Guatemala)	Dome of Almolonga	1402-04=
Huitepec (México)	Lava dome (None) Pleistocene	
Huixian (China-E)	Unknown (None) Quaternary	
Huiztomayo, Cerro (México)	Cone of Chichinautzin	1401-08=
Hukeno-yu [Fukeno-yu] (Honshu-Japan)	Thermal feature of Hachimantai	0803-25=
Hukue-zima (Kyushu-Japan)	Synonym of Fukue-jima	0802-091
Hukutoku-okanoba (Volcano Is-Japan)	Synonym of Fukutoku-Okanoba	0804-13=
Hukuzin-kaizan (Volcano Is-Japan)	Synonym of Fukujin	0804-133
Hukuzin-Okaba (Volcano Is-Japan)	Synonym of Fukujin	0804-133
Hukuzin-Okanoba (Volcano Is-Japan)	Synonym of Fukujin	0804-133
Hule, Cerro de (Honduras)	Shield volcano (None) Quaternary	
Hule, Laguna [Bosque Alegre] (Costa Rica)	Maar of Poás	1405-04=
Hulu (New Britain-SW Pac)	Dome of Lolobau	0502-13=
Hulubelu (Sumatra)	Caldera (None) Fumarolic	**0601-28=**
Huluhulu, Puu (Hawaiian Is)	Cone of Kilauea	1302-01-
Hululongwan (China-E)	Crater of Longgang Group	1005-05-
Hulumajang (Sumatra)	Synonym of Hutapanjang	0601-172
Humarata (Chile-N)	Stratovolcano of Acotango	
Humaredas, Cerro las (México)	Dome of Azufres, Los	
Humaredas, Las (México)	Synonym of Humeros, Los	1401-093
Humbab (Ethiopia)	Synonym of As-Ali	
Humeros, Los (México)	Calderas (None) Holocene?	**1401-093**
Humilladeros, Montaña de los (Canary Is)	Cinder cone of Hierro	1803-02-
Humingbird Fumarole (US-New Mexico)	Thermal feature of Valles Caldera	
Hummerich (Germany)	Cone of East Eifel Volc Field	
Hunagata (Honshu-Japan)	Synonym of Funagata	
Hunahpu (Guatemala)	Synonym of Agua	1402-10=
Hunahpu (Guatemala)	Synonym of Fuego	1402-09=
Hunga Tonga-Hunga Ha'apai (Tonga)	Submarine volcano (4, 2009) Historical	**0403-04=**
Hunglushan (Taiwan)	Tuff cone of Tatun Group	0801-032
Huniho (New Ireland-SW Pacific)	Stratovolcano of Lihir	0504-01=
Hunihuni, Puu (Hawaiian Is)	Cone of Kauai	
Hunter Island (SW Pacific)	Stratovolcano (4, 1903) Historical	**0508-02=**
Hunt's Hole (US-New Mexico)	Maar of Potrillo Volc Field	
Huoshan [Heishan] (SE Asia)	Cone of Tengchong	0705-11-
Huoshaoshan (China-E)	Cone of Wudalianchi	1005-03-
Huppusi [Fuppushi] (Hokkaido-Japan)	Stratovolcano of Akan	0805-07=
Huppusi-dake [Fuppushi-dake] (Japan)	Stratovolcano of Shikotsu	0805-04=
Hurano-dake (Hokkaido-Japan)	Stratovolcano of Tokachi	0805-05=
Hurata, Tavani (Vanuatu-SW Pacific)	Cone of Kuwae	0507-07=
Hurebetu [Furebetsu] (Hokkaido-Japan)	Stratovolcano of Akan	0805-07=
Huri (Africa-E)	Shield volcano (None) Pleistocene	
Hurricane Hill (W Indies)	Dome of Nevis Peak	1600-04=
Hurricane Ridge (Antarctica)	Fissure vent of Morning, Mt.	1900-020
Huru-dake [Furu-take] (Ryukyu Is)	Stratovolcano of Kuchinoerabu-jima	0802-05=
Hurus, Jabal al (Arabia-W)	Cone of Rahat, Harrat	0301-07=
Husa (New Britain-SW Pac)	Cone of Oto Group	
Hut Point Peninsula (Antarctica)	Scoria cones (None) Pleistocene	
Hutago (Kyushu-Japan)	Synonym of Futago	
Hutamah, Harrat al (Arabia)	Synonym of Hutaymah, Harrat	
Hutamata (Honshu-Japan)	Synonym of Futamata	

Name (Subregion)	Type (Eruptions, Most Recent) Status / Relation to Named Volcano	Volcano Number
Hutapanjang (Sumatra)	Stratovolcano (None) Holocene	**0601-172**
Hutaym, Harrat (Arabia-W)	Synonym of Ithnayn, Harrat	0301-05=
Hutaymah, Harrat (Arabia)	Volcanic field (None) Quaternary	....
Hutchinson Hill (Alaska-W)	Shield volcano of St. Paul Island	1104-01-
Hutchison (Kermadec Is)	Stratovolcano of Raoul Island	0402-03=
Hutt Peak (Antarctica)	Shield volcano of Bursey, Mt.	....
Huzi (Honshu-Japan)	Synonym of Fuji	0803-03=
Hvannadalshnjúkur (Iceland-SE)	Dome of Öraefajökull	1704-01=
Hvannstod (Iceland-NE)	Crater Row of Krafla	1703-08=
Hveradalahraun (Iceland-SW)	Crater Row of Hengill	1701-05=
Hveradalur (Iceland-NE)	Thermal feature of Kverkfjöll	1703-05=
Hveragerdi (Iceland-S)	Thermal feature of Grensdalur	....
Hveragil (Iceland-NE)	Crater of Krafla	1703-08=
Hveravellir (Iceland-SW)	Subglacial volcano (6, 950) Radiocarbon	**1701-08=**
Hverfjall (Iceland-NE)	Tuff ring of Krafla	1703-08=
Hweiain (Kamchatka)	Synonym of Ichinsky	1000-28=
Hwniindi K'elt'aeni (Alaska-E)	Synonym of Sanford	1105-01-
Hyalo Ridge (Canada)	Tuya of Wells Gray-Clearwater	1200-15-
Hydewell, Mt. (Australia)	Shield volcano Newer Volcanics Prov	0509-01-
Hydrographers Range (New Guinea)	Stratovolcano (None) Holocene	**0503-011**
Hyogowan (Izu Is-Japan)	Crater of Tori-shima	0804-09=
Hyotan-yama (Izu Is-Japan)	Cone of Miyake-jima	0804-04=
Hypipamee (Australia)	Vent of Atherton Volc Province	....
Hyuuga-dake (Kyushu-Japan)	Dome of Tsurumi	0802-13=

I

Name (Subregion)	Type (Eruptions, Most Recent) Status / Relation to Named Volcano	Volcano Number
I Monticelli (Italy)	Vent of Vesuvius	0101-02=
Ia Bang Mount [La Bang Mount] (SE Asia)	Crater of Pleiku-Bantour Volc Field	....
Iahu (Iahue, Iahul) (Vanuatu-SW Pacific)	Synonym of Yasur	0507-10=
Ialibu, Mt. (New Guinea)	Stratovolcano (None) Pleistocene	....
Iamalele (D'Entrecasteaux Is)	Lava domes (None) Holocene	**0503-05=**
Iamelele (D'Entrecasteaux Is)	Synonym of Iamalele	0503-05=
Iasur (Vanuatu-SW Pacific)	Synonym of Yasur	0507-10=
Iavinskiy (Kamchatka)	Synonym of Yavinsky	1000-021
Ibayl, Jabal (Arabia-W)	Dome of Khaybar, Harrat	0301-06=
Ibex Mountain Cone (Canada)	Cone of Alligator Lake	1200-02-
Ibi [Galloseulo] (New Britain-SW Pac)	Stratovolcano of Hargy	0502-10=
Iblean Volc Complex (Italy)	Synonym of Iblei	....
Iblei (Italy)	Shield volcano? (None) Pleistocene	....
Iboe (Halmahera-Indonesia)	Synonym of Ibu	0608-03=
Ibu (Halmahera-Indonesia)	Stratovolcano (5, 2010) Historical	**0608-03=**
Ibul, Bukit (Sumatra)	Synonym of Telor, Bukit	....
Ibungu Hills (Africa-E)	Cone of Kieyo	0202-17=
Ibusuki Volc Field (Kyushu-Japan)	Calderas (23, 885) Historical	**0802-07=**
Ice Peak (Canada)	Stratovolcano of Edziza	1200-06-
Ice Spring (US-Utah)	Crater of Black Rock Desert	1207-05-
Icefall (Canada)	Cone of Edziza	1200-06-
Icha (Kamchatka)	Synonym of Ichinsky	1000-28=

Lee Siebert (Smithsonian)

Wilson Butte, the northermost lava dome of the **Inyo Craters** in California, is seen from the Obsidian Flow lava dome. The Inyo Craters are a 12-km-long chain of silicic lava domes, lava flows, and explosion craters along the eastern margin of Sierra Nevada near the town of Mammoth. The latest eruptions at Inyo Craters took place about 600 years ago.

Name (Subregion)	Type (Eruptions, Most Recent) Status / Relation to Named Volcano	Volcano Number
Ichino-ike (Honshu-Japan)	Crater of Norikura	0803-06=
Ichino-ike (Honshu-Japan)	Crater of On-take	0803-04=
Ichinomegata (Honshu-Japan)	Maar of Megata	0803-262
Ichino-take (Kyushu-Japan)	Dome of Kinpo	....
Ichinsky (Kamchatka)	Stratovolcano (14, 1740) Historical	**1000-28=**
Ida (Honshu-Japan)	Stratovolcano of Daruma	....
Ida Ridge (Canada)	Cone of Wells Gray-Clearwater	1200-15-
Idak, Mount (Aleutian Is)	Cone of Okmok	1101-29-
Idamdehe (Halmahera-Indonesia)	Caldera of Jailolo	0608-051
Idjen, Kawah (Java)	Synonym of Ijen	0603-35=
Ido-dake (Honshu-Japan)	Cone of Hakkoda Group	0803-28=
Idolo, Cerro el (México)	Cone of Zitácuaro-Valle de Bravo	1401-061
Idolos, Los (Colombia)	Pyroclastic cone San Augustín-Isnos	....
Idup, Kawah (Java)	Thermal feature of Salak	0603-05=
Idwa, Jebel (Africa-N)	Cone of Marra, Jebel	0205-03-
Ie Joe (Sumatra)	Thermal feature of Seulawah Agam	0601-02=
Iegata-yama (Honshu-Japan)	Cone of Azuma	0803-18=
Iettunup (Kamchatka)	Shield volcanoes (None) Holocene?	**1000-71-**
Ifagao (Luzon-Philippines)	Thermal feature of Pocdol Mountains	0703-02=
Ifwoka (Africa-E)	Cone of Ngozi	0202-164
Igatono-yama (Honshu-Japan)	Cone of Fuji	0803-03=
Igaya (Izu Is-Japan)	Fissure vent of Miyake-jima	0804-04=
Igek (Alaska Peninsula)	Synonym of Veniaminof	1102-07-
Igir Binem [Binem] (Java)	Cone of Dieng Volc Complex	0603-20=
Igla Mountain (Kuril Is)	Stratovolcano of Goriaschaia Sopka	0900-17=
Iglesia, La (México)	Dome of Mispía	....
Iglesias (Costa Rica)	Shield volcano of Coco, Isla del	....
Ignaignaru, Mt. (Vanuatu-SW Pacific)	Cone of Paama Island	....
Igolki (Kamchatka)	Shield volcanoes (None) Pleistocene	....
Igorevsky Volcano (Kamchatka)	Synonym of Dzenzursky	1000-11=
Igorewskiy (Kamchatka)	Synonym of Dzenzursky	1000-11=
Igualata (Ecuador)	Stratovolcano (None) Pleistocene	....
Iguan (Ecuador)	Stratovolcano (None) Pleistocene	....
Iguana, Loma (El Salvador)	Cinder cone of San Diego	1403-001
Iguanero, Cerro (Guatemala)	Cinder cone of Ixtepeque	1402-18-
Igwisi Hills (Africa-E)	Tuff cones (None) Holocene	**0202-161**
Ih-Chia-shan (China-E)	Synonym of Yijiashan	....
Ihumatao [Maungataketake] (New Zealand)	Cone of Auckland Field	0401-02=
Iiji (Honshu-Japan)	Stratovolcano (None) Pleistocene	....
Iilewa (Hawaiian Is)	Cone of Kilauea	1302-01-
Iimori-yama (Kyushu-Japan)	Dome of Imuta	....
Iimori-yama (Kyushu-Japan)	Stratovolcano of Kirishima	0802-09=
Iiusu (Kuril Is)	Synonym of Baransky	0900-08=
Iizi (Honshu-Japan)	Synonym of Iiji	....
Iizuna (Honshu-Japan)	Stratovolcano (None) Pleistocene	....
Ija (Lesser Sunda Is)	Synonym of Iya	0604-11=
Ijang-Argapura (Java)	Synonym of Iyang-Argapura	0603-33=
Ijen (Java)	Stratovolcanoes (9, 1999) Historical	**0603-35=**
Ijen, Kawah (Java)	Synonym of Ijen	0603-35=
Ikanmikot (Kuril Is)	Stratovolcano (None) Pleistocene	....
Ikapo (Africa-E)	Maar of Kieyo	0202-17=
Ikarma (Kuril Is)	Synonym of Ekarma	0900-27=
Ikathiwik Crater (Alaska-W)	Cone of Nunivak Island	1104-02-
Ika-Togo-Ula (Mongolia)	Pyroclastic cones (None) Quaternary	....
Ikeda-Higashi (Honshu-Japan)	Cone of Izu-Tobu	0803-01=
Ikeda-ko (Kyushu-Japan)	Caldera of Ibusuki Volc Field	0802-07=
Ikenohara (Honshu-Japan)	Synonym of Nanzaki	....
Ikenokubo (Kyushu-Japan)	Tuff ring of Aso	0802-11=
Ikenosawa (Izu Is-Japan)	Caldera of Aoga-shima	0804-06=
Ikezoko (Kyushu-Japan)	Maar of Ibusuki Volc Field	0802-07=
Ikh Togo Uul (Mongolia)	Cinder cone of Khanuy Gol	1003-02-
Ikha-Togo-Ula [Ikh Togo Uul] (Mongolia)	Cinder cone of Khanuy Gol	1003-02-
Iki Volc Group (Kyushu-Japan)	Pyroclastic cones (None) Pleistocene	....
Ikincilgol Tepe (Turkey)	Cone of Nemrut Dagi	0103-02=
Iktunup (Kamchatka)	Shield volcanoes (None) Holocene?	**1000-67-**
Ilaemaen (Ilaemanschen) (Alaska-SW)	Synonym of Iliamna	1103-02-
Ilaló (Ecuador)	Stratovolcano (None) Pleistocene	....
Ilamatepec (El Salvador)	Synonym of Santa Ana	1403-02=
Ilchulbong (Korea)	Tuff cone of Halla	1006-04-
Ildborg [Eldborg] (Iceland-W)	Cone of Ljósufjöll	1700-03=
Ile (French for Island) see proper name (e.g. Cendres, Ile des)		
Ilheu Dos Mosteiros (Azores)	Cone of Sete Cidades	1802-08=
Iliamna (Alaska-SW)	Stratovolcano (7, 1876) Historical	**1103-02-**
Iliberapun (Lesser Sunda Is)	Unknown (None) Post-Miocene	....
Iliboleng (Lesser Sunda Is)	Stratovolcano (20, 1993) Historical	**0604-22=**
Ilibotong (Lesser Sunda Is)	Dome of Ilimuda	0604-17=
Iliburak (Lesser Sunda Is)	Synonym of Leroboleng	0604-20=
Iligripe (Lesser Sunda Is)	Dome of Iliwerung	0604-25=
Iliinskaia, Sopka (Kamchatka)	Synonym of Ilyinsky	1000-03=
Iliinskaya (Iliinsky) (Kamchatka)	Synonym of Ilyinsky	1000-03=
Ilikedang (Lesser Sunda Is)	Unknown (None) Post-Miocene	....
Ilikedeka (Lesser Sunda Is)	Stratovolcano (None) Pleist.-Fumarolic	....
Ililabalekan (Lesser Sunda Is)	Stratovolcano (None) Fumarolic	**0604-24=**
Ililamarap (Ililamararap) (Lesser Sunda Is)	Synonym of Ililabalekan	0604-24=
Ililawuung (Lesser Sunda Is)	Unknown (None) Post-Miocene	....
Ililewoto (Ililewotolo) (Lesser Sunda Is)	Synonym of Lewotolo	0604-23=
Ilimangga (Lesser Sunda Is)	Cone of Ililawuung	....
Iliminggar (Lesser Sunda Is)	Stratovolcano (None) Post-Miocene	....
Ilimoeda (Lesser Sunda Is)	Synonym of Ilimuda	0604-17=
Ilimonjet (Lesser Sunda Is)	Dome of Iliwerung	0604-25=
Ilimuda (Lesser Sunda Is)	Stratovolcano (None) Fumarolic	**0604-17=**
Ilina (Kamchatka)	Synonym of Ilyinsky	1000-03=
Ilinitza (Ecuador)	Synonym of Illiniza	1502-041
Iliniza (Ecuador)	Synonym of Illiniza	1502-041
Ilinsky (Kamchatka)	Synonym of Ilyinsky	1000-03=
Ilipasengdaeng (Lesser Sunda Is)	Unknown (None) Post-Miocene	....
Ilipenutun (Lesser Sunda Is)	Dome of Iliwerung	0604-25=
Ilipetrus [Iligripe] (Lesser Sunda Is)	Dome of Iliwerung	0604-25=
Ilipoegora (Lesser Sunda Is)	Synonym of Iliwerung	0604-25=
Iliseburi (Lesser Sunda Is)	Unknown (None) Post-Miocene	....
Ilitebulele (Lesser Sunda Is)	Cone of Ililabalekan	0604-24=
Iliwaitami (Lesser Sunda Is)	Unknown (None) Post-Miocene	....
Iliweroeng (Lesser Sunda Is)	Synonym of Iliwerung	0604-25=
Iliwerung (Lesser Sunda Is)	Complex volcano (12, 1999) Historical	**0604-25=**
Iliwokar (Lesser Sunda Is)	Cone of Lewotobi	0604-18=

Name (Subregion)	Type (Eruptions, Most Recent) Status . . Relation to Named Volcano	Volcano Number
Iliyin Sopka (Kamchatka)	Synonym of Ilyinsky	1000-03=
Illahraun (Iceland-SW)	Crater Row of Hofsjökull	1701-09=
Illahraun (Iceland-SW)	Crater Row of Reykjanes	1701-02=
Illano (Mindanao-Philippines)	Synonym of Makaturing	0701-04=
Illano (Mindanao-Philippines)	Synonym of Ragang	0701-06=
Illascar (Chile-N)	Synonym of Láscar	1505-10=
Illi, Puu O (Hawaiian Is)	Cone of Haleakala	1302-06-
Illihnúkur (Iceland-S)	Tuya of Torfajökull	1702-05=
Illiniza (Ecuador)	Stratovolcano (None) Holocene	**1502-041**
Illiniza Norte (Ecuador)	Stratovolcano of Illiniza	1502-041
Illiniza Sur (Ecuador)	Stratovolcano of Illiniza	1502-041
Illvidrahnjukahraun (Iceland-SW)	Fissure vent of Hofsjökull	1701-09=
Ilongo (Africa-E)	Dome of SW Usangu Basin	0202-163
Ilopango (El Salvador)	Caldera (2, 1880) Historical	**1403-06=**
Ilyaminskaya (Alaska-SW)	Synonym of Iliamna	1103-02-
Ilyinsky (Kamchatka)	Stratovolcano (6, 1901) Historical	**1000-03=**
Imac Hill (Luzon-Philippines)	Cone of San Pablo Volc Field	0703-06=
Imagination Peak (US-Oregon)	Pyroclastic cone (None) Pleistocene	....
Imbabura (Ecuador)	Compound volc. (1, -5550) Radiocarbon	**1502-004**
Imbing (Mindanao-Philippines)	Stratovolcanoes (None) Pleistocene	....
Immeruta (Italy)	Thermal feature of Lipari	0101-042
Imorigashiro (Kyushu-Japan)	Dome of Tsurumi	0802-13=
Imperial (Chile-C)	Synonym of Llaima	1507-11=
Imun (Sumatra)	Unknown (None) Holocene?	**0601-101**
Imuruk Lake (Alaska-W)	Shield volcanoes (1, 300) Radiocarbon	**1104-06-**
Imuta (Kyushu-Japan)	Lava domes (None) Pleistocene	....
In Ezzane Volc Field (Africa-N)	Volcanic field (None) Holocene?	**0205-003**
In Teria Volc Field (Africa-N)	Tuff rings (None) Quaternary	....
Inaboshi-yama (Kyushu-Japan)	Dome of Kuju	0802-12=
Inaccessible Island (Atlantic-S)	Stratovolcano (None) Pleistocene	....
Inakir (Ethiopia)	Fissure vent of Manda-Inakir	0201-122
Inamba-jima (Izu Is-Japan)	Lava dome (None) Pleistocene	....
Inamura-dake (Ryukyu Is)	Cone of Kikai	0802-06=
Inanba-jima (Izu Is-Japan)	Synonym of Inamba-jima	....
Inao-yama (Kyushu-Japan)	Dome of Unzen	0802-10=
Inarichi (Russia-SE)	Cinder cone of Udokan Plateau	1002-03-
Inatori Group (Honshu-Japan)	Crater of Izu-Tobu	0803-01=
Inca Camacha (Bolivia)	Stratovolc. Rochaculla-Inca Camacha	....
Incaguasi (Chile-N)	Unknown (None) Pleistocene	....
Incahuasi, Nevado de (Chile-N)	Stratovolcanoes (None) Holocene?	**1505-125**
Incapillo (Argentina)	Caldera (None) Pleistocene	....
Incaquasi (Chile-N)	Synonym of Incaguasi	....
Incekaya (Turkey)	Tuff cone of Nemrut Dagi	0103-02=
Inde (SE Asia)	Crater of Lower Chindwin	0705-09-
Indefatigable (Galápagos)	Synonym of Santa Cruz	1503-091
Indian Butte (US-California)	Cone of Medicine Lake	1203-02-
Indian Butte (US-Oregon)	Cone of Newberry	1202-11-
Indian Butte (US-Oregon)	Dome of Newberry	1202-11-
Indian Heaven (US-Washington)	Shield volcanoes (1, -6250) Radiocarbon	**1201-07-**
Indian Pass (US-Washington)	Cinder cone of Glacier Peak	1201-02-
Indian Pond (US-Wyoming)	Crater of Yellowstone	1205-01-
Indigirsky (Indighirsky) (Russia-NE)	Synonym of Balagan-Tas	....
Indio, Domo del (Chile-N)	Dome of Tres Cruces	....
Indooli Mountain (Alaska-W)	Cone of Nunivak Island	1104-02-
Indrapura, Peak of (Sumatra)	Synonym of Kerinci	0601-17=
Ine Rua (Lesser Sunda Is)	Thermal feature of Poco Leok	0604-07=
Ineri (Lesser Sunda Is)	Synonym of Inierie	0604-08=
Infantes, Los [Siete Fuentes] (Canary Is)	Cinder cone of Tenerife	1803-03-
Inferno (US-Idaho)	Cone of Craters of the Moon	1204-02-
Infiernillo (Argentina)	Volcanic field (1, -6890) Radiocarbon	**1507-041**
Infiernillos Ciegos de Candelario San Vicente	Thermal feature of San Vicente	1403-07=
Infiernillos de Chinameca (El Salvador)	Thermal feature of Chinameca	1403-09=
Infiernitos, Fumarole (Guatemala)	Thermal feature of Piedra Grande	....
Ingakslugwat Hills (Alaska-W)	Cinder cones (None) Holocene	**1104-03-**
Ingamakit (Russia-SE)	Dome of Udokan Plateau	1002-03-
Ingenio, El [Cerro la Celosa] (Chile-N)	Cone of Ollagüe	1505-06=
Ingilofotsy (Madagascar)	Dome of Itasy Volc Field	0303-014
Inglés, Pico [Guararí] (Costa Rica)	Cinder cone of Barva	1405-05=
Ingo (Africa-C)	Cone of Karisimbi	0203-04-
Ingri Butte (Alaska-W)	Cone of Nunivak Island	1104-02-
Ingrichuak Hills (Alaska-W)	Cinder cones (None) Pleistocene	....
Ingrijoak Hills (Alaska-W)	Cone of Nunivak Island	1104-02-
Ingrilukat-Naskorat Hill (Alaska-W)	Cone of Nunivak Island	1104-02-
Ingriruk Hill (Alaska-W)	Cone of Nunivak Island	1104-02-
Inie Lika (Lesser Sunda Is)	Synonym of Inielika	0604-09=
Inie Rie (Lesser Sunda Is)	Synonym of Inierie	0604-08=
Inielika (Lesser Sunda Is)	Complex volcano (2, 2001) Historical	**0604-09=**
Inielika, Wolo (Lesser Sunda Is)	Crater of Inielika	0604-09=
Inierie (Lesser Sunda Is)	Stratovolcano (1, -8050) Radiocarbon	**0604-08=**
Inman Nunatak (Antarctica)	Cone of Hudson Mountains	1900-028
Inn, Cerro (Galápagos)	Cone of Santiago	1503-09=
Innaccesible Cones (US-Oregon)	Cinder cone of Belknap	1202-06-
Inndalsmoya-Stakken (Atlantic-N-Jan Mayen)	Dome of Jan Mayen	1706-01=
Inrerow Atamwan (Vanuatu-SW Pacific)	Stratovolcano of Aneityum	0507-11-
Inskip Hill (US-California)	Pyroclastic cones (None) Pleistocene	....
Inukura-yama (Honshu-Japan)	Stratovolcano of Iwate	0803-24=
Inunumuri (New Britain-SW Pac)	Cone of Dakataua	0502-04=
Inusuzumi-yama (Honshu-Japan)	Cone of Fuji	0803-03=
Inyenyese (Africa-E)	Cone of Kieyo	0202-17=
Inyo Craters (US-California)	Lava domes (3, 1380) Radiocarbon	**1203-13-**
Inzolfata (Italy)	Thermal feature of Lipari	0101-042
Io [Kudriavy] (Kuril Is)	Stratovolcano of Medvezhia	0900-10=
Io San [Cherny] (Kuril Is)	Stratovolcano of Chirpoi	0900-15=
Io-sima (Volcano Is-Japan)	Synonym of Ioto [Iwo-jima]	0804-12=
Ioto (Volcano Is-Japan)	Synonym of Ioto [Iwo-jima]	0804-12=
Ioto [Iwo-jima] (Volcano Is-Japan)	Caldera (18, 2001) Historical	**0804-12=**
Io-Tori-sima (Ryukyu Is)	Synonym of Iwo-Tori-shima	0802-02=
Io-yama (Kuril Is)	Synonym of Ebeko	0900-38=
Io-yama [Iyuzan] (Honshu-Japan)	Pyroclastic cone of Izu-Tobu	0803-01=
Iozima-sinto [Showa-Iwo-jima] (Ryukyu Is)	Dome of Kikai	0802-06=
Ipala (Guatemala)	Stratovolcano (None) Holocene	**1402-19-**
Ippeki-ko (Honshu-Japan)	Maar of Izu-Tobu	0803-01=
Ipswoot Butte (US-Oregon)	Cone of Newberry	1202-11-
Iqfah, Jabal (Arabia)	Tuff ring of Hutaymah, Harrat	....
Irada (Luzon-N of)	Synonym of Iraya	0704-06-
Iramba (Africa-E)	Maar of Kieyo	0202-17=
Irarhraun (Iceland-S)	Fissure vent of Eyjafjallajökull	1702-02=
Iraya (Luzon-N of)	Stratovolcano (3, 1454) Historical	**0704-06-**

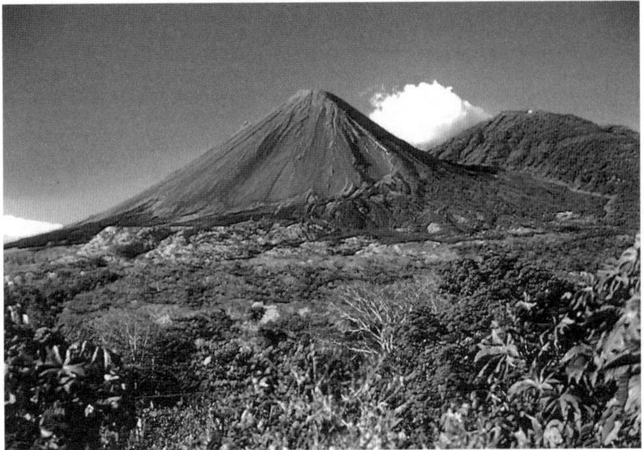

Lee Siebert (Smithsonian)

A network of lava flows, mostly erupted from flank vents, circles the base of **Izalco**, El Salvador's youngest volcano. Since the birth of Izalco in 1770 AD, the summit of the volcano grew about 650 m above its original vent on the southern flank of Santa Ana volcano, hidden behind the clouds, before eruptive activity ceased in 1966.

Name (Subregion)	Type (Eruptions, Most Recent) Status . . Relation to Named Volcano	Volcano Number
Irazú (Costa Rica)	Stratovolcano (25, 1994) Historical	**1405-06=**
Iriga (Luzon-Philippines)	Stratovolcano (None) Holocene	**0703-041**
Irind (Armenia)	Cone of Aragats	0104-06-
Iriomote-jima (Ryukyu Is)	Submarine volcano (1, 1924) Historical	**0802-01=**
Iriomotezima (Ryukyu Is)	Synonym of Iriomote-jima	0802-01=
Irish Mountain (US-Oregon)	Shield volcano (None) Pleistocene	....
Iron Trig Cone (Alaska Peninsula)	Cinder cone Savonovski River Cluster	....
Irosin (Luzon-Philippines)	Pleistocene caldera of Bulusan	0703-01=
Irruputunco (Chile-N)	Synonym of Irruputuncu	1505-04=
Irruputuncu (Chile-N)	Stratovolcano (1, 1995) Historical	**1505-04=**
Irta Ale (Ethiopia)	Synonym of Erta Ale	0201-08=
Iruputuncu (Chile-N)	Synonym of Irruputuncu	1505-04=
Isabel, Isla (México)	Tuff cones (None) Holocene?	**1401-023**
Isabella (Africa-W)	Cone of Cameroon	0204-01=
Isannach (Isannachotski) (Aleutian Is)	Synonym of Isanotski	1101-37-
Isanotski (Aleutian Is)	Stratovolcano (Uncertain)	**1101-37-**
Isarog (Luzon-Philippines)	Stratovolcano (None) Fumarolic	**0703-042**
Isau-Isau (Sumatra)	Unknown (None) Quaternary	....
Isbil, Jabal (Arabia-S)	Stratovolcano of Dhamar, Harras of	0301-12-
Ischdschea, Harret [Hala-'l-'Ishqua] (Arabia)	Tuff cone of 'Uwayrid, Harrat	0301-02=
Ischia (Italy)	Complex volcano (23, 1302) Historical	**0101-03=**
Ischia, Isola dell' (Italy)	Synonym of Ischia	0101-03=
Ishibora (Honshu-Japan)	Fissure vent of Akita-Komaga-take	0803-23=
Ishi-mine (Kyushu-Japan)	Dome of Ibusuki Volc Field	0802-07=
'Ishqua, Hala-'l- (Arabia-W)	Tuff cone of 'Uwayrid, Harrat	0301-02=
Iskut Canyon [Iskut River] (Canada)	Cone of Iskut-Unuk River Cones	1200-09-
Iskut River (Canada)	Cone of Iskut-Unuk River Cones	1200-09-
Iskut-Unuk River Cones (Canada)	Cinder cones (7, 1800) Radiocarbon	**1200-09-**
Isla del Cerro [Cerro Grande] (El Salvador)	Dome of Coatepeque Caldera	1403-041
Isla, Islota, Isola (Spanish and Italian for Island) see proper name (e.g. San Luis, Isla)		
Island Fissue (US-Oregon)	Fissure vent of North Sister Field	1202-07-
Island Park (US-Wyoming)	Pleistocene caldera of Yellowstone	1205-01-
Isleta (US-New Mexico)	Maar of Cat Hills	....
Isleta, La (Canary Is)	Cone of Gran Canaria	1803-04-
Isleta, La (Canary Is)	Fissure vent of Gran Canaria	1803-04-
Islonga (Isluca) (Chile-N)	Synonym of Isluga	1505-03=
Isluga (Chile-N)	Stratovolcano (7, 1913) Historical	**1505-03=**
Isotochniky (Kamchatka)	Cinder cone of Tolbachik	1000-24=
Issaikyo (Honshu-Japan)	Cone of Azuma	0803-18=
Issanakski (Aleutian Is)	Synonym of Isanotski	1101-37-
Isspah Butte (Canada)	Tuya of Kawdy Metah	....
Isthmus (Greece)	Synonym of Susaki	0102-01=
Istmo (Italy)	Thermal feature of Vulcano	0101-05=
Isuan [Maquiling] (Luzon-Philippines)	Stratovolcano of San Pablo Volc Field	0703-06=
Itam (Java)	Thermal feature of Ungaran	0603-23=
Itamba (Africa-E)	Maar of Kieyo	0202-17=
Itankioi (Kuril Is)	Synonym of Prevo Peak	0900-19=

Name (Subregion)	Type (Eruptions, Most Recent) Status / Relation to Named Volcano	Volcano Number
Itashibeoni-Iwo-zan (Hokkaido-Japan)	Synonym of Shiretoko-Iwo-zan	0805-09=
Itasibeoni-Iwo-zan (Hokkaido-Japan)	Synonym of Shiretoko-Iwo-zan	0805-09=
Itasy Volc Field (Madagascar)	Scoria cones (2, -6050) Radiocarbon	**0303-014**
Itcha Range (Canada)	Shield volcano (None) Pleistocene	....
Itende (Africa-E)	Maar of Kieyo	0202-17=
Itete (Africa-E)	Cone of Kieyo	0202-17=
Ithnain (Arabia-W)	Synonym of Ithnayn, Harrat	0301-05=
Ithnayn, Harrat (Arabia-W)	Volcanic field (None) Holocene	**0301-05=**
Ithundu (Africa-E)	Cone of Chyulu Hills	0202-13=
Itibisinai (Kuril Is)	Synonym of Golovnin	0900-01=
Itino-ike [Ichino-ike] (Honshu-Japan)	Crater of Norikura	0803-06=
Itino-ike [Ichino-ike] (Honshu-Japan)	Crater of On-take	0803-04=
Itinomegata [Ichinomegata] (Honshu-Japan)	Maar of Megata	0803-262
Itschinskij (Kamchatka)	Synonym of Ichinsky	1000-28=
Ittisa (Ethiopia)	Cone of Gedamsa	0201-23-
I-T'ung (China-E)	Synonym of Yitong Group	....
Iult (Kamchatka)	Stratovolcano (None) Pleistocene	....
Ivan Grozny (Kuril Is)	Somma volcano of Grozny Group	0900-07=
Ivanov (Kamchatka)	Dome of Bolshoi Semiachik	1000-15=
Ivanpah Volc Field (US-California)	Synonym of Cima Lava Field	....
Ivao Group (Kuril Is)	Cinder cones (None) Holocene	**0900-111**
Iverson Creek Volc Field (Canada)	Volcanic field of Tuya Volc Field	1200-031
IVth National Volc Congress (Kamchatka)	Fissure vent of Kliuchevskoi	1000-26=
Iwagokekodani (Honshu-Japan)	Shield volcano Washiba-Kumonotaira	0803-071
Iwaigo-dake (Kyushu-Japan)	Dome of Kuju	0802-12=
Iwaki (Honshu-Japan)	Stratovolcano (13, 1863) Historical	**0803-27=**
Iwaki-san (Honshu-Japan)	Dome of Iwaki	0803-27=
Iwale (Africa-E)	Crater of Kieyo	0202-17=
Iwanai-dake (Hokkaido-Japan)	Cone of Raiden	....
Iwanokubo (Honshu-Japan)	Cone of Izu-Tobu	0803-01=
Iwanokubo (Honshu-Japan)	Tuff ring of Izu-Tobu	0803-01=
Iwano-yama (Honshu-Japan)	Dome of Izu-Tobu	0803-01=
Iwaonupuri (Hokkaido-Japan)	Dome of Niseko	0805-031
Iwate (Honshu-Japan)	Complex volcano (26, 1919) Historical	**0803-24=**
Iwate-fuji (Iwate-Huzi) (Honshu-Japan)	Synonym of Iwate	0803-24=
Iwa-yama (Kuril Is)	Synonym of Smirnov	0900-021
Iwikau (New Zealand)	Vent of Ruapehu	0401-10=
Iwo-dake (Ryukyu Is)	Cone of Iwo-Tori-shima	0802-02=
Iwo-dake (Ryukyu Is)	Dome of Kikai	0802-06=
Iwo-dake (Honshu-Japan)	Synonym of Yake-dake	0803-07=
Iwo-jima-shinto [Showa-Iwo-jima] (Ryukyu Is)	Dome of Kikai	0802-06=
Iwo-Tori-shima (Ryukyu Is)	Complex volcano (9, 1968) Historical	**0802-02=**
Iwo-yama (Honshu-Japan)	Synonym of Adatara	0803-17=

Jose Luis Macías (UNAM)

The summit of **Iztaccíhuatl**, a massive 450 km³ stratovolcano SE of Mexico City, is composed of several overlapping volcanoes, including the northernmost peak, La Cabeza (left), the snow-capped high point El Pecho, and Las Rodillas, below the lower Ayoloco glacier at the right-center. Glacial moraines are visible at the left-center.

Name (Subregion)	Type (Eruptions, Most Recent) Status / Relation to Named Volcano	Volcano Number
Iwo-yama (Kyushu-Japan)	Dome of Kirishima	0802-09=
Iwo-yama (Izu Is-Japan)	Cone of Tori-shima	0804-09=
Iwo-zan (Kuril Is)	Synonym of Ebeko	0900-38=
Iwo-zima (Volcano Is-Japan)	Synonym of Ioto [Iwo-jima]	0804-12=
Ixhuatán (Guatemala)	Complex volcano (None) Pleistocene	....
Ixpaco, Laguna (Guatemala)	Tuff ring of Tecuamburro	1402-12=
Ixtaccíhuatl (México)	Synonym of Iztaccíhuatl	1401-082
Ixtepece (Guatemala)	Synonym of Ixtepeque	1402-18-
Ixtepeque (Guatemala)	Lava domes (None) Holocene	**1402-18-**
Ixtetal (México)	Dome of Cumbres, Las	1401-098
Ixtlán, Geysers de (México)	Therm. feature Michoacán-Guanajuato	1401-06=
Iya (Lesser Sunda Is)	Stratovolcano (8, 1969) Historical	**0604-11=**
Iyang-Argapura (Java)	Complex volcano (Uncertain) Holocene	**0603-33=**
Iyuzan (Honshu-Japan)	Pyroclastic cone of Izu-Tobu	0803-01=
Iyu-zan (Honshu-Japan)	Cone of Izu-Tobu	0803-01=
Izalco (El Salvador)	Stratovolcano (51, 1966) Historical	**1403-03=**
Izopo, Montaña de (Honduras)	Shield volcanoes (None) Quaternary	....
Izote, Cerro (México)	Dome of San Pedro	....
Iztaccíhuatl (México)	Stratovolcano (None) Holocene	**1401-082**
Iztactépetl (México)	Synonym of Iztaccíhuatl	1401-082
Iztaltetlac, Cerro (México)	Cinder cone of Papayo	1401-081
Izu (Izu Is-Japan)	Crater of Miyake-jima	0804-04=
Izumbwe-Mpoli (Africa-E)	Pyroclastic cones (None) Holocene	**0202-165**
Izumiga-take (Honshu-Japan)	Stratovolcano of Funagata	....
Izu-Oshima (Izu Is-Japan)	Synonym of Oshima	0804-01=
Izu-Tobu (Honshu-Japan)	Pyroclastic cones (6, 1989) Historical	**0803-01=**
Izu-Tori-shima (Izu Is-Japan)	Synonym of Tori-shima	0804-09=

J

Name (Subregion)	Type (Eruptions, Most Recent) Status / Relation to Named Volcano	Volcano Number
J Cone [Vulcan] (US-New Mexico)	Cone of Albuquerque	....
Jabal (Arabic for Mt.) see proper name (e.g. Haylan, Jabal)		
Jabalí, Cerros del (México)	Cinder cone of Michoacán-Guanajuato	1401-06=
Jabalí, El (El Salvador)	Stratovolcano of San Salvador	1403-05=
Jabalincito, El [Sitio Grande] (El Salvador)	Crater of San Salvador	1403-05=
Jabel-Jubeiq (Jordan)	Volcanic field (None) Post-Miocene	....
Jable, Montaña del (Canary Is)	Cinder cone of Hierro	1803-02-
Jaboncillo, Cerro (Guatemala)	Cinder cone of Agua	1402-10=
Jabut, Bukit [Bukit Cabut] (Sumatra)	Cone of Besar	0601-25=
Jacal de Piedra, Cerro (México)	Dome of Northern Guadalajara Mesa	....
Jackies Butte (US-Oregon)	Volcanic field (None) Quaternary	....
Jackmosky (Kuril Is)	Synonym of Chikurachki	0900-36=
Jack's Jump (Canada)	Cone of Wells Gray-Clearwater	1200-15-
Jacques Lake (Canada)	Cone of Quesnel Cone Group	....
Jade Mines (SE Asia)	Synonym of Namyong	....
Jadi, Gunung (Java)	Former dome of Galunggung	0603-14=
Jae Panas Hot Spring (Lesser Sunda Is)	Thermal feature of Bratan	0604-001
Jag Peak (Aleutian Is)	Cone of Okmok	1101-29-
Jagüel del Moro, Loma (Argentina)	Shield volcano of Unnamed	....
Jagüey, El (México)	Maar of Durango Volc Field	1401-022
Jahsaya, Cerro (Perú)	Stratovolcano of Firura, Nevados	....
Jailolo (Halmahera-Indonesia)	Stratovolcano (None) Holocene	**0608-051**
Jaisa (Honshu-Japan)	Synonym of Jaishi	....
Jaishi (Honshu-Japan)	Shield volcano (None) Pleistocene	....
Jajarana, Cerro (Perú)	Cinder cone of Andahua-Orcopampa	1504-004
Jalajala (Luzon-Philippines)	Thermal feature of Laguna Caldera	0703-08=
Jalapasquillo [Cerro Tepexitl] (México)	Tuff ring of Serdán-Oriental	1401-092
Jalapasquillo [Xalapasquillo] (México)	Maar of Serdán-Oriental	1401-092
Jali [Jalli] (Greece)	Synonym of Yali	0102-051
Jalilagua (Ecuador)	Dome of Casitagua	....
Jalua (Ethiopia)	Stratovolcano (None) Holocene	**0201-03=**
Jamakatan (Africa-E)	Cone of Paka	0202-053
Jambangan (Java)	Crater of Iyang-Argapura	0603-33=
Jambangan (Java)	Caldera of Semeru	0603-30=
Jambul, Bukit (Sumatra)	Unknown (None) Post-Miocene	....
James (Galápagos)	Synonym of Santiago	1503-09=
James Ross Island (Antarctica)	Shield volcano (None) Pleistocene	....
Jan Mayen (Atlantic-N-Jan Mayen)	Stratovolcano (7, 1985) Historical	**1706-01=**
Janduli (Africa-E)	Cone of Katete	....
Jang (Java)	Synonym of Iyang-Argapura	0603-33=
Janghudi (Jangudi) (Ethiopia)	Synonym of Yangudi	0201-151
Janoo (Kyushu-Japan)	Cone of Aso	0802-11=
Japati (Java)	Crater of Guntur	0603-13=
Japones (Chile-C)	Crater of Llaima	1507-11=
Jara Mesa, La (US-New Mexico)	Cone of Taylor Volc Field	....
Jara, Cerro La (US-New Mexico)	Dome of Valles Caldera	....
Jaraguay Volc Field (México)	Cinder cones (None) Holocene	**1401-004**
Jarapena, Volcán la (México)	Crater of Pinacate	1401-001
Jar'atain, Harra of (Arabia-W)	Cone of Yar, Jabal	0301-08-
Jardbadsholar [Bjarnarflag] (Iceland-NE)	Crater Row of Krafla	1703-08=
Jarian, Kawah (Java)	Crater of Tangkubanparahu	0603-09=
Jarilloso (Chile-C)	Tuff cone of Llancanelo Volc Field	....
Jarra (Arabia-W)	Synonym of Yar, Jabal	0301-08-
Jarvis (Alaska-E)	Unknown (None) Pleistocene	....
Jatun (Perú)	Cinder cone of Andahua-Orcopampa	1504-004
Jawalo (Lesser Sunda Is)	Crater of Paluweh	0604-15=
Jayu Khota, Laguna (Bolivia)	Maars (None) Holocene	**1505-035**
Jayu Kkota (Bolivia)	Synonym of Jayu Khota, Laguna	1505-035
Jean (Indian O.-W)	Crater of Fournaise, Piton de la	0303-02=
Jeaneton, Morne (W Indies)	Dome of Northern Chain	....
Jebel, Jibal, Jibbel (Arabic for Mt.) see proper name (e.g. Marra, Jebel)		
Jechapita, Volcán (Perú)	Cinder cone of Andahua-Orcopampa	1504-004
Jefferson (US-Oregon)	Stratovolcano (2, 950) Varve Count	**1202-02-**
Jeju (Korea)	Synonym of Halla	1006-04-
Jellicoe Park (New Zealand)	Cone of Auckland Field	0401-02=
Jemez Springs (US-New Mexico)	Thermal feature of Valles Caldera	....
Jemez Volc Field (US-New Mexico)	Synonym of Valles Caldera	....
Jenchana, Volcán (Perú)	Cinder cone of Andahua-Orcopampa	1504-004
Jenoy (Colombia)	Pleistocene caldera of Galeras	1501-08=
Jeremine (Indian O.-W)	Crater of Fournaise, Piton de la	0303-02=
Jero (Java)	Crater of Arjuno-Welirang	0603-29=
Jervis (Galápagos)	Synonym of Rábida	....
Jesús de Monte, Cerro (México)	Cinder cone of Comondú-La Purísima	1401-012
Jesús Grande, Isla de (Nicaragua)	Lava cone of Zapatera	1404-111
Jgorewskij (Kamchatka)	Synonym of Dzenzursky	1000-11=
Jiacong (China-E)	Shield volcano (None) Pleistocene	....
Jianghui Group (China-E)	Cinder cone (None) Pleistocene	....
Jianshan (China-E)	Dome of Fanjiatung Group	....
Jianshan (China-E)	Shield volcano (None) Quaternary	....
Jianshuidingzi (China-E)	Cone of Longgang Group	1005-05-
Jiaoshan (SE Asia)	Cone of Tengchong	0705-11-
Jicalán, Cerro de (México)	Cinder cone of Michoacán-Guanajuato	1401-06=
Jigabo (Luzon-Philippines)	Thermal feature of Malinao	....

Name (Subregion)	Type (Eruptions, Most Recent) Status Relation to Named Volcano	Volcano Number
Jigoku (Kyushu-Japan)	Thermal feature of Aso	0802-11=
Jigoku (Honshu-Japan)	Crater of On-take	0803-04=
Jigoku (Honshu-Japan)	Thermal feature of Osore-yama	0803-29=
Jigoku Spa (Kyushu-Japan)	Vent of Aso	0802-11=
Jigoku Yama [Trezubetz] (Kuril Is)	Somma volcano of Kolokol Group	0900-12=
Jigoku-ato (Kyushu-Japan)	Crater of Unzen	0802-10=
Jigoku-dani (Hokkaido-Japan)	Pyroclastic cone of Kuttara	0805-034
Jigoku-dani (Honshu-Japan)	Crater of Tate-yama	0803-08=
Jigoku-no-oana (Honshu-Japan)	Crater of Haku-san	0803-05=
Jigoku-numa (Honshu-Japan)	Crater of Hakkoda Group	0803-28=
Jii-dake (Honshu-Japan)	Shield volcano Washiba-Kumonotaira	0803-071
Jilguero, Cerro el (México)	Dome of Azufres, Los	....
Jiloá [Xiloá] (Nicaragua)	Caldera of Apoyeque	1404-091
Jim Jim, the (Australia)	Cone of Newer Volcanics Prov	0509-01-
Jimat (Java)	Cone of Dieng Volc Complex	0603-20=
Jimo (China-E)	Unknown (None) Quaternary	....
Jinaka-yama (Izu Is-Japan)	Dome of Nii-jima	0804-02=
Jinamar, Montana (Canary Is)	Cone of Gran Canaria	1803-04-
Jinetsu Hot Springs (Honshu-Japan)	Thermal feature of Kusatsu-Shirane	0803-12=
Jing-bei (Jingbohu, Jingpohu) (China-E)	Synonym of Jingbo	1005-04-
Jingbo (China-E)	Volcanic field (3, -520) Radiocarbon	**1005-04-**
Jinggo, Kepundan (Sumatra)	Crater of Marapi	0601-14=
Jinglongdingzi (China-E)	Pyroclastic cone of Longgang Group	1005-05-
Jingyishan (China-E)	Cone of Kuandian	....
Jinjinshansi (China-E)	Cone of Datong-Fengzen	....
Jinshan (China-E)	Cone of Datong-Fengzen	....
Jirou-Uemontsuka (Honshu-Japan)	Cone of Fuji	0803-03=
Jiskooksnuk Hill (Alaska-W)	Cone of Nunivak Island	1104-02-
Jiyunling (SE Asia)	Cone of Leizhou Bandao	0705-01-
Jizo Hot Springs (Honshu-Japan)	Thermal feature of Kusatsu-Shirane	0803-12=
Jizo-dake (Honshu-Japan)	Dome of Akagi	0803-13=
Jizodo Group (Honshu-Japan)	Vent of Izu-Tobu	0803-01=
Jizono-yu (Kyushu-Japan)	Thermal feature of Tsurumi	0802-13=
Jizo-san (Honshu-Japan)	Dome of Zao	0803-19=
Jliamna (Alaska-SW)	Synonym of Iliamna	1103-02-
Joao Fernandes, Pico (Azores)	Cone of Agua de Pau	1802-09=
Job, Mt. (Canada)	Cone of Meager	1200-18-
Joboshi (Honshu-Japan)	Cinder cone of Izu-Tobu	0803-01=
Jocotillo, Cerro el (Guatemala)	Cinder cone of Cuilapa-Barbarena	1402-111
Jocotitlán (México)	Stratovolcano (2, 1270) Radiocarbon	**1401-062**
Joe's Hill (Atlantic-S)	Cinder cone of Inaccessible Island	....
Joglo, Mt. (Java)	Dome of Muria	0603-251
Jogo-yama (Izu Is-Japan)	Dome of Kozu-shima	0804-03=
Johann Albrecht Hafen (New Britain-SW Pac)	Caldera of Garove	0502-03=
John, Morne (W Indies)	Dome of Watt, Morne	1600-101
Johnson Glacier (Alaska-SW)	Dome of Iliamna	1103-02-
Jökulstallar (Iceland-SW)	Shield volcano of Hveravellir	1701-08=
Jolo (Sulu Is-Philippines)	Pyroclastic cones (1, 1897) Historical	**0700-01=**
Jolo (Sulu Is-Philippines)	Synonym of Jolo	0700-01=
Jolom, Cerro (Guatemala)	Dome of Santo Tomás	....
Jolotepec, Cerro los (México)	Cinder cone of Gloria, La	1401-097
Jonassen Island (Antarctica)	Cone of Tabarin Peninsula	....
Jonggring Seloko (Java)	Crater of Semeru	0603-30=
Jorcada (Bolivia)	Stratovolcano (None) Pleistocene	....
Jorda, Puig (Spain)	Cone of Olot Volc Field	0100-03-
Jordan Craters (US-Oregon)	Volcanic field (1, -1250) Radiocarbon	**1202-19-**
Jorgencal (Jorjencal) (Chile-N)	Synonym of Putana	1505-09=
Jormajan, Mt. (Luzon-Philippines)	Dome of Bulusan	0703-01=
Jornada del Muerto (US-New Mexico)	Shield volcano (None) Pleistocene	....
Jorobado (Chile-S)	Synonym of Corcovado	1508-05=
Jorullo (México)	Cinder cone of Michoacán-Guanajuato	1401-06=
Jörundur (Iceland-NE)	Dome of Krafla	1703-08=
Jose Butte (US-New Mexico)	Cone of Raton-Clayton	....
Josephine, Mt. (Canada)	Cone of Tuya Volc Field	1200-031
Joshu-Hotaka (Honshu-Japan)	Synonym of Hotaka	....
Joya de Limón, Cerrito (Guatemala)	Cinder cone of Cuilapa-Barbarena	1402-111
Joya de los Contreras, La (México)	Maar of Santo Domingo Volc Field	....
Joya Honda, La (México)	Maar of Ventura Volc Field	....
Joya Prieta, La (México)	Maar of Santo Domingo Volc Field	....
Joya, Cerro la (México)	Cinder cone of Chichinautzin	1401-08=
Joya, Cerro la (México)	Cinder cone of Comondú-La Purísima	1401-012
Joya, La (México)	Cinder cone of Cofre de Perote	1401-096
Joya, La (Colombia)	Crater of Galeras	1501-08=
Joya, La (Nicaragua)	Vent of Granada	1404-101
Joya, La (Nicaragua)	Maar of Pilas, Las	1404-08=
Joya, La (El Salvador)	Cinder cone of San Salvador	1403-05=
Joyuela (México)	Tuff cone of Ventura Volc Field	....
Jrbashyana (Armenia)	Cone of Ghegam Ridge	0104-07-
Juan Murillo (Costa Rica)	Cinder cone of Platanar	1405-034
Juan Perdomo, Montana de (Canary Is)	Cone of Lanzarote	1803-06-
Juanacanla (México)	Cone of Zitácuaro-Valle de Bravo	1401-061
Juanoy (Colombia)	Unknown (None) Post-Miocene	....
Juban, Mt. (Luzon-Philippines)	Cone of Bulusan	0703-01=
Jubilee [Yubileinoye] (Kamchatka)	Fissure vent of Kliuchevskoi	1000-26=
Jucuapa (El Salvador)	Synonym of Tigre, El	1403-082
Jueockack (Korea)	Cone of Halla	1006-04-
Julan, Montañas de (Canary Is)	Cinder cone of Hierro	1803-02-
Julien, Morne (W Indies)	Cone of Pelée	1600-12=
Jumay Volc Field (Guatemala)	Stratovolcano (None) Quaternary	....
Jumay, Volcán (Guatemala)	Stratovolcano of Jumay Volc Field	....
Jumaytepeque (Guatemala)	Stratovolcano (None) Holocene?	**1402-121**
Jumbo Dome (Alaska-W)	Lava dome (None) Pleistocene	....
Jumento (México)	Cinder cone of Chichinautzin	1401-08=
Jumes, Puy de (France)	Cone of Chaîne des Puys	0100-02-
Junacanila, Cerro (México)	Cinder cone Zitácuaro-Valle de Bravo	1401-061
Junga-ike (Honshu-Japan)	Crater of Yake-dake	0803-07=
Junior's Kop (Indian O.-S)	Cinder cone of Marion Island	0304-07-
Junquillo Norte, Cerro el (Guatemala)	Cinder cone of Cuilapa-Barbarena	1402-111
Junquillo Sur, Cerro el (Guatemala)	Cinder cone of Cuilapa-Barbarena	1402-111
Junquillo, Cerro (El Salvador)	Cinder cone of San Diego	1403-001
Junquillo, Cerro el (Guatemala)	Cinder cone of Redondo, Cerro	....
Junta, Cerro la (México)	Cinder cone of Comondú-La Purísima	1401-012
Jurang Siunik (Sumatra)	Crater of Sorikmarapi	0601-12=
Jurig, Kawah (Java)	Crater of Tangkubanparahu	0603-09=
Juriques, Volcán (Chile-N)	Stratovolcano of Licancabur	1505-092
Jute, Cerro del (Guatemala)	Cinder cone of Moyuta	1402-13-
Jutiapa Group (Guatemala)	Synonym of Santiago, Cerro	1402-15-
Jyobu Hot Springs (Honshu-Japan)	Thermal feature of Kusatsu-Shirane	0803-12=
Jyogahana (Ryukyu Is)	Stratovolcano of Kuchinoerabu-jima	0802-05=

Large areas of hydrothermally altered ground occur at the **Jigoku-dani** ("Valley of Hell") thermal area of Kuttara volcano in Hokkaido, a popular resort area.

Tom Simkin (Smithsonian)

K

Name (Subregion)	Type (Eruptions, Most Recent) Status Relation to Named Volcano	Volcano Number
Ka Moa O Pele (Hawaiian Is)	Cone of Haleakala	1302-06-
Kaaba (Sumatra)	Synonym of Kaba	0601-22=
Kaalkoppie (Indian O.-S)	Tuff cone of Marion Island	0304-07-
Kaba (Sumatra)	Stratovolcano (11, 2000) Historical	**0601-22=**
Kaba (Indonesian for Crater) see proper name (e.g. Baru, Kaba)		
Kabalan (Kamchatka)	Synonym of Kobalan	....
Kabara (Fiji Is-SW Pacific)	Unknown (None) Pleistocene	....
Kabargin Oth Group (Georgia)	Cinder cones (None) Holocene	**0104-03-**
Kabarugi (Africa-C)	Crater of Bunyaruguru	0203-004
Kabhegy (Hungary)	Shield volcano of Balaton Highland	....
Kabinlangan (Luzon-Philippines)	Thermal feature of Cagua	0703-09=
Kabiranjuma (Africa-C)	Crater of Muhavura	0203-06-
Kabiu [Kombiu] (New Britain-SW Pac)	Stratovolcano of Rabaul	0502-14=
Kabujutan [Kabuyutan] (Java)	Crater of Guntur	0603-13=
Kabun Bungo [Kebun Bungo] (Sumatra)	Crater of Marapi	0601-14=
Kabuto-yama (Honshu-Japan)	Cone of Azuma	0803-18=
Kabuyutan (Java)	Crater of Guntur	0603-13=
Kadiendi Nae (Lesser Sunda Is)	Dome of Tambora	0604-04=
Kadjor [Kajor] (Java)	Fissure vent of Merbabu	0603-24=
Kadogo (Africa-C)	Cone of Nyamuragira	0203-02=
Kadono (Honshu-Japan)	Cinder cone of Izu-Tobu	0803-01=
Kadovar (New Guinea-NE of)	Stratovolcano (Uncertain) Holocene	**0501-002**
Kadowaki-kaikyu (Honshu-Japan)	Submarine vent of Izu-Tobu	0803-01=
Kadyr-Sugskii (Russia-SE)	Shield volcano of Azas Plateau	1002-07-
Kadyr-Tayga (Russia-SE)	Shield volcano of Azas Plateau	1002-07-
Kaeo (Hawaiian Is)	Cone of Niihau	....
Ka-er-Daxi [Ashi Shan] (China-W)	Cinder cone of Kunlun Volc Group	1004-03-
Kagamil (Aleutian Is)	Stratovolcano (1, 1929) Historical	**1101-26-**
Kagano (Africa-C)	Cone of Nyamuragira	0203-02=
Kagode (Africa-C)	Tuff cone of Fort Portal	0203-001
Kago-yama (Honshu-Japan)	Dome of Adatara	0803-17=
Kagusa Hot Springs (Honshu-Japan)	Thermal feature of Kusatsu-Shirane	0803-12=
Kaguyak (Alaska Peninsula)	Lava domes (2, -3850) Holocene	**1102-25-**
Kahala (Hawaiian Is)	Synonym of Kohala	....
Kahaualea, Puu (Hawaiian Is)	Cone of Kilauea	1302-01-
Kahe Kahe (Tonga-SW Pacific)	Synonym of Falcon Island	0403-05=
Kahekahe Tangata (Tonga-SW Pacific)	Synonym of Metis Shoal	0403-07=
Kahepuku (New Zealand)	Synonym of Kakepuku	....
Kaholua O Kahawali (Hawaiian Is)	Cone of Kilauea	1302-01-
Kahongole (Africa-C)	Cone of Nyamuragira	0203-02=
Kahoolawe (Hawaiian Is)	Shield volcano (None) Pleistocene	....
Kahualoa (Hawaiian Is)	Tuff cone of Koolau	....
Kahuwai (Hawaiian Is)	Pit crater of Kilauea	1302-01-
Kaia [Tavurvur] (New Britain-SW Pac)	Stratovolcano of Rabaul	0502-14=
Kaiamu (New Britain-SW Pac)	Maar of Sulu Range	0502-09=
Kaibun [Kaimon] (Kyushu-Japan)	Stratovolcano of Ibusuki Volc Field	0802-07=
Kaikata Seamount (Volcano Is-Japan)	Submarine volcano (None) Fumarolic	**0804-097**
Kaikohe (New Zealand)	Cone of Kaikohe-Bay of Islands	0401-01=

Name (Subregion)	Type (Eruptions, Most Recent) Status / Relation to Named Volcano	Volcano Number
Kaikohe-Bay of Islands (New Zeal.)	Volcanic field (1, 400) Radiocarbon	**0401-01=**
Kaileney (Kamchatka)	Shield volcano (None) Holocene?	**1000-62-**
Kailia (Greece)	Thermal feature of Nisyros	0102-05=
Kailupa (Halmahera-Indonesia)	Cone of Jailolo	0608-051
Kaimai (New Zealand)	Volcanic field (None) Pleistocene?	....
Kaimaloo (Hawaiian Is)	Cone of Haleakala	1302-06-
Kaimanawa (New Zealand)	Dome of Maroa	0401-061
Kaimeni [Kameno Vouno] (Greece)	Dome of Methana	0102-02=
Kaimon (Kyushu-Japan)	Stratovolcano of Ibusuki Volc Field	0802-07=
Kaino-Semiachik [Ceno-Semiachik]	Stratovolcano of Maly Semiachik	1000-14=
Kairuru (New Zealand)	Dome of Reporoa	0401-06-
Kaiseinishinoba (Volcano Is-Japan)	Submarine vent of Ioto [Iwo-jima]	0804-12=
Kaisenoba (Volcano Is-Japan)	Synonym of Kita-Fukutokutai	0804-121
Kaiser Wilhelm Mountain (Indian O.-S)	Synonym of Heard	0304-01=
Kaishio (Honshu-Japan)	Vent of Kamitakara	....

Yuri Doubik (Inst. Volc., Petropavlovsk)

Sharp-topped **Kamen** volcano in Kamchatka was truncated by a Holocene edifice collapse; symmetrical **Kliuchevskoi** volcano was formed during the past 6000 years.

Name (Subregion)	Type (Eruptions, Most Recent) Status / Relation to Named Volcano	Volcano Number
Kaitake (New Zealand)	Stratovolcano (None) Pleistocene	....
Kaitoku Kaizan (Volcano Is-Japan)	Synonym of Kaitoku Seamount	0804-10=
Kaitoku Seamount (Volcano Is-Japan)	Submarine volcano (2, 1984) Historical	**0804-10=**
Kaitoku-okanoba (Volcano Is-Japan)	Synonym of Kaitoku Seamount	0804-10=
Kajang Plateau, Bukit (New Guinea)	Unknown (None) Quaternary	....
Kajiana (Izu Is-Japan)	Crater of To-shima	0804-011
Kajongo (Africa-C)	Tuff cone of Fort Portal	0203-001
Kajor (Java)	Fissure vent of Merbabu	0603-24=
Kakambui (Africa-E)	Cone of Chyulu Hills	0202-13=
Kakapiko Lookout (New Zealand)	Dome of Kapenga	....
Kakaramea (New Zealand)	Stratovolc. of Northern Tongariro Group	....
Kakepuku (New Zealand)	Lava cones (None) Pleistocene	....
Kakhtana (Kamchatka)	Shield volcano of Voyampolsky	1000-72-
Kako (Africa-C)	Crater of Bunyaruguru	0203-004
Kakolan Island (New Britain-SW Pac)	Cone of Likuruanga	....
Kakorinya (Africa-E)	Shield volcano of Barrier, The.	0202-03=
Kakuto (Kyushu-Japan)	Caldera (None) Pleistocene	....
Kaladis (Mindanao-Philippines)	Stratovolcano (None) Pleistocene	....
Kalaieha, Puu (Hawaiian Is)	Cone of Mauna Kea	1302-03-
Kalalua (Hawaiian Is)	Cone of Kilauea	1302-01-
Kalama (Hawaiian Is)	Cone of Koolau	....
Kalambis (Philippines-C)	Thermal feature of Biliran	0702-08=
Kalamos (Greece)	Thermal feature of Mílos	0102-03=
Kalang (Java)	Synonym of Karang	0603-02=
Kalatungan (Mindanao-Philippines)	Stratovolcano (None) Holocene?	**0701-061**
Kalaupapa (Hawaiian Is)	Shield volcano of East Molokai	....
Kalawangan (Luzon-Philippines)	Thermal feature of Pinatubo	0703-083
Kale Tepe (Turkey)	Dome of Nemrut Dagi	0103-02=
Kaleci (Turkey)	Dome of Acigöl-Nevsehir	0103-004
Kaledong-Haruman (Java)	Lava domes (None) Post-Miocene	....
Kaleetan Butte (US-Oregon)	Dome of South Sister	1202-08-
Kalem (Germany)	Cone of West Eifel Volc Field	0100-01-
Kalepeamoa, Puu (Hawaiian Is)	Cone of Mauna Kea	1302-03-
Kalfadalshraun (Iceland-SW)	Crater Row of Brennisteinsfjöll	1701-04=
Kalfellshraun (Iceland-SW)	Crater Row of Reykjanes	1701-02=
Kalfsholar (Iceland-SW)	Crater Row of Grímsnes	1701-06=
Kalgauch (Kamchatka)	Stratovolcano (None) Pleistocene	....
Kalgnitunup (Kamchatka)	Stratovolcano of Kebeney	1000-50-
Kaliango [Kalyango] (Africa-C)	Tuff cone of Fort Portal	0203-001
Kalikiir (Lesser Sunda Is)	Crater of Sirung	0604-27=
Kaliu (Hawaiian Is)	Cone of Kilauea	1302-01-
Kalkani Cone (Australia)	Cone of McBride Volc Province	....
Kalnang'i Springs (Africa-E)	Thermal feature of Silali	0202-052
Kalolenyang (Africa-E)	Shield volcano of Barrier, The.	0202-03=
Kaluaiki (Hawaiian Is)	Cone of Haleakala	1302-06-
Kalubu Crater [Doro Api] (Lesser Sunda Is)	Cone of Sangeang Api	0604-05=
Kaluu O Ka Oo (Hawaiian Is)	Cone of Haleakala	1302-06-
Kalvaria (Slovakia)	Cone of Central Slovakia	....
Kalyango (Africa-C)	Tuff cone of Fort Portal	0203-001
Kamabuse-yama (Honshu-Japan)	Dome of Osore-yama	0803-29=

Name (Subregion)	Type (Eruptions, Most Recent) Status / Relation to Named Volcano	Volcano Number
Kamado-jigoku (Kyushu-Japan)	Thermal feature of Tsurumi	0802-13=
Kamafuse-yama (Honshu-Japan)	Synonym of Osore-yama	0803-29=
Kamakaia (Hawaiian Is)	Shield volcano of Kilauea	1302-01-
Kamakaiauka (Hawaiian Is)	Cone of Kilauea	1302-01-
Kamakaiawaena (Hawaiian Is)	Cone of Kilauea	1302-01-
Kamane (Izu Is-Japan)	Maar of Miyake-jima	0804-04=
Kamaoli (Hawaiian Is)	Cone of Haleakala	1302-06-
Kamari (Greece)	Pleistocene caldera of Kos	....
Kama-yama (Honshu-Japan)	Pyroclastic cone of Asama	0803-11=
Kambalnaia, Sopka (Kamchatka)	Synonym of Kambalny	1000-01=
Kambalny (Kamchatka)	Stratovolcano (1, 1350) Historical	**1000-01=**
Kamchatka Peak (Kamchatka)	Synonym of Bakening	1000-123
Kamchatskaia Gora (Kamchatka)	Synonym of Kliuchevskoi	1000-26=
Kamchatsky Vulkan (Kamchatka)	Synonym of Kliuchevskoi	1000-26=
Kamega-ike (Honshu-Japan)	Crater of Norikura	0803-06=
Kamega-ike (Honshu-Japan)	Crater of Norikura	0803-06=
Kamegawa (Kyushu-Japan)	Thermal feature of Tsurumi	0802-13=
Kamehame Hill (Hawaiian Is)	Cone of Kilauea	1302-01-
Kameishi-yama (Kyushu-Japan)	Cone of Hane-yama	....
Kamen (Kamchatka)	Stratovolcano (None) Holocene	**1000-251**
Kamen (Kamchatka)	Stratovolcano (None) Pleistocene	....
Kamen Avos (Kuril Is)	Synonym of Avos' Rocks	....
Kamenae (Greece)	Dome of Santorini	0102-04=
Kameni [Kameno Vouno] (Greece)	Dome of Methana	0102-02=
Kamenistaya (Kamchatka)	Cone of Ksudach	1000-05=
Kamenistaya (Kamchatka)	Cinder cone of Tolbachik	1000-24=
Kamenisty (Kamchatka)	Stratovolcano (None) Pleistocene	....
Kameno Vouno (Greece)	Dome of Methana	0102-02=
Kamerungebirge (Africa-W)	Synonym of Cameroon	0204-01=
Kamibori (Honshu-Japan)	Crater of Yake-dake	0803-07=
Kami-Horokamettoku-yama (Japan)	Stratovolcano of Tokachi	0805-05=
Kamiji-yama (Honshu-Japan)	Synonym of Fuji	0803-03=
Kaminakia (Greece)	Vent of Nisyros	0102-05=
Kaminoroka (Honshu-Japan)	Unknown (None) Pleistocene	....
Kamisano (Honshu-Japan)	Cinder cone of Kannabe	....
Kamitakara (Honshu-Japan)	Unknown (None) Pleistocene	....
Kami-yama (Honshu-Japan)	Dome of Hakone	0803-02=
Kami-Yuzawa (Kyushu-Japan)	Dome of Kuju	0802-12=
Kammena Vourla (Greece)	Dome of Volos-Atalanti	....
Kammerbuhl [Komorni Hurka] (Czech)	Cinder cone of Cheb Basin	....
Kammourta (Ethiopia)	Cone of Manda-Inakir	0201-122
Kamoamoa, Puu (Hawaiian Is)	Cone of Kilauea	1302-01-
Kamodjan (Kamojan) (Java)	Synonym of Kamojang, Kawah	....
Kamojang, Kawah (Java)	Stratovolcanoes (None) Pleist.-Fumarolic	....
Kamoshika (Honshu-Japan)	Thermal feature of Zao	0803-19=
Kamtschatskaja (Kamchatka)	Synonym of Kliuchevskoi	1000-26=
Kamui (Kuril Is)	Cone of Demon	0900-11-
Kamuinupuri (Hokkaido-Japan)	Stratovolcano of Mashu	0805-081
Kamuishi (Hokkaido-Japan)	Dome of Mashu	0805-081
Kamuishuto [Kamuishi] (Hokkaido-Japan)	Dome of Mashu	0805-081
Kamuissyuto [Kamuishi] (Hokkaido-Japan)	Dome of Mashu	0805-081
Kamunzukwa (Africa-C)	Crater of Bunyaruguru	0203-004
Kamuro (Honshu-Japan)	Stratovolcano of Ganto-Kamuro	....
Kana (Canada)	Cone of Edziza	1200-06-
Kana Keoki (Solomon Is-SW Pacific)	Submarine volcano (None) Holocene	**0505-052**
Kanaga (Aleutian Is)	Stratovolcano (16, 1995) Historical	**1101-11-**
Kanaga-take (Honshu-Japan)	Stratovolcano of Kurofuji	....
Kanagioi (New Guinea-NE of)	Stratovolcano of Karkar	0501-03=
Kanakaleonui, Puu (Hawaiian Is)	Cone of Mauna Kea	1302-03-
Kanakana (New Zealand)	Dome of Okataina	0401-05=
Kanamharagi (Africa-C)	Cone of Nyamuragira	0203-02=
Kanaso (Izu Is-Japan)	Maar of Miyake-jima	0804-04=
Kanaton (Aleutian Is)	Shield volcano of Kanaga	1101-11-
Kanava (Greece)	Thermal feature of Mílos	0102-03=
Kancana (Java)	Stratovolcano (None) Quaternary	....
Kancana (Java)	Stratovolcano (None) Pleistocene	....
Kandidushka (Russia-SE)	Cinder cone of Vitim Plateau	1002-04-
Kando-yama (Izu Is-Japan)	Crater of Hachijo-jima	0804-05=
Kane Nui O Hamo (Hawaiian Is)	Shield volcano of Kilauea	1302-01-
Kaneda (Honshu-Japan)	Dome of Omanago Group	0803-142
Kanekolo, Mt. (Solomon Is-SW Pacific)	Unknown (None) Post-Miocene	....
Kangaroo Hill (Australia)	Cone of Newer Volcanics Prov	0509-01-
Kangirinyang (Africa-E)	Maar of Emuruangogolak	0202-051
Kani-numa (Honshu-Japan)	Crater of Akita-Yake-yama	0803-26=
Kanjal (Russia-SW)	Fissure vent (None) Quaternary	....
Kan-K'uei (China-E)	Synonym of Gankui Group	....
Kanlaon (Philippines-C)	Stratovolcano (27, 2006) Historical	**0702-02=**
Kannabe (Honshu-Japan)	Shield volcano (None) Quaternary	....
Kannabe-yama (Honshu-Japan)	Cinder cone of Kannabe	....
Kannawa-jigoku (Kyushu-Japan)	Thermal feature of Tsurumi	0802-13=
Kannone Kaikyu (Ryukyu Is)	Submarine vent of Yokoate-jima	0802-021
Kannone-jima (Ryukyu Is)	Cone of Yokoate-jima	0802-021
Kannon-mori (Honshu-Japan)	Cone of Chokai	0803-22=
Kannonyama-Higashi (Honshu-Japan)	Cone of Izu-Tobu	0803-01=
Kanpo-dake (Hokkaido-Japan)	Cinder cone of Oshima-Oshima	0805-01=
Kanpu (Honshu-Japan)	Stratovolcano (None) Pleistocene	....
Kansu-yama (Honshu-Japan)	Cone of Fuji	0803-03=
Kantjana (Java)	Synonym of Kancana	....
Kantjana (Java)	Synonym of Kancana	....
Kanyambuzi (Africa-C)	Cone of Nyiragongo	0203-03=
Kanymagashu (Africa-C)	Cone of Nyiragongo	0203-03=
Kao (Tonga-SW Pacific)	Stratovolcano (None) Holocene	**0403-061**
Kaohikaipu (Hawaiian Is)	Cone of Koolau	....
Kaolkhon (Kamchatka)	Synonym of Ichinsky	1000-28=

Name (Subregion)	Type (Eruptions, Most Recent) Status / Relation to Named Volcano	Volcano Number
Kapayahan (Mindanao-Philippines)	Crater of Paco	0701-09-
Kapberg (New Britain-SW Pac)	Stratovolcano of Lolo	0502-071
Kapedo Hot Springs (Africa-E)	Thermal feature of Silali	0202-052
Kapellugigar (Iceland-SW)	Crater Row of Krísuvík	1701-03=
Kapenga (New Zealand)	Calderas (None) Pleistocene	....
Kapi Fumarole Field (Sumatra)	Thermal feature of Kembar	....
Kapkai (New Ireland-SW Pacific)	Thermal feature of Ambitle	0504-02=
Kapkan (Kamchatka)	Synonym of Kopkan	....
Kapoho (Hawaiian Is)	Tuff cone of Kilauea	1302-01-
Kapor, Piton (Indian O.-W)	Fissure vent of Fournaise, Piton de la	0303-02=
Kapundan (Indonesian for Crater) see proper name (e.g. Bongsu, Kapundan)		
Kapusikeju (Africa-E)	Cone of Emuruangogolak	0202-051
Kar, Las (Chile-N)	Synonym of Láscar	1505-10=
Kara Divlit Tepe (Turkey)	Cinder cone of Kula	0103-00-
Karabuki (Honshu-Japan)	Thermal feature of Kusatsu-Shirane	0803-12=
Karaca Dag (Turkey)	Shield volcano (None) Holocene	**0103-011**
Karacalidag (Turkey)	Synonym of Karaca Dag	0103-011
Kara-gama (Honshu-Japan)	Crater of Kusatsu-Shirane	0803-12=
Karagülü Tepe (Turkey)	Dome of Erciyes Dagi	0103-01=
Karaha, Kawah (Java)	Fumarole field (Uncertain) Fumarolic	**0603-16=**
Karai, Mount [Ruckenberg] (New Britain)	Dome of Sulu Range	0502-09=
Karakuli (Kamchatka)	Dome of Diky Greben	1000-022
Karakuni-dake (Kyushu-Japan)	Stratovolcano of Kirishima	0802-09=
Karama (Africa-E)	Cone of Nyambeni Hills	0202-056
Karamu (New Zealand)	Cone of Pirongia	....
Karan (Kamchatka)	Dome of Shiveluch	1000-27=
Karang (Java)	Stratovolcano (None) Holocene?	**0603-02=**
Karangetang [Api Siau] (Indonesia)	Stratovolcano (49, 2010) Historical	**0607-02=**
Karapetiana [Uochtepeh] (Armenia)	Pyroclastic cone of Ghegam Ridge	0104-07-
Karapinar Field (Turkey)	Cinder cones (None) Holocene	**0103-001**
Karapiti [Craters of the Moon] (New Zealand)	Thermal feature of Maroa	0401-061
Karasivri Tepe (Turkey)	Cone of Erciyes Dagi	0103-01=
Karatala (Indian O.-W)	Synonym of Karthala	0303-01=
Karavia Bay (New Britain-SW Pac)	Stratovolcano of Rabaul	0502-14=
Karaviotis (Greece)	Dome of Nisyros	0102-05=
Kara-yama (Kyushu-Japan)	Stratovolcano of Ibusuki Volc Field	0802-07=
Kare-numa (Honshu-Japan)	Crater of Akita-Yake-yama	0803-26=
Kariang (Halmahera-Indonesia)	Stratovolcano of Dukono	0608-01=
Kariba (Hokkaido-Japan)	Stratovolcano (None) Pleistocene	....
Karimkotan (Kuril Is)	Synonym of Kharimkotan	0900-30=
Karimsky (Kamchatka)	Synonym of Karymsky	1000-13=
Karimui, Mt. (New Guinea)	Stratovolcano (None) Pleistocene	....
Karioi (New Zealand)	Stratovolcano (None) Pleistocene	....
Karisimbi (Africa-C)	Stratovolcano (1, -8050) K-Ar	**0203-04-**
Karita-dake (Honshu-Japan)	Synonym of Zao	0803-19=
Kariya (Africa-C)	Crater of Bunyaruguru	0203-004
Karkar (New Guinea-NE of)	Stratovolcano (11, 1979) Historical	**0501-03=**
Karlovy Vary (Czech)	Thermal feature of Cheb Basin	....
Karlsbad [Karlovy Vary] (Czech)	Thermal feature of Cheb Basin	....
Karmelenberg (Germany)	Cone of East Eifel Volc Field	....
Karniyarik (Turkey)	Dome of Acigöl-Nevsehir	0103-004
Karniyarik (Turkey)	Cone of Ararat	0103-04-
Karniyarik Tepeler (Turkey)	Cone of Erciyes Dagi	0103-01=
Karolero (Africa-C)	Crater of Bunyaruguru	0203-004
Karpinskii (Kuril Is)	Synonym of Karpinsky Group	0900-35=
Karpinskiy (Kamchatka)	Fissure vent of Kliuchevskoi	1000-26=
Karpinsky Group (Kuril Is)	Cones (1, 1952) Historical	**0900-35=**
Kars Plateau (Turkey)	Volcanic field (Uncertain) Holocene?	**0103-05-**
Karsa Kile (Africa-E)	Maar of Marsabit	0202-021
Karso, Kawah (Java)	Thermal feature of Galunggung	0603-14=
Kartala (Indian O.-W)	Synonym of Karthala	0303-01=
Karthala (Indian O.-W)	Shield volcano (34, 2007) Historical	**0303-01=**
Kartin Dag (Turkey)	Dome of Erciyes Dagi	0103-01=
Kartola (Indian O.-W)	Synonym of Karthala	0303-01=
Karua (Vanuatu-SW Pacific)	Submarine vent of Kuwae	0507-07=
Karymshina (Kamchatka)	Pleist. caldera of Bolshe-Bannaya	1000-087
Karymskaia Sopka (Kamchatka)	Synonym of Karymsky	1000-13=
Karymskaya River Springs (Kamchatka)	Thermal feature of Akademia Nauk	1000-125
Karymskoe, Lake (Kamchatka)	Synonym of Akademia Nauk	1000-125
Karymsky (Kamchatka)	Maar of Akademia Nauk	1000-125
Karymsky (Kamchatka)	Stratovolcano (48, 2010) Historical	**1000-13=**
Karymsky Lake (Kamchatka)	Synonym of Akademia Nauk	1000-125
Karymsky Lake (Kamchatka)	Pleistocene caldera of Akademia Nauk	1000-125
Karymsky Springs (Kamchatka)	Thermal feature of Karymsky	1000-13=
Kasaga-take (Honshu-Japan)	Shield volcano of Shiga	0803-121
Kasakat Hill (Africa-E)	Cone of Paka	0202-053
Kasatochi (Aleutian Is)	Stratovolcano (2, 2008) Historical	**1101-13-**
Kasavu (Fiji Is-SW Pacific)	Cone of Waikama	....
Kasa-yama (Honshu-Japan)	Cinder cone of Abu	0803-001
Kasa-yama (Honshu-Japan)	Dome of Iizuna	....
Kasbek (Georgia)	Stratovolcano (2, -750) Tephrochron	**0104-02-**
Kase, Mt. (New Guinea)	Cone of Darai Hills	....
Kasega-dake (Kyushu-Japan)	Dome of Ibusuki Volc Field	0802-07=
Kasekere (Africa-C)	Tuff cone of Fort Portal	0203-001
Kasenyi (Africa-C)	Tuff cone of Katwe-Kikorongo	0203-003
Kashaka (Africa-C)	Cone of Nyiragongo	0203-03=
Kashimine (Ryukyu Is)	Stratovolcano of Kuchinoerabu-jima	0802-05=
Kasiboi (Philippines-C)	Cone of Mahagnao	0702-07=
Kasidia (Africa-C)	Crater of Bunyaruguru	0203-004
Kasolali (New Britain-SW Pac)	Thermal feature of Pago	0502-08=
Kasshi-Asahi-dake (Honshu-Japan)	Stratovolcano of Nasu	0803-15=
Kassigie [Kassijie] (Madagascar)	Cone of Itasy Volc Field	0303-014
Kassijie (Madagascar)	Cone of Itasy Volc Field	0303-014
Kastanas (Greece)	Thermal feature of Mílos	0102-03=
Kastriulya (Kamchatka)	Shield volcano of Zaozerny	1000-48-
Kasuga (Volcano Is-Japan)	Submarine volcano (1, 1959) Historical	**0804-134**
Kasuga 1 (Volcano Is-Japan)	Synonym of Kasuga	0804-134
Kasuga 2 (Volcano Is-Japan)	Synonym of Minami Kasuga	0804-135
Kasugaba (Volcano Is-Japan)	Synonym of Kasuga	0804-134
Kasuga-kaizan (Volcano Is-Japan)	Synonym of Kasuga	0804-134
Kasuga-Minaminoba (Volcano Is-Japan)	Synonym of Minami Kasuga	0804-135
Katabuta-yama N (Honshu-Japan)	Cone of Fuji	0803-03=
Katabuta-yama S (Honshu-Japan)	Cone of Fuji	0803-03=
Katafaga (Fiji Is-SW Pacific)	Unknown (None) Pleistocene	....
Katahelu (Ethiopia)	Cone (None) Pleistocene	....
Katakura-yama (Honshu-Japan)	Cone of Akita-Komaga-take	0803-23=
Katalim (Africa-E)	Cone of Paka	0202-053
Katanuma (Honshu-Japan)	Crater of Narugo	0803-20=
Katasu Hill (Canada)	Cone of Milbanke Sound Group	1200-12-
Katete (Africa-E)	Stratovolcano (None) Post-Miocene	....
Katinda (Africa-C)	Crater of Bunyaruguru	0203-004
Katkatkono (Africa-N)	Crater of Meidob Volc Field	0205-05-
Katla (Iceland-S)	Subglacial volcano (128, 1918) Historical	**1702-03=**
Katlar (Iceland-SW)	Crater Row of Krísuvík	1701-03=
Katlogiaa (Iceland-S)	Synonym of Katla	1702-03=
Katmai (Alaska Peninsula)	Stratovolcano (1, 1912) Historical	**1102-17-**
Ka-Tsung (China-E)	Synonym of Jiacong	....
Katsu-yama (Hokkaido-Japan)	Crater of Okushiri-Katsuma-yama	....
Katsu-yama Nishi (Hokkaido-Japan)	Crater of Okushiri-Katsuma-yama	....
Katt, Cuddia del (Italy)	Cone of Pantelleria	0101-071
Katta-dake (Honshu-Japan)	Dome of Zao	0803-19=
Katuba (Africa-C)	Crater of Bunyaruguru	0203-004
Katubui (Africa-E)	Crater of Kieyo	0202-17=
Katumbuan (Mindanao-Philippines)	Dome of Leonard Range	0701-031
Katunga (Africa-C)	Tuff cone (None) Holocene	**0203-005**
Katwe (Africa-C)	Maar of Katwe-Kikorongo	0203-003
Katwe-Kikorongo (Africa-C)	Tuff cones (None) Holocene	**0203-003**
Katy Hill (W Indies)	Dome of Centre Hills	....
Kauai (Hawaiian Is)	Shield volcano (None) Pleistocene	....
Kauffman Volcano (Antarctica)	Shield volcano of Andrus	1900-023
Kauhako (Hawaiian Is)	Crater of East Molokai	....
Kauka, Puu (Hawaiian Is)	Cone of Kilauea	1302-01-
Kaula (Hawaiian Is)	Shield volcano (None) Pleistocene	....
Kaulet el-Hauri (Arabia-S)	Crater of Arhab, Harra of	0301-09-
Kaulet Hattab (Arabia-S)	Tuff cone of Arhab, Harra of	0301-09-
Kaumuki (Hawaiian Is)	Cone of Kilauea	1302-01-
Kaunnai (Hokkaido-Japan)	Cone of Tomuraushi Volc Group	....
Kaupo (Hawaiian Is)	Cone of Koolau	....
Kaupulehu (Hawaiian Is)	Cone of Hualalai	1302-04-
Kavachi (Solomon Is-SW Pacific)	Submarine volcano (30, 2007) Historical	**0505-06=**
Kavaklidag (Turkey)	Dome of Erciyes Dagi	0103-01=
Kaveterang (Africa-E)	Tuff ring of Silali	0202-052
Kavychinsky (Kamchatka)	Unknown (None) Pleistocene	....
Kawa (Luzon-Philippines)	Synonym of Cagua	0703-09=
Kawagodaira (Honshu-Japan)	Maar of Izu-Tobu	0803-01=
Kawah (Indonesian for Crater) see proper name (e.g. Baru, Kawah)		
Kawahkamojang (Java)	Synonym of Kamojang, Kawah	....

Chris Nye (Alaska DGGS/AVO)

Snowcapped symmetrical **Kanaga** stratovolcano in Alaska's Aleutian Islands was constructed within the large breached **Kanaton** caldera formed by edifice collapse. An eruptive period from mid-1993 through 1995 produced the two freshest-looking lava flows, which reached the coast on either side of the sea cliffs at the lower center.

Name (Subregion)	Type (Eruptions, Most Recent) Status / Relation to Named Volcano	Volcano Number
Kawahkaraha (Java)	Synonym of Karaha, Kawah	0603-16=
Kawaihoa (Hawaiian Is)	Tuff cone of Niihau	....
Kawak Butte (US-Oregon)	Cone of Newberry	1202-11-
Kawana-Minami (Honshu-Japan)	Cone of Izu-Tobu	0803-01=
Kawayu-Iwo-zan [Atosanupuri] (Japan)	Dome of Kutcharo	0805-08=
Kawdy Metah (Canada)	Volcanic field (None) Pleistocene	....
Kawdy Mountain (Canada)	Cone of Kawdy Metah	....
Kawdy Mountain South (Canada)	Tuya of Kawdy Metah	....
Kawdy Peaks (Canada)	Synonym of Kawdy Metah	....
Kawerau (New Zealand)	Thermal feature of Okataina	0401-05=
Kawi-Butak (Java)	Stratovolcanoes (None) Holocene	**0603-281**
Kawiti (New Zealand)	Cone of Kaikohe-Bay of Islands	0401-01=
Kayabenobori (Hokkaido-Japan)	Synonym of Komaga-take	0805-02=
Kayaga-take (Honshu-Japan)	Stratovolcano of Kurofuji	....
Kayalitepe (Turkey)	Cone of Nemrut Dagi	0103-02=

Name (Subregion)	Type (Eruptions, Most Recent) Status / Relation to Named Volcano	Volcano Number
Kayo (Honshu-Japan)	Stratovolcano (None) Pleistocene	....
Kazaana (Kyushu-Japan)	Dome of Unzen	0802-10=
Kazafuki-dake (Honshu-Japan)	Dome of Shirouma-Oike	....
Kazahaya (Izu Is-Japan)	Fissure vent of Miyake-jima	0804-04=
Kazbek (Georgia)	Synonym of Kasbek	0104-02-
Kazurahata (Honshu-Japan)	Cinder cone of Ogino-Sen	....
Kealaalea Hills (Hawaiian Is)	Shield volcano of Kilauea	1302-01-
Keanakakoi (Hawaiian Is)	Pit crater of Kilauea	1302-01-
Kebenei (Kamchatka)	Synonym of Kebeney	1000-50-
Kebeney (Kamchatka)	Shield volcano (None) Holocene?	**1000-50-**
Kebioka (Honshu-Japan)	Cinder cone of Ogino-Sen	....
Kebongo (Africa-E)	Cone of Korosi	0202-054
Kebrit Ale (Ethiopia)	Synonym of Gada Ale	0201-05=
Kebun Bungo (Sumatra)	Crater of Marapi	0601-14=

Nicolas Villenueve (Univ. Réunion)

The ~ 300-m-diameter Chahalé crater occupies the summit caldera complex of **Karthala** volcano on Grand Comore Island in the Indian Ocean. Karthala is the southernmost and largest of the two shield volcanoes forming Grand Comore (also known as Ngazidja Island) and contains a 3 x 4 km summit caldera generated by repeated collapse.

Name (Subregion)	Type (Eruptions, Most Recent) Status / Relation to Named Volcano	Volcano Number
Kechii [Kuraiswa] (Africa-E)	Vent of Korosi	0202-054
Kechucavi of Molina (Chile-S)	Synonym of Minchinmávida	1508-04=
Kecil, Danau (Sumatra)	Crater of Talang	0601-16=
Kecil, Kaba [Baru, Kaba] (Sumatra)	Crater of Kaba	0601-22=
Keciri, Gunung (Java)	Pleist. caldera of Tengger Caldera	0603-31=
Keelung (Taiwan)	Synonym of Chilung Group	....
Kefeli (Turkey)	Cone of Erciyes Dagi	0103-01=
Kefenli Tepe (Turkey)	Cone of Erciyes Dagi	0103-01=
Keigetsu-dake (Hokkaido-Japan)	Dome of Daisetsu	0805-06=
Keigetsu-dake [Keigetsu-dake] (Japan)	Dome of Daisetsu	0805-06=
Keilambete, Lake (Australia)	Maar of Newer Volcanics Prov	0509-01-
Keizuka-yama (Honshu-Japan)	Shield volcano of Nikko-Shirane	0803-14=
Kekau, Gunung [Bukit Melayu] (Indonesia)	Cone of Gamalama	0608-06=
Kekep, Gunung (Java)	Cone of Sundoro	0603-21=
Kekexili (China-W)	Caldera of Unnamed	1004-04-
Kekuk Crater (Kamchatka)	Crater of Bolshoi-Kekuknaysky	1000-36-
Kekuknaysky (Kamchatka)	Shield volcano Bolshoi-Kekuknaysky	1000-36-
Kekurny (Kamchatka)	Shield volcanoes (None) Holocene?	**1000-41-**
Kelakirana Tepe (Turkey)	Cone of Nemrut Dagi	0103-02=
Kelalang (Sumatra)	Cone of Kembar	....
Kelang, Mt. (Sulawesi-Indonesia)	Cone of Klabat	0606-12=
Kelbey's Ridge (W Indies)	Dome of Saba	1600-01=
Kelbey's Ridge (W Indies)	Dome of Saba	1600-01=
Kelibara (Lesser Sunda Is)	Cone of Kelimutu	0604-14=
Kelido (Lesser Sunda Is)	Cone of Kelimutu	0604-14=
Kelimutu (Lesser Sunda Is)	Complex volcano (3, 1968) Historical	**0604-14=**
Kell (Kamchatka)	Stratovolcanoes (None) Holocene	**1000-041**
Kell (Kamchatka)	Fissure vent of Kliuchevskoi	1000-26=
Kelly Butte (US-Oregon)	Cone of Boring Lava	....
Kelly Butte (US-Oregon)	Cone of Newberry	1202-11-
Kellya (Kamchatka)	Synonym of Kell	1000-041
Keloet (Keluit) (Java)	Synonym of Kelut	0603-28=
Kelsay Point (US-Oregon)	Cinder cone of Cinnamon Butte	1202-15-
K'elt'aeni (Alaska-E)	Synonym of Wrangell	1105-02-
Kelud (Keloed) (Java)	Synonym of Kelut	0603-28=
Keluo Group (China-E)	Pyroclastic cones (None) Holocene	**1005-02-**
Keluonanshan [Nanshan] (China-E)	Cinder cone of Keluo Group	1005-02-
Kelut (Java)	Stratovolcano (36, 2008) Historical	**0603-28=**
Kembang, Gunung (Java)	Cone of Slamet	0603-18=
Kembang, Gunung (Java)	Cone of Sundoro	0603-21=
Kembar (Sumatra)	Shield volcano (None) Pleist.-Fumarolic	....
Kembar North (Java)	Cone of Arjuno-Welirang	0603-29=
Kembar South (Java)	Cone of Arjuno-Welirang	0603-29=
Kembar, Gunung (Java)	Cone of Arjuno-Welirang	0603-29=
Kemenesalja (Hungary)	Volcanic field (None) Pleistocene	....
Kemmerling (Java)	Crater of Semeru	0603-30=
Kemoentjoep, Gunung [Gunung Kemuncup]	Dome of Penanggungan	0603-291
Kemulan (Java)	Stratovolcano of Dieng Volc Complex	0603-20=
Kemuncup, Gunung (Java)	Dome of Penanggungan	0603-291
Kena (Canada)	Cone of Edziza	1200-06-
Kenashi (Honshu-Japan)	Stratovolcano (None) Pleistocene	....
Kenashi-yama (Honshu-Japan)	Dome of Iizuna	....
Kenashi-yama (Honshu-Japan)	Dome of Okiura	....
Kendalisodo, Gunung (Java)	Cone of Ungaran	0603-23=
Kendang (Java)	Stratovolcano (None) Holocene	**0603-11=**
Kendeng (Java)	Caldera of Ijen	0603-35=
Kendeng (Java)	Synonym of Kendang	0603-11=
Kendeng (Java)	Stratovolcano (None) Quaternary	....
Kendil (Java)	Dome of Dieng Volc Complex	0603-20=
Kendil, Gunung (Java)	Cone of Telomoyo	0603-231
Kendrick Peak (US-Arizona)	Cone of San Francisco Volc Field	....
Kenfield Nunatak (Antarctica)	Cone of Hudson Mountains	1900-028
Kengamine (Honshu-Japan)	Dome of Haku-san	0803-05=
Kenga-mine (Hokkaido-Japan)	Cone of Akan	0805-07=
Kennedy Hot Springs (US-Washington)	Thermal feature of Glacier Peak	1201-02-
Kent Crater (Indian O.)	Tuff cone of Prince Edward Island	0304-06-
Kenton, Cerro (México)	Cinder cone of San Quintín Volc Field	1401-002
Kenze (Africa-E)	Cone of Chyulu Hills	0202-13=
Keo Peak (Lesser Sunda Is)	Synonym of Ebulobo	0604-10=
Keonehunehune (Hawaiian Is)	Cone of Haleakala	1302-06-
Keonenelu (Hawaiian Is)	Cone of Haleakala	1302-06-
Kepala, Gunung [Gunung Kepolo] (Java)	Stratovolcano of Semeru	0603-30=
Kepez Tepe (Turkey)	Dome of Erciyes Dagi	0103-01=
Kepolo, Gunung (Java)	Stratovolcano of Semeru	0603-30=
Kepundan (Indonesian for Crater) see proper name (e.g. Tuo, Kepundan)		
Keramat, Bukit (Halmahera-Indonesia)	Cone of Gamalama	0608-06=
Keraroa (New Guinea)	Synonym of Victory	0503-03=
Keravia [Vulcan] (New Britain-SW Pac)	Pumice cone of Rabaul	0502-14=
Kerekerdo (Hungary)	Vent of Nográd	....
Kerekere, Vuti (Vanuatu-SW Pacific)	Cone of Aoba	0507-03=
Kerem (Turkey)	Cone of Erciyes Dagi	0103-01=
Kerewa (New Guinea)	Stratovolcano (None) Pleistocene	....
Kerguelen Islands (Indian O.-S)	Stratovolcanoes (None) Holocene?	**0304-02=**
Kerholl (Iceland-SW)	Crater of Grímsnes	1701-06=
Keri (New Zealand)	Cone of Kaikohe-Bay of Islands	0401-01=
Kerid (Iceland-SW)	Maar of Grímsnes	1701-06=
Kerimasi (Africa-E)	Stratovolcano (None) Pleistocene	....
Kerinci (Sumatra)	Stratovolcano (30, 2009) Historical	**0601-17=**
Kerintji (Sumatra)	Synonym of Kerinci	0601-17=
Kerkorumiksi Tepe (Turkey)	Cone of Nemrut Dagi	0103-02=
Kerkur (Turkey)	Dome of Nemrut Dagi	0103-02=
Kerlingardynga (Iceland-NE)	Shield volcano of Fremrinamur	1703-07=
Kerlingarfjöll (Iceland-SW)	Stratovolcano of Hofsjökull	1701-09=
Kerlingarholar (Iceland-NE)	Fissure vent of Krafla	1703-08=
Kerlingarholl (Iceland-SW)	Crater Row of Grímsnes	1701-06=
Keruar (New Guinea-NE of)	Synonym of Kadovar	0501-002
Kesemaru-yama (Honshu-Japan)	Stratovolcano of Sukai-Kesemaru	....
Keten (Halmahera-Indonesia)	Synonym of Moti	0608-063
Ketetahi (New Zealand)	Thermal feature of Tongariro	0401-08=
Ketil [Ketildyngja] (Iceland-NE)	Shield volcano of Fremrinamur	1703-07=
Ketildyngja (Iceland-NE)	Shield volcano of Fremrinamur	1703-07=
Ketjil, Danau [Danau Kecil] (Sumatra)	Crater of Talang	0601-16=
Ketjil, Kaba [Baru, Kaba] (Sumatra)	Crater of Kaba	0601-22=
Keto Keto, Maunga (Chile-Is)	Pyroclastic cone of Easter Island	1506-011
Ketoi (Kuril Is)	Stratovolcano (3, 1960) Historical	**0900-20=**
Ketoi-jima (Ketoy) (Kuril Is)	Synonym of Ketoi	0900-20=
Ketredeguin (Chile-C)	Synonym of Lonquimay	1507-10=
Ketrudehuin (Chile-C)	Synonym of Callaqui	1507-091
Ketumbeine (Africa-E)	Shield volcano (None) Pleistocene	....
Keveney (Kamchatka)	Shield volcano (None) Pleistocene	....
Keveneytunup (Kamchatka)	Shield volcano of Bely	1000-64-
Keyhole Explosion Crater (US-Oregon)	Crater of Diamond Craters	1202-17-
Keyocc, Cerro (Perú)	Cinder cone of Huambo	1504-005
Khadutka (Kamchatka)	Synonym of Khodutka	1000-053
Khaggiar (Italy)	Dome of Pantelleria	0101-071
Khaginak ? (Aleutian Is)	Synonym of Roundtop	1101-38-
Khaibar, Harrat el- (Arabia-W)	Synonym of Khaybar, Harrat	0301-06=
Khaiber, Harrat el- (Arabia-W)	Synonym of Khaybar, Harrat	0301-06=
Khailyulya (Kamchatka)	Unknown (None) Pleistocene	....
Khala [Pechan] (China-W)	Cone of Tianshan Volc Group	1004-02-
Khalzan-Shapochka (Kamchatka)	Shield volcano (None) Pleistocene	....
Khamar-Daban (Russia-SE)	Volcanic field (None) Quaternary	....
Khamchenskaya, Sopka (Kamchatka)	Synonym of Gamchen	1000-21=
Khamma, Cuddia (Italy)	Shield volcano of Pantelleria	0101-071
Khamsara-Biykhem Plateau (Russia-SE)	Synonym of Azas Plateau	1002-07-
Khamsara-Bol'shoi Yenisei (Russia-SE)	Synonym of Azas Plateau	1002-07-
Khangar (Kamchatka)	Stratovolcano (10, 1500) Radiocarbon	**1000-272**
Khangura (Russia-SE)	Cone of Udokan Plateau	1002-03-
Khanuy Gol (Mongolia)	Volcanic field (None) Holocene	**1003-02-**
Khao Phloi Waen (SE Asia)	Cone of Chanthaburi	....
Khara Laguna (Bolivia)	Synonym of Chascon, Cerro	....
Khara-Boldok (Russia-SE)	Cone of Tunkin Depression	1002-05-
Kharchinsky (Kamchatka)	Stratovolcano (None) Pleistocene	....
Kharimkotan (Kuril Is)	Stratovolcano (6, 1933) Historical	**0900-30=**
Khartibucale (Italy)	Cone of Pantelleria	0101-071
Khaybar, Harrat (Arabia-W)	Volcanic field (1, 650) Historical	**0301-06=**
Khaynanj (SE Asia)	Synonym of Hainan Dao	0705-001
Khebrit, Djebel (Red Sea)	Synonym of Tair, Jebel at	0201-01=
Khetik (Kamchatka)	Shield volcano of Ostanets	1000-055
Khloridnoe Lake (Kamchatka)	Maar of Uzon	1000-17=
Khoashen (Kamchatka)	Synonym of Ichinsky	1000-28=

Name (Subregion)	Type (Eruptions, Most Recent) Status Relation to Named Volcano	Volcano Number
Khobok Group (Russia-SE)	Cone of Tunkin Depression	1002-05-
Khodukta Springs (Kamchatka)	Thermal feature of Khodutka	1000-053
Khodutka (Kamchatka)	Stratovolcanoes (3, -300) Radiocarbon	**1000-053**
Khodutkinsky (Kamchatka)	Maar of Khodutka	1000-053
Khoiokhongen (Kamchatka)	Synonym of Khodutka	1000-053
Khonarassar (Armenia)	Cone of Porak	0104-09-
Khorog (Mongolia)	Cinder cone of Taryatu-Chulutu	1003-01-
Khubsugal Region (Mongolia)	Volcanic field (None) Quaternary	....
Khulugayshi (Russia-SE)	Explosion crater (None) Quaternary	....
Khurai-Tsakir (Russia-SE)	Cinder cone of Dgida Basin	....
Khurdj El-Aisar (Arabia-S)	Tuff cone of Haylan, Jabal	0301-11-
Khutsi (Honshu-Japan)	Synonym of Fuji	0803-03=
Khutza-Ula (Mongolia)	Unknown (None) Pleistocene?	....
Khuvkhoitun (Kamchatka)	Complex volcano (None) Pleistocene	....
Kialagvik (Alaska Peninsula)	Stratovolcano (None) Holocene	**1102-12-**
Kiamis, Gunung (Java)	Dome of Kendang	0603-11=
Kiapu (Hawaiian Is)	Cone of Kilauea	1302-01-
Kiaraberes (Java)	Crater of Perbakti-Gagak	0603-04=
Kibati (Africa-C)	Cone of Nyiragongo	0203-03=
Kibikoni (Africa-E)	Dome of Olkaria	0202-09=
Kibithewa (Africa-E)	Pyroclastic cone of Nyambeni Hills	0202-056
Kibo (Africa-E)	Stratovolcano of Kilimanjaro	0202-15=
Kibongoto (Africa-E)	Cone of Kilimanjaro	0202-15=
Kibreale (Ethiopia)	Synonym of Gada Ale	0201-05=
Kichpinitsch (Kamchatka)	Synonym of Kikhpinych	1000-18=
Kichwambe Volc Field (Africa-C)	Synonym of Bunyaruguru	0203-004
Kick 'em Jack (W Indies)	Submarine vent of Kick 'em Jenny	1600-16=
Kick 'em Jenny (W Indies)	Submarine volcano (13, 2001) Historical	**1600-16=**
Kicker Rock (Galápagos)	Tuff cone of San Cristóbal	1503-12-
Kie Besi (Halmahera-Indonesia)	Synonym of Makian	0608-07=
Kiematabu, Bukit (Halmahera-Indonesia)	Stratovolcano of Tidore	0608-061
Kieyo (Africa-E)	Stratovolcano (1, 1800) Historical	**0202-17=**
Kiezu-ike (Honshu-Japan)	Crater of Norikura	0803-06=
Kifune (Honshu-Japan)	Cinder cone of Mutsure-jima	....
Kigalgin (Aleutian Is)	Synonym of Carlisle	1101-23-
Kigamil (Kigamiljach) (Aleutian Is)	Synonym of Kagamil	1101-26-
Kigere (Africa-C)	Tuff cone of Fort Portal	0203-001
Kigezi (Africa-C)	Crater of Bunyaruguru	0203-004
Kigo-yama (Honshu-Japan)	Dome of Tomuro	....
Kiguga Warm Springs (Aleutian Is)	Thermal feature of Moffett	1101-111
Kijongo Kalema (Africa-C)	Tuff cone of Fort Portal	0203-001
Kijongo Katabyire (Africa-C)	Tuff cone of Fort Portal	0203-001
Kikai (Ryukyu Is)	Caldera (22, 2004) Historical	**0802-06=**
Kikaiga-shima (Ryukyu Is)	Synonym of Kikai	0802-06=
Kikdooli Butte (Alaska-W)	Cone of Nunivak Island	1104-02-
Kikhiikhylkhangei (Kamchatka)	Cone (None) Pleistocene	....
Kikhpinych (Kamchatka)	Synonym of Bolshoi Semiachik	1000-15=
Kikhpinych (Kamchatka)	Stratovolcanoes (8, 1550) Radiocarbon	**1000-18=**
Kikikyak Hill (Alaska-W)	Cone of Nunivak Island	1104-02-
Kikombe (Africa-C)	Cone of Karisimbi	0203-04-
Kikorongo (Africa-C)	Tuff cone of Katwe-Kikorongo	0203-003
Kilauea (Hawaiian Is)	Shield volcano (95, 2010) Historical	**1302-01-**
Kilauea (Hawaiian Is)	Caldera of Kilauea	1302-01-
Kilauea Iki (Hawaiian Is)	Pit crater of Kilauea	1302-01-
Kilbourne Hole (US-New Mexico)	Maar of Potrillo Volc Field	....
Kilchu-Myongch'on (Korea)	Volcanic field (None) Pleistocene	....
Kilema (Africa-E)	Cone of Kilimanjaro	0202-15=
Kileo (Africa-E)	Cone of Kilimanjaro	0202-15=
Kilian Cratere (France)	Dome of Chaîne des Puys	0100-02-
Kilima Dscharo (Kilima Njaro) (Africa-E)	Synonym of Kilimanjaro	0202-15=
Kilimandjaro (Africa-E)	Synonym of Kilimanjaro	0202-15=
Kilimanjaro (Africa-E)	Stratovolcano (None) Holocene	**0202-15=**
Kilohana Crater (Hawaiian Is)	Shield volcano of Kauai	....
Kilole (Ethiopia)	Tuff ring of Bishoftu Volc Field	0201-22-
Kilombe Caldera (Africa-E)	Caldera (None) Pleistocene?	....
Kimanura (Africa-C)	Cone of Nyamuragira	0203-02=
Kimbe (New Britain-SW Pac)	Stratovolcano (None) Post-Miocene	....
Kimen-zan (Honshu-Japan)	Dome of Adatara	0803-17=
Kimera (Africa-C)	Cone of Nyamuragira	0203-02=
Kimijooksuk Butte (Alaska-W)	Cone of Nunivak Island	1104-02-
Kimiksthek Hill (Alaska-W)	Cone of Nunivak Island	1104-02-
Kimikthak Hills (Alaska-W)	Cone of Nunivak Island	1104-02-
Kimilos (Greece)	Cone of Mílos	0102-03=
Kimitina (Kamchatka)	Stratovolcano (None) Pleistocene	....
Kimpo (Kyushu-Japan)	Synonym of Kinpo	....
Kimsachata (Perú)	Synonym of Quimsachata	1504-00-
Kinami (New Ireland-SW Pacific)	Stratovolcano of Lihir	0504-01=
Kinanga (Africa-E)	Cone of Kilimanjaro	0202-15=
Kinchokla (Kamchatka)	Synonym of Nikolka	....
Kinenin (Kamchatka)	Maar (1, 850) Radiocarbon	**1000-551**
King Creek (Canada)	Cone of Iskut-Unuk River Cones	1200-09-
King Mountain Fissure (US-Washington)	Fissure vent of Adams	1201-04-
Kingiri (Africa-E)	Maar of Kieyo	0202-17=
King's Bowl Rift (US-Idaho)	Fissure vent of Wapi Lava Field	1204-03-
Kinia River (Alaska-W)	Cinder cones (None) Post-Miocene	....
Kiniha (Africa-C)	Cone of Nyiragongo	0203-03=
Kino Crater (México)	Maar of Pinacate	1401-001
Kinpo (Kyushu-Japan)	Stratovolcano (None) Pleistocene	....
Kinpo-san (Honshu-Japan)	Synonym of Tokuyama-Mitake	....
Kinrara (Australia)	Cone of McBride Volc Province	....
Kinugasa (Kyushu-Japan)	Stratovolcano of Unzen	0802-10=
Kinunuma-Nenakusa (Honshu-Japan)	Lava domes (None) Pleistocene	....

Tom Casadevall (USGS)

The renowned double crater lakes of **Kelimutu** volcano on Indonesia's Flores Island display variable water colors and are separated by a narrow septum about 35 m high. Phreatic eruptions have occurred from the left-hand lake in the 19th and 20th centuries, and continuous upwelling occurs at both lakes.

Name (Subregion)	Type (Eruptions, Most Recent) Status / Relation to Named Volcano	Volcano Number
Kinyach [Getang] (Africa-E)	Crater of Korosi	0202-054
Kinyambatsha (Africa-C)	Cone of Nyiragongo	0203-03=
Kinyamuaga (Africa-C)	Cone of Nyamuragira	0203-02=
Kinyangaki (Africa-C)	Cone of Karisimbi	0203-04-
Kioga (Africa-E)	Cone of Kieyo	0202-17=
Kiolik Hill (Alaska-W)	Cone of Nunivak Island	1104-02-
Kipuka Hill (Atlantic-S)	Cinder cone of Tristan da Cunha	1806-01=
Kipyascheye lake (Kuril Is)	Crater of Golovnin	0900-01=
Kipyashchaya (Kuril Is)	Pleistocene caldera of Baransky	0900-08=
Kiraro (Africa-E)	Cone of Nyambeni Hills	0202-056
Kirauea (Hawaiian Is)	Synonym of Kilauea	1302-01-
Kirchweiler (Germany)	Maar of West Eifel Volc Field	0100-01-
Kirerema (Africa-C)	Cone of Karisimbi	0203-04-
Kireunsky (Kamchatka)	Cinder cone of Alney-Chashakondzha	1000-45-
Kireunsky (Kamchatka)	Shield volcano (None) Pleistocene	....
Kirgurich (Kamchatka)	Fissure vent of Kliuchevskoi	1000-26=
Kirifuki (Kuril Is)	Synonym of Asyrmintar	0900-33=
Kirigamine (Honshu-Japan)	Shield volcano (None) Pleistocene	....
Kirikiripu (New Zealand)	Cone of Karioi	....
Kirima-Itune (Africa-E)	Cone of Nyambeni Hills	0202-056
Kirishima (Kyushu-Japan)	Shield volcano (74, 2008) Historical	**0802-09=**
Kirisima (Kyushu-Japan)	Synonym of Kirishima	0802-09=
Kirkjufell (Iceland-S)	Tuya of Torfajökull	1702-05=
Kirkjufell [Eldfell] (Iceland-S)	Fissure vent of Vestmannaeyjar	1702-01=
Kirkor Dagi [Kerkur] (Turkey)	Dome of Nemrut Dagi	0103-02=
Kirmizi Tepe (Turkey)	Cone of Erciyes Dagi	0103-01=
Kirtik (Russia-SW)	Unknown (None) Quaternary	....
Kirunga Cha Nina Gongo (Africa-C)	Synonym of Nyiragongo	0203-03=
Kirunga I (Africa-C)	Cone of Nyiragongo	0203-03=
Kirunga Visoke (Africa-C)	Synonym of Visoke	0203-05-
Kirunge Cha Niragongo (Africa-C)	Synonym of Nyiragongo	0203-03=
Kirunge Ya Gongo (Africa-C)	Synonym of Nyiragongo	0203-03=
Kirungo Cha Gongo (Africa-C)	Synonym of Nyiragongo	0203-03=
Kirungu Tscha Gongo (Africa-C)	Synonym of Nyiragongo	0203-03=
Kirungu Tscha Gongwe (Africa-C)	Synonym of Nyiragongo	0203-03=
Kirutale [Kituharu] (Africa-C)	Cone of Nyamuragira	0203-02=
Kisangasi (Africa-E)	Cone of Katete	....
Kishb, Harrat (Arabia-W)	Volcanic field (None) Holocene	**0301-071**
Kishima-dake (Kyushu-Japan)	Stratovolcano of Aso	0802-11=
Kisir Dagi (Turkey)	Unknown (None) Pleistocene	....
Kiska (Aleutian Is)	Stratovolcano (4, 1990) Historical	**1101-02-**
Kisko (Hungary)	Cone of Nográd	....
Kislaz [Nagylaz] (Hungary)	Vent of Balaton Highland	....
Kislyi Klyuch (Russia-SE)	Cone of Udokan Plateau	1002-03-
Kiso-ontake (Honshu-Japan)	Synonym of On-take	0803-04=
Kissalgovar (Hungary)	Cone of Nográd	....
Kissoba (Africa-E)	Crater of Kieyo	0202-17=
Kissomlo (Hungary)	Cone of Kemenesalja	....
Kissomlyo (Hungary)	Cone of Nográd	....

Katia and Maurice Krafft

A cluster of nested craters occupies the summit of 5895-m-high **Kilimanjaro**, Africa's highest volcano. This view looks ESE to Mawenzi, a dissected stratovolcano that is one of three forming the broad Kilimanjaro massif. The low ridge above the crater complex at the left is part of the rapidly disappearing, steep-sided summit icecap.

Name (Subregion)	Type (Eruptions, Most Recent) Status / Relation to Named Volcano	Volcano Number
Kisszilvasko (Hungary)	Cone of Nográd	....
Kista (Iceland-SW)	Crater Row of Brennisteinsfjöll	1701-04=
Kistufell (Iceland-SW)	Fissure vent of Brennisteinsfjöll	1701-04=
Kistufell (Iceland-NE)	Tuya (None) Pleistocene	....
Kistufellsgjoska (Iceland-NE)	Fissure vent of Askja	1703-06=
Kistufellshraun (Iceland-NE)	Crater Row of Askja	1703-06=
Kita Yatsuga-take (Honshu-Japan)	Stratovolcanoes (2, 1200) Radiocarbon	**0803-031**
Kita-Bayonnaise (Izu Is-Japan)	Synonym of Myojin Knoll	0804-061
Kitabud (Mindanao-Philippines)	Unknown (None) Pleistocene	....
Kita-Chirippu (Kuril Is)	Synonym of Chirip	0900-09=
Kita-dake (Kyushu-Japan)	Stratovolcano of Sakura-jima	0802-08=
Kita-dake (Hokkaido-Japan)	Crater of Shiretoko-Iwo-zan	0805-09=
Kita-Fukutokutai (Volcano Is-Japan)	Submarine volcano (1, 1954) Historical	**0804-121**
Kitagawa (Honshu-Japan)	Thermal feature of Kusatsu-Shirane	0803-12=
Kita-Hiyoshi (Volcano Is-Japan)	Submarine vent of Minami-Hiyoshi	0804-131
Kitaio (Kuril Is)	Synonym of Kuntomintar	....
Kita-Iwo-dake (Kuril Is)	Synonym of Kuntomintar	....
Kita-Iwo-jima (Volcano Is-Japan)	Stratovolcano (3, 1945) Historical	**0804-11=**
Kita-Kansu-yama (Honshu-Japan)	Cone of Fuji	0803-03=
Kita-Kori-ike (Honshu-Japan)	Vent of Fuji	0803-03=
Kitanohara-Higashi (Honshu-Japan)	Maar of Izu-Tobu	0803-01=
Kita-Senrigahama (Kyushu-Japan)	Crater of Kuju	0802-12=
Kita-Tajima Volc Group (Honshu-Japan)	Synonym of Kannabe	....
Kita-Tirippu (Kuril Is)	Synonym of Chirip	0900-09=
Kita-yama (Hokkaido-Japan)	Cone of Akan	0805-07=
Kita-yama (Hokkaido-Japan)	Stratovolcano of Shikotsu	0805-04=
Kita-Yatsuga-take (Honshu-Japan)	Synonym of Kita Yatsuga-take	0803-031
Kita-Yatuga-take (Honshu-Japan)	Synonym of Kita Yatsuga-take	0803-031
Kita-Zao (Honshu-Japan)	Synonym of Ganto-Kamuro	....
Kitazungurwa (Africa-C)	Cone of Nyamuragira	0203-02=
Kitema (Africa-E)	Cone of Kieyo	0202-17=
Kithetu Hill (Africa-E)	Pyroclastic cone of Nyambeni Hills	0202-056
Kitia (Madagascar)	Dome of Itasy Volc Field	0303-014
Kitkhoysky (Kamchatka)	Shield volcanoes (None) Pleistocene	....
Kitombold (Madagascar)	Cone of Itasy Volc Field	0303-014
Kitshimbany [Kitsimbanyi] (Africa-C)	Cone of Nyamuragira	0203-02=
Kitsimbanyi (Africa-C)	Cone of Nyamuragira	0203-02=
Kittiwake Pond (Aleutian Is)	Maar of Buldir	1101-01-
Kituharu (Africa-C)	Cone of Nyamuragira	0203-02=
Kitumbeine (Africa-E)	Synonym of Ketumbeine	....
Kituro [Gituro] (Africa-C)	Cone of Nyamuragira	0203-02=
Kivandimwe (Africa-C)	Cone of Nyamuragira	0203-02=
Kiyomi-dake (Kyushu-Japan)	Dome of Ibusuki Volc Field	0802-07=
Kizdagi (Turkey)	Dome of Süphan Dagi	0103-021
Kizil Tepe (Turkey)	Cone of Acigöl-Nevsehir	0103-004
Kizil Tepe (Turkey)	Cinder cone of Erciyes Dagi	0103-01=
Kizilkuyu Tepe (Turkey)	Cone of Erciyes Dagi	0103-01=
Kizima-dake [Kishima-dake] (Kyushu-Japan)	Stratovolcano of Aso	0802-11=
Kizimen (Kamchatka)	Stratovolcano (10, 1928) Historical	**1000-23=**
Kizinen (Kamchatka)	Synonym of Kizimen	1000-23=
Kjalhraun (Iceland-SW)	Shield volcano of Hveravellir	1701-08=
Klabat (Sulawesi-Indonesia)	Stratovolcano (None) Fumarolic	**0606-12=**
Klak Butte (US-Oregon)	Cinder cone of Bachelor	1202-09-
Klakah, Ranu (Java)	Maar of Lamongan	0603-32=
Klastline (Canada)	Cone of Edziza	1200-06-
Klastline Group (Canada)	Cinder cones (None) Pleistocene	....
Klawhop Butte (US-Oregon)	Cinder cone of Newberry	1202-11-
Kleine Ssemjatschik (Kamchatka)	Synonym of Karymsky	1000-13=
Kleshnya (Kamchatka)	Cinder cone of Tolbachik	1000-24=
Klinkit Creek Peak (Canada)	Tuya of Tuya Volc Field	1200-031
Klinkit Lake Volc Field (Canada)	Volcanic field of Tuya Volc Field	1200-031
Kliuchef (Aleutian Is)	Stratovolcano of Atka	1101-16-
Kliuchevskaia Sopka (Kamchatka)	Synonym of Kliuchevskoi	1000-26=
Kliuchevskoi (Kamchatka)	Stratovolcano (102, 2010) Historical	**1000-26=**
Kliuchevskoy [Kliuchef] (Aleutian Is)	Stratovolcano of Atka	1101-16-
Kljutschew (Kamchatka)	Synonym of Kliuchevskoi	1000-26=
Kljutschewskaja Ssopka (Kamchatka)	Synonym of Kliuchevskoi	1000-26=
Kloet (Java)	Synonym of Kelut	0603-28=
Klofningahraun (Iceland-SW)	Crater Row of Reykjanes	1701-02=
Klone Butte (US-Oregon)	Cinder cone of Newberry	1202-11-
Kluchev (Kamchatka)	Synonym of Kliuchevskoi	1000-26=
Klumba (Kuril Is)	Cone of Vetrovoi Isthmus Caldera	....
Klutlan Glacier (Alaska-E)	Synonym of Churchill	1105-03-
Klyuchevskaya (Kamchatka)	Synonym of Kliuchevskoi	1000-26=
Km 14, Cerro (Nicaragua)	Cinder cone of Nejapa-Miraflores	1404-092
Knappafellsjokull (Iceland-SE)	Synonym of Öraefajökull	1704-01=
Kniazeff (Mindanao-Philippines)	Dome of Leonard Range	0701-031
Kniazeff 2 (Mindanao-Philippines)	Dome of Leonard Range	0701-031
Knife Peak (Alaska Peninsula)	Synonym of Griggs	1102-19-
Knoll, the (Antarctica)	Cone of Terror, Mt.	....
Ko (New Britain-SW Pac)	Stratovolcano of Oto Group	....
Koa (Lesser Sunda Is)	Thermal feature of Paluweh	0604-15=
Koa [Ko] (New Britain-SW Pac)	Stratovolcano of Oto Group	....
Koa [Southern Dome] (New Zealand)	Dome of Okataina	0401-05=
Koae, Puu (Hawaiian Is)	Cone of Kilauea	1302-01-
Koang, Mt. (Australia)	Cone of Newer Volcanics Prov	0509-01-
Ko-Asama-yama (Honshu-Japan)	Dome of Asama	0803-11=
Ko-Atosanupuri (Hokkaido-Japan)	Stratovolcano of Kutcharo	0805-08=
Kobalan (Kamchatka)	Stratovolcano (None) Pleistocene	....
Kobandai (Honshu-Japan)	Stratovolcano of Bandai	0803-16=
Kobayashi (Kyushu-Japan)	Pleistocene caldera of Kakuto	....
Kobe-yama (Izu Is-Japan)	Dome of Kozu-shima	0804-03=
Kobinai (Honshu-Japan)	Stratovolcano (None) Pleistocene	....
Kobi-sho (Ryukyu Is)	Stratovolcano (None) Pleistocene	....
Kobu-yama (Hokkaido-Japan)	Cone of Akan	0805-07=
Kocadag Tepe (Turkey)	Dome of Acigöl-Nevsehir	0103-004
Kocatepe [Kocadag Tepe] (Turkey)	Dome of Acigöl-Nevsehir	0103-004
Kocdagi (Turkey)	Stratovolcano of Erciyes Dagi	0103-01=
Kocher [Huoshaoshan] (China-E)	Cone of Wudalianchi	1005-03-
Kod Ali (Ethiopia)	Crater of Dubbi	0201-10=
Ko-dake (Honshu-Japan)	Cone of Akita-Komaga-take	0803-23=
Kodda Ginni Koma (Djibouti)	Tuff cone of Ardoukôba	0201-126
Koe-Koe (Chile-Is)	Fissure vent of Easter Island	1506-011
Koekoesan [Kukusan] (Java)	Cone of Ijen	0603-35=
Koenjit (Sumatra)	Synonym of Kunyit	0601-171
Koerinci (Koerintji) (Sumatra)	Synonym of Kerinci	0601-17=
Koerner Bluff (Antarctica)	Shield volcano of Bursey, Mt.	....
Koersi, Gunung [Gunung Kursi] (Java)	Cinder cone of Tengger Caldera	0603-31=
Koetlegiaa (Iceland-S)	Synonym of Katla	1702-03=

Name (Subregion)	Type (Eruptions, Most Recent) Status Relation to Named Volcano	Volcano Number
Ko-Fuji (Honshu-Japan)	Stratovolcano of Fuji	0803-03=
Kogaja-jima (Ryukyu Is)	Lava domes (None) Holocene?	**0802-041**
Koganegahara (Hokkaido-Japan)	Cone of Tomuraushi Volc Group	
Kohala (Hawaiian Is)	Shield volcano (None) Pleistocene	
Koh-i Bazman (Iran)	Synonym of Bazman	0302-03-
Koh-i Sultan (Pakistan)	Synonym of Sultan	
Koh-i Taftan (Iran)	Synonym of Taftan	0302-05-
Ko-Hiyoshi (Volcano Is-Japan)	Submarine vent of Minami-Hiyoshi	0804-131
Kohuora (New Zealand)	Tuff cone of Auckland Field	0401-02=
Koike (Honshu-Japan)	Vent of Izu-Tobu	0803-01=
Koilonga (Africa-E)	Cone of Sultan Hamud-Simba	
Koinaka-yama (Honshu-Japan)	Synonym of Fuji	0803-03=
Koizumi-dake (Hokkaido-Japan)	Stratovolcano of Daisetsu	0805-06=
Ko-jima (Izu Is-Japan)	Stratovolcano of Hachijo-jima	0804-05=
Kojin-yama (Honshu-Japan)	Dome of Chokai	0803-22=
Kok-Hem (Russia-SE)	Shield volcano of Azas Plateau	1002-07-
Kok-Hemskii [Kok-Hem} (Russia-SE)	Shield volcano of Azas Plateau	1002-07-
Kokhera (China-E)	Synonym of Wudalianchi	1005-03-
Kokh-i-Sultan (Pakistan)	Synonym of Sultan	
Kokkino Vouno (Greece)	Cinder cone of Santorini	0102-04=
Koko (Hawaiian Is)	Tuff cone of Koolau	
Koko Head (Hawaiian Is)	Tuff cone of Koolau	
Kokon (Banda Sea)	Synonym of Nila	0605-06=
Kokon-empung (Sulawesi-Indonesia)	Synonym of Lokon-Empung	0606-10=
Kokongo (New Zealand)	Cone of South Auckland	
Kokoolau (Hawaiian Is)	Cone of Kilauea	1302-01-
Kokor, Wai (Lesser Sunda Is)	Thermal feature of Poco Leok	0604-07=
Koksan-Singye (Korea)	Shield volcano (None) Pleistocene	
Kolanh Dag (Turkey)	Cone of Erciyes Dagi	0103-01=
Kolanli Dag (Turkey)	Dome of Erciyes Dagi	0103-01=
Kolbeinsey Ridge (Iceland-N of)	Submarine volcano (2, 1755) Historical	**1705-01=**
Kolbo, Gof (Africa-E)	Maar of Marsabit	0202-021
Kolchon (Kamchatka)	Synonym of Ichinsky	1000-28=
Koldukvislarhraun (Iceland-NE)	Fissure vent of Bárdarbunga	1703-03=
Kole, Puu (Hawaiian Is)	Cone of Mauna Kea	1302-03-
Kolekole (Hawaiian Is)	Cone of Haleakala	1302-06-
Kolekole, Puu (Hawaiian Is)	Cone of Kilauea	1302-01-
Kolgrafarholl (Iceland-SW)	Cone of Grímsnes	1701-06=
Kollóttadyngja (Iceland-NE)	Shield volcano of Askja	1703-06=
Kolo (Solomon Is-SW Pacific)	Synonym of Kanekolo, Mt.	
Kolob (US-Utah)	Volcanic field (None) Pleistocene	
Kolob Peak (US-Utah)	Cinder cone of Kolob	
Kolobochon (Africa-E)	Tuff ring of Korosi	0202-054
Kolokol (Kuril Is)	Stratovolcano of Kolokol Group	0900-12=
Kolokol Group (Kuril Is)	Somma volcanoes (9, 1973) Historical	**0900-12=**
Kolombangara (Solomon Is-SW Pacific)	Stratovolcano (None) Pleistocene	
K'o-lo-Nan-shan (China-E)	Synonym of Keluo Group	1005-02-
Kolumbangara (Solomon Is-SW Pacific)	Synonym of Kolombangara	
Koma Kulshan (US-Washington)	Synonym of Baker	1201-01=
Koma-dake (Honshu-Japan)	Synonym of Akita-Komaga-take	0803-23=
Komaga-take (Honshu-Japan)	Dome of Hakone	0803-02=
Komaga-take (Hokkaido-Japan)	Stratovolcano (19, 2000) Historical	**0805-02=**
Komaga-take (Honshu-Japan)	Synonym of Kurikoma	0803-21=
Komakata-yama (Honshu-Japan)	Synonym of Akita-Komaga-take	0803-23=
Komanago (Honshu-Japan)	Dome of Omanago Group	0803-142
Komarov (Kamchatka)	Stratovolcano (2, 950) Radiocarbon	**1000-22=**
Komarova (Kamchatka)	Synonym of Komarov	1000-22=
Kombang (Java)	Dome of Kelut	0603-28=
Kombiu (New Britain-SW Pac)	Stratovolcano of Rabaul	0502-14=
Kömboro (Solomon Is-SW Pacific)	Stratovolcano (None) Post-Miocene	
Kombosi (New Britain-SW Pac)	Dome of Unea	
Kombung (Admiralty Is-SW Pacific)	Cone of St. Andrew Strait	0500-01=
Kometsuka (Kyushu-Japan)	Cone of Aso	0802-11=
Komia (Greece)	Thermal feature of Milos	0102-03=
Komikasa-yama (Honshu-Japan)	Cone of On-take	0803-04=
Komitake (Honshu-Japan)	Stratovolcano of Fuji	0803-03=
Komochi-Onoko (Honshu-Japan)	Stratovolcanoes (None) Pleistocene	
Komochi-yama (Honshu-Japan)	Stratovolcano of Komochi-Onoko	
Komochi-yama (Izu Is-Japan)	Cone of Tori-shima	0804-09=
Komolion (Africa-E)	Vent of Korosi	0202-054
Komorni Hurka (Czech)	Cinder cone of Cheb Basin	
Komoti-Onoko (Honshu-Japan)	Synonym of Komochi-Onoko	
Komoti-yama [Komochi-yama] (Izu Is-Japan)	Cone of Tori-shima	0804-09=
Kompira-yama (Hokkaido-Japan)	Dome of Usu	0805-03=
Komuro-yama (Honshu-Japan)	Cone of Izu-Tobu	0803-01=
Kone (Ethiopia)	Calderas (1, 1820) Historical	**0201-20-**
Konechnaya (Kamchatka)	Shield volcano (None) Pleistocene	
Kongolo (Africa-E)	Dome of SW Usangu Basin	0202-163
Kongsfell (Iceland-SW)	Crater Row of Brennisteinsfjöll	1701-04=
Koni (Ethiopia)	Synonym of Kone	0201-20-
Konia (Aleutian Is)	Stratovolcano of Korovin	1101-161
Koniuji (Aleutian Is)	Stratovolcano (3, -1150) Ar/Ar	**1101-14-**
Koniushi (Aleutian Is)	Synonym of Koniuji	1101-14-
Kono (Honshu-Japan)	Crater of Akagi	0803-13=
Konocti, Mt. (US-California)	Dome of Clear Lake	1203-10-
Konpira-yama [Kompira-yama] (Japan)	Dome of Usu	0805-03=
Konradi (Kamchatka)	Stratovolcano (None) Pleistocene	
Konsei-zan (Honshu-Japan)	Dome of Nikko-Shirane	0803-14=
Kontaro (Greece)	Dome of Milos	0102-03=
Konwonsavaro (Vanuatu-SW Pacific)	Crater of Suretamatai	0507-01=
Kookooligit Mountains (Alaska-W)	Shield volcano (None) Holocene	**1104-05-**
Kookoolit Hill (Alaska-W)	Cone of Kookooligit Mountains	1104-05-
Koolau (Hawaiian Is)	Shield volcano (None) Pleistocene	
Kooper [Laguna Río Cuarto] (Costa Rica)	Maar of Poás	1405-04=

Name (Subregion)	Type (Eruptions, Most Recent) Status Relation to Named Volcano	Volcano Number
Kopacsihegy (Hungary)	Cone of Balaton Highland	
Kopan (Slovakia)	Cone of Filakovo-Salgotarjan	
Kopeng (Java)	Fissure vent of Merbabu	0603-24=
Kopkan (Kamchatka)	Shield volcanoes (None) Pleistocene	
Koponui (New Zealand)	Cone of Pirongia	
Kopukairoa (New Zealand)	Dome of Kaimai	
Korakia (Greece)	Dome of Milos	0102-03=
Koranga (New Guinea)	Maar (None) Holocene	**0503-003**
Korath Range (Ethiopia)	Tuff cones (None) Holocene?	**0201-32-**
Koriaka (Koriaksky) (Kamchatka)	Synonym of Koryaksky	1000-09=
Koriana (Honshu-Japan)	Vent of Fuji	0803-03=
Koriatzkaia, Sopka (Kamchatka)	Synonym of Koryaksky	1000-09=
Kori-ike (Honshu-Japan)	Vent of Fuji	0803-03=
Korinci (Korintji) (Sumatra)	Synonym of Kerinci	0601-17=
Korjaka (Korjazkij) (Kamchatka)	Synonym of Koryaksky	1000-09=

Sharp-peaked Takachiho-mine (center) of the **Kirishima** volcanic complex is flanked on the east (right) by Ohachi, with its broad summit crater. Kirishima is a large group of more than 20 Quaternary volcanoes that is the centerpiece of Kirishima National Park in Kyushu.

Name (Subregion)	Type (Eruptions, Most Recent) Status Relation to Named Volcano	Volcano Number
Koro (Fiji Is-SW Pacific)	Cinder cones (None) Holocene?	**0405-02-**
Korona (Kamchatka)	Dome of Bolshoi Semiachik	1000-15=
Koroninokonoko (Fiji Is-SW Pacific)	Cone of Waikama	
Korosi (Africa-E)	Shield volcano (None) Holocene	**0202-054**
Korotyshka (Kuril Is)	Cinder cone of Medvezhia	0900-10=
Korovin (Aleutian Is)	Stratovolcanoes (8, 2007) Historical	**1101-161**
Korowinsky (Aleutian Is)	Synonym of Korovin	1101-161
Korretsberg (Germany)	Cone of East Eifel Volc Field	
Korudagi (Turkey)	Dome of Acigöl-Nevsehir	0103-004
Koryaka (Kamchatka)	Synonym of Koryaksky	1000-09=
Koryakskaya Sopka (Kamchatka)	Synonym of Koryaksky	1000-09=
Koryaksky (Kamchatka)	Stratovolcano (7, 2009) Historical	**1000-09=**
Kos (Greece)	Calderas (None) Pleist.-Fumarolic	
Kosanbe (Honshu-Japan)	Dome of Sanbe	0803-002
Koschelewa (Kamchatka)	Synonym of Koshelev	1000-02=
Koschelewa Peak (Kamchatka)	Synonym of Opala	1000-08=
Kosciusko (Antarctica)	Shield volcano of Andrus	1900-023
Kosekumaru (Honshu-Japan)	Cone of Fuji	0803-03=
Koshegochek (Kamchatka)	Shield volcano (None) Pleistocene	
Koshelev (Kamchatka)	Stratovolcano (4, 1690) Historical	**1000-02=**
Kosheleva, Sopka (Kamchatka)	Synonym of Koshelev	1000-02=
Koshelevsky (Kamchatka)	Synonym of Koshelev	1000-02=
Koshiki (Izu Is-Japan)	Crater of Miyake-jima	0804-04=
Koshiki-ana (Izu Is-Japan)	Crater of Miyake-jima	0804-04=
Koshiki-dake (Kyushu-Japan)	Cone of Kirishima	0802-09=
Koshikirizuka (Honshu-Japan)	Cone of Fuji	0803-03=
Koshin-zan (Honshu-Japan)	Cone of Sukai-Kesemaru	
Kosiki-dake [Koshiki-dake] (Kyushu-Japan)	Cone of Kirishima	0802-09=
Kosinge Reef (Solomon Is-SW Pacific)	Thermal feature of Simbo	0505-05=
Kostakan (Kamchatka)	Cinder cones (6, 1350) Holocene	**1000-122**
Kostal (Canada)	Cone of Wells Gray-Clearwater	1200-15-
Kotamoi [Tebenkov] (Kuril Is)	Stratovolcano of Grozny Group	0900-07=
Kotchlonga (Kamchatka)	Synonym of Ichinsky	1000-28=
Kotengu-dake (Hokkaido-Japan)	Stratovolcano of Nipesotsu-Maruyama	0805-061
Kothraunskula (Iceland-W)	Cone of Ljósufjöll	1700-03=
Kotiato San (Kuril Is)	Synonym of Rasshua	0900-22=
Kotkhlonga (Kamchatka)	Synonym of Ichinsky	1000-28=
Kotlugja (Iceland-S)	Synonym of Katla	1702-03=
Ko-Tokachi-dake (Hokkaido-Japan)	Stratovolcano of Tokachi	0805-05=
Kou, Puu (Hawaiian Is)	Shield volcano of Kilauea	1302-01-
Kou'a, Maunga (Chile-Is)	Pyroclastic cone of Easter Island	1506-011
Koudiat, El (Africa-N)	Cone of Azrou Volc Field	
Kouh-e-Shahsavaran (Iran)	Synonym of Shahsavaran	
Koussi, Emi (Africa-N)	Pyroclastic shield (None) Holocene	**0205-021**
Ko-Usu (Hokkaido-Japan)	Dome of Usu	0805-03=
Koutsounorachi (Greece)	Dome of Milos	0102-03=
Kovachi (Solomon Is-SW Pacific)	Synonym of Kavachi	0505-06=
Koveshegy (Hungary)	Cone of Balaton Highland	
Kovrizhka (Russia-SE)	Cone of Tunkin Depression	1002-05-
Koya-jigoku (Kyushu-Japan)	Thermal feature of Tsurumi	0802-13=
Ko-yama [Taka-yama] (Honshu-Japan)	Cone of Azuma	0803-18=
Kozei Group (Kamchatka)	Fissure vent of Kliuchevskoi	1000-26=

Name (Subregion)	Type (Eruptions, Most Recent) Status Relation to Named Volcano	Volcano Number
Kozel [Kozelskiy] (Kamchatka)	Stratovolcano of Avachinsky	1000-10=
Kozelskiy (Kamchatka)	Stratovolcano of Avachinsky	1000-10=
Ko-zima [Ko-jima] (Izu Is-Japan)	Stratovolcano of Hachijo-jima	0804-05=
Kozin-yama [Kojin-yama] (Honshu-Japan)	Dome of Chokai	0803-22=
Kozuka-yama (Honshu-Japan)	Dome of Hakone	0803-02=
Kozukushi-yama (Honshu-Japan)	Dome of Osore-yama	0803-29=
Kozukusi-yama [Kozukushi-yama] (Japan)	Dome of Osore-yama	0803-29=
Kozu-shima (Izu Is-Japan)	Lava domes (4, 838) Historical	**0804-03=**
Kozu-sima (Izu Is-Japan)	Synonym of Kozu-shima	0804-03=
Kozyrevskii (Kuril Is)	Cone of Vernadskii Ridge	0900-37-
Kozyrevsky (Kamchatka)	Shield volcano (None) Holocene?	**1000-33-**
Krab (Kamchatka)	Dome of Kikhpinych	1000-18=
Kraeduborgir (Iceland-NE)	Fissure vent of Fremrinamur	1703-07=
Kraevedchesky (Kamchatka)	Thermal feature of Dzenzursky	1000-11=
Krafakholahraun (Iceland-S)	Fissure vent of Hekla	1702-07=
Krafla (Iceland-NE)	Caldera (30, 1984) Historical	**1703-08=**
Krainy (Kamchatka)	Stratovolcano (None) Pleistocene	
Krainy (Kamchatka)	Shield volcano (None) Holocene?	**1000-40-**
Krakagigar (Iceland-S)	Fissure vent of Hekla	1702-07=
Krakar (New Guinea-NE of)	Synonym of Karkar	0501-03=
Krakatao (Indonesia)	Synonym of Krakatau	0602-00=
Krakatau (Indonesia)	Caldera (50, 2009) Historical	**0602-00=**
Krakatoa (Indonesia)	Synonym of Krakatau	0602-00=
Krakshraun (Iceland-SW)	Fissure vent of Hveravellir	1701-08=
Krákshraun (Iceland-SW)	Shield volcano of Hveravellir	1701-08=
Kramosan (Java)	Dome of Kelut	0603-28=
Krasheninnikov (Kamchatka)	Fissure vent of Kliuchevskoi	1000-26=
Krasheninnikov (Kamchatka)	Caldera (31, 1550) Radiocarbon	**1000-19=**
Krasheninnikov (Kuril Is)	Crater of Vernadskii Ridge	0900-37-
Krasnaya (Kamchatka)	Dome of Shiveluch	1000-27=
Krasnukh, Mt. (Kuril Is)	Cone of Vernadskii Ridge	0900-37-
Krasny (Kamchatka)	Cinder cone of Kostakan	1000-122
Kratioti (Greece)	Dome of Nisyros	0102-05=
Krayniy (Kamchatka)	Synonym of Krainy	1000-40-
Krenitzyn Peak (Kuril Is)	Stratovolcano of Tao-Rusyr Caldera	0900-31=
Kreppuhraun (Iceland-NE)	Fissure vent of Kverkfjöll	1703-05=
Krepputunguhraun (Iceland-NE)	Fissure vent of Kverkfjöll	1703-05=
Krestovskaya [Krestovsky] (Kamchatka)	Stratovolcano of Ushkovsky	1000-261
Krestovskii [Krestovsky] (Kamchatka)	Stratovolcano of Ushkovsky	1000-261
Krestovsky (Kamchatka)	Stratovolcano of Ushkovsky	1000-261
Krikahraun (Iceland-S)	Fissure vent of Katla	1702-03=
Krincing (Java)	Cone of Iyang-Argapura	0603-33=
Kringluhraun (Iceland-S)	Crater Row of Hekla	1702-07=
Krísuvík (Iceland-SW)	Crater rows (11, 1340) Historical	**1701-03=**
Kroflueldar (Iceland-NE)	Crater Row of Krafla	1703-08=
Krokagilsolduhraun (Iceland-S)	Fissure vent of Hekla	1702-07=
Krokahraun (Iceland-S)	Fissure vent of Hekla	1702-07=
Krokur (Kamchatka)	Maar of Krasheninnikov	1000-19=
Kromyonia (Greece)	Synonym of Susaki	0102-01=
Kroner Lake (Antarctica)	Maar of Deception Island	1900-03=
Kronotsky (Kamchatka)	Stratovolcano (3, 1923) Historical	**1000-20=**
Kronotzkaia Sopka (Kamchatka)	Synonym of Kronotsky	1000-20=
Kronotzky (Kronozky) (Kamchatka)	Synonym of Kronotsky	1000-20=
Kropotkin (Russia-SE)	Cinder cone of Oka Plateau	1002-06-
Krotiraki (Greece)	Dome of Mílos	0102-03=
Krug (Kamchatka)	Fissure vent of Kliuchevskoi	1000-26=
Kruglaya (Kamchatka)	Dome of Uzon	1000-17=
Kruglenky (Kamchatka)	Shield volcano of Kopkan	
Kruglenky (Kamchatka)	Cinder cone of Tolbachik	1000-24=
Krugliy (Kamchatka)	Shield volcano (None) Pleistocene	
Krummel (New Britain-SW Pac)	Stratovolcano of Garbuna Group	0502-07=
Krümmel (Germany)	Cone of West Eifel Volc Field	0100-01-
Krutaya Mountain (Kuril Is)	Cone of Ivao Group	0900-111
Krutoi (Kamchatka)	Dome of Bolshoi Semiachik	1000-15=
Krutoi (Kuril Is)	Dome of Golovnin	0900-01=
Kryshanovskogo [Kryzhanovskiy]	Fissure vent of Kliuchevskoi	1000-26=
Krysuvik (Iceland-SW)	Synonym of Krísuvík	1701-03=
Krysuvik (Iceland-SW)	Thermal feature of Krísuvík	1701-03=
Kryzhanovskii (Kuril Is)	Caldera of Tao-Rusyr Caldera	0900-31=
Kryzhanovskiy (Kamchatka)	Fissure vent of Kliuchevskoi	1000-26=
Kskhudach (Kamchatka)	Synonym of Ksudach	1000-05=
Ksudach (Kamchatka)	Stratovolcano (15, 1907) Historical	**1000-05=**
Ksudatsch (Kamchatka)	Synonym of Ksudach	1000-05=
Ktenas (Greece)	Dome of Santorini	0102-04=
Kuandian (China-E)	Pyroclastic cones (None) Quaternary	
Kuani Hill (Africa-E)	Cone of Nyambeni Hills	0202-056
Kuantan (SE Asia)	Volcanic field (None) Pleistocene	
K'uan-tien (China-E)	Synonym of Kuandian	
Kuan-Tzo-Ling (China-E)	Cone of Longgang Group	1005-05-
Kuanyinshan (Taiwan)	Dome of Tatun Group	0801-032
Kuba-jima (Ryukyu Is)	Synonym of Kobi-sho	
Kuccharo (Hokkaido-Japan)	Synonym of Kutcharo	0805-08=
Kuchierabu-jima (Ryukyu Is)	Synonym of Kuchinoerabu-jima	0802-05=
Kuchinoerabu-jima (Ryukyu Is)	Stratovolcanoes (24, 1980) Historical	**0802-05=**
Kuchino-shima (Ryukyu Is)	Stratovolcanoes (4, 1190) Radiocarbon	**0802-043**
Kucuk Ararat (Turkey)	Cone of Ararat	0103-04-
Kucuk Kefeli (Turkey)	Cone of Erciyes Dagi	0103-01=
Kucukmedet Tepe (Turkey)	Cone of Karapinar Field	0103-001
Kudari-yama (Honshu-Japan)	Fissure vent of Fuji	0803-03=
Kudriavy (Kuril Is)	Stratovolcano of Medvezhia	0900-10=
Kueishantao (Taiwan-E of)	Stratovolcano (1, 1785) Historical	**0801-031**
Kugak (Kugat) (Alaska Peninsula)	Synonym of Kukak	1102-23-
Kugidach-Jagutscha [Pogromni] (Aleutian Is)	Stratovolcano of Westdahl	1101-34-
Kuharua (New Zealand)	Dome of Taupo	0401-07=
Kuh-e Bazman (Iran)	Synonym of Bazman	0302-03-
Kuh-e Sultan (Pakistan)	Synonym of Sultan	
Kuh-e Taftan (Iran)	Synonym of Taftan	0302-05-
Kuh-e-Sahand (Iran)	Synonym of Sahand	0302-001
Kuhha-ye Sabalan (Iran)	Synonym of Sabalan	0302-002
Kuh-i-Daftan (Iran)	Synonym of Taftan	0302-05-
Kuirau Park (New Zealand)	Thermal feature of Rotorua	
Kuju (Kyushu-Japan)	Stratovolcanoes (13, 1996) Historical	**0802-12=**
Kuju Naka-dake (Kyushu-Japan)	Dome of Kuju	0802-12=
Kujyu Group (Kyushu-Japan)	Synonym of Kuju	0802-12=
Kukai, Puu (Hawaiian Is)	Cone of Kilauea	1302-01-
Kukak (Alaska Peninsula)	Stratovolcano (None) Fumarolic	**1102-23-**
Kukii, Puu [Puu Kukai] (Hawaiian Is)	Cone of Kilauea	1302-01-
Kukusan (Java)	Cone of Ijen	0603-35=
Kukusan (Sumatra)	Unknown (None) Post-Miocene	
Kukusan (Java)	Cone of Semeru	0603-30=
Kula (Turkey)	Cinder cones (None) Holocene	**0103-00-**
Kula Divlit (Turkey)	Cone of Kula	0103-00-
Kulabu (Sumatra)	Cone of Sorikmarapi	0601-12=
Kulakov (Kamchatka)	Dome of Bolshoi Semiachik	1000-15=
Kulal (Africa-E)	Shield volcano (None) Pleistocene	
Kulan Spring (Mindanao-Philippines)	Thermal feature of Apo	0701-03=
Kulanapahu (Hawaiian Is)	Cone of Haleakala	1302-06-
Ku-lao-rhe (SE Asia)	Synonym of Cù-Lao Ré Group	0705-02-
Kulich (Kamchatka)	Dome of Bezymianny	1000-25=
Kulichi (Kuril Is)	Dome of Medvezhia	0900-10=
Kulkev (Kamchatka)	Shield volcano (None) Holocene?	**1000-37-**
Kulkul (New Guinea-NE of)	Synonym of Ritter Island	0501-07=
Kulshan (US-Washington)	Synonym of Baker	1201-01=
Kulshan Caldera (US-Washington)	Pleistocene caldera of Baker	1201-01=
Kulua, Puu (Hawaiian Is)	Cone of Mauna Loa	1302-02=
Kuma, Maunga (Chile-Is)	Pyroclastic cone of Easter Island	1506-011
Kuma-dake (Hokkaido-Japan)	Stratovolcano of Daisetsu	0805-06=
Kumaneshiri (Hokkaido-Japan)	Stratovolcanoes (None) Pleistocene	
Kumaneshiri-dake (Hokkaido-Japan)	Stratovolcano of Kumaneshiri	
Kumano-dake (Honshu-Japan)	Synonym of Zao	0803-19=
Kumano-dake (Honshu-Japan)	Dome of Zao	0803-19=
Kuma-Otoshi (Hokkaido-Japan)	Crater of Kutcharo	0805-08=
Kuma-Otosi [Kuma-Otoshi] (Hokkaido-Japan)	Crater of Kutcharo	0805-08=
Kumbang (Java)	Therm. feature of Dieng Volc Complex	0603-20=
Kumbang (Sumatra)	Stratovolcano (None) Pleistocene	
Kumbolo, Ranu (Java)	Maar of Semeru	0603-30=
Kumboro (Solomon Is-SW Pacific)	Synonym of Kömboro	
Kumbu (New Britain-SW Pac)	Dome of Unea	
Kumburi [Kombosi] (New Britain-SW Pac)	Dome of Unea	
Kummen (Atlantic-N-Jan Mayen)	Cone of Jan Mayen	1706-01=
Kumono-taira (Honshu-Japan)	Shield volcano Washiba-Kumonotaira	0803-071
Kumu, Puu (Hawaiian Is)	Cone of Haleakala	1302-06-
Kuna Butte (US-Idaho)	Cinder cones (None) Pleistocene	
Kunashiri-Rausu (Kuril Is)	Synonym of Mendeleev	0900-02=
Kundi-Baruklingting-Sapikerep (Java)	Pleistocene caldera Tengger Caldera	0603-31=
Kung-po (SE Asia)	Synonym of Tengchong	0705-11-
Kuniang, Kapundan [Kepundan Kuniang]	Crater of Marapi	0601-14=
Kuniang, Kepundan (Sumatra)	Crater of Marapi	0601-14=
Kunii [Kunir] (Java)	Dome of Dieng Volc Complex	0603-20=
Kuninofuka-yama (Honshu-Japan)	Synonym of Fuji	0803-03=
Kunir (Java)	Dome of Dieng Volc Complex	0603-20=
Kunjit (Sumatra)	Synonym of Kunyit	0601-171
Kunkhilok (Kamchatka)	Stratovolcano (None) Pleistocene	
Kunlun Volc Group (China-W)	Pyroclastic cones (1, 1951) Historical	**1004-03-**
Kuntomintar (Kuril Is)	Hydrotherm. field (None) Pleist.-Fumarolic	
Kunua (Bougainville-SW Pacific)	Stratovolcano of Emperor Range	
Kunumi-dake (Kyushu-Japan)	Dome of Unzen	0802-10=
Kunuweri (Banda Sea)	Synonym of Teon	0605-05=
Kunyit (Sumatra)	Stratovolcano (None) Fumarolic	**0601-171**
Kupaianaha (Hawaiian Is)	Shield volcano of Kilauea	1302-01-
Kupenui (New Zealand)	Cone of Whangarei	0401-011
Kupol (Kamchatka)	Stratovolcano (None) Pleistocene	
Kupol Skalisty (Kamchatka)	Dome of Bolshoi Semiachik	1000-15=
Kupreanof (Alaska Peninsula)	Stratovolcano (1, 1987) Historical	**1102-06-**
Kuraishi-dake (Honshu-Japan)	Synonym of Zao	0803-19=
Kuraiswa (Africa-E)	Vent of Korosi	0202-054
Kurasaki (Izu Is-Japan)	Stratovolcano of Aoga-shima	0804-06=
Kurdj Ayman (Arabia-S)	Cone of Haylan, Jabal	0301-11-
Kurgannaya (Kamchatka)	Unknown (None) Pleistocene	
Kurikoma (Honshu-Japan)	Stratovolcano (7, 1950) Historical	**0803-21=**
Kuril Lake (Kamchatka)	Synonym of Kurile Lake	1000-023
Kurile Lake (Kamchatka)	Caldera (2, -6440) Radiocarbon	**1000-023**
Kurilskoe, Lake (Kamchatka)	Synonym of Kurile Lake	1000-023
Kurino-dake (Kyushu-Japan)	Stratovolcano of Kirishima	0802-09=
Kuro-dake (Hokkaido-Japan)	Dome of Daisetsu	0805-06=
Kuro-dake (Kyushu-Japan)	Dome of Kuju	0802-12=
Kuro-dake (Kuril Is)	Synonym of Sinarka	0900-29=
Kurodani (Honshu-Japan)	Crater of Yake-dake	0803-07=
Kurofuji (Honshu-Japan)	Stratovolcanoes (None) Pleistocene	
Kurofu-yama (Honshu-Japan)	Stratovolcano of Asama	0803-11=
Kurohime (Honshu-Japan)	Stratovolcano (None) Pleistocene	
Kuroi (Kuroisi) (Kuril Is)	Synonym of Tao-Rusyr Caldera	0900-31=
Kuroishi-dake (Kuril Is)	Synonym of Tao-Rusyr Caldera	0900-31=
Kuroishimori (Honshu-Japan)	Dome of Akita-Yake-yama	0803-26=
Kuroiwa-yama (Kyushu-Japan)	Cone of Kuju	0802-12=
Kuro-jima (Kyushu-Japan)	Cone of Fukue-jima	0802-091
Kurokawa (Kyushu-Japan)	Thermal feature of Kuju	0802-12=
Kurose (Kyushu-Japan)	Volcanic neck (None) Pleistocene	

Name (Subregion)	Type (Eruptions, Most Recent) Status / Relation to Named Volcano	Volcano Number
Kurose Hole (Izu Is-Japan)	Submarine volcano (None) Holocene?	**0804-042**
Kuro-shima (Ryukyu Is)	Stratovolcano (None) Pleistocene	....
Kurotsuka (Honshu-Japan)	Cone of Fuji	0803-03=
Kursi, Gunung (Java)	Cinder cone of Tengger Caldera	0603-31=
Kurttepe (Turkey)	Thermal feature of Hasan Dagi	0103-002
Kurub (Ethiopia)	Shield volcano (None) Holocene	**0201-12=**
Kurub Koba [Kurub Koma] (Ethiopia)	Synonym of Kurub	0201-12=
Kurum (New Guinea-NE of)	Crater of Karkar	0501-03=
Kurumiga-dake (Honshu-Japan)	Dome of Narugo	0803-20=
Kururi (New Guinea)	Cinder cone of Managlase Plateau	0503-021
Kurweeton, Mt. (Australia)	Cone of Newer Volcanics Prov	0509-01-
Kusatsu-Shirane (Honshu-Japan)	Stratovolcanoes (27, 1983) Historical	**0803-12=**
Kusatu-Sirane (Honshu-Japan)	Synonym of Kusatsu-Shirane	0803-12=
Kusenbu (Kyushu-Japan)	Stratovolcano of Unzen	0802-10=
Kusenrigahama (Kyushu-Japan)	Pyroclastic cone of Aso	0802-11=
Kushiga-mine (Honshu-Japan)	Stratovolcano of Bandai	0803-16=
Kushuihuan-Beishan (China-W)	Cone of Unnamed	1004-04-
Kusigamine [Kushigamine] (Honshu-Japan)	Stratovolcano of Bandai	0803-16=
Kuska (Aleutian Is)	Synonym of Kiska	1101-02-
Kussharo (Hokkaido-Japan)	Synonym of Kutcharo	0805-08=
Kust (Kamchatka)	Cinder cone of Tolbachik	1000-24=
Kusuku (Ryukyu Is)	Dome of Iwo-Tori-shima	0802-02=
Kutali, Tavani [Pomare] (Vanuatu-SW Pacific)	Stratovolcano of Epi	0507-06=
Kutcharo (Hokkaido-Japan)	Caldera (6, 1320) Tephrochronology	**0805-08=**
Kutierabu-zima (Ryukyu Is)	Synonym of Kuchinoerabu-jima	0802-05=
Kutina (Kamchatka)	Synonym of Spokoiny	1000-671
Kutinoerabu-zima (Ryukyu Is)	Synonym of Kuchinoerabu-jima	0802-05=
Kutino-sima (Ryukyu Is)	Synonym of Kuchino-shima	0802-043
Kutinskaya Group [Kutinsky Group] (Russia)	Cone of Tunkin Depression	1002-05-
Kutinsky Group (Russia-SE)	Cone of Tunkin Depression	1002-05-
Kutlyukhat (Alaska Peninsula)	Synonym of Kukak	1102-23-
Kuttara (Hokkaido-Japan)	Stratovolcanoes (3, 1820) Tephrochron	**0805-034**
Kuttyaro (Hokkaido-Japan)	Synonym of Kutcharo	0805-08=
Kutum Volc Field (Africa-N)	Scoria cones (None) Holocene?	**0205-04-**
Kuwae (Vanuatu-SW Pacific)	Caldera (12, 1974) Historical	**0507-07=**
Kuwakidaira (Izu Is-Japan)	Caldera of Miyake-jima	0804-04=
Kuwanoki-daira (Izu Is-Japan)	Cone of Miyake-jima	0804-04=
Kuyup (Kamchatka)	Shield volcano of Uksichan	1000-35-
Kuzanek (Kamchatka)	Shield volcano (None) Pleistocene	....
Kuzay (Turkey)	Dome of Acigöl-Nevsehir	0103-004
Kuzheten (Kamchatka)	Shield volcano (None) Pleistocene	....
Kuzyu Volcano Group (Kyushu-Japan)	Synonym of Kuju	0802-12=
Kverkfjallaranamyndun (Iceland-NE)	Crater Row of Kverkfjöll	1703-05=
Kverkfjöll (Iceland-NE)	Stratovolcano (8, 1968) Historical	**1703-05=**
Kviahnjukur (Iceland-W)	Cone of Snaefellsjökull	1700-01=
Kvostof Island (Aleutian Is)	Synonym of Davidof	1101-04-
Kwa Mikungu (Africa-E)	Cone of Kilimanjaro	0202-15=
Kwadisha (Africa-E)	Cone of Chyulu Hills	0202-13=
Kwamwiga (Africa-C)	Crater of Bunyaruguru	0203-004
Kwangeta (Africa-E)	Cone of Sultan Hamud-Simba	....
Kwankaiji-onsen (Kyushu-Japan)	Thermal feature of Tsurumi	0802-13=
Kwaraha (Africa-E)	Stratovolcano (None) Pleistocene	....
Kweo Butte (US-Oregon)	Cone of Newberry	1202-11-
Kweteon (Vanuatu-SW Pacific)	Cone of Gaua	0507-02=
Kwinnum Butte (US-Oregon)	Cone of Newberry	1202-11-
Kwitintog (Vanuatu-SW Pacific)	Stratovolcano of Suretamatai	0507-01=
Kwohl Butte (US-Oregon)	Shield volcano of Bachelor	1202-09-
Kyamweru (Africa-C)	Crater of Bunyaruguru	0203-004
Kyatwa (Africa-C)	Tuff cones (None) Holocene?	**0203-002**
Kyaukka (SE Asia)	Vent of Lower Chindwin	0705-09-
Kyaukmyet (SE Asia)	Vent of Lower Chindwin	0705-09-
Kyeganywa (Africa-C)	Tuff cone of Fort Portal	0203-001
Kyema (Africa-C)	Crater of Bunyaruguru	0203-004
Kyiwin Taung (SE Asia)	Vent of Lower Chindwin	0705-09-
Kyle Cone (Antarctica)	Cone of Terror, Mt.	....
Kyoga (Africa-C)	Crater of Bunyaruguru	0203-004
Kyoga-take (Honshu-Japan)	Stratovolcanoes (None) Pleistocene	....
Kyowa-yama (Honshu-Japan)	Dome of Chokai	0803-22=

L

La see proper name (e.g. Corona, La)

Name (Subregion)	Type (Eruptions, Most Recent) Status / Relation to Named Volcano	Volcano Number
La Bang Mount (SE Asia)	Crater of Pleiku-Bantour Volc Field	....
La Palma (Canary Is)	Stratovolcanoes (13, 1971) Historical	**1803-01-**
La Roja (Italy)	Thermal feature of Vulcano	0101-05=
Laacher Kopf (Germany)	Cone of East Eifel Volc Field	....
Laacher See (Germany)	Maar of East Eifel Volc Field	....
Labo (Luzon-Philippines)	Compound volc. (None) Pleist.-Hot Springs	....
Labor, Ausoles de la (El Salvador)	Thermal feature of Apaneca Range	1403-01=
Labronzo (Italy)	Crater of Stromboli	0101-04=
Laco (Chile-N)	Lava dome (None) Pleistocene?	....
Lacona (Vanuatu-SW Pacific)	Synonym of Gaua	0507-02=
Lacroix, Fumerolle (W Indies)	Thermal feature Soufrière Guadeloupe	1600-06=
Lacroix, Piton (W Indies)	Dome of Carbets, Pitons de	....
Lacroix, Piton (Indian O.-W)	Cinder cone of Fournaise, Piton de la	0303-02=
Ladolam (New Ireland-SW Pacific)	Thermal feature of Lihir	0504-01=
Laena (Solomon Is-SW Pacific)	Unknown (None) Post-Miocene	....
Lagafell (Iceland-SW)	Shield volcano of Reykjanes	1701-02=
Lagenda (New Britain-SW Pac)	Synonym of Garua Harbour	0502-06=
Lagerny (Kamchatka)	Dome of Akademia Nauk	1000-125
Lagerny (Kamchatka)	Shield volcano of Bely	1000-64-
Lagerny (Kuril Is)	Cinder cone of Medvezhia	0900-10=
Lagerny (Kamchatka)	Cinder cone of Tolbachik	1000-24=

Name (Subregion)	Type (Eruptions, Most Recent) Status / Relation to Named Volcano	Volcano Number
Laghetto (Italy)	Maar of Alban Hills	0101-004
Laghetto (Italy)	Cinder cone of Etna	0101-06=
Lago, Lagoa, Laguna (Portuguese and Spanish for Lake) see proper name		
Lagoinha (Azores)	Dome of Terceira	1802-05=
Lagrímas, Las (Argentina)	Cinder cone of Atuel, Caldera del	1507-023
Lagula, Mt. (Luzon-Philippines)	Cone of San Pablo Volc Field	0703-06=
Lagumishera (Africa-E)	Cone of Kilimanjaro	0202-15=
Laguna (Halmahera-Indonesia)	Crater of Gamalama	0608-06=
Laguna (US-New Mexico)	Fissure vent of Zuni-Bandera	1210-02-
Laguna Caldera (Luzon-Philippines)	Caldera (None) Fumarolic	**0703-08=**
Laguna Volc Field (Luzon-Philippines)	Synonym of San Pablo Volc Field	0703-06=
Laguna, Alto de la (Colombia)	Dome of Ruiz, Nevado del	1501-02=
Laguna, Caldera de (Canary Is)	Cinder cone of Fuerteventura	1803-05-
Laguna, De la (Argentina)	Vent of Unnamed	....
Laguna, La (México)	Dome of Zitácuaro-Valle de Bravo	1401-061

Carlos Felipe Ramírez (courtesy O. González-Ferrán, Univ. Chile)

Prominent lateral levees mark a steep-sided lava flow (center) and another ~7000-year-old lava flow descending from the left side of the summit crater of **Lascár** volcano in central Chile. Light-colored pyroclastic-flow deposits from a 1993 eruption are in the foreground.

Name (Subregion)	Type (Eruptions, Most Recent) Status / Relation to Named Volcano	Volcano Number
Laguna-Pulacayo, Cerro (Chile-N)	Unknown (None) Post-Miocene	....
Lagunas, Las [Monte de la Cruz] (Costa Rica)	Cinder cone of Barva	1405-05=
Lagunillas, Las (Chile-C)	Cinder cone of Chillán, Nevados de	1507-07=
Lagunita, La [Laguna las Ninfas] (El Salv.)	Crater of Apaneca Range	1403-01=
Lahendong (Sulawesi-Indonesia)	Maar of Tondano Caldera	0606-07-
Laher, Kawah (Java)	Thermal feature of Kendang	0603-11=
Laifengshan (SE Asia)	Cone of Tengchong	0705-11-
Laigongkenshan (Taiwan)	Dome of Tatun Group	0801-032
Laika (Vanuatu-SW Pacific)	Cone of Kuwae	0507-07=
Laika Bank [Karua] (Vanuatu-SW Pacific)	Submarine vent of Kuwae	0507-07=
Laimana, Puu (Hawaiian Is)	Cone of Kilauea	1302-01-
Laina, Puu (Hawaiian Is)	Cone of West Maui	....
Laja (Chile-C)	Synonym of Antuco	1507-08=
Laja los Cerritos, Cerro la [La Laja] (México)	Shield volcano of Northern Atenguillo	....
Laja, La (México)	Shield volcano of Northern Atenguillo	....
Lajara (Chile-C)	Synonym of Mocho-Choshuenco	1507-13=
Lajas, Cerro las (México)	Shield volcano of Cofre de Perote	1401-096
Lajas, Las (Nicaragua)	Shield volcano (None) Holocene?	**1404-133**
Lajas, Montañas las (Canary Is)	Fissure vent of Tenerife	1803-03-
Lakagigar [Laki] (Iceland-NE)	Crater Row of Grímsvötn	1703-01=
Lake see proper name (e.g. Wisdom, Lake)		
Lake Hill (Alaska-W)	Cinder cone of St. Paul Island	1104-01-
Lakeshore Cone (Aleutian Is)	Cone of Semisopochnoi	1101-06-
Lakeview Mountain (US-Oregon)	Shield volcano of Red Top Mountain	....
Laki (Iceland-NE)	Crater Row of Grímsvötn	1703-01=
Lakona (Vanuatu-SW Pacific)	Synonym of Gaua	0507-02=
Lakwa, Vuti (Vanuatu-SW Pacific)	Cone of Aoba	0507-03=
Lalala (New Britain-SW Pac)	Cone of Dakataua	0502-04=
Lalasho, Ol Doinyo (Africa-E)	Cone of Chyulu Hills	0202-13=
Laloanea (Samoa-SW Pacific)	Cone of Upolu	0404-03-
Lalolalo (SW Pacific)	Crater of Wallis Islands	0404-05-
Laluai (Bougainville-SW Pacific)	Pleistocene caldera of Loloru	0505-03=
Lam Teuba (Sumatra)	Pleist. caldera of Seulawah Agam	0601-02=
Lama Heru (Lesser Sunda Is)	Synonym of Iliwerung	0604-25=
Lama, Kaba (Sumatra)	Crater of Kaba	0601-22=
Lamatelang (Lesser Sunda Is)	Synonym of Iliboleng	0604-22=
Lamb, Mt. (Australia)	Cone of McBride Volc Province	....
Lambadalshraun (Iceland-S)	Crater Row of Hekla	1702-07=
Lambafit (Iceland-S)	Fissure vent of Hekla	1702-07=
Lambafjöll (Iceland-NE)	Fissure vents (None) Pleistocene	....
Lambagai, Ol Doinyo (Africa-E)	Cone of Chyulu Hills	0202-13=
Lambagigar [Lambafit] (Iceland-S)	Fissure vent of Hekla	1702-07=
Lambahraun (Iceland-SW)	Fissure vent of Hofsjökull	1701-09=
Lambahraun (Iceland-SW)	Shield volcano of Hveravellir	1701-08=
Lambavatnsgigar (Iceland-NE)	Fissure vent of Grímsvötn	1703-01=
Lambo (Lesser Sunda Is)	Unknown (None) Post-Miocene	....
Lambuwu, Doro (Lesser Sunda Is)	Stratovolcano (None) Quaternary	....
Lamington (New Guinea)	Stratovolcano (3, 1956) Historical	**0503-01=**
Lamins Hill (Australia)	Cone of Atherton Volc Province	....
Lamona [Lamonai] (D'Entrecasteaux Is)	Stratovolcano of Dawson Strait Group	0503-06=

Name (Subregion)	Type (Eruptions, Most Recent) Status / Relation to Named Volcano	Volcano Number
Lamonai (D'Entrecasteaux Is)	Stratovolcano of Dawson Strait Group	0503-06=
Lamonai-Oiau Group (D'Entrecasteaux Is)	Synonym of Dawson Strait Group	0503-06=
Lamongan (Java)	Stratovolcano (41, 1898) Historical	**0603-32=**
Lampang (SE Asia)	Unknown (None) Pleistocene	
Lamutsky (Kamchatka)	Shield volcano of Iettunup	1000-71-
Lanai (Hawaiian Is)	Shield volcano (None) Pleistocene	
Lanang (Java)	Crater of Gede	0603-06=
Lanang, Kawah [Kawah Upas] (Java)	Crater of Tangkubanparahu	0603-09=
Landayao (Mindanao-Philippines)	Cone of Matutum	0701-02=
Landes Cleaver (US-Washington)	Vent of Baker	1201-01=
Lane, Mt. (New Guinea)	Cone of Darai Hills	
Lang, Mount (Australia)	Cone of McBride Volc Province	
Langagrunn (Iceland-SW)	Submarine vent of Reykjanes	1701-02=
Langalanga, Mt. (New Britain-SW Pac)	Cone of Dakataua	0502-04=
Lange, Crater (New Britain-SW Pac)	Crater of Garove	0502-03=
Langenberg (Germany)	Cone of East Eifel Volc Field	
Langfois, Le (Indian O.-W)	Crater of Fournaise, Piton de la	0303-02=
Langholl (Iceland-SW)	Shield volcano of Reykjanes	1701-02=
Langila (New Britain-SW Pac)	Complex volcano (24, 2009) Historical	**0502-01=**
Langjökull (Iceland-SW)	Synonym of Hveravellir	1701-08=
Langla (New Britain-SW Pac)	Synonym of Langila	0502-01=
Langoan (Sulawesi-Indonesia)	Thermal feature of Tondano Caldera	0606-07-
Langtutkin (Kamchatka)	Shield volcano (None) Pleistocene	
Langudi (Ethiopia)	Synonym of Yangudi	0201-151
Languishan (China-E)	Cone of Datong-Fengzen	
Langviuhraun (Iceland-S)	Crater Row of Hekla	1702-07=
Lanín (Chile-C)	Stratovolcano (8, 560) Radiocarbon	**1507-122**
Lanituli (SW Pacific)	Crater of Wallis Islands	0404-05-
Lano (SW Pacific)	Cone of Wallis Islands	0404-05-
Lano-o-Lepa (Samoa-SW Pacific)	Cone of Upolu	0404-03-
Lano-o-Moa (Samoa-SW Pacific)	Cone of Upolu	0404-03-
Lanquimay (Chile-C)	Synonym of Lonquimay	1507-10=
Lansa, Bukit (Halmahera-Indonesia)	Stratovolcano of Bibinoi	0608-073
Lantegy, Puy de (France)	Cone of Chaîne des Puys	0100-02-
Lanteh, Batu (Lesser Sunda Is)	Unknown (None) Quaternary	
Lantik (Sumatra)	Unknown (None) Post-Miocene	
Lanuata'ata (Samoa-SW Pacific)	Cone of Upolu	0404-03-
Lanumahu (SW Pacific)	Crater of Wallis Islands	0404-05-
Lanutavake (SW Pacific)	Crater of Wallis Islands	0404-05-
Lanuto'o, Lake (Samoa-SW Pacific)	Cone of Upolu	0404-03-
Lanza, La (México)	Dome of Mispía	
Lanzarote (Canary Is)	Fissure vents (4, 1824) Historical	**1803-06-**
Laoguipo (SE Asia)	Cone of Tengchong	0705-11-
Laoheidingzi (China-E)	Shield volcano of Changbaishan	1005-06-
Laoheishan (China-E)	Cone of Wudalianchi	1005-03-

Frederick Belton (Tennessee State Univ.)

These fresh, dark-colored lava flows in the summit crater of Ol Doinyo **Lengai** volcano in Tanzania were erupted in July 2004 from the steep-sided spatter cones (about 12 meters high) at the upper left. The unusual chemistry of these carbonatite lava flows causes rapid alteration of the flows, which can give them a light-colored surface within a few days of their eruption.

Name (Subregion)	Type (Eruptions, Most Recent) Status / Relation to Named Volcano	Volcano Number
Lao-Hei-Ting-Tzu [Laoheidingzi] (China-E)	Shield volcano of Changbaishan	1005-06-
Lapac (Sulu Is-Philippines)	Cone of Jolo	0700-01=
Lapas, Caldera de las (Canary Is)	Cinder cone of Lanzarote	1803-06-
Laposo (Sulawesi-Indonesia)	Stratovolcano (None) Quaternary	
Laqueca, Cerro (Bolivia)	Stratovolcano (None) Post-Miocene	
Larancagua (Chile-N)	Stratovolcano (None) Pleistocene?	
Larch Mountain (US-Oregon)	Shield volcano of Boring Lava	
Lardarello (Italy)	Synonym of Larderello	0101-001
Larderello (Italy)	Explosion craters (1, 1282) Historical	**0101-001**
Larderllo-Travale (Italy)	Synonym of Larderello	0101-001
Larga, Loma (El Salvador)	Synonym of Lolotique, Cerro	
Larga, Loma (México)	Cinder cone of Michoacán-Guanajuato	1401-06=
Largo, Cerro (Guatemala)	Shield volcano of Redondo, Cerro	
Larsen (Antarctica)	Cone of Seal Nunataks Group	1900-05=
Larur Kouy (Chile-N)	Stratovolcano (None) Post-Miocene	
Las see proper name (e.g. Pilas, Las)		
Las Tetillas, Cerros (México)	Dome of Acoculco	
Láscar (Chile-N)	Stratovolcanoes (29, 2007) Historical	**1505-10=**
Laschamp, Puy de (France)	Cone of Chaîne des Puys	0100-02-
Lasem (Java)	Stratovolcano (None) Pleistocene	
Laskar (Chile-N)	Synonym of Láscar	1505-10=
Laso (Africa-E)	Cone of Kilimanjaro	0202-15=
Lassen Peak (US-California)	Dome of Lassen Volc Center	1203-08-
Lassen Volc Center (US-California)	Stratovolcano (5, 1917) Historical	**1203-08-**
Lassolas, Puy de (France)	Cone of Chaîne des Puys	0100-02-
Lastarria (Chile-N)	Synonym of Copiapó	1505-14-
Lastarria (Chile-N)	Stratovolcano (None) Holocene	**1505-12=**
Lata (Samoa-SW Pacific)	Pleistocene caldera of Ta'u	0404-001
Latarana, Cerro (Chile-N)	Unknown (None) Post-Miocene	
Late (Tonga-SW Pacific)	Stratovolcano (2, 1854) Historical	**0403-09=**
Latera (Italy)	Pleistocene caldera of Vulsini	0101-003
Lathrop Wells (US-Nevada)	Cinder cone of Crater Flat	
Latial (Italy)	Synonym of Alban Hills	0101-004
Latimodjong [Latimojong] (Indonesia)	Stratovolcano Rantemario-Latimojong	
Latimojong (Sulawesi-Indonesia)	Stratovolcano Rantemario-Latimojong	
Latour Butte (US-California)	Lava cone (None) Pleistocene	
Lattani, Monte (Italy)	Dome of Roccamonfina	
Latte (Tonga-SW Pacific)	Synonym of Late	0403-09=
Latukan (Mindanao-Philippines)	Stratovolcano (None) Holocene?	**0701-05=**
Lau (Lesser Sunda Is)	Cone of Mapi Group	
Lauaan (Philippines-C)	Dome of Biliran	0702-08=
Lauchachan (Kamchatka)	Shield volcano (None) Pleistocene	
Lauchan (Kamchatka)	Shield volcano of Prodolny	
Laufafell (Iceland-S)	Dome of Torfajökull	1702-05=
Laufahraun (Iceland-S)	Fissure vent of Torfajökull	1702-05=
Laugahraun (Iceland-S)	Crater Row of Torfajökull	1702-05=
Laugarfjall (Iceland-SW)	Dome of Geysir	
Laughlin Peak (US-New Mexico)	Cone of Raton-Clayton	
l'Aumone, Puy de (France)	Dome of Chaîne des Puys	0100-02-
Launiupoko (Hawaiian Is)	Dome of West Maui	
Lautaro (Chile-S)	Stratovolcano (9, 1979) Historical	**1508-06=**
Lauti (Samoa-SW Pacific)	Cone of Upolu	0404-03-
Lava Butte (US-Oregon)	Shield volcanoes (None) Pleistocene	
Lava Butte (US-Oregon)	Cinder cone of Newberry	1202-11-
Lava Divide (US-Washington)	Stratovolcano of Baker	1201-01=
Lava Fork (Canada)	Cone of Iskut-Unuk River Cones	1200-09-
Lava Mountain (US-Oregon)	Cone of Squaw Ridge Lava Field	1202-13-
Lava Mountains Volc Field (US)	Lava domes (None) Pleistocene?	
Lava Peak (Aleutian Is)	Cone of Akutan	1101-32-
Lava Pit Crater (US-Oregon)	Shield volcano of Diamond Craters	1202-17-
Lava Plastered Cones (Hawaiian Is)	Cone of Kilauea	1302-01-
Lava Point (Aleutian Is)	Cone of Akutan	1101-32-
Lava Top Butte (US-Oregon)	Cone of Newberry	1202-11-
Lavic Lake (US-California)	Volcanic field (None) Holocene?	**1203-19-**
Lavovy Shish (Kamchatka)	Cone of Ushkovsky	1000-261
Lavovy Shysh [Lavovy Shish] (Kamchatka)	Cone of Ushkovsky	1000-261
Lavoyi Shish (Kamchatka)	Lava cone of Kliuchevskoi	1000-26=
Lawalaclough (US-Washington)	Synonym of St. Helens	1201-05-
Lawaluk (Australia)	Vent of Newer Volcanics Prov.	0509-01-
Lawarkawra (Laworkawra) (Banda Sea)	Synonym of Nila	0605-06=
Lawelatla (US-Washington)	Synonym of St. Helens	1201-05-
Lawoe (Java)	Synonym of Lawu	0603-26=
Lawu (Java)	Stratovolcano (1, 1885) Historical	**0603-26=**
Laxa (Chile-C)	Synonym of Antuco	1507-08=
Laziale, Vulcano (Italy)	Synonym of Alban Hills	0101-004
Le see proper name (e.g. Touo, Le)		
Le Brun, Mt. (Australia)	Cone of Bundaberg-Boyne Province	
Leal (Chile-C)	Synonym of Resago	1507-065
L'Eau, Piton de (Indian O.-W)	Cinder cone of Fournaise, Piton de la	0303-02=
Lebakdjero [Lebakjero] (Java)	Crater of Talagabodas	0603-15=
Lebakjero (Java)	Crater of Talagabodas	0603-15=
Lebetobi (Lesser Sunda Is)	Synonym of Lewotobi	0604-18=
Lebo Raja (Sumatra)	Synonym of Rajabasa	0601-29=
Le'ele (Samoa-SW Pacific)	Pyroclastic cone of Savai'i	0404-04=
Lefulufulua (Samoa-SW Pacific)	Dome of Tutuila	0404-02-
Lega, Wolo (Lesser Sunda Is)	Crater of Inielika	0604-09=
Legatala (Legelala, Legetala) (Banda Sea)	Synonym of Serua	0605-07=
Leggjabrjótur (Iceland-SW)	Shield volcano of Hveravellir	1701-08=
Leggjarbrjotur [Solkatla] (Iceland-SW)	Shield volcano of Hveravellir	1701-08=
Lehnsessel (El Salvador)	Synonym of Taburete	1403-072
Lehu, Puu (Hawaiian Is)	Cone of Mauna Kea	1302-03-
Lehua Island (Hawaiian Is)	Tuff cone of Niihau	
Lehua, Puu (Hawaiian Is)	Cone of Hualalai	1302-04-
Leihufeng (SE Asia)	Pyroclastic cone of Hainan Dao	0705-001
Leihuling (SE Asia)	Pyroclastic cone of Hainan Dao	0705-001
Leila (Samoa-SW Pacific)	Dome of Tutuila	0404-02-
Leirhafnarskord (Iceland-NE)	Vent of Fremrinamur	1703-07=
Leirhnjukur (Iceland-NE)	Crater Row of Krafla	1703-08=
Leirhnukagigar [Leirhnjukur] (Iceland-NE)	Crater Row of Krafla	1703-08=
Leirhnukur [Leirhnjukur] (Iceland-NE)	Crater Row of Krafla	1703-08=
Leitin (Iceland-SW)	Shield volcano of Brennisteinsfjöll	1701-04=
Leizhou Bandao (SE Asia)	Volcanic field (None) Holocene	**0705-01-**
Lejas, Montaña (Canary Is)	Cone of Tenerife	1803-03-
Lejía (Chile-N)	Stratovolcano (None) Pleistocene	
Leker (Java)	Cone of Semeru	0603-30=
Leliakina (Kamchatka)	Shield volcano of Khuvkhoitun	
Lema (New Guinea)	Synonym of Doma Peaks	0503-00-
Lema, Mt. (New Guinea)	Cone of Darai Hills	
Lemagarut (Africa-E)	Stratovolcano (None) Post-Miocene	
Lemei Rock (US-Washington)	Shield volcano of Indian Heaven	1201-07-

Name (Subregion)	Type (Eruptions, Most Recent) Status / Relation to Named Volcano	Volcano Number
Lemongan (Java)	Synonym of Lamongan	0603-32=
Lemongo (Africa-E)	Cone of Kilimanjaro	0202-15=
Lemrika (Africa-E)	Cone of Kilimanjaro	0202-15=
Leña, La (Argentina)	Dome of Northern Mendoza Volc Field	....
L'Enclos Fouqué (Indian O.-W)	Caldera of Fournaise, Piton de la	0303-02=
Lengai, Ol Doinyo (Africa-E)	Stratovolcano (21, 2010) Historical	**0202-12=**
L'Engai, Oldonyo (Africa-E)	Synonym of Lengai, Ol Doinyo	0202-12=
Lengkoan (Sulawesi-Indonesia)	Cone of Tondano Caldera	0606-07-
Lenglet, Morne (W Indies)	Cinder cone of Soufrière Guadeloupe	1600-06=
Leng-shuei-keng (Taiwan)	Thermal feature of Tatun Group	0801-032
Lengua de Vulcano (Chile-C)	Dome of Descabezado Grande	1507-05=
Leningradets [Kekuknaysky] (Kamchatka)	Shield volcano Bolshoi-Kekuknaysky	1000-36-
Lentia (Italy)	Dome of Vulcano	0101-05=
Lentiscal, Montana (Canary Is)	Cone of Gran Canaria	1803-04-
Leon Dormiente, El (Galápagos)	Tuff cone of San Cristóbal	1503-12-
León, Cerro (México)	Cone (None) Pleistocene	....
Leon, Cerro del (Chile-N)	Stratovolcanoes (None) Pleistocene	....
Leona, Cerro la (El Salvador)	Cinder cone of Coatepeque Caldera	1403-041
Leonard East (Mindanao-Philippines)	Dome of Leonard Range	0701-031
Leonard Kniazeff (Mindanao-Philippines)	Synonym of Leonard Range	0701-031
Leonard North (Mindanao-Philippines)	Dome of Leonard Range	0701-031
Leonard Range (Mindanao-Philippines)	Stratovolcano (3, 120) Radiocarbon	**0701-031**
Leonard, Lake (Mindanao-Philippines)	Caldera of Leonard Range	0701-031
Leone, Valle del (Italy)	Caldera of Etna	0101-06=
Leones, Los (Argentina)	Pyrocl. cone Northern Mendoza Field	....
Leper's Island (Vanuatu-SW Pacific)	Synonym of Aoba	0507-03=
Lepre, Monte (Italy)	Cinder cone of Etna	0101-06=
Lepshka (Kamchatka)	Fissure vent of Kliuchevskoi	1000-26=
Lepu'e (Samoa-SW Pacific)	Cone of Ta'u	0404-001
Lereboleng (Lesser Sunda Is)	Synonym of Leroboleng	0604-20=
Lerek (Lesser Sunda Is)	Caldera of Iliwerung	0604-25=
Leroboleng (Lesser Sunda Is)	Complex volcano (4, 2003) Historical	**0604-20=**
Lerongo (Africa-E)	Cone of Kilimanjaro	0202-15=
Leshe (SE Asia)	Crater of Lower Chindwin	0705-09-
Leshnaya (Kamchatka)	Cinder cone of Tolbachik	1000-24=
Leskov Island (Antarctica)	Stratovolcano (None) Fumarolic	**1900-12=**
Lesnoi (Kamchatka)	Fissure vent of Kliuchevskoi	1000-26=
Lesong (Lesser Sunda Is)	Stratovolcano of Bratan	0604-001
Lesson Island (New Guinea-NE of)	Synonym of Bam	0501-01=
L'etang Sec, Caldeira de (W Indies)	Crater of Pelée	1600-12=
Letecia, Santa (Colombia)	Pyroclastic cone of Unnamed	....
Letha Taung (SE Asia)	Synonym of Singu Plateau	0705-10-
Letpadaung (SE Asia)	Cone of Lower Chindwin	0705-09-
Lette (Tonga-SW Pacific)	Synonym of Late	0403-09=
Leucite Hills (US-Wyoming)	Volcanic field (None) Pleistocene	....
Leura, Mt. (Australia)	Tuff ring of Newer Volcanics Prov.	0509-01-
Leutak, Kawah (Java)	Thermal feature of Kamojang, Kawah	....
Leutik, Kawah (Java)	Crater of Gede	0603-06=
Leutongey (Kamchatka)	Shield volcano (None) Holocene?	**1000-53-**
Levashov (Kamchatka)	Fissure vent of Kliuchevskoi	1000-26=
Level Mountain (Canada)	Shield volcano (None) Holocene?	**1200-05-**
Level, The (W Indies)	Dome of Saba	1600-01=
Levera Hill (W Indies)	Dome of St. Catherine	1600-17=
Levera Island (W Indies)	Dome of St. Catherine	1600-17=
Levera Pond (W Indies)	Crater of St. Catherine	1600-17=
Leviy Koshegochek (Kamchatka)	Shield volcano (None) Pleistocene	....
Levyi Barun-Khobol (Russia-SE)	Cinder cone of Dgida Basin	....
Leweno (Lewero, Leweroh) (Lesser Sunda Is)	Synonym of Leroboleng	0604-20=
Lewetobi (Lesser Sunda Is)	Synonym of Lewotobi	0604-18=
Lewetobi Perampuan [Lewetobi Perempuan]	Stratovolcano of Lewotobi	0604-18=
Lewetobi Perempuan (Lesser Sunda Is)	Stratovolcano of Lewotobi	0604-18=
Lewobunga (Lesser Sunda Is)	Unknown (None) Post-Miocene	....
Lewolaga (Lesser Sunda Is)	Unknown (None) Post-Miocene	....
Lewolembwi (Vanuatu-SW Pacific)	Maar of Ambrym	0507-04=
Lewono (Leworoh) (Lesser Sunda Is)	Synonym of Leroboleng	0604-20=
Lewotobi (Lesser Sunda Is)	Stratovolcanoes (22, 2003) Historical	**0604-18=**
Lewotobi Lakilaki (Lesser Sunda Is)	Stratovolcano of Lewotobi	0604-18=
Lewotolo (Lesser Sunda Is)	Stratovolcano (8, 1951) Historical	**0604-23=**
Lexone (Chile-N)	Lava domes (None) Pleistocene	....
Lho Balohan Ceunokot (Sumatra)	Thermal feature of Pulau Weh	....
Lho Balohan Tjeunokot [Lho Bal. Ceunokot]	Thermal feature of Pulau Weh	....
Liado Hayk (Ethiopia)	Maars (None) Holocene?	**0201-172**
Liamuiga (W Indies)	Stratovolcano (3, 160) Radiocarbon	**1600-03=**
Lianbanshan [Huoshaoshan] (China-E)	Cone of Wudalianchi	1005-03-
Liangbanshan [Huoshaoshan] (China-E)	Cone of Wudalianchi	1005-03-
Liatsikas (Greece)	Dome of Santorini	0102-04=
Liborio, Cerro (México)	Cinder cone of Naolinco Volc Field	1401-095
Libtong (Philippines-C)	Thermal feature of Biliran	0702-08=
Licancabur (Chile-N)	Stratovolcano (None) Holocene	**1505-092**
Licancaur (Chile-N)	Synonym of Licancabur	1505-092
Lichades [Likhades] (Greece)	Dome of Volos-Atalanti	....
Lichtmess Insel (Antarctica)	Synonym of Candlemas Island	1900-10=
Lickades (Greece)	Dome of Volos-Atalanti	....
Licto (Ecuador)	Scoria cones (None) Holocene?	**1502-081**
Lidhogda (Atlantic-N-Jan Mayen)	Cone of Jan Mayen	1706-01=
Lien Khang Mount (SE Asia)	Caldera of Haut Dong Nai	0705-04-
Lierweisen (Germany)	Maar of West Eifel Volc Field	0100-01-
Lieskow Island (Antarctica)	Synonym of Leskov Island	1900-12=
Liferfe, Montaña (Canary Is)	Cinder cone of Tenerife	1803-03-
Lifos Tepe (Turkey)	Dome of Erciyes Dagi	0103-01=
Lihir (New Ireland-SW Pacific)	Compound volcano (None) Holocene	**0504-01=**
Lijskow Island (Antarctica)	Synonym of Leskow Island	1900-12=
Likaiu East (Africa-E)	Shield volcano of Barrier, The	0202-03=
Likaiu West (Africa-E)	Shield volcano of Barrier, The	0202-03=

Name (Subregion)	Type (Eruptions, Most Recent) Status / Relation to Named Volcano	Volcano Number
Likayu [Likaiu] (Africa-E)	Shield volcano of Barrier, The	0202-03=
Likuruanga (New Britain-SW Pac)	Stratovolcano (None) Pleistocene	....
Lila, Cerro (Argentina)	Stratovolcano of Antofalla	....
Liley (Germany)	Cone of West Eifel Volc Field	0100-01-
Lillooet Cones (Canada)	Synonym of Bridge River Cones	1200-17-
Limas (Java)	Cone of Wilis	0603-27=
Limay, Mt. (Luzon-Philippines)	Cone of Mariveles	0703-081
Limbo, Cerro el (El Salvador)	Cinder cone of Chinameca	1403-09=
Limitrofe [Volcán Barrancas] (Chile-C)	Dome of Maule, Laguna del	1507-061
Limon, Cerro el (México)	Dome of San Pedro	....
Limones Volc Field, Los (El Salvador)	Cinder cones (None) Pleistocene	....
Lina (Banda Sea)	Synonym of Nila	0605-06=
Linan (Mindanao-Philippines)	Thermal feature of Matutum	0701-02=
Linau-Balui Plateau (New Guinea-W)	Unknown (None) Quaternary	....
Lindahraun (Iceland-NE)	Fissure vent of Askja	1703-06=

The small, steep-walled,1.8-km-wide summit caldera of **Longonot** volcano in Kenya is flanked by a symmetrical cone with a circular crater erupted along a N-S fissure on the upper flanks of the volcano. Fissures lower on the north flank produced the youngest eruption of the volcano during the 19th century.

Name (Subregion)	Type (Eruptions, Most Recent) Status / Relation to Named Volcano	Volcano Number
Lindahraun (Iceland-NE)	Fissure vent of Kverkfjöll	1703-05=
Lindenberg Island (Antarctica)	Cone of Seal Nunataks Group	1900-05=
Lindero, El (Argentina)	Cinder cone of Unnamed	....
Lineas, Las (México)	Dome of Humeros, Los	1401-093
Lineinyi Crater (Kuril Is)	Cone of Vernadskii Ridge	0900-37-
Lingker, Gunung (Java)	Cone of Ijen	0603-35=
Lingshi (SE Asia)	Cone of Leizhou Bandao	0705-01-
Linosa (Italy)	Cinder cones (None) Pleistocene	....
Linow Lahendong [Lahendong] (Indonesia)	Maar of Tondano Caldera	0606-07-
Linqu (China-E)	Unknown (None) Quaternary	....
Linzor (Chile-N)	Stratovolcano (None) Pleistocene	....
Liou-huang-ku (Taiwan)	Thermal feature of Tatun Group	0801-032
Lipari (Italy)	Stratovolcanoes (3, 1230) Radiocarbon	**0101-042**
Lir (New Ireland-SW Pacific)	Synonym of Lihir	0504-01=
Lirang (Java)	Dome of Kelut	0603-28=
Liria, Caldera de (Canary Is)	Cinder cone of Fuerteventura	1803-05-
Liserser (Vanuatu-SW Pacific)	Stratovolcano of Suretamatai	0507-01=
Listado, Volcán Cerro (Chile-C)	Stratovolcano of Maipo	1507-021
Liston, El (Nicaragua)	Stratovolcano of Telica	1404-04=
Litla Eldborg undir Geitlahlid (Iceland-SW)	Crater Row of Brennisteinsfjöll	1701-04=
Litladyngja (Iceland-NE)	Shield volcano of Askja	1703-06=
Litlahraun (Iceland-SW)	Crater Row of Hengill	1701-05=
Little Aspen Butte (US-Oregon)	Shield volcano of Mountain Lakes	....
Little Barrier (New Zealand)	Stratovolcano (None) Pleistocene	....
Little Bear Mountain (Canada)	Tuya of Hoodoo Mountain	1200-08-
Little Belknap (US-Oregon)	Shield volcano of Belknap	1202-06-
Little Black Peak (US-New Mexico)	Cone of Carrizozo	1210-01-
Little Brother (US-Oregon)	Shield volcano of North Sister Field	1202-07-
Little Cache Mountain (US-Oregon)	Cinder cone of Washington	....
Little Cones (US-Nevada)	Cone of Crater Flat	....
Little Deer Mountain (US-California)	Cone of Whaleback	....
Little Donald (New Zealand)	Crater of White Island	0401-04=
Little Eagle (Canada)	Cone of Dark Mountain	....
Little Glass Mountain (US-California)	Dome of Medicine Lake	1203-02-
Little Hanish Island (Red Sea)	Cone of Hanish	0201-022
Little Hebe (US-California)	Crater of Ubehebe Craters	1203-16-
Little Hill (Australia)	Cone of Newer Volcanics Prov	0509-01-
Little Hot Creek (US-California)	Thermal feature of Long Valley	....
Little Hot Springs Valley (US-California)	Thermal feature of Lassen Volc Center	1203-08-
Little Inskip Hill (US-California)	Cone of Inskip Hill	....
Little Iskut (Canada)	Shield volcano of Spectrum Range	1200-07-
Little Meru (Africa-E)	Stratovolcano of Meru	0202-16=
Little Morne, the (Vanuatu-SW Pacific)	Cone of Epi	0507-06=
Little Mountain (W Indies)	Stratovolcano of Quill, The	1600-02=
Little Mt. Adams (US-Washington)	Cinder cone of Adams	1201-04-
Little Mt. Gulu (New Britain-SW Pac)	Cone of Lotomgan Group	....
Little Mt. Hoffman (US-California)	Cone of Medicine Lake	1203-02-
Little Mt. Worri (New Britain-SW Pac)	Cone of Garua Harbour	0502-06=
Little Nash Crater (US-Oregon)	Cinder cone of Sand Mountain Field	1202-04-

Name (Subregion)	Type (Eruptions, Most Recent) Status Relation to Named Volcano	Volcano Number
Little Odell Butte (US-Oregon)	Cinder cone of Davis Lake	1202-10-
Little Pavlof (Alaska Peninsula)	Cone of Pavlof	1102-03-
Little Potato Butte (US-California)	Cinder cone of Potato Butte	....
Little Rangitoto (New Zealand)	Cone of Auckland Field	0401-02=
Little Sand Butte (US-California)	Cone of Medicine Lake	1203-02-
Little Sitchin (Aleutian Is)	Synonym of Little Sitkin	1101-05-
Little Sitkin (Aleutian Is)	Stratovolcano (2, 1830) Historical	**1101-05-**
Little Soda Lake (US-Nevada)	Maar of Soda Lakes	1206-01-
Little Springs (US-Arizona)	Cinder cone of Uinkaret Field	1209-01-
Little Whitney (US-California)	Cinder cone of Golden Trout Creek	1203-17-
Liuchow Peninsula (SE Asia)	Synonym of Leizhou Bandao	0705-01-
Liuhuangdaban (China-W)	Cinder cone of Kunlun Volc Group	1004-03-
Livingston-Greenwich Is (Antarctica)	Tuff cones (None) Pleistocene	....
Liwowo (Africa-W)	Cone of Cameroon	0204-01=
Ljosakridha (Iceland-W)	Cone of Snaefellsjökull	1700-01=
Ljosufjallahraun (Iceland-NE)	Crater Row of Bárdarbunga	1703-03=
Ljósufjöll (Iceland-W)	Fissure vents (5, 960) Anthropology	**1700-03=**
Ljotipollur (Iceland-NE)	Crater of Bárdarbunga	1703-03=
Llafenco Group (Chile-C)	Crater of Villarrica	1507-12=
Llagdeguin (Chile-C)	Synonym of Callaqui	1507-091
Llaima (Chile-C)	Stratovolcano (56, 2009) Historical	**1507-11=**
Llallicupe (Chile-C)	Synonym of Sollipulli	1507-111
Llancahue, Volcanes de (Chile-C)	Cinder cone of Quetrupillan	1507-121
Llancanelo Volc Field (Chile-C)	Scoria cones (None) Pleistocene	....
Llanganate (Ecuador)	(None) Not a Volcano	1502-07=
Llangorse Mountain (Canada)	Cone of Atlin Volc Field	1200-03-
Llangorse Volc Field (Canada)	Synonym of Atlin Volc Field	1200-03-
Llanillos, Los (Canary Is)	Cinder cone of Hierro	1803-02-
Llano Del Banco (Canary Is)	Fissure vent of La Palma	1803-01-
Llano Grande (México)	Pleistocene caldera of Iztaccíhuatl	1401-082
Llano Grande (México)	Vent of Primavera, Sierra la	....
Llano, Cerro el (Nicaragua)	Dome of Zapatera	1404-111
Llano, El (Nicaragua)	Caldera of Zapatera	1404-111
Llanos, Los [Tacande] (Canary Is)	Cinder cone of La Palma	1803-01-
Llanquihue (Chile-S)	Synonym of Osorno	1508-01=
Llao Bay (US-Oregon)	Shield volcano of Crater Lake	1202-16-
Llao Rock (US-Oregon)	Vent of Crater Lake	1202-16-
Llaymas (Chile-C)	Synonym of Llaima	1507-11=
L'Liet, Piton de (Indian O.-W)	Cinder cone of Fournaise, Piton de la	0303-02=
Llimpi (Ecuador)	Stratovolcano (None) Pleistocene	....
Llolli, Baños de (Chile-C)	Thermal feature of Calabozos	1507-042
Llullaillaco (Chile-N)	Stratovolcano (3, 1877) Historical	**1505-11=**
Loa, Mt. (Hawaiian Is)	Synonym of Mauna Loa	1302-02=
Loa, Puu (Hawaiian Is)	Cone of Mauna Kea	1302-03-
Loaloa, Puu (Hawaiian Is)	Cone of Mauna Kea	1302-03-
Lobetobi (Lesser Sunda Is)	Synonym of Lewotobi	0604-18=
Lobo Radja (Lobo Raja) (Sumatra)	Synonym of Rajabasa	0601-29=
Loboa (Vanuatu-SW Pacific)	Stratovolcano of North Vate	0507-081
Lobobutu (Lesser Sunda Is)	Pleistocene caldera of Inielika	0604-09=

Marco Fulle (Stromboli Online)

Charred vegetation marks the path of a pyroclastic flow that swept to the sea on the SW flank of **Lopevi** volcano on February 19, 2000 and formed a 300-m-wide delta. Many historical eruptions at this basaltic-to-andesitic volcano, one of the most active in Vanuatu, have occurred along the same NW-SE-trending fissure that cuts across the island.

Name (Subregion)	Type (Eruptions, Most Recent) Status Relation to Named Volcano	Volcano Number
Loboleke, Wolo (Lesser Sunda Is)	Crater of Inielika	0604-09=
Lobos, Cerro (México)	Dome of San Pedro	....
Lobos, Cerro los (México)	Dome of Michoacán-Guanajuato	1401-06=
Lobos, Isla de (Canary Is)	Crater of Fuerteventura	1803-05-
Lobos, Montana (Canary Is)	Cone of Lanzarote	1803-06-
Lockit Butte (US-Oregon)	Cone of Newberry	1202-11-
Lodhmundur (Iceland-SW)	Dome of Hofsjökull	1701-09=
Lodo Prieto, Cerro (México)	Dome of Zitácuaro-Valle de Bravo	1401-061
Loemoet Balai, Boekit (Sumatra)	Synonym of Lumut Balai, Bukit	0601-24=
Loeroes (Java)	Synonym of Lurus	0603-321
Loewinsson-Lessin (Kamchatka)	Fissure vent of Kliuchevskoi	1000-26=
Lofia (Tonga-SW Pacific)	Cone of Tofua	0403-06=
Lofos (Greece)	Dome of Nisyros	0102-05=
Logkipi Geyser (Africa-E)	Thermal feature of Barrier, The	0202-03=
Logothetis (Greece)	Vent of Nisyros	0102-05=
Logudoro (Italy)	Volcanic field (None) Pleistocene	....
Loi Han Hun (SE Asia)	Lava dome (None) Pleistocene	....
Loihi (Hawaiian Is)	Submarine volcano (4, 1996) Historical	**1302-00-**
Loijme, Mt. (SE Asia)	Synonym of Loiyme, Mt.	....
Loinyoliunguso (Africa-E)	Cone of Sultan Hamud-Simba	....
Loiyme, Mt. (SE Asia)	Lava dome (None) Post-Miocene	....
Lokhmaty (Kamchatka)	Dome of Bezymianny	1000-25=
Loki (Iceland-NE)	Fissure vent of Bárdarbunga	1703-03=
Loki-Fögrufjöll (Iceland-NE)	Submarine vent of Bárdarbunga	1703-03=
Lokippi [Suguta-Logkipi] (Africa-E)	Thermal feature of Barrier, The	0202-03=
Lokon (Sulawesi-Indonesia)	Cone of Lokon-Empung	0606-10=
Lokon Wallenaure [Tompaluan] (Indonesia)	Crater of Lokon-Empung	0606-10=
Lokon-empoeng (Sulawesi-Indonesia)	Synonym of Lokon-Empung	0606-10=
Lokon-Empung (Sulawesi-Indonesia)	Stratovolcano (25, 2003) Historical	**0606-10=**
Lokris (Greece)	Dome of Volos-Atalanti	....
Lokukus (Africa-E)	Vent of Paka	0202-053
Lolah Butte (US-Oregon)	Cinder cone of Bachelor	1202-09-
Lolaru (Bougainville-SW Pacific)	Synonym of Loloru	0505-03=
Lolatolo [Kasolali] (New Britain-SW Pac)	Thermal feature of Pago	0502-08=
Lolco, Volcan (Chile-C)	Cone of Tolguaca	1507-093
Lolco, Volcán (Chile-C)	Cinder cone of Lonquimay	1507-10=
Lollo (New Britain-SW Pac)	Synonym of Lolo	0502-071
Lolo (New Britain-SW Pac)	Stratovolcano (None) Holocene?	**0502-071**
Lolo Butte (US-Oregon)	Cinder cone of Bachelor	1202-09-
Lolobau (New Britain-SW Pac)	Caldera (3, 1912) Historical	**0502-13=**
Loloda (Halmahera-Indonesia)	Synonym of Tobaru	0608-02-
Loloru (Bougainville-SW Pacific)	Pyroclastic shield (6, -1050) Radiocarbon	**0505-03=**
Lolotique, Cerro (El Salvador)	Unknown (None) Quaternary	....
Lolrupande, Ol Doinyo (Africa-E)	Cone of Chyulu Hills	0202-13=
Lolwai (Vanuatu-SW Pacific)	Tuff cone of Aoba	0507-03=
Lom Kot (SE Asia)	Crater of Bokeo Volc Field	....
Loma (Spanish for Hill) see proper name (e.g. Achacara, Loma)		
Loma Negra, Volcan (Argentina)	Vent of Infiernillo	1507-041
Loman Volcano Group (Afghanistan)	Lava domes (None) Quaternary	....
Lomas (Costa Rica)	Shield volcano of Sierpe, Lomas de	....
Lombenben (Vanuatu-SW Pacific)	Shield volcano of Aoba	0507-03=
Lombok (Lesser Sunda Is)	Synonym of Rinjani	0604-03=
Lomo Negro, Volcán de (Canary Is)	Cinder cone of Hierro	1803-02-
Lomonosov Group (Kuril Is)	Cinder cones (None) Holocene	**0900-351**
Lompobatang (Sulawesi-Indonesia)	Stratovolcano (None) Quaternary	....
Londolovit (New Ireland-SW Pacific)	Stratovolcano of Lihir	0504-01=
London, Isla (Chile-S)	Synonym of Fueguino	1508-09-
Lone Butte (US-Washington)	Tuya of Indian Heaven	1201-07-
Long Island (New Guinea-NE of)	Complex volcano (11, 1993) Historical	**0501-05=**
Long Valley (US-California)	Caldera (None) Pleist.-Fumarolic	....
Longaví, Nevado de (Chile-C)	Stratovolcano (1, -4890) Radiocarbon	**1507-063**
Long-fong-ku (Taiwan)	Thermal feature of Tatun Group	0801-032
Longgang Group (China-E)	Cinder cones (1, 350) Radiocarbon	**1005-05-**
Longhai (China-E)	Unknown (None) Quaternary	....
Longhushan (SE Asia)	Cone of Tengchong	0705-11-
Longhuxiaoshan (SE Asia)	Cone of Tengchong	0705-11-
Longlang (SE Asia)	Pyroclastic cone of Hainan Dao	0705-001
Longonot (Africa-E)	Stratovolcano (3, 1863) Anthropology	**0202-10=**
Longtan (SE Asia)	Cone of Tengchong	0705-11-
Longuen, Nevado de (Chile-C)	Synonym of Longaví, Nevado de	1507-063
Longwan Group (China-E)	Synonym of Longgang Group	1005-05-
Lonpuimay (Chile-C)	Synonym of Lonquimay	1507-10=
Lonquen, Nevado de (Chile-C)	Synonym of Longaví, Nevado de	1507-063
Lonquimay (Chile-C)	Stratovolcano (4, 1990) Historical	**1507-10=**
Lookout Butte (US-Oregon)	Cone of Crater Lake	1202-16-
Lookout Butte (US-California)	Cone of Medicine Lake	1203-02-
Lookout Butte (US-Wyoming)	Dome of Yellowstone	1205-01-
Lookout Mountain (US-Oregon)	Shield volcano of Bachelor	1202-09-
Lookout Mountain (US-California)	Dome of Long Valley	....
Lookout Point [Kakapiko Lookout]	Dome of Kapenga	....
Loolmalasin (Africa-E)	Unknown (None) Pleistocene?	....
Loolsuni (Banda Sea)	Synonym of Wurlali	0605-04=
Loomalasin (Africa-E)	Synonym of Loolmalasin	....
Loowit Boulder Basin Hot Springs (US)	Thermal feature of St. Helens	1201-05-
Loowit Source Hot Springs (US-Washington)	Thermal feature of St. Helens	1201-05-
Loowit Travertine Hot Springs (US-Wash.)	Thermal feature of St. Helens	1201-05-
Loowitlatkla (US-Washington)	Synonym of St. Helens	1201-05-
Lopatina (Loputin) (Russia-SE)	Cinder cone of Vitim Plateau	1002-04-
Lopevi (Vanuatu-SW Pacific)	Stratovolcano (29, 2007) Historical	**0507-05=**
López de Villalobos, Cerro (México-Is)	Dome of Bárcena	1401-02=
Loreto, Cerro (México)	Cone of Chichinautzin	1401-08=
Lorusio Hot Springs (Africa-E)	Thermal feature of Silali	0202-052
Los see proper name (e.g. Votos, Los)		
Losetom (Africa-E)	Tuff cone of Emuruangogolak	0202-051
Losloyo (Chile-N)	Stratovolcano (None) Pleistocene	....
Losolava-Tarasag (Vanuatu-SW Pacific)	Cone of Gaua	0507-02=
Lost Jim (Alaska-W)	Cone of Imuruk Lake	1104-06-
Lost Lake Butte (US-Oregon)	Shield volcano (None) Pleistocene	....
Lost Lake Group (US-Oregon)	Cinder cone of Sand Mountain Field	1202-04-
Lost Woman (US-New Mexico)	Cone of Zuni-Bandera	1210-02-
Lotigelli (Africa-E)	Cone of Kilimanjaro	0202-15=
Lotin Island (New Guinea-NE of)	Synonym of Crown Island	....
Lotomgan Group (New Britain-SW Pac)	Pyroclastic cones (None) Quaternary	....
Lot's Wife (New Zealand)	Former crater of White Island	0401-04=
Lot's Wife Rock (Izu Is-Japan)	Synonym of Sofugan	0804-091
Lou (Admiralty Is-SW Pacific)	Synonym of St. Andrew Strait	0500-01=
Louchadiere, Puy de (France)	Cone of Chaîne des Puys	0100-02-
Louse (Kuril Is)	Synonym of Mendeleev	0900-02=
Loutra Methana (Greece)	Thermal feature of Methana	0102-02=

Name (Subregion)	Type (Eruptions, Most Recent) Status / Relation to Named Volcano	Volcano Number
Low Island (Red Sea)	Cone of Hanish	0201-022
Low Island (Red Sea)	Cone of Zubair, Jebel	0201-02=
Lower Chindwin (SE Asia)	Volcanic field (None) Holocene?	**0705-09-**
Lower Geyser Basin (US-Wyoming)	Thermal feature of Yellowstone	1205-01-
Lower Glacier Valley (Aleutian Is)	Thermal feature of Makushin	1101-31-
Lower Maruanot (Luzon-Philippines)	Thermal feature of Pinatubo	0703-083
Lowetobi (Lesser Sunda Is)	Synonym of Lewotobi	0604-18=
Lowullo Butte (US-Oregon)	Cone of Newberry	1202-11-
Lquilla, Cerro (Chile-N)	Dome of Lexone	....
Lua (Hawaiian for Crater) see proper name (e.g. Hohonu, Lua)		
Lualaititi (Samoa-SW Pacific)	Pit crater of Ta'u	0404-001
Luamakami (Hawaiian Is)	Cone of Hualalai	1302-04-
Lua-o-Fafine (Samoa-SW Pacific)	Cone of Upolu	0404-03-
Lua-o-Tane (Samoa-SW Pacific)	Cone of Upolu	0404-03-
Luatele (Samoa-SW Pacific)	Shield volcano of Ta'u	0404-001
Lubbock, Mount (Antarctica)	Cone of Daniell Peninsula	....
Lubuk Raja (Sumatra)	Synonym of Lubukraya	0601-111
Lubukraya (Sumatra)	Stratovolcano (None) Holocene?	**0601-111**
Lubwa (Africa-E)	Dome of Nyambeni Hills	0202-056
Lucaret (Romania)	Dome of Beritia	....
Lucero (US-New Mexico)	Volcanic field (None) Pleistocene	....
Lucifer Hill (Antarctica)	Cone of Candlemas Island	1900-10=
Ludent (Iceland-NE)	Tuff ring of Krafla	1703-08=
Ludentsborgir (Iceland-NE)	Crater Row of Krafla	1703-08=
Lugad (Philippines-C)	Crater of Kanlaon	0702-02=
Lugugugut [Andrew's Cone] (Africa-E)	Stratovolcano of Barrier, The	0202-03=
Luise (New Ireland-SW Pacific)	Stratovolcano of Lihir	0504-01=
Lujongo (Africa-C)	Crater of Bunyaruguru	0203-004
Lukovitsa (Kamchatka)	Dome of Gamchen	1000-21=
Lukuka (Africa-C)	Cone of Karisimbi	0203-04-
Luligi (New Britain-SW Pac)	Cone of Lotomgan Group	....
Lulukan (Mindanao-Philippines)	Synonym of Latukan	0701-05=
Lulunurcu (Ecuador)	Dome of Casitagua	....
Lumanto, Cerro (Chile-C)	Cinder cone of Carrán-Los Venados	1507-14=
Lumbung Selajur [Lumbung Selayur] (Java)	Crater of Lawu	0603-26=
Lumbung Selayur (Java)	Crater of Lawu	0603-26=
Lummerfeld (Germany)	Maar of East Eifel Volc Field	....
Lumrun Butte (US-Oregon)	Cinder cone of Bachelor	1202-09-
Lumut Balai, Bukit (Sumatra)	Stratovolcano? (None) Fumarolic	**0601-24=**
Lumut, Bukit (Sumatra)	Stratovolcano of Lumut Balai, Bukit	0601-24=
Lumutdaun, Bukit (Sumatra)	Synonym of Daun, Bukit	0601-21=
Luna Butte (US-Oregon)	Cone of Newberry	1202-11-
Luna, Volcán la (México)	Crater of Pinacate	1401-001
Lunaiyir, Harrat (Arabia-W)	Synonym of Lunayyir, Harrat	0301-04-
Lunar Crater Field (US-Nevada)	Cinder cones (None) Pleistocene	....
Lunas, Los (US-New Mexico)	Vent of Cat Hills	....
Lunayyir, Harrat (Arabia-W)	Volcanic field (1, 1000) Historical	**0301-04-**
Lung-wan Group (China-E)	Synonym of Longgang Group	1005-05-
Lun-Ula (Mongolia)	Cone of Dariganga Volc Field	1003-04-
Luogangling (SE Asia)	Cone of Leizhou Bandao	0705-01-
Lurbun (Russia-SE)	Cinder cone of Udokan Plateau	1002-03-
Lurus (Java)	Complex volcano (None) Holocene?	**0603-321**
Lusiba (Africa-E)	Crater of Rungwe	0202-166
Lusitobe North (Lesser Sunda Is)	Crater of Iliwerung	0604-25=
Lusitobe South (Lesser Sunda Is)	Crater of Iliwerung	0604-25=
Luxsar, Cerro (Bolivia)	Stratovolcano of Pampa Luxsar	1505-042
Lvinaya Past (Kuril Is)	Stratovolcano (1, -7480) Radiocarbon	**0900-041**
L'vinaya Pasti (Kuril Is)	Synonym of Lvinaya Past	0900-041
Lyeskov Island (Antarctica)	Synonym of Leskov Island	1900-12=
Lynces Crater (Australia)	Cone of Atherton Volc Province	....
Lyngdalsheidi (Iceland-SW)	Shield volcano (None) Pleistocene	....
Lynn, Mt. (Australia)	Cone of McBride Volc Province	....
Lyons Peak (US-California)	Cone of Medicine Lake	1203-02-
Lysuhóll (Iceland-W)	Synonym of Helgrindur	1700-02=
Lysuhyrna (Iceland-W)	Vent of Helgrindur	1700-02=
Lysuskard (Iceland-W)	Synonym of Helgrindur	1700-02=
Lyzyk (Kamchatka)	Unknown (None) Pleistocene	....

M

Name (Subregion)	Type (Eruptions, Most Recent) Status / Relation to Named Volcano	Volcano Number
Ma Alalta (Ethiopia)	Stratovolcano (None) Holocene	**0201-111**
Ma'a. Mt. (New Guinea)	Cone of Darai Hills	....
Maalsom (Luzon-Philippines)	Thermal feature of Isarog	0703-042
Maanling (SE Asia)	Pyroclastic cone of Hainan Dao	0705-001
Maanshan (SE Asia)	Pyroclastic cone of Hainan Dao	0705-001
Maanshan (SE Asia)	Cinder cone of Tengchong	0705-11-
Maanshan (China-E)	Dome of Yitong Group	....
Maar see proper name (e.g. Estivadoux, Maar D')		
Maasok (Luzon-Philippines)	Thermal feature of Cagua	0703-09=
Mabda (Ethiopia)	Dome of Dubbi	0201-10=
Mabilog, Mt. (Luzon-Philippines)	Cone of San Pablo Volc Field	0703-06=
Mabollo Spring (Mindanao-Philippines)	Thermal feature of Apo	0701-03=
Mabuani (Africa-E)	Cone of Chyulu Hills	0202-13=
Maca (Chile-S)	Stratovolcano (1, 410) Radiocarbon	**1508-056**
Macanze, Cerro (El Salvador)	Cinder cone of Guazapa	1403-052
Macaque, Morne [Micotrin] (W Indies)	Dome of Trois Pitons, Morne	1600-10=
Macas, Volcan de (Ecuador)	Synonym of Sangay	1502-09=
Macauley Island (Kermadec Is)	Caldera (1, -4360) Radiocarbon	**0402-021**
Maccotta, Cuddia (Italy)	Shield volcano of Pantelleria	0101-071
Macdonald (Austral Is-C Pacific)	Submarine volcano (12, 1989) Historical	**1303-06-**
Macdougal (México)	Maar of Pinacate	1401-001
Macey Cone (Indian O.-S)	Cone of Heard	0304-01=
Machekh (Kuril Is)	Crater of Grozny Group	0900-07=
Machekha [Machekh] (Kuril Is)	Crater of Grozny Group	0900-07=
Machín (Colombia)	Stratovolcano (7, 1180) Radiocarbon	**1501-04=**
Machioto (Africa-E)	Dome of SW Usangu Basin	0202-163
Machmel River (Canada)	Cone of Silverthrone	1200-16-
Machuca (Chile-N)	Synonym of Putana	1505-09=
Macico da Agualva [Guilherme Moniz]	Stratovolcano of Terceira	1802-05=
MacKenney (Guatemala)	Cone of Pacaya	1402-11=
Macolod (Luzon-Philippines)	Stratovolcano of Taal	0703-07=
Macon, Cerros de (Chile-N)	Stratovolcano of Purico Complex	1505-094
Macouba, Morne (W Indies)	Crater of Pelée	1600-12=
Macuturin (Macutusing) (Philippines)	Synonym of Makaturing	0701-04=
Madahraun (Iceland-NE)	Fissure vent of Bárdarbunga	1703-03=
Madarao (Honshu-Japan)	Stratovolcano (None) Pleistocene	....
Madden's Mount (W Indies)	Dome of Nevis Peak	1600-04=
Madeira (Azores)	Shield volcano (1, -4500) Radiocarbon	**1802-12-**

Marion Island in the Indian Ocean, South Africa's only Holocene volcano, first erupted historically in 1980. The 1230-m-high island is dotted by about 150 cinder cones, smaller scoria cones, and coastal tuff cones.

Ian Meiklejohn (Univ. Pretoria)

Name (Subregion)	Type (Eruptions, Most Recent) Status / Relation to Named Volcano	Volcano Number
Madeleine (W Indies)	Dome of Soufrière Guadeloupe	1600-06=
Madera, La (Nicaragua)	Synonym of Maderas	1404-13-
Maderas (Nicaragua)	Stratovolcano (Uncertain) Holocene	**1404-13-**
Madiena, Bukit [Bukit Keramat] (Indonesia)	Cone of Gamalama	0608-06=
Madiera (Azores)	Synonym of Madeira	1802-12-
Madilogo (New Guinea)	Pyroclastic cone (None) Holocene	**0503-004**
Madinah, Harrat [Harrat Rashid] (Arabia-W)	Volcanic field of Rahat, Harrat	0301-07=
Madrepore (Italy)	Submarine vent C. Flegrei Mar Sicilia	0101-07=
Madrón, El (México)	Dome of Primavera, Sierra la	....
Mae-dake (Ryukyu Is)	Dome of Kuchino-shima	0802-043
Mae-dake [Mayu-yama] (Kyushu-Japan)	Dome of Unzen	0802-10=
Maeeboshi-dake (Honshu-Japan)	Stratovolcano of Zao	0803-19=
Maega-take (Honshu-Japan)	Stratovolcano of Adatara	0803-17=
Maekake-yama (Honshu-Japan)	Stratovolcano of Asama	0803-11=
Maelifell (Iceland-S)	Tuya of Hrómundartindur	1701-051
Maelifellshraun (Iceland-S)	Fissure vent of Katla	1702-03=
Maenir (Iceland-SW)	Dome of Hofsjökull	1701-09=
Maer Volc Province (Australia)	Pyroclastic cones (None) Pleistocene	....
Maestras, Las (Spain)	Maar of Calatrava Volc Field	0100-04-
Maetambe (Solomon Is-SW Pacific)	Unknown (None) Pleistocene?	....
Mae-Tokachi-dake (Hokkaido-Japan)	Stratovolcano of Tokachi	0805-05=
Mae-yama (Honshu-Japan)	Dome of Numazawa	0803-151
Mafane (Samoa-SW Pacific)	Cone of Savai'i	0404-04=
Mafarem (Luzon-N of)	Synonym of Matarem	....
Mafra, Pico de (Azores)	Cone of Sete Cidades	1802-08=
Mafura Craters (Africa-C)	Crater of Bunyaruguru	0203-004
Maga (Samoa-SW Pacific)	Cone of Savai'i	0404-04=
Maga Point (Samoa-SW Pacific)	Cone of Ofu-Olosega	0404-01=
Magadini (Africa-E)	Cone of Kilimanjaro	0202-15=
Magaso (Magasu) (Philippines-C)	Synonym of Cuernos de Negros	0702-01=
Magasu (Mindanao-Philippines)	Synonym of Ragang	0701-06=
Magdgo (Africa-C)	Crater of Bunyaruguru	0203-004
Magee Peak (US-California)	Stratovolcano (None) Pleistocene	....
Mageik (Alaska Peninsula)	Stratovolcano (8, -500) Radiocarbon	**1102-15-**
Maggiore, Monte (Italy)	Cone of Sabatini Complex	....
Magne, Cratere (Indian O.-W)	Crater of Fournaise, Piton de la	0303-02=
Magneto, El (Chile-S)	Cone of Cayutué-La Viguería	1508-012
Mago (Fiji Is-SW Pacific)	Scoria cones (None) Pleistocene	....
Magolo (Mindanao-Philippines)	Cone of Matutum	0701-02=
Magrafil (Luzon-Philippines)	Thermal feature of Cagua	0703-09=
Magsuyuan (Mindanao-Philippines)	Dome of Paco	0701-09-
Ma-gu-li? [Makuli] (China-E)	Dome of Sung-Hua-Chiang	....
Magusa-dake (Honshu-Japan)	Stratovolcano of Kurikoma	0803-21=
Maguskin (Kamchatka)	Cinder cone of Tolbachik	1000-24=
Mahagnao (Philippines-C)	Stratovolcano (Uncertain) Fumarolic	**0702-07=**
Mahagnaw (Philippines-C)	Synonym of Mahagnao	0702-07=
Mahameru (Java)	Synonym of Semeru	0603-30=

Name (Subregion)	Type (Eruptions, Most Recent) Status / Relation to Named Volcano	Volcano Number
Mahatua, Volcán (Chile-Is)	Pyroclastic cone of Easter Island	1506-011
Mahawoe (Sulawesi-Indonesia)	Synonym of Mahawu	0606-11=
Mahawu (Sulawesi-Indonesia)	Stratovolcano (7, 1977) Historical	**0606-11=**
Mahega (Africa-C)	Tuff cone of Katwe-Kikorongo	0203-003
Mahengetang (Sangihe Is-Indonesia)	Synonym of Banua Wuhu	0607-03=
Mahoe, Puu (Hawaiian Is)	Cone of Haleakala	1302-06-
Mahokdum (Mindanao-Philippines)	Crater of Paco	0701-09-
Mahukona (Hawaiian Is)	Submarine volcano (None) Pleistocene	....
Maichín, Cerro (Chile-C)	Stratovolcano (None) Pleistocene	....
Maiden Hill (Australia)	Cone of Newer Volcanics Prov	0509-01-
Maiden Peak (US-Oregon)	Shield volcanoes (None) Pleistocene	....
Maidu (US-California)	Stratovolcano (None) Pleistocene	....
Maile (Samoa-SW Pacific)	Cone of Savai'i	0404-04=
Maile, Puu (Hawaiian Is)	Cone of Haleakala	1302-06-
Maillard (Indian O.-W)	Crater of Fournaise, Piton de la	0303-02=
Main Crater (Antarctica)	Crater of Erebus	1900-02=
Main Endeavour (Pacific-NE)	Thermal feature of Endeavour Ridge	1301-01-
Mainit [Maquiling] (Luzon-Philippines)	Stratovolcano of San Pablo Volc Field	0703-06=
Mainit Hot Springs (Luzon-Philippines)	Thermal feature of Banahaw	0703-05=
Maioro (Kuril Is)	Synonym of Medvezhia	0900-10=
Maipo (Chile-C)	Caldera (4, 1912) Historical	**1507-021**
Maipo (Chile-C)	Synonym of San José	1507-02=
Maipu (Chile-C)	Synonym of Maipo	1507-021
Maipu (Chile-C)	Synonym of San José	1507-02=
Maish Nunatak (Antarctica)	Cone of Hudson Mountains	1900-028
Maitabi (Solomon Is-SW Pacific)	Synonym of Maetambe	....
Maitambe (Solomon Is-SW Pacific)	Synonym of Maetambe	....
Maitara (Halmahera-Indonesia)	Cone of Tidore	0608-061
Maitei (Africa-E)	Cone of Nyambeni Hills	0202-056
Maitland, Mount (W Indies)	Stratovolcano of St. Catherine	1600-17=
Majadas, Las (Guatemala)	Stratovolcano of Santa María	1402-03=
Majaijai (Luzon-Philippines)	Synonym of Banahaw	0703-05=
Majak (Russia-NE)	Dome of Balagan-Tas	....
Majatepec, Volcán (México)	Cinder cone San Sebastián Volc Field	....
Majdel Shams (Syria)	Cone of Golan Heights	0300-03-
Maji ja Moto (Africa-C)	Synonym of May-ya-moto	0203-01=

Jaime Incer

The floor of Nicaragua's steep-sided Santiago crater of **Masaya** volcano is covered by recent lava flows that are cut by a small inner crater. Crater walls expose stacked lava flows, truncated lava lakes, and pyroclastic material erupted from earlier vents.

Name (Subregion)	Type (Eruptions, Most Recent) Status / Relation to Named Volcano	Volcano Number
Majitaka-yama (Honshu-Japan)	Dome of Oetaka-yama	....
Majúa, Montaña (Canary Is)	Dome of Tenerife	1803-03-
Maka (Tonga-SW Pacific)	Submarine vent of Tafu-Maka	0403-12-
Makalia, Mt. (New Britain-SW Pac)	Shield volcano of Dakataua	0502-04=
Makanaka, Puu (Hawaiian Is)	Cone of Mauna Kea	1302-03-
Makanru Island (Kuril Is)	Stratovolcano (None) Pleistocene	....
Makanruru (Kuril Is)	Synonym of Brontona Island	....
Makanrushi Islands (Kuril Is)	Synonym of Makanru Island	....
Makara Mountain (Kamchatka)	Synonym of Kikhiikhylkhangei	....
Makatiti (New Zealand)	Dome of Okataina	0401-05=
Makaturing (Mindanao-Philippines)	Stratovolcano (2, 1882) Historical	**0701-04=**
Makhahnas (Mariana Is-C Pacific)	Submarine vent of Farallon de Pajaros	0804-14=
Makian (Halmahera-Indonesia)	Stratovolcano (8, 1988) Historical	**0608-07=**
Makiling [Maquiling] (Luzon-Philippines)	Stratovolcano of San Pablo Volc Field	0703-06=
Makiling, Mt. (Luzon-Philippines)	Stratovolcano of Taal	0703-07=
Makinku [Mwailo] (Africa-E)	Cone of Chyulu Hills	0202-13=
Makinoto (Kyushu-Japan)	Thermal feature of Kuju	0802-12=
Makjan (Halmahera-Indonesia)	Synonym of Makian	0608-07=
Makko-dai (Ryukyu Is)	Stratovolcano of Suwanose-jima	0802-03=
Maklaks Crater (US-Oregon)	Cinder cone of Crater Lake	1202-16-
Maklaks Mountain (US-Oregon)	Shield volcano of Maiden Peak	....
Makome (Africa-C)	Dome of Fort Portal	0203-001
Makouchine (Aleutian Is)	Synonym of Makushin	1101-31-
Makua, Puu (Hawaiian Is)	Cone of Haleakala	1302-06-
Makuli (China-E)	Dome of Sung-Hua-Chiang	....
Makulot [Macolod] (Luzon-Philippines)	Stratovolcano of Taal	0703-07=
Makuopuhi (Hawaiian Is)	Pit crater of Kilauea	1302-01-
Makura (Vanuatu-SW Pacific)	Cone of Emae	....
Makushin (Aleutian Is)	Stratovolcano (19, 1995) Historical	**1101-31-**
Makushin Valley (Aleutian Is)	Thermal feature of Makushin	1101-31-
Makuwan-Chisappu (Hokkaido-Japan)	Dome of Kutcharo	0805-08=
Makuwan-Tisappu [Makuwan-Chisappu]	Dome of Kutcharo	0805-08=
Makwet (Africa-W)	Cone of Oku Volc Field	0204-03-
Makyan (Halmahera-Indonesia)	Synonym of Makian	0608-07=
Malabar (Java)	Stratovolcano (None) Holocene?	**0603-081**
Malabsing, Mt. (Luzon-N of)	Dome of Camiguin de Babuyanes	0704-01=
Malacara (Guatemala)	Cinder cone of Chingo	1402-17-
Malacara (Chile-C)	Tuff cone of Llancanelo Volc Field	....
Malacara (El Salvador)	Stratovolcano of Santa Ana	1403-02=
Malacara (El Salvador)	Cinder cone of Singüil, Cerro	1403-002
Malacate, Cerro el (México)	Cone of Zitácuaro-Valle de Bravo	1401-061
Malagsom, Lake (Philippines-C)	Crater of Mahagnao	0702-07=
Malaia Semiachik (Kamchatka)	Synonym of Maly Semiachik	1000-14=
Malaia Udina [Malaya Udina] (Kamchatka)	Stratovolcano of Udina	1000-241
Malaja Katepana (Kamchatka)	Synonym of Malaya Ketepana	....
Malala, Mount [Mt. Makalia] (New Britain)	Shield volcano of Dakataua	0502-04=
Malanda (Australia)	Cone of Atherton Volc Province	....
Malang (Java)	Crater of Tangkubanparahu	0603-09=
Malang Ii, Gunung (Java)	Cone of Slamet	0603-18=
Malang Plain (Java)	Maars (None) Holocene	**0603-292**
Malang, Gunung (Java)	Cone of Slamet	0603-18=
Malaspina (Philippines-C)	Synonym of Kanlaon	0702-02=
Malaya Ipelka (Kamchatka)	Complex volcano (None) Pleistocene	....
Malaya Ketepana (Kamchatka)	Shield volcano (None) Pleistocene	....
Malaya Ploskaya [Krestovsky] (Kamchatka)	Stratovolcano of Ushkovsky	1000-261
Malaya Udina (Kamchatka)	Stratovolcano of Udina	1000-241
Malenkiy (Kamchatka)	Fissure vent of Kliuchevskoi	1000-26=
Malenky (Kamchatka)	Cinder cone of Tolbachik	1000-24=
Malen'ky (Kamchatka)	Cone of Bolshoi Semiachik	1000-15=
Malepunyo (Luzon-Philippines)	Stratovolcano (None) Pleistocene	....
Malespina (Philippines-C)	Synonym of Kanlaon	0702-02=
Maletto, Monte (Italy)	Cinder cone of Etna	0101-06=
Malgretoute (W Indies)	Dome of Qualibou	1600-14=
Malha (Africa-N)	Maar of Meidob Volc Field	0205-05-
Malheur Maar (US-Oregon)	Maar of Diamond Craters	1202-17-
Malil (Bolivia)	Stratovolcano of Ocaña	....
Malinao (Luzon-Philippines)	Stratovolcano (None) Pleist.-Fumarolic	....
Malinche, Cerro de la (México)	Cone of San Borja Volc Field	1401-007
Malinche, La (México)	Stratovolcano (7, -1170) Radiocarbon	**1401-091**
Malindang (Mindanao-Philippines)	Stratovolcano (None) Holocene	**0701-071**
Malindig (Luzon-Philippines)	Stratovolcano (None) Hot Springs	**0703-044**
Maling (Sulawesi-Indonesia)	Unknown (None) Quaternary	....
Malingtang (Sumatra)	Synonym of Melintang	....
Malintang (Sumatra)	Stratovolcano (None) Holocene	**0601-121**
Maliota (Samoa-SW Pacific)	Cone of Upolu	0404-03-
Malisbog (Philippines-C)	Thermal feature of Silay	0702-04=
Malishi (Kamchatka)	Cinder cone of Tolbachik	1000-24=
Malitawan (Philippines-C)	Stratovolcano of Biliran	0702-08=
Malja Glat (Greece)	Dome of Methana	0102-02=
Malja Khoriou (Greece)	Dome of Methana	0102-02=
Malja Skurti (Greece)	Dome of Methana	0102-02=
Maljsa (Greece)	Dome of Methana	0102-02=
Mallahle (Ethiopia)	Stratovolcano (None) Holocene?	**0201-102**
Mallali (Ethiopia)	Synonym of Mallahle	0201-102
Mallard Lake (US-Wyoming)	Dome of Yellowstone	1205-01-
Mallola, Volcà (Spain)	Cone of Olot Volc Field	0100-03-
Malo (New Britain-SW Pac)	Cone of Lolobau	0502-13=
Malo Passo (Italy)	Vent of Stromboli	0101-04=
Malobago (Luzon-Philippines)	Dome of Bulusan	0703-01=
Malobu, Mount [Malopu] (New Britain)	Cone of Sulu Range	0502-09=
Maloepang Magiwe [Malupang Magiwe]	Crater of Dukono	0608-01=
Maloepang Wariang [Malupang Wariang]	Stratovolcano of Dukono	0608-01=
Malopu, Mount (New Britain-SW Pac)	Cone of Sulu Range	0502-09=
Malpais (México)	Synonym of Michoacán-Guanajuato	1401-06=

Name (Subregion)	Type (Eruptions, Most Recent) Status . . Relation to Named Volcano	Volcano Number
Malpais (US-New Mexico)	Tuff ring of Potrillo Volc Field	....
Malpais Volc Field (US-New Mexico)	Synonym of Zuni-Bandera	1210-02-
Malpais, Cerro [Cerro el Brujo] (México)	Shield volcano of Serdán-Oriental	1401-092
Malpaís, Cerro el (México)	Dome of Mascota Volc Field	1401-031
Malpais, The (US-New Mexico)	Synonym of Carrizozo	1210-01-
Malpaís, Volcán (México)	Cinder cone of Mascota Volc Field	1401-031
Malpaisillo (Nicaragua)	Pyroclastic shield (None) Pleistocene	....
Malpasillo (Nicaragua)	Maar of Pilas, Las	1404-08=
Malpaso (Canary Is)	Cinder cone of Hierro	1803-02-
Maluatia (Samoa-SW Pacific)	Cone of Ta'u	0404-001
Malupang Magiwe (Halmahera-Indonesia)	Crater of Dukono	0608-01=
Malupang Wariang (Halmahera-Indonesia)	Stratovolcano of Dukono	0608-01=
Maly Alney (Kamchatka)	Stratovolcanoes (None) Pleistocene	....
Maly Anyuy (Russia-NE)	Cinder cone of Anjuisky	....
Maly Chekchebonay (Kamchatka)	Shield volcano (None) Pleistocene	....
Maly Payalpan (Kamchatka)	Shield volcanoes (None) Holocene?	**1000-29-**
Maly Roudny (Czech)	Cone of Unnamed	....
Maly Semiachik (Kamchatka)	Synonym of Karymsky	1000-13=
Maly Semiachik (Kamchatka)	Caldera (23, 1952) Historical	**1000-14=**
Maly Semyachik (Kamchatka)	Synonym of Maly Semiachik	1000-14=
Malyi Sitkin (Aleutian Is)	Synonym of Little Sitkin	1101-05-
Malyj Semjatschik (Kamchatka)	Synonym of Maly Semiachik	1000-14=
Malysh (Kuril Is)	Cone of Grozny Group	0900-07=
Malysh (Kamchatka)	Fissure vent of Kliuchevskoi	1000-26=
Mamane, Puu (Hawaiian Is)	Cone of Haleakala	1302-06-
Mamaon (Mindanao-Philippines)	Dome of Leonard Range	0701-031
Mambacho (Nicaragua)	Synonym of Mombacho	1404-11=
Mambajao (Mindanao-Philippines)	Stratovolcano of Camiguin	0701-08=
Mameles, Les (W Indies)	Dome of Northern Chain	....
Mamelon Central (Indian O.-W)	Former dome of Fournaise, Piton de la	0303-02=
Mammamur (New Guinea-NE of)	Synonym of Manam	0501-02=
Mammoth Crater (US-California)	Crater of Medicine Lake	1203-02-
Mammoth Hot Springs (US-Wyoming)	Thermal feature of Yellowstone	1205-01-
Mammoth Knolls (US-California)	Dome of Mammoth Mountain	1203-15-
Mammoth Mountain (US-California)	Lava domes (2, 1260) Radiocarbon	**1203-15-**
Mammoth Mountain Fumarole (US-California)	Thermal feature of Long Valley	....
Mamot (Luzon-Philippines)	Thermal feature of Pinatubo	0703-083
Mamrut Dagh (Turkey)	Synonym of Nemrut Dagi	0103-02=
Mamuil Malal (Chile-C)	Dome of Lanín	1507-122
Mamuja, Gunung [Gunung Mamuya]	Stratovolcano of Dukono	0608-01=
Mamuya, Gunung (Halmahera-Indonesia)	Stratovolcano of Dukono	0608-01=
Mana [Manna] (New Guinea)	Dome of Managlase Plateau	0503-021
Manacagan [Kasiboi] (Philippines-C)	Cone of Mahagnao	0702-07=
Managlase Plateau (New Guinea)	Volcanic field (None) Anthropology	**0503-021**
Manam (New Guinea-NE of)	Stratovolcano (38, 2009) Historical	**0501-02=**
Manamur (New Guinea-NE of)	Synonym of Manam	0501-02=
Manana (Hawaiian Is)	Tuff cone of Koolau	....
Manantial Pelado (Chile-C)	Stratovolcano of Descabezado Grande	1507-05=
Manantial, Volcán del (Argentina)	Synonym of Peinado	1505-20-
Mana'omia (Samoa-SW Pacific)	Cone of Savai'i	0404-04=
Manareyjar (Iceland-N of)	Submarine vent Tjörnes Fracture Zone	1703-10=
Manareyjar Ridge (Iceland-N of)	Synonym of Tjörnes Fracture Zone	1703-10=
Manaring (Luzon-Philippines)	Thermal feature of Cagua	0703-09=
Manaro Ngoru (Vanuatu-SW Pacific)	Crater of Aoba	0507-03=
Manat (Mindanao-Philippines)	Thermal feature of Leonard Range	0701-031
Manchas, Las [Llano del Banco] (Canary Is)	Fissure vent of La Palma	1803-01-
Manda (Ethiopia)	Fissure vent of Manda-Inakir	0201-122
Manda Gargori (Ethiopia)	Fissure vents (None) Anthropology	**0201-120**
Manda Hararo (Ethiopia)	Shield volcanoes (2, 2009) Historical	**0201-115**
Manda-Inakir (Ethiopia)	Fissure vents (1, 1928) Historical	**0201-122**
Mandalagan (Philippines-C)	Complex volcano (None) Fumarolic	**0702-03=**
Mandalagiri (Java)	Stratovolcano (None) Quaternary	....
Mandalawangi-Haruman (Java)	Stratovolcano (None) Quaternary	....
Mandanji (Africa-E)	Dome of Kieyo	0202-17=
Mandasawu, Gunung [Pocok Mandosawu]	Dome of Ranakah	0604-071
Mandasowu, Gunung (Lesser Sunda Is)	Cone of Ranakah	0604-071
Mandegugusu (Solomon Is-SW Pacific)	Synonym of Simbo	0505-05=
Mandible Cirque (Antarctica)	Caldera of Daniell Peninsula	....
Mandosawu, Pocok (Lesser Sunda Is)	Dome of Ranakah	0604-071
Manengouba (Africa-W)	Stratovolcano (None) Holocene?	**0204-02-**
Manenguba (Africa-W)	Synonym of Manengouba	0204-02-
Manga Afi [Mauga Afi] (Samoa-SW Pacific)	Fissure vent of Savai'i	0404-04=
Mangakino (New Zealand)	Caldera (None) Pleistocene	....
Manga-ma-loba (Africa-W)	Synonym of Cameroon	0204-01=
Manganamu (New Zealand)	Dome of Taupo	0401-07=
Mangatawhiri (New Zealand)	Cone of Kariol	....
Mangatoetoe (New Zealand)	Dome of Maroa	0401-061
Mangatutu (New Zealand)	Dome of Maroa	0401-061
Mangawhakamana (New Zealand)	Dome of Okataina	0401-05=
Mangere Lagoon (New Zealand)	Tuff ring of Auckland Field	0401-02=
Mangere Mountain (New Zealand)	Cone of Auckland Field	0401-02=
Manginangina (New Zealand)	Cone of Kaikohe-Bay of Islands	0401-01=
Manguf (Ethiopia)	Cone of Mega Basalt Field	0201-33-
Mangwa (Africa-E)	Cone of Sultan Hamud-Simba	....
Manieula (Hawaiian Is)	Cone of Kauai	....
Manindjau (Sumatra)	Synonym of Maninjau	....
Maninjau (Sumatra)	Caldera (None) Pleistocene	....
Manita, La (El Salvador)	Lava cone of Tigre, El	1403-082
Manito (Luzon-Philippines)	Thermal feature of Pocdol Mountains	0703-02=
Manlayao (Mindanao-Philippines)	Synonym of Paco	0701-09-
Manna (New Guinea)	Dome of Managlase Plateau	0503-021
Mano de Diablo (Chile-S)	Cone of Reclus	1508-063
Manoek (Banda Sea)	Synonym of Manuk	0605-08=
Manoek, Kawah [Kawah Manuk] (Java)	Thermal feature of Kendang	0603-11=

Name (Subregion)	Type (Eruptions, Most Recent) Status . . Relation to Named Volcano	Volcano Number
Manoelaloe [Manulalu} (Lesser Sunda Is)	Cone of Inierie	0604-08=
Manokami-dake (Honshu-Japan)	Stratovolcano of Zao	0803-19=
Manteca (México)	Cinder cone of Chichinautzin	1401-08=
Manthe, Mount (Antarctica)	Stratovolcano of Hudson Mountains	1900-028
Manu, Lua (Hawaiian Is)	Pit crater of Kilauea	1302-01-
Manuhonohono Hill (Hawaiian Is)	Cone of Kauai	....
Manuk (Banda Sea)	Stratovolcano (None) Fumarolic	**0605-08=**
Manuk, Kawah (Java)	Thermal feature of Kamojang, Kawah	....
Manuk, Kawah (Java)	Thermal feature of Kendang	0603-11=
Manuk, Kawah (Java)	Thermal feature of Papandayan	0603-10=
Manuk, Kawah (Java)	Thermal feature of Wayang-Windu	0603-08=
Manuka (Fiji Is-SW Pacific)	Cone of Taveuni	0405-01-
Manulalu (Lesser Sunda Is)	Cone of Inierie	0604-08=
Manum (Manun) (New Guinea-NE of)	Synonym of Manam	0501-02=
Manumudar (New Guinea-NE of)	Synonym of Manam	0501-02=

El Misti, Perú's best known volcano, is a symmetrical stratovolcano that towers above the city of Arequipa. Historical eruptions date back to the 15th century.

Name (Subregion)	Type (Eruptions, Most Recent) Status . . Relation to Named Volcano	Volcano Number
Manupirua Springs (New Zealand)	Thermal feature of Rotorua	....
Manurewa (New Zealand)	Cone of Auckland Field	0401-02=
Manyatta [Sampu Olkuo] (Africa-E)	Cinder cone of Suswa	0202-11=
Manza Hot Springs (Honshu-Japan)	Thermal feature of Kusatsu-Shirane	0803-12=
Manzaz Volc Field (Africa-N)	Scoria cones (None) Holocene	**0205-006**
Maoniu Shan (China-W)	Cinder cone of Kunlun Volc Group	1004-03-
Mapana, Mt. (New Britain-SW Pac)	Cone of Du Faure	....
Mapi Group (Lesser Sunda Is)	Unknown (None) Post-Miocene	....
Maquilan [Maquiling] (Luzon-Philippines)	Stratovolcano of San Pablo Volc Field	0703-06=
Maquiling (Luzon-Philippines)	Stratovolcano of San Pablo Volc Field	0703-06=
Mar, Puig de (Spain)	Cone of Olot Volc Field	0100-03-
Mar, Río (Panamá)	Crater of Valle, El	1406-03-
Maraemanuka (New Zealand)	Dome of Maroa	0401-061
Maragong-Ong (Mindanao-Philippines)	Dome of Paco	0701-09-
Marapi (Sumatra)	Complex volcano (59, 2004) Historical	**0601-14=**
Marapi, Gunung (Sumatra)	Stratovolcano of Dempo	0601-23=
Marawer Spring (Mindanao-Philippines)	Thermal feature of Apo	0701-03=
Marbas (Perú)	Cinder cone of Huambo	1504-005
Marbas Chico (Perú)	Cinder cone of Huambo	1504-005
Marbas Grande, Cerro (Perú)	Cinder cone of Huambo	1504-005
Marble Mountain (US-Washington)	Shield volcano (None) Pleistocene	....
Marca, Loma la (Ecuador)	Dome of Pululagua	1502-011
March (Kamchatka)	Fissure vent of Kliuchevskoi	1000-26=
Marchena (Galápagos)	Shield volcano (1, 1991) Historical	**1503-08=**
Marciana, Valle (Italy)	Maar of Alban Hills	0101-004
Marco, Cratere (Indian O.-W)	Crater of Fournaise, Piton de la	0303-02=
Marcondas, Pica das (Azores)	Dome of Furnas	1802-10=
Mardja (Africa-W)	Crater of Ngaoundere Plateau	0204-04-
Mare (Halmahera-Indonesia)	Stratovolcano (None) Holocene	**0608-062**
Mare (Halmahera-Indonesia)	Cone of Moti	0608-063
Marecocco (Italy)	Dome of Ischia	0101-03=
Mareoroa Springs (New Zealand)	Thermal feature of Rotorua	....
Mareta, Caldera de la (Canary Is)	Crater of Hierro	1803-02-
Mareta, La (Canary Is)	Cone of Tenerife	1803-03-
Marga Bajoer [Marga Bayur] (Sumatra)	Thermal feature of Besar	0601-25=
Marga Bajur [Marga Mayur] (Sumatra)	Thermal feature of Besar	0601-25=
Marga Bayur (Sumatra)	Thermal feature of Besar	0601-25=
Margaret, Mt. (Australia)	Cone of McBride Volc Province	....
Margaritas, Volcancito (Guatemala)	Cinder cone of Moyuta	1402-13-
Margosa Tubig (Mindanao-Philippines)	Cone of Imbing	....
Marha, Jabal el- (Arabia-S)	Tuff cone (None) Holocene?	**0301-10-**
Maria, Doro (Lesser Sunda Is)	Unknown (None) Quaternary	....
Marian Lazne (Czech)	Thermal feature of Cheb Basin	....
Mariana, Pico da (Azores)	Cone of Agua de Pau	1802-09=
Marianbald [Marian Lazne] (Czech)	Thermal feature of Cheb Basin	....
Maribaya (Java)	Thermal feature of Tangkubanparahu	0603-09=
Mariñaqui, Laguna (Chile-C)	Cinder cones (None) Holocene	**1507-092**
Marion Island (Indian O.-S)	Shield volcanoes (2, 2004) Historical	**0304-07-**
Marion Mountain (US-Oregon)	Cone of Three Fingered Jack	....
Marion Peak (US-Oregon)	Cone of Three Fingered Jack	....
Maripipi (Philippines-C)	Unknown (None) Quaternary	....

Name (Subregion)	Type (Eruptions, Most Recent) Status / Relation to Named Volcano	Volcano Number
Marishiten (Honshu-Japan)	Crater of Norikura	0803-06=
Marishiten (Honshu-Japan)	Crater of On-take	0803-04=
Mariveles (Luzon-Philippines)	Stratovolcano (1, -2050) Radiocarbon	**0703-081**
Markagunt Plateau (US-Utah)	Volcanic field (1, 1050) Dendrochronology	**1207-04-**
Markarfljot (Iceland-S)	Dome of Torfajökull	1702-05=
Market Lake Craters (US-Idaho)	Synonym of Menan Buttes	....
Marlanga (Luzon-Philippines)	Synonym of Malindig	0703-044
Marmolejo (Chile-C)	Stratovolcano of San José	1507-02=
Maroa (New Zealand)	Calderas (2, 180) Tephrochronology	**0401-061**
Maroa North (New Zealand)	Dome of Maroa	0401-061
Maroa South (New Zealand)	Dome of Maroa	0401-061
Maroa West (New Zealand)	Dome of Maroa	0401-061
Maroanui (New Zealand)	Dome of Maroa	0401-061
Marotiri (New Zealand)	Dome of Taupo	0401-07=
Maroum [Marum] (Vanuatu-SW Pacific)	Crater of Ambrym	0507-04=
Marqués, Cerro el (México)	Cone of Chichinautzin	1401-08=
Marra, Jebel (Africa-N)	Volcanic field (1, -2000) Radiocarbon	**0205-03-**
Marsabit (Africa-E)	Shield volcano (None) Holocene?	**0202-021**
Martana, Isola (Italy)	Cone of Vulsini	0101-003
Marte (Colombia)	Crater of Galeras	1501-08=
Marteles, Caldera de (Canary Is)	Maar of Gran Canaria	1803-04-
Martignano (Italy)	Crater of Sabatini Complex	....
Martimbang (Sumatra)	Stratovolcano (None) Pleistocene	....
Martin (Alaska Peninsula)	Stratovolcano (4, 1953) Historical	**1102-14-**
Martin [San Martín] (Canary Is)	Cinder cone of La Palma	1803-01-
Martín Perez, Isla (El Salvador)	Cinder cone of Zacatillo, Isla	....
Martin Vaz (Atlantic-C)	Stratovolcano (None) Pleistocene	....
Martinya, Puig de (Spain)	Cone of Olot Volc Field	0100-03-
Maruata (New Zealand)	Cone of Whangarei	0401-011
Marum (Vanuatu-SW Pacific)	Crater of Ambrym	0507-04=
Marumliglar (Vanuatu-SW Pacific)	Crater of Ambrym	0507-04=
Marumori (Honshu-Japan)	Cone of Nyuto-Takakura	....
Maruno-yama (Honshu-Japan)	Cinder cone of Izu-Tobu	0803-01=
Maruoka-yama (Kyushu-Japan)	Cone of Kirishima	0802-09=
Marushima-yama (Izu Is-Japan)	Dome of Nii-jima	0804-02=
Marusima-yama [Marushima-yama] (Japan)	Dome of Nii-jima	0804-02=
Maruyama (Honshu-Japan)	Cone of Bandai	0803-16=
Maru-yama (Hokkaido-Japan)	Cone of Akaigawa	....
Maru-yama (Izu Is-Japan)	Cone of Aoga-shima	0804-06=
Maru-yama (Kyushu-Japan)	Stratovolcano of Aso	0802-11=
Maru-yama (Honshu-Japan)	Cone of Dainichiga-take	....
Maru-yama (Hokkaido-Japan)	Synonym of E-san Maru-yama	....
Maru-yama (Honshu-Japan)	Cone of Fuji	0803-03=
Maru-yama (Honshu-Japan)	Cone of Izu-Tobu	0803-01=
Maru-yama (Hokkaido-Japan)	Dome of Kutcharo	0805-08=
Maru-yama (Hokkaido-Japan)	Dome of Nipesotsu-Maruyama	0805-061
Maru-yama (Hokkaido-Japan)	Synonym of Oshima Maru-yama	....
Maru-yama (Honshu-Japan)	Dome of Osore-yama	0803-29=
Maru-yama (Honshu-Japan)	Synonym of Ryohaku Maru-yama	....
Maru-yama (Kyushu-Japan)	Synonym of Satsuma Maru-yama	....

Ichio Moriya (Kanazawa Univ.)

A fissure eruption from the SW flank of **Miyake-jima** volcano in the Izu Islands produced lava flows that destroyed portions of Ako town, burying 400 houses. The fissure extended to below sea level, producing submarine phreatomagmatic explosions.

Name (Subregion)	Type (Eruptions, Most Recent) Status / Relation to Named Volcano	Volcano Number
Maru-yama (Honshu-Japan)	Dome of Sengoku	....
Maru-yama (Hokkaido-Japan)	Cone of Tokachi	0805-05=
Mary Bay (US-Wyoming)	Crater of Yellowstone	1205-01-
Mary's Glory (W Indies)	Cone of Northern Centres	....
Mary's Glory (W Indies)	Stratovolcano of Quill, The	1600-02=
Mary's Point Mountain (W Indies)	Dome of Saba	1600-01=
Marysville Buttes (US-California)	Synonym of Sutter Buttes	....
Mas a Fuera (Chile-Is)	Synonym of Alexander Selkirk	....
Mas a Tierra (Chile-Is)	Synonym of Robinson Crusoe	1506-02=
Mas, Kawah (Java)	Thermal feature of Papandayan	0603-10=
Masa (Samoa-SW Pacific)	Cone of Savai'i	0404-04=
Masahuat Volc Field (El Salvador)	Stratovolcano (None) Pleistocene	....
Masakari-yama (Kuril Is)	Synonym of Ebeko	0900-38=
Masalakot (Luzon-Philippines)	Dome of Banahaw	0703-05=
Masaraga (Luzon-Philippines)	Stratovolcano (None) Holocene	**0703-031**
Masarang (Sulawesi-Indonesia)	Cone of Mahawu	0606-11=
Masatepeque, Cerro (El Salvador)	Cinder cone of San Diego	1403-001
Masaya (Nicaragua)	Caldera (34, 2008) Historical	**1404-10=**
Mascota Volc Field (México)	Cinder cones (None) Holocene	**1401-031**
Mase (Solomon Is-SW Pacific)	Unknown (None) Post-Miocene	....
Masecha (Africa-C)	Crater of Bunyaruguru	0203-004
Masem, Kawah (Sulawesi-Indonesia)	Crater of Sempu	0606-04=
Mashiga (Africa-C)	Cone of Nyamuragira	0203-02=
Mashkovtsev (Kamchatka)	Stratovolcano (None) Holocene	**1000-001**
Mashu (Hokkaido-Japan)	Caldera (7, 1080) Radiocarbon	**0805-081**
Mashumangabo (Africa-C)	Cone of Nyamuragira	0203-02=
Masigit (Java)	Crater of Guntur	0603-13=
Masigit (Java)	Crater of Talagabodas	0603-15=
Masigit, Gunung (Java)	Stratovolcano of Kamojang, Kawah	....
Masipelid (Mindanao-Philippines)	Dome of Paco	0701-09-
Maskhorne Hill (W Indies)	Dome of Saba	1600-01=
Mason Spur (Antarctica)	Fissure vent of Morning, Mt.	1900-020
Mason Spurr (Antarctica)	Lava domes (None) Pleistocene	....
Massako (Africa-E)	Maar of Kieyo	0202-17=
Masseria Bosco del Monaco (Italy)	Vent of Vesuvius	0101-02=
Massif (French for Mountain Range) see proper name (e.g. Guynemer, Massif)		
Masteiro, Caldeira (Azores)	Crater of Flores	1802-001
Masugata (Honshu-Japan)	Pyroclastic cone (None) Pleistocene	....
Masyu (Hokkaido-Japan)	Synonym of Mashu	0805-081
Mat Ala (Ethiopia)	Crater of Borawli	0201-107
Mat Ala (Ethiopia)	Shield volcano (None) Holocene	**0201-105**
Mata Ahogado (Panamá)	Crater of Valle, El	1406-03-
Mata das Feiticeiras (Azores)	Cone of Picos Volc System	1802-081
Mata Ole Afi (Samoa-SW Pacific)	Crater of Savai'i	0404-04=
Mata Uta (SW Pacific)	Tuff cone of Wallis Islands	0404-05-
Mata'aga (Samoa-SW Pacific)	Cone of Savai'i	0404-04=
Mataba (Luzon-Philippines)	Dome of Pinatubo	0703-083
Matafa (Samoa-SW Pacific)	Cone of Savai'i	0404-04=
Matafao (Samoa-SW Pacific)	Dome of Tutuila	0404-02-
Matahawra (New Zealand)	Dome of Okataina	0401-05=
Matakarua (New Zealand)	Cone of Auckland Field	0401-02=
Mataleloch (New Britain-SW Pac)	Stratovolcano of Oto Group	....
Mataloko (Lesser Sunda Is)	Thermal feature of Inierie	0604-08=
Mataltepe, Cerro (Guatemala)	Cone of Suchitán	1402-16-
Matambe (Solomon Is-SW Pacific)	Synonym of Maetambe	....
Ma'tan, Jabal (Arabia-W)	Cone of Rahat, Harrat	0301-07=
Matanding (Sulu Is-Philippines)	Cinder cone of Jolo	0700-01=
Mataorochi-dake (Hokkaido-Japan)	Cone of Musa	....
Matarem (Luzon-N of)	Compound volcano (None) Pleistocene	....
Mataulano (Samoa-SW Pacific)	Cinder cone of Savai'i	0404-04=
Matavanu (Samoa-SW Pacific)	Cone of Savai'i	0404-04=
Matawha Point (New Zealand)	Cone of Karioi	....
Mateer (Africa-W)	Crater of Cameroon	0204-01=
Matehegy (Hungary)	Cone of Balaton Highland	....
Mateliane (W Indies)	Stratovolcano of Axial Chain	....
Mathaioni (Africa-E)	Cone of Chyulu Hills	0202-13=
Matheu (Mathew) (SW Pacific)	Synonym of Matthew Island	0508-01=
Mathewson Point (Antarctica)	Tuff cone of Shepard Island	....
Mati (Java)	Crater of Arjuno-Welirang	0603-29=
Mati, Lake (Halmahera-Indonesia)	Maar of Ibu	0608-03=
Matiankanina (Madagascar)	Cone of Itasy Volc Field	0303-014
Matlalcueye [Matlacueyatl] (México)	Synonym of Malinche, La	1401-091
Ma-tsao (Taiwan)	Thermal feature of Tatun Group	0801-032
Matsugakubo (Kyushu-Japan)	Maar of Ibusuki Volc Field	0802-07=
Matsugamine (Honshu-Japan)	Dome of Narugo	0803-20=
Matsukawa (Honshu-Japan)	Thermal feature of Hachimantai	0803-25=
Matsukawa Spa (Honshu-Japan)	Thermal feature of Iwate	0803-24=
Matsumae-Ko-jima (Hokkaido-Japan)	Synonym of Oshima-Ko-jima	....
Matsuwa-jima (Kuril Is)	Synonym of Sarychev Peak	0900-24=
Matsuyamahana (Izu Is-Japan)	Dome of Kozu-shima	0804-03=
Matthew Island (SW Pacific)	Stratovolcano (3, 1956) Historical	**0508-01=**
Matthieu Lakes Fissure (US-Oregon)	Fissure vent of North Sister Field	1202-07-
Matua-jima (Kuril Is)	Synonym of Sarychev Peak	0900-24=
Matuffa Crater (Africa-E)	Cone of Meru	0202-16=
Matugamine [Matsugamine] (Honshu-Japan)	Dome of Narugo	0803-20=
Matupi [Tavurvur] (New Britain-SW Pac)	Stratovolcano of Rabaul	0502-14=
Matupit Island (New Britain-SW Pac)	Cone of Rabaul	0502-14=
Matutan (Mindanao-Philippines)	Synonym of Matutum	0701-02=
Matutum (Mindanao-Philippines)	Stratovolcano (3, 1290) Radiocarbon	**0701-02=**
Mau [Loboa] (Vanuatu-SW Pacific)	Stratovolcano of North Vate	0507-081
Maug Islands (Mariana Is-C Pacific)	Stratovolcano (None) Fumarolic	**0804-143**
Mauga Afi (Samoa-SW Pacific)	Fissure vent of Savai'i	0404-04=
Mauga Ali'i (Samoa-SW Pacific)	Cone of Upolu	0404-03-
Mauga Mu (Samoa-SW Pacific)	Cinder cone of Savai'i	0404-04=

Name (Subregion)	Type (Eruptions, Most Recent) Status Relation to Named Volcano	Volcano Number
Mauga Silisili (Samoa-SW Pacific)	Cinder cone of Savai'i	0404-04=
Maugaloa (Samoa-SW Pacific)	Pyroclastic cone of Savai'i	0404-04=
Mauga-o-Savai'i (Samoa-SW Pacific)	Cone of Upolu	0404-03-
Maughan, Lake (Mindanao-Philippines)	Synonym of Parker	0701-011
Maui, Puu O (Hawaiian Is)	Cone of Haleakala	1302-06-
Mauku (New Zealand)	Cone of South Auckland	....
Maule, Domos del (Chile-C)	Dome of Maule, Laguna del	1507-061
Maule, Laguna del (Chile-C)	Caldera (None) Holocene	**1507-061**
Mauna Haleakala (Hawaiian Is)	Synonym of Haleakala	1302-06-
Mauna Hina (Hawaiian Is)	Cone of Haleakala	1302-06-
Mauna Iki (Hawaiian Is)	Shield volcano of Kilauea	1302-01-
Mauna Kea (Hawaiian Is)	Shield volcano (6, -2460) Radiocarbon	**1302-03-**
Mauna Loa (Hawaiian Is)	Shield volcano (109, 1984) Historical	**1302-02=**
Mauna Loa (Hawaiian Is)	Synonym of West Molokai	....
Mauna Ulu (Hawaiian Is)	Shield volcano of Kilauea	1302-01-
Maunga (Polynesian for Mt.) see proper name (e.g. Kuma, Maunga)		
Maungaiti (New Zealand)	Dome of Maroa	0401-061
Maungakakaramea (New Zealand)	Cone of Okataina	0401-05=
Maungakaramea (New Zealand)	Cone of Whangarei	0401-011
Maungakawakawa (New Zealand)	Cone of Kaikohe-Bay of Islands	0401-01=
Maungaku (New Zealand)	Stratovolc. Northern Tongariro Group	....
Maunganamu (New Zealand)	Dome of Taupo	0401-07=
Maungaongaonga (New Zealand)	Cone of Okataina	0401-05=
Maungataketake (New Zealand)	Cone of Auckland Field	0401-02=
Maungatapere (New Zealand)	Cone of Whangarei	0401-011
Maungaturoto (New Zealand)	Cone of Kaikohe-Bay of Islands	0401-01=
Maunu (New Zealand)	Cone of Whangarei	0401-011
Mauras, Cerro (Perú)	Cinder cone of Andahua-Orcopampa	1504-004
Maurelle Island of 1781 ? (Tonga-SW Pacific)	Synonym of Metis Shoal	0403-07=
Maurice and Katia Krafft Crater (Indian O.-W)	Crater of Fournaise, Piton de la	0303-02=
Mauritius (Indian O.-W)	Shield volcano (None) Pleistocene	....
Mavahlidargigir (Iceland-SW)	Crater Row of Krísuvík	1701-03=
Mavro Vouni (Greece)	Dome of Mílos	0102-03=
Mavros Kavos (Greece)	Dome of Mílos	0102-03=
Mawenzi (Africa-E)	Stratovolcano of Kilimanjaro	0202-15=
Mawra Cremna (Greece)	Thermal feature of Mílos	0102-03=
Maxwell Butte (US-Oregon)	Shield volcano of Three Fingered Jack	....
Mayabobo (Luzon-Philippines)	Cone of Banahaw	0703-05=
Mayal, Cerro [Volcán Sillanegra] (Argentina)	Pyroclastic cone Cochiquito Volc Group	1507-071
Maye-yama [Mayu-yama] (Kyushu-Japan)	Dome of Unzen	0802-10=
Mayon (Luzon-Philippines)	Stratovolcano (59, 2010) Historical	**0703-03=**
Mayondon Point (Luzon-Philippines)	Cone of San Pablo Volc Field	0703-06=
Mayor Island (New Zealand)	Shield volcano (2, -5060) Radiocarbon	**0401-021**
Mayor, Pico (Guatemala)	Synonym of Acatenango	1402-08=
Mayotepe, Cerro [Cerro Moyotepe] (Nica.)	Stratovolcano of San Cristóbal	1404-02=
Mayotte Island (Indian O.-W)	Shield volcano (None) Pleistocene	....
Mayugata (Hokkaido-Japan)	Crater of Komaga-take	0805-02=
Mayu-yama (Kyushu-Japan)	Dome of Unzen	0802-10=
May-ya-moto (Africa-C)	Fumarole field (None) Fumarolic	**0203-01=**
Mazama, Mt. (US-Oregon)	Synonym of Crater Lake	1202-16-
Mazatepec (México)	Cone of Chichinautzin	1401-08=
Mazatepec, Cerro (México)	Cone of Acatlán Volc Field	....
Mazhang (SE Asia)	Cone of Leizhou Bandao	0705-01-
Mazik Dagi (Turkey)	Dome of Nemrut Dagi	0103-02=
Mazo, Mount (México)	Cinder cone of San Quintín Volc Field	1401-002
Mazo, Volcán de [Caldera Roja de Mazo]	Cinder cone of Lanzarote	1803-06-
Mazrub, Jebel (Africa-N)	Cone of Bayuda Volc Field	0205-06-
Maztaloya (México)	Cone of Humeros, Los	1401-093
Mazzacaruso, Monte (Italy)	Stratovolcano of Lipari	0101-042
Mbaniata (Solomon Is-SW Pacific)	Stratovolcano (None) Post-Miocene	....
Mbareke (Solomon Is-SW Pacific)	Stratovolcano (None) Pleistocene	....
Mbati (Africa-C)	Cone of Nyiragongo	0203-03=
Mbatnou (Africa-W)	Cone of Oku Volc Field	0204-03-
Mbenumbenu (Fiji Is-SW Pacific)	Cone of Taveuni	0405-01-
Mborokua (Solomon Is-SW Pacific)	Stratovolcano (None) Post-Miocene	....
Mborukua (Solomon Is-SW Pacific)	Synonym of Mborokua	....
Mbuelesu [Mbwelesu] (Vanuatu-SW Pacific)	Crater of Ambrym	0507-04=
Mbuga (Africa-C)	Maar of Katwe-Kikorongo	0203-003
Mbuyuni (Africa-E)	Cone of Kilimanjaro	0202-15=
Mbuzi (Africa-C)	Tuff cone of Fort Portal	0203-001
Mbwelesu (Vanuatu-SW Pacific)	Crater of Ambrym	0507-04=
Mcall Kop (Indian O.)	Cone of Prince Edward Island	0304-06-
McBride Volc Province (Australia)	Shield volcanoes (None) Pleistocene	....
McCartys (US-New Mexico)	Fissure vent of Zuni-Bandera	1210-02-
Mccauley Spring (US-New Mexico)	Thermal feature of Valles Caldera	....
Mcconnell Creek Volc Province (Canada)	Synonym of Hogum Range	....
Mccormick Island (Antarctica)	Cone of Adare Peninsula	....
McCoy (US-Colorado)	Scoria cones (None) Pleistocene	....
Mcculloch Peak (Aleutian Is)	Former dome of Bogoslof	1101-30-
McDonald Islands (Indian O.-S)	Complex volcano (4, 2005) Historical	**0304-011**
Mcintyre, Mt. (Australia)	Cone of Newer Volcanics Prov	0509-01-
McKay Butte (US-Oregon)	Dome of Newberry	1202-11-
Mckee (SW Pacific)	Cone of Wallis Islands	0404-05-
Mckenzie Butte (US-California)	Dome of Shasta	1203-01-
Mckenzie Highway Lava Field (US-Oregon)	Synonym of Belknap	1202-06-
Mckinney Butte (US-Idaho)	Cone of Shoshone Lava Field	1204-01-
Mclean Volc Province (Australia)	Scoria cones (None) Pleistocene	....
Mclennan's Hill (New Zealand)	Cone of Auckland Field	0401-02=
Mcleod Hill (Canada)	Tuya of Wells Gray-Clearwater	1200-15-
McLoughlin (US-Oregon)	Stratovolcano (None) Pleistocene	....
Mcloughlin's Hill [Matukurua] (New Zealand)	Cone of Auckland Field	0401-02=
Mcmasters, Mt. (Australia)	Cone of McBride Volc Province	....
Mcnish Bay Cone (Indian O.)	Tuff cone of Prince Edward Island	0304-06-
Meager (Canada)	Complex volcano (1, -400) Radiocarbon	**1200-18-**
Meager Creek Hot Spring (Canada)	Thermal feature of Meager	1200-18-
Meager Creek Volc Field (Canada)	Synonym of Meager	1200-18-
Me-Akan (Hokkaido-Japan)	Stratovolcano of Akan	0805-07=
Meanguera, Isla (El Salvador)	Stratovolcanoes (None) Quaternary	....
Me-dake (Honshu-Japan)	Cone of Akita-Komaga-take	0803-23=
Medam, Jabal (Arabia-S)	Crater of Arhab, Harra of	0301-09-
Medaw Island (SE Asia)	Fissure vents (None) Pleistocene	....
Media Luna (Panamá)	Cinder cone of Yeguada, La	....
Media Luna, La (Nicaragua)	Cinder cone of Masaya	1404-10=
Media Luna, Volcán (Chile-C)	Cone of Carrán-Los Venados	1507-14=
Media Montaña (Canary Is)	Cone of Tenerife	1803-03-
Medicine Lake (US-California)	Shield volcano (9, 1080) Radiocarbon	**1203-02-**
Medicine Lake Highland (US-California)	Synonym of Medicine Lake	1203-02-
Medina, Harrat el- [Harrat Rashid] (Arabia-W)	Volcanic field of Rahat, Harrat	0301-07=
Medio, Cerro del [Quizapu] (Chile-C)	Crater of Azul, Cerro	1507-06=

Laguna Grande de Mojanda occupies the caldera of **Mojanda** volcano, one of the largest volcanoes of Ecuador's northern Interandean Depression.

Name (Subregion)	Type (Eruptions, Most Recent) Status Relation to Named Volcano	Volcano Number
Medio, Cerro el (Chile-C)	Cone of Calabozos	1507-042
Medio, Cerro El (US-New Mexico)	Dome of Valles Caldera	....
Medio, Del (Argentina)	Pyrocl. cone Northern Mendoza Field	....
Medja [Pui] (Lesser Sunda Is)	Cone of Iya	0604-11=
Mednyi (Kuril Is)	Stratovolcano of Tao-Rusyr Caldera	0900-31=
Medves (Hungary)	Vent of Nográd	....
Medvevezhy (Kamchatka)	Stratovolcano of Leutongey	1000-53-
Medvezhia (Kuril Is)	Somma volcano (5, 1999) Historical	**0900-10=**
Medvezhii (Kuril Is)	Synonym of Medvezhia	0900-10=
Medvezhii (Kuril Is)	Stratovolcano of Medvezhia	0900-10=
Meehaz Mountain (Canada)	Cone of Kawdy Metah	....
Meerfelder (Germany)	Maar of West Eifel Volc Field	0100-01-
Meetia (Society Is-C Pacific)	Synonym of Mehetia	1303-04-
Mega Basalt Field (Ethiopia)	Pyroclastic cones (None) Holocene	**0201-33-**
Megalo Vouno (Greece)	Cinder cone of Santorini	0102-04=
Megalos Polybotes [Polyvotis Megalos]	Vent of Nisyros	0102-05=
Megata (Honshu-Japan)	Maars (2, -2050) Tephrochronology	**0803-262**
Mehetia (Society Is-C Pacific)	Stratovolcano (Uncertain) Anthropology	**1303-04-**
Meidob Volc Field (Africa-N)	Scoria cones (6, -2950) Holocene	**0205-05-**
Meiji-Shinzan (Hokkaido-Japan)	Dome of Usu	0805-03=
Meinhuahsü (Taiwan)	Synonym of Mienhuayu	....
Meizi-Sinzan [Meiji Shinzan] (Japan)	Dome of Usu	0805-03=
Meja [Pui] (Lesser Sunda Is)	Cone of Iya	0604-11=
Meke Dag (Turkey)	Cone of Karapinar Field	0103-001
Mekegolu (Turkey)	Crater of Karapinar Field	0103-001
Mekeobruk (Turkey)	Crater of Karapinar Field	0103-001
Meketia (Society Is-C Pacific)	Synonym of Mehetia	1303-04-
Mekuninai (Hokkaido-Japan)	Cone of Niseko	0805-031
Mekunnai-dake (Hokkaido-Japan)	Cone of Raiden	....
Melalo, Bukit (Sumatra)	Unknown (None) Post-Miocene	....
Melamete (Africa-W)	Cone of Cameroon	0204-01=
Melan Oros (Arabia-S)	Synonym of Sawâd, Harra es-	0301-16-
Melaten, Gunung (Java)	Cone of Ijen	0603-35=
Melayu, Bukit (Halmahera-Indonesia)	Cone of Gamalama	0608-06=
Melbourne (Antarctica)	Stratovolcano (1, 1750) Tephrochron	**1900-015**
Melholl (Iceland-SW)	Crater Row of Krísuvík	1701-03=
Melholl (Iceland-SW)	Crater Row of Reykjanes	1701-02=
Melimoto (Melimoya) (Chile-S)	Synonym of Melimoyu	1508-052
Melimoyu (Chile-S)	Stratovolcano (2, 200) Radiocarbon	**1508-052**
Melintang (Sumatra)	Stratovolcano (None) Quaternary	....
Melkum, Mt. (Vanuatu-SW Pacific)	Stratovolcanoes (None) Pleistocene	....
Melón, Volcán (México)	Dome of Mascota Volc Field	1401-031
Melón, Volcán el (México)	Cinder cone of Michoacán-Guanajuato	1401-06=
Melón, Volcán el (México)	Cinder cone San Sebastián Volc Field	....
Melrakkahraun (Iceland-SW)	Crater Row of Krísuvík	1701-03=
Meluak (Sumatra)	Cone of Kembar	....
Melville (Antarctica)	Stratovolcano (None) Quaternary	....
Melvin Butte (US-Oregon)	Dome of Tumalo	....
Menan Buttes (US-Idaho)	Tuff cones (None) Pleistocene	....
Mencenares, Cerro (México)	Lava domes (None) Pleistocene	....
Mencheca (Chile-C)	Stratovolcano Puyehue-Cordón Caulle	1507-15=

Name (Subregion)	Type (Eruptions, Most Recent) Status / Relation to Named Volcano	Volcano Number
Menco, Cerro el (Nicaragua)	Cone of Zapatera	1404-111
Mendana (Santa Cruz Is-SW Pacific)	Cone of Tinakula	0506-01=
Mendeleev (Kuril Is)	Stratovolcano (2, 1880) Historical	**0900-02=**
Mendeleyev (Kuril Is)	Synonym of Mendeleev	0900-02=
Menengai (Africa-E)	Shield volcano (2, -6050) Tephrochron	**0202-06=**
Menjer (Java)	Crater of Dieng Volc Complex	0603-20=
Menmarubi (Honshu-Japan)	Vent of Fuji	0803-03=
Menner (Kamchatka)	Shield volcano of Gamchen	1000-21=
Menshiy Brat [Menshoi Brat] (Kuril Is)	Dome of Medvezhia	0900-10=
Menshoi Brat (Kuril Is)	Dome of Medvezhia	0900-10=
Mentolat (Chile-S)	Stratovolcano (2, 1710) Historical	**1508-054**
Menuma (Honshu-Japan)	Crater of Azuma	0803-18=
Mera Lava (Vanuatu-SW Pacific)	Synonym of Mere Lava	0507-021
Merah, Danau (Sumatra)	Crater of Sorikmarapi	0601-12=
Meralab (Vanuatu-SW Pacific)	Synonym of Mere Lava	0507-021

The irregular summit of Nicaragua's **Mombacho** volcano resulted from edifice collapse, which left the horseshoe-shaped depression in the center of the photo and produced a large debris avalanche, one of several such events at the volcano.

Jaime Incer

Name (Subregion)	Type (Eruptions, Most Recent) Status / Relation to Named Volcano	Volcano Number
Merapi (Java)	Stratovolcano of Ijen	0603-35=
Merapi (Sumatra)	Synonym of Marapi	0601-14=
Merapi (Java)	Stratovolcano (99, 2007) Historical	**0603-25=**
Merbaboe (Java)	Synonym of Merbabu	0603-24=
Merbabu (Java)	Stratovolcano (2, 1797) Historical	**0603-24=**
Merbuk (Lesser Sunda Is)	Unknown (None) Quaternary	....
Mercadel, Montaña de (Canary Is)	Cinder cone of Hierro	1803-02-
Mercedes, Cerro las (Costa Rica)	Cinder cone (None) Pleistocene	....
Mercer (New Zealand)	Tuff ring of South Auckland	....
Mercimek Tepe (Turkey)	Cone of Acigöl-Nevsehir	0103-004
Mercoeur, Puy de (France)	Cone of Chaîne des Puys	0100-02-
Mercury Islands (New Zealand)	Volcanic field (None) Pleistocene	....
Merdada (Java)	Cone of Dieng Volc Complex	0603-20=
Merdodo [Merdada] (Java)	Cone of Dieng Volc Complex	0603-20=
Mere Lava (Vanuatu-SW Pacific)	Stratovolcano (Uncertain) Holocene	**0507-021**
Mere, Wai (Lesser Sunda Is)	Unknown (None) Post-Miocene	....
Meremberg (Colombia)	Stratovolcano of Unnamed	....
Mergi, Gunung (Java)	Cone of Ungaran	0603-23=
Merig (Vanuatu-SW Pacific)	Stratovolcano (None) Pleistocene	....
Merker Kegel [Ash Cone] (Africa-E)	Cone of Meru	0202-16=
Merkurhraun (Iceland-S)	Fissure vent of Torfajökull	1702-05=
Merrem Peak (Antarctica)	Caldera of Berlin	1900-022
Merriam Cone (US-Oregon)	Cinder cone of Crater Lake	1202-16-
Merriam Cone (US-Arizona)	Cone of San Francisco Volc Field	....
Merriam Point (US-Oregon)	Dome of Crater Lake	1202-16-
Mersidat (Africa-N)	Cone of Bayuda Volc Field	0205-06-
Meru (Africa-E)	Stratovolcano (4, 1910) Historical	**0202-16=**
Merubai (Sumatra)	Unknown (None) Post-Miocene	....
Mesa (Argentina)	Stratovolc. of Northern Mendoza Field	....
Mesa Chivato (US-New Mexico)	Cone of Taylor Volc Field	....
Mesa de Huanárucua (México)	Lava cone of Michoacán-Guanajuato	1401-06=
Mesa de San Jerónimo (México)	Cone of Zitácuaro-Valle de Bravo	1401-061
Mesa de Zirimondiro (México)	Lava cone of Michoacán-Guanajuato	1401-06=
Mesa el Bosque (México)	Dome of Azufres, Los	....
Mesa el Burro (México)	Dome of Primavera, Sierra la	....
Mesa el Carpintero (México)	Dome of Azufres, Los	....
Mesa el Chiquihuitillo (México)	Dome of Primavera, Sierra la	....
Mesa el León (México)	Dome of Primavera, Sierra la	....
Mesa el Majaguate [Mesa el Najahuete]	Dome of Primavera, Sierra la	....
Mesa el Najahuete (México)	Dome of Primavera, Sierra la	....
Mesa el Rosario (México)	Dome of Azufres, Los	....
Mesa la Lobera (México)	Dome of Primavera, Sierra la	....
Mesa Nevada de Herveo (Colombia)	(None) Not a Volcano	1501-01=
Mesa, Cerro de La (Luzon-Philippines)	Tuff cone of San Pablo Volc Field	0703-06=
Mesa, La (México)	Cone of Chichinautzin	1401-08=
Mesa, La (Panamá)	Pleistocene caldera of Valle, El	1406-03-
Mesah (Banda Sea)	Synonym of Teon	0605-05=
Mesaka (Honshu-Japan)	Cinder cone of Kannabe	....
Mesas, Cerro las (El Salvador)	Cinder cone of Cinotepeque, Cerro	1403-051
Mesas, Volcán las (México)	Dome of Mascota Volc Field	1401-031

Name (Subregion)	Type (Eruptions, Most Recent) Status / Relation to Named Volcano	Volcano Number
Meseta (Guatemala)	Stratovolcano of Fuego	1402-09=
Meso-Semiachik (Kamchatka)	Stratovolcano of Maly Semiachik	1000-14=
Mess Creek Hot Spring (Canada)	Thermal feature of Spectrum Range	1200-07-
Mess Lake Hot Springs (Canada)	Thermal feature of Spectrum Range	1200-07-
Mess Lake Lava Field (Canada)	Vent of Spectrum Range	1200-07-
Mesurai-Ulu Nino (Sumatra)	Unknown (None) Post-Miocene	....
Meszah Peak (Canada)	Cone of Level Mountain	1200-05-
Metahag Creek Ne (Canada)	Tuya of Kawdy Metah	....
Metahag Creek Nw (Canada)	Tuya of Kawdy Metah	....
Metate, Cerro el (México)	Shield volc. of Michoacán-Guanajuato	1401-06=
Metcalf Domes (Aleutian Is)	Former dome of Bogoslof	1101-30-
Metepec (México)	Cone of Chichinautzin	1401-08=
Methana (Greece)	Lava domes (1, -258) Historical	**0102-02=**
Metis Shoal (Tonga-SW Pacific)	Submarine volcano (9, 1995) Historical	**0403-07=**
Metlalcueyatle (México)	Synonym of Malinche, La	1401-091
Metrogoon Lake (Aleutian Is)	Synonym of Fisher	1101-35-
Mets Tsougloukh (Armenia)	Cone of Ghegam Ridge	0104-07-
Meugeurinceng (Sumatra)	Fissure vents (None) Pleistocene	....
Mey, Puy de (France)	Cone of Chaîne des Puys	0100-02-
Meyers Nunatak (Antarctica)	Cone of Hudson Mountains	1900-028
Mezarliktepe (Turkey)	Cone of Nemrut Dagi	0103-02=
Mezhdusopochny (Kamchatka)	Shield volcano (None) Holocene?	**1000-57-**
Mfomben (Africa-W)	Cone of Oku Volc Field	0204-03-
Mgahinga [Gahinga] (Africa-C)	Cone of Muhavura	0203-06-
Miantianshan (Taiwan)	Dome of Tatun Group	0801-032
Michael (Antarctica)	Stratovolcano (12, 2006) Historical	**1900-09=**
Michico, Cerro (Argentina)	Cone of Tromen	1507-072
Michincha, Cerro (Chile-N)	Stratovolcano of Olca-Paruma	1505-05=
Michinmahuida (Michinmavida) (Chile-S)	Synonym of Minchinmávida	1508-04=
Michoacán-Guanajuato (México)	Cinder cones (7, 1952) Historical	**1401-06=**
Micos, Cerro de los (El Salvador)	Dome of Ilopango	1403-06=
Micotrin (W Indies)	Dome of Trois Pitons, Morne	1600-10=
Micros Polybotes [Polyvotis Micros] (Greece)	Vent of Nisyros	0102-05=
Microthebe (Greece)	Dome of Volos-Atalanti	....
Mida, Cuddia (Italy)	Vent of Pantelleria	0101-071
Midagahara (Honshu-Japan)	Synonym of Tate-yama	0803-08=
Midashi-yama (Honshu-Japan)	Synonym of Fuji	0803-03=
Middle Gobi (Mongolia)	Cinder cones (None) Holocene?	**1003-05-**
Middle Hill (Australia)	Cone of McBride Volc Province	....
Middle Hill [Mt. Patukio] (Solomon Is)	Cone of Simbo	0505-05=
Middle Range (W Indies)	Stratovolcano of Liamuiga	1600-03=
Middle Sister (US-Oregon)	Stratovolcano of North Sister Field	1202-07-
Midfell (Iceland-S)	Tuya of Hrómundartindur	1701-051
Midhdalsjokull (Iceland-S)	Synonym of Katla	1702-03=
Midkvislarhraun (Iceland-S)	Fissure vent of Katla	1702-03=
Midori (Honshu-Japan)	Cinder cone of Kannabe	....
Midori (Honshu-Japan)	Cinder cone of Ogino-Sen	....
Midori (Kuril Is)	Synonym of Zavaritzki Caldera	0900-18=
Midoriga-ike (Honshu-Japan)	Crater of Haku-san	0803-05=
Midoriiko (Kuril Is)	Synonym of Zavaritzki Caldera	0900-18=
Midskalarheidarhraun (Iceland-S)	Fissure vent of Eyjafjallajökull	1702-02=
Mienhuayu (Taiwan)	Stratovolcano (None) Pleistocene	....
Mie-yama (Honshu-Japan)	Synonym of Fuji	0803-03=
Migong Shan (China-W)	Cinder cone of Kunlun Volc Group	1004-03-
Migong Shan (China-W)	Cinder cone of Kunlun Volc Group	1004-03-
Migululu (Africa-E)	Cone of Chyulu Hills	0202-13=
Mihaga (Africa-C)	Cone of Nyamuragira	0203-02=
Mihara (Izu Is-Japan)	Pleistocene caldera of Hachijo-jima	0804-05=
Miharashi-yama (Honshu-Japan)	Dome of Akagi	0803-13=
Mihara-yama (Izu Is-Japan)	Cone of Oshima	0804-01=
Mihonga (Africa-C)	Cone of Nyamuragira	0203-02=
Mihunzheng (China-E)	Cinder cone of Jingbo	1005-04-
Mi-ike (Kyushu-Japan)	Maar of Kirishima	0802-09=
Miike-dake (Honshu-Japan)	Dome of Hiuchi	0803-131
Mikage-san (Honshu-Japan)	Synonym of Fuji	0803-03=
Mikami-yama (Honshu-Japan)	Synonym of Fuji	0803-03=
Mikasa-yama (Honshu-Japan)	Stratovolcano of On-take	0803-04=
Mikeno (Africa-C)	Stratovolcano (None) Pleistocene	....
Mikombe (Africa-C)	Cone of Nyamuragira	0203-02=
Mikros Polybotes [Polyvotis Micros] (Greece)	Vent of Nisyros	0102-05=
Mikura-jima (Izu Is-Japan)	Stratovolcano (2, -4100) Tephrochron	**0804-041**
Mikurigaike (Honshu-Japan)	Crater of Tate-yama	0803-08=
Milbanke Sound Group (Canada)	Cinder cones (None) Holocene	**1200-12-**
Milky River (Aleutian Is)	Thermal feature of Atka	1101-16-
Miller Knoll (US-Utah)	Cone of Markagunt Plateau	1207-04-
Milliri, Cerro (Chile-N)	Cone of Copa, Cerro	....
Milne (Kuril Is)	Somma volcano (None) Holocene	**0900-161**
Mílos (Greece)	Stratovolcanoes (1, 140) Radiocarbon	**0102-03=**
Milt's Pond Hot Springs (US-Washington)	Thermal feature of St. Helens	1201-05-
Milu Tatu (Africa-E)	Cone of Nyambeni Hills	0202-056
Mimata-yama (Kyushu-Japan)	Dome of Kuju	0802-12=
Mimot (SE Asia)	Cone of Snoul	....
Mina Azufral (Galápagos)	Thermal feature of Negra, Sierra	1503-05=
Mina, Volcán la (México)	Cinder cone of Michoacán-Guanajuato	1401-06=
Minabul (Luzon-N of)	Cone of Camiguin de Babuyanes	0704-01=
Minakami (Honshu-Japan)	Lava dome (None) Pleistocene	....
Minami Kasuga (Volcano Is-Japan)	Submarine volcano (None) Holocene	**0804-135**
Minami-Chirippu [Bogdan Khmelnitskii]	Stratovolcano of Chirip	0900-09=
Minami-dake (Hokkaido-Japan)	Stratovolcano of Akan	0805-07=
Minami-dake (Kyushu-Japan)	Stratovolcano of Sakura-jima	0802-08=
Minami-dake (Hokkaido-Japan)	Crater of Shiretoko-Iwo-zan	0805-09=
Minami-Gassan (Honshu-Japan)	Stratovolcano of Nasu	0803-15=
Minami-Hiyoshi (Volcano Is-Japan)	Submarine volcano (1, 1975) Historical	**0804-131**
Minami-Hiyoshi Kaizan (Volcano Is-Japan)	Synonym of Minami-Hiyoshi	0804-131

Name (Subregion)	Type (Eruptions, Most Recent) Status / Relation to Named Volcano	Volcano Number
Minami-Iwo-dake (Kuril Is)	Synonym of Kuntomintar	....
Minami-Iwo-jima (Volcano Is-Japan)	Synonym of Fukutoku-Okanoba	0804-13=
Minami-Tirippu [Bogdan Khmelnitskii]	Stratovolcano of Chirip	0900-09=
Minami-Yatsuga-take (Honshu-Japan)	Synonym of Yatsuga-take	....
Minami-Zao (Honshu-Japan)	Stratovolcano of Zao	0803-19=
Minardo, Monte (Italy)	Cinder cone of Etna	0101-06=
Minasguilca Chico [Ninahuilca] (Ecuador)	Dome of Atacazo	1502-021
Minchenmadon (Minchinmadon) (Chile-S)	Synonym of Minchinmávida	1508-04=
Minchinmávida (Chile-S)	Stratovolcano (5, 1835) Historical	**1508-04=**
Mineji (Izu Is-Japan)	Dome of Nii-jima	0804-02=
Mineral Mts-Cove Fort (US-Utah)	Volcanic field (None) Pleistocene	....
Minezi [Mineji] (Izu Is-Japan)	Dome of Nii-jima	0804-02=
Miniayao (Mindanao-Philippines)	Dome of Paco	0701-09-
Miñiques (Chile-N)	Stratovolcanoes (None) Holocene?	**1505-102**
Minletaung (SE Asia)	Cone of Wuntho	....
Minma (SE Asia)	Cone of Lower Chindwin	0705-09-
Minnei (Vanuatu-SW Pacific)	Crater of Ambrym	0507-04=
Minoan caldera (Greece)	Caldera of Santorini	0102-04=
Minokol Hill (Mindanao-Philippines)	Dome of Camiguin	0701-08=
Minopoli (Italy)	Crater of Campi Flegrei	0101-01=
Minowa-yama (Honshu-Japan)	Stratovolcano of Adatara	0803-17=
Miogataira (Izu Is-Japan)	Crater of Miyake-jima	0804-04=
Mippana (Izu Is-Japan)	Crater of Miyake-jima	0804-04=
Mirador (Chile-C)	Cinder cone of Carrán-Los Venados	1507-14=
Mirador (Chile-C)	Crater of Llaima	1507-11=
Mirador, Cerro del (México)	Tuff cone of Isabel, Isla	1401-023
Miraflores (Nicaragua)	Dome of Apoyeque	1404-091
Miraflores (Chile-S)	Cone of Palena Volc Group	1508-051
Miraflores (Guatemala)	Stratovolcano of Tecuamburro	1402-12=
Miraflores-Nejapa (Nicaragua)	Synonym of Nejapa-Miraflores	1404-092
Miraibta, Jebel El (Africa-N)	Cone of Bayuda Volc Field	0205-06-
Miranda (Alaska-SW)	Synonym of Iliamna	1103-02-
Mirando (Alaska-SW)	Synonym of Redoubt	1103-03-
Miravalles (Costa Rica)	Stratovolcano (2, 1946) Historical	**1405-03=**
Misahuana Mauras, Volcán (Perú)	Cinder cone of Andahua-Orcopampa	1504-004
Misaki (Honshu-Japan)	Synonym of Oki-Dogo	0803-003
Miscanti (Chile-N)	Stratovolcano (None) Pleistocene	....
Miseno, Cabo (Italy)	Tuff cone of Campi Flegrei	0101-01=
Misery Peak, Mount (W Indies)	Dome of Liamuiga	1600-03=
Misodo-ana (Izu Is-Japan)	Crater of Miyake-jima	0804-04=
Mispía (México)	Lava domes (None) Pleistocene	....
Misterio, del [Laguna Río Cuarto]	Maar of Poás	1405-04=
Misterios, Laguna de los [Laguna Río Cuarto]	Maar of Poás	1405-04=
Misti, El (Perú)	Stratovolcano (15, 1985) Historical	**1504-01=**
Mitad, El (Guatemala)	Vent of Santa María	1402-03=
Mi-take (Ryukyu Is)	Dome of Akuseki-jima	0802-022
Mi-take [Kita-dake] (Kyushu-Japan)	Stratovolcano of Sakura-jima	0802-08=
Mitake-yama (Honshu-Japan)	Synonym of Tokuyama-Mitake	....
Mitan, Morne (W Indies)	Thermal feature Soufrière Guadeloupe	1600-06=
Mitchell, Mt. (Australia)	Cone of Newer Volcanics Prov	0509-01-
Miter (US-Utah)	Crater of Black Rock Desert	1207-05-
Mitoribata (Izu Is-Japan)	Fissure vent of Miyake-jima	0804-04=
Mitsu-dake (Honshu-Japan)	Dome of Omanago Group	0803-143
Mitsugo-jima (Mitugo-zima) (Izu Is-Japan)	Synonym of Tori-shima	0804-09=
Mitsugo-yama (Honshu-Japan)	Dome of Oetaka-yama	....
Mitsuishi-yama (Honshu-Japan)	Stratovolcano of Iwate	0803-24=
Mituisi-yama [Mitsuishi-yama] (Japan)	Stratovolcano of Iwate	0803-24=
Miyake-jima (Izu Is-Japan)	Stratovolcano (38, 2009) Historical	**0804-04=**
Miyazuka-yama (Izu Is-Japan)	Dome of Nii-jima	0804-02=
Mizu-gama (Honshu-Japan)	Crater of Kusatsu-Shirane	0803-12=
Mizunashi (Kyushu-Japan)	Maar of Ibusuki Volc Field	0802-07=
Mizutamari (Izu Is-Japan)	Maar of Miyake-jima	0804-04=
Mocho, Cordillera el (Chile-C)	Stratovolcano of Quetrupillan	1507-121
Mocho, El (Chile-C)	Stratovolcano of Mocho-Choshuenco.	1507-13=
Mocho-Choshuenco (Chile-C)	Stratovolcanoes (2, 1937) Historical	**1507-13=**
Moctezuma Volc Field (México)	Volcanic field (None) Pleistocene	....
Modenda (Africa-C)	Cone of Karisimbi	0203-04-
Modoc-Medicine Lake Field (US-California)	Synonym of Medicine Lake	1203-02-
Moeder-en-Kind (Indian O.)	Cone of Prince Edward Island	0304-06-
Moengker, Gunung [Gunung Mungker] (Java)	Cone of Arjuno-Welirang	0603-29=
Moerangi (New Zealand)	Dome of Kapenga	....
Moe-shima (Ryukyu Is)	Synonym of Suwanose-jima	0802-03=
Moetelong, Boer (Sumatra)	Synonym of Telong, Bur ni	0601-05=
Mofete (Italy)	Crater of Campi Flegrei	0101-01=
Moffett (Aleutian Is)	Stratovolcano (3, -1600) Radiocarbon	**1101-111**
Moffit Butte (US-Oregon)	Tuff ring of Fort Rock Volc Field	....
Mogote de Corrales, Cerro (México)	Cinder cone of Moctezuma Volc Field	....
Mogote de las Pilas, Cerro el (Nicaragua)	Cone of Concepción	1404-12=
Mogote, Cerro (Costa Rica)	Stratovolcano of Miravalles	1405-03=
Mogote, Loma el (Nicaragua)	Cinder cone of Concepción	1404-12=
Moheli Island (Indian O.-W)	Shield volcano (None) Pleistocene	....
Moikeha (Hawaiian Is)	Submarine vent of Mauna Loa	1302-02=
Moikeshi (Kuril Is)	Synonym of Lvinaya Past	0900-041
Moina (Ethiopia)	Synonym of Dabbahu	0201-113
Moiro, Cerro (Bolivia)	Scoria cone (None) Pleistocene?	....
Mojados, Los (Argentina)	Pyrocl. cone Northern Mendoza Field	....
Mojanda (Ecuador)	Stratovolcanoes (None) Holocene?	**1502-005**
Mojón, Cerro (Guatemala)	Cinder cone of Jumay Volc Field	....
Mojon, Montana del (Canary Is)	Cone of Lanzarote	1803-06-
Moka, Pico do (Africa-W)	Synonym of San Joaquin	0204-003
Moka, Piton (Indian O.-W)	Cinder cone of Fournaise, Piton de la	0303-02=
Mokai (New Zealand)	Dome of Maroa	0401-061
Mokapalin (SE Asia)	Synonym of Thaton	....
Mokhnataya (Kamchatka)	Cinder cone of Tolbachik	1000-24=
Mokohinau Islands (New Zealand)	Volcanic field (None) Pleistocene	....
Mokoia (New Zealand)	Dome of Rotorua	....
Mokst Butte (US-Oregon)	Cinder cone of Newberry	1202-11-
Mokuaweoweo (Hawaiian Is)	Caldera of Mauna Loa	1302-02=
Mokundo (Africa-W)	Cone of Cameroon	0204-01=
Mokuyo Seamount (Izu Is-Japan)	Submarine volcano (None) Fumarolic	**0804-094**
Molabushan (China-E)	Cone of Wudalianchi	1005-03-
Molara (Italy)	Crater of Ischia	0101-03=
Molcajete (México)	Cone of Zitácuaro-Valle de Bravo	1401-061
Molcajete Galope, Volcán (México)	Dome of Mascota Volc Field	1401-031
Molcajete Grande, Volcán (México)	Cinder cone of Ceboruco	1401-03=
Molcajete, El (México)	Cone of Chichinautzin	1401-08=
Molcajete, Volcán (México)	Cinder cone of Mascota Volc Field	1401-031
Molcajete, Volcán [Ceboroquito] (México)	Cinder cone of Ceboruco	1401-03=
Molcajete, Volcán el (México)	Cinder cone of Mascota Volc Field	1401-031
Molcajete, Volcán el (México)	Dome of Mascota Volc Field	1401-031
Molengraaff Caldera (Lesser Sunda Is)	Synonym of Batur	0604-01=
Molijingshan [Moliqingshan] (China-E)	Dome of Yitong Group	....
Molina Crater (México)	Maar of Pinacate	1401-001
Molino (Italy)	Cone of Vulsini	0101-003
Molino, Cerro el (México)	Stratovolcano Southern Guadalajara	....
Moliqingshan (China-E)	Dome of Yitong Group	....
Molo (Lesser Sunda Is)	Cone of Tambora	0604-04=
Molodoi (Kamchatka)	Stratovolcano of Gamchen	1000-21=
Molodoi Kikhpinych (Kamchatka)	Synonym of Kikhpinych	1000-18=
Molodoy (Kamchatka)	Vent of Krasheninnikov	1000-19=
Molodoy Sheveluch (Kamchatka)	Dome of Shiveluch	1000-27=
Molokini Islet (Hawaiian Is)	Tuff cone of Haleakala	1302-06-
Mombacho (Nicaragua)	Stratovolcano (Uncertain) Holocene	**1404-11=**
Momisawa-dake (Honshu-Japan)	Unknown (None) Pleistocene	....
Momotombito, Volcán (Nicaragua)	Lava cone of Momotombo	1404-09=
Momotombo (Nicaragua)	Stratovolcano (18, 1905) Historical	**1404-09=**
Monaco Bank (Azores)	Submarine volcano (2, 1911) Historical	**1802-11=**
Monastero (Italy)	Shield volcano of Pantelleria	0101-071
Monastero [Cinque Denti] (Italy)	Pleistocene caldera of Pantelleria	0101-071
Monastyr (Kamchatka)	Synonym of Avachinsky	1000-10=
Monastyr (Kamchatka)	Cone of Avachinsky	1000-10=
Mondaca [Lengua de Vulcano] (Chile-C)	Dome of Descabezado Grande	1507-05=
Mondilibi (Australia)	Vent of Newer Volcanics Prov.	0509-01-
Mongibello (Italy)	Synonym of Etna	0101-06=
Mongibello (Italy)	Shield volcano of Etna	0101-06=
Mongogogura (Africa-E)	Synonym of Lengai, Ol Doinyo	0202-12=
Mongo-ma-loba (Africa-W)	Synonym of Cameroon	0204-01=

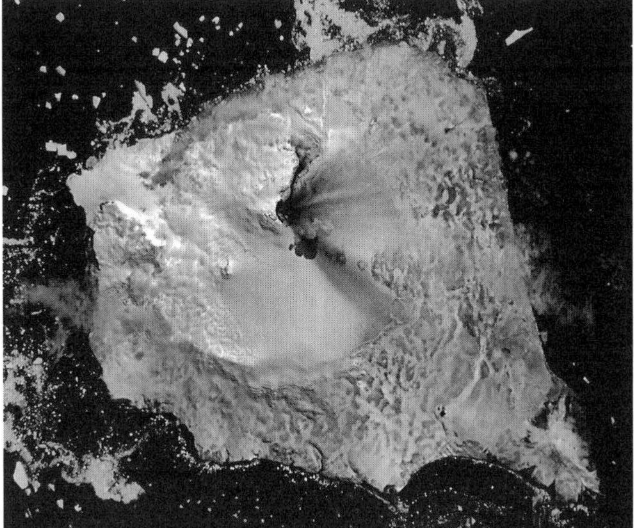

An ash plume rises from a central cone of **Montagu** volcano, the largest in the South Sandwich Islands, and ashfall deposits discolor snow on this December 7, 2003 ASTER satellite image. The summit is cut by a 6-km-wide ice-filled caldera.

Name (Subregion)	Type (Eruptions, Most Recent) Status / Relation to Named Volcano	Volcano Number
Mongomane (Africa-C)	Cone of Karisimbi	0203-04-
Mongoy, Cerro (Guatemala)	Cinder cone of Chingo	1402-17-
Moni River (New Guinea)	Synonym of Musa River	0503-02=
Monje, El (Guatemala)	Vent of Santa María	1402-03=
Monkey Hill (W Indies)	Dome of South East Range	....
Monkul (Admiralty Is-SW Pacific)	Cone of St. Andrew Strait	0500-01=
Monni (Russia-NE)	Cinder cone of Anjuisky	....
Mono Blanco, Cerro (México)	Cinder cone of San Martín	1401-11=
Mono Craters (US-California)	Lava domes (11, 1350) Radiocarbon	**1203-12-**
Mono Lake Islands (US-California)	Synonym of Mono Lake Volc Field	1203-11-
Mono Lake Volc Field (US-California)	Cinder cones (4, 1790) Tephrochron	**1203-11-**
Monolith Vent (Pacific-NE)	Thermal feature of Cleft Segment	1301-03-
Monono Island (Samoa-SW Pacific)	Lava cone of Upolu	0404-03-
Monosa (Slovakia)	Vent of Filakovo-Salgotarjan	....
Monosa-Velina (Slovakia)	Vent of Filakovo-Salgotarjan	....
Monoun, Lake (Africa-W)	Maar of Oku Volc Field	0204-03-

Name (Subregion)	Type (Eruptions, Most Recent) Status. Relation to Named Volcano	Volcano Number
Monowai Seamount (Kermadec Is)	Submarine volcano (20, 2008) Historical	**0402-05-**
Monpeloso (Italy)	Cinder cone of Etna	0101-06=
Monpilieri, Monte (Italy)	Cinder cone of Etna	0101-06=
Mons Gibel Utlamat (Italy)	Synonym of Etna	0101-06=
Monserrat, Cerro (Chile-C)	Stratovolcano of Tinguiririca	1507-03=
Mont, Montagne, Montana, Monte, Morne, Mount, Mt. see proper name		
Montagnola, La (Italy)	Dome of Amiata	
Montagnola, La (Italy)	Cinder cone of Etna	0101-06=
Montagnone-Maschiata (Italy)	Dome of Ischia	0101-03=
Montagu Island (Antarctica)	Shield volcano (1, 2007) Historical	**1900-081**
Montalto (Italy)	Dome of Vico-Cimino Complex	
Montanha (Azores)	Stratovolcano of Pico	1802-02=
Montanosa, Cerro la (Costa Rica)	Stratovolcano of Miravalles	1405-03=
Montchal, Puy de (France)	Cone of Chaîne des Puys	0100-02-
Montchatre, Maar de (France)	Maar of Chaîne des Puys	0100-02-
Montchier, Puy (France)	Cone of Chaîne des Puys	0100-02-
Montcineyre, Puy de (France)	Cone of Chaîne des Puys	0100-02-
Monte, Cerro de (Nicaragua)	Dome of Lajas, Las	1404-133
Monte, Cuddia del (Italy)	Cone of Pantelleria	0101-071
Montecchio (Italy)	Dome of Vico-Cimino Complex	
Montefiascone (Italy)	Cone of Vulsini	0101-003
Montenard, Puy de (France)	Cone of Chaîne des Puys	0100-02-
Monterosa (Italy)	Submarine vent of Lipari	0101-042
Montezuma, Cerro (Costa Rica)	Stratovolcano of Tenorio	1405-031
Montgy, Puy de (France)	Cone of Chaîne des Puys	0100-02-
Monticelli (Italy)	Crater of Campi Flegrei	0101-01=
Montículo Cinerítico (México-Is)	Tuff cone of Bárcena	1401-02=
Montione, Mt. (Italy)	Cone of Vulsini	0101-003
Montjugeat, Puy de (France)	Cone of Chaîne des Puys	0100-02-
Montolivet, Volcà (Spain)	Cone of Olot Volc Field	0100-03-
Monton de Trigo (Chile-S)	Crater of Osorno	1508-01=
Montoso, Cerro (Nicaragua)	Cinder cone of Masaya	1404-10=
Montoso, Cerro (Nicaragua)	Stratovolcano of Momotombo	1404-09=
Montoso, Cerro (Nicaragua)	Cone of Telica	1404-04=
Montsacopa, Volcà (Spain)	Cone of Olot Volc Field	0100-03-
Montuso (Colombia)	Pyroclastic cone San Augustín-Isnos	
Monumento (Atlantic-C)	Dome of Trindade	1805-051
Moolort, Mt. (Australia)	Cone of Newer Volcanics Prov	0509-01-
Moon Crater (México)	Maar of Pinacate	1401-001
Moorea (Pacific-C)	Shield volcano (None) Pleistocene	
Moorookyle, Mt. (Australia)	Cone of Newer Volcanics Prov	0509-01-
Mora Volc Field (US-New Mexico)	Synonym of Ocate	
Morabu (Africa-C)	Crater of Bunyaruguru	0203-004
Morado (Argentina)	Stratovolc. of Northern Mendoza Field	
Morado (Argentina)	Pyrocl. cone Northern Mendoza Field	
Morado (Argentina)	Cinder cone of Unnamed	
Morados Grandes, Los (Argentina)	Cone of Payún Matru	1507-066
Moraine (Canada)	Cone of Edziza	1200-06-
Morazán (Costa Rica)	Shield volcano of Sierpe, Lomas de	
More, Crater (New Britain-SW Pac)	Crater of Garove	0502-03=
Morera, Loma (Costa Rica)	Cinder cone of Platanar	1405-034
Morgabim, Piton (Indian O.-W)	Cinder cone of Fournaise, Piton de la	0303-02=
Morgan Hot Springs (US-California)	Thermal feature of Lassen Volc Center	1203-08-
Morgan Mountain (US-California)	Dome of Maidu	
Moriyoshi (Honshu-Japan)	Stratovolcano (None) Pleistocene	
Morlupo-Castelnuovo di Porto (Italy)	Cone of Sabatini Complex	
Morning, Mt. (Antarctica)	Shield volcano (None) Holocene	**1900-020**
Moro (Halmahera-Indonesia)	Crater of Ibu	0608-03=
Moro, Cuddia del (Italy)	Shield volcano of Pantelleria	0101-071
Morro (Chile-C)	Therm. feature Puyehue-Cordón Caulle	1507-15=
Morro de Azufre (Chile-C)	Synonym of Tinguiririca	1507-03=
Morro de las Atalayas (Canary Is)	Cone of Lanzarote	1803-06-
Morro Desconhecido (Atlantic-C)	Dome of Trindade	1805-051
Morro Vermelho (Atlantic-C)	Cone of Trindade	1805-051
Morro, El (Chile-S)	Crater of Osorno	1508-01=
Morro, El (Colombia)	Pyroclastic cone of Unnamed	
Mortero, El (Spain)	Maar of Calatrava Volc Field	0100-04-
Morucu (Ecuador)	Dome of Cotopaxi	1502-05=
Morzhovoi (Alaska Peninsula)	Stratovolcano of Frosty	1102-01-
Morzhovoi (Alaska Peninsula)	Stratovolcano (None) Pleistocene	
Mos (Azores)	Cone of Agua de Pau	1802-09=
Mosakiri-yama (Kuril Is)	Synonym of Ebeko	0900-38=
Mosbruch (Germany)	Maar of West Eifel Volc Field	0100-01-
Mosenberg (Germany)	Cone of West Eifel Volc Field	0100-01-
Moses (Aleutian Is)	Synonym of Shishaldin	1101-36-
Moses, Mount (Antarctica)	Stratovolcano of Hudson Mountains	1900-028
Moshkovskaya (Kamchatka)	Synonym of Mashkovtsev	1000-001
Mosimus, Mt. (Luzon-Philippines)	Twin volcano of Ambalatungan Group	0703-088
Mosonik (Africa-E)	Stratovolcano (None) Pliocene	
Mosquito Mound (Canada)	Tuya of Wells Gray-Clearwater	1200-15-
Mosquito Mountain (W Indies)	Dome of Diablotins, Morne	1600-09=
Mosquito, Cerro el (El Salvador)	Cinder cone of Cinotepeque, Cerro	1403-051
Mostaza, Montaña (Canary Is)	Cinder cone of Tenerife	1803-03-
Mostyn (New Guinea-W)	Fissure vents? (None) Quaternary	
Mota (Vanuatu-SW Pacific)	Stratovolcano (None) Pleistocene	
Mota Lava (Vanuatu-SW Pacific)	Synonym of Motlav	0507-001
Motastepe, Cerro (Nicaragua)	Cinder cone of Nejapa-Miraflores	1404-092
Mother Goose (Alaska Peninsula)	Thermal feature of Chiginagak	1102-11-
Mother, the [Kombiu] (New Britain-SW Pac)	Stratovolcano of Rabaul	0502-14=
Mothra (Pacific-NE)	Thermal feature of Endeavour Ridge	1301-01-
Moti (Halmahera-Indonesia)	Stratovolcano (None) Holocene	**0608-063**
Motianling Group (China-E)	Volcanic field (None) Quaternary	
Motir (Halmahera-Indonesia)	Synonym of Moti	0608-063
Motlav (Vanuatu-SW Pacific)	Stratovolcano (None) Holocene	**0507-001**

Name (Subregion)	Type (Eruptions, Most Recent) Status. Relation to Named Volcano	Volcano Number
Motmot (New Guinea-NE of)	Cone of Long Island	0501-05=
Motodori (Honshu-Japan)	Lava dome (None) Pleistocene	
Motonupuri (Kuril Is)	Cone of Grozny Group	0900-07=
Moto-Shirane (Honshu-Japan)	Cone of Kusatsu-Shirane	0803-12=
Moto-yama (Volcano Is-Japan)	Stratovolcano of Ioto [Iwo-jima]	0804-12=
Mottaga-dake (Honshu-Japan)	Dome of Aono-yama	
Motu Lahi (Tonga-SW Pacific)	Cone of Niuafo'ou	0403-11=
Motu Molimoli (Tonga-SW Pacific)	Cone of Niuafo'ou	0403-11=
Motuapu (New Zealand)	Dome of Taupo	0401-07=
Motuhora Island (New Zealand)	Synonym of Whale Island	
Motukaiko (New Zealand)	Dome of Taupo	0401-07=
Motukorea (New Zealand)	Cone of Auckland Field	0401-02=
Motuma (New Zealand)	Dome of Taupo	0401-07=
Motuopuhi Island (New Zealand)	Cone of Northern Tongariro Group	
Moua Pihaa (Society Is-C Pacific)	Submarine volcano (2, 1970) Seismicity	**1303-03-**
Moumoukai (Kermadec Is)	Stratovolcano of Raoul Island	0402-03=
Mouna Huararai (Hawaiian Is)	Synonym of Hualalai	1302-04-
Moundhill (Aleutian Is)	Lava cone of Seguam	1101-18-
Mountain Lakes (US-Oregon)	Volcanic field (None) Quaternary	
Mountain Top (W Indies)	Dome of Plat Pays, Morne	1600-11=
Mousa Alli (Ethiopia)	Stratovolcano (None) Holocene	**0201-123**
Mousgou, Ehi (Africa-N)	Stratovolcano of Voon, Tarso	0205-02=
Moussa Alli (Ethiopia)	Synonym of Mousa Alli	0201-123
Moustabismen, Piton de (Indian O.-W)	Cinder cone of Fournaise, Piton de la	0303-02=
Moustique, Morne (W Indies)	Stratovolcano of Axial Chain	
Mowna Roa (Hawaiian Is)	Synonym of Mauna Loa	1302-02=
Mowna Worrarar (Hawaiian Is)	Synonym of Hualalai	1302-04-
Moye (Ethiopia)	Synonym of Tullu Moje	0201-25-
Moyoro-dake [Kudriavy] (Kuril Is)	Stratovolcano of Medvezhia	0900-10=
Moyotepe, Cerro (Nicaragua)	Stratovolcano of San Cristóbal	1404-02=
Moyuta (Guatemala)	Stratovolcano (None) Hot Springs	**1402-13-**
Mpoli (Africa-E)	Cone of Izumbwe-Mpoli	0202-165
Mrit-Ment Volc Field (Africa-N)	Volcanic field (None) Quaternary	
Muaga Mua [Mauga Afi] (Samoa-SW Pacific)	Fissure vent of Savai'i	0404-04=
Muangakatote (New Zealand)	Stratovolc. Northern Tongariro Group	
Mubonyakya (Africa-E)	Cone of Chyulu Hills	0202-13=
Mucu (Lesser Sunda Is)	Thermal feature of Poco Leok	0604-07=
Mud Bay (D'Entrecasteaux Is)	Cone of Goodenough	0503-041
Mud Hill (US-New Mexico)	Cone of Raton-Clayton	
Mud Spring (US-Nevada)	Cone of Aurora-Bodie	
Mue (Africa-E)	Cone of Kilimanjaro	0202-15=
Mueggen, Cuddia (Italy)	Shield volcano of Pantelleria	0101-071
Muerto, Isla el (Nicaragua)	Cone of Zapatera	1404-111
Muerto, Volcán el (Chile-N)	Stratovolc. Ojos del Salado, Nevados	1505-13=
Mugara (Africa-C)	Cone of Nyiragongo	0203-03=
Mugogo (Africa-C)	Cone of Visoke	0203-05-
Muhabura (Africa-C)	Synonym of Muhavura	0203-06-
Muhavura (Africa-C)	Stratovolcano (None) Holocene	**0203-06-**
Muhavuru (Africa-C)	Synonym of Muhavura	0203-06-
Muhlenberg (Germany)	Cone of West Eifel Volc Field	0100-01-
Muhoti (Africa-C)	Tuff cone of Fort Portal	0203-001
Muhuboli (Africa-C)	Vent of Nyamuragira	0203-02=
Muirhead, Mt. (Australia)	Cone of Newer Volcanics Prov	0509-01-
Muja (Africa-C)	Cone of Nyiragongo	0203-03=
Mukaimachi (Honshu-Japan)	Caldera (None) Pleistocene	
Mukai-yama (Izu Is-Japan)	Dome of Nii-jima	0804-02=
Muko-yama [Mukai-yama] (Izu Is-Japan)	Dome of Nii-jima	0804-02=
Mukuani Hill (Africa-E)	Dome of Nyambeni Hills	0202-056
Mulas, Alto de las (Chile-C)	Fissure vent of Descabezado Grande	1507-05=
Mulata (Azores)	Cone of Sete Cidades	1802-08=
Mulcares Soufriere (W Indies)	Thermal feature of Soufrière Hills	1600-05=
Mulderi (Africa-C)	Crater of Karisimbi	0203-04-
Mule Mountain (US-Oregon)	Dome of Cinnamon Butte	1202-15-
Mule Peak (US-Oregon)	Cone of Cappy Mountain	
Mule, Cerro la (Nicaragua)	Cinder cone of Negro, Cerro	1404-07=
Mulimauga (Samoa-SW Pacific)	Cone of Savai'i	0404-04=
Mulino De Valentano (Italy)	Cone of Vulsini	0101-003
Mullet Island (US-California)	Dome of Salton Buttes	1203-20-
Mulukroko [Ilitebulele] (Lesser Sunda Is)	Cone of Ililabalekan	0604-24=
Mululus (New Britain-SW Pac)	Stratovolcano of Oto Group	
Munana, Mt. (Australia)	Cone of McBride Volc Province	
Mundafell (Iceland-S)	Fissure vent of Hekla	1702-07=
Mundagigar [Mundafell] (Iceland-S)	Fissure vent of Hekla	1702-07=
Mundi (Africa-E)	Cone of Paka	0202-053
Munding, Kawah (Java)	Thermal feature of Kamojang, Kawah	
Mundo Nueva (Colombia)	Crater of Cumbal	1501-10=
Mundo, Cerro (Galápagos)	Cone of San Cristóbal	1503-12-
Mundua (New Britain-SW Pac)	Complex volcano (None) Holocene	**0502-021**
Munduzhyak (Russia-SE)	Dome of Udokan Plateau	1002-03-
Mungker, Gunung (Java)	Cone of Arjuno-Welirang	0603-29=
Mungogo wa Bogwe (Africa-E)	Synonym of Lengai, Ol Doinyo	0202-12=
Mungo-ma-loba (Africa-W)	Synonym of Cameroon	0204-01=
Munlulu (New Britain-SW Pac)	Crater of Langila	0502-01=
Munlulu, Mount (New Britain-SW Pac)	Cone of Langila	0502-01=
Muntango (Africa-C)	Pit crater of Karisimbi	0203-04-
Munyanyangi (Africa-C)	Tuff cone of Katwe-Kikorongo	0203-003
Munyinya (Africa-C)	Crater of Karisimbi	0203-04-
Murakami-yama (Honshu-Japan)	Dome of Eboshi	
Murambe (Africa-C)	Crater of Bunyaruguru	0203-004
Murara (Africa-C)	Cone of Nyamuragira	0203-02=
Murcondas, Pica das [Marcondas] (Azores)	Dome of Furnas	1802-10=
Murdoch (Antarctica)	Cone of Seal Nunataks Group	1900-05=
Muria (Java)	Stratovolcano (1, -160) Holocene	**0603-251**
Muriah (Java)	Synonym of Muria	0603-251

Name (Subregion)	Type (Eruptions, Most Recent) Status Relation to Named Volcano	Volcano Number
Murniau (Africa-E)	Tuff cone of Barrier, The	0202-03=
Muro de las Lagrimas (Galápagos)	Pyroclastic cone of Negra, Sierra	1503-05=
Murphy, Mt. (Antarctica)	Shield volcano (None) Pleistocene	....
Murray Island (Solomon Is-SW Pacific)	Synonym of Mborokua	....
Murray, Mt. (Australia)	Cone of Mclean Volc Province	....
Murray, Mt. (New Guinea)	Stratovolcano (None) Pleistocene	....
Murronga Crater (Australia)	Cone of McBride Volc Province	....
Muruese (Africa-E)	Cone of Paka	0202-053
Murumuli (Africa-C)	Maar of Katwe-Kikorongo	0203-003
Musa (Hokkaido-Japan)	Stratovolcanoes (None) Pleistocene	....
Musa Ali (Ethiopia)	Synonym of Mousa Alli	0201-123
Musa River (New Guinea)	Hydrothermal field (None) Hot Springs	**0503-02=**
Musanula (Africa-C)	Cone of Karisimbi	0203-04-
Museau De Tanche (Indian O.-S)	Cone of Amsterdam Island	0304-001
Mushketova (Mushketov) (Russia-SE)	Cinder cone of Vitim Plateau	1002-04-
Mushushwe (Africa-C)	Cone of Nyiragongo	0203-03=
Muside (Africa-C)	Cone of Visoke	0203-05-
Musonge (Africa-W)	Cone of Cameroon	0204-01=
Mussa-ali (Ethiopia)	Synonym of Mousa Alli	0201-123
Musuan (Mindanao-Philippines)	Lava dome (1, 1886) Historical	**0701-07=**
Muta do Leal (Azores)	Cone of Picos Volc System	1802-081
Mutelong, Bur (Sumatra)	Synonym of Telong, Bur ni	0601-05=
Muti (Africa-C)	Cone of Nyiragongo	0203-03=
Mutju [Mucu] (Lesser Sunda Is)	Thermal feature of Poco Leok	0604-07=
Mutnaia, Sopka (Mutnaja) (Kamchatka)	Synonym of Mutnovsky	1000-06=
Mutnovskaia, Sopka (Kamchatka)	Synonym of Mutnovsky	1000-06=
Mutnovsky (Kamchatka)	Complex volcano (45, 2000) Historical	**1000-06=**
Mutnowskij (Kamchatka)	Synonym of Mutnovsky	1000-06=
Mutny (Kamchatka)	Shield volcano (None) Pleistocene	....
Mutonaju (Africa-E)	Cone of Chyulu Hills	0202-13=
Mutsa [Muja] (Africa-C)	Cone of Nyiragongo	0203-03=
Mutsu-Hiuchi-dake (Honshu-Japan)	Stratovolcano (None) Pleist.-Fumarolic	....
Mutsure-jima (Honshu-Japan)	Cinder cones (None) Pleistocene	....
Mutu (Lesser Sunda Is)	Synonym of Kelimutu	0604-14=
Muvo (Africa-C)	Cone of Nyamuragira	0203-02=
Muweilih (Africa-N)	Crater of Bayuda Volc Field	0205-06-
Mwailo (Africa-E)	Cone of Chyulu Hills	0202-13=
Mwali (Indian O.-W)	Synonym of Moheli Island	....
Myayeik (SE Asia)	Cone of Lower Chindwin	0705-09-
Myoban (Kyushu-Japan)	Thermal feature of Tsurumi	0802-13=
Myoe [Nyey] (Iceland-SW)	Submarine vent of Reykjanes	1701-02=
Myoga-take (Honshu-Japan)	Cone of Fuji	0803-03=
Myohoji (Izu Is-Japan)	Cone of Hachijo-jima	0804-05=
Myojin Knoll (Izu Is-Japan)	Submarine volcano (None) Holocene?	**0804-061**
Myojin-sho (Izu Is-Japan)	Dome of Bayonnaise Rocks	0804-07=
Myoken-dake (Kyushu-Japan)	Stratovolcano of Unzen	0802-10=
Myoken-dake (Kyushu-Japan)	Dome of Unzen	0802-10=
Myoko (Honshu-Japan)	Stratovolcano (10, -750) Radiocarbon	**0803-10=**
Myoko-dake (Honshu-Japan)	Stratovolcano of Iwate	0803-24=
Myoko-san (Honshu-Japan)	Synonym of Fuji	0803-03=
Myoko-san (Honshu-Japan)	Dome of Myoko	0803-10=
Myoro-dake [Kudriavy] (Kuril Is)	Stratovolcano of Medvezhia	0900-10=
Myozin-syo [Myojin-sho] (Izu Is-Japan)	Dome of Bayonnaise Rocks	0804-07=
Myrdalsjokull (Iceland-S)	Synonym of Katla	1702-03=
Myrdalsjökull (Iceland-S)	Stratovolcano of Katla	1702-03=
Myriam, Volcán (Guatemala)	Stratovolcano of Moyuta	1402-13-
Mytina (Czech)	Maar of Cheb Basin	....
Myvatnseldar (Iceland-NE)	Crater Row of Krafla	1703-08=
Myvetningahraun (Iceland-NE)	Fissure vent of Askja	1703-06=

N

Name (Subregion)	Type (Eruptions, Most Recent) Status Relation to Named Volcano	Volcano Number
Na Puu O Na Elemakule (Hawaiian Is)	Cone of Kilauea	1302-01-
Nabbeo (Ethiopia)	Synonym of Nabro	0201-101
Nabedao (Ryukyu Is)	Stratovolcano of Suwanose-jima	0802-03=
Nabelberg [Pusukbukit] (Sumatra)	Stratovolcano of Toba	0601-09=
Nabemori (Honshu-Japan)	Dome of Chokai	0803-22=
Nabeshima-dake (Kyushu-Japan)	Dome of Ibusuki Volc Field	0802-07=
Nabe-yama (Honshu-Japan)	Dome of Abu	0803-001
Nabe-yama (Honshu-Japan)	Dome of Aono-yama	....
Nabe-yama (Kyushu-Japan)	Cone of Sakura-jima	0802-08=
Naboiyoton [Nabuyatom] (Africa-E)	Tuff cone of Barrier, The	0202-03=
Nabro (Ethiopia)	Stratovolcano (None) Holocene?	**0201-101**
Nabugando (Africa-C)	Tuff cone of Katwe-Kikorongo	0203-003
Nabukelevu (Fiji Is-SW Pacific)	Lava domes (3, 1660) Radiocarbon	**0405-03-**
Nabuyatom (Africa-E)	Tuff cone of Barrier, The	0202-03=
Nacanze, Cerro [Cerro Macanze] (El Salv.)	Cinder cone of Guazapa	1403-052
Nachikinsky (Kamchatka)	Unknown (None) Pleistocene	....
Nacolcol (Luzon-Philippines)	Thermal feature of Pinatubo	0703-083
Nadugdugan (Luzon-Philippines)	Dome of Labo	....
Nadug-Kholdonger (China-E)	Synonym of Wudalianchi	1005-03-
Naeba (Honshu-Japan)	Stratovolcano (None) Pleistocene	....
Nafanua (Samoa-SW Pacific)	Lava cone of Vailulu'u	0404-00-
Naftilos (Greece)	Dome of Santorini	0102-04=
Nagaita (Honshu-Japan)	Cinder cone of Ogino-Sen	....
Nagane (Izu Is-Japan)	Fissure vent of Miyake-jima	0804-04=
Nagano (Honshu-Japan)	Vent of Izu-Tobu	0803-01=
Nagano-Higashi (Honshu-Japan)	Vent of Izu-Tobu	0803-01=
Nagao-yama (Honshu-Japan)	Cone of Fuji	0803-03=
Nagaramasaina (Africa-E)	Synonym of Barrier, The	0202-03=
Nagat (Vanuatu-SW Pacific)	Cone of Traitor's Head	0507-09=
Naga-yama (Honshu-Japan)	Cone of Fuji	0803-03=
Nagayama-dake (Hokkaido-Japan)	Stratovolcano of Daisetsu	0805-06=
Nagcarlang, Mt. (Luzon-Philippines)	Cone of San Pablo Volc Field	0703-06=
Nage (Lesser Sunda Is)	Thermal feature of Inierie	0604-08=
Nagira Mwaiten (Africa-E)	Cone of Barrier, The	0202-03=
Naglagbong (Luzon-Philippines)	Thermal feature of Malinao	....
Naglegbeng [Naglagbong] (Philippines)	Thermal feature of Malinao	....
Nagodang, Jebel (Sumatra)	Cone of Saut-Nagodang	....
Nagyko (Hungary)	Cone of Nográd	....
Nagylaz (Hungary)	Vent of Balaton Highland	....
Nagysomlo (Hungary)	Cone of Kemenesalja	....
Nahaha, Puu (Hawaiian Is)	Cone of Hualalai	1302-04-
Nahimbi (Africa-C)	Cone of Nyamuragira	0203-02=
Nahto (Canada)	Cone of Spectrum Range	1200-07-
Nahuistepec (El Salvador)	Dome of San Vicente	1403-07=
Naigonesoit (Africa-E)	Dome of Meru	0202-16=
Naio, Puu (Hawaiian Is)	Cone of Haleakala	1302-06-
Nairai (Fiji Is-SW Pacific)	Complex volcano (None) Pleistocene	....
Najo, El (Nicaragua)	Thermal feature of Telica	1404-04=
Naka-Azuma (Honshu-Japan)	Cone of Azuma	0803-18=
Naka-dake (Ryukyu Is)	Stratovolcano of Akuseki-jima	0802-022
Naka-dake (Kyushu-Japan)	Stratovolcano of Aso	0802-11=
Naka-dake (Kyushu-Japan)	Stratovolcano of Kirishima	0802-09=
Naka-dake (Kyushu-Japan)	Stratovolcano of Sakura-jima	0802-08=
Naka-dake (Hokkaido-Japan)	Cone of Shiretoko-Iwo-zan	0805-09=
Naka-Hiyoshi (Volcano Is-Japan)	Submarine vent of Minami-Hiyoshi	0804-131
Naka-Iwo-zima (Volcano Is-Japan)	Synonym of Ioto [Iwo-jima]	0804-12=
Naka-jima (Hokkaido-Japan)	Dome of Kutcharo	0805-08=
Naka-jima (Hokkaido-Japan)	Dome of Usu	0805-03=
Nakamachineshiri (Hokkaido-Japan)	Crater of Akan	0805-07=
Nakamaru-yama (Honshu-Japan)	Stratovolcano of Zao	0803-19=
Nakamatineshiri [Nakamachineshiri] (Japan)	Crater of Akan	0805-07=
Nakanogo (Izu Is-Japan)	Cone of Hachijo-jima	0804-05=
Nakano-shima (Ryukyu Is)	Stratovolcanoes (1, 1914) Historical	**0802-04=**
Nakano-sima (Ryukyu Is)	Synonym of Nakano-shima	0802-04=
Nakanoumi (Honshu-Japan)	Caldera of Towada	0803-271
Nakao-toge (Honshu-Japan)	Crater of Yake-dake	0803-07=
Nakitsura-yama (Hokkaido-Japan)	Cone of Yokotsu	....
Nakonomine (Honshu-Japan)	Dome of Iizuna	....
Nakot (Africa-E)	Cone of Emuruangogolak	0202-051
Nakwa, Mount (Ethiopia)	Cone of Korath Range	0201-32-
Nalachevsky (Kamchatka)	Shield volcano of Kitkhoysky	....

Tom Bretz (courtesy, W. Melson, Smithsonian)

An eruption plume rises above the summit crater of Nicaragua's **Cerro Negro** volcano in November 1968, while smoke rises from a vent (L) at the southern base of the cone that fed a lava flow. Fresh lava flows from the flank vent (lower center) were erupted in 1957.

Name (Subregion)	Type (Eruptions, Most Recent) Status Relation to Named Volcano	Volcano Number
Nama Salah (Sumatra)	Unknown (None) Pleistocene	....
Nama, Mt. (Vanuatu-SW Pacific)	Cone of Paama Island	....
Námafjall (Iceland-NE)	Thermal feature of Krafla	1703-08=
Namafjall-Kröfluhals (Iceland-NE)	Crater Row of Krafla	1703-08=
Namagura (New Britain-SW Pac)	Thermal feature of Pago	0502-08=
Namako-yama (Hokkaido-Japan)	Dome of Shiretoko-Iwo-zan	0805-09=
Namana O Ke Akua (Hawaiian Is)	Cone of Haleakala	1302-06-
Namang (Lesser Sunda Is)	Synonym of Egon	0604-16=
Namarunu (Africa-E)	Shield volcano (1, -6550) Tephrochron	**0202-04-**
Nambroque [San Juan] (Canary Is)	Fissure vent of La Palma	1803-01-
Nambroque, Pico del (Canary Is)	Synonym of La Palma	1803-01-
Nambu (Honshu-Japan)	Caldera of Akita-Komaga-take	0803-23=
Nambu-fuji (Nambu-Huzi) (Honshu-Japan)	Synonym of Iwate	0803-24=
Namlagira (Africa-C)	Synonym of Nyamuragira	0203-02=
Namshraun (Iceland-S)	Crater Row of Torfajökull	1702-05=

Ichio Moriya (Kanazawa Univ.)

The ash cone and crater in the foreground were formed during an eruption on the caldera floor of **Nisyros** volcano in the Aegean Islands in 1871. Five explosion craters pocket the 800 x 1400 m caldera floor. Post-caldera lava domes form the horizon.

Name (Subregion)	Type (Eruptions, Most Recent) Status Relation to Named Volcano	Volcano Number
Namu'a (Samoa-SW Pacific)	Tuff ring of Upolu	0404-03-
Namui, Vusi (Vanuatu-SW Pacific)	Cone of Aoba	0507-03=
Namur (New Britain-SW Pac)	Cone of Tangi	....
Namurinyang (Africa-E)	Tuff cone of Barrier, The	0202-03=
Namyong (SE Asia)	Fissure vents (None) Pleistocene	....
Nanashigure (Honshu-Japan)	Lava dome (None) Pleistocene	....
Nanawarez (Vanuatu-SW Pacific)	Stratovolcano of Aneityum	0507-11-
Nandatunshan (Taiwan)	Dome of Tatun Group	0801-032
Nangarabat Springs (Africa-E)	Thermal feature of Emuruangogolak	0202-051
Nangelaqiushan (China-E)	Cone of Wudalianchi	1005-03-
Nangetsu-yama (Honshu-Japan)	Stratovolcano of Nasu	0803-15=
Nangila (New Britain-SW Pac)	Synonym of Langila	0502-01=
Nangklak, Kawah (Java)	Crater of Papandayan	0603-10=
Nangoena (Sulawesi-Indonesia)	Synonym of Colo [Una Una]	0606-01=
Nani [Motmot] (New Guinea-NE of)	Cone of Long Island	0501-05=
Nan-Ko-la-shan [Nangelaqiushan] (China-E)	Cone of Wudalianchi	1005-03-
Nanla (New Britain-SW Pac)	Synonym of Langila	0502-01=
Nanlongwan (China-E)	Maar of Longgang Group	1005-05-
Nanook (Canada)	Dome of Edziza	1200-06-
Nanshan (China-E)	Cinder cone of Keluo Group	1005-02-
Nantai (Honshu-Japan)	Stratovolcano (1, -9540) Radiocarbon	**0803-141**
Nanti, Bukit (Sumatra)	Unknown (None) Quaternary	....
Nanum River (New Ireland-SW Pacific)	Thermal feature of Ambitle	0504-02=
Nanwaksjiak (Alaska-W)	Maar of Nunivak Island	1104-02-
Nanxing (SE Asia)	Cone of Leizhou Bandao	0705-01-
Nanzaki (Honshu-Japan)	Pyroclastic cone (None) Pleistocene	....
Nanzal, Cerro (El Salvador)	Cinder cone of Usulután	1403-081
Naolinca de Victoria Volc Field (México)	Synonym of Naolinco Volc Field	1401-095
Naolinco Volc Field (México)	Pyroclastic cones (1, -1200) Radiocarbon	**1401-095**
Napa, Cerro (Chile-N)	Stratovolcano (None) Pleistocene	....
Napau (Hawaiian Is)	Pit crater of Kilauea	1302-01-
Naperito (Africa-E)	Tuff cone of Barrier, The	0202-03=
Napier, Mt. (Australia)	Cone of Newer Volcanics Prov	0509-01-
Napoleon, Cratere (W Indies)	Crater of Soufrière Guadeloupe	1600-06=
Nappatecuhtlan (México)	Synonym of Cofre de Perote	1401-096
Nappe ee Lave ee Damar (Arabia-S)	Synonym of Dhamar, Harras of	0301-12-
Nar, Djebel en- (Arabia-S)	Synonym of Nar, Jabal an	0301-14-
Nar, Harrat en- (Arabia-W)	Synonym of 'Uwayrid, Harrat	0301-02=
Nar, Jabal an (Arabia-S)	(None) Not a Volcano	0301-14-
Narage (New Britain-SW Pac)	Stratovolcano (None) Pleist.-Geysers	....
Naranjo, El (México)	Cone of Zitácuaro-Valle de Bravo	1401-061
Naranjos, Cerro los (El Salvador)	Stratovolcano of Apaneca Range	1403-01=
Narao-dake (Kyushu-Japan)	Stratovolcano of Aso	0802-11=
Narata (Fiji Is-SW Pacific)	Cone of Taveuni	0405-01-
Narborough (Galápagos)	Synonym of Fernandina	1503-01=
Narcondam (Andaman Is-Indian O)	Synonym of Narcondum	0600-001
Narcondum (Andaman Is-Indian O)	Stratovolcano (None) Holocene	**0600-001**
Narega (New Britain-SW Pac)	Synonym of Narage	....
Nari (Korea)	Caldera of Ulreung	1006-03-
Narikawa (Kyushu-Japan)	Maar of Ibusuki Volc Field	0802-07=
Narioka (Honshu-Japan)	Pleistocene caldera of Futamata	....
Nariz, La (Argentina)	Cone of Payún Matru	1507-066
Narove Island (Solomon Is-SW Pacific)	Synonym of Simbo	0505-05=
Narraga (Narrage) (New Britain-SW Pac)	Synonym of Narage	....
Narse D'ampoix (France)	Maar of Chaîne des Puys	0100-02-
Narse D'espinsasse (France)	Maar of Chaîne des Puys	0100-02-
Narugo (Honshu-Japan)	Caldera (5, 837) Historical	**0803-20=**
Naruko (Honshu-Japan)	Synonym of Narugo	0803-20=
Narusawatakane (Honshu-Japan)	Synonym of Fuji	0803-03=
Nash Crater (US-Oregon)	Cinder cone of Sand Mountain Field	1202-04-
Naso (Honshu-Japan)	Synonym of Nasu	0803-15=
Nasu (Honshu-Japan)	Stratovolcanoes (20, 1963) Historical	**0803-15=**
Nasu-yama (Honshu-Japan)	Synonym of Nasu	0803-15=
Nasu-Yumoto Spa (Honshu-Japan)	Thermal feature of Nasu	0803-15=
Natalia (Chile-C)	Stratovolcano of Tinguiririca	1507-03=
Natib (Luzon-Philippines)	Stratovolcano (None) Holocene?	**0703-082**
Natividad, Cerro (Guatemala)	Cinder cone of Güistepeque Volc Field	....
Natorotoro (Vanuatu-SW Pacific)	Thermal feature of Kuwae	0507-07=
Natugnos (Luzon-Philippines)	Thermal feature San Pablo Volc Field	0703-06=
Natyin Taung (SE Asia)	Cone of Lower Chindwin	0705-09-
Naucampatépetl (México)	Synonym of Cofre de Perote	1401-096
Naue, Puu (Hawaiian Is)	Cone of Haleakala	1302-06-
Nauga (Chile-S)	Synonym of Calbuco	1508-02=
Nauhcampta-tépetl (México)	Synonym of Cofre de Perote	1401-096
Nauthunilawe (Fiji Is-SW Pacific)	Cone of Taveuni	0405-01-
Navajas, Las (México)	Shield volcano (None) Pleistocene	....
Navenchauc (México)	Dome of Apas-Navenchauc	....
Navidad (Chile-C)	Cinder cone of Lonquimay	1507-10=
Navolivoli (Fiji Is-SW Pacific)	Cone of Taveuni	0405-01-
Nawasif, Harrat (Arabia)	Volcanic field (None) Post-Miocene	....
Nayavuloa (Fiji Is-SW Pacific)	Cone of Taveuni	0405-01-
Naydi (Luzon-N of)	Stratovolcano of Babuyan Claro	0704-03=
Nazko (Canada)	Cinder cones (1, -5220) Radiocarbon	**1200-14-**
Ndabibi (Africa-E)	Dome of Olkaria	0202-09=
Ndakaza (Africa-C)	Crater of Nyamuragira	0203-02=
Ndale (Africa-C)	Synonym of Kyatwa	0203-002
Ndamukoro (Africa-C)	Cone of Nyiragongo	0203-03=
Ndana (Fiji Is-SW Pacific)	Cone of Taveuni	0405-01-
Ndeke (Africa-C)	Tuff cone of Fort Portal	0203-001
Ndelaitho (Fiji Is-SW Pacific)	Cone of Waikama	....
Ndelaivonda (Fiji Is-SW Pacific)	Cone of Waikama	....
Ndete Napu (Lesser Sunda Is)	Fumarole field (None) Fumarolic	**0604-13=**
Ndetu Napu (Ndetoe Napoe)	Synonym of Ndete Napu	0604-13=
Ndiru (Africa-E)	Cone of Homa Mountain	0202-07=
Ndobwa (Africa-E)	Dome of Nyambeni Hills	0202-056
Ndoinyolendikir (Africa-E)	Cone of Sultan Hamud-Simba	....
Ndonyu Yuki Hill (Africa-E)	Pyroclastic cone of Nyambeni Hills	0202-056
Ndughore (Solomon Is-SW Pacific)	Dome of Kolombangara	....
Ndwati (Africa-E)	Crater of Rungwe	0202-166
NE Anatahan (Mariana Is-C Pacific)	Submarine vent of Anatahan	0804-20=
Ne Ch'e Ddhawa (Canada)	Cone of Fort Selkirk	1200-01-
NE Lau Speading Center (Tonga-SW Pacific)	Synonym of Tafu-Maka	0403-12-
Ne, Mt. (New Guinea)	Stratovolcano of Kerewa	....
Neapolitan Yellow Tuff (Italy)	Pleistocene caldera of Campi Flegrei	0101-01=
Near Island (Red Sea)	Cone of Zukur	0201-021
Neck, the (Canada)	Cone of Edziza	1200-06-
Nedostupny (Kamchatka)	Cinder cone of Tolbachik	1000-24=
Negami-dake [Nabedao] (Ryukyu Is)	Stratovolcano of Suwanose-jima	0802-03=
Negit Island (US-California)	Cone of Mono Lake Volc Field	1203-11-
Negop-Ghang (Africa-W)	Maar of Oku Volc Field	0204-03-
Negra, La (Argentina)	Cinder cone of Unnamed	....
Negra, Montaña [Siete Fuentes] (Canary Is)	Cinder cone of Tenerife	1803-03-
Negra, Montaña [Volcán de Garachico]	Cinder cone of Tenerife	1803-03-
Negra, Montaña [Volcán Nuevo del Fuego]	Cinder cone of Lanzarote	1803-06-
Negra, Sierra (Chile-C)	Synonym of Blancas, Lomas	1507-064
Negra, Sierra (Galápagos)	Shield volcano (17, 2005) Historical	**1503-05=**
Negra, Sierra (México)	Stratovolcano of Orizaba, Pico de	1401-10=
Negras, Montañas de (Canary Is)	Fissure vent of Tenerife	1803-03-
Negras, Montañetas las (Canary Is)	Fissure vent of Tenerife	1803-03-
Negrillar de Ensenada, Volcanes el (Chile-S)	Fissure vent of Osorno	1508-01=
Negrillar, El (Chile-N)	Pyroclastic cones (None) Holocene	**1505-106**
Negrillar, La (Chile-N)	Pyroclastic cones (None) Holocene?	**1505-108**
Negritas, Las (México)	Therm. feature Michoacán-Guanajuato	1401-06=
Negro (Chile-S)	Cinder cone of Palei-Aike Volc Field	1508-08-
Negro (Argentina)	Cinder cone of Unnamed	....
Negro de Mayasquer, Cerro	Stratovolcano (1, 1936) Holocene?	**1501-11=**
Negro del Tromen, Cerro (Argentina)	Stratovolcano of Tromen	1507-072
Negro, Cerro (Chile-C)	Cinder cone of Carrán-Los Venados	1507-14=
Negro, Cerro (Chile-C)	Pleist. caldera of Chillán, Nevados de	1507-07=
Negro, Cerro (Chile-S/Argentina)	Cinder cone Crater Basalt Volc Field	1508-025
Negro, Cerro (Bolivia)	Synonym of Moiro, Cerro	....
Negro, Cerro (Costa Rica)	Shield volcano (None) Pleistocene	....
Negro, Cerro (Nicaragua)	Cinder cones (23, 1999) Historical	**1404-07=**
Negro, Cerro (Bolivia)	Maar of Pampa Luxsar	1505-042
Negro, Cerro (Chile-N)	Dome of Purico Complex	1505-094
Negro, Cerro Volcan (Argentina)	Shield volcano Northern Mendoza Field	....
Negro, Crater (Chile-C)	Crater of Maule, Laguna del	1507-061
Negro, El (México)	Cinder cone of Chichinautzin	1401-08=
Negro, Laguna (Chile-C)	Maar of Carrán-Los Venados	1507-14=
Negro, Montagnon (Canary Is)	Cone of Gran Canaria	1803-04-
Negron, Mount (Luzon-Philippines)	Dome of Pinatubo	0703-083
Negros de Aras (Chile-N)	Synonym of Negrillar, El	1505-106
Nejapa (Nicaragua)	Maar of Nejapa-Miraflores	1404-092

Name (Subregion)	Type (Eruptions, Most Recent) Status / Relation to Named Volcano	Volcano Number
Nejapa-Miraflores (Nicaragua)	Fissure vents (8, 710) Tephrochronology	**1404-092**
Nejapa-Ticoma (Nicaragua)	Synonym of Nejapa-Miraflores	1404-092
Nekhe Khota (Bolivia)	Maar of Jayu Khota, Laguna	1505-035
Nekhe Kkota [Nekhe Khota] (Bolivia)	Maar of Jayu Khota, Laguna	1505-035
Neko-dake (Kyushu-Japan)	Stratovolcano of Aso	0802-11=
Nekoma (Honshu-Japan)	Stratovolcano (None) Pleistocene	....
Nekomaga-take (Honshu-Japan)	Synonym of Nekoma	....
Nel Cannestrà (Italy)	Fissure vent of Stromboli	0101-04=
Nellie's Hump (Atlantic-S)	Cinder cone of Tristan da Cunha	1806-01=
Nelma Plateau Volc Field (Russia-SE)	Fissure vent of Sikhote-Alin	1002-01-
Nelruna [Volcano Mountain] (Canada)	Cone of Fort Selkirk	1200-01-
Nelson, Piton (Indian O.-W)	Cinder cone of Fournaise, Piton de la	0303-02=
Nemashi (Africa-E)	Cone of Chyulu Hills	0202-13=
Nemi (Italy)	Maar of Alban Hills	0101-004
Nemo Peak (Kuril Is)	Caldera (11, 1938) Historical	**0900-32=**
Nemo-san (Kuril Is)	Synonym of Nemo Peak	0900-32=
Nemours-Nedroma (Africa-N)	Volcanic field (None) Pleistocene	....
Nemrut Boynu (Turkey)	Fissure vent of Nemrut Dagi	0103-02=
Nemrut Dagi (Turkey)	Stratovolcano (26, 1650) Historical	**0103-02=**
Nemrut Kale [Nemrutbasi] (Turkey)	Cone of Nemrut Dagi	0103-02=
Nemrutbasi (Turkey)	Cone of Nemrut Dagi	0103-02=
Nenakusa-yama (Honshu-Japan)	Dome of Kinunuma-Nenakusa	....
Neostromboli (Italy)	Stratovolcano of Stromboli	0101-04=
Neozhidannyi (Kuril Is)	Cone of Ebeko	0900-38=
Neozhidannyi (Russia-SE)	Cinder cone of Udokan Plateau	1002-03-
Nepriyatnaya (Kamchatka)	Dome of Diky Greben	1000-022
Neptune Cone (Aleutian Is)	Stratovolcano of Fisher	1101-35-
Nereuantop (Vanuatu-SW Pacific)	Thermal feature of Suretamatai	0507-01=
Nerita [Giulia-Ferdinandeo] (Italy)	Submarine vent C. Flegrei Mar Sicilia	0101-07=
Nerita Bank (Italy)	Submarine vent C. Flegrei Mar Sicilia	0101-07=
Nero delle Concazze, Monte (Italy)	Cinder cone of Etna	0101-06=
Nero, Monte (Italy)	Cinder cone of Etna	0101-06=
Nesige (Kuril Is)	Synonym of Nemo Peak	0900-32=
Nesjahraun (Iceland-SW)	Fissure vent of Hengill	1701-05=
Nesjavellir (Iceland-SW)	Thermal feature of Hengill	1701-05=
Nevada de Lagunas Bravas, Sierra (Chile-N)	Synonym of Nevada, Sierra	1505-123
Nevada, Sierra (Chile-C)	Stratovolcano (None) Pleistocene	....
Nevada, Sierra (Chile-N)	Complex volcano (None) Holocene	**1505-123**
Nevado (Spanish for Mt.) see proper name (e.g. Cumbal, Nevado de)		
Nevado [Cerro Blanco] (Chile-C)	Stratovolcano of Chillán, Nevados de.	1507-07=
Nevidimka (Kamchatka)	Fissure vent of Kliuchevskoi	1000-26=
Nevis Peak (W Indies)	Stratovolcano (None) Holocene?	**1600-04=**
New Amsterdam (Indian O.-S)	Synonym of St. Paul	0304-002
New Bogoslof [Fire Island] (Aleutian Is)	Former dome of Bogoslof	1101-30-
New Cone (Alaska Peninsula)	Cone of Aniakchak	1102-09-
New Crater, The (W Indies)	Crater of Soufrière St. Vincent	1600-15=
Newberry (US-Oregon)	Shield volcano (11, 690) Radiocarbon	**1202-11-**
Newberry (US-Oregon)	Dome of South Sister	1202-08-
Newer Volcanics Prov (Australia)	Shield volcanoes (4, -2900) Radiocarbon	**0509-01-**
Nexpayantla (México)	Stratovolcano of Popocatépetl	1401-09=
Nezametnaya (Kamchatka)	Dome of Ksudach	1000-05=
Nezametnyi (Kuril Is)	Cone of Ebeko	0900-38=
Nezametnyi (Kamchatka)	Fissure vent of Kliuchevskoi	1000-26=
Nfou, Lake (Africa-W)	Maar of Oku Volc Field	0204-03-
Nfouet, Lake (Africa-W)	Maar of Oku Volc Field	0204-03-
Ngabone (Africa-E)	Cone of Sultan Hamud-Simba	....
Ngadisari (Java)	Pleist. caldera of Tengger Caldera	0603-31=
Ngahewa, Lake (New Zealand)	Crater of Reporoa	0401-06-
Ngahuha (New Zealand)	Cone of Kaikohe-Bay of Islands	0401-01=
Ngai, Donyo (Africa-E)	Synonym of Lengai, Ol Doinyo	0202-12=
Ngai, Duenjo (Africa-E)	Synonym of Lengai, Ol Doinyo	0202-12=
Ngalata (Africa-E)	Cone of Chyulu Hills	0202-13=
Ngalupala (Africa-E)	Dome of SW Usangu Basin	0202-163
Ngangiho (New Zealand)	Dome of Maroa	0401-061
Nganha (Africa-W)	Stratovolcano of Ngaoundere Plateau	0204-04-
Ngaoundere Plateau (Africa-W)	Volcanic field (None) Holocene?	**0204-04-**
Ngapi (Lesser Sunda Is)	Synonym of Lewotolo	0604-23=
Ngapouri, Lake (New Zealand)	Crater of Reporoa	0401-06-
Ngapuna (New Zealand)	Thermal feature of Rotorua	....
Ngaramo (Africa-E)	Crater of Kieyo	0202-17=
Ngatamariki (New Zealand)	Thermal feature of Maroa	0401-061
Ngatoro Cone (New Zealand)	Stratovolcano of White Island	0401-04=
Ngatutura Volc Field (New Zealand)	Synonym of South Auckland	....
Ngauruhoe (New Zealand)	Stratovolcano of Tongariro	0401-08=
Ngautuku (New Zealand)	Dome of Maroa	0401-061
Ngawha Hot Springs (New Zealand)	Thermal feature Kaikohe-Bay of Islands	0401-01=
Ngawkasoli [Paraso] (Solomon Is-SW Pacific)	Thermal feature of Nonda	....
Ngazani (Africa-E)	Cone of Chyulu Hills	0202-13=
Ngebel, Lake (Java)	Crater of Wilis	0603-27=
Ngere Kwon (Vanuatu-SW Pacific)	Stratovolcano of Suretamatai	0507-01=
Ngesong (Java)	Stratovolcano of Dieng Volc Complex	0603-20=
Ngezi (Africa-C)	Cone of Visoke	0203-05-
Nggatokae (Solomon Is-SW Pacific)	Stratovolcano (None) Pleistocene	....
Ngongotaha (New Zealand)	Dome of Rotorua	....
Ngorongoro (Africa-E)	Caldera (None) Pleistocene	....
Ngozi (Africa-E)	Caldera (3, 1450) Radiocarbon	**0202-164**
Ngulia Hills [Chaimu] (Africa-E)	Cone of Chyulu Hills	0202-13=
Nguna [Tabutera] (Vanuatu-SW Pacific)	Stratovolcano of North Vate	0507-081
Ngurdoto (Africa-E)	Caldera (None) Post-Miocene	....
Ngurdoto Crater (Africa-E)	Cone of Meru	0202-16=
Ngusuna (Solomon Is-SW Pacific)	Crater of Simbo	0505-05=
Nguu (Africa-E)	Cone of Sultan Hamud-Simba	....
Ngwala Rock (Vanuatu-SW Pacific)	Tuff cone of Aoba	0507-03=
Ngwangu (Africa-E)	Cone of Ngozi	0202-164

Name (Subregion)	Type (Eruptions, Most Recent) Status / Relation to Named Volcano	Volcano Number
Niafu (Tonga-SW Pacific)	Synonym of Niuafo'ou	0403-11=
Nianiau, Puu (Hawaiian Is)	Cone of Haleakala	1302-06-
Niawuan (Sulawesi-Indonesia)	Crater of Mahawu	0606-11=
Niblinto, Volcán (Chile-C)	Cinder cone of Chillán, Nevados de	1507-07=
Nibushi-Oyakotsu (Hokkaido-Japan)	Dome of Kutcharo	0805-08=
Nibusi-Oyakotu [Nibushi-Oyakotsu] (Japan)	Dome of Kutcharo	0805-08=
Nicanor, Cerro (Chile-C)	Cinder cone of Maipo	1507-021
Nicholson, Cerro (Perú)	Cinder cone (None) Holocene	**1504-008**
Nickens, Mount (Antarctica)	Cone of Hudson Mountains	1900-028
Nick's Cone (Aleutian Is)	Cone of Fisher	1101-35-
Nicolson Rock (Antarctica)	Cone of Toney Mountain	1900-026
Nido, Del (Argentina)	Cinder cone of Unnamed	....
Niebla, Cerro de la (Chile-N)	Compound volcano (None) Pleistocene?	....
Nieges, Piton des (Indian O.-W)	Shield volcano (None) Pleistocene	....
Nieuwerkerk (Banda Sea)	Submarine volcano? (Uncertain)	**0605-02=**
Nightingale Island (Atlantic-S)	Stratovolcano (1, 2004) Historical	**1806-011**
Nigorigawa (Hokkaido-Japan)	Hydrotherm. field (None) Pleist.-Fumarolic	....
Nigorikawa (Hokkaido-Japan)	Synonym of Nigorigawa	....
Nihonmatsurei (Honshu-Japan)	Synonym of Adatara	0803-17=
Nihuil (Argentina)	Pyrocl. cone Northern Mendoza Field	....
Niigata-Yake-yama (Honshu-Japan)	Lava dome (20, 1998) Historical	**0803-09=**
Niihau (Hawaiian Is)	Shield volcano (None) Pleistocene	....
Nii-jima (Izu Is-Japan)	Lava domes (5, 886) Historical	**0804-02=**
Niijima-yama (Izu Is-Japan)	Dome of Nii-jima	0804-02=
Nii-yama (Honshu-Japan)	Synonym of Fuji	0803-03=
Niiyama-zawa (Honshu-Japan)	Thermal feature of Hachimantai	0803-25=
Niizima-yama [Niijima-yama] (Izu Is-Japan)	Dome of Nii-jima	0804-02=
Nika (Banda Sea)	Synonym of Nila	0605-06=
Niki (Greece)	Dome of Santorini	0102-04=
Nikia (Greece)	Thermal feature of Nisyros	0102-05=
Nikko (Volcano Is-Japan)	Submarine volcano (Uncertain) Fumarolic	**0804-132**
Nikko-ba (Nikko-kaizan) (Volcano Is-Japan)	Synonym of Nikko	0804-132
Nikko-Shirane (Honshu-Japan)	Shield volcano (11, 1952) Historical	**0803-14=**
Nikko-Sirane (Honshu-Japan)	Synonym of Nikko-Shirane	0803-14=
Nikolka (Kamchatka)	Unknown (None) Pleistocene	....

Ebisu-dake lava dome in the background and Tsuruga-ike crater lake at the lower right occupy part of the elongated summit complex of **Norikura** volcano in central Honshu. A highway leads to the summit of this 3026-m-high volcano in Japan's Chubu Sangaku National Park.

Ichio Moriya (Kanazawa Univ.)

Name (Subregion)	Type (Eruptions, Most Recent) Status / Relation to Named Volcano	Volcano Number
Nikura-yama (Honshu-Japan)	Stratovolcano of Ayame-daira	....
Nila (Banda Sea)	Stratovolcano (4, 1968) Historical	**0605-06=**
Nilahue (Chile-C)	Synonym of Carrán-Los Venados	1507-14=
Nilam, Mt. (Sumatra)	Cone of Talakmau	0601-13=
Niland Field (US-California)	Synonym of Salton Buttes	1203-20-
Nimrud Dagh (Turkey)	Synonym of Nemrut Dagi	0103-02=
Ninagongo (Africa-C)	Synonym of Nyiragongo	0203-03=
Ninahuilca (Ecuador)	Dome of Atacazo	1502-021
Ninahuilca Chico I (Ecuador)	Dome of Atacazo	1502-021
Ninahuilca Chico II (Ecuador)	Dome of Atacazo	1502-021
Nindirí (Nicaragua)	Crater of Masaya	1404-10=
Ninepin Rock (Indian O.-S)	Synonym of St. Paul	0304-002
Ninfas, Cerro de las (El Salvador)	Stratovolcano of Apaneca Range	1403-01=
Ninfas, Laguna las (El Salvador)	Crater of Apaneca Range	1403-01=
Niño de Jesus [Santiaguito] (Guatemala)	Dome of Santa María	1402-03=
Nino-ike (Honshu-Japan)	Crater of On-take	0803-04=
Ninokura (Honshu-Japan)	Stratovolcano of Towada	0803-271
Ninomegata (Honshu-Japan)	Maar of Megata	0803-262
Niolkande (Kamchatka)	Shield volcano of Tynua	....
Nipesotsu-Maruyama (Japan)	Stratovolcanoes (2, 1898) Historical	**0805-061**
Nipesotsu-yama (Hokkaido-Japan)	Stratovolcano of Nipesotsu-Maruyama	0805-061
Nipha, Mount (Antarctica)	Cone of White Island	....
Niragongo (Niragonwe) (Africa-C)	Synonym of Nyiragongo	0203-03=
Nire Co (Argentina)	Cinder cone of Unnamed	....
Nireco (Chile-C)	Crater of Callaqui	1507-091
Niri Mbwelesu (Vanuatu-SW Pacific)	Crater of Ambrym	0507-04=
Niri Mbwelesu Taten (Vanuatu-SW Pacific)	Crater of Ambrym	0507-04=
Niri Taten (Vanuatu-SW Pacific)	Crater of Ambrym	0507-04=

Name (Subregion)	Type (Eruptions, Most Recent) Status Relation to Named Volcano	Volcano Number
Nirres, Volcán los (Chile-C)	Maar of Puyehue-Cordón Caulle	1507-15=
Niseikaushuppe (Hokkaido-Japan)	Stratovolcano (None) Pleistocene	....
Niseko (Hokkaido-Japan)	Stratovolcanoes (1, -4900) Tephrochron.	**0805-031**
Niseko-Annupuri (Hokkaido-Japan)	Dome of Niseko	0805-031
Nishi Kofuji (Honshu-Japan)	Fissure vent of Fuji	0803-03=
Nishi-Asakizuka (Honshu-Japan)	Cone of Fuji	0803-03=
Nishi-Azuma (Honshu-Japan)	Cone of Azuma	0803-18=
Nishibetsu (Hokkaido-Japan)	Stratovolcano of Mashu	0805-081
Nishi-Chigasaki-kaikyu (Honshu-Japan)	Submarine vent of Izu-Tobu	0803-01=
Nishi-Chokai (Honshu-Japan)	Stratovolcano of Chokai	0803-22=
Nishi-Daiten (Honshu-Japan)	Cone of Azuma	0803-18=
Nishi-dake (Honshu-Japan)	Synonym of Adatara	0803-17=
Nishi-Futatsusuka (Honshu-Japan)	Cone of Fuji	0803-03=
Nishi-Hakuunzan (Izu Is-Japan)	Pleistocene caldera of Hachijo-jima	0804-05=
Nishi-Hitokappu [Stokap] (Kuril Is)	Stratovolcano of Bogatyr Ridge	0900-06-

Simon Carn (Michigan Tech. Univ.)

The summit of **Nyamuragira** volcano is truncated by 2 x 2.3 km wide caldera whose floor is partially covered by unvegetated historical lava flows. Africa's most active volcano, 3058-m-high Nyamuragira rises about 25 km north of Lake Kivu NW of Nyiragongo volcano.

Name (Subregion)	Type (Eruptions, Most Recent) Status Relation to Named Volcano	Volcano Number
Nishi-Iwate (Honshu-Japan)	Stratovolcano of Iwate	0803-24=
Nishi-Kagonoto-yama (Honshu-Japan)	Stratovolcano of Eboshi	....
Nishi-Kaitokuba (Volcano Is-Japan)	Cone of Kaitoku Seamount	0804-10=
Nishi-Kosekumaru (Honshu-Japan)	Cone of Fuji	0803-03=
Nishi-Kumaneshiri-dake (Hokkaido-Japan)	Stratovolcano of Kumaneshiri	....
Nishi-Kurotsuka (Honshu-Japan)	Cone of Fuji	0803-03=
Nishi-Maruyama (Hokkaido-Japan)	Dome of Usu	0805-03=
Nishimine (Ryukyu Is)	Cone of Yokoate-jima	0802-021
Nishino-shima (Volcano Is-Japan)	Caldera (1, 1974) Historical	**0804-096**
Nishi-Nupukaushinupuri (Hokkaido-Japan)	Dome of Shikaribetsu Group	0805-062
Nishi-Okuniwa (Honshu-Japan)	Cone of Fuji	0803-03=
Nishi-Tsurugi (Honshu-Japan)	Cone of Fuji	0803-03=
Nishi-Usuzuka (Honshu-Japan)	Cone of Fuji	0803-03=
Nishi-yama (Hokkaido-Japan)	Cone of Akan	0805-07=
Nishi-yama (Izu Is-Japan)	Stratovolcano of Hachijo-jima	0804-05=
Nishi-yama (Hokkaido-Japan)	Stratovolcano of Oshima-Oshima	0805-01=
Nishi-yama (Hokkaido-Japan)	Dome of Usu	0805-03=
Nishi-yama Hot Springs (Honshu-Japan)	Thermal feature of Sunagohara	....
Nishi-Zao (Honshu-Japan)	Stratovolcano of Zao	0803-19=
Nisibetu [Nishibetsu] (Hokkaido-Japan)	Stratovolcano of Mashu	0805-081
Nisida (Italy)	Tuff cone of Campi Flegrei	0101-01=
Nisino-sima (Volcano Is-Japan)	Synonym of Nishino-shima	0804-096
Nisi-yama [Nishi-yama] (Hokkaido-Japan)	Cone of Akan	0805-07=
Nisi-yama [Nishi-yama] (Izu Is-Japan)	Stratovolcano of Hachijo-jima	0804-05=
Nisyros (Greece)	Stratovolcano (4, 1888) Historical	**0102-05=**
Nitonupuri (Hokkaido-Japan)	Dome of Niseko	0805-031
Nitung (Lesser Sunda Is)	Thermal feature of Paluweh	0604-15=
Niuafo'ou (Tonga-SW Pacific)	Shield volcano (11, 1985) Historical	**0403-11=**
Niu-afu (Niua Fo'ou, Niau'fou) (Tonga)	Synonym of Niuafo'ou	0403-11=
Niullihuelco (Chile-C)	Synonym of Callaqui	1507-091
Nixtamalapan, Cerro (México)	Cinder cone of San Martín	1401-11=
Nixtamalapan, Laguna (México)	Maar of San Martín	1401-11=
Nizhne-Koshelevskie (Kamchatka)	Thermal feature of Koshelev	1000-02=
Nizhnii Lurban (Russia-SE)	Dome of Udokan Plateau	1002-03-
Njale, Gof (Africa-E)	Maar of Marsabit	0202-021
Njogoine (Africa-E)	Dome of Nyambeni Hills	0202-056
Njolimwanya (Africa-E)	Cone of Ngozi	0202-164
Nkuguti (Africa-C)	Crater of Bunyaruguru	0203-004
Nkunga, Lake (Africa-E)	Crater of Nyambeni Hills	0202-056
Nobo, Mt. (Lesser Sunda Is)	Synonym of Lewotobi	0604-18=
Nobo, Mt. [Lewotobi Lakilaki] (Indonesia)	Stratovolcano of Lewotobi	0604-18=
Noboribetsu (Hokkaido-Japan)	Thermal feature of Kuttara	0805-034
Noboribetu [Noboribetsu] (Hokkaido-Japan)	Thermal feature of Kuttara	0805-034
Noborio-Minami (Honshu-Japan)	Vent of Izu-Tobu	0803-01=
Nocarane, Cerro (Perú)	Dome of Chachani, Nevado	1504-007
Noche Buena, Cerro (Costa Rica)	Cinder cone of Irazú	1405-06=
Nocilla, Monte (Italy)	Cinder cone of Etna	0101-06=
No-dake (Kyushu-Japan)	Dome of Unzen	0802-10=
Nográd (Hungary)	Volcanic field (None) Pleistocene	....
Noike (Ryukyu Is)	Stratovolcano of Kuchinoerabu-jima	0802-05=

Name (Subregion)	Type (Eruptions, Most Recent) Status Relation to Named Volcano	Volcano Number
Noisy Nellie (New Zealand)	Crater of White Island	0401-04=
Nokogiri-dake (Hokkaido-Japan)	Stratovolcano of Tokachi	0805-05=
Nole, Puu (Hawaiian Is)	Cone of Haleakala	1302-06-
Nolf Crater (US-Oregon)	Maar of Diamond Craters	1202-17-
Nome Lake South (Canada)	Tuya of Tuya Volc Field	1200-031
Nomilo Cone (Hawaiian Is)	Cone of Kauai	....
Nomoer (China-E)	Cone of Wudalianchi	1005-03-
Nomogan-Ula (Mongolia)	Cone of Khutza-Ula	....
Nonda (Solomon Is-SW Pacific)	Stratovolcano (None) Pleist.-Fumarolic	....
Nongkojajar (Java)	Pleist. caldera of Tengger Caldera	0603-31=
Nonomori-yama (Honshu-Japan)	Stratovolcano of Zao	0803-19=
Noorat, Mt. (Australia)	Tuff ring of Newer Volcanics Prov.	0509-01-
Nord Island (New Britain-SW Pac)	Synonym of Narage	....
Nordeste (Azores)	Shield volcano of Furnas	1802-10=
Nord-Jan [Beerenberg] (Jan Mayen)	Stratovolcano of Jan Mayen	1706-01=
Nordurklettar (Iceland-S)	Fissure vent of Vestmannaeyjar	1702-01=
Norikura (Honshu-Japan)	Stratovolcanoes (3, -50) Radiocarbon	**0803-06=**
Norikura Kogen Hot Springs (Honshu-Japan)	Thermal feature of Norikura	0803-06=
Norikura-dake (Honshu-Japan)	Stratovolcano of Shirouma-Oike	....
Norman Mt. (US-Arizona)	Cone of San Francisco Volc Field	....
Noro (Honshu-Japan)	Pyroclastic cone (None) Pleistocene	....
Norris Geyser Basin (US-Wyoming)	Thermal feature of Yellowstone	1205-01-
North Brother [Cherny] (Kuril Is)	Stratovolcano of Chirpoi	0900-15=
North Butte (US-California)	Dome of Sutter Buttes	....
North caldera (Iceland-NE)	Caldera of Askja	1703-06=
North Coulee (US-California)	Dome of Mono Craters	1203-12-
North Crater (US-Idaho)	Crater of Craters of the Moon	1204-02-
North Crater (New Zealand)	Crater of Ruapehu	0401-10=
North Crater (New Zealand)	Crater of Tongariro	0401-08=
North Crater (Alaska-E)	Crater of Wrangell	1105-02-
North Daughter [Tovanumbatir] (New Britain)	Stratovolcano of Rabaul	0502-14=
North Davao (Mindanao-Philippines)	Synonym of Leonard Range	0701-031
North Deadman Creek (US-California)	Dome of Inyo Craters	1203-13-
North Devil Mountain Lake (Alaska-W)	Maar of Espenberg	....
North Efate (Vanuatu-SW Pacific)	Synonym of North Vate	0507-081
North Gorda Ridge (Pacific-NE)	Submarine volcano (3, 1996) Historical	**1301-031**
North Head (New Zealand)	Cone of Auckland Field	0401-02=
North Hill (Alaska-W)	Cinder cone of St. Paul Island	1104-01-
North Island (New Britain-SW Pac)	Synonym of Narage	....
North Island (Africa-E)	Tuff cones (None) Holocene	**0202-001**
North Killeak Lake (Alaska-W)	Maar of Espenberg	....
North Makeon (Vanuatu-SW Pacific)	Cone of Gaua	0507-02=
North Menan Butte (US-Idaho)	Tuff cone of Menan Buttes	....
North Pagan (Mariana Is-C Pacific)	Stratovolcano of Pagan	0804-17=
North Paulina Peak (US-Oregon)	Cone of Newberry	1202-11-
North Pinhead (US-Oregon)	Cinder cone of Olallie Butte	....
North Rift Zone (Pacific-NE)	Fissure vent of Axial Seamount	1301-021
North Round Island (Red Sea)	Cone of Hanish	0201-022
North Sister Field (US-Oregon)	Complex volcano (4, 440) Radiocarbon	**1202-07-**
North Son (New Britain-SW Pac)	Synonym of Likuruanga	....
North Squaw Tip (US-Oregon)	Vent of McLoughlin	....
North Twin Lake (US-Oregon)	Tuff ring of Wuksi Butte-Twin Lakes	....
North Vate (Vanuatu-SW Pacific)	Stratovolcanoes (None) Holocene	**0507-081**
North Wilson (US-Oregon)	Shield volcano of Wilson	....
Northeast Crater (Italy)	Crater of Etna	0101-06=
Northeast Rift Zone (Hawaiian Is)	Fissure vent of Mauna Loa	1302-02=
Northeast Tuva Plateau (Russia-SE)	Synonym of Azas Plateau	1002-07-
Northern Atenguillo (México)	Shield volcanoes (None) Pleistocene	....
Northern Atitlán (Guatemala)	Synonym of Tolimán	1402-07=
Northern Centres (W Indies)	Stratovolcanoes (None) Pleistocene	....
Northern Chain (W Indies)	Lava domes (None) Pleistocene	....
Northern Cone (US-Nevada)	Cone of Crater Flat	....
Northern Crater (Mindanao-Philippines)	Crater of Apo	0701-03=
Northern Crater (Italy)	Maar of Roccamonfina	....
Northern Crater (Lesser Sunda Is)	Crater of Sirung	0604-27=
Northern EPR-Segment RO2 (Pacific)	Submarine volcaño (1, -50) Magnetism	**1304-02-**
Northern EPR-Segment RO3 (Pacific)	Submarine volcano (1, -50) Magnetism	**1304-021**
Northern Guadalajara Mesa (México)	Lava domes (None) Pleistocene	....
Northern Lake Abaya Field (Ethiopia)	Synonym of Hobicha Caldera	0201-293
Northern Mendoza Volc Field (Arg.)	Volcanic field (None) Pleistocene	....
Northern Shore Springs (Kamchatka)	Thermal feature of Akademia Nauk	1000-125
Northern Summit (Antarctica)	Shield volcano of Daniell Peninsula	....
Northern Symmetrical Segment (Pacific-NE)	Synonym of Cobb Segment	1301-011
Northern Tongariro Group (New Zeal.)	Stratovolcanoes (None) Pleistocene	....
Northern Volcano (Antarctica)	Cone of Adare Peninsula	....
Northwest Dome (US-Washington)	Dome of St. Helens	1201-05-
Northwest Rift Zone (US-Oregon)	Fissure vent of Newberry	1202-11-
Nosaka-yama (Honshu-Japan)	Dome of Aono-yama	....
Nosichan (Kamchatka)	Shield volcano (None) Pleistocene	....
Nosowskoj [Pogromni] (Aleutian Is)	Stratovolcano of Westdahl	1101-34-
Nossa Senhora de Lourdes, Pico (Atlantic-C)	Dome of Trindade	1805-051
Nossi Be (Madagascar)	Synonym of Nosy-Be	0303-012
Nosy-Be (Madagascar)	Cinder cones (None) Holocene	**0303-012**
Notch Butte (US-Idaho)	Cone of Shoshone Lava Field	1204-01-
Notuco (Chile-C)	Synonym of Copahue	1507-09=
Nouveau (Indian O.-W)	Crater of Fournaise, Piton de la	0303-02=
Novagrablenova (Kamchatka)	Shield volcano of Nylgimelkin	1000-65-
Novarupta (Alaska Peninsula)	Caldera (1, 1912) Historical	**1102-18-**
Novedad (Colombia)	Fissure vent of Galeras	1501-08=
Novillero, Volcán (México)	Cinder cone of Mascota Volc Field	1401-031
Novo-Bakening (Kamchatka)	Dome of Bakening	1000-123
Novy (Kamchatka)	Dome of Bezymianny	1000-25=
Noya (Kyushu-Japan)	Thermal feature of Kuju	0802-12=
Nshenyi (Africa-C)	Crater of Bunyaruguru	0203-004

Name (Subregion)	Type (Eruptions, Most Recent) Status Relation to Named Volcano	Volcano Number
NSymm Segment (Pacific-NE)	Synonym of Cobb Segment	1301-011
Ntobe (Africa-C)	Cone of Karisimbi	0203-04-
Ntumbi (Africa-E)	Dome of SW Usangu Basin	0202-163
Nuakaju (Lesser Sunda Is)	Thermal feature of Paluweh	0604-15=
Nubalykich (Kamchatka)	Shield volcano of Uksichan	1000-35-
Nubes, Las [Las Sierras] (Nicaragua)	Pleistocene caldera of Masaya	1404-10=
Nudo de Coropuna (Perú)	Synonym of Coropuna	1504-003
Nuevo del Fuego, Volcán (Canary Is)	Cinder cone of Lanzarote	1803-06-
Nuevo Mundo (Bolivia)	Lava domes (None) Holocene?	**1505-036**
Nuevo, El (Nicaragua)	Synonym of Negro, Cerro	1404-07=
Nuevo, Volcán (Chile-C)	Dome of Chillán, Nevados de	1507-07=
Nuevo, Volcán [Quizapu] (Chile-C)	Crater of Azul, Cerro	1507-06=
Nuevo, Volcán [Tinguaton] (Canary Is)	Crater of Lanzarote	1803-06-
Nugere, Puy de la (France)	Cone of Chaîne des Puys	0100-02-
Nuha Lua (Lesser Sunda Is)	Synonym of Paluweh	0604-15=
Nui Dat (SE Asia)	Cone of Bas Dong Nai	0705-05-
Nuit, Gunung (New Guinea-W)	Synonym of Nuit, Mt.	....
Nuit, Mt. (New Guinea-W)	Unknown (None) Quaternary	....
Nukabira (Hokkaido-Japan)	Thermal feature Nipesotsu-Maruyama	0805-061
Nukita (Honshu-Japan)	Cinder cone of Ogino-Sen	....
Nukuafo (SW Pacific)	Tuff cone of Wallis Islands	0404-05-
Nukuatea (SW Pacific)	Tuff cone of Wallis Islands	0404-05-
Nukufutu (SW Pacific)	Tuff cone of Wallis Islands	0404-05-
Nukutaakimua (SW Pacific)	Tuff cone of Wallis Islands	0404-05-
Nukutapu (SW Pacific)	Tuff cone of Wallis Islands	0404-05-
Nulkande [Niolkande] (Kamchatka)	Shield volcano of Tynua	....
Nulla Volc Province (Australia)	Shield volcanoes (None) Pleistocene	....
Numa Numa (Bougainville-SW Pacific)	Stratovolcano (None) Pleistocene	....
Numajiri (Honshu-Japan)	Thermal feature of Adatara	0803-17=
Numajiri-yama (Honshu-Japan)	Synonym of Adatara	0803-17=
Numanohara (Hokkaido-Japan)	Cone of Tomuraushi Volc Group	....
Numanokami (Honshu-Japan)	Stratovolcano (None) Pleistocene	....
Numanotaira (Honshu-Japan)	Crater of Adatara	0803-17=
Numanotaira (Honshu-Japan)	Crater of Bandai	0803-16=
Numanotaira Group (Honshu-Japan)	Vent of Izu-Tobu	0803-01=
Numanuma (D'Entrecasteaux Is)	Synonym of Dawson Strait Group	0503-06=
Numazawa (Honshu-Japan)	Shield volcano (1, -3400) Radiocarbon	**0803-151**
Numazawako (Honshu-Japan)	Caldera of Numazawa	0803-151
Numundo (New Britain-SW Pac)	Maar of Garbuna Group	0502-07=
Nunatak del Viedma (Argentina)	Synonym of Viedma	1508-061
Nunivak Island (Alaska-W)	Shield volcano (None) Holocene	**1104-02-**
Nunuka (Sulawesi-Indonesia)	Unknown (None) Quaternary	....
Nunurco (Ecuador)	Dome of Chacana	1502-022
Nunziata, Monte (Italy)	Cinder cone of Etna	0101-06=
Nuovo, Monte (Italy)	Tuff cone of Campi Flegrei	0101-01=
Nuovo, Monte (Italy)	Cinder cone of Etna	0101-06=
Nupahraun (Iceland-NE)	Fissure vent of Grímsvötn	1703-01=
Nupuri-Ondo (Hokkaido-Japan)	Dome of Kutcharo	0805-08=
Nureto, Cerro de (México)	Cinder cone of Michoacán-Guanajuato	1401-06=
Nusa Kua (Lesser Sunda Is)	Synonym of Paluweh	0604-15=
Nushan (China-E)	Cone (None) Pleistocene	....
Nuso Kode (Lesser Sunda Is)	Cone of Ora, Doro	....
Nusuyu (Honshu-Japan)	Dome of Azuma	0803-18=
Nutaku Kamushupe (Hokkaido-Japan)	Synonym of Daisetsu	0805-06=
Nutaku Kamusyupe (Hokkaido-Japan)	Synonym of Daisetsu	0805-06=
Nuthinaw Mountain (Canada)	Cone of Kawdy Metah	....
Nu'u (Samoa-SW Pacific)	Tuff cone of Ofu-Olosega	0404-01=
Nu'ulua (Samoa-SW Pacific)	Tuff ring of Upolu	0404-03-
Nu'utele (Samoa-SW Pacific)	Tuff ring of Upolu	0404-03-
NW Eifuku (Volcano Is-Japan)	Submarine volcano (None) Fumarolic	**0804-136**
NW Rota-1 (Mariana Is-C Pacific)	Submarine volcano (1, 2009) Historical	**0804-211**
Nyabusa (Africa-C)	Cone of Nyiragongo	0203-03=
Nyabusozi (Africa-C)	Tuff cone of Fort Portal	0203-001
Nyagashole (Africa-C)	Cone of Nyamuragira	0203-02=
Nyamatoto (Africa-E)	Cone of Homa Mountain	0202-07=
Nyambaramo (Africa-C)	Cone of Nyamuragira	0203-02=
Nyambeni Hills (Africa-E)	Shield volcano (None) Holocene	**0202-056**
Nyamersingeri (Africa-C)	Crater of Bunyaruguru	0203-004
Nyamlagira (Africa-C)	Synonym of Nyamuragira	0203-02=
Nyamulagira (Africa-C)	Synonym of Nyamuragira	0203-02=
Nyamunuka (Africa-C)	Maar of Katwe-Kikorongo	0203-003
Nyamuragira (Africa-C)	Shield volcano (43, 2006) Historical	**0203-02=**
Nyamushwa (Africa-C)	Cone of Nyiragongo	0203-03=
Nyamutsibu (Africa-C)	Cone of Nyiragongo	0203-03=
Nyarutshiru (Africa-C)	Cone of Nyiragongo	0203-03=
Nyasanja (Africa-E)	Cone of Homa Mountain	0202-07=
Nyasheke 1 (Africa-C)	Cone of Nyamuragira	0203-02=
Nyasheke 2 (Africa-C)	Cone of Nyamuragira	0203-02=
Nyerges (Hungary)	Cone of Nográd	....
Nyey (Iceland-SW)	Submarine vent of Reykjanes	1701-02=
Nyhahraun (Iceland-S)	Submarine vent of Vestmannaeyjar	1702-01=
Nyi, Lake (Africa-W)	Maar of Oku Volc Field	0204-03-
Nyiragongo (Africa-C)	Stratovolcano (19, 2010) Historical	**0203-03=**
Nylgimelkin (Kamchatka)	Shield volcanoes (1, -3550) Radiocarbon	**1000-65-**
Nyodo-san (Honshu-Japan)	Stratovolcano of Zao	0803-19=
Nyoho-Akanagi (Honshu-Japan)	Stratovolcano (None) Pleistocene	....
Nyokie, Ol Doinyo (Africa-E)	Tuff cone (None) Pleistocene	....
Nyos, Lake (Africa-W)	Maar of Oku Volc Field	0204-03-
Nyotai-san (Honshu-Japan)	Synonym of Nikko-Shirane	0803-14=
Nyudo-san (Honshu-Japan)	Cone of Zao	0803-19=
Nyuki, Doinya La [Ol Doinyo Onyoke] (Africa)	Stratovolcano of Suswa	0202-11=
Nyukie, Ol Doinyo [Ol Doinyo Onyoke]	Stratovolcano of Suswa	0202-11=
Nyungu (Africa-C)	Crater of Bunyaruguru	0203-004
Nyushan (China-E)	Synonym of Nushan	....
Nyuto-san (Honshu-Japan)	Stratovolcano of Nyuto-Takakura	....
Nyuto-Takakura (Honshu-Japan)	Stratovolcanoes (None) Pleistocene	....
Nzongwe (Africa-E)	Cone of Ngozi	0202-164
Nzuru (Africa-C)	Cone of Nyamuragira	0203-02=

O

Name (Subregion)	Type (Eruptions, Most Recent) Status Relation to Named Volcano	Volcano Number
O Chra (SE Asia)	Vent of Pailin	....
O Koro, Maunga (Chile-Is)	Pyroclastic cone of Easter Island	1506-011
O'a Caldera (Ethiopia)	Caldera (None) Holocene	**0201-28-**
O-Akan (Hokkaido-Japan)	Stratovolcano of Akan	0805-07=
Oana (Honshu-Japan)	Crater of Azuma	0803-18=
Oana (Izu Is-Japan)	Crater of Hachijo-jima	0804-05=
Oana (Izu Is-Japan)	Crater of Miyake-jima	0804-04=
O-ana (Izu Is-Japan)	Crater of Miyake-jima	0804-04=
Oba (Vanuatu-SW Pacific)	Synonym of Aoba	0507-03=
Obama (Kyushu-Japan)	Thermal feature of Unzen	0802-10=
Obandai (Honshu-Japan)	Stratovolcano of Bandai	0803-16=
Oberwinkel (Germany)	Maar of West Eifel Volc Field	0100-01-
Obiglio, Mt. (Antarctica)	Cinder cone (None) Pleistocene	....
Obmanuvshy (Kamchatka)	Cone of Maly Semiachik	1000-14=
Obrajuelo, Laguna (Guatemala)	Cone of Ixtepeque	1402-18-
Obrinnisholar (Iceland-SW)	Crater Row of Krísuvík	1701-03=
Obrucheva (Obruchev) (Russia-SE)	Cinder cone of Vitim Plateau	1002-04-
Obruk (Turkey)	Crater of Erciyes Dagi	0103-01=
Obruk (Turkey)	Cone of Hasan Dagi	0103-002
Obruk Tepe (Turkey)	Cone of Acigöl-Nevsehir	0103-004
Observation Hill (Antarctica)	Dome of Hut Point Peninsula	....
Observatory Vent (Hawaiian Is)	Shield volcano of Kilauea	1302-01=
Obsidian (US-California)	Dome of Inyo Craters	1203-13-
Obsidian Butte (US-California)	Dome of Salton Buttes	1203-20-
Obuchi (Honshu-Japan)	Crater of Fuji	0803-03=
Ocaña (Bolivia)	Stratovolcano (None) Pleistocene	....
Ocate (US-New Mexico)	Volcanic field (None) Pleistocene	....
Occidentales, Calderas [Quemadas]	Crater of Lanzarote	1803-06-
Oceana (Antarctica)	Cone of Seal Nunataks Group	1900-05=
Oceanite, Mount (Antarctica)	Cone of Montagu Island	1900-081
Ochchamo (Kamchatka)	Shield volcano (None) Pleistocene	....
Ochenta Pesos, Cerro (Nicaragua)	Cone of Lajas, Las	1404-133
Ochki (Kamchatka)	Fissure vent of Kliuchevskoi	1000-26=
Ochkovyi (Kamchatka)	Cinder cone of Kostakan	1000-122
Ocho-zan (Honshu-Japan)	Stratovolcano of Kyoga-take	....
Oclayuca (México)	Cinder cone of Chichinautzin	1401-08=
Ocote, Cerro del (El Salvador)	Synonym of Conchagua	1403-11=
Ocotenco (México)	Maar of Serdán-Oriental	1401-092
Ocoxusco, Volcán (México)	Cinder cone of Chichinautzin	1401-08=
Ocusacayo (México)	Shield volcano of Chichinautzin	1401-08=

The 1886 eruptive fissure that cuts across the Tarawera lava-dome complex of the **Okataina** volcanic center in New Zealand was the source of a major explosive eruption that produced 2 km³ of basaltic tephra. The 8-km-long 1886 fissure cuts a group of lava domes, including the flat-topped Wahanga dome at the top of the photo, which was emplaced at the end of the Kaharoa eruption about 800 years ago.

Name (Subregion)	Type (Eruptions, Most Recent) Status Relation to Named Volcano	Volcano Number
Odaira (Honshu-Japan)	Vent of Izu-Tobu	0803-01=
O-dake [Hakkoda-odake] (Honshu-Japan)	Stratovolcano of Hakkoda Group	0803-28=
Odamoi-san [Tebenkov] (Kuril Is)	Cone of Grozny Group	0900-07=
Odell Butte (US-Oregon)	Shield volcano of Davis Lake	1202-10-
Odem, Mt. (Syria)	Cinder cone of Golan Heights	0300-03-
Odiawo (Africa-E)	Cone of Homa Mountain	0202-07=
Odinokaia (Kamchatka)	Dome of Avachinsky	1000-10=
Odnoboky (Kamchatka)	Pleistocene caldera of Akademia Nauk	1000-125
Odnostoronny (Kamchatka)	Synonym of Pirozhnikova	....
O'e Taka-yama (Honshu-Japan)	Synonym of Oetaka-yama	....
Oeloebeloe (Sumatra)	Synonym of Hulubelu	0601-28=
Oemsini (Oemtjina) (New Guinea-W)	Synonym of Umsini	0609-01=
Oena Oena (Sulawesi-Indonesia)	Synonym of Colo [Una Una]	0606-01=
Oengaran (Java)	Synonym of Ungaran	0603-23=
Oepas, Gunung [Upas] (Java)	Thermal feature Dieng Volc Complex	0603-20=

Name (Subregion)	Type (Eruptions, Most Recent) Status Relation to Named Volcano	Volcano Number
Oereparapara (Vanuatu-SW Pacific)	Synonym of Ureparapara	....
Oerteale (Ethiopia)	Synonym of Erta Ale	0201-08=
Oetaka-yama (Honshu-Japan)	Lava domes (None) Pleistocene	....
Ofu-Olosega (Samoa-SW Pacific)	Shield volcanoes (1, 1866) Historical	**0404-01=**
Ogari-yama (Hokkaido-Japan)	Dome of Usu	0805-03=
Ogasawara-lo-jima (Volcano Is-Japan)	Synonym of Ioto [Iwo-jima]	0804-12=
Oga-take (Honshu-Japan)	Dome of Narugo	0803-20=
Ogi (Honshu-Japan)	Cone of Izu-Tobu	0803-01=
Ogigahana (Kyushu-Japan)	Dome of Kuju	0802-12=
Ogino-Sen (Honshu-Japan)	Scoria cones (None) Pleistocene	....
Ogmundargigar (Iceland-SW)	Crater Row of Krísuvík	1701-03=
Ogmundur (Iceland-SW)	Dome of Hofsjökull	1701-09=
Ognedieshutshai Gora (Aleutian Is)	Synonym of Makushin	1101-31-
Ogoamas (Sulawesi-Indonesia)	Unknown (None) Quaternary	....
Ogura-yama (Honshu-Japan)	Dome of Towada	0803-271

Lee Siebert (Smithsonian)

Ichino-ike pond in the foreground is one of a series of small explosion craters that cut the broad, elongated summit of **On-take** volcano. Its first historical eruption in 1979 followed a lengthy period of quiescence. Norikura volcano forms the broad massif in the middle distance, with the northern Japan Alps in the background.

Name (Subregion)	Type (Eruptions, Most Recent) Status Relation to Named Volcano	Volcano Number
Ohaaki [Broadlands] (New Zealand)	Thermal feature of Reporoa	0401-06-
Ohachi (Honshu-Japan)	Crater of Iwate	0803-24=
Ohachi (Kyushu-Japan)	Crater of Kirishima	0802-09=
Ohachi (Honshu-Japan)	Crater of Niigata-Yake-yama	0803-09=
Ohachidaira (Hokkaido-Japan)	Pleistocene caldera of Daisetsu	0805-06=
Ohaki [Broadlands] (New Zealand)	Thermal feature of Reporoa	0401-06-
Ohakune (New Zealand)	Tuff ring of Ruapehu	0401-10=
Ohalahoum [Dalahum] (Vanuatu-SW Pacific)	Cone of Ambrym	0507-04=
Ohanabe-yama (Honshu-Japan)	Stratovolcano of Towada	0803-271
Ohata-ike (Kyushu-Japan)	Crater of Kirishima	0802-09=
Ohatano (Honshu-Japan)	Maar of Izu-Tobu	0803-01=
Ohata-yama (Kyushu-Japan)	Stratovolcano of Kirishima	0802-09=
Ohati [Ohachi] (Honshu-Japan)	Crater of Iwate	0803-24=
Ohati [Ohachi] (Kyushu-Japan)	Crater of Kirishima	0802-09=
Ohati [Ohachi] (Honshu-Japan)	Crater of Niigata-Yake-yama	0803-09=
Oheinui (New Zealand)	Dome of Maroa	0401-061
Ohinemutu (New Zealand)	Thermal feature of Rotorua	....
Ohira-yama (Honshu-Japan)	Cone of Fuji	0803-03=
Ohmachi Seamount (Izu Is-Japan)	Synonym of Omachi Seamount	0804-092
Oiakoba (Kuril Is)	Synonym of Alaid	0900-39=
Oiau, Mount (D'Entrecasteaux Is)	Stratovolcano of Dawson Strait Group	0503-06=
Oiava-Ai, Mount (D'Entrecasteaux Is)	Cone of Goodenough	0503-041
Oibor, Oldoinyo (Africa-E)	Synonym of Kilimanjaro	0202-15=
Oike (Honshu-Japan)	Vent of Izu-Tobu	0803-01=
Oike-Minami (Honshu-Japan)	Vent of Izu-Tobu	0803-01=
Oile, Puu (Hawaiian Is)	Cone of Haleakala	1302-06-
Oira (New Zealand)	Pumice cone of Mayor Island	0401-021
Oirase (Honshu-Japan)	Cone of Towada	0803-271
Ojigoku (Honshu-Japan)	Thermal feature of Iwate	0803-24=
Ojika-jima (Kyushu-Japan)	Shield volcanoes (None) Pleistocene	....
Ojima (Kyushu-Japan)	Cone of Fukue-jima	0802-091
Ojima-jima (Kyushu-Japan)	Synonym of Ojika-jima	....
Ojo de Agua de la Virgen, Cerro el (El Salv.)	Stratovolcano of Apaneca Range	1403-01=
Ojo de Agua, Cerro (El Salvador)	Cinder cone of Cinotepeque, Cerro	1403-051
Ojo de Agua, Cerro (Nicaragua)	Cinder cone of Pilas, Las	1404-08=
Ojo de Agua, Loma (Nicaragua)	Cinder cone of San Cristóbal	1404-02=
Ojo del Mar (El Salvador)	Synonym of Coatepeque Caldera	1403-041
Ojo del Salado (Chile-N)	Synonym of Ojos del Salado, Nevados	1505-13=
Ojochal, Cerro [El Bosque] (Nicaragua)	Dome of Rota	1404-06-
Ojo-dake (Kyushu-Japan)	Stratovolcano of Aso	0802-11=
Ojos del Salado, Nevados (Chile-N)	Stratovolcano (1, 700) Tephrochronology	**1505-13=**
Ojotes, Los (México)	Dome of San Pedro	....
Ok (Iceland-SW)	Shield volcano (None) Pleistocene	....
Oka Plateau (Russia-SE)	Cinder cones (None) Holocene	**1002-06-**
Oka Upland Volc Field (Russia-SE)	Synonym of Oka Plateau	1002-06-
Okaihau (New Zealand)	Cone of Kaikohe-Bay of Islands	0401-01=
Okama (Honshu-Japan)	Crater of Asama	0803-11=
Okama (Honshu-Japan)	Crater of Iwate	0803-24=

Name (Subregion)	Type (Eruptions, Most Recent) Status Relation to Named Volcano	Volcano Number
Okama (Honshu-Japan)	Crater of Zao	0803-19=
Okamado-yama (Kyushu-Japan)	Stratovolcano of Aso	0802-11=
Okaro, Lake (New Zealand)	Crater of Reporoa	0401-06-
Okata (Izu Is-Japan)	Stratovolcano of Oshima	0804-01=
Okataina (New Zealand)	Lava domes (31, 1981) Historical	**0401-05=**
Okeanskoe (Kuril Is)	Thermal feature of Baransky	0900-08=
Oke-numa (Honshu-Japan)	Crater of Azuma	0803-18=
Oki-Dogo (Honshu-Japan)	Shield volcano (None) Anthropology	**0803-003**
Okinawa-Tori-shima (Ryukyu Is)	Synonym of Iwo-Tori-shima	0802-02=
Okise (Kyushu-Japan)	Cone of Sakura-jima	0802-08=
Okiura (Honshu-Japan)	Caldera (None) Pleistocene	....
Okkata-dake (Honshu-Japan)	Synonym of Aoso	....
Okmok (Aleutian Is)	Shield volcano (18, 2008) Historical	**1101-29-**
Okoli (Africa-W)	Crater of Cameroon	0204-01=
Okoma-yama (Honshu-Japan)	Synonym of Kurikoma	0803-21=
Okpo Hill (SE Asia)	Cone of Lower Chindwin	0705-09-
Oku Volc Field (Africa-W)	Stratovolcano (Uncertain) Holocene?	**0204-03-**
Oku, Mount (Africa-W)	Stratovolcano of Oku Volc Field	0204-03-
Okuno-Fuji (Honshu-Japan)	Synonym of Iwaki	0803-27=
Okushiri-Katsuma-yama (Japan)	Shield volcano (None) Pleistocene	....
Okutai-san (Kyushu-Japan)	Dome of Futago	....
Ol Buru, Doinyo (Africa-E)	Synonym of Eburru, Ol Doinyo	0202-08=
Ol Kokwe (Africa-E)	Shield volcano (None) Holocene	**0202-055**
Ol Morouk (Africa-E)	Cone of Kilimanjaro	0202-15=
Ol Olongot (Africa-E)	Synonym of Longonot	0202-10=
Olaf (Atlantic-S)	Cone of Tristan da Cunha	1806-01=
Olai, Puu (Hawaiian Is)	Cone of Haleakala	1302-06-
Olakkran (Turkey)	Cone of Erciyes Dagi	0103-01=
Olallie Butte (US-Oregon)	Shield volcanoes (None) Pleistocene	....
Olca Sur, Cerro (Chile-N)	Stratovolcano of Olca-Paruma	1505-05=
Olca-Paruma (Chile-N)	Stratovolcanoes (1, 1867) Historical	**1505-05=**
Old Bogoslof [Castle Rock] (Aleutian Is)	Dome of Bogoslof	1101-30-
Old Booby Hill (W Indies)	Dome of Saba	1600-01=
Old Craggy (US-California)	Dome of Sutter Buttes	....
Old Crater (Java)	Thermal feature of Perbakti-Gagak	0603-04=
Old Crater, The (W Indies)	Crater of Soufrière St. Vincent	1600-15=
Old Snowy Mountain (US-Washington)	Cone of Goat Rocks	....
Oldeani (Africa-E)	Stratovolcano (None) Post-Miocene	....
Oldoinyo, Oldonyo, Ol Doinyo (Masai for Mt.) see proper name (e.g. Lengai, Ol Doinyo)		
Oldugigar (Iceland-S)	Fissure vent of Hekla	1702-07=
O'Leary Peak (US-Arizona)	Cone of San Francisco Volc Field	....
Olenguruoni (Africa-E)	Synonym of Olkaria	0202-09=
Olenguruoni (Africa-E)	Dome of Olkaria	0202-09=
Oleniy [Oleny] (Kamchatka)	Shield volcano of Zaozerny	1000-48-
Oleny (Kamchatka)	Shield volcano of Zaozerny	1000-48-
Olet Takan (Lesser Sunda Is)	Unknown (None) Post-Miocene	....
Olgaria [Olkaria Hill] (Africa-E)	Pumice cone of Olkaria	0202-09=
Olgoreti, Ol Doinyo (Africa-E)	Cone of Chyulu Hills	0202-13=
Olgurtam (Africa-E)	Cone of Chyulu Hills	0202-13=
Olibano, Mt. (Italy)	Dome of Campi Flegrei	0101-01=
Olila, Mt. (Luzon-Philippines)	Cone of San Pablo Volc Field	0703-06=
Olim (Sumatra)	Fissure vents (None) Pleistocene	....
Olivas, Cerro los (Guatemala)	Cone of Suchitán	1402-16-
Olive, Mt. (Aleutian Is)	Cone of Shishaldin	1101-36-
Olivina, La [Cerro el Salto] (México)	Cinder cone of Camargo Volc Field	....
Olka (Kamchatka)	Shield volcano of Chavycha	....
Olkaria (Africa-E)	Pumice cones (3, 1770) Radiocarbon	**0202-09=**
Olkaria Hill (Africa-E)	Pumice cone of Olkaria	0202-09=
Ölkelduháls (Iceland-S)	Thermal feature of Hrómundartindur	1701-051
Olkoviy (Kamchatka)	Shield volcano of Olkoviy Volc Group	1000-052
Olkoviy Volc Group (Kamchatka)	Volcanic field (None) Holocene	**1000-052**
Olla de Carne (Costa Rica)	Cone of Tenorio	1405-031
Olla de Flores (México)	Maar of Michoacán-Guanajuato	1401-06=
Olla de Zintora [Hoya de Cintora] (México)	Maar of Michoacán-Guanajuato	1401-06=
Olla Spring (Luzon-Philippines)	Thermal feature of Banahaw	0703-05=
Olla, Cerro la (Guatemala)	Cinder cone of Chingo	1402-17-
Olla, Cerro la (El Salvador)	Cinder cone of Santa Ana	1403-02=
Ollada de los Geisers del Tatio (Chile-N)	Synonym of Tatio, El	....
Ollada, La (Nicaragua)	Crater of San Cristóbal	1404-02=
Ollagua (Chile-N)	Synonym of Ollagüe	1505-06=
Ollagüe (Chile-N)	Stratovolcano (Uncertain) Holocene?	**1505-06=**
Olleta, La (Colombia)	Dome of Ruiz, Nevado del	1501-02=
Olmedo (Galápagos)	Synonym of Santiago	1503-09=
Olmoti (Africa-E)	Cone of Chyulu Hills	0202-13=
Olmoti (Africa-E)	Caldera (None) Quaternary	....
Oloimoti (Africa-E)	Synonym of Olmoti	....
Ololbutot (Africa-E)	Fissure vent of Olkaria	0202-09=
Ololica (México)	Cinder cone of Chichinautzin	1401-08=
Olomanu (Samoa-SW Pacific)	Cone of Ta'u	0404-001
Olomanu Tai (Samoa-SW Pacific)	Cone of Savai'i	0404-04=
Olomanu Uta (Samoa-SW Pacific)	Cone of Savai'i	0404-04=
Olomatimu (Samoa-SW Pacific)	Cone of Ta'u	0404-001
Olomoana (Samoa-SW Pacific)	Shield volcano of Tutuila	0404-02-
Olonongot (Africa-E)	Synonym of Longonot	0202-10=
Olorerer (Africa-E)	Cone of Chyulu Hills	0202-13=
Olot Volc Field (Spain)	Pyroclastic cones (None) Holocene	**0100-03-**
Olotania (Samoa-SW Pacific)	Cone of Ta'u	0404-001
Olotele (Samoa-SW Pacific)	Cone of Tutuila	0404-02-
Olympe (Indian O.-S)	Cone of Amsterdam Island	0304-001
Olympus, Mt. (Galápagos)	Cone of Floreana	....
Omachi Seamount (Izu Is-Japan)	(None) Not a Volcano	0804-092
Omae-dake (Honshu-Japan)	Cone of Akita-Komaga-take	0803-23=
Omanago Group (Honshu-Japan)	Lava domes (1, -3050) Radiocarbon	**0803-142**
Omaokoili (Hawaiian Is)	Cone of Mauna Kea	1302-03-

Name (Subregion)	Type (Eruptions, Most Recent) Status / Relation to Named Volcano	Volcano Number
Omapere (New Zealand)	Cone of Kaikohe-Bay of Islands	0401-01=
Omate (Omato) (Perú)	Synonym of Huaynaputina	1504-03=
Omba (Vanuatu-SW Pacific)	Synonym of Aoba	0507-03=
Ombligo, El (México)	Dome of Toluca, Nevado de	1401-07-
Ombus (Vanuatu-SW Pacific)	Cinder cone of Yasur	0507-10=
Omeshi-dake (Honshu-Japan)	Stratovolcano (None) Pleistocene	....
Ometepe (Nicaragua)	Synonym of Concepción	1404-12=
Omine (Kyushu-Japan)	Cinder cone of Aso	0802-11=
O-mine (Izu Is-Japan)	Pyroclastic cone of Nii-jima	0804-02=
Omo Anga, Maunga (Chile-Is)	Pyroclastic cone of Easter Island	1506-011
Omori-yama (Honshu-Japan)	Cone of Zao	0803-19=
Omoturco (Ecuador)	Dome of Atacazo	1502-021
Omsini (New Guinea-W)	Synonym of Umsini	0609-01=
Omuro (Honshu-Japan)	Crater of Iwate	0803-24=
Omuro-yama (Honshu-Japan)	Cone of Fuji	0803-03=
Omuro-yama (Honshu-Japan)	Cinder cone of Izu-Tobu	0803-01=
Omuro-yama Volcano Group (Honshu-Japan)	Synonym of Izu-Tobu	0803-01=
Omuroyama-Amagi Group (Honshu-Japan)	Synonym of Izu-Tobu	0803-01=
Onagaremaru-yama (Honshu-Japan)	Cone of Fuji	0803-03=
Onamedake [Omae-dake] (Honshu-Japan)	Cone of Akita-Komaga-take	0803-23=
Onami-ike (Kyushu-Japan)	Crater of Kirishima	0802-09=
Onas, Cerro (Argentina)	Stratovolcano of Antofalla	....
Onashiroko (Honshu-Japan)	Crater of Iwate	0803-24=
On-dake (Kyushu-Japan)	Cone of Fukue-jima	0802-091
Ondverdarnesholar (Iceland-W)	Shield volcano of Snaefellsjökull	1700-01=
One Tree Hill (New Zealand)	Cone of Auckland Field	0401-02=
One, Vusi (Vanuatu-SW Pacific)	Cone of Aoba	0507-03=
Onenor (China-E)	Vent of Motianling Group	....
Onepoto (New Zealand)	Tuff ring of Auckland Field	0401-02=
Onepoto (New Zealand)	Shield volcano of South Auckland	....
Onepu (New Zealand)	Cone of Okataina	0401-05=
Onepu Springs (New Zealand)	Thermal feature of Okataina	0401-05=
Onewhero (New Zealand)	Tuff ring of South Auckland	....
Ongarato (New Zealand)	Thermal feature of Maroa	0401-061
Onigajo (Honshu-Japan)	Dome of Akita-Yake-yama	0803-26=
Onigajo (Honshu-Japan)	Stratovolcano of Iwate	0803-24=
Onigazyo [Onigajo] (Honshu-Japan)	Dome of Akita-Yake-yama	0803-26=
Onigazyo [Onigajo] (Honshu-Japan)	Stratovolcano of Iwate	0803-24=
Onikobe (Honshu-Japan)	Caldera (None) Pleistocene-Geysers	....
Oniwa-Okuniwa (Honshu-Japan)	Cone of Fuji	0803-03=
Onmae-dake (Honshu-Japan)	Stratovolcano of Zao	0803-19=
Onnebetsu (Hokkaido-Japan)	Stratovolcano (None) Pleistocene	....
Onneto-yama [Burevestnik] (Kuril Is)	Cone of Bogatyr Ridge	0900-06-
Ono (Honshu-Japan)	Pleistocene caldera of Futamata	....
Onohara-jima (Izu Is-Japan)	Lava dome (None) Pleistocene	....
Onoko-yama (Honshu-Japan)	Stratovolcano of Komochi-Onoko	....
Onsen-dake (Hokkaido-Japan)	Dome of Tokachi-Eboshi	....
Onsen-dake (Kyushu-Japan)	Synonym of Unzen	0802-10=
On-take (Ryukyu Is)	Stratovolcano of Nakano-shima	0802-04=
On-take (Honshu-Japan)	Complex volcano (1, 1980) Historical	**0803-04=**
On-take (Ryukyu Is)	Stratovolcano of Suwanose-jima	0802-03=
On-take [Mi-take] (Ryukyu Is)	Dome of Akuseki-jima	0802-022
Ontar (Vanuatu-SW Pacific)	Cone of Gaua	0507-02=
Onu (Halmahera-Indonesia)	Cone of Todoko-Ranu	0608-05=
Onyoke, Ol Doinyo (Africa-E)	Stratovolcano of Suswa	0202-11=
O'o, Puu (Hawaiian Is)	Cone of Kilauea	1302-01-
Oojini (Africa-E)	Cone of Chyulu Hills	0202-13=
Oonami-ike [Onami-ike] (Kyushu-Japan)	Crater of Kirishima	0802-09=
Oonyu-ike (Honshu-Japan)	Crater of Norikura	0803-06=
Ooshima (Izu Is-Japan)	Synonym of Oshima	0804-01=
Oo-sima (Izu Is-Japan)	Synonym of Oshima	0804-01=
Opal Cone (Canada)	Cone of Garibaldi	1200-20-
Opala (Kamchatka)	Caldera (4, 1776) Historical	**1000-08=**
Opalinskaja (Opalnaja) (Kamchatka)	Synonym of Opala	1000-08=
Opalnaja (Kamchatka)	Synonym of Opala	1000-08=
Opalny (Kamchatka)	Dome of Bolshoi Semiachik	1000-15=
Opalskaia Sopka (Kamchatka)	Synonym of Opala	1000-08=
Ophelio, Monte (Italy)	Cone of Roccamonfina	....
Ophir (Sumatra)	Synonym of Talakmau	0601-13=
Opipi, Volcán (Chile-Is)	Pyroclastic cone of Easter Island	1506-011
Opo Bay (New Zealand)	Tuff cone of Mayor Island	0401-021
Opouri, Lake [Lake Ngapouri] (New Zealand)	Crater of Reporoa	0401-06-
Oputateshike (Hokkaido-Japan)	Dome of Kutcharo	0805-08=
Oputatesike [Oputateshike] (Hokkaido-Japan)	Dome of Kutcharo	0805-08=
Ora, Doro (Lesser Sunda Is)	Unknown (None) Quaternary	....
Öraefajökull (Iceland-SE)	Stratovolcano (2, 1728) Historical	**1704-01=**
Orakei Basin (New Zealand)	Tuff ring of Auckland Field	0401-02=
Orakeikorako (New Zealand)	Thermal feature of Maroa	0401-061
Orca (New Zealand)	Crater of White Island	0401-04=
Orchilla, Montaña de (Canary Is)	Cinder cone of Hierro	1803-02-
Orchon Gol (Mongolia)	Synonym of Orkhon Gol	....
Orcopampa Volc Field (Perú)	Synonym of Andahua-Orcopampa	1504-004
Oreja, Cerro de la (Colombia)	Synonym Negro de Mayasquer, Cerro	1501-11=
Orengingnai (Africa-E)	Pumice cone of Olkaria	0202-09=
Orfialdsjokull (Iceland-SE)	Synonym of Öraefajökull	1704-01=
Organos, Los (México)	Cinder cone of Gloria, La	1401-097
Orhon Gol (Mongolia)	Synonym of Orkhon Gol	....
Ori, Maunga (Chile-Is)	Pyroclastic cone of Easter Island	1506-011
Oricola-Carsoli (Italy)	Pyroclastic cones (None) Pleistocene	....
Orilla del Monte (México)	Shield volcano of Humeros, Los	1401-093
Orion Seamount (Kermadec Is)	Synonym of Monowai Seamount	0402-05-
Orir (Vanuatu-SW Pacific)	Crater of Suretamatai	0507-01=
Orito, Maunga (Chile-Is)	Dome of Easter Island	1506-011
Orizaba, Pico de (México)	Stratovolcano (23, 1846) Historical	**1401-10=**
Orkhon Gol (Mongolia)	Volcanic field (None) Pleistocene	....
Orlando, Mt. (Cape Verde Is)	Cone of Fogo	1804-01=
Ormus Islands (Arabia-E)	(None) Not a Volcano	0301-19-
Oro, Cerro de (Guatemala)	Dome of Cuxliquel	....
Oro, Cerro de (Guatemala)	Dome of Tolimán	1402-07=
Orofure-Raiba (Hokkaido-Japan)	Stratovolcanoes (None) Pleistocene	....
Orofure-yama (Hokkaido-Japan)	Stratovolcano of Orofure-Raiba	....
Orok, Oldoinyo (Africa-E)	Synonym of Meru	0202-16=
Orokura [Kaneda] (Honshu-Japan)	Dome of Omanago Group	0803-142
Oromboha, Doro (Lesser Sunda Is)	Synonym of Lambuwu, Doro	....
Oromontique, Cerro (El Salvador)	Lava cone of Tigre, El	1403-082
Orongatea (New Zealand)	Pumice cone of Mayor Island	0401-021
Oroscocha (Perú)	Dome of Quimsachata	1504-00-
Orosí (Costa Rica)	Stratovolcanoes (None) Holocene?	**1405-01=**
Orosí-Cacao (Costa Rica)	Synonym of Orosí	1405-01=
Orosilito, Volcán (Costa Rica)	Stratovolcano of Orosí	1405-01=
Orota (Nicaragua)	Synonym of Rota	1404-06-
Orphan Butte (US-Oregon)	Cone of Newberry	1202-11-
Oruahinawe (New Zealand)	Dome of Maroa	0401-061
Oruanui (New Zealand)	Dome of Maroa	0401-061
Oruka [Tatarinov] (Kuril Is)	Stratovolcano of Chikurachki	0900-36=
Os, Puig de l' (Spain)	Cone of Olot Volc Field	0100-03-
Osawa (Izu Is-Japan)	Dome of Kozu-shima	0804-03=
Osborne Butte (US-Wyoming)	Dome of Yellowstone	1205-01-
Oscostar (SW Pacific)	Synonym Eastern Gemini Seamount	0508-001
Oscuro, El (Argentina)	Cinder cone of Unnamed	....
Oserian (Africa-E)	Dome of Olkaria	0202-09=
Osezaki (Honshu-Japan)	Stratovolcano of Daruma	....
Oshidashizawa (Hokkaido-Japan)	Crater of Komaga-take	0805-02=
Oshima (Izu Is-Japan)	Stratovolcano (99, 1990) Historical	**0804-01=**
Oshima Maru-yama (Hokkaido-Japan)	Stratovolcano (None) Pleistocene	....
Oshima-Fuji (Hokkaido-Japan)	Synonym of Komaga-take	0805-02=
Oshima-Ko-jima (Hokkaido-Japan)	Stratovolcano (None) Quaternary	....
Oshima-Oshima (Hokkaido-Japan)	Stratovolcano (5, 1790) Historical	**0805-01=**
Osho-yama (Honshu-Japan)	Stratovolcano of Adatara	0803-17=
O-sima (Izu Is-Japan)	Synonym of Oshima	0804-01=
O-sima (Hokkaido-Japan)	Synonym of Oshima-Oshima	0805-01=
Osima-Ko-zima (Hokkaido-Japan)	Synonym of Oshima-Ko-jima	....
Osima-Osima (Hokkaido-Japan)	Synonym of Oshima-Oshima	0805-01=
Öskjuvatn (Iceland-NE)	Caldera of Askja	1703-06=
Osobaya Peak (Kuril Is)	Cone of Alaid	0900-39=
Osogot (Africa-E)	Cone of Chyulu Hills	0202-13=
Osore-yama (Honshu-Japan)	Stratovolcano (1, 1787) Historical	**0803-29=**
Osorno (Chile-S)	Stratovolcano (17, 1869) Historical	**1508-01=**
Ostanets (Kamchatka)	Fissure vent of Kliuchevskoi	1000-26=
Ostanets (Kamchatka)	Shield volcanoes (None) Holocene	**1000-055**
Ostanets (Kamchatka)	Dome of Uzon	1000-17=
Osteifel Volc Field (Germany)	Synonym of East Eifel Volc Field	....
Ostraya (Kamchatka)	Synonym of Ostry	1000-68-
Ostraya Zimina (Kamchatka)	Stratovolcano of Zimina	1000-242
Ostriy (Kamchatka)	Synonym of Ostry	1000-68-
Ostry (Kamchatka)	Stratovolcano (1, -2050) Holocene	**1000-68-**

Gerardo Carrasco-Núñez (UNAM)

Pico de **Orizaba** (also known as Volcán Citlaltépetl), México's highest peak and North America's highest volcano, rises 4500 m above the Gulf of Mexico coastal plain. Its 5675-m-high summit contains a 500-m-wide, oval-shaped crater that is 300 m deep. The last eruption occurred during the 19th century.

Name (Subregion)	Type (Eruptions, Most Recent) Status / Relation to Named Volcano	Volcano Number
Ostry Tolbachik (Kamchatka)	Stratovolcano of Tolbachik	1000-24=
Ostúa, Cerro de (El Salvador)	Cinder cone of San Diego	1403-001
Osyo-yama [Osho-yama] (Honshu-Japan)	Stratovolcano of Adatara	0803-17=
Otake (Kyushu-Japan)	Thermal feature of Kuju	0802-12=
Otake [On-take] (Ryukyu Is)	Stratovolcano of Suwanose-jima	0802-03=
Otara Hill (New Zealand)	Cone of Auckland Field	0401-02=
Otdelniy (Kamchatka)	Shield volcanoes (None) Holocene	**1000-056**
Otei Springs (New Zealand)	Thermal feature of Okataina	0401-05=
Otkhodyashchy (Kamchatka)	Cone of Mutnovsky	1000-06=
Otkrytaya (Kamchatka)	Cone of Uzon	1000-17=
Otkrytyi (Kamchatka)	Fissure vent of Kliuchevskoi	1000-26=

Name (Subregion)	Type (Eruptions, Most Recent) Status Relation to Named Volcano	Volcano Number
Oto (New Britain-SW Pac)	Stratovolcano of Oto Group	....
Oto Group (New Britain-SW Pac)	Stratovolcanoes (None) Pleistocene	....
Otomeko-yama (Honshu-Japan)	Synonym of Fuji	0803-03=
Otoroa (New Zealand)	Cone of Kaikohe-Bay of Islands	0401-01=
Otota, Doro (Lesser Sunda Is)	Unknown (None) Quaternary	....
Otro Lado, Cerro el (Guatemala)	Cinder cone of Chiquimula Volc Field	1402-20-
Otsubo-no-ike (Honshu-Japan)	Crater of Akita-Komaga-take	0803-23=
Otsukue-yama (Honshu-Japan)	Cinder cone of Kannabe	....
Otter Island (Alaska-W)	Unknown (None) Pleistocene	....
Ottley's Level (W Indies)	Dome of South East Range	....
Ottomoi (Kuril Is)	Synonym of Ebeko	0900-38=
Otuataua (New Zealand)	Cone of Auckland Field	0401-02=
Otubo-no-ike [Otsubo-no-ike] (Japan)	Crater of Akita-Komaga-take	0803-23=
Oturu (New Zealand)	Pumice cone of Mayor Island	0401-021
Otutarara Springs (New Zealand)	Thermal feature of Rotorua	....
Otu'u, Maunga (Chile-Is)	Pyroclastic cone of Easter Island	1506-011
Otvazhny (Kuril Is)	Crater of Tiatia	0900-03=
Ouaha (New Zealand)	Dome of Taupo	0401-07=
Oujda Volc Field (Africa-N)	Volcanic field (None) Quaternary	....
Oukcem (Africa-N)	Maar of Manzaz Volc Field	0205-006
Oulenou (Vanuatu-SW Pacific)	Cone of Traitor's Head	0507-09=
Oulmes (Africa-N)	Synonym of Mrit-Ment Volc Field	....
Oulmès Volc Field (Africa-N)	Volcanic field (None) Pleistocene	....
Ounda Ginna Koma (Djibouti)	Tuff cone of Ardoukôba	0201-126
Ouson (Kamchatka)	Synonym of Uzon	1000-17=
O-Usu (Hokkaido-Japan)	Dome of Usu	0805-03=
Outcast Hill (Canada)	Cone of Spectrum Range	1200-07-
Outgui, Jebel (Africa-N)	Cone of Azrou Volc Field	....
Outhwaite Park (New Zealand)	Cone of Auckland Field	0401-02=
Outigui Volc Field (Africa-N)	Synonym of Azrou Volc Field	....
Oval Crater (US-Oregon)	Crater of Diamond Craters	1202-17-
Ovaljny (Kamchatka)	Synonym of Ovalny	....
Ovalnaya Zimina (Kamchatka)	Stratovolcano of Zimina	1000-242
Ovalny (Kamchatka)	Shield volcano (None) Pleistocene	....
Ovalnye (Kamchatka)	Dome of Bolshoi Semiachik	1000-15=
Ove (Solomon Is-SW Pacific)	Synonym of Simbo	0505-05=
Ove, Lake (Solomon Is-SW Pacific)	Crater of Simbo	0505-05=
Ovejero, Cerro el (Guatemala)	Cone of Suchitán	1402-16-
Overo, Cerro (Chile-N)	Maar (None) Holocene?	**1505-097**
Overo, Volcán (Argentina)	Stratovolcano of Atuel, Caldera del	1507-023
Ow Rig (Vanuatu-SW Pacific)	Stratovolcano of Suretamatai	0507-01=
Ow Sorlav-Ow Planmen (Vanuatu)	Stratovolcano of Suretamatai	0507-01=
Owakudani (Honshu-Japan)	Thermal feature of Hakone	0803-02=
Oxi (Iceland-S)	Fissure vent of Hekla	1702-07=
Oyagua (Chile-N)	Synonym of Ollagüe	1505-06=
Oyahue (Chile-N)	Synonym of Ollagüe	1505-06=
Oyakoba-yama (Oyakobatska) (Kuril Is)	Synonym of Alaid	0900-39=
Oyama (Izu Is-Japan)	Caldera of Miyake-jima	0804-04=

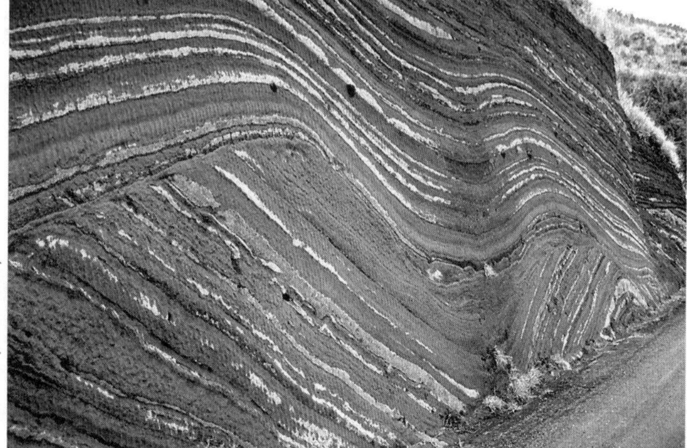

Richard Fiske (Smithsonian)

This classic outcrop at **Oshima** volcano, in the Izu Islands, south of Tokyo, shows more than 100 individual layers of pyroclastic-fall deposits produced by eruptions of Oshima volcano at fairly regular intervals over a period of about 10,000 years. A prominent unconformity in the center of the outcrop is an erosional surface that truncated deposits of the earlier eruptions.

Name (Subregion)	Type (Eruptions, Most Recent) Status Relation to Named Volcano	Volcano Number
Oyameles (México)	Dome of Humeros, Los	1401-093
Oyma (Ethiopia)	Stratovolcano (None) Pleistocene	....
Oyunuma (Hokkaido-Japan)	Crater of Kuttara	0805-034
O-Yunuma (Hokkaido-Japan)	Crater of Kuttara	0805-034
Ozernaia (Kamchatka)	Synonym of Ilyinsky	1000-03=
Ozernaya (Kamchatka)	Synonym of Ozernoy	1000-051
Ozernovsky Potok (Kamchatka)	Vent of Elovsky	1000-59-
Ozernoy (Kamchatka)	Shield volcano of Elovsky	1000-59-
Ozernoy (Kamchatka)	Cone of Krasheninnikov	1000-19=
Ozernoy (Kamchatka)	Synonym of Nachikinsky	....
Ozernoy (Kamchatka)	Shield volcano (None) Holocene	**1000-051**
Ozigoku [Ojigoku] (Honshu-Japan)	Thermal feature of Iwate	0803-24=
Ozima-zima (Kyushu-Japan)	Synonym of Ojika-jima	....
Ozukushi-yama (Honshu-Japan)	Dome of Osore-yama	0803-29=
Ozukusi-yama [Ozukushi-yama] (Japan)	Dome of Osore-yama	0803-29=
Ozyo-dake [Ojo-dake] (Kyushu-Japan)	Stratovolcano of Aso	0802-11=

P

Name (Subregion)	Type (Eruptions, Most Recent) Status Relation to Named Volcano	Volcano Number
Pa Hill (New Zealand)	Dome of Whale Island	....
Paama Island (Vanuatu-SW Pacific)	Complex volcano (None) Pleistocene	....
Pabellon Mauras, Volcán (Perú)	Cinder cone of Andahua-Orcopampa	1504-004
Pabellón, Cerro (Chile-N)	Dome of Azufre, Cerro del	1505-061
Pablo, Cerro el (México)	Cinder cone of Camargo Volc Field	....
Pabus, Bukit (Sumatra)	Unknown (None) Post-Miocene	....
Pacaracua, Cerro (México)	Shield volc. of Michoacán-Guanajuato	1401-06=
Pacaya (Guatemala)	Complex volcano (28, 2010) Historical	**1402-11=**
Pacayal, El (El Salvador)	Synonym of Chinameca	1403-09=
Pacayal, Laguna Seca el (El Salvador)	Crater of Chinameca	1403-09=
Pacha, Loma (El Salvador)	Cinder cone of Taburete	1403-072
Pacheco, Cabecos do (Azores)	Cone of Fayal	1802-01=
Pacho, Cerro (El Salvador)	Dome of Coatepeque Caldera	1403-041
Pacho, Cerro (El Salvador)	Stratovolcano of Tablas, Cerro las	....
Pachuca (México)	Dome of Zitácuaro-Valle de Bravo	1401-061
Packsaddle Mountain (US-Oregon)	Shield volcano of Williamson Mountain	....
Paco (Mindanao-Philippines)	Stratovolcano (None) Anthropology	**0701-09-**
Paddo (US-Washington)	Synonym of Adams	1201-04-
Paeh, Kawah (Java)	Thermal feature of Salak	0603-05=
P'aektu-san (China-E)	Synonym of Changbaishan	1005-06-
Pagan (Mariana Is-C Pacific)	Stratovolcanoes (17, 2006) Historical	**0804-17=**
Pagerkandang (Java)	Cone of Dieng Volc Complex	0603-20=
Pagerkandang, Kawah (Java)	Thermal feature Dieng Volc Complex	0603-20=
Pagerluhir, Gunung (Java)	Vent of Sundoro	0603-21=
Pago (New Britain-SW Pac)	Caldera (18, 2007) Historical	**0502-08=**
Pago (Samoa-SW Pacific)	Pleistocene caldera of Tutuila	0404-02-
Pahangahanga (New Zealand)	Cone of Kaikohe-Bay of Islands	0401-01=
Pahinga, Tavani [Tavani Pahunga] (Vanuatu)	Cone of Emae	....
Pahto (US-Washington)	Synonym of Adams	1201-04-
Pahunga, Tavani (Vanuatu-SW Pacific)	Cone of Emae	....
Pailas, Las (Costa Rica)	Thermal feature of Rincón de la Vieja	1405-02=
Pailin (SE Asia)	Unknown (None) Pleistocene	....
Pailoushan (China-E)	Cone of Datong-Fengzen	....
Paimún Cones (Chile-C)	Cinder cone of Lanín	1507-122
Paint Pot Crater (US-California)	Crater of Medicine Lake	1203-02-
Paisita, El (Colombia)	Crater of Galeras	1501-08=
Paisley (US-Idaho)	Cinder cone of Craters of the Moon	1204-02-
Paja I, Cerro la (Guatemala)	Cinder cone of Güistepeque Volc Field	....
Pajalitos, Loma los (El Salvador)	Cinder cone of San Diego	1403-001
Pajanales, Cerro (Chile-N)	Stratovolcano of Pular	1505-107
Pajang [Payang] (Lesser Sunda Is)	Crater of Batur	0604-01=
Pajarita, Cerro la (Guatemala)	Cone of Flores	1402-14-
Pajaritos (Chile-C)	Cone of Antillanca Group	1507-153
Pajaros (Mariana Is-C Pacific)	Synonym of Farallon de Pajaros	0804-14=
Pajas, Cerro de (Galápagos)	Cone of Floreana	....
Pajita, Cerro (Panamá)	Dome of Valle, El	1406-03-
Pajo (Luzon-Philippines)	Thermal feature of Pinatubo	0703-083
Pajonales, Cerro (Chile-N)	Stratovolcano of Pular	1505-107
Paka (Africa-E)	Shield volcano (1, -7550) Ar/Ar	**0202-053**
Pakehoolua (Hawaiian Is)	Shield volcano of Niihau	....
Pakis, Ranu (Java)	Maar of Lamongan	0603-32=
Pakis, Ranu (Java)	Maar of Semeru	0603-30=
Pakka (Africa-E)	Synonym of Paka	0202-053
Pakushin (Aleutian Is)	Cone of Makushin	1101-31-
Pakuwaja (Java)	Cone of Dieng Volc Complex	0603-20=
Pakuwodjo [Pakuwaja] (Java)	Cone of Dieng Volc Complex	0603-20=
Pakuwojo [Pakuwaja] (Java)	Cone of Dieng Volc Complex	0603-20=
Palabuno Hot Spring (Mindanao-Philippines)	Thermal feature of Balut	0701-01=
Palacpaquen, Lake (Luzon-Philippines)	Maar of San Pablo Volc Field	0703-06=
Palad (SE Asia)	Vent of Lampang	....
Palaeochori Bay (Greece)	Thermal feature of Mílos	0102-03=
Palamito (México)	Cinder cone of Chichinautzin	1401-08=
Palangiagia (New Britain-SW Pac)	Stratovolcano of Rabaul	0502-14=
Palanush Butte (US-Oregon)	Cone of Wuksi Butte-Twin Lakes	....
Palao Ragang (Mindanao-Philippines)	Synonym of Ragang	0701-06=
Palar (Chile-N)	Synonym of Pular	1505-107
Paláu, Laguna de los (México)	Maar of Ventura Volc Field	....
Paleg (Lesser Sunda Is)	Cone of Batur	0604-01=
Palei-Aike Volc Field (Chile-S)	Cinder cones (1, -5550) Anthropology	**1508-08-**
Palena Volc Group (Chile-S)	Cinder cones (None) Holocene	**1508-051**
Paleo-Semiachik (Kamchatka)	Stratovolcano of Maly Semiachik	1000-14=
Paleostromboli (Italy)	Stratovolcano of Stromboli	0101-04=
Paletera (Colombia)	Cone of Puracé	1501-06=
Palffy (Atlantic-N-Jan Mayen)	Cone of Jan Mayen	1706-01=
Pali Dome (Canada)	Dome of Cayley, Mt.	....
Palinpinon (Philippines-C)	Thermal feature of Cuernos de Negros	0702-01=
Palinuro (Italy)	Submarine volc. (1, -8040) Radiocarbon	**0101-031**
Paliorewma (Greece)	Thermal feature of Mílos	0102-03=
Paliron (Mindanao-Philippines)	Dome of Paco	0701-09-
Palizada, Volcán (Chile-C)	Stratovolc. of Descabezado Grande	1507-05=
Pallanzana, La (Italy)	Dome of Vico-Cimino Complex	....
Pallas Peak (Kuril Is)	Stratovolcano of Ketoi	0900-20=
Palma Sol Volc Field (México)	Synonym of Atlixcos, Los	1401-094
Palma Sur, Cerrito la (El Salvador)	Dome of Ilopango	1403-06=
Palma, La (Colombia)	Pyroclastic cone of Unnamed	....
Palmarola (Italy)	Cone of Pontine Islands	....
Palmas, Cerro las (México)	Cinder cone of Mascota Volc Field	1401-031
Palmas, Cerro las (El Salvador)	Stratovolcano of Tecapa	1403-08=
Palmas, Montana de las (Canary Is)	Cone of Gran Canaria	1803-04-
Palmira, Cerros (Costa Rica)	Stratovolcano of Platanar	1405-034
Palo Blanco (US-New Mexico)	Cone of Raton-Clayton	....

Name (Subregion)	Type (Eruptions, Most Recent) Status / Relation to Named Volcano	Volcano Number
Paloc (Mindanao-Philippines)	Dome of Leonard Range	0701-031
Paloe (Lesser Sunda Is)	Synonym of Paluweh	0604-15=
Palomo (Chile-C)	Stratovolcano (None) Holocene	**1507-022**
Palomos, Cerro las (Nicaragua)	Cone of Momotombo	1404-09=
Palowe (Lesser Sunda Is)	Synonym of Paluweh	0604-15=
Palsfjall (Iceland-NE)	Cone of Grímsvötn	1703-01=
Paluweh (Lesser Sunda Is)	Stratovolcano (8, 1985) Historical	**0604-15=**
Pam Lin (Admiralty Is-SW Pacific)	Cone of St. Andrew Strait	0500-01=
Pam Mandian (Admiralty Is-SW Pacific)	Cone of St. Andrew Strait	0500-01=
Pambamarca (Ecuador)	Stratovolcano (None) Pleistocene	....
Paminta (Luzon-Philippines)	Thermal feature of Cagua	0703-09=
Pamoctan (Luzon-N of)	Dome of Camiguin de Babuyanes	0704-01=
Pampa de Palacio (Perú)	Shield volcano of Chachani, Nevado	1504-007
Pampa Luxar (Bolivia)	Synonym of Pampa Luxsar	1505-042
Pampa Luxsar (Bolivia)	Volcanic field (None) Holocene?	**1505-042**
Pan de Azucar (Alaska-SW)	Synonym of Augustine	1103-01-
Pan de Azúcar (Costa Rica)	Synonym of Arenal	1405-033
Pan de Azúcar (Ecuador)	Stratovolcano (None) Pleistocene	....
Pan de Azúcar (Colombia)	Stratovolcano of Puracé	1501-06=
Pan de Azucar [Pico del Teide] (Canary Is)	Stratovolcano of Tenerife	1803-03-
Panalvía, Cerro (Guatemala)	Dome of Ipala	1402-19-
Panamao (Philippines-C)	Thermal feature of Biliran	0702-08=
Panámao (Philippines-C)	Dome of Biliran	0702-08=
Panamao, Mt. (Sulu Is-Philippines)	Crater of Jolo	0700-01=
Panandjakan [Pananjakan] (Java)	Cone of Tengger Caldera	0603-31=
Pananjakan (Java)	Cone of Tengger Caldera	0603-31=
Pana-on (Philippines-C)	Unknown (None) Pleistocene	....
Panarea (Italy)	Stratovolcano (None) Holocene?	**0101-041**
Panay (Luzon-Philippines)	Stratovolcano (None) Pleist.-Fumarolic	....
Pandan (Sumatra)	Cone of Patah Sembilan-Pandan	....
Pandan (Sumatra)	Synonym of Pendan	0601-191
Pandan I, Bukit (Sumatra)	Unknown (None) Post-Miocene	....
Pandan Ii, Bukit (Sumatra)	Unknown (None) Post-Miocene	....
Pandan, Gunung (Lesser Sunda Is)	Cone of Batur	0604-01=
Pandere Hill (Africa-E)	Cone of Kieyo	0202-17=
Pandi, Lake (Luzon-Philippines)	Maar of San Pablo Volc Field	0703-06=
Pando, Cerro (Panamá)	Dome of Tisingal	....
Pandu (Java)	Cone of Iyang-Argapura	0603-33=
Panecillo, Cerro el (Ecuador)	Dome of Mojanda	1502-005
Pangalu (New Britain-SW Pac)	Thermal feature of Garua Harbour	0502-06=
Pangasahan, Kawah (Java)	Thermal feature of Kamojang, Kawah	....
Pangasun, Mt. (Luzon-N of)	Stratovolcano of Babuyan Claro	0704-03=
Pangerango [Pangrango] (Java)	Twin volcano of Gede	0603-06=
Panggilingan, Kawah (Java)	Thermal feature of Kamojang, Kawah	....
Panggujangan Badak (Java)	Crater of Tangkubanparahu	0603-09=
Panggungan (Java)	Crater of Lawu	0603-26=
Pangguyangan Badak (Java)	Crater of Tangkubanparahu	0603-09=
Pangkalan (Java)	Pleist. caldera of Kamojang, Kawah	....
Pango (New Britain-SW Pac)	Synonym of Pago	0502-08=
Pangonan (Java)	Cone of Dieng Volc Complex	0603-20=
Pangrango (Java)	Twin volcano of Gede	0603-06=
Pangues, Los (Chile-C)	Cone of Antuco	1507-08=
Panguipulli (Chile-C)	Synonym of Mocho-Choshuenco	1507-13=
Pangujaan [Danan] (Philippines-C)	Thermal feature of Mahagnao	0702-07=
Pani, Ranu (Java)	Maar of Semeru	0603-30=
Panier, Mt. (Australia)	Shield volcano Newer Volcanics Prov	0509-01-
Panindi (Sumatra)	Unknown (None) Post-Miocene	....
Panindjanan, Bukit (Sumatra)	Cone of Garanggarag, Bukit	....
Paniri (Chile-N)	Stratovolcano (None) Pleistocene?	....
Panjang, Kapundan (Sumatra)	Crater of Talang	0601-16=
Panmure Basin (New Zealand)	Tuff ring of Auckland Field	0401-02=
Pan-Pan-Lung-wan [Banbanlongwan] (China)	Crater of Longgang Group	1005-05-
Panso [Pansol] (Luzon-Philippines)	Cone of San Pablo Volc Field	0703-06=
Pansol (Luzon-Philippines)	Cone of San Pablo Volc Field	0703-06=
Pantano Secco (Italy)	Maar of Alban Hills	0101-004
Pantar Api (Lesser Sunda Is)	Synonym of Sirung	0604-27=
Pantelleria (Italy)	Shield volcano (6, 1891) Historical	**0101-071**
Pantelleria Bank (Italy)	Submarine vent C. Flegrei Mar Sicilia	0101-07=
Pantoja, Cerro (Chile-C)	Stratovolcano (None) Holocene	**1507-152**
Panum (US-California)	Dome of Mono Craters	1203-12-
Pao de Acucar (Atlantic-C)	Dome of Trindade	1805-051
Paoha Island (US-California)	Cone of Mono Lake Volc Field	1203-11-
Papa, Gunung (Java)	Cone of Arjuno-Welirang	0603-29=
Papach's Crater (New Zealand)	Tuff cone of South Auckland	....
Papai, Puu O (Hawaiian Is)	Cone of Kauai	....
Papak, Gunung (Java)	Cone of Ijen	0603-35=
Papak, Gunung (Java)	Cone of Semeru	0603-30=
Papallacta (Ecuador)	Thermal feature of Chacana	1502-022
Papandajan (Java)	Synonym of Papandayan	0603-10=
Papandayan (Java)	Stratovolcanoes (4, 2002) Historical	**0603-10=**
Papantón de Juanacatlán, Cerro el (México)	Stratovolcano of Southern Guadalajara	....
Papanui Point (New Zealand)	Cone of Karioi	....
Papanuiti Point (New Zealand)	Tuff ring of Karioi	....
Papatele (Samoa-SW Pacific)	Dome of Tutuila	0404-02-
Papayo (México)	Lava dome (None) Holocene	**1401-081**
Papoose Hill (US-California)	Cone of Medicine Lake	1203-02-
Paquixten, Cerro (Guatemala)	Cone of San Pedro	....
Parabakti, Cipanas (Java)	Thermal feature of Perbakti-Gagak	0603-04=
Parabakti, Kawah (Java)	Thermal feature of Perbakti-Gagak	0603-04=
Parabakti, Tjipanas [Cipanas Parabakti]	Thermal feature of Perbakti-Gagak	0603-04=
Paracho, Cerros de (México)	Shield volc. of Michoacán-Guanajuato	1401-06=
Parada Norte, Cerro la (Guatemala)	Cone of Ipala	1402-19-
Parada, Cerrito la (Guatemala)	Cone of Ipala	1402-19-
Parador (Chile-C)	Cinder cone of Chillán, Nevados de	1507-07=
Paramasam (Java)	Thermal feature of Ungaran	0603-23=
Páramo de Animas (Colombia)	Synonym of Animas	....
Páramo de Miraflores (Colombia)	Unknown (None) Quaternary	....
Paramo de Ruiz (Colombia)	Synonym of Ruiz, Nevado del	1501-02=
Páramo de Santa Rosa (Colombia)	Synonym of Santa Rosa	....
Páramo de Tajumbina (Colombia)	Synonym of Doña Juana	1501-07=
Parang (Sulu Is-Philippines)	Cone of Jolo	0700-01=
Parangan (Sulu Is-Philippines)	Cone of Jolo	0700-01=
Pararoa (New Zealand)	Dome of Okataina	0401-05=
Parasa [Paraso] (Solomon Is-SW Pacific)	Thermal feature of Nonda	....
Paraso (Solomon Is-SW Pacific)	Thermal feature of Nonda	....
Paratun (Chile-S)	Synonym of Osorno	1508-01=
Parazit (Kuril Is)	Cone of Alaid	0900-39=
Paredo [Volcao do Paredao] (Atlantic-C)	Cone of Trindade	1805-051
Parehe, Maunga (Chile-Is)	Dome of Easter Island	1506-011

Lee Siebert (Smithsonian)

MacKenney cone, the historically active vent of **Pacaya** volcano in Guatemala, was constructed within a horseshoe-shaped caldera produced by collapse of the summit of an ancestral volcano about 1100 years ago. The blocky hill in the foreground is a hummock from the resulting debris avalanche, which traveled 25 km down to the Pacific coastal plain.

Name (Subregion)	Type (Eruptions, Most Recent) Status / Relation to Named Volcano	Volcano Number
Parewhaiti (New Zealand)	Dome of Okataina	0401-05=
Parícutin (México)	Cinder cone of Michoacán-Guanajuato	1401-06=
Parinacota (Chile-N)	Stratovolcano (5, 290) Surface Exposure	**1505-012**
Pario, Cerro de (México)	Cinder cone of Michoacán-Guanajuato	1401-06=
Pariou, Puy de (France)	Cone of Chaîne des Puys	0100-02-
Parish Hill (W Indies)	Dome of Saba	1600-01=
Parker (Mindanao-Philippines)	Stratovolcano (3, 1641) Historical	**0701-011**
Parmalok (Africa-E)	Tuff cone of Ol Kokwe	0202-055
Partido, Cerro (México)	Cinder cone of Flores, Los	....
Partido, Pico (Canary Is)	Cone of Lanzarote	1803-06-
Partov Cove (Aleutian Is)	Thermal feature of Recheschnoi	1101-28-
Paru, Mt. (Solomon Is-SW Pacific)	Cone of Gallego	0505-062
Parugpug (Java)	Crater of Papandayan	0603-10=
Paruma, Cerro (Chile-N)	Stratovolcano of Olca-Paruma	1505-05=
Paruma, Volcán (Chile-N)	Stratovolcano of Olca-Paruma	1505-05=
Parupujan [Parupuyan] (Java)	Crater of Guntur	0603-13=
Parupuyan (Java)	Crater of Guntur	0603-13=
Parusnaya Mountain (Kuril Is)	Cone of Golets-Tornyi Group	0900-091
Parva, La (Argentina)	Pyrocl. cone Northern Mendoza Field	....
Parva, La (Argentina)	Vent of Unnamed	....
Parvedi, Piton (Indian O.-W)	Cinder cone of Fournaise, Piton de la	0303-02=
Paryashchaya Dolina (Kamchatka)	Thermal feature of Bolshoi Semiachik	1000-15=
Paryashchyi Greben (Kamchatka)	Dome of Ksudach	1000-05=
Paryashchyi Utes (Kamchatka)	Dome of Ksudach	1000-05=
Pas des Sables, Puy (Indian O.-W)	Cinder cone of Fournaise, Piton de la	0303-02=
Pasagi (Sumatra)	Synonym of Pesagi	....
Pasaman (Sumatra)	Stratovolcano of Talakmau	0601-13=
Pasar Arbaa (Sumatra)	Stratovolcano of Talang	0601-16=
Pasarbubar (Java)	Crater of Merapi	0603-25=
Pascua, Isla de (Chile-Is)	Synonym of Easter Island	1506-011
Pasinler (Turkey)	Unknown (None) Pleistocene	....
Pasir Besar (Banda Sea)	Crater of Banda Api	0605-09=
Pasirlebar, Kawah [Kapi Fumarole Field]	Thermal feature of Kembar	....
Pasochoa (Ecuador)	Stratovolcano (None) Pleistocene	....
Pasquí, Cerro (Costa Rica)	Cinder cone of Irazú	1405-06=
Passage, Cratere du (Indian O.-W)	Crater of Fournaise, Piton de la	0303-02=
Passo del Vento (Italy)	Thermal feature of Pantelleria	0101-071
Pasto, Volcán de (Colombia)	Synonym of Galeras	1501-08=
Pastores, Cerro (México)	Cinder cone of Naolinco Volc Field	1401-095
Pastoria, Cerro la (México)	Crater of Pinacate	1401-001
Pata (Chile-S)	Synonym of Osorno	1508-01=
Pataca Kollu (Bolivia)	Volcanic field of Pucara, Cerro	....
Patah (Sumatra)	Unknown (None) Fumarolic	**0601-231**
Patah Sembilan-Pandan (Sumatra)	Unknown (None) Post-Miocene	....
Patahuille (Chile-S)	Synonym of Osorno	1508-01=
Patamban, Cerro (México)	Cone of Michoacán-Guanajuato	1401-06=
Patas (Lesser Sunda Is)	Unknown (None) Quaternary	....
Patates, Morne (W Indies)	Dome of Plat Pays, Morne	1600-11=
Patilla Pata (Bolivia)	Stratovolcano (None) Pleistocene	....

Name (Subregion)	Type (Eruptions, Most Recent) Status Relation to Named Volcano	Volcano Number
Patilo (New Guinea-NE of)	Crater of Karkar	0501-03=
Patite, Cuddie (Italy)	Shield volcano of Pantelleria	0101-071
Patoc (Luzon-Philippines)	Stratovolcano (None) Fumarolic	**0703-087**
Patoeha (Java)	Synonym of Patuha	0603-07=
Patos, Cerro (Argentina)	Stratovolcano of Antofalla	....
Patos, Islas de los (El Salvador)	Dome of Ilopango	1403-06=
Patos, Los (Chile-N)	Stratovolcano (None) Pleistocene?	....
Patricio, Cerro (Galápagos)	Cone of San Cristóbal	1503-12-
Patuha (Java)	Stratovolcano (None) Holocene	**0603-07=**
Patuha Kaler (Java)	Crater of Patuha	0603-07=
Patukio, Mt. (Solomon Is-SW Pacific)	Cone of Simbo	0505-05=
Patulul (Guatemala)	Synonym of Atitlán	1402-06=
Pauahi (Hawaiian Is)	Pit crater of Kilauea	1302-01-
Paugarani (Perú)	Synonym of Casiri, Nevados	1504-06-
Paugnat, Puy de (France)	Cone of Chaîne des Puys	0100-02-

North Pagan volcano in the Mariana Islands rises above eroded rocks of an ancestral volcano that was truncated by a 7-km-wide caldera. North Pagan volcano, the most active of two volcanoes on Pagan Island, was constructed within the past 3000 years.

U.S. Navy

Name (Subregion)	Type (Eruptions, Most Recent) Status Relation to Named Volcano	Volcano Number
Pauk (Kamchatka)	Lava cone of Krasheninnikov	1000-19=
Paukohurea (New Zealand)	Thermal feature of Kapenga	....
Paukohurea (New Zealand)	Thermal feature of Okataina	0401-05=
Paulet (Antarctica)	Cinder cone (Uncertain) Holocene	**1900-041**
Paulina Peak (US-Oregon)	Dome of Newberry	1202-11-
Paulowsky (Alaska Peninsula)	Synonym of Pavlof	1102-03-
Pauzhetka (Kamchatka)	Pleistocene caldera of Diky Greben	1000-022
Pavant Butte (US-Utah)	Tuff cone of Black Rock Desert	1207-05-
Pavas, Cerro las (El Salvador)	Stratovolcano of Ilopango	1403-06=
Pavas, Las (El Salvador)	Cinder cone of Cinotepeque, Cerro	1403-051
Pavillon, Morne [Piton Lacroix] (W Indies)	Dome of Carbets, Pitons de	....
Pavin (France)	Maar of Chaîne des Puys	0100-02-
Pavlof (Alaska Peninsula)	Stratovolcano (40, 2007) Historical	**1102-03-**
Pavlof Sister (Alaska Peninsula)	Stratovolcano (None) Holocene	**1102-04-**
Pawai (Hawaiian Is)	Pit crater of Kilauea	1302-01-
Pawenen, Gunung (Java)	Cone of Ijen	0603-35=
Pawon (Lesser Sunda Is)	Cone of Agung	0604-02=
Paxapá, Cerro (Guatemala)	Lava cone of Chiquimula Volc Field	1402-20-
Paxte, Cerro el (Guatemala)	Cone of Ipala	1402-19-
Paxton Springs (US-New Mexico)	Cone of Zuni-Bandera	1210-02-
Payachata, Nevados de (Chile-N)	Synonym of Parinacota	1505-012
Payalpan (Kamchatka)	Shield volcano of Bolshoi Payalpan	1000-30-
Payang (Lesser Sunda Is)	Crater of Batur	0604-01=
Payún Matru (Argentina)	Shield volcano (None) Holocene	**1507-066**
Payún, Cerro (Argentina)	Stratovolcano of Payún Matru	1507-066
Peak Hill (W Indies)	Dome of Saba	1600-01=
Pebble Creek Hot Spring (Canada)	Thermal feature of Meager	1200-18-
Pechan (China-W)	Cone of Tianshan Volc Group	1004-02-
Pecho, El (México)	Stratovolcano of Iztaccíhuatl	1401-082
Pecón, Cerro (Panamá)	Synonym of Tisingal	....
Pecsko (Hungary)	Cone of Nográd	....
Pecul (Guatemala)	Synonym of Pacaya	1402-11=
Pecul, Volcán (Guatemala)	Synonym of Santo Tomás	....
Pedernal, Cerro el (México)	Dome of Primavera, Sierra la	....
Pedre Barba, Montana de (Canary Is)	Cone of Lanzarote	1803-06-
Pedregal (Costa Rica)	Stratovolcano of Orosí	1405-01=
Pedregal, Cerro el (México)	Cinder cone of Michoacán-Guanajuato	1401-06=
Pedregal, El (Honduras)	Shield volcano (None) Quaternary	....
Pedregoso, Cerro (México)	Dome of Ceboruco	1401-03=
Pedrera, Cerro la (Guatemala)	Dome of Almolonga	1402-04=
Peggy's Whim (W Indies)	Thermal feature of St. Catherine	1600-17=
Pegunungan Dieng (Java)	Synonym of Dieng Volc Complex	0603-20=
Pehualtepec (México)	Cinder cone of Chichinautzin	1401-08=
Peinado (Argentina)	Stratovolcano (None) Holocene	**1505-20-**
Peishan [Pechan] (China-W)	Cone of Tianshan Volc Group	1004-02-

Name (Subregion)	Type (Eruptions, Most Recent) Status Relation to Named Volcano	Volcano Number
Peladito, El (Colombia)	Crater of Galeras	1501-08=
Pelado, Cerro (Chile-S)	Cone of Minchinmávida	1508-04=
Pelado, Cerro (Galápagos)	Pyroclastic cone of Negra, Sierra	1503-05=
Pelado, Volcán (México)	Shield volcano of Chichinautzin	1401-08=
Pelagatos, Cerro (México)	Cone of Chichinautzin	1401-08=
Pelat, Puy (France)	Cone of Chaîne des Puys	0100-02-
Pelato, Monte [Monte Pilato] (Italy)	Cone of Lipari	0101-042
Pelcoya, Cerro (Bolivia)	Stratovolcano of Talapaca, Cerro	....
Pele [Fatouleo-Kakoulo] (Vanuatu-SW Pacific)	Stratovolcano of North Vate	0507-081
Pele, Mont [Le Djungo] (Africa-W)	Cone of Tombel Graben	0204-011
Pele, Montagne (W Indies)	Synonym of Pelée	1600-12=
Pele, Puu O (Hawaiian Is)	Cone of Haleakala	1302-06-
Pelée (W Indies)	Stratovolcano (54, 1932) Historical	**1600-12=**
Pelican Butte (US-Oregon)	Shield volcano (None) Pleistocene	....
Pelicanos, Cerro de los (México)	Tuff cone of Isabel, Isla	1401-023
Pellado (Chile-C)	Stratovolcano of San Pedro-Pellado	1507-062
Pelmen (Kamchatka)	Cinder cone of Tolbachik	1000-24=
Pelon, Cerro (US-New Mexico)	Dome of Valles Caldera	....
Pelón, Cerro (México)	Cinder cone of Comondú-La Purísima	1401-012
Pelón, Cerro (México)	Cinder cone of Durango Volc Field	1401-022
Pelón, Cerro (México)	Cinder cone of Michoacán-Guanajuato	1401-06=
Pelón, Cerro (Costa Rica)	Stratovolcano of Platanar	1405-034
Pelón, Cerro (El Salvador)	Stratovolcano of Tecapa	1403-08=
Pelón, Cerro (Panamá)	Dome of Tisingal	....
Pelón, Cerro (México)	Cinder cone Zitácuaro-Valle de Bravo	1401-061
Pelón, Cerro (México)	Cinder cone Zitácuaro-Valle de Bravo	1401-061
Pelón, Cerro (México)	Dome of Zitácuaro-Valle de Bravo	1401-061
Pelón, El (Nicaragua)	Cinder cone of Masaya	1404-10=
Pelón, Volcán (México)	Synonym of San Martín Pajapan	....
Pelona, Loma la (Nicaragua)	Caldera of San Cristóbal	1404-02=
Pelota, La (Colombia)	Pyroclastic cone San Augustín-Isnos	....
Peludo, El (Argentina)	Cinder cone of Unnamed	....
Pematang Bata (Sumatra)	Crater of Suoh	0601-27=
Peña Blanca (México)	Cone of Zitácuaro-Valle de Bravo	1401-061
Peña Blanca [Ojo de Agua de la Virgen]	Stratovolcano of Apaneca Range	1403-01=
Peña Blanca, Cerro (Guatemala)	Dome of Tecuamburro	1402-12=
Penanggungan (Java)	Stratovolcano (Uncertain) Holocene	**0603-291**
Penatahan Hot Spring (Lesser Sunda Is)	Thermal feature of Bratan	0604-001
Penavallels, Altos de los (Canary Is)	Cone of Gran Canaria	1803-04-
Pencelut, Kawah (Java)	Thermal feature of Kamojang, Kawah	....
Pendan (Sumatra)	Unknown (None) Holocene	**0601-191**
Pendapuran, Kaba [Kaba Vogelsang]	Crater of Kaba	0601-22=
Pendil, Gunung (Java)	Cone of Ijen	0603-35=
Pengchiahsu (Taiwan-N of)	Stratovolcano (None) Pleist.-Fumarolic	....
Penglai (China-E)	Unknown (None) Quaternary	....
Penguin Island (Antarctica)	Stratovolcano (3, 1905) Lichenometry	**1900-031**
Penjeluang, Kaba [Kaba Vogelsang]	Crater of Kaba	0601-22=
Penoetoen (Lesser Sunda Is)	Synonym of Iliwerung	0604-25=
Peñon de los Banos (México)	Cone of Chichinautzin	1401-08=
Peñon del Marqués (México)	Cone of Chichinautzin	1401-08=
Penones, Cerro los (Perú)	Dome of Chachani, Nevado	1504-007
Pensil, El (Colombia)	Pyroclastic cone of Unnamed	....
Penta Palummo (Italy)	Cone of Campi Flegrei	0101-01=
Pentjelut, Kawah [Kawah Pencelut] (Java)	Thermal feature of Kamojang, Kawah	....
Penunggul (Java)	Dome of Tengger Caldera	0603-31=
Penville Cold Soufrière (W Indies)	Thermal feature of Diables, Morne aux	1600-08=
Penyeluang, Kaba [Kaba Vogelsang]	Crater of Kaba	0601-22=
Pequeño Cono Glacier H.P.N.I. (Chile)	Cone (None) Post-Miocene	....
Peraza, Loma (Guatemala)	Dome of Redondo, Cerro	....
Perbakti, Gunung (Java)	Stratovolcano of Perbakti-Gagak	0603-04=
Perbakti-Gagak (Java)	Stratovolcanoes (7, 1939) Historical	**0603-04=**
Perboewatan [Perbuwatan] (Indonesia)	Former crater of Krakatau	0602-00=
Perbuwatan (Indonesia)	Former crater of Krakatau	0602-00=
Perche's Mountain (W Indies)	Dome of Soufrière Hills	1600-05=
Perdidos, Los (Costa Rica)	Caldera (None) Pleistocene	....
Peremychka (Kamchatka)	Dome of Bolshoi Semiachik	1000-15=
Peremychka (Russia-SE)	Dome of Udokan Plateau	1002-03-
Peretolchin (Russia-SE)	Cinder cone of Oka Plateau	1002-06-
Pereval (Kuril Is)	Cinder cone of Medvezhia	0900-10=
Perevalny (Kamchatka)	Shield volcano (None) Pleistocene	....
Perevalovyi (Kamchatka)	Shield volcano (None) Pleistocene	....
Pereza, Cerro la (Guatemala)	Cone of Ixtepeque	1402-18-
Perfait, Piton (Indian O.-W)	Crater of Fournaise, Piton de la	0303-02=
Peridot Mesa (US-Arizona)	Tuff ring of San Carlos	....
Perikartin (Turkey)	Dome of Erciyes Dagi	0103-01=
Peristerria (Greece)	Shield volcano of Santorini	0102-04=
Perkins, Mt. (Antarctica)	Cone of Fosdick Mountains	....
Perla, La (Guatemala)	Stratovolcano of Tecuamburro	1402-12=
Perol, El (El Salvador)	Crater of Santa Ana	1403-02=
Perolitos, Los (El Salvador)	Synonym of San Miguel	1403-10=
Perpendicular Head (Pacific-S)	Tuff cone of Antipodes Island	1305-01-
Persani Mountains (Romania)	Volcanic field (None) Pleistocene	....
Pertolichina (Russia-SE)	Cinder cone of Oka Plateau	1002-06-
Peruru (Mariana Is-C Pacific)	Cone of Pagan	0804-17=
Perutarube-san (Kuril Is)	Synonym of Berutarube	0900-04=
Pervaya (Kamchatka)	Cone of Uzon	1000-17=
Pervaya (Kamchatka)	Dome of Uzon	1000-17=
Pesagi (Sumatra)	Unknown (None) Pleistocene	....
Peschanaya, Sopka (Kamchatka)	Cinder cone of Zavaritsky	1000-124
Peschanie Gorky (Kamchatka)	Cinder cone of Tolbachik	1000-24=
Peshchernyi (Kamchatka)	Fissure vent of Kliuchevskoi	1000-26=
Petacas (Colombia)	Lava dome (None) Holocene?	**1501-062**
Peter Hafen (New Britain-SW Pac)	Crater of Garove	0502-03=

Name (Subregion)	Type (Eruptions, Most Recent) Status / Relation to Named Volcano	Volcano Number
Peter I Island (Antarctica)	Shield volcano (None) Holocene	**1900-029**
Peter Simmon's Hill (W Indies)	Dome of Saba	1600-01=
Peteroa (Chile-C)	Submarine vent of Planchón-Peteroa	1507-04=
Petinos, Mount (Antarctica)	Tuff cone of Shepard Island	....
Petit Botoum (Africa-N)	Cone of Toussidé, Tarso	0205-01=
Petit Cheminee Exterieure (Indian O.-W)	Crater of Karthala	0303-01=
Petit Dadoi (Africa-N)	Cone of Toussidé, Tarso	0205-01=
Petit Hasan Dagi (Turkey)	Dome of Hasan Dagi	0103-002
Petit Piton (W Indies)	Dome of Qualibou	1600-14=
Petit Puy de Dome (France)	Cone of Chaîne des Puys	0100-02-
Petit Sarcoui (France)	Cone of Chaîne des Puys	0100-02-
Petit Suchet [Puy de l'Aumone] (France)	Dome of Chaîne des Puys	0100-02-
Petit Trou au Natron [Doon Kidimi] (Africa-N)	Crater of Toussidé, Tarso	0205-01=
Petr Shmidt Ridge (Kuril Is)	Unknown (None) Pleistocene	....
Petrel Crater (Antarctica)	Maar of Penguin Island	1900-031
Peuet Sagoee (Sumatra)	Synonym of Peuet Sague	0601-03=
Peuet Sague (Sumatra)	Complex volcano (7, 2000) Historical	**0601-03=**
Peulik (Alaska Peninsula)	Stratovolcano of Ugashik-Peulik	1102-13-
Peut Sagoe (Sumatra)	Synonym of Peuet Sague	0601-03=
Phantom Cone (US-Oregon)	Stratovolcano of Crater Lake	1202-16-
Pharaoh (Canada)	Dome of Edziza	1200-06-
Phlegethon (Greece)	Vent of Nisyros	0102-05=
Phlegraean Fields (Italy)	Synonym of Campi Flegrei	0101-01=
Phlegraean Fields of the Sicily Sea (Italy)	Synonym of Campi Flegrei Mar Sicilia	0101-07=
Phlegraeishe Felder (Italy)	Synonym of Campi Flegrei	0101-01=
Phnum Ko Ngoap (SE Asia)	Cone of Pailin	....
Phnum O Tang (SE Asia)	Cone of Pailin	....
Phnum Yat (SE Asia)	Cone of Pailin	....
Phyriplaka [Fyriplaka] (Greece)	Tuff ring of Milos	0102-03=
Pian d'Erasmo (Italy)	Cinder cone of Etna	0101-06=
Pian Di Celle (Italy)	Cone of San Venanzo	....
Piano del Lago (Italy)	Caldera of Etna	0101-06=
Piano, Caldera del (Italy)	Caldera of Etna	0101-06=
Piano, Caldera del (Italy)	Caldera of Vulcano	0101-05=
Pic, Pica, Pico, Piek (Portuguese, Spanish and Dutch for Peak) see proper name (e.g. Chico, Pico)		
Picacho (México)	Cinder cone of San Quintín Volc Field	1401-002
Picacho, Caldera el (Nicaragua)	Caldera of Pilas, Las	1404-08=
Picacho, Cerro (US-New Mexico)	Dome of Valles Caldera	....
Picacho, Cerro el (México)	Shield volc. of Michoacán-Guanajuato	1401-06=
Picacho, El (Nicaragua)	Stratovolcano of Pilas, Las	1404-08=
Picacho, El (El Salvador)	Stratovolcano of San Salvador	1403-05=
Picada, La (Chile-S)	Stratovolcano of Osorno	1508-01=
Piccolo di Monticchio, Lago (Italy)	Maar of Vulture, Monte	....
Pichagas (Bolivia)	Stratovolcano (None) Post-Miocene	....
Pichancha, La (México)	Cinder cone of Ceboruco	1401-03=
Pichares (Chile-C)	Cone of Caburgua-Huelemolle	1507-112
Pichelin (W Indies)	Dome of Plat Pays, Morne	1600-11=
Pichi Caulle (Chile-C)	Cone of Puyehue-Cordón Caulle	1507-15=
Pichi, Volcán (Chile-C)	Cinder cone of Carrán-Los Venados	1507-14=
Pi-Chia-shan [Bijiashan] (China-E)	Cone of Wudalianchi	1005-03-
Pichicha, Laguna (Nicaragua)	Crater of Zapatera	1404-111
Pichicollo, Cerro (Bolivia)	Unknown (None) Post-Miocene	....
Pichi-Gol, Volcán (Chile-C)	Maar of Puyehue-Cordón Caulle	1507-15=
Pichihua, Cerro (Perú)	Cinder cone of Andahua-Orcopampa	1504-004
Pichihuinco, Volcán (Chile-S)	Cinder cone of Osorno	1508-01=
Pichilaguna, Volcán (Chile-S)	Maar of Cayutué-La Viguería	1508-012
Pichimalla (Chile-C)	Crater of Callaqui	1507-091
Pico (Cape Verde Is)	Cone of Fogo	1804-01=
Pico (México)	Stratovolcano of Orizaba, Pico de	1401-10=
Pico (Azores)	Stratovolcano (3, 1720) Historical	**1802-02=**
Pico, Pico do (Azores)	Synonym of Pico	1802-02=
Picos Volc System (Azores)	Pyroclastic cones (7, 1652) Historical	**1802-081**
Picudo, Cerro (El Salvador)	Cinder cone of Cinotepeque, Cerro	1403-051
Picung (Java)	Crater of Guntur	0603-13=
Piebald Volc Province (Australia)	Shield volcanoes (None) Pleistocene	....
Piedmonte (Italy)	Dome of Ischia	0101-03=
Piedra de Agua, Cerro (Nicaragua)	Cone of Concepción	1404-12=
Piedra del Sal, Montana (Canary Is)	Cone of Fuerteventura	1803-05-
Piedra Grande (Guatemala)	Stratovolcanoes (None) Pleistocene	....
Piedra Herrada, Cerro (México)	Dome of Zitácuaro-Valle de Bravo	1401-061
Piedra Parada (Chile-N)	Stratovolcano (None) Pleistocene	....
Piedras Blancas (Chile-C)	Tuff ring of Llancanelo Volc Field	....
Piedras, Cerro las (Guatemala)	Shield volcano of Ixtepeque	1402-18-
Pierre Pruvost (Ethiopia)	Synonym of Ma Alalta	0201-111
Pies, El (México)	Stratovolcano of Iztaccíhuatl	1401-082
Pietra, La (Italy)	Crater of Campi Flegrei	0101-01=
Pig Beach Hill (Atlantic-S)	Cinder cone of Inaccessible Island	....
Piga, Cerro (Chile-N)	Unknown (None) Post-Miocene	....
Pigeon Mountain (New Zealand)	Cone of Auckland Field	0401-02=
Pigna San Nicola (Italy)	Crater of Campi Flegrei	0101-01=
Pihanga (New Zealand)	Stratovolc. Northern Tongariro Group	....
Piip (Kamchatka)	Thermal feature of Akademia Nauk	1000-125
Piip (Kamchatka)	Fissure vent of Kliuchevskoi	1000-26=
Piip (Kamchatka)	Shield volcano (None) Pleistocene	....
Piip (Kamchatka-E of)	Submarine volc. (1, -5050) Tephrochron.	**1000-271**
Piipa (Kamchatka-E of)	Synonym of Piip	1000-271
Pik (Kamchatka)	Stratovolcano of Kikhpinych	1000-18=
Pik (Kamchatka)	Unknown (None) Pleistocene	....
Pikesa (Greece)	Dome of Methana	0102-02=
Pilar, Lagoa do (Azores)	Cone of Sete Cidades	1802-08=
Pilas, Las (Nicaragua)	Dome of Concepción	1404-12=
Pilas, Las (Nicaragua)	Synonym of Negro, Cerro	1404-07=
Pilas, Las (Nicaragua)	Complex volcano (3, 1954) Historical	**1404-08=**
Pilato, Monte (Italy)	Cone of Lipari	0101-042
Pilato, Mt. (Italy)	Cone of Vulsini	0101-003
Pilavo (Ecuador)	Stratovolcano (None) Pleistocene	....
Pili, Cerro (Chile-N)	Synonym of Acamarachi	1505-096
Pilimbala (Colombia)	Thermal feature of Puracé	1501-06=
Pillan (Chile-S)	Synonym of Osorno	1508-01=
Pillan [El Mocho] (Chile-C)	Stratovolcano of Mocho-Choshuenco	1507-13=
Pillanilahue [Carrán] (Chile-C)	Maar of Carrán-Los Venados	1507-14=
Pillar Butte (US-Idaho)	Shield volcano of Wapi Lava Field	1204-03-
Pillow Creek (Canada)	Cone of Wells Gray-Clearwater	1200-15-
Pillow Ridge (Canada)	Vent of Edziza	1200-06-
Pilmaiquen, Crater (Chile-C)	Cinder cone of Mocho-Choshuenco	1507-13=
Pilon d'Azucar (Alaska-SW)	Synonym of Augustine	1103-01-
Pilón, Cerro (Panamá)	Dome of Valle, El	1406-03-
Pilón, Cerro el (Nicaragua)	Cone of Zapatera	1404-111
Pilón, El [Cerro los Naranjos] (El Salvador)	Stratovolcano of Apaneca Range	1403-01=
Piloncillo (México)	Dome of Zitácuaro-Valle de Bravo	1401-061
Piloncillo, Cerro el (México)	Cone of Zitácuaro-Valle de Bravo	1401-061
Pilongo (Ecuador)	Dome of Illiniza	1502-041
Pilpil Butte (US-Oregon)	Cone of Newberry	1202-11-
Pimenton (Chile-C)	Crater of Villarrica	1507-12=
Pimoe (Hawaiian Is)	Cone of Haleakala	1302-06-
Pin Gin Hill (Australia)	Cone of Atherton Volc Province	....
Piña, Cerro (Chile-N)	Cinder cone of Cariquima, Cerro	....
Pinacate (México)	Cinder cones (Uncertain) Holocene	**1401-001**
Pinacate Peak (México)	Cone of Pinacate	1401-001
Pinacate Peaks (México)	Synonym of Pinacate	1401-001
Pinachevsky (Kamchatka)	Stratovolcano of Aak	....
Pinagdalan (Luzon-Philippines)	Thermal feature San Pablo Volc Field	0703-06=
Pinal de Marquezada (México)	Dome of Zitácuaro-Valle de Bravo	1401-061
Pinar de la Venta (México)	Dome of Primavera, Sierra la	....
Pinatubo (Luzon-Philippines)	Stratovolcano (8, 1993) Historical	**0703-083**
Pinchuleu, Cerro (Chile-S/Argentina)	Cinder cone of Crater Basalt Volc Field	1508-025
Pine Butte (US-Oregon)	Cinder cone of Davis Lake	1202-10-
Pingdingshan (China-E)	Dome of Fanjiatung Group	....
Pinggang (Java)	Cone of Iyang-Argapura	0603-33=
Pinguin Bay (Indian O.-S)	Synonym of St. Paul	0304-002
Piniteddu, Monte (Italy)	Cinder cone of Etna	0101-06=
Pinnacle Peak (US-New Mexico)	Dome of Valles Caldera	....
Pinnacle Ridge (New Zealand)	Vent of Ruapehu	0401-10=
Pinnacle, the (US-Oregon)	Vent of Hood	1202-01-
Pinnacles (Alaska-SW)	Vent of Augustine	1103-01-
Pinne (Italy)	Submarine vent C. Flegrei Mar Sicilia	0101-07=
Pinne Marine [Pinne] (Italy)	Submarine vent C. Flegrei Mar Sicilia	0101-07=
Pino Hachado (Argentina)	Caldera (None) Pleistocene	....
Pino Redondo, Cerro (Guatemala)	Dome of Ixtepeque	1402-18-
Pino Solo (Argentina)	Cone of Tralihue	1507-101
Pino, Cerrito el (Guatemala)	Cinder cone of Cuilapa-Barbarena	1402-111
Pinoonan (Luzon-Philippines)	Cone of Natib	0703-082
Pinos de Galdar, Caldera de los (Canary Is)	Maar of Gran Canaria	1803-04-
Pinotaung (SE Asia)	Cone of Wuntho	....
Pinta (Galápagos)	Shield volcano (1, 1928) Historical	**1503-07=**
Pinta, El (Colombia)	Crater of Galeras	1501-08=
Pinto Basin-Salton Creek (US-Calif.)	Volcanic field (None) Pleistocene	....
Pinto, Cerro (México)	Dome of Serdán-Oriental	1401-092

A century after the catastrophic eruption that destroyed St. Pierre in 1902, Mount **Pelée**, the most active volcano of the Lesser Antilles arc, towers above the city.

Name (Subregion)	Type (Eruptions, Most Recent) Status / Relation to Named Volcano	Volcano Number
Pinto, Mt. (Sumatra)	Twin volcano of Sibayak	0601-07=
Pintos, Cerro los (Guatemala)	Cone of Ipala	1402-19-
Pintu Kecil (Banda Sea)	Crater of Banda Api	0605-09=
Pinzón (Galápagos)	Shield volcano (None) Pleistocene	....
Pioa (Samoa-SW Pacific)	Dome of Tutuila	0404-02-
Pioao (Samoa-SW Pacific)	Cone of Tutuila	0404-02-
Pipe Organ Vent (Pacific-NE)	Thermal feature of Cleft Segment	1301-03-
Pipe, Mt. [Suribachi-yama] (Japan)	Cinder cone of Ioto [Iwo-jima]	0804-12=
Pipon, Cerro (Galápagos)	Pyroclastic cone of Negra, Sierra	1503-05=
Piquet, Morne (W Indies)	Dome of Carbets, Pitons de	....
Pirana, Alto la (Colombia)	Dome of Ruiz, Nevado del	1501-02=

Name (Subregion)	Type (Eruptions, Most Recent) Status Relation to Named Volcano	Volcano Number
Piratkovsky (Kamchatka)	Stratovolcano (None) Holocene	**1000-054**
Pire (Pirepillan) (Chile-S)	Synonym of Osorno	1508-01=
Piria (Greece)	Thermal feature of Nisyros	0102-05=
Pirigallo (Chile-C)	Pleist. caldera of Chillán, Nevados de	1507-07=
Pirihueico (Argentina)	Stratovolcano of Huanquihue Group	1507-123
Pirongia (New Zealand)	Stratovolcano (None) Pleistocene	....
Piro-Piraso (Luzon-Philippines)	Cone of Taal	0703-07=
Pirozhnikova (Kamchatka)	Stratovolcano (None) Pleistocene	....
Pisambilla (Ecuador)	Synonym of Reventador	1502-01=
Pisang (Java)	Dome of Kelut	0603-28=
Pisani (Italy)	Crater of Campi Flegrei	0101-01=
Pise (Chile-S)	Synonym of Osorno	1508-01=
Pisgah Crater (US-California)	Cinder cone of Lavic Lake	1203-19-
Pisgah, Mt. (Australia)	Cone of Newer Volcanics Prov	0509-01-
Pistol Butte (US-Oregon)	Cinder cone of Bachelor	1202-09-
Pital, Loma (Costa Rica)	Cinder cone of Platanar	1405-034
Pitcairn (Pacific-C)	Shield volcano (None) Pleistocene	....
Pitjung [Picung] (Java)	Crater of Guntur	0603-13=
Pitogo (Sulu Is-Philippines)	Cone of Jolo	0700-01=
Piton (French for Peak) see proper name (e.g. Fournaise, Piton de la)		
Pitt (Pit) (US-Oregon)	Synonym of McLoughlin	....
Pitzantzi (Ecuador)	Dome of Chachimbiro	1502-002
Piuquenes (Chile-C)	Cone of Antillanca Group	1507-153
Piuquenes, Nevado de los (Chile-C)	Stratovolcano (None) Pleistocene	....
Piyakong Hill (Mindanao-Philippines)	Dome of Camiguin	0701-08=
Pizarro, Cerro (México)	Dome of Serdán-Oriental	1401-092
Pizcuaro, Cerro (México)	Dome of Azufres, Los	....
Pizzillo, Monte (Italy)	Cinder cone of Etna	0101-06=
Pizzo (Italy)	Crater of Stromboli	0101-04=
Pizzo Sopra la Fossa (Italy)	Tuff cone of Stromboli	0101-04=
Plaidter Hummerich (Germany)	Cone of East Eifel Volc Field	....
Plaisance (W Indies)	Dome of Qualibou	1600-14=
Plakes (Greece)	Dome of Mílos	0102-03=
Plan de las Ardillas (México)	Dome of Tacaná	1401-13=
Plan del Hoyo (El Salvador)	Crater of Santa Ana	1403-02=
Plancha Ladera (Ecuador)	Cone of Imbabura	1502-004
Planchón (Chile-C)	Caldera of Planchón-Peteroa	1507-04=
Planchón-Peteroa (Chile-C)	Stratovolcanoes (17, 1998) Historical	**1507-04=**
Planillas, Cerro las (México)	Vent of Primavera, Sierra la	....
Plantat (Chile-C)	Cinder cone of San José	1507-02=
Plat Pays, Morne (W Indies)	Stratovolcano (4, 1270) Radiocarbon	**1600-11=**
Plat Pays, Morne (W Indies)	Stratovolcano of Plat Pays, Morne	1600-11=
Plata (Galápagos)	Synonym of Fernandina	1503-01=
Platanar (Costa Rica)	Stratovolcanoes (None) Holocene	**1405-034**
Platanar, Cerrito el (Guatemala)	Cinder cone of Redondo, Cerro	....
Platanar, Loma el (Guatemala)	Dome of Redondo, Cerro	....
Plateau (Africa-E)	Dome of Olkaria	0202-09=

Chris Newhall (USGS)

The climactic eruptions on June 15, 1991, created a 2.5-km-wide caldera at the summit of **Pinatubo** volcano in the Philippines. The elevation of the caldera floor is more than 900 m below that of the pre-eruption summit of Pinatubo. Steam rises from fumaroles on the caldera floor in this October 4, 1991, view from the north. The outer flanks of the caldera are stripped of vegetation and covered with deposits of airfall ash and pyroclastic surges.

Name (Subregion)	Type (Eruptions, Most Recent) Status Relation to Named Volcano	Volcano Number
Plateau des Bolovens (SE Asia)	Fissure vents (None) Pleistocene	....
Plateau Dome [Kanakana] (New Zealand)	Dome of Okataina	0401-05=
Playa Hermosa (Costa Rica)	Crater of Irazú	1405-06=
Playón de Ahuachapán (El Salvador)	Thermal feature of Apaneca Range	1403-01=
Playón de Ahuachapán (El Salvador)	Thermal feature of Apaneca Range	1403-01=
Playón, El (El Salvador)	Cinder cone of San Salvador	1403-05=
Plaza de Toros (México)	Tuff ring of San Luis, Isla	1401-003
Pleiades, The (Antarctica)	Stratovolcano (1, -1050) K-Ar	**1900-013**
Pleiku Mount (SE Asia)	Crater of Pleiku-Bantour Volc Field	....
Pleiku-Bantour Volc Field (SE Asia)	Cones (None) Pleistocene	....
Plei-Monu (SE Asia)	Crater of Pleiku-Bantour Volc Field	....
Pleiones, Mount (Antarctica)	Stratovolcano of Pleiades, The	1900-013
Pleitott Mount (SE Asia)	Cone of Pleiku-Bantour Volc Field	....
Plinth Mountain (Canada)	Cone of Meager	1200-18-

Name (Subregion)	Type (Eruptions, Most Recent) Status Relation to Named Volcano	Volcano Number
Ploskaya (Russia-SE)	Shield volcano of Azas Plateau	1002-07-
Ploskaya (Kamchatka)	Synonym of Plosky	1000-63-
Ploskaya (Ploski) (Kamchatka)	Synonym of Ushkovsky	1000-261
Ploskii (Kuril Is)	Crater of Vernadskii Ridge	0900-37-
Ploskii [Ploskaya] (Russia-SE)	Shield volcano of Azas Plateau	1002-07-
Ploskiy (Kamchatka)	Stratovolcano (None) Pleistocene	....
Plosko-Kruglen'ky (Kamchatka)	Cone of Bolshoi Semiachik	1000-15=
Plosky (Kamchatka)	Stratovolcano of Bolshoi Semiachik	1000-15=
Plosky (Kamchatka)	Cone of Olkoviy Volc Group	1000-052
Plosky (Kamchatka)	Shield volcano (None) Holocene?	**1000-31-**
Plosky (Kamchatka)	Shield volcano (None) Holocene?	**1000-63-**
Plosky (Kamchatka)	Synonym of Ushkovsky	1000-261
Plosky Tolbachik (Kamchatka)	Shield volcano of Tolbachik	1000-24=
Ploskye Sopki (Kamchatka)	Synonym of Ushkovsky	1000-261
Plotina (Kamchatka)	Dome of Bezymianny	1000-25=
Plupuh, Kawah (Java)	Crater of Arjuno-Welirang	0603-29=
Poa (Lesser Sunda Is)	Crater of Paluweh	0604-15=
Poás (Costa Rica)	Stratovolcano (55, 2009) Historical	**1405-04=**
Pocdol Mountains (Luzon-Philippines)	Compound volcano (None) Fumarolic	**0703-02=**
Pochetero, Cerro (México)	Dome of Ceboruco	1401-03=
Pochnoi (Aleutian Is)	Shield volcano of Semisopochnoi	1101-06-
Pocket Basin (US-Wyoming)	Crater of Yellowstone	1205-01-
Poco Dedehg (Lesser Sunda Is)	Cone of Sano, Wai	0604-06=
Poco Leok (Lesser Sunda Is)	Stratovolcano (None) Fumarolic	**0604-07=**
Poco Rii (Lesser Sunda Is)	Stratovolcano of Poco Leok	0604-07=
Poco Sol, Laguna (Costa Rica)	Explosion crater? (None) Pleistocene	....
Pocoihuen (Chile-S)	Cone of Cayutué-La Viguería	1508-012
Pocura, Laguna (Chile-C)	Maar of Carrán-Los Venados	1507-14=
Podakan (Luzon-Philippines)	Stratovolcano of Ambalatungan Group	0703-088
Podgorny (Russia-SE)	Cone of Tunkin Depression	1002-05-
Podiok, Kawah [Kawah Pondok] (Java)	Thermal feature of Kamojang, Kawah	....
Podkova (Kamchatka)	Fissure vent of Kliuchevskoi	1000-26=
Podushechny (Kuril Is)	Dome of Golovnin	0900-01=
Poei [Pui] (Lesser Sunda Is)	Cone of Iya	0604-11=
Poelasari (Java)	Synonym of Pulosari	0603-01=
Poeloe We (Sumatra)	Synonym of Pulau Weh	....
Poendak, Gunung [Gunung Pundak] (Java)	Cone of Arjuno-Welirang	0603-29=
Poeraknja, Bukit [Bukit Puraknja] (Indonesia)	Cone of Batur	0604-01=
Poerua (New Zealand)	Cone of Kaikohe-Bay of Islands	0401-01=
Poesoek Boekit [Pusikbukit] (Sumatra)	Stratovolcano of Toba	0601-09=
Pofi (Italy)	Pyroclastic cone of Ernici, Monti	....
Poggio Biello (Italy)	Dome of Amiata	....
Poggio della Pescina (Italy)	Dome of Amiata	....
Poggio Pinzi (Italy)	Dome of Amiata	....
Poggio Pinzi (Italy)	Dome of Amiata	....
Poggio Trauzzolo (Italy)	Dome of Amiata	....
Pogpog Spring (Mindanao-Philippines)	Thermal feature of Apo	0701-03=
Pogranychny (Kamchatka)	Shield volcanoes (None) Holocene?	**1000-47-**
Pogrebennyi (Kamchatka)	Fissure vent of Kliuchevskoi	1000-26=
Pogromni (Aleutian Is)	Stratovolcano of Westdahl	1101-34-
Pogromni's Sister (Aleutian Is)	Stratovolcano of Westdahl	1101-34-
Pogrumni [Pogromni] (Aleutian Is)	Stratovolcano of Westdahl	1101-34-
Pogrumnoy [Pogromni] (Aleutian Is)	Stratovolcano of Westdahl	1101-34-
Pohakea (Hawaiian Is)	Cone of Kauai	....
Pohaturoa (New Zealand)	Dome of Maroa	0401-061
Pohaturoa (New Zealand)	Dome of Rotorua	....
Poholo, Lua (Hawaiian Is)	Pit crater of Mauna Loa	1302-02=
Poiauhtécatl [Pojautécatl] (México)	Synonym of Orizaba, Pico de	1401-10=
Poike (Chile-Is)	Shield volcano of Easter Island	1506-011
Point Kadin (Aleutian Is)	Vent of Makushin	1101-31-
Pointed Stick (Canada)	Cone of Wells Gray-Clearwater	1200-15-
Pokr Boghoutlu (Armenia)	Cone of Aragats	0104-06-
Pokuru (New Zealand)	Dome of Maroa	0401-061
Polevaya, Mt. (Russia-NE)	Cone of Unnamed	....
Poliahu, Puu (Hawaiian Is)	Cone of Mauna Kea	1302-03-
Polino (Italy)	Explosion craters (None) Pleistocene	....
Polipoli (Hawaiian Is)	Cone of Haleakala	1302-06-
Pollara (Italy)	Tuff ring of Salina	....
Pollok (Mindanao-Philippines)	Synonym of Makaturing	0701-04=
Pollok (Mindanao-Philippines)	Synonym of Ragang	0701-06=
Pollux (Antarctica)	Cone of Seal Nunataks Group	1900-05=
Polovina Hill (Alaska-W)	Cinder cone of St. Paul Island	1104-01-
Polovinka (Kamchatka)	Pleistocene caldera of Akademia Nauk	1000-125
Polovinny (Kamchatka)	Shield volcano of Maly Alney	....
Polukupol (Kamchatka)	Dome of Bolshoi Semiachik	1000-15=
Polvadera Peak (US-New Mexico)	Dome of Valles Caldera	....
Polybotes (Greece)	Vent of Nisyros	0102-05=
Polybotes Micros [Polyvotis Micros] (Greece)	Vent of Nisyros	0102-05=
Polyegos (Greece)	Cone of Mílos	0102-03=
Polytop Butte (US-Oregon)	Cone of Newberry	1202-11-
Polyvotis Megalos (Greece)	Vent of Nisyros	0102-05=
Polyvotis Micros (Greece)	Vent of Nisyros	0102-05=
Poma, Isla (México)	Tuff ring of San Luis, Isla	1401-003
Pomare (Vanuatu-SW Pacific)	Stratovolcano of Epi	0507-06=
Pomerape (Chile-N)	Stratovolcano of Parinacota	1505-012
Pomiciari, Monte (Italy)	Cinder cone of Etna	0101-06=
Ponafidin (Izu Is-Japan)	Synonym of Tori-shima	0804-09=
Pond, Mt. (W Indies)	Cone of St. Catherine	1600-17=
Pondok, Kawah (Java)	Thermal feature of Kamojang, Kawah	....
Pondona, Loma (Ecuador)	Dome of Pululagua	1502-011
Ponmachineshiri (Hokkaido-Japan)	Crater of Akan	0805-07=
Ponmatinesiri [Ponmachineshiri] (Japan)	Crater of Akan	0805-07=
Ponohohoa Chasms (Hawaiian Is)	Shield volcano of Kilauea	1302-01-

Name (Subregion)	Type (Eruptions, Most Recent) Status / Relation to Named Volcano	Volcano Number
Pontine Islands (Italy)	Lava domes (None) Pleistocene	....
Ponza (Italy)	Cone of Pontine Islands	....
Ponziane, Isola (Italy)	Synonym of Pontine Islands	....
Popa (SE Asia)	Stratovolcano (1, -442) Anthropology	**0705-08-**
Popkov (Kamchatka)	Stratovolcano of Bolshoi Semiachik	1000-15=
Poplovaya (Kuril Is)	Vent of Ebeko	0900-38=
Popocatépetl (México)	Stratovolcanoes (41, 2010) Historical	**1401-09=**
Popocatzin [Popocatepec] (México)	Synonym of Popocatépetl	1401-09=
Popolojo, Mt. (Halmahera-Indonesia)	Cone of Gamkonora	0608-04=
Popori, Mt. (Solomon Is-SW Pacific)	Cone of Gallego	0505-062
Poquintica, Cerro [Cerro Puquintica] (Chile-N)	Stratovolcano of Arintica	....
Poquis (Chile-N)	Stratovolcano (None) Pleistocene	....
Pora, Mt. (Halmahera-Indonesia)	Cone of Todoko-Ranu	0608-05=
Porak (Armenia)	Stratovolcano (2, -778) Anthropology	**0104-09-**
Porcelana (Chile-S)	Cone of Huequi	1508-03=
Pordon, Mt. (Australia)	Cone of Newer Volcanics Prov	0509-01-
Poros (Greece)	Fissure vent (None) Pleistocene	....
Poroto Ridge (Africa-E)	Synonym of Ngozi	0202-164
Porphyrion (Greece)	Dome of Volos-Atalanti	....
Porquesa (Chile-N)	Lava domes (None) Pleistocene	....
Porr (Africa-E)	Pyroclastic cone (None) Quaternary	....
Porri, Monte de (Italy)	Cone of Salina	....
Porsea (Sumatra)	Caldera of Toba	0601-09=
Port Foster (Antarctica)	Caldera of Deception Island	1900-03=
Port Resolution (Vanuatu-SW Pacific)	Synonym of Yasur	0507-10=
Porterillos (Ecuador)	Dome of Chacana	1502-022
Portezuelo, Volcanes del (Chile-C)	Cone of Chillán, Nevados de	1507-07=
Portillo, Volcán el (Chile-C)	Cone of Maule, Laguna del	1507-061
Porto D'ischia (Italy)	Vent of Ischia	0101-03=
Porto Miseno (Italy)	Crater of Campi Flegrei	0101-01=
Portrilla (Colombia)	Crater of Galeras	1501-08=
Portrillo, Los (Nicaragua)	Cone of Telica	1404-04=
Poruña, La (Chile-N)	Cone of San Pedro	1505-07=
Poruñita, La (Chile-N)	Cone of Ollagüe	1505-06=
Porvenir, Cerro (Costa Rica)	Stratovolcano of Platanar	1405-034
Porvenir, Cerro el (Guatemala)	Cinder cone of Cuilapa-Barbarena	1402-111
Posintepe, Cerro (Nicaragua)	Cone of Mombacho	1404-11=
Posos, Cerros De Los (US-New Mexico)	Dome of Valles Caldera	....
Possession, Ile de la (Indian O.-S)	Stratovolcano (None) Holocene	**0304-04-**
Post Office Hill (Antarctica)	Cone of Terror, Mt.	....
Posta Lubrano (Italy)	Dome of Ischia	0101-03=
Pot Hill [North Hill] (Alaska-W)	Cinder cone of St. Paul Island	1104-01-
Potato Butte (US-Oregon)	Cinder cone of Olallie Butte	....
Potato Butte (US-California)	Shield volcanoes (None) Pleistocene	....
Potato Hill (US-Washington)	Cinder cone of Adams	1201-04-
Potato Mountain [Morne Patates] (W Indies)	Dome of Plat Pays, Morne	1600-11=
Poteryanny (Kamchatka)	Cinder cone of Tolbachik	1000-24=
Pothole Butte (US-Oregon)	Cone of Crater Lake	1202-16-
Potio Aike, Lago (Chile-S)	Maar of Palei-Aike Volc Field	1508-08-
Potjo Dedehg [Poco Dedehg] (Indonesia)	Cone of Sano, Wai	0604-06=
Potjo Leok [Potjok Leok] (Lesser Sunda Is)	Synonym of Poco Leok	0604-07=
Potor (Chile-N)	Stratovolcano (None) Pleistocene	....
Potosí (Colombia)	Unknown (None) Post-Miocene	....
Potreros, Los (México)	Pleistocene caldera of Humeros, Los	1401-093
Potret, Kawah (Sumatra)	Crater of Telong, Bur ni	0601-05=
Potrillo (US-New Mexico)	Maar of Potrillo Volc Field	....
Potrillo Volc Field (US-New Mexico)	Cinder cones (None) Pleistocene	....
Potta (Atlantic-N-Jan Mayen)	Cone of Jan Mayen	1706-01=
Pouakai (New Zealand)	Stratovolcano (None) Pleistocene	....
Poucharet, Puy de (France)	Cone of Chaîne des Puys	0100-02-
Povoacao (Azores)	Pleistocene caldera of Furnas	1802-10=
Povorotnaia Sopka (Kamchatka)	Synonym of Mutnovsky	1000-06=
Powder Hill (US-California)	Cone of Medicine Lake	1203-02-
Powell (W Indies)	Dome of Plat Pays, Morne	1600-11=
Powell Butte (US-Oregon)	Cone of Boring Lava	....
Powers Caldera (Hawaiian Is)	Caldera of Kilauea	1302-01-
Poworotnaja Assatscha (Kamchatka)	Synonym of Mutnovsky	1000-06=
Poyauhtécatl (México)	Synonym of Orizaba, Pico de	1401-10=
Poza Rica (México)	Volcanic field (None) Pleistocene	....
Pozas, Cerro las (Guatemala)	Cone of Ixtepeque	1402-18-
Pozo (Argentina)	Crater of Northern Mendoza Volc Field	....
Pozo del Cármen (México)	Maar of Ventura Volc Field	....
Pozo, El (El Salvador)	Pit crater of Santa Ana	1403-02=
Pozo, El (Argentina)	Crater of Tromen	1507-072
Pozo, El (Argentina)	Cinder cone of Unnamed	....
Praga [Sarvaly] (Hungary)	Shield volcano of Balaton Highland	....
Prahu (Java)	Stratovolcano of Dieng Volc Complex	0603-20=
Pra-Karymsky (Kamchatka)	Stratovolcano of Karymsky	1000-13=
Prambanan (Java)	Cone of Dieng Volc Complex	0603-20=
Prambanan (Java)	Dome of Dieng Volc Complex	0603-20=
Prarauque (Chile-S)	Synonym of Osorno	1508-01=
Prata Porci (Italy)	Maar of Alban Hills	0101-004
Pravaia Mutnovskaia Sopka (Kamchatka)	Synonym of Gorely	1000-07=
Pravilny (Kamchatka)	Dome of Bezymianny	1000-25=
Pra-Visokaya (Kamchatka)	Cinder cone of Tolbachik	1000-24=
Pravyi Lurban (Russia-SE)	Dome of Udokan Plateau	1002-03-
Prawaja Mutnowskaja (Kamchatka)	Synonym of Gorely	1000-07=
Preciosa, La (México)	Maar of Serdán-Oriental	1401-092
Predskanzannyi (Kamchatka)	Fissure vent of Kliuchevskoi	1000-26=
Predvidennoye (Kamchatka)	Fissure vent of Kliuchevskoi	1000-26=
Preito, Cerro (México)	Dome of Toluca, Nevado de	1401-07-
Prek Kak (SE Asia)	Synonym of Cham	....
Prestahnukur (Iceland-SW)	Subglacial volc. (3, -3350) Radiocarbon	**1701-07=**
Preto, Pico (Atlantic-C)	Dome of Trindade	1805-051
Prevo Peak (Kuril Is)	Stratovolcano (2, 1825) Historical	**0900-19=**
Prevoste (Kuril Is)	Synonym of Prevo Peak	0900-19=
Pribrezhny (Kamchatka)	Stratovolcano (None) Pleistocene	....
Pribrezhny Severny (Kamchatka)	Stratovolcano of Pribrezhny	....
Pribrezhny Yuzhny (Kamchatka)	Stratovolcano of Pribrezhny	....
Pribrezhnyi (Kamchatka)	Fissure vent of Kliuchevskoi	1000-26=
Price Bay (Canada)	Cone of Garibaldi Lake	1200-19-
Price Island (Canada)	Cone of Milbanke Sound Group	1200-12-
Price, Mount (Canada)	Stratovolcano of Garibaldi Lake	1200-19-
Priemysh (Kamchatka)	Stratovolcano of Khodutka	1000-053
Prieto, Cerro (México)	Shield volc. of Michoacán-Guanajuato	1401-06=
Prieto, Cerro (México)	Lava dome (None) Holocene?	**1401-00-**
Prieto, Volcán (México)	Synonym of León, Cerro	....
Primavera (Colombia)	Pyroclastic cone San Augustín-Isnos	....

A narrow sand-and-gravel bar connects the picturesque fishing village of Scotts Head, the southernmost on Dominica, to the Scotts Head lava dome. The village, also known as Cachacrou, overlies volcaniclastic deposits on the SW flank of Crabier lava dome, a post-caldera dome near the southern rim of the Morne **Plat Pays** caldera.

Paul Kimberly (Smithsonian)

Name (Subregion)	Type (Eruptions, Most Recent) Status / Relation to Named Volcano	Volcano Number
Primavera, Sierra la (México)	Caldera (None) Pleistocene-Hot Springs	....
Prince Edward Island (Indian O.)	Shield volcano (None) Holocene	**0304-06-**
Prince Island (Antarctica)	Synonym of Zavodovski	1900-13=
Princess (New Zealand)	Crater of White Island	0401-04=
Princess Peak (Alaska Peninsula)	Synonym of Snowy Mountain	1102-20-
Prindle (Alaska-E)	Cinder cone (None) Pleistocene	....
Priozernaya (Russia-SE)	Shield volcano of Azas Plateau	1002-07-
Priozernyi [Priozernaya] (Russia-SE)	Shield volcano of Azas Plateau	1002-07-
Priyemysh [Priemysh] (Kamchatka)	Stratovolcano of Khodutka	1000-053
Prizrak (Kamchatka)	Pleistocene caldera of Kell	1000-041
Problematichny (Kamchatka)	Cone of Bolshoi Semiachik	1000-15=
Prodolny (Kamchatka)	Shield volcanoes (None) Pleistocene	....
Profit Elias [Profitis Ilias] (Greece)	Dome of Nisyros	0102-05=
Profitis Ilias (Greece)	Pumice cone of Mílos	0102-03=
Profitis Ilias (Greece)	Dome of Nisyros	0102-05=
Prometheus (Tonga-SW Pacific)	Vent of West Mata	0403-13-
Prongoll (Java)	Dome of Tengger Caldera	0603-31=
Propushchennyi (Kamchatka)	Fissure vent of Kliuchevskoi	1000-26=
Prospect Cone (US-Arizona)	Cinder cone of Uinkaret Field	1209-01-
Prospect Peak (US-California)	Shield volcano of Lassen Volc Center	1203-08-
Protector Shoal (Antarctica)	Submarine volcano (1, 1962) Historical	**1900-14-**
Prouty Hill [Black Hump] (US-Oregon)	Dome of North Sister Field	1202-07-
Provatas (Greece)	Thermal feature of Mílos	0102-03=
Providencia, Cerro la (México)	Dome of Azufres, Los	....
Providencia, Cerro la (Guatemala)	Cinder cone of Cuilapa-Barbarena	1402-111
Providencia, Volcán (Chile-C)	Cinder cone of Carrán-Los Venados	1507-14=
Pryor Cliff (Antarctica)	Cone of Hudson Mountains	1900-028
Psathoura (Greece)	Synonym of Sporades	....
Psorochoma (Greece)	Synonym of Susaki	0102-01=
Puai, Puu (Hawaiian Is)	Cone of Kilauea	1302-01-
Puaialua (Hawaiian Is)	Pit crater of Kilauea	1302-01-
Puas [Púas, Puás] (Costa Rica)	Synonym of Poás	1405-04=
Pucanu (Chile-C)	Synonym of Villarrica	1507-12=
Pucara, Cerro (Bolivia)	Volcanic field (None) Pleistocene	....
Puchuldiza (Chile-N)	Hydrotherm. field (None) Pleist.-Geysers	....
Puchura, Volcán (Chile-C)	Cinder cone of Carrán-Los Venados	1507-14=
Pucon (Chile-C)	Synonym of Villarrica	1507-12=
Pucu Mauras, Cerro (Perú)	Cinder cone of Andahua-Orcopampa	1504-004
Pue, Le (Samoa-SW Pacific)	Cone of Upolu	0404-03-
Pueblito, El (México)	Cinder cone of Michoacán-Guanajuato	1401-06=
Pueblo Nuevo (México)	Cone of Zitácuaro-Valle de Bravo	1401-061
Pueblo Nuevo Viñas (Guatemala)	Stratovolcano (None) Pleistocene	....
Pueblo Viejo, Cerro del (México)	Cinder cone of Michoacán-Guanajuato	1401-06=
Puelamarum [Marum] (Vanuatu-SW Pacific)	Crater of Ambrym	0507-04=
Puelche Volc Field (Chile-C)	Volcanic field (None) Pleistocene	....
Puellaro (Ecuador)	Dome of Mojanda	1502-005
Puente-Chapúa Volc Field (Argentina)	Volcanic field (None) Pleistocene	....
Puerta de la Laguna (El Salvador)	Maar of San Salvador	1403-05=

Name (Subregion)	Type (Eruptions, Most Recent) Status / Relation to Named Volcano	Volcano Number
Puerta, La (México)	Dome of Primavera, Sierra la	....
Puerta, Volcán (México)	Cinder cone of Mascota Volc Field	1401-031
Puerto, Cerro del (México)	Cinder cone of Michoacán-Guanajuato	1401-06=
Puerto, Volcán el (México)	Cinder cone of Mascota Volc Field	1401-031
Puerto, Volcán el (México)	Dome of Mascota Volc Field	1401-031
Puesto Cortaderas (Argentina)	Pyroclastic cone (None) Holocene	**1507-073**
Puet Sagu (Sumatra)	Synonym of Peuet Sague	0601-03=
Pugung (Sumatra)	Unknown (None) Post-Miocene	....
Puhimau (Hawaiian Is)	Pit crater of Kilauea	1302-01-
Puhipuhi (New Zealand)	Dome of Okataina	0401-05=
Puhuahuen (Chile-S)	Synonym of Osorno	1508-01=
Pui (Lesser Sunda Is)	Cone of Iya	0604-11=
Pu'i, Maunga (Chile-Is)	Pyroclastic cone of Easter Island	1506-011
Puia Hou [Te Mari] (New Zealand)	Crater of Tongariro	0401-08=

Hugo Delgado-Granados (UNAM)

This 1997 aerial photo shows the summit crater of México's **Popocatépetl** volcano with its floor covered by a newly extruded lava dome. Repeated lava dome growth and explosive destruction took place during a long-term eruption beginning in 1994.

Name (Subregion)	Type (Eruptions, Most Recent) Status / Relation to Named Volcano	Volcano Number
Puig (Spanish for Hill) see proper name (e.g. Subia, Puig)		
Pujajauco (Pujajen) (Chile-S)	Synonym of Osorno	1508-01=
Pujalos, Volcà (Spain)	Cone of Olot Volc Field	0100-03-
Pukaki (New Zealand)	Tuff ring of Auckland Field	0401-02=
Pukeahua (New Zealand)	Dome of Maroa	0401-061
Pukeiti (New Zealand)	Cone of Auckland Field	0401-02=
Pukeiti (New Zealand)	Cone of Kaitake	....
Pukekahu (New Zealand)	Dome of Reporoa	0401-06-
Pukekaikione (New Zealand)	Cone of Tongariro	0401-08=
Pukekaikiore (New Zealand)	Dome of Taupo	0401-07=
Pukekawa (New Zealand)	Shield volcano of South Auckland	....
Pukekawa (New Zealand)	Cone of South Auckland	....
Pukekiwiriki (New Zealand)	Tuff ring of Auckland Field	0401-02=
Pukekohe Hill (New Zealand)	Shield volcano of South Auckland	....
Pukekohe Volc Field (New Zealand)	Synonym of South Auckland	....
Pukekohu (Kermadec Is)	Crater of Raoul Island	0402-03=
Pukemoremore (New Zealand)	Dome of Maroa	0401-061
Pukeonake (New Zealand)	Cone of Ruapehu	0401-10=
Pukeonake (New Zealand)	Cone of Tongariro	0401-08=
Pukepoto (New Zealand)	Dome of Okataina	0401-05=
Pukepoto (New Zealand)	Cone of Whangarei	0401-011
Pukeroa (New Zealand)	Dome of Rotorua	....
Puketarata (New Zealand)	Dome of Maroa	0401-061
Puketutu (New Zealand)	Cone of Kaikohe-Bay of Islands	0401-01=
Puketutu Island (New Zealand)	Cone of Auckland Field	0401-02=
Puk'h'kowitz (US-Washington)	Synonym of Baker	1201-01=
Pukopuhi, Maunga (Chile-Is)	Pyroclastic cone of Easter Island	1506-011
Puku Ngaahaaha (Chile-Is)	Pyroclastic cone of Easter Island	1506-011
Pula (Luzon-Philippines)	Thermal feature of Pinatubo	0703-083
Pulacayo, Cerro (Chile-N)	Stratovolc. of Laguna-Pulacayo, Cerro	....
Pulai [Kabhegy] (Hungary)	Shield volcano of Balaton Highland	....
Pulali [Paraso] (Solomon Is-SW Pacific)	Thermal feature of Nonda	....
Pular (Chile-N)	Stratovolcanoes (Uncertain) Holocene?	**1505-107**
Pulasari (Java)	Synonym of Pulosari	0603-01=
Pulau Weh (Sumatra)	Stratovolcano (None) Pleist.-Fumarolic	....
Pule (Samoa-SW Pacific)	Cone of Savai'i	0404-04=
Pulea (Samoa-SW Pacific)	Cone of Savai'i	0404-04=
Pulo (Luzon-Philippines)	Synonym of Taal	0703-07=
Pulo Weh (Sumatra)	Synonym of Pulau Weh	....
Pulosari (Java)	Stratovolcano (None) Holocene	**0603-01=**
Púlpito, Punta (México)	Lava dome (None) Pleist.-Fumarolic	....
Pulu Betah (Lesser Sunda Is)	Synonym of Tara, Batu	0604-26=
Pulu Kambing II (Pulu Komba) (Indonesia)	Synonym of Tara, Batu	0604-26=
Pulu Weh (Sumatra)	Synonym of Pulau Weh	....
Pulucha, Cerro (Bolivia)	Stratovolcano (None) Post-Miocene	....
Pululagua (Ecuador)	Caldera (4, 290) Radiocarbon	**1502-011**
Pululahua (Ecuador)	Synonym of Pululagua	1502-011

Name (Subregion)	Type (Eruptions, Most Recent) Status / Relation to Named Volcano	Volcano Number
Pulvermaar (Germany)	Maar of West Eifel Volc Field	0100-01-
Puma Ranga, Cerro (Perú)	Cinder cone of Andahua-Orcopampa	1504-004
Pumas, Los (Chile-S)	Crater of Osorno	1508-01=
Pumice Dome (Alaska Peninsula)	Dome of Aniakchak	1102-09-
Pumice Pit Dome (US-California)	Dome of Mono Craters	1203-12-
Pumice Stone Mountain (US-California)	Cone of Medicine Lake	1203-02-
Pumire, Cerro (Chile-N)	Unknown (None) Post-Miocene	....
Pumpan, Mt. (Vanuatu-SW Pacific)	Stratovolcano (None) Pleistocene	....
Pumpkin Hill (Honduras)	Cinder cone of Utila Island	1403-16-
Puna (Samoa-SW Pacific)	Cone of Savai'i	0404-04=
Punalica, Volcán (Ecuador)	Cone of Carihuairazo	....
Punata (Chile-N)	Synonym of Guallatiri	1505-02=
Puncara [Anburo] (Ecuador)	Dome of Chachimbiro	1502-002
Punchbowl (US-California)	Dome of Mono Craters	1203-12-
Punchbowl, The (W Indies)	Crater of St. Catherine	1600-17=
Pundak, Gunung (Java)	Cone of Arjuno-Welirang	0603-29=
Pundutan North (Java)	Crater of Lawu	0603-26=
Pundutan South (Java)	Crater of Lawu	0603-26=
Pung (New Guinea-NE of)	Crater of Umboi	0501-06=
Punggur, Bukit (Sumatra)	Unknown (None) Post-Miocene	....
Puni (New Zealand)	Cone of South Auckland	....
Punikan (Lesser Sunda Is)	Unknown (None) Quaternary	....
Punón Trehue (Argentina)	Pyrocl. cone Northern Mendoza Field	
Punta Conigliara (Italy)	Thermal feature of Vulcano	0101-05=
Punta de Iacopo (Italy)	Submarine vent of Lipari	0101-042
Punta del'Arco (Italy)	Vent of Pantelleria	0101-071
Punta Della Cannuccia (Italy)	Cone of Ischia	0101-03=
Punta Gorda (Nicaragua)	Cone of Concepción	1404-12=
Punta Imperatore (Italy)	Crater of Ischia	0101-03=
Punta La Scrofa (Italy)	Cone of Ischia	0101-03=
Punta Levante (Italy)	Thermal feature of Panarea	0101-041
Punta Marmolite (Italy)	Dome of Campi Flegrei	0101-01=
Punta Serra (Italy)	Tuff ring of Campi Flegrei	0101-01=
Punta Tosca (México-Is)	Dome of Socorro	1401-021
Punta Tracino (Italy)	Vent of Pantelleria	0101-071
Punta Vincente Roca (Galápagos)	Tuff cone of Ecuador	1503-011
Punta Zacatepeque (El Salvador)	Dome of Ilopango	1403-06=
Puntas Negras, Volcán (Chile-N)	Stratovolc. Cordón de Puntas Negras	1505-101
Puntas, Cerro (Ecuador)	Stratovolcano (None) Pleistocene	....
Punteagudo, Cerro (Chile-C)	Synonym Puntiagudo-Cordón Cenizos	1507-16-
Puntiagudo, Cerro (México)	Cinder cone of San Martín	1401-11=
Puntiagudo-Cordón Cenizos (Chile)	Stratovolcano (1, 1850) Historical	**1507-16-**
Puntudo (Argentina)	Cinder cone of Unnamed	....
Puntudo, El (Argentina)	Shield volc. of Northern Mendoza Field	....
Pupandji (Sumatra)	Pyroclastic cone of Geureudong	....
Pupuke, Lake (New Zealand)	Tuff ring of Auckland Field	0401-02=
Puquentica, Cerro [Cerro Puquintica] (Chile)	Stratovolcano of Arintica	....
Puquintica, Cerro (Chile-N)	Stratovolcano of Arintica	....
Puracé (Colombia)	Stratovolcanoes (25, 1977) Historical	**1501-06=**
Purahilla (Purahuille) (Chile-S)	Synonym of Osorno	1508-01=
Purakkanginan (Lesser Sunda Is)	Crater of Batur	0604-01=
Purakkauhan (Lesser Sunda Is)	Crater of Batur	0604-01=
Puraknja, Bukit (Lesser Sunda Is)	Cone of Batur	0604-01=
Purarrahue (Chile-S)	Synonym of Osorno	1508-01=
Purau (Vanuatu-SW Pacific)	Cone of Kuwae	0507-07=
Purchas Hill (New Zealand)	Cone of Auckland Field	0401-02=
Pureora (New Zealand)	Dome of Mangakino	....
Pureora (New Zealand)	Dome of Maroa	0401-061
Purerua (New Zealand)	Cone of Kaikohe-Bay of Islands	0401-01=
Purico Complex (Chile-N)	Pyroclastic shield (None) Holocene	**1505-094**
Purkholar (Iceland-W)	Cone of Snaefellsjökull	1700-01=
Purple (Alaska Peninsula)	Synonym of Black Peak	1102-08-
Purrumbete, Lake (Australia)	Maar of Newer Volcanics Prov	0509-01-
Purupuruni, Cerros (Perú)	Lava domes (None) Pleistocene	....
Purutal (Colombia)	Pyroclastic cone San Augustín-Isnos	....
Purvine Mesa (US-New Mexico)	Fissure vent of Raton-Clayton	....
Pusukbukit (Sumatra)	Stratovolcano of Toba	0601-09=
Putahi (New Zealand)	Dome of Kaikohe-Bay of Islands	0401-01=
Putana (Chile-N)	Stratovolcano (1, 1810) Historical	**1505-09=**
Putas, Cerro (Chile-N)	Dome of Purico Complex	1505-094
Putih, Kawah (Java)	Crater of Patuha	0603-07=
Putikov Vrsok (Slovakia)	Cone of Central Slovakia	....
Puting Lupa East (Luzon-Philippines)	Thermal feature San Pablo Volc Field	0703-06=
Puting Lupa Southeast (Luzon-Philippines)	Thermal feature San Pablo Volc Field	0703-06=
Putre, Nevados de (Chile-N)	Synonym of Taapaca	1505-011
Putre, Nevados de (Chile-N)	Stratovolcano of Taapaca	1505-011
Putri, Gunung (Java)	Cone of Guntur	0603-13=
Putri-Eweranda, Gunung (Java)	Stratovolcano of Talagabodas	0603-15=
Putzalagua (Ecuador)	Lava dome (None) Pleistocene	....
Putzalahua (Ecuador)	Synonym of Putzalagua	....
Puu, Puy (Hawaiian and French for Hill) see proper name (e.g. Hualalai, Puu)		
Puulani (Hawaiian Is)	Cone of Kauai	....
Puulena (Hawaiian Is)	Pit crater of Kilauea	1302-01-
Puyehue-Aguas Calientes Hot Springs (Chile)	Thermal feature of Antillanca Group	1507-153
Puyehue-Cordón Caulle (Chile-C)	Stratovolcano (25, 1990) Historical	**1507-15=**
Puyo (Ecuador)	Scoria cones (None) Pleistocene	....
Puyuguapi (Chile-S)	Synonym of Puyuhuapi	1508-053
Puyuhuapi (Chile-S)	Cinder cones (None) Holocene	**1508-053**
Puyulek (Alaska Peninsula)	Synonym of Ugashik-Peulik	1102-13-
Pyramid (Canada)	Dome of Edziza	1200-06-
Pyramid Mountain (Canada)	Cone of Wells Gray-Clearwater	1200-15-
Pyre Peak (Aleutian Is)	Cinder cone of Seguam	1101-18-
Pyro Hill (Aleutian Is)	Maar of Fisher	1101-35-

Name (Subregion)	Type (Eruptions, Most Recent) Status / Relation to Named Volcano	Volcano Number

Q

Name (Subregion)	Type (Eruptions, Most Recent) Status / Relation to Named Volcano	Volcano Number
Qal'eh Hasan Ali (Iran)	Maars (None) Holocene?	**0302-02-**
Qeni, Tell (Syria)	Cone of Druze, Jabal ad	0300-06-
Qiangbaqian (China-W)	Shield volcano of Unnamed	1004-04-
Qidr, Jabal (Arabia-W)	Stratovolcano of Khaybar, Harrat	0301-06=
Qishr, Jabal al (Arabia-W)	Cinder cone of Lunayyir, Harrat	0301-04-
Qixingling (SE Asia)	Cone of Leizhou Bandao	0705-01-
Qol, Jabal (Arabia-S)	Crater of Arhab, Harra of	0301-09-
Qualibou (W Indies)	Caldera (1, 1766) Historical	**1600-14=**
Quanshuigou (China-W)	Cinder cone of Kunlun Volc Group	1004-03-
Quarry (Ethiopia)	Dome of Dawa Ale-Quarry	....
Quartz Mountain (US-Oregon)	Lava dome (None) Pleistocene	....
Quatre Gueules (Indian O.-W)	Crater of Fournaise, Piton de la	0303-02=
Quatro Hermanos, Los (Galápagos)	Tuff cone of Negra, Sierra	1503-05=
Quebrada del Azufre Grande (Ecuador)	Thermal feature of Antisana	1502-03=
Quebrada Seca (Colombia)	Caldera of Bravo, Cerro	1501-012
Quechucabi of Ovalle (Chile-S)	Synonym of Minchinmávida	1508-04=
Quechulac (México)	Maar of Serdán-Oriental	1401-092
Queen Mary (Atlantic-S)	Cinder cone of Tristan da Cunha	1806-01=
Queen's Park (W Indies)	Crater of St. Catherine	1600-17=
Queimado, Cerro (Azores)	Dome of Agua de Pau	1802-09=
Quelguenco (Argentina)	Stratovolcano of Huanquihue Group	1507-123
Quellaipe (Quellaype) (Chile-S)	Synonym of Calbuco	1508-02=
Quemada de Orzola, La (Canary Is)	Crater of Lanzarote	1803-06-
Quemada, Montana (Canary Is)	Cone of Fuerteventura	1803-05-
Quemada, Montaña [Caldera Rajada]	Cinder cone of Lanzarote	1803-06-
Quemada, Montana [Tacande] (Canary Is)	Cinder cone of La Palma	1803-01-
Quemadas, Islas (El Salvador)	Dome of Ilopango	1403-06=
Quemadas, Las Calderas (Canary Is)	Crater of Lanzarote	1803-06-
Quemadas, Los (Costa Rica)	Thermal feature of Tenorio	1405-031
Quemado [Riñinahue] (Chile-C)	Maar of Carrán-Los Venados	1507-14=
Quemado Volc Field (US-New Mexico)	Synonym of Red Hill	....
Quemado, Cerro (Guatemala)	Dome of Almolonga	1402-04=
Quemado, Cerro (México)	Cinder cone of Camargo Volc Field	....
Quemado, Cerro (El Salvador)	Cinder cone of San Diego	1403-001
Quemado, Cerro (Bolivia)	Synonym of Tambo Quemado	1505-021
Quemado, Volcán de el (Canary Is)	Crater of Lanzarote	1803-06-
Quemados, Cerro de (Costa Rica)	Cinder cone of Irazú	1405-06=
Quemados, Cerros [Islas Quemadas]	Dome of Ilopango	1403-06=
Quepil, Cerro (México)	Dome of Chichinautzin	1401-08=
Quesada (Costa Rica)	Cone of Platanar	1405-034
Quesnel Cone Group (Canada)	Pyroclastic cones (None) Quaternary	....
Quesnel Lake (Canada)	Cone of Quesnel Cone Group	....
Questrodugun (Chile-C)	Synonym of Sollipulli	1507-111
Quetena (Bolivia)	Fissure vent (None) Pleistocene?	....
Quetrodugon (Chile-C)	Synonym of Sollipulli	1507-111
Quetrupe (Chile-S)	Synonym of Osorno	1508-01=

Lee Siebert (Smithsonian)

The Pitons, the dramatic landmarks of **Qualibou** volcano on the West Indies island of St. Lucia, are the eroded plugs of two Pleistocene lava domes. Gros Piton (L) and the even steeper Petit Piton (R) are pre-caldera domes of the late-Pleistocene Qualibou caldera.

Name (Subregion)	Type (Eruptions, Most Recent) Status / Relation to Named Volcano	Volcano Number
Quetrupillan (Chile-C)	Stratovolcano (1, 1872) Historical	**1507-121**
Quetzaltenango, Volcán de [C. Quemado]	Dome of Almolonga	1402-04=
Queva, Nevado (Argentina)	Unknown (None) Pleistocene	....
Quezaltepeque (Guatemala)	Volcanic field (None) Holocene	**1402-21-**
Quezaltepeque [El Boquerón] (El Salvador)	Stratovolcano of San Salvador	1403-05=
Quezon (Mindanao-Philippines)	Lava domes (None) Pleistocene	....
Quick-Sman-Ik (US-Washington)	Synonym of Baker	1201-01=
Quilatoa (Ecuador)	Synonym of Quilotoa	1502-06=
Quilindana (Ecuador)	Stratovolcano of Chalupas	....
Quill, The (W Indies)	Stratovolcano (3, 250) Radiocarbon	**1600-02=**
Quillaicahue (Chile-C)	Crater of Callaqui	1507-091
Quillayes, Crater los (Chile-C)	Crater of Azul, Cerro	1507-06=
Quilotoa (Ecuador)	Caldera (1, 1280) Radiocarbon	**1502-06=**
Quimsachata (Perú)	Lava dome (1, -4450) Radiocarbon	**1504-00-**
Quimsachata, Cerro (Chile-N)	Unknown (None) Post-Miocene	....
Quimsachata, Nevados de (Chile-N)	Synonym of Acotango	....
Quinceo (México)	Cone of Michoacán-Guanajuato	1401-06=
Quinchilca (Chile-C)	Stratovolcanoes (None) Pleistocene	....
Quindío, Nevado del (Colombia)	Stratovolcano (None) Pleistocene	....
Quinistaquillas (Perú)	Synonym of Huaynaputina	1504-03=
Quinlan, Mt. (Australia)	Cone of Atherton Volc Province	....
Quinquilil (Chile-C)	Stratovolcano of Quetrupillan	1507-121
Quirotoa (Ecuador)	Synonym of Quilotoa	1502-06=
Quirrasco, Volcán (Chile-C)	Cinder cone of Carrán-Los Venados	1507-14=
Quito, Loma (Ecuador)	Dome of Pambamarca	....
Quitralpillan (Chile-C)	Synonym of Villarrica	1507-12=
Quizapu (Chile-C)	Synonym of Azul, Cerro	1507-06=
Quizapu (Chile-C)	Crater of Azul, Cerro	1507-06=
Qummatain (Arabia-W)	Cone of Yar, Jabal	0301-08-
Quoin Hill (Vanuatu-SW Pacific)	Stratovolcano of Fatmalapa	....
Quoin Hill (New Guinea-W)	Cone (None) Quaternary	....
Quoin Island (Red Sea)	Cone of Hanish	0201-022
Quoin Island (Red Sea)	Cone of Zubair, Jebel	0201-02=
Qurayn, Jabal (Arabia-W)	Cone of Birk, Harrat al	0301-072

R

Name (Subregion)	Type (Eruptions, Most Recent) Status / Relation to Named Volcano	Volcano Number
Raatu, Mt. (Vanuatu-SW Pacific)	Cone of Melkum, Mt.	....
Rabalanakaia (New Britain-SW Pac)	Cone of Rabaul	0502-14=
Rabatana [Rabalanakaia] (New Britain)	Cone of Rabaul	0502-14=
Rabaul (New Britain-SW Pac)	Pyroclastic shield (15, 2010) Historical	**0502-14=**
Rabbit Ears (US-New Mexico)	Cone of Raton-Clayton	....
Rabbit Mountain (Canada)	Unknown (None) Pleistocene	....
Rabbit Mountain (US-New Mexico)	Dome of Valles Caldera	....
Rábida (Galápagos)	Lava domes (None) Pleistocene	....
Rabot (W Indies)	Dome of Qualibou	1600-14=
Racecourse Knob (Australia)	Shield volcano McBride Volc Province	
Raco, Volcà (Spain)	Cone of Olot Volc Field	0100-03-
Radersberg (Germany)	Cone of West Eifel Volc Field	0100-01-
Radicofani (Italy)	Volcanic neck (None) Pleistocene	....
Radjabasa (Radjobaso) (Sumatra)	Synonym of Rajabasa	0601-29=
Radkevich (Kuril Is)	Crater of Tiatia	0900-03=
Ragac (Slovakia)	Cone of Filakovo-Salgotarjan	....
Ragang (Mindanao-Philippines)	Stratovolcano (7, 1873) Historical	**0701-06=**
Ragged Jack (Aleutian Is)	Synonym of Isanotski	1101-37-
Ragged Top (Aleutian Is)	Cone of Semisopochnoi	1101-06-
Ragtown Craters (US-Nevada)	Synonym of Soda Lakes	1206-01-
Ragtown Ponds (US-Nevada)	Synonym of Soda Lakes	1206-01-
Raha, Harrat er- (Arabia-W)	Synonym of Rahah, Harrat ar	0301-01=
Raha, Harrat er- (Arabia-W)	Synonym of Rahat, Harrat	0301-07=
Rahah, Harrat ar (Arabia-W)	Volcanic field (None) Anthropology	**0301-01=**
Rahat, Harrat (Arabia-W)	Volcanic field (2, 1256) Historical	**0301-07=**
Rahoum [Dalahum] (Vanuatu-SW Pacific)	Cone of Ambrym	0507-04=
Rahtawu (Java)	Dome of Muria	0603-251
Raibe-dake (Hokkaido-Japan)	Stratovolcano of Orofure-Raiba	....
Raiden (Hokkaido-Japan)	Cone of Niseko	0805-031
Raiden (Hokkaido-Japan)	Stratovolcanoes (None) Pleistocene	....
Raihuén (Chile-C)	Crater of Antillanca Group	1507-153
Raikoke (Kuril Is)	Stratovolcano (3, 1924) Historical	**0900-25=**
Raikoketo (Raikoku) (Kuril Is)	Synonym of Raikoke	0900-25=
Rainbow Mountain (US-California)	Stratovolcano (None) Pleistocene	....
Rainbow Mtn [Maungakakaramea] (New Zeal.)	Cone of Okataina	0401-05=
Rainbow River Cone (Alaska Peninsula)	Stratovolc. of Savonovski River Cluster	....
Rainier (US-Washington)	Stratovolcano (21, 1894) Historical	**1201-03-**
Rairaindreketi (Fiji Is-SW Pacific)	Cone of Taveuni	0405-01-
Rairainiika (Fiji Is-SW Pacific)	Cone of Nairai	....
Raja (Sumatra)	Unknown (None) Pleistocene	....
Rajabasa (Sumatra)	Stratovolcano (None) Fumarolic	**0601-29=**
Rajada, Caldera (Canary Is)	Cinder cone of Lanzarote	1803-06-
Rajada, Montaña (Canary Is)	Dome of Tenerife	1803-03-
Rajada, Montaña [Caldera Rajada]	Cinder cone of Lanzarote	1803-06-
Rajaderas, Volcán (Chile-C)	Stratovolcano Descabezado Grande	1507-05=
Raja-Sabanda (Sumatra)	Unknown (None) Post-Miocene	....
Rajobaso (Sumatra)	Synonym of Rajabasa	0601-29=
Rakata (Indonesia)	Stratovolcano of Krakatau	0602-00=
Raker Peak (US-California)	Cone of Lassen Volc Center	1203-08-
Rakhohkko (Kuril Is)	Synonym of Raikoke	0900-25=
Rakihan (Sumatra)	Cone of Besar	0601-25=
Rakutak, Gunung (Java)	Stratovolcano of Kamojang, Kawah	....
Ralkokeshima (Kuril Is)	Synonym of Raikoke	0900-25=
Raluan [Vulcan] (New Britain-SW Pac)	Pumice cone of Rabaul	0502-14=
Ramírez, Cerro (El Salvador)	Cinder cone of San Vicente	1403-07=
Ramirez, Cerro de los [Cerro Cerrón]	Dome of Apastepeque Field	1403-071
Ramu, Doro (Lesser Sunda Is)	Unknown (None) Post-Miocene	....
Ranakah (Lesser Sunda Is)	Lava domes (2, 1991) Historical	**0604-071**
Ranakah, Pocok (Lesser Sunda Is)	Dome of Ranakah	0604-071
Ranas, Cerro las (El Salvador)	Stratovolcano of Apaneca Range	1403-01=
Ranas, Laguna Seca de la (El Salvador)	Crater of Apaneca Range	1403-01=
Ranau (Sumatra)	Caldera (Uncertain) Holocene?	**0601-251**
Rancagua (Chile-C)	Synonym of Tinguiririca	1507-03=
Rancheria River Volc Field (Canada)	Volcanic field of Tuya Volc Field	1200-031
Rancho la Poma (México)	Cinder cone of Moctezuma Volc Field	....
Ranco (Chile-C)	Synonym of Puyehue-Cordón Caulle	1507-15=
Randazzo, Cuddia (Italy)	Cone of Pantelleria	0101-071
Rangararanga Hill (Australia)	Cone of McBride Volc Province	....
Rangataua Lakes (New Zealand)	Maar of Ruapehu	0401-10=
Rangitahua (Kermadec Is)	Crater of Raoul Island	0402-03=
Rangitoto (New Zealand)	Cone of Auckland Field	0401-02=

Name (Subregion)	Type (Eruptions, Most Recent) Status Relation to Named Volcano	Volcano Number
Rangitukua (New Zealand)	Dome of Taupo	0401-07=
Rano Aroi (Chile-Is)	Pyroclastic cone of Easter Island	1506-011
Rano Aroi (Chile-Is)	Fissure vent of Easter Island	1506-011
Rano Kau (Chile-Is)	Shield volcano of Easter Island	1506-011
Rano Kulo (Sulawesi-Indonesia)	Thermal feature of Tondano Caldera	0606-07-
Rano Randang (Sulawesi-Indonesia)	Thermal feature of Tondano Caldera	0606-07-
Rano Raraku (Chile-Is)	Pyroclastic cone of Easter Island	1506-011
Rano Sapet (Sulawesi-Indonesia)	Thermal feature of Tondano Caldera	0606-07-
Ranomafana (Madagascar)	Thermal feature of Ankaratra Field	0303-015
Ranquil del Sur, Volcán (Argentina)	Pyroclastic cone of Cochiquito Group	1507-071
Ranquil, Crater (Chile-C)	Cinder cone of Mocho-Choshuenco	1507-13=
Rantai-Betung (Sumatra)	Unknown (None) Post-Miocene	....
Rante (Java)	Stratovolcano of Ijen	0603-35=
Rantemario-Latimojong (Indonesia)	Stratovolcanoes (None) Quaternary	....
Rantop, Mt. (Vanuatu-SW Pacific)	Cone of Traitor's Head	0507-09=
Ranu (Halmahera-Indonesia)	Caldera of Todoko-Ranu	0608-05=
Raoeng (Java)	Synonym of Raung	0603-34=

Lee Siebert (Smithsonian)

The massive 4392-m-high glacier-mantled Mount **Rainier** forms the highest peak of the Cascade Range, with Mount Adams volcano in the distance. Two young overlapping cinder cones, their rims kept free of snow by high heat flow, form the flat summit of Rainier.

Name (Subregion)	Type (Eruptions, Most Recent) Status Relation to Named Volcano	Volcano Number
Raoul Island (Kermadec Is)	Stratovolcano (17, 2006) Historical	**0402-03=**
Rapa Nui (Chile-Is)	Synonym of Easter Island	1506-011
Rapanui (New Zealand)	Dome of Maroa	0401-061
Rapogi (Africa-E)	Cone of Homa Mountain	0202-07=
Rarotonga (Pacific-C)	Shield volcano (None) Pleistocene	....
Rasa, Caldeira (Azores)	Crater of Flores	1802-001
Rasa, Lagoa (Azores)	Pumice ring of Sete Cidades	1802-08=
Rasberry Hills (W Indies)	Dome of Soufrière Hills	1600-05=
Raschlenenny (Kamchatka)	Dome of Bezymianny	1000-25=
Rashid, Harrat (Arabia-W)	Volcanic field of Rahat, Harrat	0301-07=
Rashowa (Kuril Is)	Synonym of Rasshua	0900-22=
Rasshua (Kuril Is)	Stratovolcano (2, 1957) Historical	**0900-22=**
Rassoshina (Kamchatka)	Shield volcano of Titila	1000-56-
Rasuyacu [Tishigcuchi] (Ecuador)	Dome of Illiniza	1502-041
Rasyova (Kuril Is)	Synonym of Rasshua	0900-22=
Ratanakiri (SE Asia)	Synonym of Bokeo Volc Field	....
Ratas, Las (México)	Cinder cone of Chichinautzin	1401-08=
Rataschenny (Kamchatka)	Cinder cone of Tolbachik	1000-24=
Ratieng (Africa-E)	Cone of Homa Mountain	0202-07=
Raton Mesa Volc Field (US-New Mexico)	Synonym of Raton-Clayton	....
Raton-Clayton (US-New Mexico)	Volcanic field (None) Pleistocene	....
Ratu (Java)	Crater of Gede	0603-06=
Ratu, Kawah (Java)	Thermal feature of Salak	0603-05=
Ratu, Kawah (Java)	Crater of Tangkubanparahu	0603-09=
Raudahalsar (Iceland-W)	Cone of Ljósufjöll	1700-03=
Raudahraun (Iceland-S)	Fissure vent of Eyjafjallajökull	1702-02=
Raudakula (Iceland-W)	Cone of Ljósufjöll	1700-03=
Raudakula-Horgsholtshraun (Iceland-W)	Cone of Ljósufjöll	1700-03=
Raudakular (Iceland-W)	Cone of Helgrindur	1700-02=
Raudakula-Svelgarhraun (Iceland-W)	Cone of Ljósufjöll	1700-03=
Raudfossafjöll (Iceland-S)	Tuya of Torfajökull	1702-05=
Raudfossahraun (Iceland-S)	Crater Row of Hekla	1702-07=
Raudhalsar (Iceland-W)	Cone of Ljósufjöll	1700-03=
Raudholar (Iceland-NE)	Fissure vent of Fremrinamur	1703-07=
Raudholar (Iceland-SW)	Crater of Grímsnes	1701-06=
Raudholar (Iceland-NE)	Fissure vent of Grímsvötn	1703-01=
Raudholar (Iceland-SW)	Crater Row of Reykjanes	1701-02=
Raudholar (Iceland-W)	Cone of Snaefellsjökull	1700-01=
Raudholl (Iceland-NE)	Crater Row of Grímsvötn	1703-01=
Raudholl-Hafnarfjordur (Iceland-SW)	Crater Row of Krísuvík	1701-03=
Raudibotn (Iceland-S)	Crater of Katla	1702-03=
Raudimelur (Iceland-SW)	Crater Row of Krísuvík	1701-03=
Raudkembingur (Iceland-S)	Fissure vent of Hekla	1702-07=
Raudkollar (Iceland-S)	Fissure vent of Hekla	1702-07=
Raudölduhraun (Iceland-S)	Crater Row of Hekla	1702-07=
Raudoldur (Iceland-S)	Crater of Hekla	1702-07=
Raudubjallar (Iceland-S)	Fissure vent of Hekla	1702-07=
Rauduborgir (Iceland-NE)	Fissure vent of Fremrinamur	1703-07=

Name (Subregion)	Type (Eruptions, Most Recent) Status Relation to Named Volcano	Volcano Number
Rauduhnukagigir (Iceland-SW)	Crater Row of Brennisteinsfjöll	1701-04=
Raukoke (Kuril Is)	Synonym of Raikoke	0900-25=
Raung (Java)	Stratovolcano (62, 2008) Historical	**0603-34=**
Rausu (Hokkaido-Japan)	Stratovolcano (5, 1800) Radiocarbon	**0805-082**
Rausu-dake (Kuril Is)	Synonym of Mendeleev	0900-02=
Rausu-dake (Hokkaido-Japan)	Synonym of Rausu	0805-082
Ravenshoe (Australia)	Cone of Atherton Volc Province	....
Raventhorpe (New Zealand)	Tuff cone of South Auckland	....
Raveti (Solomon Is-SW Pacific)	Unknown (None) Post-Miocene	....
Rawon (Java)	Synonym of Raung	0603-34=
Ray Mountain (Canada)	Fissure vent of Wells Gray-Clearwater	1200-15-
Ray, Mount (US-Oregon)	Shield volcano of Fuji Mountain	....
Raya (Sumatra)	Synonym of Raja	....
Rayhuen [Raihuén] (Chile-C)	Crater of Antillanca Group	1507-153
Raykoke (Kuril Is)	Synonym of Raikoke	0900-25=
Raymond, Puys (Indian O.-W)	Cinder cone of Fournaise, Piton de la	0303-02=
Razlaty (Kamchatka)	Dome of Bezymianny	1000-25=
Razlaty (Kamchatka)	Stratovolcano (None) Pleistocene	....
Razorback, Mt. (Australia)	Cone of McBride Volc Province	....
Razrushennyi [Raschlenenny] (Kamchatka)	Dome of Bezymianny	1000-25=
Razval, Mount (Kuril Is)	Cone of Rasshua	0900-22=
Razzano, Monte (Italy)	Tuff cone of Sabatini Complex	....
Reading Peak (US-California)	Dome of Lassen Volc Center	1203-08-
Realenco, El [Cerro el Cerrito] (El Salvador)	Cinder cone of San Salvador	1403-05=
Reaumur, Mt. (New Guinea-NE of)	Stratovolcano of Long Island	0501-05=
Rebanada, Caldera de (Canary Is)	Cinder cone of Fuerteventura	1803-05-
Rebeke, Jebel (Arabia-S)	Tuff cone of Haylan, Jabal	0301-11-
Rebunshiri (Kuril Is)	Cone of Grozny Group	0900-07=
Recess Nunatak (Antarctica)	Cone of Fosdick Mountains	....
Recherche, La (Kermadec Is)	Synonym of Raoul Island	0402-03=
Recheschnoi (Aleutian Is)	Stratovolcano (None) Holocene	**1101-28-**
Reck (Greece)	Dome of Santorini	0102-04=
Reclus (Chile-S)	Cinder cone (4, 1908) Historical	**1508-063**
Red Bomb Crater (US-Oregon)	Cinder cone of Diamond Craters	1202-17-
Red Butte (US-Washington)	Cinder cone of Adams	1201-04-
Red Butte (US-Oregon)	Cone of Three Fingered Jack	....
Red Cap Mountain (US-California)	Cone of Medicine Lake	1203-02-
Red Cinder Butte (US-Oregon)	Cinder cone of Cinnamon Butte	1202-15-
Red Cliff (W Indies)	Dome of Nevis Peak	1600-04=
Red Cone (US-Nevada)	Cone of Crater Flat	....
Red Cone (US-Oregon)	Vent of Crater Lake	1202-16-
Red Cone (US-Oregon)	Cinder cone of Thielsen	....
Red Cones (Hawaiian Is)	Cone of Kilauea	1302-01-
Red Cones (US-California)	Cinder cone of Mammoth Mountain	1203-15-
Red Crater (US-Oregon)	Cinder cone of Bachelor	1202-09-
Red Crater (New Zealand)	Crater of Tongariro	0401-08=
Red Hill (Hawaiian Is)	Cone of Haleakala	1302-06-
Red Hill (US-California)	Cone of Medicine Lake	1203-02-
Red Hill (US-New Mexico)	Volcanic field (None) Pleistocene	....
Red Hill (Galápagos)	Cone of Santa Cruz	1503-091
Red Hill (US-New Mexico)	Cinder cone of Taos Plateau	....
Red Hill [South Fork] (US-California)	Cinder cone of Golden Trout Creek	1203-17-
Red Hill Cone (US-New Mexico)	Cone of Red Hill	....
Red Hill Maar (US-New Mexico)	Maar of Red Hill	....
Red Island (Indian O.-S)	Cone of Heard	0304-01=
Red Island (US-California)	Dome of Salton Buttes	1203-20-
Red Knoll (US-Utah)	Cone of Mineral Mts-Cove Fort	....
Red Lake Mountain (US-California)	Cinder cone (None) Pleistocene	....
Red Lake Mountain (US-California)	Cinder cone of Table Mountain	....
Red Mountain (US-Washington)	Shield volcano of Indian Heaven	1201-07-
Red Mountain (US-New Mexico)	Cone of Raton-Clayton	....
Red Mountain (US-Arizona)	Cone of San Francisco Volc Field	....
Red Mountain (US-California)	Cinder cone of Table Mountain	....
Red Mountain [Mt. Price] (Canada)	Stratovolcano of Garibaldi Lake	1200-19-
Red Mountain [Ol Doinyo Onyoke] (Africa-E)	Stratovolcano of Suswa	0202-11=
Red Mountain-Big Lava Bed (US-Wash.)	Synonym of Indian Heaven	1201-07-
Red Rock (Australia)	Maar of Newer Volcanics Prov	0509-01-
Red Rock Hill (US-California)	Cone of Twin Buttes	1203-04-
Red Rock Valley (US-Montana)	Stratovolcano (None) Pleistocene	....
Red Shale Butte (US-California)	Cone of Medicine Lake	1203-02-
Red Top Mountain (US-Oregon)	Shield volcanoes (None) Pleistocene	....
Redcloud (US-Oregon)	Vent of Crater Lake	1202-16-
Rededonda (México)	Dome of Zitácuaro-Valle de Bravo	1401-061
Redonda, Loma (Guatemala)	Dome of Redondo, Cerro	....
Redondo de la Cruz, Cerro [Monte de la Cruz]	Cinder cone of Barva	1405-05=
Redondo Peak (US-New Mexico)	Dome of Valles Caldera	....
Redondo, Cerro (Guatemala)	Cinder cone of Chingo	1402-17-
Redondo, Cerro (Guatemala)	Cinder cone of Cuilapa-Barbarena	1402-111
Redondo, Cerro (Guatemala)	Cinder cone of Güistepeque Volc Field	....
Redondo, Cerro (Guatemala)	Shield volcanoes (None) Quaternary	....
Redondo, Cerro Monte (Guatemala)	Cinder cone of Pueblo Nuevo Viñas	....
Redondo, Volcán (Chile-C)	Cone of Caburgua-Huelemolle	1507-112
Redondo, Volcán (Chile-C)	Cone of Sollipulli	1507-111
Redoubt (Alaska-SW)	Stratovolcano (16, 2009) Historical	**1103-03-**
Rees, Mount (Antarctica)	Cone of Crary Group	....
Refinería (Nicaragua)	Crater of Nejapa-Miraflores	1404-092
Reforma, La (México)	Caldera (None) Pleistocene	....
Regolo, Monte (Italy)	Cone of Sabatini Complex	....
Regulo, Ranu (Java)	Maar of Semeru	0603-30=
Rehai (SE Asia)	Thermal feature of Tengchong	0705-11-
Reicho-sen (Kyushu-Japan)	Thermal feature of Tsurumi	0802-13=
Reini (Bougainville-SW Pacific)	Stratovolcano of Billy Mitchell	0505-011
Rejo te Kavachi (Solomon Is-SW Pacific)	Synonym of Kavachi	0505-06=
Rekkame Volc Field (Africa-N)	Explosion craters (None) Pleistocene	....

Name (Subregion)	Type (Eruptions, Most Recent) Status . . Relation to Named Volcano	Volcano Number
Relibuentu (Chile-S)	Synonym of Huequi	1508-03=
Renatura (Italy)	Cinder cone of Etna	0101-06=
Rendall, Mt. (Cape Verde Is)	Cone of Fogo	1804-01=
Rendija, Cerro (US-New Mexico)	Cone of Zuni-Bandera	1210-02-
Rendova (Solomon Is-SW Pacific)	Stratovolcano (None) Pleistocene	....
Renegado, Volcán (Chile-C)	Stratovolcano of Chillán, Nevados de.	1507-07=
Renihue (Chile-C)	Synonym of Mocho-Choshuenco	1507-13=
Renón, El (Nicaragua)	Cinder cone of Masaya	1404-10=
Rentoul, Mt. (New Guinea)	Synonym of Sisa	....
Reoka (Solomon Is-SW Pacific)	Thermal feature of Savo	0505-07=
Reparo, Cerro el (Guatemala)	Cone of Suchitán	1402-16-
Repas, Volcà (Spain)	Cone of Olot Volc Field	0100-03-
Reporoa (New Zealand)	Caldera (1, 1180) Tephrochronology	**0401-06-**
Rerewhakaaitu (New Zealand)	Tuff cone of Okataina	0401-05=
Rerewhakaaitu (New Zealand)	Fissure vent of Okataina	0401-05=
Resago (Chile-C)	Cinder cone (None) Holocene	**1507-065**
Reschuelos, El (US-New Mexico)	Dome of Valles Caldera	....
Resolana, Crater la (Chile-C)	Crater of Azul, Cerro	1507-06=
Resources, Morne les (W Indies)	Dome of Diablotins, Morne	1600-09=
Restinga (Canary Is)	Cinder cone of Hierro	1803-02-
Retana Caldera (Guatemala)	Caldera of Suchitán	1402-16-
Retchechnoi (Aleutian Is)	Synonym of Recheschnoi	1101-28-
Retes, Cerro (Costa Rica)	Cone of Irazú	1405-06=
Retiro, Cerro el (El Salvador)	Cinder cone of Santa Ana	1403-02=
Retu, Maunga (Chile-Is)	Pyroclastic cone of Easter Island	1506-011
Reunion, Volcan de la (Indian O.-W)	Synonym of Fournaise, Piton de la	0303-02=
Reusch Pit (Africa-E)	Crater of Kilimanjaro	0202-15=
Reventada, Montaña (Canary Is)	Cinder cone of Tenerife	1803-03-
Reventador (Ecuador)	Stratovolcano (28, 2010) Historical	**1502-01=**
Reventador, El (Ecuador)	Synonym of Reventador	1502-01=
Revillagigedo Island (Alaska-E)	Synonym of Behm Canal-Rudyerd Bay	1105-07-
Revire Nganga (Africa-C)	Synonym of Nyiragongo	0203-03=
Reydarvatnshraun (Iceland-S)	Fissure vent of Hekla	1702-07=
Reyeheico, Volcanes de (Chile-C)	Cinder cone of Quetrupillan	1507-121
Reykjafellsgigir (Iceland-SW)	Crater Row of Hengill	1701-05=
Reykjanes (Iceland-SW)	Crater rows (23, 1879) Historical	**1701-02=**
Reykjaneshyggur (Iceland-SW)	Fissure vent of Reykjanes	1701-02=
Reynifellshraun (Iceland-S)	Crater Row of Hekla	1702-07=
Rf Crater (New Zealand)	Former crater of White Island	0401-04=
Rhododendron Cone (Alaska-W)	Cone of Imuruk Lake	1104-06-
Rial (Argentina)	Cinder cone of Unnamed	....
Riang Kotang (Lesser Sunda Is)	Thermal feature of Ilikedeka	....
Ribiera Dos Tambores (Azores)	Thermal feature of Furnas	1802-10=
Riccò, Monti (Italy)	Cinder cone of Etna	0101-06=
Richard-Foy, Mt. (Indian O.-S)	Cone of Cochons, Ile aux	0304-05-
Richardson, Mount (Antarctica)	Cone of Fosdick Mountains	....
Richmond, Mt. (New Zealand)	Cone of Auckland Field	0401-02=
Richthofen [Galloseulo] (New Britain)	Stratovolcano of Hargy	0502-10=
Rico, Cerro de Monte (Guatemala)	Cone of Ipala	1402-19-
Ridge (Canada)	Cone of Edziza	1200-06-
Ridge Dome (New Zealand)	Dome of Okataina	0401-05=
Ridge Wall (Alaska-W)	Cinder cone of St. Paul Island	1104-01-
Ridubidubina, Lake (New Guinea)	Cone of Victory	0503-03=
Riley, Mt. (US-New Mexico)	Maar of Potrillo Volc Field	....
Rimdo (Korea)	Dome of Halla	1006-04-
Rinatu, Monte (Italy)	Cinder cone of Etna	0101-06=
Rincón Chico (México)	Dome of Zitácuaro-Valle de Bravo	1401-061
Rincón de la Cerca, El (Canary Is)	Cinder cone of Hierro	1803-02-
Rincón de la Vieja (Costa Rica)	Complex volcano (21, 1998) Historical	**1405-02=**
Rincón de Parangüeo (México)	Maar of Michoacán-Guanajuato	1401-06=
Rincón, El (México)	Thermal feature of Aguajito, El	....
Rincón, El (México)	Maar of Michoacán-Guanajuato	1401-06=
Rinconada Cerro Bayo (Chile-N)	Cone of Bayo, Cerro	1505-122
Rindjani (Lesser Sunda Is)	Synonym of Rinjani	0604-03=
Ringgit (Java)	Synonym of Raung	0603-34=
Ringgit (Java)	Stratovolcano (None) Pleistocene	....
Ringgit (Java)	Dome of Tengger Caldera	0603-31=
Ringgit I (Sumatra)	Cone of Ringgit, Bukit	....
Ringgit, Bukit (Sumatra)	Unknown (None) Post-Miocene	....
Ringgit, Gunung (Java)	Stratovolcano of Arjuno-Welirang	0603-29=
Ringgit, Gunung (Java)	Cone of Ijen	0603-35=
Ringgit-besar (Java)	Synonym of Ringgit	....
Ringitt Ii (Sumatra)	Cone of Ringgit, Bukit	....
Ringo Butte (US-Oregon)	Shield volcano of Davis Lake	1202-10-
Rinihue (Chile-C)	Synonym of Mocho-Choshuenco	1507-13=
Riñinahue (Chile-C)	Maar of Carrán-Los Venados	1507-14=
Rinjani (Lesser Sunda Is)	Stratovolcano (15, 2009) Historical	**0604-03=**
Río Colorado (Chile-C)	Pleist. caldera of San Pedro-Pellado	1507-062
Rio Corbore (Italy)	Crater of Ischia	0101-03=
Río Cuarto, Laguna (Costa Rica)	Maar of Poás	1405-04=
Río Curinhuas (Nicaragua)	Synonym of Azul, Volcán	1404-14-
Río Frio, Volcán (Costa Rica)	Synonym of Arenal	1405-033
Río Hondo, Laguna de [Laguna Río Cuarto]	Maar of Poás	1405-04=
Río Ibáñez (Chile-S)	Cinder cone of Hudson, Cerro	1508-057
Río Lori Domes (Costa Rica)	Synonym of Dúrika	....
Río Murta (Chile-S)	Pyroclastic cones (None) Holocene?	**1508-058**
Río Negro, Cerro de (Chile-N)	Stratovolcano (None) Pleistocene	....
Río Salado (México)	Dome of Primavera, Sierra la	....
Rione delle Mofete [Mofete] (Italy)	Crater of Campi Flegrei	0101-01=
Rione Terra (Italy)	Crater of Campi Flegrei	0101-01=
Risco Plateado (Argentina)	Stratovolcano (None) Holocene?	**1507-024**
Rishiri (Hokkaido-Japan)	Dome of Kutcharo	0805-08=
Rishiri (Hokkaido-Japan)	Stratovolcano (1, -5830) Radiocarbon	**0805-041**
Risiri (Hokkaido-Japan)	Synonym of Rishiri	0805-041

Name (Subregion)	Type (Eruptions, Most Recent) Status . . Relation to Named Volcano	Volcano Number
Risiri [Rishiri] (Hokkaido-Japan)	Dome of Kutcharo	0805-08=
Riso Patrón (Chile-C)	Cinder cone of Maipo	1507-021
Ritter (Galápagos)	Cone of Floreana	....
Ritter Island (New Guinea-NE of)	Stratovolcano (8, 2007) Historical	**0501-07=**
Rittmann, Monte (Italy)	Cinder cone of Etna	0101-06=
Riva (Greece)	Pleistocene caldera of Santorini	0102-04=
Riveroll, Cerro (México)	Cinder cone of San Quintín Volc Field	1401-002
Rivi (Italy)	Stratovolcano of Salina	....
Riviera Ridge (Antarctica)	Fissure vent of Morning, Mt.	1900-020
Rjupnadyngjur (Iceland-SW)	Shield volcano of Brennisteinsfjöll	1701-04=
Roa (Tonga-SW Pacific)	Synonym of Late	0403-09=
Robert Meyer (Africa-W)	Crater of Cameroon	0204-01=
Roberts Mountain (Alaska-W)	Cone of Nunivak Island	1104-02-
Robertson, Mt. (New Zealand)	Cone of Auckland Field	0401-02=
Robertson's Hill (Australia)	Cone of Newer Volcanics Prov	0509-01-
Robertson's Thumb (Vanuatu-SW Pacific)	Cone of Melkum, Mt.	....
Robinson Crusoe (Chile-Is)	Shield volcanoes (1, 1835) Historical	**1506-02=**
Robinson Mountain (US-New Mexico)	Cone of Raton-Clayton	....
Robledo (Argentina)	Caldera (None) Holocene	**1505-21-**
Roca Challenger (México-Is)	Dome of Bárcena	1401-02=
Roca Negra, Volcà (Spain)	Cone of Olot Volc Field	0100-03-
Roca Redonda (Galápagos)	Shield volcano (None) Quaternary	....
Rocamel, Cerro (Honduras)	Cone of Zacate Grande, Isla	1403-14-
Rocard (Society Is-C Pacific)	Submarine volcano (3, 1972) Seismicity.	**1303-02-**
Rocas Trinidad (México-Is)	Dome of Bárcena	1401-02=
Rocca Capra (Italy)	Cinder cone of Etna	0101-06=
Rocca de Papa (Italy)	Cone of Alban Hills	0101-004
Rocca Romana (Italy)	Cone of Sabatini Complex	....
Roccamonfina (Italy)	Stratovolcano (None) Pleistocene	....
Rocche Rosse (Italy)	Vent of Lipari	0101-042
Rocchetta (Italy)	Dome of Vico-Cimino Complex	....
Rochaculla-Inca Camacha (Bolivia)	Stratovolcanoes (None) Pleistocene?	....
Rocher du Diamant (W Indies)	Dome of Unnamed	....
Roche's Bluff (W Indies)	Dome of Soufrière Hills	1600-05=
Roche's Mountain [Perche's Mountain]	Dome of Soufrière Hills	1600-05=
Rock Hill (US-California)	Dome of Salton Buttes	1203-20-
Rock Mesa (US-Oregon)	Dome of South Sister	1202-08-
Rockeskyll-SW (Germany)	Tuff ring of West Eifel Volc Field	0100-01-
Rockne Volcano (Samoa-SW Pacific)	Synonym of Vailulu'u	0404-00-
Rocky Butte (US-Oregon)	Cone of Boring Lava	....
Rocky Butte (US-Oregon)	Synonym of Lava Butte	....
Rocky Hill (Australia)	Cone of McBride Volc Province	....
Rocky Island (Red Sea)	Cone of Hanish	0201-022
Rocky Peak (US-California)	Dome of Maidu	....
Rodde, Puy de la (France)	Cone of Chaîne des Puys	0100-02-
Rodderberg (Germany)	Cinder cone (None) Pleistocene	....
Rodeo (Argentina)	Pyrocl. cone Northern Mendoza Field	....
Rodeo, El (México)	Dome of Cumbres, Las	1401-098
Rodeopampa, Loma (Ecuador)	Dome of Chachimbiro	1502-002
Rodeos, Montana (Canary Is)	Cinder cone of Lanzarote	1803-06-
Rodillas (México)	Stratovolcano of Iztaccíhuatl	1401-082
Rodley Butte (US-Oregon)	Cone of Bailey	....
Rodney, Mt. (W Indies)	Dome of St. Catherine	1600-17=

The complex summit region of **Rincón de la Vieja**, the largest volcano in NW Costa Rica, includes the steaming, lake-filled Cráter Activo (L) and the shallow 1895-m-high Von Seebach crater (upper right). Prominent erosional gulleys cut unvegetated ash deposits.

Name (Subregion)	Type (Eruptions, Most Recent) Status . . Relation to Named Volcano	Volcano Number
Rodrigo (Chile-N)	Caldera of Tres Cruces	....
Rodriguez (Chile-S)	Cone of Palena Volc Group	1508-051
Rodriguez Island (Indian O.-W)	Shield volcano (None) Pleistocene	....
Roeang (Sangihe Is-Indonesia)	Synonym of Ruang	0607-01=
Roemengan (Sulawesi-Indonesia)	Synonym of Mahawu	0606-11=
Roewang (Sangihe Is-Indonesia)	Synonym of Ruang	0607-01=
Rofubodi (Iceland-S)	Submarine vent of Vestmannaeyjar	1702-01=
Rogers Head (Indian O.-S)	Cone of Heard	0304-01=
Roisa (Italy)	Fissure vent of Stromboli	0101-04=
Roja de Mazo, Caldera (Canary Is)	Cinder cone of Lanzarote	1803-06-
Roja, Calderilla de (Canary Is)	Crater of Fuerteventura	1803-05-
Roka Piek (Lesser Sunda Is)	Synonym of Inierie	0604-08=
Rokatenda (Lesser Sunda Is)	Crater of Paluweh	0604-15=
Rokatinda [Rokatenda] (Lesser Sunda Is)	Crater of Paluweh	0604-15=
Rokka Peak (Lesser Sunda Is)	Synonym of Inierie	0604-08=

Name (Subregion)	Type (Eruptions, Most Recent) Status Relation to Named Volcano	Volcano Number
Rokkannon-Mi-ike (Kyushu-Japan)	Maar of Kirishima	0802-09=
Rokko (Kuril Is)	Caldera of Urbich Caldera	....
Rolles Peak (New Zealand)	Stratovolcano of Maroa	0401-061
Rollizos (Chile-S)	Cone of Cayutué-La Viguería	1508-012
Romani Hill (Africa-E)	Dome of Nyambeni Hills	0202-056
Romano (Italy)	Crater of Campi Flegrei	0101-01=
Romanovka (Kamchatka)	Stratovolcano (None) Holocene?	**1000-34-**
Rombongan, Gunung (Lesser Sunda Is)	Dome of Rinjani	0604-03=
Romeral (Colombia)	Stratovolcano (1, -5950) Radiocarbon	**1501-011**
Romo, Volcán (México)	Maar of Pinacate	1401-001
Rond, Piton (Indian O.-W)	Cinder cone of Fournaise, Piton de la	0303-02=
Ronde, Ile de (W Indies)	Vent of Kick 'em Jenny	1600-16=
Rongo (Africa-E)	Cone of Homa Mountain	0202-07=
Roodja [Rooja] (Lesser Sunda Is)	Cone of Iya	0604-11=
Rooja (Lesser Sunda Is)	Cone of Iya	0604-11=

Tom Simkin (Smithsonian)

Mud oozing from a miniature vent in a thermal area of the **Rotorua** caldera in New Zealand mimics a lava flow with minature flow ridges perpendicular to the direction of movement. Dessication cracks cut the surface of the older surrounding mud.

Name (Subregion)	Type (Eruptions, Most Recent) Status Relation to Named Volcano	Volcano Number
Rooke Island (New Guinea-NE of)	Synonym of Umboi	0501-06=
Rook's Bay (Indian O.-S)	Tuff cone of Marion Island	0304-07-
Roque de Infierno (Canary Is)	Cone of Lanzarote	1803-06-
Roque Grande (Canary Is)	Cinder cone of Hierro	1803-02-
Roques Blancos (Canary Is)	Dome of Tenerife	1803-03-
Roquillo, Montaña del [Volcán de Fasnia]	Cinder cone of Tenerife	1803-03-
Rosamel Island (Antarctica)	Tuff cone of Tabarin Peninsula	....
Rosario, Baños del (Guatemala)	Thermal feature of Almolonga	1402-04=
Rosario, Cerro del (El Salvador)	Dome of Ilopango	1403-06=
Rosario, Cerro el (Guatemala)	Cinder cone of Redondo, Cerro	....
Rosario, Cerro el (México)	Cinder cone Zitácuaro-Valle de Bravo	1401-061
Rosario, El (México)	Vent of Northern Atenguillo	....
Rosarito Volc Field, El (México)	Synonym of San Borja Volc Field	1401-007
Rosas, Montaña de las (Canary Is)	Cinder cone of Hierro	1803-02-
Rose Garden (Pacific-E)	Thermal feature of Galápagos Rift	1304-07-
Rose Island (Samoa-SW Pacific)	Shield volcano (None) Pleistocene	....
Rosebud (Pacific-E)	Thermal feature of Galápagos Rift	1304-07-
Rosey, Mt. (Australia)	Cone of McBride Volc Province	....
Roskill, Mt. (New Zealand)	Cone of Auckland Field	0401-02=
Ross Rocks (Indian O.)	Tuff cone of Prince Edward Island	0304-06-
Ross, Mount (Indian O.-S)	Stratovolcano of Kerguelen Islands	0304-02=
Rosse, Cuddie (Italy)	Cone of Pantelleria	0101-071
Rosso, Monte (Italy)	Cinder cone of Etna	0101-06=
Rosso, Monte (Italy)	Cone of Vulcano	0101-05=
Rosso, Mt. (Italy)	Cone of Vulsini	0101-003
Rosto de Cao (Azores)	Tuff cone of Picos Volc System	1802-081
Rota (Nicaragua)	Stratovolcano (None) Holocene	**1404-06-**
Rotaro (Italy)	Dome of Ischia	0101-03=
Rotoatua, Lake (New Zealand)	Crater of Okataina	0401-05=
Rotoehu, Lake [Rotoma Geothermal Fd]	Thermal feature of Okataina	0401-05=
Rotoiti (New Zealand)	Pleistocene caldera of Okataina	0401-05=
Rotoiti (New Zealand)	Thermal feature of Rotorua	....
Rotokakahi (New Zealand)	Dome of Kapenga	....
Rotokakahi (New Zealand)	Dome of Okataina	0401-05=
Rotokaua (New Zealand)	Thermal feature of Maroa	0401-061
Rotokawa [Rotokaua] (New Zealand)	Thermal feature of Maroa	0401-061
Rotokawa, Lake (New Zealand)	Thermal feature of Rotorua	....
Rotokawau, Lake (New Zealand)	Maar of Okataina	0401-05=
Rotokohu (New Zealand)	Dome of Okataina	0401-05=
Rotoma (New Zealand)	Pleistocene caldera of Okataina	0401-05=
Rotoma Geothermal Field (New Zealand)	Thermal feature of Okataina	0401-05=
Rotomahana (New Zealand)	Dome of Okataina	0401-05=
Rotomahana (New Zealand)	Thermal feature of Okataina	0401-05=
Rotopounamu, Lake (New Zealand)	Crater of Northern Tongariro Group	....
Rotorua (New Zealand)	Vent of Okataina	0401-05=
Rotorua (New Zealand)	Caldera (None) Pleistocene-Geysers	....
Rotorua Geothermal Field (New Zealand)	Thermal feature of Rotorua	....
Rouge, Morne (Indian O.-S)	Cone of Cochons, Ile aux	0304-05-
Rouge, Morne (W Indies)	Cone of Plat Pays, Morne	1600-11=
Rouge, Morne (W Indies)	Dome of Plat Pays, Morne	1600-11=
Rouge, Piton (Indian O.-W)	Cinder cone of Fournaise, Piton de la	0303-02=
Round Head (Aleutian Is)	Cone of Kanaga	1101-11-
Round Hill (Atlantic-S)	Cinder cone of Inaccessible Island	....
Round Hill (W Indies)	Dome of Nevis Peak	1600-04=
Round Hill (W Indies)	Synonym of Quill, The	1600-02=
Round Island (Red Sea)	Cone of Hanish	0201-022
Round Mountain (US-California)	Cone of Clear Lake	1203-10-
Round Mountain (Canada)	Vent of Garibaldi	1200-20-
Round Top (Hawaiian Is)	Cone of Koolau	....
Roundhead, Mt. (Solomon Is-SW Pacific)	Cone of Gallego	0505-062
Roundtop (Aleutian Is)	Stratovolcano (1, -7600) Radiocarbon	**1101-38-**
Roundtop Mountain (US-California)	Cone of Clear Lake	1203-10-
Roung (Java)	Synonym of Raung	0603-34=
Rouse (Kuril Is)	Synonym of Mendeleev	0900-02=
Rowo, Gunung (Java)	Maar of Muria	0603-251
Royal Society Range (Antarctica)	Cinder cones (None) Holocene?	**1900-021**
Royce (New Zealand)	Crater of White Island	0401-04=
Royce Mountain (US-Oregon)	Shield volcano of Davis Lake	1202-10-
Ruagare (Africa-C)	Cone of Karisimbi	0203-04-
Ruahine Springs (New Zealand)	Thermal feature of Rotorua	....
Ruamata (New Zealand)	Pumice cone of Mayor Island	0401-021
Ruang (Sangihe Is-Indonesia)	Stratovolcano (12, 2002) Historical	**0607-01=**
Ruapahu (New Zealand)	Synonym of Ruapehu	0401-10=
Ruapehu (New Zealand)	Stratovolcano (64, 2007) Historical	**0401-10=**
Ruawahia (New Zealand)	Dome of Okataina	0401-05=
Rubio, Cerro (US-New Mexico)	Dome of Valles Caldera	....
Rubona (Africa-C)	Cone of Nyiragongo	0203-03=
Ruby (Mariana Is-C Pacific)	Submarine volcano (2, 1995) Historical	**0804-202**
Ruby Creek (Canada)	Vent of Atlin Volc Field	1200-03-
Ruby Mountain (Canada)	Cone of Atlin Volc Field	1200-03-
Rucharu (Kuril Is)	Synonym of Vetrovoi Isthmus Caldera	....
Ruckenberg, Mount (New Britain-SW Pac)	Dome of Sulu Range	0502-09=
Rucu Pichincha (Ecuador)	Stratovolcano of Guagua Pichincha	1502-02=
Rudakov (Kuril Is)	Stratovolcano (None) Holocene?	**0900-112**
Ruddy Mountain (Alaska-E)	Dome of Drum	....
Ruderbüsch (Germany)	Cone of West Eifel Volc Field	0100-01-
Rudich's Cone (Kamchatka)	Dome of Uzon	1000-17=
Rudolf (New Zealand)	Former crater of White Island	0401-04=
Ruedas, Cerro las (Guatemala)	Cone of Ipala	1402-19-
Rugarama (Africa-C)	Cone of Nyamuragira	0203-02=
Rugarambiro (Africa-C)	Cone of Nyamuragira	0203-02=
Rugged Island (Red Sea)	Cone of Zubair, Jebel	0201-02=
Ruhara (Africa-C)	Cone of Karisimbi	0203-04-
Ruik, Lake (New Britain-SW Pac)	Crater of Du Faure	....
Ruivo, Pico (Azores)	Cinder cone of Madeira	1802-12-
Ruiz, Nevado del (Colombia)	Stratovolcano (18, 1991) Historical	**1501-02=**
Ruk Island (New Guinea-NE of)	Synonym of Umboi	0501-06=
Ruko (Kuril Is)	Synonym of Ebeko	0900-38=
Rukondja (Africa-C)	Cone of Karisimbi	0203-04-
Rumble I (New Zealand)	Submarine volcano (None) Quaternary	....
Rumble II West (New Zealand)	Submarine volcano (None) Fumarolic	**0401-131**
Rumble III (New Zealand)	Submarine volcano (6, 2008) Historical	**0401-13-**
Rumble IV (New Zealand)	Submarine volcano (None) Fumarolic	**0401-12-**
Rumble V (New Zealand)	Submarine volcano (None) Fumarolic	**0401-11-**
Rumengan (Sulawesi-Indonesia)	Synonym of Mahawu	0606-11=
Rumicola (Perú)	Cone of Huambutillo-Rumicola	....
Rumiñahui (Ecuador)	Stratovolcano (None) Pleistocene?	....
Rumoka (Africa-C)	Cone of Nyamuragira	0203-02=
Runcing (Sumatra)	Unknown (None) Quaternary	....
Rungapapa Knoll (New Zealand)	Submarine volcano (None) Quaternary	....
Rungu (Africa-C)	Cone of Karisimbi	0203-04-
Rungwe (Africa-E)	Stratovolcano (2, -50) Radiocarbon	**0202-166**
Runu, Wolo (Lesser Sunda Is)	Crater of Inielika	0604-09=
Ruru, Tavani (Vanuatu-SW Pacific)	Stratovolcano of Kuwae	0507-07=
Rurui (Kuril Is)	Stratovolcano of Smirnov	0900-021
Rurutu (Pacific-C)	Shield volcano (None) Pleistocene	....
Rusa Raja (Rusa Radja) (Lesser Sunda Is)	Synonym of Paluweh	0604-15=
Rusciello, Monte (Italy)	Crater of Campi Flegrei	0101-01=
Rusekere [Kasekere] (Africa-C)	Tuff cone of Fort Portal	0203-001
Rush Hill (Alaska-W)	Cinder cone of St. Paul Island	1104-01-
Rushashu (Africa-C)	Cone of Karisimbi	0203-04-
Rushayo (Africa-C)	Cone of Nyiragongo	0203-03=
Russel Peak (Antarctica)	Synonym of Sturge Island	1900-012
Rutoke (Africa-C)	Cone of Nyiragongo	0203-03=
Rutudagi (Turkey)	Dome of Süphan Dagi	0103-021
Rwamisega (Africa-C)	Cone of Karisimbi	0203-04-
Rwenkuba (Africa-C)	Tuff cone of Fort Portal	0203-001
Ryohaku Maru-yama (Honshu-Japan)	Stratovolcano (None) Pleistocene	....
Ryoshi-dake (Kyushu-Japan)	Cone of Kuju	0802-12=
Ryoun-dake (Hokkaido-Japan)	Dome of Daisetsu	0805-06=
Ryponkicha (Kuril Is)	Synonym of Ushishur	0900-21=
Ryuzan (Honshu-Japan)	Stratovolcano of Zao	0803-19=

S

Name (Subregion)	Type (Eruptions, Most Recent) Status Relation to Named Volcano	Volcano Number
Saar, Kawah (Java)	Thermal feature of Kamojang, Kawah	....
Saat, Kawah (Java)	Thermal feature of Talagabodas	0603-15=
Saavedra, Cerro los (México)	Cone of Tequila	....
Saba (W Indies)	Stratovolcano (1, 1640) Historical	**1600-01=**
Saba Island (Red Sea)	Cone of Zubair, Jebel	0201-02=
Sabalan (Iran)	Stratovolcano (None) Holocene	**0302-002**
Sabale (Halmahera-Indonesia)	Caldera of Tidore	0608-061
Sabana Redonda (Costa Rica)	Cone of Poás	1405-04=

Name (Subregion)	Type (Eruptions, Most Recent) Status Relation to Named Volcano	Volcano Number
Sabancaya (Perú)	Stratovolcanoes (10, 2003) Historical	**1504-006**
Sabanda, Bukit (Sumatra)	Cone of Raja-Sabanda	....
Sabanetas, Las [Laguna Seca] (Nicaragua)	Maar of Pilas, Las	1404-08=
Sabangan (Mindanao-Philippines)	Dome of Apo	0701-03=
Sabatini Complex (Italy)	Stratovolcanoes (None) Pleistocene	....
Sabinosa (Canary Is)	Cinder cone of Hierro	1803-02-
Sabinyo (Africa-C)	Stratovolcano (None) Pleistocene	....
Sabober (Ethiopia)	Tuff ring of Fentale	0201-19=
Saboke, Doro (Lesser Sunda Is)	Unknown (None) Quaternary	....
Saboma (Admiralty Is-SW Pacific)	Crater of Baluan	0500-02-
Sabrana, La [Cerro Alegría] (El Salvador)	Cone of Tecapa	1403-08=
Sabu, Ol Doinyo (Africa-E)	Cone of Nyambeni Hills	0202-056
Sabyinyo (Africa-C)	Synonym of Sabinyo	....
Sacabaya (Bolivia)	Synonym of Tambo Quemado	1505-021
Sachiusu-dake (Kuril Is)	Synonym of Baransky	0900-08=
Sacrofano (Italy)	Caldera of Sabatini Complex	....
Saddle (New Ireland-SW Pacific)	Thermal feature of Ambitle	0504-02=
Saddle Butte (US-Oregon)	Volcanic field (None) Pleistocene	....
Saddle Hill (W Indies)	Dome of Nevis Peak	1600-04=
Saddle Island (Red Sea)	Cone of Zubair, Jebel	0201-02=
Saddle Mount (New Britain-SW Pac)	Lava dome (None) Post-Miocene	....
Saddle Mountain (US-Oregon)	Shield volcano of Sprague River Valley	....
Saddle Mountain (US-Oregon)	Cone of Three Fingered Jack	....
Saddle Point (Indian O.-S)	Cone of Heard	0304-01=
Sadier (China-E)	Synonym of Shatu	....
Sadiman (Africa-E)	Stratovolcano (None) Pleistocene?	....
Saefell (Iceland-S)	Tuff cone of Vestmannaeyjar	1702-01=
Saefell (Iceland-S)	Tuff ring of Vestmannaeyjar	1702-01=
Safont, Puig (Spain)	Cone of Olot Volc Field	0100-03-
Saga, Wolo (Lesser Sunda Is)	Crater of Inielika	0604-09=
Sagan (Russia-SE)	Cone of Azas Plateau	1002-07-
Saghegy (Hungary)	Cone of Kemenesalja	....
Sago (Sumatra)	Synonym of Melintang	....
Sagoatoa (Ecuador)	Stratovolcano (None) Pleistocene	....
Saguta Swamp [Suguta-Logkipi] (Africa-E)	Thermal feature of Barrier, The	0202-03=
Sahach (Kamchatka)	Synonym of Kuzheten	....
Sahand (Iran)	Stratovolcano (None) Holocene	**0302-001**
Saho Brani (Halmahera-Indonesia)	Crater of Dukono	0608-01=
Sahu (Halmahera-Indonesia)	Cone of Todoko-Ranu	0608-05=
Saing (Java)	Cone of Iyang-Argapura	0603-33=
Sainokawara Hot Springs (Honshu-Japan)	Thermal feature of Kusatsu-Shirane	0803-12=
Saint see St. (e.g. St. Helens)		
Saint-Hippolyte, Cratere de (France)	Maar of Chaîne des Puys	0100-02-
Sairecabur (Chile-N)	Stratovolcanoes (None) Holocene	**1505-091**
Sajaka (Aleutian Is)	Stratovolcano of Tanaga	1101-08-
Sajaka Two (Aleutian Is)	Cone of Tanaga	1101-08-
Sajama, Nevado del (Bolivia)	Stratovolcano (None) Pleistocene	....
Sajiki-yama (Honshu-Japan)	Dome of Eboshi	....
Sajiki-yama (Honshu-Japan)	Cone of Fuji	0803-03=

Name (Subregion)	Type (Eruptions, Most Recent) Status Relation to Named Volcano	Volcano Number
Saka (Africa-C)	Tuff cone of Fort Portal	0203-001
Sakar (New Guinea-NE of)	Stratovolcano (None) Holocene?	**0501-08=**
Sakarat, Kawah (Java)	Thermal feature of Kamojang, Kawah	....
Sakuchi (Ryukyu Is)	Caldera of Suwanose-jima	0802-03=
Sakura-jima (Kyushu-Japan)	Stratovolcano (47, 2010) Historical	**0802-08=**
Sakura-zima (Kyushu-Japan)	Synonym of Sakura-jima	0802-08=
Sala y Gómez (Chile-Is)	Shield volcano? (None) Pleistocene	....
Salaita (Africa-E)	Cone of Kilimanjaro	0202-15=
Salak (Java)	Stratovolcano (5, 1938) Historical	**0603-05=**
Salal Creek (Canada)	Synonym of Bridge River Cones	1200-17-
Salal Glacier (Canada)	Synonym of Bridge River Cones	1200-17-
Salal Glacier (Canada)	Cone of Bridge River Cones	1200-17-
Salar de Antofalla (Argentina)	Volcanic field Antofagasta de la Sierra	1505-18-
Salasi (Sumatra)	Synonym of Talang	0601-16=
Saleleloga (Samoa-SW Pacific)	Cone of Savai'i	0404-04=
Salgotarjan (Hungary)	Synonym of Nográd	....
Salgovar (Hungary)	Cone of Nográd	....
Salina (Italy)	Stratovolcanoes (None) Pleistocene	....
Salitre de Cerro, El (México)	Dome of Zitácuaro-Valle de Bravo	1401-061
Salt Lake (D'Entrecasteaux Is)	Thermal feature of Iamalele	0503-05=
Salt Lake (Hawaiian Is)	Tuff cone of Koolau	....
Salt Lake (Galápagos)	Crater of Santiago	1503-09=
Salt Pond Peninsula (W Indies)	Dome of Liamuiga	1600-03=
Salteberg (Germany)	Cone of East Eifel Volc Field	....
Salto del Corvo, Monte (Italy)	Cinder cone of Etna	0101-06=
Salto, Cerro el (México)	Cinder cone of Camargo Volc Field	....
Salton Buttes (US-California)	Lava domes (1, -6450) Hydration Rind	**1203-20-**
Salton Creek (US-California)	Vent of Pinto Basin-Salton Creek	....
Saltos, Montana de los (Canary Is)	Cone of Fuerteventura	1803-05-
Salty Dawg (Pacific-NE)	Thermal feature of Endeavour Ridge	1301-01-
Salvatierra (México)	Synonym of San Luis, Isla	1401-003
Sama (Africa-E)	Crater of Rungwe	0202-166
Samakkenupuri (Hokkaido-Japan)	Stratovolcano (None) Pleistocene	....
Samara, Montaña (Canary Is)	Fissure vent of Tenerife	1803-03-
Samarga Plateau [Nelma Plateau Volc Field]	Fissure vent of Sikhote-Alin	1002-01-
Samat, Mt. (Luzon-Philippines)	Cone of Mariveles	0703-081
Samau (Samoa-SW Pacific)	Cone of Savai'i	0404-04=
Sambe (Honshu-Japan)	Synonym of Sanbe	0803-002
Sambinongko (Java)	Dome of Tengger Caldera	0603-31=
Sambu, Ol Doinyo (Africa-E)	Cone of Chyulu Hills	0202-13=
Sambu, Oldonyo (Africa-E)	Cone of Meru	0202-16=
Sampaloc Lake (Luzon-Philippines)	Maar of San Pablo Volc Field	0703-06=
Sampaloc Warm Springs (Luzon-Philippines)	Thermal feature of Banahaw	0703-05=
Sampeanwani (Lesser Sunda Is)	Maar of Batur	0604-01=
Sampu Olkuo (Africa-E)	Cinder cone of Suswa	0202-11=
Samra as Safra (Arabia)	Tuff ring of Hutaymah, Harrat	....
San Agustín, Cerro (Bolivia)	Stratovolcano (None) Holocene?	....
San Alessandro (Volcano Is-Japan)	Synonym of Kita-Iwo-jima	0804-11=
San Alfonso (Ecuador)	Dome of Chachimbiro	1502-002

Dick Stoiber (Dartmouth College)

Sakura-jima volcano on the southern Japanese island of Kyushu entered a period of frequent but intermittent moderate explosive eruptions in October 1955 that has continued until the present. Ashfall from the active vent at Minami-dake has often disrupted life at Kagoshima, southern Kyushu's largest city, located just 7 km across the bay.

Name (Subregion)	Type (Eruptions, Most Recent) Status Relation to Named Volcano	Volcano Number
San Andrés, Cerro de (México)	Dome of Azufres, Los	....
San Andres, Montana de (Canary Is)	Cone of Fuerteventura	1803-05-
San Andrés, Sierra de (México)	Therm. feature Michoacán-Guanajuato	1401-06=
San Angelo, Monte (Italy)	Stratovolcano of Lipari	0101-042
San Antonio (Philippines-C)	Thermal feature of Biliran	0702-08=
San Antonio (Canary Is)	Cinder cone of La Palma	1803-01-
San Antonio (México)	Stratovolcano of Tacaná	1401-13=
San Antonio (Italy)	Dome of Vico-Cimino Complex	....
San Antonio Hot Springs (US-New Mexico)	Thermal feature of Valles Caldera	....
San Antonio I, Cerro (Guatemala)	Cinder cone of Santiago, Cerro	1402-15-
San Antonio Mountain (US-New Mexico)	Dome of Valles Caldera	....
San Antonio, Cerro (Nicaragua)	Cinder cone of Granada	1404-101
San Antonio, Cerro (México)	Shield volc. of Michoacán-Guanajuato	1401-06=
San Augustín-Isnos (Colombia)	Volcanic field (None) Quaternary	....
San Bartolo (Ecuador)	Stratovolcano of Mojanda	1502-005
San Bartolo (Italy)	Vent of Stromboli	0101-04=
San Bartolo (México)	Dome of Zitácuaro-Valle de Bravo	1401-061
San Bartolo, Cerro (Guatemala)	Cinder cone of Chingo	1402-17-

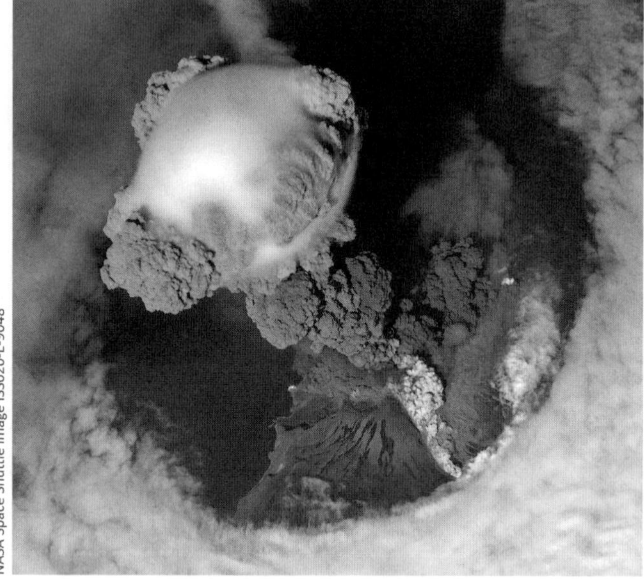

NASA Space Shuttle image ISS020-E-9048

This NASA Space Shuttle view on June 12, 2009 shows an eruption plume from **Sarychev Peak** that rose to 16-21 km altitude and pyroclastic flows that reached the sea and extended the shoreline during one of the largest historical eruptions in the Kuril Islands.

Name (Subregion)	Type (Eruptions, Most Recent) Status Relation to Named Volcano	Volcano Number
San Bartolo, Cerro (México)	Cinder cone of Southern Guadalajara	....
San Benedicto Island (México-Is)	Synonym of Bárcena	1401-02=
San Bernardino (US-Arizona)	Synonym of Geronimo	....
San Borja Volc Field (México)	Cinder cones (None) Holocene	**1401-007**
San Bras, Lagoa de (Azores)	Maar of Agua de Pau	1802-09=
San Carlos (El Salvador)	Thermal feature of Apaneca Range	1403-01=
San Carlos (Africa-W)	Shield volcano (None) Holocene	**0204-002**
San Carlos (US-Arizona)	Volcanic field (None) Pleistocene	....
San Carlos, Crateres de (Chile-C)	Cinder cone of Mocho-Choshuenco	1507-13=
San Cristobal (Luzon-Philippines)	Stratovolcano of Banahaw	0703-05=
San Cristóbal (Galápagos)	Shield volcano (None) Holocene	**1503-12-**
San Cristóbal (Nicaragua)	Stratovolcano (18, 2009) Historical	**1404-02=**
San Diego (El Salvador)	Volcanic field (None) Holocene	**1403-001**
San Diego Spring (Luzon-Philippines)	Thermal feature of Banahaw	0703-05=
San Félix (Chile-Is)	Shield volcano (None) Holocene	**1506-01=**
San Fernando (Nicaragua)	Cone of Zapatera	1404-111
San Fernando [Masaya] (Nicaragua)	Crater of Masaya	1404-10=
San Francisco (Chile-N)	Stratovolcano (None) Pleistocene	....
San Francisco (Guatemala)	Dome of Tecuamburro	1402-12=
San Francisco (Nicaragua)	Dome of Zapatera	1404-111
San Francisco (México)	Crater of Zitácuaro-Valle de Bravo	1401-061
San Francisco Peak (US-Arizona)	Cone of San Francisco Volc Field	....
San Francisco Volc Field (US-Ariz.)	Stratovolcanoes (None) Pleistocene	....
San Fransisco (Perú)	Synonym of Misti, El	1504-01=
San Gaspar, Cerro (Guatemala)	Cinder cone of Ixtepeque	1402-18-
San Gerónimo (México)	Maar of Michoacán-Guanajuato	1401-06=
San Giacomo (Italy)	Crater of Campi Flegrei	0101-01=
San Ignacio del Bosque, Lomas [El Bosque]	Dome of Rota	1404-06-
San Ignacio Volc Field (México)	Volcanic field (None) Pleistocene	....
San Ildefonso, Cerro (Nicaragua)	Cone of Lajas, Las	1404-133
San Isidro (México)	Cinder cone of Colima	1401-04=
San Isidro, Loma (Nicaragua)	Cone of San Cristóbal	1404-02=
San Jacinto [Santa Clara] (Nicaragua)	Stratovolcano of Telica	1404-04=
San Jacinto Viejo, Cerro (Nicaragua)	Synonym of San Jacinto, Cerro	....
San Jacinto, Cerro (El Salvador)	Dome of Ilopango	1403-06=
San Jacinto, Cerro (Nicaragua)	Stratovolcano (None) Pleistocene?	....
San Jacinto, Hervideros de (Nicaragua)	Thermal feature of Telica	1404-04=
San Joaquin (Africa-W)	Shield volcano (None) Holocene	**0204-003**
San Joaquin Jaripeo (México)	Shield volc. of Michoacán-Guanajuato	1401-06=

Name (Subregion)	Type (Eruptions, Most Recent) Status Relation to Named Volcano	Volcano Number
San Jorge (Ecuador)	Dome of Mojanda	1502-005
San Jorge (Azores)	Fissure vent (6, 1907) Historical	**1802-03=**
San Jorge, Cerro de (El Salvador)	Cone of San Diego	1403-001
San José (El Salvador)	Thermal feature of Apaneca Range	1403-01=
San José (Luzon-Philippines)	Thermal feature of Cagua	0703-09=
San José (Chile-C)	Stratovolcano (7, 1960) Historical	**1507-02=**
San Jose de Maipo (Chile-C)	Synonym of San José	1507-02=
San Juan (Canary Is)	Fissure vent of La Palma	1803-01-
San Juan (Nicaragua)	Crater of Masaya	1404-10=
San Juan (Hispaniola)	Cinder cones (None) Pleistocene	....
San Juan (México)	Stratovolcanoes (None) Pleistocene	....
San Juan (México)	Synonym of Sangangüey	1401-024
San Juan Cuecuelco, Cerro (México)	Cinder cone of Gloria, La	1401-097
San Juan de Amatitlán (Guatemala)	Synonym of Pacaya	1402-11=
San Juan, Cerro (Guatemala)	Cinder cone of Santiago, Cerro	1402-15-
San Juan, Loma (Nicaragua)	Stratovolcano of Cosigüina	1404-01=
San Lázaro, Cerro (El Salvador)	Dome of Apaneca Range	1403-01=
San Lorenzo (El Salvador)	Pit crater of Apastepeque Field	1403-071
San Lucas (Guatemala)	Synonym of Tolimán	1402-07=
San Lucas (México)	Cone of Zitácuaro-Valle de Bravo	1401-061
San Lucas, Loma (Nicaragua)	Cone of San Cristóbal	1404-02=
San Luis Atexcac [Laguna Atexcac] (México)	Maar of Serdán-Oriental	1401-092
San Luis el Alto (México)	Dome of Zitácuaro-Valle de Bravo	1401-061
San Luis, Cerro (US-New Mexico)	Dome of Valles Caldera	....
San Luis, Isla (México)	Tuff cone (None) Holocene	**1401-003**
San Marcelino (El Salvador)	Cinder cone of Santa Ana	1403-02=
San Marta, Volcán (México)	Synonym of San Martín Pajapan	....
San Martín (Canary Is)	Cinder cone of La Palma	1803-01-
San Martín (México)	Shield volcano (12, 1796) Historical	**1401-11=**
San Martín (México)	Cinder cone of San Quintín Volc Field	1401-002
San Martín Pajapan (México)	Stratovolcanoes (None) Pleistocene	....
San Martín Tuxtla (México)	Synonym of San Martín	1401-11=
San Martín, Cerro (Guatemala)	Cinder cone of Redondo, Cerro	....
San Martín, Cerro (México)	Stratovolc of Southern Guadalajara	....
San Martino (Italy)	Crater of Campi Flegrei	0101-01=
San Martino (Italy)	Dome of Campi Flegrei	0101-01=
San Martino, Isolotto di (Italy)	Dome of Campi Flegrei	0101-01=
San Miguel (Nicaragua)	Cinder cone of Negro, Cerro	1404-07=
San Miguel (El Salvador)	Stratovolcano (31, 2002) Historical	**1403-10=**
San Miguel, Cerro (México)	Vent of Primavera, Sierra la	....
San Miguel, Cerro (Costa Rica)	Lava dome (None) Pleistocene	....
San Nicola, Monte (Italy)	Cinder cone of Etna	0101-06=
San Nicolás (México)	Cone of Chichinautzin	1401-08=
San Nicolás (México)	Maar of Michoacán-Guanajuato	1401-06=
San Pablo (Chile-N)	Twin volcano of San Pedro	1505-07=
San Pablo Volc Field (Philippines)	Stratovolcano (1, 1350) Anthropology	**0703-06=**
San Pedro (Nicaragua)	Crater of Masaya	1404-10=
San Pedro (Chile-N)	Stratovolcanoes (6, 1960) Historical	**1505-07=**
San Pedro (Guatemala)	Stratovolcano (None) Quaternary	....
San Pedro (México)	Caldera (None) Pleistocene	....
San Pedro (Chile-C)	Stratovolcano of San Pedro-Pellado	1507-062
San Pedro, Laguna de (Guatemala)	Maar of Suchitán	1402-16-
San Pedro, Lomas de (El Salvador)	Dome of Ilopango	1403-06=
San Pedro-Pellado (Chile-C)	Stratovolcanoes (None) Holocene	**1507-062**
San Pedro-Tatara (Chile-C)	Synonym of San Pedro-Pellado	1507-062
San Quintín Volc Field (México)	Cinder cones (None) Holocene?	**1401-002**
San Rafael (México)	Caldera of Tacaná	1401-13=
San Rafael, Cerro (Nicaragua)	Cinder cone of Estelí	1404-131
San Rafael, Cerro (Guatemala)	Cinder cone of Moyuta	1402-13-
San Román, Volcán (Chile-N)	Cinder cone of Copiapó	1505-14-
San Roque (Colombia)	Pyroclastic cone of Unnamed	....
San Roque, Cerro (Costa Rica)	Dome of Rincón de la Vieja	1405-02=
San Roque, Cerro (Bolivia)	Cone (None) Post-Miocene	....
San Salvador (El Salvador)	Stratovolcano (6, 1917) Historical	**1403-05=**
San Salvador (Galápagos)	Synonym of Santiago	1503-09=
San Sebastián (El Salvador)	Cone of Masahuat Volc Field	....
San Sebastián Volc Field (México)	Cinder cones (None) Pleistocene	....
San Sebastián, Cerro de (El Salvador)	Cinder cone of Apastepeque Field	1403-071
San Valentino (Italy)	Dome of Vico-Cimino Complex	....
San Venanzo (Italy)	Maar (None) Pleistocene	....
San Vicente (Luzon-Philippines)	Dome of Labo	....
San Vicente (Costa Rica)	Dome of Rincón de la Vieja	1405-02=
San Vicente (El Salvador)	Stratovolcano (None) Holocene	**1403-07=**
San Vicente Spring (Luzon-Philippines)	Thermal feature of Banahaw	0703-05=
San Vicente, Ausoles de [Agua Agria]	Thermal feature of San Vicente	1403-07=
San Vito (Italy)	Vent of Pantelleria	0101-071
Sana'a Volc Field (Arabia-S)	Synonym of Arhab, Harra of	0301-09-
Sana'a-Amran Volc Field (Arabia-S)	Synonym of Arhab, Harra of	0301-09-
Sanagay (Ecuador)	Synonym of Sangay	1502-09=
Sanambo, Cerro (México)	Shield volc. of Michoacán-Guanajuato	1401-06=
Sanaroa Island (D'Entrecasteaux Is)	Cone of Dawson Strait Group	0503-06=
Sanbangsan (Korea)	Dome of Halla	1006-04-
Sanbe (Honshu-Japan)	Stratovolcano (3, 650) Radiocarbon	**0803-002**
Sanbonyari (Honshu-Japan)	Stratovolcano of Nasu	0803-15=
Sand Butte (US-Oregon)	Cone of Newberry	1202-11-
Sand Mountain Cones (US-Oregon)	Cinder cone of Sand Mountain Field	1202-04-
Sand Mountain Field (US-Oregon)	Cinder cones (5, 70) Radiocarbon	**1202-04-**
Sandawa (Mindanao-Philippines)	Synonym of Apo	0701-03=
Sandey (Iceland-SW)	Tuff cone of Hengill	1701-05=
Sandfell (Iceland-W)	Cone of Snaefellsjökull	1700-01=
Sandfellsgigir (Iceland-SW)	Crater Row of Hengill	1701-05=
Sandfellshaed (Iceland-SW)	Shield volcano of Reykjanes	1701-02=
Sandfellsklofagigir (Iceland-SW)	Crater Row of Krísuvík	1701-03=
Sandsea (Java)	Caldera of Tengger Caldera	0603-31=

Name (Subregion)	Type (Eruptions, Most Recent) Status / Relation to Named Volcano	Volcano Number
Sandy Point Hill (W Indies)	Dome of Liamuiga	1600-03=
Sanford (Alaska-E)	Shield volcano (None) Holocene?	**1105-01-**
Sanford, Mt. (Canada)	Cone of Atlin Volc Field	1200-03-
Sangai (Ecuador)	Synonym of Sangay	1502-09=
Sangangüey (México)	Stratovolcano (Uncertain) Holocene	**1401-024**
Sangay (Ecuador)	Stratovolcano (3, 2010) Historical	**1502-09=**
Sangay (Luzon-Philippines)	Unknown (None) Pleistocene	....
Sangean Api (Lesser Sunda Is)	Synonym of Sangeang Api	0604-05=
Sangeang Api (Lesser Sunda Is)	Complex volcano (18, 1999) Historical	**0604-05=**
Sangga Rudang, Dolok (Sumatra)	Dome of Lubukraya	0601-111
Sanggabuana (Java)	Stratovolcano (None) Quaternary	....
Sangiang Buruan (Java)	Crater of Guntur	0603-13=
Sangiang Djarian [Sangiang Jarian] (Java)	Crater of Guntur	0603-13=
Sangiang Jarian (Java)	Crater of Guntur	0603-13=
Sangiran (Java)	Crater of Lawu	0603-26=
Sanguil (Sanguili) (Mindanao-Philippines)	Synonym of Balut	0701-01=
Sangula (Africa-E)	Dome of SW Usangu Basin	0202-163
Sangumburi (Korea)	Cone of Halla	1006-04-
Sanjianshan [Bijiashan] (China-E)	Cone of Wudalianchi	1005-03-
Sanjiaolongwan (China-E)	Maar of Longgang Group	1005-05-
Sankakuten-yama [Noike] (Ryukyu Is)	Stratovolcano of Kuchinoerabu-jima	0802-05=
Sankaku-yama (Honshu-Japan)	Cone of Nyuto-Takakura	....
Sannak (Aleutian Is)	Synonym of Isanotski	1101-37-
Sanno-Boshi (Honshu-Japan)	Dome of Omanago Group	0803-142
Sannohara-Kita (Honshu-Japan)	Cone of Izu-Tobu	0803-01=
Sanno-ike (Honshu-Japan)	Crater of On-take	0803-04=
Sannomegata (Honshu-Japan)	Maar of Megata	0803-262
Sannotake-Ninotake (Kyushu-Japan)	Stratovolcano of Kinpo	....
Sano, Wai (Lesser Sunda Is)	Caldera (None) Holocene	**0604-06=**
Sanpokojin-san (Honshu-Japan)	Stratovolcano of Zao	0803-19=
Sans Nom (W Indies)	Dome of Pelée	1600-12=
Sans Toucher (W Indies)	Stratovolcano of Axial Chain	....
Sanshichi-yama (Izu Is-Japan)	Fissure vent of Miyake-jima	0804-04=
Sansiquismunde [Saquicismunde] (México)	Thermal feature of Púlpito, Punta	....
Santa Ana (México)	Synonym of Aguajito, El	....
Santa Ana (El Salvador)	Stratovolcano (12, 2005) Historical	**1403-02=**
Santa Angelo (Italy)	Dome of Ischia	0101-03=
Santa Angelo, Monte (Italy)	Tuff cone of Sabatini Complex	....
Santa Barbara (Ecuador)	Dome of Cotopaxi	1502-05=
Santa Barbara (Azores)	Stratovolcano of Terceira	1802-05=
Santa Catalina, Caldera de (Canary Is)	Crater of Lanzarote	1803-06-
Santa Catarina Mita (Guatemala)	Synonym of Suchitán	1402-16-
Santa Clara (México)	Synonym of Pinacate	1401-001
Santa Clara (México)	Shield volcano of Pinacate	1401-001
Santa Clara (US-Utah)	Volcanic field (None) Holocene?	**1207-01-**
Santa Clara (Nicaragua)	Stratovolcano of Telica	1404-04=
Santa Clara [Casita] (Nicaragua)	Stratovolcano of San Cristóbal	1404-02=
Santa Clara, Cerrito de (El Salvador)	Cinder cone of Apastepeque Field	1403-071
Santa Croce, Monte (Italy)	Dome of Roccamonfina	....
Santa Cruz (Ecuador)	Stratovolcano (None) Pleistocene	....
Santa Cruz (Galápagos)	Shield volcano (None) Holocene	**1503-091**
Santa Elena (El Salvador)	Cone of Usulután	1403-081
Santa Elena, Cerrito de (Guatemala)	Cinder cone of Cuilapa-Barbarena	1402-111
Santa Elena, Cerro (Honduras)	Shield volcano of Izopo, Montaña de	....
Santa Elena, Cerro (Guatemala)	Cinder cone of Redondo, Cerro	....
Santa Fe (Galápagos)	Shield volcano (None) Pleist.-Fumarolic	....
Santa Gertrudis, Volcán (Chile-C)	Cone of Chillán, Nevados de	1507-07=
Santa Isabel (Africa-W)	Shield volcano (3, 1923) Historical	**0204-004**
Santa Isabel (Colombia)	Shield volcano (4, -850) Radiocarbon	**1501-021**
Santa Julia, Sierra (Nicaragua)	Dome of Zapatera	1404-111
Santa Luce (Italy)	Cone of Vulsini	0101-003
Santa Margarida, Volcà (Spain)	Cone of Olot Volc Field	0100-03-
Santa Maria (Galápagos)	Synonym of Floreana	....
Santa Maria (Vanuatu-SW Pacific)	Synonym of Gaua	0507-02=
Santa María (Costa Rica)	Stratovolcano of Miravalles	1405-03=
Santa María (Costa Rica)	Cone of Rincón de la Vieja	1405-02=
Santa María (Guatemala)	Stratovolcano (3, 2010) Historical	**1402-03=**
Santa María (México)	Cone of Southern Guadalajara	....
Santa María del Oro (México)	Maar (None) Pleistocene	....
Santa Maria Di Sala (Italy)	Cone of Vulsini	0101-003
Santa María, Volcán (Argentina)	Cone of Payún Matru	1507-066
Santa Martha (México)	Stratovolcano of San Martín Pajapan	....
Santa Matilde (Nicaragua)	Cinder cone of Pilas, Las	1404-08=
Santa Michele (Italy)	Crater of Ischia	0101-03=
Santa Pancrazio (Italy)	Dome of Ischia	0101-03=
Santa Rita, Cerro (El Salvador)	Dome of Apastepeque Field	1403-071
Santa Rita, Cerro (El Salvador)	Cinder cone of Cinotepeque, Cerro	1403-051
Santa Rita, Mt. (Luzon-Philippines)	Cone of Natib	0703-082
Santa Rosa (Perú)	Cinder cone of Andahua-Orcopampa	1504-004
Santa Rosa (México)	Maar of Michoacán-Guanajuato	1401-06=
Santa Rosa (Colombia)	Shield volcano (None) Pleistocene	....
Santa Rosa Hill (Indian O.-S)	Cone of Marion Island	0304-07-
Santa Rosa, Cerro (US-New Mexico)	Dome of Valles Caldera	....
Santa Rosalina (Philippines-C)	Thermal feature of Biliran	0702-08=
Santa Teresa (México)	Cinder cone of Michoacán-Guanajuato	1401-06=
Santa Teresa, Monte (Italy)	Crater of Campi Flegrei	0101-01=
Santa Ursula (El Salvador)	Pit crater of Apastepeque Field	1403-071
Santabárbara Mortal de la Naturalez	Synonym of Irazú	1405-06=
Sant'angelo (Italy)	Dome of Ischia	0101-03=
Sant'Angelo, Monte (Italy)	Cone of Campi Flegrei	0101-01=
Santano, Alto de (Colombia)	Dome of Ruiz, Nevado del	1501-02=
Sant'Elmo, Monte (Italy)	Cone of Pantelleria	0101-071
Santiago (Nicaragua)	Crater of Masaya	1404-10=
Santiago (Galápagos)	Shield volcano (3, 1906) Historical	**1503-09=**
Santiago (Canary Is)	Fissure vent of Tenerife	1803-03-
Santiago [Santiaguito] (Guatemala)	Dome of Santa María	1402-03=
Santiago del Monte (México)	Dome of Zitácuaro-Valle de Bravo	1401-061
Santiago Volc Field, Valle de (México)	Maar of Michoacán-Guanajuato	1401-06=
Santiago, Cerro (El Salvador)	Cinder cone of Cinotepeque, Cerro	1403-051
Santiago, Cerro (Guatemala)	Volcanic field (None) Holocene	**1402-15-**
Santiago, Cerro el (México)	Cone of Chichinautzin	1401-08=
Santiago, El Cerro de (México)	Dome of Chichinautzin	1401-08=
Santiago, Lagoa de (Azores)	Pumice ring of Sete Cidades	1802-08=
Santiaguito (Guatemala)	Dome of Santa María	1402-03=
Santidad, Montana de (Canary Is)	Cone of Gran Canaria	1803-04-
Santo Antao (Cape Verde Is)	Stratovolcano (None) Pleistocene	....
Santo Domingo Volc Field (México)	Maars (None) Pleistocene	....
Santo Domingo, Cerro (Chile-N)	Dome of Guayaques	1505-093
Santo Domingo, El (México)	Maar of Santo Domingo Volc Field	....
Santo Tomas (Luzon-Philippines)	Stratovolcano (None) Uncertain	**0703-086**
Santo Tomás (Guatemala)	Stratovolcanoes (None) Pleist.-Fumarolic	....
Santo Tomás - Zunil (Guatemala)	Synonym of Santo Tomás	....
Santo Tomas, Volcan (Galápagos)	Synonym of Negra, Sierra	1503-05=
Santontón (México)	Dome of Mispía	....
Santop, Mt. (Vanuatu-SW Pacific)	Cone of William, Mt.	....
Santorini (Greece)	Shield volcanoes (12, 1950) Historical	**0102-04=**
Sao Bonifacio, Pico (Atlantic-C)	Dome of Trindade	1805-051
Sao Jorge (Azores)	Synonym of San Jorge	1802-03=
Sao Nicolau (Cape Verde Is)	Stratovolcano (None) Pleistocene	....
Sao Roque Peidade (Azores)	Fissure vent of Pico	1802-02=
Sao Thome (Africa-W)	Synonym of Sao Tome	0204-001
Sao Tiago, Lagoa de [Lagoa Santiago]	Pumice ring of Sete Cidades	1802-08=
Sao Tome (Africa-W)	Shield volcano (None) Holocene?	**0204-001**
Sao Vicente (Cape Verde Is)	Stratovolcano (None) Holocene	**1804-03-**
Sapajos, Cerro (Bolivia)	Stratovolcano (None) Post-Miocene	....
Sapaleri (Chile-N)	Synonym of Zapaleri, Cerro	....
Sapichu (México)	Cinder cone of Michoacán-Guanajuato	1401-06=
Sapien, Cerro (México)	Cinder cone of Michoacán-Guanajuato	1401-06=
Sap'o [Bora] (Ethiopia)	Pumice cone of Bora-Bericcio	0201-24-
Sapporo (Hokkaido-Japan)	Shield volcano (None) Pleistocene	....
Saquicismunde (México)	Thermal feature of Púlpito, Punta	....
Saquigua, Loma (Ecuador)	Cone of Santa Cruz	....
Sara Sara (Perú)	Stratovolcano (None) Holocene	**1504-002**
Sarabwe (Africa-E)	Cone of Kieyo	0202-17=
Saraceno, Monte (Italy)	Cone of Vulcano	0101-05=
Sarajukh (Iran)	Dome of Bijar Volc Field	....
Sarangan (Java)	Crater of Lawu	0603-26=
Sarangani (Mindanao-Philippines)	Synonym of Balut	0701-01=
Sarangsong (Sulawesi-Indonesia)	Thermal feature of Tondano Caldera	0606-07-
Sari Gol (Turkey)	Crater of Erciyes Dagi	0103-01=
Saria (Kamchatka)	Synonym of Avachinsky	1000-10=
Sarichef (Aleutian Is)	Stratovolcano of Atka	1101-16-
Saridag (Turkey)	Cone of Erciyes Dagi	0103-01=
Sarigan (Mariana Is-C Pacific)	Stratovolcano (None) Holocene	**0804-192**
Sarik-Gajah (Sumatra)	Pyroclastic cones (None) Holocene?	**0601-131**
Sarnicheff (Kuril Is)	Synonym of Sarychev Peak	0900-24=

Rick Wunderman (Smithsonian)

Lagoa Verde (Green Lake) in the foreground and Lagoa Azul (Blue Lake) fill the 5-km-wide summit caldera of Sete Cidades volcano on Sao Miguel Island in the Azores. A nearly circular ring of six Holocene pyroclastic cones occupies the caldera floor. **Sete Cidades** is one of the most active Azorean volcanoes, with historical eruptions dating back to the 15th century.

Name (Subregion)	Type (Eruptions, Most Recent) Status / Relation to Named Volcano	Volcano Number
Sarnoso (Chile-C)	Stratovolcano of Antillanca Group	1507-153
Sarskrateret (Atlantic-N-Jan Mayen)	Cone of Jan Mayen	1706-01=
Sartania (Italy)	Crater of Campi Flegrei	0101-01=
Saruana (Honshu-Japan)	Crater of Chokai	0803-22=
Saruha-yama (Kyushu-Japan)	Dome of Unzen	0802-10=
Sarukura-yama (Honshu-Japan)	Stratovolcano of Zao	0803-19=
Sarutschew [Sarichef] (Aleutian Is)	Stratovolcano of Atka	1101-16-
Sarutschew-Sergief (Aleutian Is)	Synonym of Sergief	1101-15-
Sarvaly (Hungary)	Shield volcano of Balaton Highland	....
Sarychev Peak (Kuril Is)	Stratovolcano (15, 2009) Historical	**0900-24=**
Sarytchev [Sarichef] (Aleutian Is)	Stratovolcano of Atka	1101-16-
Sasamori-yama (Honshu-Japan)	Cone of Nyuto-Takakura	....

Name (Subregion)	Type (Eruptions, Most Recent) Status Relation to Named Volcano	Volcano Number
Sashiusu-dake (Kuril Is)	Synonym of Baransky	0900-08=
Saso, Volcán (Chile-C)	Cone of Maule, Laguna del	1507-061
Sasquatch (Pacific-NE)	Thermal feature of Endeavour Ridge	1301-01-
Sastres, Las (Nicaragua)	Cinder cone of Masaya	1404-10=
Sat Agomara (Ethiopia)	Synonym of Erta Ale	0201-08=
Satah Mountain (Canada)	Volcanic field (None) Holocene	**1200-13-**
Satak (Java)	Synonym of Salak	0603-05=
Satélite (Nicaragua)	Crater of Nejapa-Miraflores	1404-092
Sa-ti-erh (China-E)	Synonym of Shatu	....
Satormal (Hungary)	Cone of Balaton Highland	....
Satsuma Maru-yama (Kyushu-Japan)	Lava dome (None) Pleistocene	....
Satsuma-Fuji [Kaimon] (Kyushu-Japan)	Stratovolcano of Ibusuki Volc Field	0802-07=
Satsuma-Iwo-jima (Ryukyu Is)	Synonym of Kikai	0802-06=
Sattomonai (Hokkaido-Japan)	Cone of Birao	....
Satuma-Huzi [Kaimon] (Kyushu-Japan)	Stratovolcano of Ibusuki Volc Field	0802-07=
Sauce, El (El Salvador)	Thermal feature of Apaneca Range	1403-01=
Saucer, the (Canada)	Cone of Edziza	1200-06-
Sauda, Harra es- (Arabia-S)	Synonym of Sawâd, Harra es-	0301-16-
Sa'umane (Samoa-SW Pacific)	Cone of Ta'u	0404-001
Saunders Island Volcano (Antarctica)	Synonym of Michael	1900-09=
Saut d'Eau (Hispaniola)	Synonym of Vigie, Morne la	....
Saut-Nagodang (Sumatra)	Unknown (None) Post-Miocene	....
Sauvetage, Piton (Indian O.-W)	Cinder cone of Fournaise, Piton de la	0303-02=
Savai'i (Samoa-SW Pacific)	Shield volcano (12, 1911) Historical	**0404-04=**
Savai'i, Tafua (Samoa-SW Pacific)	Tuff cone of Savai'i	0404-04=
Savalan (Iran)	Synonym of Sabalan	0302-002
Savan (Kamchatka)	Shield volcano (None) Pleistocene	....
Savana, Volcán de la [Cuyotepe] (El Salv.)	Cone of Apaneca Range	1403-01=
Savich (Kamchatka)	Stratovolcano of Kikhpinych	1000-18=
Savigan (Mariana Is-C Pacific)	Synonym of Sarigan	0804-192
Savo (Solomon Is-SW Pacific)	Stratovolcano (3, 1847) Historical	**0505-07=**
Savonovski River Cluster (Alaska)	Stratovolcanoes (None) Pleistocene	....
Sawâd, Harra es- (Arabia-S)	Volcanic field (1, 1253) Historical	**0301-16-**
Sawadowsky (Antarctica)	Synonym of Zavodovski	1900-13=
Sawal (Java)	Stratovolcano (None) Quaternary	....
Sawan-Chisappu (Hokkaido-Japan)	Dome of Kutcharo	0805-08=
Sawan-Tisappu [Sawan-Chisappu] (Japan)	Dome of Kutcharo	0805-08=
Sawara-dake (Hokkaido-Japan)	Synonym of Komaga-take	0805-02=
Sawara-yama (Honshu-Japan)	Cone of Fuji	0803-03=
Sawtooth Mountain (US-Oregon)	Shield volcano of Cowhorn Mountain	....
Sawtooth Mountain (US-Washington)	Shield volcano of Indian Heaven	1201-07-
Saxholar (Iceland-W)	Cone of Snaefellsjökull	1700-01=
Sayhua, Cerro (Perú)	Cinder cone of Andahua-Orcopampa	1504-004
Scara (Azores)	Pit crater of Sete Cidades	1802-08=
Scarlet Hill (Indian O.-S)	Cone of Heard	0304-01=
Scarrupo (Italy)	Cone of Ischia	0101-03=
Scauri, Cuddia di (Italy)	Shield volcano of Pantelleria	0101-071
Scenery, Mount (W Indies)	Dome of Saba	1600-01=
Schalkenmehren (Germany)	Maar of West Eifel Volc Field	0100-01-

KVERT

The summit of the isolated massif of **Shiveluch** volcano in Kamchatka is truncated by a broad 9-km-wide, late-Pleistocene horseshoe-shaped caldera. Frequent collapse of lava-dome complexes has produced numerous large debris avalanches, most recently in 1964.

Name (Subregion)	Type (Eruptions, Most Recent) Status Relation to Named Volcano	Volcano Number
Schank, Mt. (Australia)	Cone of Newer Volcanics Prov	0509-01-
Schapinskaia Sopka (Kamchatka)	Synonym of Kizimen	1000-23=
Schildkrote [Skjaldbaka] (Iceland-NE)	Shield volcano of Fremrinamur	1703-07=
Schinopi (Greece)	Thermal feature of Milos	0102-03=
Schischel (Kamchatka)	Synonym of Shishel	1000-58-
Schiwelutsch (Kamchatka)	Synonym of Shiveluch	1000-27=
Schleuther, Mount (New Britain-SW Pac)	Cone of Garua Harbour	0502-06=
Schmidt (Kamchatka)	Shield volcano (None) Holocene	**1000-201**
Schonchin Butte (US-California)	Cinder cone of Medicine Lake	1203-02-
Schreibers Meadow Cone (US-Washington)	Cinder cone of Baker	1201-01=
Schtjubelja [Stubel] (Kamchatka)	Maar of Ksudach	1000-05=
Schtschapinskij (Kamchatka)	Synonym of Kizimen	1000-23=
Schuberts Fairy (New Zealand)	Former crater of White Island	0401-04=
Schuvelutsch (Kamchatka)	Synonym of Shiveluch	1000-27=
Sciara (Italy)	Vent of Stromboli	0101-04=
Scircca [Giulia-Ferdinandeo] (Italy)	Submarine vent C. Flegrei Mar Sicilia	0101-07=
Sciuvechi, Cuddia (Italy)	Shield volcano of Pantelleria	0101-071
Scott (Atlantic-N-Jan Mayen)	Cone of Jan Mayen	1706-01=
Scott Cone (Antarctica)	Cone of Buckle Island	1900-01=
Scott Mountain (US-Oregon)	Shield volcano (None) Pleistocene	....
Scott, Mount (US-Oregon)	Cone of Boring Lava	....
Scott, Mt. (US-Oregon)	Stratovolcano of Crater Lake	1202-16-
Scotts Head (W Indies)	Dome of Plat Pays, Morne	1600-11=
Scout Hill (US-Oregon)	Cone of Crater Lake	1202-16-
Se, Pico da (Azores)	Stratovolcano of Flores	1802-001
Seal Nunataks Group (Antarctica)	Pyroclastic cones (Uncertain)	**1900-05=**
Sealandia Bank (Mariana Is-C Pacific)	Synonym of Zealandia Bank	0804-191
Seamount X (Mariana Is-C Pacific)	Submarine volcano (None) Fumarolic	**0804-23-**
Seara Cerrado de Ladeira (Azores)	Pumice cone of Sete Cidades	1802-08=
Sebain, Djebel (Red Sea)	Synonym of Tair, Jebel at	0201-01=
Seca, Caldeira (Azores)	Crater of Flores	1802-001
Seca, Caldeira (Azores)	Pumice ring of Sete Cidades	1802-08=
Seca, Laguna (El Salvador)	Pit crater of Apastepeque Field	1403-071
Seca, Laguna (Nicaragua)	Maar of Pilas, Las	1404-08=
Seca, Laguna (Nicaragua)	Crater of San Cristóbal	1404-02=
Seca, Laguna (El Salvador)	Pit crater of Santa Ana	1403-02=
Secca dei Pesci (Italy)	Dome of Panarea	0101-041
Secca D'ischia (Italy)	Cone of Ischia	0101-03=
Seco, Cerro (US-New Mexico)	Dome of Valles Caldera	....
Second Canyon (Canada)	Cone of Iskut-Unuk River Cones	1200-09-
Second Crater (Antarctica)	Crater of Hut Point Peninsula	....
Sedaeng (Java)	Dome of Tengger Caldera	0603-31=
Sedakeling (Java)	Stratovolcano (None) Quaternary	....
Sedanka Dol (Kamchatka)	Synonym of Sedankinsky	1000-52-
Sedankinsky (Kamchatka)	Shield volcano (1, -7050) Radiocarbon	**1000-52-**
Sedlo (Kamchatka)	Fissure vent of Kliuchevskoi	1000-26=
Seemalik Butte (Alaska-W)	Cone of Nunivak Island	1104-02-
Seeng, Kawah (Java)	Thermal feature of Wayang-Windu	0603-08=
Segara Anak (Lesser Sunda Is)	Caldera of Rinjani	0604-03=
Segara Munjak (Lesser Sunda Is)	Crater of Rinjani	0604-03=
Segara Muntjar [Segara Munjar] (Indonesia)	Crater of Rinjani	0604-03=
Segarawedi Kedul (Java)	Crater of Tengger Caldera	0603-31=
Segarawedi Kidul [Segarawedi Kedul] (Java)	Crater of Tengger Caldera	0603-31=
Segarawedi Lor (Java)	Crater of Tengger Caldera	0603-31=
Segehiki (Honshu-Japan)	Vent of Izu-Tobu	0803-01=
Segererua Plateau (Africa-E)	Pyroclastic cones (None) Holocene	**0202-05-**
Segoro Bandjaran [Segoro Banjaran] (Java)	Crater of Sundoro	0603-21=
Segoro Banjaran (Java)	Crater of Sundoro	0603-21=
Segoro Wedi (Java)	Crater of Sundoro	0603-21=
Seguam (Aleutian Is)	Stratovolcanoes (11, 1993) Historical	**1101-18-**
Segula (Aleutian Is)	Stratovolcano (None) Holocene	**1101-03-**
Sehittepe (Turkey)	Dome of Süphan Dagi	0103-021
Sekiguchi Group (Honshu-Japan)	Crater of Izu-Tobu	0803-01=
Sekiguchigawa-Joryu (Honshu-Japan)	Vent of Izu-Tobu	0803-01=
Sekincau Belirang (Sumatra)	Calderas (None) Fumarolic	**0601-26=**
Sekintjau Belirang (Sumatra)	Synonym of Sekincau Belirang	0601-26=
Sekison-zan (Honshu-Japan)	Dome of Asama	0803-11=
Sekita (Honshu-Japan)	Stratovolcano? (None) Pleistocene	....
Sela (Java)	Crater of Gede	0603-06=
Selawajan (Sumatra)	Synonym of Seulawah Agam	0601-02=
Selawajanten (Selawajanten) (Sumatra)	Synonym of Seulawah Agam	0601-02=
Selawik Hills (Alaska-W)	Cinder cones (None) Pleistocene	....
Selendi (Turkey)	Unknown (None) Quaternary	....
Selholl North (Iceland-SW)	Crater Row of Grímsnes	1701-06=
Selholl South (Iceland-SW)	Crater of Grímsnes	1701-06=
Selhraunsgigir (Iceland-SW)	Crater Row of Krísuvík	1701-03=
Selimkartini (Turkey)	Cone of Erciyes Dagi	0103-01=
Sella [Saddle Island] (Red Sea)	Cone of Zubair, Jebel	0201-02=
Sella, Monti (Italy)	Cinder cone of Etna	0101-06=
Sellandafjall (Iceland-NE)	Tuya (None) Pleistocene	....
Sellota (Bolivia)	Synonym of Sillota	....
Selokaki (Java)	Stratovolcano (None) Quaternary	....
Selsundshraun North (Iceland-S)	Fissure vent of Hekla	1702-07=
Selsundshraun South (Iceland-S)	Fissure vent of Hekla	1702-07=
Selva Del Lamone (Italy)	Cone of Vulsini	0101-003
Selva del Napolitano (Italy)	Dome of Ischia	0101-03=
Selvogsheidi (Iceland-SW)	Shield volcano of Hengill	1701-05=
Sembrano, Mt. (Luzon-Philippines)	Stratovolcano of Laguna Caldera	0703-08=
Sembuang, Gunung (Sumatra)	Explosion crater (None) Pleistocene	....
Sembung, Gunung (Java)	Cone of Slamet	0603-18=
Semeroe (Java)	Synonym of Semeru	0603-30=
Semeru (Java)	Cone of Iyang-Argapura	0603-33=
Semeru (Java)	Crater of Iyang-Argapura	0603-33=
Semeru (Java)	Stratovolcano (58, 2010) Historical	**0603-30=**
Semi Crater (US-California)	Crater of Medicine Lake	1203-02-
Seminung, Gunung (Sumatra)	Stratovolcano of Ranau	0601-251
Semisopochnoi (Aleutian Is)	Stratovolcano (2, 1987) Historical	**1101-06-**
Semkarok (Kamchatka)	Dome of Shiveluch	1000-27=
Semongkrong, Gunung (Java)	Cone of Tengger Caldera	0603-31=
Semonte, Mt. (Italy)	Cone of Vulsini	0101-003
Sempoe (Sulawesi-Indonesia)	Synonym of Sempu	0606-04=
Sempu (Sulawesi-Indonesia)	Caldera (Uncertain) Fumarolic	**0606-04=**
Sendai (Kyushu-Japan)	Pyroclastic cone (None) Pleistocene	....
Senda-yama (Kyushu-Japan)	Dome of Ibusuki Volc Field	0802-07=
Sendoro (Java)	Synonym of Sundoro	0603-21=
Senga, Monte (Italy)	Cone of Campi Flegrei	0101-01=
Sengereti (Africa-E)	Cone of Kieyo	0202-17=
Sengoku (Honshu-Japan)	Lava domes (None) Pleistocene	....
Sengoku-dake (Honshu-Japan)	Dome of Sengoku	....
Senhora, Pica da (Azores)	Cone of Furnas	1802-10=

Name (Subregion)	Type (Eruptions, Most Recent) Status / Relation to Named Volcano	Volcano Number
Sennin-zan (Honshu-Japan)	Synonym of Fuji	0803-03=
Sensumori (Honshu-Japan)	Dome of Chokai	0803-22=
Sentinel Plain (US-Arizona)	Volcanic field (None) Pleistocene	....
Sentinel Rock (US-Oregon)	Stratovolcano of Crater Lake	1202-16-
Sentinel, The (US-Idaho)	Cinder cone of Craters of the Moon	1204-02-
Sen-yama (Honshu-Japan)	Pyroclastic cone of Oetaka-yama	....
Seonginbong (Korea)	Synonym of Ulreung	1006-03-
Seoul-wonson (Korea)	Synonym of Ch'uga-ryong	1006-02-
Sepanas (Sumatra)	Crater of Lumut Balai, Bukit	0601-24=
Sepultura (Argentina)	Pyrocl. cone Northern Mendoza Field	....
Seraja (Lesser Sunda Is)	Unknown (None) Quaternary	....
Serangani (Serangano) (Philippines)	Synonym of Balut	0701-01=
Serawerna (Banda Sea)	Synonym of Teon	0605-05=
Serdán-Oriental (México)	Tuff cones (None) Holocene	**1401-092**
Serdtze Alaida (Kamchatka)	Dome of Kurile Lake	1000-023
Sereh, Gunung (Lesser Sunda Is)	Synonym of Sirung	0604-27=
Seret Berapi (Sumatra)	Synonym of Sorikmarapi	0601-12=
Seretmat (Vanuatu-SW Pacific)	Synonym of Suretamatai	0507-01=
Serga (Kamchatka)	Cinder cone of Tolbachik	1000-24=
Sergeeva (Kamchatka)	Shield volcano of Bely	1000-64-
Sergein (Africa-N)	Cone of Bayuda Volc Field	0205-06-
Sergief (Aleutian Is)	Stratovolcano (None) Uncertain	**1101-15-**
Serguejeyski (Aleutian Is)	Synonym of Sergief	1101-15-
Seroea (Banda Sea)	Synonym of Serua	0605-07=
Serpovidny (Kamchatka)	Cinder cone of Kostakan	1000-122
Serra do Moriao [Guilherme Moniz] (Azores)	Stratovolcano of Terceira	1802-05=
Serra Giannicola Grande (Italy)	Cinder cone of Etna	0101-06=
Serra Gorda (Azores)	Cone of Picos Volc System	1802-081
Serra Pizzuta Calvarina, Monte (Italy)	Cinder cone of Etna	0101-06=
Serra Pizzuta, Monte (Italy)	Cinder cone of Etna	0101-06=
Serrania (Bolivia)	Stratovolcano (None) Post-Miocene	....
Serreta Ridge (Azores)	Submarine vent of Terceira	1802-05=
Serua (Banda Sea)	Stratovolcano (10, 1921) Historical	**0605-07=**
Sery, Cratere (Indian O.-W)	Crater of Fournaise, Piton de la	0303-02=
Sesarga (Solomon Is-SW Pacific)	Synonym of Savo	0505-07=
Sesegara Hills (New Guinea)	Synonym of Sessagara	0503-031
Sessagara (New Guinea)	Pyroclastic cones (None) Holocene	**0503-031**
Sesshogawara (Honshu-Japan)	Thermal feature of Kusatsu-Shirane	0803-12=
Sessho-ishi (Honshu-Japan)	Thermal feature of Nasu	0803-15=
Sessyo-isi [Sessho-ishi] (Honshu-Japan)	Thermal feature of Nasu	0803-15=
Sestrenka (Kamchatka)	Dome of Uzon	1000-17=
Sete Cidades (Azores)	Stratovolcano (16, 1880) Historical	**1802-08=**
Seto-yama (Izu Is-Japan)	Dome of Nii-jima	0804-02=
Setupa (Java)	Crater of Lawu	0603-26=
Seuga (Samoa-SW Pacific)	Cone of Upolu	0404-03-
Seulawah Agam (Sumatra)	Stratovolcano (2, 1839) Historical	**0601-02=**
Seulawah Inong (Sumatra)	Unknown (None) Quaternary	....
Seulawaih Agam (Seulawain Agam)	Synonym of Seulawah Agam	0601-02=
Seulawaihinong (Sumatra)	Synonym of Seulawah Inong	....
Sevckar (Armenia)	Pyroclastic cone of Ghegam Ridge	0104-07-
Seven Sisters (Australia)	Cone of Atherton Volc Province	....
Severgin (Kuril Is)	Cone of Kharimkotan	0900-30=
Severgina (Kuril Is)	Synonym of Kharimkotan	0900-30=
Severno-Koshelevskie [Verkne-Koshelevskie]	Thermal feature of Koshelev	1000-02=
Severny (Kamchatka)	Shield volcano (1, -1550) Radiocarbon	**1000-70-**
Severny Cherpuk (Kamchatka)	Cone of Cherpuk Group	1000-273
Severny Gamchen (Kamchatka)	Stratovolcano of Gamchen	1000-21=
Seydisholar (Iceland-SW)	Crater Row of Grímsnes	1701-06=
Sfinks (Kamchatka)	Dome of Ksudach	1000-05=
Shabubembe (Africa-C)	Crater of Nyamuragira	0203-02=
Shachi (Tonga-SW Pacific)	Synonym of Curacoa	0403-102
Shadeershan (China-E)	Synonym of Shatu	....
Shadwell, Mt. (Australia)	Cone of Newer Volcanics Prov	0509-01-
Shaheru (Africa-C)	Stratovolcano of Nyiragongo	0203-03=
Shahsavaran (Iran)	Volcanic field (None) Quaternary	....
Shaitani (Africa-E)	Cone of Chyulu Hills	0202-13=
Shakunage Hot Springs (Honshu-Japan)	Thermal feature of Kusatsu-Shirane	0803-12=
Shala (Ethiopia)	Synonym of O'a Caldera	0201-28-
Shalla (Ethiopia)	Synonym of O'a Caldera	0201-28-
Shalman, Jabal (Arabia-W)	Dome of Kishb, Harrat	0301-071
Sham Hill (Canada)	Cone of Bridge River Cones	1200-17-
Shamah (Arabia)	Volcanic field (None) Post-Miocene	....
Shamao (Taiwan)	Dome of Tatun Group	0801-032
Shamrock Hill (Antarctica)	Cone of Hodson	1900-11=
Shamuhiro (Africa-C)	Cone of Nyamuragira	0203-02=
Shandun (SE Asia)	Synonym of Leizhou Bandao	0705-01-
Shangri-La (Chile-C)	Dome of Chillán, Nevados de	1507-07=
Shapochka (Kamchatka)	Synonym of Khalzan-Shapochka	....
Sharat Kovakab (Syria)	Volcanic field (None) Holocene	**0300-01-**
Shari (Hokkaido-Japan)	Stratovolcano (None) Pleistocene	....
Shark Island (Red Sea)	Cone of Zukur	0201-021
Sharp Peak (Luzon-Philippines)	Stratovolcano of Bulusan	0703-01=
Sharp Peak (US-Oregon)	Dome of Crater Lake	1202-16-
Shasta (US-California)	Stratovolcano (23, 1786) Historical	**1203-01-**
Shasta Butte (US-California)	Synonym of Shasta	1203-01-
Shastina (US-California)	Dome of Shasta	1203-01-
Shatu (China-E)	Cinder cones (None) Quaternary	....
Sha-t'u (China-E)	Synonym of Shatu	....
Shavaryn-Tsaram (Mongolia)	Cone of Taryatu-Chulutu	1003-01-
Shchapinskaya (Kamchatka)	Synonym of Kizimen	1000-23=
Sheep Trail Butte (US-Idaho)	Cinder cone of Craters of the Moon	1204-02-
She-huang-ping (Taiwan)	Thermal feature of Tatun Group	0801-032
Shejiushan [Maanshan] (SE Asia)	Cinder cone of Tengchong	0705-11-
Sheldon-Antelope (US-Nevada)	Volcanic field (None) Quaternary	....

Name (Subregion)	Type (Eruptions, Most Recent) Status / Relation to Named Volcano	Volcano Number
Shell Mountain (Alaska-E)	Stratovolcano of Edgecumbe	1105-04-
Sheltowskij (Kamchatka)	Synonym of Zheltovsky	1000-04=
Shemodogan (Kamchatka)	Shield volcano (None) Pleistocene	....
Shenglidaban (China-W)	Cinder cone of Kunlun Volc Group	1004-03-
Shepard Island (Antarctica)	Tuff cones (None) Pleistocene	....
Shepherd Dome (Antarctica)	Cone of Hudson Mountains	1900-028
Shepherd Knoll (Australia)	Cone of Nulla Volc Province	....
Sheridan Mountain (US-Oregon)	Shield volcano of Bachelor	1202-09-
Sherman Crater (US-Washington)	Crater of Baker	1201-01=
Sherokhvotaya (Kamchatka)	Dome of Shiveluch	1000-27=
Sherwood Butte (US-Oregon)	Cone of Bailey	....
Shestakov, Mt. (Kuril Is)	Stratovolcano (None) Pleistocene	....
She-Toe-shan [Maanshan] (SE Asia)	Cinder cone of Tengchong	0705-11-
Sheveluch (Kamchatka)	Synonym of Shiveluch	1000-27=
Shibaseki (Kyushu-Japan)	Thermal feature of Tsurumi	0802-13=
Shibetoro (Kuril Is)	Synonym of Tsirk	....

Paul Kimberly (Smithsonian)

La Soufrière lava dome, forming the summit of **Soufrière Guadeloupe** volcano in the Lesser Antilles, was emplaced at the end of a major eruption about the mid-15th century.

Name (Subregion)	Type (Eruptions, Most Recent) Status / Relation to Named Volcano	Volcano Number
Shibetsu-dake (Hokkaido-Japan)	Stratovolcano of Samakkenupuri	....
Shibuno-yu (Kyushu-Japan)	Thermal feature of Tsurumi	0802-13=
Shichiho-yama (Honshu-Japan)	Synonym of Fuji	0803-03=
Shield Nunatak (Antarctica)	Cone of Melbourne	1900-015
Shiga (Honshu-Japan)	Shield volcanoes (None) Holocene?	**0803-121**
Shiga-Kogen (Honshu-Japan)	Synonym of Shiga	0803-121
Shihailongwan (China-E)	Maar of Longgang Group	1005-05-
Shih-Men-Tzu-shan [Shimenzishan] (China)	Cone of Longgang Group	1005-05-
Shihorei (Hokkaido-Japan)	Pyroclastic cone of Kuttara	0805-034
Shiitokoro (Hokkaido-Japan)	Lava dome (None) Pleistocene	....
Shikanokashira (Honshu-Japan)	Cone of Fuji	0803-03=
Shikaribetsu Group (Hokkaido-Japan)	Lava domes (None) Holocene?	**0805-062**
Shikine-jima (Izu Is-Japan)	Dome of Nii-jima	0804-02=
Shikinonaru-yama (Honshu-Japan)	Synonym of Fuji	0803-03=
Shikotsu (Hokkaido-Japan)	Caldera (41, 1981) Historical	**0805-04=**
Shikuma (Honshu-Japan)	Lava domes (None) Pleistocene	....
Shikumaga-take (Honshu-Japan)	Dome of Shikuma	....
Shilin-Bogdo (Mongolia)	Cone of Dariganga Volc Field	1003-04-
Shimabara (Kyushu-Japan)	Thermal feature of Unzen	0802-10=
Shimagare-yama (Honshu-Japan)	Dome of Kita Yatsuga-take	0803-031
Shimanomine (Kyushu-Japan)	Dome of Unzen	0802-10=
Shimenzishan (China-E)	Cone of Longgang Group	1005-05-
Shimobori (Honshu-Japan)	Crater of Yake-dake	0803-07=
Shimokita-Hiuchi (Honshu-Japan)	Synonym of Mutsu-Hiuchi-dake	....
Shin-Beppu (Kyushu-Japan)	Thermal feature of Tsurumi	0802-13=
Shin-dake (Ryukyu Is)	Stratovolcano of Kuchinoerabu-jima	0802-05=
Shin-Fuji (Honshu-Japan)	Stratovolcano of Fuji	0803-03=
Shin-Funkako (Hokkaido-Japan)	Crater of Tokachi	0805-05=
Shining Mountain (Africa-E)	Synonym of Kilimanjaro	0202-15=
Shin-Io-jima (Volcano Is-Japan)	Synonym of Fukutoku-Okanoba	0804-13=
Shin-Iwo-jima (Volcano Is-Japan)	Synonym of Fukutoku-Okanoba	0804-13=
Shin-Iwo-jima [Showa-Iwo-jima] (Ryukyu Is)	Dome of Kikai	0802-06=
Shinmetaung (SE Asia)	Cone of Wuntho	....
Shinmio (Izu Is-Japan)	Maar of Miyake-jima	0804-04=
Shinmiyo-ike (Izu Is-Japan)	Crater of Miyake-jima	0804-04=
Shinmoe-dake (Kyushu-Japan)	Stratovolcano of Kirishima	0802-09=
Shino-ike (Honshu-Japan)	Crater of On-take	0803-04=
Shino-yu (Kyushu-Japan)	Thermal feature of Tsurumi	0802-13=
Shinsheridake (Kuril Is)	Synonym of Prevo Peak	0900-19=
Shinshiru Fuji (Kuril Is)	Synonym of Prevo Peak	0900-19=
Shinshiru-dake (Kuril Is)	Synonym of Goriaschaia Sopka	0900-17=
Shin-yama [Myoko-san] (Honshu-Japan)	Dome of Myoko	0803-10=
Shin-zan (Honshu-Japan)	Dome of Chokai	0803-22=
Shiobara (Honshu-Japan)	Caldera of Takahara	0803-143
Ship Rock (Aleutian Is)	Former dome of Bogoslof	1101-30-
Ship Rock (Indian O.)	Tuff cone of Prince Edward Island	0304-06-
Shipunegamori (Izu Is-Japan)	Dome of Mikura-jima	0804-041
Shira (Africa-E)	Stratovolcano of Kilimanjaro	0202-15=
Shirahata Hot Springs (Honshu-Japan)	Thermal feature of Kusatsu-Shirane	0803-12=
Shirai-dake (Honshu-Japan)	Dome of Sengoku	....

Name (Subregion)	Type (Eruptions, Most Recent) Status / Relation to Named Volcano	Volcano Number
Shiraishi-dake (Honshu-Japan)	Synonym of Zao	0803-19=
Shiramizu (Honshu-Japan)	Crater of Yake-dake	0803-07=
Shirane (Izu Is-Japan)	Submarine vent of Smith Rock	0804-08=
Shirane-san (Honshu-Japan)	Cone of Kusatsu-Shirane	0803-12=
Shirane-san (Honshu-Japan)	Dome of Nikko-Shirane	0803-14=
Shiranezawa (Honshu-Japan)	Thermal feature of Kusatsu-Shirane	0803-12=
Shiranutanoike (Honshu-Japan)	Maar of Izu-Tobu	0803-01=
Shirataka (Honshu-Japan)	Stratovolcano (None) Pleistocene	....
Shiratani-yama (Honshu-Japan)	Stratovolcano of Yake-dake	0803-07=
Shiratori-yama (Kyushu-Japan)	Stratovolcano of Kirishima	0802-09=
Shiretoko (Hokkaido-Japan)	Stratovolcano (None) Pleistocene	....
Shiretoko-Io-zan (Hokkaido-Japan)	Synonym of Shiretoko-Iwo-zan	0805-09=
Shiretoko-Iwo-zan (Hokkaido-Japan)	Stratovolcano (6, 1936) Historical	**0805-09=**
Shiribetsu (Hokkaido-Japan)	Stratovolcano (None) Pleistocene	....
Shirinki (Kuril Is)	Stratovolcano (None) Holocene	**0900-331**
Shiriyajiri-dake (Shiriyaziri) (Kuril Is)	Synonym of Fuss Peak	0900-34=
Shirogane (Hokkaido-Japan)	Thermal feature of Tokachi	0805-05=
Shirokoe Plateau (Kamchatka)	Dome of Uzon	1000-17=

Mark Davies (MVO)

Several generations of lava-dome growth can be seen in this January 27, 1997 aerial photo of **Soufrière Hills** volcano on Montserrat. Ash is venting from a small dome that began growing in December 1996 within a scarp formed by collapse of an October 1996 lava dome. This dome was constructed within the outer dome-collapse scarp at the lower left.

Name (Subregion)	Type (Eruptions, Most Recent) Status / Relation to Named Volcano	Volcano Number
Shirotsuka (Honshu-Japan)	Cone of Fuji	0803-03=
Shirouma-Norikura (Honshu-Japan)	Synonym of Shirouma-Oike	....
Shirouma-Oike (Honshu-Japan)	Stratovolcanoes (None) Pleistocene	....
Shish (Kamchatka)	Cone (None) Pleistocene	....
Shishaldin (Aleutian Is)	Stratovolcano (37, 2004) Historical	**1101-36-**
Shisheika (Kamchatka)	Lava dome (1, -2240) Radiocarbon	**1000-511**
Shishejka (Kamchatka)	Synonym of Shisheika	1000-511
Shishel (Kamchatka)	Shield volcano (None) Holocene?	**1000-58-**
Shishido-dake (Kyushu-Japan)	Stratovolcano of Kirishima	0802-09=
Shishimuta (Kyushu-Japan)	Synonym of Yabakei	....
Shiste, Cerro el (El Salvador)	Lava cone of San Diego	1403-001
Shiveluch (Kamchatka)	Stratovolcano (102, 2010) Historical	**1000-27=**
Shivit-Tayga (Russia-SE)	Stratovolcano of Azas Plateau	1002-07-
Shiwanshan (SE Asia)	Cone of Leizhou Bandao	0705-01-
Shiyinling (SE Asia)	Cone of Leizhou Bandao	0705-01-
Shlen (Kamchatka)	Shield volcano (None) Pleistocene	....
Shmalev (Kamchatka)	Fissure vent of Kliuchevskoi	1000-26=
Shoal Bay (New Zealand)	Tuff cone of Auckland Field	0401-02=
Sho-Chirippu [Ivan Grozny] (Kuril Is)	Somma volcano of Grozny Group	0900-07=
Sho-Fuji [Kaimon] (Kyushu-Japan)	Stratovolcano of Ibusuki Volc Field	0802-07=
Shohapinsky (Kamchatka)	Synonym of Kizimen	1000-23=
Shoji-yama (Honshu-Japan)	Dome of Osore-yama	0803-29=
Shokurohime (Honshu-Japan)	Cone of Kurohime	....
Shoshone Geyser Basin (US-Wyoming)	Thermal feature of Yellowstone	1205-01-
Shoshone Lava Field (US-Idaho)	Shield volcano (1, -8400) Holocene	**1204-01-**
Shoshuenco [Choshuenco] (Chile-C)	Stratovolcano of Mocho-Choshuenco	1507-13=
Shotgun Peak (US-California)	Cone of Medicine Lake	1203-02-
Shove (Africa-C)	Cone of Nyamuragira	0203-02=
Showa (Kyushu-Japan)	Crater of Sakura-jima	0802-08=
Showa (Hokkaido-Japan)	Crater of Tokachi	0805-05=
Showa-Iwo-jima (Ryukyu Is)	Dome of Kikai	0802-06=
Showa-Shinzan (Hokkaido-Japan)	Dome of Usu	0805-03=
Shtyubel' [Stubel] (Kamchatka)	Maar of Ksudach	1000-05=
Shuangshan (China-E)	Cone of Datong-Fengzen	....
Shukash Butte (US-Oregon)	Cone of Wuksi Butte-Twin Lakes	....
Shuli (Africa-C)	Cone of Nyamuragira	0203-02=
Shupanowskij (Kamchatka)	Synonym of Zhupanovsky	1000-12=
Shuqra Volc Field (Arabia-S)	Synonym of Sawâd, Harra es-	0301-16-
Shurado (Honshu-Japan)	Crater of Narugo	0803-20=
Shushaldinskaya (Aleutian Is)	Synonym of Shishaldin	1101-36-
Shuteye, Mt. (Australia)	Cone of McBride Volc Province	....
Siah Butte (US-Oregon)	Cinder cone of Bachelor	1202-09-
Siang (Java)	Crater of Galunggung	0603-14=
Siangtianshan (Taiwan)	Dome of Tatun Group	0801-032
Siaoguanyinshan (Taiwan)	Dome of Tatun Group	0801-032
Siaoyoukeng (Taiwan)	Tuff ring of Tatun Group	0801-032
Siao-you-keng (Taiwan)	Thermal feature of Tatun Group	0801-032
Siasar (Sumatra)	Unknown (None) Post-Miocene	....
Siassi Island (New Guinea-NE of)	Synonym of Umboi	0501-06=
Sibajak (Sumatra)	Synonym of Sibayak	0601-07=
Sibandung (Sumatra)	Caldera of Toba	0601-09=
Sibanggor Djulu [Sibangor Julu] (Sumatra)	Thermal feature of Sorikmarapi	0601-12=
Sibangor Julu (Sumatra)	Thermal feature of Sorikmarapi	0601-12=
Sibanteng (Java)	Thermal feature Dieng Volc Complex	0603-20=
Sibayak (Sumatra)	Stratovolcanoes (1, 1881) Historical	**0601-07=**
Sibetoro (Kuril Is)	Stratovolcano of Tsirk	....
Sibinal (México)	Caldera of Tacaná	1401-13=
Sibualbuali (Sumatra)	Stratovolcano (None) Holocene?	**0601-11=**
Sibulaboalie (Sumatra)	Synonym of Sibualbuali	0601-11=
Sibuland Spring (Mindanao-Philippines)	Thermal feature of Apo	0701-03=
Sibutan, Dolok (Sumatra)	Stratovolcano of Toba	0601-09=
Sicuín, Cerro de (México)	Cinder cone of Michoacán-Guanajuato	1401-06=
Sidas (Canada)	Cone of Edziza	1200-06-
Side Crater (Antarctica)	Crater of Erebus	1900-02=
Sidole (Sulawesi-Indonesia)	Unknown (None) Quaternary	....
Siemsen, Volcán (Chile-C)	Cone of Chillán, Nevados de	1507-07=
Sierpe, Lomas de (Costa Rica)	Shield volcanoes (None) Pleistocene	....
Sierra (Spanish for Mountain Range) see proper name (e.g. San Andrés, Sierra de)		
Sierras, Las (Nicaragua)	Pleistocene caldera of Masaya	1404-10=
Siete Cerros, Loma Los (Guatemala)	Cone of Chingo	1402-17-
Siete Fuentes (Canary Is)	Cinder cone of Tenerife	1803-03-
Siete Orejas (Guatemala)	Stratovolcano (None) Quaternary	....
Siete, Cerro el (Costa Rica)	Stratovolcano of Platanar	1405-034
Sifford Mountain (US-California)	Shield volcano (None) Pleistocene	....
Siga (Honshu-Japan)	Synonym of Shiga	0803-121
Sigadjah [Sigajah] (Java)	Thermal feature Dieng Volc Complex	0603-20=
Siga'ele (Samoa-SW Pacific)	Cone of Upolu	0404-03-
Sigajah (Java)	Thermal feature Dieng Volc Complex	0603-20=
Sigala, Batu (Sumatra)	Crater of Sinabung	0601-08=
Siglagah (Java)	Thermal feature Dieng Volc Complex	0603-20=
Sigluduk (Java)	Cone of Dieng Volc Complex	0603-20=
Signal Butte (US-California)	Cone of Shasta	1203-01-
Signal de L'Enclos (Indian O.-W)	Crater of Fournaise, Piton de la	0303-02=
Signal Hill (W Indies)	Cone of Northern Centres	....
Signal Hill (W Indies)	Stratovolcano of Quill, The	1600-02=
Signal Peak (US-Washington)	Cone of Simcoe	....
Sigolduhraun (Iceland-NE)	Fissure vent of Bárdarbunga	1703-03=
Siguam (Aleutian Is)	Synonym of Seguam	1101-18-
Sigurd (Spitsbergen)	Explosion crater (None) Pleistocene	....
Sigurdbreen (Atlantic-N-Jan Mayen)	Cone of Jan Mayen	1706-01=
Sigurdfjellet (Spitsbergen)	Synonym of Sigurd	....
Siharslan Tepe (Turkey)	Cone of Erciyes Dagi	0103-01=
Sihmiran Tepe (Turkey)	Cone of Nemrut Dagi	0103-02=
Sihsihdagi (Turkey)	Dome of Süphan Dagi	0103-021
Sikhote-Alin (Russia-SE)	Volcanic field (None) Holocene	**1002-01-**
Sikidang (Java)	Thermal feature Dieng Volc Complex	0603-20=
Sikine-zima [Shikine-jima] (Izu Is-Japan)	Dome of Nii-jima	0804-02=
Sikotu (Hokkaido-Japan)	Synonym of Shikotsu	0805-04=
Sikuma (Honshu-Japan)	Synonym of Shikuma	....
Sikunang (Java)	Cone of Dieng Volc Complex	0603-20=
Sil (Africa-E)	Synonym of Barrier, The	0202-03=
Silago (Philippines-C)	Unknown (None) Pleistocene	....
Silali (Africa-E)	Shield volcano (3, -5050) Ar/Ar	**0202-052**
Silamuk (Java)	Pyroclastic cone of Muria	0603-251
Silanga Hot Spring (New Britain-SW Pac)	Thermal feature of Sulu Range	0502-09=
Silangan (Luzon-Philippines)	Cone of Natib	0703-082
Silaung (SE Asia)	Vent of Lower Chindwin	0705-09-
Silawaih Agam (Sumatra)	Synonym of Seulawah Agam	0601-02=
Silay (Philippines-C)	Stratovolcano (None) Fumarolic	**0702-04=**
Sile [Sili] (New Britain-SW Pac)	Cone of Lolobau	0502-13=
Silenge Island (New Britain-SW Pac)	Cone of Mundua	0502-021
Silent Cone (US-Idaho)	Cinder cone of Craters of the Moon	1204-02-
Silent Hill (Australia)	Cone of McBride Volc Province	....
Sileri (Java)	Cone of Dieng Volc Complex	0603-20=
Sili (New Britain-SW Pac)	Cone of Lolobau	0502-13=
Sili (Samoa-SW Pacific)	Shield volcano of Ofu-Olosega	0404-01=
Silla (México)	Dome of Zitácuaro-Valle de Bravo	1401-061
Silla de Pando, Cerro [Cerro Pando] (Panamá)	Dome of Tisingal	....
Silla, Cerro la (Panamá)	Dome of Valle, El	1406-03-
Silla, Cerro la (México)	Cone of Zitácuaro-Valle de Bravo	1401-061
Sillajguai, Cerro (Chile-N)	Stratovolcano (None) Post-Miocene	....
Sillajhuay (Chile-N)	Synonym of Sillajguai, Cerro	....
Sillanegra, Volcán (Argentina)	Pyroclastic cone of Cochiquito Group	1507-071
Sillatepec (México)	Dome of Cumbres, Las	1401-098
Sillón Abajo, Cerrito el (Guatemala)	Lava cone of Chiquimula Volc Field	1402-20-
Sillón, Cerrito el (Guatemala)	Lava cone of Chiquimula Volc Field	1402-20-
Sillota (Bolivia)	Stratovolcano (None) Post-Miocene	....
Silueta, Cerro La (Chile-S)	Unknown (None) Post-Miocene	....
Siluman, Kawah (Java)	Crater of Tangkubanparahu	0603-09=
Silva, La (México)	Cinder cone of Chichinautzin	1401-08=
Silver Creek (US-Oregon)	Volcanic field (None) Pleistocene?	....
Silver Hills (W Indies)	Lava domes (None) Pleistocene	....
Silver Lake (US-California)	Cinder cones (None) Holocene?	**1203-05-**
Silver Lake (US-Wyoming)	Dome of Yellowstone	1205-01-
Silverthrone (Canada)	Caldera (None) Holocene	**1200-16-**
Silvestri, Monte (Italy)	Cinder cone of Etna	0101-06=
Simabara (Kyushu-Japan)	Synonym of Unzen	0802-10=

Name (Subregion)	Type (Eruptions, Most Recent) Status Relation to Named Volcano	Volcano Number
Simacak, Uruk (Sumatra)	Stratovolcano of Sibayak	0601-07=
Simagh, Jabal (Arabia-W)	Maar of Kishb, Harrat	0301-071
Simanobori (Kuril Is)	Synonym of Mendeleev	0900-02=
Simba (Africa-E)	Cone of Sultan Hamud-Simba	....
Simba, Volcan [Aguas Calientes] (Chile-N)	Stratovolcano of Láscar	1505-10=
Simbi, Lake (Africa-E)	Maar of Homa Mountain	0202-07=
Simbo (Solomon Is-SW Pacific)	Stratovolcanoes (1, 1910) Anthropology	**0505-05=**
Simbolon (Sumatra)	Stratovolcano (None) Pleistocene	....
Simcoe (US-Washington)	Volcanic field (None) Pleistocene	....
Siminyng [Gunung Seminung] (Sumatra)	Stratovolcano of Ranau	0601-251
Simokita-Hiuti (Honshu-Japan)	Synonym of Mutsu-Hiuchi-dake	....
Simone, Monte (Italy)	Cinder cone of Etna	0101-06=
Sims Butte (US-Oregon)	Cinder cone of North Sister Field	1202-07=
Simusiru Fudzi (Kuril Is)	Synonym of Prevo Peak	0900-19=
Sin Nombre (Chile-S)	Cone of Cayutué-La Viguería	1508-012
Sin Nombre, Crater (Chile-C)	Crater of Azul, Cerro	1507-06=
Sin Nombre, Nevado (Chile-C)	Stratovolcano of Tupungatito	1507-01=
Sinaboeng (Sumatra)	Synonym of Sinabung	0601-08=
Sinabun (Sumatra)	Synonym of Sinabung	0601-08=
Sinabung (Sumatra)	Stratovolcano (Uncertain) Holocene	**0601-08=**
Sinai, Mt. (W Indies)	Stratovolcano of St. Catherine	1600-17=
Sinarka (Kuril Is)	Stratovolcano (4, 1878) Historical	**0900-29=**
Sinarko (Kuril Is)	Synonym of Sinarka	0900-29=
Sincholagua (Ecuador)	Stratovolcano (None) Pleistocene	....
Sin-dake [Shin-dake] (Ryukyu Is)	Stratovolcano of Kuchinoerabu-jima	0802-05=
Sindoro (Java)	Synonym of Sundoro	0603-21=
Singgalang (Sumatra)	Twin volcano of Tandikat	0601-15=
Singgalang, Dolok (Sumatra)	Cone of Toba	0601-09=
Singiro (Africa-C)	Cone of Nyamuragira	0203-02=
Singu Plateau (SE Asia)	Fissure vents (None) Holocene	**0705-10-**
Singüil, Cerro (El Salvador)	Cinder cones (None) Holocene	**1403-002**
Sin-Hunkako [Shin-Funkako] (Japan)	Crater of Tokachi	0805-05=
Sini (Russia-SE)	Cone of Udokan Plateau	1002-03-
Sinila (Java)	Cone of Dieng Volc Complex	0603-20=
Sin-Io-jima (Sin-Iwo-zima) (Volcano Is-Japan)	Synonym of Fukutoku-Okanoba	0804-13=
Sinitiope, Loma de (Nicaragua)	Dome of Concepción	1404-12=
Sinker Butte (US-Idaho)	Shield volcano (None) Pleistocene	....
Sinmiyo [Shinmio] (Izu Is-Japan)	Maar of Miyake-jima	0804-04=
Sinmoe-dake [Shinmoe-dake] (Japan)	Stratovolcano of Kirishima	0802-09=
Sino-ike [Shino-ike] (Honshu-Japan)	Crater of On-take	0803-04=
Sintumbi (Africa-E)	Cone of Ngozi	0202-164
Sinumaan (Sulu Is-Philippines)	Cone of Jolo	0700-01=
Sin-zan [Shin-zan] (Honshu-Japan)	Dome of Chokai	0803-22=
Sio Tsirarippu [Ivan Grozny] (Kuril Is)	Somma volcano of Grozny Group	0900-07=
Siope (Samoa-SW Pacific)	Cone of Savai'i	0404-04=
Siosiorena (D'Entrecasteaux Is)	Thermal feature Dawson Strait Group	0503-06=
Sipandu (Java)	Thermal feature Dieng Volc Complex	0603-20=
Sipisopiso [Dolok Tandukbenua] (Sumatra)	Cone of Toba	0601-09=
Siple (Antarctica)	Shield volcano (None) Holocene?	**1900-025**
Sirahata (Kuril Is)	Synonym of Ketoi	0900-20=
Sirane-san [Shirane-san] (Honshu-Japan)	Dome of Nikko-Shirane	0803-14=
Siratani-yama [Shiratani-yama] (Japan)	Stratovolcano of Yake-dake	0803-07=
Siratori-yama [Shiratori-yama] (Japan)	Cone of Kirishima	0802-09=
Siren Rock (Antarctica)	Cone of Hudson Mountains	1900-028
Sirenevy (Kamchatka)	Cone of Dzenzursky	1000-11=
Sirenevy (Kuril Is)	Stratovolcano of Medvezhia	0900-10=
Siretoko (Hokkaido-Japan)	Synonym of Shiretoko	....
Siretoko-io-zan (Hokkaido-Japan)	Synonym of Shiretoko-Iwo-zan	0805-09=
Siretoko-Iwo-zan (Hokkaido-Japan)	Synonym of Shiretoko-Iwo-zan	0805-09=
Siriadziri (Kuril Is)	Synonym of Fuss Peak	0900-34=
Siroeng (Lesser Sunda Is)	Synonym of Sirung	0604-27=
Sironemuri (Kuril Is)	Synonym of Ketoi	0900-20=
Sirouma-Norikura (Honshu-Japan)	Synonym of Shirouma-Oike	....
Sirouma-oike (Honshu-Japan)	Synonym of Shirouma-Oike	....
Sirung (Lesser Sunda Is)	Complex volcano (8, 1970) Historical	**0604-27=**
Sisa (New Guinea)	Stratovolcano (None) Pleistocene	....
Sisaguk (Aleutian Is)	Synonym of Shishaldin	1101-36-
Sisel (Kamchatka)	Synonym of Shishel	1000-58-
Sisi Butte (US-Oregon)	Shield volcano of Olallie Butte	....
Sisido-dake [Shishido-dake] (Kyushu-Japan)	Stratovolcano of Kirishima	0802-09=
Sisquk (Sissagjuk) (Aleutian Is)	Synonym of Shishaldin	1101-36-
Sisters, the (Alaska-W)	Cone of St. Michael	1104-04-
Sitarinda (Sumatra)	Unknown (None) Post-Miocene	....
Sitchin (Aleutian Is)	Synonym of Great Sitkin	1101-12-
Sitchin (Sitignak?) (Aleutian Is)	Synonym of Little Sitkin	1101-05-
Sitgreaves Peak (US-Arizona)	Cone of San Francisco Volc Field	....
Sitignak ? (Aleutian Is)	Synonym of Little Sitkin	1101-05-
Sitio Grande (El Salvador)	Crater of San Salvador	1403-05=
Sitio Hornillas (Costa Rica)	Thermal feature of Rincón de la Vieja	1405-02=
Sitios, Los (Guatemala)	Stratovolcano of Piedra Grande	....
Sitkei Herceghegy (Hungary)	Maar of Kemenesalja	....
Sitkum Butte (US-Oregon)	Cinder cone of Bachelor	1202-09-
Six Shooter Butte (US-California)	Cone of Medicine Lake	1203-02-
Sixbit Point (US-Oregon)	Cone of Williamson Mountain	....
Sixmile Hill (US-California)	Cone of Cinder Butte	....
Siyut (Mindanao-Philippines)	Synonym of Makaturing	0701-04=
Siyut (Mindanao-Philippines)	Synonym of Ragang	0701-06=
Sizmos (Kamchatka)	Fissure vent of Kliuchevskoi	1000-26=
Sjadukta (Kamchatka)	Synonym of Ksudach	1000-05=
Sjonarholl (Iceland-W)	Cone of Snaefellsjökull	1700-01=
Skafta [Laki] (Iceland-NE)	Crater Row of Grímsvötn	1703-01=
Skalafell (Iceland-SW)	Shield volcano of Reykjanes	1701-02=
Skalaralda (Iceland-NE)	Crater of Askja	1703-06=
Skalistaya (Kamchatka)	Dome of Opala	1000-08=
Skalistaya (Kamchatka)	Synonym of Skalistiy	....
Skalistaya (Kamchatka)	Synonym of Skalistiy	....
Skalistiy (Kamchatka)	Unknown (None) Pleistocene	....
Skalistiy (Kamchatka)	Shield volcano (None) Pleistocene	....
Skaptarjökull [Laki] (Iceland-NE)	Crater Row of Grímsvötn	1703-01=
Skardsmyrarhraun (Iceland-SW)	Crater Row of Hengill	1701-05=
Skaros (Greece)	Shield volcano of Santorini	0102-04=
Skeifuhraun (Iceland-NE)	Fissure vent of Bárdarbunga	1703-03=
Skerjahraun (Iceland-S)	Fissure vent of Eyjafjallajökull	1702-02=
Ski Heil Peak (US-California)	Dome of Lassen Volc Center	1203-08-
Skinner Hill (New Zealand)	Dome of Taranaki [Egmont]	0401-03=
Skjaldbaka (Iceland-NE)	Shield volcano of Fremrinamur	1703-07=
Skjaldbreidur (Iceland-SW)	Shield volcano of Prestahnukur	1701-07=
Skoflunger (Iceland-SW)	Shield volcano of Prestahnukur	1701-07=
Skotuhryggur (Iceland-S)	Submarine vent of Vestmannaeyjar	1702-01=
Skrukkefjellet (Atlantic-N-Jan Mayen)	Dome of Jan Mayen	1706-01=
Skrukkelia (Atlantic-N-Jan Mayen)	Cone of Jan Mayen	1706-01=
Skuggadyngja (Iceland-NE)	Shield volcano of Fremrinamur	1703-07=
Skuridin (Kamchatka)	Fissure vent of Kliuchevskoi	1000-26=
Skyrtunna (Iceland-W)	Crater of Ljósufjöll	1700-03=
Sladen Boiling Springs (Vanuatu-SW Pacific)	Thermal feature of Gaua	0507-02=
Slag Hill (Canada)	Cone of Cayley, Mt.	....
Slamat (Java)	Synonym of Slamet	0603-18=
Slamet (Java)	Stratovolcano (41, 2009) Historical	**0603-18=**
Slattudalshraun (Iceland-SW)	Crater Row of Brennisteinsfjöll	1701-04=
Sleet (Canada)	Cone of Edziza	1200-06-
Slettahraun (Iceland-S)	Fissure vent of Torfajökull	1702-05=
Sloping Hummock (Australia)	Vent of Bundaberg-Boyne Province	....
Slunina (Kamchatka)	Shield volcano of Khuvkhoitun	....
Slusher Nunatak (Antarctica)	Cone of Hudson Mountains	1900-028
Slyunin (Kamchatka)	Fissure vent of Kliuchevskoi	1000-26=
Smahraunakula (Iceland-W)	Cone of Ljósufjöll	1700-03=
Smales Hill [Otara Hill] (New Zealand)	Cone of Auckland Field	0401-02=
Small Baguio (Luzon-Philippines)	Dome of Labo	....
Smart, Mt. (New Zealand)	Cone of Auckland Field	0401-02=
Smbatassar (Armenia)	Cone of Dar-Alages	0104-08-
Smeaton Hill (Australia)	Cone of Newer Volcanics Prov	0509-01-
Smelter Knolls (US-Utah)	Lava domes (None) Pleistocene	....
Smeroe (Smeru) (Java)	Synonym of Semeru	0603-30=
Smirnov (Kuril Is)	Stratovolcano (None) Holocene	**0900-021**
Smiroe (Java)	Synonym of Semeru	0603-30=
Smith (Greece)	Dome of Santorini	0102-04=
Smith Butte (US-Washington)	Cinder cone of Adams	1201-04-
Smith Crater (Kermadec Is)	Crater of Raoul Island	0402-03=
Smith Rock (Izu Is-Japan)	Submarine volcano (2, 1916) Historical	**0804-08=**
Smith Volcano (Luzon-N of)	Cinder cone of Babuyan Claro	0704-03=
Smoking Moses (Aleutian Is)	Synonym of Shishaldin	1101-36-
Smoky Mountain (Alaska Peninsula)	Synonym of Ugashik-Peulik	1102-13-
Smyt Bank I (Italy)	Submarine vent C. Flegrei Mar Sicilia	0101-07=

The broad, low-angle **Skjaldbreidur** basaltic shield volcano rising beyond Thingvallavatn lake is a classic example of an Icelandic-style shield volcano. Tuff cones of the Hengill volcanic system form islands in the lake.

Lee Siebert (Smithsonian)

Name (Subregion)	Type (Eruptions, Most Recent) Status Relation to Named Volcano	Volcano Number
Smyt Bank II (Italy)	Submarine vent C. Flegrei Mar Sicilia	0101-07=
Snaefell (Iceland-SE)	Stratovolcano (None) Pleistocene	....
Snaefellsjökull (Iceland-W)	Stratovolcano (10, 200) Radiocarbon	**1700-01=**
Snaehetta (Iceland-SE)	Stratovolcano of Esjufjöll	1704-02=
Snaekollur (Iceland-SW)	Dome of Hofsjökull	1701-09=
Snag Hill (US-California)	Cone of Medicine Lake	1203-02-
Snegovoy (Kamchatka)	Shield volcano (None) Holocene?	**1000-69-**
Snezhnaya (Kamchatka)	Synonym of Snezhniy	1000-66-
Snezhniy (Kamchatka)	Shield volcano (None) Holocene?	**1000-66-**
Snider Peak (Alaska-E)	Dome of Drum	....
Snipes Mountain (US-Washington)	Cinder cone of Adams	1201-04-

Name (Subregion)	Type (Eruptions, Most Recent) Status / Relation to Named Volcano	Volcano Number
Snippaker Creek (Canada)	Cone of Iskut-Unuk River Cones	1200-09-
Snou [Snow] (Kuril Is)	Stratovolcano of Chirpoi	0900-15=
Snoul (SE Asia)	Unknown (None) Pleistocene	
Snow (Kuril Is)	Stratovolcano of Chirpoi	0900-15=
Snow Mountain (US-California)	Stratovolcano (None) Pleistocene	
Snowshoe Lava Field (Canada)	Vent of Edziza	1200-06-
Snowy Mountain (Alaska Peninsula)	Stratovolcanoes (1, 1710) Radiocarbon	**1102-20-**
Soal (New Guinea-NE of)	Stratovolcano of Umboi	0501-06=
Soboliny (Kamchatka)	Stratovolcano of Maly Semiachik	1000-14=
Sobor (Africa-N)	Synonym of Voon, Tarso	0205-02=
Soborom (Africa-N)	Thermal feature of Voon, Tarso	0205-02=
Sobouroun (Africa-N)	Synonym of Voon, Tarso	0205-02=
Soche (Ecuador)	Stratovolcano (1, -6650) Radiocarbon	**1502-001**
Sochól, Cerro (México)	Cone of Chichinautzin	1401-08=
Socompa (Chile-N)	Stratovolcano (1, -5250) Radiocarbon	**1505-109**
Soconusco (México)	Synonym of Tacaná	1401-13=
Socorro (México-Is)	Shield volcano (3, 1994) Historical	**1401-021**
Socrière, La (W Indies)	Dome of Plat Pays, Morne	1600-11=
Soda Dam (US-New Mexico)	Thermal feature of Valles Caldera	
Soda Lakes (US-Nevada)	Maars (None) Holocene	**1206-01-**
Soda Peak (US-Washington)	Cinder cone of West Crater	1201-06-
Sodore (Ethiopia)	Pyroclastic cones (None) Holocene	**0201-222**
Soekaria Caldera (Lesser Sunda Is)	Synonym of Sukaria Caldera	0604-12=
Soeket [Suket] (Java)	Stratovolcano of Raung	0603-34=
Soelasih (Sumatra)	Synonym of Talang	0601-16=
Soelheimajokull (Iceland-S)	Synonym of Katla	1702-03=
Soembing (Java)	Synonym of Sumbing	0603-22=
Soembing (Sumatra)	Synonym of Sumbing	0601-18=
Soenda Caldera [Sunda Caldera] (Java)	Pleist. caldera of Tangkubanparahu	0603-09=
Soendoro (Java)	Synonym of Sundoro	0603-21=
Soengpanack (Korea)	Vent of Halla	1006-04-
Soeoh-Senke (Sumatra)	Synonym of Suoh	0601-27=
Sofugan (Izu Is-Japan)	Stratovolcano (Uncertain)	**0804-091**
Sofunobori (Kuril Is)	Synonym of Tiatia	0900-03=
Sogagigir (Iceland-SW)	Crater Row of Krísuvík	1701-03=
Sohu-gan (Izu Is-Japan)	Synonym of Sofugan	0804-091
Soi-Tayga (Russia-SE)	Cone of Azas Plateau	1002-07-
Sokol (Kamchatka)	Stratovolcano (None) Pleistocene	
Sol de Mañana (Bolivia)	Thermal feature of Volcanes, Cerro	
Solander Island (New Zealand)	Synonym of Hautere	
Solander Island (New Zealand)	Stratovolcano (None) Pleistocene	
Solchiaro (Italy)	Tuff ring of Campi Flegrei	0101-01=
Soledad, Cerro la (Guatemala)	Dome of Tecuamburro	1402-12=
Solfatara (Italy)	Crater of Campi Flegrei	0101-01=
Solfatara Pool (Luzon-Philippines)	Thermal feature of Pinatubo	0703-083
Solforoso, Monte (Italy)	Cone of Sabatini Complex	
Soliman (Canary Is)	Cinder cone of Hierro	1803-02-
Solimana (Perú)	Stratovolcano (None) Pleistocene	
Solís (México)	Maar of Michoacán-Guanajuato	1401-06=
Solitario, El (México)	Dome of Iztaccíhuatl	1401-082
Solkatla (Iceland-SW)	Shield volcano of Hveravellir	1701-08=
Sólkatla (Iceland-SW)	Crater of Hveravellir	1701-08=

Ice-clad **Snæfellsjökull** volcano towers above Breidavík bay at the western tip of the isolated Snæfellsnes Peninsula in western Iceland. Numerous pyroclastic cones dot the flanks of the 1448-m-high stratovolcano,and Holocene lava flows extend to the sea over the entire western half of the volcano.

Name (Subregion)	Type (Eruptions, Most Recent) Status / Relation to Named Volcano	Volcano Number
Sollipulli (Chile-C)	Caldera (2, 1240) Radiocarbon	**1507-111**
Solo (Sulu Is-Philippines)	Synonym of Jolo	0700-01=
Solo (Argentina)	Pyrocl. cone Northern Mendoza Field	
Solo, El (Chile-N)	Stratovolcano (None) Holocene	**1505-131**
Solowa Agam (Solawaik Agam) (Sumatra)	Synonym of Seulawah Agam	0601-02=
Sombutang (Lesser Sunda Is)	Crater of Sirung	0604-27=
Somhegy [Kabhegy] (Hungary)	Shield volcano of Balaton Highland	
Somlyo (Hungary)	Vent of Nográd	
Somma Crater (W Indies)	Crater of Soufrière St. Vincent	1600-15=
Somma, Monte (Italy)	Stratovolcano of Vesuvius	0101-02=
Sommata, La (Italy)	Cone of Vulcano	0101-05=
Somma-Vesuviana (Italy)	Synonym of Vesuvius	0101-02=
Somoskovar (Hungary)	Cone of Nográd	
Somosomo (Fiji Is-SW Pacific)	Cone of Waikama	
Sona, Monte (Italy)	Cinder cone of Etna	0101-06=
Sonae (Honshu-Japan)	Cinder cone of Ogino-Sen	
Soncco Orcco, Cerro (Perú)	Stratovolcano of Firura, Nevados	
Sone (Kyushu-Japan)	Pyroclastic cone (None) Pleistocene	
Sonequera (Bolivia)	Synonym of Sunequera	
Sonetaung (SE Asia)	Unknown (None) Post-Miocene	
Songa (Halmahera-Indonesia)	Stratovolcano of Bibinoi	0608-073
Songaksan (Korea)	Tuff ring of Halla	1006-04-
Songan (Lesser Sunda Is)	Dome of Batur	0604-01=
Songe (Africa-E)	Dome of Meru	0202-16=
Song-Hua-Chiang (China-E)	Synonym of Sung-Hua-Chiang	
Songyaung (SE Asia)	Crater of Lower Chindwin	0705-09-
Soniquera (Bolivia)	Synonym of Sunequera	
Sonne Cone (Indian O.-W)	D of Fournaise, Piton de la	0303-02=
Sopas, Las (Chile-C)	Therm. feature Puyehue-Cordón Caulle	1507-15=
Sopka (Russian for Volcano) see proper name (e.g. Goriaschaia, Sopka)		
Sopochnaia (Kamchatka)	Synonym of Ichinsky	1000-28=
Sopoetan (Sulawesi-Indonesia)	Synonym of Soputan	0606-03=
Soporo (Perú)	Cinder cone of Andahua-Orcopampa	1504-004
Sopotschnaja (Kamchatka)	Synonym of Ichinsky	1000-28=
Soputan (Sulawesi-Indonesia)	Stratovolcano (35, 2008) Historical	**0606-03=**
Soranuma (Hokkaido-Japan)	Shield volcano (None) Pleistocene	
Soraramba (New Ireland-SW Pacific)	Stratovolcano of Tabar	
Sorcali (Ethiopia)	Synonym of Sork Ale	0201-103
Sorc-ali (Sorc-alli) (Ethiopia)	Synonym of Mallahle	0201-102
Sordo Lucas (Chile-C)	Stratovolcano (None) Pleistocene	
Sordo, El (Guatemala)	Stratovolcano of Piedra Grande	
Sorea (Banda Sea)	Synonym of Serua	0605-07=
Soriano (Italy)	Dome of Vico-Cimino Complex	
Sorieq Berapi (Sumatra)	Synonym of Sorikmarapi	0601-12=
Sorikmalintang (Sumatra)	Synonym of Malintang	0601-121
Sorikmarapi (Sumatra)	Stratovolcano (7, 1986) Historical	**0601-12=**
Sorikmerapi (Sumatra)	Synonym of Sorikmarapi	0601-12=
Soritimeat (Vanuatu-SW Pacific)	Synonym of Suretamatai	0507-01=
Sor-Jan (Atlantic-N-Jan Mayen)	Cone of Jan Mayen	1706-01=
Sork Ale (Ethiopia)	Stratovolcano (None) Holocene?	**0201-103**
Soropati (Java)	Stratovolcano of Telomoyo	0603-231
Sorug Chushku-Uzu (Russia-SE)	Shield volcano of Azas Plateau	1002-07-
Sosed (Kamchatka)	Cinder cone of Tolbachik	1000-24=
Sosneado, Volcán (Argentina)	Stratovolcano of Atuel, Caldera del	1507-023
Sosso, Ehi (Africa-N)	Stratovolcano of Toussidé, Tarso	0205-01=
Sotará (Colombia)	Stratovolcano (None) Holocene	**1501-061**
Soufrière Guadeloupe (W Indies)	Stratovolcano (20, 1977) Historical	**1600-06=**
Soufrière Hills (W Indies)	Stratovolcano (5, 2010) Historical	**1600-05=**
Soufrière St. Vincent (W Indies)	Stratovolcano (21, 1979) Historical	**1600-15=**
Soufrière Volc Centre (W Indies)	Synonym of Qualibou	1600-14=
Soufrière, La (W Indies)	Dome of Soufrière Guadeloupe	1600-06=
Sounkyo (Hokkaido-Japan)	Thermal feature of Daisetsu	0805-06=
Sounzan (Honshu-Japan)	Thermal feature of Hakone	0803-02=
Sour Creek (US-Wyoming)	Dome of Yellowstone	1205-01-
Source Hill (Canada)	Fissure vent of Spectrum Range	1200-07-
Souretamati (Vanuatu-SW Pacific)	Synonym of Suretamatai	0507-01=
Sousaki (Greece)	Synonym of Susaki	0102-01=
South Auckland (New Zealand)	Shield volcanoes (None) Pleistocene	
South Belknap (US-Oregon)	Cinder cone of Belknap	1202-06-
South Butte (US-Washington)	Cinder cone of Adams	1201-04-
South Butte (US-California)	Dome of Sutter Buttes	
South Cinder Peak (US-Oregon)	Cinder cone of Jefferson	1202-02-
South Coromandel Penin. (New Zeal.)	Volcanic field (None) Pleistocene	
South Coulee (US-California)	Dome of Mono Craters	1203-12-
South Daughter [Turangunan] (New Britain)	Stratovolcano of Rabaul	0502-14=
South Devil Mountain Lake (Alaska-W)	Maar of Espenberg	
South East Mountain (W Indies)	Stratovolcano of St. Catherine	1600-17=
South East Range (W Indies)	Stratovolcano (None) Pleistocene	
South Fork (US-California)	Cinder cone of Golden Trout Creek	1203-17-
South Group (US-Oregon)	Cinder cone of Sand Mountain Field	1202-04-
South Hill (Atlantic-S)	Dome of Inaccessible Island	
South Island (Africa-E)	Stratovolcano (1, 1888) Historical	**0202-02=**
South Killeak Lake (Alaska-W)	Maar of Espenberg	
South Menan Butte (US-Idaho)	Tuff cone of Menan Buttes	
South Mountain (US-New Mexico)	Dome of Valles Caldera	
South Pagan (Mariana Is-C Pacific)	Stratovolcano of Pagan	0804-17=
South Pinhead (US-Oregon)	Shield volcano of Olallie Butte	
South Pit (Hawaiian Is)	Pit crater of Mauna Loa	1302-02=
South Rift Vent Field (Pacific-NE)	Thermal feature of Axial Seamount	1301-021
South Rift Zone (Pacific-NE)	Fissure vent of Axial Seamount	1301-021
South Rift Zone (Hawaiian Is)	Fissure vent of Mauna Kea	1302-03-
South Sister (US-Oregon)	Complex volcano (2, -50) Radiocarbon	**1202-08-**
South Son (New Britain-SW Pac)	Synonym of Bamus	0502-11=
South Soufriere Hills (W Indies)	Stratovolcano of Soufrière Hills	1600-05=
South Squaw Tip (US-Oregon)	Vent of McLoughlin	
South Twin (Alaska-SW)	Dome of Iliamna	1103-02-
South Twin Lake (US-Oregon)	Tuff ring of Wuksi Butte-Twin Lakes	
Southeast crater (Mariana Is-C Pacific)	Crater of Anatahan	0804-20=
Southeast Crater (Italy)	Crater of Etna	0101-06=
South-East Volcanics (W Indies)	Volcanic field of Grand Bonhomme	
Southern Crater (Mindanao-Philippines)	Crater of Apo	0701-03=
Southern Crater (Philippines-C)	Crater of Kanlaon	0702-02=
Southern Dome (New Zealand)	Dome of Okataina	0401-05=
Southern EPR-Segment I (Pacific-E)	Submarine volcano (3, 1915) Magnetism	**1304-14-**
Southern EPR-Segment J (Pacific-E)	Submarine volcano (2, 1890) Magnetism	**1304-13-**
Southern EPR-Segment K (Pacific-E)	Submarine volcano (5, 1990) Historical	**1304-12-**
Southern Guadalajara (México)	Volcanic field (None) Pleistocene	

Name (Subregion)	Type (Eruptions, Most Recent) Status / Relation to Named Volcano	Volcano Number
Southern Sikhote-Alin (Russia-SE)	Synonym of Sikhote-Alin	1002-01-
Southern Tuya (Canada)	Tuya of Tuya Volc Field	1200-031
Southern Volcano (Antarctica)	Cone of Adare Peninsula	....
Southwest Hill [Volcán Sudoeste] (México)	Cinder cone of San Quintín Volc Field	1401-002
Southwest Rift Zone (Pacific-NE)	Fissure vent of Axial Seamount	1301-021
Southwest Rift Zone (Hawaiian Is)	Fissure vent of Kilauea	1302-01-
Southwest Rift Zone (Hawaiian Is)	Fissure vent of Mauna Loa	1302-02=
Southwest Trident (Alaska Peninsula)	Stratovolcano of Trident	1102-16-
Sovgavan Plateau Volc Field (Russia-SE)	Fissure vent of Sikhote-Alin	1002-01-
Sozan (Honshu-Japan)	Dome of Numazawa	0803-151
SP Crater (US-Arizona)	Cone of San Francisco Volc Field	....
Spaccata, Montagna (Italy)	Crater of Campi Flegrei	0101-01=
Spanish Bonk (Canada)	Cone of Wells Gray-Clearwater	1200-15-
Spanish Creek [Spanish Lake] (Canada)	Cone of Wells Gray-Clearwater	1200-15-
Spanish Lake (Canada)	Cone of Wells Gray-Clearwater	1200-15-
Spanish Mump (Canada)	Cone of Wells Gray-Clearwater	1200-15-
Spectrum Range (Canada)	Shield volcano (None) Holocene	**1200-07-**
Spence Hot Spring (US-New Mexico)	Thermal feature of Valles Caldera	....
Spendlove Knoll (US-Utah)	Cinder cone of Kolob	....
Sphinx (Canada)	Dome of Edziza	1200-06-
Sphinx Moraine (Canada)	Vent of Garibaldi Lake	1200-19-
Spina, Monte (Italy)	Dome of Campi Flegrei	0101-01=
Spinaio, Mt. (Italy)	Cone of Vulsini	0101-003
Spitaksar (Armenia)	Dome of Ghegam Ridge	0104-07-
Split Butte (US-Idaho)	Cone of Craters of the Moon	1204-02-
Split Butte (US-Idaho)	Maar of Wapi Lava Field	1204-03-
Spokoiny (Kamchatka)	Stratovolcano (1, -3450) Radiocarbon	**1000-671**
Sporades (Greece)	Lava dome (None) Pleistocene	....
Sprague River Valley (US-Oregon)	Shield volcanoes (None) Pleistocene	....
Spring Butte (US-Oregon)	Cone of Newberry	1202-11-
Spring Ghaut Soufriere (W Indies)	Thermal feature of Soufrière Hills	1600-05=
Spring Hill (Australia)	Cone of Newer Volcanics Prov	0509-01-
Spring Hill (US-California)	Cone of Shasta	1203-01-
Springerville (US-Arizona)	Volcanic field (None) Pleistocene	....
Sprinker (Germany)	Maar of West Eifel Volc Field	0100-01-
Spurr (Alaska-SW)	Stratovolcano (7, 1992) Historical	**1103-04-**
Squamish (Canada)	Volcanic field (None) Pleistocene	....
Squaw Lake (US-Wyoming)	Crater of Yellowstone	1205-01-
Squaw Ridge Lava Field (US-Oregon)	Volcanic field (None) Holocene?	**1202-13-**
Sredni (Kuril Is)	Stratovolcano of Medvezhia	0900-10=
Srednii (Kuril Is)	Submarine volc. (Uncertain) Holocene	**0900-211**
Sredniy (Kuril Is)	Crater of Ebeko	0900-38=
Sredniy Koshegochek (Kamchatka)	Shield volcano (None) Pleistocene	....
Sredny (Kamchatka)	Shield volcano of Tuzovsky	1000-54-
Sredny (Kamchatka)	Stratovolcano of Ushkovsky	1000-261
Srednyaya [Sredny] (Kamchatka)	Stratovolcano of Ushkovsky	1000-261
Srezannaia Mountain (Kamchatka)	Synonym of Maly Semiachik	1000-14=
Srezannyi (Kamchatka)	Fissure vent of Kliuchevskoi	1000-26=
Srodjo [Sroja] (Java)	Cone of Dieng Volc Complex	0603-20=
Sroja (Java)	Cone of Dieng Volc Complex	0603-20=
Srongga, Bukit (Lesser Sunda Is)	Cone of Batur	0604-01=
Ssawadowski (Antarctica)	Synonym of Zavodovski	1900-13=
St. Allouran (Indian O.-S)	Cone of Kerguelen Islands	0304-02=
St. Andrew Strait (Admiralty Is)	Complex volcano (4, 1957) Historical	**0500-01=**
St. Antony Peak (Kuril Is)	Synonym of Tiatia	0900-03=
St. Augustine (Alaska-SW)	Synonym of Augustine	1103-01-
St. Catherine (W Indies)	Stratovolcano (None) Holocene	**1600-17=**
St. Dolmat (Alaska Peninsula)	Synonym of Fourpeaked	1102-26-
St. George (Alaska-W)	Volcanic field (None) Pleistocene	....
St. George's Harbor (W Indies)	Crater of St. Catherine	1600-17=
St. George's Hill (W Indies)	Stratovolcano of Soufrière Hills	1600-05=
St. Helens (US-Washington)	Stratovolcano (40, 2008) Historical	**1201-05-**
St. Heliers (New Zealand)	Tuff ring of Auckland Field	0401-02=
St. Hyacinthe, Mt. (Alaska-E)	Synonym of Edgecumbe	1105-04-
St. John, Mt. (New Zealand)	Cone of Auckland Field	0401-02=
St. John's Flat (W Indies)	Dome of Saba	1600-01=
St. Joseph's Mt. [Lassen Peak] (US-Calif.)	Dome of Lassen Volc Center	1203-08-
St. Marys Crater (New Zealand)	Maar of Auckland Field	0401-02=
St. Michael (Alaska-W)	Shield volcanoes (None) Anthropology	**1104-04-**
St. Michael Mountain (Alaska-W)	Cone of St. Michael	1104-04-
St. Paul (Indian O.-S)	Stratovolcano (1, 1793) Historical	**0304-002**
St. Paul Island (Alaska-W)	Shield volcano (1, -1280) Radiocarbon	**1104-01-**
St. Paulo (Indian O.-S)	Synonym of St. Paul	0304-002
St. Peter's Dome (US-New Mexico)	Dome of Valles Caldera	....
St. Thomas (Africa-W)	Synonym of Sao Tome	0204-001
Stakahraun (Iceland-S)	Fissure vent of Hekla	1702-07=
Stampar (Iceland-SW)	Crater Row of Reykjanes	1701-02=
Stangarhals (Iceland-SW)	Fissure vent of Hengill	1701-05=
Star Peak (Vanuatu-SW Pacific)	Synonym of Mere Lava	0507-021
Starbuck Crater (Antarctica)	Crater of Bursey, Mt.	....
Starichky (Kamchatka)	Cinder cone of Tolbachik	1000-24=
Stary Kikhpinych (Kamchatka)	Stratovolcano of Kikhpinych	1000-18=
Stary Sheveluch (Kamchatka)	Stratovolcano of Shiveluch	1000-27=
State President Swart Peak (Indian O.-S)	Cone of Marion Island	0304-07-
Staughtons Hill (Australia)	Maar of Newer Volcanics Prov	0509-01-
Steamboat Springs (US-Nevada)	Lava domes (None) Pleist.-Fumarolic	....
Steaming Hill Lake (Vanuatu-SW Pacific)	Synonym of Gaua	0507-02=
Steamy Gulch Hot Springs (US-Washington)	Thermal feature of St. Helens	1201-05-
Steere, Mount (Antarctica)	Shield volcano of Crary Group	....
Stefanos (Greece)	Vent of Nisyros	0102-05=
Steinaholl (Iceland-SW)	Submarine vent of Reykjanes	1701-02=
Steller (Kamchatka)	Fissure vent of Kliuchevskoi	1000-26=
Steller (Alaska Peninsula)	Stratovolcano (None) Holocene	**1102-22-**
Stena (Kamchatka)	Dome of Ksudach	1000-05=
Stena (Kamchatka)	Stratovolcano of Maly Semiachik	1000-14=
Step Canyon Hot Springs (US-Washington)	Thermal feature of St. Helens	1201-05-
Step Sister [Black Hump] (US-Oregon)	Dome of North Sister Field	1202-07-
Stephanos [Stefanos] (Greece)	Vent of Nisyros	0102-05=
Stephen Island (Australia)	Cone of Maer Volc Province	....
Stephens Hill (Alaska-W)	Cone of St. Michael	1104-04-
Stepovak Bay 1 (Alaska Peninsula)	Stratovolcano (None) Pleistocene	....
Stepovak Bay 2 (Alaska Peninsula)	Cinder cone (None) Holocene	**1102-051**
Stepovak Bay 3 (Alaska Peninsula)	Cinder cone (None) Holocene?	**1102-052**
Stepovak Bay 4 (Alaska Peninsula)	Stratovolcano (None) Pleistocene	**1102-053**
Sterna Gambru (Greece)	Dome of Methana	0102-02=

Snow-mantled **Sunset Crater** (left-center), is the youngest volcanic feature of the San Francisco Mountain volcanic field, which covers a vast area of northern Arizona between Flagstaff and the Grand Canyon. The Sunset Crater eruption began about 1100 AD.

Name (Subregion)	Type (Eruptions, Most Recent) Status / Relation to Named Volcano	Volcano Number
Ste-Rose, Piton (Indian O.-W)	Cinder cone of Fournaise, Piton de la	0303-02=
Sterpeto (Italy)	Dome of Vico-Cimino Complex	....
Stikine River Volc Field (Canada)	Synonym of Klastline Group	....
Stockmans Hill (Australia)	Cone of McBride Volc Province	....
Stockyard Hill (Australia)	Tuff ring of Newer Volcanics Prov.	0509-01-
Stokap (Kuril Is)	Stratovolcano of Bogatyr Ridge	0900-06-
Stolovaya (Kamchatka)	Dome of Opala	1000-08=
Stone Mountain [Little Glass Mountain] (US)	Dome of Medicine Lake	1203-02-
Stony Beach Hills (Atlantic-S)	Cinder cone of Tristan da Cunha	1806-01=
Stony Hill (Atlantic-S)	Dome of Tristan da Cunha	1806-01=
Stony Hill Group (Atlantic-S)	Cinder cone of Tristan da Cunha	1806-01=
Stora Eldborg undir Geitlahlid (Iceland-SW)	Crater Row of Brennisteinsfjöll	1701-04=
Storahversmor (Iceland-NE)	Shield volcano of Theistareykjarbunga	1703-09=
Storaviti (Iceland-NE)	Shield volcano of Theistareykjarbunga	1703-09=
Storhofdi (Iceland-SE)	Cone of Öraefajökull	1704-01=
Stórhöfdi (Iceland-S)	Tuff cone of Vestmannaeyjar	1702-01=
Stori Bolli (Iceland-SW)	Crater Row of Brennisteinsfjöll	1701-04=
Stori-Brandur (Iceland-SW)	Submarine vent of Reykjanes	1701-02=
Storm (Canada)	Cone of Edziza	1200-06-
Stoves of Nero (Italy)	Crater of Campi Flegrei	0101-01=
Strariy (Russia-SE)	Cinder cone of Oka Plateau	1002-06-
Strawberry Knolls (US-Utah)	Cone of Markagunt Plateau	1207-04-
Streloshnaia Sopka (Kamchatka)	Synonym of Koryaksky	1000-09=
Strelotschnaja (Kamchatka)	Synonym of Koryaksky	1000-09=
Strohn (Germany)	Maar of West Eifel Volc Field	0100-01-
Stromboli (Italy)	Stratovolcano (22, 2010) Historical	**0101-04=**
Strombolicchio (Italy)	Cone of Stromboli	0101-04=
Strompar (Iceland-SW)	Shield volcano of Brennisteinsfjöll	1701-04=
Stronghyle [Riva] (Greece)	Pleistocene caldera of Santorini	0102-04=
Strongyle (Italy)	Synonym of Stromboli	0101-04=
Strútur (Iceland-S)	Tuya (None) Pleistocene	....
Strytuhraun (Iceland-SW)	Shield volcano of Hveravellir	1701-08=
Stuart Hill (Alaska-W)	Shield volcano of St. Michael	1104-04-
Stuart Hill [Stuert Hill] (Honduras)	Cinder cone of Utila Island	1403-16-
Stubel Crater (Kamchatka)	Maar of Ksudach	1000-05=
Stuert Hill (Honduras)	Cinder cone of Utila Island	1403-16-
Stufe di Kazen (Italy)	Cone of Pantelleria	0101-071
Stupenchaty (Kamchatka)	Dome of Bezymianny	1000-25=
Stupenchaty Bastion (Kamchatka)	Stratovolcano of Maly Semiachik	1000-14=
Sturge Island (Antarctica)	Stratovolcano (None) Uncertain	**1900-012**
Sturgeon Volc Province (Australia)	Shield volcanoes (None) Pleistocene	....
Styaks Swamp (New Zealand)	Cone of Auckland Field	0401-02=
Suachu (Kamchatka)	Synonym of Avachinsky	1000-10=
Suaru, Mt. (New Guinea)	Stratovolcano (None) Pleistocene	....
Subai [Kudriavy] (Kuril Is)	Stratovolcano of Medvezhia	0900-10=
Subia, Puig (Spain)	Cone of Olot Volc Field	0100-03-
Suchiltepequez (Guatemala)	Synonym of Atitlán	1402-06=
Suchioc Chico (México)	Cinder cone of Chichinautzin	1401-08=
Suchioc Grande (México)	Cinder cone of Chichinautzin	1401-08=
Suchitán (Guatemala)	Stratovolcanoes (Uncertain) Holocene	**1402-16-**
Suchitepequez (Guatemala)	Synonym of Atitlán	1402-06=
Sudoeste, Volcán (México)	Cinder cone of San Quintín Volc Field	1401-002

Name (Subregion)	Type (Eruptions, Most Recent) Status / Relation to Named Volcano	Volcano Number
Sudsohn (New Britain-SW Pac)	Synonym of Bamus	0502-11=
Sudurey (Iceland-S)	Cone of Vestmannaeyjar	1702-01=
Sudurgigar (Iceland-S)	Fissure vent of Hekla	1702-07=
Sueindani (Honshu-Japan)	Vent of Momisawa-dake	....
Suelich (Kamchatka)	Synonym of Shiveluch	1000-27=
Suelich (Kamchatka)	Former dome of Shiveluch	1000-27=
Suemez Strait (Alaska-E)	Vent of Tlevak Strait-Suemez Is.	1105-06-
Sugar Bowl (US-Washington)	Dome of St. Helens	1201-05-
Sugar Loaf (Hawaiian Is)	Tuff cone of Koolau	....
Sugar Loaf [Levera Island] (W Indies)	Dome of St. Catherine	1600-17=
Sugarloaf (Aleutian Is)	Cone of Makushin	1101-31-
Sugarloaf (W Indies)	Dome of Quill, The	1600-02=
Sugarloaf (New Guinea)	Volcanic field (None) Pleistocene	....
Sugarloaf Mountain (US-California)	Dome of Coso Volc Field	1203-18-
Sugarloaf Peak (US-California)	Shield volcano of Potato Butte	....
Sugarloaf Peak (Aleutian Is)	Stratovolcano of Semisopochnoi	1101-06-
Sugarpine Butte (US-Oregon)	Cinder cone of Newberry	1202-11-

Yukio Hayakawa (Gunma Univ.)

A steam plume rises above On-take, the summit crater of **Suwanose-jima** volcano in Japan's Ryukyu Islands. Suwanose-jima, one of Japan's most frequently active volcanoes, has been in a state of intermittent strombolian activity since 1949.

Name (Subregion)	Type (Eruptions, Most Recent) Status / Relation to Named Volcano	Volcano Number
Sugatamino-ike (Hokkaido-Japan)	Crater of Daisetsu	0805-06=
Sugigamine (Honshu-Japan)	Stratovolcano of Zao	0803-19=
Sugobo [Andrew's Cone] (Africa-E)	Cone of Barrier, The	0202-03=
Suguta River Hot Springs (Africa-E)	Thermal feature of Emuruangogolak	0202-051
Suguta-Logkipi (Africa-E)	Thermal feature of Barrier, The	0202-03=
Suiro (Philippines-C)	Dome of Biliran	0702-08=
Suiyo Seamount (Izu Is-Japan)	Submarine volcano (None) Fumarolic	**0804-093**
Sujut (Mindanao-Philippines)	Synonym of Makaturing	0701-04=
Sujut (Mindanao-Philippines)	Synonym of Ragang	0701-06=
Sukadana (Sumatra)	Shield volcano (None) Pleistocene	....
Sukai-Kesemaru (Honshu-Japan)	Stratovolcanoes (None) Pleistocene	....
Sukaria Caldera (Lesser Sunda Is)	Caldera (None) Fumarolic	**0604-12=**
Sukawa-dake (Honshu-Japan)	Synonym of Kurikoma	0803-21=
Suket (Java)	Stratovolcano of Raung	0603-34=
Sukhoi (Kamchatka)	Stratovolcano of Maly Semiachik	1000-14=
Sukumo-yama (Honshu-Japan)	Cone of Izu-Tobu	0803-01=
Sukuta See [Suguta-Logkipi] (Africa-E)	Thermal feature of Barrier, The	0202-03=
Sulfur Cones (Antarctica)	Cone of Hut Point Peninsula	....
Sulfur Hill [Jalajala] (Luzon-Philippines)	Thermal feature of Laguna Caldera	0703-08=
Sulfur Springs (W Indies)	Thermal feature of Plat Pays, Morne	1600-11=
Sulfur Works (US-California)	Thermal feature of Lassen Volc Center	1203-08-
Sulfureo, Lago [Lago Veccienna] (Italy)	Crater of Larderello	0101-001
Sulla Tacomi [Tolire Jaha] (Indonesia)	Crater of Gamalama	0608-06=
Sulnasker (Iceland-S)	Cone of Vestmannaeyjar	1702-01=
Sulphur Bank (Hawaiian Is)	Thermal feature of Kilauea	1302-01-
Sulphur Cone (Hawaiian Is)	Cone of Mauna Loa	1302-02=
Sulphur Creek (New Britain-SW Pac)	Crater Row of Rabaul	0502-14=
Sulphur Hot Springs (US-Washington)	Thermal feature of Glacier Peak	1201-02-
Sulphur Island (Volcano Is-Japan)	Synonym of Ioto [Iwo-jima]	0804-12=
Sulphur Lagoon [Lower Te Mari] (New Zeal.)	Crater of Tongariro	0401-08=
Sulphur Lake (D'Entrecasteaux Is)	Thermal feature of Iamalele	0503-05=
Sulphur Springs (W Indies)	Vent of Qualibou	1600-14=
Sulphur Springs (W Indies)	Thermal feature of Qualibou	1600-14=
Sulphur Springs (US-New Mexico)	Thermal feature of Valles Caldera	....
Sulphur Valley (New Zealand)	Thermal feature of Whale Island	....
Sultan (Pakistan)	Volcanic field (None) Pleistocene	....
Sultan Hamud-Simba (Africa-E)	Volcanic field (None) Pleistocene	....
Sulu (Sulu Is-Philippines)	Synonym of Jolo	0700-01=
Sulu Hills (New Britain-SW Pac)	Synonym of Sulu Range	0502-09=
Sulu Range (New Britain-SW Pac)	Stratovolcanoes (None) Fumarolic	**0502-09=**
Sumaco (Ecuador)	Stratovolcano (1, 1895) Historical	**1502-04=**
Sumber Panas (Java)	Thermal feature of Perbakti-Gagak	0603-04=
Sumbing (Java)	Dome of Kelut	0603-28=
Sumbing (Java)	Stratovolcano (1, 1730) Historical	**0603-22=**
Sumbing (Sumatra)	Stratovolcano (2, 1921) Historical	**0601-18=**
Sumisu Dai-ichi Knoll (Izu Is-Japan)	Submarine vent of Smith Rock	0804-08=
Sumisu Dai-ni Knoll (Izu Is-Japan)	Submarine vent of Smith Rock	0804-08=
Sumisu Knoll No. 1 [Sumisu Dai-ichi Knoll]	Submarine vent of Smith Rock	0804-08=
Sumisu Knoll No. 2 [Sumisu Dai-ni Knoll]	Submarine vent of Smith Rock	0804-08=

Name (Subregion)	Type (Eruptions, Most Recent) Status / Relation to Named Volcano	Volcano Number
Sumisu-jima (Izu Is-Japan)	Cone of Smith Rock	0804-08=
Sumisu-jima (Sumisu-sho) (Izu Is-Japan)	Synonym of Smith Rock	0804-08=
Sumiyoshi-ike (Kyushu-Japan)	Maars (2, -6200) Radiocarbon	**0802-081**
Summit Butte (US-Oregon)	Shield volcano of Wilson	....
Summit Rock (US-Oregon)	Cone of Thielsen	....
Sumon (Honshu-Japan)	Stratovolcano (None) Pleistocene	....
Sumur (Java)	Crater of Dieng Volc Complex	0603-20=
Sumur Bandung (Java)	Crater of Arjuno-Welirang	0603-29=
Sumur Tinggi, Bukit (Sumatra)	Unknown (None) Post-Miocene	....
Sunagohara (Honshu-Japan)	Caldera (None) Pleistocene	....
Sunda Caldera (Java)	Pleist. caldera of Tangkubanparahu	0603-09=
Sunday Island (Kermadec Is)	Synonym of Raoul Island	0402-03=
Sundhnukar (Iceland-SW)	Crater Row of Reykjanes	1701-02=
Sundoro (Java)	Stratovolcano (11, 1971) Historical	**0603-21=**
Sunequera (Bolivia)	Shield volcano (None) Pleistocene	....
Sunflower Flat (US-California)	Dome of Lassen Volc Center	1203-08-
Sungal (Sulu Is-Philippines)	Cinder cone of Jolo	0700-01=
Sungay, Mt. (Luzon-Philippines)	Stratovolcano of Taal	0703-07=
Sung-Hua-Chiang (China-E)	Lava domes (None) Quaternary	....
Sunrise (Izu Is-Japan)	Thermal feature of Myojin Knoll	0804-061
Sunset (US-Idaho)	Cinder cone of Craters of the Moon	1204-02-
Sunset Crater (US-Arizona)	Cinder cone (1, 1075) Dendrochronology	**1209-02-**
Suoh (Sumatra)	Calderas (1, 1933) Historical	**0601-27=**
Suou-ana (Izu Is-Japan)	Crater of Miyake-jima	0804-04=
Süphan Dagi (Turkey)	Stratovolcano (1, -8050) Holocene	**0103-021**
Supply Reef (Mariana Is-C Pacific)	Submarine volc. (2, 1989) Hydrophonic	**0804-142**
Suretamatai (Vanuatu-SW Pacific)	Complex volcano (3, 1966) Historical	**0507-01=**
Suretametai (Vanuatu-SW Pacific)	Synonym of Suretamatai	0507-01=
Suribachi-Kakokyu (Hokkaido-Japan)	Cone of Tokachi	0805-05=
Suribachi-yama (Volcano Is-Japan)	Cinder cone of Ioto [Iwo-jima]	0804-12=
Suribachi-yama (Honshu-Japan)	Cone of Utsukushigahara	....
Suribati-yama [Suribachi-yama] (Japan)	Cinder cone of Ioto [Iwo-jima]	0804-12=
Surice (Slovakia)	Vent of Central Slovakia	....
Surprise Lake Volc Field (Canada)	Synonym of Atlin Volc Field	1200-03-
Surtsey (Iceland-S)	Tuff cone of Vestmannaeyjar	1702-01=
Surúndaro, Cerro de (México)	Cinder cone of Michoacán-Guanajuato	1401-06=
Susah, Kawah (Java)	Thermal feature of Salak	0603-05=
Susaki (Greece)	(None) Not a Volcano	0102-01=
Susaki (Ryukyu Is)	Cone of Suwanose-jima	0802-03=
Susua (Africa-E)	Synonym of Suswa	0202-11=
Susung Malaki (Luzon-Philippines)	Dome of Labo	....
Suswa (Africa-E)	Shield volcano (None) Holocene	**0202-11=**
Sutarengga (Java)	Dome of Muria	0603-251
Sutdonduran (Turkey)	Cone of Erciyes Dagi	0103-01=
Sutter Buttes (US-California)	Lava domes (None) Pleistocene	....
Suwa Fuji [Tateshina-yama} (Honshu-Japan)	Stratovolcano of Kita Yatsuga-take	0803-031
Suwanose-jima (Ryukyu Is)	Stratovolcanoes (24, 2010) Historical	**0802-03=**
Suwanose-jima Oki (Ryukyu Is)	Submarine vent of Suwanose-jima	0802-03=
Suwanose-zima (Ryukyu Is)	Synonym of Suwanose-jima	0802-03=
Suwoh (Sumatra)	Synonym of Suoh	0601-27=
Suwolbong (Korea)	Tuff ring of Halla	1006-04-
Suyama-dake (Honshu-Japan)	Synonym of Kurikoma	0803-21=
Suyelich [Suelich] (Kamchatka)	Former dome of Shiveluch	1000-27=
Suyul Hanish (Red Sea)	Cone of Hanish	0201-022
Suzanna Mount (SE Asia)	Cone of Bas Dong Nai	0705-05-
Suzuga-take (Honshu-Japan)	Dome of Akagi	0803-13=
Svalaskardshraun (Iceland-S)	Crater Row of Hekla	1702-07=
Svalthufa (Iceland-W)	Cone of Snaefellsjökull	1700-01=
Svartadyngja (Iceland-NE)	Shield volcano of Askja	1703-06=
Svartahraun (Iceland-SW)	Crater Row of Hveravellir	1701-08=
Svartihryggur (Iceland-SW)	Crater Row of Brennisteinsfjöll	1701-04=
Svartikrokur (Iceland-NE)	Crater Row of Bárdarbunga	1703-03=
Svartsengi (Iceland-SW)	Fissure vent of Reykjanes	1701-02=
Sveifluglr (Iceland-SW)	Crater Row of Krísuvík	1701-03=
Sveinagja (Iceland-NE)	Fissure vent of Askja	1703-06=
Sveinar (Iceland-NE)	Fissure vent of Fremrinamur	1703-07=
Sverre (Spitsbergen)	Synonym of Sverrefjell	....
Sverrefjell (Spitsbergen)	Cinder cone (None) Pleistocene	....
Sviagigur (Iceland-NE)	Synonym of Grímsvötn	1703-01=
Svinhofdarhraun (Iceland-S)	Fissure vent of Hekla	1702-07=
Svortuborgir (Iceland-NE)	Crater Row of Krafla	1703-08=
Svortutindar (Iceland-W)	Cone of Snaefellsjökull	1700-01=
Svyashchennaya (Russia-SE)	Cone of Tunkin Depression	1002-05-
SW Usangu Basin (Africa-E)	Lava domes (None) Holocene	**0202-163**
Swamp Wells Butte (US-Oregon)	Cone of Newberry	1202-11-
Swartkop Point (Indian O.-S)	Tuff cone of Marion Island	0304-07-
Swinton Creek (Canada)	Cone of Dark Mountain	....
Syari (Hokkaido-Japan)	Synonym of Shari	....
Sykes (México)	Maar of Pinacate	1401-001
Symonds Street (New Zealand)	Cone of Auckland Field	0401-02=
Syni [Sini] (Russia-SE)	Cone of Udokan Plateau	1002-03-
Syowa-Iwo-zima [Showa-Iwo-jima] (Ryukyu Is)	Dome of Kikai	0802-06=
Syowa-Sinzan [Showa-Shinzan] (Japan)	Dome of Usu	0805-03=
Syozi-yama [Shoji-yama] (Honshu-Japan)	Dome of Osore-yama	0803-29=
Syrdri Raudamelskula (Iceland-W)	Cone of Ljósufjöll	1700-03=
Syrfellshraun (Iceland-SW)	Crater Row of Reykjanes	1701-02=
Syrkhissar (Georgia)	Dome of Kasbek	0104-02-
Syurado [Shurado] (Honshu-Japan)	Crater of Narugo	0803-20=
Szebike (Hungary)	Shield volcano of Balaton Highland	....
Szigliget (Hungary)	Cone of Balaton Highland	....
Szilvasko (Hungary)	Cone of Nográd	....
Sziwan, Djebel (Red Sea)	Synonym of Tair, Jebel at	0201-01=
Szt. Gyorgyhegy (Hungary)	Shield volcano of Balaton Highland	....

T

Name (Subregion)	Type (Eruptions, Most Recent) Status / Relation to Named Volcano	Volcano Number
Taal (Luzon-Philippines)	Caldera (34, 1977) Historical	**0703-07=**
Taapaca (Chile-N)	Complex volcano (8, -320) Radiocarbon	**1505-011**
Tababara (Ecuador)	Dome of Chachimbiro	1502-002
Tabac, Mt. (W Indies)	Stratovolcano of Qualibou	1600-14=
Tabaquillo (México)	Lava cone of Chichinautzin	1401-08=
Tabar (New Ireland-SW Pacific)	Stratovolcano (None) Pleistocene	....
Tabarin Peninsula (Antarctica)	Shield volcano? (None) Pleistocene	....
Tabaro, Mt. (Luzon-Philippines)	Vent of Taal	0703-07=
Tabashine-yama (Honshu-Japan)	Synonym of Zao	0803-19=
Tabernacle Hill (US-Utah)	Tuff cone of Black Rock Desert	1207-05-
Tablas, Cerro (El Salvador)	Cinder cone of Singüil, Cerro	1403-002
Tablas, Cerro las (El Salvador)	Stratovolcanoes (None) Pleistocene	....
Table de l'Institut (Indian O.-S)	Pleist. caldera of Kerguelen Islands	0304-02=
Table Mountain (New Zealand)	Cone of South Coromandel Peninsula	....
Table Mountain (US-California)	Stratovolcano (None) Pleistocene	....
Table Mt. Crater (Galápagos)	Crater of Santa Cruz	1503-091
Table Peak (Red Sea)	Cone of Zubair, Jebel	0201-02=
Table Rock (US-Oregon)	Tuff cone of Fort Rock Volc Field	....
Table Top (Aleutian Is)	Cinder cone (None) Pleistocene	....
Table Vent (Pacific-NE)	Thermal feature of Cleft Segment	1301-03-
Table, the (Canada)	Tuya of Garibaldi Lake	1200-19-
Tabletop, Mt. (Australia)	Cone of McBride Volc Province	....
Tablón del Conacaste (Guatemala)	Cinder cone of Güistepeque Volc Field	....
Tablón el Rodeo, Cerro el (Guatemala)	Cinder cone of Güistepeque Volc Field	....
Tablón, Cerro el (Honduras)	Cone of Pedregal, El	....
Tablón, Loma del (Guatemala)	Shield volcano of Redondo, Cerro	....
Tabonal Negro (Canary Is)	Dome of Tenerife	1803-03-
Tabonal, El (Canary Is)	Cone of Tenerife	1803-03-
Tabon-Tabon, Mt. (Luzon-Philippines)	Stratovolcano of Bulusan	0703-01=
Tabor, Monte (Italy)	Dome of Ischia	0101-03=
Tabor, Mount (US-Oregon)	Cinder cone of Boring Lava	....
Tabun Urtu-Ula (Mongolia)	Unknown (None) Pleistocene	....
Taburete (El Salvador)	Stratovolcano (None) Holocene?	**1403-072**
Taburiente, Caldera de (Canary Is)	Stratovolcano of La Palma	1803-01-
Tabutera (Vanuatu-SW Pacific)	Stratovolcano of North Vate	0507-081
Tacaná (México)	Stratovolcano (10, 1986) Historical	**1401-13=**
Tacande (Canary Is)	Cinder cone of La Palma	1803-01-
Tacanistes, Cerro (Nicaragua)	Cone of Pilas, Las	1404-08=
Tachibana (Hokkaido-Japan)	Crater of Kuttara	0805-034
Tachibana Hot Springs (Honshu-Japan)	Thermal feature of Kusatsu-Shirane	0803-12=
Tachipegue, Cerro (El Salvador)	Cone of Singüil, Cerro	1403-002
Tacó Arriba, Cerrito de (Guatemala)	Lava cone of Chiquimula Volc Field	1402-20-
Taco, Montaña de (Canary Is)	Cone of Tenerife	1803-03-
Tacoma, Mt. (Tacoman) (US-Washington)	Synonym of Rainier	1201-03-
Tacora (Chile-N)	Stratovolcano (Uncertain) Fumarolic	**1505-01=**
Tadekho Hill (Canada)	Cone of Spectrum Range	1200-07-
Tafadek (Africa-N)	Thermal feature of Todra Volc Field	0205-001
Tafahi (Tonga-SW Pacific)	Stratovolcano (None) Holocene?	**0403-101**
Tafira, Montana (Canary Is)	Cone of Gran Canaria	1803-04-
Tafna Beni Saf (Africa-N)	Volcanic field (None) Pleistocene	....
Taftan (Iran)	Stratovolcano (Uncertain) Holocene	**0302-05-**
Tafu (Tonga-SW Pacific)	Submarine vent of Tafu-Maka	0403-12-
Tafu-Maka (Tonga-SW Pacific)	Submarine volcano (1, 2008) Historical	**0403-12-**
Taga (Honshu-Japan)	Stratovolcano of Izu-Tobu	0803-01=
Taga (Honshu-Japan)	Stratovolcano (None) Pleistocene	....
Tagabo Hills (Africa-N)	Synonym of Kutum Volc Field	0205-04-
Taghum Butte (US-Oregon)	Cone of Newberry	1202-11-
Tagiri (Kyushu-Japan)	Cone of Sakura-jima	0802-08=
Taglabunga [Talabunga] (Iceland-NE)	Shield volcano of Fremrinamur	1703-07=
Taglgigahraun (Iceland-S)	Fissure vent of Hekla	1702-07=
Tagotala (Samoa-SW Pacific)	Cone of Savai'i	0404-04=
Tagus (Galápagos)	Tuff cone of Darwin	1503-03=
Tahalra Volc Field (Africa-N)	Pyroclastic cones (None) Holocene	**0205-004**
Tahe (Lesser Sunda Is)	Cone of Tambora	0604-04=
Taheke (New Zealand)	Thermal feature of Rotorua	....
Tahiti (Pacific-C)	Synonym of Tahiti-Nui	....
Tahiti-Iti (Pacific-C)	Shield volcano (None) Pleistocene	....
Tahiti-Nui (Pacific-C)	Shield volcano (None) Pleistocene	....
Tahoma Peak (Aleutian Is)	Former dome of Bogoslof	1101-30-
Tahonelatclah (US-Washington)	Synonym of St. Helens	1201-05-
Tahoranui (New Zealand)	Cone of Kaikohe-Bay of Islands	0401-01=
Tahua (Bolivia)	Synonym of Tupua	....
Tahual (Guatemala)	Stratovolcano (None) Holocene	**1402-141**
Tahual, Volcán (Guatemala)	Stratovolcano of Suchitán	1402-16-
Tahunatara (New Zealand)	Dome of Taupo	0401-07=
Tahuya (Canary Is)	Cinder cone of La Palma	1803-01-
Taian (China-E)	Unknown (None) Quaternary	....
Taiarapu (Pacific-C)	Synonym of Tahiti-Iti	....
Taifang Range (China-E)	Synonym of Taihangshanlu	....
Taihangshanlu (China-E)	Unknown (None) Quaternary	....
Taihei-zan (Honshu-Japan)	Dome of Sanbe	0803-002
Taihei-zan (Kyushu-Japan)	Dome of Tsurumi	0802-13=
Tair, Jebel at (Red Sea)	Stratovolcano (5, 2008) Historical	**0201-01=**
Tairaga-dake (Hokkaido-Japan)	Stratovolcano of Tokachi	0805-05=
Tairoike [Furumio] (Izu Is-Japan)	Maar of Miyake-jima	0804-04=
Taisen-Minami (Kyushu-Japan)	Dome of Kuju	0802-12=
Taisen-zan (Kyushu-Japan)	Cone of Kuju	0802-12=
Taisetsu-zan (Hokkaido-Japan)	Synonym of Daisetsu	0805-06=
Ta-i-shan [Dayishan] (China-E)	Cone of Longgang Group	1005-05-
Taisho (Honshu-Japan)	Crater of Yake-dake	0803-07=
Taisho-kako (Hokkaido-Japan)	Crater of Tokachi	0805-05=
Taisyo-kako [Taisho-kako] (Hokkaido-Japan)	Crater of Tokachi	0805-05=
Taito'elau (Samoa-SW Pacific)	Cone of Upolu	0404-03-
Tajo, Cerro el (México)	Vent of Primavera, Sierra la	....
Tajumbina (Colombia)	Unknown (None) Post-Miocene	....
Tajumulco (Guatemala)	Stratovolcano (Uncertain) Holocene	**1402-02=**
Takachihomine (Kyushu-Japan)	Stratovolcano of Kirishima	0802-09=
Taka-dake (Kyushu-Japan)	Stratovolcano of Aso	0802-11=
Takadekki (Honshu-Japan)	Dome of Iizuna	....
Takadomori (Ryukyu Is)	Stratovolcano of Kuchinoerabu-jima	0802-05=
Takado-yama (Izu Is-Japan)	Dome of Kozu-shima	0804-03=
Takahachi-yama (Honshu-Japan)	Cone of Fuji	0803-03=
Takahara (Hokkaido-Japan)	Thermal feature of Daisetsu	0805-06=
Takahara (Honshu-Japan)	Stratovolcano (1, -4570) Holocene	**0803-143**
Takahe (Antarctica)	Shield volcano (3, -5550) Ice Core	**1900-027**
Takahinata (Honshu-Japan)	Dome of Onikobe	....
Takahira-yama (Kyushu-Japan)	Cone of Tsurumi	0802-13=
Takaiwa-yama (Kyushu-Japan)	Dome of Unzen	0802-10=
Takakura-yama (Honshu-Japan)	Stratovolcano of Nyuto-Takakura	....
Takamaka, Piton (Indian O.-W)	Cinder cone of Fournaise, Piton de la	0303-02=
Takamatsu (Honshu-Japan)	Stratovolcano (None) Pleistocene	....
Takamine-yama (Honshu-Japan)	Stratovolcano of Eboshi	....
Takamuro-yama (Honshu-Japan)	Cone of Izu-Tobu	0803-01=
Takane-sho (Izu Is-Japan)	Cone of Bayonnaise Rocks	0804-07=
Takanoobane (Kyushu-Japan)	Cone of Aso	0802-11=
Takanosu (Kyushu-Japan)	Dome of Kuju	0802-12=
Takara (Honshu-Japan)	Synonym of Kamitakara	....
Takara (Honshu-Japan)	Shield volcano (None) Pleistocene	....
Takashi-yama (Honshu-Japan)	Synonym of Fuji	0803-03=
Takatihomine [Takachihomine] (Japan)	Stratovolcano of Kirishima	0802-09=
Takatsuka-yama (Honshu-Japan)	Cinder cone of Izu-Tobu	0803-01=
Takatsuka-yama (Honshu-Japan)	Cinder cone of Tsuruta	....
Takawangha (Aleutian Is)	Stratovolcano (1, 1550) Radiocarbon	**1101-09-**
Taka-yama (Honshu-Japan)	Cone of Azuma	0803-18=
Taka-yama (Honshu-Japan)	Cone of Fuji	0803-03=
Taka-yama (Honshu-Japan)	Synonym of Zao	0803-19=
Takayashiro (Honshu-Japan)	Stratovolcano (None) Pleistocene	....
Takayu (Honshu-Japan)	Dome of Azuma	0803-18=
Takefjellet (Atlantic-N-Jan Mayen)	Dome of Jan Mayen	1706-01=
Takenohira (Izu Is-Japan)	Cone of Oshima	0804-01=
Takenotsugi (Kyushu-Japan)	Pyroclastic cone of Iki Volc Group	....
Takenoyu (Kyushu-Japan)	Thermal feature of Kuju	0802-12=
Taketomi (Kuril Is)	Crater of Alaid	0900-39=
Taketori-yama (Honshu-Japan)	Synonym of Fuji	0803-03=
Takeura (Hokkaido-Japan)	Stratovolcano of Kuttara	0805-034
Take-yama (Kyushu-Japan)	Dome of Ibusuki Volc Field	0802-07=
Takit (Luzon-Philippines)	Synonym of Malinao	....
Takor (Sumatra)	Synonym of Takur-Takur	....
Takou (New Zealand)	Cone of Kaikohe-Bay of Islands	0401-01=
Takuan Group (Bougainville-SW Pac.)	Compound volcano (None) Holocene	**0505-021**
Takumi-yama (Honshu-Japan)	Cone of Oki-Dogo	0803-003
Takura (Honshu-Japan)	Synonym of Takara	....
Takur-Takur (Sumatra)	Unknown (None) Pleistocene	....
Ta-ku-Shan-tzu [Dayishan] (China-E)	Cone of Longgang Group	1005-05-

The compound **Taapaca** massif in northern Chile consists of Pleistocene-to-Holocene stratovolcano and lava domes that rise above block-and-ash flow deposits at its base.

Name (Subregion)	Type (Eruptions, Most Recent) Status / Relation to Named Volcano	Volcano Number
Tala (Halmahera-Indonesia)	Synonym of Dukono	0608-01=
Tala (Luzon-Philippines)	Dome of Natib	0703-082
Talabunga (Iceland-NE)	Shield volcano of Fremrinamur	1703-07=
Talagabodas (Java)	Stratovolcano (None) Fumarolic	**0603-15=**
Talakmau (Sumatra)	Complex volcano (Uncertain) Holocene	**0601-13=**
Talamau (Sumatra)	Synonym of Talakmau	0601-13=
Talamitan, Mt. (Luzon-Philippines)	Synonym of Cariliao	....
Talang (Sumatra)	Stratovolcano (13, 2007) Historical	**0601-16=**
Talang, Danau (Sumatra)	Crater of Talang	0601-16=
Talao, Vuti (Vanuatu-SW Pacific)	Cone of Aoba	0507-03=
Talapaca, Cerro (Bolivia)	Stratovolcano (None) Post-Miocene	....
Talasea Government Station (New Britain)	Thermal feature of Garua Harbour	0502-06=

Name (Subregion)	Type (Eruptions, Most Recent) Status / Relation to Named Volcano	Volcano Number
Talasea Harbour (New Britain-SW Pac)	Synonym of Garua Harbour	0502-06=
Talatak (Luzon-Philippines)	Dome of Bulusan	0703-01=
Talawe, Mount (New Britain-SW Pac)	Stratovolcano of Langila	0502-01=
Talaya Group (Russia-SE)	Cone of Tunkin Depression	1002-05-
Talbot Bank (Italy)	Submarine vent C. Flegrei Mar Sicilia	0101-07=
Talim Island (Luzon-Philippines)	Stratovolcano of Laguna Caldera	0703-08=
Talimasa, Tavani (Vanuatu-SW Pacific)	Cone of Emae	....
Talines, Mt. (Philippines-C)	Cone of Cuernos de Negros	0702-01=
Talipao, Mt. (Sulu Is-Philippines)	Cinder cone of Jolo	0700-01=
Talisay (Luzon-Philippines)	Caldera of Taal	0703-07=
Tallang (Sumatra)	Synonym of Talang	0601-16=
Talléa (Ethiopia)	Cone of Gufa	0201-124
Talo (New Guinea-NE of)	Stratovolcano of Umboi	0501-06=
Talolinga, Loma (Nicaragua)	Cinder cone of San Cristóbal	1404-02=
Talopu Hot Spring (New Britain-SW Pac)	Thermal feature of Sulu Range	0502-09=
Talpetate, Cerro (Nicaragua)	Dome of Apoyeque	1404-091
Talquian [Chichuj] (México)	Stratovolcano of Tacaná	1401-13=
Talu (Sumatra)	Unknown (None) Post-Miocene	....
Ta-Lung-wan [Dalongwan] (China-E)	Maar of Longgang Group	1005-05-
Talutu, Mount (New Britain-SW Pac)	Dome of Sulu Range	0502-09=
Tama Lakes (New Zealand)	Crater of Ruapehu	0401-10=
Tamacite, Montana (Canary Is)	Cone of Fuerteventura	1803-05-
Tamagastepec [Tamages] (El Salvador)	Cone of Santa Ana	1403-02=
Tamagawa (Honshu-Japan)	Caldera (None) Pleistocene	....
Tamagawa Spa (Honshu-Japan)	Thermal feature of Akita-Yake-yama	0803-26=
Tamages (El Salvador)	Cone of Santa Ana	1403-02=
Tamami (Santa Cruz Is-SW Pacific)	Synonym of Tinakula	0506-01=
Taman Gedang (Sumatra)	Crater of Kunyit	0601-171
Taman Saat (Java)	Crater of Patuha	0603-07=
Taman, Kawah (Java)	Thermal feature of Perbakti-Gagak	0603-04=
Tamangoni (New Britain-SW Pac)	Dome of Unea	....
Tamanhidup (Java)	Crater of Iyang-Argapura	0603-33=
Tamankering (Java)	Crater of Iyang-Argapura	0603-33=
Tamankring (Java)	Cone of Iyang-Argapura	0603-33=
Tamano-ike (Honshu-Japan)	Crater of Chokai	0803-22=
Tamansari Group (Lesser Sunda Is)	Crater of Batur	0604-01=
Tamarii Seamount (Austral Is-C Pacific)	Synonym of Macdonald	1303-06-
Tambanan (Lesser Sunda Is)	Unknown (None) Quaternary	....
Tambo Quemado (Bolivia)	Pyroclastic shield (None) Holocene	**1505-021**
Tambor Grande (Nicaragua)	Caldera (None) Quaternary	....
Tambora (Lesser Sunda Is)	Stratovolcano (7, 1967) Historical	**0604-04=**
Tambunarakwe, Viti (Vanuatu-SW Pacific)	Cone of Aoba	0507-03=
Tamertiou, Tarso (Africa-N)	Cone of Toussidé, Tarso	0205-01=
Tamia, Montana (Canary Is)	Cone of Lanzarote	1803-06-
Tamlang, Mt. (Luzon-Philippines)	Cone of San Pablo Volc Field	0703-06=
Tamojang [Tamoyang] (Lesser Sunda Is)	Crater of Sirung	0604-27=
Tamoyang (Lesser Sunda Is)	Crater of Sirung	0604-27=
Tampad (Mindanao-Philippines)	Cone of Matutum	0701-02=
Tampomas (Java)	Stratovolcano (None) Holocene	**0603-131**

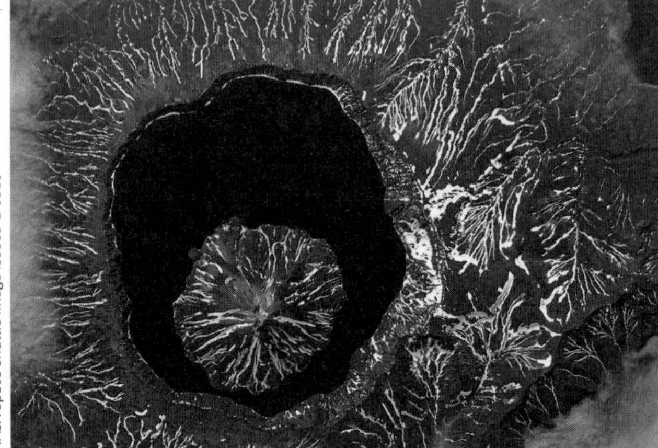

Summer snow remnants highlight dendritic drainages cutting pyroclastic-flow deposits on the flanks of lake-filled **Tao-Rusyr** caldera in the Kuril Islands; post-caldera Krenitzyn Peak stratovolcano partially fills the caldera lake.

Name (Subregion)	Type (Eruptions, Most Recent) Status / Relation to Named Volcano	Volcano Number
Tampusu [Tompusu] (Sulawesi-Indonesia)	Cone of Tondano Caldera	0606-07-
Tana (Aleutian Is)	Stratovolcanoes (None) Holocene	**1101-241**
Tana (Vanuatu-SW Pacific)	Synonym of Yasur	0507-10=
Tanaba (Honshu-Japan)	Stratovolcano (None) Pleistocene	....
Tanada (Alaska-E)	Shield volcano (None) Pleistocene	....
Tanaga (Aleutian Is)	Stratovolcanoes (6, 1914) Historical	**1101-08-**
Tanah Lapang (Halmahera-Indonesia)	Crater of Dukono	0608-01=
Tanak-Angunak (Aleutian Is)	Synonym of Carlisle	1101-23-
Tancítaro, Volcán (México)	Stratovolc. of Michoacán-Guanajuato	1401-06=
Tandic (Mindanao-Philippines)	Dome of Leonard Range	0701-031
Tandikai (Sumatra)	Synonym of Tandikat	0601-15=
Tandikat (Sumatra)	Stratovolcanoes (3, 1924) Historical	**0601-15=**
Tandukbenua, Dolok (Sumatra)	Cone of Toba	0601-09=
Tandurek (Turkey)	Synonym of Tendürek Dagi	0103-03=
Tanemakishiro (Honshu-Japan)	Crater of Iwaki	0803-27=
Tanemakisiro [Tanemakishiro] (Japan)	Crater of Iwaki	0803-27=
Tanga (New Ireland-SW Pacific)	Stratovolcano (None) Pleist.-Hot Springs	....
Tanganasoga (Canary Is)	Cinder cone of Hierro	1803-02-
Tangano (Africa-E)	Shield volcano of Ngozi	0202-164
Tangaroa (New Zealand)	Submarine volcano (None) Fumarolic	**0401-102**
Tangaroa, Maunga (Chile-Is)	Pyroclastic cone of Easter Island	1506-011
Tanggamus (Sumatra)	Stratovolcano (None) Quaternary	....
Tangi (New Britain-SW Pac)	Stratovolcano (None) Pleistocene	....
Tangkoeban Prahoe (Java)	Synonym of Tangkubanparahu	0603-09=
Tangkoko (Sulawesi-Indonesia)	Synonym of Tongkoko	0606-13=
Tangkuban Parahu (Java)	Synonym of Tangkubanparahu	0603-09=
Tangkuban Perahu (Java)	Synonym of Tangkubanparahu	0603-09=
Tangkubanparahu (Java)	Stratovolcano (18, 1983) Historical	**0603-09=**
Tanglup, Mount (New Guinea-NE of)	Cone of Umboi	0501-06=
Tang-Shui-Chang (China-E)	Thermal feature of Changbaishan	1005-06-
Tanguerres (Colombia)	Synonym of Azufral	1501-09=
Tangues, Piton (Indian O.-W)	Cinder cone of Fournaise, Piton de la	0303-02=
Tanguna (Ecuador)	Dome of Chachimbiro	1502-002
Tangwangi, Vuti (Vanuatu-SW Pacific)	Cone of Aoba	0507-03=
Tangy'n (China-E)	Unknown (None) Quaternary	....
Tanjung Tiramana (Lesser Sunda Is)	Thermal feature of Paluweh	0604-15=
Tank Farm (New Zealand)	Tuff ring of Auckland Field	0401-02=
Tanna (Vanuatu-SW Pacific)	Synonym of Yasur	0507-10=
Tanodourek (Turkey)	Synonym of Tendürek Dagi	0103-03=
Tansei (Honshu-Japan)	Dome of Nantai	0803-141
Tantalus (Hawaiian Is)	Tuff cone of Koolau	....
Tao, Volcan de (Canary Is)	Cone of Lanzarote	1803-06-
Tao-Rusyr Caldera (Kuril Is)	Stratovolcano (2, 1952) Historical	**0900-31=**
Taos Plateau (US-New Mexico)	Volcanic field (None) Pleistocene	....
Tapa (Argentina)	Vent of Unnamed	....
Tapahoro (New Zealand)	Dome of Okataina	0401-05=
Tapak (Lesser Sunda Is)	Stratovolcano of Bratan	0604-001
Tapaquilcha, Volcano (Bolivia)	Stratovolcano (None) Post-Miocene	....
Tapeixte, Cerro (México)	Cinder cone of Chichinautzin	1401-08=
Ta-Ping-shan (China-E)	Synonym of Dabingshan	....
Tapirag, Mt. (Alaska Peninsula)	Synonym of Fourpeaked	1102-26-
Tapu'ele'ele (Samoa-SW Pacific)	Cone of Savai'i	0404-04=
Tapungho (Luzon-Philippines)	Dome of Pinatubo	0703-083
Tapunikandi, Vuti (Vanuatu-SW Pacific)	Cone of Aoba	0507-03=
Taputapu (Samoa-SW Pacific)	Shield volcano of Tutuila	0404-02-
Tar River Soufriere (W Indies)	Thermal feature of Soufrière Hills	1600-05=
Tar, Djebel (Red Sea)	Synonym of Tair, Jebel at	0201-01=
Tara (Lesser Sunda Is)	Cone of Mapi Group	....
Tara, Batoe (Lesser Sunda Is)	Synonym of Tara, Batu	0604-26=
Tara, Batu (Lesser Sunda Is)	Stratovolcano (2, 2010) Historical	**0604-26=**
Tara-dake (Kyushu-Japan)	Stratovolcano (None) Pleistocene	....
Tarakan (Halmahera-Indonesia)	Pyroclastic cones (None) Holocene	**0608-001**
Tarakan Itji (Halmahera-Indonesia)	Cone of Tarakan	0608-001
Tarakan Lamo (Halmahera-Indonesia)	Cone of Tarakan	0608-001
Taranaki [Egmont] (New Zealand)	Stratovolcano (43, 1854) Historical	**0401-03=**
Taranaki Point (New Zealand)	Cone of Kariori	....
Tarascan Volc Field (México)	Synonym of Michoacán-Guanajuato	1401-06=
Taratimi (New Zealand)	Tuff ring of Mayor Island	0401-021
Tarawera (New Zealand)	Fissure vent of Okataina	0401-05=
Tardarfjoll (Iceland-SW)	Crater Row of Krísuvík	1701-03=
Tarewakoura (New Zealand)	Dome of Mayor Island	0401-021
Tari (Chile-Is)	Pyroclastic cone of Easter Island	1506-011
Tariat Volc Field (Mongolia)	Synonym of Taryatu-Chulutu	1003-01-
Tariat-Choloot (Mongolia)	Synonym of Taryatu-Chulutu	1003-01-
Taro (Honshu-Japan)	Dome of Omanago Group	0803-142
Taroeb [Tarub] (Java)	Stratovolcano of Lamongan	0603-32=
Taroka Group (Bougainville-SW Pacific)	Cone of Loloru	0505-03=
Tarosero (Africa-E)	Stratovolcano (None) Post-Miocene	....
Tarranosa (Mindanao-Philippines)	Cone of Imbing	....
Tarso (Chad term for Mountain) see proper name (e.g. Voon, Tarso)		
Tartaret (France)	Cone of Chaîne des Puys	0100-02-
Tarub (Java)	Stratovolcano of Lamongan	0603-32=
Tarucun, Cerro (México)	Cinder cone of Michoacán-Guanajuato	1401-06=
Tarugo Corral (Ecuador)	Dome of Cayambe	1502-006
Taruki-Higashi (Kyushu-Japan)	Dome of Unzen	0802-10=
Tarumai (Hokkaido-Japan)	Stratovolcano of Shikotsu	0805-04=
Tarutama (Kyushu-Japan)	Thermal feature of Aso	0802-11=
Taryatu-Chulutu (Mongolia)	Volcanic field (1, -2980) Radiocarbon	**1003-01-**
Tashats-sar (Armenia)	Cone of Ghegam Ridge	0104-07-
Tashiro (Honshu-Japan)	Stratovolcano (None) Pleistocene	....
Tasiro (Honshu-Japan)	Synonym of Tashiro	....
Taskesik Tepe (Turkey)	Dome of Acigöl-Nevsehir	0103-004
Tasovi, Vusi (Vanuatu-SW Pacific)	Cone of Aoba	0507-03=
Tat Ali (Ethiopia)	Shield volcano (None) Holocene	**0201-106**
Tata Sabaya (Bolivia)	Stratovolcano (None) Holocene	**1505-032**
Tatajachura, Cerro (Chile-N)	Stratovolcano (None) Pleistocene	....
Tatara (Chile-C)	Shield volcano of San Pedro-Pellado	1507-062
Tatara-San Pedro (Chile-C)	Synonym of San Pedro-Pellado	1507-062
Tatarinov (Kuril Is)	Stratovolcano of Chikurachki	0900-36=
Tatariwan (Sulawesi-Indonesia)	Cone of Lokon-Empung	0606-10=
Tatascamital, Cerro (Guatemala)	Dome of Ixhuatán	....
Tatchu-san (Kyushu-Japan)	Dome of Kuju	0802-12=
Tateshina-yama (Honshu-Japan)	Stratovolcano of Kita Yatsuga-take	0803-031
Tate-yama (Honshu-Japan)	Stratovolcano (5, 1839) Historical	**0803-08=**
Tatika [Sarvaly] (Hungary)	Shield volcano of Balaton Highland	....
Tatio, El (Chile-N)	Hydrotherm. field (None) Pleist.-Geysers	....
Tatio, Volcán (Chile-N)	Stratovolcano (None) Pleistocene	....
Tatodomji (Africa-N)	Cone of Toussidé, Tarso	0205-01=
Ta-T'un (China-E)	Synonym of Fanjiatung Group	....
Tatun Group (Taiwan)	Lava domes (1, -4100) Radiocarbon	**0801-032**

Name (Subregion)	Type (Eruptions, Most Recent) Status / Relation to Named Volcano	Volcano Number
Ta-tung (Taiwan)	Synonym of Tatun Group	0801-032
Ta-t'ung (China-E)	Synonym of Datong-Fengzen	....
Tau (Samoa-SW Pacific)	Dome of Tutuila	0404-02-
Ta'u (Samoa-SW Pacific)	Shield volcano (None) Holocene	**0404-001**
Tauanui (New Zealand)	Cone of Kaikohe-Bay of Islands	0401-01=
Tauga Point (Samoa-SW Pacific)	Tuff cone of Ofu-Olosega	0404-01=
Tauhara (New Zealand)	Dome of Taupo	0401-07=
Tauhara-Taupo (New Zealand)	Thermal feature of Taupo	0401-07=
Taulevu (Fiji Is-SW Pacific)	Cone of Taveuni	0405-01-
Taungbyauk (SE Asia)	Crater of Lower Chindwin	0705-09-
Taunggala (SE Asia)	Cone of Popa	0705-08-
Taunshits (Kamchatka)	Stratovolcano (2, -550) Radiocarbon	**1000-16-**
Taupe, Puy de la (France)	Cone of Chaîne des Puys	0100-02-
Taupo (New Zealand)	Caldera (25, 260) Radiocarbon	**0401-07=**
Tavai Ruro [Tavani Ruru] (Vanuatu-SW Pac.)	Stratovolcano of Kuwae	0507-07=
Tavakik [Tavani Puhanga] (Vanuatu-SW Pac.)	Cone of Emae	....
Tavalapa (Vanuatu-SW Pacific)	Cone of Kuwae	0507-07=
Tavani (Melanesian word for Mountain) see proper name (e.g. Kutali, Tavani)		
Tavanpainga [Tavani Tipikal] (Vanuatu)	Cone of Emae	....
Tavansisak [Tavani Talimasa] (Vanuatu)	Cone of Emae	....
Taveuni (Fiji Is-SW Pacific)	Shield volcano (34, 1550) Radiocarbon	**0405-01-**
Tavoka (Solomon Is-SW Pacific)	Thermal feature of Savo	0505-07=
Tavui (New Britain-SW Pac)	Submarine volcano (None) Quaternary	....
Tavui (New Britain-SW Pac)	Caldera (1, -5150) Radiocarbon	**0502-15-**
Tavurvur (New Britain-SW Pac)	Stratovolcano of Rabaul	0502-14=
Tavuyanga (Fiji Is-SW Pacific)	Cone of Taveuni	0405-01-
Taweh Hot Springs (Canada)	Thermal feature of Edziza	1200-06-
Tayawan (Luzon-Philippines)	Pleistocene caldera of Pinatubo	0703-083
Taye Poule, Piton (Indian O.-W)	Crater of Fournaise, Piton de la	0303-02=
Ta-Yen-Chih-Feng [Dayanzhifeng] (China-E)	Cone of Changbaishan	1005-06-
Taygete Cone (Antarctica)	Dome of Pleiades, The	1900-013
Tay-in-shan [Dayingshan] (SE Asia)	Stratovolcano of Tengchong	0705-11-
Tayir, Djebel (Red Sea)	Synonym of Tair, Jebel at	0201-01=
Taylor Butte (US-Oregon)	Cinder cone of Sprague River Valley	....
Taylor Butte (US-Oregon)	Shield volcano (None) Pleistocene	....
Taylor Valley (Antarctica)	Cinder cones (None) Pleistocene	....
Taylor Volc Field (US-New Mexico)	Stratovolcano (None) Pleistocene	....
Taylor, Mount (US-New Mexico)	Stratovolcano of Taylor Volc Field	....
Taylors Hill (New Zealand)	Cone of Auckland Field	0401-02=
Tayr, Jabal al (Red Sea)	Synonym of Tair, Jebel at	0201-01=
Taza, Cerro la (Chile-C)	Cinder cone of Carrán-Los Venados	1507-14=
Taza, Cerro la (México)	Cinder cone of Michoacán-Guanajuato	1401-06=
Taza, La (Chile-C)	Cone of Antillanca Group	1507-153
Tazawa (Honshu-Japan)	Caldera? (None) Pleistocene?	....
Tazenat (France)	Maar of Chaîne des Puys	0100-02-
Tazumal, Cerrito de (El Salvador)	Cinder cone of Singüil, Cerro	1403-002
Tchegulach (Aleutian Is)	Synonym of Chagulak	1101-20-
Tchobbe (Ethiopia)	Synonym of Corbetti Caldera	0201-29-
Te Ahuahu (New Zealand)	Cone of Kaikohe-Bay of Islands	0401-01=
Te Ananui (New Zealand)	Tuff ring of Mayor Island	0401-021
Te Araaka (New Zealand)	Tuff ring of Mayor Island	0401-021
Te Haehaenga (New Zealand)	Thermal feature of Okataina	0401-05=
Te Hapeotoroa (New Zealand)	Dome of Okataina	0401-05=
Te Hoata (New Zealand)	Thermal feature of Taupo	0401-07=
Te Horo (New Zealand)	Tuff ring of Mayor Island	0401-021
Te Horoa (New Zealand)	Dome of Okataina	0401-05=
Te Kahu Rea, Maunga (Chile-Is)	Pyroclastic cone of Easter Island	1506-011
Te Kauhanga (Chile-Is)	Pyroclastic cone of Easter Island	1506-011
Te Kawa (New Zealand)	Cone of Kakepuku	....
Te Kopia (New Zealand)	Thermal feature of Kapenga	....
Te Kopia (New Zealand)	Thermal feature of Okataina	0401-05=
Te Kukuta (New Zealand)	Vent of Mayor Island	0401-021
Te Kumete (New Zealand)	Dome of Okataina	0401-05=
Te Maari [Te Mari] (New Zealand)	Crater of Tongariro	0401-08=
Te Manavai (Chile-Is)	Crater of Easter Island	1506-011
Te Manavai (Chile-Is)	Dome of Easter Island	1506-011
Te Mari (New Zealand)	Crater of Tongariro	0401-08=
Te Paritu (New Zealand)	Vent of Mayor Island	0401-021
Te Pene (New Zealand)	Cone of Kaikohe-Bay of Islands	0401-01=
Te Puha Roa, Maunga (Chile-Is)	Pyroclastic cone of Easter Island	1506-011
Te Puke (New Zealand)	Cone of Kaikohe-Bay of Islands	0401-01=
Te Pupu (New Zealand)	Thermal feature of Taupo	0401-07=
Te Terata (New Zealand)	Dome of Maroa	0401-061
Te Toto Gorge (New Zealand)	Cone of Karioi	....
Te Uku (New Zealand)	Cone of Karioi	....
Te Whau (New Zealand)	Cone of Kaikohe-Bay of Islands	0401-01=
Te Whekau (New Zealand)	Crater of Okataina	0401-05=
Teahitia (Society Is-C Pacific)	Submarine volcano (4, 1985) Seismicity	**1303-01-**
Teanzul (Guatemala)	Synonym of Piedra Grande	....
Tea-Tea, Maunga (Chile-Is)	Dome of Easter Island	1506-011
Teau (Banda Sea)	Synonym of Teon	0605-05=
Tebel Hebeish (Africa-N)	Crater of Bayuda Volc Field	0205-06-
Tebel Qurein (Africa-N)	Cone of Bayuda Volc Field	0205-06-
Tebel Umm Arafibia (Africa-N)	Stratovolcano (None) Post-Miocene	....
Tebenkov (Kuril Is)	Stratovolcano of Grozny Group	0900-07=
Tecapa (El Salvador)	Stratovolcano (Uncertain) Holocene	**1403-08=**
Tecapa-Laguna de Alegría (El Salvador)	Cone of Tecapa	1403-08=
Tecchiena (Italy)	Pyroclastic cone of Ernici, Monti	....
Tecolote (México)	Cinder cone of Pinacate	1401-001
Tecolote, Cerro (Guatemala)	Cinder cone of Moyuta	1402-13-
Tecoluca, Cerro (El Salvador)	Dome of Ilopango	1403-06=
Tecomate, Cerro (México)	Dome of Mascota Volc Field	1401-031
Tecomatepe, Cerro (El Salvador)	Stratovolcano of Guazapa	1403-052
Teconto (México)	Cinder cone of Chichinautzin	1401-08=

Name (Subregion)	Type (Eruptions, Most Recent) Status / Relation to Named Volcano	Volcano Number
Tecuamburro (Guatemala)	Stratovolcano (1, -960) Radiocarbon	**1402-12=**
Tecuán, Cerro (El Salvador)	Stratovolcano of Cinotepeque, Cerro	1403-051
Tecuán, Cerro (El Salvador)	Lava cone of San Diego	1403-001
Tecuitlapa (México)	Maar of Serdán-Oriental	1401-092
Tecún Umán, Cerro (Guatemala)	Dome of Almolonga	1402-04=
Tedders (Africa-N)	Synonym of Mrit-Ment Volc Field	....
Te'elagi (Samoa-SW Pacific)	Cone of Savai'i	0404-04=
Teer, Gebel (Red Sea)	Synonym of Tair, Jebel at	0201-01=
Teeters Nunatak (Antarctica)	Stratovolcano of Hudson Mountains	1900-028
Teeuw (Banda Sea)	Synonym of Teon	0605-05=
Teide, Pico del (Canary Is)	Stratovolcano of Tenerife	1803-03-
Teir, Djebel (Red Sea)	Synonym of Tair, Jebel at	0201-01=

Snow-capped **Taranaki** (Egmont) volcano dominates the western coast of New Zealand's North Island. Taranaki has collapsed repeatedly during the late Pleistocene and Holocene, producing large debris avalanches whose deposits ring the volcano.

Name (Subregion)	Type (Eruptions, Most Recent) Status / Relation to Named Volcano	Volcano Number
Teishi Knoll [Teishi Kaikyu] (Honshu-Japan)	Submarine vent of Izu-Tobu	0803-01=
Teishi-Kaikyu (Honshu-Japan)	Submarine vent of Izu-Tobu	0803-01=
Teixcal [San Marcelino] (El Salvador)	Cinder cone of Santa Ana	1403-02=
Tekai (Honshu-Japan)	Synonym of Chokai	0803-22=
Tekletunup (Kamchatka)	Shield volcano (None) Pleistocene	....
Tel Avital (Syria)	Cinder cone of Golan Heights	0300-03-
Tel Bental (Syria)	Cinder cone of Golan Heights	0300-03-
Telagabodas (Java)	Synonym of Talagabodas	0603-15=
Telagakuning (Java)	Crater of Lawu	0603-26=
Telagapui (Lesser Sunda Is)	Unknown (None) Post-Miocene	....
Telagaranu (Halmahera-Indonesia)	Synonym of Todoko-Ranu	0608-05=
Telagawaru (Java)	Crater of Ijen	0603-35=
Telago, Gunung (Sumatra)	Unknown (None) Pleistocene	....
Telapón (México)	Stratovolcano (None) Pleistocene	....
Telcampana (México)	Cinder cone of Colima	1401-04=
Telefon Bay Cones (Antarctica)	Tuff cone of Deception Island	1900-03=
Teleki's Cone (Africa-E)	Cone of Barrier, The	0202-03=
Telemojo (Java)	Synonym of Telomoyo	0603-231
Telica (Nicaragua)	Stratovolcanoes (39, 2008) Historical	**1404-04=**
Telogo Ketjil [Telogokecil] (Sumatra)	Crater of Daun, Bukit	0601-21=
Telogokecil (Sumatra)	Crater of Daun, Bukit	0601-21=
Telogopasir (Java)	Crater of Dieng Volc Complex	0603-20=
Telogoterus (Java)	Thermal feature of Dieng Complex	0603-20=
Telogowuro (Java)	Crater of Lawu	0603-26=
Telomojo (Java)	Synonym of Telomoyo	0603-231
Telomoyo (Java)	Stratovolcano (None) Holocene	**0603-231**
Telon (Java)	Dome of Muria	0603-251
Telong, Bur ni (Sumatra)	Stratovolcano (5, 1937) Historical	**0601-05=**
Telor, Bukit (Sumatra)	Pyroclastic cone (None) Pleistocene	....
Telori (Halmahera-Indonesia)	Crater of Dukono	0608-01=
Tembargena, Montaña (Canary Is)	Cinder cone of Hierro	1803-02-
Tembergena (Canary Is)	Cinder cone of Hierro	1803-02-
Temerejeque, Montana (Canary Is)	Cone of Fuerteventura	1803-05-
Tempang (Sulawesi-Indonesia)	Cone of Tondano Caldera	0606-07-
Tempaso [Tempang] (Sulawesi-Indonesia)	Cone of Tondano Caldera	0606-07-
Tempisque, Cerro (Guatemala)	Dome of Ipala	1402-19-
Tenaca, Montaña (Canary Is)	Cinder cone of Hierro	1803-02-
Tenagatu Humun (Lesser Sunda Is)	Unknown (None) Post-Miocene	....
Tenango [Cerro Tetépetl] (México)	Lava cone of Chichinautzin	1401-08=
Tenaroh, Bukit (Sumatra)	Unknown (None) Pleistocene	....
Tenas Peak (US-Oregon)	Cinder cone of Cinnamon Butte	1202-15-
Tenayo, Cerro (México)	Cinder cone of Chichinautzin	1401-08=
Tenbo-san (Hokkaido-Japan)	Dome of Shikaribetsu Group	0805-062
Tencho-zan (Hokkaido-Japan)	Fissure vent of Rausu	0805-082
Tenchun (SE Asia)	Synonym of Tengchong	0705-11-
Tendurek Dag (Turkey)	Synonym of Tendürek Dagi	0103-03=
Tendürek Dagi (Turkey)	Shield volcano (2, 1855) Historical	**0103-03=**
Tenduruk Dagi (Turkey)	Synonym of Tendürek Dagi	0103-03=
Tenduruk Golu (Turkey)	Crater of Tendürek Dagi	0103-03=
Teneguia (Canary Is)	Cinder cone of La Palma	1803-01-
Tenerife (Canary Is)	Stratovolcano (42, 1909) Historical	**1803-03-**
Tenerife, Montaña (Canary Is)	Cinder cone of Hierro	1803-02-

Name (Subregion)	Type (Eruptions, Most Recent) Status Relation to Named Volcano	Volcano Number
Tenesedra, Montaña (Canary Is)	Cinder cone of Hierro	1803-02-
Tenga, Kepundan [Verbeek] (Sumatra)	Crater of Marapi	0601-14=
Teng-Chia-Wang [Tengjiawangshan] (China)	Cone of Longgang Group	1005-05-
Tengchong (SE Asia)	Pyroclastic cones (1, -5750) U-series	**0705-11-**
Tengger Caldera (Java)	Stratovolcanoes (62, 2004) Historical	**0603-31=**
Tengjiawangshan (China-E)	Cone of Longgang Group	1005-05-
Tengu (Honshu-Japan)	Cone of Dainichiga-take	....
Tengu-dake (Honshu-Japan)	Dome of Iizuna	....
Tengu-dake (Hokkaido-Japan)	Stratovolcano of Nipesotsu-Maruyama	0805-061
Tengu-Hirayama (Hokkaido-Japan)	Stratovolcanoes (None) Pleistocene	....
Tengu-yama (Honshu-Japan)	Dome of Tate-yama	0803-08=
Teng-yueh (SE Asia)	Synonym of Tengchong	0705-11-
Tenjin-yama (Honshu-Japan)	Cone of Fuji	0803-03=
Tenjo-san (Izu Is-Japan)	Dome of Kozu-shima	0804-03=
Tennena (Canada)	Cone of Edziza	1200-06-
Tenorio (Costa Rica)	Stratovolcanoes (None) Holocene	**1405-031**

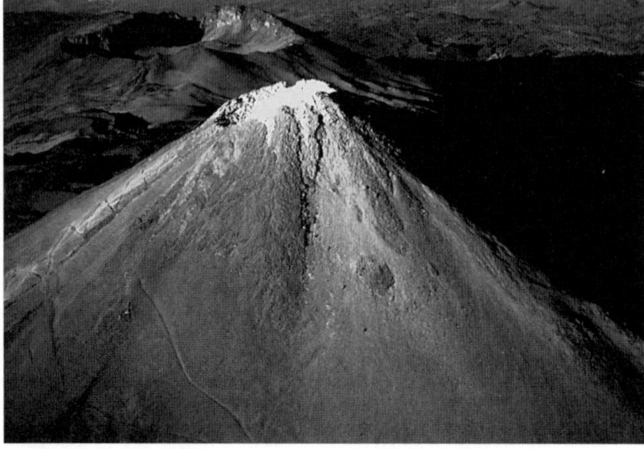

Katia and Maurice Krafft

Pico de **Teide**, the highest peak in the Atlantic Ocean, towers 1700 m above the floor of Las Cañadas caldera on **Tenerife**. Pico Viejo, another post-caldera stratovolcano capped by a 750-m-wide crater, appears in the background.

Name (Subregion)	Type (Eruptions, Most Recent) Status Relation to Named Volcano	Volcano Number
Tenshi (Honshu-Japan)	Stratovolcano of Izu-Tobu	0803-01=
Tenshi (Honshu-Japan)	Stratovolcano (None) Pleistocene	....
Tentolomatinan (Sulawesi-Indonesia)	Unknown (None) Quaternary	....
Tenusset, Puy de (France)	Cone of Chaîne des Puys	0100-02-
Tenzyo-san [Tenjo-san] (Izu Is-Japan)	Dome of Kozu-shima	0804-03=
Teodoro Wolf, Isla (Ecuador)	Dome of Cuicocha	1502-003
Teon (Banda Sea)	Stratovolcano (5, 1904) Historical	**0605-05=**
Teou (Banda Sea)	Synonym of Teon	0605-05=
Tepecik Tepe (Turkey)	Cone of Erciyes Dagi	0103-01=
Tepecingo (México)	Cone of Chichinautzin	1401-08=
Tepesidelik Damlaru (Turkey)	Vent of Erciyes Dagi	0103-01=
Tepetiltic (México)	Stratovolcano (None) Pleistocene	....
Tepetl (México)	Cinder cone of Chichinautzin	1401-08=
Tepetlapan (México)	Cinder cone of Chichinautzin	1401-08=
Tepexitl, Cerro (México)	Tuff ring of Serdán-Oriental	1401-092
Tepezingo (México)	Cinder cone of Chichinautzin	1401-08=
Tepi (Ethiopia)	Shield volcano (None) Holocene	**0201-292**
Tequila (México)	Stratovolcano (None) Pleistocene	....
Ter, Djebel (Red Sea)	Synonym of Tair, Jebel at	0201-01=
Terbang, Gunung (Java)	Cone of Slamet	0603-18=
Terceira (Azores)	Stratovolcanoes (15, 2000) Historical	**1802-05=**
Teresa (Mindanao-Philippines)	Dome of Leonard Range	0701-031
Terevaka, Maunga (Chile-Is)	Shield volcano of Easter Island	1506-011
Termas (Chile-C)	Thermal feature Chillán, Nevados de	1507-07=
Termas (Spanish for Spa) see proper name (e.g. Chanchoco, Termas de)		
Termas, Las (Chile-C)	Stratovolcano of Chillán, Nevados de	1507-07=
Terminal Geyser (US-California)	Thermal feature of Lassen Volc Center	1203-08-
Termópilas, Las (El Salvador)	Thermal feature of Apaneca Range	1403-01=
Tern (Alaska-W)	Cone of Kinia River	....
Ternate (Halmahera-Indonesia)	Synonym of Gamalama	0608-06=
Terpuk (Kamchatka)	Shield volcano (1, -800) Radiocarbon	**1000-512**
Terra Murata (Italy)	Tuff ring of Campi Flegrei	0101-01=
Terra Nova, Mount (Antarctica)	Cone of Terror, Mt.	....
Terrace (US-Utah)	Crater of Black Rock Desert	1207-05-
Terrang, Lake (Australia)	Tuff ring of Newer Volcanics Prov.	0509-01-
Terre Blanche (W Indies)	Dome of Qualibou	1600-14=
Terre de Bas (W Indies)	Stratovolcanoes (None) Pleistocene	....
Terre Elm [Sulfur Springs] (W Indies)	Thermal feature of Plat Pays, Morne	1600-11=
Terribile Bank (Italy)	Submarine vent C. Flegrei Mar Sicilia	0101-07=
Terror, El (Nicaragua)	Cone of Zapatera	1404-111
Terror, Mt. (Antarctica)	Shield volcano (None) Pleistocene	....
Teski Group (Chile-S)	Crater of Osorno	1508-01=
Tesoro (Canary Is)	Cinder cone of Hierro	1803-02-
Testaccio (Italy)	Crater of Ischia	0101-03=
Teta, Loma la (Nicaragua)	Dome of San Cristóbal	1404-02=
Tetecon (México)	Cone of Chichinautzin	1401-08=
Teteltzingo (México)	Crater of Orizaba, Pico de	1401-10=
Tetépetl, Cerro (México)	Lava cone of Chichinautzin	1401-08=
Tetequillo (México)	Lava cone of Chichinautzin	1401-08=
Tetera, Cerro [La Tetra] (US-New Mexico)	Cone of Zuni-Bandera	1210-02-
Tetide (Italy)	Submarine vent C. Flegrei Mar Sicilia	0101-07=
Tetillas, Cerro las (México)	Dome of San Pedro	....
Tetillas, Las (México)	Cinder cone of Gloria, La	1401-097
Tetitlán, Cerro (México)	Dome of San Pedro	....
Tetra, La (US-New Mexico)	Cone of Zuni-Bandera	1210-02-
Tetsu-zan (Honshu-Japan)	Stratovolcano of Adatara	0803-17=
Tetu-zan [Tetsu-zan] (Honshu-Japan)	Stratovolcano of Adatara	0803-17=
Tetyaev (Kamchatka)	Cone of Dzenzursky	1000-11=
Teu Minas (Sumatra)	Stratovolcano (None) Pleistocene	....
Teuctépetl (México)	Synonym of Orizaba, Pico de	1401-10=
Teudeuk, Gunung (Sumatra)	Synonym of Tudeuk, Gunung	....
Teufelsnadel [Devil's Needle] (Africa-E)	Vent of Lengai, Ol Doinyo	0202-12=
Teuhtli, Volcán (México)	Shield volcano of Chichinautzin	1401-08=
Teun (Banda Sea)	Synonym of Teon	0605-05=
Teupin Iboih (Sumatra)	Thermal feature of Pulau Weh	....
Teupin Krueng Madun (Sumatra)	Thermal feature of Pulau Weh	....
Teutli, Volcán [Volcán Teuhtli] (México)	Shield volcano of Chichinautzin	1401-08=
Texontepec (México)	Lava cone of Chichinautzin	1401-08=
Teyotl Peak (México)	Stratovolcano of Iztaccíhuatl	1401-082
Teyr, Djebel (Red Sea)	Synonym of Tair, Jebel at	0201-01=
Teziolo, Cerro el (México)	Cone of Chichinautzin	1401-08=
Tezontal (México)	Cinder cone of Colima	1401-04=
Tezontle (México)	Cinder cone of Chichinautzin	1401-08=
Tezontle, Volcán (México)	Cinder cone of San Pedro	....
Tezoyo, Cerro el (México)	Cone of Chichinautzin	1401-08=
Teztontle, Volcán (México)	Cone of Tepetiltic	....
Thais Hill (W Indies)	Dome of Saba	1600-01=
Thaton (SE Asia)	Fissure vents (None) Pleistocene?	....
Thaw Hill (Canada)	Cone of Spectrum Range	1200-07-
Thazi (SE Asia)	Vent of Lower Chindwin	0705-09-
The see proper name (e.g. Father, the)		
Thebes (Greece)	Dome of Volos-Atalanti	....
Theistareykir (Iceland-NE)	Synonym of Theistareykjarbunga	1703-09=
Theistareykjahraun (Iceland-NE)	Fissure vent of Theistareykjarbunga	1703-09=
Theistareykjarbunga (Iceland-NE)	Shield volcano (3, -900) Tephrochron	**1703-09=**
Thera (Greece)	Synonym of Santorini	0102-04=
Thera (Greece)	Shield volcano of Santorini	0102-04=
Therasia-Oia (Greece)	Shield volcano of Santorini	0102-04=
Thiafi Bay (Greece)	Thermal feature of Methana	0102-02=
Thielsen (US-Oregon)	Shield volcano (None) Pleistocene	....
Thierry (Indian O.-W)	Crater of Fournaise, Piton de la	0303-02=
Thiolet, Puy (France)	Cone of Chaîne des Puys	0100-02-
Thira (Greece)	Synonym of Santorini	0102-04=
Thirasia-Oia [Therasia-Oia] (Greece)	Shield volcano of Santorini	0102-04=
Thirsty Point (US-Oregon)	Cinder cone of Cinnamon Butte	1202-15-
Thjofahraun (Iceland-SW)	Fissure vent of Hengill	1701-05=
Tholothi (Fiji Is-SW Pacific)	Cone of Taveuni	0405-01-
Thomazeau (Hispaniola)	Pyroclastic cones (None) Pleistocene	....
Thompson Island (Atlantic-S)	Submarine volcano? (Uncertain)	**1806-03-**
Thórdarhyrna (Iceland-NE)	Stratovolcano of Grímsvötn	1703-01=
Thorisjökull (Iceland-SW)	Subglacial volcano (None) Pleistocene	....
Thorsarhraun (Iceland-NE)	Fissure vent of Bárdarbunga	1703-03=
Thrainsskjöldur (Iceland-SW)	Shield volcano of Reykjanes	1701-02=
Three Creek Butte (US-Oregon)	Dome of Tumalo	....
Three Fingered Jack (US-Oregon)	Shield volcanoes (None) Pleistocene	....
Three Kings (New Zealand)	Tuff ring of Auckland Field	0401-02=
Three Sisters (US-California)	Cone of Medicine Lake	1203-02-
Three Sisters Cones (Antarctica)	Cone of Erebus	1900-02=
Three Trappers (US-Oregon)	Cinder cone of Bachelor	1202-09-
Three-Quarter Cone (Aleutian Is)	Cone of Semisopochnoi	1101-06-
Threngslaborgir (Iceland-NE)	Crater Row of Krafla	1703-08=
Thridrangar (Iceland-S)	Submarine vent of Vestmannaeyjar	1702-01=
Thrihnukar (Iceland-SW)	Fissure vent of Brennisteinsfjöll	1701-04=
Throskuldshraun (Iceland-NE)	Crater Row of Bárdarbunga	1703-03=
Thule Island (Antarctica)	Submarine vent of Thule Islands	1900-07=
Thule Islands (Antarctica)	Stratovolcanoes (1, 1975) Historical	**1900-07=**
Thumb, The (Canada)	Vent of Hogum Range	....
Thumb, The (New Guinea)	Dome of Victory	0503-03=
Thwanthuku (Africa-E)	Cone of Sultan Hamud-Simba	....
Tianchi (China-E)	Caldera of Changbaishan	1005-06-
Tiang-San Pablo Hot Springs (Philippines)	Thermal feature of Banahaw	0703-05=
Tiangyang (SE Asia)	Stratovolcano of Leizhou Bandao	0705-01-
Tianshan Volc Group (China-W)	Volcanic field (2, 650) Historical	**1004-02-**
Tiantishan (SE Asia)	Cone of Tengchong	0705-11-
Tiata Imbabura (Ecuador)	Dome of Imbabura	1502-004
Tiatala (Samoa-SW Pacific)	Cone of Upolu	0404-03-
Tiatia (Kuril Is)	Stratovolcano (4, 1981) Historical	**0900-03=**
Tiau (Tiauw) (Banda Sea)	Synonym of Teon	0605-05=
Tiawir (Luzon-Philippines)	Dome of Natib	0703-082
Tibane (Mindanao-Philippines)	Dome of Camiguin	0701-08=
Tibas (Costa Rica)	Stratovolcano of Barva	1405-05=
Ticab, Lake (Luzon-Philippines)	Maar of Banahaw	0703-05=
Ticoma [Ticomo] (Nicaragua)	Crater of Nejapa-Miraflores	1404-092
Ticomo (Nicaragua)	Crater of Nejapa-Miraflores	1404-092
Ticsani (Perú)	Lava domes (1, 1800) Tephrochronology	**1504-031**
Tidichi, Ehi (Africa-N)	Synonym of Toussidé, Tarso	0205-01=
T'ido Hayk (Ethiopia)	Crater of Bilate River Field	0201-291
Tidore (Halmahera-Indonesia)	Stratovolcano (None) Holocene	**0608-061**
Tieguoshan (SE Asia)	Cone of Tengchong	0705-11-
Tien-Chi [Tianchi] (China-E)	Caldera of Changbaishan	1005-06-
Tiendilla (Costa Rica)	Cone of Turrialba	1405-07=
Tierra Colorado, Cerro (Guatemala)	Cone of Suchitán	1402-16-

Name (Subregion)	Type (Eruptions, Most Recent) Status Relation to Named Volcano	Volcano Number
Tigalalu (Halmahera-Indonesia)	Stratovolcano (None) Holocene	**0608-071**
Tigalate [San Martín] (Canary Is)	Cinder cone of La Palma	1803-01-
Tighe Rock (Antarctica)	Cone of Hudson Mountains	1900-028
Tigilsky (Kamchatka)	Shield volcano (None) Pleistocene	....
Tigre, El (El Salvador)	Stratovolcano (None) Holocene	**1403-082**
Tigre, Isla el (Honduras)	Stratovolcano (None) Holocene	**1403-13-**
Tihanyi Felsziget (Hungary)	Maar of Balaton Highland	....
Tihia (New Zealand)	Cone of Northern Tongariro Group	....
Tiho (Djibouti)	Fumarole field (None) Pleistocene	....
Tihuya [Tahuya] (Canary Is)	Cinder cone of La Palma	1803-01-
Tiis, Kawah (Java)	Thermal feature of Patuha	0603-07=
Tijaw (Banda Sea)	Synonym of Teon	0605-05=
Tikhegy [Agarteto] (Hungary)	Shield volcano of Balaton Highland	....
Tikitere (New Zealand)	Thermal feature of Rotorua	....
Tikorangi (New Zealand)	Dome of Okataina	0401-05=
Tikorangi (New Zealand)	Tuff cone of South Auckland	....
Tikura (Kuril Is)	Synonym of Chikurachki	0900-36=
Tilapa (México)	Cone of Chichinautzin	1401-08=
Tilapia Lake (Africa-E)	Crater of Central Island	0202-01=
Tilarán, Cerro (Costa Rica)	Shield volcano (None) Pleistocene	....
Tilhue, Cerro (Argentina)	Stratovolcano of Tromen	1507-072
Tiling (Java)	Crater of Lawu	0603-26=
Tillman, Mt. (Alaska-E)	Synonym of Wrangell	1105-02-
Tilmbeg (Vanuatu-SW Pacific)	Cone of Motlav	0507-001
Tilocalar (Chile-N)	Stratovolcanoes (None) Holocene?	**1505-105**
Tilocálar Norte (Chile-N)	Stratovolcano of Tilocalar	1505-105
Tilocálar Sur (Chile-N)	Stratovolcano of Tilocalar	1505-105
Tilu (Java)	Stratovolcano (None) Pleistocene	....
Timanfaya Antigua (Canary Is)	Cone of Lanzarote	1803-06-
Timanfaya, Montanas del (Canary Is)	Synonym of Lanzarote	1803-06-
Timbang (Java)	Cone of Dieng Volc Complex	0603-20=
Timber Crater (US-Oregon)	Shield volcano of Crater Lake	1202-16-
Timber Mountain (US-California)	Cone of Hackamore	....
Timbered Crater (US-California)	Tuff ring of Brushy Butte	1203-03-
Timbered Peak (US-Washington)	Cone of West Crater	1201-06-
Timborombo, Montaña de (Canary Is)	Cinder cone of Hierro	1803-02-
Timi, Ehi (Africa-N)	Stratovolcano of Toussidé, Tarso	0205-01=
Timpa Rossa, Monte (Italy)	Cinder cone of Etna	0101-06=
Timpone Carrubbo (Italy)	Stratovolcano of Lipari	0101-042
Timpone del Fuoco (Italy)	Shield volcano of Stromboli	0101-04=
Timpone Ospedale (Italy)	Stratovolcano of Lipari	0101-042
Timpone Pataso (Italy)	Stratovolcano of Lipari	0101-042
Timpoong [Mambajao] (Philippines)	Stratovolcano of Camiguin	0701-08=
Tin Can Island (Tonga-SW Pacific)	Synonym of Niuafo'ou	0403-11=
Tin Taralle Volc Field (Africa-N)	Volcanic field (None) Pleistocene	....
Tin Zaouatene Volc Field (Africa-N)	Volcanic field (None) Holocene	**0205-002**
Tinaja de los Papagos [Volcán Romo] (Méx.)	Maar of Pinacate	1401-001
Tinaja, Volcán la (México)	Cone of Zitácuaro-Valle de Bravo	1401-061
Tinajas, Cerro las (México)	Cone of Zitácuaro-Valle de Bravo	1401-061
Tinajas, Isla (Nicaragua)	Tuff ring of Zapatera	1404-111
Tinajita, Volcán el (México)	Maar of Pinacate	1401-001
Tinakoro (Santa Cruz Is-SW Pacific)	Synonym of Tinakula	0506-01=
Tinakula (Santa Cruz Is-SW Pacific)	Stratovolcano (21, 2007) Historical	**0506-01=**
Tinaroh (Sumatra)	Synonym of Tenaroh, Bukit	....
Tindaya, Montana (Canary Is)	Cone of Fuerteventura	1803-05-
Tindfjallajökull (Iceland-S)	Stratovolcano (None) Holocene?	**1702-04=**
Tindfjoll (Iceland-S)	Synonym of Tindfjallajökull	1702-04=
Tindfjöll (Iceland-S)	Stratovolcano of Tindfjallajökull	1702-04=
Tindima (Africa-E)	Cone of Chyulu Hills	0202-13=
Tindur (Iceland-SW)	Dome of Hofsjökull	1701-09=
Tinga, Montana de (Canary Is)	Cone of Lanzarote	1803-06-
Tinguaton (Canary Is)	Crater of Lanzarote	1803-06-
Tinguiririca (Chile-C)	Stratovolcano (1, 1917) Historical	**1507-03=**
Tiñor (Canary Is)	Shield volcano of Hierro	1803-02-
Tintero, El (US-New Mexico)	Cone of Taylor Volc Field	....
Tioca (México)	Cinder cone of Chichinautzin	1401-08=
Tioquitas (México)	Cinder cone of Chichinautzin	1401-08=
Tipas (Argentina)	Complex volcano (None) Holocene	**1505-22-**
Tipikal, Tavani (Vanuatu-SW Pacific)	Cone of Emae	....
Tipkal, Tavani [Tavani Tipikal] (Vanuatu)	Cone of Emae	....
Tipsoo Peak (US-Oregon)	Cinder cone of Thielsen	....
Tipt Pon (Sulu Is-Philippines)	Synonym of Jolo	0700-01=
Tir, Jibbel (Red Sea)	Synonym of Tair, Jebel at	0201-01=
Tirac (Luzon-Philippines)	Dome of Natib	0703-082
Tiranus (Kamchatka)	Fissure vent of Kliuchevskoi	1000-26=
Tirba, Montana (Canary Is)	Cone of Fuerteventura	1803-05-
Ti-re-ku (Taiwan)	Thermal feature of Tatun Group	0801-032
Tirihoi [Brat Chirpoev] (Kuril Is)	Stratovolcano of Chirpoi	0900-15=
Tirihoigaku [Brat Chirpoev] (Kuril Is)	Stratovolcano of Chirpoi	0900-15=
Tirinkatar (Armenia)	Pyroclastic cone of Aragats	0104-06-
Tirinkotan (Kuril Is)	Synonym of Chirinkotan	0900-26=
Tirohanga (New Zealand)	Dome of Maroa	0401-061
Tironi (Italy)	Vent of Vesuvius	0101-02=
Tisate, Hervideros de (Nicaragua)	Thermal feature of Telica	1404-04=
Tiscapa, Laguna de (Nicaragua)	Maar of Nejapa-Miraflores	1404-092
Tischó, Cerro (Perú)	Cinder cone of Andahua-Orcopampa	1504-004
Tishigcuchi (Ecuador)	Dome of Illiniza	1502-041
Tisingal (Panamá)	Stratovolcano (None) Pleistocene	....
Tison Lake [Mardja] (Africa-W)	Crater of Ngaoundere Plateau	0204-04-
Titila (Kamchatka)	Shield volcanoes (1, -550) Radiocarbon	**1000-56-**
Titiraupenga (New Zealand)	Dome of Mangakino	....
Tiwi (Luzon-Philippines)	Thermal feature of Malinao	....
Tiwongo (New Britain-SW Pac)	Cone of Lolobau	0502-13=
Tiwu Ata Mbupu (Lesser Sunda Is)	Crater of Kelimutu	0604-14=
Tiwu Ata Polo (Lesser Sunda Is)	Crater of Kelimutu	0604-14=
Tiwu Nua Muri Kooh Tai (Lesser Sunda Is)	Crater of Kelimutu	0604-14=
Tiwu Nua Muri Koohi Fah	Crater of Kelimutu	0604-14=
Tiyaw (Banda Sea)	Synonym of Teon	0605-05=
Tizayuca Volc Field (México)	Volcanic field of Apan-Tezontepec	....
Tjakrabuana (Java)	Synonym of Cakrabuana	....
Tjalantjang (Java)	Synonym of Canlancang	....
Tjaldstadagja (Iceland-SW)	Crater Row of Reykjanes	1701-02=
Tjanar [Canar] (Java)	Crater of Talagabodas	0603-15=
Tjareme (Java)	Synonym of Cereme	0603-17=
Tjarnahnukur (Iceland-SW)	Crater Row of Hengill	1701-05=
Tjarnarholar (Iceland-SW)	Crater Row of Grímsnes	1701-06=
Tjatoe [Catu] (Lesser Sunda Is)	Crater of Batur	0604-01=
Tjatur Caldera (Lesser Sunda Is)	Synonym of Bratan	0604-001
Tjemara, Gunung [Gunung Cemera] (Java)	Cone of Ijen	0603-35=
Tjereme (Tjeremai, Tjerme) (Java)	Synonym of Cereme	0603-17=
Tjiangkuang [Cangkuang] (Java)	Crater of Salak	0603-05=
Tjiaw (Banda Sea)	Synonym of Teon	0605-05=
Tjibeureum [Cibeureum] (Java)	Thermal feature of Kamojang, Kawah	....
Tjibeureum [Cibeureum] (Java)	Thermal feature of Perbakti-Gagak	0603-04=
Tjibeureum Palasari [Cibeureum Palasari]	Thermal feature of Perbakti-Gagak	0603-04=
Tjibodas, Kawah [Kawah Cibodas] (Java)	Thermal feature of Perbakti-Gagak	0603-04=
Tjibodas, Kawah [Kawah Cibodas] (Java)	Thermal feature of Salak	0603-05=
Tjibodas, Tjipanas [Cipanas Cibodas] (Java)	Thermal feature of Perbakti-Gagak	0603-04=
Tjiboerial [Ciburial] (Java)	Thermal feature of Kamojang, Kawah	....
Tjibolang, Kawah [Kawah Cibolang] (Java)	Thermal feature of Wayang-Windu	0603-08=
Tjibugis (Java)	Synonym of Cibugis	....
Tjibuliran [Ciburial] (Java)	Thermal feature of Kamojang, Kawah	....
Tjibuni, Kawah [Kawah Cibuni] (Java)	Thermal feature of Patuha	0603-07=
Tjigamea, Kawah [Kawah Cigamea] (Java)	Thermal feature of Salak	0603-05=
Tjigupakan [Cigupakan] (Java)	Thermal feature of Kendang	0603-11=
Tjihideung, Tjipanas [Cipanas Cihideung]	Thermal feature of Salak	0603-05=
Tjikaluwung Putri, Kawah [Cikaluwung] (Java)	Thermal feature of Salak	0603-05=
Tjikaluwung, Tjipanas [Cipanas Cikaluwung]	Thermal feature of Perbakti-Gagak	0603-04=
Tjikaluwungherang, Kawah [Cikaluwungherang]	Thermal feature of Perbakti-Gagak	0603-04=
Tjikuraj (Java)	Synonym of Cikuray	....
Tjilik, Gunung [Gunung Cilik] (Java)	Cone of Ijen	0603-35=
Tjipamatutan [Cipamatutan] (Java)	Thermal feature of Perbakti-Gagak	0603-04=
Tjipanas (Dutch: of Indonesian word for Hot Spring) see proper name (e.g. Tjibodas, Tjipanas)		
Tjipanas, Kawah [Kawah Cipanas] (Java)	Thermal feature of Salak	0603-05=
Tjipengasahan, Kawah [Kawah Cipengasahan]	Thermal feature of Kamojang, Kawah	....
Tjiremai (Java)	Synonym of Cereme	0603-17=
Tjisalada, Kawah [Kawah Cisalada] (Java)	Thermal feature of Salak	0603-05=
Tjisalada, Tjipanas [Cipanas Cisalada] (Java)	Thermal feature of Salak	0603-05=
Tjisekati, Tjipanas [Cipanas Cisekati] (Java)	Thermal feature of Perbakti-Gagak	0603-04=
Tjiseupan, Tjipanas [Cipanas Ciseupan]	Thermal feature of Perbakti-Gagak	0603-04=
Tjiwidei, Kawah [Kawah Ciwidei] (Java)	Thermal feature of Patuha	0603-07=
Tjolo, Gunung (Sulawesi-Indonesia)	Synonym of Colo [Una Una]	0606-01=
Tjondrodimuko [Condrodimuko] (Java)	Thermal feature Dieng Volc Complex	0603-20=
Tjondrodimuko, Kawah [Kawah Condrodimuko]	Thermal feature of Merbabu	0603-24=
Tjondrokemuko, Kawah	Thermal feature of Merbabu	0603-24=
Tjörnes Fracture Zone (Iceland-N of)	Submarine volcano (1, 1868) Historical	**1703-10=**
Tjundung Kelam, Bukit (Sumatra)	Synonym of Cundung Kelam, Bukit	....
Tjupu, Gunung [Gunung Cupu} (Java)	Cone of Lamongan	0603-32=
Tlacotenco (México)	Fissure vent of Chichinautzin	1401-08=

Stora-Viti crater caps the low **Theistareykjarbunga** shield volcano in NE Iceland.

Name (Subregion)	Type (Eruptions, Most Recent) Status Relation to Named Volcano	Volcano Number
Tlacotepec (México)	Lava cone of Chichinautzin	1401-08=
Tlacuallcli (México)	Cinder cone of Chichinautzin	1401-08=
Tlacuayol, Cerro (México)	Cone of Chichinautzin	1401-08=
Tláloc (México)	Stratovolcano (None) Pleistocene	....
Tlaloc, Volcán (México)	Shield volcano of Chichinautzin	1401-08=
Tlamacas (México)	Dome of Popocatépetl	1401-09=
Tlamacasco (México)	Lava cone of Chichinautzin	1401-08=
Tlapexcua, Volcán (México)	Cone of Chichinautzin	1401-08=
Tlevak Strait-Suemez Is. (Alaska-E)	Volcanic field (None) Holocene	**1105-06-**
Tman Hidup (Java)	Cone of Iyang-Argapura	0603-33=
To'a (Samoa-SW Pacific)	Tuff cone of Ta'u	0404-001
Toa Toa, Maunga (Chile-Is)	Pyroclastic cone of Easter Island	1506-011

Name (Subregion)	Type (Eruptions, Most Recent) Status. Relation to Named Volcano	Volcano Number
To'aga (Samoa-SW Pacific)	Cone of Ofu-Olosega	0404-01=
Toaza (Ecuador)	Stratovolcano of Guagua Pichincha	1502-02=
Toba (Sumatra)	Caldera (None) Holocene	**0601-09=**
Tobacco Hill (Australia)	Cone of Atherton Volc Province	....
Tobal (New Britain-SW Pac)	Cone of Lolobau	0502-13=
Tobaru (Halmahera-Indonesia)	Synonym of Ibu	0608-03=
Tobaru (Halmahera-Indonesia)	Unknown (None) Holocene	**0608-02-**
Tobeltsen (Kamchatka)	Cinder cone of Severny	1000-70-
Tobón (Guatemala)	Cone of Jumay Volc Field	....
Tobu volcano group (Honshu-Japan)	Stratovolcano of On-take	0803-04=
Toco, Cerro (Chile-N)	Stratovolcano of Purico Complex	1505-094
Tocomar (Argentina)	Unknown (None) Pleistocene	....
Toconado (Toconao) (Chile-N)	Synonym of Láscar	1505-10=
Toconse (Chile-N)	Stratovolcano of Leon, Cerro del	....
Tocopuri, Cerro de (Chile-N)	Synonym of Tocorpuri, Cerros de	....
Tocorpuri, Cerros de (Chile-N)	Stratovolcano (None) Pleistocene	....
Todako (Todoekoe, Todoke) (Indonesia)	Synonym of Todoko-Ranu	0608-05=
Todoke, Lake (Halmahera-Indonesia)	Maar of Ibu	0608-03=
Todoko (Halmahera-Indonesia)	Caldera of Todoko-Ranu	0608-05=
Todoko-Ranu (Halmahera-Indonesia)	Calderas (None) Holocene	**0608-05=**
Todra Volc Field (Africa-N)	Cinder cones (None) Holocene	**0205-001**
Toduoko, Lake (Halmahera-Indonesia)	Maar of Ibu	0608-03=
Toebaroe (Halmahera-Indonesia)	Synonym of Ibu	0608-03=
Toedoe [Tudu] (Lesser Sunda Is)	Crater of Paluweh	0604-15=
Toeroen, Gunung [Gunung Turun] (Java)	Cone of Ungaran	0603-23=
Tofooa (Tonga-SW Pacific)	Synonym of Tofua	0403-06=
Tofua (Tonga-SW Pacific)	Caldera (10, 2009) Historical	**0403-06=**
Toga (Honshu-Japan)	Maar of Megata	0803-262
Togasa-yama (Honshu-Japan)	Cinder cone of Izu-Tobu	0803-01=
Togatta Hot Spring (Honshu-Japan)	Thermal feature of Zao	0803-19=
Togawan [Toga] (Honshu-Japan)	Maar of Megata	0803-262
Togiak Valley (Alaska-W)	Volcanic field (None) Pleistocene	....
Togo (Mongolia)	Cinder cone of Khanuy Gol	1003-02-
Tôh, Tarso (Africa-N)	Volcanic field (None) Holocene	**0205-009**
To'iavea (Samoa-SW Pacific)	Cinder cone of Savai'i	0404-04=
Tokaanu (New Zealand)	Thermal feature of Taupo	0401-07=

Yuri Doubik (Inst. Volc., Petropavlovsk)

Ash clouds and incandescent lava fragments are ejected from a new cinder cone at **Tolbachik** volcano in 1975 during the largest historical basaltic eruption in the Kuril-Kamchatka arc. The "Great Tolbachik Fissure Eruption" began at a point 18 km south of the summit on July 6, producing a major explosive and effusive eruption that continued until December 1976.

Name (Subregion)	Type (Eruptions, Most Recent) Status. Relation to Named Volcano	Volcano Number
Tokachi (Hokkaido-Japan)	Stratovolcanoes (27, 2004) Historical	**0805-05=**
Tokachi-dake (Hokkaido-Japan)	Synonym of Tokachi	0805-05=
Tokachi-Eboshi (Hokkaido-Japan)	Lava domes (None) Pleistocene	....
Tokachimitsumata (Hokkaido-Japan)	Pleist. caldera of Nipesotsu-Maruyama	0805-061
Tokachi-Mitsumata (Hokkaido-Japan)	Caldera (None) Pleistocene	....
Tokajain (Lesser Sunda Is)	Synonym of Lewotolo	0604-23=
Tokara Hirase (Ryukyu Is)	Unknown (None) Quaternary	....
Tokara-Iwo-jima (Ryukyu Is)	Synonym of Kikai	0802-06=
Tokati (Hokkaido-Japan)	Synonym of Tokachi	0805-05=
Tokishirazu-yama (Honshu-Japan)	Synonym of Fuji	0803-03=
Tokiwa-yama (Honshu-Japan)	Synonym of Fuji	0803-03=
Tokoko (Sulawesi-Indonesia)	Synonym of Tongkoko	0606-13=
Tokolotai, Viti (Vanuatu-SW Pacific)	Cone of Aoba	0507-03=
Tokuoko (Halmahera-Indonesia)	Synonym of Todoko-Ranu	0608-05=
Tokushumbetsu (Hokkaido-Japan)	Stratovolc. Horohoro-Tokushumbetsu	....
Tokuyama-Mitake (Honshu-Japan)	Lava dome (None) Pleistocene	....
Tola, Cerro la (Ecuador)	Cone of Cusín	....
Tolav [Tow Lav] (Vanuatu-SW Pacific)	Stratovolcano of Suretamatai	0507-01=
Tolbachik (Kamchatka)	Shield volcano (57, 1976) Historical	**1000-24=**
Tolbachinskaia Sopka (Kamchatka)	Synonym of Tolbachik	1000-24=
Tolbatschinskaja Ssopka (Kamchatka)	Synonym of Tolbachik	1000-24=
Toledo (US-New Mexico)	Caldera of Valles Caldera	....
Toledo, Cerro (US-New Mexico)	Dome of Valles Caldera	....
Tolguaca (Chile-C)	Stratovolcano (None) Holocene	**1507-093**
Tolhuaca (Chile-C)	Synonym of Tolguaca	1507-093
Tolima, Nevado del (Colombia)	Stratovolcano (12, 1943) Historical	**1501-03=**
Tolimán (Guatemala)	Stratovolcano (None) Holocene	**1402-07=**
Tolire Djaha [Tolire Jaha] (Indonesia)	Crater of Gamalama	0608-06=
Tolire Jaha (Halmahera-Indonesia)	Crater of Gamalama	0608-06=
Tolire Kecil (Halmahera-Indonesia)	Crater of Gamalama	0608-06=
Tolire Ketjil [Tolire Kecil] (Indonesia)	Crater of Gamalama	0608-06=
Tollnerodden (Atlantic-N-Jan Mayen)	Cone of Jan Mayen	1706-01=
Tollocci, Cerro (Bolivia)	Stratovolcano (None) Post-Miocene	....
Tolmachev (Kamchatka)	Stratovolcanoes (None) Pleistocene	....
Tolmachev Dol (Kamchatka)	Cinder cones (2, 300) Radiocarbon	**1000-082**
Tolmachev Valley (Kamchatka)	Synonym of Tolmachev Dol	1000-082
Tolmacheva (Kamchatka)	Synonym of Tolmachev	....
Tolo (Halmahera-Indonesia)	Synonym of Dukono	0608-01=
Tolo Mountain (US-Oregon)	Cone of Cappy Mountain	....
Tolokembu (New Britain-SW Pac)	Cone of Lotomgan Group	....
Tolokiwa (New Guinea-NE of)	Stratovolcano (None) Quaternary	....
Tolong (Sumatra)	Unknown (None) Post-Miocene	....
Toluach (Kamchatka)	Synonym of Tolbachik	1000-24=
Toluca, Nevado de (México)	Stratovolcano (1, -1350) Radiocarbon	**1401-07-**
Tom Mackay Creek (Canada)	Cone of Iskut-Unuk River Cones	1200-09-
Tomari-yama (Kuril Is)	Synonym of Golovnin	0900-01=
Tomasillo, Cerro (México)	Stratovolcano of Tequila	....
Tomasquillo (México)	Cone of Chichinautzin	1401-08=
Tombel Graben (Africa-W)	Cinder cones (None) Holocene	**0204-011**
Tombel Plain (Africa-W)	Synonym of Tombel Graben	0204-011
Tomboro (Lesser Sunda Is)	Synonym of Tambora	0604-04=
Tombuluan (Sulawesi-Indonesia)	Cone of Mahawu	0606-11=
Tompaluan (Sulawesi-Indonesia)	Crater of Lokon-Empung	0606-10=
Tompasso (Sulawesi-Indonesia)	Thermal feature of Tondano Caldera	0606-07-
Tompusu (Sulawesi-Indonesia)	Cone of Tondano Caldera	0606-07-
Tomu (Lesser Sunda Is)	Thermal feature of Paluweh	0604-15=
Tomuraushi (Hokkaido-Japan)	Dome of Tomuraushi Volc Group	....
Tomuraushi Volc Group (Japan)	Stratovolcanoes (None) Pleistocene	....
Tomuro (Honshu-Japan)	Lava domes (None) Pleistocene	....
Tomuro-yama (Honshu-Japan)	Dome of Tomuro	....
Tonchesberg (Germany)	Cone of East Eifel Volc Field	....
Tondachi (Ryukyu Is)	Cone of Suwanose-jima	0802-03=
Tondano Caldera (Sulawesi-Indonesia)	Caldera (None) Fumarolic	**0606-07-**
Tondati [Tondachi] (Ryukyu Is)	Cone of Suwanose-jima	0802-03=
Tondourek (Turkey)	Synonym of Tendürek Dagi	0103-03=
Toney Mountain (Antarctica)	Shield volcano (None) Holocene?	**1900-026**
Tongama (Ryukyu Is)	Crater of Suwanose-jima	0802-03=
Tongariki (Chile-Is)	Pyroclastic cone of Easter Island	1506-011
Tongariro (New Zealand)	Stratovolcanoes (74, 1977) Historical	**0401-08=**
Tongkoko (Sulawesi-Indonesia)	Stratovolcano (7, 1880) Historical	**0606-13=**
Tonglon (Luzon-Philippines)	Synonym of Santo Tomas	0703-086
Tongue Island (Red Sea)	Cone of Zukur	0201-021
Tonkaya (Kamchatka)	Dome of Ksudach	1000-05=
Tonkoko (Sulawesi-Indonesia)	Synonym of Tongkoko	0606-13=
Tonohetsuri (Honshu-Japan)	Pleistocene caldera of Futamata	....
Tontog (Vanuatu-SW Pacific)	Cone of Motlav	0507-001
Tony Mountain (Antarctica)	Synonym of Toney Mountain	1900-026
To-Od Grande (Philippines-C)	Thermal feature of Mahagnao	0702-07=
To-Od Pequena (Philippines-C)	Thermal feature of Mahagnao	0702-07=
Toomba (Australia)	Cone of Nulla Volc Province	....
Toowa Valley (US-California)	Synonym of Golden Trout Creek	1203-17-
Toozaza Peak (Canada)	Cone of Tuya Volc Field	1200-031
Topaki, Gunung (Lesser Sunda Is)	Stratovolcano of Sirung	0604-27=
Topakkaya Tepe (Turkey)	Cinder cone of Erciyes Dagi	0103-01=
Tope de Coroa (Cape Verde Is)	Stratovolcano of Santo Antao	....
Topilejo-Xicomulco Volc Field (México)	Synonym of Chichinautzin	1401-08=
Topo (Azores)	Shield volcano of Pico	1802-02=
Topolnika (Kamchatka)	Synonym of Veer	1000-121
Toppgig (Iceland-W)	Cone of Snaefellsjökull	1700-01=
Toppgigur (Iceland-S)	Fissure vent of Hekla	1702-07=
Topping Cone (Antarctica)	Cone of Terror, Mt.	....
Toppo San Pablo (Italy)	Dome of Vulture, Monte	....
Topso Butte (US-Oregon)	Cone of Newberry	1202-11-
Tordillo (Argentina)	Cinder cone of Unnamed	....

Name (Subregion)	Type (Eruptions, Most Recent) Status / Relation to Named Volcano	Volcano Number
Tore (Bougainville-SW Pacific)	Lava cone (None) Holocene	**0505-00-**
Torfajökull (Iceland-S)	Stratovolcano (10, 1477) Historical	**1702-05=**
Torikabuto (Honshu-Japan)	Stratovolcano (None) Pleistocene	....
Torikabuto-yama (Kyushu-Japan)	Dome of Unzen	0802-10=
Torikabuto-yama (Honshu-Japan)	Dome of Zao	0803-19=
Torinoko-yama (Honshu-Japan)	Synonym of Fuji	0803-03=
Torinoumi (Honshu-Japan)	Crater of Chokai	0803-22=
Torinoumi (Honshu-Japan)	Crater of Iwaki	0803-27=
Tori-shima (Izu Is-Japan)	Stratovolcano (6, 2002) Historical	**0804-09=**
Tori-sima (Izu Is-Japan)	Synonym of Tori-shima	0804-09=
Toritate-yama (Honshu-Japan)	Stratovolcano of Kyoga-take	....
Torn, Volcà el (Spain)	Cone of Olot Volc Field	0100-03-
Tornyi (Kuril Is)	Cone of Golets-Tornyi Group	0900-091
Toro Pugro (Ecuador)	Dome of Chacana	1502-022
Toroeng Prong (SE Asia)	Cinder cone (None) Holocene?	**0705-03-**
Toroni (Chile-N)	Stratovolcano of Sillajguai, Cerro	....
Torre Alfina (Italy)	Volcanic neck (None) Pleistocene	....
Torre Cappella (Italy)	Crater of Campi Flegrei	0101-01=
Torre Gaveta (Italy)	Cone of Campi Flegrei	0101-01=
Torrens Point (W Indies)	Dome of Saba	1600-01=
Torrent, Volcà el (Spain)	Cone of Olot Volc Field	0100-03-
Torres (Galápagos)	Synonym of Marchena	1503-08=
Torrione (Italy)	Vent of Stromboli	0101-04=
Torta, Cerro la (Chile-N)	Dome of Tocorpuri, Cerros de	....
Tortik (Kamchatka)	Dome of Uzon	1000-17=
Tortuga, Isla (Galápagos)	Tuff cone of Negra, Sierra	1503-05=
Tortuga, Isla (México)	Shield volcano (None) Holocene	**1401-011**
Tortuguero (Costa Rica)	Pyroclastic cone (None) Pleistocene	....
Tosa Sucha (Ethiopia)	Cinder cones (None) Holocene	**0201-31-**
Tosamoshibe (Hokkaido-Japan)	Dome of Kutcharo	0805-08=
Tosamosibe [Tosamoshibe] (Hokkaido-Japan)	Dome of Kutcharo	0805-08=
Toshichi Spa (Honshu-Japan)	Thermal feature of Hachimantai	0803-25=
To-shima (Izu Is-Japan)	Stratovolcano (1, -4550) Tephrochron	**0804-011**
Tositi Spa [Toshichi Spa] (Honshu-Japan)	Thermal feature of Hachimantai	0803-25=
Tot Mountain (US-Oregon)	Cinder cone of Bachelor	1202-09-
Totepec, Cerro (México)	Cone of Acatlán Volc Field	....
Totihegy (Hungary)	Cone of Balaton Highland	....
Totogan Malang (Java)	Cone of Semeru	0603-30=
Totonicapán (Guatemala)	Synonym of Cuxliquel	....
Totuma, Cerro (Panamá)	Dome of Tisingal	....
Toumb (Armenia)	Pyroclastic cone of Ghegam Ridge	0104-07-
Touo, Le [Woosantapaliplip] (Vanuatu)	Cone of Ambrym	0507-04=
Toupe, Puy de la (France)	Cone of Chaîne des Puys	0100-02-
Tour, La [Woosantapaliplip] (Vanuatu)	Cone of Ambrym	0507-04=
Tourkal, Piton (Indian O.-W)	Cinder cone of Fournaise, Piton de la	0303-02=
Toussidé, Tarso (Africa-N)	Stratovolcano (None) Holocene	**0205-01=**
Tovanumbatir (New Britain-SW Pac)	Stratovolcano of Rabaul	0502-14=
Tovar, Cerro (Costa Rica)	Synonym of Tilarán, Cerro	....
Tow Alesere (Vanuatu-SW Pacific)	Stratovolcano of Suretamatai	0507-01=
Tow Lav (Vanuatu-SW Pacific)	Stratovolcano of Suretamatai	0507-01=
Tow Maravrig (Vanuatu-SW Pacific)	Crater of Suretamatai	0507-01=
Tow Markong (Vanuatu-SW Pacific)	Crater of Suretamatai	0507-01=
Tow Mear (Vanuatu-SW Pacific)	Crater of Suretamatai	0507-01=
Tow Vetam (Vanuatu-SW Pacific)	Stratovolcano of Suretamatai	0507-01=
Towada (Honshu-Japan)	Caldera (8, 915) Historical	**0803-271**
Towada-ko (Honshu-Japan)	Caldera of Towada	0803-271
Towada-yama (Honshu-Japan)	Stratovolcano of Towada	0803-271
Towari-yama (Honshu-Japan)	Stratovolcano of Towada	0803-271
Towawasag (Vanuatu-SW Pacific)	Stratovolcano of Suretamatai	0507-01=
Tower (Galápagos)	Synonym of Genovesa	1503-081
Tower Hill (Australia)	Maar of Newer Volcanics Prov	0509-01-
Tower Peak [Woosantapaliplip] (Vanuatu)	Cone of Ambrym	0507-04=
Towndrow Peak (US-New Mexico)	Cone of Raton-Clayton	....
Towon Gar (Vanuatu-SW Pacific)	Stratovolcano of Suretamatai	0507-01=
Toya (Hokkaido-Japan)	Pleistocene caldera of Usu	0805-03=
Toyagamori (Honshu-Japan)	Dome of Narugo	0803-20=
Toyatsuka (Honshu-Japan)	Cone of Fuji	0803-03=
Tracey Seamount (Mariana Is-C Pac.)	Submarine volcano (None) Quaternary	....
Trachilas (Greece)	Cone of Mílos	0102-03=
Trachylas [Trachilas] (Greece)	Cone of Mílos	0102-03=
Trachytovyi (Russia-SE)	Cone of Udokan Plateau	1002-03-
Trader Mountain (Alaska Peninsula)	Stratovolcano (None) Pleistocene	....
Trafalgar (New Guinea)	Stratovolcano (None) Pleistocene	....
Trahuiles (Chile-C)	Therm. feature Puyehue-Cordón Caulle	1507-15=
Traitor's Head (Vanuatu-SW Pacific)	Stratovolcano (1, 1881) Historical	**0507-09=**
Trakhitovyi (Russia-SE)	Cone of Udokan Plateau	1002-03-
Tralihue (Argentina)	Stratovolcano (None) Holocene	**1507-101**
Trampa, Cerro la (México)	Stratovolcano of Iztaccíhuatl	1401-082
Transdanubia (Hungary)	Synonym of Balaton Highland	....
Transverso, Monte (México)	Tuff cone of Isabel, Isla	1401-023
Trapa-Trapa (Chile-C)	Caldera of Copahue	1507-09=
Trapezina (Greece)	Dome of Nisyros	0102-05=
Trapichito, Cerro (Guatemala)	Cinder cone of Cuilapa-Barbarena	1402-111
Trautrén, Cerro (Chile-C)	Stratovolcanoes (None) Pleistocene	....
Trautzberger (Germany)	Maar of West Eifel Volc Field	0100-01-
Traversa Campana (Italy)	Crater of Campi Flegrei	0101-01=
Tre Monti (Italy)	Cinder cone of Etna	0101-06=
Trebol, Volcán el (México)	Crater of Pinacate	1401-001
Trentaremi (Italy)	Crater of Campi Flegrei	0101-01=
Tres Chicas, Las (México)	Caldera of Zitácuaro-Valle de Bravo	1401-061
Tres Cruces (México)	Cinder cone of Chichinautzin	1401-08=
Tres Cruces (Chile-N)	Stratovolcano (None) Pleistocene	....
Tres Cruces, Cerro (México)	Cinder cone of Chichinautzin	1401-08=
Tres Cumbres, Cerro (México)	Cone of Chichinautzin	1401-08=

Name (Subregion)	Type (Eruptions, Most Recent) Status / Relation to Named Volcano	Volcano Number
Tres Hermanas [Yepocapa] (Guatemala)	Stratovolcano of Acatenango	1402-08=
Tres Marías [Yepocapa] (Guatemala)	Stratovolcano of Acatenango	1402-08=
Tres Marias Hills (Mindanao-Philippines)	Dome of Camiguin	0701-08=
Tres Marías, Las (Costa Rica)	Synonym of Barva	1405-05=
Tres Vírgenes (México)	Stratovolcanoes (Uncertain) Holocene?	**1401-01=**
Treschina (Kamchatka)	Cinder cone of Tolbachik	1000-24=
Tressous, Puy de (France)	Cone of Chaîne des Puys	0100-02-
Tretiy (Kamchatka)	Fissure vent of Kliuchevskoi	1000-26=
Tretiya Rechka (Kamchatka)	Synonym of Tretya Rechka	....
Tretya Rechka (Kamchatka)	Shield volcano (None) Pleistocene	....
Treugolny Zub (Kamchatka)	Dome of Bezymianny	1000-25=
Trezubetz (Kuril Is)	Somma volcano of Kolokol Group	0900-12=
Tri Sestry (Kuril Is)	Stratovolcano (None) Holocene?	**0900-113**

NASA Space Shuttle image STS111-367-29

Dark lava flows radiate across the desert floor from **Toussidé** volcano in the Tibesti Range in Chad, Toussidé stratovolcano was constructed within the large Pleistocene ignimbritic caldera of Yirrigue, whose eastern scarp is seen right of Toussidé.

Name (Subregion)	Type (Eruptions, Most Recent) Status / Relation to Named Volcano	Volcano Number
Triades (Greece)	Dome of Mílos	0102-03=
Triangle (Canada)	Dome of Edziza	1200-06-
Triangle Hill (US-Oregon)	Cinder cone of Tumalo	....
Trident (Alaska Peninsula)	Stratovolcano (15, 1974) Historical	**1102-16-**
Trident I (Alaska Peninsula)	Stratovolcano of Trident	1102-16-
Trifoglietto (Italy)	Shield volcano of Etna	0101-06=
Trilope (Chile-C)	Synonym of Copahue	1507-09=
Trindade (Atlantic-C)	Stratovolcano (None) Holocene	**1805-051**
Trindade, Pico (Atlantic-C)	Dome of Trindade	1805-051
Trinityberget (Atlantic-N-Jan Mayen)	Cone of Jan Mayen	1706-01=
Triplex (Canada)	Cone of Edziza	1200-06-
Trippabjallar (Iceland-S)	Fissure vent of Hekla	1702-07=
Trippafjoll [Trippabjallar] (Iceland-S)	Fissure vent of Hekla	1702-07=
Trippodi, Monte (Italy)	Dome of Ischia	0101-03=
Tristan da Cunha (Atlantic-S)	Shield volcano (2, 1962) Historical	**1806-01=**
Triton (Greece)	Dome of Santorini	0102-04=
Tritriva (Madagascar)	Cone of Ankaratra Field	0303-015
Trocon (Argentina)	Lava domes (None) Holocene?	**1507-081**
Troina, Monte (Italy)	Cinder cone of Etna	0101-06=
Trois Pitons, Morne (W Indies)	Complex volcano (2, 920) Radiocarbon	**1600-10=**
Trois Rivières-Madeleine (W Indies)	Volcanic field of Soufrière Guadeloupe	1600-06=
Trois Sols, Puy des [Puy de Tressous] (Fran.)	Cone of Chaîne des Puys	0100-02-
Trois Tetes, Piton (Indian O.-W)	Cinder cone of Fournaise, Piton de la	0303-02=
Troitsky (Kamchatka)	Crater of Maly Semiachik	1000-14=
Troitzky [Troitsky] (Kamchatka)	Crater of Maly Semiachik	1000-14=
Trolladyngja (Iceland-NE)	Synonym of Askja	1703-06=
Trolladyngja (Iceland-NE)	Shield volcano of Bárdarbunga	1703-03=
Trolladyngja (Iceland-SW)	Crater Row of Krísuvík	1701-03=
Trolladyngjukerfid (Iceland-SW)	Synonym of Krísuvík	1701-03=
Trollagigar (Iceland-NE)	Crater Row of Bárdarbunga	1703-03=
Tröllaskógahraun (Iceland-S)	Crater Row of Hekla	1702-07=
Trolope (Chile-C)	Synonym of Copahue	1507-09=
Tromen (Argentina)	Stratovolcanoes (2, 1822) Historical	**1507-072**
Trompeta, Cerro el (México)	Dome of Michoacán-Guanajuato	1401-06=
Tronador (Chile-S)	Stratovolcano (None) Holocene?	**1508-011**
Tronador, El (El Salvador)	Thermal feature of Tecapa	1403-08=
Trophy Mountain (Canada)	Cone of Wells Gray-Clearwater	1200-15-
Trou Au Natron (Africa-N)	Pleistocene caldera of Toussidé, Tarso	0205-01=
Trou Au Natron Au Koussi [Era Kohor] (Africa)	Caldera of Koussi, Emi	0205-021
Trout Creek Butte (US-Oregon)	Shield volcano of Black Crater	....
Trout Creek Hill (US-Washington)	Shield volcano of West Crater	1201-06-
Troy (W Indies)	Dome of Saba	1600-01=
Trumbull, Mt. (US-Arizona)	Cinder cone of Uinkaret Field	1209-01-
Tsanzergwe (Africa-C)	Cone of Karisimbi	0203-04-
Tsaolingshan (Taiwan)	Shield volcano (None) Pleistocene	....
Tschachotsch (Kamchatka)	Synonym of Koshelev	1000-02=
Tseax River Cone (Canada)	Pyroclastic cone (2, 1690) Radiocarbon	**1200-10-**
Tsekone Ridge (Canada)	Vent of Edziza	1200-06-
Tsentralny [Centralny] (Kamchatka)	Shield volcano of Pogranychny	1000-47-

Name (Subregion)	Type (Eruptions, Most Recent) Status / Relation to Named Volcano	Volcano Number
Tsentralnyy Semiachik [Zentralny Semiachik]	Stratovolcano of Bolshoi Semiachik	1000-15=
Tsepochka (Kamchatka)	Cinder cone of Tolbachik	1000-24=
Tserber (Aleutian Is)	Synonym of Semisopochnoi	1101-06-
Tshabwato (Africa-C)	Cone of Nyiragongo	0203-03=
Tshambene (Africa-C)	Vent of Nyamuragira	0203-02=
Tshania (Africa-C)	Cone of Visoke	0203-05-
Tshegere, Ile (Africa-C)	Cone of Nyiragongo	0203-03=
Tshibinda (Africa-C)	Cinder cones (None) Holocene	**0203-08-**
Tshove [Shove] (Africa-C)	Cone of Nyamuragira	0203-02=
Tsiatsia (Kuril Is)	Synonym of Tiatia	0900-03=
Tsifajavona (Madagascar)	Cone of Itasy Volc Field	0303-014
Tsikura (Kuril Is)	Synonym of Chikurachki	0900-36=
Tsingrado-Provatas (Greece)	Tuff cone of Mílos	0102-03=
Tsirk (Kuril Is)	Caldera (None) Pleistocene	....
Tskhouk-Karckar (Armenia)	Pyroclastic cones (1, -3000) Tephrochron	**0104-10-**

Jose Luis Macías (UNAM)

Multiple volcanic centers along a SW-NE line form the **Tres Vírgenes** volcanic group in the Baja Peninsula. Thick, rhyodacitic lava flows form prominent ridges on the left flank.

Name (Subregion)	Type (Eruptions, Most Recent) Status / Relation to Named Volcano	Volcano Number
Tsubame (Honshu-Japan)	Thermal feature of Myoko	0803-10=
Tsubunegamori (Izu Is-Japan)	Dome of Mikura-jima	0804-041
Tsuchiurazawa (Honshu-Japan)	Stratovolcano of On-take	0803-04=
Tsuetate (Kyushu-Japan)	Thermal feature of Kuju	0802-12=
Tsugamori (Honshu-Japan)	Stratovolcano of Akita-Yake-yama	0803-26=
Tsugao-yama (Honshu-Japan)	Cone of Fuji	0803-03=
Tsugaru-Fuji (Honshu-Japan)	Synonym of Iwaki	0803-27=
Tsujino-dake (Kyushu-Japan)	Dome of Ibusuki Volc Field	0802-07=
Tsukahara (Kyushu-Japan)	Thermal feature of Tsurumi	0802-13=
Tsukumo-jima (Kyushu-Japan)	Crater of Unzen	0802-10=
Tsukushi-Fuji [Kaimon] (Kyushu-Japan)	Stratovolcano of Ibusuki Volc Field	0802-07=
Tsuruga-ike (Honshu-Japan)	Crater of Norikura	0803-06=
Tsurugi-dake (Honshu-Japan)	Cone of Hakkoda Group	0803-28=
Tsurugi-dake (Honshu-Japan)	Dome of Kurikoma	0803-21=
Tsurugi-yama (Honshu-Japan)	Dome of Osore-yama	0803-29=
Tsurumi (Kyushu-Japan)	Lava domes (3, 867) Historical	**0802-13=**
Tsurumi-dake (Kyushu-Japan)	Dome of Tsurumi	0802-13=
Tsuruta (Honshu-Japan)	Scoria cones (None) Pleistocene	....
Tuahu (New Zealand)	Dome of Maroa	0401-061
Tuahu (New Zealand)	Tuff cone of Okataina	0401-05=
Tuanshan (SE Asia)	Cone of Tengchong	0705-11-
Tuanzishan (China-E)	Cinder cone of Keluo Group	1005-02-
Tubaru (Halmahera-Indonesia)	Synonym of Ibu	0608-03=
Tuber Hill (Canada)	Stratovolcano of Bridge River Cones	1200-17-
Tuchiyu (Honshu-Japan)	Dome of Azuma	0803-18=
Tuchov Crater (Kamchatka)	Synonym of Zarechny	....
Tucle, Cerro (Chile-N)	Synonym of Tujle, Cerro	1505-103
Tuddahraun (Iceland-S)	Fissure vent of Katla	1702-03=
Tudeuk, Gunung (Sumatra)	Lava dome (None) Pleistocene	....
Tudjuh, Danau (Sumatra)	Synonym of Tujuh	....
Tudu (Lesser Sunda Is)	Crater of Paluweh	0604-15=
Tudu (Lesser Sunda Is)	Thermal feature of Paluweh	0604-15=
Tufton Hall (W Indies)	Thermal feature of St. Catherine	1600-17=
Tugamori [Tsugamori] (Honshu-Japan)	Stratovolcano of Akita-Yake-yama	0803-26=
Tugaru-Huzi (Honshu-Japan)	Synonym of Iwaki	0803-27=
Tugle, Cerro (Chile-N)	Synonym of Tujle, Cerro	1505-103
Tugumynk (Kamchatka)	Dome of Kurile Lake	1000-023
Tuhingamata (New Zealand)	Dome of Taupo	0401-07=
Tuhua (New Zealand)	Synonym of Mayor Island	0401-021
Tui Lake (Kermadec Is)	Crater of Raoul Island	0402-03=
Tuila [Tuyla] (Kamchatka)	Fissure vent of Kliuchevskoi	1000-26=
Tujle, Cerro (Chile-N)	Maar (None) Holocene	**1505-103**
Tujuh (Sumatra)	Stratovolcano (None) Quaternary	....
Tukad Kladi Hot Spring (Lesser Sunda Is)	Thermal feature of Bratan	0604-001
Tukang Kalo (Luzon-Philippines)	Dome of Labo	....
Tukap (Kuril Is)	Stratovolcano of Medvezhia	0900-10=
Tukay (Sulu Is-Philippines)	Cone of Jolo	0700-01=
Tukosmeru (Vanuatu-SW Pacific)	Stratovolcano of Yasur	0507-10=
Tukullum (US-Washington)	Synonym of Baker	1201-01=
Tukuyu (Africa-E)	Shield volcano (None) Post-Miocene	....
Tulabug, Cerro (Ecuador)	Cinder cone of Licto	1502-081

Name (Subregion)	Type (Eruptions, Most Recent) Status / Relation to Named Volcano	Volcano Number
Tulaman [Tuluman] (Admiralty Is-SW Pacific)	Cone of St. Andrew Strait	0500-01=
Tule, Cerro el (México)	Shield volc. of Michoacán-Guanajuato	1401-06=
Tule, Cerro el (México)	Dome of Primavera, Sierra la	....
Tule, Cerro el (El Salvador)	Cone of San Diego	1403-001
Tulik (Aleutian Is)	Stratovolcano of Okmok	1101-29-
Tullu Moje (Ethiopia)	Pumice cone (2, 1900) Anthropology	**0201-25-**
Tulu Billa (Ethiopia)	Cinder cone of O'a Caldera	0201-28-
Tulu Fike (Ethiopia)	Pyroclastic cone of O'a Caldera	0201-28-
Tulu Moje (Ethiopia)	Synonym of Tullu Moje	0201-25-
Tuluach (Kamchatka)	Synonym of Tolbachik	1000-24=
Tululusia (Africa-E)	Dome of Meru	0202-16=
Tuluman (Admiralty Is-SW Pacific)	Cone of St. Andrew Strait	0500-01=
Tumac Mountain (US-Washington)	Cinder cone (None) Pleistocene	....
Tumalo (US-Oregon)	Lava domes (None) Pleistocene	....
Tumanniy (Kamchatka)	Shield volcano (None) Pleistocene	....
Tumanov (Kamchatka)	Stratovolcano of Asacha	1000-058
Tumatangas (Sulu Is-Philippines)	Cinder cone of Jolo	0700-01=
Tumayhini (Africa-C)	Cone of Nyamuragira	0203-02=
Tumba del Buey, La [Crater del Buey] (Chile)	Crater of Mocho-Choshuenco	1507-13=
Tumble Buttes (US-California)	Cinder cones (None) Holocene?	**1203-06-**
Tumengjiang (China-E)	Synonym of Dunhua	....
Tumisa (Chile-N)	Stratovolcano (None) Pleistocene	....
Tumpak (Java)	Crater of Kelut	0603-28=
Tumrok (Kamchatka)	Shield volcano (None) Pleistocene	....
Tumunui (New Zealand)	Dome of Kapenga	....
Tumusun (Tumusunskii) (Russia-SE)	Cone of Khamar-Daban	....
Tunas, Cerro las (El Salvador)	Cinder cone of Cinotepeque, Cerro	1403-051
Tunas, Cerro las (México)	Cinder cone of Durango Volc Field	1401-022
Tunaumuri (New Britain-SW Pac)	Maar of Dakataua	0502-04=
Tundroviy (Kamchatka)	Shield volcano of Otdelniy	1000-056
Tung-Chiao-te-Pu-shan [Dongjiaodebushan]	Cone of Wudalianchi	1005-03-
Tunggul, Bukit (Java)	Stratovolcano of Tangkubanparahu	0603-09=
Tung-Heng-Tao-shan [Donghengdaoshan]	Cone of Longgang Group	1005-05-
Tungkat, Bukit (Sumatra)	Unknown (None) Post-Miocene	....
Tung-Lung-Men-shan [Donglongmenshan]	Cone of Wudalianchi	1005-03-
Tung-Lung-wan [Donglongwan] (China-E)	Maar of Longgang Group	1005-05-
Tungnaárfjöll (Iceland-NE)	Fissure vents (None) Pleistocene	....
Tungnafellsjökull (Iceland-NE)	Stratovolcano (None) Holocene	**1703-04=**
Tungnarbotnahraun (Iceland-NE)	Fissure vent of Bárdarbunga	1703-03=
Tung-shan [Dongshan] (China-E)	Cone of Erkeshan	....
Tunguragua (Ecuador)	Synonym of Tungurahua	1502-08=
Tungurahua (Ecuador)	Stratovolcano (26, 2009) Historical	**1502-08=**
Tun-Hua (China-E)	Synonym of Dunhua	....
Tunipilyakum (Kamchatka)	Shield volcano of Iktunup	1000-67-
Tunisa (Chile-N)	Synonym of Tumisa	....
Tunisset, Puy de [Puy de Tenusset] (France)	Cone of Chaîne des Puys	0100-02-
Tunka Depression (Russia-SE)	Synonym of Tunkin Depression	1002-05-
Tunkin Depression (Russia-SE)	Volcanic field (None) Holocene?	**1002-05-**
Tunnel Cone (US-California)	Cinder cone of Golden Trout Creek	1203-17-
Tunoa (Samoa-SW Pacific)	Shield volcano of Ta'u	0404-001
Tuo, Kapundan [Kepundan Tuo] (Sumatra)	Crater of Marapi	0601-14=
Tuo, Kepundan (Sumatra)	Crater of Marapi	0601-14=
Tuoroisischi (Italy)	Crater of Roccamonfina	....
Tuororame (Italy)	Dome of Roccamonfina	....
Tupinier (New Guinea-NE of)	Synonym of Sakar	0501-08=
Tupua (Bolivia)	Stratovolcano (None) Post-Miocene	....
Tupungatito (Chile-C)	Stratovolcano (18, 1987) Historical	**1507-01=**
Tupungato (Chile-C)	Stratovolcano (None) Pleistocene	....
Turangunan (New Britain-SW Pac)	Stratovolcano of Rabaul	0502-14=
Turbid Lake (US-Wyoming)	Crater of Yellowstone	1205-01-
Turchio, Monte (Italy)	Cinder cone of Etna	0101-06=
Turello (Italy)	Dome of Vico-Cimino Complex	....
Turfan (China-W)	Cone (1, 1120) Historical	**1004-01-**
Turitea (New Zealand)	Cone of Pirongia	....
Turkey Ridge (US-New Mexico)	Dome of Valles Caldera	....
Turoro Piccolo (Italy)	Cone of Roccamonfina	....
Turpentine Peak (US-Oregon)	Shield volcano of Three Fingered Jack	....
Turquoise Cone (Aleutian Is)	Stratovolcano of Fisher	1101-35-
Turrah, Harrat (Arabia-W)	Volcanic field of Rahat, Harrat	0301-07=
Turrialba (Costa Rica)	Stratovolcano (11, 1866) Historical	**1405-07=**
Turú (Costa Rica)	Stratovolcano of Barva	1405-05=
Turuga-ike [Tsuruga-ike] (Honshu-Japan)	Crater of Norikura	0803-06=
Turugi-dake [Tsurugi-dake] (Honshu-Japan)	Cone of Hakkoda Group	0803-28=
Turugi-yama [Tsurugi-dake] (Honshu-Japan)	Dome of Kurikoma	0803-21=
Turugi-yama [Tsurugi-yama] (Honshu-Japan)	Dome of Osore-yama	0803-29=
Turumi (Kyushu-Japan)	Synonym of Tsurumi	0802-13=
Turumi-dake [Tsurumi-dake] (Kyushu-Japan)	Dome of Tsurumi	0802-13=
Turun, Gunung (Java)	Cone of Ungaran	0603-23=
Tuscolana-Artemisio (Italy)	Pleistocene caldera of Alban Hills	0101-004
Tuscolano-Artemisio (Italy)	Stratovolcano of Alban Hills	0101-004
Tusi al Yamani, Jabal at (Arabia-W)	Cone of Birk, Harrat al	0301-072
Tusi ash Shami, Jabal at (Arabia-W)	Cone of Birk, Harrat al	0301-072
Tutaeheka (New Zealand)	Dome of Kapenga	....
Tutaeheka (New Zealand)	Dome of Okataina	0401-05=
Tute, Cerro El (El Salvador)	Dome of Apastepeque Field	1403-071
Tutong, Gunung (Sumatra)	Synonym of Telong, Bur ni	0601-05=
Tutsingale Mountain (Canada)	Cone of Kawdy Metah	....
Tutuila (Samoa-SW Pacific)	Tuff cones (None) Holocene	**0404-02-**
Tutukau (New Zealand)	Dome of Maroa	0401-061
Tutultepeque, Cerro (El Salvador)	Cinder cone of Cinotepeque, Cerro	1403-051
Tutung, Gunung (Sumatra)	Dome of Peuet Sague	0601-03=
Tutupaca (Perú)	Stratovolcano (None) Holocene	**1504-04=**
Tuvio, Mont (Vanuatu-SW Pacific)	Cone of Ambrym	0507-04=
Tuvurvur [Tavurvur] (New Britain-SW Pac)	Stratovolcano of Rabaul	0502-14=

Name (Subregion)	Type (Eruptions, Most Recent) Status / Relation to Named Volcano	Volcano Number
Tuxpan (México)	Shield volc. of Zitácuaro-Valle de Bravo	1401-061
Tuxtepec (México)	Cinder cone of Chichinautzin	1401-08=
Tuxtla, Volcán de (México)	Synonym of San Martín	1401-11=
Tuya #2 (Canada)	Tuya of Tuya Volc Field	1200-031
Tuya Butte (Canada)	Tuya of Tuya Volc Field	1200-031
Tuya Butte Volc Field (Canada)	Synonym of Tuya Volc Field	1200-031
Tuya Lake Volc Field (Canada)	Synonym of Tuya Volc Field	1200-031
Tuya Volc Field (Canada)	Volcanic field (None) Holocene	**1200-031**
Tuya Volcano Group (Canada)	Synonym of Dark Mountain	....
Tuyajto, Cerro (Chile-N)	Stratovolc. Cordón de Puntas Negras	1505-101
Tuyio [Mont Tuvio] (Vanuatu-SW Pacific)	Cone of Ambrym	0507-04=
Tuyla (Kamchatka)	Fissure vent of Kliuchevskoi	1000-26=
Tuzgle, Cerro (Argentina)	Stratovolcano (None) Holocene?	**1505-15-**
Tuzovsky (Kamchatka)	Shield volcanoes (None) Holocene?	**1000-54-**
Tv1 (New Zealand)	Crater of White Island	0401-04=
Tvibollar (Iceland-SW)	Crater Row of Brennisteinsfjöll	1701-04=
Tvilling (Atlantic-N-Jan Mayen)	Cone of Jan Mayen	1706-01=
Tvitunup (Kamchatka)	Shield volcano of Tuzovsky	1000-54-
Twiddler Hill (Australia)	Cone of Atherton Volc Province	....
Twin (Canada)	Cone of Edziza	1200-06-
Twin Buttes (US-Oregon)	Cone of Squaw Ridge Lava Field	1202-13-
Twin Buttes (US-California)	Cinder cones (None) Holocene?	**1203-04-**
Twin Calderas (Alaska-W)	Shield volcano of Imuruk Lake	1104-06-
Twin Crater (New Britain-SW Pac)	Crater of Langila	0502-01=
Twin Craters (US-Oregon)	Cinder cone of Belknap	1202-06-
Twin Craters (US-New Mexico)	Crater of Zuni-Bandera	1210-02-
Twin Knolls (US-Arizona)	Cone of Springerville	....
Twin Mountain (Alaska-W)	Cone of Nunivak Island	1104-02-
Twin Mountain (US-New Mexico)	Cone of Raton-Clayton	....
Twin Peaks (W Indies)	Dome of Diables, Morne aux	1600-08=
Twin Peaks (US-California)	Dome of Sutter Buttes	....
Twindaung (SE Asia)	Crater of Lower Chindwin	0705-09-
Twins Crater (Australia)	Crater of Sturgeon Volc Province	....
Twins, The (US-Oregon)	Shield volcano of Maiden Peak	....
Twinywa (SE Asia)	Crater of Lower Chindwin	0705-09-
Two Point Butte (US-Idaho)	Cinder cone of Craters of the Moon	1204-02-
Twunamuri (New Britain-SW Pac)	Maar of Dakataua	0502-04=
Tyatya (Kuril Is)	Synonym of Tiatia	0900-03=
Tyausu-dake [Chausu-dake] (Honshu-Japan)	Dome of Nasu	0803-15=
Tyausu-yama (Honshu-Japan)	Synonym of Niigata-Yake-yama	0803-09=
Tygilsky (Kamchatka)	Synonym of Tigilsky	....
Tynua (Kamchatka)	Shield volcanoes (None) Pleistocene	....
Tyokai (Honshu-Japan)	Synonym of Chokai	0803-22=
Tyositiro-yama [Choshichiro-yama] (Japan)	Dome of Akagi	0803-13=
Tyubetu-dake (Hokkaido-Japan)	Synonym of Chubetsu	....
Tyuo-Kakokyu [Chuo-Kakokyu] (Japan)	Cone of Tokachi	0805-05=
Tzanjuyub (Guatemala)	Pleistocene caldera of Santo Tomás	....
Tzapotlán (México)	Synonym of Colima	1401-04=
Tzempoli (México)	Cinder cone of Chichinautzin	1401-08=
Tzintzungo, Cerro de (México)	Cinder cone of Michoacán-Guanajuato	1401-06=

U

Name (Subregion)	Type (Eruptions, Most Recent) Status / Relation to Named Volcano	Volcano Number
Uachlar (Uakhlar) (Kamchatka)	Synonym of Ichinsky	1000-28=
Uau en Namus (Africa-N)	Synonym of Wau-en-Namus	0205-008
Ubakura-yama (Honshu-Japan)	Stratovolcano of Iwate	0803-24=
Ubayu (Honshu-Japan)	Dome of Azuma	0803-18=
Ubehebe Craters (US-California)	Maars (1, -4050) Anthropology	**1203-16-**
Ubia, Mount (New Britain-SW Pac)	Dome of Sulu Range	0502-09=
Ubina, Cerro (Bolivia)	Stratovolcano (None) Post-Miocene	....
Ubinas (Perú)	Stratovolcano (20, 2009) Historical	**1504-02=**
Ubur-Khangay (Mongolia)	Volcanic field (None) Pleistocene	....
Ucanca (Canary Is)	Pleistocene caldera of Tenerife	1803-03-
Uchino (Honshu-Japan)	Cinder cone of Izu-Tobu	0803-01=
Uchiura-dake (Hokkaido-Japan)	Synonym of Komaga-take	0805-02=
Uchi-yama (Kyushu-Japan)	Dome of Tsurumi	0802-13=
Uchkoren (Kamchatka)	Unknown (None) Pleistocene	....
Uchtapoliar (Armenia)	Cone of Ghegam Ridge	0104-07-
Uchuchei (Russia-SE)	Cone of Udokan Plateau	1002-03-
Uchuy (Perú)	Cinder cone of Andahua-Orcopampa	1504-004
Uctepeler (Turkey)	Cone of Erciyes Dagi	0103-01=
Ucuk Dagi (Turkey)	Cone of Erciyes Dagi	0103-01=
Ud'ale (Ethiopia)	Synonym of Assab Volc Field	0201-125
Udina (Kamchatka)	Stratovolcanoes (None) Holocene	**1000-241**
Udo (Korea)	Tuff cone of Halla	1006-04-
Udochka (Kamchatka)	Shield volcano (None) Pleistocene	....
Udokan Plateau (Russia-SE)	Pyroclastic cones (5, -220) Radiocarbon	**1002-03-**
Udone-Jima (Izu Is-Japan)	Stratovolcano (None) Pleistocene	....
Uea Island (SW Pacific)	Synonym of Wallis Islands	0404-05-
Ueno (Honshu-Japan)	Shield volcano (None) Pleistocene	....
Uetawara-yama (Honshu-Japan)	Stratovolcano of On-take	0803-04=
Ugashik (Alaska Peninsula)	Pleistocene caldera of Ugashik-Peulik	1102-13-
Ugashik-Peulik (Alaska Peninsula)	Stratovolcano (4, 1814) Historical	**1102-13-**
Ugos (Mindanao-Philippines)	Dome of Leonard Range	0701-031
Uguilla, Cerro (Bolivia)	Stratovolcano (None) Post-Miocene	....
Uhambule (Africa-E)	Dome of SW Usangu Basin	0202-163
Uhay, Mt. (Mindanao-Philippines)	Cone of Camiguin	0701-08=
Uhlirsky Vrch (Czech)	Cone of Unnamed	....
Uilyuchinsky (Kamchatka)	Synonym of Vilyuchik	1000-083
Uinkaret Field (US-Arizona)	Volcanic field (1, 1100) Anthropology	**1209-01-**
Uiun-Kholdongi (China-E)	Synonym of Wudalianchi	1005-03-
Ujakushatsch (Alaska-SW)	Synonym of Redoubt	1103-03-
Ujansi (Bolivia)	Unknown (None) Post-Miocene	....
Ujun-Holdongi (China-E)	Synonym of Wudalianchi	1005-03-
Ujuxté, Cerrito de (Guatemala)	Lava cone of Redondo, Cerro	....
Uka (Kamchatka)	Shield volcano (None) Holocene?	**1000-61-**
Uk'eledi (Alaska-E)	Synonym of Wrangell	1105-02-
Ukho (Kamchatka)	Cinder cone of Yavinsky	1000-021
Ukinrek Maars (Alaska Peninsula)	Maars (2, 1977) Historical	**1102-131**
Uksichan (Kamchatka)	Shield volcano (None) Holocene?	**1000-35-**
Uku-jima (Kyushu-Japan)	Stratovolcano of Ojika-jima	....
'Ukwatain (Arabia-W)	Cone of Yar, Jabal	0301-08-
Ulag-Arginskii [Ulug-Arginsky] (Russia-SE)	Cinder cone of Azas Plateau	1002-07-
Ulag-Arginsky [Ulug-Arginsky] (Russia-SE)	Cinder cone of Azas Plateau	1002-07-
Ulakaia Hill (Alaska-W)	Cone of St. George	....
Ulaula, Puu (Hawaiian Is)	Cone of Kilauea	1302-01-
Ulaula, Puu (Hawaiian Is)	Cone of Mauna Loa	1302-02=
Ulawon (New Britain-SW Pac)	Synonym of Ulawun	0502-12=
Ulawun (New Britain-SW Pac)	Stratovolcano (33, 2007) Historical	**0502-12=**
Ule'eg (Vanuatu-SW Pacific)	Stratovolcano of Suretamatai	0507-01=
Uliaegan (Aleutian Is)	Synonym of Uliaga	1101-25-
Uliaga (Aleutian Is)	Synonym of Carlisle	1101-23-
Uliaga (Aleutian Is)	Stratovolcano (None) Holocene	**1101-25-**
Ullung-do (Korea)	Synonym of Ulreung	1006-03-
Ulmener (Germany)	Maar of West Eifel Volc Field	0100-01-
Ulo [Paraso] (Solomon Is-SW Pacific)	Thermal feature of Nonda	....
Ulreung (Korea)	Stratovolcano (3, -2990) Radiocarbon	**1006-03-**
Ulreung-do (Korea)	Synonym of Ulreung	1006-03-
Ulreuno-do (Korea)	Synonym of Ulreung	1006-03-
Ultimo Puesto (Chile-C)	Cone of Antillanca Group	1507-153
Ulu Majur, Bukit (Sumatra)	Cone of Punggur, Bukit	....
Ulu Palik, Bukit (Sumatra)	Unknown (None) Post-Miocene	....
Ulug-Arga (Russia-SE)	Cone of Azas Plateau	1002-07-
Ulug-Arginsky (Russia-SE)	Cinder cone of Azas Plateau	1002-07-
Ulug-Art-Tayga (Russia-SE)	Cone of Azas Plateau	1002-07-
Uluinggalau (Fiji Is-SW Pacific)	Cone of Taveuni	0405-01-
Ululu, Mount (New Britain-SW Pac)	Cone of Sulu Range	0502-09=
Ulumam (New Guinea-NE of)	Cone of Karkar	0501-03=
Uluman, Mt. (New Guinea-NE of)	Synonym of Karkar	0501-03=
Ulumbu (Lesser Sunda Is)	Thermal feature of Poco Leok	0604-07=
Ulu-Nino (Sumatra)	Cone of Mesurai-Ulu Nino	....
Uluwun (New Britain-SW Pac)	Synonym of Ulawun	0502-12=
Ulvaney (Kamchatka)	Shield volcano (None) Pleistocene	....
Ulyaborskiy [Khara-Boldok] (Russia-SE)	Cone of Tunkin Depression	1002-05-
Um El Garanigh (Africa-N)	Shield volcano of Haruj	0205-007
Umani (Africa-E)	Cone of Chyulu Hills	0202-13=
Umbaba (Ethiopia)	Synonym of As-Ali	....
Umboi (New Guinea-NE of)	Complex volcano (None) Holocene	**0501-06=**
Umboi, Lake (New Britain-SW Pac)	Crater of Du Faure	....
Umcen (Umcina) (New Guinea-W)	Synonym of Umsini	0609-01=
Umi-jigoku (Kyushu-Japan)	Thermal feature of Tsurumi	0802-13=
Umm ad Dulu, Jabal (Arabia-W)	Maar of Kishb, Harrat	0301-071
Umm Arafieb, Jebel (Africa-N)	Shield volcano (None) Holocene?	**0205-07-**
Umm Khandag, Jebel (Africa-N)	Cone of Bayuda Volc Field	0205-06-
Umm Qureinat (Africa-N)	Cone of Bayuda Volc Field	0205-06-

Lee Siebert (Smithsonian)

Ubehebe craters are an isolated group of maar volcanoes erupted through non-volcanic sediments of Death Valley National Park in California. The contact between pre-eruption sedimentary rocks and overlying black ash deposits can be seen at the upper part of the western wall of the 800-m-wide, 235-m-deep Ubehebe crater.

Name (Subregion)	Type (Eruptions, Most Recent) Status / Relation to Named Volcano	Volcano Number
Umm Ruqubah, Jabal (Arabia-W)	Dome of Rahat, Harrat	0301-07=
Ummuna (Ethiopia)	Synonym of Ale Bagu	0201-09=
Umsini (New Guinea-W)	(None) Not a Volcano	0609-01=
Una Una (Sulawesi-Indonesia)	Synonym of Colo [Una Una]	0606-01=
Unabetsu (Hokkaido-Japan)	Stratovolcano (None) Pleistocene	....
Unabetu (Hokkaido-Japan)	Synonym of Unabetsu	....
Unagi (Kyushu-Japan)	Maar of Ibusuki Volc Field	0802-07=
Unalavquen (Chile-C)	Synonym of Callaqui	1507-091
Unamuncho (Ecuador)	Cone of Sagoatoa	....
Unana (Kamchatka)	Stratovolcano (None) Pleistocene	....
Unda Hararo (Ethiopia)	Shield volcano of Manda Hararo	0201-115
Undaga Island (New Britain-SW Pac)	Cone of Mundua	0502-021

Name (Subregion)	Type (Eruptions, Most Recent) Status Relation to Named Volcano	Volcano Number
Undaka Island [Undaga Island] (New Britain)	Cone of Mundua	0502-021
Undara (Australia)	Shield volcano McBride Volc Province	
Unea (New Britain-SW Pac)	Caldera (None) Quaternary	
Ungaran (Java)	Stratovolcano (None) Holocene	**0603-23=**
Ungin, Mt. (Vanuatu-SW Pacific)	Cone of Melkum, Mt.	
Ungulungwak Hill (Alaska-W)	Shield volcano of Ingrichuak Hills	
Union Peak (US-Oregon)	Cone of Crater Lake	1202-16-
Unnamed (Admiralty Is-SW Pacific)	Submarine volc (1, 1972) Hydrophonic	**0500-03-**
Unnamed (Africa-C)	Fissure vents (None) Post-Miocene	
Unnamed (Africa-E)	Pyroclastic cone (None) Holocene	**0202-162**
Unnamed (Alaska Peninsula)	Lava dome (None) Holocene	**1102-132**
Unnamed (Aleutian Is)	(None) Not a Volcano	1101-17-
Unnamed (Antarctica)	Submarine volcano (None) Holocene?	**1900-016**
Unnamed (Antarctica)	Unknown (None) Quaternary	
Unnamed (Antarctica)	Scoria cones (None) Holocene?	**1900-014**

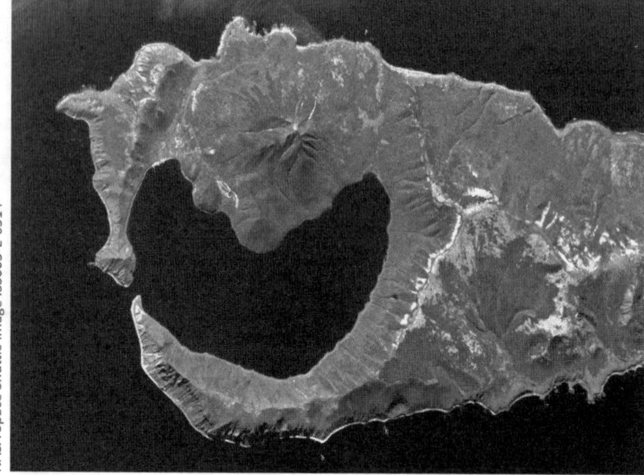

NASA Space Shuttle image ISS005-E-6514

A narrow gap in the NNE rim of 7.5-km-wide Pleistocene Brouton caldera on **Urataman** volcano allows access of the sea into Brouton Bay. The caldera floor lies 250 m beneath the sea surface, and the rim rises 450 m above it. A central cone, andesitic Urataman volcano, has grown to a height of 678 m during the Holocene in the SE part of the caldera.

Name (Subregion)	Type (Eruptions, Most Recent) Status Relation to Named Volcano	Volcano Number
Unnamed (Antarctica)	(None) Not a Volcano	1900-051
Unnamed (Arabia)	Cones (None) Post-Miocene	
Unnamed (Arabia)	Cones (None) Post-Miocene	
Unnamed (Arabia-S)	Submarine volcano (None) Uncertain	**0301-15-**
Unnamed (Arctic Ocean)	Submarine volcano? (Uncertain)	**1707-01-**
Unnamed (Arctic Ocean)	Submarine volcano (Uncertain) Holocene	**1707-02-**
Unnamed (Argentina)	Pyroclastic cone (None) Holocene?	**1505-161**
Unnamed (Argentina)	Volcanic field (None) Pleistocene	
Unnamed (Armenia)	Volcanic field (None) Pleistocene	
Unnamed (Armenia)	Volcanic field (None) Pleistocene	
Unnamed (Armenia)	Volcanic field (None) Pleistocene	
Unnamed (Armenia)	Volcanic field (None) Pleistocene	
Unnamed (Atlantic-C)	Submarine volcano (Uncertain)	**1805-03=**
Unnamed (Atlantic-C)	Submarine volcano (Uncertain)	**1805-02=**
Unnamed (Atlantic-C)	Submarine volcano (Uncertain)	**1805-04=**
Unnamed (Atlantic-C)	Submarine volcano? (Uncertain)	**1805-01=**
Unnamed (Atlantic-N)	(None) Not a Volcano	1801-01=
Unnamed (Atlantic-N)	Submarine volcano (1, 1884) Historical	**1801-02=**
Unnamed (Atlantic-N)	Submarine volcano (Uncertain)	**1801-03=**
Unnamed (Atlantic-N)	Submarine volcano (1, 1865) Historical	**1801-04=**
Unnamed (Chile-Is)	Submarine volcano (Uncertain)	**1506-04=**
Unnamed (China-E)	Unknown (None) Quaternary	
Unnamed (China-E)	Unknown (None) Quaternary	
Unnamed (China-E)	Cones (None) Pleistocene	
Unnamed (China-E)	Unknown (None) Quaternary	
Unnamed (China-E)	Cinder cones (None) Pleistocene	
Unnamed (China-E)	Unknown (None) Quaternary	
Unnamed (China-E)	Volcanic field (None) Post-Miocene	
Unnamed (China-E)	Volcanic field (None) Quaternary	
Unnamed (China-E)	Shield volcanoes (None) Post-Miocene	
Unnamed (China-E)	Volcanic field (None) Post-Miocene	
Unnamed (China-E)	Cinder cones (None) Post-Miocene	
Unnamed (China-W)	Unknown (None) Post-Miocene	
Unnamed (China-W)	Unknown (None) Post-Miocene	
Unnamed (China-W)	Unknown (None) Quaternary	
Unnamed (China-W)	Volcanic field (None) Post-Miocene	
Unnamed (China-W)	Volcanic field (None) Uncertain	**1004-04-**
Unnamed (Colombia)	Volcanic field (None) Quaternary	
Unnamed (Czech)	Volcanic field (None) Pleistocene	
Unnamed (El Salvador)	Volcanic field (None) Pleistocene	
Unnamed (Ethiopia)	Fissure vents (None) Holocene	**0201-251**
Unnamed (Ethiopia)	Pyroclastic cones (None) Holocene	**0201-201**
Unnamed (Ethiopia)	Cinder cones (None) Holocene	**0201-311**
Unnamed (Ethiopia)	Fissure vents (None) Holocene	**0201-221**
Unnamed (Georgia)	Shield volcano (None) Pleistocene	
Unnamed (Georgia)	Lava cones (None) Holocene	**0104-05-**
Unnamed (Georgia)	Cinder cones (None) Holocene	**0104-04-**

Name (Subregion)	Type (Eruptions, Most Recent) Status Relation to Named Volcano	Volcano Number
Unnamed (Hawaiian Is)	Submarine volcano? (Uncertain)	**1302-08-**
Unnamed (Hawaiian Is)	Submarine volcano (1, 1955) Historical	**1302-09-**
Unnamed (Hungary)	Volcanic field (None) Post-Miocene	
Unnamed (Indian O.-E)	Submarine volcano? (Uncertain)	**0305-01=**
Unnamed (Iran)	Unknown (None) Quaternary	
Unnamed (Iran)	Volcanic field (None) Holocene	**0302-00-**
Unnamed (Iran)	Unknown (None) Post-Miocene	
Unnamed (Iran)	Volcanic field (None) Holocene?	**0302-04-**
Unnamed (Iran)	Unknown (None) Quaternary	
Unnamed (Iran)	Unknown (None) Quaternary	
Unnamed (Iran)	Unknown (None) Quaternary	
Unnamed (Israel)	Cone (None) Post-Miocene	
Unnamed (Israel)	Cone (None) Post-Miocene	
Unnamed (Jordan)	Volcanic field (None) Post-Miocene	
Unnamed (Jordan)	Volcanic field (None) Post-Miocene	
Unnamed (Jordan)	Volcanic field (None) Post-Miocene	
Unnamed (Jordan)	Volcanic field (None) Pleistocene	
Unnamed (Kamchatka)	Shield volcanoes (None) Pleistocene	
Unnamed (Kamchatka)	Stratovolcano (None) Pleistocene	
Unnamed (Kamchatka)	Shield volcanoes (None) Holocene	**1000-085**
Unnamed (Kamchatka)	Lava domes (None) Pleistocene	
Unnamed (Kamchatka)	Shield volcano (None) Quaternary	
Unnamed (Kamchatka)	Shield volcano (None) Pleistocene	
Unnamed (Kamchatka)	Lava domes (None) Pleistocene	
Unnamed (Kamchatka)	Lava domes (None) Pleistocene	
Unnamed (Kamchatka)	Shield volcanoes (None) Pleistocene	
Unnamed (Kamchatka)	Shield volcano (None) Pleistocene	
Unnamed (Kamchatka)	Shield volcano (None) Holocene?	**1000-43-**
Unnamed (Kamchatka)	Stratovolcanoes (None) Pleistocene	
Unnamed (Kamchatka)	Cinder cones (None) Pleistocene	
Unnamed (Kamchatka)	Cinder cone (None) Holocene	**1000-081**
Unnamed (Kamchatka)	Shield volcano (None) Pleistocene	
Unnamed (Kamchatka)	Lava domes (None) Pleistocene	
Unnamed (Kamchatka)	Shield volcanoes (None) Holocene	**1000-086**
Unnamed (Kamchatka)	Shield volcano (None) Pleistocene	
Unnamed (Kamchatka)	Shield volcano (None) Pleistocene	
Unnamed (Kamchatka)	Cinder cones (None) Holocene?	**1000-232**
Unnamed (Kuril Is)	Submarine volcano (Uncertain)	**0900-061**
Unnamed (Kuril Is)	Submarine volc (1, 1972) Hydrophonic	**0900-16-**
Unnamed (Kuril Is)	Submarine volcano (1, 1924) Historical	**0900-23=**
Unnamed (Kuril Is)	Submarine volcano? (Uncertain)	**0900-13-**
Unnamed (Lesser Sunda Is)	Unknown (None) Post-Miocene	
Unnamed (Lesser Sunda Is)	Unknown (None) Post-Miocene	
Unnamed (Lesser Sunda Is)	Unknown (None) Post-Miocene	
Unnamed (Lesser Sunda Is)	Unknown (None) Post-Miocene	
Unnamed (Lesser Sunda Is)	Unknown (None) Post-Miocene	
Unnamed (Lesser Sunda Is)	Unknown (None) Post-Miocene	
Unnamed (Luzon-N of)	Submarine volcano (3, 1854) Historical	**0704-05=**
Unnamed (Mariana Is-C Pacific)	Submarine volcano? (Uncertain)	**0804-138**
Unnamed (Mariana Is-C Pacific)	Submarine volcano? (Uncertain)	**0804-139**
Unnamed (Mongolia)	Volcanic field (None) Pleistocene	
Unnamed (Mongolia)	Volcanic field (None) Pleistocene	
Unnamed (Mongolia)	Volcanic field (None) Pleistocene	
Unnamed (Mongolia)	Cones (None) Pleistocene	
Unnamed (Mongolia)	Cone (None) Pleistocene	
Unnamed (México)	Submarine volcano? (Uncertain)	**1401-008**
Unnamed (New Britain-SW Pac)	Submarine volcano? (Uncertain)	**0502-001**
Unnamed (New Britain-SW Pac)	Submarine volcano? (Uncertain)	**0502-131**
Unnamed (New Guinea-NE of)	Submarine volcano? (Uncertain)	**0501-04=**
Unnamed (Pacific-E)	Submarine volcano (17, 2006) Historical	**1304-05-**
Unnamed (Pacific-E)	Submarine volcano (1, 1969) Historical	**1304-10-**
Unnamed (Pacific-E)	Submarine volcano (1, 2003) Historical	**1304-04-**
Unnamed (Pacific-NE)	Submarine volcano? (Uncertain)	**1301-05-**
Unnamed (Pacific-S)	Submarine volcano (Uncertain)	**1305-03-**
Unnamed (Pacific-S)	Submarine volcano (Uncertain)	**1305-02-**
Unnamed (Romania)	Volcanic field (None) Pleistocene	
Unnamed (Russia-NE)	Fissure vents (None) Quaternary	
Unnamed (Russia-NE)	Explosion craters (None) Quaternary	
Unnamed (Russia-NE)	Unknown (None) Pleistocene	
Unnamed (Russia-NE)	Explosion craters (None) Quaternary	
Unnamed (Russia-NE)	Unknown (None) Pleistocene	
Unnamed (Russia-NE)	Unknown (None) Pleistocene	
Unnamed (Russia-NE)	Unknown (None) Quaternary	
Unnamed (Russia-NE)	Explosion craters (None) Quaternary	
Unnamed (Russia-NE)	Unknown (None) Quaternary	
Unnamed (Russia-NE)	Unknown (None) Quaternary	
Unnamed (Russia-SE)	Fissure vent (None) Quaternary	
Unnamed (Russia-SW)	Volcanic field (None) Pleistocene	
Unnamed (SE Asia)	Cone (None) Pleistocene	
Unnamed (SE Asia)	Cone (None) Pleistocene	
Unnamed (SW Pacific)	Submarine volc (1, 1964) Hydrophonic	**0508-03-**
Unnamed (Sangihe Is-Indonesia)	Submarine volcano? (Uncertain)	**0607-05=**
Unnamed (Solomon Is-SW Pacific)	Submarine volcanoes (None) Holocene	**0505-061**
Unnamed (Syria)	Cones (None) Pleistocene	
Unnamed (Syria)	Volcanic field (1, -2670) Radiocarbon	**0300-04-**
Unnamed (Syria)	Cones (None) Pleistocene	
Unnamed (Syria)	Volcanic field (1, 1222) Historical	**0300-02-**
Unnamed (Syria)	Cones (None) Pleistocene	
Unnamed (Syria)	Cone (None) Quaternary	
Unnamed (Syria)	Cones (None) Pleistocene	
Unnamed (Syria)	Cone (None) Pleistocene	
Unnamed (Taiwan-E of)	Submarine volcano? (Uncertain)	**0801-01=**
Unnamed (Taiwan-E of)	Submarine volcano? (Uncertain)	**0801-011**
Unnamed (Taiwan-E of)	Submarine volcano (Uncertain)	**0801-02=**

Name (Subregion)	Type (Eruptions, Most Recent) Status / Relation to Named Volcano	Volcano Number
Unnamed (Taiwan-E of)	Submarine volcano (1, 1853) Historical	**0801-03=**
Unnamed (Taiwan-N of)	Submarine volcano (Uncertain)	**0801-04=**
Unnamed (Tonga-SW Pacific)	Submarine volcano (1, 2001) Historical	**0403-091**
Unnamed (Tonga-SW Pacific)	Submarine volcano (None) Fumarolic	**0403-001**
Unnamed (Tonga-SW Pacific)	Submarine volcano (3, 1999) Historical	**0403-03=**
Unnamed (Tonga-SW Pacific)	(None) Not a Volcano	0403-02=
Unnamed (Tonga-SW Pacific)	Submarine volcano (2, 1932) Historical	**0403-01=**
Unnamed (Tonga-SW Pacific)	Submarine volcano (None) Holocene	**0403-011**
Unnamed (US-California)	(None) Not a Volcano	1203-21-
Unnamed (Vanuatu-SW Pacific)	Stratovolcanoes (None) Holocene?	**0507-08-**
Unnamed (Vanuatu-SW Pacific)	Submarine volcano (None) Quaternary	....
Unnamed (Volcano Is-Japan)	Submarine volcano? (Uncertain)	**0804-101**
Unnamed (W Indies)	Volcanic field (None) Pleistocene	....
Unnamed (W Indies)	(None) Not a Volcano	1600-07=
Unsen-dake (Kyushu-Japan)	Synonym of Unzen	0802-10=
Unuk River [Second Canyon] (Canada)	Cone of Iskut-Unuk River Cones	1200-09-
Unzen (Kyushu-Japan)	Complex volcano (11, 1996) Historical	**0802-10=**
Unzen (Kyushu-Japan)	Thermal feature of Unzen	0802-10=
Uochtepeh (Armenia)	Pyroclastic cone of Ghegam Ridge	0104-07-
Uoive Group (Uoivi) (New Guinea)	Synonym of Managlase Plateau	0503-021
Upas (Java)	Thermal feature Dieng Volc Complex	0603-20=
Upas, Kawah (Java)	Crater of Tangkubanparahu	0603-09=
Upepesanke (Hokkaido-Japan)	Dome of Nipesotsu-Maruyama	0805-061
Upolu (Samoa-SW Pacific)	Shield volcano (None) Holocene	**0404-03-**
Upolu, Tafua (Samoa-SW Pacific)	Cinder cone of Upolu	0404-03-
Upper Atiamuri (New Zealand)	Dome of Maroa	0401-061
Upper Biykhem Plateau (Russia-SE)	Synonym of Azas Plateau	1002-07-
Upper Bol'shoi Enisey (Russia-SE)	Synonym of Azas Plateau	1002-07-
Upper Bol'shoy Yenisey (Russia-SE)	Synonym of Azas Plateau	1002-07-
Upper Dome (US-California)	Dome of Mono Craters	1203-12-
Upper Geyser Basin (US-Wyoming)	Thermal feature of Yellowstone	1205-01-
Upper Glacier Valley (Aleutian Is)	Thermal feature of Makushin	1101-31-
Upper Maruanot (Luzon-Philippines)	Thermal feature of Pinatubo	0703-083
Upsal Hogback (US-Nevada)	Cinder cone of Soda Lakes	1206-01-
Uquila, Cerro (Bolivia)	Stratovolcano of Pampa Luxsar	1505-042
Uracas (Uraccas) (Mariana Is-C Pacific)	Synonym of Farallon de Pajaros	0804-14=
'Urais, Jabal (Arabia-S)	Cone of Sawâd, Harra es-	0301-16-
Urajigoku (Hokkaido-Japan)	Crater of Kuttara	0805-034
Urataman (Kuril Is)	Somma volcano (None) Holocene	**0900-191**
Urbich Caldera (Kuril Is)	Calderas (None) Pleistocene	....
Urdalshraun Eystri (Iceland-NE)	Crater Row of Kverkfjöll	1703-05=
Urdalshraun Vestari (Iceland-NE)	Crater Row of Kverkfjöll	1703-05=
Ureparapara (Vanuatu-SW Pacific)	Stratovolcano (None) Pleistocene	....
Urikomam (Ethiopia)	Synonym of Alayta	0201-112
Urji (Ethiopia)	Cone of Corbetti Caldera	0201-29-
'Urr, Jabal el- (Arabia-S)	Cone of Dhamar, Harras of	0301-12-
Uruf, Jebel (Africa-N)	Cone of Bayuda Volc Field	0205-06-
Uruk (Indonesian for Mt.) see proper name (e.g. Simacak, Uruk)		
Urumombetsu (Kuril Is)	Synonym of Urbich Caldera	....
Urun Dush (Mongolia)	Cinder cone of Khanuy Gol	1003-02-
Urup-Fuji [Kolokol] (Kuril Is)	Stratovolcano of Kolokol Group	0900-12=
Uruppu Fudzi [Kolokol] (Kuril Is)	Stratovolcano of Kolokol Group	0900-12=
Urvich (Kuril Is)	Synonym of Urbich Caldera	....
Usami (Honshu-Japan)	Stratovolcano of Izu-Tobu	0803-01=
Usami (Honshu-Japan)	Stratovolcano (None) Pleistocene	....
Usasyr (Kuril Is)	Synonym of Ushishur	0900-21=
Ushakovskaya (Kamchatka)	Thermal feature of Akademia Nauk	1000-125
Ushcud (Ecuador)	Cone of Calpi	....
Ushigakubo (Honshu-Japan)	Vent of Fuji	0803-03=
Ushiro-Asahi-dake (Hokkaido-Japan)	Stratovolcano of Daisetsu	0805-06=
Ushiroeboshi-dake (Honshu-Japan)	Stratovolcano of Zao	0803-19=
Ushishiru (Kuril Is)	Synonym of Ushishur	0900-21=
Ushishur (Kuril Is)	Caldera (4, 1884) Historical	**0900-21=**
Ushkinskaya (Ushkovskaya) (Kamchatka)	Synonym of Ushkovsky	1000-261
Ushkovsky (Kamchatka)	Compound volcano (3, 1890) Historical	**1000-261**
Usiro-Asahi-dake [Ushiro-Asahi-dake]	Stratovolcano of Daisetsu	0805-06=
Usisiru (Kuril Is)	Synonym of Ushishur	0900-21=
Uskovskii (Kamchatka)	Synonym of Ushkovsky	1000-261
Usmajac (México)	Cinder cone of Colima	1401-04=
Uson (Kamchatka)	Synonym of Uzon	1000-17=
Usori (Honshu-Japan)	Pleistocene caldera of Osore-yama	0803-29=
Usori-yama (Honshu-Japan)	Synonym of Osore-yama	0803-29=
Uspensky (Kamchatka)	Unknown (None) Pleistocene	....
Ustica (Italy)	Stratovolcanoes (None) Pleistocene	....
Ust'-Ozernoy (Kamchatka)	Synonym of Tretya Rechka	....
Ustup (Kamchatka)	Cone of Opala	1000-08=
Usu (Hokkaido-Japan)	Stratovolcano (13, 2001) Historical	**0805-03=**
Usulután (El Salvador)	Stratovolcano (None) Holocene	**1403-081**
Usun Apau Plateau (New Guinea-W)	Unknown (None) Quaternary	....
Usu-Shinzan (Hokkaido-Japan)	Dome of Usu	0805-03=
Usu-yama (Honshu-Japan)	Cone of Fuji	0803-03=
Utal, Cerro del (Guatemala)	Cinder cone of Chingo	1402-17-
Utama, Kawah (Lesser Sunda Is)	Crater of Paluweh	0604-15=
Utaschut (Utashut) (Kamchatka)	Synonym of Zheltovsky	1000-04=
Utes (Kamchatka)	Stratovolcano of Tolmachev	....
Utesiki u Sukhogo (Kamchatka)	Synonym of Veer	1000-121
Utila Island (Honduras)	Pyroclastic cones (None) Holocene	**1403-16-**
Utiura-dake (Hokkaido-Japan)	Synonym of Komaga-take	0805-02=
Uti-yama [Uchi-yama] (Kyushu-Japan)	Dome of Tsurumi	0802-13=
Utone-jima (Izu Is-Japan)	Synonym of Udone-Jima	....
Utsubo-shima [Kaimon] (Kyushu-Japan)	Stratovolcano of Ibusuki Volc Field	0802-07=
Utsukushigahara (Honshu-Japan)	Shield volcano (None) Pleistocene	....
Utsuryo-to (Korea)	Synonym of Ulreung	1006-03-
Utuloka Point (SW Pacific)	Cone of Wallis Islands	0404-05-
Utupua (Santa Cruz Is-SW Pacific)	Unknown (None) Post-Miocene	....
Uturuncu (Bolivia)	Stratovolcano (None) Pleist.-Fumarolic	....
Uva, Cerrito de la (Nicaragua)	Dome of Lajas, Las	1404-133
Uvea Island (SW Pacific)	Synonym of Wallis Islands	0404-05-
Uvera'a (Vanuatu-SW Pacific)	Stratovolcano of Suretamatai	0507-01=
Uvillas (Uvinas) (Perú)	Synonym of Ubinas	1504-02=
'Uwayrid, Harrat (Arabia-W)	Volcanic field (1, 640) Anthropology	**0301-02=**
'Uweirizh, Harrat el- (Arabia-W)	Synonym of 'Uwayrid, Harrat	0301-02=
Uyakuzhach (Kuril Is)	Synonym of Alaid	0900-39=
Uyuca, Cerro de (Honduras)	Cone of Izopo, Montaña de	....
Uyunhordongi (China-E)	Synonym of Wudalianchi	1005-03-
Uyun-Kholdongi (China-E)	Synonym of Wudalianchi	1005-03-
Uzon (Kamchatka)	Calderas (4, 200) Radiocarbon	**1000-17=**
Uzon-Geysernaya [Uzon-Geyzernaya]	Synonym of Uzon	1000-17=

V

Name (Subregion)	Type (Eruptions, Most Recent) Status / Relation to Named Volcano	Volcano Number
Vaalkop (Indian O.)	Tuff cone of Prince Edward Island	0304-06-
Vache, Puy de la (France)	Cone of Chaîne des Puys	0100-02-
Vaghramassar (Armenia)	Cone of Ghegam Ridge	0104-07-
Vahilskaia, Sopka (Kamchatka)	Synonym of Zhupanovsky	1000-12=
Vai a Heva, Maunga (Chile-Is)	Dome of Easter Island	1506-011
Vai Fo (Tonga-SW Pacific)	Cone of Niuafo'ou	0403-11=
Vaiala (Samoa-SW Pacific)	Cone of Savai'i	0404-04=
Vailoatai (Samoa-SW Pacific)	Tuff cone of Tutuila	0404-02-
Vailulu'u (Samoa-SW Pacific)	Submarine volcano (3, 2003) Historical	**0404-00-**
Vaiolo (Samoa-SW Pacific)	Cone of Savai'i	0404-04=
Vaiyots-Sar (Armenia)	Cone of Dar-Alages	0104-08-
Vaka, Maunga (Chile-Is)	Pyroclastic cone of Easter Island	1506-011
Vakak Group (Afghanistan)	Volcanic field (None) Holocene?	**0302-07-**
Vakat (Russia-SE)	Cinder cone of Udokan Plateau	1002-03-
Vakhilskaya (Kamchatka)	Synonym of Zhupanovsky	1000-12=
Vakhul'skaya Sopka (Kamchatka)	Synonym of Zhupanovsky	1000-12=
Valagja (Iceland-S)	Fissure vent of Hekla	1702-07=
Valdalda (Iceland-NE)	Shield volcano (None) Pleistocene	....
Valdivia (Chile-C)	Synonym of Mocho-Choshuenco	1507-13=
Valentano (Italy)	Cone of Vulsini	0101-003
Valentin (Kamchatka)	Cone of Koshelev	1000-02=
Valle de Antón, El (Panamá)	Pleistocene caldera of Valle, El	1406-03-
Valle de Bravo (México)	Volcanic field Zitácuaro-Valle de Bravo	1401-061
Valle Nuevo (Hispaniola)	Volcanic field (None) Pleistocene	....
Valle, El (Panamá)	Stratovolcano (None) Holocene?	**1406-03-**
Valle, Valley see proper name (e.g. Leone, Valle del)		
Valle, Volcán del (Guatemala)	Cinder cone of Santa María	1402-03=
Valles Caldera (US-New Mexico)	Caldera (None) Pleist.-Fumarolic	....
Valletta, Cuddia (Italy)	Shield volcano of Pantelleria	0101-071
Vambu Island (New Britain-SW Pac)	Cone of Mundua	0502-021
Van Heutsz Crater (Sumatra)	Crater of Seulawah Agam	0601-02=
Van Zinderen Bakker Peak (Indian O.)	Cone of Prince Edward Island	0304-06-
Vana Kei Vuna (Fiji Is-SW Pacific)	Cone of Taveuni	0405-01-

An eruption column rises above the town of Heimaey from a fissure extending from Eldfell cinder cone (right) during the 1973 eruption of **Vestmannaeyjar** volcano off the southern coast of Iceland. The eruption produced a lava flow that overran part of the town and almost blocked the harbor critical to the economic livelihood of the fishing industry; an extensive water pumping operation was implemented attempting to slow the advance of the flow.

Name (Subregion)	Type (Eruptions, Most Recent) Status / Relation to Named Volcano	Volcano Number
Vancori (Italy)	Stratovolcano of Stromboli	0101-04=
Vanei Vollohulu (Vanuatu-SW Pacific)	Synonym of Lopevi	0507-05=
Vangori (New Britain-SW Pac)	Synonym of Bola	0502-05=
Vangunu, Mt. (Solomon Is-SW Pacific)	Stratovolcano (None) Pleistocene	....
Vanikolo (Santa Cruz Is-SW Pacific)	Unknown (None) Post-Miocene	....
Vanua Lava (Vanuatu-SW Pacific)	Synonym of Suretamatai	0507-01=
Vao, Maunga (Chile-Is)	Pyroclastic cone of Easter Island	1506-011
Vapour Col (Antarctica)	Tuff cone of Deception Island	1900-03=
Varadouro (Azores)	Thermal feature of Fayal	1802-01=
Varu, Maunga [Te Kauhanga] (Chile-Is)	Pyroclastic cone of Easter Island	1506-011
Varzea, Pico do (Azores)	Cone of Sete Cidades	1802-08=
Varzin, Mount (New Britain-SW Pac)	Stratovolcano of Rabaul	0502-14=

Name (Subregion)	Type (Eruptions, Most Recent) Status Relation to Named Volcano	Volcano Number
Vasset, Puy (France)	Dome of Chaîne des Puys	0100-02-
Vateliero (Italy)	Crater of Ischia	0101-03=
Vatia (Samoa-SW Pacific)	Dome of Tutuila	0404-02-
Vatnafjöll (Iceland-S)	Fissure vent of Hekla	1702-07=
Vatnaoldur (Iceland-NE)	Crater Row of Bárdarbunga	1703-03=
Vatnsheidi (Iceland-SW)	Shield volcano of Reykjanes	1701-02=
Vatr (New Britain-SW Pac)	Synonym of Ulawun	0502-12=
Vatulasawa (Fiji Is-SW Pacific)	Cone of Waikama	
Vavalaci (Italy)	Pleistocene caldera of Etna	0101-06=
Vaxin, Cerro (México)	Cinder cone of San Martín	1401-11=
Ve'a (Samoa-SW Pacific)	Cone of Savai'i	0404-04=
Vecchia, La (Italy)	Pleistocene caldera of Pantelleria	0101-071
Vecchienna, Lago (Italy)	Crater of Larderello	0101-001
Vedurhalshraun (Iceland-S)	Fissure vent of Katla	1702-03=
Veer (Kamchatka)	Cinder cones (1, 390) Tephrochronology	**1000-121**

The word volcano derives its name from **Vulcano** in Italy's Aeolian Islands. The Fossa cone, seen here, has been active throughout the Holocene, and has been the source of most of the historical eruptions of Vulcano.

Katia and Maurice Krafft

Name (Subregion)	Type (Eruptions, Most Recent) Status Relation to Named Volcano	Volcano Number
Vega de Castellanos (Spain)	Maar of Calatrava Volc Field	0100-04-
Vega de la Caña, Cerro la (El Salvador)	Cinder cone of San Diego	1403-001
Vega, Cerrito la (Guatemala)	Cinder cone of Cuilapa-Barbarena	1402-111
Vega, Cerro los (Guatemala)	Cinder cone of Cuilapa-Barbarena	1402-111
Veggjabunga (Iceland-NE)	Shield volcano of Askja	1703-06=
Veidivötn (Iceland-NE)	Crater Row of Bárdarbunga	1703-03=
Veitskopf (Germany)	Cone of East Eifel Volc Field	
Velain (Indian O.-W)	Crater of Fournaise, Piton de la	0303-02=
Velha, Caldeira (Azores)	Thermal feature of Agua de Pau	1802-09=
Velie Nunatak (Antarctica)	Cone of Hudson Mountains	1900-028
Velky Bucon (Slovakia)	Vent of Filakovo-Salgotarjan	
Velky Roudny (Czech)	Cone of Unnamed	
Vella Lavella Sulfur Field [Paraso] (Solomons)	Thermal feature of Nonda	
Velluda, Sierra (Chile-C)	Stratovolcano of Antuco	1507-08=
Venada, Loma la (México)	Cinder cone of Camargo Volc Field	
Venados, Cerro los (México)	Cone of Camargo Volc Field	
Venados, Los (Chile-C)	Fissure vent of Carrán-Los Venados	1507-14=
Venere, Monte (Italy)	Stratovolcano of Vico-Cimino Complex	
Veniaminof (Alaska Peninsula)	Stratovolcano (21, 2008) Historical	**1102-07-**
Vent Mountain (Alaska Peninsula)	Cone of Aniakchak	1102-09-
Ventana, Cerro (Chile-S/Argentina)	Vent of Crater Basalt Volc Field	1508-025
Ventanillas (Ecuador)	Dome of Chachimbiro	1502-002
Ventanita (El Salvador)	Pit crater of Apastepeque Field	1403-071
Ventarrón, El (Nicaragua)	Caldera of Masaya	1404-10=
Ventisqueros, Cerro de los (Chile-S)	Synonym of Hudson, Cerro	1508-057
Ventotene (Italy)	Stratovolcanoes (None) Pleistocene	
Ventura Volc Field (México)	Maars (None) Pleistocene	
Venture Hydrothermal Fields (Pacific-E)	Thermal feature of Unnamed	1304-05-
Venus (Indian O.-S)	Cone of Amsterdam Island	0304-001
Venusina Sopka (Czech)	Cone of Unnamed	
Venustiano Carranza (México)	Dome of Mispía	
Vepe (Italy)	Pleistocene caldera of Vulsini	0101-003
Verbeek, Kawah (Sumatra)	Crater of Marapi	0601-14=
Verde, Cabeco (Azores)	Cone of Fayal	1802-01=
Verde, Cerro (US-New Mexico)	Shield volcano of Lucero	
Verde, Cerro (El Salvador)	Cinder cone of Santa Ana	1403-02=
Verde, Cerro (El Salvador)	Cone of Taburete	1403-072
Verde, Cerro (México)	Cinder cone of Ventura Volc Field	
Verde, Laguna (El Salvador)	Stratovolcano of Apaneca Range	1403-01=
Verde, Laguna (Chile-N)	Stratovolcano (None) Pleistocene	
Verde, Volcán Laguna (Chile-C)	Cone of Tolguaca	1507-093
Verdeloma (Ecuador)	Stratovolcano of Sangay	1502-09=
Verdugo, Volcán el (México)	Maar of Pinacate	1401-001
Verdugo, Volcán el [Macdougal] (México)	Maar of Pinacate	1401-001
Verkhne-Ingamakitsky (Russia-SE)	Cinder cone of Udokan Plateau	1002-03-
Verkhne-Koshelevskie (Kamchatka)	Thermal feature of Koshelev	1000-02=
Verkhneye (Kamchatka)	Thermal feature of Mutnovsky	1000-06=
Verkhneye Thermal Field (Kamchatka)	Thermal feature of Bolshoi Semiachik	1000-15=
Verkhovoy (Kamchatka)	Shield volcano (None) Holocene?	**1000-44-**
Vermelho, Pico (Azores)	Cone of Agua de Pau	1802-09=
Vermillion Chasm (US-Idaho)	Fissure vent of Craters of the Moon	1204-02-
Vernadskii Crater (Kuril Is)	Cone of Vernadskii Ridge	0900-37-
Vernadskii Ridge (Kuril Is)	Cinder cones (None) Holocene	**0900-37-**
Vernadskiy (Kamchatka)	Fissure vent of Kliuchevskoi	1000-26=
Vernon Harcourt, Mt. [Mt. Harcourt] (Antarctica)	Stratovolcano of Hallett Peninsula	
Verrieres, Puy de [Puy Thiolet] (France)	Cone of Chaîne des Puys	0100-02-
Vershinnyi Barun-Khobol (Russia-SE)	Cinder cone of Dgida Basin	
Vershinsky (Kamchatka)	Stratovolcano (None) Pleistocene	
Vert, Morne (W Indies)	Dome of Plat Pays, Morne	1600-11=
Vesbius (Italy)	Synonym of Vesuvius	0101-02=
Veslessa (Atlantic-N-Jan Mayen)	Cone of Jan Mayen	1706-01=
Vestasti Urdarhalsgigur (Iceland-NE)	Crater Row of Kverkfjöll	1703-05=
Vestisnuten (Atlantic-N-Jan Mayen)	Cone of Jan Mayen	1706-01=
Vestmannaeyjar (Iceland-S)	Submarine volcs. (10, 1973) Historical	**1702-01=**
Vesubio, Cerro de (Nicaragua)	Cinder cone of Estelí	1404-131
Vesuve (Vesuvio) (Italy)	Synonym of Vesuvius	0101-02=
Vesuvius (Italy)	Somma volcano (54, 1944) Historical	**0101-02=**
Veteran (SE Asia)	Submarine volc. (Uncertain) Fumarolic	**0705-07-**
Vetlam (Vanuatu-SW Pacific)	Cone of Ambrym	0507-04=
Vetmwan (Vanuatu-SW Pacific)	Cone of Motlav	0507-001
Vetore, Monte (Italy)	Cinder cone of Etna	0101-06=
Vetrovoi Isthmus Caldera (Kuril Is)	Caldera (None) Pleistocene	
Vetrovoy (Kamchatka)	Shield volcano of Yanpat	
Vetta, La [Monte Amiata] (Italy)	Dome of Amiata	
Veyer (Kamchatka)	Synonym of Veer	1000-121
Veyo Volcano (US-Utah)	Cone of Santa Clara	1207-01-
Vezzi, Monte di (Italy)	Dome of Ischia	0101-03=
Viai (New Guinea-NE of)	Stratovolcano (None) Quaternary	
Viatoa (Samoa-SW Pacific)	Cone of Upolu	0404-03-
Viboras, Montaña las (El Salvador)	Cinder cone of San Salvador	1403-05=
Viboras, Volcán las (Guatemala)	Shield volcano of Chingo	1402-17-
Vica, Montaña la (Canary Is)	Cone of Tenerife	1803-03-
Vichatel, Puy de (France)	Cone of Chaîne des Puys	0100-02-
Vico (Italy)	Caldera of Vico-Cimino Complex	
Vico, Monte (Italy)	Dome of Ischia	0101-03=
Vico-Cimino Complex (Italy)	Stratovolcanoes (None) Pleistocene	
Victoria Volc Field (Australia)	Synonym of Newer Volcanics Prov	0509-01-
Victoria, Mt. (New Zealand)	Cone of Auckland Field	0401-02=
Victoriaberg (Africa-W)	Synonym of Cameroon	0204-01=
Victory (New Guinea)	Stratovolcano (1, 1935) Historical	**0503-03=**
Vicuñas, Domo las (Chile-N)	Dome of Tres Cruces	
Vidal, Cerrito de los (Guatemala)	Lava cone of Chiquimula Volc Field	1402-20-
Vidaurre, Volcán (Chile-C)	Cone of Chillán, Nevados de	1507-07=
Vidrios, Volcán los (México)	Maar of Pinacate	1401-001
Viedma (Argentina)	Subglacial volcano (1, 1988) Historical	**1508-061**
Viejo Cayambe (Ecuador)	Stratovolcano of Cayambe	1502-006
Viejo, El (Colombia)	Crater of Galeras	1501-08=
Viejo, El (Nicaragua)	Synonym of San Cristóbal	1404-02=
Viejo, El (México)	Stratovolcano of Tres Vírgenes	1401-01=
Viejo, Pico (Canary Is)	Stratovolcano of Tenerife	1803-03-
Viejo, Volcán (Chile-C)	Stratovolcano of Chillán, Nevados de	1507-07=
Viejona, Ausoles la [Volcancito] (El Salvador)	Thermal feature of Chinameca	1403-09=
Viento, Montana del (Canary Is)	Cone of Gran Canaria	1803-04-
Viesokaia (Alaska-SW)	Synonym of Redoubt	1103-03-
Vietlam [Vetlam] (Vanuatu-SW Pacific)	Cone of Ambrym	0507-04=
Vigía, Cerro (México)	Cinder cone of San Martín	1401-11=
Vigía, El (Honduras)	Cone of Tigre, Isla el	1403-13-
Vigia, Pico do (Atlantic-C)	Dome of Trindade	1805-051
Vigie, Morne la (Hispaniola)	Scoria cone (None) Pleistocene	
Vigie, Morne la [Morne la Vue] (W Indies)	Dome of Plat Pays, Morne	1600-11=
Vigla Tepe (Turkey)	Dome of Acigöl-Nevsehir	0103-004
Vigna Vecchia (Italy)	Cone of Stromboli	0101-04=
Vigueria, La (Chile-S)	Cone of Cayutué-La Viguería	1508-012
Vikahraun (Iceland-NE)	Fissure vent of Askja	1703-06=
Vikraborgir (Iceland-NE)	Crater of Askja	1703-06=
Vilacollo (Chile-N)	Cinder cones (None) Pleistocene	
Vilfilfellshraun (Iceland-SW)	Crater Row of Brennisteinsfjöll	1701-04=
Viliuchinskaya (Kamchatka)	Synonym of Vilyuchik	1000-083
Viliuchinsky (Kamchatka)	Synonym of Vilyuchik	1000-083
Villa Rica (Chile-C)	Synonym of Villarrica	1507-12=
Villa Santo Stefano (Italy)	Pyroclastic cone of Ernici, Monti	
Villalobos, Cerro (México)	Cinder cone of Moctezuma Volc Field	
Villarrica (Chile-C)	Stratovolcano (84, 2010) Historical	**1507-12=**
Villars, Maar de (France)	Maar of Chaîne des Puys	0100-02-
Villele, Cratere de (Indian O.-W)	Crater of Fournaise, Piton de la	0303-02=
Vilyams, Mount (Kuril Is)	Cone of Smirnov	0900-021
Vilyuchik (Kamchatka)	Stratovolcano (1, -8050) Tephrochron	**1000-083**
Vilyuchinskaya (Kamchatka)	Synonym of Vilyuchik	1000-083
Vina, La (Canary Is)	Cinder cone of Hierro	1803-02-
Viñas, Cerrito las (Guatemala)	Cinder cone of Cuilapa-Barbarena	1402-111
Vindication Island (Antarctica)	Cone of Candlemas Island	1900-10=
Vindicatory Island [Vindication Island]	Cone of Candlemas Island	1900-10=
Vine (Kamchatka)	Synonym of Ilyinsky	1000-03=
Vini [Nu'utele] (Samoa-SW Pacific)	Tuff ring of Upolu	0404-03-
Vinkh-Linkh (SE Asia)	Cone (None) Pleistocene	
Viola, La (México)	Cone of Humeros, Los	1401-093
Virgen, Cono de la (Ecuador)	Pyroclastic cone of Cayambe	1502-006
Virgen, La (México)	Stratovolcano of Tres Vírgenes	1401-01=
Virgen, Montaña de la (Canary Is)	Cinder cone of Hierro	1803-02-
Virgenes, Volcán las (México)	Synonym of Tres Vírgenes	1401-01=
Visiones, Cerro las (El Salvador)	Stratovolcano of Tablas, Cerro las	
Visokaya (Kamchatka)	Cinder cone of Tolbachik	1000-24=
Visoke (Africa-C)	Stratovolcano (2, 1957) Historical	**0203-05-**
Visokiy (Kamchatka)	Stratovolcano (None) Holocene	**1000-059**

Name (Subregion)	Type (Eruptions, Most Recent) Status / Relation to Named Volcano	Volcano Number
Visokoi Volcano (Antarctica)	Synonym of Hodson	1900-11=
Vita Fumo (Italy)	Dome of Campi Flegrei	0101-01=
Viti (Iceland-NE)	Crater of Askja	1703-06=
Viti (Iceland-NE)	Maar of Krafla	1703-08=
Vitim Plateau (Russia-SE)	Cinder cones (None) Holocene	**1002-04-**
Vitorchiano (Italy)	Dome of Vico-Cimino Complex	....
Vitu (New Britain-SW Pac)	Synonym of Garove	0502-03=
Viudita, La (Ecuador)	Dome of Atacazo	1502-021
Vivara (Italy)	Tuff ring of Campi Flegrei	0101-01=
Vneshnii (Kuril Is)	Dome of Golovnin	0900-01=
Vodorazdelny (Kamchatka)	Shield volcano of Pogranychny	1000-47-
Vodorazdelny (Kamchatka)	Unknown (None) Pleistocene	....
Vogelenzang [Kaba Vogelsang] (Sumatra)	Crater of Kaba	0601-22=
Vogelsang, Kaba (Sumatra)	Crater of Kaba	0601-22=
Voghala (Solomon Is-SW Pacific)	Thermal feature of Savo	0505-07=
Vohitra (Madagascar)	Cone of Ankaratra Field	0303-015
Vohon, Tarso (Africa-N)	Synonym of Voon, Tarso	0205-02=
Vokeo (New Guinea-NE of)	Stratovolcano (None) Pleistocene	....
Voladero I, Cerro el (Guatemala)	Cinder cone of Ixtepeque	1402-18-
Volarna (Czech)	Cone of Unnamed	....
Volcan (Mindanao-Philippines)	Synonym of Musuan	0701-07=
Volcán (Nicaragua)	Synonym of Maderas	1404-13-
Volcan Island (New Guinea-NE of)	Synonym of Manam	0501-02=
Volcán, Cerro (Chile-S/Argentina)	Cinder cone Crater Basalt Volc Field	1508-025
Volcán, Cerro el (Nicaragua)	Cinder cone of Estelí	1404-131
Volcán, Cerro el (Perú)	Dome of Huaynaputina	1504-03=
Volcán, Cerro el (Honduras)	Lava cone of Yojoa, Lake	1403-15-
Volcan, El (Perú)	Synonym of Misti, El	1504-01=
Volcán, El (Chile-N)	Stratovolcano (None) Pleistocene	....
Volcán, Montaña del [Siete Fuentes]	Cinder cone of Tenerife	1803-03-
Volcan, Volca, Volcancito, Volcano see proper name (e.g. Fuego, Volcan de)		
Volcancillo, Cerro el (Perú)	Cone of Chachani, Nevado	1504-007
Volcancillo, El (México)	Cinder cone of Cofre de Perote	1401-096
Volcancito (Guatemala)	Cone of Pacaya	1402-11=
Volcancito, Ausoles del (El Salvador)	Thermal feature of Chinameca	1403-09=
Volcancitos (Costa Rica)	Thermal feature of Rincón de la Vieja	1405-02=
Volcanes del Tatio, Geiseres de los (Chile-N)	Synonym of Tatio, El	....
Volcanes, Cerro (Bolivia)	Unknown (None) Post-Miocene	....
Volcanes, Los (México)	Thermal feature of Púlpito, Punta	....
Volcanes, Los (México)	Volcanic field (None) Pleistocene	....
Volcania (Greece)	Thermal feature of Kos	....
Volcanic Creek Cone (Canada)	Cinder cone of Atlin Volc Field	1200-03-
Volcanicito, El (México)	Dome of Colima	1401-04=
Volcanico, Cerro [Fonck] (Chile-S)	Cinder cone of Tronador	1508-011
Volcano Butte (US-California)	Cone of Coso Volc Field	1203-18-
Volcano Island (Luzon-Philippines)	Synonym of Taal	0703-07=
Volcano Mountain (Canada)	Cone of Fort Selkirk	1200-01-
Volcano Peak (US-California)	Cone of Coso Volc Field	1203-18-
Volcano Vent (Canada)	Shield volcano of Tuya Volc Field	1200-031
Volcano W (Kermadec Is)	Submarine volcanoes (None) Fumarolic	**0402-001**
Volckner Rocks (New Zealand)	Dome of White Island	0401-04=
Volodavets (Kuril Is)	Crater of Tiatia	0900-03=
Volos-Atalanti (Greece)	Volcanic field (None) Pleistocene	....
Volsini (Italy)	Synonym of Vulsini	0101-003
Volvic, Maar de (France)	Maar of Chaîne des Puys	0100-02-
von Drasche, Cratere (Indian O.-W)	Crater of Fournaise, Piton de la	0303-02=
von Frantzius (Costa Rica)	Stratovolcano of Poás	1405-04=
von Hohnel Island (Africa-E)	Synonym of South Island	0202-02=
Von Seebach (Costa Rica)	Cone of Rincón de la Vieja	1405-02=
Voniuchi Khrebet (Kamchatka)	Synonym of Ksudach	1000-05=
Vonyuchi Khrebet (Kamchatka)	Synonym of Ksudach	1000-05=
Voon, Tarso (Africa-N)	Stratovolcano (None) Fumarolic	**0205-02=**
Voragine, La (Italy)	Crater of Etna	0101-06=
Vordufellsborgir (Iceland-SW)	Fissure vent of Brennisteinsfjöll	1701-04=
Vordufellshraun (Iceland-S)	Fissure vent of Tindfjallajökull	1702-04=
Vosmyorka (Kamchatka)	Fissure vent of Kliuchevskoi	1000-26=
Vostochnaya Khodutka (Kamchatka)	Shield volcanoes (None) Pleistocene	....
Vostochny Barany (Kamchatka)	Stratovolcano of Bolshoi Semiachik	1000-15=
Vostochny Thermal Field (Kamchatka)	Thermal feature of Uzon	1000-17=
Vostok (Kuril Is)	Cinder cone of Medvezhia	0900-10=
Votos [Botos] (Costa Rica)	Stratovolcano of Poás	1405-04=
Votos, Los (Costa Rica)	Synonym of Poás	1405-04=
Voui, Lake (Vanuatu-SW Pacific)	Crater of Aoba	0507-03=
Vourka (Greece)	Thermal feature of Kos	....
Voyampolsky (Kamchatka)	Shield volcanoes (None) Holocene?	**1000-72-**
Vromotopos (Greece)	Thermal feature of Kos	....
Vsevidof (Aleutian Is)	Stratovolcano (3, 1878) Historical	**1101-27-**
Vtoraia Mutnovskaia Sopka (Kamchatka)	Synonym of Gorely	1000-07=
Vue, Morne la (W Indies)	Dome of Plat Pays, Morne	1600-11=
Vuelta Kopper (Costa Rica)	Cinder cone of Platanar	1405-034
Vui, Lake [Lake Voui] (Vanuatu-SW Pacific)	Crater of Aoba	0507-03=
Vuitavoa, Vusi (Vanuatu-SW Pacific)	Cone of Aoba	0507-03=
Vulcain (Indian O.-S)	Cone of Amsterdam Island	0304-001
Vulcan (US-New Mexico)	Cone of Albuquerque	....
Vulcan (New Britain-SW Pac)	Pumice cone of Rabaul	0502-14=
Vulcan Dome (Alaska Peninsula)	Dome of Aniakchak	1102-09-
Vulcan Island (New Britain-SW Pac)	Cone of Rabaul	0502-14=
Vulcan Nunatak (Antarctica)	Cone of Fosdick Mountains	....
Vulcan, Mt. (Mindanao-Philippines)	Dome of Camiguin	0701-08=
Vulcanello (Italy)	Cone of Vulcano	0101-05=
Vulcano (Italy)	Stratovolcanoes (37, 1890) Historical	**0101-05=**
Vulcano Island (New Guinea-NE of)	Synonym of Ritter Island	0501-07=
Vulcano Laziale (Italy)	Pleistocene caldera of Alban Hills	0101-004
Vulcans Castle (US-California)	Dome of Lassen Volc Center	1203-08-
Vulcan's Throne (US-Arizona)	Cinder cone of Uinkaret Field	1209-01-
Vulcan's Thumb (Canada)	Stratovolcano of Cayley, Mt.	....
Vulcao (Cape Verde Is)	Synonym of Fogo	1804-01=
Vulcao de Lagoa do Fogo (Azores)	Synonym of Agua de Pau	1802-09=
Vulcao do Paredao (Atlantic-C)	Cone of Trindade	1805-051
Vulkan [Ashi Shan] (China-W)	Cinder cone of Kunlun Volc Group	1004-03-
Vulsini (Italy)	Caldera (1, -104) Historical	**0101-003**
Vulture, Monte (Italy)	Stratovolcano (None) Pleistocene	....
Vunakanau (New Britain-SW Pac)	Cone of Rabaul	0502-14=
Vunakokor [Varzin, Mount] (New Britain)	Stratovolcano of Rabaul	0502-14=
Vunuweri (Banda Sea)	Synonym of Teon	0605-05=
Vusi, Vuti (Melanesian for Hill) see proper name (e.g. Namui, Vusi)		
Vutusuala (Solomon Is-SW Pacific)	Thermal feature of Savo	0505-07=
Vuvungana, Vuti (Vanuatu-SW Pacific)	Cone of Aoba	0507-03=
Vysokaya (Kamchatka)	Cone of Gorely	1000-07=
Vysokii (Kamchatka)	Synonym of Visokiy	1000-059
Vysokii (Kamchatka)	Stratovolcano (None) Pleistocene	....
Vysokii (Kamchatka)	Synonym of Vysoky	1000-221
Vysoky (Kamchatka)	Stratovolcano (1, -550) Radiocarbon	**1000-221**

W

Name (Subregion)	Type (Eruptions, Most Recent) Status / Relation to Named Volcano	Volcano Number
Waawaa, Puu (Hawaiian Is)	Cone of Hualalai	1302-04-
Wacht-i-Navar Group (Afghanistan)	Lava domes (None) Quaternary	....
Wada (Honshu-Japan)	Cinder cone of Ogino-Sen	....
Wada-toge (Honshu-Japan)	Dome of Kirigamine	....
Wade (New Zealand)	Crater of White Island	0401-04=
Wadon (Java)	Crater of Gede	0603-06=
Waesche (Antarctica)	Shield volcanoes (None) Holocene?	**1900-024**
Wagifa Island [Wagipa Island]	Cone of Goodenough	0503-041
Wagio (Sulawesi-Indonesia)	Crater of Mahawu	0606-11=
Wagipa Island (D'Entrecasteaux Is)	Cone of Goodenough	0503-041
Wago, Mt. (New Britain-SW Pac)	Cone of Du Faure	....
Wago-zan (Honshu-Japan)	Synonym of Fuji	0803-03=
Waha Pele (Hawaiian Is)	Cone of Hualalai	1302-04-
Wahanga (New Zealand)	Dome of Okataina	0401-05=
Wahanga-Waimangu (New Zealand)	Fissure vent of Okataina	0401-05=
Wahi, Gunung [Tempang] (Indonesia)	Cone of Tondano Caldera	0606-07-
Wahlers Bay (Antarctica)	Maar of Deception Island	1900-03=
Wai (Indonesian for Stream) see proper name (e.g. Asam, Wai)		
Waianae (Hawaiian Is)	Shield volcano (None) Pleistocene	....
Waier Island (Australia)	Cone of Maer Volc Province	....
Waihi-Tokaanu (New Zealand)	Thermal feature of Taupo	0401-07=
Waihlup (Sumatra)	Cone of Kembar	....
Waikama (Fiji Is-SW Pacific)	Complex volcano (None) Pleistocene	....
Waikaretu (New Zealand)	Cone of South Auckland	....
Waikite (New Zealand)	Thermal feature of Kapenga	....

The Schalkenmehren maar is one of about 240 volcanic vents forming the **West Eifel** volcanic field in western Germany. The crater, now partially occupied by a lake, farmland, and the town of Schalkenhren, was formed by explosive eruptions through non-volcanic bedrock that created a low, 1-km-wide crater rim of volcanic ejecta.

Katia and Maurice Krafft

Name (Subregion)	Type (Eruptions, Most Recent) Status / Relation to Named Volcano	Volcano Number
Waikite (New Zealand)	Thermal feature of Okataina	0401-05=
Waikoro (Lesser Sunda Is)	Crater of Paluweh	0604-15=
Waikoro (Lesser Sunda Is)	Thermal feature of Paluweh	0604-15=
Wailagi Cones (D'Entrecasteaux Is)	Cone of Goodenough	0503-041
Waimangu (New Zealand)	Thermal feature of Okataina	0401-05=
Waimaori (New Zealand)	Cone of Karioi	....
Waimate (New Zealand)	Cone of Kaikohe-Bay of Islands	0401-01=
Waimimiti (New Zealand)	Cone of Kaikohe-Bay of Islands	0401-01=
Wai'oa (New Guinea)	Synonym of Waiowa	0503-04=
Waiora Valley (New Zealand)	Thermal feature of Maroa	0401-061
Waiotapu (New Zealand)	Thermal feature of Reporoa	0401-06-
Waiowa (New Guinea)	Pyroclastic cone (1, 1944) Historical	**0503-04=**
Waipa (New Zealand)	Thermal feature of Rotorua	....
Wairakei (New Zealand)	Thermal feature of Maroa	0401-061
Waishuhorun (Hokkaido-Japan)	Cone of Niseko	0805-031
Waitangi Soda Springs (New Zealand)	Thermal feature of Okataina	0401-05=

Name (Subregion)	Type (Eruptions, Most Recent) Status. Relation to Named Volcano	Volcano Number
Waita-yama (Kyushu-Japan)	Cone of Kuju	0802-12=
Waitomokia (New Zealand)	Maar of Auckland Field	0401-02=
Waiwhakapa [Ridge Dome] (New Zealand)	Dome of Okataina	0401-05=
Wajang-windu (Java)	Synonym of Wayang-Windu	0603-08=
Wakak Group (Afghanistan)	Synonym of Vakak Group	0302-07-
Wakala Hill (D'Entrecasteaux Is)	Cone of Goodenough	0503-041
Wakamiko (Kyushu-Japan)	Pleistocene caldera of Sakura-jima	0802-08=
Wake Butte (US-Oregon)	Cinder cone of Bachelor	1202-09-
Wakiong (Halmahera-Indonesia)	Synonym of Makian	0608-07=
Wakka (Lesser Sunda Is)	Synonym of Iliboleng	0604-22=
Wakoto-Oyakotu (Hokkaido-Japan)	Dome of Kutcharo	0805-08=
Walang (Java)	Synonym of Wayang-Windu	0603-08=
Waldau (Africa-W)	Crater of Cameroon	0204-01=
Waldsdorfer (Germany)	Maar of West Eifel Volc Field	0100-01-
Walelang (Sulawesi-Indonesia)	Crater of Sempu	0606-04=
Walkout Creek (Canada)	Cone of Edziza	1200-06-
Wallenaure [Tompaluan] (Indonesia)	Crater of Lokon-Empung	0606-10=
Wallis Islands (SW Pacific)	Shield volcanoes (None) Holocene	**0404-05-**
Walo (New Britain-SW Pac)	Thermal feature of Sulu Range	0502-09=
Walrus Island (Alaska-W)	Unknown (None) Pleistocene	....
Walter Penk, Cerro (Argentina)	Synonym of Tipas	1505-22-
Wambu Island [Vanbu Island] (New Britain)	Cone of Mundua	0502-021
Wanawana, Puu (Hawaiian Is)	Cone of Kauai	....
Wangi, Gunung (Java)	Dome of Penanggungan	0603-291
Wangkong (Java)	Dome of Muria	0603-251
Wangore (New Britain-SW Pac)	Synonym of Bola	0502-05=
Wantianfeng (China-E)	Shield volcano (None) Post-Miocene	....
Wapi Lava Field (US-Idaho)	Shield volcano (1, -300) Radiocarbon	**1204-03-**
Wara, Wai (Lesser Sunda Is)	Thermal feature of Poco Leok	0604-07=
Waramung Plantation (New Ireland)	Thermal feature of Ambitle	0504-02=
Wargess (Africa-E)	Tuff cone of Barrier, The	0202-03=
Warirang (Java)	Crater of Galunggung	0603-14=
Warm River Butte (US-Wyoming)	Dome of Yellowstone	1205-01-
Warm Springs Dome (US-New Mexico)	Dome of Valles Caldera	....
Warrenhelp, Mt. (Australia)	Cone of Newer Volcanics Prov	0509-01-
Warrnambool, Mt. (Australia)	Tuff ring of Newer Volcanics Prov.	0509-01-
Wartgesberg (Germany)	Cone of West Eifel Volc Field	0100-01-
Warudani-yama (Honshu-Japan)	Stratovolcano of Yake-dake	0803-07=
Washiba-ike (Honshu-Japan)	Crater of Washiba-Kumonotaira	0803-071
Washiba-Kumonotaira (Japan)	Shield volcanoes (None) Holocene	**0803-071**
Washibetsu (Hokkaido-Japan)	Stratovolcano (None) Pleistocene	....
Washigamine (Kyushu-Japan)	Stratovolcano of Aso	0802-11=
Washiga-take (Honshu-Japan)	Cone of Eboshi-Washigatake	....
Washington (US-Oregon)	Shield volcano (None) Pleistocene	....
Washington, Mt. (Fiji Is-SW Pacific)	Dome of Nabukelevu	0405-03-
Washinoko-yama (Honshu-Japan)	Dome of Aono-yama	....
Washio-dake (Kyushu-Japan)	Dome of Ibusuki Volc Field	0802-07=
Washungwe (Africa-C)	Cone of Nyiragongo	0203-03=
Wasiba-Kumonotaira (Honshu-Japan)	Synonym of Washiba-Kumonotaira	0803-071

USGS geologist W. C. Mendenhall viewed smoke and vapor columns and ash-covered snow during a 1902 expedition in the Mount **Wrangell** area in east-central Alaska. The photograph shows a steam (and ash?) column rising above the summit crater, and ash darkens the snow over a wide area of the upper southern slopes of the volcano.

Name (Subregion)	Type (Eruptions, Most Recent) Status. Relation to Named Volcano	Volcano Number
Wassiljew [Laoheishan] (China-E)	Cone of Wudalianchi	1005-03-
Wasurezuno-yama (Honshu-Japan)	Synonym of Zao	0803-19=
Wataluma Hill (D'Entrecasteaux Is)	Cone of Goodenough	0503-041
Watangan, Gunung (Java)	Cone of Tengger Caldera	0603-31=
Watchman, The (US-Idaho)	Cone of Craters of the Moon	1204-02-
Waterhouse, Mt. (Pacific-S)	Cone of Antipodes Island	1305-01-
Watom (New Britain-SW Pac)	Stratovolcano (None) Post-Miocene	....
Watom Island (New Britain-SW Pac)	Cone of Rabaul	0502-14=
Watt Mountain (W Indies)	Synonym of Watt, Morne	1600-101
Watt, Morne (W Indies)	Stratovolcanoes (5, 1997) Historical	**1600-101**
Watts Point (Canada)	Cone of Squamish	....
Watu, Gunung (Java)	Cone of Sundoro	0603-21=
Watusumbul (Java)	Dome of Dieng Volc Complex	0603-20=
Wau-en-Namus (Africa-N)	Caldera (None) Holocene?	**0205-008**
Waw an Namous (Africa-N)	Synonym of Wau-en-Namus	0205-008
Wawolika, Wolo (Lesser Sunda Is)	Crater of Inielika	0604-09=
Wayang-Windu (Java)	Lava dome (None) Fumarolic	**0603-08=**
Wazin Taung (SE Asia)	Cone of Lower Chindwin	0705-09-
Weambi (Africa-W)	Cone of Cameroon	0204-01=
Weatherboard Hill (Australia)	Cone of Newer Volcanics Prov	0509-01-
Weaver, Mt. (Antarctica)	Synonym of Unnamed	....
Webb, Mt. (Australia)	Cone of Piebald Volc Province	....
Webber Nunatak (Antarctica)	Cone of Hudson Mountains	1900-028
Wedon, Gunung (Java)	Cone of Arjuno-Welirang	0603-29=
Wehe (Africa-E)	Cone of Katete	....
Wehr (Germany)	Crater of East Eifel Volc Field	....
Wei-Chou-Tao (SE Asia)	Synonym of Weizhoudao	....
Weinfelder (Germany)	Maar of West Eifel Volc Field	0100-01-
Weishan (China-E)	Cone of Wudalianchi	1005-03-
Weizhoudao (SE Asia)	Shield volcano (None) Pleistocene?	....
Wejer (Kamchatka)	Synonym of Veer	1000-121
Wekui, Puu (Hawaiian Is)	Cone of Mauna Kea	1302-03-
Welcker (New Britain-SW Pac)	Stratovolcano of Garbuna Group	0502-07=
Welirang (Java)	Stratovolcano of Arjuno-Welirang	0603-29=
Welirang, Kawah (Java)	Crater of Karang	0603-02=
Well Bay Hot Spring (W Indies)	Thermal feature of Saba	1600-01=
Welleys Island (Antarctica)	Synonym of Hodson	1900-11=
Wellington, Mt. (New Zealand)	Cone of Auckland Field	0401-02=
Wells Gray-Clearwater (Canada)	Cinder cones (2, 1550) Dendrochron	**1200-15-**
Weng-Chuan [Wengjuan] (China-E)	Cone of Longgang Group	1005-05-
Wengjuan (China-E)	Cone of Longgang Group	1005-05-
Wenjaminow (Alaska Peninsula)	Synonym of Veniaminof	1102-07-
Wenman (Galápagos)	Shield volcano (None) Pleistocene	....
Wensaoro (Vanuatu-SW Pacific)	Crater of Suretamatai	0507-01=
Werimba, Mt. (Australia)	Cone of Atherton Volc Province	....
Wesley Rock (Tonga-SW Pacific)	Synonym of Metis Shoal	0403-07=
Wesselow (Aleutian Is)	Synonym of Makushin	1101-31-
West Butte (US-California)	Dome of Sutter Buttes	....
West Cabrit (W Indies)	Dome of Diables, Morne aux	1600-08=
West Crater (US-Washington)	Crater of Rainier	1201-03-
West Crater (US-Washington)	Volcanic field (2, -5750) Radiocarbon	**1201-06-**
West Crater (New Zealand)	Crater of White Island	0401-04=
West Crater (Alaska-E)	Crater of Wrangell	1105-02-
West Crater [Crater Lake] (New Zealand)	Crater of Ruapehu	0401-10=
West Dome (Alaska Peninsula)	Dome of Aniakchak	1102-09-
West Dome [Pa Hill] (New Zealand)	Dome of Whale Island	....
West Eifel Volc Field (Germany)	Maars (2, -8300) Radiocarbon	**0100-01-**
West Hill (Alaska-W)	Cone of St. Michael	1104-04-
West Losolava (Vanuatu-SW Pacific)	Cone of Gaua	0507-02=
West Maar (Alaska Peninsula)	Maar of Ukinrek Maars	1102-131
West Mata (Tonga-SW Pacific)	Submarine volcano (1, 2009) Historical	**0403-13-**
West Maui (Hawaiian Is)	Shield volcano (None) Pleistocene	....
West Molokai (Hawaiian Is)	Shield volcano (None) Pleistocene	....
West Pinhead (US-Oregon)	Shield volcano of Olallie Butte	....
West Prospect Peak (US-California)	Shield volcano of Lassen Volc Center	1203-08-
West Sakukan (Russia-SE)	Cinder cone of Udokan Plateau	1002-03-
West Thumb (US-Wyoming)	Pleistocene caldera of Yellowstone	1205-01-
West Trident (Alaska Peninsula)	Stratovolcano of Trident	1102-16-
West Twin Crater (US-Oregon)	Maar of Diamond Craters	1202-17-
West Umboi Island (New Guinea-NE of)	Synonym of Umboi	0501-06=
West Vent (Canada)	Shield volcano of Tuya Volc Field	1200-031
Westdahl (Aleutian Is)	Stratovolcano? (7, 1992) Historical	**1101-34-**
Western Crater (Antarctica)	Crater of Erebus	1900-02=
Western Dome (New Zealand)	Dome of Okataina	0401-05=
Western Victoria Volc Field (Australia)	Synonym of Newer Volcanics Prov	0509-01-
West-Matthew (SW Pacific)	Cone of Matthew Island	0508-01=
Wests Butte (US-Oregon)	Cinder cone of Wilson	....
Wetalth Ridge (Canada)	Cone of Spectrum Range	1200-07-
Whakaari (New Zealand)	Synonym of White Island	0401-04=
Whakamaru (New Zealand)	Pleistocene caldera of Maroa	0401-061
Whakapaka (New Zealand)	Cone of Ruapehu	0401-10=
Whakapapataringa (New Zealand)	Dome of Maroa	0401-061
Whakapoungakau (New Zealand)	Dome of Okataina	0401-05=
Whakarewarewa (New Zealand)	Thermal feature of Rotorua	....
Whale Bay (New Zealand)	Cone of Karioi	....
Whale Island (New Zealand)	Complex volc. (None) Pleist.-Fumarolic	....
Whaleback (US-California)	Shield volcano (None) Pleistocene	....
Whangarei (New Zealand)	Cinder cones (None) Holocene?	**0401-011**
Wharauroa (New Zealand)	Cone of Karioi	....
Wharauroa (New Zealand)	Cone of Pirongia	....
Whataipu (New Zealand)	Cone of Karioi	....
Whatitiri (New Zealand)	Shield volcano of Whangarei	0401-011
Wheat Mountain (US-New Mexico)	Cone of Taylor Volc Field	....
Wheeler, Mt. (Australia)	Cone of McBride Volc Province	....
White Chuck (US-Washington)	Cinder cone of Glacier Peak	1201-02-
White Creek (Canada)	Cinder cone of Satah Mountain	1200-13-
White Island (Antarctica)	Shield volcanoes (None) Pleistocene	....
White Island (New Zealand)	Stratovolcanoes (32, 2001) Historical	**0401-04=**
White Mountain (US-Utah)	Dome of Black Rock Desert	1207-05-
White Mountain (Africa-E)	Synonym of Kilimanjaro	0202-15=
White Mountain Hot Springs [Mammoth H.S.]	Thermal feature of Yellowstone	1205-01-
White River (Alaska-E)	Synonym of Churchill	1105-03-
White Rock (Luzon-Philippines)	Dome of Arayat	0703-084
Whitefish Lake (Alaska-W)	Maar of Espenberg	....
Whitehorse Bluffs (Canada)	Cone of Wells Gray-Clearwater	1200-15-
Whitford's Solfatara (Vanuatu-SW Pacific)	Thermal feature of Suretamatai	0507-01=
Whitmore Hot Springs (US-California)	Thermal feature of Long Valley	....
Whitney Butte (US-California)	Cone of Medicine Lake	1203-02-
Whiton, Mt. (Galápagos)	Synonym of Wolf	1503-02=

Name (Subregion)	Type (Eruptions, Most Recent) Status / Relation to Named Volcano	Volcano Number
Widadaren (Java)	Cone of Ijen	0603-35=
Wide Bay (Aleutian Is)	Cinder cone (None) Pleistocene	....
Widodaren [Arjuno] (Java)	Stratovolcano of Arjuno-Welirang	0603-29=
Widodaren, Gunung (Java)	Cinder cone of Tengger Caldera	0603-31=
Widu (New Britain-SW Pac)	Synonym of Garove	0502-03=
Wilcox (Aleutian Is)	Stratovolcano of Seguam	1101-18-
Wilhelmplataet (Atlantic-S)	Caldera of Bouvet	1806-02-
Wilis (Java)	Stratovolcano (Uncertain) Holocene	**0603-27=**
William, Mt. (W Indies)	Dome of St. Catherine	1600-17=
William, Mt. (Vanuatu-SW Pacific)	Stratovolcano (None) Pleistocene	....
Williams (Canada)	Cinder cone of Edziza	1200-06-
Williams Crater (US-Oregon)	Crater of Crater Lake	1202-16-
Williams, Mt. (Galápagos)	Synonym of Darwin	1503-03=
Williamson Mountain (US-Oregon)	Shield volcanoes (None) Pleistocene	....
Willow Butte (US-Oregon)	Cone of Newberry	1202-11-
Willow Park (US-Wyoming)	Dome of Yellowstone	1205-01-
Willow Peak (US-Colorado)	Cinder cone (None) Quaternary	....
Willow Wash Lava Field (US-California)	Synonym of Cima Lava Field	....
Wilson (US-Oregon)	Shield volcanoes (None) Pleistocene	....
Wilson Butte (US-California)	Dome of Inyo Craters	1203-13-
Wind Mesa (US-New Mexico)	Shield volcano of Cat Hills	....
Windu (Java)	Twin volcano of Wayang-Windu	0603-08=
Windward Island (Pacific-S)	Cone of Antipodes Island	1305-01-
Wine (Kamchatka)	Synonym of Ilyinsky	1000-03=
Wingol (Vanuatu-SW Pacific)	Stratovolcano of Motlav	0507-001
Wingoru [Goru] (New Britain-SW Pac)	Crater of Mundua	0502-021
Wiri Mountain [Manurewa] (New Zealand)	Cone of Auckland Field	0401-02=
Wisdom, Lake (New Guinea-NE of)	Caldera of Long Island	0501-05=
Wissoke (Africa-C)	Synonym of Visoke	0203-05-
Witori (New Britain-SW Pac)	Caldera of Pago	0502-08=
Wittmerberg [Mt. Olympus] (Galápagos)	Cone of Floreana	....
Witu (New Britain-SW Pac)	Synonym of Garove	0502-03=
Wizard Island (US-Oregon)	Cinder cone of Crater Lake	1202-16-
Wodong-Glaak (Lesser Sunda Is)	Unknown (None) Post-Miocene	....
Woearlili (Woeloer, Woeloer) (Banda Sea)	Synonym of Wurlali	0605-04=
Woeroeng, Kawah [Kawah Wurung] (Java)	Crater of Ijen	0603-35=
Wohushan (China-E)	Cone of Wudalianchi	1005-03-
Wolf (Galápagos)	Shield volcano (12, 1982) Historical	**1503-02=**
Wolf Island (Galápagos)	Synonym of Wenman	....
Wolf Mountain (US-Arizona)	Dome of Springerville	....
Wolfsbeuel (Germany)	Cone of West Eifel Volc Field	0100-01-
Wolkberg (Indian O.)	Cone of Prince Edward Island	0304-06-
Wolo (Indonesian for Mt.) see proper name (e.g. Lega, Wolo)		
Wolo Bobo (Lesser Sunda Is)	Stratovolcano of Inierie	0604-08=
Wolokroko [Ilitebulele] (Lesser Sunda Is)	Cone of Ililabalekan	0604-24=
Wongabel (Australia)	Cone of Atherton Volc Province	....
Wonjutschij Chrebet (Kamchatka)	Synonym of Ksudach	1000-05=
Woodford (México)	Cinder cone of San Quintín Volc Field	1401-002
Woodleigh (New Zealand)	Cone of South Auckland	....
Woosantapaliplip (Vanuatu-SW Pacific)	Cone of Ambrym	0507-04=
Woosantapaliplip (Vanuatu-SW Pacific)	Vent of Ambrym	0507-04=
Wootten's Cone [Ne Ch'e Ddhawa] (Canada)	Cone of Fort Selkirk	1200-01-
Wormous, Mt. (Vanuatu-SW Pacific)	Vent of William, Mt.	....
Woro, Kawah (Java)	Thermal feature of Merapi	0603-25=
Worri [Krummel] (New Britain-SW Pac)	Stratovolcano of Garbuna Group	0502-07=
Wotten Waven (W Indies)	Pleist. caldera of Trois Pitons, Morne	1600-10=
Wrangell (Alaska-E)	Shield volcano (8, 2002) Historical	**1105-02-**
Wuarlapna, Gunung (Banda Sea)	Dome of Serua	0605-07=
Wuchagou (China-E)	Cone of Motianling Group	....
Wudalianchi (China-E)	Volcanic field (2, 1776) Historical	**1005-03-**
Wudaogou (China-E)	Cinder cone of Jingbo	1005-04-
Wuisokij Island (Antarctica)	Synonym of Hodson	1900-11=
Wuksi Butte-Twin Lakes (US-Oreg.)	Volcanic field (None) Pleistocene	....
Wulai (New Britain-SW Pac)	Stratovolcano (None) Post-Miocene	....
Wulu Wolor Field (Lesser Sunda Is)	Thermal feature of Ilikedeka	....
Wuluke Shan (China-W)	Cinder cone of Kunlun Volc Group	1004-03-
Wum, Lake (Africa-W)	Maar of Oku Volc Field	0204-03-
Wuntho (SE Asia)	Unknown (None) Post-Miocene	....
Wurlali (Banda Sea)	Stratovolcano (1, 1892) Historical	**0605-04=**
Wurung, Kawah (Java)	Crater of Ijen	0603-35=
Wu-ta-Lien-Ch'ih (China-E)	Synonym of Wudalianchi	1005-03-
Wuzi (Africa-E)	Dome of SW Usangu Basin	0202-163
Wyeast (US-Oregon)	Synonym of Hood	1202-01-

X

Name (Subregion)	Type (Eruptions, Most Recent) Status / Relation to Named Volcano	Volcano Number
Xalapasco, Cerro (México)	Tuff cone of Serdán-Oriental	1401-092
Xalapasquillo (México)	Maar of Serdán-Oriental	1401-092
Xalapazco, El (México)	Pleistocene caldera of Humeros, Los	1401-093
Xalista (México)	Dome of Cumbres, Las	1401-098
Xalliquehuac (México)	Synonym of Popocatépetl	1401-09=
Xaltepec (México)	Cone of Chichinautzin	1401-08=
Xianjindao (Korea)	Unknown (Uncertain)	**1006-01-**
Xiao Xing-Anling (China-E)	Cone of Shatu	....
Xiaogushan (China-E)	Cone of Longgang Group	1005-05-
Xiaogushan (China-E)	Cone of Wudalianchi	1005-03-
Xiaogushan (China-E)	Dome of Yitong Group	....
Xiaokeshan (China-E)	Cone of Erkeshan	....
Xiaokongshan (SE Asia)	Cone of Tengchong	0705-11-
Xiaokushan (China-E)	Cone of Longgang Group	1005-05-
Xiao-ku-shan [Xiaogushan] (China-E)	Cone of Longgang Group	1005-05-
Xiaoliuchong (SE Asia)	Cone of Tengchong	0705-11-
Xiaolongwan (China-E)	Crater of Longgang Group	1005-05-
Xiaomipo (SE Asia)	Cone of Tengchong	0705-11-
Xiaotuanshan (SE Asia)	Cone of Tengchong	0705-11-
Xiaowengjuan (China-E)	Cone of Longgang Group	1005-05-
Xiaoyanzhifeng (China-E)	Cone of Changbaishan	1005-06-
Xiaoyishan (China-E)	Cinder cone of Keluo Group	1005-02-
Xiaoyishan (China-E)	Cone of Longgang Group	1005-05-
Xiayiluo (SE Asia)	Cone of Tengchong	0705-11-
Xibaizilongwan (China-E)	Crater of Longgang Group	1005-05-
Xico (México)	Tuff ring of Chichinautzin	1401-08=
Xicomulco (México)	Lava cone of Chichinautzin	1401-08=
Xicontle (México)	Cinder cone of Chichinautzin	1401-08=
Xihengdaoshan (China-E)	Cone of Longgang Group	1005-05-
Xihuokou (China-W)	Cinder cone of Kunlun Volc Group	1004-03-

Lee Siebert (Smithsonian)

Xitle cinder cone is the youngest of the broad Chichinautzin volcanic field. Xitle produced voluminous lava flows about 1600 years ago that traveled up to 13 km to the north into the location of present-day Mexico City, covering 80 km².

Name (Subregion)	Type (Eruptions, Most Recent) Status / Relation to Named Volcano	Volcano Number
Xijianshan (China-E)	Dome of Yitong Group	....
Xijiaodebushan (China-E)	Cone of Wudalianchi	1005-03-
Xiloá (Nicaragua)	Caldera of Apoyeque	1404-091
Xilongmenshan (China-E)	Cone of Wudalianchi	1005-03-
Xinantécatl (México)	Synonym of Toluca, Nevado de	1401-07-
Xingannanshan (China-E)	Cone of Longgang Group	1005-05-
Xiping (China-E)	Cone of Datong-Fengzen	....
Xishan (China-E)	Cone of Erkeshan	....
Xishan (China-E)	Cinder cone of Keluo Group	1005-02-
Xitle (México)	Cinder cone of Chichinautzin	1401-08=
Xitli [Xitle] (México)	Cinder cone of Chichinautzin	1401-08=
Xizijulebac (China-E)	Cone of Datong-Fengzen	....
Xoxocol (México)	Cinder cone of Chichinautzin	1401-08=
Xoyacán, Cerro (México)	Cone of Chichinautzin	1401-08=
Xuan Loc Plateau (SE Asia)	Synonym of Bas Dong Nai	0705-05-

Y

Name (Subregion)	Type (Eruptions, Most Recent) Status / Relation to Named Volcano	Volcano Number
Ya Lom (SE Asia)	Cone of Bokeo Volc Field	....
Ya Om (SE Asia)	Crater of Bokeo Volc Field	....
Ya Ra (SE Asia)	Crater of Bokeo Volc Field	....
Yabagang (China-E)	Cone of Longgang Group	1005-05-
Yabakei (Kyushu-Japan)	Caldera (None) Pleistocene	....
Ya-dake (Kyushu-Japan)	Dome of Unzen	0802-10=
Yaema [Mizutamari] (Izu Is-Japan)	Maar of Miyake-jima	0804-04=
Yaglica Dag (Turkey)	Cone of Kars Plateau	0103-05-
Yahazu-yama (Honshu-Japan)	Dome of Izu-Tobu	0803-01=
Yahi, Jabal (Arabia-W)	Dome of Kishb, Harrat	0301-071
Yahuarato, Cerro (México)	Shield volc. of Michoacán-Guanajuato	1401-06=
Yaima (Yaimas) (Chile-C)	Synonym of Llaima	1507-11=
Yakebitai (Honshu-Japan)	Cone of Kenashi	....
Yake-dake (Honshu-Japan)	Stratovolcanoes (38, 1995) Historical	**0803-07=**
Yakeishi (Honshu-Japan)	Stratovolcano (None) Pleistocene	....
Yake-yama (Honshu-Japan)	Synonym of Akita-Yake-yama	0803-26=
Yake-yama (Honshu-Japan)	Synonym of Niigata-Yake-yama	0803-09=
Yake-yama (Honshu-Japan)	Synonym of Osore-yama	0803-29=
Yake-yama [Ivan Grozny] (Kuril Is)	Somma volcano of Grozny Group	0900-07=
Yaki (Kuril Is)	Synonym of Goriaschaia Sopka	0900-17=
Yaki [Menshoi Brat] (Kuril Is)	Dome of Medvezhia	0900-10=
Yaksha (Russia-SE)	Cinder cone of Vitim Plateau	1002-04-
Yakushi-dake (Honshu-Japan)	Stratovolcano of Iwate	0803-24=
Yakutsk (Yakutskii, Yakhutskij) (Russia-SE)	Dome of Udokan Plateau	1002-03-
Yakutsk (Yakutskii, Yakutskij) (Russia-SE)	Cinder cone of Udokan Plateau	1002-03-
Yali (Greece)	Lava domes (None) Holocene	**0102-051**
Yalwa ? (Ethiopia)	Synonym of Jalua	0201-03=
Yamakawa (Kyushu-Japan)	Maar of Ibusuki Volc Field	0802-07=
Yamamio (Izu Is-Japan)	Maar of Miyake-jima	0804-04=
Yambo, Lake (Luzon-Philippines)	Maar of San Pablo Volc Field	0703-06=
Yana Mauras, Volcán (Perú)	Cinder cone of Andahua-Orcopampa	1504-004
Yanamauras, Cerro (Perú)	Cinder cone of Andahua-Orcopampa	1504-004
Yanaurcu (Ecuador)	Cone of Calpi	....

Name (Subregion)	Type (Eruptions, Most Recent) Status Relation to Named Volcano	Volcano Number
Yanaurcu de Piñán (Ecuador)	Stratovolcano (None) Pleistocene	....
Yang (Java)	Synonym of Iyang-Argapura	0603-33=
Yangudi (Ethiopia)	Complex volcano (None) Holocene	**0201-151**
Yankee Volcano (US-New Mexico)	Cone of Raton-Clayton	....
Yankicha (Kuril Is)	Synonym of Ushishur	0900-21=
Yanpat (Kamchatka)	Shield volcanoes (None) Pleistocene	....
Yanshan (China-E)	Cinder cone of Arshan	1005-011
Yantales (Chile-S)	Synonym of Yanteles	1508-050
Yantarni (Alaska Peninsula)	Stratovolcano (1, -800) Tephrochron	**1102-10-**
Yanteles (Chile-S)	Stratovolcanoes (2, -6650) Radiocarbon	**1508-050**
Yao-Chuan-shan [Yaoquanshan] (China-E)	Cone of Wudalianchi	1005-03-
Yaoquanshan (China-E)	Cone of Wudalianchi	1005-03-
Ya-pa-Kang [Yabagang] (China-E)	Cone of Longgang Group	1005-05-
Yapoah Crater (US-Oregon)	Cinder cone of North Sister Field	1202-07-
Yaponcha (US-Arizona)	Crater of Sunset Crater	1209-02-

Lee Siebert (Smithsonian)

An eruption of Old Faithful, perhaps the world's best known geyser, rises above **Yellowstone's** Upper Geyser Basin in Wyoming. Old Faithful is a periodic geyser, with eruptions to heights of about 40 m at intervals of 30 to 100 minutes.

Name (Subregion)	Type (Eruptions, Most Recent) Status Relation to Named Volcano	Volcano Number
Yar, Jabal (Arabia-W)	Volcanic field (1, 1810) Historical	**0301-08-**
Yarangalu (Ecuador)	Dome of Chacana	1502-022
Yasour (Yasowa) (Vanuatu-SW Pacific)	Synonym of Yasur	0507-10=
Yasukajigamori (Izu Is-Japan)	Dome of Mikura-jima	0804-041
Yasur (Vanuatu-SW Pacific)	Stratovolcano (4, 2010) Historical	**0507-10=**
Yatake (Kyushu-Japan)	Stratovolcano of Kirishima	0802-09=
Yatakijo-zan (Honshu-Japan)	Dome of Oetaka-yama	....
Yate (Chile-S)	Stratovolcano (None) Holocene	**1508-022**
Yatsuga-take (Honshu-Japan)	Stratovolcanoes (None) Pleistocene	....
Yatuga-take (Honshu-Japan)	Synonym of Yatsuga-take	....
Yautepemes, Los (México)	Dome of Iztaccíhuatl	1401-082
Yavinsky (Kamchatka)	Stratovolcano (1, -4050) Tephrochron	**1000-021**
Yawushan (SE Asia)	Cone of Tengchong	0705-11-
Yayantique, Cerro (El Salvador)	Volcanic field (None) Pleistocene	....
Yedo Peak (Canada)	Cone of Spectrum Range	1200-07-
Yegua, La (Argentina)	Cinder cone of Unnamed	....
Yeguada, La (Panamá)	Stratovolcano (None) Pleist.-Fumarolic	....
Yeguas, Las [San Pedro] (Chile-C)	Stratovolcano of San Pedro-Pellado	1507-062
Yelia (New Guinea)	Stratovolcano (None) Holocene?	**0503-002**
Yellow Cone (Hawaiian Is)	Cone of Kilauea	1302-01-
Yellowstone (US-Wyoming)	Calderas (4, -1350) Tephrochronology	**1205-01-**
Yellowstone Plateau (US-Wyoming)	Synonym of Yellowstone	1205-01-
Yenkahe (Vanuatu-SW Pacific)	Caldera of Yasur	0507-10=
Yenkahe Main Cone (Vanuatu-SW Pacific)	Stratovolcano of Yasur	0507-10=
Yen-Pei-shan [Xiaogushan] (China-E)	Cone of Wudalianchi	1005-03-
Yepocapa (Guatemala)	Stratovolcano of Acatenango	1402-08=
Yerakh, Jabal (Arabia-S)	Cone of Dhamar, Harras of	0301-12-
Yerbabuena, Cerro la (México)	Cinder cone of Comondú-La Purísima	1401-012
Yerovi, Isla (Ecuador)	Dome of Cuicocha	1502-003
Yersey (Lesser Sunda Is)	Submarine volcano? (None) Uncertain	**0604-28=**
Yezh (Kamchatka)	Dome of Bolshoi Semiachik	1000-15=
Yi Shan (China-W)	Cinder cone of Kunlun Volc Group	1004-03-
Yiali (Greece)	Synonym of Yali	0102-051
Yichuan (China-E)	Volcanic field (None) Quaternary	....
Yijiashan (China-E)	Cone (None) Post-Miocene	....
Yilanli Dag (Turkey)	Dome of Erciyes Dagi	0103-01=
Yilanli Dagi (Turkey)	Cone of Hasan Dagi	0103-002
Yilanobrugu (Turkey)	Crater of Karapinar Field	0103-001
Yilband Dag (Turkey)	Dome of Erciyes Dagi	0103-01=
Yilbat (Turkey)	Cone of Erciyes Dagi	0103-01=
Yingbeishan [Xiaogushan] (China-E)	Cone of Wudalianchi	1005-03-
Yingfengling (SE Asia)	Stratovolcano of Leizhou Bandao	0705-01-
Yiongxing (SE Asia)	Pyroclastic cone of Hainan Dao	0705-001
Yirrigue (Africa-N)	Pleistocene caldera of Toussidé, Tarso	0205-01=
Yitong Group (China-E)	Lava domes (None) Quaternary	....
Yi-Yerra (Africa-N)	Thermal feature of Koussi, Emi	0205-021
Yjakushatsch (Alaska-SW)	Synonym of Redoubt	1103-03-
Yodono-san (Honshu-Japan)	Dome of Gassan	....
Yoichizaka (Honshu-Japan)	Vent of Izu-Tobu	0803-01=
Yojoa, Lake (Honduras)	Volcanic field (None) Holocene	**1403-15-**
Yojualtajapán, Volcán (México)	Stratovolcano of San Martín Pajapan	....
Yokoate-jima (Ryukyu Is)	Stratovolcanoes (1, 1835) Historical	**0802-021**
Yokoate-sho (Ryukyu Is)	Submarine vent of Yokoate-jima	0802-021
Yoko-dake (Honshu-Japan)	Dome of Kita Yatsuga-take	0803-031
Yoko-dake (Ryukyu Is)	Stratovolcano of Kuchino-shima	0802-043
Yokokura-yama (Honshu-Japan)	Stratovolcano of Zao	0803-19=
Yokote (Honshu-Japan)	Scoria cones (None) Pleistocene	....
Yokote-yama (Honshu-Japan)	Shield volcano of Shiga	0803-121
Yokotsu (Hokkaido-Japan)	Stratovolcano (None) Pleistocene	....
Yokotu (Hokkaido-Japan)	Synonym of Yokotsu	....
Yolotepec (México)	Dome of Cumbres, Las	1401-098
Yolye, Volcán (Chile-C)	Cinder cone of Carrán-Los Venados	1507-14=
Yomba (New Guinea-NE of)	Submarine volcano? (None) Uncertain	**0501-041**
Yomine-yama (Kyushu-Japan)	Stratovolcano of Aso	0802-11=
Yonekubo (Kyushu-Japan)	Crater of Kuju	0802-12=
Yonemaru (Kyushu-Japan)	Maar of Sumiyoshi-ike	0802-081
Yongbocuo (China-W)	Shield volcano of Unnamed	1004-04-
Yongmeori (Korea)	Tuff ring of Halla	1006-04-
Yoran, Mt. (US-Oregon)	Shield volcano of Diamond Peak	....
Yoridai-zawa (Izu Is-Japan)	Crater of Miyake-jima	0804-04=
York (Galápagos)	Synonym of Santiago	1503-09=
Yoro-yama (Honshu-Japan)	Synonym of Fuji	0803-03=
Yosua (Yosur) (Vanuatu-SW Pacific)	Synonym of Yasur	0507-10=
Yotei (Hokkaido-Japan)	Stratovolcano (2, -1050) Tephrochron	**0805-032**
Yotsuga-take (Honshu-Japan)	Dome of Norikura	0803-06=
Yotuga-take [Yotsuga-take] (Honshu-Japan)	Dome of Norikura	0803-06=
Youkou (Africa-W)	Crater of Ngaoundere Plateau	0204-04-
Young Island (Antarctica)	Stratovolcano (None) Fumarolic	**1900-011**
Youtlkut Butte (US-Oregon)	Cone of Newberry	1202-11-
Yoyolica, Volcán (México)	Cinder cone of Chichinautzin	1401-08=
Yrtri Raudamelskula (Iceland-W)	Cone of Ljósufjöll	1700-03=
Yuba-no-Tonbu (Izu Is-Japan)	Crater of Aoga-shima	0804-06=
Yubatake Hot Springs (Honshu-Japan)	Thermal feature of Kusatsu-Shirane	0803-12=
Yubileinoye (Kamchatka)	Fissure vent of Kliuchevskoi	1000-26=
Yubi-yama (Kyushu-Japan)	Dome of Kuju	0802-12=
Yucamane (Perú)	Stratovolcanoes (6, 1902) Historical	**1504-05-**
Yucamani (Perú)	Synonym of Yucamane	1504-05-
Yueya Shan (China-W)	Cinder cone of Kunlun Volc Group	1004-03-
Yufu-dake (Kyushu-Japan)	Dome of Tsurumi	0802-13=
Yufuin (Kyushu-Japan)	Thermal feature of Tsurumi	0802-13=
Yu-gama (Honshu-Japan)	Crater of Kusatsu-Shirane	0803-12=
Yuga-mine (Honshu-Japan)	Lava dome (None) Pleistocene	....
Yugaoka (Honshu-Japan)	Vent of Izu-Tobu	0803-01=
Yugawara (Honshu-Japan)	Stratovolcano (None) Pleistocene	....
Yuhu-dake [Yufu-dake] (Kyushu-Japan)	Dome of Tsurumi	0802-13=
Yujiadashan (SE Asia)	Cone of Tengchong	0705-11-
Yumboloma (Ecuador)	Cone of Calpi	....
Yumi-ike (Honshu-Japan)	Maar of Kusatsu-Shirane	0803-12=
Yumi-Itsuka (Honshu-Japan)	Cone of Fuji	0803-03=
Yumori-yama (Honshu-Japan)	Cone of Nyuto-Takakura	....
Yumoto-Shiobara (Honshu-Japan)	Fissure vent of Takahara	0803-143
Yumurtadag (Turkey)	Cone of Nemrut Dagi	0103-02=
Yumurtatepe (Turkey)	Cone of Nemrut Dagi	0103-02=
Yunaska (Aleutian Is)	Shield volcano (3, 1937) Historical	**1101-21-**
Yunohira (Kyushu-Japan)	Dome of Sakura-jima	0802-08=
Yunomaru-yama (Honshu-Japan)	Stratovolcano of Eboshi	....
Yunotani (Kyushu-Japan)	Dome of Aso	0802-11=
Yunotani (Kyushu-Japan)	Thermal feature of Aso	0802-11=
Yunotani-dake (Kyushu-Japan)	Stratovolcano of Kirishima	0802-09=
Yunque, El (Chile-Is)	Stratovolcano of Robinson Crusoe	1506-02=
Yunuma (Hokkaido-Japan)	Crater of Tokachi	0805-05=
Yupiltepeque, Cerro de (Guatemala)	Cinder cone of Chingo	1402-17-
Yupiter (Kamchatka)	Cinder cone of Tolbachik	1000-24=
Yurdawa (Russia-SE)	Shield volcano of Azas Plateau	1002-07-
Yurievsky (Kamchatka)	Cone of Dzenzursky	1000-11=
Yurro Hondo, Laguna de [Laguna Río Cuarto]	Maar of Poás	1405-04=
Yushny (Kamchatka)	Cone of Maly Semiachik	1000-14=
Yutian (China-W)	Synonym of Kunlun Volc Group	1004-03-
Yuyiehu (China-W)	Cone of Unnamed	1004-04-
Yuzawa-yama (Kyushu-Japan)	Dome of Kuju	0802-12=
Yuzhny (Kamchatka)	Vent of Krasheninnikov	1000-19=
Yuzhny [Yushny] (Kamchatka)	Cone of Maly Semiachik	1000-14=
Yuzhny Cherpuk (Kamchatka)	Cone of Cherpuk Group	1000-273
Yuzhny Gamchen (Kamchatka)	Stratovolcano of Gamchen	1000-21=
Yves Rocard (Society Is-C Pacific)	Synonym of Rocard	1303-02-
Ywatha (SE Asia)	Vent of Lower Chindwin	0705-09-
Yztactépetl (México)	Synonym of Iztaccíhuatl	1401-082

Z

Name (Subregion)	Type (Eruptions, Most Recent) Status Relation to Named Volcano	Volcano Number
Zabytaya, Mt. (Kamchatka)	Lava cone of Kliuchevskoi	1000-26=
Zabytyi (Kamchatka)	Fissure vent of Kliuchevskoi	1000-26=
Zacapu, Volcanes de (México)	Cone of Michoacán-Guanajuato	1401-06=
Zacarias, Cerro (Guatemala)	Cone of Ipala	1402-19-
Zacate Grande, Isla (Honduras)	Stratovolcano (None) Holocene	**1403-14-**
Zacatillo, Isla (El Salvador)	Cinder cones (None) Pleistocene	....
Zakura Misaka (Honshu-Japan)	Stratovolcano of Towada	0803-271
Zametny (Kamchatka)	Cinder cone of Krasheninnikov	1000-19=
Zamok (Kamchatka)	Dome of Ksudach	1000-05=
Zanetti, Mount (Alaska-E)	Cinder cone of Wrangell	1105-02-
Zannone (Italy)	Cone of Pontine Islands	....
Zao (Honshu-Japan)	Complex volcano (43, 1940) Historical	**0803-19=**

Name (Subregion)	Type (Eruptions, Most Recent) Status Relation to Named Volcano	Volcano Number
Zao Spa (Honshu-Japan)	Thermal feature of Zao	0803-19=
Zao-numa [Okama] (Honshu-Japan)	Crater of Zao	0803-19=
Zaozerny (Kamchatka)	Shield volcanoes (None) Holocene?	**1000-48-**
Zapadnaya Khodutka (Kamchatka)	Stratovolcano Vostochnaya Khodutka	....
Zapadny (Kamchatka)	Cone of Kikhpinych	1000-18=
Zapadny Barany (Kamchatka)	Stratovolcano of Bolshoi Semiachik	1000-15=
Zapaleri, Cerro (Chile-N)	Stratovolcano (None) Pleistocene?	....
Zapatera (Nicaragua)	Shield volcano (None) Holocene	**1404-111**
Zapatera, Laguna de (Nicaragua)	Maar of Zapatera	1404-111
Zapetón (Zapatero) (Nicaragua)	Synonym of Zapatera	1404-111
Zapotitlán (Guatemala)	Synonym of Atitlán	1402-06=
Zapovedny (Kamchatka)	Synonym of Komarov	1000-22=
Zapovedny [Severny Gamchen] (Kamchatka)	Stratovolcano of Gamchen	1000-21=
Zapretny (Kamchatka)	Cinder cone of Tolbachik	1000-24=
Zara (Italy)	Dome of Ischia	0101-03=
Zardolou Group (Afghanistan)	Lava domes (None) Quaternary	....
Zarechny (Kamchatka)	Somma volcano (None) Pleistocene	....
Zarzona, Cerro de (Guatemala)	Lava cone of Ipala	1402-19-
Zasipannie (Kamchatka)	Cinder cone of Tolbachik	1000-24=
Zatoplennyi (Kamchatka)	Fissure vent of Kliuchevskoi	1000-26=
Zavaritsky (Kamchatka)	Fissure vent of Kliuchevskoi	1000-26=
Zavaritsky (Kamchatka)	Cinder cones (2, -800) Radiocarbon	**1000-124**
Zavaritzki Caldera (Kuril Is)	Caldera (2, 1957) Historical	**0900-18=**
Zavodovski (Antarctica)	Stratovolcano (1, 1819) Historical	**1900-13=**
Zawadowski (Antarctica)	Synonym of Zavodovski	1900-13=
Zazen-yama (Honshu-Japan)	Dome of Nikko-Shirane	0803-14=
Zbev-Bunanya (Kamchatka)	Shield volcano of Uksichan	1000-35-
Zealandia Bank (Mariana Is-C Pacific)	Stratovolcano (None) Fumarolic	**0804-191**
Zebayir, Jebel (Red Sea)	Synonym of Zubair, Jebel	0201-02=
Zebib, Jabal (Arabia-S)	Tuff cone of Arhab, Harra of	0301-09-
Zein Umm Araysh, Jebel (Africa-N)	Cone of Bayuda Volc Field	0205-06-
Zelezna Hurka (Czech)	Cinder cone of Cheb Basin	....
Zempoala (México)	Stratovolcano of Chichinautzin	1401-08=
Zengyu (Taiwan-N of)	Submarine volcano (Uncertain)	**0801-05=**
Zenigame (Hokkaido-Japan)	Synonym of Zenikame	....
Zenikame (Hokkaido-Japan)	Submarine volcano (None) Pleistocene	....
Zentralny Semiachik (Kamchatka)	Stratovolcano of Bolshoi Semiachik	1000-15=
Zenzur (Kamchatka)	Synonym of Dzenzursky	1000-11=
Zephyria (Greece)	Thermal feature of Mílos	0102-03=
Zeuctépetl (México)	Synonym of Orizaba, Pico de	1401-10=
Zeutongei (Kamchatka)	Synonym of Leutongey	1000-53-
Zhanjiang (SE Asia)	Cone of Leizhou Bandao	0705-01-
Zheltaya (Kamchatka)	Dome of Uzon	1000-17=
Zheltaya (Kamchatka)	Synonym of Zheltiy	....
Zheltaya Sopka (Kamchatka)	Cone of Kikhpinych	1000-18=

Name (Subregion)	Type (Eruptions, Most Recent) Status Relation to Named Volcano	Volcano Number
Zheltiy (Kamchatka)	Stratovolcano (None) Pleistocene	....
Zheltovskaia, Sopka (Kamchatka)	Synonym of Zheltovsky	1000-04=
Zheltovsky (Kamchatka)	Stratovolcano (4, 1923) Historical	**1000-04=**
Zheltyi (Kamchatka)	Stratovolcano of Asacha	1000-058
Zhupanovskaia, Sopka (Kamchatka)	Synonym of Zhupanovsky	1000-12=
Zhupanovskiye Vostriyaky (Kamchat.)	Stratovolcano (None) Pleistocene	....
Zhupanovsky (Kamchatka)	Compound volcano (12, 1959) Historical	**1000-12=**
Zhuzishan (Taiwan)	Dome of Tatun Group	0801-032
Zigoku [Jigoku] (Honshu-Japan)	Crater of On-take	0803-04=
Zigoku [Jigoku] (Honshu-Japan)	Thermal feature of Osore-yama	0803-29=
Zigoku [Trezubetz] (Kuril Is)	Somma volcano of Kolokol Group	0900-12=
Zigoku-no-oana [Jigoku-no-oana] (Japan)	Crater of Haku-san	0803-05=
Zikwala (Ethiopia)	Stratovolcano (None) Pleistocene	....
Zimina (Kamchatka)	Stratovolcanoes (None) Holocene	**1000-242**
Zin, Jabal (Arabia-S)	Stratovolcano of Arhab, Harra of	0301-09-
Zinaka-yama [Jinaka-yama] (Izu Is-Japan)	Dome of Nii-jima	0804-02=
Zini (Greece)	Dome of Kos	....
Zitacuaro, Hoyo de (México)	Crater of Zitácuaro-Valle de Bravo	1401-061
Zitácuaro-Valle de Bravo (México)	Caldera (1, -3050) Ar/Ar	**1401-061**
Zizo-dake [Jizo-dake] (Honshu-Japan)	Dome of Akagi	0803-13=
Zmeya (Kamchatka)	Crater of Kostakan	1000-122
Zoceyuca, Cerro (México)	Cinder cone of Chichinautzin	1401-08=
Zoe (Indian O.-W)	Cinder cone of Fournaise, Piton de la	0303-02=
Zoo-dake (Honshu-Japan)	Synonym of Zao	0803-19=
Zoomie (Aleutian Is)	Synonym of Okmok	1101-29-
Zorro (Argentina)	Pyrocl. cone Northern Mendoza Field	....
Zoutpan (Africa-S)	Pyroclastic cone (None) Post-Miocene	....
Zoyazál, Volcán (México)	Cone of Chichinautzin	1401-08=
Zubair, Jebel (Red Sea)	Shield volcano (1, 1824) Historical	**0201-02=**
Zubchatka (Kamchatka)	Stratovolcano of Bolshoi Semiachik	1000-15=
Zugar (Red Sea)	Synonym of Zukur	0201-021
Zukur (Red Sea)	Shield volcano (None) Holocene	**0201-021**
Zuni Salt Lake (US-New Mexico)	Maar of Red Hill	....
Zuni-Bandera (US-New Mexico)	Volcanic field (2, -1170) Anthropology	**1210-02-**
Zunil (Guatemala)	Dome of Santo Tomás	....
Zunil Geothermal Field (Guatemala)	Thermal feature of Almolonga	1402-04=
Zuquala (Ethiopia)	Synonym of Zikwala	....
Zurn Peak (Antarctica)	Cone of Toney Mountain	1900-026
Zurquí (Costa Rica)	Stratovolcano of Barva	1405-05=
Zuwayr, Jabal (Arabia-W)	Vent of Kishb, Harrat	0301-071
Zvezda (Kamchatka)	Cinder cone of Tolbachik	1000-24=
Zwavelberg (Lesser Sunda Is)	Synonym of Lewotolo	0604-23=
Zyaisa (Honshu-Japan)	Synonym of Jaishi	....
Zyanoo [Janoo] (Kyushu-Japan)	Cone of Aso	0802-11=
Zyogoro-yama [Jogo-yama] (Izu Is-Japan)	Dome of Kozu-shima	0804-03=

Anonymous photographer (Wikimedia)

Lake-filled Okama crater at **Zao** volcano, the most active in northern Honshu, Japan, has been the source of many phreatic eruptions during historical time. White mud deposited on the lake floor is periodically disturbed by gas emission, changing the color of the lake water.

References

Abbreviations Used in Citations

Abs - Abstract
Acad - Academy
Akad - Akademiia
Amer - America, American
Ann - Annual
Arch - Archaeology
Ariz - Arizona
Assoc - Association
Astron - Astronomy, Astronomical
Aust - Australia
Auth - Authority
Bol - Boletin
Boll - Bolletino
Brit - Britain, British
Bull - Bulletin
Bur - Bureau
Calif - California
Can - Canada, Canadian
Chpt - Chapter
Circ - Circular
Comm - Commision
Conf - Conference
Cong - Congress
Contr - Contribution(s)
Dept - Department, Departmento
Deut - Deutsche
Devel - Development
Div - Division
Earthq - Earthquake
Econ - Economic
Ed(s) - Editor(s)
Envir - Environmental
Excur - Excursion
Expl - Exploration
Fac - Faculty
Geochem - Geochemical, Geochemistry
Geodynam - Geodynamics
Geog - Geography, Geographic, Geograficos
Geol - Geology, Geologic, Geological, Geologique, Geologische, Geologie, Geologia, Geologico
Geophys - Geophysics, Geophysical, Geophysique, Geofisica
Geosurv - Geosurvey
Geotherm - Geothermal
Ges - Gesellschaft
His - History, Historical
IAVCEI - International Association of Volcanology and Chemistry of the Earth's Interior
Ind - Industry, Industrial
Info - Information
Inst - Institute, Institution
Internac - Internacional
Internatl - International
Invest - Investigation
Is - Islands
IUGG - International Union of Geodesy and Geophysics
IUGS - International Union of Geological Sciences
Jahrb - Jahrbuch
Jour - Journal
Lett - Letter(s)
MA - Master of Arts
Mag - Magazine
Mech - Mechanical
Mem - Memoir, Memorie
Min - Mines
Mineral - Mineral, Mineralogist, Mineralogical, Mineralogy, Mineria
MSci - Master of Science
Mtg - Meeting
N - North, Northern
Nac - Nacional
Nat - Natural
Natl - National
New Zeal - New Zealand
Newsl - Newsletter
No - Number
NOAA - National Oceanic and Atmospheric Administration
Observ - Observatory
Occ Pap - Occasional Paper
P - Page
Paleont - Paleontology
Pap - Paper
Petr - Petrology, Petrologist, Petrological
Petrol - Petroleum
PhD - Doctor of Philosophy
Phil - Philosophical
Phys - Physical, Physique
Planet - Planetary
Proc - Proceedings
Prof Pap - Professional Paper
Prog - Program
Proj - Project
Pub - Publication, Publishers
Quart - Quarterly
Rec - Record
Reg - Regional
Res - Research
Resour - Resource(s)
Rev - Review
Roy - Royal
Rpt - Report
S - South, Southern
Sci - Science, Scientific
Sec - Section
Seism - Seismological
Ser - Series
Serv - Service, Servicio
Sess - Session
Soc - Society, Sociedad, Societa
Spec - Special
Sta - Station
Suppl - Supplement
Surv - Survey
Symp - Symposium
Tech - Technology
Trans - Transactions
U S - United States
Univ - University, Universidad
Unpub - Unpublished
V - Volume
Volc - Volcanological, Volcanologie, Volcanology, Volcanism
Vulkanol - Vulkanologicheskikh
Wash - Washington
Zeit - Zeitschr

GLOBAL REFERENCES

Anonymous, 1879. Volcanic phenomena and earthquakes during 1878. *Nature*, 20: 378-379

Baille M G L, Munro M A R, 1988. Irish tree-rings, Santorini and volcanic dust veils. *Nature*, 332: 344-346

Castellano E, Becagli S, Hansson M, Hutterli M, Petit J R, Rampino M R, Severi M, Steffensen J P, Traversi R, Udisti R, 2005. Holocene volcanic history as recorded in the sulfate stratigraphy of the European Project for Ice Coring in Antarctica Dome C (EDC96) ice core. *J Geophys Res*, 110: D06114, doi:10.1029/2004JD005259

Decker R W, 1971. Table of Active Volcanoes of the World. *Unpublished 41 page table*, compiled primarily from IAVCEI catalogs with revisions by many volcanologists

Delmas R J, Kirchner S, Palais J M, Petit J-R, 1992. 1000 years of explosive volcanism at the South Pole. Tellus, 44B: 335-350

Fierstein J, Nathenson M, 1992. Another look at the calculation of fallout tephra volumes. *Bull Volc*, 54: 156-167

Green J, Short N M, 1971. *Volcanic Landforms and Surface Features: a Photographic Atlas and Glossary*. New York: Springer-Verlag, 519 p

Gushchenko I I, 1979. *Eruptions of Volcanoes of the World: A Catalog*. Moscow: Nauka Pub, *Acad Sci USSR Far Eastern Sci Center*, 474 p (in Russian)

Gutenberg B, Richter C F, 1954. *Seismicity of the Earth and Related Phenomena*. Princeton, New Jersey: Princeton Univ Press, 310 p

Hammer C U, Clausen H B, Langway CC Jr, 1997. 50,000 years of recorded global volcanism. *Climate Change*, 35:1-15

Hantke G, 1939a. Ubersicht uber die Vulkanische Tatigkeit vom Januar 1937 bis Marz 1938. *Zeit Deut Geol Ges*, 91: 160-168

Hantke G, 1939b. Ubersicht uber die Vulkanische Tatigkeit vom April bis Dezember 1938. *Zeit Deut Geol Ges*, 91: 757-765

Hantke G, 1951. Ubersicht uber die Vulkanische Tatigkeit 1941-1947. *Bull Volc*, 11: 161-208

Hantke G, 1953. Ubersicht uber die Vulkanische Tatigkeit 1948-1950. *Bull Volc*, 14: 151-180

Hantke G, 1955. Ubersicht uber die Vulkanische Tatigkeit 1951-1953. *Bull Volc*, 16: 71-114

Hantke G, 1959. Ubersicht uber die Vulkanische Tatigkeit 1954-1956. *Bull Volc*, 20: 3-36

Hantke G, 1962. Ubersicht uber die Vulkanische Tatigkeit 1957-1959. *Bull Volc*, 24: 321-348

Hedervari P, 1963. On the energy and magnitude of volcanic eruptions. *Bull Volc*, 25: 373-386

Hedervari P, 1968. Volcanophysical investigations on the energetics of the Minoan eruption of volcano Santorin. *Bull Volc*, 32: 435-468

Hedervari P, 1983. Catalog of submarine volcanoes and hydrological phenomena associated with volcanic events 1500 B.C. to Dec 31, 1899. *NOAA World Data Center A Rpt*, SE-36: 1-75

Hedervari P, 1986. Catalog of submarine volcanoes and hydrological phenomena associated with volcanic events. *NOAA World Data Center A Rpt*, 35 p

Humboldt A von, 1869. *Cosmos: A Sketch of a Physical Description of the Universe, V.* New York: Harper Brothers, 462 p

Humboldt A von, 1872. *Cosmos: A Sketch of a Physical Description of the Universe, I.* New York: Harper Brothers, 375 p

IAVCEI, 1973-80. Post-Miocene Volcanoes of the World. *IAVCEI Data Sheets, Rome: Internatl Assoc Volc Chemistry Earth's Interior.*

Katsui Y (ed), 1971. List of the World Active Volcanoes. *Volc Soc Japan draft ms*, (limited circulation), 160 p

Kennedy W Q, Richey J E, 1947. Catalogue of the Active Volcanoes of the World. *Bull Volc*, 7: 1-11

Kurbatov A V, Zielinski G A, Dunbar N W, Mayewski P A, Meyerson E A, Sneed S B, Taylor K C, 2006. A 12,000 year record of explosive volcanism in the Siple Dome ice core, West Antarctica. *J Geophys Res*, 111: D12307, doi:10.1029/2005JD006072

Lamb H H, 1970. Volcanic dust in the atmosphere; with a chronology and assessment of its meteorological significance. *Phil Trans Roy Soc London*, Ser A, 266: 425-533

Lamb H H, 1977. Supplementary Dust Veil Index assessments. *Climate Monitor*, 6: 57-67

Latter J H, 1975b. The history and geography of active and dormant volcanoes. A worldwide catalogue and index of active and potentially active volcanoes, with an outline of their eruptions. *Unpublished manuscript*, unpaginated

Latter J H, 1981a. Tsunamis of volcanic origin: summary of causes, with particular reference to Krakatoa, 1883. *Bull Volc*, 44: 467-490

Macdonald G A, 1972. *Volcanoes.* Englewood Cliffs, New Jersey: Prentice-Hall, 510 p

Moore J G, 1967. Base surge in recent volcanic eruptions. *Bull Volc*, 30: 337-363

Neumann van Padang M, 1938. Uber die Unterseevulkane der Erde. *Ing Ned-Indie*, 4(5&6): 69-83 & 85-104

Newhall C G, Dzurisin D, 1988. Historical unrest at large calderas of the world. *U S Geol Surv Bull*, 1855: 1108 p, 2 vol

Newhall C G, Melson W G, 1983. Explosive activity associated with the growth of volcanic domes. *J Volc Geotherm Res*, 17: 111-132

Pyle D M, 1989. The thickness, volume and grainsize of tephra fall deposits. *Bull Volc*, 51: 1-15

Rampino M R, Self S, Fairbridge R W, 1979. Can rapid climatic change cause volcanic eruptions? *Science*, 206: 826-829

Rittmann A, 1962. *Volcanoes and Their Activity.* New York: John Wiley, 305 p

Sapper K, 1917. *Katalog der Geschichtlichen Vulkanausbruche*. Strasbourg: Karl J Trubner, 358 p

Sapper K, 1927. *Vulkankunde.* Stuttgart: J Engelhorns Nachf, 424 p

Scrope G P, 1825. *Considerations on Volcanos.* London: W Phillips, 270 p

Scrope G P, 1862. *Volcanoes: The Character of Their Phenomena, Their Share in the Structure and Composition of the Surface of the Globe and Their Relation to its Internal Forces.* London: Longman, Green, Longmans & Roberts (2nd edition), 490 p

Shimozuru D (ed), 1974. Compiled list of dangerous volcanoes and associated information. *Bull Volc*, 38: 1-81

Siebert L, Glicken H, Ui T, 1987. Volcanic hazards from Bezymianny- and Bandai-type eruptions. *Bull Volc*, 49: 435-459

Smith W H F, Sandwell D T, 1997. Global seafloor topography from satellite altimetry and ship depth soundings. *Science*, 277: 1957-1962

Smithsonian Institution-CSLP, 1968-75. [Event notification cards]. *Center for Short-Lived Phenomena (CSLP) Event Cards*

Smithsonian Institution-GVN, 1990-. [Monthly event reports]. *Bull Global Volc Network*, v 15-33

Smithsonian Institution-SEAN, 1975-89. [Monthly event reports]. *Bull Scientific Event Alert Network (SEAN)*, v 1-14

Smithsonian Institution-USGS, 2000-. [Weekly volcanic activity reports]. *http://www.volcano.si.edu/reports/*

Tanguy J C, Ribiere C, Scarth A, Tjetjep W S, 1998. Victims from volcanic eruptions: a revised database. *Bull Volc*, 60: 137-144

Volcanological Society of Japan, 1960-96. *Bull Volc Eruptions*, no 1-33. [Annual reports issued 1 to 3 years after event year, published since 1986 in *Bull Volc*]

Von Wolff F, 1929. *Der Volcanismus II Band: Spezieller Teil 1 Teil Die Neue Welt (Pazifische Erdhalfte) der Pazifische Ozean und Seine Randgebiete.* Stuttgart: Ferdinand Enke, 828 p

Witham C S, 2005. Volcanic disasters and incidents: a new database. *J Volc Geotherm Res*, 148: 191-233

Zielinski G A, Mayewski P A, Meeker L D, Whitlow S, Twickler M S, 1996. A 11,000-yr record of explosive volcanism from the GISP2 (Greenland) ice core. *Quat Res*, 45: 109-118

Zielinski G A, Mayewski P A, Meeker L D, Whitlow S, Twickler M S, Morrison M, Meese D A, Gow A J, Alley R B, 1994. Record of volcanism since 7000 B.C. from the GISP2 Greenland ice core and implications for the volcano-climate system. *Science*, 264: 948-952

ITALY (0101)

Acocella V, Funiciello R, 1999. The interaction between regional and local tectonics during resurgent doming: the case of the island of Ischia, Italy. *J Volc Geotherm Res*, 88: 109-123

Albore Livadie C, 1986. Considerations sur l'homme prehistorique et son environment dans le territoire Phlegreen. *In*: Albore Livadie C (ed) *Tremblements de Terre, Eruptions Volcaniques et Vie des Hommes dans la Campanie Antique*, Naples: Centre Jean Berard, p 189-205

Albore Livadie C, D'Alessio G, Mastrolorenzo G, Rolandi G, 1986. Le eruzioni del Somma-Vesuvio in epoca protohistorica. *In*: Albore Livadie C (ed) *Tremblements de Terre, Eruptions Volcaniques et Vie des Hommes dans la Campanie Antique*, Naples: Centre Jean Berard, p 55-66

Alfano G B, Friedlander I, 1929. *La Storia del Vesuvio*. Naples: K Holm, 71 p, 107 plates

Alparone S, Andronico D, Giammanco S, Lodato L, 2004. A multidisciplinary approach to detect active pathways for magma migration and eruption at Mt. Etna (Sicily, Italy) before the 2001 and 2002-2003 eruptions. *J Volc Geotherm Res*, 136: 121-140

Amato A, Chiarabba C, Cocco M, di Bona M, Selvaggi G, 1994. The 1989-1990 seismic swarm in the Alban Hills volcanic area, central Italy. *J Volc Geotherm Res*, 61: 225-237

Andronico D, Branca S, Calvari S, Burton M, Caltabiano T, Corsaro R A, Del Carlo P, Garfi G, Lodato L, Miraglia L, Mure F, Neri M, Pecora E, Pompilio M, Salerno G, Spampinato L, 2005. A multi-disciplinary study of the 2002-03 Etna eruption: insights into a complex plumbing system. *Bull Volc*, 67: 314-330

Andronico D, Cioni R, 2002. Contrasting styles of Mount Vesuvius activity in the period between the Avellino and Pompeii plinian eruptions, and some implications for assessment of future hazards. *Bull Volc*, 64: 372-391

Andronico D, Cristaldi A, Scollo S, 2008. The 4-5 September 2007 lava fountain at South-East Crater of Mt Etna, Italy. *J Volc Geotherm Res*, 173: 325-328

Anzidei M, Baldi P, Casula G, Galvani A, Riguzzi F, Zanutta A, 1998. Evidence of active crustal deformation of the Colli Albani volcanic area (central Italy) by GPS surveys. *J Volc Geotherm Res*, 80: 55-65

Anzidei M, Carapezza M L, Esposito A, Giordano G, Lelli M, Tarchini L, 2008. The Albano Maar Lake high resolution bathymetry and dissolved CO budget (Colli Albani volcano, Italy): constraints to hazard evaluation. *J Volc Geotherm Res*, 171: 258-268

Armienti P, Barberi F, Bizouard H, Clocchiatti R, Innocenti F, Metrich N, Rosi M, Sbrana A, 1983. The Phlegrean Fields: magma evolution within a shallow chamber. *J Volc Geotherm Res*, 17: 289-311

Armienti P, D'Orazio M, Innocenti F, Tonarini S, Villari L, 1996. October 1995-February 1996 Mt. Etna explosive activity: trace element and isotopic constraints on the feeding system. *Acta Vulc*, 8: 1-6

Arrighi S, Principe C, Rosi M, 2001. Violent strombolian and subplinian eruptions at Vesuvius during post-1631 activity. *Bull Volc*, 63: 126-150

Arrighi S, Rosi M, Tanguy J-C, Courtillot V, 2004. Recent eruptive history of Stromboli (Aeolian Islands, Italy) determined from high-accuracy archeomagnetic dating. *Geophys Res Lett*, 35: L19603, doi:10.1029/2004GL020627

Arrighi S, Tanguy J-C, Rosi M, 2006. Eruptions of the last 2200 years at Vulcano and Vulcanello (Aeolian Islands, Italy) dated by high-accuracy archeomagnetism. *Phys Earth Planet Int*, 159: 225-233

Baldi P, Coltelli M, Fabris M, Marsella M, Tommasi P, 2008. High precision photogrammetry for monitoring the evolution of the NW flank of Stromboli volcano during and after the 2002-2003 eruption. *Bull Volc*, 70: 703-715

Barberi F, Bertagnini A, Landi P (eds), 1990. Mt. Etna: the 1989 eruption. CNR-Gruppo Nazionale Vulcanologia Italy, 75 p

Barberi F, Brondi F, Carapezza M L, Cavarra L, Murgia C, 2003. Earthen barriers to control lava flows in the 2001 eruption of Mt. Etna. *J Volc Geotherm Res*, 123: 231-243

Barberi F, Carapezza M L, Valenza M, Villari L, 1993. The control of lava flow during the 1991-1992 eruption of Mt. Etna. *J Volc Geotherm Res*, 56: 1-34

Barberi F, Cioni R, Rosi M, Santacroce R, Sbrana A, Vecci R, 1989. Magmatic and phreatomagmatic phases in explosive eruptions of Vesuvius as deduced by grain-size and component analysis of the pyroclastic deposits. *J Volc Geotherm Res*, 38: 287-307

Barberi F, Civetta L, Rosi M, Scandone R, 2009. Chronology of the 2007 eruption of Stromboli and the activity of the Scientific Synthesis Group. *J Volc Geotherm Res*, 182: 123-130

Barberi F, Innocenti F, Landi P, Rossi U, Saitta M, Santacroce R, Villa I M, 1984. The evolution of Latera caldera (Central Italy) in the light of subsurface data. *Bull Volc*, 47: 125-143

Barberi F, Rosi M, Sodi A, 1993. Volcanic hazard assessment at Stromboli based on review of historical data. *Acta Vulc*, 3: 173-187

Barberi F, Villari L, 1994. Volcano monitoring and civil protection problems during the 1991-1993 Etna eruption. *Acta Vulc*, 4: 157-165

Barbieri M, Cristofolini R, Delitala M C, Fornaseri M, Romano R, Taddeucci A, Tolomeo L, 1993. Geochemical and Sr-isotope data on historic lavas of Mount Etna. *J Volc Geotherm Res*, 56: 57-69

Beccaluva L, Derieu M, Macciotta G, Savelli C, Venturelli G, 1977. Geochronology and magmatic character of the Pliocene-Pleistocene volcanism in Sardinia (Italy). *Bull Volc*, 40: 153-168

Behncke B, 2002. Italy's volcanoes - the cradle of volcanology. http://boris.vulcanoetna.it/ (accessed February 11, 2002)

Behncke B, Calvari S, Giammanco S, Neri M, Pinkerton H, 2008. Pyroclastic density currents resulting from the interaction of basaltic magma with hydrothermally altered rock: an example from the 2006 summit eruption of Mount Etna, Italy. *Bull Volc*, 70: 1249-1268

Behncke B, Neri M, 2003. The July-August 2001 eruption of Mt. Etna (Sicily). *Bull Volc*, 65: 461-476

Behncke B, Neri M, Carniel R, 2003. An exceptional case of endogenous lava dome growth spawning pyroclastic avalanches: the 1999 Bocca Nuova eruption of Mt. Etna (Italy). *J Volc Geotherm Res*, 124: 115-128

Behncke B, Neri M, Nagay A, 2005. Lava flow hazard at Mount Etna (Italy): new data from a GIS-based study. *In*: Manga M, Ventura G (eds) Kinematics and dynamics of lava flows, *Geol Soc Amer Spec Pap*, 396: 189-208

Behncke B, Neri M, Pecora E, Zanon V, 2006. The exceptional activity and growth of the Southeast Crater, Mount Etna (Italy), between 1996 and 2001. *Bull Volc*, 69: 149-173

Behncke B, Pshenichny C A, 2009. Modeling unusual behavior of Mt. Etna, Italy, by means of event bush. *J Volc Geotherm Res*, 185: 157-171

Bellani S, Brogi A, Lazzarotto A, Liotta D, Ranalli G, 2004. Heat flow, deep temperatures and extensional structures in the Larderello geothermal field (Italy): constraints on geothermal fluid flow. *J Volc Geotherm Res*, 132: 15-29

Berrino G, 1997. Gravity changes and present-day dynamics of the island of Pantelleria (Sicily Channel-Italy). *J Volc Geotherm Res*, 78: 289-296

Bertagnini A, Landi P, 1996. The Secche di Lazzaro pyroclastics of Stromboli volcano: a phreatomagmatic eruption related to the Sciara del Fuoco sector collapse. *Bull Volc*, 58: 239-245

Bertagnini A, Landi P, Rosi M, Vigliargio A, 1998. The Pomici de Base plinian eruption of Somma-Vesuvius. *J Volc Geotherm Res*, 83: 219-239

Billi A, Acocella V, Funiciello R, Giordano G, Lanzafame G, Neri M, 2003. Mechanisms for ground-surface fracturing and incipient slope failure associated with the 2001 eruption of Mt. Etna, Italy: analysis of ephemeral field data. *J Volc Geotherm Res*, 122: 281-294

Blanc A C, 1953. Excursion au Mont Circe. *Internatl Quat Assoc (INQUA) Guidebook*, p 5-19

Blanco-Montenegro I, De Ritis R, Chiappini M, 2007. Imaging and modelling the subsurface structure of volcanic calderas with high-resolution aeromagnetic data at Vulcano (Aeolian Islands, Italy). *Bull Volc*, 69: 643-659

Boari E, Avanzinelli R, Melluso L, Giordano G, Mattei M, De Benedetti A A, Morra V, Conticelli S, 2009. Isotope geochemistry (Sr-Nd-Pb) and petrogenesis of leucite-bearing volcanic rocks from "Colli Albani" volcano, Roman Magmatic Province, Central Italy: inferences on volcano evolution and magma genesis. *Bull Volc*, 71: 977-1005

Bonadonna C, Houghton B F, 2005. Total grain-size distribution and volume of tephra-fall deposits. *Bull Volc*, 67: 441-456

Bosman A, Chiocci F L, Romagnoli C, 2009. Morpho-structural setting of Stromboli volcano revealed by high-resolution bathymetry and backscatter data of its submarine portions. *Bull Volc*, 71: 1007-1019

Boyce A J, Fulignati P, Sbrana A, 2003. Deep hydrothermal circulation in a granite intrusion beneath Larderello geothermal area (Italy): constraints from mineralogy, fluid inclusions and stable isotopes. *J Volc Geotherm Res*, 126: 243-262

Branca S, Del Carlo P, 2005. Types of eruptions of Etna volcano AD 1670-2003: implications of short-term eruptive activity. *Bull Volc*, 67: 732-742

Branca S, Del Carlo P, Lo Castro M D, De Beni E, Wijbrans J, 2009. The occurrence of Mt Barca flank eruption in the evolution of the NW periphery of Etna volcano (Italy). (Bull Volc, 71: 79-94

Brown R J, Orsi G, de Vita S, 2008. New insights into Late Pleistocene explosive volcanic activity and caldera formation on Ischia (southern Italy). *Bull Volc*, 70: 583-603

Bruno P P, 2004. Structure and evolution of the Bay of Pozzuoli (Italy) using marine seismic relflection data: implications for collapse of the Campi Flegrei caldera. *Bull Volc*, 66: 342-355

Bruno P P G, Rapolla A, 1999. Study of the sub-surface structure of Somma-Vesuvius (Italy) by seismic reflection data. *J Volc Geotherm Res*, 92: 373-387

Buchner G, 1986. Eruzione vulcaniche fenomeni vulcano-tettonica di eta prehistorica e storica nell'Isola s'Ischia. *In*: Albore Livadie C (ed) *Tremblements de Terre, Eruptions Volcaniques et Vie des Hommes dans la Campanie Antique*, Naples: Centre Jean Berard, p 145-188

Budetta G, Carbone D, 1998. Temporal variations in gravity at Mt. Etna (Italy) associated with the 1989 and 1991 eruptions. *Bull Volc*, 59: 311-326

Budetta G, del Negro C, 1995. Magnetic field changes on lava flow to detect lava tubes. *J Volc Geotherm Res*, 65: 237-248

Bullard F M, 1976. *Volcanoes of the Earth*. Austin: Univ Texas Press, 579 p

Burton M R, Neri M, Andronico D, Branca S, Caltabiano T, Calvari S, Cosaro R A, Del Carlo P, Lanzafame G, Lodato L, Miraglia L, Salerno G, Spampinato L, 2005. Etna 2004-2005: an archetype for geodynamically-controlled effusive eruptions. *Geophys Res Lett*, 32: L09303, doi:10.1029/2005GL022527.2005

Cadoux A, Pinti D L, 2009. Hybrid character and pre-eruptive events of Mt Amiata volcano (Italy) inferred from geochronological, petro-chemical and isotopic data. *J Volc Geotherm Res*, 179: 169-190

Calanchi N, Capaccioni B, Martini M, Tassi F, Valentini L, 1995. Submarine gas-emission from Panarea Island (Aeolian Archipelago): distribution of inorganic and organic compounds and inferences about source conditions. *Acta Vulc*, 7: 43-48

Calanchi N, De Rosa R, Mazzuoli R, Rossi P, Santacroce R, 1993. Silicic magma entering a basaltic magma chamber: eruptive dynamics and magma mixing-an example from Salina (Aeolian Islands, Southern Tyrrhenian Sea). *Bull Volc*, 55: 504-522

Calanchi N, Dinelli E, Gasparotto G, Lucchini F, 1996. Etnean tephra layer in Albano Lake and Adriatic Sea cores: new findings of Y1-layer in the central Mediterranean area. *Acta Vulc*, 8: 7-13

Calanchi N, Peccerillo A, Tranne C A, Lucchini F, Rossi P L, Kempton P, Barbieri M, Wu T W, 2002. Petrology and geochemistry of volcanic rocks from the island of Panarea: implications for mantle evolution beneath the Aeolian island arc (southern Tyrrhenian Sea). *J Volc Geotherm Res*, 115: 367-395

Calanchi N, Tranne C A, Lucchini F, Rossi P L, Villa I M, 1999. Explanatory notes to the geological map (1:10,000) of Panarea and Basiluzzo islands (Aeolian arc, Italy). *Acta Vulc*, 11: 223-243.

Calvari S, Coltelli M, Muller W, Pompilio M, Scribano V, 1994b. Eruptive history of South-Eastern Crater of Mount Etna, from 1971 to 1994. *Acta Vulc*, 5: 11-14

Calvari S, Coltelli M, Neri M, Pompilio M, Scribano V, 1994a. The 1991-1993 Etna eruption: chronology and lava flow-field evolution. *Acta Vulc*, 4: 1-14

Calvari S, Groppelli G, 1996. Relevance of the Chiancone volcaniclastic deposit in the recent history of Etna volcano (Italy). *J Volc Geotherm Res*, 72: 239-258

Calvari S, Groppelli G, Pasquare G, 1994. Preliminary geological data on the south-western wall of the Valle del Bove, Mt. Etna, Sicily. *Acta Vulc*, 5: 15-30

Calvari S, Muller W, Scribano V, 1998. Eruptive activity and morphology evolution of Bocca Nuova, one of the four of Etna's summit craters, from 1988 to 1995. *Acta Vulc*, 10: 27-31

Calvari S, Neri M, Pinkerton H, 2003. Effusion rate estimations during the 1999 summit eruption on Mount Etna, and growth of two distinct lava flow fields. *J Volc Geotherm Res*, 119: 107-123

Calvari S, Neri M, Pompilio M, Scribano V, 1994. Etna: 1. Eruptive activity. *Acta Vulc*, 6: 1-3

Calvari S, Neri M, Pompilo M, Scribano V, 1991. Etna: the eruptive activity between October 1989 and December 1990. *Acta Vulc*, 1: 257-260

Calvari S, Neri M, Pompilo M, Scribano V, 1993. Etna: 1. Eruptive activity. *Acta Vulc*, 3: 311-314

Calvari S, Pinkerton H, 2002. Instabilities in the summit region of Mount Etna during the 1999 eruption. *Bull Volc*, 63: 526-535

Calvari S, Pinkerton H, 2004. Birth, growth and morphologic evolution of the 'Laghetto' cinder cone during the 2001 Etna eruption. *J Volc Geotherm Res*, 132: 225-239

Calvari S, Spampinato L, Lodato L, 2006. The 5 April 2003 vulcanian paroxysmal explosion at Stromboli volcano (Italy) from field observations and thermal data. *J Volc Geotherm Res*, 149: 160-175

Calvari S, Tanner L H, Groppelli G, 1998. Debris-avalanche deposits of the Milo Lahar sequence and the opening of the Valle del Bove on Etna volcano (Italy). *J Volc Geotherm Res*, 87: 193-209

Capaccioni B, Nappi G, Renzulli A, 1994. Stratigraphy, eruptive mechanisms and depositional processes of the Pitigliano Formation (Latera volcanic complex), Vulsini District, Italy. *Acta Vulc*, 5: 31-39

Capaldi G, Civetta L, Gasparini P, 1976-77. Volcanic history of the island of Ischia (south Italy). *Bull Volc*, 40: 11-22

Capaldi G, Civetta L, Gillot P Y, 1985. Geochronology of Plio-Pleistocene volcanic rocks from southern Italy. *Rendiconti Soc Italiana Min Petr*, 40: 25-44

Capaldi G, Guerra I, Lo Bascio A, Luongo G, Pece R, Rapolla A, Scarpa R, Del Pezzo E, Martini M, Ghiara M R, 1978. Stromboli and its 1975 eruption. *Bull Volc*, 41: 259-285

Chester D K, Duncan A M, 2007. Lieutenant-Colonel Delme-Radcliffe's report on the 1906 eruption of Vesuvius, Italy. *J Volc Geotherm Res*, 166: 204-216

Chiarabba C, Amato A, Delaney P T, 1997. Crustal structure, evolution, and volcanic unrest of the Alban Hills, central Italy. *Bull Volc*, 59: 161-170

Chiocci F L, de Alteriis G, 2006. The Ischia debris avalanche: first clear submarine evidence in the Mediterranean of a volcanic island prehistorical collapse. *Terra Nova*, 18: 202-209

Chiodini G, Cioni R, Guidi M, Marini L, 1991. Geochemical variations at Fossa Grande crater fumaroles (Vulcano Island, Italy) in summer 1988. *Acta Vulc*, 1: 179-192

Cimarelli C, De Rita D, 2006. Structural evolution of the Pleistocene Cimini trachytic volcanic complex (Central Italy). *Bull Volc*, 68: 538-548

Cimarelli C, De Rita D, Dolfi D, Procesi M, 2008. Coeval strombolian and vulcanian-type explosive eruptions at Panarea (Aeolian Islands, Southern Italy). *J Volc Geotherm Res*, 177: 797-811

Cioni R, Marianelli P, Sbrana A, 1991. Dynamics of the A.D. 79 eruption: stratigraphic, sedimentological and geochemical data on the successions from the Somma-Vesuvius southern and eastern sectors. *Acta Vulc*, 2: 109-123

Cioni R, Santacroce R, Sbrana A, 1999. Pyroclastic deposits as a guide for reconstructing the multi-stage evolution of the Somma-Vesuvius caldera. *Bull Volc*, 61: 207-222

Cioni R, Sulpizo R, Garruccio N, 2003. Variability of the eruption dynamics during a subplinian event: the Greenish Pumice eruption of Somma-Vesuvius (Italy). *J Volc Geotherm Res*, 124: 89-114

Civetta L, Cornette Y, Gillot P Y, Orsi G, 1988. The eruptive history of Pantelleria (Sicily Channel) in the last 50 ka. *Bull Volc*, 50: 47-57

Civetta L, Santacroce R, 1991. Steady state magma supply in the last 3400 years of Vesuvius activity. *Acta Vulc*, 2: 147-159

Clocchiatti R, Del Moro A, Gioncada A, Joron J L, Mosbah M, Pinarelli L, Sbrana A, 1994.

Assessment of a shallow magmatic system: the 1888-90 eruption, Vulcano Island, Italy. *Bull Volc*, 56: 466-486

Clover F M, 1983. Olympiodorus of Thebes and the Historia Augusta. *Antiquitas Beitrage Hist-Augusta-Forschung*, 15: 127-156

Colantoni P, Lucchini F, Rossi P L, Sartori R, Savelli C, 1981. The Palinuro volcano and magmatism of the southeastern Tyrrhenian Sea (Mediterranean). *Marine Geol*, 39: 1-12

Cole P D, Guest J E, Duncan A M, Chester D K, Bianchi R, 2002. Post-collapse volcanic history of calderas on a composite volcano: an example from Roccamonfina, southern Italy. *Bull Volc*, 54: 253-266

Coltelli M, Del Carlo P, Pompilio M, 2000a. Etna: 1. Eruptive activity. *Acta Vulc*, 12: 63-67

Coltelli M, Del Carlo P, Pompilio M, 2000b. Vulcano and Stromboli: 1. Eruptive activity (Stromboli). *Acta Vulc*, 12: 93-95

Coltelli M, Del Carlo P, Vezzoli L, 2000. Stratigraphic constraints for explosive activity in the past 100 ka at Etna volcano, Italy. *Internatl J Earth Sci*, 89: 665-677

Coltelli M, Garduno V H, Neri M, Pasquare G, Pompilio M, 1994. Geology of the northern wall of Valle del Bove, Mt. Etna (Sicily). *Acta Vulc*, 5: 55-68

Coltelli M, Pompilio M, Del Carlo P, Calvari S, Pannucci S, Scribano V, 1998. Etna: 1. Eruptive activity. *Acta Vulc*, 10: 141-148

Coltelli M, del Carlo P, Vezzoli L, 1998. Discovery of a Plinian basaltic eruption of Roman age at Etna volcano, Italy. *Geology*, 26: 1095-1098

Colucci Pescatori G, 1986. Fonti antiche relative alle eruzioni Vesuviane ed altri fenomeni vulcanici successivi 79 DC. *In*: Albore Livadie C (ed) *Tremblements de Terre, Eruptions Volcaniques et Vie des Hommes dans la Campanie Antique*, Naples: Centre Jean Berard, p 134-141

Corazzato C, Tibaldi A, 2006. Fracture control on type, morphology and distribution of parasitic volcanic cones: an example from Mt. Etna, Italy. *J Volc Geotherm Res*, 158: 177-194

Cornette Y, Crisci G M, Gillot P Y, Orsi G, 1983. Recent volcanic history of Pantelleria: a new interpretation. *J Volc Geotherm Res*, 17: 361-374

Corsaro R A, Cristofolini R, 1996. Origin and differentiation of recent basaltic magmas from Mount Etna. *Mineral Petr*, 57: 1-21

Corsaro R A, Cristofolini R, Patane L, 1996. The 1669 eruption at Mount Etna: chronology, petrology and geochemistry, with inferences on the magma sources and ascent mechanisms. *Bull Volc*, 58: 348-358

Corsaro R A, Pompilio M, 2004. Magma dynamics in the shallow plumbing system of Mt. Etna as recorded by compositional variations in the volcanics of recent summit activity (1995-1999). *J Volc Geotherm Res*, 137: 55-71

Cortes J A, Wilson M, Condliffe E, Francalanci L, Chertkoff D G, 2005. The evolution of the magmatic system of Stromboli volcano during the Vancori period (26-13.8 ky). *J Volc Geotherm Res*, 147: 1-38

Cortese M, Frazzetta G, La Volpe L, 1986. Volcanic history of Lipari (Aeolian Islands, Italy) during the last 10,000 years. *J Volc Geotherm Res*, 27: 117-135

Costa A, Dell'Erba F, Di Vito M A, Isaia R, Macedonio G, Orsi G, Pfeiffer T, 2009. Tephra fallout hazard assessment at the Campi Flegrei caldera (Italy). *Bull Volc*, 71: 259-273

Crisci G M, De Rosa R, Esperanca S, Mazzuoli R, Sonnino M, 1991. Temporal evolution of a three component system: the island of Lipari (Aeolian Arc, southern Italy). *Bull Volc*, 53: 207-221

Crisci G M, Di Gregorio S, Rongo R, Scarpelli M, Spataro W, Calvari S, 2003. Revisiting the 1669 Etnean eruptive crisis using a cellular automata model and implications for volcanic hazards in the Catania area. *J Volc Geotherm Res*, 123: 211-230

Cubellis E, Ferri M, Luongo G, 1995. Internal structures of the Campi Flegrei caldera by gravimetric data. *J Volc Geotherm Res*, 65: 147-156

Cumin G, 1954. L'eruzione laterale Etnea del Novembre 1950-Dicembre 1951. *Bull Volc*, 15: 3-70

D'Oriano C, Poggianti E, Bertagnini A, Cioni R, Landi P, Polacci M, Rosi M, 2005. Changes in eruptive style during the A.D. 1538 Monte Nuovo eruption (Phlegrean Fields, Italy): the role of syn-eruptive crystallization. *Bull Volc* 67: 601-621

Davi M, De Rosa R, Barca D, 2009. A LA-ICP-MS study of minerals in the Rocche Rosse magmatic enclaves: evidence of a mafic input triggering the latest silicic eruption of Lipari Island (Aeolian Arc, Italy). *J Volc Geotherm Res*, 182: 45-56

De Astis G, Dellino P, De Rosa R, La Volpe L, 1997. Eruptive and emplacement mechanisms of widespread fine-grained pyroclatic deposits on Vulcano Island (Italy). *Bull Volc*, 59: 87-102

De Astis G, La Volpe L, 1997. Volcanological and petrological evolution of Vulcano island (Aeolian Arc, southern Tyrrhenian Sea). *J Geophys Res*, 102: 8021-8050

De Benedetti A A, Funiciello R, Giodano G, Diano G, Caprilli E, Paterne M, 2008. Volcanology, history and myths of the Lake Albano maar (Colli Albani volcano, Italy). *J Volc Geotherm Res*, 176: 387-406

De Rita D, Funiciello R, Rosa C, 1991. Volcanic activity and drainage network evolution of the Alban Hills area (Rome, Italy). *Acta Vulc*, 2: 185-198

De Rita D, Funiciello R, Rossi U, Sposato A, 1983. Structure and evolution of the Sacrofano-Baccano caldera, Sabatini volcanic complex, Rome. *J Volc Geotherm Res*, 17: 219-236

De Rita D, Giordano G, Esposito A, Fabbri M, Rodani S, 2002. Large volume phreatomagmatic ignimbrites from the Colli Albani volcano (Middle Pleistocene, Italy). *J Volc Geotherm Res*, 118: 77-98

De Rita D, Giordano G, Mili S, 1997. Forestepping-backstepping stacking pattern of volcaniclastic successions: Roccamonfina volcano, Italy. *J Volc Geotherm Res*, 78: 267-288

De Rosa R, Donato P, Gioncada A, Masetti M, Santacroce R, 2003. The Monte Guardia eruption (Lipari, Aeolian Islands): an example of a reversely zoned magma mixing sequence. *Bull Volc*, 65: 530-543

De Rosa R, Guillou H, Mazzuoli R, Ventura G, 2003. New unspiked K-Ar ages of volcanic rocks of the central and western sector of the Aeolian Islands: reconstruction of the volcanic stages. *J Volc Geotherm Res*, 120: 161-178

Deino A L, Orsi G, de Vita S, Piochi M, 2004. The age of the Neapolitan Yellow Tuff caldera-forming eruption (Campi Flegrei caldera - Italy) assessed by 40Ar/39Ar dating method. *J Volc Geotherm Res*, 133: 157-170

de Vita S, Orsi G, Civetta L, Carandente A, D'Antonio M, Deino A, di Cesare T, Di Vito M A, Fisher R V, Isaia R, Marotta E, Necco A, Ort M, Pappalardo L, Piochi M, Southon J, 1999. The Agnano-Monte Spina eruptions (4100 years BP) in the restless Campi Flegrei caldera (Italy). *J Volc Geotherm Res*, 91: 269-301

Del Carlo P, Branca S, 1998. Tephrostratigraphic dating of the pre-1300 AD SE flank eruptions of Mt Etna. *Acta Vulc*, 10: 33-37

Delibrias G, Di Paola G M, Rosi M, Santacroce R, 1979. La storia eruttiva del complesso vulcanico Somma Vesuvio ricostruita dalle successioni piroclastiche del Monte Somma. *Rendiconti Soc Italiana Min Petr*, 35: 411-438

Dellino P, Isaia R, La Volpe L, Orsi G, 2001. Statistical analysis of textural data from complex pyroclastic sequences: implications for fragmentation processes of the Agnano-Monte Spine Tephra (4.1 ka), Phlegrean Fields, southern Italy. *Bull Volc*, 63: 443-461

Dellino P, Isaia R, La Volpe L, Orsi G, 2004. Interaction between particles transported by fallout and surge in the deposits of the Agnano-Monte Spina eruption (Campi Flegrei, southern Italy). *J Volc Geotherm Res*, 133: 193-210

Dellino P, La Volpe L, 1995. Fragmentation versus transportation mechanism in the pyroclastic sequence of Monte Pilato-Rocche Rosse (Lipari, Italy). *J Volc Geotherm Res*, 64: 211-231

Develle A-L, Williamson D, Gasse F, WAtler-Simonnet W, 2009. Early Holocene volcanic ash fallout in the Yammouneh lacustric basin (Lebanon): tephrochronological implications for the Near East. *J Volc Geotherm Res*, 186: 416-425

Di Girolamo P, Ghiara M R, Lirer L, Munno R, Rolandi G, Stanzione D, 1984. Vulcanologia e petrologia dei Campi Flegrei. *Bol Soc Geol Italia*, 103: 394-413

Di Roberto A, Bertagnini A, Pompilio M, Gamberi F, Marani M P, 2008. Newly discovered submarine flank eruption at Stromboli volcano (Aeolian Islands, Italy). *Geophys Res Lett*, 35: L16310, doi:10.1029/2008GL034824

Di Roberto A, Bertagnini A, Pompilio M, Gamberi F, Marani M P, Rosi A M, 2008. Newly discovered submarine flank eruption at Stromboli volcano (Aeolian Islands, Italy). *Geophys Res Lett*, 35: L16310, doi:10.1029/2008GL034824

Di Vito M A, Isaia R, Orsi G, Southon J, de Vita S, D'Antonio M D, Pappalardo L, Piochi M, 1999. Volcanism and deformation since 12,000 years at the Campi Flegrei caldera (Italy). *J Volc Geotherm Res*, 91: 221-246

Di Vito M A, Sulpizio R, Zanchetta G, D'Orazio M, 2008. The late Pleistocene pyroclastic deposits of the Campanian Plain: new insights into the explosive activity of Neapolitan volcanoes. *J Volc Geotherm Res*, 177: 19-48

Di Vito M, Lirer L, Mastrolorenzo G, Rolandi G, 1987. The 1538 Monte Nuovo eruption (Campi Flegrei, Italy). *Bull Volc*, 49: 608-615

Esposito A, Giordano G, Anzidei M, 2006. The 2002-2003 submarine gas eruption at Panarea volcano (Aeolian Islands, Italy): volcanology of the seafloor and implications for hazards scenario. *Marine Geol*, 227: 119-134

Falsaperla S, Privitera E, Spampinato S, Cardaci C, 1994. Seismic activity and volcanic tremor related to the December 14, 1991 Mt. Etna eruption. *Acta Vulc*, 4: 63-73

Favalli M, Karatson D, Mazzuoli R, Pareschi M T, Ventura G, 2005. Volcanic geomorphology and tectonics of the Aeolian archipelago (Southern Italy) based on integrated DEM data. *Bull Volc*, 68: 157-170

Fedele L, Scarpati C, Lanphere M, Melluso L, Morra V, Perrotta A, Ricci G, 2008. The Breccia Museo formation, Campi Flegrei, southern Italy: geochronology, chemostratigraphy and relationship with the Campanian Ignimbrite eruption. *Bull Volc*, 70: 1189-1219

Ferlito C, Coltorti M, Cristofolini R, Giacomoni P P, 2009. The contemporaneous emission of low-K and high-K trachybasalts and the role of the NE Rift during the 2002 eruptive event, Mt. Etna, Italy. *Bull Volc*, 71: 575-587

Ferrari L, Conticelli S, Burlamacchi L, Manetti P, 1996. Volcanological evolution of the Monte Amiata, southern Tuscany: new geological and petrochemical data. *Acta Vulc*, 8: 41-56

Finizola A, Sortino F, Lenat J-F, Aubert M, Ripepe M, Valenza M, 2003. The summit hydrothermal system of Stromboli. New insights from self-potential, temperature, CO2 and fumarolic fluid measurements, with structural and monitoring implications. *Bull Volc*, 65: 486-504

Fisher R V, Orsi G, Ort M, Heiken G, 1993. Mobility of a large-volume pyroclastic flow - emplacement of the Campanian ignimbrite, Italy. *J Volc Geotherm Res*, 56: 205-220

Forgione G, Luongo G, Romano R, 1989. Mt. Etna (Sicily): volcanic hazard assessment. *In*: Latter J H (ed), *Volcanic Hazards - Assessment and Monitoring*, Berlin: Springer-Verlag, p 137-150

Francalanci L, Tommasini S, Conticelli S, 2004. The volcanic activity of Stromboli in the 1906-1998 AD period: mineralogical, geochemical and isotope data relevant to the understanding of the plumbing problem. *J Volc Geotherm Res*, 131: 179-211

Francis P W, 1995. Fire and water. *Geol Today*, 11: 27-31

Frazzetta G, Gillot P Y, La Volpe L, Sheridan M F, 1984. Volcanic hazards at Fossa of Vulcano: data from the last 6000 years. *Bull Volc*, 47: 105-125

Frazzetta G, La Volpe L, 1991. Volcanic history and maximum expected eruption at "La Fossa de Vulcano" (Aeolian Islands, Italy). *Acta Vulc*, 1: 107-113

Frazzetta G, La Volpe L, Sheridan M F, 1983. Evolution of the Fossa cone, Vulcano. *J Volc Geotherm Res*, 17: 329-360

Freda C, Gaeta M, Karner D B, Marra F, Renne P R, Taddeucci J, Scarlato P, Christensen J N, Dallai L, 2006. Eruptive history and petrologic evolution of the Albano multiple maar (Alban Hills, Central Italy). *Bull Volc*, 68: 567-591

Freda C, Gaeta M, Palladino D M, Trigila R, 1997. The Villa Senni eruption (Alban Hills, central Italy: the role of H20 and CO2 on the magma chamber evolution and on the eruptive scenario. *J Volc Geotherm Res*, 78: 103-120

Fulignati P, Marianelli P, Proto M, Sbrana A, 2004. Evidences for disruption of a crystallizing front in a magma chamber during caldera collapse: an example from the Breccia Museo (Campanian Ignimbrite eruption, Italy). *J Volc Geotherm Res*, 133: 141-155

Fulignati P, Marinelli P, Metrich N, Santacroce R, Sbrana A, 2004. Towards a reconstruction of the magmatic feeding system of the 1944 eruption of Mt Vesuvius. *J Volc Geotherm Res*, 133: 13-22

Funiciello R, Giodano G, De Rita D, 2003. The Albano maar lake (Colli Albani volcano, Italy): recent volcanic activity and evidence of pre-Roman age catastrophic lahar events. *J Volc Geotherm Res*, 123: 43-61

Gabbianelli G, Gillot P Y, Lanzafame G, Romagnoli C, Rossi P L, 1990. Tectonic and volcanic evolution of Panarea (Aeolian Islands, Italy). *Marine Geol*, 92: 313-326

Gabbianelli G, Romagnoli C, Rossi P L, Calanchi N, 1993. Marine geology of the Panarea - Stromboli area (Aeolian Archipelago, southeastern Tyrrhenian Sea). *Acta Vulc*, 3: 11-20

Gamberi F, 2001. Volcanic facies associations in a modern volcaniclastic apron (Lipari and Vulcano offshore, Aeolian Island Arc). *Bull Volc*, 63: 264-273

Gamberi Fl, Marani M, Savelli C, 1997. Tectonic, volcanic and hydrothermal featues of a submarine portion of the Aeolian arc (Tyrrhenian Sea). *Marine Geol*, 140: 167-181

Garduno V H, Neri M, Pasquare G, Borgia A, Tibaldi A, 1997. Geology of the NE-Rift of Mount Etna (Sicily, Italy). *Acta Vulc*, 9: 91-100

Gehring I, 2004. The use of grain-size dependent magnetic susceptibility and gamma-ray measurements for the detailed reconstruction of volcanostratigraphy: the case of La Fossa di Vulcano, S. Italy. *J Volc Geotherm Res*, 138: 163-183

Giaccio B, Marra F, Hajdas I, Karner D B, Renne P R, Sposato A, 2009. 40Ar/39Ar and 14C geochronology of the Albano maar deposits: implications for defining the age and eruptive style of the most recent explosive activity at Colli Albani volcanic district, Central Italy. *J Volc Geotherm Res*, 185: 203-213

Giannetti B, De Casa G, 2000. Stratigraphy, chronology, and sedimentology of ignimbrites from the white trachytic tuff, Roccomonfina volcano, Italy. *J Volc Geotherm Res*, 96: 243-295

Gillot P-Y, Keller J, 1993. Radiochronological dating of Stromboli. *Acta Vulc*, 3: 69-77

Gillot P-Y, Kieffer G, Romano R, 1994. The evolution of Mount Etna in the light of potassium-argon dating. *Acta Vulc*, 5: 81-87

Gioncada A, Mazzuoli R, Bisson M, Pareschi M T, 2003. Petrology of volcanic products younger than 42 ka on the Lipari-Vulcano complex (Aeolian Islands, Italy): an example of volcanism controlled by tectonics. *J Volc Geotherm Res*, 122: 191-220

Giordano G, De Benedetti A A, Diana A, Diano G, Gaudioso F, Marasco F, Miceli M, Mollo S, Cas R A F, Funiciello R, 2006. The Colli Albani mafic caldera (Roma, Italy): stratigraphy, structure and petrology. *J Volc Geotherm Res*, 155: 49-80

Giordano G, De Rita D, Cas R, Rodani S, 2002. Valley pond and ignimbrite veneer deposits in the small-volume phreatomagmatic `Peperino Albano' basic ignimbrite, Lago Albano maar, Colli Albani volcano, Italy: influence of topography. *J Volc Geotherm Res*, 118: 131-144

Giordano G, Porreca M, Musacchio P, Mattei M, 2008. The Holocene Secche de Lazzaro phreatomagmatic succession (Stromboli, Italy): evidence of pyroclastic density current origin deduced by facies analysis and AMS flow directions. *Bull Volc*, 70: 1221-1236

Gresta S, Longo V, 1994. An attempt at identifying seismological precursors for flank eruptions at Mt. Etna volcano. *Acta Vulc*, 5: 187-191

Gresta S, Ripepe M, Marchetti E, D'Amico S, Coltelli M, Harris A J L, Privitera E, 2004. Seismoacoutstic measurements during the July-August 2001 eruption of Mt. Etna volcano, Italy. *J Volc Geotherm Res*, 137: 219-230

Grindley G W, 1976. Relation of volcanism to earth movements, Bay of Naples, Italy. *In*: Gonzalez-Ferran O (ed) *Proc Symp Andean & Antarctic Volcanology Problems (Santiago, Chile, Sept 1974)*, Rome: IAVCEI, p 598-612

Gruppo Nazionale Vulcanologia-CNR, 1986. Phlegraean Fields: eruptive history and the 1538 Monte Nuovo eruption. Gruppo Nazionale Vulcanologia CNR Italia, 1 sheet

Guest J E, 1982. Styles of eruptions and flow morphology on Mt. Etna. *Mem Soc Geol Italiana*, 23: 49-67

Guest J E, Huntingdon A T, Wadge G, Brander J L, Booth B, Carter S, Duncan A, 1974. Recent eruption of Mount Etna. *Nature*, 250: 385-387

Guest J E, Murray J, Kilburn C, Lopes R, 1980. Eruptions on Mount Etna during 1979. *Earthq Inf Bull*, 12: 155-160

Guidoboni E, Ciuccarelli C, 2008. First historical evidence of a significant Mt. Etna eruption in 1224. *J Volc Geotherm Res*, 178: 693-700

Gurioli L, Houghton B R, Cashman K V, Cioni R, 2005. Complex changes in eruptive dynamics during the 79 AD eruption of Vesuvius. *Bull Volc*, 67: 144-159

Harris A J L, Neri M, 2002. Volumetric observations during paroxysmal eruptions at Mount Etna: pressurized drainage of a shallow chamber or pulsed supply? *J Volc Geotherm Res*, 116: 79-95

Harris A, Dehn J, Patrick M, Calvari S, Ripepe M, Lodato L, 2005. Lava effusion rates from hand-held thermal infrared imagery: an example from the June 2003 effusive activity at Stromboli. *Bull Volc*, 68: 107-117

Hornig-Kjarsgaard I, Keller J, Koberski U, Stadlbauer E, Francalanci L, Lenhart R, 1993. Geology, stratigraphy and volcanological evolution of the island of Stromboli, Aeolian arc, Italy. *Acta Vulc*, 3: 21-68

Houghton B F, Wilson C J N, Del Carlo P, Coltelli M, Sable J E, Carey R, 2004. The influence of conduit processes on changes in style of basaltic Plinian eruptions: Tarawera 1886 and Etna 122 BC. *J Volc Geotherm Res*, 137: 1-14

Imbo G, 1965. Italy. *Catalog of Active Volcanoes of the World and Solfatara Fields*, Rome: IAVCEI, 18: 1-72 ***(regional reference)***

Imbo G, Luongo G, 1968. Contribution to the knowledge of the magmatic evolution by the study of the variation of the coefficient of viscosity. *Bull Volc*, 32: 365-376

Isaia R, D'Antonio M, Dell'Erba F, Di Vito M, Orsi G, 2004. The Astroni volcano: the only example of closely spaced eruptions in the same vent area during the recent history of the Campi Flegrei caldera (Italy). *J Volc Geotherm Res*, 133: 171-192

Italiano F, Nuccio P M, 1991. Preliminary investigations on the underwater gaseous manifestations of Vulcano and Lipari. *Acta Vulc*, 1: 243-248

Johnson J B, 2005. Source location variability and volcanic vent mapping with a small-aperture infrasound array at Stromboli volcano, Italy. *Bull Volc*, 67: 1-14

Karner D B, Marra F, Renne P R, 2001. The history of the Monti Sabatini and Alban Hills volcanoes: groundwork for assessing volcanic-tectonic hazards for Rome. *J Volc Geotherm Res*, 107: 185-219

Keller J, 1970a. Datierung der Obsidiane und Bimstuffe von Lipari. *Neues Jahrb Geol Palaont Monatsh*, 1970(2): 90-101

Keller J, 1970b. Die Historischen Eruptionen von Vulcano und Lipari. *Zeit Deut Geol Ges*, 121: 179-185

Keller J, 1974. Quaternary maar volcanism near Karapinar in central Anatolia. *Bull Volc*, 38: 378-396

Keller J, 1980. The island of Vulcano. *Soc Italiana Min Petr*, 36: 368-413

Keller J, Ryan W B F, Ninkovich D, Altherr R, 1978. Explosive volcanic activity in the Mediterranean over the past 200,000 years as recorded in deep-sea sediments. *Geol Soc Amer Bull*, 89: 591-604

Keller W D, 1946. The natural steam at Larderello, Italy. *J Geol*, 54: 327-334

Kieffer G, 1979. L'activite de l'Etna pendant les derniers 20,000 ans. *CR Acad Sci Paris*, Ser-D, 288: 1023-1026

Kieffer G, 1982. L'eruption du 17 au 22 Mars 1981 de l'Etna; sa signification dans l'evolution actuelle du volcan. *Geol Mediterraneenne*, 9: 59-67

Kokelaar, Romagnoli C, 1995. Sector collapse, sedimentation and clast population evolution at an active island-arc volcano: Stromboli, Italy. *Bull Volc*, 57: 240-262

Krafft M, 1974. *Guide des Volcans d'Europe*. Neuchatel: Delachaux & Niestle, 412 p ***(regional reference)***

Krafft M, Dominique de Larouziere F, 1991. *Guide des Volcans d'Europe et des Canaries*. Lausanne, Switzerland: Delachaux and Niestle, 455 p

Krautschick S, 1985. An eruption of the Vesuvius not noticed up to now. *Mitteilschen Geograph Gesell*, 31/32: 581-582

La Delfa S, Patane G, Clocchiatti R, Joron J L, Tanguy J C, 2001. Activity of Mount Etna preceding the February 1999 fissure eruption: inferred mechanism from seismological and geochemical data. *J Volc Geotherm Res*, 105: 121-139

La Volpe L, Patella D, Rapisardi L, Tramacere A, 1984. The evolution of the Monte Vulture volcano (southern Italy): inferences from volcanological, geological and deep dipole electrical soundings data. *Bull Volc*, 22: 147-162

LaBerge R D, Giordano G, Cas R A F, Ailleres L, 2006. Syn-depositional substrate deformation produced by the shear force of a pyroclastic density current: an example from the Pleistocene ignimbrite at Monte Cimino, northern Lazio, Italy. *J Volc Geotherm Res*, 158: 307-320

Lacroix A, 1907. Eruption of Vesuvius April 1906. *Smithsonian Inst Rpt*, 1754: 223-248

Landi P, Francalanci L, Pompilio M, Rosi M, Corsaro R A, Petrone C M, Nardini I, Miraglia L, 2006. The December 2002-July 2003 effusive event at Stromboli volcano, Italy: insights into the shallow plumbing system by petrochemical studies. *J Volc Geotherm Res*, 155: 263-284

Lautze N C, Harris A J L, Bailey J E, Ripepe M, Calvari S, Dehn J, Rowland S K, Evans-Jones K, 2004. Pulsed lava effusion at Mount Etna during 2001. *J Volc Geotherm Res*, 137: 231-246

Lirer L, Luongo G, Scandone R, 1987. On the volcanological evolution of Campi Flegrei. *Eos, Trans Amer Geophys Union*, 68: 226-227, 229, 231, 233-234

Lirer L, Munno R, Postiglione I, Vinci A, Vitelli L, 1997. The A.D. 79 eruption as a future explosive scenario in the Vesuvian area: evaluation of associated risk. *Bull Volc*, 59: 112-124

Lirer L, Pescatore T, Booth B, Walker G P L, 1973. Two Plinian pumice-fall deposits from Somma-Vesuvius, Italy. *Geol Soc Amer Bull*, 84: 759-772

Lirer L, Petrosino P, Alberico I, 2001. Hazard assessment at volcanic fields: the Campi Flegrei case history. *J Volc Geotherm Res*, 112: 53-73

Lirer L, Petrosino P, Alberico I, Postiglione I, 2001. Long-term volcanic hazard forecasts based on Somma-Vesuvio past eruptive activity. *Bull Volc*, 63: 45-60

Lodato L, Spampinato L, Harris A, Calvari S, Dehn J, Patrick M, 2007. The morphology and evolution of the Stromboli 2002-2003 lava flow field: an example of a basaltic flow field emplaced on a steep slope. *Bull Volc*, 69: 661-679

Lucchi F, Tranne C A, Calanchi N, Rossi P L, 2007. Late Quaternary deformation history of the volcanic edifice of Panarea, Aeolian Arc, Italy. *Bull Volc*, 69: 239-257

Lucchi F, Tranne C A, De Astis G, Keller J, Losito R, Morche W, 2008. Stratigraphy and significance of Brown Tuffs on the Aeolian Islands (southern Italy). *J Volc Geotherm Res*, 177: 49-70

Luhr J F, Giannetti B, 1987. The Brown Leucitic Tuff of Roccamonfina volcano (Roman Region, Italy). *Contr Mineral Petr*, 95: 420-436

Luongo G, Coppola G, Cubellis E, Ferri M, Forgione G, Orbrizzo F, Ricciardi G P, Romano R, 1986. Richio vulcanico - Vesuvio, Campi Flegrei, Ischia, Etna, Stromboli, Vulcano. *Rivista dell' Amministrazione Provinciale Napoli*, 8: 34-61

Luongo G, Perrotta A, Scarpati C, 2003. Impact of the AD 79 explosive eruption on Pompeii, I. Relations amongst the depositional mechanisms of the pyroclastic products, the framework of the buildings and the associated destructive events. *J Volc Geotherm Res*, 126: 201-223

Luongo G, Perrotta A, Scarpati C, De Carolis E, Patricelli G, Ciarallo A, 2003. Impact of the AD 79 explosive eruption on Pompeii, II. Causes of death of the inhabitants inferred by stratigraphic analysis and areal distribution of the human casualties. *J Volc Geotherm Res*, 126: 169-200

Mahood G A, Hildreth W, 1986. Geology of the peralkaline volcano at Pantelleria, Strait of Sicily. *Bull Volc*, 48: 143-172

Manzo M, Ricciardi G P, Casu F, Ventura G, Zeni G, Borgstrom S, Berardino P, Del Gaudio C, Lanzari R, 2006. Surface deformation analysis in the Ischia Island (Italy) based on spaceborne radar interferometry. *J Volc Geotherm Res*, 151: 399-416

Marianelli P, Metrich N, Sbrana A, 1999. Shallow and deep reservoirs involved in magma supply of the 1944 eruption of Vesuvius. *Bull Volc*, 61: 48-63

Marinelli G, 1969. Some geological data on the geothermal areas of Tuscany. *Bull Volc*, 33: 319-333

Marra F, Freda C, Scarlato P, Taddeucci J, Karner D B, Renne P R, Gaeta M, Palladino D M, Trigila R, Cavarretta G, 2003. Post-caldera activity in the Alban Hills volcanic district (Italy): 40Ar/39Ar geochronology and insights into magma evolution. *Bull Volc*, 65: 227-247

Marra F, Karner D B, Freda C, Gaeta M, Renne P, 2009. Large mafic eruptions at Alban Hills volcanic district (Central Italy): chronostratigraphy, petrography and eruptive behavior. *J Volc Geotherm Res*, 179: 217-232

Mastrolorenzo G, 1994. Averno tuff ring in Campi Flegrei (south Italy). *Bull Volc*, 56: 561-572

Mastrolorenzo G, Lirer L, Di Vito M, Rolandi G, Scandone R, 1988. The eruptive dynamic in Campi Flegrei and Roccamonfina volcanic areas (southern Italy). *Kagoshima Internatl Conf Volc Abs*, p 330

Mastrolorenzo G, Munno R, Rolandi G, 1993. Vesuvius 1906: a case study of a paroxysmal eruption and its relation to eruption cycles. *J Volc Geotherm Res*, 58: 217-237

Mastrolorenzo G, Petrone P P, Pagano M, Incoronato A, Baxter P J, Canzanella A, Fattore L, 2001. Herculaneum victims of Vesuvius in AD 79. *Nature*, 410: 769-770

Mastrolorenzo G, Petrone P, Pappalardo L, Sheridan M F, 2006. The Avellino 3780-yr-B.P. catastrophe as a worst-case scenario for a future eruption at Vesuvius. *Proc Nat Acad Sci*, 103: 4366-4370

McGregor A D, Lees J M, 2004. Vent discrimination at Stromboli volcano, Italy. *J Volc Geotherm Res*, 137: 169-185

Melluso L, Morra V, Perrotta A, Scarpati C, Adabbo M, 1995. The eruption of The Breccia Museo (Campi Flegrei, Italy): fractional crystallization processes in a shallow, zoned magma chamber and implications for the eruptive dynamics. *J Volc Geotherm Res*, 68: 325-339

Milia A, Mirabile L, Torrente M M, Dvorak J J, 1998. Volcanism offshore of Vesuvius volcano in Naples Bay. *Bull Volc*, 59: 404-413

Molin P, Acocella V, Funiciello R, 2003. Structural, seismic and hydrothermal features at the border of an active intermittent resurgent block: Ischia Island (Italy). *J Volc Geotherm Res*, 121: 65-81

Montalto A, 1996. Signs of potential renewal of eruptive activity at La Fossa (Vulcano, Aeolian Islands). *Bull Volc*, 57: 483-492

Mulargia F, Tinti S, Boschi E, 1985. A statistical analysis of flank eruptions on Mount Etna volcano. *J Volc Geotherm Res*, 23: 263-272

Murray J B, Stevens N F, 2000. New formulae for estimating lava flow volumes at Mt. Etna volcano, Sicily. *Bull Volc*, 61: 515-526

Nappi G, 1976. Recent activity of Stromboli. *Nature*, 261: 119-120

Nappi G, 1977. Rischio vulcanico e sorveglianza nei Campi Flegrei e nell'Isola di Stromboli. *Bol Serv Geol Italia*, 98: 141-156

Nappi G, Capaccioni B, Mattioli M, Mancini E, Valentini L, 1994. Plinian fall deposits from Vulsini District (Central Italy). *Bull Volc*, 56: 502-515

Nazzaro A, 1986. Il Vesuvio: storia naturale dal 1631 al 1944. *Bol Soc Nat Napoli*, 94: 1-26

Neri M, Acocella V, 2006. The 2004-2005 Etna eruption: implications for flank deformation and structural behavior of the volcano. *J Volc Geotherm Res*, 158: 195-206

Neri M, Acocella V, Behncke B, 2004. The role of the Pernicana Fault System in the spreading of Mt. Etna (Italy) during the 2002-2003 eruption. *Bull Volc*, 66: 417-430

Orsi G, Civetta L, D'Antonio M D, Di Girolamo P, Piochi M, 1995. Step-filling and development of a three-layer magma chamber: the Neapolitan Yellow Tuff case history. *J Volc Geotherm Res*, 67: 291-312

Orsi G, D'Antonio M, de Vita S, Gallo G, 1992. The Neapolitan Yellow Tuff, a large-magnitude trachytic phreatoplinian eruption: eruptive dynamics, magma withdrawal and caldera collapse. *J Volc Geotherm Res*, 53: 275-287

Orsi G, De Vita S, di Vito M, 1996. The restless, resurgent Campi Flegrei nested caldera (Italy): constraints on its evolution and configuration. *J Volc Geotherm Res*, 74: 179-214

Orsi G, Di Vito M A, Isaia R, 2004. Volcanic hazard assessment at the restless Campi Flegrei caldera. *Bull Volc*, 66: 514-530

Orsi G, Gallo G, Heiken G, Wohletz K, Yu E, Bonani G, 1992. A comprehensive study of pumice formation and dispersal: the Cretaio Tephra of Ischia (Italy). *J Volc Geotherm Res*, 53: 329-354

Orsi G, Gallo G, Zanchi A, 1991. Simple-shearing block resurgence in caldera depressions. A model from Pantelleria and Ischia. *J Volc Geotherm Res*, 47: 1-11

Orsi G, Piochi M, Campajola L, D'Onofrio A, Gialanella L, Terrasi F, 1996. 14C geochronological constraints for the volcanic history of the island of Ischia (Italy) over the last 5000 years. *J Volc Geotherm Res*, 71: 249-257

Palladino D M, Agosta E, 1997. Pumice fall deposits of the western Vulsini volcanoes (central Italy). *J Volc Geotherm Res*, 78: 77-102

Palladino D M, Gaeta M, Marra F, 2001. A large K-foiditic hydromagmatic eruption from the early activity of the Alban Hills volcanic district, Italy. *Bull Volc*, 63: 345-359

Palladino D M, Simei S, 2002. Three types of pyroclastic currents and their deposits: examples from the Vulsini Volcanoes, Italy. *J Volc Geotherm Res*, 116: 97-118

Palladino D M, Simei S, 2005. Eruptive dynamics and caldera collapse during the Onano eruption, Vulsini, Italy. *Bull Volc*, 67: 423-440

Palladino D M, Valentine G A, 1995. Coarse-tail vertical and lateral grading in pyroclastic flow deposits of the Latera volcanic complex (Vulsini, central Italy): origin and implications for flow dynamics. *J Volc Geotherm Res*, 69: 343-364

Pasquare G, Francalanci L, Garduno V H, Tibaldi A, 1993. Structure and geologic evolution of the Stromboli volcano, Aeolian Islands, Italy. *Acta Vulc*, 3: 79-89

Peccerillo A, 2005. *Plio-Quaternary Volcanism in Italy*. Berlin: Springer, 365 p

Peccerillo A, Poli G, Tolomeo L, 1984. Genesis, evolution and tectonic significance of K-rich volcanics from the Alban Hills (Roman comagmatic region) as inferred from trace element geochemistry. *Contr Mineral Petr*, 86: 230-240

Perini G, Francalanci L, Davidson J P, Conticelli S, 2004. Evolution and genesis of magmas from Vico volcano, Central Italy: multiple differentiation pathways and variable parental magmas. *J Petr*, 45: 139-182

Perrotta A, Scarpati C, 1994. The dynamics of the Breccia Museo eruption (Campi Flegrei, Italy) and the significance of spatter clasts associated with lithic breccias. *J Volc Geotherm Res*, 59: 335-355

Perrotta A, Scarpati C, Luongo G, Aoyagi M, 2006. Burial of Emperor Augustus' villa at Somma Vesuviana (Italy) by post-79 AD Vesuvius eruptions and reworked (lahars and stream flow) deposits. *J Volc Geotherm Res*, 158: 445-466

Petrucci E, Sheppard S M F, Turi B, 1993. Water/rock interaction in the Larderello geothermal field (southern Tuscany, Italy): an 18O/16O and D/H isotope study. *J Volc Geotherm Res*, 59: 145-160

Petteruti Lieberknecht A M, Fedele L, d Amelio F, Lustrino M, Melluso L, Morra V, 2003. Plio-Pleistocene igneous activity in Sardinia (Italy). *Geophy Res Abstr*, 5: 07260

Pichler H, 1970. Volcanism in eastern Sicily and the Aeolian Islands. *In*: Alvarez W, Gohbrandt K H A (eds) *Geol and Hist of Sicily*, Petrol Explor Soc Libya, p 261-281

Pichler H, 1980. The island of Lipari. *Rendiconti Soc Italiana Min Petr*, 36: 415-440

Pinkerton H, Sparks R S J, 1976. Formation of the 1975 subterminal compound lava flow, Mount Etna. *J Volc Geotherm Res*, 1: 167-182

Poli S, Chiesa S, Gillot P-Y, Gregnanin A, Guichard F, 1987. Chemistry versus time in the volcanic complex of Ischia (Gulf of Naples, Italy): evidence of successive magmatic cycles. *Contr Mineral Petr*, 95: 322-335

Porreca M, Mattei M, MacNiocaill C, Giordano G, McClelland E, Funiciello R, 2008. Palemagnetic evidence for low-temperature emplacement of the phreatomagmatic Peperino Albano ignimbrite (Colli Albani volcano, Central Italy). *Bull Volc*, 70: 877-893

Principe C, Marini L, 2008. Evolution of the Vesuvius magmatic-hydrothermal system before the 16 December 1631 eruption. *J Volc Geotherm Res), 171: 311-306*

Principe C, Tanguy J-C, Arrighi S, Paiotti A, Le Goff M, Zoppi U, 2004. Chronology of Vesuvius' activity from A.D. 79 to 1631 based on archaeomagnetism of lavas and historical sources. *Bull Volc*, 66: 703-724

Prosperini N, Perugini D, Poli G, Manetti P, 2000. Magmatic enclaves within the Khaggiar lava dome (Pantelleria, Italy): implications for magma chamber dynamics and eruption. *Acta Vulc*, 12: 37-47

Pyle D M, van Andel T H, Paschos P, van den Bogaard P, 1998. An exceptionally thick middle Pleistocene tephra layer from Epirus, Greece. *Quat Res*, 49: 280-286

Quidelleur X, Gillot P-Y, Filoche G, Lefevre J-C, 2005. Fast geochemical changes and rapid lava accumulation at Stromboli Island (Italy) inferred from K-Ar dating and paleomagnetic variations recorded at 60 and 40 ka. *J Volc Geotherm Res*, 141: 177-193

Renzulli A, Santi P, 1997. Sub-volcanic crystallization of Stromboli (Aeolian Islands, southern Italy) preceding the Sciara del Fuoco sector collapse: evidence from monzonite lithic suite. *Bull Volc*, 59: 10-20

Rittmann A, 1964. Vulkanismus und Tektonik des Aetna. *Geol Rundschau*, 53: 788-800

Rodwell G F, 1878. *Etna: A History of the Mountain and of its Eruptions*. London: C Kegan Paul & Co, 146 p

Rolandi G, Barrella A M, Borrelli A, 1993. The 1631 eruption of Vesuvius. *J Volc Geotherm Res*, 58: 183-202

Rolandi G, Maraffi S, Petrosino P, Lirer L, 1993. The Ottaviano eruption of Somma-Vesuvio (8000 y B.P.): a magmatic alternating fall and flow-forming eruption. *J Volc Geotherm Res*, 58: 43-65

Rolandi G, Mastrolorenzo G, Barrella A M, Borrelli A, 1993. The Avellino plinian eruption of Somma-Vesuvius (3760 y B.P.): the progressive evolution from magmatic to hydromagmatic style. *J Volc Geotherm Res*, 58: 67-88

Rolandi G, Munno R, Postiglione I, 2004. The A.D. 472 eruption of the Somma volcano. *J Volc Geotherm Res*, 129: 291-319

Rolandi G, Paone A, De Lascio M, Stefani G, 2008. The 79 AD eruption of Somma: the relationship between the date of the eruption and the southeast tephra dispersion. *J Volc Geotherm Res*, 169: 87-98

Rolandi G, Petrosino P, McGeehin J, 1998. The interplinian activity at Somma-Vesuvius in the last 3500 years. *J Volc Geotherm Res*, 82: 19-52

Romagnoli C, Kokelaar P, Rossi P L, Sodi A, 1993. The submarine extension of Sciara del Fuoco feature (Stromboli Is.): morphologic characterization. *Acta Vulc*, 3: 91-98

Romano R (ed), 1982. Mount Etna volcano. *Mem Soc Geol Italiana*, 23: 1-205

Romano R, Sturiale C, 1971. L'Isola di Ustica - studio geo-vulcanologica e magmatologico. *Rev Min Siciliana*, 32: 3-61

Romano R, Sturiale C, Lentini F, 1979. *Geological Map of Mount Etna*. CNR Istit Internatl Vulc, Catania, 1:50,000 geol map

Rosi M, 1980. Isola Stromboli. *Rendiconti Soc Italiana Min Petr*, 36: 345-368

Rosi M, Bertagnini A, Landi P, 2000. Onset of the persistent activity at Stromboli volcano (Italy). *Bull Volc*, 62: 294-300

Rosi M, Principe C, Vecci R, 1993. The 1631 Vesuvius eruption. A reconstruction based on historical and stratigraphical data. *J Volc Geotherm Res*, 58: 151-182

Rosi M, Santacroce R, 1983. The AD 472 "Pollena" eruption: volcanological and petrological data for this poorly-known, Plinian-type event at Vesuvius. *J Volc Geotherm Res*, 17: 249-271

Rosi M, Santacroce R, 1984. Volcanic hazard assessment in the Phlegraean Fields: a contribution based on stratigraphic and historical data. *Bull Volc*, 47: 359-371

Rosi M, Santacroce R, Sbrana A, 1987. *Geological Map of Somma-Vesuvius Volcanic Complex*. CNR Progetto Finalizzato Geodinamica, Rome

Rosi M, Santacroce R, Sheridan M, 1981. Volcanic hazards of Vesuvius (Italy). *Bull BRGM*, 4: 169-179

Rosi M, Sbrana A, 1987. *Consiglio Nazionale delle Ricerche Quaderni de "la Ricerca Scientifica."* CNR Progetto Finalizzato Geodinamica, Rome, v 9

Rosi M, Sbrana A, Principe C, 1983. The Phlegrean Fields: structural evolution, volcanic history and eruptive mechanisms. *J Volc Geotherm Res*, 17: 273-288

Rosi M, Vezzoli L, Aleotti P, De Censi M, 1996. Interaction between caldera collapse and eruptive dynamics during the Campanian Ignimbrite eruption, Phelegraean Fields, Italy. *Bull Volc*, 57: 541-554

Rosi M, Vezzoli L, Castelmenzano A, Grieco G, 1999. Plinian pumice fall deposit of the Campanian Ignimbrite eruption (Phlegraean Fields, Italy). *J Volc Geotherm Res*, 91: 179-198

Rothery D A, Coltelli M, Pirie D, Wooster M J, Wright R, 2001. Documenting surface magmatic activity at Mount Etna using ATSR remote sensing. *Bull Volc*, 63: 387-397

Rouchon V, Gillot P Y, Quidelleur X, Chiesa S, Floris B, 2008. Temporal evolution of the Roccamonfina volcanic complex (Pleistocene), Central Italy. *J Volc Geotherm Res*, 177: 500-514

Ruggieri G, Gianelli G, 1999. Multi-stage fluid circulation in a hydraulic fracture breccia of the Larderello geothermal field (Italy). *J Volc Geotherm Res*, 90: 241-261

Rymer H, Cassidy J, Locke C A, Murray J B, 1995. Magma movements in Etna volcano associated with the major 1991-93 lava eruption: evidence from gravity and deformation. *Bull Volc*, 57: 451-461

Sandri L, Guidoboni E, Marzocchi W, Selva J, 2009. Bayesian event tree for eruption forecasting (BET_EF) at Vesuvius, Italy: a retrospective forward application to the 1631 eruption. *Bull Volc*, 71: 729-745

Santacroce R, 1983. A general model for the behavior of the Somma-Vesuvio volcanic complex. *J Volc Geotherm Res*, 17: 237-248

Santacroce R, Cioni R, Marianelli P, Sbrana A, Sulpizio R, Zanchetta G, Donahue D J, Joron J L, 2008. Age and whole rock-glass compositions of proximal pyroclastics from the major explosive eruptions of Somma-Vesuvius: a review as a tool for distal tephrochronology. *J Volc Geotherm Res*, 177: 1-18

Savelli C, Marini M, Gamberi F, 1999. Geochemistry of metalliferous, hydrothermal deposits in the Aeolian arc (Tyrrhenian Sea). *J Volc Geotherm Res*, 88: 305-323

Scandone R, Giacomelli L, Gasparini P, 1993. Mount Vesuvius: 2000 years of volcanological observations. *J Volc Geotherm Res*, 58: 5-26

Scandone R, Giacomelli L, Speranza F F, 2008. Persistent activity and violent strombolian eruptions at Vesuvius between 1631 and 1944. *J Volc Geotherm Res*, 170: 167-180

Scandone R, D'Amato J, Giacomelli L, 2010. The relevance of the 1198 eruption of Solfatara in the Phlegraean Fields (Campi Flegrei) as revealed by medieval manuscripts and historical sources. *J Volc Geotherm Res*, 189: 202-206

Scott S C, 1983. Variations in lava composition during the March 1981 eruption of Mount Etna and the implications of a compositional comparison with earlier historic eruptions. *Bull Volc*, 46: 393-412

Siani G, Sulpizio R, Paterne M, Sbrana A, 2004. Tephrostratigraphy study for the last 18,000 14C years in a deep-sea sediment sequence for the South Adriatic. *Quat Sci Rev*, 23: 2485-2500

Sigurdsson H, Carey S N, Cornell W, Pescatore T, 1985. The eruption of Vesuvius in AD 79. *Natl Geog Res*, 1: 332-387

Sigurdsson H, Cashdollar S, Sparks S R J, 1982. The eruption of Vesuvius in AD 79: reconstruction from historical and volcanological evidence. *Amer J Arch*, 86: 39-51

Slejko F F, Petrini R, Orsi G, Piochi M, Forte C, 2004. Water speciation and Sr isotopic exchange during water-melt interaction: a combined NMR-TIMS study on the Cretaio Tephra (Ischia Island, south Italy). *J Volc Geotherm Res*, 133: 311-320

Sollevanti F, 1983. Geologic, volcanologic, and tectonic setting of the Vico-Cimino area, Italy. *J Volc Geotherm Res*, 17: 203-217

Spampinato L, Calvari S, Oppenheimer C, Lodato L, 2008. Shallow magma transport for the 2002-3 Mt. Etna eruption inferred from thermal infrared surveys. *J Volc Geotherm Res*, 177: 301-312

Sparks R S J, 1975. Stratigraphy and geology of the ignimbrites of Vulsini volcano, central Italy. *Geol Rundschau*, 64: 497-523

Speranza F, Pompilio M, D'Ajello Caracciolo F, Sagnoti L, 2008. Holocene eruptive history of the Stromboli volcano: constraints from paleomagnetic dating. *J Geophys Res*, 113: B09101, doi:1029/2007JB005139

Squarci P, Gianelli G, Grassi S, Mussi M, D'Amore G, 1994. Preliminary results of geothermal prospecting on the island of Pantelleria (Italy). *Acta Vulc*, 5: 117-123

Stevens N F, Murray J B, Wadge G, 1997. The volume and shape of the 1991-1993 lava flow field of Mount Etna, Italy. *Bull Volc*, 58: 449-454

Stevenson R J, Wilson L, 1997. Physical volcanology and eruption dynamics of peralkaline agglutinates from Panterlleria. *J Volc Geotherm Res*, 79: 97-122

Stoppa F, Cundari A, 1995. A new Italian carbonatite occurrence at Cupanello (Rieti) and its genetic significance. *Contr Mineral Petr*, 122: 275-288

Stoppa F, Sforna S, 1995. Geological map of the San Venanzo volcani (Central Italy): explanatory notes. *Acta Vulc*, 7: 85-91

Stothers R B, Rampino M R, 1983. Volcanic eruptions in the Mediterranean before AD 630 from written and archaeological sources. *J Geophys Res*, 88: 6357-6371

Sulpizio R, Mele D, Dellino P, La Volpe L, 2005. A complex, subplinian-type eruption from low-viscosity, phonolitic to tephri-phonolitic magma: the AD 472 (Pollena) eruption of Somma-Vesuvius. *Bull Volc*, 67: 743-767

Taddeucci J, Pompilio M, Scarlato P, 2004. Conduit processes during the July-August 2001 explosive activity of Mt. Etna (Italy): inferences from glass chemistry and crystal size distribution of ash particles. *J Volc Geotherm Res*, 137: 33-54

Tanguy J C, 1979a. The storage and release of magma on Mount Etna: a discussion. *J Volc Geotherm Res*, 6: 179-188

Tanguy J C, 1979b. Sur l'eruption de l'Etna en 1879 (Mont Umberto-Margherita). *CR Acad Sci Paris*, 288: 1453-1456

Tanguy J C, 1981. Les eruptions historiques de l'Etna: chronologie et localisation. *Bull Volc*, 44: 585-640

Tanguy J C, Kieffer G, 1976-77. The 1974 eruption of Mount Etna. *Bull Volc*, 40: 239-252

Tanguy J C, Kieffer G, Patane G, 1996. Dynamics, lava volume and effusion rate during the 1991-1993 eruption of Mount Etna. *J Volc Geotherm Res*, 71: 259-265

Tanguy J-C, Condomines M, Le Goff M, Chillemi V, La Delfa S, Patane G, 2007. Mount Etna eruptions of the last 2,750 years: revised chronology and location through archeomagnetic and 226Ra-230Th dating. *Bull Volc*, 70: 55-83

Tanguy J-C, Le Goff M, Principe C, Arrighi S, Chillemi V, Paiotti A, La Delfa S, Patane G, 2003. Archeomagnetic dating of Mediterranean volcanics of the last 2100 years: validity and limits. *Earth Planet Sci Lett*, 211: 111-124

Tanner L H, Calvari S, 2004. Unusual sedimentary deposits on the SE side of Stromboli volcano, Italy: products of a tsunami caused by the ca. 5000 years BP Sciara del Fuoco collapse? *J Volc Geotherm Res*, 137: 329-340

Tedesco C, 1965. Main lines of the history of the Roccamonfina volcano. *Bull Volc*, 28: 119-138

Tibaldi A, 2001. Multiple sector collapses at Stromboli volcano, Italy: how they work. *Bull Volc*, 63: 112-125

Tibaldi A, 2003. Influence of cone morphology on dykes, Stromboli, Italy. *J Volc Geotherm Res*, 126: 79-95

Tinti S, Maramai A, Armigliato A, Granziani L, Manucci A, Pagnoni G, Zaniboni F, 2006. Observations of physical effects from tsunamis of December 30, 2002 at Stromboli volcano, southern Italy. *Bull Volc*, 68: 450-461

Tonarini S, Armienti P, D'Orazio M, Innocenti F, Pompilo M, Petrini R, 1995. Geochemical and isotopic monitoring of Mt. Etna 1989-1993 eruptive activity: bearing on the shallow feeding system. *J Volc Geotherm Res*, 64: 95-115

Trigila R, De Benedetti A A, 1993. Petrogenesis of Vesuvius historical lavas constrained by Pearce element ratios analysis and experimental phase equilibria. *J Volc Geotherm Res*, 58: 315-343

Uchrin G, 1990. Olympiodorus's eruption of Mount Etna. *Eos, Trans Amer Geophys Union*, 71: 329 & 334

Valentini L, Capaccioni B, Rossi P L, Scandone R, Sarocchi D, 2008. Vent area and depositional mechanism of the Upper Member of the Neapolitan Yellow Tuff (Campi Flegrei, Italy): new insights from directional fabric through image analysis. *Bull Volc*, 70: 1087-1101

Van Bergen M J, 1985. Common trace-element characteristics of crustal- and mantle-derived K-rich magmas at Mt. Amita (Central Italy). *Chem Geol*, 48: 125-135

Varekamp J C, 1980. The geology of the Vulsinian area, Lazio, Italy. *Bull Volc*, 43: 487-504

Ventura G, 1994. Tectonics, structural evolution and caldera formation on Vulcano Island (Aeolian Archipelago, southern Tyrrheanian Sea). *J Volc Geotherm Res*, 60: 207-224

Vezzoli L, 1986. *Geologic Map of the Island of Ischia*. CNR Progetto Finalizzato Geodinamica, Rome

Vezzoli L, Principe C, Malfatti J, Arrighi S, Tanguy J-C, Le Goff M, 2009. Modes and times of caldera resurgence: the <10 ka evolution of ischia caldera, Italy, from high-precision archeomagnetic dating. *J Volc Geotherm Res*, 186: 305-319

Villa I M, Buettner A, 2009. Chronostratigraphy of Monte Vulture volcano (southern Italy): secondary mineral microtextures and 39Ar-40Ar systematics. *Bull Volc*, 71: 1195-1208

Villa I M, Calanchi N, Dinelli E, Lucchini F, 1999. Age and evolution of the Albano crater lake (Roman Volcanic Province). *Acta Vulc*, 11: 305-310

Villa I M, Riggieri G, Puxeddu M, Bertini G, 2006. Geochronology and isotope transport systematics in a subsurface granite from the Larderello-Travale geothermal system (Italy). *J Volc Geotherm Res*, 152: 20-50

Vinciguerra S, Latora V, Bicciato S, Kamimura R T, 2001. Identifying and discriminating seismic patterns leading flank eruptions at Mt. Etna volcano during 1981-1986. *J Volc Geotherm Res*, 106: 211-228

Voltaggio M, Branca M, Tuccimei P, Tecce F, 1995. Leaching procedure used in dating young potassic volcanic rocks by the 226Ra/230Th method. *Earth Planet Sci Lett*, 136: 123-131

Wadge G, 1977. The storage and release of magma on Mount Etna. *J Volc Geotherm Res*, 2: 361-384

Wadge G, 1979. The storage and release of magma on Mount Etna: a reply to a discussion by J. C. Tanguy. *J Volc Geotherm Res*, 6: 189-195

Wagner B, Sulpizio R, Zanchetta G, Wulf S, Wessels M, Daut G, Nowaczyk N, 2008. The last 40 ka tephrostratigraphic record of Lake Ohrid, Albania and Macedonia: a very distal rchive for ash dispersal from Italian volcanoes. *J Volc Geotherm Res*, 177: 71-80

Walker G P L, 1968. Mount Etna. *Geog Mag*, 11: 929-935

Washington H S, 1909. The submarine eruptions of 1831 and 1891 near Pantelleria. *Amer J Sci*, 27: 130-150

Watkins S D, Giordano G, Cas R A F, De Rita D, 2002. Emplacement processes of the mafic Villa Senni Eruption Unit (VSEU) ignimbrite succession, Colli Albani volcano, Italy. *J Volc Geotherm Res*, 118: 173-203

Wohletz K, Orsi G, de Vita S, 1995. Eruptive mechanisms of the Neapolitan Yellow Tuff interpreted from stratigraphic, chemical, and granulometric data. *J Volc Geotherm Res*, 67: 263-290

Wright R, Flynn L P, Harris A J L, 2001. Evolution of lava flow-fields at Mount Etna, 27-28 October 1999, observed by Landsat 7 ETM+. *Bull Volc*, 63: 1-7

Wright R, Rothery D A, Blake S, Pieri D C, 2000. Visualising active volcanism with high spatial resolution satellite data: the 1991-1993 eruption of Mount Etna. *Bull Volc*, 62: 256-265

Zanella E, De Astis G, Lanza R, 2001. Palaeomagnetism of welded, pyroclastic-fall scoriae at Vulcano, Aeolian Archipelago. *J Volc Geotherm Res*, 107: 71-86

EUROPE TO CAUCASUS (0100, 0102-04)

Ager D V, 1980. *The Geology of Europe*. New York: Halsted Press, 576 p

Alici P, Temel A, Gourgaud A, 2002. Pb-Nd-Sr isotope and trace element geochemistry of Quaternay extension-related volcanism: a case study of Kula region (western Anatolia, Turkey). *J Volc Geotherm Res*, 115: 487-510

Alici P, Temela A, Gourgaud A, Kieffer G, Gundogdu M N, 1998. Petrology and geochemistry of potassic rocks in the Golcuk area (Isparta, SW Turkey): genesis of enriched alkaline magmas. *J Volc Geotherm Res*, 85: 423-446

Allen S R, 2001. Reconstruction of a major caldera-forming eruption from pyroclastic deposit characteristics: Kos Plateau Tuff, eastern Aegean Sea. *J Volc Geotherm Res*, 105: 141-162

Allen S R, Cas R A F, 1998. Lateral variations within coarse co-ignimbrite lithic breccias of the Kos Plateau Tuff, Greece. *Bull Volc*, 59: 356-377

Allen S R, Cas R A F, 2001. Transport of pyroclastic flows across the sea during the explosive, rhyolitic eruption of the Kos Plateau Tuff, Greece. *Bull Volc*, 62: 441-456

Allen S R, McPhie J, 2001. Syn-eruptive chaotic breccia on Kos, Greece, associated with an energetic pyroclastic flow. *Bull Volc*, 63: 421-432

Antonopoulos J, 1992. The great Minoan eruption of Thera volcano and the ensuing tsunami in the Greek archipelago. *Nat Hazards*, 5: 153-168

Arana V, Aparicio A, Martin Escorza C, Garcia Cacho L, Ortiz R, Vaquer R, Barberi F, Ferrara G, Albert J, Gassiot X, 1983. El volcanismo Neogeno-Cuaternario de Catalunya: caracteres estructurales, petrologicos y geodinamicos. *Acta Geol Hispanica*, 18: 1-17

Aydar E, 1998. Early Miocene to Quaternary evolution of volcanism and the basin formation in western Anatolia: a review. *J Volc Geotherm Res*, 85: 69-82

Aydar E, Gourgaud A, 1998. The geology of Mount Hasan stratovolcano, central Anatolia, Turkey. *J Volc Geotherm Res*, 85: 129-152

Aydar E, Gourgaud A, Ulusoy I, Digonnet F, Labazuy P, Sen E, Bayhan H, Kurttas T, Tolluoglu A U, 2003. Morphological analysis of active Mount Nemrut stratovolcano, eastern Turkey: evidences and possible impact areas of future eruption. *J Volc Geotherm Res*, 123: 301-312

Baales M, Joris O, Street M, Bittmann F, Weniger B, Wiethold J, 2002. Impact of the Late Glacial eruptions of the Laacher See volcano, central Rhineland, Germany. *Quat Res*, 58: 273-288

Barton M, Huijsmans J P P, 1986. Post-caldera dacites from the Santorini volcanic complex, Aegean Sea, Greece: an example of the eruption of lavas of near-constant composition over a 2,200 year period. *Contr Mineral Petr*, 94: 472-495

Bigazzi G, Yegingil Z, Ercan T, Oddone M, Ozdogan M, 1993. Fission track dating obsidians in central and northern Anatolia. *Bull Volc*, 55: 588-595

Bleahu M D, Boccaletti M, Manetti P, Peltz S, 1973. Neogene Carpathian arc: a continental arc displaying the features of an 'island arc'. *J Geophys Res*, 78: 5025-5032

Blumenthal M M, van der Kaaden G, Vlodavetz V I, 1964. Turkey & Caucasus. *Catalog of Active Volcanoes of the World and Solfatara Fields*, Rome: IAVCEI, 17: 1-23 ***(regional reference)***

Boccaletti M, Manetti P, Peltz S, 1973. Evolution of the upper Cretaceous and Cenozoic magmatism in the Carpathian arc: geodynamic significance. *Soc Geol Italiana Rome*, 12: 267-277

Bonadonna C, Houghton B F, 2005. Total grain-size distribution and volume of tephra-fall deposits. *Bull Volc*, 67: 441-456

Bond A, Sparks R S J, 1976. The Minoan eruption of Santorini, Greece. *J Geol Soc London*, 132: 1-16

Borsi S, Ferrara G, Innocenti F, Mazzuoli R, 1972. Geochronology and petrology of recent volcanics in the eastern Aegean Sea (west Anatolia and Lesvos Island). *Bull Volc*, 36: 473-496

Brinkmann R, 1976. *Geology of Turkey*. Amsterdam: Elsevier, 158 p

Brombach T, Caliro S, Chiodini G, Fiebig J, Hunziker J C, Raco B, 2003. Geochemical evidence for mixing of magmatic fluids with seawater, Nisyros hydrothermal system, Greece. *Bull Volc*, 65: 505-516

Brousse R, 1973. Le volcanisme Quaternaire en France-chronologie des differentes phase eruptives de la Chaine des Puys au Quaternaire recent. *Internatl Quat Assoc (INQUA) Cong*, 9: 105-109

Brousse R, Delibrias G, Labeyrie J, Rudel A, 1969. Elements de chronologie des eruptions de la Chaine des Puys. *Bull Soc Geol France*, 7: 770-793

Buchel G, Lorenz V, 1982. Zum Alter des Maarvulkanismus der Westeifel. *Neues Jahrb Geol Palaont Abh*, 163: 1-22

Bunbury J M, Hall L, Anderson G J, Stannard A, 2001. The determination of fault movement history from the interaction of local drainage with volcanic epidsodes. *Geol Mag*, 138: 185-192

Caliro S, Chiodini G, Galluzzo D, Granieri D, La Rocca M, Saccorotti G, Ventura G, 2005. Recent study of Nisyros volcano (Greece) inferred from structural, geochemical and seismological data. *Bull Volc*, 67: 358-369

Campos Venuti M, Rossi P L, 1996. Depositional facies in the Fyriplaka rhyolitic tuff ring, Milos Island (Cyclades, Greece). *Acta Vulc*, 8: 173-190

Cebria J M, Lopez-Ruiz J, Doblas M, Oyarzun R, Hertogen J, Benito R, 2000. Geochemistry of the Quaternary alkali basalts of Garrotxa (NE Volcanic Province, Spain): a case of double enrichment of the mantle lithosphere. *J Volc Geotherm Res*, 102: 217-235

D'Alessandro W, Brusca L, Kyriakopoulos K, Michas G, Papadakis G, 2008. Methana, the westernmost active volcanic system of the south Aegean arc (Greece): insight from fluids geochemistry. *J Volc Geotherm Res*, 178: 818-828

de Goer A, Boivin P, Camus G, Gourgaud A, Kieffer G, Mergoil J, Vincent P M, 1991. Volcanologie de la Chaine des Puys. *Paris: Inst Geog Natl*, 127 p and 1:25,000 geol map

Degens E T, Wong H K, Kempe S, Kurtman F, 1984. A geological study of Lake Van, eastern Turkey. *Geol Rundschau*, 73: 701-734

Deniel C, Aydar E, Gourgaud A, 1998. The Hasan Dagi stratovolcano (Central Anatolia, Turkey): evolution from calc-alkaline to alkaline magmatism in a collision zone. *J Volc Geotherm Res*, 87: 275-302

Develle A-L, Williamson D, Gasse F, WAtler-Simonnet W, 2009. Early Holocene volcanic ash fallout in the Yammouneh lacustric basin (Lebanon): tephrochronological implications for the Near East. *J Volc Geotherm Res*, 186: 416-425

Di Paola G M, 1974. Volcanology and Petrology of Nisyros Island (Dodecanese, Greece). *Bull Volc*, 38: 944-987

Djanelidze C P, 1975. On the middle Holocene age of the last eruption of Kazbek volcano. *Geomorphologia*, 2: 75-77

Dominey-Howes D, 2004. A re-analysis of the Late Bronze Age eruption and tsunami of Santorini, Greece, and the implications for the volcano-tsunami hazard. *J Volc Geotherm Res*, 130: 107-132

Druitt T H, Brenchley P J, Gokten Y E, Francaviglia V, 1995. Late Quaternary rhyolitic eruptions from Acigol Complex, central Turkey. *J Geol Soc London*, 152: 655-667

Druitt T H, Edwards L, Mellors R M, Pyle D M, Sparks R S J, Lanphere M, Davies M, Barreirio B, 1999. Santorini volcano. *Geol Soc London Mem*, 19: 1-165 and 1:20,000 geol map

Druitt T H, Francaviglia V, 1992. Caldera formation on Santorini and the physiography of the islands in the late Bronze age. *Bull Volc*, 54: 484-493

Druitt T H, Mellors R A, Pyle D M, Sparks R S J, 1989. Explosive volcanism on Santorini, Greece. *Geol Mag*, 126: 95-126

Ercan T, Oztunali O, 1982. Characteristic features and "base surges" bed forms of Kula volcanics. *Bull Geol Soc Turkey*, 25: 117-125 (in Turkish with English abs)

Feraud J, Ozkocak O, 1993. Les volcans actifs de Turquie: guide geologique et itineraires de'excursions. *L'Assoc Volc Europeenne (LAVE)*, 2: 1-82

Fouque F, 1879. Santorini et ses Eruptions. Masson G (ed), Libraire l'Academie de Medicine, Paris, 440 p (English translation by A R McBirney published by Johns Hopkins Univ Press, 1998)

Francalanci L, Varekamp J C, Vougioukalakis G, Defant M J, Innocenti F, Manetti P, 1995. Crystal retention, fractionation and crustal assimilation in a convecting magma chamber, Nisyros volcano, Greece. *Bull Volc*, 56: 601-620

Friedrich W L, 2000. *Fire in the Sea, The Santorini Volcano: Natural History and the Legend of Atlantis*. London: Cambridge Univ Press, 258 p

Friedrich W L, Kromer B, Friedrich M, Heinemeier J, Pfeiffer T, Talamo S, 2006. Santorini eruption radiocarbon dated to 1627-1600 B.C. *Science*, 312: 548

Froger J-L, Lenat J-F, Chorowicz J, Le Pennec J-L, Bourdier J-L, Kose O, Zimitoglu O, Gundogdu N M, Gourgaud A, 1998. Hidden calderas evidenced by multisource geophysical data; an example of Cappadocian calderas, central Anatolia. *J Volc Geotherm Res*, 85: 99-128

Fytikas M, Innocenti F, Kolios N, Manetti P, Mazzuoli R, Poli G, Rita F, Villari L, 1986. Volcanology and petrology of volcanic products from the island of Milos and neighbouring islets. *J Volc Geotherm Res*, 28: 297-318

Fytikas M, Innocenti F, Manetti P, Mazzuoli R, Peccerillo A, Villari L, 1984. Tertiary to Quaternary evolution of volcanism in the Aegean region. *In*: Dixon J E and Robertson A H F (eds) *The Geological Evolution of the Eastern Mediterranean*, Geol Soc London Spec Pub 17: 687-701

Fytikas M, Kolios N, Vougioukalakis G, 1990. Post-Minoan volcanic activity of the Santorini volcano: volcanic hazard and risk, forecasting possibilities. *In*: Hardy D (ed) *Thera and the Aegean World III*, London: Thera Foundation, 2: 183-198

Gencalioglu-Kuscu G, Atilla C, Cas R A F, Kuscu I, 2007. Base surge deposits, eruption history, and depositional processes of a wet phreatomagmatic volcano in Central Anatolia (Cora Maar). *J Volc Geotherm Res*, 159: 198-209

Georgalas G C, 1962. Greece. *Catalog of Active Volcanoes of the World and Solfatara Fields*, Rome: IAVCEI, 12: 1-40 ***(regional reference)***

Gertisser R, Preece K, Keller J, 2009. The plinian Lower Pumice 2 eruption, Santorini, Greece: magma evolution and volatile behavior. *J Volc Geotherm Res*, 186: 387-406

Geunet P, 1986. Datation par l'analyse pollinique de l'explosion des volcans du groupe Pavin (Besse-en-Chandesse, Puy-de-Dome, France). *11 Reun Ann Sci Terre, Clermont-Ferrand, Ed Soc Geol France*, p 85

Gonzalez Cardenas E, Gosalvez Rey R U, Escobar Lahoz E, Becerra Ramirez R, 2007. Condiciones medioambientales en el Holoceno medio del Campo de Calatrava (Ciudad Real, Espana): resultados preliminares. *Actas Cong Nac Biogeogr*, in press

Gorshkov G S, 1966. The structure of Aragatz volcano and its ignimbrites. *In*: Cook E F (ed) *Tuff Lavas and Ignimbrites, a Survey of Soviet Studies*, New York: Elsevier, 212 p

Guenet P, 1986. Datation par l'analyse pollinique de l'explosion des volcans du groupe du Pavin (Besse-en-Chandesse, Puy-de-Dome, France). *11eme Reunion Sci Terre, Clermont-Ferrand, Soc Geol France*, p 85

Guerin G, 1989. La thermoluminescence des plagioclases, methode de datation du volcanisme. Application au domaine volcanique Francais: Chaine des Puys, Monts-Dore, Cezallier, Bas-Vivarais. *Unpublished PhD thesis*, Univ Pierre et Marie Curie, 253 p

Guner Y, 1984. Geology, geomorphology and evolution of the Nemrut volcano. *Jeomorfoloji Dergisi*, 12: 23-65 (in Turkish with English abs)

Hardy D (ed), 1990. *Thera and the Aegean World III*. London: Thera Foundation

Haroutiunian R A, 2006. The historical volcanoes of Armenia and adjacent areas revisited. *J Volc Geotherm Res*, 155: 334-337

Hedervari P, 1971. Energetical calculations concerning the Minoan eruption of Santorini. *In*: Kaloyeropoyloy A (ed) *Acta 1st Internatl Sci Cong on the Volcano of Thera*, Athens: Arch Serv Greece, p 257-276

Heiken G, McCoy F, 1984. Caldera development during the Minoan eruption, Thira, Cyclades Greece. *J Geophys Res*, 89: 8441-8462

Hetier J M, Guillet B, Brousse R, Delibrias G, Maury R C, 1983. 14-C dating of buried soils in the volcanic Chaine des Puys (France). *Bull Volc*, 46: 193-202

Higgins M D, 1996. Magma dynamics beneath Kameni volcano, Thera, Greece, as revealed by crystal size and shape measurements. *J Volc Geotherm Res*, 70: 37-48

Holness M B, Bunbury J M, 2006. Insights into continental rift-related magma chambers: cognate nodules from the Kula volcanic province, western Turkey. *J Volc Geotherm Res*, 153: 241-261

Innocenti F, Mazzuoli R, Pasquare G, Radicati di Brozolo F, Villari L, 1975. The Neogene calcalkaline volcanism of central Anatolia: geochronological data on the Kayseri-Nigde area. *Geol Mag*, 112: 349-360

Innocenti F, Mazzuoli R, Pasquare G, Radicati di Brozolo F, Villari L, 1982. Tertiary and Quaternary volcanism of the Erzurum-Kars area (eastern Turkey): geochronological data and geodynamic evolution. *J Volc Geotherm Res*, 13: 223-240

Innocenti F, Mazzuoli R, Pasquare G, Serri G, Villari L, 1980. Geology of the volcanic area north of Lake Van (Turkey). *Geol Rund*, 69: 292-323

Juvigne E, Bastin B, Beaulieu J L de, Etlicher M, Gewelt M, Gilot E, Goeury C, Janssen C R, Milcamps V, Van Leeuwen J, 1990. Tephrostratigraphy of the late glacial and the Holocene of the French Massif Central based on investigations in peat-bogs. *IAVCEI 1990 Internatl Volc Cong, Mainz, Abs*, (unpaginated)

Kaloyeropoyloy A (ed), 1971. *Acta of the 1st International Science Congress on the Volcano of Thera, held in Greece, 15th-23rd September, 1969*. Athens: Arch Serv Greece, 436 p

Karakhanian A, Djrbashian R, Trifonov V, Philip H, Arakelian S, Avagian A, 2002. Holocene-historical volcanism and active faults as natural risk factors for Armenia and adjacent countries. *J Volc Geotherm Res*, 113: 319-344

Karakhanian A, Jrbashyan R, Trifonov V, Philip H, Arakelian S, Avagyan A, Baghdassaryan H, Davtian V, 2006. Historical volcanoes of Armenia and adjacent areas: what is revisited? *J Volc Geotherm Res*, 155: 338-345

Karakhanian A, Jrbashyan R, Trifonov V, Philip H, Arakelian S, Avagyan A, Baghdassaryan H, Davtian V, Ghoukassyan Y, 2003. Volcanic hazards in the region of the Armenian nuclear power plant. *J Volc Geotherm Res*, 126: 31-62

Keller J, 1971. The major volcanic events in recent eastern Mediterranean volcanism and their bearing on the problem of Santorini ash layers. *In*: Kaloyeropoyloy A (ed) *Acta 1st Internatl Sci Cong on the Volcano of Thera*, Athens: Arch Serv Greece, p 152-169

Keller J, 1974. Quaternary maar volcanism near Karapinar in central Anatolia. *Bull Volc*, 38: 378-396

Keller J, 1980. The island of Vulcano. *Soc Italiana Min Petr*, 36: 368-413

Keller J, 1982. Mediterranean Island Arcs. *In*: Thorpe R S (ed) *Andesites*, New York: John Wiley Sons, p 307-326

Keller J, Rehren T, Stadlbauer E, 1990. Explosive volcanism in the Hellenic arc: a summary and review. *In*: Hardy D (ed) *Thera and the Aegean World III*, London: Thera Foundation, 2: 13-26

Keyser M, Ritter J R R, Jordan M, 2002. 3D shear-wave velocity structure of the Eifel plume, Germany. *Earth Planet Sci Lett*, 203: 59-82

Krafft M, 1974. *Guide des Volcans d'Europe*. Neuchatel: Delachaux & Niestle, 412 p ***(regional reference)***

Kurkcuoglu B, Sen E, Aydar E, Gourgaud A, Gundogdu N, 1998. Geochemical approach to magmatic evolution of Mt. Erciyes stratovolcano, central Anatolia, Turkey. *J Volc Geotherm Res*, 85: 473-494

Kuzucuoglu C, Pastre J-F, Black S, Ercan T, Fontugne M, Guillou H, Hatte C, Karabiyikoglu M, Orth P, Turkecan A, 1998. Identification and dating of tephra layers from Quaternary sedimentary sequences of Inner Anatolia, Turkey. *J Volc Geotherm Res*, 85: 153-172

Lagios E, Sakkas V, Parcharidis I, Dietrich V, 2005. Ground deformation of Nisyros volcano (Greece) for the period 1995-2002: results from DInSAR and DGPS observations. *Bull Volc*, 68: 201-214

Lambert R S J, Holland J G, Owen P F, 1974. Chemical petrology of a suite of calc-alkaline lavas from Mount Ararat, Turkey. *J Geol*, 82: 419-438

Limburg E M, Varekamp J C, 1991. Young pumice deposits on Nisyros, Greece. *Bull Volc*, 54: 68-77

Lopez-Ruiz J, Maria Cebria J, Doblas M, 2002. Cenozoic volcanism I: the Iberian peninsula. *In*: Gibbons W, Moreno T (eds) *The Geology of Spain*, Geol Soc London, 649 p

Lorenz V, Buchel G, 1978. Phreatomagmatische Vulkane in der Sudlichen Westeifel, Ihr Alter und Ihre Beziehung zum Talnetz (abs). *Nachrichten Deut Geol Gesellschaft*, 19: 30

Mallarach J M, 1985. Geologic map of the Olot volcanic zone-lithology and geomorphology. *Realitacio Cartografica*, 1:250,000 geol map

Manning S W, 1990. *The eruption of Thera; date and implications*. *In*: Thera and the Aegean world, Hardy D A, Renfrew A C (ed), London: Thera Foundation, v 3, p 1-29

Manning S W, Ramsey C B, Kutschera W, Higham T, Kromer B, Steier P, Wild E M, 2006. Chronology for the Aegean Late Bronze Age 1700-1400 B.C. *Science*, 312: 565-569

Marini L, Principe C, Chiodini G, Cioni R, Fytikas M, Marinelli G, 1993. Hydrothermal eruptions of Nisyros (Dodecanese, Greece). Past events and present hazard. *J Volc Geotherm Res*, 56: 71-94

McCoy F W, Heiken G, 2000. The late-Bronze age explosive eruption of Thera (Santorini), Greece: regional and local effects. *In*: McCoy F W, Heiken G (eds), *Volcanic Hazards and Disasters in Human Antiquity*, *Geol Soc Amer Spec Pap*, 345: 43-70

Meece S, 2006. A bird's eye view - of a leopard's spots, The Catalhoyuk 'map' and the development of cartographic representation in prehistory. *Anatolian Studies*, 56: 1-16

Melekestsev I V, Miller T P, 1997. On the origin of the 1645 B.C. oxygen peak in the Greenland ice sheet. *Volc Seism*, 19: 163-166 (English translation)

Mellaart J, 1967. *Catal Huyuk a Neolithic Town in Anatolia*. New York: McGraw Hill, 232 p

Mellaart J, 1993. Descriptions (picturales) d'eruptions recentes du Hasan Dagi par les hommes du neolithique a Catal Hoyuk. *L'Assoc Volc Europeenne (LAVE)*, 42: 17-30

Mertes H, Schmincke H-U, 1983. Age distribution of volcanoes in the West-Eifel. *Neues Jahrb Geol Palaont Monatsh*, 166: 260-293

Mrlina J, Kampf H, Kroner C, Mingram J, Stebich M, Brauer A, Geissler W H, Kallmeyer J, Matthes H, Seidl M, 2009. Discovery of the first Quaternary maar in the Bohemian Massif, Central Europe, based on combined geophysical and geological surveys. *J Volc Geotherm Res*, 182: 97-112

Neumann van Padang M, 1971. Two catastrophic eruptions in Indonesia, comparable with the Plinian outburst of the volcano of Thera (Santorini) in Minoan time. *In*: Kaloyeropoyloy A (ed) *Acta 1st Internatl Sci Cong on the Volcano of Thera*, Athens: Arch Serv Greece, p 51-63

Ozpeker I, 1973. Volcanological evolution of Nemrut Dagi. *4th Symp Mech Sci Res Center Turkey*, p 1-17 (in Turkish)

Pallidino D M, Simei S, Kyriakopoulos K, 2008. On magma fragmentation by conduit shear stress: evidence from Kos Plateau Tuff, Aegean volcanic arc. *J Volc Geotherm Res*, 178: 807-817

Pasquare G, 1968. Geology of the Cenozoic volcanic area of Central Anatolia. *Roma Accad Nazionale Lincei Mem*, 9: 55-204

Pe-Piper G, Piper D J W, Perissoratis C, 2005. Neotectonics and the Kos Plateau Tuff eruption of 161 ka, South Aegean arc. *J Volc Geotherm Res*, 139: 315-338

Pearce J A, Bender J F, de Long S E, Kidd W S F, Low P J, Guner Y, Saroglu F, Yilmaz Y, Moorbath S, Mitchell J G, 1990. Genesis of collision volcanism in eastern Anatolia, Turkey. *J Volc Geotherm Res*, 44: 184-229

Pelletier H, Delibrias G, Labeyrie J, Perquis M T, Rudel A, 1959. Mesure de l'age d'une des coulees volcaniques issues du Puy de la Vache (Puy de Dome) par la methode du carbone 14. *CR Acad Sci Paris, Series-D*, 214: 2221

Pfeiffer T, 2001. Vent development during the Minoan eruption (1640 BC) of Santorini, Greece, as suggested by ballistic blocks. *J Volc Geotherm Res*, 106: 229-242

Platevoet B, Scaillet S, Guillou H, Blamart D, Nomade S, Massault M, Poisson A, Elitok O, Ozgur N, Yagmurlu F, Yilmaz K, 2008. Pleistocene eruptive chronology of the Golcuk volcano, Ispata Angle, Turkey. *Quaternaire*, 19: 147-156

Poka T, 1988. Neogene and Quaternary volcanism of the Carpathian-Pannonian region: changes in chemical composition and its relationship to basin formation. *Amer Assoc Petrol Geol Mem*, 45: 257-277

Pyle D M, 1990. New estimates for the volume of the Minoan eruption. *In*: Hardy D (ed) *Thera and the Aegean World III*, London: Thera Foundation, 2: 113-121

Ritter J R R, Jordan M, Christensen U R, Achauer U, 2000. A mantle plume below the Eifel volcanic fields, Germany. *Earth Planet Sci Lett*, 186: 7-14

Rutten M G, 1969. *The Geology of Western Europe*. Amsterdam: Elsevier, 520 p

Sachpazi M, Kontoes C, Voulgaris N, Laigle M, Vougioukalakis G, Sikioti O, Stavrakakis G, Baskoutas J, Kalogeras J, Lepine J C, 2002. Seismological and SAR signature of unrest at Nisyros caldera, Greece. *J Volc Geotherm Res*, 116: 19-33

Schmincke H-U, Park C, Harms E, 1999. Evolution and environmental impacts of the eruption of Laacher See volcano (Germany) 12,900 a BP. *Quat Internatl*, 61: 61-72

Sen E, Kurkcuoglu B, Aydar E, Gourgaud A, Vincent P M, 2003. Volcanological evolution of Mount Erciyes stratovolcao and origin of the Valibaba Tepe ignimbrite (Central Anatolia, Turkey). *J Volc Geotherm Res*, 125: 225-246

Shaw C S J, 2004. The temporal evolution of three magmatic systems in the West Eifel volcanic field, Germany. *J Volc Geotherm Res*, 131: 213-240

Sigurdsson H, Carey S, Alexandri M, Vougioukalaki G, Croff K, Roman C, Sakellariou D, Angagnostsu C, Rousakis G, Ioakim C, Gogou A, Ballas D, Misaridis T, Nomikou P, 2006. Marine investigations of Greece's Santorini volcanic field. *Eos, Trans Amer Geophys Union*, 87: 337, 342

Sigurdsson H, Carey S, Devine J D, 1990. Assessment of mass, dynamics and environmental effects of the Minoan eruption of Santorini volcano. *In*: Hardy D (ed) *Thera and the Aegean World III*, London: Thera Foundation, 2: 100-112

Stewart A L, McPhie J, 2006. Facies architecture and Late Pliocene - Pleistocene evolution of a felsic volcanic island, Milos, Greece. *Bull Volc*, 68: 703-726

Stothers R B, Rampino M R, 1983. Volcanic eruptions in the Mediterranean before AD 630 from written and archaeological sources. *J Geophys Res*, 88: 6357-6371

Sviatlovsky A E, 1959. *Atlas of Volcanoes of the Soviet Union*. Moscow: Akad Nauk SSSR, 170 p (in Russian with English summary) ***(regional reference)***

Szakacs A, Harangi S, 2005. Volcanic hazards in the Carpathian-Pannonian region: a discussion. *European Geosci Union, Geophys Res Abstr*, 7: 07913

Taddeucci J, Wohletz K H, 2001. Temporal evolution of the Minoan eruption (Santorini, Greece), as recorded by its Plinian fall deposit and interlayered ash flow beds. *J Volc Geotherm Res*, 109: 299-317

Tchalenko J S, 1977. A reconnaissance of the seismicity and tectonics at the northern border of the Arabian Plate (Lake Van region). *Rev Geog Phys Geol Dynam*, 19: 189-208

Tibaldi A, Pasquare F A, Papanikolaou D, Nomikou P, 2008. Discovery of a huge sector collapse at the Nisyros volcano, Greece, by on-land and offshore geological-structure data. *J Volc Geotherm Res*, 177: 485-499

Toprak V, 1998. Vent distribution and its relation to regional tectonics, Cappadocian Volcanics, Turkey. *J Volc Geotherm Res*, 85: 55-67

Traineau H, Dalabakis P, 1989. Mise en evidence d'une eruption phreatique historique sur l'ile de Milos (Grece). *Compte Rendus Acad Sci Paris*, Ser II, 308: 247-252

Ulusoy I, Labazuy P, Aydar E, Ersoy O, Cubukcu E, 2008. Structure of the Nemrut caldera (Eastern Anatolia, Turkey) and associated hydrothermal fluid circulation. *J Volc Geotherm Res*, 174: 269-283

Umran Dogan A, Dogan M, Kilinc A, Locke D, 2008. An isobaric-isenthalpic magma mixing model for the Hasan Dagi volcano, Central Anatolia, Turkey. *Bull Volc*, 70: 797-804

Valsami-Jones E, Baltatzis E, Bailey E H, Boyce A J, Alexander J L, Magganas A, Anderson L, Waldron S, Ragnarsdottir K V, 2005. The geochemistry of fluids from an active shallow submarine hydrothermal system: Milos Island, Hellenic volcanic arc. *J Volc Geotherm Res*, 148: 130-151

Vespa M, Keller J, Gertisser R, 2006. Interplinian explosive activity of Santorini volcano (Greece) during the past 150,000 years. *J Volc Geotherm Res*, 153: 262-286

Vink B W, Schuilling R D, 1971. Estimates of the various types of energy released by the eruption of Thera, Greece, at about 1400 B.C. *In*: Kaloyeropoyloy A (ed) *Acta 1st Internatl Sci Cong on the Volcano of Thera*, Athens: Arch Serv Greece, p 288-292

Vinkler A P, Harangi S, Ntaflos T, Szakacs A, 2005. Geochemistry of the 20-30 ka dacitic volcanic products from the Ciomadul volcano, Carpathian-Pannonian region - petrogenetic implications. *European Geosci Union, Geophys Res Abstr*, 7: 07820

Vougioukalakis G, 1996. Santorini, Guide to "The Volcano." Institute for the Study and Monitoring of the Santorini Volcano, 82 p

Washington H S, 1924. Notes on the Solfatara of Sousaki (Greece), a recent eruption at Methana (Greece), and recent Maccalube at Vulcano. *J Geol*, 32: 460-462

Watkins N D, Sparks R S J, Sigurdsson H, Huang T C, Federman A, Carey S, Ninkovich D, 1978. Volume and extent of the Minoan tephra from Santorini volcano: new evidence from deep-sea sediment cores. *Nature*, 271: 122-126

Westaway R, Pringle M, Yurtmen S, Demir T, Bridgeland D, Rowbotham G, Maddy D, 2004. Pliocene and Quaternary regional uplift in western Turkey: the Gediz River terrace staircase and the volcanism at Kula. *Tectonophysics*, 391: 121-169

Yilmaz Y, 1990. Comparison of young volcanic associations of western and eastern Anatolia formed under a compressional regime: a review. *J Volc Geotherm Res*, 44: 69-87

Yilmaz Y, Guner Y, Saroglu F, 1998. Geology of the Quaternary volcanic centers of the east Anatolia. *J Volc Geotherm Res*, 85: 173-210

Zolitschka B, Negendank J F W, Lottermoser B G, 1995. Sedimentological proof and dating of the early Holocene volcanic eruption of Ulmener Maar (Vulkaneifel, Germany). *Geol Rundschau*, 84: 213-219

AFRICA: EAST & CENTRAL (0201-03)

Acocella V, Korme T, Salvini F, Funiciello R, 2003. Elliptic calderas in the Ethiopian Rift: control of pre-existing structures. *J Volc Geotherm Res*, 119: 189-203

Audin J, Vellutini P J, Coulon C, Piguet P, Vincent J, 1990. The 1928-1929 eruption of Kammourta volcano - evidence of tectono-magmatic activity in the Manda-Inakir rift and comparison with the Asal Rift, Afar depression, Republic of Djibuti. *Bull Volc*, 52: 551-561

Bailey K, Lloyd F, Kearns S, Stoppa F, Eby N, Woolley A, 2005. Melilitite at Fort Portal, Uganda: another dimension to the carbonate volcanism. *Lithos*, 85: 15-25

Baker B H, 1975. Geology and geochemistry of the Ol Doinyo Nyokie trachyte ignimbrite vent complex, south Kenya rift valley. *Bull Volc*, 39: 420-440

Barberi F, Ferrara G, Santacroce R, Treuil M, Varet J, 1975. A transitional basalt-pantellerite sequence of fractional crystallization, the Boina Centre (Afar Rift, Ethiopia). *J Petr*, 16: 22-56

Barberi F, Varet J, 1970. The Erta Ale volcanic range (Danakill depression, Northern Afar, Ethiopia). *Bull Volc*, 34: 848-917

Barker D S, Nixon P H, 1989. High-Ca, low-alkali carbonatite volcanism at Fort Portal, Uganda. *Contr Mineral Petr*, 103: 166-177

Bell K, Dawson J B, 1995. Nd and Sr isotope systematics of the active carbonatite volcano, Ol Doinyo Lengai. *In*: Bell K, Keller J (eds), *Carbonatite Volcanism, Oldoinyo Lengai and the Petrogenesis of Natrocarbonatites*, Berlin: Springer-Verlag, p. 100-112

Berg E, 1959. Volcanic eruption in Belgian Congo. *J Geophys Res*, 64: 580

Berhe S M, 1978. Geological map of the Nazret area. *Ethiopian Mapping Agency*, 1:250,000

Bizouard H, Di Paola G M, 1978. Minerology of the Tullu Mose active volcano area (Arussi: Ethiopian Rift Valley). *In*: Neuman E-R and Ramberg I B (eds) *Petrology and Geochemistry of Continental Rifts*, Dordrecht, Holland: D Reidel, p 87-92

Bloomer S H, Curtis P C, Karson J A, 1989. Geochemical variation of Quaternary basaltic volcanoes in the Turkana Rift, northern Kenya. *J African Earth Sci*, 8: 511-532

Brotzu P, Morbidelli L, Piccirillo E M, Traversa G, 1980. Volcanological and magmatological evidence of the Boseti volcanic complex (Main Eithiopian Rift). *In*: Geodynamic Evolution of the Afro-Arabian Rift System, Roma: Accademia Nazionale dei Lincei, p 317-365

Brousse R, Caron J-P, Kampunzu A B, Lubala R T, Musengie M K, Vellutini P-J, 1981. Eruption et nature de la lave du Gasenyi: un nouveau volcan (Janvier-Fevrier 1980) au flanc nord du Nyamulagira (Kivu, Zaire). *CR Acad Sci Paris*, Ser-II, 292: 1413-1416

Brown F H, Carmichael I S E, 1969. Quaternary volcanics of the Lake Rudolf Region, 1. The Korath Range. *Lithos*, 2: 239-260

Brown F H, Carmichael I S E, 1971. Quaternary volcanoes of the Lake Rudolf region: II. The lavas of North Island, South Island and The Barrier. *Lithos*, 4: 305-323

Burgi P-Y, Caillet M, Haefeli S, 2002. Field measurements at Erta'Ale lava lake, Ethiopia. *Bull Volc*, 64: 472-485

Burt M L, Wadge G, Scott W A, 1994. Simple stochastic modelling of the eruption history of a basaltic volcano: Nyamuragira, Zaire. *Bull Volc*, 56: 87-97

CNR-CNRS, 1975. *Geological Maps of Afar: 1, Northern Afar (1971); 2, Central and Southern Afar* (1975). La Celle St Cloud, France: Geotechnip

CNR-CNRS Afar Team, 1973. Geology of northern Afar (Ethiopia). *Rev Geog Phys Geol Dynam*, 15: 443-490

Campbell Smith W, 1938. Petrographic description of volcanic rocks from Turkana, Kenya Colony, with notes on their field occurrence from the manscript of Mr. A.M. Champion. *Quart J Geol Soc London*, 94: 528-531

Cattermole P, 1982. Meru - A rift valley giant. *Volcano News*, 11: 1-3

Cavendish H S H, 1898. Through Somaliland and around and south of Lake Rudolf. *Geog Jour*, 11: 372-293

Champion A M, 1935. Teleki's volcano and the lava fields at the southern end of Lake Rudolf. *Geog Jour*, 85: 322-341

Charsley T J, 1987a. Geology of the Laisamis area. *Rpt Mines Geol Dept Kenya*, 106: 1-70

Charsley T J, 1987b. Geology of the North Horr area. *Rpt Mines Geol Dept Kenya*, 110: 1-40

Cole J W, 1969. Gariboldi volcanic complex, Ethiopia. *Bull Volc*, 33: 566-578

Coleman R G, Fleck R J, Hedge C E, Ghent E D, 1975. The volcanic rocks of southwest Saudi Arabia and the opening of the Red Sea. *DGMR (Jeddah) Bull*, 22: D1-D30

Combe A D, 1937. The Katunga volcano, southwest Uganda. *Geol Mag*, 74: 190-200

Davidson A, 1983. The Omo River project - reconnaissance geology and geochemistry of parts of Ilubabor, Kefa, Gemu Gofa, and Sidamo, Ethiopia. *Ethiopian Inst Geol Surv Bull*, 2: 1-89

Dawson J B, 1962. The geology of Oldoinyo Lengai. *Bull Volc*, 24: 349-387

Dawson J B, 1992. Neogene tectonics and volcanicity in the North Tanzania sector of the Gregory Rift Valley: contrasts with the Kenya sector. *Tectonophysics*, 204: 81-92

Dawson J B, 1994. Quaternary kimberlitic volcanism on the Tanzania craton. *Contr Mineral Petr*, 116: 473-485

Dawson J B, Bowden P, Clark G C, 1968. Activity of the carbonatite volcano Oldoinyo Lengai, 1966. *Geol Rundschau*, 57: 865-879

Dawson J B, Keller J, Nyamweru C, 1995. Historic and recent eruptive activity of Oldoinyo Lengai. *In*: Bell K, Keller J (eds), *Carbonatite Volcanism, Oldoinyo Lengai and the Petrogenesis of Natrocarbonatites*, Berlin: Springer-Verlag, p. 4-22

Dawson J B, Pinkerton H, Pyle D M, Nyamweru C, 1994. June 1993 eruption of Oldoinyo Lengai, Tanzania: exceptionally viscous and large carbonatite lava flows and evidence for coexisting silicate and carbonate magmas. *Geology*, 22: 799-802

De Fino M, La Volpe L, Lirer L, 1978. Geology and volcanology of the Edd-Bahar Assoli area (Ethiopia). *Bull Volc*, 41: 32-42

De Fino M, La Volpe L, Lirer L, Varet J, 1973. Geology and petrology of Manda-Inakir range and Moussa Alli volcano, central eastern Afar (Ethiopia and TFAI). *Rev Geog Phys Geol Dynam*, 15: 373-386

de Mulder M, 1985. The Karisimbi volcano. *Annales Musee Roy Afrique Central Ser 8 Sci Geol*, 90: 1-101

Delibrias G, Marinelli G, Stieltjes L, 1975. Spreading rate of the Asal Rift: A geological approach. *In*: Pilger A and Rosler A (eds) *Afar Depression of Ethiopia*, Inter-Union Comm Geodynam Sci Rpt, 14: 214-221, Stuttgart: E Schweizerbart'sche

Demant A, Lestrade P, Lubala R T, Kampunzu A B, Durieux J, 1994. Volcanological and petrological evolution of Nyiragongo volcano, Virunga volcanic field, Zaire. *Bull Volc*, 56: 47-61

Denaeyer M E, 1969. Nouvelles donnees lithologiques sur les volcans actifs des Virunga (Afrique centrale). *Bull Volc*, 33: 1128-1144

Di Paola G M, 1971. Geology of the Corbetti Caldera (main Ethiopian rift valley). *Bull Volc*, 35: 497-506

Di Paola G M, 1972. The Ethiopian Rift Valley (between 7° 00' and 8° 40' lat north). *Bull Volc*, 36: 517-560

Dodson R G, 1963. Geology of the South Horr area. *Geol Surv Kenya Rpt*, 60: 1-53

Downie C, Wilkinson P, 1972. *The Geology of Kilimanjaro*. England: Univ Sheffield Dept Geol, 253 p

Duffield W A, Bullen T D, Clynne M A, Fournier R O, Janik C J, Lanphere M A, Lowenstern J, Smith J G, W/Giorgis L, Kahsai G, W/Mariam K, Tesfai T, 1997. Geothermal potential of the Alid volcanic center, Danakil Depression, Eritrea. *U S Geol Surv Open-File Rpt*, 97-291: 1-62

Dunkley P N, Smith M, Allen D A, Darling W G, 1993. The geothermal activity and geology of the northern sector of the Kenya Rift Valley. *Brit Geol Surv Res Rpt*, SC/93/1: 1-185

Ebinger C J, Deino A L, Drake R E, Tesha A L, 1989. Chronology of volcanism and rift basin propagation: Rungwe volcanic province, East Africa. *J Geophys Res*, 94: 15,785-15,803

Ebinger C J, Yemane T, WoldeGabriel G, Aronson J L, Walter R C, 1993. Late Eocene-Recent volcanism and faulting the southern main Ethiopian rift. *J Geol Soc London*, 150: 99-108

Eckhardt S, Prata A J, Seibert P, Stebel K, Stohl A, 2008. Estimation of the vertical profile of sulfur dioxide injection into the atmosphere by a volcanic eruption using satellite column measurements and inverse transport modeling. *Atmos Chem Phys Discuss*, 8: 3761-3805

Emilia D A, Last B J, Wood C A, Dakin F M, 1976-77. Geophysics and geology of an explosion crater in the Ethiopian Rift Valley. *Bull Volc*, 40: 133-140

Favalli M, Chirico G D, Papale P, Pareschi M T, Boschi E, 2009. Lava flow hazard at Nyiragongo volcano, D.R.C. 1. Model calibration and hazard mapping. *Bull Volc*, 71: 363-374

Ferguson A J D, Harbott B J, 1982. Geographical, physical and chemical aspects of Lake Turkana. *In*: Hopson A J (ed) *Lake Turkana: a Report on the Findings of the Lake Turkana Project 1972-75*, London: Rpt Overseas Devel Admin, p 1-107

Ferguson A K, Cundari A, 1975. Petrological aspects and evolution of the leucite bearing lavas from Bufumbira, south west Uganda. *Contr Mineral Petr*, 50: 25-46

Fontijn K, Ernst G G, Elburg M A, Williamson D, Jacobs P, 2009. Recent explosive eruptions in the Rungwe volcanic province, Tanzania. *Eos, Trans Amer Geophys Union*, 89: Fall Meet Suppl, abstr V11G-07

Francis P W, Rothery D A, 1987. Using the Landsat Thematic Mapper to detect and monitor active volcanoes: an example from Lascar volcano, northern Chile. *Geology*, 15: 614-617

Gass I G, Mallick D I J, Cox K G, 1973. Volcanic islands of the Red Sea. *J Geol Soc London*, 129: 275-310

Gianelli G, Teklemariam M, 1993. Water-rock interaction process in the Aluto-Langano geothermal field (Ethiopia). *J Volc Geotherm Res*, 56: 429-445

Gibson I L, 1967. Preliminary account of the volcanic geology of Fantale, Shoa, Ethiopia. *Bull Geophys Observ Addis Ababa*, 10: 59-68

Gibson I L, 1969. The structure and volcanic geology of an axial portion of the main Ethiopian Rift. *Tectonophysics*, 8: 561-565

Gouin P, 1979. Earthquake history of Ethiopia and the Horn of Africa. *Internatl Devel Res Centre (Canada)*, 118E: 259

Guest N J, 1956. The volcanic activity of Oldonyo l'Engai, 1954. *Rec Geol Surv Tanganyika*, 4: 56-59

Guest N J, Leedal G P, 1953. The volcanic activity of Mt. Meru. *Tanganyika Geol Surv Div Rec*, 3: 40-47

Hackman B D, 1988. Geology of the Baringo-Laikipia area. *Rpt Mines Geol Dept Kenya*, 104: 1-79

Hackman B D, Charsley T J, Kagasi J, Key R M, Siambi W S, Wilkinson A F, 1989. Geology of the Isiolo area. *Rpt Mines Geol Dept Kenya*, 103: 1-88

Hamaguchi H (ed), 1983. *Volcanoes Nyiragongo and Nyamuragira: Geophysical Aspects*. Sendai: Tohoku Univ Fac Sci, 130 p

Harkin D A, 1960. The Rungwe volcanics at the northern end of Lake Nyasa. *Geol Surv Tanganyika Mem*, 2: 1-172

Harris A J L, Carniel R, Jones J, 2005. Identification of variable convective regimes at Erta Ale lava lake. *J Volc Geotherm Res*, 142: 207-223

Haug G H, Strecker M R, 1995. Volcano-tectonic evolution of the Chyulu Hills and implications for the regional stress field in Kenya. *Geology*, 23: 165-16

Hay R L, 1989. Holocene carbonatite nephelinite tephra deposits of Oldoinyo Lengai, Tanzania. *J Volc Geotherm Res*, 37: 77-91

Heumann A, Davies G R, 2002. U-Th disequilibrium and Rb-Sr age constraints on the magmatic evolution of peralkaline rhyolites from Kenya. *J Petr*, 43: 557-577

Hobley C W, 1906. Notes on the geography and people of the Baringo district of the East Africa Protectorate. *Geog Jour*, 28: 471-481

Hobley C W, 1918. A volcanic eruption in East Africa. *J East Africa & Uganda Nat Hist Soc*, 3: 339-342

Holmes A, 1950. Petrogenesis of katungite. *Amer Mineral*, 35: 772-792

Holmes A, Harwood H F, 1932. Petrology of the volcanic fields east and south-east of Ruwenzori, Uganda. *Quart J Geol Soc London*, 88: 370-442

Jack E M, 1913. The Bufumbiro Mountains. *Geog Jour*, 41: 532-550

Johnson R W, 1969. Volcanic geology of Mount Suswa, Kenya. *Phil Trans Roy Soc London*, 265: 383-412

Kampunzu A B, Lubala R T, Brousse R, Caron J P-H, Cluzel D, Lenoble L, Vellutini P J, 1984. Sur l'eruption du Nyamulagira de Decembre 1981 a Janvier 1982: cone et coulee du Rugarambiro (Kivu, Zaire). *Bull Volc*, 47: 79-105

Karson J A, Curtis P C, 1994. Axial Quaternary volcanic centers in the Turkana rift, N. Kenya. *J African Earth Sci*, 18: 15-35

Kasahara M, Zana N, 1988. Recent volcanism of Nyiragongo and Nyamuragira. *In*: Tanaka K (ed), *Geophysical Studies of Volcanoes Nyiragongo and Nyamuragira*, Hirosaki, Japan: Fac Sci, Hirosaki Univ, p 4-15 (in Japanese with English abs)

Kervyn M, Ernst G G J, Klaudius J, Keller J, Kervyn F, Mattsson H B, Belton F, Mbede E, Jacobs P, 2008. Voluminous lava flows at Oldoinyo Lengai in 2006: chronology of events and insights into the shallow magmatic system. *Bull Volc*, 70: 1069-1086

Key R M, 1987a. Geology of the Maralal area. *Rpt Mines Geol Dept Kenya*, 105: 1-93

Key R M, 1987b. Geology of the Marsabit area. *Rpt Mines Geol Dept Kenya*, 108: 1-42

Key R M, Rop B P, Rundle C C, 1987. The development of the late Cenozoic alkali basaltic Marsabit shield volcano, northern Kenya. *J African Earth Sci*, 6: 475-491

Key R M, Watkins R T, 1988. Geology of the Sabarei area. *Rpt Mines Geol Dept Kenya*, 111: 1-57

Krafft M, 1990. *Fuhrer zu den Virunga-Vulkanen*. Stuttgart: Ferdinand Enke, 187 p

Lahitte P, Gillot P-Y, Courtillot V, 2003a. Silicic central volcanoes as precursors to rift propagation: the Afar case. *Earth Planet Sci Lett*, 207: 103-116

Lahitte P, Gillot P-Y, Kidane T, Courtillot V, 2003b. New age constraints on the timing of volcanism in central Afar, in the presence of propagating rifts. *J Geophys Res*, 108: doi: 10.1029/2001JB001689

Le Bas M J, 1977. *Carbonatite-Nephelinite Volcanism*. New York: John Wiley, 347 p

Leat P T, 1984. Geological evolution of the trachytic caldera volcano Menengai, Kenya Rift Valley. *J Geol Soc London*, 141: 1057-1069

Leat P T, Macdonald R, Smith R L, 1984. Geochemical evolution of the Menengai Caldera volcano, Kenya. *J Geophys Res*, 89: 8571-8592

Lloyd F E, Wooley A R, Stoppa F, Eby G N, 2002. Phlogopite-biotite paragenses from the K-mafic-carbonatite effusive magmatic association of Katwe-Kikorongo, SW Uganda. *Mineral Petr*, 74: 299-322

MacKay M E, Rowland S K, Mouginis-Mark P J, Garbeil H, 1998. Thick lava flows of Karisimbi volcano, Rwanda: insight from SIR-C interferometric topography. *Bull Volc*, 60: 239-251

Macdonald R, Davies G R, Upton B G, Dunkley P N, Smith M, Leat P T, 1995. Petrogenesis of Silali volcano, Gregory Rift, Kenya. *J Geol Soc London*, 152: 703-720

Macdonald R, Navarro J M, Upton B G J, Davies G R, 1994. Strong compositional zonation in peralkaline magma: Menengai, Kenya Rift Valley. *J Volc Geotherm Res*, 60: 301-325

Marcelot G, Rancon J P, Demange J, 1985. The potassic series of Karisimbi volcano (Virunga Range, Rwanda): volcanological and petrological aspects. *J Volc Geotherm Res*, 26: 99-129

Marshall A S, Hinton R W, Macdonald R, 1998. Phenocryst flourite in peralkaline rhyolites, Olkaria, Kenya Rift Valley. *Mineral Mag*, 62: 477-486

Marshall A S, Macdonald R, Rogers N W, Fitton J G, Tindle A G, Nejbert K, Hinton R W, 2009. Fractionation of peralkaline silicic magmas: the Greater Olkaria volcanic complex, Kenya Rift Valley. *J Petr*, 50: 323-359

Mattsson H B, Vuorinen J, 2009. Emplacement and inflation of natrocarbonatitic lava flows during the March-April 2006 eruption of Oldoinyo Lengai, Tanzania. *Bull Volc*, 71: 301-311

McCall G J H, Bristow C M, 1965. An introductory account of Suswa volcano, Kenya. *Bull Volc*, 28: 333-367

McHenry L J, Mollel G F, Swisher III C C, 2008. Compositional and textural correlations between Olduvai Gorge Bed I tephra and volcanic sources in the Ngorongoro Volcanic Highlands, Tanzania. *Quat Internatl*, 178: 306-319

Mohr P A, 1961. The geology, structure, and origin of the Bishoftu explosion craters. *Bull Geophys Observ Addis Ababa*, 2: 65-101

Mohr P A, Mitchell J G, Raynolds R G H, 1980. Quaternary volcanism and faulting at O'a caldera, central Ethiopian Rift. *Bull Volc*, 43: 173-190

Mohr P A, Wood C A, 1976. Volcano Spacings and Lithospheric Attenuation in the Eastern Rift of Africa. *Earth Planet Sci Lett*, 33: 126-144

Nash W P, Carmichael I S E, Johnson R W, 1969. The mineralogy and petrology of Mount Suswa, Kenya. *J Petr*, 10: 409-439

Needham H D, Choukroune P, Cheminee J L, Le Pichon X, Francheteau J, Tapponnier P, 1976. The accreting plate boundary: Ardoukoba Rift (Northeast Africa) and the oceanic rift valley. *Earth Planet Sci Lett*, 28: 439-453

Nixon P H, 1973. Kimberlitic volcanoes in East Africa. *Overseas Geol Min Res*, 41: 119-138

Nixon P H, Hornung G, 1973. The carbonatite lavas and tuffs near Fort Portal, western Uganda. *Overseas Geol Min Res*, 41: 168-179

Nonnotte P, Guillou H, Le Gall B, Benoit M, Cotten J, Scaillet S, 2008. New K-Ar age determinations of Kilimanjaro volcano in the North Tanzanian diverging rift, East Africa. *J Volc Geotherm Res*, 173: 99-112

Nyamweru C, 1988. Activity of Ol Doinyo Lengai volcano, Tanzania, 1983-1987. *J African Earth Sci*, 7: 603-610

Nyamweru C, 1989. Report on activity in the northern crater of Ol Doinyo Lengai, 24th June to 1st July 1988. *J East Africa Nat Hist Soc and Natl Musuem*, 79: 1-15

Nyamweru C, 1990. Observations on changes in the active crater of Ol Doinyo Lengai from 1960 to 1988. *J African Earth Sci*, 11: 385-390

Nyamweru C, 1997. Changes in the crater of Oldoinyo Lengai: June 1993 - February 1997. *J African Earth Sci*, 25: 43-53

Ochieng J O, Wilkinson A F, Kagasi J, Kimomo S, 1988. Geology of the Loiyangalani area. *Rpt Mines Geol Dept Kenya*, 107: 1-53

Oppenheimer C, Francis P, 1998. Implications of longeval lava lakes for geomorphological and plutonic processes at Erta 'Ale volcano, Afar. *J Volc Geotherm Res*, 80: 101-111

Peccerillo A, Barberio M R, Yirgu G, Ayalew D, Barbieri M, Wu T W, 2003. Relationships betweem mafic and peralkaline silicic magmatism in continental rift settings: a petrological, geochemical and isotopic study of the Gedemsa volcano, Central Ethiopian Rift. *J Petr*, 44: 2003-2032

Platz T, Foley S F, Andre L, 2004. Low-pressure fractionation of the Nyiragongo volcanic rocks, Virunga Province, D.R. Congo. *J Volc Geotherm Res*, 136: 269-295

Pottier Y, 1978. Premiere eruption historique du Nyiragongo et manifestations adventives simultanees du Volcan Nyamulagira (Chaine des VIrunga - Kivu - Zaire: Dec. 76 - Jiun 77). *Mus Roy Afr Centr, Tervuren (Belg), Dept Geol Mineral, Rapp Ann 1977*, p 157-175

Pouclet A, 1975. Activites du Volcan Nyamuragira (rift ouest de l'Afrique centrale), evaluation des volumes de materiaux emis. *Bull Volc*, 39: 466-478

Pouclet A, 1977. Contribution l'etude structurale de l'aire volcanique des Virunga, rift de l'Afrique centrale. *Rev Geog Phys Geol Dynam*, 19: 115-124

Pouclet A, Villeneuve M, 1972. L'eruption du Rugarama (Mars-Mai 1971) au Volcan Nyamuragira (rep. Zaire). *Bull Volc*, 36: 200-221

Reece A W, 1955. The Bunyaruguru volcanic field. *Rec Geol Surv Dept Uganda (1953)*, p 29-47

Richard J J, 1942. Oldoinyo Lengai-the 1940-41 eruption volcanological observations in East Africa. *J East Africa & Uganda Nat Hist Soc*, 16: 89-108

Richard J J, Neumann van Padang M, 1957. Africa and the Red Sea. *Catalog of Active Volcanoes of the World and Solfatara Fields*, Rome: IAVCEI 4: 1-118 ***(regional reference)***

Rogers N W, Evans P J, Blake S, Scott S C, Hawkesworth C J, 2004. Rates and timescales of fractional crystallization from 238U-230Th-226Ra disequilibria in trachyte lavas from Longonot volcano, Kenya. *J Petr*, 45: 1747-1776

Rogers N W, James D, Kelley S P, De Mulder M, 1998. The generation of potassic lavas from the eastern Virunga province, Rwanda. *J Petr*, 39: 1223-1247

Saggerson E P, 1963. Geology of the Simba-Kibwezi area. *Geol Surv Kenya Rpt*, 58: 1-70

Sahama T G, 1978. The Nyiragongo main cone. *Musee Roy l'Afrique Centrale, Tuervuren, Belgique Annales, Ser In-8, Sci Geol*, 81: 1-88

Sampson D N, 1956. The volcanic hills at Igwisi. *Rec Geol Surv Tanganyika 1953*, p 48-53

Scott S C, 1980. The geology of Longonot volcano, Central Kenya: a question of volumes. *Phil Trans Roy Soc London*, Ser A, 296: 438-466

Simmons W C, 1930. Notes on the petrology of the Bufumbira volcanic rocks of Uganda. *Geol Mag*, 67: 491-499

Skilling I P, 1993. Incremental caldera collapse of Suswa volcano, Gregory Rift Valley, Kenya. *J Geol Soc London*, 150: 885-896

Skinner N J, Iles W, Brock A, 1975. The recent secular variation of declination and inclination in Kenya. *Earth Planet Sci Lett*, 25: 338-346

Smith M, Dunkley P N, Deino A, Williams L A J, McCall G J H, 1995. Geochronology, stratigraphy and structural evolution of Silali volcano, Gregory Rift, Kenya. *J Geol Soc London*, 152: 297-310

Spath A, Le Roex A P, Opiyo-Akech N, 2001. Plume-lithosphere interaction and the origin of continental rift-related alkaline volcanism-the Chyulu Hills volcanic province, southern Kenya. *J Petr*, 42: 765-787

Stieltjes L, 1974. Geologic map of the Asal Rift. *Bur Recherches Geol Minieres France*, 1:50,000

Stoppa F, Woolley A R, Lloyd F E, Eby N, 2000. Carbonate lapilli-bearing tuff and a dolomite carbonatite bomb from Murumuli crater, Katwe volcanic field, Uganda. *Min Mag*, 64: 641-650

Tanaka K (ed), 1988. *Geophysical Studies of Volcanoes Nyiragongo and Nyamuragira*. Hirosaki: Hirosaki Univ Fac Sci, 78 p (in Japanese with English abs)

Tazieff H, 1976-77. An exceptional eruption: Mt. Niragongo, Jan 10th, 1977. *Bull Volc*, 40: 189-200

Tazieff H, 1979. *Nyiragongo the Forbidden Volcano*. Woodbury, New York: Barrons Educational Ser, 287 p

Tazieff H, 1984. Mt Niragongo: renewed activity of the lava lake. *J Volc Geotherm Res*, 20: 267-280

Thompson A O, Dodson R G, 1963. Geology of the Naivasha area. *Geol Surv Kenya Rpt*, 55: 1-80

Tinkler K J, 1971. Statistical analysis of tectonic patterns in areal volcanism: the Bunyaruguru volcanic field in West Uganda. *Mathematical Geol*, 3: 335-355

Ueki S, 1983. Recent volcanism of Nyamuragira and Nyiragongo. *In*: Hamaguchi H (ed) *Volcanoes Nyamuragira and Nyiragongo: Geophys Aspects*, Japan: Tohoku Univ, Sendai, p 7-18

United Nations, 1973. Geology, geochemistry and hydrology of hot springs of the East African Rift system within Ethiopia. *United Nations Tech Rpt*, New York, DP/SF/UN 116: 1-220

Varet J, 1978. Geology of central and southern Afar (Ethiopia and Djibouti Republic). CNRS, Paris, 124 p

Varet M J, 1971. Sur l'activite recente de l'Erta Ale (Dankalie, Ethiopie). *CR Acad Sci Paris*, Ser-D, 272: 1964-1967

Vaughan R G, Kervyn M, Realmuto V, Abrams M, Hook S J, 2008. Satellite measurements of recent volcanic activity at Oldoinyo Lengai, Tanzania. *J Volc Geotherm Res*, 173: 196-206

Verhaeghe M, 1958. L'eruption du Volcan Mugogo an Kivu. *CR Acad Sci Paris*, Ser-D, 246: 2917-2920

Vinogradov V I, Krasnov A A, Kuleshov V N, Sulerzhitskiy L D, 1980. C13/C12 and O18/O16 ratios and C14 concentration in carbonatites of the Kaliango volcano (East Africa). *Internatl Geol Rev*, 22: 51-57

Weaver S D, 1976-77. The Quaternary caldera volcano Emuruangogolak, Kenya Rift, and the petrology of a bimodal ferrobasalt pantelleritic trachyte association. *Bull Volc*, 40: 209-230

Wiart P, Oppenheimer C, 2000. Largest known historical eruption in Africa: Dubbi volcano, Eritrea, 1861. *Geology*, 28: 291-294

Wiart P, Oppenheimer C, 2005. Large magnitude silicic volcanism in north Afar: the Nabro volcanic range and Ma'alalta volcano. *Bull Volc*, 67: 99-115

Wilkinson A F, 1988. Geology of the Allia Bay area. *Rpt Mines Geol Dept Kenya*, 109: 1-54

Wilkinson P, Mitchell J G, Cattermole P J, Downie C, 1986. Volcanic chronology of the Meru-Kilimanjaro region, northern Tanzania. *J Geol Soc London*, 143: 601-605

Williams L A J, 1970. The volcanics of the Gregory Rift Valley, East Africa. *Bull Volc*, 34: 439-465

Williams L A J, Macdonald R, Chapman G R, 1984. Late Quaternary caldera volcanoes of the Kenya Rift Valley. *J Geophys Res*, 89: 8553-8570

WoldeGabriel G, 1986. The Awasa caldera in the main Ethiopian Rift (MER). *IAVCEI 1986 Cong, New Zeal, Abs*, p 351

Wright T J, Ebinger C, Biggs J, Ayele A, Yirgu G, Keier D, Stork A, 2006. Magma-induced rift segmentation at continental rupture in the 2005 Afar dyking episode. *Nature*, doi:10.1038/nature04978

Zana N, Kasahara M, Kasereka M, Azangi M, Wafula M, 1993. Surface formations and seismic activities related to the 1991-1992 Nyamuragira eruption. *IAVCEI 1993 Canberra Mtg Abs*, p 127

AFRICA: WEST & NORTH (0204-05)

Almond D C, 1974. The composition of basaltic lavas from Bayuda, Sudan and their place in the Cainozoic volcanic history of north-east Africa. *Bull Volc*, 38: 345-360

Almond D C, Ahmed F, Khalil B E, 1969. An excursion to the Bayuda volcanic field of northern Sudan. *Bull Volc*, 33: 549-565

Almond D C, Kheir O M, Poole S, 1984. Alkaline basalt volcanism in northeastern Sudan: a comparison of the Bayuda and Gedaref areas. *J African Earth Sci*, 2: 233-245

Assouni-Sekkal A, Bonin B, Benhallou A, Yahiaoui R, Liegeois J-P, 2007. Cenozoic alkaline volcanism of the Atakor massif, Hoggar, Algeria. *In*: Beccaluva L, Bianchini G, Wilson M (eds) Cenozoic Volcanism in the Mediterranean Area, *Geol Soc Amer Spec Pap*, 418: 321-340

Ateba B, Dorbath C, Dorbath L, Ntepe N, Frogneux M, Aka F T, Hell J V, 2009. Eruptive and earthquake activities related to the 2000 eruption of Mount Cameroon volcano (West Africa). *J Volc Geotherm Res*, 179: 206-216

Ateba B, Ntepe N, 1997. Post-eruptive seismic activity of Mount Cameroon (Cameroon), West Africa: a statistical analysis. *J Volc Geotherm Res*, 79: 25-45

Barberi F, Chelini W, Marinelli G, Martini M, 1989. The gas cloud of Lake Nyos (Cameroon, 1986): results of the Italian technical mission. *J Volc Geotherm Res*, 39: 125-134

Bederman S H, 1966. Mount Cameroon: West Africa's active volcano. *Nigerian Geog J*, 9: 115-128

Burton A N, Wickens G E, 1966. Jebel Marra volcano, Sudan. *Nature*, 210: 1146-1147

Cotel A J, 1999. A trigger mechanism for the Lake Nyos disaster. *J Volc Geotherm Res*, 88: 343-347

Coulon C, Megartsi M, Fourcade S, Maury R C, Bellon H, Louni-Hacini A, Cotten J, Coutelle A, Hermitte D, 2002. Post-collisional transition from calc-alkaline to alkaline volcanism during the Neogene in Oranie (Algeria): magmatic expression of a slab breakoff. *Lithos*, 62: 87-110

Dalrymple G B, Lockwood J P, 1990. 40Ar/39Ar laser probe evidence concerning the age and associated hazards of the Lake Nyos maar, Cameroon. *Nat Hazards*, 3: 373-378

Dautria J M, Dostal J, Dupuy C, Liotard J M, 1988. Geochemistry and petrogenesis of alkali basalts from Tahalra (Hoggar, northwest Africa). *Chem Geol*, 69: 17-35

Dautria J M, Dupuy C, Takherist D, Dostal J, 1992. Carbonate metasomatism in the lithospheric mantle: peridotitic xenoliths from a melilititic district of the Sahara basin. *Contr Mineral Petr*, 111: 37-52

Davidson J P, Wilson I R, 1989. Evolution of an alkali basalt-trachyte suite from Jebel Marra volcano, Sudan, through assimilation and fractional crystallization. *Earth Planet Sci Lett*, 95: 141-160

Deruelle B, Kambou R, Joron J-L, 1990. New petrological data on volcanic rocks of Bioko Island (Equatorial Guinea). *IAVCEI 1990 Internatl Volc Cong, Mainz, Abs*, (unpaginated)

Deruelle B, N'ni J, Kambou R, 1987. Mount Cameroon: an active volcano of the Cameroon Line. *J African Earth Sci*, 6: 197-214

Fitton G, 1984. Mt. Cameroon, W. Africa. *Volcano News*, 18: 2-3

Fitton J G, 1987. The Cameroon line, West Africa: a comparison between oceanic and continental alkaline volcanism. *In*: Fitton J G and Upton B G J (eds) *Alkaline Igneous Rocks*, Geol Soc Amer Spec Pub 30: 273-291

Fitton J G, Dunlop H M, 1985. The Cameroon line, West Africa, and its bearing on the origin of oceanic and continental alkali basalt. *Earth Planet Sci Lett*, 72: 23-38

Fitton J G, Kilburn C R J, Thirlwall M F, Hughes D J, 1983. The 1982 eruption of Mount Cameroon, West Africa. *Nature*, 306: 327-332

Francis P W, Thorpe R S, Ahmed F, 1973. Setting and significance of Tertiary-Recent volcanism in the Darfur Province of western Sudan. *Nature*, 243: 30-32

Franz G, Breitkreuz C, Coyle D A, Bushra El Hur, Heinrich W, Paulick H, Pudlo D, Smith R, Steiner G, 1997. The alkaline Meidob volcanic field (Late Cenozoic, northwest Sudan). *J African Earth Sci*, 25: 263-921

Freeth S J, 1993. On the problems of translation in the investigation of the Lake Nyos disaster. *J Volc Geotherm Res*, 54: 353-336

Freeth S J, Rex D C, 2000. Constraints on the age of Lake Nyos, Cameroon. *J Volc Geotherm Res*, 97: 261-269

Geze B, 1953. Les volcans du Cameroun occidental. *Bull Volc*, 13: 63-92

Geze B, Hudeley H, Vincent P, Wacrenier P, 1959. Les volcacans du Tibesti (Sahara du Tchard). *Bull Volc*, 22: 135-172

Gourgaud A, Vincent P M, 2004. Petrology of two continental alkaline intraplate series at Emi Koussi volcano, Tibesti, Chad. *J Volc Geotherm Res*: 129: 261-290

Harmand C, Cantagrel J M, 1984. Le volcanisme alcalin Tertiaire et Quaternaire du Moyen Atlas (Maroc); chronologie K/Ar et cadre geodynamique. *J African Earth Sci*, 2: 51-55

Hasselo H N, Swarbrick J T, 1960. The eruption of the Cameroon Mountain in 1959. *J West African Sci Assoc*, 6: 96-101

Hinchingbrooke J, 1968. Trek to the Tibesti Range. *Geog Mag*, 11: 1024-1033

Kling G W, Clark M A, Compton H R, Devine J D, Evans W C, Humphrey E J, Koenigsberg E J, Lockwood J P, Tuttle M L, Wagner G N, 1987. The 1986 Lake Nyos gas disaster in Cameroon, West Africa. *Science*, 236: 169-175

Kling G W, Tuttle M L, Evans W C, 1989. The evolution of thermal structure and water chemistry in Lake Nyos. *J Volc Geotherm Res*, 39: 151-165

Klitzsch E, 1968. Der Basaltvulkanismus des Djebel Haroudj Ostfezzan/Libyen. *Geol Rundschau*, 57: 585-601

Liegeois J-P, Benhallou A, Azzouni-Sekkal A, Yahiaoui R, Bonin B, 2005. The Hoggar swell and volcanism: reactivation of the Precambrian Tuareg shield during Alpine convergence and West African Cenozoic volcanism. *In*: Foulger G R, Natland H H, Presnall D C, Anderson D L (eds) Plates, Plumes, and Paradigms, *Geol Soc Amer Spec Pap*, 388: 379-400

Liniger-Goumaz M, 1988. *Historical Dictionary of Equatorial Guinea*. Metuchen, New Jersey: Scarecrow Press, African Historical Dictionaries, no 21

Lockwood J P, Costa J E, Tuttle M L, Nni J, Tebor S G, 1988. The potential for catastrophic dam failure at Lake Nyos maar, Cameroon. *Bull Volc*, 50: 340-349

Lockwood J P, Rubin M, 1989. Origin and age of the Lake Nyos maar, Cameroon. *J Volc Geotherm Res*, 39: 117-124

Martin U, Nemeth K, 2006. How Strombolian is a "Strombolian" scoria cone? Some irregularities in scoria cone architecture from the Transmexican Volcanic Belt, near Volcan Ceboruco, (Mexico) and Al Haruj (Libya). *J Volc Geotherm Res*, 155: 104-118

Marzoli A, Piccirillo E M, Renne P R, Bellieni G, Iacumin M, Nyobe J B, Tongwa T, 2000. The Cameroon Volcanic Line revisited: petrogenesis of continental basaltic magmas from lithospheric and asthenospheric mantle source. *J Petr*, 41: 87-109

Marzoli A, Renne P R, Piccirillo E M, Francesca C, Bellieni G, Melfi A J, Nyobe J B, N'ni J, 1999. Silicic magmas from the continental Cameroon volcanic line (Oku, Bambouto and Ngaoundere): 40Ar-39Ar dates, petrology, Sr-Nd-O isotopes and their petrogenetic significance. *Contr Mineral Petr*, 135: 133-150

Mitchell-Thome R C, 1970. *Geology of the South Atlantic islands*. Berlin: Gebruder Borntraeger, 350 p ***(regional reference)***

Nkouathio D G, Menard J-J, Wandji P, Bardintzeff J-M, 2002. The Tombel graben (West Cameroon): a recent monogenetic volcanic field of the Cameroon Line. *J African Earth Sci*, 35: 285-300

Nkoumbou C, Deruelle B, Velde D, 1995. Petrology of Mt Etinde nephelinite series. *J Petr*, 36: 373-395

Paulick H, Franz G, 1997. The color of pumice: case study on a trachytic fall deposit, Meidob volcanic field, Sudan. *Bull Volc*, 59: 171-185

Paulick H, Franz G, Urlacher G, Breitkreuz C, Smith R, Volker F, 1993. The alkaline Meidob volcanic field, Pliocene to Holocene, W Sudan. *In*:, Duggan M B, Knutson, J (eds) *IAVCEI abstracts; Ancient volcanism & modern*, Australia: Australian Geological Survey Organisation), p 84

Permenter J L, Oppenheimer C, 2007. Volcanoes of the Tibesti massif (Chad, northern Africa). *Bull Volc*, 69: 609-626

Pesce A, 1966. Uau en Namus. *South-central Libya and northern Chad*, Petrol Explor Soc Libya, Annu Field Conf, 8th, p 47-51

Richard J J, Neumann van Padang M, 1957. Africa and the Red Sea. *Catalog of Active Volcanoes of the World and Solfatara Fields*, Rome: IAVCEI 4: 1-118 ***(regional reference)***

Sato H, Aramaki S, Kusakabe M, Hirabayashi J-I, Sano Y, Nojiri Y, Tchoua F, 1990. Geochemical difference of basalts between polygenetic and monogenetic volcanoes in the central part of the Cameroon volcanic line. *Geochem J*, 24: 357-370

Sigurdsson H, Devine J D, Tchoua F M, Presser T S, Pringle M K W, Evans W C, 1987. Origin of the lethal gas burst from Lake Monoun Cameroun. *J Volc Geotherm Res*, 31: 1-16

Suh C E, Luhr J F, Njome M S, 2008. Olivine-hosted glass inclusions from scoriae erupted in 1954-2000 at Mount Cameroon volcano, West Africa. *J Volc Geotherm Res*, 169: 1-33

Suh C E, Sparks R S J, Fitton J G, Ayonghe S N, Annen C, Nana R, Luckman A 2003. The 1999 and 2000 eruptions of Mount Cameroon: eruption behaviour and petrochemistry of lava. *Bull Volc*, 65: 267-281

Tazieff H, 1989. Mechanisms of the Nyos carbon dioxide disaster and of so-called phreatic stream eruptions. *J Volc Geotherm Res*, 39: 109-116

Tchoua F M, 1971. Le volcanisme Strombolien de la plaine de Tombel (Cameroun). *Annales Fac Sci, Yaounde, Cameroun*, 7-8: 53-78

Tchoua F M, 1983. Les explosions magmatophreatiques de Monoun. *Rev Sci Tech*, 3: 87-97

Vail J R, 1972. Jebel Marra, a dormant volcano in Darfur Province, western Sudan. *Bull Volc*, 36: 251-268

Vincent P M, 1963. Les volcans Tertiares et Quaternaires de Tibesti occidental et central (Sahara du Tchad). *Mem Bur Recherche Geol Min*, 23: 1-307

Vincent P M, 1980. Geologie et volcanologie du Mont Cameroun. *Unpublished Rpt*, ELF Aquitaine, 18 p

Wiart P, Oppenheimer C, 2000. Largest known historical eruption in Africa: Dubbi volcano, Eritrea, 1861. *Geology*, 28: 291-294

MIDDLE EAST (0300-02)

Abou-Deeb J M, Otaki M M, Tarling D H, Abdeldayem A L, 1999. A palaeomagnetic study of Syrian volcanic rocks of Miocene to Holocene age. *Geof Internac*, 38: 17-26

Aghanabati A, 1986. Geological map of the Middle East. *Geol Surv Iran*, 1:5,000,000 scale

Anonymous, 1963. Geologic map of the Arabian Peninsula. *U S Geol Surv, Arabian Amer Oil Co*, 1:2,000,000 scale

Baker J A, Menzies M A, Thirlwall M F, Macpherson C G, 1997. Petrogenesis of Quaternary intraplate volcanism, Sana'a, Yemen: implications for plume-lithosphere interaction and polybaric melt hybridization. *J Petr*, 38: 1359-1390

Baker P E, Brosset R, Gass I G, Neary C R, 1973. Jebel al Abyad: a recent alkalic volcanic complex in western Saudi Arabia. *Lithos*, 6: 291-314

Barberi F, Capaldi G, Gasperini P, Marinelli G, Santacroce R, Scandone R, Treuil M, Varet J, 1980. Recent basaltic volcanism of Jordan and its implications on the geodynamic history of the Dead Sea shear zone. *Accademia Nazionale Lincei, Atti Convegni Lincei*, 47: 667-683

Bender F, 1975. Geology of the Arabian Peninsula - Jordan. *U S Geol Surv Prof Pap*, 560-I: 1-36

Blumenthal M M, van der Kaaden G, Vlodavetz V I, 1964. Turkey & Caucasus. *Catalog of Active Volcanoes of the World and Solfatara Fields*, Rome: IAVCEI, 17: 1-23 ***(regional reference)***

Boccaletti M, Innocenti F, Manetti P, Mazzuoli R, Motamed A, Pasquare G, Radicati di Brozolo F, Sobhani E Amin, 1976-77. Neogene and Quaternary volcanism of the Bijar area (western Iran). *Bull Volc*, 40: 121-132

Brown G F, Schmidt D L, Huffman A C Jr, 1984. Geology of the Arabian Peninsula western shield area. *U S Geol Surv, Open-File Rpt*, 84:203: 1-217

Camp V E, Hooper P R, Roobol M J, White D L, 1987. The Madinah eruption, Saudi Arabia: magma mixing and simultaneous extrusion of the three basaltic chemical types. *Bull Volc*, 49: 489-508

Camp V E, Roobol M J, 1989. The Arabian continental alkali basalt province: Part I. Evolution of Harrat Rahat, Kingdom of Saudi Arabia. *Geol Soc Amer Bull*, 101: 71-95

Camp V E, Roobol M J, 1991. Geologic map of the Cenozoic lava field of Harrat Rahat, Kingdom of Saudi Arabia. *Saudi Arabia Directorate Gen Min Res*, Map GM-123, 1:250,000 geol map and text

Camp V E, Roobol M J, Hooper P R, 1991. The Arabia continental alkali basalt province: Part II. Evolution of Harrats Khaybar, Ithnayn, and Kura, Kingdom of Saudi Arabia. *Geol Soc Amer Bull*, 103: 363-391

Camp V E, Roobol M J, Hooper P R, 1992. The Arabian continental alkali basalt province: Part III. Evolution of Harrat Kishb, Kingdom of Saudia Arabia. *Geol Soc Amer Bull*, 104: 379-396

Capaldi G, Chiesa S, Conticelli S, Manetti P, 1987. Jabal an Nar: an upper Miocene volcanic center near Al Mukha. *J Volc Geotherm Res*, 31: 345-352

Cox K G, Gass I G, Mallick D I J, 1977. Western Part of Shuqra volcanic field, South Yemen. *Lithos*, 10: 185-192

Davidson J, Hassanzadeh J, Berzins R, Stockli D F, Bashukooh B, Turrin B, Pandamouz A, 2004. The geology of Damavand volcano, Alborz Mountains, northern Iran. *Geol Soc Amer Bull*, 116: 16-29

Davison I, Al-Kadasi M, Al-Khirbash S, Al-Subbary A K, Baker J, Blakey S, Bosence D, Dart C, Heaton R, McClay K, Menzies M, Nichols G, Owen L, Yelland A, 1994. Geological evolution of the southeastern Red Sea Rift margin, Republic of Yemen. *Geol Soc Amer Bull*, 106: 1474-1493

Dowgiallo J, 1986. Thermal waters of the Yemen Arab Republic. *Geothermics*, 15: 63-76

Gansser A, 1966. Iran. *Catalog of Active Volcanoes of the World and Solfatara Fields*, Rome: IAVCEI, 17: 1-20 ***(regional reference)***

Girod M, Conrad G, 1975. Les formations volcaniques recentes du sud de l'Iran (Kouth-E-Shahsavaran): donnees petrologiques preliminaires; implications structurale. *Bull Volc*, 39: 495-511

Guba I, Mustafa H, 1988. Structural control of young basaltic fissure eruptions in the plateau basalt area of the Arabian Plate, northeastern Jordan. *J Volc Geotherm Res*, 35: 319-334

Ilani S, Harlavan Y, Tarawneh K, Rabba I, Weinberger R, Ibrahim K, Peltz S Stenitz G, 2001. New K-Ar ages of basalts from the Harrat Ash Shaam volcanic field in Jordan: implications for the span and duration of the upper-mantle upwelling beneath the western Arabian Plate. *Geology*, 29: 171-174

Innocenti F, Manetti P, Mazzuoli R, Pasquare G, Villari L, 1982. Anatolia and north-western Iran. *In*: Thorpe R S (ed) *Andesites*, New York: John Wiley, p 327-349

Jung D, Kursten M O C, Tarkian M, 1976. Post-Mesozoic volcanism in Iran and its relation to the subduction of the Afro-Arabian under the Eurasian plate. *In*: Pilger A and Rosler A (eds) *Afar between Continental and Oceanic Rifting*, Inter-Union Comm Geodynam Sci Rpt, 16: 175-181

Karakhanian A, Djrbashian R, Trifonov V, Philip H, Arakelian S, Avagian A, 2002. Holocene-historical volcanism and active faults as natural risk factors for Armenia and adjacent countries. *J Volc Geotherm Res*, 113: 319-344

Krienitz M-S, Haase K M, Mezger K, Eckardt V, Shaikh-Mashail M A, 2006. Magma genesis and crustal contamination of continental intraplate lavas in northwestern Syria. *Contr Mineral Petr*, 151: 698-716

Krienitz M-S, Haase K M, Mezger K, Shaikh-Mashail M A, 2007. Magma genesis and mantle dynamics at the Harrat Ash Shamah volcanic field (southern Syria). *J Petr*, 48: 1513-1542

Lander A H S, 1902. Across Coveted Lands or a Journey from Flushing (Holland) to Calcutta Overland. London: MacMillan and Co., 2 volumes

Lapparent A F de, Lavigne Saint Suzanne J de, Bordet P, 1965. Sur l'importance et l'extension du volcanisme recent de Nawar (Afghanistan). *Bull Volc*, 28: 107-118

Milton D J, 1976-77. Qal'eh Hasan Ali maars, Central Iran. *Bull Volc*, 40: 201-208

Mouty M, Delaloye M, Fontignie D, Piskin O, Wagner J-J, 1992. The volcanic activity in Syria and Lebanon between Jurassic and Actual. *Schweiz Mineral Petrogr Mitt*: 72: 91-105

Neumann van Padang M, 1963a. Arabia and the Indian Ocean. *Catalog of Active Volcanoes of the World and Solfatara Fields*, Rome: IAVCEI, 16: 1-64 ***(regional reference)***

Poirier J P, Taher M A, 1980. Historical seismicity in the Near and Middle East, North Africa, and Spain from Arabic documents (7th-18th century). *Bull Seism Soc Amer*, 70: 2185-2202

Roobol M J, Camp V E, 1991. Geologic map of the Cenozoic lava field of Harrat Kishb, Kingdom of Saudi Arabia. *Saudi Arabia Directorate Gen Min Res*, Map GM-132, 1:250,000 Geol map and text

Roobol M J, Camp V E, 1991. Geologic map of the Cenozoic lava fields of Harrats Khaubar, Ithnayn, and Kura, Kingdom of Saudi Arabia. *Saudi Arabia Min Petrol Mineral Resour*, 1:250,000 geol map

Shakeri A, Moore F, Kompani-Zare M, 2008. Geochemistry of the thermal springs of Mount Taftan, southeastern Iran. *J Volc Geotherm Res*, 178: 829-836

Shaw J E, Baker J A, Menzies M A, Thirlwall M F, Ibrahim K M, 2003. Petrogenesis of the largest intraplate volcanic field on the Arabian Plate (Jordan): a mixed lithosphere-asthenosphere source activated by lithospheric extension. *J Petr*, 44: 1657-1679

Sondhi V P, 1947. The Makran earthquake, 28th November 1945, the birth of new islands. *Indian Minerals*, 1: 147-154

Thornber C R, 1990. Geologic map of Harrat Hutaymah, with petrologic classification and distribution of ultramafic inclusions, Saudi Arabia. *U S Geol Surv map*, MF-2129 (1:100,000 scale geol map)

Trifonov V G, 2007. The Bible and geology: destruction of Sodom and Gomorrah. *In*: Piccardi L, Masse W B (eds), Myth and Geology, *Geol Soc London Spec Publ*, 273: 133-142

United States Geological Survey, 1963. Geologic map of the Arabian Peninsula. *U S Geol Surv Map*, I-270 A, 1:2,000,000 (compiled with the Arabian Oil Company)

Weinstein Y, 2007. A transition from strombolian to phreatomagmatic activity induced by a lava flow damming water in a valley. *J Volc Geotherm Res*, 159: 267-284

White R S, Ross D A, 1979. Tectonics of the western Gulf of Oman. *J Geophys Res*, 84: 3479-3489

Zahran H M, McCausland W A, Pallister J S, Lu Z, El-Hadidy S, Aburukba A, Schawali Kadi J K, Youssef A, Ewert J W, White R A, Lundgren P, Mufti M, Stewart I C, 2009. Stalled eruption or dike intrusion at Harrat Lunayyir, Saudi Arabia? *Eos, Trans Amer Geophys Union*, 89: Fall Meet Suppl, abstr V13E-2072

INDIAN OCEAN (0303-05)

Abchir A M, Semet M P, Boudon G, Ildefonse P, Bachelery P, Clocchiatti R, 1998. Huge hydrothermal explosive activity on Piton de la Fournaise, Reunion Island: the Bellecombe Member, 2700 BC. *In*: Casale R, Fytikas M, Sigvaldasson G, Vougioukalakis G (eds), The European laboratory volcanoes, Proc 2nd Workshop, Santorini, Greece 2-4 May 1996, European Comm, p 447-455

Albarede F, Tamagnan V, 1988. Modelling the recent geochemical evolution of the Piton de la Fournaise Volcano, Reunion Island, 1931-1986. *J Petr*, 29: 997-1030

Bachelery P, Blum P A, Cheminee J L, Chevallier L, Gaulon R, Girardin N, Juapart C, Lalanne F, Le Mouel J L, Ruegg J C, Vincent P, 1982. Eruption at Le Piton de la Fournaise volcano on 3 February 1981. *Nature*, 297: 395-397

Ballestracci R, Nougier J, 1984. Detection by infrared thermography and modelling of an icecapped geothermal system in Kerguelen Archipelago. *J Volc Geotherm Res*, 20: 85-100

Barling J, Goldstein S L, Nicholls I A, 1994. Geochemistry of Heard Island (Southern Indian Ocean): Characterization of an enriched mantle component and implications for enrichment of the sub-Indian Ocean mantle. *J Petr*, 35: 1017-1053

Battaglia J, Aki K, Ferrazzini V, 2005. Location of tremor sources and estimation of lava output using tremor source amplitude on the Piton de la Fournaise volcano 2. Estimation of lava output. *J Volc Geotherm Res*, 147: 291-308

Battaglia J, Bachelery P, 2003. Dynamic dyke propagation deduced from tilt variations preceding the March 9, 1998, eruption of the Piton de la Fournaise volcano. *J Volc Geotherm Res*, 120: 289-310

Battistini R, 1962. Le massif volcanique de l'Itasy (Madagascar). *Annales Geog*, 384: 167-178

Bellair P, 1964. Recent data on the geology of Isles Crozet. *In*: Adie R J (ed) *Antarctic Geol, Proc 1st Internatl Symp Antarctic Geol*, Amsterdam: Elsevier, p 3-7

Benard R, Krafft M, 1977. *La Fournaise, Volcan Actif de l'Ile de la Reunion*. Strasbourg: Istra, 121 p

Benard R, Krafft M, 1986. *Au Cour de la Fournaise*. Mahe, Seychelle Islands: Editions Nourault/Benard (& Air France), 220 p

Besairie H J, 1973. Precis de geologie Malgache. *Annales Geol Madagascar*, 36: 1-141

Bory de St. Vincent J B G M, 1805. *Voyage to, and Travels Through the Four Principal Islands of the African Seas*. London: Richard Phillips, 71 St Paul's Church

Bret L, Fevre Y, Join J-L, Robineau B, Bachelery P, 2003. Deposits related to degradation processes on Piton des Neiges volcano (Reunion Island): overview and geological hazard. *J Volc Geotherm Res*, 123: 25-41

Carter A, van Wyk de Vries B, Kelfoun K, Bachelery P, Briole P, 2007. Pits, rifts and slumps: the summit structure of Piton de la Fournaise. *Bull Volc*, 69: 741-756

Coppola D, Staudacher Th, Cigolini C, 2005. The May-July 2003 eruption at Piton de la Fournaise (La Reunion): volume, effusion rates, and emplacement mechanisms inferred from thermal imaging and Global Positioning System (GPS) survey. *In*: Manga M, Ventura G (eds) Kinematics and dynamics of lava flows, *Geol Soc Amer Spec Pap*, 396: 103-124

Debeuf D, Bachelery P, Sigmarsson O, 2003. Two contemporaneous magma series on Mayotte Island, Comores Archipelago, Indian Ocean. *EGS-AGU-EUG Joint Assemb, Nice, France, 6-11 April 2003*, abstr 9625

Delorme H, Bachelery P, Blum P A, Cheminee J L, Delarue J F, Delmond J C, Hirn A, Lepine J C, Vincent P M, Zlotnicki J, 1989. March 1986 eruptive episodes at Piton de la Fournaise volcano (Reunion Island). *J Volc Geotherm Res*, 36: 189-208

Duffield W A, Stieltjes L, Varet J, 1982. Huge landslide blocks in the growth of Piton de la Fournaise, Reunion, and Kilauea volcano, Hawaii. *J Volc Geotherm Res*, 12: 147-160

Esson J, Flower M F J, Strong D F, Upton B G J, Wadsworth W J, 1970. Geology of the Comores Archipelago. *Geol Mag*, 107: 549-557

Flower M F J, 1972. Petrology of volcanic rocks from Anjouan, Comores Archipelago. *Bull Volc*, 36: 238-250

Flynn L, Wright R, Garbeil H, Harris A, Pilger E, 2002. A global thermal alert system using MODIS: initial results from 2000-2001. *Advances Environ Monitoring Modelling*, 1: 37-69

Fretzdorff S, Paterne M, Stoffers P, Ivanova E, 2000. Explosive activity of the Reunion Island volcanoes through the past 260,000 years as recorded in deep-sea sediments. *Bull Volc*, 62: 266-277

Gagnevin D, Ethien R, Bonin B, Moine B, Feraud G, Gerbe M C, Cottin J Y, Michon G, Tourpin S, Mamias G, Perrache C, Giret A, 2003. Open-system processes in the genesis of silica-oversaturated alkaline rocks of the Rallier-du-Baty Peninsula, Kerguelen Archipelago (Indian Ocean). *J Volc Geotherm Res*, 123: 267-300

Gillot P-Y, Nativel P, 1989. Eruptive history of the Piton de la Fournaise volcano, Reunion Island, Indian Ocean. *J Volc Geotherm Res*, 36: 53-65

Gunn B M, Abranson E C, Nougier J, Watkins N D, Hajash A, 1971. Amsterdam Island, an isolated volcano in the southern Indian Ocean. *Contr Mineral Petr*, 32: 79-92

Gunn B M, Abranson E C, Watkins N D, Nougier J, 1972. Petrology and geochemistry of Iles

Crozet: a summary. *In*: Adie R J (ed) *Antarctic Geol and Geophys*, IUGS Ser-B(1): 825-829

Johnson K T M, Graham D W, Rubin K H, Nicolaysen K, Scheirer D S, Forsyth D W, Baker E T, Douglas-Priebe L M, 2000. Boomerang Seamount: the active expression of the Amsterdam-St. Paul hotspot, Southeast Indian Ridge. *Earth Planet Sci Lett*, 183: 245-259

Kieffer G, Tricot B, Vincent P M, 1977. An unusual eruption (April 1977) at Piton de la Fournaise (Reunion Island): its volcanological and structural consequence. *CR Acad Sci Paris*, Ser-D, 285: 957-960

Krafft M, 1982. L'eruption volcanique du Kartala en Avril 1977 (Grande Comore, Ocean Indien). *CR Acad Sci Paris*, Ser-II, 294: 753-758

Krafft M, 1983. Guide des volcans de la Grande Comore. *Unpublished manuscript*, 101 p

Krafft M, Gerente A, 1977a. Volcanic activity of "Piton de la Fournaise" between November 1975 and April 1976 (Reunion Island, Indian Ocean). *CR Acad Sci Paris*, Ser-D, 284: 2091-2094

Krafft M, Gerente A, 1977b. Volcanic activity of "Piton de la Fournaise" between October 1972 and May 1973 (Reunion Island, Indian Ocean). *CR Acad Sci Paris*, Ser-D, 284: 607-610

Lameyre J, Nougier J, 1982. Geology of Ile de l'Est, Crozet archipelago (TAAF). *In*: Craddock C (ed) *Antarctic Geoscience*, Madison: Univ Wisconsin Press, p 767-770

LeMasurier W E, Thomson J W (eds), 1990. *Volcanoes of the Antarctic Plate and Southern Oceans*. Washington, D C: Amer Geophys Union, 487 p ***(regional reference)***

Lenat J-F, Bachelery P, Bonneville A, Hirn A, 1989. The beginning of the 1985-1987 eruptive cycle at Piton de la Fournaise (la Reunion); new insights in the magmatic and volcano-tectonic systems. *J Volc Geotherm Res*, 36: 209-232

Lenat J-F, Bachelery P, Bonneville A, Tarits P, Cheminee J-L, Delorme H, 1989. The December 4, 1983 to February 18, 1984 eruption of Piton de la Fournaise (la Reunion, Indian Ocean); description and interpretation. *J Volc Geotherm Res*, 36: 87-112

Lenat J-F, Boivin P, Deniel C, Gillot P-Y, Bachelery P, Fournaise 2 Team, 2009. Age and nature of deposits on the submarine flanks of Piton de la Fournaise (Reunion Island). *J Volc Geotherm Res*, 184: 199-207

Lenat J-F, Vincent P, Bachelery P, 1989. The off-shore continuation of an active basaltic volcano: Piton de la Fournaise (Reunion Island, Indian Ocean); structural and geomorphological interpretation from SEABEAM mapping. *J Volc Geotherm Res*, 36: 1-36

Longpre M-A, Staudacher T, Stix J, 2007. The November 2002 eruption at Piton de la Fournaise volcano, La Reunion Island: ground deformation, seismicity, and pit crater collapse. *Bull Volc*, 69: 511-525

Ludden J N, 1977. Eruptive patterns for the volcano Piton de la Fournaise, Reunion Island. *J Volc Geotherm Res*, 2: 385-396

Malengreau B, Lenat J-F, Froger J-L, 1999. Structure of Reunion Island (Indian Ocean) inferred from the interpretation of gravity anomalies. *J Volc Geotherm Res*, 88: 131-146

McDougall I, Verwoerd W, Chevallier L, 2001. K-Ar geochronology of Marion Island, Southern Ocean. *Geol Mag*, 138: 1-17

Melluso L, Morra V, 2000. Petrogenesis of Late Cenozoic mafic alkaline rocks of the Nosy Be archipelago (northern Madagascar): relationships with the Comorean magmatism. *J Volc Geotherm Res*, 96: 129-142

Michon L, Cayol V, Letourneur L, Peltier A, Villeneuve N, Staudache T, 2009. Edifice growth, deformation and rift zone development in basaltic setting: Insights from Piton de la Fournaise shield volcano (Reunion Island). *J Volc Geotherm Res*, 184: 14-30

Michon L, Staudacher T, Ferrazzini V, Bachelery P, Marti J, 2007. April 2007 collapse of Piton de la Fournaise: a new example of caldera formation. *Geophys Res Lett*, 34: L21301, doi:10.1029/2007GL031248

Montaggioni L, Nativel P, Billard G, 1972. L'activite actuelle du Piton de la Fournaise (Ile de la Reunion, Ocean Indien). *CR Acad Sci Paris*, Ser-D, 275: 2615-2618

Neumann van Padang M, 1963a. Arabia and the Indian Ocean. *Catalog of Active Volcanoes of the World and Solfatara Fields*, Rome: IAVCEI, 16: 1-64 ***(regional reference)***

Nougier J, 1972. Geochronology of the volcanic activity in Iles Kerguelen. *In*: Adie R J (ed) *Antarctic Geol and Geophys*, IUGS Ser-B(1): 803-808

Nougier J, 1982. Volcanism of Saint Paul and Amsterdam Islands (TAAF): some aspects of volcanism along plate margins. *In*: Craddock C (ed) *Antarctic Geoscience*, Madison: Univ Wisconsin Press, p 755-765

Oehler J-F, Labazuy P, Lenat J-F, 2004. Recurrence of major flank landslides during the last 2-Ma history of Reunion Island. *Bull Volc*, 66: 585-598

Oehler J-F, Lenat J-F, Labazuy P, 2008. Growth and collapse of the Reunion Island volcanoes. *Bull Volc*, 70: 717-742

Paul D, Kemenetsky V S, Hofmann A W, Stracke A, 2007. Compositional diversity among primitive lavas of Mauritius, Indian Ocean: implications for mantle sources. *J Volc Geotherm Res*, 164: 76-94

Peltier A, Bachelery P, Staudacher T, 2009. Magma transport and storage at Piton de La Fournaise (La Reunion) between 1972 and 2007: a review of geophysical and geochemical data. *J Volc Geotherm Res*, 184: 93-108

Savin C, Grasso J-R, Bachelery P, 2005. Seismic signature of a phreatic explosion: hydrofracturing damage at Karthala volcano, Grand Comore Island, Indian Ocean. *Bull Volc*, 67: 717-731

Sigmarsson O, Condomines M, Bachelery P, 2005. Magma residence time beneath the Piton de la Fournaise volcano, Reunion Island, from U-series disequilibria. *Earth Planet Sci Lett*, 234: 223-234

Spath A, Le Roex A P, Duncan R A, 1996. The geochemistry of lavas from the Comores Archipelago, western Indian Ocean: petrogenesis and mantle source region characteristics. *J Petr*, 97: 961-991

Staudacher T, 2010. Field observations of the 2008 summit eruption at Piton de la Fournaise (Ile de La R'eunion) and implications for the 2007 Dolomieu collapse. *J Volc Geotherm Res*, 191: 60-68

Staudacher T, Ferrazzini V, Peltier A, Kowalski P, Boissier P, Catherine P, Lauret F, Massin F, 2009. The April 2007 eruption and the Dolomieu crater collapse, two major events at Piton de la Fournaise (La Reunion Island, Indian Ocean). *J Volc Geotherm Res*, 184: 126-137

Stieltjes L, 1985. Carte des coulees historiques du volcan de la Fournaise. *Bur Recherches Geol Minieres France*, 1:50,000

Stieltjes L, Moutou P, 1989. A statistical and probabilistic study of the historic activity of Piton de la Fournaise, Reunion Island, Indian Ocean. *J Volc Geotherm Res*, 36: 67-86

Strong D F, 1972. Petrology of the island of Moheli, western Indian Ocean. *Geol Soc Amer Bull*, 83: 389-406

Strong D F, Jacquot C, 1970. The Karthala caldera, Grande Comore. *Bull Volc*, 34: 663-680

Upton B G J, Wadsworth W J, Latrille E, 1974. The 1972 eruption of Kartala volcano, Grand Comore. *Bull Volc*, 38: 136-148

Upton B G J, Wadsworth W J, Newman T C, 1967. The petrology of Rodriguez Island, Indian Ocean. *Geol Soc Amer Bull*, 78: 1495-1506

Verwoerd W J, 1971. Geology of Marion and Prince Edward Islands. *In*: Bakker E M, et al (eds) *Marion and Prince Edward Islands*, Cape Town, South Africa: A A Balkema, p 40-62

Verwoerd W J, Chevallier L, 1987. Contrasting types of surtseyan tuff cones on Marion and Prince Edward islands, southwest Indian Ocean. *Bull Volc*, 49: 399-413

Verwoerd W J, Langenegger O, 1967. Marion and Prince Edward Islands geological studies. *Nature*, 213: 231-232

Verwoerd W J, Russell S, Berruti A, 1981. 1980 volcanic eruption reported on Marion Island. *Earth Planet Sci Lett*, 54: 153-156

Weis D, Frey F A, Giret A, Cantagrel J-M, 1998. Geochemical characteristics of the youngest volcano (Mount Ross) in the Kerguelen Archipelago: inferences for magma flux, lithosphere assimilation and composition of the Kerguelen plume. *J Petr*, 39: 973-994

Zlotnicki J, Le Mouel J L, Delmond J C, Pambrun C, Delorme H, 1993. Magnetic variations on Piton de la Fournaise volcano. Volcanomagnetic signals associated with the November 6 and 30, 1987, eruptions. *J Volc Geotherm Res*, 56: 281-296

NEW ZEALAND & KERMADEC IS (0401-02)

Allen L R, 1948. Activity at Ngauruhoe, April - May, 1948. *New Zeal J Sci Tech*, 30: 187-193

Allis R G, 1984. The 9 April 1983 steam eruption at Craters of the Moon thermal area, Wairakei. *New Zeal Dept Sci Ind Res Rpt*, 196: 1-25

Alloway B V, Pillans B J, Carter L, Naish T R, Westgate J A, 2005. Onshore-offshore correlation of Pleistocene rhyolitic eruptions from New Zealand: implications for TVZ eruptive history and paleoenvironmental construction. *Quat Sci Rev*, 24: 1601-1622

Alloway B, Neall V E, Vucetich C G, 1995. Late Quaternary (post 28,000 year B.P.) tephrostratigraphy of northeast and central Taranaki, New Zealand. *J Roy Soc New Zeal*, 25: 385-458

Ashcroft J, 1986. The Kerikeri Volcanics: a basalt-Pantellerite association in Northland. *Roy Soc New Zeal Bull*, 23: 48-63

Beetham R D, Nairn I A, Otway P M, 1980. Ruapehu Crater Lake outflow investigations, 27 June 1980. *New Zeal Geol Surv Preliminary Rpt*

Beresford S W, Cole J W, 2000. Kaingaroa Ignimbrite, Taupo volcanic zone, New Zealand: evidence for asymmetric caldera subsidence of the Reporoa caldera. *New Zeal J Geol Geophys*, 43: 471-481

Bonadonna C, Houghton B F, 2005. Total grain-size distribution and volume of tephra-fall deposits. *Bull Volc*, 67: 441-456

Briggs R M, 1986. Volcanic rocks of the Waikato region, western North Island, and some possible petrologic and tectonic constraints on their origin. *Roy Soc New Zeal Bull*, 23: 76-91

Brooker M R, Houghton B F, Wilson C J N, Gamble J A, 1993. Pyroclastic phases of a rhyolitic dome-building eruption: Puketarata tuff ring, Taupo volcanic zone, New Zealand. *Bull Volc*, 55: 395-406

Brown S J A, Wilson C J N, Cole J W, Wooden J, 1998. The Whakamaru Group ignimbrites, Taupo Volcanic Zone, New Zealand: evidence for reverse tapping of a zoned silicic magmatic system. *J Volc Geotherm Res*, 84: 1-37

Buck M D, 1985. An assessment of volcanic risk on and from Mayor Island, New Zealand. *New Zeal J Geol Geophys*, 28: 283-298

Buck M D, Briggs R M, Nelson C S, 1981. Pyroclastic deposits and volcanic history of Mayor Island. *New Zeal J Geol Geophys*, 24: 449-468

Burt R M, Cole J W, Vroon P Z, 1996. Volcanic geology and geochemistry of Motuhora (Whale Island), Bay of Plenty, New Zealand. *New Zeal J Geol Geophys*, 39: 565-580

Carroll L D, Gamble J A, Houghton B F, Thordarson T, Higham T F G, 1997. A radiocarbon age determination for Mount Edgecumbe (Putauaki) volcano, Bay of Plenty, New Zealand. *New Zeal J Geol Geophys*, 40: 559-562

Carter L, Nelson C S, Froggatt P C, 1995. Correlation, dispersal, and preservation of the Kawakawa Tephra and other late Quaternary tephra layers in the southwest Pacific Ocean. *New Zeal J Geol Geophys*, 38: 29-46

Cassidy J, France S J, Locke C A, 2007. Gravity and magnetic investigation of maar volcanoes, Auckland volcanic field, New Zealand. *J Volc Geotherm Res*, 159: 153-163

Clark R H, 1970. Volcanic activity on White Island, Bay of Plenty, 1966-69 Part 1. Chronology and crater floor level changes. *New Zeal J Geol Geophys*, 13: 565-574

Clark R H, 1973. Surveillance of White Island volcano, 1968-1972. Part 1 - Volcanic events and deformation of the crater floor. *New Zeal J Geol Geophys*, 16: 949-957

Clark R H, Cole J W, 1986. White Island. *Roy Soc New Zeal Bull*, 23: 169-178

Cole J W, Brown S J A, Burt R M, Beresford S W, Wilson C J N, 1998. Lithic types in ignimbrites as a guide to the evolution of a caldera complex, Taupo volcanic centre, New Zealand. *J Volc Geotherm Res*, 80: 217-237

Cole J W, Graham I J, Hackett W R, Houghton B F, 1986. Volcanology and petrology of the Quaternary composite volcanoes of the Tongariro volcanic centre, Taupo volcanic zone. *Roy Soc New Zeal Bull*, 23: 224-250

Cole J W, Hochstein M P, Skinner D N B, Briggs R M, 1986. Tectonic setting of North Island Cenozoic volcanism (Tour Guide C1). *New Zeal Geol Surv Rec*, 11: 5-60

Cole J W, Thordarson T, Burt R M, 2000. Magma origin and evolution of White Island (Whakaari) volcano, Bay of Plenty, New Zealand. *J Petr*, 41: 867-895

Cronin S J, Neall V E, Lecointre J A, Hedley M J, Loganathan P, 2003. Environmental hazards of flouride in volcanic ash: a case study from Ruapehu volcano, New Zealand. *J Volc Geotherm Res*, 121: 271-291

Cronin S J, Neall V E, Lecointre J A, Palmer A S, 1997. Changes in Whangaehu river lahar characteristics during the 1995 eruption sequence, Ruapehu volcano, New Zealand. *J Volc Geotherm Res*, 76: 47-61

Cronin S J, Neall V E, Stewart R B, Palmer A S, 1996. A multiple-parameter approach to andesitic tephra correlation, Ruapehu volcano, New Zealand. *J Volc Geotherm Res*, 72: 199-215

de Ronde C E J, Stoffers P, Garbe-Schonberg D, Christenson B W, Jones B, Manconi R, Browne P R L, Hissmann K, Botz R, Davy B W, Schmitt M, Battershill C N, 2002. Discovery of active hydrothermal venting in Lake Taupo, New Zealand. *J Volc Geotherm Res*, 115: 257-275

de Ronde, C E J, Baker E T, Massoth G J, Lupton J E, Wright I C, Feely R A, Greene R R, 2001. Intra-oceanic subduction-related hydrothermal venting, Kermadec volcanic arc, New Zealand. *Earth Planet Sci Lett*, 193: 359-369

Donoghue S L, Gamble J A, Palmer A S, Stewart R B, 1995. Magma mixing in an andesite pyroclastic flow of the Pourahu Member, Ruapehu volcano, New Zealand. *J Volc Geotherm Res*, 68: 177-191

Donoghue S L, Neall V E, Palmer A S, Stewart R B, 1997. The volcanic history of Ruapehu during the past 2 millenia based on the record of Tufa Trig tephras. *Bull Volc*, 59: 136-146

Donoghue S, Palmer A S, McClelland E, Hobson K, Stewart R B, Neall V E, Lecointre J, Price R, 1999. The Taurewa eruptive episode: evidence for climactic eruptions at Ruapehu volcano, New Zealand. *Bull Volc*, 61: 223-240

Downey W S, Kellett R J, Smith I E M, Price R C, Stewart R B, 1994. New paleomagnetic evidence for the recent eruptive activity of Mt. Taranaki, New Zealand. *J Volc Geotherm Res*, 60: 15-27

Ewart A, Taylor S R, Capp A C, 1968. Geochemistry of the pantellerites of Mayor Island, New Zealand. *Contr Mineral Petr*, 17: 116-140

Froggatt P C, 1981a. Karapiti tephra formation: a 10,000 years B.P. rhyolitic tephra from Taupo. *New Zeal J Geol Geophys*, 24: 95-98

Froggatt P C, 1981b. Motutere tephra formation and redefinition of Hinemaiaia tephra formation, Taupo volcanic centre, New Zealand. *New Zeal J Geol Geophys*, 24: 99-106

Froggatt P C, 1981c. Stratigraphy and nature of Taupo pumice formation. *New Zeal J Geol Geophys*, 24: 231-248

Froggatt P C, Lowe D J, 1990. A review of late Quaternary silicic and some other tephra formations from New Zealand: their stratigraphy, nomenclature, distribution, volume, and age. *New Zeal J Geol Geophys*, 33: 89-109

Gamble J A, Price R C, Smith I E M, McIntosh W C, Dunbar N W, 2003. 40Ar/39Ar geochronology of magmatic activity, magma flux and hazards at Ruapehu volcano, Taupo Volcanic Zone, New Zealand. *J Volc Geotherm Res*, 120: 271-287

Gottsmann J, Dingwell D B, 2002. The thermal history of a spatterfed lava flow: the 8-ka pantellerite flow of Mayor Island, New Zealand. *Bull Volc*, 64: 410-422

Graham I J, Hackett W R, 1987. Petrology of calc-alkaline lavas from Ruapehu volcano and related vents, Taupo Volcanic Zone, New Zealand. *J Petr*, 28: 531-567

Gregg D R, 1956. Eruption of Ngauruhoe 1954-1955. *New Zeal J Sci Tech*, 37: 675-688

Gregg D R, 1960. Volcanoes of Tongariro National Park. *New Zeal Geol Soc Handbook Inf Ser*, 28: 1-82

Haase K M, Stroncik N, Garbe-Schonberg D, Stoffers P, 2006. Formation of island arc dacite magmas by extreme crystal fractionation: an example from Brothers Seamount, Kermedec island arc (SW Pacific). *J Volc Geotherm Res*, 152: 316-330

Hackett W R, Houghton B F, 1986. Active composite volcanoes of Taupo volcanic zone (Tour Guide C4). *New Zeal Geol Surv Rec*, 11: 61-114

Hackett W R, Houghton B F, 1989. A facies model for a Quaternary andesitic composite volcano: Ruapehu, New Zealand. *Bull Volc*, 51: 51-68

Hall L H, 1985. Rumble IV Seamount - no rumble? *New Zeal J Geol Geophys*, 28: 569

Hamilton W M, Baumgart I L, 1959. White Island. *New Zeal Dept Sci Ind Res Bull*, 127: 1-84

Healy J, 1956. New Zealand: report of the standing committee on volcanology. *Proc 8th Pacific Sci Cong*, 2: 27-30

Healy J, 1973. Volcano observations, 1971. *New Zeal Volc Rec*, 1: 10-18

Heming R F, 1980. Patterns of Quaternary basaltic volcanism in the northern North Island, New Zealand. *New Zeal J Geol Geophys*, 23: 335-344

Heming R F, Barnet P R, 1986. The petrology and petrochemistry of the Auckland volcanic field. *Roy Soc New Zeal Bull*, 23: 64-75

Hewson C A Y, Nairn I A, 1974. Ngauruhoe: observed activity and seismic data. *New Zeal Volc Rec*, 2: 32-34

Hobden B J, Houghton B F, Lanphere M A, Nairn I A, 1996. Growth of the Tongariro volcanic complex: new evidence from K-Ar age determinations. *New Zeal J Geol Geophys*, 39: 151-154

Hobden B J, Houghton B F, Nairn I A, 2002. Growth of a young, frequently active composite cone: Ngauruhoe volcano, New Zealand. *Bull Volc*, 64: 392-409

Horwell C J, Patterson J E, Gamble J A, Allen A G, 2005. Monitoring and mapping of hydrogen sulphide emissions across an active geothermal field: Rotorua, New Zealand. *J Volc Geotherm Res*, 139: 259-269

Houghton B F, Latter J H, Hackett W R, 1987. Volcanic hazard assessment for Ruapehu composite volcano, Taupo volcanic zone, New Zealand. *Bull Volc*, 49: 737-751

Houghton B F, Nairn I A, 1991. The 1976-1982 Strombolian and phreatomagmatic eruptions of White Island, New Zealand: eruptive and depositional mechanisms at a 'wet' volcano. *Bull Volc*, 54: 25-49

Houghton B F, Weaver S D, Wilson C J N, Lanphere M A, 1992. Evolution of a Quaternary peralkaline volcano: Mayor Island, New Zealand. *J Volc Geotherm Res*, 51: 217-236

Houghton B F, Wilson C J N, 1986. Explosive rhyolite volcanism: the case studies of Mayor Island and Taupo volcanoes (Tour Guide A1). *New Zeal Geol Surv Rec*, 12: 33-100

Houghton B F, Wilson C J N, Del Carlo P, Coltelli M, Sable J E, Carey R, 2004. The influence of conduit processes on changes in style of basaltic Plinian eruptions: Tarawera 1886 and Etna 122 BC. *J Volc Geotherm Res*, 137: 1-14

Houghton B F, Wilson C J N, McWilliams M O, Lanphere M A, Weaver S D, Briggs R M, Pringle M S, 1995. Chronology and dynamics of a large silicic magmatic system: Central Taupo Volcano Zone, New Zealand. *Geology*, 23: 13-16

Houghton B F, Wilson C J N, Rosenberg M D, Smith I E M, Parker R J, 1996. Mixed deposits of complex magmatic and phreatomagmatic volcanism: an example from Crater Hill, Auckland, New Zealand. *Bull Volc*, 58: 59-66

Jaggar T A, 1928a. Recent activities in New Zealand. *Volcano Lett*, 200: 1

Johnson R W, Knutson J, Taylor S R (eds), 1989. *Intraplate Volcanism in Eastern Australia and New Zealand*. Cambridge, England: Cambridge Univ Press, 408 p ***(regional reference)***

Jurado-Chichay Z, Walker G P L, 2000. Stratigraphy and dispersal of the Mangaone Subgroup pyroclastic deposits, Okataina volcanic centre, New Zealand. *J Volc Geotherm Res*, 104: 319-383

Jurado-Chichay Z, Walker G P L, 2001. The intensity and magnitude of the Mangaone subgroup plinian eruptions from Okataina volcanic centre, New Zealand. *J Volc Geotherm Res*, 111: 219-237

Kear D, Thompson B N, 1964. Volcanic risk in Northland. *New Zeal J Geol Geophys*, 7: 87-93

Kibblewhite A C, 1966. The acoustic detection and location of an underwater volcano. *New Zeal J Sci*, 9: 178-199

Kibblewhite A C, 1967. Note on another active seamount in the south Kermadec Ridge group. *New Zeal J Sci*, 10: 68-70

Kibblewhite A C, Denham R N, 1967. The bathymetry and total magnetic field of the south Kermadec ridge seamounts. *New Zeal J Sci*, 10: 52-67

Kissling W M, Weir G J, 2005. The spatial distribution of the geothermal fields in the Taupo volcanic zone, New Zealand. *J Volc Geotherm Res*, 145: 136-150

Latter J H, 1975a. Note on inferred submarine eruption, Rumble No. 3 volcano. *New Zeal Volc Rec*, 3: 58

Latter J H, 1977. Volcanic tremor, and A- and B-type earthquakes at Ruapehu and Ngauruhoe during 1976. *New Zeal Volc Rec*, 6: 24-31

Latter J H, 1980. Volcano-seismic activity at Ruapehu volcano during 1979. *New Zeal Volc Rec*, 9: 23-29

Latter J H, 1981b. Volcano-seismic activity at Ruapehu during 1980. *New Zeal Volc Rec*, 10: 23-29

Latter J H, Lloyd E F, Smith I E M, Nathan S, 1992. Volcanic hazards in the Kermadec Islands, and at submarine volcanoes between southern Tonga and New Zealand. *New Zeal Ministry Civil Defense, Volc Hazards Inf Ser*, 4: 1-45

Lecointre J A, Neall V E, Cleland Wallace R, Prebble W M, 2002. The 55- to 60-ka Te Whaiau Formation: a catastrophic, avalanche-induced, cohesive debris-flow deposit from Proto-Tongariro volcano, New Zealand. *Bull Volc*, 63: 509-525

Leonard G S, Cole J W, Nairn I A, Self S, 2002. Basalt triggering of the c. AD 1305 Kaharoa rhyolite eruption, Tarawera volcanic complex, New Zealand. *J Volc Geotherm Res*, 115: 461-486

Locke C A, Cassidy J, 1997. Egmont volcano, New Zealand: three-dimensional structure and its implications for evolution. *J Volc Geotherm Res*, 76: 149-161

Lowe D J, 1986. Revision of the age and stratigraphic relationships of Hinemaiaia tephra and Whakatane ash, North Island, New Zealand, using distal occurrences in organic deposits. *New Zeal J Geol Geophys*, 29: 61-73

Lowe D J, Shane P A R, Allowayc B V, Newnham R M, 2008. Fingerprints and age models for widespread New Zealand tephra marker beds erupted since 30,000 years ago: a framework for NZ-INTIMATE. *Quat Sci Rev*,

Lube G, Cronin S J, Platz T, Freundt A, Proctor J N, Henderson C, Sheridan M F, 2007. Flow and deposition of pyroclastic granular flows: a type example from the 1975 Ngauruhoe eruption, New Zealand. *J Volc Geotherm Res*, 161: 165-186

Manning D A, 1996. Middle-late Pleistocene tephrostratigrapy of the eastern Bay of Plenty, New Zealand. *Quat Internatl*, 34-36: 3-12

Manville V, Hodgson K A, Houghton B F, Keys J R, White J D L, 2000. Tephra, snow and water: complex sedimentary responses at an active snow-capped stratovolcano, Ruapehu, New Zealand. *Bull Volc*, 62: 278-293

Massoth G J, de Ronde C E J, Lupton J E, Feely R A, Baker E T, Lebon G T, Maenner S M, 2003. Chemically rich and diverse submarine hydrothermal plumes of the southern Kermadec volcanic arc (New Zealand). *Geol Soc London Spec Pub*, 219: 119-139

McClelland E, Erwin P S, 2003. Was a dacite dome implicated in the 9,500 b.p. collapse of Mt Ruapehu? A palaeomagnetic investigation. *Bull Volc*, 65: 294-305

McClelland E, Wilson C J N, Bardot L, 2004. Paleotemperature determinations for the 1.8-ka Taupo ignimbrite, New Zealand, and implications for the emplacement history of a high-velocity pyroclastic flow. *Bull Volc*, 66: 492-513

Milner D M, Cole J W, Wood C P, 2002. Asymmetric, multiple-block collapse at Rotorua caldera, Taupo Volcanic Zone, New Zealand. *Bull Volc*, 64: 134-149

Milner D M, Cole J W, Wood C P, 2003. Mamaku Ignimbrite: a caldera-forming ignimbrite erupted from a compositionally zoned magma chamber in Taupo Volcanic Zone, New Zealand. *J Volc Geotherm Res*, 122: 243-264

Mongillo M A, Wood C P, 1995. Thermal infrared mapping of White Island volcano, New Zealand. *J Volc Geotherm Res*, 69: 59-71

Mortimer N, Gans P B, Mildenhall D C, 2008. A middle-late Quaternary age for the adakitic arc volcanics of Hautere (Solander Island), Southern Ocean. *J Volc Geotherm Res*, 178: 701-707

NIWA/NOAA Vents Program, 2005. New Zealand American submarine ring of fire 2005 Kermadec arc submarine volcanoes. New Zeal Nat Inst Water Atmosph Res/NOAA Vents Program final cruise report (http://www.oceanexplorer.noaa.gov/explorations/05fire/logs/leg2_summary/media/srof05_cruisereport_final.pdf)

Nairn I A, 1974. Volcanological observations, individual volcanoes, Raupehu, observations and inspections. *New Zeal Volc Rec*, 2: 11-15

Nairn I A, 1975. Volcanological observations: individual volcanoes, Ruapehu, observations and inspections. *New Zeal Volc Rec*, 4: 27-30

Nairn I A, 1989. Mount Tarawera. *New Zeal Geol Surv*, 1:50,000 geol map sheet V16 AC and 55 p text

Nairn I A, 1991. Volcanic hazards at Okataina Volcanic Centre. *New Zeal Ministry Civil Defense, Volc Hazards Inf Ser*, 2: 1-29

Nairn I A, Cole J W, 1975. New Zealand. *Catalog of Active Volcanoes of the World and Solfatara Fields*, Rome: IAVCEI, 22: 1-156 ***(regional reference)***

Nairn I A, Cole J W, Houghton B F, Wilson C J N, 1986. Tarawera 1886 eruption. *New Zeal Internatl Volc Cong Handbook*, p 111-121

Nairn I A, Hedenquist J W, Villamor P, Berryman K R, Shane P A, 2005. The ~AD1315 Tarawera and Waiotapu eruptions, New Zealand: contemporaneous rhyolite and hydrothermal eruptions driven by an arrested basalt dike system? *Bull Volc*, 67: 186-193

Nairn I A, Houghton B F, Cole J F, 1991. Volcanic hazards at White Island. *New Zeal Ministry Civil Defense, Volc Hazards Inf Ser*, 3: 1-25

Nairn I A, Kobayashi T, Nakagawa M, 1998. The ~10 ka multiple vent pyroclastic eruption sequence at Tongariro volcanic centre: Taupo volcanic zone, New Zealand: Part 1. Eruptive processes during regional extension. *J Volc Geotherm Res*, 86: 19-44

Nairn I A, Self S, 1978. Explosive eruptions and pyroclastic avalanches from Ngauruhoe in February 1975. *J Volc Geotherm Res*, 3: 39-60

Nairn I A, Self S, Cole J W, Leonard G S, Scutter C, 2001. Distribution, stratigraphy, and history of proximal deposits from the C. AD 1305 Kaharoa eruptive episode at Tarawera volcano, New Zealand. *New Zeal J Geol Geophys*, 44: 467-484

Nairn I A, Shane P R, Cole J W, Leonard G J, Self S, Pearson N, 2004. Rhyolite magma processes of the ~ AD 1315 Kaharoa eruption episode, Tarawera volcano, New Zealand. *J Volc Geotherm Res*, 131: 265-294

Nairn I A, Wood C P, Bailey R A, 1994. The Reporoa caldera, Taupo Volcanic Zone: source of the Kaingaroa Ignimbrites. *Bull Volc*, 56: 529-537

Nairn I A, Wood C P, Hewson C A Y, 1979. Phreatic eruptions of Ruapehu: April 1975. *New Zeal J Geol Geophys*, 22: 155-169

Nakagawa M, Wada K, Thordarson T, Wood C P, Gamble J A, 1999. Petrologic investigations of the 1995 and 1996 eruptions of Ruapehu volcano, New Zealand: formation of discrete and small magma pockets and their intermittent discharge. *Bull Volc*, 61: 15-31

Neall V E, 1971. Volcanic domes and lineations in Egmont National Park. *New Zeal J Geol Geophys*, 14: 71-81

Neall V E, 1972. Tephrochronology and tephrostratigraphy of western Taranaki (N108-109), New Zealand. *New Zeal J Geol Geophys*, 15: 507-557

Neall V E, 1974. *The Volcanic History of Taranaki*. Egmont National Park, 14 p

Neall V E, 1979. New Plymouth, Egmont North, Egmont South and Manaia. *New Zeal Dept Sci Ind Res*, 1:50,000 geol map, 3 sheets and notes

Neall V E, Alloway B V, 1986. Quaternary volcaniclastics and volcanic hazards of Taranaki (Tour Guide C3). *New Zeal Geol Surv Rec*, 12: 101

Neall V E, Alloway B V, 1991. Volcanic hazards at Egmont volcano. *New Zeal Ministry Civil Defense, Volc Hazards Inf Ser*, 1: 1-31

Neall V E, Stewart R B, Smith I E M, 1986. History and petrology of the Taranaki volcanoes. *Roy Soc New Zeal Bull*, 23: 257-263

Platz T, Cronin S J, Cashman K V, Stewart R B, Smith I E M, 2007. Transition from effusive to explosive phases in andesite eruptions - a case-study from the AD1655 eruption of Mt. Taranaki, New Zealand. *J Volc Geotherm Res*, 161: 15-34

Price R C, McCulloch M T, Smith I E M, Stewart R B, 1992. Pb-Nd-Sr isotopic compositions and trace element characteristics of young volcanic rocks from Egmont volcano and comparisons with basalts and andesites from the Taupo volcanic zone, New Zealand. *Geochim Cosmochim Acta*, 56: 941-953

Reay A, 1986. Andesites from Solander Island. *Roy Soc New Zeal Bull*, 23: 337-343

Rout D J, Cassidy J, Locke C A, Smith I E M, 1993. Geophysical evidence for temporal and structural relationships within the monogenetic basalt volcanoes of the Auckland volcanic field, northern New Zealand. *J Volc Geotherm Res*, 57: 71-83

Sable J E, Houghton B F, Wilson C J N, Carey R J, 2006. Complex proximal sedimentation from Plinian plumes: the example of Tarawera 1886. *Bull Volc*, 69: 89-103

Scott B J, 1978. Observed activity at Ngauruhoe. *New Zeal Volc Rec*, 7: 44

Shane P, 2005. Towards a comprehensive distal andesitic tephrostratigraphic framework for New Zealand based on eruptions from Egmont volcano. *J Quat Sci*, 20: 45-57

Shane P, Doyle L R, Nairn I A, 2008. Hetergeneous andesite-dacite ejecta in 26-16.6 ka pyroclastic deposits of Tongariro volcano, New Zealand: the product of multiple magma-mixing events. *Bull Volc*, 70: 517-536

Shane P, Hoverd J, 2002. Distal record of multi-sourced tephra in Onepoto Basin, Auckland, New Zealand: implications for volcanic chronology, frequency and hazards. *Bull Volc*, 64: 441-454

Shane P, Martin S B, Smith V C, Beggs K F, Darragh M B, Cole J W, Nairn I A, 2007. Multiple rhyolite magmas and basalt injection in the 17.7 ka Rerewhakaaitu eruption episode from Tarawera volcanic complex, New Zealand. *J Volc Geotherm Res*, 164: 1-26

Shane P, Sikes E L, Guilderson T P, 2006. Tephra beds in deep-sea cores off northern New Zealand: implications for the history of Taupo Volcanic Zone, Mayor Island and White Island volcanoes. *J Volc Geotherm Res*, 154: 276-290

Shane P, Smith V C, Nairn I A, 2005. High temperature rhyodacites of the 36 ka Hauparu pyroclastic eruption, Okataina volcanic centre, New Zealand: change in a silicic magmatic system following caldera collapse. *J Volc Geotherm Res*, 147: 357-376

Skinner D N B, 1986. Neogene volcanism of the Hauraki volcanic region. *Roy Soc New Zeal Bull*, 23: 21-47

Smith G A, Grubensky M J, Geissman J W, 1999. Nature and origin of cone-forming volcanic breccias in the Te Herenga Formation, Ruapehu, New Zealand. *Bull Volc*, 61: 64-82

Smith I E M, Allen S R, 1993. Volcanic hazards at the Auckland Volcanic Field. *New Zeal Ministry Civil Defense, Volc Hazards Inf Ser*, 5: 1-34

Smith I E, Day R A, Ashcroft J, 1986. Volcanic associations of Northland (Tour Guide A4). *New Zeal Geol Surv Rec*, 12: 5-32

Smith R T, Houghton B F, 1995. Vent migration and changing eruptive style during the 1800a Taupo eruption: new evidence from the Hatepe and Rotongaio phreatoplinian ashes. *Bull Volc*, 57: 432-439

Smith V C, Shane P, Nairn I A, 2005. Trends in rhyolite geochemistry, mineralogy, and magma storage during the last 50 kyr at Okataina and Taupo volcanic centres, Taupo volcanic zone, New Zealand. *J Volc Geotherm Res*, 148: 372-406

Smith V C, Shane P, Nairn I A, Williams C M, 2006. Geochemistry and magmatic properties of eruption episodes from Haroharo linear vent zone, Okataina Volcanic Centre, New Zealand during the last 10 kyr. *Bull Volc*, 69: 57-88

Spinks K D, Acocella V, Cole J W, Bassett K N, 2005. Structural control of volcanism and caldera development in the transtensional Taupo Volcanic Zone, New Zealand. *J Volc Geotherm Res*, 144: 7-22

Spinks K D, Cole J W, Leonard G S, 2004. Caldera volcanism in the Taupo Volcanic Zone. *Geol Soc New Zeal, New Zeal Geophys Soc, 26th New Zeal Geotherm Workshop, 6th-9th Dec 2004, Great Lake Centre, Taupo*, Field Trip Guides, 7: 110-135

Sporli K B, Eastwood V R, 1997. Elliptical boundary of an intraplate volcanic field, Auckland, New Zealand. *J Volc Geotherm Res*, 79: 169-179

Stevenson R J, Briggs R M, Hodder A P W, 1993. Emplacement history of a low-viscosity, fountain-fed pantelleritic lava flow. *J Volc Geotherm Res*, 57: 39-56

Stevenson R J, Dingwell D B, Bagdassarov N S, Manley C R, 2001. Measurement and implication of "effective" viscosity for rhyolite flow emplacement. *Bull Volc*, 63: 227-237

Sutton A N, Blake S, Wilson C J N, 1995. An outline geochemistry of rhyolite eruptives from Taupo volcanic centre, New Zealand. *J Volc Geotherm Res*, 68: 153-175

Takano B, Ohsawa S, Glover R B, 1994. Surveillance of Ruapehu crater lake, New Zealand, by aqueous polythionates. *J Volc Geotherm Res*, 60: 29-57

Talbot J P, Self S, Wilson C J N, 1994. Dilute gravity current and rain-flushed ash deposits in the 1.8 km Hatepe Plinian deposit, Taupo, New Zealand. *Bull Volc*, 56: 538-551

Thompson B N, 1961. Geological map of New Zealand Sheet 2A-Whangarei. *New Zeal Geol Surv*, 1:250,000 geol map and text

Thompson B N, Kermode L O, Ewart A, 1965. New Zealand volcanology-central volcanic region. *New Zeal Geol Surv Handbook Inf Ser*, no 50

Thomson J A, 1926. Volcanoes of the New Zealand-Tonga volcanic zone-a record of eruptions. *New Zeal J Sci Tech*, B8: 354-371 ***(regional reference)***

Topping W W, 1973. Tephrostratigraphy and chronology of late Quaternary eruptives from the Tongariro volcanic centre, New Zealand. *New Zeal J Geol Geophys*, 16: 397-423

Topping W W, Kohn B P, 1973. Rhyolitic tephra marker beds in the Tongariro area, North Island, New Zealand. *New Zeal J Geol Geophys*, 16: 375-395

Turner M B, Bebbington M S, Cronin S J, Stewart R B, 2009. Merging eruption datasets: building an integrated Holocene eruptive record for Mt Taranaki, New Zealand. *Bull Volc*, 71: 903-918

Turner M B, Cronin S J, Bebbington M S, Platz T, 2008a. Developing probabilistic eruption forecasts for dormant volcanoes: a case study from Mt Taranaki, New Zealand. *Bull Volc*, 70: 507-515

Turner M B, Cronin S J, Smith I E, Stewart R B, Neall V E, 2008b. Eruption episodes and magma recharge events in andesitic systems: Mt Taranaki, New Zealand. *J Volc Geotherm Res*, 177: 1063-1076

Ui T, Kawachi S, Neall V E, 1986. Fragmentation of debris avalanche material during flowage; evidence from the Pungarehu Formation, Mount Egmont, New Zealand. *J Volc Geotherm Res*, 27: 255-264

Vandemeulebrouck J, Hurst A W, Scott B J, 2008. The effects of hydrothermal eruptions and a tectonic earthquake on a cycling crater lake (Inferno Crater Lake, Waimangu, New Zealand). *J Volc Geotherm Res*, 178: 271-275

Vucetich C G, Pullar W A, 1973. Holocene tephra formations erupted in the Taupo Area, and interbedded tephras from other volcanic sources. *New Zeal J Geol Geophys*, 16: 745-780

Walker G P L, 1980. The Taupo pumice: product of the most powerful known (ultraplinian) eruption? *J Volc Geotherm Res*, 8: 69-94

Walker G P L, 1981. The ground layer of the Taupo ignimbrite: a striking example of sedimentation from a pyroclastic flow. *J Volc Geotherm Res*, 10: 1-12

Walker G P L, Self S, Wilson L, 1984. Tarawera 1886, New Zealand - A basaltic Plinian fissure eruption. *J Volc Geotherm Res*, 21: 61-78

Ward G A, 1922. White Island. *New Zeal J Sci Tech*, 5: 220-226

White J D L, Houghton B F, Hodgson K A, Wilson C J N, 1997. Delayed sedimentary response to the A.D. 1886 eruption of Tarawera, New Zealand. *Geology*, 25: 459-462

Wilson C J N, 1993. Stratigraphy, chronology, styles and dynamics of late Quaternary eruptions from Taupo volcano, New Zealand. *Phil Trans Roy Soc London*, Ser A, 343: 205-306

Wilson C J N, 2001. The 26.5 ka Oruanui erupption, New Zealand: an introduction and overview. *J Volc Geotherm Res*, 112: 133-174

Wilson C J N, Ambraseys N N, Bradley J, Walker G P L, 1980. A new date for the Taupo eruption, New Zealand. *Nature*, 288: 252-253

Wilson C J N, Blake S, Charlier B L A, Sutton A N, 2006. The 26.5 ka Oruanui eruption, Taupo volcano, New Zealand: development, characteristics and evacuation of a large rhyolitic magma body. *J Petr*, 47: 35-69

Wilson C J N, Gravley D M, Leonard G S, Rowland J V, 2009. Volcanism in the central Taupo Volcanic Zone, New Zealand: tempo, styles and controls. *In*: Thordarson T, Self S, Larsen G, Rowland S K, Hoskuldsson A (eds), *Studies in Volcanology: The Legacy of George Walker*. Geol Soc London, p 225-247

Wilson C J N, Houghton B F, Kamp P J J, McWilliams M O, 1995b. An exceptionally widespread ignimbrite with implications for pyroclastic flow emplacement. *Nature*, 378: 605-607

Wilson C J N, Houghton B F, Lloyd E F, 1986. Volcanic history and evolution of Maroa-Taupo area, central North Island. *Roy Soc New Zeal Bull*, 23: 194-223

Wilson C J N, Houghton B F, McWilliams M O, Lanphere M A, Weaver S D, Briggs R M, 1995a. Volcanic and structural evolution of Taupo Volcanic Zone, New Zealand: a review. *J Volc Geotherm Res*, 68: 1-28

Wilson C J N, Houghton B F, Pillans B J, Weaver S D, 1995. Taupo Volcanic Zone calc-alkaline tephras on the peralkaline Mayor Island volcano, New Zealand: identification and uses as marker horizons. *J Volc Geotherm Res*, 69: 303-311

Wilson C J N, Rogan A M, Smith I E M, Northey D J, Nairn I A, Houghton B F, 1984. Caldera volcanoes of the Taupo volcanic zone, New Zealand. *J Geophys Res*, 89: 8463-8484

Wilson C J N, Walker G P L, 1985. The Taupo eruption, New Zealand. I. General aspects. *Phil Trans Roy Soc London*, Ser A, 314: 199-228

Wood C P, Browne P R L, 1996. Chlorine-rich pyrometamorphic magma at White Island volcano, New Zealand. *J Volc Geotherm Res*, 72: 21-35

Wright I C, Chadwick W W Jr, de Ronde C E J, Reymond D, Hyvernaud O, Gennerich H-H, Stoffers, P, Mackay K, Dunkin M A, Bannister S C, 2008. Collapse and reconstruction of Monowai submarine volcano, Kermadec arc, 1990-2004. *J Geophys Res*, doi:10.1029/2007JB005138

Wright I C, Gamble J A, 1999. Southern Kermadec submarine caldera arc volcanoes (SW Pacific): caldera formation by effusive and pyroclastic eruption. *Marine Geol*, 161: 207-227

Wright I C, Gamble J A, Shane P A R, 2003. Submarine silicic volcanism of the Healy caldera, southern Kermadec arc (SW Pacific): I - volcanology and eruption mechanisms. *Bull Volc*, 65: 15-29

Wright I C, Worthington T J, Gamble J A, 2006. New multibeam mapping and geochemistry of the 30°-35° S sector, and overview, of southern Kermadec arc volcanism. *J Volc Geotherm Res*, 149: 263-296

TONGA, SAMOA, & FIJI (0403-05)

Anderson T, 1910. The volcano of Matavanu in Savaii. *Quart J Geol Soc London*, 66: 621-639

Baker S W, 1885. A description of the new volcano in the Friendly Islands, near Tongatabu. *Trans New Zeal Inst*, 18: 41-46

Bauer G R, 1970. The geology of Tofua Island, Tonga. *Pacific Sci*, 24: 333-350

Brodie J W, 1970. Notes on the volcanic activity at Fonualei Tonga. *New Zeal J Geol Geophys*, 13: 30-38

Bryan S E, Cook A, Evans J P, Colls P W, Wells M G, Lawrence M G, Jell J S, Greig A, Leslie R, 2004. Pumice rafting and faunal dispersion during 2001-2002 in the Southwest Pacific: record of a dacitic submarine explosive eruption from Tonga. *Earth Planet Sci Lett*, 227: 135-154

Bryan W B, Stice G D, Ewart A, 1972. Geology, petrology, and geochemistry of the volcanic islands of Tonga. *J Geophys Res*, 77: 1566-1585

Cole J W, Graham I J, Gibson I L, 1990. Magmatic evolution of Late Cenozoic volcanic rocks of the Lau Ridge, Fiji. *Contr Mineral Petr*, 104: 540-554

Coulson F I E, 1976. Geology of the Lomaiviti and Moala Island Groups. *Fiji Min Res Div Bull*, 2: 1-162

Cronin S J, Bebbeington M, Lai C D, 2001. A probabalistic assessment of eruption recurrence on Taveuni volcano, Fiji. *Bull Volc*, 63: 274-288

Cronin S J, Ferland M A, Terry J P, 2004. Nabukelevu volcano (Mt. Washington), Kadavu - a source of hitherto unknown volcanic hazard in Fiji. *J Volc Geotherm Res*, 131: 371-396

Cronin S J, Neall V E, 2000. Impacts of volcanism in pre-European inhabitants of Taveuni, Fiji. *Bull Volc*, 62: 199-213

Cronin S J, Neall V E, 2001. Holocene volcanic geology, volcanic hazard, and risk on Taveuni, Fiji. *New Zeal J Geol Geophys*, 44: 417-437

Ewart A, Brothers R N, Mateen A, 1977. An outline of the geology and geochemistry, and the possible petrogenetic evolution of the volcanic rocks of the Tonga-Kermadec-New Zealand island arc. *J Volc Geotherm Res*, 2: 205-250

Ewart A, Bryan W B, Gill J B, 1973. Mineralogy and geochemistry of the younger volcanic islands of Tonga, southwest Pacific. *J Petr*, 14: 429-465

Frost E L, 1974. Taveuni, Fiji. *Asian Pacific Arch Ser*, 6: 1-175

Hart S R, Staudigel H, Koppers A A P, Blusztajn J, Baker E T, Workman R, Jackson M, Hauri E, Kurz M, Sims K, Fornari D, Saal A, Lyons S, 2000. Vailulu'u undersea volcano: The New Samoa. *Geochem Geophys Geosyst*, 1: paper 2000GC000108

Hekinian R, Muhe R, Worthington T J, Stoffers P, 2008. Geology of a submarine volcanic caldera in the Tonga Arc: dive results. *J Volc Geotherm Res*, 176: 571-582

Hoffmeister J E, Ladd H S, Alling H L, 1929. Falcon Island. *Amer J Sci*, 18: 461-471

Jaggar T A, 1930b. The island volcano of Niuafoou. *Volcano Lett*, 312: 1-3

Jaggar T A, 1931b. Geology and geography of Niuafoou volcano. *Volcano Lett*, 318: 1-3

Jensen H I, 1906. The geology of Samoa, and the eruptions in Savaii. *Proc Linnean Soc New South Wales*, 31: 641-672

Kear D, Wood B L, 1959. The geology and hydrology of western Samoa. *New Zeal Geol Surv Bull*, 63: 1-92

Konter J G, Staudigel H, Hart S R, Shearer P M, 2004. Seafloor seismic monitoring of an active submarine volcano: local seismicity at Vailulu'u Seamount, Samoa. *Geochem Geophys Geosyst*, 5: Q06007, doi: 10.1029/2004GC000702

Latter J H, 1976. Variations in stress release preceding and accompanying a submarine eruption in northern Tonga. *In*: Johnson R W (ed) *Volcanism in Australasia*, Amsterdam: Elsevier, p 355-374

Macdonald G A, 1948. Notes on Niuafo'ou. *Amer J Sci*, 246: 65-77

Macdonald G A, 1968. A contribution to the petrology of Tutuila, American Samoa. *Geol Rundschau*, 57: 821-837

Melson W G, Jarosewich E, Lundquist C A, 1970. Volcanic eruption at Metis Shoal, Tonga, 1967-1968: description and petrology. *Smithsonian Contr Earth Sci*, 4: 1-18

Nemeth K, Cronin S J, 2009. Volcanic structures and oral traditions of volcanism of Western Samoa (SW Pacific) and their implications for hazard education. *J Volc Geotherm Res*, 186: 223-237

Nemeth K, Cronin S J, Lolo F, Leavasa M, Solomona D S, Nelson F, 2007. Volcanic evolution, oral traditions of volcanism of Western Samoa (SW Pacific) and their volcanic hazard implications. *Geol Soc New Zeal, New Zeal Geophys Soc Joint Annual Conf, Prog Abs*, p 113

Pacific Islands Pilot, 1956. [Unnamed Tonga submarine volcano]. *Pacific Islands Pilot*, 2: 396

Phillips C, 1898. The volcanoes of the Pacific. *Trans New Zeal Inst*, 31: 510-551

Price R C, Maillet P, McDougall I, Dupont J, 1991. The geochemistry of basalts from the Wallis Islands, northern Melanesian borderland: evidence for a lithospheric origin for Samoan-type basaltic magmas? *J Volc Geotherm Res*, 45: 267-288

Richard J J, 1962. Kermadec, Tonga and Samoa. *Catalog of Active Volcanoes of the World and Solfatara Fields*, Rome: IAVCEI, 13: 1-38 ***(regional reference)***

Rubin K H, Embley R W, Clague D A, Resing J A, Michael P J, Keller N S, Baker E T, 2009. Lavas from active boninite and very recent basalt eruptions at two submarine NE Lau Basin sites. *Eos, Trans Amer Geophys Union*, 89: Fall Meet Suppl, abstr V43I-05

Spennemann D H R, 2003. The June 1846 eruption of Fonualei volcano, Tonga, an historical analysis. *Charles Sturt Univ, The Johnstone Centre Rpt*, 196: 1-30

Staudigel H, Hart S R, Koppers A A P, Constable C, Workman R, Kurz M, Baker E T, 2004. Hydrothermal venting at Vailulu'u Seamount: the smoking end of the Samoan chain. *Geochem Geophys Geosyst*, 5: Q02003, doi: 10.1029/2003GC000626

Stearns H T, 1944. Geology of the Samoan Islands. *Geol Soc Amer Bull*, 55: 1279-1332

Stearns H T, 1945. Geology of the Wallis Islands. *Geol Soc Amer Bull*, 56: 849-860

Stice G D, 1968. Petrology of the Manu'a Islands, Samoa. *Contr Mineral Petr*, 19: 343-357

Stice G D, McCoy F W, 1968. The geology of the Manu'a Islands, Samoa. *Pacific Sci*, 22: 427-457

Stoffers P, Worthington T J, Schwarz-Schampera U, Hannington M D, Massoth G J, Hekinian R, Schmidt M, Lundsten L J, Evans L J, Vaiomo'unga R, Kerby T, 2006. Submarine volcanoes and high-temperature hydrothermal venting on the Tonga arc, southwest Pacific. *Geology*, 34: 453-456

Taylor P, 2002. New submarine volcano (west of Vava'u). *Aust Volc Invest Occ Rpt*, 02/01: 1-7

Taylor P, 2003. Unreported submarine activity at Metis Shoal, June 1991 and the risk from future activity. *Aust Volc Invest Occ Rpt*, 03/05: 1-9

Taylor P W, 1991. The geology and petrology of Niuafo'ou Island, Tonga: subaerial volcanism in an active back-arc basin. *Unpublished MSci thesis*, Maquarie Univ

Taylor P W, 1999. A volcanic hazards assessment following the January 1999 eruption of Submarine Volcano III Tofua volcanic arc, Kingdom of Tonga. *Aust Volc Invest Occ Rpt*, 99/01: 1-8

Taylor P W, Ewart A, 1997. The Tofua Volcanic Arc, Tonga, SW Pacific: a review of historic volcanic activity. *Aust Volc Invest Occ Rpt*, 97/01: 1-58

Thomson J A, 1926. Volcanoes of the New Zealand-Tonga volcanic zone-a record of eruptions. *New Zeal J Sci Tech*, B8: 354-371 ***(regional reference)***

Vaughan R G, Abrams M J, Hook S J, Pieri D C, 2007. Satellite observations of new volcanic island in Tonga. *Eos, Trans Amer Geophys Union*, 88: 37,41

Walker G P L, Eyre P R, 1995. Dike complexes in American Samoa. *J Volc Geotherm Res*, 69: 241-254

Wendt J I, Regelous M, Collerson K D, Ewart A, 1997. Evidence for a contribution from two mantle plumes to island-arc lavas from northern Tonga. *Geology*, 25: 611-614

Woodhall D, 1985. Geology of Taveuni, Qamea, Laucala, Cikobia and adjacent islands. *Mineral Resour Dept Fiji*, 1:50,000 geol map

NEW GUINEA, NEW BRITAIN, & SOLOMONS (0500-06)

Arculus R J, Johnson R W, Chappell B W, McKee C D, Sakai H, 1983. Ophiolite-contaminated andesites, trachybasalts, and cognate inclusions of Mount Lamington, Papua New Guinea: anhydrite-amphibole-bearing lavas and the 1951 cumulodome. *J Volc Geotherm Res*, 18: 215-247

Baker E T, Massoth G J, de Ronde C E J, Lupton J E, McInnes B I A, 2002. Observations and sampling of an ongoing subsurface eruption of Kavachi volcano, Solomon Islands, May 2000. *Geology*, 30: 975-978

Baker G, 1946. Preliminary note on volcanic eruptions in the Goropu Mountains, south-eastern Papua, during the period December, 1943 to August 1944. *J Geol*, 54: 19-31

Ball E E, Johnson R W, 1976. Volcanic history of Long Island, Papua New Guinea. *In*: Johnson R W (ed) *Volcanism in Australasia*, Amsterdam: Elsevier, p 133-148

Blake D H, 1968. Post Miocene volcanoes on Bougainville Island, Territory of Papua and New Guinea. *Bull Volc*, 32: 121-140

Blake D H, 1976. Madilogo, late Quaternary volcano near Port Moresby, Papua New Guinea. *In*: Johnson R W (ed) *Volcanism in Australasia*, Amsterdam: Elsevier, p 253-258

Blake D H, Bleeker P, 1970. Volcanoes of the Cape Hoskins area, New Britain, Territory of Papua and New Guinea. *Bull Volc*, 34: 385-405

Blake D H, Loffler E, 1971. Volcanic and glacial landforms on Mount Giluwe, Territory of Papua and New Guinea. *Geol Soc Amer Bull*, 82: 1605-1614

Blake D H, McDougall I, 1973. Ages of the Cape Hoskins volcanoes, New Britain, Papua New Guinea. *J Geol Soc Aust*, 20: 199-204

Blake D H, Miezitis Y, 1967. Geology of Bougainville and Buka Islands, New Guinea. *Aust Bur Min Resour Geol Geophys Bull*, 93: 1-56

Blong R, 2003. Building damage in Rabaul, Papua New Guinea, 1994. *Bull Volc*, 65: 43-54

Blong R J, 1979. Huli legends and volcanic eruptions, Papua New Guinea. *Search*, 10: 93-94

Blong R J, 1982. *The Time of Darkness Local Legends and Volcanic Reality in Papua New Guinea*. Canberra: Aust Natl Univ Press, 257 p

Blong R, Aislabie C, 1988. The impact of volcanic hazards at Rabaul Papua New Guinea. *Papua New Guinea Inst Natl Affairs, Discussion Pap*, no 33

Branch C D, 1965. Volcanic activity at Lake Dakataua caldera, New Britain. *Aust Bur Min Resour*

Geol Geophys Rec, 1965/67: 1-8

Branch C D, 1967. Short papers from the Vulcanological Observatory, Rabual, New Britain. *Aust Bur Min Resour Geol Geophys Rpt*, 107: 1-42

Bultitude R J, 1976. Eruptive history of Bagana volcano, Papua New Guinea, between 1882 and 1975. *In*: Johnson R W (ed) *Volcanism in Australasia*, Amsterdam: Elsevier, p 317-336

Bultitude R J, 1979. Bagana volcano, Bouganiville Island geology, petrology and summary of eruptive history between 1875 and 1975. *Geol Surv Papua New Guinea Mem*, 6: 1-35

Bultitude R J, 1981. Literature search for pre-1945 sightings of volcanoes and their activity on Bougainville Island. *Geol Surv Papua New Guinea Mem*, 10: 227-242

Bultitude R J, Cooke R J S, 1981. Note on activity from Bagana volcano from 1975 to 1980. *Geol Surv Papua New Guinea Mem*, 10: 243-248

Coleman P J, 1960. An introduction to the geology of the island of Choiseul in the Western Solomons, 1957. *In*: Grover J C (ed) *Rpts on Invest Geol Min Resour Protectorate*, Brit Solomon Is Geol Rec 1957-58 Rpt no 4: 16-26

Cooke R J S, 1977. Rabaul Volcanological Observatory and Geophysical Surveillance of the Rabaul volcano. *Aust Physicist*, Feb, p 27-30

Cooke R J S, 1981a. Eruptive history of the volcano at Ritter Island. *Geol Surv Papua New Guinea Mem*, 10: 115-124

Cooke R J S, 1981b. Eruptions at Pago volcano, 1911-1933. *Geol Surv Papua New Guinea Mem*, 10: 135-146

Cooke R J S, 1981c. Notes on the activity of Ulawun volcano, 1700-1958: results of literature search. *Geol Surv Papua New Guinea Mem*, 10: 147-152

Cooke R J S, Baldwin J T, Sprod T J, 1976. Recent volcanoes and mineralization in Papua New Guinea. *25th Internatl Geol Cong, Sydney, Excur Guide*, 53: 1-30

Cooke R J S, Johnson R W, 1978. Volcanoes and volcanology in Papua New Guinea. *Geol Surv Papua New Guinea Rpt*, 78/2: 1-46 ***(regional reference)***

Cooke R J S, Johnson R W, 1981. Bam volcano: morphology, geology, and reported eruptive history. *Geol Surv Papua New Guinea Mem*, 10: 13-22

Cooke R J S, McKee C O, Dent V F, Wallace D A, 1976. Striking sequence of volcanic eruptions in the Bismarck volcanic arc, Papua New Guinea, in 1972-75. *In*: Johnson R W (ed) *Volcanism in Australasia*, Amsterdam: Elsevier, p 149-172

Crook K A W, Musgrave R J, 1989. Triple-junction tectonics, NE Woodlark Basin: construction of "near-trench" of island arc volcanoes on Indo-Australian plate and their transfer to the Pacific plate (abs). *Eos, Trans Amer Geophys Union*, 70: 1319

Eissen J-P, Blot C, Louat R, 1991. Chronologie de l'activite volcanique historique de l'arc insulaire des Nouvelles-Hebrides de 1595 a 1991. *ORSTOM Rapports Sci Tech Sci Terre Geol-Geophys*, 2: 1-69

Emeleus T G, 1981. Palaeomagnetic directions in lava flows of the Rabaul volcanic complex: preliminary application to dating. *Geol Surv Papua New Guinea Mem*, 10: 201-207

Exon N F, Johnson R W, 1986. The elusive Cook volcano and other submarine forearc volcanoes in the Solomon Islands. *Aust Bur Min Resour Geol Geophys J*, 10: 77-83

Exon N F, Johnson R W, 1989. Reply: The elusive Cook volcano and other submarine forearc volcanoes in the Solomon Islands. *Aust Bur Min Resour Geol Geophys J*, 11: 121

Finlayson D M, Gudmundsson O, Itikarai I, Nishimura Y, Shimamura H, 2003. Rabaul volcano, Papua New Guinea: seismic tomographic imaging of an active caldera. *J Volc Geotherm Res*, 124: 153-171

Fisher N H, 1939a. Geology and volcanology of Blanche Bay and the surrounding area, New Britain. *New Guinea Geol Bull*, 1: 1-53

Fisher N H, 1957. Melanesia. *Catalog of Active Volcanoes of the World and Solfatara Fields*, Rome: IAVCEI, 5: 1-105 ***(regional reference)***

Fisher N H, 1976. 1941-42 eruption of Tavurvur volcano, Rabaul, Papua New Guinea. *In*: Johnson R W (ed) *Volcanism in Australasia*, Amsterdam: Elsevier, p 201-210

Fisher N H, Branch C D, 1981. Late Cainozoic volcanic deposits of the Morobe goldfield. *Geol Surv Papua New Guinea Mem*, 10: 249-256

Greene H G, Tiffin D L, McKee C O, 1986. Structural deformation and sedimentation in an active caldera, Rabaul, Papua New Guinea. *J Volc Geotherm Res*, 30: 327-356

Grover J C, 1955. Geology, mineral deposits and prospects of mining development in the British Solomon Islands Protectorate. *Interim Geol Surv Brit Solomon Is Mem*, 1: 1-151

Grover J C, 1958. The Solomon Islands-geological exploration and research 1953-1956. *Geol Surv Brit Solomon Is Mem*, 2: 1-150

Grover J C, 1968. Submarine volcanoes and oceanographic observations in the New Georgia Group, 1963-64. *Brit Solomon Is Geol Rec, 1963-67 Rpt*, 96: 116-125

Gust D A, Johnson R W, 1981. Amphibole-bearing inclusions from Boisa Island, Papua New Guinea: evaluation of the role of fractional crystallization in an andesitic volcano. *J Geol*, 89: 219-232

Hackman B D, 1980. The geology of Guadalcanal, Solomon Islands. *Brit Inst Geol Sci Overseas Mem*, no 6

Hall L H, 1989. Discussion: The elusive Cook volcano and other submarine forearc volcanoes in the Solomon Islands. *Aust Bur Min Resour Geol Geophys J*, 11: 119-120

Heming R F, 1974. Geology and petrology of Rabaul Caldera, Papua New Guinea. *Geol Soc Amer Bull*, 85: 1253-1264

Heming R F, Carmichael I S E, 1973. High-temperature pumice flows from the Rabaul caldera, Papau, New Guinea. *Contr Mineral Petr*, 38: 1-20

Hughes G W, Craig P M, Dennis R A, 1981. Geology of the eastern Outer Islands. *Solomon Is Geol Surv Bull*, 4: 1-33

Jaggar T A, 1937. Eruptions at Rabaul, New Guinea. *Volcano Lett*, 448: 1-6

Jakes P, Smith I E, 1970. High potassium calc-alkaline rocks from Cape Nelson, Eastern Papua. *Contr Mineral Petr*, 28: 259-271

Johnson R W, 1971. Bamus volcano, Lake Hargy area, and Sulu Range, New Britain: volcanic geology and petrology. *Aust Bur Min Resour Geol Geophys Rec*, 1971/55: 1-36

Johnson R W, 1987. Large-scale volcanic cone collapse: the 1888 slope failure of Ritter volcano, and other examples from Papua New Guinea. *Bull Volc*, 49: 669-679

Johnson R W, Arculus R J, 1978. Volcanic rocks of the Witu Islands, Papua New Guinea: the origin of magmas above the deepest part of the New Britain Benioff zone. *Bull Volc*, 41: 609-655

Johnson R W, Blake D H, 1972. The Cape Hoskins area, southern Willaumez Peninsula, the Witu Islands, and associated volcanic centres, New Britain: volcanic geology and petrology. *Aust Bur Min Resour Geol Geophys Rec*, 1972/133: 1-102

Johnson R W, Davies R A, 1972. Volcanic geology of the St. Andrew Strait Islands, Bismarck Sea, Papua New Guinea. *Geol Surv Papua New Guinea, Note on Invest*, 72-002: 1-29

Johnson R W, Davies R A, Palfreyman W D, 1971. Cape Gloucester Area, New Britain' volcanic geology, petrology, and eruptive history of Langila Craters up to 1970. *Aust Bur Min Resour Geol Geophys Rec*, 1971/14: 1-34

Johnson R W, Davies R A, White A J R, 1972. Ulawun volcano, New Britain. *Aust Bur Min Resour Geol Geophys Bull*, 142: 1-42

Johnson R W, Everingham I B, Cooke R J S, 1981. Submarine volcanic eruptions in Papua New Guinea: 1878 activity of Vulcan (Rabaul) and other examples. *Geol Surv Papua New Guinea Mem*, 10: 167-180

Johnson R W, Jaques A L, Hickey R L, McKee C O, Chappell B W, 1985. Manam Island, Papua New Guinea: petrology and geochemistry of a low-TiO2 basaltic island-arc volcano. *J Petr*, 26: 283-323

Johnson R W, Macnab R P, Arculus R J, Ryburn R J, Cooke R J S, 1983. Bamus volcano, New Guinea: dormant neighbour of Ulawun, and magnesian-andesite locality. *Geol Rundschau*, 72: 207-237

Johnson R W, Taylor G A M, Davies R A, 1972. Geology and petrology of Quaternary volcanic islands off the north coast of New Guinea. *Aust Bur Min Resour Geol Geophys Rec*, 1972/21: 1-127

Johnson R W, Threlfall N A, 1985. *Volcano Town: the 1937-43 Rabaul Eruptions*. Bathurst, Australia: Robert Brown & Assoc, 151 p

Johnson R W, Tuni D, 1987. Kavachi, an active forearc volcano in the western Solomon Islands: reported eruptions between 1950 and 1982. *In*: Taylor B and Exon N F (eds) *Marine Geology, Geophysics, and Geochemistry of the Woodlark Basin, Solomon Islands*, Circum-Pacific Council Energy Min Resour Earth Sci Ser, 7: 89-112

Kennedy A K, Grove T L, Johnson R W, 1990. Experimental and major element constraints on the evolution of lavas from Lihir Island, Papua New Guinea. *Contr Mineral Petr*, 104: 722-734

Licence P S, Terrill J E, Fergusson L J, 1987. Epithermal gold mineralization, Ambitle Island, Papua New Guinea. *Proc Pacific Rim Cong 1987*, 1: 273-278

Lolok D, McKee C O, 1993. Eruption History, Stratigraphy and Petrology of the Pyroclastic Sequence at Hargy Volcano, Papua New Guinea. *IAVCEI, 1993 Canberra Mtg Abs*, p 63

Lowder G G, Carmichael I S E, 1970. The volcanoes and caldera of Talasea, New Britain: geology and petrology. *Geol Soc Amer Bull*, 81: 17-38

Lowenstein P L, 1982. Problems of volcanic hazards in Papua New Guinea. *Geol Surv Papua New Guinea Rpt*, 82/7: 1-62 ***(regional reference)***

Machida H, Blong R J, Specht J, Moriwaki H, Torrence R, Hayakawa Y, Talai B, Lolok D, Pain C F, 1996. Holocene explosive eruptions of Witori and Dakatau caldera volcanoes in west New Britain, Papua New Guinea. *Quat Internatl, 34-36: 65-78*

Mackenzie D E, Johnson R W, 1984. Pleistocene volcanoes of the western Papua New Guinea Highlands: morphology, geology, petrography, and modal and chemical analyses. *Aust Bur Min Resour Geol Geophys Rpt*, 246: 1-271

McKee C O, 1976. Investigations at Mount Lamington 1960-75. *Geol Surv Papua New Guinea Rpt*, 76/21

McKee C O, 1981. Geomorphology, geology, and petrology of Manam volcano. *Geol Surv Papua New Guinea Mem*, 10: 23-38

McKee C O, 1983. Volcanic hazards at Ulawun volcano. *Geol Surv Papua New Guinea Rpt*, 83/13: 1-20

McKee C O, Almond R A, Cooke R J S, Talai B, 1981. Basaltic pyroclastic avalanches and flank effusion from Ulawun volcano in 1978. *Geol Surv Papua New Guinea Mem*, 10: 153-166

McKee C O, Cooke R J S, Wallace D A, 1976. 1974-75 eruptions of Karkar volcano, Papua New Guinea. *In*: Johnson R W (ed) *Volcanism in Australasia*, Amsterdam: Elsevier, p 173-196

McKee C O, Johnson R W, Lowenstein P L, Riley S J, Blong R J, de Saint Ours P, Talai B, 1985. Rabaul Caldera, Papua New Guinea: volcanic hazards, surveillance, and eruption contingency planning. *J Volc Geotherm Res*, 23: 195-238

McKee C O, Johnson R W, Patia H, 1989. Assessment of volcanic hazards on Bougainville Island, Papua New Guinea (abs). *New Mexico Bur Mines Min Resour Bull*, 131: 182

McKee C O, Johnson R W, Rogerson R, 1990. Explosive volcanism on Bougainville Island: ignimbrites, calderas, and volcanic hazards. *Proc Pacific Rim Cong 1990*, 2: 237-245

McKee C O, Patia H, Johnson R W, 1988. Contrasting eruptive styles at the adjacent volcanoes Bagana and Billy Mitchell on Bouganville Island, Papua New Guinea. *Proc Kagoshima Internatl Conf Volc*, p 131-134

McKee C O, Wallace D A, 1981. Lava fields in the inner caldera of Karkar volcano. *Geol Surv Papua New Guinea Mem*, 10: 49-62

McKee C O, Wallace D A, Almond R A, Talai B, 1981. Fatal hydro-eruption of Karkar volcano in 1979: development of maar-like crater. *Geol Surv Papua New Guinea Mem*, 10: 63-84

Mennis M R, 1981. Yomba Island: real or mythical volcano? *Geol Surv Papua New Guinea Mem*, 10: 95-100

Mennis M R, 2005. Yomba Island (Hankow Reef), Atlantis of the South Pacific. *unpublished manuscript*, 40 p

Mori J, McKee C, Talai B, Itikarai I, 1989. A summary of precursors to volcanic eruptions in Papua New Guinea. *In*: Latter J H (ed), *Volcanic Hazards - Assessment and Monitoring*, Berlin: Springer-Verlag, p 260-291

Nairn I A, McKee C O, Talai B, Wood C P, 1995. Geology and eruptive history of the Rabaul Caldera area, Papua New Guinea. *J Volc Geotherm Res*, 69: 255-284

Nairn I A, Talai B, Wood C P, McKee C O, 1989. Rabaul Caldera, Papua New Guinea - 1:25,000 reconnaissance geological map and eruption history. *New Zeal Geol Surv Dept Sci Ind Res*, geol map

Neall V E, Wallace R C, Torrence R, 2008. The volcanic environment for 40,000 years of human occupation on the Willaumez Isthmus, West New Britain, Papua New Guinea. *J Volc Geotherm Res*, 176: 330-343

Neumann van Padang M, 1951. Indonesia. *Catalog of Active Volcanoes of the World and Solfatara Fields*, Rome: IAVCEI, 1: 1-271 ***(regional reference)***

Okrugin V M, 1985. Information note on the results of the 7th cruise of the R/V 'Vulcanolog' in the vicinity of the Solomon Islands. *Solomon Is Geol Div File Rpt*, unpublished rpt

Pain C F, 1981. Stratigraphy and chronology of volcanic-ash beds on Lou Island. *Geol Surv Papua New Guinea Mem*, 10: 221-226

Pain C F, Blong R J, McKee C O, 1981. Pyroclastic deposits and eruptive sequences of Long Island. Part 1: Lithology, stratigraphy, and volcanology. *Geol Surv Papua New Guinea Mem*, 10: 101-107

Pain C F, McKee C O, 1981. Late Quaternary eruptive history of Karkar Island. *Geol Surv Papua New Guinea Mem*, 10: 39-48

Palfreyman W D, Cooke R J S, 1976. Eruptive history of Manam volcano, Papua New Guinea. *In*: Johnson R W (ed) *Volcanism in Australasia*, Amsterdam: Elsevier, p 117-132

Palfreyman W D, Wallace D A, Cooke R J S, 1981. Langila volcano: summary of reported eruptive history, and eruption periodicity from 1961 to 1972. *Geol Surv Papua New Guinea Mem*, 10: 125-134

Patia H, McKee C O, 1993. Lolobau volcano, Papua New Guinea - cyclic basaltic to rhyodacitic eruptions and phreatomagmatic activity. *IAVCEI 1993 Canberra Conf Abs*, (revised abs)

Petterson M G, Wallace S, Tolia D, 2001. Explosive Surtseyan eruptions from Kavachi, Solomon Islands in 1961, 1970, 1976, 1991, 1998, and 1999. *Unpublished manuscript*, 8 p

Petterson M, Cronin S, Taylor P, Tolia D, Papabatu A, Toba T, Qopoto C, 2003. The eruptive history and volcanic hazards of Savo, Solomon Islands. *Bull Volc*, 65: 165-181

Pichler T, Dix G R, 1996. Hydrothermal venting within a coral reef ecosystem, Ambitle Island, Papua New Guinea. *Geology*, 24: 435-438

Pigram C J, Johnson R W, Taylor G A M, 1977. Investigation of hot gas emissions from Koranga volcano, Papua New Guinea, in 1967. *Aust Bur Min Resour Geol Geophys Jour*, 2: 59-62

Reche O, 1954. *Ergebnisse der Sudsee Expedition 1908-1910*. Hamburg: Appel, II Ethnographie: A Melanesien, 4: 94

Reynolds M A, Best J G, 1976. Summary of the 1953-57 eruption of Tuluman volcano, Papua New Guinea. *In*: Johnson R W (ed) *Volcanism in Australasia*, Amsterdam: Elsevier, p 287-296

Reynolds M A, Best J G, Johnson R W, 1980. 1953-57 eruption of Tuluman volcano: rhyolitic volcanic activity in the northern Bismarck Sea. *Geol Surv Papua New Guinea Mem*, 7: 1-44

Ridgway J, Coulson F I E, 1987. The geology of Choiseul and the Shortland Islands, Solomon Islands. *Brit Geol Surv Overseas Mem*, no 8

Rogerson R J, Hilyard D B, Finlayson E J, Johnson R W, Mckee C O, 1989. The geology and mineral resources of Bougainville and Buka Islands, Papua New Guinea. *Geol Surv Papua New Guinea Mem*, no 16

Rothery D A, Coppola D, Saunders C, 2005. Analysis of volcanic activity patterns using MODIS thermal alerts. *Bull Volc*, 67: 539-556

Ruxton B P, 1966b. Correlation and stratigraphy of dacitic ash-fall layers in northeastern Papua. *J Geol Soc Aust*, 13: 41-67

Saint Ours P de, 1982. Potential volcanic hazards at Manam Island. *Geol Surv Papua New Guinea Rpt*, 82/22: 1-19

Sillitoe R H, Baker E M, Brook W A, 1984. Gold deposits and hydrothermal eruption breccias associated with a maar volcano at Wau, Papua New Guinea. *Econ Geol*, 79: 638-655

Silver E, Day S, Ward S, Hoffmann G, Llanes P, Driscoll N, Appelgate B, Saunders S, 2009. Volcano collapse and tsunami generation in the Bismarck Volcanic Arc, Papua New Guinea. *J Volc Geotherm Res*, 186: 210-222

Simmons S F, Brown K L, 2006. Gold in magmatic hydrothermal solutions and the rapid formation of a giant ore deposit. *Science*, 314: 288-291

Smith I E, 1969. Notes on the volcanoes Mount Bagana and Mount Victory, Territory of Papua and New Guinea. *Aust Bur Min Resour Geol Geophys Rec*, 1968/12: 1-21

Smith I E M, 1976. Peralkaline rhyolites from the d'Entrecasteaux Islands, Papua New Guinea. *In*: Johnson R W (ed) *Volcanism in Australasia*, Amsterdam: Elsevier, p 275-285

Smith I E M, 1981. Young volcanoes in eastern Papua. *Geol Surv Papua New Guinea Mem*, 10: 257-265

Smith I E, Davies H L, 1976. Geology of the southeast Papuan mainland. *Bur Min Resour Geol Geophys Bull* 165: 1-86

Solomon Islands Geological Survey, 1982. Vella Lavella Island. *New Georgia Geol Map*, sheet no 1, 1:100,000

Taylor B, 1982. Active submarine volcano sampled. *Eos, Trans Amer Geophys Union*, 63: 609

Taylor B, 1987. A geophysical survey of the Woodlark-Solomons region. *In*: Taylor B and Exon N F (eds) *Marine Geology, Geophysics, and Geochemistry of the Woodlark Basin, Solomon Islands*, Circum-Pacific Council Energy Min Resour Earth Sci Ser, 7: 25-48

Taylor G A, 1953. Notes on Ritter, Sakar, Umboi and Long Island volcanoes. *Aust Bur Min Resour Geol Geophys Rec*, 1953/43: 1-5

Taylor G A, 1955. Report on Bam Island volcano and an inspection of Kadovar and Blup Blup. *Aust Bur Min Resour Geol Geophys Rec*, 1955/73: 1-9

Taylor G A, 1958a. The 1951 eruption of Mount Lamington, Papua. *Aust Bur Min Resour Geol Geophys Bull*, 38: 1-117

Taylor G A, 1958b. The eruptive trend of Manam volcano. *Aust Bur Min Resour Geol Geophys Rec*, 1958/73: 1-11

Taylor G A, 1960. An experiment in volcanic prediction. *Aust Bur Min Resour Geol Geophys Rec*, 1960/74: 1-17

Taylor G A, 1963. Seismic and tilt phenomena preceding a Pelean type eruption from a basaltic volcano. *Bull Volc*, 26: 5-11

Taylor G R, 1976. Residual volcanic emanations from the British Solomon Islands. *In*: Johnson R W (ed) *Volcanism in Australasia*, Amsterdam: Elsevier, p 343-354

Tiffin D L, Taylor B D, Tufar W, Itikarai I, 1990. *A Seabeam and Sampling Survey of Newly Discovered Tavui Caldera near Rabaul, Papua New Guinea.* South Pacific Applied Geoscience Comm (SOPAC) Cruise Rpt 132, 17 p

Tiffin D L, Taylor B, Crook K A W, Sinton J, Frankel E, 1986. *Surveys in the Solomon Islands and Papua New Guinea using SEAMARC II-A Cruise Report of the R/V Moana Wave, November 29, 1985 - January 9, 1986.* CCOP/SOPAC Cruise Rpt 117 (unpublished)

Turner C C, 1975. The geology of Mborokua. *Solomon Is Geol Div Rpt*, G10: 1-14

Walker G P L, Heming R F, Sprod T J, Walker H R, 1981. Latest major eruptions of Rabaul volcano. *Geol Surv Papua New Guinea Mem*, 10: 181-194

Wallace D A, Cooke R J S, Dent V F, Norris D J, Johnson R W, 1981. Kadovar volcano and investigations of an outbreak of thermal activity in 1976. *Geol Surv Papua New Guinea Mem*, 10: 1-12

Wallace D A, Johnson R W, Chappell B W, Arculus R J, Perfit M R, Crick I H, 1983. Cainozoic volcanism of the Tabar, Lihir, Tanga, and Feni Islands, Papua New Guinea: geology, whole-rock analyses, and rock-forming mineral compositions. *Aust Bur Min Resour Geol Geophys Rpt*, 243: 1-62

Williams C E F, Warden A J, 1964. *Progress Report of the Geological Survey for the Period 1959-1962.* New Hebrides: British Service, 75 p

Wood C P, Nairn I A, McKee C O, Talai B, 1995. Petrology of the Rabaul Caldera area, Papua New Guinea. *J Volc Geotherm Res*, 69: 285-302

Woodhead J D, Eggins S M, Johnson R W, 1998. Magma genesis in the New Britain island arc: further insights into melting and mass transfer processes. *J Petr*, 39: 1641-1668

VANUATU AREA (0507-08)

Allen S R, 2005. Complex spatter- and pumice-rich pyroclastic deposits from an andesitic caldera-forming eruption: the Siwi pyroclastic sequence, Tanna, Vanuatu. *Bull Volc*, 67: 27-41

Arculus R J, Shipboard Scientists, 2006. Coriolis Troughs and southern New Hebrides arc: primary tectonic results from the CoTroVE (SS06/2004) research voyage. *AESC2006, Melbourne, Australia*, 5 p

Ash R P, 1971. Vanua Lava. *New Hebrides Geol Surv Ann Rpt 1970*, p 7-12

Ash R P, Carney J N, Macfarlane A, 1980. Geology of the northern Banks Islands. *New Hebrides Geol Surv Reg Rpt*, 49 p

Atkin J, 1868. On volcanoes in the New Hebrides and Bank's Islands. *Proc Geol Soc London*, 24: 305-307

Bani P, Oppenheimer C, Tsanev V I, Carn S A, Cronin S J, Crimp R, Calkins J A, Charley D, Lardy M, Roberts T R, 2009. Surge in sulphur and halogen degassing from Ambrym volcano, Vanuatu. *Bull Volc*, 71: 1159-1168

Bani P, Oppenheimer C, Varekamp J C, Quinou T, Lardy M, Carn S, 2009. Remarkable geochemical changes and degassing at Voui crater lake, Ambae volcano, Vanuatu. *J Volc Geotherm Res*, 188: 347-357

Blot C, Priam R, 1963. Volcanisme et seismicite dans l'Archipel des Nouvelles-Hebrides. *Bull Volc*, 26: 167-180

Carney J N, Macfarlane A, 1979. Geology of Tanna, Aneityum, Futuna and Aniwa. *New Hebrides Geol Surv Reg Rpt*, 81 p

Carniel R, Di Cecca M, Rouland D, 2003. Ambrym, Vanuatu (July-August 2000): spectral and dynamical transitions on the hours-to-days timescale. *J Volc Geotherm Res*, 128: 1-13

Colley H, Ash R P, 1971. The geology of Erromango. *New Hebrides Condominium Geol Surv Reg Rpt*, 112 p

Crawford A J, Greene H G, Exon N F, 1988. Geology, petrology and geochemistry of submarine volcanoes around Epi Island, New Hebrides island arc. *In*: Greene H G and Wong F L (eds) *Geology and Offshore Resources of Pacific Island Arcs-Vanuatu Region*, Circum-Pacific Council Energy Min Resour Earth Sci Ser, 8: 301-327

Cronin S J, Gaylord D R, Charley D, Alloway B V, Wallez S, Esau J W, 2004. Participatory methods of incorporating scientific with traditional knowledge for volcanic hazard management on Ambae Island, Vanuatu. *Bull Volc*, 66: 652-668

Delmelle P, Bernard A, 2000. Volcanic lakes. *In*: Sigurdsson H (ed), *Encylopedia of Volcanoes*, San Diego: Academic Press, p. 877-896

Eissen J-P, Blot C, Louat R, 1991. Chronologie de l'activite volcanique historique de l'arc insulaire des Nouvelles-Hebrides de 1595 a 1991. *ORSTOM Rapports Sci Tech Sci Terre Geol-Geophys*, 2: 1-69

Eissen J-P, Monzier M, Robin C, Picard C, Douglas C, 1990. Report on the volcanological field work on Ambrym and Tanna Islands (Vanuatu) from 2 to 25 September 1990. *Orstom (Noumea) Rapport Missions Sci Terre Geol-Geophys*, 22: 1-22

Fisher N H, 1957. Melanesia. *Catalog of Active Volcanoes of the World and Solfatara Fields*, Rome: IAVCEI, 5: 1-105 ***(regional reference)***

Gregory J W, 1917. The Ambrym eruptions of 1913-14. *Geol Mag*, 4: 529-540

Kibblewhite A C, 1966. The acoustic detection and location of an underwater volcano. *New Zeal J Sci*, 9: 178-199

Macfarlane A, Carney J N, Crawford A J, Greene H G, 1988. Vanuatu-A review of the onshore geology. *In*: Greene H G and Wong F L (eds) *Geology and Offshore Resources of Pacific Island Arcs-Vanuatu Region*, Circum-Pacific Council Energy Min Resour Earth Sci Ser, 8: 45-91

Maillet P, Monzier M, Lefevre C, 1986. Petrology of Matthew and Hunter volcanoes, south New Hebrides island arc (southwest Pacific). *J Volc Geotherm Res*, 30: 1-27

Mallick D I J, 1971. Southern Banks Islands. *New Hebrides Geol Surv Ann Rpt 1970*, p 12-16

Mallick D I J, Ash R P, 1970. Gaua. *New Hebrides Geol Surv Ann Rpt 1968*, p 27-29

Mallick D I J, Ash R P, 1975. Geology of the southern Banks Islands. *New Hebrides Condominium Geol Surv Reg Rpt*, 33 p

McCall G J H, LeMaitre R W, Malahoff A, Robinson G P, Stephenson P J, 1970. The geology and geophysics of the Ambrym Caldera, New Hebrides. *Bull Volc*, 34: 681-696

Monzier M, Danyushevsky L V, Crawford A J, Bellon H, Cotton J, 1993. High-Mg andesites from the southern termination of the New Hebrides island arc (SW Pacific). *J Volc Geotherm Res*,

57: 193-217

Monzier M, Robin C, Eissen J-P, 1994. Kuwae (~1425 A.D.): the forgotten caldera. *J Volc Geotherm Res*, 59: 207-218

Nemeth K, Cronin S J, Charley D, Harrison M, Garae E, 2006. Exploding lakes in Vanuatu - "Surtseyan-style" eruptions witnessed on Ambae Island. *Episodes*, 29: 87-92

Nemeth K, Cronin S J, White J D L, 2007. Kuwae caldera and climate confusion. *Open Geol J*, 1: 7-11

New Hebrides Geological Survey, 1972. Geology of the Central Islands. *New Hebrides Geol Surv*, 1:100,000 geol map sheet 8

New Hebrides Geological Survey, 1973. Geology of Efate and offshore islands. *New Hebrides Geol Surv*, 1:100,000 geol map sheet 9

New Hebrides Geological Survey, 1974. Geology of Erromango. *New Hebrides Geol Surv*, 1:100,000 geol map sheet 10

New Hebrides Geological Survey, 1976. Geology of Pentecost and Ambrym. *New Hebrides Geol Surv*, 1:100,000 geol map sheet 6

New Hebrides Geological Survey, 1978a. Geology of the Banks Islands. *New Hebrides Geol Surv*, 1:100,000 geol map sheet 2

New Hebrides Geological Survey, 1978b. Geology of Tanna, Aneityum, Futuna and Aniwa. *New Hebrides Geol Surv*, 1:100,000 geol map sheet 11

New Hebrides Geological Survey, 1979. Geology of Aoba and Maewo. *New Hebrides Geol Surv*, 1:100,000 geol map sheet 5

Phillips C, 1898. The volcanoes of the Pacific. *Trans New Zeal Inst*, 31: 510-551

Priam R, 1964a. Contribution a la connaissance du Volcan de l'Ilot Matthew (sud des Nouvelles-Hebrides). *Bull Volc*, 27: 331-340

Priam R, 1964b. Une nouvelle eruption du Volcan de Lopevi (Nouvelle-Hebrides) et son analogie sismique avec les eruptions precedentes. *Bull Volc*, 27: 341-346

Priam R, Charley D, Lardy M, 1999. Lopevi-resume de l'activite historieque et de l'activite recente. *L'Assoc Volc Europeenne (LAVE)*, 77: 11-13

Purey-Cust H E, 1896. The eruption of Ambrym Island, New Hebrides, south-west Pacific, 1894. *Geog Jour*, 8: 585-602

Raos A M, Crawford A J, 2004. Basalts from the Efate Island group, central section of the Vanuatu arc, SW Pacific: geochemistry and petrogenesis. *J Volc Geotherm Res*, 134: 35-56

Raos A M, McPhie J, 2003. The submarine record of a large-scale explosive eruption in the Vanuatu arc: ~1 Ma Efate Pumice Formation. *In*: White J D L, Smellie J L, Clague D A (eds), Explosive Subacqueous Volcanism, *Amer Geophys Union, Geophy Monogr*, 140: 273-283

Robin C, Eissen J-P, Monzier M, 1993. Giant tuff cone and 12-km-wide associated caldera at Ambrym volcano (Vanuatu, New Hebrides arc). *J Volc Geotherm Res*, 55: 225-238

Robin C, Eissen J-P, Monzier M, 1994. Ignimbrites of basaltic andesite and andesite composition from Tanna, New Hebrides Arc. *Bull Volc*, 56: 10-22

Robin C, Monzier M, Crawford A J, Eggins S M, 1993. The geology, volcanology, petrology-geochemistry, and tectonic evolution of the New Hebrides island arc, Vanuatu. *IAVCEI Canberra 1993 excursion guide, Aust Geol Surv Org*, Rec 1993/59, 86 p

Robin C, Monzier M, Eissen J-P, 1994. Formation of the mid-fifteenth century Kuwae caldera (Vanuatu) by an initial hydroclastic and subsequent ignimbritic eruption. *Bull Volc*, 56: 170-183

Rothery D A, Coppola D, Saunders C, 2005. Analysis of volcanic activity patterns using MODIS thermal alerts. *Bull Volc*, 67: 539-556

Stephenson P J, McCall G J H, LeMaitre R W, Robinson G P, 1968. The Ambrym Island Research Project. *New Hebrides Geol Surv Ann Rpt 1966*, p 9-15

Taylor G A, 1956. Australian National Committee on Geodesy and Geophysics. Report of the Sub-Committee on Vulcanology, 1953 Review of volcanic activity in the Territory of Papua-New Guinea, the Solomon and New Hebrides Islands, 1951-53. *Bull Volc*, 18: 25-38

Warden A J, 1967a. Distribution and development of the volcanoes of the Central Islands. *New Hebrides Geol Surv Ann Rpt 1965*, p 27-33

Warden A J, 1967b. The geology of the Central Islands. *New Hebrides Condominium Geol Surv Reg Rpt*, 5: 1-108

Warden A J, 1967c. The 1963-65 eruption of Lopevi volcano (New Hebrides). *Bull Volc*, 30: 277-318

Warden A J, 1970. Evolution of Aoba Caldera volcano, New Hebrides. *Bull Volc*, 34: 107-140

Williams C E F, Warden A J, 1964. *Progress Report of the Geological Survey for the Period 1959-1962*. New Hebrides: British Service, 75 p

Witter J B, Self S, 2007. The Kuwae (Vanuatu) eruption of AD 1452: potential magnitude and volatile release. *Bull Volc*, 69: 301-318

Wong F L, Greene H G, 1988. Geologic hazards in the central basin region, Vanuatu. *In*: Greene H G and Wong F L (eds) *Geology and Offshore Resources of Pacific Island Arcs-Vanuatu Region*, Circum-Pacific Council Energy Min Resour Earth Sci Ser, 8: 225-251

AUSTRALIA (0509)

Blackburn G, Allison G B, Leaney F W J, 1982. Further evidence on the age of tuff at Mt. Gambier, South Australia. *Trans Roy Soc S Aust*, 106: 163-167 (plus vol 108: 130 errata)

Gill E D, 1964. Rocks contiguous with the basaltic cuirass of western Victoria. *Proc Roy Soc Victoria*, 77: 331-355

Gill E D, 1971. Applications of radiocarbon dating in Victoria, Australia. *Proc Roy Soc Victoria*, 84: 71-85

Johnson R W, Knutson J, Taylor S R (eds), 1989. *Intraplate Volcanism in Eastern Australia and New Zealand*. Cambridge, England: Cambridge Univ Press, 408 p ***(regional reference)***

Selby J, Sheard M J, 1979. Volcanoes of the Mount Gambier area. *South Aust Dept Mines Energy Min Inf Ser*, 12 p

Sheard M J, 1978. The volcanic history of the Mount Gambier volcanic complex, southeast South Australia. *Trans Roy Soc S Aust*, 102: 125-139

Sheard M J, 1986. Some volcanological observations at Mount Schank, southeast South Australia. *South Aust Geol Surv, Quart Geol Notes*, 100: 14-20

Singleton O P, Joyce E B, 1969. Cainozoic volcanicity in Victoria. *Geol Soc Aust Spec Pub*, 2: 145-154

Smith B W, Prescott J R, 1987. Thermoluminescence dating of the eruption at Mt. Schank, South Australia. *Aust J Earth Sci*, 34: 335-342

Stephenson P J, Griffin T J, 1976. Some long basaltic lava flows in North Queensland. *In*: Johnson R W (ed) *Volcanism in Australasia*, Amsterdam: Elsevier, p 41-52

Thomas L, 1976. Geothermal resources in Australia. *In*: *Proc 2nd United Nations Symp Devel Use Geotherm Resour, San Francisco*, Washington D C: U S Government Printing Office, 1: 273-274

ANDAMAN IS (0600)

Haldar D, Laskar T, Bandyopadhyay P C, Sarkar N K, Biswas J K, 1992. Volcanic eruption of the Barren Island volcano, Andaman Sea. *J Geol Soc India*, 39: 411-419

Krishnan M S, 1957. Volcanic episodes in Indian geology. *J Madras Univ*, 27: 193-209

Luhr J F, Haldar D, 2006. Barren Island volcano (NE Indian Ocean): island-arc high-alumina basalts produced by troctolite contamination. *J Volc Geotherm Res*, 149: 177-212

Mallet F R, 1885. The volcanoes of Barren Island and Narcondam, in the Bay of Bengal. *Geol Surv India Mem*, 21(4): 251-286

Mallet F R, 1895. Some early allusions to Barren Island; with a few remarks thereon. *Geol Surv India Mem*, 28(1): 22-34

Neumann van Padang M, 1951. Indonesia. *Catalog of Active Volcanoes of the World and Solfatara Fields*, Rome: IAVCEI, 1: 1-271 ***(regional reference)***

Pal T, Mitra S K, Sengupta S, Katari A, Bandopadhyay P C, Bhattacharya A K, 2007. Dacite-andesites of Narcondam volcano in the Andaman Sea - an imprint of magma mixing in the inner arc of the Andaman-Java subduction system. *J Volc Geotherm Res*, 168: 93-113

Raina V K, 1987. A note on sulfur occurrence in the volcanoes of Bay of Bengal. *Indian Minerals*, 41: 79-86

Shanker R, Haldar D, Absar A, Chakraborty S C, 2001. Pictorial Monograph of the Barren Island Volcano. Kolkata: Geol Surv India, 87 p

Sheth H C, Ray J S, Bhutani R, Kumar A, Smitha R S, 2009. Volcanology and eruptive styles of Barren Island: an active mafic stratovolcano in the Andaman Sea, NE Indian Ocean. *Bull Volc*, 71: 1021-1039

INDONESIA: SUMATRA & JAVA (0601-03)

Abdurachman E K, Bourdier J-L, Voight B, 2000. Nuees ardentes of 22 November 1994 at Merapi volcano, Java, Indonesia. *J Volc Geotherm Res*, 100: 345-361

Adreastuti S D, Alloway B V, Smith I E M, 2000. A detailed tephrostratigraphic framework at Merapi volcano, central Java, Indonesia: implications for eruption predictions and hazard assessment. *J Volc Geotherm Res*, 100: 51-67

Aldiss D T, Whandoyo R, Ghazali S A, Kusyono, 1983. Geologic map of the Sidikalang and (part of) Sinabang quadrangles, Sumatra. *Geol Res Devel Centre Indonesia*, 1:250,000 scale map and 41 p text

Aldiss D T, Whandoyo R, Sjaefudien A G, Kusyono, 1983. The Geology of the Sidikalang quadrangle, Sumatra. *Geol Res Devel Centre Indonesia*, 1:250,000 scale map and 41 p text

Alzwar M, 1985. Gunung Kelut. *Bull Volc Surv Indonesia*, 108: 1-60 (in Indonesian)

Asmoro P, Wachyudin D, Mulyadi E, 1989. Geologic map of Papandayan volcano, Garut, West Java. *Volc Surv Indonesia*, geol map

Aspden J A, Kartawa W, Aldiss D T, Djunuddin A, Whandoyo R, Diatma D, Clarke M C G, Harahap H, 1982. Geologic map of the Padangsidempuan and Sibolga quadrangles, Sumatra. *Geol Res Devel Centre Indonesia*, 1:250,000 scale map and 34 p text

Bellier O, Bellon H, Sebrier M, Sutanto, Maury R C, 1999. K-Ar age of the Ranau Tuffs: implications for the Ranau caldera emplacement and slip-partitioning in Sumatra (Indonesia). *Tectonophysics*, 312: 347-359

Bemmelen R W van, 1937. The volcano-tectonic structure of the residency of Malang (eastern Java). *Ing Ned-Indie*, 4: 159-172

Bemmelen R W van, 1941. Bulletin of the East Indian Volcanology Survey for the year 1941. *East Indian Volc Surv Bull*, 95-98: 1-110

Bemmelen R W van, 1949a. Report on the volcanic activity and volcanological research in Indonesia during the period 1936-1948. *Bull Volc*, 9: 3-30

Bemmelen R W van, 1949b. *The Geology of Indonesia*. The Hague: Government Printing Office, v 1, 732 p

Bemmelen R W van, 1956. The influence of geologic events on human history (an example from central Java). *Verh Kon Ned Geol Mijnb Genoot Geol*, 16: 20-36

Bemmelen R W van, 1971. Four volcanic outbursts that influenced human history. Toba, Sunda, Merapi, and Thera. *In*: Kaloyeropoyloy A (ed) *Acta 1st Internatl Sci Cong on the Volcano of Thera*, Athens: Arch Serv Greece, p 5-50

Bennett J D, Bridge D M, Cameron N R, Djunuddin A, Ghazali S A, Jeffery D H, Keats W, Rock N M S, Thompson S J, Whandoyo R, 1981. Geologic map of the Banda Aceh quadrangle, North Sumatra. *Geol Res Devel Centre Indonesia*, 1:250,000 scale

Boudon G, Camus G, Gourgaud A, Lajoie J, 1993. The 1984 nuee-ardente deposits of Merapi volcano, Central Java, Indonesia: stratigraphy, textural characteristics, and transport mechanisms. *Bull Volc*, 55: 327-342

Bourdier J-L, Abdurachman E K, 2001. Decoupling of small-volume pyroclastic flows and related hazards at Merapi volcano, Indonesia. *Bull Volc*, 63: 309-325

Bourdier J-L, Pratomo I, Thouret J-C, Boudon G, Vincent P M, 1997. Observations, stratigraphy and eruptive processes of the 1990 eruption of Kelut volcano, Indonesia. *J Volc Geotherm Res*, 79: 181-203

Bronto S, 1989. Volcanic geology of Galunggung, West Java, Indonesia. *Unpublished PhD thesis*, Univ Canterbury, 490 p

Bronto S, Situmorang T, Effendi W, 1986. Geologic map of Lamongan volcano, Lumajang, East

Java. *Volc Surv Indonesia*, 1:50,000 geol map

Bronto S, Zaennudin A, Erfan R D, 1985. Geologic map of Arjuno-Welirang volcanoes, East Java. *Volc Surv Indonesia*, 1:70,000 map

Cameron N R, Aspden J A, Bridge D M, Djunuddin A, Ghazali S A, Harahap H, Hariwidjaja S, Johari, Kartawa W, Keats W, Ngabito H, Rock N M S, Whandoyo R, 1982. Geologic map of the Medan quadrangle, Sumatra. *Geol Res Devel Centre Indonesia*, 1:250,000 map and 26 p text

Cameron N R, Bennett J D, Bridge D M, Clarke M C G, Djunuddin A, Ghazali S A, Harahap H, Jeffery D H, Kartawa W, Keats W, Ngabito H, Rock N M S, Thompson S J, 1983. Geologic map of the Takengon quadrangle, Sumatra. *Geol Res Devel Centre Indonesia*, 1:250,000 scale map and 26 p text

Camus G, Gourgaud A, Mossand-Berthommier P-C, Vincent P-M, 2000. Merapi (central Java, Indonesia): an outline of the structural and magmatological evolution, with a special emphasis to the major pyroclastic events. *J Volc Geotherm Res*, 100: 139-163

Camus G, Gourgaud A, Vincent P M, 1987. Petrologic evolution of Krakatau (Indonesia): Implications for a future activity. *J Volc Geotherm Res*, 33: 299-316

Carey S, Morelli D, Sigurdsson H, Bronto S, 2001. Tsunami deposits from major explosive eruptions: an example from the 1883 eruption of Krakatau. *Geology*, 29: 347-350

Carey S, Sigurdsson H, Mandeville C, Bronto S, 1996. Pyroclastic flows and surges over water: an example from the 1883 Krakatau eruption. *Bull Volc*, 57: 493-511

Carey S, Sigurdsson H, Mandeville C, Bronto S, 2000. Volcanic hazards from pyroclastic flow discharge into the sea: examples from the 1883 eruption of Krakatau, Indonesia. *In*: McCoy R W, Heiken G (eds), *Volcanic Hazards and Disasters in Human Antiquity*, *Geol Soc Amer Spec Pap*, 345: 1-14

Carn S A, 1999. Application of synthetic aperture radar (SAR) imagery to volcano mapping in the humid tropics: a case study in East Java, Indonesia. *Bull Volc*, 61: 92-105

Carn S A, Pyle D M, 2001. Petrology and geochemistry of the Lamongan volcanic field, east Java, Indonesia: primitive Sunda arc magmas in a extensional tectonic setting? *J Petr*, 42: 1643-1683

Casadevall T J, de Neve G, Kaswanda O, MacLeod N S, 1989. The 1988 eruption of Anak Krakatau, Indonesia: a return to the pre-1981 compositions (abs). *New Mexico Bur Mines Min Resour Bull*, 131: 46

Charbonnier S J, Gertisser R, 2008. Field observations and surface characteristics of pristine block-and-ash flow deposits from the 2006 eruption of Merapi volcano, Java, Indonesia. *J Volc Geotherm Res*, 177: 971-982

Chesner C A, Rose W I, 1991. Stratigraphy of the Toba tuffs and the evolution of the Toba caldera complex, Sumatra, Indonesia. *Bull Volc*, 53: 343-356

Clarke M C G, Ghazali S A, Harahap H, Kusyono, Stephenson B, 1982. Geologic map of the Pematangsiantar quadrangle, Sumatra. *Geol Res Devel Centre Indonesia*, 1:250,000 scale map and 26 p text

de Neve G A, 1985a. Earlier eruptive activities of Krakatau in historic time and during the Quaternary. *In*: Sastrapradja D et al (eds) *Proc Symp on 100 Years Devel of Krakatau and its Surroundings*, Jakarta: Lembaga Ilmu Pengetahuan Indonesia, 1: 35-46

de Neve G A, 1985b. *Volcanoes and Volcanology of Indonesia. Unpublished manuscript*, unpaginated

de Waard D, Klompe H F, 1952. The recent activity of G. Marapi in central Sumatra. *Nat Tijd Ned-Indie*, 108: 131-140

Decker R W, Hadikusumo D, 1961. Results of the 1960 expedition to Krakatau. *J Geophys Res*, 66: 3497-3511

Delmelle P, Bernard A, 2000. Volcanic lakes. *In*: Sigurdsson H (ed), *Encylopedia of Volcanoes*, San Diego: Academic Press, p. 877-896

Deplus C, Bonvalot S, Dahrin D, Diament M, Harjono H, Dubois J, 1995. Inner structure of the Krakatau volcanic complex (Indonesia) from gravity and bathymetry data. *J Volc Geotherm Res*, 64: 23-52

Djumarma A, Bronto S, Bahar I, Suparban F X, Sukhyar R, Newhall C G, Holcomb R T, Banks N G, Torley R, Lockwood J P, Tilling R I, Rubin M, del Marmol M A, 1986. Did Merapi volcano (central Java) erupt catastrophically in 1006 A.D.? *IAVCEI 1986 Cong, New Zeal, Abs*, p 236

Dvorak J, Matahelumual J, Okamura A T, Said H, Casadevall T J, Mulyadi D, 1990. Recent uplift and hydrothermal activity at Tangkuban Parahu volcano, west Java, Indonesia. *Bull Volc*, 53: 20-28

Effendi A C, Bronto S, Sukhyar R, 1986. Geologic map of Krakatau volcano complex, Sunda Strait, Lampung Province. *Volc Surv Indonesia*, 1:25,000 geol map

Gasparon M, 2005. Quaternary volcanicity. *In*: Baker A, Crow M J, Milson J S (eds) Sumatra: geology, resources and tectonic evolution *Geol Soc London Mem*, 31: 120-130

Gerbe M -C, Gourgaud A, Sigmarsson O, Harmon R S, Joron J -L, Provost A, 1992. Mineralogical and geochemical evolution of the 1982-1983 Galunggung eruption (Indonesia). *Bull Volc*, 54: 284-298

Gertisser R, Keller J, 2003. Temporal variations in magma composition at Merapi volcano (Central Java, Indonesia): magmatic cycles during the past 2000 years of explosive activity. *J Volc Geotherm Res*, 123: 1-23

Gourgaud A, Thouret J-C, Bourdier J-L, 2000. Stratigraphy and textural characteristics of the 1982-1983 tephra of Galunggung volcano (Indonesia): implications for volcanic hazards. *J Volc Geotherm Res*, 104: 169-186

Hadikusumo D, 1976. A preliminary report on volcanic eruptions during the first half of 1976 in Indonesia. *Unpublished manuscript*, 6 p

Hadisantono R D, 1990. The Sukapura, and other ignimbrites, in the Sapikerep-Sukapura valley and their relationship to caldera formation, of Bromo Tengger volcanic complex, East Java, Indonesia. *Unpublished MSci thesis*, Victoria Univ Wellington

Hadisantono R D, Dirasutisna S, Djuhara A, Martono A, 1993. Volcanic hazard map of Sundoro volcano, central Java. *Volc Surv Indonesia*, 1:50,000

Hamidi S, Djuhara A, Martono A, 1993. Volcanic hazard map of Ciremai volcano, West Java. *Volc Surv Indonesia*, 1:100,000 map

Hammer J E, Cashman K V, Voight B, 2000. Magmatic processes revealed by textural and compositional trends in Merapi dome lavas. *J Volc Geotherm Res*, 100: 165-192

Hartmann M, 1934. The volcanic activity of Merapi volcano (central Java) in its eastern summit area between 1902 and 1908. *Ing Ned-Indie*, 1: 61-73

Jaggar T A, 1928b. Poisonous gases in Java. *Volcano Lett*, 201: 1

Jaggar T A, 1932c. Eruption of Merapi (Java) 1930. *Volcano Lett*, 387: 1

Judd J W, 1888. On the volcanic phenomena of the eruption, and on the nature and distribution of the ejected materials. *In*: Symons G J (ed) *The Eruption of Krakatoa and Subsequent Phenomena*, London: Tribner & Co, Roy Soc London Rpt: 1-56

Judd J W, 1889. The earlier eruptions of Krakatoa. *Nature*, 40:365-366

Juwarna H, Wirakusumah A D, Soetoyo, Bronto S, 1986. Geologic map of Galunggung volcano, West Java. *Volc Surv Indonesia*, 1:50,000 geol map

Kartadinata M N, Okuno M, Nakamura T, Kobayashi T, 2002. Eruptive history of Tangkuban Perahu volcano, west Java, Indonesia: a preliminary report. *J Geog (Japan)*, 113: 404-409

Kastowo, Leo G W, 1973. Geologic map of the Padang quadrangle, Sumatra. *Geol Surv Indonesia*, 1:250,000 scale

Katili J A, Sudradjat A, 1984a. The devastating 1983 eruption of Colo volcano, Una-Una Island, central Sulawesi, Indonesia. *Geol Jahrb*, 75: 27-47

Katili J A, Sudradjat A, 1984b. *Galunggung: the 1982-1983 eruption*. Bandung: Volc Surv Indonesia, 102 p

Keats W, Cameron N R, Djunuddin A, Ghazali S A, Harahap H, Kartawa W, Ngabito H, Rock N M S, Thompson S J, Whandoyo R, 1981. Geologic map of the Lhokseumawe quadrangle, Sumatra. *Geol Res Devel Centre Indonesia*, 1:250,000 scale map and 13 p text

Knight M D, Walker G P L, Ellwood B B, Diehl J F, 1986. Stratigraphy, paleomagnetism, and magnetic fabric of the Toba Tuffs: constraints on the sources and eruptive styles. *J Geophys Res*, 91: 10,355-10,382

Kuenen P H, 1935. Contributions to the geology of the East Indies from the Snellius expedition, part 1, volcanoes. *Leidsche Geol Meded*, 7: 273-283

Kusumadinata K, 1979. *Data Dasar Gunungapi Indonesia*. Bandung: Volc Surv Indonesia, 820 p ***(regional reference)***

Lavigne F, Thouret J C, Voight B, Suwa H, Sumaryono A, 2000. Lahars at Merapi volcano, central Java: an overview. *J Volc Geotherm Res*, 100: 423-456

Le Guern F, Tazieff H, Faivre Pierret R, 1982. An example of health hazard: people killed by gas during a phreatic eruption: Dieng Plateau (Java Indonesia), Feb 20th 1979. *Bull Volc*, 45: 153-156

Leo G W, Hedge C E, Marvin R F, 1980. Geochemistry, strontium isotope data, and potassium-argon ages of the andesite-rhyolite association in the Padang area, West Sumatra. *J Volc Geotherm Res*, 7: 139-156

Lesage P, Surono, 1995. Seismic precursors of the February 10, 1990 eruption of Kelut volcano, Java. *J Volc Geotherm Res*, 65: 135-146

Mandeville C W, Carey S, Sigurdsson H, 1996. Sedimentology of the Krakatau 1883 submarine pyclastic deposits. *Bull Volc*, 57: 512-529

Mazot A, Bernard A, Fischer T, Inguaggiato S, Sutawidjaja I S, 2008. Chemical evolution of thermal waters and changes in the hydrothermal system of Papandayan volcano (West Java, Indonesia) after the November 2002 eruption. *J Volc Geotherm Res*, 178: 276-286

McBirney A R, Serva L, Guerra M, Conner C B, 2003. Volcanic and seismic hazards at a proposed nuclear power site in central Java. *J Volc Geotherm Res*, 126: 11-30

Miyake R A, 1930. The eruption of Krakatoa, 1883. *Volcano Lett*, 306: 1-2

Moore J N, Allis R, Renner J L, Mildenhall D, McCulloch J, 2002. Petrologic evidence for boiling to dryness in the Karaha-Telaga Bodas geothermal system, Indonesia. *Proc 27th Workshop Geotherm Res Ing, Stanford Univ, Jan 28-30, 2002*, SGP-TR171, 10 p

Mulyadi E, 1992. Le complexe de Bromo-Tengger (Est Java, Indonesie): estude structurale et volcanologique. *Unpublished PhD thesis*, Univ Blaise Pascal

Mulyadi E, Zaennudin, Wahyudin D, Dana I N, 2000. Guide book for field excursion at Lamongan, Semeru, Bromo-Tengger volcanic complex, East Java, 13-17 July 2000. *IAVCEI General Assembly, Bali 2000 Excursion Guide*, 28 p

Neumann van Padang M, 1934. Haben bei den Ausbruchen des Slametvulkans Eruptionsregen Stattgefunden? *Leidsche Geol Meded*, 6: 79-97

Neumann van Padang M, 1937a. Bestaat er Verband Tusschen den Regenval op den de Vulkanen Semeroe en Lamongan en Hunne Uitbarstingen. *Ing Ned-Indie*, 4: 1-7

Neumann van Padang M, 1937b. De uitbarsting van den Tjerimai in 1937. *Ing Ned-Indie*, 4: 211-227

Neumann van Padang M, 1951. Indonesia. *Catalog of Active Volcanoes of the World and Solfatara Fields*, Rome: IAVCEI, 1: 1-271 ***(regional reference)***

Neumann van Padang M, 1963b. The temperatures in the crater region of some Indonesian volcanoes before the eruption. *Bull Volc*, 26: 319-336

Neumann van Padang M, 1983. History of volcanology in the former Netherlands East Indies. *Scripta Geol*, 71: 1-76

Newhall C G, Bronto S, Alloway B, Banks N G, Bahar I, del Marmol M A, Hadisantono R D, Holcomb R T, McGeehin J, Miksic J N, Rubin M, Sayudi S D, Sukhyar R, Andreastuti S, Tilling R I, Torley R, Trimble D, Wirakusumah A D, 2000. 10,000 years of explosive eruptions of Merapi volcano, central Java: archaeological and modern implications. *J Volc Geotherm Res*, 100: 9-50

Nichols I A, Whitford D J, 1983. Potassium-rich volcanic rocks of the Muriah complex, Java, Indonesia: products of multiple magma sources? *J Volc Geotherm Res*, 18: 337-359

Oba N, Tomita K, Yamamoto M, Istidjab M, Badrunddin M, Parlin M, Sadjiman, Djuwandi A, Sudradjat A, Suhanda T, 1982. Geochemical study of lava flows, ejecta and pyroclastic flow from the Krakatau group, Indonesia. *Rep Fac Sci Kagoshima Univ*, 15: 41-76

Petroeschevsky W A, 1952. The volcanic activity in Indonesia during the period 1942-1948. *Berita Gunung Berapi*, 1: 17-30; 3-4: 9-31

Petroeschevsky W A, Klompe T H F, 1951. Vulcanological Investigations in Indonesia. *Organization Sci Res Indonesia Pub*, 23: 187-204 ***(regional reference)***

Posavec M, Taylor D, Van Leeuwen T, Spector A, 1973. Tectonic controls of volcanism and complex movements along the Sumatran fault system. *Geol Soc Malaysia Bull*, 6: 43-60

Purbo-Hadiwidjoyo M M, Suryo I, 1980. Distribution pattern of the Merapi volcanic debris, south central Java with special reference to the period since 1900. *Seminar Volcanic Debris Flow*, Yogjakarta, 13-14 March 1980, p 276-291

Rampino M R, Ambrose S H, 2000. Volcanic winter in the Garden of Eden: the Toba supereruption and the late Pleistocene human population crash. *In*: McCoy R W, Heiken G (eds), *Volcanic Hazards and Disasters in Human Antiquity*, *Geol Soc Amer Spec Pap*, 345: 71-82

Ratdomopurbo A, Poupinet G, 2000. An overview of the seismicity of Merapi volcano (Java, Indonesia), 1983-1994. *J Volc Geotherm Res*, 100: 193-214

Reubi O, Nicholls I A, Kamenetsky V S, 2003. Early mixing and mingling in the evolution of basaltic magmas: evidence from phenocryst assemblages, Slamet Volcano, Java, Indonesia. *J Volc Geotherm Res*, 119: 225-274

Rock N M S, Aldiss D T, Aspden J A, Clarke M C G, Djunuddin A, Kartawa W, Miswar S J, Thompson R, Whandoyo, 1983. Geologic map of the Lubuksikaping quadrangle, Sumatra. *Geol Res Devel Centre Indonesia*, 1:250,000 map and 60 p text

Rock N M S, Syah H H, Davis A E, Hutchison D, Styles M T, Lena R, 1982. Permian to Recent volcanism in northern Sumatra, Indonesia: a preliminary study of its distribution, chemistry, and peculiarities. *Bull Volc*, 45: 127-152

Rose W I, Chesner C A, 1990. Worldwide dispersal of ash and gases from earth's largest known eruption: Toba, Sumatra, 75 ka. *Palaeogeog, Palaeoclimat, Palaeoecol*, 89: 269-275

Rosidi H M D, Tjokrosapoetro S, Pendowo B, 1976. Geologic map of the Painan and northeastern part of the Muarasiberut quadrangles, Sumatra. *Geol Surv Indonesia*, 1:250,000 scale

Rothery D A, Coppola D, Saunders C, 2005. Analysis of volcanic activity patterns using MODIS thermal alerts. *Bull Volc*, 67: 539-556

Schwarzkopf L M, Schmincke H-U, Cronin S J, 2005. A conceptual model for block-and-ash flow basal avalanche transport and deposition, based on deposit architecture of 1998 and 1994 Merapi flows. *J Volc Geotherm Res*, 139: 117-134

Self S, Rampino M R, 1981. The 1883 eruption of Krakatau. *Nature*, 294: 699-704

Sieh K, Natawidjaja D, 2009. Neotectonics of the Sumatran fault, Indonesia. *J Geophys Res*, 105: 28,295-28,326

Silitonga P H, Kastowo, 1975. Geologic map of the Solok quadrangle, Sumatra. *Geol Surv Indonesia*, 1:250,000 scale

Simkin T, Fiske R S, 1983. *Krakatau 1883: The Volcanic Eruption and its Effects*. Washington, D C: Smithsonian Inst Press, 464 p

Siswowidjoyo S, 1985. The renewed activity of Krakatau volcano after its catastrophic eruption in 1883. *In*: Sastrapradja D et al (eds) *Proc Symp on 100 Years Devel of Krakatau and its Surroundings*, Jakarta: Lembaga Ilmu Pengetahuan Indonesia, 1: 192-198

Siswowidjoyo S, Sudarsono U, Wirakusumah A D, 1995. The threat of hazards in Semeru volcano, East Java, Indonesia. *Eight Regional Conf GEOSEA '95, Manilla, Philippines, 14-18 Feb 1995*, 17 p

Siswowidjoyo S, Suryo I, Yokoyama I, 1995. Magma eruption rates of Merapi volcano, Central Java, Indonesia during one century (1890-1992). *Bull Volc*, 57: 111-116

Situmorang T, Hadisantono R D, 1992. Geologic map of Gede volcano, Cianjur, West Java. *Volc Surv Indonesia*, 1:50,000 geol map

Soetoyo, Hadisantono R D, 1992. Geologic map of Tangkubanparahu volcano (Sunda Complex volcano), West Java. *Volc Surv Indonesia*, 1:50,000 scale

Sriwana T, van Bergen M J, Varekamp J C, Sumarti S, Takano B, van Os B J H, Leng M J, 2000. Geochemistry of the acid Kawah Putih lake, Patuha volcano, west Java, Indonesia. *J Volc Geotherm Res*, 97: 77-104

Stehn C E, 1927. Die Vulkanicshen Ereignisse in Niederlandisch-Indien in den Jahren 1924-1926. *Zeit Vulk*, 11: 41-52

Stehn C E, 1928. Volcanological work in the Dutch East Indies during 1923-1926. *Proc 3rd Pacific Sci Cong*, 1: 718-734

Stehn C E, 1929a. Kawah Komodjang. *4th Pacific Sci Cong Java*, Excur C2, 13 p

Stehn C E, 1929b. Keloet. *4th Pacific Sci Cong Java*, Excur 2A, p 3-23

Stehn C E, 1929c. Tangkoeban Prahoe. *4th Pacific Sci Cong Java*, Excur B3, 22 p

Stimac J, Sugiaman F, 2000. The Awi 1-2 core research program: Part 1, Geologic overview of the Awibengkok geothermal field. *Proc World Geotherm Cong 2000, Kyushu-Tohoku, Japan, May 28 - June 10, 2000*, p 2221-2226

Sudarman S, Boedihardi M, Pudyastuti K, Bardan, 1995. Kamojang geothermal field: 10 year operation experience. *Proc World Geotherm Cong, Florence, Italy, 18-31 May 1995*, 3:1773-1777

Sudarman S, Pujianto R, Budiarjo B, 1986. The Gunung Wayang-Windu geothermal area in west Java. *Proc Indonesian Petrol Assoc, 15th Ann Convention, October 1986*, p 141-153

Sujanto, Syarifuddin M Z, Sitorus K, 1988. Geological map of the Ijen caldera complex, East Java. *Volc Surv Indonesia*, 1:50,000 geol map

Sukhyar R, 1989. Geochemistry and petrogenesis of arc rocks from Dieng, Sundoro and Sumbing volcanic complexes, central Java, Indonesia. *Unpublished PhD thesis*, Monash University, 319 p

Sukhyar R, Sumartadipura N S, Effendi W, 1986. Geologic map of Dieng volcano complex, central Java. *Volc Surv Indonesia*, geol map

Sukhyar R, Sumartadipura N S, Erfan R D, 1992. Geologic map of Sundoro volcano, central Java. *Volc Surv Indonesia*, 1:50,000 geol map

Suparman, 1992. G. Kunyit (B). *Berita Berkala Vulkanologi*, no. 198: 1-8 (in Indonesian)

Suryo I, 1985. Report on the volcanic activity in Indonesia during the period 1964-1970. *Bull Volc Surv Indonesia*, 106: 1-150

Suryo I, 1986. G Semeru. *Bull Volc Surv Indonesia*, 111: 1-52 (in Indonesian)

Sutawidjaja I S, Aswin D, Sitorus K, 1985. Geologic map of Slamet volcano, Central Java. *Volc Surv Indonesia*, 1:50,000 geol map

Taverne N J M, 1926. Vulkanstudien op Java. *Vulk Meded*, 7: 1-132

Thouret J-C, Abdurachman K E, Bourdier J-L, Bronto S, 1998. Origin, characteristics, and behavior of lahars following the 1990 eruption of Kelud volcano, eastern Java (Indonesia). *Bull Volc*, 59: 460-480

Thouret J-C, Lavigne F, Kelfoun K, Bronto S, 2000. Toward a revised hazard assessment at Merapi volcano, central Java. *J Volc Geotherm Res*, 100: 479-502

Thouret J-C, Lavigne F, Suwa H, Sukatja-Surono B, 2007. Volcanic hazards at Mount Semeru, East Java (Indonesia), with emphasis on lahars. *Bull Volc*, 70: 221-244

Van Bergen M J, Bernard A, Sumarti S, Sriwana T, Sitorus K, 2000. Crater lakes of Java: Dieng, Kelud, Ijen. *IAVCEI General Assembly, Bali 2000 Excursion Guide*, 42 p

Van Gestel J T, 1895. The Krakatoa eruption: described for the first time by an eye-witness of its horrors. *The Cosmopolitan*, 18: 719-727

Verbeek R D M, 1885. *Krakatau*. Batavia: Landsdrukkerij, 495 p

Voight B, Constantine E K, Siswowidjoyo S, Torley R, 2000. Historical eruptions of Merapi volcano, central Java, Indonesia, 1768-1998. *J Volc Geotherm Res*, 100: 69-138

Voight B, Young K D, Hidayat D, Subandrio, Purbawinata M A, Ratdomopurbo A, Suharna, Panut, Sayudi D S, LaHusen R, Marso J, Murray T L, Dejean M, Iguchi M, Ishihara K, 2000. Deformation and seismic precursors to dome-collapse and fountain-collapse nuees ardentes at Merapi volcano, Java, Indonesia, 1994-1998. *J Volc Geotherm Res*, 100: 261-287

Volc Surv Indonesia, 1984. Tangkubanparahu excursion. *Unpublished manuscript*, 14 p

Volc Surv Indonesia, 1986a. Annual report of the Volcanological Survey 1983-1984. Bull Volc Surv Indonesia, no 112

Volc Surv Indonesia, 1986b. Annual report of the Volcanological Survey 1984-1985. Bull Volc Surv Indonesia, no 113

Vukadinovic D, Nichols I A, 1989. The petrogenesis of island arc basalts from Gunung Slamet volcano, Indonesia: trace element and 87Sr/86Sr constraints. *Geochim Cosmochim Acta*, 53: 2349-2363

Wahyudin D, 1990. Volcanology and petrology of Mt. Semeru volcanic complex, East Java - Indonesia. *Unpublished undergraduate thesis*, Victoria University of Wellington, 131 p

Westerveld J, 1952. Quaternary volcanism on Sumatra. *Geol Soc Amer Bull*, 63: 561-594

Wheller G E, Varne R, Foden J D, Abbott M J, 1987. Geochemistry of Quaternary volcanism in the Sunda-Banda arc, Indonesia, and three-component genesis of island-arc basaltic magmas. *J Volc Geotherm Res*, 32: 137-160

Whittome A J, Salveson J O, 1990. Exploration and evaluation of the Darajat geothermal field, west Java, Indonesia. *Trans Geotherm Res Council*, 14: 999-1005

Wikartadipura S, Sumpena A D, Djuhara A, Santoso M S, Phillips, 1993. Volcanic hazard map of Guntur volcano, West Java. *Volc Surv Indonesia*, 1:50,000 map

Wirakusumah A D, 1991. Some studies of volcanology, petrology and structure of Mt. Kelut, East Java, Indonesia. *Unpublished PhD thesis*, Victoria Univ of Wellington, 460 p

Wirakusumah A D, Juwarna H, Loebis H, 1989. Geologic map of Merapi volcano, Central Java. *Volc Surv Indonesia*, 1:50,000 geol map

Young K D, Voight B, Subandriyo, Sajiman, Miswanto, Casadevall T J, 2000. Ground deformation at Merapi volcano, Java, Indonesia: distance changes, June 1988-October 1995. *J Volc Geotherm Res*, 100: 233-259

Zaennudin A, Dana I N, Wahyudin D, 1992. Geologic map of Kelut volcano, East Java. *Volc Surv Indonesia*, 1:50,000 geol map

Zaennudin A, Sutawidjadja I S, Aswin D, 1993. Geological map of Salak volcano, West Java. *Volc Surv Indonesia*, 1:50,000 geol map

Zen M T, 1970. Growth and state of Anak Krakatau in September 1968. *Bull Volc*, 34: 205-215

Zen M T, Hadikusumo D, 1964. Recent changes in the Anak-Krakatau volcano. *Bull Volc*, 27: 259-268

INDONESIA: EAST & NORTH (0604-10)

Apandi T, Sudana D, 1980. Geologic map of the Ternate quadrangle, north Maluku. *Geol Res Devel Centre Indonesia*, 1:250,000 scale map and 9 p text

Barberi F, Bigioggero B, Boriani A, Cattaneo M, Cavallin A, Cioni R, Eva C, Gelmini R, Giorgetti F, Iaccarino S, Innocenti F, Marinelli G, Slejko D, Sudradjat A, 1987. The island of Sumbawa: a major structural discontinuity in the Indonesia arc. *Bol Soc Geol Italy*, 106: 547-620

Bemmelen R W van, 1949a. Report on the volcanic activity and volcanological research in Indonesia during the period 1936-1948. *Bull Volc*, 9: 3-30

Bemmelen R W van, 1949b. *The Geology of Indonesia*. The Hague: Government Printing Office, v 1, 732 p

Boerema J, 1929. A new undersea volcano. *Proc 4th Pacific Sci Cong*, 2B: 919-920

Bronto S, Hadisantono R D, Lockwood J P, 1982. Geologic map of Gamalama volcano, Ternate, North Maluku. *Volc Surv Indonesia*, 1:25,000 geol map

Casadevall T J, Pardyanto L, Abas H, Tulus, 1989. The 1988 eruption of Banda Api volcano, Maluku, Indonesia. *Geol Indonesia*, 12: 603-635

Cole-Dai J, Ferris D, Lanciki A, Savarino J, Baroni M, Thiemens M H, 2009. Cold decade (AD 1810-1819) caused by Tambora (1815) and another (1809) stratospheric volcanic eruption. *Geophys Res Lett*, 36: L22703, doi:10.1029/2009GL040882

Davis T A, 1982. Report on visits of volcano affected areas of Mt. Soputan of Minahasa District, North Sulawesi Province. *Unpublished manuscript*, 5 p

De Neve G A, 1985b. *Volcanoes and Volcanology of Indonesia*. *Unpublished manuscript*, unpaginated

Effendi A C, 1976. Geologic map of the Manado quadrangle, north Sulawesi. *Volc Surv Indonesia*, geol map

Foden J, 1986. The petrology of Tambora Volcano, Indonesia: A model for the 1815 eruption. *J Volc Geotherm Res*, 27: 1-41

Foden J D, 1983. The petrology of the calcalkaline lavas of Rindjani volcano, east Sunda arc: a model for island arc petrogenesis. *J Petr*, 24: 98-130

Gogarten E, 1918. Die Vulkane der Nordlichen Molukken. *Zeit Vulk*, 2: 1-298

Hadikusumo D, 1976. A preliminary report on volcanic eruptions during the first half of 1976 in

Indonesia. *Unpublished manuscript*, 6 p

Jaggar T A, 1928c. The Rokatinda eruption. *Volcano Lett*, 207: 1

Jaggar T A, 1929. The Bali eruption 1926. *Volcano Lett*, 215: 1

Jezek P, 1979. Volcano resume-Ibu. *Volcano News*, 1: 7

Jezek P A, Hutchison C S, 1978. Banda Arc of Eastern Indonesia: petrology and geochemistry of volcanic rocks. *Bull Volc*, 41: 586-608

Kasbani, Browne P R L, Johnstone R D, Kahsai K, Utami P, Wangge A, 1997. Subsurface hydrothermal alteration in the Ulumbu geothermal field, Flores, Indonesia. *Proc 22nd Workshop Geotherm Res Eng, Stanford Univ, 1997*, 7 p

Katili J A, Kartaadiputra L, Surio, 1963. Magma type and tectonic position of the Una-Una Island, Indonesia. *Bull Volc*, 26: 431-454

Katili J A, Sudradjat A, 1984a. The devastating 1983 eruption of Colo volcano, Una-Una Island, central Sulawesi, Indonesia. *Geol Jahrb*, 75: 27-47

Kemmerling G L L, 1923. De vulkanen van de Sangi-Archipel en van de Minahassa. *Vulk Seism Meded Dienst Mijnw Ned-Indie*, 5: 1-157

Kemmerling G L L, 1929. Vulkanen van Flores. *Vulk Seism Meded Dienst Mijnw Ned-Indie*, 10: 1-138

Kirk H J C, 1968. The igneous rocks of Sarawak and Sabah. *Geol Surv Borneo Region Malasia Bull*, 5: 1-220

Kusumadinata K, 1964. Notes on general observations of effusive activity in 1963 in the Batur caldera (Bali), parts 1 and 2. Direktorate Geol, unpublished ms (in Indonesian)

Kusumadinata K, 1977. Data on the Dukono volcano. *Berita Direktorat Geol Geosurv Newsl*, 9: 183

Kusumadinata K, 1979. *Data Dasar Gunungapi Indonesia*. Bandung: Volc Surv Indonesia, 820 p ***(regional reference)***

Lockwood J P, Melson W G, Lanphere M A, Bronto S, 1981. Petrology and eruptive characteristics of Gamalama volcano, Ternate Island, Indonesia. *IAVCEI, 1981 Tokyo Mtg Abs*, p 207

Manalu L, 1986. G Karangetang. *Bull Volc Surv Indonesia*, 109: 1-48

Marinelli G, Tazieff H, 1968. L'Ignimbrite et la caldera de Batur (Bali, Indonesia). *Bull Volc*, 32: 89-120

Matahelumual J, 1985. G Awu. *Bull Volc Surv Indonesia*, 107: 1-51 (in Indonesian)

Matahelumual J, 1986a. G Makian. *Bull Volc Surv Indonesia*, 110: 1-37 (in Indonesian)

Matahelumual J, 1986b. G Lokon-Empung. *Bull Volc Surv Indonesia*, 114: 1-52 (in Indonesian)

Morrice M G, Jezek P A, Gill J B, Whitford D J, Monoarfa M, 1983. An introduction to the Sangihe arc: volcanism accompanying arc-arc collision in the Molucca Sea, Indonesia. *J Volc Geotherm Res*, 19: 135-165

Morris J D, Jezek P A, Hart S R, Gill J B, 1983. The Halmahera Island arc, Molucca Sea collision zone, Indonesia: a geochemical survey. *In*: Hayes D E (ed) The Tectonic and Geologic Evolution of Southeast Asia Seas and Islands, part 2, *Amer Geophys Union, Geophys Monogr*, 27: 373-387

Muraoka H, Yasukawa K, Urai M, Takahashi M, Nasution A, Takashima I, 2002. 2001 fissure-forming eruption of Inie Lika volcano, central Flores, Indonesia. *Bull Geol Surv Japan*, 53: 175-182

Nasution A, Takashima I, Muraoka H, Takahashi H, Matsuda K, Akasako H, Futagoishi M, Kusnadi D, Nanlohi F, 2000. The geology and geochemistry of Mataloko-Nage-Bobo geothermal areas, central Flores, Indonesia. *Proc World Geotherm Cong 2000, Kyushu-Tohoku, Japan, May 28-June 10, 2000*, p 2165-2170

Neumann van Padang M, 1930. Padoweh. *Vulk Seism Meded Dienst Mijnw Ned-Indie*, 11: 1-141

Neumann van Padang M, 1951. Indonesia. *Catalog of Active Volcanoes of the World and Solfatara Fields*, Rome: IAVCEI, 1: 1-271 ***(regional reference)***

Neumann van Padang M, 1959. Changes in the top of Mount Ruang (Indonesia). *Geol en Mijnbouw*, 21: 113-118

Neumann van Padang M, 1983. History of volcanology in the former Netherlands East Indies. *Scripta Geol*, 71: 1-76

Pasternack G B, Varekamp J C, 1994. The geochemistry of the Keli Mutu crater lake, Flores, Indonesia. *Geochem J*, 28: 243-262

Petroeschevsky W A, 1952. The volcanic activity in Indonesia during the period 1942-1948. *Berita Gunung Berapi*, 1: 17-30; 3-4: 9-31

Petroeschevsky W A, Klompe T H F, 1951. Vulcanological Investigations in Indonesia. *Organization Sci Res Indonesia Pub*, 23: 187-204 ***(regional reference)***

Purbo-Hadiwidjojo M M, 1971. Geological map of Bali. *Geol Surv Indonesia*, 1:250,000 scale

Ratman N, Yasin A, 1978. Geologic map of Komodo quadrangle, Nusatenggar. *Geol Surv Indonesia*, 1:250,000 scale

Reubi O, Nicholls I A, 2004. Variability in eruptive dynamics associated with caldera collapse: an example from two successive eruptions at Batur volcanic field, Bali, Indonesia. *Bull Volc*, 66: 134-148

Ross J T, 1816. Narrative of the effects of the eruption from the Tomboro Mountain in the Island of Sumbawa on the 11th and 12th of April, 1815. *Lembaga Kebudajaan Indonesia Vehandelingen*, 8: 343-460

Self S, King A J, 1996. Petrology and sulfur and chlorine emissions of the 1963 eruption of Gunung Agung, Bali, Indonesia. *Bull Volc*, 58: 263-285

Self S, Rampino M R, Newton M S, Wolff J A, 1984. Volcanological Study of the Great Tambora eruption of 1815. *Geology*, 12: 659-663

Sigurdsson H, Carey S, 1989. Plinian and co-ignimbrite tephra fall from the 1815 eruption of Tambora volcano. *Bull Volc*, 51: 243-270

Sigurdsson H, Carey S, 1992. Eruptive history of Tambora volcano, Indonesia. *In*: Degens E T, Wong H K, Zen M T (eds) *The Sea off Mount Tambora*, Mitteilschen Geol-Palaont Inst Univ Hamburg, 70: 187-206

Stehn C E, 1927. Die Vulkanicshen Ereignisse in Niederlandisch-Indien in den Jahren 1924-1926. *Zeit Vulk*, 11: 41-52

Stehn C E, 1928. Volcanological work in the Dutch East Indies during 1923-1926. *Proc 3rd Pacific Sci Cong*, 1: 718-734

Stolz A J, Varne R, Davies, G R, Wheller G E, Foden J D, 1990. Magma source components in an arc-continent collision zone: the Flores-Lembata sector, Sunda arc, Indonesia. *Contr Mineral Petr*, 105: 585-601

Stolz A J, Varne R, Wheller G E, Foden J D, Abbott M J, 1988. The geochemistry and petrogenesis of K-rich alkaline volcanics from the Batu Tara volcano, eastern Sunda arc. *Contr Mineral Petr*, 98: 374-389

Stothers R B, 1984. The great Tambora eruption in 1815 and its aftermath. *Science*, 224: 1191-1198

Sucipta I G B E, Takashima I, Muraoka H, 2006. Morphometric age and petrological characteristics of volcanic rocks from the Bajawa cinder cone complex, Flores, Indonesia. *J Mineral Petr Sci*, 101: 48-68

Sulasdi D, 1996. Exploration of Ulumbu geothermal field, Flores-East Nusa Tenggara Indonesia. *Proc 21st Workshop Geotherm Res Eng, Stanford Univ, Jan 22-24, 1996*, SGP-TR-151: 51-54

Sumartadipura A S, 1977. Photo interpretation of Umsini volcano. *Geosurv Newsl*, 9: 99-101

Supriatna S, 1980. Geologic map of Morotai quadrangle, north Maluku. *Geol Res Devel Centre Indonesia*, 1:250,000 scale map and 10 p text

Sutawidjaja I S, 2000. A guide to the geological phenomena of Batura caldera, Bali, Indonesia. *IAVCEI General Assembly, Bali 2000 Excursion Guide*, 33 p

Sutawidjaja I S, Chaniago R, Kamal S, 1992. Geologic map of Batur caldera, Bali, Indonesia. *Volc Surv Indonesia*, 1:50,000

Tatsumi Y, Murasaki M, Arsadi E M, Nohda S, 1991. Geochemistry of Quaternary lavas from NE Sulawesi: transfer of subduction components into the mantle wedge. *Contr Mineral Petr*, 107: 137-149

Tjia H D, Hadian R, Sumailani A R, Martono A, 1980. The nature of Umsini volcano, Irian Jaya, Indonesia. *Bull Volc*, 43: 595-600

Turner S, Foden J, George R, Evans P, Varne R, Elburg M, Jenner G, 2003. Rates and processes of potassic magma evolution beneath Sangeang Api volcano, East Sunda Arc, Indonesia. *J Petr*, 44: 491-515

Van Bergen M J, Vroon P Z, Varekamp J C, Poorter R P E, 1992. The origin of the potassic rock suite from Batu Tara volcano (East Sunda Arc, Indonesia). *Lithos*, 28: 261-282

Varekamp J C, Snellius II Shipboard Party, 1984. The Banda arc volcanoes, eastern Indonesia (abs). *Eos, Trans Amer Geophys Union*, 65: 1135

Varekamp J C, van Bergen M J, Vroon P Z, Poorter R P E, Wirakusumah A D, Erfan R, Suharyono K, Sriwana T, 1989. Volcanism and tectoinics in the eastern Sunda arc, Indonesia. *Netherlands J Sea Res*, 24: 303-312

Varne R, Foden J D, 1986. Geochemical and isotopic systematics of eastern Sunda arc volcanics; implications for mantle sources and mantle mixing processes. *In*: F-C Wezel (ed), *The Origin of Arcs*, Amsterdam: Elsevier, 159-189

Verstappen H Th, 1964. Some volcanoes of Halmahera (Moluccas) and their geomorphological setting. *Ned Aardr Gen*, 81: 297-316

Volc Surv Indonesia, 1986a. Annual report of the Volcanological Survey 1983-1984. Bull Volc Surv Indonesia, no 112

Volc Surv Indonesia, 1986b. Annual report of the Volcanological Survey 1984-1985. Bull Volc Surv Indonesia, no 113

Vroon P Z, 1992. Subduction of continental material in the Banda Arc, eastern Indonesia: Sr-Nd-Pb isotope and trace element evidence from volcanics and sediments. *Fac Aardwetenschappen Rijksuniversiteit Utrecht*, 205 p

Wheller G E, 1986. Petrogenesis of Batur caldera, Bali, and the geochemistry of Sunda-Banda arc basalts. *Unpublished PhD thesis*, Univ Tasmania, 156 p

Wheller G E, Varne R, 1986. Genesis of dacitic magmatism at Batur volcano, Bali, Indonesia: implications for the origins of stratovolcano calderas. *J Volc Geotherm Res*, 28: 363-378

Wheller G E, Varne R, Foden J D, Abbott M J, 1987. Geochemistry of Quaternary volcanism in the Sunda-Banda arc, Indonesia, and three-component genesis of island-arc basaltic magmas. *J Volc Geotherm Res*, 32: 137-160

Wichmann A, 1902. Der Vulkan der Insel Una-Una (Nanguna) in Busen von Tomini, Celebes. *J German Geol Soc*, 54: 144-158

Yasin A, 1980. Geologic map of the Bacan quadrangle, north Makalu. *Geol Res Devel Centre Indonesia*, 1:250,000 scale map and 10 p text

Zelenov K K, 1964. The submarine volcano Banua Wuhu, Indonesia. *Bandung Inst Tech Dept Geol Contr*, 55: 19-34

Zen M T, Hadikusumo D, 1964. Recent changes in the Anak-Krakatau volcano. *Bull Volc*, 27: 259-268

PHILIPPINES (0700-04)

Aguila L G, Newhall C G, Miller C D, Listanco E L, 1986. Reconnaissance geology of a large debris avalanche from Iriga volcano, Philippines. *Philippine J Volc*, 3: 54-72

Alcaraz A, Abad L F, Quema J C, 1952. Hibok-Hibok volcano, Philippine Islands, and activity since 1948. *Volcano Lett*, 516: 1-6 & 517: 1-4

Alcaraz A, Abad L F, Tupas M H, 1956. The Didicas submarine volcano. *Proc 8th Pacific Sci Cong*, 2: 139-156

Alvir A D, 1956. A cluster of little known Philippine volcanoes. *Proc 8th Pacific Sci Cong*, 2: 205-206

Andal E S, Yumul G P Jr, Listanco E L, Tamayo R A Jr, Dimalanta C B, Ishii T, 2005. Characterization of the Pleistocene volcanic chain of the Bicol arc, Philippines: implications for geohazard assessment. *Terr Atmos Ocean Sci*, 16: 865-883

Balmes C P, 2000. The geochemistry of the Mt. Balut Island geothermal prospect, Davao del Sur, Philippines. *Proc World Geotherm Cong 2000, Kyushu-Tohoku, Japan, May 28-June 10, 2000*, p 959-964

Bau M, Knittel U, 1993. Significance of slab-derived partial melts and aqueous fluids for the genesis of tholeiitic and calc-alkaline island-arc basalts: evidence from Mt. Arayat, Philippines. *Chem Geol*, 105: 233-251

Bautista L P, 1988. The 1988 Bulusan volcano activity. *Phivolcs Observer*, 4: 1-3

Castillo P R, Janney P E, Solidum R U, 1999. Petrology and geochemistry of Camiguin Island, southern Philippines: insights to the source of adakites and other lavas in a complex arc setting. *Contr Mineral Petr*, 134: 33-51

Castillo P R, Newhall C G, 2004. Geochemical constraints on possible subduction components in lavas of Mayon and Taal volcanoes, southern Luzon, Philippines. *J Petr*, 45: 1089-1108

Castillo P R, Solidum R U, Punongbayan R S, 2002. Origin of high field strength element enrichment in the Sulu Arc, southern Philippines, revisited. *Geology*, 30: 707-710

Catane S G, Taniguchi H, Goto A, Givero A P, Mandanas A A, 2005. Explosive volcanism in the Philippines. *CNEAS Monograph Ser, Tohoku Univ*, 18: 1-146

COMVOL, 1981. Catalogue of Philippine volcanoes and solfataric areas. *Philippine Comm Volc*, 87 p

Corpuz E G, 1985. Chronology of the September-October 1984 eruption of Mayon volcano, Philippines. *Philippine J Volc*, 2: 36-51

Daag A S, Dolan M T, Laguerta E P, Meeker G P, Newhall C G, Pallister J S, Solidum R U, 1996. Growth of a postclimactic lava dome at Mount Pinatubo, July-October 1992. *In*: Newhall C G, Punongbayan R S (eds) *Fire and Mud: Eruptions and Lahars of Mount Pinatubo, Philippines.* Quezon City, Philippines: Philippine Inst Volc Seism, and Seattle: Univ Wash Press, p 647-664

Defant M J, Jacques D, Maury R C, de Boer J, Joron J-L, 1989. Geochemistry and tectonic setting of the Luzon arc, Philippines. *Geol Soc Amer Bull*, 101: 663-672

Defant M J, Maury R C, Joron J, Feigenson M D, Leterrier J, Bellon H, Jacques D, Richard M, 1990. The geochemistry and tectonic setting of the northern section of the Luzon arc (the Philippines and Taiwan). *Tectonophysics*, 183: 187-205

Defant M J, Maury R C, Ripley E M, Feigenson M D, Jacques D, 1991. An example of island-arc petrogenesis: geochemistry and petrology of the southern Luzon arc, Philippines. *J Petr*, 32: 455-500

Delfin F G Jr, Newhall C G, Martinez M L, Salonga N D, Bayon F E B, Trimble D, Solidum R, 1997. Geological, 14C, and historical evidence for a 17th century eruption of Parker volcano, Mindanao, Philippines. *J Geol Soc Philippines*, 52: 25-42

Delfin F G Jr, Villarosa H G, Layugan D B, Clemente V C, Candelaria M R, Ruaya J R, 1996. Geothermal exploration of the pre-1991 Mount Pinatubo hydrothermal system. *In*: Newhall C G, Punongbayan R S (eds) *Fire and Mud: Eruptions and Lahars of Mount Pinatubo, Philippines.* Quezon City, Philippines: Philippine Inst Volc Seism, and Seattle: Univ Wash Press, p 197-212

Ebasco Services, 1977. Preliminary safety analysis report, Philippine Nuclear Power Plant #1. *Philippine Atomic Energy Comm Open-File Rpt and response to questions*

Faustino L A, 1934. Taal volcano and its eruptions. *Proc 5th Pacific Sci Cong*, 3: 2377-2378

Geronimo-Catane S, 1994. Mode of emplacement of two debris-avalanche deposits at Banahao volcano, southern Luzon, Philippines. *Bull Volc Soc Japan (Kazan)*, 39: 113-127

Hoblitt R P, Wolfe E W, Scott W E, Couchman M R, Pallister J S, Javier D, 1996. The preclimactic eruptions of Mount Pinatubo, June 1991. *In*: Newhall C G, Punongbayan R S (eds) *Fire and Mud: Eruptions and Lahars of Mount Pinatubo, Philippines.* Quezon City, Philippines: Philippine Inst Volc Seism, and Seattle: Univ Wash Press, p 457-511

Koyaguchi T, 1996. Volume estimation of tephra-fall deposits from the June 15, 1991 eruption of Mount Pinatubo by theoretical and geological methods. *In*: Newhall C G, Punongbayan R S (eds) *Fire and Mud: Eruptions and Lahars of Mount Pinatubo, Philippines.* Quezon City, Philippines: Philippine Inst Volc Seism, and Seattle: Univ Wash Press, p 583-600

Ku Y-P, Chen C-H, Newhall C G, Song S-R, Yang T F, Iizuka Y, McGeehin J, 2008. Determining an age for the Inararo Tuff eruption of Mt. Pinatubo, based on correlation with a distal ash layer in core MD97-2142, South China Sea. *Quat Internatl*, 178: 138-145

Lagmay A M F, Rodolfo K S, Siringan F P, Uy H, Remotigue C, Zamora P, Lapus M, Rodolfo R, Ong J, 2007. Geology and hazard implications of the Maraunot notch in the Pinatubo caldera, Philippines. *Bull Volc*, 69: 797-809

Macdonald G A, 1955. Hawaiian Islands. *Catalog of Active Volcanoes of the World and Solfatara Fields*, Rome: IAVCEI, 3: 1-37 ***(regional reference)***

Macdonald G A, Alcaraz A, 1954. Philippine volcanoes during 1953 and 1954. *Volcano Lett*, 523: 1-5

Macdonald G A, Alcaraz A, 1956. Nuees ardentes of the 1948-1953 eruption of Hibok-Hibok. *Bull Volc*, 18: 169-178

Magalit C T, Ruelo H B, 1985. Features and characteristics of the 1984 Mayon lava flows. *Philippine J Volc*, 2: 52-67

Maturgo O, Zaide-Delfin M, Layugan D, Catane J P, 2000. Characteristics of the volcanic-hydrothermal system in Mt. Labo, Philippines: implications to development. *Proc World Geotherm Cong 2000, Kyushu-Tohoku Japan, May 28-June 10, 2000*, p 1431-1436

McDermott F, Delfin F G Jr, Defant M J, Turner S, Maury R, 2005. The petrogenesis of volcanics from Mt. Bulusan and Mt. Mayon in the Bicol arc, Philippines. *Contr Mineral Petr*, 150: 652-670

McDermott F, Defant M J, Hawkesworth C J, Maury R C, Joron J L, 1993. Isotope and trace element evidence for three component mixing in the genesis of the North Luzon arc lavas (Philippines). *Contr Mineral Petr*, 113: 9-23

Miklius A, Flower M F J, Huijsmans J P P, Mukasa S B, Castillo P, 1991. Geochemistry of lavas from Taal Volcano, southwest Luzon, Philippines. *J Petr*, 32: 593-627

Mirabueno M H T, Okuno M, Nakamura T, Laguerta E P, Newhall C G, Kobayashi T, 2007. AMS radiocarbon dating of a charcoal fragment from the Irosin Ignimbrite, Sorsogon Province, southern Luzon, Philippines. *Bull Volc Soc Japan (Kazan)*, 52: 241-244

Moore J G, Melson W G, 1969. Nuees ardentes of the 1968 eruption of Mayon volcano, Philippines. *Bull Volc*, 33: 600-620

Moore J G, Nakamura K, Alcaraz A, 1966. The 1965 eruption of Taal volcano. *Science*, 151: 955-960

Nakamura K, 1966. The magmatophreatic eruption of Taal volcano in 1965, Phillippines. *J Geog Tokyo Geog Soc*, 75: 33-44 (in Japanese with English abs)

Neumann van Padang M, 1953. Philippine Islands and Cochin China. *Catalog of Active Volcanoes of the World and Solfatara Fields*, Rome: IAVCEI, 2: 1-49 ***(regional reference)***

Newhall C G, 1977. Geology and petrology of Mayon volcano, southeastern Luzon, Philippines. *Unpublished MSci thesis*, Univ Calif (Davis), 292 p

Newhall C G, 1979. Temporal variation in the lavas of Mayon volcano, Philippines. *J Volc Geotherm Res*, 5: 61-84

Newhall C G, Daag A S, Delfin F G Jr, Hoblitt R P, McGeehin J, Pallister J S, Regalado T M, Rubin M, Tubianosa B S, Tamayo R A Jr, Umbal J V, 1996. Eruptive history of Mount Pinatubo. *In*: Newhall C G, Punongbayan R S (eds) *Fire and Mud: Eruptions and Lahars of Mount Pinatubo, Philippines.* Quezon City, Philippines: Philippine Inst Volc Seism, and Seattle: Univ Wash Press, p 165-195

Newhall C G, Punongbayan R S (eds), 1996. *Eruptive history of Mount Pinatubo.* Quezon City, Philippines: Philippine Inst Volc Seism, and Seattle: Univ Wash Press, 1126 p

Nielson D L, Clemente W C, Moore J N, Powell T S, 1996. Fracture permiability in the Matalibong-25 corehole, Tiwi geothermal field, Philippines. *Proc 21st Workshop Geotherm Reservoir Eng, Stanford Univ, Calif, Jan 22-24, 1996*, p 209-216

Ozawa A, Tagami T, Listance E L, Arpa C B, Sudo M, 2004. Initiation and propogation of subduction along the Philippine trench: evidence for temporal and spatial distribution. *J Asian Earth Sci*, 23: 105-111

Packard R L, 1900. Remarkable volcanic eruptions in the Philippines. *Popular Sci Monthly*, 56: 374-379

Paguican E M R, Lagmay A M F, Rodolfo K S, Rodolfo R S, Tengonciang A M P, Lapus M R, Baliatan E G, Obille Jr E C, 20009. Extreme rainfall-induced lahars and dike breaching, 30 November 2006, Mayon volcano, Philippines. *Bull Volc*, 71: 845: 857

Paladio-Melosantos L O, Solidum R U, Scott W E, Quiambao R B, Umbal J V, Rodolfo K S, Tubianosa B S, Delos Reys P J, Alonso R A, Ruelo H B, 1996. Tephra falls of the 1991 eruption of Mount Pinatubo. *In*: Newhall C G, Punongbayan R S (eds) *Fire and Mud: Eruptions and Lahars of Mount Pinatubo, Philippines.* Quezon City, Philippines: Philippine Inst Volc Seism, and Seattle: Univ Wash Press, p 513-535

Pallister J S, Hoblitt R P, Meeker G P, Knight R J, Siems D F, 1996. Magma mixing at Mount Pinatubo: petrographic and chemical evidence from the 1991 deposits. *In*: Newhall C G, Punongbayan R S (eds) *Fire and Mud: Eruptions and Lahars of Mount Pinatubo, Philippines.* Quezon City, Philippines: Philippine Inst Volc Seism, and Seattle: Univ Wash Press, p 687-731

Peno O, 1978. Notes on Mayon eruption from May 3-July 4, 1978 and COMVOL's role in "Operation Mayon." *COMVOL Lett*, 10(3-4): 1-3

PHIVOLCS, 1986. Close monitoring and surveillance of Canlaon volcano. *Nat Sci Tech Auth Ann Rpt*, p 2

PHIVOLCS, 1991. *Volcanoes of the Philippines.* Manila: PHIVOLCS Press, 41 p

PHIVOLCS, 2003. Annual Report 2003. *Dept Sci Tech, Phil Inst Volc Seism*, 18 p

PHIVOLCS, 2004-. Volcanoes. *http://www.phivolcs.dost.gov.ph/Volcanolist/*

Pierson T C, Janda R J, Umbal J V, Daag A S, 1992. Immediate and long-term hazards from lahars and excess sedimentation in rivers draining Mt. Pinatubo, Philippines. *U S Geol Surv, Water Resour Invest Rpt*, 92-4039: 1-35

Pinatubo Volcano Observatory Team, 1991. Lessons from a major eruption: Mt. Pinatubo, Philippines. *Eos, Trans Amer Geophys Union*, 72: 545, 552-553, 555

Punongbayan R S, 1985. An approach for estimating ages of active volcanoes. *Philippine J Volc*, 2: 191-205

Rae A J, Cooke D R, Phillips D, Zaide-Delfin M, 2004. The nature of magmatism at Palinpinon geothermal field, Negros Island, Philippines: implications for geothermal activity and regional tectonics. *J Volc Geotherm Res*: 129: 321-342

Ramos S, Zaide-Delfin M, Takashima I, Bayrante L, Panem C, Pioquinto W, 2000. Thermoluminescence dating in Mt. Labo and North Davao, Philippines: implications on geothermal wells. *Proc World Geotherm Cong 2000, Kyushu-Tohoku Japan, May 28-June 10, 2000*, p 1617-1622

Ramos-Villarta S C, Corpuz E G, Newhall C G, 1985. Eruptive history of Mayon volcano, Philippines. *Philippine J Volc*, 2: 1-35

Richard M, Maury R C, Bellon H, Stephan J F, Boirat J M, Calderon A, 1986. Geology of Mt. Iraya volcano and Batan Island, northern Philippines. *Philippine J Volc*, 3: 1-27

Rodolfo K S, Umbal J V, 2008. A prehistoric lahar-dammed lake and eruption of Mount Pinatubo described in a Philippine aborigine legend. *J Volc Geotherm Res*, 176: 432-437

Rosi M, Paladio-Melosantos M L, Di Muro A, Leoni R, Bacolcol T, 2001. Fall vs flow activity during the 1991 climactic eruption of Pinatubo volcano (Philippines). *Bull Volc*, 62: 549-566

Ruaya J R, Panem C C, 1991. Mt. Natib, Philippines: a geochemical model of a caldera-hosted geothermal system. *J Volc Geotherm Res*, 45: 255-265

Ruelo H B, 1983. Morphological and crater development of Mt. Tabaro eruption site, Taal volcano, Philippines. *Philippine J Volc*, 1: 19-68

Sajona F G, Bellon H, Maury R C, Pubellier M, Cotten J, Rangin C, 1994. Magmatic response to abrupt changes in geodynamic settings: Pliocene-Quaternary calc-alkaline and Nb-enriched lavas from Mindanao, Philippines. *Tectonophysics*, 237: 47-72

Sajona F G, Bellon H, Maury R C, Pubellier M, Querbral R D, Cotten J, Bayon F E, Pagado E, Pematian P, 1997. Tertiary and Quaternary magmatism in Mindanao and Leyte (Philippines): geochronology, geochemistry and tectonic setting. *J Asian Earth Sci*, 15: 121-153

Sajona F G, Maury R C, Prouteau G, Cotten J, Schiano P, Bellon H, Fontaine L, 2000. Slab melt as metasomatic agent in island arc magma mantle sources, Negros and Bataan (Philippines). *The Island Arc*, 9: 472-486

Salise P C, Manzano J A, Sierra J, Barela H, 1991. Geo-environmental hazard investigation of Malindang Range volcanic complex and risk assessment of town centres, Misamis Occidental. *Geol Soc Philippines 4th Ann Geol Conv Abs*, p 16-17

Santos G G, Wainerdi R E, 1969. Notes on the 1965 Taal volcanic eruptions. *Bull Volc*, 33: 503-529

Scott W E, Hoblitt R P, Torres R C, Self S, Martinez M L, Nillos T Jr, 1996. Pyroclastic flows of the June 15, 1991, climactic eruption of Mount Pinatubo. *In:* Newhall C G, Punongbayan R S (eds) *Fire and Mud: Eruptions and Lahars of Mount Pinatubo, Philippines.* Quezon City, Philippines: Philippine Inst Volc Seism, and Seattle: Univ Wash Press, p 545-570

Selga M, 1937. Las erupciones de Mayon en 1853. *Bol Soc Sism It*, 35: 165-167

Sincioco J, 1988. The 1988 eruptive activity of Canlaon volcano. *Phivolcs Observer*, 3: 3

Solidum R U, Castillo P R, Hawkins J W, 2003. Geochemistry of lavas from Negros Arc, west central Philippines: insights into the contribution from the subducting slab. *Geochem Geophys Geosyst*, 4: doi:10.1029/2003GC00513

Stimac J A, Goff F, Counce D, Larocque A C L, Hilton D R, Morgenstern U, 2004. The crater lake and hydrothermal system of Mount Pinatubo, Philippines: evolution in the decade after eruption. *Bull Volc*, 66: 149-167

Torres R, Mouginis-Mark P, Self S, Garbeil H, Kallianpur K, Quiambao R, 2004. Monitoring the evolution of the Pasig-Potrero alluvial fan, Pinatubo volcano, using a decade of remote sensing data. *J Volc Geotherm Res*, 138: 371-392

Von Biedersee H, Pichler H, 1995. The Canlaon and its neighbouring volcanoes in the Negros Belt/Philippines. *J Southeast Asian Earth Sci*, 11: 111-123

Waters A C, Fisher R V, 1971. Base surges and their deposits: Capelinhos and Taal volcanoes. *J Geophys Res*, 76: 5596-5614

Wiesner M G, Wetzel A, Catane S G, Listanco E L, Mirabueno H T, 2004. Grain size, areal thickness distribution and controls on sedimentation of the 1991 Mount Pinatubo tephra layer in the South China Sea. *Bull Volc*, 66: 226-242

Wolfe E W, Hoblitt R P, 1996. Overview of the eruption. *In:* Newhall C G, Punongbayan R S (eds) *Fire and Mud: Eruptions and Lahars of Mount Pinatubo, Philippines.* Quezon City, Philippines: Philippine Inst Volc Seism, and Seattle: Univ Wash Press, p 3-20

Wolfe J A, Self S, 1983. Structural lineaments and Neogene volcanism in southwestern Luzon. *In:* Hayes D E (ed) *The Tectonic and Geological Evolution of Southeast Asian Seas and Islands: Part 2*, Amer Geophys Union Monograph 27

Worcester D C, 1912. Taal volcano and its recent destructive eruption. *Natl Geog*, 23: 313-368

SOUTHEAST ASIA (0705)

Barr S M, James D E, 1990. Trace element characteristics of Upper Cenozoic basaltic rocks of Thailand, Kampuchea and Vietnam. *J Southeast Asian Earth Sci*, 4: 233-242

Bondarenko V I, Nadezhnyi A M, 1985. Main structural features and morphology of the volcanic zone and individual submarine volcanoes in the vicinity of the Catwic-Phu Quy islands on the Vietnamese shelf as revealed by continuous seismic profiling data. *Volc Seism*, 1985(5): 34-43 (English translation 1989, 7: 701-716)

Chen S (ed), 1986. *Atlas of Geo-Science, Analysis of Landsat Imagery in China*. Beijing: Chinese Acad Sci Press, 228 p

Du J, Liu C, Fu B, Ninomiya Y, Zhang Y, Wang C, Wang H, Sun Z, 2005. Variations of geothermometry and chemical-isotopic compositions of hot spring fluids in the Rehai geothermal field, southwestern China. *J Volc Geotherm Res*, 142: 243-261

Geographical Journal, 1923. Two new volcanic islands in the China Sea. *Geog Jour*, 62: 135-138

Liu J, Taniguchi H, 2001. Active volcanoes in China. *Tohoku Asian Studies*, 6: 173-189

Markov Y D, 1994. Recent sedimentogenesis on the Ile des Cendres volcanoes and adjacent shelf, South China Sea. *Volc Seism*, 15: 565-578 (English translation)

Neumann van Padang M, 1953. Philippine Islands and Cochin China. *Catalog of Active Volcanoes of the World and Solfatara Fields*, Rome: IAVCEI, 2: 1-49 ***(regional reference)***

Patte E, 1925. Etude de l'Ile des Cendres, volcan apparu au large de la Cote d'Annam. *Bull Serv Geol Indochina*, 13: 5-19

Saurin E, 1967. La neotectonique de l'Indochine. *Rev Geog Phys Geol Dynam*, 9: 143-152

Stephenson D, Marshall T R, 1984. The petrology and mineralogy of Mt. Popa volcano and the nature of the late-Cenozoic Burma volcanic area. *J Geol Soc London*, 141: 747-762

Tong W, Mu Z, Liu S, Zhang M, 1988. Late Cenozoic volcanoes and active geothermal systems in China. *Proc Kagoshima Internatl Conf Volc*, p 847-850

Wang F, Peng Z, Chen W, Wang Z, Yang J, Zhang Z, Hu T, 2000. High-precision thermal ionization mass spectrometry dating of young volcanic rocks by using U-series method. *Chinese Sci Bull*, 45: 83-87

Wang F, Peng Z, Zhu R, He H, Yang L, 2006. Petrogenesis and magma residence time of lavas from Tengchong volcanic field (China): evidence from U series disequilibria and 40Ar/39Ar dating. *Geochem Geophys Geosyst*, 7, doi:10.1029/2005GC001023

Wei H, Sparks R S J, Liu R, Fan Q, Wang Y, Hong H, Zhang H, Chen H, Jiang C, Dong J, Zheng Y, Pan Y, 2003. Three active volcanoes in China and their hazards. *J Asian Earth Sci*, 21: 515-526

Whitford-Stark J L, 1987. A survey of Cenozoic volcanism on mainland Asia. *Geol Soc Amer Spec Pap*, 213: 1-74

Yu J-H, O'Reilly S Y, Griffin W L, Xu X, Zhang M, Zhou X, 2003. The thermal state and composition of the lithospheric mantle beneath the Leizhou Peninsula, South China. *J Volc Geotherm Res*, 122: 165-189

Zhang X, Shi Z, 1999. Study on relationship between historical volcanic eruptions and historical strong earthquakes in China and its adjacent regions. *Acta Seism Sinica*, 12: 109-116

TAIWAN & SW JAPAN (0801-02)

Anonymous, 1925. Submarine eruption in the Yaeyama-Retto, Okinawa. *Chikyu*, 3: 249-250 (in Japanese)

Aoki K, 2008. Revised age and distribution of ca. 87 ka Aso-4 tephra based on new evidence from the northwest Pacific Ocean. *Quat Internatl*, 178: 100-118

Aramaki S, 1984. Formation of the Aira caldera, southern Kyushu, 22,000 years ago. *J Geophys Res*, 89: 8485-8501

Aramaki S, Fukuyama H, Kamo K, Kamada M, 1981. Sakurajima volcano. *In:* Kubotera A (ed) *Symp Arc Volc Field Excur Guide to Sakurajima, Kirishima and Aso Volcanoes, Part 1*, Tokyo: Volc Soc Japan, p 1-17

Aramaki S, Yamasaki M, 1963. Pyroclastic flows in Japan. *Bull Volc*, 26: 89-99

Belousov A, Belousova M, Chen C, 2010. Recent eruptive history of the Tatun volcanic group, Northern Taiwan: hazard-related issues. *J Volc Geotherm Res*, 191: 205-221

Chen C, 1978. Petrochemistry and origin of Pleistocene volcanic rocks from northern Taiwan. *Bull Volc*, 41: 513-528

Chen C H, 1981. Petrochemical aspects and tectonic implication of Pleistocene andesitic rocks of northern Taiwan and off-shore islets. *IAVCEI 1981 Tokyo Mtg Abs*, p 50-51

Chen C H, Lin S B, 2002. Eruptions younger than 20 ka of the Tatun volcano group as viewed from the sediments of the Sungshan Formation in Taipei Basin. *West Pac Earth Sci*, 2: 191-204

Chen C H, Shen J J-S, 2005. A refined historical record of volcanic eruptions around Taiwan: tectonic implications in the arc-continent collision area. *Terrestrial, Atmosph, Oceanic Sci*, 16: 331-343

Chen C-H, Lee T, Shieh Y-N, Chen C-H, Hsu W-Y, 1995. Magmatism at the onset of back-arc basin spreading in the Okinawa Trough. *J Volc Geotherm Res*, 69: 313-322

Chen S (ed), 1986. *Atlas of Geo-Science, Analysis of Landsat Imagery in China*. Beijing: Chinese Acad Sci Press, 228 p

Fujii J, Nakajima T, Kamata H, 2001. Paleomagnetic directions of the Aso pyroclastic-flow and the Aso-4 co-ignimbrite ash-fall deposits in Japan. *Earth, Planets, Space*, 53: 1137-1150

Fujii T, Nakada S, 1999. The 15 September 1991 pyroclastic flows at Unzen volcano (Japan): a flow model for associated ash-cloud surges. *J Volc Geotherm Res*, 89: 159-172

Fujisawa Y, Ueno H, Kobayashi T, 2001. 2.2 ka eruption study on the emplacement temperature of pyroclastic deposits of Yufu volcano, Japan. *Bull Volc Soc Japan (Kazan)*, 46: 187-203 (in Japanese with English abs)

Furuyama K, Daishi M, Nagao K, Eguchi M, 2002. The discovery of young dacite lava in Akuseki-jima Island, Tokara Islands, Japan. *Bull Volc Soc Japan (Kazan)*, 47: 751-755

Geshi N, Kobayashi T, 2006. Volcanic activities of Kuchinoerabujima volcano within the last 30,000 years. *Bull Volc Soc Japan (Kazan)*, 51: 1-20 (in Japanese with English abs)

Hayakawa Y, 1994a. A catalog of the volcanic eruptions during the last 2000 years in Japan. *Sci Rpt Fac Education Gumma Univ* (in Japanese with English abs) ***(regional reference)***

Hayashida A, Kamata H, Danhara T, 1996. Correlation of widespread tephra deposits based on paleomagnetic directions: link between a volcanic field and sedimentary sequences in Japan. *Quat Internatl*, 34-36: 89-98

Hedenquist J W, Aoki M, Shinohara H, 1994. Flux of volatiles and ore-forming metals from the magmatic-hydrothermal system of Satsuma Iwojima volcano. *Geology*, 22: 585-588

Ho C S, 1988. An introduction to the geology of Taiwan; explanatory text of the geologic map of Taiwan. Taipei: *Central Geol Surv, Ministry Economic Affairs*, 192 p

Honma F, 1926. Beppu, the Hot-Spring City. *Pan-Pacific Sci Cong Guidebook Excur*, E-1.5: 1-16

Hoshizumi H, Uto K, Watanabe K, 1999. Geology and eruptive history of Unzen volcano, Shimabara Peninsula, Kyushu, SW Japan. *J Volc Geotherm Res*, 89: 81-94

Ikebe S, Fujioka M, 2001. "Yunotani Catastrophe" of 1816, in Aso volcano, southwest Japan-historical records of steam explosion. *Bull Volc Soc Japan (Kazan)*, 46: 147-163 (in Japanese with English abs)

Ikebe S, Watanabe K, Miyabuchi Y, 2008. The sequence and style of the 1988-1995 eruptions of Nakadake Aso volcano, Kyushu, Japan. *Bull Volc Soc Japan (Kazan)*, 53: 15-33 (in Japanese with English abs)

Iki T, 1926. Geological notes on the Aso volcano. *Pan-Pacific Sci Cong Guidebook Excur*, E-4: 1-14

Iki T, Tsuboi S, 1926. Notes on the great eruption of Sakura-jima volcano in 1914. *Pan-Pacific Sci Cong Guidebook Excur*, E-4.5: 1-12

Imura R, 1992. Minor phreatic activity of Shinmoedake, Kirishima volcano, in 1991-92. *Bull Volc Soc Japan (Kazan)*, 37: 281-283 (in Japanese)

Imura R, 1998. Reconstruction of the sequence of the An-ei eruptions of Sakurajima volcano (A.D. 1779-1782) using the historical records. *Bull Volc Soc Japan (Kazan)*, 43: 373-383 (in Japanese with English abs)

Imura R, Kobayashi T, 1991. Eruptions of Shinmoedake volcano, Kirishima volcano group, in the last 300 years. *Bull Volc Soc Japan (Kazan)*, 36: 135-148 (in Japanese)

Inoue K, 1988. The growth history of Takachiho composite volcano in the Kirishima volcano group. *Ganko (Petr Min)*, 83: 26-41 (in Japanese with English abs)

Jaggar T A, 1924. Sakurajima, Japan's greatest volcanic eruption: a convulsion of nature whose ravages were minimized by scientific knowledge, compared with the terrors and destruction of the recent Tokyo earthquake. *Natl Geog*, 65: 441-470

Japan Association Quaternary Research, 1987. *Quaternary Maps of Japan: Landforms, Geology, and Tectonics*. Tokyo: Univ Tokyo Press

Japan Meteorological Agency, 1975. *National Catalogue of the Active Volcanoes in Japan*. Tokyo: Japan Meteorological Agency, 119 p (in Japanese) ***(regional reference)***

Japan Meteorological Agency, 1996. *National Catalogue of the Active Volcanoes in Japan (second edition)*. Tokyo: Japan Meteorological Agency, 502 p (in Japanese)

Japan Meteorological Agency, 2003. Volcanoes-monitoring and disaster reduction. Tokyo: Japan Meteorological Agency, 32 p (in Japanese)

Kagoshima Prefectural Museum, 1988. *The 1914 eruption of Sakurajima, Japan*. Kagoshima, Japan: Kagoshima Prefectural Museum, 64 p

Kamata H, Kobayashi T, 1997. The eruptive rate and history of Kuju volcano in Japan during the past 15,000 years. *J Volc Geotherm Res*, 76: 163-171

Kamata K, 1989. Shishimuta caldera, the buried source of the Yabakei pyroclastic flow in the Hohi volcanic zone, Japan. *Bull Volc*, 51: 41-50

Kaneko K, Kamata H, Koyaguchi T, Yoshikawa M, Furukawa K, 2007. Repeated large-scale eruptions from a single compositionally stratified magma chamber: an example from Aso volcano, Southwest Japan. *J Volc Geotherm Res*, 167: 160-180

Kaneko T, Martin J, Wooster M J, Nakada S, 2002. Exogenous and endogenous growth of the Unzen lava dome examined by satellite infrared image analysis. *J Volc Geotherm Res*, 116: 151-160

Kano K, Yamamoto T, Ono K, 1996. Subaqueous eruption and emplacement of the Shinjima Pumice, Shinjima (Moeshima) Island, Kagoshima Bay, SW Japan. *J Volc Geotherm Res*, 71: 187-206

Katayama N, 1974. Old records of natural phenomena concerning the Shimabara catastrophe. *Sci Rpt Shimabara Volc Observ, Fac Sci Kyushu Univ*, 9: 1-45 (in Japanese with English abs)

Kato Y, 1982. Position and amount of erupted pumice from the Iriomote submarine volcano, Ryukyu Islands. *Ryukyu Is Geol Studies*, 6: 41-47

Kawakatsu H, Kaneshima S, Matsubayashi H, Ohminato T, Sudo Y, Tsutsui T, Uhira K, Yamasato H, Ito H, Legrand D, 2000. Aso94: Aso seismic observation with broadband instruments. *J Volc Geotherm Res*, 101: 129-154

Kobayashi T, 1982. Geology of Sakurajima volcano: a review. *Bull Volc Soc Japan (Kazan)*, 27: 277-292 (in Japanese with English abs)

Kobayashi T, Aramaki S, Watanabe T, Kamada M, 1981. Kirishima volcano. *In*: Kubotera A (ed) *Symp Arc Volc Field Excur Guide to Sakurajima, Kirishima and Aso Volcanoes, Part 2*, Tokyo: Volc Soc Japan, p 18-32

Kobayashi T, Ishihara K, Hirabayashi J, 1988. A guidebook for Sakurajima volcano. *In*: Aramaki S, Kamo K, Kamada M (eds), Kagoshima:Kagoshima Prefectural Government, 88 p

Konstantinou K I, Lin C H, Liang W T, 2007. Seismicity characteristics of a potentially active Quaternary volcano: the Tatun volcano group, northern Taiwan. *J Volc Geotherm Res*, 160: 300-318

Kudo T, Hoshizumi H, 2006-. Catalog of eruptive events within the last 10,000 years in Japan, database of Japanese active volcanoes. Geol Surv Japan, AIST, http://riodb02.ibase.aist.go.jp/db099/eruption/index.html ***(regional reference)***

Kuno H, 1962. Japan, Taiwan and Marianas. *Catalog of Active Volcanoes of the World and Solfatara Fields*, Rome: IAVCEI, 11: 1-332 ***(regional reference)***

Kyoto Univ Disaster Prevention Institute, 1987. *Research on Eruptions-Prediction of Volcanic Eruptions and the Role of Universities*. Kyoto Univ Disaster Prevention Inst and Natl Univ Res Group for Volcanoes

Lan T F, Yang T F, Lee H-F, Chen Y-G, Chen C-H, Song S-R, Tsao S, 2007. Compositions and flux of soils in Liu-Huang-Ku hydrothermal area, northern Taiwan. *J Volc Geotherm Res*, 165: 27-45

Lee H-F, Yang T F, Lan T F, Chen C-H, Song S-R, Tsao S, 2008. Temporal variations of gas compositions of fumaroles in the Tatun volcano group, northern Taiwan. *J Volc Geotherm Res*, 178: 624-635

Liu J, Taniguchi H, 2001. Active volcanoes in China. *Tohoku Asian Studies*, 6: 173-189

Machida H, 1976. Stratigraphy and chronology of late Quaternary marker-tephras in Japan. *Tokyo Metropolitan Univ Geog Rpt*, 11: 109-132

Machida H, 1990. Frequency and magnitude of catastrophic explosive volcanism in the Japan region during the past 130 ka: implications for human occupance of volcanic regions. *Geol Soc Aust Symp Proc*, 1: 27-36

Machida H, Arai F, 1981. Late Quaternary large eruptions recorded in distal areas around Japan. *IAVCEI Tokyo Mtg Abs*, p 214-215

Machida H, Arai F, 1992. *Atlas of tephra in and around Japan*. Tokyo: Univ Tokyo Press, 276 p ***(regional reference)***

Machida H, Arai F, 2003. *Atlas of Tephra in and around Japan*. Tokyo, Univ Tokyo Press, 338 p

Maeno F, Taniguchi H, 2005. Eruptive history of Satsuma Iwo-jima Island, Kikai caldera, after a 6.5 ka caldera-forming eruption. *Bull Volc Soc Japan (Kazan)*, 50: 71-85 (in Japanese with English abs)

Maeno F, Taniguchi H, 2006. Silicic lava dome growth in the 1934-1935 Showa Iwo-jima eruption, Kikai caldera, south of Kyushu, Japan. *Bull Volc*, 68: 673-688

Maeno F, Taniguchi H, 2007. Spatiotemporal evolution of a marine caldera-forming eruption, generating a low-aspect ratio pyroclastic flow, 7.3 ka, Kikai caldera, Japan: implication from near-vent eruptive deposits. *J Volc Geotherm Res*, 167: 212-238

Masuda N, Watanabe K, Miyabuchi Y, 2004. Rhyolite to dacite lava flows newly-discovered on the western slope of Aso Central Cones, southwestern Japan. *Bull Volc Soc Japan (Kazan)*, 49: 119-128 (in Japanese with English abs)

Matsushima N, Kazahaya K, Saito G, Shinohara H, 2003. Mass and heat flux of volcanic gas discharging from the summit crater of Iwodake volcano, Satsuma-Iwojima, Japan, during 1996-1999. *J Volc Geotherm Res*, 126: 285-301

Miki D, 1999. Estimate of the ages of lava flows at Sakurajima volcano, Kyushu, Japan; inferred from paleomagnetic directions and paleointensities. *Bull Volc Soc Japan (Kazan)*, 44: 111-122 (in Japanese with English abs)

Milne J, 1886. The volcanoes of Japan. *Trans Seism Soc Japan*, 9: 1-184 ***(regional reference)***

Minakami T, 1950. Report on the volcanic activities in Japan during 1939-1947. *Bull Volc*, 10: 45-58

Minakami T, 1962. Report on volcanic activity in Japan for the period from 1957 to 1959. *Bull Volc*, 24: 7-22

Minakami T, Sakuma S, 1953. Report on volcanic activities and volcanological studies concerning them in Japan during 1948-1951. *Bull Volc*, 14: 79-132

Minakami T, Shimozuru D, Miyazaki T, Hiraga S, Yamaguti M, 1968. The 1959 eruption of Simmoe-dake and the 1961 Iimori-yama earthquake swarm. *Bull Earthq Res Inst, Univ Tokyo*, 46: 965-992

Miyabuchi Y, 1999. Deposits associated with the 1990-1995 eruption of Unzen volcano, Japan. *J Volc Geotherm Res*, 89: 139-158

Miyabuchi Y, Hoshizumi H, Takada H, Watanabe K, Xu S, 2003. Pumice-fall deposits from Aso volcano during the past 90,000 years, southwestern Japan. *Bull Volc Soc Japan (Kazan)*, 48: 195-214 (in Japanese with English abs)

Miyabuchi Y, Hoshizumi H, Watanabe K, 2004. Lat-Pleistocene tephrostratigraphy of Aso volcano, southwestrn Japan, after deposition of AT Ash. *Bull Volc Soc Japan (Kazan)*, 49: 51-64 (in Japanese with English abs)

Miyabuchi Y, Ikebe S, 2008. The February 2008 ash deposit from the Nakadake crater, Aso volcano, Japan. *Bull Volc Soc Japan (Kazan)*, 53: 201-206 (in Japanese with English abs)

Miyabuchi Y, Ikebe S, Watanabe K, 2008. Geological constraints on the 2003-2005 ash emissions from the Nakadake crater lake, Aso volcano, Japan. *J Volc Geotherm Res*, 178: 169-183

Miyabuchi Y, Masuda N, Watanabe K, 2004. Geologic history of the western part of post-caldera central cones of Aso volcano, southwestern Japan, based on stratigraphic relationships between lava flows and airfall tephra layers. *Bull Volc Soc Japan (Kazan)*, 49: 267-282 (in Japanese with English abs)

Miyabuchi Y, Watanabe K, 1997. Eruption ages of Holocene tephras from Aso volcano, southwestern Japan, inferred from 14C ages of buried andisols. *Bull Volc Soc Japan (Kazan)*, 42: 403-408 (in Japanese with English abs)

Miyabuchi Y, Watanabe K, 2000. Phreatic explosions and ejecta around Jigoku Spa, southwestern part of the central cones of Aso volcano, Japan. *Bull Volc Soc Japan (Kazan)*, 45: 25-32 (in Japanese with English abs)

Miyabuchi Y, Watanabe K, Egawa Y, 2006. A pyroclastic flow deposit occurring at the northeastern foot of Nakadake, Aso volcano (Japan) and its stratigraphic significance. *Bull Volc Soc Japan (Kazan)*, 51: 231-243 (in Japanese with English abs)

Moriwaki H, Machida H, Hatsumi Y, Matsushima Y, 1986. Phreatomagmatic eruptions affected by postglacial transgression in the northern coastal area of Kagoshima Bay, southern Kyushu, Japan. *Chigaku Zasshi (Jour Geog)*, 95: 24-43 (in Japanese with English abs)

Murayama I, 1990. *Volcanoes of Japan (III)*. Tokyo: Daimedo, 259 p (in Japanese) ***(regional reference)***

Nakada S, Fujii T, 1993. Preliminary report of the activity at Unzen volcano (Japan), November 1990-November 1991: dacite lava domes and pyroclastic flows. *J Volc Geotherm Res*, 54: 319-333

Nakada S, Miyake Y, Sato H, Oshima O, Fujinawa A, 1995. Endogenous growth of dacite dome at Unzen volcano (Japan), 1993-1994. *Geology*, 23: 157-160

Nakada S, Shimizu H, Ohta K, 1999. Overview of the 1990-95 eruption at Unzen volcano. *J Volc Geotherm Res*, 89: 1-22

Nakamura M, 1967. On the volcanic products and history of Kaimon-dake volcano. *Bull Volc Soc Japan (Kazan)*, 12: 119-131

Nakamura M, 1980. Possibility of new volcanic activity at Ibusuki volcanic field, Kyushu, Japan. *Bull Volc Soc Japan (Kazan)*, 25: 195-205 (in Japanese with English abs)

Nakano S, Yamamoto T, Iwaya T, Itoh J, Takada A, 2001-. *Quaternary Volcanoes of Japan*. Geol Surv Japan, AIST, http://www.aist.go.jp/RIODB/strata/VOL_JP/ ***(regional reference)***

Naruo H, 1988. The influence of the earliest eruption of Kaimon Dake volcano on a society of the latter term of the Jomon era (ca 4000 BP) in southern Kyushu. *Kagoshima Internatl Conf Volc Abs*, p 562

Neumann van Padang M, 1953. Philippine Islands and Cochin China. *Catalog of Active Volcanoes of the World and Solfatara Fields*, Rome: IAVCEI, 2: 1-49 ***(regional reference)***

Notsu K, Nakai S, Igarashi G, Ishibashi J, Mori T, Suzuki M, Wakita H, 2001. Spatial distribution and temporal variation of 3He/4He in hot spring gas released from Unzen volcanic area, Japan. *J Volc Geotherm Res*, 111: 89-98

Ohmi S, Lees J M, 1995. Three-dimensional P- and S-wave velocity structure below Unzen volcano. *J Volc Geotherm Res*, 65: 1-26

Ohta T, Hasenaka T, Fujimaki H, 1990. Geology and petrography of Yufu-Tsurumi volcano group, Oita Prefecture. *J Min Petr Econ Geol*, 85: 113-129 (in Japanese with English abs)

Onishi K, 1930. Eruption of Sakurajima 1914. *Volcano Lett*, 308: 1-3

Ono K, Kubotera A, Ota K, 1981. Aso volcano. *In*: Kubotera A (ed) *Symp Arc Volc Field Excur Guide to Sakurajima, Kirishima and Aso Volcanoes, Part 3*, Tokyo: Volc Soc Japan, p 33-52

Ono K, Soya T, Hosono T, 1982. Geology of the Satsuma-Io-Jima district. *Geol Surv Japan*, 1:50,000 geol map and text (in Japanese)

Ono K, Soya T, Mimura K, 1981. Volcanoes of Japan. *Geol Surv Japan Map Ser*, no 11, 2nd edition, 1:2,000,000

Ono K, Watanabe K, 1985. Geologic map of Aso volcano. *Geol Surv Japan*, 1:50,000 geol map and text (in Japanese with English summary)

Ono K, Watanabe K, Hoshizumi H, Ikebe S, 1995. Ash eruption of the Naka-dake crater, Aso volcano, southwestern Japan. *J Volc Geotherm Res*, 66: 137-148

Ota K, 1984. Unzen volcano. *Nagasaki Prefecture*, 98 p (in Japanese)

Ozeki N, Okuno M, Kobayashi T, 2005. Growth history of Mayuyama, Unzen volcano, Kyushu, southwest Japan. *Bull Volc Soc Japan (Kazan)*, 50: 441-454 (in Japanese with English abs)

Saito G, Kazahaya K, Shinohara H, Stimac J, Kawanabe Y, 2001. Variation of volatile concentration in a magma system of Satsuma-Iwojima volcano deduced from melt inclusion analyses. *J Volc Geotherm Res*, 108: 11-31

Saito T, Kamata H, Ishikawa N, 2000. Lithofacies and thermoremanent magnetism of the Ikeshiro pyroclastic-flow deposit and the Ikeshiro-Hokubu volcaniclastic deposit in the Yufu-Tsurumi volcano group. *Bull Volc Soc Japan (Kazan)*, 45: 217-224 (in Japanese with English abs)

Shimano T, Koyaguchi T, 2001. Eruption styles and degassing process of ascending magma of the 1813 eruption of Suwanose-jima volcano, southwest Japan. *Bull Volc Soc Japan (Kazan)*, 46: 53-70 (in Japanese with English abs)

Sudo Y, Ono H, Hurst A W, Tsutsui T, Mori T, Nakaboh M, Matsumoto Y, Sako M, Yoshikawa S, Tanaka M, Kobayashi Y, Hashimoto T, Hoka T, Yamada T, Masuda H, Kikuchi S, 1998. Seismic activity and ground deformation associated with 1995 phreatic eruption of Kuju volcano, Kyushu, Japan. *J Volc Geotherm Res*, 81: 245-267

Sumi K, Takashima I, 1976. Absolute ages of the hydrothermal alteration halos and associated volcanic rocks in some Japanese geothermal fields. *In*: *Proc 2nd United Nations Symp Devel Use Geotherm Resour, San Francisco*, Washington D C: U S Government Printing Office 1: 625-634

Suwa A, 1978. The surveillance of volcanic activities in Japan. *Bull Volc Soc Japan (Kazan)*, 23: 83-89 (in Japanese with English abs)

Takashima I, Watanabe K, 1994. Thermoluminescence age determination of lava flows/domes and collapsed materials at Unzen volcano, SW Japan. *Bull Volc Soc Japan (Kazan)*, 39: 1-12

Tanaka Y, 1993. Eruption mechanism as inferred from geomagnetic changes with special attention to the 1989-1990 activity of Aso volcano. *J Volc Geotherm Res*, 56: 319-338

Tanakadate H, 1931. Volcanic activity in Japan and vicinity during the period between 1924 and 1931. *Japan J Astron Geophys*, 9: 47-64

Tanakadate H, 1934. Volcanic activity in Japan during the period between June 1931 and June 1934. *Japan J Astron Geophys*, 12: 89-108

Tateyama H, Hoshizumi H, Watanabe K, 2002. Stratigraphy and eruptive history of Nodake volcano, Unzen, Kyushu, Japan. *Bull Volc Soc Japan (Kazan)*, 47: 739-749 (in Japanese with English abs)

Toshida K, Uto K, Matsumoto A, 2006. K-Ar dating of Kimpo volcano, northern Ryukyu Arc. *Bull Volc Soc Japan (Kazan)*, 51: 31-40 (in Japanese with English abs)

Tsukui M, Nakano S, Saito K, 2008. Eruptions and earthquakes occurred along Amurian Plate eastern margin in the 9th century. *Bull Volc Soc Japan (Kazan)*, 53: 79-91 (in Japanese with English abs)

Tsukui M, Okuno M, Kobayashi T, 2007. Eruptive history of Ohachi volcano, Kirishima volcano group, southern Kyushu, Japan. *Bull Volc Soc Japan (Kazan)*, 52: 1-21 (in Japanese with English abs)

Tsuya H, Minakami T, 1940. Minor activity of volcano Sakura-zima in October, 1939. *Bull Earthq Res Inst, Univ Tokyo*, 18: 319-339 (in Japanese with English abs)

Tsuya H, Morimoto R, 1963. Types of volcanic eruptions in Japan. *Bull Volc*, 26: 209-222

Ui T, Kobayashi T, 1988. Catastrophic pyroclastic flow eruption at Kikai caldera, 6300 years ago. *Kagoshima Internatl Conf Volc Abs*, p 396

Ui T, Matsuwo N, Sumita M, Fujinawa A, 1999. Generation of block and ash flows during the 1990-1995 eruption of Unzen volcano, Japan. *J Volc Geotherm Res*, 89: 123-137

Volcanological Society of Japan, 1999. Report on volcanic activities and volcanological studies in Japan for the period from 1995 to 1998. *Bull Volc Soc Japan (Kazan)*, 44(Suppl): 1-76

Volcanological Society of Japan, 2003. Report on volcanic activities and volcanological studies in Japan for the period from 1999 to 2002. *Bull Volc Soc Japan (Kazan)*, 48(Suppl): 1-94

Wang K L, Chung S L, Chen C H, Shinjo R, Yang T F, Chen C H, 1999. Post-collisional magmatism around northern Taiwan and its relation with opening of the Okinawa Trough. *Tectonophysics*, 308: 363-376

Watanabe K, Ono K, Sakaguchi K, Takada A, Hoshizumi H, 1999. Co-ignimbrite ash-fall deposits of the 1991 eruptions of Fugen-dake, Unzen volcano, Japan. *J Volc Geotherm Res*, 89: 95-112

Yamagata T, Takashima I, Watanabe K, Izawa E, 2004. Thermoluminescence dating of the latest lava domes at Unzen volcano, NW Kyushu, Japan. *Bull Volc Soc Japan (Kazan)*, 49: 73-81 (in Japanese with English abs)

Yamasaki T, Hayashi M, 1976. Geologic background of Otake and other geothermal areas in north-central Kyushu, southwestern Japan. *In*: *Proc 2nd United Nations Symp Devel Use Geotherm Resour, San Francisco*, Washington D C: U S Government Printing Office, 1: 673-684

Yamashina K, 1998. Pre-eruptive process and the beginning of the 1914 Taisho eruption of Sakurajima volcano based on documentary records. *Bull Volc Soc Japan (Kazan)*, 43: 385-401 (in Japanese with English abs)

Yamashina K, 1999. Volcanic cloud height of the 1914 eruption at Sakurajima volcano-discussions on documentary records and photographs. *Bull Volc Soc Japan (Kazan)*, 44: 71-82 (in Japanese with English abs)

Zhang X, Shi Z, 1999. Study on relationship between historical volcanic eruptions and historical strong earthquakes in China and its adjacent regions. *Acta Seism Sinica*, 12: 109-116

JAPAN: HONSHU (0803)

Aramaki S, 1956. The 1783 activity of Asama volcano, part 1. *Japan J Geol Geog*, 27: 189-229

Aramaki S, 1957. The 1783 activity of Asama volcano, part 2. *Japan J Geol Geog*, 28: 11-33

Aramaki S, 1963. Geology of Asama volcano. *Univ Tokyo Fac Sci J*, 14: 229-443

Aramaki S, 1993. Geological map of Asama volcano. *Geol Surv Japan*, 1:50,000 geol map and text (in Japanese with English summary)

Aramaki S, Hamuro K, 1977. Geology of the Higashi-Izu monogenetic volcano group. *Bull Earthq Res Inst, Univ Tokyo*, 52: 235-278 (in Japanese with English abs)

Aramaki S, Shimozuru D, Ossaka J, 1981. Asama volcano. *In*: Aramaki S (ed) *Symp Arc Volcano Field Excur Guide to Fuji, Asama, Kusatsu-Shirane and Nantai Volcanoes*, Tokyo: Volc Soc Japan, 1: 23-48

Aramaki S, Yamasaki M, 1963. Pyroclastic flows in Japan. *Bull Volc*, 26: 89-99

Ban M, Hayashi S, Takaoka N, 2001. K-Ar dating of the Chokai volcano, northeast Japan arc-a compound volcano composed of continuously established three stratovolcanoes. *Bull Volc Soc Japan (Kazan)*, 46: 317-333 (in Japanese with English abs)

Ban M, Hirotani S, Wako A, Suga T, Iai Y, Kagashima S, Shuto K, Kagami H, 2007. Origin of feslic magmas in a large-caldera-related stratovolcano in the central part of NE Japan - petrogenesis of the Takamatsu volcano. *J Volc Geotherm Res*, 167: 100-118

Ban M, Takahashi K, Horie T, Toya N, 2005. Petrogenesis of mafic inclusions in rhyolitic lavas from Narugo volcano, northeastern Japan. *J Petr*, 46: 1543-1563

Ban M, Yamamoto T, 2002. Petrological study of the Nasu-Chausudake volcano (ca. 16 ka to Present), northeastern Japan. *Bull Volc*, 64: 100-116

Chiba T, Tomita Y, Suzuki Y, Arai K, Fujii N, Miyaji N, Koizumi S, Nakashima K, 2007. Analysis of micro topography of the Aokigahara Lava flows, Fuji volcano, by the Light Detection and Ranging System. *In*: Aramaki S, Fujii T, Nakada S, Miyaji N (eds), Fuji volcano. Yamanashi Inst Environ Sci, p 349-363

Endo K, 1985. Peat deposits and volcanic ashes on Haku-san volcano. *Hakusan Nature Conservation Center, Rpt of Sci Res on the Alpine Zone of Mt Hakusan*, p 11-30 (in Japanese)

Endo K, Koyaguchi T, Miyaji N, Tajima Y, Takahashi M, Ukawa M, Yasui M, 2003. Asama and Fuji volcanoes. IUGG 2003 Field Trip Guidebook, *Volc Soc Japan*, p 37-65

Fujita K, Ogawa Y, Ichiki M, Yamaguchi S, Makino Y, 1999. Audio frequency magneto-telluric survey of Norikura volcano in central Japan. *J Volc Geotherm Res*, 90: 209-217

Fujinawa A, 1988. Tholeiitic and calc-alkaline magma series at Adatara volcano, Northeast Japan: 1. geochemical constraints on their origin. *Lithos*, 22: 135-158

Fujinawa A, Fujita K, Takahashi M, Umeda K, Hayashi S, 2001. Development history of Kurikoma volcano, northeast Japan. *Bull Volc Soc Japan (Kazan)*, 46: 269-284 (in Japanese with English abs)

Fujinawa A, Hayashi S, Umeda K, 2001. K-Ar ages for lava samples of Adatara volcano: reexamination of formation history of the volcano. *Bull Volc Soc Japan (Kazan)*, 46: 95-106 (in Japanese with English abs)

Fujinawa A, Kamoshida T, Tanase A, Tanimoto K, Nakamura Y, Kontani K, 2006. Reconsideration of the 1900 explosive eruption at Adatara volcano, northeastern Japan. *Bull Volc Soc Japan (Kazan)*, 51: 311-325 (in Japanese with English abs)

Hakamata K, Sugiyama S, Imanaga I, Mannen K, Oki Y, 2005. K-Ar ages of Hakone volcano, Japan. *Bull Volc Soc Japan (Kazan)*, 50: 285-299 (in Japanese with English abs)

Hamuro K, 1977. C-14 ages of Chikubo Central Cone scoria fall, Kawagodaira pyroclastic flow, Omuroyama-Amagi lateral volcano groups, Izu Peninsula. *Bull Volc Soc Japan (Kazan)*, 22: 277-278 (in Japanese)

Hamuro K, 1985. Petrology of the Higashi-Izu monogenetic volcano group. *Bull Earthq Res Inst, Univ Tokyo*, 60: 335-400

Hasebe N, Fukutani A, Sudo M, Tagami T, 2001. Transition of eruptive style in an arc-arc collision zone: K-Ar dating of Quaternary monogenetic and polygenetic volcanoes in the Higashi-Izu region, Izu Peninsula, Japan. *Bull Volc*, 63: 377-386

Hasenaka T, Ui T, Nakamura Y, Hayashi S, 1992. Traverse of Quaternary volcanoes in Japan. *29th Internatl Geol Cong, Kyoto, Field Trip A06*, 74 p

Hayakawa Y, 1983. Chuseri tephra formation from Towada volcano, Japan. *Bull Volc Soc Japan (Kazan)*, 28: 263-273 (in Japanese with English abs)

Hayakawa Y, 1985. Pyroclastic geology of Towada volcano. *Bull Earthq Res Inst, Univ Tokyo*, 60: 507-592

Hayakawa Y, 1994a. A catalog of the volcanic eruptions during the last 2000 years in Japan. *Sci Rpt Fac Education Gumma Univ*, in press (in Japanese with English abs) ***(regional reference)***

Hayakawa Y, 1994b. Discovery of an eruption product of ca. 500 years ago at Hiuchigatake. *Bull Volc Soc Japan (Kazan)*, 39: 243-246 (in Japanese)

Hayakawa Y, Aramaki S, Shimozuru D, Ossaka J, 1981. Kusatsu-Shirane volcano. *In*: Aramaki S (ed) *Symp Arc Volcano Field Excur Guide to Fuji, Asama, Kusatsu-Shirane and Nantai Volcanoes*, Tokyo: Volc Soc Japan, 1: 49-63

Hayakawa Y, Koyama M, 1992. Eruptive history of the Higashi Izu monogenetic volcano field 1: 0-32 ka. *Bull Volc Soc Japan (Kazan)*, 37: 167-181 (in Japanese with English abs)

Hayakawa Y, Nakajima H, 1998. Volcanic eruptions and hazards of Asama written in historical records. *Bull Volc Soc Japan (Kazan)*, 43: 213-221 (in Japanese with English abs)

Hayakawa Y, Soda T, Arai F, 1993. Asama and Haruna volcanoes: recent eruptions and hazards. *Climatic impact of explosive volc conf, Tokyo, Dec 3-4, 1993*, 28 p guidebook

Hayakawa Y, Yui M, 1989. Eruptive history of the Kusatsu Shirane volcano. *Quat Res*, 28: 1-17 (in Japanese with English abs)

Hayashi S, 1998. False eruption record of the 1810 Kampu eruption created by Akita Clan Office at Edo (Tokyo). *Bull Volc Soc Japan (Kazan)*, 43: 207-212 (in Japanese with English abs)

Hayatsu K, 1976. Geologic study on the Myoko volcanoes, central Japan - Part 1. Stratigraphy. *Kyoto Univ Ser Geol Min*, 42: 131-170

Hayatsu K, 1985. *Myoko volcano group - its geology and history*. Tokyo: Daiichi-Shuppan, 344 p (in Japanese)

Hayatsu K, 1987. Pyroclastic flows erupted in medieval time at Niigata-Yakeyama volcano, Japan. *Bull Volc Soc Japan (Kazan)*, 32: 77-80 (in Japanese)

Hayatsu K, 1994. The activity and age of Niigata-Yakeyama volcano, central Japan. *J Geog*, 103: 149-165 (in Japanese)

Hayatsu K, Arai F, 1980. Tephrochronological study on the Myoko volcano tephra layers and their relation to activity of the volcano. *J Geol Soc Japan*, 86: 243-263 (in Japanese with English abs)

Hayatsu K, Shimizu S, Itaya T, 1994. Volcanic history of the Myoko volcano group, central Japan; a poly-generation volcano. *J Geogr*, 103: 207-220 (in Japanese with English abs)

Higashino T, 1989. *The Documented Record of the Historic Activity of Mt. Hakusan*. Ishikawa Prefecture: Hakusan Nature Conservation Center, 8 p

Hirotani S, Ban M, 2006. Origin of silicic magma and magma feeding system of the Shirataka volcano, NE Japan. *J Volc Geotherm Res*, 156: 229-251

Hori S, Hasegawa A, 1999. Distinct S-wave reflector detected in the uppermost mantle beneath Osoresan volcano, NE Japan. *Bull Volc Soc Japan (Kazan)*, 44: 83-91 (in Japanese with English abs)

Hunter A G, Blake S, 1995. Petrogenetic evolution of a transitional tholeiitic-Calc-alkaline series: Towada volcano, Japan. *J Petr*, 36: 1579-1605

Ichimura T, 1951. Geological investigations on the Zao volcanoes. 1. Goshikidake, a central cone of the Zao proper. *Bull Earthq Res Inst, Univ Tokyo*, 39: 327-339

Ida Y, Osada N, Sawada M, Koyama E, Kagiyama T, 1989. Seismological study based on recently installed permanent stations and a small eruptive event on January 6, 1989 at Kusatsu-Shirane volcano. *Bull Earthq Res Inst, Univ Tokyo*, 64: 325-345 (in Japanese with English abs)

Ishii T, Watanabe M, Ishizuka T, Ohta S, Sakai H, Haramura H, Shikazono N, Togashi K, Minai Y, Tominaga T, Chinzei K, Horikoshi M, Matsumoto E, 1988. Geological study with the "Shinkai 2000" in the West Sagami Bay including Calyptogena colonies. *In*: *Technical Reports of the Japan Marine Science and Technology Center*, p. 189-218

Ishikawa H, Ohba T, Fujimaki H, 2007. Sr isotope diversity of hot spring and volcanic lake waters from Zao volcano, Japan. *J Volc Geotherm Res*, 166: 7-16

Ishikawa T, Minato M, Kuno H, Matsumoto T, Yagi K, 1957. Welded tuffs and deposits of pumice flow and nuee ardente in Japan. *20th Internatl Geol Cong, Mexico City*, Sec 1: 137-150

Itoh H, Hayatsu K, Suzuki K, 2000. Small scale eruptions of Niigata-Yakeyama volcano 1997-1998. *Bull Volc Soc Japan (Kazan)*, 45: 181-186 (in Japanese)

Itoh J, 1998. The eruption history of Iwate volcano in the Edo period, based on the historical documents. *Bull Volc Soc Japan (Kazan)*, 43: 467-481 (in Japanese with English abs)

Jaggar T A, 1931c. Japanese volcanoes arranged in series. *Volcano Lett*, 323: 1-3

Jaggar T A, 1932b. Recent eruptions in Japan. *Volcano Lett*, 372: 1-3

Japan Association Quaternary Research, 1987. *Quaternary Maps of Japan: Landforms, Geology, and Tectonics*. Tokyo: Univ Tokyo Press

Japan Meteorological Agency, 1975. *National Catalogue of the Active Volcanoes in Japan*. Tokyo: Japan Meteorological Agency, 119 p (in Japanese) ***(regional reference)***

Japan Meteorological Agency, 1982. List of the Active Volcanoes in Japan. *Volc Bull Japan Meteorological Agency*, 20: 2 ***(regional reference)***

Japan Meteorological Agency, 1996. *National Catalogue of the Active Volcanoes in Japan (second edition)*. Tokyo: Japan Meteorological Agency, 502 p (in Japanese)

Kano K, Ohguchi T, 2004. Pyroclastic deposits of unknown source, discovered in the Tamagawa Welded Tuffs, west of Hachiman-Tai volcano, NE Japan. *Bull Volc Soc Japan (Kazan)*, 49: 283-297 (in Japanese with English abs)

Kano K, Takarada S, 2007. Cone-building block-and-ash flows: the Senyama volcanic products of O'e Takayama volcano, SW Japan. *Bull Volc*, 69: 563-575

Kataoka K, Nagahashi Y, Yoshikawa S, 2001. An extremely large magnitude eruption close to the Plio-Pleistocene boundary: reconstruction of eruptive style and history of the Ebisutoge-Fukuda tephra, central Japan. *J Volc Geotherm Res*, 107: 47-69

Katsui Y, Oba Y, Soya T, 1978. Records of volcanic eruptions in historic times and estimation of future eruptions. *Bull Volc Soc Japan (Kazan)*, 23: 41-52 (in Japanese with English abs)

Kawachi S, Hayatsu K, 1994. Debris avalanche and lahar deposits in the Yatsugatake volcanic chain and Myoko volcano, central Japan. *J Nat Disaster Sci*, 16: 55-69

Kawachi S, Nakaya S, Muraki K, 1978. YPm-IV pumice bed in Northern Yatsugatake, Yatsugatake volcanic chain, central Japan. *Bull Geol Surv Japan*, 29: 793-805

Kawano Y, Aoki K-I, 1960. Petrology of Hachimantai and surrounding volcanoes, North-eastern Japan. *Sci Rpt Tohoku Univ, Ser III*, 6: 409-429

Kimura J-I, Nagahashi Y, 2007. Origin of a voluminous iron-enriched high-K rhyolite magma erupted in the North Japan Alps at 1.75 Ma: evidence for upper crust melting. *J Volc Geotherm Res*, 167: 81-99

Kobayashi M, Mannen K, Okuno M, Nakamura, Hakamata K, 2006. The Owakidani tephra group: a newly discovered post-magmatic eruption product of Hakano volcano, Japan. *Bull Volc Soc Japan (Kazan)*, 51: 245-256 (in Japanese with English abs)

Kobayashi M, Okuno M, Nakamura T, 1997. 14C ages of pyroclastic-flow deposits from central cones on the western slope of Old Somma of Hakone volcano, central Japan. *Bull Volc Soc Japan (Kazan)*, 42: 355-358 (in Japanese)

Kobayashi T, Oikawa J, Tsuji H, Koyama E, 2003. Volcanic tremor associated with the Asama volcano eruption on February 6, 2003. *Bull Volc Soc Japan (Kazan)*, 48: 479-484 (in Japanese with English abs)

Kobayshi K, Nakamura E, 2001. Geochemical evolution of Akagi volcano, NE Japan: implications for interaction between island-arc magma and lower crust, and generation of isotopically various magmas. *J Petr*, 42: 2303-2331

Koyaguchi T, 1986. Textural and compositional evidence for magma mixing and its mechanism, Abu volcano group, Southwestern Japan. *Contr Mineral Petr*, 93: 33-45

Koyaguchi T, 1986. Life-time of a stratified magma chamber recorded in ultramafic xenoliths from Ichinomegata volcano, northeastern Japan. *Bull Volc*, 48: 313-323

Koyama M, 1998a. Reevaluation of the eruptive history of Fuji volcano, Japan, mainly based on historical documents. *Bull Volc Soc Japan (Kazan)*, 43: 323-347 (in Japanese with English abs)

Koyama M, 1998b. Reevaluation of the 800-802 eruption of Fuji volcano, Japan, and its influence on the ancient traffic network around the volcano, based on eruptive deposits and historical records. *Bull Volc Soc Japan (Kazan)*, 43: 349-371 (in Japanese with English abs)

Koyama M, Hayakawa Y, Arai F, 1995. Eruptive history of the Higashi-Izu monogenetic volcano field 2: mainly on volcanoes older than 32,000 years ago. *Bull Volc Soc Japan (Kazan)*, 40: 191-209 (in Japanese with English abs)

Kudo T, 2008. Radiocarbon ages of the eruptive products from the eruptive episodes E and G, Towada volcano, northeast Japan. *Bull Volc Soc Japan (Kazan)*, 53: 193-199 (in Japanese with English abs)

Kudo T, Hoshizumi H, 2006-. Catalog of eruptive events within the last 10,000 years in Japan, database of Japanese active volcanoes. Geol Surv Japan, AIST, http://riodb02.ibase.aist.go.jp/db099/eruption/index.html ***(regional reference)***

Kudo T, Okuno M, Ohba T, Kitade Y, Nakamura T, 2000. The eruptive products from Jigoku-numa hot pool in Kita-Hakkoda volcano group, northeast Japan: eruption style, magnitude and age. *Bull Volc Soc Japan (Kazan)*, 45: 315-322 (in Japanese with English abs)

Kuno H, 1962. Japan, Taiwan and Marianas. *Catalog of Active Volcanoes of the World and Solfatara Fields*, Rome: IAVCEI, 11: 1-332 ***(regional reference)***

Kuno H, Oki Y, Ogino K, Hirota S, 1970. Structure of the Hakone caldera as revealed by drilling. *Bull Volc*, 34: 713-725

Kusakabe M, Hayashi N, Kobayashi T, 1983. Genesis of banded sulfur sediments at Jigokudani valley, Tateyama volcano, Japan. *Bull Volc Soc Japan (Kazan)*, 28: 245-261 (in Japanese with English abs)

Kusano T, Nakayama K, 1999. Preliminary report on the depositional processes of block-and-ash flow deposits; an example from the Taiheizan pyroclastic flow deposits at Sambe volcano, southwest Japan. *Bull Volc Soc Japan (Kazan)*: 44: 143-156 (in Japanese with English abs)

Kuwabara T, Yamazaki H, 2001. Tephrostratigraphy and eruptive history during the last 450,000 years at Osore-zan volcano, Shimokita Peninsula, northeast Japan. *Bull Volc Soc Japan (Kazan)*, 46: 37-52 (in Japanese with English abs)

Kyoto Univ Disaster Prevention Institute, 1987. *Research on Eruptions-Prediction of Volcanic Eruptions and the Role of Universities*. Kyoto Univ Disaster Prevention Inst and Natl Univ Res Group for Volcanoes

Machida H, 1964. Tephrochronological study of volcano Fuji and adjacent areas. *Chigaku Zasshi (Jour Geog)*, 73: 293-308, 337-350 (in Japanese with English abs)

Machida H, 1967. The recent development of the Fuji volcano, Japan. *Tokyo Metropolitan Univ Geog Rpt*, 2: 11-20

Machida H, 1976. Stratigraphy and chronology of late Quaternary marker-tephras in Japan. *Tokyo Metropolitan Univ Geog Rpt*, 11: 109-132

Machida H, Arai F, 1992. *Atlas of tephra in and around Japan*. Tokyo: Univ Tokyo Press, 276 p ***(regional reference)***

Machida H, Arai F, 2003. *Atlas of Tephra in and around Japan*. Tokyo, Univ Tokyo Press, 338 p

Matsumoto A, Kobayashi T, 1999. K-Ar ages of the Older Ontake volcanic products, Ontake volcano, Central Japan: reappraisal of the volcanic history based on radiometric data. *Bull Volc Soc Japan (Kazan)*, 44: 1-12 (in Japanese with English abs)

Matsumoto A, Uto K, Togashi S, 1988. Measuring ages of volcanoes (radiometric dating), II. Application to active volcanoes. *Kagoshima Internatl Conf Volc Abs*, p 406

Miki K, Fujiwara A, Hashimoto Y, 1988. Debris-flow generation and its counter measures nearby Yakeyama volcano in Niigata Japan. *Kagoshima Internatl Conf Volc Abs*, p 540

Milne J, 1886. The volcanoes of Japan. *Trans Seism Soc Japan*, 9: 1-184 ***(regional reference)***

Mimura K, Endo H, 1997. Repeated collapse and reconstruction of Bandai volcano as revealed in the large outcrop of debris deposits on the southwest foot. *Bull Volc Soc Japan (Kazan)*, 42: 3321-330 (in Japanese with English abs)

Minakami T, 1935. The explosive activities of volcano Asama in 1935 (Part 1.). *Bull Earthq Res Inst*, 13: 629-644

Minakami T, 1938. Magnetic surveys of volcano Kusatu-Sirane. *Bull Earthq Res Inst, Univ Tokyo*, 16: 117-124

Minakami T, 1950. Report on the volcanic activities in Japan during 1939-1947. *Bull Volc*, 10: 45-58

Minakami T, 1956. Report on volcanic activities and volcanological studies in Japan for the period from 1951 to 1954. *Bull Volc*, 18: 39-76

Minakami T, Hiraga S, 1951. The minor activity of volcano Azuma in February 1950. *Bull Earthq Res Inst, Univ Tokyo*, 39: 383-391

Minakami T, Mogi K, 1959. Report on volcanic activities in Japan for the period from 1954 to 1957. *Bull Volc*, 21: 127-152

Miura K, Ban M, Yagi H, 2008. The tephra layers distributed around the eastern foot of the Zao volcano-ages and volumes of the Za-To 1 to 4 tephras. *Bull Volc Soc Japan (Kazan)*, 53: 151-157

Miyagi I, 2004. On the eruption age of the Hijiori caldera, based on more accurate and reliable radiocarbon data. *Bull Volc Soc Japan (Kazan)*, 49: 201-205

Miyagi I, 2007. Stratigraphy and volcanic activities of Hijiori volcano, northeastern Japan arc. *Bull Volc Soc Japan (Kazan)*, 52: 311-333 (in Japanese with English abs)

Miyaji N, 1988. History of Younger Fuji volcano. *J Geol Soc Japan*, 94: 433-452 (in Japanese with English abs)

Miyaji N, Endo K, Togashi S, Uesugi Y, 1992. Tephrochronological history of Mt. Fuji. *29th Internatl Geol Cong, Kyoto, Field Trip*, C12: 75-109

Miyaji N, Togashi S, Chiba T, 2004. A large-scale collapse event at the eastern slope of Fuji volcano about 2900 years ago. *Bull Volc Soc Japan (Kazan)*, 49: 237-248 (in Japanese with English abs)

Miyake Y, Ossaka J, 1998. Steam explosion of Feburary 11th, 1995 at Nakanoyu Hot Spring, Nagano Prefecture, central Japan. *Bull Volc Soc Japan (Kazan)*, 43: 113-121 (in Japanese with English abs)

Miyake Y, Saito M, Takeshita Y, Oikawa T, Saito T, 2009. A newly found pyroclastic flow deposit around 10 ka at Nikko Nantai volcano, northeast Japan. *Bull Volc Soc Japan (Kazan)*, 54: 163-173 (in Japanese with English abs)

Moriya I, 1970. History of Akagi volcano. *Bull Volc Soc Japan (Kazan)*, 15: 120-131 (in Japanese with English abs)

Moriya I, Togashi S, 1984. Eruptions of Kusatsu volcano in the last 10,000 years. *Bull Volc Soc Japan (Kazan)*, 29: 330 (in Japanese)

Murai I, 1962. A brief note on the eruption of the Yake-dake volcano of June 17, 1962. *Bull Earthq Res Inst, Univ Tokyo*, 40: 805-814

Murai I, Hosoya Y, 1964. The eruptive activity of Mt. Asama from 1958 to 1961 and the associated minor pyroclastic flows. *Bull Earthq Res Inst, Univ Tokyo*, 42: 203-236

Murayama I, 1987. *Volcanoes of Japan (I)*. Tokyo: Daimedo, 315 p (2nd edition, in Japanese) ***(regional reference)***

Murayama I, 1989. *Volcanoes of Japan (II)*. Tokyo: Daimedo, 285 p (in Japanese) ***(regional reference)***

Murayama I, 1990. *Volcanoes of Japan (III)*. Tokyo: Daimedo, 259 p (in Japanese) ***(regional reference)***

Nakagawa H, Chuman N, Ishida T, Matsuyama T, Nanasaki O, Oide K, Oike S, Takahashi H, 1972. Historical development of Towada volcano-an outline. *Tohoku Univ Inst Geol Paleont Contr*, 73: 7-18 (in Japanese with English abs)

Nakamura Y, 1978. Geology and petrology of Bandai and Nekoma volcanoes. *Tokyo Univ Sci Rpt*, 14: 67-119

Nakano S, Yamamoto T, Iwaya T, Itoh J, Takada A, 2001-. *Quaternary Volcanoes of Japan*. Geol Surv Japan, AIST, http://www.aist.go.jp/RIODB/strata/VOL_JP/ ***(regional reference)***

Nishimura T, Ichihara M, Ueki S, 2006. Investigation of the Onikobe geyser, NE Japan, by observing the ground tilt and flow parameters. *Earth, Planets, Space*, 58: e21-e24

Ohba T, Kitade Y, 2005. Subvolcanic hydrothermal systems: implications from hydrothermal minerals in hydrovolcanic ash. *J Volc Geotherm Res*, 145: 249-262

Ohba T, Taniguchi H, Miyamoto T, Hayashi S, Hasenaka T, 2007. Mud plumbing system of an isolated phreatic eruption at Akita Yakeyama volcano, northern Honshu, Japan. *J Volc Geotherm Res*, 161: 35-46

Oikawa T, Nishiki K, 2005. K-Ar ages of the lavas from Kirigamine volcano, central Japan. *Bull Volc Soc Japan (Kazan)*, 50: 143-148

Oki Y, Aramaki S, Nakamura K, Hakamata K, 1978. *Volcanoes of Hakone, Izu and Oshima*.

Hakone: Hakone Town Office, 59 p

Okuno M, Moriya I, Tanaka K, Nakamura T, 1997. 6500 cal yr BP eruption of Takahara volcano, north Kanto, central Japan. *Bull Volc Soc Japan (Kazan)*, 42: 393-402 (in Japanese with English abs)

Okuno M, Nakamura T, Moriya I, Hayakawa Y, 1994. Radiocarbon ages of wood charcoal just below the Kuraigahara tephra from Norikura-dake volcano, central Japan. *Bull Nagoya Univ Furukawa Museum*, 10: 71-77 (in Japanese with English abs)

Ono K, Soya T, Mimura K, 1981. Volcanoes of Japan. *Geol Surv Japan Map Ser*, no 11, 2nd edition, 1:2,000,000

Oshima O, 1981. The latest dacitic eruption of Haruna volcano, Japan: compositional varation of minerals. *IAVCEI 1981 Tokyo Mtg Abs*, p 283

Powers S, 1915. The eruption of Yake-dake, central Japan, 1915. *Zeit Vulk*, 3: 34-35

Saito T, Takahashi S, Wada H, 2003. 14C ages of Omuroyama volcano, Izu Peninsula. *Bull Volc Soc Japan (Kazan)*, 48: 215-219 (in Japanese with English abs)

Sekiya S, Kikuchi Y, 1889. The eruption of Bandai-San. *J College Sci Imperial Univ Japan*, 3: 91-172

Shimozuru D, Kagiyama T, 1978. A newly devised infra-red ground scanner and its application to geothermal research in volcanoes. *J Volc Geotherm Res*, 4: 251-264

Sumi K, Takashima I, 1976. Absolute ages of the hydrothermal alteration halos and associated volcanic rocks in some Japanese geothermal fields. *In: Proc 2nd United Nations Symp Devel Use Geotherm Resour, San Francisco*, Washington D C: U S Government Printing Office 1: 625-634

Suwa A, 1978. The surveillance of volcanic activities in Japan. *Bull Volc Soc Japan (Kazan)*, 23: 83-89 (in Japanese with English abs)

Suzuki T, 1990. Tephrochronological study on the 200,000 years eruptive history of Akagi volcano in north Kanto, central Japan. *Chigaku Zasshi (Jour Geog)*, 99: 60-75 (in Japanese with English abs)

Suzuki T, 1992. Tephrochronological study on Nasu volcano. *Bull Volc Soc Japan (Kazan)*, 37: 251-263 (in Japanese with English abs)

Suzuki T, 1996. Discharge rates of fallout tephra and frequency of plinian eruptions during the last 400,000 years in the southern Northeast Japan arc. *Quat Internatl*, 34-36: 79-87

Suzuki T, Eden D, Danhara T, Fujiwara O, 2005. Correlation of the Hakkoda-Kokumoto Tephra, a widespread middle Pleistocene tephra erupted from th Hakkoda caldera, northeast Japan. *The Island Arc*, 14: 666-678

Suzuki T, Nakayama T, 2007. A 2.0 Ma widespread tephra associated with a large-scale pyroclastic flow from the Sengan geothermal area, northeast Japan arc. *Bull Volc Soc Japan (Kazan)*, 52: 23-38 (in Japanese with English abs)

Takahashi E, 1978. Petrologic model of the crust and upper mantle of the Japanese island arcs. *Bull Volc*, 41: 529-547

Takahashi K, 2004. Geology and volcanic history of Mt. Eboshidake and its adjacent area, northeastern Nagano Prefecture, central Japan. *Bull Volc Soc Japan (Kazan)*, 49: 83-102 (in Japanese with English abs)

Takahashi K, Miyake Y, 2004. K-Ar ages of lavas from the Mount Eboshi-dake, Johshin district, central Japan. *Bull Volc Soc Japan (Kazan)*, 49: 207-212 (in Japanese with English abs)

Takashima I, 1999. Thermoluminescence age determination of Fujisan lava dome, Takahara volcano, North Kanto, Central Japan. *Bull Volc Soc Japan (Kazan)*, 44: 275-277 (in Japanese)

Tanaka S, Hamaguchi H, Ueki S, Sato M, Nakamichi H, 2002. Migration of seismic activity during the 1998 volcanic unrest at Iwate volcano, northeastern Japan, with reference to P and S wave velocity anomaly and crustal deformation. *J Volc Geotherm Res*, 113: 399-414

Tanakadate H, 1931. Volcanic activity in Japan and vicinity during the period between 1924 and 1931. *Japan J Astron Geophys*, 9: 47-64

Tanakadate H, 1934. Volcanic activity in Japan during the period between June 1931 and June 1934. *Japan J Astron Geophys*, 12: 89-108

Tomita T, 1969. Volcanic geology of the Cenozoic alkaline petrographic province of eastern Asia. *In:* Ogura T (ed) *Geology and Mineral Resources of the Far East*, Tokyo: Univ Tokyo Press, p 139-179

Tsuboi S, Sugi K, 1926. Geological guide to the Nikko district. *Pan-Pacific Sci Cong Guidebook Excur*, B-1: 4-25

Tsukui M, Nakano S, Saito K, 2008. Eruptions and earthquakes occurred along Amurian Plate eastern margin in the 9th century. *Bull Volc Soc Japan (Kazan)*, 53: 79-91 (in Japanese with English abs)

Tsuya H, 1955. Geological and petrological studies of volcano Fuji. Part 5: on the 1707 eruption of volcano Fuji. *Bull Earthq Res Inst, Univ Tokyo*, 33: 341-383

Tsuya H, Machida H, Shimozuru D, 1988. Geologic map of Mt. Fuji. *Geol Surv Japan*, geol map and 24 p text, 2nd printing

Tsuya H, Morimoto R, 1963. Types of volcanic eruptions in Japan. *Bull Volc*, 26: 209-222

Ueki S, Aoki K, 1981. Chokai-San. *Nat Disaster Res Rpt*, Japan Ministry Education, A-56-1: 33-41 (in Japanese)

Ui T, Nakamura K, Shibahashi K, 1976-77. 1974 activity of Chokai volcano, Japan. *Bull Volc*, 40: 231-238

Ukawa M, 1993. Excitation mechanism of large-amplitude volcanic tremor associated with the 1989 Ito-oki submarine eruption, central Japan. *J Volc Geotherm Res*, 55: 33-50

Uto K, Hayakawa Y, Aramaki S, Ossaka J, 1983. Geologic map of Kusatsu-Shirane volcano. *Geol Surv Japan*, 1:25,000 geol map

Uto K, Takahashi E, Nakamura E, Kaneoka I, 1994. Geochronology of alkali volcanism in Oki-Dogo Island, Southwest Japan: geochemical evolution of basalts related to the opening of the Japan Sea. *Geochem J*, 28: 431-449

Wachi T, Doi N, Koshiya S, 1997. Tephra stratigraphy and eruptive activities of the Akita-Komagatake volcano. *Bull Volc Soc Japan (Kazan)*, 42: 17-34 (in Japanese with English abs)

Watanabe S, Widom E, Ui T, Miyaji N, Roberts A M, 2006. The evolution of a chemically zoned magma chamber: the 1707 eruption of Fuji volcano, Japan. *J Volc Geotherm Res*, 152: 1-19

Yagi K, 1971. Some genetic problems of the calderas in Japan. *In:* Kaloyeropoyloy A (ed) *Acta 1st Internatl Sci Cong on the Volcano of Thera*, Athens: Arch Serv Greece, p 73-87

Yagi K, Takeshita H, Oba Y, 1972. Petrological study on the 1970 eruption of Akita-Komagatake volcano, Japan. *Hokkaido Univ Fac Sci Jour*, 15: 109-138

Yamamoto T, 1995. Two contrasting styles of pyroclastic flows of Numazawa volcano, NE Japan: stratigraphy of the Numazawako and Mizunuma pyroclastic deposits. *Bull Volc Soc Japan (Kazan)*, 40: 67-81 (in Japanese with English abs)

Yamamoto T, 1997. Eruptive history of Nasu-Chausudake volcano, NE Japan, based on tephrostratigraphy. *J Geol Soc Japan*, 103: 676-691 (in Japanese with English abs)

Yamamoto T, 1998. Holocene Sukawa lahar deposits at the western foot of Adatara volcano, NE Japan. *Bull Volc Soc Japan (Kazan)*, 43: 61-68 (in Japanese with English abs)

Yamamoto T, 1999. Plinian fall deposits in the Fukushima-Tochigi area during 0.3-0.1 Ma: stratigraphy of marker tephra layers erupting from Numazawa, Hiuchigatake, Kinunuma, and Sunagohara volcanoes. *Bull Geol Surv Japan*, 50: 743-767

Yamamoto T, 2007. A rhyolite to dacite sequence of volcanism directly from the heated lower crust: late Pleistocene to Holocene Numazawa caldera. *J Volc Geotherm Res*, 167: 119-133

Yamamoto T, 2007. Tephrostratigraphy of Middle Pleistocene Iiji volcano, Niigata Prefecture: geochronological relationship between the Iiji-Moka tephra and the seal-level change at MIS 7 in the northern Kanto region, NE Japan. *Bull Geol Surv Japan*, 58: 117-132

Yamamoto T, Ban M, 1997. Geological map of Nasu volcano. *Geol Surv Japan*, 1:30,000 geologic map and text

Yamamoto T, Nakamura Y, Glicken H, 1999. Pyroclastic density currents from the 1888 phreatic eruption of Bandai volcano, NE Japan. *J Volc Geotherm Res*, 90: 191-207

Yamamoto T, Sakaguchi K, 2000. Eruptive history of Adatara volcano, NE Japan, during last 250,000 years based on tephrostratigraphy. *Bull Jeol Soc Japan*, 106: 865-882 (in Japanese with English abs)

Yamamoto T, Soya T, Suto S, Uto K, Takada A, Sakaguchi K, Ono K, 1991. The 1989 submarine eruption off eastern Izu Peninsula, Japan: ejecta and eruption mechanisms. *Bull Volc*, 53: 301-308

Yamamoto T, Suto S, 1996. Eruptive history of Bandai volcano, NE Japan, based on tephrastratigraphy. *Bull Geol Surv Japan*, 47: 335-359 (in Japanese with English abs)

Yamamoto T, Takada A, Ishizuka Y, Miyaji N, Tajima Y, 2005. Basaltic pyroclastic flows of Fuji volcano, Japan: characteristics of the deposits and their origin. *Bull Volc*, 67: 622-633

Yamasaki M, 1981. Nantai and adjacent volcanoes in the Nikko region. *In:* Aramaki S (ed) *Symp Arc Volcano Field Excur Guide to Fuji, Asama, Kusatsu-Shirane and Nantai Volcanoes*, Tokyo: Volc Soc Japan, 1: 64-75,

Yamasaki M, Nakanishi N, Kaseno Y, 1964. Nuee ardente deposit of Hakusan volcano. *Sci Rpt Kanazawa Univ*, 9: 189-201

Yamasaki M, Nakanishii N, Miyata K, 1966. History of Tateyama volcano. *Sci Rpt Kanazawa Univ*, 11: 73-92

Yamasaki M, Shimizu S, Moriya I, Togashi S, Endo K, Higashino T, 1988. Evolution of Hakusan volcano, Central Japan, during the last 10000 years and the volcanic disasters in future. *Proc Kagoshima Internatl Conf Volc*, p 445-447

Yamawaki T, Tanaka S, Ueki S, Hamaguchi H, Nakamichi H, Nishimura T, Oikawa J, Tsutsui T, Nishi K, Shimizu H, Yamaguchi S, Miyamachi H, Yamasato H, Hayashi Y, 2004. Three-dimensional P-wave velocity structure of Bandai volcano in northeastern Japan inferred from active seismic survey. *J Volc Geotherm Res*, 138: 267-282

Yasui M, Koyaguchi T, 2004. Sequence and eruptive style of the 1783 eruption of Asama volcano, central Japan: a case study of an andesitic explosive eruption generating fountain-fed lava flow, pumice fall, scoria flow and forming a cone. *Bull Volc*, 66: 243-262

Yokoyama S, 1981. Base surge deposits in Japan. *In:* Self S and Sparks R (eds) *Tephra Studies*, Dordrecht, Holland: Reidel, p 427-432

Yoshimoto M, Koyama E, Hirabayashi J, Nakada S, 2005. The 2004 eruption of Asama volcano, Central Japan. *Bull Volc Soc Japan*, 50: 417-420

IZU IS, VOLCANO IS, & MARIANA IS (0804)

Amma-Miyasaka M, Nakagawa M, 2002. Origin of anorthite and olivine megacrysts in island-arc tholeiites: petrological study of 1940 and 1962 ejecta from Miyake-jima volcano, Izu-Mariana arc. *J Volc Geotherm Res*, 117: 263-283

Aramaki S, Hayakawa Y, Fujii T, Nakamura K, Fukuoka T, 1986. The October 1983 eruption of Miyakejima volcano. *J Volc Geotherm Res*, 29: 203-230

Banks N G, Koyanagi R Y, Sinton J M, Honma K T, 1984. The eruption of Mount Pagan volcano, Mariana Islands, 15 May 1981. *J Volc Geotherm Res*, 22: 225-270

Bloomer S H, Stern R J, Fisk E, Geschwind C H, 1989. Shoshonitic volcanism in the northern Mariana Arc 1. Mineralogic and major and trace element characteristics. *J Geophys Res*, 94: 4469-4496

Bloomer S H, Stern R J, Smoot N C, 1989. Physical volcanology of the submarine Mariana and Volcano arcs. *Bull Volc*, 51: 210-224

Chadwick W W Jr, Embley R W, Johnson P D, Merle S G, Ristau S, Bobbitt A, 2005. The submarine flanks of Anatahan volcano, commonwealth of the Northern Mariana Islands. *J Volc Geotherm Res*, 146: 8-25

Chadwick W W, Embley R W, de Ronde C E, Stern R J, Hein J, Merle S, Ristau S, 2004. The geologic setting of hydrothermal vents at Mariana Arc submarine volcanoes: high-resolution bathymetry and ROV observations (abs). *Eos, Trans Amer Geophys Union*, Fall Meeting 2004, V43F-06

Chadwick W W Jr, Cashman K V, Embley R, Matsumoto H, Dziak R P, de Ronde C E J, Lau T A, Deardorff N D, Merle S M, 2008. Direct video and hydrophone observations of submarine explosive eruptions at NW Rota-1 volcano, Mariana Arc. *J Geophys Res*, doi:10.1029/2007JB005215

Corwin G, 1971. Quaternary volcanics of the Mariana Islands. *Unpublished manuscript*, 137 p

Corwin G, Foster H L, 1959. The 1957 explosive eruption on Iwo Jima, Volcano Islands. *Amer J Sci*, 257: 161-171

Dixon T H, Stern R J, 1983. Petrology, chemistry, and isotopic composition of submarine volcanoes in the southern Mariana arc. *Geol Soc Amer Bull*, 94: 1159-1172

Earthquake Research Institute, 1988. The 1986-1987 eruption of Izu-Oshima volcano. *Earthq Res Inst, Univ Tokyo*, 62 p

Embley R W, Baker E T, Chadwick W W Jr, Lupton J E, Resing J A, Massoth G J, Nakamura K, 2004. Explorations of Mariana Arc volcanoes reveal new hydrothermal systems. *Eos, Trans Amer Geophys Union*, 85: 37 and 40

Embley R W, Chadwick W W Jr, Baker E T, Butterfield D A, Resing J A, de Ronde C E J, Tunnicliffe V, Lupton J E, Juniper S K, Rubin K H, Stern R J, Lebon G T, Nakamura K, Merle S G, Hein J R, Wiens D A, Tamura Y, 2006. Long-term eruptive activity at a submarine arc volcano. *Nature*, 441: 494-497

Embly B, Resing J, Chadwick B, 2003. The Thomas G. Thompson explores Maug caldera. *Nat Oceanic Atmosph Admin (NOAA*, http://oceanexplorer.noaa.gov/explorations/03fire/logs/feb24/ (accessed July 25, 2003)

Fiske R S, Cashman K V, Shibata A, Watanabe K, 1998. Tephra dispersal from Myojinsho, Japan, during its shallow submarine eruption of 1952-1953. *Bull Volc*, 59: 262-275

Fiske R S, Naka J, Iizasa K, Yuasa M, 1995. Caldera-forming submarine pyroclastic eruption at Myojin Knoll, Izu-Bonin Arc. *JAMSTEC J Deep Sea Res*, 11: 315-322

Fiske R S, Naka J, Iizasa K, Yuasa M, Klaus A, 2001. Submarine silicic caldera at the front of the Izu-Bonin arc, Japan: voluminous seafloor eruptions of rhyolite pumice. *Geol Soc Amer Bull*, 113: 813-824

Foster H L, 1954. Volcanic activity in Japan. *Volcano Lett*, 526: 7

Fryer P, Gill J B, Jackson M C, 1997. Volcanological and tectonic evolution of the Kasuga seamounts, northern Mariana Trough: Alvin submersible investigations. *J Volc Geotherm Res*, 79: 277-311

Geshi N, Oikawa T, 2008. Phreatomagmatic eruptions associated with the caldera collapse during the Miyakejima 2000 eruption. *J Volc Geotherm Res*, 176: 457-468

Geshi N, Shimano T, Chiba T, Nakada S, 2002. Caldera collapse during the 2000 eruption of Miyakejima volcano, Japan. *Bull Volc*, 64: 55-68

Gorshkov A P, Gavrilenko G M, Seliverstov N I, Scripko K A, 1982. Geologic structure and fumarolic activity of the Esmeralda submarine volcano. *In*: Schmincke H-U, Baker P E, Forjaz V H (eds) *Proc Symp Activity Oceanic Volcanoes*, Arquipelago, Revista Univ Dos Acores, 3: 271-298

Hayakawa Y, 1994a. A catalog of the volcanic eruptions during the last 2000 years in Japan. *Sci Rpt Fac Education Gumma Univ*, in press (in Japanese with English abs) ***(regional reference)***

Isshiki N, 1964. Mode of eruption of Miyake-jima volcano in historic times. *Bull Volc*, 27: 29-48

Jaggar T A, 1931c. Japanese volcanoes arranged in series. *Volcano Lett*, 323: 1-3

Japan Association Quaternary Research, 1987. *Quaternary Maps of Japan: Landforms, Geology, and Tectonics*. Tokyo: Univ Tokyo Press

Japan Meteorological Agency, 1975. *National Catalogue of the Active Volcanoes in Japan*. Tokyo: Japan Meteorological Agency, 119 p (in Japanese) ***(regional reference)***

Japan Meteorological Agency, 1982. List of the Active Volcanoes in Japan. *Volc Bull Japan Meteorological Agency*, 20: 2 ***(regional reference)***

Japan Meteorological Agency, 1996. *National Catalogue of the Active Volcanoes in Japan (second edition)*. Tokyo: Japan Meteorological Agency, 502 p (in Japanese)

Johnson C G, 1953. Activity in the Marianas and Volcano Islands. *Volcano Lett*, 520: 7

Johnson R H, 1973. Acoustic observations of nonexplosive submarine volcanism. *J Geophys Res*, 78: 6093-6096

Kaneko T, Sudo N, Wooster M J, Geshi N, Shimano T, Nagai M, Nakada S, 2001. RADARSAT determination of the outlines of the successively collapsing caldera at the Miyakejima 2000 eruption. *Bull Volc Soc Japan (Kazan)*, 46: 205-209

Kaneko T, Wooster M J, 2005. Satellite thermal analysis of the 1986 Izu-Oshima lava flows. *J Volc Geotherm Res*, 148: 355-371

Kaneko T, Yasuda A, Shimano T, Nakada S, Fujii T, Kanazawa T, Nishizawa A, Matsumoto Y, 2005. Submarine flank eruption preceding caldera subsidence during the 2000 eruption of Miyakejima volcano, Japan. *Bull Volc*, 67: 243-253

Koyaguchi T, 1986. Evidence for two-stage mixing in magmatic inclusions and rhyolitic lava domes on Niijima Island, Japan. *J Volc Geotherm Res*, 29: 71-98

Kudo T, Hoshizumi H, 2006-. Catalog of eruptive events within the last 10,000 years in Japan, database of Japanese active volcanoes. Geol Surv Japan, AIST, http://riodb02.ibase.aist.go.jp/db099/eruption/index.html ***(regional reference)***

Kuno H, 1962. Japan, Taiwan and Marianas. *Catalog of Active Volcanoes of the World and Solfatara Fields*, Rome: IAVCEI, 11: 1-332 ***(regional reference)***

Kyoto Univ Disaster Prevention Institute, 1987. *Research on Eruptions-Prediction of Volcanic Eruptions and the Role of Universities*. Kyoto Univ Disaster Prevention Inst and Natl Univ Res Group for Volcanoes

Lupton J, Butterfield D, Lilley M, Evans L, Nakamura K, Chadwick W Jr, Resing J, Embley R, Olson E, Proskurowski G, Baker E, de Ronde C, Roe K, Greene R, Lebon G, Young C, 2006. Submarine venting of liquid carbon dioxide on a Mariana Arc volcano. *Geochem Geophys Geosyst*, 7: Q08007, doi:10.1029/2005GC001152

Massoth G, Chadwick B, 2003. Submarine arc volcanoes. *Nat Oceanic Atmosph Admin (NOAA*, http://oceanexplorer.noaa.gov/explorations/03fire (accessed April 25, 2003)

Meijer A, Reagan M, 1981. Petrology and geochemistry of the island of Sarigan in the Mariana arc: calc-alkaline volcanism in an oceanic setting. *Contr Mineral Petr*, 77: 337-354

Meijer A, Reagan M, 1983. Origin of K2O-SiO2 trends in volcanoes of the Mariana arc. *Geology*, 11: 67-71

Milne J, 1886. The volcanoes of Japan. *Trans Seism Soc Japan*, 9: 1-184 ***(regional reference)***

Minakami T, 1950. Report on the volcanic activities in Japan during 1939-1947. *Bull Volc*, 10: 45-58

Minakami T, 1962. Report on volcanic activity in Japan for the period from 1957 to 1959. *Bull Volc*, 24: 7-22

Minakami T, 1964. The 1962 eruption of Miyake-Sima, one of the seven Izu Islands, Japan. *Bull Volc*, 27: 225-236

Minakami T, Sakuma S, 1953. Report on volcanic activities and volcanological studies concerning them in Japan during 1948-1951. *Bull Volc*, 14: 79-132

Moore R B, Trusdell F A, 1993. Geologic map of Alamagan volcano, northern Mariana Islands. *U S Geol Surv Map I-2408*, 1:12,500 scale

Murayama I, 1989. *Volcanoes of Japan (II)*. Tokyo: Daimedo, 285 p (in Japanese) ***(regional reference)***

Murayama I, 1990. *Volcanoes of Japan (III)*. Tokyo: Daimedo, 259 p (in Japanese) ***(regional reference)***

NOAA Vents Program, 2004. Submarine ring of fire 2004, Mariana arc submarine volcanoes, R/V Thomas G. Thompson Cruise TN167, March 27 - April 17. NOAA Vents Program final cruise report (http://oceanexplorer.noaa.gov/explorations/04fire/logs/summary/media/marianas2004cruisereport.pdf)

Nagata T, 1938. Geophysical studies of Mihara volcano, Oosima Island, IV, a minor activity of volcano Mihara, August 11, 1938. *Bull Earthq Res Inst, Univ Tokyo*, 16: 702-720

Nakada S, Matsushima T, Yoshimoto M, Sugimoto T, Kato T, Watanabe T, Chong R, Camacho J T, 2005. Geological aspects of the 2003-2004 eruption of Antahan volcano, Northern Mariana Islands. *J Volc Geotherm Res*, 146: 226-240

Nakada S, Nagai M, Kaneko T, Nozawa A, Suzuki-Kamata K, 2005. Chronology and products of the 2000 eruption of Miyakejima volcano, Japan. *Bull Volc*, 67: 205-218

Nakamura K, 1964. Volcano-stratigraphic study of Oshima volcano, Izu. *Bull Earthq Res Inst, Univ Tokyo*, 42: 649-728

Nakano S, Yamamoto T, Iwaya T, Itoh J, Takada A, 2001-. *Quaternary Volcanoes of Japan*. Geol Surv Japan, AIST, http://www.aist.go.jp/RIODB/strata/VOL_JP/ ***(regional reference)***

Niino H, 1953. Report on the submarine eruption of Myojin-sho, Part 2. The second survey of Myojin-sho. *Tokyo Univ Fisheries*, 40: 33-43 and 5 plates

Niino H, Kumagori T, Tsuya H, Morimoto R, Ossaka G, Hamaguchi H, Tatsumoto M, Matsue Y, Komai Y, Arihasa C, Ebina K, Takagi K, 1953. Report on the submarine eruption of Myojin-sho, Part 1. First survey of Myojin-sho. *Tokyo Univ Fisheries*, 40: 1-32 and 24 plates

Noguchi S, Toramaru A, Shimano T, 2006. Crystallization of microlites and degassing during magma assent: constraints on the fluid mechanical behavior of magma during the Tenjo eruption on Kozu Island, Japan. *Bull Volc*, 68: 432-449

Norris R A, Johnson R H, 1969. Submarine volcanic eruptions recently located in the Pacific by SOFAR hydrophones. *J Geophys Res*, 74: 650-664

Notsu K, Sugiyama K, Hosoe M, Uemura A, Shimoike Y, Tsunomori F, Sumino H, Yamamoto J, Mori T, Hernandez P A, 2005. Diffuse CO2 efflux from Iwojima volcano, Izu-Ogasawara arc, Japan. *J Volc Geotherm Res*, 139: 147-161

Oki Y, Aramaki S, Nakamura K, Hakamata K, 1978. *Volcanoes of Hakone, Izu and Oshima*. Hakone: Hakone Town Office, 59 p

Ono K, Soya T, Mimura K, 1981. Volcanoes of Japan. *Geol Surv Japan Map Ser*, no 11, 2nd edition, 1:2,000,000

Rowland S K, Lockwood J P, Trusdell F A, Moore R B, Sako M K, Koyanagi R Y, Kojima G, 2005. Anatahan, Northern Mariana Islands: reconnaissance geological observations during and after the volcanic crisis of spring 1990, and monitoring prior to the May 2003 eruption. *J Volc Geotherm Res*, 146: 26-59

Sano Y, Gamo T, Notsu K, Wakita H, 1995. Secular variations of carbon and helium isotopes at Izu-Oshima volcano, Japan. *J Volc Geotherm Res*, 64: 83-94

Shimano T, Nakada S, 2006. Vesiculation path of ascending magma in the 1983 and the 2000 eruptions of Miyakejima volcano, Japan. *Bull Volc*, 68: 549-566

Shukuno H, Tamura Y, Tani K, Chang Q, Suzuki T, Fiske R S, 2006. Origin of silicic magmas and the compositional gap at Sumisu submarine caldera, Izu-Bonin arc, Japan. *J Volc Geotherm Res*, 156: 187-216

Soya T, Sakaguchi K, Uto K, Nakano S, Hoshizumi H, Kamata H, Sumii T, Kaneko N, Yamamoto T, Tsuchiya N, Suto S, Yamazaki H, Yamaguchi Y, Okumura K, Togashi S, 1987. The 1986 eruption and products of Isu-Oshima volcano. *Geol Surv Japan Bull*, 38: 609-630 (in Japanese with English abs)

Stern R J, 1978. Agrigan: an introduction to the geology of an active volcano in the Northern Mariana Island Arc. *Bull Volc*, 41: 43-55

Stern R J, Basu N K, Kohut E, Hein J, Embley R W, 2004. Petrology and geochemistry of igneous rocks collected in association with ROV investigations of three hydrothermal sites in the Mariana arc (abs). *Eos, Trans Amer Geophys Union*, 2004 Fall Mtg, V43F-07

Stern R J, Bibee L D, 1984. Esmeralda Bank: geochemistry of an active submarine volcano in the Mariana Island Arc. *Contr Mineral Petr*, 86: 159-169

Suga K, 1994. Volcanic history of Higashiyama, Hachijojima. *Bull Volc Soc Japan (Kazan)*, 39: 13-24

Suga K, Miyazaki Y, Chigira M, Endo K, Murakami H, 2003. Age of Takodoyama volcano, Kozushima, Izu Islands. *Bull Volc Soc Japan (Kazan)*, 48: 499-505 (in Japanese with English abs)

Sugimoto T, Ishibashi H, Matsushima T, 2005. Petrological study of Torishima volcani, Izu Islands, Japan. *Bull Volc Soc Japan (Kazan)*, 50: 87-101 (in Japanese with English abs)

Sumita M, 1985. Ring-shaped cone formed during the 1983 Miyake-jima eruption. *Bull Volc Soc Japan (Kazan)*, 30: 11-32 (in Japanese with English abs)

Sumner J M, 1998. Formation of clastogenic lava flows during fissure eruption and scoria cone collapse: the 1986 eruption of Izu-Oshima volcano, eastern Japan. *Bull Volc*, 60: 195-212

Sun C-H, Stern R J, 2001. Genesis of Mariana shoshonites: contribution of the subduction component. *J Geophys Res*, 106: 589-608

Suwa A, 1978. The surveillance of volcanic activities in Japan. *Bull Volc Soc Japan (Kazan)*, 23: 83-89 (in Japanese with English abs)

Suzuki Y, Tsukui M, 1997. New radiocarbon dates for pyroclastics erupted from Miyakejima volcano. *Bull Volc Soc Japan (Kazan)*, 42: 307-311 (in Japanese)

Takada A, Murakami F, Yuasa M, 1994. Geological maps of Aogashima volcano and submarine volcanoes south of Izu Islands. *Geol Surv Japan*, 1:10,000 geologic map

Takada A, Oshima O, Aramaki S, Ono K, Yoshida T, Kajima K, 1992. Geology of Aogashima volcano, Izu Islands, Japan. *Bull Volc Soc Japan (Kazan)*, 37: 233-250

Tamura Y, Tani K, Ishizuka O, Chang Q, Shukuno H, Riske R S, 2005. Are arc basalts dry, wet, or both? Evidence from the Sumisu caldera volcano, Izu-Bonin Arc, Japan. *J Petr*, 46: 1769-1803

Tanakadate H, 1931. Volcanic activity in Japan and vicinity during the period between 1924 and 1931. *Japan J Astron Geophys*, 9: 47-64

Tani K, Fiske R S, Tamura Y, Kido Y, Naka J, Shukuno H, Takeuchi R, 2008. Sumisu volcano, Izu-Bonin arc, Japan: site of a silicic caldera-forming eruption from a small open-ocean island. *Bull Volc*, 70: 547-562

Togashi S, 1984. 14-C ages of charcoal from pyroclastics of Tenjosan volcano, Kozushima, the Izu Islands, Japan. *Bull Volc Soc Japan (Kazan)*, 29: 277-283 (in Japanese with English abs)

Trusdell F A, Moore R B, Sako M K, 2006. Preliminary geologic map of Mount Pagan volcano, Pagan Island, Commonwealth of the Northern Mariana Islands. *U S Geol Surv Open-File Rep*, 2006-1386: 1-32

Trusdell F A, Moore R B, Sako M, White R A, Koyanagi S K, Chong R, Camacho J T, 2005. The 2003 eruption of Anatahan volcano, Commonwealth of the Northern Mariana Islands: chronology, volcanology, and deformation. *J Volc Geotherm Res*, 146: 184-207

Tsuchide M, Kato S, Uchida A, Sato H, Konishi N, Ossaka J, Hirabayashi J, 1985. Submarine volcanic activity at the Kaitoku seamount in 1985. *Rpt Hydrographic Res*, 20: 47-82 (in Japanese with English abs)

Tsukui M, Hoshino K, 2002. Magmatic differentiation of Hachijo-Nishiyama volcano, Izu Islands, Japan. *Bull Volc Soc Japan (Kazan)*, 47: 57-72 (in Japanese with English abs)

Tsukui M, Moriizumi M, Suzuki M, 1991. Eruptive history of the Higashiyama volcano, Hachijo Island during the last 22,000 years. *Bull Volc Soc Japan (Kazan)*, 36: 345-356 (in Japanese with English abs)

Tsukui M, Saito K, Hayashi K, 2006. Frequent and intensive eruptions in the 9th century, Izu Islands, Japan: revision of volcano-stratigraphy based on tephras and historical documents. *Bull Volc Soc Japan (Kazan)*, 51: 327-338 (in Japanese with English abs)

Tsukui M, Suzuki Y, 1998. Eruptive history of Miyakejima volcano during the last 7000 years. *Bull Volc Soc Japan (Kazan)*, 43: 149-166 (in Japanese with English abs)

Ueda Y, Onodera K, Ootani Y, Suzuki A, 2001. Geophysical structure of the Myojin-sho caldera and its volcanological interpretation. *Bull Volc Soc Japan (Kazan)*, 46: 175-185 (in Japanese with English abs)

Ukawa M, Fujita E, Ueda H, Kumagai T, Nakajima H, Morita H, 2006. Long-term geodetic measurements of large scale deformation at Iwo-jima caldera, Japan. *J Volc Geotherm Res*, 150: 98-118

Volcanological Society of Japan, 2003. Report on volcanic activities and volcanological studies in Japan for the period from 1999 to 2002. *Bull Volc Soc Japan (Kazan)*, 48(Suppl): 1-94

Wade J A, Plank T, Stern R J, Tollstrup D L, Gill J B, O'Leary J C, Eiler J M, Moore R B, Woodhead J D, Trusdell F, Fischer T P, Hilton D R, 2005. The May 2003 eruption of Anatahan volcano, Mariana Islands: geochemical evolution of a silicic island-arc volcano. *J Volc Geotherm Res*, 146: 139-170

Wright R, Carn S A, Flynn L P, 2005. A satellite chronology of the May-June 2003 eruption of Anatahan volcano. *J Volc Geotherm Res*, 146: 102-116

Yamamoto T, 2006. Pyroclastic density current from the caldera-forming eruption of Izu-Oshima volcano, Japan: restudy of the Sashikiji 2 member based on stratigraphy, lithofacies, and eruption age. *Bull Volc Soc Japan (Kazan)*, 51: 257-271 (in Japanese with English abs)

Yokoyama S, 1981. Base surge deposits in Japan. *In*: Self S and Sparks R (eds) *Tephra Studies*, Dordrecht, Holland: Reidel, p 427-432

Yokoyama S, Arai T, 1976. C-14 ages of Tairoike and Yaema lateral explosion craters, Miyake-Jima volcano, Izu. *Bull Volc Soc Japan (Kazan)*, 21: 57-58 (in Japanese)

Yokoyama S, Tokunaga T, 1978. Base surge deposits of Mukaiyama volcano, Nii-Jima, Izu Islands. *Bull Volc Soc Japan (Kazan)*, 23: 249-262 (in Japanese with English abs)

Yokoyama T, Shimada A, Umemura T, Toyoda S, 2004. ESR ages of rhyolitic monogenetic volcanoes in Kozushima, Japan. *Bull Volc Soc Japan (Kazan)*, 49: 23-32 (in Japanese with English abs)

Yuasa M, 1995. Myojin Knoll, Izu-Ogasawara Arc: submersible study of submarine pumice volcano. *Bull Volc Soc Japan (Kazan)*, 40: 277-284 (in Japanese with English abs)

Yuasa M, Murakami F, Saito E, Watanabe K, 1991. Submarine topography of seamounts on the volcanic front of the Izu-Ogasawara (Bonin) Arc. *Bull Geol Surv Japan*, 42: 703-743

Yuasa M, Nishimura A, Niida K, Ishizuka O, 1998. A serpentine diapir forming part of the Ohmachi Seamount near the volcanic front of the Izu-Ogasawara arc (SHINKAI 6500 #31). *JAMSTEC J Deep Sea Res*, 14: 269-277

Yuasa M, Nohara M, 1992. Petrographic and geochemical along-arc variations of volcanic rocks on the volcanic front of the Izu-Ogasawara (Bonin) Arc. *Bull Geol Surv Japan*, 43: 421-456

Zobin V M, 1972. Focal mechanism of volcanic earthquakes. *Bull Volc*, 36: 561-571

JAPAN: HOKKAIDO (0805)

Fujitani T, Masuda A, 1982. Wholly compatible and complementary patterns of rare-earth elements in Quaternary volcanic rocks from Oshima-Oshima and Oshima-Kojima isles, Japan. *Geochem J*, 16: 23-31

Fujiwara S, Nakagawa M, Hasegawa S, Komatsu D, 2007. Eruptive history of Tokachi-dake volcano during the last 3,300 years, central Hokkaido, Japan. *Bull Volc Soc Japan (Kazan)*, 52: 253-271 (in Japanese with English abs)

Furukawa R, Yoshimoto M, Yamagata K, Wada K, Ui T, 1997. Did Komagatake volcano erupt in 1694? *Bull Volc Soc Japan (Kazan)*, 42: 269-279 (in Japanese with English abs)

Hasegawa T, Ishii E, Nakagawa M, 2008. Correlations of distal ash layers in the Akan pyroclastic deposits, eastern Hokkaido, with large-scale pyroclastic flow deposits distributed in central Hokkaido, Japan. *J Geol Soc Japan*, 114: 366-381 (in Japanese with English abs)

Hasegawa T, Nakagawa M, 2007. Stratigraphy of Early to Middle Pleistocene pyroclastic deposits around Akan caldera, eastern Hokkaido, Japan. *J Geol Soc Japan*, 113: 53-72 (in Japanese with English abs)

Hayakawa Y, 1994a. A catalog of the volcanic eruptions during the last 2000 years in Japan. *Sci Rpt Fac Education Gumma Univ*, in press (in Japanese with English abs) ***(regional reference)***

Ishii E, Nakagawa M, Saito H, Yamamoto A, 2008. The Pleistocene Tokachimitsumata caldera and associated pyroclastic flow deposits in central Hokkaido, Japan: correlation of large-scale pyroclastic flow deposits with source calderas. *J Geol Soc Japan*, 114: 348-365 (in Japanese with English abs)

Ishii E, Nakagawa M, Saito H, Yamamoto A, 2008. The Pleistocene Tokachimistumata caldera and associated pyroclastic flow deposits in central Hokkaido, Japan: correlation of large-scale pyroclastic flow deposits with source calderas. *J Geol Soc Japan*, 114: 348-365 (in Japanese with English abs)

Ishikawa T, 1950. New eruption of Usu volcano, Hokkaido, Japan, during 1943-1945. *Hokkaido Univ Fac Sci Jour*, 7: 237-260

Ishikawa T, Katsui Y, Oba Y, Satoh H, 1969. Some problems of the calderas in Hokkaido. *Bull Volc Soc Japan (Kazan)*, 14: 97-108

Ishizuka Y, 1999. Eruptive history of Rishiri volcano, northern Hokkaido, Japan. *Bull Volc Soc Japan (Kazan)*, 44: 23-40 (in Japanese with English abs)

Jaggar T A, 1931a. The lava dome eruption of Tarumai. *Volcano Lett*, 317: 1-3

Jaggar T A, 1931c. Japanese volcanoes arranged in series. *Volcano Lett*, 323: 1-3

Jaggar T A, 1932b. Recent eruptions in Japan. *Volcano Lett*, 372: 1-3

Japan Association Quaternary Research, 1987. *Quaternary Maps of Japan: Landforms, Geology, and Tectonics*. Tokyo: Univ Tokyo Press

Japan Meteorological Agency, 1975. *National Catalogue of the Active Volcanoes in Japan*. Tokyo: Japan Meteorological Agency, 119 p (in Japanese) ***(regional reference)***

Japan Meteorological Agency, 1996. *National Catalogue of the Active Volcanoes in Japan (second edition)*. Tokyo: Japan Meteorological Agency, 502 p (in Japanese)

Jousset P, Mori H, Okada H, 2003. Elastic models for the magma intrusion associated with the 2000 eruption of Usu volcano, Hokkaido, Japan. *J Volc Geotherm Res*, 125: 81-106

Kadomura H, Okada H, Araya T (eds), 1988. *1977-82 Volcanism and environmental hazards of Usu volcano*. Sapporo, Japan: Hokkaido University Press, 259 p

Kano K, Yoshimura Y, Ishiyama D, Orton G J, Ohguchi T, 2006. Eruption products and structure of Katsuma-yama volcano, Okushiri Island, Hokkaido, northern Japan. *Bull Volc Soc Japan (Kazan)*, 51: 211-229 (in Japanese with English abs)

Katsui Y, 1988. Historic eruptions in Hokkaido and associated volcanic disasters. *Kagoshima Internatl Conf Volc Abs*, p 334

Katsui Y, Ando S, Inaba K, 1975. Formation and magmatic evolution of Mashu volcano, east Hokkaido, Japan. *Hokkaido Univ Fac Sci Jour*, 16: 533-552

Katsui Y, Kawachi S, Aramaki S, Kondo Y, 1989. The 1988-89 eruption of Tokachi-dake, its sequence and mechanisms. *Rpt Nat Disaster Sci Res*, no B-63-5 (in Japanese with English abs)

Katsui Y, Kawachi S, Kondo Y, Ikeda Y, Nakagawa M, Gotoh Y, Yamagishi H, Yamazaki T, Sumita M, 1990. The 1988-1989 explosive eruption of Tokachi-dake, central Hokkaido, its sequence and mode. *Bull Volc Soc Japan (Kazan)*, 35: 111-129

Katsui Y, Komuro H, 1984. Formation of fractures in Komagatake volcano, Hokkaido. *Hokkaido Univ Fac Sci Jour*, 21: 183-195

Katsui Y, Komuro H, Uda T, 1985. Development of faults and growth of Usu-Shinzan cryptodome in 1977-1982 at Usu volcano, north Japan. *Hokkaido Univ Fac Sci Jour*, 21: 339-362

Katsui Y, Oba Y, Onuma K, Suzuki T, Kondo Y, Watanabe T, Niida K, Uda T, Hagiwara S, Nagao T, Nishikawa K, Yamamoto M, Ikeda Y, Katagawa H, Tsuchiya N, Shrahase M, Nemoto S, Yokoyama S, Soya T, Fujita T, Inaba K, Koide K, 1978. Preliminary report of the 1977 eruption of Usu volcano. *Hokkaido Univ Fac Sci Jour*, 18: 385-408

Katsui Y, Oba Y, Soya T, 1978. Records of volcanic eruptions in historic times and estimation of future eruptions. *Bull Volc Soc Japan (Kazan)*, 23: 41-52 (in Japanese with English abs)

Katsui Y, Suzuki T, Soya T, Yoshihisa Y, 1989. Geological map of Hokkaido-Komagatake volcano. *Geol Surv Japan*, 1:50,000 geol map

Katsui Y, Yamamoto M, 1981. The 1741-1742 activity of Oshima-Oshima volcano, north Japan. *Hokkaido Univ Fac Sci Jour*, 19: 527-536

Katsui Y, Yokoyama I, Fujita T, Ehara S, 1975. *Komagatake. Report of the Volcanoes in Hokkaido, Part 4*. Sapporo: Committee Prevention Natural Disasters Hokkaido, 194 p (in Japanese)

Katsui Y, Yokoyama I, Murozumi M, 1981a. Tarumai volcano. *In*: Katsui Y (ed) *Symp Arc Volc Field Excur Guide to Usu and Tarumai Volcanoes and Noboribetsu Spa, Part 2*, Tokyo: Volc Soc Japan, p 38-54

Katsui Y, Yokoyama I, Murozumi M, 1981b. Noboribetsu Spa. *In*: Katsui Y (ed) *Symp Arc Volc Field Excur Guide to Usu and Tarumai Volcanoes and Noboribetsu Spa, Part 3*, Tokyo: Volc Soc Japan, p 55-64

Katsui Y, Yokoyama I, Watanabe H, Murozumi M, 1981. Usu volcano. *In*: Katsui Y (ed) *Symp Arc Volc Field Excur Guide to Usu and Tarumai Volcanoes and Noboribetsu Spa, Part 1*, Tokyo: Volc Soc Japan, p 1-37

Kishimoto H, Hasegawa T, Nakagawa M, Wada K, 2009. Tephrostratigraphy and eruption style of Mashu volcano, during the last 14,000 years, eastern Hokkaido, Japan. *Bull Volc Soc Japan (Kazan)*, 54: 15-36 (in Japanese with English abs)

Kudo T, Hoshizumi H, 2006-. Catalog of eruptive events within the last 10,000 years in Japan, database of Japanese active volcanoes. Geol Surv Japan, AIST, http://riodb02.ibase.aist.go.jp/db099/eruption/index.html ***(regional reference)***

Kuno H, 1962. Japan, Taiwan and Marianas. *Catalog of Active Volcanoes of the World and Solfatara Fields*, Rome: IAVCEI, 11: 1-332 ***(regional reference)***

Kurozumi H, Doi N, 2003. Inner structure of the Nigorikawa caldera, Hokkaido, Japan. *Bull Volc Soc Japan (Kazan)*, 48: 259-274 (in Japanese with English abs)

Machida H, 1976. Stratigraphy and chronology of late Quaternary marker-tephras in Japan. *Tokyo Metropolitan Univ Geog Rpt*, 11: 109-132

Machida H, Arai F, 1992. *Atlas of tephra in and around Japan*. Tokyo: Univ Tokyo Press, 276 p ***(regional reference)***

Milne J, 1886. The volcanoes of Japan. *Trans Seism Soc Japan*, 9: 1-184 ***(regional reference)***

Mimatsu M, 1995. *Showa-Shinzan Diary: Expanded Reprint*. Sobetsu, Hokkaido: Sobetsu Town Office, 179 p

Minakami T, 1956. Report on volcanic activities and volcanological studies in Japan for the period from 1951 to 1954. *Bull Volc*, 18: 39-76

Minakami T, 1962. Report on volcanic activity in Japan for the period from 1957 to 1959. *Bull Volc*, 24: 7-22

Minakami T, Ishikawa T, Yagi K, 1951. The 1944 eruption of volcano Usu in Hokkaido, Japan. *Bull Volc*, 11: 46-157

Miyaji N, Nakagawa M, Yoshida M, 1995. Tephrochronology of Rausu volcano during past 2,000 years. *Joint Mtg Earth Sci, 1995, Abs*, (in Japanese)

Miyaji N, Nakagawa M, Yoshida M, 2000. Eruptive history of Rausudake volcano during the last 2200 years. *Bull Volc Soc Japan (Kazan)*, 45: 75-85 (in Japanese with English abs)

Moriizumi M, 1998. The growth history of the Kuttara volcanic group, Hokkaido, Japan. *Bull Volc Soc Japan (Kazan)*, 43: 95-111 (in Japanese with English abs)

Murayama I, 1987. *Volcanoes of Japan (I)*. Tokyo: Daimedo, 315 p (2nd edition, in Japanese) ***(regional reference)***

Nakagawa M, Furukawa R, Yoshimoto M, 2003. Calderas and active volcanoes in southwestern Hokkaido. IUGG 2003 Field Trip Guidebook, *Volc Soc Japan*, p 1-35

Nakagawa M, Masuda K, Katsui Y, 1994. Recent eruptions of Eniwa volcano, post-Shikotsu caldera, southwestern Hokkaido. *Bull Volc Soc Japan (Kazan)*, 39: 237-241

Nakagawa M, Matsumoto A, Tajika J, Hirose W, Ohtsu T, 2005. Re-investigation of eruption history of Usu volcano, Hokkaido, Japan: finding of pre-Meiwa eruption (late 17th century) between Kanbun (1663) and Meiwa (1769) eruptions. *Bull Volc Soc Japan (Kazan)*, 50: 39-52 (in Japanese with English abs)

Nakagawa M, Nogami K, Ishizuka Y, Yoshimoto M, Takahashi R, Ishii E, Egusa M, Miyamura J, Shiga T, Okazaki N, Ishimaru S, 2001. The 2000 eruption of Hokkaido-Komagatake volcano and its significance: evidence for increasing effect of magma deduced from temporal variations of eruptive materials and adhered gas component on ash. *Bull Volc Soc Japan (Kazan)*, 46: 295-304 (in Japanese with English abs)

Nakamura Y, Marumo M, Hirakawa K, Sawagaki T, 2008. Holocene tephrostratigraphy in the Shiretoko Peninsula, Hokkaido, Japan. *Quat Res*, 47: 39-49 (in Japanese with English abs)

Nakano S, Yamamoto T, Iwaya T, Itoh J, Takada A, 2001-. *Quaternary Volcanoes of Japan*. Geol Surv Japan, AIST, http://www.aist.go.jp/RIODB/strata/VOL_JP/ ***(regional reference)***

Niida K, Katsui Y, Suzuki T, Kondo Y, 1980. The 1977-1978 eruption of Usu volcano. *Hokkaido Univ Fac Sci Jour*, 19: 357-394

Oba Y, 1966. Geology and petrology of Usu volcano, Hokkaido, Japan. *Hokkaido Univ Fac Sci Jour*, 13: 185-236

Oinouye Y, 1917. A few interesting phenomena on the eruption of Usu. *J Geol*, 25: 258

Okumura K, Sangawa A, 1984. Age and distribution of Toya pyroclastic flow. *Bull Volc Soc Japan (Kazan)*, 29: 338 (in Japanese)

Ono K, Soya T, Mimura K, 1981. Volcanoes of Japan. *Geol Surv Japan Map Ser*, no 11, 2nd edition, 1:2,000,000

Satake K, Kato Y, 2001. The 1741 Oshima-Oshima eruption: extent and volume of submarine debris avalanche. *Geophys Res Lett*: 28: 427-430

Sawada Y, Tanaka Y, Seino M, 1989. Volcanic activity in Japan monitored by the Japan Meteorological Agency using detected precursory phenomena. *In*: Latter J H (ed), *Volcanic Hazards - Assessment and Monitoring*, Berlin: Springer-Verlag, p 246-259

Soya T, Katsui Y, 1981. The Zenkoji debris avalanche of Usu volcano, Hokkaido, Japan. *IAVCEI 1981 Tokyo Mtg Abs*, p 347

Soya T, Katsui Y, Niida K, Sakai K, 1981. Geological map of Usu volcano. *Geol Surv Japan*, 1:25,000 scale

Sumi K, Takashima I, 1976. Absolute ages of the hydrothermal alteration halos and associated volcanic rocks in some Japanese geothermal fields. *In*: *Proc 2nd United Nations Symp Devel Use Geotherm Resour, San Francisco*, 1: 625-634

Suwa A, 1978. The surveillance of volcanic activities in Japan. *Bull Volc Soc Japan (Kazan)*, 23: 83-89 (in Japanese with English abs)

Suzuki T, Nakayama T, 2007. A 2.0 Ma widespread tephra associated with a large-scale pyroclastic flow from the Sengan geothermal area, northeast Japan arc. *Bull Volc Soc Japan (Kazan)*, 52: 23-38 (in Japanese with English abs)

Takahashi R, Nakagawa M, Nakanishi K, Yoshimoto M, 2004. The 1942 eruption of Hokkaido-Komagatake volcano was phreatomagmatic. *Bull Volc Soc Japan (Kazan)*, 49: 129-142 (in Japanese with English abs)

Takeuchi S, Nakamura M, 2001. Role of precursory less-viscous mixed magma in the eruption of phenocryst-rich magma: evidence from the Hokkaido-Komagatake 1929 eruption. *Bull Volc*, 63: 365-376

Tamada J, Nakagawa M, 2009. Eruption history of Oakan volcano, eastern Hokkaido, Japan. *Bull Volc Soc Japan (Kazan)*, 54: 147-162 (in Japanese with English abs)

Tanakadate H, 1931. Volcanic activity in Japan and vicinity during the period between 1924 and 1931. *Japan J Astron Geophys*, 9: 47-64

Tanakadate H, 1934. Volcanic activity in Japan during the period between June 1931 and June 1934. *Japan J Astron Geophys*, 12: 89-108

Tomiya A, Takahashi E, 1995. Reconstruction of an evolving magma chamber beneath Usu volcano since the 1663 eruption. *J Petr*, 36: 617-636

Tsuya H, 1930. The volcano Komagatake, Hokkaido: its geology, activity, and petrography. *Bull Earthq Res Inst, Univ Tokyo*, 8: 238-270

Tsuya H, Morimoto R, 1963. Types of volcanic eruptions in Japan. *Bull Volc*, 26: 209-222

Ui T, Ikeda Y, Koyama M, Suzuki-Kamata K, Okada H, Niida K, 2002. Pyroclastic surges occurred during the 2000 eruption of Usu volcano. *Bull Volc Soc Japan (Kazan)*, 47: 333-337 (in Japanese with English abs)

Ui T, Nakagawa M, Inaba C, Yoshimoto M, Hayashi S, and Geological Party, Joint Research Group for the Usu 200 eruption, 2002. Sequence of the 2000 eruption, Usu volcano. *Bull Volc Soc Japan (Kazan)*, 47: 105-117 (in Japanese with English abs)

Ui T, Yoshimoto M, Furukawa R, Ishizuka Y, Yoshida M, Miyaji N, Katsui Y, Kito N, Ganzawa Y, Nogami K, 1997. March 1996 eruption of Hokkaido-Komagatake, northern Japan. *Bull Volc Soc Japan (Kazan)*, 42: 141-151 (in Japanese with English abs)

Volcanological Society of Japan, 1999. Report on volcanic activities and volcanological studies in Japan for the period from 1995 to 1998. *Bull Volc Soc Japan (Kazan)*, 44(Suppl): 1-76

Volcanological Society of Japan, 2003. Report on volcanic activities and volcanological studies in Japan for the period from 1999 to 2002. *Bull Volc Soc Japan (Kazan)*, 48(Suppl): 1-94

Wada K, 1995. Fractal structure of heterogeneous ejecta from the Me-akan volcano, eastern Hokkaido, Japan: implications for mixing mechanism in a volcanic conduit. *J Volc Geotherm Res*, 66: 69-79

Yagi K, 1971. Some genetic problems of the calderas in Japan. *In*: Kaloyeropoyloy A (ed) *Acta 1st Internatl Sci Cong on the Volcano of Thera*, Athens: Arch Serv Greece, p 73-87

Yamagishi H, Feebrey C, 1994. Ballistic ejecta from the 1988-1989 andesitic Vulcanian eruptions of Tokachidake volcano, Japan: morphological features and genesis. *J Volc Geotherm Res*, 59: 269-278

Yokoyama I, Katsui Y, Abiko T, 1983. The 1979-1982 activities of Usu volcano. *In*: *Report on Volcanic Activities and Volcanological Studies in Japan for the Period 1979-1982*, Bull Volc Soc Japan, 28: 15-19

Yoshida M, 1995. Stratigraphy and lithofacies of the 1977-1989 pyroclastics near the crater of Usu volcano, southwestern Hokkaido. *Bull Volc Soc Japan (Kazan)*, 40: 249-262 (in Japanese with English abs)

Yoshida M, Nishimura Y, 2004. Temporal variation of eruption rate during the 1978 activity of Usu volcano, northern Japan, revealed by the eruptive deposits and volcanic tremor. *J Volc Geotherm Res*, 135: 285-298

Yoshimoto M, Ui T, 1998. The 1640 sector collapse of Hokkaido Komagatake volcano, northern Japan. *Bull Volc Soc Japan (Kazan)*, 43: 137-148 (in Japanese with English abs)

KURIL IS (0900)

Abdurakhmanov A I, Fedorchenko V I, 1976. On volcanic activity in the Kurile Islands in 1973 and some previously undescribed eruptions. *Trudy Sakhalin Complex Res Inst*, 48: 114-118 (in Russian)

Belousova M, 1996. The 1933 large scale sector failure and accompanying eruption of Harimkotan volcano (Kurile Islands). *Pan-Pacific Hazards Conf, Vancouver, Abs*

Botcharnikov R E, Shmulovich K I, Tkachenko S I, Korzhinsky M A, Rybin A V, 2003. Hydrogen isotope geochemistry and heat balance of a fumarolic system: Kudriavy volcano, Kuriles. *J Volc Geotherm Res*, 124: 45-66

Braitseva O A, Melekestsev I V, Ponomareva V V, Sulerzhitsky L D, 1995. Ages of calderas, large explosive craters and active volcanoes in the Kuril-Kamchatka region, Russia. *Bull Volc*, 57: 383-402

Dvigalo V N, Andreev V I, Gavrilenko G M, Ovsyannikov A A, Razina A A, Chirkov A M, 1988. Activity of the southeast Kamchatka and north Kuriles volcanoes in 1985-1986. *Volc Seism*, 1988(3): 13-20 (English translation 1990, 10: 347-359)

Erlich E N, 1986. Geology of the calderas of Kamchatka and Kurile Islands with comparison to calderas of Japan and the Aleutians, Alaska. *U S Geol Surv Open-File Rpt*, 86-291: 1-300 ***(regional reference)***

Erlich E N, Melekestsev I V, 1972. Evolution of Quaternary volcanism and tectonics in the western part of the Pacific Ring. *Pacific Geol*, 4: 1-22

Ermakov V A, Steinberg G S, 1999. Kudryavyi volcano and the evolution of Medveshiya caldera (Iturup I, Kuril Is.). *Volc Seism*, 21: 307-338 (English translation)

Fedotov S A, Ivanov B V, Avdeyko G P, Flerov G B, Andreyev V N, Dvigalo V N, Dubik Y M, Cherkov A M, 1981. 1981 eruption of the Alaid volcano. *Volc Seism*, 1981(5): 82-87 (in Russian)

Firstov P P, Ivanov B V, Karpukhina Y V, 1979. Temporal and energetical regularities of volcanic eruptions of Kurile-Kamchatka region in 1956-1976. *Akad Nauk SSSR, Sibirsk Otdeleniye Byull Vulk Stantsii*, 57: 3-11 (in Russian)

Gorshkov G S, 1958. Kurile Islands. *Catalog of Active Volcanoes of the World and Solfatara Fields*, Rome: IAVCEI, 7: 1-99 ***(regional reference)***

Gorshkov G S, 1970. *Volcanism and the Upper Mantle; Investigations in the Kurile Island Arc*. New York: Plenum Publishing Corp, 385 p ***(regional reference)***

Gurenko A A, Belousov A B, Trumbull R B, Sobolev A V, 2005. Explosive basaltic volcanism of the Chikurachki volcano (Kurile arc, Russia): insights on pre-eruptive magmatic conditions and volatile budget revealed from phenocryst-hosted melt inclusions and groundmass glasses. *J Volc Geotherm Res*, 147: 203-232

Hayakawa Y, 1994a. A catalog of the volcanic eruptions during the last 2000 years in Japan. *Sci Rpt Fac Education Gumma Univ*, in press (in Japanese with English abs) ***(regional reference)***

Ivanov B V, Andreev V N, Bogoyavlenskaya G E, Doubik Y M, Kirsanov I T, Rulenko O P, Firstov P P, Chirkov A M, 1982. The activity of volcanoes of Kamchatka and Kurile Islands in 1981. *Volc Seism*, 1982(4): 103-108 (in Russian)

Ivanov B V, Chirkov A M, Dubik Y M, Gavrilov V A, Stepanov V V, Rulenko O P, Firstov P P, 1981. The state of volcanoes in Kamchatka and Kurile Islands in 1980. *Volc Seism*, 1981(3): 99-103 (in Russian)

Ivanov B V, Chirkov A M, Dubik Y M, Khrenov A P, Dvigalo V N, Razina A A, Stepanov V V, Chubarova O S, 1984. Active volcanoes of Kamchatka and Kuril Islands: status in 1982. *Volc Seism*, 1984(4): 104-110 (English translation 1988, 6: 623-634)

Japan Meteorological Agency, 1996. *National Catalogue of the Active Volcanoes in Japan (second edition)*. Tokyo: Japan Meteorological Agency, 502 p (in Japanese)

Kirianov V Y, Egorova I A, Litasova S N, 1986. Volcanic ash on Bering Island (Commander Islands) and Kamchatka Holocene eruptions. *Volc Seism*, 1986(6): 18-28 (English translation 1990, 8: 850-868)

Larin N V, Bindeman I N, Simakin A G, 1997. Petrology of Bogdan Khmelnitskiy volcano (Iturup Island, the Kurils): a model of fractionation and mixing in the magma chamber. *Volc Seism*, 18: 529-546 (English translation)

Markhinin E K, 1983. On the state of Kunashir Island volcanoes (March, 1974-May, 1982). *Volc Seism*, 1983(1): 43-51 (English translation 1984, 5: 45-52)

McGimsey R G, Neal C A, 1997. 1996 volcanic activity in Alaska and Kamchatka: summary of events and response of the Alaska Volcano Observatory. *U S Geol Surv, Open-File Rpt*, 97-433: 1-34

McGimsey R G, Neal C A, Dixon J P, 2007. 2005 volcanic activity in Alaska and Kamchatka: summary of events and response of the Alaska Volcano Observatory. *U S Geol Surv, Open-File Rpt*, 20075269: 1-93

McGimsey R G, Neal C A, Girina O, 2005. 2003 volcanic activity in Alaska and Kamchatka: summary of events and response of the Alaska Volcano Observatory. *U S Geol Surv, Open-File Rpt*, 2005-1310: 1-58

Melekestsev I V, Braitseva O A, 1984. Gigantic rockslide avalanches on volcanoes. *Volc Seism*, 1984(4): 14-23 (English translation 1988, 4: 495-508)

Melekestsev I V, Braitseva O A, Kiryanov V Y, 1990. History of eruptive activity and predicting impending eruptions of the peak Nemo volcano on the Onekotan Island, Kuriles. *IAVCEI 1993 Internatl Volc Cong, Mainz, Abs*, (unpaginated)

Melekestsev I V, Braitseva O A, Sulerzhitskiy L D, 1988. Catastrophic explosive volcanic eruptions in Kamchatka and the Kurile Islands in late Pleistocene-early Holocene time. *Trans (Doklady) USSR Acad Sci Earth Sci*, 300: 55-59

Melekestsev I V, Dvigalo V N, Kiryanov V Y, Kurbatov A V, Nesmachnyi I A, 1994. Ebeko volcano, Kuril Islands: eruptive history and potential volcanic hazards, Part II. *Volc Seism*, 15: 411-430 (English translation)

Melekestsev I V, Volynets O N, Antonov A Y, 1997. Nemo III caldera (Onekotan I, the northern Kuriles): Structure, 14C age, dynamics of the caldera-forming eruption, evolution of juvenile products. *Volc Seism*, 19: 41-64 (English translation)

Menyailov I A, Nikitina L P, Budnikov V A, 1992. Activity of Ebeko volcano in 1987-1991: character of eruptions, composition of erupted material, volcanic hazard for Severo-Kurilsk. *Volc Seism*, 1992(5-6): 21-33 (English translation 1993, 14: 515-531)

Menyailov I A, Nikitina L P, Shapar V N, 1981. Possibility of forecasting phreatic eruptions of island-arc andesitic volcanoes. *IAVCEI 1981 Tokyo Mtg Abs*, p 234

Menyailov I A, Ovsyannikov A A, Shirokov V A, 1988. Eruption of Ebeko volcano in October-December 1987. *Volc Seism*, 1988(3): 105-108 (English translation 1990, 10: 493-498)

Murayama I, 1987. *Volcanoes of Japan (I)*. Tokyo: Daimedo, 315 p (2nd edition, in Japanese) ***(regional reference)***

Nakano S, Yamamoto T, Iwaya T, Itoh J, Takada A, 2001-. *Quaternary Volcanoes of Japan*. Geol Surv Japan, AIST, http://www.aist.go.jp/RIODB/strata/VOL_JP/ ***(regional reference)***

Neal C A, McGimsey R G, Dixon J, Melnikov D, 2005. 2004 volcanic activity in Alaska and Kamchatka: summary of events and response of the Alaska Volcano Observatory. *U S Geol Surv, Open-File Rpt*, 2005-1308: 1-67

Ono K, Soya T, Mimura K, 1981. Volcanoes of Japan. *Geol Surv Japan Map Ser*, no 11, 2nd edition, 1:2,000,000

Ovsyannikov A A, Muraviev Y D, 1992. The 1986 eruption of Chikurachki volcano. *Volc Seism*, 1992(5-6): 3-20 (English tranlation 1993, 14: 493-514)

Raszhigaeva N G, Korokty A M, Sulerzhitsky L D, Grebennikova T A, Ganzei L A, Bazarova V B, 1999. Late Pleistocene tephra around Golovnin volcano, Kunashir I. (Kuril Islands). *Volc Seism*, 20: 127-254 (English translation)

Raszhigaeva N G, Korotky A M, Sulerzhitsky L D, Grebennikova T A, Ganzei L A, Mokhova L M, Bazarova V B, 1998. Holocene tephra of Kunashir I. (Kuril Islands). *Volc Seism*, 20: 48-63 (English translation)

Rychagov S N, Stepanov I I, 1994. Hydrothermal system of Baransky volcano, Iturup Island: mercury behavior. *Volc Seism*, 16: 133-144 (English translation)

Sazonov A P, Gavrilenko G M, 1995. Lithology and geochemistry of bottom sediments in the crater bay, Ushishir volcanic island, Kuril Islands. *Volc Seism*, 16: 387-400 (English translation)

Suwa A, 1978. The surveillance of volcanic activities in Japan. *Bull Volc Soc Japan (Kazan)*, 23: 83-89 (in Japanese with English abs)

Tanakadate H, 1931. Volcanic activity in Japan and vicinity during the period between 1924 and 1931. *Japan J Astron Geophys*, 9: 47-64

Tanakadate H, 1934. Volcanic activity in Japan during the period between June 1931 and June 1934. *Japan J Astron Geophys*, 12: 89-108

Vlasov G M, 1967. Kamchatka, Kuril, and Komandorskiye Islands: geological description. *In*: *Geol of the USSR*, Moscow, 31: 1-827

KAMCHATKA (1000)

Adushkin V V Zykov Y N, Fedotov S A, 1995. Mechanism of volcanic slope failure. Assessment of potential collapse and debris avalanches at Klyuchevskoi volcano. *Volc Seism*, 16: 667-684 (English translation)

Alidibirov M A, Bogoyavlenskaya G E, Kirsanov I T, Firstov P P, Girina O A, Belousov A B, Zhkanova E Y, Malyshev A I, 1988. The 1985 eruption of Bezymianny. *Volc Seism*, 1988(6): 3-17 (English translation 1990, 10: 839-863)

Andreev V I, Litasov N E, Puzankov Y M, 1988. Radioactivity of the basalt-dacite and andesite suites of the Gamchen volcanotectonic structure. *Vulc Seism*, 7: 219-233 (English translation)

Andrews B J, Gardner J E, Tait S, Ponomareva V, Melekestsev I V, 2007. Dynamics of the 1800 14C yr BP caldera-forming eruption of Ksudach volcano, Kamchatka, Russia. *In*: Eichelberger J, Gordeev E, Izbekov P, Kasahara M, Lees J (eds), Volcanism and Subduction: the Kamchatka Region, *Amer Geophys Union, Geophys Monogr*, 172: 325-342

Babansky A D, Pevzner M M, Volynets A O, 2006. Petrology, geochemistry and geodynamics of Holocene volcanism in the Elovka River basin (North Kamchatka). All Russian Symposium "Volcanism and Geodynamics" September, 2006, Ulan-Ude, Russia, abs

Basharina L A, 1965. Gases of Kamchatka volcanoes. *Bull Volc*, 28: 95-106

Bazanova L I, Pevzner M M, 2001. Khangar: one more active volcano in Kamchatka. *Dokl Akad Nauk*, 377a: 307-309

Belousov A, 1996. Deposits of the 30 March 1956 directed blast at Bezymianny volcano, Kamchkatka, Russia. *Bull Volc*, 57: 649-662

Belousov A B, 1995. The Shiveluch volcanic eruption of 12 November 1964-explosive eruption provoked by failure of the edifice. *J Volc Geotherm Res*, 66: 357-365

Belousov A B, 1999. Comments on paper by O. A. Braitseva "Phreatomagmatic eruption in Lake Karymskoe (East Kamchatka) ~6500 14C years B.P. and Holocene episodes of basalt magma injection under the Karymsky area." *Volc Seism*, 20: 179-182 (English translation)

Belousov A B, Belousov M G, Zhdanova E Y, 1996. Northern Group of Kamchatka volcanoes: activity in 1990-1992. *Volc Seism*, 18: 161-170 (English translation)

Belousov A B, Belousova M G, 1995. The 1964 eruption of Shiveluch (Kamchatka) - a plinian eruption preceded by a voluminous slide of the cone top. *Volc Seism*, 17: 497-508 (English translation)

Belousov A B, Belousova M G, 1998. Bezymyannyi eruption on March 30, 1956 (Kamchatka): sequence of events and debris-avalanche deposits. *Volc Seism*, 20: 29-47 (English translation)

Belousov A B, Bogoyavlenskaya G E, 1988. Debris avalanche of the 1956 Bezymianny eruption. *Proc Kagoshima Internatl Conf Volc*, p 460-462

Belousov A B, Firstov P P, Zhdanova E Y, 1999. Eruptions at Bezymyannyi in 1993-1995. *Volc Seism*, 20: 321-333 (English translation)

Belousov A, Belousova M, Voight B, 1999. Multiple edifice failures, debris avalanches and associated eruptions in the Holocene history of Shiveluch volcano, Kamchatka, Russia. *Bull Volc*, 61: 324-342

Belousov A, Voight B, Belousov M, 2007. Directed blasts and blast-generated pyroclastic density currents: a comparison of the Bezymianny 1956, Mount St Helens 1980, and Soufriere Hills, Montserrat 1997 eruptions and deposits. *Bull Volc*, 69: 701-740

Belousov A, Voight B, Belousova M, Petukhin A, 2002. Pyroclastic surges and flows from the 8-10 May 1997 explosive eruption of Bezymianny volcano, Kamchatka, Russia. *Bull Volc*, 64: 455-471

Belousov V I, Grib E N, Leonov V L, 1983. The geological setting of the hydrothermal systems in the geysers valley of Uzon caldera. *Volc Seism*, 1983(1): 65-79 (English translation 1984, 5: 67-82)

Bindeman I N, 1992. Petrology of Dikiy Greben volcano, southern Kamchatka. *Volc Seism*, 1992(4): 33-55 (English translation 1993, 14: 386-410)

Bindeman I N, Leonov V L, Izbekov P E, Ponomareva V V, Watts K E, Shipley N K, Perepelov A B, Bazanova L I, Jicha B R, Singer B S, Schmitt A K, Portnyagin M V, Chen C H, 2010. Large-volume silicic volcanism in Kamchatka: Ar-Ar and U- Pb ages, isotopic, and geochemical characteristics of major pre-Holocene caldera-forming eruptions. *J Volc Geotherm Res*, 189: 57-80

Bogdanova O Y, Gorshkov A I, Baranov B V, Seliverstov N I, Sivstov A V, 1990. Hydrothermal deposits from Piip submarine volcano, Komandorskii Basin. *Volc Seism*, 11: 354-373 (English translation)

Bogoyavlenskaya G E, Braitseva O A, Melekestsev I V, Kiriyanov V Y, Miller C D, 1985. Catastrophic eruptions of the directed-blast type at Mount St. Helens, Bezymianny and Shiveluch volcanoes. *J Geodynam*, 3: 189-218

Braitseva O A, 1998. Phreatomagmatic eruption in Lake Karymskoe (East Kamchatka) ~6500 14C years B.P. and Holocene episodes of basalt magma injection under the Karymsky area. *Volc Seism*, 19: 685-692 (English translation)

Braitseva O A, 1999. Reply to A. B. Belousov's comments on paper by O. A. Braitseva "Phreatomagmatic eruption in Lake Karymskoe (East Kamchatka) ~6500 14C years B.P. and Holocene episodes of basalt magma injection under the Karymsky area." *Volc Seism*, 20: 183-186 (English translation)

Braitseva O A, Bazanova L I, Melekestsev I V, Sulerzhitskiy L D, 1998. Large Holocene eruptions of Avacha volcano, Kamchatka (7250- 3700 years B. P.). *Volc Seism*, 20:1-27 (English translation)

Braitseva O A, Egorova I A, Sulerzhitsky L D, 1979. Tephrochronological investigations of the Karymsky volcano. *Volc Seism*, 1979(1): 48-58 (in Russian)

Braitseva O A, Florenskii I V, Ponomareva V V, Litasova S N, 1985. The history of the activity of Kikhpinych volcano in the Holocene. *Volc Seism*, 1985(6): 3-19 (English translation 1989, 7: 845-872)

Braitseva O A, Kirianov V Y, 1982. On the past activity of Bezymianny volcano as shown by data of tephrochronological studies. *Volc Seism*, 1982(6): 44-55 (in Russian)

Braitseva O A, Kirianov V Y, Sulerzhitskiy L D, 1985. Marker intercalations of Holocene tephra in the eastern volcanic zone of Kamchatka. *Volc Seism*, 1985(5): 80-96 (English translation 1989, 7: 785-814)

Braitseva O A, Melekestsev I V, 1991. Eruptive history of Karymsky volcano, Kamchatka, USSR, based on tephra stratigraphy and 14C dating. *Bull Volc*, 53: 195-206

Braitseva O A, Melekestsev I V, Bogoyavlenskaya G E, Maksimov A P, 1990. Bezymiannyi volcano: eruptive history and dynamics. *Volc Seism*, 1990(2): 3-22 (English translation 1991, 12: 165-194)

Braitseva O A, Melekestsev I V, Ponomareva V V, Kirianov V Y, 1996. The caldera-forming eruption of Ksudach volcano about cal. A.D. 240: the greatest explosive event of our era in Kamchatka, Russia. *J Volc Geotherm Res*, 70: 49-65

Braitseva O A, Melekestsev I V, Ponomareva V V, Kiryanov V Y, 1995. The last caldera-forming eruption in Kamchatka: Ksudach volcano, 1700-1800 14C-years ago. *Volc Seism*, 17: 147-168 (English translation)

Braitseva O A, Melekestsev I V, Ponomareva V V, Litasova S N, Sulerzhitsky L D, 1981. Tephrochronological and geochronological studies of Tolbachik regional zone of scoria cones. *Volc Seism*, 1981(3): 14-28 (in Russian)

Braitseva O A, Melekestsev I V, Ponomareva V V, Sulerzhitsky L D, 1995. Ages of calderas, large explosive craters and active volcanoes in the Kuril-Kamchatka region, Russia. *Bull Volc*, 57: 383-402

Braitseva O A, Pevzner M M, 2001. Novo-Bakening volcano of Kamchatka: its age and tephra stratigraphy. *Volc Seism*, 22: 581-594 (English translation)

Braitseva O A, Sulerzhitskii L D, Litasova S N, Grebzdy E I, 1984. Radiocarbon dating of soils and pyroclastic deposits in Klyuchevskoi group of volcanoes. *Volc Seism*, 1984(2): 110-115 (English translation 1988, 6: 317-325)

Braitseva O, Ponomareva V, Melekestsev I, Sulerzhitsky L, Pevzner M, 2002-. Holocene Kamchatka volcanoes. http://www.kscnet.ru/ivs/volcanoes/holocene/main/main.htm

Budnikov V A, 1988. The eruption of Gorelyi volcano in April 1986. *Volc Seism*, 1988(4): 99-103 (English translation 1990, 10: 650-658)

Bursik M I, Melekestsev I V, Braitseva O A, 1991. Preliminary stratigraphic and grain size data for most recent fall deposits of Ksudach volcano, Kamchatka (abs). *Eos, Trans Amer Geophys Union*, 72: 569

Carter A, Ramsey M S, Belousov A B, 2007. Detection of a new summit crater on Bezymianny volcano lava dome: satellite and field-based thermal data. *Bull Volc*, 69: 811-815

Delemen I F, 1995. Gravitational instability mechanisms in volcanic cones (with reference to Klyuchevskoi volcano). *Volc Seism*, 16: 649-666 (English translation)

Dirksen O V, Bazanova L I, Pletchov P Y, Portnyagin M V, Bychkov K A, 2004. Volcanic activity at Sedankinsky Dol lava field, Sredinny Ridge during the Holocene (Kamchatka, Russia). IV Internatl Biennial Workshop on Subduction Processes, Petropavlovsk-Kamchatsky, August 21-27, 2004, Abs

Dirksen O V, Melekestsev I V, 1999. Chronology, evolution and morphology of Plateau Basalt eruptive centers in Avacha River area, Kamchatka, Russia. *Volc Seism*, 21: 1-28 (English translation)

Dirksen O, Humphreys M C S, Pletchov P, Melnik O, Demyanchuk Y, Spartks R S J, Mahony S, 2006. The 2001-2004 dome-forming eruption of Shiveluch volcano, Kamchatka: observation, petrological investigation and numerical modelling. *J Volc Geotherm Res*, 155: 201-226

Dorendorf F, Churikova T, Koloskov A, Worner G, 2000. Late Pleistocene to Holocene activity at Bakening volcano and surrounding monogenetic centers (Kamchatka): volcanic geology and geochemical evolution. *J Volc Geotherm Res*, 104: 131-151

Doubik P, Hill B E, 1999. Magmatic and hydromagmatic conduit development during the 1975 Tolbachik eruption, Kamchatka, with implications for hazards assessment at Yucca Mountain, NV. *J Volc Geotherm Res*, 91: 43-64

Doubik Y M, Sheridan M F, Macias J L, 1991. Deposits of the giant 1907 blast of Ksudach volcano, Kamchatka (abs). *Eos, Trans Amer Geophys Union*, 72: 569

Droznin V A, Muraviev Y D, 1994. Heat energy and environmental impact of January 1991 Avacha eruption, Kamchatka. *Volc Seism*, 16: 225-242 (English translation)

Dvigalo V N, 1984. Growth of a dome in the crater of Shiveluch volcano in 1980-1981 from photogrammetry data. *Volc Seism*, 1984(2): 104-109 (English translation 1988, 6: 307-315)

Dvigalo V N, Andreev V I, Gavrilenko G M, Ovsyannikov A A, Razina A A, Chirkov A M, 1988. Activity of the southeast Kamchatka and north Kuriles volcanoes in 1985-1986. *Volc Seism*, 1988(3): 13-20 (English translation 1990, 10: 347-359)

Dvigalo V N, Melekestsev I V, 2000. Recent large-scale downfalls on the cone of Klyuchevskoi volcano: a revision of the consequences of the events of 1944-1945, 1984-1985, and 1994. *Volc Seism*, 22: 1-23 (English translation)

Egorov Y O, Gavrilenko G M, Osipenko A B, Weidmann Y, Adank M, Perre C, Sergeeva S V, 1999. State of the acid crater lake of Gorelyi volcano, Kamchatka, in the summer of 1996. *Volc Seism*, 20: 713-719 (English translation)

Egorova I A, 1993. Age and paleogeography of the formation of volcano-sedimentary deposits in the Uzon-Geizernaya caldera depression, Kamchatka (according to palynological data). *Volc Seism*, 15: 157-176

Erlich E N, 1986. Geology of the calderas of Kamchatka and Kurile Islands with comparison to calderas of Japan and the Aleutians, Alaska. *U S Geol Surv Open-File Rpt*, 86-291: 1-300 ***(regional reference)***

Erlich E N, Gorshkov G S (eds), 1979. Quaternary volcanism and tectonics in Kamchatka. *Bull Volc*, 42:1-4

Erlich E N, Melekestsev I V, 1972. Evolution of Quaternary volcanism and tectonics in the western part of the Pacific Ring. *Pacific Geol*, 4: 1-22

Erlich E N, Melekestsev I V, Tarakanovsky A A, Zubin M I, 1972. Quaternary calderas of Kamchatka. *Bull Volc*, 36: 222-237

Fazlullin S M, Ushakov S V, Shuvalov R A, Aoki M, Nikolaeva A G, Lupikina E G, 2000. The 1996 subaqueous eruption at Academii Nauk volcano (Kamchatka) and its effects on Karymsky lake. *J Volc Geotherm Res*, 97: 181-193

Fedotov S A, 1998. Study and mechanism of the simultaneous 1996 Karymsky volcano and Akademii Nauk caldera eruptions in Kamchatka. *Volc Seism*, 19: 525-566 (English translation)

Fedotov S A, Andreev V N, Bogoyavlenskaya G E, Dvigalo V N, Khrenov A P, Zharinov N A, 1990. Main eruptions of Kamchatka volcanoes in 1985-1990. *IAVCEI 1990 Internatl Volc Cong, Mainz, Abs*, (unpaginated)

Fedotov S A, Gorel'chik V I, Stepnov V V, 1977. Seismologic data on magma chambers, mechanisms, and evolution of the 1975 Tolbachik basalt fissure eruption on Kamchatka. *Trans (Doklady) USSR Acad Sci Earth Sci*, 228: 93-96

Fedotov S A, Ivanov B V, Dvigalo V N, Kirsanov I T, Murav'ev Y D, Ovsyannikov A A, Razina A A, Seliversov N I, Stepanov V V, Khrenov A P, Chirkov A M, 1985. Activity of the volcanoes of Kamchatka and the Kuril Islands in 1984. *Volc Seism*, 1985(5): 3-23 (English translation 1989, 7: 647-682)

Fedotov S A, Khrenov A P, Chirkov A M, 1977. The great fissure eruption at Tolbachik, Kamchatka. *Trans (Doklady) USSR Acad Sci Earth Sci*, 228: 87-89

Fedotov S A, Khrenov A P, Zharinov N A, 1987. The activity of Klyuchevskoi volcano in the years 1932-1986 and the prospects for the future. *Volc Seism*, 1987(4): 1-16 (English translation 1990, 9: 501-521)

Fedotov S A, Markhinin Y K (eds), 1983. *The Great Tolbachik Fissure Eruption*. Cambridge, England: Cambridge Univ Press, 341 p

Fedotov S A, Masurenkov Y P (eds), 1991. *Active Volcanoes of Kamchatka*. Moscow: Nauka Pub, 2 volumes

Firstov P P, Gavrilov V A, Zhdanvova E Y, Kiriyanov V Y, 1995. New extrusive eruption of Shiveluch in April 1993. *Volc Seism*, 16: 371-386 (English translation)

Firstov P P, Ivanov B V, Karpukhina Y V, 1979. Temporal and energetical regularities of volcanic eruptions of Kurile-Kamchatka region in 1956-1976. *Akad Nauk SSSR, Sibirsk Otdeleniye Byull Vulk Stantsii*, 57: 3-11 (in Russian)

Florenskii I V, 1984. On the age of Uzon and Krasheninnikov calderas. *Volc Seism*, 1984(1): 102-106 (English translation 1988, 6: 147-154)

Gavrilov V A, Gordeev E I, Ivanov V V, Ivshin V M, Stepanov V V, Farberov A I, Shirokov V A, Yashchuk V V, 1984. Volcanic tremor and earthquakes associated with the 1980-1981 eruption of Gorelyi volcano. *Volc Seism*, 1984(6): 3-17 (English translation 1988, 6: 795-813)

Gavrilov V A, Ivanov V V, Trukhin Y P, Shuvalov R A, Yashchuk V V, 1986. The activation of Gorelyi volcano in August-September 1984. *Volc Seism*, 1986(5): 90-92 (English translation 1990, 8: 794-799)

Girina O A, 1994. Pyroclastic deposits of the 1984-1989 eruptions of Bezymiannyi volcano. *Volc Seism*, 15: 479-490 (English translation)

Gordeev E I, Senyukov S L, 1999. Renewal of seismic activity on Koriaksky volcano in 1994: hybrid seismic events and their use for volcanic hazard assessment. *Volc Seism*, 20: 507-524 (Enlish translation)

Gordeev E I, Senyukov S L, 2003. Seismic activity at Koryakski volcano in 1994: hybrid seismic events and their implications for forecasting volcanic activity. *J Volc Geotherm Res*, 128: 225-232

Gorel'chik V I, 1969. On the earthquake series in the region of Aag volcano. *Akad Nauk SSSR, Sibirsk Otdeleniye Byull Vulk Stantsii*, 45: 32-38 (in Russian)

Gorelchik V I, Shirokov V A, Firstov P P, Chubarova O S, 1997. Shiveluch volcano: seismicity, deep structure and forecasting eruptions (Kamchatka). *J Volc Geotherm Res*, 78: 121-132

Gorshkov G S, 1958. Kurile Islands. *Catalog of Active Volcanoes of the World and Solfatara Fields*, Rome: IAVCEI, 7: 1-99 ***(regional reference)***

Gorshkov G S, 1959. Gigantic eruption of the volcano Bezymianny. *Bull Volc*, 20: 77-109

Gorshkov G S, Dubik Y M, 1970. Gigantic directed blast at Shiveluch volcano (Kamchatka). *Bull Volc*, 34: 261-288

Gorshkov G S, Kirsanov I T, 1968. Eruption of Piip Crater (Kamchatka). *Bull Volc*, 32: 269-282

Grib V N, Leonov V L, 1994. Ignimbrites of the Uzon-Geizernaya volcano-tectonic depression, Kamchatka: geologic sequences, compositions, and formation conditions. *Volc Seism*, 15: 527-548 (English translation)

Ivanov A V, Perepelov A B, Puzankov M Y, Yasnygina T A, Malykh, Y M, Rasskazov S V, 2004. Rift- and arc-type basaltic volcanism of the Sredinny Ridge, Kamchatka: case study of the Payalpan volcano-tectonic structure. *In*: Kahnchuk A I et al. (eds), *Metallogeny of the Pacific Northwest: Tectonics, Magmatism and Metallogeny of Active Continental Margins. Vladavostok: Dalnauka, p 345-349*

Ivanov B V, Andreev V N, Bogoyavlenskaya G E, Doubik Y M, Kirsanov I T, Rulenko O P, Firstov P P, Chirkov A M, 1982. The activity of volcanoes of Kamchatka and Kurile Islands in 1981. *Volc Seism*, 1982(4): 103-108 (in Russian)

Ivanov B V, Chirkov A M, Dubik Y M, Gavrilov V A, Stepanov V V, Rulenko O P, Firstov P P, 1981. The state of volcanoes in Kamchatka and Kurile Islands in 1980. *Volc Seism*, 1981(3): 99-103 (in Russian)

Ivanov B V, Chirkov A M, Dubik Y M, Khrenov A P, Dvigalo V N, Razina A A, Stepanov V V, Chubarova O S, 1984. Active volcanoes of Kamchatka and Kuril Islands: status in 1982. *Volc Seism*, 1984(4): 104-110 (English translation 1988, 6: 623-634)

Ivanov B V, Flerov G B, Masurenkov Y P, Kiriyanov V Y, Melekestsev I V, Taran Y A, Ovsyannikov A A, 1995. The 1991 eruption of Avacha volcano: dynamics and the composition of eruptive products. *Volc Seism*, 17: 369-394 (English translation)

Ivanov B V, Gavrilenko G M, Dvigalo V N, Ovsyannikov A A, Ozerov A Y, Razina A A, Tokarev P I, Khrenov A P, Chirkov A M, 1984. Activity of volcanoes in Kamchatka and the Kuril Islands in 1983. *Volc Seism*, 1984(6): 114-121 (English translation 1988, 6: 959-972)

Jaggar T A, 1930b. The island volcano of Niuafoou. *Volcano Lett*, 312: 1-3

Jaggar T A, 1931e. Kamchatka volcanoes in 1931. *Volcano Lett*, 353: 1-3

Johnson J B, Aster R C, Ruiz M C, Malone S D, McChesney P J, Lees J M, Kyle P R, 2003. Interpretation and utility of infrasonic records from erupting volcanoes. *J Volc Geotherm Res*, 121: 15-63

Johnson J B, Lees J M, 2000. Plugs and chugs-seismic and acoustic observations of degassing explosions at Karymsky, Russia and Sangay, Ecuador. *J Volc Geotherm Res*, 101: 67-82

Kardanova O F, Dubrovskaya I K, 1994. Staryi Kikhpinych Crater: state in 1980-1989. *Volc Seism*, 16: 19-33 (English translation)

Khrenov A P, Doubik Y M, Ovsyannikov A A, Pilipenko V P, Taran Y A, Firstov P P, Chirkov A M, 1982. Eruptive activity of Karymsky volcano over the period of 10 years (1970-1980). *Volc Seism*, 1982(4): 29-48 (in Russian)

Khrenov A P, Ozerov A Y, Litasov N E, Slezin Y B, Murav'ev Y D, Zharinov N A, 1985. Parasitic eruption of Klyuchevskoi volcano (Preskazannyi eruption, 1983). *Volc Seism*, 1985(1): 3-20 (English translation 1988, 7: 1-24)

Khubunaya S A, Zharinov N A, Muraviev Y D, Ivanov V V, Bogoyavlenskaya G E, Novgorodtseva T U, Demyanckuk Y V, Budnikov V A, Fazlullin S M, 1995. 1993 eruption of Shiveluch volcano. *Volc Seism*, 17: 1-19 (English translation)

Kirianov V Y, Egorova I A, Litasova S N, 1986. Volcanic ash on Bering Island (Commander Islands) and Kamchatka Holocene eruptions. *Volc Seism*, 1986(6): 18-28 (English translation 1990, 8: 850-868)

Kirsanov I T, 1968. Eruption of Klyuchevskoi volcano in 1966 and the outbreak of the lateral Piip craters. *Akad Nauk SSSR, Sibirsk Otdeleniye Byull Vulk Stantsii*, 44: 11-29 (Thornton translation)

Kirsanov I T, Ozerov A Y, 1983. Composition of products and energy yield of the 1980-1981 Gorelyi volcano eruption. *Volc Seism*, 1983(1): 25-42 (English translation 1984, 5: 23-44)

Kirsanov T P, Melekestsev I V, 1984. On the origin and age of Khodutka thermal springs. *Volc Seism*, 1984(5): 49-59 (English translation 1988, 6: 711-725)

Kozhemyaka N N, 1979. Quaternary pumice, tuff-ignimbrite fields and centers of eruption in southern Kamchatka. *Akad Nauk SSSR, Sibirsk Otdeleniye Byull Vulk Stantsii*, 57: 26-38 (in Russian)

Kozhemyaka N N, 1995. Active volcanoes of Kamchatka: types and growth time of cones, total volumes of erupted material, productivity, and composition of rocks. *Volc Seism*, 16: 581-594 (English translation)

Kozhemyaka N N, 1996. Long-lived volcanic centers of Kamchatka: types of cones, growth time spans, volumes of erupted material, productivities, rock proportions, and tectonic settings. *Volc Seism*, 17: 621-636 (English translation)

Kozhemyaka N N, Litasov N E, Vazheevskaya A A, 1984. The Asacha group of volcanoes in Kamchatka. *Volc Seism*, 1984(3): 14-24 (English translation 1988, 6: 365-378)

Krasheninnikov S P, 1755. *Explorations of Kamchatka*. Portland: Oregon Hist Soc, English translation by E A P Crownhart-Vaughan, 371 p

Krijanovsky N, 1934. Volcanoes of Kamchatka. *Geol Soc Amer Bull*, 45: 529-549 ***(regional reference)***

Leonov V L, 1995. Lineaments, tectonic fractures, and mechanical behavior of Klyuchevskoi volcano. *Volc Seism*, 16: 627-648 (English translation)

Leonov V L, Grib E N, 1999. Calderas and ignimbrites in the Uzon-Semyachik area of Kamchatka: new data from field work on the Shirokoe Plateau. *Volc Seism*, 20: 299-320 (English translation)

Leonov V L, Grib Y N, 2005. Late-Pleistocene geology and structural control of the Karymsky volcanic center geothermal fields, Kamchatka: evidence for evolution of magmatic. *Proc World Geotherm Cong 2005, Antalya, Turkey, 24-29 April 2005*, p 1-8

Lotze F, Niedermeier G, 1969. Notizen zur Aktuo-Geologie: 205 Bericht Endogene Dynamik April bis Juni 1967. *Neues Jahrb Geol Palaont Monatsh*, 31: 54-56

Luchitsky I V (ed), 1974. *History of the Development of Relief of Siberia and the Far East. Kamchatka, Kurile and Komander Islands*. Moscow: Nauka Pub, 439 p (in Russian)

Macias J L, Sheridan M F, 1995. Products of the 1907 eruption of Shtyubel' volcano, Ksudach caldera, Kamchatka, Russia. *Geol Soc Amer Bull*, 107: 969-986

Maksimov A P, Firstov P P, Girina O A, Malyshev A I, 1991. The June 1986 eruption of Bezymiannyi. *Volc Seism*, 1991(1): 3-20 (English translation 1992, 13: 1-20)

Malyshev A I, 1995. Evolution of Bezymyannyi eruptive activity in 1986-1987. *Volc Seism*, 17: 257-269 (English translation)

Malyshev A I, 1998. Directed-blast eruption of Besymyannyi on March 30, 1956: problems of interpretation. *Volc Seism*, 19: 311-319 (English translation)

Masurenkov Y P (ed), 1980. *Volcanic Center: Structure, Dynamics and Products*. Moscow: Nauka Pub, 299 p (in Russian)

McGimsey R B, Neal C A, 1996. 1995 volcanic activity in Alaska and Kamchatka: summary of events and response of the Alaska Volcano Observatory. *U S Geol Surv, Open-File Rpt*, 96-738: 1-23

McGimsey R G, Neal C A, 1997. 1996 volcanic activity in Alaska and Kamchatka: summary of events and response of the Alaska Volcano Observatory. *U S Geol Surv, Open-File Rpt*, 97-433: 1-34

McGimsey R G, Neal C A, Dixon J P, 2007. 2005 volcanic activity in Alaska and Kamchatka: summary of events and response of the Alaska Volcano Observatory. *U S Geol Surv, Open-File Rpt*, 20075269: 1-93

McGimsey R G, Neal C A, Girina O, 2003. 1998 volcanic activity in Alaska and Kamchatka: summary of events and response of the Alaska Volcano Observatory. *U S Geol Surv, Open-File Rpt*, 03-0423: 1-35

McGimsey R G, Neal C A, Girina O, 2004. 1999 volcanic activity in Alaska and Kamchatka: summary of events and response of the Alaska Volcano Observatory. *U S Geol Surv Open-File Rpt*, 2004-1033: 1-45

McGimsey R G, Neal C A, Girina O, 2004. 2001 volcanic activity in Alaska and Kamchatka: summary of events and response of the Alaska Volcano Observatory. *U S Geol Surv, Open-File Rpt*, 2004-1453: 1-53

McGimsey R G, Neal C A, Girina O, 2005. 2003 volcanic activity in Alaska and Kamchatka: summary of events and response of the Alaska Volcano Observatory. *U S Geol Surv, Open-File Rpt*, 2005-1310: 1-58

McGimsey R G, Wallace K L, 1999. 1997 volcanic activity in Alaska and Kamchatka: summary of events and response of the Alaska Volcano Observatory. *U S Geol Surv, Open-File Rpt*, 99-448: 1-42

Melekestsev I V, 1996. Koriaksky volcano, Kamchatka: eruption of 1895-1896 was a misinterpretation. *Volc Seism*, 18: 237-242 (English translation)

Melekestsev I V, Braitseva O A, Bazanova L I, Ponomareva V V, Sulerzhitskiy L D, 1996. A particular type of catastrophic explosive eruptions with reference to the Holocene subcaldera eruptions at Khangar, Khodutka Maar, and Baraniy Amfiteatr volcanoes in Kamchatka. *Volc Seism*, 18: 135-160 (English translation)

Melekestsev I V, Braitseva O A, Dvigalo V N, Bazanova L I, 1994a. Historical eruptions of Avacha volcano, Kamchatka: Attempt of modern interpretation and classification for long-term prediction of the types and parameters of future eruptions. Part 1 (1737-1909). *Volc Seism*, 15: 649-666 (English translation)

Melekestsev I V, Braitseva O A, Dvigalo V N, Bazanova L I, 1994b. Historical eruptions of Avacha volcano, Kamchatka: Attempt of modern interpretation and classification for long-term prediction of the types and parameters of future eruptions. Part 2 (1926-1991). *Volc Seism*, 16: 93-114 (English translation)

Melekestsev I V, Braitseva O A, Ponomareva V V, 1987. Holocene activity dynamics of Mutnovskii and Gorelyi volcanoes and the volcanic risk for adjacent areas (as indicated by tephrochronological studies). *Volc Seism*, 1987(3): 3-18 (English translation 1990, 9: 337-362)

Melekestsev I V, Braitseva O A, Ponomareva V V, 1989. Prediction of volcanic hazards on the basis of the study of dynamics of volcanic activity, Kamchatka. *In*: Latter J H (ed), *Volcanic Hazards - Assessment and Monitoring*, Berlin: Springer-Verlag, p 10-35

Melekestsev I V, Braitseva O A, Ponomareva V V, Sulerzhitskiy L D, 1995. Holocene catastrophic caldera-forming eruptions of Ksudach volcano, Kamchatka. *Volc Seism*, 17: 395-422 (English translation)

Melekestsev I V, Braitseva O A, Ponomareva V V, Sulerzhitsky L D, 1990. Ages and dynamics of development of the active volcanoes of the Kurile-Kamchatka region. *Internatl Geol Rev*, 32: 436-448

Melekestsev I V, Braitseva O A, Sulerzhitskiy L D, 1988. Catastrophic explosive volcanic eruptions in Kamchatka and the Kurile Islands in late Pleistocene-early Holocene time. *Trans (Doklady) USSR Acad Sci Earth Sci*, 300: 55-59

Melekestsev I V, Dirksen O V, Girina O A, 1999. A giant landslide-explosion cirque and a debris avalanche at Bakening volcano, Kamchatka. *Volc Seism*, 20: 265-279 (English translation)

Melekestsev I V, Felitsyn S B, Kiryanov V Y, 1991. The eruption of Opala in A.D. 500 - the largest explosive eruption in Kamchatka in the Christian era. *Volc Seism*, 1991(1): 21-34 (English translation 1992, 13: 21-36)

Melekestsev I V, Kiryanov V Y, 1984. When will Avacha volcano in Kamchatka erupt? *Volc Seism*, 1984(6): 107-110 (English translation 1988, 6: 943-951)

Melekestsev I V, Ponomareva V V, Volynets O N, 1995. Kizimen volcano, Kamchatka - a future Mount St. Helens? *J Volc Geotherm Res*, 65: 205-226

Melekestsev I V, Sulerzhitskiy L D, Bazanova L I, Braitseva O A, Florenskaya N I, 1995. Holocene catastrophic lahars at Avacha and Koriakskiy volcanoes in Kamchatka. *Volc Seism*, 17: 561-570 (English translation)

Melekestsev I V, Sulerzhitsky L D, 1987. Ksudach volcano (Kamchatka) over the last ten thousand years. *Volc Seism*, 1987(4): 28-39 (English translation 1990, 9: 537-556)

Muraviev Y D, Fedotov S A, Budnikov V A, Ozerov A Y, Maguskin M A, Dvigalo V N, Andreev V I, Ivanov V V, Kartasheva I A, Markov I A, 1998. Volcanic activity in the Karymsky center in 1996: summit eruption at Karymsky and phreatomagmatic eruption in the Akademii Nauk caldera. *Volc Seism*, 19: 567-604 (English translation)

Neal C A, McGimsey R G, Chubarova O, 2004. 2000 volcanic activity in Alaska and Kamchatka: summary of events and response of the Alaska Volcano Observatory. *U S Geol Surv Open-File Rpt*, 2004-1034: 1-34

Neal C A, McGimsey R G, Dixon J, Melnikov D, 2005. 2004 volcanic activity in Alaska and Kamchatka: summary of events and response of the Alaska Volcano Observatory. *U S Geol Surv, Open-File Rpt*, 2005-1308: 1-67

Neal C A, McGimsey R G, Girina O, 2005. 2002 volcanic activity in Alaska and Kamchatka: summary of events and response of the Alaska Volcano Observatory. *U S Geol Surv, Open-File Rpt*, 2004-1058: 1-51

Ogorodov N V, Kozhemyaka N N, Vazheevskaya A A, Ogorodov A S, 1972. *Volcanoes and the Quaternary Volcanism of the Sredinny Ridge in Kamchatka*. Moscow: Nauka Pub, 190 p (in Russian)

Ogorodov N V, Volynets O N, Koloskov A V, Polytov E Y, 1978. Dikiy Greben'. *Akad Nauk SSSR, Sibirsk Otdeleniye Byull Vulk Stantsii*, 54: 75-88 (in Russian)

Ozerov A Y, Demyanchuk Y V, Storcheus A V, Karpov G A, 1996. Eruption of Bezymyannyi volcano, Kamchatka, on October 6-8, 1995. *Volc Seism*, 18: 363-366 (English translation)

Ozerov A Y, Karpov G A, Droznin V A, Dvigalo V N, Demyanchuk Y V, Ivanov V V, Belousov A B, Firstov P P, Gavrilov V A, Yashchuk V V, Okrugina A M, 1997. The September 7 - October 2, 1994 eruption of Klyuchevskoi volcano, Kamchatka. *Volc Seism*, 18: 501-516 (English translation)

Ozerov A, Ispolatov I, Lees J, 2003. Modeling Strombolian eruptions of Karymsky volcano, Kamchatka, Russia. *J Volc Geotherm Res*, 122: 265-280

Pevzner M M, 2004a. The first geolgical data on the chronology of Holocene eruptive activity in the Ichinskii volcano (Sredinnyi Ridge, Kamchatka). *Trans (Doklady) USSR Acad Sci Earth Sci*, 395: 507-510

Pevzner M M, 2004b. New data on Holocene monogenetic volcanism of the northern Kamchatka: ages and space distribution. IV Internatl Biennial Workshop on Subduction Processes, Petropavlovsk-Kamchatsky, August 21-27, 2004, Abs

Pevzner M M, 2006. Holocene volcanism of Northern Kamchtaka: the spatiotemporal aspect. *Trans (Doklady) USSR Acad Sci Earth Sci*, 409: 648-651

Pevzner M M, Melekestsev I V, Volynets O N, Melkii V A, 2000. South Cherpuk and North Cherpuk - the largest Holocene monogenetic volcanoes on the Sredinnyi Range of Kamchatka. *Volc Seism*, 21: 667-681 (English translation)

Polak B G, 1967. An energy appraisal of volcanic and hydrothermal phenomena (on the example of Kamchatka). *Bull Volc*, 30: 129-138

Ponomareva V V, 1987. The history of Krasheninnikov volcano and the dynamics of its activity. *Volc Seism*, 1987(5): 28-44 (English translation 1990, 9: 714-741)

Ponomareva V V, Braitseva O A, 1990. Volcanic hazards for the area of the Kronotsky Lake - Uzon, Geizerny Valley. *Volc Seism*, 1990(1) p 27-44 (English translation 1991, 12: 42-69)

Ponomareva V V, Kyle P R, Melekestsev I V, Rinkleff P G, Dirksen O V, Sulerzhitsky L D, Zaretskaia N E, Rourke R, 2004. The 7600 (14C) year BP Kurile Lake caldera-forming eruption, Kamchatka, Russia: stratigraphy and field relationships. *J Volc Geotherm Res*, 136: 199-222

Ponomareva V V, Melekestsev I V, Dirksen O V, 2006. Sector collapses and large landslides on late Pleistocene-Holocene volcanoes in Kamchatka, Russia. *J Volc Geotherm Res*, 158: 117-138

Ponomareva V V, Pevzner M M, Melekestsev I V, 1998. Large debris avalanches and associated eruptions in the Holocene eruptive history of Shiveluch volcano, Kamchatka. *Bull Volc*, 59: 490-505

Ponomareva V V, Tsyurupa A A, 1985. Extended liquid acidic lava flows at Krasheninnikov volcano. *Volc Seism*, 1985(3): 85-92 (English translation 1988, 7: 447-458)

Ponomareva V, Kyle P, Pevzner M, Sulerzhitsky L, Hartman M, 2007a. Holocene eruptive history of Shiveluch volcano, Kamchatka Peninsula, Russia. *In*: Eichelberger J, Gordeev E, Izbekov P, Kasahara M, Lees J (eds), Volcanism and Subduction: the Kamchatka Region, *Amer Geophys Union, Geophys Monogr*, 172: 263-282

Ponomareva V, Melekestsev I, Braitseva O, Churikova T, Pevzner M, Sulerzhitsky L, 2007b. Late Pleistocene-Holocene volcanism on the Kamchatka Peninsula, northwest Pacific region. *In*: Eichelberger J, Gordeev E, Izbekov P, Kasahara M, Lees J (eds), Volcanism and Subduction: the Kamchatka Region, *Amer Geophys Union, Geophys Monogr*, 172: 165-198

Popruzhenko S V, 1984. On the formation of the Opala caldera. *Volc Seism*, 1984(6): 111-113 (English translation 1988, 6: 953-958)

Ramsey M, Dehn J, 2004. Spaceborne observations of the 2000 Bezymianny, Kamchatka eruption: the integration of high-resolution ASTER data into near real-time monitoring using AVHRR. *J Volc Geotherm Res*, 135: 127-146

Rose S, Ramsey M, 2009. The 2005 eruption of Kliuchevskoi volcano: chronology and processes derived from ASTER spaceborne and field-based data. *J Volc Geotherm Res*, 184: 367-380

Seleznev B V, Dvigalo V N, Gusev N A, 1983. Evolution of Bezymyannai volcano from stereoscopic plotting of aerial photographs of 1950, 1967 and 1976-1981. *Volc Seism*, 1983(1): 52-64 (English translation 1984, 5: 53-66)

Seliverstov N I, Avdeiko G P, Ivanenko A N, Shkira V A, Khubunaya S A, 1986. A new submarine volcano in the west of the Aleutian island arc. *Volc Seism*, 1986(4): 3-16 (English translation 1990, 8: 473-495)

Seliverstov N I, Gavrilenko G M, Kirianov V Y, 1989. Modern activity of Piip submarine volcano, Komandorsky Basin. *Volc Seism*, 1989(6): 3-18 (English translation 1990, 11: 757-779)

Selyangin O B, 1987. Geological structure and evolution of the calderas of Ksudach volcano. *Volc Seism*, 1987(5): p 16-27 (English translation 1990, 9: 690-713)

Selyangin O B, 1993. Mutnovskiy volcano, Kamchatka: new evidence on structure, evolution, and future activity. *Volc Seism*, 1993(1): 17-35 (English translation 1993, 15: 17-38)

Selyangin O B, Ponomareva V V, 1999. Gorelovsky volcanic center, South Kamchatka: structure and evolution. *Volc Seism*, 21: 163-194 (English translation)

Shirokov V A, 1983. The influence of the 19-year tidal cycle on large-scale eruptions and earthquakes in Kamchatka, and their long-term prediction. *In*: Fedotov S A and Markhinin Y K (eds) *The Great Tolbachik Fissure Eruption, Geol and Geophys Data 1975-1976*, p 232-242

Steinberg G S, 1981. Kliuchevskoy volcano eruption of 1980 and eruption cyclicity. *Volcano News*, 8: 2-3

Sviatlovsky A E, 1959. *Atlas of Volcanoes of the Soviet Union*. Moscow: Akad Nauk SSSR, 170 p (in Russian with English summary) ***(regional reference)***

Tokarev P I, 1978. Prediction and characteristics of the 1975 eruption of Tolbachik volcano, Kamchatka. *Bull Volc*, 41: 251-258

Tokarev P I, 1985a. Prediction of lateral eruption of Klyuchevskoy volcano in March 1983. *J Volc Geotherm Res*, 25: 173-180

Tokarev P I, 1985b. The March-June 1984 eruption of Klyuchevskoi and its present state as estimated from ongoing observations. *Volc Seism*, 1985(1): 106-108 (English translation 1988, 7: 143-148)

Tomkeieff S I, 1949. The volcanoes of Kamchatka. *Bull Volc*, 8: 87-114

Ushakov S V, Fazlullin S M, 1998. Morphometric characteristics of Lake Karymskoe after an underwater eruption. *Volc Seism*, 19: 675-683 (English translation)

Vakin E A, Pilipenko G F, 1998. Hydrothermal activity in Lake Karymskoe after the 1996 underwater eruption. *Volc Seism*, 19: 737-767 (English translation)

Vlasov G M, 1967. Kamchatka, Kuril, and Komandorskiye Islands: geological description. *In*: *Geol of the USSR*, Moscow, 31: 1-827

Vlodavetz V I, 1947. The volcanoes of the Karymsky Group. *Acad Sci USSR Trans Kamchatka Volc Station*, 3: 47 (in Russian with English abs)

Vlodavetz V I, Piip B I, 1959. Kamchatka and Continental Areas of Asia. *Catalog of Active Volcanoes of the World and Solfatara Fields*, Rome: IAVCEI, 8: 1-110 ***(regional reference)***

Volynets O N, Melekestsev I V, Ponomareva V V, Yogodzinski G M, 1999. Kharchinsky and Zarechnyi volcanoes-unique centers of late Pleistocene magnesian basalts in Kamchatka: structural setting, morphology, geologic structure and age. *Volc Seism*, 20: 383-399 (English translation)

Volynets O N, Ponomareva V V, Braitseva O A, Melekestsev I V, Chen C H, 1999. Holocene eruptive history of Ksudach volcanic massif, South Kamchatka: evolution of a large magmatic chamber. *J Volc Geotherm Res*, 91: 23-42

Volynets O N, Ponomareva V V, Tsyurupa A A, 1989. Petrological and tephrochronological studies of Krasheninnikov volcano, Kamchatka. *Internatl Geol Rev*, 30: 1107-1122

Yogodzinski G M, Volynets O N, Koloskov A V, Seliverstov N I, Matvenkov V V, 1994. Magnesian andesites and the subduction component in a strongly calc-alkaline series at Piip Volcano, Far Western Aleutians. *J Petr*, 35: 163-204

Zharinov N A, Bogoyavlenskaya G E, Khubunaya S A, Demyanchuk Y V, 1995. Shiveluch volcano: a new eruptive cycle of 1980-1993. *Volc Seism*, 17: 21-30 (English translation)

Zharinov N A, Zhdanova E Y, Belousov A B, Belousova M G, Ivanov A P, Malyshev A I, Khanzutin V P, 1988. Activity of north Kamchatka volcanoes in 1985. *Volc Seism*, 1988(3): 3-12 (English translation 1990, 10: 331-346)

Zobin V M, Levina V I, Maguskin M A, 2003. Seismicity and crustal deformation preceding the January 1996 eruptions at Karymsky volcanic center, Kamchatka. *Bull Volc*, 65: 477-485

Zolotarev B P, Karpov G A, Eroshchev-Shak V A, Artamonov A V, Grigoriev V S, Pokrovsky B G, 1999. Evolution of volcanism in the Uzon caldera, Kamchatka. *Volc Seism*, 20: 675-694 (English translation)

MAINLAND ASIA (1001-06)

Bai Z, Tian M, Wu F, Xu D, Li T, 2005. Yanshan, Gaoshan-two active volcanoes of the volcanic cluster in Arshan, Inner Mongolia. *Earthq Res China*, 19(4): 402-408

Barry T L, Saunders A D, Kempton P D, Windley B F, Pringle M S, Dorjnamjaa D, Saandar S, 2003. Petrogenesis of Cenozoic basalts from Mongolia: evidence for the role of asthenospheric versus metasomatized lithospheric mantle sources. *J Petr*, 44: 55-91

Chasovitin M D, 1963. New information about the intracontinental Quaternary volcanoes of Northeastern Asia. *Doklady Akad Nauk SSSR*, 152: 39-41

Chen H, Ren J, Wu X, 1999. Volcanic eruptive processes and characteristics of the current volcanoes in the Wudalianchi volcano clusters known from Manchurian-language historical archives discovered at present (in Chinese with English abs). *Geol Rev*, 45(Suppl): 409-413

Chen S (ed), 1986. *Atlas of Geo-Science, Analysis of Landsat Imagery in China*. Beijing: Chinese Acad Sci Press, 228 p

Chough S K, Sohn Y K, 1990. Depostional mechanics and sequences of base surges, Songaksan tuff ring, Cheju Island, Korea. *Sedimentology*, 37: 1115-1135

Devyatkin Y V, Smelov S B, 1979. Position of basalts in the Cenozoic sedimentary sequence of Mongolia. *Internatl Geol Rev*, 22: 307-317

Dunlap C E, Gill J B, Palacz Z A, 1992. U/Th disequilibria in the large-volume chemically-zoned eruption of Baitoushan, 1010 AD (abs). *Eos, Trans Amer Geophys Union*, 73: 611

Fan Q, Sun Q, Li N, Wang T, 2006. Holocene volcanic rocks in Jingbo Lake region-diversity of magmatism. *Progress Nat Sci*, 16: 65-71

Feng M, 1982. The eruptions of Wudalianchi volcanoes of China. *Volcano News*, 10: 4-5

Feng M, Keyi G, Wang F, 1979. *Wudalianchi Volcanoes in China*. Shanghai: Shanghai Sci Tech Publishers, 85 p

Feng M, Whitford-Stark J L, 1986. The 1719-1721 eruptions of potassium-rich lavas at Wudalianchi, China. *J Volc Geotherm Res*, 30: 130-148

Gorodinskiy M Y, Dovgal' Y M, Sterligova V Y, 1967. The Aluchin group of late Quaternary volcanoes in western Chukotka. *Internatl Geol Rev*, 10: 1045-1054

Hasenaka T, Litasov Y, Taniguchi H, Miyamoto T, Fujimaki H, 1999. Cenozoic volcanism in Siberia: a review. *Center for Northeast Asian Studies, Tohoku Univ*, no 3, p 249-272

Horn S, Schmincke H, 2000. Voltatile emission during the eruption of Baitoushan volcano (China/North Korea) ca. 969 AD. *Bull Volc*, 61: 537-555

Ignatiev V A, 1994. Structural setting of Quaternary volcanoes in western Chukotka. *Volc Seism*, 15: 667-678 (English translation)

Johnson J S, Gibson S A, Thompson R N, Nowell G M, 2005. Volcanism in the Vitim volcanic field, Siberia: geochemical evidence for a mantle plume beneath the Baikal Rift Zone. *J Petr*, 46: 1309-1344

Lee D S, 1981. Volcanic activity in the southwest part of Choogaryong Rift Valley, Korea. *IAVCEI, 1981 Tokyo Mtg Abs*, p 200-202

Lee M W, 1982. Petrology and geochemistry of Jeju volcanic island, Korea. *Sci Rpt Tohoku Univ*, Ser 3, 15: 177-256

Lim C, Ikehara K, Toyoda K, 2008. Cryptotephra detection using high-resolution trace-element analysis of Holocene marine sediments, southwest Japan. *Geochim Cosmochim Acta*, 72: 5022-5036

Litasov Y, Hasenaka T, Litasov K, Yarmolyuk V, Sugorakova A, Lebedev V, Sasaki M, Taniguchi H, 2001. Petrologic characteristics of Cenozoic alkaline basalts from the Azas Plateau, Northeast Tuva (Russia). *Center for Northeast Asian Studies, Tohoku Univ*, no 3, p 201-226

Liu J, Maimaiti Y, 1989. Distribution and ages of Ashikule volcanoes on the West Kunlun Mountains, West China. *Bull Glacier Res*, 7: 187-190

Liu J, Taniguchi H, 2001. Active volcanoes in China. *Tohoku Asian Studies*, 6: 173-189

Liu R, Wei H, Li J, 1992. Volcano at Tianci Lake, Changbaishan Mt.-the potentially most dangerous volcano in Chinese mainland. *29th Internatl Geol Cong, Kyoto, abs*, 2: 501

Machida H, 1990. Frequency and magnitude of catastrophic explosive volcanism in the Japan region during the past 130 ka: implications for human occupance of volcanic regions. *Geol Soc Aust Symp Proc*, 1: 27-36

Machida H, Arai F, 1983. Extensive ash falls in and around the Sea of Japan from large, late Quaternary eruptions. *J Volc Geotherm Res*, 18: 151-164

Machida H, Moriwaki H, Zhao D, 1990. The recent major eruption of Changbai volcano and its environmental effects. *Geog Rpt Tokyo Metropolitan Univ*, 25: 1-25

Moriwaki H, Machida H, Da-Chang Z, Arai F, 1988. Great eruption of Baegdu (Changbai) volcano occurred around a thousand years ago. *Kagoshima Internatl Conf Volc Abs*, p 400

Ogura T, 1969. Volcanoes in Manchuria. *In*: Ogura T (ed) *Geology and Mineral Resources of the Far East*, Tokyo: Univ Tokyo Press, 2: 373-413

Rasskazov S V, 1994. Magmatism related to the eastern Siberia Rift system and the geodynamics. *Bull Centres Rech Explor-Prod Elf Aquitaine*, 18(2): 437-452

Rasskazov S V, 1999. A middle Holocene stress change in the Udokan Range volcanic zone, eastern Siberia. *Volc Seism*, 21: 261-267 (English translation)

Rasskazov S V, Boven A, Andre L, Liegeois J-P, Ivanov A V, Punzalan L, 1997. Evolution of magmatism in the Northeastern Baikal Rift System. *Petrology*, 5: 101-120 (English translation)

Rasskazov S V, Kunk M J, Luhr J F, Bowring S A, Brandt I S, Brandt S B, Ivanov A V, 1996. Episodes of eruptions and composition variations of the Quaternary lavas in the Baikal Rift System (Ar-Ar and K-Ar dating of volcanism in the Dzhida River area). *Russian Geol Geophys*, 37(6): 1-12

Sakhno V G, 2007. Chronology of eruptions, composition, and magmatic evolution of the Paektusan volcano: evidence from K-Ar, 87Sr/86Sr, and delta18O isotope data. *Doklady Earth Sci*, 412: 22-28

Sengor A M C, Kidd W S F, 1979. Post-collisional tectonics of the Turkish-Iranian Plateau and a comparison with Tibet. *Tectonophysics*, 55: 361-376

Shen Y, Wang X, 1983. Volcanic rocks in Jingbo Lake and its tectonic setting. *IUGG, 18th General Assembly, Hamburg*, 2: 573

Shi Z, Lee Q, Wu H, Yang Y, 1986. A possible historical slow earthquake in eastern China. *Roy Soc New Zeal Bull*, 24: 547-552

Shilov V N, 1997a. Comparison of Neogene-Quaternary volcanism on Sakhalin and in the East Sikhote Alin: 2. Late Cenozoic volcanism in the East Sikhote Alin. *Volc Seism*, 18: 517-528 (English translation)

Shilov V N, 1997b. Comparison of Neogene-Quaternary volcanism in Sakhalin and the East Sikhote Alin: 3. A comparative study of the rock chemistries. *Volc Seism*, 18: 667-672 (English translation)

Sohn Y K, 1996. Hydrovolcanic processes forming basaltic tuff rings and cones on Cheju Island,

Korea. *Geol Soc Amer Bull*, 108: 1199-1211

Sohn Y K, Chough S K, 1989. Depositional processes of the Suwolbong tuff ring, Cheju Island (Korea). *Sedimentology*, 36: 837-855

Sohn Y K, Park J B, Khim B K, Park K H, Koh G W, 2003. Stratigraphy, petrochemistry and Quaternary depositional record of the Songaksan tuff ring, Jeju Island, Korea. *J Volc Geotherm Res*, 119: 1-20

Sohn Y K, Park K H, 2005. Composite tuff ring/cone complexes in Jeju Island, Korea: possible consequences of substrate collapse and vent migration. *J Volc Geotherm Res*, 141: 157-175

Tapponnier P, Molnar P, 1977. Active faulting and tectonics in China. *J Geophys Res*, 82: 2905-2930

Tomita T, 1969. Volcanic geology of the Cenozoic alkaline petrographic province of eastern Asia. *In*: Ogura T (ed) *Geology and Mineral Resources of the Far East*, Tokyo: Univ Tokyo Press, p 139-179

Tong W, Mu Z, Liu S, Zhang M, 1988. Late Cenozoic volcanoes and active geothermal systems in China. *Proc Kagoshima Internatl Conf Volc*, p 847-850

Ustiev E K, 1959. Aniusky volcano and localization problems of Quaternary volcanism in north-eastern Asia. *Bull Volc*, 20: 155-172

Vlodavetz V I, Piip B I, 1959. Kamchatka and Continental Areas of Asia. *Catalog of Active Volcanoes of the World and Solfatara Fields*, Rome: IAVCEI, 8: 1-110 ***(regional reference)***

Wei H, Sparks R S J, Liu R, Fan Q, Wang Y, Hong H, Zhang H, Chen H, Jiang C, Dong J, Zheng Y, Pan Y, 2003. Three active volcanoes in China and their hazards. *J Asian Earth Sci*, 21: 515-526

Whitford-Stark J L, 1987. A survey of Cenozoic volcanism on mainland Asia. *Geol Soc Amer Spec Pap*, 213: 1-74

Zhang M, Suddaby P, Thompson R N, Thirwall M F, Menzies M A, 1995. Potassic volcanic rocks in NE China: geochemical constraints on mantle sources and magma genesis. *J Petr*, 36: 1275-1303

Zhang X, Shi Z, 1999. Study on relationship between historical volcanic eruptions and historical strong earthquakes in China and its adjacent regions. *Acta Seism Sinica*, 12: 109-116

Zhang Z, Li Z, 1999. Sr, Nd and Pb isotopic compositions of Quaternary basalts in the Jingpo Lake area and characteristics of the mantle source. *Geog Rev*, 45 (Suppl): 349-357 (in Chinese with English abs)

ALASKA: ALEUTIAN ARC (1101-03)

Alaska Volcano Observatory, 2005-. Volcanoes. *http://www.avo.alaska.edu/volcanoes.php*

Alaska Volcano Observatory Staff, 1990. The 1989-1990 eruption of Redoubt volcano. *Eos, Trans Amer Geophys Union*, 71: 265-275

Becker G F, 1898. Reconnaissance of the gold fields of southern Alaska, with some notes on general geology. *U S Geol Surv 18th Ann Rpt*, Part 3: 13-14 ***(regional reference)***

Beget J E, Kienle J, 1992. Cyclic formation of debris avalanches at Mount St. Augustine volcano. *Nature*, 356: 701-704

Beget J E, Kowalik Z, 2006. Confirmation and calibration of computer modeling of tsunamis produced by Augustine volcano, Alaska. *Sci Tsunami Hazards*, 24: 257-266

Beget J E, Larson J F, Neal C A, Nye C J, Schaefer J R, 2005. Preliminary volcano-hazard assessment for Okmok volcano, Umnak Island Alaska. *Alaska Dept Nat Resour Div Geol Geophys Surv, Rep Invest*, 2004-3: 1-32

Beget J E, Nye C J, 1994. Postglacial eruption history of Mt. Redoubt, Alaska. *J Volc Geotherm Res*, 62: 31-54

Beget J E, Nye C J, Bean K W, 2000. Preliminary volcano-hazard assessment for Makushin volcano, Alaska. *Alaska Div Geol Geophys Surv, Rpt Invest*, 2000-4: 1-22

Beget J E, Nye C J, Schaefer J R, Stelling P L, 2003. Preliminary volcano-hazard assessment for Shishaldin volcano, Alaska. *Alaska Dept Nat Resour Div Geol Geophys Surv, Rep Invest*, 2002-4: 1-28

Beget J E, Stihler S D, Stone D B, 1994. A 500-year-long record of tephra falls from Mt. Redoubt and other volcanoes in upper Cook Inlet, Alaska. *J Volc Geotherm Res*, 62: 55-67

Beget J, Gardner C, Davis K, 2008. Volcanic tsunamis and prehistorical cultural transitions in Cook Inlet, Alaska. *J Volc Geotherm Res*, 176: 377-386

Bindeman I A, Fournelle J H, Valley J W, 2001. Low-delta 18O tephra from a compositionally zoned magma body: Fisher caldera, Unimak Island, Aleutians. *J Volc Geotherm Res*, 111: 35-53

Bonadonna C, Houghton B F, 2005. Total grain-size distribution and volume of tephra-fall deposits. *Bull Volc*, 67: 441-456

Bradley C C, 1948. Geologic notes on Adak Island and the Aleutian chain, Alaska. *Amer J Sci*, 246: 214-240

Brantley S R (ed), 1990. The eruptions of Redoubt volcano, Alaska December 14, 1989 - August 31, 1990. *U S Geol Surv Circ*, 1061: 1-33

Brophy J G, 1987. The Cold Bay volcanic center, Aleutian volcanic arc. II. Implications for fractionation and mixing mechanism in calc-alkaline andesite genesis. *Contr Mineral Petr*, 97: 378-388

Burgisser A, 2005. Physical volcanology of the 2,050 BP caldera-forming eruption of Okmok caldera, Alaska. *Bull Volc*, 67: 497-525

Burk C A, 1965. Geology of the Alaska Peninsula-island arc and continental margin (Part 1). *Geol Soc Amer Mem*, 99: 1-250

Byers F M, 1959. Geology of Umnak and Bogoslof Islands, Aleutian Islands, Alaska. *U S Geol Surv Bull*, 1028-L: 267-365

Byers F M, 1961. Petrology of three volcanic suites, Umnak and Bogoslof Islands, Aleutian Island, Alaska. *Geol Soc Amer Bull*, 72: 93-128

Byers F M, Barth T F W, 1953. Volcanic activity on Akun and Akutan Islands, Alaska. *Proc 7th Pacific Sci Cong*, 2: 382-397

Caplan-Auerbach J, McNutt S R, 2003. New insights into the 1999 eruption of Shishaldin volcano, Alaska, based on acoustic data. *Bull Volc*, 65: 405-417

Carson E C, Fournelle J H, Miller T P, Mickelson D M, 2002. Holocene tephrochonology of the Cold Bay area, southwest Alaska. *Quat Sci Rev*, 21: 2213-2228

Coats R R, 1950. Volcanic activity in the Aleutian Arc. *U S Geol Surv Bull*, 974-B: 35-47

Coats R R, 1951. Geology of Buldir Island, Aleutian Islands, Alaska. *U S Geol Surv Bull*, 989-A: 1-26

Coats R R, 1956a. Geology of northern Adak Island, Alaska. *U S Geol Surv Bull*, 1028-C: 47-66

Coats R R, 1956b. Geology of northern Kanaga Island, Alaska. *U S Geol Surv Bull*, 1028-D: 69-81

Coats R R, 1956c. Reconnaissance geology of some western Aleutian islands, Alaska. *U S Geol Surv Bull*, 1028-E: 83-100

Coats R R, 1959a. Geologic reconnaissance of Semisopochnoi Island western Aleutian Islands Alaska. *U S Geol Surv Bull*, 1028-O: 477-519

Coats R R, 1959b. Geologic reconnaissance of Gareloi Island, Aleutian Islands, Alaska. *U S Geol Surv Bull*, 1028-J: 249-256

Coats R R, Nelson W H, Lewis R Q, Powers H A, 1961. Geologic reconnaissance of Kiska Island, Aleutian Islands, Alaska. *U S Geol Surv Bull*, 1028-R: 563-581

Coombs M L, Eichelberger J C, Rutherford M J, 2000. Magma storage and mixing conditions for the 1953-1974 eruptions of Southwest Trident volcano, Katmai National Park, Alaska. *Contr Mineral Petr*, 140: 99-118

Coombs M L, McGimsey R G, Browne B L, 2007a. Preliminary volcano-hazard assessment for the Tanaga volcanic cluster, Tanaga Island, Alaska. *U S Geol Surv, Sci Invest Rpt*, 2007-5094: 1-35

Coombs M L, White S M, Scholl D W, 2007b. Massive edifice failure at Aleutian arc volcanoes. *Earth Planet Sci Lett*, 256: 403-418

Curtis G H, 1968. The stratigraphy of the ejecta from the 1912 eruption of Mount Katmai and Novarupta, Alaska. *Geol Soc Amer Mem*, 116: 153-210

Dean K G, Dehn J, Papp K R, Smith S, Izbekov P, Peterson R, Kearney C, Steffke A, 2004. Integrated satellite observations of the 2001 eruption of Mt. Cleveland, Alaska. *J Volc Geotherm Res*, 135: 51-73

Decker R W, 1967. Investigations at active volcanoes. *Eos, Trans Amer Geophys Union*, 48: 639-647

Dehn J, Dean K G, Engle K, Izbekov P, 2002. Thermal precursors in satellite images of the 1999 eruption of Shishaldin volcano. *Bull Volc*, 64: 525-534

Delong S E, Perfit M R, McCulloch M T, Ach J, 1985. Magmatic evolution of Semisopochnoi Island, Alaska: trace-element and isotopic constraints. *J Geol*, 93: 609-618

Detterman R L, 1968. Recent volcanic activity on Augustine Island, Alaska. *U S Geol Surv Prof Pap*, 600-C: 126-129

Detterman R L, Wilson F H, Yount M E, Miller T P, 1987. Quaternary geologic map of the Ugashik, Bristol Bay, and western part of Karluk quadrangles, Alaska. *U S Geol Surv Map*, I-1801

Doroshin P, 1870. Some volcanoes, their eruptions, and earthquakes in the former Russian holdings in America. *Verh Russ Kais Mineral Ges St Petersberg, Zweite Ser*, p 25-44, (in Russian) ***(regional reference)***

Dreher S T, Eichelberger J C, Larsen J F, 2005. The petrology and geochemistry of the Aniakchak caldera-forming ignmbrite, Aleutian Arc, Alaska. *J Petr*, 46: 1747-1763

Drewes H, Fraser G D, Snyder G L, Barnett H F, 1961. Geology of Unalaska Island and adjacent insular shelf, Aleutian Islands, Alaska. *U S Geol Surv Bull*, 1028-S: 583-676

Eichelberger J C, Keith T E C, Miller T P, Nye C J, 1995. The 1992 eruptions of Crater Peak vent, Mount Spurr volcano, Alaska: chronology and summary. *U S Geol Surv Bull*, 2139: 1-18

Fenner C N, 1930. Mount Katmai and Mount Mageik. *Zeit Vulk*, 13: 1-24

Fierstein J, 2007. Explosive eruptive record in the Katmai region, Alaska Peninsula: an overview. *Bull Volc*, 69: 469-509

Fierstein J, Hildreth W, 1992. The Plinian eruptions of 1912 at Novarupta, Katmai National Park, Alaska. *Bull Volc*, 54: 646-684

Fierstein J, Hildreth W, 2008. Kaguyak dome field and its Holocene caldera, Alaska Peninsula. *J Volc Geotherm Res*, 177: 301-312

Fierstein J, Houghton B F, Wilson C J N, Hildreth W, 1997. Complexities of plinian fall deposition at vent: an example from the 1912 Novarupta eruption (Alaska). *J Volc Geotherm Res*, 76: 215-227

Finch R H, 1934. Shishaldin volcano. *Proc 5th Pacific Sci Cong*, 3: 2369-2376

Fournelle J H, 1988. The geology and petrology of Shishaldin volcano, Unimak Island, Aleutian arc, Alaska. *Unpublished PhD thesis*, John Hopkins Univ, 507 p

Gardner C A, Cashman K V, Neal C A, 1998. Tephra-fall deposits from the 1992 eruption of Crater Peak, Alaska: implications of clast textures for eruptive processes. *Bull Volc*, 59: 537-555

Gardner C A, Neal C A, Waitt R B, Janda R J, 1994. Proximal pyroclastic deposits from the 1989-1990 eruption of Redoubt volcano Alaska-stratigraphy, distribution, and physical characteristics. *J Volc Geotherm Res*, 62: 213-250

Henning R A, Rosenthal C H, Olds B, Reading E (eds), 1976. Alaska's volcanoes, northern link in the ring of fire. *Alaska Geog*, 4: 1-88

Hildreth W, 1983. The compositionally zoned eruption of 1912 in the Valley of Ten Thousand Smokes, Katmai National Park, Alaska. *J Volc Geotherm Res*, 18: 1-56

Hildreth W, 1987. New perspectives on the eruption of 1912 in the Valley of Ten Tousand Smokes, Katmai National Park, Alaska. *Bull Volc*, 49: 680-693

Hildreth W, 1991. The timing of caldera collapse at Mount Katmai in response to magma withdrawal toward Novarupta. *Geophys Res Lett*, 18: 1541-1544

Hildreth W E, Fierstein J, Lanphere M A, Siems D F, 2001. Snowy Mountain: a pair of small andesite-dacite stratovolcanoes in Katmai National Park. *In*: Gough L P, Wilson F H (eds) Geologic Studies in Alaska by the U.S. Geological Survey, 1999, *U S Geol Surv Prof Pap*, 1633: 13-34

Hildreth W, Fierstein J, 2000. Katmai volcanic cluster and the great eruption of 1912. *Geol Soc Amer Bull*, 112: 1594-1620

Hildreth W, Fierstein J, Calvert A T, 2007. Blue Mountain and the Gas Rocks: rear-arc dome clusters on the Alaska Peninsula. *In*: Haeussler P J, Galloway J P (eds), Studies by the U.S. Geological Survey, *U S Geol Surv Prof Pap*, 1739-A: 1-27

Hildreth W, Fierstein J, Lanphere M A, Siems D F, 1999. Alogogshak volcano: a Pleistocene andesite-dacite stratovolcano in Katmai National Park. *In*: Kelly K D (ed), Geologic Studies in Alaska by the U. S. Geological Survey, 1997 *U S Geol Surv Prof Pap*, 1614: 105-113

Hildreth W, Fierstein J, Lanphere M A, Siems D F, 2000. Mount Mageik: a compound stratovolcano in Katmai National Park. *In*: Kelly K D, Gough L P (eds), Geologic Studies in Alaska by the U. S. Geological Survey, 1998 *U S Geol Surv Prof Pap*, 1615: 23-41

Hildreth W, Fierstein J, Lanphere M A, Siems D F, 2002. Mount Griggs: a compositionally distinctive Quaternary stratovolcano behind the main volcanic line in Katmai National Park. *In*: Wilson R H, Galloway J P (eds), Geologic Studies in Alaska by the U. S. Geological Survey, 2000 *U S Geol Surv Prof Pap*, 1662: 87-112

Hildreth W, Fierstein J, Lanphere M A, Siems D F, 2003a. Trident volcano: four contiguous stratocones adjacent to Katmai Pass, Alaska Peninsula. Studies by the U.S. Geological Survey in Alaska, 2001 *U S Geol Surv Profl Pap*, 1678: 153-180

Hildreth W, Lanphere M A, Fierstein J, 2003b. Geochronology and eruptive history of the Katmai volcanic cluster, Alaska Peninsula. *Earth Planet Sci Lett*, 214: 93-114

Holasek R E, Rose W I, 1991. Anatomy of 1986 Augustine volcano eruptions as recorded by multispectral image processing of digital AVHRR weather satellite data. *Bull Volc*, 53: 420-435

Holden E S, 1898. A catalogue of earthquakes on the Pacific Coast 1769 to 1897. *Smithsonian Inst Misc Coll*, no 1087

Houghton B F, Wilson C J N, Fierstein J, Hildreth W, 2004. Complex proximal deposition during the Plinian eruptions of 1912 at Novarupta, Alaska. *Bull Volc*, 66: 95-133

Hubbard B R, 1931. World inside a mountain: Aniakchak, the new volcanic wonderland of the Alaska Peninsula, is explored. *Natl Geog*, 60: 319-345

Huggel C, Caplan-Auerbach J, Waythomas C F, Wessels R L, 2007. Monitoring and modeling ice-rock avalanches from ice-capped volcanoes: a case study of frequent large avalanches of Iliamna volcano, Alaska. *J Volc Geotherm Res*, 168: 114-136

Jacob K H, Hauksson E, 1983. A seismotectonic analysis of the seismic and volcanic hazards in the Pribilof Islands - Eastern Aleutian Islands Region of the Bering Sea. *Lamont-Doherty Geol Observ Columbia Univ Ann Rpt* NOAA 03-5-022-70: 1-224

Jaggar T A, 1927a. Three press reports. *Volcano Lett*, 108: 1

Jaggar T A, 1927b. The Aleutian Islands. *Volcano Lett*, 116: 1

Jaggar T A, 1927c. Eruption of Mageik in Alaska. *Volcano Lett*, 147: 1

Jaggar T A, 1930a. Recent activity of Bogoslof volcano. *Volcano Lett*, 275: 1-3

Jaggar T A, 1932a. Aleutian eruptions 1930-1932. *Volcano Lett*, 375: 1-3

Jicha B R, 2009. Holocene volcanic activity at Koniuji Island, Aleutians. *J Volc Geotherm Res*, 185: 214-222

Jicha B R, Singer B S, 2006. Volcanic history and magmatic evolution of Seguam Island, Aleutian Island arc, Alaska. *Geol Soc Amer Bull*, 118: 805-822

Johnson K E, Harmon R S, Richardson J M, Moorbath S, Strong D F, 1996. Isotope and trace element geochemistry of Augustine volcano, Alaska: implications for magmatic evolution. *J Petr*, 37: 95-115

Johnston D A, 1979. Volcanic gas studies at Alaskan volcanoes. *U S Geol Surv Circ*, 804-B: 83-84

Johnston D A, Detterman R L, 1979. Revision of the recent eruption history of Augustine volcano - elimination of the "1902 eruption." *U S Geol Surv Circ*, 804-B: 80-83

Jones A E, 1952. Aleutian volcanoes. *Volcano Lett*, 516: 8-9

Kamata H, Johnston D A, Waitt R B, 1991. Stratigraphy, chronology, and character of the 1976 pyroclastic eruption of Augustine volcano, Alaska. *Bull Volc*, 53: 407-419

Kay S M, Kay R W, Citron G P, 1982. Tectonic controls on tholeiitic and calc-alkaline magmatism in the Aleutian arc. *J Geophys Res*, 87: 4051-4072

Keller A S, Reiser H N, 1959. Geology of the Mt. Katmai Area, Alaska. *U S Geol Surv Bull*, 1058-G: 264-268

Keller F, Meuschke J L, Alldredge L R, 1954. Aeromagnetic surveys in the Aleutian, Marshall, and Bermuda Islands. *Eos, Trans Amer Geophys Union*, 35: 558-572

Kennedy G C, Waldron H H, 1955. Geology of Pavlof volcano and vicinity Alaska. *U S Geol Surv Bull*, 1028-A: 1-18

Kienle J, Forbes R B, 1976. Augustine: evolution of a volcano. *Alaska Univ Geophys Inst 1975-76 Ann Rpt*, p 26-48

Kienle J, Kowalik Z, Murty T S, 1987. Tsunamis generated by eruptions from Mount St. Augustine volcano, Alaska. *Science*, 236: 1442-1447

Kienle J, Kyle P R, Self S, Motyka R J, Lorenz V, 1980. Ukinrek Maars, Alaska, I. April 1977 eruption sequence, petrology and tectonic setting. *J Volc Geotherm Res*, 7: 11-37

Kienle J, Swanson S E, 1980. Volcanic hazards from future eruptions of Augustine volcano, Alaska. *Univ Alaska Geophys Inst*, UAG R-275, 122 p

Kienle J, Swanson S E, 1983. Volcanism in the eastern Aleutian Arc: late Quaternary and Holocene centers, tectonic setting and petrology. *J Volc Geotherm Res*, 17: 393-432

Lamb D, Linneman S R, Myers J D, Nicolaysen K E, 1992. Caldera formation on Yunaska Island, central Aleutian arc (abs). *Eos, Trans Amer Geophys Union*, 73: 645

Larsen J F, Neal C, Neal C, Schaefer J, Beget J, Nye C, 2007. Late Pleistocene and Holocene caldera-forming eruptions of Okmok caldera, Aleutian Islands, Alaska. *In*: Eichelberger J, Gordeev E, Izbekov P, Kasahara M, Lees J (eds), *Volcanism and Subduction: the Kamchatka Region*, Amer Geophys Union Geophys Monograph, 172: 343-364

Lu Z, Mann D, Freymueller J, 1998. Satellite radar interferometry measures deformation at Okmok volcano. *Eos, Trans Amer Geophys Union*, 79: 461-468

Marsh B D, Leitz R E, 1979. Geology of Amak Island, Aleutian Islands, Alaska. *J Geol*, 87: 715-723

Mauk F J, Kienle J, 1973. Microearthquakes at St. Augustine volcano, Alaska, triggered by Earth tides. *Science*, 182: 386-389

McGimsey R B, Neal C A, 1996. 1995 volcanic activity in Alaska and Kamchatka: summary of events and response of the Alaska Volcano Observatory. *U S Geol Surv, Open-File Rpt*, 96-738: 1-23

McGimsey R G, Neal C A, 1997. 1996 volcanic activity in Alaska and Kamchatka: summary of events and response of the Alaska Volcano Observatory. *U S Geol Surv, Open-File Rpt*, 97-433: 1-34

McGimsey R G, Neal C A, Dixon J P, 2007. 2005 volcanic activity in Alaska and Kamchatka: summary of events and response of the Alaska Volcano Observatory. *U S Geol Surv, Open-File Rpt*, 20075269: 1-93

McGimsey R G, Neal C A, Girina O, 2003. 1998 volcanic activity in Alaska and Kamchatka: summary of events and response of the Alaska Volcano Observatory. *U S Geol Surv, Open-File Rpt*, 03-0423: 1-35

McGimsey R G, Neal C A, Girina O, 2004. 1999 volcanic activity in Alaska and Kamchatka: summary of events and response of the Alaska Volcano Observatory. *U S Geol Surv Open-File Rpt*, 2004-1033: 1-45

McGimsey R G, Neal C A, Girina O, 2004. 2001 volcanic activity in Alaska and Kamchatka: summary of events and response of the Alaska Volcano Observatory. *U S Geol Surv, Open-File Rpt*, 2004-1453: 1-53

McGimsey R G, Neal C A, Girina O, 2005. 2003 volcanic activity in Alaska and Kamchatka: summary of events and response of the Alaska Volcano Observatory. *U S Geol Surv, Open-File Rpt*, 2005-1310: 1-58

McGimsey R G, Wallace K L, 1999. 1997 volcanic activity in Alaska and Kamchatka: summary of events and response of the Alaska Volcano Observatory. *U S Geol Surv, Open-File Rpt*, 99-448: 1-42

McGimsey R G, Waythomas C F, Neal C A, 1994. High strand and catastrophic draining of intracaldera Surprise Lake, Aniakchak volcano, Alaska. *In:* Till A B, Moore T E (eds) *Geologic Studies in Alaska by the U. S. Geological Survey in 1993*, U S Geol Surv Bull 2017: 59-71

McNutt S R, 1987. Eruption characteristics and cycles at Pavlof volcano, Alaska, and their relation to regional earthquake activity. *J Volc Geotherm Res*, 31: 239-267

McNutt S R, 1989. Some seismic precursors to eruptions at Pavlof volcano, Alaska, October 1973 - April 1986. *In*: Latter J H (ed) *Volcanic Hazards*. Berlin: Springer-Verlag, 1: 463-485

McNutt S R, Beavan R J, 1987. Eruptions of Pavlof volcano and their possible modulation by ocean load and tectonic stresses. *J Geophys Res*, 92: 11,509-11,523

McNutt S R, Davis C M, 2000. Lightning associated with the 1992 eruptions of Crater Peak, Mount Spurr volcano, Alaska. *J Volc Geotherm Res*, 102: 45-65

McNutt S R, Miller T P, Taber J J, 1991. Geological and seismological evidence of increased explosivity during the 1986 eruptions of Pavlof volcano, Alaska. *Bull Volc*, 53: 86-98

Melekestsev I V, Miller T P, 1997. On the origin of the 1645 B.C. oxygen peak in the Greenland ice sheet. *Volc Seism*, 19: 163-166 (English translation)

Meyer D F, Trabant D C, 1995. Lahars from the 1992 eruptions of Crater Peak, Mount Spurr volcano, Alaska. *U S Geol Surv Bull*, 2139: 183-198

Miller T P, 1984. Two-stage volcanism at the Ugashik-Peulik volcanic center, Alaska Peninsula. *Geol Soc Amer Abs Prog*, 16: 322

Miller T P, 1994. Dome growth and destruction during the 1989-1990 eruption of Redoubt volcano. *J Volc Geotherm Res*, 62: 197-212

Miller T P, 1999. Newly identified early Holocene caldera-forming druption from Roundtop volcano, Unimak Island, Alaska. *Eos, Trans Amer Geophys Union*, 1999 Fall Mtg, abs V51B-17

Miller T P, 2004. Geology of the Ugashik-Mount Peulik volcanic center, Alaska. *U S Geol Surve Open-File Rpt*, 2004-1009: 1-19

Miller T P, Chertkoff D G, Eichelberger J C, Coombs M L, 1999. Mount Dutton volcano, Alaska: Aleutian arc analog to Unzen volcano, Japan. *J Volc Geotherm Res*, 89: 275-301

Miller T P, Chouet B A, 1994. The 1989-1990 eruptions of Redoubt volcano: an introduction. *J Volc Geotherm Res*, 61: 1-10

Miller T P, McGimsey R G, Richter D H, Riehle J R, Nye C J, Yount M E, Dumoulin J A, 1998. Catalogue of the historically active volcanoes of Alaska. *U S Geol Surv Open-File Rpt*, 98-582: 1-104 ***(regional reference)***

Miller T P, Neal C A, Waitt R B, 1995. Pyroclastic flows of the 1992 Crater Peak eruptions: distribution and origin. *U S Geol Surv Bull*, 2139: 81-87

Miller T P, Smith R L, 1975. Ash flows on the Alaska Peninsula: a preliminary report on their distribution, composition and age (abs). *Geol Soc Amer Abs Prog*, 7: 1201

Miller T P, Smith R L, 1977. Spectacular mobility of ash flows around Aniakchak and Fisher Calderas, Alaska. *Geology*, 5: 173-176

Miller T P, Smith R L, 1987. Late Quaternary caldera-forming eruptions in the eastern Aleutian arc, Alaska. *Geology*, 15: 434-438

Motyka R J, Liss S A, Nye C J, Moorman M A, 1993. Geothermal resources of the Aleutian arc. *Alaska Div Geol Geophys Surv, Prof Rpt*, no 114, 17 p and 4 map sheets

Muller E H, Juhle W, Coulter H W, 1954. Current volcanic activity in Katmai National Monument, Alaska. *Science*, 119: 319-321

Myers J D, 1994. *The Geology, Geochemistry and Petrology of the recent Magmatic Phase of the Central and Western Aleutian Arc. Unpublished manuscript*, unpaginated

Myers J D, Frost C D, 1994. A petrologic re-investigation of the Adak volcanic center, central Aleutian arc, Alaska. *J Volc Geotherm Res*, 60: 109-146

Myers J D, March B D, Sinha A K, 1985. Strontium isotopic and selected trace element variations between two Aleutian volcanic centers (Adak and Atka): implications for the development of arc volcanic plumbing systems. *Contr Mineral Petr*, 91: 221-234

Myers J D, Marsh B D, Frost C D, Linton J A, 2002. Petrologic constraints on the spatial distribution of crustal magma chambers, Atka volcanic center, central Aleutian arc. *Contr Mineral Petr*, 143: 567-586

Nakamura K, Jacob K H, Davies J N, 1977. Volcanoes as possible indicators of tectonic stress orientation Aleutians and Alaska. *Pure Applied Geophys*, 115: 87-112

Neal C A, Doukas M P, McGimsey R B, 1995. 1994 volcanic activity in Alaska: summary of events and response of the Alaska Volcano Observatory. *U S Geol Surv, Open-File Rpt*, 95-0271: 1-18

Neal C A, McGimsey R B, Doukas M P, 1996. 1993 volcanic activity in Alaska: summary of events and response of the Alaska Volcano Observatory. *U S Geol Surv, Open-File Rpt*, 96-0024: 1-21

Neal C A, McGimsey R G, Dixon J, Melnikov D, 2005. 2004 volcanic activity in Alaska and Kamchatka: summary of events and response of the Alaska Volcano Observatory. *U S Geol Surv, Open-File Rpt*, 2005-1308: 1-67

Neal C A, McGimsey R G, Gardner C A, Harbin M L, Nye C J, 1995. Tephra-fall deposits from the 1992 eruptions of Crater Peak, Mount Spurr volcano, Alaska: a preliminary report on distribution, stratigraphy, and composition. *U S Geol Surv Bull*, 2139: 65-79

Neal C A, McGimsey R G, Girina O, 2005. 2002 volcanic activity in Alaska and Kamchatka: summary of events and response of the Alaska Volcano Observatory. *U S Geol Surv, Open-File Rpt*, 2004-1058: 1-51

Neal C A, McGimsey R G, Miller T P, Riehle J R, Waythomas C F, 2001. Preliminary volcano-hazard assessment for Aniakchak volcano, Alaska. *U S Geol Surv Open-File Rpt*, 00-519: 1-35

Nelson W H, 1959. Geology of Segula, Davidof, and Khvostof Islands, Alaska. *U S Geol Surv Bull*, 1028-K: 257-266

Nicolaysen K E, Myers J D, Linneman S R, Lamb D, 1992. Geologic relations of the Yunaska volcanic complex, central Aleutian arc (abs). *Eos, Trans Amer Geophys Union*, 73: 645

Norris R A, Johnson R H, 1969. Submarine volcanic eruptions recently located in the Pacific by SOFAR hydrophones. *J Geophys Res*, 74: 650-664

Nye C J, Beget J E, Motyka R J, Layer P W, 1992. Geology and geochemistry of Mt. Douglas volcano, eastern Aleutian arc, Alaska (abs). *Eos, Trans Amer Geophys Union*, 73: 645

Nye C J, Keith T E C, Eichelberger J C, Miller T P, McNutt S R, Moran S, Schneider D J, Dehn J, Schaefer J R, 2002. The 1999 eruption of Shishaldin volcano, Alaska: monitoring a distant eruption. *Bull Volc*, 64: 507-519

Nye C J, McGimsey G, Power J, 1998. Volcanoes of Alaska. *Alaska Div Geol Geophys Surv, Inf Circ*, 38

Nye C J, Turner D L, 1990. Petrology, geochemistry, and age of the Spurr volcanic complex, eastern Aleutian arc. *Bull Volc*, 52: 205-226

Okimura H, 1930. The eruption of Katmai, Alaska, 1912. *Volcano Lett*, 305: 1-3

Patrick M R, Dehn J, Papp K R, Lu Z, Dean K, Moxey L, Izbekov P, Guritz R, 2003. The 1997 eruption of Okmok volcano, Alaska: a synthesis of remotely sensed imagery. *J Volc Geotherm Res*, 127: 87-105

Petersen T, McNutt S R, 2007. Seismo-acoustic signals associated with degassing explosions recorded at Shishaldin Volcano, Alaska, 2003-2004. *Bull Volc*, 69: 527-536

Power J A, Jolly A D, Nye C J, Harbin M L, 2002. A conceptual model of the Mount Spurr magmatic system from seismic and geochemical observations of the 1992 Crater Peak eruption sequence. *Bull Volc*, 64: 206-218

Powers H A, 1958. Alaska Peninsula-Aleutian Islands. *In*: Williams H (ed) *Landscapes of Alaska*, Los Angeles: Univ Calif Press, p 62-75

Reed B L, Lanphere M A, Miller T P, 1992. Double Glacier volcano, a 'new' Quaternary volcano in the eastern Aleutian volcanic arc. *Bull Volc*, 54: 631-637

Reeder J W, 1983a. Caption to cover photo [Okmok and Akutan]. *Eos, Trans Amer Geophys Union*, 64: 50 & 451

Reeder J W, 1983b. Preliminary dating of the caldera-forming Holocene volcanic events for the eastern Aleutian Islands (abs). *Geol Soc Amer Abs Prog*, 15: 638

Reeder J W, 1985. Hydrothermal manifestations of the northern part of Atka Island of the Aleutian arc, and their geologic and tectonic setting. *IAVCEI 1985 Scientific Assembly Potassic Volc Mt Etna Volcano, Abs*, p 195-196

Richter D H, Waythomas C F, McGimsey R G, Stelling P L, 1998. Geologic map of Akutan Island, Alaska. *U S Geol Surv Open-File Rpt*, 98-135, 1:48,000 scale map and 22 p text

Riehle J R, 1985. A reconnaissance of the major Holocene tephra deposits in the Upper Cook Inlet Region, Alaska. *J Volc Geotherm Res*, 26: 37-74

Riehle J R, Kienle J, Emmel K S, 1981. Lahars in Crescent River valley, lower Cook Inlet, Alaska. *Alaskan Geol Geophys Surv Geol Rpt*, 53: 1-10

Riehle J R, Waitt R B, Meyer C E, Calk L C, 1998. Age of formation of Kaguyak caldera, eastern Aleutian arc, Alaska, estimated by tephrochronology. *In*: Gray J E, Riehle J R (eds) *Geologic studies in Alaska by the U.S. Geological Survey, 1996*, US Geol Surv Prof Pap, 1595: 161-168

Riehle J R, Yount M E, Miller T P, 1987. Petrography, chemistry, and geologic history of Yantarni volcano, Aleutian volcanic arc, Alaska. *U S Geol Surv Bull*, 1761: 1-27

Roach A L, Benoit J P, Dean K G, McNutt S R, 2001. The combined use of satellite and seismic monitoring during the 1996 eruption of Pavlof volcano, Alaska. *Bull Volc*, 62: 385-399

Robinson G D, 1948. Exploring Aleutian volcanoes. *Natl Geog*, 94: 509-528

Roman D C, Power J A, Moran S C, Cashman K V, Doukas M P, Neal C A, Gerlach T M, 2004. Evidence for dike emplacement beneath Iliamna volcano, Alaska in 1996. *J Volc Geotherm Res*, 130: 265-284

Romick J D, Kay S M, Kay R W, 1992. The influence of amphibole fractionation on the evolution of calc-alkaline andesite and dacite tephra from the central Aleutians, Alaska. *Contr Mineral Petr* 112: 101-118

Romick J D, Perfit M R, Swanson S E, Shuster R D, 1990. Magmatism in the eastern Aleutian arc: temporal characteristics of igneous activity on Akutan Island. *Contr Mineral Petr*, 104: 700-721

Rymer M J, Sims J D, 1976. Preliminary survey of modern glaciolacustrine sediments for earthquake-induced deformational structures, south-central Alaska. *U S Geol Surv Open-File Rpt*, 76-373: 1-31

Scott W E, McGimsey R G, 1994. Character, mass, distribution, and origin of tephra-fall deposits of the 1989-1990 eruption of Redoubt volcano, Alaska. *J Volc Geotherm Res*, 62: 251-172

Siebert L, Beget J E, Glicken H, 1995. The 1883 and late-prehistoric eruptions of Augustine volcano, Alaska. *J Volc Geotherm Res*, 66: 367-395

Siebert L, Glicken H, Kienle J, 1989. Debris avalanches and lateral blasts at Mount St. Augustine volcano, Alaska. *Natl Geog Res*, 5: 232-249

Simons F S, Mathewson D E, 1955. Geology of Great Sitkin Island, Alaska. *U S Geol Surv Bull*, 1028-B: 29-32

Singer B S, Myers J D, Frost C D, 1992. Mid-Pleistocene lavas from the Seguam volcanic center, central Aleutian arc: closed-system fractional crystallization of a basalt to rhyodacite eruptive suite. *Contr Mineral Petr*, 110: 87-112

Smith R L, Shaw H R, 1975. Igneous-related geothermal systems. *U S Geol Surv Circ*, 726: 58-83

Smith R L, Shaw H R, Luedke R G, Russell S L, 1978. Comprehensive tables giving physical data and thermal energy estimates for young igneous systems of the United States. *U S Geol Surv Open-File Rpt*, 78-925: 1-25

Smith W R, 1925. Aniakchak Crater, Alaska Peninsula. *U S Geol Surv Prof Pap*, 132-J: 139-149

Smith W R, Baker A A, 1922. The Cold Bay-Chignik district, Alaska. *U S Geol Surv Bull*, 755-D: 156-157 & 191-192

Snyder G L, 1954. Eruption of Trident volcano, Katmai National Monument, Alaska, February-June 1953. *U S Geol Surv Circ*, 318: 1-7

Snyder G L, 1959. Geology of Little Sitkin Island, Alaska. *U S Geol Surv Bull*, 1028-H: 169-210

Stelling P, Beget J, Nye C, Gardner J, Devine J D, George R M M, 2002. Geology and petrology of ejecta from the 1999 eruption of Shishaldin volcano, Alaska. *Bull Volc*, 64: 548-561

Stelling P, Gardner J E, Beget J, 2005. Eruptive history of Fisher caldera, Alaska, USA. *J Volc Geotherm Res*, 139: 163-183

Sumner L, 1951. Magnificent Katmai. *Sierra Club Bull*, 37: 29-51

Swanson S E, Kienle J, 1988. The 1986 eruption of Mount St. Augustine: field test of a hazard evaluation. *J Geophys Res*, 93: 4500-4520

Till A B, Yount M E, Bevier M L, 1994. The geologic history of Redoubt volcano, Alaska. *J Volc Geotherm Res*, 62: 11-30

Vergniolle S, Caplan-Auerbach C, 2006. Basaltic thermals and subplinian plumes: constraints from measurements at Shishaldin volcano, Alaska. *Bull Volc*, 68: 611-630

Waitt R B, 1995. Hybrid wet flows formed by hot pyroclasts interacting with snow during the 1992 eruptions of Crater Peak, Mount Spurr volcano, Alaska. *U S Geol Surv Bull*, 2139: 107-118

Waitt R B, Beget J E, 1996. Provisional geologic map of Augustine volcano, Alaska. *U S Geol Surv Open-File Rpt*, 96-516: 1-44

Waldron H H, 1961. Geological reconnaissance of Frosty Peak volcano and vicinity, Alaska. *U S Geol Surv Bull*, 1028-T: 677-708

Ward P L, Matumoto T, 1967. A summary of volcanic and seismic activity in Katmai National Monument, Alaska. *Bull Volc*, 31: 107-130

Waythomas C F, 1999. Stratigraphic framework of Holocene volcaniclastic deposits, Akutan volcano, east-central Aleutians Islands, Alaska. *Bull Volc*, 61: 141-161

Waythomas C F, Dorava J M, Miller T P, Neal C A, McGimsey R G, 1998. Preliminary volcano-hazard assessment for Redoubt volcano, Alaska. *U S Geol Surv Open-File Rpt*, 97-857: 1-40

Waythomas C F, Miller T P, 1999. Preliminary volcano-hazard assessment for Iliamna volcano, Alaska. *U S Geol Surv Open-File Rpt*, 99-373: 1-31

Waythomas C F, Miller T P, Beget J E, 2000. Record of late Holocene debris avalanches and lahars at Iliamna volcano, Alaska. *J Volc Geotherm Res*, 104: 97-130

Waythomas C F, Miller T P, Mangan M T, 2006. Preliminary volcano hazard assessment for the Emmons Lake volcanic center, Alaska. *U S Geol Surv, Sci Invest Rpt*, 2006-5248: 1-33

Waythomas C F, Miller T P, Nye C J, 2003. Geology and late Quaternary eruptive history of Kanaga volcano, a calc-alkaline stratovolcano in the western Aleutian Islands, Alaska. Studies by the U.S. Geological Survey in Alaska, 2001 *U S Geol Surv Profl Pap*, 1678: 181-197

Waythomas C F, Neal C A, 1998. Tsunami generation by pyroclastic flow during the 3500-yr B.P. caldera-forming eruption of aniakchak vlcano, Alaska. *Bull Volc*, 60: 110-124

Waythomas C F, Power J A, Richter D H, McGimsey R G, 1998. Preliminary volcano-hazard assessment for Akutan volcano, east-central Aleutian Islands, Alaska. *U S Geol Surv Open-File Rpt*, 98-360: 1-36

Waythomas C F, Waitt R B, 1998. Preliminary volcano-hazard assessment for Augustine volcano, Alaska. *U S Geol Surv Open-File Rpt*, 98-106: 1-39

Wilcox R E, 1959. Some effects of recent volcanic ash falls with special reference to Alaska. *U S Geol Surv Bull*, 1028-N: 409-476

Wilson C R, Forbes R B, 1969. Infrasonic waves from Alaskan volcanic eruptions. *J Geophys Res*, 74: 4511-4522

Wilson F H, 1989. Geologic setting, petrology, and age of Pliocene to Holocene volcanoes of the Stepovak Bay Area, Western Alaska Peninsula. *U S Geol Surv Bull*, 1903: 84-95

Wilson F H, Detterman R L, Miller J W, Case J E, 1995. Geologic map of the Port Moller, Stepovak Bay, and Simeonof Island quadrangles, Alaska Peninsula, Alaska. *US Geol Surv Misc Invest Ser Map I-2272, unpaged, 2 sheets, scale 1:24,000*

Wong L J, Larsen J F, 2010. The Middle Scoria sequence: a Holocene violent strombolian, subplinian and phreatomagmatic eruption of Okmok volcano, Alaska. *Bull Volc*, 72: 17-31

Wood C A, Kienle J (eds), 1990. *Volcanoes of North America*. Cambridge, England: Cambridge Univ Press, 354 p ***(regional reference)***

Wright T L, 1971b. Investigations at active volcanoes. *In*: *Volcanology, Geochemistry, and Petrology*, U.S. National Report, l967-1971, Fifteenth General Assembly, IUGG: Eos, Trans Amer Geophys Union, 52(5): 57-62

Yount M E, Miller T P, Emanuel R P, Wilson F H, 1985. Eruption in an ice-filled caldera, Mount Veniaminof, Alaska Peninsula. *In*: Bartsch-Winkler S, Reed K M (eds), The United States Geological Survey in Alaska: Accomplishments in 1983, *U S Geol Surv Circ*, 945: 59-60

Yount M E, Miller T P, Gamble B M, 1987. The 1986 eruptions of Augustine volcano, Alaska: hazards and effects. *U S Geol Surv Circ*, 998: 4-13

Yount M E, Wilson F H, Miller J W, 1985. Newly discovered Holocene volcanic vents, Port Moller and Stepovak Bay quadrangles. *In*: Bartsch-Winkler S, Reed K M (eds), The United States Geological Survey in Alaska: Accomplishments in 1983, *U S Geol Surv Circ*, 945: 60-62

ALASKA: W, E, & SE (1104-05)

AVO, 2005-. Alaska Volcano Observatory. *http://www.avo.alaska.edu/index.php*

Alaska Volcano Observatory, 2005-. Volcanoes. *http://www.avo.alaska.edu/volcanoes.php*

Athey J E, Newberry R J, Werdon M B, Freeman L K, Smith R L, Szumigala D J, 2006. Bedrock geologic map of the Liberty Bell area, Fairbanks A-4 Quadrangle, Bonnifield mining district, Alaska. *Alaska Div Geol Geophys Surv Rpt Invest 2006-2*, v. 1.0.1, 98 p, 1 sheet, scale 1:50,000

Barker J C, 1985. Sampling and analytical results of a reconnaissance in the Selawik Hills areas, northwestern Alaska. *U S Bur Mines Open-File Rep*, 43-85: 1-67

Barth T F W, 1956. Geology and petrology of the Pribilof Islands, Alaska. *U S Geol Surv Bull*, 1028-F: 101-160

Becker G F, 1898. Reconnaissance of the gold fields of southern Alaska, with some notes on general geology. *U S Geol Surv 18th Ann Rpt*, Part 3: 13-14 ***(regional reference)***

Beget J E, Hopkins D M, Charron S D, 1996. The largest known maars on Earth, Seward Peninsula, northwest Alaska. *Arctic*, 49: 62-69

Beget J E, Motyka R J, 1998. New dates on late Pleistocene dacitic tephra from the Mount Edgecumbe volcanic field, southeastern Alaska. *Quat Res*, 49: 123-125

Benson C S, Motyka R J, 1979. Glacier - volcano interactions on Mt. Wrangell, Alaska. *Univ Alaska Geophys Inst Ann Rpt*, 1977-78: 1-25

Berg H C, Elliott R L, Koch R D, 1988. Geologic map of the Ketchikan and Prince Rupert quadrangles, southeastern Alaska. *U S Geol Surv Map*, I-1807, 1:250,000 scale and 27 p text

Brew D A, Karl S M, Tobey E F, 1985. Re-interpretation of the age of the Kuiu-Etolin belt volcanic rocks, Kupreanof Island, southeastern Alaska. *In*: Bartsch-Winkler S, Reed K M (eds) *The United States Geological Survey in Alaska: accomplishments during 1983*, U S Geol Surv Circ, 945: 86-88

Brew D A, Muffler L J P, Loney R A, 1969. Reconnaissance geology of the Mount Edgecumbe volcanic field, Kruzof Island, southeastern Alaska. *U S Geol Surv Prof Pap*, 650-D: 1-18

Buddington A F, Chapin T, 1929. Geology and mineral deposits of southeastern Alaska. *U S Geol Surv Bull*, 800: 278-279

Clauge J J, Evans S G, Rampton V N, Woodsworth G J, 1995. Improved age estimates for the White River and Bridge River tephras, western Canada. *Can J Earth Sci*, 32: 1172-1179

Collier A J, Hess F L, Smith P S, Brooks A H, 1908. The gold placer of parts of Seward Peninsula. *U S Geol Surv Bull*, 328: 103

Coonrad W L, 1957. Geologic reconnaissance in the Yukon Kuskokwim Delta region, Alaska. *U S Geol Surv Map*, I-223, 1:500,000

Cox A, Hopkins D M, Dalrymple G B, 1966. Geomagnetic polarity epochs: Pribilof Islands, Alaska. *Geol Soc Amer Bull*, 77: 883-910

Crosby W O, 1907. Volcanic activity in Alaska. *Science*, 24: 78

Feeley T C, Winer G S, 2009. Volcano hazards and potential risks on St. Paul Island, Pribilof Islands, Bering Sea, Alaska. *J Volc Geotherm Res*, 182: 57-66

Foster H L, Forbes R B, Ragan D M, 1966. Granulite and peridotite inclusions from Prindle volcano, Yukon-Tanana Upland, Alaska. *U S Geol Surv Prof Pap*, 550-B: 115-119

Henning R A, Rosenthal C H, Olds B, Reading E (eds), 1976. Alaska's volcanoes, northern link in the ring of fire. *Alaska Geog*, 4: 1-88

Hoare J M, Condon W H, Cox A, Dalrymple G B, 1968. Geology, paleomagnetism and potassium-argon ages of basalts [Nunivak Island]. *Geol Soc Amer Mem*, 116: 377-414

Jaggar T A, 1931d. St. Paul Island in the Pribilof Group. *Volcano Lett*, 335: 1-4

Karl S M, Haeussler P J, McCafferty A, 1999. Reconnaissance geologic map of the Duncan Canal-Zarembo Island area, southeastern Alaska. *U S Geol Surv Open-File Rpt*, 99-168

Kosco D G, 1981. The Mt. Edgecumbe volcanic field, Alaska: an example of tholeiitic and calc-alkaline volcanism. *J Geol*, 89: 459-478

Lerbekmo J F, Campbell F A, 1969. Distribution, Composition, and Source of the White River Ash, Yukon Territory. *Can J Earth Sci*, 6: 109-116

Lerbekmo J F, Westgate J A, Smith D G W, Denton G H, 1975. New data on the character and history of the White River volcanic eruption, Alaska. *In*: Suggate R P and Cresswell M M (eds) *Quaternary Studies*, Wellington: Roy Soc New Zeal, p 203-209

McGimsey R G, Neal C A, Girina O, 2004. 1999 volcanic activity in Alaska and Kamchatka: summary of events and response of the Alaska Volcano Observatory. *U S Geol Surv Open-File Rpt*, 2004-1033: 1-45

McGimsey R G, Richter D H, DuBois G D, Miller T P, 1992. A postulated new source for the White River Ash, Alaska. *U S Geol Surv Bull*, 1999: 212-218

Mendenhall W C, 1903. The Wrangell Mountains, Alaska. *Natl Geog*, 14: 395-407

Mendenhall W C, 1905. Geology of the central Copper River region, Alaska. *U S Geol Surv Prof Pap*, 41: 54-62

Mertie J B, 1931. A geologic reconnaissance of the Dennison Fork District, Alaska. *U S Geol Surv Bull*, 827: 39-40

Miller T P, McGimsey R G, Richter D H, Riehle J R, Nye C J, Yount M E, Dumoulin J A, 1998. Catalogue of the historically active volcanoes of Alaska. *U S Geol Surv Open-File Rpt*, 98-582: 1-104 ***(regional reference)***

Moffit F H, 1905. The Fairhaven gold placers, Seward, Alaska. *U S Geol Surv Bull*, 247: 34

Neal C A, McGimsey R G, Girina O, 2005. 2002 volcanic activity in Alaska and Kamchatka: summary of events and response of the Alaska Volcano Observatory. *U S Geol Surv, Open-File Rpt*, 2004-1058: 1-51

Richter D H, Moll-Stalcup E J, Miller T P, Lanphere M A, Dalrymple G B, Smith R L, 1994. Eruptive history and petrology of Mount Drum volcano, Wrangell Mountains, Alaska. *Bull Volc*, 56: 29-46

Richter D H, Preece S J, McGimsey R G, Westgate J A, 1995. Mount Churchill, Alaska: source of the late Holocene White River Ash. *Can J Earth Sci*, 32: 741-748

Richter D H, Rosenkrans D S, Steigerwald M J, 1995. Guide to the volcanoes of the western Wrangell Mountains, Alaska-Wrangell-St. Elias National Park and Preserve. *U S Geol Surv Bull*, 2072: 1-31

Riehle J R, 1996. The Mount Edgecumbe volcanic field: a geologic history. *U S Dept Agriculture*, 42 p

Riehle J R, Brew D A, 1984. Explosive Holocene activity of the Mount Edgecumbe volcanic field, Alaska. *U S Geol Surv Circ*, 939: 111-115

Riehle J R, Brew D A, Lanphere M A, 1989. Geologic map of the Mount Edgecumbe volcanic field, Kruzof Island, southeastern Alaska. *U S Geol Surv Map*, I-1983

Riehle J R, Champion D E, Brew D A, Lanphere M A, 1992. Pyroclastic deposits of the Mount Edgecumbe volcanic field, southeast Alaska: eruptions of a stratified magma chamber. *J Volc Geotherm Res*, 53: 117-143

Riehle J R, Mann D H, Peteet D M, Engstrom D R, Brew D A, Meyer C E, 1992. The Mount Edgecumbe tephra deposits, a marker horizon in southeastern Alaska near the Pleistocene-Holocene boundary. *Quat Res*, 37: 183-202

Robinson S D, 2001. Extending the Late Holocene White River Ash distribution, northwestern Canada. *Arctic*, 54: 157-161

Rossman D L, 1959. Geology and ore deposits of northwestern Chichagof Island, Alaska. *U.S. Geol Surv Bull*, 1058-E: 139-216

Smith R L, Shaw H R, 1975. Igneous-related geothermal systems. *U S Geol Surv Circ*, 726: 58-83

Smith R L, Shaw H R, Luedke R G, Russell S L, 1978. Comprehensive tables giving physical data and thermal energy estimates for young igneous systems of the United States. *U S Geol Surv Open-File Rpt*, 78-925: 1-25

Wanek A A, Callahan J E, 1971. Geologic reconnaissance of a proposed powersite at Lake Grace, Revillagigedo Island southeastern Alaska. *U S Geol Surv Bull*, 1211-E: 1-24

Waythomas C F, Wallace K L, 2002. Flank collapse at Mount Wrangell, Alaska, recorded by volcanic mass-flow deposits in the Copper River lowland. *Can J Earth Sci*, 39: 1257-1279

Winer G S, Feeley T C, Cosca M A, 2004. Basaltic volcanism in the Bering Sea: geochronology and volcanic evolution of St. Paul Island, Pribilof Islands, Alaska. *J Volc Geotherm Res*, 134: 277-301

Winkler G R, 2000. A geologic guide to Wrangell-Saint Elias National Park and Preserve, Alaska. *U S Geol Surv Prof Pap*, 1616: 1-166

Wood C A, Kienle J (eds), 1990. *Volcanoes of North America*. Cambridge, England: Cambridge Univ Press, 354 p ***(regional reference)***

CANADA (1200)

Aitken J D, 1959. Atlin map-area, British Columbia. *Geol Surv Can Mem*, 307: 1-89

Allen C C, Jercinovic M J, Allen J S B, 1982. Subglacial volcanism in north-central British Columbia and Iceland. *J Geol*, 90: 699-715

Aumento F, Souther J G, 1973. Fission track dating of Late Tertiary and Quaternary volcanic glass from the Mount Edziza volcano, British Columbia. *Can J Earth Sci*, 10: 1156-1163

Baer A J, 1973. Bella Coola-Laredo Sound map areas, British Columbia. *Geol Surv Can Mem*, 372: 1-122

Bevier M L, 1983. Regional stratigraphy and age of Chilcotin Group basalts, south-central British Columbia. *Can J Earth Sci*, 20: 515-524

Blake W, 1985. Geological Survey of Canada radiocarbon dates XXV. *Geol Surv Can Pap*, 85: 19

Bostock H S, 1936. Carmacks District, Yukon. *Geol Surv Can Mem*, 189: 1-67

Bostock H S, 1952. Geology of Northwest Shakwak Valley, Yukon Territory. *Geol Surv Can Mem 54*, 267

Brooks G R, Friele P A, 1992. Bracketing ages for the formation of the Ring Creek lava flow, Mount Garibaldi volcanic field, southwestern British Columbia. *Can J Earth Sci*, 29: 2425-2428

Campbell R B, 1961. Quesnel Lake, west half, British Columbia. *Geol Surv Can Map*, 3-1961

Campbell R B, 1963. Quesnel Lake, east half, British Columbia. *Geol Surv Can Map*, 1-1963

Campbell R B, 1967. Canoe River, west half, British Columbia. *Geol Surv Can Map*, 15-1967

Campbell R B, Tipper H W, 1971. Geology of Bonaparte Lake map-area, British Columbia. *Geol Surv Can Mem*, 363: 1-100

Casey J J, Scarfe C M, 1978. Geology of the Heart Peaks volcanic centre, northwestern British Columbia. *Geol Surv Can Pap*, 78-1A: 87-89

Charland A, Francis D, Ludden J, 1993. Stratigraphy and geochemistry of the Itcha Volcanic Complex, central British Columbia. *Can J Earth Sci*, 30: 132-144

Church B N, McAdam K A, 1983. Geothermal potential map of British Columbia. *Brit Columbia Ministry Energy Mines Petrol Resour*, 1:2,000,000 scale

Clague J J, 1981. Late Quaternary geology and geochronology of British Columbia. Part 2: Summary and discussion of radiocarbon-dated Quaternary history. *Geol Surv Can Pap*, 80-35: 1-41

Clague J J, Evans S G, Rampton V N, Woodsworth G J, 1995. Improved age estimates for the White River and Bridge River tephras, western Canada. *Can J Earth Sci*, 32: 1172-1179

Davis N F G, 1930. Clearwater Lake area, British Columbia. *Geol Surv Can Summary Rpt*, Part A: 274-293

Dolmage V, 1921. Coast and islands of British Columbia between Burke and Douglas Channels. *Geol Surv Can Summary Rpt*, no 29

Dolmage V, 1924. Post-Pleistocene volcanics of the British Columbia coast. *J Geol*, 32: 36-48

Dolmage V, 1928. Gun Creek map-area, British Columbia. *Geol Surv Can Summary Rpt*, Part A: 78-93

Edwards B R, Edwards G, Russell J K, 1995. Revised stratigraphy for the Hoodoo Mountain volcanic centre, northwestern British Columbia. *Geol Surv Can, Current Res. 1995-A*: 105-115

Edwards B R, Hamilton T S, Nicholls J, Stout M Z, Russell J K, Simpson K, 1996. Late Tertiary to Quaternary volcanism in the Atlin area, northwestern British Columbia. *Geol Surv Can, Current Res 1996-A*: 29-36

Edwards B R, Russell J K, 1994. Preliminary stratigraphy of Hoodoo Mountain volcanic centre, northwestern British Columbia. *Geol Surv Can Pap*, 94-1A: 69-76

Edwards B R, Russell J K, 2000. Distribution, nature, and origin of Neogene-Quaternary magmatism in the northern Cordilleran volcanic province, Canada. *Geol Soc Amer Bull*, 112: 1280-1295

Edwards B R, Russell J K, Anderson R G, 2002. Subglacial, phonolitic volcanism at Hoodoo Mountain volcano, northern Canadian Cordillera. *Bull Volc*, 64: 254-272

Edwards B R, Russell J K, Anderson R G, Harder M, 2003. Overview of Neogene to Recent volcanism in the Atlin volcanic district, Northern Cordilleran province, northwestern British Columbia. *Geol Surv Canada, Current Res*, 2003-A8: 1-6

Eiche G E, Francis D M, Ludden J N, 1987. Primary alkaline magmas associated with the Quaternary Alligator Lake volcanic complex, Yukon Territory, Canada. *Contr Mineral Petr*, 95: 191-201

Elliott R L, Koch R D, Robinson S W, 1981. Age of basalt flows in the Blue River valley, Bradfield Canal quadrangle. *U S Geol Surv Circ*, 823-B: 115-116

Francis D, Ludden J, 1990. The mantle source for olivine nephelinite, basanite, and alkaline olivine basalt at Fort Selkirk, Yukon, Canada. *J Petr*, 31: 371-400

Fulton F J, 1971. Radiocarbon geochronology of southern British Columbia. *Geol Surv Can Pap*, 71-37: 1-28

Gabrielse H, 1962. Cry Lake, British Columbia. *Geol Surv Can Map*, 29-1962

Gabrielse H, 1969. Geology of Jenning River map-area. *Geol Surv Can Pap*, 68-55: 1-37

Gabrielse H, Souther J G, 1962. Dease Lake, British Columbia. *Geol Surv Can Map*, 21-1962

Green N L, 1981. Geology and petrology of Quaternary volcanic rocks, Garibaldi Lake area, southwestern British Columbia summary. *Geol Soc Amer Bull*, 92: 697-702

Green N L, 1990. Late Cenozoic volcanism in the Mount Garibaldi and Garibaldi Lake volcanic fields, Garibaldi volcanic belt, southwestern British Columbia. *Geosci Can*, 17: 171-174

Green N L, Armstrong R L, Harakal J E, Souther J G, Read P B, 1988. Eruptive history and K-Ar geochronology of the late Cenozoic Garibaldi volcanic belt, southwestern British Columbia. *Geol Soc Amer Bull*, 100: 563-579

Grove E W, 1976. Deglaciation a possible triggering mechanism for recent volcanism. *In*: Gonzalez-Ferran O (ed) *Proc Symp Andean & Antarctic Volcanology Problems (Santiago, Chile, Sept 1974)*, Rome: IAVCEI, p 88-97

Hamilton T S, Scarfe C M, 1977. Preliminary report on the petrology of the Level Mountain Volcanic Centre, northwest British Columbia. *Geol Surv Can Pap*, 77-1A: 429-433

Harder M, Russell J K, 2007. Basanite glaciovolcanism at Llangorse Mountain, northern British Columbia, Canada. *Bull Volc*, 69: 329-340

Hauksdottir S, Enegren E G, Russell J K, 1994. Recent basaltic volcanism in the Iskut-Unuk rivers area, northwestern British Columbia. *Geol Surv Can Pap*, 94-1A: 57-67

Hickson C J, 1986. Quaternary volcanism in the Wells Grey-Clearwater area, east central British Columbia. *Unpublished PhD thesis*, Univ British Columbia, 357 p

Hickson C J, Edwards B R, 2001. Volcanoes and Volcanic Hazards in Canada. *In*; Brooks G R (ed) *A Synthesis of Geological Hazards in Canada*, Geol Surv Can Bull, 548: 1-248

Hickson C J, Russell J K, Stasiuk M V, 1999. Volcanology of the 2350 B.P. eruption of Mount Meager volcanic complex, British Columbia, Canada: implications for hazards form eruptions in topographically complex terrain. *Bull Volc*, 60: 489-507

Hickson C J, Soos A, Wright R, 1994. Catalogue of Canadian volcanoes. *Geol Surv Canada Open-File Rpt* ***(regional reference)***

Hickson C J, Souther J G, 1984. Late Cenozoic volcanic rocks of the Clearwater-Wells Gray area, British Columbia. *Can J Earth Sci*, 21: 267-277

Higgins M D, 2009. The Cascadia megathrust earthquake of 1700 may have rejuvenated an isolated basalt volcano in western Canada: age and petrographic evidence. *J Volc Geotherm Res*, 179: 149-156

Hildreth W E, 2007. Quaternary magmatism in the Cascades-geologic perpectives. *U S Geol Surv Prof Pap*, 1744: 1-125

Holland S S, 1976. Landforms of British Columbia, a physiographic outline. *Brit Columbia Dept Mines Petrol Resour Bull*, 48: 1-138 (2nd printing)

Jackson L E, 1989. Pleistocene subglacial volcanism near Fort Selkirk, Yukon Territory. *Geol Surv Can Pap*, 89-1E: 251-256

Jackson L E, Stevens W, 1992. A recent eruptive history of Volcano Mountain, Yukon Territory. *Geol Surv Can Pap*, 92-1A: 33-39

Kerr F A, 1948. Lower Stikine and western Iskut River areas, British Columbia. *Geol Surv Can Mem*, 246: 1-94

Lawrence R B, Armstrong R L, Berman R G, 1984. Garibaldi Group volcanic rocks of the Salal Creek area, southwestern British Columbia: alkaline lavasw on the fringe of the predominately calc-alkaline Garibaldi (Cascade) volcanic arc. *J Volc Geotherm Res*, 21: 255-276

Lewis T J, Souther J G, 1978. Meager Mountain, B.C.- A possible geothermal energy resource. *Energy Mines Resour Can, Geotherm Ser*, 9: 1-17

Lord C S, 1948. McConnell Creek map area, Cassiar District, British Columbia. *Geol Surv Can Mem*, 251: 1-72

Mathews W H, 1958. Geology of the Mt. Garibaldi map-area, S.W. British Columbia. *Geol Soc Amer Bull*, 69: 186

Mathews W H, 1988. Neogene geology of the Okanagan Highland, British Columbia. *Can J Earth Sci*, 25: 725-731

Mathews W H, 1989. Neogene Chilcotin basalts in south-central British Columbia: geology, ages, and geomorphic history. *Can J Earth Sci*, 26: 969-982

Metcalf P, 1987. Petrogenesis of Quaternary alkaline lavas in Wells Gray Provincial Park, B.C. and constraints on the petrology of the subcordilleran mantle. *Unpublished PhD thesis*, Univ Alberta, 395 p

Michol K A, Russel J K, Andrews G D M, 2008. Welded block and ash flow deposits from Mount Meager, British Columbia, Canada. *J Volc Geotherm Res*, 169: 121-144

Muller J E, 1967. Kluane Lake map-area, Yukon Territory (115G, 115F, E 1/ 2). *Geol Surv Can Mem*, 340: 1-137

Nasmith H, Mathews W H, Rouse G E, 1967. Bridge River ash and some other Recent ash beds in British Columbia. *Can J Earth Sci*, 4: 163-170

Read P B, 1977. Meager Creek volcanic complex, southwestern British Columbia. *Geol Surv Can Pap*, 77-1A: 277-285

Read P B, 1978. Meager Creek geothermal area. *Geol Surv Can, Open-File 603*, 1:20,000 geol map and text

Read P B, 1990. Mount Meager complex, Garibaldi belt, southwestern British Columbia. *Geosci Can*, 17: 167-170

Read P B, Brown R L, Psutka J F, Moore J M, Journeay M, Lane L S, Orchard M J, 1989. Geology of parts of Snippaker Creek (104B/10), Forrest Kerr Creek (104B/15), Bob Quinn Lake (104B/16), Iskut River (104G/1) and More Creek (104G/2). *Geol Surv Can Open File*, no 2094, map and text, 2 sheets

Simpson K, Edwards B, Wetherell K, 2006. Documentation of a Holocene volcanic cone in the Tuya-Teslin volcanic field, northern British Columbia. *Geol Surv Canada, Current Res*, 2006-A1: 1-7

Souther J G, 1966. Cordilleran volcanic study. *Geol Surv Can Pap*, 66-1: 87-89

Souther J G, 1967. Cordilleran volcanic project. *Geol Surv Can Pap*, 68-1A: 42-43

Souther J G, 1970. Volcanism and its relationship to recent crustal movements in the Canadian Cordillera. *Can J Earth Sci*, 7: 553-568

Souther J G, 1971. Geology and mineral deposits of Tulsequah map-area, British Columbia. *Geol Surv Can Mem*, 362: 1-64

Souther J G, 1972. Telegraph Creek map-area British Columbia. *Geol Surv Can Pap*, 71-44: 1-38

Souther J G, 1973. Cordilleran volcanic project Spectrum Range. *Geol Surv Can Pap*, 73-1: 46-48

Souther J G, 1976. Geothermal potential of western Canada. *In*: *Proc 2nd United Nations Symp Devel Use Geotherm Resour, San Francisco*, Washington D C: U S Government Printing Office, 1: 259-267

Souther J G, 1977a. Volcanism and tectonic environments in the Canadian Cordillera, a second look. *Geol Assoc Can Spec Pap*, 16: 3-24

Souther J G, 1977b. Volcano fly-by. *Geol Assoc Can 1977 Ann Mtg, Vancouver, Fieldtrip Guidebook 16*, 15 p

Souther J G, 1980. Geothermal reconnaissance in the central Garibaldi belt, British Columbia. *Geol Surv Can Pap*, 80-1A: 1-11

Souther J G, 1992. The late Cenozoic Mount Edziza volcanic complex, British Columbia. *Geol Surv Can Mem*, 420: 1-320

Souther J G, Clague J J, Mathewes R W, 1987. Nazko cone: a Quaternary volcano in the eastern Anahim belt. *Can J Earth Sci*, 24: 2477-2485

Souther J G, Lambert M B, 1972. Volcanic rocks of the northern Canadian Cordillera. *24th Internatl Geol Cong, Montreal, Guidebook*, Sec 2: 1-54

Souther J G, Symons D T A, 1974. Stratigraphy and paleomagnetism of Mount Edziza volcanic complex, northwestern British Columbia. *Geol Surv Can Pap*, 73-32: 1-48

Souther J G, Weiland I, 1993. Crow Lagoon tephra-new evidence of recent volcanism in west-central British Columbia. *Geol Surv Can Pap*, 93-1A: 57-62

Stasiuk M V, Russell J K, 1990. Quaternary volcanic rocks of the Iskut River region, northwestern British Columbia. *Geol Surv Can Pap*, 90-1E: 153-157

Stasiuk M V, Russell J K, Hickson C J, 1994. Influence of magma chemistry on eruption behavior from the distribution and nature of the 2400 B.P. eruption products of Mount Meager, British Columbia. *Geol Surv Can Open-File*, 2843: 1-38 and 1:50,000 geol map

Sutherland-Brown A, 1969. Aiyansh lava flow, British Columbia. *Can J Earth Sci*, 6: 1460-1468

Tipper H W, 1959. Quesnel Cariboo District, British Columbia. *Geol Surv Can Map*, 12-1959

Tipper H W, 1969. Anahim Lake area, British Columbia. *Geol Surv Can Map*, 1202A

Tipper H W, 1971. Glacial geomorphology and Pleistocene history of central British Columbia. *Geol Surv Can Bull*, 196: 1-89

Westgate J A, 1977. Identification and significance of late Holocene tephra from Otter Creek, southern British Columbia, and localities in west-central Alberta. *Can J Earth Sci*, 14: 2593-2600

Wetherell K, Edwards B, Simpson K, 2005. Preliminary results of field mapping, petrography, and GIS spatial analysis of the West Tuyu lava field, northwestern British Columbia. *Geol Surv Canada, Current Res*, 2005-A2: 1-10

Wheeler J O, 1961. Whitehorse map-area, Yukon Territory, 105D. *Geol Suv Can Mem*, 312: 1-156

Wood C A, Kienle J (eds), 1990. *Volcanoes of North America*. Cambridge, England: Cambridge Univ Press, 354 p ***(regional reference)***

Wright F E, 1906. Unuk River mining region. *Ann Rpt Ministry Mines, Brit Columbia (1905)*, p 68-74

Wuorinen V, 1978. Age of Aiyansh volcano, British Columbia. *Can J Earth Sci*, 15: 1037-1038

USA: PACIFIC NW (1201-02)

Anderson S W, Fink J H, Rose W I, 1995. Mount St. Helens and Santiaguito lava domes; the effect of short-term eruption rate on surface texture and degassing processes. *J Volc Geotherm Res*, 69: 105-116

Bacon C R, 1983. Eruptive history of Mount Mazama and Crater Lake caldera, Cascade Range, U S A. *J Volc Geotherm Res*, 18: 57-116

Bacon C R, 2008. Geologic map of Mount Mazama and Crater Lake caldera, Oregon. *U S Geol Surv Sci Invest Map*, I-2832, 1:24,000 scale, 4 sheets and 45 p text

Bacon C R, Druitt T H, 1988. Compositional evolution of the zoned calcalkaline magma chamber of Mount Mazama, Crater Lake, Oregon. *Contr Mineral Petr*, 98: 224-256

Bacon C R, Lanphere M A, 2006. Eruptive history and geochronology of Mount Mazama and the Crater Lake region, Oregon. *Geol Soc Amer Bull*, 118: 1331-1359

Barnett B, Korosec M A, 1986. Geothermal exploratory drilling by the State of Washington in 1985. *Wash Geol Newsl*, 14: 21-28

Beget J E, 1981. Early Holocene glacier advance in the north Cascade Range, Washington. *Geology*, 9: 409-413

Beget J E, 1982. Recent volcanic activity at Glacier Peak. *Science*, 215: 1389-1390

Beget J E, 1983. Glacier Peak, Washington: a potentially hazardous Cascade volcano. *Environ Geol*, 5: 83-92

Belousov A, Voight B, Belousov M, 2007. Directed blasts and blast-generated pyroclastic density currents: a comparison of the Bezymianny 1956, Mount St Helens 1980, and Soufriere Hills, Montserrat 1997 eruptions and deposits. *Bull Volc*, 69: 701-740

Benedict E, 2000. Diamond Craters, Oregon's geologic gem. *U S Bur Land Management* brochure BLM/OR/WA/GI-00/027-1122.32

Benson G T, 1965. The age of Clear Lake, Oregon. *Ore Bin*, 27: 1-4

Blinman E, Mehringer P J, Shephard J C, 1979. Pollen influx and the depositon of Mazama and Glacier Peak tephra. *In*: Sheets P D and Grayson D K (eds) *Volcanic Activity and Human Ecology*, New York: Academic Press, p 393-425

Brophy J G, Dreher S T, 2000. The origin of composition gaps at South Sister volcano, central Oregon: implications for fractional crystallization processes beneath active calc-alkaline volcanoes. *J Volc Geotherm Res*, 102: 287-307

Byman J, Vallance J W, 2001. An early Holocene eruptive period at Mount Rainier, Washington. *Eos, Trans Amer Geophys Union*, 82(47): abs V42C-1042

Calder E S, Sparks R S J, Woods A W, 1997. Dynamics of co-ignimbrite plumes generated from pyroclastic flows of Mount St. Helens (7 August 1980). *Bull Volc*, 58: 432-440

Cameron K A, Pringle P, 1986. Post-glacial lahars of the Sandy River basin, Mount Hood, Oregon. *Northwest Sci*, 60: 255-237

Cameron K A, Pringle P T, 1987. A detailed chronology of the most recent major eruptive period at Mount Hood, Oregon. *Geol Soc Amer Bull*, 99: 845-851

Cameron K A, Pringle P T, 1991. Prehistoric buried forests of Mount Hood. *Oregon Geol*, 53: 34-43

Carey S, Gardner J, Sigurdsson H, 1995. The intensity and magnitude of Holocene plinian eruptions from Mount St. Helens volcano. *J Volc Geotherm Res*, 66: 185-202

Castro J, Cashman K, Joslin N, Olmsted B, 2002. Structural origin of large gas cavities in the Big Obsidian Flow, Newberry volcano. *J Volc Geotherm Res*, 114: 313-330

Champion D E, 1983. Paleomagnetic "dating" of Holocene volcanic activity at Mount Mazama, Crater Lake, Oregon (abs). *Geol Soc Amer Abs Prog*, 15: 331

Chitwood L A, 1994. Inflated basaltic lava-examples of processes and landforms from central and southeast Oregon. *Oregon Geol*, 56: 11-21

Chitwood L A, Jensen R A, Groh E A, 1977. The age of Lava Butte. *Ore Bin*, 39: 157-164

Christiansen R L, 1980. Eruption of Mt. St. Helens: volcanology. *Nature*, 285: 531-533

Ciesiel R F, Wagner N S, 1969. Lava-tube caves in the Saddle Butte area of Malheur County, Oregon. *Ore Bin*, 31: 153-171

Coombs H A, 1939. Mount Baker, a Cascade volcano. *Geol Soc Amer Bull*, 50: 1493-1510

Coombs H A, Howard A D, 1960. United States of America. *Catalog of Active Volcanoes of the World and Solfatara Fields*, Rome: IAVCEI, 9: 1-68 ***(regional reference)***

Crandell D R, 1969. The geologic story of Mount Rainier. *U S Geol Surv Bull*, 1292: 1-43

Crandell D R, 1971. Postglacial lahars from Mount Rainier volcano, Washington. *U S Geol Surv Prof Pap*, 677: 1-75

Crandell D R, 1980. Recent eruptive history of Mount Hood, Oregon, and potential hazards from future eruptions. *U S Geol Surv Bull*, 1492: 1-81

Crandell D R, 1987. Deposits of pre-1980 pyroclastic flows and lahars from Mount St. Helens volcano, Washington. *U S Geol Surv Prof Pap*, 1444: 1-93

Crandell D R, Mullineaux D R, 1973. Pine Creek volcanic assemblage at Mount St. Helens, Washington. *U S Geol Surv Bull*, 1383-A: 1-23

Crandell D R, Mullineaux D R, 1978. Potential hazards from future eruptions of Mount St. Helens volcano, Washington. *U S Geol Surv Bull*, 1383-C: 1-26

Crandell D R, Mullineaux D R, Miller C D, 1979. Volcanic-hazards studies in the Cascade Range of the western United States. *In*: Sheets P D and Grayson D K (eds) *Volcanic Activity and Human Ecology*, New York: Academic Press, p 195-219

Crandell D R, Mullineaux D R, Rubin M, 1975. Mount St. Helens volcano: recent and future behavior. *Science*, 187: 438-441

Cribb J W, Barton M, 1997. Significance of crustal and source region processes on the evolution of compositionally similar calc-alkaline lavas, Mt. Hood, Oregon. *J Volc Geotherm Res*, 76: 229-249

Criswell C W, 1987. Chronology and pyroclastic stratigraphy of the May 18, 1980, eruption of Mount St. Helens, Washington. *J Geophys Res*, 92: 10,237-10,266

Evarts R C, Ashley R P, Smith J G, 1987. Geology of the Mount St. Helens area: record of discontinuous volcanic and plutonic activity in the Cascade Arc of southern Washington. *J Geophys Res*, 92: 10,155-10,169

Fisher R V, Glicken H X, Hoblitt R P, 1987. May 18, 1980, Mount St. Helens deposits in South Coldwater Creek, Washington. *J Geophys Res*, 92: 10,267-10,283

Fiske R S, Hopson C A, Waters A C, 1963. Geology of Mount Rainier National Park, Washington. *U S Geol Surv Prof Pap*, 444: 1-93

Folsom M M, 1970. Volcanic eruptions: the pioneers' attitude on the Pacific Coast from 1800 to 1875. *Ore Bin*, 32: 61-80

Frank D, 1983. Origin, distribution, and rapid removal of hydrothermally formed clay at Mount Baker, Washington. *U S Geol Surv Prof Pap*, 1022-E: 1-31

Frank D, 1995. Surficial extent and conceptual model of hydrothermal system at Mount Rainier, Washington. *J Volc Geotherm Res*, 65: 51-80

Friedman I, 1971. Obsidian hydration dates in the Newberry volcano area, Oregon. *U S Geol Surv Prof Pap*, 750-A: A-117

Friedman I, 1977. Hydration dating of volcanism at Newberry Crater Oregon. *U S Geol Surv J Res*, 5: 337-342

Friedman I, Obradovich J, 1981. Obsidian hydration dating of volcanic events. *Quat Res*, 16: 37-47

Friedman I, Peterson N, 1971. Obsidian hydration dating applied to dating of basaltic volcanic activity. *Science*, 172: 1028

Gallino G L, Pierson T C, 1985. Polallie Creek debris flow and subsequent dam-break flood of 1980, East Fork Hood River Basin, Oregon. *U S Geol Surv Water-Supply Pap*, 2273: 1-22

Gardner C A, Scott K M, Miller C D, Myers B, Hildreth W, Pringle P T, 1995. Potential volcanic hazards from future activity of Mount Baker, Washington. *U S Geol Surv Open-File Rpt*, 95-498: 1-16

Gardner J E, Carey S, Sigurdsson H, 1998. Plinian eruptions at Glacier Peak and Newberry volcanoes, United States: implications for volcanic hazards in the Cascade Range. *Geol Soc Amer Bull*, 110: 173-187

Greeley R, Hyde J H, 1972. Lava tubes of the Cave basalt, Mount St. Helens, Washington. *Geol Soc Amer Bull*, 83: 2397-2418

Greene R C, 1968. Petrography and petrology of volcanic rocks in the Mount Jefferson area, High Cascade Range, Oregon. *U S Geol Surv Bull*, 1251-G: 1-48

Hammond P E, 1984. Indian Heaven, S. Washington Cascade Range a basaltic volcanic field supplied by a central magma system? (abs). *Geol Soc Amer Abs Prog*, 16: 528

Hammond P E, Anderson J L, Manning K J, 1980. Guide to the geology of the Upper Clackamas and North Santiam Rivers area, northern Oregon Cascade Range. *Oregon Dept Geol Min Ind Bull*, 101: 133-167

Hammond P E, Pedersen S A, Hopkins K D, Aiken D, Harle D S, Danes Z F, Konicek D L, Stricklin C R, 1976. Geology and gravimetry of the Quaternary basaltic volcanic field, southern Cascade Range, Washington. *In: Proc 2nd United Nations Symp Devel Use Geotherm Resour, San Francisco*, Washington D C: U S Government Printing Office, 1: 397-405

Harris S L, 1976. *Fire and Ice, the Cascade Volcanoes*. Seattle: The Mountaineers, 320 p ***(regional reference)***

Harris S L, 1983. In the shadow of the mountains. *Pacific Northwest*, 17: 24-33

Harris S L, 1988. *Fire Mountains of the West: the Cascade and Mono Lake Volcanoes*. Missoula, MT: Mountain Press, 379 p ***(regional reference)***

Hart W K, Mertzman S A, 1983. Late Cenozoic stratigraphy of the Jordan Valley area, southeastern Oregon. *Oregon Geol*, 45: 15-19

Heiken G H, Fisher R V, Peterson N V, 1981. A field trip to the maar volcanoes of the Fort Rock - Christmas Lake valley basin, Oregon. *In*: Johnston D A, Donnelly-Nolan J (eds) *Guides to some volcanic terranes in Washington, Idaho, Oregon, and northern California*, U S Geol Surv Circ 838: 119-140

Higgins M W, 1969. Airfall ash and pumice lapilli deposits from Central Pumice Cone, Newberry Caldera, Oregon. *U S Geol Surv Prof Pap*, 650-D: 26-32

Higgins M W, 1973. Petrology of Newberry volcano, central Oregon. *Geol Soc Amer Bull*, 84: 455-488

Hildreth W E, 2007. Quaternary magmatism in the Cascades-geologic perpectives. *U S Geol Surv Prof Pap*, 1744: 1-125

Hildreth W E, Fierstein J, Lanphere M, 2003. Eruptive history and chronology of the Mount Baker volcanic field, Washington. *Geol Soc Amer Bull*, 115: 729-764

Hildreth W, Fierstein J, 1997. Recent eruptions of Mount Adams, Washington Cascades, USA. *Bull Volc*, 58: 472-490

Hildreth W, Lanphere M A, 1994. Potassium-argon geochronology of a basalt-andesite-dacite arc system: the Mount Adams volcanic field, Cascade Range of southern Washington. *Geol Soc Amer Bull*, 106: 1413-1429

Hildreth W, Lanphere M A, Champion D E, Fierstein J, 2004. Rhyodacites of Kulshan caldera, North Cascades of Washington: postcaldera lavas that span the Jaramillo. *J Volc Geotherm Res*, 130: 227-264

Hoblitt R P, Crandell D R, Mullineaux D R, 1980. Mount St. Helens eruptive behavior during the past 1500 years. *Geology*, 8: 555-559

Holmes K L, 1955. Mount St. Helens' recent eruptions. *Ore Hist Quart*, 56: 197-210

Hopkins K D, 1976. Geology of the south and east slopes of Mount Adams volcano, Cascade Range, Washington. *Unpublished PhD thesis*, Univ Washington, 143 p

Hopson C A, Melson W G, 1990. Compositional trends and eruptive cycles at Mount St. Helens. *Geosci Can*, 17: 131-141

Hopson C A, Waters A C, Bender V R, Rubin M, 1962. The latest eruptions from Mount Rainier volcano. *J Geol*, 70: 635-647

Hyde J H, Crandell D R, 1978. Postglacial volcanic deposits at Mount Baker, Washington, and potential hazards from future eruptions. *U S Geol Surv Prof Pap*, 1022-C: 1-17

Jensen R A, 1995. *Roadside Guide to the Geology of Newberry volcano*. Bend, Oregon: The Press Pro's, 155 p

Jillson W R, 1917. The volcanic activity of Mount St. Helens and Mt. Hood in historical times. *Geol Rev*, 3: 481-485

John D A, Sisson T W, Breit G N, Rye R O, Vallance J W, 2008. Characteristics, extent and origin of hydrothermal alteration at Mount Rainier Volcano, Cascades Arc, USA: implications for debris-flow hazards and mineral deposits. *J Volc Geotherm Res*, 175: 289-314

Kamata H, Suzuk-Kamata K, Bacon C R, 1993. Deformation of the Wineglass Welded Tuff and the timing of caldera collapse at Crater Lake, Oregon. *J Volc Geotherm Res*, 56: 253-266

Kashman K V, Cronin S J, 2008. Welcoming a monster to the world: myths, oral tradition, and modern societal response to volcanic disasters. *J Volc Geotherm Res*, 176: 407-418

Korosec M A, 1987. Geologic map of Mount Adams. *Wash Div Geol Earth Sci*, 1:100,000 geol map

Kuehn S C, Foit F F Jr, 2006. Correlation of widespread Holocene and Pleistocene tephra layers from Newberry volcano, Oregon, USA, using glass compositions and numerical analysis. *Quat Internatl*, 148: 113-137

Kuehn S C, Froese D G, Carrara P E, Foit Jr F F, Pearce N J G, Rotheisler P, 2009. Major- and trace-element characterization, expanded distributions, and a new chronology for the latest Pleistocene Glacier Peak tephras in western North America. *Quat Res*, 71: 201-216

Lipman P W, Mullineaux D R (eds), 1981. The 1980 eruptions of Mount St. Helens, Washington. *U S Geol Surv Prof Pap*, 1250: 1-844

Luedke R G, Smith R L, 1982. Map showing distribution, composition, and age of late Cenozoic volcanic centers in Oregon and Washington. *U S Geol Surv Map*, I-1091-D

MacLeod N S, Sherrod D R, 1988. Geologic evidence for a magma chamber beneath Newberry volcano, Oregon. *J Geophys Res*, 93: 10,067-10,079

MacLeod N S, Sherrod D R, Chitwood L A, 1982. Geologic map of Newberry volcano, Deschutes, Klamath, and Lake Counties, Oregon. *U S Geol Surv Open-File Rpt*, 82-847: map and 27 p text

MacLeod N S, Sherrod D R, Chitwood L A, McKee E H, 1981. Newberry volcano, Oregon. *U S Geol Surv Circ*, 838: 85-91

Mack R N, Okazaki R, Valastro S, 1979. Bracketing dates for two ash falls from Mount Mazama. *Nature*, 279: 228-229

Majors H M, 1980. Three newly discovered accounts of activity on Mount St. Helens. *Northwest Discovery*, 1: 36-41

Majors H M (ed), 1978. *Mount Baker: a Chronicle of its Historic Eruptions and First Ascent.* Seattle: Northwest Press, 221 p

Majors H M, McCollum R C, 1981a. Mount Rainier: the tephra eruption of 1894. *Northwest Discovery*, 2: 334-381

Majors H M, McCollum R C, 1981b. Mount St. Helens the 1844-1857 eruptions. *Northwest Discovery*, 2: 541-550

Mehringer P J, Blinmae E, Petersen K L, 1977. Pollen influx and volcanic ash. *Science*, 198: 257-261

Moxham R M, Crandell D R, Marlatt W E, 1965. Thermal features at Mount Rainier, Washington, as revealed by infrared surveys. *U S Geol Surv Prof Pap*, 525-D: 93-100

Mullineaux D R, 1974. Pumice and other pyroclastic deposits in Mount Rainier National Park, Washington. *U S Geol Surv Bull*, 1326: 1-83

Mullineaux D R, 1986. Summary of pre-1980 tephra-fall deposits erupted from Mount St. Helens, Washington State, USA. *Bull Volc*, 48: 17-27

Mullineaux D R, Hyde J H, Rubin M, 1975. Widespread late glacial and postglacial tephra deposits from Mount St. Helens volcano, Washington. *U S Geol Surv J Res*, 3: 329-336

Mullineaux D R, Sigafoos R S, Hendricks E L, 1969. A historic eruption of Mt. Rainier, Wash. *U S Geol Surv Prof Pap*, 650-B: 15-18

Myers B, 1992. Small explosions interupt 3-year quiescence of Mount St. Helens, Washington. *Earthq Volcanoes*, 23: 58-7

Nelson C H, Bacon C R, Robinson S W, Adam D P, Bradbury J P, Barber J H Jr, Schwartz D, Vagenas G, 1994. The volcanic, sedimentologic, and paleolimnologic history of the Crater Lake caldera floor, Oregon: evidence for small caldera evolution. *Geol Soc Amer Bull*, 106: 684-704

Otto B R, Hutchison D A, 1977. The geology of the Jordan Craters, Malhuer County, Oregon. *Ore Bin*, 39: 125-140

Peterson N V, Groh E A, 1963. Recent volcanic landforms in central Oregon. *Ore Bin*, 25: 1-15

Peterson N V, Groh E A, 1966. Lunar Geological Field Conference guidebook. *Oregon Dept Geol Min Ind*, 51 p

Peterson N V, Groh E A, 1969. The ages of some Holocene volcanic eruptions in the Newberry volcano area, Oregon. *Ore Bin*, 31: 73-87

Peterson N V, Groh E A, Taylor E M, Stensland D E, 1976. Geology and mineral resources of Deschutes County Oregon. *Oregon Dept Geol Min Ind Bull*, 89: 1-62

Priest G R, 1983. A field trip guide to the central Oregon Cascades. *Oregon Geol*, 45: 133-141

Pringle P T, 1993. Roadside geology of Mount St. Helens National Volcanic Monument and vicinity. *Wash Dept Nat Resour, Div Geol Earth Resour Inf Circ*, 88: 1-119

Pringle P T, 2008. Roadside geology of Mount Rainier National Park and vicinity. *Wash State Dept Nat Resour*, Inf Circ 107, 200 p

Reid M E, Sisson T W, Brien D L, 2001. Volcano collapse produced by hydrothermal alteration and edifice shape, Mount Rainier, Washington. *Geology*, 29: 779-782

Rose W I, Wunderman R L, Hoffman M F, Gale L, 1983. A volcanologist's review of atmospheric hazards of volcanic activity; Fuego and Mount St. Helens. *J Volc Geotherm Res*, 17: 133-157

Russell J K, Nicholls J, 1987. Early crystallization history of alkali olivine basalts, Diamond Craters, Oregon. *Geochim Cosmochim Acta*, 51: 143-154

Sarna-Wojcicki A M, Champion D E, Davis J O, 1983. Holocene volcanism in the conterminous United States and the role of silicic volcanic ash layers in correlation of latest Pleistocene and Holocene deposits. *In*: Wright H E (ed) *Late-Quaternary Environments of the United States*, Minneapolis: Univ Minnesota Press, 2: 52-77

Schasse H W, 1987. Geologic map of the Mount Rainier quadrangle, Washington. *Wash Div Geol Earth Resour Open-File Rpt*, 87-16: 43

Schmidt M E, Grunder A L, 2009. The evolution of North Sister: a volcano shaped by extension and ice in the central Oregon Cascade Arc. *Geol Soc Amer Bull*, 121: 643-662

Scott K M, Hildreth W E, Gardner C A, 2000. Mount Baker-living with an active volcano. *U S Geol Surv Fact Sheet*, 059-00: 1-4

Scott W E, 1977. Quaternary glaciation and volcanism, Metolius River area, Oregon. *Geol Soc Amer Bull*, 88: 113-124

Scott W E, 1987. Holocene rhyodacite eruptions on the flanks of South Sister volcano, Oregon. *Geol Soc Amer Spec Pap*, 212: 35-53

Scott W E, Gardner C A, 1990. Field trip guide to the central Oregon High Cascades, Part 1: Mount Bachelor-South Sister area. *Oregon Geol*, 52: 99-140

Scott W E, Gardner C A, 1992. Geologic map of the Mount Bachelor volcanic chain and surrounding area, Cascade Range, Oregon. *U S Geol Surv Misc Invest Ser Map*, I-1967, 1:50,000 geol map

Scott W E, Gardner C A, Sarna-Wojcicki A M, 1989. Guidebook for field trip to the Mount Bachelor-South Sister-Bend area, central Oregon High Cascades. *U S Geol Surv Open-File Rpt*, 89-645: 1-68

Scott W E, Sherrod D R, Gardner C A, 2008. Overview of the 2004 to 2006, and continuing, eruption of Mount St. Helens, Washington. *U S Geol Surv Prof Pap*, 1750: 3-22

Sherrod D, 1991. Geologic map of a part of the Cascade Range between latitutdes 43°-44°, central Oregon. *U S Geol Surv, Misc Invest Ser*, Map I-1891, 1:125,000 scale

Sherrod D R, MacLeod N S, 1979. The last eruptions at Newberry volcano, central Oregon (abs). *Geol Soc Amer Abs Prog*, 11: 127

Sherrod D R, Minor S A, Vercoutere T L, 1989. Geologic map of the Sheepshead Mountains, Harney and Malheur counties, Oregon. *U S Geol Surv Misc Invest Map*, MF-2079, 1:50,000 scale

Sherrod D R, Scott W E, Stauffer P H (eds), 2008. A volcano revisted: the renewed eruption of Mount St. Helens, 2004-2006. *U S Geol Surv Prof Pap*, 1750: 1-856

Sherrod D R, Smith J G, 1990. Quaternary extrusion rates of the Cascade Range, northwestern United States and southern British Columbia. *J Geophys Res*, 95: 19,465-19,474

Sherrod D R, Taylor E M, Ferns M L, Scott W E, Conrey R M, Smith G A, 2004. Geologic map of the Bend 30- x 60-minute quadrangle, central Oregon. *U S Geol Surv Map*, I-2683, 1:100,000 scale and 48 p text

Shevenell L, Goff F, 1995. Evolution of hydrothermal waters at Mount St. Helens, Washington, USA. *J Volc Geotherm Res*, 69: 73-94

Simmons G C, Van Noy R M, Zilka N T, 1983. Mineral resources of the Cougar Lakes-Mount-Aix study area, Yakima and Lewis Counties, Washington. *U S Geol Surv Bull*, 1504: 1-81

Sisson T, 1995. Blast ashfall deposit of May 18, 1980 at Mount St. Helens, Washington. *J Volc Geotherm Res*, 66: 203-216

Sisson T W, Vallance J W, 2009. Frequent eruptions of Mount Rainier over the last ~2,600 years. *Bull Volc*, 71: 595-618

Smith J G, 1988. Geologic map of the Pelican Butte quadrangle, Klamath County, Oregon. *U S Geol Surv Map*, G Q-1653, 1:62,500

Smith R L, Shaw H R, 1975. Igneous-related geothermal systems. *U S Geol Surv Circ*, 726: 58-83

Smith R L, Shaw H R, Luedke R G, Russell S L, 1978. Comprehensive tables giving physical data and thermal energy estimates for young igneous systems of the United States. *U S Geol Surv Open-File Rpt*, 78-925: 1-25

Smith W D, 1927. Contribution to the geology of southeastern Oregon (Steens and Pueblo Mountains). *J Geol*, 35: 421-440

Stockstill K R, Vogel T A, Sisson T W, 2003. Origin and emplacement of the andesite of Burroughs Mountain, a zoned, large-volume lava flow at Mount Rainier, Washington, USA. *J Volc Geotherm Res*, 119: 275-296

Swanson D A, Cameron K A, Evarts R C, Pringle P T, Vance J A, 1989. Excursion 1A: Cenozoic volcanism in the Cascade Range and Columbia Plateau, southern Washington. *New Mexico Bur Mines Min Resour Mem*, 47: 1-50

Swanson D A, Casadevall T J, Dzurisin D, Malone S D Newhall C G, Weaver C S, 1983. Predicting eruptions at Mount St. Helens, June 1980 through Dec 1982. *Science*, 221: 1369-1376

Swanson D A, Dzurisin D, Holcomb R T, Iwatsubo E Y, Chadwick W W, Casadevall T J, Ewert J W, Heliker C C, 1987. Growth of the lava dome at Mount St. Helens, Washington, (USA), 1981-1983. *Geol Soc Amer Spec Pap*, 212: 1-16

Tabor R W, Crowder D F, 1969. On batholiths and volcanoes: intrusion and eruption of late Cenozoic magmas in the Glacier Peak area, North Cascades, Washington. *U S Geol Surv Prof Pap*, 604: 1-67

Taylor E M, 1965. Recent volcanism between Three Fingered Jack and North Sister Oregon Cascade Range. *Ore Bin*, 27: 121-148

Taylor E M, 1968. Roadside geology, Santiam and McKenzie Pass Highways, Oregon. *Oregon Dept Geol Min Ind Bull*, 62: 3-34

Taylor E M, 1978. Field geology of SW Broken Top quadrangle, Oregon. *Oregon Dept Geol Min Ind Spec Pap*, 2: 1-50

Taylor E M, 1981. Roadlog for central High Cascade geology, Bend, Sisters, McKenzie Pass, and Santiam Pass, Oregon. *U S Geol Surv Circ*, 838: 59-83

Tucker D S, Scott K M, 2009. Structures and facies associated with a flow of subaerial basaltic lava into a deep freshwater lake: the Sulphur Creek lava flow, North Cascades, Washington. *J Volc Geotherm Res*, 185: 311-322

Vallance J W, Scott W E, 1997. The Osceola mudflow from Mount Rainier: sedimentology and hazard implications of a huge clay-rich debris flow. *Geol Soc Amer Bull*, 109: 143-163

Vallance J W, Sisson T, Gardner C A, McGeehin J P, Champion D E, Byman, J A, 2001. Late Holocene eruptions of Mount Rainier, Washington. *Eos, Trans Amer Geophys Union*, 82(47): abs V42C-1043

Venezky D Y, Rutherford M J, 1997. Preeruption conditions and timing of dacite-andesite magma mixing in the 2.2 ka eruption at Mount Rainier. *J Geophys Res*, 102: 20,069-20,086

Walker G W, Greene R C, Pattee E C, 1966. Mineral resources of the Mount Jefferson primitive area, Oregon. *U S Geol Surv Bull*, 1230-D: 1-32

Werner C, Evans W C, Poland M, Tucker D S, Doukas M P, 2009. Long-term changes in quiescent degassing at Mount Baker volcano, Washington, USA; evidence for a stalled intrusion in 1975 and connection to a deep magma source. *J Volc Geotherm Res*, 186: 379-386

Williams D A, Kadel S D, Greeley R, Lesher C M, Clynne M A, 2004. Erosion by flowing lava: geochemical evidence in the Cave Basalt, Mount St. Helens, Washington. *Bull Volc*, 66: 168-181

Williams H, 1942. The geology of Crater Lake National Park, Oregon. *Carnegie Inst Wash Pub*, 540: 1-162

Williams H, 1944. Volcanoes of the Three Sisters region, Oregon Cascades. *Univ Calif Pub Geol Sci*, 27: 37-84

Williams H, 1957. A geologic map of the Bend Quadrangle, Oregon and a reconnaissance geologic map of the central portion of the High Cascade Mountains. *Oregon Dept Geol Min Ind*, 1:125,000 and 1:250,000 scale

Williams H, Goles G, 1968. Volume of the Mazama ash-fall and origin of Crater Lake caldera. *Oregon Dept Geol Min Ind Bull*, 62: 37-41

Wise W S, 1968. Geology of the Mount Hood volcano. *Oregon Dept Geol Min Ind Bull*, 62: 81-98

Wise W S, 1969. Geology and petrology of the Mount Hood area: a study of High Cascades volcanism. *Geol Soc Amer Bull*, 80: 969-1006

Wise W S, 1970. Cenozoic volcanism in the Cascade Mountains of southern Washington. *Wash Dept Nat Resour Bull*, 60: 1-45

Wood C A, Kienle J (eds), 1990. *Volcanoes of North America*. Cambridge, England: Cambridge Univ Press, 354 p ***(regional reference)***

Wozniak K C, Taylor E M, 1981. Late Pleistocene summit construction and Holocene flank eruptions of South Sister volcano, Oregon (abs). *Eos, Trans Amer Geophys Union*, 62: 61

Yamaguchi D K, 1983. New tree-ring dates for recent eruptions of Mount St. Helens. *Quat Res*, 20: 246-250

Yamaguchi D K, 1985. Tree-ring evidence for a two-year interval between Recent prehistoric explosive eruptions of Mount St. Helens. *Geology*, 13: 554-557

Yamaguchi D K, Hoblitt R P, Lawrence D B, 1990. A new tree-ring date for the "floating island" lava flow, Mount St. Helens, Washington. *Bull Volc*, 52: 545-550

Yamaguchi D K, Lawrence D B, 1993. Tree-ring evidence for 1842-1843 eruptive activity at the Goat Rocks dome, Mount St. Helens, Washington. *Bull Volc*, 55: 264-272

Zdanowicz C M, Zielinski G A, Germani M S, 1999. Mount Mazama eruption: calendrical age verified and atmospheric impact assessed. *Geology*, 27: 621-624

Zimbelman D R, Rye R O, Landis G P, 2000. Fumaroles in ice caves on the summit of Mount Rainier-preliminary stable isotope, gas, and geochemical studies. *J Volc Geotherm Res*, 97: 457-473

USA: CALIFORNIA (1203)

Anderson C A, 1936. Volcanic history of the Clear Lake area, Calif. *Geol Soc Amer Bull*, 47: 629-664

Anderson C A, 1940. Hat Creek lava flow. *Amer J Sci*, 238: 477-492

Anderson C A, 1941. Volcanoes of the Medicine Lake Highland California. *Univ Calif Pub Geol Sci*, 25: 347-422

Bailey R A, 1989. Geologic map of Long Valley caldera, Mono-Inyo Craters volcanic chain, and vicinity, eastern California. *U S Geol Surv Map*, I-1933, 11 p text

Bailey R A, Dalrymple G B, Lanphere M A, 1976. Volcanism, structure, and geochronology of Long Valley Caldera, Mono County, California. *J Geophys Res*, 81: 725-744

Bailey R A, Miller C D, Sieh K, 1989. Excursion 13B: Long Valley caldera and Mono-Inyo Craters volcanic chain. *New Mexico Bur Mines Min Resour Mem*, 47: 227-254

Bassett A M, Kupfer D H, 1964. A geologic reconnaissance in the southeastern Mojave Desert, California. *Calif Div Mines Geol Spec Rpt*, 83: 1-43

Bateman P C, Wahrhaftig C, 1966. Geology of the Sierra Nevada. *Calif Div Mines Geol Bull*, 190: 107-172

Bursik M, 1993. Subplinian eruption mechanisms inferred from volatile and clast dispersal data. *J Volc Geotherm Res*, 57: 57-70

Bursik M, 2002-. Long Valley tephra database. http://www.volcano.buffalo.edu:9090/mmvz

Bursik M, Reid J, 2004. Lahar in Glass Creek and Owens River during the Inyo eruption, Mono-Inyo Craters, California. *J Volc Geotherm Res*, 131: 321-331

Bursik M, Sieh K, 1989. Range front faulting and volcanism in the Mono Basin, eastern California. *J Geophys Res*, 94: 15, 585-15,609

Cagnoli B, Russell J K, 2000. Imaging the subsurface stratigraphy in the Ubehebe hydrovolcanic field (Death Valley, California) using ground penetrating radar. *J Volc Geotherm Res*, 96: 45-56

Cagnoli B, Ulrych T J, 2001. Ground penetrating radar images of unexposed climbing dune-forms in the Ubehebe hydrovolcanic field (Death Valley, California). *J Volc Geotherm Res*, 109: 279-298

California Div. Mines and Geology, 1958-69. Geologic atlas of California, 1:250,0000 scale. *Calif Div Mines Geol*

Chesterman C W, 1955. Age of the obsidian flow at Glass Mountain, Siskiyou County, California. *Amer J Sci*, 253: 418-424

Chesterman C W, 1971. Volcanism in California. *Calif Geol*, 24: 139-147

Chesterman C W, 1982. Potentially active volcanic zones in California. *Calif Dept Conservation Div Mines Geol Spec Pub*, 63: 9-16

Christiansen R L, Clynne M A, Muffler L J P, 2002. Geologic map of the Lassen Peak, Chaos Crags, and Upper Hat Creek area, California. *U S Geol Surv Geol Invest Ser* I-2723, 1:24,000 scale geol map and 17 p text

Christiansen R L, Miller C D, 1976. Volcanic evolution of Mt. Shasta, California (abs). *Geol Soc Amer Abs Prog*, 8: 360-361

Clynne M A, 1990. Stratigraphic, lithologic, and major element geochemical constraints on magmatic evolution at Lassen volcanic center, California. *J Geophys Res*, 95: 19,651-19,669

Clynne M A, Champion D E, Trimble D A, Hendley J W II, Stauffer P H, 2000. How old is "Cinder Cone"?-solving a mystery in Lassen Volcanic National Park, California. *U S Geol Surv Fact Sheet*, 023-00, 4 p

Clynne M A, Christiansen R L, Muffler L J P, Ramsey D, 2000. Field Trip Guide: Lassen Volcanic National Park and vicinity. Volcanism in National Parks: U.S. Geological Survey-National Park Service Workshop, Sept 26-29, 2000, Redding and Lassen Volcanic National Park, 16 p

Coombs H A, Howard A D, 1960. United States of America. *Catalog of Active Volcanoes of the World and Solfatara Fields*, Rome: IAVCEI, 9: 1-68 ***(regional reference)***

Crandell D R, Miller C D, Glicken H X, Christiansen R L, Newhall C G, 1984. Catastrophic debris avalanche from ancestral Mount Shasta volcano, California. *Geology*, 12: 143-146

Crandell D R, Mullineaux D R, Miller C D, 1979. Volcanic-hazards studies in the Cascade Range of the western United States. *In*: Sheets P D and Grayson D K (eds) *Volcanic Activity and Human Ecology*, New York: Academic Press, p 195-219

Crandell D R, Mullineaux D R, Sigafoos R S, Rubin M, 1974. Chaos Crags eruptions and rockfall-avalanches, Lassen Volcanic National Park, California. *U S Geol Surv J Res*, 2: 49-59

Crowe B M, Fisher R V, 1973. Sedimentary structures in base-surge deposits with special reference to cross-bedding, Ubehebe Craters, Death Valley, California. *Geol Soc Amer Bull*, 84: 663-682

Donnelly-Nolan J M, Champion D E, 1987. Geologic map of Lava Beds National Monument, northern California. *U S Geol Surv Map*, I-1804

Donnelly-Nolan J M, Champion D E, Miller C D, Grove T L, Trimble D A, 1990. Post-11,000-year volcanism at Medicine Lake volcano, Cascade Range, northern California. *J Geophys Res*, 95: 19,693-19,704

Donnelly-Nolan J M, Champion D E, Miller C D, Trimble D A, 1989. Implications of post-11,000-year volcanism at Medicine Lake volcano, northern California Cascade Range. *In*: Muffler L J P and Weaver C S (eds) *Geology, Geophysics and Tectonic Setting of the Cascade Range*, U S Geol Surv, Open-File Rpt 89-178: 556-580

Donnelly-Nolan J M, Grove T L, Lanphere M A, Champion D E, Ramsey D W, 2008. Eruptive history and tectonic setting of Medicine Lake volcano, a large rear-arc volcano in the southern Cascades. *J Volc Geotherm Res*, 177: 313-328

Donnelly-Nolan J M, Hearn B C Jr, Curtis G H, Drake R E, 1981. Geochronology and evolution of the Clear Lake volcanics. *In*: McLaughlin R J, Donnelly-Nolan J M (eds) Research in the Geysers-Clear Lake geothermal area, northern California. *U S Geol Surv Prof Pap*, 1141: 47-60

Donnelly-Nolan J M, Nathenson M, Champion D E, Ramsey D W, Lowenstern J B, Ewert J W, 2007. Volcano hazards assessment for Medicine Lake volcano, northern California. *U S Geol Surv Sci Invest Rpt*, 2007-5174-A: 1-26

Duffield W A, Bacon C R, 1981. Geologic map of the Coso volcanic field and adjacent areas, Inyo County, California. *U S Geol Surv Misc Invest Ser Map*, I-1200, 1:50,000

Duffield W A, Bacon C R, Dalrymple G B, 1980. Late Cenozoic volcanism, geochronology, and structure of the Coso Range, Inyo County, California. *J Geophys Res*, 85: 2381-2404

Eppler D B, 1987. The May 1915 eruptions of Lassen Peak, II: May 22 volcanic blast effects, sedimentaology and stratigraphy of blast and lahar deposits, and characteristics of the blast cloud. *J Volc Geotherm Res*, 31: 65-85

Eppler D B, Fink J, Fletcher R, 1987. Rheologic properties and kinematics of emplacement of the Chaos Jumbles rockfall avalanche, Lasen Volcanic National Park. *J Geophys Res*, 92: 3623-3633

Eppler D B, Malin M C, 1989. The May 1915 eruptions of Lassen Peak, California, 1: characteristics of events occurring on 19 May. *In*: Latter J H (ed) *Volcanic Hazards*. Berlin: Springer-Verlag, 1: 180-200

Finch R H, 1928. Possible 1851 lava flow at Lassen Cinder Cone. *Volcano Lett*, 199: 1

Finch R H, 1937. A tree ring calendar for dating volcanic events at Cinder Cone, Lassen National Park, California. *Amer J Sci*, 33: 140-146

Fink J H, 1983. Structure and emplacement of a rhyolite obsidian flow: Little Glass Mountain, Medicine Lake Highland, northern California. *Geol Soc Amer Bull*, 94: 362-380

Friedman I, 1968. Hydration rind dates rhyolite flows. *Science*, 159: 878-880

Friedman I, Obradovich J, 1981. Obsidian hydration dating of volcanic events. *Quat Res*, 16: 37-47

Garrison L E, 1972. Geothermal steam in the Geysers-Clear Lake region, California. *Geol Soc Amer Bull*, 83: 1449-1468

Guffanti M, Clynne M A, Smith J G, Muffler L J P, Bullen T D, 1990. Late Cenozoic volcanism, subduction, and extension in the Lassen region of California, southern Cascade Range. *J Geophys Res*, 95: 19,453-19,464

Hammersley L, DePaolo D J, 2006. Isotopic and geophysical constraints on the structure and evolution of the Clear Lake volcanic system. *J Volc Geotherm Res*, 153: 331-356

Harkness H W, 1875. A recent volcano in Plumas County. *Calif Acad Sci Proc*, 5: 408-412

Harris S L, 1976. *Fire and Ice, the Cascade Volcanoes*. Seattle: The Mountaineers, 320 p ***(regional reference)***

Hearn B C Jr, Donnelly-Nolan J M, Goff F E, 1981. The Clear Lake volcanics: tectonic setting and magma sources. *In*: McLaughlin R J, Donnelly-Nolan J M (eds) Research in the Geysers-Clear Lake geothermal area, northern California. *U S Geol Surv Prof Pap*, 1141: 25-45

Hearn B C Jr, Donnelly-Nolan J M, Goff F E, 1995. Geologic map and structure sections of the Clear Lake volcanics, Northern California. *U S Geol Surv Map*, I-2362

Heiken G, 1978a. Characteristics of tephra from Cinder Cone, Lassen Volcanic National Park, California. *Bull Volc*, 41: 119-130

Heiken G, 1978b. Plinian-type eruptions in the Medicine Lake Highland, California, and the nature of the underlying magma. *J Volc Geotherm Res*, 4: 375-402

Hildreth W, 2004. Volcanological perspectives on Long Valley, Mammoth Mountain, and Mono Craters: several contiguous but discrete systems. *J Volc Geotherm Res*, 136: 169-198

Hildreth W E, 2007. Quaternary magmatism in the Cascades-geologic perpectives. *U S Geol Surv Prof Pap*, 1744: 1-125

Hill D P, Bailey R A, Ryall A S, 1985. Active tectonic and magmatic processes beneath Long Valley caldera, eastern California: an overview. *J Geophys Res*, 90: 11,111-11,120

Hill D P, Prejean S, 2005. Magmatic unrest beneath Mammoth Mountain, California. *J Volc Geotherm Res*, 146: 257-283

Howell D G, Vedder J G, 1981. Structural implications of stratigraphic discontinuities across the southern California borderland. *In*: Ernst W G (ed) *The geotectonic development of California*, Englewood Cliffs, New Jersey: Prentice-Hall, Inc, p 536-558

Huber N K, Eckhardt W W, 1985. Devils Postpile story. *Sequoia Nat Hist Assoc*, 30 p

Huber N K, Rinehart C D, 1967. Cenozoic volcanic rocks of the Devils Postpile quadrangle, eastern Sierra Nevada California. *U S Geol Surv Prof Pap*, 554-D: 1-21

Ingebritson S E, Galloway D L, Colvard E M, Sorey M L, Mariner R H, 2001. Time-variation of hydrothermal discharge at selected sites in the western United States: implications for monitoring. *J Volc Geotherm Res*, 111: 1-23

James D E, 1966. Geology and rock magnetism of Cinder Cone lava flows, Lassen Volcanic National Park, California. *Geol Soc Amer Bull*, 77: 303-312

Kent D V, Hemming S R, Turrin B D, 2002. Laschamp excursion at Mono Lake? *Earth Planet Sci Lett*, 197: 151-164

Kilbourne R T, 1982. Chronology of eruptions in California during the last 2,000 years. *Calif Dept Conservation Div Mines Geol Spec Pub*, 63: 29-40

Kilbourne R T, Anderson C L, 1981. Volcanic history and "active" volcanism in California. *Calif Geol*, 34: 159-168

Kilbourne R T, Chesterman C W, Wood S H, 1980. Recent volcanism in the Mono Basin-Long Valley Region of Mono County, California. *Calif Div Mines Geol Spec Rpt*, 150: 7-22

Luedke R G, Smith R L, 1981. Map showing distribution, composition, and age of late Cenozoic volcanic centers in California and Nevada. *U S Geol Surv Map*, I-1091-C

Macdonald G A, 1966. Geology of the Cascade Range and Modoc Plateau. *Calif Div Mines Geol Bull*, 190: 65-95

Macdonald G A, Lydon P A, 1972. Geologic map of the Whitmore quadrangle California. *U S Geol Surv map*, GQ-993, 1:62,500 geol map

Mertz S A Jr, 1977. Recent volcanism at Schonchin and Cinder Buttes, northern California. *Contr Mineral Petr*, 61: 231-243

Miller C D, 1978. Holocene pyroclastic-flow deposits from Shastina and Black Butte, west of Mount Shasta, California. *U S Geol Surv J Res*, 6: 611-624

Miller C D, 1980. Potential hazards from future eruptions in the vicinity of Mount Shasta volcano, northern California. *U S Geol Surv Bull*, 1503: 1-43

Miller C D, 1985. Holocene eruptions at the Inyo volcanic chain, California: implications for possible eruptions in Long Valley caldera. *Geology*, 13: 14-17

Miller C D, 1989. Potential hazards from future volcanic eruptions in California. *U S Geol Surv Bull*, 1847: 1-17

Monastero F C, 2002. Model for sucess: an overview of industry-military cooperation in the development of power operations at the Coso geothermal field in southern California. *Geotherm Res Council Bull*, 31: 188-195

Moore J G, Lanphere M, 1983. Age of the Golden Trout Creek volcanic field, Sierra Nevada, California (abs). *Eos, Trans Amer Geophys Union*, 64: 895

Parker R B, 1963. Recent volcanism at Amboy Crater, San Bernardino County, California. *Calif Div Mines Geol Spec Rpt*, 76: 7-21

Peterson J A, Martin L M, 1980. Geologic map of the Baker-Cypress BLM roadless area and Timbered Crater RARE II Areas, Modoc, Shasta, and Siskiyou Counties, California. *U S Geol Surv Map*, MF-1214-A, 1:62,500 geol map

Phillips F M, 2003. Cosmogenic 36Cl ages of Quaternary basalt flows in the Mojave Desert, California, USA. *Geomorphology*, 53: 199-208

Rinehart C D, Huber N K, 1965. The Inyo Crater Lakes-a blast in the past. *Calif Div Mines Geol Min Inf Serv*, 18: 169-172

Rinehart C D, Ross D C, 1964. Geology and mineral deposits of the Mount Morrison quadrangle Sierra Nevada, California. *U S Geol Surv Prof Pap*, 385: 1-106

Robinson P T, Elders W A, Muffler L J P, 1976. Quaternary volcanism in the Salton Sea geothermal field, Imperial Valley, California. *Geol Soc Amer Bull*, 87: 347-360

Rundle J B, Eichelberger J C, 1983. Caption to cover photo. *Eos, Trans Amer Geophys Union*, 64: 11

Sampson D E, Cameron K L, 1987. The geochemistry of the Inyo volcanic chain: multiple magma systems in the Long Valley region, eastern California. *J Geophys Res*, 92: 10,403-10,421

Sarna-Wojcicki A M, Champion D E, Davis J O, 1983. Holocene volcanism in the conterminous United States and the role of silicic volcanic ash layers in correlation of latest Pleistocene and Holocene deposits. *In*: Wright H E (ed) *Late-Quaternary Environments of the United States*, Minneapolis: Univ Minnesota Press, 2: 52-77

Schmitt A K, Hulen J B, 2008. Buried rhyolites within the active, high-temperature Salton Sea geothermal system. *J Volc Geotherm Res*, 178: 708-718

Schmitt A K, Vazquez J A, 2006. Alteration and remelting of nascent oceanic crust during continental rupture: evidence from zircon geochemistry of rhyolites and xenoliths from the Salton Trough, California. *Earth Planet Sci Lett*, 252: 260-274

Sharp R P, 1957. Geomorphology of Cima Dome, Mojave Desert, California. *Geol Soc Amer Bull*, 68: 273-290

Sharp R P, Glazner A F, 1997. *Geology Underfoot in Death Valley and Owens Valley*. Missoula, MT: Mountain Press, 321 p

Sherrod D R, Smith J G, 1990. Quaternary extrusion rates of the Cascade Range, northwestern United States and southern British Columbia. *J Geophys Res*, 95: 19,465-19,474

Sieh K, Bursik M, 1986. Most recent eruption of the Mono Craters, eastern central California. *J Geophys Res*, 91: 12,539-12,571

Smith R L, Shaw H R, 1975. Igneous-related geothermal systems. *U S Geol Surv Circ*, 726: 58-83

Smith R L, Shaw H R, Luedke R G, Russell S L, 1978. Comprehensive tables giving physical data and thermal energy estimates for young igneous systems of the United States. *U S Geol Surv Open-File Rpt*, 78-925: 1-25

Sorey M L, Evans W C, Kennedy B M, Farrar C D, Hainsworth L J, Hausback B, 1998. Carbon dioxide and helium emissions from a reservoir of magmatic gas beneath Mammoth Mountain, California. *J Geophys Res*, 103: 15,303-15,323

Townley S D, Maxwell W A, 1939. Descriptive catalog of earthquakes of the Pacific Coast of the United States 1769 to 1928. *Bull Seism Soc Amer*, 29: 83

Turrin B D, Christiansen R L, Clynne M A, Champion D E, Gerstel W J, Muffler L J P, Trimble D A, 1998. Age of Lassen Peak, California, and implications for the ages of late Pleistocene glaciations in the southern Cascade Range. *Geol Soc Amer Bull*, 110: 931-945

Ui T, Glicken H, 1986. Internal structural variations in a debris-avalanche deposit from ancestral Mount Shasta, California, USA. *Bull Volc*, 48: 189-194

van den Bogaard P, Schirnick C, 1995. 40Ar/39Ar laser probe ages of Bishop Tuff quartz phenocrysts substantiate long-lived silicic magma chamber at Long Valley, United States. *Geology*, 23: 759-762

Waters A C, Donnelly-Nolan J M, Rogers B W, 1990. Selected caves and lava-tube systems in and near Lava Beds National Monument, California. *U S Geol Surv Bull*, 1673: 1-102 and 6 plates

Webb R W, 1950. Volcanic geology of Toowa valley, southern Sierra Nevada, California. *Geol Soc Amer Bull*, 61: 349-357

Wells S G, McFadden L D, Renault C E, Crowe B M, 1990. Geomorphic assessment of late Quaternary volcanism in the Yucca Mountain area, southern Nevada: implications for the proposed high-level radioactive waste repository. *Geology*, 18: 549-553

Williams H, 1932. Geology of the Lassen Volcanic National Park, California. *Univ Calif Pub Geol Sci*, 21: 195-385

Williams H, 1942. The geology of Crater Lake National Park, Oregon. *Carnegie Inst Wash Pub*, 540: 1-162

Williams H, 1949. Geology of the Macdoel quadrangle (California). *Calif Div Mines Geol Bull*, 151: 7-60

Wood C A, Kienle J (eds), 1990. *Volcanoes of North America*. Cambridge, England: Cambridge Univ Press, 354 p ***(regional reference)***

Wood S H, 1977. Distribution, correlation, and radiocarbon dating of late Holocene tephra, Mono and Inyo Craters, eastern California. *Geol Soc Amer Bull*, 88: 89-95

Wood S H, Brooks R, 1979. Panum crater tephra dated 640 +/- 40 radiocarbon Y.B.P., Mono Craters, California (abs). *Geol Soc Amer Abs Prog*, 11: 543

USA: WESTERN INTERIOR (1204-10)

Arculus R J, Gust D A, 1995. Regional petrology of the San Francisco Volcanic Field, Arizona, USA. *J Petr*, 36: 827-861

Bailey R A, Smith R L, 1978. Volcanic geology of the Jemez Mountains, New Mexico. *New Mexico Bur Mines Socorro Circ*, 163: 184-196

Bass N W, Northrop S A, 1963. Geology of Glenwood Springs quadrangle and vicinty, northwestern Colorado. *U S Geol Surv Bull*, 1142-J: 1-74

Best M G, Brimhall W H, 1974. Late Cenozoic alkalic basaltic magmas in the western Colorado Plateaus and the Basin and Range transition zone, U.S.A., and their bearing on mantle dynamics. *Geol Soc Amer Bull*, 85: 1677-1690

Biek F R, Willis G C, Hylland M D, Doelling H H, 2003. Geology of Zion National Park, Utah. *In*: Sprinkel D A, Chidsey T C Jr, Anderson P B (eds) *Geology of Utah's Parks and Monuments*, Utah Geol Assoc Publ, 28: 107-137

Brand B D, White C M, 2007. Origin and stratigraphy of phreatomagmatic deposits at the Pleistocene Sinker Butte volcano, western Snake River Plain. *J Volc Geotherm Res*, 160: 319-339

Christiansen R L, 1984. Yellowstone magmatic evolution: its bearing on understanding large-volume explosive volcanism. *In*: *Explosive Volcanism: Inception, Evolution, and Hazards*, Washington, D C: Natl Acad Press, p 84-95

Christiansen R L, 2001. The Quaternary and Pliocene Yellowstone Volcanic Field of Wyoming, Idaho, and Montana. *U S Geol Surv Prof Pap*, 729-G: 1-145

Christiansen R L, Lowenstern J B, Smith R B, Heasler H, Morgan L A, Nathenson M, Mastin L G, Muffler L J P, Robinson J E, 2007. Preliminary assessment of volcanic and hydrothermal hazards in Yellowstone National Park and vicinity. *U S Geol Surv, Open-File Rpt*, 2007-1071: 1-94

Colton H S, 1967. The basaltic cinder cones and lava flows of the San Francisco Mountain volcanic field, Flagstaff, Arizona. *Museum of North Arizona*, 58 p

Condie K C, Barsky C K, 1972. Origin of Quaternary basalts from the Black Rock Desert region, Utah. *Geol Soc Amer Bull*, 83: 333-352

Coombs H A, Howard A D, 1960. United States of America. *Catalog of Active Volcanoes of the World and Solfatara Fields*, Rome: IAVCEI, 9: 1-68 ***(regional reference)***

Creighton D N, 1987. Menan Buttes, southeastern Idaho. *Geol Soc Amer, Centennial Field Guide, Rocky Mountain Sec*, 2: 109-111

Crumpler L S, 1982. Volcanism in the Mount Taylor region. *New Mexico Geol Soc Guidebook*, 33rd Field Conf, p 291-297

Dalrymple G B, Hamblin W K, 1998. K-Ar ages of Pleistocene lava dams in the Grand Canyon in Arizona. *Proc Nat Acad Sci*, 95: 9744-9749

Davis G H, Pollock G L, 2003. Geology of Bryce Canyon National Park, Utah. *In*: Sprinkel D A, Chidsey T C Jr, Anderson P B (eds) *Geology of Utah's Parks and Monuments*, Utah Geol Assoc Publ, 28: 37-60

Dunbar N, 1999. Cosmogenic 36Cl-determined age of the Carrizozo lava flows, south-central New Mexico. *New Mex Geol*, 21(2): 25-29

Dunbar N W, Phillips F M, 2004. Cosmogenic 36Cl ages of lava flows in the Zuni-Bandera volcanic field, north-central New Mexico, U.S.A. *New Mex Bur Geol Geophys Bull*, 160: 309-317

Dungan M A, Thompson R A, Stormer J S, O'Neill J M, 1989. Rio Grande Rift volcanism: northeastern Jemez zone, New Mexico. *New Mexico Bur Mines Min Resour Mem*, 46: 435-486

Dzurisin D, Yamashita K M, Kleinman J K, 1994. Mechanism of crustal uplift and subsidence at the Yellowstone caldea, Wyoming. *Bull Volc*, 56: 261-270

Elson M D, Ort M H, Hesse S J, Duffield W A, 2002. Lava, corn, and ritual in the northern Southwest. *Amer Antiquity*, 67: 119-135

Fenton C R, Webb R H, Pearthree P A, Cerling T E, Poreda R J, 2001. Displacement rates on the Toroweap and Hurricane faults: implications for Quaternary downcutting in the Grand Canyon, Arizona. *Geology*, 29: 1035-1038

Finn C A, Morgan L A, 2002. High-resolution aeromagnetic mapping of volcanic terrain, Yellowstone National Park. *J Volc Geotherm Res*, 115: 207-231

Fournier R O, Christiansen R L, Hutchinson R A, Pierce K L, 1994. A field-trip guide to Yellowstone National Park, Wyoming, Montana, and Idaho-volcanic, hydrothermal, and glacial activity in the region. *U S Geol Surv Bull*, 2099: 1-46

Garside L F, Shevenell L A, Snow J H, Hess R H, 2002. Status of Nevada geothermal resource development - Spring 2002. *Trans Geotherm Res Council*, 26: 527-532

Garside L J, Schilling J H, 1979. Thermal waters of Nevada. *Nev Bur Mines Geol Bull*, 91: 1-167

Goff F, Gardner J N, Baldridge W S, Hulen J B, Neilsen D L, Vaniman D, Heiken G, Dungan M A, Brixton D, 1989. Excursion 17B: volcanic and hydrothermal evolution of Valles caldera and Jemez volcanic field. *New Mexico Bur Mines Min Resour Mem*, 46: 381-434

Greeley R, Black D (eds), 1977. Abstracts for the Planetary Geology Field Conference on the Snake River Plain, Idaho. *NASA TM-78, 436, Abs Snake River Conf*, 39 p

Greeley R, King J S (eds), 1977. Volcanism of the eastern Snake River Plain, Idaho: a comparative planetary geology guidebook. *NASA (Washington, DC)*, CR-154621: 1-308

Gregory H E, 1949. Geologic and geographic reconnaissance of Eastern Markagunt Plateau, Utah. *Geol Soc Amer Bull*, 60: 969-998

Gregory H E, 1950. Geology and geography of the Zion Park region Utah and Arizona. *U S Geol Surv Prof Pap*, 220: 1-200

Gregory H E, 1951. The geology and geography of the Paunsaugant region, Utah. *U S Geol Surv Prof Pap*, 226: 1-116

Hamblin W K, 1974. Late Cenozoic volcanism in the western Grand Canyon. *In*: Breed W J and Roat E C (eds) *Geol of the Grand Canyon*, Flagstaff: Museum of Northern Arizona, p 142-185

Hamblin W K, 1987. Late Cenozoic volcanism in the St. George basin, Utah. *Geol Soc Amer Centennial Field Guide, Rocky Mountain Section*, 2: 291-294

Hamilton W L, Bailey A L, Minor D R, 1992. Holocene Yellowstone tephras: progress in locating possible source vent and dating (abs). *Eos, Trans Amer Geophys Union*, 73: 637

Hamilton W, Myers W B, 1963. Menan Buttes, cones of glassy basalt in the Snake River Plain, Idaho. *U S Geol Surv Prof Pap*, 450 E2: 114-118

Hatfield S C, Rowley P D, Sable E G, Maxwell D J, Cox B V, McKell M D, Kiel D E, 2003. Geology of Cedar Breaks National Monument, Utah. *In*: Sprinkel D A, Chidsey T C Jr, Anderson P B (eds) *Geology of Utah's Parks and Monuments*, Utah Geol Assoc Publ, 28: 139-154

Heiken G, Goff F, Stix J, Tamanyu S, Shafiqullah M, Garcia S, Hagan R, 1986. Intracaldera volcanic activity, Toledo caldera and embayment, Jemez Mountains, New Mexico. *J Geophys Res*, 91: 1799-1816

Hewett D F, 1956. Geology and mineral resources of the Ivanpah Quadrangle, California and Nevada. *U.S. Geol Surv Prof Pap*, 275: 1-172

Higgins J M, 2003. Geology of Snow Canyon State Park, Utah. *In*: Sprinkel D A, Chidsey T C Jr, Anderson P B (eds) *Geology of Utah's Parks and Monuments*, Utah Geol Assoc Publ, 28: 479-494

Hildreth W, Christiansen R L, O'Neal J R, 1984. Catastrophic isotopic modification of rhyolitic magma at times of caldera subsidence, Yellowstone Plateau volcanic field. *J Geophys Res*, 89: 8339-8369

Holm R F, Moore R B, 1987. Holocene scoria cone and lava flows at Sunset Crater, northern Arizona. *In*: Bues S S (ed) *Geol Soc Amer Centennial Field Guide, Rocky Mountain Sec*, 2: 1-475

Hoover J D, 1974. Periodic Quaternary volcanism in the Black Rock Desert, Utah. *Brigham Young Univ Geol Studies*, 21: 3-72

Hughes S S, Smith R P, Hackett W R, Anderson S R, 1999. Mafic volcanism and environmental geology of the eastern Snake River Plain. *In*: Hughes S S, Thackray G D (eds), *Guidebook to the Geology of eastern Idaho*, Pocatello, Idaho: Idaho Musuem of Nat Hist, p 143-168

Hughes S S, Smith R P, Hackett W R, McCurry M, Anderson S R, Ferdock G C, 1997. Bimodal magmatism, basaltic volcanic styles, tectonics, and geomorphic processes of the eastern Snake River Plain, Idaho. *Brigham Young Univ Geol Studies*, 42: 423-458

Hutchinson R A, Westphal J A, Kieffer S W, 1997. In situ observations of Old Faithful Geyser. *Geology*, 25: 875-878

Karlo J F, Clemency C V, 1980. Picrite xenoliths from the eastern Snake River Plain, Idaho. *Contr Mineral Petr*, 73: 173-178

Keszthelyi L P, Pieri D C, 1993. Emplacement of the 75-km-long Carrizozo lava flow field, south-central New Mexico. *J Volc Geotherm Res*, 59: 59-75

Kleinhampl F J, Davis W E, Silberman M L, Chesterman C W, Chapman R H, Gray C H, 1975. Aeromagnetic and limited gravity studies and generalized geology of the Bodie Hills region, Nevada and California. *U S Geol Surv Bull*, 1384: 1-38

Kuntz M A, Champion D E, Lefebvre R H, Covington H R, 1988. Geologic map of the Craters of the Moon, Kings Bowl, and Wapi lava fields and the Great Rift volcanic rift zone, south-central Idaho. *U S Geol Surv Misc Invest Ser Map*, I:1632, 1:100,000 scale geol map

Kuntz M A, Champion D E, Spiker E C, Lefebvre R H, 1986. Contrasting magma types and steady-state, volume predictable, basaltic volcanism along the Great Rift, Idaho. *Geol Soc Amer Bull*, 97: 579-594

Kuntz M A, Champion D E, Spiker E C, Lefebvre R H, McBroome L A, 1982. The Great Rift and the evolution of the Craters of the Moon lava field, Idaho. *In*: Bonnichsen B, Breckenridge R M (eds), *The Great Rift and the Evolution of the Craters of the Moon Lava Field, Idaho*, Idaho Bur Mines Geol Bull, 26: 423-437

Kuntz M A, Covington H R, Schorr L J, 1992. An overview of basaltic volcanism of the eastern Snake River Plain. *In*: Link P K, Kuntz M A, Platt L B (eds), *Regional Geology of Eastern Idaho and Western Wyoming*, Geol Soc Amer Mem, 179: 227-267

Kuntz M A, Spiker E C, Rubin M, Champion D E, Lefebvre R H, 1986. Radiocarbon studies of latest Pleistocene and Holocene lava flows of the Snake River Plain, Idaho: data, lessons, interpretations. *Quat Res*, 25: 163-176

Larson E E, Ozima M, Bradley W C, 1975. Late Cenozoic basic volcanism in northwestern Colorado and its implications concerning tectonism and the origin of the Colorado River system. *Geol Soc Amer Mem*, 144: 115-178

Laughlin A W, Brookins D G, Causey J D, 1972. Late Cenozoic basalts from the Bandera lava field, Valencia County, New Mexico. *Geol Soc Amer Bull*, 83: 1543-1552

Laughlin A W, Poths J, Healey H A, Reneau S, WoldeGabriel G, 1994. Dating of Quaternary basalts using the cosmogenic 3He and 14C methods with implications for excess 40Ar. *Geology*, 22: 135-138

Leat P T, Thompson R N, Dickin A P, Morrison M A, Hendry G L, 1989. Quaternary volcanism in northwestern Colorado: implications for the roles of asthenosphere and lithosphere in the genesis of continental basalts. *J Volc Geotherm Res*, 37: 291-310

Lipman P W, Moench R H, 1972. Basalts of the Mount Taylor volcanic field, New Mexico. *Geol Soc Amer Bull*, 83: 1335-1344

Luedke R G, Smith R L, 1978. Map showing distribution, composition, and age of late Cenozoic volcanic centers in Colorado, Utah, and southwestern Wyoming. *U S Geol Surv Misc Invest Ser Map*, I-1091-B

Luedke R G, Smith R L, 1981. Map showing distribution, composition, and age of late Cenozoic volcanic centers in California and Nevada. *U S Geol Surv Map*, I-1091-C

Malde H E, Powers H A, Marshall C H, 1963. Reconnaissance geologic map of west-central Snake River Plain, Idaho. *U S Geol Surv Map*, I-373, 1:125,000

Maxwell C H, 1982. El Malpais. *New Mexico Geol Soc Guidebook*, 33rd Field Conf, p 299-301

Maxwell C H, 1986. Geologic map of El Malpais lava field and surrounding areas, Cibola County, New Mexico. *U S Geol Surv Map*, I-1595

McKee E D, Hamblin K W, Damon P E, 1968. K-Ar age of lava dam in Grand Canyon. *Geol Soc Amer Bull*, 79: 133-136

Minor D R, Hamilton W L, 1992. Deposits and landforms produced by the Mary Bay and Turbid Lake hydrothermal explosions, Yellowstone National Park, Wyoming (abs). *Eos, Trans Amer Geophys Union*, 73: 637

Moore R B, Wolfe E W, 1987. Geologic map of the east part of the San Francisco volcanic field, north-Central Arizona. *U S Geol Surv Map*, MF-1960, 46 p text

Morgan L A, Shanks W C III, Lovalvo D A, Johnson S Y, Stephenson W J, Pierce K L, Harlan S S, Finn C A, Lee G, Webring M, Schulze B, Duhn J, Sweeney R, Balistrieri L, 2003. Exploration and discovery in Yellowstone Lake: results from high-resolution sonar imaging, seismic reflection profiling, and submersible studies. *J Volc Geotherm Res*, 122: 221-242

Morrison R B, 1964. Late Lahontan: geology of southern Carson desert, Nevada. *U S Geol Surv Prof Pap*, 401

Nichols R L, 1946. McCartys basalt flow, Valencia County, New Mexico. *Geol Soc Amer Bull*, 57: 1049-1086

Nielson R L, 1974. The geomorphic evolution of the Crater Hill volcanic field of Zion National Park. *Brigham Young Univ Geol Studies*, 24: 55-70

Ort M H, Elson M D, Anderson K C, Duffield W A, Hooten J A, Champion D E, Waring G, 2008b. Effects of scoria-cone eruptions upon nearby human communities. *Geol Soc Amer Bull*, 120: 476-486

Ort M H, Elson M D, Anderson K C, Duffield W A, Samples T L, 2008a. Variable effects of cinder-cone eruptions on prehistoric agrarian human populations in the American southwest. *J Volc Geotherm Res*, 176: 363-376

Oviatt C G, 1991. Quaternary geology of the Black Rock Desert, Millard County, Utah. *Utah Geol Min Surv Spec Studies*, 73: 1-23

Pardee J T, 1950. Late Cenozoic block faulting in western Montana. *Geol Soc Amer Bull*, 61: 359-406

Pierce K L, Cannon K P, Meyer G A, Trebesch M J, Watts R D, 2002. Post-glacial inflation-deflation cycles, tilting, and faulting in the Yellowstone caldera based on Yellowstone Lake shorelines. *U S Geol Surv Open-File Rpt*, 02-0142: 1-62

Price J G, LaPointe D D, 1998. Ancient lakes and volcanoes near Fallon. *Nev Bur Mines Geol Educ Ser* E-28: 1-4; also online at http://www.nbmg.unr.edu/dox/e28/guide.htm

Prinz M, 1970. Idaho rift system, Snake River Plain, Idaho. *Geol Soc Amer Bull*, 81: 941-948

Reneau S L, Gardner J N, Forman S L, 1996. New evidence for the age of the youngest eruptions in the Valles caldera, New Mexico. *Geology*, 24: 7-10

Riggs N R, Duffield W A, 2008. Record of complex scoria cone eruptive activity at Red Mountain, Arizona, USA, and implications for monogenetic mafic volcanoes. *J Volc Geotherm Res*, 178: 763-776

Robinson P T, McKee E H, Moiola R J, 1968. Cenozoic volcanism and sedimentation, Silver Peak region western Nevada and adjacent California. *Geol Soc Amer Mem*, 116: 577-612

Sarna-Wojcicki A M, Champion D E, Davis J O, 1983. Holocene volcanism in the conterminous United States and the role of silicic volcanic ash layers in correlation of latest Pleistocene and Holocene deposits. *In*: Wright H E (ed) *Late-Quaternary Environments of the United States*, Minneapolis: Univ Minnesota Press, 2: 52-77

Sayre W O, Ort M H, Graham D, 1995. Capulin volcano is approximately 59,100 years old. *Park Science*, 15: 10-11

Scott D H, Trask N J, 1971. Geology of the Lunar Crater volcanic field, Nye County, Nevada. *U S Geol Surv Prof Pap*, 599-I: 11-122

Self S, Amos R C, 1982. Large magnitude strombolian eruptions: the example of Sunset Crater, Arizona (abs). *Workshop in Explosive Volcanism (Prog & Abs)*, Consig Naziona Delle Ricerche & Nat Sci Foundation

Self S, Wolff J A, 2005. Outstanding issues about relationships between large-scale calderas, ignimbrite volumes, and magma body shape and longevity. *Workshop Caldera Volcanism: Analysis, Modelling and Response, Parador de las Canadas, 16-22 October, 2005*, Abs, p 15

Self S, Wolff J A, Spell T L, Skuba C E, Morrissey M M, 1991. Revisionst to the stratigraphy and volcanology of the Post-0.5 Ma units and the volcanic section of VC-1 core hole, Valles caldera, New Mexico. *J Geophys Res*, 96: 4107-4116

Shepard M K, Arvidson R E, Caffee M, Finkel R, Harris L, 1995. Cosmogenic exposure ages of basalt flows: Lunar Crater volcanic field, Nevada. *Geology*, 23: 21-24

Smiley T L, 1958. The geology and dating of Sunset Crater, Flagstaff, Arizona. *New Mexico Geol Soc Guidebook*, 9th Field Conf, p 186-190

Smith R B, Braile L W, 1984. Crustal structure and evolution of an explosive silicic volcanic system at Yellowstone National Park. *In*: *Explosive Volcanism: Inception, Evolution, and Hazards*, Washington D C: Nat Acad Press, p 96-109

Smith R B, Braile L W, 1993. Topographic signature, space-time evolution, and physical properties of the Yellowstone-Snake River Plain volcanic system: the Yellowstone hotspot. *In*: Snoke A W, Steidtmann J R, Roberts S M (eds), *Geology of Wyoming*, Geol Surv Wyoming Mem: 5: 694-754

Smith R B, Braile L W, 1994. The Yellowstone hotspot. *J Volc Geotherm Res*, 61: 121-187

Smith R B, Siegel L J, 2000. *Windows into the Earth: The Geologic Story of Yellowstone and Grand Teton National Parks*. Oxford: Oxford Univ Press, 242 p

Smith R L, Bailey R A, 1968. Resurgent cauldrons. *Geol Soc Amer Mem*, 116: 613-662

Smith R L, Shaw H R, 1975. Igneous-related geothermal systems. *U S Geol Surv Circ*, 726: 58-83

Stearns H T, Crandall L, Steward W G, 1938. Geology and ground-water resources of the Snake River Plain in southeastern Idaho. *U S Geol Surv Water Supply Pap*, 774: 1-268

Stoeser D B, Senterfit M K, Zelten J E, 1989. Mineral resources of the Little Black Peak and Carrizozo Lava Flow wilderness study areas, Lincoln County, New Mexico. *U S Geol Surv Bull*, 1734-4: 1-20

Stormer J C, 1972. Mineralogy and petrology of the Raton-Clayton volcanic field, northeastern New Mexico. *Geol Soc Amer Bull*, 83: 3299-3322

Valentine G A, Krier D J, Perry F V, Heiken G, 2007. Eruptive and geomorphic processes at the Lathrop Wells scoria cone volcano. *J Volc Geotherm Res*, 161: 57-80

Waring G A, Blankenship R R, Bentall R, 1965. Thermal springs of the United States and other countries of the world, a summary. *U S Geol Surv Prof Pap*, 492: 1-383

Wells S G, McFadden L D, Renault C E, Crowe B M, 1990. Geomorphic assessment of late Quaternary volcanism in the Yucca Mountain area, southern Nevada: implications for the proposed high-level radioactive waste repository. *Geology*, 18: 549-553

White D E, Thompson G A, Sandberg C H, 1964. Rocks structure and geologic history of Steamboat Spring thermal area Washoe County Nevada. *U S Geol Surv Prof Pap*, 458-B: 1-62

White J D L, 1996. Pre-emergent construction of a lacustrine basaltic volcano, Pavant Butte, Utah (USA). *Bull Volc*, 58: 249- 262

Wolff J A, Gardner J N, 1995. Is the Valles caldera entering a new cycle of activity? *Geology*, 23: 411-414

Wood C A, Kienle J (eds), 1990. *Volcanoes of North America*. Cambridge, England: Cambridge Univ Press, 354 p ***(regional reference)***

USA: HAWAII (1302)

Bergmanis E C, Sinton J M, Trusdell F A, 2000. Rejuvenated volcanism along the southwest rift zone, East Maui, Hawai'i. *Bull Volc*, 62: 239-255

Brigham W T, 1868. Eruption at Mauna Loa on the Hawaiian Islands. *Boston Soc Nat Hist Proc*, 12: 82-83

Brigham W T, 1909. The volcanoes of Kilauea and Mauna Loa. *Mem B P Bishop Museum*, 2: 1-222

Calvert A T, Lanphere M A, 2006. Argon geochronology of Kilauea's early submarine history. *J Volc Geotherm Res*, 151: 1-18

Casadevall T J, Dzurisin D, 1987. Stratigraphy and petrology of the Uwekahuna Bluff section, Kilauea Caldera, Hawaii. *U S Geol Surv Prof Pap*, 1350: 351-375

Clague D A, Davis A S, Bischoff J L, Dixon J E, Geyer R, 2000. Lava bubble-wall fragments formed by submarine hydrovolcanic explosions on Loi'hi Seamount and Kilauea volcano. *Bull Volc*, 61: 437-449

Clague D A, Hagstrum J T, Champion D E, Beeson M H, 1999. Kilauea summit overflows: their ages and distribution in the Puna District, Hawai'i. *Bull Volc*, 61: 363-381

Crandell D R, 1983. Potential hazards from future volcanic eruptions on the island of Maui, Hawaii. *U S Geol Surv Map*, I-1442

Decker R W, Christiansen R L, 1984. Explosive eruptions of Kilauea volcano, Hawaii. *In*: *Explosive Volcanism: Inception, Evolution, and Hazards*, Washington, D C: Natl Acad Press, p 122-132

Duffield W A, Christiansen R L, Koyanagi R Y, Peterson D W, 1982. Storage, migration, and eruption of magma at Kilauea volcano, Hawaii, 1971-1972. *J Volc Geotherm Res*, 13: 273-307

Dzurisin D, Lockwood J P, Casadevall T J, Rubin M, 1995. The Uwekahuna Ash Member of the the Puna Basalt: product of violent phreatomagmatic eruptions at Kilauea volcano, Hawaii, between 2800 and 2100 14C years ago. *J Volc Geotherm Res*, 66: 163-184

Eakins B W, Robinson J E, 2006. Submarine geology of Hana Ridge and Haleakala volcano's northeast flank, Maui. *J Volc Geotherm Res*, 151: 229-250

Fiske R S, Koyanagi R Y, 1968. The December 1965 eruption of Kilauea volcano, Hawaii. *U S Geol Surv Prof Pap*, 607: 1-21

Fiske R S, Rose T R, Swanson D A, Champion D E, McGeehin J P, 2009. Kulanaokuaiki Tephra (ca. A.D. 400-1000): newly recognized evidence for highly explosive eruptions at Kilauea volcano, Hawaii. *Geol Soc Amer Bull*, 121: 712-728

Flynn L P, Mouginis-Mark P J, Horton K A, 1994. Distribution of thermal areas of an active lava flow field: Landsat observations of Kilauea, Hawaii, July 1991. *Bull Volc*, 56: 284-296

Fornari D J, Garcia M O, Tyce R C, Gallo D G, 1988. Morphology and structure of Loihi seamount based on SEABEAM sonar mapping. *J Geophys Res*, 93: 15,227-15,238

Garcia M O, Davis M G, 2001. Submarine growth and internal structure of ocean island volcanoes based on submarine observations of Mauna Loa volcano, Hawaii. *Geology*, 29: 163-166

Garcia M O, Kurz M D, Muenow D W, 1990. Mahukona: the missing Hawaiian volcano. *Geology*, 18: 1111-1114

Garcia M O, Rhodes J M, Trusdell F A, Pietruszka A J, 1996. Petrology of lavas from the Puu Oo eruption of Kilauea volcano: III. The Kupaianaha episode (1986-1992). *Bull Volc*, 58: 359-379

Garcia M O, Rubin K H, Norman M D, Rhodes J M, Graham D W, Muenow D W, Spencer K, 1998. Petrology and geochronology of basalt breccia from the 1996 earthquake swarm of Loihi seamount, Hawaii: magmatic history of its 1996 eruption. *Bull Volc*, 59: 577-592

Green W L, 1887. *Vestiges of the Molten Globe*. Honolulu: Hawaiian Gazette Pub Co, 337 p

Guest J E, Spudis P D, Greeley R, Taylor G J, Baloga S M, 1995. Emplacement of xenolith nodules in the Kaupulehu lava flow, Hualalai volcano, Hawaii. *Bull Volc*, 57: 179-184

Guillou H, Garcia M O, Turpin L, 1997. Unspiked K-Ar dating of young volcanic rocks from Loihi and Pitcairn hot spot seamounts. *J Volc Geotherm Res*, 78: 239-249

Hammer J E, Coombs M L, Shamberger P J, Kimura J-I, 2006. Submarine sliver in North Kona: a window into the early magmatic and growth history of Hualalai volcano, Hawaii. *J Volc Geotherm Res*, 151: 157-188

Harris A J L, Thornber C R, 1999. Complex effusive events at Kilauea as documented by GOES satellite and remote cameras. *Bull Volc*, 61: 382-395

Heliker C C, Mangan M T, Mattox T N, Kauahikaua J P, Helz R T, 1998. The character of long-term eruptions: inferences from episodes 50-53 of the Pu'u 'O'o-Kupaianaha eruption of Kilauea volcano. *Bull Volc*, 59: 381-393

Heliker C, Griggs J D, Takahashi T J, Wright T L, 1986. Volcano Monitoring at the U.S. Geological Survey's Hawaiian Volcano Observatory. *Earthq Volcanoes*, 18: 3-71

Hitchcock C H, 1909. *Hawaii and its Volcanoes*. Honolulu: Hawaiian Gazette Pub Co, 306 p

Holcomb R T, 1987. Eruptive history and long-term behavior of Kilauea volcano, Hawaii. *U S Geol Surv Prof Pap*, 1350: 261-350

Jackson M C, Frey F A, Garcia M O, Wilmoth R A, 1999. Geology and geochemistry of basaltic lava flows and dikes from the Trans-Koolau tunnel, Oahu, Hawaii. *Bull Volc*, 60: 381-401

Jaggar T A, 1947. Origin and developement of craters. *Geol Soc Amer Mem*, 21: 1-508

Jurado-Chichay Z, Rowland S K, 1995. Channel overflows of the Pohue Bay flow, Mauna Loa, Hawai'i: examples of the contrast between surface and interior lava. *Bull Volc*, 57: 117-126

Jurado-Chichay Z, Rowland S K, Walker G P L, 1996. The formation of circular littoral cones from tube-fed pahoehoe, Mauna Loa, Hawai'i. *Bull Volc*, 57: 471-482

Kauahikaua J, Camara B, 2000. Most recent eruptions of Hualalai volcano, Hawai'i: geological evidence from the historical record. *In*: McCoy F W, Heiken G (eds), *Volcanic Hazards and Disasters in Human Antiquity, Geol Soc Amer Spec Pap*, 345: 25-32

Kauahikaua J, Cashman K V, Clague D A, Champion D, Hagstrum J T, 2002. Emplacement of the most recent lava flows on Hualalai volcano, Hawai'i. *Bull Volc*, 64: 229-253

Kauahikaua J, Mangan M, Heliker C, Mattox T, 1996. A qualitative look at the demise of a basaltic vent: the death of Kupaianaha, Kilauea volcano, Hawai'i. *Bull Volc*, 57: 641-648

Klein F W, 1982. Earthquakes at Loihi submarine volcano and the Hawaiian hot spot. *J Geophys Res*, 87: 7719-7726

Klein F W, Koyanagi R Y, 1979. Seismicity of Kilauea and Loihi volcanoes, Hawaii (abs). *Hawaii Symp Intraplate Volc & Submarine Volc, Hilo, Hawaii, Abs*, p 124

Langenheim V A M, Clague D A, 1987. The Hawaiian-Emperor volcanic chain, Part II: Stratigraphic framework of volcanic rocks of the Hawaiian Islands. *U S Geol Surv Prof Pap*, 1350: 55-84

Leslie S C, Moore G F, Morgan J K, 2004. Internal structure of Puna Ridge: evolution of the submarine East Rift Zone of Kilauea volcano, Hawai'i. *J Volc Geotherm Res*, 129: 237-259

Lipman P W, 1995. Declining growth of Mauna Loa during the last 10,000 years: rates of lava accumulation vs. gravitational subsidence. *In*: Rhodes J M, Lockwood J P (eds), Mauna Loa Revealed. Structure, Composition, History, and Hazards. *Amer Geophys Union, Geophys Monogr,* 92: 45-80

Lipman P W, Coombs M L, 2006. North Kona slump: submarine flank failure during the early(?) tholeiitic shield stage of Hualalai volcano. *J Volc Geotherm Res*, 151: 189-216

Lipman P W, Sisson T W, Coombs M L, Calvert A, Kimura J-I, 2006. Piggyback tectonics: long-term growth of Kilauea on the south flank of Mauna Loa. *J Volc Geotherm Res*, 151: 73-108

Lockwood J P, Dvorak J J, English T T, Koyanagi R Y, Okamura A T, Summers M L, Tanigawa W R, 1987. Mauna Loa 1974-1984: A decade of intrusive and extrusive activity. *U S Geol Surv Prof Pap*, 1350: 537-570

Lockwood J P, Lipman P W, 1987. Holocene eruptive history of Mauna Loa volcano. *U S Geol Surv Prof Pap*, 1350: 509-535

Lockwood J P, Rubin M, 1986. Distribution and age of the Uwekahuna Ash, Kilauea volcano, Hawaii. *IAVCEI 1986 Cong, New Zeal, Abs*, p 112

Lockwood J P, Tilling R I, Holcomb R T, Klein F, Okamura A, Peterson D W, 1999. Magma migration and resupply during the 1974 summit eruptions of Kilauea volcano, Hawai'i. *U S Geol Surv Prof Pap*. 613: 1-37

Macdonald G A, 1944. The 1840 eruption and crystal differentiation in the Kilauean magma column. *Amer J Sci*, 242: 177-189

Macdonald G A, 1954. The 1942 eruption of Mauna Loa, Hawaii. *Amer J Sci*, 241: 241-256

Macdonald G A, 1955. Hawaiian Islands. *Catalog of Active Volcanoes of the World and Solfatara Fields*, Rome: IAVCEI, 3: 1-37 ***(regional reference)***

Macdonald G A, 1959. The activity of Hawaiian volcanoes during the years 1951-1956. *Bull Volc*, 22: 3-70

Macdonald G A, 1962. The 1959 and 1960 eruptions of Kilauea volcano, Hawaii, and the construction of walls to restrict the spread of the lava flows. *Bull Volc*, 24: 249-294

Macdonald G A, 1978. Geologic map of the crater section of Haleakala National Park, Maui, Hawaii. *U S Geol Surv Map*, I-1088, 8 p text

Macdonald G A, Abbott A T, 1970. *Volcanoes in the Sea*. Honolulu: Univ Hawaii Press, 441 p ***(regional reference)***

Macdonald G A, Hubbard D H, 1975. Volcanoes of the National Parks in Hawaii. *Hawaii Nat Hist Assoc*, 60 p

Malahoff A, 1987. Geology of the summit of Loihi submarine volcano. *U S Geol Surv Prof Pap*, 1350: 133-144

Mangan M T, Heliker C C, Mattox T N, Kauahikaua J P, Heltz R T, 1995. Episode 49 of the Pu'u 'O'o-Kupaianaha eruption of Kilauea volcano - breakdown of a steady-state eruptive era. *Bull Volc*, 57: 127-135

Mangan M T, Heliker C C, Mattox T N, Kauahikaua J P, Helz R T, 1995. Episode 49 of the Pu'u 'O'o-Kupaianaha eruption of Kilauea volcano - breakdown of a steady-state eruptive era. *Bull Volc*, 57: 127-135

Mastin L G, 1997. Evidence for water influx from a caldera lake during the explosive hydromagmatic eruption of 1790, Kiauea volcano, Hawaii. *J Geophys Res*, 102: 20,093-20,109

Mastin L G, Christiansen R L, Thornber C, Lowenstern J, Beeson M, 2004. What makes hydromagmatic eruptions violent? Some insights from the Keanakako'i Ash, Kilauea volcano, Hawai'i. *J Volc Geotherm Res*, 137: 15-31

Mattox T N, Heliker C, Kauahikaua J, Hon K, 1993. Development of the 1990 Kalapana flow field, Kilauea volcano, Hawaii. *Bull Volc*, 55: 407-413

McPhie J, Walker G P L, Christiansen R L, 1990. Phreatomagmatic and phreatic fall and surge deposits from explosions at Kilauea volcano, Hawaii, 1790 A.D.: Keanakakoi Ash Member. *Bull Volc*. 52: 334-354

Moore J G, Clague D A, Holcomb R T, Lipman P W, Normark W R, Torresan M E, 1989. Prodigous submarine landslides on the Hawaiian Ridge. *J Geophys Res*, 94: 17,465-17,484

Moore J G, Clague D A, Normark W R, 1982. Diverse basalt types from Loihi seamount, Hawaii. *Geology*, 10: 88-92

Moore J G, Koyanagi R Y, 1969. The October 1963 eruption of Kilauea volcano, Hawaii. *U S Geol Surv Prof Pap*, 614-C: 1-13

Moore J G, Krivoy H L, 1964. The 1962 flank eruption of Kilauea volcano and structure of the East Rift Zone. *J Geophys Res*, 69: 2033-2045

Moore J G, Normark W R, Lipman P W, 1979. Loihi seamount-a young submarine Hawaiian volcano (abs). *Hawaii Symp Intraplate Volc & Submarine Volc, Hilo, Hawaii, Abs*, p 127

Moore R B, Clague D A, Rubin M, Bohrson W A, 1987. Hualalai volcano: a preliminary summary of geologic, petrologic, and geophysical data. *U S Geol Surv Prof Pap*, 1350: 571-585

Moore R B, Helz R T, Dzurisin D, Eaton G P, Koyanagi R Y, Lipman P W, Lockwood J P, Puniwai G S, 1980. The 1977 eruption of Kilauea volcano, Hawaii. *J Volc Geotherm Res*, 7: 189-210

Moore R B, Trusdell F A, 1991. Geologic map of the lower east rift zone of Kilauea volcano, Hawaii. *U S Geol Surv Misc Invest Ser Map*, I-2225, 1:24,000 geol map

Mullineaux D R, Peterson D W, Crandell D R, 1987. Volcanic hazards in the Hawaiian Islands. *U S Geol Surv Prof Pap*, 1350: 599-621

Okubo C H, 2004. Rock mass strength and slope stability of the Hilina slump, Kilauea volcano, Hawai'i. *J Volc Geotherm Res*, 138: 43-76

Ozawa A, Tagami T, Garcia M O, 2005. Unspiked K-Ar dating of Honolulu rejuvenated and Ko'olau shield volcanism on O'ahu, Hawai'i. *Earth Planet Sci Lett*, 232: 1-11

Parfitt E A, Wilson L, 1994. The 1983-86 Pu'u 'O'o eruption of Kilauea volcano, Hawaii: a study of dike geometry and eruption mechanisms for a long-lived eruption. *J Volc Geotherm Res*, 59: 179-205

Peterson D W, Moore R B, 1987. Geologic history and evolution of geologic concepts, island of Hawaii. *U S Geol Surv Prof Pap*, 1350: 149-189

Porter S C, 1973. Stratigraphy and chronology of late Quaternary tephra along the South Rift Zone of Mauna Kea volcano, Hawaii. *Geol Soc Amer Bull*, 84: 1923-1940

Reber G, 1959. Age of lava flows on Haleakala, Hawaii. *Geol Soc Amer Bull*, 70: 1245-1246

Riker J M, Cashman K V, Kauahikaua J P, Montierth C M, 2009. The length of channelized lava flows: Insight from the 1859 eruption of Mauna Loa volcano, Hawaii. *J Volc Geotherm Res*, 183: 139-156

Robinson J E, Eakins B W, 2006. Calculated volumes of individual shield volcanoes at the young end of the Hawaiian Ridge. *J Volc Geotherm Res*, 151: 309-317

Sano H, Sherrod D R, Tagami T, 2006. Youngest volcanism about 1 million years ago at Kahoolawe Island, Hawaii. *J Volc Geotherm Res*, 152: 91-96

Sharp R P, Dzurisin D, Malin M C, 1987. An early nineteenth century reticulite pumice from Kilauea volcano. *U S Geol Surv Prof Pap*, 1350: 395-404

Sherrod D R, McGeehin J P, 1999. New radiocarbon ages from Haleakala crater, island of Maui, Hawai'i. *U S Geol Surv Open-File Rpt*, 99-143: 1-14

Sherrod D R, Murai T, Tagami T, 2007. New K-Ar ages for calculating end-of-shield extrusion rates at West Maui volcano, Hawaiian island chain. *Bull Volc*, 69: 627-642

Soule S A, Cashman K V, Kauahikaua J P, 2004. Examining flow emplacement through the surface morphology of three rapidly emplaced, solidified lava flows, Kilauea volcano, Hawai'i. *Bull Volc*, 66: 1-14

Stearns H T, 1926. The Keaina or 1823 lava flow from Kilauea volcano, Hawaii. *J Geol*, 34: 336-351

Stearns H T, 1946. Geology of the Hawaiian Islands. *Hawaii Div Hydrography Bull*, 8: 1-105

Stearns H T, 1966. *Geology of the State of Hawaii*. Palo Alto, California: Pacific Books Pub, 266 p

Swanson D A, 2008. Hawaiian oral tradition describes 400 years of volcanic activity at Kilauea. *J Volc Geotherm Res*, 176: 427-431

Swanson D A, Christiansen R L, 1973. Tragic base surge in 1790 at Kilauea volcano. *Geology*, 1: 83-86

Swanson D A, Duffield W A, Jackson D B, Peterson D W, 1979. Chronological narrative of the 1969-71 Mauna Ulu eruption of Kilauea volcano, Hawaii. *U S Geol Surv Prof Pap*, 1056: 1-55

U S Geol Surv, 1999. Youngest lava flows on East Maui probably older than A.D. 1790. *http://hvo.wr.usgs.gov/volcanowatch/1999/99_09_09.html*

U S Geol Surv, 2002. Tables of new volcano-related radiocarbon ages for East Maui (Haleakala volcano) as of 2002. *http://hvo.usgs.gov/volcanoes/halakala.c14ages_2002.pdf*

Wanless V D, Garcia M O, Rhodes J M, Weis D, Norman M D, 2006. Shield-stage alkalic volcanism on Mauna Loa volcano, Hawaii. *J Volc Geotherm Res*, 151: 141-155

Weinstein J P, Fodor R V, Bauer G R, 2004. Koolau shield basalt as xenoliths entrained during rejuvenated-stage eruptions: perspectives on magma mixing. *Bull Volc*, 66: 182-199

Wolfe E W, Wise W S, Dalrymple B, 1997. The geology and petrology of Mauna Kea volcano, Hawaii-a study of postshield volcanism. *U S Geol Surv Prof Pap*, 1557: 1-129

Wood H O, 1917. On cyclical variations in eruption at Kilauea. *Rpt Hawaiian Volcano Observ*, 2: 1-59

Wright T L, 1971a. Chemistry of Kilauea and Mauna Loa in space and time. *U S Geol Surv Prof Pap*, 735: 1-40

Wright T L, Helz R T, 1996. Differentiation and magma mixing on Kilauea's east rift zone: a further look at the eruptions of 1955 and 1960. Part II. The 1960 lavas. *Bull Volc*, 57: 602-630

Wright T L, Kinoshita W T, Peck D L, 1968. March 1965 eruption of Kilauea volcano and the formation of Makaopuhi lava lake. *J Geophys Res*, 73: 3181-3205

Wright T L, Takahashi T J, Griggs J D, 1992. *Hawai'i Volcano Watch: a Pictorial History, 1779-1991*. Honolulu: Univ Hawaii Press, 162 p

Yokose H, Lipman P W, 2004. Emplacement mechanisms of the South Kona slide complex, Hawaii Island: sampling and observations by remotely operated vehicle Kaiko. *Bull Volc*, 66: 569-584

Zimbelman J R, Garry W B, Johnston A K, Williams S H, 2008. Emplacement of the 1907 Mauna Loa basalt flow as derived from precision topography and satellite imaging. *J Volc Geotherm Res*, 177: 837-847

MEXICO (1401)

Abrams M J, Siebe C, 1994. Cerro Xalapaxco: an unusual tuff cone with multiple explosion craters, in central Mexico (Puebla). *J Volc Geotherm Res*, 63: 183-199

Aguirre-Diaz G J, Jaimes-Vierra M C, Nieto-Obregon J, 2006. The Valle de Bravo volcanic field: geology and geomorphometric parameters of a Quaternary monogenetic field at the front of the Mexican Volcanic Belt. *In*: Siebe S, Macias J-L, Aguirre-Diaz G J (eds) Neogone-Quaternary continental margin volcanism: a perspective from Mexico, *Geol Soc Amer Spec Pap*, 402: 139-154

Alonso H, 1976. Geothermal potential of Mexico. *In*: *Proc 2nd United Nations Symp Devel Use Geotherm Resour, San Francisco*, Washington D C: U S Government Printing Office, 1: 621-624

Aranda-Gomez J J, Housh T B, Luhr J F, Noyola-Medrano C, Rojas-Beltrán M A, 2009. Origin and formation of neck in a basin landform: examples from the Camargo volcanic field, Chihuahua (Mexico). *J Volc Geotherm Res*, doi:10.1016/j.jvolgeores.2009.08.004

Aranda-Gomez J J, Luhr J F, 1996. Origin of the Joya Honda maar, San Luis Potosi, Mexico. *J Volc Geotherm Res*, 74: 1-18

Aranda-Gomez J J, Luhr J F, Housh T B, Conner C B, Becker T, Henry C D, 2003. Synextensional Pliocene-Pleistocene eruptive activity in the Camargo volcanic field, Chihuahua, Mexico. *Geol Soc Amer Bull*, 115: 298-313

Aranda-Gomez J J, Luhr J F, Pier J G, 1992. The La Brena - El Jaguey maar complex, Durango, Mexico: I. Geological evolution. *Bull Volc*, 54: 393-404

Arce J L, Cervantes K E, Macias J L, Mora J C, 2005. The 12.1 ka Middle Toluca Pumice: a dacitic plinian-subplinian eruption of Nevado de Toluca in Central Mexico. *J Volc Geotherm Res*, 147: 125-143

Arce J L, Macias J L, Vazquez-Selem L, 2003. The 10.5 ka plinian eruption of Nevado de Toluca volcano, Mexico: stratigraphy and hazard implications. *Geol Soc Amer Bull*, 115: 230-248

Arce J L, Macias R, Palomo A G, Capra L, Macias J L, Layer P, Rueda H, 2008. Late Pleistocene flank collapse of Zempoala volcano (Central Mexico) and the role of fault reactivation. *J Volc Geotherm Res*, 177: 944-958

Arciniega-Ceballos A, Chouet B, Dawson P, 2003. Long-period events and tremor at Popocatepetl volcano (1994-2000) and their broadband characteristics. *Bull Volc*, 65: 124-135

Arciniega-Ceballos A, Valdes-Gonzalez C, Dawson P, 2000. Temporal and spectral characteristics of seismicity observed at Popocatepetl Volcano, central Mexico. *J Volc Geotherm Res*, 102: 207-216

Armienta M A, De la Cruz-Reyna S, 1995. Some hydro-geochemical fluctuations observed in Mexico related to volcanic activity. *Applied Geochem*, 10: 215-227

Armienta M A, De la Cruz-Reyna S, Macias J L, 2000. Chemical characteristics of the crater lakes of Popocatepetl, El Chichon, and Nevado de Toluca volcanoes, Mexico. *J Volc Geotherm Res*, 97: 105-125

Arreola J M, 1903. The recent eruptions of Colima. *J Geol*, 11: 749-761

Atl, 1922. L'attivita del Popocatepetl. *Zeit Vulk*, 6: 183-191

Ban M, Hasenaka T, Delgado G H, Takaoka N, 1992. K-Ar ages of lavas from shield volcanoes in the Michoacan-Guanajuato volcanic field, Mexico. *Geof Internac*, 31: 467-473

Barragan-R R M, Birkle P, Portugal-M E, Arrellano-G V M, Alvarez-R J, 2001. Geochemical survey of medium temperature geothermal resources from the Baja California Peninsula and Sonora, Mexico. *J Volc Geotherm Res*, 110: 101-119

Batiza R, 1977. Petrology and chemistry of Guadalupe Island: an alkalic seamount on a fossil ridge crest. *Geology*, 5: 760-764

Batiza R, 1978. Geology, petrology, and geochemistry of Isla Tortuga, a recently formed tholeiitic island in the Gulf of California. *Geol Soc Amer Bull*, 89: 1309-1324

Batiza R, Futa K, Hedge C E, 1979. Trace element and strontium isotope characteristics of volcanic rocks from Isla Tortuga: a young seamount in the Gulf of California. *Earth Planet Sci Lett*, 43: 269-278

Beal C H, 1948. Reconnaissance of the geology and oil possibilities of Baja California, Mexico. *Geol Soc Amer Mem*, 31: 1-138

Bellon H, Aguillon-Robles A, Calmus T, Maury R C, Bourgois J, Cotten J, 2006. La Purisima volcanic field, Baja California Sur (Mexico): Miocene to Quaternary volcanism related to subduction and opening of an asthenospheric window. *J Volc Geotherm Res*, 152: 253-272

Bellotti F, Capra L, Groppelli G, Norini G, 2006. Tectonic evolution of the central-eastern sector of Trans Mexican Volcanic Belt and its influence on the eruptive history of the Nevado de Toluca volcano (Mexico). *J Volc Geotherm Res*, 158: 21-36

Blatter D L, Carmichael I S E, 1998. Hornblende peridotite xenoliths from central Mexico reveal the highly oxidized nature of subarc upper mantle. *Geology*, 26: 1035-1038

Blatter D L, Carmichael I S E, 1998. Plagioclase-free andesites from Zitacuaro (Michoacan), Mexico; petrology and experimental constraints. *Contr Mineral Petr*, 132: 121-138

Blatter D L, Carmichael I S E, Deino A L, Renne P R, 2001. Neogene volcanism at the front of the central Mexican volcanic belt; basaltic andesites to dacites, with contemporaneous shoshonites and high-TiO2 lava. *Geol Soc Amer Bull*, 113: 1324-1342

Bloomfield K, 1973. The age and significance of the Tenango basalt, central Mexico. *Bull Volc*, 37: 586-595

Bloomfield K, 1975. A late-Quaternary monogenetic volcano field in central Mexico. *Geol Rundschau*, 64: 476-496

Bloomfield K, Valastro S, 1977. Late Quaternary tephrochronology of Nevado de Toluca volcano, central Mexico. *Overseas Geol Min Res*, 46: 1-15

Bohrson W A, Reid M R, 1995. Petrogenesis of alkaline basalts from Socorro Island, Mexico; trace element evidence for contamination of ocean island basalt in the shallow ocean crust. *J Geophys Res*, 100: 24,555-24,576

Bohrson W A, Reid M R, 1997. Genesis of silicic peralkaline volcanic rocks in an ocean island setting by crustal melting and open-system processes; Socorro Island, Mexico. *J Petr*, 38: 1137-1166

Bohrson W A, Reid M R, Grunder A L, Heizler M T, Harrison T M, Lee J, 1996. Prolonged history of silicic peralkaline volcanism in the eastern Pacific Ocean. *J Geophys Res*, 101: 11,457-11,474

Boudal C, Robin C, 1988. Relations entre dynamismes eruptifs et realimentations magmatiques d'origine profonde au Popocatepetl. Translated Title: Relations between eruption dynamics and deep magmatic replenishment of Popocatepetl. *Can J Earth Sci*, 25: 955-971

Boudal C, Robin C, 1989. Volcan Popocatepetl: recent eruptive history, and potential hazards and risks in future eruptions. *In*: Latter J H (ed), *Volcanic Hazards - Assessment and Monitoring*, Berlin: Springer-Verlag, p 110-128

Breton-Gonzalez M, Ramirez J J, Navarro C, 2002. Summary of the historical eruptive activity of Volcan de Colima, Mexico 1519-2000. *J Volc Geotherm Res*, 117: 21-46

Browne B L, Gardner J E, 2004. The nature and timing of caldera collapse as indicated by accidental lithic fragments from the AD ~1000 eruption of Volcan Ceboruco, Mexico. *J Volc Geotherm Res*, 130: 93-105

Browne B L, Gardner J E, 2005. Transport and deposition of pyroclastic material from the ~1000 A.D. caldera-forming eruption of Volcan Ceboruco, Nayarit, Mexico. *Bull Volc*, 67: 469-489

Bryan W B, 1966. History and mechanism of eruption of soda-rhyolite and alkali basalt Socorro Island, Mexico. *Bull Volc*, 29: 453-480

Bryan W B, 1976. A basalt - pantellerite association from Isla Socorro, Islas Revillagigedo, Mexico. *In*: Aoki H, Iizuka S (eds), *Volcanoes and Tectonosphere*, Tokyo: Tokai Univ Press, p 75-91

Cabral-Cano E, Armienta-Hernandez M A, Urrutia-Fucugauchi J, 1990. Reconocimiento geologico y paleomagnetico en la Isla Isabel, Narayit, Mexico. *Rev Geofis*, 31: 161-184

Calanchi N, Lucchini F, Navarro O C, Rossi P L, Sanchez P J, 1995. The magmatic evolution of the "modern" activity of the Nevado de Colima Volcano in relation to the Colima volcanic complex activity (Mexico). *Acta Vulc*, 7: 75-84

Calmus T, Aguillon-Robles A, Maury R C, Bellon H, Benoit M, Cotten J, Bourgois J, Michaud F, 2003. Spatial and temporal evolution of basalts and magnesian andesites ("bajaites") from Baja California, Mexico: the role of slab melts. *Lithos*, 66: 77-105

Campos-Enriquez J O, Arredondo-Fragoso J J, 1992. Gravity study of Los Humeros caldera complex, Mexico; structure and associated geothermal system. *J Volc Geotherm Res*, 49: 69-90

Campos-Enriquez J O, Garduno-Monroy V H, 1995. Los Azufres silicic center (Mexico): inference of caldera structural elements from gravity, aeromagnetic, and geoelectric data. *J Volc Geotherm Res*, 67:123-152

Camprubi, A, Canet C, Rodriquez-Diaz A A, Prol-Ledesma R M, Blanco-Florido D, Villanueva R E, Lopez-Sanchez A, 2008. Geology, ore deposits and hydrothermal venting in Bahia Concepcion, Baja California Sur, Mexico. *Island Arc*, 17: 6-25

Canon-Tapia E, Walker G P L, Herrero-Bervera E, 1995. Magnetic fabric and flow direction in basaltic pahoehoe lava of Xitle Volcano, Mexico. *J Volc Geotherm Res*, 65: 249-263

Cantagrel J-M, Gourgaud A, Robin C, 1984. Repetitive mixing events and Holocene pyroclastic activity at Pico de Orizaba and Popocatepetl (Mexico). *Bull Volc*, 47: 735-748

Cantagrel J-M, Robin C, Vincent P, 1981. Les grandes etapes d'evolution d'un volcan andesitique composite: exemple du Nevado de Toluca (Mexique). *Bull Volc*, 44: 177-188

Capra L Carreras L M, Arce J L, Macias J L, 2006. The Lower Toluca Pumice: a ca. 21,700 yr B.P. plinian eruption of Nevado de Toluca volcano, Mexico. *In*: Siebe S, Macias J-L, Aguirre-Diaz G J (eds) Neogone-Quaternary continental margin volcanism: a perspective from Mexico, *Geol Soc Amer Spec Pap*, 402: 155-173

Capra L, Macias J L, 2000. Pleistocene cohesive debris flows at Nevado de Toluca volcano, central Mexico. *J Volc Geotherm Res*, 102: 149-168

Capra L, Macias J L, 2002. The cohesive Naranjo debris-flow deposit (10 km3): a dam breakout flow derived from the Pleistocene debris-avalanche deposit of Nevado de Colima volcano (Mexico). *J Volc Geotherm Res*, 117: 215-235

Capra L, Macias J L, Espindola J M, Siebe C, 1998. Holocene plinian eruption of La Virgen volcano, Baja California, Mexico. *J Volc Geotherm Res*, 80: 239-266

Capra L, Macias J L, Garduno V H, 1997. The Zitacuaro volcanic complex, Michoacan, Mexico: magmatic and eruptive history of a resurgent caldera. *Geof Internac*, 36: 161-179

Capra L, Macias J L, Scott K M, Abrams M, Garduno-Monroy V H, 2002. Debris avalanches and debris flows transformed from collapses in the Trans-Mexican Volcanic Belt, Mexico - behavior, and implications for hazard assessment. *J Volc Geotherm Res*, 113: 81-110

Capra L, Norini G, Groppelli G, Macias J L, Arce J L, 2008. Volcanic hazard zonation of the Nevado de Toluca volcano, Mexico. *J Volc Geotherm Res*, 176: 469-484

Capra L, Poblete M A, Alvarado R, 2004. The 1997 and 2001 lahars of Popocatepetl volcano (central Mexico): textural and sedimentological constraints on their origin and hazards. *J Volc Geotherm Res*, 131: 351-369

Carey S, Sigurdsson H, 1986. The 1982 eruptions of El Chichon volcano, Mexico (2): Observations and numerical modelling of tephra-fall distribution. *Bull Volc*, 48: 127-142

Carmichael I S E, Frey H M, Lange R A, Hall C M, 2006. The Pleistocene cinder cones surrounding Volcan Colima, Mexico revisited: eruption ages and volumes, oxidation states, and sulfur content. *Bull Volc*, 68: 407-419

Carmichael I S E, Lange R A, Luhr J F, 1996. Quaternary minettes and associated volcanic rocks of Mascota, western Mexico: a consequence of plate extension above a subduction modified mantle wedge. *Contr Mineral Petr*, 124: 302-333

Carr M J, 1984. Symmetrical and segmented variation of physical and geochemical characterisitics of the Central American volcanic front. *J Volc Geotherm Res*, 20: 231-252

Carrasco-Nunez G, 1997. Lava flow growth inferred from morphometric parameters: a case study of Citlaltepetl volcano, Mexico. *Geol Mag*, 134: 151-162

Carrasco-Nunez G, 1999. Holocene block-and-ash flows from summit dome activity of Citlaltepetl volcano, Eastern Mexico. *J Volc Geotherm Res*, 88: 47-66

Carrasco-Nunez G, 2000. Structure and proximal stratigraphy of Citlaltepetl volcano (Pico de Orizaba), Mexico. *In*; Delgado-Granados H, Aguirre-Diaz G J, Stock J M (eds), *Cenozoic Tectonics and Volcanism of Mexico, Geol Soc Amer Spec Pap*, 334: 247-262

Carrasco-Nunez G, Ban M, 1994. Geologic map and structure sections of the Citlaltepetl volcano summit area, Mexico. Univ Nac Auton Mexico, Cartas Geologicas Mineras no. 9

Carrasco-Nunez G, Branney M J, 2005. Progressive assembly of a massive layer of ignimbrite with a normal-to-reverse compositional zoning: the Zaragoza ignimbrite of central Mexico. *Bull Volc*, 68: 3-20

Carrasco-Nunez G, Diaz-Castellon R, Siebert L, Hubbard B, Sheridan M F, Rodriguez S R, 2006. Multiple edifice-collapse events in the Eastern Mexican Volcanic Belt: the role of sloping substrate and implications for hazard assessment. *J Volc Geotherm Res*, 158: 151-176

Carrasco-Nunez G, Gomez-Tuena A, 1997. Volcanogenic sedimentation around Citlaltepetl (Pico de Orizaba) volcano and surroundings, Veracruz, Mexico. *In*: Aguirre G J, Aranda J J, Carrasco G, Ferrari L (eds) *Magmatism and tectonics of central and northwestern Mexico - a selection of the 1997 IAVCEI General Assembly excursions*, Mexico, D F: UNAM, Inst Geol, p 131-151

Carrasco-Nunez G, Ort M H, Romero C, 2007. Evolution and hydrological conditions of a maar volcano (Atexcac crater, Eastern Mexico). *J Volc Geotherm Res*, 159: 179-197

Carrasco-Nunez G, Riggs N R, 2008. Polygenetic nature of a rhyolitic dome and implications for hazard assessment: Cerro Pizarro volcano, Mexico. *J Volc Geotherm Res*, 171: 307-315

Carrasco-Nunez G, Righter K, Chesley J, Siebert L, Aranda-Gomez J-J, 2005. Contemporaneous eruption of calc-alkaline and alkaline lavas in a continental arc (eastern Mexican volcanic belt); chemically heterogeneous but isotopically homogeneous source. *Contr Mineral Petr*, 150: 423-440

Carrasco-Nunez G, Rose W I, 1995. Eruption of a major Holocene pyroclastic flow at Citlaltepetl volcano (Pico de Orizaba), Mexico, 8.5-9.0 ka. *J Volc Geotherm Res*, 69: 197-215

Carrasco-Nunez G, Siebert L, Diaz-Castellon R, Vazquez-Selem L, Capra L, 2009. Evolution and hazards of a long-quiescent compound shield-like volcano: Cofre de Perote, Eastern Trans-Mexican Volcanic Belt. *J Volc Geotherm Res*, doi:10.1016/j.jvolgeores.2009.08.010

Carrasco-Nunez G, Vallance J W, Rose W I, 1993. A voluminous avalanche-induced lahar from Citlaltepetl volcano, Mexico: implications for hazard assessments. *J Volc Geotherm Res*, 59: 35-46

Casadevall T J, De la Cruz-Reyna S, Rose W I, Bagley S, Finnegan D L, Zoller W H, 1984. Crater Lake and post-eruption hydrothermal activity, El Chichon volcano, Mexico. *J Volc Geotherm Res*, 23: 169-191

Casadevall T J, Rose W I Jr, Fuller W H, Hunt W H, Hart M A, Moyers J L, Woods D C, Chuan R L, Friend J, 1984. Sulfur dioxide and particles in quiescent volcanic plumes from Poas, Arenal, and Colima volcanos, Costa Rica and Mexico. *J Geophys Res*, 89: 9633-9641

Castro-Govea R, Siebe C, 2007. Late Pleistocene-Holocene stratigraphy and radiocarbon dating of La Malinche volcano, central Mexico. *J Volc Geotherm Res*, 162: 20-42

Cervantes P, Wallace P, 2003. Magma degassing and basaltic eruption styles: a case study of ~2000 year BP Xitle volcano in central Mexico. *J Volc Geotherm Res*, 120: 249-270

Cortes A, Macías J L, Capra L, Garduno-Monroy V H, 2009. Sector collapse of the SW flank of Volcan de Colima, Mexico: The 3600 yr BP La Lumbre-Los Ganchos debris avalanche and associated debris flows. *J Volc Geotherm Res*, doi:10.1016/j.jvolgeores.2009.11.013

Crausaz W, 1993. *Pico de Orizaba or Citlaltepetl: geology, archaeology, history, natural history, and mountaineering routes*. Amherst, Ohio: Geopress Internatl, 594 p

de Boer J Z, 1980. Paleomagnetism of the Quaternary Cerro Prieto, Crater Elegante, and Salton Buttes volcanic domes in the northern part of the Gulf of California rhombochasm. *Proc 2nd Symp Cerro Prieto Geotherm Field, Baja Calif, Mexico*, p 91-102

de Cserna Z, Aranda-Gomez J J, Mitre-Salazar L M, 1988. Mapa fotogeologico preliminar: secciones estructurales y resumen de la historia eruptiva del Volcan Tacana, Mexico y Guatemala. *Inst Geofis, Univ Nac Autonoma Mexico*, Cartas Geolgicas Mineras no 7

De la Cruz-Martinez V, Castillo-H D, 1986. Geologia de la zona geotermica de la Caldera de Acoculco, Puebla. Translated Title: Geology of the geothermal zone of the Acoculco Caldera, Puebla. *Geotermia*, 2: 245-254

De la Cruz-Reyna S, 1993. Random patterns of occurrence of explosive eruptions at Colima volcano, Mexico. *J Volc Geotherm Res*, 55: 51-68

De la Cruz-Reyna S, Carrasco-Nunez G, 2002. Probabilistic hazard analysis of Citlaltepetl (Pico de Orizaba) Volcano, eastern Mexican Volcanic Belt. *J Volc Geotherm Res*, 113: 307-318

De la Cruz-Reyna S, Mena M, Segovia N, Chalot J F, Seidel J L, Monnin M, 1985. Radon emanometry in soil gases and activity in ashes from El Chichon volcano. *Pure Applied Geophys*, 123: 407-421

De la Cruz-Reyna S, Quezada J L, Pena C, Zepeda O, Sanchez T, 1995. Historia de la actividad reciente del Volcan Popocatepetl. *In*: *Volcan Popocatepetl Estudios Realizados durante la Crisis de 1994-1995*, Mexico City: SINAPROC-CENEPRED-UNAM, p 3-22

De la Cruz-Reyna S, Siebe C, 1997. Volcanology; the giant Popocatepetl stirs. *Nature*, 388: 227

Delgado H, Arana-Salinas L, Nieto-Obregon J, Mendoza-Rosales C, Silva-Romo G, 1997. Pelado volcano in southern Mexico City, a young monogenetic volcano (<1000 years old) and its possible impact on human settlements. *IAVCEI General Assembly, Puerto Vallarta, Mexico, January 19-24, 1997, Abs*, p 123

Delgado H, Romero-Taran E, Cervantes P, Molinero R, Nieto-Obregon J, Mendoza-Rosales C, Silva-Romo G, 1997. Volcan Ajusco (Mexico): evolution, collapse and volcano-tectonic relations, regional transition from polygenetic to monogenetic volcanism. *IAVCEI General*

Assembly, Puerto Vallarta, Mexico, January 19-24, 1997, Abs, p 124

Delgado-Granados H, Cardenas-Gonzalez L, Piedad-Sanchez N, 2001. Sulfur dioxide emissions from Popocatepetl Volcano (Mexico); case study of a high-emission rate, passively degassing erupting volcano. *J Volc Geotherm Res*, 108: 107-120

Delgado-Granados H, Carrasco-Nunez G, Urrutia-Fucugauchi J, Casanova B M, 1988. Analysis of the eruptive records of the Popocatepetl volcano, Mexico. *Proc Kagoshima Internatl Conf Volc*, p 510-513

Dobson P F, Mahood G A, 1985. Volcanic stratigraphy of the Los Azufres geothermal area, Mexico. *J Volc Geotherm Res*, 25: 273-287

Dominguez T, Zobin V M, Reyes-Davilla G A, 2001. The fracturing in volcanic edifice before an eruption; the June-July 1998 high-frequency earthquake swarm at Volcan de Colima, Mexico. *J Volc Geotherm Res*, 105: 65-75

Duffield W A, 2001. At least Noah had some warning. *Eos, Trans Amer Geophys Union*, 82: 305, 309

Duffield W A, Tilling R I, Canul R, 1984. Geology of El Chichon volcano, Chiapas, Mexico. *J Volc Geotherm Res*, 20: 117-132

Erlund E J, Cashman K V, Wallace P J, Pioli L, Rosi M, Johnson E, Delgado Granados H, 2009. Compositional evolution of magma from Paricutin Volcano, Mexico: the tephra record. *J Volc Geotherm Res*, doi:10.1016/j.jvolgeores.2009.09.015

Espinasa-Perena R, Martin-del Pozzo A L, 2006. Morphostratigraphic evolution of Popocatepetl volcano, Mexico. *In*: Siebe S, Macias J-L, Aguirre-Diaz G J (eds) Neogone-Quaternary continental margin volcanism: a perspective from Mexico, *Geol Soc Amer Spec Pap*, 402: 115-137

Espindola J M, Zamora-Camacho A, Godinez M L, Schaaf P, Rodríguez S R, 2009. The 1793 eruption of San Martin Tuxtla volcano, Veracruz, Mexico. *J Volc Geotherm Res*, doi:10.1016/j.jvolgeores.2009.08.005

Espindola J M, Macias J L, Tilling R I, Sheridan M F, 2000. Volcanic history of El Chichon Volcano (Chiapas, Mexico) during the Holocene, and its impact on human activity. *Bull Volc*, 62: 90-104

Ferrari L, Tagami T, Eguchi M, Orozco-Esquivel M T, Petrone C M, Jacobo-Albarran J, Lopez-Martinez M, 2005. Geology, geochronology and tectonic setting of late Cenozoic volcanism along the southwestern Gulf of Mexico: the Eastern Alkaline Province revisited. *J Volc Geotherm Res*, 146: 284-306

Ferrari L, Nelson S A, Rosas-Elguera J, Aguirre G, 1997. Tectonics and volcanism of the western Mexican volcanic belt. IAVCEI General Assembly, Puerto Vallarta, Mexico, January 19-24, 1997, Fieldtrip Guidebook, Excursion no 12, 61 p

Ferrari L, Pasquare G, Venegas-Salgado S, Romero-Rios F, 2000. Geology of the western Mexican Volcanic Belt and adjacent Sierra Madre Occidental and Jalisco block. *In*; Delgado-Granados H, Aguirre-Diaz G J, Stock J M (eds), *Cenozoic Tectonics and Volcanism of Mexico, Geol Soc Amer Spec Pap*, 334: 85-97

Ferriz H, Mahood G A, 1984. Eruption rates and compositional trends at Los Humeros Volcanic Center, Puebla Mexico. *J Geophys Res*, 89: 8511-8524

Ferriz H, Mahood G A, 1987. Strong compositional zonation in a silicic magmatic system: Los Humeros, Mexican neovolcanic belt. *J Petr*, 28: 171-209

Foshag W F, Gonzalez-Reyna J, 1956. Birth and development of Paricutin volcano. *U S Geol Surv Bull*, 965-D: 355-489

Freundt A, Kutterolf S, Schmincke H-U, Hansteen T, Wehrmann H, Perez W, Strauch W, Navarro M, 2006. Volcanic hazards in Nicaragua: past, present, and future. *In*: Rose W I, Bluth G J S, Carr M J, Ewert J W, Patino L C, Vallance J W (eds), Volcanic hazards in Central America, *Geol Soc Amer Spec Pap*, 412: 141-165

Frey H M, Lange R A, Hall C H, Delgado-Granados H, 2004. Magma eruption rates constrained by 40Ar/39Ar chronology and GIS for the Ceboruco-San Pedro volcanic field, western Mexico. *Geol Soc Amer Bull*, 116: 259-276

Fries C Jr, 1953. Volumes and weights of pyroclastic material, lava, and water erupted by Paricutin Volcano, Michoacan, Mexico. *Eos, Trans Amer Geophys Union*, 34: 603-616

Fries C Jr, Guiterrez C, 1950a. Activity of Paricutin Volcano [Mexico] from August 1, 1948 to June 30, 1949. *Eos, Trans Amer Geophys Union*, 31: 406-418

Fries C Jr, Gutierrez C, 1950b. Activity of Paricutin volcano from July 1 to December 31, 1949. *Eos, Trans Amer Geophys Union*, 31: 732-740

Fries C Jr, Gutierrez C, 1951a. Activity of Paricutin volcano from July 1 to December 31, 1951. *Eos, Trans Amer Geophys Union*, 32: 572-581

Fries C Jr, Gutierrez C, 1951b. Activity of Paricutin volcano from January 1 to June 30, 1950. *Eos, Trans Amer Geophys Union*, 32: 212-221

Fries C Jr, Gutierrez C, 1952a. Activity of Paricutin volcano from January 1 to June 30, 1951. *Trans Am Geophys Union*, 33 (1): 91-100

Fries C Jr, Gutierrez C, 1952b. Activity of Paricutin volcano from July 1 to December 31, 1951. *Trans Am Geophys Union*, 33 (5): 725-733

Fries C Jr, Gutierrez C, 1954. Activity of Paricutin volcano in 1952. *Eos, Trans Amer Geophys Union*, 35: 486-494

Gadow H, 1930. *Jorullo*. London: Cambridge Univ Press, 100 p

Galbraith F W, 1959. Craters of the Pinacates. *Ariz Geol Soc, Southern Ariz Guidebook*, 2: 161-164

Galindo I, Dominguez T, 2002. Near real-time satellite monitoring during the 1997-2000 activity of Volcan de Colima (Mexico) and its relationship with seismic monitoring. *J Volc Geotherm Res*, 117: 91-104

Garcia-Palomo A, Macias J L, Arce J L, Capra L, Garduno V H, Espindola J M, 2002. Geology of Nevado de Toluca volcano and surrounding areas, central Mexico. *Geol Soc Amer Map & Chart Ser*, MCH080

Garcia-Palomo A, Macias J L, Arce J L, Mora J C, Hughes S, Saucedo R, Espindola J M, Escober R, Layer P, 2006. Geological evolution of the Tacana volcanic complex, Mexico-Guatemala. *In*: Rose W I, Bluth G J S, Carr M J, Ewert J W, Patino L C, Vallance J W (eds), Volcanic hazards in Central America, *Geol Soc Amer Spec Pap*, 412: 39-57

Garcia-Palomo A, Macias J L, Espindola J M, 2004. Strike-slip faults and K-alkaline volcanism at El Chichon volcano, southeastern Mexico. *J Volc Geotherm Res*, 136: 247-268

Garcia-Palomo A, Macias J L, Garduno V H, 2000. Miocene to Recent structural evolution of the Nevado de Toluca volcano region, central Mexico. *Tectonophysics*, 318: 281-302

Garcia-Palomo A, Macias J L, Mena M, 2000. El campo volcanico Apan-Tezontepec (CVAT) estados de Hidalgo, Tlaxacala y Mexico. *Colima Volcano Seventh Internatl Mtg Abs*, p. 74

Gardner J E, Tait S, 2000. The caldera-forming eruption of Volcan Ceboruco, Mexico. *Bull Volc*, 62: 20-33

Garduno-Monroy V H, Corona-Chavez P, Israde-Alcantara I, Mennella L, Arreygue E, Bigioggero B, Chiesa S, 1999. Carta Geologica de Michoacan. *Univ Michoacana de San Nicolás de Hidalgo*, 1:250,000 scale

Garduno-Monroy V H, Vargas-Ledezma H, Campos-Enriquez J O, 1993. Preliminary geologic studies of Sierra El Aguajito (Baja California, Mexico): a resurgent-type caldera. *J Volc Geotherm Res*, 59: 47-58

Gastil R G, Krummenacher D, Minch J, 1979. The record of Cenozoic volcanism around the Gulf of California. *Geol Soc Amer Bull*, 90: 839-857

Gastil R G, Phillips R P, Allison E C, 1975. Reconnaissance geology of the State of Baja California. *Geol Soc Amer Mem*, 140: 1-170

Goff F, Love S, Warren R G, Counce D, Obenholzner J, Siebe C, Schmidt S C, 2001. Passive infrared remote sensing evidence for large, intermittent CO2 emissions at Popocatepetl Volcano, Mexico. *Chem Geol*, 177: 133-156

Gomez-Tuena A, Carrasco-Nunez G, 1999. Fragmentation, transport and deposition of a low-grade ignimbrite; the Citlaltepetl Ignimbrite, eastern Mexico. *Bull Volc*, 60: 448-464

Gomez-Tuena A, Carrasco-Nunez G, 2000. Cerro Grande Volcano; the evolution of a Miocene stratocone in the early Trans-Mexican volcanic belt. *Tectonophysics*, 318:249-280

Gomez-Tuena, LaGatta A B, Langmuir C H, Goldstein S L, Ortega-Gutierrez F, Carrasco-Nunez G, 2003. Temporal control of subduction magmatism in the eastern Trans-Mexican Volcanic Belt: mantle sources, slab contributions, and crustal contamination. *Geochem Geophys Geosyst*, 4(8): 1-33

Gonzalez S, Pastrana A, Siebe C, Duller G, 2000. Timing of the prehistoric eruption of Xitle Volcano and the abandonment of Cuicuilco Pyramid, southern basin of Mexico. *In*: McGuire W J, Griffiths D, Stewarts I (eds) *Geol Soc Spec Pub*, 171: 205-224

Gonzalez-Partida E, Birkle P, Torres-Alvarado I S, 2000. Evolution of the hydrothermal system at Los Azufres, Mexico, based on petrologic, fluid inclusion and isotopic data. *J Volc Geotherm Res*, 104: 277-296

Gonzalez-Reyna J, 1956. A new volcano [possible Baha Peninsula submarine volcano]. *Proc 8th Pacific Sci Cong*, 2: 25

Guilbaud M-N, Siebe C, Agustin-Flores J, 2009. Eruptive style of the young high-Mg basaltic-andesite Pelagatos scoria cone, southeast of Mexico City. *Bull Volc*, 71: 859-880

Gutierrez-Coutino R, Moreno-Corzo M, Cruz-Borraz C, 1983. Determinacion del volumen del material arrojado y grado de explosivadad alcanzado por el Volcan Chichonal, Estado De Chipas. *In*: *El Volcan Chichonal*, Mexico City: Univ Nac Auton Mexico Inst Geol, p 68-80

Gutierrez-Negrin L C A, 1988. The La Primavera, Jalisco, Mexico, geothermal field. *Trans Geotherm Res Council*, 12: 161-165

Gutmann J G, 2002. Strombolian and effusive activity as precursors to phreatomagmatism: eruptive sequence at maars of the Pinacate volcanic field, Sonora, Mexico. *J Volc Geotherm Res*, 113: 345-356

Gutmann J T, 1976. Geology of Crater Elegante, Sonora, Mexico. *Geol Soc Amer Bull*, 87: 1718-1729

Gutmann J T, Sheridan M F, 1978. Geology of the Pinacate volcanic field. *In*: Burt D M, Pewe T L (eds), *Guidebook to the Geology of Central Arizona, Ariz Bur Geol Mineral Tech*, 2: 47-60

Hasenaka T, 1994. Size, distribution, and magma output rate for shield volcanoes of the Michoacan-Guanajuato volcanic field, Central Mexico. *J Volc Geotherm Res*, 63: 13-31

Hasenaka T, Carmichael I S E, 1985. The cinder cones of Michoacan-Guanajuato, central Mexico: their age, volume and distribution, and magma discharge rate. *J Volc Geotherm Res*, 25: 105-124

Haukwa C, Bodvarsson G S, Lippmann M J, Mainieri A, 1992. Preliminary reservoir engineering studies of the Miravalles geothermal field, Costa Rica. *Proc 17th Stanford Geotherm Workshop*, p 127-137

Hausback B P, 1984. Cenozoic volcanic and tectonic evolution of Baja California Sur, Mexico. *In*: Frizzell V A Jr (ed) *Geology of the Baja California Peninsula*, SEPM, 39: 219-236

Herzig C T, 1990. Geochemistry of igneous rocks from the Cerro Prieto geothermal field, northern Baja California, Mexico. *J Volc Geotherm Res*, 42: 261-271

Hooper D M, 1995. Computer-simulation models of scoria cone degradation in the Colima and Michoacan-Guanajuato volcanic field, Mexico. *Geof Internac*, 34: 321-340

Hoskuldsson A, 2001. Late Pleistocene subglacial caldera formation at Cerro las Cumbres, eastern Mexico. *Jokull*, 50: 49-64

Hoskuldsson A, Robin C, 1993. Late Pleistocene to Holocene eruptive activity of Pico de Orizaba, Eastern Mexico. *Bull Volc*, 55: 571-587

Housh T B, Aranda-Gomez J J, Luhr J F, 2009. Isla Isabel (Nayarit, Mexico): Quaternary alkalic basalts with mantle xenoliths erupted in the mouth of the Gulf of California. *J Volc Geotherm Res*, doi:10.1016/j.jvolgeores.2009.06.011

Ives R L, 1956. Age of Cerro Colorado Crater, Pinacate, Sonora, Mexico. *Eos, Trans Amer Geophys Union*, 37: 221-223

Ives R L, 1962. Dating of the 1746 eruption of Tres Virgenes volcano, Baja California del Sur, Mexico. *Geol Soc Amer Bull*, 73: 647-648

Ives R L, 1964. The Pinacate Region, Sonora, Mexico. *Calif Acad Sci Occ Pap*, 47: 1-43

Ivlev L S, Galindo I, Kudryashov V I, 1995. Estudio de aerosoles y cenizas dispersados durante la erupcion del Volcan Popocatepetl del 21 de Diciembre de 1994 - resultados prelimarares. *In*: *Volcan Popocatepetl Estudios Realizados durante la Crisis de 1994-1995*, Mexico City: SINAPROC-CENEPRED-UNAM, p 257-284

Jimenez Z, Espindola V H, Espindola J M, 1999. Evolution of the seismic activity from the 1982 eruption of El Chichon volcano, Chiapas, Mexico. *Bull Volc*, 61: 411-422

Jimenez Z, Reyes G, Espindola J M, 1995. The July 1994 episode of seismic activity at Colima Volcano, Mexico. *J Volc Geotherm Res*, 64: 321-326

Julio-Miranda P, Delgado-Granados H, Huggel C, Kaab A, 2008. Impact of the eruptive activity on glacier evolution at Popocatepetl volcano (Mexico) during 1994-2004. *J Volc Geotherm Res*, 170: 86-98

Kennedy G C, 1946. Activity of Paricutin Volcano [Mex.] from April 12 to May 3, 1946. *Eos, Trans Amer Geophys Union*, 27: 410-411

Kirianov V Y, Koloskov A V, De la Cruz-Reyna S, Martin del Pozzo A L, 1990. Main stages of the most recent volcanism in the Chichinautzin zone, Mexico volcanic belt. *Trans (Doklady) USSR Acad Sci Earth Sci*, 311: 81-83

Komorowski J C, Navarro C, Cortes A, Saucedo R, Gavilanes J C, Siebe C, Espindola J M, Rodriguez S, 1997. The Colima volcanic complex: Part I: Quaternary multiple debris-avalanche deposits, Part II: Historical pyroclastic sequences (1913, 1991, 1994). IAVCEI General Assembly, Puerto Vallarta, Mexico, January 19-24, 1997, Fieldtrip Guidebook, Excursion no 3

Krauskopf K B, Williams H, 1946. The activity of Paricutin during its third year. *Trans Am Geophys Union*, 27 (3): 406-410

Lange R A, Carmichael I S E, 1990. Hydrous basaltic andesites associated with minette and related lavas in western Mexico. *J Petr*, 31: 1225-1259

Lange R A, Carmichael I S E, 1991. A potassic volcanic front in western Mexico: the lamprophyric and related lavas of San Sebastian. *Geol Soc Amer Bull*, 103: 928-940

Lopez Loera H, Aranda-Gomez J J, Arzate J A, Molina-Garza R S, 2008. Geophysical surveys of the Joya Honda maar (Mexico) and surroundings: volcanic implications. *J Volc Geotherm Res*, 170: 135-152

Lugo-Hupb J, Ortiz-Perez M A, Palacio-Prieto J L, Bocco-Verdinelli G, 1985. Las zonas mas activas en el Cinturon Volcanico Mexicano (entre Michoacan y Tlaxcala). *Geof Internac*, 24: 83-96

Luhr J F, 1981. Colima: history and cyclicity of eruptions. *Volcano News*, 7: 1-3

Luhr J F, 2000. The geology and petrology of Volcan San Juan (Nayarit, Mexico) and the compositionally zoned Tepic pumice. *J Volc Geotherm Res*, 95: 109-156

Luhr J F, 2002. Petrology and geochemistry of the 1991 and 1998-1999 lava flows from Volcan de Colima, Mexico: implications for the end of the current eruptive cycle. *J Volc Geotherm Res*, 117: 169-194

Luhr J F, Aranda-Gomez J J, Housh T B, 1995. San Quintin volcanic field, Baja California Norte, Mexico: geology, petrology, and geochemistry. *J Geophys Res*, 100: 10,353-10,380

Luhr J F, Aranda-Gomez J J, Housh T B, Conner C B, Stamatakos J A, 1997. The Camargo volcanic field, Chihuahua, Mexico: Plio-Pleistocene extension-related basanites in the central Basin and Range province. *Eos, Trans Amer Geophys Union*, 78(suppl): 843

Luhr J F, Aranda-Gomez J J, Pier J G, 1989. Spinel-lherzolite-bearing Quaternary volcanic centers in San Luis Potosi, Mexico, 1. Geology, mineralogy, and petrology. *J Geophys Res*, 94: 7916-7940

Luhr J F, Carmichael I S E, 1980. The Colima volcanic complex, Mexico I. Post caldera andesites from Volcan Colima (and unpub list: History of eruptions of Volcan Colima). *Contr Mineral Petr*, 71: 343-372

Luhr J F, Carmichael I S E, 1981. The Colima volcanic complex, Mexico: II. Late Quaternary cinder cones. *Contr Mineral Petr*, 76: 127-147

Luhr J F, Carmichael I S E, 1982. The Colima volcanic complex, Mexico: III. Ash- and scoria-fall deposits from the upper slopes of Volcan Colima. *Contr Mineral Petr*, 80: 262-275

Luhr J F, Carmichael I S E, 1985. Jorullo volcano, Michoacan, Mexico (1759-1774): the earliest stages of fractionation in calc-alkaline magmas. *Contr Mineral Petr*, 90: 142-161

Luhr J F, Carmichael I S E, 1990. Geology of Volcan de Colima. *Univ Nac Auton Mexico, Inst Geol Bol*, 107: 1-101

Luhr J F, Carmichael I S E, 1990. Petrological monitoring of cyclical eruptive activity at Volcan Colima, Mexico. *J Volc Geotherm Res*, 42: 235-260

Luhr J F, Carmichael I S E, Varekamp J C, 1984. The 1982 eruptions of El Chichon Volcano, Chiapas, Mexico; mineralogy and petrology of the anhydrite-bearing pumices. *J Volc Geotherm Res*, 23: 69-108

Luhr J F, Delgado-Granados H, 1997. Aerial examination of volcanoes along the front of the western Trans-Mexican volcanic belt and a visit to Paricutin. IAVCEI General Assembly, Puerto Vallarta, Mexico, January 19-24, 1997, Fieldtrip Guidebook, Excursion no 9, 38 p

Luhr J F, Kimberly P G, Siebert L, Aranda-Gomez J J, Housh T B, Kysar Mattietti G, 2006. Quaternary volcanic rocks: insights from the MEXPET petrological and geochemical database. *In*: Siebe S, Macias J-L, Aguirre-Diaz G J (eds) *Neogene-Quaternary continental margin volcanism: a perspective from Mexico, Geol Soc Amer Spec Pap*, 402: 1-44

Luhr J F, Lazaar P, 1985. The Southern Guadalajara volcanic chain, Jalisco, Mexico. *Geof Internac*, 24: 691-700

Luhr J F, Navarro-Ochoa C, Savov I P, 2009. Tephrochronology, petrology and geochemistry of Late-Holocene pyroclastic deposits from Volcan de Colima, Mexico. *J Volc Geotherm Res*, doi: 10.1016/j.jvolgeores.2009.11.007

Luhr J F, Prestegaard K L, 1988. Caldera formation at Volcan Colima, Mexico, by a large Holocene volcanic debris avalanche. *J Volc Geotherm Res*, 35: 335-348

Luhr J F, Simkin T (eds), 1993. *Paricutin: The Volcano Born in a Mexican Cornfield*. Phoenix: Geoscience Press, 427 p

Lynch D J, Gutmann J T, 1988. Volcanic structures and alkaline rocks in the Pinacate volcanic field of Sonora, Mexico. *In*: Davis G H, VandenDolder E M (eds) *Geologic diversity of Arizona and its margins: excursions to choice areas*, Arizona Bur Geol Mineral Tech, 5: 309-322

Lynch D J, Musselman T E, Gutmann J T, Patchett P J, 1993. Isotopic evidence for the origin of Cenozoic volcanic rocks in the Pinacate volcanic field, northwestern Mexico. *Lithos*, 29: 295-302

Macias J L, Arce J L, García-Palomo A, Mora J C, Layer P W, Espindola J M, 2010. Late-Pleistocene flank collapse triggered by dome growth at Tacana volcano, Mexico-Guatemala, and its relationship to the regional stress regime. *Bull Volc*, 72: 32-53

Macias J L, Capra L, Arce J L, Espindola J M, Garcia-Palomo A, Sheridan M F, 2008. Hazard map of El Chichon volcano, Chiapas, Mexico: constraints posed by eruptive history and computer simulations. *J Volc Geotherm Res*, 175: 444-458

Macias J L, Carrasco G, Delgado H, Martin del Pozzo A L, Siebe C, Hoblitt R, Sheridan M F, Tilling R I, 1995. Mapa de peligros volcanicos del Popocatepetl. *Pub especial Inst Geofis, Univ Nac Auton Mexico*

Macias J L, Carrasco G, Siebe C, 1995. Zonificacion de peligros volcanicos del Popocatepetl. *In*: *Volcan Popocatepetl Estudios Realizados durante la Crisis de 1994-1995*, Mexico City: SINAPROC-CENEPRED-UNAM, p 79-92

Macias J L, Espindola J M, Bursik M, Sheridan M F, 1998. Development of lithic-breccias in the 1982 pyroclastic flow deposits of El Chichon Volcano, Mexico. *J Volc Geotherm Res*, 83: 173-196

Macias J L, Espindola J M, Garcia-Palomo A, Scott K M, Hughes S, Mora J C, 2000. Late Holocene Pelean-style eruption at Tacana volcano, Mexico and Guatemala: past, present, and future hazards. *Geol Soc Amer Bull*, 112: 1234-1249

Macias J L, Espindola J M, Taran Y, Sheridan M F, Garcia A, 1997. Explosive volcanic activity during the last 3,500 years at El Chichon volcano, Mexico. *IAVCEI Puerto Vallarta, Mexico Plenary Assembly, Excursion no. 6 Field Guide*, p. 1-53

Macias J L, Garcia A, Arce J L, Siebe C, Espindola J M, Komorowski J-C, Scott K, 1997a. Late Pleistocene-Holocene cataclysmic eruptions at Nevado de Toluca and Jocotitlan volcanoes, central Mexico. *IAVCEI Puerto Vallarta, Mexico Plenary Assembly, Excursion no. 14 Field Guide*, p. 1-63

Macias J L, Garcia A, Arce J L, Siebe C, Espindola J M, Komorowski J-C, Scott K, 1997b. Late Pleistocene-Holocene cataclysmic eruptions at Nevado de Toluca and Jocotitlan volcanoes, central Mexico. *Brigham Young Univ Geol Studies*, 42(1): 493-528

Macias J L, Sheridan M F, Espindola J M, 1997. Reappraisal of the 1982 eruptions of El Chichon volcano, Chiapas, Mexico: new data from proximal deposits. *Bull Volc*, 58: 459-471

Macias J L, Siebe C, 2005. Popocatepetl's crater filled to the brim: significance for hazard evaluation. *J Volc Geotherm Res*, 141: 321-330

Mahood G A, 1980. Geological evolution of a Pleistocene rhyolitic center - Sierra La Primavera, Jalisco, Mexico. *J Volc Geotherm Res*, 8: 199-230

Mahood G A, 1981. A summary of the geology and petrology of the Sierra La Primavera, Jalisco, Mexico. *J Geophys Res*, 86: 10,137-10,152

Mahood G A, Drake R E, 1982. K-Ar dating young rhyolitic rocks: a case study of the Sierra La Primavera, Jalisco, Mexico. *Geol Soc Amer Bull*, 93: 1232-1241

Marquez A, Verma S P, Anguita F, Oyarzun R, Brandle J L, 1999. Tectonics and volcanism of Sierra Chichinautzin: extension at the front of the Central Trans-Mexican Volcanic Belt. *J Volc Geotherm Res*, 93: 125-140

Martin U, Nemeth K, 2006. How Strombolian is a "Strombolian" scoria cone? Some irregularities in scoria cone architecture from the Transmexican Volcanic Belt, near Volcan Ceboruco, (Mexico) and Al Haruj (Libya). *J Volc Geotherm Res*, 155: 104-118

Martin del Pozzo A L, 1982. Monogenetic volcanism in Sierra Chichinautzin, Mexico. *Bull Volc*, 45: 9-24

Martin del Pozzo A L, 1993. Potential hazards from Popocatepetl and Chichinautzin monogenetic volcanoes near Mexico City. *IAVCEI 1993 Canberra Mtg Abs*, p 68

Martin del Pozzo A L, Cifuentes-Nava G, Cabral-Cano E, Sanchez-Rubio G, Reyes M, Martinez-Bringas A, Garcia E, Arango-Galvan C, 2002. Volcanomagnetic signals during the recent Popocatepetl (Mexico) eruptions and their relation to eruptive activity. *J Volc Geotherm Res*, 113: 415-428

Martin del Pozzo A L, Espinasa R, Lugo J, Barba L, Lopez J, Plunkett P, Urunuela G, Manzanilla L, 1997. Volcanic impact in central Mexico. IAVCEI General Assembly, Puerto Vallarta, Mexico, January 19-24, 1997, Fieldtrip Guidebook, 31 p

Martin del Pozzo A L, Espinasa-Perena E, Armienta M A, Aguayo A, Reyes M, Sanchez G, Cruz O, Ceniceros N, Lugo J, Gonzalez V, Butron M A, Villareal M, 1995. La emision de cenizas y variaciones geoquimicas durante Diciembre-Marzo en el Volcan Popocatepetl. *In*: *Volcan Popocatepetl Estudios Realizados durante la Crisis de 1994-1995*, Mexico City: SINAPROC-CENEPRED-UNAM, p 285-294

Martin del Pozzo A L, Sheridan M, 1995. Potential hazards from Colima volcano, Mexico. *Geof Internac*, 34: 363-376

Martin del Pozzo A L, Sheridan M F, Barrera D, Hubp J L, Selem L V, 1995. Mapa de Peligros Volcan de Colima. *Inst Geofis, Univ Nac Autonoma Mexico*, geologic map

Martin-Del Pozzo A L, Cifuentes G, Cabral-Cano E, Bonifaz R, Correa F, Mendiola I F, 2003. Timing magma ascent at Popocatepetl volcano, Mexico, 2000-2001. *J Volc Geotherm Res*, 125: 107-120

Martin-Del Pozzo A L, Gonzalez-Moran T, Espinasa-Perena R, Butron M A, Reyes M, 2008. Characterization of the recent ash emissions at Popocatepetl volcano, Mexico. *J Volc Geotherm Res*, 170: 61-75

Martinez-S R G, Jacquier B, Arnold M, 1996. The delta 34S composition of sulfates and sulfides at the Los Humeros geothermal system, Mexico and their application to physicochemical fluid evolution. *J Volc Geotherm Res*, 73: 99-118

Martinez-Serrano R G, Schaaf P, Solis-Pichardo G, del Sol Hernandez-Bernal M, Hernandez-Trevino T, Morales-Contreras J J, Macias J L, 2004. Sr, Nd and Pb isotope and geochemical data from the Quaternary Nevado de Toluca volcano, a source of recent adakitic magmatism, and the Tenango volcanic field, Mexico. *J Volc Geotherm Res*, 138: 77-110

McGee J J, Tilling R I, Duffield W A, 1987. Petrologic characteristics of the 1982 and pre-1982 eruptive products of El Chichon Volcano, Chiapas, Mexico. *Geof Internac*, 26: 85-108

Medina F, Gonzalez L, Gutierrez C, Aguilera R, Espindola J M, 1992. Analysis of the seismic activity related to the 1982 eruptions of the El Chichon volcano, Mexico. *In*: Gasparini P, Aki K (eds) *Volcanic Seismology*, Proc Volc, 3: 97-108

Medina F, Suarez F, Espindola J M, 1989. Historic and Holocene volcanic centers in NW Mexico. *Bull Volc Eruptions*, 26: 91-93

Medina-Martinez F, 1983. Analysis of the eruptive history of the Volcan de Colima, Mexico (1560-1980). *Geof Internac*, 22: 157-178

Mercado R, Rose W I, 1992. Reconocimiento geologico y evaluacion preliminar de peligrosidad del volcan Tacana, Guatemala/Mexico. *Geof Internac*, 31: 205-237

Mooser F H, 1972. The Mexican Volcanic Belt: structure and tectonics. *Geof Internac*, 12: 55-70

Mooser F, Maldonado-Koerdell M, 1963. State of the volcanoes-Colima volcano. *Mexican Natl Rpt on volcanology*, General Assembly IUGG, Berkeley, CA, 13, 7 p

Mooser F, Meyer-Abich H, McBirney A R, 1958. Central America. *Catalog of Active Volcanoes of the World and Solfatara Fields*, Rome: IAVCEI, 6: 1-146 ***(regional reference)***

Mooser F, Nairn A E M, Negendank J F W, 1974. Palaeomagnetic investigations of the Tertiary and Quaternary igneous rocks: VIII, A paleomagnetic and petrologic study of volcanics of the Valley of Mexico. *Geol Rundschau*, 63: 451-483

Mora J C, Jaimes-Viera M C, Garduno-Monroy V H, Layer P W, Pompa-Mera V, Godinez M L, 2007. Geology and geochemistry characteristics of the Chiapanecan volcanic arc (central area), Chiapas Mexico. *J Volc Geotherm Res*, 162: 43-72

Mora J C, Macias J L, Garcia-Palomo A, Arce J L, Espindola J M, Manetti P, Vaselli O, Sanchez J M, 2004. Petrology and geochemistry of the Tacana volcanic complex, Mexico-Guatemala: evidence for the last 40 000 yr of activity. *Geof Internac*, 43: 331-359

Mora J C, Macias J L, Saucedo R, Orlando A, Manetti P, Vaselli O, 2002. Petrology of the 1998-2000 products of Volcan de Colima, Mexico. *J Volc Geotherm Res*, 117: 195-212

Mullerried F K G, Scheuble H, 1925-26. Uber die Tatigkeit des Popocatepetl (Mexico) vom November 1923 bis Marz 1924. *Zeit Vulk*, 9: 52-55

Murray J B, Ramirez-Ruiz J J, 2002. Long-term predictions of the time of eruptions using remote distance measurement at Volcan de Colima, Mexico. *J Volc Geotherm Res*, 117: 79-89

Murray J B, Wooler L K, 2002. Persistent summit subsidence at Volcan de Colima, Mexico, 1982-1999. *J Volc Geotherm Res*, 117: 69-78

Navarro-Ochoa C, Gavilanes-Ruiz J C, Cortes-Cortes A, 2002. Movement and emplacement of lava flows at Volcan de Colima, Mexico: Nov. 1998 - Feb. 1999. *J Volc Geotherm Res*, 117: 155-167

Negendank J F W, Emmermann R, Krawczyk R, Mooser F, Tobschall H, Werle D, 1985. Geological and geochemical investigations on the eastern Trans-Mexican Volcanic Belt. *Geof Internac*, 24: 477-575

Nelson S A, 1980. Geology and petrology of Volcan Ceboruco, Nayarit, Mexico - Summary. *Geol Soc Amer Bull*, 91: 639-643

Nelson S A, 1986. Geologia del Volcan Ceboruco, Nayarit, con una estimacion de riesgos de erupciones futuras. *Univ Nac Auton Mexico, Inst Geol Rev*, 6: 243-258

Nelson S A, 1990. Volcanic hazards in Mexico-a summary. *Univ Nac Auton Mexico Inst Geol, Rev*, 9: 71-81

Nelson S A, Carmichael I S E, 1984. Pleistocene to Recent alkalic volcanism in the region of Sanganguey volcano, Nayarit, Mexico. *Contr Mineral Petr*, 85: 321-335

Nelson S A, Gonzalez-Caver E, 1992. Geology and K-Ar dating of the Tuxtla volcanic field, Veracruz, Mexico. *Bull Volc*, 55: 85-96

Nelson S A, Gonzalez-Caver E, Kyser T K, 1995. Constraints on the origin of alkaline and calc-alkaline magmas from the Tuxtla volcanic field, Veracruz, Mexico. *Contr Mineral Petr*, 122: 191-211

Nelson S A, Hegre J, 1990. Volcan Las Navajas, a Pliocene-Pleistocene trachyte/peralkaline rhyolite volcano in the northwestern Mexican volcanic belt. *Bull Volc*, 52: 186-204

Nelson S A, Livieres R A, 1986. Contemporaneous calc-alkaline and alkaline volcanism at Sanganguey volcano, Nayarit, Mexico. *Geol Soc Amer Bull*, 97: 798-808

Nelson S A, Sanchez-Rubio G, 1986. Trans Mexican volcanic belt field guide. *Geol Assoc Can*, 108 p ***(regional reference)***

Nixon G T, 1989. The geology of Iztaccihuatl volcano and adjacent areas of the Sierra Nevada and Valley of Mexico. *Geol Soc Amer Spec Pap*, 219: 1-58

Nunez-Cornu F J, Sanchez-Mora C, 1999. Stress field estimations for Colima Volcano, Mexico, based on seismic data. *Bull Volc*, 60: 568-580

Nunez-Cornu F, Nava F A, De la Cruz-Reyna S, Jimenez Z, Valencia C, Garcia-Arthur R, 1994. Seismic activity related to the 1991 eruption of Colima volcano, Mexico. *Bull Volc*, 56: 228-237

Ordonez M E, 1906. De Mexico a Jalapa. *10th Internatl Geol Cong, Mexico, Excur Guide*, 1: 1-11

Ort M H, Carrasco-Nunez G, 2009. Lateral vent migration during phreatomagmatic and magmatic eruptions at Tecuitlapa maar, east-central Mexico. *J Volc Geotherm Res*, 181: 67-77

Ort M H, Elson M D, Anderson K C, Duffield W A, Hooten J A, Champion D E, Waring G, 2008b. Effects of scoria-cone eruptions upon nearby human communities. *Geol Soc Amer Bull*, 120: 476-486

Ortega-Rivera A, Bohnel H, Lee J, 2004. The San Quintin volcanic field-40Ar/39Ar geochronology and paleomagnetism. *Proc Geol Soc Amer Penrose Conf, Metepec, Puebla, Mexico, Abs*, p 59

Owenby S E, Lange R A, Hall C M, 2008. The eruptive history of the Mascota volcanic field, western Mexico: age and volume constraints on the origin of andesite among a diverse suite of lamprophyric and calc-alkaline lavas. *J Volc Geotherm Res*, 177: 1077-1091

Ownby S, Delgado Granados H, Lange R A, Hall C M, 2007. Volcan Tancitaro, Michoacan, Mexico, 40Ar/39Ar constraints on its history of sector collapse. *J Volc Geotherm Res*, 161:1-14

Paz Moreno F A, Demant A, Cocheme J-J, Dostal J, Montigny R, 2003. The Quaternary Moctezuma volcanic field: a theoleiitic to alkali basaltic episode in the central Sonoran Basin and Range Province. *In*: Johnson S E, Paterson S R, Fletcher J M, Girty G H, Kimbrough D L, Martin-Barajas A (eds), Tectonic evolution of northwestern Mexico and the southwestern USA, *Geol Soc Amer Spec Pap*, 374: 439-455

Paz Moreno F A, Demant A, 1999. The Recent Isla San Luis volcanic centre: petrology of a rift-related volcanic suite in the northern Gulf of California, Mexico. *J Volc Geotherm Res*, 93: 31-52

Petrone C M, Francalanci L, Ferrari L, Schaaf P, Conticelli S, 2006. The San Pedro-Cerro Grande volcanic complex (Nayarit, Mexico): inferences on volcanology and magma evolution. *In*: Siebe S, Macias J-L, Aguirre-Diaz G J (eds) Neogone-Quaternary continental margin volcanism: a perspective from Mexico, *Geol Soc Amer Spec Pap*, 402: 65-98

Pier J G, Luhr J F, Podosek F A, Aranda-Gomez J J, 1992. The La Brena El Jaguey Maar Complex, Durango, Mexico: II. Petrology and geochemistry. *Bull Volc*, 54: 405-428

Pradal E, Robin C, 1994. Long-lived magmatic phases at Los Azufres volcanic center, Mexico. *J Volc Geotherm Res*, 63: 201-215

Prol-Ledesma R M, 1998. Pre- and post-exploitation variations in hydrothermal activity in Los Humeros geothermal field, Mexico. *J Volc Geotherm Res*, 83: 313-333

Ramirez-Ruiz J J, Santiago-Jimenez H, Alatorre-Chavez E, Breton-Gonzalez M, 2002. EDM deformation monitoring of the 1997-2000 activity at Volcan de Colima. *J Volc Geotherm Res*, 117: 61-67

Reed M J, 1976. Geology and hydrothermal metamorphism in the Cerro Prieto geothermal field, Mexico. *In*: *Proc 2nd United Nations Symp Devel Use Geotherm Resour, San Francisco*, Washington D C: U S Government Printing Office, 1: 539-547

Reed M J, 1984. Relationship between volcanism and hydrothermal activity at Cerro Prieto, Mexico. *Trans Geotherm Res Council*, 8: 217-221

Reinhardt B K, 1991. Volcanology of the younger volcanic sequence and volcanic hazards study of the Tuxtla volcanic field, Veracruz, Mexico. *Unpublished MSci thesis*, Tulane Univ, 147 p

Reyes-Davila G A, De la Cruz-Reyna S, 2002. Experience in the short-term eruption forecasting at Volcan de Colima, Mexico, and public response to forecasts. *J Volc Geotherm Res*, 117: 121-127

Richards A F, 1959. Geology of the Islas Revillagigedo, Mexico 1. Birth and development of Volcan Barcena, Isla San Benedicto. *Bull Volc*, 22: 73-124

Richards A F, 1965. Geology of the Islas Revillagigedo, 3. Effects of erosion on Isla San Benedicto 1952-61 following the birth of Volcan Barcena. *Bull Volc*, 28: 381-403

Richards A F, 1966. Geology of the Islas Revillagigedo, Mexico, 2. Geology and petrography of Isla San Benedicto. *Proc Calif Acad Sci*, 33: 361-414

Riggs N R, Carrasco-Nunez G, 2004. Evolution of a complex isolated dome system, Cerro Pizarro, central Mexico. *Bull Volc*, 66: 322-335

Righter K, Carmichael I S E, 1992. Hawaiites and related lavas in the Atenguillo graben, western Mexican volcanic belt. *Geol Soc Amer Bull*, 104: 1592-1607

Robin C, 1984. Le Volcan Popocatepetl (Mexique): structure, evolution petrologique et risques. *Bull Volc*, 47: 1-25

Robin C, Boudal C, 1987. A gigantic Bezymianny-type event at the beginning of modern Volcan Popocatepetl. *J Volc Geotherm Res*, 31: 115-130

Robin C, Camus G, Gourgaud A, 1991. Eruptive and magmatic cycles at Fuego de Colima Volcano (Mexico). *J Volc Geotherm Res*, 45: 209-225

Robin C, Cantagrel J M, 1982. Le Pico de Orizaba (Mexique): structure et evolution d'un grand volcan andesitique complexe. *Bull Volc*, 45: 299-315

Robin C, Komorowski J C, Boudal C, Mossand P, 1990. Mixed-magma pyroclastic surge deposits associated with debris avalanche deposits at Colima volcanoes, Mexico. *Bull Volc*, 52: 391-403

Robin C, Mossand P, Camus G, Cantagrel J-M, Gourgaud A, Vincent P M, 1987. Eruptive history of the Colima Volcanic Complex (Mexico). *J Volc Geotherm Res*, 31: 99-113

Robin C, Tournon J, 1978. Spatial relations of andesitic and alkaline provinces in Mexico and Central America. *Can J Earth Sci*, 15: 1633-1641

Rodriguez S R, Morales-Barrera W, Layer P, Gonzalez-Mercado E, 2009. A quaternary monogenetic volcanic field in the Xalapa region, eastern Trans-Mexican volcanic belt: geology, distribution and morphology of the volcanic vents. *J Volc Geotherm Res*, doi:10.1016/j.jvolgeores.2009.08.003

Rodriguez S-R, Siebe C, Komorowski J-C, Abrams M, 2002. The Quetzalapa Pumice: a voluminous late Pleistocene rhyolite deposit in the eastern Trans-Mexican Volcanic Belt. *J Volc Geotherm Res*, 113: 177-212

Rodriguez-Elizarraras S, Komorowski J-C, Jimenez V, Siebe C, 1993. *Libro-guia de la excursion geologica al volcan Paricutin, Estado de Michoacan, Mexico. Translated Title: Guidebook for a field trip to Paricutin Volcano, Michoacan, Mexico.* Mexico City, Mexico: Univ Nac Auton Mex, Inst Geol, 130 p

Rodriguez-Elizarraras S, Siebe C, Komorowski J-C, Espindola J M, Saucedo R, 1991. Field observations of pristine block- and ash-flow deposits emplaced April 16-17, 1991 at Volcan de Colima, Mexico. *J Volc Geotherm Res*, 48: 399-412

Rodriquez L A, Watson M W, Rose W I, Branan Y K, Bluth G J S, Chigna G, Matias O, Escobar D, Carn S A, Fischer T P, 2004. SO2 emissions to the atmosphere from active volcanoes in Guatemala and El Salvador, 1999-2002. *J Volc Geotherm Res*, 138: 325-344

Rogers G, Saunders A D, Terrell D J, Verma S P, Marriner G F, 1985. Geochemistry of Holocene volcanic rocks associated with ridge subduction in Baja California, Mexico. *Nature*, 315: 389-392

Rose W I, Bornhorst T J, Halsor S P, Capaul W A, Plumley P J, De la Cruz-Reyna S, Mena M, Mota R, 1984. Volcan El Chichon, Mexico: pre-1982 S-rich eruptive activity. *J Volc Geotherm Res*, 23: 147-168

Rossotti A, Carrasco-Nunez G, Rosi M, Di Muro A, 2006. Eruptive dynamics of the "Citlalteptel Pumice" at Citlaltepetl volcano, eastern Mexico. *J Volc Geotherm Res*, 158: 401-429

Rueda H, Arce J, Macias J, Garcia-Palomo A, 2006. A ~31 ka plinian-subplinian eruption at Tlaloc volcano, Sierra Nevada, Mexico. *Eos, Trans Amer Geophys Union*, Fall meeting 2006, abst #V33B-0668

Saucedo R, Macias J L, Bursik M, 2004. Pyroclastic flow deposits of the 1991 eruption of Volcan de Colima, Mexico. *Bull Volc*, 66: 291-306

Saucedo R, Macias J L, Bursik M, Mora J C, Gavilanes J C, Cortes A, 2002. Emplacement of pyroclastic flows during the 1998-1999 eruption of Volcan de Colima, Mexico. *J Volc Geotherm Res*, 117: 129-153

Saucedo R, Macias J L, Gavilanes J C, Arce J L, Komorowski J C, Gardner J, Valdez-Moreno G, 2010. Eyewitness, stratigraphy, chemistry, and eruptive dynamics of the 1913 Plinian eruption of Volcan de Colima, Mexico. *J Volc Geotherm Res*, 191: 149-166

Saucedo R, Macias J L, Sheridan M F, Bursik M I, Komorowski J C, 2005. Modeling of pyroclastic flows of Colima volcano, Mexico: implications for hazard assessments. *J Volc Geotherm Res*, 139: 103-115

Saunders A D, Rogers G, Marriner G F, Terrell D J, Verma S P, 1987. Geochemistry of Cenozoic volcanic rocks, Baja California, Mexico: implications for the petrogenesis of post-subduction magmas. *J Volc Geotherm Res*, 32: 223-245

Savov I P, Luhr J F, Navarro-Ochoa C, 2008. Petrology and geochemistry of lava and ash erupted from Volcán Colima, Mexico, during 1998-2005. *J Volc Geotherm Res*, 174: 241-256

Sawlan M G, 1991. Magmatic evolution of the Gulf of California rift. *In*: Dauphin J P and Simoneit B A (eds) *The Gulf and Peninsular Province of the Californias*, Amer Assoc Petrol Geol Mem, 47: 301-369

Schmitt A K, Stockli D F, Hausback B P, 2006. Eruption and magma crystallization ages of Las Tres Virgenes (Baja California) constrained by combined 230Th/238U and (U-Th)/He dating of zircon. *J Volc Geotherm Res*, 158: 281-295

Segerstrom K, 1950. Erosion studies at Paricutin, State of Michoacan, Mexico. *U S Geol Surv Bull*, 965-A: 1-164

Segerstrom K, 1966. Paricutin, 1965; aftermath of eruption. *U S Geol Surv Prof Pap*, 550-C: 93-101

Segerstrom K, Gutierrez C, 1947. Activity of Paricutin Volcano from May 4 to September 8, 1946. *Eos, Trans Amer Geophys Union*, 28: 559-566

Segovia N, De la Cruz-Reyna S, Mena M, Ramos E, Monnin M, Seidel J L, 1989. Radon in soil anomaly observed at Los Azufres geothermal field, Michoacan; a possible precursor of the 1985 Mexico earthquake (Ms = 8.1). *Nat Hazards*, 1: 319-329

Sheridan M F, Carrasco-Nunez G, Hubbard B E, Siebe C, Rodriguez-Elizarraraz S, 2001. Mapa de peligros del Volcan Citlalteptel (Pico de Orizaba). Inst Geog, Univ Nac Autonoma Mexico, 1:250,000 scale

Sheridan M F, Hubbard B, Bursik M I, Siebe C, Abrams M, Macias J L, Delgago-Granados H, 2001. Gauging short-term volcanic hazards at Popocatepetl. *Eos, Trans Amer Geophys Union*, 82: 185-188

Sheridan M F, Macias J L, 1995. Estimation of risk probability for gravity-driven pyroclastic flows at Volcan Colima, Mexico. *In*: Ida Y, Voight B (eds) *J Volc Geotherm Res*, 66: 251-256

Siebe C, 2000. Age and archaeological implications of Xitle volcano, southwestern Basin of Mexico-City. *J Volc Geotherm Res*, 104: 45-64

Siebe C, Abrams M, Macias J L, 1995. Derrumbes gigantes, depositos de avalancha de escombros y edad del actual. *In*: *Volcan Popocatepetl Estudios Realizados durante la Crisis de 1994-1995*, Mexico City: SINAPROC-CENEPRED-UNAM, p 195-220

Siebe C, Abrams M, Macias J L, Obenholzner J, 1996. Repetitive volcanic disasters in Prehispanic time at Popocatepetl, central Mexico: past key to the future? *Geology*, 24: 399-402

Siebe C, Abrams M, Sheridan M F, 1993. Major Holocene block-and-ash fan at the western slope of ice-capped Pico de Orizaba volcano, Mexico: Implications for future hazards. *J Volc Geotherm Res*, 59: 1-33

Siebe C, Arana-Salinas L, Abrams M, 2005. Geology and radiocarbon ages of Tlaloc, Tlacotenco, Cuauhtzin, Hijo del Cuauhtzin, and Ocusacayo monogenetic volcanoes in the central part of the Sierra Chichinautzin, Mexico. *J Volc Geotherm Res*, 141: 225-243

Siebe C, Komorowski J-C, Navarro C, McHone J F, Delgado H, Cortes A, 1995. Submarine eruption near Socorro Island, Mexico; geochemistry and scanning electron microscopy studies of floating scoria and reticulite. *J Volc Geotherm Res*, 68: 239-271

Siebe C, Komorowski J-C, Sheridan M F, 1992. Morphology and emplacement of an unusual debris-avalanche deposit at Jocotitlan volcano, central Mexico. *Bull Volc*, 54: 573-589

Siebe C, Macias J L, Abrams M, Obenholzner J, 1996. La destruccion de Cacaxtla y Cholula: un suceso en la historia eruptiva del Popocatepetl. *Rev Cienc, Fac Cienc, UNAM*, 41: 36-45

Siebe C, Macias J L, Abrams M, Rodriguez S, Castro R, 1997. Catastrophic prehistoric eruptions at Popocatepetl and Quaternary explosive volcanism in the Serdan-Oriental Basin, east-central Mexico. IAVCEI General Assembly, Puerto Vallarta, Mexico, January 19-24, 1997, Fieldtrip Guidebook, Excursion no 4, 88 p

Siebe C, Macias J-L, 2006. Volcanic hazards in the Mexico City metropolitan area from eruptions at Popocatepetl, Nevado de Toluca, and Jocotitlan stratovolcanoes and monogenetic scoria cones in the Sierra Chichinautzin volcanic field. *In*: Siebe S, Macias J-L, Aguirre-Diaz G J (eds) Neogone-Quaternary continental margin volcanism: a perspective from Mexico, *Geol Soc Amer Spec Pap*, 402: 253-329

Siebe C, Schaaf P, Urrutia-Fucugauchi J, 1999. Mammoth bones embedded in a late Pleistocene lahar from Popocatepetl Volcano, near Tocuila, central Mexico. *Geol Soc Amer Bull*, 111: 1550-1562

Siebe C, Verma S P, 1988. Major element geochemistry and tectonic setting of Las Derrumbadas rhyolitic domes, Puebla, Mexico. *Chem Erde*, 48: 177-189

Siebe S, Rodriguez-Lara V, Schaaf P, Abrams M, 2004a. Radiocarbon ages of Holocene Pelado, Guespalapa, and Chichinautzin scoria cones, south of Mexico City: implications for archaeology and future hazards. *Bull Volc*, 66: 203-225

Siebe S, Rodriguez-Lara V, Schaaf P, Abrams M, 2004b. Geochemistry, Sr-Nd isotope composition, and tectonic setting of Holocene Pelado, Guespalapa and Chichinautzin scoria cones, south of Mexico City. *J Volc Geotherm Res*, 130: 197-226

Siebert L, Alvarado G E, Vallance J W, van Wyk de Vries B, 2006. Large-volume volcanic edifice failures in Central America and associated hazards. *In*: Rose W I, Bluth G J S, Carr M J, Ewert J W, Patino L C, Vallance J W (eds), Volcanic hazards in Central America, *Geol Soc Amer Spec Pap*, 412: 1-26

Siebert L, Carrasco-Nunez G, 2002. Late-Pleistocene to precolumbian behind-the-arc mafic volcanism in the eastern Mexican Volcanic Belt; implications for future hazards. *J Volc Geotherm Res*, 115: 179-205

Sigurdsson H, Carey S N, Espindola J M, 1984. The 1982 eruptions of El Chichon volcano, Mexico: stratigraphy of pyroclastic deposits. *J Volc Geotherm Res*, 23: 11-38

Sigurdsson H, Carey S N, Fisher R V, 1987. The 1982 eruption of El Chichon Volcano, Mexico; 3, Physical properties of pyroclastic surges. *Bull Volc*, 49: 467-488

Sobota-Knoll F, 1988. Estudios sobre el ciclo del la actividad del Volcan de Colima, Jalisco en los anos 1894-1966. Guadalajara: Unidad Editorial, 53 p

Spinnler J, Garduno V H, Ceragioli E, 2000. Stratigraphic and structural relations between the Trans-Mexican Volcanic Belt and the Sierra Madre Occidental in the Guadalajara region, Jalisco, Mexico. *In*; Delgado-Granados H, Aguirre-Diaz G J, Stock J M (eds), *Cenozoic Tectonics and Volcanism of Mexico, Geol Soc Amer Spec Pap*, 334: 85-97

Stoopes G R, Sheridan M F, 1992. Giant debris avalanches from the Colima volcanic complex, Mexico; implications for long-runout landslides >100 km and hazard assessment. *Geology*, 20(4): 299-302

Taran Y A, Fischer T P, Pokrovsky B, Sano Y, Aurora-Armienta M, Macias J L, 1998. Geochemistry of the volcano-hydrothermal system of El Chichon volcano, Chiapas, Mexico. *Bull Volc*, 59: 436-449

Taran Y, Gavilanes J C, Cortes A, 2002. Chemical and isotopic composition of fumarolic gases and the SO2 flux from Volcan de Colima, Mexico, between the 1994 and 1998 eruptions. *J Volc Geotherm Res*, 117: 105-119

Thorpe R S, Gibson I L, Vizcaino J S, 1977. Andesitic pyroclastic flows from Colima volcano. *Nature*, 265: 724-725

Tilling R I, Rubin M, Sigurdsson H, Carey S, Duffield W A, Rose W I, 1984. Holocene eruptive activity of El Chichon volcano, Chiapas, Mexico. *Science*, 224: 747-749

Torres-Rodriguez M A, Flores-Armenta M, 1998. Pressure and enthalpy evolution in wells of the Los Azufres geothermal field. *Trans Geotherm Res Council*, 22: 339-358

Turin B D, Gutmann J T, Swisher C C III, 2008. A 13 +/- 3 ka age determination of a tholeiite, Pinacate volcanic field, Mexico, and improved methods for 40Ar/39Ar dating of young basaltic rocks. *J Volc Geotherm Res*, 177: 848-856

Uribe-Cifuentes R M, Urrutia-Fucugauchi J, 1999. Paleomagnetic study of the Valle de Santiago volcanics, Michoacan-Guanajuato volcanic field, Mexico. *Geof Internac*, 38: 217-230

Urrutia-Fucugauchi J, 1996. Palaeomagnetic study of the Xitle-Pedregal de San Angel lava flow, southern Basin of Mexico. *Phys Earth Planet Interior*, 97: 177-196

Valdes C, Gonzalez G, Arciniega A, Guzman M, Nava E, Gutierrez C, Santoyo M, 1995. Sismicidad del Volcan Popocatepetl. *In*: *Volcan Popocatepetl Estudios Realizados durante la Crisis de 1994-1995*, Mexico City: SINAPROC-CENEPRED-UNAM, p 129-138

Varekamp J C, Luhr J F, Prestegaard K L, 1984. The 1982 eruptions of El Chichon volcano (Chiapas, Mexico): character of the eruptions, ash-fall deposits, and gas phase. *J Volc Geotherm Res*, 23: 39-68

Verma S P, 1983. Magma genesis and chamber processes at Los Humeros Caldera, Mexico; Nd and Sr isotope data. *Nature*, 302: 52-55

Verma S P, 1984. Alkali and alkaline earth element geochemistry of Los Humeros Caldera, Puebla, Mexico. *J Volc Geotherm Res*, 20: 21-40

Verma S P, 1985. Heat source in Los Humeros geothermal area, Puebla, Mexico. *Trans Geotherm Res Council*, 9(Part 1): 521-526

Verma S P, 1999. Geochemistry of evolved magmas and their relationship to subduction-unrelated mafic volcanism at the volcanic front of the central Mexican volcanic belt. *J Volc Geotherm Res*, 93: 151-171

Verma S P, 2000a. Geochemical evidence for a lithospheric source for magmas from Los Humeros caldera, Puebla, Mexico. *Chem Geol*, 164: 35-60

Verma S P, 2000b. Geochemistry of the subducting Cocos plate and the origin of subduction-unrelated mafic volcanism at the volcanic front of the central Mexican Volcanic Belt. *In*; Delgado-Granados H, Aguirre-Diaz G J, Stock J M (eds), *Cenozoic Tectonics and Volcanism of Mexico, Geol Soc Amer Spec Pap*, 334: 195-222

Verma S P, 2001. Geochemical evidence for a lithospheric source for magmas from Acoculco caldera, eastern Mexican Volcanic Belt. *Internatl Geol Rev*, 43: 31-51

Verma S P, 2003. Geochemical and Sr-Nd isotope evidence for rift-related origin of magmas in Tizayuca volcanic field, central Mexican Volcanic Belt. *J Geol Soc India*, 61: 257-276

Verma S P, Lopez-Martinez M, 1982. Geochemistry of Los Humeros caldera, Puebla, Mexico. *Bull Volc*, 45: 63-79

Verma S P, Nelson S A, 1989. Isotopic and trace element constraints on the origin and evolution of alkaline and calc-alkaline magmas in the northwestern Mexican volcanic belt. *J Geophys Res*, 94: 4531-4544

Verma S P, Salazar V A, Negendank J F W, Milan M, Navarro L I, Besch T, 1993. Caracteristicas petrograficas y geoquimicas de elementos mayores del Campo Volcanico de los Tuxtlas, Veracruz, Mexico. Translated Title: Petrography and geochemistry of the major elements in Los Tuxtlas volcanic field, Veracruz, Mexico. *Geof Internac*, 32: 237-248

Waitz P, 1906. Les geysers d'Ixtlan. *10th Internatl Geol Cong, Mexico, Excur Guide*, 12: 1-22

Waitz P, 1921. Popocatepetl again in activity. *Amer J Sci*, 5: 81-87

Waitz P, 1932. Datos historicos y bibliograficos acerca del Volcan de Colima. *Mem Soc Cient Antonio Alzate (Mexico)*, 53: 349-384

Walker G P L, Wright J V, Clough B J, Booth B, 1981. Pyroclastic geology of the rhyolitic volcano of La Primavera, Mexico. *Geol Rundschau*, 70: 1100-1118

Wallace P J, Carmichael I S E, 1992. Alkaline and calc-alkaline lavas near Los Volcanes, Jalisco, Mexico: geochemical diversity and its significance in volcanic arcs. *Contr Mineral Petr*, 111: 423-439

Wallace P J, Carmichael I S E, 1994. Petrology of Volcan Tequila, Jalisco, Mexico: disequilibrium phenocryst assemblages and evolution of the subvolcanic magma system. *Contr Mineral Petr*, 117: 345-361

Wallace P J, Carmichael I S E, 1999. Quaternary volcanism near the Valley of Mexico: implications for subduction zone magmatism and the effects of crustal thickness variation of primitive magma compositions. *Contr Mineral Petr*, 135: 291-314

Wallace P J, Carmichael I S E, Righter K, Becker T A, 1992. Volcanism and tectonism in western Mexico: a contrast of style and substance. *Geology*, 20: 625-628

White S E, 1984. Popocatepetl - the ever-burning torch. *Volcano News*, 17: 1-3

White S E, 1986. Iztaccihuatl, Mexico. *Volcano News*, 23: 1-3

Wilcox R E, 1947. Activity of Paricutin volcano from December 1, 1946 to March 31, 1947. *Trans Am Geophys Union*, 28 (5): 725-731

Wilcox R E, 1948a. Activity of Paricutin volcano from April 1 to July 31, 1947. *Trans Am Geophys Union*, 29 (1): 69-74

Wilcox R E, 1948b. Activity of Paricutin volcano from December 1, 1947 to March 31, 1948. *Trans Am Geophys Union*, 29 (3): 355-360

Wilcox R E, Gutierrez C, 1948. Activity of Paricutin volcano from April 1 to July 31, 1948. *Trans Am Geophys Union*, 29 (6): 877-881

Wilcox R E, Shoup-Oropeza S, 1948. Activity of Paricutin volcano from August 1 to November 30, 1947. *Trans Am Geophys Union*, 29: 74-79

Williams H, 1950. Volcanoes of the Paricutin region Mexico. *U S Geol Surv Bull*, 965-B: 165-279

Wood C A, 1974. Reconnaissance geophysics and geology of the Pinacate craters, Sonora, Mexico. *Bull Volc*, 38: 149-172

Woodford A O, 1928. The San Quintin volcanic field, lower California. *Amer J Sci*, 15: 337-345

Wright J V, Walker G P L, 1981. Eruption, transport and deposition of ignimbrite: a case study from Mexico. *J Volc Geotherm Res*, 9: 111-131

Yarza de De la Torre E, 1971. *Volcanes de Mexico*. Mexico City, Mexico: Aguilar, 237 p ***(regional reference)***

Yokoyama I, De la Cruz-Reyna S, 1990. Precursory earthquakes of the 1943 eruption of Paricutin Volcano, Michoacan, Mexico. *J Volc Geotherm Res*, 44: 265-281

Yokoyama I, De la Cruz-Reyna S, Espindola J M, 1992. Energy partition in the 1982 eruption of El Chichon Volcano, Chiapas, Mexico. *J Volc Geotherm Res*, 51: 1-21

Yokoyama I, Mena M, 1991. Structure of La Primavera Caldera, Jalisco, Mexico, deduced from gravity anomalies and drilling results. *J Volc Geotherm Res*, 47: 183-193

Zimbelman D R, Watters R J, Firth I R, Breit G N, Carrasco-Nunez G, 2004. Stratovolcano stability assessment methods and results from Citlaltepetl, Mexico. *Bull Volc*, 66: 66-79

Zobin V M, Gonzalez-Amezcua M, Reyes-Davila G A, Dominguez T, Cerda-Chacon J C, Chavez-Alvarez J M, 2002. Comparative characteristics of the 1997-1998 seismic swarms preceding the November 1998 eruption of Volcan de Colima, Mexico. *J Volc Geotherm Res*, 117: 47-60

Zobin V M, Luhr J F, Taran Y A, Breton M, Cortes A, De la Cruz-Reyna S, Dominguez D, Galindo I, Gavilanes J C, Muniz J J, Navarro C, Ramirez J J, Reyes G A, Ursua M, Velasco J, Alatorre E, Santiago H, 2002. Overview of the 1997-2000 activity of Volcan de Colima, Mexico. *J Volc Geotherm Res*, 117: 1-19

Zobin V M, Orozco-Rojas J, Reyes-Davila G A, Navarro C, 2005. Seismicity of an andesitic volcano during block-lava effusion: Volcan de Colima, Mexico, November 1998-January 1999. *Bull Volc*, 67: 679-688

CENTRAL AMERICA: NORTHERN (1402-03)

Adams M C, Mink L L, Moore J N, White L D, Caicedo A A, 1990. Geochemistry and hydrology of the Zunil geothermal system. *Trans Geotherm Resour Council*, 14: 837-844

Aiuppa A, Rotolo S G, Villa I M, 1999. Stratigraphy, geochemistry and geochronology of a Quaternary pyroclastic sequence of the Chichontepec volcano, El Salvador. *Rev Geol Amer Central*, 22: 75-86

Anderson E B, Jacobo H R, Ussher G N H, 1994. The Berlin geothermal system - from the surface to the magma chamber. *Proc 16th New Zeal Geotherm Workshop, Auckland*, p 127-132

Anderson S W, Fink J H, Rose W I, 1995. Mount St. Helens and Santiaguito lava domes; the effect of short-term eruption rate on surface texture and degassing processes. *J Volc Geotherm Res*, 69: 105-116

Anderson T, 1908. The volcanoes of Guatemala. *Roy Geog Soc*, 31: 473-489

Barberi F, Rotolo S G, Aiuppa A, 1995. Petrology of Chichontepeque volcano (El Salvador). *Periodico Mineral*, 64: 89-91

Bardintzeff J M, Deniel C, 1992. Magmatic evolution of Pacaya and Cerro Chiquito volcanological complex, Guatemala. *Bull Volc*, 54: 267-283

Basset T, 1996. Histoire eruptive et evaluation des aleas du volcan Acatenango (Guatemala). *Terre & Environnement, Univ Geneve*, 3: 1-305

Bernard A, Escobar C D, Mazot A, Gutierrez R E, 2004. The acid volcanic lake of Santa Ana volcano, El Salvador. *In*: Rose W I, Bommer J J, Lopez D L, Carr M J, Major J J (eds), Natural Hazards in El Salvador, *Geol Soc Amer Spec Pap*, 375: 121-133

Bluth G J S, Rose W I, 2004. Observations of eruptive activity at Santiaguito volcano, Guatemala. *J Volc Geotherm Res*, 136: 297-302

Bonadonna C, Houghton B F, 2005. Total grain-size distribution and volume of tephra-fall deposits. *Bull Volc*, 67: 441-456

Bonis S, 1993. Geologic map of Guatemala, Guatemala. Instituto Geog Militar, 1:250,000 scale

Bonis S, Salazar O, 1973. The 1971 and 1973 eruptions of volcano Fuego, Guatemala, and some socio-economic considerations for the volcanologist. *Bull Volc*, 37: 394-400

Bornhorst T J, Rose W I, Chesner C A, 1982. Quaternary Barahona caldera complex, Guatemala (abs). *Eos, Trans Amer Geophys Union*, 63: 1155

Bosc E, 1979. Geologic map of Guatemala, San Agustin Acasaguastlan. Instituto Geog Nac, 1:50,000 quad

Bullard F M, 1957. Active volcanoes of Central America. *20th Internatl Geol Cong, Mexico City*, Sec 1: 351-371

Cameron B I, Walker J A, Carr M J, Patino L C, Matias O, Feigenson M D, 2003. Flux versus decompression melting at stratovolcanoes in southeastern Guatemala. *J Volc Geotherm Res*, 119: 21-50

Carr M J, 1984. Symmetrical and segmented variation of physical and geochemical characterisitics of the Central American volcanic front. *J Volc Geotherm Res*, 20: 231-252

Carr M J, Pontier N K, 1981. Evolution of a young parasitic cone towards a mature central vent; Izalco and Santa Ana volcanoes in El Salvador, Central America. *J Volc Geotherm Res*, 11: 277-292

Carr M J, Rose W I Jr, 1987. CENTAM; a database of Central American volcanic rocks. *J Volc Geotherm Res*, 33: 239-240

Chesner C A, Halsor S, 1997. Geochemical trends of sequential lava flows from Meseta Volcano, Guatemala. *J Volc Geotherm Res*, 78: 221-237

Chesner C A, Halsor S P, 2006. The Escuintla and La Democracia debris avalanche deposits, Guatemala: constraining their sources. *In*: Rose W I, Bluth G J S, Carr M J, Ewert J W, Patino L C, Vallance J W (eds), Volcanic hazards in Central America, *Geol Soc Amer Spec Pap*, 412: 105-120

Chesner C A, Pullinger C R, Escobar C D, 2004. Physical and chemical evolution of San Miguel volcano, El Salvador. *In*: Rose W I, Bommer J J, Lopez D L, Carr M J, Major J J (eds), Natural Hazards in El Salvador, *Geol Soc Amer Spec Pap*, 375: 213-226

Chesner C A, Rose W I, 1984. Geochemistry and evolution of the Fuego volcanic complex, Guatemala. *J Volc Geotherm Res*, 21: 25-44

Comision Ejecutiva Hidroelectrica de Rio Lempa (CEL), 1994. Campo Geotermico de Berlin. Inf Invest Geovulcanologicas Adicionales, unpublished rpt, 51 p

Conway F M, Diehl J F, Matias O, 1992. Paleomagnetic constraints on eruption patterns at the Pacaya composite volcano, Guatemala. *Bull Volc*, 55: 25-32

Conway F M, Diehl J F, Rose W I, Matias O, 1994. Age and magma flux of Santa Maria volcano, Guatemala; correlation of paleomagnetic waveforms with the 28,000 to 25,000 yr B.P. Mono Lake excursion. *J Geol*, 102: 11-24

Conway F M, Vallance J W, Rose W I, Johns G W, Paniagua S, 1992. Cerro Quemado, Guatemala: the volcanic history and hazards of an exogenous volcanic dome complex. *J Volc Geotherm Res*, 52: 303-323

Coombs H A, Howard A D, 1960. United States of America. *Catalog of Active Volcanoes of the World and Solfatara Fields*, Rome: IAVCEI, 9: 1-68 ***(regional reference)***

Davies D K, Quearry M W, Bonis S B, 1978. Glowing avalanches from the 1974 eruption of the volcano Fuego, Guatemala. *Geol Soc Amer Bull*, 89: 369-384

Dozy J J, 1949. Some notes on the volcanoes of Guatemala. *Bull Volc*, 8: 47-68

Duffield W A, 2001. At least Noah had some warning. *Eos, Trans Amer Geophys Union*, 82: 305, 309

Duffield W A, Heiken G H, Wohletz K H, Maassen L W, Dengo G, Mckee E H, 1989. Geology and geothermal potential of the Tecuamburro volcano area of Guatemala. *Trans Geotherm Res Council*, 13: 125-131

Duffield W A, Heiken G H, Wohletz K H, Maassen L W, Dengo G, Pinzon O, 1991. Geologic map of Tecuamburro volcano and surrounding area, Guatemala. *U S Geol Surv Map*, I-2197, 1:50,000 geol map

Dull R, 2004. Lessons from the mud, lessons from the Maya: paleoecological records of the Tierra Blanca Joven eruption. *In*: Rose W I, Bommer J J, Lopez D L, Carr M J, Major J J (eds), Natural Hazards in El Salvador, *Geol Soc Amer Spec Pap*, 375: 237-244

Dull R A, Southon J R, Sheets P, 2001. Volcanism, ecology and culture: a reassessment of the Volcan Ilopango TBJ eruption in the southern Maya realm. *Latin Amer Antiquity*, 12: 25-44

Dunn H, 1828. *Guatemala in 1827-28*. New York: G & C Carvill, 318 p

Eggers A A, 1971. The geology and petrology of the Amatitlan quadrangle, Guatemala. *Unpublished PhD thesis*, Dartmouth College, Hanover, New Hampshire, 221 p

Eggers A A, 1983. Temporal gravity and elevation changes at Pacaya Volcano, Guatemala. *J Volc Geotherm Res*, 19: 223-237

Eggers A A, Chavez D, 1979. Temporal gravity variations at Pacaya volcano, Guatemala. *J Volc Geotherm Res*, 6: 391-402

Eggers A, Krausse J, Rush H, Ward J, 1976. Gravity changes accompanying volcanic activity at Pacaya Volcano, Guatemala. *J Volc Geotherm Res*, 1: 229-236

Fairbrothers G E, Carr M J, Mayfield D G, 1978. Temporal magmatic variation at Boqueron Volcano, El Salvador. *Contr Mineral Petr*, 67: 1-9

Feldman L H, 1986. Master list of historic (pre-1804) earthquakes and volcanic eruptions in Central America. *In*: Claxton R H (ed) *Investigating Natural Hazards in Latin American History*, West Georgia College: Studies Social Sci, 25: 63-105

Feldman L H, 1993. *Mountains of Fire, Lands that Shake: Earthquakes and Volcanic Eruptions In the Historic Past of Central America (1505-1899)*. Culver City, Calif: Labyrinthos, 295 p

Flynn T, Goff F, Van Eeckhout E, Goff S, Ballinger J, Suyama J, 1991. Catastrophic landslide at Zunil I geothermal field, Guatemala. *Geotherm Res Council Trans*, 15: 425-433

Francis P W, 1973. Cannonball bombs, a new kind of volcanic bomb from the Pacaya Volcano, Guatemala. *Geol Soc Amer Bull*, 84: 2791-2793

Gall F, 1966. *Cerro Quemado Volcan de Quezaltenango*. Guatemala: Ministerio De Educacion, 115 p

Goff F, Janik C J, Fahlquist L S, Adams A, Roldan A, Revolorio M, Trujillo P E, Counce D, 1991. A reevaluation of the Moyuta geothermal system, southern Guatemala. *Bull Geotherm Resour Council*, 20: 290-298

Goff S J, Goff F, Janik C J, 1992. Tecuamburro volcano, Guatemala: exploration geothermal gradient drilling and results. *Geothermics*, 21: 483-502

Golombek M P, Carr M J, 1978. Tidal triggering of seismic and volcanic phenomena during the 1879-1880 eruption of Islas Quemadas volcano in El Salvador, Central America. *J Volc Geotherm Res*, 3: 299-308

Gonzalez Partida E, Torres Rodriguez V, Birkle P, 1997. Plio-Pleistocene volcanic history of the Ahuachapan geothermal system, El Salvador: the Concepcion de Ataco caldera. *Geothermics*, 26: 555-575

Gonzalez-Partida E, Renteria-T D, Faz-P P, Garduno-M V H, Canul-D R, Contreras-L E, Guevara-G M, Izquierdo-M G, 1991. Informe final del estudio geovulcanologico. *Comision Ejecutiva Hidoelectrica del Rio Lempa (CEL)*, unpublished internal rpt, 114 p

Haapala J M, Escobar Wolf R, Vallance J W, Rose W I, Griswold J P, Schilling S P, Ewert J W, Mota M, 2006. Volcanic hazards at Atitlan volcano, Guatemala. *U S Geol Surv Open-File Rpt*, 2005-1403

Halsor S P, Rose W I, 1988. Common characteristics of paired volcanoes in northern Central America. *J Geophys Res*, 93: 4467-4476

Halsor S, Rose W I, 1991. Mineralogical relations and magma mixing in calc-alkaline andesites from Lake Atitlan, Guatemala. *Mineral Petr*, 45: 47-67

Handal S, Barrios L A, 2004. Hydrothermal eruptions in El Salvador: a review. *In*: Rose W I, Bommer J J, Lopez D L, Carr M J, Major J J (eds), Natural Hazards in El Salvador, *Geol Soc Amer Spec Pap*, 375: 245-255

Harris A J L, Flynn L P, Matias O, Rose W I, Cornejo J, 2004. The evolution of an active silicic lava flow field: an ETM+ perspective. *J Volc Geotherm Res*, 135: 147-168

Harris A J L, Flynn L, Matias O, Rose W I, 2002. The thermal stealth flows of Santiaguito Dome, Guatemala; implications for the cooling and emplacement of dacitic block-lava flows. *Geol Soc Amer Bull*, 114: 533-546

Harris A J L, Rose W I, Flynn L P, 2003. Temporal trends in lava dome extrusion at Santiaguito 1922-2000. *Bull Volc*, 65: 77-89

Harris A J L, Vallance J W, Kimberly P, Rose W I, Matias O, Bunzendahl E, Flynn L P, Garbeil H, 2006. Downstream aggradation owing to lava dome extrusion and rainfall runoff at Volcan Santiaguito, Guatemala. *In*: Rose W I, Bluth G J S, Carr M J, Ewert J W, Patino L C, Vallance J W (eds), Volcanic hazards in Central America, *Geol Soc Amer Spec Pap*, 412: 85-104

Hart W J E, 1983. Classic to postclassic tephra layers exposed in archeological sites, eastern Zapotitan Valley. *In*: Sheets P D (ed) *Archeology and Volcanism in Central America*, Austin: Univ Texas Press, p 44-51

Hart W J E, Steen-McIntyre V, 1983. Tierra Blanca Joven tephra from the AD 260 eruption of Ilopango caldera. *In*: Sheets P D (ed), *Archeology and Volcanism in Central America*, Austin: Univ Texas Pess, p 14-34

Heiken G, Duffield W, 1990. An evaluation of the geothermal potential of the Tecuamburro volcano area of Guatemala. *Central Amer Energy Resour Project*, LA-11906-MS, Los Alamos Natl Lab, Los Alamos, NM 87545, 37 p

Hughes J M, 1978. Geology and petrology of the Caldera Tzanjuyub, western Guatemala. *Unpublished Master's thesis*, Dartmouth College, 123 p

Hughes J M, Stoiber R E, Ide G M, Maynard S R, Mackay A M, 1980. Quaternary volcanism east of the Zunil Fault Zone, west Guatemala (abs). *Eos, Trans Amer Geophys Union*, 61: 69

Incer J, 1988. Central American volcanic events (1524-1924). *Unpublished manuscript*, 52 p

Jaggar T A, 1925b. Izalco volcano. *Volcano Lett*, 19: 1

Jaggar T A, 1931f. Eruption of Santa Maria [Guatemala] November 1929. *Volc Lett*, 356: 1-4

Jaggar T A, 1931g. Volcano activity of Central America. *Volcano Lett*, 355: 1-3

Janik C J, Goff F, Fahlquist L, Adams A I, Roldan-M A, Chipera S J, Trujillo P E, Counce D, 1992. Hydrogeochemical exploration of geothermal prospects in the Tecuamburro volcano region, Guatemala. *Geothermics*, 21: 447-481

Jordan J N, Martinez M, 1984. Seismic history of El Salvador. *Unpublished manuscript*, 25 p

Katayama S, Matias O, 1995. Tephra stratigraphic approach to the eruptive history of Pacaya volcano, Guatemala. *Sci Rpt Tohoku Univ, 7th Ser (Geog)*: 45: 1-41

Kutterolf S, Freundt A, Perez W, 2008. Pacific offshore record of plinian arc volcanism in Central America: 2. Tephra volumes and eruptive masses. *Geochem Geophys Geosyst*, 8: Q02S02, doi:10.1029/2007GC001791

Lima Lobato E M, Fujino T, Palma Ayala J C, 2000. Amatitlan geothermal field in Guatemala. *Bull Geotherm Resour Council*, 29: 215-220

Lima Lobato E M, Palma J, Roldan Manzo A R, 2003. Geothermal Guatemala. Past, present, and future development of geothermal energy in Guatemala. *Geotherm Res Council Bull*, 32: 117-121

Lyons J J, Waite G P, Rose W I, Chigna G, 2010. Patterns in open vent, strombolian behavior at Fuego volcano, Guatemala, 2005-2007. *Bull Volc*, 72: 1-15

Major J J, Schilling S P, Pullinger C R, Escobar C D, 2004. Debris-flow hazards at San Salvador, San Vicente, and San Miguel volcanoes, El Salvador. *In*: Rose W I, Bommer J J, Lopez D L, Carr M J, Major J J (eds), Natural Hazards in El Salvador, *Geol Soc Amer Spec Pap*, 375: 89-108

Major J J, Schilling S P, Pullinger C R, Escobar C D, Chesner C A, Howell M M, 2001. Lahar-hazard zonation for San Miguel volcano, El Salvador. *U S Geol Surv Open-File Rpt*, 01-395: 1-14

Major J J, Schilling S P, Pullinger C R, Escobar C D, Howell M M, 2001. Volcano-hazard zonation for San Vicente volcano, El Salvador. *U S Geol Surv Open-File Rpt*, 01-367: 1-21

Major J J, Schilling S P, Sofield D J, Escobar CD, Pullinger C R, 2001. Volcano hazards in the San Salvador region, El Salvador. *U S Geol Surv Open-File Rpt*, 01-366: 1-23

Mann C P, Stix J, Vallance J W, Richer M, 2004. Subaqueous intracaldera volcanism, Ilopango caldera, El Salvador, Central America. *In*: Rose W I, Bommer J J, Lopez D L, Carr M J, Major J J (eds), Natural Hazards in El Salvador, *Geol Soc Amer Spec Pap*, 375: 159-174

Marden L, 1944. Coffee is king in El Salvador. *Natl Geog*, 84: 575-616

Martin D P, 1979. The historic activity of Fuego volcano, Guatemala: constraints on the subsurface magma bodies and processes therein. *Unpublished MSci thesis*, Michigan Tech Univ, 87 p

Martin D P, Rose W I, 1981. Behavioral patterns of Fuego volcano, Guatemala. *J Volc Geotherm Res*, 10: 67-81

Martinez-H M A, 1977. The eruption of 2 December 1976 of San Miguel volcano, Republic of El Salvador, Central America. *Center Geotech Invest, El Salv Ministry Public Works*, unpublished rpt, 4 p

McBirney A R, Bass M N, 1969. Geology of Bay Islands, Gulf of Honduras. *Amer Assoc Petrol Geol Mem*, 11: 229-243

Mercado R, Rose W I, Matias O, 1988. Eruptive history and volcanic hazard assessment of Fuego, Guatemala (abs). *Eos, Trans Amer Geophys Union*, 69: 506

Mercado R, Rose W I, Matias O, Giron J, 1988. November 1929 dome collapse and pyroclastic flow at Santiaguito dome, Guatemala (abs). *Eos, Trans Amer Geophys Union*, 69: 1487

Meyer-Abich H, 1956. Los volcanes activos de Guatemala y El Salvador. *Anales Serv Geol Nac El Salv*

Miller C D, 2002. Volcanology, stratigraphy, and effects on structures. *In*: Sheets P (ed), *Before the Volcano Erupted: The Ancient Ceren Village in Central America*. Austin: Univ Texas Press, p 11-23

Momita M, Fujino T, Lima Lobato E M, Palma J, 2002. Conceptual model of Amatitlan, Guatemala. *Chinetsu*, 39: 11-32

Montessus de Ballore F, 1884. *Temblores y Erupciones Volcanicas en Centro-America*. San Salvador: F Sagrini, 246 p ***(regional reference)***

Mooser F, Meyer-Abich H, McBirney A R, 1958. Central America. *Catalog of Active Volcanoes of the World and Solfatara Fields*, Rome: IAVCEI, 6: 1-146 ***(regional reference)***

Newhall C G, 1987. Geology of the Lake Atitlan region, western Guatemala. *J Volc Geotherm Res*, 33: 23-55

Newhall C G, Paull C K, Bradbury J P, Higuera-Gundy A, Poppe L J, Self S, Bonar Sharpless N, Ziagos J, 1987. Recent geologic history of Lake Atitlan, a caldera lake in western Guatemala. *J Volc Geotherm Res*, 33: 81-107

Nieva D, Verma M P, Santoyo E, Portugal E, Campos A, 1997. Geothermal exploration of the Chipilapa geothermal field, El Salvador. *Geothermics*, 26: 589-612

Parini M, Pisani P, Monterrosa M, 1995. Resource assessment at the Berlin geothermal field, El Salvador. *Proc World Geotherm Cong*, 3: 1537-1542

Patrier P, Papapanagiotou P, Beaufort D, Traineau H, Bril H, Rojas J, 1996. Role of permeability versus temperature in the distribution of the fine (<0.2 mu m) clay fraction in the Chipilapa geothermal system (El Salvador, Central America). *J Volc Geotherm Res*, 72: 101-120

Penfield G T, Rose W I, Halsor S, 1986. Geology of the Lake Atitlan volcanoes. *Geol Soc Amer Map and Chart Ser*, 55 1:49,212 scale map

Peterson P S, Rose W I Jr, 1985. Explosive eruptions of the Ayarza calderas, southeastern Guatemala. *J Volc Geotherm Res*, 25: 289-307

Pough F H, Mulford J W, 1957. The Cranbook Central American volcano expedition. *Cranbook Inst Sci Newsl*, 27: 10-29

Powers S, 1918. Letter concerning San Salvador eruption. *Zeit Vulk*, 4: 201

Pullinger C, 1998. Evolution of the Santa Ana volcanic complex, El Salvador. *Unpublished MSci thesis*, Michigan Tech Univ, 151 p

Reynolds J H, 1987. Timing and sources of Neogene and Quaternary volcanism in south-central Guatemala. *J Volc Geotherm Res*, 33: 9-22

Richer M, Mann C P, Stix J, 2004. Mafic magma injection triggering eruption at Ilopango caldera, El Salvador, Central America. *In*: Rose W I, Bommer J J, Lopez D L, Carr M J, Major J J (eds), Natural Hazards in El Salvador, *Geol Soc Amer Spec Pap*, 375: 175-189

Rodriquez J A, Herrara A, 2003. Geothermal El Salvador. *Geotherm Res Council Bull*, 32: 159-162

Rodriquez L A, Watson M W, Rose W I, Branan Y K, Bluth G J S, Chigna G, Matias O, Escobar D, Carn S A, Fischer T P, 2004. SO2 emissions to the atmosphere from active volcanoes in Guatemala and El Salvador, 1999-2002. *J Volc Geotherm Res*, 138: 325-344

Rolo R, Bommer J J, Houghton B F, Vallance J W, Berdousis P, Mavrommati C, Murphy W, 2004. Geologic and engineering characterization of Tierra Blanca pyroclastic ash deposits. *In*: Rose W I, Bommer J J, Lopez D L, Carr M J, Major J J (eds), Natural Hazards in El Salvador, *Geol Soc Amer Spec Pap*, 375: 55-67

Romagnoli P, Cuellar G, Jimenez M, Ghezzi G, 1976. Hydrogeological characteristics of the geothermal field of Ahuachapan, El Salvador. *In*: *Proc 2nd United Nations Symp Devel and Use Geotherm Resour, San Francisco*, 1: 571-574

Rose W I, 1972a. Notes on the 1902 eruption of Santa Maria volcano, Guatemala. *Bull Volc*, 36: 29-45

Rose W I, 1973. Pattern and mechanism of volcanic activity at the Santiaguito volcanic dome, Guatemala. *Bull Volc*, 37: 73-94

Rose W I, 1987a. Santa Maria, Guatemala: biomodal soda-rich calc-alkalic stratovolcano. *J Volc Geotherm Res*, 33: 109-129

Rose W I, 1987b. Volcanic activity at Santiaguito volcano, 1976-1984. *Geol Soc Amer Spec Pap*, 212: 17-27

Rose W I Jr, 1972b. Santiaguito Volcanic Dome, Guatemala. *Geol Soc Amer Bull*, 83: 1413-1433

Rose W I Jr, 1974. Nuee ardente from Santiaguito Volcano April 1973. *Bull Volc*, 37: 365-371

Rose W I Jr, Grant N K, Hahn G A, Lange I M, Powell J L, Easter J, Degraff J M, 1977. The evolution of Santa Maria Volcano, Guatemala. *J Geol*, 85: 63-87

Rose W I Jr, Pearson T, Bonis S, 1977. Nuee ardente eruption from the foot of a dacite lava flow, Santiaguito Volcano, Guatemala. *Bull Volc*, 40: 23-38

Rose W I Jr, Stoiber R E, Bonis S B, 1970. Volcanic activity at Santiaguito volcano, Guatemala, June 1968-August 1969. *Bull Volc*, 34: 295-307

Rose W I, Anderson A T, Woodruff L G, Bonis S, 1978. The October 1974 basaltic tephra from Fuego volcano Guatemala: description and history of the magma body. *J Volc Geotherm Res*, 4: 3-53

Rose W I, Bonis S, Stoiber R E, Keller M, Bickford T, 1973. Studies of volcanic ash from two recent Central American eruptions. *Bull Volc*, 37: 338-364

Rose W I, Conway F M, Pullinger C R, Deino A, MacIntosh W C, Svitil K A, 1999. An improved age framework for late Quaternary silicic eruptions in northern Central America. *Bull Volc*, 61: 106-120

Rose W I, Mercado R, Matias O, Giron J, 1989. Evaluation de riesgos del domo de Santiaguito, Guatemala (informe preliminar). INSIVUMEH, Guatemala, 21 p

Rose W I, Newhall C G, Bornhorst T J, Self S, 1987. Quaternary silicic pyroclastic deposits of Atitlan caldera, Guatemala. *J Volc Geotherm Res*, 33: 57-80

Rose W I, Penfield G T, Drexler J W, Larson P B, 1980. Geochemistry of the andesite flank lavas of three composite cones within the Atitlan Cauldron, Guatemala. *Bull Volc*, 43: 131-154

Rose W I, Self S, Murrow P J, Bonadonna C, Durant A J, Ernst G G J, 2008. Nature and significance of small volume fall deposits at composite volcanoes: insights from the October 14, 1974 Fuego eruption, Guatemala. *Bull Volc*, 70: 1043-1067

Rose W I, Stoiber R E, 1969. The 1966 eruption of Izalco volcano, El Salvador. *J Geophys Res*, 74: 3119-3130

Rose W I, Wunderman R L, Hoffman M F, Gale L, 1983. A volcanologist's review of atmospheric hazards of volcanic activity; Fuego and Mount St. Helens. *J Volc Geotherm Res*, 17: 133-157

Rotolo S G, Aiuppa A, Pullinger C R, Parello F, Tenorio-Mejia J, 1998. An introduction to San Vicente (Chichontepec) volcano, El Salvador. *Rev Geol Amer Central*, 21: 25-36

Rotolo S G, Castorina F, 1998. Transition from mildly-tholeiitic to calc-alkaline suite: the case of Chichontepec volcanic centre, El Salvador, Central America. *J Volc Geotherm Res*, 86: 117-136

Sapper K, 1925. *The Volcanoes of Central America*. Halle: Verlag Max Niemeyer, 144 p ***(regional reference)***

Schilling J W, Vallance J W, Matias O, Howell M M, 2001. Lahar hazards at Agua volcano, Guatemala. *U S Geol Surv Open-File Rpt*, 01-432: 1-8

Schneider K, 1911. *Die Vulkanischen Erscheinungen der Erde*. Berlin: Gebruder Borntraeger, 272 p

Schwartz D P, 1978. Geologic map of Guatemala, Zacapa 1:50,000 quadrangle. Instituto Geog Nac

Scolamacchia T, Pullinger C, Caballero L, Montalvo F, Beramendi Orosco L E, Gonzalez Hernandez G, 2010. The 2005 eruption of Ilamatepec (Santa Ana) volcano, El Salvador. *J Volc Geotherm Res*, 189: 291-318

Sheets P (ed), 2002. *Before the Volcano Erupted: The Ancient Ceren Village in Central America*. Austin: Univ Texas Press, 226 p

Sheets P D, 1979. Environmental and cultural effects of the Ilopango eruption in Central America. *In*: Sheets P D and Grayson D K (eds) *Volcanic Activity and Human Ecology*, New York: Academic Press, p 525-564

Sheets P D, 1992. *The Ceren Site, a Prehistoric Village Buried by Volcanic Ash in Central America*. Fort Worth, Tx: Harcourt Brace College Pub, 150 p

Sheets P D, 2004. Apocalypse then: social science approaches to volcanism, people, and cultures in the Zapotitan Valley, El Salvador. *In*: Rose W I, Bommer J J, Lopez D L, Carr M J, Major J J (eds), Natural Hazards in El Salvador, *Geol Soc Amer Spec Pap*, 375: 109-120

Siebert L, Alvarado G E, Vallance J W, van Wyk de Vries B, 2006. Large-volume volcanic edifice failures in Central America and associated hazards. *In*: Rose W I, Bluth G J S, Carr M J, Ewert J W, Patino L C, Vallance J W (eds), Volcanic hazards in Central America, *Geol Soc Amer Spec Pap*, 412: 1-26

Siebert L, Kimberly P, Pullinger C R, 2004. The voluminous Acajutla debris avalanche from Santa Ana volcano, western El Salvador, and comparison with other Central American edifice-failure events. *In*: Rose W I, Bommer J J, Lopez D L, Carr M J, Major J J (eds), Natural Hazards in El Salvador, *Geol Soc Amer Spec Pap*, 375: 5-23

Sofield D, 2004. Eruptive history and volcanic hazards of Volcan San Salvador. *In*: Rose W I, Bommer J J, Lopez D L, Carr M J, Major J J (eds), Natural Hazards in El Salvador, *Geol Soc Amer Spec Pap*, 375: 147-158

Squier E G, 1851. On the volcanoes of Central America and the geographical and topographical features, as connected with the proposed interoceanic canal. *Amer Assoc Adv Sci Proc*, 4: 101-122 ***(regional reference)***

Stoiber R E, 1975. Eruption of Volcan Fuego; October 14th, 1974. *Bull Volc*, 38(4): 863-869

Stoiber R E, Carr M J, 1973. Quaternary volcanic and tectonic segmentation of Central America. *Bull Volc*, 37: 304-325

Stoiber R E, Rose W I, 1970. The geochemistry of Central American volcanic gas condensates. *Geol Soc Amer Bull*, 81: 2891-2912

Stoiber R E, Rose W I Jr, 1969. Recent volcanic and fumarolic activity at Santiaguito volcano, Guatemala. *Bull Volc*, 33: 475-502

Vallance J W, Schilling S P, Matias O, Rose W I, Howell M M, 2001. Volcano hazards at Fuego and Agua, Guatemala. *U S Geol Surv Open-File Rpt*, 01-431: 1-23

Vallance J W, Siebert L, Rose W I, Giron J R, Banks N G, 1995. Edifice collapse and related hazards in Guatemala. *J Volc Geotherm Res*, 66: 337-355

Vazquez de Espinosa A, 1942. Compendium and description of the West Indies. *Smithsonian Inst Misc Coll*, 862 p

Walker J A, 1981. Petrogenesis of lavas from cinder cone fields behind the volcanic front of Central America. *J Geol*, 89: 721-739

Walker J A, Patino L C, Cameron B I, Carr M J, 2000. Petrogenetic insights provided by compositional transects across the Central American Arc; southeastern Guatemala and Honduras. *J Geophys Res*, 105: 18,949-18,963

Weber H S, Wiesemann G, 1978. Mapa Geologico de la Republica de El Salvador/America Central. Bundesanstalt fur Geowissenschaften und Rohstoffe, Hannover, Germany, 1:100,000 scale geologic map in 6 sheets

Weyl R, 1952. *Estudios Geologicos de la Region del Rio Comalapa, El Salvador*. Communic Itic Ano I, San Salvador

Williams H, 1960. Volcanic history of the Guatemalan Highlands. *Univ Calif Pub Geol Sci*, 38: 1-86

Williams H, McBirney A R, 1969. Volcanic history of Honduras. *Univ Calif Pub Geol Sci*, 85: 1-101

Williams H, McBirney A R, Dengo G, 1964. Geologic reconnaissance of southeastern Guatemala. *Univ Calif Pub Geol Sci*, 50: 1-62

Williams H, Meyer-Abich H, 1954. Historia volcanica del de Coatepeque (El Salvador) y sus alrededores. *El Salv Univ Inst Tropical Invest Cient Comun*, 3: 107-120

Williams H, Meyer-Abich H, 1955. Volcanism in the southern part of El Salvador with particular reference to the collapse basins of Lakes Coatepeque and Ilopango. *Univ Calif Pub Geol Sci*, 32: 1-64

Williams S N, Self S, 1983. The October 1902 Plinian eruptions of Santa Maria volcano, Guatemala. *J Volc Geotherm Res*, 16: 33-56

Woodruff L G, Rose W I Jr, Rigot W, 1979. Contrasting fractionation patterns for sequential magmas from two calc-alkaline volcanoes in Central America. *J Volc Geotherm Res*, 6: 217-240

Wunderman R L, Rose W I, 1984. Amatitlan, an actively resurging cauldron 10 km south of Guatemala City. *J Geophys Res*, 89: 8525-8539

Yuan A, McNutt S R, Harlow D H, 1984. Seismicity and eruptive activity at Fuego Volcano, Guatemala; February 1975 - January 1977. *J Volc Geotherm Res*, 21: 277-296

CENTRAL AMERICA: SOUTHERN (1404-06)

Alvarado G E, 1989. *Los Volcanes de Costa Rica*. San Jose, Costa Rica: Universidad Estatal a Distancia, 175 p

Alvarado G E, 1993. Volcanology and petrology of Irazu volcano, Costa Rica. *Unpublished PhD thesis*, Christian-Albrechts Univ, 261 p

Alvarado G E, 2000. *Volcanes de Costa Rica: su geologia, historia y riqueza natural*. San Jose, Costa Rica: EUNED, 269 p

Alvarado G E, Carr M J, 1993. The Platanar-Aguas Zarcas volcanic centers, Costa Rica: spatial-temporal association of Quaternary calc-alkaline and alkaline volcanism. *Bull Volc*, 55: 443-453

Alvarado G E, Carr M J, Turrin B D, Swisher CC III, Schmincke H-U, Hudnut K W, 2006. Recent volcanic history of Irazu volcano, Costa Rica: alternation and mixing of two magma batches, and pervasive mixing. *In*: Rose W I, Bluth G J S, Carr M J, Ewert J W, Patino L C, Vallance J W (eds), Volcanic hazards in Central America, *Geol Soc Amer Spec Pap*, 412: 259-276

Alvarado G E, Kussmaul S, Chiesa S, Gillot P-Y, Appel H, Worner G, Rundle C, 1992. Resumen cronoestratigrafico de las rocas igneas de Costa Rica basado en dataciones radiometricas. *J South Amer Earth Sci*, 6: 151-168

Alvarado G E, Soto G J, 2002. Pyroclastic flow generated by crater-wall collapse and outpouring of the lava pool of Arenal volcano, Costa Rica. *Bull Volc*, 63: 557-568

Alvarado G E, Soto G J, 2008. Volcanoes in the pre-Columbian life, legend, and archaeology of Costa Rica (Central America). *J Volc Geotherm Res*, 176: 356-362

Alvarado G E, Soto G J, Schmincke H-U, Blge L L, Sumita M, 2006. The 1968 andesitic lateral blast eruption at Arenal volcano, Costa Rica. *J Volc Geotherm Res*, 157: 9-33

Alvarado G E, Vega E, Chaves J, Vasquez M, 2004. Los grandes deslizamientos (volcanicos y no volcanicos) de tip debris avalanche en Costa Rica. *Rev Geol Amer Central*, 30: 83-99

Alvarado G, Acevedo A P, Monsalve M L, Espindola J M, Gomez D, Hall M, Naranjo J A, Pulgarin B, Raigosa J, Sigaran C, Van der Laat R, 1999. El desarrollo de la vulcanologia en Latinoamerica en el ultimo cuarto del siglo XX. *Rev Geofis*, 51: 185-241

Alvarado-Induni G E, 2005. *Costa Rica, Land of Volcanoes*. San Jose, Costa Rica: EUNID, 306 p

Badilla E, Chaves I, Linkimer L, Zuniga H, Alvarado G E, 2001. Fotogeologia de los complejos volcanicos El Hoyo y Asososca (Nicaragua). *Rev Geol Amer Central*, 24: 79-86

Barquero Hernandez J, 1976. *El Volcan Irazu y su Actividad*. San Jose, Costa Rica: Escula de Ciencias Geograficas, 63 p

Barquero J, de Dios Segura J, 1983. La actividad del Volcan Rincon de la Vieja. *Univ Nac Bol Vulc*, 13: 5-10

Barquero-H J, 1998a. *Volcan Poas*. San Jose, Costa Rica: privately published, 42 p

Barquero-H J, 1998b. *Volcan Irazu*. San Jose, Costa Rica: privately published, 50 p

Barquero-H J, Saenz-R R, 1987. Aparatos volcanicos de Costa Rica. *Heredia, Costa Rica: OVSICORI-UNA*, 1:750,000 map and volcano list

Behling H, 2000. A 2860-year high-resolution pollen and charcoal record from the cordillera de Talamanca in Panama: a history of human and volcanic forest disturbance. *Holocene*, 10: 387-393

Bellon H, Tournon J, 1978. Contribution de la geochronometrie K/Ar a letude du magmatisme de Costa Rica, Amerique Centrale. *Bull Soc Geol France*, 20: 955-959

Bice D C, 1980. Tephra stratigraphy and physical aspects of recent volcanism near Managua, Nicaragua. *Unpublished PhD thesis*, Univ Calif Berkeley, 422 p

Bice D C, 1985. Quaternary volcanic stratigraphy of Managua, Nicaragua; correlation and source assignment for multiple overlapping plinian deposits. *Geol Soc Amer Bull*, 96: 553-566

Bolge L L, Carr M J, Feigenson M D, Alvarado G E, 2006. Geochemical stratigraphy and magmatic evolution at Arenal volcano, Costa Rica. *J Volc Geotherm Res*, 157: 34-48

Bolge L L, Carr M J, Feigenson M D, Borgia A, 2004. Geochemistry and magmatic evolution of explosive tephras ET3 and ET4 from Arenal volcano, Costa Rica. *Rev Geol Amer Central*, 30: 127-135

Borgia A, Linneman S, Spencer D, Diego M L, Brenes A J, 1983. Dynamics of lava flow fronts, Arenal Volcano, Costa Rica. *J Volc Geotherm Res*, 19: 303-329

Borgia A, Poore C, Carr M J, Melson W G, Alvarado G E, 1988. Structural, stratigraphic, and petrologic aspects of Arenal-Chato volcanic system, Costa Rica: evolution of a young stratovolcanic complex. *Bull Volc*, 50: 86-105

Borgia A, van Wyk de Vries B, 2003. The volcano-tectonic evolution of Concepcion, Nicaragua. *Bull Volc*, 65: 248-265

Boudon G, Rancon J-P, Kieffer G, Soto G J, Traineau H, Rossignol J-C, 1995. Estilo eruptivo actual del volcan Rincon de la Vieja: evidencias de los productos de las erupciones de 1966-70 y 1991-92. *Rothschildia*, 2(2): 10-13

Boudon G, Rancon J-P, Kieffer G, Soto G J, Traineau H, Rossignol J-C, 1996. Les eruptions de 1966-1970 et 1991-92 du volcan Rincon de la Vieja, Costa Rica: exemple d'activite recurrente d'un systeme hydromagmatique. *Compte Rendus Acad Sci Paris*, Ser II, 332: 101-108

Branan Y K, Harris A, Watson I M, Phillips J C, Horton K, Williams-Jones G, Garbeil H, 2008. Investigation of at-vent dynamics and dilution using thermal infrared radiometers at Masaya volcano, Nicaragua. *J Volc Geotherm Res*, 169: 34-47

Bullard F M, 1956. Volcanic activity in Costa Rica and Nicaragua in 1954. *Eos, Trans Amer Geophys Union*, 37: 75-82

Bullard F M, 1957. Active volcanoes of Central America. *20th Internatl Geol Cong, Mexico City*, Sec 1: 351-371

Burton M R, Oppenheimer C, Horrocks L A, Francis P W, Polet J, Kanamori H, 2000. Remote sensing of CO2 and H2O emission rates from Masaya Volcano, Nicaragua. *Geology*, 28: 915-918

Bush M B, Colinvaux P A, 1990. A pollen record of a complete glacial cycle from lowland Panama. *J Vegetation Sci*, 1: 105-118

Caldcleugh A, 1836. Some account of the volcanic eruption of Coseguina. *Phil Trans Roy Soc London*, Part I: 27-36

Carr M J, 1984. Symmetrical and segmented variation of physical and geochemical characterisitics of the Central American volcanic front. *J Volc Geotherm Res*, 20: 231-252

Carr M J, Chesner C A, Gemmell J B, 1986. Nuevos analisis de lavas y bombas del volcan Rincon de la Vieja, Costa Rica. *Bol Vulc Univ Nac Costa Rica*, 16: 23-26

Carr M J, Rose W I Jr, 1987. CENTAM; a database of Central American volcanic rocks. *J Volc Geotherm Res*, 33: 239-240

Carr M J, Stoiber R E, 1973. Intermediate depth earthquakes and volcanic eruptions in Central America 1961-1972. *Bull Volc*, 37: 326-337

Carr M J, Walker J A, 1987. Intra-eruption changes in composition of some mafic to intermediate tephras in Central America. *J Volc Geotherm Res*, 33: 147-159

Casadevall T J, Rose W I Jr, Fuller W H, Hunt W H, Hart M A, Moyers J L, Woods D C, Chuan R L, Friend J, 1984. Sulfur dioxide and particles in quiescent volcanic plumes from Poas, Arenal, and Colima volcanos, Costa Rica and Mexico. *J Geophys Res*, 89: 9633-9641

Casertano L, Borgia A, Cigolini C, 1983. El Volcan Poas, Costa Rica: cronologia y caracteristicas de la actividad. *Geof Internac*, 22: 215-236

Casertano L, Borgia A, Cigolini C, Morales L D, Montero W, Gomez M, Fernandez J F, 1987. An integraded dynamic model for the volcanic activity at Poas Volcano, Costa Rica. *Bull Volc*, 49: 588-598

Castillo P, Batiza R, Vanko D, Malavassi E, Barquero J, Fernandez E, 1988. Anomalously young volcanoes on old hot-spot traces: I. Geology and petrology of Cocos Island. *Geol Soc Amer Bull*, 100: 1400-1414

Cecchi E, van Wyk de Vries B, Lavest J-M, 2005. Flank spreading and collapse of weak-cored volcanoes. *Bull Volc*, 67: 72-91

Chamberlain P W, 1903. The volcanoes of Nicaragua. *U S 57th Cong 2nd Sess, Senate Document*, 131: 27-33

Chiesa S, 1987. La mayor erupcion pliniana del Volcan Arenal, Costa Rica. *Rev Geol Amer Central*, 6: 25-41

Chiesa S, Alvarado G E, Pecchio M, Corella M, Zanchi A, 1994. Contribution to petrological and stratigraphical understanding of the Cordillera de Guanacaste lava flows, Costa Rica. *Rev Geol Amer Central*, 17: 19-43

Chiesa S, Bettoni M, Confortini F, Invernici N, Madesani R, Suardi M, 1996. Breva resena sobre la geologia de los Parques Nacionales Santa Rosa y Guanacaste. *Rothschildia*, 3(1): 1-5

Chiesa S, Civelli G, Gillot P-Y, Mora A, Alvarado G E, 1992. Rocas piroclasticas asociadas con la formacion de la caldera de Guayabo, Cordillera de Guanacaste, Costa Rica. *Rev Geol Amer Central*, 14: 59-75

Chiesa S, Confortini F, Madesani R, 1998. Geologia del Area de Conservacion de Guanacaste. *Rothschildia*, 5(2): 1-36

Cigolini C, Borgia A, Casertano L, 1984. Intra-crater activity, aa-block lava, viscosity and flow dynamics; Arenal Volcano, Costa Rica. *J Volc Geotherm Res*, 20: 155-176

Cigolini C, Kudo A M, Brookins D G, Ward D, 1991. The petrology of Poas Volcano lavas; basalt-andesite relationship and their petrogenesis with the magmatic arc of Costa Rica. *J Volc Geotherm Res*, 48(3-4): 367-384

Cole P D, Fernandez E, Duarte E, Duncan A M, 2005. Explosive activity and generation mechanisms of pyroclastic flows at Arenal volcano, Costa Rica between 1987 and 2001. *Bull Volc*, 67: 695-716

Connor C B, Hill B E, LaFemina, Navarro M, Conway M, 1996. Soil 222Rn pulse during the initial phase of the June-August 1995 eruption of Cerro Negro, Nicaragua. *J Volc Geotherm Res*, 73: 119-127

Costantini L, Bonadonna C, Houghton B F, Wehrmann H, 2009. New physical characterization of the Fontana Lapilli basaltic Plinian eruption, Nicaragua. *Bull Volc*, 71: 337-355

Deering C D, Vogel T A, Patino L C, Alvarado G E, 2007. Origin of distinct silicic magma types from the Guachipelin caldera, NW Costa Rica: evidence for magma mixing and protracted subvolcanic residence. *J Volc Geotherm Res*, 165: 103-126

Defant M J, Clark L F, Stewart R H, Drummond M S, de Boer J Z, Maury R C, Bellon H, Jackson T E, Restrepo J F, 1991. Andesite and dacite genesis via contrasting processes; the geology and geochemistry of El Valle Volcano, Panama. *Contr Mineral Petr*, 106: 309-324

Defant M J, Richerson P M, de Boer J Z, Stewart R H, Maury R C, Bellon H, Drummond M S, Feigenson M K, Jackson T E, 1991. Dacite genesis via both slab melting and differentiation: petrogenesis of La Yeguada volcanic complex, Panama. *J Petr*, 32: 1101-1142

Delmelle P, Stix J, Baxter P J, Garcia-Alvarez J, Barquero J, 2002. Atmospheric dispersion, environmental effects and potential health hazard associated with the low-altitude gas plume of Masaya volcano, Nicaragua. *Bull Volc*, 64: 423-434

Diaz F, Ponce F, Reyes E, 2000. Advanced pre-feasibility studies of El Valle de Anton geothermal field. *Proc World Geotherm Cong 2000, Kyushu - Tohoku, Japan, May 28-June 10, 2000*, p 159-168

Duffell H J, Oppenheimer C, Pyle D M, Galle B, McGonigle A J S, Burton M R, 2003. Changes in gas composition prior to a minor explosive eruption at Masaya volcano, Nicaragua. *J Volc Geotherm Res*, 126: 327-339

Feldman L H, 1986. Master list of historic (pre-1804) earthquakes and volcanic eruptions in Central America. *In*: Claxton R H (ed) *Investigating Natural Hazards in Latin American History*, West Georgia College: Studies Social Sci, 25: 63-105

Feldman L H, 1993. *Mountains of Fire, Lands that Shake: Earthquakes and Volcanic Eruptions In the Historic Past of Central America (1505-1899)*. Culven City, Calif: Labyrinthos, 295 p

Francis P W, Thorpe R S, Brown G C, Glasscock J, 1980. Pyroclastic sulphur eruption at Poas volcano, Costa Rica. *Nature*, 283: 754-756

Freundt A, Kutterolf S, Schmincke H-U, Hansteen T, Wehrmann H, Perez W, Strauch W, Navarro M, 2006. Volcanic hazards in Nicaragua: past, present, and future. *In*: Rose W I, Bluth G J S, Carr M J, Ewert J W, Patino L C, Vallance J W (eds), Volcanic hazards in Central America, *Geol Soc Amer Spec Pap*, 412: 141-165

Freundt A, Kutterolf S, Wehrmann H, Schmincke H-U, Strauch W, 2006. Eruption of the dacite to andesite zoned Mateare Tephra, and associated tsunamis in Lake Managua, Nicaragua. *J Volc Geotherm Res*, 149: 103-123

Frullani A, 1987a. Estudio de reconocimiento geotermico nacional area de Valle de Anton. *IRHE - BID - OLADE*, 74 p

Frullani A, 1987b. Estudio de reconocimiento geotermico nacional area Chitra-Calobre. *IRHE - BID - OLADE*, 67 p

Fudali R F, Melson W G, 1972. Ejecta velocities, magma chamber pressure and kinetic energy associated with the 1968 eruption of Arenal volcano. *Bull Volc*, 35: 383-401

Ghigliotti M, Frullani A, Alvarado G E, Soto G J, 1991. Distribucion areal y caracteristics de los depositos de tefra mas recientes (1080-1968 dC). Bol Obs Vulc Arenal 4(8): 11-33

Ghigliotti M, Frullani A, Soto G J, Alvarado G E, 1992. Tefroestratigrafia, historia y ciclos eruptivos del Volcan Arenal. *Bol Obs Vulc Arenal*, 5(9-10): 52-96

Gillot P-Y, Chiesa S, Alvarado G E, 1994. Chronostratigraphy of upper Miocene-Quaternary volcanism in northern Costa Rica. *Rev Geol Amer Central*, 17: 45-53

Girard G, van Wyk de Vries B, 2005. The Managua Graben and Las Sierras-Masaya volcanic complex (Nicaragua): pull-apart localization by an intrusive complex: results from analog modeling. *J Volc Geotherm Res*, 144: 37-57

Hallinan S, 1993. Nonchaotic collapse at funnel calderas; gravity study of the ring fractures at Guayabo caldera, Costa Rica. *Geology*, 21: 367-370

Hallinan S, Brown G, 1995. Incremental collapse and stratocone growth within a funnel-shaped caldera, Guayabo, Costa Rica. *J Volc Geotherm Res*, 67: 101-122

Hannah R S, Vogel T A, Patino L C, Alvarado G E, Perez W, Smith D R, 2002. Origin of silicic rocks in central Costa Rica: a study of a chemically variable ash-flow sheet in the Tiribi Tuff. *Bull Volc*, 64: 117-133

Harris A J L, 2009. The pit-craters and pit-crater-filling lavas of Masaya volcano. *Bull Volc*, 71: 541-588

Hazlett R W, 1987. Geology of the San Cristobal volcanic complex, Nicaragua. *J Volc Geotherm Res*, 33: 223-230

Hidalgo P J, 2007. Petrology and geochemistry of El Hato silicic ignimbrite, El Valle volcano, Panama. *Unpublished MSci thesis*, Michigan Tech Univ, 218 p

Hidalgo P J, Alvarado G E, Linkimer L, 2004. La Lavina del Valle Central (Costa Rica): lahar o debris avalanche? *Rev Geol Amer Central*, 30: 101-109

Hill B E, Conner C B, Jarzemba M S, La Femina P C, Navarro M, Strauch W, 1998. 1995 eruptions of Cerro Negro volcano, Nicaragua, and risk assessment for future eruptions. *Geol Soc Amer Bull*, 110: 1231-1241

Horn S P, 2001. The age of the Laguna Hule explosion crater, Costa Rica, and the timing of subsequent tephra eruptions; evidence from lake sediments. *Rev Geol Amer Central*, 24: 57-65

Hradecky P, 1997. Estudio geologico para reconocimiento de riesgo natural y vulnerabilidad geologica en el area de Managua. *Cesky Geologicky Ustav Praha, Instituto Nicaraguense de Estudios Territoriales, Managua (INETER)*, 81 p

INETER, 1995. Mapa Geologico Minero de la Republica de Nicaragua. *Instituto Nicaraguense de Estudios Territoriales, Managua (INETER)*, 1:500,000 geologic map, 5 sheets

INETER, 1999-. Volcanoes en Nicaragua. *Inst Nicaraguense Estudios Territoriales* (http://www.ineter.gob.ni/geofisica/vol/dep-vol.html)

IRHE, 1987. Final report on the reconnaissance study of geothermal resources in the Republic of Panama. *IRHE - OLADE - BID*, 72 p

Incer J, 1970. *Nuevo Geografia de Nicaragua*. Mangua: Talere S de Editorial Recalde, 582 p

Incer J, 1988. Central American volcanic events (1524-1924). *Unpublished manuscript*, 52 p

Incer J, 1990. *Nicaragua: Viajes Rutas y Encuentros 1502-1838*. San Jose, Costa Rica: Libro Libre, 638 p

Innocenti F, 1985a. Estudio de reconocimiento geotermico nacional informe petrografico. *IRHE - OLADE*, upublished rpt, 34 p and tables

Innocenti F, 1985b. Petrografia de la region Baru-Colorado. *IRHE - OLADE*, upublished rpt, unpaginated

Innocenti F, 1986. Estudios petrologicos adicionales de algunas vulcanitas del sistema Baru y Valle de Anton. *IRHE - OLADE*, unpublished rpt, 22 p and tables

Jaggar T A, 1931e. Kamchatka volcanoes in 1931. *Volcano Lett*, 353: 1-3

Kempter K A, Benner S G, Williams S N, 1996. Rincon de la Vieja volcano, Guanacaste province, Costa Rica: geology of the southwestern flank and hazards implications. *J Volc Geotherm Res*, 71: 109-127

Kempter K A, Rowe G L, 2000. Leakage of active crater lake brine through the north flank at Rincon de la Vieja Volcano, Northwest Costa Rica, and implications for crater collapse. *J Volc Geotherm Res*, 97: 143-159

Kerle N, van Wyk de Vries B, 2001. The 1998 debris avalanche at Casita Volcano, Nicaragua; investigation of structural deformation as the cause of slope instability using remote sensing. *J Volc Geotherm Res*, 105: 49-63

Kerle N, van Wyk de Vries B, Oppenheimer C, 2003. New insight into the factors leading to the 1998 flank collapse and lahar disaster at Casita volcano, Nicaragua. *Bull Volc*, 65: 331-345

Kirianov V Y, Melekestsev I V, Ovsyannikov A A, Andreev V N, 1988. Reconstruction of the eruptive activity of Momotombo volcano (Nicaragua) to assess volcanic hazards. *Proc Kagoshima Internatl Conf Volc*, p 495-498

Knutsen K L, 2009. La Yeguada volcanic complex: an assessment of the geologic hazards using new Ar40/Ar39 ages. *Unpublished MSci thesis*, Michigan Tech Univ

Krushensky R D, Escalante G, 1967. Activity of Irazu and Poas volcanoes, Costa Rica, November 1964-July 1965. *Bull Volc*, 31: 75-84

Kutterolf S, Freundt A, Perez W, 2008. Pacific offshore record of plinian arc volcanism in Central America: 2. Tephra volumes and eruptive masses. *Geochem Geophys Geosyst*, 8: Q02S02, doi:10.1029/2007GC001791

Kutterolf S, Freundt A, Perez W, Wehrman H, Schmincke H-U, 2007. Late Pleistocene to Holocene temporal succession and magnitudes of highly-explosive volcanic eruptions in west-centeral Nicaragua. *J Volc Geotherm Res*, 163: 55-82

La Femina P C, Conner C B, Hill B E, Strauch W, Armando Saballos J, 2004. Magma-tectonic interactions in Nicaragua: the 1999 seismic swarm and eruption of Cerro Negro volcano. *J Volc Geotherm Res*, 137: 187-199

Linares O F, Sheets P D, Rosenthal E J, 1975. Prehistoric agriculture in tropical highlands. *Science*, 187: 137-145

Mainieri Protti A, 1976. Proyecto geotermico de Guanacaste: informe de previabilidad tecnica. *Inst Costarricense de Electricidad (ICE)*, 97 p

Mainieri Protti A, 2003. Costa Rica geothermal update. *Geotherm Res Council Bull*, 32: 157-158

Marini L, Yock Fung A, Sanchez E, 2003. Use of reaction path modeling to identify the process governing the generation of netrual Na-Cl and acidic Na-Cl-SO4 deep geothermal liquids at Miravalles geothermal system, Costa Rica. *J Volc Geotherm Res*, 128: 363-387

Martinez M, Fernandez E, Valdes J, Barboza V, van der Laat R, Duarte E, Malavassi E, Sandoval L, Barquero J, Marino T, 2000. Chemical evolution and volcanic activity of the active crater lake of Poas Volcano, Costa Rica, 1993-1997. *J Volc Geotherm Res*, 97: 127-141

McBirney A R, 1955a. Thoughts on the eruption of the Nicaraguan volcano Las Pilas. *Bull Volc*, 17: 113-118

McBirney A R, 1955b. The origin of the Nejapa pits near Managua, Nicaragua. *Bull Volc*, 17: 145-154

McBirney A R, 1956. The Nicaraguan volcano Masaya and its caldera. *Eos, Trans Amer Geophys Union*, 37: 83-96

McBirney A R, Williams H, 1965. Volcanic history of Nicaragua. *Univ Calif Pub Geol Sci*, 55: 1-65

McKnight S B, Williams S N, 1997. Old cinder cone or young composite volcano? The nature of Cerro Negro, Nicaragua. *Geology*, 25: 339-342

Melson W G, 1982. Alternation Between Acidic and Basic Magmas in major explosive eruptions of Arenal volcano, Costa Rica. *Bol Vulc Univ Nac Costa Rica*, p 1-9

Melson W G, 1984. Prehistoric eruptions of Arenal volcano, Costa Rica. *Vinculos*, 10: 34-59

Melson W G, 1988. Major explosive eruptions of Costa Rican volcanoes: update for Costa Rican volcanism workshop. *Costa Rica Volc Workshop, Smithsonian Inst*, Nov 1988, 6 p

Melson W G, 1994. The eruption of 1968 and tephra stratigraphy of Arenal Volcano. *In*: Sheets P D, McKee B R (eds) *Archaeology, Volcanism, and Remote Sensing in the Arenal Region, Costa Rica*, Austin, TX: Univ Texas Press, p 24-47

Melson W G, Barquero-H J, Saenz-R R, Fernandez E, 1986. Erupciones explosivas de importancia en volcanes de Costa Rica. *Bol Vulc Univ Nac Costa Rica*, 16: 15-20

Melson W G, Saenz R, 1973. Volume, energy and cyclicity of eruptions of Arenal volcano, Costa Rica. *Bull Volc*, 37: 416-437

Melson W G, Saenz-R R, Barquero-H J, Fernandez-S E, 1988. Edad relativa de las erupciones del Cerro Congo y Laguna Hule. *Bol Vulc Univ Nac Costa Rica*, 19: 8-10

Mendez J, Hidalgo P J, 2004. Descripcion geologica del deposito de debris avalanche El Coyol, Formacion Barva, Costa Rica. *Rev Geol Amer Central*, 30: 199-202

Merla A, 1995. Integracion de los estudios geocientificos en las zonas geotermicas Valle de Anton y Chitra-Calobre. *IRHE - BID*, 29 p

Michigan Tech Univ, 1996. Rincon de la Vieja, Costa Rica. http://www.geol.mtu.edu/~boris/RINCON.html (28 February 2001)

Montessus de Ballore F, 1884. *Temblores y Erupciones Volcanicas en Centro-America*. San Salvador: F Sagrini, 246 p ***(regional reference)***

Mooser F, Meyer-Abich H, McBirney A R, 1958. Central America. *Catalog of Active Volcanoes of the World and Solfatara Fields*, Rome: IAVCEI, 6: 1-146 ***(regional reference)***

Mora S, 1977. Estudio geologico del Cerro Chopo. *Rev Geol Amer Central*, 5-6: 189-199

Murata K J, Dondoli C, Saenz R, 1966. The 1963-65 eruption of Irazu volcano, Costa Rica. *Bull Volc*, 29: 765-793

Obando L G, Soto G J, 1993. La turbera del rio Silencio (El Cairo, Siguirres, Costa Rica): paleoambientes lagunares influenciados por las ceniza del volcan Turrialba. *Rev Geol Amer Central*, 15: 41-48

Oppenheim V, 1970. Eruption of Arenal, Costa Rica. *Texas J Sci*, 22: 88-90

Ostapenko S V, Spektor S V, Netesov Y P, 1998. San Jacinto-Tizate geothermal field, Nicaragua: exploration and conceptual model. *Geothermics*, 27: 361-378

Ostapenko S V, Spektor S, Netesov Y, Romero F, 1997. Geothermal exploration of El Najo field Nicaragua. *Stanford Geotherm Prog Proc*, 22: 511-518

Paniagua-P S, Soto-B G, 1986. Reconocimiento de los riesgos volcanicos potenciales de la Cordillera Central de Costa Rica, America Central. *Unpublished manuscript, Simposio Internac sobre Neotectonica y Riesgos Volcanicos*, Bogota, 1986, 29 p

Pardo N, Avellan D R, Macias J L, Scolamacchia T, Rodriguez D, 2008. The ~1245 yr BP Asososca maar: new advances on recent volcanic stratigraphy of Managua (Nicaragua) and hazard implications. *J Volc Geotherm Res*, 176: 493-512

Pardo N, Macias J L, Giordano G, Cianfarra P, Avellan D R, Ballatreccia F, 2009. The ~1245 yr BP Asososca maar eruption: the youngest event along the Nejapa-Maraflores volcanic fault, western Managua, Nicaragua. *J Volc Geotherm Res*, 184: 292-312

Parsons Corporation, 1972. The Geology of Western Nicaragua. *Nicaragua Tax Improvement and Natural Resources Inventory Project*, Final Technical Rpt, v. IV

Perez W, Alvarado G E, Gans P B, 2006. The 322 ka Tiribi Tuff: stratigraphy, geochronology and mechanisms of deposition of the largest and most recent ignimbrite in the Valle Central, Costa Rica. *Bull Volc*, 69: 25-40

Perez W, Freundt A, 2006. The youngest highly explosive basaltic eruptions from Masaya caldera (Nicaragua): stratigraphy and hazard assessment. *In*: Rose W I, Bluth G J S, Carr M J, Ewert J W, Patino L C, Vallance J W (eds), Volcanic hazards in Central America, *Geol Soc Amer Spec Pap*, 412: 189-207

Perez W, Freundt A, Kutterolf S, Schmincke H-U, 2009. The Masaya Triple Layer: a 2100 year old basaltic multi-episodic plinian eruption from the Masaya caldera complex (Nicaragua). *J Volc Geotherm Res*, 179: 191-205

Plank T, Balzer V, Carr M, 2002. Nicaraguan volcanoes record paleoceanographic changes accompanying closure of the Panama gateway. *Geology*, 30: 1087-1090

Prosser J T, 1983. The geology of Poas volcano, Costa Rica. *Unpublished MA thesis*, Dartmouth College

Prosser J T, 1985. Geology and medium-term temporal magmatic variation found at the summit region of Poas volcano, Costa Rica. *Bol Vulc Univ Nac Costa Rica*, 15: 21-39

Raccichini S, Bennett F D, 1977. Nuevos aspectos de las erupciones del Volcan Poas. *Rev Geog Amer Central*, 5-6: 37-53

Rausch J, Schmincke H-U, 2010. Nejapa Tephra: The youngest (ca. 1 ka BP) highly explosive hydroclastic eruption in western Managua (Nicaragua). *J Volc Geotherm Res*, doi: 10.1016/j.jvolgeores.2010.02.010

Reagan M K, 1988. An outline of the recent eruptive history of Turrialba volcano, Costa Rica. *Costa Rica Volc Workshop, Smithsonian Inst*, Nov 1988, 33 p

Reagan M K, Gill J B, 1989. Coexisting calcalkaline and high-niobium basalts from Turrialba volcano, Costa Rica: implications for residual titanates in arc magma sources. *J Geophys Res*, 94: 4619-4633

Reagan M K, Gill J B, Malavassi E, Garcia M O, 1987. Changes in magma composition at Arenal Volcano, Costa Rica, 1968-1985; real-time monitoring of open-system differentiation. *Bull Volc*, 49: 415-434

Reagan M, Durate E, Soto G J, Fernandez E, 2006. The eruptive history of Turrialba volcano, Costa Rica, and potential hazards from future eruptions. *In*: Rose W I, Bluth G J S, Carr M J, Ewert J W, Patino L C, Vallance J W (eds), Volcanic hazards in Central America, *Geol Soc Amer Spec Pap*, 412: 235-257

Rose W I, 1972a. Notes on the 1902 eruption of Santa Maria volcano, Guatemala. *Bull Volc*, 36: 29-45

Rose W I, Bonis S, Stoiber R E, Keller M, Bickford T, 1973. Studies of volcanic ash from two recent Central American eruptions. *Bull Volc*, 37: 338-364

Rowe G L Jr, Brantley S L, Fernandez J F, Borgia A, 1995. The chemical and hydrologic structure of Poas Volcano, Costa Rica. *J Volc Geotherm Res*, 64: 233-267

Rowe G L Jr, Brantley S L, Fernandez M, Fernandez J F, Borgia A, Barquero J, 1992. Fluid-volcano interaction in an active stratovolcano; the crater lake system of Poas Volcano, Costa Rica. *J Volc Geotherm Res*, 49: 23-51

Rowe G L Jr, Ohsawa S, Takano B, Brantley S L, Fernandez J F, Barquero J, 1992. Using crater lake chemistry to predict volcanic activity at Poas Volcano, Costa Rica. *Bull Volc*, 54: 494-503

Rymer H, Cassidy J, Locke C A, Barboza M V, Barquero J, Brenes J, van der Laat R, 2000. Geophysical studies of the recent 15-year eruptive cycle at Poas Volcano, Costa Rica. *J Volc Geotherm Res*, 97: 425-442

Rymer H, van Wyk de Vries B, Stix J, Williams-Jones G, 1998. Pit crater structure and processes governing persistent activity at Masaya volcano, Nicaragua. *Bull Volc*, 59: 345-355

Saenz R, Barquero J, Malavassi E, 1984. Excursion al Volcan Irazu. *Bol Vulc Univ Nac Costa Rica*, 14: 109-116

Sanford W E, Konikow L F, Rowe G L Jr, Brantley S L, 1995. Groundwater transport of crater-lake brine at Poas Volcano, Costa Rica. *J Volc Geotherm Res*, 64: 269-293

Sapper K, 1925. *The Volcanoes of Central America*. Halle: Verlag Max Niemeyer, 144 p ***(regional reference)***

Schmincke H-U, Kutterolf S, Perez W, Rausch J, Freundt A, 2009. Walking through volcanic mud: the 2,100-year-old Acahualinca footprints (Nicaragua) I: Stratigraphy, lithology, volcanology and age of the Acahualinca section. *Bull Volc*, 71: 479-493

Scott K C, Reagan M K, Trimble D A, 2006. Tephra deposits for the past 2600 years from Irazu volcano, Costa Rica. *In*: Rose W I, Bluth G J S, Carr M J, Ewert J W, Patino L C, Vallance J W (eds), Volcanic hazards in Central America, *Geol Soc Amer Spec Pap*, 412: 225-234

Scott W E, Gardner C, Devoli G, Alvarez A, 2006. The A.D. 1835 eruption of Volcan Cosiguina, Nicaragua: a guide for assessing local hazards. *In*: Rose W I, Bluth G J S, Carr M J, Ewert J W, Patino L C, Vallance J W (eds), Volcanic hazards in Central America, *Geol Soc Amer Spec Pap*, 412: 167-187

Self S, Rampino M R, Carr M J, 1989. A reappraisal of the 1835 eruption of Cosiguina and its atmospheric impact. *Bull Volc*, 52: 57-65

Shea T, van Wyk de Vries B, Pilato M, 2008. Emplacement mechanisms of contrasting debris avalanches at Volcan Mombacho (Nicaragua), provided by structural and facies analysis. *Bull Volc*, 70: 899-921

Sheets P D, 2004. Apocalypse then: social science approaches to volcanism, people, and cultures in the Zapotitan Valley, El Salvador. *In*: Rose W I, Bommer J J, Lopez D L, Carr M J, Major J J (eds), Natural Hazards in El Salvador, *Geol Soc Amer Spec Pap*, 375: 109-120

Sheets P D, McKee B R, 1994. *Archaeology, volcanism, and remote sensing in the Arenal region, Costa Rica*. Austin, TX: Univ Texas Press, 350 p

Sherrod D R, Vallance J W, Tapi Espinosa A, McGeehin J P, 2008. Volcan Baru-eruptive history and volcano-hazards assessment. *U S Geol Surv Open-File Rpt*, 2007-1401: 1-33, 1 plate, scale 1:100,000.

Shevenell L, 1989. Preliminary evaluation of thermal and nonthermal waters at selected sites in Panama, Central America. *Los Alamos Nat Lab*, LA-11103-MS: 1-27

Siebert L, Alvarado G E, Vallance J W, van Wyk de Vries B, 2006. Large-volume volcanic edifice failures in Central America and associated hazards. *In*: Rose W I, Bluth G J S, Carr M J, Ewert J W, Patino L C, Vallance J W (eds), Volcanic hazards in Central America, *Geol Soc Amer Spec Pap*, 412: 1-26

Soto G, 1988. Estructuras volcano-tectonicas del Volcan Turrialba, Costa Rica, America Central. *Actas Quinto Cong Geol Chileno, Santiago, 8-12 de agosto de 1988*, 3: I 163- I 165

Soto G J, Alvarado G E, 2006. Eruptive history of Arenal volcano, Costa Rica, 7 ka to present. *J Volc Geotherm Res*, 157: 254-269

Soto G J, Alvarado G E, Ghigliotti M, 1998. El registro eruptivo del Arenal en el lapso 3000 - 7000 anos antes del presente y nuevas deducciones sobre la edad del volcan. *Bol OSIVAM, San Jose, Costa Rica*, 9: 19-49

Soto G J, Alvarado G E, Madrigal L A, 1996. Las posibles erupciones del Volcan Arenal en 1915 y 1922. *Bol Obs Vulc Arenal*: 6: 45-52

Soto G J, Sjobohm L, 2005. Sobre el mapeo de los peligros volcanicos del Arenal (Costa Rica) como una herramienta para la planificacion del uso del suelo y la mitigacion de desastres. *Mem VIII Seminario Ingenieria Estructural Sismica, San Jose, Costa Rica, Septiembre 2005*, 26 p

Soto G, Alvarado G E, Goold S, 2003. Erupciones <3800 a.P. del volcan Rincon de la Vieja, Costa Rica. *Rev Geol Amer Central*, 29: 67-86

Soto-B G J, 1988. Geologia y volcanologia del Volcan Turrialba, Costa Rica. *Costa Rica Volc Workshop, Smithsonian Inst*, Nov 1988, 13 p

Squier E G, 1851. On the volcanoes of Central America and the geographical and topographical features, as connected with the proposed interoceanic canal. *Amer Assoc Adv Sci Proc*, 4: 101-122 ***(regional reference)***

Stine C M, Banks N G, 1991. Costa Rica volcano profile. *U S Geol Surv Open-File Rpt*, 67 p

Stix J, 2007. Stability and instability of quiescently active volcanoes: the case of Masaya, Nicaragua. *Geology*, 35: 535-538

Stoiber R E, Carr M J, 1973. Quaternary volcanic and tectonic segmentation of Central America. *Bull Volc*, 37: 304-325

Stoiber R E, Rose W I, 1970. The geochemistry of Central American volcanic gas condensates. *Geol Soc Amer Bull*, 81: 2891-2912

Sussman D, 1985. Apoyo Caldera, Nicaragua: a major Quaternary silicic eruptive center. *J Volc Geotherm Res*, 24: 249-282

Thorpe R S, Brown G, Rymer H, Barritt S, Randal M, 1985. Recent volcano monitoring in Costa Rica. *Earthq Inf Bull*, 17: 44-49

Thorpe R S, Locke C A, Brown G C, Francis P W, Randal M, 1981. Magma chamber below Poas volcano, Costa Rica. *J Geol Soc London*, 138: 367-373

Ui T, 1972. Recent volcanism in Masaya-Granada area, Nicaragua. *Bull Volc*, 36: 174-190

Universidad Tecnologica Panama, 1992. Evaluacion de la amenaza, estimacion de la vulnerabilidad y del factor costo de riesgo del Volcan Baru, Republica de Panama. *Univ Tecnologica Panama, Fac Ingenieria Civil - CEPREDENAC*, 129 p and 1:100,000 scale map

Vallance J W, Schilling S P, Devoli G, 2001. Lahar hazards at Mombacho volcano, Nicaragua. *U S Geol Surv Open-File Rpt*, 01-455: 1-14

Vallance J W, Schilling S P, Devoli G, Howell M M, 2001. Lahar hazards at Concepcion volcano, Nicaragua. *U S Geol Surv Open-File Rpt*, 01-457: 1-33

Vallejos-Ruiz O, Sanchez-Rivera E, Gonzalez-Vargas C, 2005. Reservoir management at the Miravalles geothermal field, Costa Rica. *Proc World Geotherm Cong 2005, Antalya, Turkey, 24-29 April 2005 CD-ROM*, 8 p

van Wyk de Vries B, 1993. Tectonics and magma evolution of Nicaraguan volcanic systems. *Unpublished PhD thesis*, Open Univ, Milton Keynes, 328 p

van Wyk de Vries B, Borgia A, 1996. The role of basement in volcano deformation. *In*: McGuire W J, Jones A P and Neuberg J (eds) *Volcano Instability on the Earth and Other Planets*, Geol Soc London Spec Pub, 110: 95-110

van Wyk de Vries B, Francis P W, 1997. Catastrophic collapse at stratovolcanoes induced by gradual volcano spreading. *Nature*, 387: 387-390

van Wyk de Vries B, Kerle N, Petley D, 2000. Sector collapse forming at Casita volcano, Nicaragua. *Geology*, 28: 167-170

Vargas F, Alfaro A, 1992. Presencia de serpentinitas, basaltos alcalinos y rocas volcanicas acidas en la zona Norte-Atlantica de Costa Rica. *Rev Geol Amer Central*, 14: 105-107

Vazquez de Espinosa A, 1942. Compendium and description of the West Indies. *Smithsonian Inst Misc Coll*, 862 p

Vega Zuniga E, Chavarria Rojas L, Barrantes Viquez M, Molina Zuniga F, Hakanson E C, Mora Protti O, 2005. Geologic model of the Miravalles geothermal field, Costa Rica. *Proc World Geotherm Cong 2005, Antalya, Turkey, 24-29 April 2005 CD-ROM*, 5 p

Viramonte J G, Di Scala L, 1970. Summary of the 1968 eruption of Cerro Negro, Nicaragua. *Bull Volc*, 34: 347-351

Viramonte J G, Incer-Barquero J, 2008. Masaya, the "Mouth of Hell," Nicaragua: volcanological interpretation of the myths, legends and anecdotes. *J Volc Geotherm Res*, 176: 419-426

Viramonte J G, Navarro Collado M, Malavasi Rojas E, 1997. Nicaragua-Costa Rica Quaternary volcanic chain. IAVCEI General Assembly, Puerto Vallarta, Mexico, January 19-24, 1997, Fieldtrip Guidebook, 17 p

Viramonte J G, Ubeda E, Martinez M, 1971. The 1971 eruption of Cerro Negro volcano, Nicaragua. *Smithsonian Inst Center Short-Lived Phenomena*, 28 p

Vogel T A, Patino L C, Alvarado G E, Gans P B, 2004. Silicic ignimbrites within the Costa Rican volcanic front: evidence for the formation of continental crust. *Earth Planet Sci Lett*, 226: 149-159

Wadge G, 1983. The magma budget of Volcan Arenal, Costa Rica from 1968 to 1980. *J Volc Geotherm Res*, 19: 281-302

Wadge G, Oramas Dorta D, Cole P D, 2006. The magma budget of Volcan Arenal, Costa Rica from 1980 to 2004. *J Volc Geotherm Res*, 157: 60-74

Walker J A, 1984. Volcanic rocks from the Nejapa and Granada cinder cone alignments, Nicaragua, Central America. *J Petr*, 25: 299-342

Walker J A, Carr M J, 1986. Compositional variations caused by phenocryst sorting at Cerro Negro Volcano, Nicaragua. *Geol Soc Amer Bull*, 97: 1156-1162

Walker J A, Williams S N, Kalamarides R I, Feigenson M D, 1993. Shallow open-system evolution of basaltic magma beneath a subduction zone volcano: the Masaya Caldera Complex, Nicaragua. *J Volc Geotherm Res*, 56: 379-400

Wehrmann H, Bonadonna C, Freundt A, Houghton B F, Kutterolf S, 2006. Fontana Tephra: a basaltic plinian eruption in Nicaragua. *In*: Rose W I, Bluth G J S, Carr M J, Ewert J W, Patino L C, Vallance J W (eds), Volcanic hazards in Central America, *Geol Soc Amer Spec Pap*, 412: 209-223

Williams H, 1952. The great eruption of Coseguina, Nicaragua in 1835. *Univ Calif Pub Geol Sci*, 29: 21-45

Williams R L (ed), 1972. The geology of western Nicaragua. *Parsons Corp Final Technical Rpt*, 4:1-221

Williams S N, 1983. Plinian airfall deposits of basaltic composition. *Geology*, 11: 211-214

Williams S N, 1985. La erupcion de los volcanes Telica, Nicaragua, 1982. *Bol Vulc Univ Nac Costa Rica*, 15: 10-19

Williams-Jones G, Rymer H, Rothery D A, 2003. Gravity changes and passive SO2 degassing at the Masaya caldera complex, Nicaragua. *J Volc Geotherm Res*, 123: 137-160

Williams-Jones G, Stix J, Heiligmann M, Barquero J, Fernandez E, Gonzalez E D, 2001. A model of degassing and seismicity at Arenal Volcano, Costa Rica. *J Volc Geotherm Res*, 108: 121-139

Zuniga A, 2003. Geothermal Nicaragua. *Geotherm Res Council Bull*, 32: 163-165

COLOMBIA & ECUADOR (1501-02)

Almeida E, Cruz M, 1986. Estudio geologico del Volcan Reventador. *Inst Ecuatoriano Electrificacion (INECEL), Quito*, unpublished rpt, 43 p

Almeida E, Ramon P, 1991. Las erupciones historicas del Volcan Tungurahua. *Bol Geol Ecuatoriano*, 2: 89-138

Andrade D, Molina I, 2006. Pululahua caldera. *Fourth Conf Cities on Volcanoes, IAVCEI, Quito, Ecuador, 2006*, Excursion A3: 1-11

Banks N G, Calvache-V M L, Williams S N, 1997. 14C ages and activity for the past 50 ka at Volcan Galeras, Colombia. *J Volc Geotherm Res*, 77: 39-55

Barba D, Robin C, Samaniego P, Eissen J-P, 2008. Holocene recurrent explosive activity at Chimborazo volcano (Ecuador). *J Volc Geotherm Res*, 176: 27-35

Barberi F, Caruso P, Macedonio G, Pareschi M T, Rosi M, 1991. Reconstruction and numerical simulation of the lahar of the 1877 eruption of Cotopaxi volcano (Ecuador). *Acta Vulc*, 2: 35-44

Barberi F, Coltelli M, Frullani A, Rosi M, Almeida E, 1995. Chronology and dispersal characteristics of recently (last 5000 years) erupted tephra of Cotopaxi (Ecuador): implications for long-term eruptive forecasting. *J Volc Geotherm Res*, 69: 217-239

Barberi F, Ghigliotti M, Macedonio G, Orellana H, Pareschi M T, Rosi M, 1992. Volcanic hazard assessment of Guagua Pichincha (Ecuador) based on past behavior and numerical models. *J Volc Geotherm Res*, 49: 53-68

Barragan R, Geist D, Hall M, Larson P, Kurz M, 1998. Subduction controls on the compositions of lavas from the Ecuadorian Andes. *Earth Planet Sci Lett*, 154: 153-166

Beate B, 1989. The Chalupas ignimbrite (abs). *New Mexico Bur Mines Min Resour Bull*, 131: 18

Beate B, 1990. Sequence of explosive products of the Chachimbiro volcanic complex, Ecuador, South America. *IAVCEI 1990 Internatl Volc Cong, Mainz, Abs*, (unpaginated)

Beate B, Salgado R, 2005. Geothermal country update for Ecuador, 2000-2005. *Proc World Geotherm Cong 2005, Antalya, Turkey, 24-29 April 2005*, 5 p

Beate B, von Hillebrandt-M C G, Hall M L, 1990. Mapa de los peligros volcanicos potenciales asociados con el volcan Chimborazo. *Inst Geof Escuela Politecnica Nac Ecuador*, 1:50,000 map and text

Bernard B, van Wyk de Vries B, Barba D, Leyrit H, Robin C, Alcaraz S, Samaniego P, 2008. The Chimborazo sector collapse and debris avalanche: deposit characteristics as evidence of emplacment mechanisms. *J Volc Geotherm Res*, 176: 36-43

Borrero C A, Castillo H, 2006. Vulcanitas del S-SE de Colombia: retro-arco alcalino y su posible relacion con una ventana astenosferica. *Bol Geol*, 28(2): 23-34

Borrero C, Castillo H, Ossa C, 2007. Extension of the unknown alkaline volcanism in the southeastern Colombia. *Cities on Volcanoes 5, Shimabara, Japan, Nov 19-23, 2007*, abs, p 133

Bourdon E, Eissen J-P, Monzier M, Robin C, Martin H, Cotten J, Hall M L, 2002. Adakite-like lavas from Antisana volcano (Ecuador): evidence for slab metasomatism beneath the Andean Northern Volcanic Zone. *J Petr*, 43: 199-217

Calvache-V M L, 1990. Geology and volcanology of the recent evolution of Galeras volcano, Colombia. *Unpublished MSci thesis*, Louisiana State Univ, 172 p

Calvache-V M L, Cortes-J G P, Williams S N, 1997. Stratigraphy and chronology of the Galeras volcanic complex, Colombia. *J Volc Geotherm Res*, 77: 5-19

Calvache-V M L, Williams S N, 1997. Geochemistry and petrology of the Galeras volcanic complex, Colombia. *J Volc Geotherm Res*, 77: 21-38

Calvache-V M L, Williams S N, 1997. Emplacement and petrological evolution of the andesitic dome of Galeras volcano, 1990-1992. *J Volc Geotherm Res*, 77: 57-69

Cepeda H, Monsalve M L, Pulgarin B, 1991. Origen y mecanismo eruptivo del flujo piroclastico de Agua Blanca, Volcan Purace. *Simposio Magmatismo Andino Marco Tectonico, Univ Caldas, Memorias*, 2: 40-57

Cepeda H, Munoz F, Acevedo A P, Gil F, Pulgarin B, Nieto A, Londono A, Mejia I, Calvache M L, Mora H, Carvajal C A, Banks N, 1989. Reactivacion del Volcan Galeras, Colombia, Suramerica. *Unpublished manuscript*, 6 p

Cepeda H, Pulgarin B A, Correa A M, 1997. The Nevado del Huila volcanic complex, Colombia, S.A. *IAVCEI 1997 General Assembly, Puerto Vallarta, Mexico, Abs*, p 156

Clapperton C M, 1990. Glacial and volcanic geomorphology of the Chimborazo-Carihuairazo massif, Ecuadorian Andes. *Trans Roy Soc Edinburgh: Earth Sci*, 81: 91-116

Cortes-J G P, Raigosa-A J, 1997. A synthesis of the recent activity of Galeras volcano, Colombia: seven years of continuous surveillance, 1989-1995. *J Volc Geotherm Res*, 77: 101-114

Cuellar-Rodriguez J V, Ramirez-Lopez C, 1987. Descripcion de los volcanes Colombianos. *Rev CIAF, Bogota*, p 189-222 ***(regional reference)***

Di Muro A, Rosi M, Aguilera E, Barbieri R, Massa G, Mundula F, Pieri F, 2008. Transport and sedimentation dynamics of transitional explosive eruption columns: the example of the 800 BP Quilotoa plinian eruption (Ecuador). *J Volc Geotherm Res*, 174: 307-324

Eissen J-P, Barba D, Bernard B, 2006. Chimborazo volcano: late Pleistocene and Holocene activity. *Cities on Volcanoes 4, Quito, Ecuador, 23-27 Jan, 2006*, Field trip A2: 1-23

Espinosa B A, 1990. *Datos Preliminares Sobre la Actividad Historica del Volcan Nevado del Huila*. Popoyan, Colombia: INGEOMINAS, 5 p

Fontaine E, 1991. Evolution petrologique et geochimique du complexe de domes du volcan Azufral Colombie (Amerique du Sud). *Undergraduate proj*, Univ Montreal, 58 p

Friedlander I, 1927. Uber Einige Vulkane Columbiens (I & II Teil). *Zeit Vulk*, 10: 159-172, 223-231

Garcia-Aristizabal A, Kumagai H, Samaniego P, Mothes P, Yepes H, Monzier M, 2007. Seismic, petrologic, and geodectic analysis of the 1999 dome-forming eruption of Guagua Pichincha volcano, Ecuador. *J Volc Geotherm Res*, 161: 333-351

Hall M L, 1977. *El Volcanismo en El Ecuador*. Quito: Biblioteca Ecuador, 120 p ***(regional reference)***

Hall M L, 1980. El Reventador, Ecuador, un volcan activo de los Andes septentrionales. *Rev Politecnica, Quito*, 5: 123-136

Hall M L, 1987. Peligros potenciales de las erupciones futuras del volcan Cotopaxi. *Rev Politecnica, Quito*, 12: 41-80

Hall M L, Mothes P, 1997. Chacana caldera-the largest rhyolitic eruptive center in the northern Andes. *IAVCEI 1997 General Assembly, Puerto Vallarta, Mexico, Abs*, p 14

Hall M L, Mothes P A, 2008a. Quilotoa volcano-Ecuador: an overview of young dacitic volcanism in a lake-filled caldera. *J Volc Geotherm Res*, 176: 44-55

Hall M L, Mothes P A, 2008b. Volcanic impediments in the progressive development of pre-Columbian civilizations in the Ecuadorian Andes. *J Volc Geotherm Res*, 176: 344-355

Hall M L, Robin C, Beate B, Mothes P, Monzier M, 1999. Tungurahua volcano, Ecuador: structure, eruptive history and hazards. *J Volc Geotherm Res*, 91: 1-21

Hall M L, Vera R, 1985. La actividad volcanica del volcan Tungurahua: sus peligros y sus riesgos volcanicos. *Rev Politecnica, Quito*, 10: 91-144

Hall M, Mothes P, 2008. The rhyolitic-andesitic eruptive history of Cotopaxi volcano, Ecuador. *Bull Volc*, 70: 675-702

Hall M, Ramon P, Mothes P, LePennec J L, Garcia A, Samaniego P, Yepes H, 2004. Volcanic eruptions with little warning: the case of Volcan Reventador's surprise November 3, 2002 eruption, Ecuador. *Rev Geol Chile*, 31: 349-358

Hantke G, Parodi I, 1966. Colombia, Ecuador and Peru. *Catalog of Active Volcanoes of the World and Solfatara Fields*, Rome: IAVCEI, 19: 1-73 ***(regional reference)***

Herd D G, 1982. Glacial and volcanic geology of the Ruiz - Tolima volcanic complex Cordillera Central, Colombia. *Pub Geol Especiales INGEOMINAS*, Bogata, 8: 1-48

Herd D G, Comite de Estudios Vulcanologicos, 1986. The 1985 Ruiz volcano disaster. *Eos, Trans Amer Geophys Union*, 67: 457-460

Hidalgo S, Monzier M, ALmeida E, Chazot G, Eissen J-P, van der Plicht J, Hall M L, 2008. Late Pleistocene and Holocene activity of the Atacazo-Ninahuilca volcanic complex (Ecuador). *J Volc Geotherm Res*, 176: 16-26

Hidalgo S, Monzier M, Martin H, Chazot G, Eissen J-P, Cotten J, 2007. Adakitic magmas in the Ecuadorian volcanic front: petrogenesis of the Iliniza volcanic complex (Ecuador). *J Volc Geotherm Res*, 159: 366-392

Hillebrandt-M C G von, 1989. The evolution of Cuicocha volcano and the volcanic hazards associated with it (abs). *New Mexico Bur Mines Min Resour Bull*, 131: 283

Hoffer G, Eissen J-P, Beate B, Bourdon E, Fornari M, Cotten J, 2008. Geochemical and petrological constraints on rear-arc magma genesis processes in Ecuador: the Puyo cones and Mera lavas volcanic formations. *J Volc Geotherm Res*, 176: 107-108

Huggel C, Cegballos J L Pulgarin B, Ramirez J, Thouret J-C, 2007. Review and reassessment of hazards owing to volcano-glacier interactions in Colombia. *Annals Glaciology*, 45: 128-136

Hulbert C, 1827. *Volcanic Wonders, and Scenes of Astonishment*. Shrewsbury: C Hulbert, Second Edition, 68 p

Hurtado-Artunduaga A D, Cortez-Jimenez G P, 1997. Third version of the hazard map of Galeras volcano, Colombia. *J Volc Geotherm Res*, 77: 89-100

INECEL, 1980. Estudio de reconocimiento de los recursos geotermicos de la Republica del Ecuador. *Inf Geovulcanologico Realirado Aquater/BRGM/OLADE*, unpublished rpt

INECEL, 1987. Estudio de prefactibilidad del "Projecto Geotermico Binacional Tufino-Chiles-Cerro Negro." *Inf Geovulcanologico Realirado Aquater/BRGM/OLADE*, unpublished rpt

Johnson J B, Aster R C, Ruiz M C, Malone S D, McChesney P J, Lees J M, Kyle P R, 2003. Interpretation and utility of infrasonic records from erupting volcanoes. *J Volc Geotherm Res*, 121: 15-63

Johnson J B, Lees J M, 2000. Plugs and chugs-seismic and acoustic observations of degassing explosions at Karymsky, Russia and Sangay, Ecuador. *J Volc Geotherm Res*, 101: 67-82

Johnson J, Ramon P, Andrade D, Hall M L, 2006. Reventador volcano: 2002 to present, explosive and effusive activity. *Cities on Volcanoes 4, Quito, Ecuador, 23-27 Jan, 2006*, Field trip A5: 1-15

Kilian R, Pichler H, 1987. El Chimborazo de Humboldt y el desarrollo de otros volcanes grandes en el Ecuador. *In*: *Investigaciones Alemanas Recientes en America Latina*, Bonn: Geol Deut Ferschungsgemeinschaft, p 25-34

Le Pennec J-L, Hall M L, Robin C, Bartomioli E, 2006. Tungurahua volcano: late Holocene activity. *Cities on Volcanoes 4, Quito, Ecuador, 23-27 Jan, 2006*, Field trip A1: 1-23

Le Pennec J-L, Jaya D, Samaniego P, Ramon P, Moreno Yanez S, Egred J, van der Plicht J, 2008. The AD 1300-1700 eruptive periods at Tungurahua volcano, Ecuador, revealed by historical narratives, stratigraphy and radiocarbon dating. *J Volc Geotherm Res*, 176: 70-81

Le Pennec J-L, Ruiz-P A G, 2006. Late Pleistocene to Holocene activity of Imbabura volcano. *Cities on Volcanoes 4, Quito, Ecuador, 23-27 Jan, 2006*, Field trip C2: 1-8

Lescinsky D T, 1990. Geology, volcanology, and petrology of Cerro Bravo, a young, dacitic stratovolcano in west-central Colombia. *Unpublished MSci thesis*, Lousiana State Univ, 244 p

Lewicki J L, Fischer T, Williams S N, 2000. Chemical and isotopic compositions of fluids at Cumbal volcano, Colombia: evidence for magmatic contribution. *Bull Volc*, 62: 347-361

Lewis G E, 1950. El Sangay, fire-breathing giant of the Andes. *Natl Geog*, 98: 117-138

Lewis G E, Tschopp H J, Marks J G, 1956. Ecuador. *In*: Jenks W F (ed) *Handbook of South American Geol*, Geol Soc Amer Mem 65: 249-292

Mendez Fajury R A, 1989. Catalogo de los volcanes activos en Colombia. *Bol Geol INGEOMINAS, Colombia*, 30: 1-75

Miller C D, Mullineaux D R, Hall M L, 1978. Reconnaissance map of potential volcanic hazards from Cotopaxi volcano, Ecuador. *U S Geol Surv Map*, I-1072

Monsalve M L, 1993. Caracteristicas geoquimicas y dataciones en episodios tipo San Vincente en el Volcano Purace. *Bol Geol INGEOMINAS, Colombia*, 33: 3-17

Monzier M, Robin C, Samaniego P, Hall M L, Cotten J, Mothes P, Arnaud N, 1999. Sangay volcano, Ecuador: structural development, present activity and petrology. *J Volc Geotherm Res*, 90: 49-79

Mothes P A, Hall M L, 2008. The plinian fallout associated with Quilotoa's 800 yr BP eruption, Ecuadorian Andes. *J Volc Geotherm Res*, 176: 56-69

Mothes P A, Hall M L, Janda R J, 1998. The enormous Chillos Valley Lahar: an ash-flow-generated debris flow from Cotopaxi volcano, Ecuador. *Bull Volc*, 59: 233-244

Mothes P, Hall M L, Andrade D, Samaniego P, Pierson T C, Ruiz A G, Yepes H, 2004. Character, stratigraphy and magnitude of historical lahars of Cotopaxi volcano (Ecuador). *Acta Vulc*, 16: 85-108

Murcia H F, Hurtado B O, Cortes G P, Macías J L, Cepeda H, 2008. The ~2500 yr B.P. Chicoral non-cohesive debris flow from Cerro Machín Volcano, Colombia. *J Volc Geotherm Res*, 171: 201-214

Oppenheim V, 1950. The volcano Purace. *Amer J Sci*, 248: 171-179

Ordonez M I, Cepeda H, 1997. Morphological changes of the active cone of Galeras volcano, Colombia, during the last century. *J Volc Geotherm Res*, 77: 71-87

Padron E, Hernandez P A, Toulkeridis T, Perez N M, Marrero R, Melian G, Virgili G, Notsu K, 2008. Diffuse CO2 emission rate from Pululahua and the lake-filled Cuicocha calderas, Ecuador. *J Volc Geotherm Res*, 176: 163-169

Papale P, Rosi M, 1993. A case of no-wind plinian fallout at Pululagua caldera (Ecuador): implications for models of clast dispersal. *Bull Volc*, 55: 523-535

Parra E, Cepeda H, 1990. Volcanic hazard maps of the Nevado del Ruiz volcano, Colombia. *J Volc Geotherm Res*, 42: 117-127

Paulo A, Narebski W, Bakun-Czubarow N, Prochazka K, Wichrowoski Z, 1979. Geology, geochemistry and petrogenesis of volcanics of Cotopaxi (Ecuador). *Prace Mineralalogiczne*, 61: 1-62

Pierson T C, Janda R J, Thouret J-C, Borrero C A, 1990. Perturbation and melting of snow and ice by the 13 November 1985 eruption of Nevado del Ruiz, Colombia, and consequent mobilization, flow and deposition of lahars. *J Volc Geotherm Res*, 41: 17-66

Pinilla A, Rios P A, Borrero C A, 2006. Romeral volcano: a new source of pyroclastic fall deposits at the Ruiz-Tolima volcanic complex, central Colombia. *Cities on Volcanoes 4, Quito, Ecuador, 23-27 Jan, 2006*, Abs, p 26

Robin C, Eissen J-P, Samaniego P, Martin H, Hall M, Cotten J, 2009. Evolution of the late Pleistocene Mojanda-Fuya Fuya volcanic complex (Ecuador), by progressive adakitic involvement in mantle magma sources. *Bull Volc*, 71: 233-258

Robin C, Hall M, Jiminez M, Monzier M, Escobar P, 1997. Mojanda volcanic complex (Ecuador): development of two adjacent contemporaneous volcanoes with contrasting eruptive styles and magmatic suites. *J South Amer Earth Sci*, 10: 345-359

Robin C, Samaniego P, Le Pennec J-L, Mothes P, van der Plicht J, 2008. Late Holocene phases of dome growth and plinian activity at Guagua Pichincha volcano (Ecuador). *J Volc Geotherm Res*, 176: 7-15

Rosi M, Di Muro A, Aguilera E, 2006. Eruptive dynamics during the 800 yr BP Quilotoa eruption. *IAVCEI Commission on Explosive Volcanism Field Workshop, Cities on Volcanoes 4, Quito, Ecuador 23-27 Jan, 2006*, 30 p

Rosi M, Landi P, Polacci M, Di Muro A, Zandomeneghi D, 2004. Role of conduit shear on ascent of the crystal-rich magma feeding the 800-year-B.P. Plinian eruption of Quilotoa volcano (Ecuador). *Bull Volc*, 66: 307-321

Samaniego P, Eissen J-P, Le Pennec J-L, Hall M L, Monzier M, Mothes P, Ramon P, Robin C, Egred J, Molina I, Yepes H, 2003. Los peligros volcanicos asociados con el Tungurahua. *Inst Geofis Escuela Politecnica Nac, Inst Recherche Devel*, 1: 1-108

Samaniego P, Eissen J-P, Le Pennec J-L, Robin C, Hall M L, Mothes P, Chavrit D, Cotten J, 2008. Pre-eruptive physical conditions of El Reventador volcano (Ecuador) inferred from the petrology of the 2002 and 2004-2005 eruptions. *J Volc Geotherm Res*, 176: 82-93

Samaniego P, Eissen J-P, Monzier M, Robin C, Alvarado A, Yepes H, 2004. Los peligros volcanicos asociados con el Cayambe. *Corporacion Editora Nac IG-EPN, IRD*, 94 p

Samaniego P, Martin H, Monzier M, Robin C, Fornari M, Eissen J-P, Cotten J, 2005. Temporal evolution of magmatism in the Northern Volcanic Zone of the Andes: the geology and petrology of Cayambe volcanic complex (Ecuador). *J Petr*, 46: 2225-2252

Samaniego P, Monzier M, Robin C, Hall M L, 1998. Late Holocene eruptive activity at Nevado Cayambe volcano, Ecuador. *Bull Volc*, 59: 451-459

Samaniego P, Robin C, Monzier M, Mothes P, Beate B, Garcia A, 2006. Guagua Pichincha volcano: Holocene and late Pleistocene activity. *Cities on Volcanoes 4, Quito, Ecuador, 23-27 Jan, 2006*, Field trip A4: 1-15

Shanker R, Haldar D, Absar A, Chakraborty S C, 2001. Pictorial Monograph of the Barren Island Volcano. Kolkata: Geol Surv India, 87 p

Steimle U, 1989. The Dona Juana volcano, Departamento de Narino, southern Colombia. *Unpublished MSci thesis*, Eberhard Karls Univ, 97 p

Thouret J-C, Cantagrel J-M, Robin C, Murcia A, Salinas R, Cepeda H, 1995. Quaternary eruptive history and hazard-zone model at Nevado del Tolima and Cerro Machin volcanoes, Colombia. *J Volc Geotherm Res*, 66: 397-426

Thouret J-C, Cantagrel J-M, Salinas R, Murcia A, 1990. Quaternary eruptive history of Nevado del Ruiz (Colombia). *J Volc Geotherm Res*, 41: 225-251

Thouret J-C, Salinas R, Murcia A, 1990. Eruption and mass-wasting-induced processes during the late Holocene destructive phase of Nevado del Ruiz volcano, Colombia. *J Volc Geotherm Res*, 41: 203-224

Thouret J-C, Vatin-Perignon N, Cantagrel J M, Salinas R, Murcia A, 1985. Le Nevado el Ruiz (Cordillere Centrale des Andes de Colombie): stratigraphie, structures et dynamisme d'un appareil volcanique andesitique, compose et polygenique. *Rev Geog Phys Geol Dynam*, 26: 257-271

Vatin-Perignon N, Goemans P, Oliver R A, Parra Palacio E, 1990. Evaluation of magmatic processes for the products of the Nevado del Ruiz volcano, Colombia from geochemical and petrological data. *J Volc Geotherm Res*, 41: 153-176

Voight B, 1990. The 1985 Nevado del Ruiz volcano catastrophe: anatomy and retrospection. *J Volc Geotherm Res*, 44: 349-386

Wolf T, 1904. Cronica de los fenomenos volcanicos y terremotos del Ecuador, con algunas noticias sobre otros paises del la America Central y Meridional, desde 1533 a 1797. *Annales Univ Central, Quito*, 8: 1-120

Young R H, 1991. Eruption dynamics and petrology of the most recent eruptions of Nevado del Ruiz volcano, Colombia, South America. *Unpublished MSci thesis*, Louisiana State Univ, 121 p

GALAPAGOS (1503)

Allan J F, Simkin T, 2000. Fernandina volcano's evolved, well-mixed basalts: mineralogical and petrological constraints on the nature of the Galapagos plume. *J Geophys Res*, 105: 6017-6041

Chadwick W W, De Roy T, Carrasco A, 1991. The September 1988 intracaldera avalanche and eruption at Fernandina volcano, Galapagos Islands. *Bull Volc*, 53: 276-286

Cox A, 1971. Paleomagnetism of San Cristobal Island, Galapagos. *Earth Planet Sci Lett*, 11: 152-160

Cox A, 1983. Ages of the Galapagos Islands. *In*: Bowman R I, Berson M, Leviton A E (eds) *Patterns of Evolution in Galapagos Organisms*, San Francisco: Amer Asso Adv Sci, p 11-23

Delaney J R, Colony W E, Gerlach T M, Nordlie B E, 1973. Geology of the Volcan Chico area on Sierra Negra volcano, Galapagos Islands. *Geol Soc Amer Bull*, 84: 2455-2470

Geist D J, Harpp K S, Naumann T R, Poland M, Chadwick W W, Hall M, Rader E, 2008. The 2005 eruption of Sierra Negra volcano, Galapagos, Ecuador. *Bull Volc*, 70: 655-673

Geist D J, McBirney A R, Duncan R A, 1985. Geology of Santa Fe Island: the oldest Galapagos volcano. *J Volc Geotherm Res*, 26: 203-212

Geist D J, McBirney A R, Duncan R A, 1986. Geology and petrogenesis of lavas from San Cristobal Island, Galapagos archipelago. *Geol Soc Amer Bull*, 97: 555-566

Geist D J, Naumann T R, Standish J J, Kurz M D, Harpp K S, White W M, Fornari D J, 2005. Wolf volcano, Galapagos archipelago: melting and magmatic evolution at the margins of a mantle plume. *J Petr*, 46: 2197-2224

Geist D, Harpp K, Reynolds B, 2006. A field trip guide to the geology of the Galapagos Islands. *Cities on Volcanoes 4, Quito, Ecuador, 23-27 Jan, 2006*, Field Trip Guide, 30 p

Geist D, Howard K A, Jellinek A M, Rayder S, 1994. The volcanic history of Volcan Alcedo, Galapagos Archipelago: a case study of rhyolitic oceanic volcanism. *Bull Volc*, 56: 243-260

Geist D, Howard K A, Larson P, 1994. The generation of oceanic rhyolites by crystal fractionation: the basalt-rhyolite association at Volcan Alceda, Galapagos Archipelago. *J Petr*, 36: 965-982

Geist D, White W M, Albarede F, Harpp K, Reynolds R, Blichert-Toft J, Kurz M D, 2002. Volcanic evolution in the Galapagos: the dissected shield of Volcan Ecuador. *Geochem Geophys Geosyst*, 3(10): 1-32

Goff F, McMurtry G M, Counce D, Simac J A, Roldan-Manzo A R, Hilton D R, 2000. Contrasting hydrothermal activity at Sierra Negra and Alcedo volcanoes Galapagos Archipelago, Ecuador. *Bull Volc*, 62: 34-52

Hall M L, 1983. Origin of Espanola Island and the age of terrestrial life on the Galapagos Islands. *Science*, 221: 545-547

Harpp K, Geist D, 2002. Wolf-Darwin lineament and plume-ridge interaction in northern Galapagos. *Geochem Geophys Geosyst*, 3: 1-19

Heyerdahl T, 1963. Archaeology in the Galapagos Islands. *Calif Acad Sci Occ Pap*, 44: 45-51

Jonnsson S, Zebker H, Amelung F, 2005. On trapdoor faulting at Sierra Negra volcano, Galapagos. *J Volc Geotherm Res*, 144: 59-71

Kurz M D, Geist D, 1999. Dynamics of the Galapagos hotspot from helium isotope geochemistry. *Geochim Cosmochim Acta*, 63: 4139-4156

Martinez N G, 1934. *Impressions de un Viaje a Galapagos*. Quito: Talleres Geog Nac, 182 p

McBirney A R, Williams H, 1969. Geology and petrology of the Galapagos Islands. *Geol Soc Amer Mem*, 118: 1-197 ***(regional reference)***

Mouginis-Mark P J, Rowland S K, Garbeil H, 1996. Slopes of western Galapagos volcanoes from airborne interferometric radar. *Geophys Res Lett*, 23: 3767-3770

Mouginis-Mark P J, Snell H, Ellisor R, 2000. GOES satellite and field observations of the 1998 eruption of Volcan Cerro Azul, Galapagos Islands. *Bull Volc*, 62: 188-198

Naumann T, Geist D, 2000. Physical volcanology and structural development of Cerro Azul volcano, Isabela Island, Galapagos: implications for the development of Galapagos-type shield volcanoes. *Bull Volc*, 61: 497-514

Naumann T, Geist D, Kurtz M, 2002. Petrology and geochemistry of Volcan Cerro Azul: petrologic diversity among the western Galapagos volcanoes. *J Petr*, 43: 859-883

Reynolds R W, Geist D, Kurz M D, 1995. Physical volcanology and structural development of Sierra Negra volcano, Isabela Island, Galapagos Archipelago. *Geol Soc Amer Bull*, 107: 1398-1410

Richards A F, 1957. Volcanism in Eastern Pacific Ocean Basin: 1945-1955. *20th Internatl Geol Cong, Mexico City*, Sec 1: 19-31

Richards A F, 1962. Archipelago de Colon, Isla San Felix and Islas Juan Fernandez. *Catalog of Active Volcanoes of the World and Solfatara Fields*, Rome: IAVCEI, 14: 1-50 ***(regional reference)***

Rowland S K, Harris A J L, Wooster M J, Amelung F, Garbeil H, Wilson L, Mouginis-Mark P J, 2003. Volumetric characteristics of lava flows from interferometric radar and multispectral satellite data: the 1995 Fernandina and 1998 Cerro Azul eruptions in the western Galapagos. *Bull Volc*, 65: 311-330

Rowland S K, Munro D C, 1992. The caldera of Volcan Fernandina: a remote sensing study of its structure and recent activity. *Bull Volc*, 55: 97-109

Rowland S K, Munro D C, Perez-Oviedo V, 1994. Volcan Ecuador, Galapagos Islands: erosion as a possible mechanism for the generation of steep-sided basaltic volcanoes. *Bull Volc*, 56: 271-283

Simkin T, 1984. Geology of Galapagos Islands. *In*: Perry R (ed) *Galapagos*, Oxford: Pergamon, p 15-41

Simkin T, Howard K A, 1970. Caldera collapse in the Galapagos Islands, 1968. *Science*, 169: 429-437

Slevin J R, 1959. The Galapagos Islands, a history of their exploration. *Calif Acad Sci Occ Pap*, 25: 1-150

Standish J, Geist D, Harpp K, Kurz M D, 1998. The emergence of a Galapagos shield volcano, Roca Redonda. *Contr Mineral Petr*, 133: 136-148

Swanson F J, Baitis H W, Lexa J, Dymond J, 1974. Geology of Santiago, Rabida, and Pinzon Islands, Galapagos. *Geol Soc Amer Bull*, 85: 1803-1810

Teasdale R, Geist D, Kurz M, Harpp K, 2005. 1998 eruption at Volcan Cerro Azul, Galapagos Islands: 1. Syn-eruptive petrogenesis. *Bull Volc*, 67: 170-185

Vicenzi E P, McBirney A R, White W M, Hamilton M, 1990. The geology and geochemistry of Isla Marchena, Galapagos Archipelago: an ocean island adjacent to a mid-ocean ridge. *J Volc Geotherm Res*, 40: 291-315

White W M, McBirney A R, Duncan R A, 1993. Petrology and geochemistry of the Galapagos Islands: Portrait of a pathological mantle plume. *J Geophys Res*, 98: 19,533-19,563

PERU, N CHILE & BOLIVIA (1504-06)

Adams N K, de Silva S L, Self S, Salas G, Schubring S, Permenter J L, Arbesman K, 2001. The physical volcanology of the 1600 eruption of Huaynaputina, southern Peru. *Bull Volc*, 62: 493-518

Baker P E, 1979. Geological aspects of volcano prediction. *J Geol Soc London*, 136: 341-345

Baker P E, Buckley F, Holland J G, 1974. Petrology and geochemistry of Easter Island. *Contr Mineral Petr*, 44: 85-100

Baker P E, Gonzalez-Ferran O, Rex D C, 1987. Geology and geochemistry of the Ojos del Salado volcanic region, Chile. *J Geol Soc London*, 144: 85-96

Baker P E, Keyvan-Scocouhi F A, 1982. Petrology and geochemistry of the Juan Fernandez Islands, south east Pacific. *In*: Schmincke H-U, Baker P E, Forjaz V H (eds) *Proc Symp Activity Oceanic Volcanoes*, Arquipelago, Revista Univ Dos Acores, 3: 255-264

Bonhomme M G, Fornari M, Laubacher G, Sebrier M, Vivier G, 1988. New Cenozoic K-Ar ages on volcanic rocks from the eastern High Andes, southern Peru. *J South Amer Earth Sci*, 1: 179-183

Bruggen J, 1950. *Fundamentals of the Geology of Chile*. Santiago: Editado por el Instituto Geografico Militar, p 1-374 ***(regional reference)***

Bullard F M, 1962. Volcanoes of Southern Peru. *Bull Volc*, 24: 443-453

Calder E S, Sparks R S J, Gardeweg M C, 2000. Erosion, transport and segregation of pumice and lithic clasts in pyroclastic flows inferred from ignimbrite at Lascar volcano, Chile. *J Volc Geotherm Res*, 104: 201-235

Casertano L, 1963a. Chilean Continent. *Catalog of Active Volcanoes of the World and Solfatara Fields*, Rome: IAVCEI, 15: 1-55 ***(regional reference)***

Casertano L, 1963b. General characteristics of active Andean volcanoes and a summary of their activities during recent centuries. *Bull Seism Soc Amer*, 53: 1415-1433

Clark J G, Dymond J, 1977. Geochronology and petrochemistry of Easter and Sala y Gomez Islands: implications for the origin of the Sala y Gomez ridge. *J Volc Geotherm Res*, 2: 29-48

Clavero J E, Sparks R J S, Polanco E, Pringle M S, 2004. Evolution of Parinacota volcano, Central Andes, Northern Chile. *Rev Geol Chile*, 31: 317-347

Clavero J E, Sparks R S J, Huppert H E, Dade W B, 2002. Geological constraints on the emplacement mechanism of the Parinacota debris avalanche, northern Chile. *Bull Volc*, 64: 40-54

Clavero J E, Sparks R S J, Pringle M S, Polanco E, Gardeweg M C, 2004. Evolution and volcanic hazards of Taapaca Volcanic Complex, Central Andes of Northern Chile. *J Geol Soc London*, 161: 603-618

Clavero J, Polanco E, Godoy E, Aguilar G, Sparks R S J, van Wyk de Vries B, Perez de Arce C, Matthews S, 2004. Substrata influence in the transport and emplacement mechanism of the Ollagüe debris avalanche (northern Chile). *Acta Vulc*, 16: 59-76

Coira B, Kay S M, 1993. Implications of Quaternary volcanism at Cerro Tuzgle for crustal and mantle evolution of the Puna Plateau, Central Andes, Argentina. *Contr Mineral Petr*, 113: 40-58

Davidson J P, McMillan N J, Moorbath S, Worner G, Harmon R S, Lopez-Escobar L, 1990. The Nevados de Payachata volcanic region (18° S/69° W, N. Chile) II. Evidence for widespread crustal involvement in Andean magmatism. *Contr Mineral Petr*, 105: 412-432

Davidson J P, de Silva S L, 1992. Volcanic rocks from the Bolivian Altiplano: insights into crustal structure, contamination, and magma genesis in the central Andes. *Geology*, 20: 1127-1130

Davidson J P, de Silva S L, 1995. Late Cenozoic magmatism of the Bolivian Altiplano. *Contr Mineral Petr*, 119: 387-408

de Silva S L, Alzueta J, Salas G, 2000. The socioeconomic consequences of the A.D. 1600 eruption of Huaynaputina, southern Peru. *In*: McCoy F W, Heiken G (eds), *Volcanic Hazards and Disasters in Human Antiquity*, Geol Soc Am Spec Pap, 345: 15-24

de Silva S L, Davidson J P, Croudace I W, Escobar A, 1993. Volcanological and petrological evolution of Volcan Tata Sabaya, SW Bolivia. *J Volc Geotherm Res*, 55: 305-335

de Silva S L, Francis P W, 1990. Potentially active volcanoes of Peru - observations using Landsat Thematic Mapper and Space Shuttle imagery. *Bull Volc*, 52: 286-301

de Silva S L, Francis P W, 1991. *Volcanoes of the Central Andes*. Berlin: Springer-Verlag, 216 p ***(regional reference)***

de Silva S L, Self S, Francis P W, Drake R E, Ramirez R R, 1994. Effusive silicic volcanism in the Central Andes: the Chao dacite and other young lavas of the Altiplano-Puna volcanic complex. *J Geophys Res*, 99: 17,805-17,825

de Silva S L, Zielinski G A, 1998. Global influence of the AD 1600 eruption of Huaynaputina, Peru. *Nature*, 393: 455-458

de Silva S, Gosnold W D, 2007. Episodic construction of batholiths: insights from the spatiotemporal development of an ignimbrite flare-up. *J Volc Geotherm Res*, 167: 320-335

Delacor A, Gerbe M-C, Thouret J-C, Worner G, Paquereau-Lebti P, 2007. Magma evolution of Quaternary minor volcanic centres in southern Peru, Central Andes. *Bull Volc*, 69: 581-608

Farley K A, Basu A R, Craig H, 1993. He, Sr and Nd isotopic variations in lavas from the Juan Fernandez archipelago, SE Pacific. *Contr Mineral Petr*, 115: 75-87

Feeley T C, Davidson J P, 1994. Petrology of calc-alkaline lavas at Volcan Ollague and the origin of compositional diversity at central Andeam stratovolcanoes. *J Petr*, 35: 1295-1340

Feeley T C, Davidson J P, Armendia A, 1993. The volcanic and magmatic evolution of Volcan Ollague, a high-K, late Quaternary stratovolcano in the Andean Central Volcaniz Zone. *J Volc Geotherm Res*, 54: 221-245

Fernandez-C A, Hormann P K, Kussmaul S, Meave J, Pichler H, Subieta T, 1973. First petrologic data on young volcanic rocks of SW-Bolivia. *Tschermaks Min Petr Mitt*, 19: 149-172

Finizola A, Lenat J-F, Macedo O, Ramos D, Thouret J-C, Sortino F, 2004. Fluid circulation and structural discontinuities inside Misti volcano (Peru) inferred from self-potential measurements. *J Volc Geotherm Res*, 135: 343-360

Francis P W, 1982. The Cerro Galan caldera, Argentina. *Earthq Inf Bull*, 14: 124-133

Francis P W, Gardeweg M, Ramirez C F, Rothery D A, 1985. Catastrophic debris avalanche deposit of Socompa volcano, northern Chile. *Geology*, 13: 600-603

Francis P W, Hammill M, Kretzschmar G, Thorpe R S, 1978. The Cerro Galan caldera, north-west Argentina and its tectonic setting. *Nature*, 274: 749-751

Francis P W, McDonough W F, Hammill M, O'Callaghan L J, Thorpe R S, 1984. The Cerro Purico shield complex, north Chile. *In*: Harmon R S and Barreiro B A (eds) *Andean Magmatism - Chemical and Isotopic Constraints*, Cheshire, UK: Shiva Pub, p 106-123

Francis P W, Roobol M J, Walker G P L, Cobbold P R, Coward M, 1974. The San Pedro and San Pablo volcanoes of northern Chile and their hot avalanche deposits. *Geol Rundschau*, 63: 357-388

Francis P W, Rothery D A, 1987. Using the Landsat Thematic Mapper to detect and monitor active volcanoes: an example from Lascar volcano, northern Chile. *Geology*, 15: 614-617

Francis P W, Sparks R S J, Hawkesworth C J, Thorpe R S, Pyle D M, Tait S R, Mantovani M S, McDermott F, 1989. Petrology and geochemistry of volcanic rocks of the Cerro Galan caldera, northwest Argentina. *Geol Mag*, 126: 515-547

Francis P W, Wells G L, 1988. Landsat thematic mapper observations of debris avalanche deposits in the central Andes. *Bull Volc*, 50: 258-278

Gardeweg M C, Sparks R S J, Matthews S J, 1998. Evolution of Lascar volcano, northern Chile. *J Geol Soc London*, 155: 89-104

Gardeweg M, Lindsay J, 2004. Lascar volcano and La Pacana caldera. *IAVCEI Gen Assembly 2004 Pucon, Chile Field Trip Guide* A2, 32 p

Gerbe M-C, Thouret J-C, 2004. Role of magma mixing in the petrogenesis of tephra erupted during the 1990-98 explosive activity of Nevado Sabancaya, southern Peru. *Bull Volc*, 66: 541-561

Glaze L S, Francis P W, Self S, Rothery D A, 1989. The 16 September 1986 eruption of Lascar volcano, north Chile: satellite investigations. *Bull Volc*, 51: 149-160

Gonzalez-Ferran O, 1972. Distribucion del volcanismo activo de Chile y la reciente erupcion del Volcan Villarrica. *Instituto Geog Militar Chile*, O/T 3491 ***(regional reference)***

Gonzalez-Ferran O, 1974. Arica - Nevados de Payachata. *IAVCEI Andean Antarctic Volc Problems Guide Book - Excursion A-1*, 3-35

Gonzalez-Ferran O, 1990. Huaynaputina volcano: the biggest historical dacitic eruption in the central Andes of South America, on February 19, 1600. *IAVCEI 1990 Internatl Volc Cong, Mainz, Abs*, (unpaginated)

Gonzalez-Ferran O, 1995. *Volcanes de Chile*. Santiago: Instituto Geografico Militar, 635 p ***(regional reference)***

Gonzalez-Ferran O, Mazzuoli R, Lahsen A, 2004. Geologia del complejo volcanico Isla de Pascua Rapa Nui. *Centro Estudios Volc, Santiago - Chile*, 1:30,000 geol map

Goss A R, Kay S M, Mpodozis C, Singer B S, 20090. The Incapillo caldera and dome complex (~28° S, Central Andes): a stranded magma chamber over a dying arc. *J Volc Geotherm Res*, 184: 389-404

Guest J E, Sanchez-R J, 1969. A large dacitic lava flow in northern Chile. *Bull Volc*, 33: 778-790

Guzman S R, Petrinovic I A, Brod J A, 2006. Pleistocene mafic volcanoes in the Puna-Cordillera Oriental boundary, NW-Argentina. *J Volc Geotherm Res*, 158: 51-69

Haase K M, Stoffers P, Garbe-Schonberg C-D, 1997. The petrologic evolution of lavas from Easter Island and neighbouring seamounts, near-ridge hot spot volcanoes in the SE Pacific. *J Petr*, 38: 785-813

Hantke G, Parodi I, 1966. Colombia, Ecuador and Peru. *Catalog of Active Volcanoes of the World and Solfatara Fields*, Rome: IAVCEI, 19: 1-73 ***(regional reference)***

Hawkesworth C J, Hammill M, Gledhill A R, van Calsteren P, Rogers G, 1982. Isotope and trace element evidence for late-stage intra-crustal melting in the High Andes. *Earth Planet Sci Lett*, 58: 240-254

Hormann P K, Pichler H, Zeil W, 1973. New data on the young volcanism in the Puna of NW-Argentina. *Geol Rundschau*, 62: 397-405

Jaggar T A, 1925a. Chilean volcanoes. *Volcano Lett*, 1: 1

Jenks W F (ed), 1956. Handbook of South American geology, an evaluation of the geologic map of South America. *Geol Soc Amer Mem*, 65: 1-378

Kaneoka I, Katsui Y, 1985. K-Ar ages of volcanic rocks from Easter Island. *Bull Volc Soc Japan*, 30: 33-36

Katsui Y, Gonzalez-Ferran O, 1968. Geologia del area neovolcanica de los Nevados de Payachata. *Chile Univ Inst Geol Pub*, 29: 1-161

Kelfoun K, Druitt T, van Wyk de Vries B, Guilbaud M-N, 2008. Topographic reflection of the Socompa debris avalanche, Chile. *Bull Volc*, 70: 1169-1187

Klemetti E W, Grunder A L, 2008. Volcanic evolution of Volcan Aucanquilcha: a long-lived dacite volcano in the Central Andes of northern Chile. *Bull Volc*, 70: 633-650

Klinck B A, Ellison R A, Hawkins M P, 1986. The geology of the Cordillera Occidental and Altiplano west of Lake Titicaca southern Peru. *Brit Geol Surv Open-File Rpt*, 353 p

Kussmaul S, Hormann P K, Ploskonka E, Subieta T, 1977. Volcanism and structure of southwestern Bolivia. *J Volc Geotherm Res*, 2: 73-111

Lavallee Y, de Silva S L, Salas G, Byrnes J M, 2006. Explosive volcanism (VEI 6) without caldera formation: insight from Huaynaputina volcano, southern Peru. *Bull Volc*, 68: 333-348

Lavallee Y, de Silva S L, Salas G, Byrnes J M, 2009. Structural control on volcanism at the Ubinas, Huaynaputina, and Ticscani Volcanic Group (UHTVG), southern Peru. *J Volc Geotherm Res*, 186: 253-264

Legros F, 2001. Tephra stratigraphy of Misti volcano, Peru. *J South Amer Earth Sci*, 14: 15-29

Matthews S J, Gardeweg M C, Sparks R S J, 1997. The 1984 to 1996 cyclic activity of Lascar volcano, northern Chile: cycles of dome growth, dome subsidence, degasssing and explosive eruptions. *Bull Volc*, 59: 72-82

Matthews S J, Jones A P, Gardeweg M C, 1994. Lascar volcano, northern Chile; evidence for steady-state disequilibrium. *J Petr*, 35: 401-432

Naranjo J A, 1985. Sulphur flows at Lastarria volcano in the north Chilean Andes. *Nature*, 313: 778-780

Naranjo J A, 1992. Chemistry and petrological evolution of the Lastarria volcanic complex in the north Chilean Andes. *Geol. Mag*, 129: 723-740

Natland J H, 2003. Capture of helium and other volatiles during the growth of olivine phenocrysts in picritic basalts from the Juan Fernandez Islands. *J Petr*, 44: 421-456

O'Callaghan L J, Francis P W, 1986. Volcanological and petrological evolution of San Pedro volcano, Provincia El Loa, north Chile. *J Geol Soc London*, 143: 275-286

Oppenheimer C, Francis P W, Rothery D A, Carlton R W T, 1993. Infrared image analysis of volcanic thermal features: Lascar volcano, Chile, 1984-1992. *J Geophys Res*, 98: 4269-4286

Paquereau Lebti P, Thouret J-C, Worner G, Fornari M, 2006. Neogene and Quaternary ignimbrites in the area of Arequipa, southern Peru: stratigraphical and petrological correlations. *J Volc Geotherm Res*, 154: 251-275

Paquereau-Lebti P, Fornari M, Roperch P, Thouret J-C, Macedo O, 20008. Paleomagnetism, magnetic fabric, and 40Ar/39Ar dating of Pliocene and Quaternary ignimbrites in the Arequipa area, southern Peru. *Bull Volc*, 70: 977-997

Parodi-I A, 1975. Volcanes del Peru. *Soc Geog Lima Bull*, 94: 20-23

Petit-Breuilh M E, 1994. Tabla resumen de la actividad eruptiva del Volcan Lascar. *Serv Nac Geol Min Chile*, unpublished rpt

Petrinovic I A, Colombo Pinol F, 2006. Phreatomagmatic and phreatic eruptions in locally extensive settings of Southern Central Andes: the Tocomar volcanic centre (24° 10' S-66° 34' W), Argentina. *J Volc Geotherm Res*, 158: 37-50

Pichler H, Zeil W, 1971. The Cenozoic rhyolite-andesite association of the Chilean Andes. *Bull Volc*, 35: 424-452

Pritchard M, Simons M, 2002. A satellite geodetic survey of large-scale deformation of volcanic centres in the Central Andes. *Nature*, 418: 167-170

Richards A F, 1962. Archipelago de Colon, Isla San Felix and Islas Juan Fernandez. *Catalog of Active Volcanoes of the World and Solfatara Fields*, Rome: IAVCEI, 14: 1-50 ***(regional reference)***

Richards J P, Ullrich T, Kerrich R, 2006. The Late Miocene-Quaternary Antofalla volcanic complex, southern Puna, Argentina: protracted history, diverse petrology, and economic potential. *J Volc Geotherm Res*, 152: 197-239

Richards J P, Villeneuve M, 2001. The Llullaillaco volcano, northwest Argentina: construction by Pleistocene volcanism and destruction by edifice collapse. *J Volc Geotherm Res*, 105: 77-105

Richards J P, Villeneuve M, 2002. Characteristics of late Cenozoic volcanism along the Archibarca lineament from Cerro Llullaillaco to Corrida de Cori, northwest Argentina. *J Volc Geotherm Res*, 116: 161-200

Rivera M, Marino J, 2006. Volcanic hazards evaluation of Yucamane volcano, southern Peru. *Cities on Volcanoes 4, Quito, Ecuador, 23-27 Jan, 2006*, Abs, p 71

Roobol M J, Francis P W, Ridley W I, Rhodes M, Walker G P, 1976. Physio-chemical characteristics of the Andean volcanic chain between latitudes 21° and 22° south. *In*: Gonzalez-Ferran O (ed) *Proc Symp Andean & Antarctic Volcanology Problems (Santiago, Chile, Sept 1974)*, Rome: IAVCEI, p 450-464

Rudolph W E, 1955. Licancabur: mountain of the Atacamenos. *Geog Rev*, 45: 151-171

Ruprecht P, Worner G, 2007. Variable regimes in magma systems documented in plagioclast zoning patterns: El Misti stratovolcano and Andahua monogenetic cones. *J Volc Geotherm Res*, 165: 142-162

Schmidt A K, de Silva S L, Trumbull R B, Emmermann R, 2001. Magma evolution in the Purico ignimbrite complex, northern Chile: evidence for zoning of a dacitic magma by injection of rhyolitic melts. *Contr Mineral Petr*, 140: 680-700

Schwab K, Lippolt H, 1976. K-Ar mineral ages and late Cenozoic history of the Salar de Cauchari area (Argentine Puna). *In*: Gonzalez-Ferran O (ed) *Proc Symp Andean & Antarctic Volcanology Problems (Santiago, Chile, Sept 1974)*, Rome: IAVCEI, p 698-714

Shippee R, 1932. Lost valleys of Peru: results of the Shippee-Johnson Peruvian expedition. *Geog Rev*, 22: 562-581

Siebe C, Schaaf P, Carlotto V, Gomez J C, 2006. Radiocarbon ages and composition of Holocene-Late Pleistocene monogenetic Kimsachata and Oroscocha volcanoes in Cusco, Peru. *Cities on Volcanoes 4, Quito, Ecuador, 23-27 Jan, 2006*, Abs, p 73

Sorensen E V, Holm P M, 2008. Petrological inferences on the evolution of magmas erupted in the Adagua Valley, Peru (Central Volcanic Zone). *J Volc Geotherm Res*, 177: 378-396

Spann H, 1956. El Volcan Ubinas. *Proc 8th Pacific Sci Cong*, 2: 56-59

Sparks R S J, Gardeweg M C, Calder E S, Matthews S J, 1997. Erosion by pyroclastic flows of Lascar volcano, Chile. *Bull Volc*, 58: 557-565

Stuessy T F, Foland K A, Sutter J F, Sanders R W, Silva-O M, 1984. Botanical and geological significance of Potassium-Argon dates from the Juan Fernandez islands. *Science*, 225: 49-51

Thornber C R, 1990. Geologic map of Harrat Hutaymah, with petrologic classification and distribution of ultramafic inclusions, Saudi Arabia. *U S Geol Surv map*, MF-2129 (1:100,000 scale geol map)

Thouret J-C, Davila J, Eissen J-P, 1999. Largest explosive eruption in historical time in the Andes at Huaynaputina volcano, A.D. 1600, southern Peru. *Geology*, 27: 435-438

Thouret J-C, Finizola A, Fornari M, Legeley-Padovani A, Suni J, Frechen M, 2001. Geology of El Misti volcano near the city of Arequipa, Peru. *Geol Soc Amer Bull*, 113: 1593-1610

Thouret J-C, Juvigne E, Gourgaud A, Boivin P, Davila J, 2002. Reconstruction of the AD 1600 Huaynaputina eruption based on the correlation of geologic evidence with early Spanish chronicles. *J Volc Geotherm Res*, 115: 529-570

Thouret J-C, Juvigne E, Marino J, Moscol M, Legeley-Padovani A, Loutsch I, Davila J, Lamadon S, Rivera M, 2002. Late Pleistocene and Holocene tephro-stratigraphy and chronology in southern Peru. *Bol Soc Geol Peru*, 93: 45-61

Thouret J-C, Rivera M, Worner G, Gerbe M-C, Finizola A, Fornari M, Gonzales K, 2005. Ubinas: the evolution of the historically most active volcano in southern Peru. *Bull Volc*: 67: 557-589

Tort A, Finizola A, 2005. The buried caldera of Misti volcano, Peru, revealed by combining a self-potential survey with elliptic Fourier function analysis of topography. *J Volc Geotherm Res*, 141: 283-297

van Wyk de Vries B, Self S, Francis P W, Keszthelyi L, 2001. A gravitational spreading model for the Socompa debris avalanche. *J Volc Geotherm Res*, 105: 225-247

Vazquez de Espinosa A, 1942. Compendum and description of the West Indies. *Smithsonian Inst Misc Coll*, 862 p

Venturelli G, Fragipane M, Weibel M, Antiga D, 1978. Trace element distribution in the Cainozoic lavas of Nevado Coropuna and Andagua Valley, Central Andes of southern Peru. *Bull Volc*, 41: 213-228

Vezzoli L, Acocella V, 2009. Easter Island, SE Pacific: an end-member type of hotspot volcanism. *Geol Soc Amer Bull*, 121: 869-886

Vezzoli L, Tibaldi A, Renzullic A, Mennac M, Flude S, 2008. Faulting-assisted lateral collapses and influence on shallow magma feeding system at Ollagüe volcano (Central Volcanic Zone, Chile-Bolivia Andes). *J Volc Geotherm Res*, 171: 137-159

Wadge G, Francis P W, Ramirez C F, 1995. The Socompa collapse and avalanche event. *J Volc Geotherm Res*, 66: 309-336

Watts R B, de Silva S L, Jimenez de Rios G, Croudace I, 1999. Effusive eruption of viscous silicic magma triggered and driven by recharge: a case study of the Cerro Chascon-Runtu Jarita dome complex in southwest Bolivia. *Bull Volc*, 61: 241-264

Willis B, Washington H S, 1924. San Felix and San Ambrosio: their geology and petrology. *Geol Soc Amer Bull*, 35: 365-384

Wilson C J N, Houghton B F, Kamp P J J, McWilliams M O, 1995b. An exceptionally widespread ignimbrite with implications for pyroclastic flow emplacement. *Nature*, 378: 605-607

Wooster M J, Rothery D A, 1997. Thermal monitoring of Lascar volcano, Chile, using infrared data from the along-track scanning radiometer: a 1992-1995 time series. *Bull Volc*, 58: 566-579

Worner G, Hammerschmidt K, Henjes-Kunst F, Lezaun J, Wilke H, 2000. Geochronology (40Ar/39Ar, K-Ar and He-exposure ages) of Cenozoic magmatic rocks from Northern Chile (18-22° S): implications for magmatism and tectonic evolution of the central Andes. *Rev Geol Chile*, 27: 205-240

Worner G, Harmon R S, Davidson J, Moorbath S, Turner D L, McMillan N, Nye C, Lopez-Escobar L, Moreno H, 1988. The Nevados de Payachata volcanic region, I: geological, geochemical, and isotopic observations. *Bull Volc*, 50: 287-303

CHILE & ARGENTINA (1507-08)

Anonymous, 1992. Hudson volcanic eruption of August 12-15, 1991: ash fall characteristics and natural disaster assessment in Patagonia, Argentina. *Episodes*, 15: 280

Auer V, 1959. The Pleistocene of Fuego-Patagonia Part 3: Shoreline displacements. *Suomalainen Tiedeakatemia Helsingfors Toimituksia*, Ser A-3, 60: 1-247

Auer V, 1965. The Pleistocene of Fuego-Patagonia Part 4: bog profiles. *Suomalainen Tiedeakatemia Helsingfors Toimituksia*, Ser A-3, 80: 1-160

Bertotto G W, Bjerg E A, Cingolani C A, 2006. Hawaiian and strombolian style monogenetic volcanism in the extra-Andean domain of central-west Argentina. *J Volc Geotherm Res*, 158: 430-444

Bertotto G W, Bjerg E A, Cingolani C A, 2006. Hawaiian and strombolian style monogenetic volcanism in the extra-Andea domain of central-west Argentina. *J Volc Geotherm Res*, 158: 430-444

Bitschene P R, 1995. Environmental impact and hazard assessment of the August 1991 eruption of Mt. Hudson (Patagonian Andes). *In*: Bitschene P R, Mendia J (eds) *The August 1991 eruption of the Hudson volcano (Patagonian Andes): a thousand days after*, Univ Nac de la Patagonia San Juan Bosco, Serv Nac Geol, p. 2-15

Bonadonna C, Houghton B F, 2005. Total grain-size distribution and volume of tephra-fall deposits. *Bull Volc*, 67: 441-456

Branney M J, Gilbert J S, 1995. Ice-melt collapse pits and associated features in the 1991 lahar deposits of Volcan Hudson, Chile: criteria to distinguish eruption-induced glacier melt. *Bull Volc*, 57: 293-302

Bruggen J, 1950. *Fundamentals of the Geology of Chile*. Santiago: Editado por el Instituto Geografico Militar, p 1-374 ***(regional reference)***

Caldcleugh A, 1836b. An account of the great earthquake in Chile on the 20th of February, 1835; with a map. *Phil Trans Roy Soc London*, 126: 21-26

Carn S A, Pallister J S, Lara L, Ewert J W, Watt S, Prata A J, Thomas R J, Villarosa G, 2009. The unexptected awakening of Chaiten volcano, Chile. *Eos, Trans Amer Geophys Union*, 90: 205-206

Casertano L, 1963a. Chilean Continent. *Catalog of Active Volcanoes of the World and Solfatara Fields*, Rome: IAVCEI, 15: 1-55 ***(regional reference)***

Casertano L, 1963b. General characteristics of active Andean volcanoes and a summary of their activities during recent centuries. *Bull Seism Soc Amer*, 53: 1415-1433

Corbella H, Susana Alonso M, 1987. Post-glacial hydroclastic and pyroclastic deposits in the Lanin National Park, north Patagonian cordillera, Nequen, Argentina. *Andean Volc Internatl Symp, Tucaman, Argentina*, 9 p

Costa F, Singer B, 2002. Evolution of Holocene dacite and compositionally zoned magma, Volcan San Pedro, Southern Volcanic Zone, Chile. *J Petr*, 43: 1571-1593

D'Orazio M, Agostini S, Mazzarini F, Innocenti F, Manetti P, Haller M J, Lahsen A, 2000. The Pali Aike volcanic field, Patagonia: slab-window magmatism near the tip of South America. *Tectonophysics*, 321: 407-427

Davidson J P, Ferguson K M, Colucci M T, Dungan M A, 1988. The origin and evolution of magmas from the San Pedro-Pellado volcanic complex, S. Chile: multicomponent sources and open system evolution. *Contr Mineral Petr*, 100: 429-445

Deruelle B, Deruelle J, 1975. Geologie des volcans Quaternaires des Nevados de Chillan (Chili). *Bull Volc*, 38: 425-444

Dixon H J, Murphy M D, Sparks S J, Chavez R, Naranjo J A, Dunkley P N, Young S R, Gilbert J S, Pringle M R, 1999. The geology of Nevados de Chillan volcano, Chile. *Rev Geol Chile*, 26: 227-253

Drake R E, 1976a. Chronology of Cenozoic igneous and tectonic events in the central Chilean Andes-latitudes 35.5 to 36° S. *J Volc Geotherm Res*, 1: 265-284

Drake R E, 1976b. The chronology of Cenozoic igneous and tectonic events in the central Chilean Andes. *In*: Gonzalez-Ferran O (ed) *Proc Symp Andean & Antarctic Volcanology Problems (Santiago, Chile, Sept 1974)*, Rome: IAVCEI, p 670-697

Dungan M A, Wulff A, Thompson R, 2001. Eruptive stratigraphy of the Tatara-San Pedro complex, 36° S, Southern Volcanic Zone, Chilean Andes: reconstruction method and implications for magma evolution at long-lived arc volcanic centers. *J Petr*, 42: 555-626

Feeley T C, Dungan M A, Frey F A, 1998. Geochemical constraints on the origin of mafic and silicic magmas at Cordon el Guadal, Tatara-San Pedro complex, central Chile. *Contr Mineral Petr*, 131: 393-411

Ferguson K M, Dungan M A, Davidson J P, Colucci M T, 1992. The Tatara-San Pedro volcano, 36° S, Chile: a chemically variable, dominantly mafic magmatic system. *J Petr*, 33: 1-43

Folguera A, Bottesi G, Zapata T, Ramos V A, 2008. Crustal collapse in the Andean backarc since 2 Ma: Tromen volcanic plateau, southern Central Andes (36° 40'-37° 30' S). *Tectonophysics*, 459: 140-160

Folguera A, Naranjo J A, Orihashi Y, Sumino H, Nagao K, Polanco E, Ramos V A, 2009. Retroarc volcanism in the northern San Rafael Block (34°-35° 30' S), southern Central Andes: occurrence, age, and tectonic setting. *J Volc Geotherm Res*, 186: 169-185

Frey F A, Gerlach D C, Hickey R L, Lopez-Escobar L, Munizaga-Villavicencio F, 1984. Petrogenesis of the Laguna del Maule volcanic complex, Chile (36°). *Contr Mineral Petr*, 88: 133-149

Fuenzalida R, Etchart H, 1976. Evidencias de migracion volcanica reciente desde la linea de volcanes de la Patagonia Chilena. *In*: Gonzalez-Ferran O (ed) *Proc Symp Andean & Antarctic Volcanology Problems (Santiago, Chile, Sept 1974)*, Rome: IAVCEI, p 392-397

Fuenzalida-Ponce R, 1976. The Hudson volcano. *In*: Gonzalez-Ferran O (ed) *Proc Symp Andean & Antarctic Volcanology Problems (Santiago, Chile, Sept 1974)*, Rome: IAVCEI, p 78-87

Galland O, Hallot E, Cobbold P R, Ruffet G, de Bremond d'Ars J, 2007. Volcanism in a compressional Andean setting: a structural and geochronological study of Tromen volcano (Neuquen province, Argentina). *Tectonics*, 26: doi:10.1029/2006TC002011

Gardeweg M, Lara L, Matthews S, Polanco E, 2004. Pucon-Carburgua. *IAVCEI Gen Assembly 2004 Pucon, Chile Field Trip Guide* B3, 11 p

Gerlach D C, Frey F A, Moreno H, Lopez-Escobar L, 1988. Recent volcanism in the Puyehue-Cordon Caulle region, southern Andes, Chile (40.5° S): petrogenesis of evolved lavas. *J Petr*, 29: 333-382

Germa A, Quidelleur X, Gillot P-Y, Tchilinguirian P, 2007. Volcanic evolution of the back-arc complex of Payun Matru (Argentina) and its geodyanmic implications for caldera-forming eruption in a complex slab geometry setting. *IUGG 2007, Perugia*, abstr 6761

Gilbert J S, Stasiuk M V, Lane S J, Adam C R, Murphy M D, Sparks R S J, Naranjo J A, 1996. Non-explosive, constructional evolution of the ice-filled caldera at Volcan Sollipulli, Chile. *Bull Volc*, 58: 67-83

Gonzalez-Ferran O, 1972. Distribucion del volcanismo activo de Chile y la reciente erupcion del Volcan Villarrica. *Instituto Geog Militar Chile*, O/T 3491 ***(regional reference)***

Gonzalez-Ferran O, 1995. *Volcanes de Chile*. Santiago: Instituto Geografico Militar, 635 p ***(regional reference)***

Gonzalez-Ferran O, Vergara M, 1962. Reconocimiento geologico de la Cordillera de los Andes entre los paralelos 35° y 38° latitud sur. *Chile Univ Inst Geol Pub*, 24: 1-121

Grunder A L, Mahood G A, 1988. Physical and chemical models of zoned silicic magmas: the Loma Seca Tuff and Calabozos caldera, southern Andes. *J Petr*, 29: 831-867

Guivel C, Morata D, Pelleter E, Espinoza F, Maury R C, Lagabrielle Y, Polve M, Bellon H, Cotten J, Benoit M, Suarez M, de la Cruz R, 2006. Miocene to Late Quaternary patagonian basalts (46-47° S): geochronometric and geochemical evidence for slab tearing due to active spreading ridge subduction. *J Volc Geotherm Res*, 149: 346-370

Gutierrez F, Giocada A, Gonzalez Ferran O, Lahsen A, Mazzuoli R, 2005. The Hudson volcano and surrounding monogenetic centres (Chilean Patagonia): an example of volcanism associated with ridge-trench collision environment. *J Volc Geotherm Res*, 145: 207-233

Haberle S G, Lumley S H, 1998. Age and origin of tephras recorded in postglacial lake sediments to the west of the southern Andes, 44° to 47° S. *J Volc Geotherm Res*, 84: 239-256

Harrington R, Amini H, Stern C R, Charrier R, 1984. The Maipo stratovolcano-caldera complex in the southern Andes of central Chile (abs). *Eos, Trans Amer Geophys Union*, 65: 1136

Hickey-Vargas R, Moreno H, Lopez-Escobar L, Frey F A, 1989. Geochemical variations in Andean basaltic and silicic lavas from the Villarrica-Lanin volcanic chain (39.5° S): an evaluation of source heterogeneity, fractional crystallization and crustal assimilation. *Contr Mineral Petr*, 103: 361-386

Hildreth W, Drake R E, 1992. Volcan Quizapu, Chilean Andes. *Bull Volc*, 54: 93-125

Hildreth W, Drake R, Godoy E, Munizaga F, 1991. Bobadilla caldera and 1.1 Ma ignimbrite at Laguna del Maule, Southern Chile. *VI Congreso Geológico Chileno*, Abs, p 62-63

Hildreth W, Fierstein J, Godoy E, Drake R E, Singer B, 1999. The Puelche volcanic field: extensive Pleistocene rhyolitic lava flows in the Andes of Central Chile. *Rev Geol Chile*, 26: 275-309

Hildreth W, Grunder A L, Drake R E, 1984. The Loma Seca tuff and the Calabozos caldera: a major ash-flow and caldera complex in the southern Andes of Chile. *Geol Soc Amer Bull*, 95: 45-54

Hildreth W, Moorbath S, 1988. Crustal contribution to arc magmatism in the Andes of central Chile. *Contr Mineral Petr*, 98: 455-489

Holmberg E, 1976. Descripcion geologica de la Hoja 32c, Buta Ranquil. *Servicio Geol Nac Argentina Bol*, 152: 1-86

Inbar M, Risso C, 2001. A morphological and morphometeric analysis of a high density cinder cone volcanic field - Payun Matru, south-central Andes, Argentina. *Zeit Geomorph*, 45: 321-343

Inbar M, Risso C, Parica C, 1995. The morphological development of a young lava flow in the south western Andes - Neuquen, Argentina. *Zeit Geomorph*, 39: 479-487

Jaggar T A, 1925a. Chilean volcanoes. *Volcano Lett*, 1: 1

Katsui Y, Katz H R, 1967. Lateral fissure eruptions in the southern Andes of Chile. *Hokkaido Univ Fac Sci Jour*, 13: 443-448

Kay S M, Burns W M, Copeland P, Mancilla O, 2006. Upper Cretaceous to Holocene magmatism and evidence for transient Miocene shallowing of the Andean subduction zone under the northern Neuquen basin. *In*: Kay S M, Ramos V (eds), Evolution of an Andean Margin: A Tectonic and Magmatic View from the Andes to the Neuquen basin (35 deg-39 deg lat.). *Geol Soc Amer Spec Pap*, 407: 19-60

Kilian R, 1991. A volcanic eruption of 1988 on the Viedma glacier in the Patagonian Andes (49° 22' S). Preprint from unknown journal

Kilian R, Hohner M, Biester H, Wallrabe-Adams H J, Stern C R, 2003. Holocene peat and lake sediment tephra record from the southernmost Chilean Andes (53-55° S). *Rev Geol Chile*, 30: 23-37

Klohn E, 1963. The February 1961 eruption of Calbuco volcano. *Bull Seism Soc Amer*, 53: 1435-1436

Kratzmann D J, Carey S, Scasso R, Naranjo J-A, 2009. Compositional variations and magma mixing in the 1991 eruptions of Hudson volcano, Chile. *Bull Volc*, 71: 419-439

Lara L E, Clavero J (eds), 2004. Villarrica volcano (39.5° S), Southern Andes, Chile. *Servicio Geol Nac Argentina Bol*, 61: 1-66

Lara L E, Lavenu A, Cembrano J, Rodriguez C, 2006b. Structural controls of volcanism in transversal chains: resheared faults and neotectonics in the Cordon Caulle-Puyehue area (40.5° S), Southern Andes. *J Volc Geotherm Res*, 158: 70-86

Lara L E, Moreno H, Naranjo J A, Matthews S, Perez de Arce C, 2006a. Magmatic evolution of the Puyehue-Cordon Caulle volcanic complex (40° S), Southern Andean Volcanic Zone: from shield to unusual rhyolitic fissure volcanism. *J Volc Geotherm Res*, 157: 343-366

Lara L E, Naranjo J A, Moreno H, 2004. Rhyodacitic fissure eruption in Southern Andes (Cordon Caulle; 40.5° S) after the 1960 (Mw:9.5) Chilean earthquake: a structural interpretation. *J Volc Geotherm Res*, 138: 127-138

Lara L E, Naranjo J E, Moreno H, 2004. Lanin volcano (39.5° S), Southern Andes: geology and morphostructural evolution. *Rev Geol Chile*, 31: 241-257

Lara L, Rodriguez C, Moreno H, Perez de Arce C, 2001. Geocronologia K-Ar y geoquimica del volcanismo plioceno superior-pleistoceno de los Andes del sur (39-42° S). *Rev Geol Chile*, 28: 67-90

Lliboutry L, 1999. Glaciers of the Wet Andes. *In*: Williams R J Jr, Ferringo J G (eds) Glaciers of South America, *U S Geol Surv Prof Pap*, 1386-I: 148-206

Lopez-Escobar L, Parada M A, Moreno H, Frey F A, Hickey-Vargas R L, 1992. A contribution to the petrogenesis of Osorno and Calbuco volcanoes, Southern Andes (41° 00' - 41° 30' S). *Rev Geol Chile*, 19: 211-226

Lopez-Escobar L, Vergara M, Frey F A, 1981. Petrology and geochemistry of lavas from Antuco volcano, a basaltic volcano of the southern Andes (37° 25' S). *J Volc Geotherm Res*, 11: 329-352

Martinic-B M, 1988. Actividad volcanica historica en la region de Magellenes. *Rev Geol Chile*, 15: 181-186

Massaferro G I, Haller M J, D'Orazio M, Alric V I, 2006. Sub-recent volcanism in northern Patagonia: a tectonomagmatic approach. *J Volc Geotherm Res*, 155: 227-243

Mazzarini F, D'Orazio M, 2003. Spatial distribution of cones and satellite-detected lineaments in the Pali Aike volcanic field (southernmost Patagonia): insights into the tectonic setting of a Neogene rift system. *J Volc Geotherm Res*, 125: 291-305

McMillan N J, Harmon R S, Moorbath S, Lopez-Escobar L, Strong D F, 1989. Crustal sources involved in continental arc magmatism: a case study of volcan Mocho-Choshuenco, southern Chile. *Geology*, 17: 1152-1156

Mee K, Gilbert J S, McGarvie D W, Naranjo J A, Pringle M S, 2009. Palaeoenvironment reconstruction, volcanic evolution and geochronology of the Cerro Blanco subcomplex, Nevados de Chillan volcanic complex, central Chile. *Bull Volc*, 71: 933-952

Mee K, Tuffen H, Gilbert J S, 2006. Snow-contact volcanic facies and their use in determining past eruptive environments at Nevados de Chillan volcano, Chile. *Bull Volc*, 68: 363-376

Mella M, Munoz J, Vergara M, Klohn E, Farmer L, Stern C R, 2005. Petrogenesis of the Pleistocene Tronador volcanic group, Andean Southern Volcanic Zone. *Rev Geol Chile*, 32: 131-154

Moreno H, 1974. Airplane flight over active volcanoes of central-south Chile. *Internatl Symp Volc Andean & Antarctic Volc Problems Guidebook*, Excur D-3, 56 p ***(regional reference)***

Moreno H, 1976. The upper Cenozoic volcanism in the Andes of southern Chile (from 40°00' to 41°30' lat S). *In*: Gonzalez-Ferran O (ed) *Proc Symp Andean & Antarctic Volcanology Problems (Santiago, Chile, Sept 1974)*, Rome: IAVCEI, p 143-171

Moreno H, 1980. La erupcion del Volcan Mirador en Abril-Mayo de 1979, Lago Ranco-Rininahue, Andes del Sur. *Communicaciones Univ Chile*, 28: 1-23

Moreno H, 1992. Estudio preliminar del riesgo volcanico del area de Ralco. *Proyecto Ralco, INGENDESA, Chile*, unpublished rpt

Moreno H, 1993. Volcan Villarica, geologia y evaluacion del riesgo volcanico, regiones IX y X, 39°25' S. *Serv Nac Geol Min Chile*, 1:50,000 geol map and 112 p text

Moreno H, 2004. Osorno-Calbuco. *IAVCEI Gen Assembly 2004 Pucon, Chile Field Trip Guide* C4, 14 p

Moreno H, Gardeweg M C, 1989. La erupcion reciente en el complejo volcanico Lonquimay (Diciembre 1988-), Andes del Sur. *Rev Geol Chile*, 16: 93-117

Moreno H, Naranjo J A, 1991. The southern Andes volcanoes (33°-41° 30' S), Chile. *6th Geol Cong Chile, Excur PC-3*, 26 p

Motoki A, Orihashi Y, Naranjo J A, Hirata D, Scvarca P, Anma R, 2006. Geologic reconnaissance of Lautaro volcano, Chilean Patagonia. *Rev Geol Chile*, 33: 177-187

Muller G, Veyl G, 1957. The birth of Nilahue, a new maar type volcano at Rininahue, Chile. *20th Internatl Geol Cong, Mexico City*, Sec 1: 375-396

Naranjo J A, Haller M J, 2002. Erupciones holocenas principalmente explosivas del volcan Planchon, Andes del sur (35° 15' S). *Rev Geol Chile*, 29: 93-113

Naranjo J A, Lara L E, 2004. August-September 2003 small vulcanian eruption at the Nevados de Chillan volcanic complex (36° 50' S), Southern Andes, Chile. *Rev Geol Chile*, 31: 359-366

Naranjo J A, Moreno H, 1991. Actividad explosiva postglacial en el volcan Llaima, Andes del Sur (38° 45' S). *Rev Geol Chile*, 18: 69-80

Naranjo J A, Moreno H, Emparan C, Murphy M, 1993. Volcanismo explosivo reciente en la caldera del volcan Sollipulli, Andes del Sur (39° S). *Rev Geol Chile*, 20: 167-191

Naranjo J A, Moreno R, Banks N G, 1993. La erupcion del volcan Hudson en 1991 (46° S), region XI, Aisen, Chile. *Bol Serv Nac Geol Min Chile*, 44: 1-50

Naranjo J A, Polanco E, 2004. The 2000 AD eruption of Copahue volcano, southern Andes. *Rev Geol Chile*, 31: 279-292

Naranjo J A, Stern C R, 1998. Holocene explosive activity of Hudson volcano, southern Andes. *Bull Volc*, 59: 291-306

Naranjo J A, Stern C R, 2004. Holocene tephrochronology of the southernmost part (42° 30' - 45° S) of the Andean Southern Volcanic Zone. *Rev Geol Chile*, 31: 225-240

Naranjo J, Singer B, Moreno H, Lara L, Jicha B, 2008. Holocene tephrochronology of Puyehue and Casablanca volcanoes, southern Andes. *IAVCEI Iceland Gen Assembly, Reykjavik 2008*, abs 2-a P12 and poster

Narranjo J A, Sparks R S J, Stasiuk M V, Moreno H, Ablay G J, 1992. Morphological, structural and textural variations in the 1988-1990 andesite lava of Lonquimay volcano, Chile. *Geol Mag*, 129: 657-678

Orihashi Y, Naranjo J A, Motoki A, Sumino H, Hirata D, Anma R, Nagao K, 2004. Quaternary volcanic activity of Hudson and Lautaro volcanoes, Chilean Patagonia: new constraints from K-Ar ages. *Rev Geol Chile*, 31: 207-224

Ortiz R, Moreno H, Garcia A, Fuentealba G, Astiz M, Pena P, Sanchez N, Tarraga M, 2003. Villarrica volcano (Chile): characteristics of the volcanic tremor and forecasting of small explosions by means of a material failure method. *J Volc Geotherm Res*, 128: 247-259

Pasquare G, Bistacchi A, Francalanci L, Bertotto G W, Boari E, Massironi M, Rossotti A, 2008. Very long pahoehoe inflated basaltic lava flows in the Payena volcanic province (Mendoza and La Pampa, Argentina). *Rev Asso Geol Argentina*, 63: 131-149

Petit-Breuilh M E, 1993. Chronologia eruptiva historica del volcan Llaima. *Serv Nac Geol Min Chile*, unpublished rpt

Pichler H, Zeil W, 1971. The Cenozoic rhyolite-andesite association of the Chilean Andes. *Bull Volc*, 35: 424-452

Puig A, Herve M, Suarez M, Saunders A D, 1984. Calc-alkaline and alkaline Miocene and calc-alkaline recent volcanism in the southernmost Patagonian Cordillera, Chile. *J Volc Geotherm Res*, 21: 149-163

Ramos V A, 1981. Descripcion geologica de la Hoja 33c, Los Chihuidos Norte. *Servicio Geol Nac Argentina Bol*, 182: 1-103

Riffo P, Fuentealba G, Urra L H, 1987. Sintesis historica de als erupciones del Volcan Villarrica, Chile. *Bol Vulc Univ Nac Costa Rica*, 18: 8-11

Risso C, Nemeth k, Combina A M, Nullo F, Drosina M, 2008. The role of phreatomagmatism in Plio-Pliestocene high-density scoria cone field: Llancanelo volcanic field (Mendoza), Argentina. *J Volc Geotherm Res*, 169: 61-86

Scasso R A, Corbella H, Tiberi P, 1994. Sedimentological analysis of the tephra from the 12-15 August 1991 eruption of Hudson volcano. *Bull Volc*, 56: 121-132

Selles D, Rodriguez A C, Dungan M A, Naranjo J A, Gardeweg M, 2004. Geochemistry of Nevado de Longavi volcano (36.2° S): a compositionally atypical arc volcano in the Southern Volcanic Zone of the Andes. *Rev Geol Chile*, 31: 293-315

Shipton E, 1960. Volcanic activity on the Patagonian ice cap. *Geog Jour*, 126: 389-396

Singer B S, Jicha B R, Haper M A, Naranjo J A, Lara L E, Moreno-Roa H, Lara L, 2008. Eruptive history, geochronology, and magmatic evolution of the Puyehue-Cordon Caulle volcanic complex, Chile. *Geol Soc Amer Bull*, 120: 599-618

Singer B S, Thompson R A, Dungan M A, Feeley T C, Nelson S T, Pickens J C, Brown L L, Wulff A W, Davidson J P, Metzger J, 1997. Volcanism and erosion during the past 930 k.y. at the Tatara-San Pedro complex, Chilean Andes. *Geol Soc Amer Bull*, 109: 127-142

Skewes M A, Stern C R, 1979. Petrology and geochemistry of alkali basalts and ultramafic inclusions from the Palei-Aike volcanic field in southern Chile and the origin of the Patagonian plateau lavas. *J Volc Geotherm Res*, 6: 3-25

Sruoga P, Llambias E J, Fauque L, Schonwandt D, Repol D G, 2005. Volcanological and geochemical evolution of the Diamante caldera-Maipo volcano complex in the southern Andes of Argentina (34° 10' S). *J South Amer Earth Sci*, 19: 399-414

Stern C R, 1990. Tephrochronology of southernmost Patagonia. *Natl Geog Res*, 6: 110-126

Stern C R, 2008. Holocene tephrochronology record of large explosive eruptions in the southernmost Patagonian Andes. *Bull Volc*, 70: 435-454

Stern C R, Amini H, Charrier R, Godoy E, Herve F, Varela J, 1984, 1984. Petrochemistry and age of rhyolitic pyroclastics flows which occur along the drainage valleys of the Rio Maipo and Rio Cachapoal (Chile) and the Rio Chaucha and Rio Papagayos (Argentina). *Rev Geol Chile*, no 23: 39-52

Stern C R, Naranjo J A, 1995. Summary of the Holocene eruptive history of the Hudson volcano. *In*: Bitschene P R, Mendia J (eds) *The August 1991 eruption of the Hudson volcano (Patagonian Andes): a thousand days after*, Univ Nac de la Patagonia San Juan Bosco, Serv Nac Geol, p. 160-164

Stone J B, 1930. Two active volcanoes of Chile. *Volcano Lett*, 284: 1-3

Stone J B, 1935. The volcanoes of southern Chile. *Zeit Vulk*, 16: 81-97

Stone J B, Ingerson E, 1934. Some volcanoes of Southern Chile. *Amer J Sci*, 28: 269-287

Tormey D R, Frey F A, Lopez Escobar L, 1989. Geologic history of the active Azufre-Planchon-Peteroa volcanic center (35° 15' S, southern Andes), with implications for the development of compositional gaps. *Asoc Geol Argentina Rev*, 44: 420-430

Tunstall C, Folguera A, 2005. Control estructural en el desarrollo de una concentracion anomala de calderas en los Andes de Neuquen: Complejo Volcanico Pino Hachado (38° 30' S y 71° 0). *Rev Asoc Geol Argentina*, 60: 731-741

Varekamp J C, Maarten deMoor J, Merrill M D, Colvin A S, Goss A R, Vroon P Z, Hilton D R, 2006. Geochemistry and isotopic characteristics of the Caviahue-Copahue volcanic complex, province of Neuquen, Argentina. *In*: Kay S M, Ramos V A (eds) Evolution of an Andean margin: a tectonic and magmatic view from the Andes to the Neuquen Basin (35°-39° S lat), *Geol Soc Amer Spec Pap*, 407: 317-342

Varekamp J C, Ouimette A P, Herman S W, Bermudez A, Delpino D, 2001. Hydrothermal element fluxes from Copahue, Argentina: a "beehive" volcano in turmoil. *Geology*, 29: 1059-1062

Watt S F L, Pyle D M, Mather T A, Martin R S, Matthews N E, 2009. Fallout and distribution of volcanic ash over Argentina following the May 2008 explosive eruption of Chaiten, Chile. *J Geophys Res*, 114: doi:10.1029/2008JB006219

Watt S F L, Pyle D M, Naranjo J A, Mather T A, 2009. Landslide and tsunami hazard at Yate volcano, Chile as an example of edifice destruction on strike-slip fault zones. *Bull Volc*, 71: 559-574

Witter J B, Kress V C, Delmelle P, Stix J, 2004. Volatile degassing, petrology, and magma dynamics of the Villarica lava lake, southern Chile. *J Volc Geotherm Res*, 134: 303-337

Zollner W, Amos A J, 1973. Descripcion geologica de la Hoja 32b, Chos Malal. *Servicio Geol Nac Argentina Bol*, 143: 1-91

WEST INDIES (1600)

Anderson T, 1908. The volcanoes of Guatemala. *Roy Geog Soc*, 31: 473-489

Anderson T, Flett J S, 1903. Report on the eruptions of the Soufriere, in St. Vincent, in 1902, and on a visit to Montagne Pelee, Martinique. - Part I. *Phil Tran Roy Soc London*, Ser A, 200: 353-553

Anonymous, 2009. La saviez vous? L'existence encore intacte d un appareil volcanique en Haiti? *Bur Mines L'Energie Haiti*, 6 p brochure (pdf available online)

Arculus R J, 1976. Geology and geochemistry of the alkali basalt-andesite association of Grenada, Lesser Antilles island arc. *Geol Soc Amer Bull*, 87: 612-624

Aspinall W P, Sigurdsson H, Shepherd J B, 1973. Eruption of Soufriere volcano on St. Vincent Island, 1971-1972. *Science*, 181: 117-124

Baker P E, 1985. Volcanic hazards on St. Kitts and Montserrat, West Indies. *J Geol Soc London*, 142: 279-295

Baker P E, Buckley F, Padfield T, 1980. Petrology of the volcanic rocks of Saba, West Indies. *Bull Volc*, 43: 337-346

Barrabe L, Jolivet J, 1958. Les recentes manifestations d'activite de la Guadeloupe (Petites Antilles). *Bull Volc*, 19: 143-158

Baxter P J, Boyle R, Cole P, Neri A, Spence R, Zuccaro G, 2005. The impact of pyroclastic surges on buildings at the eruption of the Soufriere Hills volcano, Montserrat. *Bull Volc*, 67: 292-313

Bellon H, 1988. Reconnaissance chronologique des deux premieres phases d'activite volcanique en Dominique (Petites Antilles). *Compte Rendus Acad Sci Paris*, 306: 1487-1492

Belousov A, Voight B, Belousov M, 2007. Directed blasts and blast-generated pyroclastic density currents: a comparison of the Bezymianny 1956, Mount St Helens 1980, and Soufriere Hills, Montserrat 1997 eruptions and deposits. *Bull Volc*, 69: 701-740

Besson P, Poirier J-P, 1994. The 3100 BP eruption of the Soufriere of Guadeloupe - A transmission electron microscopy study of the cryptodome andesite. *Bull Volc*, 56: 184-192

Boudon G, Le Friant A, Villemant B, Viode J-P, 2005. Martinique. *In*: Lindsay J M, Robertson R E A, Shepherd J B, Ali S (eds). *Volcanic Hazard Atlas of the Lesser Antilles*, Trinidad and Tobago, Seismic Res Unit, Univ West Indies, p 127-146

Boudon G, Semet M P, Vincent P M, 1987. Magma and hydrothermally driven sector collapses: The 3,100 and 11,500 y.b.p. eruptions of la Grande Decouverte (la Soufriere) volcano, Guadaloupe, French West Indies. *J Volc Geotherm Res*, 33: 317-323

Boudon G, Semet M P, Vincent P M, 1989. The evolution of la Grande Decouverte (la Soufriere) volcano, Guadalope (FWI). *In*: Latter J H (ed), *Volcanic Hazards - Assessment and Monitoring*, Berlin: Springer-Verlag, p 86-109

Bourdier J L, Boudon G, Gourgaud A, 1989. Stratigraphy of the 1902 and 1929 nuee-ardente deposits, Mt. Pelee, Martinique. *J Volc Geotherm Res*, 38: 77-96

Bouysse P, 1980-81. Sur l'existence d'un volcan sous-marin dans l'archipel de la Guadeloupe. *Bull BRGM*, Ser 2: 3-14

Bouysse P, Sigurdsson H, 1982. The "Hodder" phenomenon of 1902: no submarine volcano off St. Lucia (Lesser Antilles). *Marine Geol*, 50: M29-M36

Carn S A, Watts R B, Thompson G, Norton G E, 2004. Anatomy of a lava dome collapse: the 20 March 2000 event at Soufriere Hills volcano, Montserrat. *J Volc Geotherm Res*, 131: 241-264

Chiodini G, Cioni R, Frullani A, Guidi M, Marini L, Prati F, Raco B, 1996. Fluid geochemistry of Montserrat Island, West Indies. *Bull Volc*, 58: 380-392

Chretien S, Brousse R, 1989. Events preceeding the great eruption of 8 May, 1902 at Mount Pelee, Martinique. *J Volc Geotherm Res*, 38: 67-75

Cole P D, Calder E S, Sparks R S J, Clarke A B, Druitt T H, Young S R, Herd R A, Harford C L, Norton G E, 2002. Deposits from dome-collapse and fountain-collapse pyroclastic flows at Soufriere Hills volcano, Montserrat. *In*; Druitt T H, Kokellar B P (eds), The eruption of Soufriere Hills volcano, Montserrat, from 1995 to 1999, *Geol Soc London Mem*, 21: 231-262

Defant M J, Sherman S, Maury R C, Bellon H, de Boer J, Davidson J, Kepezhinskas P, 2001. The geology, petrology, and petrogenesis of Saba Island, Lesser Antilles. *J Volc Geotherm Res*, 107: 87-111

Deplus C, Le Friant A, Boudon G, Komorowski J-C, Villemant B, Harford C, Segoufin J, Cheminee J-L, 2001. Submarine evidence for large-scale debris avalanches in the Lesser Antilles arc. *Earth Planet Sci Lett*, 192: 145-157

Devine J D, 1995. Petrogenesis of the basalt-andesite-dacite association of Grenada, Lesser Antilles island arc, revisited. *J Volc Geotherm Res*, 69: 1-33

Devine J D, Sigurdsson H, 1995. Petrology and eruption styles of Kick-'em-Jenny submarine volcano, Lesser Antilles island arc. *J Volc Geotherm Res*, 69: 35-58

Dorel J, Eschenbrenner S, Feuillard M, 1972. Les volcans actifs de la Guadeloupe et de la Martinique, Petites Antilles. *Bull Volc*, 36: 359-381

Druitt T H, Kokellar B P (eds), 2002. The eruption of Soufriere Hills volcano, Montserrat from 1995 to 1999. *Geol Soc London Mem*, 21: 1-645

Druitt T H, Young S R, Baptie B, Bonadronna C, Calder E S, Clarke A B, Cole P D, Harford C L, Herd R A, Luckett R, Ryan G, Voight B, 2002. Episodes of cyclic Vulcanian explosive activity with fountain collapse at Soufriere Hills volcano, Montserrat. *In*; Druitt T H, Kokellar B P (eds), The eruption of Soufriere Hills volcano, Montserrat, from 1995 to 1999, *Geol Soc London Mem*, 21: 281-306

Edmonds M, Herd R A, Strutt M H, 2006. Tephra deposits associated with a large lava dome collapse, Soufriere Hills volcano, Montserrat, 12-15 July 2003. *J Volc Geotherm Res*, 153: 313-330

Feuillard M, Allegre C J, Brandeis G, Gaulon R, Le Mouel J L, Mercier J C, Pozzo J P, Semet M P, 1983. The 1975-1977 crisis of La Soufriere de Guadeloupe (FWI): a still-born magmatic eruption. *J Volc Geotherm Res*, 16: 317-334

Fichaut M, Maury R C, Traineau H, Westercamp D, Joron J L, Gourgaud A, Coulon C, 1989. Magmatology of Mt. Pelee (Martinique, F.W.I.). III. Fractional crystallization versus magma mixing. *J Volc Geotherm Res*, 38: 189-213

Gourgaud A, Fichaut M, Joron J -L, 1989. Magmatology of Mt. Pelee (Martinique, F.W.I.). I: Magma mixing and triggering of the 1902 and 1929 Pelean nuees ardentes. *J Volc Geotherm Res*, 38: 143-169

Halama R, Boudon G, Villemant B, Joron J-L, Le Friant A, Komorowski J-C, 2006. Pre-eruptive crystallization conditions of mafic and silicic magmas at the Plat Pays volcanic complex, Dominica (Lesser Antilles). *J Volc Geotherm Res*, 153: 200-220

Harford C L, Pringle M S, Sparks R S J, Young S R, 2002. The volcanic evolution of Montserrat using 40Ar/39Ar geochronology. *In*; Druitt T H, Kokellar B P (eds), The eruption of Soufriere Hills volcano, Montserrat, from 1995 to 1999, *Geol Soc London Mem*, 21: 93-113

Harkness D D, Roobol M J, Smith A L, Stipp J J, Baker P E, 1994. Radiocarbon redating of contaminated samples from a tropical volcano: the Mansion 'Series' of St Kitts, West Indies. *Bull Volc*, 56: 326-334

Hart K, Carey S, Sigurdsson H, Sparks R S J, Robertson R E A, 2004. Discharge of pyroclastic flows into the sea during the 1996-1998 eruptions of the Soufriere Hills volcano, Montserrat. *Bull Volc*, 66: 599-614

Hay R L, 1959. Formation of the crystal-rich glowing avalanche deposits of St. Vincent B W I. *J Geol*, 67: 540-562

Heath E, Macdonald R, Belkin H, Hawkesworth C, Sigurdsson H, 1998. Magmagenesis at Soufriere volcano, St Vincent, Lesser Antilles Arc. *J Petr*, 39: 1721-1764

Herd R A, Edmonds M, Bass V A, 2005. Catastrophic lava dome failure at Soufriere Hills volcano, Montserrat, 12-13 July 2003. *J Volc Geotherm Res*, 148: 234-252

Hincks T, Sparks S, Dunkely P, Cole P, 2005. Montserrat. *In*: Lindsay J M, Robertson R E A, Shepherd J B, Ali S (eds). *Volcanic Hazard Atlas of the Lesser Antilles*, Trinidad and Tobago, Seismic Res Unit, Univ West Indies, p 147-167

Juang W S, Bellon H, 1984. K-Ar geochronology of volcanic rocks of St. Vincent, the Lesser Antilles. *Bull Cent Geol Surv*, 3: 31-43

Kokelaar B P, 2002. Setting, chronology and consequences of the eruption of Soufriere Hills volcano, Montserrat (1995-1999). *In*; Druitt T H, Kokellar B P (eds), The eruption of Soufriere Hills volcano, Montserrat, from 1995 to 1999, *Geol Soc London Mem*, 21: 1-43

Komorowski J-C, Boudon G, Semet M, Beauducel F, Antenor-Habazac C, Bazin S, Hammouya G, 2005. Guadeloupe. *In*: Lindsay J M, Robertson R E A, Shepherd J B, Ali S (eds). *Volcanic Hazard Atlas of the Lesser Antilles*, Trinidad and Tobago, Seismic Res Unit, Univ West Indies, p 67-105

Lacroix A, 1904. *La Montagne Pelee et ses eruptions*. Paris: Masson et Cie, 662 p

Le Friant A, Boudon G, Arnulf A, Robertson R E A, 2009. Debris avalanche deposits offshore St. Vincent (West Indies): impact of flank-collapse events on the morphological evolution of the island. *J Volc Geotherm Res*, 179:1-10

Le Friant A, Boudon G, Deplus C, Villemant B, 2003. Large-scale flank collapse events during the activity of Montagne Pelee, Martinique, Lesser Antilles. *J Geophys Res*, 108: 2055, doi:10.1029/2001JB001624

Le Guern F, Bernard A, Chevrier R M, 1980. Soufriere of Guadeloupe, 1976-1977 eruption mass and energy transfer and volcanic health hazards. *Bull Volc*, 43: 577-594

Lindsay J M, 2005. Saint Lucia. *In*: Lindsay J M, Robertson R E A, Shepherd J B, Ali S (eds). *Volcanic Hazard Atlas of the Lesser Antilles*, Trinidad and Tobago, Seismic Res Unit, Univ West Indies, p 218-238

Lindsay J M, Robertson R E A, Shepherd J B, Ali S (eds), 2005a. *Volcanic Hazard Atlas of the Lesser Antilles*. Trinidad and Tobago, Seismic Res Unit, Univ West Indies, 279 p ***(regional reference)***

Lindsay J M, Shepherd J B, 2005. Kick 'em Jenny & Ile de Caille. *In*: Lindsay J M, Robertson R E A, Shepherd J B, Ali S (eds). *Volcanic Hazard Atlas of the Lesser Antilles*, Trinidad and Tobago, Seismic Res Unit, Univ West Indies, p 107-126

Lindsay J M, Shepherd J B, Wilson D, 2005. Volcanic and scientific activity at Kick 'em Jenny submarine volcano 2001-2002: implications for volcanic hazard in the southern Grenadines, Lesser Antilles. *Nat Hazards*, 34: 1-24

Lindsay J M, Smith A L, Roobol M J, Stasiuk M V, 2005b. Dominica. *In*: Lindsay J M, Robertson R E A, Shepherd J B, Ali S (eds). *Volcanic Hazard Atlas of the Lesser Antilles*, Trinidad and Tobago, Seismic Res Unit, Univ West Indies, p 1-47

Lindsay J M, Stasiuk M V, Shepherd J B, 2003. Geological history and potential hazards of the late-Pleistocene to Recent Plat Pays volcanic complex, Dominica, Lesser Antilles. *Bull Volc*, 65: 201-220

Lindsay J M, Trumbull R B, Siebel W, 2005c. Geochemistry and petrogenesis of late Pleistocene to Recent volcanism in southern Dominica, Lesser Antilles. *J Volc Geotherm Res*, 148: 253-294

Loughlin S C, Baxter P J, Aspinall W P, Darroux B, Harford C L, Miller A D, 2002. Eyewitness accounts of the 25 June 1997 pyroclastic flows and surges at Soufreiere Hills volcano, Montserrat, and implications for disaster mitigation. *In*; Druitt T H, Kokellar B P (eds), The eruption of Soufriere Hills volcano, Montserrat, from 1995 to 1999, *Geol Soc London Mem*, 21: 211-230

Loughlin S C, Calder E S, Clarke A, Cole P D, Luckett R, Mangan M T, Pyle D M, Sparks R S J, Boight B, Watts R B, 2002. Pyroclastic flows and surges generated by the 25 June 1997 dome collapse, Soufriere HIlls volcano, Montserrat. *In*; Druitt T H, Kokellar B P (eds), The eruption of Soufriere Hills volcano, Montserrat, from 1995 to 1999, *Geol Soc London Mem*, 21: 191-209

Mas A, Guisseau D, Patrier Mas P, Beaufort D, Genter A, Sanjuan B, Girard J P, 2006. Clay minerals related to the hydrothermal activity of the Bouillante geothermal field (Guadeloupe). *J Volc Geotherm Res*, 158: 380-400

Mattiioli G S, Jansma P E, Jaramillo L, Smith A L, 1996. A desktop image processing and photogrammetric method for rapid volcanic hazard mapping: application to air-photo interpretation of Mount Pelee, Martinique. *Bull Volc*, 58: 401-410

Nicholls H A A, 1880. The volcanic eruption in Dominica. *Nature*, 21: 372-373

Perret F A, 1937. The eruption of Mt. Pelee 1929-1932. *Carnegie Inst Wash Pub*, 458: 1-126

Roberston R, 2005a. St. Kitts. *In*: Lindsay J M, Robertson R E A, Shepherd J B, Ali S (eds). *Volcanic Hazard Atlas of the Lesser Antilles*, Trinidad and Tobago, Seismic Res Unit, Univ West Indies, p 204-217

Robertson R, 2005. Grenada. *In*: Lindsay J M, Robertson R E A, Shepherd J B, Ali S (eds). *Volcanic Hazard Atlas of the Lesser Antilles*, Trinidad and Tobago, Seismic Res Unit, Univ West Indies, p 49-66

Robertson R, 2005b. St. Vincent. *In*: Lindsay J M, Robertson R E A, Shepherd J B, Ali S (eds). *Volcanic Hazard Atlas of the Lesser Antilles*, Trinidad and Tobago, Seismic Res Unit, Univ West Indies, p 240-261

Robertson R E A, 1995. An assessment of the risk from future eruptions of the Soufriere volcano of St. Vincent, West Indies. *Nat Hazards*, 11: 163-191

Robson G R, Tomblin J, 1966. West Indies. *Catalog of Active Volcanoes of the World and Solfatara Fields*, Rome: IAVCEI, 20: 1-56 ***(regional reference)***

Roobol M J, Smith A L, 1975. A comparison of the recent eruptions of Mt. Pelee, Martinique and Soufriere, St Vincent. *Bull Volc*, 39: 14-20

Roobol M J, Smith A L, 1976. A pattern of alternating eruptive styles. *Geology*, 4: 521-524

Roobol M J, Smith A L, 1989. Volcanic and associated hazards in the Lesser Antilles. *In*: Latter J H (ed), *Volcanic Hazards - Assessment and Monitoring*, Berlin: Springer-Verlag, p 57-85

Roobol M J, Smith A L, 1998. Pyroclastic stratigraphy of the Soufriere Hills volcano, Montserrat - implications for the present eruption. *Geophys Res Lett*, 25: 3393-3396

Roobol M J, Smith A L, 2004. *Volcanology of Saba and St. Eustatius, northern Lesser Antilles.* Amsterdam: Royal Netherlands Academy of Arts and Letters, 320 p

Roobol M J, Smith A L, Wright J V, 1981. Revisions in the pyroclastic stratigraphy of Mt. Misery volcano, St. Kitts, Lesser Antilles: 14-C ages and recognition of pyroclastic flow deposits. *J Geol Soc London*, 138: 713-718

Roobol M J, Smith A L, Wright J V, 1985. Dispersal and characteristics of pyroclastic fall deposits from Mt. Misery volcano, West Indies. *Geol Rundschau*, 74: 321-335

Roobol M J, Wright J V, Smith A L, 1983. Calderas of gravity-slide structures in the Lesser Antilles Island Arc? *J Volc Geotherm Res*, 19: 121-134

Rowley K C, 1978. Stratigraphy and geochemistry of the Soufriere volcano, St. Vincent, West Indies. *Unpublished PhD thesis*, Univ West Indies, 282 p

Samper A, Quidelleur X, Boudon G, Le Friant A, Komorowski J C, 2008. Radiometric dating of three large volume flank collapses in the Lesser Antilles arc. *J Volc Geotherm Res*, 176: 485-492

Seismic Research Unit, 2001. Seismo-volcanic activity in Dominica (updated July 11, 2001). Seismic Res Unit, Univ West Indies (http://www.uwiseismic.com/dominica.html)

Shepherd J B, 1989. Eruptions, eruption precursors and related phenomena in the Lesser Antilles. *In*: Latter J H (ed), *Volcanic Hazards - Assessment and Monitoring*, Berlin: Springer-Verlag, p 292-311

Shepherd J B, 2001. Volcanoes of the eastern Caribbean: past activity and future hazards. Paper presented at the Workshop on Volcanic and Seismic Hazards in the eastern Caribbean, May 28- June 1, 2001, 57 p

Shepherd J B, Aspinall W P, Rowley K C, Pereira J, Sigurdsson H, Fiske R S, Tomblin J F, 1979. The eruption of Soufriere volcano, St. Vincent April-June 1979. *Nature*, 282: 24-28

Shepherd J B, Sigurdsson H, 1982. Mechanism of the 1979 explosive eruption of Soufriere volcano, St. Vincent. *J Volc Geotherm Res*, 13: 119-130

Shepherd J B, Tomblin J F, Woo D A, 1971. Volcano-seismic crisis in Montserrat, West Indies. *Bull Volc*, 35: 143-163

Sheridan M F, 1980. Pyroclastic block flow from the September, 1976, eruption of La Soufriere volcano, Guadeloupe. *Bull Volc*, 43(2): 397-402

Sigurdsson H, 1972. Partly-welded pyroclast flow deposits in Dominica, Lesser Antilles. *Bull Volc*, 36: 148-163

Sigurdsson H, 1982. Tephra from the 1979 Soufriere explosive eruption. *Science*, 216: 1106-1108

Sigurdsson H, Shepherd J B, 1974. Amphibole-bearing basalts from the submarine volcano Kick'em Jenny in the Lesser Antilles Island Arc. *Bull Volc*, 38: 891-910

Sigurdsson H, Sparks R S J, 1979. An active submarine volcano. *Nat Hist*, 88: 38-43

Simpson K, 2005. Nevis. *In*: Lindsay J M, Robertson R E A, Shepherd J B, Ali S (eds). *Volcanic Hazard Atlas of the Lesser Antilles*, Trinidad and Tobago, Seismic Res Unit, Univ West Indies, p 169-178

Smith A L, Roobol M J, 1990. Mont Pelee, Martinique-A study of an active island arc volcano. *Geol Soc Amer Mem*, 175: 114 p

Smith A L, Roobol M J, 2005a. Saba. *In*: Lindsay J M, Robertson R E A, Shepherd J B, Ali S (eds). *Volcanic Hazard Atlas of the Lesser Antilles*, Trinidad and Tobago, Seismic Res Unit, Univ West Indies, p 179-190

Smith A L, Roobol M J, 2005b. St. Eustatius. *In*: Lindsay J M, Robertson R E A, Shepherd J B, Ali S (eds). *Volcanic Hazard Atlas of the Lesser Antilles*, Trinidad and Tobago, Seismic Res Unit, Univ West Indies, p 192-202

Sparks R S J, Barclay J, Calder E S, Herd A, Komorowski J-C, Luckett R, Norton G E, Ritchie L J, Voight B, Woods A W, 2002. Generation of a debris avalanche and violent pyroclastic density current on 26 December (Boxing Day) 1997 at Soufriere Hills volcano, Montserrat. *In*: Druitt T H, Kokellar B P (eds), The eruption of Soufriere Hills volcano, Montserrat, from 1995 to 1999, *Geol Soc London Mem*, 21: 409-434

Sparks R S J, Young S R, 2002. The eruption of Soufriere Hills volcano, Montserrat (1995-1999): overview of scientific results. *In*; Druitt T H, Kokellar B P (eds), The eruption of Soufriere Hills volcano, Montserrat, from 1995 to 1999, *Geol Soc London Mem*, 21: 45-69

Tanguy J C, 1994. The 1902-1905 eruptions of Montagne Pelee, Martinique: anatomy and retrospection. *J Volc Geotherm Res*, 60: 87-107

Tanguy J-C, 2004. Rapid dome growth at Montagne Pelee during the early stages of the 1902-1905 eruption: a reconstruction from Lacroix's data. *Bull Volc*, 66: 615-621

Tomblin J F, 1975. The Lesser Antilles and Aves Ridge. *In*: Nairn A E M, Stehli F G (eds) *The Ocean Basins and Margins*, 3: 467-500

Traineau H, Westercamp D, Bardintzeff J-M, Miskovsky J-C, 1989. The recent pumice eruptions of Mt. Pelee volcano, Martinique, Part I: depositional sequences, description of pumiceous deposits. *J Volc Geotherm Res*, 38: 17-32

Univ West Indies Seismic Res Unit, 1999-. Kick 'em Jenny submarine volcano. http://www.uwiseismic.com/kejtitle.html (20 April 2001, 25 Mar 2003)

Vincent P M, Bourdier J L, Boudon G, 1989. The primitive volcano of Mount Pelee: Its construction and partial destruction by flank collapse. *J Volc Geotherm Res*, 38: 1-15

Voight B, Komorowski J-C, Norton G E, Belousov A B, Belousova M, Boudon G, Francis P W, Franz W, Heinrich P, Sparks R S J, Young S R, 2002. The 26 December (Boxing Day) 1997 sector collapse and debris avalanche at Soufriere Hills volcano, Montserrat. *In*; Druitt T H, Kokellar B P (eds), The eruption of Soufriere Hills volcano, Montserrat, from 1995 to 1999, *Geol Soc London Mem*, 21: 363-407

Wadge G, 1985. Morne Patates volcano, southern Dominica, Lesser Antilles. *Geol Mag*, 122: 253-260

Wadge G, Isaacs M C, 1988. Mapping the volcanic hazards from Soufriere Hills volcano, Montserrat, West Indies using an image processor. *J Geol Soc London*, 145: 541-551

Wadge G, Wooden J L, 1982. Late Cenozoic alkaline volcanism in the northwestern Caribbean: tectonic setting and Sr isotopic characteristics. *Earth Planet Sci Lett*, 57: 35-46

Watts R B, Herd R A, Sparks R S J, Young S R, 2002. Growth patterns and emplacement of the andesitic lava dome at Soufriere Hills volcano, Montserrat. *In*; Druitt T H, Kokellar B P (eds), The eruption of Soufriere Hills volcano, Montserrat, from 1995 to 1999, *Geol Soc London Mem*, 21: 115-152

Westercamp D, 1980. Une methode d'evaluation et de zonation des risques volcaniques a la Soufriere de Guadeloupe, Antilles Francaises. *Bull Volc*, 43: 431-452

Westercamp D, Traineau H, 1983. The past 5,000 Years of volcanic activity at Mt. Pelee, Martinique, (FWI): implications for assessment of volcanic hazards. *J Volc Geotherm Res*, 17: 159-186

Wohletz K, Heiken G, Ander M, Goff F, Vuataz F-D, Wadge G, 1986. The Qualibu caldera, St. Lucia, West Indies. *J Volc Geotherm Res*, 27: 77-117

Young S R, Sparks R S J, Aspinall W P, Lynch L L, Miller A D, Roberston R E, Shepherd J B, 1998. Overview of the eruption of Soufriere HIlls volcano, Montserrat, 18 July 1995 to December 1997. *Geophys Res Lett*, 25: 3389-3392

Zellmer G F, Hawkesworth C J, Sparks R S J, Thomas L E, Harford C L, Brewer T S, Loughlin S C, 2003. Geochemical evolution of the Soufriere Hills volcano, Montserrat, Lesser Antilles volcanic arc. *J Petr*, 44: 1349-1374

Zlotnicki J, Boudon G, Viode J P, Delarue J F, Mille A, Bruere F, 1998. Hydrothermal circulation beneath Mount Pelee inferred by self potential surveying. Structural and tectonic implications. *J Volc Geotherm Res*, 84: 73-91

ICELAND (1700-05)

Andrew R E B, Gudmundsson A, 2007. Distribution, structure, and formation of Holocene lava shields in Iceland. *J Volc Geotherm Res*, 168: 137-154

Baldridge W S, McGretchin T R, Frey F A, 1973. Magmatic evolution of Heckla, Iceland. *Contr Mineral Petr*, 42: 245-258

Bardason T, 1990. Lava flows near Snaefellsjokull. *Rannsoknarverkefni Hakoli Islands*, 17 p (in Icelandic)

Barth T F W, 1950. Volcanic geology, hot springs, and geysers of Iceland. *Carnegie Inst Wash Pub*, 587: 1-126

Benjaminsson J, 1981. Tephra layer-A. *In*: Self S and Sparks R (eds) *Tephra Studies*, Dordrecht, Holland: Reidel, p 331-336

Berninghausen W H, 1964. A checklist of Icelandic volcanic activity. *Bull Seism Soc Amer*, 54: 443-450

Bjornsson A, Saemundsson K, Einarsson P, Tryggvason E, Gronvold K, 1977. Current rifting episode in North Iceland. *Nature*, 266: 318-323

Bjornsson H, Einarsson P, 1990. Volcanoes beneath Vatnajokull, Iceland: evidence from radio echo-sounding, earthquakes and jokulhlaups. *Jokull*, 40: 147-168

Bjornsson H, Kristmannsdottir H, 1984. The Grimsvotn geothermal area, Vatnajokull, Iceland. *Jokull*, 34: 25-50

Bjornsson H, Palsson F, Gudmundsson M T, 2000. Surface and bedrock topography of the Myrdalsjokull ice cap, Iceland: the Katla caldera, eruptions sites and routes of jokulhlaups. *Jokull*, 49: 29-46

Bonadonna C, Houghton B F, 2005. Total grain-size distribution and volume of tephra-fall deposits. *Bull Volc*, 67: 441-456

Botz R, Winckler G, Bayer R, Schmitt M, Schmidt M, Garbe-Schonberg D, Stoffers P, Kristjansson J K, 1999. Origin of trace gases in submarine hydrothermal vents of the Kolbeinsey Ridge, north Iceland. *Earth Planet Sci Lett*, 171: 83-93

Bourgeois O, Dauteuil O, Van Vliet-Lanoe B, 1998. Pleistocene subglacial volcanism in Iceland: tectonic implications. *Earth Planet Sci Lett*, 164: 165-178

Brandsdottir B, 1984. Seismic activity in Vatnajokull in 1900-1982 with special reference to

Skeidararhlaups, Skaftarhlaups and Vatnajokull eruptions. *Jokull*, 34: 141-150

Calderone G M, Gronvold K, Oskarsson N, 1990. The welded air-fall tuff layer at Krafla, northern Iceland: a composite eruption triggered by injection of basaltic magma. *J Volc Geotherm Res*, 44: 303-314

Carey R J, Houghton B F, Thordarson T, 2008. Contrasting styles of welding observed in the proximal Askja 1875 eruption deposits I: Regional welding. *J Volc Geotherm Res*, 171: 1-19

Clifton A E, Sigmundsson F, Feigl K L, Gudmundsson G, Arnadottir T, 2002. Surface effects of faulting and deformation resulting from magma accumulation at the Hengill triple junction, SW Iceland, 1994-1998. *J Volc Geotherm Res*, 115: 233-255

Coppola D, Staudacher Th, Cigolini C, 2005. The May-July 2003 eruption at Piton de la Fournaise (La Reunion): volume, effusion rates, and emplacement mechanisms inferred from thermal imaging and Global Positioning System (GPS) survey. *In*: Manga M, Ventura G (eds) Kinematics and dynamics of lava flows, *Geol Soc Amer Spec Pap*, 396: 103-124

de Zeeuw-van Dalfsen E, Rymer H, Sigmundsson F, Sturkell E, 2005. Net gravity decrease at Askja volcano, Iceland: constrainsts on processes responsible for continuous caldera deflation, 1988-2003. *J Volc Geotherm Res*, 139: 227-239

Eason D E, Sinton J M, 2009. Lava shields and fissure eruptions of the Western Volcanic Zone, Iceland: evidence for magma chambers and crustal interaction. *J Volc Geotherm Res*, 186: 331-348

Einarsson E H, Larsen G, Thorarinsson S, 1980. The Solheimar tephra layer and the Katla eruption of ca. 1357. *Acta Nat Islandica*, 3: 1-24

Einarsson S, Johannesson H, 1989. The age of Arnarsetur lava on the Reykjanes Peninsula. *Fjolrit Natturufraedistofnunar*, no 8 (in Icelandic with English summary)

Einarsson T, 1960. The geology of Hellisheidi. *Natturufraedingurinn*, 30: 151-175 (in Icelandic)

Einarsson T, 1974. *The Heimaey Eruption in Words and Pictures*. Reykjavik: Heimskringla, 88 p

Eliasson S, 1979. Kerlingarholar, old eruptive fissures on the Krafla fault swarm. *Natturufraedingurinn*, 49: 51-63 (in Icelandic with English summary)

Flude S, Burgess R, McGarvie D W, 2008. Silicic volcanism at Ljosufjoll, Iceland: insights into evolution and eruptive history from Ar-Ar dating. *J Volc Geotherm Res*, 169: 154-175

Foulger G R, 1995. The Hengill geothermal area, Iceland: variation of temperature gradients deduced frm the maximum depth of seismogenesis. *J Volc Geotherm Res*, 65: 119-133

Gilbert J S, Stasiuk M V, Lane S J, Adam C R, Murphy M D, Sparks R S J, Naranjo J A, 1996. Non-explosive, constructional evolution of the ice-filled caldera at Volcan Sollipulli, Chile. *Bull Volc*, 58: 67-83

Gronvold K, 1984. Myvatn fires 1724-1729, chemical composition of the lava. *Nordic Volc Inst Univ Iceland*, no 8401, 24p

Gronvold K, Johannesson H, 1984. Eruption in Grimsvotn 1983; course of events and chemical studies of tephra. *Jokull*, 34: 1-11

Gronvold K, Larsen G, Einarsson P, Thorarinsson S, Saemundsson K, 1983. The Hekla eruption of 1980-1981. *Bull Volc*, 46: 349-364

Gudmundsson A T, 1986a. Eruptions at Dyngjuhals in the 18th century. *Natturufraedingurinn*, 56: 43-48 (in Icelandic with English summary)

Gudmundsson A T, 1986b. *Iceland-Fires*. Reykjavik: Vaka-Helgafell, 168 p ***(regional reference)***

Gudmundsson A, Backstrom K, 1991. Structure and development of the Sveinagja graben, northeast Iceland. *Tectonophysics*, 200: 111-125

Gudmundsson M T, Bjornsson H, 1991. Eruptions in Grimsvotn, Vatnajokull, Iceland, 1934-1991. *Jokull*, 41: 21-45

Gudmundsson A, Oskarsson N, Gronvold K, Saemundsson K, Sigurdsson O, Stefansson R, Gislason S R, Einarsson P, Brandsdottir B, Larsen G, Johannesson H, Thordarson T, 1992. The 1991 eruption of Hekla, Iceland. *Bull Volc*, 54: 238-246

Gudmundsson G, Saemundsson K, 1980. Statistical analysis of damaging earthquakes and volcanic eruptions in Iceland from 1550-1978. *J Geophys Res*, 47: 99-109

Gudmundsson M T, Larsen G, Hoskuldsson A, Gylfason A G, 2008. Volcanic hazards in Iceland. *Jokull*, 58: 251-268

Gudmundsson M T, Sigmundsson F, Bjornsson H, 1997. Ice-volcano interaction of the 1996 Gjalp subglacial eruption, Vatnajokull, Iceland. *Nature*, 389: 954-957

Gudmundsson M T, Sigmundsson F, Bjornsson H, Hognadottir T, 2004. The 1996 eruption at Gjalp, Vatnajokull ice cap, Iceland: efficiency of heat transfer, ice deformation and subglacial water pressure. *Bull Volc*, 66: 46-65

Gunnarsson B, Marsh B D, Taylor H P Jr, 1998. Generation of Icelandic rhyolites: silicic lavas from the Torfajokull central volcano. *J Volc Geotherm Res*, 83: 1-45

Gunnlaugsson G A, Gudbergsson G M, Thorarinsson S, Rafnsson S, Einarsson T (eds), 1984. *Skaftareldar 1783-1784*. Reykjavik: Mal og Menning, 442 p (in Icelandic, with English summaries)

Hammer C U, 1984. Traces of Icelandic eruptions in the Greenland ice sheet. *Jokull*, 34: 51-65

Hansteen T H, 1991. Multi-stage evolution of the picritic Maelifell rocks, SW Iceland: constraints from mineralogy and inclusions of glass and fluid in olivine. *Contr Mineral Petr*, 109: 225-239

Hjartardottir A R, Páll Einarsson P, Sigurdsson H, 2009. The fissure swarm of the Askja volcanic system along the divergent plate boundary of N Iceland. *Bull Volc*, 71: 961-975

Hjartarson A, 1988. The Thorsa lava-the largest Holocene lava flow on earth. *Natturufraedingurinn*, 58: 1-16 (in Icelandic with English summary)

Holm F, Tronnes R G, Gronvold K, Torfason H, 2003. Petrology and geochemistry of the Esjufjoll central volcano, SE Iceland. *Summer School Tectonic-Magmatic Interaction, 31 August - 8 September, 2003, Geysir, South Iceland, Abs vol, Nordic Volc Inst Rep 0303*, p 20-21

Hoskuldsson A, Oskarsson N, Pedersen R, Gronvold K, Vogfjord K, Olafsdottir R, 2007. The millennium eruption of Hekla in February 2000. *Bull Volc*, 70: 169-182

Hoskuldsson A, Sparks R S J, Carroll M R, 2006. Constraints on the dynamics of subglacial basalt eruptions from geological and geochemical observations at Kverkfjoll, NE-Iceland. *Bull Volc*, 68: 689-701

Hunton D E, Viggiano A A, Miller T M, Ballenthin J O, Reeves J M, Wilson J C, Lee S-H, Anderson B E, Brune W H, Harder H, Simpas J B, Oskarsson N, 2005. In-situ aircraft observations of the 2000 Mt. Hekla volcanic cloud: compostion and chemical evolution in the Arctic lower stratosphere. *J Volc Geotherm Res*, 145: 23-34

Ivarsson G, 1998. Fumarole gas geochemistry in estimating subsurface temperatures at Hengill in southwestern Iceland. *In*: Arehart G B, Hulston J R (eds), *Water-Rock Interaction*, Rotterdam: Balkema, p 459-462

Jakobsson S P, 1966. The Grimsnes lavas SW-Iceland. *Acta Nat Islandica*, 2: 6-30

Jakobsson S P, 1972. Chemistry and distribution pattern of recent basaltic rocks in Iceland. *Lithos*, 5: 365-386

Jakobsson S P, 1974. Eruption at Eldeyjarbodi. *Natturufraedingurinn*, 44: 22-40 (in Icelandic with English summary)

Jakobsson S P, 1976. The age of the Grimsnes lavas. *Natturufraedingurinn*, 46: 153-162 (in Icelandic)

Jakobsson S P, 1979. Petrology of recent basalts of the eastern volcanic zone, Iceland. *Acta Nat Islandica*, 26: 1-103

Jakobsson S P, Jonasson K, Sigurdsson I A, 2008. The three igneous rock series of Iceland. *Jokull*, 58: 117-138

Jakobsson S P, Jonsson J, Shido F, 1978. Petrology of the western Reykjanes Peninsula, Iceland. *J Petr*, 19: 669-705

Jakobsson S P, Pedersen A K, Ronsbo J G, Melchior Larsen L, 1973. Petrology of mugearite-hawaiite: early extrusives in the 1973 Heimaey eruption, Iceland. *Lithos*, 6: 203-214

Jarosch A, Gudmundsson M T, Hognadottir T, Axelsson G, 2008. Progressive cooling of the hyaloclastic ridge at Gjalp, Iceland, 1996-2005. *J Volc Geotherm Res*, 170: 218-229

Jenness M H, Clifton A E, 2009. Controls on the geometry of a Holocene crater row: a field study from southwest Iceland. *Bull Volc*, 71: 715-528

Johannesson H, 1977. There is not the farm, where now is the Eldborg crater. *Natturufraedingurinn*, 47: 129-141 (in Icelandic with English summary)

Johannesson H, 1982. Summary of the geology of Snaefellsnes. *Arbok Ferdafelags Islands 1982*, p 151-172 (in Icelandic)

Johannesson H, 1983. Submarine eruption off the Vestmannaeyjar Islands in 1637-38. *Natturufraedingurinn*, 52: 33-36 (in Icelandic with English summary)

Johannesson H, 1984. The Grimsvotn eruption 1933 and more from that year. *Jokull*, 34: 151-158 (in Icelandic with English summary)

Johannesson H, 1985. The endless lavas at the foot of Eyjafjoll and glaciers of the last glaciation. *Jokull*, 35: 83-95 (in Icelandic with English summary)

Johannesson H, 1987. Grimsvotn eruption in 1816. *Natturufraedingurinn*, 57: 157-159 (in Icelandic with English summary)

Johannesson H, 1989. Age of the Hallmundarhraun lava flow in Borgarfjordur. *Fjolrit Natturufraedistofnunar*, 9: 1-12 (in Icelandic with English summary)

Johannesson H, Einarsson S, 1988a. Krisuvik eruptions 1. Age of the Ogmundarhraun lava flow and the medieval tephra layer, Reykjanes Peninsula, southwest Iceland. *Jokull*, 38: 71-87 (in Icelandic with English summary)

Johannesson H, Einarsson S, 1988b. The age of Illahraun at Svartsengi. *Fjolrit Natturufraedistofnunar*, 7: 1-11 (in Icelandic with English summary)

Johannesson H, Flores R M, Jonsson J, 1981. A short account of the Holocene tephrochronology of the Snaefellsjokull central volcano, western Iceland. *Jokull*, 9: 23-30

Johannesson H, Jakobsson S P, Saemundsson K, 1982. Geological map of Iceland, sheet 6, south Iceland. *Icelandic Museum Nat Hist & Iceland Geodetic Surv*, 1:250,000 geol map, 2nd edition

Johannesson H, Saemundsson K, 1998. Geological map of Iceland, 1:500,000. Tectonics. *Icelandic Inst Nat Hist, Reykjavik*

Johannesson H, Saemundsson K, 1998. Geological map of Iceland 1:500,000, Tectonics. *Icelandic Inst Nat Hist, Reykjavik*

Johannsdottir G E, Thordarson T, Larsen G, 2004. The widespread ~10 ka Saksunarvatn tephra: a product of large-scale basaltic phreatoplinian eruption? *IAVCEI Chile Gen Assembly, Pucon 2004*, abs S12_o_03

Johannsson M, 1959. An autumn excursion to Vatnajokull 1959. *Jokull*, 9: 41-42

Jonasson K, 1994. Rhyolite volcanism in the Krafla central volcano, north-east Iceland. *Bull Volc*, 56: 516-528

Jonasson K, 2005. Magmatic evolution of the Heidarspordur ridge, NE-Iceland. *J Volc Geotherm Res*, 147: 109-124

Jonsson J, 1972. Eldborgir undir Geitahlid. *Natturufraedingurinn*, 42: 59-66 (in Icelandic)

Jonsson J, 1974. Obrinnisholar. *Natturufraedingurinn*, 44: 109-119 (in Icelandic)

Jonsson J, 1975. A few datings. *Natturufraedingurinn*, 45: 27-20 (in Icelandic)

Jonsson J, 1977a. Reykjafellsgigir and Skardsmnyrihraun on Hellisheidi. *Natturufraedingurinn*, 47: 17-26 (in Icelandic)

Jonsson J, 1977b. Tvi-Bollar and Tvibollahraun. *Natturufraedingurinn*, 47: 103-109 (in Icelandic)

Jonsson J, 1978. Geology of the Reykjanes Peninsula. *Orkustofnun Jardhitadeild*, OS-JHD-7831, Geol maps and 303 p text (in Icelandic)

Jonsson J, 1979a. On the age of the Svinahraun lava flow. *Natturufraedingurinn*, 49: 46-50 (in Icelandic with English summary)

Jonsson J, 1979b. Volcanoes and lava flows in Skaftafellssysla. *Natturufraedingurinn*, 48: 196-232 (in Icelandic with English summary)

Jonsson J, 1983. Volcanic eruptions in historical time on the Reykjanes Peninsula, southwest Iceland. *Natturufraedingurinn*, 52: 127-139 (in Icelandic with English summary)

Jonsson J, 1986. The lava flow at Lanbagja. *Natturufraedingurinn*, 56: 209-212 (in Icelandic with English summary)

Jonsson J, 1987. The Eldgjar eruption and the Landbrot lava. *Natturufraedingurinn*, 57: 1-20 (in Icelandic with English summary)

Kjartansson G, 1964. *Geological Map of Iceland, Sheet 5, Central Iceland*. Reykjavik: Museum Nat Hist Dept Geol Geog, 1:250,000 geol map

Kjartansson G, 1966. The volume of shield volcano lavas. *Natturufraedingurinn*, 36: 125 (in Icelandic)

Kjartansson G, 1968. Geological map of Iceland, sheet 2, west-central Iceland. *Icelandic Museum Nat Hist*, 1:250,000 geol map

Kjartansson G, 1972. The Burfellshraun lava flow and its age. *Natturufraedingurinn*, 42: 159-183 (in Icelandic with English summary)

Konstantinou K I, Nolet G, Morgan W J, Allen R M, Pritchard M J, 2000. Seismic phenomena associated with the 1996 Vatnajokull eruption, central Iceland. *J Volc Geotherm Res*, 102: 169-187

Krafft M, 1974. *Guide des Volcans d'Europe*. Neuchatel: Delachaux & Niestle, 412 p ***(regional reference)***

Krafft M, Dominique de Larouziere F, 1991. *Guide des Volcans d'Europe et des Canaries*. Lausanne, Switzerland: Delachaux and Niestle, 455 p

Kristmannsdottir H, Bhornsson A, Palsson S, Sveinbjornsdottir A E, 1999. The impact of the 1996 subglacial volcanic eruption in Vatnajokull on the river Jokulsa a Fjollum, North Iceland. *J Volc Geotherm Res*, 92: 359-372

Lacasse C, Garbe-Schonberg C-D, 2001. Explosive silicic volcanism in Iceland and the Jan Mayen area during the last 6 Ma: sources and timing of major eruptions. *J Volc Geotherm Res*, 107: 113-147

Lacasse C, Karlsdottir S, Larsen G, Soosalu H, Rose W I, Ernst G G J, 2004. Weather radar observations of the Hekla 2000 eruption cloud, Iceland. *Bull Volc*, 66: 457-473

Lacasse C, Sigurdsson H, Carey S N, Johannesson H, Thomas L E, Rogers N W, 2007. Bimodal volcanism at the Katla subglacial caldera, Iceland: insight into the geochemistry and petrogenesis of rhyolitic magmas. *Bull Volc*, 69: 373-399

Lacasse C, Sigurdsson H, Johannesson H, Paterne M, Carey S, 1995. Source of Ash Zone 1 in the North Atlantic. *Bull Volc*, 57: 18-32

Lackschewitz K S, Dehn J, Wallrabe-Adams H-J, 1994. Volcaniclastic sediments from mid-oceanic Kolbeinsey Ridge, north of Iceland: evidence for submarine volcanic fragmentation processes. *Geology*, 22: 975-978

Larsen G, 1979. The age of Eldgja lavas. *Natturufraedingurinn*, 49: 1-26 (in Icelandic with English summary)

Larsen G, 1984. Recent volcanic history of the Veidivotn fissure swarm, southern Iceland - an approach to volcanic risk assessment. *J Volc Geotherm Res*, 22: 33-58

Larsen G, 1986. Phreatomagmatic eruptions in Iceland: two case histories. *IAVCEI 1986 Cong, New Zeal, Abs*, p 110

Larsen G, 2000. Holocene eruptions within the Katla volcanic system, south Iceland: characteristics and environmental impact. *Jokull*, 49: 1-28

Larsen G, Eriksson J, 2008. Holocene tephra archives and tephrochronology in Iceland - a brief overview. *Jokull*, 58: 229-250

Larsen G, Gronvold K, Thorarinsson S, 1979. Volcanic eruption through a geothermal borehole at Namafjall, Iceland. *Nature*, 278: 707-710

Larsen G, Gudmundsson M T, Bjornsson H, 1998. Eight centuries of periodic volcanism at the center of the hotspot revealed by glacier tephrostratigraphy. *Geology*, 26: 943-946

Larsen G, Newton A J, Dugmore A J, Vilmundardottir E G, 2001. Geochemistry, dispersal, volumes and chronology of Holocene silicic tephra layers from the Katla volcanic system, Iceland. *J Quat Sci*, 16: 119-132

Larsen G, Thorarinsson S, 1977. H4 and other acid Hekla tephra layers. *Jokull*, 27: 1-19

Leys C A, 1983. Volcanic and sedimentary processes during formation of the Saefell tuff-ring, Iceland. *Trans Roy Soc Edinburgh: Earth Sci*, 74: 15-22

MacDonald R, McGarvie D W, Pinkerton H, Smith R L, Palacz Z A, 1990. Petrogenetic evolution of the Torfajokull Volcanic Complex, Iceland I. Relationship between the magma types. *J Petr*, 31: 429-459

Mattsson H B, Hoskuldsson A, 2005. Eruption reconstruction, formation of flow-lobe tumuli and eruption duration in the 5900 BP Helgafell lava field (Heimaey), south Iceland. *J Volc Geotherm Res*, 147: 157-172

Mattsson H B, Hoskuldsson A, Hand S, 2005. Crustal xenoliths in the 6220 BP Saefell tuff-cone, south Iceland: evidence for a deep, diatreme-forming, Surtseyan eruption. *J Volc Geotherm Res*, 145: 234-248

Mattsson H, Hoskuldsson A, 2003. Geology of the Heimaey volcanic centre, south Iceland: early evolution of a central volcano in a propagating rift? *J Volc Geotherm Res*, 127: 55-71

McGarvie D M, MacDonald R, Pinkerton H, Smith R L, 1990. Petrogenetic evolution of the Torfajokull Volcanic Complex, Iceland II. The role of magma mixing. *J Petr*, 31: 461-481

McGarvie D W, Burgess R, Tindle A G, Tuffen H, Stevenson J A, 2006. Pleistocene rhyolitic volcanism at Torfajokull, Iceland: eruption ages, glaciovolcanism, and geochemical evolution. *Jokull*, 56: 57-75

Miller J, 1989. The 10th century eruption of Eldgja, southern Iceland. *Nordic Volc Inst Univ Iceland*, no 8903, 29p

Moore J G, Calk L C, 1991. Degassing and differentiation in subglacial volcanoes, Iceland. *J Volc Geotherm Res*, 46: 157-180

Mork M E, 1984. Magma mixing in the post-glacial Veidivotn fissure eruption, southeast Iceland: a microprobe study of mineral and glass variations. *Lithos*, 17: 55-75

Oladottir B A, Larsen G, Thordarson T, Sigmarsson O, 2005. The Katla volcano S-Iceland: Holocene tephra stratigraphy and eruption frequency. *Jokull*, 55: 53-74

Oladottir B A, Sigmarsson O, Larsen G, Thordarson T, 2008. Katla volcano, Iceland: magma composition, dynamics and eruption frequency as recorded by Holocene tephra layers. *Bull Volc*, 70: 475-493

Oskarsson B V, 2009. The Skerin ridge on Eyjafjallajökull, south Iceland: morphology and magma-ice interaction in an ice-confined silicic fissure eruption. *Unpublished MSci thesis*, Univ Iceland, 111 p

Pasvanoglu S, Kristmannsdottir H, Bjornsson S, Torfason H, 2000. Geochemical study of the Geysir geothermal field in Haukadalur, S-Iceland. *Proc World Geotherm Cong 2000, Kyushu - Tohoku, Japan, May 28 - June 10, 2000*, p 675-680

Pedersen R, Sigmundsson F, 2006. Temporal development of the 1999 intrusive episode in the Eyjafjallajokull volcano, Iceland, derived from InSAR images. *Bull Volc*, 68: 377-393

Pilcher J R, Hall V A, McCormac F G, 1996. An outline tephrochronology for the Holocene of the north of Ireland. *J Quat Sci*, 11: 485-494

Piper J D A, 1973. Volcanic history and tectonics of the North Langjokull region central Iceland. *Can J Earth Sci*, 10: 164-179

Riedel C, Petersen T, Theilen F, Neben S, 2003. High b-values in the leaky segment of the Tjornes Fracture Zone north of Iceland: are they evidence for shallow magmatic heat sources? *J Volc Geotherm Res*, 128: 15-29

Russell W S C, 1917. Askja, a volcano in the interior of Iceland. *Geog Rev*, 3: 212-221

Saemundsson K, 1965. On the geologic history of Thingvallavatn. *Natturufraedingurinn*, 35: 103-144 (in Icelandic with German summary)

Saemundsson K, 1967. Vulkanismus und Tektonik des Hengill-Gebietes in Sudwest-Island. *Acta Nat Islandica*, 2: 1-105

Saemundsson K, 1972. Notes on the geology of the Torfajokull central volcano. *Natturufraedingurinn*, 42: 81-89 (in Icelandic with English summary)

Saemundsson K, 1974. Evolution of the axial rifting zone in northern Iceland and the Tjornes Fracture Zone. *Geol Soc Amer Bull*, 85: 495-504

Saemundsson K, 1982. Excursion guide and road log for field trips A and B. *IAVCEI/IAGC 1982 Sci Assembly, Reykjavik, Generation of Major Basalt Types*

Saemundsson K, 1988. The geology of the Torfajokull region. *Arbok Ferdafelags Islands 1988*, p 164-180

Saemundsson K, 1991. The geology of the Krafla area. *In*: Gardarsson A and Einarsson A (eds) *Natural History of Lake Myvatn*, Reykjavik: Hid Islenska Natturufraedifelag, p 25-95 (in Icelandic)

Saemundsson K, 1992. Geology of the Thingvallavatn area. *Oikos*, 64: 40-68

Saemundsson K, Einarsson S, 1980. Geological map of Iceland, sheet 3, south-west Iceland. *Icelandic Museum Nat Hist & Iceland Geodetic Surv*, 1:250,000 geol map

Saemundsson K, Hjartarson A, 1994. Geology and erosion of Kolbeinsey north of Iceland. *In*: Vigoson G (ed), *Proc Hornafjorlur Internat Coastal Symp, Reykjavik*, p 443-451

Scharrer K, Spieler O, Mayer C, Munzer U, 2008. Imprints of sub-glacial volcanic activity on a glacier surface-SAR study of Katla volcano, Iceland. *Bull Volc*, 70: 495-506

Selbekk R S, Tronnes R G, 2007. The 1362 AD Oraefajokull eruption, Iceland: petrology and geochemistry of large-volume homogeneous rhyolite. *J Volc Geotherm Res*, 160: 42-58

Sharma K, Self S, Blake S, Thordarson T, Larsen G, 2008. The AD Oraefajokull eruption, S.E. Iceland: physical volcanology and volatile release. *J Volc Geotherm Res*, 178: 719-739

Sigbjarnarson G, 1988. *Krepputunga and Bruardalir-Explanatory Text to Geologic Map*. Reykjavik: Orkustofnun OS-88038/VOD-06, 44 p (in Icelandic with English summary)

Sigmarsson O, Condomines M, Fourcade S, 1992. A detailed Th, Sr and O isotope study of Hekla: differentiation processes in an Icelandic Volcano. *Contr Mineral Petr*, 112: 20-34

Sigmarsson O, Karlsson H R, Larsen G, 2000. The 1996 and 1998 subglacial eruptions beneath the Vatnajokull ice sheet in Iceland: contrasting geochemical and geophysical inferences on magma migration. *Bull Volc*, 61: 468-476

Sigmundsson F, Einarsson P, Rognvaldsson S T, Foulger G R, Hodgkinson K M, Gunnar Thorbergsson G, 1997. The 1994-1995 seismicity and deformation at the Hengill triple junction, Iceland: triggering of earthquakes by minor magma injection in a zone of horizontal shear stress. *J Geophys Res*, 102: 15,151-15,161

Sigurdsson H, Sparks R S J, 1978. Rifting episode in North Iceland in 1874-1875 and the eruptions of Askja and Sveinagja. *Bull Volc*, 41: 149-167

Sigurgeirsson M A, 1992. Tephra fall formations on the Reykjanes Peninsula. *Unpublished MSci thesis*, Univ Iceland, 114 p

Sigvaldason G E, 1979. Rifting, magmatic activity, and interaction between acid and basic liquids. *Nordic Volc Inst Univ Iceland*, no 7903, 43p

Sigvaldason G E, 1992. Recent hydrothermal explosion craters in an old hyaloclastite flow, central Iceland. *J Volc Geotherm Res*, 54: 53-63

Sigvaldason G E, 2002. Volcanic and tectonic processes coinciding with glaciation and crustral rebound: an early Holocene rhyolitic eruption in the Dyngjufjoll volcanic centre and the formation of the Askja caldera, Iceland. *Bull Volc*, 64: 192-205

Sigvaldason G E, Annertz K, Nilsson M, 1992. Effect of glacier loading/deloading on volcanism: postglacial volcanic production rate of the Dyngjufjoll area, central Iceland. *Bull Volc*, 54: 385-392

Sinton J, Gronvold K, Saemundsson K, 2005. Postglacial eruptive history of the Western Volcanic Zone, Iceland. *Geochem Geophys Geosyst*, 6(12): 10.1029/2005CG001021

Skilling I P, 2009. Subglacial to emergent basaltic volcanism at Hlodufell, south-west Iceland: a history of ice-confinement. *J Volc Geotherm Res*, 185: 276-289

Slater L, McKenzie D, Gronvold K, Shimizu N, 2001. Melt generation and movement beneath Theistareykir, NE Iceland. *J Petr*, 42: 321-254

Soosalu H, Einarsson P, 1997. Seismicity around the Hekla and Torfajokull volcanoes, Iceland, during a volcanically quiet period, 1991-1995. *Bull Volc*, 59: 36-48

Soosalu H, Einarsson P, 2002. Earthquake activity related to the 1991 eruption of the Hekla volcano, Iceland. *Bull Volc*, 63: 536-544

Soosalu H, Einarsson P, 2004. Seismic constraints on magma chambers at Hekla and Torfajokull volcanoes, Iceland. *Bull Volc*, 66: 276-286

Soosalu H, Einarsson P, Jakobsdottir S, 2003. Volcanic tremor related to the 1991 eruption of the Hekla volcano, Iceland. *Bull Volc*, 65: 562-577

Soosalu H, Einarsson P, Thorbjarnadottir B S, 2005. Seismic activity related to the 2000 eruption of the Hekla volcano, Iceland. *Bull Volc*, 68: 21-36

Soosalu H, Jonsdottir K, Einarsson P, 2006. Seismicity crisis at the Katla volcano, Iceland-signs of a cryptodome? *J Volc Geotherm Res*, 153: 177-186

Steinthorsson S, 1967. Two new C-14 datings on tephra from Snaefellsjokull. *Natturufraedingurinn*, 37: 236-238 (in Icelandic with English abs)

Steinthorsson S, 1977. Tephra layers in a drill core from the Vatnajokull ice cap. *Jokull*, 27: 2-27

Steinthorsson S, Oskarsson N, 1983. Chemical monitoring of jokullhlaup water in Skeidara and the geothermal system in Grimsvotn, Iceland. *Jokull*, 33: 73-86

Steinthorsson S, et al., 2002. *Catalog of Active Volcanoes of the World - Iceland. Unpublished manuscript*

Stevenson J A, McGarvie D W, Smellie J L, Gilbert J S, 2006. Subglacial and ice-contact volcanism at the Oraefajokull stratovolcano, Iceland. *Bull Volc*, 68: 737-752

Stevenson J A, Smellie J L, McGarvie D W, Gilbert J S, Cameron B I, 2009. Subglacial intermediate volcanism at Kerlingarfjoll, Iceland: magma-water interactions beneath thick ice. *J Volc Geotherm Res*, 185: 337-351

Stracke A, Zindler A, Salters V J M, McKenzie D, Gronvold K, 2003. The dynamics of melting beneath Theistareykir, northern Iceland. *Geochem Geophys Geosyst*, 4: doi:10.1029/2002GC000347

Sturkell E, Sigmundsson F, 2000. Continuous deflation of the Askja caldera, Iceland, during the 1983-1998 noneruptive period. *J Geophys Res*, 105: 25,671-25,684

Theilig E, Greeley R, 1986. Lava flows on Mars: analysis of small surface features and comparisons with terrestrial analogs. *J Geophys Res*, 91: E193-206

Thorarinsson S, 1958. The Oraefajokull eruption of 1362. *Acta Nat Islandica*, 2: 1-102

Thorarinsson S, 1965. Submarine eruptions near Iceland. *Natturufraedingurinn*, 35: 49-74 (in Icelandic with English summary)

Thorarinsson S, 1967a. *The Eruptions of Hekla in Historical Times*. Reykjavik: Societas Scientiarum Islandica, p 1-183

Thorarinsson S, 1967b. *Surtsey - The New Island in the North Atlantic*. New York: Viking Press, p 1-47

Thorarinsson S, 1968. Roadlog: Scandinavian geological excursion. *Unpublished Field Trip Guide*

Thorarinsson S, 1969. The Lakagigar eruption of 1783. *Bull Volc*, 33: 910-929

Thorarinsson S, 1970. *Hekla, a Notorious Volcano*. Reykjavik: Almenna Bokafelagid, 62 p

Thorarinsson S, 1974. *The History of Grimsvotn Eruptions and Skeidara Floods*. Reykjavik: Bokautgafa Menningarsjods, 254 p (in Icelandic)

Thorarinsson S, 1975. Katla and the annal of Katla eruptions. *Arbok Ferdafelags Islands 1975*, p 125-149

Thorarinsson S, 1979. The postglacial history of the Myvatn area. *Oikos*, 32: 17-28

Thorarinsson S (ed), 1960. On the geology and geophysics of Iceland. *21st Internatl Geol Cong, Copenhagen, Guidebook*, A2: 1-73 p

Thorarinsson S, Sigvaldason G E, 1962. The eruption in Askja, 1961, a preliminary report. *Amer J Sci*, 260: 641-651

Thorarinsson S, Sigvaldason G E, 1972. The Hekla eruption of 1970. *Bull Volc*, 36: 269-288

Thordarson T, Hoskuldsson A, 2008. Postglacial eruptions in Iceland. *Jokull*, 58: 197-228

Thordarson T, Larsen G, Hamilton C, 2008. Historical flood lava eruptions-the 1783-84 Laki and 934-40 Eldgja events. *IAVCEI Gen Assemb 2008 Conf Field Exc*, 1: 1-36

Thordarson T, Miller D J, Larsen G, Self S, Sigurdsson H, 2001. New estimates of sulfur degassing and atmospheric mass-loading by the 934 AD Eldgja eruption. *J Volc Geotherm Res*, 107: 33-54

Thordarson T, Self S, 1993. The Laki (Skaftar Fires) and Grimsvotn eruptions in 1783-1785. *Bull Volc*, 55: 233-263

Tryggvason E, 1984. Widening of the Krafla fissure swarm during the 1975-1981 volcano-tectonic episode. *Bull Volc*, 47: 47-71

Tryggvason E, 1994. Observed ground deformation at Hekla, Iceland prior to and during the eruptions of 1970, 1980-81 and 1991. *J Volc Geotherm Res*, 61: 281-291

Tuffen H, Castro J M, 2009. The emplacement of an obsidian dyke through thin ice: Hraftntinnuhryggur, Krafla Iceland. *J Volc Geotherm Res*, 185: 352-366

Tuffen H, Gilbert J, McGarvie D, 2001. Products of an effusive subglacial rhyolite eruption: Blahnukur, Torfajokull, Iceland. *Bull Volc*, 63: 179-190

Vilmundardottir E G, Gudmundsson A, Snorrason S P, 1985. Geology of the Burfell area. *Natturufraedingurinn*, 54: 97-113 (in Icelandic with English summary)

Vilmundardottir E G, Gudmundsson A, Snorrason S P, Larsen G, 1990. Geological map, Botnafjoll, 1913 IV, 1:50,000. *Iceland Geodetic Surv, Natl Energy Authority and Natl Power Company, Reykjavik*

Vilmundardottir E G, Hjartarson A, 1985. Pumice flows during Hekla eruptions. *Natturufraedingurinn*, 54: 17-30 (in Icelandic with English summary)

Vilmundardottir E G, Snorrason S P, Larsen G, Gudmundsson A, 1988. *Geological Map, Sigalda-Veidivotn 3340 B, 1:50,000*. Reykjavik: Natl Energy Authority, Hydro Power Div and Natl Power Company

Wastegard S, 2002. Early to middle Holocene silicic tephra horizons from the Katla volcanic system, Iceland: new results from the Faroe Islands. *J Quat Res*, 17: 723-730

Wilson L, Fagents S A, Robshaw L E, Scott E D, 2007. Vent geometry and eruptions conditions of the mixed rhyolite-basalt Namshraun lava flow, Iceland. *J Volc Geotherm Res*, 164: 127-141

Witham C S, Oppenheimer C, 2005. Mortality in England during the 1783-4 Laki Craters eruption. *Bull Volc*, 67: 15-26

Wohlfarth B, Blaauw M, Davies S M, Anderson M, Wastegard S, Hormes A, Possnert G, 2006. Constraining the age of Lateglacial and early Holocene pollen zones and tephra horizons in southern Sweden with Bayesian probability methods. *J Quat Sci*, 21: 321-334

Zhanxue S, Armannsson H, 2000. Gas chemistry and subsurface temperature estimation in the Hveragerdi high-temperature geothermal field, SW-Iceland. *Proc World Geotherm Cong, 2000, Kyushy-Tohoku, Japan, May 28-June 10, 2000*, p 2235-2240

JAN MAYEN & ARCTIC OCEAN (1706-07)

Birkenmajer K, 1972. Geotectonic aspects of the Beerenberg volcanic eruption 1970 Jan Mayen Island. *Acta Geol Polon*, 22: 1-15

Edwards M H, Kurras G J, Tolstoy M, Bohnenstiehl D R, Coakley B J, Cochran J R, 2001. Evidence of recent volcanic activity on the ultraslow-spreading Gakkel Ridge. *Nature*, 409: 808-812

Fitch F J, 1964. The development of the Beerenberg volcano, Jan Mayen. *Proc Geol Assoc London*, 75: 133-165

Imsland P, 1978. The geology of the volcanic island Jan Mayen, Arctic Ocean. *Nordic Volc Inst*, 78:13, 1-74

Imsland P, 1984. Petrology, mineralogy and evolution of the Jan Mayen magma system. *Visindafelag Islendinga, Reykjavik, Pub*, no 43, 332 p

Imsland P, 1986. The volcanic eruption on Jan Mayen, January 1985: interaction between a volcanic island and a fracture zone. *J Volc Geotherm Res*, 28: 45-54

Jakobsson M, Grantz A, Kristoffersen Y, Macnab R, 2003. Physiographic provinces of the Arctic Ocean seafloor. *Geol Soc Amer Bull*, 115: 1443-1455

Maaloe S, Sorensen I, Hertogen J, 1986. The trachybasaltic suite of Jan Mayen. *J Petr*, 27: 439-466

Roberts B, Hawkins T R W, 1963. The geology of the area around Nordkapp, Jan Mayen. *Nordic Polarinstituttt Arbok for 1963*, p 25-47

Semevskii D V, 1965. On the age of Sverre volcano. *In*: *Materials to the Spitsbergen Geol*, Leningrad, p 252-255

Siggerud T, 1972. The volcanic eruption on Jan Mayen 1970. *Norsk Polarinstitutt Arbok 1970*, p 5-18

Skjelkvale B-L, Amundsen H E F, O'Reilly S Y, Griffin W L, Gjelsvik T, 1989. A primitive, alkali basaltic stratovolcano and associated eruptive centres, northwestern Spitsbergen: volcanology and tectonic significance. *J Volc Geotherm Res*, 37: 1-19

Steinthorsson S, et al., 2002. *Catalog of Active Volcanoes of the World - Iceland. Unpublished manuscript*

Sylvester A G, 1975. History and surveillance of volcanic activity on Jan Mayen Island. *Bull Volc*, 39: 313-335

Vink G E, Morgan W J, Zhao W-L, 1984. Preferential rifting of continents: a source of displaced terrains. *J Geophys Res*, 89: 10,072-10,076

Wiese P K, 1992. Geochemistry and geochronology in the Eyjafjoll volcanic system, Iceland. *Unpublished MSci thesis*, Oregon State Univ, 230 p

AZORES & N ATLANTIC OCEAN (1801-02)

Azevedo J M M, Ferreira M R P, 2006. The volcanotectonic evolution of Flores Island, Azores (Portugal). *J Volc Geotherm Res*, 156: 90-102

Berninghausen W H, 1964. A checklist of Icelandic volcanic activity. *Bull Seism Soc Amer*, 54: 443-450

Bonadonna C, Houghton B F, 2005. Total grain-size distribution and volume of tephra-fall deposits. *Bull Volc*, 67: 441-456

Booth B, Croasdale R, Walker G P L, 1978. A quantitative study of five thousand years of volcanism on Sao Miguel, Azores. *Phil Trans Roy Soc London*, Ser A, 288: 271-319

Calvert A T, Moore R B, McGeehin J P, Rodrigues da Silva A M, 2006. Volcanic history and 40Ar/39Ar and 14C geochronology of Terceira Island, Azores, Portugal. *J Volc Geotherm Res*: 156: 103-115

Capaccioni B, Forjaz V H, Martini M, 1994. Pyroclastic flow hazard at Agua de Pau volcano (Sao Miguel Island, Azores archipelago) inferred from the Fogo A eruptive unit. *Acta Vulc*, 5: 41-48

Cardigos F, Colaco A, Dando P R, Avila S P, Sarradin P-M, Tempera F, Conceicao P, Pascoal A, Serrao Santos R, 2005. Shallow water hydrothermal vent field fluids and communities of the D. Joao de Castro seamount (Azores). *Chem Geol*, 224: 153-168

Cole P D, Guest J E, Duncan A M, Pacheco J-M, 2001. Capelinhos 1957-1958, Faial, Azores: deposits formed by an emergent surtseyan eruption. *Bull Volc*, 63: 204-220

Cole P D, Guest J E, Queiroz G, Wallenstein N, Pacheco J-M, Gaspar J L, Ferreira T, Duncan A M, 1999. Styles of volcanism and volcanic hazards on Furnas volcano, Sao Miguel, Azores. *J Volc Geotherm Res*, 92: 39-53

Cole P D, Queiroz G, Wallenstein N, Gaspar J L, Duncan A M, Guest J E, 1995. A historic subplinian/phreatomagmatic eruption: the 1630 AD eruption of Furnas volcano, Sao Miguel, Azores. *J Volc Geotherm Res*, 69: 117-135

Duncan A M, Queiroz G, Guest J E, Cole P D, Wallenstein N, Pacheco J M, 1999. The Povoacao Ignimbrite, Furnas volcano, Sao Miguel, Azores. *J Volc Geotherm Res*, 92: 55-65

Ferreira T, Oskarsson N, 1999. Chemistry and isotopic composition of fumarole discharges of Furnas caldera. *J Volc Geotherm Res*, 92: 169-179

Forjaz V H, Fernandes N S M, 1975. Geologic map of Ilha de San Jorge (Azores). *Servicos Geologicos Portugal*, 1:50,000 scale map with 32 p text (in Portuguese)

Franca Z T M, Tassinari C C G, Cruz J V, Aparicio A Y, Arana V, Rodrigues B N, 2006. Petrology, geochemistry and Sr-Nd-Pb isotopes of the volcanic rocks from Pico Islan-Azores (Portugal). *J Volc Geotherm Res*: 156: 71-89

Geldmacher J, Hoernle K A, 2000. The 72 Ma geochemical evolution of the Maderia hotspot (eastern North Atlantic): recycling of Paleozoic (500 Ma) oceanic lithosphere. *Earth Planet Sci Lett*, 183: 73-92

Geldmacher J, van den Bogaard P, Hoernle K, Schmincke H-U, 2000. The 40Ar/39Ar age dating of the Madeira Archipelago and hotspot track (eastern North Atlantic). *Geochem Geophys Geosyst*, 1: 1999GC00018

Gudmundsson A T, 1986b. *Iceland-Fires*. Reykjavik: Vaka-Helgafell, 168 p ***(regional reference)***

Guest J E, Gaspar J L, Cole P D, Queiroz G, Duncan A M, Wallenstein N, Ferreira T, Pacheco J-M, 1999. Volcanic geology of Furnas volcano, Sao Miguel, Azores. *J Volc Geotherm Res*, 92: 1-29

Klugel A, Walter T R, Schwarz S, Geldmacher J, 2005. Gravitational spreading causes en-echelon diking along a rift zone of Madeira Archipelago: an experimental approach and implications for magma transport. *Bull Volc*: 68: 37-46

Machado F, 1982. Excursion guide for field trip V3, Islands of Fayal and Pico. *Proc Internatl Symp Activity Oceanic Volc, Archipelago Univ Azores*, 3: 343-349

Machado F, Lemos R, 1998. Sobre uma possivel erupcao submarina no Banco D. Joao de Castro em 1997. *Acoreana* 8: 559-564 (in Portuguese with English abs)

Martins J A, 1982. Excursion guide for field trip V1, Island of Sao Miguel. *Proc Internatl Symp Activity Oceanic Volc, Archipelago Univ Azores*, 3: 315-328

Mitchell-Thome R C, 1976. *Geology of the Middle Atlantic Islands*. Berlin: Gebruder Borntraeger, 382 p ***(regional reference)***

Mitchell-Thome R C, 1981. Vulcanicity of Historic Times in the Middle Atlantic Islands. *Bull Volc*, 44: 57-70

Moore R B, 1983a. Preliminary geologic map of Sete Cidades volcano, Sao Miguel, Azores (1:18,000). *U S Geol Surv Open-File Rpt*, 83-742

Moore R B, 1983b. Preliminary geologic map of Furnas volcano, Sao Miguel, Azores (1:15,000). *U S Geol Surv Open-File Rpt*, 83-395

Moore R B, 1986. Preliminary geologic map of Agua de Pau volcano, Sao Miguel, Azores. *U S Geol Surv Open-File Rpt*, 86-192

Moore R B, 1990. Volcanic geology and eruption frequency, Sao Miguel, Azores. *Bull Volc*, 52: 602-614

Moore R B, 1991. Geologic map of Sao Miguel, Azores. *U S Geol Surv Map*, I-2007

Moore R B, Rubin M, 1991. Radiocarbon dates for lava flows and pyroclastic deposits on Sao Miguel, Azores. *Radiocarbon*, 33: 151-164

Morisseau M, Traineau H, 1985. Mise en evidence d'une activite hydromagmatique Holocene sur l'Ile de Flores (Acores). *CR Acad Sci Paris*, 301: 1309-1314

Neumann van Padang M, Richards A F, Machado F, Bravo T, Baker P E, Le Maitre R W, 1967. Atlantic Ocean. *Catalog of Active Volcanoes of the World and Solfatara Fields*, Rome: IAVCEI, 21: 1-128 ***(regional reference)***

Nunes J C, Camacho A, Franca Z, Montesinos F G, Alves M, Vieira R, Velez E, Ortiz E, 2006. Gravity anomalies and crustal signature of volcano-tectonic structures of Pico Island (Azores). *J Volc Geotherm Res*: 156: 55-70

Schwarz S, Klugel A, van den Bogaard P, Geldmacher J, 2005. Internal structure and evolution of a volcanic rift system in the eastern North Atlantic: the Desertas rift zone, Madeira archipelago. *J Volc Geotherm Res*, 141: 123-135

Self S, 1976. The recent volcanology of Terceira, Azores. *J Geol Soc London*, 132: 645-666

Self S, Gunn B M, 1976. Petrology, volume and age relations of alkaline and saturated peralkaline volcanics from Terceira, Azores. *Contr Mineral Petr*, 54: 293-313

Serrano Pinto M, 1998. Effects of eruptions on society - the case of the Azores Archipelago. A brief historical account. *In:*, Morello N (ed) *Volcanoes and History*, Genoa: Brigati, p 565-580

Shotton F W, Williams R E G, Johnson A S, 1974. [Radiocarbon dates on Terceira volcano]. *Radiocarbon*, 16: 293

Solgevik H, Mattsson H B, Hermelin O, 2007. Growth of an emergent tuff cone: fragmentation and depositional processes recored in the Capelas tuff cone, Sao Miguel, Azores. *J Volc Geotherm Res*, 159: 246-266

Steinthorsson S, et al., 2002. *Catalog of Active Volcanoes of the World - Iceland. Unpublished manuscript*

Thorarinsson S, 1965. Submarine eruptions near Iceland. *Natturufraedingurinn*, 35: 49-74 (in Icelandic with English summary)

Walker G P L, Croasdale R, 1970. Two Plinian-type eruptions in the Azores. *J Geol Soc London*, 127: 17-55

Waters A C, Fisher R V, 1971. Base surges and their deposits: Capelinhos and Taal volcanoes. *J Geophys Res*, 76: 5596-5614

Weston F S, 1964. List of recorded volcanic eruptions in the Azores with brief reports. *Bol Mus Lab Miner, Geol Fac Ciencas Lisboa*, 10: 3-18

Wunderman R W, Barriga F J A S, Nishimura C, Pacheco J M, Vogt P R, Gaspar J L, Queiroz G, Santos R S, 2003. Faults, post-1720 craters, and remains of a lava lake at Castro Bank seamount (E Azores) (abs). *Eos, Trans Amer Geophys Union*, 84(Suppl): F1559

Zbyszewski G, Candido de Medeiros A, Veiga Ferreira O da, Torre de Assuncao C, 1967. Geologic map of Ilha do Corvo. *Servicos Geologicos Portugal*, 1:25,000 scale map with 16 p text (in Portuguese)

Zbyszewski G, Candido de Medeiros A, Veiga Ferreira O da, Torre de Assuncao C, 1968. Geologic map of Ihla das Flores (Azores). *Servicos Geologicos Portugal*, 1:25,000 scale map with 31 p text (in Portuguese)

Zbyszewski G, Candido de Medeiros A, Veiga Ferreira O da, Torre de Assuncao C, 1971. Geologic map of Ilha Terceira (Azores). *Servicos Geologicos Portugal*, 1:50,000 scale map with 43 p text (in Portuguese)

Zbyszewski G, Candido de Medeiros A, Veiga Ferreira O da, Torre de Assuncao C, 1972. Geologic map of Ihla Graciosa (Azores). *Servicos Geologicos Portugal*, 1:25,000 scale map with 31 p text (in Portuguese)

Zbyszewski G, Moitinho de Almeida F, Veiga Ferreira O da, Torre de Assuncao C, 1958. Geologic map of Sao Miguel (Azores). *Servicos Geologicos Portugal*, two 1:50,000 scale maps with 22 and 37 p texts (in Portuguese)

Zbyszewski G, Moitinho de Almeida F, Veiga Ferreira O da, Torre de Assuncao C, 1959. Geologic map of Faial (Azores). *Servicos Geologicos Portugal*, 1:25,000 scale map with 25 p text (in Portuguese)

Zbyszewski G, Ribeiro Ferreira C, Veiga Ferreira O da, Torre de Assuncao C, 1963. Geological map of Ilha do Pico (Azores). *Servicos Geologicos Portugal*, two 1:50,000 scale maps with 25 and 21 p texts (in Portuguese)

CANARY IS & ATLANTIC CENTRAL & S (1803-06)

Ablay G J, Ernst G G J, Marti J, Sparks R S J, 1995. The ~2 ka subplinian eruption of Montana Blanca, Tenerife. *Bull Volc*, 57: 337-355

Ablay G J, Marti J, 2000. Stratigraphy, structure, and volcanic evolution of the Pico Teide-Pico Viejo formation, Tenerife, Canary Islands. *J Volc Geotherm Res*, 103: 175-208

Ablay G, Hurlimann M, 2000. Evolution of the north flank of Tenerife by recurrent giant landslides. *J Volc Geotherm Res*, 103: 135-159

Afonso A, 1974. Geological sketch and historic volcanoes in La Palma, Canary Islands. *Estudios Geol, V Teneguia*, p 7-13

Almeida F F M, 1961. Geologia e petrologia da Ilha da Trindade. *Dept Nac Producao Min, Rio de Janeiro*, Monografia 18, 197 p

Ancochea E, Fuster J M, Ibarrola E, Cendrero A, Coello J, Hernan F, Cantagrel J M, Jamond C, 1990. Volcanic evolution of the island of Tenerife (Canary Islands) in the light of new K-Ar data. *J Volc Geotherm Res*, 44: 231-249

Ancochea E, Hernan F, Cendrero A, Cantagrel J M, Fuster J M, Ibarrola E, Coello J, 1994. Constructive and destructive episodes in the building of a young oceanic island, La Palma, Canary Islands, and genesis of the Caldera de Taburiente. *J Volc Geotherm Res*, 60: 243-262

Ancochea E, Huertas M J, Cantagrel J M, Coello J, Fuster J M, Arnaud N, Ibarrola E, 1999. Evolution of the Canadas edifice and its implications for the origin of the Canadas caldera (Tenerife, Canary Islands). *J Volc Geotherm Res*, 88: 177-199

Arana V, Carracedo J C, 1979. *Los Volcanes de las Islas Canarias. II. Lanzarote-Fuerteventura*. Madrid: Rueda, 176 p

Baker P E, 1967. Historical and geological notes on Bouvetoya. *Brit Antarctic Surv Bull*, 13: 71-84

Baker P E, Gass I G, Harris P G, LeMaitre R W, 1964. Vulcanological report on the Royal Society expedition to Tristan de Cunha. *Phil Trans Roy Soc London*, 256: 439-578

Bell J D, Atkins F B, Baker P E, Smith D G W, 1972. Notes on the petrology and age of Ascension Island, south Atlantic (abs). *Eos, Trans Amer Geophys Union*, 53: 168

Brown R J, Barry T L, Branney M J, Pringle M S, Bryan S E, 2003. The Quaternary pyroclastic succession of southeast Tenerife, Canary Islands: explosive eruptions, related caldera subsidence, and sector collapse. *Geol Mag*, 140: 265-288

Brown R J, Branney M J, 2004. Event-stratigraphy of a caldera-forming ignimbrite eruption on Tenerife: the 273 ka Poris Formation. *Bull Volc*, 66: 392-416

Bryan S E, 2006. Petrology and geochemistry of the Quaternary caldera-forming, phonolitic Granadilla eruption, Tenerife (Canary Islands). *J Petr*, 47: 1557-1589

Bryan S E, Cas R A F, Marti J, 2000. The 0.57 Ma plinian eruption of the Granadilla Member, Tenerife (Canary Islands): an example of the complexity in eruption dynamics and evolution. *J Volc Geotherm Res*, 103: 209-238

Carracedo J C, 1994. The Canary Islands: an example of structural control on the growth of large oceanic-island volcanoes. *J Volc Geotherm Res*, 60: 225-241

Carracedo J C, 2006. *El Volcan Teide, Volcanologia, Interpretacion de Paisajes e Itinerarios Comentados*. CajaCanarias, 431 p

Carracedo J C, Badiola E R, 1991. *Lanzarote, la Erupcion Volcanica de 1730*. Lanzarote: Servicio de Publicaciones, 184 p

Carracedo J C, Badiola E R, Guillou H, de la Nuez J, Perex Torrado F J, 2001. Geology and volcanology of La Plama and El Hierro, western Canaries. *Estudios Geol Museo Nac Ciencias Nat*, 57: 175-273

Carracedo J C, Badiola E R, Guillou H, de la Nuez J, Perex Torrado F J, 2001. Geology and volcanology of La Palma and El Hierro, western Canaries. *Estudios Geol Museo Nac Ciencias Nat*, 57: 175-273

Carracedo J C, Badiola E R, Soler V, 1992. The 1730-1736 eruption of Lanzarote, Canary Islands: a long, high-magnitude basaltic fissure eruption. *J Volc Geotherm Res*, 53: 239-250

Carracedo J C, Day S J, Guillou H, Perez-Torrado F J, 1999. Giant Quaternary landslides in the evolution of La Plama and El Hierro, Canary Islands. *J Volc Geotherm Res*, 94: 169-190

Carracedo J C, Paterne M, Guillou H, Perez Torrado F J, Paris R, Rodriguex BAdiola E, Hansen A, 2003. Dataciones radiometreicas (14C y K/Ar) del Teide y el rift noroeste, Tenerife, Islas Canarias. *Estudios Geol Museo Nac Ciencias Nat*, 59: 15-29

Carracedo J C, Rodriguez Badiola E, Guillou H, Paterne M, Scaillet S, Perez Torrado F J, Paris R, Fra-Paleo U, Hansen A, 2007. Eruptive and structural history of Teide volcano and rift zones of Tenerife, Canary Islands. *Geol Soc Amer Bull*, 119: 1027-1051

Cas R, Edgar C J, Pittari A, Middleton J, Wolff J, Marti J, Olin P, Nichols H, 2005. Using the stratigraphic record to understand the nature of caldera collapse: the 1.59-present Las Canadas caldera complex, Tenerife, Spain. *Workshop Caldera Volcanism: Analysis, Modelling and Response, Parador de las Canadas, 16-22 October, 2005*, Abs, p 7-8

Chevallier L, Verwoerd W J, 1987. A dynamic interpretation of Tristan da Cunha volcano, South Atlantic Ocean. *J Volc Geotherm Res*, 34: 35-49

Cliff R A, Baker P E, Mateer N J, 1991. Geochemistry of Inacessible Island volcanics. *Chem Geol*, 92: 251-260

Coppo N, Schnegg P-A, Heise W, Falco P, Costa R, 2008. Multiple caldera collapses from the shallow electrical resistivity signature of the Las Canadas caldera, Tenerife, Canary Islands. *J Volc Geotherm Res*, 170: 153-166

Day S J, Carracedo J C, Guillou H, 1997. Age and geometry of an aborted rift flank collapse: the San Andres fault system, El Hierro, Canary Islands. *Geol Mag*, 134: 523-537

Day S J, Carracedo J C, Guillou H, Gravestock P, 1999. Recent structural evolution of the Cumbre Vieja volcano, La Palma, Canary Islands: volcanic rift zone reconfiguration as a precursor to volcano flank instability? *J Volc Geotherm Res*, 94: 135-167

Day S J, Heleno da Silva S I N, Fonseca J F B D, 1999. A past giant lateral collapse and present-day flank instability of Fogo, Cape Verde Islands. *J Volc Geotherm Res*, 94: 191-218

del Potro R, Pinkerton H, Hurlimann M, 2009. An analysis of the morphological, geological and structural features of Teide stratovolcano, Tenerife. *J Volc Geotherm Res*, 181: 89-105

Duprat H I, Friis H, Holm P M, Grandvuinet T, Sorenson R V, 2007. The volcanic and geochemical development of Sao Nicolau, Cape Verde Islands: constraints from field and 40Ar/39Ar evidence. *J Volc Geotherm Res*, 162: 1-19

Edgar C J, Wolff J A, Nichols H J, Cas R A F, Marti J, 2002. A complex Quaternary ignimbrite-forming phonolitic eruption: the Poris Member of the Diego Hernandez Formation (Tenerife, Canary Islands). *J Volc Geotherm Res*, 118: 99-130

Edgar C J, Wolff J A, Olin P H, Nichols H J, Pittari A, Cas R A F, Reiners P W, Spell T L, Marti J, 2007. The late Quaternary Diego Hernandez Formation, Tenerife: volcanology of a complex cycle of voluminous explosive phonolitic eruptions. *J Volc Geotherm Res*, 160: 59-85

Fuster J M, Arana V, Brandle J L, Navarro M, Alonso U, Aparicio A, 1968. *Geologia y Volcanologia de las Islas Canarias - Tenerife*. Madrid: Inst "Lucas Mallada," 218 p

Fuster J M, Cendrero A, Gastesi P, Ibarrola E, Lopez-Ruiz J, 1968. *Geologia y Volcanologia de las Islas Canarias - Fuerteventura.* Madrid: Inst "Lucas Mallada," 239 p

Fuster J M, Fernandez Santin S, Sagredo J, 1968. *Geologia y Volcanologia de las Islas Canarias - Lanzarote.* Madrid: Inst "Lucas Mallada," 177 p

Fuster J M, Hernandez-Pacheco A, Munoz M, Rodriguez Badiola E, Garcia Cacho L, 1968. *Geologia y Volcanologia de las Islas Canarias - Gran Canaria.* Madrid: Inst "Lucas Mallada," 243 p

Gee M J R, Masson D G, Watts A B, Mitchell N C, 2001. Offshore continuation of volcanic rift zones, El Hierro, Canary Islands. *J Volc Geotherm Res*, 105: 107-119

Girod M, Nougier J, 1972. Volcanism of the Sub-Antarctic Islands. *In*: Adie R J (ed) *Antarctic Geol and Geophys*, IUGS Ser-B(1): 777-778

Guillou H, Carracedo J C, Day S J, 1998. Dating of the Upper Pleistocene-Holocene volcanic activity of La Palma using the unspiked K-Ar technique. *J Volc Geotherm Res*, 86: 137-149

Guillou H, Carracedo J C, Duncan R, 2001. K-Ar, 40Ar/39Ar ages and magnetostratigraphy of Brunhes and Matuyama lava sequences from La Palma Island. *J Volc Geotherm Res*, 106: 175-194

Guillou H, Carracedo J C, Perez-Torrado F, Rodriguez-Badiola E, 1996. K-Ar ages and magnetic stratigraphy of a hotspot-induced, fast grown oceanic island: El Hierro, Canary Islands. *J Volc Geotherm Res*, 73: 141-155

Guillou H, Perez Torado F J, Hansen Machin A R, Carracedo J C, Gimeno D, 2004. The Plio-Quaternary volcanic evolution of Gran Canaria based on new K-Ar ages and magnetostratigraphy. *J Volc Geotherm Res*, 135: 221-246

Hansen Machin A R, Benjumea A, Perez-Torrado F J, Carracedo J C, Guillou H, Paternne M, 2003. Bandama volcanic complex: a subplinian volcanic eruption in the prehistoric record of Gran Canaria (Canary Islands). *Cities on Volcanoes 3, Hilo, Hawai'i, July 14-18, 2003, Abs*, p 55

Harris C, 1983. The petrology of lavas and associated plutonic inclusions of Ascension Island. *J Petr*, 24: 424-470

Hausen H, 1972. Outlines of the geology of Hierro (Canary Islands). *Finska Vetenskapssocietan Helsingfors, Commentationes Physico-Mathematicae*, 43: 65-148

Heleno S I N, Fonseca J F B D, 1999. A seismological investigation of the Fogo volcano, Cape Verde Islands: preliminary results. *Volc Seism*, 20: 199-217 (English translation)

Helono da Silva S I N, Day S J, Fonseca J F B D, 1999. Fogo volcano, Cape Verde Islands: seismicity-derived constraints on the mechanism of the 1995 eruption. *J Volc Geotherm Res*, 94: 219-231

Hernandez-Pacheco A, Valls M C, 1982. The historic eruptions of La Palma Island (Canaries). *Proc Internatl Symp Activity Oceanic Volc, Archipelago Univ Azores*, 3: 83-94

Huertas M J, Arnaud N O, Ancochea E, Cantagrel J M, Fuster J M, 2002. 40Ar/39Ar stratigraphy of pyroclastic units from the Canadas edifice (Tenerife, Canary Islands) and their bearing on the structural evolution. *J Volc Geotherm Res*, 115: 351-365

Klugel A, Schmincke H-U, White J D L, Hoernle K A, 1999. Chronology and volcanology of the 1949 multi-vent rift-zone eruption on La Palma (Canary Islands). *J Volc Geotherm Res*, 94: 267-282

Lamb H H, 1967. The problem of "Thompson Island" volcanic eruptions and meteorological evidence. *Brit Antarctic Surv Bull*, 13: 85-88

LeMasurier W E, Thomson J W (eds), 1990. *Volcanoes of the Antarctic Plate and Southern Oceans.* Washington, D C: Amer Geophys Union, 487 p ***(regional reference)***

Machado F, 1963. Erupcoes da Ilha de la Palma (Canarias). *Bolivia Museum Laboratory Min Geol Fac Ciencas Lisbon*, 9: 143-157

Marques L S, Ulbrich M N C, Ruberti E, Tassinari C, 1999. Petrology, geochemistry and Sr-Nd isotopes of the Trindade and Martin Vaz volcanic rocks (Southern Atlantic Ocean). *J Volc Geotherm Res*, 93: 191-216

Marti J, Gundmundsson A, 2000. The Las Canadas caldera (Tenerife, Canary Islands): an overlapping collapse caldera generated by magma-chamber migration. *J Volc Geotherm Res*, 103: 161-173

Marti J, Mitjavila J, Arana V, 1994. Stratigraphy, structure and geochronology of the Las Canadas caldera (Tenerife, Canary Islands). *Geol Mag*, 131: 715-727

Masson D G, 1996. Catastrophic collapse of the volcanic island of Hierro 15 ka ago and the history of landslides in the Canary Islands. *Geology*, 24: 231-234

Maund J G, Rex D C, le Roex A P, Reid D L, 1988. Volcanism on Gough Island: a revised stratigraphy. *Geol Mag*, 125: 175-181

Middlemost E A K, 1972. Evolution of La Palma, Canary Archipelago. *Contr Mineral Petr*, 36: 33-48

Mitchell N C, Masson D G, Watts A B, Gee M J R, Urgeles R, 2002. The morphology of the submarine flanks of volcanic ocean islands, a comparative study of the Canary and Hawaiian hotspot islands. *J Volc Geotherm Res*, 115: 83-107

Mitchell-Thome R C, 1970. *Geology of the South Atlantic islands.* Berlin: Gebruder Borntraeger, 350 p ***(regional reference)***

Mitchell-Thome R C, 1976. *Geology of the Middle Atlantic Islands.* Berlin: Gebruder Borntraeger, 382 p ***(regional reference)***

Mitchell-Thome R C, 1981. Vulcanicity of Historic Times in the Middle Atlantic Islands. *Bull Volc*, 44: 57-70

Mortensen A K, Wilson J R, Holm P M, 2009. The Cao Grande phonolitic fall deposit on Santa Antao, Cape Verde Islands. *J Volc Geotherm Res*, 179: 120-132

Munn S, Walter T R, Klugel A, 2006. Gravitational spreading controls rift zones and flank instability on El Hierro, Canary Islands. *Geol Mag*, 143: 257-268

Neumann van Padang M, Richards A F, Machado F, Bravo T, Baker P E, Le Maitre R W, 1967. Atlantic Ocean. *Catalog of Active Volcanoes of the World and Solfatara Fields*, Rome: IAVCEI, 21: 1-128 ***(regional reference)***

Nogales J, Schminke H-U, 1968. El pino enterrado de la Canada de las Arenas (Gran Canaria). *Cuadernos Botanica Canario*, 5: 23-25

Ortiz R, Arana V, Valberde C, 1986. Aproximacion al conocimiento del mecanismo de la erupcion de 1730-1736 en Lanzarote. *Sociedad Espanola Fisica, Anales Fisica*, Ser B, 82: 127-142

Pellicer M J, 1979. Estudio geoquimico del vulcanismo de la Isla del Hierro (A. Canario). *Estudios Geol*, 35: 15-21

Pittari A, Cas R A F, Marti J, 2005. The occurrence and origin of prominent massive, pumice-rich ignimbrite lobes within the Late Pleistocene Abrigo Ignimbrite, Tenerife, Canary Islands. *J Volc Geotherm Res*, 139: 271-293

Plesner S, Holmb P M, Wilson J R, 2003. 40Ar-39Ar geochronology of Santo Antao, Cape Verde Islands. *J Volc Geotherm Res*, 120: 103-121

Prestvik T, 1982. The geology, volcanic activity, and age of Bouvetoya, south Atlantic. *Proc Internatl Symp Activity Oceanic Volc, Archipelago Univ Azores*, 3: 115-123

Reagan M K, Turner S, Legg M, Sims K W W, Hards V L, 2008. 238U- and 232Th-decay series constraints on the timescales of crystal fractionation to produce the phonolite erupted in 2004 near Tristan da Cunha, South Atlantic Ocean. *Geochim Cosmochim Acta*, 72: 4367-4378

Ridley W I, 1971. The field relations of the Canadas volcanoes, Tenerife, Canary Islands. *Bull Volc*, 35: 318-334

Roa K, 2003. Nature and origin of toreva remnants and volcaniclastics from La Palma, Canary Islands. *J Volc Geotherm Res*, 125: 191-214

Romero C, 1991. *Las Manifestaciones Volcanicas Historicas del Archipielago Canario.* Tenerife: Gobierno de Canarias, 2 vol, 695 & 768 p ***(regional reference)***

Santos R N, Marques L S, 2007. Investigation of 238U-230Th226-226Ra and 232Th-228Ra-228Th radioactive disequilibria in volcanic rocks from Trindade and Martin Vaz Islands (Brazil; southern Atlantic Ocean. *J Volc Geotherm Res*, 161: 215-233

Schminke H U, 1990. Geological field guide-Gran Canaria. *IAVCEI 1990 Internatl Volc Cong, Mainz*, Excur 7BI: 1-199

Smith W H F, Sandwell D T, 1997. Global seafloor topography from satellite altimetry and ship depth soundings. *Science*, 277: 1957-1962

Solana M C, Kilburn C R J, Rodriguez Badiola E, Aparicio A, 2004. Fast emplacement of extensive pahoehoe flow-fields: the case of the 1736 flows from Montana de las Nueces, Lanzarote. *J Volc Geotherm Res*, 132: 189-207

Soler V, Carracedo J C, Heller F, 1984. Geomagnetic secular variation in historical lavas from the Canary Islands. *Geophys J Roy Astron Soc*, 78: 313-318

Soriano C, Galindo I, Marti J, Wolff J, 2006. Conduit-vent structures and related proximal deposits in the Las Canadas caldera, Tenerife, Canary Islands. *Bull Volc*, 69: 217-231

Verwoerd W J, Erlank A J, Kable E J D, 1976. Geology and geochemistry of Bouvet Island. *In*: Gonzalez-Ferran O (ed) *Proc Symp Andean & Antarctic Volcanology Problems (Santiago, Chile, Sept 1974)*, Rome: IAVCEI, p 203-237

Watts A B, Masson D G, 2001. New sonar evidence for recent catastrophic collapses of the north flank of Tenerife, Canary Islands. *Bull Volc*, 63: 8-19

White J D L, Schmincke H-U, 1999. Phreatomagmatic eruptive and depositional processes during the 1949 eruption on La Plama (Canary Islands). *J Volc Geotherm Res*, 94: 283-304

Wolff J A, Turbeville B N, 1985. Recent pyroclastic deposits on Brava, Cape Verde Islands (abs). *Eos, Trans Amer Geophys Union*, 66: 1152

ANTARCTICA & S SANDWICH IS (1900)

Adie R J, 1969. Northern Antarctic Peninsula. *In*: Bushnell V (ed) *Geol Map of Antarctica*, Antarctic Map Folio Ser, folio no 12, sheet 1, New York: Amer Geog Soc

Aristarain A L, Delmas R J, 1998. Ice record of a large eruption of Deception Island volcano (Antarctica) in the XVIIth century. *J Volc Geotherm Res*, 80: 17-25

Aster R, Mah S, Kyle P, McIntosh W, Dunbar N, Johnson J, Ruiz M, McNamara S, 2003. Very long period oscillations of Mount Erebus volcano. *J Geophys Res*, 108(B11), 2522, doi:10.1029.2002JB00201

Baker P E, 1968. Comparative volcanology and petrology of the Atlantic island arcs. *Bull Volc*, 32: 189-206

Baker P E, Davies T G, Roobol M J, 1969. Volcanic activity at Deception Island in 1967 and 1968. *Nature*, 224: 553-560

Baker P E, Gonzalez-Ferran O, Vergara M, 1973. Paulet Island and the James Ross Island volcanic group. *Brit Antarctic Surv Bull*, 32: 89-95

Baker P E, Gonzalez-Ferran O, Vergara M, 1976. Geology and geochemistry of Paulet Island and the James Ross Island volcanic group. *In*: Gonzalez-Ferran O (ed) *Proc Symp Andean & Antarctic Volcanology Problems (Santiago, Chile, Sept 1974)*, Rome: IAVCEI, p 39-47

Baker P E, McReath I, Harvey M R, Roobol M J, Davies T G, 1975. The geology of the South Shetland Islands: V. Volcanic evolution of Deception Island. *Brit Antarctic Surv Sci Rpt*, 78: 1-81

Behrendt J C, Cooper A K, Yuan A, 1987. Interpretation of marine magnetic gradiometer and multichannel seismic-reflection observations over the western Ross Sea shelf, Antarctica. *In*: Cooper A K and Davey F J (eds) *The Antarctic Continental Margin: Geol and Geophys of the Western Ross Sea*, Circum-Pacific Council Energy Mineral Resour Earth Sci Ser, 5B: 155-177

Berninghausen W H, Neumann van Padang M, 1960. Antarctica. *Catalog of Active Volcanoes of the World and Solfatara Fields*, Rome: IAVCEI, 10: 1-32 ***(regional reference)***

Birkenmajer K, 1979. Age of the Penguin Island volcano, South Shetland Islands (West Antarctica), by the Lichenometric Method. *Bull Acad Polonaise, Sci Ser Sci Terre*, 27: 69-76

Bjorck S, Sandgren P, Zale R, 1991. Late Holocene tephrochronology of the northern Antarctic Peninsula. *Quat Res*, 36: 322-328

Calkin P E, Nichols R L, 1972. Quaternary Studies in Antarctica. *In:*, Adie R J (ed) *Antarctic Geology and Geophysics*, Oslo: Internatl Union Geol Sci (IUGS), p 625-643

Coombs D S, Landis C A, 1966. Pumice from the South Sandwich eruption of March 1962 reaches New Zealand. *Nature*, 209: 289-290

Cooper A F, Adam L J, Coulter R G, Eby G N, McIntosh W C, 2007. Geology, geochronology and geochemistry of a basanitic volcano, White Island, Ross Sea, Antarctica. *J Volc Geotherm Res*, 165: 189-216

Corr H F J, Vaughan D G, 2008. A recent volcanic eruption beneath the West Antarctica ice sheet. *Nature Geosci*, 1: 122-125

Craddock C, Bastien T W, Rutford R H, 1964. Geology of the Jones Mountains area. *In*: Adie R J (ed) *Antarctic Geol, Proc 1st Internatl Symp Antarctic Geol*, Amsterdam: Elsevier, p 172-187

Csatho B, Schenk T, Kyle P, Wilson T, Krabill W B, 2008. Airborne laser swath mapping of the summit of Erebus volcano, Antarctica: applications to geological mapping of a volcano. *J Volc Geotherm Res*, 177: 531-548

Dort W, 1972. Late Cenozoic volcanism in Antarctica. *In*: Adie R J (ed) *Antarctic Geol and Geophys*, IUGS Ser-B(1): 645-652

Doumani G A, Minshew V H, 1965. General geology of the Mount Weaver area, Queen Maud Mountains, Antarctica. *In*: *Geol and Paleont of the Antarctic*, Antarctic Res Ser 6, Washington, D C: Amer Geophys Union, p 127-139

Esser R P, Kyle P R, McIntosh W C, 2004. 40Ar/39Ar dating of the eruptive history of Mount Erebus, Antarctica: volcano evolution. *Bull Volc*, 66: 671-686

Gass I G, Harris P G, Holdgate M W, 1963. Pumice eruption in the area of the south Sandwich Islands. *Geol Mag*, 100: 321-330

Giggenbach W F, Kyle P R, Lyon G L, 1973. Present volcanic activity on Mount Erebus, Ross Island, Antarctica. *Geology*, 1: 135-136

Gonzalez-Ferran O, 1972. Distribucion del volcanismo activo de Chile y la reciente erupcion del Volcan Villarrica. *Instituto Geog Militar Chile*, O/T 3491 ***(regional reference)***

Gonzalez-Ferran O, 1983. The Seal Nunataks: an active volcanic group on the Larsen Ice Shelf, West Antarctica. *In*: Oliver R L, James P R, Jago J B (eds) *Antarctic Earth Science*, New York: Cambridge Univ Press, p 334-337

Gonzalez-Ferran O, 1995. *Volcanes de Chile*. Santiago: Instituto Geografico Militar, 635 p ***(regional reference)***

Gonzalez-Ferran O, Gonzalez-Bonorino F, 1972. The volcanic ranges of Marie Byrd land between long 100° and 140° W. *In*: Adie R J (ed) *Antarctic Geol and Geophys*, IUGS Ser-B(1): 261-275

Gonzalez-Ferran O, Vergara M, 1972. Post-Miocene Volcanic Petrographic provinces of West Antarctica and their Relation to the Southern Andes of South America. *In*:, Adie R J (ed) *Antarctic Geology and Geophysics*, Oslo: Internatl Union Geol Sci (IUGS), p 187-195

Hamilton W, 1972. The Hallett volcanic province, Antarctica. *U S Geol Surv Prof Pap*, 456-C: 1-62

Harpel C J, Kyle P R, Dunbar N W, 2008. Englacial tephrostratigraphy of Erebus volcano, Antarctica. *J Volc Geotherm Res*, 177: 549-568

Harpel C J, Kyle P R, Esser R P, McIntosh W C, Caldwell D A, 2004. 40Ar/39Ar dating of the eruptive history of Mount Erebus, Antarctica: summit flows, tephra, and caldera collapse. *Bull Volc*, 66: 687-702

Johnson J B, Aster R C, Ruiz M C, Malone S D, McChesney P J, Lees J M, Kyle P R, 2003. Interpretation and utility of infrasonic records from erupting volcanoes. *J Volc Geotherm Res*, 121: 15-63

Kelly P J, Dunbar N W, Kyle P R, McIntosh W C, 2008. Refinement of the late Quaternary geologic history of Erebus volcano, Antarctica using 40Ar/39Ar and 36Cl age determinations. *J Volc Geotherm Res*, 177: 569-588

Keys J R, McIntosh W C, Kyle P R, 1983. Volcanic activity of Mount Melbourne, Northern Victoria Land. *Antarctic J U S*, 18: 10-11

Kyle P R, 1982. Volcanic geology of the Pleiades, Northern Victoria Land, Antarctica. *In*: Craddock C (ed) *Antarctic Geoscience*, Madison: Univ Wisconsin Press, p 747-754

Kyle P R, Cole J W, 1974. Structural control of volcanism in the McMurdo Volcanic Group, Antarctica. *Bull Volc*, 38: 16-25

Kyle P R, Dibble R R, Giggenbach W F, Keys J, 1982. Volcanic activity associated with the anorthoclase phonolite lava lake, Mount Erebus, Antarctica. *In*: Craddock C (ed) *Antarctic Geoscience*, Madison: Univ Wisconsin Press, p 735-745

Kyle P R, Jezek P A, 1978. Compositions of three tephra layers from the Byrd Station Ice Core, Antarctica. *J Volc Geotherm Res*, 4: 225-232

Kyle P R, McIntosh W, 1978. Observations of volcanic activity at Mt. Erebus. *Antarctic J U S*, 13: 32-34

Kyle P R, Moore J A, Thirlwall M F, 1992. Petrologic evolution of anorthoclase phonolite lavas at Mount Erebus, Ross Island, Antarctica. *J Petr*, 33: 849-875

Kyle P, Palais J, Delmas R, 1982. The volcanic record of Antarctic ice cores: preliminary results and potential for future investigations. *Annals Glaciology*, 3: 172-177

Lachlan-Cope T, Smellie J L, Ladkin R, 2001. Discovery of a recurrent lava lake on Saunders Island (South Sandwich Islands) using AVHRR imagery. *J Volc Geotherm Res*, 112: 105-116

LeMasurier W E, 1971. Spatial variation in Cenozoic volcanism of Marie Byrd Land and Ellsworth Land. *Antarctic J U S*, 6: 187-188

LeMasurier W E, 1972. Volcanic record of Cenozoic glacial history Marie Byrd Land. *In*: Adie R J (ed) *Antarctic Geol and Geophys*, IUGS Ser-B(1): 251-260

LeMasurier W E, Thomson J W (eds), 1990. *Volcanoes of the Antarctic Plate and Southern Oceans*. Washington, D C: Amer Geophys Union, 487 p ***(regional reference)***

LeMasurier W E, Wade F A, 1976. Volcanic history in Marie Byrd: implications with regard to southern hemisphere tectonic reconstructions. *In*: Gonzalez-Ferran O (ed) *Proc Symp Andean & Antarctic Volcanology Problems (Santiago, Chile, Sept 1974)*, Rome: IAVCEI, p 398-424

Lyon G L, Giggenbach W F, 1974. Geothermal activity in Victoria Land, Antarctica. *New Zeal J Geol Geophys*, 17: 511-521

Marti J, Baraldo A, 1990. Pre-caldera pyroclastic deposits of Deception Island (South Shetland Islands). *Antarctic Sci*, 2: 345-352

Mirsky A, 1969. Geology of the Ohio Range-Liv Glacier area. *In*: Bushnell V (ed) *Geol Map of Antarctica*, Antarctic Map Folio Ser, folio no 12 sheet 17, New York: Amer Geog Soc

Nathan S, Schulte F J, 1968. Geology and petrology of the Campbell-Aviator Divide, Northern Victoria Land, Antarctica, Part 1 Post Paleozoic rocks. *New Zeal J Geol Geophys*, 11: 940-975

Orheim O, 1972. Volcanic activity on Deception Island, South Shetland Islands. *In*: Adie R J (ed) *Antarctic Geol and Geophys*, IUGS Ser-B(1): 117-120

Palais J M, Kyle P R, McIntosh W C, Seward D, 1988. Magmatic and phreatomagmatic volcanic activity at Mt. Takahe, West Antarctica, based on tephra layers in the Byrd ice core and field observations at Mt. Takahe. *J Volc Geotherm Res*, 35: 295-317

Palais J M, Kyle P R, Mosley-Thompson E, Thomas E, 1987. Correlation of a 3200 year old tephra in ice cores from Vostok and South Pole Stations, Antarctica. *Geophys Res Lett*, 14: 804-807

Patrick M R, Smellie J L, Harris A J L, Wright R, Dean K, Izbekov P, Garbeil H, Pilger E, 2005. First recorded eruption of Mount Belinda volcano (Montagu Island), South Sandwich Islands. *Bull Volc*, 67: 415-422

Paulsen T S, Wilson T J, 2009. Structure and age of volcanic fissures on Mount Morning:a new constraint on Neogene to contemporary stress in the West Antarctic Rift, southern Victoria Land, Antarctica. *Geol Soc Amer Bull*, 121: 1071-1088

Prestvik T, Barnes C G, Sundvoll B, Duncan R A, 1990. Petrology of Peter I Oy (Peter I Island), west Antarctica. *J Volc Geotherm Res*, 44: 315-338

Quartermain L B, 1964. The Balleny Islands a descriptive and historical outline. *Antarctic Div Dept Sci Ind Res*, p 1-10

Riddolls B W, Hancox G T, 1968. The geology of the Upper Mariner Glacier region, North Victoria Land, Antarctica. *New Zeal J Geol Geophys*, 11: 881-899

Roobol M J, 1973. Historic volcanic activity at Deception Island. *Brit Antarctic Surv Bull*, 32: 23-30

Roobol M J, 1979. A model for the eruptive mechanism of Deception Island from 1820 to 1970. *Brit Antarctic Surv Bull*, 49: 137-156

Rowe C A, Aster R C, Kyle P R, Dibble R R, Schlue J W, 2000. Seismic and acoustic observations at Mount Erebus volcano, Ross Island, Antarctica, 1994-1998. *J Volc Geotherm Res*, 101: 105-128

Shultz C H, 1972. Eruption at Deception Island, Antarctica, August 1970. *Geol Soc Amer Bull*, 83: 2837-2842

Smellie J L, 2000. Lithostratigraphy and volcanic evolution of Deception Island, South Shetland Islands. *Antarct Sci*, 13: 188-209

Smellie J L, Hole M J, 1997. Products and processes in Pliocene-Recent, subaqueous to emergent volcanism in the Antarctic Peninsula: examples of englacial Surtseyan volcano construction. *Bull Volc*, 58: 628-646

Smellie J L, Morris P, Leat P T, Turner D B, Houghton D, 1998. Submarine caldera and other volcanic observations in Southern Thule, South Sandwich Islands. *Antarctic Sci*, 10: 171-172

Smith W H F, Sandwell D T, 1997. Global seafloor topography from satellite altimetry and ship depth soundings. *Science*, 277: 1957-1962

Tomblin J F, 1979. The South Sandwich Islands: II. The geology of Candlemas Island. *Brit Antarctic Surv Sci Rpt*, 92: 1-33

Treves S B, Kyle P R, 1973. Renewed volcanic activity of Mt. Erebus, Antarctica. *Antarctic J U S*, 8: 156

Weaver S D, Saunders A D, Pankhurst R J, Tarney J, 1979. A geochemical study of magmatism associated with the initial stages of back-arc spreading. *Contr Mineral Petr*, 68: 151-169

Wilbanks J R, 1972. Geology of the Fosdick Mountains, Marie Byrd Land. *In*:, Adie R J (ed) *Antarctic Geology and Geophysics*, Oslo: Internatl Union Geol Sci (IUGS), p 277-283

Wilch T I, McIntosh W C, Dunbar N W, 1999. Late Quaternary volcanic activity in Marie Byrd Land: potential 40Ar/39Ar-dated time horizons in West Antarctic ice and marine cores. *Geol Soc Amer Bull*, 111: 1563-1580

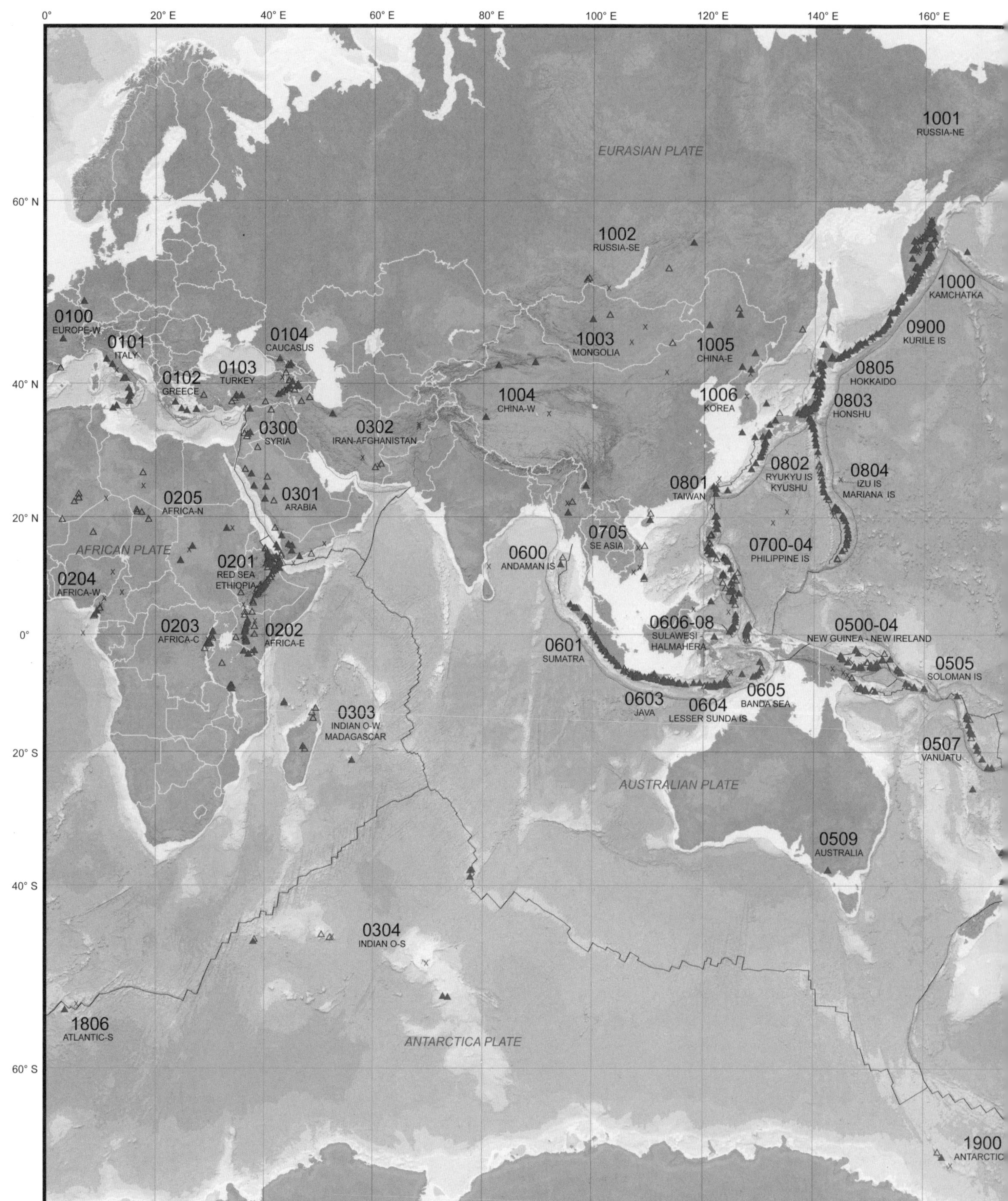

0°
20° E
40° E
60° E
80° E
100° E
120° E
140° E
160° E
60° N
40° N
20° N
0°
20° S
40° S
60° S
EURASIAN PLATE
AFRICAN PLATE
AUSTRALIAN PLATE
ANTARCTICA PLATE
1001
RUSSIA-NE
1002
RUSSIA-SE
1000
KAMCHATKA
0900
KURILE IS
0100
EUROPE-W
0101
ITALY
0104
CAUCASUS
1003
MONGOLIA
1005
CHINA-E
0102
GREECE
0103
TURKEY
0805
HOKKAIDO
1004
CHINA-W
1006
KOREA
0803
HONSHU
0300
SYRIA
0302
IRAN-AFGHANISTAN
0802
RYUKYU IS
KYUSHU
0804
IZU IS
MARIANA IS
0801
TAIWAN
0205
AFRICA-N
0301
ARABIA
0705
SE ASIA
0700-04
PHILIPPINE IS
0600
ANDAMAN IS
0201
RED SEA
ETHIOPIA
0204
AFRICA-W
0606-08
SULAWESI
HALMAHERA
0500-04
NEW GUINEA - NEW IRELAND
0203
AFRICA-C
0202
AFRICA-E
0601
SUMATRA
0505
SOLOMAN IS
0605
BANDA SEA
0603
JAVA
0604
LESSER SUNDA IS
0303
INDIAN O-W
MADAGASCAR
0507
VANUATU
0509
AUSTRALIA
0304
INDIAN O-S
1806
ATLANTIC-S
1900
ANTARCTIC